Collins

Chinese

Dictionary

HarperCollins Publishers
Westerhill Road
Bishopbriggs
Glasgow
G64 2QT
Great Britain

Second Edition 2006

Reprint 10 9 8 7 6 5 4 3

© HarperCollins Publishers 2005, 2006

ISBN 978-0-00-722391-6

Collins® and Bank of English® are
registered trademarks of HarperCollins
Publishers Limited

www.collinslanguage.com

A catalogue record for this book is available
from the British Library

HarperCollins Publishers,
10 East 53rd Street, New York, NY 10022

COLLINS CHINESE CONCISE DICTIONARY.
First US Edition 2005

ISBN 978-0-06-082200-2

www.harpercollins.com

HarperCollins books may be purchased for
educational, business, or sales promotional
use. For information, please write to:
Special Markets Department, HarperCollins
Publishers, 10 East 53rd Street, New York,
NY 10022

Typeset by Wordcraft, Glasgow

Printed in Italy by
LEGO Spa, Lavis (Trento), ITALY

Acknowledgements
We would like to thank those authors and
publishers who kindly gave permission for
copyright material to be used in the Collins
Word Web. We would also like to thank
Times Newspapers Ltd for providing
valuable data.

EDITORIAL TEAM/编辑组
吴义诚　谢曦
Marianne Davidson, Julie Kleeman, Sarah Waldram

顾凌志　顾越施　李欣　梅榕　申丕
吴乐军　於斌　赵立光
Julie Le Boulanger, Anthony Coogan, Kellie Dunn, Raphaëlle Frappin,
Bob Grossmith, Jane Goldie, Julie Helmert, Derek Hird, Cordelia Lilly,
Toby Lincoln, Duncan Marshall, Tom Mitford, Peter Offord,
Rachel Stein, Peter Terrell, Esther Tyldesley

English-Chinese translation in collaboration with Lexus Ltd

SPECIAL CONSULTANTS/特邀顾问
董琨教授, 中国社会科学院语言研究所
Professor Dong Kun, Institute of Linguistics,
Chinese Academy of Social Sciences

王立弟教授, 北京外国语大学高级翻译学院院长
Professor Wang Lidi, Graduate School of Translation and Interpretation,
Beijing Foreign Studies University

Dr David Pattinson, Department of East Asian Studies,
Leeds University

Jack Halpern, The CJK Dictionary Institute, Inc.

FOR THE PUBLISHERS/出版经理人
Jeremy Butterfield
Lorna Knight
Helen Newstead
Alison Macaulay

TYPESETTING/排版
Wordcraft

*Special thanks to Jim Kell of the Bell Educational Trust for access to the linguistic queries
sent to the China Daily 21st Century Bell Language Column between 1998 and 2002.*

William Collins' dream of knowledge for all began with the publication of his first book in 1819. A self-educated mill worker, he not only enriched millions of lives, but also founded a flourishing publishing house. Today, staying true to this spirit, Collins books are packed with inspiration, innovation and practical expertise. They place you at the centre of a world of possibility and give you exactly what you need to explore it.

Language is the key to this exploration, and at the heart of Collins Dictionaries is language as it is really used. New words, phrases and meanings spring up every day, and all of them are captured and analysed by the Collins Word Web. Constantly updated, and with over 2.5 billion entries, this living language resource is unique to our dictionaries.

Words are tools for life. And a Collins Dictionary makes them work for you.

Collins. Do more.

▼ 目录/Contents

Introduction

Compared to most European languages, learning Chinese is a challenge. However, in some ways Chinese is not particularly complicated. For example, words do not change with gender, number, case or even tense, and there are not many complicated grammatical traps for the unwary. A lot of the time, there is a pleasing directness about this fascinating and unique language. There are, however, many other things about it that make it hard for native English speakers to learn.

Chinese Pronunciation

The Four Tones

Chinese is a tonal language – that is, the pitch at which any given syllable is spoken affects the meaning of the word. There are four tones: first tone (high, even pitch); second tone (rising pitch); third tone (falling and then rising) and fourth tone (falling pitch). There is also a fifth tone (or neutral tone), generally pronounced so quietly and quickly that there is no discernible tone at all.

The tones are a very important part of the pronunciation – and wrong tones can cause real confusion.

Examples of differences in tones:				
First tone	Second tone	Third tone	Fourth tone	Neutral tone
mā	má	mǎ	mà	ma
妈	麻	马	骂	吗
mother	hemp	horse	curse; swear	[question particle]

Sometimes it can get very confusing, as below:

mǎi	mài
买	卖
buy	sell

It may seem unnatural to native speakers of English to have pitch so rigidly attached to words, but the tone is as fundamental a part of any syllable as are its vowels and consonants. While Chinese people will generally, after some thought, be able to piece together the meaning of a sentence pronounced utterly without tones, using tones (even if not 100% accurate) will at least increase the likelihood of your words sounding recognisably Chinese.

Finally, a word of warning. Although a beginner learning Chinese is likely to feel that he or she is already facing too many challenges without having to deal with tones, anyone who is considering not bothering with tones for the present may like to consider that it is *much* easier to spend a little extra time to learn the right tone than it does to un-learn a tone that you have become accustomed to using wrongly!

Pinyin

Pinyin is a phonetic system for transcribing the Chinese language, which was first introduced to help children learn to write characters, and foreigners and speakers of non-Mandarin dialects to pronounce Standard Chinese correctly. It is also very useful for dictionaries such as this one, as it means that characters can be sorted into alphabetical order, which makes it much easier to find them.

However, *pinyin* is not in common, day-to-day use, and even educated Chinese people are often not very proficient in it. This is only reasonable – after all, how many English native speakers can use the phonetic alphabet? So, although in China you may see signs written in *pinyin* from time to time, do not assume that people can read it fluently. Most Chinese people would be hard put to write their own addresses in *pinyin*. Moreover, other Chinese-speaking countries do not use the *pinyin* system at all. For this reason, it should not be regarded as a substitute for learning Chinese characters. It is, however, a good, accurate guide to pronunciation once you are used to it.

Chinese Characters

The Chinese script has a written history that goes back over three thousand years, and there are over 80,000 characters in the Chinese dictionary *Cihai*. A lot of these are archaic (some are so old that even their meanings are subject to debate), and an educated person will know roughly 4000–6000 characters. A knowledge of about 3000 characters is generally considered sufficient for basic literacy (newspapers and the like).

Each of these characters has to be learned individually – and the shape of the character, the sound of it and the meaning are learned together as a unit. This is particularly trying for westerners, who already have to deal with the unfamiliar sounds and grammatical features of the language. But if you want to learn to read and write Chinese, it is unavoidable.

Introduction

There is no way of predicting the sound and meaning of an unknown Chinese character with any degree of accuracy. This does not mean, however, that there is no system behind the characters at all. All characters contain at least one of the component parts known as "radicals", and almost all radicals have an element of meaning; if you are familiar with these, not only will using a dictionary be much easier, it will also help you identify more of the building blocks of the characters you are trying to learn. The radical of a character is not always a reliable guide to the character's meaning. For example, the radicals in the Chinese word for *rose*, 玫瑰, are the jade radical 王; and the verb *to give* 给 is based on the radical 糸 for silk. Some radicals are more dependable than others though. For example, things containing the 'rain' radical 雨 almost always have something to do with the weather, and things containing the 'tree' radical 木 are generally either to do with wood or trees.

People who grow up in China have a much better start than their overseas counterparts when it comes to learning characters, as they can see Chinese writing wherever they go, and they are already familiar with the Chinese language by the time they start school. Even so, it takes a Chinese child a good many years to master reading and writing Chinese, and the amount of memorization needed to learn enough Chinese characters to be literate colours the entire education system. This – as well as historical causes – is perhaps one reason why 8.72% of China's adult population is illiterate.

A Chinese child who is learning to read and write is given homework every evening, which will involve copying out a number of characters five or more times each, to reinforce the characters in his or her memory. Everybody has their own preferred methods for learning Chinese characters – for most, it is a combination of reading and writing exercises to reinforce the character while helping the student to understand the context in which it is used, and flashcards with the character on one side and the *pinyin* and meaning on the other.

As with all languages, the most efficient way to learn Chinese characters is little and often. Ten minutes each day spent with a few flashcards is going to be far more productive in the long run than an afternoon's cramming every fortnight – and you will be far more likely to remember it later on. It is also important to remember that Chinese people too need regular exposure to Chinese writing to keep their Chinese in top form – even highly educated people start forgetting their characters if they spend too long overseas, in an environment where they neither see nor write them.

Simplified and Complex Characters

The government of the People's Republic of China carried out a programme of simplifying the Chinese script in 1956 and another in 1964, in an effort to improve the literacy rate by making characters easier to write. It is these simplified characters which are used in this dictionary. However, for various cultural and political reasons, many regions outside the PRC did not accept these changes, and continued to use the old system. Taiwan still uses complex characters. So do Hong Kong and Singapore, although the simplified characters are now in increasingly common use. Overseas Chinese communities have tended to use complex characters, though that may change in the future, as the changes that are taking place in mainland China make it much easier for people to come to the West for work or study.

Anyone who wants to work as a translator or academic needs a working knowledge of both simplified and complex Chinese characters. But learning one form at a time is more than enough of a challenge for most learners. Which one you end up studying will depend on textbooks available, and the parts of the Chinese-speaking world with which you wish to communicate. Fortunately, the majority of characters are the same or nearly the same in both systems – it does not take long for someone who can read in one system to adjust to reading the other.

Writing Chinese

You may ask 'do I really need to learn to write Chinese?'. That depends on what you want to do with it! If you are learning it as part of a university course, you will probably be made to learn Chinese writing, whether you want to or not. If you are learning on your own, or as preparation for a stay in China, you may have no desire or time to learn the script. If you want to know a few everyday phrases to ease your way through a short holiday, then learning the script is probably not for you. If you decide not to learn characters, you should be able to navigate your way around the dictionary well enough by using *pinyin* and the four tones.

Learning Chinese is a lot easier if you do not have the extra work of memorizing characters, at least in the initial stages. On the other hand, if you do not learn the characters, you are going to find some things more confusing as you progress. A lot of Chinese characters look completely different and have totally different meanings, but sound just the same, as a quick glance at the *shi* or *yi* section of your dictionary will show.

Introduction

One of the more cheering things about learning the Chinese writing system is that most words are made up of two or more characters. This means that once you get beyond a certain point, you encounter more and more characters you know already, just in different combinations. New words and expressions consequently become easier to learn. For someone who is not learning characters, however, every new word will just be a collection of vowels, consonants and tones –the element of meaning that the characters give is lost. They also lose out on the enjoyment involved in reading and writing Chinese, which is rather like the pleasure of doing a crossword puzzle or a difficult jigsaw.

To people who do not want to learn the Chinese script, I usually say that the two most necessary characters to learn are 男 nán (male) and 女 nǚ (female), as the inability to distinguish between these two in public places can lead to severe embarrassment!

Chinese Grammar

Compared to a lot of other languages, Chinese grammar is not particularly complicated. It is not an inflected language – that is, words do not change according to gender, number or case the way they do in many European languages. Sentence structure is generally straightforward, and there are not many exceptions to the grammatical rules (unlike, say, English).

What makes the Chinese language difficult for a native speaker of English is its unfamiliarity. Not only does it sound very different from English, making it hard to guess unfamiliar words the way we often can with languages like French and German, parts of Chinese grammar are very counterintuitive to a native speaker of English. Although there is nothing very complex about Chinese grammar, it takes a while to get accustomed to it, and to learn to adapt to some of its more unfamiliar features.

Talking about Time

It is sometimes said of Chinese that it has no tenses. This is not quite true, but speakers of Chinese talk about time in a way that is quite different from ours. The English tense system is based on the idea of before and after the point of view of the narrator. Things that happened before the time in which we are talking take the past tense, those that are in the process of going on, the present, and things that have yet to take place, the future. This is shown by a change in the verbs. Chinese verbs, on the other hand, do not change with tense, but an aspect marker is placed before or after the verb. Some of the most common are 了 le (for completed actions – usually *but not always* in the past), 过 guo (for events that have already taken place), 要 yào (for things that are going to happen) and 在 zài (for things that are in the process of happening). These are no more than generalizations, however, and it is important not to use them indiscriminately as substitutes for English tenses, as that is not what they are for.

Adverbs of time are often used to show what time relation events have to each other, such as 已经 yǐjing (already), 曾经 céngjīng (once), or specific times or dates.

> 明年我去中国。
> Míngnián wǒ qù Zhōngguó.
> (literally: Next year I go China).
> I'm going to China next year.

Redundancies

Chinese is very sparing in its use of words. If a word can be guessed from the context of the surrounding text, it will seem redundant to a Chinese speaker, and so is likely to be omitted. Most languages do this to a certain extent, but speakers of Chinese will cheerfully leave out things that may seem essential to a speaker of English, such as

> 你吃晚饭了吗？
> Nǐ chī wǎnfàn le ma?
> Have you eaten supper?
> 吃了。
> Chī le.
> [I've] eaten [it].

When talking about causes and consequences, there is also a tendency to miss out the words for "if… then"

> 旧的不去，新的不来。
> Jiù de bú qù, xīn de bù laí.
> (literally: Old not go, new not come).
> If the old does not go, then the new cannot come.

This can be initially confusing, but the omissions are mostly pretty obvious and easy to follow.

Introduction

Measure Words

These are not unique to Chinese – you occasionally see something similar in English.

> a *gaggle* of geese
> a *piece* of fruit
> six *pints* of milk
> etc.

They do not occur very often in English. In Chinese, however, measure words are mandatory when giving a number of nouns. It is important to remember to put them in – and also to get them right, as there are a lot of measure words in Chinese.

一只青蛙	yī **zhī** qīngwā	one frog
三部电影	sān **bù** diànyǐng	three films
五封信	wǔ **fēng** xìn	five letters

Different measure words are used for different types of objects. 张 zhāng is used for flat things, such as tickets, sheets and tables. 条 tiáo is used to talk about long, thin things such as ribbons, or fish. There are a lot of measure words, but some are not very common, such as 匹 pǐ, the measure word for horses. The most common measure word is 个 gè, and it is a useful "default setting" for when you cannot remember the exact term you need.

Word Order

Because of the less specific nature of the Chinese view of time, the tendency to avoid redundancy and the lack of cases to show what function words have in the sentence, word order is extremely important in Chinese. It generally follows a subject-verb-object pattern, although there are certain particles or rhetorical constructions that change the order slightly. If the word order is wrong, it can be very hard to unscramble the sense of a phrase or sentence.

This leads to the question of long sentences. Textbooks introduce the learner to Chinese with short, easy sentences, sensibly laid out. However, a lot of real-life texts – especially journalistic texts and political speeches – are prone to long, convoluted sentences, with many long, linked clauses, some of which may have other clauses embedded within them. However, thanks to the strict word order of Chinese, it is possible to tell which part belongs to which from its position in the sentence. So long as the student does not panic, it is usually possible, with a bit of care and thought, to unscramble the sentences, and mentally split them into more easily manageable sections.

All this seems very intimidating to a beginner – and there is no point in trying to pass Chinese off as an easy language. However, the challenge of learning Chinese is in direct proportion to the pleasure of being able to use it. Not only is it an absorbing and intriguing language, which can express both brutal frankness and extreme delicacy, it also brings with it great opportunities to explore and understand a country and culture that is very different from that of the west. And there could be no better time to begin that exploration than now, when China is increasingly opening up.

Esther Tyldesley, University of Edinburgh

How to use the Dictionary

CHINESE-ENGLISH SIDE

1 Order

1.1 On the Chinese side, head entries are ordered traditionally, that is by single-character entries with multiple-character entries beginning with the same character nested below them.

这	zhè
这个	zhège
这里	zhèlǐ
这么	zhème
这些	zhèxiē
这样	zhèyàng
这种	zhèzhǒng
蔗	zhè
蔗糖	zhètáng

1.2 Single character entries are ordered by pinyin, that is alphabetically and then by tone. In Chinese, there are four tones, each represented by a different mark above the relevant vowel:

−	first tone	(flat tone)	mā
´	second tone	(rising tone)	má
ˇ	third tone	(falling rising tone)	mǎ
`	fourth tone	(falling tone)	mà
	light or no tone		ma

Where characters have the same pinyin and tone, they are ordered by the number of strokes in the characters, with the smallest number of strokes first.

召 zhào

兆 zhào

照 zhào

Where characters have the same pinyin, tone, and number of strokes, they are ordered by the first stroke in the character, as follows:

一 丨 丿 丶 乛

1.3 The multiple-character entries nested below single-character entries are similarly ordered by pinyin (including tone), and then by number of strokes.

蒸	zhēng
蒸馏	zhēngliú
蒸气	zhēngqì
蒸汽	zhēngqì

2 Radical and character index

If you do not know the pronunciation for the Chinese character you are looking for, you can use the index before the start of the Chinese-English side. For further information on how to use the radical index, see the introduction to that section.

3 Cross-references

Polyphones, that is characters with more than one pronunciation, are cross-referred to the alternative pinyin.

> 供 gōng [动] 1 (供应) supply 2 (提供) provide
> →另见 gòng

> 供 gòng I [动] 1 (供奉) lay (PT, PP laid) ▷供奉
> 祭品 lay offerings 2 (招供) confess ▷他供出
> 了主犯的名字。He confessed the name of the
> ...
> →另见 gōng

4 The structure of entries

On the Chinese side there are two levels of entry (single-character entries and multiple-character entries), but these are essentially structured the same way:

4.1 Pinyin

Pinyin romanization is given for all single-character and multiple-character entries.

4.2 Grammatical information

4.2.1 Parts of speech appear in square brackets after the pinyin. Where a word has more than one part of speech, Roman numerals are used:

> 早 zǎo I [名] morning II [副] a long time ago
> ▷这事我早就知道了。I knew about this a long
> time ago. III [形] early ▶早餐 breakfast ▷你
> 早点来。Come early.

For a full list of parts of speech used, see page xxxiv.

4.2.2 Parts of speech are not given for head idioms (chengyu and other idioms), since these are often phrasal.

4.3 Meaning divisions

4.3.1 Where a word or grammatical category has more than one meaning, it is divided into categories which are shown by an Arabic numeral.

> 震 zhèn I [动] 1 (震动) shake (PT shook, PP
> shaken) 2 (激动) be excited II [名] earthquake
> ▷余震 after-shock

4.3.2 Further distinctions of meaning are shown by the use of information in round brackets after the meaning category number. This information functions as a 'signpost' to help the user select the right translation when there are many different possible translations to choose from. This indicating material can be of the following kinds:

– a synonym of the headword, or superordinate:

> 症候 zhènghòu [名] 1 (症状) symptom 2 (疾病)
> disease

– a typical context for the headword, such as:

> – noun objects and subjects for verbs:

> 旺 wàng [形] 1 (火) roaring 2 (人、生意)
> flourishing 3 (花) blooming ▷十月菊花开得
> 正旺。In October the chrysanthemums are in
> full bloom.

> – noun complements for adjectives:

> 细 xì I [形] 1 (绳、线等) thin 2 (沙、粮等)
> fine 3 (声、语等) gentle 4 (节、则等) detailed
> ▶细节 details (PL) II [副] minutely ▶细看
> scrutinize ▷细问 ask in detail ▷细想 consider
> carefully

> – other words defining or restricting the headword:

> 蒸 zhēng [动] 1 (指烹饪方法) steam 2 (蒸发)
> evaporate

– a label indicating the field in which the word is used:

> 硬件 yìngjiàn [名] 1 (计算机) hardware 2 (设备)
> equipment

– a style label, which is used to mark non-neutral words and expressions as a warning to the user:

> 治学 zhìxué [动] (书) study

You will find a complete list of labels used in the dictionary on page xxxiv.

4.4 Examples

4.4.1 Word examples, as well as a few 4-character idioms (chengyu etc.), appear under meanings which function as core senses of single characters, and are preceded by a shaded arrow ▶.

4.4.2 Fuller examples are preceded by an empty arrow ▷.

4.5 **Translations**

4.5.1 In general, we have only given one translation per meaning, since we believe this is the most accurate and helpful approach.

4.5.2 In a few cases, there is no equivalent at all, and an explanation rather than a translation has to be given. In such cases it is shown in italics:

> 压岁钱 yāsuìqián [名] *traditional gifts of money*
> *given to children during the Spring Festival*

4.5.3 British and American English variants are shown where appropriate:

> 棒子 bàngzi [名] **1** (棍子) club **2** (玉米) corn (英),
> maize (美)

4.5.4 Alternative parts of translations are preceded by "或" ('or'):

> 摄影 shèyǐng [动] **1** (照相) take a photo (PT took,
> PP taken) **2** (拍电影) shoot a film (英) 或 movie
> (美) (PT, PP shot)

ENGLISH-CHINESE SIDE

Below you will find an outline of how information is presented in your dictionary. Our aim is to give you the maximum amount of detail in the clearest and most helpful way.

1 **Alphabetical order**

1.1 On the English side, strict alphabetical order applies for all headwords except for phrasal verbs (see 1.3 below). For instance, a headword with an initial capital comes before the same word with a lower-case initial.

1.2 Alphabetical order for headwords is as follows:

> upper case
> lower case
> upper case + full stop
> lower case + full stop
> upper case + numeral
> lower case + numeral
>
> **B**
> **b.**
> **B4**
> **BA** *etc.*

1.3 Phrasal verbs appear in alphabetical order at the end of the entry they belong with and before any other headwords. Thus, **buy back**, **buy in**, **buy into**, **buy off**, **buy out** and **buy up** all appear before **buyer**.

1.4 Except for phrasal verbs, all other compounds consisting of two or more words are shown as headwords in alphabetical order:

> **pedestrian**
> **pedestrian crossing**
> **pedestrianized**
> **pedestrian precinct**

2 Homonyms

2.1 Words which are written in the same way but have different pronunciations are shown as separate headwords and differentiated by the use of numbers:

> **bow¹** [bəu] N [c] **1** (*knot*) 蝴蝶结 [húdiéjié]
> **2** (*weapon*) 弓 [gōng] **3** (MUS) 琴弓 [qíngōng]
> **bow²** [bau] I N [c] **1** (*of head, body*) 鞠躬
> [jūgōng] **2** (NAUT) (*also:* **bows**) 船首

2.2 Words which are written in the same way and have the same pronunciation are treated at the same headword:

> **bear** [bɛə(r)] (*pt* **bore**, *pp* **borne**) I N [c] (*animal*)
> 熊 [xióng] II VT **1** (*liter*) (*carry*) [+ *object*] 携带
> [xiédài] **2** (*support*) [+ *weight*] 支撑 [zhīchēng]
> **3** [+ *responsibility*] 承担 [chéngdān] **4** [+ *cost*] 负
> 担 [fùdān] **5** (*tolerate*) [+ *person*] 容忍 [róngrěn]

2.3 Where the stress in a word changes according to which part of speech it is being used in, the different parts of speech are treated under the same headword, and the change of stress is indicated in the phonetic transcription:

> **escort** [*n* 'ɛskɔːt, *vb* ɪs'kɔːt]

3 Alternative forms of headwords

3.1 Part of a headword may be placed within round brackets to indicate that it is optional:

> **among(st)** [ə'mʌŋ(st)] PREP

3.2 Spelling variants of headwords are entered as headwords and cross-referred to the primary form thus:

> **maneuver** [mə'nu:və(r)] (US) VT, VI, N =
> **manoeuvre**

3.3 American spellings of words are always shown, at the headword which is spelled in the British way:

> **axe**, (US) **ax** [æks]

3.4 Past tenses of irregular verbs, and inflections of irregular nouns are shown as headwords in their own right and cross-referred to the base form:

> **went** [wɛnt] PT *of* go

> **children** [ˈtʃɪldrən] NPL *of* child

4 The structure of entries

A typical English entry in your dictionary will be made up of the following elements:

4.1 The headword

As noted above, a part of the headword may be placed in brackets to show that it is optional, or a spelling variant of the headword may also be shown directly after the headword.

4.2 Phonetic transcription

Phonetics for English words appear in square brackets immediately after the headword. They are shown using the International Phonetic Alphabet (IPA), and a complete list of the symbols used in this system can be found on page xxxvi. The pronunciation given is for British English, but the American pronunciation is also shown where the pronunciation differs significantly from the British form, eg schedule, vase.

> **vase** [vɑːz, US veɪs]

4.3 Grammatical information

4.3.1 Parts of speech appear in upper case letters after the phonetic spelling of the headword. Where a word has more than one part of speech, Roman numerals are used:

> **key** [kiː] I N [C] 1 (for lock, mechanism) 钥匙
> [yàoshi] 2 [of computer, typewriter, piano] 键
> [jiàn] 3 (MUS) 调 [diào] 4 ▶ the key (to sth)

For a full list of parts of speech used, see page xxxiv.

4.3.2 We have used the notation C, U and S and PL to show whether nouns are countable, uncountable, singular or plural. C means that the noun is countable, and has a plural form (eg *I'm reading a book; she's bought several books*). U means that the noun is not normally counted, and is not used in the plural (eg *Lesley refused to give me more information*). S (for singular noun) means the noun is always singular, and is usually preceded by *a, an* or *the* (eg *We need to persuade people to respect the environment*). PL means the noun is always plural, and is used with plural verbs or pronouns (eg *These clothes are ready to wear*).

> **hairdryer** [ˈhɛədraɪə(r)] N [C] 吹风机
> [chuīfēngjī]
> **hair gel** N [U] 发胶 [fàjiāo]
> **kick-off** [ˈkɪkɔf] (SPORT) N [S] 开场时间
> [kāichǎng shíjiān]

How to use the Dictionary

4.3.3 For phrasal verbs, the parts of speech we have used are explained below:

VI – the verb and its particle are never separated, and the meaning is intransitive:

> ▸ **melt away** VI **1** [*people +*] 逐渐散去 [zhújiàn sànqù] **2** [*doubts +*] 消除 [xiāochú]

VT – the verb and its particle can be separated by the object and the meaning is transitive.

VT FUS [不可拆分] – the verb and its particle cannot be separated, and the overall meaning is transitive:

> ▸ **laugh at** VT FUS [不可拆分] **1** (*lit*) 对···发笑 [duì···fāxiào] **2** (*fig*) (*mock*) 嘲笑 [cháoxiào]
> ▸ **laugh off** VT [*+ criticism, problem*] 对···一笑置之 [duì···yī xiào zhì zhī]

4.3.4 Information on irregular inflections of verbs and nouns is shown after the headword to enable you to use the word correctly:

> ⊙ **child** [tʃaɪld] (*pl* **children**) N [c]

> ⊙ **fly** [flaɪ] (*pt* **flew**, *pp* **flown**) I VT

4.4 Meaning divisions

4.4.1 Where a word or a grammatical category has more than one meaning, it is divided into categories which are shown by an Arabic numeral:

> **challenging** ['tʃælɪndʒɪŋ] ADJ **1** [*+ job, task*] 具有挑战性的 [jùyǒu tiǎozhànxìng de] **2** [*+ tone, look etc*] 挑衅的 [tiǎoxìn de]

4.4.2 Distinctions of meaning are shown by the use of bracketed information in italics, which can be of the following kinds:

– a synonym of the headword, which is placed in round brackets.

> **definitive** [dɪ'fɪnɪtɪv] ADJ **1** (*conclusive*) [*+ answer*] 确定的 [quèdìng de] **2** (*authoritative*) [*+ version, account*] 权威性的 [quánwēixìng de]

– a typical context for the headword, shown in square brackets, such as:

– noun objects for transitive verbs:

> **tighten** ['taɪtn] I VT **1** [*+ rope, strap*] 拉紧 [lājǐn] **2** [*+ screw, bolt*] 弄紧 [nòngjǐn] **3** [*+ grip, security, rules etc*] 加紧 [jiājǐn] II VI **1** [*grip +*] 握紧

– noun subjects for intransitive verbs:

circulate ['sɜːkjuleɪt] **I** VI [*traffic, blood* +] 循
环 [xúnhuán]; [*news, rumour* +] 散播 [sànbō];
[*person* +] (*at party*) 交际 [jiāojì] **II** VT [+ *report*]
传阅 [chuányuè]

– noun complements for adjectives:

tasteless ['teɪstlɪs] ADJ **1** [+ *food*] 无味的
[wúwèi de] **2** [+ *remark, joke*] 不雅的 [bùyǎ de]
3 [+ *furniture, decor etc*] 低俗的 [dīsú de]

– other words defining or restricting the headword:

believer [bɪ'liːvə(r)] N [C] **1** (*in idea, activity*)
笃信者 [dǔxìnzhě] **2** (REL) 信徒 [xìntú]

– a label indicating the field in which the word is used:

bishop ['bɪʃəp] N [C] **1** (REL) 主教 [zhǔjiào]
2 (CHESS) 象 [xiàng]

You will find a complete list of labels used in the dictionary on page xxxiv.

4.5 Phrases

These are shown in bold preceded by a shaded arrow ▶. Phrases include set
constructions of many different kinds, as well as exclamations and grammatical
structures:

to do something behind sb's back
back and forth
too bad!
on balance
to begin to do *or* **doing sth**

4.6 Examples

Examples are shown in italics preceded by an empty arrow ▷. The most common 500
words in English have all been given a significant number of examples to help you to
use the translations in context.

◇ **large** [lɑːdʒ] ADJ **1** (*big*) [+ *house, person etc*] 大
的 [dà de]; [+ *number, amount*] 大量的 [dàliàng
de] ▷ *We are facing a large number of problems.* 我
们面临大量的问题。▷ *a large number of people*
许多人 **2** (*serious*) [+ *problem, question*] 重大
的 [zhòngdà de] ▶ **at large** (*as a whole*) 整个
▷ *their attitude to the world at large* 他们对整个世
界的态度 ▶ **to be at large** 逍遥自在 ▷ *There*
...

4.7 Translations

In general, we have only given one translation per meaning, since we believe this is the most accurate and helpful approach. In a few cases, there is no equivalent at all, and an explanation rather than a translation has to be given.

> **au pair** ['əʊ'pɛə(r)] N [c] 为学习语言而住在当
> 地人家里并提供家政服务的外国年轻人

4.8 Pinyin

Pinyin romanization is given for all main headword and phrasal verb translations. The only exception to this is in cases, as outlined above, where there is no real Chinese equivalent and so an explanation has been given for the benefit of the Chinese user, rather than a translation.

5 Levels of formality and familiarity

It is very important to communicate with the person you are talking or writing to in a way which is appropriate to the nature of the relationship between you. You would write very differently to a business colleague and to a friend. In order to help you choose which forms of expression to use and which to avoid, we have labelled words and expressions on both sides. The full list of these labels in on page xxxv.

6 Keywords

Certain very commonly used words, such as **have** and **do**, have been treated in special depth because they constitute basic elements of English and have very many uses and meanings. We have given them a special design to make it easier to find the meaning or construction you are looking for.

> **have** [hæv] (*pt, pp* **had**) I VT 1 (*possess*) 有
> [yǒu] ▶ he has *or* he has got blue eyes/dark
> hair 他长着蓝眼睛/黑头发 ▶ do you have
> *or* have you got a car/phone? 你有车/电话
> 吗? ▶ I have *or* I have got an idea 我有个
> 主意 ▶ to have *or* have got sth to do 有必
> 须得做的事 ▶ she had her eyes closed 她
> 闭上了眼睛
> 2 (*with meals, drinks*) ▶ to have breakfast
> 吃早饭 [chī zǎofàn] ▶ to have a drink/a
> cigarette 喝一杯/抽支烟
> 3 (*with activity*) ▶ to have a swim/bath 游
> 泳/洗澡 [yóuyǒng/xǐzǎo] ▶ to have a
> meeting/party 开会/开派对
> ...

如何使用本词典

汉英部分

以下是词典中出现的主要内容的提纲。本词典旨在尽可能清晰、有效地为你提供最详尽的说明。

1 顺序
1.1 在汉语部分, 词目按传统顺序排列, 即单字词条下嵌入以相同汉字开头的多字词条。

这	zhè
这个	zhège
这里	zhèlǐ
这么	zhème
这些	zhèxiē
蔗	zhè
蔗糖	zhètáng

1.2 单字词条按拼音字母顺序排序, 再按声调顺序排序。注意, 轻声排在四声之后。同音字按笔画的多寡排列, 笔画少的在前, 笔画多的在后。

召	zhào
兆	zhào
照	zhào

笔画相同的同音字按起笔笔画排列, 顺序为：一 丨 丿 丶 乛

1.3 单字词条下的多字词条也先按照拼音(包括声调), 再按照笔画数进行排序。

蒸	zhēng
蒸馏	zhēngliú
蒸气	zhēngqì
蒸汽	zhēngqì

2 部首和汉字索引
如果使用者不知道所使用汉字的发音, 部首目录和检字表位于汉英部分之前。有关如何使用部首索引, 参见部首和汉字索引的第一部分。

3 交叉索引
多音字, 即有一个以上发音的汉字, 会标明"另见", 后接另一个发音。

供 gōng [动] 1 (供应) supply 2 (提供) provide
➡另见 gòng

供 gòng I [动] 1 (供奉) lay (PT, PP laid) ▷供奉
祭品 lay offerings 2 (招供) confess ▷他供出
了主犯的名字。He confessed the name of the
...
➡另见 gōng

4 词目构成

汉语部分的词条有两个层次, 单字词条和多字词条, 但它们的构成方式基本相同:

4.1 拼音
所有词条都标注汉语拼音。

4.2 语法结构
4.2.1 词性在方括号中用中文标注, 紧随拼音之后。如果有一个以上的词性, 用罗马数字标识:

早 zǎo I [名] morning II [副] a long time ago
▷这事我早就知道了。I knew about this a long
time ago. III [形] early ▶早餐 breakfast ▷你
早点来。Come early.

词性列表参见第xxxiv页。

4.2.2 惯用语, 包括成语和其他惯用语, 作为单独的条目列出, 但不标词性。

4.3 词义划分
4.3.1 如果一个词条有一个以上的词义, 则归入不同的意类, 用阿拉伯数字标出。

震 zhèn I [动] 1 (震动) shake (PT shook, PP
shaken) 2 (激动) be excited II [名] earthquake
▷余震 after-shock

4.3.2 当一个词条有多种含义时, 读者可以根据阿拉伯数字后圆括号中的信息找到相关的语境, 进而查到正确的翻译。圆括号中的信息起到 "路标" 的功能, 指向恰当的翻译。圆括号有如下几种功用:
主词条的同义词或近义词:

症候 zhènghòu [名] 1 (症状) symptom 2 (疾病)
disease

典型语境:在括号中显示使用主词条的典型情境, 例如:

— 动词的名词宾语或主语:

旺 wàng [形] 1 (火) roaring 2 (人、生意) flourishing 3 (花) blooming ▷十月菊花开得正旺。In October the chrysanthemums are in full bloom.

— 形容词的名词补足语:

细 xì I [形] 1 (绳、线等) thin 2 (沙、粮等) fine 3 (声、语等) gentle 4 (节、则等) detailed ▶细节 details (PL) II [副] minutely ▶细看 scrutinize ▷细问 ask in detail ▷细想 consider carefully

— 定义或用于限制主词条的其他词:

蒸 zhēng [动] 1 (指烹饪方法) steam 2 (蒸发) evaporate

— 该词使用的专业领域:

硬件 yìngjiàn [名] 1 (计算机) hardware 2 (设备) equipment

用修辞色彩缩略语标注语体色彩:

治学 zhìxué [动] (书) study

修辞色彩缩略语列表见第xxxiv页。

4.4 例子
4.4.1 以词的形式出现的例子,包括少数的四字习语(成语等),作为该汉字的核心意义出现在解释之后,前面用实心灰色箭头 ▶ 标出。
4.4.2 更完整的例子,前面用空心箭头 ▷ 标出。

4.5 翻译
4.5.1 一般情况下,作为最精确、有效的方法,每个意义只提供一个翻译。
4.5.2 在某些情况下,如果根本没有相应的翻译对等语,则提供该词的解释,而不是翻译,用斜体表示。

压岁钱 yāsuìqián [名] *traditional gifts of money given to children during the Spring Festival*

4.5.3 不规则动词的过去式和过去分词和名词的复数形式出现在英语翻译之后,便于查阅。不规则动词的过去式和过去分词形式的完整列表见第xxxvii页。

包涵 bāohán [动] forgive (PT forgave, PP forgiven) ▷招待不周, 请多包涵! Please forgive me for giving you such a poor reception.

4.5.4 以-s 结尾的名词, 若用作复数, 则标注为pl, 若用作单数, 则标注为sg

> 鬓 bìn [名] sideburns (PL)

> 丛书 cóngshū [名] series (SG)

4.5.5 必要时, 同时给出美式英语和英式英语两种翻译。

> 棒子 bàngzi [名] **1** (棍子) club **2** (玉米) corn (英), maize (美)

4.5.6 可供选择的部分前标有"或":

> 摄影 shèyǐng [动] **1** (照相) take a photo (PT took, PP taken) **2** (拍电影) shoot a film (英) 或 movie (美) (PT, PP shot)

5 语言注释

为了帮助读者更加准确、熟巧地掌握并运用英语, 我们对一些易混淆词进行了详细的比较说明。

> **person** 的复数形式通常为 **people**。*At least fifty-four people have been killed.* **persons** 通常只用于非常正式的场合, 或作为法律用语。

如何使用本词典

英汉部分

以下是词典中出现的主要内容的提纲。我们旨在尽可能清晰、有效地为你提供最详尽的说明。

1 顺序

1.1 在英语部分，除了短语动词外（见1.3），所有词条都严格按照字母顺序排列。例如，开头字母为大写的词条位于拼写相同但以小写字母开头的词条前面。

1.2 词条的排列顺序如下：

> 大写字母
> 小写字母
> 大写+句点
> 小写+句点
> 大写+数字
> 小写+数字
>
> B
> b.
> B4
> BA

1.3 短语动词出现在所属的词条末尾，其他同根词条之前。例如，**buy back**, **buy in**, **buy into**, **buy off**, **buy out** 和 **buy up** 都出现在 **buyer** 之前。

1.4 除了短语动词，两个或两个以上单词构成的复合词按照字母顺序以词条的形式出现：

> **pedestrian**
> **pedestrian crossing**
> **pedestrianized**
> **pedestrian precinct**

2 同音异义词

2.1 书写相同但发音完全不同的单词作为单独的词条出现，并且用数字上标加以区分：

> **bow¹** [bəu] N [C] **1** (*knot*) 蝴蝶结 [húdiéjié]
> **2** (*weapon*) 弓 [gōng] **3** (MUS) 琴弓 [qíngōng]
> **bow²** [bau] **I** N [C] **1** (*of head, body*) 鞠躬
> [jūgōng] **2** (NAUT) (*also:* **bows**) 船首

如上所示，数字上标明确表明该单词的发音完全不同。

2.2 书写和发音都相同的单词视作同一词条:

> **bear** [beə(r)] (*pt* **bore,** *pp* **borne**) I N [c] (*animal*)
> 熊 [xióng] II VT **1** (*liter*) (*carry*) [+ *object*] 携带
> [xiédài] **2** (*support*) [+ *weight*] 支撑 [zhīchēng]
> **3** [+ *responsibility*] 承担 [chéngdān] **4** [+ *cost*] 负
> 担 [fùdān] **5** (*tolerate*) [+ *person*] 容忍 [róngrěn]

2.3 如果单词的重音随词性的变化而变化, 不同的词性及相应的音标列在同一词条下:

> **escort** [*n* 'ɛskɔːt, *vb* ɪs'kɔːt]

3 词条的变化形式

3.1 词条的某些部分可置于圆括号中, 表明两种书写形式均可:

> **among(st)** [ə'mʌŋ(st)] PREP

3.2 单词的拼写变化也作为单独的词条录入, 并参见首先出现的拼写形式:

> **maneuver** [mə'nuːvə(r)] (US) VT, VI, N =
> **manoeuvre**

3.3 单词的美式拼写总是在括号中给出:

> **axe,** (US)**ax** [æks]

3.4 不规则动词的时态变化和不规则名词的复数形式作为单独的词条出现, 并且指示参照原形:

> **went** [wɛnt] PT *of* **go**
>
> **children** ['tʃɪldrən] NPL *of* **child**

4 词目构成

本词典中的词目通常由下列要素构成:

4.1 词条

本词典收录了500个最常用的英语单词, 并且加注特别的标志, 以帮助读者明确学习和理解的先后次序。在这些单词中, 列举了大量真实地道的例句, 有助于了解单词在真实语言环境中的用法。

> ○**decision** [dɪ'sɪʒən] N **1** [c] (*choice*) 决定
> [juédìng] ▷ *The government has announced its*
> *decision.* 政府已经宣布了决定。**2** [U] (*act of*
> *choosing*) 决心 [juéxīn] ▷ *The moment of decision*
> *can't be delayed.* 下决心的时刻不能拖了。**3** [U]
> (*decisiveness*) 决断力 [juéduànlì] ▶ **to make a**
> **decision** 作出决定

4.2 音标

英语单词的注音采用国际音标(IPA),用方括号标识。完整的音标表参见第 xxxvi页。注音以英式发音为主,当美式发音与英式发音完全不同时,加注美式发音,例如 *schedule, vase*。

vase [vɑːz, *US* veɪs]

4.3 语法结构

4.3.1 词性

词性用大写字母标注在单词的音标后。如果一个单词有　一个以上的词性,用罗马数字标识:

key [kiː] **I** N [c] **1** (*for lock, mechanism*) 钥匙
[yàoshi] **2** [*of computer, typewriter, piano*] 键
[jiàn] **3** (MUS) 调 [diào] **4** ▸ **the key (to sth)**

词性列表参见第xxxiv页。

4.3.2 名词

C, U, S 和 PL 等符号表示名词的各种形式。
C表示可数名词,并具有复数形式(例如:*I'm reading a book; she's bought several books*)。
U表示不可数名词,不具有复数形式(例如: *Lesley refused to give me more information*)。
S(用于单数名词)是指该名词总是用作单数,而且通常跟在 *a, an* 或 *the* 之后(例如: *We need to persuade people to respect the environment.*)。
PL是指该名词总是用作复数形式,并且相关的动词或代词也相应地使用复数形式(例如: *These clothes are ready to wear.*)。

hairdryer [ˈhɛədraɪə(r)] N [c] 吹风机
[chuīfēngjī]
hair gel N [u] 发胶 [fàjiāo]
kick-off [ˈkɪkɔf] (SPORT) N [s] 开场时间
[kāichǎng shíjiān]

4.3.3 短语动词的词性

VI — 用作不及物动词,动词及其小品词不可分开:

▸ **melt away** VI **1** [*people +*] 逐渐散去 [zhújiàn
sànqù] **2** [*doubts +*] 消除 [xiāochú]

VT — 用作及物动词,动词及其小品词可用宾语隔开。

VT FUS [不可拆分] — 用作及物动词,动词及其小品词不能分开的:

▸ **laugh at** VT FUS [不可拆分] **1** (*lit*) 对⋯发笑
[duì⋯fāxiào] **2** (*fig*) (*mock*) 嘲笑 [cháoxiào]
▸ **laugh off** VT [*+ criticism, problem*] 对⋯一笑置
之 [duì⋯yī xiào zhì zhī]

4.3.4 动词和名词的变体

动词和名词的不规则变化直接列在相关的词条后, 便于查阅:

child [tʃaɪld] (pl **children**) N [C]

fly [flaɪ] (pt **flew**, pp **flown**) I VT

4.4 词义划分

4.4.1 如果一个单词有一个以上的词义, 则归入不同的意类, 用阿拉伯数字标出:

challenging ['tʃælɪndʒɪŋ] ADJ **1** [+*job, task*]
具有挑战性的 [jùyǒu tiǎozhànxìng de]
2 [+*tone, look etc*] 挑衅的 [tiǎoxìn de]

4.4.2 进一步的词义区分在括号中用斜体表示, 包括下列几种情况:

同义词置于在圆括号中, 有助于拓展英语知识。

definitive [dɪ'fɪnɪtɪv] ADJ **1** (*conclusive*)
[+*answer*] 确定的 [quèdìng de] **2** (*authoritative*)
[+*version, account*] 权威性的 [quánwēixìng de]

使用词条的主要语境也置于括号中, 例如:

— 用作及物动词的名词宾语:

tighten ['taɪtn] I VT **1** [+*rope, strap*] 拉紧 [lājǐn]
2 [+*screw, bolt*] 弄紧 [nòngjǐn] **3** [+*grip, security,
rules etc*] 加紧 [jiājǐn] II VI **1** [*grip +*] 握紧

— 用作不及物动词的名词主语:

circulate ['sə:kjuleɪt] I VI [*traffic, blood +*] 循
环 [xúnhuán]; [*news, rumour +*] 散播 [sànbō];
[*person +*] (*at party*) 交际 [jiāojì] II VT [+*report*]
传阅 [chuányuè]

— 用作形容词的名词补足语:

tasteless ['teɪstlɪs] ADJ **1** [+*food*] 无味的
[wúwèi de] **2** [+*remark, joke*] 不雅的 [bùyǎ de]
3 [+*furniture, decor etc*] 低俗的 [dīsú de]

— 其他用于界定或限制该词条的单词:

believer [bɪ'li:və(r)] N [C] **1** (*in idea, activity*)
笃信者 [dǔxìnzhě] **2** (REL) 信徒 [xìntú]

用汉语标注词条的专业学科领域:

bishop ['bɪʃəp] N [C] **1** (REL) 主教 [zhǔjiào]
2 (CHESS) 象 [xiàng]

本词典中所使用的所有专业学科领域缩略词参见第xxxiv页。

4.5 短语

短语用黑体表示,并跟在实心灰色箭头标志 ▶ 后。短语包括不同种类的固定结构,感叹语和其他语法结构:

> **to do something behind sb's back**
> **back and forth**
> **too bad!**
> **on balance**
> **to begin to do** *or* **doing sth**

4.6 例子

例句用斜体表示,并跟在空心箭头标志 ▷ 后。英语中最常用的500个单词,都给出了大量的例子及在相应语境中的翻译,有助于读者在具体的语境中正确使用单词。

> **◇large** [lɑːdʒ] ADJ **1** (*big*) [+ *house, person etc*] 大
> 的 [dà de]; [+ *number, amount*] 大量的 [dàliàng
> de] ▷ *We are facing a large number of problems.* 我
> 们面临大量的问题。▷ *a large number of people*
> 许多人 **2** (*serious*) [+ *problem, question*] 重大
> 的 [zhòngdà de] ▶ **at large** (*as a whole*) 整个
> ▷ *their attitude to the world at large* 他们对整个世
> 界的态度 ▶ **to be at large** 逍遥自在 ▷ *There*
> ...

4.7 翻译

一般情况下,作为最精确、有效的方法,每个意义只提供一个翻译。
在某些情况下,如果根本没有相应的翻译对等语,则提供该词的解释,而不是翻译。

> **au pair** ['əu'pɛə(r),nе] N [C] 为学习语言而住在当
> 地人家里并提供家政服务的外国年轻人

4.8 拼音

词条及动词词组翻译都标注有拼音。如果该词条没有相应的翻译,则给出相关的解释以帮助读者理解,并省略拼音。

5 语体形式

使用正确的语体与人交流是十分重要的。给公司同事写信和给朋友写信需要使用两种不同的语体。为了帮助使用者选择正确恰当的语体,本词典在英汉和汉英两部分都对单词和表达方式作了标注。

修辞色彩缩略语列表见第xxxv页。

6 关键词

对于一些极其常用的词，例如have和do，我们给予了长篇的注释。这类词是构成英语的基本要素，语意众多，用法复杂。本词典对该类词作了特别的外观设计，便于读者查阅。

have [hæv] (*pt, pp* **had**) **I** vt **1** (*possess*) 有 [yǒu] ▶ **he has** *or* **he has got blue eyes/dark hair** 他长着蓝眼睛/黑头发 ▶ **do you have** *or* **have you got a car/phone?** 你有车/电话吗? ▶ **I have** *or* **I have got an idea** 我有个主意 ▶ **to have** *or* **have got sth to do** 有必须得做的事 ▶ **she had her eyes closed** 她闭上了眼睛
2 (*with meals, drinks*) ▶ **to have breakfast** 吃早饭 [chī zǎofàn] ▶ **to have a drink/a cigarette** 喝一杯/抽支烟
3 (*with activity*) ▶ **to have a swim/bath** 游泳/洗澡 [yóuyǒng/xǐzǎo] ▶ **to have a meeting/party** 开会/开派对
…

7 语言注释

为了帮助读者更加准确、熟巧地掌握并运用英语，我们对一些易混淆词进行了详细的比较说明。

用 **fat** 形容某人胖，显得过于直接，甚至有些粗鲁。比较礼貌而又含蓄的说法是 **plump** 或 **chubby**，后者更为正式。**overweight** 和 **obese** 暗示某人因为肥胖而有健康问题。**obese** 是医学术语，表示某人极度肥胖或超重。一般而言，应尽量避免当面使用任何表示肥胖的词语。

8 文化注释

对于英语国家中特有的文化现象，我们都加注了说明及解释。

MISS, MRS, MS

在说英语的国家中，**Mrs**（夫人）用于已婚女士的姓名前。**Miss**（小姐）用于未婚女士的姓名前。有些女士认为，让人们知道她是否结婚并不重要，所以往往用 **Ms**（女士）称呼自己。与 **Mr**（先生）类似，**Ms** 不表明任何婚姻状况。

略语表 / Reference list

▼ 词性 / PARTS OF SPEECH

abbreviation	ABBR	简
adjective	ADJ	形
adverb	ADV	副
auxiliary verb	AUX VB	助动
conjunction	CONJ	连
compound	CPD [复合词]	复合词
definite article	DEF ART	定冠词
indefinite article	INDEF ART	不定冠词
interjection	INT	叹
noun	N	名
noun abbreviation	N ABBR	名词缩写
singular noun	N SING	单数名词
noun (plural)	N(PL)	名词(复数)
noun plural	NPL	复数名词
numeral	NUM	数
plural	PL	复数
plural adjective	PL ADJ	复数形容词
plural pronoun	PL PRON	复数代词
past participle	PP	过去分词
prefix	PREFIX	前缀
preposition	PREP	介
pres part	PRES PART	现在分词
pronoun	PRON	代
past tense	PT	过去时
suffix	SUFFIX	后缀
verb	VB	动
intransitive verb	VI	不及物动词
transitive verb	VT	及物动词
indicates that particle cannot be separated from the main verb	VT FUS [不可拆分]	及物动词[不可拆分]

▼ 专业学科领域 / SUBJECT FIELD LABELS

ADMINISTRATION	ADMIN	行政		BOTANY	BOT	植
AGRICULTURE	AGR	农		BOWLS		滚木球
ANATOMY	ANAT	解剖		BOXING		拳击
ARCHITECTURE	ARCHIT	建筑		CARDS		纸牌
ART		艺术		CHEMISTRY	CHEM	化
ASTROLOGY	ASTROL	占星术		CHESS		国际象棋
ASTRONOMY	ASTRON	天文		CINEMA	CINE	电影
MOTORING	AUT	汽车		CLIMBING		登山
AVIATION	AVIAT	航空		CLOTHING		服饰
BADMINTON		羽毛球		COMMERCE	COMM	商
BASEBALL		棒球		COMPUTING	COMPUT	计算机
BIOLOGY	BIO	生物		CRICKET		板球
BOOKKEEPING		簿记		COOKING	CULIN	烹饪

DRAWING		绘画	PHILOSOPHY	PHIL	哲
DRUGS		药品	PHOTOGRAPHY	PHOT	摄影
ECONOMICS	ECON	经济	PHYSICS	PHYS	物
ELECTRICITY	ELEC	电子	PHYSIOLOGY	PHYSIOL	生理
FENCING		击剑	POLITICS	POL	政治
FINANCE	FIN	金融	POLICE		警察
FISHING		钓鱼	POST OFFICE	POST	邮政
FOOTBALL		足球	PSYCHOLOGY	PSYCH	心理
GEOGRAPHY	GEO	地理	PUBLISHING		出版
GEOLOGY	GEOL	地质	RADIO	RAD	广播
GEOMETRY	GEOM	几何	RAILWAYS	RAIL	铁路
GOLF		高尔夫	RELIGION	REL	宗
GRAMMAR	GRAM	语法	RUGBY		橄榄球
HISTORY	HIST	历史	SCIENCE	SCI	科学
INDUSTRY	IND	工业	SCHOOL	SCOL	教育
INSURANCE		保险	SEWING		缝纫
LAW		法	SOCIOLOGY	SOCIOL	社会
LINGUISTICS	LING	语言	SPACE		宇航
LITERATURE	LITER	文学	SPORT		体育
MATHEMATICS	MATH	数	TECHNICAL USAGE	TECH	术语
MEDICINE	MED	医	TELECOMMUNICATIONS	TEL	电信
METEOROLOGY	MET	气象	TENNIS		网球
MILITARY	MIL	军	TEXTING		手机短信
MINING	MIN	矿	THEATRE	THEAT	戏剧
MUSIC	MUS	音	TELEVISION	TV	电视
MYTHOLOGY	MYTH	神	UNIVERSITY	UNIV	大学
NAUTICAL	NAUT	航海	ZOOLOGY	ZOOL	动
PARLIAMENT	PARL	议会			

▼ 修辞色彩缩略语 / REGISTER LABELS

dialect		方
euphemism		婉
formal	*frm*	正式
formerly		旧
humorous		诙谐
informal	*inf*	非正式
literary	*liter*	文
offensive		侮辱
old-fashioned	*o.f.*	过时
offensive	*inf!*	疑讳 / 讳
pejorative	*pej*	贬
humble		谦
respectful		敬
slang		俚
spoken language		口
written		书
polite		客套
literal	*lit*	字
figurative	*fig*	喻

发音简表 / Guide to English phonetics

▼ 辅音 / CONSONANTS

[p]	puppy		[f]	farm raffle
[b]	baby		[v]	very rev
[t]	tent		[θ]	thin maths
[d]	daddy		[ð]	that other
[k]	cork kiss chord		[l]	little ball
[g]	gag guess		[r]	rat rare
[s]	so rice kiss		[m]	mummy comb
[z]	cousin buzz		[n]	no ran
[ʃ]	sheep sugar		[ŋ]	singing bank
[ʒ]	pleasure beige		[h]	hat reheat
[tʃ]	church		[x]	loch
[dʒ]	judge general			

▼ 半元音 / SEMIVOWELS

[j]	yet		[w]	wet

▼ 元音 / VOWELS

[iː]	heel		[ə]	over above
[ɪ]	hit pity		[əː]	urn fern work
[ɛ]	set tent		[ɔ]	wash pot
[æ]	bat apple		[ɔː]	born cork
[ɑː]	after car calm		[u]	full soot
[ʌ]	fun cousin		[uː]	pool lewd

▼ 双元音 / DIPHTHONGS

[ɪə]	beer tier		[au]	owl foul now
[ɛə]	tear fair there		[əu]	low no
[eɪ]	date plaice day		[ɔɪ]	boil boy oily
[aɪ]	life buy cry		[uə]	poor tour

不规则动词 / English irregular verbs

Present	Past tense	Past participle
arise	arose	arisen
awake	awoke	awoken
be (am, is, are; being)	was, were	been
bear	bore	born(e)
beat	beat	beaten
become	became	become
begin	began	begun
bend	bent	bent
bet	bet, betted	bet, betted
bid (at auction, cards)	bid	bid
bid (say)	bade	bidden
bind	bound	bound
bite	bit	bitten
bleed	bled	bled
blow	blew	blown
break	broke	broken
breed	bred	bred
bring	brought	brought
build	built	built
burn	burnt, burned	burnt, burned
burst	burst	burst
buy	bought	bought
can	could	(been able)
cast	cast	cast
catch	caught	caught
choose	chose	chosen
cling	clung	clung
come	came	come
cost	cost	cost
cost (work out price of)	costed	costed
creep	crept	crept
cut	cut	cut
deal	dealt	dealt
dig	dug	dug
do (does)	did	done
draw	drew	drawn
dream	dreamed, dreamt	dreamed, dreamt
drink	drank	drunk
drive	drove	driven
dwell	dwelt	dwelt
eat	ate	eaten

Present	Past tense	Past participle
fall	fell	fallen
feed	fed	fed
feel	felt	felt
fight	fought	fought
find	found	found
flee	fled	fled
fling	flung	flung
fly	flew	flown
forbid	forbad(e)	forbidden
forecast	forecast	forecast
forget	forgot	forgotten
forgive	forgave	forgiven
forsake	forsook	forsaken
freeze	froze	frozen
get	got	got, (美) gotten
give	gave	given
go (goes)	went	gone
grind	ground	ground
grow	grew	grown
hang	hung	hung
hang (execute)	hanged	hanged
have	had	had
hear	heard	heard
hide	hid	hidden
hit	hit	hit
hold	held	held
hurt	hurt	hurt
keep	kept	kept
kneel	knelt, kneeled	knelt, kneeled
know	knew	known
lay	laid	laid
lead	led	led
lean	leant, leaned	leant, leaned
leap	leapt, leaped	leapt, leaped
learn	learnt, learned	learnt, learned
leave	left	left
lend	lent	lent
let	let	let
lie (lying)	lay	lain
light	lit, lighted	lit, lighted
lose	lost	lost
make	made	made

不规则动词 / English irregular verbs

Present	Past tense	Past participle	Present	Past tense	Past participle
may	might	—	**spell**	spelt, spelled	spelt, spelled
mean	meant	meant	**spend**	spent	spent
meet	met	met	**spill**	spilt, spilled	spilt, spilled
mistake	mistook	mistaken	**spin**	spun	spun
mow	mowed	mown, mowed	**spit**	spat	spat
must	(had to)	(had to)	**spoil**	spoiled, spoilt	spoiled, spoilt
pay	paid	paid	**spread**	spread	spread
put	put	put	**spring**	sprang	sprung
quit	quit, quitted	quit, quitted	**stand**	stood	stood
read	read	read	**steal**	stole	stolen
rid	rid	rid	**stick**	stuck	stuck
ride	rode	ridden	**sting**	stung	stung
ring	rang	rung	**stink**	stank	stunk
rise	rose	risen	**stride**	strode	stridden
run	ran	run	**strike**	struck	struck
say	said	said	**strive**	strove	striven
see	saw	seen	**swear**	swore	sworn
seek	sought	sought	**sweep**	swept	swept
sell	sold	sold	**swell**	swelled	swollen, swelled
send	sent	sent	**swim**	swam	swum
set	set	set	**swing**	swung	swung
sew	sewed	sewn	**take**	took	taken
shake	shook	shaken	**teach**	taught	taught
shear	sheared	shorn, sheared	**tear**	tore	torn
shed	shed	shed	**tell**	told	told
shine	shone	shone	**think**	thought	thought
shoot	shot	shot	**throw**	threw	thrown
show	showed	shown	**thrust**	thrust	thrust
shrink	shrank	shrunk	**tread**	trod	trodden
shut	shut	shut	**wake**	woke, waked	woken, waked
sing	sang	sung	**wear**	wore	worn
sink	sank	sunk	**weave**	wove	woven
sit	sat	sat	**weave** *(wind)*	weaved	weaved
slay	slew	slain	**wed**	wedded, wed	wedded, wed
sleep	slept	slept	**weep**	wept	wept
slide	slid	slid	**win**	won	won
sling	slung	slung	**wind**	wound	wound
slit	slit	slit	**wring**	wrung	wrung
smell	smelt, smelled	smelt, smelled	**write**	wrote	written
sow	sowed	sown, sowed			
speak	spoke	spoken			
speed	sped, speeded	sped, speeded			

部 首 检 字 表
RADICAL INDEX

检字方法说明:

(1) 根据字的部首在部首目录中查到该部首所在检字表中的号码;

(2) 按此号码在检字表中找到该部首,并根据字的笔画(字的笔画数不含其部首)查到该字的汉语拼音。

How to use this index:

(1) Use pages 1 and 2 to identify the radical. Note the number preceding it.

(2) In the index on pages 3-36, use this number to find all the characters appearing in this dictionary which contain the radical. Characters are ordered according to the number of strokes. The pinyin given will lead you to the correct entry.

部 首 目 录

(63) 弓	(99) 文	(132) 老(耂)	**八 画**
(64) 子	(100) 方	(133) 耳	
(65) 女	(101) 火	(134) 西(覀)	
(66) 纟	(102) 斗	(135) 页	(166) 青
(67) 马	(103) 灬	(136) 虍	(167) 雨
(68) 幺	(104) 户	(137) 虫	(168) 齿
(69) 巛	(105) 礻	(138) 缶	(169) 隹
	(106) 心	(139) 舌	(170) 金
四 画	(107) 聿(肀)	(140) 竹(⺮)	(171) 鱼
	(108) 冊(毋母)	(141) 臼	
(70) 王		(142) 自	**九 画**
(71) 韦	**五 画**	(143) 血	
(72) 木		(144) 舟	(172) 革
(73) 犬	(109) 示	(145) 衣	(173) 骨
(74) 歹	(110) 石	(146) 羊	(174) 鬼
(75) 车	(111) 龙	(147) 米	(175) 食
(76) 戈	(112) 业	(148) 艮	(176) 音
(77) 比	(113) 目	(149) 羽	
(78) 瓦	(114) 田	(150) 糸	**十 画**
(79) 止	(115) 罒		
(80) 攴	(116) 皿	**七 画**	(177) 髟
(81) 日	(117) 钅		
(82) 曰	(118) 矢	(151) 走	**十一画**
(83) 水	(119) 禾	(152) 赤	
(84) 贝	(120) 白	(153) 豆	(178) 麻
(85) 见	(121) 瓜	(154) 酉	(179) 鹿
(86) 牛(牛)	(122) 用	(155) 辰	
(87) 手	(123) 鸟	(156) 卤	**十二画**
(88) 毛	(124) 疒	(157) 里	
(89) 气	(125) 立	(158) 足	(180) 黑
(90) 攵	(126) 穴	(159) 身	
(91) 片	(127) 衤	(160) 釆	**十三画**
(92) 斤	(128) 疋	(161) 谷	
(93) 爪(爫)	(129) 皮	(162) 豸	(181) 鼠
(94) 父	(130) 矛	(163) 角	
(95) 月		(164) 言(訁	**十四画**
(96) 欠	**六 画**	见讠)	
(97) 风		(165) 辛	(182) 鼻
(98) 殳	(131) 耒		

检 字 表

（1）
一 部

一　　　yī
一画
丁　　　dīng
七　　　qī
二画
三　　　sān
干　　gān；gàn
于　　　yú
下　　　xià
丈　　　zhàng
与　　　yǔ
才　　　cái
万　　　wàn
上　　　shàng
三画
丰　　　fēng
井　　　jǐng
开　　　kāi
夫　　　fū
天　　　tiān
无　　　wú
专　　　zhuān
丐　　　gài
五　　　wǔ
不　　　bù
屯　　　tún
互　　　hù
牙　　　yá
丑　　　chǒu
四画
末　　　mò
未　　　wèi
击　　　jī
正　　　zhēng

---

zhèng
甘　　　gān
世　　　shì
可　　　kě
丙　　　bǐng
平　　　píng
东　　　dōng
且　　　qiě
册　　　cè
丝　　　sī
五画
亚　　　yà
亘　　　gèn
更　　　lì
再　　　zài
百　　　bǎi
而　　　ér
夹　　gā；jiā；jiá
六画
严　　　yán
巫　　　wū
更　gēng；gèng
束　　　shù
两　　　liǎng
丽　　　lì
来　　　lái
求　　　qiú
七画
表　　　biǎo
事　　　shì
枣　　　zǎo
八画
奏　　　zòu
甚　　　shèn
巷　hàng；xiàng
柬　　　jiǎn
歪　　　wāi
面　　　miàn

韭　　　jiǔ
昼　　　zhòu
九画
艳　　　yàn
哥　　　gē
孬　　　nāo
十一画
棘　　　jí
十五画
噩　　　è
整　　　zhěng
臻　　　zhēn
二十一画
囊　　　náng

（2）
丨 部

三画
中　　　zhōng
　　　　zhòng
内　　　nèi
四画
北　　　běi
凸　　　tū
旧　　　jiù
甲　　　jiǎ
申　　　shēn
电　　　diàn
由　　　yóu
史　　　shǐ
央　　　yāng
冉　　　rǎn
凹　　　āo
出　　　chū
五画
师　　　shī
曳　　　yè
曲　　qū；qǔ

肉　　　ròu
六画
串　　　chuàn
七画
非　　　fēi
畅　　　chàng
八画
临　　　lín

（3）
丿 部

一画
九　　　jiǔ
匕　　　bǐ
乃　　　nǎi
二画
千　　　qiān
川　　　chuān
及　　　jí
久　　　jiǔ
三画
午　　　wǔ
升　　　shēng
夭　　　yāo
长　　　cháng
　　　　zhǎng
币　　　bì
反　　　fǎn
乏　　　fá
氏　　　shì
丹　　　dān
乌　　　wū
四画
生　　　shēng
失　　　shī
乍　　　zhà
丘　　　qiū
甩　　　shuǎi

乐	lè；yuè	**二画**		书	shū	**五画**	
五画		义	yì	**四画**		克	kè
年	nián	丸	wán	司	sī	**六画**	
朱	zhū	丫	yā	民	mín	直	zhí
丢	diū	之	zhī	**五画**		丧	sāng；sàng
乔	qiáo	**三画**		尽	jǐn；jìn	卖	mài
乒	pīng	为	wéi；wèi	买	mǎi	卓	zhuó
乓	pāng	**四画**		**六画**		卑	bēi
向	xiàng	主	zhǔ	乱	luàn	**七画**	
后	hòu	半	bàn	**七画**		南	nán
兆	zhào	头	tóu	乳	rǔ	**八画**	
六画		**五画**		肃	sù	真	zhēn
我	wǒ	州	zhōu	承	chéng	**九画**	
每	měi	兴	xīng；xìng	亟	jí；qì	乾	qián
龟	guī；jūn	农	nóng	**八画**		啬	sè
卵	luǎn	**六画**		胤	zhǐ	**十画**	
系	jì；xì	良	liáng			博	bó
七画		**七画**		**(6)**		**十二画**	
垂	chuí	学	xué	**二 部**		斡	wò
乘	guāi	**八画**				兢	jīng
秉	bǐng	叛	pàn	二	èr	**二十二画**	
质	zhì	举	jǔ	**一画**		矗	chù
周	zhōu			亏	kuī		
八画		**(5)**		**二画**		**(8)**	
拜	bài	**乙（乚ㄑ**		元	yuán	**厂 部**	
重	chóng	**ㄱ）部**		云	yún		
	zhòng	乙	yǐ	**六画**		厂	chǎng
复	fù	**一画**		些	xiē	**二画**	
九画		刁	diāo			厅	tīng
乘	chéng	了	liǎo	**(7)**		历	lì
十一画		**二画**		**十 部**		厄	è
甥	shēng	乞	qǐ			**三画**	
十三画		也	yě	十	shí	厉	lì
舞	wǔ	飞	fēi	**二画**		**四画**	
疑	yí	习	xí	支	zhī	压	yā；yà
孵	fū	子	jié	**三画**		厌	yàn
十四画		乡	xiāng	卉	huì	**五画**	
靠	kào	**三画**		古	gǔ	励	lì
		尺	chǐ	**四画**		**六画**	
(4)		巴	bā	考	kǎo	厕	cè
丶 部		予	yǔ	协	xié	**七画**	
		孔	kǒng	毕	bì	厘	lí
				华	huá	厚	hòu

八画		创	chuāng	———————		代	dài
原	yuán		chuàng	(11)		付	fù
九画		刎	wěn	**卜 部**		仙	xiān
厢	xiāng	刘	liú			仟	qiān
厩	jiù	**五画**		卜	bo；bǔ	仪	yí
十画		别	bié；biè	**三画**		他	tā
厨	chú	利	lì	卡	kǎ；qiǎ	仔	zǐ
厦	shà	删	shān	占	zhān；zhàn	**四画**	
雁	yàn	刨	bào；páo	外	wài	伟	wěi
厥	jué	判	pàn	**四画**		传	chuán
十四画		**六画**		贞	zhēn		zhuàn
赝	yàn	刺	cī；cì	**六画**		休	xiū
		到	dào	卦	guà	伍	wǔ
(9)		制	zhì	卧	wò	伎	jì
匚 部		刮	guā	**八画**		伏	fú
		刽	guì	桌	zhuō	优	yōu
二画		刹	chà；shā			伐	fá
区	qū	剁	duò	(12)		仲	zhòng
匹	pǐ	剂	jì	**冂 部**		件	jiàn
巨	jù	刻	kè			任	rèn
四画		刷	shuā；shuà	**二画**		伤	shāng
臣	chén	**七画**		冈	gāng	价	jià
匠	jiàng	荆	jīng	**四画**		伦	lún
五画		削	xiāo；xuē	同	tóng	份	fèn
匣	xiá	剐	guǎ	网	wǎng	仰	yǎng
医	yī	剑	jiàn			忼	kàng
八画		前	qián	(13)		仿	fǎng
匿	nì	剃	tì	**亻 部**		伙	huǒ
匪	fěi	**八画**		**一画**		伪	wěi
九画		剔	tī	亿	yì	仁	zhù
匮	kuì	剖	pōu	**二画**		伊	yī
		剜	wān	仁	rén	似	shì；sì
(10)		剥	bāo；bō	什	shén；shí	**五画**	
刂 部		剧	jù	仆	pú	估	gū
		九画		仇	chóu	体	tǐ
三画		副	fù	化	huà	何	hé
刊	kān	**十画**		仍	réng	佐	zuǒ
四画		剩	shèng	仅	jǐn	但	dàn
刑	xíng	割	gē	**三画**		伸	shēn
列	liè	**十一画**		仨	sā	作	zuō；zuò
划	huá；huà	剽	piāo	仕	shì	伯	bó
刚	gāng	**十三画**		仗	zhàng	伶	líng
则	zé	劐	huō				

佣	yōng;yòng	俭	jiǎn	傧	bīn	首	shǒu
低	dī	俗	sú	储	chǔ	**八画**	
你	nǐ	俘	fú	**十一画**		翁	wēng
住	zhù	信	xìn	催	cuī	益	yì
位	wèi	侵	qīn	傻	shǎ	兼	jiān
伴	bàn	侯	hóu	像	xiàng	**九画**	
伺	cì;sì	俑	yǒng	**十二画**		黄	huáng
佛	fó	俊	jùn	僚	liáo	兽	shòu
六画		**八画**		僧	sēng	**十画**	
佳	jiā	俸	fèng	**十三画**		普	pǔ
侍	shì	债	zhài	僵	jiāng	奠	diàn
佬	lǎo	借	jiè	僻	pì	曾	céng;zēng
供	gōng;gòng	偌	ruò	**十四画**		**十二画**	
使	shǐ	值	zhí	儒	rú	舆	yú
佰	bǎi	倚	yǐ			**十四画**	
例	lì	倾	qīng	**(14)**		冀	jì
侠	xiá	倒	dǎo;dào	**八 部**			
侥	jiǎo	倘	tǎng			**(15)**	
侄	zhí	俱	jù	八	bā	**人（入）部**	
侦	zhēn	倡	chàng	**二画**			
侣	lǚ	候	hòu	分	fēn;fèn	人	rén
侃	kǎn	俯	fǔ	公	gōng	入	rù
侧	cè	倍	bèi	**三画**		**一画**	
侏	zhū	倦	juàn	只	zhī;zhǐ	个	gè
侨	qiáo	健	jiàn	兰	lán	**二画**	
佩	pèi	倔	jué;juè	**四画**		介	jiè
侈	chǐ	**九画**		共	gòng	从	cóng
佼	jiǎo	做	zuò	并	bìng	今	jīn
依	yī	偃	yǎn	关	guān	仓	cāng
佯	yáng	偕	xié	**五画**		以	yǐ
七画		偿	cháng	兵	bīng	**三画**	
俨	yǎn	偶	ǒu	谷	gǔ	丛	cóng
便	biàn;pián	假	wēi	兑	duì	令	lìng
俩	liǎ	傀	kuǐ	弟	dì	**四画**	
俪	lì	偷	tōu	**六画**		全	quán
修	xiū	停	tíng	其	qí	会	huì;kuài
俏	qiào	偏	piān	具	jù	合	hé
俚	lǐ	假	jiǎ;jià	典	diǎn	企	qǐ
保	bǎo	**十画**		卷	juǎn;juàn	众	zhòng
促	cù	傲	ào	单	dān	伞	sǎn
俄	é	傅	fù	**七画**		余	tǔn
侮	wǔ	傍	bàng	养	yǎng	**五画**	
				酋	qiú	余	yú

含 hán	凫 fú	**五画**	斗 dǒu；dòu	
六画	**五画**	亨 hēng	**四画**	
舍 shě；shè	壳 ké；qiào	弃 qì	冲 chōng	
命 mìng	秃 tū	**六画**	chòng	
八画	**六画**	变 biàn	次 cì	
拿 ná	咒 zhòu	京 jīng	决 jué	
九画	凯 kǎi	享 xiǎng	冰 bīng	
盒 hé	凭 píng	夜 yè	**五画**	
十画	**十二画**	**七画**	冻 dòng	
舒 shū	凳 dèng	哀 āi	况 kuàng	
禽 qín		亭 tíng	冷 lěng	
	(18)	亮 liàng	冶 yě	
(16)	**儿 部**	帝 dì	**六画**	
勹 部		**八画**	净 jìng	
	儿 ér	衰 shuāi	**八画**	
一画	**二画**	衷 zhōng	凌 líng	
勺 sháo	允 yǔn	高 gāo	凄 qī	
二画	**三画**	离 lí	准 zhǔn	
勿 wù	兄 xiōng	旁 páng	凋 diāo	
匀 yún	**四画**	**九画**	凉 liáng；liàng	
勾 gōu；gòu	光 guāng	毫 háo	**九画**	
三画	先 xiān	烹 pēng	凑 còu	
句 jù	**八画**	商 shāng	减 jiǎn	
匆 cōng	党 dǎng	率 shuài	**十画**	
包 bāo	**九画**	**十画**	寒 hán	
四画	兜 dōu	襄 xiè	**十三画**	
旬 xún		就 jiù	凛 lǐn	
七画	**(19)**	**十一画**	**十四画**	
匍 pú	**亠 部**	禀 bǐng	凝 níng	
九画		雍 yōng		
够 gòu	**一画**	**十二画**	**(21)**	
	亡 wáng	裹 guǒ	**冖 部**	
(17)	**二画**	豪 háo		
几 部	六 liù	膏 gāo	**二画**	
	亢 kàng	**十三画**	冗 rǒng	
几 jī；jǐ	**三画**	襃 bāo	**三画**	
一画	市 shì	**十五画**	写 xiě	
凡 fán	玄 xuán	襄 xiāng	**四画**	
二画	**四画**	赢 yíng	军 jūn	
凤 fèng	交 jiāo		**五画**	
四画	产 chǎn	**(20)**	罕 hǎn	
朵 duǒ	充 chōng	**冫 部**	**七画**	
夙 sù	妄 wàng		冠 guān；guàn	

十一画		刀	dāo	助	zhù	劝	quàn
障	zhàng	**一画**		男	nán	双	shuāng
十二画		刃	rèn	努	nǔ	**三画**	
隧	suì	**二画**		劲	jìn;jìng	发	fā;fà
		切	qiē;qiè	**六画**		圣	shèng
(25)		**三画**		势	shì	对	duì
阝(在右)部		刍	chú	**七画**		**四画**	
		召	zhào	勃	bó	戏	xì
四画		**四画**		勋	xūn	观	guān
邦	bāng	负	fù	勉	miǎn	欢	huān
邪	xié	争	zhēng	勇	yǒng	**五画**	
那	nà	色	sè;shǎi	**九画**		鸡	jī
五画		**五画**		勘	kān	**六画**	
邮	yóu	免	miǎn	**十一画**		取	qǔ
邻	lín	初	chū	勤	qín	叔	shū
六画		**六画**				受	shòu
耶	yē	兔	tù	**(29)**		艰	jiān
郁	yù	券	quàn	**厶部**		**七画**	
郊	jiāo	**九画**				叙	xù
郑	zhèng	象	xiàng	**三画**		**八画**	
郎	láng	剪	jiǎn	去	qù	难	nán;nàn
八画		**十一画**		台	tái	桑	sāng
都	dōu;dū	赖	lài	**四画**		**九画**	
部	bù	**十三画**		牟	móu;mù	曼	màn
十一画		劈	pī;pǐ	**五画**		**十一画**	
鄙	bǐ			县	xiàn	叠	dié
		(28)		**六画**			
(26)		**力部**		叁	sān	**(31)**	
凵部				参	cān	**廴部**	
		力	lì		cēn		
二画		**二画**			shēn	**四画**	
凶	xiōng	办	bàn	**八画**		廷	tíng
六画		**三画**		畚	běn	延	yán
画	huà	功	gōng	能	néng	**六画**	
函	hán	夯	hāng			建	jiàn
七画		务	wù	**(30)**			
幽	yōu	加	jiā	**又部**		**(32)**	
十画		**四画**				**工部**	
凿	záo	动	dòng	又	yòu		
		劣	liè	**一画**		工	gōng
(27)		**五画**		叉	chā;chǎ	**二画**	
刀部		劫	jié	**二画**		巧	qiǎo
		劳	láo	友	yǒu	左	zuǒ

三画		坤	kūn	赫	hè	扑	pū
式	shì	垃	lā	境	jìng	扒	bā;pá
巩	gǒng	幸	xìng	**十二画**		扔	rēng
四画		坨	tuó	墩	dūn	**三画**	
贡	gòng	坡	pō	增	zēng	扛	káng
攻	gōng	垄	lǒng	墨	mò	扣	kòu
六画		**六画**		**十三画**		托	tuō
项	xiàng	型	xíng	雍	yōng	执	zhí
差	chā	垮	kuǎ	壁	bì	扩	kuò
	chà	城	chéng	**十四画**		扪	mén
	chāi	垢	gòu	壕	háo	扫	sǎo;sào
		垛	duò	壑	hè	扬	yáng
(33)		垩	è	**十六画**		**四画**	
土 部		垫	diàn	疆	jiāng	扶	fú
		垦	kěn	**十七画**		抚	fǔ
土	tǔ	垒	lěi	壤	rǎng	技	jì
三画		**七画**				抠	kōu
寺	sì	埋	mái	(34)		扰	rǎo
地	de;dì	埃	āi	**士 部**		扼	è
场	cháng	**八画**				拒	jù
	chǎng	堵	dǔ	士	shì	找	zhǎo
在	zài	域	yù	**三画**		批	pī
至	zhì	堆	duī	吉	jí	扯	chě
尘	chén	埠	bù	**四画**		抄	chāo
四画		培	péi	声	shēng	折	shé
坛	tán	基	jī	**七画**			zhē
坏	huài	堑	qiàn	壶	hú		zhé
坝	bà	堂	táng	**九画**		抓	zhuā
坎	kǎn	堕	duò	喜	xǐ	扳	bān
坍	tān	**九画**		壹	yī	抡	lūn
均	jūn	塔	dɑ;tǎ	**十画**		扮	bàn
坞	wù	堤	dī	鼓	gǔ	抢	qiǎng
坟	fén	堡	bǎo	**十一画**		抑	yì
坑	kēng	**十画**		嘉	jiā	抛	pāo
坊	fáng	填	tián	**十七画**		投	tóu
块	kuài	塌	tā	馨	xīn	抗	kàng
坚	jiān	塘	táng			抖	dǒu
坐	zuò	墓	mù	(35)		护	hù
社	shè	塑	sù	**扌 部**		抉	jué
坠	zhuì	**十一画**				扭	niǔ
五画		墙	qiáng	**一画**		把	bǎ;bà
坪	píng	墟	xū	扎	zā;zhā	报	bào
坦	tǎn			**二画**			
				打	dá;dǎ		

拟	nǐ	拷	kǎo	**八画**		援	yuán
抒	shū	拱	gǒng	捧	pěng	搀	chān
五画		挎	kuà	措	cuò	搁	gē；gé
抹	mā；mǒ	挟	xié	描	miáo	搓	cuō
拓	tuò	挠	náo	捺	nà	搂	lōu；lǒu
拢	lǒng	挡	dǎng	掩	yǎn	搅	jiǎo
拔	bá	拽	zhuài	捷	jié	握	wò
抨	pēng	挺	tǐng	排	pái	摒	bìng
拣	jiǎn	括	kuò	掉	diào	搔	sāo
担	dān；dàn	拴	shuān	掳	lǔ	揉	róu
押	yā	拾	shí	捶	chuí	**十画**	
抻	chēn	挑	tiāo；tiǎo	推	tuī	摄	shè
抽	chōu	指	zhǐ	掀	xiān	摸	mō
拐	guǎi	挣	zhēng；zhèng	授	shòu	搏	bó
拖	tuō			掏	tāo	摁	èn
拊	fǔ	挤	jǐ	掐	qiā	摆	bǎi
拍	pāi	拼	pīn	掬	jū	携	xié
拆	chāi	挖	wā	掠	lüè	搬	bān
拎	līn	按	àn	掂	diān	摇	yáo
拥	yōng	挥	huī	掖	yē；yè	搞	gǎo
抵	dǐ	挪	nuó	接	jiē	搪	táng
拘	jū	**七画**		掷	zhì	摈	bìn
抱	bào	捞	lāo	掸	dǎn	摊	tān
拉	lā；là	捕	bǔ	控	kòng	**十一画**	
拦	lán	捂	wǔ	探	tàn	撇	piē；piě
拌	bàn	振	zhèn	据	jū；jù	撩	liào
拧	níng；nìng	捎	shāo	掘	jué	摞	luò
抿	mǐn	捍	hàn	掺	chān	摧	cuī
拂	fú	捏	niē	掇	duō	摘	zhāi
拙	zhuō	捉	zhuō	**九画**		摔	shuāi
招	zhāo	捆	kǔn	揍	zòu	**十二画**	
披	pī	捐	juān	搭	dā	撵	niǎn
拨	bō	损	sǔn	搽	chá	撕	sī
择	zé；zhái	捌	bā	揠	yà	撒	sā；sǎ
抬	tái	捡	jiǎn	揩	kāi	撅	juē
拇	mǔ	挫	cuò	揽	lǎn	撩	liāo；liáo
拗	ào；niù	捋	lǚ；luō	提	dī；tí	撑	chēng
六画		换	huàn	揭	jiē	撮	cuō
拭	shì	挽	wǎn	揣	chuāi；chuǎi	撬	qiào
挂	guà	捣	dǎo	插	chā	播	bō
持	chí	捅	tǒng	揪	jiū	擒	qín
拮	jié	挨	āi；ái	搜	sōu	撞	zhuàng

撤	chè	苦	kǔ	荷	hé;hè	蓄	xù
撰	zhuàn	苛	kē	莅	lì	蒙	mēng
十三画		若	ruò	获	huò		méng
擀	gǎn	茂	mào	**八画**			Měng
撼	hàn	苹	píng	菁	jīng	蒸	zhēng
擂	lèi	苗	miáo	著	zhù	**十一画**	
操	cāo	英	yīng	菱	líng	蔫	niān
擅	shàn	苟	gǒu	萋	qī	蔷	qiáng
十四画		苑	yuàn	菲	fēi	蔽	bì
擦	cā	苞	bāo	萌	méng	暮	mù
十六画		范	fàn	萝	luó	摹	mó
攒	cuán;zǎn	茁	zhuó	菌	jūn	蔓	màn
二十画		茄	jiā;qié	萎	wěi	蔑	miè
攫	jué	茎	jīng	菜	cài	蔗	zhè
		苔	tái	菊	jú	蔼	ǎi
(36)		茅	máo	萃	cuì	蔚	wèi
艹 部		**六画**		菩	pú	**十二画**	
		茸	róng	萍	píng	蕉	jiāo
一画		茬	chá	菠	bō	蕊	ruǐ
艺	yì	荐	jiàn	萤	yíng	蔬	shū
二画		草	cǎo	营	yíng	蕴	yùn
艾	ài	茧	jiǎn	萦	yíng	**十三画**	
节	jiē;jié	茵	yīn	萧	xiāo	蕾	lěi
三画		茴	huí	菇	gū	薯	shǔ
芋	yù	荞	qiáo	**九画**		薪	xīn
芝	zhī	荏	rěn	葫	hú	薄	báo;bó;bò
四画		荟	huì	葬	zàng	**十四画**	
芙	fú	茶	chá	募	mù	藏	cáng;zàng
芜	wú	荒	huāng	董	dǒng	藐	miǎo
苇	wěi	茫	máng	葆	bǎo	**十五画**	
芸	yún	荡	dàng	葡	pú	藕	ǒu
芽	yá	荣	róng	葱	cōng	藤	téng
花	huā	荤	hūn	蒂	dì	**十六画**	
芹	qín	荧	yíng	落	là;lào;luò	蘖	niè
芥	jiè	荫	yìn	葵	kuí	蘑	mó
芬	fēn	荔	lì	**十画**		**十九画**	
苍	cāng	药	yào	蒜	suàn	蘸	zhàn
芳	fāng	**七画**		蓝	lán		
芦	lú	莽	mǎng	幕	mù	**(37)**	
芭	bā	莲	lián	蓦	mò	**寸 部**	
苏	sū	莫	mò	蓓	bèi		
五画		莴	wō	蓬	péng	寸	cùn
茉	mò						

三画		五画		四画		名	míng
寻	xún	奉	fèng	肖	xiào	四画	
导	dǎo	奔	bēn;bèn	五画		吞	tūn
四画		奇	jī;qí	尚	shàng	否	fǒu
寿	shòu	奄	yǎn	六画		呈	chéng
六画		奋	fèn	省	shěng;xǐng	呓	yì
封	fēng	态	tài	尝	cháng	呆	dāi
耐	nài	六画		八画		吱	zhī
七画		契	qì	雀	què	吠	fèi
辱	rǔ	奓	dā	常	cháng	呕	ǒu
射	shè	牵	qiān	九画		吨	dūn
九画		美	měi	辉	huī	呀	yā
尊	zūn	奖	jiǎng	赏	shǎng	吵	chǎo
十四画		七画		掌	zhǎng	呐	nà
爵	jué	套	tào	十七画		员	yuán
		奚	xī	耀	yào	听	tīng
(38)		八画				吟	yín
弋部		奢	shē	(43)		吩	fēn
		爽	shuǎng	**口部**		呛	qiāng;qiàng
六画		九画				吻	wěn
贰	èr	奥	ào	口	kǒu	吹	chuī
		十二画		二画		呜	wū
(39)		樊	fán	右	yòu	吭	háng;kēng
廾(在下)部				叶	yè	吧	bā
		(41)		叮	dīng	吮	shǔn
三画		**尢部**		号	háo;hào	吼	hǒu
异	yì			叱	chì	告	gào
四画		一画		叽	jī	吝	lìn
弄	nòng	尤	yóu	叼	diāo	启	qǐ
十一画		二画		叫	jiào	君	jūn
弊	bì	龙	lóng	另	lìng	五画	
		十画		叨	dāo	味	wèi
(40)		尴	gān	叹	tàn	哎	āi
大部				三画		咕	gū
		(42)		吁	xū;yū	呵	hē
大	dà;dài	**小部**		吐	tǔ;tù	咂	zā
一画		小	xiǎo	吓	hè;xià	呸	pēi
太	tài	一画		吊	diào	咀	jǔ
三画		少	shǎo;shào	吃	chī	呻	shēn
夸	kuā	二画		吸	xī	呷	xiā
夺	duó	尔	ěr	吗	mǎ;ma	咋	zǎ;zé;zhā
夷	yí	三画		吆	yāo		
尖	jiān	当	dāng;dàng	各	gè		

希	xī	**七画**		徐	xú	**四画**		
五画		峭	qiào	**八画**		狂	kuáng	
帖	tiē;tiě;tiè	峰	fēng	徜	cháng	犹	yóu	
帜	zhì	峻	jùn	得	dé;de;děi	**五画**		
帕	pà	**八画**		衔	xián	狙	jū	
帛	bó	崖	yá	**九画**		狐	hú	
帘	lián	崎	qí	街	jiē	狗	gǒu	
帚	zhǒu	崭	zhǎn	御	yù	狞	níng	
六画		崩	bēng	循	xún	狒	fèi	
帮	bāng	崇	chóng	**十画**		**六画**		
带	dài	崛	jué	微	wēi	狭	xiá	
八画		**九画**		**十二画**		狮	shī	
帷	wéi	嵌	qiàn	德	dé	独	dú	
九画		嵗	wǎi	**十三画**		狰	zhēng	
幅	fú	**十二画**		衡	héng	狡	jiǎo	
帽	mào	嶙	lín	**十四画**		狩	shòu	
十画		**十六画**		徽	huī	狱	yù	
幌	huǎng	巅	diān			狠	hěn	
十二画		**十七画**		(48)		**七画**		
幢	zhuàng	巍	wēi	**彡部**		狼	láng	

(46)		(47)		**四画**		**八画**		
山部		**彳部**		形	xíng	猜	cāi	
				杉	shān	猪	zhū	
山	shān	**三画**		**五画**		猎	liè	
三画		行	háng;xíng	衫	shān	猫	māo	
屿	yǔ	**四画**		**六画**		猖	chāng	
屹	yì	彻	chè	须	xū	猝	cù	
岁	suì	役	yì	**八画**		猕	mí	
岂	qǐ	彷	páng	彬	bīn	猛	měng	
四画		**五画**		彪	biāo	**九画**		
岗	gǎng	征	zhēng	彩	cǎi	猩	xīng	
岔	chà	往	wǎng	**十一画**		猥	wěi	
岛	dǎo	彼	bǐ	彰	zhāng	猾	huá	
五画		径	jìng	**十二画**		猴	hóu	
岸	àn	**六画**		影	yǐng	**十画**		
岬	jiǎ	待	dāi;dài			猿	yuán	
岭	lǐng	徇	xùn	(49)		**十三画**		
岳	yuè	衍	yǎn	**犭部**		獭	tǎ	
六画		律	lǜ	**二画**				
炭	tàn	很	hěn	犯	fàn	(50)		
峡	xiá	**七画**		**三画**		**夕部**		
峥	zhēng	徒	tú	犷	guǎng	夕	xī	

三画
多　duō
五画
罗　luó
八画
梦　mèng

（51）
夊 部

二画
处　chǔ；chù
冬　dōng
四画
麦　mài
条　tiáo
五画
备　bèi
七画
夏　xià
九画
惫　bèi

（52）
饣 部

二画
饥　jī
四画
饬　chì
饭　fàn
饮　yǐn
五画
饯　jiàn
饰　shì
饱　bǎo
饲　sì
六画
饵　ěr
饶　ráo
蚀　shí
饺　jiǎo
饼　bǐng

七画
饿　è
馁　něi
八画
馄　hún
馅　xiàn
九画
馈　kuì
馊　sōu
馋　chán
十画
馏　liù
十一画
馒　mán

（53）
丬 部

三画
壮　zhuàng
妆　zhuāng
四画
状　zhuàng
六画
将　jiāng；jiàng

（54）
广 部

广　guǎng
三画
庄　zhuāng
庆　qìng
四画
床　chuáng
库　kù
庇　bì
应　yīng；yìng
庐　lú
序　xù
五画
庞　páng
店　diàn

庙　miào
府　fǔ
底　de；dǐ
废　fèi
六画
度　dù；duó
庭　tíng
七画
席　xí
座　zuò
唐　táng
八画
庵　ān
廊　láng
庸　yōng
康　kāng
鹿　lù
十画
廉　lián
十一画
腐　fǔ
十五画
鹰　yīng

（55）
忄 部

一画
忆　yì
三画
忏　chàn
忙　máng
四画
怀　huái
怄　òu
忧　yōu
忡　chōng
怅　chàng
忱　chén
快　kuài
五画
怔　zhēng
怯　qiè

怦　pēng
性　xìng
怕　pà
怜　lián
怪　guài
怡　yí
六画
恒　héng
恢　huī
恍　huǎng
恬　tián
恤　xù
恰　qià
恪　kè
恼　nǎo
恨　hèn
七画
恭　gōng
悖　bèi
悚　sǒng
悟　wù
悄　qiāo；qiǎo
悍　hàn
悔　huǐ
悦　yuè
八画
情　qíng
惬　qiè
惜　xī
惭　cán
悼　dào
惧　jù
悸　jì
惟　wéi
惆　chóu
惊　jīng
惦　diàn
惋　wǎn
惨　cǎn
惯　guàn
九画
愤　fèn

慌	huāng	闯	chuǎng	沥	lì	**六画**	
惰	duò	**四画**		沏	qī	洼	wā
惺	xīng	闰	rùn	沙	shā	洁	jié
愕	è	闲	xián	汩	gǔ	洪	hóng
惴	zhuì	间	jiān;jiàn	汽	qì	洒	sǎ
愣	lèng	闷	mēn;mèn	沦	lún	浇	jiāo
惶	huáng	**五画**		泅	xiōng	浊	zhuó
愧	kuì	闸	zhá	泛	fàn	洞	dòng
愉	yú	闹	nào	沧	cāng	洇	yīn
慨	kǎi	**六画**		沟	gōu	测	cè
十画		闺	guī	没	méi;mò	洗	xǐ
慑	shè	闻	wén	沆	hàng	活	huó
慎	shèn	阀	fá	沉	chén	涎	xián
十一画		阁	gé	沁	qìn	派	pài
慕	mù	**七画**		**五画**		洽	qià
慢	màn	阄	jiū	沫	mò	浏	liú
慷	kāng	阅	yuè	浅	qiǎn	济	jǐ;jì
十二画		**八画**		法	fǎ	洋	yáng
懂	dǒng	阉	yān	泄	xiè	洲	zhōu
憔	qiáo	阐	chǎn	沽	gū	浑	hún
懊	ào	**九画**		河	hé	浓	nóng
憧	chōng	阑	lán	沾	zhān	津	jīn
憎	zēng	阔	kuò	沮	jǔ	**七画**	
十三画				泪	lèi	涛	tāo
懒	lǎn	(57)		油	yóu	涝	lào
憾	hàn	**氵部**		泊	bó	酒	jiǔ
懈	xiè			沿	yán	涟	lián
十四画		**二画**		泡	pào	涉	shè
懦	nuò	汁	zhī	注	zhù	消	xiāo
十五画		汇	huì	泣	qì	涓	juān
懵	měng	汉	hàn	泻	xiè	涡	wō
		三画		泌	mì	浩	hào
(56)		汗	hán;hàn	泳	yǒng	海	hǎi
门 部		污	wū	泥	ní	涂	tú
		江	jiāng	泯	mǐn	浴	yù
门	mén	汲	jí	沸	fèi	浮	fú
一画		汐	xī	沼	zhǎo	涣	huàn
闩	shuān	汛	xùn	波	bō	涤	dí
二画		池	chí	泼	pō	流	liú
闪	shǎn	汤	tāng	泽	zé	润	rùn
三画		**四画**		泾	jīng	涧	jiàn
闭	bì	汪	wāng	治	zhì	涕	tì
问	wèn	沐	mù				

浣	huàn	湖	hú	漩	xuán	灾	zāi
浪	làng	渣	zhā	漾	yàng	**五画**	
浸	jìn	渺	miǎo	演	yǎn	宝	bǎo
涨	zhǎng	湿	shī	漏	lòu	宗	zōng
	zhàng	温	wēn	**十二画**		定	dìng
涩	sè	渴	kě	潜	qián	宠	chǒng
涌	yǒng	溃	kuì	澎	péng	宜	yí
浚	jùn	湍	tuān	潮	cháo	审	shěn
八画		溅	jiàn	潸	shān	官	guān
清	qīng	滑	huá	潭	tán	宛	wǎn
添	tiān	渝	yú	潦	liáo	实	shí
鸿	hóng	湾	wān	澳	ào	**六画**	
淋	lín	渡	dù	澈	chè	宣	xuān
淅	xī	游	yóu	澜	lán	宦	huàn
渎	dú	滋	zī	潺	chán	室	shì
涯	yá	渲	xuàn	澄	chéng；dèng	宫	gōng
淹	yān	**十画**		**十三画**		宪	xiàn
渠	qú	满	mǎn	濒	bīn	客	kè
渐	jiàn	漠	mò	澡	zǎo	**七画**	
淑	shū	源	yuán	激	jī	害	hài
淌	tǎng	滤	lǜ	**十五画**		宽	kuān
混	hùn	滥	làn	瀑	pù	家	jiā
淆	xiáo	滔	tāo	**十六画**		宵	xiāo
渊	yuān	溪	xī	瀚	hàn	宴	yàn
淫	yín	溜	liū	**十七画**		宾	bīn
渔	yú	滚	gǔn	灌	guàn	宰	zǎi
淘	táo	滂	pāng			**八画**	
淳	chún	溢	yì	**(58)**		寇	kòu
液	yè	溯	sù	**宀部**		寄	jì
淬	cuì	滨	bīn			寂	jì
淤	yū	溶	róng	**二画**		宿	sù；xiǔ
淡	dàn	溺	nì	宁	níng；nìng	密	mì
淙	cóng	滩	tān	它	tā	**九画**	
淀	diàn	**十一画**		**三画**		富	fù
深	shēn	潇	xiāo	宇	yǔ	寓	yù
涮	shuàn	漆	qī	守	shǒu	**十画**	
渗	shèn	漱	shù	宅	zhái	塞	sāi；sài
涵	hán	漂	piāo	安	ān	寝	qǐn
九画			piǎo	字	zì	**十一画**	
湛	zhàn		piào	**四画**		寨	zhài
港	gǎng	漫	màn	完	wán	赛	sài
滞	zhì	滴	dī	宏	hóng	寡	guǎ
				牢	láo	察	chá

蜜	mì	迹	jì	**十一画**		**七画**	
寥	liáo	进	bèng	遭	zāo	展	zhǎn
十三画		送	sòng	遮	zhē	屑	xiè
寰	huán	迷	mí	**十二画**		**八画**	
		逆	nì	遵	zūn	屠	tú
(59)		退	tuì	**十三画**		**九画**	
辶 部		逊	xùn	邀	yāo	犀	xī
		七画		邂	xiè	属	shǔ
二画		速	sù	避	bì	屡	lǚ
边	biān	逗	dòu	**十五画**		孱	chán
辽	liáo	逐	zhú	邋	lā	**十二画**	
三画		逝	shì			履	lǚ
迂	yū	逍	xiāo	**(60)**			
达	dá	逞	chěng	**彐(彑) 部**		**(62)**	
迈	mài	造	zào			**己(巳) 部**	
过	guò	透	tòu	**二画**			
迁	qiān	途	tú	归	guī	己	jǐ
迅	xùn	逛	guàng	**四画**		已	yǐ
巡	xún	逢	féng	灵	líng	**四画**	
四画		递	dì	**五画**		忌	jì
进	jìn	通	tōng;tòng	录	lù		
远	yuǎn	**八画**		**八画**		**(63)**	
违	wéi	逻	luó	彗	huì	**弓 部**	
运	yùn	逸	yì				
还	hái;huán	逮	dǎi;dài	**(61)**		弓	gōng
连	lián	**九画**		**尸 部**		**一画**	
近	jìn	逼	bī	尸	shī	引	yǐn
返	fǎn	遇	yù	**四画**		**二画**	
迎	yíng	遏	è	层	céng	弘	hóng
这	zhè	遗	yí	屁	pì	**三画**	
迟	chí	遁	dùn	尾	wěi	弛	chí
五画		逾	yú	局	jú	**四画**	
述	shù	遒	qiú	尿	niào;suī	张	zhāng
迪	dí	道	dào	**五画**		**五画**	
迥	jiǒng	遂	suí;suì	屉	tì	弧	hú
迭	dié	遍	biàn	居	jū	弥	mí
迫	pò	遐	xiá	届	jiè	弦	xián
迢	tiáo	**十画**		屈	qū	**六画**	
六画		遨	áo	**六画**		弯	wān
选	xuǎn	遣	qiǎn	屋	wū	**七画**	
适	shì	遥	yáo	屏	bǐng;píng	弱	ruò
追	zhuī	遛	liù	屎	shǐ	**八画**	
逃	táo					弹	dàn;tán

九画		她	tā	娩	miǎn	级	jí
强	jiàng	好	hǎo;hào	娴	xián	约	yuē
	qiáng	妈	mā	娘	niáng	纪	jǐ;jì
	qiǎng	**四画**		娿	ē	纫	rèn
粥	zhōu	妥	tuǒ				
		妩	wǔ	**八画**		**四画**	
(64)		妓	jì	娶	qǔ	纬	wěi
子 部		妙	miào	婴	yīng	纯	chún
		妊	rèn	婆	pó	纰	pī
子	zǐ	妖	yāo	婊	biǎo	纱	shā
二画		姊	zǐ	娼	chāng	纲	gāng
孕	yùn	妨	fáng	婢	bì	纳	nà
三画		妒	dù	婚	hūn	纵	zòng
存	cún	**五画**		婵	chán	纷	fēn
孙	sūn	妻	qī	婶	shěn	纸	zhǐ
四画		委	wěi	婉	wǎn	纹	wén
孝	xiào	妾	qiè			纺	fǎng
孚	fú	妹	mèi	**九画**		纽	niǔ
孜	zī	姑	gū	媒	méi		
五画		姐	jiě	嫂	sǎo	**五画**	
孟	mèng	姓	xìng	媚	mèi	线	xiàn
孤	gū	姗	shān	婿	xù	练	liàn
孢	bāo	始	shǐ			组	zǔ
六画				**十画**		绅	shēn
孪	luán	**六画**		媳	xí	细	xì
孩	hái	要	yāo;yào	媲	pì	织	zhī
九画		威	wēi	嫉	jí	终	zhōng
孳	zī	耍	shuǎ	嫌	xián	绊	bàn
十四画		姜	jiāng	嫁	jià	经	jīng
孺	rú	娄	lóu	**十一画**		**六画**	
		姿	zī	嫩	nèn	绑	bǎng
(65)		娃	wá	嫖	piáo	绒	róng
女 部		姥	lǎo	嫡	dí	结	jiē;jié
		姨	yí	**十二画**		绕	rào
女	nǚ	姻	yīn	嬉	xī	绘	huì
二画		娇	jiāo	**十七画**		给	gěi;jǐ
奶	nǎi	姣	jiāo	孀	shuāng	绚	xuàn
奴	nú	姘	pīn			绛	jiàng
三画		姹	chà	**(66)**		络	luò
奸	jiān	**七画**		**纟 部**		绝	jué
如	rú	娱	yú	**二画**		绞	jiǎo
妇	fù	娟	juān	纠	jiū	统	tǒng
妃	fēi	娥	é	**三画**		**七画**	
				红	hóng	绢	juàn
				纤	qiàn;xiān		

绣	xiù	缮	shàn	**十四画**		班	bān
继	jì	**十三画**		骤	zhòu	**七画**	
八画		缰	jiāng			球	qiú
绩	jì	缴	jiǎo	**(68)**		琐	suǒ
绪	xù			**幺部**		理	lǐ
续	xù	**(67)**				望	wàng
绯	fēi	**马部**		幺	yāo	**八画**	
绰	chuò	马	mǎ	**一画**		琵	pí
绳	shéng	**二画**		幻	huàn	琴	qín
维	wéi	驭	yù	**二画**		琳	lín
绵	mián	**三画**		幼	yòu	琢	zhuó
绷	bēng	驮	duò;tuó			琥	hǔ
	běng	驯	xùn	**(69)**		**九画**	
	bèng	驰	chí	**巛部**		瑟	sè
绸	chóu	**四画**				瑞	ruì
绺	liǔ	驱	qū	**八画**		瑰	guī
综	zōng	驳	bó	巢	cháo	瑕	xiá
绽	zhàn	驴	lǘ			**十一画**	
绿	lǜ	**五画**		**(70)**		璀	cuī
九画		驾	jià	**王部**			
缄	jiān	驶	shǐ	王	wáng	**(71)**	
缅	miǎn	驹	jū	**一画**		**韦部**	
缆	lǎn	驻	zhù	玉	yù	**三画**	
缉	jī	驼	tuó	**三画**		韧	rèn
缎	duàn	**六画**		玖	jiǔ	**十画**	
缓	huǎn	骂	mà	玛	mǎ	韬	tāo
缔	dì	骄	jiāo	**四画**		**(72)**	
缕	lǚ	骆	luò	玩	wán	**木部**	
编	biān	骇	hài	环	huán		
缘	yuán	**七画**		现	xiàn	木	mù
十画		骋	chěng	玫	méi	**一画**	
缜	zhěn	验	yàn	**五画**		本	běn
缚	fù	骏	jùn	珐	fà	术	shù
缝	féng;fèng	**八画**		玷	diàn	札	zhá
缠	chán	骑	qí	玳	dài	**二画**	
缤	bīn	**九画**		珍	zhēn	朽	xiǔ
十一画		骛	wù	玲	líng	朴	pǔ
缥	piāo	骗	piàn	珊	shān	机	jī
缨	yīng	骚	sāo	玻	bō	权	quán
缩	suō	**十画**		皇	huáng	杀	shā
十二画		骗	shàn	**六画**		杂	zá
缭	liáo	骡	luó	珠	zhū		

三画

杆	gān;gǎn
杜	dù
杠	gàng
杖	zhàng
材	cái
村	cūn
杏	xìng
极	jí
杨	yáng
杈	chà
李	lǐ

四画

枉	wǎng
林	lín
枝	zhī
杯	bēi
枢	shū
柜	guì
杳	yǎo
枚	méi
析	xī
板	bǎn
松	sōng
枪	qiāng
枫	fēng
构	gòu
枕	zhěn
果	guǒ
采	cǎi

五画

某	mǒu
标	biāo
柑	gān
枯	kū
柄	bǐng
栋	dòng
查	chá
相	xiāng;xiàng
柏	bǎi
栅	zhà
柳	liǔ

栎	lì
柿	shì
栏	lán
柠	níng
枷	jiā
树	shù
亲	qīn
柒	qī
染	rǎn
架	jià
柔	róu

六画

栽	zāi
框	kuàng
桂	guì
栖	qī;xī
桎	zhì
档	dàng
株	zhū
桥	qiáo
桦	huà
栓	shuān
桃	táo
桅	wéi
格	gé
桩	zhuāng
校	jiào;xiào
核	hé
样	yàng
根	gēn
栩	xǔ
栗	lì
柴	chái
桀	jié
桨	jiǎng
案	àn

七画

械	xiè
梗	gěng
梧	wú
梢	shāo
梏	gù

梅	méi
检	jiǎn
梳	shū
梯	tī
桶	tǒng
梭	suō
梨	lí
梁	liáng

八画

棒	bàng
棱	léng
棋	qí
椰	yē
植	zhí
森	sēn
椅	yǐ
椒	jiāo
棵	kē
棍	gùn
棉	mián
棚	péng
棕	zōng
棺	guān
椰	láng
椭	tuǒ
集	jí

九画

楔	xiē
楚	chǔ
楷	kǎi
槐	huái
楼	lóu
概	gài

十画

模	mó;mú
榜	bǎng
榨	zhà

十一画

横	héng;hèng
槽	cáo
樱	yīng
橡	xiàng

樟	zhāng
橄	gǎn

十二画

橱	chú
橛	jué
橇	qiāo
橙	chéng
橘	jú

十三画

檐	yán
檀	tán

(73)

犬 部

犬	quǎn

六画

臭	chòu;xiù

九画

献	xiàn

(74)

歹 部

歹	dǎi

二画

死	sǐ

三画

歼	jiān

五画

残	cán

六画

殊	shū
殉	xùn
毙	bì

七画

殓	liàn

八画

殖	zhí

十画

殡	bìn

(75)	**十二画**	**四画**	昆　kūn
车 部	辙　zhé	瓮　wèng	昌　chāng
		六画	明　míng
车　chē；jū	**(76)**	瓶　píng	易　yì
一画	**戈 部**	瓷　cí	昂　áng
轧　yà；zhá			昏　hūn
二画	**二画**	**(79)**	**五画**
轨　guǐ	戎　róng	**止 部**	春　chūn
三画	戍　shù		昧　mèi
轩　xuān	成　chéng	止　zhǐ	是　shì
四画	**三画**	**二画**	显　xiǎn
轰　hōng	戒　jiè	此　cǐ	映　yìng
转　zhuǎn	**四画**	**三画**	星　xīng
zhuàn	或　huò	步　bù	昨　zuó
轭　è	**五画**	**四画**	昵　nì
斩　zhǎn	战　zhàn	武　wǔ	昭　zhāo
轮　lún	**六画**	歧　qí	香　xiāng
软　ruǎn	载　zǎi；zài	肯　kěn	**六画**
五画	**七画**	**六画**	晋　jìn
轱　gū	戚　qī	耻　chǐ	晒　shài
轴　zhóu	戛　jiá		晓　xiǎo
轶　yì	**八画**	**(80)**	晃　huǎng
轻　qīng	裁　cái	**攴 部**	huàng
六画	**十画**		晌　shǎng
轿　jiào	截　jié	**十画**	晕　yūn；yùn
较　jiào	**十一画**	敲　qiāo	**七画**
七画	戮　lù		匙　chí
辅　fǔ	**十三画**	**(81)**	晤　wù
辆　liàng	戴　dài	**日 部**	晨　chén
八画	**十四画**		晦　huì
辍　chuò	戳　chuō	日　rì	晚　wǎn
辈　bèi		**一画**	**八画**
九画	**(77)**	旦　dàn	暂　zàn
辐　fú	**比 部**	**二画**	晴　qíng
辑　jí	比　bǐ	早　zǎo	暑　shǔ
输　shū	**五画**	旭　xù	晰　xī
十画	皆　jiē	**三画**	量　liáng；liàng
辖　xiá	毗　pí	旱　hàn	晶　jīng
辗　zhǎn		时　shí	景　jǐng
十一画	**(78)**	旷　kuàng	晾　liàng
辘　lù	**瓦 部**	**四画**	智　zhì
	瓦　wǎ	昔　xī	**九画**
		旺　wàng	暖　nuǎn

暗	àn			赔	péi	
暇	xiá	**(84)**			**十画**	
十画		**贝 部**		赘	zhuì	
暖	ài			赚	zhuàn	
十一画		贝	bèi	**十二画**		
暴	bào	**三画**		赠	zèng	
十三画		财	cái	赞	zàn	
曙	shǔ	**四画**		**十三画**		
十五画		责	zé	赡	shàn	
曝	bào	贤	xián			
十六画		败	bài	**(85)**		
曦	xī	账	zhàng	**见 部**		
		贩	fàn			
(82)		贬	biǎn	见	jiàn	
日 部		购	gòu	**四画**		
		贮	zhù	规	guī	
二画		货	huò	觅	mì	
旨	zhǐ	贪	tān	**五画**		
四画		贫	pín	览	lǎn	
者	zhě	贯	guàn	觉	jiào; jué	
沓	dá	**五画**		**六画**		
五画		贵	guì	觊	jì	
冒	mào	贱	jiàn	**八画**		
七画		贴	tiē	靓	liàng	
冕	miǎn	贻	yí	**十一画**		
八画		贷	dài	觐	jìn	
替	tì	贸	mào			
最	zuì	费	fèi	**(86)**		
		贺	hè	**牛(牜) 部**		
(83)		**六画**		牛	niú	
水 部		贼	zéi	**三画**		
		贿	huì	牡	mǔ	
水	shuǐ	赃	zāng	**四画**		
一画		赁	lìn	牧	mù	
永	yǒng	资	zī	物	wù	
五画		**七画**		**五画**		
泵	bèng	赈	zhèn	牯	gǔ	
泉	quán	赊	shē	牲	shēng	
六画		**八画**		**六画**		
泰	tài	赋	fù	特	tè	
浆	jiāng	赌	dǔ	牺	xī	
十一画		赎	shú	**七画**		
黎	lí	赐	cì	犁	lí	

八画		
犊	dú	
犄	jī	
十画		
犒	kào	
十二画		
犟	jiàng	
(87)		
手 部		
手	shǒu	
六画		
挚	zhì	
挛	luán	
拳	quán	
八画		
掣	chè	
掰	bāi	
十一画		
摩	mó	
十五画		
攀	pān	
(88)		
毛 部		
毛	máo	
五画		
毡	zhān	
八画		
毯	tǎn	
毽	jiàn	
(89)		
气 部		
气	qì	
四画		
氛	fēn	
五画		
氢	qīng	
六画		
氧	yǎng	

腿	tuǐ	**八画**		**五画**		**六画**	
十画		飓	jù	施	shī	耿	gěng
膜	mó	**十一画**		**六画**		烤	kǎo
膊	bó	飘	piāo	旅	lǚ	烘	hōng
膀	bǎng; páng	**十二画**		**七画**		烦	fán
膑	bìn	飙	biāo	族	zú	烧	shāo
十一画				旋	xuán; xuàn	烛	zhú
膝	xī	(98)		**十画**		烟	yān
膘	biāo	**殳 部**		旗	qí	烙	lào
膛	táng			旖	yǐ	烬	jìn
十二画		**四画**				烫	tàng
膨	péng	殴	ōu	(101)		**七画**	
膳	shàn	**五画**		**火 部**		焐	wù
十三画		段	duàn			焊	hàn
朦	méng	**六画**		火	huǒ	焕	huàn
臊	sāo; sào	殷	yān; yīn	**一画**		**八画**	
臆	yì	般	bān	灭	miè	焚	fén
臃	yōng	**九画**		**二画**		焰	yàn
臀	tún	毁	huǐ	灰	huī	焙	bèi
臂	bì	殿	diàn	灯	dēng	**九画**	
		十一画		**三画**		煤	méi
(96)		毅	yì	灶	zào	煳	hú
欠 部				灿	càn	煨	wēi
		(99)		灼	zhuó	煌	huáng
欠	qiàn	**文 部**		**四画**		**十画**	
四画				炬	jù	熄	xī
欧	ōu	文	wén	炖	dùn	熔	róng
七画		**二画**		炒	chǎo	煽	shān
欲	yù	齐	qí	炊	chuī	**十一画**	
八画		**六画**		炎	yán	熨	yùn
款	kuǎn	虔	qián	炉	lú	**十二画**	
欺	qī	斋	zhāi	**五画**		燎	liáo
九画		紊	wěn	炼	liàn	燃	rán
歇	xiē	**八画**		炽	chì	燧	suì
十画		斑	bān	炯	jiǒng	**十三画**	
歌	gē	斐	fěi	炸	zhá; zhà	爆	zào
歉	qiàn			炮	bāo	**十五画**	
		(100)			páo	爆	bào
(97)		**方 部**			pào		
风 部				烁	shuò	(102)	
		方	fāng	炫	xuàn	**斗 部**	
风	fēng	**四画**		烂	làn		
五画		放	fàng				
飒	sà	房	fáng				

六画
料 liào
七画
斜 xié
九画
斟 zhēn

(103)
灬 部

四画
杰 jié
五画
点 diǎn
六画
烈 liè
热 rè
羔 gāo
八画
煮 zhǔ
焦 jiāo
然 rán
九画
照 zhào
煞 shā;shà
煎 jiān
十画
熬 áo
熙 xī
熏 xūn
熊 xióng
十一画
熟 shú
十二画
燕 yàn

(104)
户 部

户 hù
四画
所 suǒ
肩 jiān

五画
扁 biǎn;piān
六画
扇 shān;shàn
八画
扉 fēi
雇 gù

(105)
礻 部

一画
礼 lǐ
四画
视 shì
祈 qí
五画
祛 qū
祖 zǔ
神 shén
祝 zhù
祠 cí
六画
祥 xiáng
七画
祷 dǎo
祸 huò
八画
禅 chán;shàn
禄 lù
九画
福 fú
十二画
禧 xǐ

(106)
心 部

心 xīn
一画
必 bì
三画
忘 wàng
忍 rěn
四画
忠 zhōng
怂 sǒng
念 niàn
忽 hū
五画
思 sī
怎 zěn
怨 yuàn
急 jí
总 zǒng
怒 nù
怠 dài
六画
恐 kǒng
恶 ě;è;wù
虑 lǜ
恩 ēn
息 xī
恋 liàn
恣 zì
恳 kěn
恕 shù
七画
悬 xuán
患 huàn
悠 yōu
您 nín
悉 xī
八画
惹 rě
惠 huì
惑 huò
悲 bēi
惩 chéng
九画
想 xiǎng
感 gǎn
愚 yú
愁 chóu

愈 yù
意 yì
慈 cí
十画
愿 yuàn
十一画
慧 huì
憋 biē
憨 hān
慰 wèi
十二画
憩 qì

(107)
聿(聿) 部

四画
隶 lì
九画
肆 sì
肄 yì
十画
肇 zhào

(108)
毋(毋母) 部

毋 wú
一画
母 mǔ
五画
毒 dú

(109)
示 部

示 shì
六画
票 piào
祭 jì
八画
禁 jīn;jìn

		磁	cí	眠	mián		
（110）		**十画**		**六画**		**（114）**	
石 部		磕	kē	眶	kuàng	**田 部**	
		磊	lěi	眺	tiào		
石	shí	磅	bàng；páng	睁	zhēng	田	tián
三画		碾	niǎn	眯	mī；mí	**四画**	
矿	kuàng	磐	pán	眼	yǎn	畏	wèi
码	mǎ	**十一画**		眸	móu	界	jiè
四画		磺	huáng	眷	juàn	**五画**	
研	yán	磨	mó；mò	**七画**		畔	pàn
砖	zhuān	**十二画**		睐	lài	留	liú
砒	pī	礁	jiāo	鼎	dǐng	畜	chù；xù
砌	qì	磷	lín	**八画**		**六画**	
砂	shā			督	dū	略	lüè
砚	yàn	**（111）**		睛	jīng	累	léi；lěi；lèi
砍	kǎn	**龙 部**		睹	dǔ	**七画**	
五画				睦	mù	畴	chóu
砝	fǎ	**六画**		瞄	miáo	番	fān
砸	zá	聋	lóng	睫	jié	**八画**	
砰	pēng	袭	xí	睡	shuì	畸	jī
砾	lì			睬	cǎi		
础	chǔ	**（112）**		**九画**		**（115）**	
破	pò	**业 部**		睿	ruì	**罒 部**	
六画				瞅	chǒu		
硕	shuò	业	yè	**十画**		**四画**	
七画				瞌	kē	罚	fá
硬	yìng	**（113）**		瞒	mán	**五画**	
确	què	**目 部**		瞎	xiā	罢	bà
硫	liú			瞑	míng	**八画**	
八画		目	mù	**十一画**		署	shǔ
碍	ài	**二画**		瞥	piē	置	zhì
碘	diǎn	盯	dīng	瞟	piǎo	罪	zuì
碑	bēi	**三画**		瞠	chēng	罩	zhào
碎	suì	盲	máng	**十二画**		**十一画**	
碰	pèng	**四画**		瞧	qiáo	罹	lí
碗	wǎn	盹	dǔn	瞬	shùn	**十二画**	
碌	liù；lù	盼	pàn	瞳	tóng	羁	jī
九画		眨	zhǎ	瞩	zhǔ		
碧	bì	看	kān；kàn	瞪	dèng	**（116）**	
碟	dié	盾	dùn	**十三画**		**皿 部**	
碱	jiǎn	眉	méi	瞻	zhān		
碳	tàn	**五画**				**三画**	
磋	cuō	眩	xuàn			盂	yú

四画		铃	líng	锹	qiāo	私	sī
盆	pén	铅	qiān	锻	duàn	**三画**	
盈	yíng	**六画**		镀	dù	秆	gǎn
五画		铐	kào	镁	měi	季	jì
盏	zhǎn	铝	lǚ	镂	lòu	**四画**	
盐	yán	铜	tóng	**十画**		秒	miǎo
监	jiān	铠	kǎi	镍	niè	种	zhǒng
盎	àng	铡	zhá	镇	zhèn		zhòng
六画		铤	tǐng	镌	juān	秋	qiū
盔	kuī	铭	míng	镍	niè	科	kē
盛	chéng	铰	jiǎo	镑	bàng	**五画**	
	shèng	铲	chǎn	**十一画**		秤	chèng
盘	pán	银	yín	镖	biāo	租	zū
盖	gài	**七画**		镜	jìng	积	jī
盗	dào	铸	zhù	**十二画**		秧	yāng
八画		铺	pū；pù	镣	liào	秩	zhì
盟	méng	链	liàn	镩	cuān	称	chèn；chēng
十一画		铿	kēng	**十三画**		秘	mì
盥	guàn	销	xiāo	镭	léi	**六画**	
		锁	suǒ	镯	zhuó	秸	jiē
		锃	zèng	镰	lián	秽	huì
(117)		锄	chú	**十七画**		移	yí
钅部		锅	guō	镶	xiāng	**七画**	
		锈	xiù			稍	shāo；shào
二画		锉	cuò	(118)		程	chéng
针	zhēn	锋	fēng	**矢部**		稀	xī
钉	dīng；dìng	锐	ruì			税	shuì
三画		铒	láng	矢	shǐ	**八画**	
钓	diào	**八画**		**四画**		稚	zhì
金	jīn	错	cuò	矩	jǔ	稠	chóu
四画		锚	máo	**六画**		颓	tuí
钙	gài	锡	xī	矫	jiǎo	颖	yǐng
钝	dùn	锣	luó	**七画**		**九画**	
钞	chāo	锤	chuí	短	duǎn		wěn
钢	gāng	锥	zhuī	**八画**		稳	
钠	nà	锦	jǐn	矮	ǎi	**十画**	
钥	yào	锨	xiān	雉	zhì	稽	jī
钦	qīn	键	jiàn			稻	dào
钩	gōu	锯	jù	(119)		稿	gǎo
五画		锰	měng	**禾部**		**十一画**	
钱	qián	**九画**				穆	mù
钳	qián	锲	qiè	禾	hé	**十二画**	
钻	zuān；zuàn			**二画**		穗	suì
铁	tiě			秀	xiù	黏	nián

十三画	鸵	tuó	**六画**		立		lì
馥 fù	鸳	yuān	痔	zhì		**四画**	
			疵	cī	竖		shù
(120)	**六画**		痊	quán		**五画**	
白 部	鸽	gē	痒	yǎng	站		zhàn
	七画		痕	hén	竞		jìng
白 bái	鹅	é				**六画**	
二画	**八画**		**七画**		章		zhāng
皂 zào	鹊	què	痣	zhì	竟		jìng
三画	鹌	ān	痨	láo	翌		yì
的 de;dí;dì	**十画**		痘	dòu		**七画**	
六画	鹤	hè	痞	pǐ	童		tóng
皑 ái	**十一画**		痢	lì	竣		jùn
皎 jiǎo	鹦	yīng	痤	cuó		**九画**	
九画	**十二画**		痛	tòng	竭		jié
魄 pò	鹬	yù			端		duān
			八画				
(121)	**(124)**		痱	fèi		**(126)**	
瓜 部	**疒 部**		痼	gù		**穴 部**	
			痴	chī			
瓜 guā	**二画**		痒	cuì	穴		xué
十一画	疖	jiē	痰	tán		**二画**	
瓢 piáo	疗	liáo	**九画**		究		jiū
十四画	**三画**		瘟	wēn	穷		qióng
瓣 bàn	疟	nüè	瘦	shòu	空	kōng;kòng
十七画	疙	gē	瘊	hóu		**四画**	
瓤 ráng	疚	jiù	瘙	sào	突		tū
	四画		**十画**		穿		chuān
(122)	疥	jiè	瘪	biē;biě	窃		qiè
用 部	疮	chuāng	瘤	liú		**五画**	
	疯	fēng	瘠	jí	窍		qiào
用 yòng	疫	yì	瘫	tān	窄		zhǎi
四画	疤	bā	**十一画**		容		róng
甫 béng	**五画**		瘾	yǐn	窈		yǎo
	症	zhēng	瘸	qué		**六画**	
(123)		zhèng	**十二画**		窒		zhì
鸟 部	病	bìng	癌	ái	窑		yáo
	疾	jí	**十三画**			**七画**	
鸟 niǎo	疹	zhěn	癖	pǐ	窜		cuàn
四画	疼	téng	**十六画**		窝		wō
鸥 ōu	疱	pào	癫	diān	窖		jiào
鸦 yā	痂	jiā			窗		chuāng
五画	疲	pí	**(125)**				
鸭 yā	痉	jìng	**立 部**				

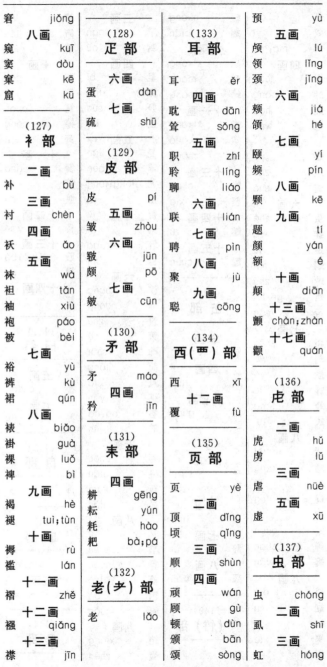

窘　jiǒng

八画
窥　kuī
窦　dòu
窠　kē
窟　kū

(127)
衤部

二画
补　bǔ
三画
衬　chèn
四画
袄　ǎo
五画
袜　wà
袒　tǎn
袖　xiù
袍　páo
被　bèi
七画
裕　yù
裤　kù
裙　qún
八画
裱　biǎo
褂　guà
裸　luǒ
裨　bì
九画
褐　hè
褪　tuì；tùn
十画
褥　rù
褴　lán
十一画
褶　zhě
十二画
襁　qiǎng
十三画
襟　jīn

(128)
疋部

六画
蛋　dàn
七画
疏　shū

(129)
皮部
皮　pí
五画
皱　zhòu
六画
皲　jūn
颇　pō
七画
皴　cūn

(130)
矛部
矛　máo
四画
矜　jīn

(131)
耒部

四画
耕　gēng
耘　yún
耗　hào
耙　bà；pá

(132)
老(耂)部
老　lǎo

(133)
耳部
耳　ěr
四画
耽　dān
耸　sǒng
五画
职　zhí
聆　líng
聊　liáo
六画
联　lián
七画
聘　pìn
八画
聚　jù
九画
聪　cōng

(134)
西(覀)部
西　xī
十二画
覆　fù

(135)
页部
页　yè
二画
顶　dǐng
顷　qǐng
三画
顺　shùn
四画
顽　wán
顾　gù
顿　dùn
颁　bān
颂　sòng

预　yù
五画
颅　lú
领　lǐng
颈　jǐng
六画
颊　jiá
颌　hé
七画
颐　yí
频　pín
八画
颗　kē
九画
题　tí
颜　yán
额　é
十画
颠　diān
十三画
颤　chàn；zhàn
十七画
颧　quán

(136)
虍部

二画
虎　hǔ
虏　lǔ
三画
虐　nüè
五画
虚　xū

(137)
虫部
虫　chóng
二画
虱　shī
三画
虹　hóng

虾	xiā	蝗	huáng	**三画**		篓	lǒu
蚁	yǐ	蝙	biān	竿	gān	箭	jiàn
蚂	mǎ;mà	**十画**		笃	dǔ	篇	piān
四画		融	róng	**四画**		**十画**	
蚕	cán	蟒	mǎng	笔	bǐ	篝	gōu
蚌	bàng	螃	páng	笑	xiào	篮	lán
蚝	háo	**十一画**		笋	sǔn	篡	cuàn
蚊	wén	螳	táng	笆	bā	篷	péng
五画		螺	luó	**五画**		篱	lí
蚯	qiū	蟑	zhāng	笺	jiān	**十一画**	
蛀	zhù	**十三画**		笨	bèn	簧	huáng
蛇	shé	蟾	chán	笼	lóng;lǒng	簌	sù
六画		蟹	xiè	笛	dí	簇	cù
蛰	zhé	**十四画**		符	fú	**十二画**	
蛙	wā	蠕	rú	第	dì	簪	zān
蛐	qū	**十五画**		笤	tiáo	**十三画**	
蛔	huí	蠢	chǔn	笞	chī	簸	bǒ;bò
蛛	zhū			**六画**		簿	bù
蛤	gé;há	(138)		筐	kuāng	**十四画**	
蛮	mán	**缶 部**		等	děng	籍	jí
七画				筑	zhù		
蜃	shèn	**三画**		策	cè	(141)	
蜗	wō	缸	gāng	筛	shāi	**臼 部**	
蛾	é	**四画**		筒	tǒng		
蜉	fú	缺	quē	筏	fá	**五画**	
蜂	fēng	**十七画**		筵	yán	舂	chōng
蜕	tuì	罐	guàn	答	dā;dá	**七画**	
八画				筋	jīn	舅	jiù
蜚	fēi	(139)		**七画**			
蜻	qīng	**舌 部**		筹	chóu	(142)	
蜡	là			签	qiān	**自 部**	
蝇	yíng	舌	shé	筷	kuài		
蜘	zhī	**五画**		简	jiǎn	自	zì
蜷	quán	甜	tián	**八画**			
蝉	chán	**七画**		箕	jī	(143)	
蜿	wān	辞	cí	箍	gū	**血 部**	
九画		**八画**		算	suàn		
蝶	dié	舔	tiǎn	箩	luó	血	xiě;xuè
蝴	hú			箔	bó	**五画**	
蝠	fú	(140)		管	guǎn	衅	xìn
蝎	xiē	**⺮(竹) 部**		**九画**			
蝌	kē	竹	zhú	箱	xiāng	(144)	
				箴	zhēn	**舟 部**	

舟	zhōu
三画	
舢	shān
四画	
舰	jiàn
舱	cāng
航	háng
五画	
舶	bó
船	chuán
舷	xián
舵	duò
六画	
艇	tǐng
七画	
艄	shāo
九画	
艘	sōu

---

(145)
衣 部

衣	yī
四画	
袅	niǎo
五画	
袋	dài
六画	
裂	liě;liè
装	zhuāng
七画	
裔	yì

---

(146)
羊 部

羊	yáng
四画	
羞	xiū
五画	
着	zhāo
	zháo
	zhuó

羚	líng
六画	
翔	xiáng
羡	xiàn
七画	
群	qún
十三画	
羹	gēng

---

(147)
米 部

米	mǐ
三画	
类	lèi
籽	zǐ
四画	
粉	fěn
五画	
粘	zhān
粗	cū
粒	lì
六画	
粟	sù
粪	fèn
七画	
粮	liáng
八画	
精	jīng
粼	lín
粹	cuì
九画	
糊	hū;hú;hù
糅	róu
十画	
糙	cāo
糖	táng
糕	gāo
十一画	
糜	mí
糟	zāo
十二画	
糨	jiàng

十四画

糯	nuò

---

(148)
艮 部

三画	
既	jì

---

(149)
羽 部

羽	yǔ
四画	
翅	chì
五画	
翎	líng
六画	
翘	qiáo;qiào
八画	
翡	fěi
翠	cuì
十画	
翱	áo
十一画	
翼	yì
十二画	
翻	fān

---

(150)
糸 部

四画	
素	sù
索	suǒ
紧	jǐn
六画	
紫	zǐ
絮	xù
十一画	
繁	fán

---

(151)
走 部

走	zǒu
二画	
赴	fù
赳	jiū
三画	
赶	gǎn
起	qǐ
五画	
越	yuè
趁	chèn
趋	qū
超	chāo
八画	
趣	qù
趟	tāng;tàng

---

(152)
赤 部

赤	chì

---

(153)
豆 部

豆	dòu
五画	
登	dēng
八画	
豌	wān

---

(154)
酉 部

三画	
酌	zhuó
配	pèi
四画	
酝	yùn
酗	xù

五画		跋	tā	蹈	dǎo		**三画**	
酣	hān	**四画**		蹊	qī;xī	豺		chái
酥	sū	距	jù	**十一画**		豹		bào
六画		趾	zhǐ	蹙	cù	**七画**		
酬	chóu	跃	yuè	蹩	bié	貌		mào
酱	jiàng	**五画**		蹦	bèng			
七画		践	jiàn	**十二画**		**(163)**		
酵	jiào	跋	bá	蹶	jué	**角 部**		
酷	kù	跌	diē	蹴	cù	角		jiǎo;jué
酶	méi	跑	pǎo	蹲	dūn	**六画**		
酿	niàng	跛	bǒ	蹭	cèng	触		chù
酸	suān	**六画**		蹿	cuān	解		jiě;jiè
八画		跨	kuà	蹬	dēng			
醋	cù	跷	qiāo	**十三画**		**(164)**		
醇	chún	跳	tiào	躁	zào	**言(言见**		
醉	zuì	踩	duò			**讠)部**		
九画		跪	guì	**(159)**		言		yán
醒	xǐng	路	lù	**身 部**		**六画**		
		跻	jī			誊		téng
(155)		跤	jiāo	身	shēn	誉		yù
辰 部		跟	gēn	**三画**		**七画**		
辰	chén	**七画**		躬	gōng	誓		shì
		踌	chóu	**四画**		**十二画**		
(156)		踉	liàng	躯	qū	警		jǐng
卤 部		踊	yǒng	**六画**		**十三画**		
卤	lǔ	**八画**		躲	duǒ	譬		pì
		踝	huái	**八画**				
(157)		踢	tī	躺	tǎng	**(165)**		
里 部		踟	chí			**辛 部**		
里	lǐ;li	踩	cǎi	**(160)**		辛		xīn
四画		踮	diǎn	**采 部**		**五画**		
野	yě	踪	zōng	**五画**		辜		gū
		踞	jù	释	shì	**六画**		
(158)		踏	tà			辟		bì;pì
足 部		**九画**		**(161)**		**七画**		
足	zú	踹	chuài	**谷 部**		辣		là
二画		踱	duó	**十画**		**九画**		
趴	pā	蹄	tí	豁	huō;huò	辨		biàn
三画		蹉	cuō			辩		biàn
趸	dǔn	蹂	róu	**(162)**		**十画**		
		十画		**豸 部**		辫		biàn
		蹑	niè					
		蹒	pán					

(166)
青 部

青	qīng
六画	
静	jìng
八画	
靛	diàn

(167)
雨 部

雨	yǔ
三画	
雪	xuě
五画	
雷	léi
零	líng
雾	wù
雹	báo
六画	
需	xū
七画	
震	zhèn
霄	xiāo
霉	méi
八画	
霖	lín
霓	ní
霍	huò
霎	shà
九画	
霜	shuāng
霞	xiá
十一画	
霭	ǎi
十三画	
霸	bà
露	lòu;lù
霹	pī

(168)
齿 部

齿	chǐ
五画	
龃	jǔ
龄	líng
龅	bāo
六画	
龇	zī
龈	yín
九画	
龋	qǔ
龌	wò

(169)
隹 部

二画	
隽	jùn
四画	
雄	xióng
雅	yǎ
五画	
雏	chú
六画	
雌	cí
八画	
雕	diāo

(170)
金 部

五画	
鉴	jiàn
八画	
鏊	zàn
十一画	
鏖	áo

(171)
鱼 部

鱼	yú
四画	
鱿	yóu
鲁	lǔ
六画	
鲜	xiān
七画	
鲢	lián
鲤	lǐ
鲨	shā
八画	
鲱	fēi
鲸	jīng
九画	
鳄	è
十画	
鳍	qí
鳏	guān
十一画	
鳖	biē
十二画	
鳝	shàn
鳞	lín

(172)
革 部

革	gé
二画	
勒	lè;lēi
四画	
靴	xuē
靶	bǎ
六画	
鞋	xié
鞍	ān
七画	
鞘	qiào
八画	
鞠	jū
九画	
鞭	biān

(173)
骨 部

骨	gū;gǔ
五画	
骷	kū
六画	
骸	hái
十二画	
髓	suǐ

(174)
鬼 部

鬼	guǐ
四画	
魂	hún
魁	kuí
五画	
魅	mèi
十一画	
魔	mó

(175)
食 部

食	shí
七画	
餐	cān

(176)
音 部

音	yīn
四画	
韵	yùn

(177)
髟 部

五画	
髯	rán

六画		八画		四画		鼠	shǔ
髻	jì	靡	mǐ	默	mò	**十画**	
八画				**五画**		鼹	yǎn
鬈	quán	(179)		黜	chù		
鬃	zōng	**鹿 部**		黝	yǒu	(182)	
十画				**八画**		**鼻 部**	
鬓	bìn	麓	lù	黩	dú		
				九画		鼻	bí
(178)		(180)		黯	àn	**三画**	
麻 部		**黑 部**				鼾	hān
				(181)			
麻	má	黑	hēi	**鼠 部**			

CHINESE-ENGLISH/汉英词典

Aa

阿 ā [前缀] (方) ▷阿爸 dad ▷阿妹 little sister →另见 ē

阿斗 Ā Dǒu [名] (喻) incompetent ▷他这个经理真是个阿斗。He's really an incompetent manager.

阿拉伯数字 Ālābó shùzì [名] Arabic numerals

阿姨 āyí [名] 1 (指年长妇女) auntie ▷李阿姨是妈妈的好朋友。Auntie Li is a good friend of Mum's. 2 (女保育员) carer

啊 ā [叹] oh ▷啊！着火了！Oh! It's caught fire! ▷啊！我考过了！Wow! I passed the exam!

啊 ǎ [叹] huh ▷啊？你在这儿干吗？Huh? What are you doing here?

啊 à [叹] 1 (表示应诺) all right ▷啊，这样可以。All right, that's fine. 2 (表示醒悟) aha ▷啊，现在我知道了。Aha! Now I understand. 3 (表示惊异或赞叹) ah ▷啊，大海！Ah, the sea!

哎 āi [叹] 1 (表示惊讶或不满) oh ▷哎！这么贵！Oh! It's so expensive! 2 (表示提醒) hey ▷哎！别踩了那朵花。Hey! Careful not to tread on that flower.

哎呀 āiyā [叹] oh ▷哎呀，这条路真难走！Oh, this road is hard going! ▷哎呀，电脑又有病毒了。Oh no, the computer has been

infected by a virus again.

哎哟 āiyō [叹] 1 (表示惊讶) oh ▷哎哟！都这么晚了！ Oh, it's so late! 2 (表示痛苦) ow 3 (表示惋惜) oh no

哀 āi I [形] (悲痛) sad II [动] 1 (悼念) mourn 2 (怜悯) pity

哀愁 āichóu [名] sorrow

哀悼 āidào [动] mourn

哀怜 āilián [名] compassion

哀求 āiqiú [动] plead ▷哀求饶命 plead for one's life

哀伤 āishāng [名] grief

哀叹 āitàn [动] sigh

哀痛 āitòng [动] grieve ▷他哀痛失去了最好的朋友。He is grieving for the loss of his best friend.

哀怨 āiyuàn [名] grief and resentment

哀乐 āiyuè [名] funeral music

埃 āi [名] dust

挨 āi [动] 1 (靠近) be next to ▷网吧挨着一家礼品店。The Internet café is next to a gift shop. ▷两个孩子挨着门坐。The two children sat by the door. 2 (逐个) ▷警察挨门搜查。The police conducted a house-to-house search. →另见 ái

挨个儿 āigèr [副] one by one ▷请大家排好队，挨个儿上车。Please will everyone line up and get on the bus one by one.

挨近 āijìn [动] be close to ▷我们学校挨近一家电影院。Our school is close to a cinema.

挨门挨户 āimén-āihù house-to-house ▷你对挨门挨户推销的做法有什么看法？What do you think of the door-to-door sales method?

唉 āi [叹] 1 (表示答应) mm 2 (表示叹息) oh →另见 ài

唉声叹气 āi shēng tàn qì sigh deeply

挨 ái [动] 1 (遭受) suffer ▷挨饿 suffer from hunger ▷挨骂 get told off 2 (艰难度过) endure ▷那么困难的年代我们都挨过来了，这不算什么。We have all endured such difficult times that this seems insignificant. 3 (拖延) put ... off (PT, PP put) →另见 āi

挨打 áidǎ [动] be beaten up

挨整 áizhěng [动] be the target of attack

皑 ái [形] 见下文

皑皑 ái'ái [形] snow-white

癌 ái [名] cancer

癌变 áibiàn [动] become cancerous (PT became, PP become)

癌症 áizhèng [名] cancer

嗳 ái [叹] oh

矮 ǎi [形] 1 (指人) short ▷我矮他一头。I'm a head shorter than him. 2 (指物) low

矮小 ǎixiǎo [形] 1 (身材) short 2 (树木、草棚等) low

矮子 ǎizi [名] dwarf

蔼 ǎi [形] friendly

霭 ǎi [名] mist

艾 ài I [名] (植) mugwort II [动] (书) end

艾滋病 àizībìng [名] AIDS

唉 ài [叹] 1 (表伤感或惋惜) oh 2 (表示回应命令) OK →另见 āi

爱 ài [动] 1 (恋) love ▷我爱你。I love you. ▷爱祖国 love one's country ▷他爱上了一个女孩。He fell in love with a girl. 2 (喜欢) enjoy ▷爱上网 enjoy surfing the net ▷爱逛街 enjoy strolling around the streets 3 (爱惜) care about ▷爱公物 respect public property 4 (容易) ▷她爱晕车。She tends to get car sick. ▷爱发脾气 be hot-tempered

爱不释手 ài bù shì shǒu be attached ▷他对那台笔记本电脑爱不释手。He's very attached to that laptop.

爱称 àichēng [名] pet name

爱戴 àidài [动] love and esteem

爱抚 àifǔ [动] fondle

爱好 àihào [动] be keen on ▷爱好集邮 be keen on stamp collecting ▷她有广泛的爱好。She has many hobbies.

爱护 àihù [动] take care of (PT took, PP taken)

爱怜 àilián [动] coo over ▷这只小狗真惹人爱怜。The puppy made everyone coo.

爱莫能助 ài mò néng zhù have one's hands tied ▷他有很多困难，但我爱莫能助。He's having a lot of problems, but my hands are tied.

爱慕 àimù [动] adore ▷她爱慕她丈夫。She adores her husband. ▷那女人爱慕虚荣。That woman is very vain.

爱情 àiqíng [名] love ▷爱情是无价的。Love is priceless.

爱屋及乌 ài wū jí wū love me, love my dog ▷他真是爱屋及乌，竟然喜欢上了女友听的音乐。This really is a case of love me, love my dog. Now he's suddenly started to like his girlfriend's music.

爱惜 àixī [动] value ▷爱惜时间 value one's time

爱心 àixīn [名] affection

隘 ài I [形] narrow ▶隘巷 narrow alley II [名] pass ▶要隘 pass

碍 ài [动] be in the way ▷你干你的，我干我的，碍你啥了？You get on with your business and I'll get on with mine. I'm not in your way, am I?

碍口 àikǒu [动] be too embarrassing for words ▷跟老师借钱真碍口！Borrowing money from a teacher is too embarrassing for words!

碍面子 ài miànzi ▷碍着上级的面子，他没啥意见。To avoid his superiors losing face, he didn't make any suggestions.

碍事 àishì I [动] matter ▷他出席不了会议不碍事。It didn't matter that he couldn't attend the meeting. II [形] serious ▷他的病不碍事。His illness isn't serious.

碍手碍脚 ài shǒu ài jiǎo get in the way ▷我正忙着呢，别在这里碍手碍脚的。I'm really busy - stop getting in the way.

碍眼 àiyǎn [形] 1 (不顺眼) ugly ▷这些花花绿绿的标牌立在校园里，怪碍眼的。These gaudy signs all over campus are a real eyesore. 2 (不便) in the way ▷人家正忙着呢，我们在这里碍眼，快走吧！Everyone's very busy. We're in the way here - let's go!

嗳 ài [叹] oh

暧 ài [形] (书) dim

暧昧 àimèi [形] 1 (含糊) vague 2 (关系) ambiguous

安 ān I [形] 1 (安定) quiet ▷坐立不安 be unable to sit still ▷心神不安 feel uneasy 2 (平安) safe ▶治安 public order ▷安抵目的地 arrive safely at one's destination II [动] 1 (使安静) calm ▶安心 calm the nerves 2 (满足) be content with ▷安于现状 be content with the way things are 3 (放置) place ▷把他安在哪里合适呢？Where would be a good place to put him? 4 (安装) fit ▷安窗户 fit a window ▷门上安把锁 fit a lock on the door 5 (设立) set ... up (PT, PP set) ▷这里安了个收费站。A toll booth has been set up here. 6 (加上) bring (PT, PP brought) ▷安罪名 bring a charge 7 (怀着) harbour (英), harbor (美) ▷安坏心 harbour (英) or harbor (美) evil intentions ▷你安的什么心？What are you plotting?

安插 ānchā [动] 1 (人) install ▷安插亲信 install in place a trusted friend 2 (东西) insert ▷安插

增刊 insert supplements

安定 āndìng I [形] stable II [动] stabilize ▷安定局面 stabilize the situation ▷安定民心 reassure the public

安顿 āndùn I [动] (表示安排妥当) (人) make arrangements for ▷安顿家小 make arrangements for the family II [形] (安稳) peaceful ▷这儿太嘈杂，我睡不安顿。It's too noisy here – I can't sleep properly.

安放 ānfàng [动] put ... in a safe place (PT, PP put) ▷把贵重物品安放好。Put your valuables in a safe place.

安分 ānfèn [形] contented

安好 ānhǎo [形] safe and sound

安家 ānjiā [动] 1 (安置家庭) settle ▷他们在北京安了家。They settled in Beijing. 2 (结婚) get married

安检 ānjiǎn [名] security check ▷经过安检 go through security ▷乘客登机前必须安检。Passengers must go through security before boarding.

安静 ānjìng [形] 1 (无声) quiet 2 (平静) peaceful ▷婴儿在小床上睡得很安静。The baby was sleeping peacefully in its cot.

安乐 ānlè [形] comfortable

安乐死 ānlèsǐ [名] euthanasia

安宁 ānníng [形] 1 (秩序正常) undisturbed 2 (宁静) calm ▷我心里天天不得安宁。I never feel at ease.

安排 ānpái [动] arrange

安全 ānquán [形] safe ▷居民区有保安巡逻，比较安全。There are security patrols in this district, so it is fairly safe. ▷安全驾驶 drive safely ▷一人出门在外，注意安全。When you are away from home, be sure to take care. ▷人身安全 personal safety

安全套 ānquántào [名] condom

安然 ānrán [形] 1 (平安) safe ▷安然无恙 safe and sound 2 (平静) peaceful ▷知道门已关好，她安然入睡了。Once she knew that the door had been locked, she fell asleep peacefully.

安身 ānshēn [动] settle down

安生 ānshēng [形] 1 (安定) peaceful 2 (安静) quiet

安慰 ānwèi I [动] comfort ▷我安慰了他几句。I said a few comforting words to him. II [形] reassured ▷听了你讲的话，我心里很安慰。After hearing what you had to say, I felt reassured.

安稳 ānwěn [形] 1 (稳当) steady 2 (方) (沉静) calm

安息 ānxī [动] 1 (休息) rest 2 (悼念用语) rest in peace

安详 ānxiáng [形] composed

安心 ānxīn [动] 1 (形容心情) stop worrying ▷得

知家中一切都好，我也就安心了。Once I knew that everything was fine at home, I stopped worrying. 2 (居心不善) plot ▷你安的什么心？What are you plotting? 3 (不分心) keep one's mind on (PT, PP kept)

安逸 ānyì [形] comfortable

安葬 ānzàng [动] bury

安置 ānzhì [动] make arrangements for

安装 ānzhuāng [动] install

庵 ān [名] 1 (书) (小草屋) hut 2 (佛寺) nunnery

谙 ān [动] (书) be familiar with

谙熟 ānshú [动] have a good knowledge of

鹌 ān 见下文

鹌鹑 ānchún [名] quail

鞍 ān [名] saddle

岸 àn I [名] edge ▷河岸 river bank ▷海岸 seashore II [形] 1 (崇高) lofty ▷伟岸 strapping 2 (骄傲) proud ▷傲岸 proud

按 àn I [动] 1 (用手压) press ▷按电钮 press a button ▷按门铃 push a doorbell ▷按手印 make a fingerprint 2 (人) push ... down ▷他把小偷按倒在地。He pushed the thief to the ground. 3 (搁下) shelve ▷按下此事不说 put the matter aside 4 (抑制) restrain ▷按不住心头怒火 be unable to restrain one's fury II [介] (依照) according to ▷按制度办事 do things by the book ▷按质定价 price on the basis of quality

按部就班 àn bù jiù bān stick to the rules ▷时间不够了，不能这样按部就班。There's not enough time, so we will have to break the rules.

按揭 ànjiē [名] mortgage

按摩 ànmó [动] massage

按捺 ànnà [动] restrain

按图索骥 àn tú suǒ jì be rigid in one's approach ▷他做什么事情都是按图索骥，效率太低。He's ineffective because his approach is too rigid.

按照 ànzhào [介] according to ▷按照课本 according to the text book ▷方案按照大家的建议修改了。The plan was changed in line with everyone's recommendations.

案 àn [名] 1 (桌子) table 2 (案件) case 3 (案卷) file 4 (提案) proposal

案件 ànjiàn [名] case

案卷 ànjuàn [名] file

案子 ànzi [名] 1 (家具) counter ▷熨衣案子 ironing board 2 (案件) case

暗 àn I [形] 1 (昏暗) dim ▷今晚月光很暗。 Tonight the moon is dim. 2 (秘密) underhand ▷明人不做暗事。 An honest person does nothing underhand. II [副] secretly

暗暗 àn'àn [副] secretly

暗藏 àncáng [动] conceal

暗淡 àndàn [形] 1 (昏暗) dim 2 (不明朗) dismal

暗害 ànhài [动] 1 (暗杀) murder 2 (陷害) stab ... in the back

暗号 ànhào [名] secret signal

暗杀 ànshā [动] assassinate

暗示 ànshì [动] hint ▷他暗示我赶快离开。 He hinted that I should leave soon. ▷他没明白我的暗示。 He didn't pick up on my hint.

暗算 ànsuàn [动] plot against ▷他总是暗算别人。 He's always plotting against people. ▷他常常遭人暗算。 He frequently falls prey to other people's machinations.

暗无天日 àn wú tiān rì anarchy ▷当时的社会暗无天日。 There was complete anarchy in society at that time.

暗语 ànyǔ [名] code word

暗中 ànzhōng I [名] the dark ▷我在暗中什么也看不见。 I couldn't see anything in the dark. II [副] surreptitiously ▷他暗中操纵选举。 He surreptitiously fixed the election.

暗自 ànzì [副] secretly

黯 àn 见下文

黯然 ànrán [形] 1 (昏暗) dim 2 (低落) dejected

肮 āng 见下文

肮脏 āngzāng [形] 1 (不干净) filthy ▷地板很肮脏。 The floor is filthy. 2 (喻) (不道德) vile ▷他思想肮脏。 His way of thinking is vile. ▷这是一笔肮脏的交易。 It's a dirty deal.

昂 áng [动] 1 (抬) lift ▷昂起头 hold one's head high 2 (高涨) be high ▷她情绪高昂。 She's high in spirits.

昂然 ángrán [形] resolute

昂首阔步 áng shǒu kuò bù stride with one's head held high ▷他昂首阔步地前进。 He strode forward with his head held high.

昂扬 ángyáng [形] upbeat

盎 àng [形] (书) abundant

盎然 àngrán [形] abundant

盎司 àngsī [量] ounce

凹 āo [形] sunken

凹陷 āoxiàn [动] sink (PT sank, PP sunk)

遨 áo 见下文

遨游 áoyóu [动] travel

嗷 áo 见下文

嗷嗷 áo'áo [拟] ▷他疼得嗷嗷叫。 He howled with pain. ▷成群的雁在头顶嗷嗷叫着。 Flocks of geese honked overhead.

熬 áo [动] 1 (煮) stew ▶熬粥 make porridge 2 (提取) decoct 3 (忍受) endure

熬煎 áojiān [名] suffering

熬夜 áoyè [动] stay up late

翱 áo 见下文

翱翔 áoxiáng [动] soar

鏖 áo 见下文

鏖战 áozhàn [动] fight hard (PT, PP fought)

袄 ǎo [名] coat ▶棉袄 padded jacket

拗 ào [动] awkward

→另见 niù

拗口 àokǒu [形] hard to pronounce

傲 ào [形] proud

傲骨 àogǔ [名] pride

傲慢 àomàn [形] arrogant

傲气 àoqì [名] arrogance ▷他有股傲气。 He is a bit arrogant.

傲然 àorán I [形] lofty II [副] proudly

奥 ào [形] profound

奥林匹克运动会 Àolínpǐkè Yùndònghuì [名] Olympic Games (PL)

奥秘 àomì [名] mystery ▷揭示大自然的奥秘 reveal Nature's mysteries

奥妙 àomiào [形] mysterious ▷这问题很好理解，其中并无奥妙。 This can be easily explained – there's nothing mysterious about it at all.

澳 ào [名] bay

懊 ào [形] 1 (后悔) regretful 2 (恼怒) annoyed

懊悔 àohuǐ [动] regret ▷他错过了这个好机会，懊悔不已。 He really regretted having missed such a good opportunity.

懊恼 àonǎo [形] upset ▷他因没考好而懊恼。 He was upset that he didn't get a better mark in the exam.

懊丧 àosàng [形] despondent ▷他因失业而懊丧。 Losing his job left him rather despondent.

Bb

八 **bā** [数] eight

八方 **bāfāng** [名] all directions

八股 **bāgǔ** [名] lifeless writing

八九不离十 **bā jiǔ bù lí shí** (口) pretty close ▷你的答案八九不离十。Your answer is pretty close.

八面玲珑 **bāmiàn línglóng** be a smooth operator

八仙过海，各显神通 **bāxiān guòhǎi, gè xiǎn shéntōng** compete to demonstrate one's talents ▷他们大搞技术创新，真是八仙过海，各显神通。They have been very innovative technically – each competing with the other to demonstrate their talents.

巴 **bā** I [动] 1 (盼望) hope ▶巴望 look forward to 2 (粘住) cling to (PT, PP clung) ▷葡萄藤巴在架子上。The vine clung to the trellis. 3 (方) (张开) open ▷巴着眼 with eyes open II [名] 1 (粘结物) crust ▶锅巴 rice crust ▶泥巴 mud 2 (器官) ▶下巴 chin ▶尾巴 tail ▶嘴巴 mouth

巴结 **bājie** [动] suck up to ▷巴结上司 suck up to the boss

巴士 **bāshì** [名] bus

巴望 **bāwàng** [动] look forward to ▷他巴望着能来信。He was looking forward to getting a letter.

巴掌 **bāzhang** [名] (手掌) palm ▷拍巴掌 clap

扒 **bā** [动] 1 (挖) dig ... up (PT, PP dug) ▷她把埋的陶器扒了出来。She dug up buried pottery. 2 (拆) pull ... down ▷扒房子 pull down a house 3 (攀缘) lean on ▷两个邻居扒在墙头上聊天。The two neighbours (英) 或 neighbors (美) leaned on the wall chatting. 4 (拨动) push ... aside 5 (剥下) take ... off (PT took, PP taken) ▷扒下袜子 take off one's socks
→另见 pá

扒拉 **bāla** [动] brush ▷把土扒拉一边去 brush the earth to one side

芭 **bā** [名] banana

芭蕉 **bājiāo** [名] banana

芭蕾舞 **bālěiwǔ** [名] ballet

吧 **bā** I [拟] crack ▷吧！枪响了。The gun went off with a crack. II [名] bar III [动] take a drag (PT took, PP taken) ▷他吧了一口烟。He took a drag on his cigarette.

吧嗒 **bādā** [拟] click ▷门吧嗒一声关上了。The door closed with a click.

吧女 **bānǚ** [名] barmaid

疤 **bā** [名] 1 (疤痕) scar ▷他脸上有疤。He had a scar on his face. 2 (痕迹) mark

疤痕 **bāhén** [名] scar ▷这件事给他心里留下一个疤痕。This event left him psychologically scarred.

捌 **bā** [数] eight

笆 **bā** [名] basketry

笆斗 **bādǒu** [名] basket

拔 **bá** [动] 1 (抽出) pull ... up ▶拔草 weed 2 (取下) pull ... out ▷拔牙 pull out a tooth 3 (吸出) draw ... out (PT drew, PP drawn) 4 (挑选) choose (PT chose, PP chosen) ▷选拔人才 select talented people 5 (提高) raise 6 (超出) exceed ▶海拔 height above sea level ▷出类拔萃 outstanding 7 (夺取) capture ▷连拔三城 capture three towns in succession 8 (冷却) cool ▷用冰水拔啤酒 cool beer in iced water

拔高 **bágāo** [动] raise ▷拔高嗓门 raise one's voice

拔河 **báhé** [名] tug-of-war

拔尖儿 **bájiānr** [形] excellent

拔苗助长 **bá miáo zhù zhǎng** damage by applying too much pressure ▷用这种方法教育孩子，简直是拔苗助长。Teaching children in this way simply means applying too much pressure and damaging them.

跋 bá I [动] cross ▶跋山 cross mountains II [名] postscript

跋扈 báhù [形] domineering

跋山涉水 bá shān shè shuǐ cross mountains and rivers

跋涉 báshè [动] trek ▷长途跋涉 make a long trek

把 bǎ I [动] 1 (握住) hold (PT, PP held) ▷把住栏杆 hold onto the rails 2 (看守) guard ▷把大门 guard the gate 3 (控制) control ▷把舵 be at the helm 4 (拿) take (PT took, PP taken) ▷别把这当回事。Don't take this too seriously. 5 (紧靠) be near to ▷把着十字路口有家超市。There is a supermarket near the crossroads. 6 (束缚) secure ▷把住裂口 secure a breach II [名] 1 (把手) handle 2 (捆) bundle ▶草把 a bundle of straw III [量] ▷一把刀 a knife ▷一把米 a handful of rice IV [介] ▷把门关好 shut the door ▷把作业做完 finish doing one's homework ▷她把书放在桌子上了。She put the book on the table. V [副] about ▷个把月 about one month
→另见 bà

把柄 bǎbǐng [名] hold ▷他抓住了我的把柄。He's got a hold over me.

把持 bǎchí [动] 1 (独占) monopolize ▷把持高位 monopolize power 2 (控制) control ▷她被伤害得这么厉害,我怕她把持不住。She has been hurt so badly, I'm worried she may not be able to keep her feelings under control.

把关 bǎguān [动] 1 (把守关口) hold a pass (PT, PP held) 2 (严守标准) ensure standards (PL) ▷把好质量关 ensure quality standards

把势 bǎshi [名] 1 (武术) martial arts (PL) 2 (能手) skilled worker ▷干庄稼活儿,他是个好把势。He is a skilled farmer.

把守 bǎshǒu [动] guard ▷把守边境 guard the border

把手 bǎshou [名] handle

把握 bǎwò I [动] grasp ▷把握实质 have a grasp of the facts ▷把握时机 seize the opportunity II [名] certainty ▷没把握 there is no certainty ▷我对自己的未来毫无把握。My future is very uncertain.

把戏 bǎxì [名] 1 (杂耍) acrobatics (PL) 2 (花招) trick ▷他耍的把戏很难看穿。It's not easy to see through his tricks.

把兄弟 bǎxiōngdì [名] sworn brothers

靶 bǎ [名] target

靶子 bǎzi [名] target ▷你还未射中靶子。You haven't hit the target yet. ▷她因犯了个错而被当作攻击的靶子。Because she made a mistake she became the target of attack.

把 bà [名] 1 (手柄) handle ▶镐把 pickaxe handle 2 (茎秆) stem ▶花把 stem 3 (话柄) butt ▶话把儿 the butt of ridicule
→另见 bǎ

把子 bàzi [名] handle ▷刀把子 knife handle

坝 bà [名] 1 (水闸) dam 2 (堤坝) dyke

爸 bà [名] father

爸爸 bàba [名] dad

耙 bà I [名] harrow II [动] harrow
→另见 pá

罢 bà [动] 1 (停) stop ▷欲罢不能 compelled to carry on 2 (免去) dismiss ▶罢免 recall 3 (完毕) finish ▷听罢,他哈哈大笑。After listening, he laughed out loud. 4 (算了) give up (PT gave, PP given)

罢工 bàgōng [动] strike (PT, PP struck) ▷工人们罢工要求增加工资。The workers are striking for higher wages.

罢了 bàle [助] ▷我的水平不高,只是尽自己的努力罢了。My average is not high, but I put in my best effort; that's all there is to it.

罢了 bàliǎo [动] let it pass (PT, PP let)

罢免 bàmiǎn [动] recall

罢手 bàshǒu [动] give up (PT gave, PP given)

罢休 bàxiū [动] give up (PT gave, PP given)

霸 bà I [名] 1 (指人) tyrant ▶恶霸 local tyrant 2 (指国家) hegemonist power ▶争霸 struggle for hegemony II [动] tyrannize ▶独霸一方 tyrannize a region III [形] tyrannical ▶霸气 domineering

霸道 bàdào [形] overbearing ▷横行霸道 tyrannize

霸道 bàdao [形] potent

霸权 bàquán [名] hegemony

霸王 bàwáng [名] despot

霸业 bàyè [名] position of supremacy

霸占 bàzhàn [动] seize

掰 bāi [动] break ... off (PT broke, PP broken) ▷农民们在田地里正掰玉米呢。The farmers are picking maize in the fields.

掰腕子 bāi wànzi [动] arm wrestle

白 bái I [形] 1 (白色) white ▶苍白 pale 2 (清楚) clear ▷真相大白 the truth has come out 3 (明

亮) bright ▶白天 daytime **4** (平淡) plain ▶白开水 boiled water **II** [动] state ▶辩白 argue **III** [副] **1** (无结果) in vain ▷我们这些试验是白做了。Our experiments were in vain. **2** (无偿地) free of charge ▷那些政客就喜欢白吃白喝。Those politicians just like eating and drinking, free of charge.

白白 báibái [副] in vain ▷不要白白浪费钱。Don't waste your money on nothing.

白璧微瑕 bái bì wēi xiá minor flaw

白菜 báicài [名] Chinese cabbage

白痴 báichī [名] **1** (病症) idiocy **2** (病人) idiot **3** (贬) (傻瓜) moron

白费 báifèi [动] waste ▷我们的努力没有白费。Our efforts have not been wasted. ▷你不要白费心思。Don't strain your brain for nothing.

白宫 Báigōng [名] the White House

白话 báihuà [名] unfounded statement

白金 báijīn [名] platinum

白净 báijìng [形] fair and clear

白酒 báijiǔ [名] clear spirit

白卷 báijuàn [名] unanswered examination paper

白领 báilǐng [名] ▷白领职员 white-collar worker

白马王子 báimǎ wángzǐ knight in shining armour (英) 或 armor (美)

白米饭 báimǐfàn [名] boiled rice

白描 báimiáo [名] **1** (指美术) line drawing **2** (指写作) straightforward style of writing

白皮书 báipíshū [名] White Paper

白热 báirè [形] white-hot

白人 báirén [名] white people (PL) ▷他是白人。He's white.

白日做梦 báirì zuò mèng daydream

白色 báisè [名] **1** (字) white **2** (喻) counterrevolutionary ▷白色政权 counterrevolutionary regime

白手起家 báishǒu qǐ jiā build up from nothing (PT, PP built) ▷他们夫妻是白手起家。The couple started out their business from scratch.

白糖 báitáng [名] white sugar

白天 báitiān [名] daytime, day

白条 báitiáo [名] IOU

白头偕老 báitóu xié lǎo live together to a ripe old age ▷祝愿这对新人白头偕老，永远幸福。May the bride and groom live happily ever after to a ripe old age.

白血病 báixuèbìng [名] leukaemia (英), leukemia (美)

白眼 báiyǎn [名] disdainful look ▷他恨遭人白眼。He hates being treated with disdain.

白银 báiyín [名] silver

白昼 báizhòu [名] daytime

白字 báizì [名] wrong character

百 bǎi **I** [数] hundred **II** [形] numerous ▷千方百计 in every way possible

百般 bǎibān [副] in every possible way

百出 bǎichū [动] be full of

百废俱兴 bǎi fèi jù xīng all neglected tasks are being dealt with

百分比 bǎifēnbǐ [名] percentage

百分点 bǎifēndiǎn [名] percentage point

百分制 bǎifēnzhì [名] percentage system

百分之百 bǎi fēn zhī bǎi absolutely ▷他百分之百会来。He will definitely come.

百花齐放 bǎi huā qí fàng blossom freely ▷我们国家的文艺事业百花齐放。Our country's literature and arts scenes are blossoming freely.

百货 bǎihuò [名] general goods (PL) ▷百货商店 department store

百科全书 bǎikē quánshū [名] encyclopaedia (英), encyclopedia (美)

百里挑一 bǎi lǐ tiāo yī one in a hundred ▷这小伙儿真是百里挑一。This lad is really one in a hundred.

百炼成钢 bǎi liàn chéng gāng experience makes you stronger ▷这支军队百炼成钢。This army has been toughened up by its experience.

百年大计 bǎinián dàjì [名] landmark event

百年树人 bǎinián shùrén it takes a long time to cultivate people

百万 bǎiwàn [数] million ▷百万富翁 millionaire

百闻不如一见 bǎi wén bù rú yī jiàn seeing is believing

百无聊赖 bǎi wú liáolài bored stiff

百姓 bǎixìng [名] the common people

百依百顺 bǎiyī bǎishùn very obedient ▷他对妻子百依百顺。He obeys his wife in everything.

百折不挠 bǎi zhé bù náo indomitable

佰 bǎi [名] hundred

柏 bǎi [名] cypress

柏油 bǎiyóu [名] tar ▷柏油路 asphalt road

摆 bǎi **I** [动] **1** (放置) arrange ▷请把桌子摆

好。Please lay the table. **2** (陈述)state **3** (显示)assume ▷他总是摆出一副官架子。He's always assuming official airs. **4** (摇动)wave ▷摆手 beckon **II** [名] **1** (部件)pendulum **2** (下幅)hem

摆布 bǎibù [动] **1** (操纵)order ... around **2** (布置)arrange

摆动 bǎidòng [动] sway

摆放 bǎifàng [动] place

摆阔 bǎikuò [动] be ostentatious

摆弄 bǎinòng [动] **1** (玩弄)fiddle with **2** (运用)manipulate ▷他善于摆弄权力。He is adept at manipulation.

摆平 bǎipíng [动] treat ... equally ▷我们对双方要摆平。We want to treat both parties equally.

摆谱儿 bǎipǔr [动] show off (PT showed, PP shown)

摆设 bǎishè [动] furnish and decorate ▷客厅里摆设得很有品位。The living room is tastefully furnished and decorated.

摆设儿 bǎisher [名] ornament

摆脱 bǎituō [动] break free from (PT broke, PP broken) ▷我们终于摆脱了贫困。We have finally broken free from poverty.

败 bài **I** [动] **1** (打败)defeat ▷大败敌人 defeat the enemy ▷我们败于主队。We lost to the home team. **2** (消除)counteract ▷败毒 counteract a poison **3** (毁坏)ruin **II** [形] withered

败北 bàiběi [动] be defeated

败笔 bàibǐ [名] artistic defect

败坏 bàihuài **I** [动] corrupt **II** [形] corrupt ▷这些人道德品质败坏。These people are morally corrupt.

败家子 bàijiāzǐ [名] spendthrift

败局 bàijú [名] defeat

败类 bàilèi [名] scum

败露 bàilù [动] be exposed

败落 bàiluò [动] decline ▷这个大家族逐渐败落了。The great family gradually went into decline.

败诉 bàisù [动] lose a lawsuit (PT, PP lost)

败仗 bàizhàng [名] defeat ▷这位将军从未打过败仗。This general has never suffered defeat.

拜 bài [动] **1** (会见)pay a visit (PT, PP paid) ▶拜会 pay an official call **2** (结拜)acknowledge ▷我拜他为师。I acknowledge him as my master. ▷结拜兄弟 sworn brothers

拜访 bàifǎng [动] call on

拜会 bàihuì [动] pay an official call (PT, PP paid)

拜年 bàinián [动] pay a New Year call (PT, PP paid)

拜托 bàituō [动] ▷拜托您给看会儿我女儿。Would you be kind enough to look after my daughter for a while.

拜谒 bàiyè [动] **1** (拜见)pay a formal visit (PT, PP paid) **2** (瞻仰)pay homage

扳 bān [动] **1** (拉动)pull ▷扳闸 pull a switch **2** (扭转)turn ▷双方扳成平局。The score is now equal.

扳子 bānzi [名] spanner

班 bān **I** [名] **1** (班级)class **2** (班组)team **3** (轮班)shift **4** (军)squad **II** [量] ▷下一班船 the next boat **III** [形] regular ▶班车 regular bus **IV** [动] deploy

班房 bānfáng [名] prison

班机 bānjī [名] **1** (指飞机)airliner **2** (指航班)scheduled flight

班级 bānjí [名] classes (PL)

班门弄斧 Bān mén nòng fǔ show oneself up in front of an expert

班子 bānzi [名] **1** (组织)group **2** (剧团)troupe

般 bān [名] sort

般配 bānpèi [动] be well matched

颁 bān 见下文

颁布 bānbù [动] promulgate

颁发 bānfā [动] **1** (发布)issue **2** (授予)award

斑 bān [名] spot

斑白 bānbái [形] greying (英), graying (美)

斑斓 bānlán [形] brightly-coloured (英), brightly-colored (美)

斑马线 bānmǎxiàn [名] zebra crossing

搬 bān [动] **1** (移动)take ... away (PT took, PP taken) ▷把这些东西搬走。Take these things away. **2** (迁移)move ▷搬家 move house **3** (套用)copy mechanically

搬弄 bānnòng [动] **1** (搬动)fiddle with ▷不要搬弄枪。Don't fiddle with the gun. **2** (挑拨)stir ... up ▷搬弄是非 make mischief **3** (炫耀)show ... off (PT showed, PP shown) ▷搬弄知识 show off one's knowledge

搬迁 bānqiān [动] relocate

搬运 bānyùn [动] transport

板 bǎn **I** [名] **1** (片状硬物)board ▷天花板 ceiling **2** (音)beat ▷有板有眼 rhythmical **II** [形] **1** (指人)stiff ▶古板 inflexible **2** (指物)hard ▷地太硬了。The ground is very hard. **III** [动] put on a stern expression (PT, PP put) ▷我

们经理老板着脸。Our manager always looks stern.

板子 bǎnzi [名] board

版 bǎn [名] 1 (底版) printing plate ▶排版 typesetting 2 (版本) edition ▶初版 first edition 3 (版面) page ▶头版 front page

版本 bǎnběn [名] edition

版权 bǎnquán [名] copyright ▷版权所有 all rights reserved

版式 bǎnshì [名] format

版税 bǎnshuì [名] royalty

版图 bǎntú [名] territory

办 bàn I [动] 1 (处理) handle ▶办事 handle affairs 2 (创设) set ... up (PT, PP set) ▷去年他们办了一个工厂。Last year they set up a factory. 3 (经营) run (PT ran, PP run) ▷校办产业 school-run industry 4 (展览) stage ▷办画展 stage an art exhibition 5 (采购) purchase 6 (惩治) punish II [名] office

办法 bànfǎ [名] way ▷想办法解决问题 find a way to solve the problem ▷这个办法可行。This is a feasible solution. ▷老师拿不努力的学生没办法。Teachers can do nothing about lazy students. ▷你办法多，帮帮我们。You always know how to sort things out – give us a hand. ▷联系办法 means of contact

办公 bàngōng [动] work

办理 bànlǐ [动] handle ▷办理丧事 handle funeral arrangements

办学 bànxué [动] run a school (PT ran, PP run)

办罪 bànzuì [动] punish

半 bàn I [数] 1 (二分之一) half ▶半价 half price 2 (很少) very few ▷他半个字都没写。He'd hardly written anything. II [名] middle ▶半夜 midnight III [副] partially ▶半新 almost new ▷他合上半开着的书。He closed the half-open book.

半半拉拉 bànbanlālā [形] (口) unfinished

半辈子 bànbèizi [名] half a lifetime ▷他当了半辈子的教师。He had spent half a lifetime as a teacher.

半壁江山 bànbì jiāngshān half the country ▷半壁江山沦落敌手。Half the country has fallen into the hands of the enemy. ▷他拥有这家公司的半壁江山。He owns half of the company.

半边天 bànbiāntiān [名] 1 (指天空) half the sky 2 (指妇女) women (PL)

半···不··· bàn...bù... neither ... nor ▶半新不旧 nearly new ▶半懂不懂 not quite clear

半成品 bànchéngpǐn [名] semi-finished product

半导体 bàndǎotǐ [名] 1 (指物质) semiconductor 2 (收音机) transistor radio

半岛 bàndǎo [名] peninsula

半吊子 bàndiàozi [名] 1 (指言行举止) blunderer 2 (指水平) incompetent ▷半吊子的老师怎么能教出好学生呢？How can that incompetent of a teacher produce good students? 3 (指处事态度) no-hoper

半斤八两 bàn jīn bā liǎng (口) six of one and half a dozen of the other ▷这两个人半斤八两，都不能胜任这份工作。They're six of one and half a dozen of the other – neither of them are competent enough to do the job.

半径 bànjìng [名] radius (PL radii)

半路出家 bànlù chūjiā (喻) have a complete career change

半瓶醋 bànpíngcù [名] (贬) ignoramus

半球 bànqiú [名] hemisphere ▷南半球 the Southern Hemisphere

半死不活 bàn sǐ bù huó lifeless

半途 bàntú [名] (书) halfway point

半途而废 bàntú ér fèi give up halfway ▷我们一定要坚持到底，不能半途而废。We must persevere – we can't give up halfway.

扮 bàn [动] 1 (饰演) play ▷他在影片中扮坏人。He played the villain in the film. 2 (指表情) pull ▷别冲我扮鬼脸。Don't pull faces at me.

扮相 bànxiàng [名] look ▷我喜欢戏中女主角的扮相。I liked the look of the female character in the play.

扮演 bànyǎn [动] act

伴 bàn I [名] company ▷我会和你做伴的。I will keep you company. ▷我和约翰搭伴去伦敦。John and I travelled to London together. II [动] accompany ▷在他的陪伴下，我回到了故乡。He accompanied me back to my hometown.

伴唱 bànchàng [动] accompany

伴侣 bànlǚ [名] 1 (爱人) partner 2 (伙伴) companion

伴娘 bànniáng [名] bridesmaid

伴随 bànsuí [动] follow

伴舞 bànwǔ [动] ▷她过去是伴舞的。She used to be a backing dancer.

伴奏 bànzòu [动] accompany ▷你唱支歌，我来给你用手风琴伴奏。Give us a song – I'll accompany you on the accordion.

拌 bàn [动] 1 (搅和) mix 2 (争吵) quarrel

拌嘴 bànzuǐ [动] quarrel

绊 bàn [动] 1 (使跌倒) trip ▷他下楼时绊脚了一跤。He tripped over on his way downstairs. 2 (妨碍) get in the way 3 (缠住) hold ... up (PT, PP held) ▷他可能又被什么事情绊住了。Maybe something's held him up again.

绊脚石 bànjiǎoshí [名] stumbling block

瓣 bàn I [名] 1 (指花儿) petal 2 (指果实或球茎) segment 3 (碎片) fragment II [量] 1 (指花、叶、果实等) ▷几瓣蒜 a few cloves of garlic ▷一瓣橘子 a segment of orange 2 (部分) part

瓣膜 bànmó [名] (医) valve

邦 bāng [名] country

邦交 bāngjiāo [名] diplomatic relations (PL) ▷断绝邦交 break off diplomatic relations

帮 bāng I [动] 1 (帮助) help ▷我帮他修改文章。I helped him to improve his essay. 2 (被雇用) be hired ▶帮短工 be hired for short-term work II [名] 1 (物体周围的面) side ▶鞋帮 shoe upper 2 (菜帮子) outer leaf (PL leaves) 3 (团伙) gang III [量] group ▷一帮小伙子 a group of young men

帮厨 bāngchú [动] help out in the kitchen

帮倒忙 bāng dàománg [动] do ... a disservice ▷他这么说其实是在给我帮倒忙。Actually what he said did me quite a disservice.

帮会 bānghuì [名] (旧) secret society

帮教 bāngjiào [动] help and teach (PT, PP taught)

帮忙 bāngmáng [动] help ▷请您帮我个忙。Please can you help me out?

帮派 bāngpài [名] faction

帮腔 bāngqiāng [动] stick up for (PT, PP stuck) ▷你为什么总给他帮腔? Why are you always sticking up for him?

帮手 bāngshǒu [名] assistant

帮凶 bāngxiōng [名] accessory

帮助 bāngzhù [动] help ▷护士长帮他做手术。The head nurse helped him carry out the operation. ▷他帮助我们渡过难关。He helped us through a difficult time. ▷水果帮助消化。Fruit aids the digestion. ▷我们需要专家的帮助。We need the help of an expert. ▷谢谢您的帮助。Thank you for your help.

帮子 bāngzi [名] outer leaf (PL leaves)

绑 bǎng [动] tie up

绑架 bǎngjià [动] kidnap

绑票 bǎngpiào [动] kidnap

榜 bǎng [名] list of names ▷光荣榜 roll of honour (英) 或 honor (美)

榜样 bǎngyàng [名] model

膀 bǎng [名] 1 (肩膀) shoulder 2 (翅膀) wing →另见 páng

膀子 bǎngzi [名] 1 (手臂上部) upper arm ▷光着膀子 be stripped to the waist 2 (翅膀) wing

蚌 bàng [名] clam

棒 bàng I [名] 1 (棍子) cudgel 2 (棍状物) rod II [形] (口) great ▷他英语说得很棒。He speaks great English.

棒槌 bàngchui [名] 1 (木棒) club 2 (外行) amateur

棒子 bàngzi [名] 1 (棍子) club 2 (玉米) corn (英), maize (美)

傍 bàng I [动] be close to II [介] near

傍大款 bàng dàkuǎn (口) be a gold-digger

傍晚 bàngwǎn [副] at dusk

谤 bàng [动] (书) slander

磅 bàng I [量] pound II [名] scales (PL) III [动] weigh →另见 páng

镑 bàng [名] pound

包 bāo I [动] 1 (包裹) wrap 2 (包围) surround 3 (包含) include ▷这笔钱只是旅费，不包食宿。This money is just for travel expenses. It doesn't include food and lodgings. 4 (承诺完成) be contracted ▷我们包下了这个工程。We've been contracted to do this project. 5 (担保) guarantee 6 (约定专用) hire ▷包车 hire a car ▷包飞机 charter a plane II [名] 1 (包裹) parcel ▶背包 backpack 2 (口袋) bag ▶钱包 wallet 3 (疙瘩) lump 4 (隆起物) hump 5 (帐篷) tent III [量] ▷一包烟 a pack of cigarettes ▷一包茶 a packet of tea

包办 bāobàn [动] 1 (单独负责) take sole charge of (PT took, PP taken) 2 (独断办理) monopolize ▷包办婚姻 arranged marriage

包庇 bāobì [动] cover up ▷包庇朋友 cover up for one's friends

包藏 bāocáng [动] harbour (英), harbor (美) ▷包藏杀机 harbour murderous intentions

包场 bāochǎng [动] make a block booking

包袱 bāofu [名] 1 (布) bundle 2 (喻) (负担) burden ▷孩子不应是成就事业的包袱。Children shouldn't get in the way of a successful career.

包干儿 bāogānr [动] see a task through (PT saw, PP seen)

包工 bāogōng I [动] contract ▷这座桥由一家北京建筑公司包工。A Beijing building company has been contracted to build the bridge. II [名] contractor

包裹 bāoguǒ [动] wrap II [名] parcel

包含 bāohán [动] contain

包涵 bāohán [动] forgive (PT forgave, PP forgiven) ▷招待不周，请多包涵！Please forgive me for giving you such a poor reception.

包括 bāokuò [动] include ▷月租450元，不包括取暖费。The rent is 450 yuan a month, but this doesn't include heating. ▷医疗队包括10个医生和一辆救护车。The medical team is comprised of ten doctors and one ambulance. ▷餐费包括百分之十的服务费。The bill includes a ten percent service charge.

包揽 bāolǎn [动] take sole charge of (PT took, PP taken)

包罗万象 bāoluó wànxiàng all-inclusive

包票 bāopiào [名] guarantee ▷我敢打包票，他肯定来。I can guarantee that he'll be coming.

包容 bāoróng [动] 1 (宽容) tolerate 2 (容纳) hold (PT, PP held)

包围 bāowéi [动] surround ▷这座城市四周被群山包围着。The city is surrounded by mountains on all sides.

包厢 bāoxiāng [名] box

包圆儿 bāoyuánr [动] 1 (全部买下) buy ... up (PT, PP bought) 2 (全部承担) finish ... off ▷这点活儿我们包圆儿了。We're going to finish this job off.

包扎 bāozā [动] bind (PT, PP bound)

包装 bāozhuāng I [动] package ... up II [名] package

苞 bāo [名] bud

苞米 bāomǐ [名] (方) corn (英), maize (美)

孢 bāo 见下文

孢子 bāozǐ [名] spore

炮 bāo [动] (烹调方法) sauté
→另见 páo, pào

胞 bāo [名] 1 (指同父母) blood ▷胞兄 full brother 2 (指同国家、同民族) fellow countryman (PL countrymen)

剥 bāo [动] peel ▷剥香蕉 peel a banana ▷剥豌豆 shell peas

龅 bāo 见下文

龅牙 bāoyá [名] buck teeth (PL)

褒 bāo [动] praise

褒贬 bāobiǎn [动] pass judgement on ▷不要随便褒贬人。You can't pass judgment on people without proper consideration.

褒奖 bāojiǎng [动] laud ▷这种行为应当受到褒奖。This kind of behaviour should be lauded.

褒扬 bāoyáng [动] praise

雹 báo [名] hail

雹子 báozi [名] hailstone

薄 báo [形] 1 (不厚) thin 2 (不浓) weak 3 (冷淡) cold ▷我对她不薄。I treat her very well. 4 (贫瘠) infertile ▷薄地 poor land
→另见 bó, bò

宝 bǎo I [名] treasure ▶国宝 national treasure II [形] precious

宝宝 bǎobǎo [名] darling

宝贝 bǎobèi [名] 1 (珍贵之物) treasure 2 (爱称) darling 3 (无能之人) idiot

宝贵 bǎoguì I [形] valuable ▷宝贵首饰 valuable jewellery ▷宝贵意见 valuable suggestion ▷宝贵文物 precious historical relics II [动] value ▷这玩意儿你不稀罕，他可宝贵得很。You don't care about it, but he values it dearly.

宝藏 bǎozàng [名] (矿产) precious minerals (PL)

宝座 bǎozuò [名] throne

饱 bǎo I [形] full ▷我吃饱了。I am full. II [副] fully ▷饱读美国文学 be well-read in American literature III [动] satisfy ▷精彩演出让观众大饱眼福。The audience feasted their eyes on the wonderful performance.

饱餐 bǎocān [动] eat one's fill (PT ate, PP eaten) ▷我们已饱餐了一顿。We've had a magnificent meal. ▷他们饱餐了一顿野味。They feasted on game.

饱尝 bǎocháng [动] 1 (吃饱) feast ▷饱尝美味佳肴 feast on fine food 2 (经历) experience

饱和 bǎohé [动] 1 (溶质) be saturated 2 (满) be full to capacity ▷政府机关的工作人员已经饱和了。The staff quota in the government organization is full. ▷冰箱的市场已经处于饱和状态。The market for refrigerators is already saturated.

饱经风霜 bǎo jīng fēngshuāng suffer hardship

饱满 **bǎomǎn** [形] **1** (丰满) plump **2** (充足) full ▷精神饱满 full of energy

饱学 **bǎoxué** [形] scholarly

保 **bǎo** I [动] **1** (保护) protect **2** (保持) keep (PT, PP kept) ▷这盒子可以用来保鲜。This box can be used to keep food fresh. **3** (保证) ensure ▷吃了这药，保你很快恢复健康。This medicine will ensure you a quick recovery. **4** (担保) stand guarantor (PT, PP stood) ▶保释 bail II [名] guarantor

保安 **bǎo'ān** [动] **1** (保治安) ensure public security **2** (保卫人身安全) ensure safety II [名] security guard

保镖 **bǎobiāo** [名] bodyguard

保藏 **bǎocáng** [动] conserve

保持 **bǎochí** [动] maintain ▷保持良好的秩序 maintain good order ▷保持警惕 stay vigilant ▷保持清醒的头脑 keep a clear head

保存 **bǎocún** [动] preserve

保单 **bǎodān** [名] insurance policy

保费 **bǎofèi** [名] (保险费) insurance premium

保管 **bǎoguǎn** I [动] (保藏管理) take care of (PT took, PP taken) II [名] storekeeper III [副] certainly ▷他做这件事保管能行。What he is doing is sure to work.

保护 **bǎohù** [动] protect ▷保护环境 protect the environment ▷保护眼睛 protect one's eyes ▷保护私人资料 data protection

保健 **bǎojiàn** [名] health care ▷保健食品 health food

保洁 **bǎojié** [动] keep the environment clean (PT, PP kept)

保龄球 **bǎolíngqiú** [名] **1** (体育运动) bowling **2** (球) bowl

保留 **bǎoliú** [动] **1** (保存不变) preserve ▷这座城市还保留着500多年前的寺庙。A temple more than 500 years old is preserved in the town. **2** (意见) hold back (PT, PP held) ▷各位可以保留自己的意见，下次开会再讨论。If everyone can hold back, we will discuss thoughts on this at the next meeting. **3** (不拿出来) retain

保密 **bǎomì** [动] keep ... secret (PT, PP kept) ▷这个消息可要保密。This information must be kept secret.

保姆 **bǎomǔ** [名] **1** (做家务的女工) domestic help **2** (保育员) nanny

保全 **bǎoquán** [动] save

保释 **bǎoshì** [动] bail

保守 **bǎoshǒu** I [动] protect II [形] conservative

保送 **bǎosòng** [动] recommend ... for a place ▷他儿子保送到清华大学。His son was recommended for admission to Qinghua University.

保外就医 **bǎo wài jiù yī** transfer a prisoner for medical attention

保卫 **bǎowèi** [动] defend

保险 **bǎoxiǎn** I [名] insurance II [形] safe III [副] certainly ▷你听我的，保险能行。If you do as I say it's sure to work.

保修 **bǎoxiū** [动] guarantee ▷这台电脑保修一年。This computer is guaranteed for one year.

保养 **bǎoyǎng** [动] **1** (身体) take care of one's health (PT took, PP taken) **2** (机器) maintain

保佑 **bǎoyòu** [动] bless

保育 **bǎoyù** [名] childcare ▷保育员 childcare worker ▷保育院 nursery school

保障 **bǎozhàng** [动] protect ▷保障公民的生命财产安全 protect people's lives and property ▷儿女多并不意味着晚年生活有保障。Having a lot of children certainly doesn't mean you will be protected in later life.

保证 **bǎozhèng** [动] guarantee ▷我保证能按时到达。I guarantee I will be there on time. ▷你的支持是我取得成功的保证。Your support is my guarantee of success.

保重 **bǎozhòng** [动] take care of oneself (PT took, PP taken)

葆 **bǎo** [动] preserve

堡 **bǎo** [名] fort

堡垒 **bǎolěi** [名] **1** (建筑物) fortress **2** (喻) (指难关) challenge **3** (指人) die-hard

报 **bào** I [动] **1** (告诉) report ▷报上级领导 report to one's superiors **2** (回答) respond ▷报以掌声 greet with applause **3** (报答) repay (PT, PP repaid) ▶报恩 repay a favour (英) 或 favor (美) **4** (报复) take revenge (PT took, PP taken) ▶报仇 take revenge II [名] **1** (报纸) newspaper ▶日报 daily **2** (刊物) periodical ▶画报 glossy magazine **3** (公告) report ▶公报 bulletin **4** (电报) telegram ▶发报 send a telegram

报案 **bào'àn** [动] report ▷接到居民报案后，警察以偷窃嫌疑将他逮捕。After a report from a local resident, the police arrested him on suspicion of theft.

报表 **bàobiǎo** [名] report form

报偿 **bàocháng** [动] repay (PT, PP repaid)

报仇 **bàochóu** [动] take revenge (PT took, PP taken)

报酬 **bàochou** [名] pay

报答 **bàodá** [动] repay (PT, PP repaid)

报到 bàodào [动] report

报道 bàodào I [动] report ▷电视台报道了这条新闻。The television station reported this item of news. II [名] report ▷一篇关于克隆人的报道 a report about human cloning ▷她负责体育新闻报道。She is in charge of sports coverage.

报废 bàofèi [动] discard ▷这辆汽车5年内报废。This car will have to be scrapped in five years.

报复 bàofù [动] retaliate

报告 bàogào I [动] report ▷有问题就向主管部门报告。If there is a problem just report it to the department responsible. II [名] report ▷在大会上作报告 give a talk at the conference

报关 bàoguān [动] declare

报价 bàojià [动] quote ▷这只手表报价500镑。This watch is quoted at £500. ▷你报价太高了。Your quotation is too high.

报捷 bàojié [动] report a success

报警 bàojǐng [动] report to the police

报刊 bàokān [名] newspapers and periodicals

报考 bàokǎo [动] take an entrance exam (PT took, PP taken)

报名 bàomíng [动] sign up ▷报名参加马拉松比赛 sign up for a marathon

报幕 bàomù [动] compere

报幕员 bàomùyuán [名] compere

报社 bàoshè [名] newspaper office

报失 bàoshī [动] report a loss ▷丢失信用卡要向警察报失。If you lose a credit card you should report it to the police.

报喜 bàoxǐ [动] give good news (PT gave, PP given) ▷报喜不报忧 give the good news but not the bad

报销 bàoxiāo [动] 1 (费用) claim for 2 (口) (除掉) demolish

报应 bàoyìng [名] just deserts ▷他迟早会遭报应。He'll get his just deserts sooner or later.

报账 bàozhàng [动] submit expenses

报纸 bàozhǐ [名] newspaper

刨 bào I [动] plane II [名] plane
→另见 páo

抱 bào [动] 1 (手臂围住) carry in one's arms 2 (儿孙) ▷我们校长等着抱孙子呢！Our head teacher is going to be a grandmother! 3 (领养) adopt 4 (方) (结合) join together ▷抱成一团 stand together 5 (心里存有) cherish

抱病 bàobìng [动] be ill

抱残守缺 bào cán shǒu quē cling to the past ▷要强化创新意识，不能抱残守缺。We must emphasize creativity, and break the pattern of clinging to the past.

抱佛脚 bào fójiǎo leave ... to the last minute ▷有些学生平时不努力，考前临时抱佛脚。Some students are lazy most of the time, and then try to cram just before the exams.

抱负 bàofù [名] ambition

抱恨 bàohèn [动] harbour (英) 或 harbor (美) regrets

抱歉 bàoqiàn [形] sorry ▷走时没来得及和你说一声，很抱歉。I'm sorry there was no time to speak with you before I left.

抱屈 bàoqū [动] feel wronged (PT, PP felt)

抱养 bàoyǎng [动] adopt

抱怨 bàoyuàn [动] complain ▷她报怨不平等的待遇。She complained about the unfair treatment. ▷小男孩报怨说爸爸脾气坏。The little boy complained that his dad had a bad temper. ▷多干点实事，少一点抱怨。Get on with it and stop grumbling.

豹 bào [名] leopard

暴 bào I [形] 1 (猛烈) violent 2 (凶狠) brutal 3 (急躁) vicious ▷她脾气很暴。She has a vicious temper. II [动] 1 (鼓起) bulge 2 (糟蹋) go to ruin (PT went, PP gone)

暴动 bàodòng [名] insurrection

暴发 bàofā [动] 1 (突然发作) break out (PT broke, PP broken) 2 (贬) (突然发财) strike it rich (PT, PP struck)

暴力 bàolì [名] violence

暴利 bàolì [名] enormous profit

暴烈 bàoliè [形] fierce

暴露 bàolù [动] reveal

暴乱 bàoluàn [名] riot

暴徒 bàotú [名] thug

暴行 bàoxíng [名] atrocity

暴躁 bàozào [形] irritable

暴卒 bàozú [动] die suddenly

爆 bào [动] 1 (猛然破裂) explode ▷炸弹爆炸了。The bomb exploded. ▷气球爆了。The balloon burst. 2 (突然发生) ▷一个无获胜希望的人爆了冷门。An outsider emerged as the winner. 3 (烹调方法) quick-fry

爆发 bàofā [动] 1 (迸发) erupt 2 (突发) break out (PT broke, PP broken)

爆满 bàomǎn [动] be completely packed

爆破 bàopò [动] blow ... up (PT blew, PP blown)

爆炸 bàozhà [动] explode

杯 bēi I [名] 1 (杯子) cup ▷玻璃杯 glass ▷酒杯 wineglass 2 (酒) drink ▷再喝杯吧！Have another drink! **3** (奖杯) cup ▶世界杯 World Cup **II** [量] cup ▶一杯咖啡 a cup of coffee ▷两杯水 two glasses of water

杯弓蛇影 bēi gōng shé yǐng suffer from imaginary fears

杯水车薪 bēi shuǐ chē xīn a drop in the ocean

卑 bēi [形] **1** (书) (谦恭) humble **2** (品质低劣) inferior

卑鄙 bēibǐ [形] contemptible

卑躬屈节 bēi gōng qū jié bow and scrape

卑贱 bēijiàn [形] **1** (地位低) lowly **2** (下贱) base

卑劣 bēiliè [形] despicable

背 bēi [动] **1** (驮) carry ... on one's back ▷她背着书包走路。She walked along the road with her schoolbag on her back. **2** (担负) take ... on (PT took, PP taken) ▷政治家背起了重大的责任。The politician has taken on great responsibility.
→另见 bèi

背包袱 bēi bāofu have a load on one's mind

背负 bēifù [动] **1** (驮) carry on one's back **2** (担负) take ... on (PT took, PP taken) ▷他背负着父母的期望。He has taken on his parents' aspirations.

背黑锅 bēi hēiguō carry the can

悲 bēi [形] **1** (悲伤) sad **2** (怜悯) compassionate ▷大慈大悲 infinitely merciful

悲哀 bēi'āi [形] sad

悲惨 bēicǎn [形] miserable

悲愤 bēifèn [名] grief and anger

悲观 bēiguān [形] pessimistic

悲伤 bēishāng [形] sad

悲天悯人 bēi tiān mǐn rén be concerned about corruption and social welfare

悲痛 bēitòng [形] sorrowful

悲壮 bēizhuàng [形] solemn and stirring

碑 bēi [名] tablet ▷纪念碑 monument ▷墓碑 tombstone

北 běi **I** [名] north ▶北方 the North **II** [动] (书) be defeated ▷败北 be defeated

北斗星 běidǒuxīng [名] the Plough (英), the Big Dipper (美)

北极 běijí [名] the North Pole

贝 bèi [名] shellfish

贝壳 bèiké [名] shell

备 bèi **I** [动] **1** (具备) have (PT, PP had) ▷柜台

上备有样品。Samples are available on the counter. **2** (准备) prepare ▷佐料备齐了。The seasoning is prepared. **3** (防备) provide against **II** [名] equipment **III** [副] to the utmost ▷备受煎熬 endure the utmost suffering

备查 bèichá [动] be at hand for reference

备份 bèifèn [动] (计算机) keep a backup copy (PT, PP kept)

备件 bèijiàn [名] spare part

备考 bèikǎo **I** [名] notes (PL) **II** [动] be at hand for reference ▷这个文件要录以备考。This document should be copied for future reference.

备课 bèikè [动] prepare a lesson ▷上完课后，老师又在备课了。When class was over the teacher prepared another lesson.

备料 bèiliào [动] **1** (准备材料) get materials ready ▷建这栋房子要备很多料。We have to get a lot of materials for building this house. **2** (准备饲料) prepare animal feed

备忘录 bèiwànglù [名] **1** (记事本) notepad **2** (外交文书) memorandum

备用 bèiyòng [动] backup ▷备用光盘 backup CD

备注 bèizhù [名] **1** (表格的栏) space for comments **2** (注解说明) notes (PL)

背 bèi **I** [名] back ▶背疼 backache ▶椅背 chairback **II** [动] **1** (指反向) have one's back to ▷他背着门站着。He is standing with his back to the door. **2** (离开) leave (PT, PP left) **3** (躲避) hide from (PT hid, PP hidden) ▷她有些背人的事。She has something to hide from people. ▷他总是背着父母说他们的坏话。He is always speaking badly of his parents behind their backs. **4** (背诵) recite ▷背首诗 recite a poem **5** (违背) go against (PT went, PP gone) **III** [形] **1** (偏僻) out-of-the-way **2** (口) (倒霉) unlucky **3** (听觉不灵) hard of hearing
→另见 bēi

背道而驰 bèi dào ér chí go in the opposite direction

背井离乡 bèi jǐng lí xiāng be forced to leave one's home

背景 bèijǐng [名] **1** (布景) scenery **2** (指景物、情况) background ▷这张照片的背景是连绵的山脉。The photo shows a chain of mountains in the background. ▷我不知道他们的背景。I know nothing about their background.

背靠背 bèikàobèi back-to-back

背离 bèilí [动] **1** (离开) depart from **2** (违背) deviate from

背叛 bèipàn [动] betray ▷背叛祖国 betray one's country ▷回国之后他就变了心，背叛了女友。After coming back from abroad he ditched his girlfriend.

背弃 bèiqì [动] abandon ▷背弃信仰 abandon one's beliefs ▷背弃誓言 go back on one's word

背时 bèishí [形] (方) 1 (过时) outmoded 2 (倒霉) unlucky

背诵 bèisòng [动] recite

背信弃义 bèi xìn qì yì break faith with

背影 bèiyǐng [名] ▷我注视着他远去的背影。I gazed at his distant receding figure.

背运 bèiyùn I [名] bad luck II [动] be unlucky

悖 bèi I [动] (书) be contrary to II [形] perverse

悖谬 bèimiù [形] (书) irrational

被 bèi I [名] quilt ▶棉被 cotton-padded quilt II [动] meet with (PT, PP met) ▷被灾 meet with disaster III [介] ▷他被哥哥打了一顿。He was beaten up by his elder brother. IV [助] ▷被陷害 be framed ▷被跟踪 be followed

被动 bèidòng [形] passive

被告 bèigào [名] defendant

被迫 bèipò [动] be forced ▷她被迫卖掉首饰。She was forced to sell her jewellery.

倍 bèi I [名] times ▷这本书的厚度是那本书的3倍。This book is three times thicker than that one. ▷物价涨了两倍。Prices have doubled. II [形] double ▷事半功倍 get twice the result with half the effort

焙 bèi [动] dry ... over heat

焙烧 bèishāo [动] bake

辈 bèi [名] 1 (辈分) generation 2 (类) ▷无能之辈 people of no ability

辈出 bèichū [动] come forward in great numbers (PT came, PP come)

辈分 bèifen [名] seniority ▷我辈分比他小。I am junior to him in the family.

惫 bèi [形] exhausted

蓓 bèi 见下文

蓓蕾 bèilěi [名] bud

奔 bēn [动] 1 (急跑) speed (PT, PP sped) 2 (赶忙) hurry 3 (逃) flee (PT, PP fled)
→另见 bèn

奔波 bēnbō [动] dash around

奔驰 bēnchí [动] speed (PT, PP sped) ▷汽车在高速公路上奔驰。The car is speeding along the motorway. ▷马在田野上奔驰。The horse is galloping across the fields.

奔放 bēnfàng [形] bold and unrestrained

奔赴 bēnfù [动] hurry towards

奔流 bēnliú I [动] rush II [名] swift current

奔忙 bēnmáng [动] rush around

奔命 bēnmìng [动] be always on the go

奔跑 bēnpǎo [动] dash

奔丧 bēnsāng [动] go home for a funeral (PT went, PP gone)

奔腾 bēnténg [动] 1 (奔跑) gallop 2 (奔流) surge

奔走 bēnzǒu [动] 1 (急走) run (PT ran, PP run) 2 (到处活动) rush about

本 běn I [名] 1 (根) root ▶木本 tree root 2 (根源) basis (PL bases) ▷本末倒置 put the cart before the horse 3 (本钱) capital ▶亏本 lose money in business 4 (本子) book ▶笔记本 notebook 5 (版本) edition ▶手抄本 hand-written copy 6 (底本) master copy ▶剧本 script II [形] 1 (主要) main ▶本部 headquarters (PL) 2 (原来) original ▶本意 original meaning 3 (自己的) one's own ▶本身 itself ▶本校 this school 4 (现今) this ▶本月 this month III [副] originally ▷我本想亲自去一趟。I originally wanted to go myself. IV [量] ▷几本书 some books

本部 běnbù [名] headquarters

本地 běndì [名] locality ▷本地货 local goods ▷她是本地人。She is a native of this place.

本分 běnfèn I [名] duty II [形] dutiful

本行 běnháng [名] profession

本金 běnjīn [名] principal

本科 běnkē [名] undergraduate course ▷他本科毕业。He graduated with a bachelor's degree. ▷本科生 undergraduate

本来 běnlái I [形] original II [副] 1 (原先) at first 2 (理所当然) of course

本领 běnlǐng [名] skill

本末 běnmò [名] 1 (从头到尾) the whole story 2 (主要的和次要的) ▷本末倒置 put the cart before the horse

本能 běnnéng [名] instinct

本钱 běnqián [名] 1 (钱财) capital 2 (资历) prerequisite

本人 běnrén [名] 1 (我) I 2 (自己) oneself ▷我本人来处理这事。I will handle it myself. ▷你本人必须参加。You must take part yourself. ▷身份证要他本人来办。He has to apply for an ID card himself.

本色 běnsè [名] character

本色 běnshǎi [名] natural colour (英) 或 color (美)

本身 běnshēn [名] itself

本事 běnshi [名] ability

本土 běntǔ [名] (乡土) native land

本位 běnwèi [名] 1 (经济) (标准) standard 2 (自

己的岗位) post

本性 běnxìng [名] nature

本义 běnyì [名] original meaning

本意 běnyì [名] intention

本职 běnzhí [名] job

本质 běnzhì [名] essence

畚 běn I [名] scoop II [动] (方) scoop up

畚箕 běnjī [名] (方) 1 (用于铲谷物) scoop 2 (用于扫垃圾) dustpan

奔 bèn I [动] 1 (走) head for ▷直奔教室 head straight for the classroom 2 (近) be getting on for ▷我是奔40的人了。I'm getting on for forty. II [介] towards
→另见 bēn

奔命 bènmìng [动] rush

奔头儿 bèntour [名] prospect

笨 bèn [形] 1 (不聪明) stupid 2 (不灵巧) clumsy ▷他嘴很笨。He's quite inarticulate. 3 (笨重) cumbersome

笨蛋 bèndàn [名] (侮辱) idiot

笨口拙舌 bèn kǒu zhuō shé inarticulate

笨手笨脚 bèn shǒu bèn jiǎo clumsy ▷看你笨手笨脚的，我来做吧。Look how clumsy you are, let me do it.

笨重 bènzhòng [形] heavy ▷笨重的家具 heavy furniture ▷笨重的体力劳动 heavy physical work

笨拙 bènzhuō [形] 1 (不灵巧) clumsy 2 (不聪明) stupid

崩 bēng [动] 1 (倒塌) collapse ▷雪崩 avalanche 2 (破裂) burst (PT, PP burst)

崩溃 bēngkuì [动] collapse ▷失恋后，她精神处于崩溃边缘。After the break-up she was close to nervous breakdown.

崩塌 bēngtā [动] collapse

绷 bēng [动] 1 (拉紧) pull ... tight ▷绳子绷紧了。The string is taut. 2 (弹) spring (PT sprang, PP sprung)
→另见 běng, bèng

绷带 bēngdài [名] bandage

嘣 bēng [拟] bang ▷除夕晚上鞭炮嘣嘣响。On New Year's Eve there were lots of bangs from firecrackers. ▷他紧张得心里嘣嘣直跳。His heart was pounding with nervousness.

甭 béng [副] (方) ▷你甭去了。Don't bother going.

绷 běng [动] (方) scowl
→另见 bēng, bèng

绷脸 běngliǎn [动] pull a long face

迸 bèng [动] spout

迸发 bèngfā [动] burst out (PT, PP burst) ▷老师的幽默使学生迸发出阵阵笑声。The teacher's jokes made the students burst out laughing.

泵 bèng [名] pump

绷 bèng [动] crack ▷木头门绷了几条缝。The wooden door has cracked in a few places.
→另见 bēng, běng

蹦 bèng [动] leap

逼 bī [动] 1 (强迫) force 2 (强取) press for ▷逼债 press for repayment of a debt 3 (逼近) close in on

逼供 bīgòng [动] extract a confession

逼近 bījìn [动] close in on ▷敌军已逼近城门。The enemy have already closed in on the city gates.

逼迫 bīpò [动] force

逼债 bīzhài [动] press for repayment of a debt

逼真 bīzhēn [形] 1 (像真的) lifelike 2 (真切) distinct

鼻 bí [名] 1 (鼻子) nose 2 (书) (首创) initiation ▷鼻祖 originator

鼻孔 bíkǒng [名] nostril

鼻梁 bíliáng [名] bridge of the nose

鼻涕 bítì [名] mucus

鼻子 bízi [名] nose

鼻祖 bízǔ [名] originator

匕 bǐ [名] 见下文

匕首 bǐshǒu [名] dagger

比 bǐ I [动] 1 (比较) compare ▷比比过去，我们现在的生活好多了。Life now is much better compared to the past. 2 (较量) compete ▷他们要比比谁游得快。They are competing to see who swims the fastest. 3 (比拟) compare ▷中国人喜欢把大地比作母亲。The Chinese like to compare the earth to a mother. 4 (仿照) copy ▷孩子们在比着图纸做飞机模型。The children are making model planes from diagrams. 5 (比画) gesture ▷她连说带比。She gesticulates as she talks. II [介] 1 (指程分) ▷两队最终以零比零战平。The two teams finally drew nil-nil. 2 (相对) ▷今年冬天比去年冷。It is colder this winter than last winter.

比比皆是 bǐbǐ jiēshì ubiquitous

比方 bǐfang I [名] analogy ▷她打了个比方，把学英语比作建房子了。She drew an analogy between learning English and building a house. II [连] ▷你会有机会买房的，比方你中了彩。You would have the chance to buy a house – supposing you won the lottery.

比分 bǐfēn [名] score

比画 bǐhuà [动] gesture ▷英语老师讲课时爱比画。The English teacher likes making gestures when he is teaching. ▷裁缝拿布料在我胸前比画着。The dressmaker held the material in front of me to take a measurement.

比基尼 bǐjīní [名] bikini

比价 bǐjià [名] exchange rate

比较 bǐjiào I [动] compare ▷让我们比较一下两个民族的风俗习惯。Let us compare for a moment the customs of the two peoples. II [介] ▷国民生产总值比去年有所增长。Compared to last year, gross national product has increased somewhat. III [副] relatively ▷这里的水果比较新鲜。The fruit here is relatively fresh. ▷广州的夏天比较热。Summers in Guangzhou are quite hot.

比例 bǐlì [名] 1 (指倍数) proportion 2 (指制图) scale ▷按比例制模型 make a scale model

比率 bǐlǜ [名] ratio

比拟 bǐnǐ [动] match

比如 bǐrú [连] for instance ▷小事情可以成为大新闻，比如人咬了狗。Small things can become big news, for instance if a person bites a dog. ▷有些人不适合做老师，比如小王。Some people are not suited to teaching, Xiao Wang for instance.

比赛 bǐsài [名] match ▷足球比赛 football match ▷演讲比赛 public speaking competition

比上不足，比下有余 bǐ shàng bùzú, bǐ xià yǒuyú reasonably well ▷咱们过的日子比上不足，比下有余。We have been living reasonably well.

比试 bǐshi [动] 1 (较量) have a competition 2 (做姿势) flourish ▷拿把剑比试一下 flourish a sword

比喻 bǐyù I [动] compare II [名] analogy

比照 bǐzhào [动] 1 (按照) base ... on ▷教练比照对手的特点制订了一个方案。The coach based his strategy on the opponent's particular strengths and weaknesses. 2 (对照) contrast

比值 bǐzhí [名] ratio

比重 bǐzhòng [名] (比值) proportion

彼 bǐ [代] 1 (那个) that 2 (对方) the other side

彼岸 bǐ'àn [名] the opposite shore

彼此 bǐcǐ [代] 1 (双方) both sides ▷这对混双选手彼此并不太了解。This mixed-doubles pair don't know each other well. 2 (谦) ▷"你这次考得不错啊！""彼此彼此！" You did really well in the exam! – You too! ▷"你看上去很棒啊！""彼此彼此！" You look great! – Likewise!

笔 bǐ I [名] 1 (工具) pen ▷圆珠笔 ball-point pen 2 (笔法) calligraphic technique 3 (笔画) brush stroke 4 (话语) ▷文章结尾处应该再添几笔。The conclusion of the essay needs fleshing out a bit. II [动] write (PT wrote, PP written) ▶亲笔 one's own handwriting III [量] 1 (款项) ▷一笔钱 a sum of money 2 (书画) ▷一笔好字 a good hand

笔调 bǐdiào [名] tone

笔法 bǐfǎ [名] artistic technique

笔杆子 bǐgǎnzi [名] 1 (笔) shaft 2 (指写作) pen 3 (指作家) skilled writer

笔画 bǐhuà [名] brush stroke

笔迹 bǐjì [名] handwriting

笔记 bǐjì I [动] take down (PT took, PP taken) II [名] 1 (记录) note ▷记笔记 take notes 2 (指体裁) ▷笔记小说 literary sketches

笔记本电脑 bǐjìběn diànnǎo [名] laptop

笔名 bǐmíng [名] pen name

笔墨 bǐmò [名] words (PL) ▷写文章忌浪费笔墨。When writing an essay you should not waste words.

笔试 bǐshì [名] written examination

笔挺 bǐtǐng I [形] neatly pressed ▷笔挺的西装 a neatly pressed suit II [副] erect ▷卫兵们笔挺地站着。The guards stood erect.

笔头儿 bǐtóur [名] 1 (笔尖) nib 2 (写字) writing 3 (写作) writing ability

笔误 bǐwù [名] slip of the pen

笔译 bǐyì [名] written translation

笔者 bǐzhě [名] the author

笔直 bǐzhí [形] straight

鄙 bǐ I [形] 1 (粗俗) mean ▶卑鄙 mean 2 (自称) (谦) ▶鄙人 my humble self II [动] despise

鄙薄 bǐbó [动] despise

鄙陋 bǐlòu [形] shallow

鄙视 bǐshì [动] despise

币 bì [名] coin ▶货币 currency ▶外币 foreign currency

必 bì [副] 1 (必然) certainly 2 (必须) ▷必修科目 compulsory subjects

必定 bìdìng [副] surely ▷他必定知道真相。He

surely knew the truth.

必恭必敬 bì gōng bì jìng very deferential

必然 bìrán I [形] inevitable II [名] necessity

必修课 bìxiūkè [名] compulsory course

必须 bìxū [副] ▷你们必须准时来上班。You must start work on time. ▷记者们必须撤离战区。The journalists have to evacuate the war zone.

必需 bìxū [动] need ▷考试时别忘带上必需的文具用品。Don't forget to bring the writing materials you need for the exam.

必要 bìyào [形] essential ▷开展反腐行动是必要的。It's essential that we start a campaign against corruption.

闭 bì [动] 1 (关上) close 2 (堵塞) stop ... up ▷闭气 airtight

闭路电视 bìlùdiànshì [名] closed-circuit television

闭门羹 bìméngēng [名] ▷吃闭门羹 be left out in the cold

闭门造车 bì mén zào chē divorce oneself from reality

闭幕 bìmù [动] 1 (指舞台) lower the curtain 2 (指会议) conclude

闭塞 bìsè [动] 1 (堵塞) obstruct 2 (不方便) be inaccessible

毕 bì I [动] finish II [副] fully

毕恭毕敬 bì gōng bì jìng 见 '必恭必敬'

毕竟 bìjìng [副] actually ▷和过去相比，我们的生活水平毕竟有了提高。If you compare with the past, actually our standard of living has improved.

毕生 bìshēng [名] lifetime

毕业 bìyè [动] graduate ▷她毕业于牛津大学法律系。She graduated in law from Oxford University.

毕业论文 bìyè lùnwén [名] thesis (PL theses)

庇 bì [动] shelter ▷包庇 shield

庇护 bìhù [动] shelter

陛 bì [名] (书) flight of steps

陛下 bìxià [名] Your Majesty

毙 bì [动] 1 (死) die 2 (口) (枪杀) shoot (PT, PP shot)

毙命 bìmìng [动] meet a violent death (PT, PP met)

敝 bì [形] 1 (破烂) ragged 2 (谦) (自己的) ▷敝人姓李。My surname is Li.

敝帚自珍 bì zhǒu zì zhēn attach sentimental

value to

婢 bì [名] slave girl

婢女 bìnǚ [名] slave girl

裨 bì [名] (书) benefit

裨益 bìyì [名] (书) benefit ▷您的建议对我公司的发展大有裨益。Your recommendation will be of great benefit to the development of our company.

辟 bì [动] (书) ward ... off
→另见 pì

辟邪 bìxié [动] exorcize

碧 bì I [形] bluish green II [名] (书) green jade

碧绿 bìlǜ [形] dark green

碧玉 bìyù [名] jasper

蔽 bì [动] shelter ▷蔽雨 shelter from the rain

弊 bì [名] 1 (蒙骗) fraud ▷考试作弊 cheat in an exam 2 (害处) disadvantage

弊病 bìbìng [名] 1 (弊端) evil 2 (毛病) disadvantage

弊端 bìduān [名] abuse ▷市场经济和计划经济各有弊端。Abuses occur in both market and planned economies.

避 bì [动] 1 (躲开) avoid 2 (防止) prevent

避风 bìfēng [动] 1 (躲风) shelter from the wind 2 (躲麻烦) lie low (PT lay, PP lain)

避风港 bìfēnggǎng [名] haven

避免 bìmiǎn [动] avoid

避难 bìnàn [动] take refuge (PT took, PP taken)

避暑 bìshǔ [动] 1 (指去凉爽地方) go to a summer resort (PT went, PP gone) 2 (避免中暑) prevent sunstroke

避嫌 bìxián [动] avoid arousing suspicion

避孕 bìyùn [动] use contraceptives ▷避孕药 the pill

避重就轻 bì zhòng jiù qīng focus on small things, ignoring what's important ▷开会时我避重就轻，只谈小问题。At the meeting, I avoided the important issues, and spoke only about minor points. ▷首相答记者问时，老是避重就轻。When the prime minister answers journalists' questions he always evades the issue.

壁 bì [名] 1 (墙) wall 2 (山石) cliff

壁橱 bìchú [名] built-in cupboard (英) 或 closet (美)

壁灯 bìdēng [名] wall lamp

壁挂 bìguà [名] hanging

壁画 bìhuà [名] mural

壁垒 bìlěi [名] rampart ▷贸易壁垒 trade barrier

壁毯 bìtǎn [名] tapestry

壁纸 bìzhǐ [名] wallpaper

臂 bì [名] arm

臂膀 bìbǎng [名] arm

边 biān [名] 1 (边线) side ▷街两边 both sides of the street 2 (边缘) edge ▷碗边儿 edge of a bowl ▷路边 roadside ▷帽边儿 brim of a hat 3 (边界) border ▷边城 border town 4 (界限) limit ▷宇宙浩瀚无边。The universe is limitless.

边…边… biān…biān… ▷边吃边谈 talk while eating

边陲 biānchuí [名] (书) frontier

边防 biānfáng [名] border defence (英) 或 defense (美)

边关 biānguān [名] border pass

边际 biānjì [名] limit

边疆 biānjiāng [名] border area

边界 biānjiè [名] border

边境 biānjìng [名] border ▷边境冲突 border conflict

边卡 biānqiǎ [名] border checkpoint

边缘 biānyuán I [名] edge ▷这个国家正处于经济危机的边缘。This country is on the verge of economic crisis. II [形] marginal ▷边缘人群 fringe group

边缘科学 biānyuán kēxué [名] borderline science

边远 biānyuǎn [形] outlying

编 biān I [动] 1 (编织) weave (PT wove, PP woven) 2 (编排) organize ▷编组 put into groups 3 (编辑) edit ▷编词典 compile a dictionary 4 (创作) write (PT wrote, PP written) ▷编歌词 write lyrics 5 (捏造) fabricate II [名] book

编程 biānchéng [动] program

编辑 biānjí I [动] edit II [名] editor

编码 biānmǎ [动] encode ▷编码指令 coded instructions

编目 biānmù [动] catalogue

编排 biānpái [动] arrange

编审 biānshěn I [动] read and edit (PT, PP read) II [名] senior editor

编写 biānxiě [动] 1 (编著) compile 2 (创作) write (PT wrote, PP written)

编译 biānyì I [动] translate and edit II [名] translator-editor

编造 biānzào [动] 1 (报表、名册等) draw … up (PT drew, PP drawn) ▷编造预算 draw up a budget 2 (故事、谎言等) invent ▷编造谎言 invent a lie

编者 biānzhě [名] editor

编织 biānzhī [动] 1 (毛衣等) knit 2 (地毯等) weave (PT wove, PP woven)

编制 biānzhì I [动] 1 (编织) weave (PT wove, PP woven) 2 (制做) draw … up (PT drew, PP drawn) II [名] personnel quota ▷控制政府人员的编制 restrict the quota of government employees

编著 biānzhù [动] compile

编撰 biānzhuàn [动] compile

编组 biānzǔ [动] put into groups (PT, PP put)

编纂 biānzuǎn [动] compile

蝙 biān 见下文

蝙蝠 biānfú [名] bat

鞭 biān I [名] 1 (鞭子) whip 2 (教鞭) pointer 3 (爆竹) firecracker II [动] whip

鞭策 biāncè [动] spur on

鞭长莫及 biān cháng mòjí be beyond one's influence

鞭笞 biānchī [动] (书) flog

鞭打 biāndǎ [动] whip

鞭炮 biānpào [名] firecracker

鞭辟入里 biān pì rù lǐ incisive

鞭挞 biāntà [动] lash out at

贬 biǎn [动] 1 (降低) reduce ▷快要过期的食品会贬价出售。Foodstuffs getting close to their sell-by date need to be reduced in price. 2 (评价低) belittle ▷不要把别人贬得太低。You shouldn't belittle other people.

贬斥 biǎnchì [动] 1 (书) (降职) demote 2 (排斥) denigrate

贬义词 biǎnyì cí [名] derogatory expression

贬值 biǎnzhí [动] 1 (购买力下降) depreciate 2 (兑换率降低) devalue

扁 biǎn [形] flat
→ 另见 piān

扁担 biǎndan [名] carrying pole

褊 biǎn [形] (书) narrow

褊狭 biǎnxiá [形] (书) cramped ▷住房褊狭 cramped living conditions ▷气量褊狭 small-minded

变 biàn I [动] 1 (改变) change ▷小城的面

貌变了。The appearance of the town has changed. **2** (变成) become (PT became, PP become) ▷他变成熟了。He's become quite grown up. **3** (转换) transform ▷变乡村为城市 urbanize **II** [名] turn of events ▷情况可能有变。There may have been a change in circumstances.

变本加厉 biàn běn jiā lì become aggravated

变动 biàndòng [动] alter ▷会议安排变动了。The arrangements for the conference have altered.

变革 biàngé [动] transform ▷中国正在经历巨大的社会变革。China is currently undergoing a massive social transformation.

变更 biàngēng [动] modify

变故 biàngù [名] unforeseen event

变卦 biànguà [动] go back on one's word (PT went, PP gone)

变化 biànhuà [动] change

变幻 biànhuàn [动] fluctuate

变换 biànhuàn [动] vary

变脸 biànliǎn [动] turn hostile

变量 biànliàng [名] variable

变卖 biànmài [动] sell ... off (PT, PP sold)

变迁 biànqiān [动] change

变色龙 biànsèlóng [名] chameleon

变数 biànshù [名] variable

变态 biàntài **I** [名] (生物) metamorphosis **II** [形] abnormal

变天 biàntiān [动] **1** (指天气变化) ▷早上还有太阳，下午就变天了。It was sunny in the morning, but the weather changed in the afternoon. **2** (指政局变化) stage a comeback

变通 biàntōng [动] be flexible

变戏法 biàn xìfǎ [动] conjure

变相 biànxiàng [动] disguise

变心 biànxīn [动] cease to be loyal ▷他对女朋友变心了。He ceased to be loyal to his girlfriend.

变形 biànxíng [动] become deformed (PT became, PP become)

变性 biànxìng [动] **1** (化) denature **2** (改变性别) change sex

变异 biànyì [名] variation

变质 biànzhì [动] go bad (PT went, PP gone) ▷牛奶变质了。The milk has gone off.

便 biàn **I** [形] **1** (方便) convenient ▶轻便 portable **2** (简单) simple ▶便饭 simple meal **II** [名] **1** (方便之时) convenience ▷何时来讲学，悉听尊便。Please come and speak to us at your own convenience. **2** (粪便) excretion **III** [动] excrete ▶小便 urinate ▶大便 defecate **IV** [副] ▷稍等片刻演唱会便开始。The performance is about to start in a moment. →另见 pián

便当 biàndang [形] (口) handy

便道 biàndào [名] **1** (近路) shortcut **2** (人行道) pavement **3** (临时道路) temporary road

便饭 biànfàn [名] quick meal

便服 biànfú [名] **1** (平常服装) everyday clothes **2** (中式服装) Chinese dress

便捷 biànjié [形] **1** (直捷方便) quick and convenient **2** (轻快敏捷) nimble

便利 biànlì **I** [形] convenient **II** [动] facilitate

便士 biànshì [量] pence

便条 biàntiáo [名] note

便携式 biànxiéshì [形] portable

便衣 biànyī [名] **1** (指服装) plain clothes **2** (指人) plain-clothes policeman

便于 biànyú [动] be easy to ▷便于联系 be easy to contact

遍 biàn **I** [副] all over ▷我把柜子翻了个遍也没找着。I searched all through my wardrobe but couldn't find it. **II** [量] ▷我说了两遍。I said it twice.

遍布 biànbù [动] be found everywhere

遍地 biàndì [名] everywhere

遍及 biànjí [动] spread all over (PT, PP spread)

遍体鳞伤 biàn tǐ lín shāng beaten black and blue

辨 biàn [动] distinguish

辨别 biànbié [动] distinguish

辨认 biànrèn [动] identify

辨析 biànxī [动] discriminate ▷辨析同义词 discriminate between synonyms

辩 biàn [动] debate ▶争辩 contend

辩白 biànbái [动] plead innocence

辩驳 biànbó [动] refute

辩才 biàncái [名] eloquence

辩护 biànhù [动] **1** (辩解) defend **2** (申辩) plead ▷为被告人辩护 plead on the behalf of the accused

辩护人 biànhùrén [名] counsel

辩解 biànjiě [动] offer an explanation ▷不要为自己的错误行为辩解。Don't try to make excuses for your mistakes.

辩论 biànlùn [动] argue ▷我不想就这个问题与你辩论。I don't want to argue with you about this.

辫 biàn [名] plait

辫子 biànzi [名] 1 (发辫) plait 2 (把柄) handle

标 biāo I [名] 1 (记号) mark 2 (标准) standard 3 (奖品) prize 4 (出价) bid 5 (皮毛) symptom II [动] mark

标榜 biāobǎng [动] (贬) 1 (宣扬) flaunt 2 (吹捧) flatter

标本 biāoběn [名] 1 (样品) specimen 2 (代表) sample 3 (指问题、病) cause and effect ▷我们对这个问题得标本兼治。We need to tackle both the cause and the effect of this problem.

标兵 biāobīng [名] (喻) (榜样) example

标底 biāodǐ [名] minimum bid

标的 biāodì [名] 1 (指合同) objective 2 (靶子) target

标点 biāodiǎn I [名] punctuation II [动] punctuate

标杆 biāogān [名] 1 (样板) model 2 (指测量工具) measuring pole

标记 biāojì [名] mark

标价 biāojià [名] marked price ▷这套西装标价为500镑。This suit is priced at £500.

标明 biāomíng [动] mark

标签 biāoqiān [名] label

标枪 biāoqiāng [名] (体育) javelin

标题 biāotí [名] 1 (指文章、书) title 2 (指新闻) headline

标新立异 biāo xīn lì yì break the mould

标语 biāoyǔ [名] slogan

标志 biāozhì I [名] sign II [动] mark

标致 biāozhì [形] beautiful

标准 biāozhǔn [名] I standard ▷道德标准 moral standard ▷不能把钱作为衡量幸福的惟一标准。You can't take money as the only standard for happiness. ▷当警察要达到一定的身高标准。In order to be a policeman you have to meet certain height requirements. ▷录取标准 entry requirements II [形] standard ▷标准时间 standard time ▷标准音 standard pronunciation

彪 biāo [名] (书) tiger cub

彪炳千古 biāobǐng qiāngǔ timeless

彪悍 biāohàn [形] valiant

彪形大汉 biāoxíng dàhàn [名] strapping man

膘 biāo [名] fat

镖 biāo [名] dart

飙 biāo [名] (书) whirlwind

飙升 biāoshēng [动] shoot up (PT, PP shot)

表 biǎo I [名] 1 (计时器) watch ▶手表 wristwatch 2 (计量器) meter ▶电表 electricity meter 3 (表格) form 4 (外表) appearance 5 (指亲戚) cousin ▶表哥 cousin 6 (榜样) model II [动] express

表白 biǎobái [动] express

表层 biǎocéng [名] surface

表达 biǎodá [动] express ▷他的表达能力很强。He's very good at expressing himself.

表格 biǎogé [名] form

表功 biǎogōng [动] (贬) talk oneself up ▷在经理面前，他使劲表功。When he was with his manager he did his best to talk himself up.

表决 biǎojué [动] vote

表里 biǎolǐ [名] (喻) (言行和思想) ▷这人表里不一。This man isn't what he appears. ▷她很可靠，表里如一。You can rely on her – what you see is what you get.

表露 biǎolù [动] reveal

表面 biǎomiàn [名] surface ▷我们不应只处理问题的表面。We shouldn't just be tackling the surface of the problem.

表面文章 biǎomiàn wénzhāng go through the motions ▷没有人真正遵守新规定，都在做表面文章。No one really respects the new regulations – they're all just going through the motions.

表明 biǎomíng [动] show (PT showed, PP shown)

表亲 biǎoqīn [名] cousin

表情 biǎoqíng [名] expression

表示 biǎoshì I [动] 1 (表达) express ▷表示衷心感谢 express heartfelt gratitude ▷表示歉意 express regret ▷举手表示赞成 raise one's hand to express approval 2 (显示) indicate ▷路上结冰了，表示温度是零下。The road is iced up, which indicates that the temperature is below zero. II [名] 1 (言行或表情) gesture ▷他们不友好的表示激怒了我们。Their unfriendly gesture infuriated us. 2 (意见) attitude ▷对于这个决定，他还未做明确的表示。He still hasn't given a clear indication of his attitude towards the decision.

表述 biǎoshù [动] express

表率 biǎoshuài [名] model

表态 biǎotài [动] make one's position known ▷在会上，每个人都要对这个问题表态。Everyone at the meeting had to make known their position on the problem.

表现 biǎoxiàn I [动] 1 (显出) show (PT showed, PP shown) 2 (贬) (炫耀) show off (PT showed, PP shown) II [名] (指行为、作风) performance

表演 **biǎoyǎn** [动] **1** (演出) perform ▷演员们的精彩表演赢得了观众的喝彩。The actors' wonderful performance won the audience's acclaim. **2** (演示) demonstrate

display 是公共演出或其他意在娱乐大众的活动。它可能在室外进行。*a firework display... gymnastic displays...* **exhibition** 是指图片、雕塑、史料或者其他艺术品的展示，例如在博物馆或者美术馆举办的展览。*an exhibition of modern art...* **performance** 或 **show** 是指演唱、舞蹈或者其他娱乐观众的表演形式。**performance** 通常指某个具体的活动，而 **show** 可能是在一段时期内每晚上进行的演出。**show** 经常包含不同的项目，譬如音乐、舞蹈或者喜剧表演。*They were giving a performance of Bizet's opera "Carmen"... How about going shopping and seeing a show in London?* **show** 也用来表示电视或者广播中的某个节目。*I had my own TV show.*

表扬 **biǎoyáng** [动] praise
表彰 **biǎozhāng** [动] commend

婊 biǎo 见下文
婊子 **biǎozi** [名] (贬) whore

裱 biǎo [动] mount
裱糊 **biǎohú** [动] paper

憋 biē [动] **1** (抑制) suppress **2** (憋闷) feel suffocated (PT, PP felt) ▷总呆在屋里憋得慌。Staying indoors all day will make you feel absolutely suffocated.
憋闷 **biēmen** [名] depression
憋气 **biēqì** [动] **1** (呼吸困难) feel suffocated (PT, PP felt) **2** (无法发泄) be frustrated

瘪 biē 见下文
➔另见 biě
瘪三 **biēsān** [名] (方) layabout

鳖 biē [名] soft-shelled turtle

别 bié I [动] **1** (离开) say goodbye (PT, PP said) ▶告别 part **2** (区分) differentiate ▶区别 distinguish **3** (固定) pin ▷胸针可以再别高一点。The brooch could be pinned a little bit higher. ▷他腰间别着一支枪。A gun was strapped round his waist. II [名] **1** (类别) category ▷填写你的年龄、性别及政治派别。Please complete all parts of the form including age, gender and political party. **2** (差别) ▷天壤之别 worlds apart III [形] (其他) other ▶别人 other people IV [副] **1** (不要)

▷别听信谣言。Don't listen to gossip. ▷别忘了关灯。Don't forget to turn off the light. **2** (莫非) maybe ▷他肯定在家的，你别是敲错门了吧？I'm sure he's at home. Maybe you knocked on the wrong door.
➔另见 biè

别称 **biéchēng** [名] alternative name
别出心裁 **bié chū xīncái** be original ▷朱莉别出心裁，想要徒步走新疆。Julie had the original idea of touring Xinjiang on foot.
别号 **biéhào** [名] alternative name
别具匠心 **bié jù jiàngxīn** be completely original ▷他的画总是别具匠心。His paintings are always completely original.
别具一格 **bié jù yī gé** have a unique style ▷这座小城市有浓郁的地方特色，别具一格。This small town is rich in local specialities, which gives it its own unique style.
别开生面 **bié kāi shēng miàn** innovative
别离 **biélí** [动] leave (PT, PP left) ▷他别离了妻子，外出打工。He left his wife and went to look for work elsewhere.
别名 **biémíng** [名] alternative name
别人 **biérén** [名] other people ▷家里只有我，没有别人。There's only me at home, nobody else.
别树一帜 **bié shù yī zhì** found a new school of thought
别墅 **biéshù** [名] villa
别无长物 **bié wú chángwù** **1** (表示俭朴) own the mere bare necessities **2** (表示贫穷) not have a penny to one's name
别有风味 **bié yǒu fēngwèi** be unique
别有用心 **bié yǒu yòngxīn** have something up one's sleeve
别针 **biézhēn** [名] safety pin
别致 **biézhì** [形] unique ▷这辆车看上去很别致。This car has a unique look.
别字 **biézì** [名] misspelling

蹩 bié 见下文
蹩脚 **biéjiǎo** [形] shoddy ▷他写的文章很蹩脚。His essay was a pretty shoddy piece of work.

瘪 biě [形] **1** (表面下陷) dented ▷他把车头撞瘪了。He dented the front of the car. **2** (不饱满) shrivelled ▷大多数谷子已经瘪了。Most of the crop has shrivelled up.
➔另见 biē

别 biè [动] (方) talk ... out of ▷这个人很倔强，我恐怕别不过他。This guy is too stubborn – I'm afraid I won't be able to talk him out of it.
➔另见 bié

别扭 bièniu I [形] 1 (指人、工具) difficult ▷在这种人手下工作真别扭。This kind of man is always difficult to work for. ▷这钳子用起来很别扭。These pliers are very difficult to use. 2 (指文章、说话) awkward ▷这篇文章读起来有点别扭。This essay reads a little awkwardly. II [名] spat ▷他在和老板闹别扭。He's having a spat with his boss.

宾 bīn [名] guest
宾馆 bīnguǎn [名] hotel
宾客 bīnkè [名] guest
宾至如归 bīn zhì rú guī feel at home ▷好的旅馆服务让游客有宾至如归的感觉。Good hotel service will make guests feel at home.

彬 bīn 见下文
彬彬有礼 bīnbīn yǒulǐ courteous

傧 bīn 见下文
傧相 bīnxiàng [名] 1 (伴娘) chief bridesmaid (英), maid of honour (美) 2 (伴郎) best man

滨 bīn I [名] ▶海滨 seashore II [动] border

缤 bīn 见下文
缤纷 bīnfēn [形] (书) ▷五彩缤纷 a dazzling array of colour

濒 bīn [动] 1 (紧挨) border on ▷濒临大海 border on the sea 2 (临近) be on the point of ▶濒死 on the point of death
濒临 bīnlín [动] border ▷中国濒临太平洋。China borders the Pacific.
濒危 bīnwēi [动] be endangered

摈 bìn [动] reject
摈除 bìnchú [动] discard
摈弃 bìnqì [动] abandon

殡 bìn [名] funeral ▶出殡 funeral procession
殡仪馆 bìnyíguǎn [名] funeral parlour (英) 或 parlor (美)
殡葬 bìnzàng [动] hold a funeral (PT, PP held)

膑 bìn [名] kneecap

鬓 bìn [名] sideburns (PL)
鬓发 bìnfà [名] sideburns (PL)
鬓角 bìnjiǎo [名] sideburns (PL)

冰 bīng I [名] ice II [动] 1 (使感觉寒冷) be freezing ▷这水冰手。This water is freezing. 2 (冰镇) cool ▷你去冰冷饮，我来煮咖啡。You cool the drinks and I'll make the coffee.
冰川 bīngchuān [名] glacier
冰点 bīngdiǎn [名] freezing point
冰冷 bīnglěng [形] freezing
冰凉 bīngliáng [形] ice-cold
冰淇淋 bīngqílín [名] ice cream
冰清玉洁 bīng qīng yù jié as pure as jade
冰霜 bīngshuāng [名] coldness
冰炭不相容 bīngtàn bù xiāng róng be completely incompatible
冰糖 bīngtáng [名] rock sugar
冰天雪地 bīng tiān xuě dì mind-numbingly cold
冰消瓦解 bīng xiāo wǎ jiě fall apart ▷头子被捕后，这个黑社会集团很快就冰消瓦解了。After their leader was caught, the underground gang soon fell apart.
冰镇 bīngzhèn [形] iced ▷冰镇啤酒 ice-cold beer

兵 bīng [名] 1 (军队) the army ▷骑兵 cavalry ▷当兵 join the army 2 (士兵) soldier 3 (兵器) arms (PL) ▷坚甲利兵 military strength 4 (兵法) military strategy ▷纸上谈兵 be an armchair strategist
兵变 bīngbiàn [名] mutiny
兵不血刃 bīng bù xuè rèn win without firing a shot
兵不厌诈 bīng bù yàn zhà all's fair in love and war
兵法 bīngfǎ [名] military tactics (PL)
兵荒马乱 bīng huāng mǎ luàn the turmoil of war
兵器 bīngqì [名] arms (PL)
兵强马壮 bīng qiáng mǎ zhuàng military might
兵团 bīngtuán [名] military corps (PL military corps)
兵役 bīngyì [名] military service ▷服兵役 do military service
兵营 bīngyíng [名] barracks (PL)
兵种 bīngzhǒng [名] military division

丙 bǐng [名] third ▷丙组的运动员先上。The athletes in group three are to go first. ▷甲、乙、丙组 groups A, B and C

秉 bǐng [动] 1 (书) (拿) hold (PT, PP held) 2 (书) (掌握) preside over ▶秉权 be in power ▷康熙皇帝executes61年。The Emperor Kangxi ruled for 61 years. 3 (书) (根据) be in accordance with

秉承 bǐngchéng [动] **1** (传统) carry ... on ▷我们要秉承公司的优秀传统。We must carry on the company's excellent traditions. **2** (意见) adopt

秉公 bǐnggōng [动] be impartial ▷秉公执法的法官 a judge who is impartial in enforcing the law ▷法制人员要秉公办事。Legal staff must be impartial about their work.

秉性 bǐngxìng [名] nature ▷她秉性坚强。She is strong by nature.

柄 bǐng [名] **1** (器物) handle **2** (喻) (指言行) handle ▶笑柄 laughing stock ▷别让任何人抓住你的把柄。Don't let anyone get a handle on you. **3** (指植物) stem

饼 bǐng [名] **1** (指面食) cake ▶月饼 moon cake **2** (饼状物) ▶铁饼 discus ▷土豆饼 potato bread

饼干 bǐnggān [名] biscuit (英), cookie (美)

屏 bǐng [动] **1** (气、呼吸) hold (PT, PP held) **2** (除去) get rid of ▷屏弃坏习惯 get rid of bad habits →另见 píng

屏除 bǐngchú [动] discard

屏息 bǐngxī [动] hold one's breath (PT, PP held)

禀 bǐng [动] (书) consult

禀报 bǐngbào [动] (书) report

禀承 bǐngchéng [动] 见'秉承'

禀赋 bǐngfù [名] gift ▷他运动禀赋很高。He has a real gift for sports.

禀告 bǐnggào [动] (书) report

禀性 bǐngxìng [名] nature

并 bìng I [动] **1** (合并) merge ▷把两个部门并成一个 merge two departments into one **2** (并拢) bring ... together (PT, PP brought) ▷把脚并起来 bring your feet together II [副] **1** (平排) side by side ▷齐头并进 progress side by side **2** (同) simultaneously ▷人类能左右脑并用。Humans can use the left and right sides of their brains simultaneously. ▶相提并论 mention in the same breath **3** (表示强调) really ▷他今晚并不想出去。He really doesn't want to go out this evening. III [连] and ▷他会说法语,并在学习西班牙语。He can speak French, and he is studying Spanish at the moment.

并存 bìngcún [动] coexist

并蒂莲 bìngdìlián [名] (喻) (夫妻) devoted married couple

并发 bìngfā [动] develop into ▷他得了流感,现在并发了肺炎。He caught the flu, and now it has developed into pneumonia.

并发症 bìngfāzhèng [名] complication

并轨 bìngguǐ [动] merge ▷两种体制并轨。The two systems have merged.

并驾齐驱 bìng jià qí qū be on a level pegging ▷两国的经济发展并驾齐驱。The two countries are on a level pegging in terms of economic development.

并肩 bìngjiān [副] side by side ▷我们并肩在桥上走着。We were walking side by side on the bridge.

并举 bìngjǔ [动] develop simultaneously

并列 bìngliè [动] be equal ▷她俩期末考试并列第一。They came equal first in the end of term exams. ▷他俩并列冠军。They are joint champions.

并排 bìngpái [副] side by side ▷三个人并排骑着自行车。The three of them were cycling side by side.

并且 bìngqiě [连] **1** (和) and ▷她聪明并且用功。She is clever and diligent. **2** (此外) also ▷我们有信心,并且有实力赢得这场比赛。We have the confidence and also the ability to win the match.

并吞 bìngtūn [动] swallow ... up

并行 bìngxíng [动] **1** (指位置) run side by side (PT ran, PP run) **2** (指时间) run concurrently

并重 bìngzhòng [动] attach equal importance to

病 bìng I [名] **1** (疾病) disease ▶心脏病 heart disease **2** (错误) fault ▷这句话有语病。This sentence is not grammatical. ▷发音不好是这班同学的通病。Bad pronunciation is a common fault among students in this class. II [动] be ill ▷他病得不轻。He was seriously ill.

病变 bìngbiàn [名] pathological changes (PL)

病毒 bìngdú [名] virus

病房 bìngfáng [名] ward

病故 bìnggù [动] die of an illness

病号 bìnghào [名] patient

病句 bìngjù [名] ungrammatical sentence

病菌 bìngjūn [名] bacteria

病理 bìnglǐ [名] pathology

病历 bìnglì [名] medical record

病例 bìnglì [名] case ▷非典型病例 an atypical case

病魔 bìngmó [名] serious illness

病情 bìngqíng [名] condition ▷孩子的病情有好转。The child's condition has improved a lot.

病人 bìngrén [名] **1** (指医院里) patient **2** (指家里) invalid

病入膏肓 bìng rù gāo huāng beyond help

病态 bìngtài [名] illness ▷肥胖症是一种病态。Obesity is an illness.
病征 bìngzhēng [名] symptom
病症 bìngzhèng [名] illness

摒 bìng [动] exclude
摒弃 bìngqì [动] abandon

波 bō [名] 1 (指水、声音、电) wave 2 (喻) (意外变化) unexpected turn of events
波动 bōdòng [动] fluctuate
波段 bōduàn [名] wave
波及 bōjí [动] affect
波澜 bōlán [名] waves (PL) ▷情感的波澜 waves of emotion
波澜壮阔 bōlán zhuàngkuò magnificent
波浪 bōlàng [名] wave
波涛 bōtāo [名] billow
波折 bōzhé [名] setback

拨 bō I [动] 1 (号码) dial 2 (琴弦) pluck 3 (频道) change over to ▷请拨到中央一台好吗？Can you change over to CCTV1 please? 4 (算盘) flick 5 (火) poke 6 (配给) allocate II [量] 1 (指人) group ▷我们公司为了新项目招了一拨人。Our company recruited a group of people for the new project. 2 (指物) batch ▷这两拨货昨天已经发出去了。The two batches of goods were sent out yesterday.
拨款 bōkuǎn [动] allocate funds ▷政府拨款兴建了100所小学。The government allocated funds for the setting up of 100 primary schools. ▷教育拨款已经到位。The funding for education is already in place.
拨弄 bōnong [动] 1 (琴弦) pluck 2 (算盘) flick 3 (指用器具) poke around ▷我用筷子拨弄着鸡块。I poked at the chicken pieces with my chopsticks. 4 (挑拨) stir ... up

玻 bō 见下文
玻璃 bōli [名] glass

剥 bō 见下文
→另见 bāo
剥夺 bōduó [动] strip ... of ▷他被剥夺政治权利5年。He was stripped of his political rights for five years.
剥离 bōlí [动] come off (PT came, PP come)
剥削 bōxuē [动] exploit ▷残酷的剥削 ruthless exploitation ▷废除剥削制度 abolish exploitative systems

菠 bō 见下文

菠菜 bōcài [名] spinach
菠萝 bōluó [名] pineapple

播 bō [动] 1 (电视、收音机) broadcast (PT, PP broadcast) 2 (播种) sow (PT sowed, PP sown)
播放 bōfàng [动] broadcast (PT, PP broadcast)
播弄 bōnong [动] 见 '拨弄'
播送 bōsòng [动] broadcast (PT, PP broadcast)
播音 bōyīn [动] broadcast (PT, PP broadcast)
播音员 bōyīnyuán [名] broadcaster
播种 bōzhǒng [动] sow (PT sowed, PP sown)
播种 bōzhòng [动] sow (PT sowed, PP sown) ▷农民在田里播种小麦。Farmers are sowing the field with wheat.

伯 bó [名] 1 (伯父) uncle 2 (大哥) eldest brother 3 (伯爵) earl
伯伯 bóbo [名] 1 (伯父) uncle 2 (用于称呼) uncle

uncle 有时可作为对跟父亲同辈且年纪较大的男子的称呼，但不常用。伯伯后通常跟姓氏，例如：李伯伯；而 Uncle 后跟名字，例如：Uncle Tom。

伯乐 Bólè [名] talent scout
伯仲 bózhòng [名] (书) ▷他俩不分伯仲。There's little to choose between them. ▷他们的英语能力在伯仲之间。Their English is equally good.

驳 bó [动] refute
驳斥 bóchì [动] refute
驳杂 bózá [形] mixed

泊 bó [动] 1 (停靠) moor ▶泊船 moor a boat 2 (停留) stop over
泊位 bówèi [名] berth

帛 bó [名] (书) silks (PL)

勃 bó [形] (书) thriving
勃勃 bóbó [形] exuberant
勃然 bórán [副] suddenly

舶 bó [名] ocean liner
舶来品 bóláipǐn [名] import

脖 bó [名] neck

博 bó I [动] 1 (通晓) possess a wide knowledge of 2 (取得) gain II [形] abundant
博爱 bó'ài [名] universal love ▷自由、平等、博爱 liberty, equality and fraternity
博大精深 bó dà jīng shēn deep
博导 bódǎo [名] doctoral supervisor

博览 **bólǎn** [动] read widely (PT, PP read)

博览会 **bólǎnhuì** [名] fair

博士 **bóshì** [名] doctor

博士后 **bóshìhòu** [名] ▷我正在做博士后研究。I'm doing postdoctoral research at the moment.

博闻强记 **bó wén qiáng jì** be learned

博物 **bówù** [名] natural sciences (PL)

博物馆 **bówùguǎn** [名] museum

博学 **bóxué** [形] learned

搏 **bó** [动] 1 (搏斗) fight (PT, PP fought) 2 (跳动) beat (PT beat, PP beaten)

搏动 **bódòng** [动] beat (PT beat, PP beaten)

搏斗 **bódòu** I [动] 1 (对打) fight (PT, PP fought) 2 (斗争) struggle II [名] battle

箔 **bó** [名] foil ▷金箔 gold leaf

膊 **bó** [名] arm

薄 **bó** I [形] 1 (不健壮) weak 2 (少) meagre 3 (不厚道) mean 4 (不庄重) frivolous II [动] (轻视) look down on
→另见 **báo, bò**

薄利 **bólì** [名] small profit

薄命 **bómìng** [形] ill-fated

薄情 **bóqíng** [形] heartless

薄弱 **bóruò** [形] weak

跛 **bǒ** [形] lame

跛子 **bǒzi** [名] ▷他是个跛子。He has a limp.

簸 **bǒ** [动] 1 (扬去) fan 2 (上下颠动) be bumpy
→另见 **bò**

簸荡 **bǒdàng** [动] bump up and down

簸箩 **bǒluo** [名] wicker basket

薄 **bò** 见下文
→另见 **báo, bó**

薄荷 **bòhe** [名] peppermint

簸 **bò** 见下文
→另见 **bǒ**

簸箕 **bòji** [名] (器具) dustpan

卜 **bǔ** [动] practice divination

补 **bǔ** [动] 1 (衣服、鞋、车胎、袜子) mend 2 (牙) fill 3 (增加) add ▷请把邮编补上。Please add the postcode. 4 (滋补) nourish

补办 **bǔbàn** [动] ▷我的身份证丢了，得去补办。I've lost my identity card and must replace

it. ▷我错过了注册的时间，得以后补办。I missed the deadline for registration and had to deal with that at a later date.

补偿 **bǔcháng** [动] 1 (损失) compensate ▷补偿费 compensation 2 (欠缺、差额) make up for ▷公司给他5,000美元以补偿他的损失。The company gave him US$5,000 in compensation for his injury.

补充 **bǔchōng** [动] add ▷补充说明 additional explanation

补丁 **bǔding** [名] patch

补给 **bǔjǐ** [名] supply

补救 **bǔjiù** [动] remedy ▷我们必须采取补救措施。We must adopt remedial measures.

补考 **bǔkǎo** [动] resit (PT, PP resat) ▷她下学期得补考数学。She has to resit her maths exam next term. ▷我下个月要参加补考。I will be taking resits next month.

补品 **bǔpǐn** [名] tonic

补贴 **bǔtiē** I [动] subsidize II [名] subsidy

补习 **bǔxí** [动] take extra lessons (PT took, PP taken)

补休 **bǔxiū** [名] time off in lieu

补养 **bǔyǎng** [动] nourish

补药 **bǔyào** [名] tonic

补助 **bǔzhù** [名] subsidy ▷学校每月补助他们200美元。The school gives them a subsidy of 200 dollars every month.

捕 **bǔ** [动] catch (PT, PP caught)

捕风捉影 **bǔ fēng zhuō yǐng** listen to hearsay

捕获 **bǔhuò** [动] capture

捕捞 **bǔlāo** [动] fish ▷捕捞牡蛎 fish for oysters

捕猎 **bǔliè** [动] hunt

捕捉 **bǔzhuō** [动] 1 (抓住) seize ▷捕捉良机 seize a golden opportunity 2 (捉拿) hunt down ▷捕捉逃犯 hunt down a convict

哺 **bǔ** [动] feed (PT, PP fed)

哺乳 **bǔrǔ** [动] breast-feed (PT, PP breast-fed)

哺乳动物 **bǔrǔ dòngwù** [名] mammal

哺育 **bǔyù** [动] 1 (喂养) feed (PT, PP fed) 2 (培养) nurture

不 **bù** [副] 1 (用于否定句) not ▷我不喜欢游泳。I don't like swimming. ▶不法 illegal ▶不轨 undisciplined ▶不诚实 dishonest ▶不人道 inhumane ▷他不抽烟。He doesn't smoke. 2 (用于否定回答) no ▷"你累了吧？""不，不累。" Are you tired? – No, I'm not. ▷"你不忙吧？"—"不，很忙"。You're not busy, are you? – Yes, I am. 3 (表示不能) ▷我吃不下。I can't eat it. ▷你找不到她吗？Can't you find her? ▷他中文学不好。He's not good at Chinese. **4** (方)(用于问句) ▷你饿不? Are you hungry? **5** (跟'就是'搭配) ▷周末，她不是购物，就是看电视。If she doesn't go shopping at the weekend she'll watch TV. **6** (客套)(不用) ▷不客气。Please don't mention it. ▷不谢。You're welcome.

不安 bù'ān [形] **1** (指局势) unstable **2** (指情绪) uneasy **3** (客套)(表示歉意) ▷让您花这么多钱，真是不安。I'm sorry to make you spend so much money.

不白之冤 bù bái zhī yuān injustice

不卑不亢 bù bēi bù kàng neither overbearing nor self-effacing ▷他待人的态度一向不卑不亢。His manner with people is neither overbearing nor self-effacing.

不必 bùbì [副] ▷明天早上你们不必再来了。You don't have to come again tomorrow morning.

不⋯不⋯ bù...bù... **1** (表示强式否定) ▷不知不觉 unwittingly ▷不慌不忙 unhurriedly ▷不折不扣 one hundred percent **2** (既不⋯也不⋯) neither ... nor ... ▷不亏不盈 neither too little nor too much ▷不大不小 just the right size ▷不死不活 half dead **3** (如果不⋯就不⋯) unless ... then not ▷不破不立 without destruction there can be no construction ▷不见不散。See you there.

不测 bùcè I [形] (预料不到的) unexpected II [名] (意外) contingency

不曾 bùcéng [副] never ▷我不曾见过你。I've never met you.

不耻下问 bù chǐ xià wèn learn from those beneath one ▷老教授不耻下问，令人敬佩。It's admirable that the old professor is willing to learn from those beneath him.

不但 bùdàn [连] not only ▷这辆车的设计不但美观，而且实用。The design of this car is not only beautiful, it's also practical.

不当 bùdàng [形] inappropriate ▷用词不当 use inappropriate words ▷有不当之处，谨请包涵。Please excuse any improprieties.

不得了 bùdéliǎo [形] **1** (表示惊讶) My God! ▷不得了，着火了! My God! It's on fire. ▷带孩子去酒吧，那可不得了。Taking children into bars is a shocking thing to do. **2** (表示程度) ▷这孩子淘气得不得了。This child is terribly naughty. ▷他难劝说得不得了。It is incredibly difficult to persuade him.

不得已 bùdéyǐ [动] have no alternative but to ▷这也是不得已而为之的事情。This is one of those things we have no alternative but to do.

不定 bùdìng I [副] ▷这货他们还不定要不要呢。It's still not certain whether they want

these goods or not. II [形] 风向不定。The wind direction is changeable. ▷游移不定的目标 moving target

不断 bùduàn [副] continually ▷汽车不断减价。Cars are continually coming down in price. ▷沙漠不断扩大。The desert is expanding all the time. ▷人们的生活水平不断提高。The quality of people's lives goes on getting better.

不⋯而⋯ bù...ér... ▷不劳而获 acquire without working ▷不言而喻 it goes without saying ▷不胫而走 spread like wildfire

不乏 bùfá [动] ▷这当中不乏知情者。There is no shortage of people in the know about this.

不凡 bùfán [形] extraordinary

不妨 bùfáng [副] ▷你不妨先说说你的想法。There's no harm in saying what you think.

不服 bùfú [动] not accept ▷你如果不服判决还可以上诉。If you don't accept the verdict, you can still appeal.

不敢 bùgǎn [动] not dare ▷她不敢说实话。She doesn't dare tell the truth.

不公 bùgōng [形] unfair

不苟 bùgǒu [形] careful ▷不苟言笑 serious in manner

不管 bùguǎn [连] ▷不管那女人怎么欺负我们，我们都不在乎。No matter how that woman bullies us, we just don't care. ▷不管你去什么地方，请一定和我保持联系。Wherever you go, please do keep in touch with me. ▷不管什么人求你帮忙，你不要拒绝他们。Whoever asks you for help, you shouldn't refuse them. ▷不管出什么事，我们都要保持镇定。Whatever happens, we must remain calm. ▷不管有多少人反对，他们都坚持原计划。It doesn't matter how many people disagree, they insist on implementing the original plan.

不轨 bùguǐ [形] irregular ▷这些人行为不轨引起了警察的注意。The irregular conduct of these people has attracted the attention of the police.

不过 bùguò I [副] **1** (仅仅) only ▷不过是点小伤，过几天就好了。It's only a slight injury. It'll be fine in a few days. ▷宝宝不过6个月大。The baby is only six months old. **2** (非常) ▷你要能帮忙，那就再好不过了! If you were able to help, that couldn't be better. ▷这是最简单不过的方法。This is much the easiest method. II [连] but ▷他很喜欢新学校，不过离家太远了。He really likes his new school, but it's a very long way from home.

不及 bùjí [动] **1** (不如) be not as good as **2** (来不及) be too late

不计其数 bù jì qí shù countless

不假思索 **bù jiǎ sīsuǒ** without hesitation ▷他不假思索地给出了正确答案。He gave the correct answer without hesitation.

不禁 **bùjīn** [动] cannot help ▷我不禁失笑。I couldn't help laughing. ▷众人不禁欢呼起来。The crowd were unable to restrain a cheer.

不仅 **bùjǐn** [副] **1** (不止) not just ▷这不仅是学校的问题。This is not just the school's problem. **2** (不但) not only ▷这地毯不仅质量好，而且价格便宜。Not only is the carpet good quality, it's also cheap.

不胫而走 **bù jìng ér zǒu** spread like wildfire

不久 **bùjiǔ** [名] ▷在不久的将来 in the near future ▷这片田地不久前刚开垦。This land has only just been cultivated. ▷他们不久就要结婚了。They are getting married soon.

不拘 **bùjū** I [动] **1** (不拘泥) not confine oneself **2** (不计较) not worry about II [连] regardless of ▷不拘什么人，他都以礼相待。Regardless of who someone is, he is always polite.

不拘一格 **bùjū yī gé** not be limited to one type ▷选用人才要不拘一格。When selecting staff you mustn't be limited to just one type.

不堪 **bùkān** I [动] **1** (承受不了) cannot stand ▷不堪其苦 can't stand the hardship **2** (不能) not able ▷不堪设想 be inconceivable II [形] extreme

不可 **bùkě** [动] **1** (不可以) ▷不可一概而论。You can't generalize. ▷植物生长，水和阳光两者缺一不可。For plants to grow they must have both sun and water. ▷我们不可忽视年轻人的心理健康。We shouldn't overlook the mental health of young people. ▷我们对这些疾病不可不防。We mustn't fail to take steps against such diseases. **2** (与"非"连用) ▷今天非下雨不可。It will certainly rain today. ▷你非挨批不可。You are bound to be criticized. ▷我们非得解决这个问题不可。We absolutely have to sort this problem out.

不可救药 **bù kě jiù yào** be beyond help

不可思议 **bù kě sīyì** unbelievable

不可一世 **bù kě yī shì** be insufferably arrogant

不快 **bùkuài** [形] unhappy

不愧 **bùkuì** [动] be worthy of

不力 **bùlì** [形] **1** (不尽力) ▷领导常常批评他办事不力。The boss frequently criticizes him for not doing his best. **2** (不得力) incompetent

不利 **bùlì** [形] **1** (不好) disadvantageous **2** (不顺) unsuccessful

不了了之 **bù liǎo liǎo zhī** leave unresolved ▷由于找不到嫌疑人，这个案件只能不了了之。Since the suspect hasn't been found, the case simply had to be left unresolved.

不料 **bùliào** [动] not anticipate ▷不料下午下雨。I didn't anticipate it would rain in the afternoon. ▷我们本想和她开个玩笑，不料她却当真了。We had just wanted to have a laugh with her – we hadn't appreciated that she was serious.

不论 **bùlùn** [连] no matter ▷不论是谁，都必须遵守法规。No matter who you are, you have to abide by the regulations. II [动] not consider

不满 **bùmǎn** [形] dissatisfied

不免 **bùmiǎn** [副] inevitably ▷竞争不免要有淘汰。In competitions there is inevitably elimination.

不明飞行物 **bùmíng fēixíngwù** [名] UFO

不谋而合 **bù móu ér hé** happen to coincide

不平 **bùpíng** I [形] unfair II [名] **1** (不公) injustice **2** (愤怒) resentment III [动] feel resentful (PT, PP felt)

不巧 **bùqiǎo** [形] unfortunate ▷你来得真不巧，王医生不在。Unfortunately, you haven't come at a good time – Dr Wang isn't here.

不求甚解 **bù qiú shèn jiě** be content with a superficial understanding ▷他学习一向不求甚解。He studies only to have a superficial understanding.

不屈 **bùqū** [动] not yield

不然 **bùrán** I [形] not so ▷这两件事看似一样，其实不然。These two seem the same, but in fact it is not so. II [连] otherwise ▷他家有老人，不然咱们倒可以去他家聚会。There is an elderly person in his family – otherwise we could get together at his house.

不忍 **bùrěn** [动] not bear

不如 **bùrú** [动] not be as good as ▷论跑步你不如她。You are not as good as her at running. ▷城里太吵，不如住在郊区。The city is too noisy – it's better living in the suburbs.

不三不四 **bù sān bù sì** **1** (不正经) shady **2** (不像样) neither one thing nor the other

不少 **bùshǎo** [形] a lot of ▷她有不少好朋友。She has a lot of good friends.

不胜 **bùshèng** I [动] cannot bear ▷不胜其苦 be unable to bear any more hardship ▷他不胜酒力，终于醉倒了。He had no tolerance for alcohol, and in the end fell down dead drunk. II [副] deeply ▷我对你的帮助不胜感激。I am deeply grateful for your help.

不是 **bùshi** [名] fault

不速之客 **bù sù zhī kè** uninvited guest ▷她是晚会上的不速之客。She was an uninvited guest at the party. ▷昨晚我家来了一位

不速之客。Yesterday evening we had an unexpected guest.

不同 bù tóng [形] different

不同凡响 bù tóng fánxiǎng outstanding

不外 bùwài [动] be limited to

不闻不问 bù wén bù wèn be indifferent ▷对与己无关的事情一概不闻不问。He's indifferent to anything that doesn't have a bearing on him.

不相上下 bù xiāng shàng xià be about the same

不屑 bùxiè [动] disdain ▷不屑一顾 disdain to look at ▷他不屑金钱的诱惑。He's scornful of the temptations of money. ▷不屑的神情 a disdainful expression

不幸 bùxìng I [形] 1 (不幸运) unhappy 2 (出人意料) unfortunate ▷不幸被言中了。Unfortunately, it turned out to be true. II [名] disaster

不修边幅 bù xiū biānfú scruffy

不朽 bùxiǔ [形] immortal

不学无术 bù xué wú shù ignorant and incompetent ▷不学无术的人怎么能当校长？How can someone ignorant and incompetent be head teacher?

不宜 bùyí [动] not be suitable for ▷这种菜不宜生食。This kind of vegetable is not suitable for serving raw.

不遗余力 bù yí yú lì do one's utmost ▷足球俱乐部不遗余力地引进外国球星。The football team did its utmost to attract foreign football stars.

不翼而飞 bù yì ér fēi disappear without trace

不约而同 bù yuē ér tóng happen to coincide ▷大家不约而同地投了赞成票。Everybody happened to vote in favour.

不择手段 bù zé shǒuduàn (贬) go to any lengths ▷为了发财，他不择手段。He'll go to any lengths to get rich.

不折不扣 bù zhé bù kòu through and through ▷他是不折不扣的球迷。He's a football fan through and through.

不知所措 bù zhī suǒ cuò be at a loss

不止 bùzhǐ [副] 1 (不停地) incessantly ▷大笑不止 laugh incessantly 2 (多于) more than ▷不止一次 on more than one occasion

不至于 bùzhìyú [副] ▷你不至于骗我吧？You won't go so far as to cheat me, will you?

不自量力 bù zì liàng lì overestimate one's abilities

布 bù I [名] cloth ▷布娃娃 rag doll II [动] 1 (宣告) publicize 2 (散布) spread (PT, PP spread) 3 (布置) arrange

布丁 bùdīng [名] pudding

布告 bùgào I [名] notice II [动] put up a notice (PT, PP put)

布景 bùjǐng [名] set

布局 bùjú [动] 1 (指结构) design ▷房间布局合理。The room is designed sensibly. ▷花园的布局很精巧。The layout of the garden is ingenious. 2 (指下棋) deploy

布匹 bùpǐ [名] cloth

布置 bùzhì [动] decorate

步 bù I [名] 1 (脚步) step 2 (阶段) stage 3 (地步) situation II [动] step III [量] move

步调 bùdiào [名] step ▷步调一致 stay in step

步伐 bùfá [名] pace ▷加快步伐 quicken one's pace

步人后尘 bù rén hòu chén follow in other people's footsteps

步行 bùxíng [动] go on foot (PT went, PP gone)

步骤 bùzhòu [名] step

部 bù I [名] 1 (部分) part ▷局部 part ▷头部 head 2 (部门) department ▷教育部 education department ▷总部 headquarters (PL) ▷分部 branch 3 (指军队) headquarters (PL) ▷司令部 army headquarters II [量] ▷一部字典 a dictionary ▷一部新型手机 a new style of mobile phone

部队 bùduì [名] armed forces (PL) ▷特种部队 special forces

部分 bùfen [名] part ▷我们只完成了项目的第一部分。We have only finished the first part of the project. ▷部分学生没有参加运动会。Some students didn't attend the sports meeting. ▷你要承担自己的那部分责任。You should shoulder your share of the responsibility. ▷我部分地同意他的观点。I partially agree with his view.

部件 bùjiàn [名] parts (PL)

部落 bùluò [名] tribe

部门 bùmén [名] department ▷政府部门 government department ▷邮政部门 post room ▷农业部门 department of agriculture

部署 bùshǔ [动] deploy

部位 bùwèi [名] place ▷手术部位 the place operated on

部下 bùxià [名] subordinate

埠 bù [名] port

簿 bù [名] book ▷练习簿 exercise book

簿子 bùzi [名] notebook

Cc

擦 cā [动] 1 (抹) wipe ... clean ▷擦眼镜 wipe one's glasses clean ▷擦汗 wipe away one's sweat 2 (指用水) wash 3 (皮鞋) polish 4 (摩擦) rub ▷摩拳擦掌 be itching for a fight 5 (涂) apply ▷她粉底擦得太厚了。She has applied too much foundation. 6 (火柴) strike (PT, PP struck) 7 (破) scrape ▷擦伤 scrape 8 (挨着) brush ▷排球没发过去，擦网了。The volleyball didn't make it's way over – it just brushed the net. 9 (瓜果) shred
擦拭 cāshì [动] wipe ... clean ▷擦拭窗户 wipe a window clean ▷擦拭银器 polish silverware

猜 cāi [动] 1 (猜测) guess 2 (猜疑) suspect
猜测 cāicè I [动] speculate ▷大家都在猜测谁能得奖。Everybody was speculating about who was going to win the prize. II [名] speculation
猜忌 cāijì [动] be suspicious
猜谜儿 cāimèir [动] guess
猜拳 cāiquán [动] play a finger guessing game
猜想 cāixiǎng [动] suppose
猜疑 cāiyí [动] have unfounded suspicions about

才 cái I [名] 1 (才能) ability ▷多才多艺 multi-talented 2 (人才) talent ▶奇才 extraordinary talent II [副] 1 (刚) just ▷我才到家，电话就响了。Just as I arrived home, the phone rang. 2 (表示晚) not...until ▷路上堵车，我10点才到单位上班。Because of the traffic jam, I did not arrive at work until ten. 3 (表示条件) only...if ▷学生只有用功，才能取得好成绩。Students will only be able to do well if they study hard. 4 (表示情况改变) only after ▷他解释后，我才明白了他为什么那么难过。It was only after he explained that I understood why he was so sad. 5 (程度低) only ▷他才学会上网。He has only just learned how to use the Internet. 6 (表示强调) really ▷他才不愿意见你呢！He really doesn't want to see you!
才干 cáigàn [名] ability
才华 cáihuá [名] talent
才貌 cáimào [名] ability and appearance
才能 cáinéng [名] ability ▷施展才能 put one's abilities to use ▷他有领导才能。He has leadership qualities.
才气 cáiqì [名] talent
才识 cáishí [名] ability and insight ▷他具有卓越的政治才识。He is a man of outstanding political ability and insight.
才学 cáixué [名] ability and learning
才子 cáizǐ [名] talented man (PL men)

材 cái [名] 1 (指物) material ▶建材 building material ▶教材 teaching material 2 (人才) talented person
材料 cáiliào [名] 1 (原料) material ▷建筑材料公司 building materials company ▷这件大衣是用什么材料做的？What material is this coat made of? 2 (资料) material ▷我正为毕业论文搜集材料。I'm in the process of gathering material for my dissertation. 3 (人才) talent ▷我不是经商的材料。I have no talent for business.

财 cái [名] wealth
财宝 cáibǎo [名] treasure
财阀 cáifá [名] tycoon
财富 cáifù [名] wealth
财经 cáijīng [名] finance and economics ▷财经学院 Institute of Finance and Economics
财路 cáilù [名] road to riches
财贸 cáimào [名] trade and finance
财神 cáishén [名] the god of wealth
财团 cáituán [名] consortium
财务 cáiwù [名] financial affairs (PL)
财物 cáiwù [名] assets (PL)
财政 cáizhèng [名] finance
财主 cáizhu [名] rich man (PL men)

裁 cái [动] 1 (衣服、纸) cut (PT, PP cut) 2 (减) cut (PT, PP cut) ▶ 裁员 cut staff 3 (判断) decide

裁定 cáidìng [动] adjudicate

裁缝 cáifeng [名] 1 (指男装) tailor 2 (指女装) dressmaker

裁决 cáijué [动] adjudicate

裁判 cáipàn I [名] judgment II [动] make a decision ▷ 我们要公平裁判这件事。We should make a fair decision on this matter.

裁员 cáiyuán [动] make redundancies ▷ 信息产业内刮起了一阵裁员风暴。There have been a wave of redundancies in the IT industry.

采 cǎi I [动] 1 (摘) pick 2 (选) choose (PT chose, PP chosen) 3 (开采) extract ▶ 采油 extract oil 4 (采集) gather II [名] spirit ▶ 风采 bearing

采伐 cǎifá [动] fell ▷ 过度的采伐会破坏森林。Excessive felling will destroy the forest.

采访 cǎifǎng [动] interview ▷ 记者采访了一位著名作家。The reporter interviewed a famous writer. ▷ 她已经做了十几年的新闻采访工作。She has already been working in investigative journalism for over ten years.

采购 cǎigòu I [动] purchase II [名] buyer

采光 cǎiguāng [名] lighting

采集 cǎijí [动] collect

采纳 cǎinà [动] adopt

采取 cǎiqǔ [动] adopt ▷ 政府采取紧急措施防止病毒传播。The government is adopting urgent measures to prevent the spread of disease. ▷ 我们采取主动，首先和新客户联络。We took the initiative and contacted the new client first.

采用 cǎiyòng [动] adopt ▷ 老师采用互动教学方式。The teacher has adopted an interactive method of teaching.

采摘 cǎizhāi [动] pick

彩 cǎi [名] 1 (颜色) colour (英), color (美) 2 (欢呼声) cheer 3 (花样) variety 4 (博彩) winnings (PL) ▶ 彩票 lottery ticket 5 (血) blood ▶ 挂彩 be wounded

彩电 cǎidiàn [名] colour (英) 或 color (美) TV

彩卷 cǎijuǎn [名] colour (英) 或 color (美) film

彩礼 cǎilǐ [名] wedding present

彩排 cǎipái [动] rehearse

彩票 cǎipiào [名] lottery ticket

彩色 cǎisè [名] colour (英), color (美)

睬 cǎi [动] take notice of (PT took, PP taken) ▷ 他太没人缘，晚上没人睬他。He's not very good with people and no one takes any notice of him at parties.

踩 cǎi [动] 1 (脚) step on ▷ 跳舞时，我踩到他的脚了。During the dance I stepped on his foot. ▷ 我踩在椅子上擦窗户。I stood on a chair and cleaned the window. 2 (贬低) put ... down (PT, PP put) ▷ 他不会夸人，只会踩人。He never praises people – he only puts them down.

菜 cài [名] 1 (植物) vegetable 2 (饭食) dish

菜单 càidān [名] menu

菜篮子 càilánzi [名] 1 (指买菜用的) shopping basket 2 (食品供应) food supply

菜谱 càipǔ [名] 1 (菜单) menu 2 (指书) cookbook

菜肴 càiyáo [名] dish

参 cān [动] 1 (加入) join ▶ 参军 enlist 2 (参考) refer to
→ 另见 cēn, shēn

参拜 cānbài [动] bow before

参半 cānbàn [动] halve

参观 cānguān [动] tour ▷ 我们参观了故宫博物院。We toured the Forbidden City museum.

参加 cānjiā [动] take part in (PT took, PP taken) ▷ 参加演讲比赛 take part in a public speaking competition ▷ 参加新年晚会 attend a New Year's party ▷ 去年他参加了民主党。Last year he joined the Democratic Party.

参军 cānjūn [动] enlist ▷ 参军使他成熟了很多。Joining the army made him a lot more mature.

参考 cānkǎo I [动] consult ▷ 为了写毕业论文，我参考了几十本书。For my dissertation I had to consult dozens of different books. II [名] reference ▷ 参考书 reference book ▷ 以上观点仅供参考。The above advice is only for reference.

参谋 cānmóu I [名] 1 (顾问) advisor 2 (指军职) staff officer II [动] give advice (PT gave, PP given) ▷ 你帮我参谋一下，看他俩谁更优秀。I need you to give me some advice – who do you think is the best out of those two?

参数 cānshù [名] parameter

参议员 cānyìyuán [名] senator

参与 cānyù [动] participate in ▷ 参与竞选活动 participate in campaign activities ▷ 参与决策制定 participate in policy formulation ▷ 我参赛的态度是 "重在参与，不重输赢"。My attitude towards competitions is: "It's not the winning, it's the taking part that counts."

参赞 cānzàn [名] attaché ▷ 美国大使馆文化参赞 the cultural attaché to the American embassy

参照 cānzhào [动] act in accordance with ▷ 我

参照导师的意见修改了我的论文。I acted in accordance with the advice of my supervisor, and amended my thesis.

餐 cān I [名] meal II [量] meal

餐车 cānchē [名] 1 (指推车) food trolley 2 (指车厢) buffet (英) 或 dining (美) car

餐巾 cānjīn [名] napkin

餐具 cānjù [名] eating utensils (PL)

餐厅 cāntīng [名] canteen

残 cán I [形] 1 (指器物) defective 2 (指人或动物) disabled ▷这是匹好马，可惜残了。This is a good horse. It's a shame it's lame. 3 (剩余) remaining 4 (凶恶) cruel II [动] treat viciously

残暴 cánbào [形] cruel ▷侵略者的残暴 the cruelty of the invaders

残存 cáncún [动] survive ▷这是惟一残存的中国清代陶器样品。This is the only surviving example of Qing dynasty pottery in China. ▷公司里仍残存着性别歧视现象。Sexual discrimination still goes on in the company.

残废 cánfèi [动] be disabled ▷他中风后残废了。He was disabled by his stroke. ▷车祸使她成了残废。The car accident left her disabled.

残骸 cánhái [名] wreckage

残害 cánhài [动] devastate ▷战争残害了无数的人民。The war devastated the lives of countless people.

残疾 cánjí [名] disability ▷残疾人 people with disabilities ▷欢迎有残疾的人报名参加。People with disabilities are particularly encouraged to apply.

残局 cánjú [名] mess ▷公司倒闭后，只有经理在收拾残局。When the company closed only the manager was left to clear up the mess.

残酷 cánkù [形] brutal ▷残酷的市场竞争 brutal market competition ▷ 他被敌人残酷地杀害了。He was brutally murdered by the enemy.

残年 cánnián [名] final years (PL) ▷老人无儿无女，只能孤单单地度过残年。The old man had no children, and lived out his final years in loneliness.

残缺 cánquē [形] deficient

残忍 cánrěn [形] cruel

残杀 cánshā [动] brutally kill

残余 cányú [形] remaining ▷战败后，残余的部队逃回老家。After their defeat, the remaining troops fled home.

蚕 cán [名] silkworm

蚕豆 cándòu [名] broad (英) 或 fava (美) bean

蚕食 cánshí [动] encroach on ▷沙皇俄国对邻国采取了蚕食政策。Tsarist Russia adopted a policy of encroaching on its neighbours.

惭 cán 见下文

惭愧 cánkuì [形] ashamed

惨 cǎn [形] 1 (悲惨) tragic 2 (厉害) severe 3 (凶恶) cruel

惨案 cǎn'àn [名] massacre

惨败 cǎnbài [动] suffer a disastrous defeat

惨不忍睹 cǎn bù rěn dǔ too horrible to look at

惨淡 cǎndàn [形] 1 (暗淡) dim 2 (萧条) dismal ▷几年的惨淡经营后，生意终于出现了转机。After several years' hard work, the business finally turned around.

惨绝人寰 cǎn jué rén huán horrific

惨痛 cǎntòng [形] bitter

惨无人道 cǎn wú rén dào barbaric

惨重 cǎnzhòng [形] disastrous

灿 càn 见下文

灿烂 cànlàn [形] glorious

仓 cāng [名] store ▶仓房 storehouse

仓储 cāngchǔ [动] store

仓促 cāngcù [形] hasty

仓皇 cānghuáng [形] panic-stricken

仓库 cāngkù [名] storehouse

苍 cāng [形] 1 (指天空) deep blue 2 (指植物) dark green 3 (指鬓发) grey (英), gray (美)

苍白 cāngbái [形] 1 (脸色) pale 2 (文章、表演等) bland

苍苍 cāngcāng [形] 1 (指天空) deep blue 2 (指植物) dark green 3 (指鬓发) grey (英), gray (美)

苍劲 cāngjìng [形] 1 (树) mighty 2 (书画) bold

苍老 cānglǎo [形] old

苍茫 cāngmáng [形] vast

苍生 cāngshēng [名] (书) the masses (PL)

苍天 cāngtiān [名] the heavens (PL)

苍蝇 cāngyíng [名] fly

沧 cāng [名] deep blue

沧海 cānghǎi [名] the sea

沧海桑田 cāng hǎi sāng tián radical changes ▷多年后重返故乡，真有种沧海桑田的感觉。Returning home after so many years, I had the impression that the place had undergone a complete transformation.

沧海一粟 cāng hǎi yī sù a drop in the ocean

沧桑 cāngsāng [名] all that life has to offer ▷在外漂泊了几十年，他已经饱经沧桑。He spent years drifting about, and has experienced all that life has to offer.

舱 cāng [名] 1 (用于载人) cabin ▶头等舱 first-class cabin 2 (用于装物) hold ▶货舱 cargo hold

藏 cáng [动] 1 (隐藏) hide (PT hid, PP hidden) 2 (储存) store 3 (收集) collect ▶藏书 collect books
→另见 zàng

藏龙卧虎 cáng lóng wò hǔ hidden talent ▷人才招聘市场里藏龙卧虎。There is a lot of hidden talent on the job market.

藏匿 cángnì [动] conceal

藏书 cángshū I [动] collect books II [名] book collection

藏污纳垢 cáng wū nà gòu ▷这个地区真是个藏污纳垢之地。It's a really unsavoury area.

藏拙 cángzhuō [动] keep one's limitations to oneself (PT, PP kept) ▷他从不当众唱歌，只是为了藏拙。He never sings in public – he prefers to keep his limitations to himself. ▷她用化妆来藏拙。She uses make-up to cover her blemishes.

操 cāo I [动] 1 (拿) hold (PT, PP held) 2 (掌握) control 3 (从事) engage in 4 (语言、口音) speak (PT spoke, PP spoken) II [名] 1 (体育活动) exercise ▶早操有益于学生的身体健康。Morning exercises are beneficial to students' health. 2 (品行) conduct

操办 cāobàn [动] make arrangements ▷他父母给他操办婚礼。His parents made all the arrangements for his wedding.

操场 cāochǎng [名] sports ground

操持 cāochí [动] 1 (处理) take charge of (PT took, PP taken) 2 (筹办) make arrangements for

操劳 cāoláo [动] work hard ▷校长为学生操劳过度，病倒了。The headteacher worked excessively hard for the pupils, and fell ill.

操练 cāoliàn [动] drill ▷教官正在操练新兵。The officer is putting the new soldiers through the drill.

操心 cāoxīn [动] concern ▷父母为他的身体操心。His parents were concerned about his health.

操行 cāoxíng [名] behaviour (英), behavior (美)

操之过急 cāo zhī guò jí be in too much of a rush ▷我们慢慢解决这个问题，不可操之过急。Let's take our time over this problem. We don't want to be in too much of a rush.

操纵 cāozòng [动] 1 机器、仪器) operate 2 (贬) manipulate

操作 cāozuò [动] operate ▷工人熟练地操作着机器。The workers are operating the machine skilfully (英) 或 skillfully (美). ▷所有办公人员都能操作电脑。Everyone in the office knows how to use a computer. ▷操作说明 operating instructions (PL) ▷操作方法 how to use ▷安全操作手册 safety handbook

糙 cāo [形] poor ▷这条裤子做得太糙。These trousers are very poorly made. ▷这书印得太糙了。This book has been printed so shoddily.

嘈 cáo 见下文
嘈杂 cáozá [形] noisy

槽 cáo [名] 1 (下凹) groove 2 (用于盛液体) channel 3 (用于装饲料) trough

草 cǎo I [名] 1 (植物) grass 2 (用作材料) straw II [形] 1 (字) illegible 2 (初步) draft

草案 cǎo'àn [名] draft

草包 cǎobāo [名] 1 (人) waster 2 (物) straw sack

草本 cǎoběn [形] herbal

草草 cǎocǎo [副] hastily ▷我草草看了一遍笔记，就进了考场。I glanced hastily at my notes and went into the examination hall. ▷因为观众不多，所以演唱会草草收场了。Because there weren't enough people in the audience, the performance was brought to an abrupt end. ▷我们不能就这样草草了事，一定要找出问题的根源。This isn't something that we can just dash off – we're going to have to get to the root of the problem.

草创 cǎochuàng [动] set ... up (PT, PP set) ▷我们市场部还处于草创阶段。Our marketing department is still just being set up.

草稿 cǎogǎo [名] rough draft

草菅人命 cǎo jiān rénmìng set little store by human life

草帽 cǎomào [名] straw hat

草莓 cǎoméi [名] strawberry

草木皆兵 cǎo mù jiē bīng be panic-stricken ▷战争即将打响，全国上下草木皆兵。Just before the war, the whole country was panic-stricken.

草拟 cǎonǐ [动] draft

草签 cǎoqiān [动] initial

草书 cǎoshū [名] cursive writing

草率 cǎoshuài [形] rash ▷他没有认真考虑，就草率地做了答复。He didn't think about it properly and came up with a careless reply. ▷写作文前要仔细构思，不要草率动笔。There's no point putting pen to paper before

you have organised your thoughts. ▷结婚是人
生大事，绝不能草率。Marriage is a big deal.
You should never go into it rashly.

草图 cǎotú [名] sketch

草原 cǎoyuán [名] grasslands (PL)

草纸 cǎozhǐ [名] rough paper

册 cè I [名] book ▶手册 handbook ▶相册
photo album II [量] 1 (指同一本书) copy 2 (指
不同本书) volume

册子 cèzi [名] brochure

厕 cè [名] toilet ▶公厕 public toilet

厕所 cèsuǒ [名] toilet

侧 cè I [名] side ▷步行街两侧是大大小小的商
店。On either side of the pedestrian walkway
there are shops of various sizes.
II [动] turn ... away ▷我侧过脸去，不再理睬
他。I turned my face away, and didn't take any
more notice of him.

侧面 cèmiàn I [形] 1 (非官方) unofficial ▷侧
面消息证实他已经提交了辞呈。Unofficial
sources have confirmed that he has already
handed in his notice. 2 (指方位) side ▷侧面的
大楼是另外一个公司的。The building to the
side here belongs to another company.
II [名] side ▷船身的侧面遭到了猛烈的攻
击。The side of the ship was heavily attacked.
▷我们从多个侧面分析市场的发展现状。We
are looking at current market developments
from many different angles.

侧目 cèmù [动] 1 (贬) shock ▷他无礼的行为令
人侧目。Her rudeness shocked people. 2 (褒)
surprise ▷泳坛小将的出色表现引起了老
将的侧目。The outstanding performance
by the new swimmers surprised the more
experienced contenders.

侧身 cèshēn [动] turn sideways ▷她只能侧身
过门。She had to turn sideways to get through
the door.

侧重 cèzhòng [动] emphasize

测 cè [动] 1 (测量) measure 2 (推测) predict

测定 cèdìng [动] measure

测量 cèliáng I [动] measure II [名] survey

测评 cèpíng [动] evaluate ▷测评系统
evaluation system

测试 cèshì I [动] test II [名] test

测验 cèyàn I [动] test II [名] test

策 cè I [名] suggestion II [动] whip

策动 cèdòng [动] stir ... up

策划 cèhuà I [动] design II [名] planning

策略 cèlüè I [名] strategy II [形] strategic

策源地 cèyuándì [名] starting place ▷内战的
策源地 the place where the civil war started

参 cēn 见下文
→另见 cān, shēn

参差 cēncī [形] uneven ▷纪录片的质量参差不
齐。The documentaries are uneven in quality.

层 céng I [量] 1 (指建筑物) floor ▷这幢摩天
大楼有50层。This skyscraper is 50 floors
high. 2 (指覆盖物) layer ▷电脑屏幕上有一
层灰。There's a layer of dust on the computer
screen. 3 (步) step ▷我们需要进一层研究。
We need to investigate this further. 4 (指含
义) layer ▷他的话还有一层深意。There is
another layer of meaning in what he says.
II [名] (指物、状态) layer ▷飞机穿过云层。The
plane passed through layers of cloud.

> 在英式英语里，**ground floor** 是指紧贴
> 地面的那个楼层。它上面的一层叫做
> **first floor**。在美式英语中，**first floor**
> 是指紧贴地面的楼层，它上面的一层
> 是 **second floor**。

层出不穷 céng chū bù qióng come thick
and fast

层次 céngcì [名] 1 (指语言、文章) ▷他说话层次
清楚。He speaks very clearly. ▷这篇报道层次
混乱。This report has been put together very
sloppily. 2 (指程度) level

层面 céngmiàn [名] 1 (范围) range ▷杂志的
读者层面很广。Magazine readership is very
broad. 2 (方面) aspect

曾 céng [副] once
→另见 zēng

曾经 céngjīng [副] once ▷我曾经想出国留
学。I once wanted to study abroad.

蹭 cèng [动] 1 (摩擦) rub ▷他在门垫上把鞋
底的泥蹭掉了。He rubbed the mud off his
shoe onto the doormat. 2 (沾上) smear ▷他
离得太近，袖子上蹭到了油漆。He got
too close to the wet paint and got his sleeve
smeared. 3 (指速度) creep along (PT, PP crept)
▷路上很挤，她一点一点地往前蹭。The
roads were packed, so she crept along at a
snail's pace. 4 (占便宜) scrounge ▷她已经工
作了，可是还去父母家蹭饭吃。She has a job
now, but still goes back to her parents' house to
scrounge food.

叉 chā I [名] 1 (器具) fork 2 (餐具) fork 3 (符号)
cross II [动] spear
→另见 chǎ

叉腰 chāyāo [动] put one's hands on one's hips ▷她站着的时候习惯叉腰。When she was standing she liked to put her hands on her hips.

叉子 chāzi [名] 1 (符号) cross 2 (餐具) fork

差 chā [名] difference ▷这两个数的差是多少？What's the difference between these two numbers?
➝另见 chà, chāi

差别 chābié [名] difference

差错 chācuò [名] 1 (错误) mistake 2 (意外) accident ▷万一他出了什么差错，他父母可承受不了。If he were ever to have any kind of accident, his parents wouldn't be able to bear it.

差额 chā'é [名] difference

差价 chājià [名] price difference

差距 chājù [名] difference

差强人意 chā qiáng rényì just passable ▷公司去年的效益差强人意。Last year the company's results were only just passable.

差异 chāyì [名] difference ▷中英文差异很大。The differences between Chinese and English are huge.

插 chā [动] insert ▷插插销 insert a plug ▷我能不能插一句？Can I interrupt just a second? ▷他开始插手公司事务。He started meddling in the company's affairs.

插话 chāhuà I [动] interrupt II [名] interruption

插科打诨 chā kē dǎ hùn joke around

插曲 chāqǔ [名] 1 (音乐) incidental music 2 (事件) interlude

插入 chārù [动] insert

插手 chāshǒu [动] involve oneself in ▷雇主不应该插手职员的私事。Employers should not involve themselves in the private affairs of their staff.

插图 chātú [名] illustration

插销 chāxiāo [名] 1 (闩) bolt 2 (插头) electrical plug

插页 chāyè [名] insert

插足 chāzú [动] involve oneself in

插嘴 chāzuǐ [动] interrupt

插座 chāzuò [名] socket (英), outlet (美)

喳 chā 见下文
➝另见 zhā

喳喳 chāchā [拟] whisper

茬 chá [名] 1 (根茎) stubble 2 (次数) crop

茶 chá [名] tea ▷红茶 black tea ▷泡茶 make tea

茶点 chádiǎn [名] refreshments (PL)

茶话会 cháhuàhuì [名] tea party

茶具 chájù [名] tea set

茶叶 cháyè [名] tea leaves (PL)

茶余饭后 chá yú fàn hòu over a cup of tea ▷这个笑话成了茶余饭后的谈资。The joke became dinner-party material.

茶座 cházuò [名] tea house

查 chá [动] 1 (检查) inspect 2 (调查) investigate ▷这个案子还需要查一查。This case needs further investigation.

查抄 cháchāo [动] confiscate

查点 chádiǎn [动] check the quantity of ▷查点车上装载物品 check the quantity of goods in a vehicle

查对 cháduì [动] verify

查访 cháfǎng [动] make inquiries ▷查访民情 sound out public feeling

查封 cháfēng [动] seal ... up

查号台 cháhàotái [名] directory inquiries (SG) (英) 或 assistance (美)

查看 chákàn [动] examine

查问 cháwèn [动] interrogate ▷警察正在查问嫌疑犯。The police are interrogating the suspect right now.

查询 cháxún [动] inquire about ▷网上查询 search the web

查阅 cháyuè [动] look ... up ▷我去图书馆查阅资料。I'm going to the library to look up some information. ▷写论文前必须查阅大量书刊。Before writing a thesis it is necessary to consult a lot of material.

查账 cházhàng [动] check accounts

查找 cházhǎo [动] look for

查证 cházhèng [动] verify

搽 chá [动] apply ▷搽化妆品 apply cosmetics

察 chá [动] check ▷观察 observe

察访 cháfǎng [动] make inquiries

察觉 chájué [动] detect

察看 chákàn [动] examine ▷察看事故发生现场 examine the scene of the accident ▷察看工地 inspect a building site

察言观色 chá yán guān sè read people ▷他善于察言观色，讨好上司。He's very good at reading people and ingratiating himself with his superiors.

叉 chǎ [动] cross ▷叉着腿 with legs crossed

→另见 chā

杈 chà [名] branch

岔 chà **I** [名] **1** (岔路) fork ▷三岔路口 a fork in the road **2** (毛病) accident ▶岔子 accident **II** [动] **1** (偏离方向) turn off ▷出租汽车岔上了小道。The taxi turned off onto a narrow track. **2** (分开) diverge ▶岔开 diverge

岔子 chàzi [名] **1** (岔路) side road **2** (事故) accident

刹 chà [名] Buddhist temple
→另见 shā

刹那 chànà [名] instant ▷刹那间 in an instant

诧 chà [动] be surprised

诧异 chàyì [动] be surprised ▷他突然辞职，大家都很诧异。When he suddenly resigned everybody was very surprised.

差 chà **I** [动] **1** (不相同) ▷你和他比差得远了。You are not nearly as good as him. **2** (缺欠) ▷差3个人 be three people short ▷他还差我10镑钱。He still owes me ten pounds. **II** [形] **1** (错误) mistaken **2** (不好) poor ▷这些鞋的质量很差。These shoes are of poor quality.
→另见 chā, chāi

差不多 chà bu duō **I** [形] very similar ▷这两块布颜色差不多。The colour (英) 或 color (美) of these two pieces of material is very similar. **II** [副] almost ▷晚饭差不多快做好了。Dinner is almost ready.

差劲 chàjìn [形] bad

姹 chà [形] beautiful

姹紫嫣红 chà zǐ yān hóng beautiful flowers (PL)

拆 chāi [动] **1** (打开) tear ... open (PT tore, PP torn) ▷拆信 tear open a letter **2** (拆毁) dismantle ▷拆房子 demolish a house

拆穿 chāichuān [动] expose

拆毁 chāihuǐ [动] demolish

拆台 chāitái [动] undermine

差 chāi [动] send (PT, PP sent) ▷校长差他去参加研讨会。The principal is sending him to attend the seminar. ▶出差 go on a business trip
→另见 chā, chà

差旅费 chāilǚfèi [名] travel expenses (PL)

差遣 chāiqiǎn [动] dispatch

差使 chāishǐ [动] assign

差使 chāishi [名] position

差事 chāishi [名] **1** (任务) assignment **2** (差使) position

柴 chái [名] firewood

柴火 cháihuo [名] firewood

柴油 cháiyóu [名] diesel

豺 chái [名] jackal

豺狼 cháiláng [名] **1** (豺和狼) jackals and wolves (PL) **2** (喻) (恶人) cruel and evil people (PL)

掺 chān [动] mix

搀 chān **1** (搀扶) support ... by the arm ▷老两口相互搀着散步。The couple go walking arm in arm to support each other. **2** (混合) mix ▷咖啡里搀牛奶味道更佳。Coffee tastes nicer with milk.

搀扶 chānfú [动] support ... by the arm

搀和 chānhuo [动] mix

搀杂 chānzá [动] mix

婵 chán 见下文

婵娟 chánjuān **I** [形] beautiful **II** [名] moon

谗 chán [动] slander

谗言 chányán [名] slander

馋 chán [形] greedy

馋涎欲滴 chánxián yù dī drool ▷牛肉的香味使我馋涎欲滴。The delicious smell of the beef made my mouth water.

禅 chán [名] (宗) **1** (静坐) meditation **2** (指佛事) ▶禅林 Buddhist temple
→另见 shàn

禅宗 chánzōng [名] Zen

孱 chán [形] frail

孱弱 chánruò [形] (书) **1** (瘦弱) frail **2** (软弱) weak **3** (薄弱) faint

缠 chán [动] **1** (缠绕) twine **2** (纠缠) pester ▷别老缠着我，自己玩儿去。Stop pestering me, and go and play on your own. **3** (方) (应付) deal with (PT, PP dealt)

缠绵 chánmián [形] **1** (摆脱不开) lingering **2** (婉转动人) moving

蝉 chán [名] cicada

蝉联 chánlián [动] continue to hold a post ▷蝉联奥运会冠军 be the reigning Olympic champion

潺 chán 见下文
潺潺 chánchán [拟] babble ▷溪水潺潺 a babbling stream

蟾 chán [名] toad
蟾蜍 chánchú [名] toad

产 chǎn [动] 1 (生育) give birth to (PT gave, PP given) 2 (出产) produce ▷这里产石油。Oil is produced here. ▷荔枝产在南方。Lychees are grown in the South.
产地 chǎndì [名] producing area ▷菠萝产地 pineapple producing area
产妇 chǎnfù [名] woman who is in labour or who has just given birth
产量 chǎnliàng [名] yield
产品 chǎnpǐn [名] product ▷产品质量 product quality
产权 chǎnquán [名] property rights (PL) ▷知识产权 intellectual property
产生 chǎnshēng [动] produce ▷产生结果 produce a result ▷他的小说在读者中产生了很大反响。His novel created a big stir among readers. ▷他对电脑产生了浓厚的兴趣。He's become deeply interested in computers.
产物 chǎnwù [名] product
产业 chǎnyè [名] 1 (财产) property 2 (工业生产) industry ▷产业革命 the Industrial Revolution
产值 chǎnzhí [名] output value

谄 chǎn [动] flatter
谄媚 chǎnmèi [动] flatter

铲 chǎn I [名] shovel II [动] shovel
铲除 chǎnchú [动] eradicate

阐 chǎn [动] explain
阐明 chǎnmíng [动] expound
阐释 chǎnshì [动] explain ▷他对合同条款作了详细的阐释。He gave a detailed explanation of the clauses in the contract.
阐述 chǎnshù [动] expound

忏 chàn [动] repent
忏悔 chànhuǐ [动] repent

颤 chàn [动] tremble
→另见 zhàn
颤抖 chàndǒu [动] shiver ▷他激动得浑身颤抖。He was trembling with excitement.
颤巍巍 chànwēiwēi [形] faltering ▷爷爷颤巍巍地端起碗。Grandpa lifted his bowl unsteadily.

昌 chāng [形] flourishing
昌明 chāngmíng [形] thriving
昌盛 chāngshèng [形] prosperous

猖 chāng [形] aggressive
猖獗 chāngjué [形] rampant
猖狂 chāngkuáng [形] fierce

娼 chāng [名] prostitute
娼妓 chāngjì [名] prostitute

长 cháng I [形] long ▷长发 long hair II [名] 1 (长度) length ▷这张桌子有两米长。This table is two metres in length. 2 (长处) strong point ▷取长补短 learn from others' strong points
→另见 zhǎng
长城 Chángchéng [名] the Great Wall
长处 chángchu [名] strong point
长此以往 cháng cǐ yǐ wǎng if things carry on this way ▷这些学生天天吸烟喝酒，长此以往肯定荒废学业。These students smoke and drink every day – if they carry on this way they'll certainly neglect their studies.
长度 chángdù [名] length
长短 chángduǎn [名] 1 (长度) length 2 (意外) accident
长方形 chángfāngxíng [名] rectangle
长话短说 cháng huà duǎn shuō cut a long story short ▷时间有限，我们就长话短说。There's not much time, so we'll keep it brief.
长假 chángjià [名] extended break
长江 Cháng Jiāng [名] the Yangtze
长久 chángjiǔ [形] long-term ▷长久之计 long-term plan
长空 chángkōng [名] vast sky
长眠 chángmián [动] (婉) die
长年累月 cháng nián lěi yuè year in year out
长跑 chángpǎo [动] go long-distance running (PT went, PP gone) ▷你参加过长跑比赛吗？Have you ever taken part in any long-distance running competitions?
长篇大论 cháng piān dà lùn be long-winded
长篇小说 chángpiān xiǎoshuō [名] full-length novel
长生不老 chángshēng bù lǎo immortality
长逝 chángshì [动] pass away
长寿 chángshòu [形] long-lived ▷祝您长寿！Here's to a long life!
长叹 chángtàn [动] sigh deeply
长途 chángtú [形] long-distance ▷长途电话 long-distance phone call ▷长途旅行 long

journey

长项 **chángxiàng** [名] strong point

长于 **chángyú** [动] be good at

长远 **chángyuǎn** [形] long-term ▷长远利益 long-term benefits ▷长远眼光 long-term view

长治久安 **cháng zhì jiǔ ān** lasting stability and peace

长足 **chángzú** [形] rapid ▷职业教育取得了长足发展。 There has been rapid development in vocational education.

场 **cháng** I [名] threshing ground II [量] ▷昨天下了一场大雨。 Yesterday there was a downpour. ▷母亲生了一场病。 Mother had an illness.
→另见 chǎng

肠 **cháng** [名] intestines (PL)

肠子 **chángzi** [名] intestines (PL)

尝 **cháng** I [动] taste ▶品尝 taste II [副] (书) ever

尝试 **chángshì** [动] try

常 **cháng** I [形] 1 (平常) common ▶常态 normality 2 (经常) frequent ▶常客 regular guest II [副] often ▷我常去看戏。 I often go to the theatre (英) 或 theater (美).

常常 **chángcháng** [副] often ▷我常常去北京出差。 I often go to Beijing on business. ▷圣诞节人们常常互送礼物。 At Christmas people usually give presents to each other.

常规 **chángguī** [名] 1 (规矩) convention ▷常规武器 conventional weapons (PL) 2 (医) routine

常轨 **chángguǐ** [名] normal practice

常客 **chángkè** [名] regular guest

常例 **chánglì** [名] common practice

常情 **chángqíng** [名] sense

常人 **chángrén** [名] ordinary person (PL people)

常任 **chángrèn** [形] permanent

常识 **chángshí** [名] 1 (非专业知识) general knowledge 2 (生活经验) common sense

常委 **chángwěi** [名] standing committee member

常务 **chángwù** [形] standing ▷常务委员会 standing committee

常言 **chángyán** [名] saying

偿 **cháng** [动] 1 (归还) repay (PT, PP repaid) ▶偿付 pay ... back 2 (满足) fulfil ▷如愿以偿 fulfil one's dreams

偿还 **chánghuán** [动] repay (PT, PP repaid)

偿命 **chángmìng** [动] pay with one's life (PT, PP paid)

徜 **cháng** 见下文

徜徉 **chángyáng** [动] (书) wander about at one's leisure

厂 **chǎng** [名] 1 (工厂) factory ▷服装厂 clothing factory (厂子) works (SG) ▷木材厂 timber yard (英), lumberyard (美)

厂家 **chǎngjiā** [名] factory

场 **chǎng** I [名] 1 (地方) ground ▶操场 sports ground ▶市场 market 2 (舞台) stage ▷上场 go on stage 3 (戏剧片段) scene ▷话剧的第一幕第二场 Act I, Scene II of the play 4 (物) field ▷电磁场 electromagnetic field II [量] ▷一场足球赛 a football match ▷一场戏 a play
→另见 cháng

场地 **chǎngdì** [名] space ▷运动场地 sports area

场合 **chǎnghé** [名] occasion

场面 **chǎngmiàn** [名] 1 (戏剧情况) scene 2 (情景) occasion 3 (排场) front ▷撑场面 keep up appearances

场所 **chǎngsuǒ** [名] place ▷公共场所 public place

敞 **chǎng** I [形] spacious ▶宽敞 spacious II [动] be open ▷大门敞着。 The main door is open.

敞亮 **chǎngliàng** [形] 1 (明亮) light and spacious 2 (喻) (开阔) clear ▷听了你的解释，我心里敞亮多了。 Having heard your explanation, I'm much clearer now.

怅 **chàng** [形] disappointed

怅然 **chàngrán** [形] disappointed

怅惘 **chàngwǎng** [形] listless

畅 **chàng** I [形] 1 (无阻碍) smooth ▶畅通 unimpeded 2 (舒适) untroubled ▷他心情不畅。 He's troubled by something. II [副] uninhibitedly ▶畅饮 drink one's fill

畅达 **chàngdá** [形] free-flowing

畅快 **chàngkuài** [形] carefree

畅所欲言 **chàng suǒ yù yán** speak freely

畅谈 **chàngtán** [动] talk happily

畅通 **chàngtōng** [动] be open ▷道路畅通 open road

畅销 **chàngxiāo** [动] have a ready market ▷这种新型洗衣机很畅销。 There is a ready market for this new type of washing machine.

畅游 **chàngyóu** [动] 1 (游览) enjoy sightseeing 2 (游泳) enjoy a swim

倡 chàng [动] initiate

倡导 chàngdǎo [动] initiate

倡议 chàngyì [动] propose ▷这项倡议得到了大家的认同。This proposal met with everyone's agreement.

唱 chàng [动] 1 (发出乐音) sing (PT sang, PP sung) ▶独唱 solo ▷合唱 chorus 2 (大叫) cry

唱段 chàngduàn [名] aria

唱反调 chàng fǎndiào [动] express a contrary opinion

唱高调 chàng gāodiào [动] speak fine-sounding words (PT spoke, PP spoken)

唱歌 chànggē [动] sing (PT sang, PP sung)

唱腔 chàngqiāng [名] aria

唱戏 chàngxì [动] perform opera

唱主角 chàng zhǔjué [动] play the lead

抄 chāo [动] 1 (誊写) copy ▷抄诗 copy out a poem 2 (抄袭) plagiarize 3 (查收) raid ▷抄家 raid a home 4 (走近路) take a short cut (PT took, PP taken) ▷抄道 take a short cut 5 (插在袖子里) fold one's arms (into one's sleeves) ▷他抄着手站在那儿。He stood there with his arms folded.

抄家 chāojiā [动] search a home and confiscate possessions

抄录 chāolù [动] make a copy

抄袭 chāoxí [动] 1 (剽窃) plagiarize 2 (照搬) copy indiscriminately 3 (绕道袭击) launch a surprise attack

钞 chāo [名] banknote

钞票 chāopiào [名] banknote

超 chāo I [动] 1 (超过) exceed ▷超额 be above quota 2 (不受限制) transcend ▷超现实 transcend reality II [形] super ▷超低温 ultra-low temperature ▷超级明星 superstar

超编 chāobiān [动] overstaff

超标 chāobiāo [动] exceed limits

超常 chāocháng [形] extraordinary

超额 chāo'é [动] be above quota

超级 chāojí [形] super ▷超级大国 superpower ▷超级市场 supermarket

超群 chāoqún [动] be pre-eminent

超然 chāorán [形] aloof

超人 chāorén [名] superman (PL supermen)

超声波 chāoshēngbō [名] ultrasonic wave

超市 chāoshì [名] supermarket

超脱 chāotuō I [形] unconventional II [动] be detached from

超越 chāoyuè [动] overcome (PT overcame, PP overcome)

超载 chāozài [动] overload

超支 chāozhī [动] overspend (PT, PP overspent)

超重 chāozhòng [动] 1 (超过载重量) overload ▷货车超重了。The truck is overloaded. 2 (超过标准量) be overweight ▷他的行李超重了。His luggage is over the limit.

巢 cháo [名] nest

巢穴 cháoxué [名] 1 (指动物) nest 2 (指匪徒) lair

朝 cháo I [名] 1 (宫廷) imperial court 2 (朝代) dynasty 3 (王朝) reign ▷康熙王朝 Kangxi's reign II [动] face III [介] towards →另见 zhāo

朝拜 cháobài [动] 1 (皇帝) pay one's respects to (PT, PP paid) 2 (神) worship

朝代 cháodài [名] dynasty

朝圣 cháoshèng [动] make a pilgrimage

朝廷 cháotíng [名] 1 (听政的地方) court 2 (统治机构) imperial government

朝向 cháoxiàng [名] exposure

朝野 cháoyě [名] the government and the people

嘲 cháo [动] ridicule

嘲讽 cháofěng [动] sneer at ▷他总爱嘲讽他的同伴。He loved to sneer at his mates. ▷她用嘲讽的眼神瞥了他一眼。She glanced at him with a sneering expression.

嘲弄 cháonòng [动] mock ▷嘲弄历史定会被历史所嘲弄。Those who mock history will be mocked by history.

嘲笑 cháoxiào [动] laugh at ▷不要嘲笑别人的短处。You shouldn't laugh at other people's weaknesses.

潮 cháo I [名] 1 (潮汐) tide 2 (社会运动) movement ▶工潮 labour (英) 或 labor (美) movement ▶思潮 Zeitgeist II [形] damp

潮流 cháoliú [名] 1 (水流) tide 2 (发展趋势) trend

潮湿 cháoshī [形] humid

潮水 cháoshuǐ [名] tidal waters (PL)

潮汐 cháoxī [名] tide

吵 chǎo I [动] 1 (发出噪音) make a racket 2 (争吵) squabble II [形] noisy

吵架 chǎojià [动] quarrel

吵闹 chǎonào [动] 1 (争吵) bicker 2 (打扰) disturb

吵嘴 chǎozuǐ [动] bicker

炒 chǎo [动] **1** (烹调) stir-fry **2** (地皮、外汇等) speculate **3** (方)(解雇) sack ▷他被老板给炒了。He was sacked by the boss.

炒股 chǎogǔ [动] speculate in stocks and shares

炒汇 chǎohuì [动] speculate in foreign currency

炒货 chǎohuò [名] roasted snacks (PL)

炒冷饭 chǎo lěngfàn [动] rehash

炒买炒卖 chǎomǎi-chǎomài make a quick buck

炒鱿鱼 chǎo yóuyú [动] ▷她被炒了鱿鱼。She was given her marching orders.

炒作 chǎozuò [动] hype ▷她歌唱得很糟，但被炒作得很好。She's a hopeless singer but she's been really hyped.

车 chē [名] **1** (运输工具) vehicle ▶小汽车 car ▶公共汽车 bus **2** (带轮的装置) wheel ▶风车 windmill **3** (机器) machine

车次 chēcì [名] **1** (火车的) train number **2** (长途汽车的) coach number

车费 chēfèi [名] fare

车祸 chēhuò [名] traffic accident

车间 chējiān [名] workshop

车库 chēkù [名] garage

车辆 chēliàng [名] vehicle

车轮 chēlún [名] wheel

车皮 chēpí [名] wagon

车水马龙 chē shuǐ mǎ lóng heavy traffic

车胎 chētāi [名] tyre (英), tire (美)

车厢 chēxiāng [名] coach

车载斗量 chē zài dǒu liáng ten a penny (英), a dime a dozen (美)

车站 chēzhàn [名] **1** (火车的) railway station **2** (汽车的) bus stop

车子 chēzi [名] **1** (小型运输车) vehicle **2** (自行车) bicycle

扯 chě [动] **1** (拉) pull ▷别扯我袖子。Stop pulling at my sleeve. **2** (撕) tear (PT tore, PP torn) **3** (闲谈) chat ▶闲扯 chat

扯谎 chěhuǎng [动] lie

扯皮 chěpí [动] wrangle

彻 chè [动] penetrate ▶透彻 penetrating ▶彻夜 all night

彻底 chèdǐ [形] thorough ▷房子打扫得很彻底。The room has been given a thorough cleaning. ▷他们的计划彻底落空了。Their plan was a complete failure.

彻头彻尾 chè tóu chè wěi outright

掣 chè [动] **1** (退) withdraw (PT withdrew, PP withdrawn) **2** (闪) flash by ▷风驰电掣 go like the wind

撤 chè [动] **1** (除去) take ... away (PT took, PP taken) ▷他的职务给撤了。He was dismissed from his job. **2** (退) move away ▷请向后撤一撤。Please move back a little.

撤除 chèchú [动] dismantle

撤换 chèhuàn [动] replace

撤离 chèlí [动] evacuate

撤诉 chèsù [动] drop charges

撤退 chètuì [动] withdraw (PT withdrew, PP withdrawn)

撤销 chèxiāo [动] **1** (职务) dismiss **2** (计划) cancel **3** (法令) rescind

撤职 chèzhí [动] dismiss (from a post)

澈 chè [形] clear

抻 chēn [动] stretch

嗔 chēn [动] **1** (生气) be angry **2** (埋怨) complain

嗔怪 chēnguài [动] rebuke

臣 chén 见下文

臣服 chénfú [动] acknowledge allegiance to

臣民 chénmín [名] subject

尘 chén [名] **1** (尘土) dirt ▶灰尘 dust **2** (尘世) the material world ▶红尘 worldly affairs (PL)

尘埃 chén'āi [名] dust

尘封 chénfēng [动] be dusty

尘世 chénshì [名] worldly affairs (PL)

尘土 chéntǔ [名] dust

辰 chén [名] **1** (星辰) heavenly body **2** (时间) birthday ▶寿辰 birthday

沉 chén I [动] **1** (向下落) sink (PT sank, PP sunk) ▷船沉到了海底。The ship sank to the bottom of the sea. **2** (指情绪) become grave (PT became, PP become) ▷遇到不如意的事，她马上就会沉下脸来。She pulls a long face as soon as anything happens to displease her. II [形] **1** (程度深) deep ▷昨晚我睡得很沉。Last night I slept very deeply. **2** (重) heavy **3** (不舒服) heavy ▷我两条腿发沉。My legs feel heavy.

沉沉 chénchén [形] **1** (重) heavy **2** (程度深) deep ▷孩子们沉沉地睡了。Children sleep deeply.

沉甸甸 chéndiāndiān [形] **1** (重) heavy **2** (喻) worried ▷任务还没完成，我心里沉甸甸的。The job is not finished, and that worries me.

沉浮 chénfú I [动] drift II [名] vicissitude

沉积 chénjī [动] silt up

沉寂 chénjì [形] 1 (十分寂静) quiet 2 (没有消息) ▷他沉寂了很久后，突然给我们来了一封信。There was no news from him for ages, and then suddenly he sent us a letter. ▷那位小说家已沉寂了多年。We've heard nothing from the novelist for years.

沉浸 chénjìn [动] immerse

沉静 chénjìng [形] 1 (肃静) quiet 2 (指性格) placid

沉沦 chénlún [动] sink into (PT sank, PP sunk)

沉闷 chénmèn [形] 1 (天气、气氛) depressing 2 (心情) depressed ▷最近我心情很沉闷。I've been feeling really depressed lately. 3 (指性格) introverted

沉湎 chénmiǎn [动] indulge in

沉没 chénmò [动] sink (PT sank, PP sunk)

沉默 chénmò I [形] taciturn II [动] be silent

沉溺 chénnì [动] indulge in

沉睡 chénshuì [动] be fast asleep

沉思 chénsī [动] ponder ▷他为此事沉思了很久。He pondered this matter for a long time. ▷他陷入了沉思。He was lost in thought.

沉痛 chéntòng [形] 1 (心情) grieving 2 (教训) bitter

沉稳 chénwěn [形] 1 (稳重) steady 2 (安稳) peaceful ▷他一向睡得沉稳。He always sleeps peacefully.

沉重 chénzhòng [形] heavy

沉着 chénzhuó [形] calm ▷他处理问题沉着冷静。He deals with problems calmly and soberly.

沉醉 chénzuì [动] be intoxicated ▷他沉醉在成功的喜悦中。He was intoxicated with success.

忱 chén [名] sincerity ▶热忱 ardour (英), ardor (美)

陈 chén I [动] 1 (陈列) set ... out (PT, PP set) 2 (陈述) state II [形] old

陈词滥调 chén cí làn diào clichés

陈腐 chénfǔ [形] dated

陈规 chénguī [名] outmoded conventions (PL)

陈旧 chénjiù [形] out-of-date

陈列 chénliè [动] display

陈年 chénnián [形] aged ▷陈年老酒 old wine

陈设 chénshè I [动] display ▷房间里陈设着几张古画。Some old pictures are on display in the room. II [名] furnishings (PL)

陈述 chénshù [动] state

晨 chén [名] morning ▶早晨 early morning ▶清晨 dawn

晨光 chénguāng [名] dawn

晨练 chénliàn [动] morning exercise

衬 chèn I [名] lining II [动] 1 (垫) line 2 (衬托) set ... off (PT, PP set) III [形] lining ▶衬布 lining material

衬托 chèntuō [动] set ... off (PT, PP set)

称 chèn [动] match ▶相称 match ▶对称 be symmetrical
→另见 chēng

称心 chènxīn [动] be satisfactory ▷这台电脑我买得称心。I am satisfied with the computer I bought.

称职 chènzhí [动] be competent ▷他担任这个职务很称职。He's very competent at his job.

趁 chèn [介] ▷趁这个机会我讲几句话。I would like to take this opportunity to say a few words. ▷趁年轻多学点知识。Learn something while you are young.

趁火打劫 chèn huǒ dǎ jié profit from other people's misfortunes

趁热打铁 chèn rè dǎ tiě strike while the iron is hot

趁势 chènshì [动] take the opportunity (PT took, PP taken)

称 chēng I [动] 1 (叫) call ▷我们都称他老王. We call him Old Wang. 2 (说) say (PT, PP said) ▶称谢 express one's gratitude 3 (测量) weigh II [名] name ▶简称 short form
→另见 chèn

称病 chēngbìng [动] plead illness

称道 chēngdào [动] praise ▷他孝敬父母值得称道。The respect he shows towards his parents is worthy of praise.

称号 chēnghào [名] title

称呼 chēnghu I [动] call ▷我不知道怎么称呼他。I don't know what I should call him. II [名] form of address

称颂 chēngsòng [动] praise

称王称霸 chēngwáng chēngbà domineer

称谓 chēngwèi [名] title

称赞 chēngzàn [动] praise

撑 chēng [动] 1 (抵住) prop ... up ▷他两手撑着下巴在深思。His chin was propped on his hands, and he was deep in thought. 2 (船) punt 3 (坚持住) keep ... up (PT, PP kept) ▷他撑不住了，到底笑了。In the end, he couldn't help laughing. **4** (张开) open **5** (容不下) fill to bursting ▷少吃点吧，别撑着！Don't eat so much, you'll burst!

撑腰 chēngyāo [动] support

瞠 chēng [动] stare

瞠目结舌 chēng mù jié shé be flabbergasted ▷他的回答令我瞠目结舌。I was flabbergasted at his reply.

成 chéng I [动] **1** (成功) accomplish ▷那件事成了。The job is done. **2** (成为) become (PT became, PP become) ▷两个人成了好朋友。The two of them became good friends. **II** [名] result **III** [形] **1** (成熟的) mature ▶成虫 adult **2** (现成的) established ▶成品 finished product **3** (表示数量) ▷成千上万 hundreds and thousands of ▷成批生产 bulk production **4** (可以) O.K. ▷成！就这么定了。O.K. – that's agreed.

成本 chéngběn [名] cost ▷生产成本 production costs (PL)

请勿混淆 **cost** 和 **costs**。某事物的 **cost** 是指用于购买、完成或者制造它所需的费用。…*the cost of the telephone call… the total cost was over a million pounds…* 企业或者家庭的 **costs** 是指保证它们继续运转所需要的费用，包括电费、修理费用和税款。…*attempts to cut costs and boost profits…*

成材 chéngcái [动] become useful (PT became, PP become)

成分 chéngfèn [名] **1** (组成部分) composition ▷化学成分 chemical composition **2** (社会阶层) status

成功 chénggōng [动] succeed ▷他这次试验获得了成功。This time his experiment was successful. ▷本届运动会开得很成功。This year's sports event was a great success.

成果 chéngguǒ [名] achievement

成活 chénghuó [动] survive

成绩 chéngjì [名] success ▷我们在环境保护方面取得了很大成绩。We have had considerable success in environmental protection. ▷他的学习成绩不理想。His school record is not satisfactory.

成家 chéngjiā [动] **1** (结婚) marry **2** (成为专家) become an authority (PT became, PP become)

成见 chéngjiàn [名] prejudice ▷他分明对我有成见。He is clearly prejudiced against me.

成交 chéngjiāo [动] strike a deal (PT, PP struck)

成就 chéngjiù I [名] achievement ▷他在事业上很有成就。He has achieved much in his career. II [动] achieve ▷他立志成就一番事业。He aspires to succeed in his career.

成立 chénglì [动] **1** (建立) found ▷联合国成立于1945年。The United Nations was founded in 1945. ▷一所新学校成立了。A new school has been established. **2** (有根据) be tenable ▷你的结论根本无法成立。Your conclusions are completely untenable.

成名成家 chéngmíng chéngjiā become an established authority

成年 chéngnián I [动] **1** (指动植物) mature **2** (指人) grow up (PP grew, PT grown) II [副] all year round

成品 chéngpǐn [名] end product

成气候 chéng qìhòu [动] get somewhere ▷这孩子将来能成气候。This child will really go places one day.

成器 chéngqì [动] grow up to be a useful person (PP grew, PT grown) ▷那孩子将来成不了器。That child is never going to get anywhere in life.

成亲 chéngqīn [动] marry

成全 chéngquán [动] help … get what he/she wants

成人 chéngrén I [名] adult II [动] grow up (PP grew, PT grown)

成人之美 chéng rén zhī měi help others achieve their goals

成熟 chéngshú [形] **1** (指果实) ripe **2** (指思想) mature **3** (指机会等) ripe

成为 chéngwéi [动] become (PT became, PP become)

成文 chéngwén I [名] existing writing ▷他抄袭成文。He is copying existing works. II [动] write (PT wrote, PP written) ▷这些规定必须成文。These provisions must be in writing.

成问题 chéng wèntí [动] be a problem

成效 chéngxiào [名] result

成心 chéngxīn [副] deliberately

成性 chéngxìng [动] become second nature (PT became, PP become)

成语 chéngyǔ [名] idiom

成员 chéngyuán [名] member ▷家庭成员 family member

成长 chéngzhǎng [动] grow up (PP grew, PT grown)

成竹在胸 chéng zhú zài xiōng have well-thought-out ideas

呈 chéng [动] **1** (呈现) assume ▷苹果呈圆型。Apples have a round form. **2** (呈送) present

呈报 chéngbào [动] submit a report

呈请 chéngqǐng [动] apply

呈现 chéngxiàn [动] appear

诚 chéng I [形] honest ▶忠诚 loyal ▶诚心 sincere II [副] really

诚惶诚恐 chéng huáng chéng kǒng in fear and trepidation

诚恳 chéngkěn [形] sincere ▷他诚恳地向她表示了感谢。He thanked her sincerely.

诚然 chéngrán [副] 1 (确实) truly ▷这孩子诚然懂礼貌。This child really does know how to be polite. 2 (固然) admittedly ▷困难诚然很多，但我们有信心克服。Admittedly there are many difficulties, but we are confident of overcoming them.

诚实 chéngshí [形] honest

诚心诚意 chéngxīn chéngyì in all sincerity

诚挚 chéngzhì [形] sincere

承 chéng [动] 1 (承受) bear (PT bore, PP borne) ▷这桥承不住这么重的货车。This bridge cannot bear the weight of such a heavy lorry. 2 (承担) undertake (PT undertook, PP undertaken) 3 (承蒙) be indebted to ▷承您夸奖。You're flattering me. 4 (继续) inherit ▶继承 be a successor to

承办 chéngbàn [动] undertake (PT undertook, PP undertaken)

承包 chéngbāo [动] contract

承保 chéngbǎo [动] underwrite (PT underwrote, PP underwritten)

承担 chéngdān [动] 1 (责任) bear (PT bore, PP borne) 2 (工作) undertake (PT undertook, PP undertaken) 3 (费用) bear (PT bore, PP borne)

承当 chéngdāng [动] bear (PT bore, PP borne) ▷一切责任都由我来承当。All responsibility will be borne by me.

承接 chéngjiē [动] 1 (接受) accept 2 (接续) continue

承揽 chénglǎn [动] contract ▷我公司承揽房屋装修业务。My company's contracted to do the decorating work.

承蒙 chéngméng [动] (书) be indebted to

承诺 chéngnuò I [动] undertake (PT undertook, PP undertaken) II [名] commitment

承认 chéngrèn [动] 1 (认可) acknowledge 2 (政权) recognize

承上启下 chéng shàng qǐ xià link the preceding and the following ▷这段起了承上启下的作用。This paragraph is a link between the one before it and the one after it.

承受 chéngshòu [动] 1 (禁受) bear (PT bore, PP borne) ▷这木板承受不住100公斤的重量。This plank cannot bear a weight of 100 kilos. 2 (经受) experience

城 chéng [名] 1 (城墙) city wall ▶城外 outside the city 2 (城市) city ▶进城 go to town 3 (城镇) town

城堡 chéngbǎo [名] castle

城府 chéngfǔ [名] shrewdness ▷他城府很深。He's very shrewd.

城区 chéngqū [名] metropolitan area

城市 chéngshì [名] city

乘 chéng [动] 1 (搭坐) travel by ▷乘火车 travel by train 2 (利用) take advantage of (PT took, PP taken) ▷乘人之危 take advantage of sb's difficulties 3 (几倍于) multiply ▷8乘5等于40。Eight times five is forty.

乘法 chéngfǎ [名] multiplication

乘方 chéngfāng [名] (数) power

乘机 chéngjī [动] seize an opportunity

乘客 chéngkè [名] passenger

乘凉 chéngliáng [动] enjoy the cool

乘人之危 chéng rén zhī wēi take advantage of others' difficulties

乘务员 chéngwùyuán [名] conductor

乘虚而入 chéngxū'érrù exploit a weakness

盛 chéng [动] 1 (装) ladle ... out ▷帮我盛碗饭。Give me a bowl of rice. 2 (容纳) contain ▷这袋子可盛50公斤。This bag can hold 50 kilos. →另见 shèng

程 chéng [名] 1 (规矩) rule ▶章程 constitution 2 (程序) procedure ▶议程 agenda ▶课程 curriculum 3 (距离) distance ▶路程 journey 4 (道路) journey ▶登程 set off

程度 chéngdù [名] 1 (水平) level 2 (限度) extent ▷在一定程度上 to some extent

程控 chéngkòng [动] automate

程式 chéngshì [名] form

程序 chéngxù [名] 1 (次序) procedure 2 (计算机) program

惩 chéng [动] punish

惩办 chéngbàn [动] punish

惩处 chéngchǔ [动] punish

惩罚 chéngfá [动] punish ▷侵略者受到了应得的惩罚。The invaders got the punishment they deserved.

惩前毖后 chéng qián bì hòu learn from the past

澄 chéng I [形] clear ▶澄空 clear sky II [动]

make ... clear ▶澄清 purify
➔另见 dèng

澄清 chéngqīng I [形] clear II [动] clear ... up
▷我们之间的误会澄清了。We have cleared
up our misunderstanding.

橙 chéng 见下文
橙子 chéngzi [名] orange

逞 chěng [动] 1 (夸耀) flaunt ▶逞威风 flaunt
one's power 2 (达到目的) succeed ▶得逞 have
one's way 3 (纵容) indulge ▶逞性 headstrong

逞能 chěngnéng [动] show off (PT showed, PP
shown) ▷他为了逞能，喝酒醉得东倒西
歪。He showed off by drinking until he was
staggering about all over the place.

逞强 chěngqiáng [动] flaunt one's superiority

逞凶 chěngxiōng [动] behave violently

骋 chěng [动] 1 (跑) gallop ▶驰骋 gallop 2 (放任)
give free rein to (PT gave, PP given)

骋目 chěngmù [动] (书) look into the distance

秤 chèng [名] balance

吃 chī [动] 1 (咀嚼吞咽) eat (PT ate, PP eaten) ▷吃
面条 eat noodles ▷吃药 take medicine ▷吃
奶 suckle 2 (就餐) eat in (PT ate, PP eaten) ▷我
中午不做饭，吃食堂。I don't cook lunch
– I eat in the canteen. 3 (依靠) live off ▷吃
劳保 live off welfare ▷吃老本 rest on one's
laurels 4 (消灭) wipe ... out ▷吃掉一个棋子
take a chess piece 5 (耗费) withstand (PT, PP
withstood) ▶吃力 strenuous ▷吃不消 unable
to withstand 6 (吸收) absorb ▷棉布吃水。
Cloth absorbs water. 7 (受) take (PT took, PP
taken) ▶吃亏 lose out ▷他胸口吃了一枪。
He took a bullet in the chest.

吃醋 chīcù [动] be jealous ▷我的女友好吃
醋。My girlfriend gets jealous easily.

吃豆腐 chī dòufu (喻) (方) be lecherous

吃官司 chī guānsi [动] be taken to court

吃喝玩乐 chī hē wán lè eat, drink and be
merry

吃紧 chījǐn [形] 1 (紧张) tense ▷前线战事吃
紧。The situation on the front line was tense.
▷节前火车票吃紧。In the run-up to the
holiday, the ticket situation was tense. 2 (重
要) important ▷做事最吃紧的是要专心。
The most important thing is to concentrate on
what you're doing.

吃惊 chījīng [动] surprise ▷她这么快就去了
澳大利亚，让人吃了一惊。The speed with
which she left for Australia surprised everyone.

吃苦 chīkǔ [动] put up with hardship (PT,
PP put) ▷儿时的经历使我很能吃苦。My
childhood experiences have helped me to put
up with all kinds of hardship.

吃亏 chīkuī 1 (受损失) lose out (PT, PP lost)
▷在谈判中我们吃亏了。We lost out in the
negotiation. 2 (条件不利) be at a disadvantage

吃里爬外 chī lǐ pá wài double-cross

吃力 chīlì [形] 1 (费力) exhausting 2 (方) (疲劳)
exhausted

吃请 chīqǐng [动] buy ... off with a meal (PT, PP
bought) ▷他为人廉洁，从不接受吃请。He's
very straight-up, and would never be bought
by a meal out.

吃素 chīsù [动] be vegetarian

吃香 chīxiāng [形] (口) popular

吃一堑，长一智 chī yī qiàn, zhǎng yī zhì
experience is the mother of all wisdom

笞 chī [动] beat (PT beat, PP beaten) ▶鞭笞 whip

嗤 chī [动] (书) sneer

嗤笑 chīxiào [动] sneer at ▷他因为是文盲而
遭人嗤笑。He was sneered at because he was
illiterate.

嗤之以鼻 chī zhī yǐ bí turn one's nose up at

痴 chī I [形] idiotic ▷别理他，他在发痴。
Don't listen to him – he's just being silly. II [名]
obsession

痴呆 chīdāi [形] idiotic ▷老年痴呆症 senile
dementia

痴迷 chīmí [形] infatuated

痴情 chīqíng I [名] passion II [形] deeply
passionate

痴人说梦 chī rén shuō mèng unrealistic
expectation

痴心妄想 chī xīn wàng xiǎng wishful
thinking

池 chí [名] 1 (池塘) pond ▷养鱼池 fish pond 2 (指
旁边高中间洼) pit ▷乐池 orchestra pit 3 (护城
河) moat ▶城池 city moat

池塘 chítáng [名] pond

池鱼之殃 chí yú zhī yāng be involved in a
disaster not of one's own making

弛 chí [动] (书) relax

弛缓 chíhuǎn I [动] calm down II [形]
slackened

驰 chí [动] 1 (跑得快) speed (PT, PP sped) ▶奔驰
gallop 2 (传播) disseminate 3 (向往) long for
▶驰想 be lost in thought

驰骋 chíchěng [动] 1 (字) (快跑) gallop ▷驰骋辽阔草原 gallop across the wide plains 2 (喻) (活跃) be very active in ▷他驰骋于歌坛多年。He has been very active in the music world for years.

驰名 chímíng [动] become famous (PT became, PP become)

驰驱 chíqū [动] (骑马快跑) go at a gallop (PT went, PP gone)

迟 chí [形] 1 (慢) slow 2 (晚) late ▷对不起，迟了10分钟。Sorry, I'm ten minutes late. 3 (久) long ▷迟迟不做决定 dither

迟到 chídào [动] be late ▷上班迟到会扣奖金。If you're late for work your bonus can be docked.

迟钝 chídùn [形] (贬) slow ▷他对股市变化反应迟钝。He was slow to react to the changes on the stock exchange.

迟缓 chíhuǎn [形] slow

迟疑 chíyí [动] hesitate ▷她毫不迟疑地离开了家。She didn't hesitate to leave home.

迟早 chízǎo [副] sooner or later ▷他胡作非为，迟早要出事。His behaviour (英) 或 behavior (美) is outrageous. Sooner or later it'll end in disaster.

持 chí [动] 1 (拿着) hold (PT, PP held) ▷他手持护照。He held a passport in his hand. 2 (支持) support ▶坚持 maintain 3 (主管) manage ▷操持家务 manage the housework 4 (对抗) oppose ▶僵持 reach a stalemate

持久 chíjiǔ [形] protracted

持平 chípíng I [形] fair II [动] be equal ▷公司今年的利润与去年持平。This year's company profits are the same as last year's.

持续 chíxù [动] go on (PT went, PP gone) ▷高温天气持续了几天。The hot weather went on for some days. ▷该电视节目的收视率持续上升。The ratings for this TV programme (英) 或 program (美) continued to rise.

持之以恒 chí zhī yǐ héng persevere ▷英语学习要持之以恒。You must persevere with your English studies.

持之有故 chí zhī yǒu gù insist with good reason

匙 chí [名] spoon

踟 chí 见下文

踟蹰 chíchú [动] waver

尺 chǐ I [量] unit of length, equal to a third of a metre II [名] ruler

尺寸 chǐcun [名] 1 (长度) size 2 (口) (分寸) sense of propriety

尺牍 chǐdú [名] letter

尺度 chǐdù [名] yardstick

尺码 chǐmǎ [名] 1 (尺寸) size 2 (标准) standard

齿 chǐ I [名] 1 (器官) tooth (PL teeth) 2 (齿状物) protrusion ▶梳齿 teeth of a comb II [动] (书) mention

齿轮 chǐlún [名] gear wheel

侈 chǐ [形] (书) 1 (浪费) wasteful ▶奢侈 extravagant 2 (夸大) exaggerated

侈谈 chǐtán (书) I [动] brag II [名] extravagant flights of fancy

耻 chǐ [名] 1 (羞愧) shame 2 (耻辱) disgrace

耻辱 chǐrǔ [名] disgrace

耻笑 chǐxiào [动] mock

叱 chì [动] (书) rebuke

叱责 chìzé [动] scold

叱咤 chìzhà [动] (书) roar

叱咤风云 chì zhà fēng yún all-powerful

斥 chì [动] 1 (责备) denounce 2 (使离开) drive ... away (PT drove, PP driven) ▶排斥 repel 3 (支付) fund 4 (扩展) expand

斥退 chìtuì [动] 1 (开除) dismiss ▷他被老板斥退了。He was dismissed by the boss. 2 (喝令退出) shout at ... to go away ▷他斥退了手下。He shouted at his subordinate to go away.

斥责 chìzé [动] denounce

斥资 chìzī [动] fund

赤 chì I [形] 1 (红色) red 2 (表示革命) revolutionary 3 (忠诚) sincere II [动] bare

赤膊上阵 chì bó shàng zhèn 1 (字) do ... bare-chested ▷参赛者身穿短裤，赤膊上阵。The competitors entered the field in shorts and with bare chests. 2 (喻) lay oneself bare (PT, PP laid)

赤诚 chìchéng [形] completely sincere

赤胆忠心 chì dǎn zhōng xīn utter devotion

赤道 chìdào [名] the equator

赤脚 chìjiǎo [动] be barefoot ▷赤脚走路 walk barefoot

赤裸裸 chìluǒluǒ [形] 1 (光身子) stark naked 2 (喻) (毫无掩饰) undisguised

赤贫 chìpín [形] utterly destitute ▷一个从赤贫走向成功的商业奇才 a commercial genius who rose from utter destitution to success

赤手空拳 chì shǒu kōng quán unarmed ▷赤

手空拳地搏斗 engage in unarmed combat

赤条条 chìtiáotiáo [形] stark naked

赤子 chìzǐ [名] 1 (初生儿) newborn baby ▷赤子之心 pure and innocent 2 (爱国的人) patriot

赤字 chìzì [名] deficit ▷财政赤字 financial deficit

饬 chì I [动] 1 (命令) order 2 (整顿) reorganize II [形] prudent

饬令 chìlìng [动] order

炽 chì [形] 1 (书) (旺) ablaze 2 (热烈) fiery

炽烈 chìliè [形] 1 (字) (指火) raging 2 (喻) passionate ▷炽烈的情感 passionate emotions

炽热 chìrè [形] red-hot

翅 chì [名] 1 (翅膀) wing 2 (鳍) fin

翅膀 chìbǎng [名] wing

敕 chì [名] edict

冲 chōng I [名] important place ▷战略要冲 place of strategic importance II [动] 1 (向前闯) rush forward ▷横冲直撞 push one's way through 2 (猛撞) clash ▶冲撞 collide 3 (浇) pour boiling water on ▷这药需用开水冲服。 This medicine should be taken mixed with boiled water. 4 (冲洗) rinse ▷冲一冲碗碟 rinse the dishes 5 (指胶片) develop ▷冲胶卷 develop a roll of film 6 (抵消) balance ▶冲账 balance the accounts
→另见 chòng

冲刺 chōngcì [动] 1 (字) sprint ▷向终点冲刺 sprint to the finishing line 2 (喻) make a final spurt

冲动 chōngdòng [动] be impulsive ▷不要冲动，理智些吧。 Don't be so impulsive – have some sense. ▷我当时有种购物的冲动。 I had an impulse to go shopping.

冲锋 chōngfēng [动] charge

冲锋陷阵 chōng fēng xiàn zhèn 1 (作战英勇) charge the enemy lines 2 (喻) fight a brave battle

冲击 chōngjī [动] 1 (撞击) pound 2 (喻) (影响) have a big impact on ▷进入世界贸易组织将会冲击中国农业。 Entering the World Trade Organisation will have a big impact on China's agriculture. 3 (冲锋) charge

冲剂 chōngjì [名] *medicine to be taken in water*

冲浪 chōnglàng [名] surf

冲天 chōngtiān [动] soar ▷怒火冲天 in a towering rage

冲突 chōngtū I [动] 1 (激烈争斗) conflict 2 (相

抵触) clash ▷英语课和法语课冲突了。 The English class clashes with the French class. II [名] (矛盾) conflict

冲洗 chōngxǐ [动] 1 (洗涤) wash ▷冲洗汽车 clean a car 2 (指胶片) develop ▷冲洗照片 develop a photograph

充 chōng [动] 1 (满) fill ▶充电 charge a battery ▶充其量 at most 2 (担任) act as ▷充当助理经理 act as assistant manager ▷充当配角 take a supporting role 3 (假装) pass ... off as ▷以次充好 pass things off as good quality

充斥 chōngchì [动] (贬) flood ▷市场上充斥着假货。 The market is flooded with fake goods.

充当 chōngdāng [动] act as ▷朋友不懂英语，我充当翻译。 My friend doesn't understand English, so I act as interpreter.

充电 chōngdiàn [动] 1 (字) charge 2 (喻) (指人) recharge one's batteries

充耳不闻 chōng ěr bù wén turn a deaf ear

充分 chōngfèn I [形] ample ▷做好充分的准备 make ample preparations II [副] fully ▷充分展示自己的才华 show one's talents to the full

充饥 chōngjī [动] alleviate one's hunger

充军 chōngjūn [动] banish ▷他被发配边疆充军。 He was banished to the border area.

充满 chōngmǎn [动] 1 (填满) fill 2 (有) brim with ▷他的话充满自信。 His speech brimmed with confidence.

充沛 chōngpèi [形] abundant

充其量 chōngqíliàng [副] at best

充实 chōngshí I [形] rich II [动] enrich

充数 chōngshù [动] make up the numbers

充裕 chōngyù [形] plentiful

充足 chōngzú [形] sufficient

忡 chōng 见下文

忡忡 chōngchōng [形] anxious ▷忧心忡忡 be worried sick

舂 chōng [动] pound ▷舂米 husk rice

憧 chōng 见下文

憧憬 chōngjǐng [动] look forward to

虫 chóng [名] insect

虫害 chónghài [名] pests (PL)

重 chóng I [动] 1 (重复) repeat ▷书买重了 buy two copies of the same book 2 (重叠) overlap II [副] again ▷他把作文重写了一遍。 He wrote his essay all over again. ▷重返英国 return to Britain III [量] layer ▷万重山 range

after range of mountains ▷一重重的困难 endless difficulties
→另见 zhòng

重唱 chóngchàng [名] ensemble ▷二重唱 duo

重蹈覆辙 chóng dǎo fù zhé make the same old mistakes

重叠 chóngdié [形] overlapping

重逢 chóngféng [动] reunite ▷和好友重逢 be reunited with a good friend

重复 chóngfù [动] repeat

重婚 chónghūn [动] commit bigamy

重申 chóngshēn [动] reiterate

重新 chóngxīn [副] again ▷我把床重新铺了一遍。I made the bed again. ▷重新命名文件 rename a file ▷重新开始 start afresh

重洋 chóngyáng [名] the ocean

重奏 chóngzòu [名] ensemble

崇 chóng I [形] high II [动] think highly of (PT, PP thought) ▶推崇 hold ... in great esteem

崇拜 chóngbài [动] worship

崇高 chónggāo [形] lofty

崇敬 chóngjìng [动] respect ▷谁是你最崇敬的人? Who do you respect most?

崇山峻岭 chóng shān jùn lǐng towering mountains

崇尚 chóngshàng [动] advocate

宠 chǒng [动] spoil

宠爱 chǒng'ài [动] dote on

宠儿 chǒng'ér [名] favourite (英), favorite (美)

宠辱不惊 chǒng rǔ bù jīng be unflappable

宠物 chǒngwù [名] pet

冲 chòng I [形] 1 (指气味刺鼻) pungent ▷大蒜味很冲。Garlic is very pungent. 2 (劲儿足) vigorous ▷他说话挺冲的。He speaks quite bluntly. II [介] 1 (对着) at ▷他冲我做了个鬼脸。He made a face at me. ▷这些意见都是冲他提的。All the criticisms were aimed at him. 2 (凭) because of ▷顾客就是冲着这家超市的良好服务而来的。Customers go to that supermarket because of the excellent service. III [动] 1 (冲压) punch 2 (口) (正对) face ▷这道门冲南。This door faces south.
→另见 chōng

冲劲儿 chòngjìnr [名] 1 (指人) vigour (英), vigor (美) 2 (刺激性) kick

抽 chōu [动] 1 (取出) take ... out (PT took, PP taken) ▷他从钱夹中抽出一张钞票。He took a note (英) 或 bill (美) out of his wallet. 2 (取出部分) take (PT took, PP taken) ▷抽时间 find

time 3 (长出) sprout ▶抽芽 sprout 4 (吸) inhale ▶抽烟 smoke ▶抽血 take blood ▷抽水 pump water 5 (抽缩) shrink (PT shrank, PP shrunk) ▷棉布洗后会抽。Cotton shrinks after washing. 6 (打) whip ▷抽鞭子 whip

抽查 chōuchá [动] do a spot-check ▷产品质量抽查 do a spot-check on product quality

抽搐 chōuchù [动] twitch

抽风 chōufēng [动] 1 (指疾病) have convulsions 2 (喻) (不合常理) lose the plot (PT, PP lost)

抽奖 chōujiǎng [动] draw prizes (PT drew, PP drawn)

抽筋 chōujīn [动] (口) (肌肉痉挛) have cramp ▷脚抽筋 have cramp in one's foot

抽空 chōukòng [动] find the time (PT, PP found)

抽泣 chōuqì [动] sob

抽签 chōuqiān [动] draw lots (PT drew, PP drawn) ▷昨天我们是抽签决定谁洗碗的。Yesterday we drew lots to decide who was going to wash the dishes.

抽水 chōushuǐ [动] 1 (吸水) pump water 2 (缩水) shrink (PT shrank, PP shrunk) ▷这种布料不会抽水。This type of cloth doesn't shrink.

抽屉 chōuti [名] drawer

抽象 chōuxiàng [形] abstract

抽烟 chōuyān [动] smoke ▷他过去抽烟。He used to smoke.

抽样 chōuyàng [动] sample

仇 chóu [名] 1 (仇敌) enemy 2 (仇恨) hatred ▶报仇 avenge

仇敌 chóudí [名] enemy

仇恨 chóuhèn [动] hate

仇视 chóushì [动] be hostile to

惆 chóu [形] grief-stricken

惆怅 chóuchàng [形] melancholy

绸 chóu [名] silk ▶丝绸 silk

绸缎 chóuduàn [名] silk and satin

畴 chóu [名] (书) (种类) variety ▶范畴 category

酬 chóu I [动] 1 (书) (敬酒) toast 2 (报答) reward 3 (往来) socialize ▷应酬 socialize 4 (实现) realize II [名] payment

酬报 chóubào [动] reward ▷酬报好心人 reward good-hearted people ▷公司给每个员工500美金作为酬报。The company gave each of its employees a bonus of five hundred US dollars.

酬宾 chóubīn [动] have a sale ▷周末百货

公司将有大酬宾活动。This weekend the department store is having a big sale.

酬金 chóujīn [名] remuneration

酬劳 chóuláo I [动] repay (PT, PP repaid) II [名] repayment

酬谢 chóuxiè [动] repay (PT, PP repaid)

稠 chóu [形] 1 (浓度大) thick 2 (稠密) dense

稠密 chóumì [形] dense

愁 chóu [动] be anxious ▶忧愁 be worried

愁眉苦脸 chóu méi kǔ liǎn pull a long face

愁闷 chóumèn [形] gloomy

筹 chóu I [名] 1 (小片) counter 2 (计策) plan ▷一筹莫展 be at one's wits end II [动] prepare

筹办 chóubàn [动] make preparations ▷筹办酒席 make preparations for a banquet

筹备 chóubèi [动] arrange

筹划 chóuhuà [动] plan

筹集 chóují [动] raise

筹码 chóumǎ [名] 1 (计数用具) counter 2 (喻) bargaining counter

踌 chóu 见下文

踌躇 chóuchú I [动] hesitate II [形] (书) complacent

踌躇满志 chóu chú mǎn zhì be full of pride

丑 chǒu [形] 1 (丑陋) ugly 2 (令人厌恶) disgraceful

丑八怪 chǒubāguài [名] (口) ▷他是个丑八怪。He's really ugly.

丑恶 chǒu'è [形] ugly

丑化 chǒuhuà [动] vilify

丑剧 chǒujù [名] farce

丑陋 chǒulòu [形] ugly

丑闻 chǒuwén [名] scandal

瞅 chǒu [动] (方) look at ▷我瞅了孩子一眼。I glanced at the child.

臭 chòu I [形] 1 (指气味) smelly 2 (惹人厌恶) disgusting 3 (拙劣) lousy II [副] severely →另见 xiù

臭虫 chòuchóng [名] bedbug

臭烘烘 chòuhōnghōng [形] foul-smelling

臭美 chòuměi [形] (贬) smug

臭名昭著 chòu míng zhāo zhù notorious

臭味相投 chòu wèi xiāng tóu be two of a kind

臭氧 chòuyǎng [名] ozone ▷臭氧层 ozone

layer

出 chū [动] 1 (与入相对) go out (PT went, PP gone) ▶出国 go abroad ▶出行 go on a journey ▶出游 go sightseeing 2 (来到) appear ▶出庭 appear in court ▷刚出台的法律 brand-new laws 3 (超出) exceed ▶出轨 derail ▷不出3天货就到了。The goods arrived within three days. 4 (给) give out (PT gave, PP given) ▷出考题 set an exam paper ▷他为此出了很多力。He put a lot of effort into this. 5 (产生) produce ▷这个学校出优秀教师。This college produces excellent teachers. 6 (发生) occur ▶出事 have an accident 7 (发出) come out (PT came, PP come) ▶出血 bleed ▶出汗 sweat 8 (显露) appear ▶出名 become famous 9 (支出) pay out (PT, PP paid) ▷量入为出 spend what one earns

出版 chūbǎn [动] publish

出殡 chūbìn [动] hold a funeral procession (PT, PP held)

出兵 chūbīng [动] dispatch troops

出差 chūchāi [动] go away on business (PT went, PP gone) ▷我经常去北京出差。I often go to Beijing on business.

出产 chūchǎn [动] produce

出丑 chūchǒu [动] make a fool of oneself ▷他演失败，当众出丑了。His performance was a failure – he made a fool of himself in front of everyone.

出处 chūchù [名] source

出道 chūdào [动] launch one's career

出动 chūdòng [动] 1 (外出活动) set off (PT, PP set) 2 (派出) dispatch

出尔反尔 chū ěr fǎn ěr go back on one's word

出发 chūfā [动] 1 (离开) set out (PT, PP set) 2 (表示着眼点) take ... as a starting point (PT took, PP taken) ▷从实际出发 take reality as one's starting point

出访 chūfǎng [动] travel on official business

出风头 chū fēngtou 1 (表示贬义) show off (PT showed, PP shown) 2 (抢眼) steal the show (PT stole, PP stolen)

出格 chūgé [动] 1 (出众) be outstanding 2 (过分) step out of line ▷你的所作所为出格了。Your behaviour (英) 或 behavior (美) is out of line.

出活 chūhuó I [动] get work done ▷他花了很长时间，但就是不出活。He spent a lot of time on it, but didn't actually get any work done. II [形] efficient

出击 chūjī [动] attack

出家 chūjiā [动] 1 (当和尚) become a monk (PT became, PP become) 2 (当尼姑) become a nun (PT became, PP become)

出嫁 chūjià [动] marry

出境 chūjìng [动] 1 (指国境) leave the country (PT, PP left) 2 (指某一区域) leave a place

出局 chūjú [动] be knocked out

出口 chūkǒu I [动] 1 (说) utter 2 (指贸易) export II [名] exit

出口成章 chū kǒu chéng zhāng eloquent and articulate

出类拔萃 chū lèi bá cuì stand out from the crowd

出力 chūlì [动] put effort into (PT, PP put) ▷他为公司的创建出力不少。He put a lot of effort into establishing the company.

出笼 chūlóng [动] 1 (指蒸笼) come out of the steamer (PT came, PP come) 2 (喻) come out (PT came, PP come) ▷新政策出笼后，倍受抨击。When the new policies came out, they were heavily criticized.

出路 chūlù [名] 1 (指道路) way out 2 (前途) prospects (PL) 3 (销路) market

出落 chūluo [动] blossom

出马 chūmǎ [动] take the lead (PT took, PP taken) ▷厂长亲自出马谈这些生意。The factory director took the lead in these business discussions.

出卖 chūmài [动] 1 (卖) sell (PT, PP sold) 2 (贬) (背弃) betray

出面 chūmiàn [动] come out (PT came, PP come) ▷由董事会出面召集会议。The board of directors came out with a request for a meeting.

出名 chūmíng [动] become famous (PT became, PP become)

出没 chūmò [动] haunt

出纳 chūnà I [动] (指财务管理) keep the books (PT, PP kept) II [名] cashier

出品 chūpǐn I [动] produce II [名] product

出奇 chūqí [形] extraordinary

出奇制胜 chū qí zhì shèng seize victory through a surprise attack

出勤 chūqín [动] 1 (按时到) show up on time (PT showed, PP shown) ▶出勤率 ratio of attendance 2 (外出办公) go away for work (PT went, PP gone)

出让 chūràng [动] sell (PT, PP sold)

出人头地 chū rén tóu dì stand out

出任 chūrèn [动] (书) take up the post of (PT took, PP taken) ▷出任总理 take up the post of prime minister

出入 chūrù I [动] come and go II [名] discrepancy

出色 chūsè [形] outstanding

出山 chūshān [动] take up a post (PT took, PP taken)

出身 chūshēn I [动] come from (PT came, PP come) ▷他出身于一个富裕的家庭。He comes from a wealthy family. II [名] background ▷他是农民出身。He comes from a farming background.

出神入化 chū shén rù huà reach perfection

出生 chūshēng [动] be born ▷她出生在英国。She was born in Britain.

出生入死 chū shēng rù sǐ risk one's life

出师 chūshī [动] 1 (期满学成) finish one's apprenticeship 2 (书) (出兵) dispatch troops

出使 chūshǐ [动] be sent on a diplomatic mission

出世 chūshì [动] 1 (出生) be born ▷刚刚出世的婴儿 a new-born baby 2 (产生) arise (PT arose, PP arisen) 3 (超脱人世) be detached from the rest of the world

出手 chūshǒu I [动] 1 (卖出) sell (PT, PP sold) 2 (拿出) give ... out (PT gave, PP given) 3 (行动) hit (PT, PP hit) II [名] (本领) skill

出售 chūshòu [动] sell (PT, PP sold)

出台 chūtái [动] 1 (上场) make an appearance 2 (公布实施) promulgate

出息 chūxi I [名] prospect II [动] come on (PT came, PP come) ▷他上大学后出息多了。He's really come on since going to university.

出席 chūxí [动] attend

出现 chūxiàn [动] appear ▷他没有出现在聚会上，朋友很失望。He didn't appear at the gathering and his friends were very disappointed. ▷她的出现令我感到意外。I was surprised by her unexpected appearance.

出血 chūxiě [动] 1 (字) bleed (PT, PP bled) 2 (喻) (花钱) blow a lot of money (PT blew, PP blown)

出洋相 chū yángxiàng [动] make a fool of oneself

出狱 chūyù [动] be released from prison

出院 chūyuàn [动] leave hospital (PT, PP left)

出众 chūzhòng [形] outstanding

出租 chūzū [动] let (PT, PP let) ▷有房出租 room to let

初 chū I [名] original ▷和好如初 become reconciled II [形] 1 (第一) first ▶初恋 first love ▷初次交往 first contact 2 (最低) primary ▶初级 primary 3 (开始) early ▶初冬 early winter

初步 chūbù [形] fundamental

初出茅庐 chū chū máolú be wet behind the ears

初级 chūjí [形] primary ▷初级阶段 initial stages

初期 chūqī [名] initial stage

初生之犊不怕虎 chū shēng zhī dú bù pà hǔ the young are fearless

初衷 chūzhōng [名] original intention

刍 chú I [名] hay II [动] (书) mow the lawn (PT mowed, PP mown) III [形] (书) (谦) meagre

刍议 chúyì [名] (谦) my humble opinion

除 chú I [动] 1 (去掉) get rid of ▶开除 dismiss ▶去除 remove 2 (指算术) divide ▶除法 division ▷16除以8等于2. Sixteen divided by eight is two. II [介] 1 (表示绝对排除关系) except ▷除彼得外大家都来了。Everyone came except Peter. 2 (表示并非惟一) apart from ▷除了珍妮，谁还去过上海？Apart from Jenny, who else has been to Shanghai?

除非 chúfēi I [连] unless ▷除非天下雨，我通常晚饭后出去散步。Unless it's raining, I normally go for a walk after dinner. ▷除非他要我去，否则我不去。I won't go unless he wants me to. II [介] other than ▷这个秘方，除非他也没人知道。Other than him, no one else knows the secret recipe.

除了 chúle [介] 1 (表示不包括) except ▷除了你其他人都参加了会议。Everyone else attended the meeting except you. 2 (除此以外) apart from ▷他除了学习英语，还学习日语。Apart from studying English, he also studies Japanese. 3 (表示非此即彼) apart from ... the only ... ▷他的生活很简单，除了工作就是睡觉。His life is pretty simple – the only thing he does apart from work is sleep.

除名 chúmíng [动] strike ... off (PT, PP struck)

除外 chúwài [动] ▷班长除外，每个人都要写份报告。Everyone had to write a report except the class monitor. ▷雨天除外，他每天步行上班。He walks to work every day, except when it rains.

除夕 chúxī [名] New Year's Eve

厨 chú [名] 1 (厨房) kitchen 2 (厨师) cook

厨师 chúshī [名] cook

锄 chú I [名] hoe II [动] 1 (松土) hoe ▶锄地 hoe the fields 2 (铲除) wipe ... out

锄头 chútou [名] hoe

雏 chú [形] (幼小) nestling

雏儿 chúr [名] (口) 1 (幼鸟) chick 2 (喻) (指人) innocent

雏形 chúxíng [名] 1 (最初形式) original state ▷公司的雏形不是这样的。The company didn't originally look like this. 2 (指模型) model

橱 chú [名] cabinet

橱窗 chúchuāng [名] 1 (指商店的展示窗) shop (英) 或 store (美) window 2 (用于展览图片等) display case

处 chǔ [动] 1 (交往) get on with 2 (在) be in ▷处于困境 be in a difficult position ▷他身处他乡，倍感孤独。When he's away from home he feels twice as lonely. 3 (办理) deal with (PT, PP dealt) 4 (处罚) penalize ▶惩处 penalize →另见 chù

处罚 chǔfá [动] punish

处方 chǔfāng [名] prescription

处分 chǔfèn I [动] punish II [名] punishment

处境 chǔjìng [名] situation

处决 chǔjué [动] 1 (执行死刑) execute 2 (决断) decide ▷提工资的事由董事会处决。Salary increases are decided on by the board of directors.

处理 chǔlǐ [动] 1 (解决) deal with (PT, PP dealt) ▷遇到问题应该及时处理。You should deal with problems as they arise. 2 (减价) sell ... at a reduced price (PT, PP sold) ▷处理品 goods sold at a discount 3 (加工) treat ▷经高温处理过的牛奶 milk pasteurized at a high temperature

处女 chǔnǚ [名] virgin ▷处女地 virgin land ▷处女航 maiden voyage

处世 chǔshì [动] conduct oneself

处心积虑 chǔ xīn jī lù plot and scheme

处治 chǔzhì [动] punish

处置 chǔzhì [动] 1 (处理) deal with (PT, PP dealt) 2 (惩治) punish

础 chǔ [名] plinth

储 chǔ [动] store

储备 chǔbèi I [动] store ... up II [名] reserve

储藏 chǔcáng [动] 1 (保藏) store 2 (蕴藏) contain ▷大量的石油储藏在这片沙漠中。Large reserves of oil are contained in this desert.

储存 chǔcún [动] stockpile

储蓄 chǔxù I [动] save II [名] savings (PL)

楚 chǔ I [名] (书) (痛苦) suffering II [形] (清晰) clear

楚楚 chǔchǔ [形] 1 (整洁) neat and tidy 2 (娇柔) dainty

处 chù [名] 1 (地方) place ▶暗处 secret place ▶益处 profit ▷四处都是人。There were people everywhere. 2 (部门) department ▷人事处 human resources department

→另见 chǔ

处所 chùsuǒ [名] area

畜 chù [名] livestock
→另见 xù

畜生 chùsheng [名] beast

触 chù [动] 1 (接触) touch 2 (触动) move

触动 chùdòng [动] 1 (碰撞) bump into 2 (损害) offend 3 (打动) stir ... up

触犯 chùfàn [动] violate

触及 chùjí [动] touch

触角 chùjiǎo [名] tentacle

触类旁通 chù lèi páng tōng reason by analogy

触摸 chùmō [动] touch ▷触摸式屏幕 touch screen

触目惊心 chù mù jīng xīn shocking

黜 chù [动] (书) dismiss

黜免 chùmiǎn [动] (书) dismiss

矗 chù [动] (书) stand straight (PT, PP stood)

矗立 chùlì [动] stand majestically (PT, PP stood)

揣 chuāi [动] conceal ... in one's clothes
→另见 chuǎi

揣 chuǎi [动] (书) surmise
→另见 chuāi

揣测 chuǎicè [动] guess

揣度 chuǎiduó [动] (书) speculate

揣摩 chuǎimó [动] speculate ▷我不停地揣摩他的心思。I kept speculating on what he might be thinking.

踹 chuài [动] 1 (踢) kick 2 (踩) tread (PT trod, PP trodden) ▷他踹到了狗屎。He trod in dog's mess.

川 chuān [名] 1 (河流) river 2 (平地) plain

川流不息 chuān liú bù xī endless streams ▷街上的人群川流不息。There were endless streams of people and cars on the road.

川资 chuānzī [名] travel expenses (PL)

穿 chuān [动] 1 (破) (纸) pierce 2 (谎言、事实) expose 3 (通过) pass through ▷周末的街头，行人穿行不息。Endless streams of people pass through the streets at the weekends. ▷穿针 thread a needle 4 (串) piece ... together ▷把线索穿起来 piece together all the clues ▷穿珍珠 string pearls together 5 (衣服、鞋袜、首饰等) wear (PT wore, PP worn) ▷她喜欢穿金

戴银。She likes to wear gold and silver. ▷他迅速穿上衣服。He put his clothes on very quickly. 6 (表示透彻) penetrate ▷看穿事情的真相 see through to the truth of a situation

穿插 chuānchā I [副] alternately ▷工作和休闲穿插进行 take turns to work and rest II [动] weave ... in (PT wove, PP woven) ▷他在论文中穿插了些引文。He wove some quotations into his essay.

穿戴 chuāndài I [名] dress ▷他不讲究穿戴。He's not particular about what he wears. II [动] dress ▷全家穿戴整齐，准备去参加宴会。The whole family dressed up very smartly in preparation for the dinner party.

穿梭 chuānsuō [动] shuttle back and forth ▷机场大巴穿梭往来于机场和火车站。The airport bus shuttles back and forth between the airport and the train station.

穿小鞋 chuān xiǎoxié [动] (喻) make things hard for

穿越 chuānyuè [动] pass through

穿凿 chuānzáo [动] give a far-fetched account (PT gave, PP given)

穿着 chuānzhuó [名] outfit

传 chuán [动] 1 (交给) hand ... down 2 (传授) pass ... on 3 (传播) spread (PT, PP spread) 4 (传导) conduct 5 (表达) express ▷传情 express one's feelings ▷他们俩在会上眉目传情。They were eyeing each other up at the meeting. 6 (命令) summon 7 (传染) infect
→另见 zhuàn

传播 chuánbō [动] disseminate

传达 chuándá I [动] pass ... on ▷传达指示 pass on an instruction II [名] receptionist ▷传达室 reception room

传单 chuándān [名] leaflet

传递 chuándì [动] extend ▷传递祝福 extend good wishes ▷传递信息 transmit information

传媒 chuánméi [名] 1 (传播媒介) media ▷新闻传媒 the news media 2 (传染媒介) medium ▷苍蝇是许多疾病的传媒。Flies are the medium of many infections.

传票 chuánpiào [名] 1 (传唤凭证) summons (SG) 2 (账目凭单) voucher

传奇 chuánqí [形] legendary ▷传奇人物 legendary figure

传染 chuánrǎn [动] infect ▷蚊子传染疟疾。Mosquitoes carry the malaria infection.

传世 chuánshì [动] hand ... down

传授 chuánshòu [动] pass ... on ▷传授经验 pass on one's experience ▷传授知识 pass on knowledge

传说 chuánshuō I [动] ▷传说几百年前，这

儿是一片海。People say that several hundred years ago this was all ocean. ▷传说他10年前就去了海外。It is said that he went abroad ten years ago. II [名] legend

传统 chuántǒng I [名] tradition II [形] 1 (世代相传) traditional ▷传统文化 traditional culture ▷传统医学 traditional medicine 2 (保守) conservative

传真 chuánzhēn [动] (指通讯方式) fax ▷我把文件传真给他了。I faxed the documents to him. ▷给我发个传真吧。Please send me a fax.

船 chuán [名] boat ▶渔船 fishing boat

船舶 chuánbó [名] shipping

船只 chuánzhī [名] vessels (PL)

喘 chuǎn I [动] gasp II [名] asthma

喘息 chuǎnxī [动] 1 (急促呼吸) pant 2 (短时休息) come up for air (PT came, PP come)

喘吁吁 chuǎnxūxū [形] puffing and panting

串 chuàn I [动] 1 (连贯) string ... together (PT, PP strung) ▷她把珍珠串了起来。She strung the pearls together. 2 (勾结) conspire 3 (指信号) get mixed up ▷电视串台了。The TV channels were all mixed up. ▷电话串线了。There was a crossed line. 4 (走动) drop by ▷他爱来我家串门。He likes to drop by my place. 5 (担任角色) act II [量] bunch ▷两串钥匙 two bunches of keys ▷一串珍珠 a string of pearls

串通 chuàntōng [动] (暗中勾结) collude ▷他俩串通作伪证。The two men colluded as false witnesses.

创 chuāng [名] wound ▶创痕 scar ▶创口 cut ▶创可贴 plaster (英), Band-Aid® (美)
→另见 chuàng

创伤 chuāngshāng [名] 1 (指肉体上的) wound 2 (指精神上的) trauma

疮 chuāng [名] 1 (指疾病) ulcer ▶口疮 mouth ulcer ▶冻疮 chilblain 2 (指外伤) cut

疮疤 chuāngbā [名] 1 (疤痕) scar 2 (喻) weak point

疮痍 chuāngyí [名] (书) trauma

窗 chuāng [名] window ▶窗子 window

窗口 chuāngkǒu [名] 1 (字) window ▶售票窗口 ticket window 2 (喻)(渠道) vehicle 3 (喻)(反映处) window ▷眼睛是心灵的窗口。The eyes are a window on the soul.

窗口行业 chuāngkǒu hángyè [名] service industry

床 chuáng I [名] bed ▶单人床 single bed ▶河床 river bed ▶机床 lathe II [量] ▷一床棉被 a quilt

床位 chuángwèi [名] bed

闯 chuǎng [动] 1 (冲) rush 2 (磨炼) steel oneself 3 (惹) stir ... up ▶闯祸 cause trouble

闯荡 chuǎngdàng [动] steel oneself to face the outside world

闯祸 chuǎnghuò [动] cause trouble

闯江湖 chuǎng jiānghú lead a nomadic lifestyle (PT, PP led)

创 chuàng [动] create ▶独创 make an original creation ▷开创新纪元 create a new era ▷今年钢铁产量又创新高。This year steel production has reached new highs.
→另见 chuāng

创见 chuàngjiàn [名] original idea

创建 chuàngjiàn [动] establish

创举 chuàngjǔ [名] pioneering work

创刊 chuàngkān [动] start publication

创立 chuànglì [动] establish ▷创立事业 establish a career ▷创立品牌 create a trademark

创始 chuàngshǐ [动] found

创业 chuàngyè [动] carve out a career

创意 chuàngyì [名] creativity

创造 chuàngzào [动] create ▷创造财富 create wealth

创作 chuàngzuò I [动] create II [名] work

吹 chuī [动] 1 (出气) blow (PT blew, PP blown) ▷吹灭蜡烛 blow out a candle 2 (演奏) play 3 (夸口) boast 4 (口)(破裂) fall through (PT fell, PP fallen) ▷他们去夏威夷的计划吹了。Their plan to go to Hawaii fell through. ▷我和女友吹了。I've broken up with my girlfriend.

吹风 chuīfēng [动] 1 (受风寒) catch a chill (PT, PP caught) 2 (吹干) blow-dry 3 (口)(透露) give advance warning (PT gave, PP given)

吹灰之力 chuī huī zhī lì [名] little effort ▷他不费吹灰之力就通过了考试。He got through the exam with very little effort.

吹毛求疵 chuī máo qiú cī find fault

吹牛 chuīniú [动] (书) brag

吹捧 chuīpěng [动] flatter

吹嘘 chuīxū [动] boast ▷吹嘘自己的长处 boast about one's strengths

炊 chuī [动] cook ▷炊具 cooking utensil ▷炊事 cooking

垂 chuí I [动] 1 (一头向下) hang down (PT, PP hung) 2 (敬) (长辈或上级) condescend 3 (书) (流传) hand ... down ▷永垂不朽 be everlasting II [副] (书) on the verge of ▶生命垂危 be on the verge of death
垂手 chuíshǒu [动] (表示恭敬) stand to attention (PT, PP stood)
垂手可得 chuí shǒu kě dé do ... with one's eyes shut
垂头丧气 chuí tóu sàng qì be crestfallen
垂直 chuízhí [形] vertical

捶 chuí [动] pound

锤 chuí I [名] hammer II [动] hammer
锤炼 chuíliàn [动] 1 (冶金) hammer ... into shape 2 (磨炼) harden ▷锤炼意志 harden one's resolve ▷锤炼孩子的思考力 sharpen a child's powers of thought 3 (钻研琢磨) refine ▷锤炼写作技巧 refine one's writing skills

春 chūn [名] 1 (春季) spring 2 (情欲) sexual desire 3 (生机) vitality
春分 chūnfēn [名] spring equinox
春风得意 chūnfēng déyì take pride in one's successes
春风化雨 chūnfēng huàyǔ (喻) inspirational teaching
春光 chūnguāng [名] spring scenes (PL)
春节 Chūn Jié [名] Chinese New Year
春卷 chūnjuǎn [名] spring roll
春联 chūnlián [名] Spring Festival couplets (PL)
春秋 chūnqiū [名] year
春天 chūntiān [名] spring
春药 chūnyào [名] aphrodisiac

纯 chún [形] 1 (纯净) pure 2 (纯熟) skilful (英), skillful (美)
纯粹 chúncuì I [形] pure II [副] purely
纯洁 chúnjié I [形] pure II [动] purify
纯净 chúnjìng [形] pure
纯利 chúnlì [名] net profit
纯真 chúnzhēn [形] wholesome
纯正 chúnzhèng [形] 1 (纯粹) pure 2 (正当) unselfish ▷动机纯正 unselfish motivation

唇 chún [名] lip
唇舌 chúnshé [名] argument
唇亡齿寒 chún wáng chǐ hán share a common fate

淳 chún [形] (书) honest

淳朴 chúnpǔ [形] simple

醇 chún I [名] 1 (烈酒) spirit 2 (化) alcohol II [形] (书) pure
醇厚 chúnhòu [形] (纯正浓厚) rich

蠢 chǔn [形] 1 (愚蠢) stupid 2 (笨拙) clumsy
蠢蠢欲动 chǔnchǔn yù dòng on the point of stirring up trouble

戳 chuō I [动] 1 (穿过) poke ▷他不小心戳到了我的眼睛。He accidentally poked me in the eye. 2 (方) (损坏) pierce II [名] seal
戳穿 chuōchuān [动] 1 (刺穿) pierce 2 (揭穿) expose
戳子 chuōzi [名] seal

啜 chuò [动] (书) 1 (喝) sip 2 (抽噎) sob
啜泣 chuòqì [动] sob

绰 chuò [形] (书) 1 (宽绰) abundant 2 (柔美) graceful
绰绰有余 chuòchuò yǒu yú more than enough ▷用我的工资支付日常的生活绰绰有余。My wages are more than enough to pay for my daily outgoings.
绰号 chuòhào [名] nickname

辍 chuò [动] stop
辍笔 chuòbǐ [动] stop ▷辍笔5年后他又开始作画。Five years after he stopped painting he started up again. ▷他40岁就辍笔了。He stopped writing at the age of forty.
辍学 chuòxué [动] give up one's studies (PT gave, PP given) ▷她被迫辍学。She was forced to give up her studies.

刺 cī [拟] whoosh
→另见 cì

疵 cī [名] flaw

词 cí [名] 1 (语句) words (PL) ▶台词 lines 2 (指语言单位) word 3 (指韵文形式) classical poetry using a set pattern
词典 cídiǎn [名] dictionary ▷双语词典 bilingual dictionary
词典学 cídiǎnxué [名] lexicography
词法 cífǎ [名] morphology
词汇 cíhuì [名] vocabulary
词语 cíyǔ [名] term
词藻 cízǎo [名] rhetoric
词组 cízǔ [名] phrase

祠 cí [名] ancestral temple
祠堂 cítáng [名] ancestral temple

瓷 cí [名] porcelain

辞 cí I [名] 1 (语言) diction 2 (文学体裁) early form of classical Chinese poetry II [动] 1 (告别) bid...farewell (PT bade, PP bidden) 2 (辞职) resign ▷他辞掉了市长的职务。He resigned from his position as mayor. 3 (辞退) dismiss ▷他被经理辞了。He was dismissed by the manager. 4 (躲避) decline
辞别 cíbié [动] bid...farewell (PT bade, PP bidden) ▷他辞别了亲人去国外打工。He bade farewell to his relatives as he left to work overseas.
辞呈 cíchéng [名] letter of resignation ▷他向老板递交了辞呈。He gave his boss his letter of resignation.
辞典 cídiǎn [名] dictionary
辞令 cílìng [名] language ▷外交辞令 diplomatic language
辞世 císhì [动] pass away ▷因病辞世 pass away due to illness
辞书 císhū [名] reference books (PL)
辞退 cítuì [动] dismiss ▷他因工作不力，被老板辞退。He wasn't hardworking enough, and so was dismissed by the boss.
辞行 cíxíng [动] bid...farewell (PT bade, PP bidden)
辞藻 cízǎo [名] rhetoric
辞章 cízhāng [名] 1 (韵文和散文) poetry and prose 2 (写作技巧) writing skills (PL)
辞职 cízhí [动] resign

请勿混淆 **resign** 和 **retire**。**resign** 表示某人在提出不愿再做某份工作后离职。*He resigned last week after a newspaper published claims that he had lied to get the job...She has threatened to resign from her well-paid job as a protest.* **retire** 表示离职并停止工作，通常此时是由于该人已达到领取养老金的年龄。*He retired in 1960...Her mum retired from her job as a teacher at the age of 60.* 当职业运动员不再从事职业体育运动，即使他们还非常年轻，也可以使用 **retire**。

慈 cí [形] kind
慈爱 cí'ài [形] affectionate
慈悲 cíbēi [名] compassion
慈善 císhàn [形] charitable
慈祥 cíxiáng [形] kind

磁 cí [名] (物) magnetism
磁场 cíchǎng [名] magnetic field
磁盘 cípán [名] disk
磁盘驱动器 cípán qūdòngqì [名] disk drive

雌 cí [形] female
雌雄 cíxióng [名] winners and losers (PL)

此 cǐ [代] (这) this (PL these) ▷此书 this book ▷此时此刻 right now ▷就此分手 part company now ▷由此向前 from now on ▷长此以往 if things continue like this
此起彼伏 cǐ qǐ bǐ fú continuously rising and falling
此外 cǐwài [连] apart from this ▷抽屉里就几件衣服，此外别无他物。There were just a few items of clothing in the drawer. Apart from that there was nothing.
此一时，彼一时 cǐ yī shí, bǐ yī shí things have changed ▷此一时，彼一时，现在家庭妇男越来越越多了。Things have changed – there are more and more house-husbands around today.

次 cì I [名] ranking ▶档次 grade ▶层次 level ▶名次 position (in a competition) II [形] 1 (第二) second ▶次子 second son ▶次日 next day 2 (差) inferior ▶次品 inferior product ▷电影拍得太次了。The film was badly made. III [量] time ▶初次 first time ▶屡次 repeatedly
次序 cìxù [名] order ▷老师按字母次序点名。The teacher read the names out in alphabetical order.
次要 cìyào [形] secondary

伺 cì 见下文
→另见 sì
伺候 cìhou [动] wait on ▷许多男人都希望老婆好好伺候他。A lot of men hope that their wives will wait on them.

刺 cì I [动] 1 (穿过) pierce 2 (刺激) irritate 3 (暗杀) assassinate 4 (侦探) spy 5 (讽刺) satirize II [名] sting
→另见 cī
刺刺不休 cì cì bù xiū go on and on ▷他对此刺刺不休地说了一下午。He went on and on about it all afternoon.
刺耳 cì'ěr [形] 1 (指声音) ear-piercing 2 (喻) (指言语) jarring
刺骨 cìgǔ [动] be piercing ▷海水冰冷刺骨。The seawater was piercingly cold.
刺激 cìjī [动] 1 (指生物现象) stimulate 2 (推动)

stimulate 3 (打击) provoke

刺客 cìkè [名] assassin

刺杀 cìshā [动] 1 (暗杀) assassinate 2 (拼杀) bayonet

刺探 cìtàn [动] spy ▷刺探商业情报 gather business intelligence

刺猬 cìwei [名] hedgehog

刺绣 cìxiù I [动] embroider II [名] embroidery

刺眼 cìyǎn [形] 1 (光线太强) dazzling 2 (扎眼) loud

赐 cì [动] 1 (赏赐) bestow ▷国王赐给他一箱黄金。The king bestowed a case of gold on him. 2 (敬) grant

赐教 cìjiào [动] (敬) give instructions (PT gave, PP given) ▷请高手赐教。Please give me instructions.

匆 cōng [副] hastily

匆匆 cōngcōng [形] hasty

匆促 cōngcù [形] hasty

匆忙 cōngmáng [形] hurried

葱 cōng I [名] spring onion II [形] green

葱翠 cōngcuì [形] lush green

聪 cōng I [名] hearing II [形] 1 (指听力) acute 2 (聪明) clever

聪明 cōngmíng [形] clever

从 cóng I [动] 1 (跟随) follow ▷从众 follow the crowd ▷从俗 follow convention 2 (顺从) comply with ▷服从 obey ▷言听计从 blindly follow 3 (从事) participate in ▷从戎 enlist 4 (采取) ▷从严治理 govern according to tougher principles ▷一切从简 do everything simply II [名] follower ▷仆从 attendant III [形] (从属) subordinate ▷从犯 accessory IV [介] 1 (起于) from ▷从前到后 from front to back ▷从明天起 from tomorrow onwards ▷从山顶向远处眺望 look out into the distance from the top of the mountain ▷从东到西 from east to west 2 (经过) ▷轮船从桥下经过。The boat passed underneath the bridge. ▷飞机从我们头顶飞过。The plane passed over our heads. V [副] ▷从未 never ▷他从未见过大海。He's never seen the sea. ▷她从未到过苏格兰。She's never been to Scotland.

从此 cóngcǐ [副] after that ▷他们从此不再贫穷。After that they were no longer poor.

从而 cóng'ér [连] thus ▷公司决定裁员，从而削减成本。The company decided to lay people off, and thus reduce their costs.

从犯 cóngfàn [名] accessory

从军 cóngjūn [动] enlist

从来 cónglái [副] ▷我从来没去过美国。I've never been to the States. ▷她从来未说过。She never said it.

从命 cóngmìng [动] obey orders

从前 cóngqián [名] 1 (过去) ▷希望你比从前快乐。I hope you are happier than you were before. 2 (很久很久以前) once upon a time

从容 cóngróng [形] 1 (镇静) calm ▷神态从容 calm manner ▷从容应对 respond calmly 2 (宽裕) ample ▷时间从容。There's ample time.

从善如流 cóng shàn rú liú take good advice

从事 cóngshì [动] 1 (投身) undertake (PT undertook, PP undertaken) 2 (处理) deal with (PT, PP dealt)

从速 cóngsù [副] as soon as possible

从业 cóngyè [动] be employed ▷她从业于教育界。She is employed as a teacher.

丛 cóng I [动] crowd together II [名] 1 (指草木) thicket 2 (指人或物) crowd

丛书 cóngshū [名] series (SG)

淙 cóng 见下文

淙淙 cóngcóng [拟] gurgling

凑 còu [动] 1 (聚集) gather ... together 2 (碰) encounter 3 (接近) approach

凑合 còuhe [动] 1 (聚集) gather ... together 2 (拼凑) improvise 3 (将就) get by

凑巧 còuqiǎo [形] lucky ▷真不凑巧，没带多少现金。How unlucky – I didn't bring enough cash. ▷我凑巧也搭乘那趟火车。I happened to take the same train.

凑数 còushù [动] 1 (凑足数额) make enough ▷几个月的工资积攒下来凑数买了台电脑。My months of saving gave me enough to buy a computer. 2 (滥竽充数) make up the numbers ▷这张唱片中没有一首凑数之作。Not one song on this album is there just to make up the numbers.

粗 cū I [形] 1 (横剖面大) thick 2 (颗粒大) coarse 3 (指声音) gruff 4 (粗糙) crude 5 (疏忽) careless 6 (鲁莽) reckless II [副] sketchily ▷粗知一二 have a sketchy understanding

粗暴 cūbào [形] rough ▷他态度粗暴。He has a rough manner.

粗糙 cūcāo [形] 1 (不光滑) rough 2 (不细致) crude

粗茶淡饭 cū chá dàn fàn simple fare

粗放 cūfàng [形] extensive

粗犷 cūguǎng [形] 1 (粗野) crude 2 (粗豪)

forthright

粗话 cūhuà [名] obscene language

粗粮 cūliáng [名] coarse grain

粗鲁 cūlǔ [形] crude

粗疏 cūshū [形] careless

粗俗 cūsú [形] obscene

粗心 cūxīn [形] careless

粗野 cūyě [形] rough

粗枝大叶 cū zhī dà yè slapdash

粗制滥造 cū zhì làn zào shoddy

促 cù I [形] urgent II [动] 1 (催) press ▶ 敦促 press 2 (靠近) be near

促成 cùchéng [动] bring about (PT, PP brought)

促进 cùjìn [动] promote

促使 cùshǐ [动] press for ▷ 促使经济快速发展 press for speedy economic development

猝 cù [副] suddenly

猝然 cùrán [副] all of a sudden

醋 cù [名] 1 (指调味品) vinegar 2 (嫉妒) jealousy

簇 cù I [动] cluster II [量] bunch ▷ 一簇花 a bunch of flowers

簇新 cùxīn [形] brand new

簇拥 cùyōng [动] cluster round

蹙 cù I [形] urgent II [动] tighten ▶ 蹙额 knit one's brow

蹴 cù [动] 1 (踢) kick 2 (踏) tread (PT trod, PP trodden)

汆 cuān [动] blanch

镩 cuān I [名] ice pick II [动] hack

蹿 cuān [动] leap

攒 cuán [动] assemble
→ 另见 zǎn

攒动 cuándòng [动] huddle together

蹿 cuàn [动] 1 (乱跑) rush about 2 (改动) falsify

窜改 cuàngǎi [动] falsify

篡 cuàn [动] usurp

篡夺 cuànduó [动] usurp

篡改 cuàngǎi [动] falsify

催 cuī [动] 1 (敦促) hurry 2 (加快) speed ... up (PT, PP speeded)

催促 cuīcù [动] hurry ▷ 你不要老是催我。You've got to stop hurrying me all the time.

催化 cuīhuà [动] catalyze

催眠 cuīmián [动] hypnotize

摧 cuī [动] destroy

摧残 cuīcán [动] destroy

摧毁 cuīhuǐ [动] destroy

摧枯拉朽 cuī kū lā xiǔ with incredible ease

摧折 cuīzhé [动] 1 (折断) break (PT broke, PP broken) 2 (折磨) devastate ▷ 百姓饱受战火的摧折。The people were devastated by the war.

璀 cuǐ 见下文

璀璨 cuǐcàn [形] dazzling

脆 cuì [形] 1 (易碎) brittle 2 (指食物) crispy 3 (声音) crisp

脆弱 cuìruò [形] fragile

萃 cuì I [动] assemble II [名] gathering

萃集 cuìjí [动] cream ... off

啐 cuì [动] spit (PT, PP spat)

淬 cuì 见下文

淬火 cuìhuǒ [动] quench

瘁 cuì [形] (书) overwhelmed with work

粹 cuì I [形] pure II [名] essence

翠 cuì I [形] green II [名] jadeite

翠绿 cuìlǜ [形] emerald green

村 cūn I [名] village II [形] rustic

村落 cūnluò [名] village

村野 cūnyě I [名] countryside II [形] rustic

村庄 cūnzhuāng [名] village

皴 cūn [动] chapped

存 cún [动] 1 (存在) exist 2 (储存) store 3 (储蓄) save 4 (寄存) check ... in ▷ 存行李 check in one's bags 5 (保留) retain 6 (结存) be leftover ▷ 3年后公司净结存为零。After three years the company was left with nothing. 7 (心里怀着) harbour (英), harbor (美)

存储 cúnchǔ [动] store

存档 cúndàng [动] file

存放 cúnfàng [动] deposit ▷ 他将手提箱存放在朋友处。He deposited his suitcase at his friend's place.

存盘 cúnpán [动] save ▷ 打完文件后注意存

盘。Make sure that you save your file after you've finished your keying in.

存心 cúnxīn **I** [动] ▷他对她存心不良。He has designs on her. **II** [副] deliberately ▷她存心叫我出丑。She deliberately made a fool of me.

存在 cúnzài [动] exist ▷这颗行星上可能存在生命。Life may exist on this planet. ▷企业管理存在严重的缺陷。There are serious failings in the management of this enterprise. ▷各国政府在这个问题上存在分歧。Each country differs on this point. ▷他沉浸在往事的追忆中，忘记了我的存在。He was immersed in his recollection of the past and forgot about my existence.

存折 cúnzhé [名] passbook

寸 cùn **I** [量] unit of length approximately 3 cm **II** [形] tiny

寸步 cùnbù [名] tiny step

寸草不留 cùn cǎo bù liú raze to the ground

寸心 cùnxīn [名] **1** (内心) heart **2** (心意) feelings (PL)

搓 cuō [动] rub

磋 cuō [动] consult

磋商 cuōshāng [动] discuss

撮 cuō **I** [动] **1** (聚集) scoop ... up **2** (摘取) summarize **3** (方) (吃) grab a bite ▷上馆子撮一顿吧。Let's go to a restaurant to grab a bite to eat. **II** [量] **1** (指物) pinch ▷一撮面粉 a pinch of flour **2** (指人) clique

撮合 cuōhe [动] matchmake (PT, PP matchmade) ▷朋友撮合的婚姻 a marriage matchmaded by friends

蹉 cuō 见下文

蹉跎 cuōtuó [动] waste time

痤 cuó 见下文

痤疮 cuóchuāng [名] acne

挫 cuò [动] **1** (挫折) defeat **2** (降低) wear ... down (PT wore, PP worn)

挫折 cuòzhé [名] setback

措 cuò [动] **1** (安排) handle **2** (筹划) make plans

措辞 cuòcí [动] diction

措施 cuòshī [名] measure ▷采取环保措施 take measures to protect the environment ▷预防措施 preventative measures

措手不及 cuò shǒu bù jí be caught off-guard

锉 cuò **I** [名] file **II** [动] file

错 cuò **I** [形] **1** (参差) interlocking **2** (不正确) incorrect **3** (糟糕) bad **II** [动] **1** (摩擦) grind (PT, PP ground) **2** (避开) miss ▷错过机会 miss an opportunity **3** (使不冲突) stagger ▷把上课和开会时间错开 stagger the time between classes and meetings **III** [名] fault

错爱 cuò'ài [动] (谦) ▷承蒙您错爱。You are too kind.

错怪 cuòguài [动] blame ... wrongly ▷对不起，是我错怪你了。Please accept my apologies for having wrongly blamed you.

错觉 cuòjué [名] illusion

错乱 cuòluàn [形] cluttered

错位 cuòwèi [动] displace

错误 cuòwù **I** [形] wrong **II** [名] mistake

错综复杂 cuòzōng fùzá complex ▷错综复杂的经济现象 complex economic phenomenon

Dd

→另见 dá

答理 dāli [动] **1** (理睬) bother ▷她从不答理她不喜欢的人。She never bothers with people she doesn't like. ▷他性格古怪，别答理他。Don't take any notice of him – he's weird. **2** (打招呼) acknowledge ▷他跟我打招呼，我没答理他。He said hello to me, but I didn't acknowledge him.

答应 dāying [动] **1** (回答) answer **2** (同意) agree ▷我答应借他钱。I agreed to lend him money. **3** (承诺) promise

打 dá [量] dozen
→另见 dǎ

达 dá [动] **1** (数量、目标) reach **2** (指时间) last ▷长达两个小时的报告 a report lasting two hours **3** (通) ▷这趟火车直达北京。This train is going direct to Beijing. ▷你要坐直达火车还是直达班机？Are you going by express train or direct flight? **4** (表示) express ▶转达 convey ▷请尽快把我的话转达给她。Please convey my message to her as soon as possible.

达标 dábiāo [动] reach a standard

达到 dádào [动] **1** (要求、水平、目的) achieve ▷达到目的 achieve an aim ▷达到要求 satisfy requirements **2** (指过程) reach ▷剧情达到高潮。The plot reached its climax.

达观 dáguān [形] philosophical

沓 dá [量] pile ▷一沓信 a pile of letters ▷两沓文件夹 two piles of files

答 dá [动] **1** (回答) answer ▷认真答题！Answer the question properly! **2** (还报) repay (PT, PP repaid) ▶报答 repay ▷我怎么才能答谢你的帮助呀？How can I repay you for all your help?
→另见 dā

答案 dá'àn [名] answer

答辩 dábiàn [动] defend ▷法庭答辩 defend at court ▷我明天论文答辩。Tomorrow I have the viva for my thesis.

答复 dáfù [动] respond ▷等我仔细考虑后再答复你。I'll get back to you after I've thought it over. ▷这不是个令人满意的答复。This is not a satisfactory response.

答卷 dájuàn I [名] answer sheet II [动] answer exam questions

答谢 dáxiè [动] express appreciation

答疑 dáyí [动] take questions (PT took, PP taken)

耷 dā 见下文

耷拉 dāla [动] droop ▷她的眼皮耷拉着。Her eyelids were drooping.

搭 dā [动] **1** (建造) put ... up (PT, PP put) ▷搭帐篷 put up a tent **2** (挂) hang (PT, PP hung) ▷我把大衣搭在胳膊上。I hung my overcoat over my arm. **3** (坐) take (PT took, PP taken) ▷他每个月搭飞机去上海。He takes the plane to Shanghai every month. ▷搭便车 get a lift **4** (连接) join ▶搭伙 join forces ▷两家公司终于搭上了关系。The two companies finally joined forces. **5** (加上) come up with (PT came, PP come) ▷再搭上点钱，我就能买辆新汽车。If I can come up with a bit more money, I'll be able to buy a new car. **6** (抬) carry ▷帮我把餐桌搭到厨房去。Help me carry the dining table into the kitchen.

搭档 dādàng I [名] partner II [动] team up ▷这个项目我和大卫搭档。I teamed up with David on the project. ▷咱们搭档开饭馆吧！Let's open a restaurant together!

搭救 dājiù [动] rescue

搭配 dāpèi [动] **1** (安排) combine **2** (配合) pair up **3** (指语言) collocate

搭腔 dāqiāng [动] respond

答 dā [动] answer

打 dǎ I [动] **1** (指暴力) hit (PT, PP hit) ▶殴打 beat up **2** (敲) beat (PT beat, PP beaten) ▷打鼓 beat a drum **3** (破) break (PT broke, PP broken)

▷我把暖瓶给打了。I broke the Thermos flask*. **4** (发出) send (PT, PP sent) ▷打信号 send a signal ▷打电话 make a phone call ▷打手电 shine a torch **5** (做游戏) play ▷打篮球 play basketball **6** (表示动作) ▶打喷嚏 sneeze ▷小狗在雪堆里打滚。The little dog rolled about in the snow. **7** (建造) build (PT, PP built) **8** (涂抹) polish ▷鞋子得打油了。These shoes need a polish. ▷明天我要给汽车打蜡。Tomorrow I'm going to wax the car. **9** (交涉) deal with (PT, PP dealt) ▷我再也不和他打交道了。I don't want to have to deal with him any more. ▷打官司 file a lawsuit **10** 制造) make (PT, PP made) ▷打家具 make furniture **11** (搅拌) beat (PT beat, PP beaten) ▷打两个鸡蛋 beat two eggs **12** (编织) knit ▷打毛衣 knit a sweater **13** (捕捉) catch (PT, PP caught) ▶打猎 go hunting ▷他打了两只麻雀。He caught two sparrows. **14** (画) draw (PT drew, PP drawn) ▷打草稿 draw up a draft ▷他在纸上打横线。He drew horizontal lines on the paper. **15** (举) hold (PT, PP held) ▷打伞 hold an umbrella **16** (除去) get rid of **17** (买) buy (PT, PP bought) ▷请帮我去打瓶料酒。Please buy me a bottle of cooking wine. **18** (揭) open ▷打开礼物 open a present **19** (穿凿) dig (PT, PP dug) ▷打油井 dig an oil well ▷打耳洞 pierce one's ears **20** (证明、介绍信) issue **21** (舀) spoon out ▷你能帮我打碗汤吗？Can you spoon me out a bowl of soup? **22** (收割) gather ▷打柴 gather firewood **23** (从事) do (PT did, PP done) ▶打杂儿 do odd jobs **24** (用) make (PT, PP made) ▷打比喻 make a comparison **25** (定罪名) convict ▷他被打成反动派。He was convicted of being a reactionary. **26** (捆) pack ▷打行李 pack one's bags **27** (计算) calculate ▷这笔费用应计入成本。This expenditure has to be factored into our costs. **28** (拨动) flick ▷他算盘打得很快。He's very quick with his abacus. **II** [介] from ▷打今儿起 from today ▷打这儿左转。Turn left just here.
→另见 dá

打靶 dǎbǎ [动] practice shooting ▷打靶练习 target practice

打败 dǎbài [动] defeat

打扮 dǎban **I** [动] make oneself up **II** [名] look

打抱不平 dǎ bàobùpíng defend against an injustice

打草惊蛇 dǎ cǎo jīng shé give the game away

打岔 dǎchà [动] interrupt

打倒 dǎdǎo [动] **1** (击倒在地) knock down **2** (指口号) down with ▷打倒帝国主义！Down with imperialism! **3** (推翻) overthrow

打的 dǎ dī [动] take a taxi (PT took, PP taken)

打点 dǎdian [动] **1** (收拾) organize ▷公司全靠他打点。The company left him to organize everything. ▷打点行装 pack one's bags **2** (贿赂) bribe

打动 dǎdòng [动] move

打赌 dǎdǔ [动] bet (PT, PP bet)

打发 dǎfa [动] **1** (时间) while away **2** (哄走) get rid of **3** (派) send (PT, PP sent)

打非 dǎfēi [动] crack down on illegal publications

打工 dǎgōng [动] temp ▷他在我们公司打了一个月的工。He temped in our company for a month. ▷打工妹 female migrant worker

打官司 dǎ guānsi [动] take legal action (PT took, PP taken)

打黑 dǎhēi [动] combat criminal organizations

打火 dǎhuǒ [动] **1** (发动) start ▷他的摩托车不打火。His motorbike wouldn't start. **2** (点燃) light (PT, PP lit)

打火机 dǎhuǒjī [名] lighter

打击 dǎjī **I** [名] **1** (指精神上) blow ▷高考落榜对他是一个沉重的打击。It was a big blow when he failed to pass the college entrance exams. **2** (指音乐) percussion ▷打击乐器 percussion instrument

打家劫舍 dǎ jiā jié shè loot

打假 dǎjiǎ [动] crack down on counterfeiting ▷打假行动 a campaign to crack down on counterfeiting

打架 dǎjià [动] have a fight

打搅 dǎjiǎo [动] **1** (扰乱) disturb **2** (婉) disturb ▷对不起，打搅您一下！Sorry, may I disturb you for just a second?

打卡 dǎkǎ [动] **1** (指上班) clock in **2** (指下班) clock out **3** (付费) swipe

打开 dǎkāi [动] **1** (开启) open ▷请打开车门。Please open the car door. **2** (扩展) expand ▷打开局面 expand operations **3** (开) turn ... on ▷打开空调 turn on the air conditioning

打捞 dǎlāo [动] salvage

打量 dǎliang [动] size up

打猎 dǎliè [动] hunt

打乱 dǎluàn [动] disrupt ▷公司的计划被打乱了。The company's plans were disrupted.

打埋伏 dǎ máifu **1** (隐藏) lie in ambush **2** (隐瞒) cover-up

打破沙锅问到底 dǎpò shāguō wèn dào dǐ get to the bottom of things

打气 dǎqì [动] **1** (球、轮胎) inflate **2** (人) encourage

打趣 dǎqù [动] tease ▷别打趣我了。Don't tease me.

打拳 **dǎquán** [动] do shadow boxing

打扫 **dǎsǎo** [动] clean ▷妈妈花了整个下午在打扫厨房。Mum spent an entire afternoon cleaning the kitchen.

打手 **dǎshou** [名] hired thug

打算 **dǎsuan** I [动] plan ▷你明天打算干什么？What are you planning to do tomorrow? II [名] plan

打听 **dǎtīng** [动] ask about

打消 **dǎxiāo** [动] give up (PT gave, PP given) ▷我打消了去参加晚会的念头。I gave up the idea of going to the party.

打小报告 **dǎ xiǎobàogào** (贬) tell tales

打雪仗 **dǎ xuězhàng** [动] have a snowball fight

打印 **dǎyìn** [动] print

打印机 **dǎyìnjī** [名] printer

打油诗 **dǎyóushī** [名] doggerel

打游击 **dǎ yóujī** [动] 1 (不固定) drift ▷他没有固定工作，四处打游击。He has no fixed work – he just drifts about. ▷他没钱租房子，到朋友家打游击。He doesn't have enough money to rent a flat so just drifts between friends' houses. 2 (战斗) fight a guerrilla war (PT, PP fought)

打杂儿 **dǎ zár** [动] do odd jobs

打仗 **dǎzhàng** [动] fight a war (PT, PP fought) ▷打败仗 be defeated ▷打胜仗 win a war

打招呼 **dǎ zhāohu** [动] 1 (问好) greet ▷他笑呵呵地和每个到场的人打招呼。He cheerily greeted everyone who came. 2 (通知) inform

打折扣 **dǎ zhékòu** [动] 1 (指做事情) fall short of a requirement (PT fell, PP fallen) 2 (降价) discount

大 **dà** [形] 1 (数量、体积、面积) big 2 (指力气) great ▷他劲儿真大！He's so strong! 3 (重要) important ▷法国是葡萄酒大国。France is an important wine-producing country. 4 (强) strong ▷大风 strong wind 5 (指声音) loud ▷音乐声太大，请关小一点。The music's too loud – could you turn it down a bit please? 6 (雨、雪) heavy ▷大雨 heavy rain 7 (指年龄) old ▷你多大了？How old are you? ▷他比我大。He's older than me. 8 (指程度) ▷大笑 roar with laughter ▷大吃一惊 take a big shock ▷大哭 sob one's heart out 9 (老大) eldest ▷大姐 eldest sister 10 (敬) (名字、作品等) ▷请问尊姓大名？Would you be kind enough to tell me your name?

→另见 **dài**

> big, large 和 great 都用来表示大小。一般而言，large 比 big 正式，而 great 又比 large 更为正式。big 和 large 通常用于描述物体。big 还表示某事物很重要

或给人印象深刻。...his influence over the big advertisers... great 通常用于强调某人或某事物的重要性。...the great artist, Van Gogh... great 还可以暗示某事物因其大小而给人深刻的印象。The great bird of prey soared into the sky. 表示数量大可以用 large 或 great, 但不能用 big。...a large amount of blood on the floor...the arrival of tourists in great numbers... big 和 great 都可用于表示程度, great 比 big 更正式。Most of them act like big fools... It gives me great pleasure to welcome you. 注意, great 除了表示大小外还有其他的含义, 比如它可以表示某事物很独特, 非常好, 或很有趣。

大本营 **dàběnyíng** [名] base

大不了 **dàbùliǎo** I [副] at the worst II [形] serious ▷没考好没什么大不了, 再努力点就是了。If you don't do well in your exams it's not serious – you'll just have to work a bit harder.

大步流星 **dà bù liú xīng** at a stride ▷老师大步流星地走进教室。The teacher came striding into the classroom.

大材小用 **dà cái xiǎo yòng** waste of talent

大吹大擂 **dà chuī dà léi** make a great noise

大打出手 **dà dǎ chūshǒu** come to blows

大胆 **dàdǎn** [形] bold

大刀阔斧 **dà dāo kuò fǔ** boldly

大抵 **dàdǐ** [副] generally

大地 **dàdì** [名] the land

大动干戈 **dà dòng gāngē** make a big fuss

大凡 **dàfán** [副] generally speaking

大方 **dàfang** [形] 1 (慷慨) generous 2 (不拘束) natural 3 (不俗气) tasteful ▷她穿着文雅大方。She dresses tastefully and elegantly.

大概 **dàgài** I [名] general idea II [形] approximate III [副] probably

大纲 **dàgāng** [名] outline

大公无私 **dà gōng wú sī** impartial

大功告成 **dà gōng gào chéng** complete successfully

大锅饭 **dàguōfàn** [名] extreme egalitarianism

大海捞针 **dà hǎi lāo zhēn** look for a needle in a haystack

大亨 **dàhēng** [名] magnate

大户 **dàhù** [名] important customer

大伙儿 **dàhuǒr** [代] everybody ▷我们大伙儿一起做饭。Everybody cooks together.

大惑不解 **dà huò bù jiě** be very puzzled

大家 **dàjiā** I [名] master ▷国画大家 a master of traditional Chinese painting II [代] everybody ▷大家都很喜欢这部电影。

Everyone really likes this film. ▷大家都认为她是个好老师。Everybody thought she was a good teacher. ▷大家都会上网吗？Does everybody know how to get on to the Internet? ▷我们大家必须继续努力。We must all keep on trying.

大惊小怪 dà jīng xiǎo guài make a mountain out of a molehill

大局 dàjú [名] overall picture

大举 dàjǔ [形] large-scale

大快人心 dà kuài rén xīn to everybody's satisfaction

大款 dàkuǎn [名] (贬) moneybags (SG)

大理石 dàlǐshí [名] marble

大量 dàliàng [形] 1 (数量多) large amount of ▷这家公司吸引了大量的资金。This company attracted a large amount of investment. ▷公司准备大量裁员。The company is preparing to lay off a large number of people. 2 (气量大) generous ▷宽宏大量 broadminded

大陆 dàlù [名] 1 (指各大洲) continent ▷亚洲大陆 the Asian continent 2 (指中国) the mainland ▷中国大陆 mainland China

大路货 dàlùhuò [名] basic goods (PL)

大名 dàmíng [名] 1 (名字) full name 2 (名气) great reputation

大名鼎鼎 dàmíng dǐngdǐng celebrated

大模大样 dà mú dà yàng haughtily

大逆不道 dà nì bù dào traitorous

大年 dànián [名] (丰年) bumper year

大排档 dàpáidàng [名] (方) market ▷夜间大排档 night market

大牌 dàpái I [形] hotshot ▷大牌影星 hotshot movie star II [名] 1 (品牌) famous brand 2 (威风) airs and graces (PL)

大盘 dàpán [名] market index

大片 dàpiān [名] blockbuster

大起大落 dà qǐ dà luò wild fluctuations ▷股票价格大起大落。Share prices are fluctuating wildly.

大气 dàqì I [名] 1 (气体) atmosphere 2 (呼吸) heavy breathing II [形] open-minded

大气候 dàqìhòu [名] climate

大器晚成 dà qì wǎn chéng great talent takes time to develop ▷她是位大器晚成的作家。She's a writer who will take time to develop.

大千世界 dàqiān-shìjiè the boundless universe

大人 dàren [名] adult

大赦 dàshè [动] amnesty

大失所望 dà shī suǒ wàng to one's great disappointment

大师 dàshī [名] master

大师傅 dàshifu [名] head chef

大使 dàshǐ [名] ambassador

大事 dàshì I [名] important event II [副] greatly

大势所趋 dàshì suǒ qū in tune with the general trend

大手笔 dàshǒubǐ [名] 1 (作品) masterpiece 2 (作家) well-known writer

大手大脚 dà shǒu dà jiǎo be extravagant ▷他花钱大手大脚。He's very extravagant with money.

大提琴 dàtíqín [名] cello

大体 dàtǐ I [名] fundamental principle II [副] more or less ▷两国意见大体一致。The opinions of the two countries are more or less the same.

大庭广众 dà tíng guǎng zhòng in broad daylight

大同小异 dà tóng xiǎo yì much the same ▷他的新书和上本书大同小异。His new book is much the same as his last one.

大腕 dàwàn [名] big name ▷大腕级导演 a big-name director ▷他是歌坛的大腕。He's a big name in the singing world.

大喜过望 dà xǐ guò wàng pleased beyond expectation ▷她没有想到会得到这份工作，因此她大喜过望。She never thought she'd get the job, and so was pleased beyond all expectation.

大显身手 dà xiǎn shēnshǒu use one's talents to the full

大相径庭 dà xiāng jìngtíng as different as chalk and cheese

大小 dàxiǎo I [名] 1 (尺寸) size 2 (辈分) seniority ▷这女孩子说话真没大小！The way this girl talks is so disrespectful! ▷全校不分大小，公平竞争。There are no distinctions of seniority at all on this campus - everyone competes on an equal footing. 3 (人口) people (PL) ▷全家大小共三口人。There are three people in my family altogether. 4 (大的和小的) total ▷我市大小超市有上百家。Our city has a total of over one hundred supermarkets. II [副] anyway ▷他大小是个经理，说话算数。Anyway, he's a manager so it's his word that counts.

大写 dàxiě I [名] 1 (指字母) capital letter 2 (指数字) Chinese numeral written in full form II [动] write in capitals (PT wrote, PP written)

大兴土木 dà xīng tǔmù carry out major building works

大型 dàxíng [形] large-scale ▷大型企业 large-scale enterprises ▷大型艺术展 large-scale art exhibition

大选 dàxuǎn [名] general election

大学 dàxué [名] university (英), college (美) ▷大学毕业 graduate from university (英) 或 college (美) ▷上大学 go to university (英) 或 college (美)

大学生 dàxuéshēng [名] university (英) 或 college (美) student

大雪 dàxuě [名] heavy snow ▷昨天下了场大雪。It snowed heavily yesterday.

大雅 dàyǎ [名] elegance

大言不惭 dà yán bù cán brag shamelessly

大意 dàyì [名] general idea

大意 dàyi [形] careless

大有作为 dà yǒu zuòwéi make the most of one's abilities

大雨 dàyǔ [名] downpour

大约 dàyuē [副] 1 (指数量) approximately ▷我大约有200块钱。I have approximately 200 yuan. 2 (可能) probably ▷他大约在上网。He's probably on the Internet.

大杂烩 dàzáhuì [名] 1 (指事物) mishmash 2 (指食物) hotchpotch

大张旗鼓 dà zhāng qí gǔ with great fanfare

大丈夫 dàzhàngfu [名] true man (PL men)

大致 dàzhì [副] 1 (大体上) approximately ▷两个人的水平大致相同。They are both at approximately the same level. 2 (大约) probably ▷他看上去大致20岁。By the look of him he's probably around 20 years old.

大众 dàzhòng [名] the people (PL) ▷大众文学 popular literature ▷大众品味 popular tastes

大众化 dàzhònghuà [名] popularization

大自然 dàzìrán [名] nature

大作 dàzuò [名] (敬) masterpiece

呆 dāi I [形] 1 (傻) slow-witted 2 (发愣) blank 3 (吓、惊) dumbstruck II [动] stay

呆板 dāibǎn [形] stiff

呆若木鸡 dāi ruò mù jī dumbstruck

呆账 dāizhàng [名] bad debt

呆子 dāizi [名] fool ▷书呆子 bookworm ▷他真是个呆子！He's such a fool!

待 dāi [动] stay ▷你再多待一会儿。Do stay a little longer. ▷她成天待在家里。She stays at home all day.
→另见 dài

歹 dǎi [形] evil

歹毒 dǎidú [形] vicious

歹徒 dǎitú [名] gangster

逮 dǎi [动] catch (PT, PP caught)
→另见 dài

大 dài 见下文

大夫 dàifu [名] doctor
→另见 dà

代 dài I [动] 1 (替) do ... on behalf of ▷经理病了，经理助理代他在会上发言。As the manager was ill, his assistant spoke on his behalf. ▷我代她在合同上签了字。I signed the contract on her behalf. 2 (指问候) ▷你见到他时，代我问好。When you see him, say hello from me. 3 (代理) act as ▷代校长 acting headmaster II [名] 1 (时代) times (PL) ▷古代 ancient times 2 (辈分) generation 3 (朝代) dynasty

代办 dàibàn [动] take ... over (PT took, PP taken)

代笔 dàibǐ [动] write on behalf of (PT wrote, PP written) ▷我为他代笔写申请信。I wrote the application on his behalf.

代表 dàibiǎo I [名] representative ▷谈判代表 the delegate to the negotiations II [动] 1 (代替) stand in for (PT, PP stood) ▷副主任代表主任主持会议。The deputy director stood in for the director as chair of the meeting. 2 (委托) represent ▷他全权代表我们公司。He has full authority to represent our company. 3 (指意义、概念) be representative of ▷他的诗代表了时代精神。His poem is representative of the spirit of the age. III [形] archetypal ▷达芬奇是文艺复兴时期的代表人物。Da Vinci was an archetypal Renaissance figure.

代词 dàicí [名] pronoun

代沟 dàigōu [名] generation gap

代号 dàihào [名] code name

代价 dàijià [名] cost

代劳 dàiláo [动] help ... out ▷打印的事就请您代劳了！Could you help me out with the printing?

代理 dàilǐ [动] 1 (暂时替代) act on behalf of ▷代理经理 acting manager ▷代理校长 acting headmaster 2 (委托) represent

代理人 dàilǐrén [名] agent

代码 dàimǎ [名] code

代数 dàishù [名] algebra

代替 dàitì [动] substitute for

代谢 dàixiè [动] metabolize

代言人 dàiyánrén [名] spokesperson

玳 dài 见下文

玳瑁 dàimào [名] tortoiseshell

带 dài I [名] 1 (长条物) strap ▶皮带 leather belt ▶磁带 cassette ▶录像带 videotape 2 (轮胎) tyre (英), tire (美) ▶车带 car tyre (英) 或 tire (美) 3 (区域) zone ▶热带 the tropics ▷长江一带 the Yangtze region II [动] 1 (携带) take (PT took, PP taken) ▷别忘了带钱包! Don't forget to take your wallet! 2 (捎带) ▷你出去时带点牛奶回来, 好吗? Can you buy some milk when you're out? ▷你去邮局时, 能帮我带几张邮票吗? If you're going to the post office, could you get me some stamps? 3 (呈现) wear (PT wore, PP worn) ▷面带笑容 wear a smile on one's face 4 (含有) have (PT, PP had) ▷这些豆子稍带苦味儿。 These beans have a slightly bitter taste. ▷他这么说, 是话里带刺儿。 His remarks smacked of sarcasm. 5 (连带) come with (PT came, PP come) ▷买电脑, 带免费打印机。 When you buy a computer the printer comes free. ▷这本书带免费光盘吗? Does the book come with a free CD? 6 (指导) direct ▷老教授带着两个博士生。 The old professor was supervising two doctoral students. 7 (领) lead (PT, PP led) ▷她带着一组学生去野营。 She led a group of students on a camping expedition. 8 (养) bring ... up (PT, PP brought) ▷她是由奶奶带大的。 She was brought up by her grandmother. 9 (带动) inspire ▷他带得我也爱运动了。 He inspired my love of sport.

带动 dàidòng [动] 1 (指进步) drive (PT drove, PP driven) ▷高科技带动社会进步。 Technology drives social progress. 2 (指机械动力) power

带劲 dàijìn [形] 1 (指兴致) interesting 2 (形容情绪高昂) energetic ▷他的演讲很带劲。 He gave an impassioned speech.

带领 dàilǐng [动] 1 (领着) guide 2 (指挥) lead (PT, PP led)

带头 dàitóu [动] take the initiative (PT took, PP taken) ▷他带头捐书给图书馆。 He took the initiative in donating books to the library.

待 dài [动] 1 (对待) treat ▶优待 treat 2 (招待) entertain 3 (等待) wait for ▷这个问题有待解决。 This problem will have to wait for a solution.
→另见 dāi

待命 dàimìng [动] await orders

待人接物 dài rén jiē wù people skills

待业 dàiyè [动] be unemployed ▷待业青年 unemployed youth

待遇 dàiyù [名] pay

贷 dài I [动] 1 (指银行) lend (PT, PP lent) ▷银行贷给公司一笔款。 The bank lent money to the company. 2 (指借钱方) take out a loan (PT took, PP taken) ▷公司向银行贷了一笔款。 The company took out a loan from the bank. II [名] loan

贷款 dàikuǎn I [动] lend (PT, PP lent) ▷他向银行贷款买房。 He took out a loan from the bank to buy a house. ▷这次银行拒绝贷款给他。 The bank refused to lend him money this time. II [名] loan

怠 dài [形] 1 (懒惰) lazy 2 (不恭敬) disrespectful

怠工 dàigōng [动] go slow (PT went, PP gone)

怠慢 dàimàn [动] slight ▷他怠慢了客人。 He slighted the guests. II [形] (谦) remiss ▷如有怠慢之处, 请多包涵。 If I have been at all remiss, please accept my full apologies.

袋 dài I [名] bag II [量] bag

袋鼠 dàishǔ [名] kangaroo

逮 dài [动] capture
→另见 dǎi

逮捕 dàibǔ [动] arrest

戴 dài [动] 1 (眼镜、帽子、小装饰品等) wear (PT wore, PP worn) 2 (拥护尊敬) support

戴罪立功 dài zuì lì gōng atone for one's crimes

丹 dān I [形] red II [名] pellet ▷灵丹妙药 panacea

丹青 dānqīng [名] (书) painting

丹心 dānxīn [名] loyalty

单 dān I [形] 1 (一个) single ▷单人床 single bed 2 (奇数) odd 3 (单独) solitary 4 (不复杂) simple 5 (薄弱) weak 6 (衣、裤) thin II [副] only ▷成功不能单凭运气。 To be successful you can't rely only on luck. III [名] 1 (单子) sheet ▶床单 bed sheet 2 (列表) list ▶菜单 menu

单薄 dānbó [形] 1 (穿得少) flimsy 2 (瘦弱) frail 3 (薄弱) weak

单车 dānchē [名] (方) (自行车) bicycle

单程 dānchéng [名] single

单纯 dānchún I [形] simple II [副] merely ▷单纯地注入资金是无法挽救公司的。 A mere cash injection isn't going to save the company.

单词 dāncí [名] word

单打 dāndǎ [名] singles (PL) ▷乒乓球女子单打 the women's table-tennis singles

单单 dāndān [副] only ▷别人都懂了, 单单他不明白。 The others all understood – only he didn't get it.

单调 **dāndiào** [形] monotonous

单独 **dāndú** [形] **1** (独自) alone **2** (独立) unaided ▷我能单独处理这事。I can handle this by myself.

单杠 **dāngàng** [名] horizontal bar

单价 **dānjià** [名] unit price

单间 **dānjiān** [名] separate room

单据 **dānjù** [名] receipt

单枪匹马 **dān qiāng pǐ mǎ** single-handedly

单亲 **dānqīn** [名] single parent ▷他来自单亲家庭。He comes from a single-parent family.

单身 **dānshēn** [名] single ▷单身汉 bachelor

单数 **dānshù** [名] **1** (指数字) odd number **2** (指词) singular ▷名词的单数形式 the singular form of the noun

单位 **dānwèi** [名] **1** (指标准量) unit ▷以平方米为测量单位 use square metres as the unit of measurement ▷单位人口密度 population density by area **2** (机构) unit ▷事业单位 work unit

单相思 **dānxiāngsī** [名] unrequited love

单一 **dānyī** [形] single

单音词 **dānyīncí** [名] monosyllabic word

单元 **dānyuán** [名] unit ▷单元房 self-contained flat (英) 或 apartment (美)

单子 **dānzi** [名] **1** (指床上用品) sheet **2** (列表) list

担 **dān** [动] **1** (挑) carry ... on one's shoulder **2** (负) take ... on (PT took, PP taken) ▷担起责任 take on a responsibility
→另见 dàn

担保 **dānbǎo** [动] guarantee ▷他为我做担保。He acted as my guarantor. ▷我能担保产品质量。I can vouch for the quality of the product.

担待 **dāndài** [动] **1** (原谅) forgive (PT forgave, PP forgiven) **2** (负责) take responsibility (PT took, PP taken) ▷出了事儿，她会担待的。If anything goes wrong, she will take responsibility for it.

担当 **dāndāng** [动] take ... on (PT took, PP taken) ▷他勇于担当重任。He has the courage to take on important tasks.

担负 **dānfù** [动] shoulder

担架 **dānjià** [名] stretcher

担任 **dānrèn** [动] hold the post of (PT, PP held) ▷她担任经理助理。She holds the post of manager's assistant.

担心 **dānxīn** [动] worry ▷他担心母亲的身体。He worried about his mother's health.

耽 **dān** 见下文

耽搁 **dānge** [动] **1** (拖延) delay ▷这事儿不能再耽搁了。This cannot be delayed any further. **2** (停留) stay ▷我不能在这儿再耽搁了。I can't stay here any longer.

耽误 **dānwu** [动] delay ▷因为机械故障，耽误了飞机的起飞。The flight was delayed because of a mechanical fault. ▷别耽误时间！Don't waste time!

胆 **dǎn** [名] **1** (指器官) gall bladder **2** (胆量) courage **3** (指器皿) liner

胆敢 **dǎngǎn** [动] dare

胆固醇 **dǎngùchún** [名] cholesterol

胆量 **dǎnliàng** [名] guts (PL)

胆怯 **dǎnqiè** [形] timid

胆识 **dǎnshí** [名] courage and insight

胆战心惊 **dǎn zhàn xīn jīng** be scared out of one's wits

胆子 **dǎnzi** [名] guts (PL) ▷他胆子不小。He's got such guts.

掸 **dǎn** [动] brush

掸子 **dǎnzi** [名] duster

旦 **dàn** [名] **1** (书) (早晨) dawn **2** (天) day

旦夕 **dànxī** [名] short while ▷危在旦夕 in imminent danger

但 **dàn** I [连] but ▷她不很聪明，但很努力。She wasn't very clever, but she was very hardworking. ▷他有驾照，但没有车。He has a driver's licence, but no car. II [副] only ▷但愿 wish ▷晴空万里，但见骄阳。In the clear and boundless sky all you could see was the blazing sun.

但凡 **dànfán** [副] ▷但凡星期天，她都去游泳。She goes swimming every Sunday. ▷但凡中国人，都知道孔子。All Chinese people know about Confucius.

但是 **dànshì** [连] but ▷工作很忙，但是她坚持锻炼。She was very busy at work, but she managed to stick to her exercise regime. ▷虽然下雨，但是不冷。Even though it's raining, it's not cold.

担 **dàn** I [名] load II [量] ▷一担水 two buckets of water
→另见 dān

担子 **dànzi** [名] **1** (扁担) shoulder pole **2** (责任) responsibility

诞 **dàn** I [动] be born II [名] birthday III [形] absurd

诞辰 **dànchén** [名] birthday

诞生 dànshēng [动] be born ▷新一代手机诞生了。A new generation of mobile phones was born.

淡 dàn [形] 1 (指味道浓淡) weak 2 (指咸淡) bland 3 (颜色浅) light 4 (稀薄) light 5 (不热情) indifferent 6 (不红火) slack ▷最近生意很清淡。Business has been very slack lately.

淡泊 dànbó [动] (书) be unconcerned about

淡薄 dànbó [形] 1 (不浓厚) indifferent 2 (模糊) faint 3 (密度小) thin

淡化 dànhuà [动] 1 (指观念、感情、问题等) water down ▷淡化政治 watered-down politics 2 (水) desalinate ▷海水淡化工程 sea water desalination project

淡季 dànjì [名] low season ▷旅游淡季 the low tourist season ▷现在是西瓜的淡季。Watermelons are currently out of season.

淡漠 dànmò [形] 1 (冷淡) indifferent 2 (记忆、印象) faded

淡然 dànrán [形] (书) indifferent

淡然处之 dànrán chǔ zhī be unruffled ▷面对困难，他淡然处之。He was unruffled in the face of difficulty.

淡忘 dànwàng [动] fade from memory

蛋 dàn [名] 1 (卵) egg ▶鸡蛋 egg 2 (球状物) ball ▶鱼蛋 fish ball

蛋白质 dànbáizhì [名] protein

蛋糕 dàngāo [名] cake

弹 dàn [名] 1 (弹子) pellet 2 (子弹) bullet 3 (炸弹) bomb ▶原子弹 atomic bomb
→另见 tán

弹丸 dànwán [名] 1 (丸) pellet 2 (书) (狭小之地) tiny place

弹药 dànyào [名] ammunition

氮 dàn [名] nitrogen

当 dāng I [助动] should ▷你有问题，当问就问。If you have questions that should be raised, then raise them. II [介] 1 (向) in front of ▶当众 in public ▷老师当着全班批评了班长。The teacher criticized the class monitor in front of the whole class. 2 (正在) ▷当我们到时，电影已开始了。When we arrived the film had already started. ▷当他在美国时，他爷爷去世了。His grandfather passed away while he was in America. III [动] 1 (担任) act as ▷当经理 act as manager 2 (承当) deserve ▷不敢当！I don't deserve it! 3 (掌管) be in charge ▶当家 rule the roost 4 (相当) match ▷门当户对 be well-matched IV [拟] 1 (指金属敲击

声) chime ▷当当的钟声 the chiming of the bell 2 (指敲门声) knock
→另见 dàng

当场 dāngchǎng [副] there and then ▷经理当场签了合同。The manager signed the contract there and then.

当初 dāngchū [名] those days ▷当初他俩就不和。Even in those days they didn't get on.

当代 dāngdài [名] the present ▷当代文学 contemporary literature

当道 dāngdào I [名] the middle of the road II [动] (贬) hold power (PT, PP held)

当地 dāngdì [名] locality ▷我在当地买了一所房子。I bought a house in the locality. ▷当地风俗 local customs

当机立断 dāng jī lì duàn make an on-the-spot decision

当即 dāngjí [副] immediately

当家 dāngjiā [动] rule the roost

当今 dāngjīn [名] the present

当局 dāngjú [名] authorities (PL)

当令 dānglìng [动] be in season ▷葡萄正当令。Grapes are currently in season.

当面 dāngmiàn [动] do ... face to face ▷当面讨论 have a face-to-face discussion

当年 dāngnián I [名] those days ▷想当年，我们都很幼稚。Thinking back to those days, we were all so naïve. II [动] be in the prime of one's life ▷三十多岁是男人正当年的时候。A man is in his prime in his thirties.

当前 dāngqián I [动] be faced with II [名] present ▷当前的目标 the present aim

当权 dāngquán [动] hold power (PT, PP held)

当然 dāngrán I [副] of course ▷"能帮个忙吗？" "当然可以！" "Can you help me? – Of course!" ▷坐公共汽车当然要买票。Of course you have to buy a ticket if you want to take the bus. II [形] natural ▷你不努力，成绩差是当然的。If you don't work hard, it's only natural that you'll get low marks.

当仁不让 dāng rén bù ràng not shirk responsibility

当时 dāngshí [名] ▷他当时不知道犯了法。At the time he didn't know he'd broken the law. ▷我当时高兴极了。I was ecstatic at the time.

当头 dāngtóu [动] 1 (迎头) take ... in the face (PT took, PP taken) ▷当头一拳 take a punch in the face 2 (在眼前) confront 3 (放在首位) prioritize ▷生意人是利字当头。Businesspeople prioritize profit above all else.

当务之急 dāng wù zhī jí top priority ▷我们的当务之急是解决资金问题。Our top priority is to resolve the issue of funding.

当心 dāngxīn [动] be careful

当选 dāngxuǎn [动] be elected ▷他当选为新一届主席。He was elected as the new chairman.

当政 dāngzhèng [动] be in power ▷他当政时，国泰民安。When he was in power the state was prosperous and the people were at peace.

当之无愧 dāng zhī wú kuì fully deserve ▷他是当之无愧的好领导。He fully deserved the title of good leader.

当中 dāngzhōng [名] 1 (中间) ▷几个人当中，只有我信任她。Out of a number of people, I was the only one who believed her. ▷讨论当中，他言辞激烈。During the discussion he spoke forcefully. 2 (正中间) the centre (英) 或 center (美) ▷他站在舞台当中。He stood in the centre of the stage.

当众 dāngzhòng [副] publicly

挡 dǎng I [动] 1 (拦) keep off (PT, PP kept) ▷请别挡路！Keep off the road! 2 (遮蔽) shelter from II [名] (排挡) gear

挡箭牌 dǎngjiànpái [名] excuse

党 dǎng [名] 1 (政党) party 2 (集团) faction

党派 dǎngpài [名] clique

党羽 dǎngyǔ [名] (贬) adherents (PL)

当 dàng I [形] appropriate ▷妥当 appropriate ▷用词不当 an inappropriate choice of words II [动] 1 (作为) treat ... as ▷我把妈妈当作最好的朋友。I treat my mother like my best friend. 2 (认为) assume ▷我当你明白了。I assumed you'd understood. 3 (抵押) pawn ▷他把手表当了。He pawned his watch. 4 (指时间和地点) ▷当天 that day ▷当场 on the spot →另见 dāng

当年 dàngnián [名] that same year

当铺 dàngpù [名] pawnshop

当时 dàngshí [名] ▷他当时就在合同上签了字。He signed the contract there and then. ▷接到他的短信，我当时就给他回了电话。I called him back as soon as I received his text.

当天 dàngtiān [名] the same day ▷我明天去天津，当天就回来。I'm going to Tianjin tomorrow, and returning the same day.

当真 dàngzhēn I [动] take ... seriously (PT took, PP taken) ▷别把他的话当真！Don't take what he said seriously! II [形] serious III [副] really ▷他当真辞职了？Did he really resign?

当作 dàngzuò [动] regard ... as ▷人们经常把狗当作最忠实的朋友。People often regard dogs as their most loyal friends.

荡 dàng I [动] 1 (摇摆) sway 2 (闲逛) loaf about 3 (清除) clear ... away II [形] 1 (广阔) vast 2 (放纵) loose in morals

荡妇 dàngfù [名] tart

荡气回肠 dàng qì huí cháng soul-stirring

荡然无存 dàngrán wú cún completely disappear

荡漾 dàngyàng [动] undulate

档 dàng [名] 1 (档案) file 2 (等级) grade

档案 dàng'àn [名] files (PL)

档次 dàngcì [名] grade

刀 dāo [名] 1 (指工具) knife (PL knives) 2 (刀状物) blade

刀枪 dāoqiāng [名] weapons (PL)

刀刃 dāorèn [名] 1 (字) knife edge 2 (喻) the most vital thing ▷他总能把钱花在刀刃上。He always spends his money on vital things.

刀山火海 dāo shān huǒ hǎi extremely dangerous place

叨 dāo 见下文

叨唠 dāolao [动] prattle on ▷别为了一点小事就叨唠。You really shouldn't prattle on about something so trivial.

导 dǎo [动] 1 (引导) guide ▷导游 guide 2 (传导) conduct 3 (开导) give guidance (PT gave, PP given) 4 (导演) direct

导播 dǎobō I [动] produce II [名] director

导弹 dǎodàn [名] missile

导电 dǎodiàn [动] conduct electricity

导购 dǎogòu [动] give shopping advice (PT gave, PP given) ▷导购小姐 salesgirl

导航 dǎoháng [动] navigate ▷雷达导航系统 radar navigation system

导火线 dǎohuǒxiàn [名] 1 (字) fuse 2 (喻) trigger

导论 dǎolùn [名] introduction

导师 dǎoshī [名] 1 (字) tutor 2 (喻) mentor

导体 dǎotǐ [名] conductor

导向 dǎoxiàng I [名] guidance II [动] lead to (PT, PP led)

导演 dǎoyǎn I [动] direct II [名] director

导游 dǎoyóu I [动] guide II [名] tour guide

导致 dǎozhì [动] lead to (PT, PP led) ▷首相的决定导致了暴动。The prime minister's decision led to rioting. ▷粗心导致她没考好。Because of her carelessness she failed the exam.

岛 dǎo [名] island ▷岛国 island nation ▷半岛

peninsula

岛屿 **dǎoyǔ** [名] islands (PL)

倒 **dǎo** I [动] **1** (横躺) fall (PT fell, PP fallen) ▶摔倒 fall down ▶卧倒 lie down ▷我倒在床上就睡 I collapsed into bed and fell asleep immediately. **2** (失败) fail ▶倒闭 go bankrupt ▷击倒竞争对手 beat a rival competitor **3** (食欲) spoil ▶倒胃口 lose one's appetite **4** (换) change ▷倒班 change shifts **5** (倒买倒卖) speculate **6** (嗓子) lose ▷歌唱家的嗓子倒了。 The singer lost her voice. II [名] (贬) wheeler-dealer

→另见 dào

倒闭 **dǎobì** [动] go bankrupt

倒戈 **dǎogē** [动] swap sides

倒买倒卖 **dǎo mǎi dǎo mài** speculate

倒霉 **dǎoméi** [形] unlucky

倒手 **dǎoshǒu** [动] **1** (换手) swap hands ▷他们着手拎行李。 He swapped the suitcase from one hand to the other. **2** (买卖货物) change hands

倒塌 **dǎotā** [动] collapse

倒台 **dǎotái** [动] fall from power (PT fell, PP fallen) ▷保守党政府倒台了。 The Conservative government fell from power.

倒腾 **dǎoteng** [动] **1** (买进卖出) deal in (PT, PP dealt) ▷他在倒腾香烟。 He deals in cigarettes. **2** (翻腾) rummage around

倒胃口 **dǎowèikou** [动] **1** (指食欲) lose one's appetite (PT, PP lost) **2** (使人生厌) put ... off (PT, PP put) ▷他的所作所为让人倒胃口。 People were really put off by what he had done.

捣 **dǎo** [动] **1** (捶打) crush **2** (搅乱) make trouble

捣鬼 **dǎoguǐ** [动] make mischief

捣毁 **dǎohuǐ** [动] destroy

捣乱 **dǎoluàn** [动] **1** (扰乱) disturb **2** (制造麻烦) make trouble

祷 **dǎo** [动] pray

祷告 **dǎogào** [动] pray

蹈 **dǎo** [动] **1** (跳动) skip ▶舞蹈 dancing **2** (书) (踩) tread (PT trod, PP trodden)

到 **dào** I [动] **1** (达到) arrive ▷火车到了。 The train has arrived. ▷我是昨天到上海的。 I arrived in Shanghai yesterday. ▷到点了, 起床！ Time to get up! **2** (去) go (PT went, PP gone) ▷我到厦门旅游。 I'm going to Xiamen on a tour. **3** (用作动词的补语) ▷听到这个消息我很吃惊。 When I heard the news I was very surprised. ▷老师没想到我们会来医院看

他。 Our teacher hadn't imagined we would visit him in hospital. ▷真想不到他会离婚。 I never would have thought he'd get divorced. ▷你的要求我办不到。 I can't handle your demands. II [形] (周到) considerate

到处 **dàochù** [名] all places (PL) ▷这种植物到处都有。 You can find this kind of plant everywhere.

到达 **dàodá** [动] arrive

到底 **dàodǐ** I [动] ▷坚持到底 keep going until the end ▷把改革进行到底 carry through reforms II [副] **1** (究竟) ▷你到底在干什么？ What on earth are you up to? ▷你到底还想不想上大学？ Do you actually want to go to university? **2** (毕竟) after all ▷他到底还是个孩子。 After all, he's still just a kid. **3** (终于) at last

到家 **dàojiā** [形] perfect

到位 **dàowèi** I [动] be in place ▷资金已经到位。 The money is already in place. ▷货物一次到位。 The goods will be sent in one go. II [形] precise ▷他回答得很到位。 He answered very precisely.

到职 **dàozhí** [动] take office (PT took, PP taken)

倒 **dào** I [动] **1** (顺倒) ▷倒数第一 the very last ▷老师倒着点名。 The teacher did the roll call in reverse order. ▷他把地图挂倒了。 He hung the map up upside down. ▷姓和名写倒了。 The first name and surname were written the wrong way round. **2** (后退) reverse ▷倒车 reverse a car **3** (倾倒) empty out ▷倒垃圾 empty the rubbish out ▷我来给您倒杯茶。 Let me pour you a cup of tea. ▷在会上, 他把所有的想法都倒了出来。 He poured out all his ideas at the meeting. II [副] **1** (表示意料之外) unexpectedly **2** (反而) instead ▷她没哭, 倒笑了。 She didn't cry, but laughed instead. **3** (表示让步) though ▷这房子地段倒好, 就是太小。 Although the location of the house is good, it's still too small. ▷这部手提电脑新倒是新, 就是太沉。 Even though this laptop is new, it's just too heavy. **4** (表示转折) ▷他其貌不扬, 倒是很聪明。 He's not very attractive, but he's clever. ▷这包不漂亮, 倒很实用。 This bag isn't very smart, but it's practical. **5** (表示不耐烦) ▷你倒快点走啊！ Can you go a bit faster? ▷你倒是说呀！ Can you get on with it please! **6** (表示责怪) ▷他说得倒漂亮, 从没见他兑现过。 He's all talk – he never lives up to his promises.

→另见 dǎo

倒彩 **dàocǎi** [名] booing ▷喝倒彩 boo

倒插门 **dàochāmén** I [动] live off one's wife's family II [名] *son-in-law living off his wife's family*

倒打一耙 dào dǎ yī pá hit back unfairly ▷他倒打一耙，要求赔偿。He hit back with an unfair demand for compensation.

倒挂 dàoguà [动] 1 (颠倒地挂) hang ... upside down (PT, PP hung) 2 (价格等) be topsy-turvy ▷市场价与出厂价倒挂。The market prices are topsy-turvy in relation to factory prices.

倒立 dàolì [动] 1 (物) be upside down 2 (人) do a handstand

倒计时 dàojìshí [动] count down ▷奥运会进入了倒计时阶段。The countdown to the Olympics has begun.

倒贴 dàotiē [动] lose money unexpectedly (PT, PP lost)

倒退 dàotuì [动] go back (PT went, PP gone) ▷倒退5年，他只是个学徒。Going back five years, he was still a trainee. ▷她被吓得倒退了几步。She was so shocked that she had to take a few steps back.

倒影 dàoyǐng [名] reflection

倒置 dàozhì [动] reverse

悼 dào [动] mourn

悼词 dàocí [名] eulogy

悼念 dàoniàn [动] mourn

盗 dào I [动] rob ▶盗窃 steal II [名] robber ▶海盗 pirate

盗版 dàobǎn I [动] pirate ▷盗版软件 pirated software II [名] pirate copy

盗匪 dàofěi [名] robber

盗汗 dàohàn [名] night sweat

盗墓 dàomù [动] rob tombs

盗窃 dàoqiè [动] steal (PT stole, PP stolen)

盗用 dàoyòng [动] misappropriate

盗贼 dàozéi [名] thieves (PL)

道 dào I [名] 1 (路) road ▶近道 shortcut 2 (方法) way ▷生财之道 the road to riches 3 (德) morals 4 (技艺) art ▷茶道 tea ceremony 5 (道教) the Tao 6 (线) (line) line ▷横道儿 horizontal line 7 (水流途径) channel ▶下水道 sewer II [量] 1 (用于长条形物体) ▷一道阳光 a beam of sunlight ▷两道泪痕 two tear streaks 2 (门、墙等) ▷第二道门 the second door ▷一道墙 a wall 3 (题目、命令) ▷三道题 three questions ▷两道命令 two orders 4 (次) ▷我还要办一道手续。I still need to complete one formality. ▷刷了两道漆 paint two coats

道别 dàobié [动] 1 (辞行) part ▷我们握手道别。We shook hands in parting. 2 (离别) say goodbye (PT, PP said) ▷临行前，他向全家道别。Before he left he said goodbye to everyone.

道德 dàodé [名] morals (PL) ▷偷东西真不道德。Stealing is so immoral.

道家 Dàojiā [名] Taoist school of thought

道教 Dàojiào [名] Taoism

道具 dàojù [名] prop

道理 dàolǐ [名] 1 (规律) principle 2 (情理) sense

道路 dàolù [名] path

道貌岸然 dàomào ànrán (贬) be sanctimonious

道歉 dàoqiàn [动] apologize ▷我向你们道歉。I apologize to you all.

道士 dàoshi [名] Taoist priest

道听途说 dào tīng tú shuō hearsay

道谢 dàoxiè [动] thank

道学 dàoxué [名] 1 (理学) Neo-Confucianism 2 (古板迂腐) old school ▷她道学气太重。She's so old-school.

道义 dàoyì [名] morality and justice

稻 dào [名] paddy

稻子 dàozi [名] rice

得 dé I [动] 1 (得到) get (PT got, PP got (英) 或 gotten (美)) ▷得奖 win a prize 2 (病) catch (PT, PP caught) ▷他得了流感。He caught flu. ▷她得了胃病。She's developed a stomach problem. 3 (计算) equal ▷四减二得二。Four minus two equals two. ▷三三得九。Three threes are nine. 4 (完成) be ready ▷晚饭得了。Dinner is ready. 5 (适合) be suitable ▶得体 appropriate II [叹] 1 (表示同意、禁止) OK ▷得，就这么决定了。OK, that's settled then. ▷得了，别再想了。That's enough. Stop thinking about it. 2 (表示无可奈何) Oh no! ▷得，我又没考及格！Oh no, I failed again! III [助动] ▷版权所有，不得转载。All rights reserved, reprinting not allowed. ▷未经许可，不得擅自播放。Not to be transmitted without permission.

→另见 de, děi

得便 débiàn [动] be convenient ▷我有个口信，请您得便转告他。I've a message – please pass it on to him when it's convenient.

得不偿失 dé bù cháng shī not be worth the effort

得逞 déchěng [动] (贬) succeed ▷他们的阴谋没能得逞。Their plot failed to succeed.

得寸进尺 dé cùn jìn chǐ be insatiably greedy

得当 dédàng [形] proper ▷这些问题处理得很得当。These issues have been dealt with properly.

得到 dédào [动] get (PT got, PP got (英) 或 gotten (美)) ▷得到表扬 win praise ▷得到奖

学金 win a scholarship ▷得到帮助 get help ▷得到一张唱片 get hold of a record ▷得到提拔 get a promotion ▷他得到了一次出国的机会。He got an opportunity to go abroad.

得法 défǎ [动] have the right technique ▷老师教学得法，学生成绩大大提高。When a teacher has the right technique, the students get much better results.

得过且过 dé guò qiě guò drift along ▷他没有责任心，得过且过。He has no sense of responsibility – he just drifts along.

得力 délì I [动] benefit from II [形] competent

得失 déshī [名] ▷他太计较个人得失。He pays too much attention to personal gain.

得势 déshì [动] (贬) be in power

得手 déshǒu I [动] succeed II [副] smoothly

得体 détǐ [形] appropriate

得天独厚 dé tiān dú hòu enjoy great natural advantages ▷香港的地理位置得天独厚。Hong Kong enjoys great natural advantages.

得心应手 dé xīn yìng shǒu be very proficient ▷有了丰富的教学经验，她教起书来得心应手。With her wealth of teaching experience, she is a very proficient teacher.

得意 déyì [形] pleased with oneself ▷他对自己的工作感到很得意。He has a high opinion of his own work.

得主 dézhǔ [名] winner

得罪 dézuì [动] offend

德 dé [名] 1 (品行) morality ▶品德 moral character ▷社会公德 public morals 2 (恩惠) kindness ▶恩德 kindness

德高望重 dé gāo wàng zhòng have integrity and a good reputation

德行 déxing [名] (贬) revolting behaviour (英) 或 behavior (美)

德育 déyù [名] ethics (SG)

地 de [助] ▷刻苦地学习 study hard ▷努力地工作 work hard ▷我们激烈地讨论了这个问题。We discussed the question heatedly. ▷委员会认真地考虑了雇员的意见。The committee took staff opinion into careful consideration. ▷学生大声地回答问题。The student answered questions loudly. ▷警察仔细地检查了小包。The police officer closely inspected the bag.
→另见 dì

的 de [助] 1 (用于定语后面的) ▷昂贵的价格 high price ▷他的哥哥 his elder brother ▷经理的秘书 the manager's secretary ▷住在那座房子里的夫妇很少出去。The couple who live in that house rarely go out. ▷你买的书真有意思。The book you bought is really interesting. ▷进行的改革有一定的效力。The reforms that were brought in had some effect. ▷我最喜欢的裙子在这儿买不到。The skirt which I like the best is not on sale here. 2 (名词化) ▷画画的 painter ▷这是你的，那是我的。This is yours and that is mine. 3 (用于是…的强调结构) ▷我的嗓子是喊哑的。I shouted myself hoarse.
→另见 dí, dì

的话 dehuà [助] ▷如果没有问题的话，会就开到这儿。If there are no questions, we can end the meeting here. ▷见到她的话，替我问好。Please give her my regards if you see her.

得 de [助] 1 (用于动词后面) ▷这种野菜吃得。This wild herb is edible. ▷这事太危险，我做不得。It's too dangerous – I shouldn't do it. 2 (动词或补语中间的) ▷她抬得动。She can carry it. ▷我写得完。I am able to finish writing it. 3 (动词和形容词后面) ▷他英语学得很快。He's learning English very quickly. ▷风大得很。The wind's very strong.
→另见 dé, děi

得 děi I [动] (口) (需要) need ▷买房得多少钱？How much money do you need to buy a house? II [助动] (口) 1 (必要) must ▷要想成功，就得艰苦奋斗。If you want to succeed, you must work hard. ▷我们6点出发。We have to leave at six. 2 (表示推测) will ▷再不听话，就得挨批评了。If you don't do as you are told, you will get a telling off. ▷快走，电影得开始了。Get a move on, the film's just about to start.
→另见 dé, de

灯 dēng [名] light ▶台灯 desk lamp ▶红绿灯 traffic lights (PL)

灯红酒绿 dēng hóng jiǔ lǜ (喻) the high life ▷这座城市是个灯红酒绿的花花世界。The city is happening and has a great nightlife.

灯火 dēnghuǒ [名] lights (PL)

灯具 dēngjù [名] lighting

灯塔 dēngtǎ [名] lighthouse

登 dēng [动] 1 (由低到高) go up (PT went, PP gone) 2 (刊登) publish 3 (踩踏板) pedal 4 (踩) get up onto 5 (裤子、鞋) put ... on (PT, PP put) ▷他登上鞋就出去了。He put his shoes on and went out.

登场 dēngchǎng [动] go on stage (PT went, PP gone)

登峰造极 dēng fēng zào jí attain the height

of perfection

登记 dēngjì [动] register

登录 dēnglù [动] log in ▷登录网站 log in to a website

登门 dēngmén [动] call by ▷明天我登门拜访你。I'll call by to see you tomorrow.

登时 dēngshí [副] immediately

登台 dēngtái [动] 1 (上场) go on stage (PT went, PP gone) ▷登台演出 perform on stage ▷登台演讲 go up to speak 2 (政治) enter politics

登载 dēngzǎi [动] publish

噔 dēng [拟] thud ▷他噔噔地跑上楼去。He thudded upstairs.

蹬 dēng [动] pedal

等 děng I [名] 1 (等级) grade ▶中等 medium ▶优等 outstanding ▷二等奖 second prize ▷一等品 first-rate goods 2 (类) kind ▷这等人 this kind of person II [动] 1 (相同) equal ▶等于 be equal to 2 (等待) wait ▷等车 wait for a bus III [连] (等到) when ▷等他来了，我们再讨论。We'll talk about it when he comes. IV [助] 1 (列举未尽的) etc. ▷他爱读诗歌、小说等等。He likes to read poems, novels, etc. 2 (煞尾的) namely ▷我喜欢足球、篮球、排球等三项运动。I enjoy three sports, namely football, basketball and volleyball.

等待 děngdài [动] wait ▷他耐心地等待时机。He patiently waited for an opportunity.

等到 děngdào [连] when

等等 děngděng [助] and so on ▷参赛国有英国、爱尔兰、法国等等。Countries taking part in the contest include Britain, Ireland, France, and so on.

等号 děnghào [名] (数) equals sign

等候 děnghòu [动] expect

等级 děngjí [名] grade

等量齐观 děng liàng qí guān equate

等式 děngshì [名] (数) equality

等同 děngtóng [动] equate

等闲 děngxián [形] (书) ordinary

等于 děngyú [动] 1 (相等于) equal 2 (等同) be equivalent to ▷保持沉默等于拒绝。To keep silent is equivalent to saying no.

凳 dèng [名] stool ▶板凳 wooden stool

澄 dèng [动] settle
→另见 chéng

澄清 dèngqīng [动] become clear (PT became, PP become)

瞪 dèng [动] 1 (表示生气) glare at 2 (睁大) open one's eyes wide

低 dī I [形] 1 (指高度、程度) low ▷房子的天花板很低。The house has a low ceiling. ▷蜻蜓飞得很低。Dragonflies fly very low. ▷水平低 low level ▷他们的工资低。Their wages are very low. ▷他喜欢低声说话。He likes to speak quietly. 2 (指等级) junior ▷她是低年级学生。She's a junior student. ▷我比她低两届。I am two years below her. II [动] (头) bend (PT, PP bent) ▷他低下了头。He bent his head.

低潮 dīcháo [名] low ebb ▷生意处于低潮。Business is at a low ebb.

低沉 dīchén [形] 1 (声音) deep ▷他声音低沉。He's got a deep voice. 2 (天空) overcast ▷低沉的夜空 an overcast night 3 (心情) ▷他情绪低沉。He's feeling a bit low.

低档 dīdàng [形] inferior

低调 dīdiào [形] low-key ▷问题处理得很低调。The problem was dealt with in a low-key way.

低谷 dīgǔ [名] doldrums (PL) ▷他的情绪陷入了低谷。He's in the doldrums.

低级 dījí [形] 1 (不高级) inferior 2 (庸俗) vulgar

低贱 dījiàn [形] humble

低廉 dīlián [形] cheap

低劣 dīliè [形] shoddy

低落 dīluò [形] depressed

低迷 dīmí [形] depressed

低能 dīnéng [名] low intelligence

低三下四 dī sān xià sì servile

低声下气 dī shēng xià qì meek

低下 dīxià [形] inferior

堤 dī [名] dyke

堤坝 dībà [名] water defences (英) 或 defenses (美) (PL)

提 dī [动] carry ▷提着行李 carry luggage
→另见 tí

提防 dīfang [动] guard against

滴 dī I [动] drip ▷汗水从脑门上往下滴。Sweat kept dripping from his forehead. ▷我给他滴了几滴眼药水。I put some eye drops in his eyes. II [名] drop ▶水滴 drop of water III [量] drop ▷几滴墨水 a few drops of ink

滴答 dīdā [拟] 1 (指水滴) drip 2 (指钟表) tick

滴水不漏 dī shuǐ bù lòu be watertight ▷她的反驳滴水不漏。Her refutation is watertight.

嘀 dī 见下文
→另见 dí
嘀嗒 dīdā [拟] 滴答

的 dí 见下文
→另见 de, dì
的确 díquè [副] really ▷这的确是事实。This really is the truth.
的士 díshì [名] taxi

迪 dí [动] (书) enlighten
迪斯科 dísīkē [名] disco

敌 dí I [名] enemy II [动] oppose III [形] equal
敌对 díduì [形] hostile
敌人 dírén [名] enemy
敌视 díshì [动] be hostile towards ▷敌视的态度 a hostile attitude
敌手 díshǒu [名] rival
敌意 díyì [名] hostility

涤 dí [动] wash

笛 dí [名] 1 (音) flute 2 (警笛) siren
笛子 dízi [名] bamboo flute

嘀 dí 见下文
→另见 dī
嘀咕 dígu [动] 1 (小声说) whisper 2 (猜疑) have misgivings ▷我对是否考及格心里直嘀咕。I have misgivings about whether I'll pass the exam.

嫡 dí [形] 1 (指血统) blood ▷嫡亲 blood relation 2 (正宗) orthodox
嫡系 díxì [名] direct line of descent

诋 dǐ [动] (书) curse
诋毁 dǐhuǐ [动] defame

底 dǐ [名] 1 (最下部分) bottom ▷湖底 the bottom of a lake 2 (内情) ▷魔术师终于露了底。The magician finally showed how the trick worked. ▷会计向我们交了底，公司只赔不赚。The accountant let us see everything – the company simply can't pay. 3 (指文件) record ▷重要文件要留底儿。Records of important documents should be kept. 4 (末尾) end ▷年底 the end of the year 5 (衬托面) background ▷白底蓝花 blue flowers on a white background
底层 dǐcéng [名] 1 (指建筑) ground floor 2 (最下部) bottom ▷没受教育的人经常留在社会底层。Those without education are often left at the bottom of heap.

底稿 dǐgǎo [名] original
底价 dǐjià [名] reserve price
底牌 dǐpái [名] hand ▷谈判对手最后亮了底牌。The other side's negotiator came clean at last.
底气 dǐqì [名] lung power
底细 dǐxì [名] ▷我没摸清他的底细。I don't get where he's coming from. ▷事情的底细她没了解。She hasn't understood how the situation came about.
底子 dǐzi [名] 1 (最下部分) ▷我的鞋底子破了。I have a hole in the sole of my shoe. ▷她化妆底子颜色不好看。Her foundation is the wrong colour. 2 (内情) inside information 3 (基础) foundation ▷他的数学底子好。He has a good grounding in maths (英) 或 math (美). 4 (草稿) draft ▷画设计图前要打底子。Before you draw a design you must make a draft. 5 (衬托面) background

抵 dǐ [动] 1 (支撑) support 2 (抵抗) resist 3 (补偿) compensate for 4 (抵押) mortgage 5 (抵消) offset 6 (代替) be equal to
抵偿 dǐcháng [动] make good ▷我来抵偿损失。I'll make good the loss. ▷他们用实物抵偿欠款。They paid off their debt.
抵触 dǐchù [动] clash ▷他们的意见相抵触。They have a difference of opinion. ▷他与我在定期考核问题上抵触。We clashed on the question of regular assessment.
抵达 dǐdá [动] reach
抵挡 dǐdǎng [动] withstand (PT, PP withstood)
抵抗 dǐkàng [动] resist ▷我们应该坚持锻炼以增强对疾病的抵抗力。We should take exercise to build up resistance to disease.
抵赖 dǐlài [动] deny
抵消 dǐxiāo [动] ▷他的勤奋抵消了经验不足。His industriousness is enough to compensate for his inexperience. ▷正、负数抵消。Positive and negative numbers cancel each other out.
抵押 dǐyā [动] mortgage
抵御 dǐyù [动] resist
抵制 dǐzhì [动] resist
抵罪 dǐzuì [动] be punished for a crime

地 dì [名] 1 (地球) the Earth ▷地心 the Earth's core 2 (陆地) land ▶地下水 ground water 3 (土地) fields (PL) ▷农民们正在地里干活。The peasants are working in the fields. 4 (地点) location ▶目的地 destination 5 (路程) ▷车刚开了3英里就抛锚了。The car had only gone three miles when it broke down. ▷他家离城有5公里地。His home is five kilometres from the

town. ▷从家到学校坐4站地。There are four
stops between home and school. **6** (衬托面)
background ▷白地儿红字 red characters on a
white background
➔另见 de

地步 dìbù [名] **1** (处境) ▷你怎么到了这个地步
了？How did you get into such a state? ▷他
竟落到沿街乞讨的地步。He was eventually
reduced to begging in the street. **2** (程度)
extent ▷她紧张到晕倒的地步。She was so
nervous that she passed out.

地产 dìchǎn [名] property (英), real estate (美)

地大物博 dì dà wù bó a vast territory with
rich resources

地带 dìdài [名] zone

地道 dìdào [名] tunnel

地道 dìdao [形] **1** (真正) genuine ▷一颗地道
的珍珠 a genuine pearl **2** (纯正) pure ▷他
的汉语说得真地道。His Chinese is very
idiomatic. **3** (指质量) well done ▷这项工作
干得真地道！The work has been really well
done.

地点 dìdiǎn [名] location

地段 dìduàn [名] area

地方 dìfāng [名] locality ▷地方政府 local
government ▷地方方言 local accent

地方 dìfang [名] **1** (区域) place ▷这个地方真
美。This place is beautiful. ▷你是哪个地方的
人？Where do you come from? **2** (空间) room
▷车里没地方了。There is no room in the
car. **3** (身体部位) ▷我这个地方酸痛。I ache
here. **4** (部分) part ▷有不明白的地方吗？Are
there any parts that are not clear?

地理 dìlǐ [名] geography ▷地理位置
geographical location

地利 dìlì [名] favourable geography

地面 dìmiàn [名] **1** (地表) the Earth's
surface **2** (指房屋) floor

地盘 dìpán [名] territory

地皮 dìpí [名] building land

地平线 dìpíngxiàn [名] horizon ▷地平线上有
一条船。There is a ship on the horizon.

地球 dìqiú [名] the Earth

地球村 dìqiúcūn [名] global village

地球仪 dìqiúyí [名] globe

地区 dìqū [名] area ▷北京地区普降大雨。The
whole Beijing area gets a lot of rain. ▷贫困地
区 poor area

地势 dìshì [名] topography

地摊 dìtān [名] stall

地毯 dìtǎn [名] carpet

地铁 dìtiě [名] **1** (地下铁道) underground (英),
subway (美) **2** (列车) underground (英) 或
subway (美) train ▷他每天坐地铁上班。
Every day he takes the underground (英) 或
subway (美) to work.

地图 dìtú [名] map

地位 dìwèi [名] position ▷学术地位 academic
position ▷国际地位 international standing
▷平等的地位 equal status ▷历史地位 place
in history

地下 dìxià [名] underground ▷地下管道
underground pipe ▷非法地下组织 an illegal
underground organization

地下室 dìxiàshì [名] basement

地形 dìxíng [名] topography

地狱 dìyù [名] hell ▷孩子过着地狱般的生活。
This child has had a hellish life.

地域 dìyù [名] **1** (领土) territory **2** (本土) locality

地震 dìzhèn [名] earthquake ▷新疆地震了。
There has been an earthquake in Xinjiang.

地址 dìzhǐ [名] address ▷通信地址 postal
address ▷家庭地址 home address ▷办公地址
business address ▷请留下您的地址。Please
leave your address.

地址簿 dìzhǐbù [名] address book

地质 dìzhì [名] geology

地质学 dìzhìxué [名] geology

地主 dìzhǔ [名] landlord

弟 dì [名] younger brother ▶表弟 cousin

弟兄 dìxiong [名] brothers (PL)

弟子 dìzǐ [名] disciple

的 dì [名] target ▶目的 goal
➔另见 de, dí

帝 dì [名] **1** (神) God **2** (君主) emperor **3** (帝国主
义) imperialism

帝国 dìguó [名] empire

帝国主义 dìguó zhǔyì [名] imperialism

帝王 dìwáng [名] emperor

递 dì **I** [动] (传送) pass ▷请把碗递给她。
Please would you pass her the bowl. ▷能给
她递个口信吗？Could you pass on a message
to her? ▷他给我递了一个眼色。He gave me a
meaningful look. **II** [副] (顺次) in succession
▶递增 progressively increase

递补 dìbǔ [动] substitute ▷甲队员由乙队员递
补。Player A was substituted by player B.

递交 dìjiāo [动] hand over

递进 dìjìn [动] progress ▷分层递进的教育方
法 a teaching method that progresses in stages

递送 dìsòng [动] deliver ▷递送邮包 deliver

parcels

第 dì [名] ▷第二次世界大战 the Second World War ▷得第一名 come first ▷第二职业 second job ▷第三产业 tertiary industry ▷第三世界 the Third World

第六感觉 dìliù gǎnjué [名] sixth sense

第三者 dìsānzhě [名] (破坏感情者) ▷因为第三者插足，他们分手了。They split up because of an affair.

第一夫人 dìyī fūrén [名] First Lady

第一手 dìyīshǒu [形] first-hand

蒂 dì [名] base

缔 dì [动] establish

缔交 dìjiāo [动] establish diplomatic relations

缔结 dìjié [动] conclude

缔约 dìyuē [动] conclude a treaty

缔造 dìzào [动] found

掂 diān [动] weigh in one's hand

掂量 diānliáng [动] 1 (字) weigh in one's hand ▷他掂量了一下邮件的重量。He weighed the mail in his hand. 2 (喻) (斟酌) consider ▷他仔细掂量了经理的话。He considered the manager's words carefully.

颠 diān [动] 1 (颠簸) jolt 2 (跌落) fall (PT fell, PP fallen)

颠簸 diānbǒ [动] toss

颠倒 diāndǎo [动] ▷这张照片上下颠倒了。The photo is upside down. ▷请把拖把颠倒过来放。Please could you put the mop the other way up.

颠覆 diānfù [动] overturn

颠扑不破 diān pū bù pò irrefutable

颠三倒四 diān sān dǎo sì incoherent ▷他说话颠三倒四的。He talks incoherently. ▷他做事颠三倒四的。When he tries to do something he always gets in a muddle.

巅 diān [名] summit

巅峰 diānfēng [名] summit

癫 diān [形] insane

癫痫 diānxián [名] epilepsy

典 diǎn I [名] 1 (标准) standard 2 (书籍) standard work ▷词典 dictionary 3 (典故) allusion 4 (礼仪) ceremony II [动] pawn

典当 diǎndàng [动] ▷她典当房子以获得10万英镑贷款。She got a mortgage of £100,000 on her house.

典范 diǎnfàn [名] model

典故 diǎngù [名] allusion

典礼 diǎnlǐ [名] ceremony ▷毕业典礼 graduation ceremony ▷开幕典礼 opening ceremony ▷闭幕典礼 closing ceremony ▷结婚典礼 wedding ceremony

典型 diǎnxíng I [名] model II [形] (代表性) representative ▷典型案例 a representative case ▷典型文学作品 typical works of literature

典雅 diǎnyǎ [形] elegant

点 diǎn I [名] 1 (时间单位) o'clock ▷他早上8点上课。He starts class at eight o'clock in the morning. 2 (钟点) ▷到点了，该开会了。It's time for the meeting. 3 (小滴液体) drop ▷雨点 raindrops 4 (痕迹) stain ▷油点儿 oil stain 5 (指字、画) dot 6 (指几何) point ▷两点之间，直线最短。Between two points, a straight line is the shortest. 7 (小数点) decimal point ▷五点六 five point six (5.6) 8 (标志) point ▷终点 end point ▷沸点 boiling point ▷(方面) point ▷优点 strong point ▷重点 focal point ▷从这点看，他是对的。From this point of view he is right. ▷我对这点毫不怀疑。I have no doubts about that. II [动] 1 (画点) make a dot 2 (头) nod ▷点头 nod one's head 3 (药水等) ▷点眼药 apply eye drops 4 (查对) check ▷点名 call the register 5 (指定) select ▷点菜 order food 6 (灯、火、烟等) light (PT, PP lit) ▷点烟 light a cigarette 7 (点缀) decorate ▷客厅里点缀着彩灯。The sitting room is decorated with coloured lights. 8 (启发) hint ▷老师一点他就明白了。He quickly took the teacher's hint. III [量] 1 (少量) a little ▷有一点儿问题。There is a bit of a problem. ▷她会说一点日语。She can speak a little Japanese. ▷请给我一点糖。Could you give me some sugar? 2 (事项) item ▷议事日程上有6点。There are six items on the agenda. ▷领导的讲话主要有3点。There are three main points in the leader's speech. ▷我们有4点建议。We have four recommendations.

点拨 diǎnbo [动] instruct

点滴 diǎndī [名] bit ▷丰富的知识是点点滴滴积累成的。In-depth knowledge is accumulated bit by bit.

点击 diǎnjī [动] click

点题 diǎntí [动] set the theme (PT, PP set) ▷这段的第一句点了题。The first sentence of this section sets the theme.

点头 diǎntóu [动] nod

点头哈腰 diǎntóu-hāyāo bow and scrape

点心 diǎnxin [名] snack

点缀 diǎnzhuì [动] decorate

点子 diǎnzi [名] 1 (关键部分) key point 2 (主意) idea

碘 diǎn [名] iodine

踮 diǎn [动] stand on tiptoe (PT, PP stood)

电 diàn I [名] 1 (能源) electricity ▶电能 electric power ▶发电站 electric power station ▷停电了。There's been a power cut. 2 (电报) telegram ▷发急电 send an urgent telegram II [动] 1 (触电) get an electric shock ▷发(电报) send a telegram (PT, PP sent) ▶电贺 congratulate by telegram

电报 diànbào [名] telegram

电波 diànbō [名] electro-magnetic wave

电池 diànchí [名] battery

电动 diàndòng [形] electric ▷电动玩具 electric toy

电荷 diànhè [名] electric charge

电话 diànhuà [名] 1 (电话机) telephone ▷办公室的电话占线(英) 或 busy(美). ▷别挂电话！ Don't hang up! 2 (打、接、回) call ▷我接到了妈妈的长途电话。I received a long-distance call from Mum. ▷上午有你的两个电话。This morning there were two calls for you.

电话号码 diànhuà hàomǎ [名] phone number

电力 diànlì [名] electricity ▷电力供应 electricity supply

电流 diànliú [名] electric current

电路 diànlù [名] electric circuit

电脑 diànnǎo [名] computer ▷台式电脑 desktop computer ▷手提电脑 laptop ▷电脑病毒 computer virus ▷他电脑专业毕业。He graduated in computing. ▷我在上电脑课。I'm taking a computer class.

电器 diànqì [名] electrical appliance ▷家用电器 home appliance

电视 diànshì [名] television, TV ▷彩色电视 colour(英) 或 color(美) television ▷卫星电视 satellite television ▷看电视 watch television ▷开电视 turn on the television ▷关电视 turn off the television

电台 diàntái [名] station

电信 diànxìn [名] telecommunications (PL)

电压 diànyā [名] voltage

电影 diànyǐng [名] film (英), movie (美)

电影院 diànyǐngyuàn [名] cinema

电源 diànyuán [名] power supply

电子 diànzǐ [名] electron ▷电子表 digital watch ▷电子游戏 electronic game ▷电子琴 electronic piano ▷电子音乐 electronic music

电子商务 diànzǐ shāngwù [名] e-commerce

电子图书 diànzǐ túshū [名] e-book

电子邮件 diànzǐ yóujiàn [名] e-mail ▷发电子邮件 send an e-mail

电阻 diànzǔ [名] resistance

店 diàn [名] 1 (商店) shop (英), store (美) 2 (旅店) hotel

店铺 diànpù [名] shop (英), store (美)

玷 diàn 见下文

玷污 diànwū [动] tarnish

垫 diàn I [名] cushion ▶椅垫 chair cushion ▶鞋垫 insole II [动] 1 (铺) insert ▷她在桌子腿下垫了点纸。She inserted a bit of paper under the table leg. 2 (付钱) pay (PT, PP paid) ▷书钱我先替你垫上。For now I'll pay for the book for you. 3 (填补) ▷吃点小菜，先垫垫肚子。Have a snack – it'll take the edge off.

淀 diàn 见下文

淀粉 diànfěn [名] starch

惦 diàn 见下文

惦记 diànjì [动] think about (PT, PP thought) ▷她老惦记着这些老人。She's always thinking about these old people.

惦念 diànniàn [动] worry about

奠 diàn [动] establish

奠定 diàndìng [动] establish

奠基 diànjī [动] lay a foundation (PT, PP laid) ▷奠基石 cornerstone

殿 diàn [名] palace ▶宫殿 palace

殿军 diànjūn [名] ▷他是殿军。He won the wooden spoon.

殿堂 diàntáng [名] hall

殿下 diànxià [名] (敬) Your Majesty

靛 diàn [名] indigo

靛蓝 diànlán [名] indigo

刁 diāo [形] 1 (狡猾) cunning 2 (方) (挑食的) fussy ▷孩子嘴真刁。The child is a really fussy eater.

刁难 diāonàn [动] make things difficult ▷他这是故意刁难我们。He is intentionally making things difficult for us.

刁钻 diāozuān [形] cunning

叼 diāo [动] have ... in one's mouth

凋 diāo [动] wither ▶凋零 wither ▷松柏常绿不凋。Pine trees are evergreen.

凋零 diāolíng [动] wither

凋谢 diāoxiè [动] wither

雕 diāo I [动] carve II [名] 1 (指艺术) sculpture ▶石雕 stone sculpture ▶浮雕 relief 2 (鸟) vulture

雕虫小技 diāo chóng xiǎo jì lesser talent

雕刻 diāokè I [动] carve II [名] carving

雕塑 diāosù [名] sculpture

雕琢 diāozhuó [动] 1 (雕刻) carve ▷用玉石雕琢成的荷花 a lotus flower carved in jade 2 (修饰) ▷这位作家爱过分雕琢文字。This writer writes in an overly ornate style.

吊 diào [动] 1 (悬挂) hang (PT, PP hung) ▷门前吊着一盏灯。A lamp is hanging at the doorway. 2 (提) hoist ... up 3 (收回) revoke ▷吊销执照 revoke a licence (英) 或 license (美) 4 (轻打) drop ▷他轻轻一吊,球过网了。He lightly dropped the ball over the net.

吊儿郎当 diào'erlángdāng fool around

吊胃口 diào wèikǒu [动] whet sb's appetite ▷这味道真吊胃口。The smell is really whetting my appetite.

吊销 diàoxiāo [动] revoke

吊唁 diàoyàn [动] express one's condolences

钓 diào [动] fish ▶钓鱼 go fishing ▷钓名利 fish for a compliment

钓饵 diào'ěr [名] bait

钓具 diàojù [名] fishing tackle

调 diào I [动] transfer ▷他被调到我们单位了。He was transferred to our unit. II [名] 1 (口音) accent ▷他说话有四川调。He has a Sichuan accent. 2 (曲调) melody ▷他唱走调了。He sings out of tune. ▷我不喜欢这个调。I don't like the melody. 3 (音) key ▷B调奏鸣曲 a sonata in the key of B 4 (声调) pitch →另见 tiáo

调兵遣将 diào bīng qiǎn jiàng deploy troops

调拨 diàobō [动] send (PT, PP sent)

调查 diàochá [动] investigate ▷这件事情一定要调查清楚。This matter must certainly be investigated and clarified.

调动 diàodòng [动] 1 (工作) transfer 2 (部队) deploy 3 (积极性) mobilize

调度 diàodù I [动] 1 (车辆) control 2 (生产、工作、人力) manage II [名] controller

调虎离山 diào hǔ lí shān entice ... out

调换 diàohuàn [动] swap

调门儿 diàoménr [名] 1 (声音) pitch ▷调门儿别太高了,我唱不上去。Don't pitch it too high. I won't be able to sing it. ▷她说话调门儿真高。She has a very high-pitched voice. 2 (论调) line ▷几篇评论文章的调门儿一样。A number of reviews took the same line.

调配 diàopèi [动] deploy

调遣 diàoqiǎn [动] assign ▷我会听从组织的调遣。I'll accept the organization's assignment.

调子 diàozi [名] 1 (音) melody 2 (喻) tone ▷他的话语中带着悲观的调子。There is a pessimistic tone to what he is saying.

掉 diào [动] 1 (落下) fall (PT fell, PP fallen) ▷树叶纷纷从树上掉下来。The leaves are gradually falling from the trees. 2 (落后) fall behind (PT fell, PP fallen) 3 (遗失) lose (PT, PP lost) ▷我的上衣掉了一个扣子。I've lost a button off my shirt. 4 (减少) reduce 5 (转回) turn ... round ▷把车头掉过来 turn the car round 6 (互换) swap ▷我们掉一下座位好吗? Let's swap seats, OK?

掉换 diàohuàn [动] swap

掉价 diàojià [动] 1 (指价格) come down in price (PT came, PP come) 2 (指身份) lose social status (PT, PP lost)

掉以轻心 diào yǐ qīng xīn treat ... lightly ▷对安全问题千万不能掉以轻心。Safety issues should never be treated lightly.

爹 diē [名] (方) dad

跌 diē [动] fall down (PT fell, PP fallen)

跌宕 diēdàng [形] (书) twisting and turning

跌跌撞撞 diēdiezhuàngzhuàng staggering ▷他喝醉了,走路跌跌撞撞的。He's drunk and is staggering.

跌落 diēluò [动] (价格、产量) fall (PT fell, PP fallen) ▷最近物价有些跌落。Recently prices have fallen somewhat.

迭 dié I [动] alternate II [副] again and again ▷这种错误迭有发生。This sort of mistake is happening again and again.

迭起 diéqǐ [动] occur frequently

谍 dié [名] 1 (谍报) espionage 2 (间谍) spy

谍报 diébào [名] intelligence report

喋 dié 见下文

喋喋不休 diédié bù xiū witter on ▷他喋喋不休地谈着对未来的设想。He witters on and on about his plans for the future.

牒 dié [名] official document ▷最后通牒 ultimatum

叠 dié [动] 1 (一层加一层) pile ... up 2 (信、纸、衣、被) fold
叠床架屋 dié chuáng jià wū duplication ▷写文章切忌叠床架屋。When you write an essay you should avoid repeating yourself.

碟 dié 见下文
碟子 diézi [名] small plate

蝶 dié [名] butterfly

丁 dīng [名] 1 (成年男子) man (PL men) 2 (人口) population 3 (小块) cube ▷肉丁 diced meat
丁当 dīngdāng [拟] 1 (瓷器、玉器) chink 2 (铃铛) tinkle 3 (指没钱) ▷他穷得丁当响。He's penniless.
丁零 dīnglíng [拟] tinkle

叮 dīng [动] 1 (蚊虫) bite (PT bit, PP bitten) 2 (叮嘱) warn
叮嘱 dīngzhǔ [动] warn ▷妈妈叮嘱我注意交通安全。Mother keeps warning me about watching the traffic.

盯 dīng [动] stare at
盯梢 dīngshāo [动] tail

钉 dīng I [名] nail II [动] 1 (紧跟) follow ... closely 2 (督促) put pressure on (PT, PP put) ▷妈妈钉着他写作业。Mother is putting pressure on him to do his homework.
→另见 dìng

顶 dǐng I [名] 1 (最高部分) top ▷头顶 top of one's head ▷山顶 mountain top II [动] 1 (指用头) carry ... on one's head ▷她头顶一个水罐。She is carrying a water pot on her head. 2 (拱起) lift ... up ▷我们把汽车顶了起来。We lifted the car up. ▷小猫把土顶起来了。The kitten is pushing the earth up. 3 (支撑) prop ... up 4 (撞) butt 5 (迎着) face ▷他们顶着烈日在训练。They do their training facing the sun. 6 (顶撞) be rude to 7 (承担) undertake (PT undertook, PP undertaken) 8 (相当) ▷他干活一个人能顶两个。He can do as much work as two people. 9 顶替 take the place of (PT took, PP taken) III [量] ▷一顶帽子 a hat ▷一顶蚊帐 a mosquito net IV [副] extremely ▷顶好 extremely good
顶点 dǐngdiǎn [名] 1 (最高点) top ▷我们爬到了山的顶点。We reached the top of the mountain. 2 (数) node

顶峰 dǐngfēng [名] summit
顶呱呱 dǐngguāguā [形] first-rate
顶礼膜拜 dǐnglǐ móbài (贬) worship
顶牛儿 dǐngniúr [动] be at loggerheads with
顶替 dǐngtì [动] 1 (替代) take the place of (PT took, PP taken) ▷他走了，谁来顶替他的岗位？After he's gone, who will take his place? 2 (冒名) pose as
顶天立地 dǐng tiān lì dì dauntless
顶头上司 dǐngtóu shàngsi direct superior
顶用 dǐngyòng [动] do the trick
顶嘴 dǐngzuǐ [动] answer back

鼎 dǐng I [名] tripod II [形] (书) (大) substantial
鼎鼎大名 dǐngdǐng dàmíng renowned
鼎沸 dǐngfèi [形] (书) tumultuous
鼎力 dǐnglì (书) make a great effort
鼎盛 dǐngshèng [形] flourishing

订 dìng [动] 1 (确立) draw ... up (PT drew, PP drawn) ▷我们必须订生产指标。We must draw up production targets. 2 (预订) order ▶订报 subscribe to a newspaper 3 (校正) revise 4 (装订) fasten ... together
订单 dìngdān [名] order form
订购 dìnggòu [动] order
订婚 dìnghūn [动] get engaged
订货 dìnghuò [动] order goods
订交 dìngjiāo [动] establish relations
订金 dìngjīn [名] deposit
订立 dìnglì [动] establish
订正 dìngzhèng [动] correct

钉 dìng [动] 1 (固定) nail 2 (缝) sew ... on (PT sewed, PP sewn)
→另见 dīng

定 dìng I [形] 1 (平静) calm ▷她好像心神不定。She doesn't seem to be in a calm state of mind. 2 (不变的) settled ▷定论 final conclusion 3 (规定的) fixed ▷定义 definition II [动] 1 (决定) decide ▷我们必须尽快定计划。We must quickly decide on a plan. 2 (固定) settle ▷他们打算定居杭州。They plan to settle in Hangzhou. 3 (预定) order ▷定报 subscribe to a newspaper ▷他定了一批货。He ordered some goods. ▷我们订了音乐会的票。We booked tickets for the concert. III [副] definitely ▷我们的事业定会成功。Our project will definitely succeed.
定案 dìng'àn [动] reach a verdict
定夺 dìngduó [动] make a final decision
定额 dìng'é I [名] quota II [动] set a quota

定稿 dìnggǎo [动] finalize a manuscript

定购 dìnggòu [动] order

定婚 dìnghūn [动] get engaged

定货 dìnghuò [动] order goods

定价 dìngjià [动] set a price (PT, PP set)

定金 dìngjīn [名] deposit

定居 dìngjū [动] settle ▷他们准备定居国外。 They are planning to settle abroad.

定局 dìngjú I [名] foregone conclusion II [动] make a final decision

定理 dìnglǐ [名] theorem

定量 dìngliàng I [动] 1 (规定数量) ration 2 (测定含量) quantify ▷我们对药物要进行定量分析。We need to do some quantitative analysis of the drugs. II [名] ration

定律 dìnglǜ [名] law

定论 dìnglùn [名] conclusion

定期 dìngqī I [动] set a date (PT, PP set) II [形] fixed

定情 dìngqíng [动] pledge one's love

定位 dìngwèi I [动] appraise II [名] position ▷我们必须找到这颗行星的定位。We must establish the exact position of the planet.

定型 dìngxíng [动] finalize a design

定性 dìngxìng [动] determine ▷我们对他的过失必须定性。We must determine what his error is.

定义 dìngyì [名] definition

定语 dìngyǔ [名] attribute

定罪 dìngzuì [动] convict

丢 diū [动] 1 (遗失) lose (PT, PP lost) 2 (扔掉) throw away (PT threw, PP thrown) 3 (投) toss ▷他丢给乞丐一便士。He tossed the beggar a penny. 4 (搁置) I can't let go of it. ▷这件事我丢不开。I've not used my Japanese for years and have now forgotten it all. 5 (留下) leave ... behind (PT, PP left) ▷我的日语丢了好多年，都忘光了。

丢丑 diūchǒu [动] lose face (PT, PP lost)

丢盔卸甲 diū kuī xiè jiǎ make a run for it

丢脸 diūliǎn [动] lose face (PT, PP lost)

丢人 diūrén [动] lose face (PT, PP lost)

丢三落四 diū sān là sì scatterbrained

丢卒保车 diū zú bǎo jū lose a pawn to save a castle

东 dōng [名] 1 (方向) east ▶东南亚 Southeast Asia ▶东风 east wind ▷中国东临太平洋。China borders on the Pacific Ocean to the east. 2 (主人) owner ▶房东 landlord ▶股东 shareholder 3 (东道主) host

东半球 dōngbànqiú [名] eastern hemisphere

东道 dōngdào [名] host

东道国 dōngdàoguó [名] host nation

东拉西扯 dōng lā xī chě rambling ▷你不要再东拉西扯了，快说正经事。Stop rambling and get to the point.

东跑西颠 dōng pǎo xī diān rush around

东拼西凑 dōng pīn xī còu scrimp and save ▷他就这样东拼西凑，硬把学费交上了。This is how he scrimped and saved, and managed to pay for the school fees.

东山再起 Dōng shān zài qǐ make a comeback

东西 dōngxī [名] east and west

东西 dōngxi [名] 1 (物品) thing ▷你把东西放在这儿吧。Why don't you leave your things here. ▷今天他买了不少东西。He did quite a bit of shopping today. 2 (家伙) ▷他这个小东西，真滑头！He's a slippery character! 3 (与'什么'一词连用) ▷我什么东西也看不见。I can't see anything. ▷他在大学里没学到什么东西。He didn't learn anything at university.

东…西… dōng … xī … ▷东倒西歪 walk unsteadily ▷他说话是东一句，西一句。He talks incoherently.

东张西望 dōng zhāng xī wàng look in all directions ▷他东张西望，也没找到出租车。He looked in all directions, but couldn't find a taxi. ▷考试时，不许东张西望。During exams it is not permitted to look around.

冬 dōng I [名] winter II [拟] knock

冬眠 dōngmián [动] hibernate

冬天 dōngtiān [名] winter

冬至 dōngzhì [名] winter solstice

董 dǒng [名] director

董事 dǒngshì [名] director

董事会 dǒngshìhuì [名] 1 (指企业) board of directors 2 (指学校) board of trustees

懂 dǒng [动] understand (PT, PP understood)

懂行 dǒngháng [动] (方) know the ropes (PT knew, PP known)

栋 dòng I [名] (书) ridgepole II [量] ▷一栋楼 a building

动 dòng [动] 1 (指改变位置) move ▷不要动我的书。Don't move my books. ▷不许动！Freeze! 2 (行动) act 3 (用作补) ▷我提不动这个大箱子。I can't lift this case. ▷她太累了，走不动。She's too tired – she can't go on. ▷他能举得动100公斤的杠铃。He can lift barbells weighing 100 kilograms. **4** (使用) use ▷我们得动脑筋，想个办法。We must use our brains and think of a way. **5** (触动) affect **6** (感动) move ▷这首歌很动人。This song is very moving.

动产 **dòngchǎn** [名] movable property

动词 **dòngcí** [名] verb

动荡 **dòngdàng** [形] unstable

动工 **dònggōng** [动] begin construction (PT began, PP begun)

动机 **dòngjī** [名] motive

动静 **dòngjìng** [名] **1** (声音) sound **2** (情况) movement ▷敌军没有什么动静。There's no activity among the enemy troops.

动力 **dònglì** [名] **1** (指机械) power **2** (力量) strength

动乱 **dòngluàn** [名] unrest

动脉 **dòngmài** [名] artery

动情 **dòngqíng** [动] **1** (激动) be moving **2** (爱上) fall for (PT fell, PP fallen)

动人 **dòngrén** [形] moving ▷动人的故事 moving story

动身 **dòngshēn** [动] begin (PT began, PP begun)

动手 **dòngshǒu** [动] **1** (开始做) get to work **2** (用手摸) touch ▷只许看，不许动手。You can look, but don't touch. **3** (打人) strike a blow (PT, PP struck) ▷到底是谁先动手的？So who struck the first blow?

动态 **dòngtài** [名] developments (PL)

动弹 **dòngtan** [动] move ▷我的腿麻了，动弹不了。My leg has gone to sleep. I can't move it.

动听 **dòngtīng** [形] ▷动听的音乐 beautiful music ▷动听的故事 interesting story

动武 **dòngwǔ** [动] use military force

动物 **dòngwù** [名] animal

动物园 **dòngwùyuán** [名] zoo

动向 **dòngxiàng** [名] trend

动心 **dòngxīn** [动] be affected

动摇 **dòngyáo** [动] shake (PT shook, PP shaken)

动议 **dòngyì** [名] motion

动用 **dòngyòng** [动] use

动员 **dòngyuán** [动] mobilize

动辄 **dòngzhé** [副] (书) readily ▷他动辄发火。He gets angry very readily.

动辄得咎 **dòng zhé dé jiù** be blamed no matter what one does

动作 **dòngzuò** I [名] movement II [动] make a move

冻 **dòng** I [动] freeze (PT froze, PP frozen) II [名] jelly

冻结 **dòngjié** [动] freeze (PT froze, PP frozen) ▷他的全部资产已被冻结。All his assets have been frozen.

洞 **dòng** I [名] **1** (孔) hole **2** (穴) cave II [副] thoroughly

洞察 **dòngchá** [动] see clearly (PT saw, PP seen)

洞房 **dòngfáng** [名] bridal suite

洞悉 **dòngxī** [动] understand ... clearly (PT, PP understood)

洞穴 **dòngxué** [名] cave

都 **dōu** [副] **1** (全部) all ▷全体成员都参加了会议。All the members attended the meeting. **2** (表示理由) all ▷都是他才酿成了车祸。The car crash was all his fault. **3** (甚至) even ▷老师待他比亲生父母都好。The teacher treated him even better than his parents. **4** (已经) already ▷都到寒冬了，他衣服还穿得很少。It's mid-winter already, but he's still lightly dressed.
→另见 dū

兜 **dōu** I [名] **1** (衣袋) pocket ▶裤兜 trouser pocket **2** (拎兜) bag ▶网兜 string bag II [动] **1** (绕) ▷她说话爱兜圈子。She tends to skirt around the subject. **2** (招揽) canvass **3** (承担) take responsibility (PT took, PP taken) ▷这样做要是有差错，我兜着。If we do it this way and it's a mistake, I will take responsibility for it.

兜底 **dōudǐ** [动] expose ▷市长的风流韵事被兜了底。The mayor's illicit affair was exposed.

兜风 **dōufēng** [动] **1** (挡风) catch the wind (PT, PP caught) **2** (游逛) go for a spin (PT went, PP gone)

兜揽 **dōulǎn** [动] **1** (招揽) drum ... up ▷小贩在街头兜揽生意。The vendor drummed up business on the street corner. **2** (包揽) take ... on (PT took, PP taken) ▷我绝不随便兜揽这事。There's no way I'm taking this on like this.

兜圈子 **dōuquānzi** [动] **1** (盘旋) circle **2** (喻) (拐弯抹角) beat about the bush (PT beat, PP beaten)

兜售 **dōushòu** [动] flog

斗 **dǒu** I [名] **1** (指容器) cup **2** (斗状物) ▶烟斗 pipe ▶漏斗 funnel **3** (北斗星) the Plough (英), the Big Dipper (美) II [量] measurement of capacity, equal to 10 litres
→另见 dòu

斗胆 **dǒudǎn** [副] (用于自谦) boldly ▷容我斗胆评论一下你的工作。May I be so bold as to pass comment on your work?

抖 dǒu [动] 1 (颤抖) shiver 2 (甩动) shake (PT shook, PP shaken) ▷她把外套在门口抖了抖。She gave her coat a good shake in the doorway. 3 (倒出) bring ... to light (PT, PP brought) ▷首相受贿的丑闻被媒体给抖了出来。The media brought to light the scandal of the prime minister taking bribes. 4 (振作) gear...up ▷队员们抖起精神迎接下一场比赛。The players geared themselves up in preparation for the next match. 5 (贬) (得意) throw one's weight about (PT threw, PP thrown) ▷他发财后抖得不得了。After he'd made his fortune, he threw his weight about like you wouldn't believe.

抖动 dǒudòng [动] 1 (振动) shake (PT shook, PP shaken) 2 (颤动) tremble

抖擞 dǒusǒu [动] rouse ▷战士们精神抖擞地开往前线。The soldiers made their way to the front line with spirits roused.

陡 dǒu I [形] steep II [副] suddenly

陡峻 dǒujùn [形] precipitous

陡峭 dǒuqiào [形] steep ▷陡峭的悬崖 steep cliff

陡然 dǒurán [副] suddenly ▷总统竞选陡然升温。The presidential election is suddenly hotting up.

斗 dòu [动] 1 (打斗) fight (PT, PP fought) ▷斗鸡 cock fighting 2 (战胜) beat (PT beat, PP beaten) →另见 dǒu

斗殴 dòu'ōu [动] fight (PT, PP fought)

斗气 dòuqì [动] nurse a grudge ▷他正在和女朋友斗气。He's nursing a grudge against his girlfriend.

斗争 dòuzhēng [动] 1 (努力战胜) struggle ▷阶级斗争 class struggle 2 (打击) combat 3 (奋斗) fight for (PT, PP fought)

斗志 dòuzhì [名] will to fight

斗嘴 dòuzuǐ [动] 1 (吵架) quarrel 2 (耍嘴皮子) exchange banter

豆 dòu [名] bean

豆蔻年华 dòukòu niánhuá teenage

豆子 dòuzi [名] 1 (豆类作物) bean 2 (豆状物) bead

逗 dòu I [动] 1 (引逗) tease 2 (招引) attract 3 (逗留) stay II [形] amusing

逗号 dòuhào [名] comma

逗留 dòuliú [动] stay ▷她在巴黎逗留了3天。She stayed in Paris for three days.

逗趣儿 dòuqùr [动] amuse ▷她是个爱逗趣儿的人。She loves to make people laugh.

痘 dòu [名] 1 (痘苗) vaccine ▷种痘 vaccinate 2 (天花) smallpox

窦 dòu [名] 1 (洞) hole ▷疑窦 doubtful point 2 (医) (指器官) sinus ▷鼻窦 sinuses

都 dū [名] 1 (首都) capital 2 (大城市) major city ▷景德镇有瓷都之称。Jingdezhen is known as the porcelain city. →另见 dōu

都市 dūshì [名] metropolis ▷都市的夜生活丰富多彩。The city's nightlife is rich and varied.

嘟 dū I [拟] honk II [动] (方) pout ▷他嘟着嘴，在一旁生气。He pouted in annoyance.

嘟囔 dūnang [动] mumble ▷他一边嘟囔着一边走了出去。He mumbled to himself as he walked out.

督 dū [动] supervise

督察 dūchá I [动] supervise II [名] supervisor

督促 dūcù [动] watch over

毒 dú I [名] poison II [形] 1 (有毒) poisonous 2 (毒辣) malicious III [动] poison

毒害 dúhài [动] poison

毒辣 dúlà [形] malicious

毒品 dúpǐn [名] drug

毒手 dúshǒu [名] treachery

独 dú I [形] only ▷他是家里的独子。He's the only son in the family. II [副] 1 (独自) alone ▷他现在独居。He lives alone. 2 (惟独) only ▷会议独缺山姆一人。Only Sam was missing from the meeting. III [名] old people without children

独霸 dúbà [动] dominate

独白 dúbái [名] soliloquy

独步 dúbù [动] 1 (无敌) be unrivalled (英) 或 unrivaled (美) ▷他在60年代独步文坛。In the sixties he was unrivalled in literary circles. 2 (独自行走) walk alone ▷他独步旅行，走遍了全国的城市。He travelled alone, visiting cities all over the country.

独裁 dúcái [动] dictate

独唱 dúchàng [名] solo

独出心裁 dú chū xīn cái be original

独创 dúchuàng [动] invent by oneself ▷他独创了新的风格。He invented this new style all by himself.

独当一面 dú dāng yī miàn take full responsibility

独到 dúdào [形] unique

独断独行 dú duàn dú xíng act autocratically

独家 dújiā [名] the only one ▷他独家生产这种设备。He's the only one who makes this equipment. ▷该报刊登了关于首相的独家新闻。The paper ran an exclusive on the prime minister.

独角戏 dújiǎoxì [名] one-man show

独具匠心 dú jù jiàngxīn have ingenuity

独揽 dúlǎn [动] have a monopoly on ▷在封建社会中，皇帝独揽大权。During feudal times, emperors had a monopoly on power.

独立 dúlì [动] 1 (指国家) declare independence ▷独立宣言 declaration of independence 2 (指个人) be independent 3 (单独站立) stand alone (PT, PP stood)

独木不成林 dú mù bù chéng lín many hands make light work

独木难支 dú mù nán zhī no one can save a difficult situation alone

独木桥 dúmùqiáo [名] 1 (字) single-plank bridge 2 (喻) rocky road

独辟蹊径 dú pì xī jìng be revolutionary

独身 dúshēn [动] be single ▷他独身多年后终于结婚了。After being single many years, he finally got married.

独树一帜 dú shù yī zhì start a trend

独特 dútè [形] distinctive

独一无二 dú yī wú èr unparalleled

独占鳌头 dú zhàn áo tóu emerge as the winner

独自 dúzì [副] alone

读 dú [动] 1 (朗读) read (PT, PP read) ▷我每天给奶奶读报。I read the newspaper to my grandmother every day. 2 (阅读) read (PT, PP read) ▷大家需要仔细读这篇文章。Everyone should read this article carefully. 3 (上学) go to school (PT went, PP gone) ▷他因家庭生活困难只读完小学。His family were poor so he only managed to get through primary school.

读书 dúshū [动] 1 (阅读) read (PT, PP read) 2 (学习) study 3 (上学) go to school (PT went, PP gone)

读物 dúwù [名] reading material

读者 dúzhě [名] reader

渎 dú I [动] (书) show disrespect (PT showed, PP shown) ▷亵渎 blaspheme II [名] (书) drain

渎职 dúzhí [动] neglect one's duty

犊 dú [名] calf

牍 dú [名] 1 (木简) wooden writing tablet 2 (文件) documents

黩 dú [动] (书) 1 (轻举妄动) act wantonly ▷黩武 warlike 2 (玷污) blacken

笃 dǔ [形] 1 (忠诚) sincere 2 (危急) critical

笃实 dǔshí [形] 1 (忠诚老实) faithful 2 (实在) sound

笃学 dǔxué [动] be studious

堵 dǔ I [动] 1 (堵塞) block ▷水管子堵了。The water pipe was blocked. ▷他们把漏水的地方给堵上了。They blocked up the leak. ▷因为车辆过多，公路上很堵。The road was blocked due to an excessive number of vehicles. 2 (发闷) suffocate ▷房间很闷，我胸口堵得很。The room was really stuffy and I felt quite suffocated. II [量] ▷一堵墙 a wall

堵截 dǔjié [动] intercept ▷他们堵截了敌人的运输车。They intercepted the enemy convoy.

堵塞 dǔsè [动] block up ▷用洗面奶清洁被堵塞的毛孔。You should use cleansing milk to clean blocked pores.

赌 dǔ [动] 1 (赌博) gamble 2 (打赌) bet (PT, PP bet)

赌博 dǔbó [动] gamble ▷他决心放弃赌博。He decided to give up gambling.

赌气 dǔqì [动] act rashly out of a sense of injustice

赌咒 dǔzhòu [动] swear (PT swore, PP sworn)

赌注 dǔzhù [名] bet

睹 dǔ [动] see (PT saw, PP seen)

睹物思人 dǔ wù sī rén ▷夫妻俩睹物思人，想起了远在他乡的儿子。The couple saw something that reminded them of their son who was far away from home.

杜 dù [动] shut ... out (PT, PP shut)

杜绝 dùjué [动] put an end to (PT, PP put)

杜撰 dùzhuàn [动] make ... up ▷这个故事纯属杜撰。This story is pure fabrication.

肚 dù [名] belly

肚子 dùzi [名] 1 (腹部) stomach 2 (圆而突起部分) ▷腿肚子 calf

妒 dù [动] envy

妒忌 dùjì [动] envy

度 dù I [名] 1 (限度) limit ▷他疲劳过度。He was totally exhausted. 2 (气量) tolerance ▷大度 magnanimous 3 (考虑) consideration

▷消防员们已把生死置之度外。The firemen didn't give a thought to their personal safety. **4** (程度) degree ▶厚度 thickness ▶亮度 brightness **II** [量] **1** (指经度或纬度) degree ▷北纬42度 latitude 42 degrees north **2** (指电量) kilowatt-hour ▷1度电 one kilowatt-hour **3** (指温度) degree ▷水的沸点为100度。The boiling point of water is 100 degrees. **4** (指弧度或角度) degree ▷直角为90度。A right-angle is 90 degrees. **5** (次) time ▷一年一度的会议 annual meeting **III** [动] spend (PT, PP spent) ▷他们要去瑞士度周末。They are going to spend the weekend in Switzerland. →另见 duó

度量 dùliàng [名] tolerance

度日如年 dù rì rú nián drag on for years

渡 dù [动] **1** (越过) cross ▷横渡英吉利海峡 cross the English Channel **2** (指用船只) ferry **3** (喻) (通过) survive

渡口 dùkǒu [名] ferry crossing

镀 dù [动] plate

镀金 dùjīn [动] **1** (字) gold-plate **2** (喻) do ... for show ▷他出国留学只不过是为镀金。His going abroad to study was really just for show.

端 duān **I** [名] **1** (头) end **2** (开头) beginning ▶开端 beginning **3** (方面) aspect **4** (理由) reason ▷他无端指责我。There was no reason for him to blame me. **II** [形] proper **III** [动] carry ▷他习惯端着碗喝汤。When he eats soup, he holds his bowl in both hands.

端倪 duānní [名] clue

端午节 Duānwǔjié [名] Dragon Boat Festival

端详 duānxiáng **I** [名] details (PL) **II** [形] dignified and serene

端详 duānxiang [动] look closely

端正 duānzhèng **I** [形] **1** (不歪斜) upright **2** (正派) proper **II** [动] correct

端庄 duānzhuāng [形] dignified

短 duǎn **I** [形] short ▷一封短信 a short letter **II** [动] owe ▷我不短你钱。I don't owe you money. **III** [名] weakness ▷揭别人的短儿 expose other people's weaknesses

短兵相接 duǎn bīng xiāng jiē **1** (字) (指搏斗) engage in close combat **2** (喻) (针锋相对) tit for tat

短处 duǎnchu [名] weakness

短促 duǎncù [形] very brief

短见 duǎnjiàn [名] **1** (短浅的见识) short-sighted view **2** (自杀) suicide

短裤 duǎnkù [名] **1** (指女式内裤) pants (PL) **2** (指男式内裤) briefs (PL) **3** (指夏装) shorts (PL)

短路 duǎnlù [名] (电子) short circuit

短命 duǎnmìng [形] short-lived

短平快 duǎn píng kuài **I** [名] smash **II** [形] ▷此类项目以短平快著称。This type of project is famous for giving quick returns on your investment.

短评 duǎnpíng [名] brief comment

短浅 duǎnqiǎn [形] narrow and shallow ▷目光短浅 short-sighted

短缺 duǎnquē [动] lack ▷短缺商品 commodities in short supply

短视 duǎnshì [形] short-sighted

短途 duǎntú [名] short distance ▷短途旅行 short-haul trip

短小 duǎnxiǎo [形] short ▷他身材短小。He's short. ▷短小精悍的文章 a concise article

短信 duǎnxìn [名] text message

短暂 duǎnzàn [形] brief ▷短暂的分别 brief parting

段 duàn [量] **1** (用于长条物) ▷一段铁轨 a section of railway ▷一段木头 a chunk of wood **2** (指时间) period ▷一段时间 a period of time **3** (指路程) stretch ▷下一段路会很难走。The next stretch of road may be difficult to walk. **4** (部分) piece ▷一段对话 a piece of dialogue

段落 duànluò [名] **1** (指文章) paragraph **2** (阶段) stage

断 duàn **I** [动] **1** (分成段) break (PT broke, PP broken) **2** (断绝) break ... off (PT broke, PP broken) **3** (判断) decide **II** [副] absolutely

断案 duàn'àn [动] settle a lawsuit

断层 duàncéng [名] **1** (指地质) fault **2** (不相衔接) gap

断代 duàndài [动] **1** (无后代) be childless **2** (喻) (后继无人) lack a successor

断代史 duàndàishǐ [名] dynastic history

断档 duàndàng [动] be sold out

断定 duàndìng [动] determine

断断续续 duànduànxùxù on and off ▷这本小说他断断续续地写了3年。He wrote the novel on and off for three years.

断交 duànjiāo [动] **1** (指国家) sever diplomatic relations ▷断交3年后，两国又重建外交关系。Three years after severing diplomatic relations, the two countries re-established their ties. **2** (指朋友) fall out (PT fell, PP fallen) ▷两人多年前就已断交了。The two friends fell out years ago.

断绝 duànjué [动] break ... off (PT broke, PP broken) ▷断绝往来 break contact

断然 duànrán I [形] resolute II [副] categorically

断送 duànsòng [动] forfeit ▷断送前程 forfeit one's future

断言 duànyán [动] assert

断章取义 duàn zhāng qǔ yì quote out of context ▷他断章取义，曲解我的本意。He quoted me out of context and quite distorted my original meaning.

缎 duàn [名] satin

锻 duàn [动] forge

锻炼 duànliàn [动] 1 (指身体) work out 2 (磨炼) toughen ▷艰苦的环境锻炼人的意志。People are toughened by difficult experiences. 3 (冶炼) temper

堆 duī I [动] pile ▷别把垃圾堆在这里。Don't pile the rubbish up here. II [名] pile III [量] pile ▷一堆石头 a pile of stones

堆放 duīfàng [动] stack ▷房间里堆放着很多书。Scores of books were stacked in the room.

堆积 duījī [动] pile ... up ▷粮食堆积如山。The grain was piled up like a mountain.

队 duì I [名] 1 (行列) line ▷列队欢迎 line up to welcome 2 (指集体) team ▷篮球队 basketball team II [量] troop ▷一队人马 an array of troops

队列 duìliè [名] formation

队伍 duìwu [名] 1 (军队) troops (PL) 2 (指集体) contingent 3 (行列) formation

对 duì I [动] 1 (回答) answer ▶对答 answer 2 (对待) treat ▷他对待他的父母很糟糕。He treated his parents horribly. 3 (朝着) face ▷对准目标 aim at the target 4 (接触) come into contact with (PT came, PP come) 5 (投合) suit ▷对脾气 suit one's temperament ▷今天的菜很对他的胃口。Today's meal was definitely to his liking. 6 (调整) adjust ▷对焦距 adjust the focus 7 (核对) check ▷对表 set one's watch 8 (加进) add ▷往酒里对点水 add some water to the alcohol II [形] 1 (对面) opposite ▷河对岸 the opposite side of the river 2 (正确) correct ▷这题我回答对了。I answered this question correctly. 3 (正常) normal III [介] 1 (朝) at ▷他对着她呵呵傻笑。He giggled at her. 2 (对于) to ▷吸烟对健康有害。Smoking is harmful to your health. ▷他对自己的未来做了详尽的规划。He planned exhaustively for his future. ▷大家对选举的结果很关心。Everyone was very concerned about the results of the election. IV [量] pair

▷一对绣花鞋 a pair of embroidered shoes ▷一对夫妻 a married couple

对白 duìbái [名] dialogue

对比 duìbǐ I [动] contrast ▷鲜明的对比 marked contrast II [名] ratio

对不起 duì bu qǐ [动] (愧疚) be sorry ▷对不起，我迟到了10分钟。Sorry, I'm ten minutes late. ▷对不起，请再说一遍。Sorry? Can you say that again please? ▷对不起，借过。Excuse me – may I just pass through?

对策 duìcè [名] countermeasure

对称 duìchèn [形] symmetrical

对答 duìdá [动] answer

对待 duìdài [动] treat

对等 duìděng [形] equal ▷两国在对等的基础上签定了条约。The two countries signed the agreement on an equal basis.

对调 duìdiào [动] swap ▷如果你不喜欢这个位置的话，我们可以对调。If you don't like your seat, we can swap.

对方 duìfāng [名] other side ▷恋爱中的男女很少介意对方的缺点。People who are in love rarely mind about their partner's weaknesses.

对付 duìfu [动] 1 (应对) deal with (PT, PP dealt) ▷对付复杂局面 deal with a complicated situation ▷他不是一个好对付的人。He isn't easy to handle. 2 (将就) make do ▷没有别的，我们只好吃点方便面对付了。There's nothing else, so we'll just have to make do with some instant noodles.

对话 duìhuà I [名] dialogue ▷两国将就边境问题对话。The two countries will have a dialogue about the border issue. II [动] hold talks (PT, PP held) ▷劳资双方终于开始对话。Employers and employees began holding talks.

对讲机 duìjiǎngjī [名] intercom

对角线 duìjiǎoxiàn [名] diagonal

对接 duìjiē [动] link ... up

对劲 duìjìn [形] 1 (合适) well-suited 2 (投缘) compatible 3 (正常) normal ▷这几天她好像不太对劲。She hasn't been altogether right these last few days.

对抗 duìkàng [动] 1 (对立) confront ▷两党之间的对抗并未消除。There are still some major disputes between the two parties. 2 (抵抗) oppose

对口 duìkǒu [动] be appropriate to ▷对口的工作 a job that is appropriate to one's training

对立 duìlì I [动] counter II [形] antagonistic

对路 duìlù [形] 1 (合适) suitable ▷该产品在法国市场不对路。This product is unsuitable for the French market. 2 (投缘) suited ▷两个人好

像不对路。These two don't seem very suited to each other.

对面 duìmiàn I [名] 1 (对过) the opposite ▷街对面有一家餐馆。There's a restaurant on the opposite side of the street. 2 (正前方) the front ▷对面跑过来一只小狗。A small dog ran up right in front of us. II [副] face to face ▷他们终于对面儿把事情说清楚了。They finally clarified the matter face to face.

对牛弹琴 duì niú tán qín preach to deaf ears

对手 duìshǒu [名] 1 (指比赛) opponent 2 (指能力) match ▷论工作能力，他根本不是你的对手。In terms of his professional abilities, he's just no match for you.

对头 duìtóu [形] 1 (正常) normal 2 (投合) compatible

对头 duìtou [名] 1 (仇人) enemy 2 (竞争对手) rival ▷她的对头也在竞争这个项目。Her rival is also competing for this project.

对象 duìxiàng [名] 1 (目标) object ▷爱丽斯是他爱慕的对象。Alice is the object of his affections. 2 (指男女朋友) partner

对应 duìyìng [动] correspond

对于 duìyú [介] ▷对于离婚，社会舆论反应不一。Society is divided in its opinion of divorce. ▷对于这篇文章，大家理解不一。Not everyone understands this article in the same way.

对照 duìzhào [动] compare

对症下药 duì zhèng xià yào use appropriate methods ▷治病要对症下药。When treating illnesses, appropriate methods must be used.

对峙 duìzhì [动] confront

兑 duì [动] 1 (互换) exchange 2 (汇兑) cash

兑付 duìfù [动] cash ▷兑付支票 cash a cheque (英) 或 check (美)

兑换 duìhuàn [动] convert ▷将欧元兑换成美元 convert euros into US dollars

兑现 duìxiàn [动] 1 (兑换现金) cash 2 (实现承诺) keep one's word (PT, PP kept)

吨 dūn [量] ton

吨位 dūnwèi [名] tonnage

敦 dūn [形] sincere

敦促 dūncù [动] urge

敦厚 dūnhòu [形] genuine

敦请 dūnqǐng [动] cordially invite

敦实 dūnshí [形] stocky ▷保镖长通常都挺敦实。Bodyguards are usually very stocky.

墩 dūn [名] 1 (堆) mound 2 (墩子) block ▶桥墩 pier

蹲 dūn [动] 1 (弯腿) squat 2 (逗留) stay

盹 dǔn [名] nap ▷我得打个盹。I must take a nap.

趸 dǔn I [名] wholesale II [动] buy ... wholesale (PT, PP bought)

趸批 dǔnpī [名] wholesale

炖 dùn [动] stew ▷土豆炖牛肉 stewed beef with potato

盾 dùn [名] (盾牌或盾形物) shield

盾牌 dùnpái [名] 1 (字) shield 2 (喻) pretext

钝 dùn [形] 1 (不锋利) blunt 2 (不灵活) dim

钝角 dùnjiǎo [名] obtuse angle

顿 dùn I [动] 1 (停顿) pause 2 (叩) kowtow ▶顿首 kowtow 3 (跺) stamp ▶顿足 stamp one's foot 4 (安置) arrange ▶安顿 settle down II [形] tired ▶劳顿 fatigued III [副] suddenly IV [量] ▷一顿饭 a meal ▷亨利昨晚挨了一顿打。Henry took quite a beating last night.

顿号 dùnhào [名] Chinese serial comma

顿时 dùnshí [副] immediately

遁 dùn [动] escape

遁词 dùncí [名] pretext

多 duō I [形] 1 (数量大) a lot of ▷很多书 a lot of books 2 (相差大) more ▷中国领土面积比日本大多了。China has a much bigger land mass than Japan. 3 (超出) too many ▷你多给了我2英镑。You gave me two pounds too much. ▷她喝多了。She drank too much. 4 (过分) excessive ▶多疑 over-suspicious II [数] ▷300多艘军舰 over three hundred warships ▷2年多前 over two years ago III [动] be more than ▷这个游戏多了2个人。We have two people too many for the game. ▷多个人就多份力量。The more people we have, the stronger we will be. IV [副] 1 (用在疑问句中) how ▷从北京到上海有多远？How far is it from Beijing to Shanghai? ▷你儿子多大了？How old is your son? 2 (表示感叹) how ▷多美的城市！How beautiful this town is! ▷这女孩儿多聪明啊！This girl is so clever! 3 (表示任何一种程度) however ▷无论多晚，她都会等他回家。However late it got, she would wait up for him to return home. ▷给我一把尺，多长都行。Give me a ruler – any length will do.

多半 duōbàn I [数] ▷这个班的学生多半英

语好。Most of the students in this class have good English. ▷他的家庭成员多半赞同他的婚事。On the whole, most of his family were happy about his marriage. **II** [副] (大概) very likely ▷今天多半要下雨。It's very likely to rain today.

多边 duōbiān [名] ▷多边贸易谈判 multilateral trade talks ▷多边协议 multilateral agreement

多才多艺 duō cái duō yì versatile

多此一举 duō cǐ yī jǔ take unnecessary action

多愁善感 duō chóu shàn gǎn oversensitive

多多益善 duō duō yì shàn the more the better ▷你给我多少我都要, 多多益善。Give me whatever you want, but the more the better.

多方 duōfāng [名] every way ▷多方协助 all manner of help

多亏 duōkuī [动] be lucky ▷多亏你把他送医院了。It's lucky that you took him to hospital. ▷多亏你告诉我们, 不然我们就迷路了。It's lucky that you told us or we would have got lost.

多媒体 duōméitǐ [名] multimedia

多米诺骨牌 duōmǐnuò gǔpái [名] dominoes (PL)

多么 duōme [副] **1** (用于询问程度) how ▷他到底有多么聪明? How clever is he really? **2** (用在感叹句) ▷多么蓝的天啊! What a clear day! ▷海洋是多么广阔啊! The ocean is so vast! **3** (表示程度深) no matter how ▷不管天气多么寒冷, 我们都要坚持锻炼。No matter how cold it gets, we must all stick to our exercise routine.

多面手 duōmiànshǒu [名] all-rounder

多谋善断 duō móu shàn duàn shrewd

多情 duōqíng [形] affectionate

多少 duōshǎo [副] **1** (或多或少) somewhat ▷经历了许多挫折后, 他多少有些变化。After all the setbacks, he's somewhat changed. ▷这笔买卖多少能赚点钱。We're bound to earn some money from this deal. **2** (稍微) slightly

多少 duōshao **I** [代] (用于询问数量) ▷这台电视机多少钱? How much is this television? ▷今天有多少人到会? How many people attended the meeting today? **II** [数] ▷你们有多少我们要多少。We want everything you've got. ▷这样的电影, 没有多少人会喜欢的。There can't be many people who like this kind of film. ▷他的棋艺实在太高, 多少人败在他的手下。He's just too good at chess – countless people have lost to him.

多事之秋 duō shì zhī qiū troubled times ▷今年真是多事之秋, 家里接二连三地出事。This year we've had really troubled times – our family has had one problem after another.

多数 duōshù [名] the majority ▷多数民众参加了公投。The majority of people voted in the referendum.

多心 duōxīn [动] be oversensitive

多样 duōyàng [形] diverse

多余 duōyú [形] **1** (超出需要量的) surplus **2** (不必要的) redundant

多嘴 duōzuǐ [动] speak out of turn (PT spoke, PP spoken)

哆 duō [动] (书) scold

哆哆逼人 duōduō bī rén overbearing

哆哆怪事 duōduō guàishì strange goings-on

哆 duō 见下文

哆嗦 duōsuo [动] tremble ▷他气得直哆嗦。He trembled with rage. ▷她冷得直哆嗦。She was so cold she was shivering.

掇 duō [动] pick ... up ▶拾掇 tidy ... up

掇弄 duōnòng [动] (方) **1** (收拾) fix **2** (怂恿) provoke

夺 duó [动] **1** (抢) seize ▷夺门而出 force one's way out **2** (争取) compete for **3** (剥夺) deprive ▷父亲剥夺了我的继承权。My father deprived me of my inheritance. **4** (决定) resolve

夺标 duóbiāo [动] **1** (夺冠) win first prize (PT, PP won) **2** (中标) win a tender (PT, PP won)

夺冠 duóguàn [动] win the championship (PT, PP won)

夺目 duómù [形] dazzling

夺取 duóqǔ [动] **1** (武力强取) capture **2** (努力争取) strive for (PT strove, PP striven)

度 duó [动] (书) surmise
→另见 dù

踱 duó [动] stroll

朵 duǒ [量] ▷朵朵白云 white clouds ▷几朵玫瑰 some roses

躲 duǒ [动] **1** (隐藏) hide (PT hid, PP hidden) **2** (避让) avoid ▶躲债 avoid a creditor

躲避 duǒbì [动] **1** (回避) run away from (PT ran, PP run) ▷躲避问题 run away from one's problems **2** (躲藏) hide (PT hid, PP hidden) ▷我不知道他躲避到哪里去了。I don't know where he had hidden himself.

躲藏 duǒcáng [动] hide (PT hid, PP hidden)

躲闪 duǒshǎn [动] dodge

驮 duò [名] load
→另见 tuó

剁 duò [动] chop

垛 duò I [动] stack II [名] stack

舵 duò [名] helm
舵手 duòshǒu [名] helmsman

堕 duò [动] fall (PT fell, PP fallen)

堕落 duòluò [动] go to the bad (PT went, PP gone)

堕胎 duòtāi [动] have an abortion ▷堕胎在一些国家还是不合法的。Abortion is still illegal in some countries.

惰 duò [形] lazy ▶懒惰 indolent
惰性 duòxìng [名] 1 (消极态度) apathy 2 (指化学性质) inertia

跺 duò [动] stamp ▷他气得直跺脚。He was so angry that he stamped his feet repeatedly.

Ee

阿 ē [动] pander to ▶ 阿谀 flatter
→另见 ā
阿谀奉承 ēyú fèngcheng creep and crawl
▷ 我讨厌那些阿谀奉承的人。I hate people
who creep and crawl to others.

婀 ē 见下文
婀娜 ēnuó [形] graceful ▷ 婀娜多姿 lithe and
graceful

讹 é I [名] error ▷ 以讹传讹 spread
misinformation II [动] extort ▷ 他绑架的目
的只是为了讹钱。He did the kidnapping as a
way of extorting money.
讹传 échuán [名] hearsay
讹诈 ézhà [动] extort

俄 é I [名] (俄罗斯) Russia II [副] suddenly
俄顷 éqǐng [副] (书) presently

娥 é [名] pretty woman (PL women)
娥眉 éméi [名] 1 (字) beautiful eyebrows 2 (喻)
(美女) beautiful woman (PL women)

鹅 é [名] goose (PL geese)
鹅毛 émáo [名] 1 (字) goose feather 2 (喻)
trivial gift

蛾 é [名] moth
蛾子 ézi [名] moth

额 é [名] 1 (额头) forehead 2 (牌匾) board 3 (规定
数目) quota
额度 édù [名] amount
额外 éwài [形] additional

恶 ě 见下文
→另见 è, wù
恶心 ěxin I [动] feel nauseous (PT, PP felt)
II [形] nauseating

厄 è I [名] 1 (书) (险要处) strategic place 2 (艰难
困苦) disaster II [动] encounter difficulties
厄运 èyùn [名] misfortune

扼 è [动] 1 (用力掐) clutch 2 (把守) guard
扼杀 èshā [动] 1 (掐死) strangle 2 (喻) stifle
扼要 èyào [形] concise
扼制 èzhì [动] control

轭 è [名] yoke

垩 è [名] chalk

恶 è I [名] evil II [形] 1 (凶恶) ferocious 2 (恶
劣) evil
→另见 ě, wù
恶霸 èbà [名] local bully
恶毒 èdú [形] vicious
恶贯满盈 è guàn mǎn yíng evil and
deserving of punishment
恶棍 ègùn [名] scoundrel
恶果 èguǒ [名] disastrous consequences (PL)
恶化 èhuà [动] deteriorate ▷ 两国关系恶
化。Relations between the two countries
deteriorated.
恶劣 èliè [形] bad
恶梦 èmèng [名] nightmare
恶魔 èmó [名] 1 (指宗教) demon 2 (喻) devil
恶习 èxí [名] vice
恶性 èxìng [形] 1 (疾病) malignant ▷ 恶性肿瘤
malignant tumour 2 (事故) horrific ▷ 恶性循
环 vicious circle
恶浊 èzhuó [形] filthy
恶作剧 èzuòjù [名] practical joke ▷ 不要再搞
恶作剧了。Don't play any more practical jokes.

饿 è I [形] hungry II [动] starve
饿虎扑食 è hǔ pū shí like a hungry tiger

遏 è [动] suppress

遏止 èzhǐ [动] check ▷民主化是不可遏止的趋势。The trend towards democracy cannot be checked. ▷遏止腐败现象 check corruption

遏制 èzhì [动] keep a check on (PT, PP kept)

愕 è [动] astound

愕然 èrán [形] (书) stunned

腭 è [名] palate

噩 è [形] terrifying

噩耗 èhào [名] devastating news (SG)

鳄 è [名] crocodile, alligator

恩 ēn [名] kindness ▶报恩 repay a favour (英) 或 favor (美)

恩爱 ēn'ài [形] loving ▷他们是一对恩爱夫妻。They are a devoted couple.

恩赐 ēncì [动] bestow ▷大丰收是上苍对我们的恩赐。A plentiful harvest is a gift from heaven.

恩德 ēndé [名] kindness

恩典 ēndiǎn I [名] favour (英), favor (美) II [动] bestow kindness on

恩惠 ēnhuì [名] favour (英), favor (美)

恩将仇报 ēn jiāng chóu bào bite the hand that feeds one

恩情 ēnqíng [名] great kindness

恩人 ēnrén [名] benefactor ▷他是我的大恩人。He is my saviour (英) 或 savior (美).

恩怨 ēnyuàn [名] a mixture of gratitude and resentment

摁 èn [动] press ▷请摁一下开关。Please press the switch.

儿 ér I [名] 1 (小孩子) child (PL children) 2 (年轻人) youngster ▶ 男儿 young man 3 (儿子) son II [形] male ▶ 儿马 stallion

儿歌 érgē [名] nursery rhyme

儿女 érnǚ [名] 1 (儿子和女儿) children 2 (青年男女) men and women (PL)

儿童 értóng [名] child (PL children)

儿戏 érxì [名] (喻) trivial thing ▷工作不是儿戏。Work is not a game.

而 ér [连] 1 (并且) and ▷美丽而聪明 beautiful and clever ▷抽烟有其害而无其利。Smoking does nothing but harm. 2 (但是) but ▷这种香水的香味儿浓而不劣。This perfume is strong but the smell is not overpowering. 3 (连接状语和谓语词) ▷夺门而逃 force the door and rush out 4 (如果) if ▷想成功而不努力,那是痴心妄想。It's just wishful thinking to imagine that you can be successful without putting in the work. 5 (到) to ▷由始而终 from start to finish

而后 érhòu [连] then ▷他去年来过一封信,而后再没联系过。Last year he sent a letter, but after that he didn't get in contact again.

而今 érjīn [名] today ▷原本荒凉的郊野,而今已是高楼林立。Today the old wasteland is a forest of skyscrapers.

而且 érqiě [连] and what's more ▷他会讲英语,而且讲得好。He can speak English, and what's more he speaks it very well. ▷他不但歌唱得好,而且还会作曲。He sings very well, and on top of that he can also write music.

而已 éryǐ [助] ▷我劝别的意思,只是提醒你而已。All I'm doing is cautioning you. ▷她只是说说而已,不会真做的。She's all talk – she won't really do it.

尔 ěr [代] (书) 1 (你) you ▶非尔之过。It's not your fault. 2 (这样) so ▶果尔 if so 3 (那) that ▷尔日 on that day ▷尔时 at that time

尔虞我诈 ěr yú wǒ zhà each trying to cheat the other

耳 ěr [名] 1 (耳朵) ear 2 (耳状物) ear 3 (指位置) side

耳边风 ěrbiānfēng [名] deaf ear ▷她把妈妈的建议当作耳边风。She turned a deaf ear to her mother's advice.

耳聪目明 ěr cōng mù míng 1 (字) have good eyesight and hearing 2 (喻) have one's wits about one ▷他耳聪目明,极少上当。He has his wits about him and is rarely fooled.

耳光 ěrguāng [名] slap in the face

耳目 ěrmù [名] 1 (见闻) information ▷耳目闭塞 ill-informed 2 (密探) spy

耳目一新 ěr mù yī xīn refreshing

耳濡目染 ěr rú mù rǎn be subtly influenced

耳熟能详 ěr shú néng xiáng ▷这个曲子我耳熟能详。I've heard this tune so many times that I know it off by heart.

耳闻目睹 ěr wén mù dǔ witness ... first-hand

耳语 ěryǔ [动] whisper

饵 ěr I [名] 1 (糕饼) cake 2 (鱼饵) bait II [动] (书) entice

饵子 ěrzi [名] bait

二 èr I [数] two ▷第二次 the second time ▷一心二用 do two things at once II [动] ▷本店不

二价。No bargaining in this shop.

二百五 èrbǎiwǔ [名] 1 (傻气的人) imbecile 2 (方) (半瓶醋) dabbler

二胡 èrhú [名] (中国乐器) erhu

二郎腿 èrlángtuǐ [名] cross-legged position ▷他坐着时老翘着二郎腿。He always sat cross-legged.

二流子 èrliúzi [名] layabout

二十 èrshí [数] twenty

二十四节气 èrshísì jiéqì [名] the twenty-four Chinese solar terms

二心 èrxīn [名] 1 (异心) disloyalty ▷他早就有了二心。He's been disloyal for a long time now. 2 (旁骛) half-heartedness

二一添作五 èr yī tiān zuò wǔ go fifty-fifty ▷我们二一添作五吧! Let's go fifty-fifty!

贰 èr [数] an elaborate form of "two", used in writing cheques etc to prevent mistakes and forgery

Ff

发 fā I [动] 1 (送出) send (PT, PP sent) ▷发
电子邮件 send an e-mail ▷发货 deliver
goods ▷发工资 pay wages 2 (发射) emit ▶发
光 shine 3 (产生) produce ▶发电 generate
electricity ▶发芽 sprout 4 (表达) express ▶发
言 speak ▷发指示 give instructions 5 (扩
大) develop ▶发扬 carry on 6 (兴旺) prosper
▶发家 make a family fortune 7 (使膨胀) ▷发
面 leaven dough ▷蛋糕发起来了。The cake
has risen. 8 (散开) spread (PT, PP spread) ▶发
散 diverge ▶发挥 bring into play 9 (揭开)
uncover ▶发现 discover ▶发掘 unearth ▶揭
发 expose 10 (变得) become ▶发霉 go mouldy
(英) 或 moldy (美) ▶发臭 smell bad 11 (流露)
▶发愁 worry ▷发脾气 lose one's temper 12 (感
到) feel (PT, PP felt) ▷发冷 feel cold 13 (起程)
leave (PT, PP left) ▶出发 set out II [量] ▷上千
发子弹 thousands of bullets
→另见 fà

发榜 fābǎng [动] post up

发报 fābào [动] send a telegram (PT, PP sent)

发表 fābiǎo [动] 1 (宣布) announce ▷发表消
息 announce the news ▷发表演说 make a
speech 2 (刊登) publish

发布 fābù [动] issue

发财 fācái [动] make a fortune

发愁 fāchóu [动] worry

发出 fāchū [动] 1 (发送) send out (PT, PP sent)
▷发出求救信号 send out an SOS ▷发出传票
issue a summons 2 (散发) give out (PT gave, PP
given) ▷发出光和热 give out light and heat

发达 fādá I [形] developed ▷他肌肉发达。He
has well-developed muscles. II [动] promote

发呆 fādāi [动] be in a daze

发电 fādiàn [动] generate electricity

发电厂 fādiànchǎng [名] power station (英),
power plant (美)

发动 fādòng [动] 1 (启动) start 2 (发起)
launch 3 (鼓动) mobilize

发抖 fādǒu [动] 1 (因恐惧等) tremble 2 (因寒冷
等) shiver

发放 fāfàng [动] grant ▷发放通行证 grant a
pass

发愤 fāfèn [动] make a determined effort

发疯 fāfēng [动] go mad (PT went, PP gone)

发福 fāfú [动] put on weight (PT, PP put)

发稿 fāgǎo [动] file a report

发号施令 fā hào shī lìng go around issuing
orders

发狠 fāhěn [动] 1 (下决心) make a determined
effort 2 (恼火) be annoyed

发还 fāhuán [动] return ▷老师把作文发还给
了学生。The teacher returned the essays to
the students.

发慌 fāhuāng [动] be nervous

发挥 fāhuī [动] 1 (充分利用) bring ... into play
(PT, PP brought) ▷这份工作使我充分发挥
了专长。This job enabled me to make full
use of my special skills. ▷发挥想象力 give
one's imagination free rein ▷发挥电脑的作
用 make the most of a computer 2 (详尽论述)
elaborate ▷这一理论需要进一步发挥。This
theory needs further elaboration.

发火 fāhuǒ [动] 1 (着火) catch fire (PT, PP
caught) 2 (爆炸) detonate 3 (发脾气) lose one's
temper (PT, PP lost)

发货 fāhuò [动] deliver goods

发迹 fājì [动] rise to power (PT rose, PP risen)

发家 fājiā [动] make a family fortune

发酵 fājiào [动] ferment ▷发酵饮料 fermented
drink

发觉 fājué [动] discover ▷她发觉有错误。
She discovered a mistake. ▷我发觉他有些不
对劲。I realized there was something wrong
with him.

发掘 fājué [动] unearth ▷发掘地下宝藏
unearth buried treasure ▷发掘潜力 discover
hidden potential

发狂 fākuáng [动] go mad (PT went, PP gone)

发困 fākùn [动] feel sleepy (PT, PP felt)

发愣 fālèng [动] be in a daze

发霉 fāméi [动] go mouldy (英) 或 moldy (美) (PT went, PP gone)

发明 fāmíng [动] invent ▷计算机的发明是对人类的巨大贡献。The invention of the computer was of great benefit to humanity.

发难 fānàn [动] revolt ▷他们向政府发难。They revolted against the government.

发怒 fānù [动] get angry

发配 fāpèi [动] banish

发票 fāpiào [名] 1 (收据) receipt 2 (发货清单) invoice

发起 fāqǐ [动] 1 (倡议) sponsor 2 (发动) launch

发情 fāqíng [动] be in heat

发热 fārè [动] 1 (发烧) have a fever 2 (发出热量) give off heat (PT gave, PP given) 3 (不冷静) be hot-headed

发人深省 fā rén shēn xǐng give food for thought

发烧 fāshāo [动] have a temperature

发射 fāshè [动] launch

发生 fāshēng [动] happen ▷这是什么时候发生的? When did this happen? ▷近年来这座城市发生了很大变化。In recent years great changes have taken place in this city. ▷发生了一起车祸。There was a car accident.

发誓 fāshì [动] vow

发售 fāshòu [动] sell (PT, PP sold)

发条 fātiáo [名] spring ▷我的表上发条了。My watch is wound up.

发问 fāwèn [动] ask

发现 fāxiàn [动] discover ▷发现一个新油田 discover a new oilfield ▷发现线索 find clues ▷他在物理学上做出了很多重要发现。He made many important discoveries in physics.

发祥地 fāxiángdì [名] birthplace

发泄 fāxiè [动] vent

发行 fāxíng [动] publish ▷发行词典 publish a dictionary ▷发行影片 release a film ▷发行股票 issue stocks

发芽 fāyá [动] sprout

发言 fāyán [动] make a speech ▷工会主席的发言很精彩。The chairman of the trade union made a wonderful speech. ▷他要在明天的会上发言。He is going to speak at the meeting tomorrow.

发言人 fāyánrén [名] spokesperson (PL spokespersons)

发炎 fāyán [动] become inflamed

发扬 fāyáng [动] carry on

发音 fāyīn [动] pronounce ▷你这个单词发音不对。You pronounced this word wrong. ▷她的发音很标准。She has standard pronunciation.

发育 fāyù [动] develop ▷这些小鸡发育正常。These chicks are developing normally. ▷你要密切注意孩子智力的发育。You need to monitor children's intellectual development closely.

发源 fāyuán [动] rise (PT rose, PP risen)

发展 fāzhǎn [动] 1 (变化) develop ▷发展友好关系 develop friendly relations ▷中国的发展是对全球的重大贡献。The development of China has a lot to offer the world. 2 (扩大) expand

发作 fāzuò [动] 1 (突发) ▷激光唱机的老毛病发作了。The CD player is playing up again. ▷爷爷的心脏病又发作了。Grandpa had another heart attack. 2 (发脾气) flare up ▷他爱为小事发作。He is liable to flare up at trivial things.

乏 fá [动] 1 (缺乏) lack 2 (疲倦) be tired

乏味 fáwèi [形] dull

伐 fá [动] 1 (砍树) cut ... down (PT, PP cut) 2 (攻打) attack ▶讨伐 suppress

罚 fá [动] punish ▶罚款 fine ▷罚输者喝酒。The loser has to drink as a forfeit.

罚金 fájīn [名] fine ▷对他应处以罚金。A fine should be imposed on him.

罚款 fákuǎn I [动] fine II [名] fine

阀 fá [名] 1 (指人或家族) ▶军阀 warlord ▶财阀 tycoon 2 (指机器部件) valve

阀门 fámén [名] valve

筏 fá [名] raft

法 fǎ [名] 1 (法律) law ▷守法 abide by the law ▷犯法 break the law 2 (方法) method ▶用法 use 3 (标准) model ▷效法 follow an example 4 (佛理) Buddhism 5 (法术) magic ▶戏法 conjuring tricks

法办 fǎbàn [动] bring to justice (PT, PP brought)

法宝 fǎbǎo [名] magic weapon

法典 fǎdiǎn [名] statutes (PL)

法定 fǎdìng [形] statutory ▷法定假日 statutory holiday ▷法定继承权 legal right of inheritance

法官 fǎguān [名] judge

法规 fǎguī [名] laws and regulations (PL)

法理 fǎlǐ [名] legal principle

法令 fǎlìng [名] decree

法律 fǎlǜ [名] law

法门 fǎmén [名] Buddhism

法术 fǎshù [名] magic

法庭 fǎtíng [名] court ▷军事法庭 military court ▷民事法庭 civil court

法学 fǎxué [名] law

法医 fǎyī [名] forensic medical expert

法院 fǎyuàn [名] court

法则 fǎzé [名] law

法制 fǎzhì [名] legal system

法治 fǎzhì [名] rule of law

法子 fǎzi [名] way

砝 fǎ 见下文

　砝码 fǎmǎ [名] weight

发 fà [名] hair ▷发辫 plait
→另见 fā

> **hair** 既可以用作可数名词也可以用作不可数名词。在描述人时，hair 通常用作不可数名词。*She has long blonde hair and blue eyes… the girl with red hair and freckles…* 然而，当强调一根根或几簇头发或毛发时，可以将它用作可数名词。*There were some blonde hairs in the car.*

发廊 fàláng [名] hairdresser's

发型 fàxíng [名] hairstyle

珐 fà 见下文

　珐琅 fàláng [名] enamel

帆 fān [名] sail

帆布 fānbù [名] canvas

帆船 fānchuán [名] sailing boat ▷帆船运动 sailing

番 fān [量] ▷我三番五次告诉他不要抽烟。I've told him time and time again he shouldn't smoke. ▷经过几番挫折他明白了许多道理。After a few false starts he picked up quite a lot. ▷他是出于一番好意才做的。He just did it out of a kind impulse. ▷这首曲子别有一番情调。This melody has an entirely different feel.

番茄 fānqié [名] tomato (PL tomatoes)

翻 fān [动] 1 (换位置) turn over ▷服务员把垫子翻过来。The staff turned the mattress over. ▷他在床上翻了个身。He turned over in bed. ▷车翻了。The car overturned. 2 (寻找) rummage ▷她正在屋里东找西翻。She is rummaging around in her room. 3 (推翻) reverse 4 (越过) get across 5 (增加) multiply 6 (翻译) translate 7 (翻脸) fall out (PT fell, PP fallen)

翻案 fān'àn [动] overturn a verdict

翻版 fānbǎn [名] reprint

翻番 fānfān [动] double

翻覆 fānfù [动] 1 (颠覆) overturn 2 (彻底变化) be transformed 3 (翻身) turn over

翻供 fāngòng [动] retract one's testimony

翻滚 fāngǔn [动] 1 (沸腾) seethe 2 (翻筋斗) roll

翻悔 fānhuǐ [动] back out ▷她说和我一起去，可又翻悔了。She said she'd go with me, but then backed out. ▷现在要翻悔你的承诺为时已晚。It's too late to go back on your promise.

翻江倒海 fān jiāng dǎo hǎi earth-shaking

翻来覆去 fān lái fù qù 1 (来回翻身) toss and turn 2 (反反复复) repeatedly

翻脸 fānliǎn [动] fall out (PT fell, PP fallen) ▷我和姐姐从没翻过脸。I've never fallen out with my sister.

翻身 fānshēn [动] 1 (转身) turn over 2 (解放) emancipate oneself

翻腾 fānténg [动] 1 (滚动) churn 2 (翻动) rummage 3 (思考) think over

翻天覆地 fān tiān fù dì earth-shattering

翻箱倒柜 fān xiāng dǎo guì search high and low

翻新 fānxīn [动] renovate ▷这所房子正在翻新。This house is being renovated. ▷皮沙发刚刚翻新过。The leather sofa has just been reconditioned. ▷花样翻新 in a new guise

翻译 fānyì I [动] translate II [名] translator

翻云覆雨 fān yún fù yǔ shifty

凡 fán I [名] 1 (人世间) mortal world 2 (大概) approximation II [形] ordinary III [副] 1 (凡是) ▷凡年满16周岁的，可申办身份证。All those who have reached the age of 16 can apply for an ID card. ▷凡坏人没有好下场。Bad people always come to a sticky end. 2 (总共) in all ▷全书凡6卷。The set contains six volumes in all.

凡人 fánrén [名] 1 (平常人) ordinary person 2 (俗人) mortal

凡是 fánshì [副] ▷凡是去过大连的人都说那儿好。Everyone who's been to Dalian says it's lovely. ▷凡是没洗干净的杯子都要放这儿。Any glasses that have not been washed properly should be put here.

烦 fán I [名] trouble ▷不厌其烦 not mind taking the trouble II [动] (谦) trouble ▷烦你给我喝杯水。May I trouble you to get me a glass of water? ▷烦请您给她捎个话儿？Could you please pass on a message to her?

III [形] (厌烦) fed up ▷我烦那些人。I am fed up with those people. ▷这事真叫人烦！It's so annoying!

烦劳 fánláo [动] trouble ▷烦劳您给孩子们读个故事。Would you mind reading a story to the children?

烦闷 fánmèn [形] depressed

烦恼 fánnǎo [形] worried ▷你不要为小事烦恼。You shouldn't worry about little things.

烦琐 fánsuǒ [形] over-elaborate

烦躁 fánzào [形] agitated

樊 fán [名] (书) fence

樊篱 fánlí [名] 1 (篱笆) fence 2 (喻) (形容限制) barrier

繁 fán I [形] numerous II [动] propagate

繁多 fánduō [形] numerous ▷名目繁多 numerous items ▷花样繁多 a great variety

繁复 fánfù [形] laborious and complicated

繁华 fánhuá [形] bustling

繁忙 fánmáng [形] busy

繁茂 fánmào [形] lush

繁荣 fánróng I [形] flourishing ▷经济在繁荣。The economy is booming. II [动] ▷繁荣市场 create a strong market

繁文缛节 fán wén rù jié bureaucracy

繁衍 fányǎn [动] multiply

繁杂 fánzá [形] diverse

繁殖 fánzhí [动] breed (PT, PP bred)

繁重 fánzhòng [形] strenuous ▷繁重的工作 strenuous work ▷繁重的任务 arduous tasks

反 fǎn I [名] 1 (相反) opposite ▷适得其反 lead to just the opposite 2 (造反) rebellion II [动] 1 (转换) turn ▷反败为胜 turn defeat into victory 2 (回) return 3 (反对) oppose 4 (背叛) rebel III [形] opposite IV [副] 1 (相反地) on the contrary ▷我觉得她不但不丑，反倒挺美。She is not ugly to me; on the contrary, I think she's beautiful. ▷他不安慰我，反伤我的感情。Instead of comforting me, he hurt my feelings. 2 (从反面) again ▶反顾 look back ▶反思 review

反驳 fǎnbó [动] refute

反差 fǎnchā [名] contrast

反常 fǎncháng [形] unusual

反衬 fǎnchèn [动] set ... off (PT, PP set) ▷绿叶将花朵反衬得更加美丽。The green leaves set off the flowers beautifully.

反唇相讥 fǎn chún xiāng jī respond sharply

反倒 fǎndào [副] ▷让她等我，她反倒上车了。I asked her to wait for me, but instead she

got on the bus. ▷雪停了，天反倒冷了。The snow has stopped, but the weather has turned colder.

反动 fǎndòng I [形] reactionary II [名] reaction

反对 fǎnduì [动] oppose

反而 fǎn'ér [副] instead ▷她不但没有平静下来，反而越来越激动。Instead of calming down, she became more and more agitated. ▷他不感到累，反而劲头更足。He didn't feel tired; on the contrary, he had even more energy.

反复 fǎnfù [副] 1 (重复) repeatedly 2 (多变) capriciously

反感 fǎngǎn [形] disgusted ▷我对他们的行为很反感。I'm disgusted by their behaviour.

反攻 fǎngōng [名] counterattack

反躬自问 fǎn gōng zì wèn ask oneself

反光 fǎnguāng I [动] reflect light II [名] reflected light

反话 fǎnhuà [名] irony

反悔 fǎnhuǐ [动] go back on one's word (PT went, PP gone) ▷答应别人的事不能反悔。You can't go back on your promise.

反击 fǎnjī [动] fight back (PT, PP fought) ▷他们决定进行有力的反击。They decided to launch a major counterattack.

反抗 fǎnkàng [动] resist ▷反抗压迫 resist oppression ▷反抗精神 spirit of resistance

反恐怖主义 fǎn kǒngbù zhǔyì [名] anti-terrorism

反馈 fǎnkuì [动] give feedback (PT gave, PP given) ▷反馈意见 feedback

反面 fǎnmiàn I [名] other side II [形] negative

反目 fǎnmù [动] turn against

反派 fǎnpài [名] villain

反叛 fǎnpàn [动] revolt

反扑 fǎnpū [动] launch a counterattack

反其道而行之 fǎn qí dào ér xíng zhī do just the opposite

反射 fǎnshè I [动] reflect II [名] reflex ▷条件反射 conditioned reflex

反思 fǎnsī [动] review ▷对这次事故我们要进行深刻的反思。We need to have a full review of this accident.

反诉 fǎnsù [动] counterclaim

反问 fǎnwèn I [动] answer a question with a question ▷他没回答我的问题，却反问我一个。He didn't reply to my question, but answered with a question of his own. II [名] rhetorical question

反响 fǎnxiǎng [名] reverberation

反省 fǎnxǐng [动] question oneself ▷我们需要反省自己的行为。We need to question our own behaviour.

反义词 fǎnyìcí [名] opposite

反应 fǎnyìng [名] 1 (反响) response ▷上级对我们的意见很快有了反应。Management made a quick response to our suggestion. ▷观众对这部影片的反应不一。Audience reaction to the film varied. ▷这孩子反应很快。The kid is quick-witted. 2 (指机体) reaction ▷过敏反应 allergic reaction 3 (指物理、化学) reaction ▷核反应 nuclear reaction

反映 fǎnyìng [动] 1 (反照) reflect 2 (汇报) report

反语 fǎnyǔ [名] irony

反正 fǎnzhèng [副] anyway ▷反正必须有人去，就让我去吧！Since someone has to go anyway, why not let me go!

反之 fǎnzhī [连] otherwise ▷努力了我们就会成功，反之就难说了。If we work hard we will succeed – otherwise we may not.

返 fǎn [动] return

返潮 fǎncháo [动] get damp

返工 fǎngōng [动] redo

返航 fǎnháng [动] return

返回 fǎnhuí [动] come back (PT came, PP come)

返老还童 fǎn lǎo huán tóng regain one's youth

犯 fàn I [动] 1 (违犯) violate 2 (侵犯) attack 3 (发作) ▷他心脏病又犯了。He had another heart attack. 4 (错误、罪行等) commit II [名] criminal

犯病 fànbìng [动] have a relapse

犯愁 fànchóu [动] worry

犯法 fànfǎ [动] break the law (PT broke, PP broken)

犯规 fànguī [动] break the rules (PT broke, PP broken)

犯忌 fànjì [动] break a taboo (PT broke, PP broken)

犯禁 fànjìn [动] violate a prohibition

犯人 fànrén [名] prisoner

犯罪 fànzuì [动] commit a crime ▷犯罪心理 criminal mind

饭 fàn [名] 1 (餐) meal ▷早饭 breakfast ▶晚饭 supper 2 (米饭) rice

饭局 fànjú [名] dinner party

饭桶 fàntǒng [名] 1 (盛饭工具) rice container 2 (饭量大的人) big eater 3 (喻) (无用的人) imbecile

饭碗 fànwǎn [名] 1 (盛饭的碗) rice bowl 2 (口)

(职业) job

泛 fàn I [动] 1 (书) (漂浮) float 2 (透出) suffuse ▷他脸上泛红。He blushed. 3 (泛滥) flood II [副] superficially

泛泛而谈 fànfàn ér tán talk generally

泛泛之交 fànfàn zhī jiāo acquaintance

泛滥 fànlàn [动] overflow

范 fàn [名] 1 (模型) model ▶典范 model 2 (范围) limit ▶规范 standard 3 (模子) pattern

范畴 fànchóu [名] category

范例 fànlì [名] example

范围 fànwéi [名] limit ▷管辖范围 limits of jurisdiction ▷势力范围 sphere of influence

范文 fànwén [名] model essay

贩 fàn I [动] deal in (PT, PP dealt) II [名] dealer

贩卖 fànmài [动] deal in (PT, PP dealt) ▷贩卖艺术品 deal in art ▷贩卖丝绸 be in the silk trade ▷贩卖人口 traffic in human beings

贩子 fànzi [名] dealer

方 fāng I [名] 1 (方向) direction ▶南方 the South 2 (方形) square ▶长方形 rectangle 3 (方面) side 4 (方法) method 5 (地方) place 6 (方子) prescription 7 (数) (乘方) power ▷3的4次方是81。Three to the power of four is 81. II [形] 1 (方形) square 2 (正直) honest III [副] 1 (书) (正当) ▶方今 nowadays ▷方兴未艾 be on the rise ▷来日方长 there is still time 2 (方才) just ▷如梦方醒 as if just awakened from a dream IV [量] 1 (指方形物) ▷一方豆腐 a piece of tofu ▷一方毛巾 a towel 2 (指平方或立方) ▷一方木材 a cubic metre of timber ▷办公室有30方。The office is 30 square metres.

方案 fāng'àn [名] plan ▷退休金方案 pension scheme ▷校长在制定本期工作方案。The head teacher is drawing up a work plan for the term.

方便 fāngbiàn [形] 1 (便利) convenient ▷上海的交通很方便。Transport in Shanghai is easy. ▷我们应把方便留给他人。We should make things easy for people. 2 (适宜) appropriate ▷这里谈话不方便。It's not appropriate to talk here.

方才 fāngcái [副] just now ▷方才的事你不要放在心上。Don't take to heart what happened just now.

方程 fāngchéng [名] equation

方寸 fāngcùn [名] (心绪) mind ▷他乱了方寸。He felt very troubled.

方法 fāngfǎ [名] method

方法论 fāngfǎlùn [名] methodology

方略 fānglüè [名] strategy

方面 fāngmiàn [名] 1 (指人) side ▷优势在我们方面。Our side has the advantage. 2 (指物) aspect ▷我们应该分析问题的所有方面。We should analyse all aspects of the problem.

方式 fāngshì [名] way ▷生活方式 way of life ▷生产方式 production method ▷她用简单的方式解决了问题。She solved the problem in a simple way.

方位 fāngwèi [名] position

方向 fāngxiàng [名] direction ▷你要朝那个方向走。You need to go in that direction. ▷他们在森林里迷失了方向。They got disoriented in the wood.

方兴未艾 fāng xīng wèi ài be on the rise

方言 fāngyán [名] dialect

方正 fāngzhèng [形] 1 (不歪斜) square 2 (正直) honest

方子 fāngzi [名] 1 (药方) prescription ▷开方子 write a prescription 2 (配方) formula

芳 fāng [名] 1 (香味) fragrance 2 (好名声) virtue

芳香 fāngxiāng [名] fragrance ▷芳香的花朵 fragrant flower

防 fáng I [动] 1 (防备) prevent ▷防冻 prevent frostbite ▷防盗 guard against theft 2 (防守) defend ▷海防 sea defences (英) 或 defenses (美) II [名] dyke

防暴 fángbào [动] ▷防暴警察 riot police

防备 fángbèi [动] guard against ▷防备敌人偷袭 guard against surprise attacks by the enemy ▷防备火灾 take precautions against fire

防不胜防 fáng bù shèng fáng be unable to defend

防范 fángfàn [动] keep a lookout (PT, PP kept)

防护 fánghù [动] protect

防患未然 fáng huàn wèi rán take preventative measures

防空 fángkōng [名] air defence (英) 或 defense (美) ▷防空导弹 air defence missile

防身 fángshēn [动] defend oneself

防微杜渐 fáng wēi dù jiàn nip in the bud

防卫 fángwèi [动] defend

防务 fángwù [名] defence (英), defense (美)

防线 fángxiàn [名] line of defence (英) 或 defense (美)

防御 fángyù [动] defend ▷修筑防御工事 construct defences (英) 或 defenses (美)

防止 fángzhǐ [动] prevent ▷防止疾病扩散 prevent disease from spreading

防治 fángzhì [动] prevent and cure

坊 fáng [名] workshop

妨 fáng [动] obstruct ▷妨碍 obstruct

妨碍 fáng'ài [动] obstruct ▷车祸妨碍了交通。The car accident obstructed the traffic. ▷嘈杂声会妨碍他人学习。The noise will disturb those who are studying.

妨害 fánghài [动] jeopardize

房 fáng [名] 1 (房子) house ▶楼房 tower block 2 (房间) room ▶书房 study ▶卧房 bedroom 3 (房子之物) ▶蜂房 beehive 4 (家族) ▷远房亲戚 a distant relative

房地产 fángdìchǎn [名] real estate

房东 fángdōng [名] landlord

房客 fángkè [名] tenant

房事 fángshì [名] sex

房屋 fángwū [名] building

仿 fǎng [动] 1 (仿效) copy 2 (类似) be like ▷他们两个人年龄相仿。They are both about the same age.

仿佛 fǎngfú I [连] as if II [形] similar

仿生学 fǎngshēngxué [名] bionics (PL)

仿效 fǎngxiào [动] imitate

仿造 fǎngzào [动] copy

仿照 fǎngzhào [动] copy ▷这个方法不错, 我们可以仿照。That's a good method – let's copy it.

仿制 fǎngzhì [动] fake ▷这是仿制品。This is a fake.

访 fǎng [动] 1 (访问) call on ▶访友 call on a friend ▶访谈 call in for a chat 2 (调查) investigate ▶访查 investigate

访问 fǎngwèn [动] visit

纺 fǎng I [动] spin (PT, PP spun) II [名] silk

纺织 fǎngzhī [动] ▷纺织品 textiles (PL) ▷纺织工业 textile industry

放 fàng [动] 1 (使自由) release ▶释放 release ▶解放 free 2 (暂时停止) ▷下周我放两天假。I'll have two days off next week. ▷放学了。School is now over. 3 (放纵) let oneself go ▷放声歌唱 sing uninhibitedly ▷放言高论 speak without restraint 4 (赶牲畜吃草) graze ▷放牛 graze cattle 5 (驱逐) expel ▶流放 banish 6 (发出) send out (PT, PP sent) ▷放炮 fire a gun ▶放风筝 fly a kite 7 (点燃) set ... off (PT, PP set) ▷放爆竹 set off firecrackers 8 (借出收息) lend (PT, PP lent) ▷放高利贷 practise (英) 或 practice (美) usury 9 (扩展) ▷把照片放大 enlarge a photo ▷把裙子放长 let down a skirt 10 (花

开) bloom **11** (搁置) put ... to one side (PT, PP put) **12** (弄倒) cut down (PT, PP cut) **13** (使处于) put (PT, PP put) ▷她把课本放在桌子上。She put the book on the table. **14** (加进) add ▷你往里放点糖就好喝。If you add some sugar it will taste better. **15** (控制自己) ▷放严肃点 become more serious **16** (放映) project ▷放电影 project a film **17** (保存) leave (PT, PP left) ▷把东西就放我这里吧。Leave your things with me.

放大 **fàngdà** [动] enlarge ▷把照片放大 enlarge a photo ▷把音量放大 turn up the volume

放荡 **fàngdàng** [形] dissipated

放风 **fàngfēng** [动] **1** (开窗通风) let in fresh air (PT, PP let) **2** (从牢房出来) let out for exercise **3** (散发消息) leak

放牧 **fàngmù** [动] graze

放屁 **fàngpì** [动] **1** (指生理现象) break wind (PT broke, PP broken) **2** (侮辱) (用来骂人) talk nonsense ▷放屁! (讳) That's complete crap!

放弃 **fàngqì** [动] give ... up (PT gave, PP given)

放晴 **fàngqíng** [动] clear up

放任 **fàngrèn** [动] ignore ▷对错误的行为不能放任不管。Bad behaviour should not be ignored. ▷放任政策 laissez-faire policy

放射 **fàngshè** [动] radiate

放射性 **fàngshèxìng** [名] **1** (指原子能) radioactivity ▷放射性灰尘 radioactive dust **2** (指医学) radiation

放生 **fàngshēng** [动] release

放肆 **fàngsì** [形] wanton

放松 **fàngsōng** [动] relax

放心 **fàngxīn** [动] set one's mind at rest (PT, PP set) ▷孩子还没回来，我不放心。My mind won't rest because the child hasn't come back yet.

放眼 **fàngyǎn** [动] survey

放逐 **fàngzhú** [动] banish

放纵 **fàngzòng** I [动] indulge ▷不要太放纵孩子。Don't be too indulgent with the children. II [形] undisciplined

飞 **fēi** I [动] (鸟、虫、飞机) fly (PT flew, PP flown) ▷这架飞机将由广州飞往北京。This plane is going from Guangzhou to Beijing. **2** (空中游动) flutter ▷叶子在空中飞着。The leaves are fluttering in the air. ▷飞雪花了。It's snowing. **3** (挥发) evaporate II [形] **1** (意外的) unexpected ▷飞祸 unexpected disaster **2** (凭空而来的) unfounded ▷流言飞语 unfounded rumours (英) or rumors (美) (PL) III [副] swiftly

飞驰 **fēichí** [动] speed (PT, PP sped)

飞碟 **fēidié** [名] UFO

飞短流长 **fēi duǎn liú cháng** tell stories

飞黄腾达 **fēi huáng téng dá** have a meteoric rise

飞机 **fēijī** [名] aeroplane (英), airplane (美)

飞快 **fēikuài** I [形] razor-sharp II [副] rapidly

飞毛腿 **fēimáotuǐ** [名] fast runner

飞速 **fēisù** [形] very fast

飞吻 **fēiwěn** [动] blow a kiss (PT blew, PP blown) ▷女孩儿给妈妈一个飞吻。The girl blew her mother a kiss.

飞翔 **fēixiáng** [动] hover

飞行 **fēixíng** [动] fly (PT flew, PP flown)

飞扬 **fēiyáng** [动] rise (PT rose, PP risen)

飞扬跋扈 **fēi yáng bá hù** pushy

飞跃 **fēiyuè** [动] leap ▷近几年，中国经济飞跃发展。China's economy has developed by leaps and bounds in recent years.

飞涨 **fēizhǎng** [动] soar

妃 **fēi** [名] concubine

非 **fēi** I [名] **1** (错误) wrong ▷是非 right and wrong **2** (非洲) Africa II [动] **1** (非议) blame ▷无可厚非 beyond reproach **2** (违反) run counter to (PT ran, PP run) ▷非法 illegal ▷非礼 impolite **3** (不是) not be ▷我非三言两语就能把这事说完的。I am not able to say it in a few words. **4** (强硬) insist on ▷他非要我参加。He insists on my taking part. ▷不行，我非得走。No, I must go. III [副] (必须) ▷我不让他去，他非去不可。I've tried to stop him, but he simply has to go. ▷要想通过考试，你非努力不行。You can't pass the exam without working hard.

非常 **fēicháng** I [形] exceptional II [副] very ▷你的同情让我非常感动。Your sympathy moved me very much. ▷这项工作非常难。This job is very hard. ▷你说的话非常重要。What you said is extremely important. ▷我非常抱歉。I'm terribly sorry.

非典 **fēidiǎn** [名] (非典型性肺炎) SARS

非法 **fēifǎ** [形] illegal

非凡 **fēifán** [形] outstanding

非…非… **fēi…fēi…** [连] neither...nor... ▷非亲非故 neither a relative nor a friend

非分 **fēifèn** [形] inappropriate

非金属 **fēijīnshǔ** [名] nonmetal

非礼 **fēilǐ** I [形] impolite II [动] sexually assault

非驴非马 **fēi lú fēi mǎ** be neither one thing nor the other

非难 fēinàn [动] censure
非人 fēirén [形] inhuman
非同小可 fēi tóng xiǎo kě no small matter
非议 fēiyì [动] reproach

绯 fēi [形] red
绯红 fēihóng [形] bright red ▷她脸蛋热得绯红。Her face was red with the heat.

扉 fēi [名] door
扉页 fēiyè [名] title page

蜚 见下文
蜚声 fēishēng [动] become famous

鲱 fēi [名] herring

肥 féi I [名] fertilizer II [动] 1 (使肥沃) fertilize 2 (暴富) get rich III [形] 1 (脂肪多) fat 2 (肥沃) fertile 3 (肥大) loose
肥大 féidà [形] 1 (宽大) loose 2 (肿大) swollen
肥料 féiliào [名] fertilizer
肥胖 féipàng [形] fat
肥沃 féiwò [形] fertile
肥皂 féizào [名] soap
肥壮 féizhuàng [形] stout

匪 fěi I [名] robber II [副] not ▷受益匪浅 gain quite significantly
匪徒 fěitú [名] gangster
匪夷所思 fěi yí suǒ sī fantastic

诽 fěi [动] slander
诽谤 fěibàng [动] slander

菲 fěi 见下文
菲薄 fěibó I [动] look down on II [形] humble

斐 fěi [形] brilliant
斐然 fěirán [形] brilliant

翡 fěi 见下文
翡翠 fěicuì [名] jadeite

吠 fèi [动] bark

肺 fèi [名] lung
肺腑 fèifǔ [名] heart ▷肺腑之言 heartfelt words ▷感人肺腑 deeply moving

狒 fèi 见下文
狒狒 fèifèi [名] baboon

废 fèi I [动] abandon II [形] 1 (不用的) waste 2 (没用的) useless 3 (残废的) disabled
废除 fèichú [动] abolish
废黜 fèichù [动] depose
废话 fèihuà [名] nonsense
废品 fèipǐn [名] 1 (不合格产品) reject 2 (废旧物品) waste
废弃 fèiqì [动] abandon
废寝忘食 fèi qǐn wàng shí forget to eat or sleep
废物 fèiwù [名] waste
废止 fèizhǐ [动] annul
废置 fèizhì [动] abandon

沸 fèi [形] boiling
沸点 fèidiǎn [名] boiling point
沸腾 fèiténg [动] 1 (汽化) boil 2 (喻) (指情绪) ▷大家沸腾起来。There was uproar.

费 fèi I [名] fee ▷车费 bus fare ▷医药费 medical expenses II [形] expensive III [动] 1 (花费) spend (PT, PP spent) ▷我费了好大的劲才明白他的意思。It was ages before I understood what he meant. ▷买这件皮大衣费了我很多钱。This leather coat cost me a lot of money. 2 (消耗过度) ▷这个牌子的冰箱很费电。This brand of refrigerator consumes too much electricity. ▷孩子们穿鞋太费。Children wear out their shoes too quickly.
费解 fèijiě [形] incomprehensible
费尽心机 fèi jìn xīnjī rack one's brains
费力 fèilì [动] take a lot of effort (PT took, PP taken) ▷我毫不费力地就把工作做完了。I got the job done without too much effort.
费神 fèishén [动] 1 (敬) ▷劳您费神把稿子看一下。Can I trouble you to take a look at this draft? 2 (耗费精神) put energy into (PT, PP put) ▷为写这篇文章我费了很大的神。I put a lot of energy into writing this article.
费事 fèishì [动] take trouble (PT took, PP taken) ▷他不怕费事，尽量做好会议的筹办工作。He is taking a lot of trouble in making arrangements for the meeting.
费心 fèixīn [动] 1 (敬) ▷您费心照看一会儿我的儿子好吗？Would you mind looking after my son for a while? ▷您费心帮我看看有没有错误。Can you check this for mistakes? 2 (耗费心思) devote a lot of care ▷我为他费了很多心。I devoted a lot of care to him.
费用 fèiyong [名] expense ▷生活费用 living expenses

痱 fèi [名] prickly heat

痱子 fèizi [名] prickly heat

分 fēn I [动] 1 (分开) divide ▷分离 separate ▷分散 scatter ▷分裂 split 2 (分配) assign ▷这些电脑已分给我们了。These computers have been assigned to us. 3 (辨别) distinguish ▷不分皂白 make no distinction between right and wrong II [名] 1 (分支) branch ▷分公司 branch of a company 2 (分数) fraction ▷分母 denominator III [量] 1 (分数) ▷四分之三 three quarters 2 (十分之一) one tenth ▷我们都怕老板三分。We are all a little afraid of the boss. 3 (长度单位) unit of length, equivalent to 3mm 4 (指货币) unit of Chinese currency, equal to a hundredth of a yuan 5 (指时间) minute ▷5点过5分 5 minutes past 5 6 (指弧度或角度) minute ▷36度20分角 36 degrees 20 minutes 7 (百分之一) per cent ▷月利1分 monthly interest of 1 per cent ▷他物理是93分。He got 93 per cent in physics.
→另见 fèn

分崩离析 fēn bēng lí xī fall to pieces

分辨 fēnbiàn [动] distinguish ▷分辨花样 distinguish one variety from another ▷我分辨不出这是什么颜色。I can't tell what colour it is.

分别 fēnbié I [动] 1 (离别) split up (PT, PP split) 2 (辨别) distinguish ▷分别善恶 distinguish the good from the bad II [名] difference

分布 fēnbù [动] distribute

分成 fēnchéng [动] divide

分词 fēncí [名] participle

分寸 fēncun [名] ▷经理说话很有分寸。The manager talks in a measured way.

分道扬镳 fēn dào yáng biāo each goes their own way

分割 fēngē [动] break apart (PT broke, PP broken)

分工 fēngōng [名] division of labour ▷社会分工 division of labour in society

分红 fēnhóng [动] get a bonus

分化 fēnhuà [动] 1 (分成) split up (PT, PP split) 2 (瓦解) break up (PT broke, PP broken) 3 (细胞、组织等) divide

分解 fēnjiě [动] 1 (数) break down (PT broke, PP broken) 2 (书) (解说) explain

分居 fēnjū [动] separate

分句 fēnjù [名] clause

分类 fēnlèi [动] classify ▷粗略的分类 rough classification

分离 fēnlí [动] 1 (分开) separate 2 (离别) part

分裂 fēnliè [动] 1 (分开) split (PT, PP split) 2 (生物) divide

分门别类 fēn mén bié lèi categorize

分泌 fēnmì [动] secrete

分娩 fēnmiǎn [动] give birth (PT gave, PP given)

分明 fēnmíng I [形] clear II [副] clearly

分派 fēnpài [动] assign

分配 fēnpèi [动] assign

分歧 fēnqí [名] difference

分散 fēnsàn [动] 1 (不集中) divert ▷不要分散你的注意力。Don't allow your attention to be diverted. 2 (散展) disperse

分身 fēnshēn [动] spare time

分神 fēnshén [动] ▷麻烦您分神帮我讲一讲这句话。Can I trouble you to help me with this speech?

分手 fēnshǒu [动] 1 (告别) say goodbye (PT, PP said) 2 (指男女关系) break up (PT broke, PP broken)

分数 fēnshù [名] fraction

分水岭 fēnshuǐlǐng [名] 1 (地理) watershed 2 (喻) (界限) dividing line

分摊 fēntān [动] share

分庭抗礼 fēn tíng kàng lǐ stand up to

分析 fēnxī [动] analyse (英), analyze (美) ▷对当前国际形势的透彻分析 a thorough analysis of recent international trends

分享 fēnxiǎng [动] share in ▷我们一起分享成功的欢乐。We will all share in the pleasure of success.

分晓 fēnxiǎo I [名] 1 (结果) solution 2 (道理) reason II [形] clear

分心 fēnxīn [动] 1 (分散注意力) be distracted 2 (费心) ▷这事让您分心了。Sorry to trouble you with this.

分忧 fēnyōu [动] ▷她始终帮我分忧。She always helps me through my problems.

分赃 fēnzāng [动] share the spoils

分支 fēnzhī [名] branch ▷学科的分支 branch of science ▷河流的分支 tributary

分子 fēnzǐ [名] 1 (数) numerator 2 (化) molecule

芬 fēn [名] fragrance ▷芬芳 fragrant

芬芳 fēnfāng [形] fragrant

吩 fēn 见下文

吩咐 fēnfù [动] instruct ▷母亲吩咐我看管好房子。Mother instructed me to look after the house.

纷 fēn [形] 1 (多) numerous ▷纷繁 numerous 2 (乱) confused ▷纷扰 confusion

纷繁 fēnfán [形] numerous

纷纷 fēnfēn I [形] diverse II [副] one after another

纷乱 fēnluàn [形] chaotic

纷纭 fēnyún [形] disorderly

纷争 fēnzhēng [名] dispute

纷至沓来 fēn zhì tà lái come thick and fast

氛 fēn [名] atmosphere

氛围 fēnwéi [名] atmosphere

坟 fén [名] grave

坟墓 fénmù [名] grave

焚 fén [动] burn

焚化 fénhuà [动] incinerate

焚烧 fénshāo [动] burn

粉 fěn I [名] 1 (粉末) powder 2 (粉丝) vermicelli II [动] 1 (成碎末) crumble ▶粉碎 crush 2 (变成粉状) pulverize III [形] 1 (白色) white 2 (粉红色) pink

粉红 fěnhóng [形] pink

粉末 fěnmò [名] powder

粉墨登场 fěn mò dēng chǎng 1 (贬) embark upon a political career 2 (产品、新人) be launched

粉饰 fěnshì [动] gloss over

粉刷 fěnshuā [动] whitewash

粉碎 fěnsuì I [形] crushed II [动] smash

分 fèn [名] 1 (成分) component ▶水分 water content 2 (限度) limit ▶过分 excessive ▶本分 duty 3 (情分) feelings (PL)
→另见 fēn

分量 fènliàng [名] weight ▷这两个西瓜是一样的分量。These two watermelons are the same weight. ▷他说的话很有分量。He speaks with authority.

分子 fènzǐ [名] ▷积极分子 activist ▷知识分子 intellectual ▷保守分子 conservative

份 fèn I [名] 1 (一部分) part ▶股份 share ▷他们把钱平分成4份。The money was divided equally between the four of them. 2 (指划分单位) ▶年份 year II [量] 1 (指食物) portion ▷一份快餐 a portion of fast food 2 (指报刊) copy

份额 fèn'é [名] share

份子 fènzi [名] share ▷出份子 club together

奋 fèn [动] 1 (振作) exert oneself ▶勤奋 diligent 2 (举起) raise

奋不顾身 fèn bù gù shēn act bravely and selflessly ▷抢险队员奋不顾身营救孩子们。The emergency worker showed great courage in rescuing the children.

奋斗 fèndòu [动] fight (PT, PP fought) ▷为前途而奋斗 fight for the future

奋发 fènfā [动] work hard

奋发图强 fèn fā tú qiáng work hard for success

奋勇 fènyǒng [动] act bravely ▷奋勇杀敌 fight the enemy bravely

粪 fèn [名] excrement

粪土 fèntǔ [名] rubbish

愤 fèn [形] indignant ▶气愤 indignant

愤慨 fènkǎi [形] indignant ▷这种无耻行为令人愤慨！This is outrageous behaviour (英) 或 behavior (美), quite infuriating!

愤怒 fènnù [形] angry ▷同事们愤怒谴责他卑鄙无耻的行径。His colleagues angrily condemned his despicable conduct.

愤世嫉俗 fèn shì jí sú detest the ways of the world

丰 fēng [形] 1 (丰富) abundant 2 (大) great 3 (貌美) good-looking

丰碑 fēngbēi [名] monument

丰富 fēngfù I [形] abundant ▷丰富多彩的生活 a full and interesting life II [动] enrich

丰功伟绩 fēng gōng wěi jì great achievements

丰厚 fēnghòu [形] abundant ▷丰厚的皮毛 thick fur ▷丰厚的薪水 a generous salary

丰满 fēngmǎn [形] 1 (指物品) plentiful 2 (指身材) well-developed ▷身体丰满匀称 a full and well-proportioned figure

丰年 fēngnián [名] good year ▷瑞雪兆丰年。Snow at the right time is a sign of a good harvest.

丰盛 fēngshèng [形] rich

丰收 fēngshōu [动] have a good harvest

丰硕 fēngshuò [形] substantial

丰衣足食 fēng yī zú shí be comfortably off

丰足 fēngzú [形] ample

风 fēng I [名] 1 (指空气流动) wind ▶狂风 gale ▷今天刮大风。It's very windy today. 2 (风气) trend 3 (景象) scene 4 (态度) manner ▷风度 bearing 5 (消息) information ▷闻风而动 respond immediately II [形] rumoured (英), rumored (美) ▷风言风语 gossip III [动] air ▷风干 air-dry

风波 fēngbō [名] storm

风采 fēngcǎi [名] 1 (神采) elegance 2 (文采)

writing talent

风餐露宿 fēng cān lù sù face the elements

风尘 fēngchén [名] (指旅行) travel weariness

风驰电掣 fēng chí diàn chè quick as lightning

风传 fēngchuán [动] be rumoured (英) 或 rumored (美)

风度 fēngdù [名] bearing

风格 fēnggé [名] 1 (气度) manner ▷高尚风格 refined manner 2 (特点) style ▷绘画风格 style of painting

风光 fēngguāng [名] scenery

风花雪月 fēng huā xuě yuè love affair

风华 fēnghuá [名] (书) elegance and talent ▷风华正茂 be in one's prime

风化 fēnghuà I [名] morals (PL) II [动] weather

风纪 fēngjì [名] discipline

风景 fēngjǐng [名] scenery

风浪 fēnglàng [名] 1 (风和波浪) rough waters (PL) 2 (遭遇) difficulties (PL) ▷久经风浪 have survived many troubles

风凉 fēngliáng [形] cool

风凉话 fēngliánghuà [名] sarcastic remark

风流 fēngliú [形] 1 (指功绩) outstanding 2 (指才学) free-spirited 3 (指男女关系) promiscuous ▷一夜风流 one night stand

风马牛不相及 fēng mǎ niú bù xiāng jí be completely at odds ▷这部电影的配乐与剧情风马牛不相及。The background music to this film is completely at odds with the storyline.

风貌 fēngmào [名] 1 (风格) style ▷民间艺术的风貌 folk-art style 2 (景象) scene

风靡一时 fēngmǐ yīshí be in fashion

风起云涌 fēng qǐ yún yǒng 1 (字) rising storm 2 (喻) upsurge ▷外资合作风起云涌 Joint ventures with foreign investment have really taken off.

风气 fēngqì [名] ▷社会风气越来越好。Social mores are improving. ▷全校出现了做早操的风气。Everyone at school has taken to doing morning exercises.

风情 fēngqíng [名] 1 (风向、风力) wind force and direction 2 (感情) expressions of love (PL) ▷卖弄风情 flirt 3 (风土人情) local customs (PL)

风趣 fēngqù [名] wit ▷他说话特别风趣。He is exceedingly witty.

风骚 fēngsāo I [名] literary brilliance II [形] flirtatious

风尚 fēngshàng [名] custom

风声 fēngshēng [名] 1 (指风) sound of the wind 2 (消息) rumour (英), rumor (美)

风水 fēngshuǐ [名] feng shui

风俗 fēngsú [名] custom

风调雨顺 fēng tiáo yǔ shùn favourable conditions

风头 fēngtou [名] 1 (情势) situation ▷看风头办事 act according to the situation 2 (出头露面) limelight ▷出风头 seek the limelight

风土 fēngtǔ [名] ▷风土人情 local landscape and customs

风味 fēngwèi [名] distinctive style ▷北京风味小吃 dishes in the Beijing style

风闻 fēngwén [动] hear a rumour (英) 或 rumor (美) (PT, PP heard)

风险 fēngxiǎn [名] risk

风向 fēngxiàng [名] wind direction

风行 fēngxíng [动] be in fashion

风雅 fēngyǎ [形] refined

风言风语 fēng yán fēng yǔ gossip

风雨 fēngyǔ [名] 1 (字) wind and rain 2 (喻) (困难) hardship

风雨同舟 fēngyǔ tóngzhōu stick together ▷风雨同舟共渡难关 stick together in difficulty

风云 fēngyún [名] turmoil ▷战争风云 the turmoil of war

风云人物 fēngyún rénwù influential person (PL people)

风韵 fēngyùn [名] charm

风姿 fēngzī [名] poise

枫 fēng [名] maple

封 fēng I [动] (封闭) seal ▷因车祸，路被封了。The road was sealed off because of the car accident. II [名] envelope III [量] ▷一封信 a letter

封闭 fēngbì [动] 1 (盖住) seal 2 (查封) seal off

封存 fēngcún [动] freeze (PT froze, PP frozen) ▷封存账号 freeze an account

封顶 fēngdǐng [动] cap ▷封顶价格 cap prices

封建 fēngjiàn I [名] feudalism II [形] feudal ▷封建社会 feudal society

封镜 fēngjìng [动] finish shooting

封杀 fēngshā [动] blacklist

封锁 fēngsuǒ [动] 1 (断绝联系) block ▷封锁经济 impose an economic blockade 2 (不能通行) seal off

疯 fēng I [形] mad II [副] madly ▷野草疯长。The weeds are out of control.

疯狂 fēngkuáng [形] crazy

疯子 fēngzi [名] lunatic ▷他是疯子。He's mad.

峰 fēng [名] **1** (山顶) peak **2** (喻) hump
峰会 fēnghuì [名] summit meeting
峰峦 fēngluán [名] a row of peaks

锋 fēng [名] **1** (尖端) point **2** (带头的) vanguard **3** (锋面) front ▶冷锋 cold front
锋利 fēnglì [形] **1** (工具) sharp **2** (言论) cutting ▷锋利的言辞 cutting remarks (PL)
锋芒 fēngmáng [名] **1** (尖利部分) the cutting edge ▷斗争锋芒直指官场腐败。The focus of attack is official corruption. **2** (才干) talent

蜂 fēng **I** [名] **1** (黄蜂) wasp **2** (蜜蜂) bee **II** [副] in swarms ▷蜂聚 gather in swarms
蜂蜜 fēngmì [名] honey
蜂拥 fēngyōng [动] swarm ▷球迷蜂拥而至。The football fans swarmed in.

逢 féng [动] come across (PT came, PP come)
逢场作戏 féng chǎng zuò xì enjoy the fun while it lasts ▷有的人把交朋友当作是逢场作戏。Some people regard friendship as a game.
逢凶化吉 féng xiōng huà jí land on one's feet
逢迎 féngyíng [动] (贬) ingratiate oneself with

缝 féng [动] sew (PT sewed, PP sewn)
→另见 fèng
缝纫 féngrèn [动] sew (PT sewed, PP sewn)

讽 fěng [动] mock ▶讥讽 satirize
讽刺 fěngcì [动] ridicule

凤 fèng [名] phoenix
凤毛麟角 fèng máo lín jiǎo as rare as hen's teeth

奉 fèng [动] **1** (献给) present **2** (接受) receive **3** (尊重) respect **4** (信仰) believe in **5** (伺候) attend to
奉承 fèngcheng [动] flatter
奉告 fènggào [动] (敬) inform
奉公守法 fèng gōng shǒu fǎ be public-spirited and respect the law
奉命 fèngmìng [动] be instructed ▷部委奉命紧急调查。Government departments were instructed to carry out an urgent investigation.
奉陪 fèngpéi [动] accompany ▷谁想下棋, 我都愿奉陪。If anyone wants to play a game of chess, I'd be glad to join them.
奉若神明 fèng ruò shén míng idolize
奉献 fèngxiàn [动] dedicate ▷为教育奉献生命 dedicate one's life to education

奉行 fèngxíng [动] pursue

俸 fèng [名] salary
俸禄 fènglù [名] official's salary

缝 fèng [名] **1** (接合处) seam ▷无缝长袜 seamless stockings **2** (缝隙) crack
→另见 féng
缝隙 fèngxì [名] crack

佛 fó [名] **1** (佛教) Buddhism **2** (佛像) Buddha
佛教 fójiào [名] Buddhism
佛学 fóxué [名] Buddhism

否 fǒu **I** [动] deny **II** [副] **1** (书)(不) no **2** (是、能、可) or not ▷他明天是否参加聚会? Is he coming to the party tomorrow or not?
否定 fǒudìng **I** [动] negate ▷事实否定了他说的话。The facts negate what he said. ▷我否定了他的建议。I refuted his suggestion. **II** [形] negative
否决 fǒujué [动] veto ▷否决提议 veto the motion
否认 fǒurèn [动] deny
否则 fǒuzé [连] otherwise ▷好好温习功课, 否则考试通不过。Revise properly, otherwise you won't pass your exams.

夫 fū [名] **1** (丈夫) husband **2** (男子) man (PL men) **3** (劳动者) manual worker
夫妇 fūfù [名] husband and wife
夫人 fūrén [名] Mrs ▷胡夫人 Mrs Hu ▷第一夫人 First Lady
夫子 fūzǐ [名] **1** (学者) scholar (贬)(陈腐的人) old fogey

肤 fū [名] skin
肤浅 fūqiǎn [形] superficial

孵 fū [动] hatch ▷孵小鸡 hatch chicks

敷 fū [动] **1** (涂) apply **2** (铺开) lay (PT, PP laid) **3** (足够) be sufficient for ▷入不敷出 income falls short of expenditure
敷设 fūshè [动] lay (PT, PP laid) ▷敷设电缆 lay an electric cable ▷敷设地雷 lay landmines
敷衍 fūyǎn [动] **1** (应付) go through the motions (PT went, PP gone) ▷敷衍了事 do a superficial job **2** (维持) get by ▷手里的钱还够敷衍几天。I have enough money to get by for a few days.

伏 fú **I** [动] **1** (趴) lean over **2** (低下去) fall (PT fell, PP fallen) **3** (隐藏) hide (PT hid, PP hidden) **4** (屈

服) concede ▷伏输 concede defeat **5** (降伏) subdue **II** [名] the height of summer

伏案 fú'àn [动] hunch over one's desk

伏笔 fúbǐ [名] foreshadowing ▷故事的开端为悲剧性的结尾埋下了伏笔。The beginning of the story foreshadows the tragic ending.

伏兵 fúbīng [名] ambush

伏法 fúfǎ [动] be executed

伏击 fújī [动] ambush

伏侍 fúshi [动] look after

伏输 fúshū [动] concede defeat

伏特 fútè [量] volt

伏天 fútiān [名] the height of summer

伏帖 fútiē [形] **1** (舒服) content **2** (平整) neat ▷衣服熨烫得很伏帖。The clothes were ironed neatly.

伏罪 fúzuì [动] plead guilty

凫 fú **I** [名] wild duck **II** [动] swim (PT swam, PP swum)

芙 fú 见下文

芙蓉 fúróng [名] (荷花) lotus

扶 fú [动] **1** (稳住) steady ▷老太太扶着栏杆使自己站稳。The old woman steadied herself by holding on to the rail. ▷姑娘扶老大爷过马路。The girl helped the old man across the road. **2** (搀起) help up ▷护士把孩子扶起来。The nurse helped the child up. **3** (扶助) help

扶持 fúchí [动] support

扶贫 fúpín [动] help the poor

扶养 fúyǎng [动] **1** provide for ▷夫妻俩努力工作以扶养父母和孩子。The couple work hard to provide for their parents and children. **2** bring up (PT, PP brought) ▷他是由奶奶扶养大的。He was brought up by his grandmother.

扶摇直上 fúyáo zhí shàng rise sharply ▷公司产量扶摇直上。The company's output rose sharply.

扶植 fúzhí [动] foster

扶助 fúzhù [动] support

孚 fú [动] inspire confidence ▷深孚众望 inspire public confidence

拂 fú [动] **1** (轻擦) brush **2** (甩动) flick

拂拭 fúshì [动] wipe

拂晓 fúxiǎo [名] dawn

拂袖而去 fúxiù'érqù storm off

服 fú **I** [名] clothes (PL) ▶校服 school uniform

II [动] **1** (吃) take (PT took, PP taken) ▶服药 take medicine **2** (担任) serve ▶服役 serve in the army **3** (服从) comply with ▷心服口服 be totally compliant **4** (使信服) convince **5** (适应) adapt ▷不服水土 not acclimatized →另见 fù

服从 fúcóng [动] obey

服毒 fúdú [动] take poison (PT took, PP taken)

服法 fúfǎ [名] directions (PL) ▷中药的服法 directions for using traditional Chinese medicine

服气 fúqì [动] accept ▷我对老师的批评感到不服气。I was unconvinced by the teacher's criticism.

服饰 fúshì [名] dress and accessories (PL)

服侍 fúshì [动] look after

服输 fúshū [动] concede

服帖 fútiē [形] **1** (驯服) docile **2** (妥当) proper ▷他把每件事安排得服服帖帖。He sorted everything into its proper place.

服务 fúwù [动] serve ▷很高兴为您服务。I am very happy to be of service to you.

服务员 fúwùyuán [名] **1** (指商店里) attendant **2** (指饭馆里) waiter, waitress **3** (指宾馆里) room attendant

服刑 fúxíng [动] serve a prison sentence ▷他在监狱中服了3年刑。He served a three-year prison sentence.

服药 fúyào [动] take medicine (PT took, PP taken)

服役 fúyì [动] serve (in the forces) ▷他的儿子在海军服役。His son is serving in the navy.

服用 fúyòng [动] (药) take (PT took, PP taken)

服装 fúzhuāng [名] clothing

俘 fú **I** [动] capture **II** [名] prisoner ▶战俘 prisoner of war

俘获 fúhuò [动] capture

俘虏 fúlǔ [名] prisoner

浮 fú **I** [动] float ▷她脸上浮现一丝笑容。She gave a faint smile. **II** [形] **1** (表面上) superficial ▶浮面 surface **2** (可移动) movable ▶浮财 movable assets (PL) **3** (暂时) temporary **4** (轻浮) slapdash **5** (空虚) empty ▶浮夸 exaggerated **6** (多余) surplus

浮沉 fúchén [动] drift ▷与世浮沉 swim with the tide ▷商海浮沉 the ups and downs of business

浮动 fúdòng [动] **1** (流动) float **2** (不稳定) fluctuate

浮光掠影 fú guāng lüè yǐng fleeting ▷浮光掠影看厦门 make a fleeting visit to Xiamen

浮华 fúhuá [形] ostentatious

浮夸 fúkuā [动] exaggerate

浮力 fúlì [名] buoyancy

浮浅 fúqiǎn [形] shallow

浮现 fúxiàn [动] come back (PT came, PP come) ▷他的音容笑貌又浮现在眼前。His voice and smiling face came back to me.

浮想联翩 fúxiǎng liánpiān many thoughts run through one's mind

浮游 fúyóu [动] float

浮躁 fúzào [形] impulsive

浮肿 fúzhǒng [动] puff up ▷一夜没睡，他的眼睛有些浮肿。After a sleepless night, his eyes are a bit puffy.

符 fú I [名] 1 (标记) mark ▶音符 musical note 2 (图形) Daoist motif ▷护身符 talisman II [动] be in keeping with ▷他说的和做的不符。His words are out of keeping with his actions.

符号 fúhào [名] mark

符合 fúhé [动] match ▷符合招生条件 meet admission requirements

幅 fú I [名] 1 (指布) width 2 (泛指大小) size ▶幅度 range ▷大幅油画 a large oil painting II [量] ▷一幅窗帘 a curtain ▷一幅照片 a photograph

幅度 fúdù [名] range ▷两臂摆动的幅度不要太大。You must not swing your arms too much. ▷此次降价的幅度非常大。This time prices fell very sharply.

幅员 fúyuán [名] size ▷中国幅员辽阔。China is vast in size.

辐 fú [名] spoke

辐射 fúshè I [动] radiate II [名] radiation

蜉 fú 见下文

蜉蝣 fúyóu [名] mayfly

福 fú [名] good fortune

福分 fúfen [名] good fortune ▷有这么好的闺女，真是你的福分。You are really fortunate to have such a good daughter.

福利 fúlì [名] welfare ▷你们公司的福利好吗？Do you have good company benefits?

福气 fúqì [名] good fortune

福音 fúyīn [名] 1 (宗)(教义) Gospel 2 (好消息) good news

蝠 fú [名] bat ▶蝙蝠 bat

抚 fǔ [动] 1 (安慰) comfort ▶抚恤 give relief to (PT gave, PP given) 2 (保护) nurture 3 (按着) stroke

抚爱 fǔ'ài [动] cherish ▷缺乏抚爱的童年 a loveless childhood

抚今追昔 fǔ jīn zhuī xī evoke memories of the past

抚摩 fǔmó [动] stroke

抚弄 fǔnòng [动] fondle

抚慰 fǔwèi [动] comfort

抚恤 fǔxù [动] give relief to (PT gave, PP given)

抚养 fǔyǎng [动] bring ... up (PT, PP brought)

抚育 fǔyù [动] 1 (人) raise 2 (动植物) tend

拊 fǔ [动] (书) clap

拊掌 fǔzhǎng [动] clap one's hands

斧 fǔ [名] axe (英), ax (美)

斧子 fǔzi [名] axe (英), ax (美)

府 fǔ [名] 1 (机关) government body ▶官府 the authorities ▶政府 government 2 (住宅) official residence

俯 fǔ [动] bend over (PT, PP bent) ▶俯伏 lie prone ▶俯冲 nose-dive

俯就 fǔjiù [动] 1 (敬)(担任) kindly accept ▷请您俯就经理一职。Please accept the position of director. 2 (迁就) go along with (PT went, PP gone)

俯瞰 fǔkàn [动] look down on ▷她从飞机上俯瞰长江。She looked down on the Yangtze from the plane.

俯拾即是 fǔ shí jí shì extremely common ▷民间故事俯拾即是。Folk tales are to be found everywhere.

俯视 fǔshì [动] look down on

俯首 fǔshǒu [动] bow one's head

俯首帖耳 fǔ shǒu tiē ěr be totally subservient ▷他对上司俯首帖耳。He's totally subservient to his boss.

釜 fǔ [名] pot

釜底抽薪 fǔ dǐ chōu xīn take drastic action

辅 fǔ [动] complement ▷相辅而行 complement each other

辅导 fǔdǎo [动] coach ▷辅导学生学习物理 coach students in physics

辅助 fǔzhù I [动] assist ▷他辅助我写这本书。He assisted me in writing this book. II [形] supplementary ▷辅助教材 supplementary teaching materials ▷辅助信

息 additional information

辅佐 fǔzuǒ [动] assist ▷辅佐朝政 assist in the affairs of state

脯 fǔ [名] 1 (肉干) dried meat 2 (蜜饯) preserved fruit

腐 fǔ I [形] rotten II [名] beancurd ▶腐竹 roll of dried beancurd

腐败 fǔbài I [动] rot ▷腐败的食物 rotten food II [形] corrupt

腐化 fǔhuà [动] 1 (堕落) corrupt ▷贪污腐化 corruption 2 (腐烂) decompose

腐烂 fǔlàn I [动] rot II [形] decadent

腐蚀 fǔshí [动] 1 (消损) corrode ▷金属工具被腐蚀了。The metal tools have corroded. 2 (堕落) corrupt

腐朽 fǔxiǔ I [动] rot II [形] decadent

腐竹 fǔzhú [名] roll of dried beancurd

父 fù [名] 1 (父亲) father 2 (指男性长辈) senior male relative ▶祖父 grandfather

父老 fùlǎo [名] elder

父亲 fùqīn [名] father

父兄 fùxiōng [名] 1 (父亲和哥哥) father and elder brothers 2 (家长) head of the family

讣 fù I [动] announce a death II [名] obituary

讣告 fùgào I [动] announce a death II [名] obituary

付 fù [动] 1 (事物) hand over ▶托付 entrust ▷付诸实施 put into effect 2 (钱) pay (PT, PP paid) ▶偿付 pay back ▷付邮资 pay postage

付排 fùpái [动] have typeset

付托 fùtuō [动] entrust ▷付托重任 entrust with a heavy responsibility

付印 fùyìn [动] 1 (指交付出版社) submit for publication 2 (指交付印刷) go to press (PT went, PP gone)

付账 fùzhàng [动] pay the bill (PT, PP paid)

付之一炬 fù zhī yī jù be consumed by fire ▷失恋的女孩儿把男朋友的信付之一炬。The jilted girl burned all her boyfriend's letters.

付之一笑 fù zhī yī xiào brush off with a smile ▷他把感情看得失, 爱与不爱都付之一笑。He treats love and loss lightly.

付诸东流 fù zhū dōng liú waste ▷巨额投资付诸东流。A huge investment was wasted.

负 fù I [动] 1 (书) (背) carry on one's back ▷负重 carry a heavy load 2 (担负) bear (PT bore, PP borne) 3 (遭受) suffer ▷负伤 be wounded 4 (享有) enjoy 5 (拖欠) be in arrears ▷负债 be in debt 6 (背弃) turn one's back on 7 (失败) lose (PT, PP lost) ▷甲队0比2负于乙队。The A team lost to the B team two-nil. II [形] negative ▶负数 negative number

负担 fùdān I [动] bear (PT bore, PP borne) II [名] burden

负荷 fùhè I [动] (书) carry II [名] load

负荆请罪 fù jīng qǐng zuì humbly apologize

负疚 fùjiù [动] feel guilty (PT, PP felt)

负面效应 fùmiàn xiàoyìng [名] negative effect

负气 fùqì [动] ▷负气出走 leave in a fit of anger

负伤 fùshāng [动] be wounded

负心 fùxīn [动] be heartless

负隅顽抗 fù yú wán kàng put up a stiff resistance

负约 fùyuē [动] 1 (违背诺言) break a promise (PT broke, PP broken) 2 (失约) miss an appointment

负责 fùzé I [动] be responsible ▷谁应对这起事故负责? Who should be held responsible for this accident? II [形] conscientious ▷他对工作很负责。He is very conscientious about his work.

负债 fùzhài [动] be in debt

负重 fùzhòng [动] 1 (背着重物) carry a heavy load 2 (承担重任) take on an important task (PT took, PP taken)

妇 fù [名] 1 (妇女) woman (PL women) ▶妇科 gynaecology (英) gynecology (美) 2 (已婚妇女) married woman (PL women) 3 (妻) wife (PL wives)

妇科 fùkē [名] gynaecology (英), gynecology (美)

妇女 fùnǚ [名] woman (PL women)

附 fù [动] 1 (附带) attach 2 (靠近) get close to 3 (依从) depend on

附带 fùdài [动] add ▷附带说一句 mention in passing

附和 fùhè [动] echo ▷随声附和别人的说法 echo the views of others

附会 fùhuì [动] make a false analogy

附加 fùjiā [动] add ▷附加手续费 additional administrative charge

附件 fùjiàn [名] 1 (文件) attachment 2 (零件) spare parts (PL)

附近 fùjìn I [形] nearby II [名] vicinity ▷附近有电话亭吗? Is there a telephone box in the vicinity?

附录 fùlù [名] appendix

附设 fùshè [动] add ▷办公楼里附设了个休息室。A new lounge has been opened in the office building.

附属 fùshǔ I [动] attach to ▷该医院附属于一所大学。This hospital is attached to a university. II [形] affiliated to

附议 fùyì [动] support a motion

附庸 fùyōng [名] dependency

附注 fùzhù [名] annotation

附着 fùzhuó [动] stick to (PT, PP stuck)

服 fù [量] dose
→另见 fú

赴 fù [动] go to (PT went, PP gone) ▷奔赴前线 rush to the front

赴任 fùrèn [动] take up a job (PT took, PP taken)

赴汤蹈火 fù tāng dǎo huǒ go through hell and high water

赴约 fùyuē [动] keep an appointment (PT, PP kept)

复 fù I [形] 1 (重复) duplicated ▷复制 reproduce 2 (繁复) complex II [动] 1 (转) turn 2 (回答) reply 3 (恢复) recover 4 (报复) take revenge (PT took, PP taken) III [副] again ▶复查 re-examine

复辟 fùbì [动] restore to power

复仇 fùchóu [动] take revenge (PT took, PP taken) ▷3年后他终于为死去的儿子复仇了。After three years, he finally avenged his son's death.

复读 fùdú [动] retake (PT retook, PP retaken)

复发 fùfā [动] recur ▷病治愈后要防止复发。After an illness is cured, you must prevent it from recurring.

复古 fùgǔ [动] go back to the old ways (PT went, PP gone)

复合 fùhé [形] compound

复活 fùhuó [动] revive

复活节 Fùhuó Jié [名] (宗) Easter

复句 fùjù [名] compound sentence

复述 fùshù [动] 1 (重复) repeat 2 (重新表达) retell (PT, PP retold)

复数 fùshù [名] plural

复苏 fùsū [动] 1 (生物体) resuscitate 2 (经济) recover

复习 fùxí [动] revise ▷为考试而复习 revise for exams ▷复习功课 go over one's lessons

复兴 fùxīng [动] revive ▷文艺复兴 the Renaissance

复议 fùyì [动] reconsider

复印 fùyìn [动] photocopy

复员 fùyuán [动] 1 (转入和平) return to peacetime conditions 2 (退役) demobilize

复原 fùyuán [动] 1 (恢复健康) recover ▷老师病后身体已经复原。Our teacher has already recovered from his illness. 2 (恢复原样) restore

复杂 fùzá [形] complex

复制 fùzhì [动] reproduce

副 fù I [形] 1 (辅助) deputy ▷副局长 deputy director 2 (附带) subsidiary ▶副业 subsidiary business ▷副作用 side effect II [名] assistant ▶大副 first mate III [动] correspond to ▷名副其实 live up to its name IV [量] 1 (套) pair ▷一副耳机 a pair of headphones ▷一副手套 a pair of gloves 2 (指表情) ▷一副冷面孔 a cold expression

副本 fùběn [名] duplicate

副词 fùcí [名] adverb

副刊 fùkān [名] supplement

副食 fùshí [名] non-staple food

副手 fùshǒu [名] assistant

副业 fùyè [名] subsidiary business

副作用 fùzuòyòng [名] side effect

赋 fù I [动] 1 compose ▷赋诗一首 compose a poem 2 bestow II [名] (旧) tax ▶田赋 land tax

赋税 fùshuì [名] tax

赋闲 fùxián [动] be out of work

赋有 fùyǒu [动] possess ▷赋有朝气 possess vitality ▷赋有个性 have individuality

赋予 fùyǔ [动] give (PT gave, PP given) ▷赋予权利 grant rights

傅 fù [名] teacher

富 fù I [形] 1 (指财产) rich 2 (丰富的) abundant II [名] wealth III [动] enrich

富贵 fùguì [形] rich and influential

富豪 fùháo [名] rich and powerful person (PL people)

富丽堂皇 fù lì táng huáng splendid

富强 fùqiáng [形] prosperous and powerful

富饶 fùráo [形] abundant

富庶 fùshù [形] rich and populous

富翁 fùwēng [名] man of means (PL men) ▷百万富翁 millionaire

富有 fùyǒu I [形] wealthy II [动] be full of ▷富有创造力 be very creative

富裕 fùyù [形] prosperous ▷富裕地区 prosperous area ▷他家很富裕。His family is very well off.

富余 fùyu [形] surplus

富足 fùzú [形] comfortable

腹 fù[名] 1 (指躯干) stomach 2 (指物体) belly 3 (内心) mind ▶腹稿 mental outline

腹背受敌 fù bèi shòu dí be attacked from all sides

腹地 fùdì[名] hinterland

腹稿 fùgǎo[名] mental outline ▷演讲前先打个腹稿。Before making a speech, first have a mental outline.

缚 fù[动] bind (PT, PP bound) ▷作茧自缚 make a noose for one's own neck

覆 fù[动] 1 (盖住) cover 2 (翻过来) overturn

覆盖 fùgài[动] cover ▷地上覆盖着厚厚的白雪。The ground was covered in thick white snow.

覆灭 fùmiè[动] wipe out ▷全军覆灭。The whole army was wiped out.

覆没 fùmò[动] 1 (书) (指船) sink (PT sank, PP sunk) 2 (被消灭) annihilate

覆辙 fùzhé[名] ▷重蹈覆辙 take the same path to disaster

馥 fù[名] (书) fragrance

馥郁 fùyù[形] strongly scented

Gg

夹 gā 见下文
→另见 jiā, jiá
夹肢窝 gāzhiwō [名] armpit

咖 gā 见下文
→另见 kā
咖喱 gālí [名] curry

嘎 gā [拟] screech ▷火车嘎的一声停了下来。
The train screeched to a halt.
嘎吱 gāzhī [拟] creak ▷小板凳被他压得嘎吱嘎吱地响。The stool creaked under his weight.

该 gāi I [动] 1 (应当) ought to 2 (轮到) be the turn of ▷这次该他主持会议了。It's his turn to chair the meeting this time. 3 (活该) serve ... right ▷他睡懒觉误了火车，活该！He overslept and missed the train – serves him right! II [助动] 1 (应该) should ▷工作明天该完成了。The work should be finished by tomorrow. 2 (表示推测) ▷他还没回来，该不是又加班了吧？He's still not back – isn't he doing overtime? ▷再不吃的话，菜都该凉了。If we keep waiting the food is only going to get colder. 3 (用于加强语气) ▷房间里放些鲜花该多温馨啊！It would be so lovely to have some flowers in the room. ▷要是他能在这儿该多好啊！It would be great if he could be here.

III [代] that, this
该当 gāidāng [动] deserve
该死 gāisǐ [形] damn

改 gǎi [动] 1 (改变) change 2 (修改) alter 3 (改正) correct
改编 gǎibiān [动] 1 (重写) adapt ▷将小说改编为电影 adapt a novel for the screen 2 (指编制) reorganise ▷改编军队 reorganize an army ▷改编预算体制 restructure a budgetary system
改变 gǎibiàn [动] change ▷安妮改变了主意，决定呆在家里。Annie changed her mind and decided to stay at home.
改朝换代 gǎi cháo huàn dài a change of regime
改动 gǎidòng [动] change
改恶从善 gǎi è cóng shàn turn over a new leaf
改革 gǎigé [动] reform ▷改革经济体制 reform the economic system
改观 gǎiguān [动] 1 (指面貌) take on a new look (PT took, PP taken) ▷城市的面貌改观了许多。The city has already taken on quite a new look. 2 (指观点) change one's attitude ▷家人对他完全改观了。His family completely changed their attitude towards him.
改过自新 gǎi guò zì xīn wipe the slate clean
改行 gǎiháng [动] change profession
改换 gǎihuàn [动] replace
改悔 gǎihuǐ [动] mend one's ways
改嫁 gǎijià [动] remarry ▷在中国封建社会里，改嫁是不被容许的。Remarriage wasn't acceptable in feudal Chinese society.
改进 gǎijìn [动] improve
改口 gǎikǒu [动] correct oneself
改良 gǎiliáng [动] 1 (改善) improve 2 (改进) reform
改善 gǎishàn [动] improve
改头换面 gǎi tóu huàn miàn make superficial changes
改弦更张 gǎi xián gēng zhāng make a fresh start
改邪归正 gǎi xié guī zhèng turn over a new leaf
改选 gǎixuǎn [动] re-elect
改造 gǎizào [动] 1 (指对自然) reclaim ▷改造农田 reclaim farmland 2 (彻底改变) transform ▷改造社会 transform society ▷改造罪犯 rehabilitate offenders
改正 gǎizhèng [动] correct ▷他改正了文中的错字。He corrected the wrong characters in

his essay. ▷改正缺点 mend one's ways

改组 gǎizǔ [动] reshuffle ▷政府改组 government reshuffle

丐 gài [名] beggar

钙 gài [名] (化) calcium

盖 gài I [名] 1 (指器皿) cover 2 (甲壳) shell II [动] 1 (蒙上) cover 2 (遮掩) cover... up ▷他们想盖住丑闻。They wanted to cover the scandal up. 3 (打上) stamp 4 (压过) block... out ▷汽车的噪音把我们的说话声盖下去了。The noise from the car blocked out the sound of our voices. 5 (建造) build (PT, PP built)

盖棺论定 gài guān lùn dìng only when a man is dead can he be judged

盖世 gàishì [动] be unparalleled ▷才华盖世 be of unparalleled talent

盖子 gàizi [名] (口) 1 (遮蔽物) lid 2 (甲壳) shell

概 gài I [名] 1 (大略) outline 2 (气度) bearing II [副] without exception

概况 gàikuàng [名] general situation

概括 gàikuò I [动] summarize II [形] brief

概率 gàilǜ [名] probability

概论 gàilùn [名] introduction

概貌 gàimào [名] general picture

概莫能外 gài mò néng wài without exception

概念 gàiniàn [名] concept

概念化 gàiniànhuà [动] conceptualize

概述 gàishù [动] summarize

概数 gàishù [名] approximate number

概要 gàiyào [名] outline

干 gān I [动] have to do with ▷干连 be responsible for ▷这不干我事。This has nothing to do with me. II [形] 1 (无水) dry 2 (不用水) dry ▷干洗 dry-clean 3 (干涸) dried-up 4 (空) empty ▷外强中干 outwardly strong but inwardly weak 5 (指非认的关系) adoptive III [名] ▷笋干 dried bamboo shoots ▷豆腐干 dried tofu ▷葡萄干 raisin IV [副] 1 (只具形式) hollowly ▷干笑 laugh hollowly 2 (白白) in vain ▷他失约了，害得我干等了半天。He failed to make the appointment and I ended up wasting a long time waiting for him.
→另见 gàn

干巴巴 gānbābā [形] 1 (干燥) dried-up 2 (不生动) bland

干杯 gānbēi [动] drink a toast (PT drank, PP drunk) ▷为我们成功的合作而干杯。Let's

drink a toast to our successful cooperation. ▷"干杯！" "Cheers!"

干瘪 gānbiě [形] 1 (不丰满) shrivelled ▷干瘪的水果 shrivelled fruit ▷干瘪的老头子 a wizened old man 2 (枯燥) dull

干脆 gāncuì I [形] direct II [副] just ▷报酬这么低，干脆别干了。There's so little money in it – just give it up.

干戈 gāngē [名] arms ▷两国为了领土问题大动干戈。The two nations went to war over a territorial dispute.

干旱 gānhàn [形] arid

干涸 gānhé [形] dried-up

干货 gānhuò [名] dried food

干净 gānjìng [形] 1 (无尘) clean 2 (利落) clear ▷他干净利落地介绍完整个项目。He gave a clear and comprehensive introduction to the project. 3 (一点不剩) complete ▷请把汤喝干净。Please finish your soup.

干枯 gānkū [形] withered ▷干枯的叶子 withered leaves

干扰 gānrǎo [动] disturb ▷别干扰他学习。Don't disturb him when he's studying.

干涉 gānshè I [动] meddle ▷干涉别人私事 meddle in other people's affairs II [名] (关系) link

干洗 gānxǐ [动] dry-clean

干系 gānxì [名] responsibility ▷这件事故和他脱不了干系。He cannot escape responsibility for the accident.

干预 gānyù [动] interfere ▷干预总统选举 interfere in a presidential election

干燥 gānzào [形] dry

甘 gān I [形] 1 (指味觉) sweet 2 (幸福) fortunate II [副] willingly ▷他甘愿在家照看孩子。He willingly stayed at home to look after the children.

甘拜下风 gān bài xià fēng throw in the towel

甘苦 gānkǔ [名] 1 (美好和艰辛) ups and downs (PL) 2 (艰辛) hardship

甘甜 gāntián [形] sweet

甘心 gānxīn [动] 1 (愿意) be willing 2 (满意) be satisfied

甘休 gānxiū [动] take... lying down (PT took, PP taken) ▷他考试非得拿A才甘休。If he doesn't get an A in the exam he's not going to take it lying down.

甘于 gānyú [动] be willing to

甘愿 gānyuàn [动] be willing to

杆 gān [名] post

→另见 gǎn

肝 **gān** [名] liver

肝胆 **gāndǎn** [名] **1** (真诚) sincerity **2** (勇气) courage

肝胆相照 **gāndǎn xiāng zhào** open one's heart

肝火 **gānhuǒ** [名] anger ▷不必为这点小事大动肝火。There is no need to get so angry over something so trivial.

肝脑涂地 **gān nǎo tú dì** lay down one's life

柑 **gān** [名] mandarin orange

竿 **gān** [名] pole

尴 **gān** 见下文

尴尬 **gāngà** [形] **1** (困难) awkward ▷尴尬的处境 an awkward situation **2** (方) (不自然) embarrassed ▷她看上去很尴尬。She looked very embarrassed.

杆 **gǎn** I [名] shaft II [量] ▷一杆笔 a pen ▷几杆枪 several guns
→另见 gān

秆 **gǎn** [名] stalk

赶 **gǎn** I [动] **1** (追) catch (PT, PP caught) ▷赶公共汽车 catch a bus ▷赶潮流 catch up with the latest fashions **2** (加快) rush ▷赶功课 rush off an assignment ▷天黑了，学生们赶着回家。It was getting dark so the students rushed home. **3** (驱赶) drive (PT drove, PP driven) ▷赶着马车进城 drive a cart into town **4** (驱逐) drive... out ▷赶走外来政权 drive out the foreign regime **5** (遇到) happen to ▷她的生日赶上是国庆节。Her birthday happened to be the same day as National Day. II [介] until ▷这株树赶明年春天再种吧。Let's not plant this tree until next spring.

赶场 **gǎnchǎng** [动] rush from one place to another

赶集 **gǎnjí** [动] go to market (PT went, PP gone)

赶紧 **gǎnjǐn** [副] quickly ▷下课后我赶紧回家。After class I quickly went home.

赶快 **gǎnkuài** [副] at once ▷我们得赶快走了！We must go at once!

赶浪头 **gǎn làngtou** follow the trend

赶路 **gǎnlù** [动] race ahead

赶忙 **gǎnmáng** [副] hurriedly

赶巧 **gǎnqiǎo** [副] by chance ▷我散步时赶巧遇见个老同学。I was out for a walk when I bumped into an old school friend. ▷他赶巧

也在那儿。By chance he happened to be there as well.

赶时髦 **gǎn shímáo** be fashionable

赶鸭子上架 **gǎn yāzi shàng jià** set an impossible challenge

敢 **gǎn** I [形] courageous II [动] **1** ((有胆量) dare **2** (有把握) be sure ▷我敢断定他在撒谎。I'm sure he is lying. **3** (谦) (请求) venture ▷敢问尊姓大名？May I ask your name?

敢于 **gǎnyú** [动] dare to ▷他敢于批评他的老板。He dared to criticize his boss.

敢作敢当 **gǎn zuò gǎn dāng** be ready to stand up and be counted

感 **gǎn** I [动] **1** (觉得) feel (PT, PP felt) **2** (感动) move ▷这个故事很感人。This story is very moving. ▷他被她的爱所感动。He was moved by her affection. ▷感人肺腑 extremely moving **3** (怀谢意) be grateful **4** (受) be affected by **5** (接触) be sensitive to II [名] sense ▷成就感 a sense of achievement ▷新鲜感 a breath of fresh air

感触 **gǎnchù** [名] emotion ▷对家乡的变化他深有感触。He was very emotional about the changes to his home town.

感动 **gǎndòng** [动] move ▷他很容易被感动。He's very easily moved.

感恩 **gǎn'ēn** [动] be grateful

感恩节 **Gǎn'ēnjié** [名] Thanksgiving

感官 **gǎnguān** [名] sense organs (PL)

感光 **gǎnguāng** [动] be light-sensitive

感化 **gǎnhuà** [动] reform

感激 **gǎnjī** [动] appreciate ▷我感激你所做的一切。I appreciate everything you have done.

感激涕零 **gǎnjī tì líng** shed tears of gratitude

感觉 **gǎnjué** I [名] feeling II [动] **1** (感到) feel (PT, PP felt) ▷感觉不舒服 feel below par ▷感觉轻松 feel relaxed **2** (认为) sense ▷他感觉到有点儿不对劲。He sensed that there was something wrong.

感慨 **gǎnkǎi** [动] sigh

感冒 **gǎnmào** [动] catch a cold (PT, PP caught)

感情 **gǎnqíng** [名] **1** (心理反应) emotion **2** (喜爱) feelings (PL) ▷他们感情一直没变。They never lost their feelings for each other.

感染 **gǎnrǎn** [动] **1** (传染) infect ▷伤口感染 The cut became infected. **2** (引起共鸣) strike a chord (PT, PP struck) ▷他的演讲感染了在场的每个人。His speech struck a chord with everyone present.

感人肺腑 **gǎn rén fèifǔ** pull at one's heartstrings ▷这本书感人肺腑。This book really pulls at people's heartstrings.

感伤 gǎnshāng [动] be inconsolable

感受 gǎnshòu I [动] feel (PT, PP felt) II [名] impression ▷重返故乡后，他感受良多。His return home left a deep impression on him.

感叹 gǎntàn [动] sigh

感悟 gǎnwù [动] come to understand (PT came, PP come)

感想 gǎnxiǎng [名] thoughts (PL) ▷你对这些评论有何感想？ Did you have any particular thoughts on these comments?

感谢 gǎnxiè [动] thank ▷感谢您的指导。Thank you for your guidance.

感性 gǎnxìng [名] perception

感应 gǎnyìng [动] 1 (物理) induce 2 (感情变化) respond

感召 gǎnzhào [动] inspire

感知 gǎnzhī [动] perceive

橄 gǎn 见下文

橄榄 gǎnlǎn [名] olive

擀 gǎn [动] roll

擀面杖 gǎnmiànzhàng [名] rolling pin

干 gàn I [名] 1 (主体) trunk ▶躯干 trunk ▷公司骨干 the backbone of the company 2 (干部) cadre II [动] 1 (做) do (PT did, PP done) ▶干活 work 2 (担任) act as ▷他干过队长。He acted as team leader. III [形] capable
→另见 gān

干部 gànbù [名] cadre

干才 gàncái [名] 1 (才能) ability 2 (指人) able person

> ability, capability 和 capacity 混淆。ability 通常表示某人有能力做好某事。He had remarkable ability as a musician… the ability to bear hardship… capability 表示某人做事的能力。…a job that was beyond the capability of one man… the film director's ideas of the capability of the actor… 如果某人有某种 capacity, 或 capacity for something, 或 capacity to do something, 表示他具备做此事的能力。capacity 比 ability 更为正式。…their capacity for hard work… his capacity to see the other person's point of view…

干将 gànjiàng [名] go-getter

干劲 gànjìn [名] vigour (英), vigor (美)

干警 gànjǐng [名] police

干练 gànliàn [形] capable and experienced

干流 gànliú [名] trunk stream

干线 gànxiàn [名] artery

冈 gāng [名] ridge

刚 gāng I [形] strong II [副] 1 (恰好) just ▷水温刚好。The temperature of the water was just right. 2 (仅仅) just ▷这儿刚放一把椅子。There is just enough room for a chair. 3 (不久以前) only just ▷小宝宝刚会走路。The baby has only just started walking.

刚愎自用 gāng bì zì yòng obstinate

刚才 gāngcái [名] just now

刚刚 gānggāng [副] just ▷我刚刚吃完晚餐。I've just finished dinner.

刚好 gānghǎo I [形] just right II [副] luckily ▷我到车站的时候刚好有车。Luckily there was a bus when I got to the station.

刚健 gāngjiàn [形] bold

刚劲 gāngjìng [形] vigorous

刚烈 gāngliè [形] fiery

刚强 gāngqiáng [形] unyielding ▷刚强的性格 unyielding personality

刚毅 gāngyì [形] determined

刚正 gāngzhèng [形] principled

刚直 gāngzhí [形] upright

肛 gāng [名] anus

纲 gāng [名] 1 (总绳) headrope 2 (主体) key part 3 (生物群) class

纲举目张 gāng jǔ mù zhāng take care of the big things and the little things will take care of themselves

纲领 gānglǐng [名] guiding principle

纲目 gāngmù [名] detailed outline

纲要 gāngyào [名] outline

钢 gāng [名] steel

钢材 gāngcái [名] steel products (PL)

钢琴 gāngqín [名] piano

钢铁 gāngtiě [名] 1 (字) steel 2 (喻) iron ▷钢铁意志 an iron will

缸 gāng [名] 1 (器物) vat ▶鱼缸 fish bowl 2 (像缸之物) jar ▶汽缸 cylinder

岗 gǎng [名] 1 (土坡) ridge 2 (岗位) post ▶下岗 be laid-off

岗哨 gǎngshào [名] 1 (指处所) lookout post 2 (指人) sentry

岗位 gǎngwèi [名] post

港 **gǎng** [名] **1** (港湾) harbour (英), harbor (美) **2** (香港) Hong Kong

港币 **gǎngbì** [名] Hong Kong dollar

港口 **gǎngkǒu** [名] port

港湾 **gǎngwān** [名] harbour (英), harbor (美)

杠 **gàng I** [名] **1** (棍子) bar **2** (直线) thick line ▷在错误的地方划上红杠。Where there is a mistake, mark it with a thick red line. **II** [动] cross out

杠子 **gàngzi** [名] **1** (棍子) carrying pole **2** (直线) thick line

高 **gāo** [形] **1** (指高度) tall ▷高楼 tall building **2** (指标准或程度) high ▷高标准 high standard **3** (指等级) senior ▷高中 senior school **4** (指声音) high-pitched **5** (指年龄) old **6** (指价格) high **7** (敬) ▷您有何高见? What is your opinion?

高矮 **gāo'ǎi** [名] height

高昂 **gāo'áng** [形] **1** (高起) elated **2** (昂贵) exorbitant

高傲 **gāo'ào** [形] arrogant

高不成，低不就 **gāo bù chéng, dī bù jiù** have ideas above one's station

高不可攀 **gāo bù kě pān** unattainable

高超 **gāochāo** [形] excellent

高潮 **gāocháo** [名] **1** (字) high tide **2** (喻) climax

高大 **gāodà** [形] **1** (字) huge **2** (喻) glorious

高档 **gāodàng** [形] top quality

高等 **gāoděng** [形] higher

高低 **gāodī** [名] **1** (高低程度) height **2** (高下) difference **3** (深浅) appropriateness

高地 **gāodì** [名] highlands (PL)

高调 **gāodiào** [名] big talk

高度 **gāodù** [名] altitude

高峰 **gāofēng** [名] summit ▷珠穆朗玛峰是世界第一高峰。Mount Qomolangma is the highest summit in the world. ▷上班高峰时间 morning rush hour

高峰会议 **gāofēng huìyì** [名] summit meeting

高峰时间 **gāofēng shíjiān** [名] rush hour

高高在上 **gāo gāo zài shàng** be superior

高官厚禄 **gāo guān hòu lù** plum job

高贵 **gāoguì** [形] **1** (指道德) dignified **2** (指地位) noble

高级 **gāojí** [形] **1** (指级别) senior ▷高级讲师 senior lecturer ▷高级法院 high court **2** (超过一般) high-quality ▷高级英语 advanced English ▷高级宾馆 luxury hotel

高架桥 **gāojiàqiáo** [名] flyover (英), overpass (美)

高见 **gāojiàn** [名] (敬) opinion

高洁 **gāojié** [形] noble

高就 **gāojiù** [动] (敬) be employed

高踞 **gāojù** [动] set oneself above (PT, PP set) ▷高踞榜首 take first place

高亢 **gāokàng** [形] resounding

高考 **gāokǎo** [名] college entrance examination

高科技园区 **gāokējì** [形] hi-tech

高科技 **gāokējì yuánqū** [形] hi-tech zone

高空 **gāokōng** [名] high altitude

高利贷 **gāolìdài** [名] usury

高龄 **gāolíng I** [名] (敬) old age **II** [形] older ▷高龄孕妇 women who are pregnant later in life

高论 **gāolùn** [名] (敬) brilliant remarks (PL)

高帽子 **gāomàozi** [名] flattery

高明 **gāomíng I** [形] wise **II** [名] expert

高攀 **gāopān** [动] be a social climber

高强 **gāoqiáng** [形] outstanding

高人 **gāorén** [名] master

高人一等 **gāo rén yī děng** regard oneself as a cut above the rest

高尚 **gāoshàng** [形] **1** (指道德) noble **2** (有意义的) respectable

高深 **gāoshēn** [形] profound

高深莫测 **gāoshēn mò cè** unfathomable

高手 **gāoshǒu** [名] expert

高寿 **gāoshòu** [名] **1** (敬) (年纪) age ▷您高寿了? May I ask how old you are? **2** (长寿) longevity

高速 **gāosù** [形] rapid ▷中国经济正高速发展。China's economy is developing rapidly.

高速公路 **gāosù gōnglù** [名] motorway (英), freeway (美)

高抬贵手 **gāo tái guì shǒu** be merciful

高谈阔论 **gāo tán kuò lùn** talk off the top of one's head

高屋建瓴 **gāo wū jiàn líng** be strategically situated

高下 **gāoxià** [名] superiority and inferiority

高兴 **gāoxìng I** [形] happy **II** [动] enjoy

高压 **gāoyā I** [名] **1** (指气压) high pressure **2** (指电压) high voltage **3** (指血压) high blood pressure **II** [形] high-handed ▷高压政策 high-handed policy

高雅 **gāoyǎ** [形] elegant

高原 **gāoyuán** [名] plateau (PL plateaux)

高瞻远瞩 **gāo zhān yuǎn zhǔ** far-sighted

高涨 **gāozhǎng** [动] rocket ▷物价高涨。Prices are rocketing.

高招 gāozhāo [名] bright ideas (PL)
高枕无忧 gāo zhěn wú yōu rest easy
高中 gāozhōng [名] (高级中学) senior school (英), high school (美)
高姿态 gāozītài [名] generous attitude

羔 gāo [名] young
羔羊 gāoyáng [名] lamb

膏 gāo [名] 1 (脂肪) grease 2 (糊状物) paste ▷药膏 ointment
膏药 gāoyao [名] plaster

糕 gāo [名] cake
糕点 gāodiǎn [名] pastries (PL)

搞 gǎo [动] 1 (干) do (PT did, PP done) 2 (弄) get (PT got, PP got (英) 或 gotten (美)) ▷搞到资金 secure funding ▷搞到消息 get information
搞定 gǎodìng [动] (口) sort... out ▷这事一定要搞定！ This has really got to be sorted out!
搞鬼 gǎoguǐ [动] be up to mischief

稿 gǎo [名] draft
稿本 gǎoběn [名] manuscript
稿费 gǎofèi [名] fee
稿件 gǎojiàn [名] manuscript
稿子 gǎozi [名] 1 (草稿) draft 2 (诗文) manuscript 3 (计划) plan

告 gào [动] 1 (陈述) tell (PT, PP told) 2 (控诉) sue 3 (请求) request 4 (表明) announce ▷告辞 take one's leave 5 (宣布) declare
告白 gàobái [名] expression
告别 gàobié [动] say goodbye (PT, PP said)
告成 gàochéng [动] accomplish
告吹 gàochuī [动] come to nothing (PT came, PP come) ▷我们去大陆投资的计划告吹了。 Our plans to invest on the mainland came to nothing.
告辞 gàocí [动] take leave (PT took, PP taken) ▷晚饭后他起身告辞。 After the meal, he stood up and took his leave.
告发 gàofā [动] prosecute
告急 gàojí [动] report an emergency
告捷 gàojié [动] 1 (获胜) triumph 2 (报告胜利) report a victory
告诫 gàojiè [动] warn ▷我告诫孩子别太晚回家。 I warned the children not to be too late home.
告警 gàojǐng [动] raise the alarm
告老还乡 gào lǎo huán xiāng retire to one's hometown

告密 gàomì [动] ▷她向当局告密说会有军事政变。 She tipped off the authorities about the coup.
告罄 gàoqìng [动] run out (PT ran, PP run) ▷门票已告罄。 There aren't any tickets left.
告饶 gàoráo [动] beg for mercy
告示 gàoshi [名] notification
告诉 gàosu [动] tell (PT, PP told)

> tell 表示告知某人某事。The manufacturer told me that the product did not contain corn. 动词 tell 通常可以带直接宾语，用来指受话方。He told Alison he was suffering from leukaemia...What did she tell you? 以下表达是错误的 'What did she tell to you?'。tell 后还可以加动词不定式，表示命令或指示。
> say 是表示某人说话最常用的词汇。请注意，在使用动词 say 时，表示受话方，应该使用介词 to。不能说 'What did she say you?'，正确的说法是 'What did she say to you?'。

告退 gàotuì [动] request to leave
告知 gàozhī [动] let... know (PT, PP let) ▷我写信告知父母我的近况。 I wrote to my parents to let them know my latest news.
告终 gàozhōng [动] end up ▷以失败告终 end up in failure
告状 gàozhuàng [动] (口) 1 (起诉) file a lawsuit 2 (抱怨) complain ▷他向老板告状说我工作不卖力。 He went to the boss to complain that I wasn't working hard enough.

疙 gē 见下文
疙瘩 gēda [名] 1 (指皮肤) pimple ▷起鸡皮疙瘩 come out in goosebumps 2 (小块) lump 3 (问题) unease ▷他们之间有点疙瘩。 There was a certain amount of unease between them.

咯 gē 见下文
咯咯 gēgē [拟] chuckle
咯吱 gēzhī [拟] creak

哥 gē [名] 1 (哥哥) elder brother 2 (亲热称呼) brother
哥儿们 gērmen [名] 1 (弟兄) brothers (PL) 2 (朋友) mate (英), buddy (美)

胳 gē 见下文
胳膊 gēbo [名] arm

鸽 gē [名] dove
鸽子 gēzi [名] dove

搁 gē [动] 1 (放) put (PT, PP put) 2 (搁置) put

aside
→另见 gé

搁笔 gēbǐ[动]stop ▷那个画家已搁笔多年。That artist stopped painting a long time ago.

搁浅 gēqiǎn[动] 1 (字) be stranded 2 (喻) come to a standstill (PT came, PP come) ▷项目搁浅了。The project came to a standstill.

搁置 gēzhì[动]shelve ▷议案被搁置。The proposal was shelved.

割 gē[动]cut (PT, PP cut)

割爱 gē'ài[动]give up what one treasures (PT gave, PP given)

割裂 gēliè[动]separate

割让 gēràng[动]cede ▷割让领土 cede territory

割舍 gēshě[动]give up (PT gave, PP given)

歌 gē I [名]song II [动]sing (PT sang, PP sung)

歌唱 gēchàng[动] 1 (唱)sing (PT sang, PP sung) 2 (颂扬)sing the praises of

歌功颂德 gē gōng sòng dé sing the praises of

歌剧 gējù[名]opera

歌曲 gēqǔ[名]tune

歌手 gēshǒu[名]singer

歌颂 gēsòng[动]sing the praises of

歌坛 gētán[名]singing circles (PL) ▷他在歌坛很有名。He's very well-known in singing circles.

歌舞 gēwǔ[名]singing and dancing

歌星 gēxīng[名]pop star

歌谣 gēyáo[名]ballad

歌咏 gēyǒng[动]sing (PT sang, PP sung)

革 gé I [名]leather II [动] 1 (改变)change 2 (开除)expel

革除 géchú[动] 1 (铲除)eliminate 2 (开除)expel

革命 gémìng[动]revolutionize ▷工业革命 industrial revolution

革新 géxīn[动]innovate

革职 gézhí[动]dismiss

阁 gé[名] 1 (指建筑)pavilion 2 (内阁)cabinet ▷内阁成员 a member of the cabinet 3 (女子的居室)boudoir 4 (架子)shelf (PL shelves)

阁下 géxià[名](敬)Your Excellency

格 gé[名] 1 (格子)check 2 (规格)standard 3 (品质)character

格调 gédiào[名] 1 (艺术特点)style 2 (书)(品格)character ▷他格调不高。He does not have a nice character.

格斗 gédòu[动]wrestle

格格不入 gé gé bù rù be incompatible

格局 géjú[名]set-up

格式 géshì[名]format

格外 géwài[副] 1 (特别)especially 2 (额外)additionally ▷店里忙的时候就得格外找帮手。When the stall is busy we need additional staff.

格言 géyán[名]maxim

格子 gézi[名]shelf (PL shelves)

搁 gé[动]withstand (PT, PP withstood) ▷刚出土的文物搁不住阳光直射。Newly excavated cultural relics are unable to withstand direct sunshine.
→另见 gē

蛤 gé[名]clam
→另见 há

蛤蜊 gélí[名]clam

隔 gé[动] 1 (阻隔)separate 2 (间隔)be apart ▷两地相隔不远。The two places aren't far apart.

隔岸观火 gé àn guān huǒ stand by and watch

隔壁 gébì[名]next door ▷隔壁邻居 neighbour (英), neighbor (美)

隔阂 géhé[名]misunderstanding ▷文化隔阂 cultural misunderstanding ▷男女朋友间难免会有些隔阂。Misunderstandings are more or less inevitable in relationships.

隔绝 géjué[动]isolate ▷他在乡村过着与世隔绝的生活。He led a completely isolated life in the countryside. ▷两家隔绝往来已久。All contact between the two families stopped a long time ago.

隔离 gélí[动]quarantine ▷病人已被隔离观察。The patient has already been quarantined and observed. ▷种族隔离 racial segregation ▷南非种族隔离 apartheid

隔膜 gémó I [名]gulf ▷距离使两人产生隔膜。Distance created a gulf between them. II [形](不了解)inept

隔墙有耳 gé qiáng yǒu ěr the walls have ears

隔靴搔痒 gé xuē sāo yǎng fail to get to the heart of a matter

隔音 géyīn[动]soundproof

嗝 gé[名] 1 (饱嗝)burp 2 (冷嗝)hiccup

个 gè I [名](指身材或大小)size II [量] 1 (表示个数) ▷6个桃子 six peaches ▷两个月 two months 2 (表示约数) ▷俩人相差个两三岁。

There's about two or three years between them. ▷她比她丈夫大个一两岁。She's about one or two years older than her husband. **3** (表示动量) ▷开个会 have a meeting ▷冲个澡 have a shower **4** (用在动补之间) ▷叫个不停 talk incessantly **III** [形] individual

个案 gè'àn [名] case ▷个案研究 case study

个别 gèbié [形] **1** (单个) individual **2** (少数) a couple ▷有个别人违反纪律。A couple of people broke the rules.

个人 gèrén **I** [名] individual **II** [代] oneself ▷就他个人而言 as far as he's concerned ▷在我个人看来，这是个好主意。As far as I'm concerned this is a good idea.

个体 gètǐ [名] **1** (指生物) individual ▷生物个体 each and every individual **2** (指经济形态) ▷个体所有制 private ownership ▷个体经营 private enterprise

个头儿 gètóur [名] **1** (指人) build ▷这男孩个头儿大。This boy is well-built. **2** (指物) size ▷大个头儿的西瓜 a big watermelon

个性 gèxìng [名] personality ▷他个性很强。He has a very strong personality.

个子 gèzi [名] stature ▷高个子女人 a tall woman

各 gè **I** [代] each ▷他们各取所好。Each of them will get what they want. **II** [副] individually

各奔前程 gè bèn qiánchéng go one's own way

各别 gèbié [形] **1** (不同) different **2** (方) (别致) unique **3** (特别) peculiar

各得其所 gè dé qí suǒ everyone in their proper place

各个 gègè **I** [代] each ▷各个成员 each member **II** [副] one by one ▷问题得各个解决。The problems need to be dealt with one by one.

各尽所能 gè jìn suǒ néng do what one can in one's role

各色 gèsè [形] all kinds of

各抒己见 gè shū jǐ jiàn everyone has their say

各行其是 gè xíng qí shì do as one pleases ▷这个部门各行其是。Everyone in this department does as they please.

各有千秋 gè yǒu qiān qiū each has its strong points

各自 gèzì [代] each

各自为政 gè zì wéi zhèng everyone does their own thing

给 gěi **I** [动] **1** (给予) give (PT gave, PP given)

▷给我勇气 give me courage **2** (让) let (PT, PP let) ▷给他看看照片 Let him see the photos. **II** [介] **1** (为) for ▷我给妻子做早餐。I made breakfast for my wife. **2** (向) to ▷留给他 leave it to him ▷递给我 pass it to me **III** [助] ▷我把开会的事给忘了。I forgot about the meeting. ▷他把钥匙给掉了。He lost the key. →另见 jǐ

给以 gěiyǐ [动] give (PT gave, PP given) ▷给以资助 give financial support

---

根 gēn **I** [名] **1** (指植物) root **2** (子孙) offspring **3** (指物体) base **4** (本原) origin ▶祸根 the root of the problem **5** (依据) grounds (PL) ▷无根之谈 groundless claims **II** [副] thoroughly ▶根除 root... out **III** [量] ▷一根绳子 a length of rope ▷几根稻草 some pieces of straw ▷一根头发 a hair

根本 gēnběn **I** [名] root **II** [形] fundamental **III** [副] **1** (完全) ▷根本没人告诉我。Nobody told me at all. **2** (彻底) thoroughly ▷根本转变态度 completely change one's attitude

根除 gēnchú [动] eliminate

根底 gēndǐ [名] **1** (基础) grounding ▷他数学根底不错。He has a good grounding in maths. **2** (底细) cause ▷灾祸的根底 the cause of the tragic accident

根基 gēnjī [名] **1** (字) foundations (PL) ▷建筑物的根基 the foundations of the building **2** (喻) foundation ▷事业的根基 the foundation of a career

根究 gēnjiū [动] get to the bottom of

根据 gēnjù **I** [介] according to **II** [名] basis (PL bases) ▷她的说法毫无根据。Her argument had absolutely no basis whatsoever. ▷文章的根据 the basis of the article

根绝 gēnjué [动] eradicate

根深蒂固 gēn shēn dì gù deep-rooted

根由 gēnyóu [名] cause

根源 gēnyuán [名] cause

根治 gēnzhì [动] bring... to an end (PT, PP brought)

根子 gēnzi [名] (口) **1** (字) root **2** (喻) source

跟 gēn **I** [名] heel **II** [动] **1** (跟随) follow **2** (嫁) marry **III** [介] **1** (同) with ▷我跟朋友去公园了。I went to the park with friends. **2** (向) ▷跟我说说这件事。Tell me what happened. ▷婚姻大事得跟父母商量。When it comes to marriage you really should talk it through with your parents. **3** (表示比较) as ▷他的教育背景跟我相似。His educational background is similar to mine. **IV** [连] and ▷珍妮跟海伦都去上课了。Jenny and Helen both went to their lectures.

跟前 gēnqián [名] ▷他走到我跟前耳语了几句。He came close and whispered a few words. ▷有只猫蹲在窗户跟前。There's a cat sitting at the window.

跟随 gēnsuí [动] follow

跟头 gēntou [名] fall ▷跌了个跟头 have a fall ▷翻跟头 do a somersault

跟踪 gēnzōng [动] tail

亘 gèn [动] stretch

亘古未有 gèn gǔ wèi yǒu unprecedented

更 gēng I [动] 1 (改变) change 2 (书)(经历) experience II [名] watch
→另见 gèng

更迭 gēngdié [动] alternate

更动 gēngdòng [动] change

更改 gēnggǎi [动] alter

更换 gēnghuàn [动] change

更生 gēngshēng [动] 1 (复兴) revive 2 (再生) regenerate ▷更生玻璃 recycled glass

更替 gēngtì [动] replace ▷这个国家政权更替频繁。This country's governments are constantly being replaced.

更新 gēngxīn [动] 1 (事物) replace ▷更新网站内容 update web content ▷更新设备 replace old equipment 2 (森林) renew

更衣 gēngyī [动] change one's clothes ▷更衣间 changing room

更正 gēngzhèng [动] correct ▷自我更正 correct oneself

耕 gēng [动] plough

耕耘 gēngyún [动] cultivate

耕作 gēngzuò [动] farm

羹 gēng [名] thick soup

羹匙 gēngchí [名] soup spoon

耿 gěng [形] upright

耿耿 gěnggěng [形] 1 (忠诚) devoted 2 (有心事) troubled

耿耿于怀 gěng gěng yú huái dwell on ▷她对同事的话一直耿耿于怀。She kept dwelling on what her colleague had said.

耿直 gěngzhí [形] upright

哽 gěng [动] choke

哽咽 gěngyè [动] choke down sobs

梗 gěng I [名] stalk II [动] 1 (挺直) straighten 2 (阻塞) obstruct

梗概 gěnggài [名] outline

梗塞 gěngsè [动] 1 (阻塞) block 2 (梗死) obstruct

梗阻 gěngzǔ [动] block

更 gèng [形] 1 (更加) even more ▷天更黑了。It's getting even darker. ▷她更漂亮了。She is becoming even more beautiful. 2 (书)(再) further
→另见 gēng

更加 gèngjiā [副] even more ▷天气更加热了。The weather got even hotter.

工 gōng I [名] 1 (指人) worker ▶童工 child labour 2 (指阶级) the working class 3 (工作或劳动) work 4 (工程) project 5 (工业) industry 6 (指时间) man-day ▷这个工程得要7个工。This project will require seven man-days. 7 (技术) skill ▶做工 workmanship ▷他的唱工很好。He's a good singer. II [动] be skilled in III [形] exquisite

工本 gōngběn [名] production cost

工厂 gōngchǎng [名] factory

工场 gōngchǎng [名] workshop

工程 gōngchéng [名] engineering project ▷大兴土木工程 launch massive construction projects

工程师 gōngchéngshī [名] engineer

工夫 gōngfu [名] 1 (时间) time ▷这份作业很花工夫。The assignment took a long time to complete. 2 (空闲) spare time ▷有工夫到我这里来。If you have any spare time do come over to my place.

工会 gōnghuì [名] trade union

工匠 gōngjiàng [名] craftsman

工具 gōngjù [名] 1 (器具) tool ▷工具箱 toolbox ▷运输工具 means of transport 2 (喻) instrument ▷语言是交流的工具。Language is a means of communication.

工力 gōnglì [名] expertise

工期 gōngqī [名] time limit

工巧 gōngqiǎo [形] exquisite

工人 gōngrén [名] worker

工时 gōngshí [名] man-hour ▷他每天干8个工时的活。He works for eight hours a day.

工事 gōngshì [名] fortifications (PL)

工薪族 gōngxīnzú [名] wage earners (PL)

工序 gōngxù [名] process

工业 gōngyè [名] industry ▷石油工业 petroleum industry

工艺 gōngyì [名] 1 (技术) technology 2 (手工艺) craft

工友 gōngyǒu [名] **1** (同事) fellow worker **2** (勤杂工) caretaker

工于心计 gōng yú xīnjì calculating

工整 gōngzhěng [形] neat

工资 gōngzī [名] pay

> **pay** 是概括性的词汇，表示通过工作从雇主处得到的报酬。专业人员和办公室职员的工资是 **salary**，通常按月支付。然而，当谈论某人的 **salary** 时，通常是指年薪。*I'm paid a salary of £15,000 a year.* 体力劳动者的工资称为 **wages**，或 **a wage**。*Every week he handed all his wages in cash to his wife.* **wages** 通常是以小时或星期计算。*...a wage of five dollars an hour...* **income** 指各种来源的收入的总和，其中也包括工资。*Only 25% of his income comes from his job, the rest is from investments.*

工作 gōngzuò [名] **1** (劳动) work ▷编译字典不是一件简单的工作。Translating and editing a dictionary is not an easy job. ▷他做任何工作都很尽力。He does his best on any work given to him. **2** (职业) job ▷我想找份好工作。I am looking for a good job. **3** (业务) work ▷科研工作 scientific research work

弓 gōng I [名] bow II [动] bend (PT, PP bent)

弓箭 gōngjiàn [名] bow and arrow

公 gōng I [形] **1** (非私有) public ▷公共服务 public service **2** (共识) general **3** (共用) international **4** (公正) fair **5** (雄性) male II [动] make... public III [名] **1** (公务) official business ▷因公出差 go on a business trip **2** (集体) authorities (PL) **3** (指爵位) duke **4** (敬) (老先生) ▷王公 Mr Wang **5** (丈夫的父亲) father-in-law

公安 gōng'ān [名] public security

公报 gōngbào [名] bulletin ▷新闻公报 news bulletin

公布 gōngbù [动] announce

公厕 gōngcè [名] public toilet

公道 gōngdào [形] fair

公德 gōngdé [名] social norms (PL)

公断 gōngduàn [动] arbitrate

公费 gōngfèi [名] public expense

公愤 gōngfèn [名] public outcry ▷他的暴行引起了公愤。There was public outcry at his atrocious behaviour.

公干 gōnggàn [名] business

公告 gōnggào [名] proclamation ▷发布公告 issue a proclamation

公共 gōnggòng [形] public

公共汽车 gōnggòng qìchē [名] bus

公共汽车站 gōnggòng qìchēzhàn [名] **1** (指总站) bus station **2** (指路边站) bus stop

公共关系 gōnggòng guānxì [名] public relations (PL)

公关 gōngguān [名] (公共关系) public relations (PL)

公海 gōnghǎi [名] the high seas (PL)

公害 gōnghài [名] **1** (指对环境) environmental hazard **2** (指对社会) public hazard

公函 gōnghán [名] official correspondence

公家 gōngjiā [名] the state

公开 gōngkāi I [形] public ▷公开演讲 public speech II [动] make public

公款 gōngkuǎn [名] public funds (PL)

公里 gōnglǐ [名] kilometre (英), kilometer (美)

公理 gōnglǐ [名] universal truth

公历 gōnglì [名] Gregorian calendar

公路 gōnglù [名] motorway

公论 gōnglùn [名] public opinion

公民 gōngmín [名] citizen

公墓 gōngmù [名] cemetery

公平 gōngpíng [形] fair

公婆 gōngpó [名] one's husband's parents

公仆 gōngpú [名] public servant

公然 gōngrán [副] openly

公认 gōngrèn [动] acknowledge ▷他是大家公认的好学生。He was generally acknowledged to be a good student.

公审 gōngshěn [动] put... on trial (PT, PP put)

公式 gōngshì [名] formula (PL formulae)

公事 gōngshì [名] official business

公司 gōngsī [名] company ▷进出口公司 import-export company

公诉 gōngsù [动] (法) publicly prosecute

公文 gōngwén [名] official document

公务 gōngwù [名] official business

公物 gōngwù [名] public property

公休 gōngxiū [名] public holiday

公演 gōngyǎn [动] perform ▷这部歌剧一个月后将公演。The opera will be performed a month from now.

公益 gōngyì [名] public welfare

公有 gōngyǒu [形] public ▷公有土地 public land

公寓 gōngyù [名] **1** (旅馆) boarding house **2** (楼房) apartment

公元 gōngyuán [名] A.D. ▷公元2003年 2003 A.D.

公园 gōngyuán [名] park

公约 gōngyuē [名] treaty

公允 gōngyǔn [形] even-handed

公债 gōngzhài [名] government bonds (PL)

公章 gōngzhāng [名] official seal

公正 gōngzhèng [形] impartial

公证 gōngzhèng [名] authentication

公职 gōngzhí [名] public employment

公众 gōngzhòng [名] public

公主 gōngzhǔ [名] princess

功 gōng [名] 1 (功劳) contribution 2 (成效) achievement 3 (技术) skill

功败垂成 gōng bài chuí chéng fall at the last hurdle

功臣 gōngchén [名] hero (PL heroes)

功到自然成 gōng dào zìrán chéng success is born out of hard work

功德 gōngdé [名] merits (PL)

功底 gōngdǐ [名] grounding

功绩 gōngjì [名] contribution

功课 gōngkè [名] homework

功亏一篑 gōng kuī yī kuì fall at the last hurdle

功劳 gōngláo [名] contribution

功能 gōngnéng [名] function ▷电视有教育功能。Television has an educational function.

功效 gōngxiào [名] efficiency

功勋 gōngxūn [名] feats (PL)

功业 gōngyè [名] exploits (PL)

功用 gōngyòng [名] function

攻 gōng [动] 1 (攻打) attack 2 (驳斥) accuse 3 (学习) study hard

攻读 gōngdú [动] study hard ▷攻读学位 study for a degree

攻关 gōngguān [动] (突破难点) tackle a key problem

攻击 gōngjī [动] 1 (进攻) attack 2 (中伤) slander

攻克 gōngkè [动] capture

攻势 gōngshì [名] offensive

攻占 gōngzhàn [动] attack and occupy

供 gōng [动] 1 (供应) supply 2 (提供) provide →另见 gòng

供给 gōngjǐ [动] supply

供求 gōngqiú [名] supply and demand

供养 gōngyǎng [动] look after

供应 gōngyìng [动] supply

宫 gōng [名] 1 (皇宫) palace 2 (庙宇) temple 3 (文化娱乐场所) club

宫殿 gōngdiàn [名] palace

宫廷 gōngtíng [名] 1 (宫殿) palace 2 (统治集团) court

恭 gōng [形] respectful

恭贺 gōnghè [动] congratulate

恭敬 gōngjìng [形] respectful ▷他对老师非常恭敬。He was very respectful towards the teacher.

恭顺 gōngshùn [动] be respectful

恭维 gōngwei [动] flatter

恭喜 gōngxǐ [动] congratulate

躬 gōng I [动] (弯下身子) bow II [副] (自身) in person

巩 gǒng 见下文

巩固 gǒnggù I [形] solid II [动] strengthen

拱 gǒng [动] 1 (两手相合) join one's hands together 2 (环绕) encircle 3 (肢体弯曲) arch 4 (顶动) push ▷拱芽 sprout ▷拱开海外市场的大门 push open the doors to overseas markets

拱手 gǒngshǒu [动] cup one's hands

共 gòng I [形] common II [动] share III [副] 1 (一齐) together ▷共唱一首歌 sing a song together 2 (总共) altogether ▷该校共有学生8,000人。This school has 8,000 students altogether. IV [名] (共产党) the communist party

共处 gòngchǔ [动] coexist ▷和平共处 peaceful coexistence

共存 gòngcún [动] coexist

共和 gònghé [名] republic

共聚一堂 gòng jù yī táng gather together ▷亲朋好友共聚一堂，祝贺他的成功。His relatives and close friends gathered together to congratulate him on his success.

共鸣 gòngmíng [名] (物) resonance 2 (指情绪) sympathy

共识 gòngshí [名] consensus

共事 gòngshì [动] work together ▷和她共事很愉快。It's great working with her.

共通 gòngtōng [形] universal

共同 gòngtóng I [形] common ▷共同愿望 common aspiration II [副] together ▷共同生活 live together

共同体 gòngtóngtǐ [名] community

共性 gòngxìng [名] similarity

贡 gòng [名] tribute

贡品 gòngpǐn [名] tribute

贡献 gòngxiàn I [动] devote ▷他把一生贡献给了科学事业。He devoted his whole life to science. II [名] contribution

供 gòng I [动] 1 (供奉) lay (PT, PP laid) ▷供奉祭品 lay offerings 2 (招供) confess ▷他供出了主犯的名字。He confessed the name of the chief culprit. II [名] 1 (供品) offerings (PL) ▷上供 lay offerings 2 (口供) confession ▷翻供 withdraw a confession
→另见 gōng

供词 gòngcí [名] confession
供奉 gòngfèng [动] make offerings to
供品 gòngpǐn [名] offerings (PL)
供认 gòngrèn [动] confess
供职 gòngzhí [动] hold a position (PT, PP held) ▷他供职于清华大学。He held a position at Tsinghua University.

勾 gōu [动] 1 (删除) cross out ▷把这句话勾掉。Cross out this sentence. 2 (描画) draw (PT drew, PP drawn) 3 (调和使黏) thicken ▷勾芡 thicken 4 (引起) evoke ▷勾起对往事的回忆 evoke memories of the past 5 (结合) gang up ▷他和坏人勾在一起。He's got in with some bad people.
→另见 gòu

勾搭 gōuda [动] 1 (串通) gang up 2 (引诱) seduce ▷他用花言巧语勾搭那个姑娘。He used all kinds of sweet talk to seduce the girl.
勾画 gōuhuà [动] sketch
勾结 gōujié [动] collude ▷他与敌人相勾结。He colluded with the enemy.
勾引 gōuyǐn [动] entice ▷勾引某人犯罪 entice sb to commit a crime

沟 gōu [名] 1 (指人工) ditch 2 (指自然的) gully 3 (浅槽) groove
沟壑 gōuhè [名] gully
沟通 gōutōng [动] communicate ▷父母与子女应该经常沟通。Parents should always communicate with their children.

钩 gōu I [名] 1 (钩子) hook 2 (汉字笔画) hooked stroke 3 (符号) tick II [动] 1 (用钩子挂) hook 2 (编织、缝) crochet
钩心斗角 gōu xīn dòu jiǎo scheme against one another

篝 gōu [名] (书) cage
篝火 gōuhuǒ [名] bonfire

苟 gǒu I [形] casual II [副] temporarily III [连] (书) provided

苟活 gǒuhuó [动] lead a dog's life (PT, PP led)
苟且 gǒuqiě [形] 1 (得过且过) drifting 2 (敷衍) perfunctory 3 (不正当) illicit
苟全 gǒuquán [动] barely manage to survive
苟同 gǒutóng [动] (书) agree without due consideration ▷你的观点我可不能苟同。I can't agree with you just like that.

狗 gǒu [名] dog
狗急跳墙 gǒu jí tiào qiáng clutch at straws ▷他狗急跳墙，口不择言。He's really clutching at straws now – he'll say whatever it takes.
狗腿子 gǒutuǐzi [名] henchman
狗血喷头 gǒuxuè pēn tóu abusively
狗仔队 gǒuzǎiduì [名] paparazzi

勾 gòu 见下文
→另见 gōu
勾当 gòudàng [名] dealings (PL) ▷罪恶勾当 criminal dealings

构 gòu I [动] 1 (组成) compose 2 (结成) form 3 (建造) construct II [名] 1 (结构) structure 2 (文艺作品) composition
构成 gòuchéng I [动] 1 (造成) constitute ▷他的行为已构成行贿。His actions already constitute bribery. 2 (组成) compose ▷氢和氧构成水。Water is composed of hydrogen and oxygen. II [名] line-up ▷这支队伍的成员构成很合理。The team line-up made a lot of sense.
构件 gòujiàn [名] component part
构思 gòusī [动] compose
构想 gòuxiǎng I [动] compose II [名] concept
构造 gòuzào [名] structure

购 gòu [动] buy (PT, PP bought)
购买 gòumǎi [动] buy (PT, PP bought) ▷购买食品和药品 buy food and medicines
购物 gòuwù [动] go shopping (PT went, PP gone) ▷她爱购物。She likes shopping. ▷我刚才去购物了。I've just been shopping.
购销 gòuxiāo [名] buying and selling
购置 gòuzhì [动] purchase ▷学校又购置了一批计算机。The school has purchased another batch of computers.

垢 gòu I [名] 1 (脏东西) filth 2 (书) (耻辱) insult II [形] (书) (污秽) filthy

够 gòu I [形] enough ▷5个就够了。Five is enough. ▷只要你满意就够了。As long as you are satisfied, that's enough. II [动] reach

▷我够不到顶层书架上的书。I can't reach the books on the top shelf. ▷这些产品不够标准。These products do not come up to standard. III [副] quite

够本 gòuběn [动] **1** (不输不赚) break even (PT broke, PP broken) **2** (喻) be worth the effort

够戗 gòuqiàng [形] (方) awful

够味儿 gòuwèir [形] (口) **1** (口味纯正) just right **2** (水平高) excellent

够意思 gòu yìsi [形] (口) wonderful

估 gū [动] guess

估计 gūjì [动] reckon ▷我估计明天能完工。I reckon we should be able to finish tomorrow. ▷这是个保守的估计。This is a conservative estimate.

估价 gūjià [动] **1** (对商品) estimate **2** (对人或事物) evaluate

估量 gūliáng [动] measure ▷这场火灾的损失难以估量。It'll be hard to measure the damage caused by the fire.

估摸 gūmo [动] (口) reckon

估算 gūsuàn [动] guess

咕 gū [拟] coo

咕咚 gūdōng [拟] splash

咕嘟 gūdū [拟] **1** (指液体) bubble **2** (指喝水声) gulp ▷他咕嘟咕嘟地喝了一大杯水。He gulped down a large glass of water.

咕唧 gūjī [动] whisper

咕噜 gūlū [拟] rumble ▷我肚子咕噜咕噜直响。My stomach rumbled.

呱 gū [拟] cry

沽 gū [动] (书) **1** (买) purchase **2** (卖) sell (PT, PP sold)

沽名钓誉 gū míng diào yù court publicity ▷他从不沽名钓誉。He never courts publicity.

姑 gū I [名] **1** (姑母) aunt **2** (丈夫的姐妹) sister-in-law **3** (尼姑) nun II [副] (姑且) for the time being

姑息 gūxī [动] appease

孤 gū [形] **1** (幼年丧父或父母双亡) orphaned **2** (孤单) alone

孤傲 gū'ào [形] aloof

孤单 gūdān [形] **1** (单薄) weak ▷工党在该选区势力孤单。Support for the Labour Party is pretty weak in this constituency. **2** (寂寞) lonely ▷他时常感到孤单。He often feels lonely.

孤独 gūdú [形] solitary

孤儿 gū'ér [名] orphan

孤芳自赏 gū fāng zì shǎng narcissistic

孤家寡人 gūjiā guǎrén loner

孤苦伶仃 gūkǔ língdīng lonely and wretched

孤立 gūlì I [形] **1** (无联系) isolated ▷这个案件绝对不是孤立的。This is definitely not an isolated case. **2** (无助) unsupported II [动] isolate

孤零零 gūlínglíng [形] alone

孤陋寡闻 gū lòu guǎ wén out of touch

孤僻 gūpì [形] antisocial

孤掌难鸣 gū zhǎng nán míng hard to achieve by oneself

孤注一掷 gū zhù yī zhì put all one's eggs in one basket ▷他从不做孤注一掷的事。He never puts all his eggs in one basket.

轱 gū 见下文

轱辘 gūlu [名] wheel

骨 gū 见下文
→另见 gǔ

骨朵儿 gūduor [名] bud

菇 gū [名] mushroom

辜 gū [名] guilt

辜负 gūfù [动] fail to live up to ▷他辜负了家长和老师对他的期望。He failed to live up to the expectations of his parents and teachers.

箍 gū I [名] hoop II [动] bind (PT, PP bound)

古 gǔ I [名] ancient times (PL) II [形] ancient ▷古文明 ancient civilization

古板 gǔbǎn [形] set in one's ways ▷他为人处事很古板。He's so set in his ways.

古代 gǔdài [名] antiquity

古典 gǔdiǎn I [名] classics (PL) II [形] classical

古董 gǔdǒng [名] **1** (古代器物) antique **2** (喻) (指人) old fogey

古怪 gǔguài [形] bizarre

古籍 gǔjí [名] ancient books (PL)

古迹 gǔjì [名] historic site

古老 gǔlǎo [形] ancient

古朴 gǔpǔ [形] simple

古色古香 gǔ sè gǔ xiāng have an antique feel ▷故宫里的建筑物古色古香。The architecture of the Forbidden City has a real antique feel to it.

古诗 gǔshī [名] ancient poetry

古玩 gǔwán [名] antiques (PL)

古往今来 gǔ wǎng jīn lái throughout the ages

古文 gǔwén [名] (文言文) classical prose

古稀 gǔxī [名] seventy years of age

古雅 gǔyǎ [形] quaint

古装 gǔzhuāng [名] ancient costume

谷
gǔ [名] 1 (山谷) valley 2 (谷类作物) grain 3 (谷子) millet 4 (方) (稻谷) unhusked rice

谷物 gǔwù [名] grain

谷子 gǔzi [名] millet

汩
gǔ [形] (书) gurgling

汩汩 gǔgǔ [拟] gurgle

股
gǔ I [名] 1 (大腿) thigh 2 (指组织单位) department 3 (指绳或线) strand 4 (股份) share II [量] 1 (指条状) ▷一股水流 a trickle of water ▷两股毛线 two strands of thread 2 (气体、气味) whiff

股东 gǔdōng [名] shareholder

股份 gǔfèn [名] share

股票 gǔpiào [名] share

股市 gǔshì [名] stock market

骨
gǔ [名] bone
→另见 gū

骨干 gǔgàn [名] 1 (解剖) backbone 2 (起重要作用的力量) core

骨骼 gǔgé [名] (解剖) skeleton

骨架 gǔjià [名] 1 (骨头架子) skeleton 2 (支架) framework

骨气 gǔqì [名] integrity

骨肉 gǔròu [名] flesh and blood ▷这个孩子是他的亲骨肉。The child is his flesh and blood.

骨头 gǔtou [名] 1 (字) bone 2 (喻) character

骨子里 gǔzilǐ [名] deep down ▷他表面答应,骨子里却另有打算。He made a show of agreement but deep down he had other ideas.

牯
gǔ [名] bull

鼓
gǔ I [名] drum II [动] 1 (敲击) ▷鼓琴 play the zither ▷鼓掌 clap one's hands 2 (扇) blow (PT blew, PP blown) 3 (振奋) rouse 4 (拍打) beat (PT beat, PP beaten) 5 (凸起, 胀大) bulge ▷他鼓着嘴。He puffed his cheeks out. III [形] bulging ▷她的书包鼓鼓的。Her schoolbag was full to bursting.

鼓吹 gǔchuī [动] 1 (宣传) advocate 2 (吹嘘) boast about ▷他鼓吹他所谓的发明。He boasted about his so-called invention.

鼓动 gǔdòng [动] rouse

鼓励 gǔlì [动] encourage

鼓舞 gǔwǔ I [动] inspire II [形] inspiring

鼓掌 gǔzhǎng [动] applaud

固
gù I [形] strong ▶坚固 solid ▶稳固 stable ▶牢固 firm II [副] 1 (坚定) firmly 2 (本来) originally III [连] (固然) no doubt ▷中餐固好, 西餐也不错。There's no doubt that Chinese food is good, but Western cuisine isn't bad either. IV [动] 1 (使坚固) solidify 2 (防卫) strengthen

固步自封 gù bù zì fēng be a stick-in-the-mud

固定 gùdìng I [形] fixed II [动] fix ▷她把锻炼的时间固定在星期六下午。She fixed the exercise time for Saturday afternoons.

固然 gùrán [连] 1 (虽然) admittedly ▷这样办固然可以,但就是需要时间。Admittedly, you can do this but it will take time. 2 (的确) no doubt ▷事业固然重要,但家庭也不可忽视。There's no doubt that work is important, but you can't neglect your family over it.

固守 gùshǒu [动] 1 (坚守) vigorously defend 2 (固执遵循) cling to (PT, PP clung) ▷固守陈规 cling to old-fashioned conventions

固体 gùtǐ [名] solid

固有 gùyǒu [形] inherent

固执 gùzhí [形] stubborn

固执己见 gùzhí jǐjiàn be stubborn

故
gù I [名] 1 (变故) incident 2 (原因) reason 3 (友情) friendship 4 (老友) old friend II [动] pass away III [形] 1 (表示老、旧) old 2 (亡故) deceased IV [副] on purpose V [连] therefore ▷他病了, 故未参加会议。He was ill, and therefore not at the meeting.

故步自封 gù bù zì fēng be complacent

故技 gùjì [名] old trick ▷故技重演 be up to one's old tricks

故居 gùjū [名] former home

故里 gùlǐ [名] home town

故弄玄虚 gù nòng xuánxū make a mystery of something ▷媒体总爱故弄玄虚。The media always likes to make a mystery out of things.

故事 gùshi [名] story

故土 gùtǔ [名] native soil

故乡 gùxiāng [名] birthplace

故意 gùyì [副] deliberately ▷他故意气他的父亲。He deliberately angered his father.

故障 gùzhàng [名] fault ▷这台机器出了故障。This machine is faulty.

故作姿态 gù zuò zītài pose ▷别故作姿态了, 赶快照吧! Stop posing and let me take the picture!

顾 **gù I** [动] **1** (看) look ▶回顾 look back ▶环顾 look around **2** (注意, 照管) attend to ▶照顾 attend to ▶兼顾 give consideration to both sides **3** (拜访) visit **4** (光临) shop at ▷他爱光顾这家书店。He likes to shop at this bookshop. **II** [副] (书) however

顾此失彼 **gù cǐ shī bǐ** let things slip

顾及 **gùjí** [动] consider

顾忌 **gùjì** [动] be guarded ▷他说话毫无顾忌。He was never guarded about what he said.

顾客 **gùkè** [名] customer

顾虑 **gùlǜ** [名] misgivings (PL) ▷顾虑重重 have serious misgivings

顾名思义 **gù míng sī yì** as the name implies

顾盼 **gùpàn** [动] look around ▷他上课的时候老是左右顾盼。He was always looking around in class.

顾全 **gùquán** [动] consider ... fully

顾问 **gùwèn** [名] consultant

顾惜 **gùxī** [动] value

顾影自怜 **gù yǐng zì lián 1** (孤独失意) self-pity **2** (自我欣赏) narcissism

梏 **gù** [名] wooden handcuffs (PL) ▶桎梏 fetters and handcuffs (PL)

雇 **gù** [动] **1** (雇佣) employ **2** (租赁) hire

雇佣 **gùyōng** [动] employ

雇员 **gùyuán** [名] employee

雇主 **gùzhǔ** [名] employer

痼 **gù** [形] **1** (难治愈) chronic **2** (难克服) inveterate

痼疾 **gùjí** [名] chronic illness

瓜 **guā** [名] (植) melon

瓜分 **guāfēn** [动] carve ... up ▷企图瓜分别国领土 plot to carve up other countries' territories

瓜葛 **guāgé** [名] association ▷我不想和这件事有任何瓜葛。I don't want to be associated with this in any way.

瓜熟蒂落 **guā shú dì luò** everything works out when the time is right

呱 **guā** 见下文

呱呱 **guāguā** [拟] croak

呱呱叫 **guāguājiào** [形] (口) fantastic

刮 **guā** [动] **1** (指用刀) shave **2** (涂抹) smear **3** (搜刮) plunder **4** (风) blow (PT blew, PP blown)

刮目相看 **guāmù xiāng kàn** look at someone with new eyes

剐 **guǎ** [动] cut (PT, PP cut)

寡 **guǎ I** [形] **1** (少) few **2** (淡而无味) bland **II** [名] **1** (寡妇) widow **2** (寡居) widowhood

寡妇 **guǎfu** [名] widow

寡廉鲜耻 **guǎ lián xiǎn chǐ** shameless

卦 **guà** [名] divinatory symbol

挂 **guà** [动] **1** (悬挂) hang **2** (中断电话) hang up ▷他愤怒地把电话挂了。He hung up angrily. **3** (接通电话) connect ▷请挂传达室。Can you please put me through to reception? **4** (钩) hitch ... up

挂彩 **guàcǎi** [动] **1** (悬挂彩带) decorate **2** (受伤) be wounded

挂齿 **guàchǐ** [动] mention

挂钩 **guàgōu I** [名] hook **II** [动] link ... up with

挂号 **guàhào** [动] register

挂靠 **guàkào** [动] be affiliated to ▷挂靠在浙江大学 be affiliated to Zhejiang University

挂历 **guàlì** [名] calendar

挂名 **guàmíng** [动] be nominal ▷我只在该公司挂名而已。I only have nominal responsibility for this company.

挂念 **guàniàn** [动] be concerned about ▷小张很挂念出国的妻子。Xiao Zhang was very concerned about his wife, who had gone abroad.

挂拍 **guàpāi** [动] retire

挂失 **guàshī** [动] report the loss of

挂帅 **guàshuài** [动] take charge (PT took, PP taken)

挂图 **guàtú** [名] wall chart

挂靴 **guàxuē** [名] retire

挂一漏万 **guà yī lòu wàn** be far from exhaustive

褂 **guà** [名] gown

乖 **guāi I** [形] **1** (听话) well-behaved **2** (机灵) clever **3** (书) (不正常) abnormal **II** [动] (书) (违反) violate

乖戾 **guāilì** [形] (书) twisted ▷他的行为乖戾。He's so twisted.

乖僻 **guāipì** [形] eccentric

乖巧 **guāiqiǎo** [形] **1** (机灵) clever **2** (惹人爱) lovable

拐 **guǎi I** [名] **1** (拐杖) walking stick **2** (拐角处) turning **3** (七) seven **II** [动] **1** (转变方向) turn ▷车从大路拐进一条小胡同。The car left the main road and turned into a small alley. **2** (拐

骗) swindle

拐卖 guǎimài [动] abduct and sell

拐骗 guǎipiàn [动] 1 (钱财) swindle 2 (妇女或儿童等) abduct

拐弯抹角 guǎi wān mò jiǎo 1 (道路不畅) twist and turn 2 (不直接) beat about the bush

怪 guài I [形] strange II [动] 1 (觉得奇怪) be surprised 2 (责怪) blame ▷这事也不能全怪他。We can't blame this entirely on him. III [副] (口) really ▷这行李怪沉的。This bag is really heavy. IV [名] monster

怪诞 guàidàn [形] uncanny

怪话 guàihuà [名] snide remark

怪模怪样 guài mú guài yàng grotesque

怪圈 guàiquān [名] strange phenomenon (PL phenomena)

怪异 guàiyì [形] weird

怪罪 guàizuì [动] blame

关 guān I [动] 1 (合拢) close ▷关窗户 close the window 2 (圈起来) imprison ▷战俘被关进集中营。The prisoners of war were imprisoned in a concentration camp. ▷别让孩子整天关在家里。Make sure the children aren't cooped up at home all day. 3 (停业) close…down ▷这家公司早就关了。The company closed down a long time ago. 4 (中断、终止) turn off ▷关灯 turn off the light 5 (牵连) concern ▷这不关他的事。This matter does not concern him. II [名] 1 (守卫处所) pass 2 (出入境收税处) customs (PL) ▷海关 customs (PL) 3 (转折点) critical point ▷手术这一关他总算闯过去了。His critical operation passed off safely. 4 (关联部分) ▶关节 joint ▶关键 key

关爱 guān'ài [动] cherish

关闭 guānbì [动] 1 (合拢) close 2 (歇业或停办) close down

关怀 guānhuái [动] be concerned about ▷关怀社会弱势群体 be concerned about disadvantaged social groups

关键 guānjiàn I [名] crux II [形] key

关节 guānjié [名] joint

关口 guānkǒu [名] 1 (必经之地) strategic pass 2 (关头) juncture

关联 guānlián [动] be interrelated ▷发展经济和保护环境是互相关联的。Developing the economy and protecting the environment are interrelated.

关卡 guānqiǎ [名] checkpoint

关切 guānqiè I [形] deeply concerned II [动] be concerned

关税 guānshuì [名] customs duty

关头 guāntóu [名] juncture

关系 guānxì I [名] 1 (联系) relation ▷外交关系 diplomatic relations 2 (意义) bearing ▷此事关系重大。This matter is of grave importance. 3 (原因) reason ▷由于健康关系，他提前退休了。He retired early for reasons of ill health. 4 (证件) identification papers ▷出门把关系带上。Take your papers with you when you go out. II [动] impact on ▷会议的决定关系到公司的未来。The decisions made at this meeting will impact on the future of the company.

关心 guānxīn [动] be concerned ▷关心股市走向 be concerned about stock market trends

关押 guānyā [动] imprison

关于 guānyú [介] on ▷关于这个问题有很多争议。There is a lot of controversy on this point.

关照 guānzhào [动] 1 (关心照顾) look after 2 (口头通知) tell

关注 guānzhù [动] pay close attention to (PT, PP paid) ▷社会都应该关注老年人问题。Society should pay close attention to the problems of the elderly.

观 guān I [动] look ▶围观 gather round to watch ▶旁观 look on II [名] view ▶景观 sight ▶奇观 spectacle

观测 guāncè [动] observe

观察 guānchá [动] observe

观点 guāndiǎn [名] point of view

观感 guāngǎn [名] impressions (PL)

观光 guānguāng [动] go sightseeing (PT went, PP gone) ▷去巴黎观光 go sightseeing in Paris

观看 guānkàn [动] watch

观摩 guānmó [动] watch and learn

观念 guānniàn [名] concept

观赏 guānshǎng [动] stand back and enjoy

观望 guānwàng [动] wait and see ▷他们采取观望的态度。They took a "wait-and-see" attitude.

观众 guānzhòng [名] spectator

官 guān [名] 1 (公职人员) official 2 (器官) organ

官场 guānchǎng [名] official circles ▷这在官场中很常见。This is very common in official circles.

官邸 guāndǐ [名] official residence

官方 guānfāng [名] official

官官相护 guān guān xiāng hù ▷这种官官相护的情况必须制止。The way that officials stick up for and protect one another has got to stop.

官吏 guānlì [名] (旧) official

官僚 guānliáo [名] bureaucrat ▷官僚作风 bureaucracy

官能 guānnéng [名] sense

官腔 guānqiāng [名] bureaucratic manner

官司 guānsi [名] lawsuit ▷和某人打官司 file a lawsuit against somebody

官员 guānyuán [名] official

官运亨通 guānyùn hēngtōng have a successful career as an official

官职 guānzhí [名] official position

冠 guān [名] 1 (帽子) hat 2 (帽状物) ▷鸡冠 crown ▷花冠 garland
→另见 guàn

冠冕堂皇 guānmiǎn tánghuáng grandiose

棺 guān [名] coffin

鳏 guān [名] widower

鳏寡孤独 guān guǎ gū dú [名] people with no family to support them

管 guǎn I [名] 1 (管子) pipe ▷水管 water pipe 2 (乐器) wind instrument ▷双簧管 oboe 3 (管状物) tube ▷晶体管 transistor 4 (医) duct II [动] 1 (负责) be in charge of ▷管销售 be in charge of sales 2 (管辖) have jurisdiction over ▷这个市管3个区和5个县。This city has jurisdiction over three districts and five counties. 3 (管教) discipline ▷把自己家的孩子管好 discipline one's children well 4 (过问) interfere ▷这事不用你管。It's no use you interfering in this. 5 (担任) be in charge of ▷她管市场部。She's in charge of the marketing department. 6 (保证) guarantee ▷管换管退。The replacement or refund of defective goods is guaranteed. 7 (提供) provide ▷管吃管住 provide food and accommodation III [形] narrow ▷管见 in my humble opinion IV [介] ▷大家管他叫"小王"。Everyone calls him "Xiao Wang".

管保 guǎnbǎo [动] guarantee

管道 guǎndào [名] pipeline ▷管道煤气 piped gas ▷石油运输管道 oil pipeline

管家 guǎnjiā [名] housekeeper

管教 guǎnjiào [动] discipline ▷管教子女是父母的责任。It's the responsibility of parents to instil a sense of discipline in their children.

管理 guǎnlǐ [动] 1 (负责) be in charge ▷管理财务 be in charge of finance 2 (保管) take care of (PT took, PP taken) ▷他管理计算机。He takes care of the computers. 3 (看管) keep guard over (PT, PP kept) ▷管理犯人 keep guard over the prisoners ▷企业管理 business management

管事 guǎnshì [动] 1 (负责) be in charge 2 (有效) be effective

管束 guǎnshù [动] discipline

管辖 guǎnxiá [动] have jurisdiction over

管弦乐 guǎnxiányuè [名] orchestral music

管用 guǎnyòng [形] effective

管制 guǎnzhì I [名] control II [动] place under surveillance

贯 guàn I [动] 1 (贯穿) pass through 2 (连贯) keep following (PT, PP kept) II [名] ancestral home ▷籍贯 place of origin

贯彻 guànchè [动] implement

贯穿 guànchuān [动] run through ▷这项政策应该贯穿于整个工程。This policy should run through the whole project. ▷这条铁路贯穿南北。The railway runs from north to south.

贯串 guànchuàn [动] permeate

贯通 guàntōng [名] 1 (理解透彻) be well versed in 2 (连接) link... up

贯注 guànzhù [动] concentrate ▷你应该全神贯注于工作。You should concentrate fully on your work.

冠 guàn I [动] crown II [名] crown
→另见 guān

冠词 guàncí [名] (语法) article

冠军 guànjūn [名] champion

惯 guàn [动] 1 (习惯) be used to ▷我吃西餐已经惯了。I'm already used to Western food. 2 (纵容) spoil

惯犯 guànfàn [名] reoffender

惯技 guànjì [名] old trick

惯例 guànlì [名] convention

惯用 guànyòng I [动] often use ▷他惯用这种方法。He often uses this sort of method. II [形] habitual

盥 guàn 见下文

盥洗 guànxǐ [动] wash (英), wash up (美)

灌 guàn [动] 1 (灌溉) irrigate 2 (注入) pour... into ▷灌热水瓶 pour water into a flask 3 (强行劝酒) force... to drink ▷他把别人都灌醉了。He got them all drunk. 4 (录音) record

灌溉 guàngài [动] irrigate

灌木 guànmù [名] (植) bush

灌输 guànshū [动] 1 (输水) divert water 2 (思想、知识) indoctrinate ▷有人向他灌输迷信思想。Someone indoctrinated him with superstitious beliefs.

灌注 guànzhù [动] pour ... into

罐 guàn 见下文
罐头 guàntou [名] tin

光 guāng I [名] 1 (指物质) light ▷月光 moonlight ▷阳光 sunlight 2 (景物) scenery ▷迷人的风光 enchanting scenery 3 (荣誉) glory ▷奥运冠军为国增光。Olympic champions bring glory to their country. 4 (明亮) glint ▷他看到金子时两眼放光。His eyes glinted when he saw the gold. 5 (好处) benefit II [动] 1 (光大) glorify ▷光耀门庭 bring glory to the family name 2 (露出) bare ▷大冬天他还光着上身。He went bare-chested even in the depths of winter. III [形] 1 (光滑) smooth 2 (露着) bare ▷光脚 barefooted 3 (穷尽) used up ▷钱都用光了。All the money's used up. IV [副] just ▷这件事光有热情是不够的。This requires more than just enthusiasm. ▷他光说不做。He's all talk.
光波 guāngbō [名] (物) light wave
光彩 guāngcǎi I [名] radiance II [形] glorious
光大 guāngdà [动] carry ... forward
光复 guāngfù [动] recover
光顾 guānggù [动] shop at ▷欢迎光顾我店。Welcome to our shop.
光怪陆离 guāng guài lù lí bizarre and fantastic
光棍 guānggùn [名] 1 (地痞) hooligan 2 (单身汉) bachelor
光滑 guānghuá [形] smooth
光辉 guānghuī I [名] radiance II [形] magnificent
光洁 guāngjié [形] bright and clean
光景 guāngjǐng I [名] 1 (情景) scene 2 (境况) situation II [副] 1 (大约) about ▷半夜光景下起了雪。It started snowing about halfway through the night. 2 (很可能) probably ▷她很努力，将来光景会出息。She's so hard-working – in the future she'll probably be very successful.
光亮 guāngliàng [形] shiny
光临 guānglín [动] be present
光溜溜 guāngliūliū [形] 1 (光滑) slippery 2 (无遮掩的) naked
光芒 guāngmáng [名] radiance
光芒万丈 guāngmáng wànzhàng resplendent
光明 guāngmíng I [名] light II [形] bright
光明正大 guāngmíng zhèngdà open and aboveboard
光盘 guāngpán [名] CD
光荣 guāngróng [形] glorious ▷光荣属于那些默默无闻的幕后工作者。The glory should go to those who go unrecognised behind the scenes.
光天化日 guāng tiān huà rì in broad daylight
光秃秃 guāngtūtū [形] barren
光线 guāngxiàn [名] light
光阴 guāngyīn [名] time
光阴似箭 guāngyīn sì jiàn time flies
光泽 guāngzé [名] gloss
光照 guāngzhào [名] light
光宗耀祖 guāng zōng yào zǔ bring glory to one's ancestors

咣 guāng [拟] bang

广 guǎng [形] 1 (宽阔) broad 2 (多) numerous
广播 guǎngbō [动] broadcast (PT, PP broadcast) ▷他们正在广播找人。They are currently broadcasting missing person announcements. ▷英语广播 English language broadcast
广博 guǎngbó [形] erudite
广场 guǎngchǎng [名] square
广大 guǎngdà [形] 1 (宽广) vast 2 (众多) numerous
广度 guǎngdù [名] range
广泛 guǎngfàn [形] wide-ranging ▷广泛的群众基础 broad popular base ▷广泛开展活动 initiate a wide range of activities
广告 guǎnggào [名] advertisement
广阔 guǎngkuò [形] broad
广义 guǎngyì [名] broad sense

犷 guǎng [形] uncouth ▶粗犷 rough and uncouth
犷悍 guǎnghàn [形] intrepid

逛 guàng [动] stroll
逛荡 guàngdang [动] loiter

归 guī [动] 1 (返回、还给) return 2 (合并) group ... together ▷我把书籍归类了。I sorted out the books. 3 (属于) be under the charge of ▷这支部队归他指挥。This team is under his charge. ▷这本书归我所有。This book belongs to him.
归并 guībìng [动] 1 (并入) merge 2 (合拢) add ... up ▷费用归并后惊人得高。When you add it all up it's prohibitively expensive.
归档 guīdàng [动] file ▷将这些资料归档备查。Please file these materials away for future reference.
归根结底 guī gēn jié dǐ in the final analysis
归功 guīgōng [动] give credit to (PT gave, PP given) ▷成绩不能都归功于一个人。You can't give one person the credit for all the success.

归还 guīhuán [动] return

归咎 guījiù [动] blame ▷不能把责任都归咎于他。You can't lay the blame entirely on him.

归纳 guīnà [动] sum... up

归属 guīshǔ [动] come under (PT came, PP come) ▷这个小组归属于人事部。This team comes under the human resources department.

归顺 guīshùn [动] swear allegiance to (PT swore, PP sworn)

归降 guīxiáng [动] surrender

归心似箭 guīxīn sì jiàn long to return home

归于 guīyú [动] 1 (属于) attribute... to ▷成功归于大家的努力。The success is down to everyone's hard work. 2 (趋于) tend to

归置 guīzhi [动] (口) tidy... up

龟 guī [名] tortoise
→另见 jūn

龟甲 guījiǎ [名] tortoiseshell

龟缩 guīsuō [动] recoil ▷遇到困难我们不应该龟缩。We shouldn't recoil in the face of difficulty.

规 guī I [名] 1 (工具) compasses (PL) 2 (规则) rule II [动] 1 (劝告) admonish ▶规劝 admonish 2 (谋划) plan ▶规划 plan

规程 guīchéng [名] rules (PL)

规定 guīdìng I [动] stipulate ▷请在规定的时间内完成。Please complete this within the specified time. II [名] directive ▷这项规定过于苛刻。This directive is excessively harsh.

规范 guīfàn [名] standard ▷良好的行为规范 standards of good conduct ▷他的汉语不规范。His Chinese is not standard. ▷一定要规范市场秩序。We must standardize the market economy.

规格 guīgé [名] specification

规划 guīhuà I [名] plan II [动] plan

规矩 guīju I [名] norm II [形] well-behaved ▷她的女儿很规矩。Her daughter is so well-behaved. ▷他办事总是规矩。He always plays by the rules.

规律 guīlǜ [名] law

规模 guīmó [名] scale

规劝 guīquàn [动] remonstrate

规则 guīzé I [名] regulation II [形] orderly

规章 guīzhāng [名] regulations (PL)

闺 guī [名] 1 (书) (门) gate 2 (闺房) boudoir

闺女 guīnü [名] 1 (未婚女子) girl 2 (女儿) daughter

瑰 guī [形] magnificent

瑰宝 guībǎo [名] treasure

瑰丽 guīlì [形] magnificent

轨 guī [名] 1 (轨道) rail 2 (秩序) course

轨道 guǐdào [名] 1 (指机车) track 2 (指天体) orbit 3 (秩序) course ▷这个项目已进入轨道。The project is now on course.

轨迹 guǐjì [名] 1 (数) locus 2 (天文) orbit

诡 guǐ [形] 1 (奸猾) scheming 2 (奇异) eerie

诡辩 guǐbiàn [动] quibble ▷你实际上是在诡辩。What you are really doing is quibbling. ▷诡辩改变不了事实。Quibbling cannot change the facts.

诡计 guǐjì [名] intrigue

诡秘 guǐmì [形] surreptitious

诡异 guǐyì [形] strange

鬼 guǐ I [名] 1 (灵魂) ghost 2 (勾当) dirty trick 3 (不良行为者) ▶酒鬼 drunkard ▶色鬼 lech 4 (表示爱称) ▶机灵鬼 smart aleck II [形] 1 (不光明) secretive 2 (恶劣) damned 3 (机灵) clever

鬼把戏 guǐbǎxì [名] dirty trick

鬼点子 guǐdiǎnzi [名] wicked idea

鬼鬼祟祟 guǐguǐ suìsuì stealthy

鬼话 guǐhuà [名] lie

鬼混 guǐhùn [动] hang around ▷不要整天和不三不四的人鬼混。You shouldn't be hanging around with such shady people.

鬼脸 guǐliǎn [名] grimace

鬼迷心窍 guǐ mí xīn qiào be obsessed

鬼使神差 guǐ shǐ shén chāi strange coincidence

柜 guì [名] 1 (柜子) cupboard ▶衣柜 wardrobe ▶保险柜 safe 2 (柜房) shop

柜台 guìtái [名] counter

刽 guì [动] cut off (PT, PP cut)

刽子手 guìzishǒu [名] 1 (死刑犯执行者) executioner 2 (屠杀者) butcher

贵 guì I [形] 1 (指价格) expensive 2 (值得珍视) valuable

贵宾 guìbīn [名] distinguished guest

贵干 guìgàn [名] business

贵人 guìrén [名] 1 (尊贵的人) eminent person 2 (好人) good person

贵重 guìzhòng [形] valuable

贵族 guìzú [名] aristocrat

桂 **guì** [名] laurel

桂冠 **guìguān** [名] laurel ▷桂冠诗人 Poet Laureate

跪 **guì** [动] kneel

跪拜 **guìbài** [动] worship on bended knee

滚 **gǔn** I [动] 1 (滚动) roll 2 (走开) get lost ▷你赶快滚! Just get lost, will you! 3 (沸腾) boil 4 (指缝纫方法) hem II [形] 1 (滚动的) rolling 2 (沸腾的) boiling III [副] very

滚动 **gǔndòng** [动] roll

滚瓜烂熟 **gǔnguā lànshú** know off by heart ▷他把那首诗背得滚瓜烂熟。He knew the whole poem off by heart.

滚滚 **gǔngǔn** [形] 1 (指河流) surging 2 (指财富) rolling ▷财源滚滚。The money is rolling in.

滚热 **gǔnrè** [形] boiling hot

滚烫 **gǔntàng** [形] boiling

滚圆 **gǔnyuán** [形] perfectly round

棍 **gùn** [名] 1 (棍子) stick 2 (地痞) ruffian

锅 **guō** [名] 1 (指炊具) pot 2 (锅状物) bowl ▶火锅 hotpot

锅巴 **guōbā** [名] rice crust

锅台 **guōtái** [名] kitchen range

国 **guó** I [名] country II [形] 1 (国家) national ▶国徽 national emblem 2 (中国) Chinese ▷国剧 Chinese opera

国宝 **guóbǎo** [名] national treasure

国宾 **guóbīn** [名] guest of the state

国策 **guócè** [名] national policy

国产 **guóchǎn** [形] domestic

国粹 **guócuì** [名] the embodiment of a country

国都 **guódū** [名] capital

国度 **guódù** [名] country

国法 **guófǎ** [名] national law

国防 **guófáng** [名] national defence (英) 或 defense (美)

国歌 **guógē** [名] national anthem

国格 **guógé** [名] national dignity

国画 **guóhuà** [名] traditional Chinese painting

国徽 **guóhuī** [名] national emblem

国会 **guóhuì** [名] parliament

国货 **guóhuò** [名] domestic goods (PL)

国籍 **guójí** [名] nationality

国计民生 **guó jì mín shēng** the national economy and the people's livelihood

国际 **guójì** [形] international ▷国际和平与稳定 international peace and stability

国家 **guójiā** [名] state

国界 **guójiè** [名] national border

国境 **guójìng** [名] 1 (指范围) national territory 2 (边境) frontier

国库 **guókù** [名] treasury

国力 **guólì** [名] national strength

国门 **guómén** [名] border

国民 **guómín** [名] citizen

国民经济 **guómín jīngjì** [名] national economy

国难 **guónàn** [名] national crisis (PL crises)

国内 **guónèi** [形] domestic ▷国内生产总值 gross domestic product

国旗 **guóqí** [名] national flag

国企 **guóqǐ** [名] (国有企业) state-owned enterprise

国情 **guóqíng** [名] the state of the country

国庆 **guóqìng** [名] national day

国色天香 **guósè tiānxiāng** stunningly beautiful

国手 **guóshǒu** [名] national champion

国书 **guóshū** [名] credentials (PL)

国税 **guóshuì** [名] national taxation

国泰民安 **guó tài mín ān** a contented people living in a country at peace

国土 **guótǔ** [名] national territory

国王 **guówáng** [名] king

国威 **guówēi** [名] national prestige

国务 **guówù** [名] domestic affairs (PL)

国宴 **guóyàn** [名] state banquet

国营 **guóyíng** [形] state-run ▷国营企业 state-run enterprises

国有 **guóyǒu** [形] state-owned

国债 **guózhài** [名] national debt

果 **guǒ** I [名] 1 (果子) fruit 2 (结局) outcome ▶效果 result ▶成果 achievement II [动] be full III [形] resolute IV [副] naturally V [连] if

果不其然 **guǒ bu qí rán** as expected ▷果不其然，他在图书馆看书。As expected, he was in the library reading books.

果断 **guǒduàn** [形] resolute

果脯 **guǒfǔ** [名] preserved fruit

果敢 **guǒgǎn** [形] resolute and daring

果品 **guǒpǐn** [名] fruit

果然 **guǒrán** [副] really

果实 **guǒshí** [名] 1 (果子) fruit 2 (成果) fruits (PL) ▷成功的果实 the fruits of success

果真 **guǒzhēn** I [副] really ▷他果真是个勤奋的年轻人。He really is a very hard-working young man. II [连] if

果子 **guǒzi** [名] fruit

裹 **guǒ** [动] **1** (缠绕) wrap ▷我把身子用毯子裹上。I wrapped myself up in a blanket. **2** (夹带) smuggle... away ▷他临走时裹走了一些首饰。When he left he smuggled away some jewellery. **3** (方) (吸) suck

裹足不前 **guǒ zú bù qián** drag one's feet

过 **guò** I [动] **1** (经过) pass through **2** (度过) spend (PT, PP spent) ▷你假期怎么过的？How did you spend your holiday? **3** (过去) pass ▷几天过去了，他还杳无音信。Several days passed and still there was no news of him. **4** (处理) go over (PT went, PP gone) ▷这段文字还得过一遍。This piece of text should be gone over again. **5** (转移到) transfer ▷过账 transfer from one account to another **6** (超过) be more than ▷工程已经过半。The project is already more than half way through. ▷年过半百 over fifty years old **7** (生活) live ▷我们过得很好。We live well. **8** (庆祝) celebrate ▷过生日 celebrate a birthday II [名] fault ▷将功补过 atone for one's crimes III [介] past ▷现在是9点过8分。It is now eight minutes past nine.

过不去 **guò bu qù** [动] **1** (堵塞) be impassable **2** (为难) make things difficult for ▷他有意和我过不去。He wanted to make things difficult for me. **3** (通不过) not get past ▷这在老板那儿一定过不去的。This definitely isn't going to get past the boss. **4** (抱歉) feel sorry

过场 **guòchǎng** [名] interlude ▷走过场 (喻) do as a formality

过程 **guòchéng** [名] process ▷理解过程 process of understanding

过错 **guòcuò** [名] fault

过道 **guòdào** [名] corridor

过得去 **guò de qù** [动] **1** (可通过) be passable **2** (不错) be passable ▷饭菜还过得去。The food is just passable. **3** (过意得去) feel at ease

过度 **guòdù** [形] excessive

过分 **guòfèn** [形] excessive

过关 **guòguān** [动] **1** (通过关口) cross a pass **2** (通过检验) pass a test

过河拆桥 **guò hé chāi qiáo** turn one's back on

过后 **guòhòu** [副] later ▷我们过后再谈。Let's talk again later.

过户 **guòhù** [动] (法) transfer ownership

过火 **guòhuǒ** [形] excessive

过激 **guòjī** [形] extreme

过继 **guòjì** [动] adopt ▷他从小就过继给了他的叔叔。He was adopted by his uncle when he was little.

过奖 **guòjiǎng** [动] flatter

过街老鼠 **guò jiē lǎoshǔ** public enemy

过节儿 **guòjiér** [名] grudge

过客 **guòkè** [名] passer-by

过来 **guòlái** [动] come over (PT came, PP come) ▷你赶快过来，大家都等你呢！Come straight over - everyone is waiting for you!

过来人 **guòláirén** [名] old hand

过量 **guòliàng** [形] excessive

过虑 **guòlù** [动] (过分担心) be overanxious ▷此事你不必过虑。There's no need for you to get overanxious about this

过滤 **guòlù** [动] filter ▷过滤杂质 filter out impurities

过门 **guòmén** [动] get married

过敏 **guòmǐn** [名] (医) allergy

过目 **guòmù** [动] look over

过目成诵 **guò mù chéng sòng** blessed with an extraordinary memory

过期 **guòqī** [动] expire

过谦 **guòqiān** [形] overly modest

过去 **guòqù** [名] the past ▷他比过去胖多了。He weighs a lot more than he used to.

过去 **guòqu** [动] pass by ▷一辆车刚过去。A car just went past.

过人 **guòrén** [动] excel

过日子 **guò rìzi** [动] live

过剩 **guòshèng** [形] excessive

过失 **guòshī** [名] mistake

过时 **guòshí** I [形] outdated II [动] pass time

过世 **guòshì** [动] pass away

过头 **guòtóu** [形] excessive

过往 **guòwǎng** [动] **1** (来去) come and go **2** (交往) associate with

过问 **guòwèn** [动] concern oneself with ▷这件事你就不必过问了。There's no need for you to concern yourself with this.

过细 **guòxì** [形] meticulous

过眼云烟 **guò yǎn yúnyān** fleeting

过瘾 **guòyǐn** [动] do to one's heart's content ▷昨天我们玩得很过瘾。Yesterday we played to our heart's content.

过硬 **guòyìng** [形] completely proficient

过于 **guòyú** [副] too

Hh

你急什么？ If even she isn't worried then why are you? **5** (居然) really ▷他这次考试还真的通过了。 He really did pass the exam this time round. **6** (早在) as early as ▷当他还在襁褓中就被父母遗弃了。 He was abandoned by his parents in infancy.

→另见 huán

> **still** 用于强调对于某事的发生或者对某事持续了如此长的时间而感到惊讶。 *She was still looking at me…There are still plenty of horses round here.* **yet** 用于否定句和疑问句中，用于强调语气，暗示说话人对某事未发生，或者晚于预期时间发生而感到惊讶。 *Have you seen it yet? …The troops could not yet see the shore …It isn't dark yet.*

还是 háishi I [副] **1** (仍然) still ▷尽管很危险，警察们还是冲了进去。 In spite of the danger, the police still rushed on in. **2** (最好) had better ▷你还是先完成作业吧。 You'd better finish your homework first. II [连] or ▷你是去巴黎还是去伦敦？ Are you going to Paris or London?

孩 hái [名] child (PL children)

孩提 háití [名] (书) early childhood

孩子 háizi [名] child (PL children)

骸 hái [名] **1** (骨) bones (PL) ▶骸骨 skeleton **2** 身体 (body) ▶形骸 human body ▶遗骸 remains (PL)

海 hǎi I [名] **1** (海洋) ocean ▶海岸线 coastline **2** (湖泊) lake **3** (喻) (指数量) sea ▶人海 sea of people ▶火海 inferno II [形] extra large ▷你先不要夸海口，事后再说。 Don't go making wild boasts just yet – let's wait until after the event.

海岸 hǎi'àn [名] shore

海拔 hǎibá [名] elevation

海报 hǎibào [名] poster

海滨 hǎibīn [名] seaside

海底捞针 hǎidǐlāozhēn look for a needle in a haystack

海港 hǎigǎng [名] harbour (英), harbor (美)

海关 hǎiguān [名] customs (PL)

海货 hǎihuò [名] seafood

海疆 hǎijiāng [名] territorial waters (PL)

海军 hǎijūn [名] the navy

海枯石烂 hǎikūshílàn forever ▷他们发誓海枯石烂不变心。 They vowed that they would always be faithful.

海阔天空 hǎikuòtiānkōng **1** (字) (指自然) boundless **2** (喻) (无拘束) anything and

---

哈 hā I [叹] aha II [拟] ha ha ▷哈哈大笑 roar with laughter III [动] breathe out ▷他冲着手哈气，好暖和些。 He breathed on his hands to warm them up.

→另见 hǎ

哈欠 hāqian [名] yawn

哈腰 hāyāo [动] **1** (字) stoop ▷哈腰捡钱包 stoop to pick up one's wallet **2** (喻) suck up to

蛤 há 见下文

→另见 gé

蛤蟆 háma [名] toad

哈 hǎ 见下文

→另见 hā

哈巴狗 hǎbagǒu [名] **1** (字) Pekin(g)ese **2** (喻) sycophant

咳 hāi [叹] oh

→另见 ké

还 hái [副] **1** (仍旧) still, yet ▷那家老饭店还很兴旺。 The old restaurant is still thriving. ▷她还没回来。 She hasn't come back yet. **2** (更加) even more ▷他比我还想家。 He's even more homesick than I am. **3** (尚) still ▷她不聪明，但还算老实。 She's no great brain, but still, she's honest. **4** (尚且) even ▷她还不着急，

everything ▷他们海阔天空地聊了起来。 They started chatting about anything and everything.

海里 hǎilǐ [名] nautical mile

海量 hǎiliàng [名] 1 (敬) (大度) magnanimity ▷多谢您海量包涵。Thank you so much for your generosity. 2 (指酒量) tolerance ▷论喝酒，我可比不了您的海量。When it comes to alcohol, my tolerance just isn't as great as yours.

海洛因 hǎiluòyīn [名] heroin

海绵 hǎimián [名] sponge

海事 hǎishì [名] 1 (指事务) maritime affairs (PL) 2 (指事故) maritime accident

海誓山盟 hǎi shì shān méng pledge everlasting love

海外 hǎiwài [名] ▷海外学子 overseas student

海味 hǎiwèi [名] seafood

海峡 hǎixiá [名] strait ▷台湾海峡 the Taiwan Straits

海鲜 hǎixiān [名] seafood

海洋 hǎiyáng [名] ocean

海域 hǎiyù [名] waters (PL)

海员 hǎiyuán [名] sailor

骇 hài [动] shock

骇然 hàirán [形] dumbstruck

骇人听闻 hài rén tīng wén shocking

害 hài I [动] 1 (损害) harm ▶害人害己 harm others as well as oneself ▷他的失误害得公司破产。His mistake forced the company into bankruptcy. 2 (杀害) kill ▶遇害 be murdered 3 (指疾病) contract ▶害病 contract an illness 4 (感到) feel uneasy (PT, PP felt) ▶害羞 be shy II [名] harm ▶自然灾害 natural disaster III [形] harmful ▶害虫 pest

害处 hàichu [名] harm ▷多吃蔬菜没有害处。It won't do you any harm to eat more vegetables.

害怕 hàipà [动] be afraid

害群之马 hài qún zhī mǎ black sheep ▷她是这个班里的害群之马。She's the black sheep of the class.

害臊 hàisào [动] feel ashamed (PT, PP felt)

害羞 hàixiū [动] be shy

酣 hān 见下文

酣畅 hānchàng [形] unrestrained ▷笔墨酣畅 free-flowing writing

憨 hān [形] 1 (傻) silly ▶憨笑 simper 2 (朴实) naive ▷憨态可掬 charmingly naive

憨厚 hānhòu [形] down-to-earth

憨笑 hānxiào [动] simper

鼾 hān [名] snore

鼾睡 hānshuì [动] be sound asleep

含 hán [动] 1 (用嘴) keep ... in the mouth (PT, PP kept) ▷把温度计含在嘴巴里。Hold the thermometer in your mouth. 2 (包含) contain ▷含氟的牙膏 toothpaste with fluoride ▷这些烟不含尼古丁。These cigarettes do not contain nicotine. 3 (怀有) hold (PT, PP held) ▶含冤 suffer a gross injustice ▶含笑 with a smile

含苞 hánbāo [动] be in bud

含糊 hánhu [形] 1 (不清楚) vague 2 (马虎) careless ▷关键之处不可含糊。Make sure not to overlook the key points.

含混 hánhùn [形] ambiguous

含量 hánliàng [名] content

含情脉脉 hánqíng mòmò full of tender affection ▷他含情脉脉地望着新娘。He gazed at his bride with tender affection.

含沙射影 hán shā shè yǐng make insinuations

含辛茹苦 hán xīn rú kǔ endure hardship ▷她含辛茹苦地养大了5个孩子。She endured a lot of hardship bringing up her five children.

含蓄 hánxù I [动] be full of ▷文章中含蓄着深意。The essay had real depth. II [形] 1 (耐人寻味) measured 2 (内敛) reserved

含义 hányì [名] implication

函 hán [名] letter ▷公函 official letter

函电 hándiàn [名] correspondence

函授 hánshòu [动] teach by correspondence (PT, PP taught)

函数 hánshù [名] function

涵 hán [动] contain ▶涵盖 cover

涵养 hányǎng I [名] self-control II [动] conserve ▷树木有助于涵养水源。Trees are helpful in water conservation.

寒 hán I [形] 1 (冷) cold ▶春寒 spring chill ▶寒风 chilly wind 2 (贫穷) poor ▶贫寒 poverty-stricken ▶寒士 poor scholar II [动] tremble with fear ▶心寒 be bitterly disappointed

寒碜 hánchen [形] 1 (丑) ugly 2 (丢脸) disgraceful ▷我考试没过，真寒碜！I failed the exam – what a disgrace! II [动] (讥笑) ridicule

寒窗 hánchuāng [名] difficult learning conditions (PL)

寒带 hándài [名] Frigid Zone

寒噤 hánjìn [名] shiver

寒冷 hánlěng [形] cold

寒流 hánliú [名] cold spell

寒酸 hánsuān [形] shabby ▷穿着寒酸 dress shabbily

寒心 hánxīn [动] be bitterly disappointed

寒暄 hánxuān [动] engage in small talk ▷我不善于与人寒暄。I'm no good at making small talk.

罕 hǎn 见下文

罕见 hǎnjiàn [形] rare

罕有 hǎnyǒu [形] rare

喊 hǎn [动] 1 (大声叫) shout ▶呼喊 yell 2 (叫) call ▷有人在喊你。Somebody's calling you.

喊叫 hǎnjiào [动] cry out

汉 hàn [名] 1 (汉族) the Han (PL) ▷汉人 the Han people (PL) 2 (男子) man (PL men) ▶庄稼汉 farmer ▶好汉 a real man

汉奸 hànjiān [名] traitor

汉学 hànxué [名] Sinology

汉语 Hànyǔ [名] Chinese

汉字 Hànzì [名] Chinese characters (PL)

汉子 hànzi [名] 1 (男子) man (PL men) 2 (方) (丈夫) husband

汉族 Hànzú [名] the Han (PL)

汗 hàn [名] sweat

汗流浃背 hàn liú jiā bèi sweat profusely

汗马功劳 hàn mǎ gōngláo distinguished service ▷他为公司的创建立下了汗马功劳。He distinguished himself in the work involved in setting up the company.

汗水 hànshuǐ [名] sweat

汗颜 hànyán [动] (书) feel ashamed (PT, PP felt)

旱 hàn [形] dry ▶旱季 dry season ▶旱田 non-irrigated land ▶旱冰 roller skating

旱涝保收 hàn lào bǎo shōu 1 (字) be sure of a stable yield 2 (喻) ensure a safe income ▷旱涝保收的工作 financially stable employment

旱灾 hànzāi [名] drought

悍 hàn [形] 1 (勇猛) brave 2 (凶狠) ferocious ▶凶悍 ferocious

悍然 hànrán [形] flagrant

捍 hàn [动] defend

捍卫 hànwèi [动] defend

焊 hàn [动] weld ▷他俩好得像是焊在了一起。The two of them go about as if they were joined at the hip.

焊接 hànjiē [动] weld

憾 hàn 见下文

憾事 hànshì [名] regret

撼 hàn [动] shake (PT shook, PP shaken)

撼动 hàndòng [动] vibrate

瀚 hàn [形] vast ▶浩瀚 vast

夯 hāng I [名] rammer ▶石夯 stone rammer II [动] 1 (砸) pound 2 (方) (击打) strike (PT, PP struck) ▷他被人用木棍夯倒了。Someone struck him down with a stick.

行 háng I [名] 1 (行列) row ▶第一行 first row ▷请把图标排成竖行。Please arrange the icons in vertical rows. 2 (行业) profession ▶同行 people in the same profession ▶行规 industry rules 3 (机构) firm ▶银行 bank ▶车行 car dealer II [动] place ▷在家你行几? Where do you come in your family? III [量] line ▷一行大雁 a line of wild geese ▷十四行诗 a sonnet
→另见 xíng

行当 hángdang [名] 1 (口) (行业) line of work 2 (角色) role ▷他在戏班子里演好几个行当。He played several roles in the opera troupe.

行话 hánghuà [名] jargon

行家 hángjia [名] expert

行列 hángliè [名] ranks (PL)

行情 hángqíng [名] market conditions (PL)

行市 hángshi [名] prices (PL)

行伍 hángwǔ [名] the ranks (PL)

行业 hángyè [名] industry ▷服务行业 service industry ▷行业规则 industry rules

吭 háng [名] throat ▷引吭高歌 belt out a song
→另见 kēng

航 háng I [名] (书) boat II [动] 1 (指船) sail ▷扬帆远航 set sail on a long voyage 2 (指飞机) fly (PT flew, PP flown) ▶航空公司 airline

航班 hángbān [名] 1 (指客轮) scheduled voyage 2 (指客机) scheduled flight

航程 hángchéng [名] voyage

航道 hángdào [名] channel

航海 hánghǎi [动] navigate

航空 hángkōng [动] fly (PT flew, PP flown) ▶航

空信 airmail

航天 hángtiān [动] fly through the air (PT flew, PP flown)

航线 hángxiàn [名] route

航向 hángxiàng [名] course

航行 hángxíng [动] 1 (指船) sail 2 (指飞机) fly (PT flew, PP flown)

沆 hàng 见下文

沆瀣一气 hàng xiè yī qì (贬) be in cahoots with

巷 hàng 见下文
→另见 xiàng

巷道 hàngdào [名] tunnel

号 háo [动] 1 (叫) yell 2 (哭) howl
→另见 hào

号啕 háotáo [动] wail

蚝 háo [名] oyster

蚝油 háoyóu [名] oyster sauce

毫 háo I [名] 1 (细毛) fine hair 2 (笔) writing brush 3 (千分之一) ▶毫米 millimetre (英), millimeter (美) ▶毫升 millilitre (英), milliliter (美) II [形] (一点儿) tiny

毫毛 háomáo [名] body hair

豪 háo I [名] giant ▶文豪 literary giant II [形] 1 (指性格) unrestrained 2 (指语言) heroic 3 (指文笔) outstanding 4 (有权势) powerful ▶豪门 dynasty

豪放 háofàng [形] uninhibited

豪富 háofù [名] tycoon ▷非豪富买不起这里的别墅。Unless you're rolling in it, you won't be able to afford a villa around here.

豪华 háohuá [形] luxurious

豪杰 háojié [名] hero (PL heroes)

豪迈 háomài [形] heroic

豪门 háomén [名] dynasty

豪爽 háoshuǎng [形] straightforward

豪言壮语 háo yán zhuàng yǔ inspirational words ▷教练发豪言壮语，保证下场比赛能赢。The coach gave a really inspirational speech, guaranteeing that they could win the next match.

壕 háo [名] (指作战) moat

壕沟 háogōu [名] 1 (指作战) trench 2 (指大沟) ditch

嚎 háo [动] 1 (大声叫) howl 2 (大声哭) wail

嚎啕 háotáo [动] wail

好 hǎo I [形] 1 (令人满意) good ▷他脾气好。He's good-natured. ▷他为班里做了很多好事。He's done a lot of good things for the class. ▷汤很好闻。The soup smells good. 2 (容易) easy ▷这件事不好办。This won't be easy to manage. ▷英语好学吗? Is English easy to learn? 3 (健康) well ▷你身体好吗? Are you keeping well? 4 (亲密) good ▷我们是好朋友。We're good friends. 5 (表示问候) ▷你好! Hello! ▷大家好。Hello everyone. 6 (表示完成) ▷工作找好了。I've found work. ▷衣服洗好了。The clothes have been washed. 7 (表示答应、结束等) ▷好，我们现在就去! OK, let's go then! ▷好了，今天课就上到这里。Right, let's finish today's lesson here. 8 (表示反语) ▷好啊! 你这下考砸了吧。Well done for going and flunking the exam. II [副] 1 (强调多或久) very ▷我等了好久她才来。I'd waited for a long time before she arrived. 2 (表示程度深) ▷好无礼的要求啊! Such a rude request! ▷他话说得好快。He speaks so quickly. III [助动] (以便) ▷准备一下，我们好出发。Get yourself ready so that we can go out. IV [名] 1 (喝彩) cheer ▷他一唱完，全场叫好。As soon as he'd finished singing, everyone cheered. 2 (问候) regards (PL) ▷请代我向你太太问好。Please send my regards to your wife.
→另见 hào

好比 hǎobǐ [动] be just like ▷情场好比战场。Affairs of the heart are just like battlefields.

好不 hǎobù [副] so ▷当时好不热闹。It was so lively then.

好处 hǎochu [名] 1 (益处) benefit 2 (利益) profit

好歹 hǎodǎi I [名] 1 (好坏) right and wrong ▷别理他，这人不知好歹。Don't listen to him – he doesn't know right from wrong. 2 (危险) the unthinkable II [副] 1 (将就) anyhow 2 (无论如何) at any rate ▷他好歹是你弟弟，这事就算了吧。At any rate, he's your brother, so just forget it.

好多 hǎoduō [形] many

好感 hǎogǎn [名] attraction ▷她对他有好感。She's attracted to him.

好汉 hǎohàn [名] brave man

好好先生 hǎohǎoxiānsheng yes man ▷他是个好好先生，谁都不想得罪。He's such a yes man – he doesn't like to offend anyone.

好久 hǎojiǔ [副] for a long time ▷我们好久没听到他的消息了。We haven't heard any news from him for a long time.

好看 hǎokàn [形] 1 (漂亮) nice-looking 2 (精彩) good ▷这本书很好看。This book is very good. 3 (光荣) proud ▷你成绩好，父母脸上

也不知有多好看。If you get good results, your parents will be so proud. **4** (难堪) embarrassed ▷我要他好看！I want to really embarrass him.

好了疮疤忘了疼 hǎole chuāngbā wàngle téng make the same mistakes all over again

好评 hǎopíng [名] high praise ▷他的小说大受好评。His novel was very highly praised.

好事 hǎoshì [名] (好事情) good deed ▷他为学校做了很多好事。He has done a lot of good deeds for the school.

好事多磨 hǎoshì duō mó it's never easy to get what you want

好手 hǎoshǒu [名] expert

好受 hǎoshòu [形] comfortable

好说 hǎoshuō [动] (没问题) be fine ▷你只要把钱交了，其他的事都好说。Just pay the fee – don't worry about the rest.

好似 hǎosì [副] ▷想起来那件事好似是昨天发生的。I think this is like what happened yesterday.

好听 hǎotīng [形] **1** (指声音、音乐) lovely **2** (指言语) nice

好像 hǎoxiàng [副] apparently ▷我们好像在哪儿见过。Apparently we've met somewhere before.

好笑 hǎoxiào [形] funny

好样儿的 hǎoyàngr de [名] ▷这些小伙子个个是好样儿的。These lads have got real guts.

好意 hǎoyì [名] kindness

好意思 hǎoyìsi [动] dare ▷这种话你也好意思说？How dare you talk like this! ▷让您久等了，真不好意思。I'm very embarrassed for making you wait so long.

好在 hǎozài [副] luckily ▷他好在还有个姐姐。Luckily he still has a sister.

好转 hǎozhuǎn [动] improve

号 hào I [名] **1** (名称) name ▶绰号 nickname **2** (商店) firm ▶商号 firm **3** (标记) sign ▶逗号 comma **4** (次序) number ▷我的座位在10号车厢。My seat is in coach ten. **5** (日期) date ▷今天几月几号？What's the date today? ▷6月1号是国际儿童节。The first of June is International Children's Day. **6** (大小) size ▷他得穿大T恤衫。He needs a large-sized T-shirt. ▷我穿36号的鞋。I wear size thirty-six shoes. **7** (命令) order ▷他总向别人发号施令。He's always giving other people orders. **8** (乐器) brass instrument ▶小号 trumpet II [动] (脉) take (PT took, PP taken) ▶号脉 take a pulse
→另见 hǎo

号称 hàochēng [动] **1** (著称) be known as **2** (声

称) claim to be ▷军队实际八十万，号称百万。The army actually has 800,000 soldiers, but it claims to have a million.

号角 hàojiǎo [名] bugle

号令 hàolìng [名] order

号码 hàomǎ [名] number

号脉 hàomài [动] take a pulse (PT took, PP taken)

号召 hàozhào [动] appeal

好 hào [动] **1** (喜爱) like ▷他爱好集邮。He likes collecting stamps. ▷他好背后议论人。He likes discussing other people behind their backs. **2** (容易) be easy ▷天太热，人好中暑。It's too hot – you could easily get sunstroke.
→另见 hǎo

好客 hàokè [形] hospitable

好奇 hàoqí [形] curious ▷好奇有时会引致灾祸。Curiosity can sometimes lead to disaster.

好强 hàoqiáng [形] ambitious

好胜 hàoshèng [形] competitive

好事 hàoshì [动] be nosy

好恶 hàowù [名] likes and dislikes (PL)

好学 hàoxué [形] studious

好逸恶劳 hào yì wù láo bone idle

耗 hào I [动] **1** (用) use **2** (方) (拖延) dawdle II [名] (坏消息) bad news (SG)

耗费 hàofèi [动] consume

耗损 hàosǔn [动] waste

耗子 hàozi [名] (方) mouse (PL mice)

浩 hào [形] **1** (大) great **2** (多) many

浩荡 hàodàng [形] mighty

浩浩荡荡 hàohào dàngdàng awesome

浩劫 hàojié [名] catastrophe

浩如烟海 hào rú yān hǎi myriad ▷中国古典诗歌浩如烟海。There are a myriad of Chinese ancient classical poems.

呵 hē [动] **1** (气) breathe out **2** (责备) scold

呵斥 hēchì [动] bawl ▷孩子还小，不要总呵斥他。The kid's still small – you shouldn't be bawling at him all the time.

呵护 hēhù [动] look after

喝 hē [动] drink (PT drank, PP drunk)
→另见 hè

喝西北风 hē xīběifēng starve ▷他没了工作，全家只能喝西北风了。He lost his job, so the whole family is going to starve.

禾 hé 见下文
禾苗 hémiáo [名] grain seedling

合 hé I [动] **1** (闭) close ▷我把书合上了。I closed the book. **2** (合在一起) join ▷合资 joint venture **3** (折合) be equal to ▷一英镑合人民币多少钱？ How much is a pound equal to in Renminbi? **4** (符合) tally with ▷他所说的不合事实。His story doesn't tally with the facts. ▷这段话不合逻辑。There's no logic in these words. II [形] whole ▷合家团聚 the whole family reunited
合并 hébìng [动] merge
合唱 héchàng [名] chorus
合成 héchéng [动] **1** (联合) merge **2** (化) synthesize
合法 héfǎ [形] legal
合格 hégé [形] qualified
合乎 héhū [动] conform to
合伙 héhuǒ [动] form a partnership
合计 héjì [动] add up to
合计 héji [动] **1** (琢磨) think (PT, PP thought) ▷他合计来合计去还是觉得不划算。He thought and thought about it and still reckoned it wasn't worth it. **2** (商量) discuss
合剂 héjì [名] mixture
合金 héjīn [名] alloy
合刊 hékān [名] combined issue
合理 hélǐ [形] rational
合流 héliú [动] (汇合) merge
合拍 hépāi I [形] in step with ▷他的生活方式与时代不太合拍。His lifestyle is not really in step with the times. II [动] co-produce
合情合理 hé qíng hé lǐ fair ▷他的做法合情合理。He has a fair way of doing things.
合群 héqún [形] gregarious
合身 héshēn [形] fitted ▷这些衣服很合身。These clothes are a good fit.
合适 héshì [形] appropriate
合算 hésuàn [动] be worthwhile
合同 hétong [名] contract
合意 héyì [形] suitable
合营 héyíng [动] co-own
合资 hézī [名] joint venture
合资公司 hézī gōngsī [名] joint venture company
合奏 hézòu [动] ensemble
合作 hézuò [动] cooperate ▷两家出版社合作出版了这套百科全书。Two publishing companies collaborated to publish this encyclopedia. ▷加强国际间的经济合作 increase international economic cooperation ▷我们是合作伙伴。We are partners in this collaboration.

何 hé [代] **1** (什么) ▷何时 when ▷何人 who **2** (哪里) ▷这消息从何而来？ Where did this information come from?
何必 hébì [副] why
何不 hébù [副] why ... not ▷何不叫你女朋友一起来？ Why don't you ask your girlfriend to come too? ▷既然有事，何不早说？ You may have had things to do, but why didn't you say so earlier?
何尝 hécháng [副] ▷我何尝不想多学些英语，实在是没时间。It's not that I don't want to study English any more. I just don't have the time.
何等 héděng [副] how ▷他们何等幸福啊！ How lucky are they!
何妨 héfáng I [动] (书) be no harm in ▷说说何妨？ What's the harm in talking? II [副] why ▷你何妨不出国留学呢？ Why don't you go abroad to study?
何苦 hékǔ [副] ▷你何苦这么做呢？ Why are you bothering to do it? ▷你何苦去那么早呢？ Why are you bothering to go so early?
何况 hékuàng [连] ▷那影片大人看了都害怕，何况儿童。Even adults find the film scary, never mind children. ▷山路很难走，何况还下着雨。The mountain pass is tricky, even when it's not raining.
何其 héqí [副] how ▷何其贪婪！ How greedy!
何以 héyǐ [副] (书) **1** (怎么) how **2** (为什么) why
何止 hézhǐ [动] be far more than

和 hé I [连] and ▷他和我是同事。He and I are colleagues. ▷工作和学习 work and study II [介] with ▷这事和你没关系。This has nothing to do with you. III [形] **1** (平和) mild ▷温和 temperate **2** (暖) warm ▷暖和 warm **3** (和睦) on good terms ▷夫妻不和。The couple are not on good terms. IV [名] **1** (和解) reconciliation ▷讲和 talk of reconciliation **2** (和平) peace ▷维和部队 peace-keeping forces **3** (总数) total ▷5与5的和是10。5 and 5 is 10. V [动] draw (PT drew, PP drawn) ▷这场比赛和了。The match was a draw.
→另见 huó, huò
和蔼 hé'ǎi [形] affable
和风 héfēng [名] light breeze
和服 héfú [名] kimono
和好 héhǎo [动] reconcile
和缓 héhuǎn I [形] gentle II [动] relax

和解 héjiě [动] settle ... differences ▷尽管国际社会的调停两国终未和解。Despite the intervention of the international community, the two countries were ultimately unable to settle their differences.

和睦 hémù [形] harmonious

和盘托出 hé pán tuō chū tell the whole truth ▷她要将秘密和盘托出。She will tell the whole truth about her secrets.

和平 hépíng [名] (指战争) peace

和气 héqi I [形] polite II [名] peace

和善 héshàn [形] kind

和尚 héshang [名] Buddhist monk

和声 héshēng [名] (指音乐) chord

和事老 héshìlǎo [名] mediator

和数 héshù [名] sum

和谐 héxié [形] harmonious

和煦 héxù [形] warm

和颜悦色 hé yán yuè sè be all sweetness and light ▷老师对学生总是和颜悦色。The teacher is all sweetness and light with the students.

和约 héyuē [名] peace treaty

河 hé [名] 1 (河) river 2 (银河) galaxy

河川 héchuān [名] river

河道 hédào [名] river's course

河流 héliú [名] river

荷 hé [名] lotus
→另见 hè

荷包蛋 hébāodàn [名] poached egg

核 hé I [名] 1 (指水果) stone 2 (指细胞、原子) nucleus II [动] examine ▶审核 examine and verify

核查 héchá [动] examine

核定 héding [动] verify

核对 héduì [动] check

核计 héjì [动] calculate

核实 héshí [动] verify

核算 hésuàn [动] calculate

核武器 héwǔqì [名] nuclear weapon

核心 héxīn [名] core

核准 hézhǔn [动] verify and approve

核子 hézǐ [名] nucleus

盒 hé [名] box

颌 hé [名] jaw

吓 hè I [动] scare II [叹] damn ▷吓，这是怎

么搞的！Damn! How has this happened?
→另见 xià

贺 hè [动] congratulate

贺词 hècí [名] congratulatory speech

贺卡 hèkǎ [名] greetings card

贺年 hènián [动] extend New Year's greetings ▷贺年卡 New Year's card

贺喜 hèxǐ [动] congratulate

荷 hè I [动] (扛) shoulder II [名] load
→另见 hé

荷枪实弹 hèqiāngshídàn [动] armed ▷荷枪实弹的警察在巡逻。Armed police are on the beat.

喝 hè [动] shout
→另见 hē

喝彩 hècǎi [动] cheer

喝倒彩 hè dàocǎi [动] boo

赫 hè I [形] conspicuous II [名] (赫兹) hertz

赫然 hèrán [副] (突然出现) impressively

赫兹 hèzī [名] hertz

褐 hè [名] (指颜色) brown

鹤 hè [名] crane

壑 hè [名] gully

黑 hēi [形] 1 (指颜色) black ▶黑板 blackboard 2 (暗) dark ▷天快黑了。It's nearly dark. 3 (秘密) secret ▶黑话 jargon 4 (狠毒) wicked ▷他的心真黑！He's so wicked! 5 (反动) ▶黑社会 gangland ▶黑手党 the Mafia

黑暗 hēi'àn [形] 1 (指光线) dark 2 (腐败) corrupt

黑白 hēibái [名] 1 (颜色) black and white ▷黑白电视机 black and white television 2 (是非) right and wrong

黑帮 hēibāng [名] bunch of gangsters

黑道 hēidào [名] 1 (指路) dark street 2 (黑社会) gangland

黑话 hēihuà [名] jargon

黑客 hēikè [名] hacker

黑名单 hēimíngdān [名] blacklist

黑幕 hēimù [名] dark secret

黑钱 hēiqián [名] dirty money

黑人 hēirén [名] black person (PL people)

黑色幽默 hēisè yōumò [名] black humour (英) 或 humor (美)

黑哨 hēishào [名] referee's biased call

黑社会 hēishèhuì [名] the underworld

黑市 hēishì [名] black market

黑手党 hēishǒudǎng [名] the Mafia
黑压压 hēiyāyā [形] masses of
黑油油 hēiyóuyōu [形] greasy
黑黝黝 hēiyōuyōu [形] shiny black

嘿 hēi I [叹] 1 (用于提起注意) hey ▷嘿，快来！Hey, come quickly! 2 (表示得意) wow 3 (表示惊异) oh II [拟] ha ha

痕 hén [名] trace
痕迹 hénjì [名] 1 (印记) imprint 2 (迹象) trace

很 hěn [副] very ▷他个子很高。He is very tall. ▷她钢琴弹得很不错。She plays the piano very well. ▷我很了解他。I understand him very well. ▷伦敦的房价贵得很。House prices in London are very high.

狠 hěn I [形] 1 (凶恶) ruthless 2 (坚决) resolute 3 (厉害) relentless II [动] harden
狠毒 hěndú [形] cruel
狠心 hěnxīn [形] heartless

恨 hèn [动] 1 (憎恶) hate ▷他恨懒惰的人。He hates lazy people. 2 (后悔) regret ▷她恨当初和他结了婚。She regretted getting married to him in the first place.
恨铁不成钢 hèn tiě bù chéng gāng be cruel to be kind
恨之入骨 hènzhīrùgǔ detest ▷他对贪官恨之入骨。He detests corruption.

亨 hēng 见下文
亨通 hēngtōng [形] smooth

哼 hēng I [拟] moan II [动] 1 (唱) hum ▷他一边走一边哼着一只小曲。He hummed a tune as he walked. 2 (叫唤) groan
哼哧 hēngchī [拟] snort

恒 héng I [形] 1 (永久) permanent 2 (平常) common II [名] perseverance
恒量 héngliàng [名] constant
恒温 héngwēn [名] constant temperature
恒心 héngxīn [名] perseverance
恒星 héngxīng [名] star

横 héng I [名] horizontal II [形] 1 (梁、线、行) horizontal ▷横线 horizontal line 2 (左右向) sideways ▷他平躺在床上。He lay sideways on the bed. 3 (南北向) lengthways 4 (指横截) transverse ▶人行横道 zebra crossing III [副] 1 (纷杂) flowingly ▷妙趣横生 sparkle with wit 2 (蛮横) flagrantly ▷横行霸道 throw

one's weight about IV [动] turn ... lengthways ▷请把桌子横过来。Please turn the table lengthways.
→另见 hèng
横冲直撞 héng chōng zhí zhuàng swerve about recklessly ▷巴士在车道里横冲直撞。The bus swerved about recklessly in the bus lane.
横七竖八 héng qī shù bā lying this way and that ▷门前横七竖八地停着很多自行车。Bicycles were lying this way and that in front of the door.
横扫 héngsǎo [动] sweep ... away (PT, PP swept) ▷秋风横扫落叶。The autumn wind swept away the fallen leaves.
横竖 héngshù [副] in any case ▷我横竖会把那笔钱还给你。I'll give you the money back in any case.
横向 héngxiàng [形] 1 (平行) horizontal 2 (指东西方向) lateral
横行 héngxíng [动] run wild (PT ran, PP run)
横行霸道 héngxíng bàdào terrorize ▷黑社会成员在社会上横行霸道。Members of the criminal underworld are terrorizing society.

衡 héng I [名] weight II [动] weigh
衡量 héngliáng [动] weigh

横 hèng [形] 1 (粗暴) harsh 2 (指意外) unexpected
→另见 héng
横财 hèngcái [名] ill-gotten gains (PL) ▷发横财 get rich by foul means

哼 hng [叹] hmmph

轰 hōng I [拟] bang II [动] 1 (指炮) bang 2 (指火药) boom 3 (指雷) rumble 4 (动物) herd 5 (人) drive (PT drove, PP driven)
轰动 hōngdòng [动] take ... by storm (PT took, PP taken) ▷轰动世界 take the world by storm
轰轰烈烈 hōnghōnglièliè vigorously ▷我们要轰轰烈烈地干一番事业。We are going to promote this cause vigorously.
轰隆 hōnglōng [拟] rumble
轰炸 hōngzhà [动] bomb
→另见 hǒng, hòng

哄 hōng [拟] (形容大笑) roar
→另见 hǒng, hòng
哄传 hōngchuán [动] spread (PT, PP spread) ▷人们在哄传地震的消息。People are spreading the news of the earthquake.
哄抢 hōngqiǎng [动] scramble for

哄堂大笑 hōngtáng dàxiào make everyone roar with laughter ▷他的笑话引得大家哄堂大笑。His joke made everyone roar with laughter.

烘 hōng [动] (烘烤) dry ▷她把衣服烘干了。She dried her clothes.

烘托 hōngtuō [动] (使突出) set ... off (PT, PP set) ▷绿叶烘托着粉红色的花朵。The greenery set off the pink flowers.

弘 hóng I [形] great II [动] expand

弘扬 hóngyáng [动] promote

红 hóng I [形] 1 (指颜色) red 2 (形容受欢迎) popular ▶走红 be popular 3 (形容成功) successful ▶红运 lucky 4 (革命) red II [名] (红利) bonus ▶分红 get a bonus

红白喜事 hóng bái xǐshì [名] weddings and funerals (PL)

红包 hóngbāo [名] 1 (作为贺礼) lucky money 2 (贿赂) dirty money

红茶 hóngchá [名] black tea

红尘 hóngchén [名] the human world

红灯区 hóngdēngqū [名] red-light district

红火 hónghuo [形] flourishing

红利 hónglì [名] bonus

红领巾 hónglǐngjīn [名] red scarf (worn by members of the Young Pioneers organization)

红绿灯 hónglùdēng [名] traffic lights (PL)

红马甲 hóngmǎjiǎ [名] stockbroker

红娘 hóngniáng [名] matchmaker

红旗 hóngqí [名] red flag

红人 hóngrén [名] rising star ▷他是剧团里的红人。He is the rising star of the theatrical troupe.

红润 hóngrùn [形] ruddy

红色 hóngsè [形] red ▷红色的头发 red hair ▷红色政权 revolutionary power

红十字会 Hóngshízìhuì [名] the Red Cross

红彤彤 hóngtōngtōng [形] scarlet

红外线 hóngwàixiàn [名] infrared rays

红眼 hóngyǎn [动] see red (PT saw, PP seen)

红眼病 hóngyǎnbìng [名] 1 (病) conjunctivitis 2 (嫉妒) jealousy

红艳艳 hóngyànyàn [形] scarlet

宏 hóng [形] great

宏大 hóngdà [形] grand

宏观 hóngguān [前缀] macro- ▷宏观经济 macroeconomics

宏论 hónglùn [名] bright idea

宏图 hóngtú [名] grand plan

宏伟 hòngwěi [形] magnificent

虹 hóng [名] rainbow

洪 hóng [名] (指洪水) flood

洪亮 hóngliàng [形] sonorous

洪水 hóngshuǐ [名] flood

鸿 hóng I [名] 1 (大雁) wild goose (PL geese) 2 (书信) letter II [形] vast

鸿沟 hónggōu [名] gap

鸿雁 hóngyàn [名] (鸟) wild goose (PL geese)

鸿运 hóngyùn [名] fortune

哄 hǒng [动] 1 (哄骗) cheat 2 (安抚) calm ▷妈妈哄小孩睡觉。The mother calmed the child so that he could sleep.
→另见 hōng, hòng

哄骗 hǒngpiàn [动] cheat

哄 hòng [动] cause an uproar
→另见 hōng, hǒng

侯 hóu [名] 1 (贵族) nobleman (PL noblemen) 2 (侯爵) marquis

喉 hóu [名] throat

喉咙 hóulóng [名] throat

喉舌 hóushé [名] mouthpiece

猴 hóu [名] monkey

猴子 hóuzi [名] monkey

瘊 hóu 见下文

瘊子 hóuzi [名] wart

吼 hǒu [动] 1 (狮子、老虎) roar 2 (人、风) howl

吼叫 hǒujiào [动] howl

后 hòu [名] 1 (背面) the back ▷房后有个车库。At the back of the house is a garage. 2 (指时间) ▶后天 the day after tomorrow ▷后来的人没有位置坐。The people who arrive late won't get seats. 3 (指次序) the last ▷我坐在后排。I'm sitting in the last row. ▷他的考试成绩在全班后十名。His test mark puts him in the last ten of the class. 4 (子孙) children 5 (君主的妻子) empress ▶皇后 empress

后备 hòubèi [名] reserve

后辈 hòubèi [名] younger generation

后代 hòudài [名] 1 (指时代) later generations (PL) 2 (子孙) offspring

后盾 hòudùn [名] backup

后方 hòufāng [名] rear

后福 hòufú [名] future fortune

后果 hòuguǒ [名] consequence

后患 hòuhuàn [名] bad consequences (PL)

后悔 hòuhuǐ [动] regret

后会有期 hòu huì yǒu qī we'll meet again someday

后继 hòujì [动] carry on

后进 hòujìn I [形] backward II [名] slowcoach

后劲 hòujìn [名] 1 (指酒) after-effects (PL) 2 (形容力量) stamina

后来 hòulái [副] afterwards ▷后来他们谁也不理谁。Afterwards they didn't talk to each other. ▷我后来再也没有见过他。I didn't see him again after that.

后路 hòulù [名] (指机会) way out

后面 hòumian I [名] back II [副] later

后怕 hòupà [动] have a lingering fear

后起之秀 hòu qǐ zhī xiù ▷他是文学界的后起之秀。He's up-and-coming in the literary world.

后勤 hòuqín [名] logistics (PL)

后人 hòurén [名] 1 (指非亲属) follower 2 (子孙) offspring

后任 hòurèn [名] successor

后事 hòushì [名] funeral

后手 hòushǒu [名] way out

后台 hòutái [名] 1 (指舞台) backstage 2 (喻) (指人或集团) backstage support

后天 hòutiān [名] the day after tomorrow

后退 hòutuì [动] retreat

后卫 hòuwèi [名] rear

后裔 hòuyì [名] descendant

后援 hòuyuán [名] reinforcements (PL)

后缀 hòuzhuì [名] suffix

厚 hòu I [形] 1 (书、衣服、脸皮) thick ▷他脸皮真厚! He's so thick-skinned! ▷厚被子 thick blanket 2 (雪、土) deep 3 (指感情) profound 4 (指性格) honourable 5 (指利润、礼品) extravagant 6 (指味道) rich 7 (指家产) loaded II [动] 1 (优待) favour (英), favor (美) 2 (重视) stress

厚爱 hòu'ài [名] adoration

厚道 hòudao [形] kind

厚望 hòuwàng [名] expectation

厚颜无耻 hòuyánwúchǐ shameless ▷厚颜无耻的叛徒 shameless turncoat

厚重 hòuzhòng [形] 1 (字典、大衣) thick 2 (奖赏、礼物) extravagant 3 (文化沉积) dignified

候 hòu I [动] 1 (等待) wait 2 (问好) inquire after II [名] 1 (时节) season 2 (情况) state

候补 hòubǔ [动] be a candidate for

候鸟 hòuniǎo [名] migratory bird

候选人 hòuxuǎnrén [名] candidate

呼 hū I [动] 1 (排气) exhale 2 (喊) shout 3 (叫) call II [拟] whistle

呼哧 hūchī [拟] pant

呼喊 hūhǎn [动] shout

呼号 hūháo [动] 1 (因悲伤) wail 2 (为求援) cry out

呼唤 hūhuàn [动] call

呼机 hūjī [名] pager

呼叫 hūjiào [动] 1 (指电台) call 2 (呼喊) shout

呼救 hūjiù [动] call for help

呼噜 hūlu [名] (口) snore

呼哨 hūshào [名] whistle

呼声 hūshēng [名] 1 (指声音) cry ▷震天动地的呼声 an earth-shattering cry 2 (意见) voice

呼吸 hūxī [动] breathe

呼啸 hūxiào [动] whistle ▷警车呼啸而过。The police car whistled past.

呼应 hūyìng [动] echo

呼吁 hūyù [动] call for ▷联合国呼吁双方停火。The United Nations is calling for a bilateral ceasefire.

忽 hū I [动] neglect II [副] suddenly

忽而 hū'ér [副] suddenly ▷远处的灯光忽而明,忽而暗。The lights in the distance flickered on and off.

忽略 hūlüè [动] overlook ▷易被忽略的细节 details that could be easily overlooked

忽然 hūrán [副] suddenly ▷天空忽然飘起了雪花。All at once the sky filled with snow.

忽视 hūshì [动] ignore

糊 hū [动] plaster
→另见 hú, hù

囫 hú 见下文

囫囵吞枣 húlún tūn zǎo read without understanding

狐 hú [名] fox

狐假虎威 hú jiǎ hǔ wēi exploit another person's power

狐疑 húyí [动] suspect

弧 hú [名] arc

弧度 húdù [名] radian

弧形 húxíng [名] arc

胡 hú I [名] 1 (髭) moustache (英), mustache (美) 2 (长在下颌、两腮) beard II [副] recklessly

胡扯 húchě [动] talk nonsense ▷他尽胡扯。He is talking complete nonsense.

胡搅蛮缠 hú jiǎo mán chán pester incessantly

胡乱 húluàn [副] 1 (随便) casually ▷她胡乱地吃了两口就出门了。She grabbed a quick bite, then went out. 2 (任意) wilfully ▷他总是胡乱地发表意见。He's always spouting off his opinions.

胡闹 húnào [动] play up ▷睡觉去吧，别胡闹了。Go to bed, and no playing up.

胡说 húshuō [动] talk nonsense

胡思乱想 hú sī luàn xiǎng let one's imagination run away with itself

胡同 hútòng [名] lane

胡言乱语 hú yán luàn yǔ talk nonsense ▷他一喝酒就会胡言乱语。Once he starts drinking he talks all sorts of nonsense.

胡子 húzi [名] 1 (髭) moustache (英), mustache (美) 2 (指长在下颌、两腮) beard 3 (方) (胡匪) bandit

胡作非为 hú zuò fēi wéi run amok

壶 hú [名] pot ▷一壶咖啡 a pot of coffee

葫 hú 见下文

葫芦 húlu [名] gourd

湖 hú [名] lake

湖泊 húpō [名] lake

煳 hú [动] burn ▷饭烧煳了。The rice is burnt.

蝴 hú 见下文

蝴蝶 húdié [名] butterfly

糊 hú [动] paste
→另见 hū, hù

糊里糊涂 húlihútú confused

糊涂 hútu [形] 1 (不明白) confused 2 (混乱) chaotic ▷办公室里乱得一塌糊涂。The office was in complete chaos.

虎 hǔ I [名] tiger II [形] vigorous

虎口余生 hǔ kǒu yú shēng narrowly escape death

虎头蛇尾 hǔ tóu shé wěi peter out after a good start

唬 hǔ [动] intimidate

琥 hǔ 见下文

琥珀 hǔpò [名] amber

互 hù [副] mutually ▷两国领导定期互访。The leaders of the two countries met one another regularly in each place.

互补 hùbǔ [动] complement one another

互动 hùdòng [动] interact ▷教与学是互动的。There is interaction between teaching and learning.

互惠 hùhuì [动] reciprocate

互利 hùlì [动] be of mutual benefit

互联网 hùliánwǎng [名] the Internet

互通有无 hù tōng yǒuwú provide what another lacks

互相 hùxiāng [副] mutually

互助 hùzhù [动] help one another out

户 hù [名] 1 (门) door 2 (住户) family ▷几百户人家 several hundred families 3 (门第) social standing ▷门当户对 be well-matched 4 (户头) bank account ▶账户 account

户籍 hùjí [名] registered permanent residence

户口 hùkǒu [名] 1 (住户人口) number of households and total population 2 (户籍) registered permanent residence ▷迁户口 change one's permanent address

护 hù [动] 1 (保护) protect 2 (庇护) take sides (PT took, PP taken)

护城河 hùchénghé [名] moat

护短 hùduǎn [动] cover up ▷你不应该给他护短。You shouldn't have covered up for him.

护航 hùháng [动] escort

护理 hùlǐ [动] nurse ▷护理伤员 nurse the wounded

护身符 hùshēnfú [名] talisman

护士 hùshi [名] nurse

护送 hùsòng [动] escort

护卫 hùwèi [动] protect

护照 hùzhào [名] passport

糊 hù [名] paste
→另见 hū, hú

糊弄 hùnong [动] (方) 1 (欺骗) fool ▷他爱编造谎言糊弄我。He loves to make up lies to fool me with. 2 (将就) make do with ▷粗茶淡饭，糊弄着吃吧。It's just simple fare, but I hope it will do.

花 huā I [名] 1 (指植物) flower 2 (花状物) ▶泪花 tear ▶雪花 snowflake ▶火花 spark 3 (烟

火)fireworks (PL) **4** (花纹) pattern ▷印花布料 patterned material ▷白底红花 a red pattern on a white background **5** (精华) pinnacle ▷艺术之花 the pinnacle of artistic achievement **6** (美女) beauty ▶校花 school beauties (PL) **7** (妓女) lady of the night ▷花街柳巷 red-light district **II** [形] **1** (多彩) multi-coloured (英), multi-colored (美) ▷花绿绿 colourful (英), colorful (美) **2** (有花的) floral ▶花篮 basket of flowers ▶花车 float **3** (模糊) blurred ▶头昏眼花 muddle-headed and bleary-eyed **4** (虚假) superficial ▶花招 trick ▷花言巧语 smooth talk **III** [动] spend (PT, PP spent) ▷花钱 spend money ▷花工夫 put in effort

花白 huābái [形] grey (英), gray (美)

花边 huābiān [名] **1** (花纹) flowery border **2** (饰带) lace

花边新闻 huābiān xīnwén [名] tabloid gossip

花草 huācǎo [名] flowers and plants (PL)

花朵 huāduǒ [名] flower

花费 huāfèi [动] spend (PT, PP spent) ▷花费心血 expend effort ▷留学的花费很大。It's very expensive to study abroad.

花好月圆 huā hǎo yuè yuán blissful harmony

花花公子 huāhuā-gōngzǐ playboy

花花绿绿 huāhuālǜlǜ [形] colourful (英), colorful (美)

花花世界 huāhuā-shìjiè world full of temptations

花卉 huāhuì [名] flowers and plants (PL)

花季 huājì [名] the flower of one's youth ▷花季少女 a young girl in the flower of her youth

花架子 huājiàzi [名] (喻) *something done merely for show*

花里胡哨 huālíhúshào **1** (鲜艳) garish (美) **2** (浮华) showy

花柳病 huāliǔbìng [名] sexually transmitted disease

花名册 huāmíngcè [名] register

花容月貌 huā róng yuè mào stunningly beautiful

花色 huāsè [名] **1** (颜色) design and colour (英) 或 color (美) **2** (种类) variety

花哨 huāshao [形] **1** (颜色鲜艳) garish **2** (花样多) complex

花生 huāshēng [名] peanut

花束 huāshù [名] bouquet

花天酒地 huā tiān jiǔ dì lead a life of debauchery

花纹 huāwén [名] decorative design

花消 huāxiao [名] cost

花言巧语 huā yán qiǎo yǔ smooth talk

花样 huāyàng [名] **1** (式样) variety **2** (花招) trick

花椰菜 huāyēcài [名] broccoli

花园 huāyuán [名] garden

花招 huāzhāo [名] trick

花枝招展 huāzhī zhāozhǎn gaudily dressed

哗 huā [拟] ▷自来水哗哗地流。The water gushed out of the tap. ▷窗帘哗的一声拉上了。The curtains were pulled closed with a swoosh.
→另见 huá

哗啦 huālā [拟] ▷他哗啦哗啦地翻着书。He sped through the book. ▷大桥哗啦一声就坍了。The bridge collapsed with a great crash.

划 huá [动] **1** (拨水) row ▶划桨 paddle **2** (合算) be worthwhile ▷划不来 not worth it **3** (擦) scratch ▷我把手指划破了。I've scratched my finger.
→另见 huà

划算 huásuàn **I** [动] calculate **II** [形] good value

华 huá **I** [形] **1** (光彩) magnificent ▶华美 gorgeous **2** (繁盛) prosperous ▶繁华 flourishing **3** (奢侈) extravagant ▶浮华 flashy **4** (花白) grey (英), gray (美) ▶华发 grey (英) 或 gray (美) hair **II** [名] **1** (精华) the cream ▷才华 talent **2** (时光) time ▷青春年华 youth **3** (中国) China ▶华人 Chinese person

华灯 huádēng [名] decorated lantern

华而不实 huá ér bù shí showy

华发 huáfà [名] grey (英) 或 gray (美) hair

华贵 huáguì [形] **1** (华丽珍贵) sumptuous **2** (豪华富贵) luxurious

华丽 huálì [形] resplendent

华美 huáměi [形] resplendent

华侨 huáqiáo [名] overseas Chinese

华人 huárén [名] Chinese

华裔 huáyì [名] *person of Chinese origin*

哗 huá [动] make a noise
→另见 huā

哗变 huábiàn [动] mutiny

哗然 huárán [形] in uproar

哗众取宠 huá zhòng qǔ chǒng play to the gallery

滑 huá **I** [形] **1** (光滑) slippery ▷路很滑。The road is very slippery. ▷她的皮肤很滑。Her skin is silky smooth. **2** (油滑) crafty **II** [动] slip

滑动 huádòng [动] slide (PT, PP slid)

滑稽 huájī [形] comical

滑溜 huáliu [形] smooth ▷滑溜的秀发 beautiful sleek hair

滑腻 huánì [形] silky-smooth

滑坡 huápō [动] 1 (字) slide (PT, PP slid) ▷昨天发生山体滑坡。Yesterday there was a landslide. 2 (喻) drop

滑润 huárùn [形] smooth

滑头 huátóu [名] sly old fox

滑翔 huáxiáng [动] glide

滑行 huáxíng [动] slide (PT, PP slid)

滑雪 huáxuě [动] ski

猾 huá [形] cunning

化 huà I [名] chemistry ▷化肥 chemical fertilizer II [动] 1 (变化) change ▷化装 make oneself up 2 (感化) convert ▷教化 educate 3 (融化) melt ▷积雪融化了。The piles of snow have melted. 4 (消化) digest ▷消化饼干 digestive biscuit 5 (烧化) burn ▷火化 cremate 6 (死) die

化工 huàgōng [名] chemical industry

化合 huàhé [动] chemically combine

化解 huàjiě [动] eliminate

化疗 huàliáo [动] treat ... with chemotherapy

化名 huàmíng [名] pseudonym

化身 huàshēn [名] embodiment

化石 huàshí [名] fossil

化险为夷 huà xiǎn wéi yí head off a disaster

化学 huàxué [名] chemistry

化验 huàyàn [动] test

化妆 huàzhuāng [动] make oneself up

化装 huàzhuāng [动] 1 (修饰) get into costume 2 (假扮) disguise oneself

划 huà [动] 1 (划分) demarcate 2 (划拨) transfer 3 (计划) plan
→另见 huá

划拨 huàbō [动] 1 (资金) transfer 2 (物品) allocate ▷政府把食品划拨给灾区。The government allocated food to the disaster zone.

划分 huàfēn [动] 1 (分成部分) divide 2 (区分) differentiate

划价 huàjià [动] get a prescription priced

划时代 huàshídài epoch-making

划一 huàyī [形] uniform

画 huà I [动] 1 (用铅笔) draw (PT drew, PP drawn) 2 (用刷状笔画) paint II [名] 1 (用铅笔) drawing 2 (用刷状笔画) painting ▷油画 oil painting 3 (笔画) stroke III [形] painted

画报 huàbào [名] pictorial

画饼充饥 huà bǐng chōng jī comfort oneself with illusions

画工 huàgōng [名] 1 (指人) painter 2 (指技法) drawing skill

画家 huàjiā [名] painter

画具 huàjù [名] painting utensil

画龙点睛 huà lóng diǎn jīng add the crowning touch

画面 huàmiàn [名] tableau (PL tableaux)

画蛇添足 huà shé tiān zú gild the lily

画坛 huàtán [名] artistic circles (PL)

画图 huàtú [名] picture

画外音 huàwàiyīn [名] voice-over

画像 huàxiàng [名] portrait

画押 huàyā [动] sign

画展 huàzhǎn [名] art exhibition

话 huà I [名] words (PL) ▷说话 talk ▷对话 conversation ▷谎话 lie II [动] talk about ▷话旧 reminisce ▷闲话家常 chat about everyday things

话别 huàbié [动] part ▷依依话别 be reluctant to part

话柄 huàbǐng [名] basis for attack

话旧 huàjiù [动] reminisce

话剧 huàjù [名] stage play

话题 huàtí [名] subject

话头 huàtóu [名] topic of conversation

话匣子 huàxiázi [名] chatterbox

话音 huàyīn [名] 1 (声音) voice 2 (言外之意) tone

话语 huàyǔ [名] words (PL)

桦 huà [名] birch

怀 huái I [名] 1 (胸前) bosom 2 (胸怀) mind ▷满怀壮志 have a head full of plans II [动] 1 (思念) think of (PT, PP thought) 2 (存有) keep ... in mind (PT, PP kept) 3 (有孕) become pregnant (PT became, PP become)

怀抱 huáibào I [动] 1 (抱在怀) hold ... in one's arms (PT, PP held) ▷女孩怀抱着猫咪。The girl held a cat in her arms. 2 (心里有) cherish II [名] bosom

怀才不遇 huái cái bù yù be unable to give full play to one's talent

怀春 huáichūn [动] have amorous thoughts

怀古 huáigǔ [动] ruminate on the past

怀恨 huáihèn [动] nurse a grudge

怀旧 huáijiù [动] ruminate on the past

怀念 huáiniàn [动] yearn for ▷怀念故乡 yearn for one's hometown

怀疑 huáiyí [动] 1 (认为是真) suspect ▷我怀疑她没说实话。I suspect that she's not telling the truth. 2 (认为不可能) doubt ▷我对他是否会来表示怀疑。I doubt he will come.

怀孕 huáiyùn [动] be pregnant

槐 huái [名] Chinese scholar tree

踝 huái [名] ankle

坏 huài I [形] 1 (不好) bad ▷坏蛋 bad egg ▷坏习惯 bad habit 2 (程度深) extreme ▷便宜的价格乐坏了顾客。The cheap prices made the customers extremely happy. II [动] go off (PT went, PP gone) ▷牛奶坏了。The milk has gone off. ▷空调坏了。The air-conditioning has broken down. III [名] dirty trick

坏处 huàichu [名] harm ▷多喝绿茶没坏处。There's no harm in drinking more green tea. ▷缺乏睡眠对身体有坏处。It's bad for you not to get enough sleep.

坏蛋 huàidàn [名] (讳) bastard

坏话 huàihuà [名] 1 (逆耳之言) honest truth ▷他好话坏话一并听。He's prepared to hear things he doesn't want to hear as well as that which is more welcome. 2 (不利的话) slur ▷他从不说老婆坏话。He never speaks ill of his wife.

坏事 huàishì I [名] bad things (PL) II [动] mess things up

坏水 huàishuǐ [名] evil idea

欢 huān [形] 1 (快乐) happy 2 (活跃) vigorous

欢畅 huānchàng [形] overjoyed

欢呼 huānhū [动] cheer

欢聚 huānjù [动] happily gather

欢快 huānkuài [形] cheerful ▷欢快的气氛 cheerful atmosphere

欢乐 huānlè [形] joyful

欢声笑语 huān shēng xiào yǔ happy chatter ▷校园里留下了我们的欢声笑语。Our happy chatter lingered in the schoolyard.

欢送 huānsòng [动] see ... off (PT saw, PP seen) ▷欢送代表团 see a delegation off

欢腾 huānténg [动] rejoice

欢天喜地 huān tiān xǐ dì with great joy ▷大家欢天喜地地迎新年。Everyone welcomed in the new year with great joy.

欢喜 huānxǐ I [形] overjoyed ▷她满心欢喜地等他回来。Her heart was full of joy as she waited for him to return. II [动] be fond of

欢心 huānxīn [名] favour (英), favor (美) ▷她拼命想讨老师的欢心。She desperately wanted to gain favour with her teacher.

欢迎 huānyíng [动] welcome ▷欢迎光临！Welcome! ▷欢迎来中国。Welcome to China.

还 huán [动] 1 (回) return ▷还乡 return to one's hometown ▷生还 survive 2 (归还) return ▷还债 repay a debt ▷请把字典还给我。Please return the dictionary to me. 3 (回报) repay (PT, PP repaid) ▷还礼 return a gift with a gift ▷还价 make a counter-offer ▷还手 strike back →另见 hái

还本 huánběn [动] repay capital (PT, PP repaid)

还击 huánjī [动] fight back (PT, PP fought) ▷驻军奋起还击。The garrison readied itself for a counterattack.

还价 huánjià [动] make a counter-offer ▷讨价还价 haggle

还手 huánshǒu [动] retaliate ▷我还手打了他一巴掌。I slapped him in retaliation.

还原 huányuán [动] 1 (恢复) restore 2 (化) reduce

还愿 huányuàn [动] 1 (对神) thank the gods for answering one's prayers 2 (对人) fulfil a promise

环 huán I [名] 1 (圆圈) ring ▷耳环 earring 2 (环节) element ▷销售是重要的一个环节。Marketing is an important element. II [动] surround ▷四面环海 be surrounded by sea on all sides

环保 huánbǎo [名] (环境保护) environmental protection

环抱 huánbào [动] surround

环顾 huángù [动] look around

环节 huánjié [名] 1 (指事物) link 2 (指动物) segment

环境 huánjìng [名] environment ▷生活环境 living conditions (PL) ▷投资环境 investment environment

环境保护 huánjìng bǎohù [名] environmental protection

环球 huánqiú I [动] go round the world (PT went, PP gone) II [名] the whole world

环绕 huánrào [动] surround

环视 huánshì [动] look around

环行 huánxíng [动] circle

寰 huán [名] world

寰球 huánqiú [名] the whole world

缓 huǎn I [形] 1 (慢) slow 2 (缓和) relaxed

II [动] **1** (推迟) delay **2** (恢复) revive

缓兵之计 huǎn bīng zhī jì delaying tactics

缓冲 huǎnchōng [动] buffer

缓和 huǎnhé [形] relaxed

缓急 huǎnjí [名] degree of urgency

缓解 huǎnjiě [动] alleviate

缓慢 huǎnmàn [形] slow

缓刑 huǎnxíng [动] suspend a sentence

幻 huàn I [形] unreal II [动] change magically

幻灯 huàndēng [名] **1** (幻灯片) slide **2** (幻灯机) slide projector

幻境 huànjìng [名] fairyland

幻觉 huànjué [名] illusion

幻灭 huànmiè [动] vanish into thin air

幻想 huànxiǎng I [动] dream ▷他幻想成为宇航员。He dreamed of becoming an astronaut. II [名] fantasy

幻影 huànyǐng [名] illusion

宦 huàn I [名] **1** (官吏) official **2** (太监) eunuch II [动] fill an office

宦官 huànguān [名] eunuch

宦海 huànhǎi [名] official circles (PL)

宦途 huàntú [名] official career

换 huàn [动] **1** (交换) exchange ▷我拿书换你的杂志。I've got this book to exchange for your magazine. ▷用美元换英镑 exchange US dollars for pounds **2** (更换) replace ▷家具换成新的了。The furniture has been replaced.

换代 huàndài [动] (产品更新) upgrade

换季 huànjì [动] change clothes for the season

换届 huànjiè [动] reappoint ▷政府官员每隔5年换届。Government officials are reappointed to their jobs every five years.

换取 huànqǔ [动] exchange ... for ▷该国用石油换取食品。The country provides oil in exchange for food.

换算 huànsuàn [动] convert ▷把外汇换算成人民币 convert foreign currency into Renminbi

换汤不换药 huàn tāng bù huàn yào make superficial changes

换血 huànxiě [动] (喻) introduce fresh blood

唤 huàn [名] summon

唤起 huànqǐ [动] **1** (号召) appeal ▷唤起民众的人权意识 appeal to people's awareness of human rights **2** (引起) call on

唤醒 huànxǐng [动] **1** (叫醒) wake up (PT woke, PP woken) ▷每天早晨闹钟把我唤醒。Every morning I am woken up by my alarm clock. **2** (使醒悟) awaken (PT awoke, PP awoken)

涣 huàn [动] vanish

涣然冰释 huànrán bīng shì melt away

涣散 huànsàn I [形] slack II [动] slacken

浣 huàn [动] wash

浣熊 huànxióng [名] racoon

患 huàn I [动] **1** (害) suffer from **2** (忧虑) worry II [名] trouble

患得患失 huàn dé huàn shī worry about personal gains and losses

患难 huànnàn [名] adversity

患者 huànzhě [名] sufferer

焕 huàn [形] shining

焕发 huànfā [动] **1** (有光彩) shine (PT, PP shone) **2** (振作) brace oneself

焕然一新 huànrán yī xīn take on an entirely new look

荒 huāng I [形] **1** (荒芜) waste **2** (荒凉) desolate **3** (短缺) short **4** (荒歉) famine **5** (非理性) ridiculous II [动] neglect III [名] wasteland

荒诞 huāngdàn [形] absurd

荒废 huāngfèi [动] **1** (没耕种) leave ... uncultivated (PT, PP left) **2** (荒疏) neglect **3** (浪费) waste

荒郊 huāngjiāo [名] wilderness

荒凉 huāngliáng [形] desolate

荒谬 huāngmiù [形] ridiculous

荒漠 huāngmò I [形] deserted II [名] desert

荒年 huāngnián [名] famine year

荒疏 huāngshū [动] neglect

荒唐 huāngtáng [形] **1** (荒谬) absurd **2** (放荡) unconventional

荒无人烟 huāng wú rén yān desolate and uninhabited

荒芜 huāngwú [形] waste

荒淫 huāngyín [形] debauched

慌 huāng [形] nervous

慌乱 huāngluàn [形] flustered

慌忙 huāngmáng [形] hurried

慌张 huāngzhāng [形] nervous

皇 huáng [名] emperor

皇帝 huángdì [名] emperor

皇宫 huánggōng [名] palace

皇后 huánghòu [名] empress
皇家 huángjiā [名] royal family
皇历 huángli [名] (口) almanac
皇亲国戚 huáng qīn guó qì relatives of the
  emperor

黄
黄 huáng I [形] 1 (指颜色) yellow 2 (色情)
  pornographic II [名] 1 (蛋黄) yolk 2 (黄金) gold
黄灿灿 huángcàncàn [形] golden
黄道吉日 huángdào jírì [名] auspicious day
黄澄澄 huángdēngdēng [形] golden
黄瓜 huánggā [名] cucumber
黄河 Huánghé [名] Yellow River
黄昏 huánghūn [名] dusk
黄金 huángjīn [名] gold
黄金时代 huángjīn shídài [名] 1 (繁荣时期)
  golden age 2 (指人生) the prime of one's life
黄粱美梦 huángliáng měimèng pipe dream
黄牛 huángniú [名] 1 (指动物) ox 2 (票贩子)
  ticket tout
黄牌 huángpái [名] yellow card
黄泉 huángquán [名] the underworld
黄色 huángsè [名] 1 (指颜色) yellow 2 (色情)
  pornographic
黄种 Huángzhǒng [名] Mongoloid race

惶
惶 huáng [名] fear
惶惶 huánghuáng [形] on tenterhooks
惶惑 huánghuò [形] apprehensive
惶恐 huángkǒng [形] terrified

煌
煌 huáng [形] bright

蝗
蝗 huáng 见下文
蝗虫 huángchóng [名] locust

磺
磺 huáng [名] (化) sulphur (英), sulfur (美)

簧
簧 huáng [名] 1 (指乐器) reed 2 (指器物) spring

恍
恍 huǎng [副] 1 (恍然) suddenly 2 (仿佛)
  seemingly
恍惚 huǎnghū [形] 1 (神志不清) absent-
  minded 2 (不真切) faint
恍然大悟 huǎngrán dàwù suddenly see the
  light
恍如隔世 huǎng rú gé shì seem like a long
  time ago

晃
晃 huǎng [动] 1 (闪耀) dazzle 2 (闪过) flash past
  →另见 huàng
晃眼 huǎngyǎn [动] 1 (耀眼) dazzle 2 (瞬间)
  happen in the blink of an eye

谎
谎 huǎng [名] lie
谎言 huǎngyán [名] lie

幌
幌 huǎng [名] (书) heavy curtain
幌子 huǎngzi [名] 1 (商品标志) shop (英) 或 store
  (美) sign 2 (名义) veneer

晃
晃 huàng [动] shake (PT shook, PP shaken)
  →另见 huǎng
晃动 huàngdòng [动] rock
晃悠 huàngyou [动] 1 (摆动) sway 2 (闲逛)
  wander about

灰
灰 huī I [名] 1 (灰烬) ash 2 (尘土) dust 3 (石灰)
  lime II [动] (消沉) be disheartened
灰暗 huī'àn [形] gloomy
灰尘 huīchén [名] dust
灰飞烟灭 huī fēi yān miè disappear
灰烬 huījìn [名] ashes (PL)
灰溜溜 huīliūliū [形] 1 (指颜色) dull grey (英) 或
  gray (美) 2 (神情沮丧) dejected
灰蒙蒙 huīmēngmēng [形] overcast
灰色 huīsè [名] 1 (指颜色) grey (英), gray
  (美) 2 (喻) (颓废) melancholy ▷灰色的心
  情 melancholy emotions ▷灰色的电影
  melancholy film
灰心 huīxīn [动] lose heart (PT, PP lost)
灰心丧气 huī xīn sàng qì down in the dumps

诙
诙 huī 见下文
诙谐 huīxié [形] humorous

恢
恢 huī [形] vast
恢复 huīfù [动] recover
恢弘 huīhóng [形] (书) extensive
恢恢 huīhuī [形] vast

挥
挥 huī [动] 1 (挥舞) wave 2 (抹掉) wipe …
  away 3 (指挥) command 4 (散出) scatter
挥发 huīfā [动] evaporate
挥汗如雨 huī hàn rú yǔ drip with sweat
挥霍 huīhuò [动] squander
挥金如土 huī jīn rú tǔ throw one's money
  about
挥舞 huīwǔ [动] wave

辉
辉 huī I [名] splendour (英), splendor (美) II [动]
  shine (PT, PP shone)
辉煌 huīhuáng [形] brilliant
辉映 huīyìng [动] reflect

徽 huī [名] badge
徽章 huīzhāng [名] badge

回 huí I [动] 1 (旋转) circle ▷ 巡回 make a circuit 2 (还) return ▷ 回国 return to one's country 3 (掉转) turn around ▶ 回头 turn one's head 4 (答复) reply ▶ 回信 reply to a letter 5 (回绝) decline ▷ 我回了他的邀请。I declined his invitation. II [量] 1 (次数) time ▷ 这是我第三回到杭州。This is my third time in Hangzhou. ▷ 我去过两回。I have been there twice. 2 (章) chapter ▷ 小说的第二回 the novel's second chapter

回报 huíbào [动] 1 (报告) report back 2 (报答) repay (PT, PP repaid) ▷ 回报父母 repay one's parents 3 (报复) retaliate

回避 huíbì [动] avoid

回肠荡气 huí cháng dàng qì soul-stirring

回潮 huícháo [动] 1 (字) get damp again 2 (喻) (重现) reappear

回车键 huíchējiàn [名] return key

回程 huíchéng [名] return (英) 或 round (美) trip

回答 huídá [动] answer

回荡 huídàng [动] reverberate

回复 huífù [动] 1 (答复) reply 2 (恢复) return ▷ 回复原状 return to a former state

回顾 huígù [动] look back

回光返照 huí guāng fǎn zhào brief revival before the end

回归 huíguī [动] return

回合 huíhé [名] round

回话 huíhuà [动] reply

回击 huíjī [动] counterattack

回敬 huíjìng [动] 1 (回报) do ... in return ▷ 回敬你一杯 raise a glass in return 2 (回击) give tit-for-tat (PT gave, PP given)

回扣 huíkòu [名] commission

回老家 huílǎojiā 1 (字) return home 2 (喻) (诙谐) kick the bucket

回笼 huílóng [动] 1 (食物) reheat ▷ 把冷包子回笼 reheat cooled buns 2 (货币) withdraw ... from circulation (PT withdrew, PP withdrawn) ▷ 货币回笼 withdraw currency from circulation

回落 huíluò [动] drop back

回马枪 huímǎqiāng [名] sudden retaliation

回迁 huíqiān [动] move back

回升 huíshēng [动] pick ... up

回生 huíshēng [动] resurrect

回声 huíshēng [名] echo (PL echoes)

回收 huíshōu [动] 1 (再利用) recycle 2 (收回) retrieve ▷ 回收成本 retrieve one's costs

回首 huíshǒu [动] 1 (回头) look back 2 (书) (回忆) recollect

回天乏术 huí tiān fá shù be unable to turn around a hopeless situation

回条 huítiáo [名] receipt

回头 huítóu I [动] 1 (转身) turn around 2 (回来) return 3 (悔悟) repent II [副] in a moment ▷ 你先休息，回头我再找你吃晚饭。You have a rest just now, and in a moment I'll come back and get you for supper. ▷ 回头见。See you later.

回头客 huítóukè [名] returning customer

回头是岸 huí tóu shì àn never too late to mend one's ways

回味 huíwèi I [名] aftertaste II [动] reflect on

回响 huíxiǎng I [动] 1 (响应) respond 2 (回声) echo II [名] echo (PL echoes)

回想 huíxiǎng [动] recall

回心转意 huí xīn zhuǎn yì change one's mind

回旋 huíxuán [动] 1 (盘旋) circle 2 (进退) have room for manoeuvre

回忆 huíyì [动] recall

回音 huíyīn [名] 1 (回声) echo (PL echoes) 2 (答复) reply

回执 huízhí [名] receipt

茴 huí 见下文
茴香 huíxiāng [名] fennel

蛔 huí 见下文
蛔虫 huíchóng [名] roundworm

悔 huǐ [动] regret
悔不当初 huǐ bù dāng chū regret a decision
悔改 huǐgǎi [动] repent
悔过自新 huǐ guò zì xīn turn over a new leaf
悔恨 huǐhèn [动] deeply regret
悔悟 huǐwù [动] repent

毁 huǐ [动] 1 (破坏) destroy 2 (烧) burn 3 (诽谤) defame
毁谤 huǐbàng [动] slander
毁害 huǐhài [动] destroy
毁坏 huǐhuài [动] destroy ▷ 蓄意毁坏公物 vandalism
毁灭 huǐmiè [动] exterminate
毁容 huǐróng [动] disfigure
毁约 huǐyuē [动] go back on one's word (PT went, PP gone)

卉 huì [名] grass

汇 huì I [动] 1 (汇合) converge 2 (聚集) gather 3 (划拨) transfer II [名] 1 (外汇) foreign exchange 2 (聚集物) collection ▶词汇 vocabulary

汇报 huìbào [动] report

汇单 huìdān [名] remittance advice

汇兑 huìduì [动] remit

汇合 huìhé [动] 1 (水流) converge 2 (人群、意志、力量) come together (PT came, PP come)

汇集 huìjí [动] collect ▷人群汇集到广场上。A crowd gathered on the square.

汇率 huìlǜ [名] exchange rate

汇总 huìzǒng [动] collect

会 huì I [动] 1 (聚合) assemble ▶会诊 have a consultation 2 (见面) meet (PT, PP met) ▶会客 receive a guest 3 (理解) understand (PT, PP understood) ▶领会 understand 4 (通晓) be able to ▷会武术 be able to do martial arts II [助动] 1 (能做) can ▷我不会下象棋。I can't play chess. 2 (擅长) ▷会过日子 know how to economize ▷能说会道 be eloquent 3 (可能) might ▷明天会更热。Tomorrow might be hotter. III [名] 1 (集会) gathering ▶茶话会 tea party 2 (团体) association ▶学生会 student union 3 (城市) city ▶大都会 metropolis 4 (时机) opportunity ▶机会 opportunity 5 (庙会) fair
→ 另见 kuài

会餐 huìcān [动] dine together

会合 huìhé [动] meet (PT, PP met)

会话 huìhuà [动] converse

会见 huìjiàn [动] meet (PT, PP met)

会聚 huìjù [动] assemble

会客 huìkè [动] receive a guest

会商 huìshāng [动] consult

会师 huìshī [动] join forces

会谈 huìtán [动] hold talks (PT, PP held)

会同 huìtóng [动] join together

会晤 huìwù [动] meet (PT, PP met)

会心 huìxīn [动] understand (PT, PP understood)

会议 huìyì [名] 1 (集会) meeting ▷首脑会议 summit meeting 2 (机构) council ▷政治协商会议 political consultation council

会员 huìyuán [名] member ▷会员注册 apply for membership

会战 huìzhàn [动] 1 (字) meet for a decisive battle (PT, PP met) 2 (喻) launch a campaign

会账 huìzhàng [动] pick up the bill

会诊 huìzhěn [动] consult

讳 huì I [动] regard ... as taboo II [名] taboo

讳疾忌医 huì jí jì yī (喻) conceal one's shortcomings for fear of criticism

讳言 huìyán [动] be afraid to speak up

荟 huì [形] (书) lush

荟萃 huìcuì [动] assemble

诲 huì [动] teach (PT, PP taught)

诲人不倦 huì rén bù juàn teach tirelessly

绘 huì [动] 1 (用铅笔) draw (PT drew, PP drawn) 2 (用刷状笔画) paint

绘画 huìhuà [动] 1 (用铅笔) draw (PT drew, PP drawn) 2 (用刷状笔画) paint

绘声绘色 huì shēng huì sè vivid

绘制 huìzhì [动] draw (PT drew, PP drawn)

贿 huì [名] bribe

贿赂 huìlù [动] bribe ▷接受贿赂 accept a bribe

彗 huì [名] (书) broom

彗星 huìxīng [名] comet

晦 huì I [形] 1 (昏暗) dark 2 (不明显) unclear II [名] night

晦气 huìqì I [形] unlucky II [名] bad luck

晦涩 huìsè [形] obscure

秽 huì [形] 1 (肮脏) filthy 2 (丑恶) abominable 3 (淫乱) promiscuous

秽闻 huìwén [名] (书) notoriety

秽行 huìxíng [名] (书) debauched behaviour (英) 或 behavior (美)

秽语 huìyǔ [名] obscene language

惠 huì [动] (书) be beneficial ▶恩惠 kindness ▷互利互惠 mutually beneficial

惠顾 huìgù [动] patronize

惠临 huìlín [动] (敬) honour (英) 或 honor (美) ...with one's presence

喙 huì [名] (书) 1 (鸟嘴) beak 2 (人嘴) mouth

慧 huì [形] intelligent

慧心 huìxīn [名] (智慧) wisdom

慧眼 huìyǎn [名] penetrating insight

昏 hūn I [名] dusk II [形] 1 (黑暗) dark 2 (迷糊) muddled III [动] faint

昏暗 hūn'àn [形] dim

昏沉 hūnchén [形] 1 (暗淡) murky 2 (昏乱) muddled

昏花 hūnhuā [形] poor ▷老眼昏花 poor eyesight in old age

昏黄 hūnhuáng [形] dim

昏厥 hūnjué [动] faint

昏聩 hūnkuì [形] (喻) (糊涂) muddle-headed

昏乱 hūnluàn [形] **1** (指头脑) confused **2** (书) (指社会) chaotic

昏迷 hūnmí [动] be unconscious

昏天黑地 hūn tiān hēi dì **1** (指天色) pitch-black **2** (神志不清) dizzy **3** (激烈) fiercely **4** (指社会混乱) chaotic

昏庸 hūnyōng [形] ineffectual

荤 hūn I [名] meat II [形] dirty ▷荤笑话 dirty jokes

荤腥 hūnxīng [名] meat

婚 hūn I [名] marriage II [动] marry

婚变 hūnbiàn [动] go through a marital breakdown

婚嫁 hūnjià [名] marriage

婚检 hūnjiǎn [动] have a pre-marital medical

婚礼 hūnlǐ [名] wedding ceremony

婚配 hūnpèi [动] get married

婚外恋 hūnwàiliàn [名] extra-marital relationship

婚姻 hūnyīn [名] marriage

浑 hún [形] **1** (浑浊) muddy **2** (糊涂) muddled **3** (天然) natural **4** (满) whole

浑蛋 húndàn [名] (讳) bastard

浑厚 húnhòu [形] **1** (指性格) straightforward **2** (指风格) powerful **3** (指声音) deep and resonant

浑浑噩噩 húnhún'è'è muddle-headed

浑朴 húnpǔ [形] straightforward

浑然一体 húnrán yītǐ completely blend in

浑水摸鱼 hún shuǐ mō yú fish in troubled waters

浑浊 húnzhuó [形] murky

馄 hún 见下文

馄饨 húntún [名] wonton

魂 hún [名] **1** (灵魂) soul **2** (精神) spirit

魂不附体 hún bù fù tǐ scared out of one's wits

魂魄 húnpò [名] soul

混 hùn I [动] **1** (搀杂) mix **2** (蒙混) pass off ...as ▷鱼目混珠 pass off something fake as genuine **3** (苟且生活) drift ▷混日子 drift through the days II [副] aimlessly

混沌 hùndùn I [名] chaos II [形] ignorant

混合 hùnhé [动] mix

混混儿 hùnhùnr [名] rascal

混乱 hùnluàn [形] **1** (无秩序) chaotic **2** (无条理) disordered

混同 hùntóng [动] mix ... up

混为一谈 hùn wéi yī tán confuse ▷你不能将这两个概念混为一谈。You mustn't lump these two concepts together.

混淆 hùnxiáo [动] confuse

混血儿 hùnxuè'ér [名] ▷马丁是个混血儿。Martin is mixed-race.

混杂 hùnzá [动] mix

混战 hùnzhàn [动] engage in long and complicated warfare

混浊 hùnzhuó [形] murky

劐 huō [动] slit (PT, PP slit)

豁 huō [动] **1** (裂开) break ... open (PT broke, PP broken) **2** (舍弃) go all out (PT went, PP gone) →另见 huò

豁口 huōkǒu [名] breach

和 huó [动] mix ... with liquid →另见 hé, huò

和面 huómiàn [动] knead dough

活 huó I [动] **1** (生存) live **2** (使生存) keep ... alive (PT, PP kept) II [形] **1** (有生命) alive **2** (不固定) flexible ▷活期账号 current account **3** (不死板) lively **4** (逼真) lifelike III [副] completely ▷他活像个白痴。He acted like a complete idiot. IV [名] **1** (工作) work **2** (产品) product

活宝 huóbǎo [名] clown

活蹦乱跳 huó bèng luàn tiào lively and energetic

活动 huódòng I [动] **1** (运动) take exercise (PT took, PP taken) ▷我想到公园活动活动。I'd like to go to the park for a spot of exercise. **2** (行动) operate ▷黑帮常在该地区活动。The gang often operates in this area. **3** (动用关系) use connections ▷她为逃脱责任到处活动。She used all the connections she could to get herself out of trouble. II [名] activity ▷文娱活动 recreational activities III [形] movable

活该 huógāi [动] (口) serve ... right ▷他和女朋友分手后很孤独——活该！He has been lonely after breaking up with his girlfriend – serves him right!

活活 huóhuó [副] when still alive

活计 huójì [名] **1** (体力劳动) manual labour (英) 或 labor (美) **2** (手工制品) handicrafts (PL)

活见鬼 huójiànguǐ preposterous

活口 huókǒu [名] 1 (指受害者) survivor 2 (指俘房、罪犯) captive

活力 huólì [名] vitality

活灵活现 huó líng huó xiàn lifelike

活路 huólù [名] 1 (指道路) through pass 2 (生存之道) means of subsistence 3 (可行之道) feasible method

活络 huóluò [形] 1 (活动) wobbly 2 (不确定) uncertain 3 (灵活) quick ▷头脑活络 quick brain

活埋 huómái [动] bury ... alive

活命 huómìng I [动] survive II [名] life (PL lives)

活泼 huópō [形] lively

活菩萨 huópúsa [名] (喻) angel

活期 huóqī [形] current ▷活期账号 current account

活塞 huósāi [名] piston

活生生 huóshēngshēng [形] 1 (真实) living 2 (活活) alive

活受罪 huóshòuzuì (口) suffer a living hell

活水 huóshuǐ [名] running water

活页 huóyè [名] ▷活页笔记本 loose-leaf notebook

活跃 huóyuè I [形] brisk II [动] 1 (使有生气) invigorate 2 (积极从事) be active

活捉 huózhuō [动] capture ... alive

活字典 huózìdiǎn [名] walking dictionary

火 huǒ I [名] 1 (火焰) fire 2 (枪支弹药) ammunition 3 (医) (指内火) internal heat 4 (喻) (愤怒) rage II [动] be in a rage III [形] 1 (红色) flaming red 2 (兴旺) prosperous IV [副] urgently

火把 huǒbǎ [名] torch

火暴 huǒbào [形] (方) 1 (暴躁) fiery 2 (旺盛) bustling

火柴 huǒchái [名] match

火车 huǒchē [名] train

火红 huǒhóng [形] 1 (指颜色) flaming red 2 (旺盛) active ▷火红的生命 an active life

火候 huǒhou [名] 1 (火力) cooking power 2 (喻) (修养) level of attainment 3 (时机) crucial moment

火化 huǒhuà [动] cremate

火急 huǒjí [形] urgent

火警 huǒjǐng [名] fire alarm

火炬 huǒjù [名] torch

火坑 huǒkēng [名] (喻) living hell

火辣辣 huǒlālā [形] 1 (表示热) burning 2 (表示疼) burning 3 (表示激动) agitated 4 (泼辣尖锐) fiery ▷火辣辣的个性 a fiery character

火力 huǒlì [名] 1 (指燃料) thermal energy 2 (指弹药) firepower

火冒三丈 huǒ mào sān zhàng burn with rage

火气 huǒqì [名] 1 (医) (指病因) internal heat 2 (怒气) temper

火器 huǒqì [名] firearm

火热 huǒrè [形] 1 (极热) burning hot 2 (热烈) powerful ▷火热的表演 a powerful performance 3 (亲热) intimate ▷双方谈得火热。The two sides engaged in intense talks. 4 (激烈) energetic ▷两人辩论得火热。The two of them engaged in an energetic debate.

火山 huǒshān [名] volcano (PL volcanoes)

火上加油 huǒ shàng jiā yóu (喻) pour oil on the flames

火烧眉毛 huǒ shāo méimao (喻) be pressing

火速 huǒsù [副] at top speed

火腿 huǒtuǐ [名] ham

火险 huǒxiǎn [名] 1 (指保险) fire insurance 2 (火灾) fire risk

火眼金睛 huǒ yǎn jīn jīng eagle-eyed

火焰 huǒyàn [名] flame

火药 huǒyào [名] gunpowder

火药味 huǒyàowèi [名] (喻) belligerence

火葬 huǒzàng [动] cremate

伙 huǒ I [名] 1 (同伴) companion 2 (集集体) partnership 3 (伙食) meals (PL) II [量] group III [副] together with

伙伴 huǒbàn [名] companion

伙房 huǒfáng [名] kitchen

伙计 huǒji [名] 1 (伙伴) partner 2 (店员) shop assistant (英), sales clerk (美)

伙食 huǒshí [名] meals (PL)

伙同 huǒtóng [动] (贬) be in league with

或 huò I (书) [副] 1 (也许) probably ▷到下周或可完成任务。The task will probably be completed by next week. 2 (稍微) remotely ▷不可或缺 indispensable II [连] or ▷无论刮风或下雨，他都准时上班。Even when it's windy or rainy, he's always at work on time. ▷今天或明天，这份功课我一定得完成。I must finish this homework today or tomorrow.

或许 huòxǔ [副] perhaps

或者 huòzhě I [副] maybe ▷再给他发封信，或者会有回音的。If you send him another letter, maybe he'll reply. II [连] or ▷周末我或者在家做饭，或者出去吃。At the weekend I

will either cook at home or go out to eat. ▷你
先发言，或者他先发言都可以。Whether you
speak first or he does doesn't really matter.

和 huò [动] mix
→另见 hé, huó

货 huò [名] 1 (货币) currency 2 (货物) goods
(PL) 3 (人) person (PL people) ▶蠢货 idiot
货币 huòbì [名] currency
货单 huòdān [名] invoice
货款 huòkuǎn [名] payment for goods
货色 huòsè [名] 1 (货物) goods (PL) 2 (贬) (指人
或言行思想) rubbish (英), garbage (美)
货物 huòwù [名] goods (PL)
货真价实 huò zhēn jià shí 1 (字) high quality
at a decent price ▷本店提供的服务货真价
实。The service in this shop (英) 或 store (美)
is of a high quality and it comes at a decent
price. 2 (喻) through and through

获 huò [动] 1 (捉住) capture 2 (得到) obtain 3 (收
割) reap ▶收获 harvest
获得 huòdé [动] gain ▷获得灵感 gain
inspiration ▷获得冠军 win the championship
获取 huòqǔ [动] obtain
获释 huòshì [动] be set free
获悉 huòxī [动] (书) learn ▷我从朋友那里获
悉他早已出国。I learned from friends that he
had already gone abroad.
获准 huòzhǔn [动] get permission

祸 huò [名] I [名] misfortune II [动] harm

祸不单行 huò bù dān xíng it never rains but
it pours
祸根 huògēn [名] root of the trouble
祸国殃民 huò guó yāng mín bring disaster
upon the country and the people
祸害 huòhài I [名] 1 (祸患) disaster 2 (指人或事
物) scourge II [动] destroy
祸患 huòhuàn [名] disaster
祸首 huòshǒu [名] chief culprit
祸水 huòshuǐ [名] (喻) culprit

惑 huò [动] 1 (疑惑) be puzzled 2 (蛊惑) delude
惑乱 huòluàn [动] befuddle

霍 huò [副] suddenly
霍地 huòdì [副] suddenly
霍霍 huòhuò I [拟] swish II [形] flash
霍乱 huòluàn [名] cholera
霍然 huòrán [副] suddenly

豁 huò I [形] 1 (指人) positive 2 (开阔) clear
II [动] be exempt
→另见 huō
豁达 huòdá [形] positive ▷妮科尔为人豁达。
Nicole is such a positive person.
豁亮 huòliàng [形] 1 (敞亮) roomy and
bright 2 (响亮) resonant
豁免 huòmiǎn [动] be exempt from ▷豁免关税
be exempt from import duty
豁然开朗 huòrán kāilǎng 1 (字) suddenly
come across a panoramic scene 2 (喻) (突然领
悟) suddenly see the light

Jj

几 jī I [名] small table ▶茶几 tea table ▷窗明几净 bright and clean II [副] (书) almost ▷当他到的时候几近3点。It was almost three o'clock by the time he arrived.
→另见 jǐ

几乎 jīhū [副] almost ▷从这儿到海边几乎有3公里。It is almost three kilometres from here to the coast. ▷他几乎就要成功了。He almost succeeded.

几率 jīlù [名] probability

讥 jī [动] mock ▷反唇相讥 retort sarcastically

讥讽 jīfěng [动] ridicule

讥笑 jīxiào [动] jeer

击 jī [动] 1 (打) strike (PT, PP struck) ▷用拳头猛击 pummel wildly ▷击鼓 beat a drum 2 (攻) attack ▷回击 launch a counterattack 3 (接触) meet (PT, PP met) ▷目击 witness ▶撞击 ram

击发 jīfā [动] fire

击掌 jīzhǎng [动] clap

击中要害 jīzhòng yàohài hit home ▷他的评论击中了要害。His review hit home.

叽 jī [拟] chirp

叽咕 jīgu [动] whisper

叽叽喳喳 jījizhāzhā [拟] chirp

饥 jī I [形] hungry II [名] famine

饥饿 jī'è [形] starving

饥荒 jīhuang [名] 1 (粮灾) famine 2 (债务) debt

机 jī I [名] 1 (机器) machine ▶起重机 crane ▶发动机 engine 2 (飞机) aeroplane (英), airplane (美) ▶客机 airliner ▶直升机 helicopter 3 (枢纽) pivot ▶转机 turning point 4 (机会) opportunity ▷见机行事 play it by ear 5 (机能) ▶有机体 organism ▷无机化学 inorganic chemistry II [形] quick-witted ▶机智 ingenious

机场 jīchǎng [名] airport

机动 jīdòng [形] 1 (传动的) motorized ▷机动车 motor vehicle 2 (灵活) flexible 3 (备用的) reserve ▷机动兵力 reserve forces

机构 jīgòu [名] 1 (指机器) mechanism ▷传动机构 transmission 2 (指机关) body ▷管理机构 administrative body ▷科研机构 scientific research institute 3 (指内部) internal structure ▷机构调整 restructuring

机关 jīguān [名] 1 (部门) department ▷政府机关 government department 2 (机械) mechanism ▷启动机关 starting mechanism 3 (计谋) scheme

机关枪 jīguānqiāng [名] machine gun

机会 jīhuì [名] opportunity ▷抓住机会 grasp an opportunity ▷错过机会 miss an opportunity

机警 jījǐng [形] alert

机灵 jīling [形] clever

机能 jīnéng [名] function

机器 jīqì [名] 1 (指装置) machine 2 (指机构) apparatus

机巧 jīqiǎo [形] dexterous

机械 jīxiè I [名] machinery II [形] rigid ▷机械搬他人的做法 copy someone else's method exactly

机械化 jīxièhuà [动] mechanize ▷农业机械化 agricultural mechanization

机要 jīyào [形] confidential

机遇 jīyù [名] opportunity

机智 jīzhì [形] resourceful

机组 jīzǔ [名] 1 (一组机器) set 2 (空勤人员) aircrew

肌 jī [名] muscle

肌肤 jīfū [名] skin

肌肉 jīròu [名] muscle

肌体 jītǐ [名] body

鸡 jī [名] chicken ▶公鸡 cock ▶母鸡 hen

鸡蛋 jīdàn [名] egg
鸡毛蒜皮 jīmáo suànpí trivial thing
鸡尾酒 jīwěijiǔ [名] cocktail

奇 jī [形] odd
➙另见 qí
奇数 jīshù [名] odd number

唧 jī [动] squirt
唧唧喳喳 jījī zhāzhā [拟] chirp

积 jī I [动] accumulate ▷积经验 accumulate experience II [形] long-standing ▷积习难改。Old habits die hard. III [名] (数) product
积存 jīcún [动] stockpile
积德 jīdé [动] do good deeds
积极 jījí [形] 1 (肯定的) positive 2 (热心的) active ▷她积极参加学校组织的活动。She takes an active part in events organized by the college. ▷他上课发言很积极。He participates actively in class.
积累 jīlěi [动] accumulate ▷资本积累 accumulation of capital
积习 jīxí [名] habit
积蓄 jīxù I [动] save II [名] savings
积压 jīyā [动] 1 (物品) overstock ▷店里积压了大量商品。The shop has overstocked on a lot of products. 2 (指情绪) ▷我积压了一肚子怒火。I have a lot of pent-up anger.
积怨 jīyuàn [名] accumulated resentment
积攒 jīzǎn [动] save ... bit by bit
积重难返 jī zhòng nán fǎn old habits die hard

基 jī I [名] base II [形] primary ▶基层 grass roots
基本 jīběn I [形] 1 (根本) basic ▷基本规律 basic norms 2 (主要) essential ▷基本特点 essential characteristics 3 (基础) elementary ▷基本知识 basic knowledge II [副] basically ▷饭菜基本准备好了。The food is basically ready.
基本功 jīběngōng [名] basic skill
基础 jīchǔ I [名] foundation II [形] basic ▷基础知识 basic knowledge
基地 jīdì [名] base ▷军事基地 military base
基点 jīdiǎn [名] starting point
基调 jīdiào [名] 1 (基本精神) keynote 2 (音) main key
基督 Jīdū [名] Jesus
基督教 Jīdūjiào [名] Christianity
基建 jījiàn [名] infrastructure development

基金 jījīn [名] fund ▷助学基金 study fund
基石 jīshí [名] cornerstone
基数 jīshù [名] 1 (数) cardinal number 2 (统计) base
基因 jīyīn [名] gene ▷基因工程 genetic engineering
基于 jīyú [介] on the basis of ▷基于确凿的证据，他被判入狱。On the basis of irrefutable evidence he was sent to jail.

犄 jī 见下文
犄角 jījiǎo [名] (角落) corner
犄角 jījiao [名] (指动物) horn

缉 jī [动] seize ▶侦缉 apprehend
缉捕 jībǔ [动] arrest
缉查 jīchá [动] raid
缉毒 jīdú [动] crack down on drug trafficking
缉拿 jīná [动] apprehend
缉私 jīsī [动] crack down on smuggling

畸 jī [形] 1 (不平衡) lopsided 2 (不正常) abnormal
畸轻畸重 jī qīng jī zhòng give more weight to one than the other
畸形 jīxíng [形] 1 (有缺陷的) deformed 2 (不正常的) unbalanced

跻 jī [动] mount
跻身 jīshēn [动] ascend

箕 jī [名] (指器具) dustpan

稽 jī [动] check ▶稽查 check
稽查 jīchá I [动] check II [名] customs officer
稽考 jīkǎo [动] ascertain

激 jī I [动] 1 (涌起) surge 2 (刺激) catch a chill (PT, PP caught) ▷他被大雨激了一下。He caught a chill in the rain. 3 (唤起) excite ▷申奥成功激起了北京市民的热情。The successful bid for the Olympic Games excited Beijingers' enthusiasm. 4 (冰) chill ▷把啤酒放凉水里激一下。Put the beer in cold water to chill it a little. II [形] violent
激昂 jī'áng [形] aroused
激荡 jīdàng [动] inspire
激动 jīdòng [动] excite ▷激动的孩子 excited child ▷令人激动的电影 exciting film
激发 jīfā [动] arouse
激愤 jīfèn [形] indignant
激光 jīguāng [名] laser
激化 jīhuà [动] intensify

激活 jīhuó [动] activate

激进 jījìn [形] radical

激励 jīlì [动] inspire

激烈 jīliè [形] intense

激怒 jīnù [动] enrage

激情 jīqíng [名] passion

激素 jīsù [名] hormone

激增 jīzēng [动] shoot up (PT, PP shot) ▷电子产品在激增。The quantity of electrical goods being produced has shot up.

羁 jī I [名] bridle II [动] 1 (拘束) restrain 2 (拦阻) delay

羁绊 jībàn [名] fetters (PL)

羁留 jīliú [动] 1 (逗留) stay 2 (拘留) detain

羁押 jīyā [动] detain

及 jí I [动] 1 (到达) reach ▷他过河时，水深及腰。When he crossed the river, the water reached his waist. 2 (比得上) be as good as ▷我的法语水平不及她。My French isn't as good as hers. 3 (赶上) be in time for ▷现在去看电影还来得及。There is still time to get to the film. II [连] and ▷老师及学生 teachers and students

及格 jígé [动] pass

及时 jíshí I [形] timely ▷这场雨下得很及时。This rain has come at the right time. II [副] without delay ▷有病要及时去就医。If you are ill you should go to the doctor without delay.

及早 jízǎo [副] as soon as possible

吉 jí [形] lucky ▶吉祥 auspicious ▷逢凶化吉 land on one's feet

吉利 jílì [形] lucky

吉庆 jíqìng [形] auspicious

吉日 jírì [名] lucky day

吉他 jítā [名] guitar

吉祥 jíxiáng [形] auspicious

吉凶 jíxiōng [名] good and bad luck

汲 jí [动] draw (PT drew, PP drawn)

汲取 jíqǔ [动] derive

级 jí I [名] 1 (等级) level ▷各级政府部门 government departments of all levels 2 (年级) year (英), grade (美) ▷三年级 third year (英) or grade (美) 3 (台阶) step ▷石级 stone step 4 (语言) degree ▷比较级 the comparative degree II [量] step ▷100多级台阶 a staircase of more than 100 steps

级别 jíbié [名] level

极 jí I [名] 1 (顶点) extreme ▷真是荒谬之极。This is absurd in the extreme. 2 (指地球或磁体) pole ▷南极 the South Pole ▷阴极 negative pole II [动] go to an extreme (PT went, PP gone) III [形] extreme ▶极限 limit IV [副] very ▷极少数 very few

极点 jídiǎn [名] 1 (极限) extreme 2 (指地球或磁体) pole

极度 jídù [副] extremely

极端 jíduān I [名] extreme ▷做什么事情都不要走极端。You should exercise moderation in all that you do. II [形] absolute ▷极端仇视 absolute hostility

极力 jílì [副] to the utmost ▷极力劝说 do one's utmost to persuade

极其 jíqí [副] extremely

极限 jíxiàn [名] limit

极刑 jíxíng [名] death penalty

即 jí I [动] 1 (书) (就是) mean (PT, PP meant) ▷对她来说，结婚即生儿育女。From her point of view, marriage means having children. 2 (靠近) approach ▷这个目标可望而不可即。This goal is unattainable. 3 (到) ▷即位 ascend the throne 4 (就着) ▷即兴演唱 ad-lib II [形] present ▶即日 this very day III [副] immediately ▷我打个电话即到。I will be there immediately – I just have to make a phone call.

即便 jíbiàn [连] even if ▷即便我忙，也要为你送行。Even though I'm busy, I'll see you off.

即将 jíjiāng [副] soon

即刻 jíkè [副] immediately

即日 jírì [副] 1 (当天) this very day 2 (近几天) the next few days

即使 jíshǐ [连] even if ▷即使他不来，我们也照样干。Even if he doesn't come, we'll go ahead as usual. ▷即使分手了，他们还是朋友。Even though they've split up they're still friends.

即位 jíwèi [动] ascend the throne

即席 jíxí [形] impromptu ▷即席发言 make an impromptu speech

即兴 jíxìng [形] impromptu

吸 jí [副] urgently

急 jí I [形] 1 (着急) anxious ▷他急着赶火车。He is anxious to catch the train. 2 (急躁) impatient 3 (猛烈) ▷雨下得真急。It's raining really hard. ▷水流很急。There's a strong current. 4 (紧急) urgent ▷这件事很急。This matter is urgent. ▷急刹车 slam on the brakes

II [名] priority ▷当务之急是解决难民的吃住问题。Our top priority is to resolve the refugee accommodation and food supply problems. **III** [动] worry ▷他还没来，真急死人了。He still hasn't arrived – we're worried to death.

急不可待 jí bù kě dài extremely anxious

急促 jícù [形] **1** (短促) rapid **2** (紧张) pressing ▷时间急促，我们赶快出发。Time is pressing – we had better go.

急功近利 jí gōng jìn lì seek short-term benefits

急救 jíjiù [动] give first-aid (PT gave, PP given)

急剧 jíjù [副] rapidly ▷那座城市的环境急剧恶化。The environment in the city is rapidly getting worse.

急忙 jímáng [副] hurriedly

急迫 jípò [形] urgent

急切 jíqiè [形] eager ▷我怀着急切的心情等他的来信。I waited eagerly for his letter.

急速 jísù [副] rapidly ▷经济形势急速恶化。The economy is deteriorating rapidly.

急性 jíxìng [形] acute

急性子 jíxìngzi [名] hothead

急于 jíyú [副] anxiously ▷他急于要走。He is anxious to go. ▷不要急于下结论。Don't be in such a hurry to pass judgment.

急躁 jízào [形] impatient

急诊 jízhěn [名] emergency treatment

急中生智 jí zhōng shēng zhì show resourcefulness in an emergency

疾 jí **I** [名] disease **II** [形] rapid

疾病 jíbìng [名] disease

棘 jí [名] thorn

棘手 jíshǒu [形] thorny

集 jí **I** [动] gather ▷集大家的智慧 draw on collective wisdom **II** [名] **1** (集市) market ▷赶集 go to market **2** (集子) anthology ▷诗集 an anthology of poems **3** (部分) part ▷该书分上下两集。This book is divided into two parts.

集合 jíhé [动] assemble

集会 jíhuì [名] assembly

集结 jíjié [动] build ... up (PT, PP built)

集权 jíquán [动] centralize

集散地 jísàndì [名] distribution centre (英) 或 center (美)

集市 jíshì [名] market

集思广益 jí sī guǎng yì pool knowledge

集体 jítǐ [名] collective

集团 jítuán [名] group

集腋成裘 jí yè chéng qiú every little helps

集镇 jízhèn [名] market town

集中 jízhōng [动] concentrate ▷大商场多集中在市中心。Most of the department stores are concentrated in the city centre.

集装箱 jízhuāngxiāng [名] container

集资 jízī [动] raise funds

辑 jí **I** [动] edit **II** [名] volume

辑录 jílù [动] compile

嫉 jí [动] envy

嫉妒 jídù [动] envy ▷你不要嫉妒他人。You shouldn't be jealous of other people.

嫉贤妒能 jí xián dù néng envy successful and talented people

瘠 jí [形] **1** (瘦弱) thin and weak **2** (瘠薄) barren

瘠田 jítián [名] infertile land

籍 jí [名] **1** (籍贯) native place **2** (书籍) book **3** (小册子) register **4** (身份) ▷国籍 nationality

籍贯 jíguàn [名] native place ▷他籍贯是福建厦门。He was born in Xiamen in Fujian.

几 jǐ [数] **1** (用于疑问句) ▷昨天来了几位客人？How many customers came yesterday? **2** (用于陈述句) ▷我在图书馆借了几本书。I borrowed several books from the library. →另见 jī

几何 jǐhé [名] geometry

几经 jǐjīng [副] ▷几经周折，他终于找到了失散多年的亲人。After much effort, he finally found the relatives he'd lost touch with for many years. ▷几经努力，她终于考上了重点大学。After much hard work, she finally got into a key university.

几时 jǐshí [代] **1** (什么时候) ▷你几时回来？When will you come back? ▷电脑几时修好？When will the computer be fixed? **2** (任何时候) any time ▷我几时也没有说过这话。I never said anything of the sort.

己 jǐ [名] self ▶自己 oneself

挤 jǐ [动] **1** (紧紧靠拢) crowd ▷公共汽车很挤。The bus is very crowded. ▷过道里挤满了人。The passageway was packed with people. **2** (事情、会议、约会) be close ▷两个会议都挤在一起。The two meetings are very close to each other. ▷事情都挤在一块儿了。Everything's happening at the same time. **3** (推人) elbow one's way ▷他挤上拥挤的汽车。He elbowed his way onto the crowded bus. **4** (贬) (指社

交) push one's way ▷她拼命想挤进上层社会。She worked hard to push her way into top society. **5** (牙膏、颜料) squeeze ... out ▷挤奶 milk **6** (时间) make (PT, PP made) ▷他挤时间学英语。He made time to study English. **7** (排斥) rob ... of ▷他的晋升机会被挤掉了。He was robbed of his opportunity for promotion.

济 jǐ 见下文
→另见 jì

济济一堂 jǐjǐ yītáng assemble ▷研讨会上全国的语言学家济济一堂。Linguists from all over the country assembled at the symposium.

给 jǐ I [动] provide ▷补给 supply II [形] sufficient
→另见 gěi

给养 jǐyǎng [名] supplies (PL)

给予 jǐyǔ [动] (书) give (PT gave, PP given) ▷他对我们给予了很大帮助。He has rendered us much help.

脊 jǐ [名] **1** (指人或动物) spine ▷脊柱 spinal column **2** (指物体) ridge ▷山脊 mountain ridge ▷书脊 spine

脊背 jǐbèi [名] back

脊梁 jǐliang [名] (脊背) back

脊髓 jǐsuǐ [名] spinal cord

脊椎 jǐzhuī [名] **1** (脊柱) spinal column ▷脊椎动物 vertebrates **2** (脊骨) vertebra (PL vertebrae)

计 jì I [动] **1** (核算) calculate ▷共计 total **2** (打算) plan **3** (考虑) bother ▷他工作不计报酬。He's not bothered about what he's paid for his work. II [名] **1** (计谋) strategy **2** (测量仪器) gauge ▷温度计 thermometer

计策 jìcè [名] strategy

计划 jìhuà I [名] plan ▷你们应制定学习计划。You should devise a study plan. II [动] plan ▷你计划不周，怎么能成功呢？If you don't plan properly, how can you succeed?

计较 jìjiào [动] **1** (在乎) bother ▷斤斤计较 quibble over every detail **2** (争论) argue ▷先不跟你计较，有空我再说。I won't argue with you now. Let's talk about it when I have time. **3** (计议) deliberate

计算 jìsuàn [动] **1** (数) calculate **2** (筹划) plan ▷做事没个计算可不行。It's no good taking action without a plan. **3** (暗算) scheme ▷小心别被人计算。Be careful others aren't scheming against you.

计算机 jìsuànjī [名] computer

计算器 jìsuànqì [名] calculator

记 jì I [动] **1** (指往事) remember **2** (写) record ▷记名字 record a name ▷记笔记 make notes ▷记账 keep accounts II [名] **1** (指事或文章) record ▷游记 travel journal ▷日记 diary **2** (标志) mark **3** (指皮肤) birthmark III [量] (方) ▷一记远射，球进了！A long shot – and it's a goal! ▷他被打了一记耳光。He got a slap in the face.

> **remember** 后接带 **to** 的不定式或者动词的 **-ing** 形式。**remember to do something** 表示记得去做某事。*He remembered to buy his wife chocolates*。**remember doing something** 则表示记得已经做过某事。*I remember reading the newspaper aloud to my father at the age of five.*

记挂 jìguà [动] be concerned about

记过 jìguò [动] give ... a black mark (PT gave, PP given) ▷他没完成任务，被记过一次。He didn't finish his work, and was given a black mark.

记号 jìhao [名] mark ▷在你不会的地方作个记号。Make a mark by the ones you are unable to do.

记录 jìlù I [动] (写下) write ... down (PT wrote, PP written) ▷请把你的心得体会记录下来。Please write down what your own understanding is. II [名] **1** (材料) record ▷请整理一下会议记录。Please tidy up the minutes of the meeting. **2** (人) secretary ▷她是这次会议的记录。She is the secretary for this meeting. **3** (成绩) record ▷他打破了男子 100 米世界纪录。He broke the world record for the men's 100 metres (英) 或 meters (美).

记名 jìmíng [动] register ▷总经理通过无记名投票选出。The general manager was elected by secret ballot.

记取 jìqǔ [动] remember

记事 jìshì I [动] keep a record (PT, PP kept) ▷记事本 notebook II [名] chronicles (PL)

记事儿 jìshìr [动] have memories ▷她打5岁起就记事儿了。Her memories start from when she was five.

记述 jìshù [动] tell (PT, PP told) ▷这部影片记述了一个真实的故事。This film tells a true story. ▷记者对此事进行了完整的记述。The journalist gave a full account of the event.

记性 jìxing [名] memory

记忆 jìyì I [动] remember II [名] memory ▷记忆犹新 the memory is fresh

记载 jìzǎi [动] record ▷这篇文章记载了当时的情况。This essay records the situation at that time. ▷请据实记载事情经过。Please write down exactly what happened.

记者 jìzhě [名] journalist ▷他是一名出色的摄影记者。He is a famous photo-journalist.

伎 jì 见下文

伎俩 jìliǎng [名] trick ▷逃票是他惯用的伎俩。Not buying tickets is his favourite trick. ▷我们识破了他的伎俩。We saw through his ploy.

纪 jì I [名] 1 (指时间) age ▶中世纪 the Middle Ages (PL) 2 (指地质) period ▶侏罗纪 the Jurassic period 3 (纪律) discipline II [动] record

纪律 jìlǜ [名] discipline

纪念 jìniàn I [动] commemorate II [名] memento ▷送给你一支钢笔作纪念。Here is a pen as a memento. ▷给我签个名留作纪念吧。Please give me your autograph as a souvenir.

纪实 jìshí [名] record ▷纪实文学 literature based on actual events

纪要 jìyào [名] summary ▷请整理好会议纪要。Please put together a summary of the meeting.

纪元 jìyuán [名] era ▶新纪元 new era ▷公历从耶稣诞生的那年开始纪元。The Western calendar begins in the year of the birth of Christ.

技 jì [名] 1 (技艺) skill ▶技能 skill ▶技巧 technique 2 (本领) ability ▶绝技 unique ability

技能 jìnéng [名] skill

技巧 jìqiǎo [名] technique

技术 jìshù [名] technology ▷我们需要不断学习国际先进技术。We need to keep up with international advances in technology. ▷生产要与技术改造同时进行。Production must go hand in hand with technological improvement.

技艺 jìyì [名] skill

系 jì [动] 1 (打结) tie 2 (扣上) fasten ▷把领扣系好。Button up your collar.
→另见 xì

忌 jì [动] 1 (嫉妒) envy ▷当领导决不能忌才。A leader should never be resentful of others' ability. 2 (害怕) fear ▶忌惮 dread 3 (避免) avoid 4 (戒除) give ... up (PT gave, PP given) ▶忌酒 give up drinking ▷为了健康，你需要忌烟。You should give up smoking for the sake of your health.

忌妒 jìdu I [动] be jealous ▷他总是忌妒别人的成功。He is always jealous of other people's success. II [名] jealousy ▷她这么做是出于忌妒。She's done that out of jealousy.

忌讳 jìhui [动] 1 (禁忌) be superstitious about 2 (避免) avoid ▷夜里我忌讳走墓地。At night I try to avoid walking by the graveyard.

际 jì [名] 1 (边缘) border ▶天际 horizon 2 (里边) interior ▶脑际 in one's mind 3 (彼此之间) ▶国际 international 4 (时候) occasion 5 (遭遇) lot

际遇 jìyù [名] (书) experience

妓 jì 见下文

妓女 jìnǚ [名] prostitute

季 jì [名] season ▶春季 spring ▶旺季 busy season ▶雨季 rainy season

季度 jìdù [名] quarter

季节 jìjié [名] season

季军 jìjūn [名] third place ▷她在这次写作大赛中获得季军。She came third in this major writing competition.

剂 jì I [名] 1 (指药、针、麻醉) preparation ▶针剂 injection 2 (指起化学物理作用) ▶杀虫剂 insecticide ▶除臭剂 deodorant II [量] (指配的汤药) dose ▶一剂药 a dose of medicine

剂量 jìliàng [名] dosage

迹 jì [名] 1 (印) trace ▶足迹 footprint ▶血迹 bloodstain 2 (遗留物) remains (PL) ▶笔迹 writing ▶古迹 historic sites (PL)

迹象 jìxiàng [名] indication ▷种种迹象表明他们不会来了。All the indications are that they won't come. ▷他还没有好转的迹象。He's still not showing any signs of improvement.

济 jì [动] 1 (渡过) cross ▷让我们同舟共济，共同努力吧。We're all in the same boat, so let's work together. 2 (救) help ▶接济 give aid 3 (有益) be of help ▷无济于事 be of no help
→另见 jǐ

济事 jìshì [动] be of use ▷你这点儿钱根本不济事。This is simply not enough money to be of any use. ▷他去了也不济事。It won't be of any use even if he does go.

既 jì I [副] already ▶既定 fixed ▶既成事实 a fait accompli II [连] 1 表示兼而有之) ▷他字写得既快又好。He writes both quickly and well. ▷他既高又壮。He's tall and strong. 2 (既然) since ▷既来之，则安之。Since we've come, let's make the best of it.

既然 jìrán [连] since ▷既然你知道错误了，为什么不及时纠正呢？Since you knew you'd made a mistake, why didn't you put it right immediately? ▷既然他执意要去，你就答应

吧。Seeing as he's determined to go, why don't you just agree to it?

既往不咎 jì wǎng bù jiù let bygones be bygones

觊 jì 见下文

觊觎 jìyú [动] (书) covet

继 jì I [副] 1 (接续) continuously ▷继任 succeed to a post 2 (接连) successively ▷相继 one after another II [动] continue

继承 jìchéng [动] 1 (遗产、文化等) inherit 2 (遗志、未成事业) take ... on (PT took, PP taken)

继而 jì'ér [副] then ▷他先是一愣，继而大笑。At first he was taken aback – then he burst out laughing.

继往开来 jì wǎng kāi lái forge ahead

继续 jìxù I [动] continue ▷你们要继续努力。You must continue to work hard. ▷我们继续昨天的话题接着谈。We'll continue with the topic we discussed yesterday. ▷身体痊愈后，他继续工作。After he recovered he went back to work. ▷我们继续往下读。Let's read on. II [名] continuation

祭 jì [动] 1 (祭祀) sacrifice ▷祭坛 sacrificial altar 2 (祭奠) hold a memorial service (PT, PP held)

祭奠 jìdiàn [动] hold a memorial service (PT, PP held)

祭祀 jìsì [动] sacrifice ▷一头小牛被用作祭祀。A young cow is used as a sacrifice.

祭文 jìwén [名] eulogy

悸 jì [动] (书) palpitate ▷想起那次历险，我到现在都心有余悸。When I think about the danger we were in, I still have palpitations.

悸动 jìdòng [动] pound

寄 jì [动] 1 (邮递) post (英), mail (美) ▷包裹已经寄走了。The package has already been posted (英) 或 mailed (美). 2 (付托) place ▷我寄希望于他。I pinned my hopes on him. 3 (依附) depend on ▷寄人篱下 be a dependant (英) 或 dependent (美)

寄存 jìcún [动] deposit ▷我把行李寄存在存包处了。I've checked my bag in.

寄放 jìfàng [动] leave (PT, PP left)

寄居 jìjū [动] live ▷她从小寄居在姑姑家。She has lived with her aunt ever since she was little.

寄生 jìshēng [动] be a parasite ▷真菌寄生在某些植物中。Fungus is a parasite on certain plants. ▷我们不能过寄生生活。We can't live as parasites.

寄宿 jìsù [动] 1 (借宿) stay ▷昨晚下大雨，我只好寄宿朋友家。With the heavy rain last night, I had no choice but to stay over at my friend's house. 2 (住校) board ▷我所在的学校是一所寄宿学校。The school I attended was a boarding school.

寄托 jìtuō [动] 1 (物品) leave (PT, PP left) 2 (理想、感情、希望) focus ▷葬礼是我们寄托感情的时刻。The funeral was an occasion for focusing our feelings. ▷她把希望寄托在女儿身上。Her hopes were pinned on her daughter.

寄养 jìyǎng [动] 1 (指人) foster 2 (指动植物) give ... to look after (PT gave, PP given) ▷我把这盆花寄养在你这儿行吗？Would it be all right if I give you this plant to look after?

寄予 jìyǔ [动] 1 (寄托) place ▷父亲对他寄予了无限希望。His father places all his hopes in him. 2 (给予) show (PT showed, PP shown) ▷全社区对他家的不幸寄予了无限的同情。The whole community showed boundless sympathy for the family's misfortunes. ▷他对年轻人寄予了无限关怀。He's deeply committed to young people.

寂 jì [形] 1 (静) quiet 2 (寂寞) lonely

寂静 jìjìng I [形] peaceful ▷尖叫声划破了寂静的夜晚。A scream broke the silence of the night. II [名] tranquillity

寂寞 jìmò [形] lonely

绩 jì [名] achievement ▷功绩 accomplishment ▷战绩 military success

髻 jì [名] chignon

冀 jì [动] (书) hope ▷冀望 long for

加 jiā [动] 1 (相加) ▷2加2等于4。Two plus two is four. ▷雪上加霜 one disaster after another 2 (增加) increase ▷老板要给我们加工资。The boss wants to increase our wages. 3 (添加) add ▷加点糖 add some sugar ▷请加一副碗筷。Can you give us another bowl and another set of chopsticks? 4 (加以) ▷我们对孩子要严加管教。We should be strict with children.

加班 jiābān [动] work overtime

加倍 jiābèi [动] double ▷下个月油价可能加倍。Next month the price of oil may double. ▷值夜班要加倍警惕。The night shift has to be doubly vigilant.

加法 jiāfǎ [名] addition

加封 jiāfēng [动] 1 (提升) grant 2 (查封) seal

加工 jiāgōng [动] 1 (制作) process 2 (完善) polish

加害 jiāhài [动] do ... harm

加紧 jiājǐn [动] step up

加剧 jiājù [动] make ... worse ▷谣言加剧了他们之间的矛盾。The allegation made the tension between them worse. ▷这项政策加剧了贫富差距。This policy exacerbates the gap between rich and poor.

加仑 jiālún [量] gallon

加码 jiāmǎ [动] 1 (加注) raise the stakes 2 (增加) increase a quota

加盟 jiāméng [动] join ▷本俱乐部欢迎青年人加盟。This club encourages young people to join.

加密 jiāmì [动] encrypt

加冕 jiāmiǎn [动] crown

加强 jiāqiáng [动] strengthen ▷加强防卫 strengthen defences (英) 或 defenses (美)

加入 jiārù [动] 1 (添加) add ▷汤里需要再加入点盐。You need to add a bit more salt to the soup. 2 (参加) join

加塞儿 jiāsāir [动] queue-jump (英), line-jump (美)

加速 jiāsù [动] accelerate

加以 jiāyǐ I [动] ▷旧的工作方法必须加以改进。The old working methods need to be improved. II [连] ▷这家商店离学校近, 加以价格便宜, 所以顾客很多。This shop is close to campus, and it's also cheap, so there are a lot of customers.

加油 jiāyóu [动] 1 (加燃料) refuel ▷飞机需要加油了。The plane needs to refuel. ▷我的汽车该加油了。I should get some petrol (英) 或 gas (美) for the car. 2 (加劲儿) make more effort ▷老板一再叮嘱大家加油干。The boss kept urging people to make more effort. ▷快, 加油! Come on, come on!

夹 jiā I [动] 1 (钳) get hold of 2 (携带) carry ... under one's arm ▷我们校长总是夹着公文包。Our head teacher always carries a briefcase under his arm. 3 (限制) ▷两边高楼夹着一条狭窄的街道。A narrow street hemmed in by tall buildings on either side. 4 (带) mix ... with ▷笑声夹杂着哭声 laughter mixed with tears II [名] folder ▷文件夹 document folder
→另见 gā, jiá

夹带 jiādài [动] smuggle

夹道 jiādào I [名] alleyway II [动] line the road

夹缝 jiāfèng [名] crevice

夹攻 jiāgōng [动] attack in a pincer movement

夹克 jiākè [名] jacket

夹生 jiāshēng [形] half-cooked

夹杂 jiāzá [动] be mixed with

茄 jiā 见下文
→另见 qié

茄克 jiākè [名] jacket

佳 jiā [形] fine ▷佳音 good news ▷她最近身体欠佳。She has recently been in poor health.

佳话 jiāhuà [名] talking point

佳节 jiājié [名] festival

佳境 jiājìng [名] beauty spot

佳丽 jiālì [名] beauty

佳偶 jiā'ǒu [名] happily married couple

佳期 jiāqī [名] wedding day

佳人 jiārén [名] beautiful woman (PL women)

佳肴 jiāyáo [名] delicacies (PL)

佳音 jiāyīn [名] good news (SG)

枷 jiā 见下文

枷锁 jiāsuǒ [名] fetters (PL)

痂 jiā [名] scab

家 jiā I [名] 1 (家庭) family 2 (住所) home ▷他一放假就回家。As soon as the holiday started he went back home. 3 (学派) school of thought 4 (指人) ▷船家 boatman (PL boatmen) ▷农家 peasant ▷专家 expert ▷歌唱家 singer ▷画家 painter II [形] 1 (饲养的) domestic ▷家畜 domestic animal 2 (嫡亲的) ▷家兄 elder brother III [量] ▷一家公司 a company

家产 jiāchǎn [名] estate

家常 jiācháng [名] domestic affairs (PL)

家丑 jiāchǒu [名] family scandal

家畜 jiāchù [名] domestic animal

家传 jiāchuán [动] hand ... down

家当 jiādàng [名] family possessions (PL)

家底 jiādǐ [名] property ▷他家底颇厚。His family is quite wealthy.

家电 jiādiàn [名] domestic electrical appliance

家伙 jiāhuo [名] 1 (工具) tool 2 (武器) weapon 3 (人) guy

家计 jiājì [名] (书) family livelihood

家教 jiājiào I [动] bring ... up (PT, PP brought) II [名] private tutor

家境 jiājìng [名] family circumstances (PL)

家具 jiājù [名] furniture
注意 furniture 只能用作不可数名词。不能说 'a furniture' 或 'furnitures'。如要具体指代桌子、椅子或床等家具, 可以用 a piece of furniture 或 an item of furniture。

家眷 jiājuàn [名] wife and children

家禽 jiāqín [名] poultry (PL)

家室 jiāshì [名] 1 (妻子) wife (PL wives) ▷他已有家室。He's married. 2 (家庭) family

家属 jiāshǔ [名] family members (PL)

家庭 jiātíng [名] family ▷他妻子很会处理家庭关系。His wife is very good at sorting out relationships within the family. ▷我的家很和睦。My household is harmonious.

家务 jiāwù [名] housework

家乡 jiāxiāng [名] hometown

家小 jiāxiǎo [名] wife and children

家业 jiāyè [名] family property

家用 jiāyòng I [名] living expenses (PL) II [形] domestic ▷家用电器 domestic electrical appliance ▷家用电脑 home computer

家喻户晓 jiā yù hù xiǎo be a household name

家园 jiāyuán [名] homeland

家长 jiāzhǎng [名] 1 (一家之长) head of the family 2 (父母) parent

家政 jiāzhèng [名] housekeeping

家族 jiāzú [名] family

嘉 jiā I [形] fine ▷嘉宾 honoured (英) 或 honored (美) guest II [动] praise

嘉宾 jiābīn [名] honoured (英) 或 honored (美) guest

嘉奖 jiājiǎng [动] commend

嘉许 jiāxǔ [动] praise

夹 jiá [形] lined ▷夹袄 padded jacket
→另见 gā, jiā

戛 jiá 见下文

戛然而止 jiá rán ér zhǐ stop suddenly

颊 jiá [名] cheek

甲 jiǎ [名] 1 (第一) ▷甲级品 A-grade 2 (动物硬壳) shell ▷龟甲 tortoiseshell 3 (角质硬壳) nail ▷指甲 fingernail 4 (装备) armour (英), armor (美) ▷装甲车 armoured (英) 或 armored (美) car

甲板 jiǎbǎn [名] deck

甲虫 jiǎchóng [名] beetle

岬 jiǎ [名] cape

岬角 jiǎjiǎo [名] headland

假 jiǎ I [形] 1 (虚伪) false ▷他表面上热情，其实特假。He gives a false impression of being friendly. 2 (不真) artificial ▷假发 wig ▷假山 rockery ▷假话 lie II [连] if ▷假如 if III [动] borrow

→另见 jià

假扮 jiǎbàn [动] dress up as

假充 jiǎchōng [动] pretend to be

假定 jiǎdìng [动] suppose ▷假定你中了大奖，你会做什么？Supposing you won the jackpot, what would you do with it? ▷有外星人的说法只是一种假定。The existence of extraterrestrials is just hypothesis.

假借 jiǎjiè [动] make use of

假冒 jiǎmào [动] pass oneself off as ▷他假冒总经理的名义诈骗银行。He passed himself off as the managing director to defraud the bank. ▷假冒伪劣产品 fake, sub-standard goods

假面具 jiǎmiànjù [名] mask

假名 jiǎmíng [名] pseudonym

假如 jiǎrú [连] if

假设 jiǎshè I [动] suppose ▷假设这是真的，我们该怎么办？Supposing it's true, what should we do? II [名] hypothesis (PL hypotheses)

假使 jiǎshǐ [连] if

假释 jiǎshì [动] release ... on parole

假象 jiǎxiàng [名] deceptive appearance ▷现在的经济繁荣只是一种假象。The current apparent economic boom is deceptive.

假惺惺 jiǎxīngxīng [形] hypocritical

假意 jiǎyì I [名] insincerity ▷谁知道她是真情还是假意？Who knows whether she is sincere or not? II [动] pretend ▷他假意吃惊。He pretended to be surprised. ▷他假意笑着向我问好。He greeted me with a false smile.

假装 jiǎzhuāng [动] pretend ▷我假装不懂他的意思。I pretended not to understand what he meant.

价 jià [名] 1 (价格) price ▷物价 price 2 (价值) value

价格 jiàgé [名] price ▷价格标签 price tag

价目 jiàmù [名] marked price

价钱 jiàqian [名] price

价值 jiàzhí [名] value ▷价值观念 values ▷商业价值 market potential

价值连城 jiàzhí liánchéng priceless

驾 jià I [动] 1 (驾驭) harness 2 (驾驶) drive (PT drove, PP driven) ▷驾车 drive a car ▷驾飞机 fly a plane II [代] (敬) ▷劳驾 excuse me III [量] ▷3驾马车 three carts

驾轻就熟 jià qīng jiù shú be a piece of cake

驾驶 jiàshǐ [动] steer

驾驭 jiàyù [动] master

驾照 jiàzhào [名] driving licence (英) 或 driver's

license (美)

架 jià I [名] 1 (架子) frame ▶书架 bookshelf ▶脚手架 scaffolding 2 (指行为) ▶吵架 quarrel ▶打架 fight II [动] 1 (撑起) support ▷架电线 carry electrical cables 2 (招架) ward ... off 3 (绑架) kidnap ▷孩子被人架走了。The child was kidnapped. 4 (搀扶) support ... under the arm ▷我们把伤员架上了救护车。Supporting the injured person under the arm, we helped him into the ambulance. III [量] ▷5架飞机 five planes ▷一架钢琴 a piano

架次 jiàcì [名] flight

架空 jiàkōng [动] build ... on stilts (PT, PP built)

架设 jiàshè [动] erect

架势 jiàshi [名] stance

架子 jiàzi [名] 1 (支撑物) rack ▷衣服架子 clothes rack 2 (指武术) position 3 (傲气) air ▷他一点都没有明星的架子。He doesn't have the air of a star at all. 4 (结构) structure ▷这篇论文我已经搭好了架子。I've already worked out the structure for this essay.

假 jià [名] holiday ▶暑假 summer holiday ▶病假 sick leave
→另见 jiǎ

假期 jiàqī [名] holiday

假日 jiàrì [名] holiday

嫁 jià [动] 1 (结婚) marry 2 (转移) shift the blame

嫁祸于人 jià huò yú rén shift the blame onto another person ▷这是你自己的错，怎么能嫁祸于人？It's your fault. How can you shift the blame onto someone else?

嫁接 jiàjiē [动] graft

嫁妆 jiàzhuang [名] dowry

尖 jiān I [形] 1 (锐利) pointed ▷这支铅笔削得太尖了。This pencil is too sharp. 2 (指声音) shrill 3 (敏感) sensitive ▷他的眼睛很尖。His eyesight is very acute. 4 (吝啬) stingy 5 (尖刻) biting II [动] ▷她尖着眼睛找别人的错。She kept her eyes peeled in the search for peoples' mistakes. ▷这孩子尖着耳朵听父母说什么。The child strained to hear what his parents were saying. III [名] 1 (尖端) tip ▶笔尖 pen tip 2 (精华) the best ▷他是我们中的尖子。Of all of us he is the best.

尖端 jiānduān I [名] point ▷长矛的尖端 spearhead II [形] cutting-edge ▷尖端科技 the cutting edge of science and technology

尖刻 jiānkè [形] acrimonious

尖利 jiānlì [形] sharp

尖锐 jiānruì [形] 1 (锋利) sharp 2 (敏锐)

penetrating ▷他的看法很尖锐。He has insightful ideas. 3 (刺耳) shrill

尖酸刻薄 jiānsuān kèbó bitterly sarcastic

尖子 jiānzi [名] the best

奸 jiān I [形] 1 (奸诈) wicked ▶奸计 trickery 2 (不忠) treacherous ▶奸臣 treacherous official II [动] ▶通奸 adultery ▶强奸 rape III [名] traitor ▶内奸 traitor

奸猾 jiānhuá [名] treachery

奸计 jiānjì [名] trickery

奸商 jiānshāng [名] shark

奸污 jiānwū [动] rape

奸细 jiānxi [名] spy

奸险 jiānxiǎn [形] malicious

奸邪 jiānxié [形] crafty and evil

奸淫 jiānyín [动] rape

奸诈 jiānzhà [形] fraudulent

歼 jiān 见下文

歼灭 jiānmiè [动] annihilate

坚 jiān I [形] hard ▶坚冰 solid ice II [名] stronghold ▷坚不可摧 indestructible III [副] firmly ▶坚信 firmly believe

坚持 jiānchí [动] go on (PT went, PP gone) ▷你应该坚持锻炼身体。You should go on taking exercise. ▷他坚持要我参加。He insisted that I take part. ▷系主任一向坚持原则。The head of department sticks to his principles.

坚定 jiāndìng [形] steadfast ▷我们要坚定地走正确的道路。We must steadfastly keep to the correct path.

坚固 jiāngù [形] solid

坚果 jiānguǒ [名] nut

坚决 jiānjué [副] resolutely

坚强 jiānqiáng [形] strong ▷他意志坚强。He is strong-willed.

坚韧 jiānrèn [形] tenacious

坚如磐石 jiān rú pánshí solid as a rock

坚实 jiānshí [形] solid

坚挺 jiāntǐng [形] strong

坚硬 jiānyìng [形] hard

坚贞 jiānzhēn [形] constant

间 jiān I [介] between ▶课间 between lessons II [名] 1 (范围) ▷晚间 in the evening ▶田间 field ▷人世间 in this world 2 (屋子) room ▶房间 room ▷洗手间 toilet ▷车间 workshop III [量] ▷两间客厅 two living rooms
→另见 jiàn

间距 jiānjù [名] distance ▷高速行驶应注意

行车间距。When driving fast you must keep your distance from other cars.

肩 jiān 见下文

肩膀 jiānbǎng [名] shoulder

肩负 jiānfù [动] shoulder ▷父亲肩负着养家活口的责任。Our father shoulders the responsibility of supporting the family. ▷他肩负了整项工程的组织工作。He has taken on the administration of the whole project.

艰 jiān [形] difficult ▶艰辛 hardship

艰巨 jiānjù [形] formidable

艰苦 jiānkǔ [形] harsh

艰难 jiānnán [形] hard ▷他们生活艰难。Their life is hard. ▷这位病人觉得走路很艰难。The invalid finds it difficult to walk.

艰深 jiānshēn [形] abstruse

艰险 jiānxiǎn [形] hard and dangerous ▷路途极其艰险。The journey is hard and dangerous.

监 jiān I [动] supervise ▶监视 keep watch II [名] 1 (监狱) prison ▶探监 visit a prison 2 (负责人) inspector ▶总监 chief-inspector

监测 jiāncè [动] monitor

监察 jiānchá [动] supervise

监督 jiāndū [动] supervise ▷舞台监督 stage manager

监工 jiāngōng I [动] oversee (PT oversaw, PP overseen) II [名] supervisor

监管 jiānguǎn [动] take charge of (PT took, PP taken)

监护 jiānhù [动] be a guardian ▷孩子由祖父母监护。The child's grandparents are its guardians.

监禁 jiānjìn [动] take ... into custody (PT took, PP taken)

监考 jiānkǎo [动] invigilate

监控 jiānkòng [动] monitor and control

监牢 jiānláo [名] prison

监视 jiānshì [动] spy on

监听 jiāntīng [动] monitor ▷警方一直在监听罪犯。The police are continuously monitoring criminals.

监狱 jiānyù [名] prison

兼 jiān [动] ▷这位董事长又兼着总经理的职位。The Chairman of the Board is also the CEO.

兼并 jiānbìng [动] acquire

兼程 jiānchéng [动] advance at the double

兼而有之 jiān ér yǒu zhī be both ... and ... ▷一次学术性与娱乐性兼而有之的活动 an activity that is both educational and fun

兼顾 jiāngù [动] be concerned about both ... and ... ▷公司执行安全与效率兼顾的原则。The company philosophy is to be concerned about both safety and efficiency.

兼任 jiānrèn [动] be concurrently

兼容 jiānróng [动] be compatible

兼容性 jiānróngxìng [名] compatibility

兼收并蓄 jiān shōu bìng xù incorporate diverse elements

兼职 jiānzhí [动] have more than one job ▷由于兼职太多，他终于累垮了。Because he had too many jobs, he eventually collapsed with exhaustion. ▷兼职教师 part-time teacher

笺 jiān [名] writing paper ▶信笺 letter paper

缄 jiān 见下文

缄口 jiānkǒu [动] (书) hold one's tongue (PT, PP held)

缄默 jiānmò [动] (书) keep silent (PT, PP kept)

煎 jiān [动] 1 (油炸) fry ▷煎鸡蛋 fry an egg 2 (水煮) decoct

煎熬 jiān'áo [动] suffer ▷他承受了许多煎熬。He's experienced a lot of suffering.

拣 jiǎn [动] choose (PT chose, PP chosen)

拣选 jiǎnxuǎn [动] select

茧 jiǎn [名] 1 (指昆虫) cocoon ▶蚕茧 silkworm cocoon 2 (指手) callus

柬 jiǎn [名] card ▶请柬 invitation

柬帖 jiǎntiě [名] card

俭 jiǎn [形] frugal

俭朴 jiǎnpǔ [形] economical

俭省 jiǎnshěng [形] frugal

捡 jiǎn [动] pick ... up ▷谁捡到了我的手表？Who picked up my watch?

检 jiǎn [动] 1 (检查) examine ▶体检 medical examination 2 (检点) show restraint (PT showed, PP shown)

检测 jiǎncè [动] determine

检查 jiǎnchá I [动] examine ▷明天我要检查身体。I'm going to be medically examined tomorrow. II [名] self-criticism

检察 jiǎnchá [名] procuratorial work

检点 jiǎndiǎn I [动] check II [形] cautious

检举 jiǎnjǔ [动] accuse

检索 jiǎnsuǒ [动] look ... up ▷我喜欢在网上检

索信息。I like to look up information on the Internet.

检讨 jiǎntǎo [动] examine

检修 jiǎnxiū [动] overhaul

检验 jiǎnyàn [动] inspect

检疫 jiǎnyì [动] quarantine

检阅 jiǎnyuè [动] inspect

减 jiǎn [动] 1 (减去) subtract ▷3减2等于1。 Three minus two is one. 2 (减少) reduce ▶裁减 cut down 3 (降低) decrease ▶减退 fail

减产 jiǎnchǎn [动] ▷战争使石油大幅度减产。The war caused a large-scale drop in oil production.

减法 jiǎnfǎ [名] subtraction

减肥 jiǎnféi [动] slim ▷减肥食谱 diet

减缓 jiǎnhuǎn [动] slow down

减免 jiǎnmiǎn [动] reduce

减轻 jiǎnqīng [动] reduce

减色 jiǎnsè [动] spoil

减少 jiǎnshǎo [动] reduce

减员 jiǎnyuán [动] cut staff (PT, PP cut)

剪 jiǎn I [名] scissors (PL) II [动] 1 (铰) cut (PT, PP cut) ▷我该剪头了。I need to get my hair cut. ▷剪羊毛 shear a sheep 2 (除去) eliminate

剪裁 jiǎncái [动] cut (PT, PP cut) ▷文章太长，需要剪裁。The article is too long – it needs cutting. ▷这条裙子是我自己剪裁的。I made this skirt myself.

剪彩 jiǎncǎi [动] cut a ribbon (PT, PP cut) ▷市长将为开幕式剪彩。The mayor is cutting the ribbon at the opening ceremony.

剪辑 jiǎnjí [动] edit ▷电影剪辑 film editing

剪贴 jiǎntiē [动] cut and paste (PT, PP cut)

剪影 jiǎnyǐng [名] silhouette

简 jiǎn I [形] simple ▶简单 simple II [动] simplify ▶简化 simplify

简报 jiǎnbào [名] briefing ▷要闻简报 news bulletin

简编 jiǎnbiān [名] concise edition

简便 jiǎnbiàn [形] handy

简称 jiǎnchēng [名] abbreviation

简单 jiǎndān [形] 1 (不复杂) simple ▷他头脑简单。He's simple-minded. ▷医生简单地处理了他的伤口。The doctor treated his wound simply. 2 (草率) casual ▷不可用简单的方式对待学生的思想变化。Changes in student attitudes shouldn't be treated lightly. ▷简单从事 treat things casually 3 (平凡) ▷这孩子能说两门外语，真不简单。It is quite

extraordinary that this child can speak two foreign languages.

简短 jiǎnduǎn [形] brief

简化 jiǎnhuà [动] simplify

简洁 jiǎnjié [形] concise

简捷 jiǎnjié [形] direct ▷这种简捷的方法真省时。The direct method really saves time. ▷他说话简捷，从不拐弯抹角。He always gets straight to the point and doesn't beat about the bush.

简介 jiǎnjiè [名] synopsis (PL synopses)

简历 jiǎnlì [名] CV (英), resumé (美)

简练 jiǎnliàn [形] concise

简陋 jiǎnlòu [形] crude

简略 jiǎnlüè [形] brief ▷他说话一贯很简略。What he says is always very sketchy. ▷他简略介绍了公司的情况。He gave a brief description of the situation at the company.

简明 jiǎnmíng [形] concise

简朴 jiǎnpǔ [形] simple ▷她穿着简朴。She dresses simply.

简体字 jiǎntǐzì [名] simplified character

简写 jiǎnxiě [动] abridge

简要 jiǎnyào [形] brief

简易 jiǎnyì [形] simple

简直 jiǎnzhí [副] simply ▷这简直是浪费口舌。This is simply a waste of breath.

简装 jiǎnzhuāng [名] standard edition

碱 jiǎn [名] alkali

见 jiàn I [动] 1 (看到) see (PT saw, PP seen) ▶常见 common ▶罕见 rare ▷我们俩好久没见了。We have not seen each other in a long time. 2 (接触) come into contact with (PT came, PP come) ▷汽油见火就着。Petrol ignites on contact with a flame. 3 (看得出) be visible ▶见效 take effect 4 (参照) see (PT saw, PP seen) ▷见上图 see the above diagram 5 (会见) meet (PT, PP met) ▶接见 receive ▷我下午见校长。I'm meeting the principal this afternoon. II [名] opinion ▶偏见 prejudice III [助动] (书) ▷请见谅。Please excuse me.

见不得 jiàn bu dé [动] 1 (不能接触) be unable to stand exposure to ▷这种细菌见不得光。This type of bacteria can't stand exposure to light. 2 (不能公开) be unmentionable ▷这个政客做了很多见不得人的事。This politician has done a lot of shameful things. 3 (不能忍受) be unable to endure ▷我见不得别人可怜的样子。I can't bear seeing others suffer.

见长 jiàncháng [动] be good at

见地 jiàndì [名] insight ▷这篇文章颇有见

地。This essay is quite insightful.

见多识广 jiàn duō shí guǎng have wide experience

见方 jiànfāng [名] square

见缝插针 jiàn fèng chā zhēn take every opportunity

见怪 jiànguài [动] take offence (英) 或 offense (美) (PT took, PP taken) ▷他说话不得体，请别见怪。He is talking inappropriately – please don't take offence.

见鬼 jiànguǐ [动] 1 (毁灭) go to hell ▷让陈旧的传统观念见鬼去吧！To hell with those old-fashioned ideas! 2 (奇怪) odd

见好 jiànhǎo [动] get better ▷他的病见好了。He is getting better.

见机行事 jiàn jī xíng shì play ... by ear ▷情况复杂，你就见机行事吧。It is a complex situation – you'd better play it by ear.

见解 jiànjiě [名] opinion

见面 jiànmiàn [动] meet (PT, PP met)

见仁见智 jiàn rén jiàn zhì have different opinions

见识 jiànshi I [动] experience II [名] experience ▷增长见识 widen one's experience

见外 jiànwài [形] treat ... as a stranger ▷大家都是朋友，请别见外。We are all friends – please don't stand on ceremony.

见微知著 jiàn wēi zhī zhù recognize telltale signs

见闻 jiànwén [名] information

见习 jiànxí [动] learn on the job ▷见习记者 trainee reporter

见笑 jiànxiào [动] laugh at

见义勇为 jiàn yì yǒng wéi stand up for what is right

见异思迁 jiàn yì sī qiān be fickle

见长 jiànzhǎng [动] shoot up (PT, PP shot)

见证 jiànzhèng I [动] witness II [名] clear proof

见证人 jiànzhèngrén [名] witness

件 jiàn I [量] item ▷一件衣裳 an item of clothing ▷两件事 two things II [名] correspondence ▷急件 urgent letter

间 jiàn I [名] space ▶间隙 interval ▷亲密无间 as thick as thieves II [动] 1 (使分隔) keep apart (PT, PP kept) ▶间隔 separate 2 (使不和) sow discord (PT sowed, PP sown) ▶离间 alienate 3 (使稀少) thin ... out
→另见 jiān

间谍 jiàndié [名] spy

间断 jiànduàn [动] interrupt ▷大雨一夜没有间断。The rain didn't let up all night.

间隔 jiàngé I [名] distance II [动] divide

间或 jiànhuò [副] (书) occasionally

间接 jiànjiē [形] indirect ▷这些经验我是间接得到的。I gained this experience indirectly.

间隙 jiànxì [名] gap ▷他们利用会议间隙到城里逛了逛。They took advantage of a gap between meetings to go into town.

间歇 jiànxiē [名] intermission

饯 jiàn 见下文

饯行 jiànxíng [动] give a farewell dinner (PT gave, PP given)

建 jiàn [动] 1 (建造) build (PT, PP built) ▶扩建 extend 2 (建立) found ▶建国 found a new state 3 (提出) propose ▶建议 propose

建交 jiànjiāo [动] establish diplomatic relations

建立 jiànlì [动] establish ▷两个国家建立了友好关系。The two countries have established friendly relations.

建设 jiànshè [动] build (PT, PP built) ▷建设未来 build for the future

建树 jiànshù [名] contribution ▷他在物理研究方面颇有建树。He has made a significant contribution to physics.

建议 jiànyì [动] propose ▷他建议重新装修办公室。He proposed that we redecorate the office. ▷她提了很多合理的建议。She made a lot of sensible proposals.

建造 jiànzào [动] build (PT, PP built)

建制 jiànzhì [名] system ▷行政建制 administrative system

建筑 jiànzhù I [动] build (PT, PP built) ▷建筑房屋 build houses II [名] building ▷高层建筑 high-rise building ▷建筑工地 building site

建筑师 jiànzhùshī [名] architect

荐 jiàn [动] recommend ▶推荐 recommend ▷推荐信 letter of recommendation

荐举 jiànjǔ [动] recommend

贱 jiàn [形] 1 (便宜) cheap 2 (地位低) lowly ▶贫贱 poor and lowly 3 (卑鄙) contemptible ▶下贱 contemptible

贱民 jiànmín [名] rabble

剑 jiàn [名] sword

剑拔弩张 jiàn bá nǔ zhāng at each other's throats

涧 jiàn [名] gully ▶山涧 mountain stream

健 jiàn I [形] ▶强健 strong and healthy ▶健全 sound II [使强健] 1 (使强健) strengthen ▶健身 keep fit 2 (善于) be good at ▶健谈 be good at small-talk

健步如飞 jiàn bù rú fēi be a good walker

健儿 jiàn'ér [名] good athlete

健将 jiànjiàng [名] great sportsman

健康 jiànkāng [形] healthy ▷奶奶身体很健康。Granny is very healthy. ▷他已经恢复了健康。He's already recovered his health.

健美 jiànměi [形] strong and handsome ▷他体格健美。His physique is very good.

健全 jiànquán [形] sound

健身 jiànshēn [动] keep fit (PT, PP kept) ▷健身运动 fitness activity

健谈 jiàntán [形] glib

健忘 jiànwàng [形] forgetful

健旺 jiànwàng [形] thriving

健在 jiànzài [动] be still alive

健壮 jiànzhuàng [形] robust

舰 jiàn [名] warship ▷巡洋舰 cruiser ▶舰队 fleet ▷航空母舰 aircraft-carrier

舰只 jiànzhī [名] naval vessel

渐 jiàn [副] gradually ▷天气渐暖。The weather is getting warmer.

渐渐 jiànjiàn [副] gradually ▷物价渐渐上涨。Prices are gradually going up.

渐进 jiànjìn [动] advance gradually ▷掌握一门语言是个渐进过程。Mastering a language is a gradual process.

渐入佳境 jiàn rù jiājìng gradually improve

践 jiàn [动] 1 (踩) trample ▶践踏 trample 2 (履行) carry out ▶实践 carry out ▷践约 keep an appointment

践踏 jiàntà [动] trample ▷请勿践踏草地！Keep off the grass!

践约 jiànyuē [动] keep an appointment (PT, PP kept)

毽 jiàn 见下文

毽子 jiànzi [名] shuttlecock

腱 jiàn [名] tendon

溅 jiàn [动] splash

溅落 jiànluò [动] splash down

鉴 jiàn I [动] 1 (照见) reflect ▷水清可鉴。The water is so clear you can see reflections in it. 2 (细看) scrutinize ▶鉴别 distinguish

II [名] warning ▷引以为鉴 take ... as a warning

鉴别 jiànbié [动] distinguish ▷鉴别是非 distinguish between right and wrong

鉴定 jiàndìng [名] appraisal ▷经理对安娜的表现做了客观的鉴定。The manager gave an objective appraisal of Anna's performance.

鉴赏 jiànshǎng [动] appreciate ▷鉴赏艺术作品 appreciate artworks

鉴于 jiànyú [连] ▷鉴于天气不好，我们决定取消比赛。Seeing that the weather was bad, we decided to cancel the competition.

键 jiàn [名] key ▶键盘 keyboard ▷琴键 key

键盘 jiànpán [名] keyboard

箭 jiàn 见下文

箭步 jiànbù [名] big stride

江 jiāng [名] 1 (大河) river 2 (长江) Yangtze

江河日下 jiāng hé rì xià go from bad to worse

江湖 jiānghú [名] rivers and lakes (PL) ▷江湖艺人 itinerant entertainer

江郎才尽 Jiāngláng cái jìn lose one's touch

江山 jiāngshān [名] 1 (江河和山岭) rivers and mountains (PL) 2 (国家) the country

将 jiāng I [副] ▷他将成为一名医生。He is going to become a doctor. II [助] ▷丑闻将传开来。News of the scandal began to spread. ▷他把一本字典扔将过去。He threw over a dictionary. III [动] 1 (下棋用语) check 2 (激) egg ... on IV [介] with ▷将功折罪 atone for a crime with good deeds ▷请将车停在路边。Please stop the car by the side of the road. ▷他将孩子送到了私立学校。He sent the child to a private school.
→另见 jiàng

将错就错 jiāng cuò jiù cuò make the best of a bad situation

将功补过 jiāng gōng bǔ guò atone for a crime with good deeds

将计就计 jiāng jì jiù jì beat someone at their own game

将近 jiāngjìn [动] be approximately ▷这位足球明星的月收入将近3万镑。This football star has a monthly income of approximately £30,000.

将就 jiāngjiu [动] make do with ▷饭菜不好，将就吃吧。The food isn't great, but we'll just have to make do with it.

将军 jiāngjūn I [名] general II [动] challenge

将来 jiānglái [名] future ▷不远的将来，人

类就能消灭艾滋病。In the not-too-distant future, we are going to be able to wipe out AIDS.

将心比心 jiāng xīn bǐ xīn have empathy for

将信将疑 jiāng xìn jiāng yí only half believe

将要 jiāngyào [副] ▷她将要做妈妈了。She is going to be a mother.

姜 jiāng [名] ginger

浆 jiāng I [名] paste ▶纸浆 pulp ▶糖浆 syrup II [动] starch ▶浆洗 starch

僵 jiāng [形] 1 (僵硬) stiff ▷我浑身冻僵了。I'm frozen. 2 (相持不下) deadlocked ▷说话注意点，别把事情弄僵了。Be careful what you say – you don't want to reach a deadlock.

僵持 jiāngchí [动] refuse to budge

僵化 jiānghuà [动] become rigid ▷他思想变得越来越僵化了。He's becoming more and more rigid in the way he thinks.

僵局 jiāngjú [名] deadlock ▷谈判陷入僵局。The talks reached a deadlock.

僵尸 jiāngshī [名] corpse

僵死 jiāngsǐ [动] be dead

僵硬 jiāngyìng [形] stiff ▷计算机前坐久了浑身会僵硬。If you sit in front of a computer a long time you get stiff.

缰 jiāng [名] rein ▶缰绳 rein

疆 jiāng [名] border ▶边疆 frontier

疆场 jiāngchǎng [名] battlefield

疆界 jiāngjiè [名] border

疆土 jiāngtǔ [名] territory

疆域 jiāngyù [名] domain

讲 jiǎng [动] 1 (说) speak (PT spoke, PP spoken) ▷讲英语 speak English 2 (解释) explain ▷他在给我们讲计算机的用法。He is explaining to us how to use the computer. 3 (谈) discuss ▷讲条件 discuss terms 4 (提及) mention ▷讲足球，他可是专家。As for football, he's quite an expert. 5 (讲求) emphasize ▷讲卫生 pay attention to hygiene

讲和 jiǎnghé [动] make peace

讲话 jiǎnghuà [动] 1 (说话) speak (PT spoke, PP spoken) ▷上课不许讲话。No talking in class. 2 (发言) address ▷校长要来给我们讲话。The principal is coming to address us.

讲解 jiǎngjiě [动] explain

讲究 jiǎngjiu I [动] be particular about II [名] art ▷养花大有讲究。Growing flowers is quite an art. III [形] exquisite ▷他穿着一向

讲究。He is always exquisitely dressed.

讲理 jiǎnglǐ [动] be reasonable ▷他这个人不讲理。He is quite unreasonable.

讲排场 jiǎng páichang [动] be ostentatious

讲评 jiǎngpíng [动] critique

讲情 jiǎngqíng [动] intercede ▷她为逃学的儿子向老师讲情。She interceded with the teacher for her son, who'd been playing truant.

讲师 jiǎngshī [名] lecturer

讲授 jiǎngshòu [动] teach (PT, PP taught)

讲述 jiǎngshù [动] relate

讲台 jiǎngtái [名] dais

讲坛 jiǎngtán [名] forum

讲学 jiǎngxué [动] give lectures (PT gave, PT given)

讲演 jiǎngyǎn [动] lecture ▷他的讲演很鼓舞人心。His lectures are inspiring.

讲义 jiǎngyì [名] teaching materials (PL)

讲座 jiǎngzuò [名] course of lectures ▷系列讲座 lecture series

奖 jiǎng I [动] encourage ▶夸奖 praise II [名] award ▶奖品 prize

奖杯 jiǎngbēi [名] cup

奖惩 jiǎngchéng [名] reward and punish

奖金 jiǎngjīn [名] bonus

奖励 jiǎnglì [动] encourage and reward ▷物质奖励 material incentive

奖牌 jiǎngpái [名] medal

奖品 jiǎngpǐn [名] trophy

奖券 jiǎngquàn [名] lottery ticket

奖赏 jiǎngshǎng [动] reward ▷他因科研成果而获得奖赏。He gained an award for his scientific achievements.

奖学金 jiǎngxuéjīn [名] scholarship

奖状 jiǎngzhuàng [名] certificate

桨 jiǎng [名] oar

匠 jiàng [名] 1 (工匠) craftsman (PL craftsmen) ▶木匠 carpenter 2 (书) (名家) master ▶文学巨匠 great literary master

匠人 jiàngrén [名] craftsman (PL craftsmen)

匠心 jiàngxīn [名] (书) craftsmanship

降 jiàng [动] 1 (落下) drop ▶降雪 snow 2 (降低) reduce ▶降价 reduce prices
→另见 xiáng

降低 jiàngdī [动] reduce ▷降低生活开支 reduce living expenses

降格以求 jiàng gé yǐ qiú compromise one's standards

降落 jiàngluò [动] land

降生 jiàngshēng [动] be born

降温 jiàngwēn [动] 1 (变天) cool ▷明天开始降温。It will start getting cooler tomorrow. 2 (缓和) wane ▷暑假结束后，旅游热开始降温。Once the summer vacation is over, interest in travel starts to wane.

将 jiàng [名] 1 (军官) general ▶上将 general 2 (总指挥) commander-in-chief →另见 jiāng

将领 jiànglǐng [名] general

将士 jiàngshì [名] officers and men

绛 jiàng [形] crimson

强 jiàng [形] stubborn ▶倔强 stubborn →另见 qiáng, qiǎng

强嘴 jiàngzuǐ [动] answer ... back

酱 jiàng I [名] 1 (调味品) soya bean (英) 或 soybean (美) paste ▶酱油 soy sauce 2 (糊状食品) paste ▶果酱 jam II [形] ▶酱肘子 knuckle of pork in soy sauce

酱菜 jiàngcài [名] vegetables in soy sauce

酱油 jiàngyóu [名] soy sauce

犟 jiàng [形] obstinate

犟劲 jiàngjìn [名] stubbornness

糨 jiàng [形] thick

糨糊 jiànghu [名] paste

交 jiāo I [动] 1 (交出) hand ... in ▷请按时交作业。Please hand in your homework on time. 2 (付给) pay (PT, PP paid) ▷这个月的房租你交了吗？Have you paid this month's rent? 3 (托付) entrust ▷我要把这事交给他办。I am going to entrust it to him. 4 (交叉) cross ▷她站立不动，双臂交于胸前。She stood still, with her arms crossed in front of her. 5 (结交) associate with ▶交友 make friends 6 (书) (到) arrive at ▷时令已交立冬。It's already the beginning of winter. II [名] 1 (交情) friendship ▷深交 deep friendship 2 (交接处) boundary ▷小镇位于两省之交。The town is situated on the boundary between the two provinces. ▷此时正是秋冬之交。We are just on the cusp between autumn and winter. III [副] ▷风雨交加的夜晚 a night of both wind and rain ▷她小时候过着饥寒交迫的生活。When she was young she experienced both hunger and cold.

交白卷 jiāo báijuàn [动] 1 (指考试) hand in a blank examination paper 2 (喻) ▷到现在还没开始，你想明天交白卷啊？You still haven't even started. You won't have done it by tomorrow, will you?

交班 jiāobān [动] hand over to the next shift

交兵 jiāobīng [动] (书) engage militarily

交叉 jiāochā I [动] 1 (相交) intersect ▷一条公路与铁路在此交叉。A highway and a railway intersect here. 2 (穿插) alternate ▷各种体育活动交叉进行，学生会更感兴趣。If sports activities alternate with each other, students will find it more fun. II [形] overlapping ▷两篇论文有交叉的内容。The two theses overlap in content. ▷交叉学科 interdisciplinary subjects

交差 jiāochāi [动] report ▷工作完不成，我们没办法向上级交差。If we don't finish the work, we'll have nothing to report to management.

交错 jiāocuò [动] (书) crisscross

交代 jiāodài [动] 1 (移交) hand ... over ▷临走前，我已经向一位同事交代了工作。Before I left I handed my work over to a colleague. 2 (说明) explain ▷你要把有关政策交代清楚。You need to explain the relevant policy clearly. 3 (嘱咐) instruct

交底 jiāodǐ [动] lay one's cards on the table (PT, PP laid)

交点 jiāodiǎn [名] intersection ▷这里是两条铁路的交点。This is the intersection of two railway lines.

交锋 jiāofēng [动] 1 (交战) engage in combat 2 (比赛) compete ▷两支足球队将在上海交锋。The two football teams will compete in Shanghai.

交付 jiāofù [动] 1 (交纳) pay (PT, PP paid) ▷房客还没有交付租金。The tenant has not yet paid his rent. 2 (交给) hand ... over ▷交付任务 hand over a task ▷那座新的办公楼即将交付使用。That new office building is about to be made available for use.

交割 jiāogē [动] complete a transaction ▷双方已将每一笔货款交割清楚。The parties have completed payment transactions for the consignments.

交互 jiāohù [副] 1 (一起) together ▷做这项工作需要两种工具交互使用。For this job you need to use the two tools together. 2 (替换) in turn ▷队员们交互上场，免得过度劳累。The players took it in turns to go on, so as not to get too tired. 3 (互相) ▷老师让我们交互批改听写。The teacher asked us to correct each other's dictations.

交换 jiāohuàn [动] exchange ▷毕业前，同学们互相交换礼物。Before graduation, students exchange presents with each other. ▷我和她交换了座位。I swapped my seat with her. ▷农民们正在市场上交换农产品。The farmers trade agricultural produce in the market.

交火 jiāohuǒ [动] engage in battle

交集 jiāojí [动] mix ▷听到这个消息，她悲喜交集。On hearing the news, she had mixed feelings of joy and sorrow.

交际 jiāojì [动] socialize ▷他不善于人交际。He is not good at socializing. ▷语言是重要的交际工具。Language is an important tool for social interaction.

交加 jiāojiā [动] ▷在一个风雪交加的夜晚，他突然出现在村头。On a night of wind and snow, he suddenly appeared in the village.

交接 jiāojiē [动] 1 (连接) ▷现正是春夏交接之际。Now is the time when spring is turning into summer. 2 (移交) hand ... over 3 (结交) associate with ▷她交接的人都是上流社会的。The people she associates with are all upper class.

交界 jiāojiè [动] share a border

交警 jiāojǐng [名] traffic police

交口称誉 jiāo kǒu chēng yù be universally praised

交流 jiāoliú [动] exchange ▷交流学习经验 exchange learning techniques ▷老师就传统教育问题交流了看法。The teachers exchanged views on traditional education.

交配 jiāopèi [动] (动物) mate

交情 jiāoqing [名] friendship

交涉 jiāoshè [动] negotiate ▷关于人质问题，双方已经过多次交涉。The two sides have negotiated several times over the hostage.

交手 jiāoshǒu [动] compete ▷我和他还从未交过手。I've never competed against him.

交谈 jiāotán [动] talk ▷两个好朋友交谈了一整夜。The two friends talked together the whole night.

交替 jiāotì [动] 1 (更换) ▷中国人常在新旧年交替时吃饺子。Chinese people often eat dumplings to see in the New Year. 2 (轮换) alternate ▷工作和休息应交替进行。One should alternate work and relaxation.

交通 jiāotōng [名] 1 (交流的工具) communications (PL) 2 (运输) traffic ▷这个地区的公路交通繁忙而有序。Road traffic in the area is heavy but well-regulated.

交头接耳 jiāo tóu jiē ěr (贬) whisper to each other ▷这俩学生在课堂上老是交头接耳。The two students are always whispering to each other in class.

交往 jiāowǎng [动] have contact ▷他与国际友人交往频繁。He is in frequent contact with international friends. ▷他交往了很多不三不四的朋友。He has relations with a lot of dubious characters. ▷这小伙子不爱交往。This young man is not very sociable. ▷我们与外界的交往日益广泛。Our contact with the outside world is becoming more and more extensive.

交响乐 jiāoxiǎngyuè [名] symphony

交椅 jiāoyǐ [名] 1 (折叠椅) folding chair 2 (喻) (地位) position ▷她在部门坐上了第一把交椅。She occupies the highest position in the department.

交易 jiāoyì I [动] trade ▷他们在交易股票。They are trading shares. ▷新产品开始上市交易。The new products have gone onto the market. ▷电子市场里交易很红火。Trade in the electronics market is flourishing. II [名] transaction ▷一笔划算的交易 a good deal

交谊 jiāoyì [名] (书) friendship

交战 jiāozhàn [动] engage in war

交织 jiāozhī [动] intertwine ▷两棵大树枝叶交织在一起。The branches of the two trees are intertwined. ▷喜悦和伤感交织在一起。Joy is mingled with sadness.

郊 jiāo [名] suburbs (PL) ▶市郊 suburbs (PL) ▶郊外 outskirts (PL) ▷他在北郊买了房子。He bought a house on the northern outskirts of the city.

郊区 jiāoqū [名] suburbs (PL) ▷他住在北京郊区。He lives in the Beijing suburbs.

浇 jiāo [动] 1 (灌溉) irrigate 2 (洒水) water ▷浇花 water the flowers 3 (浸透) soak ▷他被浇了一身雨。He was soaked in the rain. 4 (浇铸) cast (PT, PP cast)

浇灌 jiāoguàn [动] 1 (灌溉) irrigate ▷浇灌土地 irrigate the land ▷浇灌花园 water a garden 2 (灌注) pour ▷他们向墙体内浇灌了混凝土。They poured concrete into the wall frame.

娇 jiāo I [形] 1 (柔嫩) delicate ▷嫩红娇绿 delicate blossoms and leaves 2 (秀美) lovely ▷江山如此多娇。The scenery is so lovely. 3 (娇气) fragile II [动] spoil ▷这个女孩儿被父母娇坏了。The girl has been spoiled by her parents.

娇滴滴 jiāodīdī [形] coy

娇惯 jiāoguàn [动] pamper

娇贵 jiāoguì [形] fragile ▷刚走一小段路就受不了，怎么这么娇贵？Walking just a short distance is too much for you – how come you are so fragile? ▷这个花瓶很娇贵，搬的时候

要小心。This vase is fragile – be careful when you move it.

娇嫩 jiāonèn [形] delicate

娇气 jiāoqì I [形] fragile II [名] fussiness ▷我们要想法去掉这孩子的娇气。We've got to find a way of stopping the child from being so fussy.

娇生惯养 jiāo shēng guàn yǎng be pampered all one's life

娇小玲珑 jiāoxiǎo línglóng exquisite ▷她长得娇小玲珑。She looks exquisite.

娇纵 jiāozòng [动] indulge

姣 jiāo [形] (书) good-looking ▶姣美 beautiful

姣好 jiāohǎo [形] beautiful ▷她相貌姣好, 身材苗条。She has a beautiful face and a slender figure.

骄 jiāo [形] 1 (骄傲) arrogant ▶骄气 arrogance 2 (书) (猛烈) fierce ▷7月的西安, 骄阳似火。In Xi'an in July the sun is incredibly fierce.

骄傲 jiāo'ào I [形] 1 (傲慢) arrogant 2 (自豪) proud II [名] pride ▷5,000年悠久的历史是中国人民的骄傲。Their 5,000 years of history is the pride of the Chinese people.

骄横 jiāohèng [形] overbearing ▷他态度骄横, 让人无法忍受。People can't stand his overbearing attitude.

骄气 jiāoqì [名] arrogance

骄奢淫逸 jiāoshēyínyì dissipated

骄子 jiāozǐ [名] favourite (英) 或 favorite (美) son

胶 jiāo I [名] 1 (黏性物质) glue ▶万能胶 all-purpose glue ▶树胶 resin 2 (橡胶) rubber ▶胶鞋 rubber boots (PL) II [动] glue ▷请把我的皮鞋胶上吧。Could you glue my shoes back together, please.

胶合 jiāohé [动] glue ... together ▷把这两张纸胶合在一起吧。Let's glue these two pieces of paper together.

胶卷 jiāojuǎn [名] film ▷我买了一个彩色胶卷儿。I bought a roll of colour (英) 或 color (美) film.

胶囊 jiāonáng [名] capsule

胶着 jiāozhuó [动] (喻) stalemate

教 jiāo [动] teach (PT, PP taught) ▷他在中学教计算机。He teaches computing in a middle school. ▷我教孩子画画。I teach children drawing.
→另见 jiào

教学 jiāoxué [动] teach (PT, PP taught) ▷他在一个小山村教学。He teaches in a mountain village.

椒 jiāo [名] 1 (胡椒) pepper ▶胡椒 pepper 2 (辣椒) chilli ▶辣椒 chilli

焦 jiāo I [形] 1 (成黄黑色) burnt ▷米饭烧焦了。The rice is burnt. ▷孩子的衣服烤焦了。The child's clothes are scorched. ▷北京烤鸭外焦里嫩。Peking duck is charred on the outside and tender on the inside. 2 (喻) (干) dry ▷她说得口焦舌燥。She spoke until her mouth was parched. 3 (着急) agitated ▶心焦 feel agitated II [名] coke

焦点 jiāodiǎn [名] 1 (物) focal point ▶主焦点 main focus 2 (喻) (关键) focus ▷选课问题成了同学们议论的焦点。The problem of choosing courses has become a focus of discussion among the students. ▷她光彩夺目, 成了晚会的焦点。She was stunningly beautiful and became the focus of attention at the party.

焦急 jiāojí [形] anxious ▷她为母亲的健康而感到焦急。She's anxious about her mother's health. ▷她焦急地等待着丈夫归来。She waited anxiously for her husband to return.

焦距 jiāojù [名] (物) focal length

焦虑 jiāolù [形] anxious

焦头烂额 jiāo tóu làn é be in a terrible way

焦躁 jiāozào [形] restless

焦灼 jiāozhuó [形] (书) anxious

跤 jiāo [名] fall ▶摔跤 fall down

蕉 jiāo [名] banana ▶香蕉 banana

礁 jiāo [名] reef

礁石 jiāoshí [名] reef

嚼 jiáo [动] chew
→另见 jué

角 jiǎo [名] 1 (指动物) horn ▶羊角 ram's horn 2 (军号) bugle 3 (数) angle ▶直角 right angle 4 (角落) corner ▶墙角 corner of a wall
→另见 jué

角度 jiǎodù [名] 1 (数) angle 2 (视角) point of view ▷从不同角度分析 analyze from different points of view ▷我们可以从多个角度来看待这个问题。We must look at this problem from different angles.

角落 jiǎoluò [名] corner ▷屋子的角落里挂了很多蜘蛛网。There were a lot of spider webs in the corner of the room.

侥 jiǎo 见下文

侥幸 jiǎoxìng [形] lucky ▷对考试不要心存

侥幸. In exams you shouldn't put your faith in luck.

佼 jiǎo [形] (书) beautiful

佼佼 jiǎojiǎo [形] (书) outstanding ▷佼佼者 outstanding figure

狡 jiǎo [形] cunning ▶狡计 crafty trick

狡辩 jiǎobiàn [动] use specious arguments

狡猾 jiǎohuá [形] cunning

狡诈 jiǎozhà [形] deceitful

饺 jiǎo [名] Chinese dumpling ▶水饺儿 Chinese dumpling

绞 jiǎo [动] 1 (扭) twist 2 (勒死) hang (PT, PP hanged) ▶绞死 hang

绞杀 jiǎoshā [动] hang

绞刑 jiǎoxíng [名] hanging

铰 jiǎo [动] cut (PT, PP cut) ▷这张纸太大, 用 剪子铰一下. This piece of paper is too big, so let's cut it down with the scissors.

矫 jiǎo I [动] correct ▶矫正 correct ▷他现已 痛矫前非. He's cleaned up his act now. II [形] strong

矫健 jiǎojiàn [形] vigorous

矫揉造作 jiǎo róu zào zuò forced ▷那个演 员的表演矫揉造作. That actor's performance was very forced. ▷她矫揉造作的姿态令人反 感. Her affected manners are off-putting.

矫枉过正 jiǎo wǎng guò zhèng overcompensate ▷因超重而节食固然不 错, 但如果矫枉过正, 就会造成营养不良. It's good to go on a diet if you're overweight. But if you go too far you'll end up malnourished.

矫正 jiǎozhèng [动] correct ▷你应该好好矫 正一下发音. You really should correct your pronunciation.

皎 jiǎo [形] bright ▶皎月 bright moon

皎洁 jiǎojié [形] bright

脚 jiǎo [名] 1 (指人、动物) foot (PL feet) ▶脚印 footprint 2 (指物体) base ▶墙脚 base of a wall ▶山脚 foot of a mountain

脚本 jiǎoběn [名] script ▷电视剧脚本 television script

脚步 jiǎobù [名] 1 (步伐) step ▷重重的脚步声 the sound of heavy footsteps 2 (速度) pace

脚镣 jiǎoliào [名] shackles (PL)

脚踏两只船 jiǎo tà liǎng zhī chuán (喻) (贬) sit on the fence

脚踏实地 jiǎo tà shídì keep one's feet on the ground ▷我们要脚踏实地地工作. It's important to have a down-to-earth attitude towards work.

脚注 jiǎozhù [名] footnote

搅 jiǎo [动] 1 (搅拌) stir ▷把汤搅匀了再喝. Stir the soup before drinking it. 2 (混杂) mix ▷不 要把这两件事搅在一块儿. Don't mix these two things. 3 (搅扰) disturb ▷噪音搅得我 无法入睡. The noise disturbed me so much I couldn't sleep.

搅拌 jiǎobàn [动] stir ▷他往咖啡里加了点 糖, 搅拌了一下. He put some sugar in the coffee and stirred it. ▷把饺子馅儿搅拌均 匀. Mix the dumpling filling until smooth.

搅和 jiǎohuo [动] 1 (混合) mix ▷别把这两种 东西搅和在一起. Don't mix these two things together 2 (扰乱) mess...up ▷这件事全让你 给搅和了! You've completely messed it up!

缴 jiǎo [动] 1 (交纳) pay (PT, PP paid) ▷缴租金 pay the rent 2 (收缴) seize

缴获 jiǎohuò [动] seize

叫 jiào I [动] 1 (喊叫) shout ▷他们听到这个 好消息都叫了起来. When they heard the good news they shouted for joy. 2 (招呼) call ▷他被人叫出去了. Somebody called him outside. 3 (菜、车) order ▶叫菜 order food ▶叫车 order a cab 4 (称为) be called ▷洛杉 矶又叫天使之城. Los Angeles is also called the City of Angels. ▷你叫什么名字? What's your name? 5 (吩咐) order ▷大夫叫他卧床休 息. The doctor ordered him to stay in bed and rest. 6 (叫牌) bid (PT, PP bid) ▷他叫3个黑桃. He bid three spades. II [形] male ▶叫驴 male donkey III [介] by ▷词典叫汤姆拿走了. The dictionary was taken away by Tom.

叫喊 jiàohǎn [动] yell

叫花子 jiàohuāzi [名] beggar

叫唤 jiàohuan [动] cry out

叫苦 jiàokǔ [动] moan

叫骂 jiàomà [动] hurl abuse

叫卖 jiàomài [动] peddle

叫牌 jiàopái [动] bid (PT, PP bid)

叫屈 jiàoqū [动] complain of unfair treatment

叫嚷 jiàorǎng [动] shout

叫嚣 jiàoxiāo [动] yell

叫座 jiàozuò [动] attract a crowd ▷这部电 影很叫座. This show has pulled in quite an audience.

叫做 jiàozuò [动] be called

觉 jiào [名] sleep ▷希望你睡个好觉。I hope you'll have a good sleep.
→另见 jué

校 jiào [动] check
→另见 xiào
校订 jiàodìng [动] check
校对 jiàoduì I [动] proofread II [名] proofreader
校勘 jiàokān [动] cross-check
校样 jiàoyàng [名] proofs (PL)

轿 jiào [名] sedan chair
轿车 jiàochē [名] car
轿子 jiàozi [名] sedan chair

较 jiào [动] 1 (比较) compare ▶较量 test one's strength 2 (书) (计较) dispute
较劲儿 jiàojìnr [动] be competitive ▷不大的事，你较什么劲！It's not that important. Why be so competitive?
较量 jiàoliàng [动] 1 (竞争) compete ▷我们无法和他们较量。There's no way we can compete with them. 2 (计较) dispute
较真儿 jiàozhēnr [形] serious ▷什么事情你不要太较真儿。You shouldn't take everything so seriously.

教 jiào I [动] teach (PT, PP taught) ▶教导 instruct II [名] religion ▶信教 be religious
→另见 jiāo
教材 jiàocái [名] teaching materials (PL)
教程 jiàochéng [名] course
教导 jiàodǎo [动] instruct
教皇 jiàohuáng [名] the Pope
教会 jiàohuì [名] the Church
教诲 jiàohuì [名] teaching
教具 jiàojù [名] teaching aid
教科书 jiàokēshū [名] textbook
教练 jiàoliàn [名] coach
教师 jiàoshī [名] teacher ▷家庭教师 home tutor
教室 jiàoshì [名] classroom
教授 jiàoshòu I [名] professor II [动] lecture in ▷教授法学 lecture in Law
教唆 jiàosuō [动] incite
教堂 jiàotáng [名] church
教条 jiàotiáo [名] doctrine
教徒 jiàotú [名] disciple
教学 jiàoxué [名] 1 (知识传授) teaching 2 (教与学) teaching and study

教训 jiàoxun I [名] lesson ▷我从这件事中吸取了教训。I drew lessons from this. II [动] teach ... a lesson (PT, PP taught)
教养 jiàoyǎng [动] 1 (教育培养) bring ... up (PT, PP brought) ▷这孩子很有教养。The child is well brought-up. 2 (感化) reform
教益 jiàoyì [名] benefit
教育 jiàoyù I [名] education II [动] educate ▷要教育青少年遵纪守法。We must educate young people to obey the law.
教育部 jiàoyùbù [名] the Ministry of Education
教员 jiàoyuán [名] teacher

窖 jiào I [名] cellar II [动] store ... in a cellar
窖藏 jiàocáng [动] store ... in a cellar

酵 jiào [动] ferment
酵母 jiàomǔ [名] yeast

节 jiē 见下文
→另见 jié
节骨眼 jiēguyǎn [名] crucial moment

阶 jiē [名] 1 (台阶) step 2 (官阶) rank
阶层 jiēcéng [名] stratum (PL strata)
阶段 jiēduàn [名] stage ▷工程第一阶段已经完工。The first stage of the project has already been completed.
阶级 jiējí [名] class ▷有产阶级 the propertied class
阶梯 jiētī [名] 1 (梯子) ladder 2 (楼梯) flight of stairs
阶下囚 jiēxiàqiú [名] prisoner

疖 jiē [名] boil

皆 jiē [副] all ▷这个消息人人皆知。Everyone knows all about it.
皆大欢喜 jiē dà huān xǐ everyone's happy

结 jiē [动] bear (PT bore, PP borne) ▶结果 bear fruit
→另见 jié
结巴 jiēba [动] stutter
结实 jiēshi [形] 1 (坚固耐用) sturdy 2 (健壮) strong ▷我儿子体格结实。My son has a strong build.

接 jiē [动] 1 (靠近) draw near (PT drew, PP drawn) ▶接近 be close to 2 (连接) connect ▷接电线 connect a cable 3 (托住) catch (PT, PP caught) ▷接球 catch a ball 4 (接收) receive ▷接到一封信 receive a letter ▷接电话 answer the phone 5 (迎接) meet (PT, PP met) ▷去火车

站接人 meet someone at the station **6** (接替) take over (PT took, PP taken) ▷接工作 take over a job

接班 jiēbān [动] come on shift (PT came, PP come)

接触 jiēchù [动] **1** (交往) come into contact with (PT came, PP come) **2** (冲突) clash **3** (遇到) encounter

接待 jiēdài [动] receive

接二连三 jiē èr lián sān one after another ▷他接二连三来信叫我去他那里过圣诞节。 He sent one letter after another asking me to spend Christmas at his place.

接风 jiēfēng [动] hold a welcoming dinner (PT, PP held)

接管 jiēguǎn [动] take over (PT took, PP taken)

接轨 jiēguǐ [动] be brought into line with

接火 jiēhuǒ [动] **1** (射击) exchange fire **2** (接电) connect ▷照明设备安装好了，就等接火。The lights have been installed. We're just waiting for them to be connected.

接济 jiējì [动] support

接见 jiējiàn [动] have an interview with

接近 jiējìn I [动] approach II [形] approachable

接口 jiēkǒu [名] (计算机的) interface

接力 jiēlì [动] relay ▷接力赛跑 relay race

接连 jiēlián [副] in a row ▷雨接连下了3天。It rained for three days in a row.

接纳 jiēnà [动] **1** (接受) admit ▷我被俱乐部接纳为会员。I was admitted as a member of the club. **2** (采纳) accept ▷他的建议被大家所接纳。His proposal was accepted by everyone.

接洽 jiēqià [动] take up a matter with (PT took, PP taken) ▷我们将与有关部门接洽。We are taking the matter up with the relevant department.

接任 jiērèn [动] take over (PT took, PP taken)

接生 jiēshēng [动] deliver

接收 jiēshōu [动] **1** (收受) receive **2** (接管) take over (PT took, PP taken) **3** (接纳) admit ▷我们俱乐部准备接收一批新会员。Our club is getting ready to admit a new group of members.

接手 jiēshǒu [动] take over (PT took, PP taken)

接受 jiēshòu [动] accept

接替 jiētì [动] replace ▷他将接替原来的大使。He's replacing the former ambassador.

接头 jiētóu [动] **1** (连接) link up ▷两颗卫星要在太空中接头了。The two satellites will link up with one another in space. **2** (联系) contact ▷我明天和他接头。I'll contact him tomorrow.

接吻 jiēwěn [动] kiss

接应 jiēyìng [动] **1** (配合) back ... up ▷你们先干，随后我们接应。You go first, we'll act as backup. **2** (供应) supply ▷药品暂时接应不上。There's a temporary shortage of medical supplies.

接着 jiēzhe [动] **1** (用手接) catch (PT, PP caught) ▷给你一个桃子，接着！Here's a peach for you – catch! **2** (紧跟着) follow

接踵而来 jiēzhǒng ér lái a constant stream of people ▷到这里旅游的人接踵而来。There's a constant stream of tourists here.

秸 jiē [名] straw

揭 jiē [动] **1** (取下) take ... down (PT took, PP taken) ▷把墙上的画揭下来。Take the picture down from the wall. **2** (拿起) pick ... up **3** (揭露) reveal

揭穿 jiēchuān [动] expose

揭发 jiēfā [动] expose

揭竿而起 jiē gān ér qǐ rise up in arms

揭露 jiēlù [动] reveal

揭幕 jiēmù [动] unveil

揭示 jiēshì [动] **1** (发布) announce **2** (使人领会) reveal

揭晓 jiēxiǎo [动] announce

嗟 jiē [动] (书) sigh

嗟来之食 jiē lái zhī shí handouts

街 jiē [名] **1** (街道) street **2** (方) (集市) market

街道 jiēdào [名] **1** (马路) street **2** (社区) neighbourhood (英), neighborhood (美)

街坊 jiēfang [名] (口) neighbour (英), neighbor (美)

街谈巷议 jiē tán xiàng yì the talk of the town

街头巷尾 jiē tóu xiàng wěi all over town

孑 jié [形] solitary

孑然 jiérán [形] alone ▷他孑然一身。He's all alone in the world.

节 jié I [名] **1** (连接处) joint **2** (段落) paragraph **3** (节日) festival ▶圣诞节 Christmas **4** (事项) item ▶细节 details (PL) **5** (节操) moral fibre (英) 或 fiber (美) ▶气节 integrity II [动] **1** (节约) save **2** (删节) abridge III [量] ▷3节课 three classes ▷一节管子 a length of pipe
→另见 jiè

节哀 jié'āi [动] overcome one's grief (PT overcame, PP overcome)

节操 jiécāo [名] integrity

节俭 jiéjiǎn [形] frugal

节令 jiélìng [名] seasonal changes (PL) ▷吃穿跟着节令走。What we eat and wear depends on what festival it is.

节目 jiémù [名] programme (英), program (美)

节拍 jiépāi [名] beat

节气 jiéqì [名] solar term

节日 jiérì [名] festival

节省 jiéshěng [动] conserve

节外生枝 jié wài shēng zhī complicate matters ▷眼看问题就要解决了，没想到又节外生枝。We were just about to solve the problem. We hadn't imagined that there would be additional complications.

节衣缩食 jié yī suō shí scrimp and save

节余 jiéyú [名] saving

节育 jiéyù [动] practise (英) 或 practice (美) birth control

节约 jiéyuē [动] save

节制 jiézhì [动] 1 (控制) control 2 (指挥) command

节奏 jiézòu [名] rhythm

劫 jié [动] 1 (抢劫) rob ▶打劫 take ... by force 2 (胁迫) coerce ▶劫持 hijack

劫持 jiéchí [动] hijack

劫富济贫 jié fù jì pín rob the rich to give to the poor

劫后余生 jié hòu yúshēng have a close brush with death

劫机 jiéjī [动] hijack a plane

杰 jié I [名] hero (PL heroes) ▶豪杰 hero II [形] outstanding ▶杰作 masterpiece

诘 jié [动] question ... closely ▶反诘 refute

诘问 jiéwèn [动] interrogate

拮 jié 见下文

拮据 jiéjū [形] hard-up ▷他手头拮据。He's pretty hard-up.

洁 jié I [形] clean ▶整洁 clean and tidy II [动] clean

洁白 jiébái [形] pure white

洁净 jiéjìng [形] clean

洁具 jiéjù [名] cleaning materials (PL)

洁身自好 jié shēn zì hào maintain one's moral integrity

结 jié I [动] 1 (编织) tie ▶结网 weave a net 2 (结合) unite ▷两国结为联盟。The two countries formed an alliance. 3 (凝聚) freeze (PT froze, PP frozen) ▶结冰 ice up 4 (了结) settle up ▶结账 settle up II [名] 1 (绳扣) knot ▶活结 slip-knot 2 (字据) written undertaking 3 (生理) node

→另见 jiē

结案 jié'àn [动] close a case

结拜 jiébài [动] swear friendship (PT swore, PP sworn) ▷结拜兄弟 blood brothers

结伴 jiébàn [动] form groups ▷结伴而行 go in groups

结冰 jiébīng [动] ice over

结仇 jiéchóu [动] become enemies (PT became, PP become)

结党营私 jié dǎng yíng sī form a conspiracy

结发夫妻 jiéfà fūqī couple married for the first time

结构 jiégòu [名] composition ▷产品结构 composition of a product

结果 jiéguǒ I [名] result ▷结果出人预料。The result was unexpected. II [副] in the end ▷结果，他赢了比赛。In the end, he won the contest.

结合 jiéhé [动] 1 (联系) combine ▷劳逸结合 strike a balance between work and play 2 (结为夫妇) become husband and wife (PT became, PT become)

结婚 jiéhūn [动] get married ▷她和一位富商结了婚。She married a rich businessman. ▷这对夫妇结婚30多年了。This couple have been married for over thirty years.

结交 jiéjiāo [动] associate with

结晶 jiéjīng I [动] crystallize II [名] 1 (晶体) crystal 2 (成果) crystallization

结局 jiéjú [名] outcome

结论 jiélùn [名] conclusion ▷得出结论 come to a conclusion

结盟 jiéméng [动] align ▷不结盟政策 policy of non-alignment

结亲 jiéqīn [动] become related through marriage (PT became, PP become) ▷两家最近结亲了。The two families have recently become related through marriage.

结社 jiéshè [动] form an association

结识 jiéshí [动] become acquainted with (PT became, PP become)

结束 jiéshù [动] end

结算 jiésuàn [动] settle up ▷你先付账，事后我们再结算。You pay the bill, and we can settle up later.

结尾 jiéwěi [名] ending

结业 jiéyè [动] finish ▷两个月的学习班即将结业。The two-month course is about to finish.

结账 jiézhàng [动] settle up ▷饭菜我来结账。Let me pay for the meal.

桀 Jié 见下文

桀骜不驯 jié'ào bù xún stubborn and intractable

捷 jié I [形] quick ▶敏捷 nimble II [名] victory

捷报 jiébào [名] news of victory

捷径 jiéjìng [名] short cut ▷这是去公园的捷径。This is the short cut to the park. ▷他在工作上总想走捷径。He always tries to take short cuts in his work.

捷足先登 jié zú xiān dēng the early bird catches the worm

睫 jié [名] eyelash

截 jié I [动] 1 (切断) chop 2 (阻拦) block II [量] piece ▷一截木头 a piece of wood ▷半截粉笔 half a stick of chalk

截长补短 jié cháng bǔ duǎn use one's strengths to compensate for one's shortcomings

截断 jiéduàn [动] 1 (切断) cut ... off (PT, PP cut) 2 (打断) interrupt

截获 jiéhuò [动] intercept

截流 jiéliú [动] dam

截取 jiéqǔ [动] cut ... out (PT, PP cut)

截然 jiérán [副] completely ▷截然不同 completely different

截止 jiézhǐ [动] be over ▷报名已经截止了。Registration is already over.

竭 jié [动] use ... up

竭诚 jiéchéng [副] wholeheartedly

竭尽 jiéjìn [动] exert ▷他们竭尽全力完成了这项任务。They really pulled out all the stops to get the task finished.

竭力 jiélì [动] do one's utmost

竭泽而渔 jié zé ér yú kill the goose that lays the golden eggs

姐 jiě [名] elder sister

姐妹 jiěmèi [名] sisters (PL)

解 jiě [动] 1 (分开) divide ▶解剖 dissect 2 (解开) untie ▶解鞋带 untie one's shoelaces 3 (解除) relieve ▶解热 allay a fever 4 (解答) answer ▶解题 solve a problem 5 (理解) understand ▷令人不解 confusing

→另见 jiè

解除 jiěchú [动] get rid of ▷解除痛苦 get rid of suffering ▷解除婚约 break off one's engagement

解答 jiědá [动] answer

解冻 jiědòng [动] 1 (融化) thaw 2 (解除冻结) unfreeze (PT unfroze, PP unfrozen) 3 (喻) (缓和关系) thaw

解放 jiěfàng [动] liberate ▷妇女解放运动 the women's liberation movement

解雇 jiěgù [动] dismiss

解救 jiějiù [动] rescue

解决 jiějué [动] 1 (处理) resolve ▷解决问题 resolve a problem 2 (消灭) annihilate

解闷 jiěmèn [动] relieve the boredom

解囊相助 jiě náng xiāng zhù be generous to those in need ▷当他人遇到困难的时候，我们应该慷慨解囊。When others are in difficulties, we should be generous to them.

解聘 jiěpìn [动] dismiss ▷解聘某人的职务 dismiss someone from their job

解剖 jiěpōu [动] dissect

解气 jiěqì [动] let off steam (PT, PP let)

解散 jiěsàn [动] 1 (散开) disperse 2 (取消) dissolve

解释 jiěshì [动] explain

解手 jiěshǒu [动] relieve oneself

解说 jiěshuō [动] explain

解体 jiětǐ [动] disintegrate

解脱 jiětuō [动] 1 (摆脱) break away from (PT broke, PP broken) ▷他终于从逆境中解脱出来了。He finally extricated himself from the predicament. 2 (开脱) explain ... away ▷不要为自己的过失解脱。Don't go explaining away your mistakes.

解围 jiěwéi [动] 1 (解除包围) break a siege (PT broke, PP broken) 2 (摆脱窘境) save ... blushes ▷他们提拿我，你该帮我解围。If they tease me you'll have to save my blushes.

介 jiè I [动] be situated between ▷这个湖介于两座山之间。The lake is situated between the two mountains. II [形] upstanding ▶耿介 principled

介词 jiècí [名] preposition

介入 jièrù [动] intervene ▷我们不该介入他们夫妻间的争吵。We really shouldn't intervene in their marital strife.

介绍 jièshào [动] 1 (使相识) introduce ▷自我介绍 introduce oneself ▷我把妻子介绍给了同事。I introduced my wife to my colleagues. 2 (推荐) sponsor 3 (使了解) give an introduction to (PT gave, PP given) ▷导游向我们介绍了当地的风土人情。The guide gave us an introduction to local customs and culture.

介意 jièyì [动] mind ▷我打开窗户你介意吗？ Do you mind if I open the window?

戒 jiè I [动] 1 (防备) guard against 2 (戒除) give up (PT gave, PP given) ▶戒烟 give up smoking II [名] 1 (警告) warning 2 (戒律) religious discipline 3 (戒指) ring

戒备 jièbèi [动] be on the alert

戒除 jièchú [动] give up (PT gave, PP given)

戒毒 jièdú [动] come off drugs (PT came, PP come)

戒律 jièlǜ [名] religious tenets (PL)

戒严 jièyán [动] impose martial law ▷宣布戒严 declare martial law

戒指 jièzhi [名] ring

芥 jiè 见下文

芥菜 jiècài [名] mustard leaf (PL leaves)

届 jiè I [动] fall due (PT fell, PP fallen) ▶届期 at the appointed time II [量] ▷82届毕业生 the class of '82 ▷第九届人代会 the Ninth People's Congress

届时 jièshí [动] ▷届时请您光临。 When the time comes, do come and have a look around.

界 jiè [名] 1 (界限) boundary ▷国界 national boundaries (PL) 2 (阶层) circles (PL) ▷各界人士 people from all walks of life ▷新闻界 media circles 3 (范围) range ▷大开眼界 broaden one's horizons 4 (类别) category ▷动物界 the animal kingdom

界定 jièdìng [动] demarcate

界面 jièmiàn [名] interface

界限 jièxiàn [名] 1 (分界) dividing line 2 (限度) limits (PL)

界线 jièxiàn [名] 1 (边界) boundary 2 (分界线) dividing line

疥 jiè [名] scabies

诫 jiè I [动] warn ▶告诫 warn II [名] religious tenets (PL)

借 jiè [动] 1 (借入) borrow ▷我从图书馆借了几本书。 I borrowed some books from the library. 2 (借出) lend (PT, PP lent) ▷请把词典借我用一下。 Please can you lend me your dictionary a moment? 3 (假托) use ... as a means of ▷这家公司借广告欺骗消费者。 The company uses advertising as a means of cheating consumers. 4 (凭借) make use of ▷我借此机会向大家表示感谢。 May I take this opportunity to express my thanks to all of you.

借词 jiècí [名] loan word

借贷 jièdài I [动] 1 (借入) borrow money 2 (借出) lend money (PT, PP lent) II [名] debtors and creditors (PL)

借刀杀人 jiè dāo shā rén get others to do one's dirty work

借端 jièduān [动] use ... as a pretext

借故 jiègù [动] make an excuse

借光 jièguāng [动] (谦) excuse me

借鉴 jièjiàn [动] learn from ▷借鉴别人的经验 learn from other people's experiences

借酒浇愁 jiè jiǔ jiāo chóu drown one's sorrows

借据 jièjù [名] IOU

借口 jièkǒu I [动] use ... as an excuse ▷他借口有事不来上班。 He used the fact that he had things to do as an excuse not to go to work. II [名] excuse ▷他企图找借口为自己辩护。 He tried to find an excuse to justify himself.

借尸还魂 jiè shī huán hún come back in a new form

借题发挥 jiè tí fāhuī use an excuse to hold forth

借助 jièzhù [动] enlist the help of

解 jiè [动] escort
→另见 jiě

解送 jièsòng [动] escort

巾 jīn [名] cloth ▶毛巾 towel

巾帼 jīnguó [名] (书) women (PL)

斤 jīn [量] unit of weight, equal to 500 grams

斤斤计较 jīnjīn jìjiào quibble over every detail

今 jīn I [形] 1 (现在的) present 2 (当前的) current II [名] today ▷今明两天都可以来。 Come today or tomorrow, as you wish.

今后 jīnhòu [副] from now on

今年 jīnnián [名] this year ▷今年年底我父亲就要退休了。 My father will retire at the end of this year. ▷今年夏天他大学就要毕业了。 He graduates from university this summer.

今日 jīnrì [名] today ▷今日气温偏高。 It's pretty hot today.

今世 jīnshì [名] this life ▷今生今世我都不会忘记父母的恩情。 I will remember my parents' kindness for the rest of my life.

今天 jīntiān [名] today ▷今天是我的生日。 Today's my birthday. ▷今天我想去看场戏。 I want to go and see a play today.

今朝 jīnzhāo [名] today

金 jīn I [名] 1 (化) gold 2 (金属) metal ▶五金 hardware 3 (钱) money ▷奖金 prize money II [形] golden ▷金发 blonde hair

金榜 jīnbǎng [名] roll of honour (英) 或 honor (美)

金碧辉煌 jīnbì-huīhuáng magnificent

金蝉脱壳 jīnchán tuō qiào make a cunning getaway

金额 jīn'é [名] sum

金刚石 jīngāngshí [名] diamond

金黄 jīnhuáng [形] golden

金婚 jīnhūn [名] golden wedding

金科玉律 jīn kē yù lù golden rule

金口玉言 jīnkǒu-yùyán pearls of wisdom

金牌 jīnpái [名] gold medal

金钱 jīnqián [名] money

金秋 jīnqiū [名] autumn (英), fall (美)

金融 jīnróng [名] finance ▷金融行业 the financial sector

金属 jīnshǔ [名] metal

金丝猴 jīnsīhóu [名] golden monkey

金玉良言 jīnyù liángyán words of wisdom

金枝玉叶 jīn zhī yù yè aristocrat

金子 jīnzi [名] gold

金字塔 jīnzìtǎ [名] pyramid

津 jīn [名] 1 (津液) saliva 2 (汗) sweat 3 (渡口) ferry

津津乐道 jīnjīn lè dào talk with great enthusiasm ▷不要对别人的隐私津津乐道。 Don't talk about other people's private business with such enthusiasm.

津津有味 jīnjīn yǒu wèi with great enjoyment

津贴 jīntiē [名] subsidy

矜 jīn I [动] have pity on ▶矜恤 pity II [形] 1 (自大) egotistical ▶骄矜 self-important 2 (拘谨) reserved

矜持 jīnchí [形] reserved

筋 jīn [名] 1 (肌腱) tendon 2 (肌肉) muscle ▶筋骨 physique 3 (口) (静脉血管) vein ▶青筋 blue vein 4 (像筋的东西) ▶橡皮筋 rubber band

筋道 jīndao [形] (方) chewy

筋斗 jīndǒu [名] (方) somersault

筋骨 jīngǔ [名] physique

筋疲力尽 jīn pí lì jìn dog-tired

筋肉 jīnròu [名] muscle

禁 jīn [动] 1 (禁受) endure 2 (忍住) restrain 3 (耐) bear (PT bore, PP borne)
→另见 jìn

禁受 jīnshòu [动] stand (PT, PP stood) ▷我们的友谊禁受了时间的考验。Our friendship has stood the test of time.

襟 jīn [名] 1 (上衣前面) front ▶衣襟 shirt front 2 (连襟) brother-in-law (PL brothers-in-law) 3 (胸怀) mind ▷胸襟广阔 broad-minded

襟怀 jīnhuái [名] mind

仅 jǐn [副] only ▷此书仅存一本。We only keep one copy of this book.

仅仅 jǐnjǐn [副] just ▷我们的工作才仅仅开始。Our work has only just begun.

尽 jǐn I [副] 1 (尽量) as far as possible ▶尽快 as early as possible 2 (最) most ▷尽东边 the most easterly point ▷尽底下 the very bottom 3 (表示继续) constantly ▷这些天尽下两了。It's been raining non-stop for the last few days. II [动] 1 (不超过) take no more than (PT took, PP taken) ▷我们准备尽着4天把工作做完。We're planning to take no more than four days over this work. 2 (考虑在先) give priority to (PT gave, PP given) ▷他爱尽旧衣服穿。He likes wearing old clothes.
→另见 jìn

尽管 jǐnguǎn I [副] without reserve ▷有话尽管说。If there's something you'd like to say please don't hold back. II [连] even though ▷尽管在下大雨，他还是要出去。Even though it was pouring with rain, he still wanted to go out.

尽量 jǐnliàng [副] to the best of one's ability ▷你尽量早点来。Do your best to come a bit earlier.

尽早 jǐnzǎo [副] as soon as possible ▷有消息，我会尽早通知你。As soon as I have news I will contact you.

紧 jǐn I [形] 1 (不松) tight 2 (牢固) secure 3 (接近) close 4 (急迫) pressing 5 (严格) strict 6 (拮据) short of money II [动] tighten

紧巴巴 jǐnbābā [形] 1 (不松) tight 2 (拮据) hard-up

紧凑 jǐncòu [形] tight ▷日程安排得很紧凑。We're on a very tight schedule.

紧急 jǐnjí [形] urgent

紧密 jǐnmì [形] 1 (密切的) close 2 (密集的) dense

紧迫 jǐnpò [形] pressing

紧俏 jǐnqiào [形] in demand ▷紧俏商品 products in demand

紧缩 jǐnsuō [动] cut down on (PT, PP cut)

紧要 jǐnyào [形] crucial

紧张 jǐnzhāng [形] 1 (激烈) intense 2 (不安) nervous 3 (不足) in short supply ▷最近药品比较紧张。Recently, the demand for medicines has exceeded the supply.

锦 jǐn I [名] brocade II [形] glorious

锦标 jǐnbiāo [名] prize ▷锦标赛 championship

锦缎 jǐnduàn [名] brocade

锦囊妙计 jǐnnáng miàojì a masterplan

锦上添花 jǐn shàng tiān huā improve on perfection

锦绣 jǐnxiù [形] splendid

谨 jǐn [副] 1 (谨慎地) warily 2 (郑重地) solemnly

谨慎 jǐnshèn [形] wary

谨小慎微 jǐn xiǎo shèn wēi over-cautious

谨严 jǐnyán [形] meticulous

尽 jìn I [动] 1 (完) exhaust ▷我已经想尽了办法。I've exhausted all my ideas. 2 (达到极限) go to extremes (PT went, PP gone) ▷山穷水尽 at the end of one's tether 3 (充分发挥) use ... to the full ▷人尽其才 everyone uses their talents to the full 4 (努力完成) strive to accomplish (PT strove, PP striven) ▷尽职尽责 strive to fulfil one's professional responsibilities II [形] complete ▷尽人皆知 be common knowledge ▷尽收眼底 have a grandstand view →另见 jǐn

尽瘁 jìncuì [动] drive oneself to the brink of exhaustion (PT drove, PP driven)

尽力 jìnlì [动] try one's hardest ▷我们会尽力完成。We'll try our hardest to get the job done.

尽量 jǐnliàng [动] do all one can ▷我尽量不麻烦别人。I do all I can to avoid annoying other people.

尽情 jìnqíng [副] to one's heart's content ▷尽情享受 enjoy oneself to one's heart's content

尽善尽美 jìn shàn jìn měi flawless

尽头 jìntóu [名] end

尽心 jìnxīn [动] put one's heart and soul into (PT, PP put) ▷医护人员要尽心尽力抢救病人。Medical workers should put their hearts and souls into saving their patients.

尽心竭力 jìnxīn-jiélì give one's all ▷在工作上，他尽心竭力。He gave his all to the job.

尽兴 jìnxìng [副] to one's heart's content ▷大家尽兴玩吧！Have a wonderful time, everybody!

尽责 jìnzé [动] meet all one's obligations (PT, PP met)

尽职 jìnzhí [动] fulfil (英) 或 fulfill (美) one's duty

进 jìn [动] 1 (前进) advance 2 (进入) enter ▷进城 go to town 3 (接纳) bring ... in (PT, PP brought) ▷进货 stock up 4 (吃食) eat (PT ate, PP eaten) ▷他滴水不进。Not even a drop of water passed his lips. 5 (呈上) submit 6 (攻进) enter ▷进球 score a goal

进逼 jìnbī [动] press on

进补 jìnbǔ [动] pep ... up ▷喝鸡汤可进补。Drinking chicken soup can pep you up.

进步 jìnbù I [动] improve II [形] advanced

进程 jìnchéng [名] progression

进度 jìndù [名] 1 (进行速度) pace 2 (工作计划) schedule

进而 jìn'ér [连] then ▷首先我们得先测试产品，进而再推广。First we have to test the product, and then we have to promote it.

进发 jìnfā [动] set out for (PT, PP set)

进犯 jìnfàn [动] invade

进攻 jìngōng [动] attack

进贡 jìngòng [动] offer tribute

进化 jìnhuà [动] evolve ▷人类的进化 human evolution

进货 jìnhuò [动] stock up

进军 jìnjūn [动] advance ▷中国正在向现代化进军。China is advancing towards modernization.

进口 jìnkǒu [动] import

进取 jìnqǔ [动] forge ahead ▷进取精神 ambition

进入 jìnrù [动] 1 (走进) enter 2 (到了) reach 3 (到位) get inside ▷进入角色 get inside a role

进退 jìntuì [动] advance and retreat

进退维谷 jìn tuì wéi gǔ on the horns of a dilemma

进项 jìnxiang [名] income

进行 jìnxíng [动] carry ... out ▷我们正在进行改革。We're carrying out reforms. ▷会议正在进行。The meeting is in progress.

进行曲 jìnxíngqǔ [名] march

进修 jìnxiū [动] take a refresher course (PT took, PP taken)

进展 jìnzhǎn [动] make progress

近 jìn [形] 1 (不远) near ▷这两所大学离得很近。The two universities are very near one another. ▷近日 recently 2 (接近) close ▷平易近人 approachable 3 (亲近) close to ▷近邻 family and neighbours (英) 或 neighbors (美)

近代 jìndài [名] modern times (PL)

近乎 jìnhu I [动] be little short of ▷你不及格的可能性近乎为零。The chances of you failing this exam are little short of zero. II [形]

intimate

近况 jìnkuàng [名] the latest ▷你知道史蒂芬的近况吗? Have you heard the latest about Stephen?

近来 jìnlái [副] recently

近亲 jìnqīn [动] be closely related ▷近亲不能结婚。Close relatives cannot marry.

近视 jìnshì [形] short-sighted (英), near-sighted (美)

近水楼台 jìn shuǐ lóu tái be favourably (英) 或 favorably (美) situated

近似 jìnsì [形] similar ▷两种物质很近似。The two types of material are very similar.

劲 jìn [名] 1 (力气) strength 2 (情绪) spirit 3 (态度) manner 4 (趣味) fun
→另见 jìng

劲头 jìntóu [名] energy

晋 jìn [动] call on

晋级 jìnjí [动] be promoted

晋见 jìnjiàn [动] have an audience with

晋升 jìnshēng [动] promote ▷学院将他晋升为教授。The college promoted him to a professorship.

烬 jìn [名] ash

浸 jìn [动] 1 (浸泡) soak 2 (渗入) soak through ▷汗水把她的衣服浸透了。Sweat soaked through her clothes.

浸礼 jìnlǐ [名] (基督教的) baptism

浸没 jìnmò [动] immerse

浸透 jìntòu [动] drench ▷他浑身被雨水浸透了。He got drenched to the bone.

禁 jìn I [动] 1 (禁止) forbid (PT forbade, PP forbidden) ▷严禁赌博。Gambling is forbidden. 2 (监禁) imprison ▶禁闭 lock ... up II [名] taboo
→另见 jīn

禁闭 jìnbì [动] lock ... up

禁地 jìndì [名] restricted area

禁锢 jìngù [动] 1 (关押) imprison 2 (束缚) fetter

禁忌 jìnjì I [名] taboo II [动] avoid

禁令 jìnlìng [名] ban ▷政府已经解除了对这部电影的禁令。The government has lifted the ban on the film.

禁区 jìnqū [名] restricted area

禁止 jìnzhǐ [动] forbid (PT forbade, PP forbidden)

觐 jìn [动] have an audience with

觐见 jìnjiàn [动] have an audience with

噤 jìn [动] 1 (不说话) keep silent (PT, PP kept) 2 (哆嗦) shiver

噤若寒蝉 jìn ruò hán chán keep one's mouth shut

茎 jīng [名] 1 (指植物) stem 2 (茎状物) ▷刀茎 handle of a knife

京 jīng [名] 1 (首都) capital 2 (北京) Beijing

京城 jīngchéng [名] capital

京剧 jīngjù [名] Beijing opera

京腔 jīngqiāng [名] Beijing accent

泾 jīng 见下文

泾渭分明 Jīng Wèi fēnmíng entirely different

经 jīng I [名] 1 (经线) warp ▶经纱 warp 2 (指中医) channels (PL) 3 (经度) longitude 4 (经典) scripture ▶佛经 Buddhist sutra II [动] 1 (经营) run (PT ran, PP run) ▷经商 be in business 2 (经受) endure ▷她经得起折腾。She can endure suffering. 3 (经过) ▷这文章经老师一解释,我们都理解了。Once the article had been explained by the teacher, we all understood it. ▷途经西安 go via Xi'an III [形] regular ▶经常 often

经办 jīngbàn [动] handle

经常 jīngcháng I [形] day-to-day ▷经常开支 day-to-day costs II [副] often ▷我经常出差。I often go on business trips.

经典 jīngdiǎn [名] classics (PL) ▷经典著作 classical works

经度 jīngdù [名] longitude

经费 jīngfèi [名] funds (PL)

经管 jīngguǎn [动] be in charge of ▷他经管这个项目。He's in charge of this project. ▷招聘会计由我经管。Recruiting accountants is my responsibility.

经过 jīngguò I [动] 1 (通过) pass ▷这路公共汽车经过我家。This bus passes by my home. ▷我们将经过王子街。We'll go along Prince's Street. 2 (延续) ▷经过3年的恋爱,他们终于结婚了。Having been together for three years, they finally got married. 3 (经历) ▷企业经过裁员缩减了经费开支。Business expenditure was reduced through staff cutbacks. II [名] course ▷事情发生的经过 the course of events

经纪 jīngjì I [动] (管理) manage II [名] broker

经纪人 jīngjìrén [名] broker

经济 jīngjì I [名] 1 (社会生产关系) economy ▷国民经济 national economy ▷经济发展 economic development 2 (个人财政状况) financial situation ▷他家经济条件好。

His family are well-off. ▷经济拮据 hard-up

II [形] 1 (有关国民经济) economic ▷经济作物 cash crop 2 (实惠) economical ▷经济舱 economy-class cabin

经济危机 jīngjì wēijī [名] economic crisis

经济学 jīngjìxué [名] economics (SG)

经久 jīngjiǔ [形] 1 (时间长) prolonged 2 (耐久) durable

经理 jīnglǐ [名] manager

经历 jīnglì [动] experience ▷成长经历 the experience of growing up

经贸 jīngmào [名] economy and trade ▷经贸关系 economic and trade relations

经商 jīngshāng [动] be in business

经手 jīngshǒu [动] handle

经手人 jīngshǒurén [名] ▷她是这个案件的经手人。She's handling this case.

经受 jīngshòu [动] experience ▷经受折磨 experience suffering ▷经受打击 sustain an attack

经销 jīngxiāo [动] deal in (PT, PP dealt) ▷经销商 dealer

经验 jīngyàn [名] experience ▷丰富的教学经验 rich teaching experience ▷交流经验 exchange experiences

经营 jīngyíng [动] 1 (管理) run (PT ran, PP run) ▷经营一个小牧场 run a small farm ▷经营地产开发 manage a property business ▷企业经营管理 business management 2 (组织) organize an art exhibition 3 (销售) deal in (PT, PP dealt) ▷该店经营各类摄影器材。This shop deals in all sorts of photography equipment.

经传 jīngzhuàn [名] classics (PL)

荆 jīng 见下文

荆棘 jīngjí [名] 1 (字) brambles (PL) 2 (喻) difficulties (PL)

菁 jīng 见下文

菁华 jīnghuá [名] cream ▷社会的菁华 the cream of society

惊 jīng [动] 1 (紧张) start 2 (惊动) startle ▷打草惊蛇 alert the enemy

惊诧 jīngchà [动] be amazed ▷他工作效率之高让我惊诧。I was amazed at his efficiency. ▷她脸上现出惊诧的神色。A look of amazement appeared on her face.

惊动 jīngdòng [动] 1 (震动) alarm 2 (打扰) disturb

惊慌 jīnghuāng [形] scared ▷惊慌失措 be scared out of one's wits

惊厥 jīngjué [动] faint from fear

惊恐 jīngkǒng [形] terrified ▷惊恐失色 turn pale with terror

惊奇 jīngqí [形] surprised

惊人 jīngrén [形] amazing

惊世骇俗 jīng shì hài sú astounding

惊叹号 jīngtànhào [名] exclamation mark (英) 或 point (美)

惊涛骇浪 jīng tāo hài làng stormy seas (PL)

惊天动地 jīng tiān dòng dì earth-shattering

惊喜 jīngxǐ [动] be pleasantly surprised

惊险 jīngxiǎn [形] thrilling

惊心动魄 jīng xīn dòng pò horrifying

惊讶 jīngyà [形] astonished ▷听到这个消息后他感到很惊讶。He was astonished to hear the news.

晶 jīng I [形] sparkling II [名] crystal

晶体 jīngtǐ [名] crystal

晶莹 jīngyíng [形] sparkling and translucent

睛 jīng [名] eyeball ▷目不转睛 stare fixedly

兢 jīng 见下文

兢兢业业 jīngjīngyèyè meticulous ▷她工作兢兢业业。She works meticulously.

精 jīng I [形] 1 (经挑选的) refined ▶精兵 crack troops 2 (完美) excellent 3 (细密) precise ▷精打细算 careful budgeting 4 (心细) sharp ▷精明 shrewd 5 (精通) skilled ▷精于书法 be good at calligraphy II [名] 1 (精华) essence ▶酒精 alcohol 2 (精力) energy ▷聚精会神 focus all one's energies on 3 (精子) sperm 4 (妖) demon III [副] (方) extremely

精彩 jīngcǎi [形] wonderful

精粹 jīngcuì [形] succinct

精打细算 jīng dǎ xì suàn budget carefully

精当 jīngdàng [形] precise

精干 jīnggàn [形] competent

精光 jīngguāng [形] ▷她饿极了，把饭菜吃了个精光。She was so hungry, she cleaned her plate. ▷电影票卖得精光。Tickets for the film are all sold out.

精华 jīnghuá [名] cream

精力 jīnglì [名] energy

精练 jīngliàn [形] succinct

精炼 jīngliàn I [动] refine II [形] succinct

精良 jīngliáng [形] excellent

精灵 jīnglíng [名] 1 (鬼怪) spirit 2 (指人) clever thing

精美 jīngměi [形] exquisite

精密 jīngmì [形] accurate ▷ 精密仪器 precision instrument

精明 jīngmíng [形] shrewd

精疲力竭 jīng pí lì jié completely worn out

精辟 jīngpì [形] penetrating

精品 jīngpǐn [名] quality goods (PL) ▷ 精品书店 quality bookshop ▷ 民间艺术精品 fine pieces of folk art

精巧 jīngqiǎo [形] exquisite

精确 jīngquè [形] precise ▷ 这篇论文对海外市场作了精确的分析。This essay gives a thorough analysis of overseas markets.

精锐 jīngruì [形] crack ▷ 精锐部队 crack troops

精深 jīngshēn [形] profound

精神 jīngshén [名] 1 (主观世界) mind ▷ 精神负担 a load on one's mind ▷ 精神病 mental illness 2 (宗旨) gist ▷ 把握文件精神 get the gist of a document

精神 jīngshen I [名] energy II [形] energetic

精神文明 jīngshén wénmíng [名] intellectual and ideological development

精髓 jīngsuǐ [名] (喻) essence

精通 jīngtōng [动] be proficient in

精细 jīngxì [形] fine

精心 jīngxīn [形] meticulous ▷ 精心策划的阴谋 a meticulously planned plot

精选 jīngxuǎn [动] select ... carefully

精益求精 jīng yì qiú jīng always striving to improve

精英 jīngyīng [名] elite ▷ 信息技术行业的精英 the elite of the IT industry

精湛 jīngzhàn [形] exquisite

精致 jīngzhì [形] delicate

精装 jīngzhuāng [形] (指书) hard-back

精子 jīngzǐ [名] sperm

鲸 jīng [名] whale

鲸吞 jīngtūn [动] swallow up

井 jǐng I [名] 1 (用于取水) well 2 (井状物) ▷ 天井 skylight ▷ 矿井 mine shaft II [形] neat

井底之蛙 jǐng dǐ zhī wā person with limited vision

井井有条 jǐngjǐng yǒu tiáo in perfect order

井然 jǐngrán [形] orderly

阱 jǐng [名] trap

颈 jǐng [名] neck

景 jǐng I [名] 1 (风景) scenery 2 (情形) situation ▶ 背景 background 3 (布景) scene ▶ 外景 outdoor scene II [动] admire

景点 jǐngdiǎn [名] scenic spot

景观 jǐngguān [名] scenery

景况 jǐngkuàng [名] situation ▷ 他景况很不如意。His situation is not at all to his liking. ▷ 生活景况 living conditions

景气 jǐngqì I [名] boom II [形] booming

景色 jǐngsè [名] scenery

景物 jǐngwù [名] scenery

景象 jǐngxiàng [名] scene

景致 jǐngzhì [名] scenery

警 jǐng I [形] alert ▶ 警惕 on the alert II [动] 1 (使警觉) warn 2 (戒备) be on the alert III [名] 1 (危急) alarm ▶ 报警 raise the alarm 2 (警察) police ▶ 巡警 an officer on the beat

警报 jǐngbào [名] alarm

警备 jǐngbèi [动] guard

警察 jǐngchá [名] police ▷ 便衣警察 plain-clothes police

警告 jǐnggào [动] warn ▷ 警察鸣枪警告。The police fired a warning shot.

警戒 jǐngjiè [动] 1 (告诫) warn 2 (防备) guard ▷ 放松警戒 let one's guard down ▷ 采取警戒措施 take precautionary measures

警句 jǐngjù [名] epigram

警觉 jǐngjué [名] vigilance ▷ 保持警觉 maintain vigilance ▷ 一人出门在外必须提高警觉。Anyone going out alone should be extra vigilant.

警力 jǐnglì [名] police force ▷ 每天有4000警力上街巡逻。Every day 4,000 police patrol the streets.

警示 jǐngshì [名] warning

警惕 jǐngtì [动] watch out for

警卫 jǐngwèi [名] guard

警钟 jǐngzhōng [名] alarm bell

劲 jìng [形] powerful
→ 另见 jìn

劲敌 jìngdí [名] formidable opponent

径 jìng I [名] 1 (小路) path 2 (方法) way ▶ 捷径 short cut 3 (直径) diameter ▶ 半径 radius II [副] directly ▷ 径自 without letting anyone know

径赛 jìngsài [名] track event

径自 jìngzì [副] without consultation ▷ 我决定径自到她家走一趟。Without asking I decided to pay her a visit at home.

净 jìng I [形] 1 (干净) clean 2 (光) all gone ▷ 钱花净了。The money is all gone. 3 (纯) net

II [副] only ▷啥都不干，净吹牛 all talk and no action

净化 jìnghuà [动] purify

净值 jìngzhí [名] net value

净重 jìngzhòng [名] net weight

胫 jìng [名] shin

痉 jìng 见下文

痉挛 jìngluán [动] convulse

竞 jìng [动] compete

竞技 jìngjì [名] sports (PL)

竞赛 jìngsài [名] competition

竞相 jìngxiāng [动] compete

竞选 jìngxuǎn [动] run for (PT ran, PP run) ▷竞选总统 run for president

竞争 jìngzhēng [动] compete ▷竞争上岗 compete for a job

竟 jìng **I** [动] finish ▷未竟之业 unfinished task **II** [副] **1** (终于) in the end ▷有志者事竟成。Where there's a will there's a way. **2** (竟然) actually ▷谁也没想到，他竟发这么大的火。Who would have thought he would actually get this angry.

竟然 jìngrán [副] unexpectedly ▷玛莉竟然放弃事业，甘当家庭妇女。Mary unexpectedly gave up her career and became a housewife. ▷走到半路上竟然下起雨来。They were halfway down the road when, to their surprise, it began to rain.

敬 jìng **I** [动] **1** (尊重) respect **2** (恭敬地给) offer **II** [形] respectful

敬爱 jìng'ài [动] revere

敬而远之 jìng ér yuǎn zhī keep away from

敬酒 jìngjiǔ [动] propose a toast ▷主席举杯向来宾们敬酒。The chairman proposed a toast to the guests.

敬礼 jìnglǐ [动] salute

敬佩 jìngpèi [动] admire

敬畏 jìngwèi [动] be in awe of

敬仰 jìngyǎng [动] revere ▷令人敬仰的作家 a revered author

敬业 jìngyè [动] be committed to one's work

敬意 jìngyì [名] tribute ▷我们对奋战在第一线的护士表示崇高的敬意。We paid tribute to the nurses who worked on the front line.

敬重 jìngzhòng [动] have high regard for ▷他深受同事敬重。He is highly regarded by those who have worked with him.

静 jìng [形] **1** (不动) still **2** (无声) quiet

静电 jìngdiàn [名] static electricity

静脉 jìngmài [名] vein

静悄悄 jìngqiāoqiāo [形] very quiet

静态 jìngtài [名] static state

静物 jìngwù [名] still life

静止 jìngzhǐ [动] be still

静坐 jìngzuò [动] **1** (指气功) meditate **2** (指抗议) stage a sit-in

境 jìng [名] **1** (边界) border ▶国境 border **2** (地方) place ▶仙境 fairyland **3** (景况) situation ▶困境 predicament

境地 jìngdì [名] (地步) situation

境界 jìngjiè [名] **1** (界限) boundary **2** (程度) level

境况 jìngkuàng [名] condition

境遇 jìngyù [名] circumstances (PL)

镜 jìng [名] **1** (镜子) mirror **2** (光学器具) lens ▶眼镜 glasses ▶望远镜 telescope

镜头 jìngtóu [名] **1** (指装置) camera lens **2** (照相画面) shot **3** (指一系列画面) take

镜子 jìngzi [名] mirror

迥 jiǒng [形] (书) (相差大) completely different

迥然 jiǒngrán [形] completely different

炯 jiǒng 见下文

炯炯 jiǒngjiǒng [形] bright

窘 jiǒng [形] **1** (穷困) hard-up **2** (为难) embarrassed

窘况 jiǒngkuàng [名] difficult situation

窘迫 jiǒngpò [形] **1** (穷困) very poor **2** (为难) embarrassed

窘态 jiǒngtài [名] embarrassment ▷在记者的追问下，总统面露窘态。Under questioning from the journalist, the president looked embarrassed.

纠 jiū [动] **1** (缠绕) entangle **2** (集合) assemble **3** (督察) supervise **4** (改正) correct

纠察 jiūchá **I** [动] maintain order **II** [名] steward

纠缠 jiūchán [动] **1** (绕在一起) entangle ▷他们两人的关系纠缠不清。Their relationship is very complicated. **2** (找麻烦) hassle

纠纷 jiūfēn [名] dispute

纠葛 jiūgé [名] dispute

纠合 jiūhé [动] (贬) gang up ▷当地的毒贩纠合起来走私海洛因。The local drug traffickers worked together on a heroin smuggling operation.

纠正 jiūzhèng [动] correct

究 jiū I [动] investigate ▶深究 investigate thoroughly II [副] actually

究竟 jiūjìng I [名] outcome II [副] actually ▷究竟发生了什么事？What actually happened?

赳 jiū 见下文

赳赳 jiūjiū [形] valiant

阄 jiū [名] lot ▶抓阄 draw lots

揪 jiū [动] seize

揪辫子 jiū biànzi (喻) have a hold over

揪心 jiūxīn [动] worry ▷用不着揪心，他会应付的。No need to worry – he can cope.

九 jiǔ [数] 1 (指数字) nine 2 (表示多数或多次) ▷九死一生 have a narrow escape

九牛二虎之力 jiǔ niú èr hǔ zhī lì (喻) enormous effort ▷我费了九牛二虎之力将冰箱运回家。I bust a gut to get the fridge home.

九牛一毛 jiǔ niú yī máo a drop in the ocean

九泉 jiǔquán [名] the underworld ▷含笑九泉 rest happy in one's grave

九死一生 jiǔ sǐ yī shēng have a narrow escape

九霄云外 jiǔ xiāo yún wài far away ▷他早把誓言抛到了九霄云外。He has long since forgotten his promise.

久 jiǔ [形] 1 (时间长) long ▶恒久 permanent ▷久别重逢 be reunited after a long time apart 2 (时间长短) long ▷回家住了多久？How long did you go home for?

久而久之 jiǔ ér jiǔ zhī over time

久久 jiǔjiǔ [形] ▷精彩表演使观众久久不愿离去。The performance was so good that for a long time the audience didn't want to leave.

久违 jiǔwéi [动] (客套) ▷聚会上有许多久违的老友。There were loads of old friends at the party that we hadn't seen for ages. ▷久违了！近来还好吗？Long time no see! Have you been well?

久仰 jiǔyǎng [动] (客套) ▷久仰大名，幸会幸会！I'm delighted to have the opportunity to meet you at last!

久远 jiǔyuǎn [形] remote ▷久远的历史 remote history

玖 jiǔ [数] nine

韭 jiǔ 见下文

韭菜 jiǔcài [名] chive

酒 jiǔ [名] alcohol ▶葡萄酒 wine ▶敬酒 propose a toast ▶啤酒 beer ▶酒鬼 wino

酒店 jiǔdiàn [名] 1 (酒馆) bar 2 (宾馆) hotel

酒会 jiǔhuì [名] party ▶鸡尾酒会 cocktail party

酒家 jiǔjiā [名] (饭馆) restaurant

酒精 jiǔjīng [名] alcohol

酒量 jiǔliàng [名] alcohol tolerance ▷他酒量大，喝七八杯没问题。He can hold his drink well – he drinks seven or eight glasses without a problem.

酒令 jiǔlìng [名] drinking game

酒楼 jiǔlóu [名] restaurant

酒肉朋友 jiǔròu péngyǒu [名] fair-weather friend

酒窝 jiǔwō [名] dimple

酒席 jiǔxí [名] feast

旧 jiù I [形] 1 (过时) old ▷旧观念 old-fashioned idea 2 (陈旧) used ▷旧衣服 used clothes II [名] old friend

旧地 jiùdì [名] familiar place

旧观 jiùguān [名] old look

旧交 jiùjiāo [名] old friend

旧居 jiùjū [名] former residence

旧历 jiùlì [名] lunar calendar

旧情 jiùqíng [名] old friendship

旧式 jiùshì [形] old-style

咎 jiù I [名] blame ▷引咎辞职 take the blame and resign II [动] blame ▷既往不咎 let bygones be bygones

咎由自取 jiù yóu zì qǔ only have oneself to blame

疚 jiù [动] (书) be remorseful ▶内疚 have a guilty conscience

厩 jiù [名] barn

救 jiù [动] save ▶呼救 cry for help ▶救灾 provide disaster relief

救国 jiùguó [动] save the nation

救护 jiùhù [动] give first-aid (PT gave, PP given) ▷救护伤员 give first-aid to the wounded

救护车 jiùhùchē [名] ambulance

救荒 jiùhuāng [动] send relief (PT, PP sent)

救济 jiùjì [动] provide relief ▷救济灾民 provide relief to disaster victims

救命 jiùmìng [动] save a life ▷他救了我的命。

He saved my life. ▷救命啊！Help!

救生 jiùshēng [动] save a life ▶救生员 lifeguard

救世主 jiùshìzhǔ [名] the Saviour

救死扶伤 jiù sǐ fú shāng save the dying and nurse the wounded

救亡 jiùwáng [动] save a nation

救星 jiùxīng [名] saviour

救援 jiùyuán [动] go to the rescue (PT went, PP gone) ▷救援小组 rescue team ▷救援灾区 bring relief to a disaster area

救灾 jiùzāi [动] 1 (救济灾民) provide disaster relief 2 (消除灾害) perform a clean-up operation

就 jiù I [动] 1 (靠近) move close to ▷避重就轻 evade serious issues and dwell on the trivial 2 (开始) take ... up (PT took, PP taken) ▷就职 take up a position 3 (完成) accomplish 4 (趁) take the opportunity (PT took, PP taken) ▷等你看完了这本书，就手把读后感写完吧。You should write the review as soon as you've finished reading the book. 5 (搭配着吃) eat ... with (PT ate, PP eaten) ▷泡菜就稀粥 eat pickles with rice congee II [副] 1 (强调时间短) shortly ▷请稍等，我这就做完。Wait a moment, I'll be finished shortly. 2 (早已) already ▷他清晨5点就起床了。He was already up at five in the morning. 3 (表示紧接着) as soon as ▷我一回家就打电话给你。I'll call you as soon as I get home. 4 (表示条件关系) then ▷用功点就能考出好成绩。If you put in a bit of work then you'll get good exam results. 5 (强调数量多) as much as ▷他一个月写两篇文章，我一星期就写3篇。He writes two articles a month. I write as many as three a week. ▷那么多行李他一人就拎走了。He carried all that luggage by himself. 6 (仅仅) only ▷就他一人没来。He was the only one who didn't come. 7 (原本) already ▷我就知道他喜欢撒谎。I already knew he liked to tell lies. ▷裤子本来就小，洗了后更小。The trousers were already small, and after washing them they got even smaller. 8 (表示坚决) simply ▷我就不信完成不了任务。I simply don't believe I can't finish the job. 9 (强调事实) exactly ▷这里就是我童年生活过的地方。This is exactly the place where I spent my childhood. 10 (表示容忍) even though ▷衬衫难看就难看些吧，因为便宜，我就买了。Even though the shirt wasn't that nice, I bought it because it was cheap. III [连] even if ▷你就不来，我也无所谓。Even if you don't come, I really don't care. IV [介] on ▷就贸易争端进行了会谈 hold talks on trade disputes

就便 jiùbiàn [副] in passing ▷你来学校时，请就便到我办公室来一下。When you come to school, please visit my office at your convenience.

就餐 jiùcān [动] dine

就此 jiùcǐ [副] at this point ▷今天的课就此结束。We'll conclude today's class here.

就地 jiùdì [副] on the spot

就读 jiùdú [动] study ▷就读于清华大学历史系 study at Qinghua University's history department

就范 jiùfàn [动] give in (PT gave, PP given)

就近 jiùjìn [副] nearby

就寝 jiùqǐn [动] go to bed (PT went, PP gone)

就任 jiùrèn [动] take up a post (PT took, PP taken) ▷就任市长一职 take up the post of mayor

就事论事 jiù shì lùn shì confine oneself to the facts

就是 jiùshì I [副] 1 (表示赞同) exactly ▷"他索价太高。""就是！""He's asking too much."-"Exactly!" 2 (表示坚决) still ▷无论大家怎么解释，他就是不相信。No matter what everyone said, he still didn't believe them. 3 (表示强调) really ▷东立就是聪明。Dong Li is really clever. 4 (确定范围) only ▷他挺聪明的，就是不够勤勉。He's very clever, only he doesn't work hard enough. II [助] ▷我一定准时到。你放心就是了。I will definitely arrive on time – just stop worrying! ▷你干就是了，没人说你。Just go ahead and do it – no one will blame you! III [连] even if ▷你就是再努力，也没人理你。Even if you try harder, people still won't pay attention to you.

就手 jiùshǒu [副] on the way ▷出门时就手关灯。Can you turn off the lights on your way out?

就算 jiùsuàn [连] even if ▷就算你不去参加会议也没关系。Even if you don't attend the conference, it is not a problem.

就位 jiùwèi [动] be in place

就绪 jiùxù [动] be in order ▷爆破准备就绪。Preparations for the demolition are all in order.

就业 jiùyè [动] get a job ▷就业指导 careers advice ▷就业服务中心 job centre (英) 或 center (美) ▷帮助下岗工人再就业 help those laid off to find a new job

就医 jiùyī [动] go to the doctor (PT went, PP gone)

就义 jiùyì [动] die a martyr

就诊 jiùzhěn [动] see a doctor (PT saw, PP seen)

就职 jiùzhí [动] take office (PT took, PP taken) ▷新总统宣誓就职。The new president was sworn into office.

就座 jiùzuò [动] take one's seat (PT took, PP taken) ▷双方就座后，谈判就开始了。After the two sides took their seats, the talks began. ▷大型会议室能容纳500余人就座。The large conference hall can seat more than 500 people.

舅 jiù [名] 1 (舅父) uncle 2 (妻的弟兄) brother-in-law (PL brothers-in-law)

　舅舅 jiùjiu [名] uncle
　舅子 jiùzi [名] brother-in-law (PL brothers-in-law)

拘 jū I [动] 1 (逮捕) arrest 2 (拘束) restrain ▷无拘无束 free and easy 3 (拘泥) be small-minded ▷王教授是个不拘小节的人。Professor Wang isn't the type to worry about little things.

　拘捕 jūbǔ [动] arrest
　拘谨 jūjǐn [形] overcautious
　拘留 jūliú [动] detain
　拘拿 jūná [动] arrest
　拘泥 jūnì [动] stick rigidly to (PT, PP stuck)
　拘束 jūshù I [动] restrain ▷少一份拘束多一份积极 a little less restraint and a little more action II [形] restrained
　拘押 jūyā [动] take ... into custody (PT took, PP taken)

狙 jū [动] (书) watch for
　狙击 jūjī [动] snipe ▷狙击手 sniper

居 jū I [动] 1 (住) live 2 (是) be (PT was, PP been) ▷居全国第一 be number one in the country 3 (任) claim ▷居功 claim the credit 4 (积累) store ... up II [名] house

　居安思危 jū ān sī wēi be prepared for danger in times of peace
　居多 jūduō [动] be in the majority ▷这个商场里本地货居多。The majority of the goods in the store are local. ▷相册里黑白照片居多。Most of the photos in the album are black and white.
　居高临下 jū gāo lín xià occupy a commanding position
　居家 jūjiā [动] run a household (PT ran, PP run) ▷居家过日，以俭为本。In order to run an efficient household, you have to be thrifty. ▷居家生活 domestic life
　居民 jūmín [名] resident
　居然 jūrán [副] unexpectedly ▷他考试居然敢做弊！No one would have expected him to cheat in his exam.
　居室 jūshì [名] room

居心 jūxīn [动] ▷居心不良 harbour (英) 或 harbor (美) bad intentions
居心叵测 jū xīn pǒ cè have ulterior motives
居住 jūzhù [动] live

驹 jū [名] 1 (好马) fine horse 2 (驹子) foal

掬 jū [动] hold ... in both hands (PT, PP held)

鞠 jū [动] (书) bow
　鞠躬 jūgōng [动] bow
　鞠躬尽瘁 jūgōng jìn cuì devote oneself entirely to

局 jú I [名] 1 (棋盘) chessboard 2 (次) game ▶平局 a draw 3 (形势) situation ▶时局 current political situation 4 (聚会) gathering ▶赌局 gambling party ▶饭局 dinner party 5 (圈套) ruse ▶骗局 fraud 6 (部分) part 7 (机关部门) department 8 (业务机构) office 9 (商店) shop II [量] ▷我赢了这局棋。I won the chess game. ▷下一局比赛明天进行。The next match is taking place tomorrow.

　局部 júbù [名] part ▷局部麻醉 local anaesthetic (英) 或 anesthetic (美)
　局促 júcù [形] 1 (拘谨) inhibited 2 (狭小) cramped
　局面 júmiàn [名] situation ▷打破电信垄断局面 break the telecommunications monopoly
　局势 júshì [名] situation
　局限 júxiàn [动] limit
　局限性 júxiànxìng [名] limitation
　局域网 júyùwǎng [名] local area network

菊 jú [名] chrysanthemum

橘 jú [名] tangerine

咀 jǔ [动] chew
　咀嚼 jǔjué [动] 1 (嚼) chew 2 (体会) mull ... over

沮 jǔ [形] depressed
　沮丧 jǔsàng [形] depressed

矩 jǔ [名] 1 (曲尺) square 2 (规则) regulation
　矩形 jǔxíng [名] rectangle

举 jǔ I [动] 1 (往上托) raise ▶举重 weightlifting 2 (兴起) mobilize ▶举兵 dispatch troops 3 (选举) elect 4 (提出) cite ▶举例 cite an example II [名] act III [形] (书) whole

　▌请勿混淆 raise 和 rise。raise 是及物动词，其后通常要跟宾语，而 rise 是不及物动词，其后通常不跟宾语。rise 不能用在被动语态中。...the government's decision to raise prices...The number of people affected is likely to rise. raise 和 rise 都能够用作名词，表示加薪；raise 用于美式英语中，而 rise 用在英式英语中。Millions of Americans get a pay raise today...Last year she got a rise of 12 per cent.

举办 jǔbàn [动] hold (PT, PP held)

举报 jǔbào [动] report

举措 jǔcuò [名] measure

举动 jǔdòng [名] action

举国 jǔguó [名] the whole country

举荐 jǔjiàn [动] recommend

举例 jǔlì [动] give an example (PT gave, PP given) ▷举例说明 illustrate with examples

举目无亲 jǔmù wú qīn be a stranger in a strange land

举棋不定 jǔ qí bù dìng dither

举世 jǔshì [名] the whole world ▷举世闻名 world-famous ▷举世无双 unrivalled

举手之劳 jǔ shǒu zhī láo no trouble at all ▷ "谢谢你开车送我回家。" "不客气。举手之劳。" "Thanks for driving me home." – "You're welcome – it was no trouble at all."

举行 jǔxíng [动] hold (PT, PP held) ▷举行会议 hold a meeting

举一反三 jǔ yī fǎn sān extrapolate information

举止 jǔzhǐ [名] conduct

举足轻重 jǔ zú qīng zhòng play a key role

龃 jǔ 见下文

龃龉 jǔyǔ [动] (书) (喻) disagree

巨 jù [形] huge ▶巨著 monumental work ▶艰巨 onerous

巨大 jùdà [形] huge

巨额 jù'é [名] enormous amounts (PL)

巨匠 jùjiàng [名] (书) giant

巨人 jùrén [名] giant

巨头 jùtóu [名] tycoon

巨子 jùzǐ [名] giant ▷媒体巨子 media giant

句 jù I [名] sentence II [量] ▷说几句话 say a few words ▷写两句诗 write two lines of verse

句法 jùfǎ [名] 1 (句子结构) sentence structure 2 (语言法学) syntax

句号 jùhào [名] full stop (英), period (美)

句型 jùxíng [名] sentence pattern

句子 jùzi [名] sentence

拒 jù [动] 1 (抵抗) resist 2 (拒绝) refuse

拒捕 jùbǔ [动] resist arrest

拒绝 jùjué [动] refuse ▷他拒绝签合同。He refused to sign the contract. ▷婉言拒绝邀请 turn down an invitation

具 jù I [动] have (PT, PP had) ▷初具规模 begin to take shape II [名] utensil ▶餐具 tableware ▶玩具 toy ▶文具 stationery III [量] ▷一具棺材 a coffin ▷一具尸体 a corpse

具备 jùbèi [动] have (PT, PP had) ▷这手机具备收发电子信件的功能。This mobile phone has the capacity to send and receive emails.

具体 jùtǐ [形] 1 (明确) detailed 2 (特定) particular

具有 jùyǒu [动] have (PT, PP had)

炬 jù [名] torch

俱 jù [副] ▷面面俱到 attend to each and every aspect

俱乐部 jùlèbù [名] club

剧 jù I [名] drama ▶喜剧 comedy ▶丑剧 farce ▶剧团 troupe II [形] severe ▶剧变 dramatic change

剧本 jùběn [名] script

剧毒 jùdú [名] deadly poison

剧烈 jùliè [形] severe

剧目 jùmù [名] repertoire

剧务 jùwù [名] 1 (指事务) stage management 2 (指人) stage manager

剧院 jùyuàn [名] 1 (剧场) theatre (英), theater (美) 2 (剧团) company

剧种 jùzhǒng [名] genre

剧组 jùzǔ [名] crew

据 jù I [动] 1 (占据) occupy ▶盘据 forcibly occupy ▷据为己有 appropriate 2 (凭借) rely on ▶据点 stronghold II [介] according to ▷据报道 according to reports III [名] evidence ▶收据 receipt ▶论据 grounds for argument ▷真凭实据 hard evidence

据点 jùdiǎn [名] stronghold

据理力争 jù lǐ lìzhēng put forward a strong and fair argument

据说 jùshuō [动] be said ▷据说他已定居美国。It is said that he's already settled in America.

距 jù [名] distance ▷这两个城市相距不远。The distance between these two cities is not great. ▷相距遥远 far apart from each other

距离 jùlí [动] be at a distance from ▷住宅距离办公室约有3英里。The house is about 3 miles from the office. ▷俩人的观点有距离。The two of them have quite different views.

惧 jù [动] be frightened
惧怕 jùpà [动] fear ▷人人都惧怕生病。Everyone fears getting ill.

飓 jù 见下文
飓风 jùfēng [名] hurricane

锯 jù I [名] saw II [动] saw (PT sawed, PP sawn)

聚 jù [动] 1 (集合) get together ▶团聚 reunite 2 (积聚) amass ▶凝聚 condense ▷聚敛财富 amass a vast illegal fortune
聚宝盆 jùbǎopén [名] treasure trove
聚餐 jùcān [动] have a dinner party
聚合 jùhé [动] (聚集) get together
聚会 jùhuì [动] get together ▷周末有个同学聚会。At the weekend there's a get-together of classmates.
聚积 jùjī [动] accumulate ▷聚积一些钱 save a bit of money
聚集 jùjí [动] gather
聚焦 jùjiāo [动] focus ▷聚焦保险市场 focus on the insurance market
聚精会神 jù jīng huì shén focus all one's attention on
聚众 jùzhòng [动] mob

踞 jù [动] (占据) occupy
踞守 jùshǒu [动] guard

捐 juān I [动] 1 (舍弃) relinquish ▷捐躯 die for a cause 2 (捐助) donate ▶募捐 appeal for donations II [名] levy
捐款 juānkuǎn [动] donate money ▷收到一笔捐款 receive a donation
捐躯 juānqū [动] sacrifice one's life
捐献 juānxiàn [动] donate
捐助 juānzhù [动] contribute

涓 juān [名] (书) trickle
涓涓 juānjuān [形] (书) trickling

娟 juān [形] (书) beautiful
娟秀 juānxiù [形] (书) beautiful

圈 juān [动] pen ... in ▷别总把孩子圈在家里。You shouldn't keep the children penned up in the house.
→另见 juàn, quān

镌 juān [动] (书) engrave ▶镌刻 engrave

卷 juǎn I [动] 1 (裹成筒形) roll ... up 2 (撮起) sweep ... up (PT, PP swept) ▷飓风把房屋卷走了。The hurricane swept the house away. 3 (喻) (牵涉) be swept up in II [名] roll III [量] roll ▷一卷卫生纸 a roll of toilet paper
→另见 juàn
卷逃 juǎntáo [动] run off with (PT ran, PP run)
卷土重来 juǎn tǔ chóng lái stage a comeback

卷 juàn I [名] 1 (书本) book 2 (试卷) exam paper 3 (文件) document II [量] volume
→另见 juǎn
卷子 juànzi [名] exam paper ▷出卷子 set exam papers
卷宗 juànzōng [名] 1 (文件) file 2 (纸夹子) folder

隽 juàn [形] (书) meaningful ▶隽永 meaningful

倦 juàn I [形] (书) tired II [动] be tired of
倦容 juànróng [名] tired look ▷满脸倦容 look completely tired out
倦色 juànsè [名] tired look

绢 juàn [名] silk

眷 juàn I [名] family member II [动] (书) care about
眷恋 juànliàn [动] (书) be sentimentally attached to
眷念 juànniàn [动] (书) feel nostalgic about (PT, PP felt)
眷属 juànshǔ [名] 1 (亲属) family member 2 (夫妻) husband and wife

圈 juàn [名] pen ▶猪圈 pigsty
→另见 juān, quān

撅 juē [动] stick up (PT, PP stuck) ▷撅起嘴巴 pout

决 jué I [动] 1 (决定) decide ▷犹豫不决 be unable to make a decision 2 (执行死刑) execute 3 (决口) burst (PT, PP burst) 4 (定胜负) decide on a result ▶决战 decisive battle II [副] under any circumstances ▷无论多困难，我都决不放弃努力。No matter how difficult it is, I won't give up under any circumstances. III [形] decisive ▶果决 resolute
决策 juécè [动] make a strategic decision
决定 juédìng [动] 1 (打定主意) decide ▷决定远走高飞 decide to run away ▷这盘棋

决定胜负。This game of chess will be the decider. ▷作出惊人的决定 make a startling decision **2** (表示条件关系) determine ▷他的个性决定了他对职业的选择。His character was the determining factor in his choice of career.

决斗 juédòu [动] **1** (字) duel **2** (殊死的斗争) engage in a decisive battle

决断 juéduàn **I** [动] make a decision **II** [名] **1** (决定) decision **2** (指作风) decisiveness

决计 juéjì **I** [动] have made up one's mind **II** [副] definitely

决口 juékǒu [动] burst (PT, PP burst)

决裂 juéliè [动] break with (PT broke, PP broken) ▷戒毒后，他与过去的生活彻底决裂了。After giving up drugs, he made a complete break with his past life. ▷夫妻俩争吵之后彻底决裂了。After their quarrel the couple completely broke it off.

决赛 juésài [名] final ▷半决赛 semi-final ▷四分之一决赛 quarter-final

决心 juéxīn [名] determination ▷我从未见像他这样有决心的人。I've never seen anyone as determined as him.

决一雌雄 jué yī cí xióng fight it out

决议 juéyì [名] resolution

决意 juéyì [动] be determined ▷她决意要辞职。She was determined to resign.

决战 juézhàn [动] fight a decisive battle (PT, PP fought)

诀 jué **I** [名] **1** (指词句) mnemonic **2** (诀窍) knack **II** [动] part

诀别 juébié [动] bid farewell (PT bade, PP bidden)

诀窍 juéqiào [名] knack

抉 jué [动] (书) pick ... out ▶抉择 choose

角 jué **I** [名] **1** (角色) role **2** (女演员) actress **3** (男演员) actor **II** [动] fight (PT, PP fought) ▶口角 quarrel
→另见 jiǎo

角斗 juédòu [动] wrestle ▷角斗士 wrestler ▷角斗场 wrestling ring

角色 juésè [名] **1** (剧中人物) part ▷扮演主要角色 play the main part **2** (某类人) role ▷他在公司中是什么样的角色？What role does he have in the company?

角逐 juézhú [动] compete ▷权力角逐 power struggle ▷角逐诺贝尔文学奖 compete for the Nobel Prize for Literature

觉 jué **I** [动] **1** (感觉) feel (PT, PP felt) ▷穿得太少，会觉得冷的。If you don't wear enough

clothes you'll feel cold. **2** (睡醒) wake up (PT woke, PP woken) ▷大梦初觉 come to one's senses **3** (觉悟) become aware of (PT became, PP become) **II** [名] sense ▶触觉 sense of touch ▶知觉 consciousness
→另见 jiào

觉察 juéchá [动] detect

觉得 juéde [动] **1** (感到) feel (PT, PP felt) ▷觉得有点冷 feel a bit cold **2** (认为) think (PT, PP thought) ▷他觉得我不适合做这项工作。He doesn't think I'm suited for this work. ▷我觉得应该亲自去一趟。I think I should go in person.

觉悟 juéwù [名] awareness ▷觉悟到改革的重要性 become aware of the importance of reform

觉醒 juéxǐng [动] awaken ▷民族意识的觉醒 the awakening of a national consciousness

绝 jué **I** [动] **1** (断绝) cut ... off (PT, PP cut) ▶隔绝 isolate **2** (穷尽) exhaust **3** (无后代) have no descendants ▷断子绝孙 be the last in one's line **4** (死) die ▷悲痛欲绝 be torn apart with grief **II** [形] **1** (不通) hopeless ▶绝路 blind alley ▶绝地 impasse **2** (高超) superb **III** [副] **1** (最) extremely ▶绝密 top secret **2** (绝对) absolutely ▷绝无此意 have absolutely no such intentions

绝笔 juébǐ [名] **1** (最后的作品) last work **2** (最好的作品) masterpiece

绝处逢生 jué chù féng shēng make a miraculous recovery

绝代 juédài [形] (书) exceptional

绝顶 juédǐng **I** [副] extremely ▷绝顶聪明 extremely intelligent **II** [名] (书) summit

绝对 juéduì **I** [形] absolute ▷绝对真理 absolute truth **II** [副] absolutely

绝后 juéhòu [动] **1** (无后代) be childless **2** (不会再有) never to be seen again ▷空前绝后 unprecedented and unrepeatable

绝活 juéhuó [名] speciality (英), specialty (美)

绝技 juéjì [名] expertise

绝交 juéjiāo [动] **1** (指国家间) break ties (PT broke, PP broken) **2** (指个人) break up (PT broke, PP broken) ▷他背信弃义，我只好和他绝交。He was dishonest with me so I had no choice but to break up with him.

绝境 juéjìng [名] (绝望的地址) hopeless situation

绝口 juékǒu [动] **1** (住口) stop talking ▷骂不绝口 continuously insult **2** (回避不谈) not open one's mouth

绝妙 juémiào [形] brilliant

绝情 juéqíng [形] heartless

绝食 juéshí [动] go on hunger strike (PT went, PP gone)

绝望 juéwàng [动] feel desperate (PT, PP felt)

绝无仅有 jué wú jǐn yǒu unique

绝育 juéyù [动] sterilize

绝缘 juéyuán [动] (电子) insulate ▷绝缘材料 insulating materials ▷绝缘体 insulator

绝招 juézhāo [名] 1 (绝技) unique skill 2 (妙举) masterstroke

绝症 juézhèng [名] terminal illness

绝种 juézhǒng [动] become extinct (PT became, PP become) ▷保护濒临绝种的野生动物 protect wild animals on the verge of extinction

倔 jué 见下文
→另见 juè

倔强 juéjiàng [动] be stubborn

掘 jué [动] dig (PT, PP dug) ▶挖掘 excavate

崛 jué 见下文

崛起 juéqǐ [动] (书) 1 (突起) soar 2 (兴起) spring up (PT sprang, PP sprung)

厥 jué [动] faint ▶晕厥 faint

橛 jué [名] peg

爵 jué [名] peerage ▷公爵 duke

爵士 juéshì [名] 1 (作为头衔，用于全名前) Sir ▷温斯顿·丘吉尔爵士 Sir Winston Churchill 2 (指级别) knight ▷他被封为爵士。He was awarded a knighthood.

爵士乐 juéshìyuè [名] jazz

蹶 jué [动] (喻) (失败) suffer a setback ▷一蹶不振 unable to recover from a setback

嚼 jué [动] chew
→另见 jiáo

攫 jué [动] seize

攫取 juéqǔ [动] plunder

倔 juè [形] surly
→另见 jué

军 jūn I [名] 1 (军队) army ▶参军 enlist ▷海军 navy 2 (指军队编制单位) regiment 3 (指集体) forces (PL) ▷革命的后备军 revolutionary reserve forces II [形] military ▶军费 military expenditure ▶军令 military order ▶军乐 military music

军备 jūnbèi [名] arms (PL)

军队 jūnduì [名] troops (PL)

军阀 jūnfá [名] warlord

军工 jūngōng [名] 1 (军事工业) arms industry 2 (军事工程) military project

军官 jūnguān [名] officer

军国主义 jūnguó zhǔyì [名] militarism

军火 jūnhuǒ [名] ammunitions (PL) ▷军火商 arms dealer

军界 jūnjiè [名] the military

军情 jūnqíng [名] military movement ▷刺探军情 gather military intelligence

军区 jūnqū [名] military region

军人 jūnrén [名] soldier ▷退伍军人 ex-serviceman

军事 jūnshì [名] military affairs (PL) ▷军事法庭 military tribunal

军属 jūnshǔ [名] soldier's family

军衔 jūnxián [名] military rank ▷他被赐予上校军衔。He was given the rank of colonel.

军心 jūnxīn [名] troop morale

军需 jūnxū [名] military supplies (PL)

军营 jūnyíng [名] barracks

军用 jūnyòng [形] military ▷军用物资 military supplies

军长 jūnzhǎng [名] military commander

军政 jūnzhèng [名] 1 (军事和政治) military affairs and politics (PL) 2 (指军中行政工作) military administration 3 (军队和政府) army and government

军职 jūnzhí [名] military post

军种 jūnzhǒng [名] armed services (PL)

军装 jūnzhuāng [名] army uniform

均 jūn I [动] divide ... equally ▷把钱均一下。Divide the money out equally. II [形] even ▶平均 average ▷分配不均 uneven distribution III [副] 1 (都) all ▷来作客的均是老同学。All the guests were old classmates. 2 (平均) equally ▷均分利润 divide the profits equally

均等 jūnděng [形] equal ▷机会均等 equal opportunities

均分 jūnfēn [动] divide ... equally

均衡 jūnhéng [形] balanced

均势 jūnshì [名] even balance

均摊 jūntān [动] share ... equally

均匀 jūnyún [形] even ▷将咖啡牛奶搅拌均匀。Mix the coffee and milk evenly.

均沾 jūnzhān [动] share ... equally ▷利益均沾 share the profits equally

龟 jūn 见下文
→另见 guī
龟裂 jūnliè [动] 1 (指皮肤) chap ▷龟裂的嘴唇 chapped lips 2 (裂缝) crack

君 jūn [名] 1 (君主) monarch 2 (书) (指尊称) Mr. ▷李君 Mr. Li
君权 jūnquán [名] monarchical power
君王 jūnwáng [名] monarch
君主 jūnzhǔ [名] monarch
君子 jūnzǐ [名] gentleman (PL gentlemen)
君子协定 jūnzǐxiédìng [名] gentleman's agreement

菌 jūn [名] 1 (指植物) fungus ▷蘑菇是食用菌的一种。Mushrooms are a type of edible fungus. 2 (特指细菌) bacterium (PL bacteria)

皲 jūn 见下文
皲裂 jūnliè [动] chap ▷皲裂的皮肤 chapped skin

俊 jùn I [形] 1 (指女性) pretty 2 (指男性) handsome II [名] talented
俊杰 jùnjié [名] hero
俊美 jùnměi [形] beautiful
俊俏 jùnqiào [形] (口) charming
俊秀 jùnxiù [形] delicate

峻 jùn [形] 1 (高大) high 2 (严厉) harsh
峻峭 jùnqiào [形] precipitous

浚 jùn [动] dredge

骏 jùn [名] fine horse ▶骏马 steed

竣 jùn [动] complete
竣工 jùngōng [动] be complete ▷写字楼按时竣工。The office block has been completed to schedule.

Kk

咖 kā 见下文
→另见 gā

咖啡 kāfēi [名] coffee ▷咖啡豆 coffee bean ▷速溶咖啡 instant coffee ▷我想喝杯咖啡。I'd like a cup of coffee. ▷请来3杯加奶的咖啡。Three white coffees, please.

卡 kǎ I [量] (物) calorie II [名] 1 (卡片) card ▷生日卡 birthday card 2 (指录音机) cassette
→另见 qiǎ

卡车 kǎchē [名] lorry (英), truck (美)

卡拉OK kǎlā'ōukèi [名] karaoke

卡路里 kǎlùlǐ [量] calorie

卡片 kǎpiàn [名] card

卡通 kǎtōng [名] cartoon

开 kāi I [动] 1 (打开) open ▷开门 open the door 2 (开辟) open... up 3 (绽放) bloom ▷菊花开了。The chrysanthemums are in bloom. 4 (松开) come undone (PT came, PP come) ▷信封开了。The envelope has come unstuck. ▷扣子开了。The buttons have come undone. 5 (驾驶) drive (PT drove, PP driven) ▷他喜欢开汽车。He likes driving. ▷我喜欢开飞机。I like flying planes. 6 (办) run (PT ran, PP run) 7 (开始) start 8 (举行) hold (PT, PP held) 9 (写出) write... out (PT wrote,

PP written) ▷请医生开一张药方。Ask the doctor to write out a prescription. 10 (支付) pay (PT, PP paid) 11 (沸腾) boil 12 (摆出) serve ▷开饭了。Dinner is ready. 13 (指比例) be in a ratio of ▷三七开 be in a ratio of three to seven II [量] (出版) (开本) ▷这个本子是4开的。This book is in quarto format.

开办 kāibàn [动] set... up (PT, PP set) ▷他们开办了一家药店。They set up a pharmacy.

开本 kāiběn [名] ▷这本杂志是8开本的。This magazine is in octavo format.

开场 kāichǎng [动] start

开场白 kāichǎngbái [名] 1 (指演出) prologue (英), prolog (美) 2 (指话语) introduction

开诚布公 kāi chéng bù gōng frank ▷大家开诚布公地谈了自己的看法。Everyone spoke their mind.

开除 kāichú [动] dismiss ▷他被公司开除了。He was dismissed by the company.

开创 kāichuàng [动] initiate

开刀 kāidāo [动] 1 (做手术) operate on ▷她的背部开过刀。She had an operation on her back. 2 (喻) make an example of

开导 kāidǎo [动] talk... round ▷经朋友们开导, 她终于想通了。Her friends talked her round and finally she agreed.

开动 kāidòng [动] 1 (启动) start ▷请大家开动脑筋, 想想办法。Please would everyone get their brains in gear, and think of a solution. 2 (前进) get going

开端 kāiduān [名] beginning

开发 kāifā [动] 1 (开采) exploit ▷开发自然资源 exploit natural resources 2 (开垦) reclaim 3 (发现) develop

开放 kāifàng [动] 1 (展开) bloom 2 (解禁) open ▷实行对外开放政策 implement a policy of openness 3 (开朗) be open-minded

开工 kāigōng [动] 1 (指工厂) go into operation (PT went, PP gone) 2 (指工程) start

开关 kāiguān [名] 1 (指电器) switch 2 (指管道) valve

开国 kāiguó [动] found a state

开户 kāihù [动] open an account ▷公司准备在另一家银行开户。The company is going to open an account with another bank.

开花 kāihuā [动] 1 (开放) flower ▷茉莉开了花。The jasmine is in flower. 2 (喻) (破裂) split (PT, PP split) 3 (喻) (高兴) ▷她心里乐开了花。She's bursting with joy. 4 (喻) (兴起) take off (PT took, PP taken) ▷这项新技术在农村已遍地开花。The new technology has already taken off in the countryside.

开化 kāihuà [动] 1 (文明) become civilized (PT

became, PP become) (方) (融化) thaw

开怀 kāihuái [形] happy ▷乐开怀 be extremely happy ▷宴会上，大家开怀畅饮。At the dinner party everyone drank to their heart's content.

开会 kāihuì [动] have a meeting

开火 kāihuǒ [动] 1 (进攻) open fire 2 (喻) (抨击) attack

开价 kāijià [动] quote ▷这件古董开价5千美元。This antique is quoted at five thousand dollars.

开奖 kāijiǎng [动] announce the winner

开禁 kāijìn [动] lift a ban ▷那部电影终于开禁了。At last the ban on that film has been lifted.

开局 kāijú I [动] start II [名] opening

开卷有益 kāi juàn yǒu yì reading broadens the mind

开课 kāikè [动] 1 (开学) start 2 (授课) teach a course (PT, PP taught) ▷胡教授准备给研究生开课。Professor Hu will be teaching a postgraduate course.

开垦 kāikěn [动] reclaim

开口 kāikǒu [动] 1 (说话) open one's mouth ▷开会时她一直没开口。She didn't open her mouth during the meeting. 2 (开刃) sharpen 3 (裂开) split (PT, PP split)

开口子 kāi kǒuzi [动] 1 (指堤岸等) burst (PT, PP burst) ▷河堤开口子了！The dam has burst! 2 (指政策) gain a concession ▷在这件事上不能给任何人开口子。We can't allow anyone any concessions.

开阔 kāikuò [形] 1 (指地域) wide 2 (指胸怀) broad ▷他心胸开阔。He's broad-minded. ▷旅游能开阔眼界。Travel broadens the horizons.

开朗 kāilǎng [形] 1 (指空间) open 2 (指性格) cheerful

开路 kāilù [动] 1 (开辟道路) open up a path ▷我们开了一条穿山路。We opened up a path through the mountains. 2 (引路) lead the way (PT, PP led) ▷村民在森林里开路。The villager led the way into the forest.

开门见山 kāi mén jiàn shān get straight to the point ▷我写文章喜欢开门见山。When I write essays I like to get straight to the point.

开明 kāimíng [形] enlightened

开幕 kāimù [动] 1 (指演出) start 2 (指会) open

开辟 kāipì [动] 1 (开通) open... up 2 (开发) develop

开窍 kāiqiào [动] 1 (指思想) get it straight ▷无论我怎么说，她就是不开窍。No matter how often I explained, she couldn't get it

straight. 2 (指儿童) grow up (PT grew, PP grown) ▷他还没有开窍，不知道生孩子是怎么一回事。He's not yet grown-up enough to understand the facts of life.

开设 kāishè [动] set... up (PT, PP set) ▷开设工厂 set up a factory

开始 kāishǐ I [动] start, begin ▷他明天开始上班。He'll start work tomorrow. II [名] beginning

> start, begin, 和 commence 在语意上很相近，不过 commence 更为正式，通常不用于日常会话。The meeting is ready to begin/start… He tore the list up and started/began a new one… the new school term commences in September… 注意，start, begin, 和 commence 后面都可以跟名词或动词的 -ing 形式，但是，只有 start 和 begin 后面能够跟带 'to' 的动词不定式。可以说 It's starting/beginning to rain., 但不能说 'It's commencing to rain.'

开水 kāishuǐ [名] boiling water

开庭 kāitíng [动] convene ▷明天法庭要开庭审理那宗杀人案。The court is convening tomorrow to hear the murder case.

开通 kāitōng [动] 1 (通畅) clear 2 (开始使用) start to use

开通 kāitong [形] broad-minded

开头 kāitóu I [动] begin (PT began, PP begun) II [名] beginning

开脱 kāituō [动] shake... off (PT shook, PP shaken) ▷他尽力为自己开脱罪责。He did everything he could to shake off the guilt.

开拓 kāituò [动] 1 (开辟) open... up ▷开拓新市场 open up new markets 2 (开阔) broaden ▷开拓眼界 broaden one's horizons

开玩笑 kāi wánxiào [动] joke ▷我只是开玩笑。I was only joking. ▷别拿我开玩笑。Don't make fun of me.

开销 kāixiāo I [动] cover one's expenses ▷每月的工资不够他开销。His monthly salary is not enough to cover his expenses. II [名] expenses (PL) ▷旅游开销 travel expenses

开小差 kāi xiǎochāi [动] 1 (当逃兵) desert 2 (喻) (走神儿) be absent-minded

开心 kāixīn I [形] happy ▷他好像有点儿不开心。He looks a little unhappy. ▷他们玩得开心极了。They had a lot of fun. II [动] make fun of ▷他老拿别人开心。He's always making fun of people.

开眼 kāiyǎn [动] open one's eyes ▷这次旅游让我们对地方风情开了眼。The trip opened our eyes to local customs. ▷义务劳动可真叫人开眼。Voluntary work is a real eye-opener.

开业 kāiyè [动] start a business

开凿 kāizáo [动] cut (PT, PP cut)

开展 kāizhǎn [动] launch ▷他们为灾区开展募捐活动。They launched a campaign to get donations for the disaster area.

开张 kāizhāng [动] 1 (开业) open a business 2 (开门) open for business ▷这个小店每天上午9点开张。This shop opens for business at 9 a.m. every day. 3 (喻) (重新开始) start again ▷失败了不要紧，可以重打鼓另开张嘛！Don't worry about losing – you can always have another go!

开支 kāizhī [动] 1 (支付) spend (PT, PP spent) ▷她从不乱开支。She never spends extravagantly. ▷我们要节约开支。We should cut down on expenses. 2 (方) (发工资) pay wages (PT, PP paid) ▷我公司月底开支。My firm pays us at the end of the month.

揩 kāi [动] wipe ▷揩干碟子 dry the dishes ▷他用手揩揩了揩汗。He wiped away the sweat with his handkerchief.

凯 kǎi [名] triumph

凯歌 kǎigē [名] victory song

凯旋 kǎixuán [动] return in triumph

铠 kǎi [名] armour (英), armor (美)

铠甲 kǎijiǎ [名] suit of armour (英) 或 armor (美)

慨 kǎi I [动] be indignant II [形] generous

慨叹 kǎitàn [动] sigh with regret

楷 kǎi [名] (典范) model

楷模 kǎimó [名] example

刊 kān I [动] 1 (出版) publish 2 (修改) correct ▶刊误 correct printing errors II [名] periodical ▶报刊 the press ▶月刊 monthly

刊登 kāndēng [动] publish

刊物 kānwù [名] periodical

刊载 kānzǎi [动] publish ▷这份报纸正在连续刊载她的小说。This newspaper is serializing her novel.

看 kān [动] 1 (照料) look after ▷她每天在家看孩子。She's at home every day looking after the children. ▷帮我看会儿行李吧。Please could you watch my luggage? 2 (看管) watch over ▷父母不应看着孩子学习。Parents shouldn't watch over their children while they study. ▷这些囚犯不易看。Guarding these prisoners isn't easy.
→另见 kàn

看管 kānguǎn [动] 1 (看守) guard 2 (照管) look after ▷孩子需要好好看管。Children need a lot of looking after. ▷我不在时他会看管花园。He'll look after the garden while I'm away.

看护 kānhù [动] take care of (PT took, PP taken)

看家 kānjiā I [动] look after the house II [形] special ▷看家本领 special skill

看守 kānshǒu I [动] guard II [名] guard

勘 kān [动] 1 (校订) collate 2 (探测) survey ▶勘察 explore

勘测 kāncè [动] survey

勘探 kāntàn [动] explore

勘误 kānwù [动] correct printing errors

坎 kǎn [名] ridge

坎肩儿 kǎnjiānr [名] sleeveless jacket

坎坷 kǎnkě [形] 1 (坑坑洼洼) bumpy 2 (喻) (不顺利) rough ▷他经历相当坎坷。He's had a really rough ride. ▷坎坷的人生之路 the rocky road of life

侃 kǎn [动] (口) chat

侃大山 kǎn dàshān [动] (方) shoot the breeze (PT, PP shot)

侃侃而谈 kǎnkǎn'értán speak frankly and in measured tones

砍 kǎn [动] 1 (劈) chop 2 (减) cut (PT, PP cut)

砍伐 kǎnfá [动] fell

看 kàn I [动] 1 (观看) look at ▷看电视 watch TV ▷我昨天晚上去看京剧了。I went to see Beijing Opera last night. 2 (阅读) read (PT, PP read) 3 (认为) think (PT, PP thought) ▷你看这事儿怎么办？What do you think we should do about this? 4 (拜访) visit 5 (照料) look after 6 (预测) expect ▷英镑看涨。The pound is expected to rise. 7 (对待) treat ▷我把他当知己看。I treat him like a bosom friend. 8 (诊治) treat ▷昨天张医生给她看过病。Doctor Zhang treated her yesterday. ▷我要带孩子去看病。I am taking my child to see the doctor. 9 (取决于) depend on ▷"你明年买车吗？""看情况吧。" Are you going to buy a car next year? – It depends. ▷下午踢不踢球得看天气。Whether we play football this afternoon depends on the weather. II [助] (表示尝试) ▷你试试看，衣服合适不？Why don't you try on the clothes and see if they fit? ▷"这果子好吃吗？""尝尝看。" How is the fruit? – Have a taste. III [叹] (表示惊讶、责备) ▷你看！怎么又迟到了！Goodness! How come you're late again! ▷看，你又忘了锁门吧！Look, you forgot to lock the door again!

→另见 kān

look at 或 watch 表示某人注意到某个可见的事物。通常，look at 表示观看静止不动的物体，而 watch 用于移动中或者变化中的事物。*He watched David run down the stairs… I stayed up late to watch the film… I asked him to look at the picture above his bed… It is polite to look at people when they are talking to you.* look 不能够直接跟宾语，其后必须加上 at 或其他介词。*He looked at me for a long time before he spoke… I looked towards the plane.*

看不起 kàn bu qǐ [动] look down on

看待 kàndài [动] regard ▷他们把我当朋友看待。They regard me as a friend.

看法 kànfǎ [名] opinion

看好 kànhǎo [动] look good ▷今年的经济形势看好。The economic prospects look good this year.

看见 kànjiàn [动] see (PT saw, PP seen) ▷黑暗中我看见一个人影。I could make out a figure in the dark. ▷你看见过瀑布吗？ Have you ever seen a waterfall?

看来 kànlái [动] seem ▷她看来好多了。She seems much better. ▷这看来是个好主意。That seems like a good idea. ▷看来他不想来了。It seems he didn't want to come.

看破红尘 kàn pò hóngchén be disillusioned with the world ▷他因看破红尘而出家了。He became a monk because he was disillusioned with the world.

看望 kànwàng [动] visit

看重 kànzhòng [动] value

康 kāng [形] (健康) healthy (书) (富裕) well off ▷小康生活 a relatively comfortable life

康复 kāngfù [动] recover ▷祝您早日康复！I hope you get well soon.

康乐 kānglè [形] happy and peaceful

慷 kāng 见下文

慷慨 kāngkǎi [形] 1 (激昂) fervent 2 (大方) generous

扛 káng [动] shoulder ▷他能扛两百磅的袋子。He can shoulder a 200-pound bag. ▷他老板的过失由他扛着。He's shouldering the blame for the boss's mistake.

亢 kàng [形] 1 (高亢) high 2 (高傲) haughty

亢奋 kàngfèn [形] excited

伉 kàng [动] be equal

伉俪 kànglì [名] (书) married couple

抗 kàng [动] 1 (抵抗) resist ▷抗衰老 anti-aging 2 (抗拒) refuse ▶违抗 defy 3 (对等) be a match for ▶抗衡 contend with

抗衡 kànghéng [动] match ▷我们的实力无法与他们抗衡。There's no way we can match them in strength.

抗拒 kàngjù [动] resist

抗议 kàngyì [动] protest ▷他们对虐待动物的行为提出了强烈抗议。They protested vehemently against cruelty to animals.

抗争 kàngzhēng [动] resist

考 kǎo [动] 1 (测试) have an exam ▷明天我们考数学。We have our maths exam tomorrow. 2 (检查) check 3 (研究) study ▶考古 archaeology

考查 kǎochá [动] check

考察 kǎochá [动] 1 (实地调查) investigate 2 (细致观察) analyse (英), analyze (美) ▷仔细考察后，他们终于发现了问题的所在。After careful analysis they finally understood what was wrong.

考古 kǎogǔ I [动] study archaeology (英) 或 archeology (美) II [名] archaeology (英), archeology (美)

考核 kǎohé [动] check

考究 kǎojiu I [动] 1 (考察) investigate 2 (讲究) be particular about ▷她在衣着方面非常考究。She's extremely particular about her clothes. II [形] exquisite

考虑 kǎolù [动] consider ▷这个问题需要慎重考虑。This problem needs to be considered carefully. ▷这事儿你考虑了吗？ Have you thought it over? ▷我已把一切都考虑在内。I've already taken everything into consideration.

考勤 kǎoqín [动] check attendance ▷学校开始对学生加强考勤。The school is stepping up attendance checks on its pupils.

考试 kǎoshì [动] sit an exam (PT, PP sat) ▷他英语考试没及格。He failed the English exam.

考研 kǎoyán [动] sit the entrance exam for postgraduate studies (PT, PP sat)

考验 kǎoyàn [动] test ▷她想考验一下我的诚实。She wants to test my honesty. ▷经受考验 undergo an ordeal

考证 kǎozhèng [动] confirm through research

拷 kǎo [动] 1 (打) beat (PT beat, PP beaten) ▶拷打 beat 2 (拷贝) copy ▷文件已拷到光盘上了。The file has been copied to CD-ROM.

拷贝 kǎobèi I [名] copy II [动] copy

拷打 kǎodǎ [动] torture

烤 kǎo [动] **1** (指东西) roast ▷烤牛肉 roast beef **2** (指人体) warm oneself ▶烤火 warm oneself by a fire

烤炉 kǎolú [名] oven

烤面包 kǎomiànbāo [名] toast

烤鸭 kǎoyā [名] roast duck

铐 kào I [名] handcuffs (PL) II [动] handcuff

犒 kào [动] reward

犒劳 kàoláo [动] reward with a feast

靠 kào [动] **1** (倚) lean ▷梯子靠在墙上。The ladder was leaning against the wall. **2** (近) keep to (PT, PP kept) ▷请大家往这边靠一点。Could everyone keep this way please. **3** (依赖) ▷他靠自己的努力实现了梦想。He achieved his dreams through hard work. ▷不要指望别人，要靠自己。There's no use in looking to anyone else – you have to do it yourself. **4** (信赖) trust ▷他的话靠不住。You can't trust what he says.

靠拢 kàolǒng [动] draw close (PT drew, PP drawn)

靠山 kàoshān [名] (贬) patron

苛 kē [形] harsh

苛捐杂税 kējuān záshuì heavy taxation

苛刻 kēkè [形] harsh

苛求 kēqiú [动] be demanding ▷你对人不能太苛求。You shouldn't be so demanding of others.

科 kē [名] **1** (指学术) discipline ▶文科 humanities (PL) **2** (指部门) department ▶人事科 human resources (PL) **3** (生物)(指分类) family ▶猫科 cat family **4** (法律条文) law

科班 kēbān [名] professional training

科幻 kēhuàn [名] science fiction

科技 kējì [名] science and technology ▷他在科技战线工作了一辈子。He's spent a lifetime working at the forefront of science and technology.

科举 kējǔ [名] imperial examination

科目 kēmù [名] subject

科普 kēpǔ [名] popular science

科学 kēxué I [名] science II [形] scientific

科学家 kēxuéjiā [名] scientist

科研 kēyán [名] scientific research

棵 kē [量] ▷一棵稻草 a piece of straw ▷一棵水仙 a narcissus

窠 kē [名] nest

窠臼 kējiù [名] (书) set pattern

颗 kē [量] ▷一颗种子 a seed ▷一颗汗珠 a bead of sweat

颗粒 kēlì [名] **1** (指药片等) ▷这些药物颗粒颜色不一。These pills are not uniform in colour (英) 或 color (美). **2** (指粮食等) grain

磕 kē [动] **1** (碰) bump ▷我的头磕在了门框上。My head bumped against the doorframe. **2** (敲) knock out ▷她把米粒从碗里磕了出来。She knocked the grains of rice out of the bowl.

磕碰 kēpèng I [动] knock ▷玻璃器皿禁不住磕碰。Glass objects cannot be knocked about. ▷碗上有个磕碰儿。There's a crack in the bowl. II [名] clash ▷同事之间出现磕碰是难免的。It's difficult to avoid clashes between colleagues.

瞌 kē 见下文

瞌睡 kēshuì [动] doze

蝌 kē 见下文

蝌蚪 kēdǒu [名] tadpole

壳 ké [名] shell
→另见 qiào

咳 ké [动] cough
→另见 hāi

咳嗽 késou [动] cough

可 kě I [动] **1** (同意) approve ▶认可 approve **2** (适合) suit ▶可心 satisfying II [助动] **1** (可以) can ▷对我来说，房子可大可小。As far as I'm concerned, the house can be big or small. ▷参考书不可带出去。The reference sources can't be taken out. **2** (值得) ▷没什么可担心的。There's no need to worry. ▷没有什么可抱怨的。There's nothing to complain about. ▷展览的确可看。The exhibition is really worth seeing. III [连] but ▷不让他去，可他还是去了。I didn't give him permission to go, but he went anyway. IV [副] **1** (表示强调) very **2** (加强反问) ▷可不是嘛！Absolutely! ▷这个建议好是好，可谁愿意去做呢？The proposal is great but who's actually going to implement it? **3** (加强疑问) ▷这件事他可知道？Did he ever know about this? ▷这书你可看过？Have you read this book before?

可爱 kě'ài [形] adorable

可悲 kěbēi [形] lamentable

可鄙 kěbǐ [形] despicable

可耻 kěchǐ [形] disgraceful

可歌可泣 kě gē kě qì be deeply moving

可观 kěguān [形] 1 (值得看) worth seeing ▷展览馆的艺术品着实可观。The gallery's art collection is really worth seeing. 2 (程度高) considerable

可贵 kěguì [形] valuable

可恨 kěhèn [形] detestable

可见 kějiàn [连] so ▷玛丽苗条了，可见她减肥成功。Mary has slimmed down, so her diet has obviously been successful.

可见度 kějiàndù [名] visibility

可靠 kěkào [形] reliable

可可 kěkě [名] cocoa ▷可可豆 cocoa bean

可口 kěkǒu [形] tasty

可乐 kělè [名] Coke®

可怜 kělián I [形] pitiful ▷那位病人看上去很可怜。That patient looks pitiful. ▷我存的那点钱少得可怜。I've only managed to save a pitiful amount. II [动] pity

可能 kěnéng I [形] possible ▷我们实现目标是可能的。It's possible we'll realize our targets. II [副] maybe ▷他可能去重庆了。Maybe he went to Chongqing. III [名] possibility

可怕 kěpà [形] frightening

可气 kěqì [形] annoying

可巧 kěqiǎo [副] as luck would have it

可是 kěshì I [副] ▷他儿子可是真聪明。His son is really clever. ▷我可是不和他一起去。I'll definitely not be going with him. II [连] but ▷这个小镇不大，可是很热闹。This is a small town, but it's very lively.

可视电话 kěshì diànhuà [名] videophone

可塑性 kěsùxìng [名] 1 (指物) plasticity 2 (指人) flexibility

可望而不可即 kě wàng ér bù kě jí unattainable ▷登上月球，对古人来说是可望而不可即的幻想。Previous generations would never have believed that man could go to the moon.

可恶 kěwù [形] detestable

可惜 kěxī I [形] regrettable ▷错过了那个工作机会，真可惜！What a shame you missed out on that job opportunity! II [副] regrettably ▷可惜我不能参加你们的婚礼了。Unfortunately, I can't attend your wedding.

可喜 kěxǐ [形] heartening

可笑 kěxiào [形] 1 (令人耻笑) ridiculous 2 (引人发笑) funny

可行 kěxíng [形] workable

可疑 kěyí [形] suspicious

可以 kěyǐ I [助动] 1 (能够) can ▷别人能做到的，你也可以。If other people can do it, so can you. 2 (有权) may ▷这个俱乐部任何人都可以参加。Anyone may attend this club. II [形] 1 (不坏) not bad ▷他乒乓球打得还可以。He's not bad at table tennis. 2 (厉害) awful ▷今天我忙得够可以的。I'm awfully busy today.

渴 kě I [形] thirsty II [副] eagerly ▷渴慕 admire

渴求 kěqiú [动] hunger for ▷她渴求成功。She's hungry for success.

渴望 kěwàng [动] long ▷他渴望回到祖国的怀抱。He longs to return to his country.

克 kè I [动] 1 (克制) restrain ▷克己 restrain oneself 2 (战胜) overcome (PT overcame, PP overcome) ▷克敌制胜 win victory over the enemy II [量] gram

克服 kèfú [动] 1 (战胜) overcome (PT overcame, PP overcome) ▷克服困难 overcome difficulties 2 (克制) put up with (PT, PP put)

克己奉公 kè jǐ fèng gōng make sacrifices for the public good

克隆 kèlóng [动] clone

克制 kèzhì [动] restrain

刻 kè I [动] engrave II [名] 1 (雕刻物品) engraving ▷石刻 stone inscription 2 (指十五分钟) quarter ▷现在是十点一刻。It's now a quarter past ten. 3 (泛指时间) moment ▷刻不容缓 be very urgent III [形] 1 (表示程度) extreme ▷刻苦 hardworking 2 (刻薄) harsh ▷刻毒 evil

刻板 kèbǎn I [动] cut printing blocks (PT, PP cut) II [形] rigid

刻薄 kèbó [形] harsh

刻骨铭心 kè gǔ míng xīn be engraved in one's memory ▷那件事给我留下了刻骨铭心的记忆。That event is engraved in my memory.

刻画 kèhuà [动] 1 (涂抹) scribble on 2 (描绘) portray

刻苦 kèkǔ [形] hardworking

刻意 kèyì [副] painstakingly

恪 kè [形] (书) scrupulous

恪守 kèshǒu [动] (书) keep scrupulously (PT, PP kept) ▷多年来，他一直恪守诺言。He's kept his promise scrupulously for many years now.

客 kè I [名] 1 (客人) visitor ▷送客 see off a visitor 2 (旅客) traveller (英), traveler (美) ▷客

车 passenger train **3** (顾客) customer ▶客户 customer **4** (指某类人) ▶政客 politician ▶刺客 assassin **II** [动] settle down

客场 **kèchǎng** [名] ▷曼联队本周将客场作战。Manchester United are playing away this weekend.

客串 **kèchuàn** [动] be a guest performer

客观 **kèguān** [形] objective

客户 **kèhù** [名] customer ▷客户对这种新产品非常满意。The customers are very satisfied with this new product.

客气 **kèqi I** [形] polite ▷他对人总是那么客气。He's always polite to people. **II** [动] be polite ▷女主人请我们不要客气。The hostess asked us not to stand on ceremony.

客人 **kèrén** [名] guest

客套 **kètào I** [名] civility **II** [动] exchange greetings

客座 **kèzuò** [名] guest seat ▷这边是主人座位，那边是客座。These seats are for the hosts and those are for the guests. ▷他是这所大学的客座教授。He's a visiting professor at the university.

课 **kè** [名] **1** (学科) subject **2** (学时) class **3** (单元) lesson

课本 **kèběn** [名] textbook

课程 **kèchéng** [名] course

课程表 **kèchéngbiǎo** [名] timetable

课堂 **kètáng** [名] classroom

课题 **kètí** [名] **1** (论题) topic ▷研究课题 research topic **2** (难题) problem

课文 **kèwén** [名] text

肯 **kěn** [助动] be willing ▷他不肯帮我。He isn't willing to help me. ▷孩子肯接受老师的意见。The child is ready to take the teacher's advice.

肯定 **kěndìng I** [动] confirm ▷他是否同意，我不能肯定。I can't confirm whether he agrees or not. **II** [形] **1** (确定的) affirmative ▷老师的回答是肯定的。The teacher answered in the affirmative. **2** (明确的) clear ▷她没有给我肯定的答复。She didn't give me a clear reply. **III** [副] certainly

垦 **kěn** [动] cultivate

垦殖 **kěnzhí** [动] reclaim land

恳 **kěn I** [形] sincere **II** [动] request

恳切 **kěnqiè** [形] earnest

恳求 **kěnqiú** [动] beg ▷她恳求朋友陪她一起去。She begged her friend to go with her.

啃 **kěn** [动] **1** (咬) gnaw **2** (喻) pore over ▷他喜欢啃书本。He likes to pore over books.

坑 **kēng I** [名] **1** (洼) hole **2** (洞) tunnel **II** [动] cheat

坑害 **kēnghài** [动] entrap

坑坑洼洼 **kēngkengwāwā** bumpy

坑骗 **kēngpiàn** [动] cheat

吭 **kēng** [动] utter
→另见 háng

吭哧 **kēngchi I** [拟] huff and puff ▷他搬箱子时，累得吭哧吭哧的。Moving the box left him huffing and puffing with exhaustion. **II** [动] toil ▷他吭哧了半天才把活儿干完。He toiled for a long time to finish the work.

铿 **kēng** [拟] clang

铿锵 **kēngqiāng** [形] ringing

空 **kōng I** [形] empty ▷柜子里是空的。The cupboard is empty. **II** [名] sky **III** [副] for nothing ▷我们空欢喜了一场。Our happiness had no foundation.
→另见 kòng

空荡荡 **kōngdàngdàng** [形] empty

空洞 **kōngdòng I** [名] cavity **II** [形] empty

空间 **kōngjiān** [名] space ▷实验室没有足够的空间放设备。There isn't enough space for the equipment in the laboratory. ▷这个故事给读者留下了想像的空间。This story gives the reader space to use their imagination.

空军 **kōngjūn** [名] air force

空旷 **kōngkuàng** [形] spacious

空难 **kōngnàn** [名] aircrash

空气 **kōngqì** [名] **1** (大气) air **2** (气氛) atmosphere

空前绝后 **kōng qián jué hòu** unmatched ▷恺撒大帝被称为罗马历史上空前绝后的军事领袖。Julius Caesar has been called the most unmatched military general in Roman history.

空谈 **kōngtán** [动] talk idly ▷他的许诺不过是一纸空谈。His promise is just idle talk.

空袭 **kōngxí** [动] attack from the air ▷这个城市又一次遭受了空袭。The city experienced another air raid.

空想 **kōngxiǎng** [动] fantasize ▷别再空想了。Stop fantasizing. ▷这种理论纯粹是一种空想。This theory is just pure fantasy.

空虚 **kōngxū** [形] empty ▷我感到精神空虚。I feel spiritually empty.

孔 **kǒng** [名] hole ▶鼻孔 nostril

孔穴 kǒngxué [名] hole

恐 kǒng I [动] fear ▶惶恐 be frightened II [副] probably ▷恐明天要变天。The weather will probably change tomorrow. ▷此人恐不可靠。I'm afraid he's unreliable.

恐怖 kǒngbù I [形] terrifying II [名] terror ▷恐怖主义 terrorism ▷恐怖小说 horror fiction

恐吓 kǒnghè [动] threaten

恐慌 kǒnghuāng [形] frightened

恐惧 kǒngjù [动] be frightened ▷突如其来的暴风雨使我恐惧万分。The sudden thunderstorm really frightened me. ▷这条新闻引起了人们的恐惧。This news created fear among the people.

恐龙 kǒnglóng [名] dinosaur

恐怕 kǒngpà [副] 1 (担心) fearfully ▷他恐怕考不好。He's afraid that he won't do well in the exam. 2 (大概) probably ▷火车恐怕要晚点了。The train will probably be late.

空 kòng I [动] leave ... empty (PT, PP left) ▷请你把书架的第一层空出来。Please empty out the first shelf of the bookcase. II [形] vacant ▶空位 vacant seats III [名] 1 (空间) space ▷储藏室里没空放你的行李了。There's no space left in the cupboard for your luggage. 2 (时间) free time ▶有空 have free time
→另见 kōng

空白 kòngbái [名] blank ▷他们的研究成果填补了科学技术上的一项空白。The findings of their research filled a scientific and technological gap.

空缺 kòngquē [名] vacancy

空隙 kòngxì [名] 1 (指空间) gap 2 (指时间) interval 3 (指机会) opening ▷别给你的对手留下任何空隙。Don't give your opponent any kind of opening.

空闲 kòngxián [动] be free ▷等我空闲下来再去拜访你。I'll call on you when I'm free. ▷这个操场空闲两年了。This games area has been unused for two years. ▷他一有空闲就下棋。When he has free time he plays chess.

空子 kòngzi [名] 1 (空间) space ▷车里没空子了。There's no space left in the car. 2 (时间) time ▷咱们抽空子去打篮球吧。Let's find time to go and play basketball. 3 (喻)(机会) opportunity ▷他这人爱钻空子。He's a bit of an opportunist.

控 kòng [动] 1 (控制) control ▶自控 self-control 2 (控告) charge ▶指控 charge 3 (指流体) drain ▷她把瓶子里的水控干了。She drained the water from the bottle.

控告 kònggào [动] accuse ▷员工们控告公司违反劳动法。The workers accused the company of violating the labour (英) 或 labor (美) laws.

控股公司 kònggǔ gōngsī [名] holding company

控诉 kòngsù [动] denounce

控制 kòngzhì [动] control

抠 kōu I [动] 1 (挖) pick ▷他把掉在洞里的东西抠了出来。He picked out the things that had fallen into the hole. 2 (雕刻) carve 3 (探明) work out ▷我非把这道题抠出来不可。I simply have to work the problem out. II [形] (口) stingy

抠门儿 kōuménr [形] stingy

口 kǒu I [名] 1 (嘴) mouth 2 (丁) ▷家口 family member 3 (味) taste ▷口轻 not too salty 4 (指容器) rim ▷瓶口 the mouth of a bottle 5 (指端口) ▷出口 exit ▷入口 entrance ▷窗口 window 6 (缝) split 7 (刃) edge ▷刀口 the edge of a knife 8 (行) department ▶卫生口 public health department II [量] ▷两口猪 two pigs ▷一口井 one well ▷我家有五口人。There are five people in my family.

口岸 kǒu'àn [名] port

口碑 kǒubēi [名] opinion ▷他在同事中口碑很差。His colleagues have a poor opinion of him.

口才 kǒucái [名] eloquence ▷她的口才很好。She speaks eloquently.

口吃 kǒuchī [形] stammering ▷他有点儿口吃。He has a slight stammer.

口齿 kǒuchǐ [名] 1 (发音) enunciation ▷他口齿不清。He doesn't enunciate clearly. 2 (说话) ability to speak ▷这个小姑娘口齿伶俐。The little girl is very eloquent.

口供 kǒugòng [名] confession

口号 kǒuhào [名] slogan

口红 kǒuhóng [名] lipstick

口技 kǒujì [名] vocal mimicry

口角 kǒujiǎo [名] corner of the mouth

口角 kǒujué [动] quarrel

口口声声 kǒukoushēngshēng keep on saying ▷他口口声声说要参加比赛，却没报名。He kept on saying that he wanted to enter the competition but he never did enrol.

口令 kǒulìng [名] 1 (命令) verbal command 2 (暗语) password

口气 kǒuqì [名] 1 (语气) tone 2 (气势) spoken manner ▷他没什么本事，口气倒不小。He has no real ability, but his spoken manner is very imposing. **3** (含义) implication ▷听你的口气，你是不想给她道歉了？ Are you implying that you don't want to apologize to her?

口腔 kǒuqiāng [名] the inside of the mouth

口舌 kǒushé [名] **1** (纠纷) dispute **2** (话语) persuasion ▷为了她俩和解，我费了不少口舌。 I spent ages persuading them to make up.

口是心非 kǒu shì xīn fēi not say what one means ▷口是心非的人很令人厌恶。 People hate it when you don't say what you mean.

口述 kǒushù [动] dictate

口头 kǒutóu [名] **1** (嘴) word ▷他只是口头上答应了。 He agreed verbally. **2** (口语) ▷口头作文 oral composition

口头禅 kǒutóuchán [名] pet phrase

口味 kǒuwèi [名] taste ▷流行音乐不合我的口味。 Pop music is not to my taste. ▷每个人欣赏艺术品的口味不同。 Everyone has their own different taste in art. ▷她做菜口味不错。 She cooks delicious food.

口吻 kǒuwěn [名] **1** (指动物) snout **2** (口气) tone

口信 kǒuxìn [名] message

口音 kǒuyīn [名] **1** (声音) voice **2** (方音) accent

口语 kǒuyǔ [名] spoken language

口子 kǒuzi I [量] person (PL people) ▷他家有六口子。 There are six people in his family. II [名] **1** (豁口) gap ▷院墙上出了个大口子。 There's a big gap in the garden wall. **2** (喻) (指变通做法) exception

叩 kòu [动] **1** (敲) knock ▶叩门 knock at a door **2** (磕头) kowtow

叩拜 kòubài [动] kowtow

扣 kòu I [动] **1** (拉紧) fasten **2** (朝下) put ... upside down (PT, PP put) ▷孩子把碗扣在了桌子上。 The child put the bowl upside down on the table. **3** (喻) (戴) frame **4** (抓) arrest **5** (击) smash **6** (减) deduct II [名] button

扣除 kòuchú [动] deduct

扣留 kòuliú [动] arrest

扣人心弦 kòu rén xīnxián be thrilling

扣押 kòuyā [动] detain

扣子 kòuzi [名] button

寇 kòu I [动] invade II [名] invader

枯 kū [形] **1** (枯萎) withered ▶枯草 withered grass **2** (干涸) dried-up **3** (指肌肉) emaciated ▶枯瘦 skinny **4** (乏味) dull ▶枯燥 uninteresting

枯竭 kūjié [形] **1** (干涸) dried-up **2** (用尽) exhausted

枯萎 kūwěi [形] withered

枯燥 kūzào [形] dull

哭 kū [动] cry

哭鼻子 kū bízi [动] (口) snivel

哭哭啼啼 kūkūtítí sob one's eyes out ▷一晚上她都哭哭啼啼的。 She sobbed her eyes out the entire evening.

哭泣 kūqì [动] weep (PT, PP wept)

窟 kū [名] **1** (洞穴) cave **2** (聚居地) ▶匪窟 gangster hideout ▶贫民窟 slum

窟窿 kūlong [名] **1** (洞) hole **2** (亏空) deficit

骷 kū 见下文

骷髅 kūlóu [名] skeleton

苦 kǔ I [形] **1** (苦涩) bitter **2** (艰苦) hard II [动] **1** (苦害) be hard on ▷照顾6个孩子可苦了她。 Looking after six children has taken its toll on her. **2** (遭受) suffer from ▶苦旱 suffer from drought III [副] painstakingly ▶苦练 train hard IV [名] suffering ▶吃苦 bear hardships

苦处 kǔchu [名] suffering

苦干 kǔgàn [动] work hard

苦功 kǔgōng [名] hard work

苦果 kǔguǒ [名] **1** (指果实) bitter fruit **2** (指结果) unfortunate consequences

苦口婆心 kǔ kǒu pó xīn do one's best to persuade ▷父母苦口婆心地劝他，他就是不听。 His parents did their best to persuade him but he just didn't listen.

苦闷 kǔmèn [形] depressed

苦难 kǔnàn I [名] hardship II [形] hard

苦恼 kǔnǎo [形] distressed

苦涩 kǔsè [形] bitter

苦思冥想 kǔ sī míng xiǎng rack one's brains ▷他苦思冥想了一整天，仍然没有结果。 He racked his brains for the whole day to no effect.

苦头 kǔtóu [名] suffering

苦笑 kǔxiào [动] give a wry smile (PT gave, PP given)

苦心 kǔxīn I [名] pains ▷煞费苦心 take great pains II [副] painstakingly ▷他曾苦心研究过这题目。 He painstakingly researched the topic.

苦衷 kǔzhōng [名] predicament

库 kù [名] warehouse ▶国库 state treasury

库存 kùcún [名] stock

裤 kù [名] trousers (PL)(英), pants (PL)(美)
裤子 kùzi [名] trousers (PL)(英), pants (PL)(美)

酷 kù I [形] cruel II [副](书) extremely ▶酷热 extremely hot ▶酷爱 love passionately

夸 kuā [动] 1 (夸大) exaggerate 2 (夸奖) praise
夸大 kuādà [动] exaggerate
夸奖 kuājiǎng [动] praise
夸口 kuākǒu [动] boast ▷李太太总夸口说自己的女儿聪明。Mrs. Li is always boasting about how clever her daughter is. ▷他夸口说自己能得冠军。He boasted that he would become a champion.
夸夸其谈 kuā kuā qí tán hype things up ▷我们提倡脚踏实地，反对夸夸其谈。We encourage a down-to-earth manner – we don't go in for hype.
夸张 kuāzhāng I [形] exaggerated II [名] hyperbole

垮 kuǎ [动] 1 (坍塌) collapse ▷大坝被水冲垮了。The dyke burst under the weight of the water. 2 (伤身) wear down (PT wore, PP worn) ▷她因繁重的工作而垮了下来。She was worn down by the heavy work.
垮台 kuǎtái [动] collapse

挎 kuà [动] carry
挎包 kuàbāo [名] satchel

胯 kuà [名] hip
胯骨 kuàgǔ [名] hipbone

跨 kuà [动] 1 (迈步) step 2 (骑) ride (PT rode, PP ridden) ▷跨上马 ride a horse 3 (架) span ▷独木桥横跨在山谷。The single-plank bridge spans the mountain valley. 4 (超越) surpass ▶跨国 transnational 5 (附着) adhere to
跨度 kuàdù [名] span
跨越 kuàyuè [动] surpass

会 kuài [名] accounting ▶财会 finance and accounting
→另见 huì
会计 kuàijì [名] 1 (指工作) accounting 2 (指人员) accountant

块 kuài I [名] lump ▶土块 lump of earth II [量] piece ▷一块蛋糕 a piece of cake ▷一块烤面包 a slice of toast ▷一块方糖 a lump of sugar
块头 kuàitóu [名] build

快 kuài I [形] 1 (快速) fast 2 (赶快) ▷快点

儿，要不我们就迟到了。Hurry up, or we'll be late. 3 (灵敏) quick ▷她反应特别快。She responds extremely quickly. ▷他脑子快，做事效率高。He's quick-witted and does things efficiently. 4 (锋利) sharp 5 (直爽) straightforward ▶爽快 frank 6 (愉快)(书) happy II [副] soon ▷学生快毕业了。The students will graduate soon.
快餐 kuàicān [名] fast food
快感 kuàigǎn [名] delight
快活 kuàihuo [形] delighted
快件 kuàijiàn [名] 1 (指货品) express delivery ▷这件行李用快件托运。The luggage will be sent express. 2 (指邮件) express mail
快乐 kuàilè [形] happy
快马加鞭 kuài mǎ jiā biān go at top speed
快速 kuàisù [形] quick ▷面对突发事件，当地政府做出了快速反应。Local government reacted quickly to the sudden turn of events.
快要 kuàiyào [副] soon ▷路快要修好了。The road will be repaired soon.

脍 kuài (书) I [名] sliced meat II [动] slice
脍炙人口 kuài zhì rén kǒu win universal acclaim ▷他的文章脍炙人口。His article won universal acclaim.

筷 kuài [名] chopsticks (PL)

宽 kuān I [形] 1 (距离大) wide 2 (范围广) broad 3 (宽大) lenient ▶宽容 tolerant 4 (宽裕) well-off ▷日子比原来宽点儿了。We are better-off than we were before. II [动] extend ▷我们的访问时间宽至本月底。Our visit is extended until the end of the month. III [名] width ▷这条路有20米宽。The road is twenty metres wide.
宽敞 kuānchang [形] spacious
宽大 kuāndà [形] 1 (指面积) spacious 2 (宽容) lenient
宽带 kuāndài [名] broadband
宽广 kuānguǎng [形] extensive
宽宏大量 kuānhóng dàliàng generous-minded
宽厚 kuānhòu [形] 1 (指人体) muscular 2 (指为人) generous
宽阔 kuānkuò [形] 1 (指范围) wide 2 (指心胸) broad ▷心胸宽阔 broad-minded
宽容 kuānróng [形] lenient
宽松 kuānsōng [形] 1 (不拥挤) ▷这条裤子很宽松。These trousers are quite loose. ▷电影院人不多，很宽松。There aren't many people in the cinema – it's not crowded. 2 (宽畅)

relieved **3** (宽裕) well-off **4** (宽舒) relaxed

宽裕 kuānyù [形] **1** (指生活) good **2** (指时间) ample ▷不用着急，时间还很宽裕。Don't worry, there's still ample time.

宽窄 kuānzhǎi [名] width

款 kuǎn [名] **1** (项目) section ▷第1条第3款 article, section **3 2** (钱) sum of money ▷现款 cash **3** (题名) signature ▶落款 inscribe **4** (样式) style

款待 kuǎndài [动] entertain

款式 kuǎnshì [名] style

款项 kuǎnxiàng [名] **1** (钱) sum of money **2** (项目) section

诓 kuāng [动] deceive

诓骗 kuāngpiàn [动] deceive

筐 kuāng I [名] basket II [量] basket ▷一筐土豆 a basket of potatoes

狂 kuáng I [形] **1** (疯狂) crazy ▶发狂 go crazy **2** (猛烈) violent ▶狂风 gale **3** (狂妄) arrogant **4** (狂热) wild ▷欣喜若狂 be wild with joy II [副] wildly

狂暴 kuángbào [形] violent

狂欢 kuánghuān [动] have a mad time of it

狂热 kuángrè [形] fanatical

狂妄 kuángwàng [形] arrogant

旷 kuàng I [形] **1** (空阔) spacious ▶旷野 wilderness **2** (开阔) free from worry ▷心旷神怡 carefree and happy **3** (松) loose II [动] neglect ▶旷课 play truant

旷达 kuàngdá [形] (书) broad-minded

旷课 kuàngkè [动] play truant

旷日持久 kuàng rì chí jiǔ protracted ▷双方进行了旷日持久的谈判。The negotiations between the two sides were protracted.

况 kuàng I [名] situation ▶状况 condition II [连] (书) besides ▶何况 moreover

况且 kuàngqiě [连] besides

矿 kuàng [名] **1** (矿场) mine **2** (矿石) ore

矿藏 kuàngcáng [名] mineral resources (PL)

矿产 kuàngchǎn [名] mineral

矿井 kuàngjǐng [名] mine

矿山 kuàngshān [名] mine

矿石 kuàngshí [名] ore

矿物 kuàngwù [名] mineral

矿业 kuàngyè [名] mining industry

框 kuàng I [名] **1** (框架) frame **2** (方框) box II [动] **1** (画圈) box ▷我用红笔把这句话框了起来。I put a red box around the sentence. **2** (口) (限制) limit ▷我们不能把市场只框在北京。We can't limit the market to Beijing.

框架 kuàngjià [名] **1** (指建筑) frame **2** (指文书) framework

眶 kuàng [名] socket ▶眼眶 eye socket

亏 kuī I [动] **1** (亏损) lose (PT, PP lost) **2** (欠缺) lack ▶理亏 be in the wrong **3** (亏负) allow ... to suffer losses ▷公司亏不了股东。The company can't allow its shareholders to suffer losses. II [副] **1** (幸亏) luckily ▷亏你把我叫醒，要不我就迟到了。It's lucky you woke me up or I would have been late. **2** (表示讥讽) ▷这烂主意，亏你想得出来！How could you think up such a stupid idea? ▷亏他还是个经理，连这点问题都解决不了！What a joy to have him as a manager - when he can't even solve a problem as small as this!

亏待 kuīdài [动] treat ... badly ▷公司不能亏待员工。The company can't treat its workers badly.

亏空 kuīkong I [动] be in debt II [名] deficit

亏欠 kuīqiàn [动] be in arrears

亏心 kuīxīn [动] feel guilty (PT, PP felt)

盔 kuī [名] helmet

盔甲 kuījiǎ [名] suit of armour (英) 或 armor (美)

窥 kuī [动] **1** (偷看) peep **2** (窥探) pry

窥测 kuīcè [动] seek out (PT, PP sought)

窥探 kuītàn [动] pry ▷不要窥探别人的隐私。You shouldn't pry into other people's private affairs. ▷字体专家能从字体中窥探人的性格。Handwriting specialists can tell people's character from their handwriting.

葵 kuí 见下文

葵花 kuíhuā [名] sunflower

魁 kuí I [名] head ▶夺魁 win first place II [形] well-built

魁梧 kuíwú [形] tall and sturdy

傀 kuǐ 见下文

傀儡 kuǐlěi [名] puppet

匮 kuì [动] (书) be deficient

匮乏 kuìfá [形] (书) deficient ▷灾区生活用品极为匮乏。The disaster area is very low in

馈 kuì [动](书) present
馈赠 kuìzèng [动](书) present

溃 kuì [动] **1** (指伤口) fester **2** (指军队) be defeated
溃败 kuìbài [动] be defeated
溃烂 kuìlàn [动] fester

愧 kuì **I** [形] ashamed **II** [名] shame ▷问心无愧 have nothing to be ashamed of
愧疚 kuìjiù [形](书) guilty

坤 kūn [形] female
坤表 kūnbiǎo [名] lady's watch

昆 kūn 见下文
昆虫 kūnchóng [名] insect

捆 kǔn **I** [动] tie... up ▷请你把报纸捆一捆。Could you please tie up the newspapers. **II** [量] bundle ▷一捆书 a bundle of books
捆绑 kǔnbǎng [动] tie... up

困 kùn **I** [动] **1** (困扰) be stricken ▷少女为情所困。The girl was stricken by love. **2** (限制) trap **II** [形] **1** (瞌睡) sleepy **2** (困难) difficult ▶困境 predicament
困乏 kùnfá [形] tired
困惑 kùnhuò [形] confused ▷我对下一步该怎么做感到困惑。I'm confused about what to do next.

困苦 kùnkǔ [形] hard
困难 kùnnan [形] **1** (指事情) difficult ▷克服困难 overcome difficulties **2** (指经济) poor ▷他家生活困难。His family lives in poverty.
困扰 kùnrǎo [动] trouble

扩 kuò [动] expand
扩充 kuòchōng [动] expand ▷实验室需要扩充设备。The laboratory needs additional equipment.
扩大 kuòdà [动] expand ▷扩大生产 expand production ▷扩大经济影响 extend economic influence
扩散 kuòsàn [动] spread (PT, PP spread)
扩展 kuòzhǎn [动] expand
扩张 kuòzhāng [动] **1** (医)(指血管等) dilate **2** (指领土等) expand

括 kuò [动] **1** (包括) include **2** (加括号) bracket
括弧 kuòhú [名] bracket

阔 kuò [形] **1** (宽广) wide **2** (阔气) wealthy
阔别 kuòbié [动] be separated for a long time ▷他阔别故乡已多年。He hasn't seen his home town for a long time. ▷阔别多年的朋友 long-lost friend
阔步 kuòbù [动] take great strides (PT took, PP taken)
阔绰 kuòchuò [形] ostentatious
阔气 kuòqi [形] extravagant ▷他爱摆阔气。He likes to throw his money about.

LI

拉扯 lāche [动] 1 (抚养) bring ... up (PT, PP brought) 2 (拽住) stop ▷你不要拉扯他，否则他揍你。Don't stop him, or else he'll punch you. 3 (牵涉) drag ... in ▷一人做事一人当，别把我拉扯进去。This has nothing to do with me – don't drag me into it.

拉锯 lājù [动] see-saw ▶拉锯战 stalemate

拉拉队 lālāduì [名] cheering squad

拉拢 lālǒng [动] draw ... in (PT drew, PP drawn)

拉平 lāpíng [动] draw level (PT drew, PP drawn)

拉纤 lāqiàn [动] tow

邋 lā 见下文
邋遢 lātā [形] (口) scruffy

拉 lá [动] tear (PT tore, PP torn) ▷我把大衣拉了个口子。I've torn a hole in my coat.
→另见 lā

喇 lǎ 见下文
喇叭 lǎbɑ [名] 1 (管乐器) trumpet ▷吹喇叭 play the trumpet 2 (扩音器) loudspeaker

落 là [动] 1 (遗漏) be missing ▷文章结尾落了个句号。There's a full stop missing at the end of the article. 2 (忘记) leave (PT, PP left) 3 (落后) fall behind (PT fell, PP fallen) ▷快点走，别落下。You'd better walk a bit quicker – you don't want to fall behind.
→另见 lào, luò

腊 là [名] 1 (农历12月) twelfth lunar month 2 (冬天腌制的) cured meat ▶腊肠 sausage

腊味 làwèi [名] cured meat

辣 là I [形] 1 (指味道) hot ▶辣酱 chilli sauce ▶辣椒 chilli 2 (指心肠) vicious II [动] sting (PT, PP stung) ▷我被洋葱辣得直流眼泪。The onion stung my eyes and made them water.

辣手 làshǒu I [名] vicious behaviour II [形] tricky

蜡 là [名] candle

蜡烛 làzhú [名] candle

啦 la [助] ▷你回来啦！Hey – you're back!

垃 lā 见下文
垃圾 lājī [名] rubbish (英), garbage (美) ▷垃圾邮件 junk mail ▷垃圾食品 junk food

在英式英语中，表示垃圾最常用的词汇是 **rubbish**。在美式英语中，**garbage** 和 **trash** 更为常用。…the smell of rotten garbage… She threw the bottle into the trash. **garbage** 和 **trash** 有时也用于英式英语中，但语体仅限于非正式或者者有喻义。I don't have to listen to this garbage… The book was trash.

拉 lā [动] 1 (用力移动) pull ▷拉人力车 pull a rickshaw ▶拉纤 tow 2 (载运) transport ▷拉一车货 transport a truckload of goods ▷出租车司机拉我到了机场。The taxi driver took me to the airport. 3 (演奏) play ▷拉小提琴 play the violin 4 (拖长) extend ▷拉橡皮筋 stretch an elastic band ▷拉长声音 hold a note 5 (帮助) help ▷朋友遇到困难，我就拉他一把。I would always help a friend in trouble. 6 (拉拢) draw ... in (PT drew, PP drawn) ▷不是我主动加入俱乐部的，而是被拉入伙的。I didn't join the club of my own volition, I got drawn in. ▶拉关系 establish connections 7 (口) (排泄) excrete ▶拉肚子 have diarrhoea (英) 或 diarrhea (美)
→另见 lá

来 lái I [动] 1 (来到) come (PT came, PP come) ▷家里来了几个客人。Some guests came to the house. 2 (发生) happen ▷刚到家，麻烦来了。As soon as I got home, the trouble started. 3 (泛指做事) ▷请来碗面条。A bowl of noodles, please. ▷你累了，让我来。You're tired – let me do it. 4 (表示可能) can, be able to ▷她弹得来钢琴。She can play the piano. ▷芭

蕾舞我跳不来。I can't do ballet. **5** (表示要做)
▷请你来帮个忙。Can you help me with this?
▷让我们大家一起来渡难关。Together we
can get through this crisis. **6** (表示目的) ▷母亲
买了些调料来腌肉。My mother bought some
seasonings to cure the meat. ▷我要想个法子
来对付他。I must think of a way to deal with
him. **7** (表示朝向) ▷服务员很快就把饭菜端
了上来。Soon the waiter had brought the food
to the table. **II** [形] coming ▶来年 the coming
year **III** [助] **1** (表示持续) ▷几年来 in the last
few years ▷近来 lately **2** (表示概数) about
▷10来公斤重 about 10 kilos

来宾 láibīn [名] guest

来访 láifǎng [动] visit

来回 láihuí **I** [动] **1** (去了再来) make a round
trip ▷从住宅小区到市中心来回有多远?
How far is it from the residential area to town
and back? **2** (来来去去) move back and forth
II [名] round trip ▷我从学校到家一天跑两
个来回。I make the round trip from school to
home twice a day.

来历 láilì [名] past

来临 láilín [动] come (PT came, PP come) ▷你会
有好运来临。Good luck will come to you.

来龙去脉 lái lóng qù mài ins and outs

来路 láilù [名] **1** (道路) approach **2** (来历) origins
(PL) ▷不要打开来路不明的下载文件。Don't
open downloaded documents if it's not clear
where they came from.

···来···去 ···lái···qù [动] ▷跑来跑去 run back
and forth ▷眉来眼去 make eyes at each other

来日方长 lái rì fāng cháng have plenty of
time

来势 láishì [名] force

来头 láitou [名] **1** (来历) connections **2** (缘由)
reason

来往 láiwang [动] have dealings with

来由 láiyóu [名] reason

来源 láiyuán **I** [名] origin **II** [动] originate
▷小说素材来源于生活。The material for the
novel originates in real life.

来之不易 lái zhī bù yì be hard to come by

睐 lài [动] look at

赖 lài **I** [动] **1** (依靠) depend **2** (留) stay **3** (抵赖)
deny **4** (诬赖) blame ... wrongly ▷你自己做错
了事不要赖别人。You shouldn't blame others
for your mistakes. **II** [形] bad

赖皮 làipí [名] shameless behaviour (英) 或
behavior (美) ▷耍赖皮 act shamelessly

兰 lán [名] orchid

拦 lán [动] stop ▷你喜欢去就去,我不拦你。If
you want to go, just go – I won't stop you.

拦劫 lánjié [动] rob

拦截 lánjié [动] intercept

拦路虎 lánlùhǔ a stumbling block

拦腰 lányāo [动] break in half (PT broke, PP
broken) ▷狂风将大树拦腰斩断。The trees
were snapped in half by the storm.

拦阻 lánzǔ [动] block

栏 lán [名] **1** (栏杆) fence **2** (圈) shed **3** (部分版面)
column ▷备注栏 comments column

栏杆 lángān [名] fence

栏目 lánmù [名] column

阑 lán [形] (书) late

阑珊 lánshān [动] fade

蓝 lán [形] blue

蓝本 lánběn [名] original version

蓝领 lánlǐng [名] ▷蓝领工人 blue-collar worker

蓝图 lántú [名] blueprint

蓝牙 lányá [名] Bluetooth®

澜 lán [名] waves (PL)

褴 lán 见下文

褴褛 lánlǚ [形] shabby

篮 lán [名] **1** (篮子) basket **2** (球篮) hoop

篮球 lánqiú [名] basketball

览 lǎn [动] **1** (观看) see (PT saw, PP seen) ▶游览
go sightseeing **2** (阅读) read (PT, PP read) ▶阅
览 read

揽 lǎn [动] **1** (搂) hug **2** (捆) tie **3** (包揽) take ... on
(PT took, PP taken) **4** (把持) monopolize

揽活 lǎnhuó [动] take on work (PT took, PP
taken)

缆 lǎn **I** [名] **1** (粗绳) rope **2** (似缆之物) cable
II [动] moor

缆车 lǎnchē [名] cable car

懒 lǎn [形] **1** (懒惰) lazy **2** (疲倦) lethargic

懒怠 lǎndai **I** [形] lazy **II** [动] be lazy

懒得 lǎnde [动] not feel like ▷天太热,我懒得
出门。I don't feel like going out, it's too hot.

懒惰 lǎnduò [形] lazy

懒散 lǎnsǎn [形] lazy

懒洋洋 lǎnyāngyāng [形] lethargic

烂 **làn** I [形] **1** (松软) soft ▷土豆炖烂了。The potatoes are done. **2** (破烂) worn-out **3** (头绪乱) messy ▷烂摊子 a shambles II [动] be rotten ▷西瓜烂了。The watermelon has gone off.

烂漫 **lànmàn** [形] **1** (指颜色) brightly-coloured (英), brightly-colored (美) **2** (指性格) unaffected

烂熟 **lànshú** [形] **1** (煮得熟) well-cooked ▷牛肉炖得烂熟。The beef is overcooked. **2** (熟练) learn ... by heart ▷他把这首诗背得烂熟。He learned the poem off by heart.

烂摊子 **làntānzi** [名] mess

滥 **làn** I [动] flood II [副] excessively ▷滥用 squander

滥调 **làndiào** [名] cliché

滥用 **lànyòng** [动] misuse

滥竽充数 **làn yú chōng shù** be a makeweight

郎 **láng** [名] ▷放牛郎 cowherd ▷女郎 young lady

狼 **láng** [名] wolf (PL wolves)

狼狈 **lángbèi** [形] in dire straits ▷他遭遇失败，处境狼狈。He failed, and is now in dire straits.

狼狈为奸 **lángbèi wéi jiān** join in a conspiracy

狼藉 **lángjí** [形] (书) messy ▷屋子久未整理，一片狼藉。This room hasn't been tidied for ages - it's a complete mess. ▷声名狼藉 have a bad name

狼吞虎咽 **láng tūn hǔ yàn** wolf ... down ▷他狼吞虎咽地吃下了一大碗面。He wolfed down a big bowl of noodles.

廊 **láng** [名] corridor ▶走廊 corridor ▶画廊 gallery

榔 **láng** 见下文

榔头 **lángtou** [名] hammer

锒 **láng** 见下文

锒铛 **lángdāng** I [名] (书) iron chain II [拟] clink

朗 **lǎng** [形] **1** (明亮) bright **2** (响亮) clear

朗读 **lǎngdú** [动] read ... aloud (PT, PP read)

朗诵 **lǎngsòng** [动] recite

浪 **làng** I [名] wave ▶浪花 foam ▶声浪 sound wave II [形] wasteful ▶浪费 squander

浪潮 **làngcháo** [名] tide

浪荡 **làngdàng** [动] loaf around

浪费 **làngfèi** [动] waste

浪迹 **làngjì** [动] wander ▷浪迹天涯 wander to the ends of the earth

浪漫 **làngmàn** [形] romantic

浪头 **làngtou** [名] **1** (口) (波浪) wave **2** (潮流) trend

浪子 **làngzǐ** [名] prodigal

捞 **lāo** [动] **1** (取) take (PT took, PP taken) ▶捕捞 fish for **2** (攫取) wangle ▷捞好处 wangle benefits

捞取 **lāoqǔ** [动] seek (PT, PP sought)

牢 **láo** I [名] **1** (牲畜圈) pen **2** (监狱) prison II [形] firm

牢固 **láogù** [形] firm

牢靠 **láokào** [形] **1** (坚固) firm **2** (可靠) reliable

牢笼 **láolóng** [名] shackles (PL)

牢骚 **láosāo** [名] grumble ▷他一肚子牢骚。He's full of complaints. ▷他牢骚了一整天。He grumbled for the entire day.

劳 **láo** I [动] **1** (劳动) work **2** (烦劳) trouble ▷劳您帮我看下行李。Would you mind keeping an eye on my luggage? **3** (慰劳) reward II [名] **1** (劳苦) toil ▷积劳成疾 collapse from overwork **2** (功劳) service

劳动 **láodòng** [名] labour (英), labor (美) ▷脑力劳动 brain work ▷他下地劳动去了。He's gone to work in the fields.

劳动力 **láodònglì** [名] **1** (劳动能力) labour (英), labor (美) **2** (人力) workforce

劳改 **láogǎi** [动] reform through hard labour

劳驾 **láojià** [动] (客套) excuse me ▷劳驾，把盐递过来。Excuse me, would you mind passing me the salt?

劳苦 **láokǔ** [形] hard-working

劳累 **láolèi** [形] exhausted

劳力 **láolì** [名] **1** (气力) labour (英), labor (美) **2** (劳动力) labour (英) 或 labor (美) force

劳碌 **láolù** [动] toil

劳民伤财 **láo mín shāng cái** waste of manpower and resources

劳务 **láowù** [名] labour (英) 或 labor (美) service

劳役 **láoyì** [名] hard labour (英) 或 labor (美)

劳资 **láozī** [名] labour (英) 或 labor (美) and capital

唠 **láo** 见下文

唠叨 **láodao** [动] be talkative

痨 **láo** [名] TB, tuberculosis

痨病 láobìng [名]TB, tuberculosis

老 lǎo I [形] 1 (年岁大的) old ▷老婆婆
old lady 2 (有经验的) experienced ▶老手
veteran 3 (旧的) old ▷老同学 old school
friend 4 (火候大的) well-done ▷肉煮老了。
The beef is well-done. II [名] old people ▷爱
老携幼 care for and nurture the old and young
III [副] 1 (经常) always ▷他老去父母家吃
饭。 He always eats dinner at his parent's
house. 2 (长久) for a long time ▷电器老不用
就会坏。 If electrical equipment isn't used for a
long time it can break down. 3 (非常) very ▶老
远 very far

老百姓 lǎobǎixìng [名] ordinary people

老板 lǎobǎn [名] boss

老本 lǎoběn [名] capital ▷他失业后尽吃老
本。 After he lost his job, he had to use up all
his savings.

老巢 lǎocháo [名] den

老成 lǎochéng [形] mature

老大 lǎodà I [名] head ▷他是我们小组的老
大。 He is the leader of our group. II [副] very
▷今天我心里老大不高兴。 I'm feeling very
upset today.

老大难 lǎodànán [名] long-standing problem
▷交通阻塞的确是北京的老大难。
Congestion really is a long-standing problem
in Beijing.

老底 lǎodǐ [名] dubious past

老调重弹 lǎo diào chóng tán it's the same
old tune

老公 lǎogōng [名] (方) husband

老汉 lǎohàn [名] old man (PL men)

老虎 lǎohǔ [名] tiger

老化 lǎohuà [动] age ▷这些机器设备正在老
化。 These machines are getting old.

老话 lǎohuà [名] saying

老家 lǎojiā [名] home ▷回老家 return home
▷我老家在上海。 Shanghai is my hometown.

老奸巨猾 lǎo jiān jù huá sly old devil

老练 lǎoliàn [形] experienced

老迈 lǎomài [形] aged

老谋深算 lǎo móu shēn suàn ▷我们教
练老谋深算，善于利用对手的弱点。 Our
coach is a wise old bird – he's good at using the
opponents' weaknesses.

老年 lǎonián [名] old age

老牌 lǎopái [名] established brand

老婆 lǎopo [名] (口) 1 (老太太) old woman (PL
women) 2 (妻子) wife (PL wives)

老气 lǎoqì [形] 1 (指人) mature 2 (指服装) old-
fashioned

老生常谈 lǎo shēng cháng tán commonplace

老师 lǎoshī [名] teacher

老实 lǎoshi [形] 1 (诚实规矩) honest 2 (不聪明)
naive ▷你怎么这样老实，居然把实情告诉
他！ How can you be so naive? I can't believe
you told him!

老手 lǎoshǒu [名] expert ▷修车老手 expert
mechanic

老鼠 lǎoshǔ [名] mouse (PL mice)

老态龙钟 lǎotài lóngzhōng worn out with
age ▷他变得老态龙钟，牙掉了，路也走
不动。 He has aged a great deal – he's lost his
teeth and has become house-bound.

老外 lǎowài [名] foreigner

老乡 lǎoxiāng [名] fellow villager

老朽 lǎoxiǔ [形] decrepit

老爷 lǎoye [名] master

老于世故 lǎo yú shì gù worldly-wise

老账 lǎozhàng [名] old debts (PL)

老子 lǎozi [名] (口) 1 (父亲) father 2 (自称) I ▷老
子才不怕老板呢。 I'm not afraid of the boss.

老字号 lǎozìhào [名] established name

佬 lǎo [名] (贬) guy ▶乡巴佬 country bumpkin
▶阔佬 rich guy

姥 lǎo 见下文

姥姥 lǎolao [名] (口) granny

姥爷 lǎoye [名] (口) grandpa

涝 lào [名] waterlogging ▶洪涝 flood

烙 lào [动] 1 (物体) iron 2 (食品) bake

烙印 làoyìn [名] 1 (痕迹) brand 2 (印象)
impression ▷童年生活在我心底留下了深刻
烙印。 My childhood has left a deep impression
on me.

落 lào 见下文
→另见 là, luò

落价 làojià [动] drop in price

乐 lè I [形] happy II [动] 1 (乐于) take pleasure
in (PT took, PP taken) ▷幸灾乐祸 take
pleasure in the misfortunes of others 2 (笑)
laugh ▷漫画把大家逗乐了。 The cartoon
made everybody laugh.
→另见 yuè

乐观 lèguān [形] optimistic ▷保持乐观情绪
adopt an optimistic attitude

乐呵呵 lèhēhē [形] joyful

乐极生悲 lè jí shēng bēi out of extreme joy

comes extreme sorrow

乐趣 lèqù [名] delight

乐土 lètǔ [名] paradise

乐意 lèyì I [动] be willing to ▷他不乐意帮我们。He's unwilling to help us. II [形] happy

乐园 lèyuán [名] playground ▷迪斯尼乐园 Disneyland

乐滋滋 lèzīzī [形] contented

勒 lè [动] 1 (收住缰绳) rein ... in 2 (强制) force ▶勒令 order ▶勒索 extort
→另见 lēi

勒令 lèlìng [动] order

勒索 lèsuǒ [动] blackmail

勒 lēi [动] tie ... tightly ▷勒紧绳子 tie a tight knot
→另见 lè

累 léi 见下文
→另见 lěi, lèi

累累 léiléi [形] (书) countless

累赘 léizhui [形] cumbersome

雷 léi [名] 1 (雷电) thunder ▷电闪雷鸣 thunder and lightning 2 (武器) mine ▶鱼雷 torpedo

雷电 léidiàn [名] thunder and lightning

雷厉风行 léi lì fēng xíng with the speed of lightning

雷同 léitóng I [动] echo II [形] duplicate

镭 léi [名] radium

垒 lěi I [动] build (PT, PP built) II [名] rampart

垒球 lěiqiú [名] softball

累 lěi I [动] 1 (积累) accumulate 2 (牵连) involve II [形] repeated
→另见 léi, lèi

累次 lěicì [副] repeatedly ▷经过累次打击，走私得到遏制。After repeated attacks the smuggling was finally contained.

累积 lěijī [动] accumulate

累及 lěijí [动] involve

累计 lěijì [动] add up

累累 lěilěi [形] countless

磊 lěi 见下文

磊落 lěiluò [形] open and upright

蕾 lěi [名] bud

肋 lèi [名] rib

肋骨 lèigǔ [名] rib

泪 lèi [名] tear ▶眼泪 tears (PL) ▶流泪 shed tears

泪花 lèihuā [名] teardrop

泪汪汪 lèiwāngwāng [形] teary

类 lèi I [名] kind ▶分类 classify ▶另类 alternative II [动] be similar to ▶类似 similar to

类比 lèibǐ [名] analogy

类别 lèibié [名] category

类似 lèisì [形] similar

类型 lèixíng [名] type

累 lèi I [形] tired II [动] 1 (使劳累) tire ▷孩子身体弱，别累着他。The child isn't strong – be careful not to tire him out. 2 (操劳) work hard
→另见 léi, lěi

累死累活 lèi sǐ lèi huó work oneself to death

擂 lèi I [动] beat (PT beat, PP beaten) II [名] competition

擂台 lèitái [名] 1 (指拳击) ring 2 (指竞技) arena

棱 léng [名] 1 (平面连接处) edge 2 (凸起处) ridge

棱角 léngjiǎo [名] 1 (字) edges and corners (PL) ▷一张棱角分明的脸 an angular face 2 (喻) sharp-wittedness

冷 lěng [形] 1 (温度低) cold ▷我觉得好冷。I feel really cold. 2 (不热情) frosty ▷他冷冷地对我说了声再见。He said goodbye to me very coldly. 3 (寂静) silent 4 (生僻) rare 5 (不受欢迎的) unpopular 6 (暗中的) hidden ▶冷枪 a shot from a sniper

冷冰冰 lěngbīngbīng [形] cold ▷那个老师对我们总是冷冰冰的。That teacher is always cold towards us. ▷孩子们的手和脚冻得冷冰冰的。The kids' hands and feet are frozen.

冷不防 lěngbufáng [副] suddenly

冷藏 lěngcáng [动] refrigerate

冷场 lěngchǎng [动] 1 (指演出) freeze up (PT froze, PP frozen) ▷请把台词再背几遍，以免上台时冷场。You should run through your lines a few more times, to avoid drying up on stage. 2 (指开会) go silent (PT went, PP gone) ▷我们最好事先多安排几个发言人，不要在开会时冷场。We'd better organise several people to speak at the meeting – we don't want any awkward silences.

冷嘲热讽 lěng cháo rè fěng have a dig at

冷处理 lěngchǔlǐ [动] shelve temporarily ▷专家认为此问题需冷处理。Experts think this problem should be shelved temporarily.

冷淡 lěngdàn I [形] cold II [动] cold-shoulder ▷多炒几个菜，别冷淡了客人。Make sure you do enough food – we don't want our guests to feel slighted.

冷冻 lěngdòng [动] freeze (PT froze, PP frozen) ▷冷冻食品 frozen produce

冷宫 lěnggōng [名] limbo

冷静 lěngjìng [形] 1 (方)(不热闹) quiet 2 (沉着) cool-headed

冷酷 lěngkù [形] cold-blooded

冷酷无情 lěngkù wúqíng ruthless

冷冷清清 lěnglěngqīngqīng [形] deserted

冷落 lěngluò I [形] isolated II [动] isolate ▷陪他聊聊，别冷落了他。Why don't you go chat to him – you shouldn't be leaving him out.

冷门 lěngmén [名] 1 (指专业) unpopular speciality (英) 或 specialty (美) ▷我弟弟选了个冷门专业。My brother has chosen an unusual specialty. 2 (指比赛) outsider

冷漠 lěngmò [形] indifferent

冷暖 lěngnuǎn [名] changes in temperature (PL) ▷冷暖空调设备 adjustable air-conditioning equipment

冷僻 lěngpì [形] 1 (冷落偏僻) deserted 2 (不常见的) rare

冷清 lěngqīng [形] deserted ▷没有你家里变得多么冷清。The house seems so deserted without you.

冷却 lěngquè [动] cool

冷若冰霜 lěng ruò bīng shuāng icy manner

冷色 lěngsè [名] cool colour (英) 或 color (美)

冷飕飕 lěngsōusōu [形] chilly

冷笑 lěngxiào [动] smile sarcastically

冷血动物 lěngxuè dòngwù [名] 1 (指动物) cold-blooded animal 2 (指人) cold fish

冷言冷语 lěng yán lěng yǔ make sarcastic comments

冷眼 lěngyǎn [名] 1 (冷静的态度) cool detachment 2 (冷淡的待遇) cold shoulder ▷冷眼相待 give sb the cold shoulder

冷饮 lěngyǐn [名] cold drink

冷遇 lěngyù [名] the cold shoulder ▷我遭到了她的冷遇。She gave me the cold shoulder.

冷战 lěngzhàn [名] cold war

愣 lèng I [形] staggered ▷听到这个消息，大家愣住了。Everyone was staggered at the news. II [副] bluntly

厘 lí 见下文

厘米 límǐ [量] centimetre (英), centimeter (美)

离 lí [动] 1 (分离) leave (PT, PP left) ▷离乡 leave the country 2 (距离) be far away from ▷我家离办公室不太远。My home is quite near to the office. 3 (缺少) do without ▷成功离不开奋斗和自信心。There can be no achievement without diligence and self-confidence.

离别 líbié [动] part

离间 líjiàn [动] sow dissent (PT sowed, PP sown)

离谱 lípǔ [形] unreasonable

离奇 líqí [形] odd

离散 lísàn [动] be separated

离休 líxiū [动] retire

离异 líyì [动] get divorced ▷离异后她独自生活。After the divorce, she lived alone.

离子 lízǐ [名] ion

梨 lí [名] pear

犁 lí I [名] plough (英), plow (美) II [动] plough (英), plow (美)

黎 lí 见下文

黎明 límíng [名] dawn

罹 lí [动] (书) suffer from ▷罹祸 suffer misfortune

罹难 línàn [动] (书) have a fatal accident

篱 lí [名] fence

篱笆 líba [名] bamboo fence

礼 lǐ [名] 1 (仪式) ceremony 2 (表示尊敬) courtesy 3 (礼物) present

礼拜 lǐbài [名] 1 (宗) religious service 2 (星期) week 3 (天) day of the week ▷礼拜六你来我家吃饭吧！Come over for a meal on Saturday.

礼服 lǐfú [名] ceremonial robe

礼节 lǐjié [名] courtesy

礼貌 lǐmào [名] manners (PL)

礼品 lǐpǐn [名] gift

礼尚往来 lǐ shàng wǎng lái ▷朋友之间应该礼尚往来。Friends should treat each other the way they would like to be treated themselves.

礼堂 lǐtáng [名] hall

礼物 lǐwù [名] present

礼仪 lǐyí [名] etiquette

礼遇 lǐyù [动] receive special treatment

李 lǐ [名] plum

里 lǐ I [名] 1 (反面) inside ▷裤子里儿 trouser lining 2 (里边) inner ▶里屋 inner room 3 (街坊) neighbour (英), neighbor (美) ▶邻里

neighbourhood (英), neighborhood (美) **4** (家乡) hometown ▶故里 birthplace **II** [介] in ▷屋子里 in the room **III** [副] ▶这里 here ▶那里 there **IV** [量] *unit of length, equal to 500 metres*

里程 lǐchéng [名] **1** (路程) mileage **2** (发展过程) course

里程碑 lǐchéngbēi [名] milestone

里手 lǐshǒu [名] **1** (左边) left-hand side **2** (内行) expert

里应外合 lǐ yìng wài hé have inside help ▷我军与城里的部队里应外合攻下了这座城市。Our troops collaborated with troops inside the town to take the city.

俚 lǐ [名] vulgar

俚语 lǐyǔ [名] slang

理 lǐ **I** [名] **1** (条纹) texture **2** (道理) reason ▶合理 reasonable **3** (自然科学) natural science **II** [动] **1** (管理) manage ▶理财 manage the finances **2** (整理) tidy ▷理发 get one's hair cut **3** (表示态度) acknowledge ▷置之不理 ignore

理财 lǐcái [动] manage the finances

理睬 lǐcǎi [动] pay attention (PT, PP paid) ▷3个电话打了过来，他都不予理睬。Three phone calls came though, but he ignored them all.

理发 lǐfà [动] get a haircut

理会 lǐhuì [动] **1** (懂) understand (PT, PP understood) ▷我理会他的意思。I understand what he means. **2** (注意) notice ▷他下车之后，竟没有理会站在对面的我。He got out of the car, but didn't notice me standing opposite him.

理解 lǐjiě [动] understand (PT, PP understood)

理科 lǐkē [名] science

理疗 lǐliáo [名] physiotherapy

理论 lǐlùn [名] theory

理念 lǐniàn [名] principle

理事 lǐshì [名] **1** (负责人) director ▷常务理事 managing director ▷理事会 board of directors **2** (成员国) member ▷理事国 member of the UN Security Council

理所当然 lǐ suǒ dāng rán natural ▷他认为我给他礼物是理所当然的。He reckons it's entirely natural that I should give him a present.

理想 lǐxiǎng **I** [名] ideal **II** [形] ideal

理性 lǐxìng [名] reason

理由 lǐyóu [名] reason

理直气壮 lǐ zhí qì zhuàng with complete confidence

理智 lǐzhì **I** [名] intellect **II** [形] rational ▷我们一定要理智地去想想啊。We must think about this rationally.

鲤 lǐ [名] carp (PL carp) ▶鲤鱼 carp

力 lì **I** [名] **1** (物) force **2** (功能) strength ▷理解力 comprehension **3** (体力) physical strength ▷四肢无力 weak all over **II** [动] fight (PT, PP fought) ▷力争冠军 fight for the championship

力不从心 lì bù cóng xīn feel inadequate to the task

力度 lìdù [名] intensity

力量 lìliang [名] **1** (力气) strength ▷这一拳力量很大。That was a very powerful punch. **2** (能力) power ▷请尽一切力量按时完成任务。Please do everything in your power to complete the task on time. **3** (作用) strength ▷这种药的力量大。This medicine is very strong.

力排众议 lì pái zhòng yì override objections

力气 lìqi [名] strength ▷生病后我走路没力气。After the illness I didn't have enough strength to walk.

力所能及 lì suǒ néng jí do everything in one's power ▷红十字会将为战争受害者提供力所能及的援助。The Red Cross will do everything in their power to help the war victims. ▷让孩子去做一些自己力所能及的家务事。Let the child do his best with the housework.

力图 lìtú [动] strive (PT strove, PP striven) ▷新政府力图解决经济危机。The new government strove to solve the economic crisis.

力学 lìxué [名] mechanics (PL)

力争 lìzhēng [动] **1** (极力争取) strive (PT strove, PP striven) ▷力争上游 strive for progress **2** (极力争辩) argue ▷据理力争 argue on good grounds

力作 lìzuò [名] masterpiece

历 lì **I** [名] **1** (经历) experience **2** (历法) calendar **II** [形] previous

历程 lìchéng [名] course

历次 lìcì [名] all previous occasions ▷他在历次战斗中都立下了功勋。In all previous battles he has achieved glorious victories.

历代 lìdài [名] successive generations (PL)

历来 lìlái [副] always

历历在目 lìlì zài mù flood back

历史 lìshǐ [名] history ▷历史文物 historical relic

厉 lì [形] **1** (严格) strict **2** (严肃) stern

厉害 **lìhai** [形] terrible ▷他口渴得厉害。He was terribly thirsty.

立 **lì** I [动] **1** (站) stand (PT, PP stood) **2** (竖立) stand ... up (PT, PP stood) ▷请把竹竿立在角落里。Please stand the bamboo pole in the corner. **3** (建立) ▷立功 make contributions **4** (制定) set ... up (PT, PP set) ▶立法 legislate **5** (存在) exist ▷自立 stand on one's own two feet II [形] upright ▷立柜 wardrobe III [副] immediately

立场 **lìchǎng** [名] position

立春 **lìchūn** [名] the start of spring

立冬 **lìdōng** [名] the start of winter

立法 **lìfǎ** [动] legislate

立方 **lìfāng** I [名] cube ▷2的立方是8。2 cubed is 8. II [量] cubic ▷立方米 cubic metre (英) 或 meter (美)

立竿见影 **lì gān jiàn yǐng** produce instant results

立即 **lìjí** [副] immediately ▷家中有急事，我得立即回去。There's a crisis at home, I have to go back immediately. ▷听到留言后他立即回了电话。As soon as he got the message he returned the call.

立刻 **lìkè** [副] immediately ▷老师让我们立刻打扫教室卫生。The teacher told us to tidy up the classroom immediately. ▷回家后立刻给我打个电话。Give me a call as soon as you get home.

立论 **lìlùn** I [动] present one's argument II [名] argument

立秋 **lìqiū** [名] the start of autumn

立身处世 **lì shēn chǔ shì** social conduct

立体 **lìtǐ** I [名] solid II [形] solid

立体声 **lìtǐshēng** [名] stereo

立夏 **lìxià** [名] the start of summer

立项 **lìxiàng** [动] officially set up a project

立意 **lìyì** [动] **1** (打定主意) be determined ▷他立意要走。He's determined to go. **2** (命意) approach ▷文章立意独特。The article has a unique approach.

立正 **lìzhèng** [动] stand to attention (PT, PP stood)

立志 **lìzhì** [动] be determined ▷他立志当一名海军。He is determined to become a naval captain.

立足 **lìzú** [动] **1** (站得住脚) be established ▷在海外立足对她来说不容易。It wasn't easy for her to establish herself overseas. **2** (处于某立场) be based in

吏 **lì** [名] official

沥 **lì** I [动] drip II [名] drop

沥青 **lìqīng** [名] asphalt

丽 **lì** [形] beautiful ▶壮丽 magnificent

丽人 **lìrén** [名] beauty

丽质 **lìzhì** [名] beauty

励 **lì** [动] encourage ▶奖励 reward

利 **lì** I [形] **1** (锋利) sharp **2** (顺利) advantageous II [名] **1** (益处) interest ▶利弊 pros and cons (PL) **2** (利润) profit and interest ▶暴利 staggering profits (PL) ▷高利贷 high-interest loan III [动] benefit ▷利国利民 benefit both people and country ▷互惠互利 mutually beneficial

利弊 **lìbì** [名] pros and cons (PL)

利害 **lìhài** [名] advantages and disadvantages (PL) ▷利害得失 gains and losses

利害 **lìhai** [形] terrible ▷这句话真利害。That's a terrible thing to say. ▷天冷得利害。It's terribly cold today.

利率 **lìlǜ** [名] interest rate

利落 **lìluo** [形] **1** (灵活的) nimble ▷说话利落 be quick with words **2** (有条理的) orderly **3** (完毕的) settled ▷事情办利落了。The matter has been settled.

利器 **lìqì** [名] **1** (兵器) sharp weapon **2** (工具) useful tool

利润 **lìrùn** [名] profit

利税 **lìshuì** [名] profits tax

利息 **lìxī** [名] interest

利益 **lìyì** [名] benefit

利用 **lìyòng** [动] **1** (物) use ▷合理利用自然资源 use natural resources appropriately **2** (人) exploit ▷你甭想利用我，我没那么幼稚。Don't even consider taking advantage of me – I'm not that naive.

利诱 **lìyòu** [动] entice

例 **lì** I [名] **1** (例子) example ▶举例 give an example **2** (依据) precedent ▶先例 precedent ▷史无前例 without precedent **3** (事例) case **4** (规则) rule II [形] regular

例假 **lìjià** [名] public holiday

例如 **lìrú** [动] give an example (PT gave, PP given) ▷大商场货物齐全，例如服装、家电、食品等应有尽有。The big shopping centre sells all kinds of goods, for example, clothes, household appliances and food.

例外 **lìwài** [动] be an exception ▷每个人都要加班加点，头儿也不例外。Everyone had to work overtime, and the boss was no exception.

▷所有人见到市长都点头哈腰，只有他是个例外。When everyone saw the mayor, they all bowed obsequiously – he was the only exception.

例行公事 lìxíng-gōngshì mere formality

例证 lìzhèng [名] instance

隶 lì I [动] be subordinate to II [名] slave

隶属 lìshǔ [动] be subordinate to

栎 lì [名] oak

荔 lì 见下文

荔枝 lìzhī [名] lychee

俪 lì I [形] parallel II [名] couple

莅 lì [动] (书) arrive

莅临 lìlín [动] (书) arrive

栗 lì I [名] chestnut II [动] tremble

砾 lì [名] debris (SG)

砾石 lìshí [名] gravel

粒 lì I [名] grain II [量] ▷一粒珍珠 a pearl ▷三粒入球 three goals

粒子 lìzi [名] **1** (颗粒) grain ▷米粒子 a grain of rice **2** (物) granule

痢 lì 见下文

痢疾 lìji [名] dysentery

俩 liǎ [数] (口) **1** (两个) two ▷我俩 the two of us **2** (几个) some ▷多赚俩钱 make some profit

连 lián I [动] connect ▶连接 link II [副] in succession ▷连年闹水灾 be flooded several years in succession ▷连看了几眼 glance at several times III [介] **1** (包括) including ▷连他4人 four people, including him **2** (甚至) even ▷连小伙都嫌冷。Even the young men thought it was too cold.

连词 liáncí [名] conjunction

连带 liándài [动] be related

连⋯带⋯ lián⋯dài⋯ and ▷连人带车 people and cars ▷连滚带爬 roll and crawl ▷连蹦带跳 jump and skip

连贯 liánguàn [动] be coherent ▷她讲话简明、连贯、得体。She spoke concisely, coherently and appropriately.

连接 liánjiē [动] connect

连累 liánlěi [动] implicate ▷战争连累了旅游业。The war had negative implications for tourism. ▷自己做事不要连累别人。You should not involve other people in things you have done.

连忙 liánmáng [副] at once ▷孩子发烧，他连忙去请大夫。When he found out that the child had a fever, he went to call a doctor at once.

连绵 liánmián [形] continuous ▷阴雨连绵 rainy spell

连任 liánrèn [动] re-elect ▷他连任市长一职。He was re-elected as mayor for another term.

连锁 liánsuǒ [名] chain ▷连锁反应 chain reaction

连续 liánxù [动] go on without stopping (PT went, PP gone) ▷他连续干了3天，觉得没睡。He worked for three days in a row without sleeping.

连夜 liányè [副] **1** (当天夜里) that night ▷接到电话后，我连夜赶到他家去。After receiving the call, I went to his house that very night. **2** (连续几夜) nights on end ▷听说他生病了，我连夜不得安心。After hearing that he was ill, I couldn't stop worrying for nights on end.

连载 liánzǎi [动] serialize

帘 lián [名] curtain (英), drape (美)

怜 lián [动] **1** (怜悯) pity **2** (怜爱) love

怜悯 liánmǐn [动] pity

怜惜 liánxī [动] take pity on (PT took, PP taken)

涟 lián [名] **1** (波纹) waves (PL) **2** (泪痕) flow

涟漪 liányī [名] (书) ripple ▷感情涟漪 waves of emotion

莲 lián [名] lotus

莲花 liánhuā [名] lotus flower

联 lián I [动] unite ▶联赛 league match II [名] couplet

联邦 liánbāng [名] federation ▷英联邦 the British Commonwealth

联播 liánbō [动] broadcast (PT, PP broadcast) ▷新闻联播 news broadcast

联合 liánhé I [动] **1** (人) unite **2** (骨) rejoin II [形] joint ▷联合声明 joint statement

联合国 Liánhéguó [名] United Nations, UN

联欢 liánhuān [动] have a get-together ▷师生联欢 a student/teacher get-together

联结 liánjié [动] connect ▷全球由因特网连接起来了。The entire world is connected by the Internet.

联络 liánluò [动] contact ▷保持联络 maintain contact ▷联络方式 ways to maintain contact

联袂 liánmèi [副] (书) together ▷联袂出演 perform together ▷联袂提议 make a joint proposal

联盟 liánméng [名] alliance

联名 liánmíng [动] do ... jointly

联网 liánwǎng [动] network

联系 liánxì [动] connect ▷他与恐怖分子有联系。He has connections with terrorists. ▷理论联系实际 apply theory to practice ▷和老同学失去了联系 lose touch with old schoolmates ▷和上层人物联系紧密 have close relations with one's superiors ▷促进经济贸易联系 encourage economic and trade relations

联想 liánxiǎng [动] associate

联谊 liányì [动] keep up a friendship (PT, PP kept) ▷联谊会 reunion

联姻 liányīn [动] be related by marriage

廉 lián [形] 1 (廉洁) honest 2 (便宜) cheap

廉耻 liánchǐ [名] integrity

廉价 liánjià [形] cheap ▷廉价日用品 cheap everyday goods

廉洁 liánjié [形] honest

廉政 liánzhèng [动] govern honestly

鲢 lián [名] silver carp (PL silver carp)

镰 lián [名] sickle ▷镰刀 sickle

敛 liǎn [动] 1 (收起) collect ▶敛容 assume a serious expression 2 (约束) restrain ▶敛迹 lie low 3 (收集) collect

敛财 liǎncái [动] accumulate wealth

敛迹 liǎnjì [动] lie low (PT lay, PP lain) ▷刑满出狱后他有所敛迹。After he was released from jail he lay low for a while.

脸 liǎn [名] 1 (面部) face ▷洗脸 wash one's face 2 (前部) front ▶门脸 shop front (英), storefront (美) 3 (情面) face ▷脸皮厚 thick-skinned

脸蛋儿 liǎndànr [名] cheeks (PL)

脸面 liǎnmiàn [名] 1 (面部) face 2 (情面) feelings (PL)

脸皮 liǎnpí [名] 1 (情面) feelings (PL) 2 (羞耻心) skin ▷他脸皮厚，不知羞耻。He's very thick-skinned and has no sense of shame.

脸色 liǎnsè [名] 1 (气色) complexion 2 (表情) expression

练 liàn I [动] practise (英), practice (美) ▶练武 practise martial arts II [形] experienced ▶熟练 skilful (英), skillful (美)

练笔 liànbǐ [动] 1 (练习写作) practise (英) 或 practice (美) writing 2 (练习书法) practise (英) 或 practice (美) calligraphy

练兵 liànbīng [动] drill

练功 liàngōng [动] do exercises

练习 liànxí I [动] practise (英), practice (美) II [名] exercise ▷练习簿 exercise book

炼 liàn [动] 1 (锻炼) do exercise 2 (烧铸) smelt 3 (琢磨) consider

炼制 liànzhì [动] refine ▷石油炼制 petroleum refining

恋 liàn [动] 1 (恋爱) love ▶相恋 fall in love with each other 2 (想念) miss ▷恋家 be homesick

恋爱 liàn'ài [动] love ▷你和谁恋爱了？Who are you in love with? ▷谈恋爱 be in love

恋恋不舍 liànliànbùshě be reluctant to part

恋情 liànqíng [名] romantic love

恋人 liànrén [名] lover

殓 liàn [动] put ... in a coffin (PT, PP put)

链 liàn [名] chain ▶项链 necklace

链条 liàntiáo [名] chain

良 liáng I [形] good II [副] much

良好 liánghǎo [形] good ▷考试成绩良好 good exam results

良师益友 liáng shī yì yǒu [名] ▷书籍是我们的良师益友。Books are our best teachers and most faithful friends.

良心 liángxīn [名] conscience ▷昧着良心做事 act against one's conscience

良性 liángxìng [形] benign ▷良性肿瘤 benign tumour

良知 liángzhī [名] intuition

凉 liáng [形] 1 (冷) cool 2 (灰心) disappointed → 另见 liàng

凉快 liángkuai [形] cool ▷树阴下面挺凉快。It's nice and cool under the trees. ▷我去空调房里凉快凉快。I'm going into the air-conditioned room to cool off.

凉爽 liángshuǎng [形] cool

凉飕飕 liángsōusōu [形] chilly

梁 liáng [名] 1 (房梁) beam 2 (桥梁) bridge 3 (隆起物) ridge

量 liáng [动] 1 (衡量) measure ▷让我们量一量这张床的长宽高。Let's measure the bed. 2 (估量) appraise → 另见 liàng

量度 **liángdù** [动] measure
量具 **liángjù** [名] measuring tool

粮 **liáng** [名] grain
粮食 **liángshi** [名] cereals (PL)

两 **liǎng** I [数] **1** (表示具体数目) two ▷两米 two metres (英) 或 meters (美) ▷两个小时 two hours **2** (表示不定量目) a few ▷说两句 say a few words ▷敲两下门 knock several times on the door II [名] both ▷两全其美 satisfy both sides ▷势不两立 be mutually exclusive III [量] unit of weight, equal to 50 grams
两败俱伤 **liǎng bài jù shāng** lose-lose situation
两便 **liǎngbiàn** [形] be convenient for all involved ▷你去拜会老友，我去喝茶，咱们两便。You go and visit old friends, and I'll go and drink tea – that way everyone will be happy.
两可 **liǎngkě** [动] be ambiguous
两口子 **liǎngkǒuzi** [名] couple
两难 **liǎngnán** [形] difficult ▷他面临两难选择。He's facing some difficult choices.
两栖 **liǎngqī** [动] be amphibious ▷两栖作战 an amphibious military operation
两全其美 **liǎng quán qí měi** satisfy both sides ▷我有个两全其美的方法。I have a solution that will please everybody.
两袖清风 **liǎng xiù qīng fēng** be incorruptible

亮 **liàng** I [形] **1** (光线) bright **2** (声音) clear **3** (心胸) tolerant ▷心明眼亮 see and think clearly II [动] **1** (发光) shine (PT, PP shone) ▷灯还亮着。The lights are still lit. **2** (显露) show (PT showed, PP shown) ▷亮底 come clean ▷亮身份 reveal one's identity
亮光 **liàngguāng** [名] light ▷屋里透出一丝亮光。A ray of light shone through the room.
亮晶晶 **liàngjīngjīng** [形] sparkling ▷她的珠宝在烛光下显得亮晶晶的。All her jewels were sparkling in the candlelight.
亮堂 **liàngtang** [形] **1** (物体) bright **2** (胸怀) enlightened
亮相 **liàngxiàng** [动] appear on stage ▷香港歌星昨日亮相广州。Yesterday, pop stars from Hong Kong were playing Guangzhou.

凉 **liàng** [动] let ... cool (PT, PP let) ▷夏天我喜欢把西瓜放冰箱里凉凉。In summer I like to put the watermelon in the fridge to cool.
→另见 liáng

谅 **liàng** [动] understand (PT, PP understood)
谅解 **liàngjiě** [动] forgive (PT forgave, PP forgiven) ▷网站正在建设之中，不便之处，敬请谅解。This website is still under construction – please forgive us for any inconvenience.

辆 **liàng** [量] ▷一辆汽车 a car ▷两辆坦克 two tanks

靓 **liàng** [形] (方) **1** (指女性) beautiful **2** (指男性) handsome
靓女 **liàngnǚ** [名] pretty girl
靓仔 **liàngzǎi** [名] handsome man (PL men)

量 **liàng** I [名] **1** (限度) capacity **2** (数量) quantity II [动] estimate ▶量力 make an estimation of one's own abilities ▷量入为出 live within one's means
→另见 liáng
量变 **liàngbiàn** [名] quantitative change
量力 **liànglì** [动] make an estimation of one's own abilities ▷凡事须量力而行。In all matters one should act according to one's abilities.
量入为出 **liàng rù wéi chū** live according to one's means
量刑 **liàngxíng** [动] determine a penalty
量子 **liàngzǐ** [名] quantum

晾 **liàng** [动] **1** (弄干) dry ▷晾干菜 dry out vegetables **2** (晒干) air

踉 **liàng** 见下文
踉跄 **liàngqiàng** [动] stagger

撩 **liāo** [动] **1** (掀) raise ▷撩起窗帘 raise the curtain ▷撩撩头发 put one's hair up **2** (水) sprinkle
→另见 liáo

辽 **liáo** [形] distant
辽阔 **liáokuò** [形] vast ▷辽阔的土地 vast territory

疗 **liáo** [动] treat ▶治疗 treat
疗程 **liáochéng** [名] course of treatment
疗养 **liáoyǎng** [动] convalesce ▷疗养院 convalescent home

聊 **liáo** I [副] just ▷聊以自慰 just to console oneself II [动] (口) chat ▷我们经常聚在一起聊聊。We often get together for a chat.
聊赖 **liáolài** [名] interest ▷百无聊赖 bored stiff

聊天儿 liáotiānr [动] (口) chat
聊天室 liáotiānshì [名] chat room

寥 liáo [形] 1 (稀少) few ▷寥寥无几 very few 2 (静寂) silent
寥廓 liáokuò [形] (书) vast
寥寥 liáoliáo [形] few

僚 liáo [名] 1 (官吏) official ▶官僚 bureaucrat 2 (同僚) associate ▶同僚 colleague

撩 liáo [动] tease
→另见 liāo
撩拨 liáobō [动] tease

嘹 liáo 见下文
嘹亮 liáoliàng [形] clear

潦 liáo 见下文
潦草 liáocǎo [形] 1 (字迹) illegible 2 (做事) sloppy ▷办事潦草 do things sloppily
潦倒 liáodǎo [形] down on one's luck

缭 liáo [动] 1 (缠绕) curl 2 (缝纫) sew (PT sewed, PP sewn) ▷缭贴边 hem
缭乱 liáoluàn [形] (书) confused ▷眼花缭乱 dazzled
缭绕 liáorào [动] float in the air ▷烟雾缭绕。 The smoke floated into the air.

燎 liáo [动] burn ▷心急火燎 burning with impatience

了 liǎo I [动] 1 (完毕) finish ▷不了了之 finish without any concrete results ▷了账 settle a debt 2 (放在动词之后表示可能) ▷办不了 not be able to handle ▷受得了 be able to bear 3 (明白) understand (PT, PP understood) ▶明了 understand II [副] (书) ▷了无惧色 without a trace of fear ▷了无长进 no progress at all
了不得 liǎobudé [形] 1 (惊异) amazing ▷能做这样的事情真是了不得。 It's amazing to be able to do such a thing. 2 (非凡) extraordinary ▷高兴得了不得 extraordinarily happy 3 (严重) terrible
了不起 liǎobuqǐ [形] amazing
了得 liǎode [形] terrible
了结 liǎojié [动] put an end to (PT, PP put)
了解 liǎojiě [动] 1 (知道) understand (PT, PP understood) ▷我了解他的为人。 I understand his behaviour. ▷政府应推动对艾滋病的了解。 The government should promote understanding of the AIDS crisis. 2 (打听) find

...out (PT, PP found) ▷你去了解一下事情的真相。 You go and find out the truth behind this matter.
了然 liǎorán [形] clear ▷一目了然 in a flash of understanding
了如指掌 liǎo rú zhǐ zhǎng know like the back of one's hand

料 liào I [动] expect ▷我没料到你会来。 I never expected that you would be able to come. ▷世事难料。 Human affairs are hard to predict. ▷不出所料 as expected II [名] 1 (材料) material ▷木料 timber ▶燃料 fuel ▶布料 cloth 2 (谷物) feed ▶草料 fodder
料理 liàolǐ [动] manage
料想 liàoxiǎng [动] expect

撂 liào [动] (口) 1 (放下) put ... down (PT, PP put) ▷他把纸牌撂在桌上走出去了。 He put the cards down on the table and left. 2 (弄倒) knock ... down ▷他一下就把我撂倒了。 He knocked me down with one blow. 3 (抛弃) abandon ▷孩子出生后被撂掉了。 The baby was abandoned at birth.

瞭 liào 见下文
瞭望 liàowàng [动] keep a look-out (PT, PP kept)

镣 liào [名] fetters (PL)
镣铐 liàokào [名] shackles (PL)

咧 liē 见下文
→另见 liě
咧咧 liēlie [动] (方) 1 (乱说) gossip 2 (哭啼) cry

咧 liě [动] grin
→另见 liē
咧嘴 liězuǐ [动] grin

裂 liě [动] split (PT, PP split)
→另见 liè

列 liè I [动] 1 (排列) set ... out (PT, PP set) 2 (安排) list II [名] 1 (行列) rank 2 (类别) category
列兵 lièbīng [名] private
列车 lièchē [名] train
列岛 lièdǎo [名] archipelago
列举 lièjǔ [动] list
列席 lièxí [动] attend as an observer ▷列席会议 attend a meeting as an observer

劣 liè [形] bad ▷恶劣 bad ▶低劣 inferior
劣根性 liègēnxìng [名] inherent flaw
劣迹 lièjì [名] offence (英), offense (美)

劣势 lièshì [名] position of weakness

劣质 lièzhì [形] poor-quality

烈 liè I [形] 1 (强烈) strong ▶激烈 fierce ▶猛烈 violent 2 (刚正) upright ▶壮烈 heroic II [名] 1 (烈士) martyr 2 (功业) exploits (PL)

烈士 lièshì [名] martyr

烈性 lièxìng [形] 1 (指性情) fiery ▷烈性马 a spirited horse 2 (指浓度) strong ▷烈性酒 strong liquor

---

猎 liè [动] hunt ▶打猎 go hunting

猎奇 lièqí [动] seek novelty (PT, PP sought)

裂 liè [动] split (PT, PP split) ▶分裂 split ▶破裂 break
→另见 liě

裂变 lièbiàn [动] split (PT, PP split)

裂痕 lièhén [名] crack

裂口 lièkǒu [名] split

拎 līn [动] carry

邻 lín I [名] neighbour (英), neighbor (美) ▶邻居 neighbour (英), neighbor (美) II [形] neighbouring (英), neighboring (美) ▶邻邦 neighbouring (英) 或 neighboring (美) country

邻邦 línbāng [名] neighbouring (英) 或 neighboring (美) country

邻近 línjìn I [动] be close to II [名] vicinity ▷邻近就有一家超市。There's a supermarket in the vicinity.

邻居 línjū [名] neighbour (英), neighbor (美)

林 lín [名] 1 (树林) wood ▷风景林 scenic wood 2 (同类) ▷艺林 artistic circles ▷石林 the Stone Forest 3 (林业) forestry ▶林业 forestry

林立 línlì [动] cluster

林木 línmù [名] forest

林业 línyè [名] forestry

临 lín [动] 1 (靠近) face ▶临危 face danger 2 (到达) reach ▶光临 presence 3 (将要) be about to ▶临产 be in labour (英) 或 labor (美) 4 (临摹) copy

临场 línchǎng [动] enter a competition

临床 línchuáng [形] clinical

临近 línjìn [动] be close to ▷那家饭店临近机场。That restaurant is close to the airport. ▷考试临近了。The exams are approaching.

临摹 línmó [动] copy

临时 línshí [副] temporarily ▷临时措施 temporary measures

临头 líntóu [动] happen

临危 línwēi [动] 1 (即将死亡) be dying 2 (面临危险) be in mortal danger

临阵磨枪 lín zhèn mó qiāng leave things until the last moment ▷平时要努力，靠临阵磨枪不行。You should work hard all the time, not leave everything until the last moment.

临终 línzhōng [动] be on the point of death

淋 lín [动] drench

淋巴 línbā [名] lymph

淋漓尽致 línlí jìn zhì thorough

淋浴 línyù [动] take a shower (PT took, PP taken)

琳 lín [名] precious jade

琳琅满目 línláng mǎn mù a feast for the eyes

粼 lín 见下文

粼粼 línlín [形] clear

嶙 lín 见下文

嶙峋 línxún [形] 1 (指山石) jagged 2 (指人体) bony

霖 lín [名] downpour

磷 lín [名] phosphorus

鳞 lín I [名] scale II [形] scaly

鳞次栉比 lín cì zhì bǐ row upon row ▷街道两旁的建筑物鳞次栉比。On either side of the road are row upon row of houses.

凛 lǐn [形] 1 (寒冷) cold ▶凛冽 bitterly cold 2 (严肃) strict ▶凛然 stern 3 (害怕) afraid

凛冽 lǐnliè [形] bitterly cold

凛然 lǐnrán [形] stern

吝 lìn [形] miserly

吝啬 lìnsè [形] stingy

吝惜 lìnxī [动] grudge

赁 lìn [动] rent ▷房屋出赁 room for rent

赁金 lìnjīn [名] rent

伶 líng [名] (旧) actor

伶仃 língdīng [形] lonely

伶俐 línglì [形] clever

伶牙俐齿 líng yá lì chǐ articulate

灵 líng I [形] 1 (灵活) nimble ▶灵敏 agile 2 (灵验) effective II [名] 1 (灵魂) soul 2 (神灵) deity ▶精灵 spirit 3 (灵柩) bier

灵便 língbiàn [形] **1** (指身体) nimble **2** (指工具) easy

灵丹妙药 líng dān miào yào panacea

灵魂 línghún [名] soul

灵活 línghuó [形] **1** (敏捷的) agile **2** (机动的) flexible

灵机一动 língjī yī dòng have a brainwave

灵柩 língjiù [名] bier

灵敏 língmǐn [形] sensitive

灵巧 língqiǎo [形] agile

灵堂 língtáng [名] mourning hall

灵通 língtōng [形] **1** (指信息) well-informed ▷他这个人信息灵通。He is well informed about current affairs. **2** (指效果) effective

灵性 língxìng [名] aptitude

灵验 língyàn [形] **1** (有效) effective **2** (应验) accurate

囹 líng 见下文

囹圄 língyǔ [名] prison

玲 líng 见下文

玲珑 línglóng [形] **1** (精巧细致) exquisite **2** (灵活敏捷) nimble

玲珑剔透 línglóng tītòu exquisitely made

凌 líng I [动] **1** (侵犯) insult ▶欺凌 bully **2** (升高) rise (PT rose, PP risen) **3** (逼近) approach ▶凌晨 before daybreak II [名] ice ▶冰凌 icicle

凌晨 língchén [名] before daybreak

凌驾 língjià [动] look down one's nose at ▷他总是凌驾于他人之上。He always looks down his nose at other people.

凌厉 línglì [形] quick and powerful

凌乱 língluàn [形] messy

凌辱 língrǔ [动] insult

铃 líng [名] **1** (响器) bell **2** (铃状物) ▶哑铃 dumb-bell

铃铛 língdang [名] small bell

陵 líng [名] **1** (小山) mound ▶丘陵 hill **2** (陵墓) tomb

陵墓 língmù [名] tomb

陵园 língyuán [名] cemetery

羚 líng [名] antelope

羚羊 língyáng [名] antelope

聆 líng [动] listen

聆听 língtīng [动] listen attentively

菱 líng [名] water chestnut

菱形 língxíng [名] rhombus

翎 líng [名] feather

翎毛 língmáo [名] plumage

零 líng I [名] **1** (零数) zero **2** (零头) odd ▷她年纪七十有零。She's seventy-odd years old. II [形] **1** (零碎的) odd ▶零活 odd jobs (PL) ▶零钱 small change **2** (部分的) spare ▶零件 spare parts (PL) III [动] wither and fall IV [连] ▷两年零三个月 two years and three months ▷五元零二分 five yuan two fen

零部件 língbùjiàn [名] parts (PL)

零点 língdiǎn [名] midnight

零件 língjiàn [名] spare parts (PL)

零钱 língqián [名] small change

零敲碎打 líng qiāo suì dǎ do things in bits and pieces ▷我建议你把作业一次做完，别零敲碎打。I suggest that you finish your homework in one go – don't do it in bits and pieces.

零散 língsǎn [形] scattered

零食 língshí [名] snack

零售 língshòu [动] retail ▷零售店 retail shop

零碎 língsuì I [形] trivial II [名] odds and ends (PL)

零头 língtóu [名] **1** (零碎部分) remnant **2** (零钱) small change

零星 língxīng [形] **1** (零碎的) fragmentary **2** (少量的) a little **3** (零散的) scattered

零用 língyòng [动] use ... as spending money

零用钱 língyòngqián [名] pocket money (英), allowance (美)

龄 líng [名] **1** (年龄) age **2** (年限) duration

岭 líng [名] **1** (山) mountain ridge **2** (山脉) range

领 líng I [名] **1** (衣领) collar **2** (脖颈) neck **3** (大纲) outline II [动] **1** (带领) lead (PT, PP led) **2** (占有) possess ▶占领 occupy **3** (领取) get (PT got, PP got (英), gotten (美)) ▶招领 advertise lost property ▶冒领 falsely lay claim to **4** (接受) accept **5** (了解) understand (PT, PP understood) **6** (领养) adopt ▷这孩子有人领了。Someone has adopted this child. III [形] belonging to ▶领土 territory IV [量] ▷一领凉席 a summer mat ▷一领长袍 a long dress

领班 lǐngbān [名] supervisor

领导 lǐngdǎo I [动] lead (PT, PP led) ▷他领导有方。He's an effective leader. II [名] leader ▷好的领导总是承认自己的错误。A good leader always acknowledges his or her mistakes.

领地 lǐngdì [名] 1 (指私人土地) fief 2 (指国家领土) territory

领海 lǐnghǎi [名] territorial waters (PL)

领会 lǐnghuì [动] understand (PT, PP understood)

领教 lǐngjiào [动] 1 (表示客气) accept ▷你说得对，领教了！ You're right, I take your point. 2 (表示请教) ask for advice ▷有几个问题要向您领教一下，好吗？ Can I ask for your advice about a few things? 3 (表示经历) experience

领空 lǐngkōng [名] air space

领略 lǐnglüè [动] appreciate

领情 lǐngqíng [动] be grateful ▷你的帮助，我十分领情。 I am extremely grateful for your help.

领取 lǐngqǔ [动] get (PT got, PP got (英), gotten (美))

领事 lǐngshì [名] consul

领受 lǐngshòu [动] accept

领头儿 lǐngtóur [动] take the lead (PT took, PP taken)

领土 lǐngtǔ [名] territory

领悟 lǐngwù [动] comprehend

领先 lǐngxiān [动] lead (PT, PP led) ▷他在比赛中遥遥领先。 He took a runaway lead in the competition.

领衔 lǐngxián [动] 1 (领头) head a list 2 (主演) star ▷他在一部新影片中领衔主演。 He's starring in a new film.

领袖 lǐngxiù [名] leader

领有 lǐngyǒu [动] possess

领域 lǐngyù [名] 1 (区域) district 2 (范围) field ▷社会科学领域 the field of social sciences

另 lìng I [代] another II [副] separately

另当别论 lìng dāng bié lùn treat... differently ▷他的问题应该另当别论。 His problem should be treated differently.

另类 lìnglèi [名] something out of the ordinary

另起炉灶 lìng qǐ lú zào make a fresh start

另外 lìngwài I [代] other ▷我不喜欢这些衣服，我喜欢另外那些。 I don't like these clothes – I like the others. II [副] in addition ▷我去了邮局，另外还去了果蔬店。 In addition to going to the post office, I also went to the greengrocer.

另眼相看 lìng yǎn xiāng kàn look at... in a new light

令 lìng I [名] 1 (命令) order 2 (酒令) drinking game 3 (时节) season ▷时令菜 seasonal

vegetables II [动] 1 (令) order 2 (使) make (PT, PP made) III [形] 1 (美好) excellent ▷令誉 good reputation 2 (表示尊敬) your

令行禁止 lìng xíng jìn zhǐ stick to the letter of the law

溜 liū I [动] 1 (滑行) slide (PT, PP slid) 2 (走开) sneak off 3 (加热) heat 4 (熘) quick fry II [形] smooth

溜达 liūda [动] go for a stroll (PT went, PP gone)

溜须拍马 liū xū pāi mǎ toady

刘 liú 见下文

刘海儿 liúhǎir [名] fringe (英), bangs (美) (PL)

浏 liú [形] clear

浏览 liúlǎn [动] glance over

留 liú [动] 1 (不走) stay 2 (使留) keep... back (PT, PP kept) ▷挽留 persuade... to stay 3 (留意) be careful ▷留神 be careful 4 (保留) keep (PT, PP kept) 5 (积蓄) grow (PT grew, PP grown) ▷留胡子 grow a beard 6 (接受) accept 7 (遗留) leave... behind (PT, PP left) ▷他死后留下很多遗产。 When he died he left behind a considerable legacy. 8 (留学) study abroad ▷留英 study in Britain

留步 liúbù [动] stop here

留后路 liúhòulù [动] leave a way out (PT, PP left)

留后手 liúhòushǒu [名] leave room for manoeuvre (英) 或 maneuver (美) (PT, PP left)

留恋 liúliàn [动] be reluctant to leave

留念 liúniàn [动] keep as a souvenir (PT, PP kept)

留情 liúqíng [动] show mercy (PT showed, PP shown)

留任 liúrèn [动] remain in office

留神 liúshén [动] be on the alert

留宿 liúsù [动] put... up for the night (PT, PP put)

留心 liúxīn [动] take note (PT took, PP taken)

留学 liúxué [动] study abroad ▷她要到国外去留学。 She wants to go abroad to study.

留言 liúyán [动] leave a message (PT, PP left)

留意 liúyì [动] look... out

留影 liúyǐng [动] have a picture taken as a souvenir

流 liú I [动] 1 (流动) flow ▷漂流 drift 2 (传播) spread (PT, PP spread) 3 (转变) change for the worse 4 (发配) banish ▷流放 exile II [名] 1 (水流) current ▷洪流 torrent 2 (等级) grade

流弊 liúbì [名] abuse

流产 liúchǎn [动] 1 (医) have an abortion 2 (失

败) fall through (PT fell, PP fallen)

流畅 liúchàng [形] graceful

流程 liúchéng [名] 1 (指水流) course 2 (指生产) flow

流传 liúchuán [动] spread (PT, PP spread)

流窜 liúcuàn [动] go on the run (PT went, PP gone)

流动 liúdòng [动] 1 (移动) flow 2 (流离) move about ▷流动演出队 travelling (英) 或 traveling (美) performing troupe

流毒 liúdú [动] spread evil influence (PT, PP spread)

流芳百世 liúfāng bǎishì be remembered for posterity

流放 liúfàng [动] exile

流感 liúgǎn [名] the flu

流浪 liúlàng [动] roam about

流离失所 liúlí shī suǒ destitute and homeless

流利 liúlì [形] fluent ▷他讲一口非常流利的英语。He speaks completely fluent English.

流里流气 liúlǐliúqì naughty

流连忘返 liúlián wàngfǎn enjoy oneself so much that one forgets to go home ▷这里的美景令我们流连忘返。The scenery here is so lovely that I don't want to go home.

流露 liúlù [动] reveal

流落 liúluò [动] drift about

流氓 liúmáng [名] 1 (下流) perversion 2 (歹徒) hooligan

流派 liúpài [名] school

流失 liúshī [动] erode

流水 liúshuǐ [名] 1 (流动水) running water 2 (销售额) turnover

流淌 liútǎng [动] flow

流体 liútǐ [名] fluid

流通 liútōng [动] circulate ▷货币流通 circulation of money

流线型 liúxiànxíng [形] streamlined

流星 liúxīng [名] meteor

流行 liúxíng [动] be fashionable ▷这种服装开始流行起来。These clothes are becoming fashionable. ▷流行音乐 pop music

流言 liúyán [名] gossip

流域 liúyù [名] basin

硫 liú [名] sulphur (英), sulfur (美)

硫酸 liúsuān [名] sulphuric (英) 或 sulfuric acid (美)

瘤 liú [名] tumour (英), tumor (美)

瘤子 liúzi [名] tumour (英), tumor (美)

柳 liǔ [名] willow

柳树 liǔshù [名] willow

柳絮 liǔxù [名] catkin

绺 liǔ [量] hank ▷一绺头发 a lock of hair

六 liù [数] six

陆 liù [数] an elaborate form of "six" used in writing cheques etc to prevent mistakes and forgery →另见 lù

遛 liù [动] 1 (指人) take a stroll (PT took, PP taken) 2 (指动物) walk ▷我要出去遛狗。I have to go out to walk the dog.

馏 liù [动] warm ... up

龙 lóng I [名] dragon II [形] imperial ▷龙袍 imperial robe

龙飞凤舞 lóng fēi fèng wǔ lively and elegant

龙卷风 lóngjuǎnfēng [名] tornado

龙腾虎跃 lóng téng hǔ yuè bustle about

龙头 lóngtóu [名] tap (英), faucet (美)

聋 lóng [形] deaf

聋子 lóngzi [名] ▷他是个聋子。He's deaf.

笼 lóng [名] 1 (笼子) basket 2 (笼屉) steamer →另见 lǒng

隆 lóng I [形] 1 (盛大) grand ▷隆重 solemn 2 (兴盛) prosperous 3 (深厚) deep II [动] bulge

隆冬 lóngdōng [名] midwinter

隆隆 lónglóng [拟] rumble

隆重 lóngzhòng [形] solemn

拢 lǒng [动] 1 (聚拢) hold (PT, PP held) 2 (靠近) get close to 3 (总合) add ... up 4 (梳理) comb 5 (合上) close

垄 lǒng [名] 1 (土埂) ridge 2 (小路) raised path between fields

垄断 lǒngduàn [动] monopolize

笼 lǒng [动] cover →另见 lóng

笼络 lǒngluò [动] win ... over (PT, PP won)

笼统 lǒngtǒng [形] general ▷笼统地介绍 give a general introduction

笼罩 lǒngzhào [动] envelop

弄 lòng [名](方) lane
→另见 nòng
弄堂 lòngtáng [名](方) alley

搂 lōu [动] 1 (聚集) rake ... up 2 (提起) pull ... up 3 (搜刮) extort 4 (方)(扳) pull 5 (方)(核算) check
→另见 lǒu

娄 lóu I [形](方) feeble II [动](方) go bad (PT went, PP gone)
娄子 lóuzi [名](口) blunder

楼 lóu [名] 1 (楼房) tall building ▷教学楼 teaching block 2 (楼层) floor ▷语音室在二楼。The language lab is on the second floor. 3 (城楼) city gate tower
楼房 lóufáng [名] multi-storey (英) 或 multi-level (美) building
楼盘 lóupán [名] building

搂 lǒu [动] embrace
→另见 lōu
搂抱 lǒubào [动] embrace

篓 lǒu [名] basket

陋 lòu [形] 1 (难看) ugly ▶丑陋 ugly 2 (狭小) narrow 3 (粗俗) common ▶陋习 bad habit 4 (肤浅) shallow ▶浅陋 superficial
陋习 lòuxí [名] bad habit

漏 lòu [动] 1 (雨、水) leak 2 (消息、风声) divulge 3 (词、句) leave ... out (PT, PP left)
漏洞 lòudòng [名] 1 (空隙) leak 2 (破绽) loophole
漏斗 lòudǒu [名] funnel
漏网 lòuwǎng [动] slip through the net

镂 lòu I [动] engrave II [名] engraving plate
镂刻 lòukè [动] engrave

露 lòu [动] reveal
→另见 lù
露富 lòufù [动] flaunt one's wealth
露脸 lòuliǎn [动] enjoy one's moment of fame
露马脚 lòumǎjiǎo [动] give oneself away (PT gave, PP given)
露头 lòutóu [动] 1 (露出头) show one's face (PT showed, PP shown) 2 (刚出现) appear
露馅儿 lòuxiànr [动] give the game away (PT gave, PP given)

芦 lú [名] reed

芦苇 lúwěi [名] reed

庐 lú [名] cottage
庐山真面目 lúshān zhēnmiànmù true character

炉 lú [名] stove ▷煤油炉 paraffin (英) 或 kerosene (美) stove ▷炼钢炉 steel-making furnace
炉火纯青 lú huǒ chún qīng reach perfection
炉灶 lúzào [名] kitchen range

颅 lú [名] skull

卤 lǔ I [名] 1 (盐卤) bittern 2 (卤汁) thick gravy II [动] stew ... in soy sauce
卤肉 lǔròu [名] pot-stewed meat

虏 lǔ I [名] captive ▶俘虏 prisoner of war II [动] capture

掳 lǔ [动] carry ... off
掳掠 lǔlüè [动] pillage

鲁 lǔ [形] 1 (迟钝) stupid ▶愚鲁 ignorant 2 (莽撞) impetuous ▶粗鲁 coarse
鲁莽 lǔmǎng [形] rash

陆 lù [名] land
→另见 liù
陆地 lùdì [名] land
陆军 lùjūn [名] land forces (PL)
陆续 lùxù [副] one after another ▷代表团陆续抵达。The delegates arrived one after the other.

录 lù I [名] record II [动] 1 (记载) record ▶记录 take notes 2 (选取) choose (PT chose, PP chosen) ▶选录 select 3 (录音) tape-record
录取 lùqǔ [动] admit ▷她被剑桥大学录取了。She was given a place at the University of Cambridge.
录像 lùxiàng [动] video (英), videotape (美)
录音 lùyīn [动] record
录用 lùyòng [动] recruit

鹿 lù [名] deer
鹿死谁手 lùsǐshuíshǒu who will win the prize ▷到底鹿死谁手, 一会儿就见分晓了。As to who will win the prize, we'll find out soon.

禄 lù [名] official pay ▶俸禄 official's salary

碌 lù [形] 1 (平凡) ordinary ▶庸碌

mediocre **2** (繁忙) busy ▶忙碌 busy

碌碌 lùlù [形] **1** (平庸) commonplace **2** (辛苦) busy

路 lù [名] **1** (道路) road ▶路标 signpost **2** (路程) journey ▷一路平安 have a safe journey **3** (门路) means ▶财路 a means of getting rich **4** (条理) sequence ▶思路 train of thought **5** (方面) sort ▷外路货 foreign goods **6** (路线) route ▶8路车 No. 8 bus **7** (种类) kind ▷他俩是一路的。They're two of a kind. ▷他们俩不是一路人。They're two very different people.

路标 lùbiāo [名] signpost

路程 lùchéng [名] journey

路过 lùguò [动] pass through

路径 lùjìng [名] **1** (道路) route **2** (门路) means (SG)

路况 lùkuàng [名] road conditions (PL)

路线 lùxiàn [名] **1** (指交通) route **2** (指思想) line

路子 lùzi [名] way

辘 lù 见下文

辘轳 lùlu [名] winch

辘辘 lùlù [拟] rumble

戮 lù [动] **1** (杀) kill ▶杀戮 slaughter **2** (合) unite

麓 lù [名] (书) foot of a mountain ▶山麓 foot of a mountain

露 lù I [名] **1** (水珠) dew **2** (饮品) juice II [动] reveal ▶暴露 expose ▶揭露 unmask →另见 lòu

露骨 lùgǔ [形] undisguised

露宿 lùsù [动] sleep outdoors (PT, PP slept)

露天 lùtiān [名] the open air ▷露天剧场 open-air theatre (英) 或 theater (美)

露头角 lù tóujiǎo [动] show promise (PT showed, PP shown)

露营 lùyíng [动] camp out

驴 lǘ [名] donkey

驴唇不对马嘴 lǘchún bú duì mǎzuǐ incongruous

侣 lǚ [名] companion ▶情侣 lover ▶伴侣 partner

侣伴 lǚbàn [名] partner

捋 lǚ [动] stroke →另见 luō

旅 lǚ I [名] **1** (军队编制) brigade **2** (泛指军队) force II [动] travel III [副] together

旅伴 lǚbàn [名] travelling (英) 或 traveling (美) companion

旅差费 lǚchāifèi [名] travelling (英) 或 traveling (美) expenses (PL)

旅程 lǚchéng [名] itinerary

旅居 lǚjū [动] live away from home

旅客 lǚkè [名] passenger

旅途 lǚtú [名] journey ▷祝你旅途愉快！ Have a good journey!

旅行 lǚxíng [动] travel

旅游 lǚyóu [名] tour ▷旅游业 tourism ▷去国外旅游 travel abroad

铝 lǚ [名] aluminium (英), aluminum (美)

屡 lǚ [副] repeatedly

屡次 lǚcì [副] repeatedly

屡见不鲜 lǚjiànbùxiān common occurrence

屡屡 lǚlǚ [副] time and again

缕 lǚ I [名] thread II [量] wisp ▷一缕烟 a wisp of smoke

缕缕 lǚlǚ [形] continuous

履 lǚ I [名] **1** (鞋子) shoe **2** (脚步) step II [动] **1** (踩踏) walk on ▷如履薄冰 treading on thin ice **2** (执行) carry ... out

履历 lǚlì [名] personal details (PL) ▷履历表 CV (英), resumé (美)

履行 lǚxíng [动] carry ... out

律 lǜ I [名] law ▶纪律 discipline ▶定律 law II [动] restrain ▶自律 self-disciplined

律师 lǜshī [名] lawyer

在英式英语和美式英语中，lawyer 是对律师的通称，表示某人具有法律专业资格，并且能够为他人做司法代理。在美式英语中，lawyer 具有备案资格，并且可以代表其当事人上庭辩护。美式英语中，lawyer 的同义词是 attorney。在英国，由 solicitor 处理诸如遗嘱和合同之类的法律文件，并且准备上庭所需要的各类文件；由 solicitor 上庭为当事人辩护，特别是在初级法院审理的案件。在高等法院，通常由 barrister 为控辩双方辩护。在苏格兰，barrister 被称为 advocate。

虑 lǜ I [动] think about (PT, PP thought) ▶考虑 consider II [名] concern ▶忧虑 worry

绿 lǜ [形] green

绿灯 lǜdēng [名] **1** (指交通信号) green light **2** (指方便条件) the go-ahead

绿化 lǜhuà [动] make ... green ▷绿化荒山 plant trees on the mountains

绿卡 lǜkǎ [名] green card

绿油油 lǜyōuyōu [形] glossy green

绿洲 lǜzhōu [名] oasis (PL oases)

氯 lǜ [名] chlorine

滤 lǜ [动] filter ▶过滤 filter

孪 luán 见下文

孪生 luánshēng [动] be a twin ▷孪生兄弟 twin brothers

挛 luán [动] curl up ▶痉挛 convulse

卵 luǎn [名] ovum (PL ova)

卵巢 luǎncháo [名] ovary

卵子 luǎnzǐ [名] ovum (PL ova)

乱 luàn I [形] 1 (没有秩序的) disorderly ▶杂乱 muddled ▶混乱 confused 2 (心绪不宁的) disturbed II [名] 1 (指冲突) chaos ▶战乱 war chaos ▶骚乱 disturbance 2 (指男女) promiscuity ▶淫乱 licentiousness III [动] confuse ▶扰乱 disturb IV [副] carelessly

乱哄哄 luànhōnghōng [形] chaotic

乱七八糟 luànqībāzāo in a mess

乱世 luànshì [名] turbulent times (PL)

乱真 luànzhēn [动] pass ... off as genuine ▷以假乱真 pass off a fake as genuine

乱子 luànzi [名] disturbance

掠 lüè [动] 1 (掠夺) ransack ▶抢掠 plunder 2 (拂过) speed past (PT, PP sped)

掠夺 lüèduó [动] plunder

掠取 lüèqǔ [动] grab

掠影 lüèyǐng [名] panorama

略 lüè I [名] 1 (简述) summary ▶要略 summary ▶节略 outline 2 (计谋) plan ▶策略 tactic ▶方略 general plan II [动] 1 (夺取) capture ▶侵略 invade 2 (简化) simplify ▶省略 omit III [形] simple IV [副] slightly

略微 lüèwēi [副] a little

略语 lüèyǔ [名] abbreviation

抡 lūn [动] swing (PT, PP swung)

伦 lún [名] 1 (人伦) human relationships (PL) 2 (条理) order 3 (同类) match

伦比 lúnbǐ [动] rival

伦理 lúnlǐ [名] ethics (SG)

沦 lún [动] 1 (沉没) sink (PT sank, PP sunk) 2 (没落) be reduced to ▷这位前总统已沦为阶下囚。The former president was reduced to the status of a prisoner.

沦落 lúnluò [动] sink to (PT sank, PP sunk)

沦丧 lúnsàng [动] be ruined

沦陷 lúnxiàn [动] be occupied

轮 lún I [名] 1 (轮子) wheel 2 (轮状物) ▷年轮 growth ring 3 (轮船) steamship II [量] ▷一轮明月 a bright moon ▷他比我大一轮。He's a dozen years older than me.

轮船 lúnchuán [名] steamship

轮番 lúnfān [副] successively

轮换 lúnhuàn [动] take turns (PT took, PP taken) ▷他们轮换站岗。They took turns to stand guard.

轮回 lúnhuí [动] recur

轮廓 lúnkuò [名] outline

轮流 lúnliú [副] in turns ▷我们轮流辅导孩子学习。We take it in turns to coach the child.

轮椅 lúnyǐ [名] wheelchair

论 lùn I [名] 1 (文章) essay ▶立论 argument ▶社论 editorial 2 (学说) theory ▷相对论 theory of relativity II [动] 1 (分析) discuss ▷评论 comment on ▶争论 dispute 2 (看待) consider ▷不能一概而论。You can't consider everything at once. 3 (衡量) set (PT, PP set) ▷按质论价 determine price according to quality III [介] in terms of ▷论水平，他比我强。In terms of ability, he's better than I am.

论处 lùnchǔ [动] punish

论点 lùndiǎn [名] argument

论调 lùndiào [名] view

论断 lùnduàn [名] thesis (PL theses)

论据 lùnjù [名] argument

论述 lùnshù [动] set forth (PT, PP set) ▷精辟的论述 brilliant analysis

论坛 lùntán [名] forum ▷世界经济论坛 the World Economic Forum

论文 lùnwén [名] dissertation

论战 lùnzhàn [动] debate

论证 lùnzhèng I [名] proof II [动] expound

论著 lùnzhù [名] work

捋 luō [动] stroke
→另见 lǚ

罗 luó I [名] 1 (网) net 2 (筛) sieve 3 (丝织品) silk gauze II [动] 1 (捕捉) catch ... with a net (PT, PP caught) 2 (陈列) spread ... out (PT, PP spread) **3** (搜集) collect

罗锅儿 luóguōr **I** [名] hunchback **II** [形] hunchbacked ▷罗锅桥 humpbacked bridge

罗列 luóliè [动] **1** (陈列) set ... out (PT, PP set) **2** (列举) enumerate

罗马数字 Luómǎ shùzì [名] Roman numeral

罗盘 luópán [名] compass

罗网 luówǎng [名] net

罗织 luózhī [动] frame

萝 luó [名] trailing plant

萝卜 luóbo [名] turnip ▷胡萝卜 carrot

逻 luó [动] patrol

逻辑 luóji [名] logic ▷逻辑推理 logical reasoning

锣 luó [名] gong

箩 luó [名] bamboo basket

箩筐 luókuāng [名] large bamboo basket

骡 luó [名] mule

螺 luó [名] **1** (指动物) snail **2** (指指纹) whorl

螺钉 luódīng [名] screw

螺旋 luóxuán [名] **1** (曲线) spiral **2** (指简单机械) screw

裸 luǒ [动] expose

裸露 luǒlù [动] expose

裸体 luǒtǐ [形] naked

骆 luò 见下文

骆驼 luòtuo [名] camel

络 luò 见下文

络绎不绝 luòyì bù jué endless stream ▷参观的人络绎不绝。There was an endless stream of spectators.

落 luò **I** [动] **1** (掉下) fall (PT fell, PP fallen) ▷脱落 shed ▷坠落 drop **2** (下降) go down (PT went, PP gone) ▷降落 descend **3** (降下) lower **4** (衰败) decline ▷衰落 wane **5** (落后) fall behind (PT fell, PP fallen) ▷落榜 fail an examination **6** (停留) stay ▷落栈 stay at a hotel **7** (归属) fall to (PT fell, PP fallen) ▷家庭的重任落在了他的身上。The responsibilities of the household fell to him. **8** (得到) suffer ▷从政就意味着要落责难。Being a politician means laying oneself open to public censure. **9** (记录) record **II** [名] **1** (停留之地) whereabouts (PL) ▷着落 location ▷下落 whereabouts **2** (聚居之地) settlement ▷部落 tribe ▷村落 village →另见 là, lào

落榜 luòbǎng [动] fail the college entrance examination

落差 luòchā [名] drop

落成 luòchéng [动] complete

落地 luòdì [动] **1** (坠地) fall to the ground (PT fell, PP fallen) **2** (出生) be born

落后 luòhòu **I** [动] fall behind (PT fell, PP fallen) ▷落后于时代 fall behind the times **II** [形] backward

落户 luòhù [动] settle

落花流水 luò huā liú shuǐ in a sorry state

落脚 luòjiǎo [动] stay

落井下石 luò jǐng xià shí kick a man when he's down

落空 luòkōng [动] come to nothing (PT came, PP come)

落落大方 luòluò dàfāng elegant and graceful

落马 luòmǎ [动] be brought to justice

落难 luònàn [动] suffer misfortune

落魄 luòpò [形] (潦倒) (书) down-and-out

落实 luòshí **I** [形] workable **II** [动] implement

落网 luòwǎng [动] be caught

落伍 luòwǔ **I** [动] drop out **II** [形] outdated

落叶归根 luò yè guī gēn return to one's roots

落座 luòzuò [动] take one's seat (PT took, PP taken)

摞 luò **I** [动] pile ... up **II** [量] ▷一摞杂志 a stack of magazines ▷一摞碟子 a pile of plates

Mm

妈 mā [名] **1** (口) (母亲) mum (英), mom (美) **2** (长一辈妇女) ▶姑妈 aunt ▶舅妈 aunt

妈妈 māma [名] (口) mum (英), mom (美)

抹 mā [动] **1** (擦) wipe ▷我把桌子抹干净了。I wiped the table clean. **2** (拉) pull ▷他把帽檐儿往下一抹。He pulled the brim of his hat down.
→另见 mǒ

抹布 mābù [名] cloth

麻 má **I** [名] **1** (指植物) hemp ▶大麻 marijuana ▶亚麻 flax **2** (指纤维) hemp **3** (芝麻) sesame **4** (麻将牌) mahjong **II** [形] **1** (麻木) numb ▷我的脚都站麻了。My foot has gone numb from standing for so long. **2** (粗糙) rough

麻痹 mábì **I** [名] paralysis ▶小儿麻痹症 polio **II** [动] lower one's guard ▷麻痹对手 throw one's opponent off guard

麻烦 máfan **I** [形] problematic ▷入学手续很麻烦。The enrolment process was problematic. ▷申请签证很麻烦。Applying for visas can be such a hassle. **II** [名] trouble **III** [动] trouble ▷不好意思,麻烦您了。Sorry to trouble you.

麻将 májiàng [名] mahjong

麻利 máli [形] dexterous

麻木 mámù [形] **1** (指知觉) numb ▷他冻得手脚麻木了。He was so cold that his hands and feet went numb. **2** (喻) (迟钝) insensitive ▷他对别人的批评很麻木。He's insensitive to the criticisms of others.

麻木不仁 mámù bù rén (贬) **1** (反应迟钝) be insensitive **2** (不关心) uncaring

麻酥酥 másūsū [形] tingly ▷蹲了一小会儿,脚就麻酥酥的。After squatting for a short while, I got pins and needles in my feet.

麻醉 mázuì [动] **1** (医) anaesthetize (英), anesthetize (美) ▷全身麻醉 a general anaesthetic (英) 或 anesthetic (美) **2** (喻) be lulled

马 mǎ [名] horse

马不停蹄 mǎ bù tíng tí non-stop

马达 mǎdá [名] motor

马大哈 mǎdàhā **I** [形] careless **II** [名] scatterbrain

马到成功 mǎ dào chénggōng achieve immediate success

马后炮 mǎhòupào [名] ▷他总是爱放马后炮。He's always too slow to act. ▷事后才提建议,这不是马后炮嘛! Isn't it a bit late to be making suggestions after the event?

马虎 mǎhu [形] careless

马脚 mǎjiǎo [名] giveaway ▷走私者在海关露了马脚。The smugglers gave themselves away at customs.

马拉松 mǎlāsōng [名] marathon ▷马拉松式的研究 a marathon piece of research

马路 mǎlù [名] road

马匹 mǎpǐ [名] horse

马赛克 mǎsàikè [名] (建筑) mosaic

马上 mǎshàng [副] right away ▷他马上就到。He'll be here right away. ▷妈妈接到电话后,马上就走了。After getting the call, Mum left right away. ▷准备好了吗? 我们马上就走。Are you ready? We're going right now.

马戏 mǎxì [名] circus

吗 mǎ 见下文
吗啡 mǎfēi [名] morphine
→另见 ma

玛 mǎ 见下文
玛瑙 mǎnǎo [名] agate

码 mǎ **I** [名] numeral ▶数码 number ▶页码 page number **II** [量] ▷我们说的是两码事儿。We were talking about two different things. ▷这根本就是一码事儿嘛！These are basically the same thing after all **III** [动](口) stack ... up

码头 **mǎtou** [名] pier

蚂 **mǎ** 见下文
→另见 **mà**

蚂蚁 **mǎyǐ** [名] ant

蚂 **mà** 见下文
→另见 **mǎ**

蚂蚱 **màzha** [名] locust

骂 **mà** [动] **1** (侮辱) insult **2** (斥责) tell ... off (PT, PP told) ▷他因为没完成家庭作业而挨骂。He was told off for not doing his homework.

骂街 **màjiē** [动] shout and scream in public

骂名 **màmíng** [名] bad reputation

吗 **ma** [助] **1** (表示疑问) ▷你去银行吗？Are you going to the bank? **2** (表示反问) ▷你不是去过她的家吗？Haven't you been to her house before?
→另见 **mǎ**

嘛 **ma** [助] **1** (表示显而易见) ▷事实就是这样嘛！That's just the way things are! **2** (表示期望) ▷别不高兴嘛！Please don't be unhappy. **3** (表示停顿) ▷那件事情，明天再说吧！Oh that! Well, let's talk about it tomorrow.

埋 **mái** [动] **1** (盖住) bury **2** (隐藏) hide (PT hid, PP hidden) ▷隐姓埋名 go incognito
→另见 **mán**

埋藏 **máicáng** [动] bury ▷埋藏在心中的秘密 a secret buried in one's heart

埋伏 **máifú** [动] **1** lie in ambush (PT lay, PP lain) **2** ambush

埋没 **máimò** [动] **1** (埋住) cover **2** (忽视) overlook

埋头 **máitóu** [动] bury oneself in ▷埋头苦读 bury oneself in serious reading

埋葬 **máizàng** [动] bury

买 **mǎi** [动] **1** (购买) buy (PT, PP bought) ▷她爱买贵的衣服。She liked to buy expensive clothes. ▷不是每个人都买得起房。Not everyone can afford to buy a flat. ▷我去市场买东西。I'm going shopping in the market. **2** (换取) win ... over (PT, PP won) ▷收买民心 win people over ▶买通 buy ... off

买单 **mǎidān** [动] (方) pay a bill (PT, PP paid) ▷买单！The bill, please! ▷今天吃饭我来买单吧！Today the meal's on me.

买空卖空 **mǎi kōng mài kōng** speculate on the stock market

买卖 **mǎimai** [名] **1** (生意) business ▷当地市场的买卖很兴隆。Business is brisk at the local market. **2** (商店) shop (英), store (美)

买通 **mǎitōng** [动] bribe ▷为了提前出狱，他买通了监狱长。In order to get out of prison early he bribed the prison governor.

买账 **mǎizhàng** [动] buy (PT, PP bought) ▷他喜欢对别人指手画脚，但没人买他的账。He likes to try and order people around, but no one buys it.

迈 **mài** **I** [动] step ▶迈步 stride **II** [形] elderly **III** [量] mile

迈进 **màijìn** [动] stride forward (PT strode, PP stridden) ▷我们正向我们的目标迈进。We are making great strides towards our objectives.

麦 **mài** [名] **1** (麦类粮食) wheat ▶燕麦 oats (PL) **2** (小麦) wheat

麦克风 **màikèfēng** [名] microphone, mike (口)

麦秋 **màiqiū** [名] wheat-harvesting season

卖 **mài** [动] **1** (出售) sell (PT, PP sold) ▷书都卖完了。The books are all sold out. **2** (出卖) betray **3** (尽量使出) do all one can ▶卖劲儿 spare no effort **4** (故意表现) make a show of ▶装疯卖傻 play the fool

卖点 **màidiǎn** [名] selling point

卖关子 **mài guānzi** [动] keep ... guessing (PT, PP kept) ▷她说话爱卖关子。When she talks she likes to keep people guessing.

卖命 **màimìng** [动] work oneself to the bone ▷他每天卖命赚钱。He works himself to the bone every day.

卖弄 **màinong** [动] show off (PT showed, PP shown)

卖淫 **màiyín** [动] sell sex (PT, PP sold)

卖座 **màizuò** [动] attract customers ▷这个小咖啡馆儿很卖座。This small coffee house attracts a lot of customers.

脉 **mài** [名] **1** (血管) blood vessels (PL) ▶动脉 artery (PL arteries) ▶静脉 vein **2** (脉搏) pulse ▶号脉 feel a pulse **3** (脉状物) ▶山脉 mountain range ▶矿脉 mineral veins ▶叶脉 leaf veins
→另见 **mò**

脉搏 **màibó** [名] pulse

脉络 **màiluò** [名] **1** (医) blood vessels (PL) **2** (喻) (条理) train of thought ▷写文章脉络要清楚。When writing essays, the sequence of ideas must be clear.

埋 mán 见下文
→另见 mái
埋怨 mányuàn [动] **1** (指责) blame **2** (抱怨) complain

蛮 mán I [形] rough ▶野蛮 wild II [副] **1** (鲁莽) recklessly **2** (方)(很) very
蛮干 mángàn [动] act recklessly
蛮横 mánhèng [形] boorish

馒 mán 见下文
馒头 mántou [名] steamed bun

瞒 mán [动] hide the truth from (PT hid, PP hidden) ▶快告诉我们吧，别瞒着啦！Hurry up and tell us – don't keep us in the dark!
瞒天过海 mán tiān guò hǎi act in an underhand way

满 mǎn I [形] **1** (充实) full **2** (全) complete ▶满分 full marks ▶她满眼泪花。Her eyes are full of tears. II [动] **1** (使充满) fill ▶快给客人满上酒。Hurry up and fill the guests' glasses with wine. **2** (满足) be satisfied ▶他对自己的生活心满意足。He is fully satisfied with his life. III [副] fully
满不在乎 mǎn bù zàihu be indifferent to
满城风雨 mǎn chéng fēng yǔ cause a sensation
满怀 mǎnhuái I [动] be filled with ▶她满怀着伤痛，离开了家乡。She left her hometown filled with sorrow. II [名] chest ▶他们在黑暗中撞了个满怀。They bumped right into each other in the darkness.
满面春风 mǎnmiàn chūnfēng beaming with joy
满腔 mǎnqiāng [动] be filled with ▶他对工作满腔热情。He is full of enthusiasm about his work.
满意 mǎnyì [动] be satisfied
满员 mǎnyuán [动] be full
满月 mǎnyuè I [动] ▶孩子马上就满月了。The child is almost a month old. II [名] full moon
满足 mǎnzú [动] **1** (感到满意) be satisfied ▶他对生活很满足。He is very satisfied with life. ▶满足现状 satisfied with the status quo **2** (使满足) satisfy ▶产量无法满足市场需求。Output cannot satisfy the demands of the market.

曼 màn [形] **1** (轻柔) graceful **2** (长) prolonged
曼延 mànyán [动] stretch

谩 màn [形] rude
谩骂 mànmà [动] hurl abuse at

蔓 màn 见下文
蔓延 mànyán [动] spread (PT, PP spread) ▶大火迅速蔓延到整个村落。The fire spread quickly to the whole village.

漫 màn I [动] overflow II [形] all over III [副] (随便) randomly
漫不经心 màn bù jīngxīn absent-mindedly
漫步 mànbù [动] stroll
漫长 màncháng [形] endless
漫画 mànhuà [名] comic strip
漫骂 mànmà [动] rant and rave
漫山遍野 màn shān biàn yě all over the place
漫谈 màntán [动] discuss ... informally
漫天 màntiān [形] **1** (满天) filling the sky ▶云雾漫天。The sky was filled with clouds and mist. **2** (无限度) outrageous
漫延 mànyán [动] spread (PT, PP spread)
漫游 mànyóu [动] travel around ▶我希望将来能漫游全世界。I hope that in the future I will be able to travel the world.

慢 màn I [形] **1** (缓慢) slow **2** (冷漠) indifferent ▶傲慢 haughty II [动] hold on (PT, PP held) ▶且慢，我有话要说。Hold on – I have something to say.
慢慢腾腾 mànmantēngtēng sluggish
慢条斯理 màntiáo-sīlǐ in a leisurely way
慢悠悠 mànyōuyōu [形] leisurely

忙 máng I [形] busy II [动] be busy with ▶你这一段忙什么呢？What's been keeping you busy recently?
忙乎 mánghu [动] be busy ▶我忙乎着搬家呢！I'm busy moving house.
忙碌 mánglù [动] be busy ▶快考试了，同学们都很忙碌。The exams are approaching and the students are all very busy.
忙乱 mángluàn [形] rushed ▶早上总是很忙乱。Mornings are always rushed.

盲 máng [形] blind ▶文盲 illiterate
盲从 mángcóng [动] follow ... blindly
盲打 mángdǎ [动] touch-type
盲点 mángdiǎn [名] blind spot ▶法律盲点 loopholes in the law
盲动 mángdòng [动] act rashly
盲目 mángmù [形] blind ▶盲目崇拜 blind worship

盲目性 mángmùxìng [名] blindness

盲人摸象 mángrén mō xiàng mistake a part for the whole

盲文 mángwén [名] braille

茫 máng I [形] 1 (远而模糊) hazy 2 (迷惑) puzzling

茫茫 mángmáng [形] vast

茫然 mángrán [形] at a loss ▷给他解释了半天，他还是茫然地望着我。I took a long time explaining it to him but he still stared at me blankly.

莽 mǎng I [名] coarse grass II [形] rash

莽莽 mǎngmǎng [形] vast

莽撞 mǎngzhuàng [形] impetuous

蟒 mǎng [名] (动物) python

猫 māo [名] cat

猫儿腻 māornì [名] (方) trick

猫儿眼 māoryǎn [名] spyhole

毛 máo I [名] 1 (毛发) hair ▶羽毛 feather 2 (指食物上) mould (英), mold (美) ▷面包上长毛了。The bread is mouldy (英) 或 moldy (美). 3 (指墙上或衣物上) mildew 4 (指植物) ▷不毛之地 barren land ▷空气中飞着一些小毛毛。There are small bits of fluff floating in the air. II [形] 1 (粗糙) crude ▶毛坯 semi-finished product 2 (不纯) gross ▶毛重 gross weight 3 (粗率) careless 4 (小) little

毛笔 máobǐ [名] brush pen

毛病 máobìng [名] 1 (故障) problem 2 (缺点) shortcoming 3 (疾病) illness ▷他的腿有点毛病。He has something wrong with his leg.

毛糙 máocāo [形] 1 (指物) crude 2 (指人) careless ▷他干活毛糙。He's careless about his work.

毛骨悚然 máo gǔ sǒngrán make sb's flesh creep

毛孔 máokǒng [名] pore

毛利 máolì [名] gross profit

毛皮 máopí [名] fur

毛茸茸 máorōngrōng [形] 1 (指人) hairy 2 (指有羽毛物) feathered 3 (指有毛皮的动物) furry

毛手毛脚 máo shǒu máo jiǎo careless

毛遂自荐 Máo Suì zì jiàn volunteer one's services

毛重 máozhòng [名] gross weight

矛 máo [名] spear

矛盾 máodùn I [名] 1 (相抵之处) conflict 2 (哲) contradiction II [形] uncertain ▷对于选择

哪个专业，她内心很矛盾。She's uncertain about which major to choose.

矛头 máotóu [名] (喻) target ▷会上，大家把批评的矛头都指向了老赵。At the meeting, Lao Zhao was the target of everybody's criticism.

茅 máo [名] thatch

茅庐 máolú [名] thatched cottage

茅塞顿开 máo sè dùn kāi suddenly see the light

锚 máo [名] anchor ▶起锚 weigh anchor

茂 mào [形] 1 (茂盛) luxuriant 2 (丰富) abundant

茂密 màomì [形] dense

茂盛 màoshèng [形] flourishing

冒 mào I [动] 1 (往外) give ... off (PT gave, PP given) ▷锅冒烟了。The wok is giving off smoke. 2 (不顾) risk ▷冒着生命危险 putting one's life at risk 3 (假充) pretend to be ▶冒牌 bogus ▶冒认 lay false claim to II [副] falsely ▶冒进 jump the gun

冒充 màochōng [动] pass ... off as ▷这个店将商品冒充名牌出售。This store sells products which are passed off as brand names.

冒犯 màofàn [动] 1 (他人、尊严) offend 2 (纪律、规定) violate ▷无人敢冒犯军纪。No one dares to violate military discipline.

冒火 màohuǒ [动] fly into a rage (PT flew, PP flown)

冒尖儿 màojiānr [动] 1 (高出容器) brim over 2 (稍稍超出) be just over ▷他10岁冒点尖儿。He's just over ten years old. 3 (突出) be outstanding 4 (初显) emerge

冒进 màojìn [动] jump the gun

冒昧 màomèi [形] (谦) presumptuous ▷冒昧打断您一下。May I interrupt you a moment?

冒牌 màopái [动] pirate ▷冒牌商品 pirated goods

冒失 màoshi [形] abrupt

冒头 màotóu [动] emerge

冒险 màoxiǎn [动] take a risk (PT took, PP taken) ▷不要轻易去冒险。Don't take risks lightly.

贸 mào [动] trade ▶外贸 foreign trade

贸然 màorán [副] rashly

贸易 màoyì [名] trade ▷他在一家对外贸易公司工作。He works for a company that's engaged in foreign trade.

帽 mào [名] 1 (帽子) hat 2 (帽状物) ▶笔帽儿 pen cap ▶螺丝帽 screw cap

帽子 **màozi** [名] **1** (字) hat **2** (喻) (坏名义) label ▷他脱不掉捣蛋鬼的帽子。He can't shake off the label of troublemaker.

貌 **mào** [名] (相貌、外表) appearance
貌合神离 **mào hé shén lí** appear united on the outside but be troubled underneath
貌似 **màosì** [动] appear to be

没 **méi I** [动] not have ▷他们没孩子。They don't have any children. ▷屋子里没人。There's no one in the room. **II** [副] not ▷他没去美国。He did not go to America. ▷他没看过大海。He's never seen the sea before. ▷他没吃早餐就走了。He left before eating breakfast. →另见 mò
没大没小 **méi dà méi xiǎo** show no respect for one's elders
没劲 **méijìn I** [动] have no energy **II** [形] uninteresting
没精打采 **méi jīng dǎ cǎi** be out of sorts
没门儿 **méiménr** [动] (方) **1** (没门路) not have the right connections **2** (不可能) be impossible ▷不努力工作就想赚大钱？没门儿！You want to earn big bucks without hard work? Not a chance!
没谱儿 **méipǔr** [动] **1** (心里没数) not have a clue ▷论文怎么写，他根本没谱儿。He doesn't have a clue how to write his thesis. **2** (没准儿) be unreliable ▷不要听他的，他说话没谱儿。Don't listen to him – he's a loose cannon.
没趣 **méiqù** [形] put out
没完 **méiwán** [动] **1** (没结束) be unfinished ▷活儿还没完，你怎么就走了？The work isn't finished yet – how can you just leave? **2** (不罢休) not let ... drop ▷你要是不还我钱，我跟你没完！If you don't give me my money back, I won't let it drop!
没戏 **méixì** [动] (方) be a lost cause
没心没肺 **méi xīn méi fèi 1** (没良心) heartless **2** (缺心眼) thoughtless **3** (过于单纯) simple-minded
没有 **méiyǒu I** [动] **1** (不具有) not have ▷我没有手机。I don't have a mobile phone. **2** (不存在) there is not ▷办公室里没有人。There's no one in the office. **3** (全都不) ▷放心吧，没有谁敢欺负你。Relax – no one's going to dare to bully you. ▷他们中没有谁敢说谎。None of them dares to lie. ▷没有一个答案是正确的。None of the answers are correct. **4** (不如) be not as ... as ... ▷他没有你努力。He's not as hard working as you. ▷我的房子没有你的大。My house isn't as big as yours. **5** (不到) be less than ▷他们干了没有两个小时就休息

了。They had been working for less than two hours when they took a rest. **II** [副] **1** (尚未) not yet ▷庄稼还没有成熟。The crops haven't ripened yet. **2** (未曾) never before ▷我没有吃过西餐。I have never eaten Western food before.
没辙 **méizhé** [动] (方) not be able to do anything about ▷他不想去，我也没辙。He doesn't want to go, and I can't do anything about it.

玫 **méi** 见下文
玫瑰 **méigui** [名] rose

枚 **méi** [量] ▷一枚硬币 one coin ▷两枚炸弹 two bombs

眉 **méi** [名] **1** (眉毛) eyebrow **2** (书眉) top margin
眉飞色舞 **méi fēi sè wǔ** beam with joy ▷运动会上得了冠军，他高兴得眉飞色舞。His whole face lit up when he became champion at the athletics meeting.
眉开眼笑 **méi kāi yǎn xiào** beam with joy
眉目 **méimù** [名] **1** (容貌) features (PL) **2** (条理) order ▷这篇文章眉目不清。This article is badly ordered. **3** (头绪) light at the end of the tunnel
眉批 **méipī** [名] headnote
眉头 **méitóu** [名] brows (PL)

梅 **méi** [名] **1** (指树) plum tree **2** (指花) plum blossom **3** (指果) plum
梅毒 **méidú** [名] syphilis
梅花 **méihuā** [名] plum blossom

媒 **méi** [名] **1** (媒人) matchmaker ▶做媒 be a matchmaker **2** (媒介) intermediary
媒介 **méijiè** [名] intermediary
媒人 **méiren** [名] matchmaker
媒体 **méitǐ** [名] media

煤 **méi** [名] coal
煤气 **méiqì** [名] **1** (指燃料) gas **2** (指有毒气体) carbon monoxide ▷煤气中毒 carbon monoxide poisoning
煤油 **méiyóu** [名] kerosene

酶 **méi** [名] enzyme

霉 **méi** [动] **1** (指食物) mould (英), mold (美) **2** (指衣物) mildew
霉变 **méibiàn** [动] **1** (指衣物) become mildewy (PT became, PP become) **2** (指食物) go mouldy (英) 或 moldy (美) (PT went, PP gone)
霉烂 **méilàn** [动] go rotten (PT went, PP gone)

每 **měi I** [形] every, each ▷每个晚上他都要加班。He has to work overtime every evening. ▷他热爱这里的每一片土地。He loves every corner of this land. ▷她努力做好每一项工作。She worked hard on each piece of work. **II** [副] every time ▷每回答一个问题，他都增强一份信心。Every time he answers a question, he gains in confidence. ▷每逢周六他都去打工。He works every Saturday.

每况愈下 **měi kuàng yù xià** go from bad to worse

每每 **měiměi** [副] more often than not

美 **měi I** [形] **1** (美丽) beautiful ▷这幅画太美了。This painting is so beautiful. ▷京剧演员表演得真美。The Beijing Opera actress performed beautifully. **2** (好) good ▷这个店的商品物美价廉。The merchandise in this shop is good and reasonably priced. ▷我们的明天会更美。Our future will be even better. **II** [动] (方) be pleased with oneself ▷穿了身儿新衣服，看把你美的！Don't you look pleased with yourself, all dressed up in your new clothes! **III** [名] **1** (好事) good deed ▷成人之美 do a good deed **2** (美洲) North and South America **3** (美国) the USA ▷中美关系 Sino-American relations

美不胜收 **měi bù shèng shōu** indescribably beautiful ▷黄山的风景美不胜收。The scenery at Huangshan is indescribably beautiful.

美感 **měigǎn** [名] beautiful impression

美观 **měiguān** [形] beautiful

美国 **Měiguó** [名] the US, the USA

> 美国被称为 **the US** 或 **the USA**，其相应的全称为 **the United States** 和 **the United States of America**。美国还可被称为 **America** 或 **the States**，后者的语体更加不正式。

美好 **měihǎo** [形] wonderful

美化 **měihuà** [动] beautify

美丽 **měilì** [形] beautiful ▷像花儿一样美丽 as beautiful as a flower ▷美丽的人生 beautiful life

> 描述某人的外貌时，通常使用 **beautiful** 和 **pretty** 形容漂亮的妇女、女孩或婴儿。**beautiful** 比 **pretty** 的程度强烈得多。*She was a pretty little girl who grew up to be a beautiful woman.* 表示男性英俊的词是 **handsome**。*David is a very handsome man and popular with women.* **good-looking** 和 **attractive** 既可以描述女性也可以描述男性。*Not all of the boys in the class were as good-looking as John… His wife isn't particularly attractive but she's nice and has a good sense of humour.*

美满 **měimǎn** [形] perfectly satisfactory

美妙 **měimiào** [形] splendid

美容 **měiróng** [动] make oneself more beautiful ▷美容店 beauty salon ▷她做了美容手术。She's had cosmetic surgery.

美食 **měishí** [名] delicacy

美术 **měishù** [名] **1** (造型艺术) fine arts (PL) **2** (绘画) painting

美谈 **měitán** [名] legend

美味 **měiwèi** [名] delicacy

美学 **měixué** [名] aesthetics (英), esthetics (美) (PL)

美言 **měiyán** [动] put in a good word for (PT, PP put)

美元 **měiyuán** [名] US dollar

美中不足 **měi zhōng bù zú** small imperfection ▷这汤美中不足的是不够咸。The only thing wrong with the soup is that it isn't salty enough.

美滋滋 **měizīzī** [形] (口) pleased with oneself

镁 **měi** [名] magnesium

妹 **mèi** [名] **1** (指同胞) younger sister **2** (指亲戚) ▶表妹 cousin **3** (方) (指年轻女子) young girl

妹妹 **mèimei** [名] **1** (指同胞) younger sister **2** (指亲戚) ▷她是我叔伯妹妹。She's my cousin.

昧 **mèi I** [形] hazy ▶愚昧 ignorant **II** [动] **1** (隐藏) conceal **2** (违背) go against (PT went, PP gone)

昧心 **mèixīn** [形] against one's principles ▷他从不说昧心话。He never says anything that goes against his principles. ▷他从不赚昧心钱。He'll never make money dishonestly.

媚 **mèi I** [动] flatter **II** [形] charming

媚俗 **mèisú** [动] pander to public opinion

媚态 **mèitài** [名] **1** (讨好姿态) obsequiousness **2** (妩媚姿态) feminine charms (PL)

魅 **mèi** [名] demon

魅力 **mèilì** [名] charm ▷他已经50岁了，却依然魅力十足。He's already 50 but he's still utterly charming.

闷 **mēn I** [形] stuffy **II** [动] **1** (盖) cover … tightly **2** (不出声) keep silent (PT, PP kept) **3** (呆) shut oneself in (PT, PP shut) ▷星期天他也闷在教室里学习。Even on Sundays he

shuts himself in the classroom and studies.
→另见 mèn

闷热 mēnrè [形] muggy

闷头儿 mēntóur [副] silently

门 mén I [名] 1 (指出入口) door ▷北门 north gate 2 (指开关装置) switch ▶电门 switch 3 (门状物) ▷橱门 cupboard door ▷球门 goal 4 (门路) knack ▷对于修电脑，他终于摸着点门儿了。He finally got the hang of repairing computers. 5 (派别) school of thought ▶佛门 Buddhism 6 (门类) category II [量] ▷我选了5门课。I chose five courses. ▷一门技术 a skill ▷一门大炮 a cannon

门当户对 mén dāng hù duì families of equal rank ▷门当户对的婚姻未必幸福。Marrying within your own class will not necessarily make you happy.

门道 méndao [名] know-how ▷他做生意很有门道。He has excellent business know-how.

门第 méndì [名] family status

门户 ménhù [名] 1 (门) door 2 (通路) gateway 3 (家) family 4 (派别) sect

门类 ménlèi [名] category

门路 ménlu [名] 1 (窍门) knack ▷多动脑筋，就能找出门路来。If you put your mind to it you'll get the knack of it. 2 (贬)(后门儿) connection ▷他家很有门路。His family is very well-connected.

门面 ménmian [名] 1 (门脸儿) shop front (英), storefront (美) 2 (喻)(外表) appearance

门徒 méntú [名] disciple

门外汉 ménwàihàn [名] layman

门卫 ménwèi [名] guard

门诊 ménzhěn [名] outpatient department

扪 mén [动] (书) touch

扪心自问 mén xīn zì wèn examine one's conscience

闷 mèn [形] 1 (烦) low 2 (无聊) bored 3 (密闭) tightly closed ▷闷罐子 a sealed jar
→另见 mēn

闷棍 mèngùn [名] 1 (字) blow ▷一闷棍打得他眼冒金星儿。After one blow he saw stars. 2 (喻)(打击) bolt from the blue

闷闷不乐 mèn mèn bù lè be below ▷他这几天总是闷闷不乐的。These last few days he's been really low.

蒙 mēng [动] 1 (欺骗) deceive 2 (乱猜) make a wild guess
→另见 méng, Měng

蒙蒙亮 mēngmēngliàng [形] just light ▷天

刚蒙蒙亮，部队就出发了。Dawn was just breaking as the team set off.

蒙骗 mēngpiàn [动] deceive

萌 méng [动] sprout

萌动 méngdòng [动] 1 (指植物) sprout 2 (指事物) arise (PT arose, PP arisen) ▷对私家车的市场需求萌动。A demand for private cars has arisen.

萌发 méngfā [动] 1 (指种子) sprout 2 (指事物) come into being (PT came, PP come)

萌生 méngshēng [动] form ▷看到别人发了财，他就萌生了邪念。Seeing other people getting rich, wicked thoughts formed in his mind.

萌芽 méngyá [动] 1 (指植物) sprout 2 (指事物) emerge

蒙 méng I [动] 1 (遮盖) cover 2 (受到) receive II [形] ignorant ▶启蒙 enlighten
→另见 mēng, Měng

蒙蔽 méngbì [动] deceive

蒙混 ménghùn [动] deceive ▷蒙混过关 muddle through

蒙眬 ménglóng [形] sleepy

蒙昧 méngmèi [形] 1 (未开化) uncivilized 2 (无知) ignorant ▷有些人因为蒙昧无知而犯罪。Some people commit crimes through ignorance.

蒙蒙 méngméng [形] 1 指雨 drizzly 2 (指烟雾) misty

蒙受 méngshòu [动] 1 (耻辱，冤屈) suffer ▷蒙受了巨大损失 suffer a great loss 2 (恩惠) receive

蒙太奇 méngtàiqí [名] montage

盟 méng [名] 1 (同盟) alliance ▶二战盟国 the Allies 2 (指行政区) league

盟军 méngjūn [名] allied forces (PL)

盟誓 méngshì [动] swear an oath (PT swore, PP sworn)

盟约 méngyuē [名] treaty of alliance

朦 méng 见下文

朦胧 ménglóng [形] 1 (月光) hazy 2 (烟雾) misty

猛 měng I [形] 1 (凶猛) fierce 2 (勇猛) brave II [副] 1 (猛烈) fiercely 2 (忽然) suddenly

猛烈 měngliè [形] fierce

猛然 měngrán [副] suddenly

猛醒 měngxǐng [动] wake up to reality (PT woke, PP woken)

弥散 mísàn [动] disperse

蒙 Měng [名] Mongolia
→另见 mēng, méng
蒙古族 Měnggǔzú [名] Mongolian nationality

锰 měng [名] manganese

懵 měng [形] muddled
懵懵懂懂 měngmeng-dǒngdǒng muddled
▷听了他的解释，我还是懵懵懂懂。I was
still muddled, even after he had explained.

孟 mèng [形] (指排行) eldest
孟子 Mèngzǐ [名] Mencius

梦 mèng I [名] 1 (睡梦) dream 2 (幻想) illusion
II [动] dream ▷她梦到自己是电影明星。She
dreamed she was a film star.
梦话 mènghuà [名] 1 (字) ▷我听见你晚上说
梦话了。I heard you talk in your sleep. 2 (喻)
nonsense
梦幻 mènghuàn [名] illusion ▷她仿佛来到
了梦幻世界。She seemed to have entered a
dreamworld.
梦境 mèngjìng [名] dreamworld
梦寐以求 mèngmèi yǐ qiú ▷他梦寐以求的
愿望终于实现了。He finally realized his long-
cherished dream.
梦想 mèngxiǎng [动] dream ▷不奋斗就能
成功，简直是梦想！You'd be dreaming to
imagine that success can be achieved without
a struggle. ▷他梦想着开一家自己的公司。
He dreamed of opening his own company. ▷她
实现了当一名作家的梦想。She fulfilled her
dream of being a writer.

咪 mī 见下文
咪咪 mīmī [拟] miaow (英), meow (美)

眯 mī [动] 1 (眼皮微合) squint 2 (方) (小睡) take a
nap (PT took, PP taken)
→另见 mí
眯缝 mīfeng [动] squint

弥 mí I [形] full II [动] fill III [副] more
弥补 míbǔ [动] make ... up ▷我们要想方设法
弥补这一重大损失。We must think of a way
to make up for this heavy loss.
弥合 míhé [动] patch ... up ▷感情上的裂
痕是不容易弥合的。It's hard to patch up
emotional wounds.
弥留 míliú [动] (书) be on one's deathbed
弥漫 mímàn [动] pervade
弥撒 mísa [名] mass

迷 mí I [动] 1 (迷失) be lost ▷迷路 lose one's
way 2 (迷恋) become obsessed with (PT
became, PP become) 3 (迷惑) be deluded
II [名] fan ▷球迷 sports fan
迷彩服 mícǎifú [名] camouflage clothing
迷宫 mígōng [名] maze
迷糊 míhu [形] confused
迷惑 míhuò [动] 1 (不明白) be confused ▷听了
他的话，我更迷惑了。After listening to him I
was even more confused. 2 (使迷糊) baffle
迷恋 míliàn [动] be obsessed with
迷茫 mímáng [形] 1 (广阔而模糊) vast and
hazy 2 (迷离) dazed ▷他神色迷茫地望着
前方，仿佛周围的一切都不存在了。He
stared ahead in a daze as if nothing around him
existed.
迷你 mínǐ [形] mini ▷你的迷你裙真漂亮。
Your mini-skirt is really lovely.
迷失 míshī [动] lose (PT, PP lost) ▷迷失方向
lose one's bearings ▷在诱惑面前，不要迷失
了自己。You mustn't lose your head in the face
of temptation.
迷途 mítú [动] lose one's way (PT, PP lost) ▷误
入迷途 go astray
迷信 míxìn [动] 1 (鬼神) be superstitious about
▷他迷信鬼神。He has a superstitious belief in
ghosts and spirits. 2 (人或事) have blind faith
in ▷迷信可能会让人丧失理智。Superstition
may cause people to behave irrationally.

眯 mí [动] get ... into one's eye ▷沙子眯了我的
眼。The sand got into my eye.
→另见 mī

猕 mí 见下文
猕猴 míhóu [名] rhesus monkey
猕猴桃 míhóutáo [名] 1 (指植物) kiwi
plant 2 (指果实) kiwi fruit

谜 mí [名] 1 (谜语) riddle 2 (神秘) mystery
谜语 míyǔ [名] riddle

糜 mí I [名] gruel ▷肉糜 mincemeat II [形]
rotten III [动] waste
糜烂 mílàn [形] 1 (腐烂) rotten ▷他的伤口
已经糜烂。His wound has already become
infected. 2 (喻) (腐化) debauched

米 mǐ I [名] 1 (稻米) rice ▷米饭 cooked
rice 2 (去壳种子) husked seeds (PL) ▷虾米
dried shrimp ▷一袋花生米 a bag of peanuts
II [量] metre (英), meter (美)

米饭 mǐfàn [名] cooked rice

米色 mǐsè [名] beige

靡 mǐ [动] blow ... down (PT blew, PP blown) ▶风靡 be fashionable

觅 mì [动] look for

觅取 mìqǔ [动] look for

泌 mì [动] secrete

泌尿 mìniào [动] urinate ▷泌尿系统疾病 disease of the urinary system

秘 mì I [形] secret II [动] keep ... secret (PT, PP kept) III [名] secretary

秘方 mìfāng [名] secret recipe

秘诀 mìjué [名] secret ▷成功的秘诀 secret of success

秘密 mìmì [名] secret ▷一定要保守秘密！You must keep this a secret!

秘书 mìshū [名] 1 (指人) secretary 2 (指工作) secretarial work

秘书处 mìshūchù [名] secretariat

密 mì [形] 1 (空隙小) dense 2 (关系近) close 3 (精致) meticulous ▶精密 precise 4 (秘密) secret

密布 mìbù [动] be full of

密度 mìdù [名] density ▷这个地区人口密度很大。This region has a high population density.

密封 mìfēng [动] seal ... tightly ▷密封机舱 air-tight cabin

密集 mìjí [形] concentrated

密码 mìmǎ [名] 1 (口令) password 2 (符号系统) code

密密麻麻 mìmìmámá crammed ▷他笔记上的字密密麻麻的。His notebook was crammed full of writing.

密谋 mìmóu [动] conspire

密切 mìqiè [形] close ▷他俩的关系一直很密切。They've always had a very close relationship. ▷密切与欧洲的关系是十分重要的。It is important to establish close links with Europe.

密探 mìtàn [名] spy

幂 mì [名] (数) power ▷2的3次幂得8。2 to the power of 3 is 8.

蜜 mì I [名] honey II [形] sweet

蜜蜂 mìfēng [名] bee

蜜饯 mìjiàn [名] preserved fruit

蜜月 mìyuè [名] honeymoon ▷新婚夫妇一起去度蜜月了。The newly married couple went on their honeymoon. ▷两个人的关系正处在蜜月期。The two of them are going through their honeymoon period.

眠 mián [动] 1 (睡) sleep (PT, PP slept) ▶失眠 suffer from insomnia 2 (冬眠) hibernate ▶休眠 be dormant

绵 mián I [名] silk thread II [形] 1 (连绵) continuous 2 (柔软) soft

绵薄 miánbó [名] (谦) meagre effort

绵长 miáncháng [形] long ▷绵长的岁月 many years

绵里藏针 mián lǐ cáng zhēn 1 (贬) soft on the outside but ruthless within 2 (褒) an iron fist in a velvet glove

绵绵 miánmián [形] continuous

绵软 miánruǎn [形] weak

绵延 miányán [动] go on and on (PT went, PP gone) ▷绵延不断的文化传统 unbroken cultural tradition

棉 mián [名] 1 (指植物) cotton ▶棉田 cotton field 2 (棉花) cotton ▷姑娘们正在纺棉织布。The girls are weaving cotton cloth. 3 (棉状物) fibre (英), fiber (美)

棉花 miánhua [名] 1 (指植物) cotton 2 (棉絮) cotton wadding

棉衣 miányī [名] cotton-padded clothing

免 miǎn [动] 1 (除去) exempt ▶免试 be exempt from an exam ▶免费 free ▷她被免职了。She was fired from her job. 2 (避免) avoid 3 (不要) not be allowed ▷闲人免进 staff only ▷此事免谈。This matter is non-negotiable.

免除 miǎnchú [动] 1 (避免) prevent ▷机器常检修，能免除大的故障。Frequent servicing can prevent machines from having major breakdowns. 2 (免去) discharge ▷他被免除了职务。He was discharged from his post. ▷他的债务被免除了。He was relieved of his debts.

免费 miǎnfèi [动] be free of charge ▷世上没有免费午餐。There's no such thing as a free lunch in this world. ▷这里的孩子可以免费入学。Children here can attend school free of charge. ▷送你一张免费参观券。I'll give you a free visitor's ticket. ▷实行免费医疗制度 implement a system of free medical care ▷注册一个免费电子邮箱 register for free email

免检 miǎnjiǎn [动] be exempt from inspection

免俗 miǎnsú [动] do one's own thing

免疫 miǎnyì [名] immunity ▷这位病人的免疫系统受到了破坏。This patient's immune system has been destroyed.

免罪 miǎnzuì [动] be exempt from punishment

勉 miǎn [动] **1** (努力) strive ▷勉力 exert oneself **2** (勉励) encourage **3** (勉强) force ... to carry on

勉励 miǎnlì [动] encourage

勉强 miǎnqiǎng I [动] **1** (尽力) push oneself hard ▷身体不好，做事就不要太勉强。 If your health is not good, don't push yourself too hard. **2** (强迫) force ▷孩子不想学钢琴，就不要勉强他。 If the child does not want to study the piano, don't force him. II [形] **1** (不情愿) reluctant ▷我让他帮忙，他勉强答应了。 I asked him to help, and he reluctantly agreed. **2** (凑合) barely enough ▷他挣的钱勉强够自己花。 The money he earned was barely enough to support himself. **3** (牵强) far-fetched

勉为其难 miǎn wéi qí nán attempt the impossible ▷拿不到冠军也无所谓，不要勉为其难。 It doesn't matter if you don't win first prize – don't be attempting the impossible.

娩 miǎn [动] give birth (PT gave, PP given)

冕 miǎn [名] crown

缅 miǎn I [形] (书) remote II [动] (方) roll ... up

缅怀 miǎnhuái [动] cherish the memory of

腼 miǎn 见下文

腼腆 miǎntiǎn [形] bashful

面 miàn I [名] **1** (脸) face ▷面色 expression ▷面露难色 look reluctant ▷他面带笑容。 He had a smile on his face. **2** (表面) surface ▷水面 surface of the water **3** (方位) aspect ▷前面 front ▷考虑问题要全面。 We should examine every aspect of this problem. **4** (书) (当面) ▷面试 interview ▷法国签证得面签。 You have to have an interview to get a French visa. **5** (情面) self-respect ▷面子 face **6** (粉末) powder ▷辣椒面 chilli powder **7** (磨成粉的粮食) flour ▷白面 wheat flour **8** (面条) noodles (PL) II [动] (朝) face ▷面墙而坐 sit facing the wall III [量] **1** (用于扁平物) ▷一面墙 a wall ▷两面镜子 two mirrors **2** (指见面的次数) ▷我曾见过他一面。 I have met her once before.

面包房 miànbāofáng [名] bakery

面点 miàndiǎn [名] pastry

面对 miànduì [动] face ▷我们要勇于面对任何困难。 We must face any difficulties head on. ▷面对失败，他毫不气馁。 In the face of defeat he wasn't in the least disheartened.

面额 miàn'é [名] denomination

面红耳赤 miàn hóng ěr chì go red in the face

面积 miànjī [名] area

面颊 miànjiá [名] cheek

面孔 miànkǒng [名] face

面料 miànliào [名] **1** (布料) material **2** (表层材料) covering

面临 miànlín [动] face

面貌 miànmào [名] **1** (面容) features (PL) **2** (喻) appearance

面面俱到 miàn miàn jù dào cover every detail

面目 miànmù [名] **1** (相貌) appearance ▷他面目可憎。 He looks repulsive. ▷车祸后，那辆车已经面目全非。 After the accident, the car was totally unrecognizable. **2** (颜面) face

面前 miànqián [名] ▷当他出现在我面前时，我又惊又喜。 When he appeared in front of me, I was surprised and pleased. ▷在困难面前，他们没有低头。 They never admitted defeat in the face of difficulties.

面色 miànsè [名] **1** (气色) complexion **2** (神情) expression

面纱 miànshā [名] veil

面善 miànshàn [形] **1** (面熟) familiar ▷他看着面善。 He looks familiar. **2** (面容和善) kind-faced ▷面善的老婆婆 kind-faced old lady

面生 miànshēng [形] unfamiliar

面世 miànshì [动] come out (PT came, PP come)

面试 miànshì [动] have an interview

面熟 miànshú [形] familiar

面值 miànzhí [名] denomination

面子 miànzi [名] **1** (表面) outside **2** (体面) face ▷丢面子 lose face **3** (情面) feelings (PL) ▷给我点面子，你就答应吧！ Show some respect for my feelings and say yes!

喵 miāo [拟] miaow (英), meow (美)

苗 miáo [名] **1** (指植物) seedling ▷树苗 sapling **2** (指动物) young ▷鱼苗 fry **3** (指人) descendant ▷他是他家的独苗儿。 He's the only remaining descendant in his family.

苗条 miáotiao [形] slim

苗头 miáotou [名] premonition ▷他早就看出了这件事的苗头。 He had had a premonition about this a long time ago.

苗子 miáozi [名] **1** (农) seedling **2** (喻) (指人) ▷他是个当总经理的苗子。 He's a managing director in the making. ▷她是个当记者的好苗子。 She's a budding young journalist.

描 miáo [动] **1** (画) trace ▷描图纸 tracing paper **2** (涂抹) touch ... up

描绘 miáohuì [动] depict

描摹 miáomó [动] 1 (照底样写画) trace 2 (文字描绘) portray

描述 miáoshù [动] describe

描写 miáoxiě [动] describe

瞄 miáo [动] fix one's eyes on ▷瞄靶子 aim at the target

瞄准 miáozhǔn [动] 1 (对准) take aim (PT took, PP taken) 2 (专注于) focus on

秒 miǎo [量] (指时间) second

秒表 miǎobiǎo [名] stopwatch

渺 miǎo [形] 1 (远而模糊) distant 2 (微小) tiny

渺茫 miǎománg [形] 1 (远而模糊) distant 2 (难料) uncertain

渺小 miǎoxiǎo [形] tiny

藐 miǎo I [形] small II [动] treat ... with contempt

藐视 miǎoshì [动] treat ... with contempt ▷对困难既不要藐视，也不要惧怕。You should neither belittle nor fear difficulties.

藐小 miǎoxiǎo [形] tiny

妙 miào [形] 1 (好) wonderful 2 (巧妙) ingenious ▶妙举 ingenious move

妙龄 miàolíng [名] youthfulness

妙趣横生 miàoqù héngshēng sparkling with wit

妙手回春 miào shǒu huí chūn achieve a miraculous cure

庙 miào [名] temple

庙宇 miàoyǔ [名] temple

灭 miè [动] 1 (熄灭) go out (PT went, PP gone) ▷炉子里的火灭了吗？Has the fire in the stove gone out? 2 (使熄灭) extinguish ▶灭火器 fire extinguisher 3 (淹没) submerge 4 (消亡) perish 5 (消灭) kill

灭迹 mièjì [动] destroy evidence

灭绝 mièjué [动] 1 (消亡) become extinct (PT became, PP become) 2 (完全失掉) ▷灭绝人性 inhuman

灭口 mièkǒu [动] dispose of a witness

灭亡 mièwáng [动] destroy

灭种 mièzhǒng [动] 1 (指人类) be exterminated 2 (指动植物) become extinct (PT became, PP become)

蔑 miè I [形] contemptuous II [动] slander

蔑视 mièshì [动] show contempt for (PT

showed, PP shown)

民 mín [名] 1 (人民) the people 2 (人) person ▶网民 Internet user 3 (民间) folk 4 (非军方) civilian

民办 mínbàn [动] privately run ▷民办大学 private university

民兵 mínbīng [名] militia

民法 mínfǎ [名] civil law

民愤 mínfèn [名] public anger

民风 mínfēng [名] folklore

民歌 míngē [名] folk song

民间 mínjiān [名] 1 (百姓中间) folk ▷民间传说 folklore 2 (非官方) ▷民间交往 non-governmental exchanges ▷民间组织 non-governmental organization

民警 mínjǐng [名] civil police

民居 mínjū [名] private house

民情 mínqíng [名] 1 (风俗情况) conditions (PL) 2 (民意) public opinion

民权 mínquán [名] civil rights (PL)

民俗 mínsú [名] folklore

民谣 mínyáo [名] popular ballad

民营 mínyíng [动] run privately ▷民营企业 privately-run enterprise

民乐 mínyuè [名] folk music

民政 mínzhèng [名] civil administration

民众 mínzhòng [名] the common people (PL)

民主 mínzhǔ I [名] democracy II [形] democratic

民族 mínzú [名] nationality ▷少数民族 ethnic minority

抿 mǐn [动] 1 (轻轻合拢) close ... lightly ▷抿嘴一笑 smile with one's lips closed 2 (用嘴轻沾) sip

泯 mǐn [动] (书) vanish

泯灭 mǐnmiè [动] disappear

敏 mǐn [形] 1 (快) quick ▶敏感 sensitive 2 (聪明) clever ▶机敏 quick-witted

敏感 mǐngǎn [形] sensitive

敏捷 mǐnjié [形] quick ▷反应敏捷 quick reactions ▷猴子的动作非常敏捷。Monkeys are extremely agile.

敏锐 mǐnruì [形] keen

名 míng I [名] 1 (名字) name ▷书名 book title 2 (名声) reputation ▷这部名著早已名扬四海。This famous work has long enjoyed a worldwide reputation. ▷名利双收 win fame and fortune II [形] famous ▷世界名校 world-famous school ▷她抄写了一整本名人名言。

She copied out a whole book of well-known sayings of famous people. **III** [量] **1** (指人) ▷5名工人 five workers **2** (指名次) ▷期末考试她得了第一名。She came first in the end-of-term exams. **IV** [动] describe ▷她有一种不可名状的恐惧。She feels an indescribable fear.

名不副实 míng bù fù shí not live up to one's reputation

名不虚传 míng bù xū chuán live up to one's reputation

名称 míngchēng [名] name

名词 míngcí [名] noun

名次 míngcì [名] ranking

名存实亡 míng cún shí wáng exist in name only

名单 míngdān [名] list of names ▷他上了黑名单。He was blacklisted.

名额 míng'é [名] quota

名分 míngfèn [名] (书) status

名副其实 míng fù qí shí live up to the name of ▷他是一位名副其实的大科学家。He really lives up to his name as a great scientist.

名贵 míngguì [形] priceless

名家 míngjiā [名] master

名利 mínglì [名] fame and fortune

名列前茅 míng liè qiánmáo come out among the top ▷他在期末考试中名列前茅。He came out among the top candidates in the end-of-term exams.

名流 míngliú [名] celebrity

名落孙山 míng luò Sūn Shān fail to make the grade ▷这次考试他又名落孙山。Yet again he failed the exams.

名目 míngmù [名] items (PL) ▷名目众多的收费 all kinds of charges

名牌 míngpái [名] famous name ▷他从上到下穿的都是名牌。He was dressed in designer clothing from head to foot.

名片 míngpiàn [名] business card

名气 míngqi [名] fame ▷有名气 be famous

名人 míngrén [名] famous person

名声 míngshēng [名] reputation

名胜 míngshèng [名] tourist site ▷名胜古迹 sites of scenic and historical interest

名堂 míngtang [名] **1** (花样) variety **2** (花招) trick ▷你搞什么名堂！What are you up to? **3** (道理) reason ▷他这么做一定有名堂。There must be a reason why he did this. **4** (结果) achievement

名望 míngwàng [名] fame ▷老先生在学术圈里很有名望。The old gentleman is very famous in academic circles.

名义 míngyì [名] name ▷以人民的名义 in the name of the people ▷他名义上是校长，其实很多事并不由他决定。He is the College Principal in name only – in fact many decisions are not taken by him.

名誉 míngyù [名] **1** (名声) reputation **2** (名义) ▷名誉校长 honorary principal

名正言顺 míng zhèng yán shùn legitimate

名字 míngzi [名] name ▷你叫什么名字？What's your name?

明 míng **I** [形] **1** (亮) bright ▷明月 bright moon **2** (清楚) clear ▷讲明 clarify **3** (公开) open **4** (有眼力) perceptive **II** [名] **1** (视力) sight ▷他双目失明。He's lost his sight in both eyes. **2** (光明) light **III** [动] **1** (懂) understand (PT, PP understood) ▷他是个明理的人。He's an understanding person. **2** (显示) show (PT showed, PP shown) ▶表明 indicate ▷以死明志 be willing to die for one's beliefs **IV** [副] openly ▷明知故犯 openly do wrong

明白 míngbai **I** [形] **1** (清楚) clear ▷他没讲明白。He didn't explain clearly. **2** (聪明) sensible **3** (公开) explicit ▷他已明白表示不会退出比赛。He explicitly said that he wouldn't be retiring from the match. **II** [动] understand (PT, PP understood)

明察秋毫 míng chá qiū háo not miss a trick

明晃晃 mínghuānghuāng [形] gleaming

明净 míngjìng [形] clear and bright

明快 míngkuài [形] **1** (明白顺畅) lucid and lively **2** (爽快) straightforward

明朗 mínglǎng [形] **1** (明亮) bright and clear **2** (明确) clear-cut **3** (明快) bright and cheerful

明亮 míngliàng [形] **1** (亮堂) bright **2** (发亮) shining **3** (明白) clear

明媚 míngmèi [形] bright and beautiful

明明 míngmíng [副] obviously

明目张胆 míng mù zhāng dǎn brazenly

明确 míngquè [形] clear-cut ▷大会明确了今后的奋斗目标。The congress clarified the future goals to strive for.

明文 míngwén [名] written document ▷教育部明文规定，一定要减轻学生负担。The Education Department has stipulated in writing that the burden on students must be reduced.

明显 míngxiǎn [形] obvious ▷他的进步非常明显。It's obvious that he's progressed. ▷人民的生活水平明显提高了。The people's standard of living has visibly improved.

明星 míngxīng [名] star

明哲保身 míng zhé bǎo shēn keep one's distance

明智 míngzhì [形] sensible

鸣 míng [动] 1 (叫) chirp 2 (响) sound ▷仪式开始了，首先鸣礼炮20响。The ceremony began, and first a 20-gun salute was sounded. ▷电闪雷鸣 a flash of lightning and the rumble of thunder ▷鸣枪警告 fire a warning shot 3 (表达) express

冥 míng I [形] (书) 1 (昏暗) dark 2 (深沉) deep 3 (糊涂) stupid ▶冥昧 ignorant II [名] the underworld

冥思苦想 míng sī kǔ xiǎng be deep in thought

冥想 míngxiǎng [动] be deep in thought

铭 míng I [名] inscription II [动] (书) engrave

瞑 míng [动] close one's eyes

瞑目 míngmù [动] die content

命 mìng I [名] 1 (性命) life 2 (命运) fate 3 (寿命) lifespan 4 (命令) order II [动] set (PT, PP set)

命案 mìng'àn [名] murder case

命根子 mìnggēnzi [名] lifeblood ▷经理说，顾客就是我们的命根子。The manager says that the customers are our lifeblood. ▷这孩子是全家人的命根子。This child is the very life of the family.

命令 mìnglìng [动] order ▷我们还没接到上级的命令。We still haven't received the order from above.

命脉 mìngmài [名] lifeblood

命名 mìngmíng [动] name ▷这座山被命名为"英雄山"。This mountain was named Heroes' Mountain.

命题 mìngtí [动] assign ... a topic

命运 mìngyùn [名] fate

命中 mìngzhòng [动] hit the target (PT, PP hit)

谬 miù [形] false

谬论 miùlùn [名] fallacy

谬误 miùwù [名] falsehood

摸 mō [动] 1 (触摸) stroke 2 (取) fish ... out ▷他从兜儿里摸出两块钱。He fished two yuan out of his pocket. 3 (偷) pilfer ▷小偷小摸 petty theft 4 (探索) find one's way (PT, PP found) ▷别急，慢慢就能摸出门道儿来。Don't worry – slowly does it and you'll find your way. 5 (摸黑行动) feel one's way (PT, PP felt)

摸底 mōdǐ [动] make a full assessment of a situation

摸索 mōsuǒ [动] 1 (试探) grope ▷黑暗中，他摸索着上楼。He groped his way upstairs in the dark. 2 (探索) try to find out

摹 mó [动] copy

摹拟 mónǐ [动] imitate

模 mó I [名] model ▶模型 model II [动] imitate
→另见 mú

模范 mófàn [形] model ▷他是一位劳动模范。He's a model worker.

模仿 mófǎng [动] imitate

模糊 móhu [形] blurred ▷不要模糊事物之间的差别。Don't blur the distinctions between things.

模棱两可 móléng liǎngkě equivocal

模拟 mónǐ [动] imitate

模式 móshì [名] pattern ▷写文章没有固定的模式。There's no fixed pattern for essay-writing.

模特儿 mótèr [名] model

模型 móxíng [名] 1 (样品) model 2 (模具) mould (英), mold (美)

膜 mó [名] 1 (体内薄皮组织) membrane 2 (膜状物) film

膜拜 móbài [动] prostrate oneself

摩 mó [动] 1 (摩擦) rub ... together 2 (轻抚) stroke ▶按摩 massage 3 (切磋) mull ... over

摩擦 mócā I [动] rub ▷两个物体摩擦会生热。When two objects are rubbed together they will produce heat. II [名] 1 (阻力) friction 2 (冲突) conflict

摩登 módēng [形] modern

摩肩接踵 mó jiān jiē zhǒng jostle each other

摩拳擦掌 mó quán cā zhǎng itch to

摩托车 mótuōchē [名] motorbike

磨 mó [动] 1 (摩擦) rub 2 (指用磨料) grind (PT, PP ground) ▶打磨 polish ▷磨刀 sharpen a knife 3 (折磨) wear ... down (PT wore, PP worn) 4 (纠缠) pester 5 (拖延) dawdle 6 (消亡) die out
→另见 mò

磨擦 mócā [名] rub

磨蹭 móceng I [动] 1 (摩擦) rub ... lightly 2 (纠缠) be in a tangle II [形] sluggish

磨合 móhé [动] 1 (指机器) run ... in (PT ran, PP run) 2 (适应) adapt to each other 3 (协商) consult ▷经过多次磨合，双方签署了协

议。After much consultation both parties signed the agreement.

磨炼 móliàn [动] steel

磨灭 mómiè [动] obliterate ▷他的伟大功绩不可磨灭。His huge achievements cannot be obliterated.

磨难 mónàn [名] hardship

磨损 mósǔn [动] wear ... out (PT wore, PP worn)

磨洋工 mó yánggōng [动] dawdle over one's work

蘑 mó [名] mushroom

蘑菇 mógu I [名] mushroom II [动] 1 (纠缠) pester 2 (磨蹭) dawdle

魔 mó I [名] 1 (魔鬼) demon 2 (魔法) magic II [形] magic

魔法 mófǎ [名] magic

魔鬼 móguǐ [名] devil

魔力 mólì [名] charm

魔术 móshù [名] magic

魔术师 móshùshī [名] magician

魔王 mówáng [名] 1 (字) demon king 2 (喻) fiend

魔掌 mózhǎng [名] (喻) clutches (PL) ▷她终于逃出了歹徒的魔掌。She finally escaped from the clutches of the thugs.

魔爪 mózhǎo [名] (喻) claws (PL)

抹 mǒ [动] 1 (涂抹) apply 2 (擦) wipe 3 (去除) erase ▷我很难将这次经历从记忆中抹去。I'm finding it hard to erase the experience from my memory.
→另见 mā

抹黑 mǒhēi [动] (喻) blacken sb's name ▷媒体企图抹黑他的形象。The media tried to blacken his name.

抹杀 mǒshā [动] write ... off (PT wrote, PP written)

末 mò [名] 1 (尾) end ▶末梢 end ▷世纪末 the end of the century 2 (次要) minor details (PL) 3 (屑) powder ▷面包末 breadcrumbs

末端 mòduān [名] end

末了 mòliǎo [名] end

末流 mòliú [形] inferior

末日 mòrì [名] 1 (宗) Judgment Day 2 (灭亡日) end ▷侵略者的末日终于到来了。The end had finally come for the invaders.

末尾 mòwěi [名] end

没 mò [动] 1 (沉没) sink (PT sank, PP sunk) 2 (漫过) overflow 3 (隐没) disappear ▶出没 appear and disappear

→另见 méi

没落 mòluò [动] decline

没收 mòshōu [动] confiscate

沫 mò [名] foam

茉 mò 见下文

茉莉 mòlì [名] jasmine

陌 mò [名] (书) footpath

陌生 mòshēng [形] unfamiliar

陌生人 mòshēngrén [名] stranger

脉 mò 见下文
→另见 mài

脉脉 mòmò [形] affectionate

莫 mò I [代] (书) 1 (指人) nobody 2 (指物) nothing II [副] (书) 1 (不) not ▷望尘莫及 be too far behind to catch up 2 (别) ▷莫打岔 don't interrupt ▷莫生气 don't get angry

莫不 mòbù [副] ▷大家对他莫不啧啧称赞。There was no-one who did not sing his praises. ▷全家莫不为他感到骄傲。There is no-one in the family who is not proud of him.

莫大 mòdà [形] greatest

莫非 mòfēi [副] ▷莫非那对恋人分手了？Can it be that the couple have split up? ▷莫非老板要给我加工资？Is it possible that the boss is going to give me a pay rise?

莫名其妙 mò míng qí miào baffling

莫须有 mòxūyǒu fabricated

蓦 mò [副] suddenly ▶蓦然 suddenly

漠 mò I [名] desert II [副] indifferently

漠不关心 mò bù guānxīn indifferent

漠然 mòrán [形] indifferent

漠视 mòshì [动] ignore

墨 mò I [名] 1 (墨汁) ink 2 (字画) calligraphy and painting 3 (喻) (学问) learning II [形] dark ▷一副墨镜 a pair of sunglasses

墨迹 mòjì [名] 1 (字) ink mark 2 (真迹) true work

墨绿 mòlù [形] dark green

墨守成规 mò shǒu chéngguī (贬) be a stickler for routine

默 mò [动] 1 (不出声) do ... silently 2 (默写) write ... from memory (PT wrote, PP written) ▷默古诗 write classical poetry from memory ▷每个字默5遍。Write out every character five times.

默哀 mò'āi [动] pay ... silent tribute (PT, PP paid)

默默 mòmò [形] silent

默契 mòqì I [形] ▷双方合作非常默契。The cooperation between the two sides is one of tacit agreement. II [名] tacit agreement ▷我们俩之间很有默契。There's a tacit agreement between us.

默认 mòrèn [动] tacitly agree

默写 mòxiě [动] write ... from memory (PT wrote, PP written)

默许 mòxǔ [动] tacitly consent to

磨 mò I [名] mill II [动] grind (PT, PP ground) ▷磨咖啡豆 grind coffee beans
→另见 mó

磨坊 mòfáng [名] mill

牟 móu [动] seek (PT, PP sought) ▷牟私利 seek personal gain

牟取 móuqǔ [动] seek (PT, PP sought) ▷牟取巨额利润 seek a vast profit

眸 móu [名] (书) eye

眸子 móuzǐ [名] pupil

谋 móu I [名] plan ▷他是个足智多谋的人。He is a resourceful person. II [动] 1 (谋求) seek (PT, PP sought) 2 (商议) consult ▷不谋而合 agree without prior consultation

谋反 móufǎn [动] plot a rebellion

谋害 móuhài [动] 1 (谋杀) plot a murder 2 (陷害) plot against

谋划 móuhuà [动] plan

谋略 móuluè [名] strategy ▷他是个有谋略、有才智的军事家。He is a resourceful and astute strategist.

谋求 móuqiú [动] seek (PT, PP sought)

谋取 móuqǔ [动] seek (PT, PP sought)

谋杀 móushā [动] murder ▷谋杀案 murder case

谋生 móushēng [动] make a living

谋私 móusī [动] seek personal advantage (PT, PP sought) ▷以权谋私 abuse power for personal gain

谋事 móushì [动] 1 (筹划事情) plan things 2 (找工作) look for a job

某 mǒu [代] 1 (指确定的人或事) ▷张某 a certain person called Zhang 2 (指不确定的人或事) ▷找出某种办法解决问题。Find some way to solve the problem. ▷一定有某人知道这件事。Someone must know about this.

某人 mǒurén [代] (指他人) somebody

模 mú [名] mould (英), mold (美)
→另见 mó

模具 mújù [名] mould (英), mold (美)

模样 múyàng [名] 1 (相貌) looks (PL) ▷她模样不错。She is not bad-looking. 2 (表示大概) ▷这女人有40岁模样儿。This woman is about forty. ▷吃了一个小时模样了，大家就结束了。After eating for about an hour everyone has finished.

母 mǔ I [名] 1 (母亲) mother 2 (指长辈女子) ▶祖母 grandmother 3 (喻) (基础) origin ▷失败乃成功之母。Failure is the mother of success. II [形] 1 (雌性) female ▶母牛 cow 2 (指能力或作用) ▶航空母舰 aircraft carrier ▶母体 matrix

母爱 mǔ'ài [名] maternal love

母带 mǔdài [名] master tape

母公司 mǔgōngsī [名] parent company

母亲 mǔqīn [名] mother

母系 mǔxì [形] 1 (母亲方面) maternal ▷他家母亲亲属很多。He has a lot of relatives on his mother's side. 2 (母女相承) matriarchal ▷母系社会 matriarchal society

母校 mǔxiào [名] alma mater ▷我离开母校已经20年了。I left my old school twenty years ago.

母性 mǔxìng [名] maternal instinct

母语 mǔyǔ [名] (第一语言) mother tongue

牡 mǔ [形] (书) male

牡丹 mǔdan [名] peony

拇 mǔ [名] 见下文

拇指 mǔzhǐ [名] 1 (指手) thumb 2 (指脚) big toe

木 mù I [名] 1 (树) tree 2 (木材) wood II [形] 1 (僵) numb ▷天太冷，我的脚都冻木了。It's freezing, my feet are numb with cold. 2 (呆) stupid

木材 mùcái [名] timber

木工 mùgōng [名] 1 (指工作) woodwork 2 (指人) carpenter

木匠 mùjiang [名] carpenter

木刻 mùkè [名] woodcarving

木料 mùliào [名] timber

木马 mùmǎ [名] 1 (鞍马) vaulting horse 2 (跳马) vault 3 (指玩具) rocking horse

木乃伊 mùnǎiyī [名] mummy

木偶 mù'ǒu [名] puppet

木然 mùrán [形] stupefied

木头 mùtou [名] wood

木已成舟 mù yǐ chéng zhōu what's done is done

目 mù [名] 1 (眼睛) eye 2 (条目) item 3 (目录) catalogue (英), catalog (美) 4 (名) title 5 (指生物) order

目标 mùbiāo [名] 1 (对象) target ▷雾太大，看不清目标。The fog's too heavy – we can't see the target properly. ▷他们侦察了一个晚上，也没发现目标。They searched all evening, but didn't find what they were looking for. 2 (目的) goal ▷有目标的生活才有意义。Life only has meaning if you have goals.

目不识丁 mù bù shí dīng completely illiterate

目不暇接 mù bù xiá jiē too much for the eye to take in

目不转睛 mù bù zhuǎn jīng stare fixedly

目瞪口呆 mù dèng kǒu dāi be dumbstruck ▷听了那个消息，他惊得目瞪口呆。He was dumbstruck at the news.

目的 mùdì [名] 1 (指地点) destination ▷旅游目的国 tourist destination 2 (结果) aim ▷有明确的学习目的 have clear study aims ▷他终于达到了目的了。He finally achieved his goal. ▷学习的目的是为了增长知识。The purpose of study is to increase knowledge. 3 (企图) intention

目睹 mùdǔ [动] witness

目光 mùguāng [名] 1 (视线) gaze ▷大家的目光都聚集在老师身上。Everyone's gaze was focused on the teacher. 2 (眼神) look ▷他用奇怪的目光看着我。He gave me a strange look. 3 (见识) sight ▷目光敏锐 sharp-eyed

目击 mùjī [动] witness ▷目击者 eyewitness

目空一切 mù kōng yīqiè supercilious

目录 mùlù [名] 1 (指事物) catalogue (英), catalog (美) 2 (指书刊) table of contents

目前 mùqián [名] present ▷目前，全国经济形势很好。At present the country's economic situation is very good. ▷我们目前的任务是什么？What are our current duties? ▷到目前为止，公司已出售两万台电脑。To date the company has sold 20,000 computers.

目中无人 mù zhōng wú rén be condescending

沐 mù [动] (书) 1 (洗头) wash one's hair 2 (蒙受) receive

沐浴 mùyù [动] 1 (洗澡) take a bath (PT took, PP taken) 2 (喻) (沉浸) revel ▷沐浴在幸福和欢乐之中 revel in one's fortune and happiness

牧 mù [动] herd

牧民 mùmín [名] herdsman (PL herdsmen)

牧师 mùshi [名] priest

牧童 mùtóng [名] shepherd boy

牧业 mùyè [名] animal husbandry

募 mù [动] 1 (钱款) raise ▷募款 raise funds 2 (兵员) enlist

募集 mùjí [动] collect

募捐 mùjuān [动] collect donations

墓 mù [名] grave

墓碑 mùbēi [名] gravestone

墓地 mùdì [名] graveyard

幕 mù I [名] 1 (帐篷) tent 2 (帷幔) curtain ▷银幕 the silver screen II [量] act

幕后 mùhòu [名] (贬) behind the scenes ▷将军正在幕后策划一起叛乱。The General is plotting a rebellion behind the scenes.

睦 mù [动] get on ▷和睦 harmonious

睦邻 mùlín [动] get on with one's neighbours (英) 或 neighbors (美) ▷两国建立了睦邻友好关系。The two countries have built up good, neighbourly (英) 或 neighborly (美) relations.

慕 mù [动] admire

慕名 mùmíng [动] be impressed by a reputation

暮 mù [名] 1 (傍晚) dusk 2 (晚) ▷暮春时节 in late spring

暮年 mùnián [名] old age

暮气 mùqì [名] lethargy

穆 mù [形] solemn

穆斯林 mùsīlín [名] Muslim

Nn

族总是哪里有水，就迁往哪里。Nomads always move to wherever there is water. **3** (指某一地方) ▷我们应该在哪里见过。I'm sure we've met somewhere before. **4** (用于反问) ▷我哪里去过美国？ When was I supposed to have gone to America? ▷他哪里会弹钢琴？ How is he supposed to be able to play the piano? **5** (谦) ▷哪里，哪里，你过奖了。No, no, it was nothing.

哪怕 **nǎpà** [连] no matter ▷哪怕有再多的困难，我也要坚持到底。No matter how many difficulties remain, I will hold fast till the end.

哪样 **nǎyàng** [代] **1** (表示提问) what kind **2** (表示任何一种) whatever

那 **nà** I [代] **1** (指远处) that (PL those) ▷那楼是去年建的。That block was built last year. **2** (表示不确指) ▷他这也想学，那也想学。He wants to study everything. **3** (表示复指) that ▷赚钱，那个才是商人真正关心的。Making money – that's all businessmen care about. II [连] then ▷你想买，那就买吧。If you want to buy it, then buy it. ▷小明不在家，那我们就走吧。Xiao Ming is out, so we should just go.

那个 **nàge** [代] **1** (指代人、事或物) that (PL those) ▷那个是主卧。That's the master bedroom. ▷那个房间是我妹妹的。That's my sister's room. **2** (表示婉转) ▷他说话挺那个的。What he said was too much.

那里 **nàli** [代] ▷我去过那里。I've been there. ▷我也要去那里吗？ Shall I go over there as well?

那么 **nàme** [代] **1** (表示程度) ▷你不该那么相信他。You shouldn't trust him so much. **2** (表示数量) ▷再有那么七八个就够了。Another seven or so will be enough. **3** (表示方式) ▷你别那么想。Don't think in that way.

那些 **nàxiē** [代] those ▷那些书是我的。Those are my books.

那样 **nàyàng** [副] ▷我没有说过那样的话。I never said anything like that.

拿 **ná** I [动] **1** (握) hold (PT, PP held) ▷他手里拿着一本书。He's holding a book in his hand. **2** (夺) capture ▷我们拿下了敌人的阵地。We captured the enemy position. **3** (有把握) be sure ▷我拿不准他到底来不来。I'm not sure whether he's coming or not. **4** (掌握) cope with ▷家里活他样样拿得起来。He can cope with all the housework. **5** (架子、样子) put on (PT, PP put) ▷我们老板总拿架子。Our boss always puts on airs. **6** (得) get (PT got, PP got (英), gotten (美)) ▷他拿了季军。He got third prize. II [介] **1** (用) with ▷她拿毛巾把头发擦干。She dried her hair with a towel. ▷少拿这个吓唬我！ Stop trying to scare me with that stuff! **2** (把) ▷他不拿工作当回事。He doesn't take the job seriously.

拿手 **náshǒu** [动] be good at ▷做菜她很拿手。She's good at cooking.

哪 **nǎ** I [代] **1** (什么) which ▷哪是我的包裹？Which is my parcel? ▷你喜欢哪种音乐？What kind of music do you like? ▷哪个人是李先生？ Which one is Mr Li? **2** (任何一个) any ▷哪天来都行。You can come any day. II [副] how ▷不努力哪会成功？How can you be successful without hard work?

哪里 **nǎli** [代] **1** (用于问处所) ▷你住在哪里？ Where do you live? **2** (指任何地方) ▷游牧民

呐 **nà** 见下文

呐喊 **nàhǎn** [动] cheer

纳 **nà** [动] **1** (收) receive ▶出纳 cashier **2** (接受) accept ▶采纳 accept **3** (享受) enjoy **4** (放进去) put (PT, PP put) **5** (交付) pay (PT, PP paid) **6** (缝纫) sew (PT sewed, PP sewn)

纳粹 **nàcuì** [名] Nazi

纳凉 **nàliáng** [动] enjoy the shade

纳闷儿 **nàmènr** [动] (口) not see ▷我纳闷儿他为什么还没到。I don't understand why he hasn't arrived yet.

纳米技术 nàmǐ jìshù [名] nanotechnology

纳入 nàrù [动] be incorporated into ▷他的提议被纳入议事范围。His suggestion was incorporated into the agenda of the meeting.

纳税 nàshuì [动] pay taxes (PT, PP paid)

纳税人 nàshuìrén [名] taxpayer

钠 nà [名] sodium

捺 nà [动] control

乃 nǎi [动] (书) be (PT was, PP been) ▷失败乃成功之母。Failure is the mother of success.

乃至 nǎizhì [连] (书) even ▷他在国内乃至海外都很有影响。He's very influential, in his own country and even overseas.

奶 nǎi I [名] 1 (乳房) breast 2 (乳汁) milk II [动] breast-feed (PT, PP breast-fed)

奶酪 nǎilào [名] cheese

奶妈 nǎimā [名] wet nurse

奶名 nǎimíng [名] baby name

奶奶 nǎinai [名] granny

奶昔 nǎixī [名] milkshake

耐 nài [动] 1 (指人) endure 2 (指衣服) be durable 3 (指材料) be resistant ▷这种材料耐腐蚀。This material is corrosion-resistant.

耐烦 nàifán [形] patient ▷她有点不耐烦了。She's getting a bit impatient.

耐久 nàijiǔ [形] long-lasting

耐劳 nàiláo [动] not be afraid of hard work

耐力 nàilì [名] stamina

耐人寻味 nài rén xún wèi be thought-provoking

耐心 nàixīn [形] patient ▷她对孩子很有耐心。She's very patient with children.

耐性 nàixìng [名] patience

男 nán [名] 1 (男性) male 2 (儿子) son

男儿 nán'ér [名] man (PL men)

男女 nánnǚ [名] men and women (PL) ▷男女平等 equality between men and women

男人 nánrén [名] man (PL men)

男人 nánren [名] (方) husband

男士 nánshì [名] gentleman (PL gentlemen)

男性 nánxìng [名] male

男子汉 nánzǐhàn [名] man (PL men) ▷孩子已经长成了男子汉。The child has already become a man.

南 nán [名] south ▶东南 south-east ▶西南 south-west

南方 nánfāng [名] the South ▷南方风俗 a southern custom

南国 nánguó [名] (书) the South ▷南国风光 southern scenery

南腔北调 nán qiāng běi diào strong accent ▷他讲话南腔北调的。He speaks with a strong accent.

南辕北辙 nán yuán běi zhé at odds with ▷你的行为和你的承诺南辕北辙。Your actions are at odds with your words.

难 nán I [形] 1 (困难) hard 2 (不好) bad ▷难吃 unpalatable II [动] baffle
→见 nàn

难产 nánchǎn [动] 1 (医) have a difficult labour 2 (不易完成) be hard to carry out ▷我们的计划一再难产。Our plan was beset with difficulties.

难处 nánchǔ [动] be hard to get along with

难处 nánchu [名] trouble ▷各家有各家的难处。Every family has its own troubles.

难道 nándào [副] ▷你难道还不明白吗？How can you not understand? ▷难道你就不累？Aren't you tired?

难怪 nánguài I [副] ▷难怪一个人找不到，原来今天不上班。No wonder no one's here – it's a working day! II [动] be understandable

难关 nánguān [名] crisis (PL crises)

难过 nánguò I [动] have a hard time ▷他挣得不多，日子难过。He doesn't earn much – he has a hard time of it. II [形] upset

难解难分 nán jiě nán fēn 1 (形容比赛) be locked in battle 2 (形容关系) be inseparable

难堪 nánkān [形] (尴尬) embarrassed ▷他因为没钱付小费而感到难堪。He felt embarrassed at not having enough money for a tip.

难看 nánkàn [形] 1 (丑) ugly 2 (不体面) ashamed

难免 nánmiǎn [动] be unavoidable ▷年轻人犯点错误是难免的，关键要从中吸取教训。It's unavoidable that young people will make mistakes. The important thing is that they learn from them.

难能可贵 nán néng kě guì highly commendable

难受 nánshòu [动] 1 (指身体) not feel well ▷我头疼得难受。I've got a bad headache. 2 (指心情) feel down (PT, PP felt)

难说 nánshuō [动] be hard to say ▷他来不来还难说。It's hard to say if he'll come or not.

难听 nántīng [动] 1 (不悦耳) sound awful 2 (粗俗) be crude 3 (不体面) be shameful

难为情 nánwéiqíng [形] 1 (难堪)

embarrassed 2 (过意不去) awkward

难为 nánwei [动] 1 (使人为难) embarrass 2 (客套) put ... out (PT, PP put) ▷帮我打扫房间，真难为你了。Thank you for helping me with the cleaning – I know I've really put you out. 3 (指做难事) be tough ▷一个人把几个孩子拉扯大，真难为她了。It must have been very tough for her, bringing up all those children on her own.

难言之隐 nán yán zhī yǐn be reluctant to discuss ▷他似乎有难言之隐。He seemed reluctant to discuss the subject.

难以 nányǐ [副] hard ▷难以启齿 not know where to start ▷难以置信 hard to believe

难于 nányú [副] hard ▷没有本科学历，难于找工作。Without an undergraduate degree it can be hard to find work.

难 nàn I [名] trouble II [动] blame ▶非难 blame
→另见 nán

难民 nànmín [名] refugee

难兄难弟 nànxiōng-nàndì fellow sufferers (PL) ▷大家都是难兄难弟，应该互相关照。Everyone's in the same boat – we should be looking after each other.

囊 náng [名] 1 (口袋) bag 2 (袋状物) pocket ▶胆囊 gall bladder

囊括 nángkuò [动] 1 (包罗) encompass 2 (指比赛) win (PT, PP won)

孬 nāo [形] (方) (怯懦) cowardly

孬种 nāozhǒng [名] coward

挠 náo [动] 1 (轻抓) scratch 2 (阻止) prevent ▶阻挠 hinder 3 (屈服) yield

挠头 náotóu [形] troublesome

恼 nǎo [形] 1 (生气) angry ▷气恼 get angry 2 (不痛快) unhappy ▶烦恼 worried

恼火 nǎohuǒ [形] annoyed

恼羞成怒 nǎo xiū chéng nù fly off the handle

脑 nǎo [名] 1 (生理) brain 2 (脑筋) brain ▷他不爱动脑。He's not in the habit of using his brain. 3 (头部) head 4 (头领) leader ▶首脑 head

脑袋 nǎodai [名] head

脑海 nǎohǎi [名] mind

脑筋 nǎojīn [名] 1 (指思考能力) brain 2 (指思想) mind ▷他脑筋灵活。He's got a quick mind.

脑力 nǎolì [名] brain power ▷脑力劳动 brain work

闹 nào I [形] noisy II [动] 1 (吵闹) have a row 2 (发泄) vent 3 (病、灾难) suffer from ▷他家乡闹了地震。His hometown suffered an earthquake. ▷前两天她闹胃炎。A couple of days ago she had a bout of gastritis. 4 (玩) go out (PT went, PP gone)

闹别扭 nào bièniu [动] 1 (吵架) fall out (PT fell, PP fallen) ▷夫妻俩闹别扭了。The couple have fallen out. 2 (合不来) be at loggerheads ▷两国就贸易问题闹别扭。The two countries are at loggerheads over trading issues.

闹肚子 nào dùzi [动] have diarrhoea (英) 或 diarrhea (美)

闹鬼 nàoguǐ [动] be haunted

闹哄哄 nàohōnghōng [形] noisy

闹剧 nàojù [名] farce ▷你们的闹剧也该收场了。You should put a stop to this nonsense.

闹情绪 nào qíngxù [动] take things badly (PT took, PP taken)

闹市 nàoshì [名] busy commercial area

闹腾 nàoteng [动] 1 (吵闹) make a row 2 (大声说笑) make a din

闹钟 nàozhōng [名] alarm clock

呢 ne [助] 1 (表示疑问) ▷你们都走，我呢？If you all go, what about me? ▷我到底错在哪儿呢？What did I actually do wrong? 2 (表示陈述) ▷离北京还远着呢。Beijing is still quite far. ▷他导演的电影好着看呢。The film he directed is actually really good. 3 (表示持续) ▷老师还在办公室呢。The teacher is still in the office. ▷警察正在搜索逃犯呢。The police are hunting down the escaped convict. 4 (表示停顿) ▷如今呢，我们住上了大房子。Nowadays, we live in a big house.
→另见 ní

馁 něi [形] disheartened

内 nèi [名] 1 (里头) inside ▷他躲在大楼内。He hid inside the building. ▷保龄球是室内运动。Bowling is an indoor sport. ▷他在一个月内完成了任务。He finished the task within a month. 2 (指妻子的亲属) in-laws (PL) ▷内弟 brother-in-law (PL brothers-in-law)

内部 nèibù [形] internal

内存 nèicún [名] memory

内地 nèidì [名] the interior ▷很多港澳同胞到内地旅游参观。Many tourists from Hong Kong, Macao and Taiwan come to mainland China for sightseeing.

内定 nèidìng [动] be appointed internally

内分泌 nèifēnmì [名] endocrine system

内服 nèifú [动] take orally (PT took, PP taken) ▷此药可内服。This medicine is to be taken orally.

内阁 nèigé [名] cabinet

内涵 nèihán [名] connotation

内行 nèiháng I [名] expert II [形] expert

内河 nèihé [名] inland river

内讧 nèihòng [名] internal conflict

内疚 nèijiù [动] feel guilty (PT, PP felt) ▷我为失职而内疚。I felt guilty about my unprofessional behaviour. ▷他被内疚折磨着。He is tortured by guilt.

内科 nèikē [名] internal medicine ▷内科病房 medical ward ▷内科医生 physician

内陆 nèilù [形] inland

内乱 nèiluàn [名] civil conflict

内幕 nèimù [名] inside story

内勤 nèiqín I [形] office-based II [名] office staff

内容 nèiróng [名] content

内务 nèiwù [名] (国内事务) internal affairs (PL)

内线 nèixiàn [名] 1 (指人) mole 2 (指电话) internal line ▷内线电话 internal phone call

内向 nèixiàng [形] introverted

内销 nèixiāo [动] sell on the domestic market (PT, PP sold)

内心 nèixīn [名] mind ▷谁知道他内心怎么想的? Who knows what he's thinking deep down?

内秀 nèixiù [形] quietly intelligent ▷我的男朋友长相平平，但很内秀。My boyfriend looks pretty ordinary, but he's intelligent in an understated way.

内应 nèiyìng [名] mole

内在 nèizài [形] internal ▷内在规律 intrinsic law

内脏 nèizàng [名] internal organs (PL)

内债 nèizhài [名] internal debt

内政 nèizhèng [名] domestic affairs (PL)

嫩 nèn [形] 1 (指皮肤) delicate 2 (指食品) tender 3 (指颜色) light 4 (口) (指阅历) green

能 néng I [名] 1 (能力) ability ▷无才无能 untalented and incapable 2 (物) (能量) energy ▷核能 nuclear energy II [形] capable III [助动] can ▷我能照顾好自己。I can take care of myself.

能动 néngdòng [形] active ▷我们能动地改造世界。We are working actively to change the world.

能够 nénggòu [动] be able to ▷飞机一个小时后能够起飞。The flight will be able to take off in an hour. ▷有谁能够帮我解决这个问题? Who can help me solve this problem?

请勿混淆 able 和 capable。这两个词都可以表示某人能做某事。如果说某人 able to do something，表示他有能力做某事，因为他具做此事所需的知识或技能，或条件允许可以做此事。*He wondered if he would be able to climb over the rail… They were able to use their profits for new investments.* 注意，如果时态是过去时，则表示某人事实上已经做了某事。*We were able to reduce costs.* 如果某人 capable of doing something，表示他具备做某事的知识和技能，或者他有可能去做某事。*The workers are perfectly capable of running the organization themselves… She was quite capable of ruining the project if it didn't please her.* 可以说某人 capable of 某种感情或行为。*He's capable of loyalty… I don't believe it's capable of murder.* 也可以用 capable of 表示汽车或机器的性能。*The car was capable of 110 miles per hour.* 如果将某人描述为 able 或者 capable，说明他能力很强。*His father was an able golfer…She's certainly a capable gardener.*

能力 nénglì [名] ability

请勿混淆 ability, capability 和 capacity。ability 表示某人有能力做好某事。*He had remarkable ability as a musician… the ability to bear hardship…* 某人的 capability 是指他所能完成的工作量及工作质量的好坏。*…a job that was beyond the capability of one man… the film director's ideas of the capability of the actor…* 如果某人具有某种特殊的 capacity，或 a capacity for something，或 a capacity to do something，说明他具备做该事所需的能力。capacity 比 ability 更为正式。*…their capacity for hard work… his capacity to see the other person's point of view…*

能量 néngliàng [名] (物) energy

能耐 néngnai [名] ability

能人 néngrén [名] ▷我们要让个能人来处理这件事。We should let somebody competent take care of this.

能手 néngshǒu [名] expert

能源 néngyuán [名] source of energy ▷能源短缺 energy shortage

呢 ní [名] woollen cloth
→另见 ne

呢子 nízi [名] woollen cloth ▷呢子大衣

woollen overcoat

泥 ní [名] 1 (指土) mud 2 (泥状物) paste ▷土豆泥 mashed potato

泥泞 nínìng I [形] muddy II [名] mud

泥潭 nítán [名] marsh

霓 ní 见下文

霓虹灯 níhóngdēng [名] neon light

拟 nǐ [动] 1 (起草) draft 2 (打算) plan

拟订 nǐdìng [动] draft

拟人 nǐrén [名] personification

拟声词 nǐshēngcí [名] onomatopoeia

你 nǐ [代] 1 (称对方) you ▷你是我最好的朋友。You are my best friend. 2 (你的) ▷你家有几口人？How many people are there in your family?

你们 nǐmen [代] you (PL)

昵 nì [形] intimate ▶亲昵 affectionate

昵称 nìchēng [名] pet name

逆 nì I [形] adverse II [动] go against (PT went, PP gone)

逆差 nìchā [名] deficit

逆耳 nì'ěr [形] hard to take ▷忠言逆耳 the truth hurts

逆反心理 nìfǎn xīnlǐ [名] rebellious mentality

逆境 nìjìng [名] adversity

逆来顺受 nì lái shùn shòu resign oneself to

逆流 nìliú I [动] go against the trend (PT went, PP gone) II [名] (喻) unhealthy trend ▷我们一定要抵制这股社会逆流。We must fight this unhealthy social trend.

逆水行舟 nì shuǐ xíng zhōu go against the stream

逆子 nìzǐ [名] disobedient son

匿 nì [动] (书) conceal ▶隐匿 secrete

匿迹 nìjì [动] go into hiding (PT went, PP gone) ▷他怎么销声匿迹了？Why has he vanished from the scene?

匿名 nìmíng [形] anonymous

腻 nì I [形] 1 (太油) oily 2 (厌烦) fed-up 3 (细致) meticulous II [名] dirt

腻烦 nìfan [动] 1 (厌烦) be bored ▷这个电影我看了3遍也没有腻烦。I've seen this film three times and I'm still not bored of it. 2 (厌恶) loathe

腻味 nìwei [动] 1 (方) (厌烦) be bored ▷这纪录片真腻味人。This documentary is so boring. 2 (方) (厌恶) dislike

溺 nì [动] 1 (淹没) drown 2 (过分) indulge in ▶溺爱 overindulge

蔫 niān [形] 1 (枯萎) withered ▷花因为缺水都蔫了。The flowers withered from lack of water. 2 (萎靡不振) listless

年 nián I [名] 1 (时间单位) year ▷今年 this year 2 (元旦或春节) New Year ▷过年 celebrate Spring Festival 3 (岁数) age ▷年过半百 over fifty years old 4 (阶段) age ▷老年 old age ▶童年 childhood 5 (时代) era ▷明朝末年 the end of the Ming dynasty ▷近年来 in recent years 6 (年成) harvest II [形] annual ▷年薪 annual salary

年表 niánbiǎo [名] chronology

年成 niáncheng [名] harvest

年代 niándài [名] 1 (时代) period 2 (十年) decade

年度 niándù [名] year ▷年度预算 annual budget

年份 niánfèn [名] a particular year ▷这两笔支出不在一个年份。These two expenses were not incurred in the same year.

年富力强 nián fù lì qiáng in the prime of life

年关 niánguān [名] the end of the year

年华 niánhuá [名] (书) years (PL)

年会 niánhuì [名] annual meeting

年货 niánhuò [名] Spring Festival goods

年级 niánjí [名] year (英), grade (美)

年纪 niánjì [名] age ▷他年纪不大。He's quite young.

年鉴 niánjiàn [名] yearbook

年景 niánjǐng [名] 1 (年成) harvest 2 (过年景象) holiday atmosphere

年龄 niánlíng [名] age

年迈 niánmài [形] (书) old

年谱 niánpǔ [名] chronology

年青 niánqīng [形] young

年轻 niánqīng [形] young

年头 niántóu [名] 1 (年份) year 2 (多年时间) years (PL) ▷他从事翻译有年头了。He's been doing translation for years. 3 (时代) times (PL) ▷那年头，日子不好过。In those days, life was hard.

年限 niánxiàn [名] time limit ▷贷款偿还年限 mortgage repayment period

年月 niányue [名] (书) years (PL)

黏 nián [形] glutinous

黏糊 niánhu [形] **1** (指东西) sticky ▷这粥黏糊了。The rice porridge has thickened. **2** (指人) languid

黏着 niánzhuó [动] stick together (PT, PP stuck)

碾 niǎn I [名] roller II [动] **1** (使粉碎) grind (PT, PP ground) **2** (使平坦) flatten

撵 niǎn [动] drive ... away (PT drove, PP driven) ▷我们把他撵走了。We drove him away.

念 niàn I [动] **1** (读) read (PT, PP read) **2** (上学) study **3** (想念) miss II [名] idea

念叨 niàndao [动] **1** (唠叨) nag **2** (谈论) discuss ▷我有些事想念念叨叨。There's something I want to discuss with you.

念旧 niànjiù [动] be nostalgic

念念不忘 niànniàn bù wàng always remember ▷他对老师的帮助念念不忘。He always remembered his teacher's help.

念头 niàntou [名] idea

娘 niáng [名] **1** (方) (母亲) mum **2** (指年长妇女) auntie

娘家 niángjia [名] a married woman's parents' home ▷她要带孩子回娘家。She wants to take her child back to her parents' home.

娘胎 niángtāi [名] womb

酿 niàng I [动] **1** (葡萄酒、蜜) make (PT, PP made) **2** (啤酒) brew **3** (祸事) lead to (PT, PP led) ▷酒后驾车会酿成大祸。Drink-driving can lead to disaster. II [名] alcohol

酿造 niàngzào [动] **1** (葡萄酒、醋、酱油) make (PT, PP made) **2** (啤酒) brew

鸟 niǎo [名] bird

鸟瞰 niǎokàn I [动] get a bird's-eye view ▷从山顶可以鸟瞰全城。From the mountain top you get a bird's-eye view of the whole city. II [名] (书) overview

鸟语花香 niǎo yǔ huā xiāng the sounds and scents of nature

袅 niǎo [形] (书) delicate

袅袅 niǎoniǎo [形] **1** (书) (指烟雾) curling **2** (书) (指声音) lingering

尿 niào I [名] urine ▶排尿 urinate II [动] urinate
→另见 suī

捏 niē [动] **1** (拿) hold (PT, PP held) **2** (饺子) make (PT, PP made) **3** (泥人) mould (英), mold (美)

镊 niè I [名] tweezers (PL) II [动] pick ... up

镍 niè [名] nickel

蹑 niè [动] creep

蹑手蹑脚 niè shǒu niè jiǎo creep ▷他蹑手蹑脚地走进教室。He crept into the classroom.

孽 niè [名] sin

孽种 nièzhǒng [名] (旧) undutiful child (PL children)

您 nín [代] you ▷您慢走！Mind how you go!

宁 níng [形] peaceful
→另见 nìng

宁静 níngjìng [形] quiet

拧 níng [动] **1** (毛巾、衣服) wring (PT, PP wrung) ▷你洗完衣服后，把它们拧一下。When you've washed the clothes, wring them out. **2** (皮肤) pinch
→另见 nìng

狞 níng [形] (书) ferocious ▶狰狞 savage

狞笑 níngxiào [名] evil laugh

柠 níng 见下文

柠檬 níngméng [名] lemon

凝 níng [动] **1** (凝结) congeal **2** (集中注意力) gaze

凝固 nínggù [动] solidify

凝结 níngjié [动] **1** (指气体) liquefy **2** (指液体) solidify

凝聚 níngjù [动] embody

凝练 ningliàn [形] (书) concise

凝视 níngshì [动] gaze

凝重 níngzhòng [形] (书) imposing

宁 nìng [副] ▷我们宁早勿晚。We'd rather be early than late.
→另见 níng

宁可 nìngkě [副] ▷我宁可回家。I'd rather go home.

宁肯 nìngkěn [副] ▷我宁肯熬夜，也不要迟交作业。I'd rather work all night than hand my homework in late.

宁缺毋滥 nìng quē wù làn place quality over quantity ▷对于买衣服，我的原则是宁缺毋滥。When buying clothes, I go by the principle of quality over quantity.

宁死不屈 nìng sǐ bù qū rather die than surrender

宁愿 nìngyuàn [副] ▷我宁愿走也不乘公交车。I'd rather walk than take the bus.

拧 nìng [形] stubborn
→另见 níng

牛 niú [名] 1 (指动物) cow ▶公牛 bull 2 (指肉) beef

牛犊 niúdú [名] calf (PL calves)

牛劲 niújìn [名] 1 (大力气) great strength ▷这小子还真有股牛劲。This child is really strong. 2 (牛脾气) obstinacy

牛皮 niúpí [名] 1 (牛的皮) leather 2 (大话) boast

牛脾气 niúpíqi [名] stubbornness

牛市 niúshì [名] bull market

牛头不对马嘴 niú tóu bù duì mǎ zuǐ incongruous

牛仔裤 niúzǎikù [名] jeans (PL)

扭 niǔ [动] 1 (掉转) turn around 2 (拧) twist 3 (崴) sprain 4 (指走路) sway 5 (指打架) wrestle

扭打 niǔdǎ [动] wrestle

扭捏 niǔnie [形] coy ▷他扭捏地说话。He spoke coyly.

扭曲 niǔqū [动] twist ▷扭曲事实 twist the facts ▷扭曲的灵魂 twisted soul

扭转 niǔzhuǎn [动] turn ... around ▷他扭转船头。He turned the boat around. ▷她突然扭转身子。Suddenly, she turned round. ▷最后的进球扭转了整个局面。The last goal turned the whole game around.

纽 niǔ [名] (扣子) button

纽带 niǔdài [名] tie ▷建立起友谊的纽带 establish ties of friendship

拗 niù [形] obstinate ▷他脾气拗得很。He's terribly obstinate. ▷我可拗不过他。I won't be able to persuade him.
→另见 ào

农 nóng [名] 1 (农业) agriculture 2 (农民) farmer

农产品 nóngchǎnpǐn [名] agricultural produce

农场 nóngchǎng [名] farm

农村 nóngcūn [名] the countryside

农活 nónghuó [名] farm work

农具 nóngjù [名] farm tools (PL)

农历 nónglì [名] lunar calendar

农贸市场 nóngmào shìchǎng [名] farmer's market

农民 nóngmín [名] farmer

农药 nóngyào [名] pesticide

农业 nóngyè [名] agriculture ▷农业现代化 agricultural modernisation

农作物 nóngzuòwù [名] crops (PL)

浓 nóng [形] 1 (指气味、味道) strong 2 (指烟雾) thick ▷浓烟 thick smoke 3 (指兴趣) great ▷他对语言有很浓的兴趣。He has a great interest in languages.

浓度 nóngdù [名] 1 (化) concentration 2 (指酒) strength ▷威士忌酒浓度高。Whisky is strong.

浓厚 nónghòu [形] 1 (指烟雾、云层) thick 2 (指色彩、气氛、意识) strong 3 (指兴趣) great

浓烈 nóngliè [形] strong

浓缩 nóngsuō I [动] condense II [形] condensed

浓郁 nóngyù [形] strong

浓重 nóngzhòng [形] strong

脓 nóng [名] pus

脓包 nóngbāo [名] boil

弄 nòng [动] 1 (搞) make (PT, PP made) ▷我要把问题弄清楚。I'd like to clarify this issue. ▷别把衣服弄脏了。Don't get your clothes dirty. 2 (设法取得) get (PT got, PP got (英), gotten (美)) 3 (摆弄) play with
→另见 lòng

弄巧成拙 nòng qiǎo chéng zhuō be too clever for one's own good

弄虚作假 nòng xū zuò jiǎ falsify

奴 nú [名] slave

奴才 núcai [名] flunkey

奴隶 núlì [名] slave

奴仆 núpú [名] servant

奴役 núyì [动] enslave

努 nǔ [动] 1 (劲儿) make an effort ▷我们再努把力。Let's make one last effort. 2 (嘴) pout ▷他努了下嘴，摆出不在乎的样子。He pouted, making a big show of not caring.

努力 nǔlì [动] try hard ▷他不努力工作。He doesn't work hard. ▷我会尽最大努力。I'll try my very best.

怒 nù I [形] 1 (生气) angry ▶恼怒 furious 2 (指气势) powerful ▷玫瑰在怒放。The roses are in full bloom. II [名] anger ▷发怒 lose one's temper

怒斥 nùchì [动] (书) reproach

怒吼 nùhǒu [动] roar

怒火 nùhuǒ [名] fury ▷强压怒火 curb one's fury

女 nǚ [名] 1 (女子) woman (PL women) ▷女科

学家 female scientist ▷女演员 actress **2** (女儿) daughter ▷长女 eldest daughter ▶子女 children (PL)

女儿 nǚ'ér [名] daughter

女郎 nǚláng [名] girl ▷封面女郎 cover girl

女强人 nǚqiángrén [名] superwoman (PL superwomen)

女权 nǚquán [名] women's rights (PL) ▷女权运动 Women's Movement

女人 nǚrén [名] woman (PL women)

女人 nǚren [名] **1** (妻子) wife (PL wives) **2** (口) (情妇) mistress

女色 nǚsè [名] feminine charm ▷他贪图女色。 He chases after women.

女士 nǚshì [名] **1** (指称呼) Ms. ▷王女士，你好！ Hello, Ms. Wang! **2** (对妇女的尊称) lady

女性 nǚxìng [名] **1** (指性别) the female sex **2** (指女人) woman (PL women)

女婿 nǚxu [名] son-in-law (PL sons-in-law)

女子 nǚzǐ [名] woman (PL women)

暖 nuǎn **I** [形] warm **II** [动] warm ▷天气暖起来了。 The weather has become warmer.

暖和 nuǎnhuo **I** [形] warm **II** [动] warm up

暖流 nuǎnliú [名] **1** (地理) warm current **2** (喻) (指感觉) glow

暖色 nuǎnsè [名] warm colour (英) 或 color (美)

暖水瓶 nuǎnshuǐpíng [名] Thermos flask®

暖洋洋 nuǎnyángyáng [形] balmy

疟 nüè 见下文

疟疾 nüèji [名] malaria

虐 nüè [形] cruel ▶暴虐 brutality ▷虐政 tyranny

虐待 nüèdài [动] ill-treat

挪 nuó [动] move

挪动 nuódong [动] move

挪用 nuóyòng [动] **1** (移作别用) divert **2** (公款) misappropriate

诺 nuò [动] promise ▶承诺 undertake

诺言 nuòyán [名] promise

懦 nuò [形] weak ▶怯懦 timid

懦夫 nuòfū [名] coward

懦弱 nuòruò [形] cowardly

糯 nuò [形] glutinous

糯米 nuòmǐ [名] glutinous rice

Oo

哦 ó [叹] oh ▷哦，他也来了。Oh, he's come too.
→另见 ò

嚄 ǒ [叹] oh ▷嚄，你竟然也在。Oh, you're actually in.

哦 ò [叹] oh ▷哦，我明白了。Oh, now I understand.
→另见 ó

讴 ōu 见下文
讴歌 ōugē [动] (书) sing the praises of (PT sang, PP sung) ▷这篇报道讴歌了白衣天使。This report sings the praises of doctors and nurses.

欧 ōu [名] 1 (欧洲) Europe 2 (欧姆) ohm
欧元 ōuyuán [名] euro

殴 ōu [动] beat ...up (PT beat, PP beaten) ▶斗殴 fight
殴打 ōudǎ [动] beat ...up (PT beat, PP beaten)

鸥 ōu [名] gull

呕 ǒu [动] vomit
呕吐 ǒutù [动] vomit
呕心沥血 ǒu xīn lì xuè work one's heart out

偶 ǒu I [名] 1 (人像) image ▶木偶 puppet 2 (双数) even number 3 (配偶) mate II [形] chance ▷我们的相识是由于一次偶遇。We met through a chance encounter.
偶尔 ǒu'ěr [副] occasionally ▷我偶而去游泳。Occasionally I go swimming.
偶然 ǒurán [形] chance ▷我偶然发现了这则消息。I found out this piece of news by chance.
偶然性 ǒuránxìng [名] chance
偶数 ǒushù [名] even number
偶像 ǒuxiàng [名] idol

藕 ǒu [名] lotus root
藕断丝连 ǒu duàn sī lián separated but still together in spirit

怄 òu [动] (方) annoy
怄气 òuqì [动] (方) be annoyed

Pp

趴 pā [动] 1 (卧倒) lie prone (PT lay, PP lain) 2 (伏靠) bend over (PT, PP bent) ▷上课别趴在桌子上。Don't lean on the desk during class.

趴伏 pāfú [动] lie prone (PT lay, PP lain)

啪 pā [拟] bang ▷字典啪地一声掉在地上。The dictionary dropped to the floor with a bang.

扒 pá [动] 1 (搂) rake 2 (方)(挠) scratch ▷扒痒 scratch an itch 3 (偷) steal (PT stole, PP stolen) ▷我的钱包被扒走了。My wallet has been stolen.
→另见 bā

扒窃 páqiè [动] steal (PT stole, PP stolen)

扒手 páshǒu [名] pickpocket

爬 pá [动] 1 (前移) crawl 2 (上移) climb ▷爬山 climb a mountain 3 (起床) get up 4 (升迁) be promoted ▷他靠巴结老板往上爬。He got promoted by sucking up to the boss.

爬格子 pá gézi write (PT wrote, PP written)

爬升 páshēng [动] rise (PT rose, PP risen) ▷飞机爬升到万米高空。The plane rose to an altitude of 10,000 metres. ▷物价的不断爬升令人担忧。Continual price rises are worrying. ▷近两年，他爬升很快。He's risen very fast in the last two years.

爬行 páxíng [动] crawl

耙 pá [名] rake
→另见 bà

耙子 pázi [名] rake

帕 pà [名] handkerchief

怕 pà [动] 1 (惧怕) fear 2 (担心) be afraid ▷我怕这么做不合适。I'm afraid it's not appropriate to do it this way. 3 (估计) may be ▷我们怕有3年没见面了。It might be three years since we last met.

怕生 pàshēng [动] be shy

怕羞 pàxiū [动] be shy ▷在生人面前，她很怕羞。She's very shy in front of strangers.

拍 pāi I [动] 1 (击打) beat (PT beat, PP beaten) ▷我拍掉了鞋上的泥。I knocked the mud off my shoes. 2 (拍摄) shoot (PT, PP shot) ▷他最近拍了一部电影。He's recently shot a film. 3 (发) send (PT, PP sent) 4 (拍马屁) flatter II [名] 1 (用具) bat (英), paddle (美) 2 (节奏) beat

拍板 pāibǎn I [名] 1 (指乐器) clappers (PL) 2 (决定) final say ▷没有老板的拍板，谁也不敢行动。No one will want to act without the go-ahead from the boss. II [动] 1 (字)(成交) clinch a deal ▷又一批生意拍板成交了。Another business deal has been clinched. 2 (喻)(同意) give the OK (PT gave, PP given) ▷这个方案老板还没拍板。The boss still hasn't given the proposal the OK.

拍击 pāijī [动] strike (PT, PP struck)

拍马屁 pāi mǎpì [动] suck up ▷他很善于拍马屁。He's very good at sucking up to people.

拍卖 pāimài [动] auction

拍摄 pāishè [动] shoot (PT, PP shot)

拍手称快 pāi shǒu chēng kuài applaud ▷犯罪分子落网，人人拍手称快。Everyone applauded when the criminals were caught.

拍照 pāizhào [动] take a photograph (PT took, PP taken)

拍子 pāizi [名] 1 (用具) bat (英), paddle (美) ▷网球拍子 tennis racket 2 (节奏) beat ▷打拍子 beat time

排 pái I [动] 1 (摆放) put ... in order (PT, PP put) ▷请把椅子排好。Please arrange the chairs. 2 (排演) rehearse 3 (除去) drain II [名] 1 (行列) row ▷我坐在教室的前排。I sit in the front row in class. 2 (指军队) platoon 3 (指水运) raft III [量] row ▷两排桌子 two rows of tables

排比 páibǐ [名] parallelism

排场 **páichǎng** [名] ostentation ▷他们的婚宴办得真排场。Their wedding was very ostentatious.

排斥 **páichì** [动] exclude

排除 **páichú** [动] remove

排放 **páifàng** [动] discharge

排挤 **páijǐ** [动] squeeze ... out ▷她被排挤出了决策层。She was squeezed out of policy-making.

排解 **páijiě** [动] 1 (调解) mediate ▷朋友排解了他们的纠纷。Friends mediated between them in the dispute. 2 (消除) dispel

排练 **páiliàn** [动] rehearse

排列 **páiliè** [动] arrange ▷人名按字母顺序排列。People's names have been put in alphabetical order.

排遣 **páiqiǎn** [动] shake ... off (PT shook, PP shaken) ▷我无法排遣心中郁闷。I can't shake off these gloomy feelings.

排山倒海 **pái shān dǎo hǎi** overwhelming

排外 **páiwài** [动] be xenophobic ▷排外阻碍了这个国家的发展。Xenophobia hindered the country's development.

排泄 **páixiè** [动] 1 (指雨水、污水) discharge 2 (指新陈代谢) excrete

排演 **páiyǎn** [动] rehearse

排印 **páiyìn** [动] typeset and print (PT, PP typeset)

排忧解难 **pái yōu jiě nàn** sort out problems

牌 **pái** [名] 1 (标志板) board ▶广告牌 hoarding ▶门牌 house number ▶招牌 shop sign 2 (商标) brand

牌号 **páihào** [名] 1 (字号) store name 2 (商标) brand

牌价 **páijià** [名] list price

牌照 **páizhào** [名] 1 (指车辆) registration number 2 (指商业) licence (英), license (美)

牌子 **páizi** [名] 1 (标志板) board 2 (商标) brand

派 **pài** I [名] 1 (帮派) group ▶学派 school of thought 2 (风度) manner II [动] 1 (分配) set (PT, PP set) ▷他派给我一大堆活。He set me a huge pile of work. 2 (委派) send (PT, PP sent) 3 (安排) assign ▷他们派我去机场接客人。They assigned me to go to the airport to meet people. 4 (分摊) apportion 5 (指摘) expose III [形] stylish IV [量] 1 (帮) school of thought ▷这两派总是意见不一。The two parties never agree. 2 (用于景色、语言) ▷一派新气象 a new scene ▷一派胡言 a pack of lies

派别 **pàibié** [名] school of thought

派对 **pàiduì** [名] party

派遣 **pàiqiǎn** [动] dispatch

派生 **pàishēng** [动] derive ▷许多英语词汇是拉丁文的派生。Many English words are derived from Latin.

派头 **pàitóu** [名] style ▷你穿这件夹克很有派头。You look very stylish in this jacket.

派系 **pàixì** [名] faction

攀 **pān** [动] 1 (向上爬) climb ▶攀岩 rock-climbing 2 (指关系) seek friends in high places (PT, PP sought) ▶高攀 be a social climber 3 (拉扯) chat

攀比 **pānbǐ** [动] compete

攀登 **pāndēng** [动] scale

攀附 **pānfù** [动] 1 (指植物) climb 2 (指人) try to get in with

攀谈 **pāntán** [动] chat

盘 **pán** I [名] 1 (盘子) tray ▶茶盘 tea tray 2 (盘状物) ▶棋盘 chessboard 3 (行情) quotation II [动] 1 (绕) wind (PT, PP wound) ▶盘旋 wind 2 (检查) examine ▶盘问 interrogate 3 (清点) make an inventory ▶盘货 stocktake 4 (转让) transfer III [量] 1 (指物量) ▷一盘电线 a coil of wire ▷三盘录像带 three videotapes 2 (指动量) game ▷我再跟你下盘棋。I'll play another game of chess with you.

盘查 **pánchá** [动] interrogate

盘点 **pándiǎn** [动] stocktake

盘根错节 **pán gēn cuò jié** knotty

盘根究底 **pán gēn jiū dǐ** get to the heart of the matter

盘踞 **pánjù** [动] occupy

盘绕 **pánrào** [动] wind ... round (PT, PP wound)

盘算 **pánsuàn** [动] figure ... out

盘问 **pánwèn** [动] interrogate

盘旋 **pánxuán** [动] 1 (环绕) circle ▷飞机在上空盘旋。The plane circled overhead. 2 (萦绕) linger ▷这个想法一直在他脑子里盘旋。The thought lingered in his mind.

盘子 **pánzi** [名] plate

磐 **pán** 见下文

磐石 **pánshí** [名] huge rock

蹒 **pán** 见下文

蹒跚 **pánshān** [形] limp

判 **pàn** I [动] 1 (分辨) distinguish ▶判明 ascertain 2 (评定) judge ▷判卷子 mark exams 3 (裁决) sentence ▶审判 try II [副] clearly

判别 pànbié [动] distinguish ▷判别是非 tell right from wrong

判处 pànchǔ [动] sentence

判定 pàndìng [动] judge ▷法院判定他无罪。 The court found him not guilty.

判断 pànduàn [动] judge

判决 pànjué [动] 1 (裁定) come to a verdict (PT came, PP come) ▷法院的判决已经出来了。 The court has already come to a verdict. 2 (判断) judge

判若两人 pàn ruò liǎng rén become a completely different person ▷他一工作起来简直判若两人。 When he's working he's a completely different person.

盼 pàn [动] 1 (盼望) long ▷我盼着见到亲人。 I long to see my loved ones. 2 (看) look ▷左顾右盼 look around

盼头 pàntou [名] good prospects (PL)

盼望 pànwàng [动] long ▷人们盼望战争早日结束。 The people longed for the war to be over soon.

叛 pàn [动] betray

叛变 pànbiàn [动] betray

叛离 pànlí [动] betray

叛乱 pànluàn [名] revolt

叛逆 pànnì [动] rebel ▷他从小就是个叛逆的人。 He has been a rebel ever since he was young.

畔 pàn [名] 1 (旁边) bank 2 (田边) boundary ▷田畔 edge of a field

乓 pāng [拟] bang ▷门乓地一声关上了。 The door banged shut.

滂 pāng 见下文
滂沱 pāngtuó [形] torrential

彷 páng 见下文
彷徨 pánghuáng [动] hesitate

庞 páng I [形] 1 (体积大) huge 2 (多而杂) innumerable and disordered II [名] face ▷脸庞 face

庞大 pángdà [形] huge

庞然大物 pàngrán dà wù giant

庞杂 pángzá [形] jumbled up

旁 páng I [名] side ▷他站在了我身旁。 He stood by my side. II [形] (口) other ▷我还有旁的事儿要做。 I still have other things to do.

旁观 pángguān [动] look on

旁敲侧击 páng qiāo cè jī make oblique references

旁若无人 páng ruò wú rén oblivious of others

旁听 pángtīng [动] 1 (指开会) sit in on (PT, PP sat) ▷他旁听了昨天的董事会。 He sat in on yesterday's board meeting. 2 (指上课) take (PT took, PP taken) ▷他旁听夜校的课。 He's taking evening classes.

旁征博引 páng zhēng bó yǐn cite extensive sources

旁证 pángzhèng [名] circumstantial evidence

膀 páng 见下文
→另见 bǎng
膀胱 pángguāng [名] bladder

磅 páng 见下文
→另见 bàng
磅礴 pángbó [形] majestic

螃 páng 见下文
螃蟹 pángxiè [名] crab

胖 pàng [形] fat

胖墩儿 pàngdūnr [名] chubby little thing

胖乎乎 pànghūhū [形] fat

胖子 pàngzi [名] fatty

抛 pāo [动] 1 (投掷) throw (PT threw, PP thrown) 2 (丢下) leave ... behind (PT, PP left) ▷他把别的车手远远抛在了后面。 He left the other drivers far behind him. 3 (暴露) bare ▷抛头露面 appear in public 4 (脱手) dispose of

抛光 pāoguāng [动] polish

抛锚 pāomáo [动] 1 (指船) cast anchor (PT, PP cast) 2 (指车) break down (PT broke, PP broken) ▷我的车半路上抛锚了。 My car broke down on the way.

抛弃 pāoqì [动] desert ▷抛弃妻子 desert one's wife ▷抛弃旧观念 give up on one's old ideas

抛售 pāoshòu [动] dispose of

抛头露面 pāo tóu lù miàn (贬) appear in public ▷他是个经常抛头露面的公众人物。 He is a highly visible public figure.

抛砖引玉 pāo zhuān yǐn yù (谦) get the ball rolling

刨 páo [动] 1 (挖掘) dig (PT, PP dug) 2 (除去) exclude
→另见 bào
刨除 páochú [动] deduct
刨根问底 páo gēn wèn dǐ get to the root of

things

咆 páo 见下文
咆哮 páoxiào [动] roar

炮 páo 见下文
→另见 bāo, pào
炮制 páozhì [动] concoct

袍 páo [名] gown ▶旗袍 cheongsam

跑 pǎo [动] 1 (奔) run (PT ran, PP run) ▷小男孩跑向妈妈。The little boy ran to his mother. 2 (逃) escape 3 (奔波) run around (PT ran, PP run) ▷我为这事跑了好几天。I've been running around trying to sort this out for several days. 4 (漏) leak ▷车胎跑气了。The tyre (英) 或 tire (美) is flat.
跑步 pǎobù [动] run (PT ran, PP run) ▷我每天跑步去学校。I run to school every day. ▷他喜欢跑步。He likes jogging.
跑买卖 pǎo mǎimai [动] travel on business
跑题 pǎotí [动] stray from the topic
跑腿 pǎotuǐ [动] do the legwork (PT did, PP done)

泡 pào I [名] 1 (指气体) bubble 2 (指泡状) ▶灯泡 light bulb ▷我的脚上磨起了泡。I've got blisters on my feet from the rubbing. II [动] 1 (浸) soak 2 (消磨) dawdle 3 (沏) infuse ▶泡茶 make tea
泡吧 pàobā [动] go clubbing (PT went, PP gone)
泡沫 pàomò [名] foam
泡影 pàoyǐng [名] lost hope ▷他的一切希望都化为泡影。All his hopes came to nothing.

炮 pào [名] 1 (武器) cannon 2 (爆竹) firecracker
→另见 bāo, páo
炮火 pàohuǒ [名] gunfire
炮筒子 pàotǒngzi [名] 1 (指物) barrel 2 (指人) ▷他像个炮筒子。He's always shooting his mouth off.

疱 pào [名] blister

呸 pēi [叹] bah

胚 pēi 见下文
胚胎 pēitāi [名] 1 (生物) (指动物) embryo 2 (雏形) embryonic form ▷欧共体是欧盟的胚胎。The EEC was the EU in embryonic form.

陪 péi [动] 1 (相伴) go with (PT went, PP gone) ▷我要陪母亲去医院。I have to go to the hospital with my mother. ▷我不用你陪。

You don't need to come with me. 2 (协助) assist ▶陪考 assistant examiner
陪伴 péibàn [动] keep ... company (PT, PP kept) ▷她常常陪伴在奶奶身边。She often keeps her grandma company.
陪衬 péichèn [动] set off (PT, PP set)
陪同 péitóng I [动] accompany ▷他陪同中外宾参观了工厂。He accompanied the foreigners visiting the factory. II [名] guide

培 péi [动] foster
培训 péixùn [动] train ▷新教师需要培训。New teachers need training.
培养 péiyǎng [动] cultivate ▷培养细菌 cultivate bacteria
培育 péiyù [动] 1 (培植养育) cultivate ▷培育幼苗 cultivate seedlings 2 (培养教育) nurture

赔 péi [动] 1 (赔偿) make good ▷损失应该你来赔。You should make good the loss. 2 (亏本) make a loss ▷这次生意我们赔了。We've made a loss in this transaction.
赔本 péiběn [动] make a loss
赔偿 péicháng [动] compensate ▷他应该赔偿我们的损失。He should compensate us for the loss. ▷他们得到了及时的赔偿。They received prompt compensation.
赔了夫人又折兵 péile fūrén yòu zhé bīng pay a double penalty
赔罪 péizuì [动] apologize

佩 pèi [动] 1 (佩带) wear (PT wore, PP worn) ▷他腰佩一支手枪。He carries a pistol at his belt. 2 (佩服) admire ▶钦佩 esteem
佩带 pèidài [动] wear (PT wore, PP worn) ▷他胸前佩带着一枚勋章。He is wearing a medal on his chest.
佩服 pèifú [动] admire

配 pèi I [动] 1 (指两性) marry 2 (指动物) mate 3 (调和) mix ▶配药 make up a prescription 4 (分派) allocate ▶配售 ration 5 (补充) ▶配钥匙 have a key made ▷配货 replace goods 6 (衬托) match 7 (符合) fit ▷她的穿着和身份很相配。She dresses to fit her role. II [名] spouse
配备 pèibèi I [动] provide ▷公司给他配备了一辆轿车。The company provided him with a car. II [名] equipment
配餐 pèicān I [动] ▷配餐要讲究营养均衡。Planning meals demands particular attention to nutritional balance. II [名] meal
配方 pèifāng I [动] dispense prescriptions II [名] prescription

配合 pèihé [动] cooperate ▷他们善于相互配合。They are good at cooperating with each other.

配合 pèihe [形] complementary

配角 pèijué [名] supporting role

配偶 pèi'ǒu (书) [名] spouse

配套 pèitào I [动] be a set ▷所有的家具都要配套。The furniture should all be from the same range. II [形] coherent

配制 pèizhì 1 (调制) make...up ▷他在酒吧里配制鸡尾酒。He mixes cocktails in a bar. 2 (附衬) add ▷他为这本书配制了插图。He added illustrations to the book.

配置 pèizhì [动] deploy

喷 pēn [动] gush ▷油井终于喷油了。Finally oil gushed from the well.
→另见 pèn

喷发 pēnfā [动] erupt

喷泉 pēnquán [名] fountain

喷洒 pēnsǎ [动] spray

喷嚏 pēntì [名] sneeze

喷泻 pēnxiè [动] gush

喷嘴 pēnzuǐ [名] nozzle

盆 pén [名] 1 (盛具) basin ▶脸盆 washbasin 2 (盆状物) ▶骨盆 pelvis

盆地 péndì [名] basin

盆盆罐罐 pénpén-guànguàn [名] household utensils (PL)

喷 pèn 见下文
→另见 pēn

喷香 pènxiāng [形] delicious

抨 pēng 见下文

抨击 pēngjī [动] attack

怦 pēng [拟] thump ▷我吓得心怦怦直跳。My heart is thumping with fear.

砰 pēng [拟] bang

烹 pēng [动] cook

烹饪 pēngrèn [动] cook ▷他擅长烹饪。He's an excellent cook.

烹调 pēngtiáo [动] cook

朋 péng [名] friend

朋党 péngdǎng [名] clique

朋友 péngyǒu [名] 1 (指友谊) friend 2 (女友) girlfriend 3 (男友) boyfriend

棚 péng [名] awning ▷自行车棚 bicycle shed

蓬 péng I [形] dishevelled (英), disheveled (美) II [量] clump ▷一蓬草 a clump of grass

蓬勃 péngbó [形] vigorous

蓬松 péngsōng [形] fluffy

蓬头垢面 péng tóu gòu miàn unkempt appearance

鹏 péng 见下文

鹏程万里 péng chéng wàn lǐ go far ▷祝你鹏程万里，事业有成。I hope your undertaking succeeds and that you go far.

澎 péng 见下文

澎湃 péngpài [形] 1 (指波涛) surging 2 (指心情) racing

篷 péng [名] 1 (顶) covering ▶篷车 wagon 2 (帆) sail

膨 péng [动] expand

膨化 pénghuà [动] pop

膨胀 péngzhàng [动] 1 (指体积) expand 2 (指事物) inflate ▷政府有效地抑制了通货膨胀。The government controlled inflation effectively.

捧 pěng I [动] 1 (托) hold...in both hands (PT, PP held) ▷他手捧一束鲜花。He held a bouquet of flowers in both hands. 2 (奉承) flatter II [量] handful ▷一捧花生 a handful of peanuts

捧场 pěngchǎng [动] support ▷感谢各位的捧场。Thanks for everyone's support.

捧腹 pěngfù [动] split one's sides laughing (PT, PP split) ▷这段小品令人捧腹。This sketch is side-splittingly funny.

碰 pèng [动] 1 (撞击) hit (PT, PP hit) 2 (遇见) bump into ▷我在街上碰到了一位老同学。I bumped into an old classmate in the street. 3 (试探) take a chance (PT took, PP taken)

碰壁 pèngbì [动] hit a brick wall (PT, PP hit)

碰钉子 pèng dīngzi [动] be rebuffed

碰巧 pèngqiǎo [副] by chance ▷我碰巧遇见他。I met him by chance.

碰头 pèngtóu [动] meet (PT, PP met)

碰一鼻子灰 pèng yī bízi huī meet with a rebuff

碰撞 pèngzhuàng [动] 1 (撞击) collide 2 (冒犯) offend

批 pī I [动] 1 (批示) comment ▶批示 comment 2 (批评) criticize II [名] wholesale ▷我们将成批购进材料。We are going to buy the materials wholesale. III [量] ▷一批大学生 a group of university students ▷新到的一批货 a new batch of goods

批驳 pībó [动] rebut

批发 pīfā [动] 1 (成批出售) sell ... wholesale (PT, PP sold) ▷他专门批发建筑材料。He specializes in selling building materials wholesale. 2 (批准转发) be authorized for dispatch

批复 pīfù [动] respond to ▷总经理批复了我们的申请。The managing director has responded to our request.

批改 pīgǎi [动] correct

批量 pīliàng [名] batch

批判 pīpàn [动] 1 (驳斥) repudiate 2 (批评) criticize

批评 pīpíng [动] criticize ▷接受批评 accept criticism

批示 pīshì [动] comment ▷文件上有校长的亲笔批示。The document contained comments from the principal himself.

批准 pīzhǔn [动] approve ▷没有我的批准，谁也不许离开。No one may leave without my approval.

纰 pī [动] unravel

纰漏 pīlòu [名] slip

披 pī [动] 1 (搭) drape ... over one's shoulders ▷他披上了大衣。He draped the coat over his shoulders. ▷她披着白色披肩。She's wrapped in a white shawl. 2 (开裂) split (PT, PP split)

披风 pīfēng [名] cape

披肝沥胆 pī gān lì dǎn loyal and sincere

披肩 pījiān [名] 1 (指饰物) scarf 2 (指衣服) cape

披荆斩棘 pī jīng zhǎn jí clear away obstacles

披露 pīlù [动] 1 (公布) announce 2 (表露) reveal

披星戴月 pī xīng dài yuè day and night

砒 pī 见下文

砒霜 pīshuāng [名] arsenic

劈 pī I [动] 1 (砍) chop ▷他把木头劈成了两半。He chopped the wood in two. 2 (裂开) split (PT, PP split) 3 (雷击) strike (PT, PP struck) II [形] (方) hoarse ▷他嗓子喊劈了。He's shouted himself hoarse. III [介] right in ▶劈脸 in one's face ▷他一进门劈脸就问我干了什么。As soon as he came in he asked me straight out what I was doing.

→另见 pǐ

劈波斩浪 pī bō zhǎn làng weather a storm

劈里啪啦 pīlipālā [拟] pitter-patter

劈头 pītóu [副] 1 (朝头上) right on the head 2 (迎面) in one's face ▷我一出门，劈头遇上了老王。As soon as I went out, I came face to face with Lao Wang. 3 (开头) at the very start ▷他劈头第一句话就问出了什么事。His first words were to ask what was up.

劈头盖脸 pī tóu gài liǎn in one's face

霹 pī 见下文

霹雳 pīlì [名] thunderbolt

皮 pí I [名] 1 (表皮) skin 2 (皮革) leather 3 (外皮) covering ▶漆皮 coat of paint 4 (表面) surface 5 (薄片) sheet ▶奶皮儿 skin on the milk 6 (指橡胶) rubber II [形] 1 (韧) thick-skinned 2 (变韧的) rubbery 3 (顽皮) naughty

皮尺 píchǐ [名] tape measure

皮肤 pífū [名] skin

皮革 pígé [名] leather

皮货 píhuò [名] fur

皮开肉绽 pí kāi ròu zhàn be horrifically beaten

皮毛 pímáo [名] 1 (指兽皮) fur 2 (指知识) superficial knowledge

皮实 píshí [形] 1 (结实) sturdy 2 (耐用) durable

皮试 píshì [动] have a skin test

皮笑肉不笑 pí xiào ròu bù xiào (贬) put on a false smile ▷他皮笑肉不笑的样子真可恶。His false smile is really unbearable.

皮子 pízi [名] hide

毗 pí 见下文

毗连 pílián [动] border on ▷美国的北部跟加拿大毗连。The United States borders on Canada to the north.

疲 pí [形] 1 (疲劳) tired ▷筋疲力尽 be exhausted 2 (厌倦) tired of

疲惫 píbèi [形] weary

疲乏 pífá [形] tired

疲倦 píjuàn [形] tired

疲劳 píláo [形] 1 (劳累) weary 2 (衰退) weakened

疲软 píruǎn [形] 1 (怠倦) weary 2 (不景气) weak

疲塌 píta [形] slack

疲于奔命 pí yú bēn mìng be constantly on the run

啤 pí 见下文

啤酒 píjiǔ [名] beer

琵 pí 见下文
琵琶 pípá [名] Chinese lute

脾 pí [名] spleen
脾气 píqi [名] **1** (怒气) temper **2** (性情) temperament
脾性 píxìng [名] (方) character

匹 pǐ **I** [动] match **II** [量] **1** (指动物) ▷三匹马 three horses ▷几匹骡子 some mules **2** (指布料) bolt ▷两匹绸缎 two bolts of silk **III** [形] single
匹敌 pǐdí [动] match
匹夫 pǐfū [名] the man on the street
匹配 pǐpèi [动] match

痞 pǐ 见下文
痞子 pǐzi [名] hooligan

劈 pī [动] **1** (分开) split (PT, PP split) ▷他把线劈成了两股。He split the thread into two strands. **2** (分裂) break off (PT broke, PP broken) **3** (叉开) open very wide
→另见 pǐ
劈叉 pǐchà [动] do the splits
劈柴 pǐchái [动] chop firewood

癖 pǐ [名] addiction
癖好 pǐhào [名] favourite (英) 或 favorite (美) hobby
癖性 pǐxìng [名] inclination

屁 pì **I** [名] wind ▶放屁 fart **II** [形] meaningless ▶屁事 trivialities (PL)
屁股 pìgu [名] **1** (指人) bottom **2** (指后部) rear
屁滚尿流 pì gǔn niào liú (贬) scare the hell out of
屁话 pìhuà [名] (讳) rubbish

辟 pì **I** [动] **1** (开辟) open ... up ▷这里将辟为工业园区。This will be opened up as industrial land. ▷新辟一块菜地 start a vegetable patch **2** (驳斥) repudiate ▶辟谣 deny a rumour (英) 或 rumor (美) **II** [形] incisive ▶透辟 penetrating
→另见 bì

媲 pì 见下文
媲美 pìměi [动] rival

僻 pì [形] **1** (僻静) secluded ▶偏僻 out-of-the-way **2** (古怪) eccentric **3** (不常见) rare
僻静 pìjìng [形] secluded

譬 pì [名] analogy ▶譬如 for example ▶譬喻 metaphor
譬如 pìrú [动] take ... for example (PT took, PP taken) ▷譬如饮食习惯，南北各不相同。Taking eating habits as an example, there are big differences between the north and the south.
譬喻 pìyù [名] analogy

片 piān 见下文
→另见 piàn
片子 piānzi [名] **1** (电影) film (英), movie (美) **2** (X光) X-ray **3** (唱片) record

扁 piān 见下文
→另见 biǎn
扁舟 piānzhōu [名] skiff

偏 piān [形] **1** (倾斜的) slanting **2** (不公的) biased
偏爱 piān'ài [动] show favouritism (英) 或 favoritism (美) to (PT showed, PP shown)
偏差 piānchā [名] **1** (指方向) deviation **2** (指工作) error
偏废 piānfèi [动] give unequal emphasis to (PT gave, PP given) ▷经济增长与环境保护，二者不可偏废。Economic growth and environmental protection should be given equal emphasis.
偏激 piānjī [形] extreme
偏见 piānjiàn [名] prejudice ▷你对他有偏见。You're prejudiced against him.
偏劳 piānláo [动] (敬) go to trouble (PT went, PP gone) ▷让您偏劳，谢谢了。Thanks for going to so much trouble.
偏离 piān lí [动] deviate from ▷飞机偏离了航线。The plane went off course.
偏僻 piānpì [形] remote
偏偏 piānpiān [副] **1** (表示主观) persistently ▷别人都同意，他偏偏唱反调。Everyone else agreed, but he was persistent in his disagreement. **2** (表示客观) contrary to expectation ▷我去找他，他偏偏离开了。I went to see him, but he happened to be out. **3** (表示范围) only ▷大家我都想到了，偏偏把他给漏了。I thought of everyone, but of all people I left him out.
偏颇 piānpō [形] (书) biased ▷您这种看法有点偏颇。You're a bit biased in your outlook.
偏巧 piānqiǎo [副] **1** (刚好) as luck would have it ▷我正要去找他，偏巧，他来了。I was just going to see him when, as luck would have it, he turned up. **2** (偏偏) as it happens ▷我找他有事，偏巧他不在。I went to see him about

something, but as it happens he was out.

偏袒 piāntǎn [动] side with ▷爸爸总是偏袒弟弟。Dad always sides with my younger brother.

偏向 piānxiàng I [动] 1 (袒护) favour (英), favor (美) ▷你不能这么偏向他。You shouldn't favour him like this. 2 (倾向) prefer to II [名] deviation

偏心 piānxīn [动] be biased ▷经理的偏心引起了员工的不满。The manager's bias created dissatisfaction among the workers.

偏重 piānzhòng [动] emphasize

篇 piān I [名] 1 (文章) writing ▶篇章 sections (PL) 2 (单张纸) sheet ▶歌篇儿 song sheet II [量] ▷一篇作文 a composition ▷三篇文章 three essays

篇幅 piānfu [名] 1 (指文章长度) length ▷文章篇幅不要过长。The essay shouldn't be overlong. 2 (指页数量) space ▷报纸用整版篇幅登载了这条消息。The newspaper gave this story a whole page.

篇目 piānmù [名] 1 (标题) title 2 (目录) contents (PL)

篇章 piānzhāng [名] sections (PL) ▷篇章布局 structure of an article

便 pián 见下文
→另见 biàn

便便 piánpián [形] fat ▷他大腹便便。He's got a pot-belly.

便宜 piányi I [形] cheap II [名] small gains (PL) III [动] let ... off lightly (PT, PP let) ▷你不能这么便宜了他。You shouldn't let him off so lightly.

片 piàn I [名] 1 (指薄度) piece ▶纸片儿 scraps of paper 2 (指地区) area II [动] slice III [形] 1 (不全) incomplete ▷片面 one-sided 2 (简短) brief IV [量] 1 (指片状物) ▷两片药 two tablets ▷几片树叶 some leaves 2 (指水陆) stretch ▷一片沼泽地 a stretch of marsh 3 (指声音、心意等) ▷一片忠心 in all sincerity ▷一片掌声 a burst of applause
→另见 piān

片段 piànduàn [名] extract

片断 piànduàn I [名] 1 (零碎) fragment 2 (片段) extract II [形] fragmentary

片刻 piànkè [名] instant ▷昨晚,我片刻也没离开房间。Last night I didn't leave my room for a moment.

片面 piànmiàn I [名] one side ▷不要听信他的片面之词。You shouldn't listen to his one-sided account. II [形] one-sided

片言只语 piàn yán zhī yǔ just a few words

▷你要经常给我发电邮,哪怕片言只语也好。You should email me often – just a few words will do.

片子 piànzi [名] 1 (薄片) piece ▷玻璃片子 pieces of glass 2 (名片) namecard

骗 piàn [动] 1 (欺瞒) deceive 2 (骗得) swindle ▶骗钱 swindle

骗局 piànjú [名] swindle

骗取 piànqǔ [动] ▷他骗取了上级的信任。He wormed his way into his boss's confidence. ▷你骗取不了我的同情。You can't trick me into sympathizing with you.

骗术 piànshù [名] trick

骗子 piànzi [名] swindler

剽 piāo I [动] rob II [形] agile

剽悍 piāohàn [形] agile and brave

剽窃 piāoqiè [动] plagiarize

漂 piāo [动] 1 (浮) float 2 (流动) drift
→另见 piǎo, piào

漂泊 piāobó [动] 1 (指船舶) float 2 (指生活) drift

漂浮 piāofú I [动] float II [形] superficial

漂流 piāoliú [动] drift

漂移 piāoyí [动] drift

漂游 piāoyóu [动] 1 (浮动) float 2 (漂泊) drift

缥 piāo 见下文

缥缈 piāomiǎo [形] indistinct

飘 piāo [动] 1 (飞扬) flutter 2 (指腿、脚) wobble

飘荡 piāodàng [动] 1 (浮动) float 2 (漂泊) drift

飘动 piāodòng [动] drift

飘零 piāolíng [动] 1 (坠落) fall (PT fell, PP fallen) 2 (流浪) wander

飘飘然 piāopiāorán [形] 1 (轻飘飘) floating 2 (很得意) smug

飘洒 piāosǎ [动] fall (PT fell, PP fallen)

飘洒 piāosa [形] graceful

飘扬 piāoyáng [动] flutter

飘摇 piāoyáo [动] sway

飘逸 piāoyì I [形] (书) graceful II [动] drift

嫖 piáo [动] visit prostitutes

嫖客 piáokè [名] client (of a prostitute)

瓢 piáo [名] ladle

瓢泼大雨 piáopōdàyǔ downpour

漂 piǎo [动] 1 (漂白) bleach 2 (冲洗) rinse
→另见 piāo, piào

漂白 piǎobái [动] bleach
漂洗 piǎoxǐ [动] rinse

瞟 piǎo [动] give a sidelong look (PT gave, PP given)

票 piào [名] **1** (作凭证) ticket **2** (指钞票) note (英), bill (美) **3** (指戏曲) amateur performance
票房价值 piàofáng jiàzhí [名] box office takings (PL)
票据 piàojù [名] **1** (汇票) note (英), bill (美) **2** (凭证) voucher
票子 piàozi [名] (口) note (英), bill (美)

漂 piāo 见下文
→另见 piāo, piǎo
漂亮 piàoliang [形] **1** (好看) good-looking ▷过年了，孩子们穿上了漂亮衣服。At New Year, the children wore beautiful clothes. ▷你女儿真漂亮。Your daughter is very pretty. **2** (精彩) wonderful ▷这场球踢得漂亮。It was a brilliant football match.

撇 piē [动] **1** (弃) cast ... aside (PT, PP cast) ▷他撇下家庭，外出创业。He cast aside his family and went off to make a new career for himself. **2** (舀) skim
→另见 piě

瞥 piē [动] shoot a glance at (PT, PP shot) ▷他瞥了我一眼。He shot me a glance.
瞥视 piēshì [动] glance at

撇 piě I [动] **1** (扔) throw (PT threw, PP thrown) **2** (扭) curl ▶撇嘴 curl one's lip II [量] tuft ▷两撇胡子 two tufts of facial hair
→另见 piē
撇开 piěkāi [动] leave ... aside (PT, PP left) ▷撇开成见 leave one's prejudices aside
撇嘴 piězuǐ [动] curl one's lip

拼 pīn [动] **1** (合) join together ▷我们把两张桌子拼了起来。We joined the two tables together. ▷拼图游戏 jigsaw puzzle **2** (竭尽全力) go all out (PT went, PP gone) ▶拼命 with all one's might **3** (字、词) spell ▷你能拼一下这个词吗？Can you spell this word?
拼搏 pīnbó [动] go all out (PT went, PP gone) ▷经过90分钟的拼搏，我们终于赢得了那场足球赛。By going all out for ninety minutes, we finally won the football match.
拼凑 pīncòu [动] piece ... together
拼命 pīnmìng [动] **1** (不要命) risk one's life ▷歹徒见她要拼命转身跑掉了。When the thugs saw that she was ready to fight to the death,

they turned and fled. **2** (努力) go all out (PT went, PP gone) ▷他为了给父亲治病拼命挣钱。He went all out to earn the money to cure his father.
拼盘 pīnpán [名] cold platter
拼死 pīnsǐ [动] risk one's life
拼写 pīnxiě [动] spell
拼音 pīnyīn [名] Pinyin

姘 pīn [动] (贬) have an affair ▶姘妇 lover ▶姘夫 lover
姘头 pīntou [名] (贬) lover

贫 pín I [形] **1** (穷) poor ▶贫民 the poor **2** (少) deficient ▶贫血 anaemia (英), anemia (美) II [动] (方) be a chatterbox
贫乏 pínfá [形] lacking ▷自然资源贫乏 lacking in natural resources
贫寒 pínhán [形] (书) impoverished
贫瘠 pínjí [形] poor
贫苦 pínkǔ [形] poverty-stricken
贫困 pínkùn [形] impoverished
贫民 pínmín [名] the poor (PL)
贫民窟 pínmínkū [名] slums (PL)
贫穷 pínqióng [形] poor ▷贫穷是造成犯罪的原因之一。Poverty is one of the causes of crime.
贫嘴 pínzuǐ [形] (方) garrulous

频 pín [副] frequently ▷他频频旷课。He frequently plays truant.
频道 píndào [名] channel
频繁 pínfán [形] frequent
频率 pínlǜ [名] **1** (物) frequency **2** (指心脏) rate
频频 pínpín [副] frequently

品 pǐn I [名] **1** (物品) article ▶商品 merchandise **2** (等级) grade ▶精品 special product **3** (种类) type ▶品种 variety **4** (品质) character ▶品德 moral character II [动] taste
品尝 pǐncháng [动] savour (英), savor (美)
品德 pǐndé [名] moral character
品格 pǐngé [名] character
品级 pǐnjí [名] grade
品貌 pǐnmào [名] appearance
品牌 pǐnpái [名] brand
品评 pǐnpíng [动] (书) judge
品头论足 pǐn tóu lùn zú make personal remarks
品位 pǐnwèi [名] **1** (质量) quality **2** (喜好) taste
品味 pǐnwèi [动] **1** (尝) taste **2** (体会) appreciate ▷品味古典音乐 appreciate classical music

品行 pǐnxíng [名] character and conduct

品性 pǐnxìng [名] nature

品质 pǐnzhì [名] 1 (品德) character 2 (质量) quality ▷这些种子品质优良。These are top-quality seeds.

品种 pǐnzhǒng [名] 1 (动) breed 2 (植) species 3 (指产品) kind ▷超市里货物品种齐全。There are all kinds of products in the supermarket.

聘 pìn [动] engage

聘礼 pìnlǐ [名] betrothal gift

聘请 pìnqǐng [动] invite

聘任 pìnrèn [动] engage

聘用 pìnyòng [动] engage

乒 pīng I [拟] bang ▷乒的一声气球爆了。The balloon exploded with a bang. II [名] (乒乓球) table tennis ▷世乒赛 Table Tennis World Championships

乒乓 pīngpāng I [拟] bang ▷隔壁一天到晚的乒乓声不断。There was an incessant banging noise next door. II [名] ping-pong

平 píng I [形] 1 (平坦) flat ▶平原 plain 2 (安定) calm ▷心平气和 even-tempered 3 (普通) ordinary 4 (平均) even ▶平分 fifty-fifty 5 (指比分) ▶平局 a draw II [动] 1 (夷平) level 2 (指成绩) equal 3 (镇压) suppress

平安 píng'ān [形] safe and sound

平常 píngcháng I [形] common II [副] usually

平淡 píngdàn [形] 1 (语气、文章) flat 2 (谈话、生活) dull

平等 píngděng [形] equal

平定 píngdìng [动] 1 (叛乱、暴乱) put ... down (PT, PP put) 2 (情绪) calm ... down

平凡 píngfán [形] uneventful

平反 píngfǎn [动] overturn a sentence ▷他被平反了。His sentence was overturned.

平方 píngfāng [名] 1 (数) square 2 (平方米) square metre (英) or meter (美)

平房 píngfáng [名] single-storey house

平分 píngfēn [动] divide equally ▷咱们一起干，赚了钱平分。Let's do the work together, and go halves on the money we earn.

平和 pínghé [形] 1 (指人) placid 2 (指药物) mild

平衡 pínghéng [名] balance ▷保持平衡 maintain a balance ▷平衡收支 balance revenue and expenditure

平缓 pínghuǎn [形] gentle

平静 píngjìng [形] calm

平均 píngjūn [形] average

平米 píngmǐ [名] square metre (英) 或 meter (美)

平民 píngmín [名] the common people (PL)

平平 píngpíng [形] mediocre

平铺直叙 píng pū zhí xù pedestrian ▷这篇文章虽然平铺直叙，但十分感人。Although this essay is a little pedestrian, it's deeply moving all the same.

平起平坐 píng qǐ píng zuò be on an equal footing ▷他和总经理平起平坐。He's on an equal footing with the general manager.

平日 píngrì [名] the usual

平生 píngshēng [名] one's whole life ▷这是他平生最大的遗憾。This is the greatest regret of his whole life.

平时 píngshí [副] usually

平手 píngshǒu [名] draw ▷我看这场拳击会成平手。I think the fight will end in a draw.

平台 píngtái [名] platform

平坦 píngtǎn [形] flat

平稳 píngwěn [形] 1 (稳定) stable 2 (不摇晃) steady

平息 píngxī [动] quieten (英) 或 quiet (美) down

平心而论 píng xīn ér lùn in all fairness

平心静气 píng xīn jìng qì calmly

平行 píngxíng [形] parallel

平易 píngyì [形] amiable

平庸 píngyōng [形] mediocre

平原 píngyuán [名] plain

平整 píngzhěng I [动] level II [形] neat

评 píng [动] 1 (评论) criticize ▶批评 criticize ▶书评 book review ▷他的新书获得好评。His new book was well received. 2 (评判) judge ▶评分 mark 3 (选) select

评比 píngbǐ [动] appraise

评定 píngdìng [动] assess

评估 pínggū [动] evaluate

评价 píngjià [动] evaluate ▷后人对他的一生给予了高度的评价。He was very much revered by later generations.

评介 píngjiè [动] review

评论 pínglùn [动] review

评判 píngpàn [动] judge

评书 píngshū [名] storytelling

评述 píngshù [动] comment on

评说 píngshuō [动] evaluate

评头论足 píng tóu lùn zú make personal remarks

评选 píngxuǎn [动] select ▷印度小姐被大众评选为新一届世界小姐。The public selected Miss India as the new Miss World.

评议 píngyì [动] consult
评语 píngyǔ [名] comment

坪 píng [名] level ground ▷草坪 lawn

苹 píng 见下文
苹果 píngguǒ [名] apple

凭 píng I [动] rely on ▷他总是凭经验解决
难题。He relies on experience to solve his
problems. ▷他是凭能力当上市长的。He
became mayor thanks to his own ability.
II [介] ▷减价商品能凭礼券购买。Cut-price
products can be paid for with gift vouchers.
▷你凭什么说我们的产品不合格? On what
basis are you saying that our products are
not up to standard? III [名] evidence ▷凭据
credentials (PL) ▷真凭实据 hard evidence
IV [连] no matter ▷凭他怎么叫，也没人答
理他。No matter what he asked for, no one
took any notice of him.
凭借 píngjiè [动] be based on ▷公司凭借
高质量的产品占领市场。The company's
domination of the market is based on the high
quality of its products.
凭据 píngjù [名] credentials (PL)
凭空 píngkōng [副] out of thin air ▷小报凭空
捏造最荒谬的新闻。The tabloids make up the
most ridiculous stories out of thin air.
凭仗 píngzhàng [动] rely on
凭证 píngzhèng [名] evidence

屏 píng [名] (屏风) screen
→另见 bǐng
屏蔽 píngbì [名] screen
屏风 píngfēng [名] screen
屏幕 píngmù [名] screen
屏障 píngzhàng [名] barrier

瓶 píng [名] bottle

萍 píng 见下文
萍水相逢 píng shuǐ xiāng féng have a
chance encounter ▷我和他在巴黎萍水相
逢。I had a chance encounter with him in Paris.

坡 pō [名] slope ▷山坡 slope
坡度 pōdù [名] gradient

泼 pō I [动] splash II [形] shrewish ▷泼妇
harridan
泼辣 pōla [形] bold
泼冷水 pō lěngshuǐ [动] ▷他有信心的时候，
不要给他泼冷水。Don't dampen his spirits

when he's feeling confident.

颇 pō [副] rather

婆 pó [名] 1 (老年妇女) old lady ▷老太婆 old
lady 2 (丈夫的母亲) mother-in-law (PL mothers-
in-law) ▷公婆 parents-in-law (PL)
婆家 pójia [名] husband's family
婆婆妈妈 pópomāmā fussy

迫 pò I [动] 1 (逼迫) force 2 (接近) approach
II [形] urgent ▷迫不及待 cannot wait
迫不得已 pò bù dé yǐ have no alternative
▷市长迫不得已向市民道歉。The mayor
had no alternative but to apologize to the
townspeople.
迫不及待 pò bù jí dài be unable to wait ▷她
迫不及待地把房子卖掉。She couldn't wait to
sell the house.
迫害 pòhài [动] persecute
迫降 pòjiàng [动] crash-land
迫近 pòjìn [动] approach
迫切 pòqiè [形] pressing
迫使 pòshǐ [动] necessitate
迫在眉睫 pò zài méi jié be imminent ▷解决
交通堵塞迫在眉睫。A solution to the traffic
jam problem is imminent.

破 pò I [形] 1 (受损) broken ▷裤子都被穿
破了。The trousers were completely worn
out. 2 (烂) lousy ▷没人愿做那破工作。No
one is willing to do that lousy job. II [动]
1 (受损) cut ▷他的膝盖破了。He's cut his
knee. 2 (破除) break (PT broke, PP broken)
▷破例 make an exception ▷我不想把10镑
钱破开。I don't want to have to break a ten
pound note. ▷破世界记录 break a world
record 3 (钱、工夫) spend (PT, PP spent) 4 (揭
穿) expose ▷破案 solve a case 5 (打败) defeat
破败 pòbài [形] 1 (家族、经济) declining 2 (房
子、城市建筑) run-down
破产 pòchǎn [动] go bankrupt (PT went, PP
gone)
破除 pòchú [动] do away with
破费 pòfèi [动] spend money (PT, PP spent)
破釜沉舟 pò fǔ chén zhōu burn one's bridges
破格 pògé [动] break a rule (PT broke, PP broken)
破罐破摔 pò guàn pò shuāi not learn from
one's mistakes ▷他失业后破罐破摔。After
he lost his job, he learned nothing from his
mistakes.
破坏 pòhuài [动] 1 (建筑、环境、文物、公物)
destroy 2 (团结、社会秩序) undermine 3 (协

定、法规、规章) violate **4** (计划) bring ... down (PT, PP brought) **5** (名誉) damage

破解 pòjiě [动] decipher

破镜重圆 pò jìng chóng yuán get back together

破旧 pòjiù [形] shabby

破烂 pòlàn **I** [形] ragged **II** [名] scrap

破例 pòlì [动] make an exception

破裂 pòliè [动] **1** (谈判) break down (PT broke, PP broken) **2** (感情) break up **3** (外交关系) break off

破落 pòluò [形] declining

破灭 pòmiè [动] destroy

破碎 pòsuì **I** [动] **1** (破成碎块) smash **2** (指梦想) break (PT broke, PP broken) **II** [形] broken

破天荒 pòtiānhuāng be unprecedented ▷他破天荒地给妻子买了一束玫瑰。 In an unprecedented move, he bought his wife a bouquet of roses.

破译 pòyì [动] crack

破折号 pòzhéhào [名] dash

魄 pò [名] **1** (精神) spirit ▶魂魄 soul **2** (魄力) courage ▶气魄 verve

魄力 pòlì [名] courage

剖 pōu [动] **1** (破开) cut open (PT, PP cut) ▶解剖 dissect **2** (分析) analyse (英), analyze (美)

剖白 pōubái [动] explain oneself

剖面 pōumiàn [名] section

剖析 pōuxī [动] analyse (英), analyze (美)

扑 pū [动] **1** (冲向) rush at ▷狮子猛地向猎物扑过去。 The lion rushed after its prey. **2** (专注于) devote ▷他一心扑在工作上。 He's totally devoted to his work. **3** (扑打) swat ▷他用树枝扑蜻蜓。 He used a branch to swat at dragonflies. **4** (翅膀) beat (PT beat, PP beaten)

扑鼻 pūbí [动] be pungent ▷香水味扑鼻。 The smell of the perfume was pungent.

扑哧 pūchī [拟] **1** (指笑声) chuckle **2** (指撒气) hiss

扑打 pūdǎ [动] beat (PT beat, PP beaten)

扑救 pūjiù [动] put ... out (PT, PP put)

扑克 pūkè [名] poker

扑空 pūkōng [动] come away empty-handed (PT came, PP come)

扑灭 pūmiè [动] put ... out (PT, PP put)

扑朔迷离 pūshuò mílí complicated and confusing

扑簌 pūsù [形] streaming ▷听到那个消息，他的眼泪就扑簌簌地落了下来。 When he heard the news, tears streamed from his eyes.

扑腾 pūtēng [拟] thud

扑腾 pūteng [动] **1** (打水) splash **2** (跳动) flop

扑通 pūtōng [拟] plop

铺 pū [动] **1** (摊开) spread (PT, PP spread) **2** (铺设) lay (PT, PP laid)
→另见 pù

铺垫 pūdiàn [动] **1** (垫子) cushion **2** (指叙事) foreshadow

铺盖 pūgài [动] cover

铺盖 pūgai [名] bedroll

铺设 pūshè [动] lay (PT, PP laid)

铺天盖地 pū tiān gài dì all over the place

铺张 pūzhāng [形] extravagant

仆 pú [动] (旧) servant

仆人 púrén [名] servant

匍 pú 见下文

匍匐 púfú [动] grovel

菩 pú 见下文

菩萨 púsà [名] **1** (宗) bodhisattva **2** (善人) saint ▷老婆婆像菩萨一样善良。 The old lady is as kind as a saint.

葡 pú 见下文

葡萄 pútao [名] grape

朴 pǔ 见下文

朴实 pǔshí [形] **1** (简朴) simple **2** (诚实) honest

朴素 pǔsù [形] **1** (衣着) plain **2** (生活) simple **3** (语言) plain

圃 pǔ [名] garden

普 pǔ [形] general

普遍 pǔbiàn **I** [形] common **II** [副] commonly

普及 pǔjí [动] **1** (传布) spread (PT, PP spread) **2** (推广) popularize

普通 pǔtōng [形] common

谱 pǔ **I** [名] **1** (指烹饪) book **2** (指音乐) score **3** (指棋) manual **4** (指家族) family records (PL) **5** (口) (把握) confidence ▷这项工程需要多少钱他心里有谱儿。 He is fairly confident about how much money this project will require. **II** [动] set to music (PT, PP set)

谱写 pǔxiě [动] compose

谱子 pǔzi [名] score

铺 pù [名] **1** (商店) shop ▶杂货铺 general store **2** (床) plank bed ▶卧铺 berth

→另见 pū

铺面 pùmiàn [名] shop front

铺位 pùwèi [名] bunk

铺子 pùzi [名] (口) shop

瀑 pù [名] waterfall

瀑布 pùbù [名] waterfall

曝 pù [动] (书) expose ... to the sun

曝露 pùlù [动] (书) expose

曝晒 pùshài [动] expose ... to strong sunlight

七 qī [数] seven ▷七年 seven years
七零八落 qī líng bā luò scattered around ▷屋子里七零八落地放着一些书。Books were scattered around the room.
七上八下 qī shàng bā xià be agitated
七十二行 qīshí'èr háng [名] all sorts of occupations (PL)
七手八脚 qī shǒu bā jiǎo with great commotion

沏 qī [动] brew ▷她沏了壶茶。She made a pot of tea.

妻 qī [名] wife (PL wives) ▷未婚妻 fiancée
妻小 qīxiǎo [名] wife and children
妻子 qīzi [名] wife (PL wives)

柒 qī [数] an elaborate form of "seven", used in writing cheques etc to prevent mistakes and forgery

栖 qī [动] perch ▷两栖动物 amphibian
栖身 qīshēn [动] (书) inhabit
栖息 qīxī [动] roost

凄 qī [形] (书) 1 (寒冷) cold 2 (萧条) miserable ▷凄凉 desolate 3 (悲伤) sad
凄惨 qīcǎn [形] tragic

凄厉 qīlì [形] (书) 1 (风声) howling 2 (叫声) shrill
凄凉 qīliáng [形] dreary

萋 qī 见下文
萋萋 qīqī [形] (书) luxuriant

戚 qī [名] (亲人) relative ▷亲戚 relative

期 qī I [名] 1 (预定时间) time limit ▷到期 expire 2 (一段时间) period of time ▷假期 holiday II [量] 1 (指训练班) class 2 (指杂志、报纸) edition III [动] expect
期待 qīdài [动] await
期货 qīhuò [名] futures (PL)
期刊 qīkān [名] periodical
期盼 qīpàn [动] await
期望 qīwàng I [名] expectations (PL) II [动] expect
期限 qīxiàn [名] time limit

欺 qī [动] 1 (欺骗) deceive 2 (欺负) bully
欺负 qīfu [动] bully
欺行霸市 qī háng bà shì monopolize
欺凌 qīlíng [动] humiliate
欺骗 qīpiàn [动] deceive
欺生 qīshēng [动] take advantage of a fresh face (PT took, PP taken)
欺侮 qīwǔ [动] (书) bully
欺压 qīyā [动] tyrannize
欺诈 qīzhà [动] swindle ▷欺诈他人钱财 swindle people out of their money

漆 qī I [名] lacquer ▷油漆 paint II [动] paint
漆黑 qīhēi [形] pitch-black ▷房间里一片漆黑。The room was in complete darkness.

蹊 qī 见下文
蹊跷 qīqiāo [形] odd

齐 qí I [形] 1 (整齐) neat 2 (一致) joint 3 (完备) ready ▷人都到齐了。Everyone is present. II [动] 1 (达到) reach ▷水深齐腰。The water is waist deep. 2 (取齐) level III [副] at the same time
齐备 qíbèi [形] ready
齐全 qíquán [形] complete
齐心 qíxīn [动] be of one mind ▷大家齐心了，事情就好办了。With everyone working together, everything will be well managed.
齐心协力 qí xīn xié lì join forces
齐整 qízhěng [形] neat

其 qí [代] (书) 1 (他的) his ▷他是演员，其父也

是演员。He's an actor, and his father is also an actor. **2** (她的) her **3** (它的) its **4** (他们的、她们的、它们的) their **5** (他) him **6** (她) her **7** (它) it ▷我们应尽量促其成功。We must make sure that it is successful. **8** (他们、她们、它们) them **9** (那个) that

其次 **qícì** [代] **1** (下一个) ▷其次要做的事是什么？What are we going to do next? **2** (次要的) the second

其貌不扬 **qí mào bù yáng** plain

其实 **qíshí** [副] actually ▷其实不然。Actually, it wasn't like that. ▷他看起来很壮，其实身体不好。He looks very strong, but he's actually in poor health.

其它 **qítā** [代] other

其他 **qítā** [代] other ▷除了看书，他还有很多其他爱好。Apart from reading, he has a lot of other hobbies. ▷我不知道，你问其他人吧。I don't know, ask someone else. ▷还有其他事情没有？Is there anything else?

其余 **qíyú** [代] the rest

其中 **qízhōng** [名] ▷他有六套西服，其中两套是黑色的。He has six suits, of which two are black. ▷学校有50位老师，其中10位是男老师。The school has 50 teachers, and ten of them are male.

奇 **qí** I [形] **1** (非常少见的) strange ▶奇闻 fantastic story ▶奇事 miracle **2** (出人意料的) unexpected ▶奇袭 surprise attack ▶奇遇 lucky encounter II [动] surprise ▶惊奇 surprise ▷不足为奇 be not at all surprising III [副] unusually ▷天气奇冷。The weather is unusually cold.
→另见 jī

奇才 **qícái** [名] genius ▷足球奇才 footballing genius

奇耻大辱 **qí chǐ dà rǔ** a crying shame

奇怪 **qíguài** [形] strange

奇观 **qíguān** [名] wonder ▷世界七大奇观 the seven wonders of the world

奇迹 **qíjì** [名] miracle

奇妙 **qímiào** [形] wonderful

奇缺 **qíquē** [动] be very short of

奇特 **qítè** [形] peculiar

奇闻 **qíwén** [名] incredible story ▷简直是天下奇闻！That really is the most incredible story!

奇形怪状 **qí xíng guài zhuàng** grotesque

奇异 **qíyì** [形] **1** (奇怪) strange **2** (惊异) astonished ▷他用奇异的目光看着我。He looked at me in astonishment.

奇遇 **qíyù** [名] chance encounter

祈 **qí** [动] (书) **1** (祈祷) pray **2** (希望) wish ▶祈求 invoke

歧 **qí** [形] **1** (途、路) forked **2** (不一致) different

歧路 **qílù** [名] (书) (喻) wrong turning ▷他走上了条人生歧路。He took a wrong turning in life.

歧视 **qíshì** [动] discriminate ▷种族歧视 racial discrimination ▷不要歧视残疾人。Don't discriminate against handicapped people.

歧途 **qítú** [名] wrong path ▷误入歧途 go astray

歧义 **qíyì** [名] ambiguity

脐 **qí** [名] navel

脐带 **qídài** [名] (生理) umbilical cord

崎 **qí** 见下文

崎岖 **qíqū** [形] rugged

骑 **qí** I [动] ride (PT rode, PP ridden) II [名] cavalry

棋 **qí** [名] chess ▶围棋 go (board game)

棋子 **qízǐ** [名] piece

旗 **qí** [名] flag ▶锦旗 silk banner

旗鼓相当 **qí gǔ xiāngdāng** be well-matched

旗开得胜 **qí kāi dé shèng** win in the first contest

旗袍 **qípáo** [名] cheongsam

旗帜 **qízhì** [名] **1** (旗子) banner **2** (立场) stand **3** (榜样) model

鳍 **qí** [名] fin

乞 **qǐ** [动] beg ▶行乞 go begging

乞丐 **qǐgài** [名] beggar

乞求 **qǐqiú** [动] beg ▷乞求宽恕 beg for forgiveness

乞讨 **qǐtǎo** [动] beg

岂 **qǐ** [副] (书) how ▷工作很多，岂敢懈怠！With so much on, how can you dare be so lazy!

岂敢 **qǐgǎn** [动] dare ▷我岂敢不承担责任？Do I dare shirk the responsibility?

岂有此理 **qǐ yǒu cǐ lǐ** outrageous

企 **qǐ** [动] look forward to

企鹅 **qǐ'é** [名] penguin

企及 **qǐjí** [动] hope ▷这个目标无法企及。There's no hope for this cause.

企盼 **qǐpàn** [动] (书) wait in hope

企求 **qǐqiú** [动] (书) seek (PT, PP sought)

企图 qǐtú I [动] plan II [名] (贬) plan

企业 qǐyè [名] enterprise ▷国有企业 state-owned enterprise

启

启 qǐ [动] 1 (打开) open ▶开启 open 2 (开导) enlighten ▶启发 enlighten 3 (开始) start

启程 qǐchéng [动] set out (PT, PP set)

启迪 qǐdí [动] enlighten ▷他的话给了我们很多启迪。We found his words very enlightening.

启动 qǐdòng [动] start

启发 qǐfā I [动] inspire ▷我从这个故事里得到很大启发。I drew a lot of inspiration from this story. II [名] inspiration

启蒙 qǐméng [动] 1 (促使思想进步) enlighten 2 (传授基本知识) impart rudimentary knowledge ▷启蒙读物 early learning materials

启示 qǐshì [动] enlighten ▷她从这则寓言中得到了启示。She was very inspired by the parable.

启事 qǐshì [名] announcement ▷寻人启事 missing persons announcement

启用 qǐyòng [动] start using

启运 qǐyùn [动] begin shipping (PT began, PP begun)

起

起 qǐ I [动] 1 (起来) rise (PT rose, PP risen) ▶起立 stand up 2 (取出) remove ▷起瓶盖 remove a bottle top 3 (长出) form ▷脚上起泡 form a blister on one's foot 4 (产生) become (PT became, PP become) ▷起疑心 become suspicious 5 (拟订) sketch out ▶起草 draft 6 (建立) establish ▷白手起家 make a fortune from nothing II [量] 1 一起交通事故 a traffic accident ▷一起火灾 a fire

起步 qǐbù [动] get going ▷我们的事业才刚刚起步。Our careers have only just got going.

起草 qǐcǎo [动] draft

起程 qǐchéng [动] set out (PT, PP set) ▷我们起程前往巴黎。We set out in the direction of Paris.

起初 qǐchū [名] origin ▷他起初在班里排名第一。Originally he was top of the class.

起点 qǐdiǎn [名] starting point

起动 qǐdòng [动] start

起飞 qǐfēi [动] take off (PT took, PP taken) ▷飞机准时起飞。The plane took off on time. ▷中国经济起飞了。China's economy has taken off.

起伏 qǐfú [动] undulate

起哄 qǐhòng [动] 1 (捣乱) create a disturbance 2 (开玩笑) mock

起家 qǐjiā [动] build ... up (PT, PP built) ▷他靠卖服装起家。He built himself up by selling clothes.

起见 qǐjiàn [动] be for ▷为方便起见 for the sake of convenience ▷为安全起见 for safety's sake

起劲 qǐjìn [形] enthusiastic

起居 qǐjū [名] everyday life

起来 qǐlái [动] 1 (站起或坐起) get up ▷赶快起来，来客人了。Get up quick, there's a visitor. 2 (起床) get up ▷起来吧，天都亮了。Time to get up – it's already light.

起立 qǐlì [动] stand up (PT, PP stood)

起落 qǐluò [动] rise and fall (PT rose and fell, PP risen and fallen)

起码 qǐmǎ [形] minimum ▷起码的常识 the minimum of common sense ▷一本词典起码要50块。A dictionary should cost at least fifty yuan.

起色 qǐsè [名] improvement

起身 qǐshēn [动] set out (PT, PP set) ▷我明天天亮就起身。I am setting out at first light tomorrow.

起誓 qǐshì [动] swear (PT, PP sworn)

起死回生 qǐ sǐ huí shēng bring ... back from the dead

起诉 qǐsù [动] sue ▷向法院起诉 take a case to court

起头 qǐtóu I [动] start II [名] the beginning ▷我们起头遇到些困难，后来就好多了。We encountered some difficulties at the beginning, but later things got a lot better.

起先 qǐxiān [名] the beginning

起义 qǐyì [动] revolt ▷农民起义 peasant revolt

起因 qǐyīn [名] cause

起用 qǐyòng [动] employ

起源 qǐyuán I [动] originate ▷这种舞起源于亚洲。This type of dancing originated in Asia. II [名] origin ▷生命的起源 the origins of life

起早贪黑 qǐ zǎo tān hēi work from dawn until dusk

起子 qǐzi [名] 1 (开瓶盖) bottle opener 2 (螺丝刀) screwdriver

气

气 qì I [名] 1 (气体) gas ▶毒气 poison gas 2 (空气) air ▷这球没气了。This ball is deflated. 3 (气息) breath ▷上气不接下气 out of breath 4 (精神) mood ▷垂头丧气 be dejected 5 (气味) smell ▶臭气 stink 6 (习气) manner ▶孩子气 childishness ▶书生气 scholarly manner 7 (怒气) anger ▷忍下这口气 put up with someone's attitude 8 (医) qi II [动] 1 (生气) be angry 2 (使生气) provoke

▷别气我！Don't provoke me!

气冲冲 qìchōngchōng [形] furious

气度 qìdù [名] bearing

气氛 qìfēn [名] atmosphere

气愤 qìfèn [形] angry ▷我们对这种恶劣行为十分气愤。We got extremely angry about this terrible behaviour.

气概 qìgài [名] spirit

气功 qìgōng [名] qigong

气候 qìhòu [名] climate

气急败坏 qìjí bàihuài exasperated

气力 qìlì [名] strength

气量 qìliàng [名] tolerance

气流 qìliú [名] air flow

气恼 qìnǎo [形] sulky

气派 qìpài [名] impressive manner

气魄 qìpò [名] imposing manner

气球 qìqiú [名] balloon

气色 qìsè [名] complexion

气势 qìshì [名] imposing manner

气体 qìtǐ [名] gas

气味 qìwèi [名] smell

气息 qìxī [名] 1 (呼吸) breath 2 (气味) smell ▷春天的气息 the smell of spring 3 (指时代、生活) sign ▷时代气息 a sign of the times

气象 qìxiàng [名] 1 (大气现象) weather 2 (气象学) meteorology 3 (情景) atmosphere

气压 qìyā [名] air pressure

气质 qìzhì [名] disposition

弃 qì [动] abandon

弃权 qìquán [动] abstain ▶弃权票 abstention

汽 qì [名] 1 (气体) vapour (英), vapor (美) 2 (蒸气) steam

汽车 qìchē [名] car ▶公共汽车 bus

汽化 qìhuà [动] (物) vaporize

汽水 qìshuǐ [名] fizzy drink

汽油 qìyóu [名] petrol (英), gasoline (美)

泣 qì [动] (书) weep (PT, PP wept)

泣不成声 qì bù chéng shēng choke with tears ▷她哭得泣不成声。She was crying so much that she couldn't get the words out.

契 qì I [动] agree ▶默契 tacit agreement II [名] deed

契合 qìhé [动] agree with

契约 qìyuē [名] contract

砌 qì [动] build (PT, PP built) ▷他在房子后面砌了堵墙。He has built a wall at the back of the house.

器 qì [名] 1 (器具) utensil ▶乐器 musical instrument ▶瓷器 china 2 (器官) organ

器材 qìcái [名] equipment

器官 qìguān [名] organ

器具 qìjù [名] utensil

器量 qìliàng [名] tolerance

器皿 qìmǐn [名] container

器械 qìxiè [名] instrument ▷手术器械 surgical instruments

器重 qìzhòng [动] think highly of (PT, PP thought) ▷上司很器重他。The boss thinks highly of him.

憩 qì [动] (书) rest

掐 qiā [动] 1 (截断) pinch 2 (按住) throttle

掐算 qiāsuàn [动] count ... on one's fingers

卡 qiǎ I [动] 1 (不能动) get stuck 2 (脖子) wedge 3 (阻挡) block II [名] 1 (指夹东西) fastener ▶发卡 hairpin 2 (关卡) checkpoint ▶边卡 border checkpoint →另见 kǎ

卡壳 qiǎké [动] get stuck

洽 qià I [形] harmonious II [动] consult ▶洽谈 hold talks

洽谈 qiàtán [动] hold talks (PT, PP held)

恰 qià [副] 1 (适当) appropriately 2 (刚好) exactly

恰当 qiàdàng [形] appropriate

恰好 qiàhǎo [副] luckily ▷他恰好也在。Luckily he's here as well.

恰恰 qiàqià [副] exactly ▷这恰恰是我们不想看到的。This is exactly what we didn't want to see.

恰巧 qiàqiǎo [副] luckily ▷恰巧我带着这本书。Luckily I had the book with me.

恰如其分 qià rú qí fèn appropriate

千 qiān I [数] thousand II [形] many

千差万别 qiān chā wàn bié different in every possible way

千方百计 qiān fāng bǎi jì do everything in one's power ▷医护人员千方百计抢救病人。The hospital staff did everything in their power to save the patient.

千古 qiāngǔ [名] ▷千古名言 ancient wisdom ▷千古遗恨 eternal regret

千金 qiānjīn [名] (敬) daughter

千钧一发 qiān jūn yī fà at the crucial moment

千里迢迢 qiān lǐ tiáotiáo from far away

千篇一律 qiān piān yīlù follow the same pattern

千万 qiānwàn I [数] ten million II [副] ▷你千万要记住老师的话。Be sure to remember what the teacher said. ▷你千万别做傻事。You absolutely mustn't do anything stupid.

仟 qiān [数] *an elaborate form of "thousand", used in writing cheques etc to prevent mistakes and forgery*

迁 qiān [动] 1 (迁移) move 2 (转变) change

迁就 qiānjiù [动] make allowances ▷我们不能迁就这么多错误。We cannot make allowances for so many mistakes.

迁怒 qiānnù [动] ▷不要迁怒于他人。Don't take your anger out on others.

迁徙 qiānxǐ [动] migrate

迁移 qiānyí [动] move

牵 qiān [动] 1 (拉住) pull 2 (牵涉) involve

牵扯 qiānchě [动] involve ▷这起案件牵扯到许多人。This case has involved a lot of people.

牵动 qiāndòng [动] influence

牵挂 qiānguà [动] worry ▷她牵挂孩子。She worried about her children.

牵就 qiānjiù [动] yield to

牵累 qiānlěi [动] 1 (牵制) tie … down 2 (连累) implicate

牵连 qiānlián [动] 1 (连累) implicate 2 (联系) connect ▷不要把两件事故意牵连到一起。You shouldn't deliberately connect the two issues.

牵强 qiānqiǎng [形] far-fetched

牵涉 qiānshè [动] involve

牵引 qiānyǐn [动] draw (PT drew, PP drawn) ▷火车由内燃机牵引。Trains are drawn by internal combustion engines.

铅 qiān [名] (化) lead

铅笔 qiānbǐ [名] pencil

谦 qiān [形] modest

谦卑 qiānbēi [形] modest

谦恭 qiāngōng [形] courteous

谦和 qiānhé [形] modest and gentle

谦让 qiānràng [动] modestly decline

谦虚 qiānxū I [形] modest ▷谦虚是一种美德。Modesty is a virtue. II [动] speak modestly (PT spoke, PP spoken) ▷他谦虚了一下，最后接受了礼物。He was shy about it at first, but in the end he accepted the present.

谦逊 qiānxùn [形] unassuming

签 qiān I [动] 1 (名字) sign 2 (意见) endorse II [名] 1 (指占卜、赌博、比赛) lot ▷抽签决定 draw lots 2 (标志) label ▶书签 bookmark 3 (细棍子) stick ▶牙签 toothpick

签到 qiāndào [动] sign in

签名 qiānmíng [动] sign

签署 qiānshǔ [动] sign

签约 qiānyuē [动] sign

签证 qiānzhèng [名] visa

签字 qiānzì [动] sign one's name

前 qián I [形] 1 (正面的) front ▶前门 front door 2 (指次序) first ▶前几名 the front-runners 3 (从前的) former ▶前市长 the former mayor ▶前夫 ex-husband 4 (未来的) future II [动] advance ▷勇往直前 take the bull by the horns

前辈 qiánbèi [名] older generation

前程 qiánchéng [名] future

前方 qiánfāng [名] 1 (前面) front 2 (前线) the front

前锋 qiánfēng [名] (体育) forward

前功尽弃 qián gōng jìn qì a waste of effort

前后 qiánhòu [名] 1 (时间接近) ▷春节前后 around the time of the Spring Festival ▷暑假前后 summer holiday time 2 (自始至终) ▷创作这部小说，前后用了3年时间。Creating the story took three years from start to finish. 3 (总共) ▷他前后去过3次欧洲。He's been to Europe three times altogether. 4 (前面和后面) the front and the back

前进 qiánjìn [动] 1 (向前走) advance 2 (发展) make progress

前景 qiánjǐng [名] prospects (PL)

前科 qiánkē [名] criminal record

前列 qiánliè [名] 1 (指排、列) front row 2 (指带头) forefront

前驱 qiánqū [名] pioneer

前人 qiánrén [名] predecessor

前身 qiánshēn [名] previous existence ▷这所大学的前身是一所女子师范学校。In a previous existence, this university was a ladies' teaching college.

前提 qiántí [名] precondition

前途 qiántú [名] future

前往 qiánwǎng [动] be bound for

前卫 qiánwèi I [名] forward II [形] fashionable

前夕 qiánxī [名] eve ▷圣诞节前夕 Christmas Eve

前线 qiánxiàn [名] front line
前言 qiányán [名] foreword
前沿 qiányán [名] front line
前兆 qiánzhào [名] omen
前缀 qiánzhuì [名] (语言) prefix
前奏 qiánzòu [名] (音) prelude

虔 qián 见下文
虔诚 qiánchéng [形] devout

钱 qián [名] money ▷挣钱 make money
钱财 qiáncái [名] money

钳 qián [名] pliers (PL)
钳子 qiánzi [名] pliers (PL)

乾 qián 见下文
乾坤 qiánkūn [名] (书) the universe

潜 qián I [动] 1 (入水) dive 2 (隐藏) hide (PT hid,
PP hidden) ▷潜伏 lurk II [形] latent ▷潜能
potential III [副] secretly ▷潜逃 abscond
潜藏 qiáncáng [动] hide (PT hid, PP hidden)
潜伏 qiánfú [形] hidden
潜力 qiánlì [名] potential
潜台词 qiántáicí [名] (喻) implication
潜移默化 qián yí mò huà exert a subtle
influence over
潜意识 qiányìshí [名] the subconscious
潜在 qiánzài [形] latent

浅 qiǎn [形] 1 (指深度) shallow 2 (指难度)
easy 3 (指学识) lacking 4 (指颜色) light ▷浅
蓝色 light blue ▷浅绿色 pale green 5 (指时
间) short
浅薄 qiǎnbó [形] superficial
浅近 qiǎnjìn [形] (书) simple
浅显 qiǎnxiǎn [形] obvious

遣 qiǎn [动] send (PT, PP sent) ▷派遣 dispatch
遣返 qiǎnfǎn [动] repatriate
遣送 qiǎnsòng [动] deport

谴 qiǎn [动] censure
谴责 qiǎnzé [动] condemn

欠 qiàn [动] 1 (钱、情) owe 2 (缺乏) lack 3 (移动)
raise ... slightly
欠缺 qiànquē [动] lack
欠身 qiànshēn [动] lift oneself up

纤 qiàn [名] towrope
→另见 xiān

纤夫 qiànfū [名] tracker

堑 qiàn [名] 1 (沟) moat ▷堑壕 trench 2 (挫折)
setback

嵌 qiàn [动] inlay

歉 qiàn I [形] poor ▷歉收 poor harvest II [名]
apology ▷抱歉 apologize
歉疚 qiànjiù [动] regret
歉收 qiànshōu [动] have a poor harvest
歉意 qiànyì [名] apology

呛 qiāng [动] choke
→另见 qiàng

枪 qiāng [名] 1 (旧兵器) spear 2 (兵器) gun ▷手
枪 pistol
枪毙 qiāngbì [动] 1 (打死) execute (by firing
squad) 2 (否定) turn down
枪手 qiāngshǒu [名] gunman (PL gunmen)
枪手 qiāngshou [名] someone who sits in for
someone else in an exam
枪械 qiāngxiè [名] weapons (PL)
枪支 qiāngzhī [名] firearms (PL)

腔 qiāng [名] 1 (指身体) cavity 2 (曲调) tune 3 (指
口音) accent

强 qiáng I [形] 1 (力量大) strong 2 (程度高)
able 3 (好) better ▷现在的生活是一年比一
年强。Life is getting better year by year. 4 (略
多于) extra ▷三分之一强 a third extra II [动]
force
→另见 jiàng, qiǎng
强暴 qiángbào I [形] violent II [动] rape
强大 qiángdà [形] powerful
强盗 qiángdào [名] robber
强调 qiángdiào [动] stress ▷强调重点 stress
the important points
强度 qiángdù [名] intensity
强固 qiánggù [形] solid
强悍 qiánghàn [形] valiant
强化 qiánghuà [动] strengthen ▷强化地板
reinforced floor
强奸 qiángjiān [动] rape
强健 qiángjiàn [形] strong
强劲 qiángjìng [形] powerful
强烈 qiángliè [形] intense ▷强烈地震 a
powerful earthquake
强权 qiángquán [名] power
强身 qiángshēn [动] work out ▷强身健体 get
fit by working out

强盛 **qiángshèng** [形] powerful and prosperous

强手 **qiángshǒu** [名] talent

强项 **qiángxiàng** [名] forte

强行 **qiángxíng** [动] force

强硬 **qiángyìng** [形] tough ▷采取强硬的态度 take a tough stance

强有力 **qiángyǒulì** [形] forceful

强制 **qiángzhì** [动] force ▷采取强制手段 adopt forceful measures

强壮 **qiángzhuàng** [形] strong

墙 **qiáng** [名] wall

蔷 **qiáng** 见下文

蔷薇 **qiángwēi** [名] rose

抢 **qiǎng** [动] 1 (抢劫) rob 2 (抢夺) grab 3 (抢先) forestall 4 (赶紧) rush

抢夺 **qiǎngduó** [动] loot ▷抢夺市场 seize a market

抢购 **qiǎnggòu** [动] panic-buy (PT, PP panic-bought)

抢劫 **qiǎngjié** [动] rob ▷抢劫银行 rob a bank

抢手 **qiǎngshǒu** [形] in great demand ▷这种商品在市场上很抢手。These products are in great demand on the market.

抢先 **qiǎngxiān** [动] be the first ▷抢先报道新闻 be the first to report the news

抢眼 **qiǎngyǎn** [形] striking

强 **qiǎng** [动] 1 (勉强) make an effort ▷强装笑脸 force a smile 2 (迫使) force
→另见 jiàng, qiáng

强词夺理 **qiǎng cí duó lǐ** argue irrationally

强迫 **qiǎngpò** [动] force

强求 **qiǎngqiú** [动] insist on

襁 **qiǎng** [名] swaddling clothes (PL)

襁褓 **qiǎngbǎo** [名] swaddling clothes (PL)

呛 **qiàng** [动] irritate
→另见 qiāng

悄 **qiāo** 见下文
→另见 qiǎo

悄悄 **qiāoqiāo** [副] 1 (悄然无声) quietly ▷天黑了，到处静悄悄的。As darkness fell everything became very quiet. 2 (不让知道) stealthily

跷 **qiāo** [名] (高跷) stilt

跷跷板 **qiāoqiāobǎn** [名] seesaw

锹 **qiāo** [名] spade

敲 **qiāo** [动] 1 (击) knock ▷他使劲敲门。He knocked hard on the door. ▷这事给我们敲了警钟。This rang alarm bells with us. 2 (敲诈) blackmail ▷他想敲我一笔钱。He wants to blackmail some money out of me.

敲打 **qiāodǎ** [动] beat (PT beat, PP beaten)

敲定 **qiāodìng** [动] determine

敲诈 **qiāozhà** [动] extort ▷敲诈他人钱财 extort money

橇 **qiāo** [名] sledge

乔 **qiáo** [形] tall

乔木 **qiáomù** [名] (植) arbour (英), arbor (美)

乔迁 **qiáoqiān** [动] (书) move ▷乔迁新居 move to a new house

乔装 **qiáozhuāng** [动] disguise

侨 **qiáo** I [动] live abroad II [名] expatriate ▶华侨 overseas Chinese

侨胞 **qiáobāo** [名] *fellow countryman living abroad*

侨居 **qiáojū** [动] emigrate

侨眷 **qiáojuàn** [名] *relatives of nationals living abroad*

侨民 **qiáomín** [名] emigrant

荞 **qiáo** 见下文

荞麦 **qiáomài** [名] (农) buckwheat

桥 **qiáo** [名] bridge

桥梁 **qiáoliáng** [名] bridge

桥牌 **qiáopái** [名] bridge

翘 **qiáo** [动] raise
→另见 qiào

翘盼 **qiáopàn** [动] long for

憔 **qiáo** 见下文

憔悴 **qiáocuì** [形] haggard

瞧 **qiáo** [动] look ▶瞧病 see a doctor

巧 **qiǎo** [形] 1 (手、口) nimble 2 (有技能的) skilful (英), skillful (美) 3 (恰好) coincidental 4 (虚浮的) false ▷花言巧语 falsehood

巧合 **qiǎohé** [名] coincidence

巧克力 **qiǎokèlì** [名] chocolate

巧妙 **qiǎomiào** [形] clever ▷巧妙地拒绝 cleverly deny

悄 qiǎo 见下文
→另见 qiāo
悄然 qiǎorán [副] (书) quietly

壳 qiào [名] shell ▶地壳 the earth's crust
→另见 ké

俏 qiào [形] 1 (漂亮) pretty 2 (畅销) saleable
俏货 qiàohuò [名] saleable goods (PL)
俏丽 qiàolì [形] beautiful
俏皮 qiàopi [形] witty

峭 qiào [形] steep ▶陡峭 steep
峭壁 qiàobì [名] precipice
峭立 qiàolì [形] steep

窍 qiào [名] 1 (窟窿) hole 2 (关键) crux ▶开窍
enlighten ▶诀窍 knack
窍门 qiàomén [名] knack

翘 qiào [动] 1 (仰起) stick up (PT, PP stuck)
2 (腿、拇指) raise
→另见 qiáo

撬 qiào [动] prise ▷她把门撬开了。She prised
the door open.

鞘 qiào [名] scabbard

切 qiē [动] cut (PT, PP cut) ▷请把土豆切成块
儿。Please cut the potatoes into pieces.
切除 qiēchú [动] excise
切磋 qiēcuō [动] compare notes
切割 qiēgē [动] cut (PT, PP cut)
切削 qiēxiāo [动] cut (PT, PP cut)

茄 qié [名] aubergine (英), eggplant (美)
→另见 jiā
茄子 qiézi [名] aubergine (英), eggplant (美)

且 qiě I [副] for the time being ▷这件事且
放放。Leave this for the time being. ▷先别
急，且听我说。Stop worrying: listen to me a
moment. II [连] 1 (尚且) even ▷既便宜且实
用 cheap and useful 2 (而且) and

切 qiè I [动] correspond to ▷他的想法不切实
际。His ideas don't correspond to reality.
II [形] eager III [副] definitely
切合 qièhé [动] correspond to ▷切合实际
correspond to reality
切记 qièjì [动] bear ... in mind (PT bore, PP borne)
切身 qièshēn [形] personal ▷切身利益
personal gain ▷切身经历 personal experience

切实 qièshí I [形] realistic II [副] conscientiously
切中 qièzhòng [动] hit (PT, PP hit) ▷你的批评
切中要害。Your criticism hits the mark.

妾 qiè [名] concubine

怯 qiè [形] timid ▶胆怯 timid
怯场 qièchǎng [动] get stage fright
怯懦 qiènuò [形] over-cautious
怯弱 qièruò [形] timid and weak-willed
怯生生 qièshēngshēng [形] shy

窃 qiè I [动] steal (PT stole, PP stolen) II [副]
surreptitiously
窃取 qièqǔ [动] steal (PT stole, PP stolen)
窃听 qiètīng [动] eavesdrop
窃贼 qièzéi [名] thief (PL thieves)

惬 qiè 见下文
惬意 qièyì [形] pleased

锲 qiè [动] carve
锲而不舍 qiè ér bù shě persevering

钦 qīn 见下文
钦佩 qīnpèi [动] admire

侵 qīn [动] invade
侵犯 qīnfàn [动] infringe ▷侵犯著作权
infringe copyright
侵害 qīnhài [动] 1 (权利、利益) violate 2 (指自
然) encroach on
侵略 qīnlüè [动] invade
侵权 qīnquán [动] violate rights
侵入 qīnrù [动] invade ▷侵入他国领空 violate
another country's airspace
侵蚀 qīnshí [动] erode ▷土壤侵蚀 soil erosion
侵吞 qīntūn [动] 1 (非法占有) embezzle 2 (武力
吞并) annex
侵袭 qīnxí [动] invade ▷台风侵袭东南沿海
地区。The typhoon has struck the south-east
coastal area.
侵占 qīnzhàn [动] seize

亲 qīn I [名] 1 (父母) parent 2 (亲戚)
relative 3 (婚姻) marriage ▶定亲
engagement 4 (新娘) bride II [形] 1 (指血缘
近) blood ▷亲兄弟 blood brothers 2 (指感情
好) intimate III [副] personally IV [动] 1 (亲
吻) kiss ▷她亲了一下孩子的脸。She gave the
child a kiss on the cheek. 2 (亲近) be close to
亲爱 qīn'ài [形] dear
亲笔 qīnbǐ I [动] write ... personally (PT wrote,

PP written) **II** [名] personal inscription

亲近 qīnjìn [形] close ▷ 大家都愿意亲近她。 Everyone wants to be close to her.

亲眷 qīnjuàn [名] relatives (PL)

亲密 qīnmì [形] close ▷ 亲密朋友 close friend ▷ 亲密无间 be as thick as thieves

亲昵 qīnnì [形] very intimate

亲戚 qīnqi [名] relative

亲切 qīnqiè [形] warm

亲热 qīnrè [形] affectionate

亲人 qīnrén [名] close relative

亲身 qīnshēn [形] personal

亲生 qīnshēng [形] one's own ▷ 亲生父母 one's own parents

亲事 qīnshì [名] marriage

亲属 qīnshǔ [名] relatives (PL)

亲吻 qīnwěn [动] kiss

亲眼 qīnyǎn [副] with one's own eyes ▷ 他亲眼看到了事情的经过。He witnessed the whole event.

亲自 qīnzì [副] personally

芹 qín 见下文

芹菜 qíncài [名] celery

琴 qín [名] ▷ 钢琴 piano ▷ 小提琴 violin

禽 qín [名] birds (PL)

禽兽 qínshòu [名] **1** (字) birds and animals (PL) **2** (喻) beast

勤 qín **I** [形] hard-working **II** [副] regularly **III** [名] **1** (勤务) duty ▷ 值勤 be on duty **2** (到场) attendance ▷ 考勤 check attendance

勤奋 qínfèn [形] diligent

勤俭 qínjiǎn [形] hard-working and thrifty

勤恳 qínkěn [形] hard-working and conscientious

勤快 qínkuai [形] hard-working

勤劳 qínláo [形] hard-working

勤勉 qínmiǎn [形] hard-working

擒 qín [动] capture

擒拿 qínná [动] **1** (格斗) immobilize **2** (捉拿) catch (PT, PP caught)

噙 qín [动] **1** (叼) hold ... in the mouth (PT, PP held) ▷ 老板总是噙着雪茄。The boss always has a cigar in his mouth. **2** (含) ▷ 她眼里噙着泪花。Her eyes are full of tears.

寝 qín **I** [动] sleep (PT, PP slept) **II** [名] **1** (指卧室) bedroom **2** (指陵墓) tomb

沁 qìn [动] ooze

沁人心脾 qìn rén xīn pí be refreshing

青 qīng **I** [形] **1** (指绿色) green **2** (指黑色) black **3** (指年纪) young ▷ 青年 youth **II** [名] **1** (指青草) grass **2** (指庄稼) unripe crops

青出于蓝而胜于蓝 qīng chū yú lán ér shèng yú lán the student surpasses the teacher

青春 qīngchūn [名] youth ▷ 充满青春活力 full of youthful energy

青春期 qīngchūnqī [名] youth

青红皂白 qīng hóng zào bái the rights and wrongs ▷ 他不分青红皂白就批评人。He just started to criticize people, without taking any interest in the rights and wrongs of the matter.

青黄不接 qīng huáng bù jiē temporary shortage ▷ 大学师资出现了青黄不接现象。There is a temporary shortage of university teachers.

青年 qīngnián [名] youth

青山绿水 qīngshān lǜshuǐ [名] beautiful landscape

青丝 qīngsī [名] black hair ▷ 她的青丝已成白发。Her black hair has gone grey.

青天 qīngtiān [名] **1** (蓝天) blue sky **2** (清官) unbiased judge

轻 qīng **I** [形] **1** (指重量) light **2** (指数量或程度) ▷ 他们年纪很轻。They are quite young. ▷ 他的病可不轻。His illness is very serious. **3** (指无足轻重) not important ▷ 任务轻 light task **4** (指轻松愉快) relaxed ▷ 轻音乐 light music **II** [副] **1** (指少用力) gently ▷ 这只箱子得轻拿轻放。This box should be handled with care. **2** (轻率) rashly ▷ 不要轻信他人。Don't trust people too readily. **III** [动] disparage

轻便 qīngbiàn [形] portable ▷ 轻便电视机 portable TV

轻薄 qīngbó [形] frivolous

轻车熟路 qīng chē shú lù a piece of cake ▷ 干这项工作，他是轻车熟路。This job is a piece of cake for him.

轻而易举 qīng ér yì jǔ without effort

轻浮 qīngfú [形] frivolous

轻举妄动 qīng jǔ wàng dòng act rashly

轻快 qīngkuài [形] **1** (轻捷) brisk **2** (轻松) light-hearted

轻慢 qīngmàn [动] treat ... disrespectfully ▷ 不要轻慢客人。Be sure not to treat the guests disrespectfully.

轻描淡写 qīng miáo dàn xiě brush over

轻蔑 qīngmiè [形] disdainful ▷ 他轻蔑地瞪了我一眼。He stared disdainfully at me.

轻飘飘 qīngpiāopiāo [形] light

轻巧 qīngqiǎo [形] 1 (灵巧) handy 2 (灵活) dexterous 3 (容易) simple

轻柔 qīngróu [形] gentle ▷轻柔的音乐 gentle music

轻生 qīngshēng [动] commit suicide

轻声 qīngshēng [副] in a gentle voice

轻视 qīngshì [动] look down on ▷轻视他人 look down on others

轻率 qīngshuài [形] hasty

轻松 qīngsōng [形] relaxing

轻佻 qīngtiāo [形] frivolous

轻闲 qīngxián [形] free

轻信 qīngxìn [动] be credulous ▷不要轻信谣传。Don't believe rumours (英) 或 rumors (美) too readily.

轻易 qīngyì [副] 1 (容易) easily ▷这些资料不是轻易能得到的。These materials are not easily obtained. 2 (随便) rashly ▷不要轻易下结论。Don't jump to rash conclusions.

轻音乐 qīngyīnyuè [名] light music

轻盈 qīngyíng [形] graceful

氢 qīng [名] (化) hydrogen

氢弹 qīngdàn [名] hydrogen bomb

倾 qīng I [动] 1 (斜) lean ▷房子的墙有点往外倾。The walls of the house lean outwards slightly. 2 (塌) collapse 3 (倒出) empty out 4 (用尽) exhaust II [名] tendency

倾巢 qīngcháo [动] turn out in full force

倾倒 qīngdǎo [动] 1 (倒下) topple 2 (佩服) fall for (PT fell, PP fallen) ▷大家都为她的美貌而倾倒。Everyone fell for her good looks.

倾倒 qīngdào [动] empty ▷倾倒垃圾 empty the rubbish (英) 或 garbage (美)

倾覆 qīngfù [动] overturn

倾家荡产 qīng jiā dàng chǎn be ruined ▷赌博使他倾家荡产。Gambling ruined him.

倾慕 qīngmù [动] admire

倾盆大雨 qīngpén dàyǔ downpour ▷昨天下了场倾盆大雨。There was a downpour yesterday.

倾诉 qīngsù [动] pour ... out ▷倾诉衷肠 pour out one's feelings

倾吐 qīngtǔ [动] pour out ▷倾吐心中的苦水 pour out one's pain

倾向 qīngxiàng I [动] incline to ▷这两种观点我倾向于前者。I incline to the first of these two views. II [名] tendency ▷他有发胖的倾向。He has a tendency to put on weight.

倾销 qīngxiāo [动] dump

倾斜 qīngxié [动] slant

倾泻 qīngxiè [动] come down in torrents (PT came, PP come)

倾心 qīngxīn [动] 1 (爱慕) have a soft spot for ▷她倾心于那个戴眼镜的老师。She likes that teacher with the glasses. 2 (尽心) be sincere ▷老师和学生在倾心交谈。The teacher is having a heart-to-heart talk with his student.

倾注 qīngzhù [动] 1 (流泻) pour ▷山洪向河里倾注。The mountain torrents poured into the river. 2 (集中) throw into (PT threw, PP thrown) ▷他把自己的精力都倾注在事业上。He threw all his energy into the undertaking.

清 qīng I [形] 1 (纯净) clear ▷清水 clear water 2 (寂静) quiet ▷你该享受清福了。You ought to enjoy a quiet life. 3 (清楚) distinct ▷分清 distinguish 4 (完全) settled ▷把钱还清 settle the debt 5 (纯洁) pure ▷玉洁冰清 pure and virtuous II [动] 1 (清除) get rid of ▷清垃圾 get rid of the rubbish (英) 或 garbage (美) 2 (结清) settle ▷账都清了吗? Are the accounts all settled? 3 (清点) check 4 (清理) put in order (PT, PP put)

清白 qīngbái [形] clean ▷历史清白 clean record

清查 qīngchá [动] check

清场 qīngchǎng [动] clear the place ▷电影演完了,该清场了。The film's finished – the cinema should be cleared.

清除 qīngchú [动] get rid of

清楚 qīngchu I [形] clear ▷发音清楚 clear pronunciation ▷头脑清楚 clear-headed II [动] understand (PT, PP understood) ▷这个问题你清楚吗? Do you understand this question?

清脆 qīngcuì [形] melodious

清单 qīngdān [名] detailed list ▷货物清单 stock inventory

清淡 qīngdàn [形] 1 (不浓) light ▷清淡口味 delicate flavour 2 (不腻) non-oily 3 (萧条) slack ▷最近生意清淡。Business has been slack recently.

清点 qīngdiǎn [动] check ▷清点货物 do stock-taking

清高 qīnggāo [形] noble and virtuous

清规戒律 qīngguī jièlǜ excessive rules ▷我们不受某些清规戒律的束缚。We don't want to be bound by any excessive rules.

清寒 qīnghán [形] 1 (清贫) impoverished 2 (清冷) clear and crisp

清洁 qīngjié [形] clean

清净 qīngjìng [形] quiet

清静 **qīngjìng** [形] quiet

清苦 **qīngkǔ** [形] poor and honest

清朗 **qīnglǎng** [形] clear ▷清朗的月夜 a clear moonlit night ▷清朗的声音 a clear sound

清冷 **qīnglěng** [形] **1** (凉) chilly **2** (冷清) deserted

清理 **qīnglǐ** [动] tidy ... up ▷清理房间 tidy up a room

清廉 **qīnglián** [形] honest

清凉 **qīngliáng** [形] refreshing ▷清凉饮料 refreshing drink

清明 **qīngmíng** [形] **1** (清澈) clear and bright **2** (清醒) clear ▷神志清明 clear-headed

清贫 **qīngpín** [形] impoverished

清扫 **qīngsǎo** [动] sweep ... clean (PT, PP swept)

清爽 **qīngshuǎng** [形] **1** (清凉) refreshing **2** (轻松) relaxed ▷听了他的话，我心里清爽了。 Hearing his words put me more at ease.

清算 **qīngsuàn** [动] **1** (账目) settle **2** (罪行) redress

清晰 **qīngxī** [形] clear ▷口齿清晰 clear enunciation

清洗 **qīngxǐ** [动] **1** (洗净) wash ▷清洗衣物 wash clothes **2** (清除) purge

清闲 **qīngxián** [形] leisurely

清香 **qīngxiāng** [形] lightly scented

清心寡欲 **qīng xīn guǎ yù** be pure of heart and free from desire

清新 **qīngxīn** [形] refreshing

清醒 **qīngxǐng** I [形] clear-headed II [动] come to (PT came, PP come) ▷我们去看病人时，他还没有清醒。 When we went to see him, he still hadn't come to.

清秀 **qīngxiù** [形] delicate

清一色 **qīngyīsè** [形] uniform

清真 **qīngzhēn** [形] Muslim

蜻 **qīng** 见下文

蜻蜓 **qīngtíng** [名] dragonfly

蜻蜓点水 **qīngtíng diǎn shuǐ** skim over

情 **qíng** [名] **1** (感情) feeling ▶热情 warmth **2** (情面) kindness ▷求情 plead for leniency **3** (爱情) love ▷一见钟情 love at first sight **4** (性欲) passion ▶情欲 passion **5** (情况) condition ▶病情 patient's condition ▷实情 true state of affairs ▷军情 military situation

情报 **qíngbào** [名] intelligence report ▷军事情报 military intelligence

情不自禁 **qíng bù zì jīn** be unable to refrain from ▷他们情不自禁地欢呼起来。 They were unable to refrain from cheering. ▷我们情不自禁唱了起来。 We couldn't help but start singing.

情操 **qíngcāo** [名] sentiment

情敌 **qíngdí** [名] rival (in a love triangle)

情调 **qíngdiào** [名] sentiment

情窦初开 **qíngdòu chū kāi** adolescent love

情分 **qíngfèn** [名] affection ▷夫妻情分 affection between husband and wife

情感 **qínggǎn** [名] feeling

情怀 **qínghuái** [名] feelings (PL)

情节 **qíngjié** [名] **1** (内容) plot **2** (事实) circumstances (PL)

情结 **qíngjié** [名] complex ▷自卑情结 inferiority complex

情景 **qíngjǐng** [名] sight ▷感人的情景 moving sight

情况 **qíngkuàng** [名] **1** (状况) situation ▷情况危急 desperate situation ▷我父母身体情况良好。 My parents are in excellent health. **2** (变化) military development ▷前线有什么情况？ What developments are there on the front line?

情理 **qínglǐ** [名] reason ▷合乎情理 reasonable

情侣 **qínglǚ** [名] lovers (PL)

情面 **qíngmiàn** [名] feelings (PL) ▷他一点不讲情面。 He's completely ruthless.

情趣 **qíngqù** [名] interest ▷她的生活充满情趣。 She's got an interesting life.

情人 **qíngrén** [名] sweetheart

情人节 **qíngrénjié** [名] Valentine's Day

情书 **qíngshū** [名] love letter

情投意合 **qíng tóu yì hé** have a lot in common

情形 **qíngxing** [名] situation

情绪 **qíngxù** [名] **1** (心理状态) mood ▷急躁情绪 irritable mood ▷情绪低落 depressed **2** (不很开心) moodiness ▷他有点情绪。 He's a bit moody.

情义 **qíngyì** [名] affection

情谊 **qíngyì** [名] friendship

情意 **qíngyì** [名] affection

情由 **qíngyóu** [名] whys and wherefores (PL) ▷他不分情由就开始胡乱批评人。 Without asking the whys and wherefores he started to criticize people indiscriminately.

情有可原 **qíng yǒu kě yuán** forgivable ▷他这样做情有可原。 What he did is forgivable.

情愿 **qíngyuàn** [动] **1** (愿意) be willing to **2** (宁愿) prefer ▷天太热，我情愿留在家里。 It's too hot. I would prefer to stay at home.

晴 **qíng** [形] fine ▷天晴了。 It's cleared up.

晴好 **qínghǎo** [形] fine

晴朗 qínglǎng [形] sunny

晴天霹雳 qíngtiān pīlì a bolt from the blue ▷她父亲去世的消息对她来说是晴天霹雳。The news that her father had died came like a bolt from the blue.

顷 qǐng I [名] a little while II [副] just now

请 qǐng [动] 1 (请求) ask ▷请他进来。Ask him to come in. 2 (邀请) invite ▷我们将请一位知名学者来讲学。We will invite a well-known scholar to come and lecture. ▷这位教授是从国外请来的。This professor has been invited from abroad. 3 (敬) ▷请这边走。This way, please. ▷请大家安静一下。Everyone quiet, please.

请便 qǐngbiàn [动] go ahead ▷如果你现在就想吃午餐，那就请便吧。If you want to have your lunch now, do go ahead. ▷你若要退出这个项目，请便！If you want to quit this project, go ahead!

请假 qǐngjià [动] ask for leave ▷她请假10天去度假。She asked for ten days' holiday leave.

请教 qǐngjiào [动] consult

请客 qǐngkè [动] treat ▷昨晚伊芙请客吃晚餐。Last night Eve treated us to dinner. ▷今天我来请客。Today it's on me.

请命 qǐngmìng [动] plead on behalf of

请求 qǐngqiú [动] ask ▷请求谅解 ask for understanding

请示 qǐngshì [动] ask for instructions

请帖 qǐngtiě [名] invitation ▷发请帖 send out invitations

请问 qǐngwèn [动] ▷请问你几岁了？May I ask you how old you are? ▷请问怎么出去？Could you show me the way out, please?

请勿 qǐngwù [动] ▷请勿触摸。Please don't touch. ▷请勿吸烟。No smoking.

请愿 qǐngyuàn [动] petition

请罪 qǐngzuì [动] apologize

庆 qìng I [动] celebrate ▷庆新年 celebrate New Year II [名] festival ▶国庆 National Day

庆典 qìngdiǎn [名] celebration

庆贺 qìnghè [动] celebrate ▷值得庆贺的事 something worth celebrating

庆幸 qìngxìng [动] rejoice

庆祝 qìngzhù [动] celebrate ▷庆祝生日 celebrate a birthday

穷 qióng I [形] poor II [名] limit ▷无穷无尽 limitless III [副] 1 (彻底) thoroughly 2 (极端) extremely

穷苦 qióngkǔ [形] destitute

穷困 qióngkùn [形] poverty-stricken

穷年累月 qióng nián lěi yuè for years on end ▷他们穷年累月在这儿工作。They've worked here for years on end.

穷酸 qióngsuān [形] down at heel

穷乡僻壤 qióng xiāng pì rǎng remote and backward places

穷凶极恶 qióng xiōng jí è diabolical

丘 qiū [名] 1 (指土堆) mound ▶沙丘 sand dune 2 (指坟墓) grave ▶坟丘 grave

丘陵 qiūlíng [名] hill

秋 qiū [名] 1 (指季节) autumn (英), fall (美) 2 (指庄稼) harvest time 3 (指一年) year ▷千秋万代 thousands of years 4 (指厄运期) period

秋分 qiūfēn [名] autumnal equinox

秋高气爽 qiū gāo qì shuǎng crisp autumn weather

秋千 qiūqiān [名] swing

秋天 qiūtiān [名] autumn (英), fall (美)

蚯 qiū 见下文

蚯蚓 qiūyǐn [名] earthworm

囚 qiú I [动] imprison II [名] prisoner

囚犯 qiúfàn [名] prisoner

囚禁 qiújìn [动] imprison

求 qiú I [动] 1 (请求) request ▷求人帮助 request help ▷他求我办事。He asked me to handle things. 2 (追求) strive (PT strove, PP striven) ▷求和平 strive for peace ▷求进步 seek advancement II [名] demand ▷供不应求 supply doesn't meet demand ▷供大于求 supply outstrips demand

求爱 qiú'ài [动] woo

求和 qiúhé [动] 1 (指战争) sue for peace 2 (指下棋) claim a draw

求婚 qiúhūn [动] propose ▷他向她求婚。He proposed to her.

求教 qiújiào [动] seek advice (PT, PP sought)

求情 qiúqíng [动] beg for leniency ▷他为同学向老师求情。He interceded with the teacher on behalf of his classmate.

求饶 qiúráo [动] ask for forgiveness

求同存异 qiú tóng cún yì seek common ground while retaining independence

求证 qiúzhèng [动] seek verification (PT, PP sought)

求之不得 qiú zhī bù dé exactly what one's been looking for ▷你帮助我，真是求之不得

啊！Your help was exactly what I needed!

求知 qiúzhī [动] seek knowledge (PT, PP sought) ▷他把精力都放在求知上。He put all his energy into the pursuit of knowledge.

求助 qiúzhù [动] seek help (PT, PP sought)

酋 qiú [名] 1 (酋长) tribal chief 2 (头领) chief

酋长 qiúzhǎng [名] 1 (指部落首领) tribal chief 2 (指酋长国首领) sheikh

球 qiú [名] 1 (数) (球体) sphere 2 (指球状) ball ▶雪球 snowball 3 (指体育) ball ▶橡皮球 rubber ball ▶篮球 basketball ▶足球 football 4 (指比赛) ball game 5 (地球) the Earth ▶全球 the whole world ▶西半球 western hemisphere

球赛 qiúsài [名] ball game

球艺 qiúyì [名] ball skills (PL)

遒 qiú [形] powerful

遒劲 qiújìng [形] vigorous

区 qū I [动] distinguish ▶区别 distinguish II [名] 1 (地区) area ▶林区 wooded area ▷工业区 industrial area 2 (指行政单位) region ▶自治区 autonomous region ▷海淀区 Haidian District

区别 qūbié [动] distinguish ▷我看不出它们之间有什么区别。I can't see any distinction between them.

区分 qūfēn [动] differentiate ▷区分两种植物 differentiate between two kinds of plant

区区 qūqū [形] trivial

区域 qūyù [名] area ▷行政区域 administrative area

曲 qū I [形] 1 (弯曲) bent 2 (理亏) wrong ▷是非曲直 the rights and wrongs of a matter II [动] bend (PT, PP bent) III [名] 1 (弯曲处) bend ▶河曲 bend in a river 2 (发酵剂) leaven
→另见 qǔ

曲解 qūjiě [动] distort ▷你曲解了我的本意。You've distorted my original meaning.

曲线 qūxiàn [名] curve

曲折 qūzhé [形] 1 (弯曲) winding 2 (复杂) complicated

曲直 qūzhí [名] right and wrong

驱 qū [动] 1 (赶) drive (PT drove, PP driven) 2 (奔) gallop 3 (赶) expel ▶驱散 disperse

驱除 qūchú [动] drive ... away (PT drove, PP driven) ▷驱除侵略者 drive away invaders

驱动 qūdòng [动] drive (PT drove, PP driven)

驱赶 qūgǎn [动] drive ... away (PT drove, PP driven)

驱使 qūshǐ [动] 1 (迫使) order ... about 2 (推动) urge

驱逐 qūzhú [动] drive ... out (PT drove, PP driven)

屈 qū I [动] 1 (弯) bend (PT, PP bent) 2 (服) submit ▶屈服 surrender 3 (冤) wrong ▷你这样说真屈他了。What you said really wronged him. II [形] wrong III [名] injustice

屈才 qūcái [动] do work beneath one's ability

屈从 qūcóng [动] give way (PT gave, PP given)

屈服 qūfú [动] give in (PT gave, PP given)

屈辱 qūrǔ [名] humiliation

屈膝 qūxī [动] kneel (PT, PP knelt)

屈指可数 qūzhǐ kě shǔ can be counted on the fingers ▷这样的好作家屈指可数。Good authors like this are few and far between.

屈尊 qūzūn [动] lower oneself

祛 qū [动] dispel

祛除 qūchú [动] get rid of

躯 qū [名] human body ▷为国捐躯 die for one's country

躯干 qūgàn [名] trunk

躯体 qūtǐ [名] body

趋 qū [动] 1 (走) hasten ▷疾趋而过 speed past 2 (趋向) tend to become ▷大家的观点趋于一致。All our opinions are tending to unanimity.

趋势 qūshì [名] trend

趋向 qūxiàng I [动] tend to II [名] trend

趋炎附势 qū yán fù shì ingratiate oneself with influential people

蛐 qū 见下文

蛐蛐儿 qūqur [名] cricket

渠 qú [名] ditch ▷排水渠 drainage ditch

渠道 qúdào [名] 1 (水道) irrigation ditch 2 (途径) channel ▷两国应通过外交渠道解决彼此间的分歧。The two countries need to resolve their differences through diplomatic channels.

曲 qǔ [名] 1 (指歌曲) song ▷让我们高歌一曲。Let's sing a song. 2 (指乐曲) music ▷钢琴曲 piano music
→另见 qū

曲调 qǔdiào [名] melody

曲子 qǔzi [名] tune

取 qǔ 1 (拿到) take (PT took, PP taken) ▷取款

withdraw money ▷取包 collect a parcel **2** (得到) obtain ▷咎由自取 have only oneself to blame ▷取信于人 win the trust of others **3** (采取) adopt ▷取中立态度 adopt a neutral position ▷取赞成立场 give the seal of approval **4** (选取) choose (PT chose, PP chosen) ▷给孩子取个名 name a child

取材 qǔcái [动] draw material (PT drew, PP drawn) ▷这部小说取材于现实生活。This novel draws on real life.

取长补短 qǔ cháng bǔ duǎn learn from each other's strong points

取代 qǔdài [动] replace ▷许多人工劳动被计算机取代了。A lot of manual work has been replaced by computers.

取得 qǔdé [动] get (PT got, PP got (英), gotten (美)) ▷取得学位 get a degree ▷取得圆满成功 achieve complete success

取缔 qǔdì [动] ban

取而代之 qǔ ér dài zhī replace ▷老前锋受伤了，教练只能让替补球员取而代之。The original forward was injured – the coach had to replace him with a substitute player.

取经 qǔjīng [动] learn from the experience of others

取决 qǔjué [动] depend on

取名 qǔmíng [动] choose a name (PT chose, PP chosen)

取巧 qǔqiǎo [动] pull a fast one

取舍 qǔshě [动] make a choice

取消 qǔxiāo [动] cancel ▷取消比赛 cancel the competition ▷半决赛由于下雨取消了。The semi-final has been called off because of rain. ▷市政府取消了放鞭炮的禁令。The municipal government has lifted a ban on firecrackers.

取笑 qǔxiào [动] make fun of

取样 qǔyàng [动] take a sample (PT took, PP taken)

取悦 qǔyuè [动] please

取证 qǔzhèng [动] collect evidence

娶 qǔ [动] marry ▷我哥哥娶了位护士。My brother got married to a nurse.

娶亲 qǔqīn [动] get married

龋 qǔ 见下文

龋齿 qǔchǐ [名] tooth decay

去 qù I [动] **1** (到) go (PT went, PP gone) ▷从广州去北京 go from Guangzhou to Beijing ▷我们昨天去上海了。We went to Shanghai yesterday. **2** (除) get rid of **3** (距) be apart ▷相去不远 not far apart **4** (发) send (PT, PP sent) ▷去了一封信 send a letter II [形] past ▶去年 last year

去处 qùchù [名] site

去路 qùlù [名] way ▷挡住某人的去路 block someone's way

去世 qùshì [动] pass away

去向 qùxiàng [名] whereabouts (PL) ▷不知去向 nowhere to be found

趣 qù I [名] interest ▶志趣 interest ▷这个故事有趣。This is an interesting story. II [形] interesting

趣味 qùwèi [名] taste ▷低级趣味 vulgar taste

圈 quān I [名] **1** (环形物) circle ▶北极圈 Arctic Circle **2** (界) group II [动] circle ▷请圈出正确的答案。Please circle the right answer.
→另见 juān, juàn

圈点 quāndiǎn [动] **1** (加标点) punctuate **2** (标出) mark

圈套 quāntào [名] trap ▷落入圈套 fall into a trap

圈子 quānzi [名] **1** (环形) circle ▷说话绕圈子 express oneself in a roundabout way **2** (范围) ▷学生的活动圈子很小。The students socialize within a small circle. ▷她到哪儿都搞小圈子。Wherever she goes she creates little networks.

权 quán I [名] **1** (权力) power ▶当权 be in power **2** (权利) right ▶表决权 the right to vote **3** (形势) ▷主动权 initiative ▷控制权 control **4** (权宜) expediency ▷通权达变 adapt to circumstances II [副] for the time being

权衡 quánhéng [动] weigh... up ▷权衡利弊 weigh up the pros and cons

权力 quánlì [名] power ▷滥用权力 abuse power

权利 quánlì [名] right ▷受教育权利 right to education ▷民主权利 democratic rights (PL)

权且 quánqiě [副] for the time being

权势 quánshì [名] power and influence

权术 quánshù [名] political trickery ▷玩弄权术 play politics

权威 quánwēi [名] authority

权限 quánxiàn [名] jurisdiction ▷超越权限 go beyond one's jurisdiction

权宜 quányí [形] expedient

权益 quányì [名] rights and interests (PL) ▷保护消费者的权益 protect the rights and interests of consumers

全 quán I [形] 1 (齐全) complete ▷人都到全了吗？Is everyone here? 2 (整个) whole ▷全世界 the whole world II [副] entirely ▷我们班同学全去了。Our entire class went. III [动] keep ... intact (PT, PP kept) ▷两全齐美 satisfy both sides

全部 quánbù [形] whole

全才 quáncái [名] all-rounder ▷他是个全才。He's an all-rounder.

全称 quánchēng [名] full name

全程 quánchéng [名] whole journey

全副 quánfù [形] complete ▷全副武装 fully armed

全国 quánguó [形] nationwide ▷全国人口普查 nationwide census ▷全国游泳冠军 national swimming champion

全会 quánhuì [名] plenary session

全集 quánjí [名] complete works ▷莎士比亚全集 the complete works of Shakespeare

全家福 quánjiāfú [名] family photo

全局 quánjú [名] overall situation

全军覆没 quán jūn fùmò be wiped out

全力 quánlì [名] all one's strength ▷竭尽全力 spare no effort ▷全力以赴 go all out

全貌 quánmào [名] full view

全面 quánmiàn [形] comprehensive ▷全面发展 comprehensive development ▷全面出击 all-out attack

全民 quánmín [名] all the people

全能 quánnéng [形] all-round ▷全能运动员 all-round athlete

全盘 quánpán [形] overall ▷全盘否定 total denial

全球 quánqiú [名] the whole world

全权 quánquán [名] full powers (PL)

全神贯注 quán shén guàn zhù with undivided attention ▷学生们全神贯注地听老师讲课。The students listened to the teacher with undivided attention.

全速 quánsù [名] full speed ▷警车全速前进。The police car is driving at full speed.

全体 quántǐ [名] everyone

全心全意 quán xīn quán yì wholeheartedly

全自动 quánzìdòng [形] automatic ▷全自动洗衣机 automatic washing machine

诠 quán [动] (书) annotate

诠释 quánshì [动] annotate

泉 quán [名] spring ▷温泉 hot spring

泉水 quánshuǐ [名] spring water

泉源 quányuán [名] 1 (水源) spring 2 (来源) source ▷知识的泉源 source of knowledge

拳 quán [名] fist

拳打脚踢 quán dǎ jiǎo tī beat ... up

拳击 quánjī [名] boxing

拳击手 quánjīshǒu [名] boxer

痊 quán 见下文

痊愈 quányù [动] recover

蜷 quán [动] coil ▷蛇把身子蜷成一团儿。The snake coiled itself up.

蜷曲 quánqū [动] curl ▷乞丐把身体蜷曲成一团儿。The beggar curled up.

鬈 quán [形] curly

鬈曲 quánqū [形] crinkled

颧 quán 见下文

颧骨 quángǔ [名] cheekbone

犬 quǎn [名] dog ▷嗅探犬 sniffer dog

犬牙交错 quǎnyá jiāocuò jigsaw pattern

劝 quàn [动] 1 (说服) advise ▷我劝他放弃这个计划。I advised him to abandon this plan. 2 (勉励) encourage

劝导 quàndǎo [动] persuade ▷在家人的劝导下，他想通了。Under the persuasive influence of his family, he came round.

劝告 quàngào [动] advise ▷我们劝告他不要这样做。We advised him not to do it.

> 注意 advice 是不可数名词。可以说 a piece of advice 或 some advice，但不能说 'an advice' 或 'advices'。请勿混淆 advice 和 advise。advise 是与 advice 同词根的动词。

劝架 quànjià [动] mediate

劝解 quànjiě [动] 1 (劝导) reassure ▷经他人劝解，他终于想通了。With others' reassurance, he finally came round. 2 (劝架) mediate

劝诫 quànjiè [动] admonish

劝说 quànshuō [动] persuade ▷他们劝说我们去青岛度假。They persuaded us to go on holiday to Qingdao.

劝阻 quànzǔ [动] dissuade

券 quàn [名] ticket ▶奖券 lottery ticket ▶入场券 admission ticket

缺 quē I [动] 1 (缺乏) lack ▷这地方缺水。This place is short of water. 2 (残破) be incomplete ▷这本书缺两页。This book is missing two

pages. **3** (缺席) be absent ▷人全到了，一个
不缺。Everyone's here, no one's absent. **II** [名]
vacancy ▶补缺 fill a vacancy

缺德 quēdé [形] wicked

缺点 quēdiǎn [名] shortcoming

缺乏 quēfá [动] lack ▷缺乏资源 lack the
resources

缺憾 quēhàn [名] regret

缺口 quēkǒu [名] **1** (口子) gap **2** (缺额) shortfall
▷我们的资金还有很大缺口。There's still a
huge shortfall in our funds.

缺门 quēmén [名] gap

缺欠 quēqiàn [名] defect

缺勤 quēqín [动] be absent ▷他最近常缺勤。
He's been absent a lot recently.

缺少 quēshǎo [动] lack ▷我这里缺少人手。I'm
shorthanded here.

缺席 quēxí [动] be absent

缺陷 quēxiàn [名] defect ▷生理缺陷 physical
defect

瘸 qué [动] be lame
瘸子 quézi [名] ▷她是瘸子。She is lame.

却 què **I** [动] **1** (后退) step back **2** (使退却) drive
... back (PT drove, PP driven) **3** (拒绝) decline
▶推却 decline ▷盛情难却。It's difficult to
refuse such a kind offer. **4** (表示完成) ▶冷却
cool off ▶忘却 forget **II** [副] however ▷我有
许多话要说，却不知从何说起。I have a lot to
say, but don't know where to start.

却步 quèbù [动] shrink back (PT shrank, PP
shrunk)

雀 què [名] sparrow
雀跃 quèyuè [动] jump for joy

确 què [副] **1** (确实地) really ▷确有其事。
It really happened. **2** (坚定地) firmly ▶确信
firmly believe

确定 quèdìng **I** [动] determine **II** [形] definite
▷确定的证据 definite proof

确立 quèlì [动] establish

确切 quèqiè [形] precise

确认 quèrèn [动] confirm

确实 quèshí **I** [形] true **II** [副] really ▷他确实
聪明。He's really clever.

确凿 quèzáo [形] irrefutable

确诊 quèzhěn [动] diagnose

鹊 què [名] magpie

裙 qún [名] skirt
裙子 qúnzi [名] skirt

群 qún **I** [名] crowd **II** [量] ▷一群绵羊 a flock
of sheep ▷一群蜜蜂 a swarm of bees ▷一
群奶牛 a herd of cows ▷一群学生 a group of
students

群策群力 qún cè qún lì pull together

群岛 qúndǎo [名] archipelago

群起 qúnqǐ [动] rise together (PT rose, PP risen)

群情 qúnqíng [名] popular feeling

群体 qúntǐ [名] **1** (指生物) colony **2** (指社会)
group

群众 qúnzhòng [名] the masses (PL)

Rr

然 rán I [形] correct II [代] so III [连] (书) however

然而 rán'ér [连] however ▷他发了财，然而生活依然俭朴。Even after he'd made it, he led a simple and thrifty life.

然后 ránhòu [连] afterwards ▷我先看新闻，然后吃晚饭。I'm watching the news first, and I'll have supper afterwards.

髯 rán [名] side whiskers (PL)

燃 rán [动] 1 (燃烧) burn ▶易燃物 flammable substance 2 (点燃) light (PT, PP lit)

燃点 rándiǎn I [动] light (PT, PP lit) II [名] ignition point

燃放 ránfàng [动] let ... off (PT, PP let) ▷燃放烟花 let off fireworks

燃料 ránliào [名] fuel ▷炭是一种固体燃料。Coal is a form of solid fuel.

燃眉之急 rán méi zhī jí matter of extreme urgency

燃烧 ránshāo [动] burn

冉 rǎn 见下文

冉冉 rǎnrǎn [副] slowly ▷冉冉升起的太阳 the slowly rising sun

染 rǎn [动] 1 (着色) dye ▷她把头发染成了蓝色。She dyed her hair blue. 2 (感染) contract ▷他身染重病。He's contracted a serious illness. 3 (沾染) catch (PT, PP caught) ▷他染上了抽烟喝酒的习惯。He's acquired the habit of smoking and drinking.

染料 rǎnliào [名] dye

染指 rǎnzhǐ [动] take more than one's fair share (PT took, PP taken)

嚷 rāng 见下文
→另见 rǎng

嚷嚷 rāngrang [动] 1 (喧哗) shout ▷小声点儿，别嚷嚷了！Quieten down a bit – don't shout! 2 (声张) make ... widely known

瓤 ráng [名] 1 (指瓜果) flesh 2 (指物品) padding

壤 rǎng [名] 1 (土地) soil 2 (地域) region ▷穷乡僻壤 remote backwater

嚷 rǎng [动] 1 (喊叫) howl 2 (吵闹) make a racket
→另见 rāng

嚷叫 rǎngjiào [动] shout

让 ràng I [动] 1 (退让) make allowances ▷孩子小，你就让着点吧。The child's only young – you should make allowances for him. 2 (谦让) invite ▷先把客人让进屋 invite guests to enter a room first 3 (允许) let (PT, PP let) ▷老板不让我休假。My boss won't let me take any holiday. 4 (避开) make way 5 (转让) transfer ▷这张演出票能让给我吗？Can the ticket for the performance be transferred to me? II [介] by ▷大树让风吹倒了。The big tree was blown down by the wind.

让步 ràngbù [动] make a concession

让利 rànglì [动] give up a share of the profits (PT gave, PP given)

让位 ràngwèi [动] 1 (指职位) step down ▷老领导主动让位给年轻人。The old leader stepped down in favour of someone younger. 2 (指座位) give up one's seat (PT gave, PP given)

让贤 ràngxián [动] step down in favour of a worthier candidate

饶 ráo I [形] rich II [动] 1 (宽恕) forgive (PT forgave, PP forgiven) 2 (添加) add

饶命 ráomìng [动] spare a life ▷皇帝饶了他一命。The emperor spared his life. ▷小偷被打得连喊饶命。They beat the thief until he begged for mercy.

饶舌 ráoshé [动] prattle ▷快点说，别再饶舌了。Tell me quickly – no more beating about the bush.

饶恕 ráoshù [动] let ... off (PT, PP let) ▷他还
年轻，就饶恕他这一次吧！ He's still young
– can't you let him off just this once?

扰 rǎo I [动] (搅乱) disturb ▶打扰 disturb
II [形] (书) (混乱) chaotic

扰乱 rǎoluàn [动] disrupt

绕 rào [动] 1 (缠绕) wind (PT, PP wound) 2 (围
绕) go round (PT went, PP gone) ▷他每天绕
着操场跑步。 He runs several times round
the sports ground every day. 3 (迂回) make a
detour ▷前方修路，车辆绕行。 There are
road-works ahead – please take a detour.

绕口令 ràokǒulìng [名] tongue twister

绕圈子 rào quānzi [动] 1 (指走路) go round and
round in circles (PT went, PP gone) 2 (喻) (指说
话) beat about the bush (PT beat, PP beaten)

绕弯子 rào wānzi [动] (喻) beat about the bush
(PT beat, PP beaten)

绕嘴 ràozuǐ [形] awkward ▷这篇文章读起来
绕嘴。 This essay doesn't read well.

惹 rě [动] 1 (引起) stir up ▷他在单位老惹麻烦。
He's always stirring up trouble at work. 2 (触
动) provoke ▷她爱生气，你不要惹她。 She's
got a quick temper – don't provoke her. 3 (招)
make (PT, PP made) ▷他的话常常惹人发笑。
He often makes people laugh when he talks.

惹祸 rěhuò [动] stir up trouble

惹事 rěshì [动] cause trouble

惹是生非 rě shì shēng fēi stir up trouble

惹眼 rěyǎn [形] showy ▷她那件粉色衣服很惹
眼。 That pink dress of hers is very showy.

热 rè I [名] 1 (物) heat 2 (高烧) fever ▶退热
dispel a fever II [形] 1 (温度高) hot ▷今天真
热。 It's so hot today. 2 (情谊深) warm ▷她
是个热心肠。 She's very warm-hearted. 3 (羡
慕) envious 4 (走俏) popular 5 (热潮) ▷出国
热开始降温了。 The craze for going abroad is
starting to wear off. ▷西方国家兴起了汉语
热。 Studying Chinese has become all the rage
in Western countries. III [动] heat ▷把米饭
热一热再吃。 Heat up the rice before you eat it.

热爱 rè'ài [动] love ▷她非常热爱教育事业。
She loves her work as a teacher.

热潮 rècháo [名] craze

热忱 rèchén [名] enthusiasm

热诚 rèchéng [形] warm and sincere

热带 rèdài [名] the tropics (PL) ▷这些都是热带
植物。 These are all tropical plants.

热点 rèdiǎn [名] 1 (指地区) prime site ▷这

一地区已成为外商投资的热点。 This
region has become a prime site for foreign
investment. 2 (指问题) sticking point

热度 rèdù [名] 1 (冷热程度) temperature 2 (高烧)
fever 3 (热情) enthusiasm

热敷 rèfū [名] hot compress

热狗 règǒu [名] hot dog

热乎乎 rèhūhū [形] warm

热乎 rèhu [形] 1 (热) hot 2 (亲热) (指人际关系)
affectionate

热火朝天 rè huǒ cháo tiān be in full swing
▷建筑工地上，大家干得热火朝天。 On the
construction site, the work was in full swing.

热辣辣 rèlālā [形] burning hot ▷他觉得脸上热
辣辣的。 He felt his face was burning. ▷阳光
热辣辣地炙烤着大地。 The land was roasting
under the burning hot sun.

热浪 rèlàng [名] heat wave

热恋 rèliàn [动] be passionately in love ▷两
人正处于热恋之中。 They are having a
passionate love affair.

热量 rèliàng [名] amount of heat

热烈 rèliè [形] heated ▷班会上，大家讨论得
非常热烈。 At the class meeting, everyone was
having a heated discussion.

热流 rèliú [名] 1 (指气流) warm front 2 (指感受)
warmth 3 (热潮) upsurge ▷移民的热流 a rise
in emigration

热卖 rèmài [动] sell like hot cakes (PT, PP sold)

热门 rèmén [名] popularity ▷这些都是热门
专业。 These are all very popular majors.

热闹 rènao I [形] lively II [动] liven up ▷我们
准备在元旦热闹热闹。 We're getting ready for
a lively time at New Year's. III [名] spectacle

热启动 rèqǐdòng [动] reboot ▷电脑死机时，
试试热启动。 When the computer crashes, try
rebooting it.

热切 rèqiè [形] eager ▷孩子们热切地盼望
着儿童节的到来。 The children were eagerly
looking forward to Children's Day.

热情 rèqíng I [名] passion II [形] enthusiastic
▷招待客人要热情周到。 When entertaining
guests you should be enthusiastic and
attentive. ▷她对顾客非常热情。 She's very
friendly to the clients.

热身 rèshēn [动] warm ... up ▶热身赛 warm-up
match

热腾腾 rètēngtēng [形] piping hot

热线 rèxiàn [名] 1 (指电话或电报) hotline ▷这个
广播电台开通了观众热线。 This radio station
has opened an audience hotline. 2 (指交通)
busy route ▷旅游热线 busy tourist route

热销 rèxiāo [动] sell like hot cakes (PT, PP sold)

热心 rèxīn [形] warm-hearted

热血 rèxuè [名] enthusiasm ▷20年前，他还是一个热血青年。Twenty years ago he was still an enthusiastic youth.

热饮 rèyǐn [名] hot drink

热战 rèzhàn [动] open war

热中 rèzhōng [动] 1 (渴望) be desperate for ▷他热中于权势和金钱。He's desperate for power and money. 2 (爱好) be keen on ▷他热中于集邮。He's keen on stamp collecting.

人 rén [名] 1 (人类) human being 2 (某种人) person (PL people) ▶军人 soldier 3 (每人) everybody ▷这个孩子人见人爱。Everyone who sees this child likes him. 4 (成年人) adult 5 (别人) other people (PL) ▷我们要真诚待人。We must treat other people with honesty. 6 (为人) personality 7 (人手) manpower ▷我们这里活儿多，能不能派几个人？We've got so much to do here – can you send us some more manpower? ▷我们办公室缺人。Our office is short-staffed.

> person 的复数形式通常为 people。At least fifty-four people have been killed. persons 通常只用于非常正式的场合，或作为法律用语。

人才 réncái [名] 1 (指能人) talent ▷他是个难得的人才。He is an unusually talented person. 2 (指外貌) good looks (PL) ▷他长得一表人才。He's a good-looking man.

人称 rénchēng [名] person ▷"我"是第一人称。"I" is the first person.

人次 réncì [量] person time

人道 réndào [形] humane ▶人道主义 humanitarianism

人地生疏 rén dì shēngshū ▷我对这里人地生疏，请多多指教。I'm a stranger here – please give me as much advice as you can.

人多势众 rén duō shì zhòng safety in numbers

人浮于事 rén fú yú shì be overstaffed

人格 réngé [名] 1 (品质) character 2 (资格) dignity

人工 réngōng I [形] man-made II [名] manpower III [量] man-day

人和 rénhé [动] stand united (PT, PP stood)

人际 rénjì [名] ▷人际状况 personal situation ▷搞好人际关系非常重要。It's very important to have good personal relationships.

人家 rénjiā [名] 1 (住户) household 2 (家庭) family 3 (婆家) fiancé's family ▷姑娘大了，该找个人家了。The girl's grown up – should find her a husband.

人家 rénjia [代] 1 (别人) others ▷人家都去了，你怎么不去？Other people have gone, so why don't you go? 2 (他) he 3 (她) she 4 (他们) they 5 (指自己) I

人间 rénjiān [名] the world

人口 rénkǒu [名] 1 (地区人数) population ▷人口众多 large population ▷全国人口普查 national census 2 (家庭人数) ▷他家人口很多。There are a lot of people in his family. 3 (泛指人) people (PL)

人来疯 rénláifēng [动] ▷我儿子总是人来疯。My son always gets over-excited when we have guests.

人类 rénlèi [名] mankind, humankind ▷人类正面临着越来越多的挑战。Mankind is facing more and more challenges.

人力 rénlì [名] manpower

人马 rénmǎ [名] 1 (指军队) forces (PL) 2 (指机构) members (PL)

人面兽心 rén miàn shòu xīn a wolf in sheep's clothing

人民 rénmín [名] the people ▷为人民服务 serve the people ▷公务员是人民的公仆。Government officials are the servants of the people.

人命 rénmìng [名] life (PL lives)

人品 rénpǐn [名] 1 (品质) character 2 (仪表) appearance

人气 rénqì [名] popularity

人情 rénqíng [名] 1 (人的感情) human emotion 2 (情面) feelings (PL) ▷好朋友都不愿帮我，真不讲人情！None of my good friends were willing to help me – what an unfeeling bunch! 3 (礼俗) etiquette 4 (礼物) gift

人权 rénquán [名] human rights (PL)

人山人海 rén shān rén hǎi a sea of people ▷国庆节那天，天安门广场上人山人海。On National Day, Tiananmen Square was a sea of people.

人身 rénshēn [名] person (PL people)

人参 rénshēn [名] ginseng

人生 rénshēng [名] life (PL lives) ▶人生观 philosophy of life

人士 rénshì [名] figure ▷知名人士 famous figure

人世 rénshì [名] the world ▷他离开人世已经5年了。It's already five years since he passed away.

人事 rénshì [名] 1 (指人员安排) personnel 2 (指人际关系) personal relations (PL) 3 (指人情事理) the ways of the world ▷他这么大了，应该懂点人事了。At his age, he ought to know the ways of the world. 4 (指人的意识)

consciousness ▷等我赶到时，他已人事不
知。By the time I got there, he'd already lost
consciousness.

人手 rénshǒu [名] manpower ▷缺人手 lack the
manpower

人体 réntǐ [名] the human body ▷人体器官移
植 human organ transplants

人头 réntóu [名] 1 (人的头) human head 2 (人
数) people (PL) ▷按人头拨款 allocate money
according to the number of people 3 (指人际关
系) links (PL)

人为 rénwéi I [动] put in the effort (PT, PP put)
▷事在人为 human effort can achieve anything
II [形] man-made

人文科学 rénwén kēxué [名] humanities (PL)

人物 rénwù [名] 1 (能人) figure ▷他是一位有
世界影响的领袖人物。He is a figure of global
stature. 2 (艺术形象) character ▷这部小说塑
造了100多个人物。There are over a hundred
characters in this novel.

人心 rénxīn [名] 1 (感情和愿望) popular
feeling 2 (人性) conscience

人性 rénxìng [名] human nature ▷这是一种灭
绝人性的行为。This is inhuman behaviour.

人选 rénxuǎn [名] candidate

人烟 rényān [名] signs of human habitation (PL)

人员 rényuán [名] 1 (雇员) staff 2 (指某类人)
▷退休人员 retirees ▷走私人员 smugglers

人缘儿 rényuánr [名] personal relations (PL)
▷她人缘儿很好。She gets on very well with
people.

人云亦云 rén yún yì yún parrot

人造 rénzào [形] artificial ▷发射人造卫星
launch an artificial satellite

人证 rénzhèng [名] testimony

人质 rénzhì [名] hostage

人种 rénzhǒng [名] ethnic group

仁 rén [名] 1 (仁爱) benevolence 2 (果肉) kernel

仁爱 rén'ài [名] benevolence

仁慈 réncí [形] benevolent

仁义 rényì [名] benevolence and righteousness

仁至义尽 rén zhì yì jìn do everything one can
▷我对他已做到仁至义尽。I've already done
all I can for him.

忍 rěn [动] 1 (忍受) endure ▷容忍 tolerate 2 (忍
心) have the heart to ▷残忍 ruthless

忍耐 rěnnài [动] show restraint (PT showed, PP
shown)

忍气吞声 rěn qì tūn shēng suffer in silence

忍让 rěnràng [动] hold back (PT, PP held) ▷大家

都忍让一点儿。Everyone held back a bit.

忍辱负重 rěn rǔ fù zhòng ▷他忍辱负重
30年，终于完成了使命。After enduring
thirty years of humiliation, he finally
accomplished his mission.

忍受 rěnshòu [动] bear (PT bore, PP borne)

忍无可忍 rěn wú kě rěn ▷对于他们的卑
劣行为，大家已忍无可忍。Everyone is at
the end of their tether with their appalling
behaviour.

忍心 rěnxīn [动] bear (PT bore, PP borne) ▷看到
孩子受罪，你忍心吗？How can you bear to
watch the children suffer?

荏 rěn [形] weak ▷色厉内荏 all bark no bite

荏苒 rěnrǎn [动] (书) slip by

刃 rèn I [名] 1 (锋) blade 2 (刀) knife (PL knives)
II [动] (书) kill

认 rèn [动] 1 (识) know (PT knew, PP known) 2 (建
立关系) establish a relationship 3 (承认) admit
▷认输 admit defeat 4 (接受吃亏) accept ▷这
东西贵就贵吧，我认了。Never mind the
expense – I can take it.

认错 rèncuò [动] 1 (承认错误) admit one's
mistakes ▷你去向老师认个错吧。Go and tell
the teacher you admit you were wrong. 2 (误
认) mistake ... for ... (PT mistook, PP mistaken)
▷他不是你同学，你认错了人。He's not your
classmate – you've got the wrong man.

认可 rènkě [动] 1 (许可) endorse ▷他的方案已
得到上级认可。His project was endorsed by
his superiors. 2 (承认) approve ▷他的能力得
到了同事们的认可。His abilities won him the
approval of his colleagues.

认生 rènshēng [动] be shy of strangers

认识 rènshi I [动] know (PT knew, PP known)
▷他们是在一次晚会上认识的。They
got to know each other at a party. II [名]
understanding ▷他对这件事的认识是不对
的。His knowledge of this is incorrect.

认输 rènshū [动] concede defeat

认为 rènwéi [动] think (PT, PP thought) ▷你
认为这篇文章怎么样？What do you think
of this essay? ▷我们认为，这个决定是错误
的。We think that the decision is wrong.

认真 rènzhēn I [形] serious II [动] take ...
seriously (PT took, PP taken) ▷他开个玩笑，
你就认真了。He was joking, but you took him
seriously.

认证 rènzhèng [动] authenticate

认罪 rènzuì [动] plead guilty ▷证据确凿，他不
得不低头认罪。The proof was incontestable

– he had no choice but to admit defeat and plead guilty.

任 rèn I [动] 1 (聘) appoint ▶委任 appoint 2 (担当) take up (PT took, PP taken) 3 (听凭) let (PT, PP let) ▷各种款式，任你选择。There's a variety of different styles – I'll let you decide. II [名] (职责) responsibility III [量] ▷他是这个公司的第3任总裁。He's the third CEO of this company. ▷他当了两任总统。He's been president for two terms. IV [连] no matter ▷任你去哪里，我也不管。No matter where you go, I won't care.

任何 rènhé [形] any ▷你们可以从中选择任何一个。You can choose any one of them. ▷任何人都不能迟到。No one can be late. ▷任何事物都有两面性。Every coin has two sides.

任劳任怨 rèn láo rèn yuàn work hard despite other people's criticism

任命 rènmìng [动] appoint ▷他被任命为部门经理。He was appointed branch manager.

任凭 rènpíng I [动] allow ... to do as they please ▷这种情况下不能任凭你一人做主。Under these circumstances we can't let you take the decision alone. II [连] no matter ▷任凭你是谁，都不该违反规定。No matter who you are, you still can't break the rules.

任人唯贤 rèn rén wéi xián choose the best person for the job

任务 rènwu [名] task

任性 rènxìng [形] headstrong

任意 rènyì I [副] at will ▷你可以任意指派一个人做这件事。You can send anyone you like to do this job. II [形] unconditional

任用 rènyòng [动] appoint

任重道远 rèn zhòng dào yuǎn shoulder a heavy responsibility

纫 rèn [动] 1 (穿针) thread 2 (缝) sew (PT sewed, PP sewn)

韧 rèn [形] resilient ▶柔韧 pliant

韧劲 rènjìn [名] (口) tenacity

韧性 rènxìng [名] 1 (指物体) flexibility 2 (指精神) tenacity

妊 rèn 见下文

妊娠 rènshēn [动] be pregnant

扔 rēng [动] 1 (掷) throw (PT threw, PP thrown) 2 (丢) throw ... away ▷他把垃圾扔了。He threw the rubbish away.

仍 réng (书) I [动] 1 (沿袭) remain 2 (频繁) occur frequently II [副] still ▷事故仍在调查中。The accident is still under investigation. ▷困难仍未克服。The difficulties have not yet been overcome.

仍旧 réngjiù I [动] continue as before ▷此项法规仍旧。This statute will remain as it was before. II [副] still ▷我劝了半天，她仍旧不同意。I spent ages trying to persuade her, but she still wouldn't agree.

仍然 réngrán [副] 1 (表示继续) still ▷他仍然保持着老习惯。He still sticks to his old habits. 2 (表示恢复) ▷回国后，他仍然到原公司工作。After his return from overseas he went back to work in his old company.

日 rì [名] 1 (太阳) sun ▶日出 sunrise ▶日落 sunset 2 (白天) daytime ▷他们日夜不停地赶路。They travelled onwards, not stopping during the day or at night. 3 (天) day ▶明日 tomorrow 4 (每天) every day ▷城市面貌日见改善。The city looks better and better every day. 5 (泛指一段时间) days (PL) ▶往日 the past 6 (指某一天) day ▶生日 birthday 7 (日本) Japan ▷日货 Japanese goods

日常 rìcháng [形] everyday ▷日常生活用语 everyday words and expressions

日程 rìchéng [名] agenda

日后 rìhòu [名] future ▷这个问题日后再解决。This problem can be resolved at some point in the future.

日积月累 rì jī yuè lěi accumulate ...over a long period

日久天长 rì jiǔ tiān cháng year in, year out ▷只要坚持锻炼，日久天长就会有效果。You just have to keep on with the exercise – you'll see the results over time.

日理万机 rì lǐ wàn jī be occupied with important matters

日历 rìlì [名] calendar

日内 rìnèi [名] next few days (PL) ▷运动员将于日内回国。The athletes will return home within the next few days.

日期 rìqī [名] date ▷出生日期 date of birth ▷考试日期还没定下来。The date of the exam hasn't been fixed yet.

日新月异 rì xīn yuè yì change rapidly and continuously

日以继夜 rì yǐ jì yè work round the clock

日益 rìyì [副] increasingly

日用 rìyòng I [形] everyday II [名] day-to-day expenses (PL)

日子 rìzi [名] 1 (日期) date 2 (时间) day ▷近些日子，你都忙什么呢？What have you been up to these last few days? 3 (生活) life (PL lives)

▷老百姓的日子越来越好了。The lives of ordinary people are getting better and better.

戎 róng [名] army ▷戎装 military uniform

戎马 róngmǎ [名] **1** (字) war horse **2** (喻) military career

茸 róng **I** [形] downy **II** [名] young deer antlers (PL)

茸毛 róngmáo [名] down

茸茸 róngróng [形] downy

荣 róng [形] **1** (茂盛) flourishing **2** (兴旺) thriving **3** (光荣) glorious

荣华富贵 rónghuá fùguì glory and wealth

荣幸 róngxìng [形] honoured (英), honored (美) ▷认识您，我感到非常荣幸。I feel honoured to know you.

荣耀 róngyào [形] glorious

荣誉 róngyù [名] **1** (指名声) glory ▷这次比赛，他为学校赢得了荣誉。He won glory for the school in this competition. **2** (指名义上的) honour (英), honor (美) ▷荣誉市民 honoured (英) 或 honored (美) citizens

绒 róng [名] **1** (绒毛) down **2** (纺织品) ▶天鹅绒 velvet ▶灯芯绒 corduroy

绒线 róngxiàn [名] **1** (丝线) floss **2** (毛线) (方) wool ▷绒线背心 a woollen (英) 或 woolen (美) vest

容 róng **I** [动] **1** (容纳) fit ▷这个会议室容得下300人吗？Can this meeting room fit three hundred people? **2** (容忍) tolerate ▷他容不得比他强的人。He can't tolerate anyone better than him. **3** (允许) allow ▷他根本不容别人发表观点。He just doesn't allow anyone else to express their views. **II** [名] **1** (神情) facial expression **2** (相貌) appearance **3** (喻) (外观) appearance ▶市容 appearance of a city

容光焕发 róngguāng huànfā glowing with health

容积 róngjī [名] volume

容量 róngliàng [名] capacity

容貌 róngmào [名] features (PL)

容纳 róngnà [动] **1** (盛下) hold (PT, PP held) ▷这个电影院能容纳近千人。This cinema can hold almost a thousand people. **2** (接受) tolerate ▷容纳异议 tolerate different opinions

容器 róngqì [名] container

容忍 róngrěn [动] tolerate ▷她不能容忍孩子的懒惰。She couldn't tolerate the child's laziness.

容许 róngxǔ [动] allow ▷老师不容许任何人缺课。The teacher didn't allow anyone to miss class.

容易 róngyì [形] **1** (简便) easy ▷学好一门外语不容易。Learning a foreign language isn't easy. ▷英文录入比中文录入容易。It's easier to type in English than it is to type in Chinese. **2** (较可能) likely ▷天冷容易感冒。When the weather's cold it's easy to catch a cold.

溶 róng [动] dissolve

溶化 rónghuà [动] **1** (溶解) dissolve **2** (融化) melt

溶解 róngjiě [动] dissolve

溶液 róngyè [名] solution

熔 róng [动] melt

熔点 róngdiǎn [名] melting point

熔化 rónghuà [动] melt

熔炼 róngliàn [动] **1** (指物质) smelt **2** (喻) steel oneself ▷熔炼意志 steel oneself

熔炉 rónglú [名] **1** (指炉子) furnace **2** (喻) forge

融 róng [动] **1** (融化) melt **2** (融合) blend **3** (流通) circulate

融合 rónghé [动] merge ▷两种文化正在互相融合。The two cultures are merging together.

融化 rónghuà [动] melt

融会贯通 róng huì guàn tōng thoroughly master

融洽 róngqià [形] harmonious ▷他们的关系一直很融洽。Their relationship has always been very harmonious.

融资 róngzī [动] pool funds ▷这个公司通过融资解决了资金问题。The company resolved its financial problems through a pooling of funds.

冗 rǒng [形] **1** (多余) superfluous ▶冗员 redundant personnel **2** (烦琐) trivial

冗长 rǒngcháng [形] long-winded

柔 róu [形] **1** (软) soft **2** (柔和) gentle

柔肠 róucháng [名] (喻) tender feelings (PL)

柔道 róudào [名] judo

柔和 róuhé [形] **1** (温和) gentle **2** (柔软) soft

柔滑 róuhuá [形] silky

柔美 róuměi [形] gentle and beautiful

柔情 róuqíng [名] tender feelings (PL)

柔软 róuruǎn [形] soft

柔顺 róushùn [形] meek

揉 róu [动] **1** (搓) rub ▷揉伤口 rub a wound **2** (团弄) knead

揉搓 róucuo [动] 1 (搓) rub ▷别老揉搓你的衣服。Don't keep rubbing at your clothes. 2 (方) (折磨) torment ▷别老揉搓我了。Stop tormenting me.

糅 róu [动] mix ▶糅杂 mix

糅合 róuhé [动] blend ▷糅合东西方文化 blend Eastern and Western cultures

蹂 róu [动] (书) tread on (PT trod, PP trodden)

蹂躏 róulìn [动] trample on ▷饱受战争蹂躏的城市 a city trampled on by war

肉 ròu I [名] 1 (指人) flesh 2 (指动物) meat ▶猪肉 pork 3 (指瓜果) flesh II [形] (不脆) spongy

肉搏 ròubó [动] fight hand to hand (PT, PP fought)

肉麻 ròumá [形] sickening ▷不要说那么肉麻的话。Don't say such sickening things.

肉体 ròutǐ [名] the human body ▷他的精神和肉体都受到了折磨。He endured both physical and mental torture.

肉刑 ròuxíng [名] corporal punishment

肉眼 ròuyǎn [名] 1 (指视力) the naked eye ▷肉眼看到的星星很有限。A limited number of stars can be seen with the naked eye. 2 (喻) lack of perceptiveness

肉欲 ròuyù [名] sexual desires (PL)

如 rú I [动] 1 (依从) comply with 2 (好似) be like ▷她俩亲如姐妹。The two of them are as close as sisters. ▷对她来说,这话如五雷轰顶。The words hit her like a thunderbolt. 3 (比得上) be as good as ▶不如 not as good as 4 (例如) ▷北京有很多名胜,如故宫、天坛等。Beijing has many tourist attractions, such as the Forbidden City, the Temple of Heaven and so on. II [介] as III [连] if ▷如一切顺利,我们会提前到达。If everything goes well, we'll be arriving early.

如出一辙 rú chū yī zhé be exactly the same

如此 rúcǐ [代] ▷人生如此美好! Life is so beautiful! ▷他的态度竟如此恶劣。His attitude was so unpleasant. ▷听说要放10天假。一但愿如此。I've heard we're getting ten days holiday – let's hope so.

如法炮制 rú fǎ páozhì follow a set pattern

如果 rúguǒ [连] if ▷如果我是你,就接受那份工作。If I were you, I'd accept that job. ▷我想周末去爬山,如果不下雨的话。I'd like to go mountain-climbing at the weekend, as long as it doesn't rain.

如何 rúhé [代] ▷此事如何解决? How are we going to sort this out? ▷你今后如何打算?

What are your plans for the future?

如火如荼 rú huǒ rú tú magnificent

如获至宝 rú huò zhì bǎo like hitting the jackpot

如饥似渴 rú jī sì kě be hungry for ▷他如饥似渴地学习古代汉语。He threw himself eagerly into the study of classical Chinese.

如箭在弦 rú jiàn zài xián have one's finger on the trigger

如胶似漆 rú jiāo sì qī joined at the hip ▷小两口新婚燕尔,如胶似漆。That newly-wed couple are joined at the hip.

如今 rújīn [名] today

如雷贯耳 rú léi guàn ěr be a household name

如梦初醒 rú mèng chū xǐng as if woken from a dream ▷老师的一番话,使他如梦初醒。It was as if the teacher's words had woken him from a dream.

如期 rúqī [副] on time ▷工人们如期完成了生产指标。The workers achieved their production target on time.

如日中天 rú rì zhōng tiān be at the height of one's powers

如实 rúshí [副] accurately ▷如实讲述事情的经过 tell it like it is

如释重负 rú shì zhòng fù breathe a sigh of relief

如数家珍 rú shǔ jiā zhēn know ... like the back of one's hand

如数 rúshù [副] exactly the right number

如同 rútóng [动] be like

如意 rúyì [动] be satisfied ▷大家对你这么好,还不如意? Everyone's been so good to you – are you still not satisfied?

如意算盘 rúyì suànpán wishful thinking

如鱼得水 rú yú dé shuǐ (喻) like a duck to water ▷他在新公司如鱼得水。He took to his new post like a duck to water.

如愿以偿 rúyuàn yǐ cháng have one's wish granted

如醉如痴 rú zuì rú chī be entranced

如坐针毡 rú zuò zhēn zhān be on edge ▷案情毫无进展,使他如坐针毡。The case was making no progress at all, and he was completely on edge.

儒 rú [名] 1 (儒家) Confucianism 2 (旧) (读书人) scholar

儒家 Rújiā [名] Confucianism

孺 rú [名] child (PL children)

蠕 rú [动] 见下文

蠕动 rúdòng [动] wriggle

乳 rǔ I [名] 1 (乳房) breast 2 (乳汁) milk 3 (乳状物) milk ▶炼乳 condensed milk ▶豆乳 soya milk II [形] suckling ▶乳猪 suckling 或 sucking pig

乳儿 rǔ'ér [名] nursing baby

乳名 rǔmíng [名] pet name

乳臭未干 rǔxiù wèi gān wet behind the ears

乳制品 rǔzhìpǐn [名] milk products (PL)

辱 rǔ I [名] dishonour (英), dishonor (美) II [动] 1 (侮辱) insult 2 (玷污) disgrace

辱骂 rǔmà [动] call ... names

辱没 rǔmò [动] disgrace

入 rù [动] 1 (进入) enter ▶入场 enter 2 (参加) join ▶入学 enrol 3 (合乎) agree with II [名] (收入) income ▶岁入 yearly income

入不敷出 rù bù fū chū live beyond one's means

入超 rùchāo [名] import surplus

入耳 rù'ěr [形] pleasant-sounding

入股 rùgǔ [动] buy shares (PT, PP bought)

入骨 rùgǔ [动] cut to the bone (PT, PP cut)

入伙 rùhuǒ [动] 1 (参加) join 2 (搭伙) share a meal

入籍 rùjí [动] become a citizen (PT became, PP become) ▷他在美国居住10年后入籍。He was resident in America for ten years before becoming a citizen.

入境 rùjìng [动] enter a country ▷他去办理美国入境签证。He went to apply for a US visa.

入口 rùkǒu I [动] 1 (指嘴) put ... in the mouth (PT, PP put) ▷入口的东西，要注意卫生。You should make sure that you only put clean things in your mouth. 2 (指货物) import II [名] (门) entrance

入流 rùliú [动] be up to standard ▷他写的小说不入流。His novel isn't up to standard.

入门 rùmén I [动] cross the threshold II [名] introduction ▷他正在读《电脑入门》。He's reading "An Introduction to Computers".

入迷 rùmí [动] be engrossed in ▷他下棋入了迷。He was engrossed in his chess game.

入魔 rùmó [动] be obsessed ▷他玩游戏像入了魔一样。He is obsessed with playing games.

入木三分 rù mù sān fēn (喻) incisive

入侵 rùqīn [动] invade

入情入理 rù qíng rù lǐ reasonable and logical

入神 rùshén I [动] be enthralled ▷她看小说看得入了神。She was enthralled by the novel. II [形] wonderful

入时 rùshí [形] fashionable

入手 rùshǒu [动] begin (PT began, PP begun) ▷教学应该从培养孩子兴趣入手。Education should begin with encouraging the child's interests.

入网 rùwǎng [动] 1 (手机、寻呼机) have a network connection 2 (计算机) connect to the Internet

入围 rùwéi [动] be short-listed

入味 rùwèi [形] 1 (有滋味) tasty 2 (有趣味) interesting

入伍 rùwǔ [动] join the army

入乡随俗 rù xiāng suí sú when in Rome, do as the Romans do

入选 rùxuǎn [动] be selected

入眼 rùyǎn [形] eye-catching ▷这衣服不怎么入眼。These clothes don't look good.

褥 rù [名] bedding

软 ruǎn [形] 1 (柔) soft 2 (温和) gentle 3 (柔弱) weak 4 (没主见) easily swayed

软包装 ruǎnbāozhuāng [名] 1 (指材料) soft packaging 2 (指包装) soft package

软刀子 ruǎndāozi [名] (喻) underhand tactics (PL)

软骨头 ruǎngǔtou [名] (喻) spineless person

软化 ruǎnhuà [动] soften

软和 ruǎnhuo [形] soft

软件 ruǎnjiàn [名] 1 (计算机) software ▷他们正在开发更先进的软件。They're developing more advanced software. 2 (指素质、服务、水平等) staff capacity

软禁 ruǎnjìn [动] put under house arrest (PT, PP put)

软绵绵 ruǎnmiānmiān [形] 1 (柔软) soft 2 (缠绵) sentimental 3 (软弱) feeble

软盘 ruǎnpán [名] floppy disk

软弱 ruǎnruò [形] weak ▷她大病初愈，身子还有些软弱。She's just getting over a serious illness, and she's still quite weak.

软水 ruǎnshuǐ [名] soft water

软卧 ruǎnwò [名] soft sleeper

软饮料 ruǎnyǐnliào [名] soft drink

软硬兼施 ruǎn yìng jiān shī (贬) use both hard and soft tactics

软着陆 ruǎnzhuólù [动] make a soft landing ▷这颗卫星安全地实现了软着陆。The satellite safely achieved a soft landing.

蕊 ruǐ [名] pistil

锐 ruì I [形] sharp II [名] vigour (英), vigor (美)

III [副] sharply

锐不可当 ruì bù kě dāng unstoppable ▷这个球队锐不可当，一举拿下冠军。This team is unstoppable – they won the championship with one bash at it.

锐角 ruìjiǎo [名] acute angle

锐利 ruìlì [形] **1** (锋利) sharp **2** (尖锐) astute ▷锐利的辞令 astute language

锐气 ruìqì [名] drive

锐意 ruìyì [形] determined

瑞 ruì [名] good luck
瑞雪 ruìxuě [名] timely fall of snow

睿 ruì [形] (书) far-sighted
睿智 ruìzhì [形] (书) far-sighted

闰 rùn [名] 见下文
闰年 rùnnián [名] leap year
闰日 rùnrì [名] February 29th
闰月 rùnyuè [名] leap month

润 rùn **I** [形] sleek **II** [动] **1** (加油或水) lubricate **2** (修饰) polish **III** [名] profit
润滑 rùnhuá [动] lubricate
润色 rùnsè [动] polish
润泽 rùnzé **I** [形] moist **II** [动] moisten

若 ruò **I** [动] be like ▷他一副若有所失的样子。He looked as if he had lost something. **II** [连] if ▷现在若不努力，将来会后悔的。If you don't work hard now you'll regret it in the future.

若非 ruòfēi [连] if not ▷若非众人相助，哪有他的今天？If it wasn't for everybody's help, where would he be today?

若干 ruògān [数] several ▷若干人 several people

若是 ruòshì [连] if ▷若是你能参加，那就太好了。It would be great if you could join in.

若无其事 ruò wú qí shì act as if nothing is the matter ▷他心里很生气，表面上却装出若无其事的样子。Inside he was very angry, but on the outside he pretended that nothing was the matter.

若有所思 ruò yǒu suǒ sī as if lost in thought

偌 ruò 见下文
偌大 ruòdà [形] so big ▷偌大的公园，连个人影也没有。This park is so big, and yet there isn't a soul in sight.

弱 ruò [形] **1** (弱小) weak **2** (年幼) young **3** (软弱) weak
弱不禁风 ruò bù jīn fēng fragile
弱点 ruòdiǎn [名] weakness
弱化 ruòhuà [动] weaken
弱肉强食 ruò ròu qiáng shí the weak are food for the strong
弱视 ruòshì [名] lazy eye
弱项 ruòxiàng [名] Achilles' heel
弱小 ruòxiǎo [形] weak
弱智 ruòzhì [形] retarded ▷她女儿有点弱智。Her daughter has learning difficulties.

Ss

洒 **sǎ**[动] **1**(泼) sprinkle **2**(指不小心) spill
洒落 **sǎluò**[动] shower
洒脱 **sǎtuo**[形] carefree

撒 **sǎ**[动] **1**(散布) scatter ▷撒点酱油 sprinkle soy sauce **2**(散落) spill
→另见 sā
撒播 **sǎbō**[动] sow (PT sowed, PP sown)

飒 **sà** 见下文
飒爽 **sàshuǎng**[形] valiant

腮 **sāi**[名] cheek
腮帮子 **sāibāngzi**[名](口) cheek

塞 **sāi** Ⅰ [动] stuff ... into ▷我把零碎东西塞进了抽屉。I stuffed the bits and pieces into the drawer. Ⅱ [名] cork
→另见 sài
塞子 **sāizi**[名] cork

塞 **sài**[名] place of strategic importance
→另见 sāi
塞翁失马 **sài wēng shī mǎ** blessing in disguise

赛 **sài** Ⅰ [名] match ▷排球赛 volleyball match ▷演讲比赛 debating contest Ⅱ [动] outdo (PT outdid, PP outdone)
赛车 **sàichē** Ⅰ [动] race Ⅱ [名] **1**(指汽车) racing car **2**(指自行车) racer
赛程 **sàichéng**[名] **1**(指距离) distance **2**(比赛日程) programme (英), program (美) **3**(比赛进度) schedule
赛季 **sàijì**[名] season
赛跑 **sàipǎo**[动] race
赛区 **sàiqū**[名] area
赛事 **sàishì**[名] competition
赛制 **sàizhì**[名] competition rules (PL)

仨 **sā**[数](口) three ▷哥仨 three brothers

撒 **sā**[动] **1**(手、网) let ... go (PT, PP let) **2**(贬)(疯、野) lose control of oneself (PT, PP lost) ▷撒野 have a tantrum
→另见 sǎ
撒欢儿 **sāhuānr**[动](方) gambol
撒谎 **sāhuǎng**[动](口) lie
撒娇 **sājiāo**[动] behave like a spoiled child
撒泼 **sāpō**[动] make a scene
撒气 **sāqì**[动] **1**(球、车胎) get a puncture **2**(发泄怒气) take one's anger out on (PT took, PP taken) ▷别拿我撒气！Don't take your anger out on me!
撒手 **sāshǒu**[动] **1**(松手) let go (PT, PP let) **2**(不管) ignore ▷这么大的事你不能撒手不管。This matter is too important – you can't just ignore it. **3**(婉)(死) pass away
撒手锏 **sāshǒujiǎn**[名] trump card ▷不到紧急关头不要亮出撒手锏。Don't reveal your trump card before the crucial moment.
撒野 **sāyě**[动] throw a fit (PT threw, PP thrown) ▷一个醉汉在街上撒野。A man was throwing a drunken fit in the middle of the street. ▷这孩子没得到礼物，就在后院里撒野。Not having received a gift, the child had a tantrum in the back yard.

三 **sān**[数] **1**(指数目) three ▷三本书 three books **2**(表示序数) third ▷我住三层。I live on the third floor. **3**(表示多数) several ▷三思 think twice ▷三番五次 over and over again **4**(表示少数) a few ▷三言两语 in a few words ▷三三两两 in twos and threes
三百六十行 **sānbǎi liùshí háng**[名] all walks of life
三长两短 **sān cháng liǎng duǎn** accident ▷孩子要有个三长两短，父母该怎么办呢？If something happens and the child dies, what will his parents do then?
三番五次 **sān fān wǔ cì** over and over again

三伏 sānfú [名] the hottest days of summer (PL)

三更半夜 sāngēng-bànyè the middle of the night ▷你三更半夜不睡觉，跑出去干吗？ It's the middle of the night – why aren't you asleep and what are you doing outside?

三角 sānjiǎo [名] triangle ▷三角恋爱 love triangle

三九天 sānjiǔtiān [名] the coldest days of winter (PL)

三令五申 sān lìng wǔ shēn give repeated orders ▷政府三令五申司机不能在开车时打手机。 The government has given repeated orders that drivers must not use mobile phones while driving.

三明治 sānmíngzhì [名] sandwich

三亲六故 sān qīn liù gù friends and relatives (PL)

三三两两 sānsānliǎngliǎng in twos and threes ▷大家三两两地离开了办公室。 Everyone left the office in twos and threes.

三生有幸 sān shēng yǒu xìng be extremely lucky

三思而行 sān sī ér xíng think twice ▷处理这个棘手的问题，望你三思而行，切莫鲁莽。 I hope you'll think twice before you deal with this difficult issue, and not do anything rash.

三天打鱼，两天晒网 sān tiān dǎ yú, liǎng tiān shài wǎng work in fits and starts ▷你三天打鱼，两天晒网，根本练不好书法。 You lack perseverance, so you'll never get anywhere with your calligraphy.

三天两头 sān tiān liǎng tóu (口) almost every day

三围 sānwéi [名] vital statistics (PL)

三维空间 sānwéi kōngjiān [名] three-dimensional space

三五成群 sān wǔ chéng qún (口) in little groups

三下五除二 sān xià wǔ chú èr efficiently ▷他三下五除二把我交给的任务完成了。 He efficiently completed the task I gave him.

三心二意 sān xīn èr yì half-hearted ▷他工作三心二意的。 He's half-hearted about his work.

三言两语 sān yán liǎng yǔ in a few words ▷三言两语解释不清。 It's not possible to explain in a few words.

叁 sān [数] an elaborate form of "three", used in writing cheques etc to prevent mistakes and forgery

伞 sǎn [名] umbrella

伞兵 sǎnbīng [名] paratrooper

散 sǎn I [动] loosen II [形] loose
→另见 sàn

散户 sǎnhù [名] small-scale investor

散乱 sǎnluàn [形] messy

散漫 sǎnmàn [形] slack

散文 sǎnwén [名] prose

散装 sǎnzhuāng [形] loose

散 sàn [动] 1 (分离) break up (PT broke, PP broken) ▷班会散了。 The class meeting broke up. ▷乌云散了。 The dark clouds scattered. 2 (散布) give ... out (PT gave, PP given) 3 (排除) dispel
→另见 sǎn

散布 sànbù [动] 1 (传单) distribute 2 (谣言) spread (PT, PP spread)

散步 sànbù [动] go for a stroll (PT went, PP gone)

散发 sànfā [动] give ... off (PT gave, PP given) ▷她身上散发出一股香水味。 She gives off a scent of perfume. ▷散发广告单 send out flyers

散会 sànhuì [动] end a meeting ▷散会之后请把会议室打扫一下。 When the meeting is over, please tidy up the meeting room.

散伙 sànhuǒ [动] 1 (团体、组织) dissolve 2 (夫妻) split up (PT, PP split) ▷小夫妻散伙后，孩子怎么办？ When the young couple split up, what will happen to the children?

散失 sànshī [动] 1 (物品) lose (PT, PP lost) ▷一些文物在战争中散失了。 Some cultural relics were lost in the war. 2 (水分) evaporate

丧 sāng [名] funeral
→另见 sàng

丧服 sāngfú [名] mourning suit

丧事 sāngshì [名] funeral arrangements (PL)

丧葬 sāngzàng [动] bury

丧钟 sāngzhōng [名] death knell

桑 sāng [名] mulberry

桑那浴 sāngnàyù [名] sauna

嗓 sǎng [名] 1 (嗓子) throat 2 (嗓音) voice

嗓门 sǎngmén [名] voice ▷他嗓门大。 He's got a loud voice.

嗓音 sǎngyīn [名] voice

嗓子 sǎngzi [名] 1 (喉咙) throat 2 (嗓音) voice

丧 sàng [动] lose (PT, PP lost)
→另见 sāng

丧胆 sàngdǎn [动] be terrified ▷敌军闻风丧胆。 The enemy were terrified.

丧尽天良 sàng jìn tiān liáng heartless ▷她丧尽天良地为私利而贩卖奴隶。She heartlessly sold people into slavery for her own profit.

丧命 sàngmìng [动] die

丧偶 sàng'ǒu [动] be widowed

丧气 sàngqì [动] lose heart (PT, PP lost)

丧气 sàngqi [形] (口) unlucky ▷烧烤会碰上下雨，真丧气！It rained on our barbecue – what bad luck!

丧失 sàngshī [动] lose (PT, PP lost) ▷丧失尊严 lose one's dignity

丧心病狂 sàng xīn bìng kuáng frenzied

搔 sāo [动] scratch

骚 sāo I [动] disturb II [形] (贬) flirty
骚动 sāodòng I [名] disturbance ▷总统被暗杀，在全国引起骚动。The assassination of the president led to disturbances all over the country. II [动] create an uproar ▷电影放到一半突然停电，观众骚动起来。Halfway through the film there was a power cut and the audience was in an uproar.

骚乱 sāoluàn [动] riot

骚扰 sāorǎo [动] harass ▷性骚扰 sexual harassment

臊 sāo [名] foul smell
→另见 sào

扫 sǎo [动] 1 (打扫) sweep (PT, PP swept) 2 (除去) clear ... away ▶扫黄 anti-pornography campaign 3 (快速掠过) sweep (PT, PP swept) ▷演员向观众扫了一眼。The actor's gaze swept over the audience.
→另见 sào

扫除 sǎochú [动] 1 (打扫) sweep ... up (PT, PP swept) 2 (除掉) eliminate ▷扫除文盲 eliminate illiteracy

扫地出门 sǎo dì chū mén be cast out into the world with nothing to one's name ▷父母死后，她被扫地出门。After her parents died, she was cast out into the world with nothing to her name.

扫黄 sǎohuáng [动] hold an anti-pornography campaign (PT, PP held)

扫盲 sǎománg [动] eliminate illiteracy

扫描 sǎomiáo [动] scan

扫描仪 sǎomiáoyí [名] scanner

扫墓 sǎomù [动] tend a grave

扫射 sǎoshè [动] strafe

扫视 sǎoshì [动] take a quick look (PT took, PP taken) ▷他向人群扫视了一遍，开始发表演讲。He took a quick look at the audience and then began his speech.

扫尾 sǎowěi [动] wind ... up (PT, PP wound) ▷工作大体做完了，明日谁来扫尾？The work is pretty much finished. Who's going to come in tomorrow to wind things up?

扫兴 sǎoxìng [形] disappointed

嫂 sǎo [名] 1 (哥哥之妻) sister-in-law (PL sisters-in-law) 2 (泛称已婚妇女) auntie
嫂子 sǎozi [名] (口) sister-in-law (PL sisters-in-law)

扫 sào 见下文
→另见 sǎo
扫帚 sàozhou [名] broom

瘙 sào 见下文
瘙痒 sàoyǎng [动] itch

臊 sào [形] shy
→另见 sāo

色 sè [名] 1 (颜色) colour (英), color (美) 2 (脸色) expression 3 (种类) kind 4 (景象) scenery 5 (质量) quality 6 (美貌) good looks (PL)
→另见 shǎi
色彩 sècǎi [名] 1 (颜色) colour (英), color (美) 2 (指情调) tone ▷小说笼罩着悲剧色彩。The novel is tragic in tone.

色调 sèdiào [名] 1 (指色彩) shade 2 (指思想) tone

色鬼 sèguǐ [名] lecher

色狼 sèláng [名] lecher

色盲 sèmáng [名] colour (英) 或 color (美) blindness

色眯眯 sèmīmī [形] lewd

色情 sèqíng [形] pornographic

色素 sèsù [名] pigment

色相 sèxiàng [名] charm

色泽 sèzé [名] lustre (英), luster (美)

涩 sè [形] 1 (味道) astringent 2 (文句) obscure

啬 sè [形] stingy

瑟 sè [名] Chinese harp
瑟缩 sèsuō [动] huddle ▷他瑟缩在角落里抽烟。He huddled in the corner to have a smoke.

森 sēn [形] 1 (形容树多) wooded 2 (阴暗) gloomy
森林 sēnlín [名] forest
森严 sēnyán [形] heavily guarded ▷军事重

地戒备森严。The military area is heavily guarded.

僧 sēng [名] Buddhist monk
僧侣 sēnglǚ [名] Buddhist monk

杀 shā I [动] 1 (杀死) kill 2 (战斗) fight (PT, PP fought) 3 (削弱) reduce ▷杀威风 cut down to size II [助] ▷这个喜剧笑杀人。The comedy was utterly hilarious.
杀毒 shādú [动] get rid of a virus ▷杀毒软件 anti-virus software
杀风景 shā fēngjǐng spoil the mood ▷草坪上的垃圾真杀风景。The rubbish on the lawn really spoils the atmosphere.
杀害 shāhài [动] murder
杀机 shājī [名] murderous intent
杀价 shājià [动] bargain ▷我很会杀价。I'm a very good bargainer.
杀戒 shājiè [名] Buddhist prohibition against taking life
杀戮 shālù [动] massacre
杀气 shāqì [名] murderous look
杀青 shāqīng [动] be complete ▷电影杀青并进入发行阶段。The film is complete and ready for release.
杀生 shāshēng [动] kill
杀手 shāshǒu [名] killer

沙 shā I [名] 1 (石粒) sand 2 (指食品) paste II [形] hoarse
沙场 shāchǎng [名] (书) battlefield
沙尘 shāchén [名] dust
沙尘暴 shāchénbào [名] sandstorm
沙发 shāfā [名] sofa
沙锅 shāguō [名] casserole
沙化 shāhuà [动] desertify ▷草原逐渐沙化。The grasslands are gradually turning into desert. ▷沙化是自然环境的大患。Desertification is a disaster for the natural environment.
沙皇 shāhuáng [名] tsar
沙龙 shālóng [名] salon
沙漠 shāmò [名] desert
沙滩 shātān [名] beach
沙哑 shāyǎ [形] hoarse
沙眼 shāyǎn [名] trachoma
沙子 shāzi [名] sand

纱 shā [名] 1 (指材料) yarn 2 (指织品) gauze
纱布 shābù [名] gauze

刹 shā [动] brake
→另见 chà
刹车 shāchē I [动] 1 (停止机器) brake ▷他没能刹住车，撞到了树上。He didn't brake in time, and crashed into the tree. 2 (喻) (制止) put a stop to (PT, PP put) ▷这个项目成了烂摊子。赶快刹车吧。This project is turning into a real shambles. We should put a stop to it at once. II [名] brake

砂 shā [名] grit (PL grit)

煞 shā I [动] 1 (结束) stop 2 (勒紧) tighten ▷煞车 brake II [副] (书) extremely
→另见 shà
煞车 shāchē I [动] 1 (停止机器) brake 2 (喻) (制止) put a stop to (PT, PP put) II [名] brake

鲨 shā [名] shark

傻 shǎ [形] 1 (蠢) stupid 2 (死心眼) inflexible
傻瓜 shǎguā [名] fool
傻乎乎 shǎhūhū [形] simple-minded
傻气 shǎqì [形] foolish
傻笑 shǎxiào [动] giggle
傻眼 shǎyǎn [动] be stunned
傻子 shǎzi [名] fool

厦 shà [名] tall building ▷摩天大厦 skyscraper

煞 shà I [名] evil spirit II [副] extremely
→另见 shā
煞白 shàbái [形] deathly pale
煞费苦心 shà fèi kǔxīn take great pains ▷父母对孩子的教育煞费苦心。Parents take great pains over their children's education.

霎 shà [名] instant
霎时间 shàshíjiān [名] instant

筛 shāi [动] sieve
筛选 shāixuǎn [动] 1 (指用筛子) sieve 2 (挑选) select ▷筛选运动员 select athletes

色 shǎi [名] colour (英), color (美)
→另见 sè
色子 shǎizi [名] dice

晒 shài [动] 1 (阳光照射) ▷他被晒黑了。He's tanned. ▷我被晒伤了。I've got sunburn. ▷我被晒得直出汗。I was sweating constantly out in the sun. 2 (吸收光热) lie in the sun (PT lay, PP lain) ▷她躺在沙滩上晒太阳。She was lying on the beach, sunbathing. ▷我把衣服拿出去

晒。I put the clothes out to dry in the sun.

晒台 shàitái [名] roof terrace

山 shān [名] 1 (地质) mountain ▶山峦 mountain range 2 (似山之物) ▶冰山 iceberg ▷人山人海 crowds of people

山崩 shānbēng [名] landslide

山川 shānchuān [名] landscape

山村 shāncūn [名] mountain village

山洞 shāndòng [名] cave

山峰 shānfēng [名] peak

山冈 shāngāng [名] hillock

山歌 shāngē [名] folk song

山沟 shāngōu [名] 1 (流水沟) gully 2 (山谷) valley 3 (偏僻山区) mountainous area

山谷 shāngǔ [名] valley

山河 shānhé [名] (书) lands (PL)

山货 shānhuò [名] mountain delicacies (PL)

山涧 shānjiàn [名] mountain stream

山脚 shānjiǎo [名] foothills (PL)

山林 shānlín [名] wooded hill

山峦 shānluán [名] mountain range

山脉 shānmài [名] mountain range

山盟海誓 shān méng hǎi shì make a pledge of everlasting love

山南海北 shān nán hǎi běi 1 (字) far and wide 2 (喻) (指说话) far-ranging

山坡 shānpō [名] mountainside

山清水秀 shān qīng shuǐ xiù beautiful natural scenery

山穷水尽 shān qióng shuǐ jìn reach the end of the road ▷股市还没到山穷水尽的地步。The stock market still hasn't reached its lowest point.

山区 shānqū [名] mountainous area

山水 shānshuǐ [名] 1 (风景) scenery 2 (画) landscape painting

山头 shāntóu [名] mountaintop

山寨 shānzhài [名] mountain village

山珍海味 shān zhēn hǎi wèi [名] exotic delicacies (PL)

杉 shān [名] Chinese fir

删 shān [动] delete

删除 shānchú [动] delete

删改 shāngǎi [动] revise

删节 shānjié [动] abridge

衫 shān [名] shirt

姗 shān 见下文

姗姗来迟 shānshān lái chí arrive late

珊 shān 见下文

珊瑚 shānhú [名] coral

舢 shān 见下文

舢板 shānbǎn [名] sampan

扇 shān [动] 1 (扇子) fan 2 (耳光) slap →另见 shàn

扇动 shāndòng [动] flap

煽 shān [动] incite

煽动 shāndòng [动] incite ▷煽动民族仇恨 incite racial hatred

煽风点火 shān fēng diǎn huǒ (喻) stir up trouble

煽情 shānqíng I [动] stir up emotion II [形] 1 (褒) moving 2 (贬) sentimental

潸 shān [动] (书) shed tears (PT, PP shed)

潸然 shānrán [形] (书) tearful ▷潸然泪下 with tears rolling down one's cheeks

闪 shǎn I [动] 1 (闪避) dodge 2 (受伤) sprain 3 (突然出现) flash ▶流星一闪而过。The meteor flashed by. 4 (闪耀) shine (PT, PP shone) II [名] lightning

闪避 shǎnbì [动] dodge

闪电 shǎndiàn [名] lightning

闪动 shǎndòng [动] flash

闪念 shǎnniàn [动] be seized by a sudden thought

闪闪 shǎnshǎn [形] sparkling

闪身 shǎnshēn [动] sidestep

闪失 shǎnshī [名] accident

闪烁 shǎnshuò [动] 1 (忽明忽暗) twinkle ▷星星闪烁着。The stars were twinkling. 2 (吞吞吐吐) speak evasively (PT spoke, PP spoken)

闪烁其词 shǎnshuò qí cí speak evasively (PT spoke, PP spoken) ▷从他的闪烁其词能看出他分明是在掩饰什么。You can tell from his evasive language that he's got something to hide.

闪现 shǎnxiàn [动] flash

闪耀 shǎnyào [动] shine (PT, PP shone)

讪 shàn I [动] mock II [形] embarrassed

讪笑 shànxiào [动] mock

扇 shàn I [名] 1 (扇子) fan 2 (板状物) leaf (PL leaves) II [量] ▷一扇窗 a window ▷两扇门 two doors

→另见 shān

善 shàn I [形] 1 (善良) kind 2 (良好) good ▶善事 good deeds 3 (友好) friendly II [动] 1 (办好) sort ... out ▶善后 deal with the aftermath 2 (擅长) be an expert at 3 (容易) be prone to ▶善忘 forgetful III [副] well

善罢甘休 shàn bà gān xiū ▷你就这样打发他走，他绝不会善罢甘休的。If you send him away like that, he won't take it lying down.

善待 shàndài [动] treat ... well ▷善待朋友 treat friends well

善后 shànhòu [动] deal with the aftermath (PT, PP dealt) ▷处理事故的善后问题 deal with the aftermath of an accident

善举 shànjǔ [名] charitable act

善良 shànliáng [形] kind-hearted

善始善终 shàn shǐ shàn zhōng start well and end well

善意 shànyì [名] good intention ▷善意的提醒 a well-intentioned warning

善于 shànyú [动] be good at ▷善于绘画 be good at painting

善终 shànzhōng [动] 1 (老死) die a natural death 2 (做好最后工作) end well

禅 shàn [动] abdicate
→另见 chán

禅让 shànràng [动] abdicate

骟 shàn [动] neuter

缮 shàn [动] 1 (修补) repair 2 (书) (抄写) copy

缮写 shànxiě [动] copy ▷缮写文件 copy documents

擅 shàn I [动] be expert at ▷他擅辩。He's an expert debater. II [副] without leave ▷擅离职守 be absent without leave

擅长 shàncháng [动] be skilled in ▷擅长外交 be skilled in diplomacy ▷擅长武术 be skilled at martial arts

擅自 shànzì [动] take it upon oneself (PT took, PP taken) ▷上司不在，他擅自和客户签了协议。Since the boss was out, he took it upon himself to sign the agreement.

膳 shàn [名] (书) meal

膳食 shànshí [名] food

赡 shàn [动] support

赡养 shànyǎng [动] support ▷赡养父母 support one's parents

鳝 shàn [名] eel

伤 shāng I [动] 1 (身体部位) injure ▶扭伤 sprain ▷她伤了胳膊。She injured her arm. 2 (感情) hurt (PT, PP hurt) II [名] injury

伤残 shāngcán [名] the disabled (PL) ▷伤残军人 a disabled soldier

伤风 shāngfēng [动] catch a cold (PT, PP caught)

伤风败俗 shāng fēng bài sú offend public decency ▷这本小说被公认为伤风败俗。This novel was widely condemned as an offence to public decency.

伤感 shānggǎn [形] sentimental ▷一部伤感的电影 a sentimental film

伤害 shānghài [动] 1 (感情) hurt (PT, PP hurt) 2 (身体) damage ▷吸烟伤害身体。Smoking damages your health.

伤痕 shānghén [名] scar

伤口 shāngkǒu [名] wound

伤脑筋 shāng nǎojīn [动] be a headache ▷他让父母伤脑筋。He's a headache for his parents.

伤神 shāngshén [动] 1 (耗费精神) be stressful ▷你天天熬夜工作很伤神的。It's very stressful for you to stay up late working every night. 2 (伤心) be upset

伤天害理 shāng tiān hài lǐ do things that are against reason or nature

伤亡 shāngwáng [名] casualty

伤心 shāngxīn [形] sad

商 shāng I [动] discuss ▶磋商 consult ▶协商 negotiate II [名] 1 (商业) commerce ▶经商 trade 2 (商人) businessman (PL businessmen), businesswoman (PL businesswomen) ▶珠宝商 jeweller (英), jeweler (美) 3 (数) quotient ▷10被5除的商是2。Ten divided by five is two.

商标 shāngbiāo [名] trademark

商场 shāngchǎng [名] shopping centre (英) 或 mall (美)

商店 shāngdiàn [名] shop (英), store (美)

商定 shāngdìng [动] agree on ▷合同条款还未商定。The articles in the contract have not yet been agreed on.

商贩 shāngfàn [名] pedlar

商会 shānghuì [名] chamber of commerce

商机 shāngjī [名] business opportunity

商界 shāngjiè [名] business circles (PL)

商量 shāngliáng [动] discuss

商贸 shāngmào [名] commerce

商品 shāngpǐn [名] commodity ▷商品交易会

trade fair ▷进出口商品 the import and export of goods

商品房 shāngpǐnfáng [名] commercial housing

商洽 shāngqià [动] discuss ▷我们需要与制造商商洽。We need to discuss matters with the manufacturer.

商情 shāngqíng [名] market conditions (PL)

商榷 shāngquè [动] discuss

商人 shāngrén [名] businessman (PL businessmen), businesswoman (PL businesswomen)

商谈 shāngtán [动] negotiate

商讨 shāngtǎo [动] discuss

商务 shāngwù [名] business ▷商务谈判 business negotiation ▷电子商务 e-commerce

商业 shāngyè [名] commerce ▷商业合作 commercial collaboration ▷商业银行 merchant bank ▷商业信息 commercial information

商酌 shāngzhuó [动] deliberate over ▷商酌反恐怖法案 deliberate over the anti-terrorism bill

晌 shǎng [名] 1 (一段时间) moment 2 (方) (晌午) noon

晌午 shǎngwu [名] (口) noon

赏 shǎng I [动] 1 (赏赐) award ▷因为他的出色表现，公司赏他一辆车。Because of his outstanding performance, the company awarded him a car. 2 (欣赏) admire ▷赏月 look at the moon 3 (赏识) appreciate II [名] reward

赏赐 shǎngcì I [动] grant II [名] reward

赏罚分明 shǎng fá fēn míng [动] be fair in meting out rewards and punishments

赏光 shǎngguāng [动] (敬) visit ▷本人非常感谢您能赏光我的个人主页。Thank you very much for visiting my website.

赏鉴 shǎngjiàn [动] appreciate

赏脸 shǎngliǎn [动] (敬) do ... the honour (英) 或 honor (美) ▷请您赏脸收下这份礼物。Please do me the honour of accepting this gift.

赏识 shǎngshí [动] think highly of (PT, PP thought)

赏析 shǎngxī [动] appreciate

赏心悦目 shǎng xīn yuè mù aesthetically pleasing ▷一幅赏心悦目的山水画 an aesthetically pleasing landscape painting

上 shàng I [名] 1 (指方位) upper part ▷上游 upper stream ▷上层 upper layer 2 (指等级、质量) ▷上级 higher authorities (PL) ▷上品

high-quality products 3 (指时间、次序) ▷上个月 last month ▷上半年 the first half of the year II [动] 1 (向上) go up (PT went, PP gone) ▷上楼 go upstairs 2 (按点前往) go (PT went, PP gone) ▷上学 go to school ▶上班 go to work 3 (去) go to (PT went, PP gone) ▷他上天津开会去了。He went to Tianjin to attend a meeting. 4 (出场) make an entrance ▷上场时，队长先上。When a team makes its entrance, the captain leads the way. 5 (添补) fill ▶上货 restock 6 (饭、菜) serve ▷上菜 serve food 7 (安装) fix ▷上螺丝 fix a screw 8 (涂) apply ▷上涂料 apply paint 9 (登载) appear ▷上杂志 appear in a magazine 10 (拧紧) tighten ▷我的表已上弦了。I've wound up my watch. 11 (达到) reach ▷上岁数 reach a great age ▷上百艘船停靠在岸边。Over a hundred boats were moored on the bank. 12 (楼、山) go up (PT went, PP gone) 13 (表示从低到高) ▷我跑上楼梯。I ran up the stairs. ▷演员走上舞台。The performer walked onto the stage. 14 (表示达到目的) ▷考上大学 pass the university entrance exams ▷当上老师 become a teacher 15 (表示开始) ▷喜欢上古典音乐 come to like classical music ▷他干上了导游。He's started work as a tour guide. III [介] 1 (在物体表面) on ▷椅子上 on the chair 2 (表示范围) in ▷报纸上 in the newspaper 3 (表示某方面) ▷事实上 in fact

上班 shàngbān [动] go to work (PT went, PP gone)

上报 shàngbào [动] 1 (报告) report ▷这一急情况应及时上报。This urgent matter should be reported immediately. 2 (刊登) be in the newspaper

上辈 shàngbèi [名] 1 (祖先) ancestor 2 (上代) previous generation

上菜 shàngcài [动] serve food

上操 shàngcāo [动] do morning exercises

上策 shàngcè [名] the best plan

上层 shàngcéng [名] upper level ▷上层领导 upper echelons of leadership

上层建筑 shàngcéng jiànzhù [名] superstructure

上场 shàngchǎng [动] enter

上乘 shàngchéng [形] first-class ▷中国家具质量上乘。The quality of Chinese furniture is first class.

上蹿下跳 shàng cuàn xià tiào 1 (乱蹦) jump about ▷小丑上蹿下跳，把观众逗得哈哈大笑。The clown jumped about, and the audience burst into peals of laughter. 2 (贬) (指拉拢人) pull strings

上当 shàngdàng [动] be taken in ▷数次上当之

后，我不再信他的话了。After I'd been taken in several times, I stopped believing what he said.

上等 shàngděng [形] first-class

上帝 Shàngdì [名] God

上吊 shàngdiào [动] hang oneself (PT, PP hanged)

上访 shàngfǎng [动] appeal to the higher authorities

上坟 shàngfén [动] pay one's respects at a grave (PT, PP paid)

上风 shàngfēng [名] 1 (指风) windward 2 (喻) (有利地位) advantage ▷占上风 get the upper hand

上浮 shàngfú [动] raise

上岗 shànggǎng [动] take up a post (PT took, PP taken) ▷企业员工竞争上岗。The workers are competing for jobs.

上告 shànggào [动] 1 (告状) appeal ▷上告法院 appeal to a higher court 2 (报告) report

上钩 shànggōu [动] rise to the bait (PT rose, PP risen)

上古 shànggǔ [名] ancient times (PL)

上轨道 shàng guǐdào [动] be on the right track

上好 shànghǎo [形] top-quality ▷上好的丝绸 top-quality silk

上火 shànghuǒ [动] (方) (发怒) get angry

上货 shànghuò [动] stock up ▷新品上货 stock up on new goods

上机 shàngjī [动] use a computer

上级 shàngjí [名] higher authorities (PL) ▷上级机关 higher level organization

上将 shàngjiàng [名] general

上交 shàngjiāo [动] hand ... in

上缴 shàngjiǎo [动] hand ... over

上进 shàngjìn [动] make progress

上空 shàngkōng [名] ▷直升机在上空盘旋。A helicopter is hovering overhead.

上口 shàngkǒu I [动] flow well II [形] flowing

上来 shànglái [动] 1 (指动作趋向) ▷饭菜端上来了。The meal was brought to the table. ▷他从坑里爬上来了。He climbed out of the pit. 2 (表示成功) ▷这个问题我答不上来。I can't answer this question. 3 (指等级提升) promote ▷这名干部是从基层提拔上来的。This official was promoted from the grass roots.

上梁不正下梁歪 shàngliáng bù zhèng xiàliáng wāi those in subordinate positions will follow the example set by their superiors

上流 shàngliú I [名] upper reaches (PL) II [形] upper-class

上马 shàngmǎ [动] begin (PT began, PP begun)

上门 shàngmén [动] 1 (到家里) call on ▷他亲自上门向他们道谢。He called on them in person to offer his thanks. ▷送货上门 delivery service 2 (锁门) lock the door

上面 shàngmian [名] 1 (指位置高) ▷书桌上面挂着风铃。A windchime is hanging above the desk. ▷他住在我上面。He lives above me. 2 (物体表面) ▷墙上面挂着相片。Photographs were hanging on the walls. ▷袖子上面有墨迹。There are ink stains on the sleeve. 3 (以上的部分) ▷上面的例子很具说服力。The previous example is very persuasive. ▷上面我们分析了各种可能性。As can be seen above, we have made an analysis of all possibilities. 4 (方面) ▷他没时间花在看小说上面。He doesn't have time for reading novels. ▷他在音乐上面的造诣很深。His achievements in the field of music are considerable. 5 (上级) superior ▷上面来了指示。We have received instructions from our superiors.

上年纪 shàng niánji [动] get old ▷妈妈上了年纪，视力下降了。Mum's getting old – her eyesight is failing.

上品 shàngpǐn [名] top grade

上去 shàngqù [动] 1 (指由低到高) go up (PT went, PP gone) 2 (提高) improve

上任 shàngrèn [动] take up a new post (PT took, PP taken)

上色 shàngshǎi [动] colour (英), color (美)

上身 shàngshēn I [名] upper body II [动] put ... on (PT, PP put)

上升 shàngshēng [动] 1 (往高处移) ascend 2 (增加) increase

上市 shàngshì [动] appear on the market ▷明日有新股上市。Tomorrow the new stock will appear on the market. ▷8月桃子大量上市。In August, peaches are in season.

上手 shàngshǒu [动] start

上书 shàngshū [动] submit a statement ▷工人联名上书揭发厂长贪污受贿。The workers submitted a statement revealing how the plant manager had accepted bribes.

上司 shàngsi [名] superior

上诉 shàngsù [动] appeal

上溯 shàngsù [动] trace ... back

上算 shàngsuàn [形] worthwhile

上台 shàngtái [动] 1 (指舞台、讲台) appear on stage 2 (贬) (掌权) come to power (PT came, PP come) ▷新领导上台了。The new leader has come to power.

上天 shàngtiān I [动] 1 (升空) launch ▷人造卫星上天了。A man-made satellite was launched. **2** (死亡) (婉) pass away **II** [名] Heaven

上网 shàngwǎng [动] go online (PT went, PP gone) ▷上网查信 go online to check one's e-mail ▷上网聊天 go online to chat

上文 shàngwén [名] preceding paragraph ▷请见上文。Please see above.

上午 shàngwǔ [名] morning

上西天 shàng xītiān (口) (贬) kick the bucket

上限 shàngxiàn [名] upper limit

上相 shàngxiàng [形] photogenic

上演 shàngyǎn [动] perform

上瘾 shàngyǐn [动] be addicted to

上映 shàngyìng [动] show (PT showed, PP shown)

上游 shàngyóu [名] **1** (指河流) upper reaches (PL) **2** (先进) front rank

上涨 shàngzhǎng [动] rise (PT rose, PP risen)

上阵 shàngzhèn [动] pitch in ▷厂长亲自上阵抓生产。The boss pitched in personally in the struggle to increase production.

上座率 shàngzuòlǜ [名] box-office figures (PL)

尚 shàng **I** [动] esteem **II** [副] (书) still ▷现在下结论为还时尚早。It's still too early to jump to conclusions.

尚且 shàngqiě [连] ▷简单的对话他尚且都不懂,更何况难的了。He can't even understand simple conversations, let alone difficult ones. ▷宝宝尚且不会走路,更何况跑呢。The baby can't even walk, let alone run.

捎 shāo [动] deliver ▷捎口信 deliver a message

捎带 shāodài [副] in passing ▷每次出差我都捎带买些礼物。Every time I go away on business I always pick up presents.

烧 shāo [动] **1** (着火) burn ▷她把信烧掉了。She burned the letter. ▷房子烧了。The house was burned down. **2** (加热) heat ▷烧水 boil water **3** (烹) braise ▷红烧牛肉 beef braised in soy sauce **4** (烤) roast ▶烧鸡 roast chicken **5** (发烧) have a temperature ▷她烧到了39度。She has a temperature of 39 degrees.

烧毁 shāohuǐ [动] be burned down

烧烤 shāokǎo [动] barbecue

烧香 shāoxiāng [动] burn incense

烧灼 shāozhuó [动] burn

梢 shāo [名] top ▶树梢 treetop

稍 shāo [副] slightly ▷他比我稍矮点。He's slightly shorter than me.

→另见 shào

稍稍 shāoshāo [副] a little

稍微 shāowēi [副] a little

稍纵即逝 shāo zòng jí shì fleeting ▷商人要善于抓住稍纵即逝的市场机遇。Business people must be good at taking advantage of every fleeting window of opportunity.

艄 shāo [名] **1** (船尾) stern **2** (舵) rudder ▷撑艄 be at the helm

艄公 shāogōng [名] helmsman

勺 sháo [名] ladle

少 shǎo **I** [形] few ▷你要少吃甜食。You should eat fewer sweet things. ▷屋里家具太少。There is very little furniture in the room. **II** [动] **1** (缺) lack ▷汤里少了葱。There is no onion in the soup. **2** (丢) be missing ▷她发现自行车少了。She discovered that a bike was missing. **III** [副] ▷少等一会儿 Please wait a moment.

→另见 shào

少见多怪 shǎo jiàn duō guài ▷大千世界无奇不有,你用不着少见多怪。The world is full of miraculous things, you shouldn't be so easily impressed. ▷也许是我少见多怪,我觉得最美丽的地方莫过于桂林了。Perhaps I haven't seen much of the world, but I think nowhere is more beautiful than Guilin.

少量 shǎoliàng [名] a little ▷在汤里放少量盐。Put a little salt in the soup.

少陪 shǎopéi [动] (客套) ▷我得先走一步,少陪了。I'm afraid I really have to go.

少时 shǎoshí [名] ▷他少时就回来了。He came back after a short while. ▷少时雷雨停了,探险队又继续赶路。Before long the storm stopped and the exploration team continued on its way.

少数 shǎoshù [名] minority

少许 shǎoxǔ [形] (书) a little

少 shào **I** [形] young ▶少女 young girl **II** [名] teenager ▶阔少 rich kid

→另见 shǎo

少不更事 shàobùgēngshì green ▷新来的工人少不更事。The new workers are very green.

少妇 shàofù [名] young wife (PL wives)

少男少女 shàonán shàonǚ [名] teenagers (PL)

少年老成 shàonián lǎochéng mature beyond one's years

少女 shàonǚ [名] young girl

少相 shàoxiang [形] young-looking

少壮 shàozhuàng [形] young and strong

哨 shào [名] 1 (兵站) post ▶哨所 post 2 (哨子) whistle ▷吹哨 whistle

哨兵 shàobīng [名] sentry

哨卡 shàoqiǎ [名] sentry post

哨子 shàozi [名] whistle

稍 shào 见下文
→另见 shāo

稍息 shàoxī [动] stand at ease (PT, PP stood)

奢 shē [形] extravagant ▶奢靡 wasteful ▶奢望 high hopes (PL)

奢侈 shēchǐ [形] luxurious

奢华 shēhuá [形] sumptuous

奢求 shēqiú [动] make excessive demands

奢望 shēwàng [名] high hopes (PL)

赊 shē [动] buy ... on credit (PT, PP bought) ▶赊购 buy ... on credit

赊欠 shēqiàn [动] buy on credit (PT, PP bought)

赊账 shēzhàng [动] buy on credit (PT, PP bought)

舌 shé [名] tongue ▶火舌 flame

舌头 shétou [名] tongue

舌战 shézhàn [动] have a heated dispute

折 shé [动] 1 (折断) snap ▷树枝折了。The branch snapped. 2 (亏损) lose money (PT, PP lost)
→另见 zhē, zhé

折本 shéběn [动] lose money (PT, PP lost) ▷他把那批货折本卖掉了。He sold all of those goods at a loss.

蛇 shé [名] snake

舍 shě [动] 1 (舍弃) abandon ▷舍己为人 be altruistic 2 (施舍) give (PT gave, PP given) ▷他时常舍些钱给乞丐。He frequently gives to beggars.
→另见 shè

舍本逐末 shě běn zhú mò get one's priorities wrong ▷大学生过多参与社会活动其实是舍本逐末。Students who get too involved in social activities have got their priorities wrong.

舍己为人 shě jǐ wèi rén be altruistic ▷他舍己为人的精神令人感动。His sense of altruism is touching.

舍近求远 shě jìn qiú yuǎn go far afield ▷附近商店有各种装修材料，我们不必舍近求远。The local shops have all sorts of decorating

materials – there's no need for us to go far afield.

舍命 shěmìng [动] risk one's life

舍弃 shěqì [动] give up (PT gave, PP given)

舍身 shěshēn [动] give one's life (PT gave, PP given) ▷舍身救人 give one's life for others

设 shè [动] 1 (摆) set ... up (PT, PP set) ▷设宴 give a banquet 2 (想) plan ▶设计 work out a plan 3 (假定) suppose ▶设想 envisage

设备 shèbèi [名] equipment ▷办公设备 office equipment

设法 shèfǎ [动] try

设防 shèfáng [动] set up defences (英) 或 defenses (美) (PT, PP set)

设计 shèjì [动] design ▷服装设计 fashion design

设立 shèlì [动] establish

设身处地 shè shēn chǔ dì put oneself in another person's shoes

设施 shèshī [名] facilities (PL)

设想 shèxiǎng [动] 1 (想像) imagine 2 (着想) consider

设置 shèzhì [动] 1 (设立) set ... up (PT, PP set) ▷设置障碍 set up a barrier 2 (安装) install ▷起居室里设置了空调。Air conditioning has been installed in the living room.

社 shè [名] organization ▶报社 newspaper office ▶旅行社 travel agent

社会 shèhuì [名] society ▷国际社会 international community ▷社会福利 social welfare

社会主义 shèhuì zhǔyì [名] socialism

社交 shèjiāo [名] social contact ▷社交活动 social activity

社论 shèlùn [名] editorial

社区 shèqū [名] community ▷社区服务 community service

社团 shètuán [名] organization

舍 shè [名] house ▶宿舍 dormitory
→另见 shě

射 shè [动] 1 (发) shoot (PT, PP shot) ▷射箭 shoot an arrow 2 (喷) spout ▶喷射 spurt 3 (放出) emit ▶照射 shine

射程 shèchéng [名] range

射击 shèjī I [动] fire II [名] shooting

射门 shèmén [动] shoot (PT, PP shot)

射线 shèxiàn [名] 1 (电磁波) ray 2 (数) straight line

射影 shèyǐng [名] projection

涉 shè [动] 1 (渡) cross ▷跋山涉水 cross mountains and rivers 2 (经历) go through (PT went, PP gone) ▶涉险 go through dangerous situations 3 (牵涉) involve ▶涉嫌 be a suspect

涉及 shèjí [动] involve ▷走私案涉及海关和警方。 The smuggling case involves Customs and the police. ▷这个问题书里面没涉及到。 The book does not touch on this question.

涉猎 shèliè [动] 1 (浏览) browse ▷这类书只需涉猎就行了。 It's enough just to browse through a book like this. 2 (接触) touch

涉世 shèshì [动] have experience of life ▷他涉世不深，常常受骗。 He has little experience of life and is always getting cheated.

涉嫌 shèxián [动] be a suspect

赦 shè [动] pardon

赦免 shèmiǎn [动] pardon

摄 shè [动] 1 (吸取) absorb 2 (摄影) take a photo (PT took, PP taken) 3 (代理) act for

摄取 shèqǔ [动] 1 (吸收) take in (PT took, PP taken) 2 (拍摄) take a photo of

摄像 shèxiàng [动] make a video

摄影 shèyǐng [动] 1 (照相) take a photo (PT took, PP taken) 2 (拍电影) shoot a film (英) 或 movie (美) (PT, PP shot)

摄制 shèzhì [动] produce ▷摄制电影 produce a film (英) 或 movie (美)

慑 shè [动] (书) fear

慑服 shèfú [动] 1 (屈服) submit 2 (使屈服) make … submit

谁 shéi [代] 1 (表示问人) who ▷谁在门外？ Who's at the door? 2 (指任何一个人) whoever ▷谁先到谁买票。 Whoever arrives first buys the tickets.

申 shēn [动] express

申办 shēnbàn [动] 1 (申请举办) bid for (PT, PP bid) ▷申办奥运会 bid for the Olympics 2 (申请办理) apply for ▷申办寿险 apply for a pension

申报 shēnbào [动] declare

申辩 shēnbiàn [动] defend oneself

申斥 shēnchì [动] reprimand

申明 shēnmíng [动] declare

申请 shēnqǐng [动] apply ▷申请工作 apply for a job

申诉 shēnsù [动] appeal

申冤 shēnyuān [动] 1 (昭雪冤屈) get justice 2 (申诉冤屈) appeal for justice

伸 shēn [动] stretch ▶伸懒腰 stretch oneself

伸手 shēnshǒu [动] 1 (伸出手) hold out one's hand (PT, PP held) 2 (索要) ask for help

伸缩 shēnsuō [动] 1 (伸展和收缩) expand and contract 2 (变通) be flexible

伸展 shēnzhǎn [动] stretch

伸张 shēnzhāng [动] uphold (PT, PP upheld)

身 shēn I [名] 1 (身体) body ▷身强力壮 be strong and fit 2 (生命) life ▷舍身 lay down one's life 3 (自己) oneself ▷以身作则 set a good example (with one's own conduct) 4 (品德) moral character 5 (部分) body ▷车身 body (of a car) II [量] 一身新衣 a set of new clothes

身败名裂 shēn bài míng liè be utterly discredited

身不由己 shēn bù yóu jǐ not be able to help oneself ▷他社交活动太多，确实身不由己。 He's got himself involved in so many activities – he just can't help himself.

身材 shēncái [名] figure

身段 shēnduàn [名] figure

身份 shēnfen [名] 1 (地位) position 2 (尊严) dignity

身份证 shēnfènzhèng [名] identity card

身价 shēnjià [名] social status

身教 shēnjiào [动] teach by example (PT, PP taught)

身经百战 shēn jīng bǎi zhàn be seasoned ▷这位球星身经百战。 This football star is a seasoned player.

身临其境 shēn lín qí jìng actually be there ▷这幅油画使人有身临其境之感。 This painting makes you feel you are actually there.

身强力壮 shēn qiáng lì zhuàng tough

身躯 shēnqū [名] body

身世 shēnshì [名] life experience

身手 shēnshǒu [名] skill

身受 shēnshòu [动] experience … personally

身体 shēntǐ [名] body

身体力行 shēn tǐ lì xíng practise (英) 或 practice (美) what one preaches ▷当领导身体力行非常重要。 It's very important for a leader to practise what he preaches.

身外之物 shēn wài zhī wù worldly things ▷金钱和荣誉都是身外之物。 Money and fame are worldly things.

身心 shēnxīn [名] body and mind ▷身心健康 physical and mental health

身孕 shēnyùn [名] pregnancy ▷她有了身孕。 She is pregnant.

身子 shēnzi [名] (口) 1 (身体) body ▷她生病后

身子很弱。Since she became ill she has been very weak. **2** (身孕) pregnancy ▷她已有了3个月的身子。She is three months pregnant.

呻 shēn 见下文
呻吟 shēnyín [动] groan

参 shēn [名] ginseng
→另见 cān, cēn

绅 shēn [名] gentry
绅士 shēnshì [名] gentleman

深 shēn I [形] **1** (指深度) deep ▶深水 deep water **2** (距离远) remote ▶深山 remote mountain **3** (深奥) difficult ▷这本书对孩子来说太深了。This book is too difficult for children. **4** (深刻) deep ▷我对老经理的印象特别深。My old boss left a deep impression on me. **5** (密切) close ▷我和父母的感情都很深。I am very close to my parents. **6** (浓重) dark ▶深蓝 dark blue **7** (指时间久) late ▶深夜 late at night II [名] depth ▷这口井有10米深。This well is 10 metres (英) 或 meters (美) deep. III [副] very ▶深信不疑 firmly believe
深奥 shēn'ào [形] profound
深层 shēncéng [名] the depths (PL) ▷雨水渗到了土壤的深层。The rain has seeped deep into the soil. ▷深层原因 underlying reason
深沉 shēnchén [形] deep ▷暮色深沉。The dusk is deepening. ▷他的嗓音深沉。He has a deep voice. ▷我哥哥很深沉。My brother is a deep one.
深仇大恨 shēn chóu dà hèn deep hatred
深度 shēndù I [名] depth ▷测量油井的深度 gauge the depth of an oil well ▷这篇文章缺乏深度。This essay lacks depth. II [形] extreme ▷深度近视 extreme short-sightedness
深更半夜 shēngēng-bànyè in the dead of night
深广 shēnguǎng [形] broad
深厚 shēnhòu [形] **1** (浓重) deep **2** (坚实) solid
深化 shēnhuà [动] deepen
深究 shēnjiū [动] get to the bottom of
深居简出 shēn jū jiǎn chū be a recluse
深刻 shēnkè [形] deep ▷首相的讲话给我留下深刻的印象。The prime minister's speech made a deep impression on me.
深明大义 shēn míng dàyì be principled ▷父亲深明大义，送儿子去投案自首。The father was very principled: he sent his son to give himself up.
深谋远虑 shēn móu yuǎn lù think ahead ▷决策者需要深谋远虑。Policy makers need to think ahead.
深浅 shēnqiǎn [名] **1** (深度) depth **2** (分寸) sense of propriety ▷他说话没深浅。He often speaks inappropriately.
深切 shēnqiè [形] **1** (深厚) heartfelt ▷对朋友们深切的关怀我非常感谢。Many thanks to my friends for their heartfelt concern. **2** (切实) deep ▷我对这种事有深切的体会。I have a deep understanding of these things.
深情 shēnqíng [名] deep feeling
深情厚谊 shēn qíng hòu yì [名] deep friendship
深入 shēnrù I [动] penetrate II [形] thorough
深入浅出 shēn rù qiǎn chū explain difficult concepts simply
深山 shēnshān [名] remote mountains (PL)
深思 shēnsī [动] reflect on
深思熟虑 shēn sī shú lù careful consideration ▷购房时一定要深思熟虑。When buying a house you must give it careful consideration.
深邃 shēnsuì [形] **1** (距离远) deep **2** (深奥) profound
深恶痛绝 shēn wù tòng jué detest
深信 shēnxìn [动] believe deeply
深渊 shēnyuān [名] abyss
深远 shēnyuǎn [形] far-reaching
深造 shēnzào [动] pursue advanced studies
深湛 shēnzhàn [形] profound
深重 shēnzhòng [形] serious

什 shén 见下文
→另见 shí
什么 shénme [代] **1** (表示疑问) what ▷你要什么? What do you want? **2** (表示虚指) something ▷他们在商量着什么。They are discussing something. **3** (表示任指) anything ▷我什么都不怕。I'm not afraid of anything. **4** (表示惊讶、不满) what ▷什么! 他拒绝出席会议! What! He refused to attend the meeting! ▷这是什么菜! 一点都不好吃。What sort of food is this? It's disgusting. **5** (表示责难) ▷你在胡说什么! What's that rubbish? **6** (表示不同意) ▷什么不好意思? 她脸皮厚得很。What do you mean she's embarrassed? She's very thick-skinned. **7** (表示例举不尽) ▷什么水果、酸奶、糖果，她都爱吃。She likes eating things like fruit, yoghurt and sweets.
什么的 shénmede [代] ▷餐桌上摆满了香蕉、李子、苹果什么的。The dining table was loaded with bananas, plums, apples and so on.

神 shén I [名] 1 (宗) god ▶鬼神 supernatural beings (PL) 2 (精神) spirit ▶走神 be absent-minded II [形] 1 (高超) amazing ▶神奇 magical 2 (方) (聪明) clever ▷你可真神！How clever you are!

神不守舍 shén bù shǒu shè drift off ▷他在课堂上总是神不守舍。He's always drifting off in class.

神采 shéncǎi [名] demeanour

神出鬼没 shén chū guǐ mò come and go ▷那批人神出鬼没，居无定所。That bunch come and go – they don't live anywhere permanently.

神乎其神 shén hū qí shén so wonderful ▷这是一个神乎其神的传说。This is such a wonderful legend.

神化 shénhuà [动] deify

神话 shénhuà [名] myth

神魂颠倒 shén hún diān dǎo be infatuated ▷他被那女人弄得神魂颠倒。He's become infatuated with that woman.

神机妙算 shén jī miào suàn have foresight

神经 shénjīng [名] nerve ▷神经系统 nervous system

神灵 shénlíng [名] spirit

神秘 shénmì [形] mysterious

神明 shénmíng [名] god

神奇 shénqí [形] magical

神气 shénqì I [名] manner ▷他说话的神气很严肃。His manner as he spoke was serious. II [形] 1 (精神) impressive ▷他穿上西装显得很神气。He looks impressive in a suit. 2 (得意) cocky

神情 shénqíng [名] expression

神色 shénsè [名] look

神圣 shénshèng [形] sacred

神思 shénsī [名] state of mind

神似 shénsì [形] lifelike

神速 shénsù [形] incredibly fast

神态 shéntài [名] look

神通 shéntōng [名] remarkable ability

神往 shénwǎng [动] be amazed ▷桂林山水令人神往。The scenery around Guilin is amazing.

神仙 shénxiān [名] immortal

神学 shénxué [名] theology

神志 shénzhì [名] mind

审 shěn I [形] careful ▶审慎 cautious II [动] 1 (审查) go over (PT went, PP gone) ▷审稿 review 2 (审讯) try ▷审案 try a case

审查 shěnchá [动] examine

审订 shěndìng [动] revise

审定 shěndìng [动] examine and approve

审核 shěnhé [动] verify

审计 shěnjì [动] audit

审理 shěnlǐ [动] hear (PT, PP heard)

审美 shěnměi [动] appreciate

审判 shěnpàn [动] try

审批 shěnpī [动] examine and approve

审慎 shěnshèn [形] cautious

审时度势 shěn shí duó shì take stock of a situation

审视 shěnshì [动] examine ... closely

审问 shěnwèn [动] interrogate

审讯 shěnxùn [动] interrogate

审议 shěnyì [动] consider

审阅 shěnyuè [动] check

婶 shěn [名] aunt

肾 shèn [名] kidney

甚 shèn I [形] extreme ▷欺人太甚 be too high-handed II [副] very ▷这家饭店的服务甚佳。The service at this restaurant is very good.

甚至 shènzhì I [副] even ▷父亲去世后，他痛苦得甚至无法工作。After his father passed away, he was so distressed he couldn't even work. II [连] ▷对职员们的相继辞职，老板感到遗憾甚至痛苦。The boss felt regret, even distress, about the spate of resignations. ▷在巴西，不但年轻人，甚至老年人都喜欢足球。In Brazil everybody loves football, not just the young, but older people too.

渗 shèn [动] seep

渗漏 shènlòu [动] leak

渗入 shènrù 1 (液体) seep into 2 (势力等) penetrate

渗透 shèntòu [动] 1 (液体、气体) permeate 2 (抽象事物) infiltrate

蜃 shèn 见下文

蜃景 shènjǐng [名] mirage

慎 shèn [形] careful

慎重 shènzhòng [形] cautious

升 shēng I [动] 1 (由低往高) rise (PT rose, PP risen) 2 (提升) promote ▶升职 be promoted II [量] litre (英), liter (美) ▷1升牛奶 a litre of milk

升格 shēnggé [动] promote ▷他由系主任升格为校长。He was promoted from head of department to principal.

升华 shēnghuá [动] **1** (物) sublimate **2** (升级) distil (英), distill (美)

升级 shēngjí [动] **1** (升高年级) go up (PT went, PP gone) ▷我儿子将升到2年级。My son will go up into year two (英) 或 second grade (美). **2** (规模扩大) escalate ▷战争还在升级。The war continues to escalate.

升级换代 shēng jí huàn dài upgrade

升迁 shēngqiān [动] get promoted and transferred to a different department

升天 shēngtiān [动] die

升学 shēngxué [动] move to a more advanced school

升值 shēngzhí [动] appreciate

生 shēng I [动] **1** (生育) give birth to (PT gave, PP given) ▷生孩子 have a baby **2** (长) grow (PT grew, PP grown) ▷生根 take root **3** (活) live ▷生死 life and death **4** (患) get (PT got, PP got (英), gotten (美)) ▷生病 get ill **5** (点) light (PT, PP lit) ▶生火 light a fire II [名] **1** (生命) life (PL lives) ▷求生 eke out a living **2** (生平) life (PL lives) ▷今生 this life **3** (学生) student ▶新生 new student ▶小学生 primary school pupil (英), elementary school student (美) III [形] **1** (活的) living ▶生物 living things **2** (未熟的) unripe ▷生苹果 unripe apples **3** (未煮的) raw ▷生鱼片 slices of raw fish **4** (未加工的) crude ▶生铁 crude iron **5** (生疏) unfamiliar ▶生人 stranger **6** (生硬) stiff ▷这个句子是生凑的。This sentence is awkwardly put together. IV [副] very ▶生疼 very painful

生搬硬套 shēng bān yìng tào copy ... mechanically ▷对别人的学习方法不能生搬硬套。One should not mechanically copy other students' study methods.

生产 shēngchǎn [动] **1** (制造) produce **2** (生孩子) give birth to (PT gave, PP given)

生产线 shēngchǎnxiàn [名] production line

生辰 shēngchén [名] birthday

生存 shēngcún [动] survive

生动 shēngdòng [形] lively

生还 shēnghuán [动] survive

生活 shēnghuó I [名] life ▷提高生活质量 improve quality of life ▷日常生活 daily life II [动] **1** (居住) live ▷他从小和祖母一起生活。He's lived with his grandmother since he was little. **2** (生存) survive ▷没有水，人就不能生活。Without water, human beings can't survive.

生机 shēngjī [名] **1** (生存机会) lease of life ▷一线生机 a chance of survival **2** (活力) life ▷春天来了，大地充满生机。It's spring and the earth is teeming with life.

生计 shēngjì [名] make a living

生就 shēngjiù [动] be born with

生来 shēnglái [副] ▷人生来是平等的。All human beings are born equal.

生离死别 shēng lí sǐ bié part forever

生理 shēnglǐ [名] physiology

生力军 shēnglìjūn [名] **1** (指军队) new troops (PL) **2** (指人员) fresh blood

生灵 shēnglíng [名] (书) (生命) the people (PL)

生龙活虎 shēng lóng huó hǔ full of energy

生路 shēnglù [名] way out

生命 shēngmìng [名] life (PL lives) ▷挽救生命 save a life ▷生命科学 life science

生命力 shēngmìnglì [名] vitality

生命线 shēngmìngxiàn [名] lifeblood

生怕 shēngpà [副] ▷我生怕着凉，多盖了条毯子。So as not to get cold, I put on another blanket. ▷我睡觉时把钱放在枕头下，生怕贼偷了去。I slept with all my money under my pillow for fear of thieves.

生僻 shēngpì [形] obscure

生平 shēngpíng [名] one's life ▷我生平从未感到这么震惊过。I have never been so astonished in my whole life.

生气 shēngqì I [动] get angry II [名] vitality

生趣 shēngqù [名] life's pleasures

生人 shēngrén [名] stranger

生日 shēngrì [名] birthday

生色 shēngsè [动] add colour (英) 或 color (美) to

生身父母 shēngshēn fùmǔ [名] natural parents (PL)

生事 shēngshì [动] make trouble

生手 shēngshǒu [名] ▷我刚来，是个生手。I've just arrived and am new to the job.

生疏 shēngshū [形] **1** (没接触过的) unfamiliar **2** (不熟练的) rusty **3** (疏远的) distant

生死存亡 shēng sǐ cún wáng of vital importance

生死攸关 shēng sǐ yōu guān a matter of life and death

生死与共 shēng sǐ yǔ gòng live and die side by side

生态 shēngtài [名] ecology

生吞活剥 shēng tūn huó bō adopt ... wholesale ▷学习他国经验不能生吞活剥。When learning from the experience of other countries, it's no good adopting everything wholesale.

生物 shēngwù [名] living things (PL)

生物学 shēngwùxué [名] biology

生息 shēngxī [名] **1** (取得利息) bear interest (PT bore, PP borne) **2** (书) (生存) live

生肖 shēngxiào [名] animal of the Chinese zodiac

生效 shēngxiào [动] come into effect (PT came, PP come)

生性 shēngxìng [名] disposition

生涯 shēngyá [名] career

生意 shēngyi [名] business

生硬 shēngyìng [形] 1 (不自然) unnatural 2 (不柔和) rigid

生育 shēngyù [动] give birth to (PT gave, PP given)

生长 shēngzhǎng [动] 1 (植物) grow (PT grew, PP grown) 2 (生物) grow up (PT grew, PP grown)

生殖 shēngzhí [动] reproduce

生字 shēngzì [名] new word

声 shēng I [名] 1 (声音) sound ▷歌声 song 2 (名声) reputation ▷声誉 fame II [动] make a sound ▷不声不响 silent

声辩 shēngbiàn [动] argue

声波 shēngbō [名] sound wave

声称 shēngchēng [动] claim ▷他声称将把所有财产捐献给慈善机构。 He claims he will give all his money to charity.

声带 shēngdài [名] vocal cords (PL)

声调 shēngdiào [名] tone

声东击西 shēng dōng jī xī decoy tactics ▷这位将军作战时善于声东击西。 In war this general is excellent at decoy tactics.

声价 shēngjià [名] reputation

声明 shēngmíng [动] state ▷联合声明 joint statement

声色 shēngsè [名] voice and expression ▷不动声色 maintain one's composure

声势 shēngshì [名] power and influence

声嘶力竭 shēng sī lì jié hoarse

声讨 shēngtǎo [动] condemn

声望 shēngwàng [名] prestige

声息 shēngxī [名] 1 (声音) noise 2 (消息) information

声响 shēngxiǎng [名] noise

声言 shēngyán [动] declare

声音 shēngyīn [名] 1 (指人) voice 2 (指物) sound

声誉 shēngyù [名] reputation

声援 shēngyuán [动] publicly support

声乐 shēngyuè [名] (音) vocal music

声张 shēngzhāng [动] disclose

牲 shēng [名] 1 (家畜) domestic animal 2 (祭神的牲畜) animal sacrifice

牲畜 shēngchù [名] livestock

牲口 shēngkou [名] beast of burden

甥 shēng [名] nephew

甥女 shēngnǚ [名] niece

绳 shéng I [名] rope II [动] (书) restrain

绳子 shéngzi [名] rope

省 shěng I [动] 1 (节约) save ▷省钱 save money 2 (免掉) leave ... out (PT, PP left) II [名] province ▷广东省 Guangdong Province →另见 xǐng

省城 shěngchéng [名] provincial capital

省吃俭用 shěng chī jiǎn yòng live frugally

省会 shěnghuì [名] provincial capital

省略 shěnglüè [动] leave ... out (PT, PP left)

省事 shěngshì [动] save trouble ▷请人装修房子比自己动手省事很多。 Having someone else decorate your house is much simpler than doing it yourself.

省心 shěngxīn [动] save worry ▷雇了个保姆，我省心多了。 Hiring a nanny has saved me a lot of worry.

圣 shèng I [形] holy ▷神圣 sacred II [名] 1 (圣人) sage 2 (帝王) emperor

圣诞 shèngdàn [名] Christmas

圣地 shèngdì [名] 1 (宗) the Holy Land 2 (名胜) sacred place

圣洁 shèngjié [形] holy and pure

圣经 Shèngjīng [名] the Bible

圣人 shèngrén [名] sage

圣贤 shèngxián [名] saint

胜 shèng I [动] 1 (赢) win (PT, PP won) ▷这次竞赛我们胜了。 We won the competition. 2 (打败) defeat ▷曼联又胜了对手。 Manchester United again defeated their opponents. 3 (好于) be better than ▷实际行动胜过动人的言辞。 Actions speak louder than words. II [形] superb ▷胜景 wonderful scenery

胜地 shèngdì [名] scenic area

胜迹 shèngjì [名] historical site

胜利 shènglì [动] 1 (打败对方) be victorious 2 (获得成功) be successful

胜券 shèngquàn [名] confidence in one's own success

胜任 shèngrèn [动] be qualified

胜诉 shèngsù [动] win a lawsuit (PT, PP won)

盛 shèng I [形] 1 (兴盛) flourishing ▷牡丹花开得盛极了。 The peonies are in full bloom. 2 (强

烈) intense ▷森林大火烧得很盛。The forest fire is intense. **3** (盛大) grand ▶盛宴 sumptuous dinner **4** (深厚) abundant ▶盛情 great kindness **5** (盛行) popular ▷这种款式今年很盛。This style is popular this year. **II** [副] deeply ▶盛赞 highly praise
➔另见 chéng

盛产 shèngchǎn [动] produce large quantities of ▷该地区盛产煤。This region produces large quantities of coal.

盛传 shèngchuán [动] spread (PT, PP spread)

盛大 shèngdà [形] magnificent

盛典 shèngdiǎn [名] grand ceremony

盛会 shènghuì [名] grand assembly

盛举 shèngjǔ [名] grand event

盛况 shèngkuàng [名] grand occasion

盛怒 shèngnù [动] be in a rage

盛气凌人 shèng qì líng rén overbearing

盛情 shèngqíng [名] great kindness

盛世 shèngshì [名] heyday

盛夏 shèngxià [名] midsummer

盛行 shèngxíng [动] be in fashion

盛誉 shèngyù [名] fame

盛装 shèngzhuāng [名] best clothes (PL)

剩 shèng [动] be left ▷买完东西后，我还剩 10镑钱。After I'd been shopping, I still had ten pounds left.

剩余 shèngyú [动] be left

尸 shī [名] corpse

尸体 shītǐ [名] corpse

尸体解剖 shītǐ jiěpōu [名] post-mortem

失 shī **I** [动] **1** (丢失) lose (PT, PP lost) ▷他 失血过多。He lost a lot of blood. **2** (改变) deviate ▶失色 turn pale **3** (未得到) fail ▶失 望 be disappointed **4** (背弃) break (PT broke, PP broken) ▷失信 break a promise **II** [名] mistake ▶过失 error

失败 shībài [动] fail ▷卫星发射失败了。The satellite launch was unsuccessful. ▷他雅思 考试又失败了。He failed IELTS again. ▷我 军在那次战斗中遭到了失败。Our army was defeated in that battle.

失策 shīcè [动] be unwise ▷公司投资失策。The company invested unwisely.

失常 shīcháng [动] be odd ▷在学校，他的表现 失常。At school he behaves very oddly.

失传 shīchuán [动] be lost ▷造剑的手艺失传 了。The art of swordmaking has been lost.

失聪 shīcōng [动] go deaf (PT went, PP gone)

失掉 shīdiào [动] **1** (失去) lose (PT, PP lost) ▷失 掉职位 lose one's job **2** (错过) miss ▷失掉机会 miss a chance

失和 shīhé [动] become estranged (PT became, PP become)

失衡 shīhéng [动] become unbalanced (PT became, PP become) ▷因为不吃蔬菜，他营养 失衡。Because he's not eating vegetables his nutrition has become unbalanced.

失火 shīhuǒ [动] catch fire (PT, PP caught)

失控 shīkòng [动] be out of control ▷森林大火 失控了。The forest fire is out of control.

失礼 shīlǐ [动] **1** (违背礼节) be rude ▷戴手套握 手被认为是失礼。Wearing gloves to shake hands is considered rude. **2** (客套) (表示歉意) ▷让您久等了，失礼！失礼！I'm very sorry to have kept you waiting so long.

失利 shīlì [动] lose (PT, PP lost)

失恋 shīliàn [动] be jilted

失灵 shīlíng [动] not work

失落 shīluò [形] **1** (遗失的) lost ▷失落的文明 a lost civilization **2** (低沉) dejected ▷他找不到 工作，心里非常失落。He can't find a job and is feeling very dejected.

失眠 shīmián [动] be unable to sleep

失眠症 shīmiánzhèng [名] insomnia

失明 shīmíng [动] go blind (PT went, PP gone)

失陪 shīpéi [动] (客套) ▷我有事，先失陪了。I have something to do, so please excuse me if I leave now.

失窃 shīqiè [动] be stolen

失散 shīsàn [动] be separated from ▷他终于 找到了失散多年的女儿。He finally found the daughter he had been separated from for many years.

失声 shīshēng [动] **1** (指哭泣) be choked with tears **2** (指唱歌) ▷这位歌手在演唱时突然 失声。When this singer was performing, his voice suddenly cracked.

失实 shīshí [动] be false

失事 shīshì [动] have an accident

失手 shīshǒu [动] let ... slip (PT, PP let) ▷我失 手打破了花瓶。I let the vase slip and it broke. ▷上届奥运会冠军意外失手，卫冕失败。The previous Olympic champion let the contest slip through his fingers and lost the title. ▷他失手 打了哥哥。He lost control and hit his brother.

失守 shīshǒu [动] be taken

失算 shīsuàn [动] miscalculate

失态 shītài [动] forget oneself (PT forgot, PP forgotten)

失调 shītiáo [动] **1** (比例不均) lose balance (PT,

PP lost) ▷大学生男女比例失调。There is a disproportionate ratio of men to women at university. **2** (调养不当) lack proper care

失望 shīwàng **I** [形] disappointed **II** [动] lose hope (PT, PP lost) ▷球迷对中国足球队永远失望了。The fans have lost all hope in the Chinese football team.

失误 shīwù [动] slip up

失效 shīxiào [动] **1** (不起作用) stop working ▷电池失效了。The battery has run out. **2** (没有法力) be no longer valid

失信 shīxìn [动] go back on one's word (PT went, PP gone)

失学 shīxué [动] drop out of school

失业 shīyè [动] be unemployed, be out of work ▷失业人口在增加。Unemployment is rising.

失意 shīyì [形] disappointed

失约 shīyuē [动] fail to show up ▷我们约好今早见面，可她失约了。We had an arrangement to meet this morning, but she didn't show up.

失真 shīzhēn [动] be unclear ▷传真照片经常失真。Faxed photos are often unclear. ▷录音里的声音完全失真了。The recording was completely distorted.

失职 shīzhí [动] neglect one's duty

失主 shīzhǔ [名] owner (of lost property)

失踪 shīzōng [动] be missing

失足 shīzú [动] **1** (跌倒) slip **2** (犯法) go off the rails (PT went, PP gone)

师 shī [名] **1** (老师) teacher **2** (军) division

师范 shīfàn [名] (指学院) teacher training college

师父 shīfu [名] master

师傅 shīfu [名] (口) master

师长 shīzhǎng [名] teacher

师资 shīzī [名] teachers (PL)

诗 shī [名] poetry ▷自由诗 free verse

诗歌 shīgē [名] poetry ▷诗歌朗诵 poetry reading

诗篇 shīpiān [名] poem

诗人 shīrén [名] poet

诗坛 shītán [名] the poetry world

虱 shī [名] louse (PL lice)

狮 shī 见下文

狮子 shīzi [名] lion

施 shī [动] **1** (实行) carry ... out ▷施工 construct **2** (给予) exert ▶施压 exert pressure **3** (肥料) apply ▶施肥 spread fertilizer

施工 shīgōng [动] construct ▷施工现场 construction site

施加 shījiā [动] exert

施舍 shīshě **I** [动] give (PT gave, PP given) **II** [名] charity

施行 shīxíng [动] (执行) implement

施展 shīzhǎn [动] put ... to good use (PT, PP put) ▷施展本领 put one's abilities to good use

湿 shī [形] wet

湿度 shīdù [名] humidity

湿漉漉 shīlūlū [形] damp

湿润 shīrùn [形] moist

嘘 shī [叹] shush
→另见 xū

十 shí [名] ten

十恶不赦 shí è bù shè irredeemably evil ▷十恶不赦的杀人犯 evil murderer

十二分 shí'èrfēn [形] a hundred per cent ▷我对赢得比赛有十二分的信心。I'm one hundred per cent confident of winning the competition.

十分 shífēn [副] extremely ▷我十分满意。I'm extremely satisfied.

十进制 shíjìnzhì [名] decimal system

十拿九稳 shí ná jiǔ wěn practically certain ▷这场球赛，教练是十拿九稳。The coach is practically certain of winning the match.

十全十美 shí quán shí měi perfect in every way

十字架 shízìjià [名] cross

十足 shízú [形] complete ▷他是个十足的笨蛋。He's a complete idiot.

什 shí 见下文
→另见 shén

什锦 shíjǐn [形] mixed

石 shí [名] stone

石沉大海 shí chén dà hǎi elicit no response ▷我写给他的信石沉大海。The letter I wrote him elicited no response.

石窟 shíkū [名] grotto

石器时代 shíqì shídài [名] the Stone Age

石油 shíyóu [名] oil ▷石油工业 the oil industry

时 shí [名] **1** (指时间单位) hour ▷钟表要报时了。The clock is about to strike the hour. ▷营业时间是从上午9时到下午5时。Business hours are from 9 a.m. to 5 p.m. **2** (指规定时间) time ▶准时 on time **3** (时常) ▷天气时冷

时热。The weather fluctuates between hot and cold. **4** (时尚) fashion ▶入时 fashionable ▶过时 out-of-date **5** (时候) time ▶当时 at that time **6** (机会) opportunity ▶失时 miss an opportunity **7** (语法) tense ▷过去时 past tense

时差 shíchā [名] time difference

时常 shícháng [副] often

时代 shídài [名] **1** (指时期) age ▷信息时代 the information age **2** (指人生) period ▷青年时代 youth ▷少年时代 childhood

时代精神 shídài jīngshén [名] spirit of the age

时而 shí'ér [副] sometimes ▷电脑时而出故障。The computer sometimes plays up. ▷他精神失常了,时而大哭,时而大笑。He's psychologically unbalanced – one moment he's in floods of tears, the next he's laughing uncontrollably.

时光 shíguāng [名] (书) time ▷时光飞逝。Time flies.

时过境迁 shí guò jìng qiān things have changed

时候 shíhou [名] time ▷你什么时候上班? What time do you go to work? ▷时候不早了,我们该睡觉了。It's late, and we should go to bed.

时机 shíjī [名] opportunity

时间 shíjiān [名] time ▷时间到了。Time's up! ▷他不抓紧时间。He didn't make the best use of his time. ▷办公时间 working hours

时局 shíjú [名] political situation

时刻 shíkè I [名] moment ▷紧急时刻 critical moment II [副] constantly ▷士兵们时刻准备战斗。The soldiers are ready for combat at all times.

时刻表 shíkèbiǎo [名] timetable (英), schedule (美)

时来运转 shíláiyùnzhuǎn have a change of luck ▷她时来运转,当上了女主角。She's lucky enough to be playing the female lead.

时髦 shímáo [形] fashionable

时期 shíqī [名] period

时区 shíqū [名] time zone

时尚 shíshàng [名] fad

时时 shíshí [副] often

时势 shíshì [名] current trend

时事 shíshì [名] current affairs (PL)

时下 shíxià [名] current

时兴 shíxīng [动] be in fashion

时装 shízhuāng [名] fashion

识 shí I [动] know (PT knew, PP known) II [名]

knowledge

识别 shíbié [动] distinguish

识货 shíhuò [动] have a discerning eye for goods

识趣 shíqù [形] tactful

实 shí I [形] **1** (实心) solid ▷这玻璃球里面是实的。This ball is solid glass. **2** (真实) true ▶实话 truth II [名] reality

实地 shídì [副] ▷记者在进行实地报道。The journalist is reporting on the spot.

实干 shígàn [动] get on with the job

实惠 shíhuì I [名] material benefit II [形] solid

实际 shíjì I [名] reality II [形] **1** (实有的) real **2** (合乎事实的) practical

实价 shíjià [名] actual price

实践 shíjiàn I [动] practise (英), practice (美) II [名] practice

实况 shíkuàng [名] ▷电视台将实况转播世界杯决赛。The TV station will broadcast the World Cup final live.

实力 shílì [名] strength

实情 shíqíng [名] actual state of affairs ▷他一点不了解实情。He doesn't understand the actual situation at all.

实施 shíshī [动] implement

实事求是 shí shì qiú shì based on solid evidence

实体 shítǐ [名] entity

实物 shíwù [名] material object

实习 shíxí [动] practise (英), practice (美)

实习生 shíxíshēng [名] trainee

实现 shíxiàn [动] realize

实效 shíxiào [名] actual effect ▷这种教学方法很有实效。This kind of teaching method is very effective.

实心 shíxīn [形] (指物体) solid

实行 shíxíng [动] put ... into practice (PT, PP put)

实验 shíyàn I [动] test II [名] experiment

实验室 shíyànshì [名] laboratory

实业 shíyè [名] industry

实业家 shíyèjiā [名] industrialist

实用 shíyòng [形] practical

实在 shízài I [形] honest II [副] really ▷我实在不明白。I really don't understand.

实质 shízhì [名] essence ▷这两种现象实质不一样。These two phenomena are essentially different. ▷改革取得了实质的进展。The reforms have made substantial headway.

拾 shí I [动] pick ... up II [数] an elaborate form of "ten", used in writing cheques etc to prevent mistakes and forgery

拾掇 shíduo [动] (整理) tidy ... up

食 shí I [动] eat (PT ate, PP eaten) ▶食肉动物 carnivore II [名] 1 (食物) food ▶主食 staple ▶狗食 dog food 2 (指天体) eclipse ▶日食 solar eclipse

食粮 shíliáng [名] 1 (食物) grain 2 (喻) (指精神) food for the soul

食量 shíliàng [名] appetite

食品 shípǐn [名] food

食谱 shípǔ [名] recipe

食堂 shítáng [名] canteen

食物 shíwù [名] food

食言 shíyán [动] break a promise (PT broke, PP broken)

食用 shíyòng [形] edible

食欲 shíyù [名] appetite

蚀 shí [动] erode

蚀本 shíběn [动] lose one's capital (PT, PP lost)

史 shǐ [名] history

史册 shǐcè [名] (书) annals (PL)

史迹 shǐjì [名] historical remains (PL)

史料 shǐliào [名] historical data (PL)

史前 shǐqián [名] prehistory ▷史前文明 prehistoric civilization

史诗 shǐshī [名] epic

史实 shǐshí [名] historical fact

史书 shǐshū [名] historical record

史无前例 shǐ wú qián lì unprecedented

史学 shǐxué [名] history

矢 shǐ [名] (书) arrow

矢口否认 shǐkǒu fǒurèn flatly deny

使 shǐ I [动] 1 (使用) use ▷他不会使电脑。 He can't use a computer. ▷电子词典很好 使。Electronic dictionaries are very easy to use. 2 (让) make (PT, PP made) ▷服务员的 恶劣态度使顾客很不满意。The assistants' appalling attitude made the customers quite upset. ▷他使父母失望了。He disappointed his parents. II [名] envoy ▶大使 ambassador

使馆 shǐguǎn [名] embassy ▷中国驻英国使馆 the Chinese embassy in the UK

使坏 shǐhuài [动] play tricks

使唤 shǐhuan [动] order ... about

使节 shǐjié [名] envoy

使命 shǐmìng [名] mission

使用 shǐyòng [动] use ▷我使用宽带上网。

I use broadband to go online. ▷使用说明 operating instructions (PL)

始 shǐ [动] start

始末 shǐmò [名] the whole story ▷报纸登 载了 "9.11" 事件始末。The newspaper covered the whole story of 9-11.

始终 shǐzhōng [副] all along ▷我始终没有勇 气告诉他。All along I didn't have the courage to tell him.

始祖 shǐzǔ [名] earliest ancestor

驶 shǐ [动] 1 (车) drive (PT drove, PP driven) ▷疾 驶 speed 2 (船) sail ▷驶离港口 sail out of the harbour (英) 或 harbor (美)

屎 shǐ [名] 1 (粪便) excrement 2 (眼、耳) wax ▷耳屎 ear wax

士 shì [名] 1 (军人) soldier 2 (军衔) non-commissioned officer ▶中士 sergeant 3 (专业 人员) ▶护士 nurse ▶博士 doctor

士兵 shìbīng [名] private

士气 shìqì [名] morale

氏 shì [名] surname

氏族 shìzú [名] clan

示 shì [动] show (PT showed, PP shown)

示范 shìfàn [动] demonstrate

示例 shìlì [动] give a demonstration (PT gave, PP given)

示威 shìwēi [动] demonstrate ▷伦敦民众示 威反对战争。People in London demonstrated against the war.

示意 shìyì [动] signal

示众 shìzhòng [动] parade

世 shì [名] 1 (生) life ▶来世 afterlife 2 (代) generation ▶世仇 family feud 3 (时期) age ▶世纪 century 4 (世界) world ▶世上 in this world

世仇 shìchóu [名] family feud

世代 shìdài [名] generation

世道 shìdào [名] attitudes (PL) ▷世道变了。 人人都向 "钱" 看。Attitudes have changed. Everyone's just interested in money.

世风 shìfēng [名] (书) atmosphere

世故 shìgù [名] the ways of the world (PL)

世故 shìgu [形] (贬) worldly-wise

世纪 shìjì [名] century

世家 shìjiā [名] well-known family

世交 shìjiāo [名] family friend

世界 shìjiè [名] world

世贸组织 shìmào zǔzhī [名] WTO

世面 shìmiàn [名] facet of life

世人 shìrén [名] (书) the common people (PL)

世事 shìshì [名] (书) world affairs (PL)

世俗 shìsú I [名] custom II [形] secular

世态炎凉 shìtài yán liáng the hypocrisy of the world

世外桃源 shì wài Táoyuán utopia ▷世外桃源是不存在的。Utopia does not exist.

世袭 shìxí [动] inherit

仕 shì 见下文

仕途 shìtú [名] (书) official career

市 shì [名] 1 (城市) city 2 (市场) market

市场 shìchǎng [名] market

市价 shìjià [名] market price

市郊 shìjiāo [名] suburb

市侩 shìkuài [名] money-grubber

市面 shìmiàn [名] market

市民 shìmín [名] city residents (PL)

市区 shìqū [名] urban area

市容 shìróng [名] the city's appearance

市政 shìzhèng [名] municipal administration ▷市政工程 municipal projects (PL)

式 shì [名] 1 (样式) style ▷欧式家具 European-style furniture 2 (典礼) ceremony 3 (式子) formula ▶公式 formula

式样 shìyàng [名] style

式子 shìzi [名] formula (PL formulae)

似 shì 见下文

→另见 sì

似的 shìde [助] ▷她的眼睛像天空似的那么蓝。Her eyes are as blue as the sky.

事 shì [名] 1 (事情) thing ▶私事 private matter ▷我想和你说几件事。I want to talk to you about a number of things. 2 (事故) accident ▶出事 have an accident 3 (事端) trouble ▶闹事 make trouble 4 (责任) responsibility ▷这没我的事。This is not my responsibility. 5 (工作) job ▷他刚下岗，正在找事做。He's just become unemployed and is looking for a job. 6 (用于问答) problem ▷有事吗？没事。Are you OK? – I'm fine.

事变 shìbiàn [名] 1 (事件) incident 2 (事故) emergency

事出有因 shì chū yǒu yīn ▷国家队换教练事出有因。There was a good reason for the national team to change their coach.

事端 shìduān [名] incident

事故 shìgù [名] accident

事迹 shìjì [名] achievement

事件 shìjiàn [名] event

事理 shìlǐ [名] reason

事例 shìlì [名] example

事情 shìqíng [名] matter ▷他公司事情很多。He is very busy with business matters. ▷事情不会这么简单。Things can't be that simple.

事实 shìshí [名] fact ▷事实上 in fact

事态 shìtài [名] situation

事务 shìwù [名] work

事物 shìwù [名] thing

事项 shìxiàng [名] item

事业 shìyè [名] 1 (用于个人) undertaking 2 (用于社会) activity ▷她献身公益事业。She dedicated herself to welfare activities. 3 (指非企业) facilities (PL)

事业心 shìyèxīn [名] dedication

事宜 shìyí [名] (书) arrangements (PL)

事与愿违 shì yǔ yuàn wéi not go according to plan

势 shì [名] 1 (势力) force 2 (姿态) gesture 3 (地理) feature 4 (趋势) tendency

势必 shìbì [副] ▷人们对手机的需求势必会增长。People's demand for mobile phones (英) or cell phones (美) is bound to increase.

势不可挡 shì bù kě dǎng unstoppable ▷信息全球化势不可挡。The globalization of information is unstoppable.

势不两立 shì bù liǎng lì be irreconcilable ▷英格兰和苏格兰橄榄球队势不两立。The English and Scottish rugby teams are sworn enemies.

势均力敌 shì jūn lì dí equally matched

势力 shìlì [名] power ▷势力范围 sphere of influence

势利 shìlì [形] snobbish

势利眼 shìlìyǎn [名] snob

势如破竹 shì rú pò zhú inexorable ▷数字媒体的发展势如破竹。The development of digital media is inexorable.

势头 shìtóu [名] momentum

势在必行 shì zài bì xíng be imperative ▷保护知识产权势在必行。It is imperative that intellectual properties are protected.

侍 shì [动] serve

侍奉 shìfèng [动] look after

侍候 shìhòu [动] serve

侍卫 shìwèi [名] bodyguard

侍者 shìzhě [名] (旧) servant

饰 shì I [动] 1 (装饰) decorate 2 (扮演) play ▷她在歌剧中饰卡门。She plays Carmen in the opera. II [名] ornament ▶首饰 jewellery (英), jewelry (美)

饰物 shìwù [名] ornaments (PL)

饰演 shìyǎn [动] play ▷他饰演孙悟空。He plays the Monkey King.

试 shì I [动] try ▷你可以在网上试玩新游戏。You can try playing new games online. ▷我可以试一下这双鞋吗? Can I try on this pair of shoes? II [名] examination

试点 shìdiǎn I [动] do a pilot project II [名] test site

试管 shìguǎn [名] test tube ▷试管婴儿 test-tube baby

试金石 shìjīnshí [名] touchstone

试卷 shìjuàn [名] exam paper

试探 shìtàn [动] sound ... out ▷美国试探英国对美伊战争的态度。The United States sounded the British out about how they felt about the war with Iraq.

试题 shìtí [名] exam question

试行 shìxíng [动] try ... out

试验 shìyàn [动] test

试用 shìyòng [动] try ... out

试用期 shìyòngqī [名] probation ▷我还在试用期呢。I'm still on probation.

视 shì [动] 1 (看到) look at 2 (看待) look on ▷视为知己 look on as an intimate friend 3 (考察) inspect

视察 shìchá [动] inspect

视角 shìjiǎo [名] angle ▷他的研究视角很独特。He has a unique angle in his research.

视觉 shìjué [名] vision ▷DVD给人们带来全新的视觉享受。DVDs give people a brand new visual experience.

视力 shìlì [名] sight

视听 shìtīng [名] sight and hearing

视线 shìxiàn [名] 1 (指眼睛) line of vision 2 (注意力) attention

视野 shìyě [名] field of vision

柿 shì 见下文

柿子 shìzi [名] persimmon, sharon fruit

拭 shì [动] (书) wipe ... away

拭目以待 shì mù yǐ dài eagerly await ▷人们对总统大选的结果拭目以待。People were eagerly awaiting the result of the presidential election.

是 shì I [动] be (PT was, were, PP been) ▷我是学生。I am a student. ▷遍地是雪。There's snow everywhere. ▷我们是3个孩子的家。We have three children. ▷他绝不是想省钱。It's certainly not that he's trying to save money. ▷是学生就要听老师话。Every student should listen to what their teacher says. II [名] right ▶是非 right and wrong III [副] yes ▷你要见他吗? – 是, 我现在就要见他。Are you going to see him? – Yes, I'm going to see him right now.

是非 shìfēi [名] 1 (对与错) right and wrong ▷他不辨是非。He can't tell the difference between right and wrong. 2 (麻烦) trouble ▷他老惹是非。He's always making trouble.

是否 shìfǒu [副] ▷我不知道他是否同意。I don't know whether he agrees or not.

适 shì [形] 1 (适合) suitable 2 (恰好) right 3 (舒服) well ▷他最近身体不适。He's not been well recently.

适当 shìdàng [形] appropriate

适得其反 shì dé qí fǎn lead to just the opposite ▷服药过量会适得其反。Taking more than the prescribed dose will produce the opposite effect.

适度 shìdù [形] moderate

适合 shìhé [形] suitable

适可而止 shì kě ér zhǐ not go too far

适量 shìliàng [形] of an appropriate amount ▷适量用药 take medicine in appropriate doses

适龄 shìlíng [形] appropriately aged ▷适龄青年可以参军。Young people of the appropriate age can enter the army.

适时 shìshí [形] timely ▷你要适时督促他一下。You need to give him a bit of timely encouragement.

适销 shìxiāo [动] sell well (PT, PP sold)

适宜 shìyí [形] advisable ▷吃止痛药后不适宜饮酒。After taking painkillers it's not advisable to drink alcohol.

适应 shìyìng [动] adapt

适中 shìzhōng [形] moderate

室 shì [名] room ▶办公室 office

室外 shìwài [形] outdoor

逝 shì [动] 1 (人) die 2 (书) (时间等) pass

逝世 shìshì [动] (书) pass away

释 shì [动] (解释) explain

释放 shìfàng [动] release

释疑 shìyí [动] clear up doubts

释义 shìyì [动] define ▷ 老师给出生词的释义。The teacher gave a definition of the new word.

嗜 shì [动] be addicted to ▷ 嗜酒 be an alcoholic

嗜好 shìhào [名] hobby ▷ 她的最大嗜好是购物。Her favourite (英) 或 favorite (美) hobby is shopping.

誓 shì I [动] swear (PT swore, PP sworn) II [名] vow

誓不罢休 shì bù bàxiū swear not to give up ▷ 他不打赢官司, 誓不罢休。He swore not to give up until he had won the case.

誓词 shìcí [名] oath

誓死 shìsǐ [副] ▷ 他誓死报仇。He is ready to die in pursuit of revenge.

誓言 shìyán [名] oath

誓约 shìyuē [名] oath

收 shōu [动] 1 (归拢) put ... away (PT, PP put) ▶收拾 tidy ... up 2 (取回) take ... back (PT took, PP taken) ▷ 我把晾在外面的被单收了进来。I took in the sheet, which had been drying in the sun outside. 3 (收割) harvest 4 (接纳) accept 5 (约束) restrain 6 (逮捕) arrest 7 (结束) stop ▶收工 stop work 8 (获得) gain ▶收入 income

收编 shōubiān [动] incorporate

收兵 shōubīng [动] 1 (指战斗) retreat 2 (指工作) complete

收藏 shōucáng [动] collect

收场 shōuchǎng I [动] end up II [名] (贬) ending

收成 shōucheng [名] harvest

收复 shōufù [动] recapture

收割 shōugē [动] harvest

收购 shōugòu [动] 1 (买入) purchase 2 (并购) take ... over (PT took, PP taken) ▷ 由于市场竞争十分激烈, 大部分小公司被收购。As the market is very competitive, the majority of small companies have been taken over.

收获 shōuhuò [动] 1 (指庄稼) harvest 2 (指成果) gain ▷ 这次出国考察, 他的收获很大。He has gained a great deal from this trip overseas.

收集 shōují [动] collect

收据 shōujù [名] receipt

收敛 shōuliǎn [动] 1 (笑容) vanish 2 (指行为) restrain oneself

收留 shōuliú [动] take ... in (PT took, PP taken) ▷ 父母去世后, 他的一个远方亲戚收留了他。After his parents died, a distant relative took him in.

收买 shōumǎi [动] 1 (收购) purchase 2 (笼络) buy ... off (PT, PP bought)

收盘 shōupán [动] close

收入 shōurù [名] income ▷ 近几年, 人们的收入明显增加。In recent years, people's incomes have markedly increased.

收视率 shōushìlǜ [名] ratings (PL)

收拾 shōushi [动] 1 (整顿) tidy 2 (修理) repair 3 (口) (惩罚) punish ▷ 他被人收拾了。He's been punished.

收缩 shōusuō [动] 1 (指物理现象) contract 2 (紧缩) cut back (PT cut, PP cut) ▷ 公司资金紧张, 需要收缩开支。The company's under financial pressure – we have to cut back on expenditure.

收听 shōutīng [动] listen to ▷ 他的收音机能收听BBC的节目。His radio can pick up BBC programmes (英) 或 programs (美).

收尾 shōuwěi [动] conclude ▷ 这篇文章收尾仓促了些。This article concludes in a hasty fashion.

收效 shōuxiào [动] yield results

收养 shōuyǎng [动] adopt

收益 shōuyì [名] profit

收音机 shōuyīnjī [名] radio

收支 shōuzhī [名] income and expenditure

手 shǒu I [名] 1 (指人体) hand ▷ 有问题的同学请举手。Will any student who has a question please raise their hand. 2 (指人) expert ▶选手 player II [量] ▷ 他这手可真厉害！He really made a good move there!

手笔 shǒubǐ [名] 1 (手迹) handwriting 2 (造诣) literary skill

手臂 shǒubì [名] arm

手表 shǒubiǎo [名] watch

手册 shǒucè [名] 1 (记录本) handbook 2 (参考书) reference book

手电筒 shǒudiàntǒng [名] torch (英), flashlight (美)

手段 shǒuduàn [名] 1 (方法) method 2 (贬) (花招) trick

手法 shǒufǎ [名] technique

手风琴 shǒufēngqín [名] accordion

手感 shǒugǎn [名] feel ▷ 真丝面料手感很好。This silk has a really nice feel.

手稿 shǒugǎo [名] manuscript

手工 shǒugōng I [名] craft ▷ 这个包全凭手工。The bag is completely hand-made. II [动] make ... by hand

手工业 shǒugōngyè [名] cottage industry

手工艺 shǒugōngyì [名] handicraft

手机 shǒujī [名] mobile phone (英), cell phone (美)

手疾眼快 shǒu jí yǎn kuài quick off the mark ▷幸亏他手疾眼快，一下子拔掉了电源。 Luckily he was quick off the mark, and took the plug out of the socket at once.

手迹 shǒujì [名] handwriting

手脚 shǒujiǎo [名] 1 (动作) movement ▷他手脚非常敏捷。He is very agile. 2 (贬) (捣鬼) sleight of hand ▷他在账目上做了手脚。He's used sleight of hand on the accounts.

手紧 shǒujǐn [形] 1 (指不随便花钱) stingy 2 (口) (缺钱) hard-up

手绢 shǒujuàn [名] handkerchief

手铐 shǒukào [名] handcuffs (PL)

手忙脚乱 shǒu máng jiǎo luàn in a mad rush ▷他做事从容冷静，从不手忙脚乱。He does things calmly, never in a mad rush.

手气 shǒuqì [名] luck

手枪 shǒuqiāng [名] pistol

手软 shǒuruǎn [动] be soft ▷对待毒贩子决不能手软。You can't be soft on drug smugglers.

手势 shǒushì [名] sign

手术 shǒushù I [名] operation II [动] operate

手套 shǒutào [名] glove ▷一副手套 a pair of gloves

手头 shǒutóu I [副] to hand ▷我手头没有你要的这本书。I don't have the book you need to hand. II [名] financial situation ▷最近我手头比较紧。Recently, my financial situation's been bad.

手腕 shǒuwàn [名] 1 (指人体) wrist 2 (喻) (手段) trick

手舞足蹈 shǒu wǔ zú dǎo dance for joy ▷听到这个好消息，他高兴得手舞足蹈。When he heard the good news, he was so happy that he danced for joy.

手下 shǒuxià I [名] subordinate II [副] 1 (领导下) under ▷他一直在部长手下工作。He works directly under the minister. 2 (手头) on one's hands ▷我们手下有个大项目。I've got a big job on my hands.

手心 shǒuxīn [名] 1 (指手) palm 2 (喻) (控制范围) the palm of one's hand ▷她把他们控制在手心里。She has them all in the palm of her hand.

手续 shǒuxù [名] procedure

手艺 shǒuyì [名] skill

手淫 shǒuyín I [动] masturbate II [名] masturbation

手语 shǒuyǔ [名] sign language

手掌 shǒuzhǎng [名] palm

手纸 shǒuzhǐ [名] toilet paper

手指 shǒuzhǐ [名] finger

手镯 shǒuzhuó [名] bracelet

手足 shǒuzú [名] 1 (指人体) hands and feet (PL) 2 (兄弟) brother

守 shǒu [动] 1 (防卫) guard 2 (遵循) observe ▷守法 observe the law 3 (看护) nurse

守备 shǒubèi [动] be on garrison duty

守候 shǒuhòu [动] 1 (等待) wait for 2 (看护) attend

守护 shǒuhù [动] guard

守岁 shǒusuì [动] stay up to see the new year in ▷中国人有守岁的习俗。The Chinese have a tradition of staying up all night to see the new year in.

守旧 shǒujiù [动] be conservative

守口如瓶 shǒu kǒu rú píng keep one's mouth shut ▷他对此事守口如瓶。He kept his mouth shut about it.

守望 shǒuwàng [动] keep watch (PT, PP kept)

守卫 shǒuwèi [动] guard

守业 shǒuyè [动] keep a business going (PT, PP kept) ▷创业难，守业更难。It is difficult to start an enterprise, but even more difficult to keep it going.

守夜 shǒuyè [动] stay up all night

守则 shǒuzé [名] regulation

守株待兔 shǒu zhū dài tù wait for good things to drop into one's lap ▷没有人能靠守株待兔取得成功。Nobody succeeds by sitting around waiting for things to happen.

首 shǒu I [名] 1 (脑袋) head 2 (头领) leader II [形] 1 (第一) first ▷首富 the richest person 2 (最早) first ▷首发车时间为5:30。The first bus leaves at 5:30. III [量] ▷这是一首人们熟悉的古诗。This is a well-known old poem.

首创 shǒuchuàng [动] pioneer

首当其冲 shǒu dāng qí chōng bear the brunt ▷出现险情时，这支部队总是首当其冲。This unit always bears the brunt of any danger.

首都 shǒudū [名] capital

首犯 shǒufàn [名] ringleader

首富 shǒufù [名] the richest

首领 shǒulǐng [名] chief

首脑 shǒunǎo [名] head of state

首屈一指 shǒu qū yī zhǐ be second to none ▷这个大学对微生物领域的研究在全国首屈一指。This university is second to none in this country in the field of micro-organic research.

首饰 shǒushì [名] jewellery (英), jewelry (美)

首尾 shǒuwěi [名] 1 (开始和结尾) the beginning and the end ▷这部电影首尾都很出人意料。This film has an unexpected beginning and end. 2 (从头到尾) ▷整个项目,首尾经过了4年。From start to finish, the whole project took four years.

首席 shǒuxí I [名] seat of honour (英) 或 honor (美) II [形] chief ▷他是该公司的首席顾问。He's the company's chief advisor.

首先 shǒuxiān [副] 1 (最早) first ▷王教授在会上首先发言。Professor Wang spoke first in the meeting. 2 (第一) first ▷首先,我们要找到问题的根源。First, we need to find the root of the problem.

首相 shǒuxiàng [名] prime minister

首要 shǒuyào I [形] primary II [名] head

首长 shǒuzhǎng [名] commander-in-chief

寿 shòu I [名] 1 (敬) (岁数) longevity ▷您高寿?How old are you? 2 (寿命) lifespan 3 (寿辰) birthday II [形] (婉) burial ▶寿衣 burial clothes (PL)

寿辰 shòuchén [名] birthday

寿命 shòumìng [名] life ▷随着生活水平的提高,人们的寿命越来越长。Since living standards are higher, life expectancy is steadily increasing.

寿星 shòuxīng [名] 1 (神) the god of longevity 2 (指老人) very long-lived person

受 shòu [动] 1 (接受) receive ▷每个儿童都有受教育的权利。Every child has the right to receive an education. 2 (遭受) suffer ▷他受了很多打击。He suffered many setbacks. 3 (忍受) bear (PT bore, PP borne) ▷天气太热,她受不了了。The weather's too hot. She can't bear it. ▷你能受得了住在这样艰苦的环境里吗?Can you bear to live in this terrible environment?

受宠若惊 shòu chǒng ruò jīng be overwhelmed with gratitude ▷您的到来令我受宠若惊。I'm so grateful you could come.

受挫 shòucuò [动] suffer a setback

受害 shòuhài [动] 1 (受伤害) suffer injury 2 (受损害) suffer loss

受贿 shòuhuì [动] accept bribes

受惊 shòujīng [动] be startled

受精 shòujīng [动] be fertilized

受累 shòulěi [动] involve

受理 shòulǐ [动] hear a case (PT, PP heard) ▷对于此案,法院拒绝受理。The court has refused to hear the case.

受命 shòumìng [动] receive instructions

受权 shòuquán [动] be authorized

受审 shòushěn [动] stand trial (PT, PP stood)

受洗 shòuxǐ [动] be baptized

受刑 shòuxíng [动] be tortured

受益 shòuyì [动] reap the benefits of ▷她受益于英语好。She is reaping the benefits of her good English.

受用 shòuyòng [动] reap the benefits of ▷保护环境,世代受用。Future generations will reap the benefits of environmental protection.

受用 shòuyong [形] well ▷我近来身体不太受用。I haven't been well recently.

受孕 shòuyùn [动] conceive

受制 shòuzhì [动] (书) 1 (受限) be constrained 2 (受迫害) be persecuted

受罪 shòuzuì [动] 1 (指苦难) suffer 2 (指不愉快的事) have a hard time

狩 shòu 见下文

狩猎 shòuliè [动] hunt

兽 shòu [名] beast

兽行 shòuxíng [名] 1 (凶残行为) brutal act 2 (秽乱行为) bestial behaviour

兽性 shòuxìng [名] barbarity

兽医 shòuyī [名] vet

授 shòu [动] 1 (奖) award 2 (传授) instruct

授奖 shòujiǎng [动] present awards

授命 shòumìng [动] give orders (PT gave, PP given)

授权 shòuquán [动] authorize

授勋 shòuxūn [动] decorate

授意 shòuyì [动] suggest

授予 shòuyǔ [动] award

售 shòu [动] sell (PT, PP sold)

售货 shòuhuò [动] sell goods (PT, PP sold)

瘦 shòu [形] 1 (指人) thin 2 (指食用肉) lean 3 (指衣服、鞋袜) tight

瘦骨嶙峋 shòu gǔ lín xún bony

瘦弱 shòuruò [形] emaciated

瘦削 shòuxuē [形] gaunt

瘦子 shòuzi [名] thin person ▷他年轻时是个瘦子,现在发胖了。When he was young he was thin, but now he's fat.

书 shū I [动] write (PT wrote, PP written) ▶书写 write II [名] 1 (字体) handwriting 2 (册子) book ▶精装书 hardback 3 (书)(信) letter ▶情

书 love letter 4 (文件) document ▶申请书 application documents (PL)

书本 shūběn [名] book

书呆子 shūdāizi [名] bookworm

书店 shūdiàn [名] bookshop

书法 shūfǎ [名] calligraphy

书稿 shūgǎo [名] manuscript

书画 shūhuà [名] painting and calligraphy

书籍 shūjí [名] books (PL)

书记 shūjì [名] secretary

书刊 shūkān [名] books and periodicals (PL)

书面 shūmiàn [形] written

书面语 shūmiànyǔ [名] written language

书目 shūmù [名] catalogue ▷看书前我习惯先看书目。Before reading a book, I normally look at the bibliography.

书生气 shūshēngqì [名] bookishness

书香门第 shūxiāng méndì [名] scholarly family

书写 shūxiě [动] write (PT wrote, PP written)

书信 shūxìn [名] letter

书展 shūzhǎn [名] book fair

抒 shū [动] express

抒发 shūfā [动] express

抒情 shūqíng [动] express emotion

抒写 shūxiě [动] express

枢 shū [名] 1 (指门) hinge 2 (中心) centre (英), center (美)

枢纽 shūniǔ [名] hub

叔 shū [名] (指父亲的弟弟) uncle

叔叔 shūshu [名] (口) 1 (指亲戚) uncle 2 (指父辈男性) uncle

殊 shū [形] 1 (不同) different 2 (特别) special

殊荣 shūróng [名] special honour (英) 或 honor (美)

殊死 shūsǐ [形] desperate

殊途同归 shū tú tóng guī independently reach the same conclusion ▷我们俩的解题思路简直殊途同归。We have handled this problem in different ways, but we have both reached the same conclusion.

梳 shū I [名] comb II [动] comb

梳理 shūlǐ [动] 1 (头发、胡须) comb 2 (思路) put ... in order (PT, PP put)

梳妆 shūzhuāng [动] get dressed up

淑 shū [形] ladylike

淑女 shūnǚ [名] lady

舒 shū I [动] 1 (指身体) stretch out 2 (指心情) relax II [形] (书) (缓慢) leisurely

舒畅 shūchàng [形] carefree

舒服 shūfu [形] comfortable

舒适 shūshì [形] cosy (英), cozy (美)

舒坦 shūtan [形] comfortable

舒心 shūxin [形] content ▷老两口的日子越来越舒心。The old couple are increasingly content with their lives.

舒展 shūzhǎn I [动] stretch out II [形] comfortable

疏 shū I [动] 1 (清理) dredge 2 (分散) scatter II [形] 1 (指距离) distant 2 (指关系) distant 3 (粗心) neglectful

疏导 shūdǎo [动] 1 (水道) dredge 2 (交通) direct 3 (思想) guide

疏忽 shūhu I [形] careless II [动] neglect III [名] carelessness

疏解 shūjiě [动] 1 (矛盾) resolve 2 (交通) clear

疏漏 shūlòu I [动] miss II [名] slip

疏散 shūsàn I [形] (书) scattered II [动] evacuate

疏松 shūsōng I [形] loose II [动] loosen

疏通 shūtōng [动] 1 (河道) dredge 2 (关系) mediate

疏远 shūyuǎn I [形] distant II [动] become estranged from (PT became, PP become) ▷尽管他犯了错，你也不该疏远他。Although he's done wrong, you shouldn't become estranged from him.

输 shū [动] 1 (运送) transport 2 (失败) lose (PT, PP lost)

输出 shūchū [动] 1 (指从内到外) emit ▷报警器输出信号。The alarm emits a signal. 2 (出口) export

输家 shūjiā [名] loser

输理 shūlǐ [动] lose the argument (PT, PP lost)

输入 shūrù [动] 1 (指从外到内) enter ▷把数据输入计算机 enter data into a computer 2 (进口) import

输送 shūsòng [动] 1 (物品) convey 2 (人员) transfer

蔬 shū [名] vegetable

蔬菜 shūcài [名] vegetable

赎 shú [动] 1 (换回) redeem ▷他们赎回了典当的项链。They redeemed the necklace they had pawned. ▷绑匪声称100万美金才能赎

出人质。The kidnapper demanded a ransom of 1,000,000 dollars for the release of the hostage. **2** (弥补) atone for

赎金 **shújīn** [名] **1** (指抵押品) deposit **2** (指人质) ransom

赎买 **shúmǎi** [动] buy ... out (PT, PP bought)

赎罪 **shúzuì** [动] atone for one's crime ▷他会用一生来赎罪。It will take him his whole life to atone for his crimes.

熟 **shú** [形] **1** (指果实) ripe **2** (指食物) cooked **3** (熟悉) familiar ▷他对北京很熟。He knows Beijing well. **4** (熟练) skilled

熟练 **shúliàn** [形] skilled

熟门熟路 **shú mén shú lù** be on one's home ground ▷他对这儿熟门熟路。He's on his home ground here.

熟能生巧 **shú néng shēng qiǎo** practice makes perfect ▷你要反复练习弹钢琴，毕竟熟能生巧嘛。You need to constantly practice the piano. After all, practice makes perfect.

熟人 **shúrén** [名] old acquaintance

熟食 **shúshí** [名] cooked food

熟视无睹 **shú shì wú dǔ** turn a blind eye to ▷我们不能对不良社会行为熟视无睹。We can't turn a blind eye to anti-social behaviour.

熟识 **shúshi** [动] get to know ▷两个小孩儿很快就熟识起来。The two kids got to know each other really quickly.

熟悉 **shúxī** I [动] know well (PT knew, PP known) II [形] familiar

熟习 **shúxí** [动] be skilled at

熟语 **shúyǔ** [名] idiom

属 **shǔ** I [名] **1** (生物) genus **2** (家属) family member II [动] **1** (隶属) be under **2** (指属相) ▷你属什么？What sign of the Chinese zodiac are you?

属地 **shǔdì** [名] dependency

属相 **shǔxiang** [名] (口) sign of the Chinese zodiac

属性 **shǔxìng** [名] attribute

属于 **shǔyú** [动] belong to

暑 **shǔ** [名] **1** (热) heat **2** (盛夏) midsummer

暑假 **shǔjià** [名] summer holidays (PL) (英) 或 vacation (美)

暑期 **shǔqī** [名] **1** (指暑假) summer holidays (PL) (英) 或 vacation (美) **2** (指夏季) summertime

署 **shǔ** I [名] department ▷审计署 auditing department II [动] **1** (布置) arrange **2** (名字) sign

署名 **shǔmíng** [动] sign

鼠 **shǔ** [名] **1** (指家鼠) mouse (PL mice) ▷米老鼠 Mickey Mouse **2** (比家鼠大，尾巴长) rat

鼠辈 **shǔbèi** [名] (贬) scoundrel

鼠标 **shǔbiāo** [名] mouse

鼠目寸光 **shǔ mù cùn guāng** short-sighted (英) 或 near-sighted (美)

数 **shǔ** [动] **1** (数目) count **2** (指名次) rank ▷他的学习成绩在班里数第一。His marks are top of the class. **3** (列举) list
→另见 **shù**

数不胜数 **shǔ bù shèng shǔ** innumerable ▷中国近几年的变化数不胜数。In recent years, China has undergone innumerable changes.

数落 **shǔluo** [动] scold

数说 **shǔshuō** [动] **1** (列举) list **2** (责备) scold

数一数二 **shǔ yī shǔ èr** the top one or two ▷他一直是成绩数一数二的学生。His grades are in the top one or two of his class.

薯 **shǔ** [名] potato (PL potatoes)

曙 **shǔ** (书) [名] dawn

曙光 **shǔguāng** [名] first light

术 **shù** [名] **1** (技艺) skill **2** (策略) tactic

术语 **shùyǔ** [名] terminology

戍 **shù** [动] defend

束 **shù** I [动] **1** (捆) tie **2** (约束) restrain II [量] bunch ▷他送给妻子一大束鲜花。He gave his wife a big bunch of flowers. III [名] **1** (指花) bunch **2** (指光) cluster

束缚 **shùfù** [动] **1** (书) (捆绑) tie **2** (局限) restrain ▷他从不受传统思想的束缚。He has never been restrained by traditional thinking.

束手无策 **shù shǒu wú cè** be at one's wits end ▷他什么都试过了，最后还是束手无策。He'd tried everything, and in the end he was at his wits end.

束之高阁 **shù zhī gāo gé** let ... gather dust ▷很多人买了书就束之高阁。Many people buy books and just let them gather dust.

束装 **shùzhuāng** [动] pack up

述 **shù** [动] state

述评 **shùpíng** I [动] review II [名] review

述说 **shùshuō** [动] give an account (PT gave, PP given) ▷他述说着昨晚发生的事情。He gave an account of yesterday evening's incident.

述职 shùzhí [动] report ▷述职报告 work report

树 shù I [名] tree II [动] 1 (书) (培育) cultivate 2 (建立) establish

树碑立传 shù bēi lì zhuàn (贬) seek the limelight ▷我做好事不为树碑立传，而是为大家服务。I do good things not to seek the limelight, but to serve everyone.

树敌 shùdí [动] antagonize

树立 shùlì [动] establish ▷树立信心 establish confidence

树林 shùlín [名] wood

树木 shùmù [名] trees (PL)

树阴 shùyīn [名] shade

竖 shù I [形] vertical II [动] erect III [名] vertical stroke

竖立 shùlì [动] erect

恕 shù [动] forgive (PT forgave, PP forgiven)

数 shù [名] 1 (数目) number 2 (数) number 3 (语法) ▶单数 singular ▶复数 plural
→另见 shǔ

数额 shù'é [名] amount

数据 shùjù [名] data (PL)

数据库 shùjùkù [名] database

数量 shùliàng [名] quantity

数码 shùmǎ I [名] numeral II [形] digital

数码相机 shùmǎ xiàngjī [名] digital camera

数目 shùmù [名] amount

数学 shùxué [名] mathematics (SG)

数字 shùzì [名] 1 (指系统) numeral 2 (数据) figure

数字化 shùzìhuà [动] digitize ▷我们生活在数字化时代。We are living in the digital age.

漱 shù [动] gargle

漱口 shùkǒu [动] rinse one's mouth out

刷 shuā I [名] brush II [动] 1 (清除) scrub 2 (淘汰) eliminate III [拟] rustle
→另见 shuà

刷卡 shuākǎ [动] swipe a card ▷购物付款可以刷卡。Goods can be paid for by card.

刷洗 shuāxǐ [动] scrub

刷新 shuāxīn [动] 1 (字) refurbish 2 (喻) break (PT broke, PP broken) ▷他刷新了男子跳高世界记录。He broke the men's high jump world record.

刷子 shuāzi [名] brush

耍 shuǎ [动] 1 (方) (玩) play 2 (戏弄) mess ... around ▷你别想耍我们！Don't think you can mess us around! 3 (贬) (施展) play ▷别再耍小聪明了。Don't play those petty tricks again.

耍把戏 shuǎ bǎxì [动] play tricks

耍花招 shuǎ huāzhāo [动] play tricks

耍滑 shuǎhuá [动] slack off ▷我们不喜欢耍滑的人。We don't like slackers.

耍赖 shuǎlài [动] act shamelessly

耍弄 shuǎnòng [动] take ... for a ride (PT took, PP taken) ▷当心别让别人耍弄了。Be careful not to let other people take you for a ride.

刷 shuà 见下文
→另见 shuā

刷白 shuàbái [形] (方) pale

衰 shuāi I [形] declining II [动] decline

衰败 shuāibài [动] decline

衰变 shuāibiàn [动] decay

衰竭 shuāijié [形] exhausted

衰老 shuāilǎo [形] ageing ▷经常运动可以延缓衰老过程。Regular exercise can delay the ageing process. ▷她非常害怕衰老。She's really afraid of getting old.

衰落 shuāiluò [动] go downhill (PT went, PP gone)

衰弱 shuāiruò [形] weak

衰退 shuāituì [动] 1 (视力) fail 2 (经济) decline

衰亡 shuāiwáng [动] deteriorate ▷民族的衰亡关系到每个人。The nation's deterioration affects everyone.

摔 shuāi [动] 1 (跌倒) fall (PT fell, PP fallen) 2 (下落) fall out (PT fell, PP fallen) ▷他从床上摔了下来。He fell out of bed. 3 (跌坏) break (PT broke, PP broken) 4 (扔) throw (PT threw, PP thrown)

摔打 shuāidǎ [动] 1 (拍打) beat (PT beat, PP beaten) ▷他把鞋上的泥摔打掉。He beat the mud off the shoes. 2 (锻炼) toughen oneself up ▷经过几年摔打，他坚强了很多。After a few years of toughening himself up, he had become much stronger.

摔跤 shuāijiāo I [动] 1 (摔倒) fall over (PT fell, PP fallen) 2 (受挫) come to grief (PT came, PP come) ▷你这么不谦虚，会摔跤的。If you show such lack of modesty, you'll come to grief. II [名] wrestling

甩 shuǎi [动] 1 (抡) swing (PT, PP swung) 2 (扔) fling (PT, PP flung) 3 (抛开) throw off (PT threw, PP thrown) ▷你要甩开包袱。You need to throw off your burden.

甩卖 shuǎimài [动] sell at a reduced price (PT,

PP sold)

甩手 shuǎishǒu [动] 1 (指运动) swing one's arms (PT, PP swung) 2 (指工作、事情) wash one's hands of ▷这件事做了一半, 你不能甩手不管。 You're only halfway through. You can't wash your hands of the matter now.

帅 shuài I [名] commander-in-chief II [形] handsome

帅气 shuàiqi [形] handsome

率 shuài I [动] command II [形] 1 (不慎重) rash 2 (坦白) frank

率领 shuàilǐng [动] lead (PT, PP led)

率先 shuàixiān [副] ▷中国率先研制出了这种高效肥料。 China has taken the lead in developing this highly efficient fertilizer.

率真 shuàizhēn [形] sincere

率直 shuàizhí [形] forthright ▷他的率直赢得了大家的好评。 His forthrightness won everyone's approval.

闩 shuān I [名] bolt II [动] bolt

拴 shuān [动] tie

栓 shuān [名] 1 (开关机件) plug 2 (塞子) cork

涮 shuàn [动] 1 (清洗) rinse 2 (指吃法) dip-boil 3 (方) be tricked ▷这张票是假的, 我们被涮了。 This ticket is a fake – we've been tricked.

双 shuāng I [形] 1 (两个) two 2 (偶数) even ▷双数 even number 3 (加倍) double II [量] pair

双胞胎 shuāngbāotāi [名] twins (PL)

双边 shuāngbiān [形] bilateral

双重 shuāngchóng [形] double

双方 shuāngfāng [名] both sides (PL)

双杠 shuānggàng [名] parallel bars

双关 shuāngguān [名] double entendre

双管齐下 shuāng guǎn qí xià work in parallel ▷治疗和锻炼双管齐下, 他很快就会恢复健康。 With medical treatment and exercise working in parallel, he will quickly recover.

双料 shuāngliào [形] double ▷他是语言学和社会学双料博士。 He's got two PhDs – one in linguistics and the other in sociology.

双亲 shuāngqīn [名] parents (PL)

双全 shuāngquán [动] have both ... and ... ▷智勇双全 be both wise and brave

双休日 shuāngxiūrì [名] the weekend

霜 shuāng [名] frost

霜冻 shuāngdòng [名] frost

孀 shuāng [名] widow

孀居 shuāngjū [动] (书) be a widow ▷她已经孀居多年了。 She has been a widow for many years.

爽 shuǎng [形] 1 (指天气) clear 2 (指性格) frank 3 (指健康) well ▷他今天感觉身体不爽。 Today he doesn't feel well.

爽口 shuǎngkǒu [形] refreshing

爽快 shuǎngkuài [形] 1 (舒服) refreshed ▷喝一杯冰啤酒, 感觉爽快极了! After drinking a glass of cold beer, you feel very refreshed. 2 (直爽) frank

爽朗 shuǎnglǎng [形] 1 (指天气) clear 2 (指性格) open 3 (指笑声) cheerful

爽目 shuǎngmù [形] easy on the eye

爽直 shuǎngzhí [形] frank

谁 shuí [代] → shéi

水 shuǐ [名] 1 (物质) water 2 (指江河湖海) waters (PL) 3 (汁) liquid ▷消毒水 disinfectant ▷墨水 ink

水兵 shuǐbīng [名] sailor

水彩 shuǐcǎi [名] 1 (指颜料) watercolour (英), watercolor (美) 2 (指画) watercolour (英), watercolor (美)

水草 shuǐcǎo [名] 1 (植物) water weed 2 (资源) water and pasture

水产 shuǐchǎn [名] aquatic products (PL)

水到渠成 shuǐ dào qú chéng success comes naturally ▷他经验丰富, 资金充足, 开公司是水到渠成的事。 He has a lot of experience and enough capital, so when he starts up a company, success will come naturally.

水分 shuǐfèn [名] 1 (指物质) moisture content 2 (虚假成分) exaggeration

水果 shuǐguǒ [名] fruit

水火 shuǐhuǒ [名] 1 (形容对立物) opposites (PL) 2 (形容灾难) misery

水货 shuǐhuò [名] 1 (走私品) smuggled goods (PL) 2 (劣质品) inferior goods (PL)

水晶 shuǐjīng [名] crystal

水库 shuǐkù [名] reservoir

水力 shuǐlì [名] hydraulic power

水利 shuǐlì [名] (水利工程) irrigation project

水淋淋 shuǐlínlín [形] sopping wet

水灵 shuǐlíng [形] 1 (指水果) fresh and juicy 2 (指人、花) charming

水流 shuǐliú [名] 1 (江河统称) river 2 (流动的水)

current

水陆 shuǐlù [名] land and water ▷这种交通工具是水陆两用的。This is an amphibious vehicle.

水路 shuǐlù [名] waterway

水落石出 shuǐ luò shí chū get to the bottom of

水面 shuǐmiàn [名] the water's surface

水平 shuǐpíng I [名] standard ▷人们的生活水平越来越高。People's living standards are getting higher and higher. II [形] horizontal ▷箱子要保持水平。Ensure that the box is horizontal.

水禽 shuǐqín [名] aquatic birds (PL)

水渠 shuǐqú [名] ditch

水乳交融 shuǐ rǔ jiāo róng in complete harmony ▷这幅画人物和景物水乳交融，非常和谐。The figure in this picture is in complete harmony with the scenery.

水势 shuǐshì [名] current

水手 shuǐshǒu [名] sailor

水土 shuǐtǔ [名] 1 (水和土) water and land 2 (环境气候) climate

水汪汪 shuǐwāngwāng [形] 1 (形容充满水) watery 2 (指眼睛) bright

水乡 shuǐxiāng [名] region of rivers and lakes

水泄不通 shuǐ xiè bù tōng completely packed ▷汽车把这条路堵得水泄不通。The road was so packed with cars that nothing could get through at all.

水性 shuǐxìng [名] ability to swim ▷他水性很好。He's a good swimmer.

水性杨花 shuǐxìng yánghuā flirtatious ▷她不是个水性杨花的女子。She's not a flirtatious woman.

水银 shuǐyín [名] mercury

水域 shuǐyù [名] waters (PL)

水源 shuǐyuán [名] 1 (指河流) source of a river 2 (指民用水) water source

水灾 shuǐzāi [名] flood

水涨船高 shuǐ zhǎng chuán gāo ▷留学生越来越多，学费也水涨船高。The number of overseas students is continually increasing, and there has been a corresponding increase in tuition fees. ▷足球运动员出了名，其身价也水涨船高。Once a footballer has made a name for himself, his social status increases along with his fame.

水质 shuǐzhì [名] water quality

水中捞月 shuǐ zhōng lāo yuè impractical

水准 shuǐzhǔn [名] 1 (水平) standard 2 (水平面) water level

水族 shuǐzú [名] aquatic animals (PL)

说 shuì [动] persuade
→另见 shuō

税 shuì [名] tax

税法 shuìfǎ [名] tax law

税率 shuìlǜ [名] tax rate

税收 shuìshōu [名] tax revenue

税务局 shuìwùjú [名] tax office

睡 shuì [动] sleep (PT, PP slept)

睡觉 shuìjiào [动] sleep (PT, PP slept) ▷睡觉是有效的休息方式。Sleeping is an effective way of relaxing.

睡梦 shuìmèng [名] dream

睡眠 shuìmián [名] sleep

睡意 shuìyì [名] drowsiness

吮 shǔn [动] suck ▷小男孩儿吮着拇指。The little boy was sucking his thumb.

吮吸 shǔnxī [动] suck

顺 shùn I [介] 1 (指方向) with ▶顺时针 clockwise 2 (沿) along 3 (趁便) ▶顺便 on the way II [动] 1 (朝同一方向) follow 2 (使有条理) put … in order (PT, PP put) 3 (顺从) obey 4 (合意) be to one's liking ▶顺心 as one would wish III [形] successful ▷他找工作很顺。His job hunt has been very successful.

顺便 shùnbiàn [副] 1 (指乘方便) on the way ▷你去超市时顺便帮我到邮局寄封信吧。Would you mind going to the post office to post this letter for me on your way to the supermarket? 2 (说、问) by the way ▷顺便问一下，他给你回电话了吗？By the way, did he call you back?

顺差 shùnchā [名] favourable (英) 或 favorable (美) balance

顺畅 shùnchàng [形] smooth ▷交通很少有顺畅的时候。There is seldom a smooth flow of traffic.

顺从 shùncóng [动] obey

顺当 shùndàng [形] smooth

顺耳 shùn'ěr [形] pleasant to hear ▷这首歌听起来挺顺耳的。This tune is quite pleasant. ▷他一句不顺耳的话也听不进去。He won't listen to anything he doesn't want to hear.

顺风 shùnfēng [动] 1 (指风向) travel downwind 2 (指祝福) ▷祝你一路顺风。Have a safe journey! ▷一路顺风 Bon voyage!

顺境 shùnjìng [名] favourable (英) 或 favorable (美) circumstances (PL)

顺口 shùnkǒu I [形] flowing ▷这首诗念起来不太顺口。This poem doesn't flow too well. II [副] without thinking ▷他顺口把我们的秘密透露出去了。He revealed our secret without thinking.

顺理成章 shùn lǐ chéng zhāng logical and coherent

顺利 shùnlì [副] smoothly ▷你们的计划执行得顺利吗? Did your plan go smoothly?

顺路 shùnlù [副] on the way ▷下班后你能顺路到医院去看他吗? On your way home after work, would you mind going to see him in the hospital?

顺手 shùnshǒu I [形] 1 (顺利) smooth 2 (好使) easy to use ▷这些新工具都很顺手。These new tools are very easy to use. II [副] on the way ▷我顺手把灯关上。I turned out the lights as I went past.

顺手牵羊 shùn shǒu qiān yáng walk off with

顺藤摸瓜 shùn téng mō guā trace ... to its roots

顺心 shùnxīn [形] satisfactory ▷他现在日子过得很顺心。Life is going very well for him at the moment. ▷咱们出去走走, 忘掉那些不顺心的事。Let's go out for a walk and try and forget this whole mess.

顺序 shùnxù [名] order

顺延 shùnyán [动] postpone

顺眼 shùnyǎn [形] attractive ▷这套家具看起来挺顺眼。This furniture is very attractive. ▷她对男朋友看不顺眼。She had a low opinion of her boyfriend.

顺应 shùnyìng [动] follow ▷顺应时代的变化 change with the times

瞬 shùn [名] flash ▶一瞬间 in a flash

瞬息万变 shùnxī wàn biàn fast-changing

说 shuō [动] 1 (用语言表达意思) say (PT, PP said) ▷他说他不来了。He said he wouldn't come. 2 (解释) explain 3 (责备) tell ... off (PT, PP told) ▷你衣服弄得这么脏, 看你妈妈不说你。Your mum will give you a telling-off for getting your clothes so dirty.

→另见 shuì

表示"说"最常用的词汇是 say。请注意, 在使用动词 say 时, 如果想要表示说话的对象, 应该使用介词 to。'What did she say to you?' 是错误的用法。'What did she say to you?' 则是正确的表达。表示告知某人某事用 tell。The manufacturer told me that the product did not contain corn. 然而, 动词 tell 通常带直接宾语, 表示说话的对象。He told Alison he was suffering from leukaemia...What did she tell you? 'What did she tell to you?' 是错误的用法。tell 可以和带 to 的动词不定式连用, 表示命令或指示。My mother told me to shut up and eat my dinner.

说长道短 shuō cháng dào duǎn criticize

说唱 shuōchàng [名] 1 (曲艺) a form of popular entertainment consisting mostly of singing and comic dialogue 2 (音) rap ▷说唱艺人 rapper

说法 shuōfa [名] 1 (措辞) version 2 (见解) opinion ▷大家对这件事说法不一。Everybody has different opinions on this matter. 3 (公道) justification

说服 shuōfú [动] persuade

说合 shuōhe [动] 1 (指亲事) bring ... together (PT, PP brought) 2 (商量) discuss

说和 shuōhe [动] mediate

说话 shuōhuà I [动] 1 (用语言表达意思) talk 2 (闲谈) chat II [副] (马上) any minute

说教 shuōjiào [动] preach

说客 shuōkè [名] persuasive talker

说理 shuōlǐ [动] argue ▷这篇论文说理充分, 论证严谨。This essay is well argued and precisely reasoned.

说媒 shuōméi [动] act as matchmaker

说明 shuōmíng I [动] 1 (解释明白) explain 2 (证明) prove II [名] explanation ▷产品使用说明 instruction manual

说情 shuōqíng [动] plead for

说三道四 shuō sān dào sì gossip

说书 shuōshū [动] give a storytelling performance

说闲话 shuō xiánhuà gossip

说笑 shuōxiào [动] joke around

说一不二 shuō yì bù èr be a man of one's word ▷我们的女老板说一不二。Our boss is a woman of her word.

烁 shuò [形] twinkling

硕 shuò [形] large

硕果 shuòguǒ [名] success

硕士 shuòshì [名] master's degree ▷文科硕士 MA ▷理科硕士 MSc

司 sī I [动] take charge of (PT took, PP taken) ▶司机 driver ▷各司其职 each attends to their own duties II [名] department

司法 sīfǎ [名] judiciary

司机 sījī [名] driver

司空见惯 sīkōng jiàn guàn be used to

司令 sīlìng [名] commander

司仪 sīyí [名] master of ceremonies, MC

丝 sī [名] 1 (指蚕) silk 2 (像丝) thread ▷铁丝 wire ▷把土豆切成丝。Shred the potato.

丝绸 sīchóu [名] silk

丝毫 sīháo [形] slightest ▷丝毫无损 not harmed in the slightest

私 sī [形] 1 (个人的) private ▷私事 private affairs 2 (自私的) selfish ▷无私 unselfish 3 (暗地里的) secret 4 (非法的) illegal

私奔 sībēn [动] elope

私产 sīchǎn [名] private property

私党 sīdǎng [名] clique

私邸 sīdǐ [名] private residence

私房 sīfang [形] 1 (指积蓄) personal savings (PL) 2 (指话) personal matters (PL)

私愤 sīfèn [名] grudge

私活 sīhuó [名] moonlighting ▷他因利用上班时间干私活被罚没全年奖金。He lost a whole year's bonuses for moonlighting during office hours.

私交 sījiāo [名] personal connections (PL)

私立 sīlì [形] private

私了 sīliǎo [动] settle ... privately

私囊 sīnáng [名] one's own pocket ▷他用纳税人的钱中饱私囊。He was lining his own pockets with taxpayers' money.

私情 sīqíng [名] 1 (私人交情) personal considerations (PL) 2 (不正当的男女情爱) relationship

私人 sīrén [形] 1 (属于个人的) private 2 (人与人之间的) personal ▷你和老板的私人关系怎么样? How do you get on with your boss?

私生活 sīshēnghuó [名] private life

私生子 sīshēngzǐ [名] illegitimate child (PL children)

私通 sītōng [动] 1 (私下勾结) have secret communication 2 (通奸) commit adultery

私下 sīxià [副] privately

私心 sīxīn [名] selfishness

私营 sīyíng [动] privately run ▷这家工厂顺利地完成了由国营到私营的转变。The factory smoothly carried out the transformation from state ownership to private ownership.

私有 sīyǒu [形] private ▷私有化 privatization

私语 sīyǔ [动] whisper

私欲 sīyù [名] selfish desires (PL)

私自 sīzì [副] without permission

思 sī I [动] 1 (思考) think (PT, PP thought) 2 (思念) miss 3 (希望) hope II [名] thought ▷思路 train of thought

思潮 sīcháo [名] 1 (指社会) trend 2 (指个人) thought ▷他思潮起伏, 久久不能入睡。His head was full of restless thoughts, and for a long time he could not sleep.

思考 sīkǎo [动] think (PT, PP thought) ▷请给我时间思考一下你的建议。Please give me some time to think your suggestion over.

思量 sīliang [动] consider

思念 sīniàn I [动] miss II [名] longing

思路 sīlù [名] reasoning ▷你这道题的思路是对的。Your reasoning in this question is correct. ▷敲门声打断了他的思路。The knock on the door interrupted his train of thought.

思索 sīsuǒ [动] ponder

思维 sīwéi [名] thinking ▷动物有类似人的思维能力吗? Do animals have mental abilities similar to those of humans?

思乡 sīxiāng [动] be homesick

思想 sīxiǎng [名] 1 (指有体系) thought 2 (念头) idea ▷这些学生都很有自己的思想。These students all have their own ideas.

思绪 sīxù [名] state of mind

斯 sī 见下文

斯文 sīwen [形] gentle

撕 sī [动] tear (PT tore, PP torn) ▷她把信撕得粉碎。She tore the letter into pieces.

撕毁 sīhuǐ [动] tear ... up (PT tore, PP torn)

撕票 sīpiào [动] kill the hostage ▷绑架他女朋友的人威胁说不马上给钱他们就撕票。The people who had kidnapped his girlfriend threatened to kill her if he didn't immediately pay the ransom.

嘶 sī I [动] neigh II [形] hoarse

嘶哑 sīyǎ [形] hoarse

死 sǐ I [动] die II [形] 1 (死亡的) dead ▷死尸 corpse 2 (不可调和的) implacable ▷死敌 sworn enemy 3 (不能通过的) impassable ▷死胡同 dead end 4 (确切的) fixed ▷我们要把出发的时间定死。We should fix our departure time. 5 (脑筋) slow-witted 6 (规定) rigid 7 (水) still III [副] 1 (拼死) to the death ▷死战 fight to the death 2 (表示固执或坚决) stubbornly ▷死等 wait indefinitely 3 (表示达极点) extremely ▷累死我了。I'm completely exhausted.

死板 sǐbǎn [形] 1 (不活泼的) stiff 2 (不灵活的) inflexible

死不瞑目 sǐ bù míngmù die discontented

死党 sǐdǎng [名] diehard supporters (PL)

死敌 sǐdí [名] sworn enemy

死灰复燃 sǐhuī fù rán revive

死活 sǐhuó **I** [名] safety ▷煤矿主不顾矿工的死活，让他们没日没夜地工作。The mine manager didn't care at all about his employees' safety and made them work day and night. **II** [副] simply ▷交通灯变绿了但车子死活打不着火。The lights had changed to green, but the car simply wouldn't start.

死机 sǐjī [动] crash

死角 sǐjiǎo [名] (喻) untouched area ▷知识产权法中的死角 areas untouched by intellectual property laws

死结 sǐjié [名] tight knot

死劲儿 sǐjìnr [副] with all one's strength

死里逃生 sǐ lǐ táo shēng have a narrow escape

死路 sǐlù [名] **1** (走不通的路) dead end **2** (喻) (引向毁灭的道路) road to ruin

死命 sǐmìng **I** [名] doom **II** [副] desperately

死难 sǐnàn [动] die in an accident ▷这家公司向死难者家属进行了赔付。The company gave compensation to the families of the victims of the accident.

死皮赖脸 sǐ pí lài liǎn brazen

死气沉沉 sǐqì chénchén dead

死去活来 sǐ qù huó lái devastated ▷她哭得死去活来。She was crying her eyes out. ▷他爱她爱得死去活来。He was madly in love with her.

死神 sǐshén [名] Death

死尸 sǐshī [名] corpse

死水 sǐshuǐ [名] **1** (指水) stagnant water **2** (指气氛、环境) lifelessness

死亡 sǐwáng [动] die

死心 sǐxīn [动] give up on (PT gave, PP given) ▷她对出国死心了。She's given up on the idea of going abroad.

死心塌地 sǐ xīn tā dì have one's heart set on

死刑 sǐxíng [名] death penalty

死硬 sǐyìng [形] **1** (形容硬) stiff **2** (顽固) stubborn

死有余辜 sǐ yǒu yú gū death is too good for ▷这种坏人死有余辜。Death's too good for people like that.

死于非命 sǐ yú fēi mìng die a violent death

死战 sǐzhàn **I** [名] life-and-death battle **II** [动] fight to the death (PT, PP fought)

死者 sǐzhě [名] the deceased

四 sì [数] four

四不像 sìbùxiàng (喻) (不伦不类) neither one thing nor the other

四处 sìchù [名] everywhere

四方 sìfāng [名] **1** (形状) square **2** (各处) all directions

四方步 sìfāngbù [名] leisurely pace

四分五裂 sì fēn wǔ liè be torn asunder

四海 sìhǎi [名] the world

四季 sìjì [名] the four seasons (PL)

四邻 sìlín [名] neighbours (英), neighbors (美) (PL)

四平八稳 sì píng bā wěn well-balanced

四舍五入 sì shě wǔ rù round off to the nearest number ▷5.61四舍五入后得5.6。5.61 can be rounded down to 5.6.

四声 sìshēng [名] the four tones of Standard Chinese pronunciation

四通八达 sì tōng bā dá extend in all directions ▷地铁线路四通八达。The different lines of the underground link everywhere up.

四肢 sìzhī [名] limbs (PL)

四周 sìzhōu [名] all sides ▷四周都是人。There are people everywhere. ▷餐馆四周都是写字楼。The restaurant is surrounded by office buildings.

寺 sì [名] **1** (指佛教) temple ▶喇嘛寺 Tibetan Buddhist temple **2** (指伊斯兰教) mosque ▶清真寺 mosque

寺院 sìyuàn [名] temple

似 sì **I** [动] (像) be like ▷他的脸似纸一样白。His face was as white as a sheet of paper. **II** [副] apparently ▷她看似单纯，其实很成熟。She appears to be naive, but actually she's very worldly-wise. **III** [介] than ▷赛马一匹快似一匹。Each racehorse is quicker than the last.
→另见 shì

似曾相识 sì céng xiāngshí look familiar ▷他俩初次见面，但却都有似曾相识的感觉。It was the first time the two had met, and yet they felt strangely familiar.

似乎 sìhū [副] apparently

似是而非 sì shì ér fēi specious ▷他的推理似是而非。His reasoning is specious.

伺 sì [动] watch ▶窥伺 spy on
→另见 cì

伺机 sìjī [动] wait for the opportunity to ▷伺机进攻 wait for an opportunity to attack

饲 sì [动] raise ▶饲养 raise

饲料 sìliào [名] fodder

饲养 sìyǎng [动] raise

肆 sì I [动] be unrestrained II [名] an elaborate form of "four", used in writing cheques etc to prevent mistakes and forgery

肆虐 sìnüè [动] wreak havoc ▷那年蝗虫肆虐。That year locusts wreaked havoc.

肆无忌惮 sì wú jì dàn unscrupulous

肆意 sìyì [副] wantonly

松 sōng I [名] 1 (树) pine tree 2 (食品) a condiment made of finely shredded preserved meat II [动] 1 (放开) relax ▷他松开了抓着绳子的手。He relaxed his grip on the rope. 2 (鞋带、腰带) loosen III [形] loose ▷他的腰带有点松。His belt is a bit loose. ▷你管学生不能太松了。You shouldn't be too soft on the students.

松绑 sōngbǎng [动] 1 (解开绳索) untie 2 (放宽限制) relax

松弛 sōngchí [形] 1 (肌肉) limp 2 (心情) relaxed 3 (纪律) lax

松动 sōngdòng [动] 1 (牙齿、岩石、螺丝) loosen 2 (口气) relax 3 (规定) relax

松劲 sōngjìn [动] relax one's efforts

松口 sōngkǒu [动] 1 (松嘴) let go (PT, PP let) 2 (不坚持) (主张、意见) relent

松快 sōngkuai [形] 1 (指精神) relieved ▷和老师谈话后，他心里松快了许多。After he talked to his teacher, he felt much relieved. 2 (指身体) relaxed 3 (指空间上) less crowded

松软 sōngruǎn [形] 1 (指物体) soft 2 (指肢体) weak

松散 sōngsǎn [形] 1 (指结构) loose 2 (指精神) lax

松松垮垮 sōngsōngkuǎkuǎ [形] 1 (指衣着) baggy 2 (指精神) sluggish

松懈 sōngxiè [形] 1 (放松) relaxed 2 (松散) lax

怂 sǒng 见下文

怂恿 sǒngyǒng [动] provoke

耸 sǒng [动] 1 (伸向高处) tower 2 (引起注意) alarm

耸动 sǒngdòng [动] (肩膀) shrug

耸立 sǒnglì [动] tower

耸人听闻 sǒng rén tīng wén sensationalize

悚 sǒng 见下文

悚然 sǒngrán [形] terrified

讼 sòng [动] take a case to court (PT took, PP taken) ▶诉讼 lawsuit

送 sòng [动] 1 (信、邮包、外卖) deliver 2 (礼物) give (PT gave, PP given) ▷你准备送他什么结婚礼物？What are you going to give him as a wedding present? 3 (送行) see ... off (PT saw, PP seen) ▷他把女朋友送到家。He saw his girlfriend home. 4 (陪着去) take (PT took, PP taken) ▷我把客人送到机场。I took the guests to the airport.

送别 sòngbié [动] see ... off (PT saw, PP seen) ▷老师为毕业生举行了送别晚会。The teachers held a farewell banquet for the graduating students.

送命 sòngmìng [动] lose one's life (PT, PP lost)

送死 sòngsǐ [动] (口) court death

送行 sòngxíng [动] see ... off (PT saw, PP seen) ▷她到机场给朋友送行。She went to the airport to see a friend off.

送葬 sòngzàng [动] be part of a funeral procession

送终 sòngzhōng [动] 1 (临终照料) be with ... in his/her last moments 2 (安排丧事) make funeral arrangements

诵 sòng [动] 1 (大声读) read ... aloud (PT, PP read) 2 (背诵) recite

诵读 sòngdú [动] read ... aloud (PT, PP read)

颂 sòng I [动] praise II [名] ode

颂词 sòngcí [名] ode

颂歌 sònggē [名] hymn of praise

颂扬 sòngyáng [动] extol

搜 sōu [动] search

搜捕 sōubǔ [动] hunt for ▷他试图逃避警方的搜捕。He attempted to avoid the hunt organised by the police.

搜查 sōuchá [动] search ▷警察拦截住一辆可疑车辆进行搜查。The police stopped a suspicious vehicle and carried out a search.

搜刮 sōuguā [动] extort

搜集 sōují [动] gather

搜罗 sōuluó [动] recruit

搜索 sōusuǒ [动] search for

搜索引擎 sōusuǒ yǐnqíng [名] search engine

搜寻 sōuxún [动] hunt for

嗖 sōu [拟] whizz ▷一辆摩托车嗖的一声从他身边驶过。A motorbike whizzed past him.

馊 sōu [形] sour

馊主意 sōu zhǔyi [名] bad idea

艘 sōu [量] ▷3艘游艇 three yachts

嗽 sòu [动] cough ▶咳嗽 cough

苏 sū [动] revive ▶复苏 recover
苏打 sūdá [名] soda
苏醒 sūxǐng [动] come to (PT came, PP come)

酥 sū I [名] biscuit II [形] 1 (用于食物) crisp 2 (用于人体) limp
酥软 sūruǎn [形] weak ▷工作一天之后，他回到家累得浑身酥软。After a day's work, he returned home so tired that his whole body felt really weak.
酥松 sūsōng [形] loosened
酥油 sūyóu [名] butter

俗 sú I [名] 1 (风俗) custom ▶民俗 folk custom ▷入乡随俗 when in Rome, do as the Romans do 2 (没出家的) laity ▶僧俗 clergy and laity II [形] 1 (大众的) popular 2 (庸俗) vulgar
俗不可耐 sú bù kě nài as common as muck
俗话 súhuà [名] proverb
俗气 súqi [形] vulgar
俗人 súrén [名] 1 (一般人) ordinary person (PL people) 2 (庸俗的人) vulgar person (PL people)
俗套 sútào [名] 1 (无聊的礼节) conventions (PL) 2 (陈旧的格调) cliché
俗语 súyǔ [名] common saying

夙 sù [形] (书) 1 (早) early 2 (旧有的) old ▶夙怨 old grudge
夙兴夜寐 sù xīng yè mèi work day and night
夙愿 sùyuàn [名] long-cherished ambition

诉 sù [动] 1 (说给人) tell (PT, PP told) ▶诉说 tell 2 (倾吐) pour ... out ▶诉苦 complain 3 (控告) accuse ▶上诉 appeal to a higher court
诉苦 sùkǔ [动] complain
诉说 sùshuō [动] tell (PT, PP told)
诉讼 sùsòng [名] legal proceedings (PL)

肃 sù [形] 1 (恭敬的) respectful ▶肃立 stand to attention 2 (严肃) serious
肃静 sùjìng [形] silent
肃立 sùlì [动] stand to attention (PT, PP stood)
肃然起敬 sùrán qǐ jìng filled with deep respect ▷老人的宽厚让我肃然起敬。The old people's generosity filled me with deep respect.

素 sù I [形] plain II [副] always ▶平素 usually III [名] 1 (蔬菜、瓜果等食物) vegetable ▶素食者 vegetarian 2 (有根本性质的) element ▶维生素 vitamin
素材 sùcái [名] material

素餐 sùcān [名] vegetarian meal
素净 sùjìng [形] neat
素来 sùlái [副] usually ▷她素来很安静。She's usually very quiet. ▷他俩素来不和。Those two never get on.
素昧平生 sù mèi píng shēng never met ▷一位素昧平生的女孩子给她买了火车票。A girl she had never met before bought her a train ticket.
素描 sùmiáo [名] sketch
素食 sùshí [名] vegetarian food
素雅 sùyǎ [形] elegant
素养 sùyǎng [名] cultivation
素质 sùzhì [名] character

速 sù I [名] speed II [形] quick ▶速算 quick calculation
速成 sùchéng [动] take a crash course (PT took, PP taken) ▷计算机速成班 a crash course in computers
速递 sùdì [动] send by express delivery (PT, PP sent)
速度 sùdù [名] speed
速记 sùjì [动] take shorthand notes (PT took, PP taken) ▷我非常羡慕会速记的人。I really admire people who know shorthand.
速溶 sùróng [动] dissolve quickly ▷速溶咖啡 instant coffee
速效 sùxiào [名] fast action ▷用这种方法减肥有速效。You will see quick results with this diet. ▷速效止痛片 fast-acting pain killer
速写 sùxiě [名] sketch

宿 sù [动] stay
→另见 xiǔ
宿敌 sùdí [名] old enemy
宿命论 sùmìnglùn [名] fatalism
宿舍 sùshè [名] dormitory
宿营 sùyíng [动] camp
宿愿 sùyuàn [名] long-cherished ambition

粟 sù [名] millet

塑 sù I [动] model II [名] mould (英), mold (美)
塑料 sùliào [名] plastic
塑像 sùxiàng [名] statue
塑造 sùzào [动] 1 (指用物质材料制造) shape 2 (指用艺术手段制造) model

溯 sù [动] 1 (逆水走) go upstream (PT went, PP gone) 2 (回想) recollect
溯源 sùyuán [动] trace ... back to its roots

簌 sù I [拟] rustle II [形] 1 (形容眼泪) streaming 2 (形容发抖) shivering

酸 suān I [形] 1 (指味道) sour 2 (伤心) sad 3 (迂腐) pedantic 4 (疼) sore II [名] acid

酸楚 suānchǔ [形] miserable

酸溜溜 suānliūliū [形] 1 (形容味道) sour 2 (形容嫉妒) envious 3 (形容言谈举止) pedantic

酸奶 suānnǎi [名] yoghurt

酸甜苦辣 suān tián kǔ là all the pains and pleasures of life

酸性 suānxìng [名] acidity

蒜 suàn [名] garlic

蒜头 suàntóu [名] bulb of garlic

算 suàn [动] 1 (计算) calculate 2 (计算进去) count 3 (谋划) plan 》暗算 plot against 4 (当作) be considered as 5 (由某人负责) blame 6 (算数) count 7 (作罢) 》算了吧，这些小事我们就不要再管了。Forget it, we needn't worry about these small details. 》这工作今天做不完就算了，明天再说。Let's leave it for today and try again tomorrow. 8 (推测) suppose 9 (表示突出) 》几个朋友中算他最有钱。He must be the richest of that group of friends. 》全班算他最小。He has to be the youngest in the class.

算法 suànfǎ [名] algorithm

算计 suànji I [动] 1 (计算数目) calculate 2 (考虑) consider 3 (估计) guess 4 (暗中谋算) plot II [名] plan

算命 suànmìng [动] tell sb's fortune (PT, PP told) 》算命先生 fortune teller

算盘 suànpán [名] 1 (计算用具) abacus 2 (喻) (打算) scheme

算术 suànshù [名] maths (SG) (英), math (美)

算数 suànshù [动] count

算账 suànzhàng [动] 1 (计算账目) work out accounts 》年底一算账，他赚了1万多元。When he worked out his accounts at the end of the year, he had earned over ten thousand yuan. 2 (把事情扯平) get even with

尿 suī [名] piss (讳)
➜ 另见 niào

虽 suī [连] although 》他个子虽小，力气却很大。Although he isn't big, he's very strong.

虽然 suīrán [连] although

随 suí [动] 1 (跟随) follow 2 (顺从) go along with (PT went, PP gone) 3 (任凭) let ... do as they like (PT, PP let) 》孩子大了，随他去吧。The child's grown up – let him do as he wishes. 4 (方) (像) take after (PT took, PP taken) 》小女孩长得随她爸爸。The little girl takes after her father.

随便 suíbiàn I [动] do as one wishes 》这件事怎样处理你随便吧。Deal with this matter as you wish. II [形] 1 (随意) casual 2 (欠考虑的) thoughtless III [副] 》大家随便坐。Everyone can sit where they like. 》她在商店里随便逛逛。She's wandering around the shops. IV [连] no matter

随波逐流 suí bō zhú liú go with the flow

随处 suíchù [副] anywhere

随从 suícóng I [名] entourage II [动] accompany

随大溜 suí dàliù follow the crowd

随地 suídì [副] anywhere

随风倒 suífēngdǎo be easily swayed

随风转舵 suí fēng zhuǎn duò (贬) follow the prevailing wind

随和 suíhe [形] easygoing

随后 suíhòu [副] soon after

随机应变 suí jī yìng biàn change with the times

随即 suíjí [副] immediately

随口 suíkǒu [副] carelessly

随身 suíshēn [副] 》每个士兵要随身携带30多公斤物品。Every soldier must carry over 30 kilos on their back. 》乘客的随身行李不能超过10公斤。Passengers may not bring more than ten kilograms of hand luggage on board.

随身听 suíshēntīng [名] Walkman®

随声附和 suí shēng fùhè echo sb's words 》他的讲话真荒唐，但有很多人随声附和。What he says is ridiculous, yet many people echo his words.

随时 suíshí [副] at any time

随手 suíshǒu [副] on one's way 》请随手关门。Please close the door on your way. 》他随手把信放在抽屉里。He put the letter in a drawer on his way past.

随同 suítóng [动] accompany

随意 suíyì [动] do as one likes

随遇而安 suí yù ér ān adapt to changing circumstances

随着 suízhe [动] follow 》他随着父母移民加拿大了。Following his parents, he emigrated to Canada.

髓 suí [名] marrow 》骨髓 bone marrow

岁 suì I [名] year II [量] year 》他20岁了。He's 20 years old.

岁数 suìshu [名] age ▷在他这个岁数，不应该再干重体力活了。He shouldn't be doing heavy manual work at his age.

岁月 suìyuè [名] years (PL)

遂 suì [动] 1 (如意) satisfy 2 (成功) succeed ▷杀人未遂 attempted murder

遂愿 suìyuàn [动] fulfil sb's wishes

碎 suì I [动] 1 (破碎) break (PT broke, PP broken) 2 (使粉碎) smash ▶碎纸机 shredder II [形] 1 (不完整) broken 2 (说话唠叨) garrulous

隧 suì [名] tunnel

隧道 suìdào [名] tunnel

燧 suì [名] flint

燧石 suìshí [名] flint

穗 suì [名] 1 (指植物) ear ▶麦穗 ear of wheat 2 (指装饰品) tassel

孙 sūn [名] grandchild (PL grandchildren) ▷祖孙三代 three generations

孙女 sūnnǚ [名] granddaughter

孙子 sūnzi [名] grandson

损 sǔn I [动] 1 (减少) decrease 2 (损害) harm 3 (损坏) damage 4 (方)(挖苦) make fun of II [形](方) mean

损公肥私 sǔn gōng féi sī embezzle public funds

损害 sǔnhài [动] 1 (健康) damage 2 (利益) harm 3 (名誉) ruin 4 (关系) damage

损耗 sǔnhào [动] lose (PT, PP lost) ▷我们必须减少生产过程中的能源损耗。We must reduce loss of resources in the production process.

损坏 sǔnhuài [动] damage

损人利己 sǔn rén lì jǐ hurt others to benefit oneself

损失 sǔnshī I [动] lose (PT, PP lost) II [名] loss

笋 sǔn [名] bamboo shoot

唆 suō [动] instigate

唆使 suōshǐ [动] incite

梭 suō [名] shuttle

梭镖 suōbiāo [动] spear

梭巡 suōxún [动] patrol

梭子 suōzi [名] 1 (用于纺织) shuttle 2 (用于枪支) clip

缩 suō [动] 1 (收缩) contract 2 (收回去) withdraw (PT withdrew, PP withdrawn)

缩减 suōjiǎn [动] 1 (经费) cut (PT, PP cut) 2 (人员) reduce

缩略语 suōlüèyǔ [名] abbreviation

缩手缩脚 suō shǒu suō jiǎo 1 (指寒冷) shrink with cold (PT shrank, PP shrunk) 2 (形容顾虑多) be overcautious

缩水 suōshuǐ [动] shrink (PT shrank, PP shrunk) ▷这件T恤衫缩水吗？Will this T-shirt shrink in the wash?

缩写 suōxiě I [名] abbreviation ▷NATO是英文North Atlantic Treaty Organization 的缩写。NATO is the abbreviation for the North Atlantic Treaty Organization. II [动] abridge

缩影 suōyǐng [名] epitome

所 suǒ I [名] 1 (处所) place 2 (用于机构名称) office ▶派出所 local police station ▶诊所 clinic II [量] ▷一所大学 a university III [助] 1 (表示被动) ▷她被我的真诚所感动。She was deeply moved by my sincerity. ▷他被金钱所迷惑。He's obsessed with money. 2 (表示强调) ▷我所看过的影片很少有大片。Out of all the films I've seen, hardly any have been blockbusters. ▷这正是大家所不理解的。This is the bit that no-one understands.

所得税 suǒdéshuì [名] income tax

所属 suǒshǔ [名] 1 (统属之下的) subordinate 2 (自己隶属的) affiliation

所谓 suǒwèi [形] 1 (通常说的) ▷中医所谓"上火"不止是指嗓子疼一种症状。What is known in Chinese medicine as 'excess internal heat' covers a lot more than sore throats and the like. ▷所谓"网虫"，就是上网上瘾的人。The people we refer to as 'Net Worms' are addicted to the Internet. 2 (形容不认可) so-called

所向披靡 suǒ xiàng pī mǐ invincible

所以 suǒyǐ [连] 1 (表示结果) so ▷路上堵车，所以我迟到了。There was a lot of traffic, so I am late. 2 (表示突出原因) the reason why ▷她之所以成功，是因为坚持不懈。The reason for her success is her unremitting effort.

所以然 suǒyǐrán [名] the reason why

所有 suǒyǒu I [动] own II [名] possession III [形] all

所有权 suǒyǒuquán [名] proprietary rights (PL)

所有制 suǒyǒuzhì [名] ownership

所在 suǒzài [名] ▷这便是问题的症结所在。This is the crux of the matter. ▷巨大的市场是中国的魅力所在。What gives China its appeal is its enormous markets.

索 suǒ I [名] 1 (绳子) rope 2 (链子) chain II [动] 1 (找) search ▶探索 explore 2 (要) request

索赔 suǒpéi [动] claim damages ▷他的车祸索赔要求迟迟未能得到保险公司的明确答复。His claim for damages after the car accident has still not been properly dealt with by the insurance company after all this time.

索取 suǒqǔ [动] demand ▷他来索取欠款。He's come to demand the money he's owed.

索性 suǒxìng [副] might as well ▷既然已经帮助他了, 就索性帮到底。Since we've already helped him out, we might as well help until the job is done.

索引 suǒyǐn [名] index

琐 suǒ [形] petty
琐事 suǒshì [名] triviality
琐碎 suǒsuì [形] petty

锁 suǒ I [名] lock II [动] 1 (用锁锁住) lock 2 (眉) frown
锁链 suǒliàn [名] chain

Tt

他 **tā** [代] **1** (另一人) he ▷他是教师。He's a teacher. ▷他的包在书桌上。His bag is on the desk. **2** (其他) other ▷另有他故。There is another reason.

他们 **tāmen** [代] they ▷他们学习刻苦。They study hard. ▷学生应当尊敬他们的老师。Students should respect their teachers.

他人 **tārén** [名] others (PL)

他乡 **tāxiāng** [名] a place far from home

它 **tā** [代] it ▷把它扔掉。Throw it away. ▷它的牙锋利无比。Its teeth are razor sharp.

它们 **tāmen** [代] they ▷如果下周没人来认领这些东西，它们就会被销毁了。If no-one claims these items in the next week, they will be destroyed. ▷词典都在那里，把它们拿来。The dictionaries are over there, bring them here.

她 **tā** [代] she ▷她是个杰出的外交家。She's a distinguished diplomat. ▷她的裙子在衣柜里。Her skirt is in the wardrobe.

趿 **tā** 见下文

趿拉 **tāla** [动] shuffle along

塌 **tā** [动] **1** (倒塌) collapse **2** (凹下) sink (PT sank, PP sunk) ▷他瘦得连双颊都塌下去了。He's got so thin that even his cheeks are sunken. **3** (安定) settle down

塌方 **tāfāng** [动] collapse

塌实 **tāshi** [形] **1** (不浮躁) steady **2** (放心) at peace

塔 **tǎ** [名] **1** (指佛教建筑物) pagoda **2** (指塔形物) tower

塔楼 **tǎlóu** [名] tower block

獭 **tǎ** [名] otter

踏 **tà** [动] **1** (踩) step onto **2** (喻) start ▷我刚踏上工作岗位。I've just started working.

踏青 **tàqīng** [动] go on an outing in spring (PT went, PP gone)

胎 **tāi** [名] **1** (母体内的幼体) foetus (英), fetus (美) ▷怀胎 be pregnant **2** (生育次数) pregnancy **3** (轮胎) tyre (英), tire (美)

胎儿 **tāi'ér** [名] foetus (英), fetus (美)

胎记 **tāijì** [名] birthmark

胎盘 **tāipán** [名] placenta

胎生 **tāishēng** [形] viviparous ▷胎生动物 viviparous animal

台 **tái** I [名] **1** (指建筑) tower ▷观测台 observation tower **2** (指讲话、表演) stage ▷舞台 stage **3** (指作座子用) stand ▷蜡台 candlestick **4** (台形物) ▷窗台 window sill ▷站台 platform **5** (桌子或类似物) table ▷梳妆台 dressing table ▷写字台 desk **6** (指电话服务) telephone service ▷长途台 long-distance service ▷查号台 directory inquiries (SG) **7** (指广播电视) station ▷电视台 television station **8** (台湾) Taiwan II [量] **1** (指机器) ▷一台电脑 a computer **2** (指戏剧、戏曲) ▷两台京剧 two Beijing Opera performances

台布 **táibù** [名] tablecloth

台词 **táicí** [名] line

台风 **táifēng** [名] typhoon

台阶 **táijiē** [名] **1** (指建筑) step **2** (喻) way out ▷我赶快换了话题以便给他们找个台阶儿下。I hurriedly changed the subject to give them a way out.

台历 **táilì** [名] desk calendar

台球 **táiqiú** [名] **1** (指美式) pool **2** (指英式) billiards

台柱子 **táizhùzi** [名] leading figure

苔 **tái** [名] moss

苔藓 **táixiǎn** [名] moss

抬 **tái** [动] **1** (举) raise **2** (搬) carry **3** (抬杠) bicker

抬杠 táigàng [动] bicker

抬举 táiju [动] favour (英), favor (美) ▷别太抬举他了，他会骄傲的。Don't favour him too much or he'll get conceited. ▷你真不识抬举! You're so ungrateful!

抬头 táitóu [动] 1 (昂头) raise one's head 2 (喻) (势力、受压制的人) get a foothold ▷我们绝对不能让偷渡活动抬头。We must not let the people-smugglers get a foothold.

太 tài I [形] 1 (高或大) highest ▶太空 space 2 (指辈分高) senior ▶太爷爷 great-grandfather II [副] 1 (指程度过分) too ▷这部电影太长。This film is too long. 2 (指程度极高) so ▷我太高兴了。I am so happy. 3 (用于否定) that ▷她跑得不太快。She's not that fast a runner.

太极拳 tàijíquán [名] Tai-chi

太监 tàijiàn [名] eunuch

太空 tàikōng [名] space

太平 tàipíng [形] peaceful

太平间 tàipíngjiān [名] mortuary

太平无事 tàipíng wú shì all is well

太平洋 Tàipíngyáng [名] the Pacific Ocean

太太 tàitai [名] 1 (妻子) wife (PL wives) 2 (指对老年妇女) lady 3 (对已婚妇女) Mrs ▷张太太 Mrs. Zhang

太阳 tàiyáng [名] sun ▷太阳系 solar system

太子 tàizǐ [名] crown prince

态 tài [名] 1 (状态) state ▶常态 normality ▶体态 posture 2 (语言) voice

态度 tàidu [名] 1 (举止神情) manner ▷这里的服务员态度好。The service is good here. 2 (看法) attitude ▷他对这件事表明了态度。He made his attitude to the affair clear.

泰 tài [形] (平安) peaceful

泰斗 tàidǒu [名] leading authority

泰然 tàirán [形] calm

坍 tān [动] collapse

坍塌 tāntā [动] fall down (PT fell, PP fallen)

贪 tān I [动] 1 (贪污) be corrupt 2 (不满足) crave ▶贪玩 be too fond of a good time ▶贪吃 be greedy 3 (好处、便宜) covet II [形] greedy

贪杯 tānbēi [动] be too fond of alcohol

贪得无厌 tān dé wú yàn insatiably greedy

贪官污吏 tān guān wū lì corrupt official

贪婪 tānlán [形] greedy

贪恋 tānliàn [动] overindulge in

贪生怕死 tān shēng pà sǐ do anything to save one's neck

贪图 tāntú [动] covet

贪污 tānwū [动] embezzle

贪心 tānxīn I [形] greedy II [名] greed

贪赃 tānzāng [动] take bribes (PT took, PP taken)

摊 tān I [动] 1 (摆开) spread ... out (PT, PP spread) ▷摊开地图 spread out a map ▷我们把问题摊开来解决。In order to solve a problem we need to air it. 2 (指烹调) fry ▷他摊了个鸡蛋。He fried an egg. 3 (分担) share 4 (碰到) run into (PT ran, PP run) II [名] stall

摊点 tāndiǎn [名] stall

摊贩 tānfàn [名] street trader

摊牌 tānpái [动] put one's cards on the table (PT, PP put)

摊派 tānpài [动] apportion

摊位 tānwèi [名] stall

摊子 tānzi [名] 1 (摊位) stall 2 (喻) (规模) scale 3 (喻) (混乱) shambles (SG) ▷他被派来收拾烂摊子。He's been sent here to sort out this shambles.

滩 tān [名] 1 (指河、湖) bank 2 (指海) beach 3 (指水很急) rapids (PL)

瘫 tān I [名] paralysis II [形] paralysed (英), paralyzed (美)

瘫痪 tānhuàn I [名] paralysis II [动] be paralysed (英) 或 paralyzed (美)

坛 tán [名] 1 (祭坛) altar 2 (土台) raised plot ▶花坛 raised flower bed 3 (圈子) circles (PL) 4 (台子) platform ▶论坛 forum 5 (壶) jug

谈 tán I [动] talk ▷谈生意 discuss business II [名] talk ▷无稽之谈 nonsense

谈何容易 tán hé róngyì easier said than done

谈虎色变 tán hǔ sè biàn turn pale at the mention of

谈话 tánhuà [动] chat

谈论 tánlùn [动] discuss

谈判 tánpàn [动] negotiate ▷商业谈判 commercial negotiation

谈天 tántiān [动] chat

谈吐 tántǔ [名] way of talking

谈笑风生 tán xiào fēng shēng talk cheerfully

谈心 tánxīn [动] have a heart-to-heart talk

弹 tán I [动] 1 (指弹性) spring (PT sprang, PP sprung) ▷门弹了回来。The door sprang back.

▷球弹不起来了。The ball doesn't bounce. ▷香槟酒瓶盖弹上了天。The champagne cork shot into the air. **2** (棉花、羊毛) fluff ... up **3** (土、灰、球) flick **4** (乐器) play **II** [形] springy
→另见 dàn

弹劾 tánhé [动] impeach

弹簧 tánhuáng [名] spring ▶弹簧门 swing door

弹力 tánlì [名] elasticity ▶弹力裤 stretch trousers (英) 或 pants (美)

弹性 tánxìng [名] **1** (弹力) elasticity **2** (喻) flexibility ▷弹性工作制 flexible working system ▷法律是没有弹性的。The law is inflexible.

弹奏 tánzòu [动] play

痰 tán [名] phlegm

潭 tán [名] deep pool

檀 tán [名] sandalwood

忐 tǎn 见下文

忐忑 tǎntè [形] disturbed ▷忐忑不安 ill at ease

坦 tǎn [形] **1** (平整) flat **2** (直率) candid **3** (心里安定) calm ▶坦然 composed

坦白 tǎnbái **I** [形] candid **II** [动] confess

坦诚 tǎnchéng [形] frank

坦荡 tǎndàng [形] **1** (指道路) broad and smooth **2** (指心胸) magnanimous

坦然 tǎnrán [形] calm ▷他坦然面对死亡。He is facing death calmly.

坦率 tǎnshuài [形] frank ▷双方坦率地交换了意见。The two parties had a frank exchange of views.

坦途 tǎntú [名] smooth road

袒 tǎn [动] **1** (露出) expose **2** (偏心) be biased

袒护 tǎnhù [动] shield

袒露 tǎnlù [动] expose

毯 tǎn [名] **1** (指地上) carpet ▶地毯 carpet **2** (指床上) blanket ▶毛毯 wool blanket **3** (指墙上) tapestry ▶壁毯 tapestry

叹 tàn [动] **1** (叹气) sigh ▶哀叹 lament **2** (书) (吟哦) chant **3** (书) (赞美) extol ▶惊叹 marvel at

叹词 tàncí [名] exclamation

叹服 tànfú [动] gasp in admiration

叹气 tànqì [动] sigh

叹为观止 tàn wéi guān zhǐ take sb's breath away

叹息 tànxī [动] sigh

炭 tàn [名] charcoal

探 tàn **I** [动] **1** (试图发现) explore **2** (看望) visit **3** (伸出去) stick ... out (PT, PP stuck) **4** (过问) inquire ▶探究 scout **II** [名] scout ▶侦探 detective

探测 tàncè [动] survey

探查 tànchá [动] examine

探访 tànfǎng [动] **1** (搜寻) seek ... out (PT, PP sought) **2** (亲友) visit

探戈 tàngē [名] tango

探究 tànjiū [动] investigate

探亲 tànqīn [动] visit one's relatives

探求 tànqiú [动] seek (PT, PP sought)

探视 tànshì [动] visit

探索 tànsuǒ [动] probe ▷科学探索 scientific investigation

探讨 tàntǎo [动] investigate

探听 tàntīng [动] scout about

探望 tànwàng [动] **1** (看望) visit **2** (看) look around

探险 tànxiǎn [动] explore

碳 tàn [名] carbon

碳水化合物 tànshuǐ-huàhéwù [名] carbohydrate

汤 tāng [名] **1** (热水) hot water **2** (指食物) soup

汤剂 tāngjì [名] herbal medicine

汤料 tāngliào [名] stock

汤药 tāngyào [名] herbal medicine

趟 tāng [动] wade ▷我们趟过一条小河。We waded through a stream.
→另见 tàng

唐 táng [名] (唐朝) the Tang Dynasty

唐突 tángtū [形] brusque

堂 táng **I** [名] **1** (房屋) hall ▶礼堂 auditorium ▶课堂 classroom ▶教堂 church **2** (厅) hall **II** [量] ▷两堂课 two lessons

堂皇 tánghuáng [形] imposing

堂堂 tángtáng [形] dignified

塘 táng [名] **1** (堤防) embankment ▶海塘 sea wall **2** (水池) pond **3** (浴池) public bathhouse

搪 táng [动] **1** (抵挡) keep ... out (PT, PP kept) **2** (搪塞) prevaricate

搪瓷 tángcí [名] enamel

搪塞 tángsè [动] prevaricate

膛 táng [名] 1 (胸) chest 2 (中空部分) cavity ▷枪膛 bore

糖 táng [名] 1 (指做饭) sugar ▷糖醋鸡 sweet-and-sour chicken 2 (糖果) sweet

糖果 tángguǒ [名] sweet

糖衣 tángyī [名] sugar coating ▷糖衣片 sugar-coated tablet

螳 táng [名] mantis

倘 tǎng [连] if

倘若 tǎngruò [连] if

倘使 tǎngshǐ [连] if

淌 tǎng [动] drip ▷淌眼泪 shed tears

躺 tǎng [动] lie (PT lay, PP lain)

烫 tàng I [形] very hot ▷这汤真烫。This soup is boiling hot. ▷滚烫的水 boiling hot water II [动] 1 (人) scald ▷他被热水烫了。He was scalded by hot water. 2 (加热) heat ... up ▷日本清酒要烫过后再喝。Japanese wine should be heated before drinking. ▷她每天都烫脚。She bathes her feet in warm water everyday. 3 (熨) iron 4 (头发) perm

烫手 tàngshǒu [形] scalding

趟 tàng I [量] ▷我已经去了好几趟。I've made several trips. II [名] ranks (PL)
→另见 tāng

涛 tāo [名] wave

掏 tāo [动] 1 (拿出) take ... out (PT took, PP taken) 2 (挖) dig (PT, PP dug) 3 (偷) steal (PT stole, PP stolen)

滔 tāo [形] torrential

滔滔 tāotāo [形] 1 (指水势) torrential 2 (指说话) verbose ▷他说起话来是滔滔不绝。When he starts talking, he just goes on and on.

滔天 tāotiān [形] 1 (指波浪) towering 2 (指灾祸或罪恶) heinous

韬 tāo I [名] (书) art of war II [动] conceal

韬略 tāolüè [名] military strategy

逃 táo [动] 1 (逃跑) run away (PT ran, PP run) 2 (逃避) flee (PT, PP fled)

逃避 táobì [动] escape ▷逃避责任 shirk responsibility ▷逃避关税 evade customs duties

逃窜 táocuàn [动] flee (PT, PP fled)

逃犯 táofàn [名] escaped criminal

逃荒 táohuāng [动] flee from famine (PT, PP fled)

逃命 táomìng [动] run for one's life (PT ran, PP run)

逃难 táonàn [动] flee from disaster (PT, PP fled)

逃跑 táopǎo [动] escape

逃生 táoshēng [动] run for one's life (PT ran, PP run) ▷他们真是死里逃生。They had a narrow escape from death.

逃亡 táowáng [动] go into exile (PT went, PP gone)

逃之夭夭 táo zhī yāoyāo make a getaway

桃 táo [名] peach

桃李 táolǐ [名] 1 (桃和李) peaches and plums 2 (喻) (学生) student

桃色 táosè I [名] (粉红色) peach ▷她穿着一件桃色的连衣裙。She was wearing a peach-coloured dress. II [形] sexual ▷桃色新闻 sexual scandal

陶 táo I [名] pottery II [动] 1 (制陶) make pottery 2 (教育培养) mould (英), mold (美) ▷熏陶 nurture III [形] happy ▷乐陶陶 happy and contented

陶瓷 táocí [名] ceramics (SG)

陶器 táoqì [名] pottery

陶然 táorán [形] carefree

陶冶 táoyě [动] mould (英), mold (美)

陶醉 táozuì [动] be intoxicated ▷他们陶醉于成功的喜悦中。They are intoxicated with the joys of success.

淘 táo I [动] 1 (米) wash 2 (金子) pan for ▷淘金 pan for gold 3 (厕所) clean ... out II [形] naughty

淘气 táoqì [形] naughty

淘汰 táotài [动] eliminate ▷意大利足球队在第一轮就被淘汰了。The Italian football team was eliminated in the first round.

讨 tǎo [动] 1 (债) demand 2 (饭、钱) beg 3 (帮助) ask for 4 (谴责) denounce ▷声讨 censure 5 (娶) marry 6 (招惹) provoke 7 (讨论) discuss ▷探讨 inquire into

讨伐 tǎofá [动] send troops against (PT, PP sent)

讨好 tǎohǎo [动] 1 (取得欢心) curry favour with 2 (得到好效果) get a good result

讨价还价 tǎo jià huán jià haggle ▷做分给你的工作，不要讨价还价。Do the job you've been given and don't make a fuss.

讨教 tǎojiào [动] ask for advice

讨论 tǎolùn [动] discuss ▷小组展开了一次讨论。The team held a discussion.

注意 discuss 绝不能用作不及物动词。例如, 'They discussed.', 'I discussed with him.' 或 'They discussed about politics.' 都是不正确的用法。然而, 可以说跟某人就某事 have a discussion。I had a long discussion about all this with Stephen. 或者, discuss 某事物 with 某人。I discussed my essay with my teacher. 若讨论不十分正式, 可以只用动词 talk。They come here and sit for hours talking about politics…We talked all night long.

讨嫌 tǎoxián [形] annoying

讨厌 tǎoyàn I [形] 1 (可恶) disgusting 2 (指难办) nasty II [动] dislike

套 tào I [名] 1 (套子) cover ▶手套 glove ▶避孕套 condom 2 (应酬话) convention 3 (阴谋) trap II [动] 1 (罩在外面) slip … on 2 (拴) harness 3 (引出) trick … into ▷套口供 trick a suspect into making a confession 4 (模仿) copy 5 (拉拢) win … over (PT, PP won) III [量] ▷一套西装 a suit ▷两套邮票 two sets of stamps

套餐 tàocān [名] set meal

套话 tàohuà [名] cliché

套袖 tàoxiù [名] oversleeve

套用 tàoyòng [动] apply … indiscriminately

套语 tàoyǔ [名] polite formula

套装 tàozhuāng [名] suit

套子 tàozi [名] 1 (罩子) cover 2 (俗套) formula 3 (圈套) trap

特 tè I [形] special ▶特价 special price II [副] 1 (特地) especially 2 (非常) extremely III [名] secret agent

特别 tèbié I [形] peculiar ▷他的口音很特别。His accent is peculiar. II [副] 1 (格外) exceptionally ▷这种产品质量特别好。The quality of this product is exceptionally good. 2 (特地) specially ▷我们特别为你准备了你爱吃的东西。We've prepared the things you like to eat specially for you.

特别行政区 tèbié xíngzhèngqū [名] special administration region

特产 tèchǎn [名] speciality (英), specialty (美)

特长 tècháng [名] speciality (英), specialty (美)

特此 tècǐ [副] hereby ▷他是我公司职员, 特此证明。I hereby declare that he is an employee of my company.

特地 tèdì [副] especially

特点 tèdiǎn [名] characteristic

特定 tèdìng [形] specific

特技 tèjì [名] 1 (指表演) stunt 2 (指电影) special effects (PL)

特价 tèjià [名] bargain price ▷特价商品 bargain

特例 tèlì [名] special case

特区 tèqū [名] special zone ▷经济特区 special economic zone

特权 tèquán [名] privilege

特色 tèsè [名] characteristic

特赦 tèshè [动] give a special pardon to (PT gave, PP given)

特使 tèshǐ [名] special envoy

特殊 tèshū [形] special ▷特殊情况 special circumstances

特务 tèwu [名] special agent

特写 tèxiě [名] 1 (指文学) feature 2 (指电影) close-up

特性 tèxìng [名] characteristic

特许 tèxǔ [名] special permission ▷特许出口证 special export permit

特邀 tèyāo [动] specially invite ▷特邀代表 specially invited representative

特异 tèyì [形] exceptional

特意 tèyì [副] deliberately

特征 tèzhēng [名] characteristic

特种 tèzhǒng [形] special ▷特种部队 special forces

疼 téng I [形] sore ▷我牙疼。I have toothache. II [动] love

疼爱 téng'ài [动] love … dearly

腾 téng [动] 1 (奔跑) gallop 2 (跳跃) jump 3 (升到空中) rise (PT rose, PP risen) 4 (空出) vacate ▷我腾出时间学习。I make time for study. 5 (激动) excite

腾达 téngdá [动] take … off (PT took, PP taken)

腾飞 téngfēi [动] boom

腾腾 téngténg [形] seething

誊 téng [动] copy

誊写 téngxiě [动] copy

藤 téng [名] vine ▶藤椅 cane chair

剔 tī [动] 1 (牙、指甲) pick 2 (除) pick … out 3 (肉) pick meat off a bone

剔除 tīchú [动] reject

梯 tī [名] ladder ▶电梯 lift (英), elevator (美)

▶楼梯 stairs (PL)

梯形 tīxíng [名] trapezoid

踢 tī [动] kick ▷踢足球 play football

提 tí [动] 1 (拿) carry ▷他提着个箱子。He's carrying a suitcase. 2 (升) raise ▷提嗓子 raise one's voice ▷他被提为大副。He was promoted to first mate. 3 (提前) bring forward (PT, PP brought) ▷会议向前提了。The meeting has been brought forward. 4 (提出) put ... forward (PT, PP put) ▷他提了个建议。He put forward a proposal. 5 (提取) collect ▶提 炼 extract 6 (谈起) mention ▷别再提那件事 了。Don't mention that subject again.
→另见 dī

提案 tí'àn [名] motion

提拔 tíbá [动] promote

提倡 tíchàng [名] promote

提成 tíchéng [名] commission

提出 tíchū [动] put ... forward (PT, PP put) ▷提 出改革方案 put forward a proposal for reform

提纲 tígāng [名] synopsis (PL synopses)

提纲挈领 tí gāng qiè lǐng bring out the essential points

提高 tígāo [动] raise ▷提高效率 increase efficiency ▷提高管理水平 raise the standard of management

提供 tígōng [动] provide ▷提供住宿 provide accommodation

提货 tíhuò [动] take delivery of goods (PT took, PP taken)

提交 tíjiāo [动] submit

提炼 tíliàn [动] refine

提名 tímíng [动] nominate

提前 tíqián I [动] bring ... forward (PT, PP brought) II [副] early

提亲 tíqīn [动] propose marriage

提请 tíqǐng [动] put ... forward (PT, PP put)

提取 tíqǔ [动] 1 (取出) collect ▷提取现金 withdraw cash 2 (提炼) extract

提神 tíshén [动] refresh oneself

提审 tíshěn [动] 1 (审讯) bring ... to court (PT, PP brought) 2 (上一级法院审判) review

提升 tíshēng [动] 1 (指职位) promote 2 (指档次) upgrade 3 (温度、价格) raise

提示 tíshì [动] 1 (指出) point ... out 2 (提醒) remind ▷你要忘了台词, 我提示你。If you forget your lines, I'll prompt you.

提问 tíwèn [动] ask a question

提携 tíxié [动] give guidance and support (PT gave, PP given)

提心吊胆 tí xīn diào dǎn be on tenterhooks

提醒 tíxǐng [动] remind

提要 tíyào [名] synopsis (PL synopses)

提议 tíyì I [动] propose II [名] proposal

啼 tí [动] 1 (哭) cry 2 (叫) call

啼笑皆非 tí xiào jiē fēi not know whether to laugh or cry

题 tí I [名] subject ▶标题 title II [动] inscribe

题跋 tíbá [名] preface and postscript

题材 tícái [名] theme

题词 tící I [动] write a dedication (PT wrote, PP written) II [名] dedication

题库 tíkù [名] collection of past papers

题名 tímíng I [动] autograph II [名] title

题目 tímù [名] 1 (标题) title 2 (考题) question

题字 tízì I [动] inscribe II [名] inscription

蹄 tí [名] hoof (PL hooves)

体 tǐ I [名] 1 (身体) body ▶人体 human body 2 (物体) substance ▶液体 liquid 3 (指书法或文学) style 4 (语法) aspect ▷进行体 progressive aspect 5 (体制) system ▶政体 system of government II [动] 1 (亲自做) do ... personally ▷身体力行 practice what you preach 2 (为人着想) be considerate

体裁 tǐcái [名] genre

体操 tǐcāo [名] gymnastics (SG)

体察 tǐchá [动] observe

体格 tǐgé [名] physique

体会 tǐhuì I [动] come to understand (PT came, PP come) II [名] understanding

体积 tǐjī [名] volume

体检 tǐjiǎn [名] physical examination

体力 tǐlì [名] physical strength

体例 tǐlì [名] style

体谅 tǐliàng [动] show understanding (PT showed, PP shown) ▷她体谅他人的难处。She shows understanding for others' difficulties.

体面 tǐmiàn I [名] dignity II [形] 1 (荣耀) respectable 2 (好看) good-looking

体魄 tǐpò [名] physique

体态 tǐtài [名] posture

体坛 tǐtán [名] the world of sport

体贴 tǐtiē [动] show consideration for (PT showed, PP shown) ▷体贴老人 show consideration for the elderly

体统 tǐtǒng [名] decency

体温 tǐwēn [名] temperature

体无完肤 tǐ wú wán fū 1 (指人) be beaten black and blue 2 (指论点、文章) be savaged by criticism

体系 tǐxì [名] system

体现 tǐxiàn [动] embody

体形 tǐxíng [名] physique

体型 tǐxíng [名] physique

体恤 tǐxù [动] show sympathy for (PT showed, PP shown)

体验 tǐyàn [动] learn from experience

体育 tǐyù [名] 1 (课程) P. E. 2 (运动) sport ▷体育比赛 sports event

体育场 tǐyùchǎng [名] stadium

体育馆 tǐyùguǎn [名] gym

体制 tǐzhì [名] system

体质 tǐzhì [名] physique

体重 tǐzhòng [名] weight

屉 tì [名] 1 (笼屉) steamer 2 (抽屉) drawer

剃 tì [动] shave

涕 tì [名] 1 (书) (眼泪) tear 2 (鼻涕) mucus

替 tì I [动] 1 (代) replace ▷我替你看孩子。I'll look after the children for you. 2 (衰败) decline II [介] for ▷别替他操心了。Don't worry about him.

替补 tìbǔ [形] substitute

替代 tìdài [动] replace

替换 tìhuàn [动] replace

替身 tìshēn [名] body double

替罪羊 tìzuìyáng [名] scapegoat

天 tiān I [名] 1 (天空) sky ▷鸽子在天上飞。Pigeons were flying in the sky. 2 (一昼夜) day ▶昨天 yesterday ▷他3天后回来。He'll come back in three days' time. 3 (一段时间) ▷五更天 before dawn ▷天还早呢。It's still so early. 4 (季节) season ▶秋天 autumn (英), fall (美) 5 (天气) weather ▶阴天 overcast weather ▷天很热。It's a very hot day. 6 (自然) nature ▷人定胜天。Man can conquer nature. 7 (造物主) God ▷天知道！God knows! 8 (神的住所) Heaven ▷上西天 go to Heaven II [形] (指位于顶部的) overhead ▶天桥 overhead walkway

天才 tiāncái [名] 1 (才能) talent 2 (人) genius

天长地久 tiān cháng dì jiǔ eternal

天窗 tiānchuāng [名] skylight

天敌 tiāndí [名] natural enemy

天地 tiāndì [名] 1 (天和地) world ▷天地间 in this world 2 (境地) field ▷科学研究的新天地 a new field of scientific research

天鹅 tiān'é [名] swan

天翻地覆 tiān fān dì fù 1 (指变化) earth-shattering 2 (形容胡闹) upheaval

天方夜谭 tiānfāng yètán pie in the sky ▷你的想法简直就是天方夜谭。Your ideas are just pie in the sky.

天分 tiānfèn [名] talent

天赋 tiānfù I [动] be innate II [名] talent ▷他很有艺术天赋。He has a talent for art.

天高地厚 tiān gāo dì hòu 1 (恩情) profound 2 (复杂性) complex

天各一方 tiān gè yī fāng be far apart ▷夫妻俩现在是天各一方。The couple are currently far away from each other.

天寒地冻 tiān hán dì dòng freezing

天花乱坠 tiān huā luàn zhuì wild exaggeration

天昏地暗 tiān hūn dì àn 1 (指天气) a murky sky over a dark earth 2 (指政治) chaos and corruption

天机 tiānjī [名] 1 (字) mysteries of nature (PL) 2 (喻) important secret

天价 tiānjià [名] astronomical price

天经地义 tiān jīng dì yì unalterable truth

天空 tiānkōng [名] sky

天理 tiānlǐ [名] justice

天良 tiānliáng [名] conscience ▷他这样做是丧尽天良。He acted completely without conscience in this affair.

天伦 tiānlún [名] natural bonds (PL) ▷享受天伦之乐 enjoy the happiness of family life

天罗地网 tiān luó dì wǎng tight encirclement

天命 tiānmìng [名] fate

天南海北 tiān nán hǎi běi 1 (遥远) far away ▷即使身处天南海北，我们也要互相关心。Even if we are far away from one another, we must still care for each other. 2 (不同的地区) different places ▷大家来自天南海北。We all come from very different places. 3 (指话题) far-reaching

天平 tiānpíng [名] scales (PL)

天气 tiānqì [名] weather ▷天气预报 weather forecast

天然 tiānrán [形] natural

天壤之别 tiānrǎng zhī bié poles apart ▷我们之间的信仰有着天壤之别。Our beliefs are poles apart.

天日 tiānrì [名] light

天色 tiānsè [名] time of day ▷天色已晚。It's getting late.

天生 tiānshēng [形] inherent ▷这孩子天生聋

哑。This child was born deaf-mute.

天时 tiānshí [名] opportunity

天使 tiānshǐ [名] angel

天书 tiānshū [名] (喻) gobbledegook

天堂 tiāntáng [名] Heaven

天体 tiāntǐ [名] heavenly body

天文 tiānwén [名] astronomy ▷天文望远镜 astronomical telescope

天文数字 tiānwén shùzì [名] astronomical figure

天无绝人之路 tiān wú jué rén zhī lù there is always a way out

天下 tiānxià [名] the world

天仙 tiānxiān [名] 1 (男神仙) god 2 (女神仙) goddess 3 (美女) beauty

天险 tiānxiǎn [名] natural barrier

天线 tiānxiàn [名] aerial

天象 tiānxiàng [名] astronomical phenomena (PL)

天性 tiānxìng [名] nature

天旋地转 tiān xuán dì zhuàn feel dizzy ▷坐缆车使我觉得天旋地转。Sitting in the cable car, I felt as though the world was spinning.

天涯 tiānyá [名] the ends of the earth ▷浪迹天涯 wander to the ends of the earth

天衣无缝 tiān yī wú fèng flawless

天意 tiānyì [名] God's will

天有不测风云 tiān yǒu bùcè fēngyún something unexpected can always happen ▷天有不测风云，人有旦夕祸福。Life is as unpredictable as the weather.

天灾 tiānzāi [名] natural disaster

天造地设 tiān zào dì shè ideal

天真 tiānzhēn [形] innocent

天之骄子 tiān zhī jiāozǐ child of good fortune

天职 tiānzhí [名] bounden duty

天资 tiānzī [名] talent ▷天资聪颖 endowed with great intelligence

天子 tiānzǐ [名] the emperor of China

天字第一号 tiān zì dì yī hào greatest in the world ▷你是天字第一号傻瓜。You are the most stupid fool in the world.

添 tiān [动] 1 (增加) add ▷添衣服 put on more clothes 2 (生孩子) give birth to (PT gave, PP given)

添补 tiānbǔ [动] replenish

添加剂 tiānjiājì [名] additive

添枝加叶 tiān zhī jiā yè embellish the facts

添置 tiānzhì [动] acquire

田 tián [名] 1 (耕地) field 2 (开采地) field ▷油田 oilfield

田地 tiándì [名] 1 (指耕种) field 2 (地步) plight

田径 tiánjìng [名] track and field sports (PL)

田野 tiányě [名] open country

田园 tiányuán [名] countryside ▷田园风光 rural scenery

恬 tián [形] quiet ▶恬适 quiet and comfortable

恬不知耻 tián bù zhī chǐ have no sense of shame

恬静 tiánjìng [形] peaceful

甜 tián [形] 1 (指味道) sweet 2 (指睡觉) sound 3 (喻) (幸福) happy

甜点 tiándiǎn [名] dessert

甜蜜 tiánmì [形] happy ▷甜蜜的话语 honeyed words

甜食 tiánshí [名] sweet

甜丝丝 tiánsīsī [形] 1 (指味道) sweet 2 (指心情) happy

甜头 tiántou [名] 1 (指味) sweet taste 2 (指利益) benefit ▷他尝到了科学种田的甜头。He benefited from scientific farming.

甜言蜜语 tián yán mì yǔ honeyed words ▷不要为甜言蜜语所迷惑。Don't be taken in by honeyed words.

填 tián [动] 1 (塞满) fill 2 (补充) fill ▷填补空白 fill a gap 3 (填写) complete ▷填表格 fill in a form

填报 tiánbào [动] complete and submit

填充 tiánchōng [动] 1 (填上) stuff 2 (补足) fill ... in

填空 tiánkòng [动] 1 (指工作) fill a vacancy 2 (指考试) fill in the blanks

填写 tiánxiě [动] fill ... in

舔 tiǎn [动] lick

挑 tiāo [动] 1 (肩扛) carry ... on a carrying pole 2 (挑选) choose (PT chose, PP chosen) 3 (挑剔) nitpick
→另见 tiǎo

挑刺儿 tiāocìr [动] be overcritical

挑肥拣瘦 tiāo féi jiǎn shòu be picky

挑拣 tiāojiǎn [动] be particular ▷挑拣饮食 be particular about one's food

挑三拣四 tiāo sān jiǎn sì be petty ▷不要挑三拣四了，哪个都不错的。Don't be so petty, they're all OK.

挑食 tiāoshí [动] be a fussy eater

挑剔 tiāoti [动] nitpick ▷他的工作无可挑剔。You can't find fault with his work.

挑选 tiāoxuǎn [动] select

条 tiáo I [名] 1 (细树枝) twig 2 (长条) strip 3 (层次) order ▷有条有理 well-ordered 4 (分项) item ▷逐条分析 analyse (英) 或 analyze (美) item by item 5 (律令) (短书信) note II [量] 1 (用于细长东西) ▷两条腿 two legs ▷一条烟 a multipack of cigarettes ▷两条肥皂 two bars of soap 2 (指分事项的) ▷一条新闻 an item of news 3 (指与人有关) ▷一条人命 a life

条幅 tiáofú [名] scroll

条件 tiáojiàn [名] 1 (客观因素) condition ▷自然条件 natural conditions 2 (要求) requirement ▷她符合入学条件。She fits the entry requirements for the school. ▷无条件接受 accept unconditionally 3 (状况) circumstances (PL)

条款 tiáokuǎn [名] provision

条理 tiáolǐ [名] order

条例 tiáolì [名] regulations (PL)

条令 tiáolìng [名] regulations (PL)

条目 tiáomù [名] 1 (指规章) clauses (PL) 2 (指词典) entry

条条框框 tiáo tiáo kuàng kuàng conventions and restrictions

条文 tiáowén [名] article

条形码 tiáoxíngmǎ [名] bar code

条约 tiáoyuē [名] treaty

迢 tiáo [形] remote

迢迢 tiáotiáo [形] far away ▷我的家乡在迢迢千里以外。My home town is far away. ▷千里迢迢 from afar

调 tiáo I [动] 1 (使和谐) harmonize ▶失调 imbalance 2 (使均匀) blend ▷把调料调均匀。Blend in the seasoning. ▷给钢琴调音 tune a piano 3 (调解) mediate 4 (挑逗) tease 5 (挑拨) provoke
→另见 diào

调和 tiáohé I [形] harmonious II [动] 1 (调解) reconcile 2 (妥协) compromise

调剂 tiáojì [动] 1 (配药剂) make up a prescription 2 (调整) liven ... up ▷她累的时候，就去散步调剂一下。When she's tired, she livens herself up with a walk.

调教 tiáojiào [动] 1 (孩子) educate 2 (动物) train

调节 tiáojié [动] adjust

调解 tiáojiě [动] mediate ▷调解纠纷 mediate in a dispute ▷调解矛盾 resolve a conflict

调理 tiáolǐ [动] 1 (调养) recuperate 2 (管理) take care of (PT took, PP taken) ▷她身体不好，需要调理饮食。She's not in good health and has to take care with what she eats. 3 (管教) discipline

调料 tiáoliào [名] seasoning

调配 tiáopèi [动] mix

调皮 tiáopí [形] 1 (顽皮) naughty 2 (难对付) unruly

调情 tiáoqíng [动] flirt

调试 tiáoshì [动] debug

调停 tiáotíng [动] mediate

调戏 tiáoxì [动] molest

调养 tiáoyǎng [动] take care of oneself (PT took, PP taken) ▷调养身体 take care of one's health

调整 tiáozhěng [动] adjust

笤 tiáo 见下文

笤帚 tiáozhou [名] broom

挑 tiǎo [动] 1 (扯起一头) raise 2 (向上拨) prick ▷挑水泡 lance a blister 3 (挑拨) incite 4 (喻) (公开提出) bring ... out into the open (PT, PP brought)
→另见 tiāo

挑拨 tiǎobō [动] stir ... up ▷他总是挑拨他们之间的关系。He's always stirring up trouble between them. ▷挑拨是非 sow discord

挑大梁 tiǎo dàliáng [动] be the mainstay

挑动 tiǎodòng [动] provoke ▷挑动内战 provoke a civil war

挑逗 tiǎodòu [动] tease

挑唆 tiǎosuō [动] instigate

挑衅 tiǎoxìn [动] provoke ▷武装挑衅 armed provocation

挑战 tiǎozhàn [动] challenge ▷挑战体能极限 challenge the limits of one's physical abilities ▷挑战自我 set oneself a challenge ▷面临新挑战 face a new challenge

眺 tiào [动] survey ▶远眺 look far into the distance

眺望 tiàowàng [动] survey from up high ▷眺望远方 look far into the distance

跳 tiào [动] 1 (跃) jump ▷从床上跳下来 leap out of bed ▷跳上马背 jump onto a horse 2 (弹起) bounce 3 (起伏地动) beat (PT beat, PP beaten) ▷他激动得心直跳。His heart is beating with excitement. 4 (越过) jump over ▷跳过几页 skip a few pages

跳槽 tiàocáo [动] change jobs

跳动 tiàodòng [动] beat (PT beat, PP beaten)

跳高 tiàogāo [名] high jump

跳水 tiàoshuǐ [名] diving
跳舞 tiàowǔ [动] dance
跳远 tiàoyuǎn [名] long jump
跳跃 tiàoyuè [动] jump

帖 tiē I [动] obey II [形] proper
→另见 tiě, tiè

贴 tiē I [动] 1 (粘) stick (PT, PP stuck) 2 (紧挨) be close to ▷后背贴后背站着 stand back to back 3 (补贴) subsidize II [名] allowance
贴补 tiēbǔ [动] subsidize ▷挣钱贴补家用 earn money to help with the family expenses
贴金 tiējīn [动] 1 (贴金箔) gild 2 (吹捧) boast about ▷如果他不总往自己脸上贴金，他会有很多朋友。 He'd make a lot more friends if he stopped blowing his own trumpet all the time.
贴切 tiēqiè [形] suitable ▷你对他的评价很贴切。 Your appraisal of him is very apt.
贴身 tiēshēn [形] 1 (衣服) ▷贴身衣服 underclothes (PL) 2 (随从) personal ▷贴身侍卫 personal bodyguard
贴心 tiēxīn [形] intimate ▷贴心话 confidential talk

帖 tiě [名] 1 (请帖) invitation ▷发喜帖 send out wedding invitations 2 (小卡片) card
→另见 tiē, tiè
帖子 tiězi [名] 1 (请帖) invitation 2 (招贴) poster

铁 tiě [名] 1 (金属) iron 2 (武器) weapon ▷手无寸铁 unarmed 3 (喻) (坚强) toughness ▶铁人 iron man ▶铁哥们 fast friends (PL) 4 (喻) (形容强暴) ferocity 5 (喻) (确定) unshakable ▷铁的纪律 iron discipline ▷铁的事实 hard fact
铁窗 tiěchuāng [名] 1 (窗户) window with an iron grating 2 (监狱) prison
铁道 tiědào [名] railway (英), railroad (美)
铁饭碗 tiěfànwǎn [名] (喻) job for life ▷经济改革后，很多工人都失去了铁饭碗。 After the economic reforms, a lot of workers lost their job security.
铁路 tiělù [名] railway (英), railroad (美)
铁面无私 tiě miàn wú sī strict and impartial
铁器 tiěqì [名] ironware ▷铁器时代 the Iron Age
铁青 tiěqīng [形] livid ▷她气得脸色铁青。 Her face turned livid with rage.
铁石心肠 tiě shí xīncháng hard-hearted
铁丝 tiěsī [名] wire
铁腕 tiěwàn [名] iron fist ▷以铁腕统治 rule with an iron fist
铁心 tiěxīn [动] make up one's mind to

铁证 tiězhèng [名] irrefutable proof

帖 tiè [名] copybook
→另见 tiē, tiě

厅 tīng [名] 1 (大堂) hall ▶客厅 sitting room ▶餐厅 canteen 2 (机关) office 3 (省部门名称) provincial government department ▷省教育厅 Provincial Education Department

听 tīng I [动] 1 (收听) listen to ▷听广播 listen to a broadcast 2 (听从) obey ▷听老师的话 do as the teacher says 3 (判断) supervise ▷听政 administer affairs of state 4 (任凭) allow ▷听其自然 let things take their own course II [名] tin III [量] can ▷一听啤酒 a can of beer
听从 tīngcóng [动] obey
听而不闻 tīng ér bù wén turn a deaf ear
听候 tīnghòu [动] await
听话 tīnghuà I [动] obey II [形] obedient
听话儿 tīnghuàr [动] wait for a reply
听见 tīngjiàn [动] hear (PT, PP heard) ▷我现在可以听见你了。 I can hear you now.
听讲 tīngjiǎng [动] attend a lecture
听觉 tīngjué [名] hearing ▷听觉灵敏 acute hearing
听凭 tīngpíng [动] let (PT, PP let)
听其自然 tīng qí zìrán let things take their course
听取 tīngqǔ [动] listen to
听任 tīngrèn [动] (书) allow
听说 tīngshuō [动] hear (PT, PP heard) ▷我听说他结婚了。 I've heard that he's got married.
听天由命 tīng tiān yóu mìng resign oneself to one's fate
听之任之 tīng zhī rèn zhī take a laissez-faire attitude ▷我们对毒品泛滥不能听之任之。 We can't take a laissez-faire attitude to drug abuse.
听众 tīngzhòng [名] audience

廷 tíng [名] court

亭 tíng [名] 1 (亭子) pavilion 2 (小房子) kiosk ▶报亭 newspaper stand ▶电话亭 phone box (英), phone booth (美)
亭亭玉立 tíngtíng yù lì slender

庭 tíng [名] 1 (书) (厅堂) hall 2 (院子) courtyard 3 (法庭) law court
庭院 tíngyuàn [名] courtyard

停 tíng I [动] 1 (止) stop 2 (停留) stop off ▷我

在德国停了两天。I stopped off in Germany for two days. ▷这列火车在武汉停多长时间? How long does this train stop in Wuhan? **3** (停放) park ▷车就停在大门口。The car is parked at the main gate. ▷船停在港口。The boat is moored in the harbour. **II** [形] ready ▶停妥 settled

停泊 tíngbó [动] anchor

停车场 tíngchēchǎng [名] car park (英), car lot (美)

停当 tíngdang [形] ready ▷一切准备停当。Everything's ready.

停顿 tíngdùn **I** [动] **1** (中止) halt **2** (指说话) pause **II** [名] pause

停放 tíngfàng [动] park

停火 tínghuǒ [动] cease fire ▷签订停火协议 sign a cease-fire agreement

停靠 tíngkào [动] stop at ▷船停靠在码头。The ship is berthed at the quay.

停歇 tíngxiē [动] **1** (停止) stop **2** (歇息) rest

停薪留职 tíng xīn liú zhí [动] take unpaid leave (PT took, PP taken)

停业 tíngyè [动] close down ▷一批小饭店将停业整顿。Some small restaurants will be closed while being brought up to standard.

停职 tíngzhí [动] suspend

停止 tíngzhǐ [动] stop ▷停止营业 cease trading

停滞 tíngzhì [动] stagnate

挺 tǐng **I** [动] **1** (伸直) straighten **2** (凸出) stick out (PT, PP stuck) **3** (勉强支撑) endure ▷挺过了一场病 pull through an illness ▷如果头疼，别硬挺着。If you've got a headache, don't just grin and bear it. **II** [形] **1** (直) upright **2** (突出) distinguished **III** [副] very

挺拔 tǐngbá [形] **1** (直立突出) tall and straight **2** (坚强有力) forceful

挺进 tǐngjìn [动] press on ▷大军挺进前线。The army pressed on to the front line.

挺立 tǐnglì [动] stand upright (PT, PP stood)

铤 tǐng [形] (书) quick

铤而走险 tǐng ér zǒu xiǎn rush headlong into danger

艇 tǐng [名] boat ▶游艇 yacht ▶救生艇 lifeboat

通 tōng **I** [动] **1** (连接) connect with ▶通商 have trade relations with ▷这间办公室不通风。This office is poorly ventilated. ▷这条高速公路直通上海。This expressway leads directly to Shanghai. **2** (使不堵) clear ... out ▷通下水道 clear out a drain **3** (传达)

inform ▷通电报 send a telegram **4** (通晓) understand (PT, PP understood) ▷精通英语 have a good command of English **II** [名] expert **III** [形] **1** (没有障碍) open ▷电话打通了。The call has been put through. **2** (顺畅) workable ▷这个计划行不通。This plan is unworkable. ▷我怎么也想不通他为什么要这么做。I just don't understand why he would do something like that. **3** (通顺) coherent **4** (普通) common **5** (整个) overall ▷通盘规划 overall plan **IV** [副] **1** (全部) completely **2** (一般) normally

→另见 tòng

通报 tōngbào **I** [动] **1** (指对下级) circulate a notice **2** (通知) inform **II** [名] **1** (文件) notice **2** (刊物) bulletin

通病 tōngbìng [名] common failing

通才 tōngcái [名] versatile person

通常 tōngcháng **I** [形] normal **II** [名] normal circumstances (PL) ▷我通常7点起床。Under normal circumstances, I get up at seven o'clock.

通畅 tōngchàng [形] **1** (指运行) unobstructed ▷道路通畅 the road is clear **2** (流畅) smooth

通车 tōngchē [动] open to traffic ▷环路已通车。The ring road has opened to traffic.

通称 tōngchēng **I** [名] common term **II** [动] be generally known as

通达 tōngdá [动] understand (PT, PP understood)

通道 tōngdào [名] **1** (大路) route **2** (指出入) passageway ▷剧院的通道上站满了人。The aisle of the theatre (英) 或 theater (美) was full of people. ▷地下通道 tunnel

通电 tōngdiàn [动] **1** (指电器) switch ... on ▷给冰箱通电 switch on the refrigerator **2** (指用上电) be connected to the electricity grid **3** (打电报) send a telegram (PT, PP sent)

通牒 tōngdié [名] diplomatic note ▷最后通牒 ultimatum

通告 tōnggào **I** [动] announce **II** [名] announcement ▷张贴通告 put up a notice

通过 tōngguò **I** [动] **1** (经过) pass ▷通过边境线 cross the border ▷通过障碍物 pass through barriers **2** (同意) pass ▷国会议员一致通过了这个法案。The congressmen passed the bill unanimously. **II** [介] by means of ▷他通过不正当手段牟取暴利。He made enormous profits by dishonest methods.

通红 tōnghóng [形] bright red

通婚 tōnghūn [动] intermarry

通货 tōnghuò [名] currency

通货膨胀 tōnghuò péngzhàng [动] inflate ▷战后出现了大面积的通货膨胀。After the

war, there was widespread inflation.

通缉 tōngjī [动] list ... as wanted ▷通缉令 wanted notice ▷毒品犯正被通缉。The drug dealers are listed as wanted.

通奸 tōngjiān [动] commit adultery

通力 tōnglì [动] make a concerted effort

通令 tōnglìng I [动] issue a general order ▷政府通令全国进入战争状态。The government issued a general order, declaring that the nation was at war. II [名] general order

通明 tōngmíng [形] brightly lit

通盘 tōngpán [形] overall

通气 tōngqì [动] 1 (指空气) ventilate 2 (指信息) keep in touch (PT, PP kept) ▷我们朋友之间要通气。We friends should keep in touch.

通融 tōngróng [动] 1 (给人方便) make an exception ▷请你帮助通融一下。Please help us by making an exception in this case. 2 (暂时借) make a short-term loan

通商 tōngshāng [动] have commercial relations

通顺 tōngshùn I [形] coherent II [动] polish

通俗 tōngsú [形] popular

通天 tōngtiān I [形] extremely high II [动] have direct access to the highest authorities

通通 tōngtōng [副] completely

通宵 tōngxiāo [名] all night

通晓 tōngxiǎo [动] have a good knowledge of

通信 tōngxìn [动] correspond

通行 tōngxíng [动] 1 (指交通) pass through 2 (普通适用) be in general use

通讯 tōngxùn I [名] dispatch ▷新华社通讯 Xinhua News Agency dispatch II [动] communicate

通用 tōngyòng [动] be in common use

通知 tōngzhī I [名] notification ▷发出通知 issue a notice II [动] inform

同 tóng I [动] 1 (一样) be the same ▷我们个性不同。Our personalities are different. 2 (共同) do ... together ▶同居 cohabit ▷同甘苦 stick together through thick and thin II [介] 1 (跟) with ▷你最好同他谈谈这事。You had better talk about it with him. ▷他同朋友在一起吃饭。He is eating with friends. 2 (指比较) as ▷我同我哥哥一样高。I'm just as tall as my older brother.

同伴 tóngbàn [名] companion

同胞 tóngbāo [名] 1 (指同父母) brother and sister 2 (指同一国家或民族) compatriot

同病相怜 tóng bìng xiāng lián sympathize with each other

同步 tóngbù [形] 1 (字) synchronized 2 (喻) in step with ▷工业发展和环境保护要同步进行。Industrial development must be in step with environmental protection.

同窗 tóngchuāng I [动] study together II [名] fellow student

同等 tóngděng [形] of the same level ▷同等待遇 equal treatment

同犯 tóngfàn [名] accomplice

同房 tóngfáng [动] 1 (指住在一起) live together 2 (婉) have sex

同甘共苦 tóng gān gòng kǔ go through thick and thin together

同感 tónggǎn [名] sympathy

同归于尽 tóng guī yú jìn die together

同行 tóngháng [动] be in the same line of work ▷他的父母是同行，都是老师。His parents are in the same line of work – they are both teachers.

同化 tónghuà [动] assimilate

同伙 tónghuǒ I [名] accomplice II [动] conspire

同居 tóngjū [动] cohabit

同类 tónglèi I [形] of the same kind II [名] the same kind

同流合污 tóng liú hé wū associate with criminals

同盟 tóngméng [名] alliance

同谋 tóngmóu I [动] conspire II [名] conspirator

同年 tóngnián I [名] 1 (同一年) the same year 2 (同龄人) a person of the same age ▷我们同年，都属虎。We're the same age, we were both born in the Year of the Tiger. II [动] be a contemporary of ▷我们俩同年。We're the same age.

同情 tóngqíng [动] sympathize ▷我们同情那些受害者。We sympathize with the victims. ▷我们对遇难者家属表示同情。We expressed our sympathies to the families of the deceased.

同声传译 tóng shēng chuán yì [名] simultaneous interpretation

同时 tóngshí I [名] at the same time ▷同时发生 occur simultaneously II [连] besides ▷桌子太大了，同时也太贵了。Besides being expensive, the table was also too big. ▷该项目时间紧，同时工作量也很大。Time is tight on the project, and the workload is huge too.

同事 tóngshì I [动] work together II [名] colleague

同屋 tóngwū [名] roommate

同乡 tóngxiāng [名] fellow countryman ▷我们几个是同乡。We're all from the same place.

同行 tóngxíng [动] travel together

同性恋 tóngxìngliàn [名] homosexuality

同学 tóngxué [名] 1 (指同校) fellow student 2 (指同班) classmate 3 (学生) student

同样 tóngyàng [形] 1 (一样) same ▷同样的愿望 the same aspirations 2 (情况类似) similar

同一 tóngyī [形] 1 (一样) same 2 (统一的) unanimous

同义词 tóngyìcí [名] synonym

同意 tóngyì [动] agree ▷我们需要得到老板的同意。We have to obtain authorization from our boss.

同志 tóngzhì [名] comrade

同舟共济 tóng zhōu gòng jì be in the same boat

铜 tóng [名] copper

铜牌 tóngpái [名] bronze medal

铜器 tóngqì [名] bronzeware ▷铜器时代 the Bronze Age

铜墙铁壁 tóng qiáng tiě bì impassable barrier

童 tóng [名] 1 (小孩) child (PL children) ▶神童 child prodigy 2 (指未婚) virgin

童工 tónggōng [名] child worker

童话 tónghuà [名] fairy tale

童年 tóngnián [名] childhood

童声 tóngshēng [名] child's voice ▷童声合唱 children's choir

童心 tóngxīn [名] childlike innocence

童谣 tóngyáo [名] nursery rhyme

童贞 tóngzhēn [名] chastity

童真 tóngzhēn [名] innocence

瞳 tóng [名] pupil

瞳孔 tóngkǒng [名] pupil

统 tǒng I [名] ▶系统 system ▶血统 bloodline II [动] command III [副] all

统称 tǒngchēng I [动] be collectively known as II [名] general designation

统筹 tǒngchóu [动] make an overall plan ▷统筹全局 plan on the basis of the situation as a whole

统计 tǒngjì I [名] statistics (PL) ▷人口统计 census II [动] count ▷统计选票 count votes

统考 tǒngkǎo [名] unified examination ▷高考是全国统考。The university entrance exams are run on a nationwide system.

统属 tǒngshǔ [动] be subordinate to

统帅 tǒngshuài I [名] 1 (军) commander-in-chief 2 (喻) (主导) driving force II [动] command

统率 tǒngshuài [动] command

统统 tǒngtǒng [副] entirely

统辖 tǒngxiá [动] have jurisdiction over

统一 tǒngyī I [动] 1 (使成一体) unite 2 (使一致) unify ▷统一思想 reach a common understanding II [形] unified

统治 tǒngzhì [动] rule ▷推翻独裁统治 overthrow dictatorial rule

捅 tǒng [动] 1 (戳) stab ▷小心别让针捅了眼睛。Be careful not to stab yourself in the eye with that needle. ▷一次打架时他被捅了两刀。He was stabbed twice in a fight. 2 (揭穿) disclose

捅娄子 tǒnglóuzi cause trouble

捅马蜂窝 tǒng mǎfēngwō create pandemonium

桶 tǒng I [名] bucket ▷汽油桶 petrol (英) 或 gasoline (美) drum ▷啤酒桶 beer barrel II [量] barrel ▷一桶柴油 a barrel of diesel oil ▷两桶牛奶 two churns of milk

筒 tǒng [名] 1 (竹管) bamboo tube 2 (粗管状物) ▶笔筒 pen holder ▷邮筒 post box (英), mailbox (美) 3 (指衣服) ▷袖筒 sleeve ▷长筒袜 stockings (PL)

通 tòng [量] 1 (遍) ▷她一通一通地打电话。She made one phone call after another. ▷她跳了一通舞。She danced for a while. 2 (指言语) ▷老师说了他一通。The teacher gave him a telling-off.
→ 另见 tōng

痛 tòng I [动] 1 (疼) ache ▷头痛 have a headache ▷胃痛 have a stomach ache 2 (悲伤) grieve ▶哀痛 sorrow II [副] deeply ▷痛饮 swig ▷痛打 give a sound beating to

痛不欲生 tòng bù yù shēng overwhelmed with grief

痛楚 tòngchǔ [名] anguish

痛定思痛 tòng dìng sī tòng learn from bitter experience

痛改前非 tòng gǎi qián fēi make a clean break with the past

痛恨 tònghèn [动] detest

痛苦 tòngkǔ [形] painful ▷医生的首要职责是减轻病人的痛苦。The first duty of the doctor is to reduce the patient's suffering.

痛快 tòngkuài [形] 1 (高兴) joyful 2 (尽兴) to one's heart's content ▷吃个痛快 eat one's fill ▷玩个痛快 play to one's heart's content 3 (爽

快) straightforward

痛快淋漓 tòngkuài línlí with great eloquence

痛心 tòngxīn [动] be deeply distressed

痛心疾首 tòng xīn jí shǒu **1** (指痛恨) detest **2** (指伤心) be devastated

痛痒 tòngyǎng [名] **1** (疾苦) sufferings (PL) **2** (要紧事) importance ▷无关痛痒的事 a matter of no importance

偷 tōu **I** [动] **1** (窃) steal (PT stole, PP stolen) **2** (抽出) take time off (PT took, PP taken) ▷偷工夫干点私活儿 take time off to do private work **3** (苟且) muddle along **II** [名] thief (PL thieves) **III** [副] stealthily

偷盗 tōudào [动] steal (PT stole, PP stolen)

偷渡 tōudù [动] cross a border illegally ▶偷渡客 illegal immigrant

偷工减料 tōu gōng jiǎn liào produce inferior goods with shoddy materials

偷空 tōukòng [动] take time off (PT took, PP taken)

偷懒 tōulǎn [动] be lazy

偷窃 tōuqiè [动] steal (PT stole, PP stolen)

偷情 tōuqíng [动] have a secret affair

偷偷 tōutōu [副] secretly

偷偷摸摸 tōutōumōmō on the sly

偷闲 tōuxián [动] take a break (PT took, PP taken)

头 tóu **I** [名] **1** (脑袋) head ▷点头 nod one's head **2** (头发) hair ▷分头 parted hair ▶平头 crew cut ▷梳头 comb one's hair **3** (顶端) tip ▷笔头儿 pen tip ▷船头 bows **4** (开始) beginning ▷从头说起 tell the story from the beginning **5** (结尾) end **6** (剩余) remnant ▷布头儿 leftover cloth ▷烟头儿 cigarette end **7** (头目) head ▷工头 foreman ▷谁是你们的头儿? Who's your boss? **8** (方面) aspect ▷复习英语时,只顾语法一头可不行。 When you're revising English, it won't do just to concentrate on the grammar aspect of the subject. **9** (界限) boundary ▷老师批评学生过了头。 The teacher overstepped the mark when he criticized the student. **II** [形] **1** (第一) first ▶头奖 first prize **2** (领头) leading **3** (时间在前) first ▷头几年 first few years **III** [量] **1** (指动物) ▷5头公牛和3头母牛 five bulls and three cows **2** (指蒜) bulb ▷一头蒜 a bulb of garlic

头等 tóuděng [形] first class

头发 tóufa [名] hair

头角 tóujiǎo [名] (喻) talent

头领 tóulǐng [名] leader

头颅 tóulú [名] skull

头面人物 tóumiàn rénwù [名] (贬) bigwig

头目 tóumù [名] leader

头脑 tóunǎo [名] brains (PL)

头破血流 tóu pò xuè liú be beaten black and blue

头饰 tóushì [名] headdress

头头是道 tóu tóu shì dào clear and logical

头衔 tóuxián [名] title

头绪 tóuxù [名] **1** (条理) clue **2** (心思) thoughts (PL)

头重脚轻 tóu zhòng jiǎo qīng top-heavy

投 tóu [动] **1** (扔) throw (PT threw, PP thrown) **2** (放进去) put ... in (PT, PP put) **3** (跳下去) throw oneself (PT threw, PP thrown) ▷刚才有个男的投河自尽了。A man has just thrown himself into a river in an act of suicide. **4** (投射) cast (PT, PP cast) ▷投去羡慕的目光 cast an admiring glance **5** (寄) post **6** (奔向) seek ... out (PT, PP sought) ▷弃暗投明 turn from evil to good

投案 tóu'àn [动] give oneself up (PT gave, PP given)

投保 tóubǎo [动] take out insurance (PT took, PP taken)

投奔 tóubèn [动] seek refuge (PT, PP sought) ▷他无家可归,只好去投奔老朋友。He was left homeless, and had to seek refuge with an old friend.

投币电话 tóu bì diànhuà [名] payphone

投标 tóubiāo [动] tender

投产 tóuchǎn [动] go into production (PT went, PP gone)

投递 tóudì [动] deliver

投放 tóufàng [动] **1** (食物、药物) throw ... in (PT threw, PP thrown) **2** (人力、物力、财力) invest **3** (市场) supply

投合 tóuhé **I** [动] (融洽) get along **2** (迎合) cater to

投机 tóujī **I** [动] speculate **II** [形] agreeable

投靠 tóukào [动] **1** (依靠) depend on **2** (屈服) give oneself up (PT gave, PP given)

投其所好 tóuqísuǒhào cater to sb's tastes

投入 tóurù **I** [形] **1** (指专注) engrossed **2** (指逼真) realistic **II** [动] **1** (放入) put ... in (PT, PP put) ▷把球投入球篮。Put the ball through the hoop. ▷开发新产品需要很大的投入。Developing new product lines requires a considerable investment. **2** (参加) throw oneself into (PT threw, PP thrown)

投身 tóushēn [动] throw oneself into (PT threw, PP thrown)

投诉 tóusù I [动] lodge a complaint II [名] appeal

投胎 tóutāi [动] be reincarnated

投降 tóuxiáng [动] surrender ▷无条件投降 unconditional surrender

投影 tóuyǐng I [动] project II [名] 1 (影子) projection 2 (喻) reflection

投缘 tóuyuán [形] congenial

投掷 tóuzhì [动] throw (PT threw, PP thrown)

投资 tóuzī I [动] invest II [名] investment

透 tòu I [动] 1 (渗透) penetrate ▷阳光从窗户透进来。The sunlight is coming in through the windows. 2 (泄露) leak out 3 (显露) appear II [形] 1 (透彻) thorough ▷他对植物学了解很透。He has a thorough knowledge of botany. 2 (程度深) complete ▷我浑身都湿透了。I'm soaked to the skin. ▷这些芒果熟透了。These mangoes are completely ripe.

透彻 tòuchè [形] incisive

透顶 tòudǐng [形] thorough

透风 tòufēng [动] 1 (透气) ventilate 2 (透露消息) divulge a secret

透露 tòulù [动] disclose

透明 tòumíng [形] transparent

透视 tòushì [动] 1 (表立体空间) make ... three-dimensional 2 (医) X-ray 3 (喻) (看清楚) grasp the essence of

透支 tòuzhī [动] overdraw (PT overdrew, PP overdrawn) ▷透支金额 overdraft

凸 tū [形] protuberant

秃 tū [形] 1 (指毛发) bald 2 (指山) barren 3 (指树) bare 4 (不锐利) blunt 5 (指文章) incomplete

秃顶 tūdǐng I [动] be bald II [名] 1 (指人) bald man (PL men) 2 (指头顶) bald patch

秃子 tūzi [名] (口) baldy

突 tū I [动] break out (PT broke, PP broken) ▷突围 escape from a siege II [形] protruding III [副] suddenly

突变 tūbiàn [动] 1 (突然变化) change suddenly 2 (生物) mutate ▷基因突变 genetic mutation

突出 tūchū [动] give prominence to (PT gave, PP given) ▷他从不突出自己。He never pushes himself forward. II [形] 1 (明显) noticeable ▷突出的特点 prominent feature 2 (隆起) protruding

突飞猛进 tū fēi měng jìn advance by leaps and bounds

突击 tūjī I [动] 1 (突然袭击) assault 2 (加快完成) do a rush job II [副] from nowhere

突破 tūpò [动] 1 (防线、界线) break through (PT broke, PP broken) ▷突破敌人的封锁线 break through the enemy's blockade 2 (僵局、难关) make a breakthrough ▷癌症治疗上的新突破 a new breakthrough in cancer treatment 3 (限额) surpass ▷突破定额 overfulfil a quota ▷这位长跑运动员突破了他的体能极限。The long-distance runner has broken the limits of his physical endurance. 4 (记录) break (PT broke, PP broken)

突起 tūqǐ I [动] 1 (突然发生) erupt ▷家庭矛盾突起。A family conflict has erupted. 2 (高耸) tower II [名] bulge

突然 tūrán I [形] sudden II [副] suddenly

突如其来 tū rú qí lái unexpected

图 tú I [名] 1 (图画) picture ▷几何图 geometrical figure 2 (地图) map 3 (计划) plan ▶宏图 grand plan II [动] 1 (贪图) seek (PT, PP sought) ▷图一时痛快 seek momentary gratification 2 (谋划) scheme

图案 tú'àn [名] design

图表 túbiǎo [名] chart

图画 túhuà [名] picture

图解 tújiě I [名] diagram II [动] illustrate ▷图解词典 illustrated dictionary

图景 tújǐng [名] 1 (景物) image 2 (前景) prospect

图谋 túmóu I [动] 1 (阴谋策划) plot 2 (谋求) seek (PT, PP sought) ▷图谋私利 seek personal advantage II [名] plot

图书 túshū [名] books (PL)

图书馆 túshūguǎn [名] library

图腾 túténg [名] totem

图像 túxiàng [名] image

图章 túzhāng [名] seal

图纸 túzhǐ [名] drawing

徒 tú I [名] 1 (徒弟) apprentice ▶门徒 disciple 2 (指信教) believer 3 (贬) (同类人) clique ▶赌徒 gambler ▶匪徒 gangster II [动] walk ▶徒步 on foot III [形] empty ▶徒手 unarmed IV [副] 1 (仅仅) only 2 (白白地) in vain

徒弟 túdì [名] apprentice

徒劳 túláo [形] futile

徒然 túrán I [形] futile II [副] to no avail

徒手 túshǒu [形] unarmed

徒刑 túxíng [名] imprisonment ▷无期徒刑 life imprisonment

徒有虚名 tú yǒu xū míng have an undeserved reputation

途 tú [名] way ▶旅途 journey ▶前途 prospect ▷沿途 along the way

途径 tújìng [名] channel ▷通过合法途径解决 resolve through legal channels ▷通过外交途径寻求国际援助 seek international aid through diplomatic channels ▷经非法途径入境 enter a country by illegal means

涂 tú [动] 1 (抹) spread ... on (PT, PP spread) ▷涂油漆 apply paint 2 (乱写乱画) scribble 3 (改动) cross ... out

涂改 túgǎi [动] alter

涂料 túliào [名] paint

涂抹 túmǒ [动] 1 (随意写) scribble 2 (油漆、颜料) paint 3 (改动) alter

涂饰 túshì [动] 1 (上油漆) paint 2 (美化) do ... up ▷涂饰墙壁 do up the walls

涂写 túxiě [动] scribble

涂鸦 túyā [动] scrawl

涂脂抹粉 tú zhī mǒ fěn (喻) whitewash

屠 tú I [动] 1 (动物) slaughter 2 (人) massacre II [名] butcher

屠夫 túfū [名] 1 (字) butcher 2 (喻) mass murderer

屠杀 túshā [动] massacre

屠宰 túzǎi [动] slaughter

土 tǔ I [名] 1 (泥) soil 2 (土地) land ▷故土 native land ▶领土 territory 3 (鸦片) opium II [形] 1 (地方) local 2 (民间) folk 3 (不时髦) unfashionable

土包子 tǔbāozi [名] yokel

土崩瓦解 tǔ bēng wǎ jiě disintegrate

土产 tǔchǎn [名] local product

土地 tǔdì [名] 1 (田地) land 2 (疆域) territory

土豆 tǔdòu [名] potato (PL potatoes)

土法 tǔfǎ [名] traditional method

土方 tǔfāng [名] folk remedy

土话 tǔhuà [名] local dialect

土皇帝 tǔhuángdì [名] local despot

土货 tǔhuò [名] local product

土木 tǔmù [名] (土木工程) civil engineering

土气 tǔqì [形] vulgar

土壤 tǔrǎng [名] soil

土特产 tǔtèchǎn [名] local speciality (英) 或 specialty (美)

土语 tǔyǔ [名] local dialect

土政策 tǔzhèngcè [名] local policies (PL)

土著 tǔzhù [名] indigenous peoples (PL)

吐 tǔ [动] 1 (排出口外) spit (PT, PP spat) 2 (露出) put ... out (PT, PP put) ▷蚕吐丝 Silkworms spin silk. 3 (说出来) speak out (PT spoke, PP spoken)
→另见 tù

吐口 tǔkǒu [动] 1 (讲实情) tell the truth (PT, PP told) 2 (同意) agree 3 (提出要求) come out with (PT came, PP come) ▷他吐口要1000元。He came out with a demand for 1000 Yuan.

吐露 tǔlù [动] reveal

吐气 tǔqì [动] let off steam (PT, PP let)

吐 tù [动] vomit
→另见 tǔ

吐沫 tùmo [名] saliva

兔 tù [名] 1 (野兔) hare 2 (家兔) rabbit

湍 tuān I [形] (书) torrential II [名] rapids (PL)

湍急 tuānjí [形] fast-flowing

团 tuán I [名] 1 (球形物) ball ▷毛线团 ball of wool 2 (组织) group ▶剧团 drama company 3 (军) regiment 4 (政治组织) league II [动] (聚合) unite ▷团聚 reunite 2 (揉成球状) roll into a ball III [形] round IV [量] ▷一团面 a lump of dough ▷一团毛线 a ball of wool

团队 tuánduì [名] team

团伙 tuánhuǒ [名] gang

团结 tuánjié [动] unite

团聚 tuánjù [动] reunite

团体 tuántǐ [名] organization

团圆 tuányuán [动] reunite

推 tuī [动] 1 (门、窗、车) push 2 (指用工具) scrape ▶推土机 bulldozer ▷他推了个光头。He's shaved his head. 3 (开展) push forward 4 (推断) deduce 5 (辞让) decline 6 (推诿) shift 7 (推迟) postpone 8 (举荐) elect

推波助澜 tuī bō zhù lán exacerbate

推测 tuīcè [动] infer

推崇 tuīchóng [动] esteem

推辞 tuīcí [动] decline

推迟 tuīchí [动] put ... off (PT, PP put) ▷既然不是每个人都能来参加，那就把会议推迟到下周吧？Not everyone can attend the meeting, so let's put it off until next week.

推出 tuīchū [动] bring ... out (PT, PP brought) ▷HarperCollins出版社又推出了一本畅销书。HarperCollins Publishers have brought out yet another best-seller.

推导 tuīdǎo [动] derive

推动 tuīdòng [动] promote

推断 tuīduàn [动] deduce

推度 tuīduó [动] infer

推翻 tuīfān [动] 1 (推倒) overturn 2 (打垮) overthrow (PT overthrew, PP overthrown) 3 (根本否定) repudiate

推广 tuīguǎng [动] popularize

推荐 tuījiàn [动] recommend

推举 tuījǔ [动] elect

推理 tuīlǐ [动] infer

推论 tuīlùn [动] infer

推拿 tuīná [动] massage ▷用推拿疗法治疗疼痛 treat pain by massage

推敲 tuīqiāo [动] submit ... to close scrutiny

推却 tuīquè [动] decline

推让 tuīràng [动] decline

推三阻四 tuī sān zǔ sì fob ... off with excuses

推算 tuīsuàn [动] calculate

推托 tuītuō [动] make excuses

推脱 tuītuō [动] shirk

推诿 tuīwěi [动] pass the buck ▷要尽职尽责，不要相互推诿。You should do your duty and not pass the buck to each other.

推销 tuīxiāo [动] promote ▷推销新产品 promote new products

推卸 tuīxiè [动] shirk

推心置腹 tuī xīn zhì fù confide in ▷我们俩做了推心置腹的长谈。The two of us had a long, heart-to-heart talk.

推行 tuīxíng [动] implement

推选 tuīxuǎn [动] elect

推移 tuīyí [动] 1 (时间变迁) pass ▷随着时间的推移 with the passage of time 2 (发展) develop ▷随着政治局的推移，经济情况稳定了。As the current political situation develops, the economy is stabilizing.

颓 tuí I [动] decline II dispirited ▶颓废 dejected

颓废 tuífèi [形] decadent

颓唐 tuítáng [形] dejected

腿 tuǐ [名] 1 (下肢) leg ▶大腿 thigh ▶小腿 calf (PL calves) 2 (支撑物) leg ▷桌子腿儿 table leg 3 (火腿) ham

腿脚 tuǐjiǎo [名] mobility ▷这位老人的腿脚不太利索。The old man isn't very mobile.

退 tuì [动] 1 (后移) retreat 2 (使后移) cause ... to withdraw ▷他把刀从刀套里退出来。He drew the knife from its sheath. 3 (退出) quit (PT, PP quit) 4 (减退) recede 5 (减弱) fade 6 (退还) return 7 (撤销) cancel

退步 tuìbù I [动] 1 (落后) lag behind 2 (让步) give way (PT gave, PP given) II [名] leeway

退化 tuìhuà [动] degenerate

退路 tuìlù [名] 1 (道路) line of retreat 2 (余地) leeway

退却 tuìquè [动] 1 (军) retreat 2 (退缩) flinch

退让 tuìràng [动] make a concession ▷在原则问题上，我们不能让退让。We can make no concessions on matters of principle.

退缩 tuìsuō [动] hold back (PT, PP held)

退位 tuìwèi [动] abdicate

退伍 tuìwǔ [动] demobilize ▷退伍军人 ex-serviceman

退休 tuìxiū [动] retire

退役 tuìyì [动] 1 (军人) demobilize ▷退役军官 retired officer 2 (运动员) retire

蜕 tuì [动] 1 (蛇、蝉) slough 2 (鸟) moult (英), molt (美)

蜕变 tuìbiàn [动] transform

蜕化 tuìhuà [动] 1 (脱皮) slough ... off 2 (喻) (腐化堕落) degenerate

褪 tuì [动] 1 (衣服) take ... off (PT took, PP taken) 2 (毛) shed (PT, PP shed) 3 (颜色) fade →另见 tùn

吞 tūn [动] 1 (整个咽下) swallow 2 (吞并) take over (PT took, PP taken)

吞并 tūnbìng [动] annex

吞没 tūnmò [动] 1 (据为己有) misappropriate 2 (淹没) engulf

吞噬 tūnshì [动] engulf

吞吐 tūntǔ I [动] handle ▷这个港口每年可吞吐8000万吨货物。This port can handle 80 million tons of cargo every year. II [形] hesitant

吞吞吐吐 tūntūntǔtǔ hum and haw

屯 tún I [动] 1 (储存) store ... up 2 (驻扎) station ▷屯兵 be stationed II [名] village

囤 tún [动] store

囤积 túnjī [动] hoard

臀 tún [名] buttock

褪 tùn [动] take ... off (PT took, PP taken) →另见 tuì

托 tuō I [动] 1 (撑) support 2 (委托) entrust 3 (依赖) rely on II [名] tray

托词 tuōcí I [动] make an excuse II [名] excuse

托儿所 tuō'érsuǒ [名] nursery

托福 tuōfú I [动] (客套) ▷托您的福，我们都好。We're fine, thanks to you. II [名] TOEFL, Test of English as a Foreign Language

托付 tuōfù [动] entrust

托管 tuōguǎn [动] entrust to

托人情 tuō rénqíng [动] pull strings

托运 tuōyùn [动] ship ▷托运行李 checked baggage

拖 tuō [动] 1 (拉) pull 2 (地板) mop 3 (下垂) trail ▷她的长裙拖地。Her long dress trailed along the ground. 4 (拖延) delay

拖拉 tuōlā I [动] delay II [形] dilatory

拖拉机 tuōlājī [名] tractor

拖累 tuōlěi [动] 1 (成为负担) be a burden 2 (使受牵连) implicate

拖泥带水 tuō ní dài shuǐ be slapdash ▷他工作总拖泥带水。He's always slapdash in his work. ▷说话要直接，别拖泥带水。Say what you've got to say, don't beat about the bush.

拖欠 tuōqiàn [动] be in arrears

拖沓 tuōtà [形] dilatory

拖延 tuōyán [动] delay

脱 tuō [动] 1 (皮肤、毛发) shed (PT, PP shed) 2 (衣服、鞋帽) take ... off (PT took, PP taken) 3 (摆脱) escape 4 (颜色) fade 5 (油脂) skim

脱产 tuōchǎn [动] be released from one's regular work

脱稿 tuōgǎo [动] complete

脱钩 tuōgōu [动] 1 (车厢) disconnect 2 (喻) cut ties (PT, PP cut) ▷他和原单位早就脱钩了。He cut his ties with his former unit long ago.

脱轨 tuōguǐ [动] derail

脱节 tuōjié [动] be separated

脱臼 tuōjiù [动] dislocate

脱口而出 tuō kǒu ér chū the words roll off one's tongue

脱离 tuōlí [动] 1 (关系) break off (PT broke, PP broken) ▷脱离关系 break off relations 2 (危险) get away from

脱落 tuōluò [动] 1 (毛发、牙齿) lose (PT, PP lost) 2 (油漆、墙皮) come off (PT came, PP come)

脱贫 tuōpín [动] escape from poverty

脱身 tuōshēn [动] get away (PT, PP come)

脱手 tuōshǒu [动] 1 (离开手) let ... slip (PT, PP let) 2 (卖出) get rid of

脱水 tuōshuǐ [动] dehydrate

脱俗 tuōsú [形] refined

脱销 tuōxiāo [动] be sold out

脱颖而出 tuō yǐng ér chū come to the fore

驮 tuó [动] carry on one's back ▷马驮着米袋。The horse is carrying bags of rice.
→另见 duò

驼 tuó I [名] camel II [形] hunchbacked

坨 tuó I [名] lump II [动] stick together (PT, PP stuck)

鸵 tuó 见下文
鸵鸟 tuóniǎo [名] ostrich

妥 tuǒ [形] 1 (适当) appropriate 2 (停当) ready

妥当 tuǒdang [形] appropriate

妥善 tuǒshàn [形] appropriate

妥帖 tuǒtiē [形] appropriate

妥协 tuǒxié [动] compromise

椭 tuǒ 见下文
椭圆 tuǒyuán [名] oval

拓 tuò [动] open ... up

拓荒 tuòhuāng [动] open up virgin land

拓宽 tuòkuān [动] 1 (扩大) expand 2 (加宽) widen

拓展 tuòzhǎn [动] expand

唾 tuò I [名] saliva II [动] spit (PT, PP spat)

唾骂 tuòmà [动] revile

唾沫 tuòmo [名] (口) saliva

唾弃 tuòqì [动] spurn

唾手可得 tuò shǒu kě dé within easy reach ▷真是唾手可得的好机会。It really is a golden opportunity.

Ww

挖 **wā** [动] **1** (掘) dig (PT, PP dug) ▷挖洞 dig a hole ▷挖隧道 dig a tunnel **2** (耳朵、鼻子) pick

挖掘 **wājué** [动] excavate

挖空心思 **wā kōng xīnsī** (贬) rack one's brains ▷他挖空心思赚大钱。He racked his brains for ways to make a lot of money.

挖苦 **wāku** [动] have a dig at ▷他总挖苦成绩差的学生。He is always having a dig at underachieving students.

挖墙脚 **wā qiángjiǎo** (贬) undermine ▷两个党派经常互挖墙脚。The two parties are always undermining each other.

哇 **wā** [拟] **1** (指哭声) wail **2** (指呕吐声) vomit

洼 **wā** I [形] low-lying II [名] dip

洼陷 **wāxiàn** [动] dip ▷桥面洼陷。The bridge dips. ▷这儿的地面洼陷了。The ground dips here.

蛙 **wā** [名] frog

蛙泳 **wāyǒng** [名] breaststroke

娃 **wá** [名] (方) baby

娃娃 **wáwa** [名] **1** (小孩) baby **2** (玩具) doll

瓦 **wǎ** [名] tile

瓦解 **wǎjiě** [动] collapse ▷这个恐怖组织已经瓦解了。The terrorist network has already collapsed. ▷我们瓦解了敌人的阴谋。We smashed the enemy's plot.

瓦砾 **wǎlì** [名] rubble

瓦斯 **wǎsī** [名] gas

袜 **wà** [名] sock ▶长筒袜 stocking

袜子 **wàzi** [名] sock

歪 **wāi** I [形] **1** (倾斜) slanting ▷画挂歪了。The picture is crooked. **2** (坏) devious ▷他出了个歪点子。He came up with a devious suggestion. II [动] incline

歪打正着 **wāi dǎ zhèng zháo** have a stroke of good luck ▷他歪打正着中了彩票头彩。By a stroke of good luck, he won first prize in the lottery.

歪门邪道 **wāi mén xié dào** dishonest means

歪曲 **wāiqū** [动] distort

歪斜 **wāixié** [形] crooked

崴 **wǎi** [动] sprain

外 **wài** I [名] **1** (范围以外) ▷户外运动 outdoor sports ▷他把车停在门外。He parked the car outside the gate. **2** (外国) ▶外宾 foreign visitor II [形] **1** (非所属的) ▶外国 abroad **2** (疏远的) ▶外人 outsider **3** (非正式) informal ▶外号 nickname III [副] besides ▶外加 plus

外币 **wàibì** [名] foreign currency

外表 **wàibiǎo** [名] exterior ▷大楼外表很气派。The exterior of the building is very imposing. ▷人的外表不可信。Don't judge by appearances.

外宾 **wàibīn** [名] foreign visitor

外部 **wàibù** I [名] exterior II [形] external

外地 **wàidì** [名] other parts of the country ▷我们班有几个外地学生。Our class has several students from other parts of the country. ▷他去外地出差。He went away on business.

外地人 **wàidìrén** [名] person from another part of the country

外调 **wàidiào** [动] transfer ▷两位网络工程师从IT部外调到了纽约办事处。Two network engineers were transferred from the IT department to the New York office.

外敷 **wàifū** [动] apply externally

外公 **wàigōng** [名] maternal grandfather

外观 **wàiguān** [名] appearance

外行 **wàiháng** I [名] layman (PL laymen) ▷对电脑编程，我是个外行。I'm a layman where computer programming is concerned. II [形]

amateurish

外号 wàihào [名] nickname

外汇 wàihuì [名] **1** (外汇兑换) foreign exchange **2** (外币) foreign currency

外籍 wàijí [形] foreign

外交 wàijiāo [名] foreign affairs

外交部 wàijiāobù [名] Ministry of Foreign Affairs

外交部长 wàijiāo bùzhǎng [名] Minister of Foreign Affairs

外交官 wàijiāoguān [名] diplomat

外界 wàijiè [名] outside world ▷外界因素 external factors

外景 wàijǐng [名] scene shot on location

外科 wàikē [名] surgery

外科手术 wàikē shǒushù [名] surgical operation

外科医生 wàikē yīshēng [名] surgeon

外快 wàikuài [名] extra income ▷他在夜校教课赚外快。He earns some extra income by teaching evening classes.

外流 wàiliú [动] drain ▷中国的很多人才外流到国外。There is a major brain drain from China to other countries.

外露 wàilù [动] show (PT showed, PP shown) ▷我父亲的感情从不外露。My father never shows his feelings.

外卖 wàimài [名] takeaway (英), takeout (美) ▷中国餐馆提供外卖服务。Chinese restaurants provide a takeaway (英) 或 takeout (美) service.

外贸 wàimào [名] foreign trade

外貌 wàimào [名] appearance

外婆 wàipó [名] maternal grandmother

外企 wàiqǐ [名] foreign enterprise

外强中干 wài qiáng zhōng gān outwardly strong but inwardly weak

外侨 wàiqiáo [名] foreign resident

外人 wàirén [名] **1** (局外人) outsider **2** (外国人) foreigner

外伤 wàishāng [名] injury ▷他从马上摔了下来，只受了点外伤。He fell off his horse, but only had a slight injury.

外商 wàishāng [名] foreign businessman (PL businessmen)

外甥 wàisheng [名] nephew

外事 wàishì [名] foreign affairs

外孙 wàisūn [名] grandson

外套 wàitào [名] overcoat

外围 wàiwéi [名] periphery

外文 wàiwén [名] foreign language

外线 wàixiàn [名] outside line

外乡 wàixiāng [名] another part of the country ▷他在外乡遭了劫。He was robbed while away from home.

外向 wàixiàng [形] **1** (指性格) extrovert **2** (指经济) export-oriented

外销 wàixiāo [动] sell ... externally (PT, PP sold) ▷本厂产品外销到美国。The products from the factory are sold abroad to the United States.

外因 wàiyīn [名] external cause

外语 wàiyǔ [名] foreign language

外遇 wàiyù [名] extra-marital affair ▷她有外遇后，就想和丈夫离婚。After having an affair, she wanted to divorce her husband.

外援 wàiyuán [名] **1** (援助) foreign aid **2** (外国球员) foreign player

外在 wàizài [形] external

外债 wàizhài [名] foreign debt

外资 wàizī [名] foreign capital

外资企业 wàizī qǐyè [名] foreign-funded enterprise

弯 wān I [形] curved II [动] bend (PT, PP bent) ▷我弯着腰扫地。I bent down to sweep the floor. III [名] bend

弯路 wānlù [名] **1** (字) (弯曲的路) winding road **2** (喻) (曲折) tortuous route

弯曲 wānqū [形] **1** (头发) wavy **2** (小路、小河) winding

剜 wān [动] cut ... out (PT, PP cut)

湾 wān [名] bay

蜿 wān 见下文

蜿蜒 wānyán [形] **1** (路、河) winding ▷蜿蜒的长城 the winding Great Wall **2** (指蛇) wriggling

豌 wān 见下文

豌豆 wāndòu [名] pea

丸 wán I [名] **1** (球形物) ball **2** (指药) pill II [量] pill ▷他服了一丸药。He took a pill.

丸药 wányào [名] pill

完 wán I [形] whole ▶完整 complete II [动] **1** (完成) complete **2** (耗尽) run out (PT ran, PP run) ▷打印纸使完了。The printing paper has run out. **3** (了结) finish ▷他的书写完了。He's finished writing his book.

完备 wánbèi [形] complete

完毕 wánbì [动] finish

完成 wánchéng [动] complete

完蛋 wándàn [动] be finished

完好 wánhǎo [形] intact ▷这些文物保存完好。These cultural relics have been kept intact and in good condition.

完结 wánjié [动] finish

完满 wánmǎn [形] successful

完美 wánměi [形] perfect

完全 wánquán I [形] complete II [副] completely ▷我完全赞成你的观点。I completely endorse your point of view.

完善 wánshàn I [形] perfect II [动] perfect ▷法律体系需要完善。The legal system needs to be improved.

完整 wánzhěng [形] complete

玩 wán [动] 1 (玩耍) play 2 (游玩) have a good time ▷我去泰国玩了一个星期。I went to Thailand for a week's holiday. 3 (做客) visit ▷欢迎到我家来玩儿！Please come and visit me at home. 4 (表示祝愿) enjoy ▷玩得好！Enjoy yourself! 5 (耍弄) play ▷他爱对人玩花招。He likes to play tricks on people.

玩具 wánjù [名] toy

玩弄 wánnòng [动] 1 (贬) (调情) play games with ▷他老玩弄年轻女子。He is always playing games with young girls. 2 (贬) (使用) employ

玩儿命 wánrmìng [动] (口) bust a gut (PT bust, PP busted) ▷他玩儿命学英语。He put everything into learning English.

玩世不恭 wán shì bù gōng (贬) frivolous ▷他是个玩世不恭的花花公子。He is a frivolous playboy.

玩耍 wánshuǎ [动] play

玩物 wánwù [名] plaything

玩笑 wánxiào [名] joke ▷他喜欢跟人开玩笑。He likes to play jokes on people. ▷我把他的话当玩笑。I took what he said as a joke.

玩意儿 wányìr [名] (口) 1 (东西) thing 2 (人) ▷千万别和他交朋友。他不是什么好玩意儿。Whatever you do don't make friends with him. He's bad news. 3 (玩具) toy 4 (器械) gadget

顽 wán [形] 1 (难以摆脱的) stubborn 2 (淘气) naughty

顽固 wángù [形] 1 (贬) (指思想) obstinate 2 (指病) persistent 3 (指政治) diehard

顽抗 wánkàng [动] stubbornly resist

顽皮 wánpí [形] mischievous

顽强 wánqiáng [形] tenacious

顽症 wánzhèng [名] chronic illness

宛 wǎn 见下文

宛如 wǎnrú [动] (书) be just like ▷美丽的风景宛如仙境。The beautiful scenery is just like paradise.

挽 wǎn [动] 1 (拉) hold (PT, PP held) ▷他们俩经常手挽手去学校。They often go to school hand in hand. 2 (卷起) roll ... up ▷卷起袖子 roll up one's sleeves

挽回 wǎnhuí [动] redeem ▷挽回局面 redeem the situation ▷挽回面子 save face

挽救 wǎnjiù [动] save

挽留 wǎnliú [动] press ... to stay ▷老师挽留我与他共进晚餐。My teacher pressed me to stay for dinner.

晚 wǎn I [形] late ▶晚秋 late autumn ▷火车晚了10分钟。The train was ten minutes late. ▷我起晚了。I got up late. II [名] evening

晚安 wǎn'ān [形] 祝你晚安。Good night.

晚辈 wǎnbèi [名] younger generation

晚点 wǎndiǎn [动] be late

晚饭 wǎnfàn [名] dinner

晚会 wǎnhuì [名] party

晚年 wǎnnián [名] old age

晚期 wǎnqī [名] late period ▷他晚期的作品更优秀。His later works are even more outstanding.

晚上 wǎnshang [名] evening

晚熟 wǎnshú [动] develop late ▷这孩子晚熟。This child is a late developer.

惋 wǎn 见下文

惋惜 wǎnxī [动] regret ▷教练为队员受伤感到惋惜。The coach regretted the injury to the team member.

婉 wǎn [形] 1 (委婉) tactful ▶婉谢 decline 2 (柔顺) gracious ▶婉顺 docile

婉言 wǎnyán [名] tactful language ▷我婉言拒绝了他的邀请。I tactfully refused his invitation.

婉转 wǎnzhuǎn [形] 1 (温和) tactful ▷他婉转地批评了学生。He tactfully criticized the student. 2 (优美) melodious

碗 wǎn [名] bowl

碗柜 wǎnguì [名] sideboard

万 wàn I [数] ten thousand II [副] definitely ▷你万不可错失良机。You really mustn't let slip a good opportunity.

万不得已 wàn bù dé yǐ as a last resort

万分 wànfēn [副] extremely

万金油 wànjīnyóu [名] (贬) jack of all trades

万能 wànnéng [形] 1 (无所不能) omnipotent 2 (多用途的) all-purpose ▷万能钥匙 master key

万人空巷 wàn rén kōng xiàng the whole town turns out ▷这位奥斯卡得主访问上海时, 万人空巷。When the Oscar winner visited Shanghai, the whole town turned out.

万世 wànshì [名] (书) the ages ▷他的发明会流传万世。His invention will be passed on through the ages.

万岁 wànsuì [叹] long live

万万 wànwàn I [副] absolutely ▷我万万没想到他这么无礼。I had absolutely no idea that he was so rude. II [数] hundred million

万无一失 wàn wú yī shī be sure of success ▷我们为这次登山活动做了精心准备, 以确保万无一失。We made careful preparations for climbing the mountain, so as to be sure of success.

万物 wànwù [名] the whole of creation ▷春天到了, 万物复苏。Spring has arrived – everything is coming back to life.

万象 wànxiàng [名] (书) everything under the sun

万幸 wànxìng [形] very lucky

万一 wànyī I [连] if by any chance ▷万一他不在, 把信交给他的秘书。If by any chance he isn't there, give the letter to his secretary. II [名] contingency

万紫千红 wàn zǐ qiān hóng blaze of colour (英) 或 color (美)

腕 wàn [名] 1 (指手) wrist 2 (指脚) ankle

腕儿 wànr [名] (口) star

腕子 wànzi [名] 1 (指手) wrist 2 (指脚) ankle

汪 wāng I [动] collect II [拟] bark

汪汪 wāngwāng [形] tearful

汪洋 wāngyáng [名] expanse of water

亡 wáng I [动] die II [形] (书) deceased ▶亡父 late father ▶亡友 deceased friend

亡故 wánggù [动] (书) pass away

亡命徒 wángmìngtú [名] desperate criminal

亡羊补牢 wáng yáng bǔ láo better late than never

王 wáng [名] king

王八 wángba [名] (动) tortoise

王八蛋 wángbadàn [名] (讳) bastard

王朝 wángcháo [名] dynasty

王储 wángchǔ [名] crown prince

王法 wángfǎ [名] (口) law of the land

王公 wánggōng [名] aristocracy

王国 wángguó [名] kingdom

王牌 wángpái [名] ace ▷他是王牌记者。He's an ace reporter.

王室 wángshì [名] royalty

王子 wángzǐ [名] prince

网 wǎng I [名] 1 (工具) net ▶渔网 fishing net 2 (网状物) web ▶蜘蛛网 spider's web 3 (系统) network ▶互联网 the Internet ▶信息网 information network ▶交通网 communication network II [动] net

网吧 wǎngbā [名] Internet café

网点 wǎngdiǎn [名] points (PL) ▷银行在各地设有服务网点。The bank has set up service points everywhere.

网罗 wǎngluó [动] headhunt

网络 wǎngluò [名] network ▷网络服务器 network server ▷经济网络 economic network ▷他建立了广泛的人际网络。He built up a wide network of relationships.

网迷 wǎngmí [名] Internet fan

网民 wǎngmín [名] Internet user

网球 wǎngqiú [名] tennis

网球场 wǎngqiúchǎng [名] tennis court

网页 wǎngyè [名] web page

网友 wǎngyǒu [名] chat buddy

网站 wǎngzhàn [名] website

网址 wǎngzhǐ [名] web address

枉 wǎng I [动] ▶枉法 pervert the course of justice II [副] (书) in vain

枉法 wǎngfǎ [动] (书) pervert the course of justice

枉费 wǎngfèi [动] (书) waste ▷他不会听你的, 别枉费唇舌了。He won't listen, so don't waste your breath on him.

往 wǎng I [介] to ▷飞机正飞往柏林。The plane is flying to Berlin. II [形] past ▶往事 past events (PL)

往常 wángcháng [名] ▷他往常不吃早饭。He didn't use to eat breakfast.

往来 wǎnglái [动] 1 (去来) come and go 2 (交往) ▷两国往来密切。Contacts between the two countries are close.

往往 wǎngwǎng [副] often

妄 wàng [形] 1 (不合理) unreasonable 2 (随意) presumptuous

妄图 wàngtú [动] try in vain (PT, PP tried)

妄想 wàngxiǎng I [动] (贬) have a pipe dream II [名] pipe dream

妄自菲薄 wàng zì fěibó underestimate oneself

妄自尊大 wàng zì zūn dà (贬) have a high opinion of oneself

忘 wàng [动] forget (PT forgot, PP forgotten) ▷我忘了带雨伞。I forgot my umbrella.

忘恩负义 wàng ēn fù yì (贬) be ungrateful ▷他是个忘恩负义的小人。He's an ungrateful rat.

忘乎所以 wàng hū suǒ yǐ (贬) get carried way ▷他高兴得忘乎所以。He was so happy he got quite carried away.

忘怀 wànghuái [动] (书) forget (PT forgot, PP forgotten)

忘记 wàngjì [动] forget (PT forgot, PP forgotten) ▷我忘记了他的样子。I've forgotten what he looks like. ▷我忘记了给朋友写信。I forgot to write a letter to my friend.

忘年交 wàngniánjiāo [名] friend (who is significantly older or younger) ▷这位学生和老教授成了忘年交。The student and the elderly professor became friends despite their age difference.

忘却 wàngquè [动] (书) forget (PT forgot, PP forgotten)

忘我 wàngwǒ [形] selfless ▷他忘我地朝他的目标奋斗着。He worked selflessly towards his goal. ▷他忘我地研究诗歌。He lost himself in his study of poetry.

旺 wàng [形] 1 (火) roaring 2 (人、生意) flourishing 3 (花) blooming ▷十月菊花开得正旺。In October the chrysanthemums are in full bloom.

旺季 wàngjì [名] 1 (指生意) peak season ▷秋天是北京的旅游旺季。Autumn is the peak season for tourism in Beijing. 2 (指水果、蔬菜) season ▷夏天是西瓜旺季。Summer is the season for watermelons.

旺盛 wàngshèng [形] 1 (精力、生命力) full of energy 2 (植物) thriving ▷果园的桃树长得很旺盛。The peach trees in the orchard are thriving.

旺销 wàngxiāo [动] sell well (PT, PP sold)

望 wàng [动] 1 (向远处看) look into the distance 2 (察看) watch ▷望风 be on the lookout 3 (希望) hope ▷望一路顺风。I hope you have a safe journey.

望子成龙 wàng zǐ chéng lóng have high expectations of one's children ▷父母太望子成龙，会给孩子很大压力。If parents' expectations are too high it will put a lot of pressure on the children.

危 wēi I [形] dangerous II [动] endanger

危害 wēihài [动] harm ▷抽烟危害健康。Smoking damages your health.

危机 wēijī [名] crisis (PL crises)

危急 wēijí [形] critical

危难 wēinàn [名] danger ▷他有危难时，总能找同朋友帮忙。When he was in danger, he could always look to his friends for help.

危险 wēixiǎn I [形] dangerous II [名] danger ▷消防员冒着生命危险扑灭森林大火。The firefighter put his life in danger to extinguish the forest fire.

危言耸听 wēi yán sǒng tīng scare story

危在旦夕 wēi zài dàn xī be in imminent danger

威 wēi [名] power

威风 wēifēng I [名] air of authority II [形] impressive

威力 wēilì [名] power

威猛 wēiměng [形] powerful

威名 wēimíng [名] renown ▷这位医生威名远扬。This doctor is renowned far and wide.

威慑 wēishè [动] terrorize

威士忌 wēishìjì [名] whisky

威望 wēiwàng [名] prestige

威武 wēiwǔ [形] powerful

威胁 wēixié [动] threaten

威信 wēixìn [名] prestige

威严 wēiyán I [形] dignified II [名] dignity

偎 wēi [动] snuggle up to

偎依 wēiyī [动] snuggle up to

微 wēi I [形] tiny ▷微米 micron ▷微秒 microsecond ▷门缝里射出一线微光。A ray of light shone through the crack in the door. II [副] slightly ▷她们姐妹俩的性格微有不同。The two sisters were slightly different in character.

微波 wēibō [名] 1 (涟漪) ripple 2 (电子) (超短波) microwave

微波炉 wēibōlú [名] microwave oven

微薄 wēibó [形] meagre (英), meager (美)

微不足道 wēi bù zú dào not worth mentioning ▷这是件微不足道的小事。This is a trivial matter.

微风 wēifēng [名] gentle breeze

微观 wēiguān [前缀] micro- ▷微观结构 microstructure

微观世界 wēiguān shìjiè [名] microcosm

微乎其微 wēi hū qí wēi very little ▷他夺冠的可能性微乎其微。There is very little possibility of his becoming the champion.

微粒 wēilì [名] particle

微量元素 wēiliàng yuánsù [名] trace element

微妙 wēimiào [形] delicate

微弱 wēiruò [形] faint

微生物 wēishēngwù [名] micro-organism

微小 wēixiǎo [形] tiny

微笑 wēixiào [动] smile ▷她的微笑很迷人。Her smile was enchanting.

微型 wēixíng [形] mini ▷微型唱片机 MiniDisc®

煨 wēi [动] (烹饪) stew

巍 wēi 见下文

巍峨 wēi'é [形] towering

为 wéi I [动] 1 (是) be ▷一公斤为两磅。A kilo is two pounds. 2 (变成) ▷他懂得如何变弊为利。He knows how to turn a disadvantage into an advantage. 3 (充当) act as ▷他选朋友为他的代言人。He chose his friend to act as his spokesman. II [介] ▷这部老电影为大家喜爱。Everyone loves this old film.
→另见 wèi

为非作歹 wéi fēi zuò dǎi commit all kinds of crimes

为富不仁 wéi fù bù rén wealthy but uncharitable

为害 wéihài [动] cause harm

为难 wéinán I [形] embarrassed II [动] make things difficult for ▷考官出了些难题，故意为难学生。The examiner set tough questions, deliberately making things difficult for the students.

为期 wéiqī [动] be scheduled for ▷电影节为期一周。The film festival is scheduled to last a week.

为生 wéishēng [动] make a living

为数 wéishù [动] ▷抢手的房产为数不少。There is a lot of fast-selling property.

为所欲为 wéi suǒ yù wéi (贬) do just as one pleases

为伍 wéiwǔ [动] associate with

为止 wéizhǐ [动] ▷到上周末为止，我们收到了上千封求职信。By the end of last week, we had received over a thousand letters of application.

违 wéi [动] break (PT broke, PP broken) ▷违法 break the law

违背 wéibèi [动] go against (PT went, PP gone)

违法 wéifǎ I [动] break the law (PT broke, PP broken) II [形] illegal

违反 wéifǎn [动] go against (PT went, PP gone)

违犯 wéifàn [动] violate

违禁 wéijìn [形] banned

违抗 wéikàng [动] disobey

违心 wéixīn [形] ▷他违心地投了赞成票。He voted for the motion against his conscience.

违约 wéiyuē [动] break a contract (PT broke, PP broken) ▷这家公司被控违约。The company was accused of breach of contract.

违章 wéizhāng [动] break regulations (PT broke, PP broken)

围 wéi I [动] surround II [名] 1 (四周) all sides ▷外围 periphery 2 (周长) measurement ▷三围 vital statistics ▷胸围 chest measurement

围攻 wéigōng [动] 1 (用语言) attack ... from all sides 2 (用武力) besiege

围观 wéiguān [动] look on ▷他从河里救孩子时，一群人在围观。A crowd of people looked on as he rescued the child from the river. ▷围观的人越来越多。There were more and more onlookers.

围困 wéikùn [动] strand

围拢 wéilǒng [动] crowd around

围棋 wéiqí [名] go (board game)

围绕 wéirào [动] 1 (物体) revolve around 2 (话题) centre (英) 或 center (美) on ▷大家围绕着此议题展开讨论。Everyone began a discussion centred on this subject.

桅 wéi [名] mast

桅杆 wéigān [名] mast

帷 wéi [名] curtain

帷幕 wéimù [名] 1 (指舞台) curtain 2 (指事件) ▷世界杯拉开了帷幕。The World Cup has begun.

惟 wéi [副] 1 (单单) only 2 (书) (只是) but ▷他各科成绩都不错，惟数学不好。He achieved good results in all subjects but mathematics.

惟独 wéidú [副] only ▷客人都到了，惟独她没来。She was the only guest who had not arrived.

惟恐 wéikǒng [动] be afraid

惟利是图 wéi lì shì tú only interested in profit

惟妙惟肖 **wéi miào wéi xiào** remarkably true to life

惟一 **wéiyī** [形] only ▷他是班里惟一的男生。 He is the only male student in the class.

维 **wéi** I [动] 1 (连接) hold ... together (PT, PP held) 2 (保持) maintain II [名] dimension ▷三维空间 three-dimensional space

维持 **wéichí** [动] 1 (保持) maintain ▷维持交通 秩序 direct the traffic 2 (资助) support ▷他靠 卖画维持生活。He relies on selling paintings to support himself.

维护 **wéihù** [动] safeguard ▷维护和平 safeguard peace ▷维护消费者的利益 defend consumers' interests

维生素 **wéishēngsù** [名] vitamin

维系 **wéixì** [动] maintain

维修 **wéixiū** [动] maintain

伟 **wěi** [形] great

伟大 **wěidà** [形] great

伟哥 **wěigē** [名] (医) Viagra®

伟人 **wěirén** [名] great man (PL men)

伪 **wěi** [形] false ▶伪钞 counterfeit note (英) 或 bill (美)

伪君子 **wěijūnzǐ** [名] hypocrite

伪劣 **wěiliè** [形] fake and second-rate

伪善 **wěishàn** [形] hypocritical

伪造 **wěizào** [动] forge ▷他的护照是伪造的。 His passport was forged.

伪装 **wěizhuāng** I [动] disguise ▷间谍伪装成 农民，混进了城里。The spy infiltrated the city disguised as a peasant. II [名] disguise

苇 **wěi** [名] reed

尾 **wěi** [名] 1 (尾巴) tail 2 (末端) end ▶排尾 the person at the end of a row ▷他喜欢坐大巴 的车尾。He likes sitting at the back of the bus. 3 (残余) remainder ▶扫尾 finish off

尾巴 **wěiba** [名] 1 (尾部) tail 2 (残余) unfinished business ▷今天的会议留了个尾巴。Today's meeting left unfinished business. 3 (跟踪的人) ▷他发现他的车后有个尾巴。He discovered that his car was being tailed.

尾气 **wěiqì** [名] exhaust (英) tailpipe

尾声 **wěishēng** [名] 1 (文学) epilogue 2 (指 活动) end ▷国际艺术节已接近尾声。The International Arts Festival is already drawing to an end.

尾数 **wěishù** [名] (指小数点后) digits after the decimal point

尾随 **wěisuí** [动] tail

纬 **wěi** [名] 1 (地理) latitude 2 (指纺织) weft

纬度 **wěidù** [名] latitude

纬线 **wěixiàn** [名] 1 (地理) latitude 2 (指纺织) weft

委 **wěi** I [动] entrust II [名] 1 (委员) committee member 2 (委员会) committee

委派 **wěipài** [动] appoint

委培 **wěipéi** [动] send ... for training (PT, PP sent)

委屈 **wěiqu** I [名] unjust treatment II [形] aggrieved III [动] wrong

委任 **wěirèn** [动] appoint ▷董事长委任他当策 划总监。The Chairman of the Board appointed him Chief Planning Inspector.

委托 **wěituō** [动] entrust ▷我委托姐姐看了几 天孩子。I entrusted the children to my sister's care for a few days.

委婉 **wěiwǎn** [形] 1 (指言词) tactful ▷我委婉 地拒绝了他的邀请。I tactfully refused his invitation. 2 (语气) mild

萎 **wěi** [形] withered

萎靡 **wěimǐ** [形] downhearted

萎缩 **wěisuō** [动] 1 (医) atrophy 2 (经济) shrink (PT shrank, PP shrunk)

唯 **wěi** 见下文

唯唯诺诺 **wěiwěinuònuò** obsequious

猥 **wěi** 见下文

猥亵 **wěixiè** I [形] (贬) obscene II [动] (贬, 书) act indecently towards

卫 **wèi** [动] protect

卫兵 **wèibīng** [名] guard

卫冕 **wèimiǎn** [动] defend a title

卫生 **wèishēng** I [名] 1 (干净) hygiene 2 (扫除) clean-up ▷我在打扫教室卫生。I am giving the classroom a clean-up. II [形] hygienic ▷饭 前不洗手不卫生。It is unhygienic not to wash your hands before eating.

卫生间 **wèishēngjiān** [名] toilet (英), rest room (美)

卫生球 **wèishēngqiú** [名] mothball

卫生纸 **wèishēngzhǐ** [名] toilet paper (英) 或 tissue (美)

卫星 **wèixīng** [名] satellite

为 **wèi** [介] for ▷我真为你高兴！I am really happy for you! ▷为健康着想, 他每天去跑

步。He went jogging every day for the sake of his health. ▷她在为孩子唱催眠曲。She is singing lullabies to the children.
→另见 wéi

为了 wèile [介] in order to ▷为了买房子, 他把车卖了。He sold his car in order to buy a house. ▷为了联系方便, 他买了个手机。He bought a mobile phone to keep in contact more easily.

为什么 wèi shénme [副] why ▷你为什么迟到了？Why were you late?

未 wèi [副] not ▷她还未回信。She has still not written back.

未必 wèibì [副] not necessarily ▷他未必会接受邀请。He may not necessarily be able to accept the invitation.

未曾 wèicéng [副] not ... before ▷我未曾见过他。I haven't seen him before.

未尝 wèicháng [副] not ▷他未尝不想取得好成绩。It wasn't that he didn't want good results.

未成年人 wèichéngniánrén [名] minor

未婚夫 wèihūnfū [名] fiancé

未婚妻 wèihūnqī [名] fiancée

未来 wèilái [名] future ▷他能预见未来。He can foresee the future. ▷未来的几天将有沙尘暴。In the next few days there will be a sandstorm.

未免 wèimiǎn [副] rather ▷他的讲话未免太长了。His speech went on rather too long. ▷他说的未免都是对的。What he says is not always correct.

未遂 wèisuì [动] fail ▷他自杀未遂。He attempted suicide.

未知数 wèizhīshù [名] 1 (数) unknown number 2 (未知事物) ▷他能否成名还是个未知数。It is uncertain whether he will become famous or not.

位 wèi I [名] 1 (位置) location 2 (地位) position ▶岗位 post 3 (数学) digit ▷两位数 two-digit number ▷他挣六位数的工资。He earns a six-figure salary. II [量] ▷主持人请来了两位嘉宾。The host invited two guests of honour (英) 或 honor (美).

位次 wèicì [名] position ▷歌曲排行榜的位次没变。The position of the songs in the charts has not changed.

位于 wèiyú [动] be located ▷格拉斯哥位于苏格兰。Glasgow is located in Scotland.

位置 wèizhi [名] 1 (地点) location ▷这房子的位置不好。This house is not well located. 2 (地位) place ▷他在人们心中的位置很高。He has an important place in peoples' hearts.

▷他在家里没有位置。He's a nobody at home. 3 (职位) position ▷人事部有5个空位置。The Human Resources Department has five vacant positions.

位子 wèizi [名] 1 (座位) seat 2 (职位) position ▷市场部里没位子了。There are no vacancies in Marketing.

味 wèi [名] 1 (滋味) taste 2 (气味) smell ▷这花没香味。This flower has no scent.

味道 wèidao [名] 1 (滋味) taste ▷这家饭馆的菜味道不错。The food in this restaurant is delicious. 2 (感觉) ▷他越想越不是味道。The more he thinks about it, the less palatable it becomes.

味精 wèijīng [名] monosodium glutamate

畏 wèi [动] (害怕) be afraid of

畏惧 wèijù [动] be afraid of ▷他畏惧失败。He is afraid of losing.

畏缩 wèisuō [动] shrink in fear (PT shrank, PP shrunk)

畏罪 wèizuì [动] fear punishment for one's crimes

胃 wèi [名] stomach ▷我的胃不舒服。I have a stomach upset.

胃口 wèikǒu [名] 1 (食欲) appetite 2 (喜好) liking ▷这套家具不合我的胃口。This furniture is not to my liking.

谓 wèi [动] (书) call ▷此谓自食其果。This is called "reaping what you have sown".

谓语 wèiyǔ [名] predicate

喂 wèi I [动] feed (PT, PP fed) II [叹] 1 (指打电话) hello 2 (指招呼) hey

喂养 wèiyǎng [动] raise

蔚 wèi 见下文

蔚蓝 wèilán [形] azure

蔚然成风 wèirán chéng fēng become the trend

慰 wèi [动] comfort

慰劳 wèiláo [动] show appreciation (PT showed, PP shown)

慰问 wèiwèn [动] express appreciation ▷市长向医务人员表示了亲切慰问。The mayor expressed his sincere appreciation to the medical workers.

慰问信 wèiwènxìn [名] letter of support

温 wēn I [形] 1 (不冷不热) warm 2 (平和) mild

II [动] **1** (加热) warm ... up ▷你最好把剩饭温一温再吃。You'd be best to warm up the leftovers before eating them again. **2** (复习) revise **3** (回忆) recall **III** [名] temperature

温饱 wēnbǎo [名] adequate food and clothing

温差 wēnchā [名] difference in temperature

温床 wēnchuáng [名] hotbed

温带 wēndài [名] temperate zone

温度 wēndù [名] temperature

温故知新 wēn gù zhī xīn gain new insights by studying the past

温和 wēnhé [形] **1** (指性情、态度) mild **2** (指气候) temperate

温暖 wēnnuǎn [形] warm ▷温暖的阳光 warm sunshine ▷在那些困难的日子里，家人给了她很多温暖。Her family gave her a lot of warmth during those difficult times.

温情 wēnqíng [名] tenderness

温泉 wēnquán [名] hot spring

温柔 wēnróu [形] gentle

温室 wēnshì [名] greenhouse ▷温室效应 the greenhouse effect

温顺 wēnshùn [形] docile

温文尔雅 wēn wén ěr yǎ cultured

温习 wēnxí [动] revise

温馨 wēnxīn [形] cosy (英), cozy (美)

瘟 wēn **I** [名] communicable disease **II** [形] infected

瘟疫 wēnyì [名] plague

文 wén **I** [名] **1** (字) writing ▶文盲 illiterate **2** (书面语) written language ▶中文 the Chinese language **3** (文章) essay **4** (指社会产物) culture ▶文明 civilization **5** (指自然现象) ▶天文 astronomy **6** (文科) humanities (PL) ▷他是学文的。He studied the humanities. **7** (非军事) civilian **II** [形] gentle **III** [动] tattoo

文本 wénběn [名] **1** (版本) version **2** (文件) text

文笔 wénbǐ [名] style ▷他的文笔很好。He has an excellent writing style.

文不对题 wén bù duì tí go off on a tangent

文才 wéncái [名] literary talent

文采 wéncǎi [名] **1** (指文艺) literary talent **2** (指词藻) flowery language

文法 wénfǎ [名] (语法) grammar

文风 wénfēng [名] **1** (指风气) atmosphere **2** (指语言) style

文工团 wéngōngtuán [名] song and dance ensemble

文豪 wénháo [名] great writer

文化 wénhuà [名] **1** (精神财富) culture ▷他对中国茶文化很有研究。He had researched Chinese tea culture in great detail. ▷他们的文化生活很丰富。They have a rich cultural life. **2** (知识) education

文火 wénhuǒ [名] gentle heat

文集 wénjí [名] collected works (PL)

文件 wénjiàn [名] **1** (公文) document ▷这是一份机密文件。This is a classified document. **2** (计算机) file ▷把文件存放在C盘。Save the file on the C drive.

文教 wénjiào [名] culture and education

文静 wénjìng [形] gentle

文具 wénjù [名] stationery

文科 wénkē [名] humanities (PL)

文盲 wénmáng [名] **1** (无知的人) illiterate **2** (无知) illiteracy

文明 wénmíng **I** [名] civilization **II** [形] civilized

文凭 wénpíng [名] diploma

文气 wénqi [形] reserved

文人 wénrén [名] scholar

文书 wénshū [名] **1** (公文) official document **2** (文职人员) secretary

文坛 wéntán [名] literary circles (PL)

文体 wéntǐ [名] **1** (体裁) genre **2** (文娱) recreation

文物 wénwù [名] cultural relic

文献 wénxiàn [名] document

文学 wénxué [名] literature

文雅 wényǎ [形] refined

文艺 wényì [名] **1** (文学艺术) art and literature **2** (文学) literature **3** (演艺) performing arts (PL)

文娱 wényú [名] recreation

文摘 wénzhāi [名] abstract ▷她对读过的文章做了文摘。She made abstracts of the articles she read.

文章 wénzhāng [名] **1** (著作) essay **2** (含义) implication

文质彬彬 wén zhì bīnbīn gentle and refined

文绉绉 wénzhōuzhōu [形] genteel

文字 wénzì [名] **1** (指符号) script **2** (指文章) writing

纹 wén [名] line

纹理 wénlǐ [名] grain

纹丝不动 wén sī bù dòng motionless ▷一丝风都没有，树枝纹丝不动。There wasn't a breath of wind – the branches were motionless. ▷接受检阅的士兵纹丝不动地立正站着。The soldiers under inspection stood to attention without moving a muscle.

闻 wén I [动] 1 (书) (听见) hear (PT, PP heard) 2 (嗅) smell II [名] 1 (消息) news 2 (声望) reputation

闻风而动 wén fēng ér dòng act at once on hearing the news ▷记者的"嗅觉"特别灵敏，总能闻风而动。The reporter had a particularly good journalistic nose and always acted quickly on a story.

闻风丧胆 wén fēng sàng dǎn tremble with fear on hearing the news ▷这批勇猛的缉毒警令毒品贩子闻风丧胆。The drug dealers trembled with fear when they heard about the courageous drugs squad.

闻名 wénmíng I [动] be famous II [形] famous

蚊 wén [名] mosquito (PL mosquitoes)

刎 wěn [动] cut one's throat (PT, PP cut) ▷他自刎身亡。He committed suicide by cutting his own throat.

吻 wěn I [名] 1 (动物的嘴) mouth 2 (口气) tone II [动] kiss

吻合 wěnhé [形] identical

紊 wěn [形] disorderly

紊乱 wěnluàn [形] chaotic

稳 wěn I [形] 1 (平稳) steady 2 (坚定) firm 3 (稳重) composed 4 (可靠) reliable 5 (肯定) sure ▷这场足球赛我们稳赢。We're sure to win this football match. II [动] keep calm (PT, PP kept)

稳操胜券 wěn cāo shèng quàn be sure to win ▷这场比赛，红队稳操胜券。The red team are sure to win this competition.

稳当 wěndang [形] 1 (牢稳) steady ▷她的孩子两岁时就走得很稳当了。At two years old her child was very steady on his legs. 2 (妥当) reliable

稳定 wěndìng I [形] steady ▷他有份十分稳定的工作。He's got a really steady job. ▷近期，市场物价稳定。Market prices have been stable recently. II [动] settle ▷新政策有助于稳定市场价格。The new policy will help to settle market prices.

稳固 wěngù I [形] stable II [动] firm ... up ▷他稳固了政权后，又推行了一系列改革措施。After firming up his political power, he carried out another series of reforms.

稳健 wěnjiàn [形] 1 (矫健) firm 2 (沉着) calm

稳妥 wěntuǒ [形] safe

稳重 wěnzhòng [形] steady

问 wèn [动] 1 (提问) ask ▷他总是喜欢问各种问题。He likes to ask a lot of questions. 2 (问候) send regards to (PT, PP sent) ▷代我向你妈妈问好。Please send my regards to your mother. 3 (审讯) interrogate 4 (干预) ask about ▷她的父母从不过问她的工作。Her parents never asked about her work. II [介] from ▷我问他借了一支钢笔。I borrowed a pen from him. III [名] question ▶疑问 doubt

问寒问暖 wèn hán wèn nuǎn ask how things are going ▷老邻居之间总是问寒问暖。Old neighbours always ask each other how things are going.

问候 wènhòu [动] send regards to (PT, PP sent) ▷请代我问候你的爸妈。Please send my regards to your parents.

问津 wènjīn [动] (书) inquire about ▷退休人员的住房问题一直无人问津。Nobody ever inquires about the housing problems of retired people.

问世 wènshì [动] come out (PT came, PP come)

问题 wèntí [名] 1 (疑问) question ▷欢迎大家踊跃提问题。Everyone is invited to get up and ask questions. 2 (困难) problem ▷高校扩招造成了一定的就业问题。The expansion of higher education has created some employment problems. 3 (故障) fault ▷我的电脑出问题了。There's something wrong with my computer. 4 (关键) point ▷问题在于他还没意识到形势的严峻。The point is, he still hasn't realized how grim the situation is. 5 (分项) issue ▷今天开会主要讲两个问题。Today's meeting mainly concerns two issues.

问讯 wènxùn [动] 1 (打听) inquire ▷他到处问讯失散亲人的消息。He inquired all over the place about his lost relatives. 2 (审问) question

问罪 wènzuì [动] denounce

翁 wēng [名] 1 (配偶的父亲) father-in-law 2 (男性老人) old man (PL men)

嗡 wēng [拟] buzz

瓮 wèng [名] jar

莴 wō 见下文

莴笋 wōsǔn [名] asparagus lettuce

涡 wō [名] eddy

涡流 wōliú [名] whirlpool

窝 wō I [名] 1 (栖息地) nest 2 (小家) home 3 (据点) den ▷这是一个贼窝。This is a den of thieves. 4 (凹陷处) depression ▶酒窝 dimple ▷当心，这里有个小水窝。Mind the puddle. II [动] 1 (藏匿) harbour (英), harbor (美) 2 (躲

藏) hide (PT hid, PP hidden) **3** (停滞) halt **4** (郁积) contain ▶窝火 contain one's anger **5** (弯曲) bend (PT, PP bent) **III** [量] brood

窝藏 wōcáng [动] harbour (英), harbor (美)

窝火 wōhuǒ [动] seethe with anger

窝囊 wōnang [形] **1** (烦恼) annoyed **2** (软弱无能) hopeless

窝棚 wōpeng [名] shed

窝赃 wōzāng [动] conceal stolen goods

蜗 wō 见下文

蜗牛 wōniú [名] snail

我 wǒ [代] **1** (自己, 作主语) I ▷我今天下午有事, 不能开会了。I'm busy this afternoon so I can't go to the meeting. ▷她是我的同事。She's my colleague. **2** (自己, 作宾语) me ▷请帮我一下。Please give me a hand. **3** (书) (我们) we ▷我公司最近更新了设备。Our company has recently updated its equipment. **4** (书) (我方) our side ▷敌我双方的力量悬殊较大。There's a big difference in strength between us and the enemy. **5** (自己) self ▷他的忘我精神令人佩服。Everyone admired his selflessness.

我们 wǒmen [代] **1** (作主语) we ▷我们去年去了希腊。Last year we went to Greece. ▷我们一起去公园吧。Let's go to the park. ▷我们的公寓非常干净。Our flat is very clean. **2** (作宾语) us ▷老师邀请我们去他家作客。Our teacher invited us to his house. **3** (我) I ▷我们孩子特别乖。My children are really good. ▷我们在论文中引用了大量的新数据。I've used a lot of new data in my thesis.

我行我素 wǒ xíng wǒ sù do things one's own way ▷她向来我行我素, 不会因别人改变自己。She always does things her own way and doesn't change for anyone.

卧 wò **I** [动] **1** (躺) lie (PT lay, PP lain) ▷她睡觉时习惯侧卧。She tends to lie on her side when she sleeps. **2** (趴伏) sit (PT, PP sat) **II** [形] sleeping **III** [名] berth

卧病 wòbìng [动] be laid up

卧床 wòchuáng [动] stay in bed

卧底 wòdǐ [动] go undercover (PT went, PP gone)

卧铺 wòpù [名] berth

卧室 wòshì [名] bedroom

握 wò [动] **1** (抓) grasp **2** (掌握) master

握别 wòbié [动] part with a handshake

握手 wòshǒu [动] shake hands (PT shook, PP shaken)

斡 wò 见下文

斡旋 wòxuán [动] mediate ▷经过他的斡旋, 两国签署了停战协议。Following his mediation, the two countries signed an armistice.

龌 wò 见下文

龌龊 wòchuò [形] **1** (肮脏) filthy **2** (喻) (指品质) dirty **3** (书) (指气量) narrow-minded

乌 wū **I** [名] crow **II** [形] black

乌龟 wūguī [名] tortoise

乌合之众 wū hé zhī zhòng (贬) mob

乌黑 wūhēi [形] jet-black

乌纱帽 wūshāmào [名] official post

乌烟瘴气 wū yān zhàng qì foul ▷别抽烟了, 弄得房间里乌烟瘴气的。Don't smoke – it makes the room smell really foul.

乌有 wūyǒu [动] (书) not exist

乌云 wūyún [名] black cloud

污 wū **I** [名] dirt **II** [形] **1** (肮脏) dirty **2** (腐败) corrupt **III** [动] **1** (弄脏) dirty ▷当心, 别污了新衣服。Careful not to dirty your new clothes. **2** (羞辱) smear

污点 wūdiǎn [名] stain ▷他的白衬衣上有好多污点。There were stains all over his white shirt. ▷这件事成了他终生洗不掉的污点。This affair became the stain that he was never able to wash away.

污垢 wūgòu [名] dirt

污秽 wūhuì **I** [名] filth **II** [形] filthy

污蔑 wūmiè [动] **1** (侮辱) slander **2** (玷污) tarnish

污染 wūrǎn [动] pollute ▷政府采取了一系列措施治理大气污染。The government has adopted a series of measures to combat air pollution.

污辱 wūrǔ [动] **1** (侮辱) insult **2** (玷污) sully

污浊 wūzhuó [形] filthy

巫 wū [名] sorcerer

巫师 wūshī [名] wizard

巫术 wūshù [名] witchcraft

呜 wū [拟] hoot

呜咽 wūyè [动] sob

诬 wū [动] falsely accuse

诬告 wūgào [动] falsely accuse

诬蔑 wūmiè [动] slander

诬陷 wūxiàn [动] frame

屋 wū [名] 1 (房子) house 2 (房间) room

屋顶 wūdǐng [名] roof

屋子 wūzi [名] room

无 wú I [动] 1 (没有) not have ▶无效 invalid ▶无形 invisible ▷他毫无常识。He has no common sense. ▷因发烧, 我四肢无力。Because of the fever, my arms and legs were completely limp. 2 (无论) never mind ▷大家都在无日无夜地赶这个项目。Everyone worked day and night to get the project done. II [副] not ▷无论怎么解释, 他也不肯原谅我。It doesn't matter how I explain it, he won't forgive me. ▷你无须多说, 行动最有说服力。You don't need to say any more – actions speak louder than words.

无比 wúbǐ [形] incomparable

无边无际 wú biān wú jì boundless

无病呻吟 wú bìng shēnyín 1 (人) make a fuss about nothing 2 (文章) be excessively sentimental

无常 wúcháng [形] changeable

无偿 wúcháng [形] free

无耻 wúchǐ [形] shameless

无从 wúcóng [副] ▷这道题目很难, 我感到无从入手。This question is so difficult – I don't know how I'm going to tackle it.

无敌 wúdí [动] invincible

无的放矢 wú dì fàng shǐ be aimless ▷复习时要目标明确, 决不能无的放矢。When revising you need clear targets – never be aimless.

无地自容 wú dì zì róng feel too ashamed to show one's face

无动于衷 wú dòng yú zhōng be completely indifferent ▷他对妈妈的一番苦心无动于衷。He was completely indifferent to his mother's considerable efforts.

无独有偶 wú dú yǒu ǒu (贬) come in pairs ▷无独有偶, 他丢了钥匙, 钱包被偷了。These things come in pairs – just as he lost his keys, his wallet was stolen too.

无度 wúdù [形] excessive

无端 wúduān [副] for no reason ▷他无端受了批评, 感到很委屈。He was upset at being criticized for no reason.

无恶不作 wú è bù zuò commit all kinds of atrocities

无法无天 wú fǎ wú tiān be completely lawless

无妨 wúfáng I [动] be harmless II [副] may as well ▷我有没讲清楚的地方, 无妨提出来。If there's anything I haven't made clear, you

may as well say so.

无非 wúfēi [副] simply

无辜 wúgū I [动] be innocent II [名] the innocent

无关 wúguān [动] have nothing to do with ▷这件事与你无关。This has nothing to do with you.

无稽 wújī [形] absurd

无几 wújǐ [形] very little

无济于事 wú jì yú shì be of no avail ▷我们怎么劝都无济于事, 她还是哭个不停。However hard we tried to pacify her, it was to no avail – she still couldn't stop crying.

无精打采 wú jīng dǎ cǎi 1 (没有活力) be listless ▷夏天的午后, 人们总是无精打采的。People are always listless on summer afternoons. 2 (情绪低落) be dispirited ▷他们比赛输了, 个个无精打采地退了场。Having lost the game, they all left the pitch feeling very dispirited.

无拘无束 wú jū wú shù be free and easy ▷他向往无拘无束的生活。He longed for a free and easy life.

无可厚非 wú kě hòu fēi give no cause for criticism ▷她虽有点儿私心, 但也无可厚非。Although she was a little selfish, that was no cause for criticism.

无可奈何 wú kě nàihé have no alternative ▷我一再坚持, 妈妈终于无可奈何地同意让我出国读书。I persevered and persevered, and in the end my mother had no alternative but to agree to let me study abroad.

无可置疑 wú kě zhì yí be beyond doubt ▷他们夺冠的实力无可置疑。Their ability to win the championship was beyond doubt.

无孔不入 wú kǒng bù rù (贬) be everywhere ▷小偷无孔不入, 大家要提高警惕。Thieves are everywhere and everybody should be on the lookout.

无愧 wúkuì [动] be worthy of ▷他无愧于"人民英雄"的称号。He was worthy of the title of "people's hero".

无赖 wúlài I [形] shameless II [名] rascal

无理取闹 wú lǐ qǔ nào be deliberately provocative

无量 wúliàng [动] be boundless

无论 wúlùn [连] no matter what ▷无论受到什么挫折, 我们都不会退缩。No matter what setbacks we meet, we can't go back now.

无名 wúmíng [形] 1 (没名称的) unnamed 2 (不出名的) unknown 3 (匿名的) anonymous 4 (没来由的) indescribable

无奈 wúnài I [形] helpless II [连] but ▷我正

想出门，无奈朋友来访，我只好作罢。I was just about to go out, but my friend came round so I had to drop my plans.

无能为力 wú néng wéi lì be powerless ▷这件事我实在无能为力。I'm powerless to do anything about this.

无奇不有 wú qí bù yǒu full of extraordinary things ▷他的科幻小说无奇不有，引人入胜。His science fiction novel was full of extraordinary things that people found fascinating.

无情 wúqíng [形] 1 (指感情) heartless 2 (不留情) ruthless

无穷 wúqióng [形] infinite

无伤大雅 wú shāng dàyǎ not matter much ▷这是朋友聚会，穿得随意些也无伤大雅。It's just a meeting of friends, so it doesn't matter much if you dress a bit casually.

无上 wúshàng [形] highest

无师自通 wú shī zì tōng self-taught ▷他对家电维修可谓无师自通。You could say he is self-taught when it comes to repairing electrical household goods.

无事生非 wú shì shēng fēi make a fuss about nothing

无数 wúshù I [形] countless II [动] be uncertain

无所事事 wú suǒ shì shì do nothing ▷失业后，他整天呆在家里无所事事。After he lost his job he stayed at home all day doing nothing.

无所适从 wú suǒ shì cóng be unsure what to do ▷大家都帮着出主意，他反而无所适从了。Everybody helped him to come up with ideas but he was unsure what to do.

无所谓 wúsuǒwèi [动] 1 (谈不上) never mind 2 (不在乎) be indifferent ▷她对别人的看法一向都持无所谓的态度。She was always indifferent to other people's views. ▷会议不重要，你来不来无所谓。The meeting isn't important so it doesn't matter if you're there or not.

无所作为 wú suǒ zuòwéi accomplish nothing

无微不至 wú wēi bù zhì meticulous ▷父母对子女的关爱无微不至。Parents are meticulous about caring for their children.

无谓 wúwèi [形] pointless

无限 wúxiàn [形] boundless

无线电 wúxiàndiàn [名] radio

无懈可击 wú xiè kě jī unassailable ▷他的回答无懈可击。His reply was unassailable.

无心 wúxīn I [动] not be in the mood for ▷儿

子生病时，她根本无心工作。When her son was ill she wasn't in the mood to work. II [形] unintentional

无形 wúxíng I [形] imperceptible II [副] imperceptibly

无须 wúxū [副] needlessly ▷你无须多言，行动是最有力的证明。You needn't say much – actions speak a lot louder than words.

无意 wúyì I [动] have no intention of ▷我无意打断你们的谈话。I have no intention of interrupting you. II [形] inadvertent

无意识 wúyìshí [形] unconscious

无与伦比 wú yǔ lún bǐ unparalleled ▷金字塔是世界上无与伦比的建筑奇迹。The pyramids are marvels of construction that are unparalleled throughout the world.

无缘 wúyuán [动] have no luck with

无缘无故 wú yuán wú gù for no reason at all

无知 wúzhī [形] ignorant

无中生有 wú zhōng shēng yǒu make ... up ▷你这是无中生有，造谣诬陷。You're just making it up and starting false rumours (英) 或 rumors (美).

无足轻重 wú zú qīng zhòng be insignificant

毋
毋 wú [副] not
毋宁 wúnìng [副] rather

芜
芜 wú I (书) [形] 1 (指草) overgrown with weeds 2 (指文辞) miscellaneous II [名] (书) grassland
芜杂 wúzá [形] disorderly

梧
梧 wú 见下文
梧桐 wútóng [名] Chinese parasol tree

五
五 wǔ [名] five ▷他五岁时得了一场重病。When he was five, he contracted a serious illness. ▷今年的产量是去年的五倍。This year's output is five times last year's. ▷五分之一 one fifth

五大三粗 wǔ dà sān cū tall and well-built

五谷 wǔgǔ [名] crops (PL)

五官 wǔguān [名] the five sense organs

五光十色 wǔ guāng shí sè brilliantly-coloured (英) 或 colored (美)

五湖四海 wǔ hú sì hǎi all over the country ▷北京每天都迎来来自五湖四海的游客。Every day, people from all over the country come to Beijing.

五花八门 wǔ huā bā mén wide variety ▷五花八门的电视节目让我无从选择。I find it hard to select from such a wide variety of television programmes (英) 或 programs (美).

五金 wǔjīn [名] hardware

五体投地 wǔ tǐ tóu dì be lost in admiration

五味 wǔwèi [名] all sorts of flavours (英) 或 flavours (美)

五脏 wǔzàng [名] the five internal organs

午 wǔ [名] noon

午饭 wǔfàn [名] lunch

午夜 wǔyè [名] midnight

伍 wǔ [名] 1 (军队) army 2 (同辈) company ▷我不与虚伪的人为伍。I don't keep company with hypocrites. 3 (五) an elaborate form of "five", used in writing cheques etc to prevent mistakes and forgery

妩 wǔ 见下文

妩媚 wǔmèi [形] lovely

武 wǔ [形] 1 (军事的) military ▶武力 military force 2 (勇猛) valiant ▶威武 powerful

武打 wǔdǎ acrobatic fighting in Chinese opera

武断 wǔduàn [动] be arbitrary

武功 wǔgōng [名] 1 (书) military exploits (PL) 2 (武术) martial arts (PL)

武官 wǔguān [名] 1 (指军队) officer 2 (指大使馆) attaché

武警 wǔjǐng [名] armed police

武力 wǔlì [名] 1 (军事力量) military strength 2 (暴力) force

武器 wǔqì [名] weapon

武士 wǔshì [名] warrior

武术 wǔshù [名] martial arts circles (PL)

武艺 wǔyì [名] skill in martial arts

武装 wǔzhuāng I [名] 1 (武装力量) armed forces (PL) 2 (武力) arms (PL) 3 (军备) armaments (PL) II [动] 1 (用武器) arm 2 (用精神、物质) equip

侮 wǔ [动] 1 (侮辱) insult 2 (外侵) foreign aggression

侮蔑 wǔmiè I [动] scorn II [形] scornful

侮辱 wǔrǔ [动] insult

捂 wǔ [动] cover

舞 wǔ I [名] dance II [动] 1 (跳舞) dance 2 (飞舞) flutter 3 (挥舞) brandish 4 (玩弄) play with

舞弊 wǔbì [动] embezzle

舞蹈 wǔdǎo [名] dance

舞剧 wǔjù [名] ballet

舞台 wǔtái [名] stage

勿 wù [副] not ▷请勿吸烟 no smoking ▷请勿入内 no entry

勿忘草 wùwàngcǎo [名] forget-me-not

务 wù I [名] business ▷我有要务在身。I've got urgent business. ▷他负责公司内务。He's in charge of the company's internal affairs. II [动] be engaged in III [副] without fail

务必 wùbì [副] without fail

务实 wùshí [动] be pragmatic

务虚 wùxū [动] discuss principles

坞 wù [名] 1 (指地形) depression ▶村坞 village settlement ▶山坞 col 2 (指建筑) ▶花坞 sunken flowerbed ▶船坞 dock

物 wù [名] 1 (东西) thing 2 (物产) produce 3 (动物) creature 4 (指哲学) matter 5 (指法律) property 6 (指环境) the outside world 7 (内容) content

物产 wùchǎn [名] produce

物极必反 wù jí bì fǎn things go into reverse when pushed to the extreme ▷不要总是批评学生，否则，物极必反。Don't criticize the students or it may backfire on you.

物价 wùjià [名] price

物件 wùjiàn [名] article

物理 wùlǐ [名] 1 (书) (常理) laws of nature (PL) 2 (指学科) physics (SG)

物力 wùlì [名] material resources (PL)

物品 wùpǐn [名] article

物色 wùsè [动] look for

物体 wùtǐ [名] body

物业 wùyè [名] property

物证 wùzhèng [名] material evidence

物质 wùzhì [名] 1 (哲) matter 2 (非精神) material things (PL)

物种 wùzhǒng [名] species

物资 wùzī [名] material

误 wù I [名] mistake II [形] 1 (不正确) erroneous ▶误会 misunderstand 2 (非故意) accidental ▶误伤 accidentally injure III [动] 1 (耽误) miss ▷快点儿，别误了火车！Hurry up – we don't want to miss the train! 2 (损害) harm

误差 wùchā [名] error

误导 wùdǎo [动] mislead (PT, PP misled)

误会 wùhuì [动] misunderstand (PT, PP misunderstood)

误解 wùjiě [动] misunderstand (PT, PP misunderstood)

误区 wùqū [名] long-standing misunderstanding

误人子弟 wùrénzǐdì lead young people astray

误事 wùshì [动] mess things up ▷不提前做好准备，就会误事。You'll mess things up if you don't prepare in advance.

恶 wù [动] loathe
→另见 ě, è

悟 wù [动] realize

悟性 wùxìng [名] intelligence ▷他学钢琴很有悟性。He has picked up the piano very quickly.

晤 wù 见下文

晤谈 wùtán (书) [动] discuss ... face-to-face ▷他每周与导师晤谈一次。He has a face-to-face discussion with his supervisor once a week.

焐 wù [动] 1 (使变暖) warm ... up ▷冬天，她用暖水袋焐脚。During winter she uses a hot water bottle to warm her feet up. 2 (保温) keep ... warm (PT, PP kept) ▷把饭放在锅里焐着。You should keep the rice warm in the pot.

鹜 wù [动] seek (PT, PP sought)

雾 wù [名] fog

雾里看花 wù lǐ kàn huā have blurred vision ▷摘了眼镜，她看什么都好像雾里看花。When she took her glasses off everything was blurred.

雾茫茫 wùmāngmāng [形] foggy

Xx

吸收 xīshōu [动] 1 (摄取) absorb 2 (接纳) recruit ▷俱乐部吸收了一批海外球员。The club has recruited some foreign players.

吸引 xīyǐn [动] attract

汐 xī [名] evening tide ▶潮汐 morning and evening tides (PL)

希 xī I [动] hope II [形] 见 '稀'

希罕 xīhan I [形] rare II [动] cherish III [名] rarity

希奇 xīqí [形] strange

希望 xīwàng I [动] hope ▷她希望早点嫁人。She's hoping to get married soon. ▷我希望你成个大歌星。I hope you make it as a pop star. II [名] hope ▷他的病有希望了。There's hope he will recover. ▷这批小球员大有希望。These young footballers show a lot of promise.

昔 xī [名] the past

昔日 xīrì [名] former times (PL)

析 xī [动] 1 (分开) separate 2 (解释) analyse (英), analyze (美) ▶剖析 analyse

牺 xī 见下文

牺牲 xīshēng [动] 1 (献身) sacrifice oneself ▷他为救落水儿童牺牲了。He lost his life saving the drowning child. 2 (放弃) sacrifice ▷牺牲个人利益 sacrifice personal gain

息 xī I [名] 1 (呼吸) breath 2 (消息) news (SG) 3 (利息) interest II [动] 1 (休息) rest ▶歇息 have a rest 2 (停止) stop ▶息怒 calm down

息怒 xīnù [动] calm down

息事宁人 xī shì níng rén keep the peace

息息相关 xī xī xiāng guān be closely connected with ▷当今任何一个国家所发生的事情都和整个世界息息相关。Today, events in any individual country are closely connected with the rest of the world.

奚 xī 见下文

奚落 xīluò [动] mock

悉 xī I [形] ▶悉心 devote all one's attention to II [动] learn ▷获悉 learn of an event

淅 xī 见下文

淅沥 xīlì [拟] pitter-patter

夕 xī [名] 1 (傍晚) sunset 2 (晚上) evening ▶除夕 New Year's Eve

夕阳 xīyáng [名] setting sun

西 xī [名] 1 (方向) west 2 (疆域) the West

西餐 xīcān [名] Western food

西方 Xīfāng [名] the West

西服 xīfú [名] Western clothes

西化 xīhuà [动] Westernize

西洋 Xīyáng [名] the West

西药 xīyào [名] Western medicine

西医 xīyī [名] 1 (药品) Western medicine 2 (医生) doctor

西乐 xīyuè [名] Western music

西装 xīzhuāng [名] Western clothes

吸 xī [动] 1 (气、水等) draw ... in (PT drew, PP drawn) ▶吸气 breathe ▷用吸管吸酸奶 drink yoghurt with a straw 2 (吸收) absorb ▷用海绵吸水 mop up water with a sponge 3 (吸引) attract ▷异性相吸 opposites attract

吸尘器 xīchénqì [名] vacuum cleaner

吸纳 xīnà [动] attract

吸取 xīqǔ [动] absorb ▷吸取热量 absorb heat ▷吸取教训 draw a lesson ▷吸取知识 acquire knowledge

惜 xī [动] 1 (珍惜) cherish ▷惜时如命 regard one's time as precious 2 (可惜) pity ▶惋惜 feel sorry for 3 (吝惜) spare ▶吝惜 stint ▷不惜一切代价 at any price

惜别 xībié [动] part reluctantly

惜力 xīlì [动] not give one's all ▷他工作时从不惜力。He always gives his all at work.

晰 xī [形] clear ▶清晰 distinct

稀 xī [形] 1 (稀有) rare 2 (稀疏) sparse ▷奶奶的头发太稀了。Granny's hair is very thin. 3 (水多的) watery ▶稀饭 rice porridge

稀薄 xībó [形] thin

稀客 xīkè [名] infrequent visitor

稀里糊涂 xīlihútú muddle-headed

稀少 xīshǎo [形] sparse

稀疏 xīshū [形] scattered

稀松 xīsōng [形] sloppy

稀稀拉拉 xīxilālā sparse

稀有 xīyǒu [形] rare

犀 xī [名] rhinoceros

犀利 xīlì [形] penetrating ▷犀利的评论 incisive comments ▷犀利的目光 sharp eyes

犀牛 xīniú [名] rhinoceros

锡 xī [名] tin

锡箔 xībó [名] tinfoil

溪 xī [名] brook

溪流 xīliú [名] brook

熙 xī 见下文

熙熙攘攘 xīxī rǎngrǎng bustling

熄 xī [动] put ... out (PT, PP put) ▶熄灯 put out the light ▷他的车在半坡上熄火了。His car gave out halfway up the slope.

熄灭 xīmiè [动] put ... out (PT, PP put)

嘻 xī I [叹] wow ▷嘻，魔术师太神了！Wow! The magician is amazing! II [拟] ha ha

嘻嘻哈哈 xīxī hāhā laughing ▷一群年轻人坐在草地上嘻嘻哈哈地说笑。A crowd of young people sat on the grass laughing and chatting.

膝 xī [名] knee ▶屈膝 kneel

嬉 xī [动] (书) play ▶嬉戏 play

嬉皮士 xīpíshì [名] hippie

嬉皮笑脸 xī pí xiào liǎn grin cheekily

蹊 xī [名] (书) footpath
→另见 qī

蹊径 xījìng [名] (书) path

曦 xī [名] (书) sunlight ▶晨曦 early morning sunlight

习 xí I [动] 1 (学习) practise (英), practice (美) ▶习武 study martial arts 2 (熟悉) be used to ▷习以为常 become used to II [名] custom ▶习俗 custom ▶习气 bad habit

习惯 xíguàn I [动] be used to ▷我习惯早起。I'm used to getting up early. II [名] habit

习气 xíqì [名] bad habit

习俗 xísú [名] custom

习题 xítí [名] exercises (PL)

习习 xíxí [形] gently blowing

习性 xíxìng [名] habits (PL)

习以为常 xí yǐ wéi cháng become used to ▷大熊猫对人山人海的参观者已经习以为常了。The panda has long become accustomed to the huge crowds of visitors.

习语 xíyǔ [名] idiom

习作 xízuò [名] sketch

席 xí I [名] 1 (编织物) mat ▶竹席 bamboo mat 2 (座位) seat ▶席位 seat ▶出席 be present 3 (宴席) feast ▶酒席 banquet II [量] ▷一席长谈 a long chat ▷一席佳肴 a table covered with delicacies

席地 xídì [动] sit on the ground (PT, PP sat)

席卷 xíjuǎn [动] engulf

席位 xíwèi [名] seat

袭 xí [动] 1 (攻击) make a surprise attack ▶空袭 air raid 2 (仿做) follow the pattern of ▶抄袭 plagiarize

袭击 xíjī [动] attack

袭用 xíyòng [动] follow

媳 xí [名] daughter-in-law (PL daughters-in-law)

媳妇 xífù [名] 1 (儿子的妻子) daughter-in-law (PL daughters-in-law) 2 (晚辈的妻子) wife (PL wives) ▷侄媳妇 nephew's wife

媳妇儿 xífur [名] 1 (方) (妻子) wife (PL wives) 2 (妇女) married woman (PL women)

洗 xǐ [动] 1 (衣、碗等) wash ▶洗衣店 Launderette® (英), Laundromat® (美) 2 (胶卷) develop 3 (录音、录像) wipe 4 (麻将、扑克) shuffle 5 (洗礼) baptize 6 (洗劫) loot 7 (洗雪) redress ▶洗冤 redress a wrong

洗尘 xǐchén [动] give a dinner of welcome (PT gave, PP given)

洗涤 xǐdí [动] wash

洗耳恭听 xǐ ěr gōng tīng listen in respectful silence

洗劫 xǐjié [动] loot

洗礼 xǐlǐ [名] **1** (宗) baptism **2** (喻) (考验) trial

洗钱 xǐqián [动] launder money

洗刷 xǐshuā [动] **1** (地板、厕所) scrub **2** (耻辱、污点) clear oneself of

洗心革面 xǐ xīn gé miàn turn over a new leaf

洗衣机 xǐyījī [名] washing machine

洗澡 xǐzǎo [动] have a bath

喜 xǐ I [形] **1** (高兴) happy ▶欢喜 happy **2** (可贺的) celebratory II [动] **1** (爱好) like ▶喜好 like **2** (适宜) suit III [名] (口) pregnancy ▶有喜 be pregnant

喜爱 xǐ'ài [动] like

喜出望外 xǐ chū wàng wài be overjoyed at unexpected news

喜好 xǐhào [动] like

喜欢 xǐhuan [动] like

喜剧 xǐjù [名] comedy

喜庆 xǐqìng [形] joyous

喜鹊 xǐque [名] magpie

喜事 xǐshì [名] **1** (开心事) happy event **2** (婚礼) wedding ▷他俩决定从简办喜事。The couple decided on a simple wedding.

喜闻乐见 xǐ wén lè jiàn love to be entertained by ▷说书是中国人喜闻乐见的民间艺术。Story-telling is a folk art much loved by the Chinese.

喜笑颜开 xǐ xiào yán kāi light up ▷老人一见到孙子就喜笑颜开的。As soon as the old man sees his grandchild his face lights up.

喜形于色 xǐ xíng yú sè beam with pleasure

喜洋洋 xǐyángyáng [形] beaming

喜悦 xǐyuè [形] happy ▷掩饰不住内心的喜悦 be unable to hide one's happiness

禧 xǐ [名] (书) happiness ▶福禧 good fortune

戏 xì I [动] **1** (玩耍) play ▶嬉戏 have fun **2** (嘲弄) joke ▶戏弄 tease II [名] show ▶京戏 Beijing Opera ▶马戏 circus

戏法 xìfǎ [名] magic

戏剧 xìjù [名] theatre (英), theater (美)

戏弄 xìnòng [动] tease ▷他没有发觉自己是在受人戏弄。He didn't realize he was being teased.

戏曲 xìqǔ [名] Chinese opera

戏院 xìyuàn [名] theatre (英), theater (美)

系 xì I [名] **1** (系统) system ▶星系 galaxy **2** (部门) department ▶法语系 French department II [动] **1** (拴) tie ▶把绳子在树上 tie a rope

to a tree **2** (在) relate to ▷战争胜败系此一役。Success or failure in the war comes down to the campaign. **3** (书) (是) be (PT was, were, PP been) ▷纯系捏造 be pure fabrication →另见 jì

系列 xìliè [名] series (SG)

系数 xìshù [名] coefficient

系统 xìtǒng [名] system

细 xì I [形] **1** (绳、线等) thin **2** (沙、粮等) fine **3** (声、语等) gentle **4** (节、则等) detailed ▶细节 details (PL) II [副] minutely ▶细看 scrutinize ▷细问 ask in detail ▷细想 consider carefully

细胞 xìbāo [名] cell

细节 xìjié [名] details (PL)

细菌 xìjūn [名] germ

细密 xìmì [形] **1** (精细) finely woven **2** (仔细) detailed

细腻 xìnì [形] exquisite

细微 xìwēi [形] subtle

细心 xìxīn [形] careful

细则 xìzé [名] detailed rules (PL)

细枝末节 xì zhī mò jié minor details (PL)

细致 xìzhì [副] meticulously

隙 xì [名] **1** (指物体) crack ▶岩隙 crevice **2** (指情感) rift ▷二人向来有隙。There's always been disagreement between them. **3** (漏洞) opportunity

呷 xiā [动] (方) sip ▷呷一口酒 take a sip of wine

虾 xiā [名] shrimp ▶龙虾 lobster

瞎 xiā I [形] **1** (失明) blind **2** (方) (糟蹋) wasted II [副] groundlessly

瞎扯 xiāchě [动] talk nonsense

瞎话 xiāhuà [名] lie

瞎子 xiāzi [名] blind man/woman ▷她是瞎子。She is blind.

匣 xiá [名] box ▶金属匣 metal box

匣子 xiázi [名] box

侠 xiá I [名] knight II [形] chivalrous ▶侠义 chivalrous

侠客 xiákè [名] knight

峡 xiá [名] gorge ▶海峡 strait ▷三峡工程 the Three Gorges Project

峡谷 xiágǔ [名] canyon

狭 xiá [形] narrow ▶狭窄 narrow

狭隘 xiá'ài [形] narrow ▷心胸狭隘 narrow-minded

狭路相逢 xiá lù xiāng féng come into unavoidable confrontation

狭小 xiáxiǎo [形] cramped ▷狭小的空间 cramped space ▷作为领导他的气量过于狭小。He was too narrow-minded a leader.

狭义 xiáyì [名] narrow sense

狭窄 xiázhǎi [形] narrow

遐 xiá 见下文

遐迩闻名 xiá ěr wén míng (书) be known far and wide

遐想 xiáxiǎng [动] daydream

瑕 xiá [名] flaw ▷洁白无瑕 spotlessly white

瑕不掩瑜 xiá bù yǎn yú small failings do not detract from overall excellence ▷她的缺点和优点相比可以说是瑕不掩瑜。On balance, her strong points more than make up for her weaknesses.

瑕疵 xiácī [名] blemish

暇 xiá [名] time

辖 xiá [动] have jurisdiction ▶直辖 under direct jurisdiction

辖区 xiáqū [名] area of jurisdiction

辖制 xiázhì [动] control

霞 xiá [名] red sky ▶彩霞 red sky

霞光 xiáguāng [名] rays of sunlight (PL)

下 xià I [动] 1 (走下) go down (PT went, PP gone) ▶下山 go down the mountain ▶下楼 go downstairs ▷下船 disembark from a boat ▷下床 get out of bed 2 (落下) fall (PT fell, PP fallen) ▶下雨 rain ▶下雪 snow 3 (传发) issue ▶下令 issue an order 4 (下锅煮) put ... in (PT, PP put) ▷下面条 put the noodles into the boiling water 5 (给出) give (PT gave, PP given) 6 (开始) begin (PT began, PP begun) ▶下笔 start to write 7 (结束) finish ▶下班 finish work ▶下课 finish class 8 (生下) give birth to ▶下蛋 lay an egg ▷下猪崽 have a litter of piglets 9 (用于动词后，表示动作由高到低) ▷落下 fall down 10 (用于动词后，表示有些空间) ▷车里装不下这么多东西。We won't be able to fit so many things in the car. 11 (用于动词后，表示脱离物体) ▷拧下灯泡 unscrew a light bulb 12 (用于动词后，表示动作完成) ▷记录下会议内容 take the minutes at a meeting ▷他拿下了乒乓球比赛的第一局。He won the first set in table tennis.

II [名] 1 (低) ▶下层 lower level ▶下品 inferior products (PL) 2 (另) ▶下次 next time 3 (指方位或时间) ▶眼下 at the moment ▷树下 under the tree ▷楼下 downstairs 4 (指范围、情况、条件) ▷在朋友的帮助下 with help from friends ▷在权威的压力下 under pressure from authority III [量] ▷我拍了他好几下才把他叫醒。Only after slapping him a few times did I wake him up.

下班 xiàbān [动] finish work

下辈子 xià bèizi [名] the next life

下笔 xiàbǐ [动] start to write

下不为例 xià bù wéi lì not to be repeated ▷这次的事就算了，下不为例。I'll forget about it this time, but it mustn't be repeated.

下策 xiàcè [名] bad move

下层 xiàcéng [名] lower level

下场 xiàchǎng [动] 1 (退场) leave the pitch (PT, PP left) ▷大卫只踢了不到10分钟就下场了。David had been playing for less than ten minutes when he left the pitch. 2 (下舞台) go off stage (PT went, PP gone)

下场 xiàchǎng [名] end ▷悲惨的下场 a tragic end ▷你这样做不会有好下场。If you do this, the result will be disastrous.

下达 xiàdá [动] issue

下跌 xiàdiē [动] fall (PT fell, PP fallen) ▷物价在下跌。Prices are falling.

下放 xiàfàng [动] (降职) be demoted

下岗 xiàgǎng [动] 1 (完工) leave one's post (PT, PP left) 2 (失业) be laid off

下海 xiàhǎi [动] 1 (指捕鱼) go out to sea (PT went, PP gone) 2 (指经商) go into business (PT went, PP gone)

下怀 xiàhuái [名] one's heart's desire ▷正中下怀 be exactly what one wants

下级 xiàjí [名] subordinate

下贱 xiàjiàn [形] (讳) contemptible

下课 xiàkè [动] finish class ▷下课了，大家可以走了。Class is over – everyone can go.

下款 xiàkuǎn [名] signature

下来 xiàlái I [动] 1 (指由高到低) come down (PT came, PP come) ▷我上不去了，你下来吧。I won't come up – you come down. 2 (指作物成熟) be harvested 3 (用于动词后，指脱离物体) ▷那孩子从床上掉了下来。The child fell off the bed. ▷他把眼镜摘了下来。He took off his glasses. ▷他把书中的一页撕了下来。He tore a page out of the book. 4 (用于动词后，指持续时间) ▷这条老规矩是祖上传下来的。This custom has been passed down by our predecessors. ▷学习非常艰难，但他坚持下来了。Studying was arduous, but he persisted. **5** (用于动词后，表示动作完成) ▷夫妇俩的争吵平息下来了。The couple's argument petered out. ▷这道难题我们一定要拿下来。We certainly need to sort out this problem. **6** (表示出现某种状态) ▷队伍的步伐慢了下来。The pace of the team began to slow. ▷灯光暗了下来。The light started to fade.

下流 xiàliú [形] dirty ▷下流的玩笑 dirty jokes

下落 xiàluò [名] whereabouts (PL)

下马 xiàmǎ [动] **1** (指骑马) dismount **2** (喻) (停工) abandon

下马威 xiàmǎwēi [名] initial show of strength

下面 xiàmian I [副] **1** (指位置) underneath **2** (指次序) next ▷这个问题我下面会谈到的。I will discuss this question next. II [名] lower levels (PL)

下去 xiàqù I [动] **1** (指由高到低) go down (PT went, PP gone) **2** (指时间的延续) continue **3** (用于动词后，指空间上) jump ▷从楼上跳下去 jump from a building ▷把部队从前线撤下去 withdraw troops from the frontline **4** (时间上的持续) ▷这口气他忍不下去。He won't be able to go on in that vein. **5** (指数量下降) ▷高烧已经退下去了。His temperature has already gone down. **6** (指程度深化) ▷天气有可能热下去。The weather will probably go on getting hotter. ▷他狠不下去心戒毒。He's unable to endure detox any longer.

下手 xiàshǒu I [名] assistant II [动] begin (PT began, PP begun)

下属 xiàshǔ [名] subordinate

下水 xiàshuǐ I [动] **1** (入水) launch **2** (入伙) get into trouble II [名] down river

下榻 xiàtà [动] (书) stay

下台 xiàtái [动] **1** (下舞台) step down **2** (交权) step down **3** (难堪) get out of an awkward situation ▷你这样做真让我下不来台。If you do this, you'll be putting me in an awkward situation.

下网 xiàwǎng [动] **1** (撒网) cast a net (PT, PP cast) **2** (计算机) go offline (PT went, PP gone)

下文 xiàwén [名] **1** (指文章) ▷一看下文他才知道是怎么回事。As soon as he read what followed, he understood what had happened. **2** (喻) (指结果) further development

下午 xiàwǔ [名] afternoon

下限 xiàxiàn [名] ▷我们的计划最好早一点儿完成，下限不得超过月底。It would be best to complete the scheme early – at the very latest we must be finished by the end of the month.

下意识 xiàyìshí [名] subconscious

下游 xiàyóu [名] **1** (指江河) lower reaches

(PL) **2** (喻) (指地位) bottom

下载 xiàzǎi [动] download

吓 xià [动] frighten ▶惊吓 scare ▷那部电影真吓人。That film is quite frightening.
→另见 hè

吓唬 xiàhu [动] frighten

夏 xià [名] summer ▶盛夏 the height of summer

夏历 xiàlì [名] lunar calendar

夏令营 xiàlìngyíng [名] summer camp

夏天 xiàtiān [名] summer

仙 xiān [名] immortal ▶成仙 become immortal

仙境 xiānjìng [名] fairyland

仙女 xiānnǚ [名] fairy

仙人 xiānrén [名] immortal

先 xiān [形] **1** (指时间) earlier ▶事先 beforehand **2** (敬) (指人) late ▶先父 one's late father

先辈 xiānbèi [名] ancestors (PL)

先导 xiāndǎo [名] guide

先锋 xiānfēng [名] vanguard

先河 xiānhé [名] start

先后 xiānhòu I [名] ▷公司晋升不分先后，只凭个人能力。The company makes no distinction as to seniority but promotes people on the basis of ability. II [副] successively

先进 xiānjìn [形] advanced

先决 xiānjué [形] prerequisite

先前 xiānqián [名] the past

先遣 xiānqiǎn [形] advance

先驱 xiānqū [名] pioneer

先人 xiānrén [名] ancestor

先声夺人 xiān shēng duó rén show of strength

先生 xiānsheng [名] **1** (指男士) Mr ▷吴先生 Mr Wu **2** (老师) teacher **3** (丈夫) husband **4** (医生) doctor

先天 xiāntiān [名] ▷你臂上的印记是先天的吗？Is that a birth mark on your arm?

先行 xiānxíng [动] **1** (先走) go ahead (PT went, PP gone) **2** (优先) ▷本规定在部分城市先行实施。This regulation is being implemented ahead of time in just a few cities.

先兆 xiānzhào [名] omen

纤 xiān [形] fine ▶纤小 fine
→另见 qiàn

纤巧 xiānqiǎo [形] delicate

纤维 xiānwéi [名] fibre

纤细 xiānxì [形] fine

掀 xiān [动] lift ▷大风掀了房顶。The gale blew the roof off.

掀起 xiānqǐ [动] 1 (揭起) lift 2 (涌起) surge 3 (兴起) start

锨 xiān [名] shovel ▶铁锨 shovel

鲜 xiān I [形] 1 (新鲜) fresh ▶鲜桃 fresh peaches 2 (鲜美) delicious II [名] delicacy ▶海鲜 seafood

鲜活 xiānhuó [形] live

鲜货 xiānhuò [名] fresh produce

鲜美 xiānměi [形] delicious

鲜明 xiānmíng [形] 1 (鲜艳) bright 2 (突显) distinct

鲜艳 xiānyàn [形] brightly-coloured (英), brightly-colored (美)

闲 xián I [形] 1 (不忙) idle ▷他直到退休后才闲下来。Only when he retired did he start to take it easy. 2 (安静) quiet 3 (闲置) unused ▶闲房 empty house ▶闲田 fallow fields (PL) II [名] leisure

闲话 xiánhuà [名] 1 (流言) gossip 2 (废话) digression

闲情逸致 xián qíng yì zhì be in a carefree mood ▷没想到您还有钓鱼这种闲情逸致。I never expected you to be in the mood for fishing.

闲人 xiánrén [名] layabout

闲散 xiánsǎn [形] free

闲事 xiánshì [名] other people's business

闲暇 xiánxiá [名] leisure

闲言碎语 xián yán suì yǔ gossip

闲杂 xiánzá [形] miscellaneous

闲置 xiánzhì [动] be unused ▷闲置资金 unused funds

贤 xián I [形] virtuous ▶贤达 worthy II [名] virtuous person

贤惠 xiánhuì [形] kind-hearted

贤明 xiánmíng [形] wise

贤妻良母 xián qī liáng mǔ good wife and loving mother

弦 xián [名] 1 (指乐器) string ▶小提琴弦 violin string 2 (指钟表) spring 3 (数) hypotenuse

弦外之音 xián wài zhī yīn implication

咸 xián [形] salted ▶咸菜 pickled vegetables (PL) ▷这汤稍有点咸。The soup's a little salty.

涎 xián [名] saliva ▶垂涎 drool

涎皮赖脸 xián pí lài liǎn be brazen

娴 xián [形] 1 (书) (文雅) refined ▶娴雅 elegant 2 (熟练) skilled ▶娴熟 skilled

娴静 xiánjìng [形] refined

娴雅 xiányǎ [形] elegant

衔 xián I [动] 1 (嘴) hold ... in the mouth (PT, PP held) ▷她嘴里衔着一支铅笔。She had a pencil in her mouth. 2 (连) link ... up ▶衔接 link ... up II [名] rank ▶军衔 military rank

衔接 xiánjiē [动] link up

舷 xián [名] side of a boat ▶左舷 port ▶右舷 starboard ▶舷梯 gangway

嫌 xián I [动] dislike ▷我们嫌老板太挑剔。We dislike our boss because he's too fussy. ▷我抽支烟你嫌不嫌？Do you mind if I smoke? ▷他嫌这儿吵，搬走了。He found it too noisy here and moved away. II [名] 1 (嫌怨) grudge ▷二人捐了前嫌。The two of them buried old grudges. 2 (嫌疑) suspicion ▷他因涉嫌贪污被逮捕。He was arrested on suspicion of corruption.

嫌弃 xiánqì [动] cold-shoulder

嫌恶 xiánwù [动] detest

嫌疑 xiányí [名] suspicion

显 xiǎn I [动] 1 (表现) display ▷各显其能 each displaying their skill 2 (呈现) be apparent ▷她40多了，一点也不显老。She's over 40 but doesn't look it. II [形] illustrious ▶显赫 celebrated

显而易见 xiǎn ér yì jiàn obvious

显赫 xiǎnhè [形] illustrious

显露 xiǎnlù [动] appear

显然 xiǎnrán [副] obviously ▷他的成绩显然。His achievements are obvious.

显示 xiǎnshì [动] demonstrate

显眼 xiǎnyǎn [形] conspicuous ▷她的胸针很显眼。Her brooch is very showy.

显要 xiǎnyào I [形] influential II [名] influential figure

显著 xiǎnzhù [形] striking

险 xiǎn [形] 1 (要紧) strategic ▶险地 strategic position 2 (危险) dangerous ▶险境 dangerous situation 3 (狠毒) vicious ▶阴险 sinister

险恶 xiǎn'è [形] 1 (阴险恶毒) sinister 2 (危险可怕) perilous

险峻 xiǎnjùn [形] precipitous

险情 **xiǎnqíng** [名] hazard

险胜 **xiǎnshèng** [动] narrowly win (PT, PP won) ▷ 英格兰队以1比0险胜阿根廷。England narrowly beat Argentina one-nil.

险要 **xiǎnyào** [名] strategic location

险阻 **xiǎnzǔ** [名] difficulty

县 **xiàn** [名] county

现 **xiàn** I [形] 1 (现在) present ▶ 现状 present situation 2 (现有) ready ▶ 现钱 ready money II [副] on the spot III [动] reveal ▶ 现形 give oneself away IV [名] ready money ▶ 兑现 cash a cheque (英) 或 check (美)

现场 **xiànchǎng** [名] scene ▷ 犯罪现场 scene of the crime ▷ 现场报道 live report

现成 **xiànchéng** [形] ready-made ▷ 现成的解决问题的方法 a ready-made solution to the problem

现代 **xiàndài** [名] modern times (PL) ▷ 现代通讯器材 modern communications equipment

现今 **xiànjīn** [名] today ▷ 现今的生产力远非50年前可比。Production today can't be compared with that of 50 years ago.

现金 **xiànjīn** [名] cash

现身说法 **xiàn shēn shuō fǎ** cite one's own experience

现实 **xiànshí** [名] reality ▷ 现实主义 realism

现象 **xiànxiàng** [名] phenomenon (PL phenomena)

现行 **xiànxíng** [形] current

现眼 **xiànyǎn** [动] make a fool of oneself

现役 **xiànyì** I [名] active service II [形] active

现在 **xiànzài** [名] now ▷ 他要我们现在就去。He wants us to go now. ▷ 你的笔记本电脑现在不在我手里。I don't have your laptop at the moment.

> **now** 和 **at present** 都可用来表示说话时存在或发生的事物。**now** 可以指一段时间或者某个具体时刻。*She gradually built up energy and is now back to normal... I'm feeling much better now... I'm going home now.* **at present** 指一段时间，并且暗示情况可能会发生改变。语体较为正式。*I don't want to get married at present... At present there is a world energy shortage.* **presently** 表示不久，是有些过时的用法。*The Prince of Wales will be here presently... I shall have more to say presently.* **presently** 有时跟 **at present** 的用法一样，但有人认为这种用法是不正确的。*We are presently looking at ways to cut costs.*

现状 **xiànzhuàng** [名] the current situation

限 **xiàn** I [动] limit ▷ 自愿捐赠，款数不限。There are no limits on voluntary contributions. ▷ 此项权利只限本地区居民享用。This right is limited to people resident in the area. II [名] limit ▶ 权限 the limits of power (PL)

限定 **xiàndìng** [动] restrict

限度 **xiàndù** [名] limit

限量 **xiànliàng** [动] limit

限令 **xiànlìng** [动] order

限期 **xiànqī** I [动] set a deadline (PT, PP set) II [名] deadline

限制 **xiànzhì** [动] restrict ▷ 这种产品出口有限制。There are restrictions on the export of this kind of product.

线 **xiàn** I [名] 1 (指细长物品) thread ▶ 棉线 cotton thread ▶ 电线 electric wire 2 (交通干线) line ▶ 主线 main line II [量] ▷ 一线生机 a ray of hope

线路 **xiànlù** [名] 1 (指交通) route 2 (指电流等) circuit

线索 **xiànsuǒ** [名] clue

线条 **xiàntiáo** [名] (指绘画) line

宪 **xiàn** [名] constitution ▶ 立宪 constitutionalism

宪法 **xiànfǎ** [名] constitution

宪章 **xiànzhāng** [名] charter

陷 **xiàn** I [名] 1 (书) (陷阱) trap 2 (过失) fault ▶ 缺陷 defect II [动] 1 (沉入) get bogged down ▷ 小心别陷进沼泽里。Be careful not to get stuck in the marsh. 2 (凹进) sink (PT sank, PP sunk) ▷ 房子的地基陷下去了。The house's foundations have subsided somewhat. 3 (卷入) get involved ▷ 他陷在一场政治斗争中不能脱身。He's got involved in a political conflict he can't extricate himself from.

陷害 **xiànhài** [动] frame

陷阱 **xiànjǐng** [名] trap

陷落 **xiànluò** [动] 1 (下陷) sink (PT sank, PP sunk) 2 (被攻陷) be captured by the enemy

馅 **xiàn** [名] stuffing ▷ 饺子馅 jiaozi filling

馅儿饼 **xiànrbǐng** [名] pie

羡 **xiàn** [动] admire

羡慕 **xiànmù** [动] envy

献 **xiàn** [动] 1 (给) give (PT gave, PP given) ▶ 献花 give flowers ▶ 献血 donate blood 2 (表演) show (PT showed, PP shown) ▶ 献技 display one's skill

献丑 **xiànchǒu** [动] (谦) show oneself up (PT showed, PP shown)

献词 **xiàncí** [名] message of congratulation

献礼 **xiànlǐ** [动] present a gift

献身 **xiànshēn** [动] devote one's life to

献殷勤 **xiàn yīnqín** [动] be attentive ▷他拼命向姑娘献殷勤。He was very attentive to the young lady.

腺 **xiàn** [名] gland ▶泪腺 tear duct

乡 **xiāng** [名] 1 (乡村) countryside 2 (家乡) home town 3 (行政区划) township

乡村 **xiāngcūn** [名] village

乡亲 **xiāngqīn** [名] 1 (同乡) fellow townspeople 2 (当地群众) local people

乡土 **xiāngtǔ** [名] native soil

乡下 **xiāngxia** [名] countryside

相 **xiāng** I [动] evaluate ▷相对象 evaluate a prospective marriage partner ▷那种手机样式太旧，估计你相不上。That style of mobile phone is very old. I reckon you won't like it. II [副] 1 (互相) mutually ▶相差 differ 2 (对) ▷笑脸相迎 greet ... with a smile ▷好言相劝 comfort ... with kind words →另见 xiàng

相称 **xiāngchèn** [形] matching ▷他的举止和他的年龄不相称。His behaviour (英) 或 behavior (美) is not in keeping with his age.

相持 **xiāngchí** [动] lock ... in stalemate ▷双方谈判已经相持了很久。Negotiations between the two sides have already been locked in stalemate for a long time.

相处 **xiāngchǔ** [动] get along ▷大家在一起相处很融洽。Everybody gets along very well together.

相传 **xiāngchuán** [动] 1 (传说) be traditionally said ▷相传，这个湖里有个水怪。Traditionally, there is said to be a monster in this lake. 2 (传递) hand ... down ▷这项手工艺是一代代相传下来的。This handicraft has been handed down through the generations.

相当 **xiāngdāng** I [动] match ▷这几位棋手水平相当。These few chess experts are evenly matched. II [形] appropriate ▷他做这项工作正相当。This work is really appropriate for him. III [副] quite ▷昨天晚上的演出相当精彩。The performance yesterday evening was quite brilliant.

相对 **xiāngduì** I [动] be opposite II [形] 1 (非绝对的) relative 2 (比较的) comparative

相对论 **xiāngduìlùn** [名] theory of relativity

相反 **xiāngfǎn** I [形] opposite II [连] ▷她不

但没生气，相反，显得特别高兴。Not only was she not angry; on the contrary she seemed very pleased.

相仿 **xiāngfǎng** [形] similar ▷他儿子和我女儿年龄相仿。His son and my daughter are of a similar age.

相辅相成 **xiāng fǔ xiāng chéng** complement each other

相干 **xiānggān** [动] have to do with ▷这事跟我不相干。This has nothing to do with me.

相关 **xiāngguān** [动] be related ▷新出台的政策与农民的利益密切相关。The new policy has a major bearing on the welfare of farmers.

相好 **xiānghǎo** I [动] 1 (亲密) be very close 2 (恋爱) be lovers II [名] 1 (朋友) close friend 2 (情人) lover

相互 **xiānghù** I [形] mutual II [副] ▷在这个问题上，希望大家能相互理解。As regards this question, hopefully everyone will understand each other.

相继 **xiāngjì** [副] in succession ▷去年，他的爷爷、奶奶相继去世了。Last year his grandfather and grandmother died one after the other.

相敬如宾 **xiāng jìng rú bīn** treat each other with respect ▷夫妻俩多年来相敬如宾，从没红过脸。The couple have treated each other with respect for many years and have never had a heated exchange.

相配 **xiāngpèi** [形] well-matched

相亲 **xiāngqīn** [动] evaluate a prospective marriage partner

相识 **xiāngshí** [动] be acquainted ▷我们俩是老相识了。The two of us are old acquaintances.

相思 **xiāngsī** [动] be lovesick

相似 **xiāngsì** [形] similar

相提并论 **xiāng tí bìng lùn** lump ... together ▷这些概念之间没有任何联系，不能相提并论。There's no connection between these concepts – you can't lump them together.

相同 **xiāngtóng** [形] identical

相投 **xiāngtóu** [动] be compatible

相像 **xiāngxiàng** [动] be alike

相信 **xiāngxìn** [动] believe ▷他不相信任何人。He doesn't believe anyone. ▷我相信他们一定会准时到达。I'm quite sure they will arrive on time.

相形见绌 **xiāng xíng jiàn chù** pale into insignificance

相依为命 **xiāngyī wéi mìng** depend on each other for survival

相宜 **xiāngyí** [形] fitting

相应 **xiāngyìng** I [动] correspond II [形] corresponding ▷经济效益提高了，工厂的环境也得到了相应的改善。With the factory's profitability having increased, there was a corresponding improvement in the working environment.

相知 **xiāngzhī** [动] be well acquainted

相左 **xiāngzuǒ** [动] conflict ▷双方意见相左。The two parties held different views.

香 **xiāng** I [形] 1 (芬芳) fragrant 2 (美味) delicious 3 (胃口好的) ▷他病了，吃什么都不香。He's ill – he has no appetite at all. 4 (睡得熟的) sound ▷屋子里暖暖的，睡觉真香！The room was so warm so I slept very soundly. 5 (受欢迎的) popular II [名] 1 (香料) spice 2 (烧的香) incense

香波 **xiāngbō** [名] shampoo

香肠 **xiāngcháng** [名] sausage

香料 **xiāngliào** [名] spice

香喷喷 **xiāngpēnpēn** [形] delicious

香水 **xiāngshuǐ** [名] perfume

香甜 **xiāngtián** [形] 1 (指味道) fragrant 2 (指睡眠) sound

香烟 **xiāngyān** [名] 1 (卷烟) cigarette 2 (烧香的烟) incense smoke

厢 **xiāng** [名] 1 (厢房) wing 2 (像房子的空间) ▶车厢 railway carriage ▶包厢 box

厢房 **xiāngfáng** [名] wing

箱 **xiāng** [名] 1 (箱子) box 2 (箱状物) ▶信箱 postbox (英), mailbox (美)

箱子 **xiāngzi** [名] box

襄 **xiāng** 见下文

襄助 **xiāngzhù** [动] (书) assist

镶 **xiāng** [动] edge

镶嵌 **xiāngqiàn** [动] mount ▷这枚戒指上镶嵌着钻石。This ring is mounted with diamonds.

详 **xiáng** I [形] detailed II [动] 1 (细说) explain 2 (知道) know (PT knew, PP known)

详尽 **xiángjìn** [形] detailed

详情 **xiángqíng** [名] details (PL)

详实 **xiángshí** [形] full and accurate

详细 **xiángxì** [形] detailed ▷老板需要一份详细的报告。The boss requires a detailed report. ▷他详细叙述了事情发生的经过。He recounted in detail how the incident occurred.

降 **xiáng** [动] 1 (投降) surrender 2 (伏) control ▷这孩子调皮捣蛋，谁也降不住他。This child is acting up – no-one can control him. →另见 jiàng

降伏 **xiángfú** [动] subdue ▷这匹马性子烈，很难降伏。This horse has a fierce temper and is very difficult to subdue.

降服 **xiángfú** [动] surrender

祥 **xiáng** [形] auspicious

祥和 **xiánghé** [形] auspicious and harmonious

翔 **xiáng** [动] circle in the air

翔实 **xiángshí** [形] full and accurate

享 **xiǎng** [动] enjoy

享乐 **xiǎnglè** [动] lead a life of pleasure (PT, PP led)

享受 **xiǎngshòu** [动] enjoy ▷听音乐是一种精神享受。Listening to music is a kind of spiritual enjoyment.

享有 **xiǎngyǒu** [动] enjoy ▷18岁以上的公民享有选举权。Citizens above the age of eighteen enjoy the right to vote.

响 **xiǎng** I [名] 1 (回声) echo 2 (声音) sound II [动] sound ▷下课铃响了。The bell for the end of class sounded. ▷响锣 sound a gong III [形] loud

响当当 **xiǎngdāngdāng** [形] 1 (响亮) loud 2 (响) (出色) outstanding

响动 **xiǎngdong** [名] sound of movement

响亮 **xiǎngliàng** [形] loud and clear

响应 **xiǎngyìng** [动] respond ▷大家积极响应班长的倡议。Everyone responded enthusiastically to the class monitor's proposal.

想 **xiǎng** [动] 1 (思考) think (PT, PP thought) ▷你帮我想个办法吧！Help me think of a way to do it! 2 (推测) reckon ▷我想他会同意的。I reckon he'll agree. ▷我想今天可能会下雨。I reckon it might rain today. 3 (打算) want to ▷我想换个工作。I want to change jobs. 4 (想念) miss ▷孩子们很想妈妈。The children miss their mother. ▷刚到这里时，她特别想家。When she first arrived here she missed home terribly.

想必 **xiǎngbì** [副] presumably ▷他满脸不高兴，想必和老婆吵架了。He looked totally miserable – presumably he had had an argument with his wife.

想当然 **xiǎngdāngrán** [动] take ... for granted (PT took, PP taken) ▷事情不是那么简单，不能想当然。The matter's not that simple; we can't take it for granted.

想法 **xiǎngfǎ** [名] opinion

想方设法 **xiǎng fāng shè fǎ** move heaven and earth ▷她遇到困难时，朋友们想方设法帮她解决。When she encountered a difficulty, her friends moved heaven and earth to help her.

想念 **xiǎngniàn** [动] miss

想入非非 **xiǎng rù fēi fēi** take off on a flight of fancy ▷读小说时，她经常想入非非，把自己当成书中的主人公。When reading novels, she often takes off on a flight of fancy where she becomes the protagonist in the book.

想头 **xiǎngtou** [名] (口) **1** (念头) idea **2** (希望) hope

想像 **xiǎngxiàng** I [动] imagine II [名] imagination

向 **xiàng** I [名] direction ▷风向 wind direction II [动] **1** (对着) face ▷我的卧室向东。My bedroom faces east. **2** (偏袒) side with ▷妈妈老是向着妹妹。The mother always sides with her younger daughter. III [介] to ▷我向他表示了感谢。I expressed my thanks to him. IV [副] always ▷老先生对考古学向有研究。The old gentleman has always done research in archaeology.

向导 **xiàngdǎo** I [名] guide ▷山高路险，我们最好找一位向导。It's a tricky, high path; it's best we look for a guide. II [动] guide

向来 **xiànglái** [副] always

向往 **xiàngwǎng** [动] yearn ▷向往自由 yearn for freedom ▷山里的孩子向往着外面的世界看一看。The children in the mountains yearn to have a look at the outside world.

项 **xiàng** I [名] **1** (颈后部) nape ▷颈项 nape **2** (款项) sum ▷用项 expenditure ▷进项 income **3** (项目) item ▷事项 item II [量] item ▷会议讨论内容共5项。There are altogether five items to be discussed at the meeting. ▷3项要求 three requirements

项链 **xiàngliàn** [名] necklace

项目 **xiàngmù** [名] item ▷出口项目去年增加了一倍。Export items doubled last year. ▷他将参加3个运动项目的比赛。He will take part in a competition of three sporting events.

巷 **xiàng** [名] lane
→另见 **hàng**

相 **xiàng** I [动] **1** (判断) judge **2** (书) (辅助) assist II [名] **1** (相貌) appearance ▷狼狈相 sorry appearance **2** (姿势) posture ▷吃相 table manners **3** (官位) minister ▷外相 foreign minister ▷首相 prime minister **4** (相片)

photograph ▷照相 take a photograph
→另见 **xiāng**

相貌 **xiàngmào** [名] appearance

相片 **xiàngpiàn** [名] photograph

象 **xiàng** I [名] **1** (大象) elephant **2** (样子) appearance ▷景象 scene II [动] imitate

象棋 **xiàngqí** [名] Chinese chess

象牙 **xiàngyá** [名] ivory

象征 **xiàngzhēng** [动] symbolize ▷长城是中国的象征。The Great Wall is a symbol of China.

像 **xiàng** I [名] portrait ▷画像 paint portraits ▷雕像 statue II [动] **1** (相似) look like ▷他长得像妈妈。He looks like his mother. ▷这姐妹俩模样太像了。These two sisters are very similar in looks. **2** (比如) ▷像他这样的好孩子，谁不喜欢呢！Who doesn't like good children like this one! ▷像洗衣机这种家用电器，在这里还不普遍。Domestic appliances such as washing machines are still not widespread here. III [副] as if ▷门外像有人说话。It sounds as if there are people talking outside. ▷像要下雪了。It looks as if it might snow.

像话 **xiànghuà** [动] be reasonable

像模像样 **xiàng mú xiàng yàng** presentable ▷他俩都想办一个像模像样的婚礼。They both want to have a decent wedding.

像样 **xiàngyàng** [动] be decent

橡 **xiàng** [名] **1** (橡树) oak **2** (橡胶树) rubber tree

橡胶 **xiàngjiāo** [名] rubber

橡皮 **xiàngpí** [名] rubber (英), eraser (美)

削 **xiāo** [动] peel ▷削苹果 peel an apple
→另见 **xuē**

逍 **xiāo** 见下文

逍遥 **xiāoyáo** [形] carefree

逍遥法外 **xiāoyáo fǎ wài** evade capture ▷杀人犯逍遥法外10年，现在终于被抓获归案。The murderer evaded capture for ten years; now finally he's been caught and brought to justice.

消 **xiāo** [动] **1** (消失) disappear **2** (使消失) remove **3** (度过) spend (PT, PP spent) ▷消夏 pass a leisurely summer **4** (需要) take (PT took, PP taken) ▷只消一天，我们就到了。It'll only take a day, then we'll be there.

消沉 **xiāochén** [形] depressed

消除 **xiāochú** [动] eliminate

消防 **xiāofáng** [名] fire fighting

消费 xiāofèi [动] consume

消耗 xiāohào [动] consume

消化 xiāohuà [动] digest ▷这种食品不易消化。This kind of food is not easy to digest. ▷学过的东西要消化、吸收。You must digest and absorb what you study.

消极 xiāojí [形] 1 (反面) negative 2 (消沉) demoralized

消解 xiāojiě [动] dispel

消灭 xiāomiè [动] 1 (消失) die out 2 (除掉) eradicate

消磨 xiāomó [动] 1 (逐渐消耗) wear ... down (PT wore, PP worn) ▷消磨意志 wear down one's willpower 2 (排遣) while away ▷消磨时光 while away time

消遣 xiāoqiǎn [动] while away time

消散 xiāosàn [动] dissipate

消失 xiāoshī [动] vanish

消逝 xiāoshì [动] elapse

消瘦 xiāoshòu [动] become thin (PT became, PP become) ▷几个月不见，她愈加消瘦了。In the several months since I last saw her she's become even thinner.

消亡 xiāowáng [动] wither away

消息 xiāoxi [名] news (SG) ▷电台报道了战争的最新消息。The radio reported the latest news of the war. ▷分别多年，他们一直没有互通消息。In the many years they've been apart they've had no news of each other.

消闲 xiāoxián I [动] spend one's free time (PT, PP spent) II [形] carefree

消夜 xiāoyè [名] night-time snack

宵 xiāo [名] night ▶通宵 all night

萧 xiāo [形] desolate

萧瑟 xiāosè I [拟] rustle II [形] desolate

萧条 xiāotiáo [形] 1 (寂寞冷落) bleak 2 (经济) depressed

销 xiāo [动] 1 (熔化) melt 2 (除去) cancel 3 (销售) market 4 (消费) spend (PT, PP spent)

销毁 xiāohuǐ [动] 1 (熔化毁掉) destroy 2 (烧掉) burn

销魂 xiāohún [动] overwhelm

销假 xiāojià [动] report back after being on holiday

销路 xiāolù [名] market

销声匿迹 xiāo shēng nì jì disappear from sight ▷到了冬天，某些动物停止了活动，销声匿迹了。When winter arrives, some animals cease being active and disappear from sight.

销售 xiāoshòu [动] sell (PT, PP sold) ▷家电部今天销售了50台空调。The household appliances division has sold fifty air-conditioning units today. ▷他负责公司的销售工作。He is responsible for the company's sales. ▷公司在国外也打开了销售市场。The company has also opened up sales markets abroad.

销赃 xiāozāng [动] 1 (销售赃物) dispose of stolen goods 2 (销毁赃物) destroy stolen goods

潇 xiāo [形] (书) deep and clear

潇洒 xiāosǎ [形] natural and unaffected

霄 xiāo [名] clouds (PL)

嚣 xiāo [动] clamour (英), clamor (美)

嚣张 xiāozhāng [形] arrogant

淆 xiáo [形] confused

小 xiǎo I [形] 1 (不大) small ▷小毛病 small problem ▶小床 single bed ▷年龄小 young 2 (排行最末的) youngest ▷他的小女儿才两岁。His youngest daughter is only two years old. II [副] 1 (短时间) ▷小憩 take a short rest 2 (稍微) a bit ▷小有名气 have something of a reputation III [名] young children

可以用 little 形容小的事物。...a little house... little children... 但是，little 通常不用于强调某事物的体积小。例如，不能说 'The town is little.' 或 'I have a very little car.'，但是可以说 The town is small. 或 I have a very small car.。little 没有 small 那么精确，但通常暗示说话者对于所谈论的对象的态度。因此，little 通常用在其他形容词的后面。What a nice little house you've got here!... Shut up, you horrible little boy!

小辈 xiǎobèi [名] younger member

小便 xiǎobiàn I [动] urinate II [名] urine

小菜 xiǎocài [名] 1 (下酒菜) pickled vegetables (PL) 2 (喻) easy job

小册子 xiǎocèzi [名] pamphlet

小产 xiǎochǎn [名] miscarriage

小吃 xiǎochī [名] 1 (非正餐) snack 2 (冷盘) cold dish

小丑 xiǎochǒu [名] 1 (滑稽演员) clown 2 (喻) scoundrel

小聪明 xiǎocōngming [名] petty trick

小道儿消息 xiǎodàor xiāoxi [名] hearsay

小动作 xiǎodòngzuò [名] little trick

小恩小惠 xiǎo ēn xiǎo huì [名] small favours (英) 或 favors (美) (PL)

小儿科 xiǎo'érkē [名] **1** (医) paediatrics (英) 或 pediatrics (美) department **2** (喻) kid's stuff

小费 xiǎofèi [名] tip

小鬼 xiǎoguǐ [名] little devil

小伙子 xiǎohuǒzi [名] lad

小节 xiǎojié [名] **1** (小事) trifle **2** (音) bar

小姐 xiǎojiě [名] **1** (称呼) Miss ▷李小姐 Miss Li **2** (女子) young lady ▷有位小姐找你。 There's a young lady looking for you.

小金库 xiǎojīnkù [名] supplementary fund

小看 xiǎokàn [动] underestimate

小康 xiǎokāng [形] relatively well-off

小麦 xiǎomài [名] wheat

小名 xiǎomíng [名] pet name

小品 xiǎopǐn [名] short sketch

小气 xiǎoqi [形] **1** (气量小) petty **2** (吝啬) stingy

小巧玲珑 xiǎoqiǎo línglóng dainty

小区 xiǎoqū [名] housing estate

小人 xiǎorén [名] vile character

小商品 xiǎoshāngpǐn [名] small items (PL)

小时 xiǎoshí [名] hour ▷很多公司实行8小时工作制。 Lots of companies have implemented an eight-hour working day.

小市民 xiǎoshìmín [名] philistine

小说 xiǎoshuō [名] novel

小算盘 xiǎosuànpan [名] (喻) calculation ▷打小算盘 be calculating

小题大做 xiǎo tí dà zuò make a mountain out of a molehill ▷他不过是迟到了几次，老板就把他开除了，真是小题大做。 He was late no more than a few times, and the boss sacked him – that was making a mountain out of a molehill.

小提琴 xiǎotíqín [名] violin

小偷 xiǎotōu [名] thief (PL thieves)

小巫见大巫 xiǎo wū jiàn dà wū pale into insignificance

小鞋 xiǎoxié [名] (喻) ▷因为给公司提过意见，老板常常给他穿小鞋。 Because he made some complaints to the company, the boss often gives him a hard time.

小写 xiǎoxiě [名] lower case

小心 xiǎoxīn I [动] be careful ▷过马路，一定要小心。 You must be careful when crossing the road. II [形] careful

小型 xiǎoxíng [形] small-scale

小学 xiǎoxué [名] primary school (英), elementary school (美)

小学生 xiǎoxuéshēng [名] primary school pupil (英), elementary school student (美)

小意思 xiǎoyìsi [名] **1** (微薄心意) small token **2** (小事情) nothing significant

小子 xiǎozi [名] (口) **1** (男孩子) boy **2** (贬) (男性) guy

小字辈 xiǎozìbèi [名] youngster

小组 xiǎozǔ [名] group

晓 xiǎo I [名] dawn II [动] **1** (知道) know (PT knew, PP known) **2** (使人知道) tell (PT, PP told)

晓得 xiǎode [动] know (PT knew, PP known) ▷这件事你晓得不晓得？ Do you know about this matter or not?

孝 xiào I [动] be dutiful ▷孝子 a filial son II [名] filial piety

孝敬 xiàojìng [动] **1** (孝顺尊敬) show filial respect for (PT showed, PP shown) ▷孝敬父母是中华民族的美德。 Showing filial respect for one's parents is a virtue of Chinese people. **2** (献礼物) give as a present (PT gave, PP given) ▷过年了，他买了两瓶好酒孝敬爷爷。 At New Year, he bought two bottles of good wine to give as a present to his grandfather.

孝顺 xiàoshùn I [动] show filial obedience (PT showed, PP shown) ▷孝顺父母 show filial obedience to one's parents II [形] filial

肖 xiào [动] resemble

肖像 xiàoxiàng [名] portrait

校 xiào [名] **1** (学校) school **2** (军) (校官) field officer

→另见 jiào

校规 xiàoguī [名] school rules (PL)

校历 xiàolì [名] school calendar

校长 xiàozhǎng [名] principal

哮 xiào I [名] wheezing II [动] wheeze

哮喘 xiàochuǎn [名] asthma

笑 xiào [动] **1** (欢笑) laugh ▷孩子们笑得开心极了！ The children laughed with great delight! **2** (嘲笑) laugh at ▷别担心，大家不会笑你的。 Don't worry, nobody will laugh at you.

笑柄 xiàobǐng [名] laughing stock

笑话 xiàohua I [名] joke ▷他爱说笑话。 He likes to tell jokes. II [动] laugh at

笑里藏刀 xiào lǐ cáng dāo be a wolf in sheep's clothing

笑料 xiàoliào [名] laughing stock

笑眯眯 xiàomīmī [形] smiley

笑面虎 xiàomiànhǔ [名] wolf in sheep's clothing

笑容 xiàoróng [名] smile

笑嘻嘻 xiàoxīxī [形] grinning

笑逐颜开 xiào zhú yán kāi beam with pleasure

效 xiào I [名] effect II [动] 1 (仿效) imitate 2 (献出) devote ... to

效法 xiàofǎ [动] 1 (模仿) model oneself on 2 (学习) learn from ▷ 我们应该效法先进的教育制度。We ought to learn from advanced educational systems.

效果 xiàoguǒ [名] 1 (结果) effect 2 (戏剧) effects (PL)

效劳 xiàoláo [动] serve

效力 xiàolì I [动] serve II [名] effectiveness ▷ 这种药很有效力。This medicine is very effective.

效率 xiàolǜ [名] efficiency

效益 xiàoyì [名] returns (PL)

效应 xiàoyìng [名] effect

啸 xiào [动] 1 (指人) whistle 2 (指禽兽) roar 3 (指自然界) roar

些 xiē [量] 1 (不定量) some ▷ 我要去超市买些食品。I have to go to the supermarket to buy some provisions. 2 (略微) a little ▷ 这条路近些。This street is a little nearer.

楔 xiē [名] wedge

楔子 xiēzi [名] 1 (木片) wedge 2 (木钉) peg 3 (引子) prologue (英), prolog (美)

歇 xiē [动] 1 (休息) rest ▷ 太累了，我们歇会儿吧！I'm too tired, let's rest for a while! 2 (停) stop

歇脚 xiējiǎo [动] stop for a rest

歇斯底里 xiēsīdǐlǐ [名] hysteria ▷ 昨天她和一个售货员歇斯底里地大吵了一顿。Yesterday she argued hysterically with a salesman.

歇息 xiēxi [动] 1 (休息) have a rest ▷ 忙了半天了，歇息一会儿吧。We've been busy for ages, let's have a rest for a while. 2 (睡觉) go to sleep (PT went, PP gone)

蝎 xiē [名] scorpion

协 xié I [动] assist II [副] jointly ▶ 协办 jointly run ▶ 协议 agree on

协定 xiédìng [名] agreement

协会 xiéhuì [名] association

协商 xiéshāng [动] consult

协调 xiétiáo I [动] coordinate II [形] coordinated

协同 xiétóng [动] coordinate ▷ 经理助理协同经理工作。The manager's assistant coordinates his work.

协议 xiéyì [名] agreement

协助 xiézhù [动] help ▷ 在各方的协助下，展览取得了成功。Thanks to the help of all concerned, the exhibition was a great success.

协作 xiézuò [动] collaborate

邪 xié [形] 1 (不正当) evil 2 (不正常) abnormal II [名] misfortune

邪恶 xié'è [形] evil

邪教 xiéjiào [名] heresy

邪路 xiélù [名] evil ways (PL)

邪门儿 xiéménr [形] (方) abnormal

邪门歪道 xié mén wāi dào devious means (PL)

邪念 xiéniàn [名] evil thought

胁 xié I [名] side II [动] coerce

胁迫 xiépò [动] coerce

挟 xié [动] 1 (夹住) hold ... under one's arm (PT, PP held) 2 (挟制) coerce 3 (心怀) harbour (英), harbor (美)

挟持 xiéchí [动] 1 (抓住) seize by the arms 2 (威胁) hold under duress (PT, PP held)

偕 xié [动] be together with

偕老 xiélǎo [动] grow old together (PT grew, PP grown)

偕同 xiétóng [动] be together with ▷ 总理偕同政府各部官员参加了仪式。The prime minister took part in the ceremony, together with officials from each government department.

斜 xié I [形] slanting II [动] slant

斜路 xiélù [名] (喻) wrong path

斜坡 xiépō [名] slope

谐 xié [形] 1 (和谐) harmonious 2 (诙谐) humorous

谐和 xiéhé [形] harmonious

谐音 xiéyīn [动] sound the same

携 xié [动] 1 (携带) carry 2 (拉着) hold (PT, PP held)

携带 xiédài [动] carry

携手 xiéshǒu [动] 1 (字) join hands 2 (喻) collaborate ▷ 中美双方决定携手建设这个项目。China and the US decided to collaborate on the establishment of this project.

鞋 xié [名] shoes (PL)

鞋匠 xiéjiang [名] cobbler

写 xiě [动] 1 (书写) write (PT wrote, PP written) 2 (写作) write (PT wrote, PP written) 3 (描写) describe 4 (绘画) draw (PT drew, PP drawn)

写生 xiěshēng [动] sketch from nature

写实 xiěshí [动] write realistically (PT wrote, PP written)

写意 xiěyì [名] freehand brushwork

写照 xiězhào [名] portrayal

写作 xiězuò [动] write (PT wrote, PP written) ▷他上小学时就开始写作了。He first started writing when he was at primary school (英) 或 elementary school (美).

血 xiě [名] (口) blood
→ 另见 xuè

血淋淋 xiělínlín [形] blood-soaked

泄 xiè [动] 1 (排出) discharge 2 (泄露) let ... out (PT, PP let) 3 (发泄) vent

泄劲 xièjìn [动] lose heart (PT, PP lost)

泄漏 xièlòu [动] 1 (逸出) leak ▷这起火灾是由于煤气泄漏引起的。This fire was caused by a gas leak. 2 (泄露) let ... out (PT, PP let) ▷不要把这个消息泄漏出去。Don't let this news get out.

泄露 xièlòu let ... out (PT, PP let) ▷公司机密被泄露出去了。The company secrets have been let out.

泄密 xièmì [动] divulge a secret

泄气 xièqì [动] lose heart (PT, PP lost)

泻 xiè [动] 1 (流) pour down 2 (腹泻) have diarrhoea (英) 或 diarrhea (美)

卸 xiè [动] 1 (搬下) unload ▷卸车 unload a vehicle 2 (除去) remove ▷卸装 disrobe 3 (拆卸) strip ▷卸下钟表的零件 strip the parts of a clock 4 (解除) be relieved of ▷卸任 step down

卸任 xièrèn [动] step down ▷总统卸任后,去一所大学当了校长。After the president stepped down, he became vice-chancellor of a university.

卸妆 xièzhuāng [动] remove one's makeup

屑 xiè I [名] bits (PL) II [形] trivial III [动] deign to

械 xiè [名] 1 (器械) tool 2 (武器) weapon

亵 xiè I [动] be disrespectful to II [形] indecent

亵渎 xièdú [动] profane

谢 xiè [动] 1 (感谢) thank ▷帮了我大忙,多谢了! Many thanks for helping me out so much! 2 (认错) apologize 3 (拒绝) decline 4 (脱落) wither

谢绝 xièjué [动] decline

谢客 xièkè [动] decline to receive visitors

谢幕 xièmù [动] take a curtain call (PT took, PP taken)

谢谢 xièxie [动] thank you, thanks (口)

谢罪 xièzuì [动] offer an apology

邂 xiè 见下文

邂逅 xièhòu [动] meet by chance (PT, PP met)

懈 xiè [动] be lax

懈怠 xièdài [形] slack

懈气 xièqì [动] stop trying ▷失败是常有的事,不要懈气。Failure is a common occurrence: don't stop trying.

蟹 xiè [名] crab

心 xīn [名] 1 (心脏) heart 2 (思想) mind ▶用心 attentively ▶谈心 heart-to-heart talk 3 (中心) centre (英), center (美) ▶圆心 centre (英) 或 center (美) of a circle

心爱 xīn'ài [形] treasured

心安理得 xīn ān lǐ dé have a clear conscience ▷他做错事,还能心安理得。He can do wrong and still have a clear conscience.

心病 xīnbìng [名] 1 (焦虑) anxiety 2 (隐痛) sore point

心不在焉 xīn bù zài yān be absent-minded ▷他做事心不在焉,经常出错。He does things absent-mindedly and often makes mistakes.

心肠 xīncháng [名] 1 (心地) heart ▷她心肠好。She has a good heart. 2 (兴致) mood ▷我现在没心肠听音乐。I'm not in the mood for listening to music at the moment.

心驰神往 xīn chí shén wǎng yearn for

心得 xīndé [名] what one has learned

心地 xīndì [名] character

心服口服 xīn fú kǒu fú be utterly convinced

心腹 xīnfù [名] 1 (指人) trusted subordinate 2 (指事) confidence

心肝 xīngān [名] 1 (良心) conscience 2 (心爱的人) darling

心广体胖 xīn guǎng tǐ pán healthy and happy

心寒 xīn hán [形] disappointed

心怀鬼胎 xīn huái guǐ tāi harbour (英) 或

harbor(美) evil intentions

心慌意乱 xīn huāng yì luàn be nervous and flustered ▷遇到这种麻烦事，他心慌意乱，不知所措。When he comes up against this kind of problem, he gets nervous and flustered and doesn't know what to do.

心灰意懒 xīn huī yì lǎn be disheartened

心机 xīnjī [名] thinking

心计 xīnjì [名] calculation

心惊胆战 xīn jīng dǎn zhàn terrified ▷回忆起大地震时的情景，她到现在还心惊胆战。When she remembers the scene at the time of the earthquake, she still feels terrified.

心境 xīnjìng [名] state of mind

心坎 xīnkǎn [名] the bottom of one's heart ▷我从心坎上感谢你。I thank you from the bottom of my heart.

心旷神怡 xīn kuàng shén yí feel relaxed and happy

心理 xīnlǐ [名] psychology

心灵 xīnlíng I [名] mind II [形] quick-witted

心领神会 xīn lǐng shén huì understand tacitly ▷看到母亲使了个眼色，她心领神会，马上就出去了。On seeing her mother's glance, she took the hint and immediately went out.

心平气和 xīn píng qì hé in a calm state of mind ▷只要双方心平气和地谈一谈，矛盾是能够解决的。It only needs the two sides to talk calmly, and the conflict can be resolved.

心情 xīnqíng [名] frame of mind ▷这几天我心情不好。In the last few days I've not been in a good frame of mind.

心神 xīnshén [名] 1 (心情) state of mind ▷这件事搞得他心神不定。This matter made him feel uncertain. 2 (精力) effort ▷写这部书费了他不少心神。He devoted a lot of energy to writing the book.

心事 xīnshì [名] preoccupation

心思 xīnsi [名] 1 (想法) thoughts (PL) ▷对这件事，不知道她是什么心思。I don't know what her thoughts are about this. 2 (脑筋) brains (PL) ▷为赚钱，他挖空了心思。He racked his brains to think of ways of making money. 3 (兴致) mood ▷她只想着度假，工作上根本没心思。She's only thinking of her holiday – she's not in the mood for work at all.

心态 xīntài [名] mentality

心心相印 xīn xīn xiāng yìn be a kindred spirit ▷她希望找一位心心相印的伴侣。She hopes to find a partner who is a kindred spirit.

心胸 xīnxiōng [名] 1 (胸怀) broadmindedness ▷他心胸狭隘。He is narrow-minded. 2 (志向)

aspiration ▷他是个很有心胸的青年。He is a young man with great aspirations.

心绪 xīnxù [名] mood

心血 xīnxuè [名] painstaking care

心血来潮 xīnxuè lái cháo be seized by a whim

心眼儿 xīnyǎnr [名] 1 (内心) heart ▷听他这么说，她从心眼儿里不高兴。Hearing him speak in this way, she was deeply unhappy. 2 (心地) intention ▷她心眼儿好。Her intentions are good. 3 (机智) intelligence ▷这姑娘有心眼儿，样样能干。This girl is intelligent, and competent in every way. 4 (顾虑) unfounded misgivings (PL) ▷他心眼儿太多，很难打交道。He is oversensitive – it's difficult to establish a rapport with him. 5 (气量) tolerance ▷小心眼儿 intolerant

心意 xīnyì [名] 1 (情意) feelings (PL) 2 (意思) meaning

心有余悸 xīn yǒu yú jì have a lingering fear

心愿 xīnyuàn [名] one's heart's desire

心悦诚服 xīn yuè chéng fú wholeheartedly admire ▷对手的为人和能力，令他心悦诚服。He wholeheartedly admired his opponent's conduct and ability.

心脏 xīnzàng [名] heart

心照不宣 xīn zhào bù xuān have a tacit understanding

辛 xīn [形] 1 (辣) hot 2 (辛苦) laborious 3 (痛苦) bitter

辛苦 xīnkǔ I [形] laborious II [动] trouble ▷真不好意思，辛苦你了！I'm really sorry to trouble you!

辛辣 xīnlà [形] biting ▷这篇文章对官僚主义作风进行了辛辣的讽刺。This piece is a biting satire on bureaucracy.

辛劳 xīnláo [动] toil

辛勤 xīnqín [形] hardworking

辛酸 xīnsuān [形] bitter

欣 xīn [形] glad

欣然 xīnrán [副] gladly ▷老板欣然同意了我的请求。The boss gladly agreed to my request.

欣赏 xīnshǎng [动] 1 (赏识) admire ▷朋友们都非常欣赏他的才学。His friends all greatly admired his learning. 2 (享受) enjoy

欣慰 xīnwèi [形] satisfied

欣喜 xīnxǐ [形] joyful

欣欣向荣 xīnxīn xiàng róng flourishing

新 xīn I [形] 1 (跟旧相对) new ▷新家具 new furniture 2 (刚结婚的) newly-wed ▷新媳妇

newly-wed wife **II** [副] newly ▷新买的衣服 newly bought clothes

新潮 xīncháo **I** [形] fashionable **II** [名] new trend

新陈代谢 xīn chén dàixiè the old gives way to the new ▷生命就是新陈代谢的过程。Life is a process of the old giving way to the new.

新村 xīncūn [名] new estate

新大陆 Xīn Dàlù [名] the New World

新房 xīnfáng [名] bridal chamber

新欢 xīnhuān [名] new sweetheart

新近 xīnjìn [副] ▷北京新近变化很大。Great changes have taken place recently in Beijing.

新郎 xīnláng [名] bridegroom

新年 xīnnián [名] **1** (指一段时间) New Year **2** (指元旦当天) New Year's Day

新娘 xīnniáng [名] bride

新奇 xīnqí [形] novel ▷他的想法很新奇，富有创造性。He has lots of novel ideas: he's bursting with creativity.

新人 xīnrén [名] **1** (新婚夫妇) newly married couple **2** (新型人才) new talent

新式 xīnshì [形] up-to-date

新手 xīnshǒu [名] beginner

新闻 xīnwén [名] news (sc) ▷新闻记者 news reporter ▷国际新闻 international news ▷国内新闻 domestic news ▷新闻节目 news programme (英) 或 program (美) ▷最近，我们公司的新闻真不少呢！Recently, there has been a lot of news in our company!

新鲜 xīnxiān [形] **1** (指食物) fresh ▷这些水果很新鲜。This fruit is very fresh. **2** (指植物) tender ▷新鲜的嫩芽 tender shoots **3** (清新) fresh ▷新鲜空气 fresh air **4** (新奇) novel ▷新鲜经验 novel experience

新兴 xīnxīng [形] newly emerging

新型 xīnxíng [形] new-style

新秀 xīnxiù [名] rising talent

新颖 xīnyǐng [形] original

薪 xīn [名] **1** (柴火) firewood **2** (薪水) salary

薪水 xīnshui [名] salary

馨 xīn [名] strong fragrance

馨香 xīnxiāng [名] (书) **1** (芳香) fragrance **2** (烧香的香味) smell of burning incense

信 xìn **I** [动] **1** (相信) believe ▶轻信 readily believe **2** (信奉) ▷信教 be religious ▷信佛教 be a Buddhist **II** [副] at will ▷信口开河 shoot one's mouth off **III** [名] **1** (书信) letter ▶信箱 letterbox (英), mailbox (美) ▷寄信 send a letter **2** (信息) information ▶口信 verbal

message **3** (信用) trust ▶失信 lose trust **4** (凭据) proof ▶信物 evidence

信贷 xìndài [名] credit

信封 xìnfēng [名] envelope

信奉 xìnfèng [动] believe in ▷信奉基督教 be a Christian

信服 xìnfú [动] be convinced ▷他的话漏洞百出，不能让我信服。His speech was full of inconsistencies – he couldn't convince me.

信号 xìnhào [名] signal ▷接收信号 receive a signal

信件 xìnjiàn [名] letter

信口雌黄 xìn kǒu cíhuáng make irresponsible remarks ▷我们对那些记者的信口雌黄感到愤慨。We are outraged at the irresponsible comments made by the journalists.

信口开河 xìn kǒu kāi hé talk off the top of one's head

信赖 xìnlài [动] trust

信念 xìnniàn [名] belief

信任 xìnrèn [动] trust ▷他为人忠厚朴实，大家都信任他。He's loyal and honest – everybody trusts him.

信手 xìnshǒu [副] at one's fingertips

信守 xìnshǒu [动] stand by (PT, PP stood) ▷信守誓言 stand by one's word

信条 xìntiáo [名] tenet

信徒 xìntú [名] follower

信托 xìntuō [动] trust ▷信托公司 trust company

信息 xìnxī [名] information ▷传递信息 pass on information ▷信息时代 the information age

请注意，information 在任何情况下都只能用作不可数名词。不能说 'an information' 或 'informations'。For further information contact the number below. 但是，在特指从他人处获知的某一具体信息时，可以用 a piece of information 或 an item of information。We will be looking at every piece of information we receive.

信心 xìnxīn [名] faith ▷他对前途失去信心。He lost faith in his future.

信仰 xìnyǎng [动] believe in ▷他没有宗教信仰。He has no religious faith.

信用 xìnyòng [名] **1** (指信任) word ▷他一向守信用。He always keeps his word. **2** (指借贷) credit

信用卡 xìnyòngkǎ [名] credit card

信誉 xìnyù [名] reputation

衅 xìn [名] quarrel ▶挑衅 pick a quarrel

兴 xīng [动] 1 (旺盛) prosper ▶兴衰 rise and fall 2 (流行) be popular ▶时兴 fashionable 3 (使盛行) promote ▷大兴反腐败之风 heavily promote anti-corruption 4 (发动) begin (PT began, PP begun) ▶兴修 begin construction
→另见 xìng

兴办 xīngbàn [动] set ... up (PT, PP set) ▷兴办合资企业 set up a joint venture

兴奋 xīngfèn [动] be excited ▷他兴奋得跳了起来。He leaped with excitement.

兴风作浪 xīng fēng zuò làng create chaos ▷黑客兴风作浪攻击一些著名网站。Hackers have been creating chaos on some well-known websites.

兴建 xīngjiàn [动] build (PT, PP built)

兴起 xīngqǐ [动] rise up (PT rose, PP risen)

兴盛 xīngshèng [形] prosperous

兴师动众 xīng shī dòng zhòng drag in a lot of people ▷为这件小事不值得兴师动众。This little matter does not require a lot of people to be dragged in.

兴旺 xīngwàng [形] prosperous

兴许 xīngxǔ [副] (方) maybe ▷他这么晚还没到，兴许有事不来了。He's so late getting here – maybe something's come up and he can't come.

星 xīng [名] 1 (指天体) star ▶星空 a starry sky 2 (指名人) star ▶球星 football star 3 (细碎物) bit ▶火星 spark ▷星星点点 bits and pieces

星辰 xīngchén [名] star

星斗 xīngdǒu [名] stars (PL)

星火 xīnghuǒ [名] 1 (微小的火) spark 2 (流星之光) meteor

星罗棋布 xīng luó qí bù be dotted with ▷旅游区内名胜古迹星罗棋布。The tourist area is dotted with historic and scenic attractions.

星期 xīngqī [名] 1 (周) week 2 (指某天) ▶星期天 Sunday ▶星期三 Wednesday

星球 xīngqiú [名] heavenly body

星体 xīngtǐ [名] heavenly body

星系 xīngxì [名] galaxy

星移斗转 xīng yí dǒu zhuǎn the passing of time ▷星移斗转，此塔何时建造已无史料可考。With the passing of time there are no longer any records as to when this tower was built.

星座 xīngzuò [名] constellation

猩 xīng [名] orang-utan ▶黑猩猩 chimpanzee

猩红 xīnghóng [形] blood-red

惺 xīng 见下文

惺忪 xīngsōng [形] bleary

腥 xīng I [名] raw meat II [形] fishy

刑 xíng [名] 1 (刑罚) punishment ▶死刑 the death penalty 2 (体罚) corporal punishment

刑罚 xíngfá [名] punishment

刑法 xíngfǎ [名] criminal law

刑事 xíngshì [形] criminal ▷刑事案件 criminal case

行 xíng I [动] 1 (走) walk ▶步行 go on foot 2 (流通) be current ▶发行 issue 3 (做) do (PT did, PP done) ▶行医 practise (英) 或 practice (美) medicine II [助动] 1 (可以) OK ▷行，就这么说定了。OK, so that's settled. 2 (能干) capable IV [名] 1 (旅行) travel ▶行踪 track 2 (行为) conduct ▶暴行 act of cruelty
→另见 háng

行程 xíngchéng [名] journey

行动 xíngdòng [动] 1 (行走) move about ▷奶奶年纪大了，行动不便。Grandma's getting old and finding it harder to move about. 2 (活动) take action (PT took, PP taken) ▷采取行动 take action

行贿 xínghuì [动] bribe

行进 xíngjìn [动] advance

行径 xíngjìng [名] conduct

行军 xíngjūn [动] march

行李 xíngli [名] luggage

luggage 是不可数名词。可以说某人有 a piece of luggage 或 some luggage，但不能说有 'a luggage' 或 'some luggages'。在英式英语中，人们通常用 luggage 指旅行者所携带的行李。baggage 是比较专业的词汇，例如在机场或谈论旅游保险时使用。在美式英语中，luggage 是指空的旅行袋或手提箱，baggage 是指装有物品的箱包。无论是英式还是美式英语，旅行者所携带的行李都可称作 bags。美国人还将一个手提箱称为 a bag。

行人 xíngrén [名] pedestrian

行使 xíngshǐ [动] exercise

行驶 xíngshǐ [动] travel

行为 xíngwéi [名] behaviour (英), behavior (美) ▷行为不轨 improper behaviour ▷行为规范 standards of behaviour

行星 xíngxīng [名] planet

行云流水 xíng yún liú shuǐ natural and unforced

行政 xíngzhèng [名] administration

行装 xíngzhuāng [名] luggage

行踪 xíngzōng [名] whereabouts (PL) ▷他行踪不定，四海为家。His whereabouts are uncertain – he could be living anywhere.

行走 xíngzǒu [动] walk

形 xíng I [名] 1 (形状) shape 2 (形体) body II [动] 1 (显露) appear 2 (对照) compare

形成 xíngchéng [动] form ▷这种自然现象形成于几千年前。This natural phenomenon formed thousands of years ago. ▷二氧化碳形成温室效应。Carbon dioxide has caused the greenhouse effect. ▷火山的形成 volcanic formation

形骸 xínghái [名] (书) the human body

形迹 xíngjì [名] traces (PL)

形容 xíngróng [动] describe

形容词 xíngróngcí [名] adjective

形式 xíngshì [名] form

形势 xíngshì [名] situation ▷形势很严峻。The situation is grave.

形态 xíngtài [名] 1 (形状) form 2 (语言) morphology

形体 xíngtǐ [名] physique ▷形体美 physical beauty

形象 xíngxiàng [名] image

形形色色 xíngxíngsèsè of every description ▷小说描绘了形形色色的人物。The novel depicts characters of every description.

形状 xíngzhuàng [名] shape

型 xíng [名] type ▶体型 build ▶模型 model ▶血型 blood group ▶典型 typical ▶造型 mould (英), mold (美)

型号 xínghào [名] model ▷这种牌子的电脑有好几种型号。This make of computer comes in several different models.

省 xǐng [动] 1 (检查) examine oneself critically ▶反省 self-questioning 2 (探望) visit ▶省亲 visit one's relatives 3 (醒悟) be aware ▷发人深省 be enlightening →另见 shěng

省察 xǐngchá [动] examine one's conscience ▷你们要省察自己的行为。You must examine your behaviour (英) 或 behaviour (美).

醒 xǐng I [动] 1 (神志恢复) come to (PT came, PP come) ▷车祸后很久他才醒过来。After

the car crash it took him a long time to come to. ▷她还酒醉未醒。She still hasn't sobered up. 2 (睡醒) wake up (PT woke, PP woken) ▶惊醒 wake up with a start 3 (醒悟) become aware (PT became, PP become) ▶提醒 remind II [形] eye-catching

醒目 xǐngmù [形] eye-catching

醒悟 xǐngwù [动] wake up to (PT woke, PP woken) ▷多年后我才醒悟，自己当时是错误的。It wasn't until years later that it dawned on me that I'd been wrong.

兴 xìng [名] excitement →另见 xīng

兴冲冲 xìngchōngchōng [形] excited

兴高采烈 xìng gāo cǎi liè be on top of the world ▷喜讯传来，全家兴高采烈。When the good news arrived, the family was on top of the world.

兴趣 xìngqù [名] interest ▷他对集邮有浓厚的兴趣。He has a deep interest in stamp-collecting.

兴致 xìngzhì [名] interest ▷他对打牌下棋兴致不高。He has no great interest in card games or chess.

杏 xìng [名] apricot

幸 xìng I [形] lucky II [动] rejoice III [副] fortunately

幸而 xìng'ér [副] fortunately

幸福 xìngfú I [名] happiness II [形] happy

幸好 xìnghǎo [副] luckily ▷我一人在家闷得慌，幸好你来串门。I was really bored at home by myself – lucky for me you came by!

幸会 xìnghuì [动] be honoured (英) 或 honored (美) ▷久仰大名，幸会幸会！I've been looking forward to meeting you for a long time – I'm honoured!

幸亏 xìngkuī [副] fortunately

幸免 xìngmiǎn [动] survive

幸运 xìngyùn I [名] good luck II [形] lucky

幸灾乐祸 xìng zāi lè huò gloat at others' misfortunes ▷看到他家破人亡，她却幸灾乐祸地笑了。When she saw that his family was ruined, she gloated at his misfortune.

性 xìng [名] 1 (性格) character ▶品性 moral character ▶任性 stubborn 2 (性能) function ▶酸性 acidity 3 (性别) gender ▶男性 male 4 (情欲) sex ▶性关系 sexual intercourse 5 (性质) reliability ▶实用性 utility 6 (语法) gender ▶阳性 masculine

性别 xìngbié [名] sex

性感 xìnggǎn [形] sexy

性格 xìnggé [名] personality

性交 xìngjiāo [动] have sex

性命 xìngmìng [名] life (PL lives)

性能 xìngnéng [名] function

性情 xìngqíng [名] disposition ▷这女孩儿性情温和。This girl has a gentle disposition.

性骚扰 xìngsāorǎo [动] sexually harass ▷法律如何保护受到性骚扰的女性？How does the law protect women from sexual harassment?

性欲 xìngyù [名] sexual desire

性质 xìngzhì [名] character

姓 xìng I [动] ▷我姓李。My surname is Li. II [名] surname

姓名 xìngmíng [名] full name

姓氏 xìngshì [名] surname

凶 xiōng I [形] 1 (不幸的) unlucky ▷凶兆 ill omen 2 (凶恶) ferocious ▶凶相 fierce look 3 (厉害) terrible ▷俩人吵得很凶。The two men had a terrible quarrel. II [名] act of violence

凶暴 xiōngbào [形] ferocious

凶残 xiōngcán [形] savage

凶恶 xiōng'è [形] fierce

凶狠 xiōnghěn [形] vicious

凶猛 xiōngměng [形] ferocious

凶器 xiōngqì [名] weapon

凶手 xiōngshǒu [名] murderer

凶险 xiōngxiǎn [形] 1 (危险可怕) perilous ▷这条山路极其凶险。This mountain road is perilous. ▷老人病情凶险。The old man's condition is critical. 2 (凶恶阴险) ruthless

兄 xiōng [名] brother

兄弟 xiōngdì [名] brother

兄长 xiōngzhǎng [名] elder brother

汹 xiōng [动] upsurge

汹汹 xiōngxiōng [形] turbulent

汹涌澎湃 xiōng yǒng péng pài tempestuous

胸 xiōng [名] 1 (胸部) chest 2 (心胸) heart ▷胸怀大志 have a big heart

胸怀 xiōnghuái [名] heart

胸襟 xiōngjīn [名] 1 (气量) broadmindedness ▷胸襟开阔 broadminded 2 (胸部衣襟) chest

胸脯 xiōngpú [名] chest

胸有成竹 xiōng yǒu chéng zhú have a well thought-out strategy

雄 xióng I [形] 1 (公的) male 2 (有气魄的) imposing 3 (强有力的) strong II [名] very powerful person

雄辩 xióngbiàn [名] convincing argument

雄厚 xiónghòu [形] abundant

雄赳赳 xióngjiūjiū [形] gallant

雄图 xióngtú [名] grand plan

雄伟 xióngwěi [形] imposing

雄心 xióngxīn [名] ambition

雄壮 xióngzhuàng [形] majestic

熊 xióng [名] bear

熊猫 xióngmāo [名] panda

熊熊 xióngxióng [形] blazing

休 xiū I [动] 1 (停止) stop 2 (休息) rest II [副] ▷你休想得逞。Don't imagine you can win.

休克 xiūkè [名] shock

休戚相关 xiū qī xiāng guān be interconnected

休息 xiūxi [动] rest

休闲 xiūxián [动] 1 (闲置) be unused 2 (悠闲) be at leisure ▷休闲服装 casual clothes

休养 xiūyǎng [动] recuperate

休养生息 xiūyǎng shēngxī recovery ▷本届政府实行了休养生息政策。This government has pursued policies for national recovery.

休整 xiūzhěng [动] rest and reorganize

休止 xiūzhǐ [动] cease ▷对环境的破坏何时才能休止？When will the damage to the environment cease?

修 xiū [动] 1 (修饰) decorate 2 (修理) mend 3 (学习) study 4 (兴建) build (PT, PP built) 5 (剪) trim

修补 xiūbǔ [动] mend

修长 xiūcháng [形] slender

修辞 xiūcí [动] engage in rhetoric

修订 xiūdìng [动] revise ▷修订草案 revise a draft

修改 xiūgǎi [动] alter ▷修改计划 alter one's plans ▷修改文章 revise an essay

修建 xiūjiàn [动] build (PT, PP built)

修理 xiūlǐ [动] repair

修女 xiūnǚ [名] nun

修身 xiūshēn [动] improve oneself

修饰 xiūshì [动] 1 (修整装饰) decorate 2 (修改润饰) polish

修养 xiūyǎng [名] 1 (水平) accomplishments (PL) ▷文学修养 literary accomplishments 2 (指态度) gentility

修正 xiūzhèng [动] correct

羞 xiū I [形] shy II [动] disgrace III [名] shame
羞惭 xiūcán [形] ashamed
羞耻 xiūchǐ [形] ashamed
羞答答 xiūdādā [形] coy
羞愧 xiūkuì [形] ashamed
羞怯 xiūqiè [形] timid
羞辱 xiūrǔ I [名] humiliation II [动] humiliate
羞涩 xiūsè [形] shy

朽 xiǔ [动] 1 (腐烂) rot 2 (衰老) go senile (PT went, PP gone)

宿 xiǔ [量] night ▷他在旅店里住了两宿。He stayed at the guesthouse for two nights.
→另见 sù

秀 xiù I [形] 1 (清秀) elegant 2 (优异) outstanding II [名] talent ▶新秀 new talent
秀才 xiùcai [名] scholar
秀丽 xiùlì [形] beautiful
秀美 xiùměi [形] elegant
秀气 xiùqi [形] 1 (清秀) delicate 2 (文雅) refined

臭 xiù [名] smell
→另见 chòu

袖 xiù [名] sleeve
袖手旁观 xiù shǒu páng guān stand by and do nothing
袖珍 xiùzhēn [形] pocket-sized ▷袖珍收音机 pocket radio

绣 xiù I [动] embroider II [名] embroidery
绣花枕头 xiùhuā zhěntou pretty on the outside but lacking substance underneath

锈 xiù [名] rust ▶生锈 go rusty ▷刀锈了。The knife has rusted.

嗅 xiù [动] smell
嗅觉 xiùjué [名] sense of smell ▷狗的嗅觉很灵敏。Dogs have an acute sense of smell.

吁 xū [动] (书) sigh
→另见 yù
吁吁 xūxū [拟] huff and puff

须 xū I [副] ▶必须 must II [名] beard
须要 xūyào [动] need
须知 xūzhī [名] essentials (PL)

虚 xū I [形] 1 (空着) empty 2 (胆怯) timid 3 (虚假) false 4 (虚心) modest 5 (弱) weak II [副]

虚词 xūcí [名] function word
虚浮 xūfú [形] superficial
虚构 xūgòu [动] fabricate ▷故事情节纯属虚构。This story has been completely fabricated.
虚怀若谷 xū huái ruò gǔ be open-minded
虚幻 xūhuàn [形] illusory
虚假 xūjiǎ [形] false
虚惊 xūjīng [名] false alarm
虚名 xūmíng [名] undeserved reputation
虚情假意 xū qíng jiǎ yì ▷我看得出他对我只是虚情假意。I realized that his apparent friendliness to me was not genuine.
虚荣 xūróng [名] vanity
虚弱 xūruò [形] frail
虚伪 xūwěi [形] hypocritical
虚无 xūwú [形] non-existent
虚心 xūxīn [形] open-minded ▷我们要虚心向他人学习。We need to learn from others in an open-minded way.
虚张声势 xū zhāng shēngshì bluff and bluster ▷面对虚张声势的商家，如何讨个好价钱？How is it possible to bargain with shopkeepers who bluff and bluster?

墟 xū [名] ruins (PL)

需 xū I [动] need ▷去英国留学需一大笔经费。You'll need considerable funds if you want to go to Britain to study. II [名] needs (PL) ▶军需 military requirements (PL)
需求 xūqiú [名] demand ▷该地区对中药材的需求很旺盛。There is a thriving demand for Chinese medicinal herbs in this area.
需要 xūyào I [动] need ▷常人每天需要吃一定量的水果和蔬菜。Everyone needs to eat a certain amount of fruit and vegetables each day. II [名] needs (PL) ▷日常生活需要 necessities of life

嘘 xū [叹] (方) sh ▷嘘！别吵醒了他。Sh! Don't wake him!
→另见 shī

徐 xú [副] slowly
徐徐 xúxú [副] slowly

许 xǔ I [动] 1 (称赞) praise 2 (答应) promise 3 (允许) allow ▷妻子不许他抽烟喝酒。His wife doesn't allow him to smoke or drink. II [副] maybe ▷他看上去脸色苍白，许是生病了。He looks a bit pale – maybe he's ill.
许多 xǔduō [形] many ▷这套家具用了许多

年了。This furniture has been in use for many years. ▷他养了许多金鱼。He keeps a lot of goldfish.

许久 xǔjiǔ [名] ages (PL) ▷我等了许久才收到他的回信。I had to wait for ages before he replied to my letter.

许可 xǔkě [动] allow ▷如果条件许可，我就报名参赛。If circumstances allow, I'll sign up for the competition.

许诺 xǔnuò [动] promise ▷他曾许诺来看她，可是终究没来。He promised to visit her, but he never came.

许配 xǔpèi [动] marry ... off ▷父母将她许配给了一个有钱人。Her parents married her off to a rich man.

许愿 xǔyuàn [动] 1 (对神) vow 2 (对人) promise

诩 xǔ [动] (书) boast

栩 xǔ 见下文

栩栩 xǔxǔ [形] vivid

旭 xù [名] (书) sunrise

旭日 xùrì [名] the rising sun

序 xù I [名] 1 (次序) order 2 (序文) preface ▷我给这本书写了序。I wrote the preface to this book. II [形] preliminary

序列 xùliè [名] formation
序幕 xùmù [名] prologue
序曲 xùqǔ [名] overture
序数 xùshù [名] ordinal number
序言 xùyán [名] foreword

叙 xù [动] 1 (谈) chat 2 (记述) recount

叙别 xùbié [动] have a farewell talk
叙事 xùshì [动] narrate
叙述 xùshù [动] recount

恤 xù [动] 1 (怜悯) pity 2 (救济) give money (PT gave, PP given)

恤金 xùjīn [名] pension

畜 xù [动] raise
→另见 chù

畜牧 xùmù [动] rear ▷畜牧业 animal husbandry

酗 xù 见下文

酗酒 xùjiǔ [动] get drunk ▷他因酗酒斗殴被警方拘留。He was arrested because he got drunk and was involved in a fight.

绪 xù [名] 1 (开端) beginning 2 (心情) feelings (PL)

绪论 xùlùn [名] preface

续 xù [动] 1 (接连) continue 2 (延长) extend 3 (添加) add

续聘 xùpìn [动] keep ... on (PT, PP kept) ▷合同期满后，公司续聘了他。When his contract expired, the company kept him on.

絮 xù I [名] 1 (棉絮) cotton wadding 2 (絮状物) ▶柳絮 willow catkin II [动] 1 (铺衬) pad with cotton 2 (啰唆) be long-winded

絮叨 xùdāo [动] go on (PT went, PP gone) ▷她絮絮叨叨，我听得都厌烦了。How she went on! I was sick of the sound of it!

婿 xù [名] 1 (女婿) son-in-law (PL sons-in-law) 2 (丈夫) husband

蓄 xù [动] 1 (储存) store 2 (留着) grow (PT grew, PP grown) ▷蓄胡子 grow a beard 3 (存有) harbour (英), harbor (美)

蓄积 xùjī [动] store
蓄谋 xùmóu [动] premeditate
蓄意 xùyì [动] premeditate

轩 xuān [形] (书) high

轩昂 xuān'áng [形] dignified

轩然大波 xuānrán dà bō complete crisis ▷球员罢赛掀起轩然大波。The footballers' strike caused a complete crisis.

宣 xuān [动] 1 (宣布) announce 2 (疏导) lead ... off (PT, PP led) ▶宣泄 get ... off one's chest

宣布 xuānbù [动] announce
宣称 xuānchēng [动] announce
宣传 xuānchuán [动] disseminate ▷宣传工具 means of dissemination ▷宣传进步思想 promote progressive thought
宣告 xuāngào [动] proclaim
宣判 xuānpàn [动] pass judgment ▷法庭宣判被告无罪。The court declared the defendant not guilty.
宣誓 xuānshì [动] take an oath (PT took, PP taken)
宣泄 xuānxiè [动] get ... off one's chest ▷明天的讨论是给大家一个宣泄的机会。Tomorrow's discussion will be an opportunity for everyone to get things off their chests.
宣言 xuānyán [名] declaration
宣扬 xuānyáng [动] advocate
宣战 xuānzhàn [动] declare war ▷珍珠港事件后，美国向日本宣战。After Pearl Harbor the United States declared war on Japan.

喧 xuān [动] make a noise

喧宾夺主 xuān bīn duó zhǔ get one's priorities wrong

喧哗 xuānhuá I [形] riotous II [动] create a disturbance

喧闹 xuānnào [形] rowdy

喧嚣 xuānxiāo I [形] noisy II [动] cause an uproar

玄 xuán [形] 1 (深奥) deep 2 (口) (玄乎) unreliable

玄乎 xuánhu [形] (口) unreliable

玄妙 xuánmiào [形] mysterious

玄虚 xuánxū [名] mystery

悬 xuán I [动] 1 (挂) hang (PT, PP hung) 2 (设想) imagine 3 (挂念) be concerned about 4 (未定) be unresolved ▷这件事还悬着呢。This matter is still unresolved. II [形] far apart

悬案 xuán'àn [名] unsolved case

悬挂 xuánguà [动] hang (PT, PP hung)

悬念 xuánniàn [名] suspense

悬赏 xuánshǎng [动] offer a reward ▷政府悬赏百万美金捉拿要犯。The government offered a reward of a million dollars for the arrest of the perpetrator.

悬殊 xuánshū [形] distant ▷大城市里贫富悬殊。In big cities there's a huge gap between the rich and the poor.

悬崖 xuányá [名] precipice

旋 xuán I [动] 1 (旋转) revolve 2 (返回) return II [名] spiral
→另见 xuàn

旋律 xuánlù [名] melody

旋钮 xuánniǔ [名] knob

旋绕 xuánrào [动] circle ▷乐曲声在耳边旋绕不绝。The tune kept going round and round in my head.

旋涡 xuánwō [名] whirlpool

旋转 xuánzhuǎn [动] revolve ▷地球围绕太阳旋转。The earth revolves around the sun.

漩 xuán [名] whirlpool

漩涡 xuánwō [名] whirlpool

选 xuǎn I [动] 1 (挑选) choose (PT chose, PP chosen) 2 (选举) vote II [名] 1 (指人) selection ▶人选 selection of people 2 (作品集) collection ▶文选 collected works (PL)

选拔 xuǎnbá [动] select

选本 xuǎnběn [名] anthology

选材 xuǎncái [动] 1 (选人才) select talent 2 (选材料) select material

选集 xuǎnjí [名] anthology

选举 xuǎnjǔ [动] elect

选民 xuǎnmín [名] electorate

选派 xuǎnpài [动] select

选取 xuǎnqǔ [动] choose (PT chose, PP chosen)

选手 xuǎnshǒu [名] contestant

选修 xuǎnxiū [动] choose to study (PT chose, PP chosen) ▷这学期我选修了经济学。This term I've chosen to study economics. ▷选修课程 optional course

选择 xuǎnzé [动] choose (PT chose, PP chosen) ▷成千种商品供您自由选择。We have a thousand different products for you to choose from. ▷选择配偶 choose a partner ▷别无选择 have no choice ▷中文字体选择 a selection of Chinese fonts

炫 xuàn [动] 1 (晃眼) dazzle 2 (夸耀) show off (PT showed, PP shown)

炫耀 xuànyào [动] show off (PT showed, PP shown)

绚 xuàn [形] splendid

绚烂 xuànlàn [形] splendid

绚丽 xuànlì [形] gorgeous

眩 xuàn [形] (书) dizzy

眩目 xuànmù [动] dazzle

旋 xuàn [动] spin (PT, PP spun)
→另见 xuán

旋风 xuànfēng [名] whirlwind

渲 xuàn 见下文

渲染 xuànrǎn [动] exaggerate

削 xuē 见下文
→另见 xiāo

削减 xuējiǎn [动] cut (PT, PP cut) ▷削减财政开支 cut government expenditure

削弱 xuēruò [动] weaken

靴 xuē [名] boot

靴子 xuēzi [名] boot

穴 xué [名] 1 (洞) den 2 (穴位) acupuncture point

穴位 xuéwèi [名] acupuncture point

学 xué I [动] 1 (学习) study ▷学英语 learn English 2 (模仿) imitate ▷学鸟叫 imitate birdsong II [名] 1 (学问) learning ▶博学 erudition 2 (学科) science ▶数学 mathematics ▶生物学 biology ▶化学

chemistry **3** (学校) school ▶大学 university ▶中学 senior school (英), high school (美) ▶小学 primary school (英), elementary school (美)

学报 xuébào [名] academic journal

学潮 xuécháo [名] student movement

学风 xuéfēng [名] learning style

学府 xuéfǔ [名] institute of higher education

学籍 xuéjí [名] one's status as a student

学界 xuéjiè [名] educational circles (PL)

学究 xuéjiū [名] pedant

学科 xuékē [名] subject

学力 xuélì [名] level of academic attainment

学历 xuélì [名] educational background

学龄 xuélíng [名] school age ▷学龄前儿童 preschool children

学名 xuémíng [名] scientific name ▷食盐的学名是氯化钠。The scientific name for salt is sodium chloride.

学派 xuépài [名] school of thought

学生 xuésheng [名] student ▷学生会 student union

学识 xuéshí [名] knowledge

学士 xuéshì [名] **1** (读书人) scholar **2** (指学位) bachelor ▷文学学士 Bachelor of Arts, B.A.

学术 xuéshù [名] learning ▷学术论文 academic essay

学说 xuéshuō [名] theory

学位 xuéwèi [名] degree ▷硕士学位 master's degree

学问 xuéwen [名] learning

学习 xuéxí [动] study ▷学习英语语法 study English grammar ▷学习方法 study methods ▷学习发达国家的经验 learn from the experience of the developed countries

学校 xuéxiào [名] school ▷职业技术学校 vocational and technical school

学业 xuéyè [名] studies (PL) ▷你最好完成学业后再找工作。It would be best to look for work again after you've finished your studies.

学者 xuézhě [名] scholar

学子 xuézǐ [名] (书) student

雪 xuě **I** [名] snow **II** [形] bright **III** [动] avenge

雪白 xuěbái [形] snow-white

雪耻 xuěchǐ [动] avenge an insult

雪花 xuěhuā [名] snowflake

雪亮 xuěliàng [形] bright

雪中送炭 xuě zhōng sòng tàn give help when it is most needed

血 xuè [名] **1** (血液) blood **2** (刚强的气质) courage ▷血性男儿 courageous man
→另见 xiě

血本 xuèběn [名] principal

血汗 xuèhàn [名] sweat and toil

血口喷人 xuè kǒu pēn rén vicious slander

血气方刚 xuèqì fāng gāng full of youthful vigour (英) 或 vigor (美)

血肉 xuèròu [名] flesh and blood

血统 xuètǒng [名] blood relationship

血型 xuèxíng [名] blood type

血压 xuèyā [名] blood pressure

血液 xuèyè [名] **1** (血) blood **2** (主要力量) lifeblood

血缘 xuèyuán [名] blood relationship

血债 xuèzhài [名] blood debt

血战 xuèzhàn [名] bloody battle

勋 xūn [名] merit

勋章 xūnzhāng [名] medal

熏 xūn [动] **1** (烟气接触物体) ▷烟把墙熏黑了。The smoke has blackened the wall. ▷一股怪味直熏鼻子。I'm aware of a strange smell. **2** (熏制) smoke ▶熏肉 smoked meat

熏染 xūnrǎn [动] influence ▷他深得古典艺术之熏染。He has been deeply influenced by classical art.

熏陶 xūntáo [动] influence ▷他从小受到古典音乐的熏陶。He had been influenced by classical music since he was small.

旬 xún [名] **1** (十日) ten days ▶上旬 the first ten days of the month **2** (指十岁) ▷他年过7旬。He's more than seventy years old.

寻 xún [动] search

寻常 xúncháng [形] usual ▷这件事很不寻常。This is a most unusual business.

寻访 xúnfǎng [动] search for

寻呼 xúnhū [动] put out a call for (PT, PP put) ▶寻呼机 pager

寻觅 xúnmì [动] search for ▷寻觅人生伴侣 search for a life partner

寻求 xúnqiú [动] seek (PT, PP sought) ▷寻求法律帮助 seek legal assistance

寻死 xúnsǐ [动] commit suicide

寻思 xúnsi [动] ponder ▷他在寻思如何才能把问题解决好。He is pondering how to solve the problem.

寻衅 xúnxìn [动] pick a fight

寻找 xúnzhǎo [动] look for ▷寻找丢失的钱包

look for a lost purse ▷寻找人生的真谛 seek the meaning of life

巡 **xún** [动] patrol

巡查 **xúnchá** [动] patrol

巡警 **xúnjǐng** [名] policeman

巡逻 **xúnluó** [动] patrol ▷这个住宅区24小时都有警卫巡逻。This residential area is patrolled by guards 24 hours a day.

巡视 **xúnshì** [动] make a tour of inspection

询 **xún** [动] inquire

询问 **xúnwèn** [动] ask ▷母亲在信中询问我的生活情况。In her letters Mother asked how I was doing.

循 **xún** [动] abide by

循规蹈矩 **xún guī dǎo jǔ** stick to the rules

循环 **xúnhuán** [动] circulate

循序渐进 **xúnxù jiànjìn** take a progressive approach ▷我主张循序渐进的学习方法。I'd advise a study method that takes a progressive approach.

循循善诱 **xúnxún shàn yòu** teach with skill and patience

训 **xùn** I [动] 1 (教导) teach (PT, PP taught) 2 (训练) train II [名] rule

训斥 **xùnchì** [动] reprimand

训导 **xùndǎo** [动] give ... training and guidance (PT gave, PP given)

训话 **xùnhuà** [动] reprimand

训练 **xùnliàn** [动] training ▷ 职业训练 vocational training

讯 **xùn** I [动] interrogate ▶审讯 interrogate II [名] message ▶传讯 pass on a message ▶简讯 brief message ▶喜讯 good news (SG)

讯问 **xùnwèn** [动] 1 (问) ask ▷医生讯问了她的身体状况。The doctor asked about her physical condition. 2 (审问) question

汛 **xùn** [名] flood

汛期 **xùnqī** [名] flood season

汛情 **xùnqíng** [名] flood situation

迅 **xùn** [形] swift

迅猛 **xùnměng** [形] swift and violent

迅速 **xùnsù** [形] swift

驯 **xùn** I [形] tame II [动] tame

驯服 **xùnfú** I [形] tame II [动] tame ▷驯服野兽 tame wild animals

驯化 **xùnhuà** [动] domesticate

驯良 **xùnliáng** [形] docile

驯养 **xùnyǎng** [动] tame

徇 **xùn** [动] (书) give way to (PT gave, PP given)

徇情 **xùnqíng** [动] (书) be swayed by personal considerations

徇私 **xùnsī** [动] show favouritism (英) 或 favoritism (美) (PT showed, PP shown)

逊 **xùn** [形] 1 (谦虚) modest 2 (书) (差) inferior

逊色 **xùnsè** [动] be inferior to ▷你的工作成绩和他相比毫不逊色。Your achievements at work are not inferior to his.

殉 **xùn** [动] die for ▶殉情 die for love

殉难 **xùnnàn** [动] die ▷他在抗洪救灾中不幸殉难。Sadly, he died fighting the floods.

殉职 **xùnzhí** [动] die in the line of duty ▷3名消防队员在救火时殉职。Three members of the fire brigade died in the line of duty.

熏 **xùn** [动] (方) suffocate

Yy

丫 **yā** [名] **1** (分叉) fork **2** (方) (女孩子) girl

丫头 **yātou** [名] **1** (女孩子) girl **2** (旧) (丫鬟) maid

压 **yā** I [动] **1** (施力) press **2** (超越) outdo (PT outdid, PP outdone) **3** (使稳定) control **4** (压制) suppress **5** (积压) put ... off (PT, PP put) ▷上访信要及时处理，不能压着。Appeals to the authorities should be dealt with promptly – you mustn't put them off. **6** (下注) bet (PT, PP bet) II [名] pressure
→另见 **yà**

压价 **yājià** [动] force a price down

压力 **yālì** [名] **1** (物) pressure **2** (指对人) pressure ▷她承受着来自媒体的压力。She is coming under pressure from the media. **3** (负担) burden ▷沉重的生活压力 the heavy burden of existence

压迫 **yāpò** [动] **1** (压制) oppress **2** (挤压) put pressure on (PT, PP put) ▷囊肿压迫神经。Cysts put pressure on the nerves.

压岁钱 **yāsuìqián** [名] *traditional gifts of money given to children during the Spring Festival*

压缩 **yāsuō** [动] **1** (指体积) compress **2** (减少) reduce

压抑 **yāyì** [动] suppress

压制 **yāzhì** [动] **1** (抑制) suppress **2** (指制造方法) press

呀 **yā** I [叹] (表示惊异) oh ▷呀！已经12点了！Oh! It's 12 o'clock already! II [拟] creak

押 **yā** I [动] **1** (抵押) leave ... as a security (PT, PP left) **2** (拘留) detain ▷这所监狱押着几百名犯人。Several hundred convicts are held in this prison. **3** (看管) guard II [名] signature

押金 **yājīn** [名] deposit

押送 **yāsòng** [动] send ... under escort (PT, PP sent)

押韵 **yāyùn** [动] rhyme

鸦 **yā** [名] crow

鸦片 **yāpiàn** [名] opium

鸦雀无声 **yā què wú shēng** so quiet you could hear a pin drop ▷教室里鸦雀无声。It was so quiet in the classroom that you could hear a pin drop.

鸭 **yā** [名] duck

牙 **yá** [名] **1** (牙齿) tooth (PL teeth) **2** (牙状物) ▶月牙 crescent moon

牙齿 **yáchǐ** [名] tooth (PL teeth)

牙床 **yáchuáng** [名] gum

牙膏 **yágāo** [名] toothpaste

牙关 **yáguān** [名] jaw ▷我们咬紧牙关渡过了难关。We gritted our teeth through the tough times.

牙科 **yákē** [名] dental department

牙签 **yáqiān** [名] toothpick

牙刷 **yáshuā** [名] toothbrush

牙痛 **yátòng** [名] toothache

牙医 **yáyī** [名] dentist

牙龈 **yáyín** [名] gum

芽 **yá** [名] **1** (指植物) sprout **2** (芽状物) spike

涯 **yá** [名] **1** (边际) end ▶天涯 the ends of the earth **2** (喻) (极限) limit

崖 **yá** [名] cliff

哑 **yǎ** [形] **1** (不能说话) mute **2** (不说话) speechless **3** (嘶哑) hoarse

哑巴 **yǎba** [名] mute

哑剧 **yǎjù** [名] mime

哑口无言 **yǎ kǒu wú yán** be reduced to silence ▷他被质问得哑口无言。He was reduced to silence by the interrogation.

哑铃 **yǎlíng** [名] dumbbell

哑谜 **yǎmí** [名] riddle ▷你就直说吧，别打哑谜了！Tell me straight – don't talk in riddles!

哑语 yǎyǔ [名] sign language ▷第五频道可以
收看哑语新闻。You can see the news in sign
language on Channel Five.

雅 yǎ I [形] 1 (合乎规范) proper 2 (高尚) elegant
II [名] (敬) you ▶雅意 your esteemed opinion

雅观 yǎguān [形] tasteful ▷这种动作很不雅
观。Gestures like that are in really bad taste.

雅量 yǎliàng [名] 1 (大的气度) magnanimity
2 (大的酒量) tolerance for drink

雅皮士 yǎpíshì [名] yuppie

雅俗共赏 yǎ sú gòng shǎng suit all tastes

雅兴 yǎxìng [名] inspiration

雅致 yǎzhì [形] elegant

雅座 yǎzuò [名] private room

轧 yà I [动] 1 (碾) roll 2 (排挤) push out ▶倾轧
push out II [拟] creak
→另见 zhá

亚 yà I [形] inferior ▶亚热带 sub-tropical belt
▷我们的产品质量不亚于其他工厂。The
quality of our products is not inferior to any
other factory's. II [名] Asia

亚军 yàjūn [名] runner-up (PL runners-up)

亚洲 yàzhōu [名] Asia ▷她是亚洲人。She's
Asian.

压 yà 见下文
→另见 yā

压根儿 yàgēnr [副] at all ▷我压根儿就没见过
这样的事。I've never seen anything like it.

揠 yà [动] (书) pull ... up

揠苗助长 yà miáo zhù zhǎng do more harm
than good

咽 yān [名] pharynx
→另见 yàn

咽喉 yānhóu [名] 1 (字) throat 2 (喻) (险要处)
strategic pass

烟 yān I [名] 1 (指气体) smoke 2 (烟状物)
mist 3 (烟草) tobacco ▶香烟 cigarette 4 (鸦
片) opium II [动] be irritated by smoke ▷厨
房里的烟烟得人睁不开眼睛。The smoke in
the kitchen irritated our eyes so badly that we
couldn't keep them open.

烟草 yāncǎo [名] 1 tobacco plant 2 (烟草制品)
tobacco

烟花 yānhuā [名] firework ▷孩子们爱放烟
花。Kids like to set off fireworks.

烟灰缸 yānhuīgāng [名] ashtray

烟火 yānhuǒ [名] 1 (烟花) fireworks (PL) 2 (烟和
火) smoke and fire

烟卷儿 yānjuǎnr [名] cigarette

烟民 yānmín [名] smokers (PL)

烟幕 yānmù [名] smokescreen ▷他的和平演说
不过是一种烟幕。His peace talks are merely a
smokescreen.

烟消云散 yān xiāo yún sàn vanish into
thin air ▷得知真实情况后,人们的不满情
绪烟消云散了。When they found out what
was really going on, the people's feelings of
discontent vanished into thin air.

殷 yān [形] (书) dark red
→另见 yīn

殷红 yānhóng [形] dark red

胭 yān 见下文

胭脂 yānzhi [名] rouge

阉 yān I [动] castrate II [名] (书) eunuch

阉割 yāngē [动] castrate

淹 yān [动] 1 (淹没) flood 2 (浸渍) tingle

淹没 yānmò [动] 1 (漫过) submerge 2 (喻)
drown ... out ▷歌声被歌迷们尖叫声所
淹没。The song was drowned out by the
screeches of the fans. ▷她瘦小的身影很快
淹没在人海中。Her slight form was soon
drowned in the crowd.

腌 yān [动] pickle

腌制 yānzhì [动] pickle ▷腌制食品不宜多
吃。Pickled foods should not be eaten in large
quantities.

延 yán [动] 1 (延长) extend 2 (推迟) delay 3 (聘
请) employ

延长 yáncháng [动] extend

延迟 yánchí [动] delay

延年益寿 yán nián yì shòu prolong life ▷据
说少食多餐能够延年益寿。It is said that
eating little but often can prolong your life.

延伸 yánshēn [动] stretch

延误 yánwù [动] delay

延续 yánxù [动] go on (PT went, PP gone)

严 yán [形] 1 (严密) tight ▷我把门关严了。
I shut the door tightly. 2 (严格) strict 3 (形容程
度深) severe

严惩 yánchéng [动] punish ... severely

严打 yándǎ [动] crack down on ▷开展针对盗
版的严打 launch a crackdown on pirating

严格 yángé [形] strict ▷大家要严格遵守规章
制度。Everyone must strictly abide by the rules

and regulations.

严谨 yánjǐn [形] 1 (严密谨慎) meticulous 2 (严密细致) compact

严峻 yánjùn [形] rigorous

严酷 yánkù [形] 1 (严厉) stern 2 (残酷) cruel

严厉 yánlì [形] severe ▷父亲严厉地批评了他。His father gave him a severe telling-off.

严密 yánmì [形] 1 (没有缝隙) tight ▷罐头封得很严密。The tin is closed very tightly. 2 (没有疏漏) close ▷人们严密关注着事态的发展。People kept a close watch on how the situation was developing.

严明 yánmíng I [形] firm but fair II [动] be firm but fair

严肃 yánsù I [形] 1 (庄重) solemn 2 (严格认真) severe ▷对于违章人员一定要严肃处理。People who break the rules must be dealt with severely. II [动] enforce

严正 yánzhèng [形] stern but fair

严重 yánzhòng [形] serious ▷这一工程存在着严重的质量问题。There are serious problems with the quality of this project. ▷他的病情非常严重。His illness is extremely serious.

言 yán I [动] speak (PT spoke, PP spoken) ▷言之有理 sound reasonable II [名] 1 (话) speech 2 (字) words (PL)

言不由衷 yán bù yóu zhōng not say what one means ▷他的回答言不由衷。He didn't say what he meant.

言辞 yáncí [名] wording

言归正传 yán guī zhèng zhuàn get back to business ▷刚才大家闲聊了半天，现在言归正传吧。We've been chatting for ages – now let's get back to business.

言简意赅 yán jiǎn yì gāi be brief and to the point

言论 yánlùn [名] speech ▷言论自由 freedom of speech

言情片 yánqíngpiān [名] romantic film (英) 或 movie (美)

言谈 yántán [名] what one says ▷从言谈中，我了解了他的过去。From what he said, I learned a lot about his past.

言听计从 yán tīng jì cóng take people at their word ▷他对他妈妈言听计从。He took his mother at her word.

言语 yányǔ [名] language

岩 yán [名] 1 (岩石) rock 2 (山峰) crag

岩洞 yándòng [名] cave

炎 yán I [形] scorching II [名] 1 (炎症) inflammation 2 (权势) power

炎黄子孙 yánhuángzǐsūn [名] Chinese people (PL)

炎热 yánrè [形] scorching hot ▷他在北京度过了一个炎热的夏天。He spent a scorching hot summer in Beijing.

炎症 yánzhèng [名] inflammation

沿 yán I [介] along ▷沿着这条路往前走。Go straight along this road. II [动] 1 (依照) follow ▶沿袭 follow 2 (镶边) border III [名] edge

沿岸 yán'àn [名] bank

沿革 yángé [名] evolution

沿海 yánhǎi [名] coast ▷夏天，很多人到沿海城市度假。In summer, many people go to the coastal cities for their holidays.

沿袭 yánxí [动] follow

沿用 yányòng [动] continue to use

研 yán [动] 1 (细磨) grind (PT, PP ground) 2 (研究) research

研读 yándú [动] research ▷他正在研读语言学理论方面的书籍。He's researching linguistic theory from a series of books.

研究 yánjiū [动] 1 (探求) research ▷做生意首先要研究市场。When doing business, one must first research the market. ▷历史研究对今天很有借鉴意义。Much can be gained today from historical research. 2 (商讨) discuss ▷领导们正在研究职工提交的建议。The leaders are discussing the suggestions submitted by the workers. ▷这套方案有待于进一步研究。This scheme is awaiting further discussion.

研讨 yántǎo [动] discuss

研制 yánzhì [动] develop

盐 yán [名] salt

筵 yán [名] banquet

筵席 yánxí [名] banquet

颜 yán [名] 1 (字) face 2 (体面) face 3 (颜色) colour (英), color (美)

颜料 yánliào [名] colouring (英), coloring (美)

颜色 yánsè [名] 1 (色彩) colour (英), color (美) ▷她喜欢穿深颜色的衣服。She likes to wear dark colours. 2 (表情) expression 3 (指报复) revenge ▷给你点颜色看看！I'll show you!

檐 yán [名] 1 (房檐) eaves (PL) 2 (檐状物) brim

奄 yǎn 见下文

奄奄 yǎnyǎn [形] feeble

俨 yǎn [形] (书) solemn

俨然 yǎnrán I [形] (书) solemn II [副] just like ▷她走上讲台，俨然是个老师。She walked up to the podium, just like a teacher.

衍 yǎn [动] 1 (书) develop 2 (多余) be redundant

衍变 yǎnbiàn [动] evolve

衍生 yǎnshēng [动] 1 (指化合物) derive 2 (产生) give rise to (PT gave, PP given) ▷这个地方衍生了很多美丽动人的传说。This place has given rise to many beautiful and touching legends.

掩 yǎn [动] 1 (遮盖) cover 2 (关) close

掩蔽 yǎnbì I [动] take shelter (PT took, PP taken) II [名] shelter

掩藏 yǎncáng [动] hide (PT hid, PP hidden)

掩耳盗铃 yǎn ěr dào líng bury one's head in the sand

掩盖 yǎngài [动] 1 (遮盖) cover 2 (隐藏) conceal ▷陷阱用树枝掩盖起来。The trap is covered with tree branches.

掩护 yǎnhù I [动] cover for II [名] cover

掩埋 yǎnmái [动] bury

掩饰 yǎnshì [动] conceal

眼 yǎn I [名] 1 (眼睛) eye 2 (小洞) small hole 3 (关键) crux II [量] ▷村里打了两眼井。Two wells were dug in the village.

眼巴巴 yǎnbābā [形] 1 (形容急切盼望) eager ▷孩子们眼巴巴地盼着过年。The children were eagerly awaiting the New Year. 2 (形容无可奈何) helpless ▷他眼巴巴地看着自己的家被大火吞噬。He watched helplessly as he saw his house being engulfed by flames.

眼馋 yǎnchán [动] covet

眼福 yǎnfú [名] a feast for the eyes

眼高手低 yǎn gāo shǒu dī have great ambition but little talent

眼光 yǎnguāng [名] 1 (视线) gaze 2 (观察能力) vision ▷在选拔人才方面，他非常有眼光。He has real vision when it comes to promoting talent. 3 (观点) perspective ▷你不能用老眼光来评价现在的年轻人。You can't apply outdated perspectives when criticizing today's youth.

眼红 yǎnhóng I [动] be jealous II [形] furious

眼睑 yǎnjiǎn [名] eyelid

眼界 yǎnjiè [名] horizons (PL) ▷读书能扩大眼界。Reading can broaden your horizons.

眼睛 yǎnjing [名] eye ▷她的眼睛里涌出了喜悦的泪花。Tears of joy welled up in her eyes.

眼看 yǎnkàn I [动] 1 (指正在发生) look on ▷她眼看着信被风吹跑了。She looked on as the letter got blown away by the wind. 2 (任凭) allow II [副] soon ▷眼看着就到秋天了。Soon it'll be autumn.

眼泪 yǎnlèi [名] tear

眼力 yǎnlì [名] 1 (视力) eyesight 2 (鉴别能力) judgement ▷你真有眼力，买了能升值的房子。You've obviously got good judgement, buying property that's likely to go up in value.

眼色 yǎnsè [名] look ▷怕我说漏了，她赶紧给我使眼色。She shot me a look, worried that I might give the game away.

眼神 yǎnshén [名] 1 (指神态) expression 2 (方) (视力) eyesight

眼生 yǎnshēng [形] unfamiliar ▷我看她有点眼生。She doesn't look particularly familiar.

眼熟 yǎnshú [形] familiar

眼下 yǎnxià [名] ▷眼下正是大学生毕业找工作的时候。Now is the time when university graduates start looking for work.

眼睁睁 yǎnzhēngzhēng [形] helpless ▷别眼睁睁地看着他受罪。Don't just stand there watching him suffer.

眼中钉 yǎnzhōngdīng [名] thorn in one's side

偃 yǎn [动] (书) lay ... down (PT, PP laid)

偃旗息鼓 yǎn qí xī gǔ lay down one's arms

演 yǎn [动] 1 (演变) evolve 2 (发挥) bring ... into play (PT, PP brought) 3 (依照程序) follow a routine 4 (表演) perform

演变 yǎnbiàn [动] evolve

演出 yǎnchū [动] perform

演化 yǎnhuà [动] evolve

演讲 yǎnjiǎng [动] make a speech

演示 yǎnshì [动] demonstrate

演说 yǎnshuō [动] make a speech

演算 yǎnsuàn [动] work ... out ▷数学课上，老师让我们演算了10道题。In the maths class the teacher made us work out ten problems.

演习 yǎnxí [动] manoeuvre (英), maneuver (美)

演义 yǎnyì [名] historical novel

演绎 yǎnyì [名] deduction

演员 yǎnyuán [名] performer

演奏 yǎnzòu [动] perform ▷这位音乐大师演奏得非常美妙。This great musician gave an exquisite performance.

鼹 yǎn [名] mole

鼹鼠 yǎnshǔ [名] mole

厌 yàn [动] 1 (满足) be satisfied 2 (厌烦) be fed up with 3 (厌恶) detest

厌烦 yànfán [动] be sick of ▷他老打扰我，很让人厌烦。He keeps disturbing me – I'm sick of it.

厌倦 yànjuàn [动] be weary of

厌世 yànshì [动] be world-weary

厌恶 yànwù [动] loathe

砚 yàn [名] ink stone

砚台 yàntai [名] ink stone

咽 yàn [动] 1 (吞咽) swallow ▷5片药他一口就咽了下去。He swallowed down five tablets in one go. 2 (憋住) hold back (PT, PP held) →另见 yān

咽气 yànqì [动] (死) die

宴 yàn [动] host a dinner

宴会 yànhuì [名] banquet ▷他们举行宴会欢迎国际友人。They held a banquet to welcome their friends from overseas.

宴请 yànqǐng [动] invite ... to dinner ▷公司宴请了10位贵宾。The company held a dinner for ten important guests.

艳 yàn I [形] 1 (华丽) gorgeous 2 (指情爱) romantic II [动] (书) envy

艳福 yànfú [名] luck in love ▷公司最漂亮女孩儿爱上了他，真是艳福不浅呢！The prettiest girl in the office has fallen for him: he's certainly not short of luck!

艳丽 yànlì [形] gorgeous

唁 yàn [动] extend condolences ▶吊唁 offer one's condolences

唁电 yàndiàn [名] condolences (PL)

验 yàn I [动] 1 (检查) test 2 (灵验) produce the expected result II [名] result

验光 yànguāng [动] have an eye test ▷配眼镜前要先验光。Before you get new glasses you should have your eyes tested.

验尸 yànshī [动] perform an autopsy

验收 yànshōu [动] accept ... after checking

验算 yànsuàn [动] check one's calculations

验血 yànxiě [动] have a blood test

验证 yànzhèng [动] verify

谚 yàn [名] saying

谚语 yànyǔ [名] proverb

雁 yàn [名] wild goose (PL geese)

焰 yàn [名] 1 (火苗) flame 2 (喻) (气势) momentum

焰火 yànhuǒ [名] firework

燕 yàn [名] swallow

燕麦 yànmài [名] oats (PL)

燕尾服 yànwěifú [名] tailcoat

燕窝 yànwō [名] edible bird's nest

赝 yàn [形] (书) forged

赝本 yànběn [名] forgery

赝品 yànpǐn [名] fake

央 yāng I [动] plead ▷孩子央了半天，母亲才答应。The child pleaded with his mother for ages before she agreed. II [名] centre (英), center (美)

央告 yānggao [动] beg

央求 yāngqiú [动] plead

秧 yāng [名] 1 (幼苗) seedling 2 (茎) stem 3 (稻秧) rice seedling

扬 yáng I [动] 1 (高举) raise 2 (传播) spread (PT, PP spread) II [形] good-looking

扬长避短 yáng cháng bì duǎn play to one's strengths ▷在用人上要注意扬长避短。When managing people you should get them to play to their strengths.

扬长而去 yángcháng ér qù storm out ▷他把杯子摔在地上，然后扬长而去。He threw his cup onto the floor, and stormed out.

扬帆 yángfān [动] (书) set sail (PT, PP set)

扬眉吐气 yáng méi tǔ qì hold one's head up high

扬名 yángmíng [动] become famous (PT became, PP become)

扬弃 yángqì [动] (抛弃) discard

扬言 yángyán [动] (贬) spread it about (PT, PP spread) ▷他扬言要打断陶陶的腿。He was spreading it about that he was going to break Taotao's legs.

扬扬 yángyáng [形] complacent

羊 yáng [名] sheep (PL sheep) ▶山羊 goat

羊肠小道 yángcháng xiǎodào [名] narrow, winding road

羊毛 yángmáo [名] wool

羊绒衫 yángróngshān [名] cashmere

阳 yáng I [名] 1 (阴的对立面) Yang (of Yin and Yang) 2 (太阳) sun II [形] 1 (突出) protruding 2 (外露) overt 3 (带正电) positive

阳春 yángchūn [名] springtime

阳奉阴违 yáng fèng yīn wéi pretend to

obey orders ▷他阳奉阴违，最后被免了职。He pretended to obey orders without actually executing them, and in the end he was dismissed.

阳刚 yánggāng [形] masculine

阳历 yánglì [名] the Gregorian calendar

阳台 yángtái [名] balcony

阳性 yángxìng [名] **1** (医) positive **2** (语言) masculine

杨 yáng [名] poplar

杨柳 yángliǔ [名] **1** (杨树和柳树) poplars and willows (PL) **2** (柳树) willow

佯 yáng [动] feign

佯装 yángzhuāng [动] pretend

洋 yáng **I** [名] **1** (海洋) ocean **2** (洋钱) silver dollar **II** [形] **1** (盛大) vast **2** (外国的) foreign

洋白菜 yángbáicài [名] cabbage

洋葱 yángcōng [名] onion

洋货 yánghuò [名] foreign goods (PL)

洋气 yángqì [形] **1** (指有西方味的) Western **2** (贬) (时髦的) trendy

洋相 yángxiàng [名] spectacle ▷今天他在全班同学面前出了个大洋相。Today he made a real spectacle of himself in front of all his classmates.

洋洋 yángyáng [形] **1** (盛大) copious **2** (得意) smug

洋溢 yángyì [动] brim with

仰 yǎng [动] **1** (脸向上) look up **2** (敬慕) respect **3** (依赖) depend on

仰慕 yǎngmù [动] look up to

仰望 yǎngwàng [动] look up

仰仗 yǎngzhàng [动] depend on

养 yǎng **I** [动] **1** (供给) provide for **2** (饲养) keep (PT, PP kept) ▷她总爱养很多狗。She's always kept lots of dogs. ▷我爱养花。I like growing flowers. **3** (生育) give birth to (PT gave, PP given) **4** (培养) form ▷他养成了早睡早起的习惯。He had formed the habit of going to bed early and getting up early. **5** (调养) recuperate **6** (维修) maintain **7** (扶助) support **8** (保持) look after ▷你的头发太干，需要好好养养。Your hair's too dry – you need to look after it a bit. **II** [形] foster ▶养母 foster-mother ▶养子 adopted son **III** [名] cultivation

养分 yǎngfèn [名] nutrient

养护 yǎnghù [动] **1** (指物体) maintain **2** (指人体) build up one's strength (PT, PP built)

养活 yǎnghuo [动] (口) **1** (提供生活费用) support **2** (饲养) raise **3** (生育抚养) give birth to (PT gave, PP given)

养精蓄锐 yǎng jīng xù ruì conserve one's strength

养老 yǎnglǎo [动] **1** (奉养老人) care for the elderly **2** (年老休养) enjoy one's old age

养料 yǎngliào [名] nourishment

养生 yǎngshēng [动] keep fit (PT, PP kept)

养育 yǎngyù [动] bring up (PT, PP brought)

养殖 yǎngzhí [动] breed (PT, PP bred)

养尊处优 yǎng zūn chǔ yōu live a life of luxury

氧 yǎng [名] oxygen

氧化 yǎnghuà [动] oxidize

痒 yǎng [动] itch ▷他全身痒得难受。His whole body is horribly itchy. ▷见别人出国旅游，她心里也有点痒了。Seeing others travelling abroad gave her itchy feet. ▷他心里痒痒的，想马上就开始该项目。He's itching to get started on the project.

样 yàng **I** [名] **1** (模样) style **2** (标准物) sample **II** [量] type ▷她带了3样水果。She brought three types of fruit. ▷我每样菜都尝了尝。I've tasted every single dish.

样板 yàngbǎn [名] **1** (板状样品) sample **2** (板状工具) template **3** (榜样) model

样本 yàngběn [名] **1** (指商品图样) book of samples **2** (指出版物) proofs (PL)

样品 yàngpǐn [名] sample

样式 yàngshì [名] style

样子 yàngzi [名] **1** (模样) appearance ▷这个手机样子不错。This mobile phone looks good. **2** (神情) expression **3** (样板) pattern **4** (口) (情形) the look of things ▷看样子他不来了。By the look of things, he's not coming.

漾 yàng [动] **1** (水面微动) ripple **2** (向外流) overflow

幺 yāo **I** [数] one **II** [形] youngest

夭 yāo [动] die young

夭折 yāozhé [动] **1** (未成年而死) die young **2** (喻) (形容停止) come to an untimely end (PT came, PP come)

吆 yāo 见下文

吆喝 yāohe [动] call out

妖 yāo I [名] evil spirit II [形] 1 (邪恶) wicked 2 (书) (妖艳) bewitching

妖怪 yāoguài [名] monster

妖精 yāojing [名] 1 (妖怪) demon 2 (喻) scarlet woman (PL women)

妖媚 yāomèi [形] seductive

妖魔 yāomó [名] monster

妖艳 yāoyàn [形] coquettish

要 yāo [动] 1 (求) ask 2 (威胁) threaten 3 (邀请) invite
→另见 yào

要求 yāoqiú I [动] demand ▷工人们要求改善工作环境。The workers demanded improvements to their working environment. ▷要求加薪 request a pay rise II [名] request ▷航空公司满足了乘客的要求。The airline company satisfied all the passengers' requests. ▷老师的要求非常严格。The teacher's demands are very severe. ▷这些要求很难达到。These requirements are going to be difficult to meet.

要挟 yāoxié [动] threaten

腰 yāo [名] 1 (身体中部) waist ▷她疼得直不起腰来。She was in so much pain that she couldn't stand up straight. 2 (裤腰) waist ▷这条裙子腰太肥。This skirt's too big at the waist. 3 (腰包) wallet 4 (事物中段) middle

腰板儿 yāobǎnr [名] 1 (腰和背) back 2 (口) (体格) health ▷她80岁了，腰板儿还挺硬朗。She's eighty years old, but still in excellent health.

腰包 yāobāo [名] wallet

腰带 yāodài [名] belt

腰杆子 yāogǎnzi [名] 1 (口) (腰部) back 2 (靠山) backing ▷他腰杆子硬，当然什么都不怕啦！He's got very secure backing – of course he doesn't have much to fear!

腰果 yāoguǒ [名] cashew nut

腰围 yāowéi [名] waistline

腰子 yāozi [名] kidney

邀 yāo [动] 1 (邀请) invite 2 (书) (求得) seek (PT, PP sought)

邀功 yāogōng [动] take all the credit (PT took, PP taken)

邀集 yāojí [动] invite ... to a get-together ▷他经常邀集一些朋友。He often invites friends to get-togethers.

邀请 yāoqǐng [动] invite ▷她愉快地接受了邀请。She accepted the invitation readily.

肴 yáo [名] meat dishes (PL) ▷美味佳肴 delectable dishes

窑 yáo [名] 1 (用于烧砖) kiln 2 (指煤矿) pit 3 (窑洞) cave dwelling 4 (指妓院) brothel

窑洞 yáodòng [名] cave dwelling

窑子 yáozi [名] brothel

谣 yáo [名] 1 (歌谣) folk song 2 (谣言) rumour (英), rumor (美)

谣传 yáochuán I [动] be rumoured (英), rumored (美) ▷谣传罗素破产了。Rumour has it that Russell has gone bankrupt. II [名] rumour (英), rumor (美)

谣言 yáoyán [名] hearsay

摇 yáo [动] shake (PT shook, PP shaken)

摇摆 yáobǎi [动] wave

摇荡 yáodàng [动] sway

摇动 yáodòng [动] 1 (摇东西) wave 2 (晃) shake (PT shook, PP shaken)

摇滚乐 yáogǔnyuè [名] rock and roll

摇晃 yáohuàng [动] shake (PT, shook PP shaken) ▷他太醉了，走路都摇晃。He was so drunk that he was staggering around.

摇奖 yáojiǎng [动] hold a draw (PT, PP held)

摇篮 yáolán [名] cradle ▷尼罗河流域是古埃及文明的摇篮。The River Nile was the cradle of ancient Egyptian civilization.

摇旗呐喊 yáo qí nàhǎn bang the drum ▷球迷为足球队摇旗呐喊。The football fans banged the drum for their team.

摇钱树 yáoqiánshù [名] source of easy money

摇摇欲坠 yáoyáo yù zhuì hang by a thread ▷他的明星地位摇摇欲坠。His celebrity status hung by a thread. ▷这座老桥摇摇欲坠。This old bridge is on the verge of collapse.

摇曳 yáoyè [动] sway

遥 yáo [形] distant

遥感 yáogǎn [名] remote sensing

遥控 yáokòng [动] operate by remote control

遥望 yáowàng [动] gaze into the distance

遥遥 yáoyáo [形] 1 (指距离) distant 2 (指时间) lengthy

遥远 yáoyuǎn [形] 1 (指距离) distant 2 (指时间) far-off ▷遥远的将来 the far-off future

杳 yáo [形] (书) far away and out of sight

杳无音信 yǎo wú yīnxìn never heard from again ▷他20年前去了海外，至今杳无音

信。He went overseas twenty years ago, and he hasn't been heard of since.

咬 yǎo [动] 1 (指用嘴) bite (PT bit, PP bitten) 2 (夹住) grip ▷这个钳子太小，咬不住。These pliers are too small – I can't get a grip. 3 (牵扯) incriminate 4 (过分钻研) nit-pick 5 (紧追) be neck and neck

咬耳朵 yǎo ěrduo [动] (口) whisper

咬文嚼字 yǎo wén jiáo zì pay excessive attention to wording ▷咬文嚼字未必能写出好文章。Paying excessive attention to wording doesn't necessarily produce a good essay.

咬牙 yǎoyá [动] 1 (咬紧牙关) clench one's teeth 2 (磨牙) grind one's teeth (PT, PP ground)

舀 yǎo [动] ladle

舀子 yǎozi [名] ladle

窈 yǎo 见下文

窈窕 yǎotiǎo [形] (书) gentle and beautiful

药 yào I [名] 1 (指治病) medicine 2 (指化学物品) chemical II [动] 1 (书) (治疗) cure 2 (毒死) poison

药补 yàobǔ [名] drug therapy ▷药补和食补相结合对她恢复健康有好处。A combination of drug therapy and diet will help her recovery.

药材 yàocái [名] herbal medicine

药方 yàofāng [名] prescription ▷医生给我开了一张药方。The doctor wrote me out a prescription.

药理 yàolǐ [名] pharmacology

药力 yàolì [名] effects (PL)

药品 yàopǐn [名] medicine

药物 yàowù [名] medicine

药性 yàoxìng [名] medicinal properties (PL)

药学 yàoxué [名] pharmacology

要 yào I [形] important II [名] main issue III [动] 1 (想得到) want ▷我女儿要一个新书包。My daughter wants a new schoolbag. 2 (要求) ask ▷老师要我们安静。The teacher asked us to be quiet. IV [助动] 1 (应该) should ▷饭前要洗手。You should wash your hands before you eat. 2 (需要) need ▷我要上厕所。I need the toilet. ▷这台风扇要多少钱？How much is this fan? 3 (表示意志) want ▷我要学开车。I want to drive. 4 (将要) be about to ▷我们要放暑假了。We're about to break for summer vacation. 5 (用于比较) ▷姐姐比妹妹要高些。The elder sister is taller than the younger. ▷她要挣得比你多点。She earns a

bit more than you. V [连] 1 (如果) if ▷你要碰见他，替我问声好。If you meet him, say hello from me. 2 (要么) either ... or ▷要就同意，要就不同意，别模棱两可。Either you agree or you disagree – don't sit on the fence.

→ 另见 yāo

要案 yào'àn [名] major case

要不 yàobù [连] 1 (否则) otherwise ▷快点走，要不你要迟到了。Go quickly, otherwise you'll be late. 2 (表示选择) either ... or ▷我们要不去看电影，要不去咖啡厅，你说呢？We can either go to see a film or go to a coffee shop – which would you prefer?

要点 yàodiǎn [名] rudiments (PL)

要犯 yàofàn [名] main offender

要害 yàohài [名] 1 (指身体) vulnerable spot 2 (军事要地) strategic point 3 (关键) key part

要好 yàohǎo [形] 1 (感情融洽) amicable 2 (上进) eager to improve ▷你的房间总是乱糟糟的，怎么一点也不要好？Your room's always such a tip – don't you care about making it any better?

要紧 yàojǐn [形] 1 (重要) important 2 (严重) serious

要领 yàolǐng [名] 1 (要点) gist 2 (基本要求) main points (PL)

要么 yàome [连] either ... or ▷你要么学文，要么学理。You either study arts or science.

要命 yàomìng [动] 1 (使丧生) kill 2 (表示程度) be incredibly ▷这个人吝啬得要命。This man's incredibly stingy. 3 (表示抱怨) be dreadful ▷这个饭馆真要命，上菜得一个小时。This is a truly dreadful restaurant – it's taken them an hour to bring our food.

要强 yàoqiáng [形] competitive ▷她在工作上非常要强。She's very competitive at work.

要是 yàoshi [连] if ▷要是你不满意，可以随时退货。If you're not satisfied, you can return the goods at any time.

要死 yàosǐ [副] extremely ▷昨天我忙得要死。I was extremely busy yesterday.

要素 yàosù [名] key element

要职 yàozhí [名] important post

钥 yào 见下文

钥匙 yàoshi [名] key

耀 yào I [名] radiance II [动] 1 (照射) shine (PT, PP shone) 2 (炫耀) boast of III [形] brilliant

耀武扬威 yào wǔ yáng wēi flaunt one's power

耀眼 yàoyǎn [形] dazzling

耶 yē 见下文
耶稣 Yēsū [名] Jesus

掖 yē [动] tuck ▷他把信掖在了裤兜里。He tucked the letter into his trouser pocket.

椰 yē [名] coconut
椰子 yēzi [名] 1 (树) coconut tree 2 (果实) coconut

噎 yē [动] 1 (堵塞) choke ▷我吃鱼时噎住了。I choked on the fish. 2 (方) (话) reduce ... to silence

爷 yé [名] 1 (祖父) grandfather 2 (方) (父亲) dad 3 (长辈) uncle 4 (旧) (显贵) master 5 (指神、佛) god
爷爷 yéye [名] 1 (口) (祖父) granddad 2 (祖父的同辈人) ▷李爷爷常来我家下棋。Old Mr Li often comes to my house to play chess.

也 yě [副] 1 (同样) also ▷我也是名律师。I'm also a lawyer. ▷他也去过中国。He's been to China too. 2 (表示对等) ▷这条街上有中餐馆，也有西餐馆。There are Chinese restaurants on this street as well as Western restaurants. ▷他特别聪明，也很能干。He's highly intelligent, and also very competent. 3 (表示结果) ▷这道题太难，怎么想也想不出来。This question is too difficult – I just can't figure it out. ▷他太固执，谁劝也不听。He's very stubborn – he never listens to anyone who tries to give him advice. 4 (表示转折) ▷即使他来了，也帮不上忙。Even if he comes, it still won't be of any use. ▷虽然她心里不高兴，也没说什么。Although she was unhappy, she didn't say anything. 5 (表示委婉) ▷这个电影倒也不错。This film really isn't at all bad. 6 (表示强调) ▷她病了，一口饭也不想吃。She's ill – she doesn't want to eat anything at all.
也罢 yěbà [助] 1 (表示容忍) ▷也罢，我们就不等他了。All right then, we won't wait for him. 2 (表示条件) ▷你高兴也罢，不高兴也罢，反正就这样定了。We've settled the matter anyway, whether you like it or not.
也许 yěxǔ [副] perhaps ▷他还没到，也许是没赶上车。He's still not arrived – perhaps he missed the bus.

冶 yě [动] smelt ▷冶铁 smelt iron
冶炼 yěliàn [动] smelt

野 yě I [名] 1 (野外) open country ▷野餐 picnic 2 (界限) border ▷分野 dividing line 3 (民间) ▷在野 out of power II [形] 1 (野生) wild ▷野菜 wild herbs 2 (蛮横) rude ▷粗野 rough 3 (无约束) unruly
野餐 yěcān [动] have a picnic ▷周末我们去山上野餐吧！Let's go for a picnic in the mountains this weekend!
野鸡 yějī [名] 1 (雉) pheasant 2 (妓女) prostitute
野蛮 yěmán [形] 1 (蒙昧) uncivilized 2 (残暴) brutal
野生 yěshēng [形] wild
野兽 yěshòu [名] wild animal
野外 yěwài [名] open country
野味 yěwèi [名] game
野心 yěxīn [名] ambition
野性 yěxìng [名] wild nature
野营 yěyíng [名] camp

业 yè I [名] 1 (行业) industry ▷饮食业 the food and drink industry 2 (职业) job ▷就业 obtain employment ▷失业 be unemployed 3 (学业) studies (PL) ▷结业 finish one's studies ▷毕业 graduate 4 (事业) enterprise ▷功业 achievement 5 (产业) property ▷家业 family property II [副] already ▷业已 already
业绩 yèjì [名] achievement
业务 yèwù [名] profession ▷这些年轻人业务能力很强。These young people are very professional. ▷公司经常组织业务学习活动。The company often organizes professional training sessions.
业余 yèyú I [名] spare time ▷业余爱好 hobby II [形] amateurish
业主 yèzhǔ [名] owner

叶 yè [名] 1 (叶子) leaf (PL leaves) ▷叶脉 vein 2 (时期) period ▷明朝中叶 the mid-Ming period
叶落归根 yè luò guī gēn return to one's roots

页 yè I [名] page ▷活页笔记本 loose-leaf notebook II [量] page ▷这本书被撕掉了一页。A page has been torn out of this book. ▷翻开了人生新的一页 turn over a new leaf
页码 yèmǎ [名] page number

曳 yè [动] drag ▷拖曳 haul

夜 yè [名] night
夜班 yèbān [名] night shift
夜半 yèbàn [名] midnight
夜不闭户 yè bù bì hù leave one's door unlocked at night
夜长梦多 yè cháng mèng duō long delays

cause complications ▷我们争取尽早签合同，免得夜长梦多。We'll do our best to sign the contract as soon as possible, to avoid the problems that may be incurred by a delay.

夜景 yèjǐng [名] night view ▷西湖夜景，美丽迷人。The view of the West Lake by night is absolutely enchanting.

夜郎自大 Yèláng zìdà be foolishly conceited

夜猫子 yèmāozi [名] (方) 1 (猫头鹰) owl 2 (喻) (晚睡者) night owl

夜幕 yèmù [名] night

夜生活 yèshēnghuó [名] nightlife

夜市 yèshì [名] night market

夜宵 yèxiāo [名] late-night snack

夜以继日 yè yǐ jì rì day and night ▷加固堤坝的工程夜以继日地进行着。Work on reinforcing the dam continued day and night.

夜总会 yèzǒnghuì [名] nightclub

液 yè [名] liquid

液化 yèhuà [动] liquefy

液态 yètài [名] liquid

液体 yètǐ [名] liquid

腋 yè [名] (夹肢窝) armpit ▷腋毛 underarm hair

一 yī [数] 1 (指数目) one ▷一分钟 one minute 2 (相同) ▷他们是一类人。They are the same sort of people. ▷大家观点不一。Everyone has different opinions. 3 (另一) ▷传呼机一名寻呼机。Pager is another name for a beeper. 4 (全) ▷一屋子烟 full of smoke 5 (专) ▷一心一意 heart and soul 6 (表示短暂) ▷看一看 take a look 7 (与 '就' 连用) ▷我一碰杯子，它就掉地上了。I barely touched the glass, and it fell to the floor.

一把手 yī bǎ shǒu [名] 1 (一员) member 2 (能手) skilled worker 3 (负责人) boss

一败涂地 yī bài tú dì come a cropper

一般 yībān [形] 1 (一样) same ▷他们俩一般大。The two of them are the same age. 2 (普通) ordinary ▷他很不一般，工作非常出色。He is quite out of the ordinary, and his work is exceptional.

一板一眼 yī bǎn yī yǎn meticulous

一⋯半⋯ yī⋯bàn⋯ [数] ▷我看她的病一时半会儿好不了。It seems to me that she's not going to get well for a while. ▷这个问题不是一句半句能讲清楚的。This can't be explained in a few sentences.

一本正经 yī běn zhèng jīng be prim and proper

一边 yībiān I [名] 1 (一面) side ▷镜子的另一边是水银。There is mercury on the other side of this mirror. ▷今天的辩论，你认为哪一边更强？Which do you think was the strongest side in today's debate? 2 (旁边) ▷你过来帮帮忙，别在一边呆着。Come over and help－don't just hang around on the sidelines. II [副] at the same time ▷她吃着晚饭，一边还看着电视。She was eating and watching television at the same time.

一边倒 yī biān dǎo [动] predominate

一并 yībìng [副] together

一⋯不⋯ yī⋯bù⋯ [副] 1 (用于两动词之间) ▷他离家出走后一去不返。He left home, never to return. 2 (用于一名一动之间) ▷大厅明亮宽敞，一尘不染。The great hall was bright and spacious－and spotless.

一不做，二不休 yī bù zuò, èr bù xiū go the whole hog

一步登天 yī bù dēng tiān have a meteoric rise

一刹那 yīchànà [名] instant

一唱一和 yī chàng yī hè sing the same tune

一成不变 yī chéng bù biàn immutable

一筹莫展 yī chóu mò zhǎn be at one's wits end

一锤定音 yī chuí dìng yīn settle ... there and then

一蹴而就 yī cù ér jiù accomplish at one stroke

一带 yīdài [名] region

一旦 yīdàn I [名] single day ▷这座城堡竟然在一次大火中毁于一旦。The great fire destroyed this castle in a single day. II [副] ▷一旦发生核战争，整个地球将会陷入灾难。If atomic war were to break out, it would be disastrous for the whole world.

一刀切 yīdāoqiē [动] take a sweeping approach (PT took, PP taken)

一道 yīdào [副] together

一点 yīdiǎn [量] 1 (一些) some ▷你行李太多，我帮你提一点儿吧。You've got so much luggage－let me help you with some of it. 2 (很少) a little ▷我兜里就剩一点儿钱了。There's a little money left in my pocket. ▷这件事我一点儿都不知道。I know nothing about this.

一定 yīdìng I [形] 1 (规定的) definite 2 (固定的) fixed ▷她在城里做小时工，没有一定的收入和住所。She did casual work in the city, but had no fixed income or address. 3 (相当) certain ▷生活条件有了一定的改善。There has been a certain improvement in living conditions. 4 (特定) given ▷在一定条件下 under given circumstances II [副] definitely ▷放心，我一定去机场接你。Don't worry, I'll definitely pick you up at the airport.

一⋯⋯而⋯⋯ yī⋯ér⋯ [连] ... in one ... ▷满满一杯酒，他一饮而尽。The glass was full to overflowing, but he drank it down in one gulp. ▷看到警察来了，围观的人们一哄而散。On seeing the police arrive, the people who had gathered to watch scattered.

一发 yīfā [副] 1 (更加) even more ▷如不抓紧处理，局面将一发不可收拾。If we don't deal with the matter quickly, the situation will become even more unmanageable. 2 (一并) together ▷这件事情，明天会上和其他事情一发讨论。We'll deal with this matter together with other issues at the meeting tomorrow.

一发千钧 yī fà qiān jūn in imminent danger

一帆风顺 yī fān fēng shùn plain sailing

一概 yīgài [副] without exception

一共 yīgòng [副] altogether ▷参加晚会的一共有27个人。There were 27 people at the party altogether. ▷这套书一共多少本？How many books are there in this set?

一鼓作气 yī gǔ zuò qì make a push for it

一贯 yīguàn [形] consistent

一挥而就 yīhuī'érjiù dash ... off

一己 yǐjǐ [名] oneself

一见如故 yī jiàn rú gù hit it off at once

一见钟情 yī jiàn zhōng qíng love at first sight ▷爱情小说中，男女主人公常常是一见钟情。In romantic fiction, the hero and heroine often fall in love at first sight.

一箭双雕 yī jiàn shuāng diāo kill two birds with one stone

一经 yījīng [副] as soon as ▷决议一经通过，就立即执行。The resolution must be implemented as soon as it's passed.

一⋯⋯就⋯⋯ yī⋯jiù⋯ [副] as soon as ▷他一看书就打盹儿。As soon as he started reading he fell asleep.

一举 yìjǔ I [名] one action II [副] at one stroke

一蹶不振 yī jué bù zhèn be unable to recover after a setback

一览 yīlǎn [名] overview

一劳永逸 yī láo yǒng yì get things right once and for all

一连 yīlián [副] on end ▷一连下了几个月的雨。It's been raining for months on end.

一了百了 yī liǎo bǎi liǎo find a single solution ▷事情错综复杂，很难找到一个一了百了的解决办法。Matters are very complex. It's very difficult to find a single solution to all problems.

一路 yīlù I [名] 1 (行程) journey ▷一路顺利吗？Did you have a good journey? 2 (一类) a kind ▷他们俩一路货色。They are two of a kind. 3 (一起) the same way ▷明天出差，咱俩是一路。When we go on business tomorrow, we're going the same way. II [副] all the way ▷那辆红色赛车一路领先。That red racing car was in the lead all the way.

一律 yīlǜ I [形] same II [副] without exception

一马当先 yī mǎ dāng xiān take the lead

一脉相承 yī mài xiāng chéng share the same origins

一毛不拔 yī máo bù bá be very stingy ▷有些人缠绵万贯，对他人却一毛不拔。Some people have bags of money, but they're very stingy with other people.

一面 yī miàn I [名] side ▷这个规定也有合理的一面。This rule has its reasonable side. II [副] at the same time ▷她一面听音乐，一面看小说。She was listening to music and reading a novel at the same time.

一鸣惊人 yī míng jīng rén set the world on fire

一目了然 yī mù liǎo rán be clear at a glance

一诺千金 yī nuò qiān jīn one's word is one's bond

一瞥 yīpiē [动] glance

一齐 yīqí [副] simultaneously

一起 yīqǐ I [名] the same place II [副] together

一气呵成 yī qì hē chéng go without a hitch

一窍不通 yī qiào bù tōng not know the first thing about

一切 yīqiè [代] 1 (全部) all ▷承担一切责任 take full responsibility ▷消除一切困难 eliminate all difficulties 2 (全部事物) everything ▷那里的一切，她都记得很清楚。She remembers everything about the place very clearly.

一日千里 yī rì qiān lǐ at a tremendous pace ▷人类在科学技术方面的进步一日千里。Humanity has made tremendous progress in science and technology.

一日三秋 yī rì sān qiū days creep by like years

一如 yīrú [动] be just like ▷这里污染严重、环境恶劣，一如所闻。It's heavily polluted here – it's just like people say it is.

一身 yīshēn [名] 1 (全身) ▷水洒了他一身。The water splashed all over him. 2 (一人) ▷她独自一身去国外求学。She went abroad to study all on her own.

一时 yīshí I [名] 1 (一个时期) time 2 (短暂时间) moment II [副] 1 (临时) for the moment ▷书名我一时想不起来了。I can't think of the book title for the moment. 2 (时而) sometimes

一视同仁 yī shì tóng rén treat everyone the

same

一手 yīshǒu I [名] 1 (本领) skill 2 (贬)(手段) trick ▷你这一手骗不了我。You can't fool me with that trick. II [副] single-handedly

一手遮天 yī shǒu zhē tiān engage in a cover-up

一丝不苟 yī sī bù gǒu be meticulous ▷她对教学工作一丝不苟。She's meticulous in her teaching work.

一体 yītǐ [名] whole ▷全球经济一体化 the unification of the global economy

一同 yītóng [副] together

一团和气 yī tuán héqì keep on good terms

一网打尽 yī wǎng dǎ jìn round ... up in one fell swoop

一往情深 yī wǎng qíng shēn be devoted to

一味 yīwèi [副] blindly

一文不名 yī wén bù míng be penniless

一窝蜂 yīwōfēng [副](口) ▷人们一窝蜂地跑过去看热闹。People came swarming over to see the fun.

一无所有 yī wú suǒ yǒu not have a penny to one's name

一五一十 yī wǔ yī shí every last detail ▷她把事情的经过一五一十地告诉了我。She told me every last detail of the events.

一下 yīxià I [量] ▷我去问一下儿。I'll just go and ask. ▷请大家自我介绍一下儿。I'd like everybody to introduce themselves. ▷这件事我们还得商量一下儿。We still need to discuss this. II [副] at once ▷天一下儿就冷了。All at once the weather turned cold.

一线 yīxiàn I [名] the front line ▷他一直在科研第一线工作。He's always worked on the front line of scientific research. II [形] ▷一线阳光 a ray of sunlight ▷一线希望 a ray of hope

一相情愿 yī xiāng qíngyuàn wishful thinking

一向 yīxiàng [副] always ▷他做事一向拖拖拉拉。Whatever he does he always drags his feet.

一些 yīxiē [量] 1 (部分) some ▷这项工作让他也分担一些吧。Let him take responsibility for some of this work. 2 (几个) a few ▷别的都卖了，只剩这一些了。All the others have been sold – there are only these few left. ▷他曾游历过一些名山大川。He has visited several famous scenic spots. 3 (略微) a little ▷她感觉好一些了。She feels a little better.

一心 yīxīn I [形] united II [副] wholeheartedly

一行 yīxíng [名] group

一言既出，驷马难追 yī yán jì chū, sì mǎ nán zhuī what's said can't be unsaid

一言以蔽之 yī yán yǐ bì zhī in short ▷一言

以蔽之，任何一种改革都必须从实际出发。In short, any kind of reform must have a basis in reality.

一样 yīyàng [形] same ▷他俩爱好一样。They have the same hobbies. ▷两个人成绩一样好。Their results are equally good. ▷姐俩性格完全不一样。The sisters' personalities are completely different. ▷这位老人的头发像雪一样白。The old man's hair is as white as snow.

一叶知秋 yī yè zhī qiū a straw in the wind

一一 yīyī [副] in turn ▷对记者提出的问题，他一一做了回答。He replied to each of the journalist's questions in turn.

一…一… yī…yī… 1 (表示整个) ▷希望我们能一生一世在一起。I hope we will be able to spend our whole lives together. 2 (表示量少) ▷即使一分一秒她也舍不得浪费。She didn't want to waste even a second. 3 (表示对比) ▷这里多数家庭是一夫一妻，而不是一夫多妻。Most households here consist of one husband and one wife, and not one husband and several wives. 4 (表示连续) ▷他一瘸一拐地离开了足球场。He limped off the field. ▷小船一上一下地颠簸着。The little boat bobbed up and down. 5 (表示交替) ▷他俩一问一答，配合密切。Their question and answering was very tight. ▶一张一弛 alternately tense and relaxed 6 (表示对应) ▷姐妹俩一左一右挽扶着母亲。The two sisters supported their mother, one on the right and one on the left.

一衣带水 yī yī dài shuǐ be separated by a narrow strip of water

一意孤行 yī yì gū xíng go one's own way

一应 yīyīng [代] everything

一再 yīzài [副] repeatedly ▷他们一再要求改善待遇。They repeatedly demanded an improvement in their treatment.

一朝一夕 yī zhāo yī xī overnight

一针见血 yī zhēn jiàn xiě be spot on

一知半解 yī zhī bàn jiě have a smattering of knowledge

一直 yīzhí [副] 1 (不变向) straight ▷一直走到十字路口，再向右拐。Go straight ahead to the crossroads, then turn right. ▷顺着这条大街一直走500米就到了。Follow this avenue for five hundred metres and you'll be there. 2 (不间断) always ▷这个牌子的电视一直很受欢迎。This brand of TV has always been very popular. ▷大风一直刮了两天两夜。The gale blew for two days and two nights. 3 (指一定范围) all the way ▷从最北一直到最南，这股寒流袭击了整个国家。The cold current hit the country from the north all the way to the south. ▷他被雨淋得从头顶一直湿到脚底。

The rain soaked him from head to foot.

一致 yīzhì I [形] unanimous ▷他们夫妻俩在很多方面意见不一致。The couple disagreed about quite a number of things. II [副] unanimously

一字千金 yī zì qiān jīn be full of pearls of wisdom

衣 yī [名] 1 (衣服) clothing 2 (表层) cover 3 (医) afterbirth
衣服 yīfu [名] clothes (PL)
衣冠 yīguān [名] clothing
衣裳 yīshang [名] clothes (PL)
衣着 yīzhuó [名] clothing

伊 yī 见下文
伊甸园 yīdiànyuán [名] the Garden of Eden

医 yī I [名] 1 (医生) doctor ▶牙医 dentist 2 (医) medicine ▶中医 Chinese traditional medicine II [动] treat
医疗 yīliáo [动] treat ▷免费医疗制度 system of free medical care ▷改善医疗卫生条件 improve medical hygiene
医生 yīshēng [名] doctor
医术 yīshù [名] medical skill
医务 yīwù [名] ▷医务工作者 medical worker
医学 yīxué [名] medicine
医药 yīyào [名] medicine
医院 yīyuàn [名] hospital
医治 yīzhì [动] cure

依 yī I [动] 1 (依靠) depend on 2 (依从) comply with II [介] according to
依从 yīcóng [动] comply with
依存 yīcún [动] depend on
依附 yīfù [动] rely on
依旧 yījiù [副] still ▷10年了，他依旧孑然一身。It's been ten years, and he's still all alone.
依据 yījù I [动] go by (PT went, PP gone) II [名] basis (PL bases) ▷做这种判断你有什么依据吗？ Do you have any basis for this judgment?
依靠 yīkào I [动] rely on II [名] support
依赖 yīlài [动] depend on
依恋 yīliàn [动] be reluctant to leave
依然 yīrán I [副] still ▷她依然像10年前那么漂亮。She's still as beautiful as she was ten years ago.
依托 yītuō I [动] entrust II [名] support
依稀 yīxī [形] vague
依依 yīyī [形] 1 (摇摆) fluttering 2 (留恋) reluctant

依照 yīzhào [介] according to ▷依照规定，你是不能请假的。According to the regulations, you're not allowed to request leave. ▷我们就依照你的建议试一试吧。Let's try it your way.

咿 yī 见下文
咿呀 yīyā [拟] 1 (指物) squeak 2 (指人) prattle

壹 yī [数] an elaborate form of "one", used in writing cheques etc to prevent mistakes and forgery

---

仪 yí [名] 1 (外表) appearance 2 (礼节) ceremony 3 (礼物) gift 4 (仪器) meter
仪表 yíbiǎo [名] 1 (外表) appearance 2 (仪器) meter
仪器 yíqì [名] meter
仪式 yíshì [名] ceremony
仪仗队 yízhàngduì [名] guard of honour (英) 或 honor (美)

夷 yí I [形] (书) safe ▷化险为夷 head off disaster II [动] (书) 1 (破坏) raze ▷夷为平地 raze to the ground 2 (杀掉) exterminate ▶夷灭 destroy

---

怡 yí [形] (书) cheerful
怡然自得 yírán zìdé contented

宜 yí I [形] suitable II [副] ▷事不宜迟。 Matters should not be delayed.
宜人 yírén [形] pleasant

贻 yí [动] (书) 1 (赠送) present 2 (遗留) bequeath
贻误 yíwù [动] affect ... adversely
贻笑大方 yíxiào dàfāng expose oneself to ridicule

姨 yí [名] 1 (母亲的姐妹) aunt 2 (妻子的姐妹) sister-in-law (PL sisters-in-law)
姨表 yíbiǎo [名] cousin

移 yí [动] 1 (移动) move 2 (改变) change
移动 yídòng [动] move
移交 yíjiāo [动] hand ... over
移民 yímín I [动] emigrate ▷去年我移民法国。Last year I emigrated to France. II [名] immigrant ▷他是来自西班牙的移民。He's a Spanish immigrant.
移植 yízhí [动] transplant

遗 yí I [名] lost item II [动] 1 (遗失) lose (PT, PP lost) 2 (遗漏) omit 3 (留下) leave ... behind (PT, PP left) 4 (死者留下) bequeath 5 (排泄) discharge

遗产 yíchǎn [名] legacy

遗传 yíchuán [动] inherit ▷有些疾病可能会遗传。Some diseases can be hereditary.

遗存 yícún [动] survive

遗骸 yíhái [名] remains (PL)

遗憾 yíhàn I [名] regret ▷没上过大学是他终身的遗憾。It was his lifelong regret that he had not gone to university. II [动] be a pity ▷真遗憾，我没看到你的表演。It's such a pity that I didn't see your performance.

遗迹 yíjì [名] remains (PL)

遗精 yíjīng [动] emit

遗留 yíliú [动] leave (PT, PP left) ▷父亲去世后遗留了很多钱财。My father left a lot of money when he died.

遗漏 yílòu [动] omit

遗弃 yíqì [动] 1 (车、船等) abandon 2 (妻、子等) desert

遗容 yíróng [名] (死后容貌) remains (PL)

遗失 yíshī [动] lose (PT, PP lost)

遗书 yíshū [名] 1 (前人著作) posthumous papers 2 (书面遗言) last letter

遗孀 yíshuāng [名] widow

遗体 yítǐ [名] remains (PL)

遗忘 yíwàng [动] forget (PT forgot, PP forgotten)

遗址 yízhǐ [名] ruins (PL)

遗嘱 yízhǔ [名] will

颐 yí I [名] (书) cheek II [动] (书) take care of oneself (PT took, PP taken)

颐和园 Yíhéyuán [名] the Summer Palace

颐养 yíyǎng [动] (书) take care of one's health (PT took, PP taken)

疑 yí [动] doubt

疑案 yí'àn [名] 1 (疑难案件) difficult case 2 (神秘事件) mystery

疑惑 yíhuò [动] have doubts

疑难 yínán [形] knotty

疑神疑鬼 yí shén yí guǐ be extremely suspicious

疑团 yítuán [名] doubts and suspicions (PL)

疑问 yíwèn [名] question

疑心 yíxīn I [名] suspicion II [动] suspect ▷她疑心邻居偷了她的手表。She suspected that her neighbour (英) 或 neighbor (美) stole her watch.

乙 yǐ [名] second ▷乙等 second grade

已 yǐ I [动] stop ▶不已 endlessly ▷死而后已 to the end of one's days II [副] already ▷大会已于昨日闭幕。The convention ended yesterday. ▷前期工作已准备完毕。Preparations for the preliminary stage of the work are already complete.

已经 yǐjing [副] already ▷已经到深秋了。It's already late autumn.

已然 yǐrán I [动] already be a fact II [副] already

已往 yǐwǎng [名] the past ▷已往他好吃懒做，现在完全变了样。In the past he was greedy and lazy – now he's completely changed.

以 yǐ (书) I [动] use ▷以强凌弱 use one's strength to humiliate the weak II [介] 1 (依照) by ▷以新的标准衡量 judge by new standards 2 (因为) for ▷他以博学多才闻名于全校。He became well-known throughout the school for his wide-ranging academic achievements. 3 (表示界限) ▶以内 within ▶以南 to the south III [连] ▷我们要改进技术，以提高生产效率。We should improve the technology so as to increase production.

以便 yǐbiàn [连] in order that

以讹传讹 yǐ é chuán é Chinese whispers

以后 yǐhòu [名] ▷两年以后，他果然去周游世界了。Two years later, he did indeed go on a round-the-world tour. ▷以后我们去看电影。Afterwards we're going to see a film.

以及 yǐjí [连] as well as ▷夜校开设了英文班、法文班以及德文班。The night school has started up classes in English, French and German. ▷医学专家讲解了这一传染病的特点以及防治方法。The medical expert explained the peculiarities of this infectious disease, as well as the methods of prevention.

以来 yǐlái [名] ▷入冬以来，这里已经下了5场雪。There have been five snowfalls here since the beginning of the winter.

以免 yǐmiǎn [连] in case ▷做好准备，以免不必要的麻烦。Prepare yourself thoroughly in case of unnecessary trouble.

以前 yǐqián [名] ▷10年以前，这里还是一片废墟。Ten years ago this was still a complete ruin. ▷她以前是老师。She was a teacher before.

以身作则 yǐ shēn zuò zé set an example

以往 yǐwǎng [名] the past ▷他以往身体不好，现在非常健康。In the past his health wasn't too good, but he's very healthy now.

以为 yǐwéi [动] think (PT, PP thought) ▷我以为你不想来呢！I thought you didn't want to come! ▷老李以为这件事跟他没关系。Old Li reckoned that this had nothing to do with him.

以⋯为⋯ yǐ⋯wéi⋯ [动] take ... as (PT took, PP taken)

以下 yǐxià [名] **1** (低于某点) ▷这里的气温常年在20度以下。The temperature here is below twenty degrees all year round. ▷俱乐部成员多数在30岁以下。Most of the club members are under thirty. ▷这个店的玩具价格200元以下的占了80%。80% of the toys in the shop sell for less than two hundred yuan. **2** (接下来) ▷以下我来谈谈应该注意的问题。Next I will discuss the problems to which we must pay special attention. ▷以下请王先生给大家讲一讲。Now I would like to ask Mr. Wang to talk to us.

以眼还眼，以牙还牙 yǐ yǎn huán yǎn, yǐ yá huán yá an eye for an eye and a tooth for a tooth

以逸待劳 yǐ yì dài láo wait for the enemy to wear themselves out

以至 yǐzhì [连] **1** (表示延伸) ▷这项工程可能需要两年以至更长的时间。This project will perhaps require two years or even more. ▷这项政策会影响到整个国家、省以至县。This policy will effect the whole country, down to province and county level. **2** (表示结果) to such an extent that ▷他紧张得以至胃疼。He was so nervous that he got a stomachache.

以致 yǐzhì [连] so that ▷她操劳过度，以致累垮了身体。She worked so hard that she damaged her health.

蚁 yǐ [名] ant

倚 yǐ I [动] **1** (靠着) lean on **2** (仗恃) rely on II [形] biased

倚靠 yǐkào [动] **1** (斜躺) lean on **2** (依赖) depend on

倚老卖老 yǐ lǎo mài lǎo take advantage of one's seniority

倚仗 yǐzhàng [动] rely on

倚重 yǐzhòng [动] depend heavily on

椅 yǐ [名] chair

椅子 yǐzi [名] chair

旖 yǐ 见下文

旖旎 yǐnǐ [形] (书) charming

亿 yì [数] hundred million

义 yì I [名] **1** (正义) righteousness **2** (情谊) human ties (PL) **3** (意义) meaning II [形] **1** (正义的) just **2** (人工的) artificial **3** (拜认的) adopted ▶义父 adoptive father

义不容辞 yì bù róng cí be duty-bound

义愤 yìfèn [名] righteous indignation

义卖 yìmài [动] sell ... for charity (PT, PP sold) ▷义卖所得钱款已全部寄往灾区。All money raised from this charity sale has already been sent to the disaster area.

义气 yìqi I [名] loyalty II [形] loyal

义无反顾 yì wú fǎn gù be duty-bound

义务 yìwù I [名] duty II [形] compulsory

义演 yìyǎn [名] charity gala

义正词严 yì zhèng cí yán speak sternly out of a sense of justice

艺 yì [名] **1** (技能) skill ▶手艺 craftsmanship **2** (艺术) art

艺名 yìmíng [名] stage name

艺人 yìrén [名] **1** (演员) performer **2** (工人) artisan

艺术 yìshù I [名] **1** (文艺) art **2** (方法) skill ▷管理艺术 management skills II [形] artistic ▷花园的布局很艺术。The layout of the garden is very artistic.

艺术家 yìshùjiā [名] artist

忆 yì [动] remember

议 yì I [名] opinion ▶建议 propose II [动] discuss ▶商议 discuss

议案 yì'àn [名] proposal

议程 yìchéng [名] agenda

议会 yìhuì [名] parliament

议决 yìjué [动] pass a resolution

议论 yìlùn I [动] discuss II [名] talk ▷对新一届领导，人们私下里有很多议论。Privately, there was a lot of talk about the new leadership.

议题 yìtí [名] topic

议员 yìyuán [名] MP(英), congressman, congresswoman(美)

议政 yìzhèng [动] discuss politics

屹 yì [形] towering

屹立 yìlì [动] stand (PT, PP stood)

屹然 yìrán [形] towering

亦 yì [副] also ▷反之亦然 vice versa

亦步亦趋 yì bù yì qū blindly follow suit

异 yì I [形] **1** (不同) different ▶差异 difference **2** (奇异) strange **3** (惊奇) surprising ▶诧异 be surprised **4** (另外) other ▶异国 foreign country II [动] separate ▶离异 separate

异邦 yìbāng [名] foreign country

异常 yìcháng [形] unusual

异端 yìduān [名] (书) heresy

异乎寻常 yìhū xúncháng exceptional ▷ 这个月，公司的销售情况异乎寻常地顺利。This month, the company's sales have been exceptionally good.

异化 yìhuà [动] 1 (哲) alienate 2 (语言) dissimilate

异己 yìjǐ [名] dissident

异口同声 yì kǒu tóng shēng speak with one voice ▷ 大家异口同声地称赞她是个热心人。Everyone unanimously agreed that she was a really warm-hearted person.

异曲同工 yì qǔ tóng gōng employ different methods with equal success ▷ 这两座桥的设计、造型异曲同工。These two bridges were planned and built equally successfully using different methods.

异物 yìwù [名] 1 (医) foreign body 2 (奇异物品) curiosity

异乡 yìxiāng [名] foreign parts (PL)

异想天开 yì xiǎng tiān kāi have one's head in the clouds

异性 yìxìng [名] 1 (指性别) the opposite sex 2 (指性质) opposite

异议 yìyì [名] objection ▷ 如果有异议，我们可以进一步讨论。If there are any objections, we can discuss this further.

译 yì [动] translate

译文 yìwén [名] translation

译者 yìzhě [名] translator

译制 yìzhì [动] dub ▷ 很多美国电影都被译制成了中文。A lot of American movies have been dubbed into Chinese.

抑 yì [动] repress

抑扬顿挫 yīyáng dùncuò speak with a lilt

抑郁 yìyù [形] depressed

抑制 yìzhì [动] 1 (生理) inhibit 2 (控制) control

呓 yì [名] 1 (梦话) ▷ 梦呓 talk in one's sleep 2 (胡话) ravings (PL)

呓语 yìyǔ [名] ▷ 他睡觉时常说呓语。He often talks in his sleep.

役 yì I [名] 1 (劳力) labour (英), labor (美) ▷ 劳役 forced labour 2 (兵役) military service ▷ 退役 retire from the army 3 (奴仆) servant 4 (战争) battle II [动] treat as a servant ▷ 奴役 enslave

易 yì I [形] 1 (容易) easy ▷ 不讲卫生，易得传染病。If you're not careful about hygiene, it's easy to get an infection. 2 (和气) amiable ▷ 平易近人 amiable and easy to get on with II [动] 1 (改变) change 2 (交换) exchange ▷ 以物易物 barter

易如反掌 yì rú fǎn zhǎng easy as falling off a log

轶 yì [形] 1 (超群) superior 2 (散失) lost

轶事 yìshì [名] anecdote

疫 yì [名] epidemic

疫苗 yìmiáo [名] inoculation

益 yì I [名] benefit II [形] beneficial III [动] increase IV [副] increasingly

益处 yìchù [名] benefit

谊 yì [名] friendship

逸 yì I [形] 1 (安乐) leisurely 2 (散失) lost II [动] 1 (逃跑) escape 2 (超越) surpass

逸事 yìshì [名] anecdote

逸闻 yìwén [名] anecdote

翌 yì [名] the next ▷ 翌日 the next day

肄 yì [动] study

肄业 yìyè [动] study

裔 yì [名] 1 (书) (后代) descendant ▷ 华裔 foreign citizen of Chinese descent 2 (书) (边疆) border region ▷ 四裔 the frontiers (PL)

意 yì I [名] 1 (意思) meaning ▷ 他词不达意。He couldn't express what he meant. 2 (心愿) wish ▷ 好意 good intention II [动] expect

意会 yìhuì [动] sense

意见 yìjiàn [名] 1 (看法) opinion ▷ 请你发表一下意见。Please give us your opinion. ▷ 大家互相交换了意见。Everyone exchanged ideas. ▷ 对这个计划大家还有什么意见？What does everyone think of this plan? 2 (不满) objection ▷ 工人们对这件事的处理意见很大。The workers greatly objected to the way this matter was dealt with. ▷ 有意见就提出来。If you have objections, raise them.

意境 yìjìng [名] artistic conception

意料 yìliào [名] expect

意念 yìniàn [名] thought

意气 yìqì [名] 1 (气概) spirit 2 (志趣) temperament 3 (情绪) emotions (PL)

意识 yìshí I [名] consciousness II [动] realize

意思 yìsi [名] 1 (意义) meaning 2 (意见) idea

3 (愿望) wish **4** (趣味) interest ▷这个连续剧太没意思。This series is so boring. **5** (心意) token ▷这是我们的一点小意思，请收下。This is a small token of our esteem – do accept it.

意图 yìtú [名] intention

意外 yìwài **I** [名] accident **II** [形] unexpected

意味 yìwèi [名] **1** (意思) significance **2** (情调) flavour (英), flavor (美)

意向 yìxiàng [名] intention

意义 yìyì [名] **1** (含义) meaning **2** (作用) significance

意译 yìyì [动] translate freely

意愿 yìyuàn [名] wish ▷作决定要符合大多数人的意愿。The decision must accord with the wishes of the majority.

意志 yìzhì [名] will

意中人 yìzhōngrén [名] the object of one's affections

溢 yì **I** [动] overflow **II** [副] excessively

溢出 yìchū [动] overflow

溢于言表 yì yú yán biǎo an outpouring of emotion

毅 yì [形] resolute

毅力 yìlì [名] perseverance

毅然 yìrán [形] resolute

臆 yì [副] subjectively

臆测 yìcè [动] conjecture

臆断 yìduàn [动] make assumptions

臆造 yìzào [动] fabricate

翼 yì [名] **1** (翅膀) wing ▶机翼 aircraft wing **2** (侧面) side

翼翼 yìyì [形] (书) cautious

因 yīn **I** [连] because ▷因交通阻塞，他们无法准时到达。Because there was a traffic jam, they were unable to arrive on time. ▷因天气恶劣，今天的郊游取消了。Today's outing has been cancelled due to bad weather. **II** [介] because of ▷昨天他因病缺课。He missed a class yesterday because of illness. **III** [名] cause ▶外因 external cause ▶病因 cause of the illness ▷事出有因 there are reasons why things happen

因材施教 yīn cái shī jiào teach according to one's student's ability ▷教师在教学时应尽量因材施教。Teachers, when teaching, ought as far as possible to teach students according to their abilities.

因此 yīncǐ [连] so ▷他迷恋于玩游戏，因此无心学习，成绩下降。He is obsessed with playing games, so he's not interested in studying and his achievements have dropped off. ▷这种病很容易复发，因此要格外注意。It's very easy to have a relapse with this kind of illness, so you have to be exceptionally careful. ▷由于引进了先进技术，生产效率因此大大提高。The production rate has increased hugely due to imported advanced technology.

因地制宜 yīn dì zhì yí act according to local conditions

因而 yīn'ér [连] therefore ▷由于工人们加强了安全意识，因而事故发生率大大减少了。Workers have become more safety conscious, and therefore the accident rate has fallen greatly.

因果 yīnguǒ [名] **1** (原因和结果) cause and effect **2** (宗) karma

因陋就简 yīn lòu jiù jiǎn make do with what's available ▷老师们因陋就简，给孩子们建了一个小活动室。The teachers made do with what was available and built a small activity room for the children.

因势利导 yīn shì lì dǎo give advice appropriate to the situation

因素 yīnsù [名] **1** (成分) element **2** (原因) factor ▷影响学生学习成绩的因素有很多。There are many factors that influence students' grades.

因特网 yīntèwǎng [名] the Internet

因为 yīnwèi [连] because ▷因为有暴风雨，所以他们取消了航海计划。They cancelled their plans to go sailing because of the stormy weather. ▷她昨天请了一天的假，是因为孩子生病了。Yesterday she requested a day off because her child was sick.

因袭 yīnxí [动] follow traditional ways

因循 yīnxún [动] follow

因噎废食 yīn yē fèi shí give up eating for fear of choking

因缘 yīnyuán [名] **1** (宗) karma **2** (缘分) ▷他俩好像有前世因缘，一见面就坠入了情网。It seems that the two of them were destined for each other – they fell in love at first sight.

阴 yīn **I** [形] **1** (指天气) overcast ▷天阴得厉害。It's a very overcast day. **2** (隐蔽的) secret ▶阳奉阴违 support in public but undermine in secret **3** (险的) insidious ▶阴谋 plot **4** (物) negative ▶阴极 cathode **II** [名] **1** (阳的对立面) Yin (of Yin and Yang) **2** (指月亮) the moon ▶阴历 lunar calendar **3** (背面)

back **4** (阴凉处) shade ▶ 树阴 the shade

阴暗 yīn'àn [形] gloomy

阴部 yīnbù [名] private parts (PL)

阴沉 yīnchén [形] gloomy

阴错阳差 yīn cuò yáng chā unexpected mishap

阴毒 yīndú [形] sinister

阴魂 yīnhún [名] spirits of the dead (PL)

阴极 yīnjí [名] (物) **1** (指电波) negative pole **2** (指电子) cathode

阴茎 yīnjīng [名] penis

阴冷 yīnlěng [形] **1** (指天气) chilly ▶ 今天天气阴冷阴冷的。It's really raw today. **2** (指脸色) gloomy

阴历 yīnlì [名] lunar calendar

阴凉 yīnliáng [形] shady and cool

阴谋 yīnmóu [动] plot ▶ 敌人的阴谋被识破了。The enemy's plot has been uncovered.

阴森 yīnsēn [形] gloomy

阴险 yīnxiǎn [形] sinister

阴性 yīnxìng [名] **1** (医) negative **2** (语言) feminine gender

阴阳 yīnyáng [名] Yin and Yang

阴阳怪气 yīn yáng guàiqì odd ▶ 他说话老是阴阳怪气的, 让人听着别扭。He has such an odd way of speaking that it's irritating to listen to him.

阴郁 yīnyù [形] **1** (阴沉沉的) gloomy **2** (沮丧的) depressed

茵 yīn [名] mattress

音 yīn [名] **1** (声音) sound **2** (消息) news (SG) **3** (音节) syllable

音标 yīnbiāo [名] phonetic symbols (PL)

音调 yīndiào [名] pitch ▶ 他讲话时音调很高亢。He has a high-pitched voice.

音符 yīnfú [名] note

音节 yīnjié [名] syllable

音量 yīnliàng [名] volume ▶ 请把收音机的音量放大点儿。Turn up the volume on the radio a bit.

音容 yīnróng [名] face and voice

音色 yīnsè [名] timbre

音素 yīnsù [名] phoneme

音响 yīnxiǎng [名] **1** (声音) sound **2** (指设备) acoustics (PL)

音像 yīnxiàng [名] audio and video

音信 yīnxìn [名] news (SG) ▶ 最近几年, 他音信全无。There's been no news of him for several years.

音译 yīnyì [名] transliteration

音乐 yīnyuè [名] music

音乐会 yīnyuèhuì [名] concert

洇 yīn [动] saturate ▶ 纸被墨水洇透了。This paper has been saturated with ink.

姻 yīn **I** [名] marriage **II** [形] related by marriage

姻亲 yīnqīn [名] in-law

殷 yīn [形] (书) **1** (丰富) prosperous **2** (深厚) earnest **3** (殷勤) courteous → 另见 yān

殷切 yīnqiè [形] earnest

殷勤 yīnqín [形] courteous ▶ 她对待客人一向殷勤。She treats guests very courteously.

吟 yín [动] recite

吟诵 yínsòng [动] recite

银 yín **I** [名] **1** (指金属) silver **2** (指货币) money ▶ 收银台 cashier's desk **II** [形] silver

银行 yínháng [名] bank

银河 yínhé [名] the Milky Way

银灰 yínhuī [形] silvery grey (英) 或 gray (美)

银婚 yínhūn [名] silver wedding

银幕 yínmù [名] screen

银牌 yínpái [名] silver medal ▶ 他在长跑比赛中获得了银牌。He won a silver medal in the long-distance race.

银屏 yínpíng [名] (荧光屏) fluorescent screen

淫 yín [形] **1** (过多) excessive **2** (放纵) licentious **3** (淫秽) obscene

淫荡 yíndàng [形] lewd

淫秽 yínhuì [形] obscene

淫乱 yínluàn [形] debauched

龈 yín [名] gum

引 yín [动] **1** (牵引) draw (PT drew, PP drawn) **2** (引导) lead (PT, PP led) ▶ 引路 lead the way **3** (离开) leave (PT, PP left) **4** (引起) cause **5** (引用) cite

引导 yǐndǎo [动] **1** (带领) lead (PT, PP led) ▶ 校长引导我们参观了校园。The principal led us round the campus. **2** (启发诱导) guide

引渡 yǐndù [动] extradite

引发 yǐnfā [动] initiate

引见 yǐnjiàn [动] introduce

引进 yǐnjìn [动] **1** (人) recommend **2** (物) import

引经据典 yǐn jīng jù diǎn quote from the

classics ▷这篇文章引经据典，非常令人信服。This article quotes from the classics, which makes it more convincing.

引咎 yǐnjiù [动] take the blame (PT took, PP taken)

引狼入室 yǐn láng rù shì expose oneself to danger

引力 yǐnlì [名] gravitation

引起 yǐnqǐ [动] cause ▷人们担心，贫富不均可能会引起社会动荡。People are worried that inequalities in wealth might cause social unrest. ▷这一事件的发生马上引起了媒体的注意。As soon as it happened the event aroused media interest.

引擎 yǐnqíng [名] engine

引人入胜 yǐn rén rù shèng absorbing ▷这个故事悬念迭出，引人入胜。This story is full of suspense, and deeply absorbing.

引申 yǐnshēn [动] extend

引退 yǐntuì [动] retire ▷从官场引退之后，他感到无比轻松。When he retired from political life he felt incredibly relaxed.

引言 yǐnyán [名] foreword

引用 yǐnyòng [动] 1 (引述) quote 2 (任用) appoint

引诱 yǐnyòu [动] 1 (诱导) induce 2 (诱惑) tempt

引证 yǐnzhèng [动] cite

引子 yǐnzi [名] 1 (戏剧) prologue 2 (音) prelude 3 (开场白) prologue

饮 yǐn I [动] drink (PT drank, PP drunk) II [名] drink

饮料 yǐnliào [名] drink

饮食 yǐnshí [名] food and drink

饮食店 yǐnshídiàn [名] eatery

饮用水 yǐnyòngshuǐ [名] drinking water

隐 yǐn I [动] conceal II [形] hidden III [名] (书) secret

隐蔽 yǐnbì I [动] take cover (PT took, PP taken) ▷警察隐蔽在一堵墙的后面。The policeman took cover behind a wall. II [形] concealed

隐藏 yǐncáng [动] conceal

隐讳 yǐnhuì [动] hold back (PT, PP held)

隐晦 yǐnhuì [形] obscure

隐瞒 yǐnmán [动] cover ... up

隐匿 yǐnnì [动] 1 (隐瞒) cover ... up 2 (隐藏) hide (PT hid, PP hidden)

隐私 yǐnsī [名] private matters (PL)

隐退 yǐntuì [动] 1 (消失) disappear 2 (退职) retire

隐隐 yǐnyǐn [副] faintly

隐语 yǐnyǔ [名] 1 (暗示的话) riddle 2 (黑话) code words (PL)

隐约 yǐnyuē [形] faint

瘾 yǐn [名] 1 (嗜好) addiction 2 (兴趣) strong interest

印 yìn I [名] 1 (图章) stamp 2 (痕迹) print II [动] 1 (留下痕迹) print 2 (符合) be in line with

印发 yìnfā [动] print and distribute

印泥 yìnní [名] red ink paste

印刷 yìnshuā [动] print

印象 yìnxiàng [名] impression

印章 yìnzhāng [名] seal

印证 yìnzhèng [动] confirm ▷这些奖励是她努力工作最好的印证。All those prizes are the best confirmation of her hard work.

荫 yìn [形] shady

荫凉 yìnliáng [形] shady and cool

应 yīng I [动] 1 (答应) answer ▷我朝屋子里喊了两声，没人应。I shouted twice towards the room but no-one answered. ▷人家在叫你，你倒应一声儿啊！Someone's calling you, go on, answer! 2 (应允) agree ▷他们的要求，你应了吗？Have you agreed to their demands? II [助动] should ▷发现危险，应立即发出警报。If you discover danger, you should raise the alarm immediately. ▷应按照医嘱服药。You should take your medicine according to the doctor's orders.

→另见 yìng

应当 yīngdāng [助动] should ▷天太热，应当洗个冷水澡。When it's too hot you should take a cold shower.

应该 yīnggāi [助动] should ▷你不应该惹她生气。You shouldn't make her angry. ▷家长应该鼓励孩子。Parents should encourage their children.

应允 yīngyǔn [动] consent

英 yīng [名] 1 (书) (花) flower 2 (才能出众者) hero (PL heroes) 3 (英国) Britain

英镑 yīngbàng [名] pound sterling

英才 yīngcái [名] 1 (杰出才智) talent ▷他具有盖世英才。He possesses outstanding talent. 2 (杰出人才) talented person

英豪 yīngháo [名] hero (PL heroes)

英俊 yīngjùn [形] 1 (有才干的) very talented 2 (漂亮的) handsome

英明 yīngmíng [形] wise

英年 yīngnián [名] the flush of one's youth

英武 yīngwǔ [形] (书) valiant

英雄 yīngxióng I [名] hero (PL heroes) II [形] heroic

英勇 yīngyǒng [形] brave

英语 yīngyǔ [名] English

英姿 yīngzī [名] dashing appearance

婴 yīng [名] baby

婴儿 yīng'ér [名] baby

缨 yīng [名] 1 (带子) strap 2 (装饰物) tassel 3 (缨状物) tassel

樱 yīng [名] 1 (樱桃) cherry 2 (樱花) cherry blossom

樱桃 yīngtáo [名] 1 (指植物)(树) cherry tree ▷院子里种了几棵樱桃树。 Several cherry trees have been planted in the yard. 2 (果实) cherry

鹦 yīng 见下文

鹦鹉 yīngwǔ [名] parrot

鹰 yīng [名] eagle

迎 yíng [动] 1 (迎接) welcome 2 (对着) meet (PT, PP met)

迎合 yínghé [动] cater to ▷这家餐馆迎合南方人的口味。 This restaurant caters to the tastes of people from South China.

迎候 yínghòu [动] await

迎接 yíngjiē [动] welcome

迎刃而解 yíng rèn ér jiě be neatly solved

迎头 yíngtóu [动] be head-on ▷我刚进校门，迎头碰上了李教授。 Just after I came in through the school gates, I bumped right into Professor Li.

迎战 yíngzhàn [动] meet head-on (PT, PP met) ▷中国队将迎战美国队。 The Chinese team will meet the American team head-on.

荧 yíng [形] (书) luminous

荧光 yíngguāng [名] fluorescence ▷荧光灯比普通灯泡节能。 Fluorescent lights are more energy-efficient than ordinary light bulbs.

荧屏 yíngpíng [名] 1 (电子) fluorescent screen 2 (电视) television

盈 yíng [动] 1 (充满) fill 2 (增长) increase 3 (多出来) have a surplus of

盈亏 yíngkuī I [动] wax and wane II [名] profit and loss

盈利 yínglì [名] profit

盈余 yíngyú [动] profit ▷这笔生意做下来有

3万元的盈余。 If we do this business then we'll make thirty thousand dollars profit.

萤 yíng [名] firefly

萤火虫 yínghuǒchóng [名] firefly

营 yíng I [动] 1 (谋求) seek (PT, PP sought) 2 (经营) operate 3 (建造) build (PT, PP built) II [名] 1 (军队驻地) barracks (PL) 2 (军队编制) battalion 3 (营地) camp

营地 yíngdì [名] camp

营房 yíngfáng [名] barracks (PL)

营火 yínghuǒ [名] campfire

营救 yíngjiù [动] rescue

营私 yíngsī [动] feather one's nest

营销 yíngxiāo [动] sell (PT, PP sold)

营养 yíngyǎng [名] nourishment ▷大病初愈，你要好好营养一下身体。 When recovering from a serious illness, you have to nourish your body well. ▷水果中含有丰富的营养。 Fruit contains a lot of nutrients.

营业 yíngyè [动] do business ▷这家商店明天开始正式营业。 This shop will open for business tomorrow.

营造 yíngzào [动] 1 (建筑) build (PT, PP built) 2 (林木) plant 3 (气氛) create

萦 yíng [动] (书) entwine

萦怀 yínghuái [动] linger

萦绕 yíngrào [动] linger

蝇 yíng [名] fly

蝇头 yíngtóu [名] speck ▷蝇头小利 minuscule profit

赢 yíng [动] 1 (胜) win (PT, PP won) 2 (获利) gain

赢利 yínglì [名] gain

赢余 yíngyú [动] profit ▷这个月音像店盈余上万元。 This month the record shop's profit is more than ten thousand yuan. ▷除去开支，我们只有几百元的赢余。 After our expenses, we only have a few hundred yuan profit.

颖 yǐng I [名] intelligence II [形] intelligent

颖慧 yǐnghuì [形] (书) intelligent

影 yǐng I [名] 1 (影子) shadow 2 (照片) photograph 3 (电影) film (英), movie (美) II [动] copy

影片 yǐngpiàn [名] 1 (胶片) film 2 (电影) film (英), movie (美)

影射 yǐngshè [动] allude to

影视 yǐngshì [名] film and television

影坛 yǐngtán [名] the world of film

影响 yǐngxiǎng I [动] affect ▷一场大风严重影响了庄稼的长势。A large gale seriously affected the growth of the crops. ▷小声点，别影响他们的学习。Quiet! Don't disturb their studies. II [名] influence ▷有些书会使青少年受到不良影响。Some books have a bad influence on young people.

影印 yǐngyìn [动] photocopy ▷影印资料 photocopied material

应 yìng [动] 1 (回答) answer ▶回应 answer 2 (满足) respond to ▷应顾客需要，我们增开了两家分店。In response to the customers' needs, we opened two more branches. 3 (顺应) comply with 4 (应付) handle ▶应急 handle an emergency 5 (相符合) correspond to →另见 yīng

应变 yìngbiàn [动] take emergency measures (PT took, PP taken)

应标 yìngbiāo [动] bid (PT, PP bid)

应承 yìngchéng [动] agree ▷我请她帮忙，她满口应承。When I asked her to help, she readily agreed.

应酬 yìngchou I [动] socialize with ▷他去应酬客人了。He went to socialize with the guests. II [名] social engagement

应付 yìngfù [动] 1 (采取办法) handle 2 (敷衍) do half-heartedly 3 (将就) make do with ▷没有更好的衣服，就穿这件应付吧。I don't have any better clothes: I'll just make do with this.

应接不暇 yìngjiē bù xiá have more to do than one can cope with

应聘 yìngpìn [动] accept an offer

应时 yìngshí [形] seasonal

应试 yìngshì [动] 1 (应考) take exams (PT took, PP taken) 2 (适应考试) ▷应试教育不利于学生身心全面发展。Education that is geared towards exams has a bad effect on students' overall development.

应验 yìngyàn [动] come true (PT came, PP come) ▷他的很多预言都应验了。Many of his predictions have come true.

应邀 yìngyāo [动] be invited to ▷我应邀参加了昨天的宴会。I was invited to yesterday's banquet.

应用 yìngyòng I [动] apply ▷这项技术已经广泛应用于农业生产。This technology has already been widely applied to agricultural production. II [形] applied ▷应用科学 applied science

应战 yìngzhàn [动] 1 (作战) engage the enemy 2 (接受挑战) accept a challenge

映 yìng [动] reflect

映衬 yìngchèn [动] set ... off (PT, PP set)

映射 yìngshè [动] shine (PT, PP shone)

映照 yìngzhào [动] shine upon (PT, PP shone) ▷柔和的灯光映照着她美丽的面庞。The soft lighting is shining upon her beautiful face.

硬 yìng I [形] 1 (坚固) hard 2 (刚强) firm 3 (能干的) strong II [副] obstinately

硬邦邦 yìngbāngbāng [形] rock hard

硬币 yìngbì [名] coin

硬度 yìngdù [名] hardness ▷这种木头硬度不高。This kind of wood is not hard enough. ▷这种水硬度太高，不适合饮用。This kind of water is too hard: it's not suitable for drinking.

硬化 yìnghuà [动] 1 (变硬) harden 2 (喻) stiffen

硬件 yìngjiàn [名] 1 (计算机) hardware 2 (设备) equipment

硬朗 yìnglang [形] (口) sturdy

硬盘 yìngpán [名] hard disk

硬性 yìngxìng [形] inflexible

哟 yō [叹] (表示轻微的惊异或赞叹) oh ▷哟，他怎么来了？ Oh, how did he get here?

佣 yōng I [动] hire II [名] servant →另见 yòng

佣工 yōnggōng [名] servant

拥 yōng [动] 1 (抱) embrace 2 (围着) gather round 3 (拥挤) swarm 4 (拥护) support

拥抱 yōngbào [动] embrace

拥戴 yōngdài [动] support

拥护 yōnghù [动] support ▷决议草案得到了大多数议员的拥护。The draft resolution obtained the support of most of the representatives.

拥挤 yōngjǐ I [形] crowded II [动] crowd

拥有 yōngyǒu [动] have (PT, PP had)

庸 yōng I [形] 1 (平凡) commonplace 2 (不高明) mediocre II [动] need

庸才 yōngcái [名] mediocrity

庸碌 yōnglù [形] mediocre

庸人 yōngrén [名] (书) nonentity

庸俗 yōngsú [形] vulgar

雍 yōng [形] (书) harmonious

雍容 yōngróng [形] graceful

壅 yōng [动] obstruct

壅塞 yōngsè [动] block ... up

臃 yōng [形] (书) obese
臃肿 yōngzhǒng [形] 1 (指身体) obese 2 (指机构) overstaffed

永 yǒng I [形] (书) everlasting II [副] forever
永恒 yǒnghéng [形] everlasting
永久 yǒngjiǔ [形] eternal
永生 yǒngshēng I [动] live forever II [副] forever
永世 yǒngshì [副] forever ▷您的恩德，我永世不忘。I will remember your kindness forever.
永远 yǒngyuǎn [副] eternally ▷我们将永远怀念这位可敬的朋友。We will eternally cherish the memory of this respected friend. ▷他们希望一辈子生活在一起，永远不分离。They want to be together all their lives, and never part.

泳 yǒng [名] swim (PT swam, PP swum)
泳道 yǒngdào [名] lane

俑 yǒng [名] figurine

勇 yǒng [形] brave
勇敢 yǒnggǎn [形] brave
勇猛 yǒngměng [形] valiant
勇气 yǒngqì [名] courage
勇士 yǒngshì [名] warrior
勇往直前 yǒng wǎng zhí qián carry on bravely
勇于 yǒngyú [助动] have the courage to ▷勇于迎接挑战 have the courage to take on a challenge

涌 yǒng [动] 1 (冒出) gush 2 (喻) emerge
涌现 yǒngxiàn [动] emerge

踊 yǒng [动] leap
踊跃 yǒngyuè I [形] eager II [动] leap

用 yòng I [动] 1 (使用) use ▷你们可以用这个教室。You can use this classroom. 2 (需要) need ▷不用担心，他们很快就到了。There's no need to worry, they'll be here soon. ▷我自己去就行，不用你陪着。I'll go by myself; you don't have to come. 3 (消费) consume ▶用餐 have a meal ▶用茶 drink tea II [名] 1 (费用) expense ▶家用 household expenses (PL) 2 (用处) use ▶没用 useless
用场 yòngchǎng [名] use
用处 yòngchu [名] use
用功 yònggōng I [形] hardworking II [动] work hard

用户 yònghù [名] user ▷网络用户 internet user
用具 yòngjù [名] tool
用力 yònglì [动] exert oneself ▷他用力举起了大石头。He really exerted himself lifting the big stone.
用品 yòngpǐn [名] goods (PL) ▷办公用品 office goods ▷体育用品 sporting goods
用人 yòngrén [动] 1 (使用人) make the best use of staff 2 (需要人) be understaffed
用事 yòngshì [动] act
用途 yòngtú [名] use
用心 yòngxīn I [动] be careful II [形] careful ▷他做什么事都很用心。Whatever he does he's always very careful. III [名] intention
用意 yòngyì [名] intention
用语 yòngyǔ I [动] word II [名] term

佣 yòng 见下文
→另见 yōng
佣金 yòngjīn [名] commission

优 yōu I [形] 1 (优良) excellent 2 (书) (充足) abundant II [动] give ... preferential treatment (PT gave, PP given)
优待 yōudài [动] give preferential treatment (PT gave, PP given) ▷这个公司格外优待老客户。This company gives preferential treatment to old customers. ▷立功人员应得到优待。Hardworking staff should receive preferential treatment.
优点 yōudiǎn [名] strong point
优厚 yōuhòu [形] generous
优化 yōuhuà [动] optimize
优惠 yōuhuì [形] preferential
优良 yōuliáng [形] fine
优美 yōuměi [形] elegant
优胜 yōushèng I [名] victory II [形] superior
优势 yōushì [名] advantage ▷我们要尽量发挥出自己的优势。We have to do our best to give play to our own advantages.
优先 yōuxiān [动] have priority
优秀 yōuxiù [形] outstanding
优雅 yōuyǎ [形] refined
优异 yōuyì [形] outstanding
优越 yōuyuè [形] superior
优质 yōuzhì [形] high-quality

忧 yōu I [形] anxious II [动] worry III [名] anxiety
忧愁 yōuchóu [形] depressed
忧患 yōuhuàn [名] suffering
忧虑 yōulǜ [动] worry ▷他为自己的前途感到

忧虑。He was worried about his prospects.

忧伤 yōushāng [形] sad

忧郁 yōuyù [形] depressed

呦 yōu [叹] ooh!

幽 yōu I [形] 1 (暗) dim 2 (深) remote 3 (隐蔽的) hidden 4 (沉静) tranquil II [动] imprison III [名] the underworld

幽暗 yōu'àn [形] gloomy

幽会 yōuhuì [名] date ▷他们在电影院幽会。They went on a date to the cinema. ▷这对恋人经常去公园幽会。The couple often meet in the park.

幽禁 yōujìn [动] imprison

幽静 yōujìng [形] peaceful

幽灵 yōulíng [名] ghost

幽默 yōumò [形] humorous ▷他说话很幽默。He's got a very humorous way of talking.

幽情 yōuqíng [名] deep feelings (PL)

幽深 yōushēn [形] serene

幽雅 yōuyǎ [形] refined

悠 yōu I [形] 1 (久远) remote 2 (闲适) leisurely II [动] (口) swing (PT, PP swung)

悠长 yōucháng [形] drawn-out

悠久 yōujiǔ [形] long-standing

悠然 yōurán [形] carefree ▷他在乡下过着悠然的日子。He lives a carefree life in the country.

悠闲 yōuxián [形] leisurely

悠扬 yōuyáng [形] melodious

悠悠 yōuyōu [形] 1 (久远) remote 2 (从容不迫) unhurried

悠远 yōuyuǎn [形] 1 (指时间) distant 2 (指距离) far

尤 yóu [副] especially

尤其 yóuqí [副] especially ▷他爱好体育，尤其喜欢踢足球。He loves sport, especially football.

由 yóu I [动] 1 (听凭) give in to (PT gave, PP given) ▷不能什么事都由着孩子。You can't give in to children in everything. 2 (经过) go through (PT went, PP gone) ▷必由之路 the only way II [介] 1 (归) by ▷这件事由你去安排吧！This business will be dealt with by you. 2 (根据) ▷这篇论文由三个部分构成。This essay is made up of three parts. 3 (从) ▷由此可见 from this we can see... ▷由简到繁 from simple to complex ▷由上海到深圳 from Shanghai to Shenzhen 4 (由于) due to ▷她头痛是由睡眠不足引起的。Her headache is due

to lack of sleep. III [名] cause ▶理由 reason

由来 yóulái [名] origin ▷没人知道这个传说的由来。No-one knows the origins of this legend.

由于 yóuyú [介] as a result of ▷由于司机一时不慎，发生了一起重大交通事故。As a result of the driver's momentary carelessness, there was a serious accident. ▷由于不用功，他没能通过考试。Because he didn't work hard, he couldn't pass the exam.

由衷 yóuzhōng [形] heartfelt

邮 yóu I [动] post (英), mail (美) II [名] 1 (邮务) post (英), mail (美) 2 (邮票) stamp

邮递 yóudì [动] send ... by post (英) 或 mail (美) (PT, PP sent) ▷邮递印刷品很便宜。It's very cheap to send printed matter by post.

邮电 yóudiàn [名] post and telecommunications

邮寄 yóujì [动] post (英), mail (美)

邮件 yóujiàn [名] post (英), mail (美) ▷朋友之间用电子邮件联系非常方便。It's very convenient for friends to use email to keep in touch. ▷这个歌星在生日那天收到了大量邮件。The pop star received a lot of mail on his birthday.

邮局 yóujú [名] post office

邮票 yóupiào [名] stamp

邮政 yóuzhèng [名] postal service

邮资 yóuzī [名] postage

犹 yóu I [动] be like II [副] still

犹然 yóurán [副] still

犹如 yóurú [动] be like

犹豫 yóuyù [形] hesitant

油 yóu I [名] oil II [动] 1 (油漆) oil 2 (被油弄脏) stain with oil III [形] oily

油光 yóuguāng [形] shiny

油乎乎 yóuhūhū [形] oily

油滑 yóuhuá [形] slippery ▷这个人很油滑，待人没有一点诚意。This person is very slippery: he treats people completely insincerely.

油腻 yóunì I [形] greasy II [名] oily food

油漆 yóuqī I [名] varnish II [动] varnish

油腔滑调 yóu qiāng huá diào glib

油水 yóushui [名] 1 (脂肪) oil 2 (贬) (好处) profit

油头粉面 yóu tóu fěn miàn overdressed ▷他打扮得油头粉面，一看就让人不舒服。He was so overdressed that people felt uncomfortable looking at him.

油头滑脑 yóu tóu huá nǎo slick

油印 **yóuyìn** [动] mimeograph

油脂 **yóuzhī** [名] oil ▷这种小吃含油脂过多，少吃为好。This kind of snack is too oily, the less you eat the better.

鱿 **yóu** [名] squid

鱿鱼 **yóuyú** [名] squid

游 **yóu** I [动] **1** (游泳) swim (PT swam, PP swum) **2** (游览) tour II [名] reach III [形] roving

游程 **yóuchéng** [名] **1** (距离) distance ▷1,000米的游程他很快就游完了。He swam the distance of 1000 metres very quickly. **2** (路程) journey **3** (日程) itinerary

游荡 **yóudàng** [动] **1** (闲逛) wander **2** (飘荡) float

游逛 **yóuguàng** [动] stroll

游记 **yóujì** [名] travel notes (PL)

游客 **yóukè** [名] tourist

游览 **yóulǎn** [动] tour

游民 **yóumín** [名] vagrant

游牧 **yóumù** [动] live a nomadic life ▷这个民族仍然过着游牧生活。This tribe still live a nomadic life.

游刃有余 **yóu rèn yǒu yú** be more than equal to ▷他经验丰富，做这项工作游刃有余。He has plenty of experience, so he is more than equal to this task.

游手好闲 **yóu shǒu hào xián** [形] loaf about ▷一个游手好闲、不愿工作的人，很难得到尊重。It's very difficult for people who are idle and unwilling to work to gain respect.

游说 **yóushuì** [动] lobby

游戏 **yóuxì** I [名] game ▷孩子们都喜欢玩电脑游戏。Children all like to play computer games. ▷做任何事，首先要弄清游戏规则。No matter what you do, first you have to clarify the rules of the game. II [动] play ▷年轻人要珍惜生活，不要游戏人生。Young people must cherish life and mustn't play at it.

游行 **yóuxíng** [动] march

游移 **yóuyí** [动] waver

游泳 **yóuyǒng** I [动] swim (PT swam, PP swum) II [名] swimming ▷游泳是很好的健身运动。Swimming is a very good way of keeping fit.

游泳池 **yóuyǒngchí** [名] swimming pool

游子 **yóuzǐ** [名] person far from home

友 **yǒu** I [名] friend ▶男友 boyfriend II [形] friendly ▶友邦 friendly nation

友爱 **yǒu'ài** [形] affectionate

友好 **yǒuhǎo** I [形] friendly II [名] friend

友情 **yǒuqíng** [名] friendship

友人 **yǒurén** [名] friend

友善 **yǒushàn** [形] 〈书〉 amicable

友谊 **yǒuyì** [名] friendship

有 **yǒu** [动] **1** (具有) have (PT, PP had) ▷我有一套《红楼梦》。I have a set of "Dream of Red Chamber". **2** (存在) ▷院子里有一棵大树。There's a big tree in the courtyard. **3** (表示估量) ▷她有我那么大。She is as old as me. **4** (发生) occur ▷我的生活有了一些变化。A few changes have occurred in my life. **5** (表示程度) have (PT, PP had) ▷她很有修养。She has many accomplishments. ▷他特别有学问。He's extremely knowledgeable. **6** (某) ▷有一次，他得了冠军。He won a prize once. ▷有人说，这个湖里有怪兽。Some people say that there's a monster in the lake. ▷有时候他去健身房锻炼。Sometimes he goes to the gym to work out. **7** (客套) ▷有劳您给我查一下地图好吗？Could I trouble you to help me look it up on the map?

有碍 **yǒu'ài** [动] 〈书〉 obstruct

有板有眼 **yǒu bǎn yǒu yǎn** orderly ▷这位经理讲起话来不紧不慢，有板有眼。This manager speaks in a calm, orderly manner.

有备无患 **yǒu bèi wú huàn** be prepared

有偿 **yǒucháng** [形] paid

有的 **yǒude** [名] some ▷展出的作品，有的来自本土，有的来自海外。Of the articles on display, some are local, others are from overseas. ▷他说这些论文写得都很好，我看有的很一般。He says that all the essays are good, but some of them look pretty mediocre to me.

有的放矢 **yǒu dì fàng shǐ** be to the point ▷会议发言不要漫无边际，要有的放矢。Conference speeches shouldn't be rambling – they should be to the point.

有方 **yǒufāng** [形] competent ▷新经理管理有方，受到一致拥护。The new manager is very competent and enjoys universal support.

有关 **yǒuguān** [动] **1** (有关系) be relevant ▷这个案子跟某个大公司有关。This case is relevant to a certain large company. **2** (涉及到) be about ▷他写了一本有关风水方面的书。He has written a book about feng shui. ▷国家出台了一项有关计划生育问题的政策。The government has issued a policy on family planning. ▷他们讨论了有关教育制度改革的若干问题。They discussed several questions relating to reform of the education system.

有过之无不及 **yǒu guò zhī wú bù jí** go even further than ▷跟我住的地方比，这里的环境

污染程度有过之无不及。The environmental pollution here is even worse than where I live.

有机 yǒujī [形] (化) organic ▷传统理论与新思潮有机地结合。Traditional theory and new thinking are linked in one organic whole.

有口皆碑 yǒu kǒu jiē bēi be universally acclaimed

有口无心 yǒu kǒu wú xīn ▷她是个有口无心的人，你不要太计较。Don't take any of it to heart – her bark is worse than her bite.

有赖 yǒulài [动] depend on

有劳 yǒuláo [动] trouble ▷有劳您帮我咨询一下。Could I trouble you to help me make a few enquiries?

有利 yǒulì [形] favourable (英), favorable (美)

有门儿 yǒuménr [动] (口) be hopeful ▷我看李杨找工作的事有门儿。I reckon that Li Yang's search for a job is looking pretty hopeful.

有名无实 yǒu míng wú shí lack substance ▷畅销书未必都好，有些不过是有名无实。Not all bestsellers are good, some lack substance.

有目共睹 yǒu mù gòng dǔ be plain for all to see

有气无力 yǒu qì wú lì feeble ▷他有气无力地说："我想喝水。"He said feebly, "I want water."

有求必应 yǒu qiú bì yìng never refuse a request

有趣 yǒuqù [形] interesting

有如 yǒurú [动] be like ▷老太太的头发有如雪一样白。The old lady's hair is as white as snow.

有声有色 yǒu shēng yǒu sè vivid ▷文中对乡村的描写有声有色、情趣盎然。The description of the village is vivid and full of emotion.

有恃无恐 yǒu shì wú kǒng secure in the knowledge that one has backing ▷经理的秘书总是对我们指手画脚，因为她有恃无恐。The manager's secretary is always bossing us around, secure in the knowledge that she has backing.

有数 yǒushù I [动] know all about (PT knew, PP known) ▷这件事怎么做，我心中有数。I know all about how to do this. II [形] just a few ▷我们的任务必须在有数的几天内完成。Our assignment has to be completed in just a few days.

有条不紊 yǒu tiáo bù wěn methodical

有头有脸 yǒu tóu yǒu liǎn command respect ▷他在单位里可是有头有脸的，大家都服他。He commands a lot of respect at work – everyone listens to him.

有为 yǒuwéi [形] promising

有喜 yǒuxǐ [动] (口) be pregnant

有戏 yǒuxì [动] (方) look hopeful

有限 yǒuxiàn [形] limited ▷旅馆床位数量有限，请提前预订。The guesthouse has a limited number of beds – please book in advance. ▷有限的几个电脑，满足不了学生的需要。This small number of computers are insufficient for the students' needs.

有限公司 yǒuxiàn gōngsī [名] limited company

有线电视 yǒuxiàn diànshì [名] cable TV

有心 yǒuxīn I [动] be determined to ▷我有心帮朋友一把，却不知怎么做。I am determined to help my friend, but I don't know what to do. II [副] deliberately

有形 yǒuxíng [形] tangible

有幸 yǒuxìng [形] fortunate ▷她有幸获得了世界名牌大学的奖学金。She was fortunate enough to receive a scholarship from a world-class university.

有眼无珠 yǒu yǎn wú zhū be totally lacking in perception

有意 yǒuyì I [动] (有兴趣) be interested in ▷姑娘好像对那个小伙子有意。It seems as if the girl is interested in that guy. II [副] on purpose ▷你这不是有意叫我为难嘛！You're just doing this on purpose to make me feel bad!

有意识 yǒu yìshí [形] conscious

有意思 yǒuyìsi I [形] 1 (有意义) significant 2 (有趣味) interesting II [动] be interested in ▷你没看出来他对你有意思吗？Haven't you noticed he's interested in you?

有朝一日 yǒu zhāo yī rì one day ▷我希望有朝一日能到世界一流大学读书。I hope that one day I can go and study at one of the world's best universities.

黝 yǒu 见下文

黝黑 yǒuhēi [形] dark

又 yòu [副] 1 (重复) again ▷今天他又来了。He came again today. 2 (同时) ▷车开得又快又稳。The car drives fast and smoothly. ▷她是一个好教师，又是一个好妈妈。She's both a good teacher and a great mother. 3 (也) too ▷天黑了，路又滑，最好别出门。It's dark, and the roads are slippery too – you'd better not go out. 4 (另外) another ▷家里又买了一个书架。They bought another set of bookshelves for their home. ▷老师又布置了几项作业。The teacher set several more questions for homework. 5 (再加上) and ▷一又三分之二 one and two thirds ▷两个月又三天 two

months and three days **6** (可是) but ▷她想去旅游，又怕累。She wants to go travelling but she's afraid it'll tire her out. **7** (根本) even ▷又不是我的错，你怪我干吗？It's not even my fault – why are you blaming me? ▷他又不知道，你问他干什么？What are you asking him for? He has no idea.

又及 yòují [动] ▷信写完了，她在下面又添上一行字："又及…" At the end of her letter, she added another line: "PS …"

右 yòu [名] **1** (右边) right ▷请向右转。Please turn right. **2** (右翼) the Right

幼 yòu I [形] young II [名] child (PL children)
幼儿 yòu'ér [名] small child (PL children)
幼年 yòunián [名] infancy
幼小 yòuxiǎo [形] young
幼稚 yòuzhì [形] **1** (书) (年龄很小) young **2** (头脑简单) naive

囿 yòu I [名] (书) enclosure ▷鹿囿 deer park II [动] limit ▷囿于成见 be blinded by prejudice ▷囿于孤陋寡闻 be handicapped by ignorance

诱 yòu [动] **1** (诱导) guide **2** (引诱) entice
诱导 yòudǎo I [动] guide II [动] (生理) induce
诱饵 yòu'ěr [名] bait
诱发 yòufā [动] **1** (诱导启发) bring out (PT, PP brought) ▷他的鼓励大大诱发了人们的积极性。His encouragement did a lot to bring out people's initiative. **2** (导致发生) induce
诱惑 yòuhuò [动] **1** (引诱) entice **2** (吸引) attract
诱使 yòushǐ [动] lure ▷他经常诱使那几个少年去偷盗。He often lures those kids into stealing things.
诱因 yòuyīn [名] cause

迂 yū [形] **1** (指路) circuitous **2** (指人) pedantic
迂腐 yūfǔ [形] pedantic
迂回 yūhuí I [形] winding II [动] (军) outflank

淤 yū I [名] silt II [动] silt up
淤积 yūjī [动] silt up
淤泥 yūní [名] silt
淤塞 yūsè [动] silt up

于 yú I [介] **1** (在) in ▷这位老人生于1899年。This old man was born in 1899. ▷暑期班已于昨日开课。The summer-holiday class began lessons yesterday. **2** (向) from ▷问道于盲 ask the way from a blind person ▷求助于朋友 ask for help from friends **3** (对)

to ▷印刷术的发明于人类非常有益。The invention of printing was of great benefit to humanity. **4** (从) from ▷很多成语来源于历史故事。Many Chinese idioms originate from historical stories. **5** (比) than ▷大于bigger than **6** (在…方面) ▷乐于助人 delight in helping people ▷我从早到晚都忙于家务。I'm busy with household chores from morning till night.
于是 yúshì [连] so ▷同学们对学英语很感兴趣，于是成立了一个英语俱乐部。The students were very interested in English, so they started an English club.

余 yú I [动] remain ▷除去花销，尚余千元。With the costs deducted, more than a thousand yuan still remains. II [名] **1** (零头) ▷500余人 more than five hundred people ▷我导师40岁有余。My supervisor is over 40. **2** (指时间) ▷课余 extra-curricular
余波 yúbō [名] aftereffects (PL)
余地 yúdì [名] room ▷这件事已没有商量的余地。There is no longer any room for negotiation in this matter.
余悸 yújì [名] lingering fear
余力 yúlì [名] spare energy
余生 yúshēng [名] **1** (指晚年) remaining years (PL) **2** (指性命) survival
余味 yúwèi [名] aftertaste
余暇 yúxiá [名] free time
余兴 yúxìng [名] **1** (兴致) excitement **2** (文娱) entertainment

盂 yú [名] jar ▷痰盂 spittoon (英), cuspidor (美)

鱼 yú [名] fish (PL fish)
鱼贯 yúguàn [形] in single file ▷参加葬礼的人们鱼贯进入教堂。The mourners at the funeral entered the church in single file.
鱼雷 yúléi [名] torpedo (PL torpedoes)
鱼龙混杂 yú lóng hùnzá a mix of good and bad people ▷这个乐队鱼龙混杂。This band has a mixture of good and bad musicians.
鱼肉 yúròu I [名] fish II [动] (书) savagely oppress
鱼死网破 yú sǐ wǎng pò everyone is a loser
鱼跃 yúyuè [动] dive

娱 yú I [动] amuse II [名] amusement
娱乐 yúlè I [动] have fun ▷放假了，大家好好娱乐一下。The holidays are here – everyone should have some fun. II [名] entertainment

渔 yú [动] **1** (捕鱼) fish **2** (谋取) filch ▷渔利 profit

渔产 yúchǎn [名] aquatic products (PL)

渔利 yúlì I [动] profit ▷他名为帮忙，实际是想从中渔利。On the surface he was helping out, but in fact he was profiting from the situation. II [名] easy pickings (PL)

渔业 yúyè [名] fisheries (PL)

隅 yú [名] 1 (角落) corner 2 (边地) outlying area

逾 yú I [动] (书) exceed II [副] (书) even more

逾期 yúqī [动] be overdue

逾越 yúyuè [动] exceed ▷他认为自己与父母之间有不可逾越的鸿沟。He believed there was an unbridgeable gulf between him and his parents.

渝 yú [动] change ▷忠贞不渝 unswervingly loyal

愉 yú [形] happy

愉快 yúkuài [形] happy ▷祝你旅行愉快！Have a pleasant journey!

愉悦 yúyuè [形] cheerful

愚 yú I [形] foolish II [动] fool

愚笨 yúbèn [形] clumsy

愚蠢 yúchǔn [形] foolish

愚昧 yúmèi [形] ignorant

愚弄 yúnòng [动] make a fool of ▷明白自己被人愚弄之后，他决定报复。Once he realized he had been made a fool of, he resolved to get his revenge.

舆 yú I [形] popular II [名] (书) chariot

舆论 yúlùn [名] public opinion

与 yǔ I [动] give (PT gave, PP given) ▶赠与 present II [介] with ▷我永远不会与政客为友。I will never make friends with politicians. ▷与敌人决一死战 fight the enemy to the death III [连] and ▷春季与秋季 spring and autumn

与其 yǔqí [连] rather than ▷与其每天发牢骚，不如想办法改变现状。Rather than grumbling all the time, it would be better to find a way to change the situation.

与人为善 yǔ rén wéi shàn glad to help others ▷他一向与人为善，大家都很信任他。He's always glad to help people – everybody has great trust in him.

与日俱增 yǔ rì jù zēng grow day by day ▷随着经济的发展，这个国家的国力与日俱增。As the economy develops, the country is getting stronger day by day.

予 yǔ [动] give (PT gave, PP given) ▶授予 award

予以 yǔyǐ [动] give (PT gave, PP given)

屿 yǔ [名] islet ▶岛屿 islands (PL)

宇 yǔ [名] 1 (房屋) house 2 (四方) the universe 3 (风度) appearance

宇航 yǔháng I [动] travel through space II [名] space travel

宇航员 yǔhángyuán [名] astronaut

宇宙 yǔzhòu [名] universe

羽 yǔ [名] 1 (羽毛) feather 2 (翅膀) wing

羽毛 yǔmáo [名] feather

羽毛球 yǔmáoqiú [名] 1 (指运动) badminton 2 (指球体) shuttlecock

羽翼 yǔyì [名] 1 (翅膀) wing 2 (帮手) assistant

雨 yǔ [名] rain

雨后春笋 yǔ hòu chūnsǔn spring up like mushrooms

雨具 yǔjù [名] waterproofs (PL)

雨量 yǔliàng [名] rainfall

雨露 yǔlù [名] 1 (雨水和露水) rain and dew 2 (喻) (恩惠) favour (英), favor (美)

雨水 yǔshuǐ [名] (降水) rain

语 yǔ I [名] 1 (语言) language ▷他会说多种外国语。He can speak many foreign languages. ▶手语 sign language ▶旗语 semaphore 2 (谚语) saying II [动] talk

语病 yǔbìng [名] grammatical mistake

语词 yǔcí [名] words and phrases (PL)

语调 yǔdiào [名] tone

语法 yǔfǎ [名] grammar

语感 yǔgǎn [名] feel for language ▷他语感好，因此文章写得好。He has a good feel for language, and so he writes very good essays.

语境 yǔjìng [名] context

语句 yǔjù [名] sentence

语料 yǔliào [名] corpus

语气 yǔqì [名] 1 (口气) tone of voice 2 (语法) mood

语文 yǔwén [名] 1 (语言文字) language 2 (中文) Chinese 3 (语言与文学) language and literature

语无伦次 yǔ wú lúncì speak incoherently ▷他紧张得双腿发抖，说话语无伦次。He was so nervous that his legs were shaking and his speech was incoherent.

语系 yǔxì [名] language family

语序 yǔxù [名] word order

语言 yǔyán [名] language

语义 yǔyì [名] ▷这两个词语义相同，但使用场合不同。These two words are the same semantically, but they are used in different contexts.

语音 yǔyīn [名] pronunciation

语音信箱 yǔyīnxìnxiāng [名] voice mail

语种 yǔzhǒng [名] language

语重心长 yǔ zhòng xīn cháng sincere words

玉 yù [名] 1 (玉石) jade 2 (美丽) beauty 3 (敬)(指对方身体) ▶玉照 your photograph

玉米 yùmǐ [名] 1 (指植物) maize (英), corn (美) 2 (指子实) corn on the cob

玉器 yùqì [名] jadeware

玉石俱焚 yù shí jù fén destruction of both good and bad

玉照 yùzhào [名] your photograph

驭 yù [动] drive (PT drove, PP driven)

芋 yù [名] 1 (指植物) taro 2 (指块茎) tuber

芋头 yùtou [名] taro

吁 yù [动] plead
→另见 xū

吁请 yùqǐng [动] request

吁求 yùqiú [动] plead with

郁 yù [形] 1 (香气浓) strong-smelling 2 (茂盛) lush 3 (烦闷) gloomy

郁积 yùjī [动] repress ▷郁积在他心中的委屈，终于倾诉出来了。He finally poured out all the grievances that he'd kept repressed.

郁结 yùjié [动] repress

郁闷 yùmèn [形] melancholy

郁郁 yùyù [形] 1 (茂密) lush 2 (苦闷) depressed ▷近来他有点儿郁郁不乐。He's been a bit depressed lately.

育 yù I [动] 1 (生育) give birth to (PT gave, PP given) 2 (养活) raise II [名] education

育龄 yùlíng [名] childbearing age

育种 yùzhǒng [动] breed (PT, PP bred)

狱 yù [名] 1 (监狱) prison 2 (官司) lawsuit

浴 yù [动] wash

浴场 yùchǎng [名] outdoor swimming pool

浴盆 yùpén [名] bath

浴室 yùshì [名] bathroom

预 yù I [副] in advance II [动] take part in (PT took, PP taken)

预报 yùbào [动] predict ▷天气预报说今晚有霜冻。The weather forecast is for frost this evening.

预备 yùbèi [动] prepare

预测 yùcè [动] predict ▷谈判结果与人们的预测很不一样。The result of the negotiations was completely different from everyone's predictions.

预防 yùfáng [动] prevent

预感 yùgǎn [动] have a premonition ▷他买彩票时预感会中大奖，果真应验了。As he bought the lottery ticket he had a premonition that he was going to win a big prize, and sure enough it came true.

预告 yùgào [动] give advance warning (PT gave, PP given) ▷下周的电影预告你看了吗？Have you seen the trailer for next week's film?

预计 yùjì [动] estimate

预见 yùjiàn [动] foresee (PT foresaw, PP foreseen) ▷那位人类学家的预见非常准确。That anthropologist's predictions were accurate.

预警 yùjǐng [动] give advance warning (PT gave, PP given)

预科 yùkē [名] foundation course

预料 yùliào [动] predict ▷不出我的预料，他果然当上了经理。As I predicted, he did become a manager.

预算 yùsuàn [名] budget

预习 yùxí [动] prepare for lessons ▷每天的功课，他都提前预习。He always prepares every day's lesson in advance.

预先 yùxiān [副] in advance ▷租用会议室，要预先提出申请。If you want to hire the meeting room you have to submit a request in advance.

预言 yùyán [动] predict ▷他的预言果然变成了现实。It turned out that his prophecy came true.

预兆 yùzhào [名] premonition ▷出车祸的那天早晨，他就有一种不祥的预兆。The morning before the car accident, he had a premonition of disaster.

域 yù [名] region ▶领域 realm

欲 yù I [名] desire II [动] (书) want ▷为所欲为 do what one wants III [副] (书) ▷喷薄欲出 about to burst forth

欲盖弥彰 yù gài mí zhāng protest too much

欲念 yùniàn [名] sexual desire

欲速则不达 yù sù zé bù dá try to run before one can walk ▷学习外语是一个循序渐

进的过程，欲速则不达。Studying foreign languages is a progressive, gradual process – you can't run before you can walk.

欲望 yùwàng [名] desire

遇 yù I [动] meet (PT, PP met) II [名] 1 (待遇) treatment 2 (机会) opportunity

遇害 yùhài [动] be murdered

遇救 yùjiù [动] be rescued

遇难 yùnàn [动] 1 (意外死亡) be killed in an accident 2 (遭难) meet with misfortune (PT, PP met)

喻 yù [动] 1 (明白) understand (PT, PP understood) ▷知识就是力量，这个道理是不言而喻的。It goes without saying that knowledge is power. 2 (说明) explain 3 (比方) give an example (PT gave, PP given)

御 yù (书) [动] 1 (赶车) drive (PT drove, PP driven) 2 (抵挡) keep ... out (PT, PP kept)

御寒 yùhán [动] keep out the cold (PT, PP kept)

寓 yù I [动] 1 (居住) live 2 (寄托) imply II [名] residence

寓所 yùsuǒ [名] residence

寓言 yùyán [名] fable

寓意 yùyì [名] moral

裕 yù [形] plentiful

愈 yù I [形] (书) recover II [副] (书) the more ... the more ... ▷士兵们愈战愈勇。The more the soldiers fought the braver they became.

愈合 yùhé [动] heal up

愈加 yùjiā [副] increasingly ▷年轻时他就我行我素，上了年纪愈加固执。He was set in his ways when he was young, and as he got older he became increasingly stubborn.

誉 yù I [名] reputation II [动] praise

誉满全球 yù mǎn quánqiú have a worldwide reputation ▷早在古代，中国丝绸就已誉满全球。Early in antiquity, Chinese silk already had a worldwide reputation.

鹬 yù [名] snipe

鸳 yuān [名] mandarin duck

鸳鸯 yuānyāng [名] 1 (指鸟) mandarin duck 2 (指人) lovebirds (PL)

冤 yuān I [名] 1 (冤枉) injustice 2 (冤仇) enmity II [形] ▷花这么多钱买了假货，太冤了！What bad luck to spend so much money on a fake.

冤仇 yuānchóu [名] enmity

冤大头 yuāndàtóu [名] squanderer

冤家 yuānjia [名] 1 (仇人) enemy 2 (可气又可爱的人) ▷你这个小冤家，别再气我了！Stop annoying me you little devil.

冤枉 yuānwang I [动] treat unfairly ▷他没什么责任，你别冤枉他。He wasn't responsible – don't be unfair to him. II [名] wrongful treatment III [形] not worthwhile

渊 yuān I [名] ▶深渊 abyss II [形] deep

渊博 yuānbó [形] erudite

渊源 yuānyuán [名] origin

元 yuán I [名] 1 (始) first 2 (首) chief ▶元凶 chief culprit 3 (主) fundamental ▶元素 element 4 (整体) component ▶单元 unit 5 (圆形货币) coin ▶金元 gold coin II [量] yuan ▷5元钱 five yuan

元旦 Yuándàn [名] New Year's Day

元件 yuánjiàn [名] part

元老 yuánlǎo [名] founding member

元气 yuánqì [名] vitality

元首 yuánshǒu [名] head of state

元帅 yuánshuài [名] commander-in-chief

元宵 yuánxiāo [名] the Lantern Festival

元宵节 Yuánxiāo Jié [名] the Lantern Festival

元勋 yuánxūn [名] founding father

元音 yuányīn [名] vowel

园 yuán [名] 1 (指菜地或果林) garden 2 (指游乐场所) park

园地 yuándì [名] 1 (田园) garden 2 (活动范围) field

园丁 yuándīng [名] 1 (园艺工人) gardener 2 (老师) teacher

园林 yuánlín [名] garden

园艺 yuányì [名] gardening

员 yuán I [名] 1 (指工作或学习的人) ▶理发员 hairdresser ▶学员 student 2 (成员) member II [量] ▷一员大将 an able general

员工 yuángōng [名] staff (PL)

原 yuán I [形] 1 (本来的) original ▷原计划 original plan 2 (未加工的) raw ▶原油 crude oil II [动] forgive (PT forgave, PP forgiven) ▶原谅 forgive III [名] plain

原本 yuánběn I [名] 1 (原稿) original manuscript 2 (初本) first edition 3 (原书) original II [副] originally

原材料 yuáncáiliào [名] raw and processed

materials (PL)

原稿 yuángǎo [名] manuscript

原告 yuángào [名] plaintiff

原籍 yuánjí [名] native home

原来 yuánlái I [形] original ▷几十年过去, 这个小镇还是原来的样子。Decades have passed, but this town is still as it always was. II [副] 1 (起初) originally ▷我原来并不知道他们两人之间的恩恩怨怨。Originally I knew nothing about their complicated emotional history. 2 (其实) all along ▷我以为你出国了, 原来你还在国内呢! I thought you had gone abroad, and all along you were still in the country!

原理 yuánlǐ [名] principle

原谅 yuánliàng [动] forgive (PT forgave, PP forgiven) ▷我得早点走, 请原谅。I have to leave early, please excuse me. ▷我求她原谅我的过失。I begged her pardon for my mistake.

原料 yuánliào [名] (指烹饪) ingredient

原始 yuánshǐ [形] 1 (古老) primitive 2 (最初) original

原委 yuánwěi [名] full details (PL)

原先 yuánxiān I [形] original II [副] originally

原形 yuánxíng [名] true colours (英) 或 colors (美) (PL)

原因 yuányīn [名] reason ▷这次没考好, 主要原因是没重视。The main reason I didn't do well in this exam is that I didn't take it very seriously. ▷医生们尚未查出得这种病的原因。The doctors have never established the causes of this illness.

原原本本 yuányuánběnběn from start to finish ▷他把事情的经过原原本本地讲了一遍。He gave us a full and detailed account of the affair.

原则 yuánzé [名] principle ▷我们原则上同意你的观点。We agree with you in principle.

原著 yuánzhù [名] the original

原子 yuánzǐ [名] atom

圆 yuán I [形] 1 (圆形的) round ▶圆圈 circle 2 (球形的) spherical 3 (圆满的) satisfactory II [动] justify III [名] 1 (数) (圆周) circle 2 (金属货币) coin ▶银圆 silver coin

圆场 yuánchǎng [动] mediate

圆规 yuánguī [名] compasses (PL)

圆滑 yuánhuá [形] sly

圆满 yuánmǎn [形] satisfactory

圆梦 yuánmèng [动] 1 (释梦) interpret dreams 2 (实现梦想) realize one's dream ▷他一直想出国, 这次终于可以圆梦了。He's always wanted to go abroad. This time he can finally realize his dream.

圆舞曲 yuánwǔqǔ [名] waltz

援 yuán [动] 1 (牵引) pull ▶攀援 clamber 2 (引用) cite ▶援例 cite a precedent 3 (援助) help ▶支援 support

援救 yuánjiù [动] rescue

援引 yuányǐn [动] cite ▷他援引专家的结论来支持自己的观点。He cited the conclusions of the experts in support of his view.

援助 yuánzhù [动] help

缘 yuán [名] 1 (缘故) cause 2 (缘分) fate 3 (边缘) edge

缘分 yuánfèn [名] fate ▷恋爱婚姻, 要看两个人的缘分。The success of love and marriage depends on predestination.

缘故 yuángù [名] cause

缘由 yuányóu [名] cause

猿 yuán [名] ape

猿猴 yuánhóu [名] apes and monkeys (PL)

猿人 yuánrén [名] ape-man (PL ape-men)

源 yuán [名] source ▶水源 source

源泉 yuánquán [名] source

源源 yuányuán [形] continuous

源远流长 yuán yuǎn liú cháng have a long history ▷中华文明源远流长。Chinese civilization has a long history.

远 yuǎn [形] 1 (指距离) far ▷两条河相距不远。The two rivers are not far from one other. 2 (指血统) distant 3 (指程度) far ▷这本词典远比其他词典好。This dictionary is far better than other dictionaries. ▷这本小说远不如我上星期读的那本有意思。This novel is nowhere near as interesting as the one I read last week.

远程 yuǎnchéng [名] long distance ▷远程导弹 long-range missile

远程会议 yuǎnchéng-huìyì [名] teleconference

远大 yuǎndà [形] far-reaching

远方 yuǎnfāng [名] afar ▷客人们从远方来。The guests have come from afar.

远见 yuǎnjiàn [名] foresight

远近 yuǎnjìn [名] 1 (距离的长短) distance 2 (远处和近处) far and near ▷他可是远近闻名的大人物。He's known of far and wide.

远景 yuǎnjǐng [名] 1 (远处景物) distant view 2 (未来景象) future prospect

远亲 yuǎnqīn [名] distant relative

远视 yuǎnshì [名] (医) long sight ▷他是远视

眼，近处的东西看不清。He's long-sighted – he can't see anything properly close to.

远洋 yuǎnyáng [名] ocean

远征 yuǎnzhēng [动] go on an expedition (PT went, PP gone)

远走高飞 yuǎnzǒugāofēi travel far away

远足 yuǎnzú [动] hike ▷他周末远足。At the weekends he goes hiking.

苑 yuàn [名] 1 (园林) garden 2 (书) (指文艺) circles (PL) ▶艺苑 artistic circles

怨 yuàn I [动] blame II [名] resentment

怨恨 yuànhèn [动] hold a grudge against (PT, PP held) ▷他小时候没能上学，到现在还怨恨父母。He couldn't go to school when he was young, and to this day he still holds a grudge against his parents.

怨声载道 yuàn shēng zài dào ▷对于不合理的税收制度，人们怨声载道。There were many complaints about the unfair taxation system.

怨天尤人 yuàn tiān yóu rén blame everyone and everything except oneself

怨言 yuànyán [名] complaint

院 yuàn [名] 1 (院落) courtyard 2 (指机关和处所) ▶研究院 research institute ▶电影院 cinema (英), movie theater (美) 3 (学院) college 4 (医院) hospital

院落 yuànluò [名] yard

院士 yuànshì [名] fellow

愿 yuàn I [名] 1 (愿望) wish ▶愿望 desire 2 (愿心) promise II [情] ▷他愿出力，不愿出钱。He is volunteering work, not money.

愿望 yuànwàng [名] wish

愿意 yuànyì [动] 1 (同意) be willing to ▷你愿意负责这项工作吗？Are you willing to take on this project? 2 (希望) wish

约 yuē I [动] 1 (束缚) restrict 2 (商定) arrange 3 (邀请) invite 4 (节俭) economize 5 (数) (约分) reduce ▷十分之五可以约成二分之一。Five over ten can be reduced to one over two. II [形] brief ▶简约 brief III [副] about ▷这袋米约有20公斤。This sack of rice weighs about twenty kilograms.

约定俗成 yuē dìng sú chéng established by usage ▷对这种事我们有约定俗成的解决办法。We have established practice for dealing with this kind of thing.

约法三章 yuē fǎ sān zhāng establish a set of rules

约会 yuēhuì [动] make an appointment ▷今天的约会临时取消了。The appointment today has been put off.

约略 yuēluè [副] approximately ▷参加示威的人数，约略有10万人。Approximately a hundred thousand people attended the demonstration.

约束 yuēshù [动] bind (PT, PP bound) ▷法律约束人，也保护人。The law binds people but also protects them.

月 yuè [名] 1 (月球) the moon ▶满月 full moon 2 (份) month ▶3月 March 3 (每月) monthly ▶月薪 monthly salary 4 (月亮状) ▶月饼 mooncake

月份 yuèfèn [名] month

月光 yuèguāng [名] moonlight

月经 yuèjīng [名] 1 (例假) period 2 (经血) menses (PL)

月亮 yuèliang [名] the moon

月票 yuèpiào [名] monthly ticket

月食 yuèshí [名] lunar eclipse

月下老人 yuèxià lǎorén matchmaker

乐 yuè [名] music ▶器乐 instrumental music ▶民乐 folk music →另见 lè

乐队 yuèduì [名] band

乐理 yuèlǐ [名] musical theory

乐谱 yuèpǔ [名] score

乐器 yuèqì [名] musical instrument ▷他会演奏多种乐器。He can play a lot of different instruments.

乐曲 yuèqǔ [名] music

乐坛 yuètán [名] musical circles (PL)

乐团 yuètuán [名] philharmonic orchestra

乐章 yuèzhāng [名] movement

岳 yuè [名] 1 (高山) mountain 2 (妻子的父母) parents-in-law (PL)

岳父 yuèfù [名] father-in-law (PL fathers-in-law)

岳母 yuèmǔ [名] mother-in-law (PL mothers-in-law)

阅 yuè [动] 1 (看) read (PT, PP read) 2 (检阅) inspect 3 (经历) experience

阅读 yuèdú [动] read (PT, PP read)

阅览 yuèlǎn [动] read (PT, PP read)

阅历 yuèlì [名] experience

悦 yuè I [形] happy II [动] please

悦耳 yuè'ěr [形] beautiful ▷这男孩子嗓音清脆，唱起歌来悦耳动听。The boy has a clear voice – when he sings it's beautiful.

悦目 yuèmù [形] beautiful ▷这些女孩们的服装色彩悦目。These girls' clothes are a beautiful colour (英) 或 color (美).

跃 yuè [动] leap

跃跃欲试 yuèyuè yù shì itching to have a go ▷听完老师的介绍，同学们跃跃欲试。Having heard the teacher's introduction, the students were itching to have a go.

越 yuè I [动] 1 (跨过) jump over 2 (超过) exceed ▶越级 skip a grade 3 (昂扬) be in high spirits II [副] ▷这门课越学越有意思。The more you study this subject, the more interesting it gets. ▷这姑娘长得越来越漂亮了。This girl is becoming more and more beautiful.

越冬 yuèdōng [动] live through winter

越发 yuèfā [副] increasingly ▷到了晚年，他越发固执。Towards the end of his life, he became increasingly stubborn.

越轨 yuèguǐ [动] overstep the mark

越来越 yuèláiyuè [副] more and more ▷他的英语说得越来越流利了。His English is getting more and more fluent. ▷天气越来越暖和了。The weather is getting warmer and warmer.

越权 yuèquán [动] overstep one's authority

越野 yuèyě [动] go cross-country (PT went, PP gone)

越狱 yuèyù [动] escape from prison

越···越··· yuè···yuè··· [副] the more ... the more ... ▷你越说，那家伙越不听。The more you talk, the more that guy won't listen. ▷明天大家来得越早越好。The earlier everyone can come tomorrow the better.

越俎代庖 yuè zǔ dài páo meddle in other's affairs ▷这件事必须由他自己做，你不能越俎代庖。He has to do this himself – don't you go getting involved.

晕 yūn [动] 1 (晕眩) dizzy 2 (昏迷) faint →另见 yùn

晕厥 yūnjué [动] pass out

云 yún I [名] cloud II [动] say (PT, PP said)

云彩 yúncai [名] cloud

云集 yúnjí [动] converge

云雾 yúnwù [名] mist

云霄 yúnxiāo [名] the skies (PL)

匀 yún I [形] even II [动] 1 (使均匀) even ... out 2 (分) apportion

匀称 yúnchèn [形] well-proportioned

匀整 yúnzhěng [形] regular

芸 yún 见下文

芸芸众生 yúnyún zhòng shēng all living things ▷他认为自己是旷世奇才，不同于芸芸众生。He thinks he's got some sort of unique talent – that he's a cut above all other mortals.

耘 yún [动] hoe

允 yǔn I [动] allow ▶应允 assent II [形] fair

允诺 yǔnnuò [动] promise

允许 yǔnxǔ [动] allow ▷儿童饮酒是绝对不允许的。Children aren't allowed to drink alcohol.

陨 yǔn [动] (书) fall from the sky (PT fell, PP fallen)

陨落 yǔnluò [动] 1 (坠落) fall from the sky (PT fell, PP fallen) 2 (喻) (去世) die

陨石 yǔnshí [名] meteorite

孕 yùn I [动] be pregnant II [名] pregnancy

孕育 yùnyù [动] be pregnant with ▷平静的表面下孕育着一场政治风暴。Beneath the calm exterior, a political hurricane was brewing.

运 yùn I [动] 1 (运动) move 2 (搬运) transport ▶货运 transport 3 (运用) use II [名] luck ▶好运 good luck

运筹帷幄 yùnchóu wéiwò plan ... from behind the scenes

运动 yùndòng I [动] (物) move II [名] 1 (体育活动) sport ▷适量运动有益健康。A degree of sporting activity is good for the health. 2 (大规模) movement

运动鞋 yùndòngxié [名] trainer

运动员 yùndòngyuán [名] athlete

运河 yùnhé [名] canal

运气 yùnqi [名] luck

运输 yùnshū [动] transport

运算 yùnsuàn [动] calculate

运行 yùnxíng [动] move

运用 yùnyòng [动] make use of ▷应尽量把书本知识运用到实践中去。You should make practical use of what you have learned in books.

运转 yùnzhuǎn [动] 1 (指星球) orbit ▷月亮绕着地球运转。The moon orbits the earth. 2 (指机器) run (PT ran, PP run)

运作 yùnzuò [动] operate

晕 yùn I [动] feel giddy (PT, PP felt) ▶晕机 be airsick II [名] 1 (指日、月) halo ▶月晕 lunar

halo **2** (指光、色) glow ▶红晕 red glow
→另见 yūn

晕场 yùnchǎng [动] get stage fright

晕车 yùnchē [动] be carsick

晕船 yùnchuán [动] be seasick

酝 yùn [动] (书) brew

酝酿 yùnniàng [动] brew ▷这件事已经酝酿
好长时间了。This affair has been brewing for
a long time.

韵 yùn [名] **1** (声音) music **2** (情趣) charm **3** (韵
母) rhyme

韵味 yùnwèi [名] lasting appeal

蕴 yùn **I** [动] (书) contain **II** [名] (书) store

蕴藏 yùncáng [动] contain

蕴涵 yùnhán [动] contain

熨 yùn [动] iron

熨斗 yùndǒu [名] iron

Zz

扎 zā [动] tie
→另见 zhā

咂 zā [动] **1** (吸入) sip **2** (咂嘴) make noises of appreciation **3** (品味) savour (英), savor (美)
咂嘴 zāzuǐ [动] make noises of appreciation

杂 zá **I** [形] miscellaneous ▶复杂 complicated **II** [动] mix ▷棉花中间杂进其他纤维。Other fibres (英) 或 fibers (美) are mixed into the cotton.
杂感 zágǎn [名] **1** (偶感) random thoughts (PL) **2** (杂记) notes (PL)
杂烩 záhuì [名] **1** (指菜) stew **2** (拼凑) mixture
杂货 záhuò [名] groceries (PL)
杂技 zájì [名] acrobatics (PL)
杂交 zájiāo [动] hybridize ▷杂交水稻 rice hybrid
杂乱 záluàn [形] jumbled up ▷冰箱里的东西很杂乱。The things in the fridge are all jumbled up.
杂念 zániàn [名] distracting thoughts (PL)
杂牌 zápái [名] inferior brand
杂耍 záshuǎ [名] variety show
杂碎 zásui [名] entrails (PL)
杂物 záwù [名] litter

杂音 záyīn [名] **1** (干扰) static **2** (噪声) noise **3** (医) murmur
杂志 zázhì [名] magazine ▷专业杂志 technical magazine ▷学术杂志 academic journal
杂质 zázhì [名] impurity ▷这种米杂质很多。This rice has a lot of impurities in it.
杂种 zázhǒng [名] **1** (生物) hybrid **2** (侮辱) bastard

砸 zá [动] **1** (撞击) pound **2** (打破) break (PT broke, PP broken) ▷杯子砸坏了。The cup was broken. **3** (方) (失败) fail ▷戏演砸了。The performance went badly.

咋 zǎ [代] **1** (为什么) ▷你咋不回家呢？Why don't you go home? **2** (怎么) ▷那里咋样啊？How are things going there?
→另见 zé, zhā

灾 zāi [名] **1** (灾害) disaster ▶水灾 flood **2** (不幸) misfortune
灾害 zāihài [名] disaster
灾荒 zāihuāng [名] famine
灾祸 zāihuò [名] calamity
灾难 zāinàn [名] disaster
灾区 zāiqū [名] disaster area

栽 zāi [动] **1** (种) plant ▷栽花 grow flowers **2** (插) stick ... in (PT, PP stuck) **3** (强加) frame **4** (摔倒) tumble
栽培 zāipéi [动] **1** (种植) cultivate ▷水稻栽培 rice cultivation **2** (造就) nurture **3** (提拔) promote
栽赃 zāizāng [动] frame
栽种 zāizhòng [动] plant

载 zǎi **I** [名] year **II** [动] record ▶登载 publish
→另见 zài

宰 zǎi [动] **1** (管) rule ▶主宰 dominate **2** (杀) slaughter
宰割 zǎigē [动] oppress

仔 zǎi [名] **1** (儿子) son **2** (指动物) young animal ▷下仔 drop a litter

再 zài [副] **1** (又) again ▷你再说一遍。Say that again. **2** (更) more ▷你再做得认真些就更好了。If you were a bit more serious about it, it would be better. ▷请把音量放得再大些。Please turn the volume up a bit. ▷再大的风雨我也不怕。Even if the storm were worse I wouldn't be afraid. **3** (继续) ▷我不能再等了。I can't wait any longer. ▷即使再给几天，任

务也完不成。Even if we're given another few days, this job won't be done. **4** (接着) then ▷吃完饭再打电脑游戏。Eat your dinner and then you can play your computer game. ▷你做完功课再看小说。You can read your book when you've finished your homework. **5** (另外) ▷再说 besides ▷再就是 and also

再次 zàicì [副] once again ▷再次相聚 get together again

再会 zàihuì [动] say goodbye (PT, PP said)

再见 zàijiàn [动] say goodbye (PT, PP said) ▷再见！Goodbye!

再接再厉 zài jiē zài lì persevere

再就业 zàijiùyè [动] re-employ

再三 zàisān [副] again and again ▷再三叮嘱 warn ... again and again ▷再三思考 on second thoughts

再生 zàishēng [动] **1** (复活) revive **2** (回收) recycle

再现 zàixiàn [动] reappear

再造 zàizào [动] rebuild (PT, PP rebuilt)

在 zài I [动] **1** (存在) live ▷精神永在。The spirit will live forever. **2** (处于) be (PT was, PP been) ▷你的书在桌子上。Your book is on the table. ▷我父母在纽约。My parents are in New York. **3** (在于) rest with ▷和解的关键在他们。The key to reconciliation rests with them. II [副] ▷情况在改变。Things are changing. ▷他们在看电视。They're watching TV. III [介] at ▷在机场等候 wait at the airport ▷在人类历史中 in human history

在岗 zàigǎng [形] employed

在行 zàiháng [形] expert ▷他对计算机很在行。He's a computer expert.

在乎 zàihu [动] care ▷他对别人的批评满不在乎。He doesn't care about criticism.

在劫难逃 zài jié nán táo ▷这次我看他是在劫难逃。This time I see there will be no escape.

在世 zàishì [动] be alive

在逃 zàitáo [动] be on the run

在望 zàiwàng [动] **1** (可以看见) be visible **2** (即将到来) be in sight ▷胜利在望。Victory is in sight.

在位 zàiwèi [动] be in power

在押 zàiyā [动] be in prison

在业 zàiyè [形] employed

在意 zàiyì [动] care ▷你说什么我都不会在意的。Whatever you say, I just don't care.

在于 zàiyú [动] **1** (存在) lie in (PT lay, PP lain) **2** (取决于) depend on

在职 zàizhí [动] be employed ▷他是在职

研究生。He's working and also doing a postgraduate degree.

在座 zàizuò [动] be present

载 zài [动] [动] **1** (装载) carry ▷载重 load **2** (充满) be full of ▷怨声载道 complaints on all sides
→另见 zǎi

载歌载舞 zài gē zài wǔ sing and dance

载运 zàiyùn [动] transport

载重 zàizhòng [名] load ▷载重能力 loading capacity

簪 zān I [名] hairpin II [动] put ... in one's hair (PT, PP put) ▷簪花 put flowers in one's hair

咱 zán [代] **1** (咱们) we **2** (方) (我) I

咱们 zánmen [代] **1** (我们) we **2** (方) (我) I ▷咱们只是个普通劳动者。I'm just an ordinary labourer.

攒 zǎn [动] save
→另见 cuán

暂 zàn I [形] brief II [副] temporarily ▷暂住朋友那里 stay at a friend's temporarily ▷暂停 suspend

暂且 zànqiě [副] for the moment

暂时 zànshí [名] ▷暂时的需要 temporary need ▷我们暂时休息一下。We'll rest for a moment.

暂行 zànxíng [形] provisional

錾 zàn I [动] engrave II [名] chisel

赞 zàn I [动] **1** (帮助) assist ▷赞助 assistance **2** (称颂) commend II [名] eulogy

赞成 zànchéng [动] approve ▷赞成政府的决策 approve of the government's policy ▷投赞成票 cast a yes vote

赞歌 zàngē [名] paean

赞美 zànměi [动] praise

赞赏 zànshǎng [动] admire

赞颂 zànsòng [动] sing the praises of (PT sang, PP sung)

赞叹 zàntàn [动] marvel at

赞同 zàntóng [动] approve of

赞扬 zànyáng [动] pay tribute to (PT, PP paid) ▷学校赞扬学生们的勇敢行为。The school paid tribute to the students' bravery.

赞助 zànzhù [动] assist ▷为残疾人提供赞助 offer assistance to disabled people

赃 zāng [名] **1** (赃物) booty ▷分赃 share the booty **2** (贿赂) bribes (PL) ▷贪赃 take bribes

赃款 zāngkuǎn [名] dirty money

赃物 zāngwù [名] **1** (被盗物品) stolen goods (PL) **2** (受贿之物) bribe

脏 zāng [形] dirty
→另见 zàng

脏话 zānghuà [名] dirty word

脏字 zāngzì [名] swear word

脏 zàng [名] internal organ ▶心脏 heart ▶肝脏 liver ▶肾脏 kidney
→另见 zāng

脏器 zàngqì [名] organ

葬 zàng [动] bury ▶送葬 attend a funeral

葬身 zàngshēn [动] be buried

葬送 zàngsòng [动] ruin

藏 zàng [名] **1** (储存地) store **2** (经典) scriptures (PL) **3** (西藏) Tibet
→另见 cáng

藏蓝 zànglán [形] purplish blue

藏青 zàngqīng [形] dark blue

遭 zāo I [动] meet with (PT, PP met) ▶遭殃 suffer II [量] time ▷头一遭 the first time

遭际 zāojì [名] encounter

遭受 zāoshòu [动] suffer ▷遭受水灾 be hit by floods

遭殃 zāoyāng [动] suffer

遭遇 zāoyù I [动] meet with (PT, PP met) II [名] experience

遭罪 zāozuì [动] suffer

糟 zāo I [名] dregs (PL) II [动] **1** (浪费) waste ▶糟蹋 spoil **2** (腌制) flavour (英) 或 flavor (美) with alcohol III [形] **1** (腐烂) rotten **2** (弄坏) messy

糟糕 zāogāo [形] ▷真糟糕，我的钥匙丢了。Oh no, I've lost my key! ▷糟糕，庄稼给毁了。How awful! The crops have been ruined.

糟践 zāojian [动] **1** (浪费) waste **2** (侮辱) insult

糟粕 zāopò [名] rubbish

糟蹋 zāota [动] **1** (浪费) waste **2** (损坏) abuse

凿 záo I [名] chisel II [动] cut (PT, PP cut)

早 zǎo I [名] morning II [副] a long time ago ▷这事我早就知道了。I knew about this a long time ago. III [形] early ▶早餐 breakfast ▷你早点来。Come early.

早安 zǎo'ān [名] ▷早安! Good morning!

早操 zǎocāo [名] morning exercises (PL)

早产 zǎochǎn [名] (医) premature birth

早晨 zǎochen [名] morning ▷他早晨9点上班。He goes to work at 9 o'clock in the morning.

早点 zǎodiǎn [名] breakfast

早饭 zǎofàn [名] breakfast

早年 zǎonián [名] youth ▷他早年当过兵。In his youth he was a soldier.

早期 zǎoqī [名] early stage ▷他的早期作品 his early works

早上 zǎoshang [名] morning ▷早上好! Good morning!

早晚 zǎowǎn I [名] morning and evening II [副] **1** (迟早) sooner or later **2** (方) (将来) some day

枣 zǎo [名] date

枣红 zǎohóng [形] claret

澡 zǎo [动] bathe

澡盆 zǎopén [名] bathtub

澡堂 zǎotáng [名] public baths (PL)

皂 zào I [名] soap II [形] black

灶 zào [名] **1** (炊具) cooker (英), stove (美) **2** (厨房) kitchen ▷学生灶 students' canteen

灶具 zàojù [名] cooking utensil

造 zào I [动] **1** (制作) make (PT, PP made) ▷造船 build a ship **2** (瞎编) concoct ▶造谣 start a rumour (英) 或 rumor (美) **3** (书) (前往) arrive ▶造访 visit **4** (培养) train II [名] harvest

造成 zàochéng [动] cause

造反 zàofǎn [动] rebel

造访 zàofǎng [动] visit

造福 zàofú [动] benefit ▷这项新发明将造福于人类。This new invention will benefit humanity.

造化 zàohua [名] good fortune

造价 zàojià [名] cost

造就 zàojiù [动] train

造孽 zàoniè [动] do evil

造型 zàoxíng [名] model

造谣 zàoyáo [动] start a rumour (英) 或 rumor (美)

造诣 zàoyì [名] achievements (PL)

造作 zàozuò [动] make (PT, PP made)

造作 zàozuo [形] artificial

噪 zào [动] **1** (叫) chirp ▷蝉噪 noise of cicadas **2** (嚷) clamour (英), clamor (美) ▶鼓噪 create an uproar

噪音 zàoyīn [名] noise

燥 zào [形] dry ▶干燥 dry
燥热 zàorè [形] 1 (指天气) hot and dry 2 (医) dry

躁 zào [形] rash ▶烦躁 be agitated
躁动 zàodòng [动] fidget

则 zé I [名] 1 (榜样) standard ▶准则 standard 2 (规章) rule ▶总则 general principle II [量] piece ▷新闻三则 three items of news III [连] 1 (就) then ▷不战则已，战则必胜。If you don't fight, then fine. If you do fight, fight to win. 2 (却) but ▷他很虚荣，她则不然。He's very vain, but she's not. ▷南方湿润，北方则干燥。The south is humid, but the north is dry. IV [副] ▷不能让老人们干这种活儿，一则他们年纪大，二则身体差。You can't let elderly people do this kind of work. For one thing, they're too old, and for another, they're not up to it health-wise.

责 zé I [名] responsibility ▶负责 be responsible for II [动] 1 (要求) demand ▶责令 order 2 (质问) cross-examine ▶责问 call to account 3 (责备) blame ▶指责 censure
责备 zébèi [动] blame
责成 zéchéng [动] instruct ▷此事要责成人事部来办。We need to instruct the human resources department to handle this.
责怪 zéguài [动] accuse ▷他责怪孩子太粗心。He accused the child of being thoughtless.
责令 zélìng [动] order
责任 zérèn [名] responsibility ▷这件事也有你的责任。This is also your responsibility.
责无旁贷 zé wú páng dài be duty-bound

择 zé [动] choose (PT chose, PP chosen) →另见 zhái
择交 zéjiāo [动] choose one's friends (PT chose, PP chosen)
择偶 zé'ǒu [动] choose a partner (PT chose, PP chosen)
择优 zéyōu [动] choose the best (PT chose, PP chosen)

咋 zé 见下文
咋舌 zéshé [动] be speechless ▷他惊讶得直咋舌。He was left speechless with surprise. →另见 zǎ, zhā

泽 zé [名] 1 (聚水地) pool ▶沼泽 swamp 2 (潮湿) damp ▶润泽 moist 3 (光) sheen ▶色泽 colour (英) 或 color (美) and sheen ▶光泽 lustre (英),

luster (美) 4 (恩惠) kindness

啧 zé [拟] click
啧啧称赞 zézé chēngzàn shout and cheer

贼 zéi I [名] 1 (小偷) thief (PL thieves) ▶盗贼 robber 2 (叛徒) traitor II [形] 1 (邪恶) evil 2 (狡猾) cunning III [副] (方) especially ▷天贼冷。It's especially cold.
贼头贼脑 zéi tóu zéi nǎo behave furtively ▷瞧他贼头贼脑的样子就不像好人。Look at him going around so furtively – surely he's up to no good.

怎 zěn [代] (方) ▷你怎能相信他的话？How can you believe him? ▷他怎么这么小心眼？Why is he being so petty?
怎么 zěnme I [代] ▷你看这事我该怎么办？What do you think I should do about this? ▷你昨天怎么没来上课？Why weren't you in class yesterday? ▷这到底是怎么一回事？What on earth has happened here? II [副] 1 (泛指方式) ▷他愿意怎么办就让他怎么办。Let him do it however he wants. ▷我是怎么想就怎么说。I say whatever I think. ▷他最近怎么样？How has he been doing? 2 (表示程度) ▷他今天不怎么高兴。He's not that happy today. ▷这本书不怎么好看。This book isn't that interesting.
怎样 zěnyàng [副] how ▷这种情况怎样处理？How is this to be dealt with? ▷你怎样批评我都可以。Whatever criticisms you have are fine.

曾 zēng [形] ▷曾祖父母 great-grandparents →另见 céng
曾孙 zēngsūn [名] great-grandson
曾祖 zēngzǔ [名] great-grandfather

增 zēng [动] increase
增加 zēngjiā [动] increase ▷增加人民收入 increase people's income
增色 zēngsè [动] add to
增长 zēngzhǎng [动] increase ▷控制人口增长 control the increase in population
增值 zēngzhí [名] (经济) increase
增值税 zēngzhíshuì [名] VAT
增殖 zēngzhí I [名] proliferation II [动] multiply

憎 zēng [动] hate
憎恨 zēnghèn [动] detest
憎恶 zēngwù [动] loathe

锃 zèng [形] (方) shiny

锃亮 zèngliàng [形] shiny

赠 zèng [动] present ▶馈赠 present ▶捐赠 donate

赠品 zèngpǐn [名] gift

赠送 zèngsòng [动] present

赠言 zèngyán [名] advice

扎 zhā [动] 1 (刺) prick 2 (住下) set up camp (PT, PP set) ▷部队驻扎在村子里。The troops set up camp in the village. 3 (钻进) plunge into ▷他一下扎进水中。He plunged into the water.
→另见 zā

扎根 zhāgēn [动] take root (PT took, PP taken)

扎实 zhāshi [形] 1 (结实) sturdy 2 (实在) solid ▷他英语基础比较扎实。He has a solid foundation in English.

扎眼 zhāyǎn [形] 1 (刺眼) dazzling 2 (惹人注意) loud

咋 zhā 见下文
→另见 zǎ

咋呼 zhāhu [动] (方) 1 (吆喝) cry out 2 (炫耀) show off (PT showed, PP shown)

喳 zhā [拟] chatter
→另见 chā

渣 zhā [名] 1 (渣滓) residue ▶残渣 dregs (PL) 2 (碎屑) crumbs (PL)

渣滓 zhāzǐ [名] dregs (PL) ▷那些人是社会的渣滓。Those people are the dregs of society.

札 zhá [名] 1 (木片) wooden writing tablets (PL) 2 (信件) letter

札记 zhájì [名] notes (PL)

轧 zhá [动] roll
→另见 yà

轧制 zházhì [动] roll

闸 zhá I [名] 1 (水闸) sluice 2 (制动器) brake 3 (电闸) switch II [动] dam

闸门 zhámén [名] sluice

炸 zhá [动] fry
→另见 zhà

铡 zhá I [名] cutter II [动] cut (PT, PP cut)

铡刀 zhádāo [名] cutter

眨 zhǎ [动] wink

眨眼 zhǎyǎn [动] blink ▷他一眨眼工夫就不见

了。He disappeared in the blink of an eye.

乍 zhà I [副] 1 (起初) first ▷乍一看，这东西不错。On first inspection this isn't bad. 2 (忽然) suddenly II [动] spread (PT, PP spread) ▶乍翅 spread one's wings

诈 zhà [动] 1 (骗) swindle 2 (装) pretend ▶诈降 pretend to surrender 3 (诱) draw ... out (PT drew, PP drawn) ▷其实他是在诈你。Actually he's trying to draw you out.

诈唬 zhàhu [动] trick

诈骗 zhàpiàn [动] swindle

栅 zhà [名] railing

栅栏 zhàlan [名] bar

炸 zhà [动] 1 (爆破) blow ... up (PT blew, PP blown) 2 (破裂) explode ▷暖水瓶炸了。The flask exploded. 3 (逃离) run scared (PT ran, PP run)
→另见 zhá

炸弹 zhàdàn [名] bomb

炸药 zhàyào [名] explosive

榨 zhà [动] extract

榨取 zhàqǔ [动] squeeze

斋 zhāi [名] 1 (斋戒) fast 2 (素食) vegetarian diet 3 (屋子) room ▶书斋 study

斋戒 zhāijiè [动] fast

摘 zhāi [动] 1 (取) pick 2 (选) select ▶摘编 take extracts from 3 (借) borrow

摘录 zhāilù [动] take extracts (PT took, PP taken) ▷摘录新闻 take extracts from the news

摘取 zhāiqǔ [动] select

摘要 zhāiyào I [动] summarize II [名] abstract

宅 zhái [名] house ▶住宅 house

宅子 zháizi [名] house

择 zhái [动] select
→另见 zé

窄 zhǎi [形] 1 (不宽敞) narrow 2 (气量小) narrow-minded 3 (不宽裕) hard up

窄小 zhǎixiǎo [形] narrow

债 zhài [名] debt

债权 zhàiquán [名] (法) creditor's rights (PL)

债券 zhàiquàn [名] bond

债务 zhàiwù [名] debt

寨 zhài [名] 1 (村寨) stockade 2 (山寨) mountain stronghold 3 (营寨) camp

占 zhān [动] divine
→另见 zhàn

占卜 zhānbǔ [动] divine

占卦 zhānguà [动] divine

沾 zhān [动] 1 (浸) moisten 2 (被附上) stick (PT, PP stuck) ▷她身上沾的都是泥。She was covered with mud. 3 (碰) touch ▷他滴酒不沾。He doesn't touch alcohol. 4 (得) benefit from ▷他总想沾点便宜。He always wants to take advantage.

沾光 zhānguāng [动] benefit from association ▷他的提干显然是沾了他老领导的光。His promotion obviously came from his connection with his old boss.

沾染 zhānrǎn [动] be contaminated by ▷你要防止伤口沾染细菌。You must prevent the wound from becoming contaminated with germs.

沾沾自喜 zhānzhān zì xǐ pat oneself on the back

毡 zhān [名] felt

粘 zhān [动] stick (PT, PP stuck)
粘贴 zhāntiē [动] stick (PT, PP stuck)

瞻 zhān [动] look up
瞻前顾后 zhān qián gù hòu be indecisive ▷他做事总是瞻前顾后。Whatever he does he's always indecisive about it.
瞻仰 zhānyǎng [动] revere ▷瞻仰遗容 pay one's respects

斩 zhǎn [动] chop
斩草除根 zhǎn cǎo chú gēn destroy root and branch
斩钉截铁 zhǎn dīng jié tiě categorical ▷他斩钉截铁地回答对方的问题。He answered the other side's questions categorically.

盏 zhǎn I [名] small cup II [量] ▷一盏灯 an electric lamp

展 zhǎn I [动] 1 (进行) develop 2 (施展) give free rein to (PT gave, PP given) 3 (暂缓) postpone II [名] exhibition
展播 zhǎnbō [名] show
展开 zhǎnkāi [动] 1 (张开) spread (PT, PP spread) 2 (进行) develop
展览 zhǎnlǎn [名] exhibition

展品 zhǎnpǐn [名] exhibit
展示 zhǎnshì [动] reveal ▷展示个性 reveal one's personality
展望 zhǎnwàng [动] look into the distance
展现 zhǎnxiàn [动] emerge
展销 zhǎnxiāo [动] display ... for sale

崭 zhǎn 见下文
崭露头角 zhǎn lù tóujiǎo begin to make a name for oneself
崭新 zhǎnxīn [形] brand-new

辗 zhǎn [动] toss and turn
辗转 zhǎnzhuǎn [动] 1 (翻来覆去) toss and turn 2 (传来传去) pass through many different hands

占 zhàn [动] 1 (占用) occupy ▷非常抱歉，占了您很多时间。I apologize for taking up so much of your time. 2 (处于) ▷占上风 get the upper hand
→另见 zhān
占据 zhànjù [动] occupy
占领 zhànlǐng [动] capture
占用 zhànyòng [动] occupy ▷会议室已被占用了。The meeting room is already occupied.
占有 zhànyǒu [动] own

战 zhàn I [名] war ▷枪战 exchange of fire II [动] 1 (战斗) fight (PT, PP fought) 2 (发抖) shiver
战败 zhànbài [动] 1 (打败) defeat 2 (失败) be defeated
战场 zhànchǎng [名] front
战斗 zhàndòu [动] fight (PT, PP fought)
战犯 zhànfàn [名] war criminal
战俘 zhànfú [名] prisoner of war
战绩 zhànjì [名] military successes (PL)
战乱 zhànluàn [名] ravages of war (PL)
战略 zhànlüè [名] strategy ▷战略反攻 plan a counter-attack
战胜 zhànshèng [动] overcome (PT overcame, PP overcome)
战士 zhànshì [名] soldier
战术 zhànshù [名] tactics (PL)
战役 zhànyì [名] battle
战战兢兢 zhànzhànjīngjīng ▷他们非常害怕，战战兢兢地往前走。They were scared out of their wits and walked on trembling with fear.
战争 zhànzhēng [名] war

站 zhàn I [动] 1 (站立) stand (PT, PP stood) ▷我在火车上站3个多小时了。I stood on the train for more than three hours. ▷我们站在你这边。We'll stand by you. 2 (停下) stop ▷等车站稳了乘客才可以下车。When the bus comes to a stop, the passengers can get off. II [名] 1 (停车地点) stop ▷公共汽车站 bus stop 2 (服务机构) centre (英), center (美) ▷医疗站 treatment centre

站立 zhànlì [动] stand (PT, PP stood)

站台 zhàntái [名] platform

站住 zhànzhù [动] 1 (站稳) stand firm (PT, PP stood) 2 (停步) halt 3 (停留) wait 4 (合理) hold up (PT, PP held) ▷你的解释站不住。Your explanation doesn't hold up.

绽 zhàn [名] split

绽放 zhànfàng [动] bloom

湛 zhàn [形] 1 (深邃) deep 2 (清澈) crystal clear

湛蓝 zhànlán [形] azure

颤 zhàn [动] tremble
→另见 chàn

颤栗 zhànlì [动] tremble

蘸 zhàn [动] dip ... in ▷我喜欢蘸点醋吃饺子。I like to eat dumplings dipped in vinegar.

张 zhāng I [动] 1 (打开) open ▷张大嘴巴 open one's mouth wide 2 (展开) extend ▶扩张 stretch 3 (夸大) exaggerate ▶夸张 exaggerate 4 (看) look ▷东张西望 look around 5 (开业) open for business ▷商店要开张了。The shop is about to open for business. 6 (陈设) lay ... on (PT, PP laid) ▷他们结婚时不想大张筵席。When they get married, they don't want to lay on a big reception. II [量] ▷一张海报 a poster ▷一张书桌 a desk

张灯结彩 zhāng dēng jié cǎi be decorated with lanterns and streamers

张挂 zhāngguà [动] hang ... up (PT, PP hung)

张冠李戴 Zhāng guān Lǐ dài confuse one thing with another ▷他不是我们经理, 我看你是张冠李戴了。He's not our manager – you're confusing him with someone else.

张皇 zhānghuáng [形] alarmed

张口结舌 zhāng kǒu jié shé be at a loss for words

张罗 zhāngluo [动] 1 (料理) take care of (PT took, PP taken) 2 (筹划) raise ▷我得去张罗点儿钱。I need to raise some money. 3 (接待) attend to ▷赶快张罗客人吧! Go and attend to the guests!

张望 zhāngwàng [动] look around

张牙舞爪 zhāng yá wǔ zhǎo make threatening gestures

张扬 zhāngyáng [动] spread ... about (PT, PP spread) ▷这事不要到处张扬。You mustn't go spreading this about everywhere.

章 zhāng [名] 1 (作品) article ▶文章 article 2 (章节) chapter 3 (条理) order 4 (章程) regulation ▶宪章 charter 5 (图章) seal 6 (标志) badge (英), button (美)

章程 zhāngchéng [名] regulation

章法 zhāngfǎ [名] 1 (规则) regulation 2 (条理) orderliness ▷这篇文章很有章法。This essay is very well organized.

彰 zhāng I [形] obvious ▶昭彰 evident II [动] praise ▶表彰 praise

樟 zhāng [名] camphor tree

樟脑 zhāngnǎo [名] camphor

蟑 zhāng 见下文

蟑螂 zhāngláng [名] cockroach

长 zhǎng I [形] 1 (大) older ▷他年长我3岁。He's three years older than me. 2 (排行第一) oldest ▶长兄 oldest brother II [名] 1 (年长者) ▶兄长 elder brother ▶师长 teacher (头领) head ▶校长 head teacher ▷理事长 chairman of the board III [动] 1 (生) form ▷他身上长了疥疮。A sore formed on his body. 2 (发育) grow (PT grew, PP grown) ▷他长得像他爸爸。He looks like his father. 3 (增加) acquire ▷长知识 acquire knowledge
→另见 cháng

长辈 zhǎngbèi [名] elder

长进 zhǎngjìn [名] progress

长势 zhǎngshì [名] crop growth

长相 zhǎngxiàng [名] features (PL)

涨 zhǎng [动] increase
→另见 zhǎng

涨幅 zhǎngfú [名] increase ▷物价涨幅平稳。Prices are increasing, but at a steady rate.

掌 zhǎng I [名] 1 (手掌) palm 2 (人的脚部) sole 3 (动物的脚掌) foot (PL feet) ▷鸭掌 duck's foot ▷熊掌 bear's paw 4 (掌形物) ▷仙人掌 cactus 5 (U型铁) horseshoe 6 (鞋掌) sole II [动] 1 (打) slap ▷我掌了他一下。I gave him a slap. 2 (钉) sole ▷掌鞋 sole shoes 3 (主持) be in charge of ▷掌管家事 be in charge of household affairs

掌舵 zhǎngduò [动] be at the helm ▷有他掌舵我们放心。As long as he's at the helm, we feel at ease.

掌管 zhǎngguǎn [动] administer

掌柜 zhǎngguì [名] manager

掌上明珠 zhǎng shàng míngzhū be the apple of sb's eye ▷她可是父亲的掌上明珠啊！She is the apple of her father's eye!

掌握 zhǎngwò [动] control ▷掌握一门新技术 master a new skill

丈 zhàng [名] 1 (敬) old man (PL men) ▶岳丈 father-in-law 2 (丈夫) husband ▶妹丈 brother-in-law

丈夫 zhàngfu [名] husband

丈量 zhàngliáng [动] measure

丈人 zhàngrén [名] father-in-law

仗 zhàng I [名] 1 (战斗) battle ▶打仗 fight 2 (兵器) weapons (PL) II [动] 1 (拿着) be armed ▷仗刀 armed with a knife 2 (依靠) rely on

仗恃 zhàngshì [动] rely on

仗义 zhàngyì [形] righteous

仗义执言 zhàng yì zhí yán speak out from a sense of justice

杖 zhàng [名] 1 (拐杖) walking stick 2 (棒子) ▶擀面杖 rolling pin

帐 zhàng [名] curtain ▶蚊帐 mosquito net ▶营帐 tent

帐篷 zhàngpeng [名] tent

账 zhàng [名] 1 (账目) accounts (PL) 2 (账簿) ledger 3 (债务) credit ▶赊账 buy on credit

账单 zhàngdān [名] bill

账号 zhànghào [名] account number

账面 zhàngmiàn [名] statement

胀 zhàng [动] 1 (膨胀) expand 2 (肿胀) swell (PT swelled, PP swollen)

涨 zhàng [动] 1 (涨大) expand 2 (充血) flush →另见 zhǎng

障 zhàng I [名] barrier ▶屏障 screen ▶路障 blockade II [动] hinder

障碍 zhàng'ài I [动] hinder II [名] obstacle

招 zhāo I [动] 1 (挥动) beckon ▷他招手让我进里面去。He beckoned me inside. 2 (招收) recruit 3 (引来) attract 4 (惹怒) provoke 5 (坦白) confess II [名] 1 (计谋) trick 2 (指下棋) move

招标 zhāobiāo [动] invite tenders

招待 zhāodài [动] entertain ▷招待宾客 entertain guests ▷招待会 reception

招供 zhāogòng [动] confess ▷他在法庭上全都招供了。He confessed everything in court.

招呼 zhāohu [动] 1 (呼唤) call 2 (问候) greet 3 (吩咐) tell (PT, PP told) ▷请招呼他进来坐一会儿。Please tell him to come in and sit down for a while.

招集 zhāojí [动] assemble

招架 zhāojià [动] hold one's own (PT, PP held)

招揽 zhāolǎn [动] solicit

招领 zhāolǐng [动] post a 'Found' notice

招牌 zhāopai [名] sign

招聘 zhāopìn [动] advertise for ▷这家饭店要招聘服务员。The hotel wants to advertise for waiters.

招惹 zhāorě [动] cause ▷他总招惹是非。He always causes trouble.

招商 zhāoshāng [动] attract business

招式 zhāoshì [名] body language

招收 zhāoshōu [动] enrol

招数 zhāoshù [名] strategic move

招贴 zhāotiē [名] poster

招摇 zhāoyáo [动] show off (PT showed, PP shown)

招展 zhāozhǎn [动] flutter

招致 zhāozhì [动] 1 (招收) recruit 2 (引起) lead to (PT, PP led)

昭 zhāo I [形] clear ▶昭然 obvious II [动] show (PT showed, PP shown)

昭然若揭 zhāorán ruò jiē clear as day

昭雪 zhāoxuě [动] exonerate

着 zhāo [名] 1 (步) move ▷他这着棋可走错了。This move of his has really gone wrong. 2 (法) tactic ▷这下他没着了。He has no tactics beyond this.
→另见 zháo, zhuó

着数 zhāoshù [名] move

朝 zhāo [名] 1 (晨) morning 2 (天) day
→另见 cháo

朝晖 zhāohuī [名] morning sunlight

朝令夕改 zhāo lìng xī gǎi keep chopping and changing

朝气 zhāoqì [名] youthful spirit

朝三暮四 zhāo sān mù sì blow hot and cold ▷交朋友不能朝三暮四。You shouldn't blow hot and cold with your friends.

朝夕 zhāoxī [名] 1 (每天) every day 2 (时间) a

very short time

着 zháo [动] 1 (挨) touch ▷他说话总是不着边际。When he's talking he never sticks to the point. 2 (受到) be affected by ▷小心着凉。Be careful not to get cold. 3 (燃烧) be lit ▷木炭着了。The charcoal is lit. 4 (入睡) fall asleep (PT fell, PP fallen) ▷昨晚我一躺下就着了。Yesterday evening I fell asleep as soon as I lay down.
→另见 zhāo, zhuó

着急 zháojí [形] worried ▷别着急，休息几天就好了。Don't worry, you'll be fine after a few days' rest.

着迷 zháomí [动] be fanatical ▷他对足球着迷。He's fanatical about football.

爪 zhǎo [名] claw
→另见 zhuǎ

爪牙 zhǎoyá [名] flunkey

找 zhǎo [动] 1 (寻找) look for ▷他去电影院找女儿了。He went to the cinema to look for his daughter. 2 (退余额) give change (PT gave, PP given) ▶找钱 give change 3 (求见) call on ▷有事找他就行。If you encounter any problem it's fine to ask him.

找茬儿 zhǎochár [动] pick holes

找到 zhǎodào [动] find (PT, PP found)

找事 zhǎoshì [动] 1 (找工) look for a job 2 (滋事) make trouble

沼 zhǎo [名] pool

沼气 zhǎoqì [名] methane

沼泽 zhǎozé [名] marsh

召 zhào [动] summon

召唤 zhàohuàn [动] call

召集 zhàojí [动] convene

召见 zhàojiàn [动] summon

召开 zhàokāi [动] hold (PT, PP held)

兆 zhào I [名] (预兆) sign ▷病兆 the sign of an illness II [量] million ▶兆瓦 megawatt III [动] foretell (PT, PP foretold)

兆头 zhàotou [名] omen

照 zhào I [动] 1 (照射) light up (PT, PP lit) ▷阳光照得满屋亮堂堂的。The sunlight lit up the whole room. 2 (映现) reflect ▶照镜子 look at oneself in the mirror 3 (拍摄) take a photograph (PT took, PP taken) ▷这张照片照得不错。This photograph is excellent. 4 (照料) look after ▷请帮我关照一下孩子。Please can you help me and look after the children for a while. 5 (对照) contrast ▶比照 contrast 6 (遵照) refer to ▶参照 consult 7 (明白) understand (PT, PP understood) ▷心照不宣 have a tacit understanding II [名] 1 (照片) photograph 2 (执照) licence (英), license (美) III [介] 1 (按照) according to ▷照章办事 act according to the rules 2 (向着) in the direction of ▷照这个方向一直走就到了。Just keep walking in this direction and you'll find it.

照本宣科 zhào běn xuān kē go by the book

照常 zhàocháng [副] as usual ▷节日期间，商店照常营业。On holidays the shop will open for business as usual.

照顾 zhàogù [动] 1 (照料) look after 2 (考虑) consider

照会 zhàohuì I [动] deliver a note to II [名] note

照看 zhàokàn [动] look after ▷他正在照看孩子。He's looking after the children.

照例 zhàolì [副] as a rule

照料 zhàoliào [动] take care of (PT took, PP taken)

照面儿 zhàomiànr 1 [动] put in an appearance (PT, PP put) ▷他打了个照面儿就走了。He put in an appearance and then left.

照明 zhàomíng [名] lighting

照片 zhàopiàn [名] photograph

照射 zhàoshè [动] light up (PT, PP lit)

照相 zhàoxiàng [动] take a picture (PT took, PP taken)

照相机 zhàoxiàngjī [名] camera

照样 zhàoyàng [副] 1 (依照样品) in the same style 2 (依然) still ▷没有他，我们照样能做好。Even without him, we'll still be able to do it.

照耀 zhàoyào [动] illuminate

照应 zhàoyìng [动] 1 (呼应) correlate 2 (照料) look after

罩 zhào I [名] 1 (罩子) cover ▶床罩 bedcover ▶口罩 face mask 2 (罩衣) overall ▶外罩 dustcoat II [动] cover

肇 zhào [动] 1 (开始) start 2 (发生) cause

肇事 zhàoshì [动] cause trouble

折 zhē [动] 1 (翻转) roll over ▷他在床上折来折去。In bed he rolled this way and that. 2 (倒) pour ... back and forth ▷她拿两个杯子把水折几下就凉了。She poured the water from one cup to another to cool it.
→另见 shé, zhé

折腾 zhēteng [动] **1** (翻来覆去) toss and turn **2** (反复做) do ... over and over again **3** (折磨) cause suffering ▷头痛可真折腾人。Headaches can cause a lot of suffering.

蜇 zhē [动] sting (PT, PP stung) ▷他被马蜂蜇了一下。He was stung by a hornet.

遮 zhē [动] **1** (遮挡) hide ... from view (PT hid, PP hidden) ▷乌云遮住了阳光。The sun was hidden by dark clouds. **2** (阻挡) obstruct ▷遮雨 keep out the rain **3** (遮盖) conceal

遮蔽 zhēbì [动] obstruct

遮挡 zhēdǎng **I** [动] keep ... out (PT, PP kept) ▷请找个东西遮挡一下阳光。Please find something to protect us from the sun. **II** [名] cover

遮掩 zhēyǎn [动] **1** (遮蔽) obscure ▷屋子被门帘遮掩着。The room is obscured by a door curtain. **2** (掩饰) hide (PT hid, PP hidden)

折 zhé **I** [动] **1** (折断) break (PT broke, PP broken) **2** (损失) lose (PT, PP lost) **3** (弯曲) wind (PT, PP wound) **4** (回转) turn back **5** (使信服) convince ▷精湛的演出折服了观众。The audience were bowled over by the brilliant performance. **6** (折合) convert ... into **7** (折叠) fold **II** [名] **1** (折子) notebook ▷存折 bank book **2** (折扣) discount ▷所有服装在打折销售。All clothes are reduced.

➔另见 shé, zhē

折叠 zhédié [动] fold

折服 zhéfú [动] **1** (说服) subdue **2** (佩服) be bowled over by

折合 zhéhé [动] convert ... into ▷我把人民币都折合成了英镑。I've converted all my renminbi to pounds sterling.

折旧 zhéjiù [动] depreciate

折扣 zhékòu [名] discount ▷打折扣销售 sell at a discount

折磨 zhémó [动] torment ▷她身体虚弱，经常遭受疾病的折磨。She's in poor health and often tormented by illness.

折射 zhéshè [名] refraction

折算 zhésuàn [动] convert

折中 zhézhōng [动] compromise ▷折中方案 a compromise plan

哲 zhé **I** [形] wise **II** [名] sage

哲理 zhélǐ [名] philosophical theory

哲学 zhéxué [名] philosophy

辙 zhé [名] **1** (车痕) wheel track **2** (韵律) rhyme **3** (办法) way ▷这事我也没辙了。There's no way out of this.

者 zhě [名] **1** (人) ▷长者 elder ▷记者 journalist ▷作者 author ▷编者 editor ▷教育工作者 educationalist (英), educator (美) **2** (物) ▷前者 the former ▷后者 the latter

褶 zhě [名] crease

褶皱 zhězhòu [名] wrinkle

这 zhè [代] **1** (指人或事物) this (PL these) ▷这本书写得不错。This book is well-written. **2** (指时间) ▷他这才突然明白过来。He's just suddenly understood. ▷我这就过去。I'm going right now.

这个 zhège **I** [代] this ▷这个可比那个好多了。This one is much better than that one. ▷为这个他耽误了好几天工作。He put off work for several days on account of this. **II** [副] ▷瞧他这个忙啊！Look how busy he is!

这里 zhèlǐ [代] ▷这里发生了一起交通事故。A traffic accident happened here.

这么 zhème [代] **1** (指程度) ▷今天这么热。It's so hot today. **2** (指方式) ▷我看就应该这么做。I think it should be done this way.

这些 zhèxiē [代] these (PL) ▷这些事情够他忙的。These things are enough to keep him busy.

这样 zhèyàng [代] **1** (指程度) ▷乡村的风景这样美。The scenery in the countryside is so beautiful. **2** (指状态) ▷再这样下去可不行。It really won't do to carry on like this. ▷他就这样死心眼。He is just so stubborn.

这种 zhèzhǒng [代] ▷这种菜好吃。This kind of vegetable is tasty.

蔗 zhè [名] sugarcane

蔗糖 zhètáng [名] sucrose

贞 zhēn **I** [形] **1** (坚定) loyal ▷坚贞 loyal **2** (贞洁) chaste **II** [名] chastity

贞操 zhēncāo [名] **1** (贞节) chastity **2** (忠贞) loyalty

贞节 zhēnjié [名] chastity

贞洁 zhēnjié [形] chaste

针 zhēn [名] **1** (工具) needle **2** (针状物) ▷表针 hand ▷别针 safety pin **3** (针剂) injection **4** (缝合) stitch

针对 zhēnduì [动] **1** (对准) be aimed at ▷他的话不是针对你。What he said was not aimed at you. **2** (按照) have ... in mind ▷针对当前形势，我想谈谈自己的看法。With the current situation in mind, I would like to give my own views. ▷针对不同年龄用药。Vary the dose according to age.

针锋相对 zhēn fēng xiāng duì tit for tat

针灸 zhēnjiǔ [名] acupuncture

侦 zhēn [动] investigate

侦查 zhēnchá [动] investigate

侦察 zhēnchá [动] reconnoitre (英), reconnoiter (美)

侦缉 zhēnjī [动] track down and arrest

侦破 zhēnpò [动] crack

侦探 zhēntàn I [动] spy on II [名] detective ▷侦探小说 detective novel

珍 zhēn I [名] treasure ▷珍宝 jewellery (英), jewelry (美) II [动] value ▷珍惜 value III [形] valuable

珍爱 zhēn'ài [动] cherish

珍宝 zhēnbǎo [名] treasure

珍藏 zhēncáng [动] collect

珍贵 zhēnguì [形] precious

珍视 zhēnshì [动] value

珍惜 zhēnxī [动] value

珍稀 zhēnxī [形] rare

珍重 zhēnzhòng [动] value ... highly

珍珠 zhēnzhū [名] pearl

真 zhēn I [形] true ▷真话 truth ▷真品 genuine product II [副] really ▷他真勇敢。 He is really brave. ▷昨晚的电影真不错。Last night's film was really good.

真才实学 zhēn cái shí xué real knowledge and true ability

真诚 zhēnchéng [形] sincere

真谛 zhēndì [名] true meaning

真迹 zhēnjì [名] authentic work

真空 zhēnkōng [名] vacuum

真理 zhēnlǐ [名] truth

真切 zhēnqiè [形] vivid

真实 zhēnshí [形] true

真是 zhēnshi [副] really ▷我真是搞不懂，他 到底想干什么。I really can't make out what on earth he's up to. ▷真是，她把雨伞忘在 火车上了。She's gone and left her umbrella on the train.

真相 zhēnxiàng [名] true situation

真正 zhēnzhèng [形] true ▷他是我真正的朋 友。He's a true friend of mine. ▷我们要真正 对工作负责。We have to be truly responsible for the work.

真挚 zhēnzhì [形] genuine

真主 Zhēnzhǔ [名] Allah

斟 zhēn [动] pour

斟酌 zhēnzhuó [动] consider

箴 zhēn [动] advise

箴言 zhēnyán [名] advice

臻 zhēn [动] become (PT became, PP become)

诊 zhěn [动] examine ▶就诊 see a doctor

诊断 zhěnduàn [动] diagnose ▷医生把他的这 种症状诊断为胃溃疡。The doctor diagnosed his symptoms as a gastric ulcer.

诊所 zhěnsuǒ [名] clinic

枕 zhěn I [名] pillow II [动] rest one's head on ▷他枕着衣服睡着了。He fell asleep with his head resting on his clothes.

枕头 zhěntou [名] pillow

疹 zhěn [名] rash ▶湿疹 eczema ▶麻疹 measles (SG)

缜 zhěn 见下文

缜密 zhěnmì [形] meticulous

阵 zhèn I [名] 1 (军) (阵形) battle formation 2 (军) (阵地) position 3 (时间) a while II [量] ▷一阵暴雨 a burst of rain ▷一阵掌声 a burst of applause

阵地 zhèndì [名] position

阵脚 zhènjiǎo [名] position

阵容 zhènróng [名] battle formation

阵势 zhènshì [名] battle formation

阵亡 zhènwáng [动] be killed in action

阵线 zhènxiàn [名] frontline

阵营 zhènyíng [名] camp

振 zhèn [动] 1 (振动) vibrate 2 (振作) boost ▷最近我食欲不振。Recently my appetite has been poor.

振动 zhèndòng [动] vibrate

振奋 zhènfèn [动] rouse

振聋发聩 zhèn lóng fā kuì enlighten ▷这篇 报道起了振聋发聩的作用。This report had an enlightening effect.

振兴 zhènxīng [动] revitalize

振振有辞 zhènzhèn yǒu cí speak convincingly

振作 zhènzuò [动] pull oneself together ▷受挫之后他又振作起来。After this setback he pulled himself together again.

赈 zhèn [动] relieve

赈济 zhènjì [动] relieve

震 zhèn I [动] 1 (震动) shake (PT shook, PP shaken) 2 (激动) be excited II [名] earthquake ▷余震 after-shock

震荡 zhèndàng [动] shake (PT shook, PP shaken)

震动 zhèndòng [动] shake (PT shook, PP shaken)

震耳欲聋 zhèn ěr yù lóng deafening

震撼 zhènhàn [动] shake (PT shook, PP shaken)

震惊 zhènjīng [动] amaze ▷得知这个消息，人们震惊了。People were amazed to hear this news.

震慑 zhènshè [动] frighten

镇 zhèn I [名] 1 (城镇) town 2 (重地) garrison II [动] 1 (抑制) suppress 2 (守卫) guard ▶镇守 guard 3 (安定) calm ▶镇抚 calm 4 (冷却) cool III [形] calm ▶镇静 calm

镇定 zhèndìng [形] calm

镇静 zhènjìng [形] calm

镇静剂 zhènjìngjì [形] sedative

镇压 zhènyā [动] suppress

正 zhēng 见下文
→另见 zhèng

正月 zhēngyuè [名] first month of the lunar year

争 zhēng [动] 1 (争夺) contend 2 (争论) argue

争辩 zhēngbiàn [动] argue ▷她老为孩子的教育问题与丈夫争辩。She's constantly arguing with her husband about the children's education.

争吵 zhēngchǎo [动] quarrel ▷这对夫妻经常为小事争吵。The couple often quarrel about trivial things.

争斗 zhèngdòu [动] fight (PT, PP fought)

争端 zhēngduān [名] dispute

争夺 zhēngduó [动] fight for (PT, PP fought)

争光 zhēngguāng [动] win honour (英) 或 honor (美) for (PT, PP won)

争论 zhēnglùn [动] argue ▷不管什么问题，他总爱与人争论。He'll argue over anything.

争鸣 zhēngmíng [动] contend

争气 zhēngqì [动] be a credit to

争取 zhēngqǔ [动] strive for (PT strove, PP striven) ▷争取机会 grasp the opportunity ▷争取主动 grasp the initiative

争先 zhēngxiān [动] try to be the first ▷昨天的讨论会上，个个都争先发言。At yesterday's conference everyone was vying to speak.

争议 zhēngyì [名] dispute ▷对这个方案大家有许多争议。Everyone is in hot dispute over this scheme.

争执 zhēngzhí [动] quarrel ▷他们两人为此

事争执很久了。The two of them have been quarrelling for a long time over this.

征 zhēng I [动] 1 (征讨) mount a military expedition ▶征战 go on a military campaign 2 (召集) draft ▶征兵 conscript ▷应征入伍 enlist 3 (征收) levy ▶征税 levy taxes 4 (征求) solicit ▶征订 solicit subscriptions II [名] 1 (征程) journey ▶长征 the Long March 2 (迹象) sign ▶特征 feature

征调 zhēngdiào [动] draft

征服 zhēngfú [动] conquer

征购 zhēnggòu [动] procure

征集 zhēngjí [动] 1 (收集) collect 2 (征募) recruit

征求 zhēngqiú [动] solicit

征收 zhēngshōu [动] levy

征途 zhēngtú [名] journey

征用 zhēngyòng [动] requisition

征兆 zhēngzhào [名] sign

怔 zhēng [形] terror-stricken

挣 zhēng 见下文
→另见 zhèng

挣扎 zhēngzhá [动] struggle

峥 zhēng 见下文

峥嵘 zhēngróng [形] 1 (高峻) soaring 2 (非凡) remarkable

狰 zhēng 见下文

狰狞 zhēngníng [形] sinister

症 zhēng 见下文
→另见 zhèng

症结 zhēngjié [名] crux

睁 zhēng [动] open

睁眼瞎 zhēngyǎnxiā [名] illiterate

蒸 zhēng [动] 1 (指烹饪方法) steam 2 (蒸发) evaporate

蒸馏 zhēngliú [动] distil (英), distill (美)

蒸气 zhēngqì [名] vapour (英), vapor (美)

蒸汽 zhēngqì [名] steam

蒸蒸日上 zhēngzhēng rì shàng developing fast

整 zhěng I [形] 1 (完整) whole 2 (规整) tidy II [动] 1 (整理) sort ... out 2 (修理) repair 3 (刁难) punish

整顿 zhěngdùn [动] reorganize ▷整顿工作作风 reorganize working methods ▷整顿纪律

consolidate discipline

整个 zhěnggè [形] whole ▷整个假期我全给浪费了。I wasted the whole holiday.

整合 zhěnghé [动] integrate

整洁 zhěngjié [形] tidy

整理 zhěnglǐ [动] sort ... out

整齐 zhěngqí [形] 1 (有序的) orderly 2 (均匀的) even ▷整齐的步伐 march in step

整容 zhěngróng [动] have a make-over

整数 zhěngshù [名] whole number

整体 zhěngtǐ [名] whole

整形 zhěngxíng [动] carry out plastic surgery ▷面部整形手术 facial plastic surgery

整治 zhěngzhì [动] restore

整装 zhěngzhuāng [动] pack

正 zhèng I [形] 1 (不偏不斜) straight ▷这幅照片挂得不正。This photograph is not hung straight. ▷请坐端正。Please sit up straight. ▷他把靶子放在了正前方。He put the target directly ahead of him. 2 (居中的) main ▷正殿 main hall 3 (正面) right ▷纸张的正面 the right side of the paper 4 (正直) upright ▶公正 just 5 (正当) right ▷走上正轨 get on the right track 6 (纯正) pure ▷这道菜的味儿有点不正。This dish does not taste authentic. 7 (规范的) regular ▷这小伙子五官端正。This young man has regular features. 8 (主要的) principal ▶正餐 main meal 9 (指图形) regular ▷正八角形 regular octagon 10 (物) positive ▷正离子 positive ion 11 (数) (大于零的) positive ▶正数 positive number II [动] 1 (使不歪) straighten ▷他把帽子正了一正，出门了。He straightened his hat, and went out. 2 (改正) put ... right (PT, PP put) III [副] 1 (恰好) just ▷这双鞋大小正合适。This pair of shoes is just the right size. 2 (正在) right now ▷天正刮着风。It's windy right now. ▷他们正在酒店就餐。They're in the hotel eating right now.
→另见 zhēng

正版 zhèngbǎn [形] original

正本 zhèngběn [名] original

正常 zhèngcháng [形] normal

正当 zhèngdāng [形] legitimate

正道 zhèngdào [名] the right way

正点 zhèngdiǎn [名] ▷火车将正点到达。The train will arrive on schedule.

正法 zhèngfǎ [动] execute

正规 zhèngguī [形] standard

正轨 zhèngguǐ [名] right track

正襟危坐 zhèng jīn wēi zuò sit upright and attentively

正经 zhèngjīng I [形] 1 (正派) decent 2 (正当

的) serious 3 (标准的) standard II [副] really ▷这件家具正经不错。This furniture is really not bad.

正面 zhèngmiàn I [名] 1 (指方位) front ▷正面进攻 frontal attack ▷正面交锋 head-on clash 2 (主要的一面) the right II [形] positive III [副] directly

正派 zhèngpài [形] honest

正品 zhèngpǐn [名] quality products (PL)

正巧 zhèngqiǎo [副] by chance ▷我回来的时候，他正巧要出去。When I got back he happened to be heading out.

正确 zhèngquè [形] correct

正式 zhèngshì [形] official ▷正式报告 official report ▷他已被这所学校正式录取。He's been officially enrolled at this school.

正视 zhèngshì [动] face

正题 zhèngtí [名] topic

正统 zhèngtǒng I [名] orthodoxy II [形] orthodox

正文 zhèngwén [名] text

正义 zhèngyì I [名] justice II [形] just

正音 zhèngyīn I [动] correct one's pronunciation II [名] standard pronunciation

正在 zhèngzài [副] right now ▷会议正在进行。The meeting is taking place right now.

正直 zhèngzhí [形] upright

正中下怀 zhèng zhòng xià huái just what one wants ▷他父亲让他报考军校，对他来说真是正中下怀。His father let him take the entrance exam for the military academy, which is just what he wanted.

正宗 zhèngzōng I [名] orthodox school II [形] authentic

证 zhèng I [动] prove ▶证明 prove II [名] 1 (证据) evidence ▶物证 material evidence ▷出庭作证 give evidence in court 2 (证件) ▶身份证 identity card ▷驾驶证 driver's licence (英) 或 license (美)

证词 zhèngcí [名] testimony

证件 zhèngjiàn [名] certificate

证据 zhèngjù [名] evidence

证明 zhèngmíng I [动] prove ▷事实证明我的分析是对的。The facts prove my analysis is correct. II [名] certificate

证券 zhèngquàn [名] bond

证实 zhèngshí [动] confirm ▷这条消息有待于证实。This news remains to be confirmed.

证书 zhèngshū [名] certificate

证物 zhèngwù [名] exhibit

证言 zhèngyán [名] verbal evidence

郑 zhèng 见下文

郑重 zhèngzhòng [形] serious ▷对方郑重
表示愿意与我们合作。The other party is
expressing a serious desire to work with us.

政 zhèng [名] 1 (政治) politics (SG) 2 (事务) affairs
(PL)

政变 zhèngbiàn [名] coup

政策 zhèngcè [名] policy

政党 zhèngdǎng [名] political party

政法 zhèngfǎ [名] politics and law

政府 zhèngfǔ [名] government

政绩 zhèngjì [名] political achievements (PL)

政见 zhèngjiàn [名] political view

政界 zhèngjiè [名] political circles (PL)

政局 zhèngjú [名] political situation

政客 zhèngkè [名] politician

政权 zhèngquán [名] political power

政治 zhèngzhì [名] politics (SG)

政治家 zhèngzhìjiā [名] statesman,
stateswoman

挣 zhèng [动] 1 (赚得) earn ▶挣钱 earn money
▷挣口饭吃 earn a living 2 (摆脱) break free (PT
broke, PP broken) ▷挣开枷锁 break free from
one's shackles
→另见 zhēng

症 zhèng [名] disease
→另见 zhēng

症候 zhènghòu [名] 1 (症状) symptom 2 (疾病)
disease

症状 zhèngzhuàng [名] symptom

之 zhī I [代] ▷他考上了重点大学，朋友们为
之高兴。When he got into a top university, his
friends were very happy for him. II [助] 1 (的)
▷爱国之心 patriotic feeling ▷父母之爱
parental love ▷自知之明 self-awareness 2 (用
在主谓结构之间) ▷世界之大，无奇不有。
There is nothing too strange in this vast world.

之后 zhīhòu [介] after ▷看完电影之后，他们
去了附近的一家餐馆。After seeing a film,
they went to a nearby restaurant.

之间 zhījiān [介] 1 (指两者) between 2 (指三者或
三者以上) among

之前 zhīqián [介] before ▷项目结束之前，每个
人压力都很大。Before finishing the project,
everyone was very stressed.

之一 zhīyī [代] one of ▷他是他们班最用功的
学生之一。He is one of the hardest working
students in their class. ▷沈阳是中国最大的
城市之一。Shenyang is one of China's biggest
cities.

支 zhī I [名] branch ▷支公司 branch of a
company II [动] 1 (支撑) prop ... up ▷这
棚子该用东西支一下。This shed needs
something to prop it up. ▷把雨伞支开 put
up an umbrella 2 (伸出) raise ▷小兔子支起了
耳朵。The rabbit pricked up its ears. ▷他的
门牙有些往外支。His front teeth stick out a
bit. 3 (支持) bear (PT bore, PP borne) ▷她牙疼
得有点支不住了。She could hardly bear her
toothache. 4 (调度) send (PT, PP sent) ▷她
借故支走了他。She found an excuse to send
him away. 5 (付出) pay ... out (PT, PP paid) ▷上
个月家里开支很大。Last month household
expenses were very high. 6 (领取) get (PT got,
PP got (英), gotten (美)) ▷出差前，我们从财
务处支了些钱。Before going on the business
trip, we got some money from the finance
department. III [量] 1 (指乐曲) ▷一支钢琴
曲 a piano tune 2 (指细长物) ▷一支钢笔 a
pen 3 (指队伍) ▷一支部队 an army unit 4 (指
灯) ▷60支光的灯泡 60 watt bulb

支部 zhībù [名] branch

支撑 zhīchēng [动] 1 (抵挡) support 2 (维持)
maintain

支持 zhīchí [动] 1 (鼓励) support ▷他们夫妻
俩在事业上互相支持。Husband and wife
support each other in their work. 2 (支撑) hold
out (PT, PP held) ▷他走了3个小时，实在
支持不住了。After he had walked for three
hours, he really couldn't last anymore.

支出 zhīchū I [动] spend (PT, PP spent) II [名]
expenditure

支付 zhīfù [动] pay (PT, PP paid)

支解 zhījiě [动] dismember

支离破碎 zhīlí pòsuì break into fragments

支流 zhīliú [名] 1 (指江河) tributary 2 (指事物)
minor aspect

支配 zhīpèi [动] 1 (安排) allocate 2 (控制)
control

支票 zhīpiào [名] cheque (英), check (美) ▷把支
票兑付成现金 cash a cheque

支使 zhīshi [动] 1 (使唤) order ... about ▷她爱
支使人。She likes to order people about. 2 (打
发走) send ... away (PT, PP sent) ▷他让我把孩
子们支使走。He asked me to send the children
away.

支线 zhīxiàn [名] feeder

支援 zhīyuán [动] help

支柱 zhīzhù [名] pillar

只 zhī I [形] single ▷只言片语 a few words
▷形单影只 solitary II [量] ▷一只拖鞋 a

slipper ▷两只小船 two boats ▷3只小鸟 three birds
→另见 zhǐ

只身 zhīshēn [副] by oneself ▷他只身去了国外。He went abroad by himself.

只言片语 zhī yán piàn yǔ a few words

汁 zhī [名] juice ▷果汁 fruit juice ▷椰子汁 coconut milk ▷肉汁 beef extract ▷胆汁 bile

芝 zhī 见下文
芝麻 zhīma [名] sesame

枝 zhī [名] branch
枝节 zhījié [名] 1 (次要的事) minor issue 2 (麻烦的事) unexpected difficulty

知 zhī I [动] 1 (知道) know (PT knew, PP known) ▷此事我全然不知。I'm completely in the dark about this. 2 (使知道) inform ▷通知学生下午2点开会。Tell the students the meeting will start at 2 p.m. II [名] knowledge
知道 zhīdào [动] know (PT knew, PP known) ▷这事我可不知道。I really know nothing about this. ▷谁知道他想要干什么。Who knows what he wants to do?
知根知底 zhī gēn zhī dǐ know ... through and through ▷对于他我是知根知底的。I know him through and through.
知己 zhījǐ I [形] intimate II [名] bosom friend
知交 zhījiāo [名] intimate friend
知觉 zhījué [名] perception
知名 zhīmíng [形] famous
知趣 zhīqù [动] behave tactfully
知识 zhīshi [名] knowledge
知识分子 zhīshi fènzǐ [名] intellectual
知心 zhīxīn [形] intimate
知音 zhīyīn [名] bosom friend

肢 zhī [名] limb
肢解 zhījiě [动] dismember
肢体 zhītǐ [名] limbs (PL)

织 zhī [动] knit

脂 zhī [名] 1 (油脂) grease 2 (胭脂) rouge ▷唇脂 lipstick
脂肪 zhīfáng [名] fat

蜘 zhī 见下文
蜘蛛 zhīzhū [名] spider

执 zhī I [动] 1 (拿着) hold (PT, PP held) 2 (执掌)

take charge of (PT took, PP taken) ▷执教 be a teacher 3 (坚持) stick to (PT, PP stuck) 4 (执行) carry out II [名] written acknowledgment ▷回执 receipt
执法 zhífǎ [动] enforce the law
执教 zhíjiào [动] teach (PT, PP taught)
执迷不悟 zhí mí bù wù stick to one's bad old ways
执拗 zhíniù [形] obstinate
执勤 zhíqín [动] be on duty
执行 zhíxíng [动] carry out
执意 zhíyì [副] ▷他执意要请我们吃饭。He insisted on treating us to a meal.
执照 zhízhào [名] licence (英), license (美)
执政 zhízhèng [动] be in power
执著 zhízhuó [形] persevering

直 zhí I [形] 1 (不弯曲) straight ▷笔直的道路 dead straight road 2 (竖的) vertical ▷房间直里有5米。The room is 5 metres (英) 或 meters (美) long. 3 (公正) upstanding ▷他为人正直。He's an upstanding person. 4 (直爽) candid ▷她说话很直。She speaks very candidly. II [动] straighten ▷请把身子直起来。Straighten up. III [副] 1 (直接) straight ▷有话请直说吧。If you have something to say, come straight out with it! 2 (不断地) continuously ▷她直说个没完。She talked non-stop. 3 (简直) simply ▷我疼得直想死。I was simply in agony.
直观 zhíguān [形] audio-visual
直角 zhíjiǎo [名] right angle
直接 zhíjiē [形] direct ▷他将直接飞往伦敦。He will fly direct to London.
直截了当 zhíjié liǎodàng bluntly
直径 zhíjìng [名] diameter
直觉 zhíjué [名] intuition
直升机 zhíshēngjī [名] helicopter
直属 zhíshǔ I [动] be directly under ▷该市直属中央政府管辖。That town is directly under the jurisdiction of central government. II [形] subordinate to
直率 zhíshuài [形] frank
直爽 zhíshuǎng [形] forthright
直系亲属 zhíxì qīnshǔ [名] directly related family members
直辖 zhíxiá [形] directly under
直线 zhíxiàn I [名] straight line II [形] sharp ▷经济直线增长 sharp economic growth
直言 zhíyán [动] speak bluntly (PT spoke, PP spoken) ▷直言不讳 call a spade a spade
直译 zhíyì [名] literal translation

侄 zhí [名] nephew
侄女 zhínǚ [名] niece

值 zhí I [名] 1 (价值) value 2 (数) value II [动] 1 (值得) be worth ▷这事不值一提。It's not worth mentioning. 2 (碰上) just happen to be ▷我访问伦敦时，正值圣诞节。It just happened to be Christmas when I visited London. 3 (轮到) be on duty ▷值夜班 be on night duty
值班 zhíbān [动] be on duty
值得 zhídé [动] be worth ▷这书值得买。This book is worth buying.
值勤 zhíqín [动] be on duty
值日 zhírì [动] be on duty for the day ▷今天该我值日。Today it's my turn to be on duty.

职 zhí [名] 1 (职位) post 2 (职责) duty
职称 zhíchēng [名] professional title
职工 zhígōng [名] 1 (员工) staff 2 (工人) blue-collar worker
职能 zhínéng [名] function
职权 zhíquán [名] authority
职位 zhíwèi [名] post
职务 zhíwù [名] post
职业 zhíyè [名] occupation ▷职业律师 professional lawyer
职员 zhíyuán [名] member of staff
职责 zhízé [名] responsibility

植 zhí [动] 1 (栽种) plant 2 (树立) establish
植被 zhíbèi [名] vegetation
植物 zhíwù [名] plant ▷草本植物 herbs

殖 zhí [动] breed (PT, PP bred) ▷生殖 reproduce
殖民 zhímín [动] colonize ▷殖民政策 colonial policy
殖民地 zhímíndì [名] colony

止 zhǐ I [动] 1 (停止) stop ▷止住伤口流血 staunch a wound ▷终止合同 suspend a contract 2 (截止) end II [副] only ▷他不止一次欺骗我。He's deceived me on more than one occasion.
止境 zhǐjìng [名] limit

只 zhǐ [副] only ▷我只在周末有时间。I only have time at the weekend.
→另见 zhī
只顾 zhǐgù [动] 1 (专心) be absorbed in ▷他只顾看电视，连饭都没吃。He's so absorbed in watching television he's not even eating. 2 (只顾及) only care for ▷你只顾自己的眼前利益

是不对的。It's bad that you only care for your own immediate interests.
只管 zhǐguǎn [副] by all means ▷有什么问题大家只管问。If anyone has a question by all means ask.
只好 zhǐhǎo [副] ▷太晚了没有公共汽车，她只好打的回家。It was too late and there were no buses so she had to take a taxi home.
只是 zhǐshì I [副] merely ▷他只是在找托词。He's merely looking for a pretext. ▷问题肯定会解决，只是时间而已。The problem will certainly be resolved, it's merely a question of time. II [连] but ▷大家纷纷出钱，只是数额有多有少。One after another everyone offered money, but the amounts were varied.
只要 zhǐyào [连] so long as ▷只要我们有信心，就会战胜困难。As long as we have confidence, we can overcome difficulties.
只有 zhǐyǒu [副] only ▷只有发展经济才能振兴国家。The country can only be revitalized if the economy is developed.

旨 zhǐ I [名] 1 (用意) purpose ▶要旨 main point 2 (意旨) decree ▶圣旨 imperial decree II [形] tasty
旨趣 zhǐqù [名] intent

纸 zhǐ [名] paper
纸币 zhǐbì [名] note (英), bill (美)
纸巾 zhǐjīn [名] paper towel
纸上谈兵 zhǐ shàng tán bīng all talk and no action
纸张 zhǐzhāng [名] paper
纸醉金迷 zhǐ zuì jīn mí live a life of debauchery

指 zhǐ I [名] finger ▶中指 middle finger ▶无名指 ring finger II [动] 1 (对着) point to 2 (点明) point ... out 3 (针对) refer to ▷我没指他。I wasn't referring to him. 4 (依靠) rely on
指标 zhǐbiāo [名] target
指出 zhǐchū [动] point ... out
指导 zhǐdǎo [动] instruct ▷英语老师在指导学生写作。The English teacher is instructing the students in essay writing.
指点 zhǐdiǎn [动] show ... how (PT showed, PP shown)
指定 zhǐdìng [动] appoint ▷老板指定王小姐当秘书。The boss appointed Miss Wang as his secretary. ▷指定赞助商 official sponsor
指挥 zhǐhuī I [动] command II [名] 1 (指挥官) commander 2 (乐队指挥) conductor
指教 zhǐjiào [动] give advice (PT gave, PP given)

指控 zhǐkòng [动] charge ▷他被指控犯杀人罪。He was charged with murder.

指令 zhǐlìng I [动] instruct II [名] instruction

指鹿为马 zhǐ lù wéi mǎ distort the facts

指名 zhǐmíng [动] name

指南 zhǐnán [名] guide

指南针 zhǐnánzhēn [名] compass

指派 zhǐpài [动] assign ▷上司指派我做这项工作。The boss assigned me to this work.

指日可待 zhǐ rì kě dài be just round the corner

指桑骂槐 zhǐ sāng mà huái attack by innuendo

指使 zhǐshǐ [动] incite ▷他经常指使年幼无知的孩子做坏事。He often incites the young to mischief.

指示 zhǐshì [动] instruct ▷我们接到了上级的指示。We have received instructions from high up.

指手画脚 zhǐ shǒu huà jiǎo 1 (用手势示意) gesticulate 2 (轻率地批评) pick fault with

指数 zhǐshù [名] index

指望 zhǐwang I [动] count on ▷我们指望孩子将来有出息。We count on our children being successful in the future. II [名] hope

指纹 zhǐwén [名] fingerprint

指引 zhǐyǐn [动] point the way

指责 zhǐzé [动] criticize

指正 zhǐzhèng [动] 1 (纠正错误) correct mistakes 2 (客套) make comments

咫 zhǐ 见下文

咫尺 zhǐchǐ [名] (书) (喻) the immediate vicinity

咫尺天涯 zhǐchǐ tiānyá so near and yet so far

趾 zhǐ [名] 1 (脚指头) toe 2 (脚) foot (PL feet)

趾高气扬 zhǐ gāo qì yáng high and mighty

至 zhì I [动] arrive ▷我于明日至沪。I'll arrive in Shanghai tomorrow. II [介] to ▷从古至今 from ancient times to the present ▷从东至西 from east to west III [副] 1 (至于) ▷至于他什么时候回来，我不知道。As to what time he's due back, I'm just not sure. ▶甚至 even 2 (最) extremely ▶至少 at least ▷兴奋之至 extreme excitement

至高无上 zhì gāo wú shàng paramount

至交 zhìjiāo [名] best friend

至今 zhìjīn [副] so far ▷他至今已在公司里呆了10年了。So far he's been at the company for 10 years.

至理名言 zhìlǐ-míngyán [名] maxim

至亲 zhìqīn close relative

至上 zhìshàng [形] highest

至少 zhìshǎo [副] at least

至于 zhìyú [介] as to ▷我已经尽了力，至于行不行，就全凭运气了。I've done what I can, so as to whether or not it will work, all I can rely on is luck.

志 zhì I [名] 1 (志向) will 2 (记录) record 3 (记号) sign II [动] remember

志大才疏 zhì dà cái shū have ideas above one's station

志气 zhìqì [名] will

志趣 zhìqù [名] aspiration

志士 zhìshì [名] strong-willed person

志同道合 zhì tóng dào hé share one's ambitions and outlook on life ▷我喜欢结交志同道合的朋友。I'd like to make friends with someone who shares my ambitions and outlook on life.

志向 zhìxiàng [名] ambition

志愿 zhìyuàn I [名] aspiration II [动] volunteer

帜 zhì [名] flag

制 zhì I [动] 1 (制造) make (PT, PP made) 2 (拟订) work ... out 3 (约束) restrict II [名] system

制裁 zhìcái [动] impose sanctions ▷法律制裁 legal sanctions (PL)

制订 zhìdìng [动] work ... out

制定 zhìdìng [动] draw ... up (PT drew, PP drawn)

制度 zhìdù [名] system

制服 zhìfú I [名] uniform II [动] subdue

制剂 zhìjì [名] preparation

制品 zhìpǐn [名] product

制胜 zhìshèng [动] win (PT, PP won)

制约 zhìyuē [动] restrict

制造 zhìzào [动] 1 (物品) manufacture 2 (气氛、局势) create

制止 zhìzhǐ [动] prevent

制作 zhìzuò [动] make (PT, PP made) ▷制作工艺品 make handicrafts ▷制作网页 create a web page ▷制作商 manufacturer

质 zhì I [名] 1 (性质) nature ▶本质 nature 2 (质量) quality ▷高质产品 high-quality goods 3 (物质) matter ▶流质 fluid 4 (抵押品) pledge ▶人质 hostage II [形] simple ▶质朴 plain III [动] question ▶质疑 cast doubt on

质变 zhìbiàn [名] fundamental change

质地 zhìdì [名] texture

质感 zhìgǎn [名] sense of reality

质量 zhìliàng [名] **1** (物) mass **2** (优劣) quality

质问 zhìwèn [动] inquire

质疑 zhìyí [动] query

治 zhì [动] **1** (治理) control **2** (医治) cure **3** (消灭) exterminate **4** (惩办) punish **5** (研究) research

治安 zhì'ān [名] security ▶社会治安 public order

治理 zhìlǐ [动] **1** (统治管理) administer **2** (处理) manage

治疗 zhìliáo [动] cure

治学 zhìxué (书) study

桎 zhì [名] (书) shackles (PL)

桎梏 zhìgù [名] (书) shackles (PL)

挚 zhì [形] (书) sincere

挚友 zhìyǒu [名] close friend

致 zhì I [动] **1** (给与) send (PT, PP sent) **2** (集中) concentrate **3** (招致) cause **4** (以致) result in II [名] appeal III [形] fine

致力 zhìlì [动] dedicate oneself to

致命 zhìmìng [动] cause death ▷这种药可能致命。This medicine can cause death. ▷致命的打击 a fatal blow

致使 zhìshǐ [连] so that ▷航空人员违反规章制度，致使发生重大飞行事故。Flouting of the rules by airline staff led to a serious plane crash.

致意 zhìyì [动] greet

秩 zhì [名] order

秩序 zhìxù [名] sequence

掷 zhì [动] throw (PT threw, PP thrown)

痔 zhì 见下文

痔疮 zhìchuāng [名] piles (PL)

窒 zhì [动] obstruct

窒息 zhìxì [动] suffocate

智 zhì I [形] wise II [名] wisdom

智慧 zhìhuì [名] intelligence

智力 zhìlì [名] intelligence

智囊 zhìnáng [名] brain ▷智囊团 think-tank

智能 zhìnéng I [名] intelligence and ability II [形] smart

智商 zhìshāng [名] IQ

智育 zhìyù [名] intellectual education

痣 zhì [名] mole

滞 zhì [动] come to a stop (PT came, PP come)

滞后 zhìhòu [形] lagging behind ▷这个城市的服务业发展滞后。This city's service industry is lagging behind.

滞留 zhìliú [动] stay behind

滞销 zhìxiāo [动] not sell well

置 zhì [动] **1** (搁) put (PT, PP put) **2** (设立) set up (PT, PP set) **3** (购置) buy (PT, PP bought)

置换 zhìhuàn [动] exchange

置若罔闻 zhì ruò wǎng wén shut one's eyes to ▷地方官员对中央政府下文置若罔闻。Local officials shut their eyes to memos from the central government.

置身 zhìshēn [动] take up a position (PT took, PP taken)

置疑 zhìyí [动] doubt

置之度外 zhì zhī dù wài give no thought to ▷为了追求理想他将金钱置之度外。In pursuit of his dreams, he gave money no thought.

雉 zhì [名] pheasant

稚 zhì [形] young

稚嫩 zhìnèn [形] **1** (娇嫩) tender **2** (幼稚) naive

稚气 zhìqì [形] childish

中 zhōng I [名] **1** (中心) centre (英), center (美) ▶中央 central **2** (中国) China ▶中餐 Chinese food **3** (范围内) ▷人海中 amid the crowd ▷在我的印象中，他很有才华。To my mind, he's very talented. **4** (两端之间的) the middle ▶中层 mid-level **5** (不偏不倚) impartial ▶适中 moderate **6** (在过程里的) course ▷在改革中 in the course of reform ▷会议在进行中。The meeting is in progress. II [动] be suitable for ▷这套家具中看不中用。This furniture looks great, but it's no use. III [形] (方) OK ▷这件事情中不中？ Is this OK?
→另见 zhòng

中饱 zhōngbǎo [动] misappropriate

中断 zhōngduàn [动] break ... off (PT broke, PP broken)

中国 Zhōngguó [名] China

中华 Zhōnghuá [名] China ▷中华民族 the Chinese nation

中坚 zhōngjiān [形] core

中间 zhōngjiān [名] **1** (中心) middle **2** (之间) ▷我站在他俩中间。I was standing in between the both of them. ▷他是我们中间最刻苦的一个。He is the most hard-working of all of us.

中介 zhōngjiè [名] agency ▶房产中介 estate

agent

中立 zhōnglì [动] be neutral ▶中立国 neutral country ▷我方保持中立。We will remain neutral.

中流 zhōngliú I [名] (指河流) the middle reaches (of a river) II [形] mediocre

中流砥柱 zhōngliú Dǐzhù tower of strength

中年 zhōngnián [名] middle age

中秋节 Zhōngqiūjié [名] Mid-Autumn Festival

中世纪 zhōngshìjì [名] the Middle Ages (PL)

中枢 zhōngshū [名] centre (英), center (美)

中途 zhōngtú [名] ▷他中途辍学了。He abandoned his studies halfway through.

中文 Zhōngwén [名] Chinese ▷学中文 study Chinese

中午 zhōngwǔ [名] noon

中心 zhōngxīn [名] centre (英), center (美) ▷广场中心有一座雕塑。There's a statue in the centre of the square. ▷国际会议中心 international conference centre ▷北京是中国的政治文化中心。Beijing is the political and cultural heart of China.

中学 zhōngxué [名] high school (英), senior school (美)

中旬 zhōngxún [名] the middle ten days of a month ▷我们学校9月中旬开学。Our school term starts in mid-September.

中央 zhōngyāng [名] 1 (中心地) centre (英), center (美) 2 (最高机构) central government

中药 zhōngyào [名] Chinese medicine

中医 zhōngyī [名] 1 (医学) traditional Chinese medicine 2 (医生) doctor of traditional Chinese medicine

中庸 zhōngyōng [形] mediocre

中用 zhōngyòng [形] useful

中游 zhōngyóu [名] 1 (河流) the middle reaches (of a river) 2 (水平) ordinariness

中原 Zhōngyuán [名] the central Chinese plains (PL)

中止 zhōngzhǐ [动] cease

中转 zhōngzhuǎn [动] transfer

忠 zhōng [形] faithful

忠诚 zhōngchéng [形] loyal

忠厚 zhōnghòu [形] loyal and sincere

忠实 zhōngshí [形] 1 (忠诚可靠) loyal 2 (真实) true ▷译文必须忠实于原文的主旨。A translated text should be true to the purpose of the original.

忠贞 zhōngzhēn [形] faithful

终 zhōng I [动] die II [副] in the end III [形] all

▶终身 all one's life

终点 zhōngdiǎn [名] 1 (尽头) terminus (PL termini) 2 (体育) finish

终端 zhōngduān [名] terminal

终归 zhōngguī [副] in the end

终结 zhōngjié [动] end

终究 zhōngjiū [副] in the end ▷自然资源终究会枯竭。Natural resources will run out in the end.

终了 zhōngliǎo [动] end

终年 zhōngnián [名] 1 (全年) the whole year 2 (去世年龄) ▷他于1970年去世，终年85岁。He died in 1970, at the age of 85.

终日 zhōngrì [名] the whole day ▷他当了总经理后终日不得闲。After taking up the post of general manager he was busy the whole day long.

终身 zhōngshēn [名] one's whole life

终审 zhōngshěn [名] final verdict

终生 zhōngshēng [名] one's whole life

终于 zhōngyú [副] finally ▷他终于答应了我的要求。He finally agreed to my request. ▷暴雨终于停了。The storm's over at last.

终止 zhōngzhǐ [动] stop

钟 zhōng [名] 1 (响器) bell 2 (记时器) clock 3 (指时间) ▷5点钟 five o'clock

钟爱 zhōng'ài [动] adore

钟情 zhōngqíng [动] be in love ▷一见钟情 fall in love at first sight

钟头 zhōngtóu [名] hour ▷3个钟头 three hours

衷 zhōng [名] heart

衷肠 zhōngcháng [名] innermost feelings (PL)

衷情 zhōngqíng [名] emotion

衷心 zhōngxīn [形] heartfelt

肿 zhǒng [动] swell (PT swelled, PP swollen)

肿瘤 zhǒngliú [名] tumour (英), tumor (美)

种 zhǒng I [名] 1 (物种) species (PL species) ▷灭种 become extinct as a species 2 (人种) race 3 (种子) seed ▷播种 sow seeds 4 (胆量) courage ▷有种 be brave II [量] ▷各种商品 all kinds of commodities ▷3种选择 three choices → 另见 zhòng

种类 zhǒnglèi [名] type

种子 zhǒngzi [名] seed ▷小麦种子 wheat seeds ▷种子选手 seeded player

种族 zhǒngzú [名] race ▷种族歧视 racial discrimination

中 zhòng [动] 1 (对准) hit (PT, PP hit) ▷子弹打中了靶子。The bullet hit the target. ▷彩票

中了头奖。The lottery ticket won first prize. ▷他猜中了谜语。He guessed the riddle correctly. **2** (受到) be hit by ▶中毒 be poisoned ▶中暑 heatstroke ▷胸口中了颗子弹。He was hit in the chest by a bullet.
→另见 zhōng

中标 zhòngbiāo [动] make a successful bid for

中彩 zhòngcǎi [动] win the lottery (PT, PP won)

中毒 zhòngdú [动] be poisoned

中肯 zhòngkěn [形] relevant

中伤 zhòngshāng [动] slander

中意 zhòngyì [动] be ideal ▷这台洗衣机我中意。This washing machine is ideal for me.

仲 zhòng [形] intermediary

仲裁 zhòngcái [动] arbitrate

众 zhòng I [形] many ▶众人 everyone II [名] crowd ▶公众 the public

众多 zhòngduō [形] numerous

众口难调 zhòng kǒu nán tiáo tastes differ

众目睽睽 zhòng mù kuí kuí in full view of everybody ▷劫匪在众目睽睽下持刀杀人。The bandit stabbed a man to death in full view of everybody.

众叛亲离 zhòng pàn qīn lí outcast

众人 zhòngrén [名] everybody

众矢之的 zhòng shǐ zhī dì target of public criticism

众志成城 zhòng zhì chéng chéng unity is strength

种 zhòng [动] sow (PT sowed, PP sown) ▶耕种 cultivate ▶种田 farm ▶种痘 vaccinate ▷种果树 plant fruit trees
→另见 zhǒng

种瓜得瓜，种豆得豆 zhòng guā dé guā, zhòng dòu dé dòu reap what one sows

种植 zhòngzhí [动] plant

重 zhòng I [名] weight ▷这袋面粉有多重? How much does this bag of flour weigh? II [形] **1** (重量大) heavy ▷水比油重。Water is heavier than oil. **2** (程度深) strong ▷情深意重 deep affection **3** (重要) important ▶重任 important task **4** (不轻率) serious ▶稳重 staid III [动] stress ▶注重 pay attention to
→另见 chóng

重创 zhòngchuāng [动] be seriously injured

重大 zhòngdà [形] major ▷重大转变 a major change

重点 zhòngdiǎn [名] key point ▷重点政策 key policy

重工业 zhònggōngyè [名] heavy industry

重力 zhònglì [名] gravity

重量 zhòngliàng [名] weight

重任 zhòngrèn [名] important task

重视 zhòngshì [动] attach importance to

重武器 zhòngwǔqì [名] heavy weapons

重心 zhòngxīn [名] **1** (物) centre (英) 或 center (美) of gravity **2** (主要部分) core

重要 zhòngyào [形] important ▷重要文献 important document ▷发表重要讲话 give an important speech

重音 zhòngyīn [名] **1** (重读的音) stress **2** (音) accent

重镇 zhòngzhèn [名] strategic town

舟 zhōu [名] (书) boat

州 zhōu [名] **1** (自治州) autonomous prefecture **2** (美国的行政区) state ▷加利福尼亚州 the State of California

周 zhōu I [名] **1** (圈子) circle **2** (星期) week II [动] **1** (环绕) circle **2** (接济) give ... financial help (PT gave, PP given) III [形] **1** (普遍) widespread **2** (完备) thorough

周边 zhōubiān [名] periphery

周长 zhōucháng [名] perimeter

周到 zhōudào [形] thorough

周而复始 zhōu ér fù shǐ come full circle

周济 zhōujì [动] give ... financial help (PT gave, PP given)

周密 zhōumì [形] meticulous

周末 zhōumò [名] weekend

周期 zhōuqī [名] period

周全 zhōuquán I [形] thorough II [动] bring about (PT, PP brought)

周围 zhōuwéi [名] the vicinity ▷房子周围种了很多树。A number of trees were planted in the vicinity of the house. ▷周围的人都睁大眼睛看着他。The people around him stared at him in astonishment.

周旋 zhōuxuán [动] **1** (回旋) circle **2** (交际) socialize **3** (较量) compete with

周游 zhōuyóu [动] travel ▷周游世界 travel all over the world

周折 zhōuzhé [名] twists and turns (PL) ▷他费尽周折终于找到了亲生父母。After various twists and turns, he finally found his birth parents.

周转 zhōuzhuǎn [动] **1** (经济) have a turnover of ▷公司有3千万英镑供周转。The company has a turnover of thirty million pounds. **2** (调度) have enough

洲 zhōu [名] 1 (大陆) continent 2 (沙洲) island
洲际 zhōujì [名] continent

粥 zhōu [名] porridge
粥少僧多 zhōu shǎo sēng duō not enough to go round ▷毕业生到处寻找工作机会，但粥少僧多。Recent graduates are looking everywhere for work, but there aren't enough jobs to go round.

轴 zhóu I [名] 1 (零件) axle 2 (直线) axis (PL axes) 3 (器物) spool II [量] scroll ▷一轴国画 a Chinese watercolour painting
轴承 zhóuchéng [名] bearing
轴心 zhóuxīn [名] 1 (轮轴) axle 2 (联合阵线) axis (PL axes)

肘 zhǒu [名] elbow

帚 zhǒu [名] broom

咒 zhòu [动] curse
咒骂 zhòumà [动] swear at (PT swore, PP sworn)

昼 zhòu [名] daylight
昼夜 zhòuyè [名] day and night

皱 zhòu [动] wrinkle ▷丝绸易皱。Silk fabrics crease easily.
皱纹 zhòuwén [名] wrinkle

骤 zhòu I [动] gallop II [形] sudden
骤然 zhòurán [副] suddenly

朱 zhū [形] bright red
朱红 zhūhóng [名] vermilion

侏 zhū 见下文
侏儒 zhūrú [名] dwarf (PL dwarves)

珠 zhū [名] 1 (珍珠) pearl 2 (球型物) bead ▷汗珠 a bead of sweat ▷泪珠 a teardrop
珠宝 zhūbǎo [名] jewels (PL)
珠联璧合 zhū lián bì hé a good combination

株 zhū I [名] 1 (树根) stem 2 (植株) plant II [量] ▷一株幼苗 a seedling ▷三株桃树 three peach trees
株连 zhūlián [动] implicate ▷在封建社会里，一人犯罪，株连九族。In feudal times, when a man committed a crime, the whole clan was implicated.

诸 zhū [代] all

诸多 zhūduō [形] large numbers of ▷新政府面临诸多挑战。The new government is facing a number of challenges.
诸如此类 zhū rú cǐ lèi and so forth ▷我喜欢看动画、漫画诸如此类的东西。I like cartoons, caricatures, and so forth.
诸位 zhūwèi [代] you (PL)

猪 zhū [名] pig

蛛 zhū [名] spider
蛛丝马迹 zhū sī mǎ jì clues ▷大劫案的蛛丝马迹渐渐浮出水面。Clues were gradually starting to surface in the big robbery case.

竹 zhú [名] bamboo

逐 zhú I [动] 1 (追赶) chase 2 (驱逐) drive ... away (PT drove, PP driven) II [副] one after another ▷逐年 year in year out ▷大家逐个发言。The people gave one speech after another.
逐步 zhúbù [副] step by step
逐渐 zhújiàn [副] gradually
逐一 zhúyī [副] one after another

烛 zhú I [名] candle II [动] (书) illuminate
烛台 zhútái [名] candlestick

主 zhǔ I [名] 1 (接待者) host ▷东道主 host 2 (所有者) owner ▷房主 home-owner 3 (当事人) person concerned ▷事主 crime victim 4 (主见) idea ▷他慌张得心里没了主。He was in such a state that he had no idea what to do next. 5 (上帝) God II [形] main ▷主干道 main road III [动] 1 (主持) take charge (PT took, PP taken) ▷主办 take charge of 2 (主张) be in favour (英) 或 favor (美) of ▷主战 be in favour of war 3 (从自身出发) look at ... subjectively ▷主观 subjective
主持 zhǔchí [动] 1 (负责掌握) take charge of (PT took, PP taken) 2 (主张) support
主导 zhǔdǎo [动] direct
主动 zhǔdòng [形] voluntary
主犯 zhǔfàn [名] main culprit
主妇 zhǔfù [名] housewife (PL housewives)
主观 zhǔguān [形] subjective
主见 zhǔjiàn [名] opinion
主教 zhǔjiào [名] bishop
主角 zhǔjué [名] lead role ▷谁在剧中担任主角？Who's got the lead in the play?
主力 zhǔlì [名] leading player
主流 zhǔliú [名] 1 (指河流) main current 2 (指事物) general trend

主谋 zhǔmóu I [动] conspire II [名] ringleader

主权 zhǔquán [名] sovereignty

主人 zhǔrén [名] 1 (接待者) host 2 (雇佣者) master ▶ 女主人 mistress 3 (所有者) owner

主食 zhǔshí [名] staple food

主题 zhǔtí [名] subject

主体 zhǔtǐ [名] main part

主席 zhǔxí [名] chairman, chairwoman

主旋律 zhǔxuánlǜ [名] theme

主演 zhǔyǎn [动] play the lead

主要 zhǔyào [形] major ▷ 主要问题 major issue ▷ 主要原因 major cause

主页 zhǔyè [名] home page

主义 zhǔyì [名] doctrine ▶ 社会主义 socialism ▶ 浪漫主义 romanticism

主意 zhǔyi [名] 1 (办法) idea ▷ 他给我们出了个好主意。 He gave us a good idea. 2 (主见) opinion ▷ 你自己拿主意吧。 You make up your own mind.

主语 zhǔyǔ [名] subject

主宰 zhǔzǎi [动] dominate

主张 zhǔzhāng I [动] advocate II [名] standpoint

主旨 zhǔzhǐ [名] main point

主子 zhǔzi [名] master

煮 zhǔ [动] boil

嘱 zhǔ [动] admonish

嘱咐 zhǔfù [动] urge ▷ 他嘱咐儿子要好好学习。 He urged his son to study hard.

嘱托 zhǔtuō [动] entrust ... with ▷ 上司把这项重任嘱托给了我。 My boss entrusted me with this important task.

瞩 zhǔ [动] look closely

瞩目 zhǔmù [动] watch with interest

伫 zhù 见下文

伫立 zhùlì [动] (书) stand for a long time (PT, PP stood)

助 zhù [动] help

助词 zhùcí [名] auxiliary word

助动词 zhùdòngcí [名] auxiliary verb

助人为乐 zhù rén wéi lè take pleasure in helping others

助手 zhùshǒu [名] assistant

助兴 zhùxìng [动] liven things up

住 zhù [动] 1 (居住) live ▷ 他和父母住在一起。 He lives with his parents. 2 (停住) stop ▷ 住口！ Shut up! 3 (用作动词补语) ▷ 卡车停住了。 The truck stopped. ▷ 听到这消息，她一下愣住了。 She was struck dumb by the news.

住户 zhùhù [名] household

住宿 zhùsù [动] stay

住宅 zhùzhái [名] house

住址 zhùzhǐ [名] address

贮 zhù [动] store

贮藏 zhùcáng [动] store

注 zhù I [动] 1 (灌入) pour ▶ 注射 inject 2 (集中) concentrate 3 (解释) explain ▶ 批注 comment on II [名] 1 (记载) record ▶ 注册 enrol (英), enroll (美) 2 (赌注) bet

注册 zhùcè [动] enrol (英), enroll (美) ▷ 新生明天开始注册。 The new students will begin enrolling tomorrow. ▷ 注册表 register ▷ 注册会计师 chartered (英) 或 certified (美) accountant

注定 zhùdìng [动] be destined ▷ 他注定要失败。 He was destined to lose.

注解 zhùjiě [动] annotate

注目 zhùmù [动] focus

注射 zhùshè [动] inject

注视 zhùshì [动] stare ▷ 她注视着窗台上的一束鲜花。 She's staring at the bunch of fresh flowers on the windowsill.

注释 zhùshì [动] annotate

注销 zhùxiāo [动] cancel

注意 zhùyì [动] be careful ▷ 请注意交通安全。 Please be careful on the roads. ▷ 登山前特别要注意服装和鞋子。 Before you climb the mountain, be careful to kit yourself out correctly.

注音 zhùyīn [动] give a phonetic notation (PT gave, PP given)

注重 zhùzhòng [动] stress

驻 zhù [动] 1 (停留) stop 2 (设立) stay ▷ 中国驻伦敦大使馆 the Chinese embassy in London

驻地 zhùdì [名] camp

驻守 zhùshǒu [动] garrison

驻扎 zhùzhā [动] be stationed

祝 zhù [动] wish ▷ 祝你成功！ Wishing you every success! ▷ 祝你生日快乐！ Happy birthday!

祝福 zhùfú [动] wish ... luck ▷ 我们祝福你！ We wish you good luck! ▷ 祝福你万事如意！ May all your wishes come true!

祝贺 zhùhè [动] congratulate ▷ 祝贺你考上了名牌大学。 Congratulations on getting into such a prestigious university.

祝愿 zhùyuàn [动] wish ▷祝愿你早日康复。I wish you a speedy recovery.

著 zhù I [形] marked II [动] 1 (显出) show (PT showed, PP shown) 2 (写作) write (PT wrote, PP written) III [名] work

著称 zhùchēng [动] be famous ▷埃及以金字塔著称。Egypt is famous for its pyramids.

著名 zhùmíng [形] famous ▷长江三峡是中国著名的风景区。The Three Gorges are one of China's famous beauty spots.

著述 zhùshù I [动] write (PT wrote, PP written) II [名] writings (PL)

著作 zhùzuò [名] writings (PL)

蛀 zhù I [动] bore II [名] moth

蛀虫 zhùchóng [名] moth

铸 zhù [动] smelt

铸造 zhùzào [动] smelt

筑 zhù [动] build (PT, PP built)

抓 zhuā [动] 1 (拿住) grab 2 (划过) scratch 3 (捉拿) catch (PT, PP caught) 4 (着重) take control of (PT took, PP taken) 5 (吸引) attract 6 (把握住) seize

抓耳挠腮 zhuā ěr náo sāi scratch one's head

抓获 zhuāhuò [动] capture

抓紧 zhuājǐn [动] make the most of ▷我们时间不多了，你得抓紧。We don't have much time, you'd better make the most of it.

抓阄儿 zhuājiūr [动] draw lots (PT drew, PP drawn)

爪 zhuǎ [名] claw
→另见 zhǎo

拽 zhuài [动] pull

专 zhuān [动] 1 (集中) concentrate 2 (独占) dominate ▶专卖 monopoly

专长 zhuāncháng [名] speciality (英), specialty (美)

专诚 zhuānchéng [副] specially

专程 zhuānchéng [副] specially ▷他专程来到桂林拍摄记录片。He made the journey to Guilin specially to shoot a documentary.

专断 zhuānduàn [形] arbitrary

专攻 zhuāngōng [动] specialize in

专横 zhuānhèng [形] domineering

专家 zhuānjiā [名] expert ▷专家门诊 specialist clinic

专利 zhuānlì [名] patent

专门 zhuānmén I [形] specialized II [副] especially

专权 zhuānquán [动] monopolize

专任 zhuānrèn [动] work full-time ▷他专任舞蹈教师。He's a full-time dancing teacher.

专题 zhuāntí [名] special subject ▷新闻专题 special report

专心 zhuānxīn [形] single-minded

专业 zhuānyè [名] special field of study ▷英语专业 English major ▷专业人才 professionals

专一 zhuānyī [形] single-minded

专职 zhuānzhí [名] full-time work

专制 zhuānzhì [形] despotic

专注 zhuānzhù [形] concentrated on

砖 zhuān [名] brick

砖头 zhuāntou [名] brick

转 zhuǎn [动] 1 (改换) turn ▶转弯 turn a corner ▶转学 change schools 2 (传送) pass ... on ▶转送 deliver ▷请把文件转给他。Please pass this document on to him.
→另见 zhuàn

转变 zhuǎnbiàn [动] transform

转播 zhuǎnbō [动] relay

转达 zhuǎndá [动] pass ... on ▷请转达我对他的问候。Please give him my regards.

转告 zhuǎngào [动] pass ... on

转轨 zhuǎnguǐ [动] be in transition

转化 zhuǎnhuà [动] change

转换 zhuǎnhuàn [动] convert

转机 zhuǎnjī I [名] a turn for the better ▷生意已有转机。Business has taken a turn for the better. II [动] change planes

转嫁 zhuǎnjià [动] 1 (改嫁) remarry 2 (转移) transfer

转交 zhuǎnjiāo [动] pass ... on

转让 zhuǎnràng [动] transfer

转手 zhuǎnshǒu [动] resell (PT, PP resold)

转瞬 zhuǎnshùn [副] in an instant

转型 zhuǎnxíng [动] transform

转眼 zhuǎnyǎn [副] in an instant

转业 zhuǎnyè [动] change jobs

转移 zhuǎnyí [动] change

转账 zhuǎnzhàng [动] transfer accounts

转折 zhuǎnzhé [动] change dramatically ▶转折点 turning point

转正 zhuǎnzhèng [动] become a permanent member (PT became, PP become)

传 zhuàn [名] 1 (传记) biography 2 (历史故事) tale →另见 chuán
传记 zhuànjì [名] biography

转 zhuàn [动] turn ▷电风扇被摔坏，不转了。 The fan's broken – it's not turning round. ▷月亮围着地球转。 The Moon orbits the Earth. →另见 zhuǎn
转动 zhuàndòng [动] revolve
转向 zhuànxiàng [动] lose one's way (PT, PP lost)
转悠 zhuànyou [动] (口) 1 (转动) roll 2 (漫步) stroll

赚 zhuàn [动] 1 (获得利润) make a profit 2 (挣钱) earn
赚头 zhuàntou [名] (口) profit

撰 zhuàn [动] write (PT wrote, PP written)
撰述 zhuànshù [动] compose

妆 zhuāng I [动] put on make-up (PT, PP put) ▶梳妆 do one's hair and put on make-up II [名] adornments (PL)

庄 zhuāng I [名] 1 (指村庄) village ▶农庄 village 2 (指土地) manor ▶庄园 manor 3 (指商店) ▶茶庄 teahouse ▷饭庄 restaurant
庄稼 zhuāngjia [名] crops (PL)
庄严 zhuāngyán [形] solemn
庄园 zhuāngyuán [名] manor
庄重 zhuāngzhòng [形] solemn ▷首相讲话时声音庄重。 When the prime minister spoke, his tone was solemn.

桩 zhuāng I [名] pile ▶打桩 drive in a pile II [量] ▷一桩事 an issue

装 zhuāng I [动] 1 (修饰) dress up ▶装饰 decorate 2 (假装) pretend ▷装疯卖傻 play the fool 3 (装载) load ▷装车 load a truck with goods 4 (装配) install ▷我们家里装了空调。 We've had air-conditioning installed. II [名] (服装) clothing ▶套装 matching outfit
装扮 zhuāngbàn [动] 1 (打扮) dress up 2 (假装) disguise
装备 zhuāngbèi I [名] equipment II [动] equip
装点 zhuāngdiǎn [动] decorate
装订 zhuāngdìng [动] bind (PT, PP bound)
装潢 zhuānghuáng [动] decorate
装甲 zhuāngjiǎ [形] armoured (英), armored (美)
装聋作哑 zhuāng lóng zuò yǎ feign ignorance
装门面 zhuāng ménmian [动] keep up appearances (PT, PP kept)
装束 zhuāngshù [名] outfit
装修 zhuāngxiū [动] fit ... out
装置 zhuāngzhì I [动] install II [名] equipment

壮 zhuàng I [形] 1 (强壮) strong ▶健壮 robust 2 (雄壮) grand ▶壮阔 grand II [动] bolster ▶壮胆 embolden
壮大 zhuàngdà I [形] well-built II [动] expand
壮观 zhuàngguān [形] magnificent
壮举 zhuàngjǔ [名] brave feat
壮丽 zhuànglì [形] majestic
壮烈 zhuàngliè [形] heroic
壮年 zhuàngnián [名] prime of life
壮士 zhuàngshì [名] hero (PL heroes)
壮实 zhuàngshi [形] sturdy
壮志 zhuàngzhì [名] high ideals (PL)

状 zhuàng [名] 1 (形状) shape ▷奇形怪状 weirdly-shaped 2 (情况) state ▶症状 symptom 3 (诉状) complaint ▶告状 bring a case 4 (证书) certificate ▶奖状 certificate
状况 zhuàngkuàng [名] condition
状态 zhuàngtài [名] condition
状元 zhuàngyuán [名] the best ▷三百六十行，行行出状元。 No matter what career you choose, you can be the best.

撞 zhuàng [动] 1 (碰撞) collide ▷小男孩被车撞了。 The little boy was knocked down by a car. 2 (碰见) bump into ▷逛街时我撞上了老同学。 While window shopping I bumped into an old classmate. 3 (试探) try ▷撞运气 try one's luck 4 (闯) dash
撞车 zhuàngchē [动] 1 (车辆相撞) collide 2 (发生分歧) clash
撞击 zhuàngjī [动] collide
撞骗 zhuàngpiàn [动] swindle

幢 zhuàng [量] ▷一幢别墅 a villa ▷两幢楼房 two blocks of flats (英) 或 apartments (美)

追 zhuī [动] 1 (追赶) chase ▶追随 follow 2 (追究) investigate ▶追查 investigate 3 (追求) seek (PT, PP sought) ▷追名逐利 seek fame and fortune 4 (回溯) reminisce ▶追思 reminisce 5 (补办) ▶追加 supplement
追捕 zhuībǔ [动] pursue and capture
追悼 zhuīdào [动] mourn
追赶 zhuīgǎn [动] chase
追悔 zhuīhuǐ [动] regret
追击 zhuījī [动] pursue

追加 zhuījiā [动] supplement

追究 zhuījiū [动] investigate

追求 zhuīqiú [动] 1 (争取) seek (PT, PP sought) 2 (求爱) chase after

追溯 zhuīsù [动] trace

追随 zhuīsuí [动] follow

追忆 zhuīyì [动] recollect

追逐 zhuīzhú [动] 1 (追赶) chase 2 (追求) seek (PT, PP sought)

追踪 zhuīzōng [动] track

锥 zhuī [名] 1 (锥子) awl 2 (锥状物) cone

坠 zhuì I [动] 1 (书) (落) fall (PT fell, PP fallen) ▶坠落 drop 2 (垂) droop ▶下坠 droop II [名] pendant ▶耳坠 earring

坠落 zhuìluò [动] fall (PT fell, PP fallen)

惴 zhuì [形] (书) anxious

惴惴不安 zhuìzhuì bù'ān ill at ease ▷他暴虐的脾气让每个人都惴惴不安。His brutal temper made everyone feel very ill at ease.

赘 zhuì [形] superfluous

赘词 zhuìcí [名] superfluous words (PL)

谆 zhūn [形] earnest

谆谆 zhūnzhūn [形] earnest

准 zhǔn I [动] 1 (准许) allow ▶批准 ratify ▷不准随地吐痰。Spitting is prohibited. 2 (依据) be in accord with II [名] standard ▷以此为准 take this as the standard III [形] 1 (准确) accurate ▶准时 punctual 2 (类似) quasi ▶准科学 quasi-science

准备 zhǔnbèi [动] 1 (筹划) prepare ▷心理准备 psychological preparation 2 (打算) plan

准确 zhǔnquè [形] accurate

准绳 zhǔnshéng [名] benchmark

准头 zhǔntou [名] (口) accuracy

准许 zhǔnxǔ [动] permit

准予 zhǔnyǔ [动] allow

准则 zhǔnzé [名] norms (PL)

拙 zhuō [形] 1 (笨) clumsy ▶拙劣 poor 2 (谦) (自己的) ▶拙著 my writing

拙劣 zhuōliè [形] poor

捉 zhuō [动] 1 (握住) clutch 2 (捕捉) catch (PT, PP caught)

捉襟见肘 zhuō jīn jiàn zhǒu have more problems than one can cope with

捉摸 zhuōmō [动] predict

捉弄 zhuōnòng [动] play with

桌 zhuō I [名] table ▶书桌 desk II [量] table ▷一桌菜 a table covered in dishes

灼 zhuó I [动] burn ▶烧灼 burn II [形] bright

灼见 zhuójiàn [名] penetrating insight

灼热 zhuórè [形] scorching

茁 zhuó [形] thriving

茁壮 zhuózhuàng [形] sturdy

卓 zhuó [形] 1 (高而直) upright 2 (高明) eminent ▶卓越 outstanding

卓识 zhuóshí [名] good judgement

卓有成效 zhuó yǒu chéngxiào highly effective

卓越 zhuóyuè [形] outstanding

卓著 zhuózhù [形] distinguished

浊 zhuó [形] 1 (浑浊) muddy 2 (粗重) deep

酌 zhuó [动] 1 (斟酒) pour out wine (PT drank, PP drunk) 2 (饮酒) drink 3 (斟酌) consider

酌量 zhuóliàng [动] consider

酌情 zhuóqíng [动] use one's discretion

啄 zhuó [动] peck

啄木鸟 zhuómùniǎo [名] woodpecker

着 zhuó I [动] 1 (穿) wear (PT wore, PP worn) ▶着装 clothing 2 (接触) come into contact with (PT came, PP come) ▶着陆 land 3 (使接触) apply ▶着手 set about ▶着眼 keep ... in mind 4 (派遣) send (PT, PP sent) ▷着人去调查 send someone to investigate II [名] whereabouts (PL) ▷衣食无着 without food or clothing

→另见 zhāo, zháo

着力 zhuólì [动] put effort into (PT, PP put)

着陆 zhuólù [动] land

着落 zhuóluò I [名] 1 (下落) whereabouts (PL) 2 (来源) source II [动] rest with ▷这些任务着落在我们身上。The responsibility rests with us.

着实 zhuóshí [副] 1 (实在) really 2 (狠狠) severely

着手 zhuóshǒu [动] set about (PT, PP set)

着想 zhuóxiǎng [动] consider

着眼 zhuóyǎn [动] keep ... in mind (PT, PP kept) ▷大处着眼 keep the big picture in mind

着意 zhuóyì [动] take pains (PT took, PP taken)

着重 zhuózhòng [动] stress

琢 zhuó [动] carve ▶ 雕琢 carve
→另见 zuó
琢磨 zhuómó [动] polish

镯 zhuó [名] bracelet

吱 zī [拟] squeak
吱声 zīshēng [动] (方) say the word (PT, PP said)

孜 zī 见下文
孜孜不倦 zīzī bù juàn diligently

咨 zī [动] consult ▶ 咨询 seek advice from
咨询 zīxún [动] seek advice from (PT, PP sought)

姿 zī [名] 1 (容貌) looks (PL) ▶ 姿色 good
looks (PL) 2 (姿势) posture ▶ 舞姿 dancer's
movement
姿色 zīsè [名] good looks (PL)
姿势 zīshì [名] posture
姿态 zītài [名] 1 (姿势) posture 2 (态度) attitude

资 zī I [名] 1 (钱财) money ▶ 外资 foreign
capital ▶ 邮资 postage 2 (资质) ability ▶ 天
资 natural ability 3 (资格) qualifications (PL)
▶ 资历 record of service II [动] 1 (资助) aid
...financially ▶ 资敌 aid the enemy 2 (提供)
provide
资本 zīběn [名] 1 (本钱) capital 2 (优势) ▷ 他
把贵族的出身作为取得事业成功的资本。
He capitalized on his aristocratic origins to
advance his career.
资本主义 zīběn zhǔyì [名] capitalism
资产 zīchǎn [名] property
资产阶级 zīchǎn jiējí [名] bourgeoisie
资格 zīgé [名] 1 (条件) qualifications (PL) 2 (身
份) seniority
资金 zījīn [名] funds ▷ 募集资金 raise funds
资历 zīlì [名] record of service
资料 zīliào [名] 1 (必需品) means (PL) ▷ 生产资
料 means of production 2 (材料) material
资讯 zīxùn [名] data (PL) ▷ 商业资讯 trade data
资源 zīyuán [名] resources (PL) ▷ 自然资源
natural resources ▷ 资源丰富 rich in natural
resources
资助 zīzhù [动] aid ...financially

孳 zī [动] multiply
孳生 zīshēng [动] multiply

滋 zī [动] 1 (滋生) grow (PT grew, PP grown) ▶ 滋
长 grow 2 (增添) increase ▶ 滋养 nourish
滋补 zībǔ [动] nourish

滋润 zīrùn I [形] 1 (水份多) moist 2 (方) (舒服)
comfortable ▷ 日子过得挺滋润。 The days
pass very comfortably. II [动] moisten
滋生 zīshēng [动] 1 (繁殖) multiply 2 (引起)
cause
滋事 zīshì [动] cause trouble
滋味 zīwèi [名] 1 (味道) flavour (英), flavor
(美) 2 (感受) feeling ▷ 听了他的冷言冷语，我
心里不是滋味。 After hearing his cold words, I
felt very upset.
滋长 zīzhǎng [动] grow (PT grew, PP grown)

龇 zī [动] ▷ 龇着牙 bare one's teeth
龇牙咧嘴 zī yá liě zuǐ look fierce

子 zǐ I [名] 1 (儿子) son ▶ 母子 mother and
son 2 (人) person ▶ 男子 man 3 (种子) seed
▶ 瓜子 melon seed 4 (卵) egg ▶ 鱼子 fish
roe 5 (粒状物) ▶ 棋子 chess piece 6 (铜子)
coin ▷ 我身上一个子儿都没有。 I haven't got
a penny on me. II [形] 1 (幼小) young ▶ 子鸡
chick 2 (附属) affiliated ▷ 子公司 subsidiary
company
子弟 zǐdì [名] children
子公司 zǐgōngsī [名] subsidiary company
子女 zǐnǚ [名] children
子孙 zǐsūn [名] descendants (PL)
子午线 zǐwǔxiàn [名] meridian
子夜 zǐyè [名] midnight

仔 zǐ [形] young
仔细 zǐxì [形] 1 (细心) thorough 2 (小心) careful

姊 zǐ [名] sister
姊妹 zǐmèi [名] sisters (PL)

籽 zǐ [名] seed ▶ 菜籽 vegetable seed

紫 zǐ [形] purple
紫外线 zǐwàixiàn [名] ultraviolet ray

自 zì I [代] oneself ▷ 自讨苦吃 bring trouble
on oneself II [副] certainly ▷ 他这样做自有
一番用意。 In doing this he certainly has some
motive. III [介] from ▷ 他自小就聪明能
干。 From an early age he has been clever and
capable.
自爱 zì'ài [名] self-respect
自拔 zìbá [动] free oneself
自白 zìbái [动] vindicate oneself
自不量力 zì bù liàng lì overestimate one's
abilities
自成一家 zì chéng yī jiā have one's own style

自持 zìchí [动] control oneself

自从 zìcóng [介] since

自大 zìdà [形] arrogant

自得 zìdé [形] self-satisfied

自动 zìdòng [形] 1 (主动的) voluntary ▷自动让出座位 voluntarily give up one's seat 2 (机械的) automatic ▷按下电钮, 门会自动打开。When you press the button, the door will open automatically.

自动化 zìdònghuà [动] automate

自动取款机 zìdòng qǔkuǎnjī [动] cashpoint (英), ATM (美)

自发 zìfā [形] spontaneous

自负 zìfù I [形] conceited II [动] take responsibility (PT took, PP taken)

自高自大 zì gāo zì dà self-important

自告奋勇 zì gào fènyǒng volunteer ▷他自告奋勇地要为她出庭辩护。He volunteered to appear in court in her defence.

自顾不暇 zì gù bù xiá be unable to take care of oneself

自豪 zìháo [形] proud ▷我们为你获得冠军感到自豪。We are very proud that you won the championship.

自己 zìjǐ I [代] oneself ▷你要相信自己的能力。You must have faith in your own ability. ▷炮弹自己不会爆炸。The shell won't detonate by itself. ▷我能够照顾好自己。I can take care of myself. II [形] our ▷自己人 our people

自给 zìjǐ [动] be self-sufficient

自尽 zìjìn [动] commit suicide

自觉 zìjué I [动] be aware of II [形] conscientious

自绝 zìjué [动] isolate oneself

自来水 zìláishuǐ [名] tap water

自理 zìlǐ [动] take care of oneself (PT took, PP taken)

自力更生 zì lì gēng shēng self-reliant

自立 zìlì [动] support oneself ▷自立门户 become independent

自流 zìliú [动] 1 (指水) flow freely 2 (指事) develop freely 3 (指人) do as one pleases

自律 zìlǜ [动] self-disciplined

自满 zìmǎn [形] self-satisfied

自鸣得意 zì míng déyì be very pleased with oneself

自命 zìmìng [动] consider oneself ▷自命不凡 consider oneself exceptional

自欺欺人 zì qī qī rén deceive oneself and others

自然 zìrán I [名] nature II [形] natural ▷自然免疫 natural immunity ▷表情自然 natural expression III [副] naturally ▷你对他那么冷淡, 他自然不会再来了。Since you were so cold to him, he naturally won't want to come again.

自杀 zìshā [动] commit suicide

自食其果 zì shí qí guǒ reap what one has sown

自首 zìshǒu [动] give oneself up (PT gave, PP given)

自私 zìsī [形] selfish

自卫 zìwèi [动] defend oneself

自我 zìwǒ [代] self ▷自我介绍 introduce oneself

自相矛盾 zìxiāng máodùn contradictory

自信 zìxìn [形] self-confident

自行车 zìxíngchē [名] bicycle

自修 zìxiū [动] 1 (自习) study by oneself 2 (自学) teach oneself (PT, PP taught) ▷他自修了企业管理课程。He taught himself business management.

自选 zìxuǎn [形] optional ▷自选商场 supermarket

自以为是 zì yǐ wéi shì believe oneself to be infallible

自缢 zìyì [动] hang oneself (PT, PP hanged)

自由 zìyóu I [名] freedom II [形] free

自由职业者 zìyóu zhíyèzhě [名] freelancer

自圆其说 zì yuán qí shuō justify oneself

自怨自艾 zì yuàn zì yì repent

自愿 zìyuàn [动] volunteer

自在 zìzài [形] 1 (自由) free 2 (舒适) comfortable

自知之明 zì zhī zhī míng self-knowledge

自治 zìzhì [动] be autonomous

自重 zìzhòng I [形] self-possessed ▷请你自重。Please behave yourself. II [名] weight

自主 zìzhǔ [动] make decisions by oneself

自助餐 zìzhùcān [名] self-service buffet

自传 zìzhuàn [名] autobiography

自转 zìzhuàn [动] rotate

自尊 zìzūn [名] self-respect

自作自受 zì zuò zì shòu suffer as a result of one's own actions

字 zì [名] 1 (文字) character 2 (字音) pronunciation ▷字正腔圆 have perfect enunciation 3 (书法作品) calligraphy ▶字画 painting and calligraphy 4 (字体) script ▷黑体字 bold face 5 (字据) written pledge

字典 zìdiǎn [名] dictionary

字节 zìjié [名] byte

字据 zìjù [名] ▷别人向我借钱时一般都会请求立字据。When someone borrows money from me, I usually ask for an IOU. ▷我们有字据为证。We have it in writing.

字里行间 zì lǐ háng jiān between the lines

字母 zìmǔ [名] letter

字眼 zìyǎn [名] wording

恣 zì [动] act freely

恣意 zìyì [副] wantonly

宗 zōng I [名] 1 (祖宗) ancestor 2 (家族) clan ▶同宗 of the same clan 3 (宗派) school ▶正宗 orthodox school 4 (宗旨) purpose II [量] ▷一宗心事 a worrying matter

宗教 zōngjiào [名] religion

宗派 zōngpài [名] faction

宗师 zōngshī [名] master

宗旨 zōngzhǐ [名] purpose

宗族 zōngzú [名] clan

综 zōng [动] summarize ▶综述 sum ... up

综合 zōnghé I [动] synthesize II [形] comprehensive ▷综合大学 university

棕 zōng [名] 1 (棕榈) palm 2 (棕毛) palm fibre (英) 或 fiber (美)

棕榈 zōnglú [名] palm

踪 zōng [名] tracks (PL) ▶行踪 tracks (PL)

踪迹 zōngjì [名] trace

鬃 zōng [名] ▶马鬃 mane ▶猪鬃 bristles (PL)

总 zǒng I [动] gather ▶总括 sum ... up II [形] 1 (全部的) total ▷总金额 total amount of money 2 (为首的) chief ▶总部 headquarters (PL) III [副] 1 (一直) always ▷他总是迟到。He's always late. 2 (毕竟) after all ▷发生这么大的事，我总得告诉他。After all, I couldn't not tell him about an event of this importance.

总裁 zǒngcái [名] director

总得 zǒngděi [副] ▷我们也总得有个地方坐坐呀。There must be somewhere for us to sit.

总督 zǒngdū [名] governor

总而言之 zǒng ér yán zhī in brief

总纲 zǒnggāng [名] general principles (PL)

总共 zǒnggòng [副] altogether

总归 zǒngguī [副] after all

总和 zǒnghé [名] total

总计 zǒngjì [动] total

总结 zǒngjié I [动] summarize II [名] summary

总括 zǒngkuò [动] sum ... up

总理 zǒnglǐ [名] premier

总是 zǒngshì [副] always ▷你总是迟到。You're always late.

总数 zǒngshù [名] total

总算 zǒngsuàn [副] 1 (最终) finally ▷多年的心血总算没有白费。All those years of struggle have finally paid off. 2 (大体上) all things considered ▷他能这样待你总算可以了。All things considered, the way he treats you isn't bad.

总体 zǒngtǐ [名] ▷总体评估 overall evaluation ▷总体战略思路 overall strategy

总统 zǒngtǒng [名] president

总务 zǒngwù [名] 1 (指事务) general affairs (PL) 2 (指官员) general manager

总之 zǒngzhī [连] ▷你需要找好的管理人才，财务人才，总之你一个人是不够的。You need to find a good manager and accountant – in short you can't do it all on your own.

纵 zòng I [形] 1 (从南向北的) north-south ▷运河贯穿两省。The canal runs north-south through two provinces. 2 (从前到后的) 纵深 depth ▶纵向 forward direction II [动] 1 (释放) release 2 (放任) indulge ▶纵酒 drink too much 3 (纵身) jump III [副] (书) ▷纵有千辛万苦，我也毫不畏惧。Even if there are a lot of difficulties, I will not be at all afraid.

纵横 zònghéng I [动] move freely II [形] 1 (竖的和横的) vertical and horizontal 2 (奔放自如的) easy ▷笔意纵横 write with ease

纵火 zònghuǒ [动] set fire to (PT, PP set) ▷有人故意纵火烧毁了房屋。Someone deliberately set fire to the house.

纵情 zòngqíng [副] to one's heart's content ▷纵情歌唱 sing to one's heart's content

纵然 zòngrán [连] even though

纵容 zòngróng [动] connive

纵深 zòngshēn [名] depth

走 zǒu [动] 1 (行走) walk ▶走路 walk ▷出去走走 go out for a walk 2 (跑动) run (PT ran, PP run) ▶奔走 run around 3 (运行) move ▷钟不走了。The clock's stopped. 4 (离开) leave (PT, PP left) ▷我先走。I'll be off. 5 (来往) visit ▷走亲戚 visit relatives 6 (通过) go through (PT went, PP gone) ▷走这条街比较近。If we go through this street it's quicker. 7 (漏出) leak ▷走气了。There's a gas leak. 8 (改变) depart from ▷走样 deviate from 9 (去世) die ▷他聪明能干，却早早地走了。He was clever and able, but died very young.

走动 zǒudòng [动] 1 (行走) walk about 2 (来往)

visit each other

走访 zǒufǎng [动] interview

走过场 zǒu guòchǎng go through the motions

走后门 zǒu hòumén use one's connections

走火 zǒuhuǒ [动] 1 (枪支) go off accidentally (PT gone, PP went) 2 (失火) be on fire ▷房子走火了。 The house is on fire.

走江湖 zǒu jiānghú lead a nomadic life

走廊 zǒuláng [名] corridor

走漏 zǒulòu [动] 1 (泄露) leak 2 (走私漏税) smuggle and evade taxes

走路 zǒulù [动] walk ▷我每天走路上班。 I walk to work every day.

走马看花 zǒu mǎ kàn huā have a superficial understanding

走南闯北 zǒu nán chuǎng běi travel extensively

走俏 zǒuqiào [动] sell well (PT, PP sold)

走人 zǒurén [动] leave (PT, PP left)

走神 zǒushén [动] lose concentration (PT, PP lost)

走兽 zǒushòu [名] beasts (PL)

走私 zǒusī [动] smuggle

走投无路 zǒu tóu wú lù have no way out

走向 zǒuxiàng I [名] alignment II [动] move towards

走穴 zǒuxué [动] moonlight

走样 zǒuyàng [动] deviate from

走运 zǒuyùn [动] (口) be lucky

走嘴 zǒuzuǐ [动] let something slip (PT, PP let)

奏 zòu [动] 1 (演奏) play ▶奏乐 play music 2 (发生) produce ▶奏效 have effect

奏鸣曲 zòumíngqǔ [名] sonata

奏效 zòuxiào [动] have effect ▷这感冒药吃下去立即奏效。 As soon as you take this flu medicine it will have the desired effect.

揍 zòu [动] (口) beat (PT beat, PP beaten)

租 zū I [动] 1 (租用) (房屋) rent 2 (租用) (汽车, 自行车, 录像带) hire (英), rent (美) 3 (出租) rent out II [名] rent ▶房租 rent

请勿混淆 rent, hire, 和 let。 在英式英语中，hire 表示通过支付一笔费用从而能够暂时使用某物。 在美式英语中，同样情况下 rent 更为常用。 He was issued with a car... He hired a car for the weekend. 以连续付款的方式而长期使用某物，应使用 rent。 ...the apartment he had rented... He rented a TV. rent 还可以表示以收取租金的方式将房屋出租给他人。 We rented our house to an American professor. 英式英语中，也可以使用单词 let。 They were letting a room to a school teacher.

租借 zūjiè [动] rent

租赁 zūlìn [动] rent

租用 zūyòng [动] rent

足 zú I [名] foot (PL feet) ▶足迹 footprint II [形] ample ▶充足 adequate III [副] 1 (达到某种程度) as much as ▷一顿酒席足足可以花上1000块钱。 You can spend as much as a thousand yuan on a banquet. ▷他足足用了两年时间写这本书。 It took him a whole two years to write this book. 2 (足以) enough

足够 zúgòu [动] be enough

足金 zújīn [名] solid gold

足球 zúqiú [名] football

足坛 zútán [名] footballing world

足以 zúyǐ [动] be enough

足智多谋 zú zhì duō móu wise and resourceful

族 zú [名] 1 (家族) clan ▶族人 clan member 2 (种族) nationality 3 (类别) group

诅 zǔ 见下文

诅咒 zǔzhòu [动] curse

阻 zǔ [动] block ▶劝阻 dissuade from

阻碍 zǔ'ài [动] obstruct

阻挡 zǔdǎng [动] stop

阻击 zǔjī [动] block

阻拦 zǔlán [动] block

阻力 zǔlì [名] 1 (物) resistance 2 (障碍) obstruction

阻挠 zǔnáo [动] obstruct

阻塞 zǔsè [动] block ▷交通阻塞 traffic jam

阻止 zǔzhǐ [动] stop

组 zǔ I [动] form ▶组建 set ... up II [名] group ▷兴趣小组 interest group III [量] ▷几组电池 some batteries

组成 zǔchéng [动] form

组阁 zǔgé [动] form a cabinet

组合 zǔhé I [动] constitute II [名] combination

组建 zǔjiàn [动] set ... up (PT, PP set)

组织 zǔzhī I [动] organize II [名] 1 (集体) organization 2 (指器官) tissue 3 (指纱线) weave

组装 zǔzhuāng [动] assemble

祖 **zǔ**[名] **1** (祖辈) grandparent ▶祖母 grandmother **2** (祖宗) ancestor **3** (首创者) founder

祖传 **zǔchuán**[动] hand ... down

祖父 **zǔfù**[名] grandfather

祖国 **zǔguó**[名] motherland

祖籍 **zǔjí**[名] ancestral home

祖母 **zǔmǔ**[名] grandmother

祖师 **zǔshī**[名] founder

祖先 **zǔxiān**[名] ancestors (PL)

祖宗 **zǔzong**[名] ancestors (PL)

钻 **zuān**[动] **1** (打洞) drill ▶钻探 drilling **2** (穿过) go through (PT went, PP gone) **3** (钻研) bury one's head in
→另见 zuàn

钻空子 **zuān kòngzi** exploit loopholes

钻探 **zuāntàn**[动] drill

钻研 **zuānyán**[动] study ... intensively

钻营 **zuānyíng**[动] further one's own interests

钻 **zuàn**[名] **1** (工具) drill ▶电钻 electric drill **2** (钻石) diamond ▶钻戒 diamond ring
→另见 zuān

钻石 **zuànshí**[名] **1** (金刚石) diamond **2** (宝石) jewel

嘴 **zuǐ**[名] **1** (口) mouth **2** (嘴状物) ▶茶壶嘴 spout of a teapot **3** (话) words (PL) ▶插嘴 interrupt

嘴尖 **zuǐ jiān**[形] sharp-tongued ▷他不但嘴尖, 脸皮也厚。He's not just sharp-tongued but also very thick-skinned.

嘴紧 **zuǐ jǐn**[形] tight-lipped

嘴脸 **zuǐliǎn**[名] features (PL)

嘴碎 **zuǐ suì**[形] talkative

嘴甜 **zuǐ tián**[形] ingratiating

嘴硬 **zuǐ yìng**[形] stubborn

最 **zuì**[副] most ▷最难忘的海外之旅 the most unforgettable trip abroad ▷这家饭店服务最好。The service at this restaurant is the best. ▷3人中他薪水最高。He's got the highest salary of the three.

最惠国 **zuìhuìguó**[名] most-favoured (英) 或 most-favored (美) nation

最近 **zuìjìn**[形] recent ▷最近的一期杂志 a recent edition of the magazine ▷他最近发表了几篇文章。He's recently published several essays.

罪 **zuì** I [名] **1** (恶行) crime ▶犯罪 commit a crime **2** (过失) blame ▶归罪 lay the blame on others **3** (苦难) hardship ▶遭罪 encounter hardship **4** (刑罚) punishment ▶死罪 death sentence II [动] blame ▶怪罪 blame

罪恶 **zuì'è**[名] crime

罪犯 **zuìfàn**[名] criminal

罪过 **zuìguò**[名] fault

最好 **zuìhǎo**[副] ▷你最好现在就去见你的老板。You'd better go to see your manager now.

罪魁 **zuìkuí**[名] chief culprit

罪名 **zuìmíng**[名] charge

罪孽 **zuìniè**[名] sin

罪行 **zuìxíng**[名] crime

罪证 **zuìzhèng**[名] evidence of a crime

罪状 **zuìzhuàng**[名] crime

醉 **zuì** I [形] **1** (饮酒过量的) drunk ▶醉鬼 drunk **2** (用酒泡制的) steeped in wine II [动] drink too much (PT drank, PP drunk) ▶陶醉 revel in

醉生梦死 **zuì shēng mèng sǐ** drunken haze

醉翁之意不在酒 **zuì wēng zhī yì bù zài jiǔ** have an ulterior motive

醉心 **zuìxīn**[动] be engrossed in

醉醺醺 **zuìxūnxūn**[形] drunk

尊 **zūn** I [形] senior II [动] respect III [量] ▷一尊神像 an image of a deity

尊称 **zūnchēng** I [名] term of address II [动] address

尊崇 **zūnchóng**[动] revere

尊贵 **zūnguì**[形] respected

尊敬 **zūnjìng**[动] respect

尊严 **zūnyán** I [形] dignified II [名] dignity

尊重 **zūnzhòng** I [动] respect II [形] serious ▷放尊重些! Behave yourself!

遵 **zūn**[动] follow

遵从 **zūncóng**[动] follow

遵守 **zūnshǒu**[动] observe ▷遵守纪律 observe discipline ▷遵守命令 comply with orders ▷遵守法律 abide by the law

遵循 **zūnxún**[动] follow

遵照 **zūnzhào**[动] obey

作 **zuō**[名] workshop
→另见 zuò

作坊 **zuōfang**[名] workshop

昨 **zuó**[名] **1** (昨天) yesterday ▶昨日 yesterday **2** (过去) the past ▷今是昨非 repent of past actions

昨天 zuótiān [名] yesterday

琢 zuó 见下文
→另见 zhuó
琢磨 zuómo [动] ponder

左 zuǒ I [名] left ▶左边 the left II [形] 1 (相反的) conflicting ▷观点相左 conflicting opinions 2 (进步的) leftist ▶左派 left-wing
左顾右盼 zuǒ gù yòu pàn look around
左撇子 zuǒpiězi [名] ▷她是左撇子。She is left-handed.
左右 zuǒyòu I [名] 1 (左和右) left and right ▷他左右各站一名保镖。Bodyguards stood to his left and right. 2 (跟随者) attendants (PL) 3 (上下) ▷他身高1点75米左右。He is about 1.75 metres (英) 或 meters (美) tall. II [动] control ▷左右政局 control the political situation
左…右… zuǒ…yòu… again and again ▷我左一句右一句地劝他别辞职。I tried again and again to persuade him not to give up his job.
左右逢源 zuǒ yòu féng yuán succeed regardless
左右开弓 zuǒ yòu kāi gōng use each hand alternately ▷他左右开弓凌空射门。He shot first with his right foot and then with his left.
左右手 zuǒyòushǒu [名] (喻) right-hand man
左右为难 zuǒ yòu wéi nán be in a dilemma ▷去也不好，不去也不好，真让我左右为难。It's a problem if I go, but also a problem if I don't – I'm in a real dilemma.

佐 zuǒ I [动] assist II [名] assistant
佐料 zuǒliào [名] seasoning
佐证 zuǒzhèng [名] evidence

作 zuò I [动] 1 (起) rise (PT rose, PP risen) ▷鞭炮声大作。There was a sudden loud noise of firecrackers. 2 (写) write (PT wrote, PP written) ▶作家 writer ▶作曲 compose music 3 (装) pretend ▶造作 affected 4 (犯) do (PT did, PP done) ▶作案 commit a crime 5 (当) take …as (PT took, PP taken) ▶作废 become invalid 6 (发作) feel (PT, PP felt) ▶作呕 feel sick II [名] work ▶杰作 masterpiece
→另见 zuō
作罢 zuòbà [动] drop
作弊 zuòbì [动] cheat
作壁上观 zuò bì shàng guān be an onlooker
作对 zuòduì [动] 1 (为敌) oppose 2 (成对) partner
作法 zuòfǎ [名] 1 (写法) writing technique 2 (做法) method

作风 zuòfēng [名] style
作家 zuòjiā [名] writer
作假 zuòjiǎ [动] 1 (冒充) fake 2 (耍花招) play tricks 3 (故作客套) stand on ceremony (PT, PP stood)
作茧自缚 zuò jiǎn zì fù make things difficult for oneself
作践 zuòjian [动] (口) run … down (PT ran, PP run)
作乐 zuòlè [动] enjoy oneself
作美 zuòměi [动] make things easy
作难 zuònán [动] be in a quandary
作孽 zuòniè [动] commit a sin
作弄 zuònòng [动] tease
作呕 zuò'ǒu [动] feel sick (PT, PP felt)
作陪 zuòpéi [动] help entertain
作品 zuòpǐn [名] work ▷文学作品 literary work
作曲 zuòqǔ [动] compose music
作威作福 zuò wēi zuò fú act like a tyrant
作为 zuòwéi I [名] 1 (行为) action ▷我们要根据一个人的作为来评判他。We should judge a person by their actions. 2 (成绩) accomplishment ▷有所作为 considerable accomplishment 3 (干头儿) scope II [动] 1 (当作) regard … as ▷我把养花作为一种休闲方式。I regard gardening as a form of relaxation. 2 (身为) ▷作为一名母亲，抚育儿女是她的责任。As a mother, looking after one's children is one's responsibility.
作文 zuòwén [动] write an essay (PT wrote, PP written)
作物 zuòwù [名] crop
作秀 zuòxiù [动] (贬) put a positive spin on things (PT, PP put)
作业 zuòyè I [名] work ▷野外作业 fieldwork II [动] do work
作用 zuòyòng I [动] affect II [名] 1 (影响) effect 2 (活动) action
作者 zuòzhě [名] author

坐 zuò [动] 1 (坐下) sit (PT, PP sat) ▷坐在窗口 sit by the window 2 (乘坐) travel by ▷坐飞机 travel by plane
坐班 zuòbān [动] work nine to five
坐标 zuòbiāo [名] coordination
坐吃山空 zuò chī shān kōng fritter away a fortune
坐次 zuòcì [名] seating plan
坐而论道 zuò ér lùn dào sit and pontificate
坐井观天 zuò jǐng guān tiān have a restricted outlook

坐牢 zuòláo [动] be in prison

坐冷板凳 zuò lěngbǎndèng be sidelined

坐立不安 zuò lì bù ān be on tenterhooks

坐落 zuòluò [动] be located

坐位 zuòwèi [名] seat

坐享其成 zuò xiǎng qí chéng benefit from others' efforts

坐以待毙 zuò yǐ dài bì sit and await one's fate

坐镇 zuòzhèn [动] take personal command (PT took, PP taken)

座 zuò I [名] 1 (坐位) seat ▶座号 seat number 2 (垫子) stand ▷茶杯座 coaster 3 (星座) constellation ▷双子座 Gemini II [量] ▷一座山 a mountain

座上客 zuòshàngkè [名] guest of honour (英) 或 honor (美)

座谈 zuòtán [动] discuss

座位 zuòwèi [名] seat

座无虚席 zuò wú xū xí have no empty seats ▷这部影片首映的时候，电影院里座无虚席。There was a full house at the film premier.

座右铭 zuòyòumíng [名] motto (PL mottoes)

做 zuò [动] 1 (制造) make (PT, PP made) ▷做个布娃娃 make a cloth doll 2 (写作) write (PT wrote, PP written) ▷做文章 write an essay 3 (从事) do (PT did, PP done) ▷做生意 do business 4 (举行) hold (PT, PP held) ▷做寿 hold a birthday party 5 (充当) be (PT was, were, PP been) ▷做大会主席 chair a meeting 6 (用作) be used as (PT was, were, PP been) ▷这块布可以做窗帘。This piece of cloth can be used as a curtain. 7 (结成) become (PT became, PP become) ▷做朋友 become friends

做爱 zuò'ài [动] make love

做伴 zuòbàn [动] keep ... company (PT, PP kept)

做东 zuòdōng [动] be host ▷今天聚餐我做东。The meal today is my treat.

做法 zuòfǎ [名] method

做工 zuògōng I [动] work II [名] workmanship

做活儿 zuòhuór [动] work

做客 zuòkè [动] be a guest

做媒 zuòméi [动] be a matchmaker

做梦 zuòmèng [动] dream ▷你想当市长？别做梦了！You want to be mayor? Dream on!

做人 zuòrén [动] 1 (待人接物) know how to behave (PT knew, PP known) 2 (当正派人) be an upright person

做声 zuòshēng [动] make a sound

做事 zuòshì [动] 1 (办事) deal with matters (PT, PP dealt) 2 (工作) work

做手脚 zuò shǒujiǎo [动] use underhand methods

做文章 zuò wénzhāng [动] (喻) make an issue of

做戏 zuòxì [动] 1 (演戏) put on a play (PT, PP put) 2 (假装) pretend

做贼心虚 zuò zéi xīn xū have a guilty conscience

做主 zuòzhǔ [动] decide

做作 zuòzuo [形] affected

ENGLISH-CHINESE/英汉词典

Aa

A¹, a [eɪ, ə] N [C/U] (letter) 英语的第一个字母 ▶ **A shares** (BRIT: ECON) A股 ▶ **from A to B** 从一地到另一地

A² [eɪ] N [C/U] **1** (MUS) C大调音阶中的第六音 **2** (SCOL, UNIV) 优 [yōu]

○

a [eɪ, ə] (before vowel or silent h: **an**) INDEF ART **1** (article) 一个 [yīgè] ▶ **a man** 一个男人 ▶ **a girl** 一个女孩 ▶ **a mirror** 一面镜子 ▶ **an elephant** 一只大象 ▶ **she's a doctor** 她是一名医生 ▶ **what a beautiful baby!** 多么漂亮的一个小宝宝啊! ▶ **have you got a dishwasher?** 你有洗碗机吗? ▶ **they haven't got a television** 他们没有电视 ▶ **a Mrs Blair telephoned** 一位布莱尔夫人打电话了
2 (one) 一 [yī] ▶ **a year ago** 一年前 ▶ **a hundred/thousand/million pounds** 100/1000/100万英镑 ▶ **a third of the population** 三分之一的人口
3 (expressing ratios, prices etc) ▶ **five hours a day/week** 一天/一周5个小时 [yītiān/yīzhōu wǔgè xiǎoshí] ▶ **five times a day** 一天5次 ▶ **100 km an hour** 每小时100公里 ▶ **it costs £5 a person** 每人付5镑 ▶ **30p a kilo** 每公斤30便士

○ **A & E** (BRIT) N ABBR (= accident and emergency) 急诊室 [jízhěnshì] [美= ER]

aback [ə'bæk] ADV ▶ **to be taken aback** 大吃一惊 [dàchī yījīng]

abandon [ə'bændən] I VT **1** (leave) [+ person, family] 抛弃 [pāoqì] **2** [+ car] 丢弃 [diūqì] **3** (give up) [+ search, idea, research] 放弃 [fàngqì] II N ▶ **with abandon** 尽情地 [jìnqíng de] ▶ **to abandon o.s. to sth** 使自己沉溺于某事 ▶ **to abandon ship** 弃船

abandoned [ə'bændənd] ADJ **1** [+ building, vehicle] 废弃的 [fèiqì de] **2** [+ child] 被遗弃的 [bèi yíqì de]

abate [ə'beɪt] VI [storm, violence +] 减弱 [jiǎnruò]

abattoir ['æbətwɑ:(r)] (BRIT) N [C] 屠宰场 [túzǎichǎng] [美= slaughterhouse]

abbey ['æbɪ] N [C] 大修道院 [dà xiūdàoyuàn]

abbreviation [əbri:vɪ'eɪʃən] N [C] 缩写 [suōxiě] ▶ **CD is an or the abbreviation for compact disc** CD是compact disc的缩写

abdomen ['æbdəmɛn] N [C] 腹部 [fùbù]

abdominal [æb'dɔmɪnl] ADJ [+ pain] 腹部的 [fùbù de]

abduct [æb'dʌkt] VT 绑架 [bǎngjià]

abduction [æb'dʌkʃən] N [C/U] 诱拐 [yòuguǎi]

abide [ə'baɪd] VT ▶ **I can't abide it/him** 我无法忍受这事/他 [wǒ wúfǎ rěnshòu zhèshì/tā] ▶ **I can't abide living here** 住在这儿让我受不了 ▶ **abide by** VT FUS [不可拆分] [+ rule, decision] 遵守 [zūnshǒu]

ability [ə'bɪlɪtɪ] N **1** [S] (capacity) ▶ **ability (to do sth)** (做某事的) 能力 [(zuò mǒushì de) nénglì] **2** [C/U] (talent, skill) 才能 [cáinéng] ▶ **to the best of my ability/abilities** 尽我最大的努力

○ **able** ['eɪbl] ADJ **1** ▶ **to be able to do sth** (have skill, ability) 能够做某事 [nénggòu zuò mǒushì] ▷ **The giant frog is able to jump three metres.** 大青蛙能够跳3米远。; (have opportunity) 可以做某事 [kěyǐ zuò mǒushì] ▷ **You'll be able to read in peace here.** 你可以在这里安静地看书。**2** (clever) [+ pupil, player] 有才能的 [yǒu cáinéng de]
▧ 用法参见 **can**

abnormal [æb'nɔ:məl] ADJ [+ behaviour, child, situation] 反常的 [fǎncháng de]

abnormality [æbnɔ:'mælɪtɪ] N **1** [U] (abnormal nature) 变态 [biàntài] **2** [C] (abnormal feature) 异常 [yìcháng]

aboard [ə'bɔ:d] I PREP [+ ship, plane] 在…上 [zài…shang] II ADV 在飞机/船/火车上 [zài fēijī/chuán/huǒchē shang]

abolish [ə'bɔlɪʃ] VT [+ system, practice] 废止 [fèizhǐ]

abolition [æbə'lɪʃən] N [U] 废除 [fèichú]

abort [ə'bɔ:t] VT **1** [+ child, foetus] 使流产 [shǐ liúchǎn] **2** [+ plan, mission] 使中止 [shǐ zhōngzhǐ]

abortion [ə'bɔ:ʃən] (MED) N [C/U] 流产 [liúchǎn] ▶ **to have an abortion** 流产

abortive [ə'bɔ:tɪv] (frm) ADJ [+ attempt, coup] 夭折的 [yāozhé de]

about [əˈbaʊt] I PREP 1 (*relating to*) 关于 [guānyú] ▸ **a book about London** 关于伦敦的一本书 ▸ **what's it about?** 这是关于什么的？ ▸ **she knows a lot about art** 她对艺术懂得很多 ▸ **we talked about it** 我们谈到了这事 ▸ **management is about motivating people** 管理就是要激发大家的热情 ▸ **to be sorry/pleased/angry about sth** 对某事感到抱歉/开心/生气 ▸ **there's something odd about this** 这有点怪怪的 ▸ **we'll have to do something about this** 我们对此要采取点儿措施 ▸ **what** or **how about eating out?** 出去吃怎么样？ 2 (*place*) 在⋯各处 [zài⋯gèchù] ▸ **he was wandering about the garden** 他在花园里到处闲逛 ▸ **clothes scattered about the room** 扔得满屋各处都是的衣服 ▸ **it must be about here somewhere** 一定在这周围的某个地方 3 (*frm*) (*around*) 围绕 [wéirào] ▸ **a chain hung about her neck** 环绕在她脖子上的一条项链 II ADV 1 (*approximately*) 大约 [dàyuē] ▸ **about a hundred/thousand people** 大约100/1000人 ▸ **at about two o'clock** 在两点钟左右 2 (*place*) 在 [zài] ▸ **to leave things lying about** 把东西到处乱放 ▸ **to run/walk about** 到处跑/到处走 ▸ **is Paul about?** 保罗在吗？ ▸ **there's a lot of flu/money about** 正在流行流感/资金充足 ▸ **to be about to do sth** 正要做某事 ▸ **he was about to leave** 他正要离开

◦ **above** [əˈbʌv] I PREP 1 (*higher than*) 在⋯上面 [zài⋯shàngmian] 2 (*greater than, more than*) (*in number*) 超过 [chāoguò] 3 (*in rank, authority*) 级别高于 [jíbié gāoyú] 4 ▸ **to be above sth** (*better, superior*) 不属于某事 [bùxièyú mǒushì] 5 ▸ **to be above suspicion/criticism** (*beyond*) 无法猜疑/指责的 [wúfǎ cāiyí/zhǐzé de] 6 (*in loudness*) (*over*) 高过 [gāoguò] ▷ *I couldn't hear her above all the noise.* 太吵了，我听不见她在说什么。 7 (*in importance*) (*before*) 胜过 [shèngguò] II ADV 1 (*in position*) (*higher up, overhead*) 在上面 [zàishàngmian] 2 (*in amount, number*) (*greater, more*) 以上 [yǐshàng] 3 (*in authority, power*) 上级 [shàngjí] 4 (*in writing*) 在上文 [zài shàngwén] III ADJ ▸ **the above address** 上述地址 [shàngshù dìzhǐ] ▸ **above all** 首先 [shǒuxiān] ▸ **from above** 从上面 ▸ **any/none of the above** 上述中任一/无一

abrasive [əˈbreɪzɪv] I ADJ 1 [+ *substance*] 磨砂的 [móshā de] 2 [+ *person, manner*] 粗暴的 [cūbào de] II N 磨砂材料 [móshā cáiliào]

abroad [əˈbrɔːd] ADV 1 [*be* +] 在国外 [zài guówài] 2 [*go* +] 到国外 [dào guówài] ▸ **there is a feeling/rumour abroad that...** 一种情绪/谣言在到处流传⋯

abrupt [əˈbrʌpt] ADJ 1 (*sudden*) [+ *action, ending etc*] 突然的 [tūrán de] 2 (*curt*) [+ *person, manner*] 鲁莽的 [lǔmǎng de]

abruptly [əˈbrʌptlɪ] ADV 1 (*suddenly*) [*leave, end* +] 突然地 [tūrán de] 2 (*curtly*) [*speak* +] 生硬地 [shēngyìng de]

abscess [ˈæbsɪs] N [C] 脓肿 [nóngzhǒng]

absence [ˈæbsəns] N 1 [C/U] [*of person*] 缺席 [quēxí] 2 [S] [*of thing*] 缺乏 [quēfá] ▸ **in sb's absence** 在某人不在时 ▸ **in the absence of sth** 在缺乏某物的情况下

absent [*adj* ˈæbsənt, *vb* æbˈsɛnt] I ADJ 1 (*from work, school*) 缺席的 [quēxí de]; (*at home*) [+ *parent*] 不同住的 [bù tóngzhù de] 2 (*inattentive*) 心不在焉的 [xīnbùzàiyān de] II VT (*frm*) ▸ **to absent o.s. from sth** 未出席某事 [wèi chūxí mǒushì] ▸ **to be absent** 不在 ▸ **to be absent from sth** 不存在于某事 ▸ **absent without leave** (MIL) 擅离职守

absentee [æbsənˈtiː] N [C] 缺席者 [quēxízhě]

absent-minded [ˈæbsəntˈmaɪndɪd] ADJ 心不在焉的 [xīnbùzàiyān de]

absolute [ˈæbsəluːt] I ADJ 1 (*complete*) [+ *beginner, confidence*] 完全的 [wánquán de] 2 (*utter*) (*used for emphasis*) 绝对的 [juéduì de] 3 [+ *power, monarchy*] 专制的 [zhuānzhì de] 4 (*definite*) 确凿的 [quèzuò de] 5 (*universal*) [+ *truth, rule*] 绝对的 [juéduì de] II N [C] 绝对 [juéduì] ▸ **the absolute minimum/maximum** 绝对最小/最大值

absolutely [æbsəˈluːtlɪ] ADV 1 (*utterly*) (*used for emphasis*) 绝对地 [juéduì de] 2 ▸ **absolutely (not)** (*certainly*) (*used for emphasis*) 地绝对 (不是) 地 [juéduì (bùshì) de]

absorb [əbˈzɔːb] VT 1 [+ *liquid, light*] 吸收 [xīshōu] 2 [+ *shock, impact, sound*] 消减 [xiāojiǎn] 3 (*assimilate*) [+ *group, business*] 并入 [bìngrù] 4; [+ *effects, losses*] 承受 [chéngshòu]; [+ *information, facts*] 理解 [lǐjiě] ▸ **to be absorbed in a book** 专心致志地读一本书

absorbent cotton [əbˈzɔːbənt-] (US) N [U] 脱脂棉 [tuōzhīmián] [英= **cotton wool**]

absorbing [əbˈzɔːbɪŋ] ADJ [+ *book, film etc*] 引人入胜的 [yǐn rén rù shèng de]

abstain [əbˈsteɪn] VI 1 (*in vote*) 弃权 [qìquán] 2 ▸ **to abstain from eating/drinking** 节制饮食/戒酒 [jiézhì yǐnshí/jièjiǔ]

abstract [*adj, n* ˈæbstrækt, *vb* æbˈstrækt] I ADJ 1 [+ *idea, quality*] 抽象的 [chōuxiàng de] 2 (ART) 抽象派的 [chōuxiàngpài de] 3 (LING) [+ *noun*] 抽象的 [chōuxiàng de] II N [C] (*summary*) 摘要 [zhāiyào] III VT (*frm*) ▸ **to abstract sth (from)** (从⋯中) 抽取某物 [(cóng⋯zhōng) chōuqǔ mǒuwù] ▸ **in the abstract** 抽象地

absurd [əbˈsəːd] I ADJ (*ridiculous*) 荒谬的 [huāngmiù de] ▷ *That's absurd.* 岂有此理。 II N

► **the absurd** (frm) 荒诞的事 [huāngdàn de shì]

abundance [əˈbʌndəns] N [S] 丰富 [fēngfù] ► **an abundance of** 大量的 ► **in abundance** 充足的

abundant [əˈbʌndənt] ADJ 丰富的 [fēngfù de]

abuse [n əˈbjuːs, vb əˈbjuːz] I N 1 [U] (insults) 辱骂 [rǔmà] 2 [U] (ill-treatment) (physical) 虐待 [nüèdài]; (sexual) 猥亵 [wěixiè] 3 [C/U] (misuse) [of power, alcohol, drug] 滥用 [lànyòng] II VT 1 (insult) 辱骂 [rǔmà] 2 (ill-treat) (physically) 虐待 [nüèdài] 3 (sexually) [+ child] 摧残 [cuīcán] 4 (misuse) [+ power, alcohol, drug] 滥用 [lànyòng] ► **to be open to abuse** 易产生弊病的

abusive [əˈbjuːsɪv] ADJ 1 (insulting) [+ person, language] 谩骂的 [mànmà de] 2 (violent) [+ person] 残暴的 [cánbào de]; [+ relationship] 暴虐的 [bàonüè de]

abysmal [əˈbɪzməl] ADJ [+ conditions, wages, performance] 糟糕的 [zāogāo de] ► **an abysmal failure** 彻底的失败

abyss [əˈbɪs] (liter) N [C] 1 (deep hole) 无底洞 [wúdǐ dòng] 2 (gap) 深渊 [shēnyuān] 3 (gap, gulf) 鸿沟 [hónggōu]

academic [ækəˈdɛmɪk] I ADJ 1 [+ system, books, freedom] 学术的 [xuéshù de] 2 [+ person] 学究的 [xuéjiū de] 3 (pej) (irrelevant) 空谈的 [kōngtán de] II N 大学教师 [dàxué jiàoshī]

academic year N [C] 学年 [xuénián]

academy [əˈkædəmɪ] N [C] 1 (organisation) 学会 [xuéhuì] 2 (school, college) 学院 [xuéyuàn]

accelerate [ækˈsɛləreɪt] I VI 1 (process +) 加快 [jiākuài] 2 (AUT) 加速 [jiāsù] II VT [+ process] 使加快 [shǐ jiākuài]

acceleration [æksɛləˈreɪʃən] N [U] 1 [of process, change] 加快 [jiākuài] 2 (AUT) 加速 [jiāsù] 3 (PHYS) 加速度 [jiāsùdù]

accelerator [ækˈsɛləreɪtə(r)] (AUT) N [C] 加速器 [jiāsùqì]

accent [ˈæksɛnt] N [C] 1 (pronunciation) 口音 [kǒuyīn] 2 (written mark) 重音符号 [zhòngyīn fúhào] ► **to speak with an (Irish/French) accent** 讲话带(爱尔兰/法国)口音 ► **to have a strong/German accent** 带有浓重的/德国口音 ► **the accent is on...** (emphasis, stress) 重点在… ► **to put the accent on sth** 将着重点放在某事上

accentuate [ækˈsɛntjueɪt] VT (emphasize) 使突出 [shǐ tūchū]

○ **accept** [əkˈsɛpt] VT 1 [+ invitation, advice, responsibility, credit cards etc] 接受 [jiēshòu] 2 (as true, valid) [+ fact, view] 接受 [jiēshòu]; (as inevitable) [+ change, sb's death] 接受 [jiēshòu] 3 [+ person] 接纳 [jiēnà] ▷ Stephen was finally accepted into the family. 斯蒂芬最终被这个家庭所接纳。► **to accept that...** (acknowledge) 承认…

acceptable [əkˈsɛptəbl] ADJ 1 (permissible) 可接受的 [kě jiēshòu de] 2 (suitable) 合意的 [héyì de] 3 (adequate) 令人满意的 [lìng rén mǎnyì de] ► **acceptable to sb** 某人可以接受的 ► **it is acceptable for sb to do sth** 某人做某事是可以接受的

acceptance [əkˈsɛptəns] N 1 [C/U] [of an offer] 接受 [jiēshòu] 2 [U] [of an idea] 赞同 [zàntóng] 3 [U] [of a situation] 容忍 [róngrěn] 4 [U] [of something new] 认可 [rènkě] 5 [U] [of a person] 接纳 [jiēnà]

access [ˈæksɛs] I N [U] ► **access (to sth)** (to building, room) 进入(某物) [jìnrù (mǒuwù)]; (to information, papers) (某物的)使用权 [(mǒuwù de) shǐyòngquán] ► **access (to sb)** (to person) 接近(某人) [jiējìn (mǒurén)] II VT (COMPUT) 存取 [cúnqǔ] ► **to have access to sb** [+ child] 有见某人的机会 ► **to have access to sth** [+ information, library, phone] 有享用某物的机会 ► **to gain access (to sth)** 得以进入(某物)

accessible [ækˈsɛsəbl] ADJ ► **accessible (to sb)** [+ place, object] 易于(某人)接近的 [yìyú (mǒurén) jiējìn de]; [+ knowledge, service, commodity] (对某人)易获得的 [(duì mǒurén) yì dédào de]; [+ art, culture] (对某人)易理解的 [(duì mǒurén) yì lǐjiě de]

accessory [ækˈsɛsərɪ] N [C] 1 (for room, car) 附件 [fùjiàn] 2 (CLOTHING) 饰品 [shìpǐn] 3 (LAW) ► **an accessory to the crime** 犯罪同谋 [fànzuì tóngmóu]

accident [ˈæksɪdənt] N [C] 1 (involving vehicle) 事故 [shìgù] 2 (mishap) 意外 [yìwài] 3 (chance event) 偶然事件 [ǒurán shìjiàn] ► **to have an accident** 出事故 ► **to meet with an accident** 出事故 ► **by accident** (unintentionally) 无意中; (by chance) 偶然

accidental [æksɪˈdɛntl] ADJ 意外的 [yìwài de]

accidentally [æksɪˈdɛntəlɪ] ADV (unintentionally) 意外地 [yìwài de]

accident and emergency (BRIT) N [C] 急诊室 [jízhěnshì] [美= **emergency room**]

acclaim [əˈkleɪm] (frm) I VT ► **to be acclaimed (for/as sth)** (因某事/作为某事而)受赞扬 [(yīn mǒushì/zuòwéi mǒushì ér) shòu zànyáng] II N ► **to win** or **receive acclaim** 受到赞扬 [shòudào zànyáng]

accolade [ˈækəleɪd] (frm) N [C] 荣誉 [róngyù]

accommodate [əˈkɒmədeɪt] VT 1 (hold) [car, hotel etc] 容纳 [róngnà] 2 (put up) 为…提供住宿 [wèi...tígōng zhùsù] 3 (satisfy) 使满意 [shǐ mǎnyì] ► **to accommodate o.s. to sth** 使自己适应某事

accommodation [əkɒməˈdeɪʃən] I N 1 [U] (place to stay) 住处 [zhùchù] 2 [U] (frm) (space) 空位 [kòngwèi] 3 [C] (frm) (agreement) 和解 [héjiě] II **accommodations** (US) NPL = **accommodation**

accompaniment [əˈkʌmpənɪmənt] N [C] 1 (complement) 伴随物 [bànsuíwù] 2 (MUS) 伴奏 [bànzòu] ► **to the accompaniment of sth**

[+ cheers, shouting etc] 在某物的伴随下

accompany [əˈkʌmpənɪ] VT **1** (frm) (escort) 陪伴 [péibàn] **2** (complement) 与…相配合 [yǔ…xiāng pèihé] **3** (MUS) 为…伴奏 [wèi…bànzòu]

accomplice [əˈkʌmplɪs] N [C] 同谋 [tóngmóu]

accomplish [əˈkʌmplɪʃ] VT 完成 [wánchéng]

accomplished [əˈkʌmplɪʃt] ADJ [+ cook, musician etc] 有造诣的 [yǒu zàoyì de]; [+ performance] 精湛的 [jīngzhàn de]

accomplishment [əˈkʌmplɪʃmənt] N **1** [C] (achievement) 成就 [chéngjiù] **2** [C] (frm) (skill) 技能 [jìnéng] **3** [U] (completion) 完成 [wánchéng]

○ **accord** [əˈkɔːd] I N [C] (agreement, treaty) 协议 [xiéyì] ▷ the 1991 peace accord 1991年和平协议 II VT (frm) (grant) 授予 [shòuyǔ] III VI ▶ to accord with sth (frm) (correspond) 和某事相符 [hé mǒushì xiāngfú] ▶ of its own accord (by itself) 自行地 ▶ of one's own accord (voluntarily) 自愿地 ▶ in accord (with) (frm) (与…)一致 ▶ with one accord (liter) 一致地

accordance [əˈkɔːdəns] N ▶ in accordance with sth [+ sb's wishes, the law etc] 根据某事 [gēnjù mǒushì]

according [əˈkɔːdɪŋ] ▶ according to PREP [+ person] 据…所说 [jù…suǒshuō]; [+ account, information] 根据 [gēnjù] ▶ to go/work out according to plan 按计划进行/发展 ▶ the gospel according to (St) Matthew/Luke 马太/路加福音

accordingly [əˈkɔːdɪŋlɪ] ADV **1** (appropriately) 相应地 [xiāngyìng de] **2** (consequently) 因此 [yīncǐ]

accordion [əˈkɔːdɪən] N [C] 手风琴 [shǒufēngqín]; (also: piano accordion) 键盘式手风琴 [jiànpánshì shǒufēngqín]

○ **account** [əˈkaʊnt] I N [C] **1** (with bank, at shop) 账户 [zhànghù] ▷ I have an account with Barclays. 我在巴克莱银行有一个账户。 **2** (COMM) (client, customer) 客户 [kèhù] ▷ The agency has won two important new accounts. 代理公司赢得了两个重要的新客户。 **3** (report) 描述 [miáoshù] ▷ He gave an account of what happened. 他对发生的事情做了一番描述。 II accounts NPL (COMM) 账 [zhàng] ▷ He kept the accounts. 他记账。 III VT ▶ to be accounted sth (frm) 被视为某事 [bèi shìwéi mǒushì] ▶ to buy/pay for sth on account 分期付款购买某物 ▶ to give a good account of o.s. 使自己表现不错 ▶ to be brought or called or held to account for sth 被要求就某事作出解释 ▶ to be of no/little account (frm) 完全不/不大重要 ▶ on no account 绝对不 ▶ on account of 因为 ▶ to take sth into account, take account of sth 考虑到某事 ▶ by or from all accounts 根据大家所说

▶ **account for** VT FUS (不可拆分) **1** (explain) 解释 [jiěshì] ▷ How do you account for the company's

high staff turnover? 你如何解释公司如此频繁的人事变动? **2** (represent) 占 [zhàn] ▷ Software accounts for over half of our product range. 软件产品占我们产品系列的一半以上。 ▶ to be not accounted for 未解释的

accountable [əˈkaʊntəbl] ADJ ▶ to be accountable (to sb/for sth) (向某人/就某事) 负责 [(xiàng mǒurén/jiù mǒushì) fùzé] ▶ to be held accountable for sth 被认为应对某事负责

accountant [əˈkaʊntənt] N [C] 会计师 [kuàijìshī]

accumulate [əˈkjuːmjuleɪt] I VT 积累 [jīlěi] II VI 累积 [lěijī]

accumulation [əkjuːmjuˈleɪʃən] N [C/U] [of debts, evidence] 积累 [jīlěi]

accuracy [ˈækjʊrəsɪ] N [U] [of information, measurements] 准确 [zhǔnquè] **2** [of person, device] 精确 [jīngquè]

accurate [ˈækjʊrɪt] ADJ **1** [+ information, measurement, instrument] 精确的 [jīngquè de]; [+ description, account, person, aim] 准确的 [zhǔnquè de]; [+ person, work] 正确的 [zhèngquè de] **2** [+ weapon, throw] 精确的 [jīngquè de]

accurately [ˈækjʊrɪtlɪ] ADV **1** [measure, predict +] 精确地 [jīngquè de] **2** [describe, assess, report, aim +] 准确地 [zhǔnquè de]

accusation [ækjʊˈzeɪʃən] N [C/U] (criticism) 谴责 [qiǎnzé] **2** [C] (allegation) 控告 [kònggào]

accuse [əˈkjuːz] VT **1** ▶ to accuse sb of (doing) sth (of dishonesty, immorality) 指责某人(做)某事 [zhǐzé mǒurén (zuò) mǒushì] **2** ▶ to be accused of sth (of crime) 被指控某事 [bèi zhǐkòng mǒushì]

accused [əˈkjuːzd] (LAW) N ▶ the accused 被告 [bèigào]

accustomed [əˈkʌstəmd] ADJ **1** ▶ to be/become accustomed to (doing) sth 习惯于/开始习惯于(做)某事 [xíguàn yú/kāishǐ xíguàn yú (zuò) mǒushì] **2** ▶ to become/be accustomed to sth [eyes +] 开始适应/适应某事 [kāishǐ shìyìng/shìyìng mǒushì] **3** (usual) ▶ his/her accustomed response 他/她的习惯反应 [tā/tā de xíguàn fǎnyìng]

ace [eɪs] N [C] **1** A纸牌 [A zhǐpái] **2** (TENNIS) 发球得分 [fāqiú défēn] ▶ the ace of spades 黑桃A

ache [eɪk] I VI **1** [part of body +] 痛 [tòng] **2** ▶ to ache for sth/to do sth (yearn) 渴望某事/做某事 [kěwàng mǒushì/zuò mǒushì] II N [C] 疼痛 [téngtòng] ▶ I've got (a) stomach/toothache 我胃/牙痛 ▶ I'm aching all over 我浑身疼痛 ▶ aches and pains 周身不适

achieve [əˈtʃiːv] VT **1** [+ aim] 实现 [shíxiàn] **2** [+ victory, success, result] 取得 [qǔdé]

achievement [əˈtʃiːvmənt] N **1** [C] (accomplishment) [of person, organization] 成就 [chéngjiù] **2** [U] (fulfilment) 实现 [shíxiàn] ▶ it was quite an achievement 这是个了不起的成就

acid ['æsɪd] **I** N **1** [C/U] (CHEM) 酸 [suān]
2 [U] (inf) (LSD) 迷幻药 [míhuànyào] **II** ADJ
1 (CHEM) [+ soil] 酸性的 [suānxìng de] **2** (sharp)
[+ taste] 酸的 [suān de]; [+ remark, humour] 尖
刻的 [jiānkè de] ▸ **citric/hydrochloric acid** 柠
檬/盐酸 [suān de]

acidic [ə'sɪdɪk] ADJ **1** (containing acid) [+ substance]
酸性的 [suānxìng de] **2** (sharp) [+ taste, smell] 酸
的 [suān de]

acknowledge [ək'nɒlɪdʒ] VT **1** (frm) [+ fact,
situation, problem] 承认 [chéngrèn] **2** [+ person
met] 对…打招呼 [duì…dǎ zhāohu] **3** [+ letter,
parcel] (by replying) 告知收到 [gàozhī shōudào]
4 (recognize value of) [+ achievement, status] 认可
[rènkě] ▸ **to acknowledge that...** 承认…

acknowledgement [ək'nɒlɪdʒmənt] **I** N
1 [s] (acceptance) 承认 [chéngrèn] **2** [C] [of
letter, parcel] 收到通知 [shōudào tōngzhī]
3 [U] (gesture of recognition) 反应 [fǎnyìng]
II acknowledgements NPL (in book) 致谢
[zhìxiè]

acne ['æknɪ] N [U] 痤疮 [cuóchuāng]

acorn ['eɪkɔːn] N [C] 橡果 [xiàngguǒ]

acoustic [ə'kuːstɪk] ADJ **1** [+ guitar, instrument]
非电传音的 [fēi diànchuányīn de] **2** [+ signal]
声音的 [shēngyīn de]

acquaint [ə'kweɪnt] (frm) VT ▸ **to acquaint sb
with sth** (inform) 把某事通知某人 [bǎ mǒushì
tōngzhī mǒurén] ▸ **to acquaint o.s. with sth**
开始知道某事 ▸ **to be acquainted with sb/sth**
[+ person] 认识某人; [+ fact] 了解某事

acquaintance [ə'kweɪntəns] N **1** [C] (person)
熟人 [shúrén] **2** [U] (familiarity) (with person) 结
识 [jiéshí]; (with subject) 了解 [liǎojiě] ▸ **to
make sb's acquaintance** (frm) 结识某人

acquainted [ə'kweɪntɪd] ADJ **1** (frm) ▸ **to
be/get acquainted with sth** 了解/开始了
解某事 [liǎojiě/kāishǐ liǎojiě mǒushì] **2** (frm)
▸ **to be acquainted (with sb)** (和某人) 相识
[(hé mǒurén) xiāngshí] **3** ▸ **to get** or **become
acquainted (with sb)** 开始了解 (某人) [kāishǐ
liǎojiě (mǒurén)]

acquire [ə'kwaɪə(r)] VT **1** (obtain, buy) 获得
[huòdé] **2** (learn, develop) [+ skill, habit] 学到
[xuédào] **3** (gain) [+ reputation] 取得 [qǔdé]

acquisition [ækwɪ'zɪʃən] N **1** [C] (thing
obtained) 获得物 [huòdéwù] **2** [U] (getting) [of
property, goods] 获得 [huòdé]; [of habit] 形成
[xíngchéng]; [of skill] 习得 [xídé]

acquit [ə'kwɪt] VT (clear) ▸ **to acquit sb (of sth)**
(LAW) 宣判某人 (无罪) [xuānpàn mǒurén
(wúzuì)] ▸ **to acquit o.s. well/badly** (frm) 表现
良好/不好

acre ['eɪkə(r)] N [C] 英亩 [yīngmǔ]

acrobatic [ækrə'bætɪk] ADJ [+ movement, display]
杂技的 [zájì de]

acronym ['ækrənɪm] N [C] 首字母缩略词
[shǒuzìmǔ suōlüècí]

> **acronym** (首字母缩略词) 是一种特殊
> 的缩写形式, 它可以像一个普通单词那
> 样读出。例如, **NATO** (北约) 和 **AIDS**
> (艾滋病)。**acronym** 是由组成这个名称
> 的每个词的第一个字母构成。**NATO** 代
> 表 **North Atlantic Treaty Organization**
> (北大西洋公约组织); **AIDS** 代表
> **acquired immune deficiency syndrome**
> (获得性免疫缺损综合征); **DOS** 代
> 表 **disk operating system** (磁盘操作系
> 统)。首字母缩略词比全称更常用, 因为
> 它们说起来更方便。

○ across [ə'krɒs] **I** PREP **1** (moving from one side
to the other of) 穿过 [chuānguò] ▷ He walked
across the room. 他穿过这个房间。**2** (situated on
the other side of) [of street, river, room etc] 在…对
面 [zài…duìmiàn] ▷ the houses across the street
在街对面的房子 **3** (extending from one side to the
other of) 跨越 [kuàyuè] ▷ the bridge across Lake
Washington 跨越华盛顿湖的桥 **4** (over) 搭在…
上 [dāzài…shàng] ▷ Her clothes were lying across
the chair. 她的衣服正搭在椅子上。**5** (involving
different groups) 跨越 [kuàyuè] ▷ parties from
across the political spectrum 来自不同政治派别的
党派 **II** ADV **1** (to/from a particular place/person)
从/向对面 [cóng/xiàng duìmiàn] ▷ Richard
walked across to the window. 理查德向对面的窗
户走去。**2** (from one side to the other) 从一边到
另一边 [cóng yībiān dào lìngyībiān] **3** ▸ **across
from** (opposite) 在…对面 [zài…duìmiàn] ▷ They
parked across from the theatre. 他们把车停在剧
院的对面。**4** ▸ **across at/to** (towards) 朝向
[cháoxiàng] ▷ He glanced across at his wife. 他朝
他的妻子瞥了一眼。**5** (in width) 宽 [kuān] ▷ a
hole 200 metres across 200米宽的洞 ▸ **to get** or
put sth across to sb 让某人明白某事

acrylic [ə'krɪlɪk] **I** ADJ [+ material, paint] 丙烯
酸的 [bǐngxīsuān de] **II** N [U] (textile) 丙烯酸
[bǐngxīsuān] **III acrylics** NPL (paint) 丙烯酸
[bǐngxīsuān]

ACT N ABBR (= American College Test) 美国大学入
学测试 [Měiguó Dàxué Rùxué Cèshì]

○ act [ækt] **I** VI **1** (take action) 行动 [xíngdòng]
▷ We have to act quickly. 我们得立即行动起
来。**2** (behave) 举止 [jǔzhǐ] ▷ They were acting
suspiciously. 他们举止可疑。**3** ▸ **to act for** or **on
behalf of sb** (lawyer +) 代表某人行事 [dàibiǎo
mǒurén xíngshì] **4** ▸ **to act as sb/sth** 担任某职
务/充当某物 [dāndāng mǒuzhíwù/chōngdāng
mǒuwù] ▷ Mr. Tang acted as interpreter. 唐先生
担当口译工作。**5** (work) [drug, chemical +] 见效
[jiànxiào] ▷ The drug acts swiftly, preventing liver
damage. 药物很快见效, 保护肝脏免受伤害。
6 (in play, film) 演戏 [yǎnxì] ▷ I was acting in
a play in Edinburgh. 我在爱丁堡演过一出戏。
7 (pretend) 假装 [jiǎzhuāng] ▷ Ignore her, she's

just acting. 别理她，她只是假装的。II VT(in play, film) [+ part, role] 扮演 [bànyǎn] ▷ I acted the part of Malvolio. 我扮演了马尔瓦里奥这个角色。III N [C] 1 (action) 行动 [xíngdòng] ▷ the act of reading 阅读 ▷ acts of sabotage 破坏行动 2 ▶ it's (just or all) an act (pretence) 这(只)是做做样子 [zhè (zhǐ) shì zuòzuò yàngzi] ▷ His anger was real. It wasn't an act. 他真的生气了，并不是做做样子。3 (THEAT) [of play, opera] 幕 [mù]; [of performer] 节目 [jiémù] ▷ a show consisting of songs and comedy acts 一场由演唱和喜剧节目组成的演出 4 (LAW) 法令 [fǎlìng] ▷ the 1944 Education Act 1944年教育法令 ▶ to act surprised/act the innocent 装出惊讶/无辜的样子 ▶ act of God (LAW) 不可抗力 ▶ in the act of doing sth ▶ to catch sb in the act (of doing sth) 当场捉住某人（做某事） ▶ to get one's act together (inf) 有条理地筹划 ▶ act on VT FUS [不可拆分] [+ advice, information] 根据…行动 [gēnjù…xíngdòng] ▷ The police are acting on information received last night. 警察正根据昨晚收到的情报采取行动。
▶ act out VT 1 (in play) [+ event] 将…表演出来 [jiāng…biǎoyǎn chūlái] ▷ The students act out events from history. 学生们将历史事件表演出来。2 (in behaviour) [+ fantasy, desire] 用行动表达 [yòng xíngdòng biǎodá]
▶ act up (inf) VI 1 [car, TV etc +] 出故障 [chū gùzhàng] ▷ The TV is acting up again. 电视机又出故障了。2 [child +] 捣乱 [dǎoluàn]
acting ['æktɪŋ] I N [U] 1 (profession) 表演 [biǎoyǎn] 2 (art) 演技 [yǎnjì] II ADJ [+ manager, director etc] 代理的 [dàilǐ de]
○ **action** ['ækʃən] I N 1 [U] (steps, measures) 行动 [xíngdòng] ▷ We need government action to prevent these crimes. 我们需要政府采取行动防止这些罪行。2 [C] (deed) 行为 [xíngwéi] ▷ He could not be held responsible for his actions. 他不应被认为是对他的行为负责。3 [C] (movement) 动作 [dòngzuò] ▷ Their every action was recorded. 他们的每个动作都被录了下来。4 [C] (in court) 诉讼 [sùsòng] ▷ a libel action 诽谤诉讼 5 ▶ the action (inf) 精彩的活动 [jīngcǎi de huódòng] ▷ Hollywood is where the action is now. 现今精彩的活动都在好莱坞。6 [U] (MIL) 行动 [xíngdòng] ▷ military action 军事行动 II ADJ [+ movie, hero] 动作的 [dòngzuò de] ▶ to take action 采取行动 ▶ to put a plan/policy into action 将计划/政策付诸实施 ▶ to bring an action against sb (LAW) 对某人提出起诉 ▶ killed/missing/wounded in action (MIL) 在战斗中阵亡/失踪/受伤 ▶ out of action [+ person] 不能活动; [+ machine] 出故障
action replay (BRIT) N [C] 慢镜头回放 [mànjìngtóu huífàng]
activate ['æktɪveɪt] VT [+ mechanism] 使活动 [shǐ huódòng]
active ['æktɪv] I ADJ 1 [+ person, life] 活跃的

[huóyuè de] 2 (in organisation or campaign) 积极的 [jījí de] 3 (concrete, positive) [+ step, support] 积极的 [jījí de] 4 (operative) 活跃的 [huóyuè de] 5 [+ ingredient] 速效的 [sùxiào de] 6 [+ volcano] 活的 [huó de] II N ▶ the active (LING) 主动语态 [zhǔdòng yǔtài] ▶ to play an active part or role (in sth) 积极参加（某事）
actively ['æktɪvlɪ] ADV 1 (directly) [involved +] 积极地 [jījí de] 2 (positively) [encourage, discourage +] 积极地 [jījí de]
activist ['æktɪvɪst] N [C] 积极分子 [jījí fènzǐ]
activity [æk'tɪvɪtɪ] I N 1 [U] (being active) 活跃 [huóyuè] 2 [C] (pastime) 活动 [huódòng] II **activities** NPL (actions) 活动 [huódòng]
actor ['æktə(r)] N [C] 演员 [yǎnyuán]
actress ['æktrɪs] N [C] 女演员 [nǚ yǎnyuán]
actual ['æktjuəl] ADJ 1 (real, genuine) 真实的 [zhēnshí de] 2 (for emphasis) 实际上的 [shíjìshang de]
○ **actually** ['æktjuəlɪ] ADV 1 (indicating or emphasising truth) 实际地 [shíjì de] ▷ I was so bored I actually fell asleep. 我闷透了，竟然睡着了。▷ Actually, we have the same opinion. 实际上我们有同样的观点。2 (in fact) 事实上 [shìshíshang] ▷ I'm not a student, I'm a doctor, actually. 我不是个学生，事实上，我是位医生。

> actually 和 really 都用于强调陈述的内容。actually 用于强调某个情形下的确存在的事实，通常该事实出人意料，或者跟刚刚提及的事情形成对比。All the characters in the novel actually existed... He actually began to cry. 它还可以用来强调叙述的精确性或者表示对他人的更正。No one was actually drunk... We couldn't actually see the garden. 在谈话中使用 really 是为了强调正在谈论的内容。I really think he's sick. 在形容词或者副词前，really 与 very 含义相似。This is really serious.

acupuncture ['ækjupʌŋktʃə(r)] N [U] 针灸疗法 [zhēnjiǔ liáofǎ]
acupuncturist ['ækjupʌŋktʃərɪst] N [C] 针灸医生 [zhēnjiǔ yīshēng]
acute [ə'kju:t] ADJ 1 (severe) [+ embarrassment, shortage] 严重的 [yánzhòng de] 2 (MED) [+ illness, infection] 急性的 [jíxìng de] 3 (keen, sharp) [+ mind, senses, observer] 敏锐的 [mǐnruì de] 4 (MATH) ▶ acute angle 锐角 [ruìjiǎo] 5 (LING) [+ accent] 带重音符号的 [dài zhòngyīn fúhào de] ▶ e acute 尖重音e
acutely [ə'kju:tlɪ] ADV (intensely) [+ aware, conscious] 敏锐地 [mǐnruì de]; [+ embarrassing, sensitive] 剧烈地 [jùliè de]
AD ADV ABBR (= Anno Domini) 公元 [gōngyuán]
ad [æd] (inf) N (advertisement) 广告 [guǎnggào]
adamant ['ædəmənt] ADJ ▶ to be adamant about sth/that... 对某事/…抱坚决态度 [duì

mǒushì/…bào jiānjué tàidù]

adapt [ə'dæpt] I VT **1** (alter, change) 使适合
[shǐ shìhé] **2** (for television, cinema) [+ novel, play]
改编 [gǎibiān] II VI ▶ **to adapt (to)** 适应
[shìyìng] ▶ **to adapt o.s.** 使自己适应

adaptable [ə'dæptəbl] ADJ [+ person, object,
material] 适应性强的 [shìyìngxìng qiáng de]

adaptor [ə'dæptə(r)] (ELEC) N [C] 转接器
[zhuǎnjiēqì]

⊙ **add** [æd] I VT **1** (put in, put on) 加入 [jiārù]
▷ Add the grated cheese to the sauce. 把磨碎的奶
酪加入酱汁中。**2** ▶ **to add (together)** (calculate
total of) 加(起来) [jiā (qǐlái)] ▷ Add three and
fourteen. 3加14。**3** (say) 补充 [bǔchōng] **4** (give) 增添
[zēngtiān] ▷ The herbs add flavour. 香料增添特
殊风味。II VI **1** (calculate) 做加法 [zuò jiāfǎ]
2 ▶ **to add to** (increase) 增加 [zēngjiā] ▷ This all
adds to the cost. 这都增加了成本。▶ **he added
that...** 他接着说⋯
▶ **add on** VT 附加 [fùjiā] ▷ They add on 9 per cent
for service. 他们附加9%的服务费。
▶ **add up** I VI **1** (calculate) 做加法 [zuò jiāfǎ]
▷ Many young children cannot add up. 许多幼龄
儿童不会做加法。**2** (accumulate) 累积 [lěijī]
3 (appear consistent) 合情合理 [héqínghélǐ]
II VT (calculate total of) 把⋯加起来 [bǎ⋯jiā
qǐlái] ▶ **it doesn't add up** 这说不通
▶ **add up to** VT FUS [不可拆分] (amount to) 合计
达 [héjì dá]

added ['ædɪd] ADJ (extra) 额外的 [éwài de]

addict ['ædɪkt] N [C] **1** ▶ **drug/heroin addict** 吸
毒/海洛因成瘾的人 [xīdú/hǎiluòyīn chéngyǐn
de rén] **2** ▶ **TV/football addict** 电视/足球迷
[diànshì/zúqiú mí]

addicted [ə'dɪktɪd] ADJ ▶ **to be addicted to
sth** [+ drugs, drink] 对某物上瘾 [duì mǒuwù
shàngyǐn]; [+ TV, chocolate etc] 对某事入迷 [duì
mǒushì rùmí]

addiction [ə'dɪkʃən] N [C/U] **1** (to drugs, alcohol)
瘾 [yǐn] **2** (to gambling, boxing) 入迷 [rùmí]

addictive [ə'dɪktɪv] ADJ **1** [+ drug] 易上瘾的
[yì shàngyǐn de] **2** [+ activity] 使人入迷的 [shǐ
rén rùmí de]

addition [ə'dɪʃən] N **1** [U] (MATH) 加法 [jiāfǎ]
2 ▶ **(with/by) the addition of...** (通过) 添加⋯
[(tōngguò) tiānjiā⋯] **3** [C] ▶ **addition (to)** (thing
added) 增添物 [zēngtiānwù] ▶ **in addition** 另
外 ▶ **in addition to** 除⋯之外

additional [ə'dɪʃənl] ADJ 附加的 [fùjiā de]

additive ['ædɪtɪv] N [C] 添加剂 [tiānjiājì]

address [ə'drɛs] N [C] **1** (postal address) 地
址 [dìzhǐ] **2** (speech) 演说 [yǎnshuō] II VT
1 [+ letter, parcel] 在⋯上写收件人姓名地址
[zài⋯shang xiě shōujiànrén xìngmíng dìzhǐ]
2 (frm) (speak to) [+ person] 对⋯讲话 [duì⋯
shuōhuà]; [+ meeting, conference etc] 向⋯讲话

[xiàng⋯jiǎnghuà] ▶ **to give an address (to
sb/at sth)** (speech) (对某人/在某场合) 做演讲
▶ **form of address** 称呼 ▶ **to be addressed to
sb** [+ letter, parcel] 是写给某人的 ▶ **to address
a remark to sb** (frm) 对某人进行评论 ▶ **to
address sb as...** 称某人为⋯ ▶ **to address (o.s.
to) a problem** 致力于处理某个问题

address book N [C] 通讯录 [tōngxùnlù]

adept ['ædɛpt] ADJ ▶ **adept (at)** 熟练的
[shúliàn de]

adequate ['ædɪkwɪt] ADJ **1** (sufficient) 足够
的 [zúgòu de] **2** (satisfactory) 符合要求的 [fúhé
yāoqiú de] **3** (appropriate) [+ response, reply etc] 恰
当的 [qiàdàng de]

adequately ['ædɪkwɪtlɪ] ADV **1** (sufficiently)
足够地 [zúgòu de] **2** (satisfactorily) 恰当地
[qiàdàng de]

adhere [əd'hɪə(r)] VI **1** ▶ **adhere to** (frm) (stick
to) 粘附 [niánfù] **2** (fig) (abide by) [+ rule, decision,
treaty] 遵守 [zūnshǒu] **3** (hold to) [+ opinion, belief]
坚持 [jiānchí]

adhesive [əd'hiːzɪv] I N [C/U] 粘合剂
[niánhéjì] II ADJ 有粘性的 [yǒu niánxìng de]

adhesive tape N [U] **1** (BRIT) 胶带 [jiāodài]
2 (US: MED) 绊创膏 [bànchuànggāo]

adjacent [ə'dʒeɪsənt] ADJ 邻近的 [línjìn de]
▶ **adjacent to** 邻近

adjective ['ædʒɛktɪv] N [C] 形容词
[xíngróngcí]

adjoining [ə'dʒɔɪnɪŋ] ADJ [+ room, office etc] 相
邻的 [xiānglín de]

adjourn [ə'dʒəːn] I VT (break off) [+ meeting, trial]
休 [xiū] II VI (break off) [meeting +] 休会 [xiūhuì];
[trial +] 休庭 [xiūtíng] ▶ **they adjourned to the
pub** (BRIT: inf) 他们转移到酒吧去了

adjudicate [ə'dʒuːdɪkeɪt] (frm) I VT [+ claim,
dispute, contest] 裁决 [cáijué] II VI ▶ **to
adjudicate (on sth)** (就某事) 做出裁定 [(jiù
mǒushì) zuòchū cáidìng]

adjust [ə'dʒʌst] I VT **1** (change) [+ approach, policy
etc] 调整 [tiáozhěng] **2** (rearrange) [+ clothing]
整理 [zhěnglǐ] **3** [+ device, position, setting] 校准
[jiàozhǔn] **4** [+ eyes, vision] 使适应 [shǐ shìyìng]
II VI **1** (adapt) 适应 [shìyìng] **2** ▶ **to adjust to**
适应 [shìyìng] ▶ **to adjust or become adjusted
(to sth)** [eyes, vision +] 适应 (某事)

adjustable [ə'dʒʌstəbl] ADJ 可调节的 [kě
tiáojié de]

adjustment [ə'dʒʌstmənt] N [C] **1** (to machine)
校正 [jiàozhèng] **2** [of prices, wages] 调整
[tiáozhěng] **3** (in behaviour, thinking) 改变
[gǎibiàn] ▶ **to make an adjustment to sth** 对
某物作调整

admin ['ædmɪn] (inf) N 管理 [guǎnlǐ] ▶ **to do
the admin** 做杂事

administer [əd'mɪnɪstə(r)] VT **1** [+ country,
department] 掌管 [zhǎngguǎn] **2** [+ test] 监管
[jiānguǎn] **3** (frm) [+ drug] 使用 [shǐyòng] ▶ **to**

administer justice 执法

administration [ədmɪnɪs'treɪʃən] N **1** [U] (organizing, supervising) 管理 [guǎnlǐ] **2** [C] (managing body) 管理部门 [guǎnlǐ bùmén] ▶ the (Reagan/Clinton) Administration (US) (里根/克林顿)政府

administrative [əd'mɪnɪstrətɪv] ADJ [+ costs, staff, system] 行政的 [xíngzhèng de]

administrator [əd'mɪnɪstreɪtə(r)] N [C] 行政人员 [xíngzhèng rényuán]

admiral ['ædmərəl] N [C] 海军上将 [hǎijūn shàngjiàng]

admiration [ædmə'reɪʃən] N [U] 钦佩 [qīnpèi] ▶ in admiration [stare, gasp etc +] 满怀钦佩 ▶ to have great admiration for sth/sb 对某物/某人无限钦佩

admire [əd'maɪə(r)] VT **1** (like, respect) [+ person] 钦佩 [qīnpèi] **2** (look at) [+ something beautiful] 欣赏 [xīnshǎng] ▶ I admire your courage/honesty 我钦佩你的勇气/诚实

admirer [əd'maɪərə(r)] N [C] **1** ▶ an admirer of sth/sb (fan) 某物/某人的赞赏者 [mǒuwù/mǒurén de zànshǎngzhě] **2** (suitor) 爱慕者 [àimùzhě]

admission [əd'mɪʃən] N **1** [C/U] (admittance) 进入许可 [jìnrù xǔkě] **2** [C/U] (of country to organization) 加入许可 [jiārù xǔkě] **3** [C/U] (to hospital) 住院 [zhùyuàn] **4** [U] (to exhibition, night club etc) 进入 [jìnrù] **5** [U] (also: admission charge, admission fee) 入场费 [rùchǎngfèi] **6** [C/U] (confession) 承认 [chéngrèn] ▶ admission free/£2.50 免费入场/入场费2.50英镑 ▶ to gain admission (to) (frm) 获准进入 ▶ by his/her own admission 据他/她自己承认 ▶ an admission of guilt/failure 承认罪责/失败

admit [əd'mɪt] VT **1** (confess) 承认 [chéngrèn] **2** (accept) [+ defeat, responsibility] 接受 [jiēshòu] **3** (permit to enter) (to club, organization) 接纳 [jiēnà]; (to place, area) 准许⋯进入 [zhǔnxǔ⋯jìnrù] ▶ he admits that... 他承认⋯ ▶ I must admit that... 我不得不承认⋯ ▶ to be admitted to hospital 住进医院 ▶ "children not admitted" "儿童不得入内" ▶ this ticket admits two 这张票可让两人入场 ▶ admit to VT FUS [不可拆分] (confess) [+ murder etc] 承认 [chéngrèn] ▶ to admit to doing sth or having done sth 承认做过某事

admittance [əd'mɪtəns] N [U] (to building, hospital) 准许进入 [zhǔnxǔ jìnrù]; (as member, student etc) 进入权 [jìnrùquán] ▶ "no admittance" "禁止入内" ▶ to gain admittance to sth (cross threshold) 有权进入(某处); (as member, student, employee etc) 被(某处)录取

admittedly [əd'mɪtɪdlɪ] ADV 公认地 [gōngrèn de]

adolescence [ædəu'lɛsns] N [U] 青春期 [qīngchūnqī]

adolescent [ædəu'lɛsnt] I ADJ 青春期的 [qīngchūnqī de] II N [C] (teenager) 青少年 [qīngshàonián]

adopt [ə'dɔpt] VT **1** [+ plan, approach, attitude] 采用 [cǎiyòng] **2** [+ child] 收养 [shōuyǎng]

adopted [ə'dɔptɪd] ADJ **1** [+ child] 被收养的 [bèi shōuyǎng de] **2** [+ country, home] 移居的 [yíjū de]

adoption [ə'dɔpʃən] N **1** [C/U] (of child) 收养 [shōuyǎng] **2** [U] (of policy) 采用 [cǎiyòng]

adoptive [ə'dɔptɪv] ADJ **1** [+ parent, mother, father] 收养的 [shōuyǎng de] **2** [+ country, town, city etc] 移居的 [yíjū de]

adore [ə'dɔ:(r)] VT **1** [+ person] 敬慕 [jìngmù] **2** (inf) [+ film, activity, food etc] 喜爱 [xǐ'ài]

adorn [ə'dɔ:n] VT (decorate) 装饰 [zhuāngshì] ▶ adorned with 用⋯装饰的

Adriatic [eɪdrɪ'ætɪk] N ▶ the Adriatic (Sea) 亚得里亚海 [Yàdélǐyà Hǎi]

adrift [ə'drɪft] ADJ **1** [+ boat, crew] 漂浮的 [piāofú de] **2** (fig) [+ person] 漂泊无依的 [piāobó wúyī de] ▶ to come adrift (BRIT) [wire, rope, fastening etc +] 脱落 ▶ to set adrift [+ boat, crew] 使漂流

ADT (US) ABBR (= Atlantic Daylight Time) 大西洋夏令时间 [Dàxīyáng Xiàlìngshí]

adult ['ædʌlt] I N [C] **1** (person) 成年人 [chéngniánrén] **2** (animal, bird, insect) 成体 [chéngtǐ] II ADJ **1** (grown-up) [+ life] 成年的 [chéngnián de] **2** [+ animal, bird, insect] 成熟的 [chéngshú de] **3** (for adults) 成人的 [chéngrén de] **4** (explicit) [+ literature, film] 色情的 [sèqíng de]; (mature) 成熟的 [chéngshú de]

adultery [ə'dʌltərɪ] N [U] 通奸 [tōngjiān] ▶ to commit adultery 有通奸行为

adulthood ['ædʌlthud] N [U] 成年 [chéngnián]

advance [əd'vɑ:ns] I VI **1** (move forward) 前进 [qiánjìn] **2** (make progress) 进展 [jìnzhǎn] II N **1** [C/U] (development) 发展 [fāzhǎn] **2** [C/U] (movement forward) 挺进 [tǐngjìn] **3** [C] (money) 预付款 [yùfùkuǎn] III ADJ [+ notice, warning] 预先的 [yùxiān de] IV VT **1** [+ money] 预付 [yùfù] **2** (propose) [+ theory, idea] 提出 [tíchū] **3** (bring forward) 提前 [tíqián] V advances NPL ▶ to make advances to sb (o.f.) (amorously) 向某人献殷勤 [xiàng mǒurén xiàn yīnqín] ▶ troops are advancing on the capital 部队正朝首都挺进 ▶ in advance [book, prepare, plan +] 提前 ▶ in advance of (before) 在⋯之前 ▶ (to pay sb) an advance on sth 预付(某人)某事的费用 ▶ advance booking (THEAT) 提前预订

advanced [əd'vɑ:nst] ADJ **1** (highly developed) [+ system, device] 先进的 [xiānjìn de]; [+ country] 发达的 [fādá de] **2** (SCOL) [+ student, pupil] 高年级的 [gāoniánjí de]; [+ course, work] 高等的 [gāoděng de] **3** [+ stage, level] ▶ to be at/reach an advanced stage/level 到晚期的 [dào wǎnqī de] **4** (frm) [+ years, age] 老的 [lǎo de]

advantage [əd'vɑːntɪdʒ] N [c] **1** (benefit) 好处 [hǎochù] **2** (favourable factor) 有利因素 [yǒulì yīnsù] **3** (superiority) 优势 [yōushì]; (TENNIS) 优势分 [yōushìfēn] ▶ **to have the advantage of being/doing sth** 由于某事/做某事而占据优势 ▶ **to take advantage of** [+ person] 利用; [+ opportunity] 利用 ▶ **to use** or **turn sth to one's advantage** 使某事转化为对自己有利 ▶ **the advantage of x over y** x 与y相比所具有的优势 ▶ **to have an advantage over sb** 胜过某人 ▶ **to (best/good) advantage** 达到(最佳/很好的)效果

advantageous [ædvən'teɪdʒəs] ADJ 有利的 [yǒulì de] ▶ **advantageous to sb** 对某人有利的

advent ['ædvənt] N **1** ▶ **the advent of** (arrival) …的出现 […de chūxiàn] **2** (REL) ▶ **Advent** 降临节 [Jiànglín Jié]

adventure [əd'ventʃə(r)] N **1** [c] (exciting event) 冒险活动 [màoxiǎn huódòng] **2** [U] (excitement) 冒险 [màoxiǎn]

adventurous [əd'ventʃərəs] ADJ **1** (bold) [+ person] 喜欢冒险的 [xǐhuān màoxiǎn de] **2** (innovative) [+ thing] 冒险的 [màoxiǎn de]

adverb ['ædvəːb] N [c] 副词 [fùcí]

adversary ['ædvəsəri] N [c] 对手 [duìshǒu]

adverse ['ædvəːs] ADJ [+ effect, conditions] 不利的 [bùlì de]; [+ reaction, publicity] 敌对的 [díduì de]

adversity [əd'vəːsɪtɪ] N [U/C] 逆境 [nìjìng] ▶ **in the face of adversity** 面临逆境

advert ['ædvəːt] (BRIT) N 广告 [guǎnggào] [美= **ad**]

advertise ['ædvətaɪz] I VI (in newspaper, on television etc) 做广告 [zuò guǎnggào] II VT **1** [+ product, event] 为…做广告 [wèi…zuò guǎnggào] **2** [+ job] 刊登 [kāndēng] ▶ **to advertise for sth/sb** [+ staff, accommodation] 登广告征求某物/某人

advertisement [əd'vəːtɪsmənt] (COMM) N [c] (in newspaper, classified ads, on television) 广告 [guǎnggào] ▶ **to be an advertisement for sth** (ESP BRIT) 为某事做宣传

advertiser ['ædvətaɪzə(r)] N [c] (in newspaper, on television etc) 广告人 [guǎnggàorén]

advertising ['ædvətaɪzɪŋ] N [U] **1** (advertisements) 广告 [guǎnggào] **2** (industry) 广告业 [guǎnggàoyè]

advertising agency N [c] 广告公司 [guǎnggào gōngsī]

advertising campaign N [c] 宣传活动 [xuānchuán huódòng]

advice [əd'vaɪs] N [U] 忠告 [zhōnggào] ▶ **a piece of advice** 一条建议 ▶ **to ask (sb) for advice (about/on sth)** 征求(某人)(关于某事的)意见 ▶ **to take (legal) advice** (frm) 征求(律师的)意见 ▶ **take my advice** (inf) 听我的劝告

请勿将 **advice** 和 **advise** 混淆。advice 含有字母 **c**,是名词。She gave me some useful advice…Let me give you a piece of advice. advise 含有字母 **s**,是动词。The teacher advised him to study harder if he wanted to do well in his exams.

advisable [əd'vaɪzəbl] (frm) ADJ ▶ **it is/would be advisable to…** …是可取的 […shì kěqǔ de]

advise [əd'vaɪz] VT **1** (tell) ▶ **to advise sb to do sth** 劝某人做某事 [quàn mǒurén zuò mǒushì] **2** (help) ▶ **to advise sb on sth** 在某事上劝某人 [zài mǒushì shang quàn mǒurén] **3** (frm) (inform) ▶ **to advise sb of sth** 将某事通知某人 [jiāng mǒushì tōngzhī mǒurén] ▶ **to advise sb against sth/doing sth** 劝某人不要接受某事/做某事

用法参见 **advice**

adviser [əd'vaɪzə(r)] N [c] 顾问 [gùwèn]

advisory [əd'vaɪzərɪ] (frm) ADJ [+ role, capacity, body etc] 咨询的 [zīxún de] ▶ **in an advisory capacity** 以顾问身份

advocate [vb 'ædvəkeɪt, n 'ædvəkɪt] I (frm) VT (support, recommend) 拥护 [yōnghù] II N [c] **1** (barrister) 律师 [lùshī] **2** (frm) (supporter, proponent) 拥护者 [yōnghùzhě]

Aegean [iː'dʒiːən] N ▶ **the Aegean (Sea)** 爱琴海 [Àiqín Hǎi]

aerial ['ɛərɪəl] I (BRIT) N [c] 天线 [tiānxiàn] [美= **antenna**] II ADJ [+ attack, photograph] 空中的 [kōngzhōng de]

aerobics [ɛə'rəubɪks] I N [U] 有氧健身操 [yǒuyǎng jiànshēncāo] II CPD [复合词] [+ class, instructor] 健美操 [jiànměicāo]

aeroplane ['ɛərəpleɪn] (BRIT) N [c] 飞机 [fēijī] [美= **airplane**]

aerosol ['ɛərəsɔl] N [c] (can, spray) 按钮式喷雾器 [ànniǔshì pēnwùqì]

aesthetic [iːs'θetɪk] ADJ 审美的 [shěnměi de]

affable ['æfəbl] ADJ [+ person, nature] 和蔼可亲的 [hé'ǎi kěqīn de]

affair [ə'fɛə(r)] I N **1** [s] (matter, business) 事情 [shìqíng] **2** [c] (romance) 风流韵事 [fēngliú yùnshì] II **affairs** NPL **1** (matters) 事务 [shìwù] **2** (personal concerns) 私事 [sīshì] ▶ **to have an affair (with sb)** (和某人)发生暧昧关系 ▶ **that's your/my affair** 那是你/我的私事

affect [ə'fɛkt] VT **1** (influence) [+ person, object] 影响 [yǐngxiǎng] **2** (disease +) 侵袭 [qīnxí] **3** (emotionally) 感动 [gǎndòng] **4** (liter) (feign) ▶ **to affect interest/concern** 佯装感兴趣/关心 [yángzhuāng gǎn xìngqù/guānxīn]

请勿将 **affect** 和 **effect** 混淆。如果事物 affects 某人或某事,则它影响了该人或该事,或者使他们发生改变。Fitness affects you mentally and physically, and how you feel affects your relationships and your ability to cope…Noise affects *different people in different ways.* **affect** 的名词形式是 **effect**。如果某事物 **affect** 你，它对你有 **effect**。*…the effect of noise on people in factories… the effect of the anaesthetic…* **effect** 也可以用作动词。如果你 **effect** 某事，例如某个变化或修理某物，你促使该事发生或做了这件事。**effect** 作为动词时，是一个比较正式的词汇，而且比作为名词时的用法少见得多。*She had effected a few rather hasty repairs.*

affected [əˈfɛktɪd] ADJ [+ behaviour, person] 做作的 [zuòzuo de]

affection [əˈfɛkʃən] I N [U] (fondness) 喜爱 [xǐ'ài] II **affections** NPL 爱慕 [àimù] ▸ **to feel affection for sb** 喜欢某人 ▸ **to win sb's affection** 赢得某人的爱慕

affectionate [əˈfɛkʃənɪt] ADJ [+ person, kiss, animal] 有感情的 [yǒu gǎnqíng de] ▸ **to be affectionate towards sb** 钟爱某人

affinity [əˈfɪnɪtɪ] N 1 [s] (bond) ▸ **to have an affinity with sb/sth** 和某人/某物有亲近感 [hé mǒurén/mǒuwù yǒu qīnjìngǎn] 2 [c] (resemblance) 相似 [xiāngsì]

afflict [əˈflɪkt] VT ▸ **to be afflicted with** or **by sth** 被某事所折磨 [bèi mǒushì suǒ zhémó]

affluent [ˈæfluənt] ADJ (wealthy) [+ person, surroundings] 富裕的 [fùyù de]

afford [əˈfɔːd] VT 1 ▸ **to be able to afford (to buy/pay) sth** 买/支付得起某物 [mǎi/zhīfùdeqǐ mǒuwù] 2 ▸ **to be able to afford (to do) sth** (permit o.s.) 担负得起(做)某事 [dānfùdeqǐ (zuò) mǒushì] 3 (frm) (provide) [+ opportunity, protection] 提供 [tígōng]

affordable [əˈfɔːdəbl] ADJ 买得起的 [mǎideqǐ de]

Afghanistan [æfˈgænɪstæn] N 阿富汗 [Āfùhàn]

afield [əˈfiːld] ADV ▸ (from) **far afield** (来自)远方 [(láizì) yuǎnfāng] ▸ (from) **further** or **farther afield** (来自)更远的地方

afloat [əˈfləʊt] ADV ▸ **to keep sth afloat** 使某物浮在水面上 [shǐ mǒuwù fúzài shuǐmiàn shàng]; (financially) 使某物维持下去 [shǐ mǒuwù wéichí xiàqù]

afoot [əˈfʊt] ADV ▸ **there is something afoot** 某事正在进行中 [mǒushì zhèngzài jìnxíng zhōng] ▸ **plans/moves are afoot to…** 正有计划/行动…

afraid [əˈfreɪd] ADJ (frightened) 害怕的 [hàipà de] ▸ **to be afraid of sb/sth** 害怕某人/某物 ▸ **to be afraid to do sth/of doing sth** 怕做某事 ▸ **to be afraid for sb** 担心某人 ▸ **to be afraid that…** (worry, fear) 担心…; (expressing apology, disagreement) 恐怕… ▸ **don't be afraid to…** (expressing reassurance) 不要有顾虑… ▸ **I'm afraid so/not** 恐怕是/不是的

afresh [əˈfreʃ] ADV [start +] 重新 [chóngxīn]

Africa [ˈæfrɪkə] N 非洲 [Fēizhōu]

African [ˈæfrɪkən] I ADJ 非洲的 [Fēizhōu de] II N [c] (person) 非洲人 [Fēizhōurén]

African-American [æfrɪkənəˈmɛrɪkən] I N [c] 美国黑人 [Měiguó hēirén] II ADJ 美国黑人的 [Měiguó hēirén de]

⊕ **after** [ˈɑːftə(r)] I PREP 1 (in time) 在…以后 [zài…yǐhòu] ▷ *She arrived just after breakfast.* 她刚好在早饭后到到。 2 (in place, order) 在…后面 [zài…hòumiàn] ▷ *I wrote my signature after Penny's.* 我把名字签在潘妮的后面。 II ADV (afterwards) 以后 [yǐhòu] ▷ *Soon after, he began preparing the meal.* 不久以后，他开始准备饭菜。 III CONJ (once) 在…以后 [zài…yǐhòu] ▷ *They felt ill after they had eaten.* 他们吃完后感到不舒服。 ▸ **the day after tomorrow** 后天 ▸ **it's ten after eight** (US) 现在是8点过10分 [英=past] ▸ **day after day/year after year** 日复一日/年复一年 ▸ **to call/shout/stare after sb** 在某人身后叫/喊/瞪眼 ▸ **the second biggest, after Germany** 紧随德国之后的第二大 ▸ **to clean/tidy/clear up after sb** (for) 替某人打扫/整理/清理 ▸ **to be after sb** (chasing, following) 追逐某人 ▷ *The police are after him.* 警察在追捕他。 ▸ **to be after sth** (trying to get) 想得到某物 ▸ **to ask after sb** 询问某人的情况 ▸ **to be named after sb/sth** (BRIT) 以某人/某物的名字命名 ▸ **after all** 毕竟 ▸ **after you!** 您先请！ ▸ **after doing sth** 做完某事后 ▷ *after flying to London* 飞抵伦敦后

after、**afterwards** 和 **later** 用于表示某事发生在说话的时间，或者某个特定事情之后。**after** 可以和 **not long**、**shortly** 等连用。*After dinner she spoke to him… I returned to England after visiting India… Shortly after, she called me.* 在无须指明某个特定时间或事件时，可以用 **afterwards**。*Afterwards we went to a night club…You'd better come and see me later.* **afterwards** 可以和 **soon**、**shortly** 等连用。*Soon afterwards, he came to the clinic.* **later** 表示某事发生在说话之后，可以和 **a little**、**much** 或 **not much** 等连用。*I'll go and see her later…A little later, the lights went out… I learned all this much later.* 可以用 **after**、**afterwards** 和 **later** 后跟表示时间段的词语，表示某事发生的时间。*… five years after his death…She wrote me six years later/afterwards.*

aftermath [ˈɑːftəmæθ] N ▸ **(in) the aftermath (of)** (在)(…)结束后的一个时期里 [(zài)(…) jiéshù hòu de yīgè shíqī lǐ]

afternoon [ˈɑːftəˈnuːn] N [c/U] 下午 [xiàwǔ] ▸ **this afternoon** 今天下午 ▸ **tomorrow/yesterday afternoon** 明天/昨天下午 ▸ **(good) afternoon!** (goodbye) 再见！; (hello) 下午好！

after-shave (lotion) [ˈɑːftəʃeɪv-] N [U] 须后(润肤)水 [xūhòu (rùnfū) shuǐ]

aftersun [ˈɑːftə(r)ˈsʌn] N [U] 晒后修复霜 [shàihòu xiūfùshuāng]

afterwards [ˈɑːftəwədz], (US) **afterward** [ˈɑːftəwəd] ADV 以后 [yǐhòu]
▶ 用法参见 after

○again [əˈɡɛn] ADV **1** (a second or another time) 又一次地 [yòu yīcì de] ▷ He kissed her again. 他又一次吻了她。**2** (returning to previous state) 又 [yòu] ▷ She opened the door and then closed it again. 她打开门，随着又关上了。▶ **again and again/time and again** 一再 ▶ **now and again** 时而 ▶ **(but) then** or **there again** （但）另一方面

○against [əˈɡɛnst] I PREP **1** (leaning on, touching) 紧靠在 [jǐnkào zài] ▷ He stood the ladder against the wall. 他把梯子紧靠在墙上。▷ She pressed her nose against the window. 她把鼻子紧贴在窗户上。**2** (opposed to) 反对 [fǎnduì] ▷ He is against privatization. 他反对私有化。**3** (towards) (expressing hostility) 针对 [zhēnduì] ▷ violence against women 针对妇女的暴力 **4** (in game or competition) 同…对抗 [tóng…duìkàng] ▷ They'll be playing against Australia. 他们将在比赛中同澳大利亚队对抗。**5** ▶ **to protect against sth** 保护免受某种伤害 [bǎohù miǎnshòu mǒuzhǒng shānghài] ▷ The cream protects against sunburn. 这种润肤霜保护皮肤免受晒伤。**6** (compared to) 和…对比 [hé…duìbǐ] ▷ The pound has fallen against the dollar. 英镑对美元的比值有所下跌。II ADV (in opposition) 反对 [fǎnduì] ▷ 283 votes in favour and 29 against 283票赞成，29票反对 ▶ **against the law/rules** 违反法律/规则 ▶ **against sb's wishes/advice** 违背某人的意愿/忠告 ▶ **against one's will** 违背自己的意愿 ▶ **to have sth against sb** 讨厌某人 ▶ **to have nothing against sb** 并不讨厌某人 ▶ **against a background of...** 在…的背景下 ▶ **against a blue background** 衬着蓝色的背景 ▶ **(as) against** (compared to) 和…相比

○age [eɪdʒ] I N **1** [C/U] (of person, object) 年龄 [niánlíng] ▷ I'm the same age as you. 我和你同龄。**2** [U] (being old) 老年 [lǎonián] ▷ He is showing signs of age. 他开始显老了。**3** [C] (period in history) 时代 [shídài] ▷ We live in an age of uncertainty. 我们生活在一个动乱的时代。II VI [person +] 变老 [biànlǎo] ▷ He has aged a lot. 他变老了许多。III VT [+ person] 使…见老 [shǐ…jiànlǎo] ▷ The worry had aged him. 忧愁使他见老了。▶ **what age is he?** 他多大了？▶ **you don't look your age** 你看起来与你年纪不相符 ▶ **20 years of age** 20岁 ▶ **at the age of 20** 20岁时 ▶ **to be under age** [person +] 未成年 ▶ **under age smoking/drinking/sex** 未成年抽烟/喝酒/性行为 ▶ **to come of age** [person +] 达到法定年龄 ▶ **an age, ages** (inf) 很长时间 ▷ I haven't seen you for ages! 我很长时间没见到你了！▶ **the Stone/Bronze/Iron Age** 石器/铜器/铁器时代 ▶ **the age of steam/television/**

chivalry 蒸汽/电视/骑士时代 ▶ **through the ages** 历代

aged¹ [eɪdʒd] ADJ ▶ **aged 10** 10岁 [shí suì]

aged² [ˈeɪdʒɪd] I ADJ (elderly) 老年的 [lǎonián de] II N PL ▶ **the aged** 老人 [lǎorén]

age group N [C] 同一年龄的人们 [tóngyī niánlíng de rénmen] ▶ **the 40 to 50 age group** 年龄在40岁到50岁的人们

age limit N [C] 年龄限制 [niánlíng xiànzhì]

agency [ˈeɪdʒənsɪ] N [C] **1** (COMM) 代理处 [dàilǐchù] **2** (ESP US) (government body) 机构 [jīgòu]

agenda [əˈdʒɛndə] N [C] **1** [of meeting] 议程 [yìchéng] **2** (political) 议事日程 [yìshì rìchéng] ▶ **on the/sb's agenda** (for meeting) 在（某人的）议事日程中 ▶ **high on the agenda** (political) 首要事件 ▶ **to set the agenda** 设定议程 ▶ **to have one's own agenda** 有自己的专门议题 ▶ **a hidden agenda** 秘密议程

agent [ˈeɪdʒənt] N [C] **1** (representative) 代理人 [dàilǐrén] **2** (for actor, writer, musician) 经纪人 [jīngjìrén] **3** (spy) 间谍 [jiàndié] **4** (chemical) 剂 [jì] **5** ▶ **the/an agent of sth** (instrument) 某事的催化物 [mǒushì de cuīhuàwù]

age of consent N ▶ **the age of consent** 承诺年龄 [chéngnuò niánlíng] ▶ **under/over the age of consent** 未满/超过承诺年龄

aggravate [ˈæɡrəveɪt] VT **1** (make worse) [+ situation] 使恶化 [shǐ èhuà] **2** (inf) (annoy) [+ person] 激怒 [jīnù]

aggression [əˈɡrɛʃən] N [U] 侵略 [qīnlüè] ▶ **an act of aggression** 侵犯行为

aggressive [əˈɡrɛsɪv] ADJ **1** (belligerent) 好战的 [hàozhàn de] **2** (forceful) [+ salesman, campaign] 有闯劲的 [yǒu chuǎngjìn de]

aghast [əˈɡɑːst] (frm) ADJ ▶ **aghast (at)** [+ behaviour, situation] (被…)吓呆[(bèi…) xiàdāi]

agile [ˈædʒaɪl] ADJ **1** (physically) 灵活的 [línghuó de] **2** (mentally) 敏捷的 [mǐnjié de]

agitate [ˈædʒɪteɪt] I VI ▶ **to agitate for/against sth** (campaign) 鼓吹某事/鼓吹反对某事 [gǔchuī mǒushì/gǔchuī fǎnduì mǒushì] II VT **1** (upset) [+ person] 使焦虑 [shǐ jiāolù] **2** (frm) (shake) [+ liquid] 搅动 [jiǎodòng]

agitated [ˈædʒɪteɪtɪd] ADJ [+ person] 焦虑的 [jiāolù de]

AGM N ABBR (= annual general meeting) 年度会议 [niándù huìyì]

○ago [əˈɡəʊ] ADV ▶ **2 days ago** 两天前 [liǎngtiān qián] ▶ **long ago/a long time ago** 很久以前 ▶ **how long ago?** 多久以前？▶ **as long ago as 1925** 早在1925年

agonizing [ˈæɡənaɪzɪŋ] ADJ **1** [+ pain, death] 令人痛苦的 [lìng rén tòngkǔ de] **2** [+ wait] 烦人的 [fánrén de] **3** [+ decision, choice] 折磨人的 [zhémó rén de]

agony [ˈæɡənɪ] N [C/U] 痛苦 [tòngkǔ] ▶ **to be**

in agony 在极度痛苦中
○ **agree** [əˈgriː] I vi 1 *(have same opinion)* 同意 [tóngyì] ▷ *They find it hard to agree about this.* 他们觉得很难就这一点一点。2 ▸ **to agree to sth/to do sth** 同意某事/做某事 [tóngyì mǒushì/zuò mǒushì] ▷ *He has agreed to our proposal.* 他已经同意了我们的建议。3 ▸ **to agree with sth** *(approve of)* 对某事表示赞同 [duì mǒushì biǎoshì zàntóng] ▷ *I don't agree with children smoking.* 我不赞同儿童吸烟。4 ▸ **to agree (with sth)** *[figures, total +]* *(tally)* (和某事) 相符 [(hé mǒushì) xiāngfú] ▷ *This bill doesn't agree with my calculations.* 这账单和我算的结果不相符。5 ▸ **to agree (with sth)** *[account, story +]* *(be consistent)* (和某事) 一致 [(hé mǒushì) yīzhì] ▷ *His statement agrees with those of other witnesses.* 他的陈述和其他证人的完全一致。6 ▸ **agree (with sth)** *(according to grammar)* *[word +]* (和某事) 一致 [(hé mǒushì) yīzhì] ▷ *The subject must agree with the verb.* 主语必须和动词保持数的一致。II vt ▸ **to agree sth** (BRIT) *(decide)* 商定 [shāngdìng] ▷ *We have agreed a price.* 我们商定了价格。▸ **to agree with sb about sth** *[person +]* 关于某事赞成某人的看法 ▸ **I agree with what you say** 我同意你说的观点 ▸ **milk doesn't agree with me** 我喝不惯牛奶 ▸ **to agree on sth** *[+ price, arrangement]* 商定某事 ▸ **to be agreed on sth** 就某事达成协议 ▸ **to agree that...** 同意…

agreeable [əˈgriːəbl] ADJ 1 *(pleasant)* *[+ sensation]* 令人愉快的 [lìng rén yúkuài de]; *[+ person]* 容易相处的 [róngyì xiāngchǔ de] 2 *(willing)* ▸ **to be agreeable (to sth/to doing sth)** 欣然同意(某事/做某事) [xīnrán tóngyì (mǒushì/zuò mǒushì)]

agreed [əˈgriːd] ADJ *[+ time, place, price]* 约定的 [yuēdìng de]

agreement [əˈgriːmənt] N 1 [c] ▸ **an agreement (on sth)** *(decision, arrangement)* (关于某事的)协议 [(guānyú mǒushì de) xiéyì] 2 [u] ▸ **agreement (on sth)** *(concurrence)* (关于某事的)一致意见 [(guānyú mǒushì de) yīzhì yìjiàn] 3 [u] *(consent)* 同意 [tóngyì] 4 [u] *(in grammar)* 一致 [yīzhì] ▸ **to be in agreement (with sb/sth)** (与某人)意见一致/同意(某事) ▸ **to nod one's head in agreement** 点头表示同意 ▸ **to reach an agreement** 达成共识

agricultural [æɡrɪˈkʌltʃərəl] ADJ *[+ land, worker]* 农业的 [nóngyè de]

agriculture [ˈæɡrɪkʌltʃə(r)] N [u] 农业 [nóngyè]

ahead [əˈhɛd] ADV 1 *(in front) (of place)* 在前地 [zàiqián de] 2 *(in work, achievements)* 提前地 [tíqián de] 3 *(in competition)* 领先地 [lǐngxiān de] 4 *(in the future)* 在未来 [zài wèilái] ▸ **the days/months ahead** 今后几天/几个月 ▸ **to think/plan ahead** 事先考虑/计划 ▸ **ahead of** *(in front of)* 在…之前;*(before in time)* 在…面前;

(in advance of) *[+ event]* 预先;*(in ranking, progress)* 领先 ▸ **ahead of time/schedule** 提前 ▸ **to get ahead of sb** *(in front of)* 超过某人;*(in progress)* 超越 ▸ **a year ahead** *(in advance)* 提前一年 ▸ **to send sb (on) ahead** 送某人先走 ▸ **to go (on) ahead** 先走 ▸ **right** or **straight ahead** *(direction)* 笔直向前;*(location)* 正前方 ▸ **go ahead!** *(giving permission)* 干吧!

○ **aid** [eɪd] I N 1 [u] *(support) (to country, people)* 援助 [yuánzhù] 2 [u] *(frm) (assistance)* 帮助 [bāngzhù] 3 [c] *(device)* 辅助 [fǔzhù] ▷ *teaching aids* 教学辅助设备 II vt 1 *(support)* *[+ country, people]* 援助 [yuánzhù] 2 *(help)* *[+ person, organization]* 协助 [xiézhù] 3 *(facilitate)* *[+ process]* 促进 [cùjìn] ▸ **with the aid of sb/sth** 在某人/某物的帮助下 ▸ **in aid of** (ESP BRIT) *[+ charity]* 用以援助 ▸ **to come/go to sb's aid** 前来/往援助某人 ▸ **to aid and abet** (LAW) 同谋

aide [eɪd] N [c] 助手 [zhùshǒu]

AIDS [eɪdz] N ABBR (= *acquired immune deficiency syndrome*) 艾滋病 [àizībìng]

ailing [ˈeɪlɪŋ] ADJ 1 *[+ person]* 久病不起的 [jiǔbìng bùqǐ de] 2 *[+ economy, industry]* 每况愈下的 [měi kuàng yù xià de]

ailment [ˈeɪlmənt] N [c] 小病 [xiǎobìng]

aim [eɪm] I vt 1 ▸ **to aim sth (at sb/sth)** *[+ gun, camera]* 将某物瞄准(某人/某物) [jiāng mǒuwù miáozhǔn (mǒurén/mǒuwù)]; *[+ punch, kick]* 将某物对准(某人/某物) [jiāng mǒuwù duìzhǔn (mǒurén/mǒuwù)] II vi *(with weapon)* 瞄准 [miáozhǔn] III N 1 [c] *(objective)* 目标 [mùbiāo] 2 [s] *(in shooting)* 瞄准 [miáozhǔn] ▸ **to be aimed at sb** *[+ remarks, campaign]* 针对某人 ▸ **to be aimed at achieving sth** 意在获取某物 ▸ **to aim at sth** *(with weapon)* 瞄准某物 ▸ **to aim to do sth** (inf) 打算做某事 ▸ **to take aim (at sth/sb)** 向(某物/某人)瞄准

ain't [eɪnt] (inf) = **am not, aren't, isn't**

○ **air** [ɛə(r)] I N 1 [u] *(atmosphere)* 空气 [kōngqì] ▷ *He breathed in the cold night air.* 他呼吸了夜晚清凉的空气。2 [c] *(o.f.)* *(tune)* 曲调 [qǔdiào] 3 [s] *(appearance)* 神情 [shénqíng] ▷ *with an air of superiority* 摆出高人一等的神情 II vt 1 *[+ room]* 使通气 [shǐ tōngqì] 2 *[+ clothes]* 晾干 [liànggān] 3 *[+ opinions, grievances]* 发表 [fābiǎo] 4 *(broadcast)* *[+ programme]* 播放 [bōfàng] III CPD [复合词] *[+ travel]* 乘飞机 [chéng fēijī]; *[+ fare]* 飞机 ▸ **in/into/through the air** 在/进入/穿过天空 ▷ *He threw the ball (up) into the air.* 他把球抛向天空。▸ **by air** *(flying)* 乘飞机 ▸ **to clear the air** 澄清事实 ▸ **in the air** 在空中 ▸ **up in the air** *(undecided)* 悬而未决 ▸ **to be/come off (the) air** *[+ programme, station]* 停止播放 ▸ **to be/go on (the) air** *[+ programme, station]* 正在/开始播放

airbag [ˈɛəbæɡ] N [c] *(in car)* 安全气袋 [ānquán qìdài]

airbed [ˈɛəbɛd] (BRIT) N [c] 充气床垫 [chōngqì]

chuángdiàn]

air-conditioned ['ɛəkən'dɪʃənd] ADJ 装有空调的 [zhuāngyǒu kōngtiáo de]

air conditioner N [c] 空调 [kōngtiáo]

air conditioning [-kən'dɪʃənɪŋ] N [U] 空气调节 [kōngqì tiáojié]

aircraft ['ɛəkrɑːft] (pl **aircraft**) N [c] 飞行器 [fēixíngqì]

airfield ['ɛəfiːld] N [c] 停机坪 [tíngjīpíng]

air force I N [c] 空军 [kōngjūn] II CPD [复合词] [+ pilot, base] 空军 [kōngjūn] ▶ **the air force** 空军

air hostess (BRIT) N [c] 空中小姐 [kōngzhōng xiǎojiě] [美= **stewardess**]

airlift ['ɛəlɪft] I N [c] 空运 [kōngyùn] II VT 空运 [kōngyùn]

airline ['ɛəlaɪn] N [c] 航空公司 [hángkōng gōngsī]

airliner ['ɛəlaɪnə(r)] N [c] 班机 [bānjī]

airmail ['ɛəmeɪl] N [U] ▶ **by airmail** 航空邮寄 [hángkōng yóujì]

airplane ['ɛəpleɪn] (US) N [c] 飞机 [fēijī] [英= **aeroplane**]

airport ['ɛəpɔːt] N [c] 飞机场 [fēijīchǎng]

air raid N [c] 空袭 [kōngxí]

air terminal (ESP BRIT) N [c] 航空终点站 [hángkōng zhōngdiǎnzhàn]

airtight ['ɛətaɪt] ADJ 1 [+ container] 密封的 [mìfēng de] 2 (US) [+ case, alibi] 无懈可击的 [wú xiè kě jī de]

airy ['ɛərɪ] ADJ 1 [+ room, building] 通风的 [tōngfēng de] 2 (casual) [+ manner] 没头脑的 [méi tóunǎo de]

aisle [aɪl] N [c] (in church, theatre, supermarket, on plane) 过道 [guòdào] ▶ **to walk down the aisle** (get married) 结婚 ▶ **aisle seat** (on plane) 靠过道的座位

ajar [ə'dʒɑː(r)] ADJ [+ door] 微开的 [wēikāi de]

akin [ə'kɪn] ADJ ▶ **akin to** (similar to) 相似的 [xiāngsì de]

à la carte [ɑːlɑː'kɑːt] ADJ, ADV 照菜单点 [zhào càidān diǎn]

alarm [ə'lɑːm] I N 1 [U] (anxiety) 惊慌 [jīnghuāng] 2 [c] (warning device) (in house, car etc) 警报 [jǐngbào] 3 [c] (on clock) 闹钟 [nàozhōng] II VT [+ person] 使惊慌 [shǐ jīnghuāng] ▶ **to raise/sound the alarm** 拉响警报 ▶ **to view** or **regard sth with alarm** 警觉地看待某事物

alarm call N [c] 唤醒电话 [huànxǐng diànhuà]

alarm clock N [c] 闹钟 [nàozhōng]

alarmed [ə'lɑːmd] ADJ 1 [+ person] 惊恐的 [jīngkǒng de] 2 [+ house, car etc] 装有警报器的 [zhuāngyǒu jǐngbàoqì de]

alarming [ə'lɑːmɪŋ] ADJ 令人惊恐的 [lìng rén jīngkǒng de]

Albania [æl'beɪnɪə] N 阿尔巴尼亚 [Ā'ěrbāníyà]

albeit [ɔːl'biːɪt] CONJ (although) 尽管 [jǐnguǎn]

album ['ælbəm] N [c] 1 (for stamps, photos etc)

册子 [cèzi] 2 (LP) 唱片 [chàngpiàn]

alcohol ['ælkəhɔl] N [U] 1 (drink) 酒 [jiǔ] 2 (chemical) 酒精 [jiǔjīng]

alcohol-free ['ælkəhɔl'friː] ADJ [+ beer, wine] 无酒精的 [wú jiǔjīng de]

alcoholic [ælkə'hɔlɪk] I N [c] 酒鬼 [jiǔguǐ] II ADJ [+ drink] 含酒精的 [hán jiǔjīng de] ▶ **his alcoholic father** 他那嗜酒成瘾的父亲

alcoholism ['ælkəhɔlɪzəm] N [U] 酒精中毒 [jiǔjīng zhòngdú]

ale [eɪl] N [c/U] 麦酒 [màijiǔ]

alert [ə'ləːt] I ADJ 1 (wide awake) 警觉的 [jǐngjué de] 2 ▶ **alert to sth** (danger, opportunity) 对某事警觉 [duì mǒushì jǐngjué] II N [c] (situation) ▶ **a security alert** 安全警戒 [ānquán jǐngjiè] III VT [+ emotion, police] 使警觉 [shǐ jǐngjué] ▶ **to alert sb to sth** 使某人对某事警觉 ▶ **on the alert (for sth)** (对某事)警觉 ▶ **on alert** 警惕着 ▶ **to give the alert** 发出警报

A level (BRIT) N [c/U] 中学中高级考试

algebra ['ældʒɪbrə] N [U] 代数 [dàishù]

Algeria [æl'dʒɪərɪə] N 阿尔及利亚 [Ā'ěrjílìyà]

alias ['eɪlɪəs] I N [c] (of criminal) 化名 [huàmíng] II PREP ▶ **Peter Lewis, alias John Lord** 比得·路易斯,化名约翰·洛德 [Bǐdé Lùyísī, huàmíng Yuēhàn Luòdé]

alibi ['ælɪbaɪ] N [c] 不在场证据 [bùzàichǎng zhèngjù]

alien ['eɪlɪən] I N [c] 1 (foreigner) 外侨 [wàiqiáo] 2 (extra-terrestrial) 外星人 [wàixīngrén] II ADJ 1 (foreign) 异己的 [yìjǐ de] 2 (from outer space) 外星的 [wàixīng de] ▶ **alien (to)** 与…截然不同的 [yǔ…jiérán bùtóng de]

alienate ['eɪlɪəneɪt] VT [+ person] 使疏远 [shǐ shūyuǎn] ▶ **to alienate sb from sb/sth** 使某人疏远某人/某物

alight [ə'laɪt] I ADJ 1 [+ fire] 燃着的 [ránzhe de] 2 [+ eyes, face] 闪耀的 [shǎnyào de] II VI 1 (frm) [bird +] 飞落 [fēiluò] 2 [passenger +] 下来 [xiàlái] ▶ **to set sth alight** 点着某物

align [ə'laɪn] VT [+ objects] 对齐 [duìqí] ▶ **to align o.s. with sb** 与某人结盟

alike [ə'laɪk] I ADJ ▶ **to be/look alike** 是/看起来相似的 [shì/kànqǐlái xiāngsì de] II ADV (similarly) 相似地 [xiāngsì de] ▶ **winter and summer alike** 无论冬夏

alive [ə'laɪv] ADJ 1 (living) ▶ **to be alive** 活着的 [huózhe de] 2 (lively) [+ place, person] ▶ **to be/feel alive** 充满活力的 [chōngmǎn huólì de] 3 (thriving) ▶ **to be alive** 活跃的 [huóyuè de] ▶ **to be burned/buried alive** 活活烧死/活埋 ▶ **to keep sb alive** 维持某人的生命 ▶ **alive with** 充满… ▶ **alive to** 意识到 ▶ **to bring sth alive** (story, description) 使物品活灵活现; (person, place, event) 使物品活跃起来 ▶ **to come alive** (story, description) 使物品灵活现; (person, place, event) 使活跃起来 ▶ **alive and kicking** 生龙活虎的 ▶ **alive and well** 安

然无恙的

◯

all [ɔːl] **I** ADJ 所有的 [suǒyǒu de] ▶ **all day/ night** 整日/夜 ▶ **all big cities** 所有的大城 市 ▶ **all five books** 所有的5本书 ▶ **all the time/his life** 始终/他的整个一生 ▶ **all the books** 所有的书

II PRON **1** 全部 [quánbù] ▶ **it's all settled** 全都安顿好了 ▶ **all I could do was apologize** 我所能做的全部就是道歉 ▶ **all that remains is to...** 所有剩下的就是要… ▶ **I ate it all, I ate all of it** 我把它全都吃了 ▶ **have you got it all?** 你全都有了吗? ▶ **all of us** 我们中的所有人 ▶ **all of the time** 每时每刻 ▶ **all of the boys** 所有的男孩 子 ▶ **we all sat down** 我们都坐下了 ▶ **is that all?** *(anything else?)* 那就是全部吗?; *(in shop)* 就这些吗?; *(not more expensive?)* 就 这个价吗?

2 *(in expressions)* ▶ **after all** *(considering)* 毕 竟 [bìjìng]; *(regardless)* 终究 [zhōngjiū] ▶ **all but the strongest/smallest etc** *(all except for)* 只有最强壮的/最小的{等} ▶ **to have seen/done it all** 全都看了/做了 ▶ **all in** *(inf)* *(exhausted)* 筋疲力尽的; *(BRIT: inf)* *(inclusive)* 全都包括在内 ▶ **all in all** 总 之 ▶ **for all I know/care** 我一无所知/不 关我事 ▶ **in all** 总共 ▶ **best of all** 最好 不过的是

III ADV **1** *(emphatic)* 完全 [wánquán] ▶ **he was doing it all by himself** 他完全是自己 做的 ▶ **all alone** 孤零零的 ▶ **all around** 周围 ▶ **it's not as hard as all that** 不算太 难 ▶ **all the more/the better** 更加/更好 ▶ **she all but died** *(almost)* 她几乎要死掉了

2 *(in scores)* ▶ **the score is 2 all** 比分2比2平 [bǐfēn èr bǐ èr píng]

Allah [ˈælə] N 安拉 [Ānlā]

allay [əˈleɪ] VT [+ *fears*] 减轻 [jiǎnqīng]

allegation [ælɪˈgeɪʃən] N [c] 指控 [zhǐkòng] ▶ **allegations of brutality/corruption** 对暴 行/腐败的指控

allege [əˈlɛdʒ] *(frm)* VT ▶ **to allege that...** *(claim)* 宣称… [xuānchēng…] ▶ **he is alleged to have killed her** 据称他杀了她

alleged [əˈlɛdʒd] *(frm)* ADJ 据称的 [jùchēng de]

allegedly [əˈlɛdʒɪdlɪ] ADV 据说地 [jùshuō de]

allegiance [əˈliːdʒəns] N [c/U] ▶ **allegiance (to)** 忠诚 [zhōngchéng]

allergic [əˈlɜːdʒɪk] ADJ [+ *reaction, response*] 过敏 的 [guòmǐn de] ▶ **to be allergic to sth** [+ *peanuts, cats etc*] 对某物过敏; *(inf)* [+ *work, mornings etc*] 对某物反感

allergy [ˈælədʒɪ] *(MED)* N [c/U] 过敏症 [guòmǐnzhèng] ▶ **to have an allergy to sth** 对 某物有过敏症

alleviate [əˈliːvɪeɪt] VT **1** [+ *pain*] 减轻

[jiǎnqīng] **2** [+ *poverty, misery*] 缓和 [huǎnhé]

alley [ˈælɪ] N [c] *(street)* 小巷 [xiǎoxiàng]

alliance [əˈlaɪəns] N [c] **1** *(group)* 联盟 [liánméng] **2** ▶ **alliance (with)** *(relationship)* (与…)联盟 [(yǔ…) liánméng]

allied [ˈælaɪd] ADJ **1** [+ *nation*] 同盟的 [tóngméng de] **2** [+ *forces, troops*] 同盟国 的 [tóngméngguó de] **3** *(related)* [+ *industries, disciplines*] 相关的 [xiāngguān de] ▶ **allied to** 与…相关的

alligator [ˈælɪgeɪtə(r)] N [c] 短吻鳄 [duǎnwěnè]

allocate [ˈæləkeɪt] VT [+ *time, money, tasks, rooms*] 分配 [fēnpèi]

allot [əˈlɒt] VT *(allocate)* ▶ **to allot sth (to sb)** [+ *time*] 拨给(某人)某物 [bōgěi (mǒurén) mǒuwù]; [+ *money, seats*] 分配(给某人)某物 [fēnpèi (gěi mǒurén) mǒuwù] ▶ **in/within the allotted time** 在规定时间内

allotment [əˈlɒtmənt] N [c] 私人租用的,用 于种植植物或蔬菜的小片土地

▤ **ALLOTMENT**

花园和园艺是英国文化的重要方面。如果 城镇和城市居民有一个小花园或庭院都没 有园地,他们可以向当地政府租一块公 地。这些小块土地通常用来种植蔬菜和水 果,但也可以种植其他植物花草。

all-out [ˈɔːlaʊt] **I** ADJ [+ *effort, attack*] 竭尽全力 的 [jiéjìn quánlì de] **II** ADV ▶ **to go all out for sth/to do sth** 为某事竭尽全力/竭尽全力做 某事 [wèi mǒushì jiéjìn quánlì/jiéjìn quánlì zuò mǒushì] ▶ **all-out strike** 全体罢工

◯ **allow** [əˈlaʊ] VT **1** *(permit)* [+ *practice, behaviour*] 允许 [yǔnxǔ] ▷ *Henry doesn't allow smoking in his office.* 亨利不允许在他的办公室吸烟。

2 *(set aside)* [+ *sum, time, amount*] 留出 [liúchū] ▷ *Please allow 28 days for delivery.* 请留出28天的 发货期。**3** ▶ **to allow sth to happen** *(by failing to prevent sth)* 许可某事发生 [róngxǔ mǒushì fāshēng] ▷ *Don't allow the soil to dry out.* 不要 让土壤干透。▷ *We cannot allow the situation to deteriorate.* 我们不容许情况恶化。**4** ▶ **to allow sb to do sth** *(make sth possible)* 允许某人做某事 [yǔnxǔ mǒurén zuò mǒushì] ▷ *The extra money allows them to distribute more aid.* 额外的款项令 他们能够提供更多援助。**5** [+ *claim, goal*] 认 可 [rènkě] ▷ *After an appeal, the goal was allowed.* 经过申诉,这一入球得到认可。▶ **to allow sb to do sth** *(give permission for sth)* 允许某人做某 事 [yǔnxǔ mǒurén zuò mǒushì] ▷ *They allow their children to stay up late.* 他们 允许自己的孩子们晚睡。▶ **to be allowed to do sth** 被允许做某事 ▷ *The children are not allowed to watch too much TV.* 孩子们不被允许看太多电 视。▶ **smoking is not allowed** 禁止吸烟 ▶ **to allow that...** *(frm)* *(concede)* 承认…

▶ **allow for** VT FUS [不可拆分] [+ *delay, inflation, possibility*] 考虑到 [kǎolù dào] ▷ *Allow for long delays on all routes north.* 要考虑到所有向北路线的长时间阻塞。
▶ **allow of** VT FUS [不可拆分] (*permit*) 容许 [róngxǔ]

allowance [əˈlaʊəns] N [C] **1** (*welfare payment*) 津贴 [jīntiē] **2** (*allocation*) 限额 [xiàn'é] **3** (*for expenses*) 补助 [bǔzhù] **4** (US) 零用钱 [língyòngqián] [英= **pocket money**] **5** ▶ **tax allowance** 免税额 [miǎnshuì'é] ▶ **to make allowances for** [+ *thing, situation*] 顾及到; [+ *person*] 考虑到

alloy [ˈælɔɪ] N [C/U] 合金 [héjīn] ▶ **an alloy of...** …的合金

all right I ADJ **1** ▶ **to be all right** (*satisfactory*) 还不错的 [hái bùcuò de]; (*well, safe*) 安然无恙的 [ānrán wúyàng de] II ADV **1** (*well*) [*go, work out +*] 顺利地 [shùnlì de] **2** (*properly*) [*see, hear, work +*] 没问题地 [méi wèntí de] **3** (*as answer*) (*okay*) 可以 [kěyǐ] ▶ **it's** or **that's all right by me** 对我来说没问题

ally [n ˈælaɪ, vb əˈlaɪ] I N [C] **1** [*of country*] 同盟国 [tóngméngguó] **2** ▶ **the Allies** (*during World War I*) 协约国 [Xiéyuēguó]; (*during World War II*) 同盟国 [Tóngméngguó] **3** (*friend, supporter*) 死党 [sǐdǎng] II VT ▶ **to ally o.s. with sth/sb** 和某组织/某人结盟 [hé mǒu zǔzhī/mǒurén jiéméng]

almighty [ɔːlˈmaɪtɪ] I ADJ (*inf*) (*tremendous*) [+ *row, problem etc*] 巨大的 [jùdà de] II N ▶ **the Almighty** 上帝 [Shàngdì] ▶ **Almighty God** 全能的上帝

almond [ˈɑːmənd] N [C/U] **1** (*nut*) 杏仁 [xìngrén] **2** (*tree*) 杏树 [xìngshù]

○ **almost** [ˈɔːlməʊst] ADV 差不多 [chàbùduō] ▷ *I spent almost a month in China.* 我在中国待了差不多一个月。▶ **almost certainly** 几乎肯定

alone [əˈləʊn] I ADJ **1** (*not with other people*) 独自的 [dúzì de] **2** (*having no family or friends*) 孤独的 [gūdú de] **3** ▶ **to be alone together** (*with no other people*) 单独在一起 [dāndú zài yīqǐ] II ADV **1** (*unaided*) 独自地 [dúzì de] **2** ▶ **in Florida/France alone** (*merely*) (*used for emphasis*) 仅仅在佛罗里达/法国 [jǐnjǐn zài Fóluólǐdá/Fǎguó] ▶ **to leave sb/sth alone** (*undisturbed*) 不要打扰某人/某物 ▶ **to be alone with sb** 与某人独处 ▶ **let alone...** 更谈不上… ▶ **I alone survived** 只有我幸存下来

○ **along** [əˈlɒŋ] I PREP **1** (*towards one end of*) 沿着 [yánzhe] ▷ *He drove us along East Street.* 他沿着东大街开车。**2** (*on, beside*) [+ *road, corridor, river*] 沿着 [yánzhe] ▷ *the houses built along the river* 沿着河建造的房屋 II ADV 沿着 [yánzhe] ▷ *Halfway along, turn right into Hope St.* 沿着路往前走一半，往右拐到希望街。▶ **to be coming along** (*fine* or *nicely*) 进行(顺利) ▶ **to take/bring sb along** 带某人一同前往 ▶ **he was**

hopping/limping along 他跳跃/蹒跚着前行 ▶ **along with** (*together with*) 与…一起 ▶ **all along** (*all the time*) 自始至终

alongside [əˈlɒŋˈsaɪd] I PREP **1** (*next to*) 在…旁边 [zài…pángbiān] **2** (*together with*) 与…并肩 [yǔ…bìngjiān] II ADV [*come, stop +*] 并排地 [bìngpái de]

aloof [əˈluːf] ADJ (*distant*) 冷淡的 [lěngdàn de] ▶ **to stay** or **keep aloof from sth** 远离某事

aloud [əˈlaʊd] ADV [*read, speak +*] 大声地 [dàshēng de]

alphabet [ˈælfəbɛt] N ▶ **the alphabet** 字母表 [zìmǔbiǎo]

Alps [ælps] NPL ▶ **the Alps** 阿尔卑斯山脉 [Ā'ěrbèisī Shānmài]

○ **already** [ɔːlˈrɛdɪ] ADV 已经 [yǐjīng] ▷ *I have already started making dinner.* 我已经开始做晚餐了。▷ *They've spent nearly a million dollars on it already.* 他们在这上面已经花了近百万美金。▷ *He was already late for his appointment.* 他约会已经迟到了了。▶ **is it five o'clock already?** (*expressing surprise*) 已经到5点了吗?

alright [ɔːlˈraɪt] ADV = **all right**

○ **also** [ˈɔːlsəʊ] ADV **1** (*too*) 也 [yě] ▷ *a pianist who also plays guitar* 一个也会弹吉他的钢琴家 **2** (*moreover*) 同样 [tóngyàng] ▷ *Six other passengers were also injured.* 其他六个乘客同样受了伤。

> **also** 和 **too** 在语意不很接近，但是，**also** 从不用在句末，而 **too** 却常用于句末。*He was also an artist and lived at Compton... He's a singer and an actor too... I've been to Beijing and to Shanghai too... I've been to Beijing and also to Shanghai.*

altar [ˈɔːltə(r)] (REL) N [C] 祭坛 [jìtán]

alter [ˈɔːltə(r)] I VT [+ *plans, policy, situation*] 更改 [gēnggǎi] II VI 改变 [gǎibiàn]

alteration [ɔltəˈreɪʃən] N [C] 改动 [gǎidòng]

alternate [*adj* ɔlˈtəːnɪt, *vb* ˈɔːltəneɪt] I ADJ **1** (*successive*) [+ *actions, events*] 交替的 [jiāotì de] **2** (US) (*alternative*) [+ *plan, method, solution*] 供替换的 [gōng tìhuàn de] [英= **alternative**] II VI **1** ▶ **to alternate (with)** 轮流 [lúnliú] **2** ▶ **to alternate (between)** 交替 [jiāotì] ▶ **on alternate days/weeks** 隔天/周

alternative [ɔlˈtəːnətɪv] I ADJ **1** (BRIT) [+ *plan, method, solution*] 另外的 [lìngwài de] [美= **alternate**] **2** (*non-conventional*) [+ *technology, energy*] 非常规的 [fēi chángguī de]; [+ *comedy, comedian*] 另类的 [lìnglèi de] II N [C] ▶ **(an) alternative (to)** …的替代 [...de tìdài] ▶ **to have no alternative (but to)** (除…外)别无选择

alternatively [ɔlˈtəːnətɪvlɪ] ADV 或者 [huòzhě]

○ **although** [ɔːlˈðəʊ] CONJ **1** (*despite the fact that*) 尽管 [jǐnguǎn] ▷ *Although he was late he stopped for a sandwich.* 尽管已经晚了，他还是停下

来吃了一个三明治。**2** (but) 但是 [dànshì]
▷ Something was wrong, although I couldn't work out what. 有些不对头，但我不知道是什么。
■ 用法参见 **though**

altitude ['æltɪtjuːd] N [C/U] [of place, plane] 高度 [gāodù] ▶ **at an altitude of 30,000 ft** 在海拔3万英尺的高度 ▶ **at high/low altitude** 在高/低海拔处 ▶ **to gain/lose altitude** 升高/降低海拔

altogether [ɔːltə'gɛðə(r)] ADV **1** (completely) 完全 [wánquán] **2** (far) [used for emphasis] ▶ **altogether different/stronger/better** etc 全然不同/更强/更好 [等] [quánrán bùtóng/gèngqiáng/gènghǎo [děng]] **3** (in total) 总共 [zǒnggòng] **4** (on the whole, in all) 总之 [zǒngzhī] ▶ **how much is that altogether?** 总共多少钱?

aluminium [ælju'mɪnəm], (US) **aluminum** [ə'luːmɪnəm] N [U] 铝 [lǚ]

○ **always** ['ɔːlweɪz] ADV **1** (at all times) 总是 [zǒngshì] ▷ He's always late. 他总是迟到。 **2** (continuously) 一直 [yīzhí] ▷ He has always been the family solicitor. 他一直做家庭事务律师。 ▶ **you can/could always try again** 你总是可以重新开始

Alzheimer's (disease) ['æltshaɪməz-] N [U] 阿尔茨海默(病) [Ā'ěrcíhǎimò (bìng)]

AM (RAD) ABBR (= amplitude modulation) 调幅 [tiáofú]

am [æm] VB see **be**

a.m. ADV ABBR (= ante meridiem) 上午 [shàngwǔ]

amalgamate [ə'mælgəmeɪt] VI, VT [organizations, companies +] 合并 [hébìng]

amass [ə'mæs] VT [+ fortune, information] 积累 [jīlěi]

amateur ['æmətə(r)] I N [C] (non-professional) 业余爱好者 [yèyú àihàozhě] II ADJ **1** [+ boxing, athletics] 非职业的 [fēi zhíyè de] **2** [+ player, person] 业余的 [yèyú de] ▶ **amateur dramatics** 业余演出

amaze [ə'meɪz] VT 使惊讶 [shǐ jīngyà] ▶ **to be amazed (at/by/that...)** (对/被…)惊讶

amazement [ə'meɪzmənt] N [U] 惊异 [jīngyì]

amazing [ə'meɪzɪŋ] ADJ (surprising, fantastic) 令人惊讶的 [lìng rén jīngyà de]

Amazon ['æməzən] N **1** ▶ **the Amazon** (river) 亚马孙河 [Yàmǎsùn Hé] **2** [C] (woman) (in mythology) 亚马孙族女战士 [yàmǎsūnzú nǚzhànshì] **3** [C] (woman) (resembling mythological woman) 魁梧而有男子气概的女子 [kuíwú ér yǒu nánzǐ qìgài de nǚzǐ] ▶ **the Amazon jungle** 亚马孙丛林

ambassador [æm'bæsədə(r)] N [C] 大使 [dàshǐ]

amber ['æmbə(r)] I N [U] (substance) 琥珀 [hǔpò] II ADJ (in colour) 琥珀色的 [hǔpòsè de] III CPD [复合词] [+ jewellery, earrings] 琥珀 [hǔpò] ▶ **the lights are on amber** (BRIT) 黄色交通灯亮起

ambiguous [æm'bɪgjuəs] ADJ **1** (unclear, confusing) [+ word, phrase, reply] 意义不明确的 [yìyì bù míngquè de] **2** (conflicting) [+ feelings] 模棱两可的 [móléng liǎngkě de]

ambition [æm'bɪʃən] N **1** [C] ▶ **an ambition (to do sth)** (做某事的)志向 [(zuò mǒushì de) zhìxiàng] **2** [U] (desire) 抱负 [bàofù] ▶ **to achieve one's ambition** 实现自己的抱负

ambitious [æm'bɪʃəs] ADJ **1** [+ person] 雄心勃勃的 [xióngxīn bóbó de] **2** [+ idea, project] 宏大的 [hóngdà de]

ambulance ['æmbjuləns] N [C] 救护车 [jiùhùchē]

ambush ['æmbuʃ] I N [C/U] 伏击 [fújí] II VT 埋伏 [máifu] ▶ **to lie in ambush (for sb)** 埋伏着等候(某人)

amend [ə'mɛnd] I VT [+ law, text] 修正 [xiūzhèng] II N ▶ **to make amends (for sth)** (因某事)赔偿 [(yīn mǒushì) péicháng]

amendment [ə'mɛndmənt] N [C/U] **1** (to law) 修正 [xiūzhèng] **2** (US) ▶ **the First/Second Amendment** (to US Constitution) 第一/二修正案 [Dìyī/èr Xiūzhèng'àn] **3** (to letter, essay etc) 修改 [xiūgǎi]

amenities [ə'miːnɪtɪz] NPL (features, facilities) 便民设施 [biànmín shèshī] ▶ **"close to all amenities"** "毗邻便民设施"

America [ə'mɛrɪkə] N 美洲 [Měizhōu]

American [ə'mɛrɪkən] I ADJ 美国的 [Měiguó de] II N [C] (person) 美国人 [Měiguórén]

American football (BRIT) N **1** [U] (sport) 美式足球 [měishì zúqiú] [美= football] **2** [C] (ball) 橄榄球 [gǎnlǎnqiú] [美= football]

Amex ['æmɛks] N ABBR (= American Stock Exchange) 美国证券交易所 [Měiguó Zhèngquàn Jiāoyìsuǒ]

amiable ['eɪmɪəbl] ADJ [+ person] 亲切的 [qīnqiè de]

amicable ['æmɪkəbl] ADJ **1** [+ relationship] 和睦的 [hémù de] **2** [+ parting, divorce, settlement] 友好的 [yǒuhǎo de]

amid(st) [ə'mɪd(st)] PREP **1** (liter) (at the same time as) 在…当中 [zài…dāngzhōng] **2** (surrounded by) 在…中间 [zài…zhōngjiān]

amiss [ə'mɪs] I ADJ ▶ **something is amiss** 出问题了 [chū wèntí le] II (BRIT) ADV ▶ **it would not go** or **come amiss** 不会出岔子的 [bù huì chū chàzi de]

ammunition [æmju'nɪʃən] N [U] **1** (for weapon) 弹药 [dànyào] **2** (in argument) 进攻手段 [jìngōng shǒuduàn]

amnesty ['æmnɪstɪ] N **1** [C/U] (to political prisoners) 大赦 [dàshè] **2** [C] (by police for weapons etc) 宽恕期限 [kuānshù qīxiàn] ▶ **to grant amnesty to sb** 特赦某人

among(st) [ə'mʌŋ(st)] PREP **1** (surrounded by, included in) 在…当中 [zài…dāngzhōng] **2** [+ group of people] 在…当中 [zài…dāngzhōng]

3 [share, distribute +] (between) 在…当中 [zài…dāngzhōng] ▶ talking/arguing among themselves/yourselves 他们/你们自己彼此交谈/争论

> 如果指两个以上的人或物，用 among 或 amongst。如果只指两个人或物，用 between。…an area between Mars and Jupiter… an argument between his mother and another woman… an opportunity to discuss these issues amongst themselves. amongst 是有些过时的表达方式。注意，如果你 between 某些东西或某些人，他们在你的两侧。如果你 among 或 amongst 某些东西或某些人，他们在你的周围。…the bag standing on the floor between us… the sound of a pigeon among the trees…

amount [ə'maunt] I N [C/U] (quantity) 数量 [shùliàng]; [of money] 数额 [shù'é]; [of work] 总量 [zǒngliàng] II VI ▶ to amount to sth (total) 总共达到某数 [zǒnggòng dádào mǒushù]; (be same as) 相当于某事 [xiāngdāngyú mǒushì] ▶ any amount of 许多

amp [æmp] N [C] 安培 [ānpéi] ▶ a 13 amp plug 一个13安培的插头

ample ['æmpl] ADJ **1** (sufficient) [+ supplies, space, opportunity] 充足的 [chōngzú de] **2** (large) [+ stomach, bosom] 宽阔的 [kuānkuò de] ▶ this is ample 这绰绰有余

amplifier ['æmplɪfaɪə(r)] N [C] 扬声器 [yángshēngqì]

amplify ['æmplɪfaɪ] VT **1** [+ sound] 放大 [fàngdà] **2** [+ feeling, fear] 增加 [zēngjiā] **3** [+ idea, statement] 详述 [xiángshù]

amputate ['æmpjuteɪt] VT 截去 [jiéqù]

amuse [ə'mjuːz] VT **1** (make laugh) 使发笑 [shǐ fāxiào] **2** (distract, entertain) 给…消遣 [gěi…xiāoqiǎn] ▶ to amuse o.s. 自娱自乐 ▶ to keep sb amused 给某人提供消遣 ▶ to be amused at/by sth 被某事逗乐 ▶ he was not amused (by) 他对…不为所动

amusement [ə'mjuːzmənt] I N **1** [U] (mirth) 愉悦 [yúyuè] **2** [U] (entertainment) 娱乐 [yúlè] **3** [C] (pastime) 消遣 [xiāoqiǎn] II amusements NPL 娱乐活动 [yùlè huódòng] ▶ much to my amusement 令我十分开心的是

amusement arcade N [C] 游乐场 [yóulèchǎng]

amusement park (ESP US) N [C] 游乐场 [yóulèchǎng]

amusing [ə'mjuːzɪŋ] ADJ [+ story, person] 有趣的 [yǒuqù de]

an [æn, ən] DEF ART see a

anaemia, (US) **anemia** [ə'niːmɪə] N [U] 贫血症 [pínxuè zhèng]

anaemic, (US) **anemic** [ə'niːmɪk] ADJ **1** (MED) 贫血的 [pínxuè de] **2** (fig) 索然无味的 [suǒrán wúwèi de]

anaesthetic, (US) **anesthetic** [ænɪs'θetɪk] N [C/U] 麻醉剂 [mázuìjì] ▶ local anaesthetic 局部麻醉 ▶ general anaesthetic 全身麻醉 ▶ under anaesthetic 处于麻醉状态

analog(ue) ['ænəlɔg] I ADJ **1** [+ watch, display] 指针式的 [zhǐzhēnshì de] **2** [+ computer, signal] 模拟的 [mónǐ de] II (frm) N [C] ▶ an analogue of …的模拟 […de mónǐ]

analogy [ə'nælədʒɪ] N [C/U] 相似 [xiāngsì] ▶ to draw an analogy between 找出…之间的相似之处 ▶ by analogy 用类推法

analyse, (US) **analyze** ['ænəlaɪz] VT **1** [+ situation, information] 分析 [fēnxī] **2** (CHEM, MED) 解析 [jiěxī] **3** (psychoanalyse) 精神分析 [jīngshén fēnxī]

analyses [ə'næləsiːz] NPL of analysis

analysis [ə'næləsɪs] (pl **analyses**) N **1** [C/U] [of situation, statistics] 分析 [fēnxī] **2** [C/U] (CHEM, MED) 解析 [jiěxī] **3** [U] (psychoanalysis) 精神分析 [jīngshén fēnxī] ▶ in the last or final analysis 归根结底

analyst ['ænəlɪst] N [C] **1** (political, industrial) 分析者 [fēnxīzhě] **2** (psychoanalyst) 心理分析师 [xīnlǐ fēnxīshī]

analytic(al) [ænə'lɪtɪk(l)] ADJ **1** (logical) [+ mind, approach] 分析的 [fēnxī de] **2** (scientific) 解析的 [jiěxī de]

analyze ['ænəlaɪz] (US) VT = analyse

anarchy ['ænəkɪ] N [U] (chaos, disorder) 混乱 [hùnluàn]

anatomy [ə'nætəmɪ] N **1** [U] (science) 解剖学 [jiěpōuxué] **2** [C] ▶ my/his anatomy (body) 我/他的身体 [wǒ/tā de shēntǐ]

ancestor ['ænsɪstə(r)] N [C] 祖先 [zǔxiān]

ancestral [æn'sɛstrəl] ADJ 祖传的 [zǔchuán de]

anchor ['æŋkə(r)] I N [C] 锚 [máo] II VI 抛锚 [pāomáo] III VT **1** (fix) ▶ to anchor sth (to sth) 把某物固定 (在某物上) [bǎ mǒuwù gùdìng (zài mǒuwù shang)] **2** [+ boat] 停泊 [tíngbó] ▶ to drop anchor 抛锚 ▶ to weigh anchor 起锚

anchovy ['æntʃəvɪ] N [C/U] 鳀鱼 [tíyú]

ancient ['eɪnʃənt] ADJ **1** [+ Greece, Rome, monument] 古代的 [gǔdài de] **2** (very old) 古老的 [gǔlǎo de] **3** (inf) (aged, antiquated) [+ person] 老的 [lǎo de]; [+ car] 老式的 [lǎoshì de]

○ and [ænd] CONJ 和 [hé] ▶ men and women 男人和女人 ▶ we walked for hours and hours 我们几个小时几个小时接连地走 ▶ he talked and talked 他说啊说啊 ▶ better and better 越来越好 ▶ to try and do sth 试着做某事

Andes ['ændiːz] NPL ▶ the Andes 安第斯山脉 [Āndìsī Shānmài]

Andorra [æn'dɔːrə] N 安道尔 [Āndào'ěr]

anemia etc [ə'niːmɪə] (US) = anaemia etc

anesthetic [ænɪs'θetɪk] (US) = anaesthetic

anew [ə'njuː] ADV [start +] 重新 [chóngxīn]

angel ['eɪndʒəl] N [C] **1** (spirit) 天使 [tiānshǐ]
2 (kind person) 可爱的人 [kě'ài de rén]

anger ['æŋɡə(r)] I N [U] 生气 [shēngqì] II VT
使生气 [shǐ shēngqì] ▶ **words spoken in anger**
气话

angina [æn'dʒaɪnə] N [U] 心绞痛 [xīnjiǎotòng]

angle ['æŋɡl] I N [C] **1** (MATH) 角 [jiǎo]
2 (position, direction) 角度 [jiǎodù] **3** (approach)
视角 [shìjiǎo] II VI **1** (face, point) 指向
[zhǐxiàng] **2** ▶ **to angle for sth** [+ compliments]
转弯抹角地得到某物 [zhuǎn wān mǒ jiǎo de
dédào mǒuwù] III VT (position) 转换角度
[zhuǎnhuàn jiǎodù] ▶ **at an angle** 倾斜地
▶ **an angle of ninety/sixty degrees** 90度/60度
角

angler ['æŋɡlə(r)] N [C] 钓鱼的人 [diàoyú de
rén]

Anglican ['æŋɡlɪkən] I ADJ [+ church, priest,
service] 英国圣公会的 [Yīngguó Shènggōnghuì
de] II N [C] 英国圣公会教徒 [Yīngguó
Shènggōnghuì jiàotú] ▶ **the Anglican Church**
英国圣公会教堂

angling ['æŋɡlɪŋ] N [U] 钓鱼 [diàoyú]

Angola [æŋ'ɡəʊlə] N 安哥拉 [Āngēlā]

angrily ['æŋɡrɪlɪ] ADV [react, deny +] 气愤地
[qìfèn de]

angry ['æŋɡrɪ] ADJ **1** [+ person, response] 生气
的 [shēngqì de] **2** [+ wound, rash] 发炎的 [fāyán
de] ▶ **to be angry with sb/about sth** 对某
人/某事生气 ▶ **to get angry** 发怒 ▶ **to make
sb angry** 使某人生气

> angry 指在特定时间或场合的情绪
> 或感觉。如果某人经常生气，可以说他
> 是 **bad-tempered**。She's a bad-tempered
> young lady. 可以用 **furious** 描述某人非
> 常生气。Senior police officers are furious at
> the mistake. **annoyed** 或 **irritated** 表
> 示某人生气的程度不是很重。The Prime
> Minister looked annoyed but calm...a man
> irritated by the barking of his neighbour's
> dog... 如果一件事情经常或不断发生，
> 它会使人感到 **irritated**。如果某个人
> 经常感到恼火，可以用 **irritable** 形
> 容他。

anguish ['æŋɡwɪʃ] N [U] **1** (mental) 极度痛苦
[jídù tòngkǔ] **2** (physical) 剧痛 [jùtòng]

animal ['ænɪməl] I N [C] **1** (creature) 动物
[dòngwù] **2** (type of person) 与众不同的人
[yǔzhòng bùtóng de rén] **3** (pej) (brute)
禽兽 [qínshòu] II ADJ [+ fats, products, instinct,
attraction] 动物的 [dòngwù de]

animate [adj 'ænɪmɪt, vb 'ænɪmeɪt] I ADJ
(living) 有生命的 [yǒu shēngmìng de] II VT
(enliven) [+ person, face] 使有生气 [shǐ yǒu
shēngqì]

animated ['ænɪmeɪtɪd] ADJ **1** [+ person,
expression, conversation] 生气勃勃的 [shēngqì

bóbó de] **2** [film, feature] 动画的 [dònghuà de]

animation [ænɪ'meɪʃən] N **1** [C/U] (computer,
cartoon) 动画片制作 [dònghuàpiàn zhìzuò]
2 [U] (liveliness) 生气 [shēngqì]

animosity [ænɪ'mɒsɪtɪ] N [C/U] 憎恨
[zēnghèn]

aniseed ['ænɪsiːd] N [U] 茴香 [huíxiāng]

ankle ['æŋkl] (ANAT) N [C] 踝 [huái]

annex ['ænɛks] I N [C] **1** (joined to main building)
群房 [qúnfáng] **2** (separate building) 附属建筑
[fùshǔ jiànzhù] II VT (take over) [+ land, territory]
兼并 [jiānbìng]

annexe ['ænɛks] (BRIT) N = **annex**

annihilate [ə'naɪəleɪt] VT **1** (destroy) [+ people]
消灭 [xiāomiè] **2** (defeat) [+ enemy, opponent] 歼
灭 [jiānmiè]

anniversary [ænɪ'vɜːsərɪ] N [C]
1 ▶ **anniversary (of sth)** (某事的) 周年纪念
[(mǒushì de) zhōunián jìniàn] **2** (also: **wedding
anniversary**) 结婚周年纪念 [jiéhūn zhōunián
jìniàn]

○ **announce** [ə'naʊns] VT **1** (declare) [+ decision,
engagement etc] 宣布 [xuānbù] ▷ The TV presenter
announced the grave news. 电视解说员宣布了
这条重大消息。**2** (at station or airport) 通告
[tōnggào] II VI (say) 说 [shuō] ▷ "I'm going to
bed," she announced. "我要睡觉了，"她说道。
▶ **to announce that...** (in official statement, in a
clear way) 宣布···; (at airport or station) 通告
▶ **the government has announced that...** 政
府宣称···

announcement [ə'naʊnsmənt] N [C]
1 (statement) 宣布 [xuānbù] **2** (notice) (in
newspaper) 通知 [tōngzhī] **3** (at airport or station)
通告 [tōnggào] ▶ **the announcement of his
resignation/death/engagement** 他的退休/死
亡/订婚的通告 ▶ **to make an announcement**
发表声明

announcer [ə'naʊnsə(r)] N [C] (on radio, TV)
(male) 男播音员 [nán bōyīnyuán]; (female) 女播
音员 [nǚ bōyīnyuán]

annoy [ə'nɔɪ] VT 使烦恼 [shǐ fánnǎo]

annoyance [ə'nɔɪəns] N **1** [U] (feeling) 厌烦
[yànfán] **2** (annoying thing) 使人厌烦的东
西 [shǐ rén yànfán de dōngxi] ▶ **to his/my
annoyance...** 让他/我烦恼的是···

annoyed [ə'nɔɪd] ADJ 厌烦的 [yànfán de] ▶ **to
be annoyed at sth/with sb** 对某事/某人感
到厌烦 ▶ **to be annoyed about sth** 对某事厌
烦 ▶ **to get annoyed (about sth)** (对某事)感
到厌烦

> 用法参见 angry
> 请勿将 **annoyed** 和 **annoying** 混淆。
> 如果你感到 **annoyed**，表示你相当生
> 气。David could see Jane waiting for him
> outside the cinema. She looked annoyed...
> I was annoyed by his selfish behaviour. 某
> 人或某事物 **annoying**，则表示该人或

该事物令人感到非常生气或令人无法容忍。You must have found my attitude annoying... Does he have any annoying habits I should know about?

annoying [ə'nɔɪɪŋ] ADJ [+ noise, habit, person] 讨厌的 [tǎoyàn de] ▸ **how annoying!** 真是讨厌！用法参见 **annoyed**

annual ['ænjuəl] I ADJ 1 (once every year) [+ meeting, report] 每年的 [měinián de] 2 (during a year) [+ sales, income, rate] 年度的 [niándù de] II N [C] 1 (book) 年刊 [niánkān] 2 (plant) 一年生植物 [yīniánshēng zhíwù]

annually ['ænjuəlɪ] ADV 1 (once a year) 每年地 [měinián de] 2 (during a year) 一年地 [yīnián de]

annum ['ænəm] N see **per**

anonymous [ə'nɔnɪməs] ADJ 1 [+ letter, gift, phone call] 匿名的 [nìmíng de] 2 [+ person] 不知名的 [bùzhīmíng de] 3 (boring) [+ place, clothing] 无特色的 [wú tèsè de] ▸ **to remain anonymous** 不留名的

anorak ['ænəræk] N [C] 1 (jacket) 连帽防风夹克 [liánmào fángfēng jiákè] 2 (BRIT: pej) (person) 迷 [mí]

anorexia [ænə'rɛksɪə] (also: **anorexia nervosa**) (MED) N [U] 厌食症 [yànshízhèng]

anorexic [ænə'rɛksɪk] I ADJ 患厌食症的 [huàn yànshízhèng de] II N [C] 厌食症患者 [yànshízhèng huànzhě]

○ **another** [ə'nʌðə(r)] I ADJ 1 ▸ **another book** (one more) 再一本书 [zài yī běn shū] ▷ I need another book, I've finished this one. 我再需要一本书，这本已经读完了。2 (a different one) 另外的 [lìngwài de] ▷ Can I have another book, this one's torn. 能不能给我另外一本书，这本书撕坏了。3 ▸ **another 5 years/miles/kilos** 再有5年/英里/公斤 [zài yǒu wǔ nián/yīnglǐ/gōngjīn] ▷ Continue down the road for another 2 kilometres. 沿着这条路再走两公里。II PRON 1 (one more) 再一个 [zài yī gè] ▷ He had a drink, then poured another. 他喝了一杯，随后又倒了一杯。2 (a different one) 不同的一个 [bùtóng de yīgè] ▷ a civil war, with one community against another 不同群体间进行的一场内战 ▸ **one another** 相互 ▸ **one (shop) after another** 一个(商店)接着一个(商店) ▸ **another drink?** 再来一杯？

○ **answer** ['ɑːnsə(r)] I N [C] 1 (reply) (to question) 回答 [huídá]; (to letter) 回信 [huíxìn] 2 (solution) (to problem, in exam or quiz) 答案 [dá'àn] II VI (reply) (to question) 回答 [huídá]; (to telephone ringing, knock at door) 应答 [yìngdá] III VT 1 (reply to) [+ person] 答复 [dáfù]; [+ question] (asked by person, in exam or quiz) 回答 [huídá]; [+ letter] 回复 [huífù]; [+ advertisement, prayers] 回应 [huíyìng] ▷ She answered an advert for a job as a cook. 她应聘了厨师的招聘广告。2 (satisfy) [+ need] 满足 [mǎnzú] 3 = **answer to** ▸ **there was no answer** (on telephone) 无人接听；(at

door) 无人应答 ▸ **in answer to...** 回应… ▸ **to answer the phone** 接听电话 ▸ **to answer the door** 应声开门

▸ **answer back** I VI 顶嘴 [dǐngzuǐ] II VT 跟…顶嘴 [gēn…dǐngzuǐ]

▸ **answer for** VT FUS [不可拆分] [+ crimes, actions] 承受…的后果 [chéngshòu…de hòuguǒ] ▷ One of these days you will answer for your crimes. 总有一天你要为你的罪责承担后果。

▸ **answer to** VT FUS [不可拆分] [+ description] 符合 [fúhé] ▷ A man answering to his description was seen in Glasgow. 一个和他的描述相符的男人出现在格拉斯哥。

answering machine ['ɑːnsərɪŋ-] N [C] 电话答录机 [diànhuà dálùjī]

answerphone ['ɑːnsə(r)fəun] N [C] = **answering machine**

ant [ænt] N 蚂蚁 [mǎyǐ]

antagonism [æn'tægənɪzəm] N [U] 敌对 [díduì]

Antarctic [ænt'ɑːktɪk] N ▸ **the Antarctic** 南极 [Nánjí]

Antarctica [ænt'ɑːktɪkə] N 南极洲 [Nánjízhōu]

antelope ['æntɪləup] (pl **antelope** or **antelopes**) N [C] 羚羊 [língyáng]

antenatal ['æntɪ'neɪtl] ADJ [+ care, treatment] 产前的 [chǎnqián de]

antenna [æn'tɛnə] N [C] 1 (pl **antennae** [æn'tɛniː]) [of insect] 触角 [chùjiǎo] 2 (pl **antennas**) [of radio, TV] (aerial) 天线 [tiānxiàn]

anthem ['ænθəm] N [C] 赞美诗 [zànměishī]

anthology [æn'θɔlədʒɪ] N [C] [of poetry, stories etc] 选集 [xuǎnjí]

anthropology [ænθrə'pɔlədʒɪ] N [U] 人类学 [rénlèixué]

anti... ['æntɪ] PREFIX 1 (expressing opposition) 反 [fǎn] 2 (intended to destroy or prevent sth) 抗 [kàng]

antibiotic ['æntɪbaɪ'ɔtɪk] N [C] 抗生素 [kàngshēngsù]

antibody ['æntɪbɔdɪ] N [C] 抗体 [kàngtǐ]

anticipate [æn'tɪsɪpeɪt] VT 1 (expect, foresee) 预期 [yùqī] 2 (be prepared for) 提前行动 [tíqián xíngdòng] 3 (look forward to) 期望 [qīwàng] ▸ **this is worse/better than I anticipated** 这比我原先期望的要坏/好

anticipation [æntɪsɪ'peɪʃən] N [U] 1 ▸ **in anticipation of sth** (preparation for) 预期某事 [yùqī mǒushì] 2 (excitement) 期待某事 [qīdài mǒushì] ▸ **thanking you in anticipation** (frm) 预致谢意

anticlimax ['æntɪ'klaɪmæks] N [C/U] 虎头蛇尾 [hǔ tóu shé wěi]

anticlockwise ['æntɪ'klɔkwaɪz] (BRIT) ADV 按逆时针方向 [àn nì shízhēn fāngxiàng]

antics ['æntɪks] NPL 1 [of animals, children] 滑稽动作 [huájī dòngzuò] 2 [of politicians, celebrities]

丑态 [chǒutài]

anti-depressant [ˌæntɪdɪˈprɛsnt] N [C] (medicine) 抗抑郁症药 [kàng yìyùzhèng yào]; (activity, substance) 兴奋剂 [xīngfènjì]

antidote [ˈæntɪdəʊt] N [C] 1 (to poison) 解毒剂 [jiědújì] 2 ▸ an antidote to sth [+ unpleasant situation] 解决某事的良方 [jiějué mǒushì de liángfāng]

antifreeze [ˈæntɪfriːz] (AUT) N [U] 防冻剂 [fángdòngjì]

antihistamine [ˈæntɪˈhɪstəmɪn] N [C/U] 抗组织胺 [kàng zǔzhī ān]

antiquated [ˈæntɪkweɪtɪd] ADJ (outdated) 过时的 [guòshí de]

antique [ænˈtiːk] I N [C] (valuable old object) 古董 [gǔdǒng] II CPD [复合词] [+ furniture, jewellery] 古式 [gǔshì]

antiquity [ænˈtɪkwɪtɪ] N 1 [U] (the past) 古代 [gǔdài] 2 [C] (old object) 古物 [gǔwù]

antiseptic [ˌæntɪˈsɛptɪk] I N [C/U] 杀菌剂 [shājūnjì] II ADJ 杀菌的 [shājūn de]

antisocial [ˌæntɪˈsəʊʃəl] ADJ 1 (unsociable) 不喜社交的 [bù xǐ shèjiāo de] 2 (offensive) 冒犯他人的 [màofàn tārén de]

antlers [ˈæntləz] NPL 鹿角 [lù jiǎo]

anxiety [æŋˈzaɪətɪ] N 1 [C/U] (concern) 焦虑 [jiāolù] 2 [U] (MED) 焦虑症 [jiāolùzhèng] ▸ anxiety over or about sth 对某事感到焦虑 ▸ his anxiety to please/to do well (eagerness) 他急于取悦他人/好好表现的愿望

anxious [ˈæŋkʃəs] ADJ 1 (worried) [+ expression, person] 忧虑的 [yōulù de] 2 (worrying) [+ situation, time] 不安的 [bù'ān de] ▸ to be anxious to do sth (keen) 渴望做某事 ▸ to be anxious that... (keen) 极力希望··· ▸ to get or grow anxious 感到忧虑 ▸ anxious for sth 热切渴望某事

any [ˈɛnɪ] I ADJ 1 (in negatives, in questions) 一些的 [yīxiē de] ▸ I haven't any chocolate/sweets 我没有巧克力/糖果了 ▸ without any help 没有任何帮助 ▸ there was hardly any food 几乎没有食物了 ▸ there were hardly any potatoes 几乎没有土豆了 ▸ have you got any chocolate/sweets? 你有巧克力/糖果吗？ ▸ are there any others? 还有其他人吗？ 2 (in 'if' clauses) 任何的 [rènhé de] ▸ if there are any tickets left 如果有票剩下的话 3 (no matter which) 任何的 [rènhé de] ▸ take any card you like 你喜欢哪张卡就拿哪张 ▸ any excuse will do 任何一个理由都行 ▸ any teacher will tell you that... 任何一个老师都告诉诉你··· 4 (in expressions) ▸ any day now 从现在起的任何一天 [cóng xiànzài qǐ de rènhé yītiān] ▸ (at) any moment (在) 任何时

候 ▸ any time (whenever) 不论何时; (also: at any time) 在任何时候 ▷ He could be sent for (at) any time. 他可以随叫随到。 ▸ any time you feel like a chat, just call me 任何时候你想聊天，就给我打电话 ▸ the bomb could go off (at) any time 炸弹任何时候都可能爆炸 ▸ at any rate (more precisely) 至少; (whatever the case) 无论如何 ▸ she wanted to buy a dress but not just any dress 她想买件礼服，但要有点特别的那种

II PRON 1 (in negatives) 一些 [yīxiē] ▸ I didn't eat any (of it) 我一点东西也没吃 ▸ I haven't any (of them) 我一个也没有 ▸ there was nothing any of us could do to help 我们没有一个人能帮得上忙 2 (in questions) 一些 [yīxiē] ▸ have you got any? 你有吗？ ▸ can any of you sing? 你们中间有谁会唱歌？ 3 (in 'if' clauses) 任何一 [rènhé] ▸ if any of you would like to take part,... 如果你们中任何人想参加的话，… 4 (no matter which ones) 无论哪一个 [wúlùn nǎ yīgè] ▸ help yourself to any of the books 无论哪本书你随便拿

III ADV 1 (with negative) 丝毫 [sīháo] ▸ I can't see things getting any better 我看不出事情有丝毫好转 ▸ I don't play tennis any more 我不再打网球了 ▸ don't want any longer 不再等了 2 (in questions) ···一点 [...yīdiǎn] ▸ are you feeling any better? 你感觉好好一点吗？ ▸ do you want any more soup/sandwiches? 你还想要多点汤/三明治吗？ 3 (in 'if' clauses) 再···一点 [zài...yīdiǎn] ▸ if it had been any colder we would have frozen to death 如果再冷一点，我们就要被冻死了

anybody [ˈɛnɪbɒdɪ] PRON = anyone

anyhow [ˈɛnɪhaʊ] ADV 1 = anyway 2 (BRIT: inf) (haphazardly) 随随便便地 [suísuíbiànbiàn de] ▸ do it anyhow 随随便便地做 ▸ she leaves things just anyhow 她就是随随便便地乱放东西

anymore [ɛnɪˈmɔː(r)] ADV = any more see any

anyone [ˈɛnɪwʌn] PRON 1 (in negatives, 'if' clauses) 任何人 [rènhé rén] 2 (in questions) 任何一个人 [rènhé yīgè rén] 3 (no matter who) 不论什么人 [bùlùn shénme rén] ▸ I can't see anyone 我见不到任何人 ▸ did anyone see you? 有人看到你吗？ ▸ did you speak to anyone? 你对任何人说起过吗？ ▸ does anyone want a cake? 有人想要块蛋糕吗？ ▸ if anyone should phone... 如果有人打电话··· ▸ anyone could do it 任何人都能做到 ▸ anyone who is anyone 重要人物

anything [ˈɛnɪθɪŋ] PRON 1 (in negatives, questions, 'if' clauses) 任何事 [rènhé shì] 2 (no matter what) 无论何事物[wúlùn hé shìwù] ▶ I can't see anything 我什么也看不见 ▶ hardly anything 几乎没有任何东西 ▶ can you see anything? 你能看到些什么吗？ ▶ did you find anything? 你找到些什么吗？ ▶ if anything happens to me... 如果任何事情发生在我身上… ▶ he'll eat anything 他什么东西都会吃 ▶ you can say anything you like 你可以畅所欲言 ▶ anything will do 什么都行 ▶ anything between... and... 在…和…之间的样子 ▶ the lecture was anything but boring 讲座绝对不无聊 ▶ anything but! 绝对不！ ▶ I wouldn't do that for anything (inf) 我决不会那样做的 ▶ he's as clever as anything (inf) 他极其聪明 ▶ if anything 如果有什么不同的话 ▶ the painting didn't fetch anything like that much 这幅画根本没卖到那么高的价钱

anytime ['ɛnɪtaɪm] ADV 任何时候[rènhé shíhòu]

anyway ['ɛnɪweɪ] ADV **1** (besides) 无论如何[wúlùn rúhé] **2** (all the same) 还是[háishì] **3** (at least) 至少[zhìshǎo] **4** (in short) 总之[zǒngzhī] **5** (well) 不管怎样[bùguǎn zěnyàng] ▶ I shall go anyway 不论如何我要走了 ▶ why are you phoning, anyway? 你到底为什么打电话？

anywhere ['ɛnɪwɛə(r)] ADV **1** (in negatives, questions, 'if clauses) 任何地方[rènhé dìfāng] **2** (no matter where) 无论什么[wúlùn nǎlǐ] ▶ I can't see him anywhere 我哪里都见不到他 ▶ have you seen the scissors anywhere? 你在哪儿见过剪刀吗？ ▶ put your case down anywhere 把箱子放在哪儿都行 ▶ anywhere in the world 世界的任何地方 ▶ I would have known him anywhere 无论在哪儿我都认识他

apart [ə'pɑːt] ADV **1** [move, pull +] 分开[fēnkāi] **2** ▶ sit apart from the others 不和其他人坐在一起[bù hé qítā rén zuò zài yīqǐ] ▶ to be apart [couple, family +] 分开 ▶ to live apart 分居 ▶ 10 miles apart 相距10英里 ▶ a long way apart 意见迥异 ▶ with one's legs/feet apart 某人的腿/脚分开 ▶ to take sth apart 拆卸某物 ▶ to come or fall apart 崩溃 ▶ apart from (excepting) 除去；(in addition to) 除了…以外 ▶ I can't tell them apart 我不能分辨二者 ▶ set apart (from) 位于…的远处

apartment [ə'pɑːtmənt] I N [c](US) 公寓[gōngyù] [英=flat] II apartments NPL (BRIT) 房间[fángjiān]

apartment building, apartment house (US) N [c] 公寓楼[gōngyùlóu] [英=block of flats]

apathy ['æpəθɪ] N [U] 冷漠[lěngmò]

ape [eɪp] I N [c] 猿[yuán] II VT (imitate) 模仿[mófǎng]

aperitif [ə'pɛrɪtiːf] N [c] 开胃酒[kāiwèijiǔ]

aperture ['æpətʃuə(r)] N [c] **1** (frm) (hole, gap) 孔[kǒng] **2** (PHOT) 孔径[kǒngjìng]

apiece [ə'piːs] ADV (in number) 每人[měirén]; (in cost) 每个[měigè]

apologetic [əpɔlə'dʒɛtɪk] ADJ [tone, letter, person] 道歉的[dàoqiàn de] ▶ to be apologetic about... 为…感到抱歉

apologize [ə'pɔlədʒaɪz] VI 道歉[dàoqiàn] ▶ I apologize (for...) (frm) 我(为…而)道歉 ▶ to apologize to sb (for sth) 向(某人)道歉

apology [ə'pɔlədʒɪ] N [c/U] 道歉[dàoqiàn] ▶ to make (sb) an apology 向(某人)道歉 ▶ to send one's apologies (frm) (for one's absence) 致歉 ▶ to offer or make one's apologies (frm) 表达某人的歉意 ▶ please accept my apologies (frm) 请接受我的道歉 ▶ I make no apologies for what I said 我不为我所说的话感到抱歉

apostrophe [ə'pɔstrəfɪ] N [c] 撇号[piěhào]

appal, (US) **appall** [ə'pɔːl] VT (shock) 使惊骇[shǐ jīnghài]

appalled [ə'pɔːld] ADJ (horrified) 惊骇的[jīnghài de] ▶ to be appalled by/at sth 对某事物感到惊骇 ▶ to be appalled that... …使人惊骇

appalling [ə'pɔːlɪŋ] ADJ **1** (shocking) [+destruction, conditions, behaviour] 骇人听闻的[hàiréntīngwén de] **2** (great, intense) [+headache, ignorance] 严重的[yánzhòng de] ▶ she's an appalling cook (bad, poor) 她是个差劲的厨师

apparatus [æpə'reɪtəs] N [c/U] **1** (equipment) 装置[zhuāngzhì] **2** [of organization, system] 机构[jīgòu] ▶ a piece of apparatus 一件仪器

apparel [ə'pærəl] (ESP US: frm) N [U] 衣服[yīfu]

apparent [ə'pærənt] ADJ **1** (seeming) 表面上的[biǎomiànshang de] **2** (obvious) 明显的[míngxiǎn de] ▶ it is apparent that... 显然… ▶ for no apparent reason 原因不明地

apparently [ə'pærəntlɪ] ADV 表面看来[biǎomiàn kànlái]

appeal [ə'piːl] I VI **1** ▶ to appeal (to sb) (be attractive) 吸引(某人)[xīyǐn (mǒurén)] **2** (LAW) 上诉(for)(US) (decision, verdict) 上诉[shàngsù] II VT (US) (decision, verdict) 上诉[shàngsù] III N **1** [c] (request) 请求[qǐngqiú] **2** [c] (for good cause) 呼吁[hūyù] **3** [c/U] (LAW) 上诉[shàngsù] **4** [U] (attraction, charm) 吸引力[xīyǐnlì] ▶ to appeal (to sb) for sth 为某事(向某人)呼吁 ▶ he appealed for calm/silence 他请求大家平静下来/安静下来 ▶ it doesn't appeal to me 这一点也引不起我的兴趣 ▶ to appeal against a decision/verdict (BRIT) 对决定/判决进行上诉 ▶ to appeal to the Supreme Court 上诉最高法庭 ▶ right of appeal (LAW) 上诉权

appealing [ə'piːlɪŋ] ADJ **1** (attractive) [+idea, person] 吸引人的[xīyǐn rén de] **2** (pleading) [+look, tone] 恳求的[kěnqiú de]

○ appear [ə'pɪə(r)] VI **1** (seem) 看起来[kànqǐlái] ▷ He appears confident. 他看起来很有信心。 **2** (come into view, begin to develop) 出现[chūxiàn] ▷ Two men suddenly appeared at the door. 两个男人突然出现在门口。 ▷ The flowers appear in early summer. 这种花开在初夏。 **3** (become available)

问世 [wènshì] ▷ *New diet books appear every week.* 每周都有新的减肥食谱出售。**4** *(in court)* 出庭 [chūtíng] ▶ **to appear to be/have** 看起来是/有 ▷ *The aircraft appears to have crashed.* 这架飞机看起来是已经坠毁了。▶ **it appears/it would appear that…** 看起来似乎是…▶ **to appear in a play/film** 出演电视剧/电影

appearance [əˈpɪərəns] N **1** [S] *(arrival)* 出现 [chūxiàn] **2** [S] *(look, aspect)* 外表 [wàibiǎo] **3** [C] *(in public, on TV)* 露面 [lòumiàn] ▶ **to put in an appearance** *(show your face)* 露一下面 ▶ **to keep up appearances** 装门面 ▶ **to/by/from all appearances** 显然 ▶ **to make an appearance** *(on TV, in public)* 露面 ▶ **in order of appearance** *(in film, play)* 按出场顺序

appease [əˈpiːz] VT 安抚 [ānfǔ]

appendices [əˈpɛndɪsiːz] NPL *of* appendix

appendicitis [əpɛndɪˈsaɪtɪs] N [U] 阑尾炎 [lánwěiyán]

appendix [əˈpɛndɪks] *(pl* **appendices** *or* **appendixes)** N [C] **1** (ANAT) 阑尾 [lánwěi] **2** *(to publication)* 附录 [fùlù] ▶ **to have one's appendix out** 切除阑尾

appetite [ˈæpɪtaɪt] N [C/U] **1** *(desire to eat)* 食欲 [shíyù] **2** ▶ **an appetite for sth** *(desire)* 对某事的爱好 [duì mǒushì de àihào] ▶ **the walk has given me an appetite** 散步增进了我的食欲

appetizer [ˈæpɪtaɪzə(r)] N [C] *(first course)* 开胃食品 [kāiwèi shípǐn]

applaud [əˈplɔːd] I VI *(clap)* 鼓掌欢迎 [gǔzhǎng huānyíng] II VT **1** *(praise)* [+ *person, behaviour*] 称赞 [chēngzàn] **2** *(cheer)* [+ *actor, singer etc*] 鼓掌 [gǔzhǎng]

applause [əˈplɔːz] N [U] *(clapping)* 掌声 [zhǎngshēng]

apple [ˈæpl] N [C] 苹果 [píngguǒ] ▶ **she is the apple of her father's eye** 她是父亲的掌上明珠

appliance [əˈplaɪəns] *(frm)* N [C] *(device)* 器具 [qìjù]

applicable [əˈplɪkəbl] ADJ *(relevant)* ▶ **applicable (to)** 适用于 [shìyòng yú] ▶ **if/where applicable** 如果适用

applicant [ˈæplɪkənt] N [C] *(for job, place at college)* 申请人 [shēnqǐngrén]

application [æplɪˈkeɪʃən] N **1** [C] *(for job, grant etc)* 申请 [shēnqǐng] **2** [U] *(hard work)* 专心 [zhuānxīn] **3** [C/U] *(use)* [*of knowledge, theory etc*] 应用 [yìngyòng] **4** [C/U] *(applying)* [*of cream, paint etc*] 敷用 [fūyòng] **5** [C] (COMPUT) *(program)* 应用程序 [yìngyòng chéngxù] ▶ **on application** 申请之时 ▶ **the application of sth to sth** 某物对某物的应用

application form N [C] 申请表格 [shēnqǐng biǎogé]

apply [əˈplaɪ] I VI **1** ▶ **to apply (to sb)** *(be relevant)* (对某人)适用 [(duì mǒurén) shìyòng] **2** *(make application)* 提出申请 [tíchū shēnqǐng] II VT **1** *(use)* [+ *principle, technique*] 应

用 [yìngyòng] **2** [+ *paint, polish etc*] 涂 [tú] ▶ **to apply for sth** [+ *job, grant, membership*] 申请某事 ▶ **to apply to sb** [+ *council, governing body*] 向某人提出申请 ▶ **to apply to do sth** 申请做某事 ▶ **to apply the brakes** *(frm)* 刹车 ▶ **to apply o.s. (to sth)** 致力于(某事)

appoint [əˈpɔɪnt] VT ▶ **to appoint sb (to sth)** *(to post)* 任命某人(为某职) [rènmìng mǒurén (wéi mǒuzhí)]; *(to political position, post of honour)* 委任某人(为某职) [wěirèn mǒurén (wéi mǒuzhí)] ▶ **to appoint sb manager** 任命某人为经理

appointed [əˈpɔɪntɪd] ADJ ▶ **(at) the appointed time/hour** (在)约定时间/钟点 [(zài) yuēdìng shíjiān/zhōngdiǎn]

appointment [əˈpɔɪntmənt] N [C] *(arranged meeting)* *(in business, politics)* 约会 [yuēhuì]; *(with hairdresser, dentist, doctor)* 预约 [yùyuē] **2** [C/U] *(selection)* 任命 [rènmìng] **3** [C] *(post)* 职务 [zhíwù] ▶ **to make an appointment (with sb)** *(in business, politics)* (和某人)订一个约会; *(to see hairdresser, dentist, doctor)* (和某人)预约 ▶ **by appointment** 根据预约

appraisal [əˈpreɪzl] N ▶ **an appraisal (of)** (对…的)评估 [(duì…de) pínggū]

appreciate [əˈpriːʃɪeɪt] I VT **1** *(like, value)* 欣赏 [xīnshǎng] **2** *(be grateful for)* 感谢 [gǎnxiè] **3** *(understand, be aware of)* 理解 [lǐjiě] II VI *(increase in value)* [*currency, shares, property etc* +] 涨价 [zhǎngjià] ▶ **I (really) appreciate your help** 我(十分)感谢你的帮助 ▶ **I appreciate that…** 我意识到… ▶ **I'd appreciate it if…** 如蒙…我将不胜感激

appreciation [əpriːʃɪˈeɪʃən] N **1** [U] *(enjoyment)* 欣赏 [xīnshǎng] **2** [U] *(gratitude)* 感激 [gǎnjī] **3** [S/U] *(understanding)* ▶ **appreciation (of)** (对…的)了解 [(duì…de) liǎojiě] **4** [S/U] *(in value)* 涨价 [zhǎngjià]

appreciative [əˈpriːʃɪətɪv] ADJ **1** *(praising)* 赞赏的 [zànshǎng de] **2** ▶ **appreciative of** *(grateful)* 感激的 [gǎnjī de]

apprehend [æprɪˈhɛnd] VT **1** *(frm)* *(catch)* 逮捕 [dàibǔ] **2** *(liter)* *(understand)* 领会 [lǐnghuì]

apprehension [æprɪˈhɛnʃən] N **1** [C/U] *(frm)* *(fear)* 忧虑 [yōulǜ] **2** [U] *(frm)* *(arrest)* 逮捕 [dàibǔ] ▶ **in** *or* **with apprehension** 在恐惧中

apprehensive [æprɪˈhɛnsɪv] ADJ ▶ **apprehensive about** *or* **of** *(fearful)* 担心…的 [dānxīn…de]

apprentice [əˈprɛntɪs] I N [C] 学徒 [xuétú] II VT ▶ **to be apprenticed to sb** 给某人当学徒 [gěi mǒurén dāng xuétú] ▶ **an apprentice plumber/carpenter** *etc* 管子工/木匠{等}学徒

approach [əˈprəʊtʃ] I VI *(draw near)* [*person, car* +] 走近 [zǒu jìn]; [*event, time* +] 临近 [línjìn] II VT **1** *(draw near to)* [+ *place, person*] 向…靠近 [xiàng…kàojìn]; [+ *event*] 临近 [línjìn] **2** *(consult, speak to)* [+ *person*] 接洽 [jiēqià] **3** *(deal with)*

[+ *situation, problem*] 处理 [chǔlǐ] III N [C]
1 (*advance*) [*of person*] 靠近 [kàojìn] **2** (*to a problem, situation*) 方式 [fāngshì] **3** ▶ **approach to sth** (*access, path*) 通往某地的途径 [tōngwǎng mǒudì de tújìng] **4** (*proposal*) 对某事的提议 [duì mǒushì de tíyì] ▶ **to approach sb about sth** 就某事同某人接触 ▶ **the approach of Christmas/winter** 圣诞节/冬天的临近

appropriate [*adj* ə'prəuprɪɪt, *vb* ə'prəuprɪeɪt]
I ADJ (*suitable*) [+ *remarks, behaviour, clothing*] 恰当的 [qiàdàng de]; [+ *person, authority*] 相关的 [xiāngguān de] II (*firm*) (*steal*) [+ *property, materials, funds*] 盗用 [dàoyòng]; [+ *idea*] 剽窃 [piáoqiè] ▶ **it is/seems appropriate to...** …是/似乎是恰当的 ▶ **it is appropriate that...** …是恰当的 ▶ **to take appropriate action** 采取适当的行动 ▶ **appropriate for sth** 与某物相称 ▶ **appropriate for sth/sb** 适合于某物/某人

appropriately [ə'prəuprɪɪtlɪ] ADV **1** (*sensibly*) [*dress, act* +] 恰当地 [qiàdàng de] **2** (*acceptably*) 合适地 [héshì de] ▶ **appropriately enough...** (*emphasizing suitability*) 再合适不过地…

approval [ə'pruːvəl] N [U] **1** (*permission*) 批准 [pīzhǔn] **2** (*liking*) 赞成 [zànchéng] ▶ **to meet with sb's approval** [*proposal etc* +] 获得某人的赞同 ▶ **to give one's approval to sth** 对某事表示同意 ▶ **approval for sth** 对某事的批准 ▶ **on approval** 包退包换的 ▶ **seal** or **stamp of approval** 批准

approve [ə'pruːv] I VT **1** (*authorize*) [+ *publication, product, action*] 批准 [pīzhǔn] **2** (*pass*) [+ *motion, decision*] 通过 [tōngguò] II VI 赞成 [zànchéng] ▶ **to be approved by sb** (*authorized*) 被某人批准
▶ **approve of** VT FUS [不可拆分] **1** (*be pleased about*) [+ *action, event, idea*] 赞成 [zànchéng] **2** (*like, admire*) [+ *person, thing*] 称许 [chēngxǔ]

如果某当权者 **approve** 某个计划或者行动，他正式表示认可并且同意此事可以进行。例如，某委员会 **approve** 一个决议，即允许执行该决议。*At least the idea is now accepted and has even been approved by Parliament.* 若某当权者 **approve** 某物，比如某个建筑或产品，表示他们对它感到满意并允许投入使用或销售。如果某一药品被 **approved**，医生可以将它应用于临床治疗。*...premises which have been approved by the local authority.* 如果你 **approve of** 某种行为或事情，则表示你很乐意看到它已经发生或者即将发生。*I don't like the whole idea, I didn't approve of this meeting...His return to the office was widely approved of.* 如果你 **approve of** 某人或某物，例如某本书或某部电影，则表示你喜欢他它或对他它赞赏有加。*Do you think your father will approve of me?...He did not approve of my taste in pictures.*

approved [ə'pruːvd] ADJ 被认可的 [bèi rènkě de]

approx. [ə'prɔks] ABBR (= *approximately*) 大约地 [dàyuē de]

approximate [*adj* ə'prɔksɪmɪt, *vb* ə'prɔksɪmeɪt] I ADJ [+ *amount, number, age*] 近似的 [jìnsì de] II VI ▶ **to approximate to** (*resemble*) 接近于 [jiējìn yú]

approximately [ə'prɔksɪmɪtlɪ] ADV 大约地 [dàyuē de]

APR N ABBR (= *annual percentage rate*) 年度百分率 [niándù bǎifēnlù]

Apr. ABBR (= *April*) 四月 [sìyuè]

apricot ['eɪprɪkɔt] N [C/U] (*fruit*) 杏子 [xìngzi]

April ['eɪprəl] N [C/U] 四月 [sìyuè] *see also* **July**

April Fool's Day N [C/U] 愚人节 [Yúrénjié]

⊙ **APRIL FOOL'S DAY**

愚人节，英国人互相开各种各样的玩笑、搞恶作剧。谁要是上当，就称之为 **April Fools**。有时甚至也跟着凑热闹，编造新闻故事，发出骗人的报导，例如，在意大利，曾有报道说意大利面条长在树上。

apron ['eɪprən] N [C] **1** (*clothing*) 围裙 [wéiqún] **2** (*at airport*) ▶ **the apron** 停机坪 [tíngjīpíng]

apt [æpt] ADJ **1** (*suitable*) [+ *comment, description etc*] 恰当的 [qiàdàng de] **2** (*likely*) ▶ **to be apt to do sth** 易于做某事的 [yìyú zuò mǒushì de]

aptitude ['æptɪtjuːd] N [C/U] (*capability, talent*) 天资 [tiānzī] ▶ **to have an aptitude for sth** 有做某事的天分

aquarium [ə'kwɛərɪəm] (*pl* **aquariums** or **aquaria** [ə'kwɛərɪə]) N [C] **1** (*fish tank*) 养鱼缸 [yǎng yú gāng] **2** (*building*) 水族馆 [shuǐzúguǎn]

Aquarius [ə'kwɛərɪəs] N **1** [U] (*sign*) 宝瓶座 [Bǎopíng Zuò] **2** [C] (*person*) 属宝瓶座的人 [shǔ Bǎopíng Zuò de rén] ▶ **I'm (an) Aquarius** 我是宝瓶座的

aquatic [ə'kwætɪk] ADJ **1** (*living in water*) [+ *plant, animal*] 水生的 [shuǐshēng de] **2** (*relating to water*) [+ *sports, studies*] 水上的 [shuǐshang de]

Arab ['ærəb] I ADJ 阿拉伯的 [Ālābó de] II N [c] 阿拉伯人 [Ālābórén]

Arabia [ə'reɪbɪə] N 阿拉伯半岛 [Ālābó Bàndǎo]

Arabian [ə'reɪbɪən] ADJ 阿拉伯的 [Ālābó de]

Arabic ['ærəbɪk] I ADJ [+ *language, script etc*] 阿拉伯的 [Ālābó de] II N [U] (*language*) 阿拉伯语 [Ālābóyǔ] ▶ **Arabic numeral** 阿拉伯数字

arable ['ærəbl] ADJ **1** [+ *crop, farming*] 垦殖的 [kěnzhí de] **2** [+ *land*] 可耕的 [kěgēng de]

arbitrary ['ɑːbɪtrərɪ] ADJ (*random*) [+ *attack, decision*] 任意的 [rènyì de]

arbitration [ɑːbɪ'treɪʃən] N [U] (*of dispute, quarrel*) 仲裁 [zhòngcái] ▶ **the dispute went to**

arbitration 争议交付仲裁

arc [ɑ:k] N [c] **1** (curve) 弧形 [húxíng] **2** (in geometry) 弧 [hú]

arcade [ɑ:'keɪd] N [c] **1** (shopping centre) 拱廊式街道 [liángshì jiēdào] **2** (also: amusement arcade) 游乐场 [yóulèchǎng]

arch [ɑ:tʃ] I N [c] **1** (curved structure) 拱 [gǒng] **2** [of foot] 足弓 [zúgōng] II VT [+one's back] 使成弓形 [shǐ chéng gōngxíng] III VI 拱起 [gǒngqǐ] IV ADJ **1** [+expression, look] 调皮的 [tiáopí de] **2** (superior) [+tone, behaviour] 高人一等的 [gāorényīděng de]

archaeology [ɑ:kɪ'ɔlədʒɪ] N [U] 考古学 [kǎogǔxué]

archaic [ɑ:'keɪɪk] ADJ 过时的 [guòshí de]

archbishop [ɑ:tʃ'bɪʃəp] N [c] 大主教 [dà zhǔjiào]

archeology [ɑ:kɪ'ɔlədʒɪ] (US) =archaeology

archetypal [ɑ:kɪtaɪpəl] ADJ 典型的 [diǎnxíng de]

architect ['ɑ:kɪtɛkt] N [c] **1** [of building] 建筑师 [jiànzhùshī] **2** (frm) [of idea, event] 设计师 [shèjìshī]

architectural [ɑ:kɪ'tɛktʃərəl] ADJ 建筑的 [jiànzhù de]

architecture ['ɑ:kɪtɛktʃə(r)] N [U] **1** (design of buildings) 建筑学 [jiànzhùxué] **2** (style of building) 建筑风格 [jiànzhù fēnggé]

archive ['ɑ:kaɪv] I N [c] **1** (collection) [of papers, records, films etc] 档案 [dàng'àn] **2** (place) 档案馆 [dàng'àn guǎn] II ADJ [+material, film] 档案的 [dàng'àn de] III VT 把…存档 [bɑ…cúdǎng] IV archives NPL **1** (collection) [of papers, records, films etc] 档案 [dàng'àn] **2** (place) 档案室 [dàng'ànshì] ▶ archive file (COMPUT) 档案文件

Arctic ['ɑ:ktɪk] I N ▶ the Arctic 北极区 [Běijí Qū] II ADJ **1** [+ice, explorer etc] 北极的 [Běijí de] **2** (inf) (freezing) 极冷的 [jílěng de]

ardent ['ɑ:dənt] ADJ [+admirer, supporter] 热烈的 [rèliè de]

arduous ['ɑ:djuəs] ADJ (difficult and tiring) [+task] 艰巨的 [jiānjù de]; [+journey] 艰苦的 [jiānkǔ de]

are [ɑ:(r)] VB see be

○ **area** ['ɛərɪə] N **1** [c] (region, zone) 地区 [dìqū] ▷ people who live in rural areas 住在乡村地区的人 **2** [c] [of room, building etc] (used for particular activity) 区 [qū] ▷ a picnic area 野餐区 **3** [c/U] (MATH, GEOM) 面积 [miànjī] **4** [c] (part) [of surface] 部分 [bùfen] ▷ Apply cream to the affected area. 把药膏涂在患部。 **5** [c] (subject, topic) 领域 [lǐngyù] **6** [c] (aspect) 方面 [fāngmiàn] ▷ She controls every area of his life. 她控制着他生活的各个方面。 **7** ▶ the area (inf: FOOTBALL) 罚球区 [fáqiúqū] ▶ in the London area 在伦敦周边地区 ▶ in my/your area 在我/你住的地区 ▷ The schools in our area are terrible. 我们所住地区的学校很糟糕。 ▶ to cover/occupy an area of 50 sq km 占地面积50平方公里 ▶ 50 sq km in area 面积50平方公里

area code (ESP US) N [c] 区号 [qūhào] [英=dialling code]

arena [ə'ri:nə] N [c] **1** (for sport, entertainment) 竞技场 [jìngjìchǎng] **2** ▶ the political/economic arena 政治/经济舞台 [zhèngzhì/jīngjì wǔtái]

aren't [ɑ:nt] =are not

Argentina [ɑ:dʒən'ti:nə] N 阿根廷 [Āgēntíng]

Argentine ['ɑ:dʒəntaɪn] ADJ 阿根廷的 [Āgēntíng de]

Argentinian [ɑ:dʒən'tɪnɪən] I ADJ 阿根廷的 [Āgēntíng de] II N [c] (person) 阿根廷人 [Āgēntíngrén]

arguably ['ɑ:gjuəblɪ] ADV 可证明地 [kě zhèngmíng de] ▶ it is arguably... 这可以认为…

argue ['ɑ:gju:] I VI **1** (quarrel) ▶ to argue (with sb) (about sth) (为某事) (和某人) 争吵 [(wèi mǒushì) (hé mǒurén) zhēngchǎo] **2** (claim) ▶ to argue that... 论证… [lùnzhèng…] II VT (debate) [+case, point] 辩论 [biànlùn] ▶ to argue for/against sth 据理赞成/反对某事

argument ['ɑ:gjumənt] N [c/U] **1** (quarrel) 争吵 [zhēngchǎo] **2** (reason) 论点 [lùndiǎn] ▶ to get into an argument (with sb) (和某人) 开始一场争论 ▶ an argument for/against sth 赞成/反对某事的论据

Aries ['ɛəri:z] N **1** [U] (sign) 白羊座 [Báiyáng Zuò] **2** [c] (person) 属白羊座的人 [shǔ Báiyáng Zuò de rén] ▶ I'm (an) Aries 我是白羊座的

arise [ə'raɪz] (pt arose, pp arisen [ə'rɪzn]) VI **1** (emerge) [problem, difficulty etc +] 出现 [chūxiàn] **2** ▶ to arise from/out of sth (result from) 由某事引起 [yóu mǒushì yǐnqǐ] **3** ▶ to arise from sth (frm) (from sitting, kneeling) 从某处站起来 [cóng mǒuchù zhàn qǐlái]; (from bed) 起床 [qǐchuáng] ▶ if the need/opportunity arises 一旦有需要/机会

arithmetic [ə'rɪθmətɪk] N [U] **1** (MATH) 算术 [suànshù] **2** (in particular calculation) 计算 [jìsuàn] **3** ▶ the arithmetic (of particular situation) 数字 [shùzì]

○ **arm** [ɑ:m] I N [c] **1** [of person] 胳膊 [gēbo] **2** [of jacket, shirt etc] 袖子 [xiùzi] **3** [of chair] 扶手 [fúshǒu] **4** [of organization etc] 部门 [bùmén] ▷ the political arm of the movement 该运动的政治部门 II VT [+person, nation] 武装 [wǔzhuāng] III arms NPL (weapons) 武器 [wǔqì] IV CPD [复合词] arms [+dealer, trade] 军火 [jūnhuǒ] ▶ arm in arm 臂挽臂地 ▶ to cost an arm and a leg (inf) 价钱过高 ▶ at arm's length 距离一臂远的 ▶ to keep sb at arm's length 同某人保持一定距离 ▶ to welcome sb/sth with open arms 热烈欢迎某人/某事 ▶ to twist sb's arm (inf) 对某人施加压力 ▶ a shot in the arm 兴奋剂

armchair ['ɑ:mtʃeə(r)] N [c] 扶手椅 [fúshǒuyǐ]

armed [ɑ:md] ADJ **1** [+ robber, policeman etc] 武装的 [wǔzhuāng de] **2** [+ conflict, attack etc] 武力的 [wǔlì de] ▶ **the armed forces** 武装部队 ▶ **armed with a knife** 携带小刀的

armed robbery N [C/U] 持枪抢劫 [chíqiāng qiǎngjié]

Armenia [ɑ:'mi:nɪə] N 亚美尼亚 [Yàměiníyà]

armour, (US)**armor** [ˈɑːmə(r)] N [U] **1** [of knight, soldier] 盔甲 [kuījiǎ] **2** (MIL) (also: **armour-plating**) [of tank] 装甲钢板 [zhuāngjiǎ gāngbǎn]; (tanks) 装甲部队 [zhuāngjiǎ bùduì]

armpit [ˈɑːmpɪt] N [C] 腋窝 [yèwō]

armrest [ˈɑːmrɛst] N [C] 扶手 [fúshǒu]

army [ˈɑːmɪ] I N **1** ▶ **the army** 军队 [jūnduì] ▷ *He joined the army.* 他参军了。 **2** (host) ▶ **an army of sth** 一大群某物 [yīdàqún mǒuwù] ▷ *an army of volunteers* 一大群志愿者 II CPD [复合词] [+ officer, unit, uniform] 军队 [jūnduì]

A road (BRIT) N [C] 主干公路 [zhǔgàn gōnglù]

aroma [əˈrəumə] N [C/U] [of food, coffee] 香味 [xiāngwèi]; [of flower] 芳香 [fāngxiāng] ▶ **the aroma of…** …的香味

aromatherapy [ərəumə'θεrəpɪ] N [U] 芳香疗法 [fāngxiāng liáofǎ]

arose [əˈrəuz] PT of **arise**

around [əˈraund] I ADV (about) 到处 [dàochù] ▷ *They wandered around.* 他们到处闲逛。 II PREP **1** (encircling) 围绕 [wéirào] ▷ *We were sitting around a table.* 我们正围绕桌子坐着。 ▷ *It measures fifteen feet around the trunk.* 树干合抱有15英尺。 **2** (near) 在附近 [zài fùjìn] ▷ *We don't live around here.* 我们不住在附近。 **3** (about, roughly) (with numbers, weights, times, dates) 大约 [dàyuē] ▷ *There were around 200 people.* 大约有200人。 ▷ *It was around 5 o'clock.* 那时大约5点钟。 ▶ **is he around?** 他在吗?

arouse [əˈrauz] VT **1** [+ anger, interest, passion] 激起 [jīqǐ] **2** ▶ **to be aroused** (sexually) 被激起情欲 [bèi jīqǐ qíngyù] **3** (frm) (from sleep) 唤醒 [huànxǐng]

arrange [əˈreɪndʒ] I VT **1** (organize) [+ meeting, tour, appointment etc] 安排 [ānpái] **2** (put in order) [+ books, objects] 整理 [zhěnglǐ]; [+ flowers] 布置 [bùzhì] **3** ▶ **to be arranged by sb** [+ piece of music] 由某人改编 [yóu mǒurén gǎibiān] II VI ▶ **to arrange to do sth** 安排做某事 [ānpái zuò mǒushì] ▶ **it was arranged that…** 已安排好… ▶ **to arrange for sth to be done** 就做某事做好安排

arrangement [əˈreɪndʒmənt] I N [C] **1** (agreement) 约定 [yuēdìng] **2** (grouping, layout) [of books, furniture] 布置 [bùzhì] **3** (display) [of flowers] 插花 [chāhuā] **4** [of piece of music] 改编的乐曲 [gǎibiān de yuèqǔ] II **arrangements** NPL (plans, preparations) 安排 [ānpái] ▶ **to make an arrangement to do sth** 为做某事做好安排 ▶ **to come to an arrangement with sb** 和某人达成协议 ▶ **by arrangement** 根据约定 ▶ **to**

make arrangements (for sth) (为某事) 做好准备工作

array [əˈreɪ] N [C] **1** (display) ▶ **an array of things** 一排东西 [yīpái dōngxī] **2** (range) ▶ **an array of people/things** 一大批人/物 [yīdàpī rén/wù] **3** (network) 阵列 [zhènliè]

arrears [əˈrɪəz] NPL (money owed) 欠款 [qiànkuǎn] ▶ **to be in/get into arrears (with rent)** 拖欠(租金) ▶ **to be paid in arrears** 事后结算 ▶ **rent arrears** 欠租

arrest [əˈrɛst] I VT **1** (detain) 逮捕 [dàibǔ] **2** (frm) (stop) [+ process, development] 抑制 [yìzhì] II N [C/U] (detention) 拘捕 [jūbǔ] ▶ **to make an arrest** 逮捕 ▶ **to place sb under arrest** 将某人逮捕 ▶ **to be under arrest** 被逮捕 ▶ **to arrest sb's attention** (frm) 吸引某人的注意力

arrival [əˈraɪvl] N **1** [C/U] [of person, vehicle, letter] 到达 [dàodá] **2** [S] [of invention, idea, product] 出现 [chūxiàn] **3** [C] (newcomer) (in job, at place) 新到者 [xīndàozhě]

arrive [əˈraɪv] VI **1** [person, vehicle +] 到达 [dào] **2** [letter, meal +] 来 [lái]
▶ **arrive at** VT FUS [不可拆分] [+ idea, decision] 达到 [dádào]
用法参见 **reach**

arrogance [ˈærəgəns] N [U] 傲慢 [àomàn]

arrogant [ˈærəgənt] ADJ 傲慢的 [àomàn de]

arrow [ˈærəu] N [C] **1** (weapon) 箭 [jiàn] **2** (sign) 箭头标志 [jiàntóu biāozhì]

arse [ɑ:s] (BRIT: infl) N [C] 屁股 [pìgu] [美=**ass**]

arsenal [ˈɑːsɪnl] N [C] **1** (stockpile, supply) 军火储备 [jūnhuǒ chǔbèi] **2** (building) 军火库 [jūnhuǒkù]

arson [ˈɑːsn] I N [U] 纵火 [zònghuǒ] II CPD [复合词] [+ attack] 纵火 [zònghuǒ]

art [ɑ:t] I N **1** [U] (paintings, sculpture etc) 艺术 [yìshù] ▷ *an exhibition of modern art* 一场现代艺术展 **2** [U] (activity of drawing, painting etc) 美术 [měishù] ▷ *I've never been any good at art.* 我一向对美术不在行。 **3** [C] (skill) 技艺 [jìyì] II CPD [复合词] [+ exhibition, collection, student] 艺术 [yìshù] III **arts** NPL **1** ▶ **the arts** (creative activities) 艺术活动 [yìshù huódòng] **2** ▶ **a patron of the arts** 一位艺术活动赞助人 **2** (in education) 文科 [wénkē] IV CPD [复合词] [+ graduate, student, course] 文科 [wénkē] ▶ **work of art** 艺术品 ▶ **the art of survival** 生存的技巧

art college N [C] 美术学院 [měishù xuéyuàn]

artery [ˈɑːtərɪ] N [C] **1** (blood vessel) 动脉 [dòngmài] **2** (route) 要道 [yàodào]

art gallery N [C] **1** (large, national) 美术馆 [měishùguǎn] **2** (small, private) 画廊 [huàláng]

arthritis [ɑ:'θraɪtɪs] N [U] 关节炎 [guānjiéyán]

artichoke [ˈɑːtɪtʃəuk] N [C/U] **1** (also: globe artichoke) 洋蓟 [yángjì] **2** (also: Jerusalem artichoke) 菊芋 [júyù]

article [ˈɑːtɪkl] I N [C] **1** (frm) (object, item) 物品 [wùpǐn] **2** (in newspaper) 文章 [wénzhāng]

3 (in document) 条款 [tiáokuǎn] **4** (LING) 冠词 [guàncí] **II articles** (BRIT) NPL (training) (in law, accountancy) 契约 [qìyuē] ▶ **articles of clothing** 服装

articulate [adj ɑ:ˈtɪkjulɪt, vb ɑ:ˈtɪkjuleɪt] **I** ADJ **1** [+ person] 表达能力强的 [biǎodá nénglì qiáng de] **2** [+ speech, writing] 表达清楚的 [biǎodá qīngchǔ de] **II** VT **1** (frm) (express) [+ feelings, ideas] 明确表达 [míngquè biǎodá] **2** (pronounce) 清晰地发音 [qīngxī de fāyīn]

artificial [ɑːtɪˈfɪʃəl] ADJ **1** (man-made) [+ flowers, leg, lake] 人造的 [rénzào de] **2** (false) [+ conditions, situation] 人为的 [rénwéi de] **3** (affected) [+ manner, person] 矫揉造作的 [jiǎoróuzàozuo dè]

artist [ˈɑːtɪst] N [c] **1** (painter, sculptor) 画家 [huàjiā] **2** (writer, composer etc) 艺术家 [yìshùjiā] **3** (musician, actor etc) 表演艺术家 [biǎoyǎn yìshùjiā]

artistic [ɑːˈtɪstɪk] ADJ **1** [+ person] 艺术性强的 [yìshùxìng qiáng de] **2** [+ tradition, freedom] 艺术的 [yìshù de] **3** [+ design, arrangement] 精美的 [jīngměi de]

art school N = art college

artwork [ˈɑːtwɜːk] N **1** [U] (for advert, book etc) 插图 [chātú] **2** [c] (work of art) 艺术作品 [yìshù zuòpǐn]

as [æz, əz] **I** CONJ **1** (referring to time) 当…时 [dāng…shí] ▶ **he came in as I was leaving** 我离开时他进来了 ▶ **as the years went by** 随着时间的推移

2 (since, because) 因为 [yīnwéi] ▶ **as you can't come, I'll go on my own** 既然你不能来，我就自己去

3 (referring to manner, way) 像…一样 [xiàng…yíyàng] ▶ **as you can see** 如你所见到的 ▶ **as she said** 如她所说 ▶ **do as you wish** 按你的愿望去做 ▶ **it's on the left as you go in** 在你进入时的左侧

II PREP **1** (in the capacity of) 作为 [zuòwéi] ▶ **he works as a salesman** 他做推销员的工作 ▶ **as a teacher, I am very aware that...** 作为老师，我非常清楚… ▶ **she was dressed as a nun** 她穿得像个修女 ▶ **he gave it to me as a present** 他把它作为礼物送给我 ▶ **to come as a surprise/shock** 出人意料/令人震惊地来到了

III ADV **1** (in comparisons) ▶ **as big/good/easy etc as...** 像…一样大/好/容易{等} [xiàng…yíyàng dà/hǎo/róngyì {děng}] ▶ **you're as tall as he is** or **as him** 你和他一样高 ▶ **twice as big/good etc as...** …的两倍大/比…好得多 ▶ **as much money/many books as...** 同…一样多的钱/书

▶ **as much/many as...** 和…一样 ▶ **as soon as** 一…就…

2 (in expressions) ▶ **as if** or **though** 好像 [hǎoxiàng] ▶ **you think I'm lying to you? as if (I would)!** 你认为我在向你撒谎吗？(我)才不会呢！ ▶ **as from** or **of tomorrow** 从明天起 ▶ **as for** or **to that** 至于那一点 ▶ **he inquired as to what the problem was** 有关存在什么问题，他进行了了解

asap, ASAP ADV ABBR (= as soon as possible) 尽快 [jìnkuài]

asbestos [æzˈbɛstəs] N [U] 石棉 [shímián]

ascend [əˈsɛnd] **I** VT **1** [+ hill, stairs] 登 [dēng] **2** ▶ **to ascend the throne** 登上王位 [dēngshàng wángwèi] **II** VI **1** (lead) [staircase, path +] 上升 [shàngshēng] **2** (travel) [lift, vehicle etc +] 上升 [shàngshēng] **3** ▶ **to ascend to power** 掌权 [zhǎngquán] ▶ **in ascending order** 按由小到大的次序

ascent [əˈsɛnt] N [c] **1** (slope, path) 斜坡 [xiépō] **2** (climb) (by vehicle, elevator) 上升 [shàngshēng]; (by person) [of mountain] 攀登 [pāndēng]

ascertain [æsəˈteɪn] VT (frm) (establish) [+ details, facts] 查明 [chámíng] ▶ **to ascertain who/what...** 查明谁/什么… ▶ **to ascertain that...** 查明…

ASEAN [ˈæsiæn] N ABBR (= Association of South-East Asian Nations) 东盟 [Dōngméng]

ash [æʃ] **I** N **1** [U] (from fire, cigarette) 灰末 [huīmò] **2** [c/U] (tree) 白蜡树 [báilàshù] **II ashes** NPL **1** [of fire] 灰烬 [huījìn] **2** (remains) 骨灰 [gǔhuī] ▶ **to burn sth to ashes** 将某物烧为灰烬

ashamed [əˈʃeɪmd] ADJ ▶ **to be/feel ashamed** (embarrassed, guilty) 感到羞愧 [gǎndào xiūkuì] ▶ **to be ashamed of sb/sth** 对某人/某事感到羞愧 ▶ **to be ashamed of o.s. (for having done sth)** 因自己(做了某事)而感到惭愧 ▶ **to be ashamed to admit sth** 耻于承认某事

ashore [əˈʃɔː(r)] ADV **1** [be +] 在岸上 [zài àn shàng] **2** [swim, go +] 向岸边 [xiàng ànbiān]

ashtray [ˈæʃtreɪ] N [c] 烟灰缸 [yānhuīgāng]

Ash Wednesday N [c/U] 圣灰星期三 [Shènghuī Xīngqīsān]

Asia [ˈeɪʃə] N 亚洲 [Yàzhōu]

Asian [ˈeɪʃən] **I** ADJ 亚洲的 [Yàzhōu de] **II** N [c] (person) 亚洲人 [Yàzhōurén]

aside [əˈsaɪd] **I** ADV **1** ▶ **to put** or **lay sth aside** 把某物放到一边 [bǎ mǒuwù fàng dào yībiān] **2** ▶ **to stand/step/move aside** 站/走/挪到一边 [zhàn/zǒu/nuó dào yībiān] **3** ▶ **to take** or **draw sb aside** 把某人拉到一边 [bǎ mǒurén lā dào yībiān] **4** ▶ **to set** or **put sth aside** 存储某物 [cúnchǔ mǒuwù] **II** N [c] **1** (to audience, camera) 旁白 [pángbái] **2** (digression) 题外话 [tíwàihuà] ▶ **to brush** or **sweep objections aside** 对反对意见置之不理{或}不顾反对意见

aside from (ESP US) PREP 除了⋯之外 [chúle⋯zhīwài]

○ **ask** [ɑ:sk] I VT **1** ▶ **to ask (sb) a question** 问 (某人)一个问题 [wèn (mǒurén) yīgè wèntí] **2** (invite) 邀请 [yāoqǐng] ▷ I asked her to the party. 我邀请她参加聚会。 II VI [wèn] ▶ **to ask (sb) whether/why...** 问(某人)是否/为 什么⋯ ▶ **to ask sb to do sth** 请求某人做某 事 ▶ **to ask to do sth** 要求做某事 ▶ **to ask sb the time** 向某人询问时间 ▶ **to ask sb about sth** 向某人打听某事 ▶ **I asked him his name** 我问他叫什么 ▶ **to ask (for/sb's) permission/ forgiveness** 请求(某人的)许可/原谅 ▶ **to ask sb's opinion** 征询某人意见 ▶ **if you ask me** 据 我看 ▶ **to ask (about) the price** 询问价钱 ▶ **to ask sb out to dinner** 请某人出去吃饭
▶ **ask after** VT FUS [不可拆分] [+ person] 问候 [wènhòu]
▶ **ask for** VT FUS [不可拆分] **1** (ask to have) [+ thing] 要 [yào] **2** (ask to see) [+ person] 找 [zhǎo]
▶ **you're asking for trouble!** 你在自找麻烦!
▶ **you asked for it!** 你自讨苦吃!

asking price ['ɑ:skɪŋ-] N ▶ **the asking price** 索价 [suǒjià]

asleep [ə'sli:p] ADJ 睡着的 [shuìzháo de] ▶ **to be asleep** 睡着了 ▶ **to fall asleep** 入睡

AS level (BRIT: SCOL) N 介于GCSE和A level之 间的等级考试

asparagus [əs'pærəgəs] N [U] 芦笋 [lúsǔn]

aspect ['æspɛkt] N [C] **1** (element) [of subject] 方面 [fāngmiàn] **2** (quality, appearance) 面貌 [miànmào] **3** (frm) (outlook) ▶ **a south-west aspect** 朝西南方向 [cháo xīnán fāngxiàng]

aspirations [æspə'reɪʃənz] NPL 志向 [zhìxiàng] ▶ **her aspirations to a movie career** 她从事电影工作的志向

aspire [əs'paɪə(r)] VI ▶ **to aspire to** 有志于 [yǒuzhì yú]

aspirin ['æsprɪn] N **1** [U] (drug) 阿司匹林 [āsīpǐlín] **2** [C] (tablet) 阿司匹林药片 [āsīpǐlín yàopiàn]

ass [æs] N [C] **1** (animal) 驴 [lú] **2** (inf) (idiot) 傻 瓜 [shǎguā] **3** (US: inf!) (bottom) 屁股 [pìgu] [英= **arse**]

assassin [ə'sæsɪn] N [C] 刺客 [cìkè]

assassinate [ə'sæsɪneɪt] VT 暗杀 [ànshā] ▰▰▰用法参见 kill

assault [ə'sɔ:lt] I N [C/U] (attack) (on individual, by army) 攻击 [gōngjī]; (on belief, idea) 抨击 [pēngjī] II VT (attack) 袭击 [xíjī]; (sexually) 强 奸 [qiángjiān] ▶ **assault and battery** (LAW) 人 身攻击 ▶ **to be charged with assault** 被指控 侵犯人身 ▶ **an assault on sb/sth** 对某人/某 事的攻击

assemble [ə'sɛmbl] I VT **1** (gather together) [+ people, group] 集合 [jíhé] **2** (fit together) [+ machinery, object] 装配 [zhuāngpèi] II VI (gather) [people, crowd +] 聚集 [jùjí]

assembly [ə'sɛmblɪ] N **1** [C] (meeting) 集 会 [jíhuì] **2** [C] (institution) 议会 [yìhuì] **3** [U] (construction) [of vehicles etc] 装配 [zhuāngpèi] **4** [C/U] (in school) 集合 [jíhé]

assert [ə'sə:t] VT **1** [+ opinion, innocence] 宣称 [xuānchēng] **2** [+ authority] 维护 [wéihù] ▶ **to assert o.s.** 坚持己见

assertion [ə'sə:ʃən] N [C/U] (statement, claim) 断言 [duànyán]

assess [ə'sɛs] VT **1** (gauge) [+ problem, situation, abilities] 估量 [gūliàng] **2** (calculate) [+ tax, value] 估价 [gūjià] **3** [+ student, work] 评估 [pínggū]

assessment [ə'sɛsmənt] N [C/U] **1** (evaluation) [of problem, situation, abilities] 评估 [pínggū] **2** (calculation) [of tax, value] 估价 [gūjià] **3** [of student, work] 评价 [píngjià]

asset ['æsɛt] I N [C] (useful quality, person etc) 宝 贵财富 [bǎoguì cáifù] II **assets** NPL (COMM) (property, funds) 资产 [zīchǎn] ▶ **to be an asset to sb/sth** 为某人/某物的难得之材

assign [ə'saɪn] VT **1** (allocate) ▶ **to assign sth to sb** [+ task] 把某物分配给某人 [bǎ mǒuwù fēnpèi gěi mǒurén] **2** [+ cause, meaning, value] 将某物赋 予某处 [jiāng mǒuwù fùyǔ mǒuchù] ▶ **to be assigned to sth** [+ place, group] 被指派到某处 ▶ **to be assigned sb/sth** 被分配了某人/某物

assignment [ə'saɪnmənt] N [C] (task) 任务 [rènwù]; (for student) 作业 [zuòyè]

assimilate [ə'sɪmɪleɪt] I VT **1** (learn) [+ ideas, methods etc] 吸收 [xīshōu] **2** ▶ **to be assimilated** [+ immigrants] 同化 [tónghuà] II VI [immigrants +] 同化 [tónghuà]

assist [ə'sɪst] VT [+ person] 帮助 [bāngzhù]; [+ injured person] 扶助 [fúzhù]

assistance [ə'sɪstəns] N [U] 帮助 [bāngzhù] ▶ **to be of assistance** 有帮助

assistant [ə'sɪstənt] I N [C] **1** (helper) 助 手 [zhùshǒu] **2** (BRIT) (in shop) 营业员 [yíngyèyuán] II ADJ ▶ **assistant secretary/ professor** 副部长/教授 [fù bùzhǎng/jiàoshòu]

associate [vb ə'səuʃɪeɪt, n ə'səuʃɪɪt] I VT **1** (in your thoughts) 联想 [liánxiǎng] **2** ▶ **to be associated with sth** 和某事有关 [hé mǒushì yǒuguān] II VI ▶ **to associate with sb** 和某人 交往 [hé mǒurén jiāowǎng] III N [C] (at work) 同事 [tóngshì] ▶ **to associate o.s. with sth** 与 某物有联系 ▶ **associate member** 准成员 ▶ **associate director** 副主管

association [əsəusɪ'eɪʃən] N **1** [C] (group) 协会 [xiéhuì] **2** ▶ **to have associations (with sth/for sb)** (mental connection) 有(对某事/某人)的联想 [yǒu (duì mǒushì/mǒurén de) liánxiǎng] **3** [C/U] (involvement, link) 联系 [liánxì] ▶ **association (with sb/sth)** (同某人/某物的)联系 [(tóng mǒurén/mǒuwù de) liánxì] ▶ **in association with** (in collaboration with) 与⋯ 联合

assorted [ə'sɔ:tɪd] ADJ (various, mixed) 各种各 样的 [gèzhǒng gèyàng de] ▶ **in assorted sizes**

不同尺寸

assortment [ə'sɔːtmənt] N [C] ▶ **an assortment of sth** [of shapes, colours] 一批花色齐全的某物 [yīpī huāsè qíquán de mǒuwù]; [of objects, people] 各种各样的某物 [gèzhǒng gèyàng de mǒuwù]

assume [ə'sjuːm] VT **1** (suppose) 假设 [jiǎshè] **2** [+ responsibility, power] 承担 [chéngdān] **3** (adopt) [+ appearance, attitude] 呈现 [chéngxiàn]; [+ name] 采用 [cǎiyòng] ▶ **let us assume that...** 让我们假设…

assumption [ə'sʌmpʃən] N **1** [C] (supposition) 假定 [jiǎdìng] **2** [U] [of responsibility, power] 承担 [chéngdān] ▷ **the assumption of total responsibility** 承担全部责任 ▶ **on the assumption that** (on condition that) 根据⋯这一假设

assurance [ə'ʃʊərəns] N **1** [C/U] (assertion, promise) 保证 [bǎozhèng] **2** [U] ▶ **with assurance** (confidence) 有把握 [yǒu bǎwò] **3** [U] (BRIT) (insurance) 保险 [bǎoxiǎn]

assure [ə'ʃʊə(r)] VT **1** (reassure) 使确信 [shǐ quèxìn] **2** (guarantee) [+ happiness, success etc] 保证 [bǎozhèng] ▶ **the series is assured of success** 这部连续剧保证能获得成功

AST (US) ABBR (= Atlantic Standard Time) 大西洋标准时间 [Dàxīyáng Biāozhǔn Shíjiān]

asterisk ['æstərɪsk] N [C] 星号 [xīnghào]

asthma ['æsmə] N [U] 哮喘 [xiàochuǎn]

astonish [ə'stɒnɪʃ] VT 使惊讶 [shǐ jīngyà]

astonishing [ə'stɒnɪʃɪŋ] ADJ 惊人的 [jīngrén de] ▶ **I find it astonishing that...** 我对⋯感到惊讶

astonishment [ə'stɒnɪʃmənt] N [U] 惊讶 [jīngyà] ▶ **in astonishment** 惊讶地 ▶ **to my astonishment** 令我吃惊的是

astound [ə'staund] VT 使震惊 [shǐ zhènjīng]

astray [ə'streɪ] ADV ▶ **to go astray** [letter +] 丢失 [diūshī] ▶ **to lead sb astray** 将某人引入歧途

astride [ə'straɪd] PREP 骑跨 [qíkuà]

astrology [əs'trɒlədʒɪ] N [U] 占星术 [zhānxīngshù]

astronaut ['æstrənɔːt] N [C] 宇航员 [yǔhángyuán]

astronomer [əs'trɒnəmə(r)] N [C] 天文学家 [tiānwénxuéjiā]

astronomical [æstrə'nɒmɪkl] ADJ **1** (enormous) [+ odds, price] 极巨大的 [jí jùdà de] **2** [+ science] 天文学的 [tiānwénxué de]

astronomy [əs'trɒnəmɪ] N [U] 天文学 [tiānwénxué]

astute [əs'tjuːt] ADJ [+ person, decision] 精明的 [jīngmíng de]

asylum [ə'saɪləm] N **1** [U] (POL) (refuge) 避难 [bìnàn] **2** [C] (mental hospital) 精神病院 [jīngshénbìng yuàn] ▶ **to seek (political) asylum** 寻求(政治)避难 ▶ **to grant** or **give sb (political) asylum** 授予(或)给予某人(政治)避难权 ▶ **to claim (political) asylum** 要求(政治)避难

O

at [æt] PREP **1** (position, time, age) 在 [zài] ▶ **we had dinner at a restaurant** 我们在一家饭店吃了饭 ▶ **at home** 在家 ▶ **at school** 在学校 ▶ **at work** (not at home) 在工作 ▶ **at my brother's** 在我哥哥家 ▶ **at the baker's** 在面包房 ▶ **at the bus stop** 在公交车站 ▶ **what time will you arrive at the hotel?** 你几点到宾馆？ ▶ **to be sitting at a table/desk** 坐在桌边/书桌边 ▶ **there's someone at the door** 门口有人; (towards) ▶ **to throw sth at sb** 向某人扔某物 ▶ **the question was directed at me** 问题是直接针对我的 ▶ **to wave/frown at sb** 冲某人招手/皱眉 ▶ **at four o'clock** 在4点钟 ▶ **at night** 在晚上 ▶ **at Christmas** 在圣诞节 ▶ **at the weekend** 在周末 ▶ **she died at the age of 76** 她在76岁时去世了 **2** (referring to price, speed etc) 以 [yǐ] ▶ **apples at £2 a kilo** 苹果每公斤两镑 ▶ **at 50 km/h** 以每小时50公里的速度 ▶ **two at a time** 每次2个

3 (in measurements) 达 [dá] ▶ **at 110 kilos, she's very overweight** 达到110公斤, 她严重超重了

4 (referring to activity) 在⋯方面 [zài⋯fāngmiàn] ▶ **he's at work on a novel** 他正在写一本小说 ▶ **to play at cowboys** 扮演牛仔 ▶ **to be good at sth/at doing sth** 擅长某事/做某事

5 (referring to cause) 由于 [yóuyú] ▶ **shocked/surprised/annoyed at sth** 由于某事而震惊/吃惊/恼怒

6 (in expressions) ▶ **not at all** (in answer to question) 一点也不 [yīdiǎn yě bù]; (in answer to thanks) 别客气 [bié kèqi] ▶ **I'm not at all tired** 我一点儿也不累 ▶ **there's nothing at all to see** 没有任何值得看的

ate [eɪt] PT of **eat**

atheist ['eɪθɪɪst] N [C] 无神论者 [wúshénlùnzhě]

Athens ['æθɪnz] N 雅典 [Yǎdiǎn]

athlete ['æθliːt] N [C] 运动员 [yùndòngyuán]

athletic [æθ'letɪk] ADJ **1** [+ tradition, excellence etc] 体育的 [tǐyù de] **2** (sporty) [+ person] 运动的 [yùndòng de] **3** (muscular) [+ build, frame] 健壮的 [jiànzhuàng de]

athletics [æθ'letɪks] N [U] 田径运动 [tiánjìng yùndòng]

Atlantic [ət'læntɪk] **I** ADJ 大西洋的 [Dàxīyáng de] **II** N ▶ **the Atlantic (Ocean)** 大西洋 [Dàxīyáng]

atlas ['ætləs] N [C] 地图册 [dìtúcè]

ATM N ABBR (= Automated Telling Machine) 自动取款机 [zìdòng qǔkuǎnjī]

atmosphere ['ætməsfɪə(r)] N 1 [c] (of planet) 大气层 [dàqìcéng] 2 [s] (feel) (of place) 气氛 [qìfēn] 3 [c] (air) 空气 [kōngqì]

atom ['ætəm] (PHYS) N [c] 原子 [yuánzǐ]

atomic [ə'tɒmɪk] ADJ 原子的 [yuánzǐ de]

atom(ic) bomb N [c] 原子弹 [yuánzǐdàn]

atrocious [ə'trəʊʃəs] ADJ 糟透的 [zāotòu de]

atrocity [ə'trɒsɪti] N [c] (act of cruelty) 暴行 [bàoxíng]

attach [ə'tætʃ] VT 1 (fasten, join) 附上 [fùshàng] 2 [+ importance, significance etc] 把…放在 [bǎ…fàng zài] ▶ **to be attached to sb/sth** (emotionally) 喜爱某人/某物

attachment [ə'tætʃmənt] N 1 [c/u] (affection) ▶ **attachment (to sb)** (对某人的) 爱慕之情 [(duì mǒurén de) àimù zhī qíng] 2 [c] (of tool, computer file) 附件 [fùjiàn]

⊙**attack** [ə'tæk] I VT 1 (assault) [+ person] 袭击 [xíjí] 2 [+ place, troops] 攻击 [gōngjī] 3 (criticise) [+ person, idea] 抨击 [pēngjī] ▷ He attacked the press for misleading the public. 他抨击新闻界误导公众。 4 (tackle) [+ task, problem etc] 着手 [zhuóshǒu] 5 (in sport) 进攻 [jìngōng] II VI (MIL, SPORT) 进攻 [jìngōng] III N 1 [c/u] (on person) 袭击 [xíjí] 2 [c/u] (military assault) 攻击 [gōngjī] 3 [c] (criticism) 抨击 [pēngjī] 4 [c/u] (of illness) 发作 [fāzuò] ▷ an attack of asthma, an asthma attack 哮喘发作 5 [c] (in sport) 进攻 [jìngōng] ▶ **to come under attack** (assault) 遭到袭击; (criticism) 遭到抨击 ▶ **to launch an attack** (assault) 发动进攻; (criticism) 发起抨击 ▶ **an attack on sb** (assault) 袭击某人; (criticism) 抨击某人

attacker [ə'tækə(r)] N [c] 攻击者 [gōngjīzhě]

attain [ə'teɪn] VT 1 [+ state, condition] 达到 [dádào] 2 [+ ambition, rank] 获得 [huòdé] 3 [+ age] 到达 [dàodá]

⊙**attempt** [ə'tempt] I N [c] (try) 尝试 [chángshì] II VT (try) 试图 [shìtú] III VI ▶ **to attempt to do sth** 试图做某事 [shìtú zuò mǒushì] ▶ **an attempt to do sth** 做某事的企图 ▶ **an attempt on sb's life** 企图杀害某人 ▶ **to make no attempt to help** 他并未试着帮忙 ▶ **at** or **on the first attempt** 首次尝试 ▶ **he attempted a smile** 他试图挤出一丝微笑 ▶ **an attempt at humour** 试图表示幽默

attend [ə'tend] VT 1 (be member of) [+ school, church, course] 上 [shàng] 2 (take part in) [+ lecture, conference] 参加 [cānjiā] ▶ **attend to** VT FUS [不可拆分] 1 [+ needs, affairs] 处理 [chǔlǐ] 2 [+ patient, customer] 照料 [zhàoliào]

attendance [ə'tendəns] N 1 [u] (presence) 出席 [chūxí] 2 [c/u] (people present) 出席者 [chūxízhě]

attendant [ə'tendənt] I N [c] (person) 服务员 [fúwùyuán] II ADJ [+ dangers, risks, publicity] 伴随的 [bànsuí de]

attention [ə'tenʃən] I N [u] 1 (concentration) 注意 [zhùyì] 2 (care) 照料 [zhàoliào] II INT (MIL) 立正 [lìzhèng] ▶ **for the attention of…** 收件人为… ▶ **it has come to my attention that…** 我已开始注意到… ▶ **to draw sb's attention to sth** 把某人的注意力引向某事 ▶ **to stand to/at attention** (MIL) 立正站着 ▶ **to pay attention (to sth/sb)** 关注(某事/某人) ▶ **to attract sb's attention** 吸引某人的注意

attentive [ə'tentɪv] ADJ 1 (intent) [+ audience] 聚精会神的 [jù jīng huì shén de] 2 (polite, helpful) [+ person] 体贴的 [tǐtiē de]; [+ service] 周到的 [zhōudào de] ▶ **he is attentive to his wife** 他对妻子很体贴

attic ['ætɪk] N [c] 阁楼 [gélóu]

attitude ['ætɪtjuːd] N [c/u] 1 (mental view) 看法 [kànfǎ] 2 (behaviour) 态度 [tàidù] 3 (posture) 姿势 [zīshì] 4 ▶ **kids/women with attitude** (aggressive style) 争强好胜的孩子/女人 [zhēng qiáng hào shèng de háizi/nǚrén]

attorney [ə'tɜːnɪ] (US) N [c] (lawyer) 律师 [lùshī] ▶ **power of attorney** 代理权

Attorney General N [c] 1 (BRIT) 检察总长 [jiǎnchá zǒngzhǎng] 2 (US) 司法部长 [sīfǎ bùzhǎng]

attract [ə'trækt] VT 1 [+ people, animals, metal] 吸引 [xīyǐn] 2 (gain) [+ support, publicity] 获得 [huòdé]; [+ sb's interest, attention] 引起 [yǐnqǐ]

attraction [ə'trækʃən] I N [u] (charm, appeal) [of person] 吸引力 [xīyǐnlì] II **attractions** NPL (also: **tourist attractions**) (amusements) 游览胜地 [yóulǎn shèngdì] ▶ **the attraction of sth** [of place, activity etc] 某物的诱人之处

attractive [ə'træktɪv] ADJ 1 [+ man, woman] 有魅力的 [yǒu mèilì de]; [+ thing, place] 吸引人的 [xīyǐn rén de] 2 (interesting) [+ price, idea, offer] 令人感兴趣的 [lìng rén gǎn xìngqù de] ▶ **he was very attractive to women** 他对女人很有吸引力

attribute [n 'ætrɪbjuːt, vb ə'trɪbjuːt] I N [c] 特性 [tèxìng] II VT ▶ **to attribute sth to sb** [+ poem, painting, remark] 认为某物出自某人 [rènwéi mǒuwù chūzì mǒurén]; [+ quality, motive] 认为某人具有某物 [rènwéi mǒurén jùyǒu mǒuwù] ▶ **to attribute sth to sth** [+ situation, cause] 把某事归因于某事

aubergine ['əʊbəʒiːn] (BRIT) N 1 [c/u] (vegetable) 茄子 [qiézi] [美=**eggplant**] 2 [u] (colour) 紫红色 [zǐhóngsè]

auburn ['ɔːbən] ADJ [+ hair] 赤褐色的 [chìhèsè de]

auction ['ɔːkʃən] I N [c] 拍卖 [pāimài] II VT 拍卖 [pāimài] ▶ **auction off** VT 拍卖掉 [pāimài diào]

auctioneer [ɔːkʃə'nɪə(r)] N [c] 拍卖师 [pāimàishī]

audible ['ɔːdɪbl] ADJ 听得见的 [tīngdejiàn de]

audience ['ɔːdɪəns] N [C] 1 (in theatre etc) 观众 [guānzhòng] 2 (RAD, TV) 听众 [tīngzhòng] 3 (public) 读者 [dúzhě] 4 (interview) (with Queen, Pope etc) 接见 [jiējiàn]

audio ['ɔːdɪəu] ADJ [+ cassette, tape] 音响的 [yīnxiǎng de]

audio-visual ['ɔːdɪəu'vɪzjuəl] ADJ [+ materials, equipment] 视听的 [shìtīng de]

audit ['ɔːdɪt] (COMM) I VT [+ accounts] 审计 [shěnjì] II N [C] 查账 [cházhàng]

audition [ɔː'dɪʃən] I N [C] (CINE, THEAT) 试演 [shìyǎn] II VI ▶ to audition (for sth) 试演 (某剧) [shìyǎn(mǒu jù)] III VT 让…试演 [ràng…shìyǎn]

auditor ['ɔːdɪtə(r)] N [C] (accountant) 审计员 [shěnjìyuán]

auditorium [ɔːdɪ'tɔːrɪəm] N [C] (pl auditoria [ɔːdɪ'tɔːrɪə]) 1 (in theatre, concert hall) 观众席 [guānzhòngxí] 2 (US) (for concerts, lectures) 礼堂 [lǐtáng]

Aug. ABBR (= August) 八月 [bāyuè]

augment [ɔːg'mɛnt] VT [+ income, salary etc] 增加 [zēngjiā]

August ['ɔːgəst] N [C/U] 八月 [bāyuè] see also **July**

aunt [ɑːnt] N [C] (father's sister) 姑母 [gūmǔ]; (father's older brother's wife) 伯母 [bómǔ]; (father's younger brother's wife) 婶母 [shěnmǔ]; (mother's sister) 姨母 [yímǔ]; (mother's brother's wife) 舅母 [jiùmǔ]

auntie, aunty ['ɑːntɪ] (inf) N [C] = **aunt**

au pair ['əu'pɛə(r)] N [C] 为学习语言而住在当地人家里并提供家政服务的外国年轻人

aura ['ɔːrə] ▶ an aura of sth 某物的一种氛围 [mǒuwù de yīzhǒng fēnwéi]

auspicious [ɔːs'pɪʃəs] (frm) ADJ [+ opening, start, occasion] 吉利的 [jílì de]

austerity [ɔs'tɛrɪtɪ] N [U] 1 (hardship) ▶ time/ period of austerity 经济紧缩年代/时期 [jīngjì jǐnsuō niándài/shíqī] 2 (frm) (simplicity) 朴素 [pǔsù]

Australia [ɔs'treɪlɪə] N 澳大利亚 [Àodàlìyà]

Australian [ɔs'treɪlɪən] I ADJ 澳大利亚的 [Àodàlìyà de] II N [C] (person) 澳大利亚人 [Àodàlìyàrén]

Austria ['ɔstrɪə] N 奥地利 [Àodìlì]

Austrian ['ɔstrɪən] I ADJ 奥地利的 [Àodìlì de] II N [C] (person) 奥地利人 [Àodìlìrén]

authentic [ɔː'θɛntɪk] ADJ 1 (genuine) [+ cuisine] 正宗的 [zhèngzōng de]; [+ painting] 真的 [zhēn de]; [+ document] 真实的 [zhēnshí de] 2 (reliable) [+ account] 可靠的 [kěkào de]

author ['ɔːθə(r)] N [C] 1 (writer) [of novel] 作家 [zuòjiā]; [of text] 作者 [zuòzhě] 2 (originator) [of plan, scheme] 发起人 [fāqǐrén]

authoritarian [ɔːθɔrɪ'tɛərɪən] (pej) I ADJ [+ attitudes, government] 独裁主义的 [dúcái zhǔyì de] II N [C] 独裁主义者 [dúcái zhǔyì zhě]

authoritative [ɔː'θɔrɪtətɪv] ADJ 1 [+ person, manner] 命令式的 [mìnglìngshì de] 2 [+ account, study] 权威的 [quánwēi de]

O **authority** [ɔː'θɔrɪtɪ] N 1 [U] (power) 权威 [quánwēi] ▷ He had an air of authority. 他有一种权威的姿态。2 [U] (right, permission) 许可 [xǔkě] ▷ The bank closed my account without my authority. 银行未经我的许可就结了我的账户。3 ▶ an authority on sth (expert) 某方面的权威 [mǒu fāngmiàn de quánwēi] ▷ She's a world authority on heart disease. 她是位心脏病方面的世界级权威。4 [C] (government body, ruling body) 当局 [dāngjú] ▷ the local authority 地方当局 ▶ to have the authority to do sth 具有做某事的权力

authorize ['ɔːθəraɪz] VT 授权 [shòuquán] ▶ to authorize sb/to be authorized to do sth 授权某人/被授权做某事

autobiography [ɔːtəbaɪ'ɔgrəfɪ] N [C] 自传 [zìzhuàn]

autograph ['ɔːtəgrɑːf] I N [C] 亲笔签名 [qīnbǐ qiānmíng] II VT 亲笔签名于 [qīnbǐ qiānmíng yú]

automatic [ɔːtə'mætɪk] I ADJ 1 [+ process, machine] 自动的 [zìdòng de] 2 [+ reaction] 无意识的 [wú yìshi de] 3 [+ action, punishment] 必然发生的 [bìrán fāshēng de] II N [C] 1 (rifle, pistol) 自动枪 [zìdòngqiāng] 2 (car) 自动挡 [zìdòngdǎng]

automatically [ɔːtə'mætɪklɪ] ADV 1 (by itself) 自动地 [zìdòng de] 2 (without thinking) 无意识地 [wú yìshi de] 3 (as a matter of course) 自然而然地 [zìrán'érrán de]

automobile ['ɔːtəməbiːl] (US) N [C] 汽车 [qìchē]

autonomous [ɔː'tɔnəməs] ADJ 1 (self-governing) [+ country] 自治的 [zìzhì de]; [+ organization, group] 独立自主的 [dúlì zìzhǔ de] 2 (independent) [+ individual, person] 独立的 [dúlì de]

autonomy [ɔː'tɔnəmɪ] N [U] 1 (self-government) [of country] 自治 [zìzhì]; [of organization] 独立自主 [dúlì zìzhǔ] 2 (frm) (independence) [of person] 自主权 [zìzhǔquán]

autumn ['ɔːtəm] (BRIT) N [C/U] 秋季 [qiūjì] [美 = **fall**] ▶ in (the) autumn 在秋季

auxiliary [ɔːg'zɪlɪərɪ] I ADJ 1 [+ staff, service, force] 辅助的 [fǔzhù de] 2 [+ equipment] 备用的 [bèiyòng de] II N [C] 1 (person) 助手 [zhùshǒu] 2 (in grammar) 助动词 [zhùdòngcí] ▶ auxiliary verb 助动词

Av. ABBR = **Ave**.

avail [ə'veɪl] (frm) I VT ▶ to avail o.s. of sth [+ offer, opportunity, service] 利用某物 [lìyòng mǒuwù] II N ▶ to or of little avail 没多大效果 [méi duōdà xiàoguǒ] ▶ to or of no avail 没有效果

availability [əveɪlə'bɪlɪtɪ] N [U] [of goods, staff

etc] 获得的可能性 [huòdé de kěnéngxìng]

○ **available** [ə'veɪləbl] ADJ **1** (*obtainable*) [+ *article, service*] 可用的 [kě yòng de] ▷ *Breakfast is available from 6 a.m.* 从早晨6点起可用早餐。 ▷ *the best available information* 可享用的最佳信息 **2** [+ *person*] (*unoccupied*) 有空的 [yǒukòng de] ▷ *The minister was not available.* 部长没空。; (*unattached*) 单身的 [dānshēn de] **3** [+ *time*] 空闲的 [kòngxián de] ▷ *I have very few days available at the moment.* 我目前没几天是空闲的。▶ **every available means** 每个可利用的方法 ▶ **is the manager available?** 经理有空吗？▶ **he is not available for comment** 他现在无法发表意见 ▶ **to make sth available to sb** 使某人可以享用某物 ▶ **available for hire/rent/sale** 可供雇用/出租/出售

avalanche ['ævəlɑːnʃ] N **1** [C] 雪崩 [xuěbēng] **2** [s] [*of people, mail, events*] 涌现 [yǒngxiàn]

Ave. ABBR (= *avenue*) 大街 [dàjiē]

avenge [ə'vɛndʒ] VT [+ *death*] 替…报仇 [tì…bàochóu]

avenue ['ævənjuː] N [C] **1** (*lined with shops, houses*) 大街 [dàjiē]; (*tree-lined*) 林阴道 [línyīn dào] **2** (*means, solution*) 途径 [tújìng]

average ['ævərɪdʒ] I N [C] **1** (MATH) (*mean*) 平均数 [píngjūnshù] ▶ **the average (for sth/sb)** (某物/某人的)平均水平 [(mǒuwù/mǒurén de) píngjūn shuǐpíng] II ADJ **1** (MATH) 平均的 [píngjūn de] **2** (*ordinary*) 普通的 [pǔtōng de] **3** (*mediocre*) 平庸的 [píngyōng de] III VT 平均为 [píngjūn wéi] ▶ **on average** 平均 [+] ▶ **an average of ten days** 平均10天左右 ▶ **above/below (the) average** 高于/低于平均水平 ▶ **average out I** VI ▶ **to average out at/to sth** 平均为某数值 [píngjūn wéi mǒu shùzhí] II VT 得出…的平均数 [déchū…de píngjūnshù]

averse [ə'vəːs] ADJ ▶ **I'm/he's not averse to sth/doing sth** 我/他不反对某事/做某事 [wǒ/tā bù fǎnduì mǒushì/zuò mǒushì]

avert [ə'vəːt] VT **1** (*prevent*) [+ *accident, war*] 避免 [bìmiǎn] **2** (*turn away*) ▶ **to avert one's eyes/gaze from sth** 将目光/注视从某物上移开 [jiāng mùguāng/zhùshì cóng mǒuwù shang yíkāi]

avid ['ævɪd] ADJ [+ *supporter, reader*] 热切的 [rèqiè de]

avocado [ævə'kɑːdəu] (BRIT) N [C/U] (*also:* **avocado pear**) 鳄梨 [èlí]

avoid [ə'vɔɪd] VT **1** (*dodge*) [+ *person, obstacle*] 避免 [bìmiǎn] **2** (*prevent*) [+ *trouble, danger*] 防止 [fángzhǐ] **3** (*evade, shun*) 躲避 [duǒbì] ▶ **to avoid doing sth** 避免做某事

await [ə'weɪt] VT **1** (*wait for*) 等待 [děngdài] **2** (*be in store for*) 等待着 [děngdài zhe] ▶ **long awaited** [+ *event, opportunity*] 期待已久的

awake [ə'weɪk] (*pt* **awoke,** *pp* **awoken** *or* **awakened**) I ADJ ▶ **to be awake** 醒着的

[xǐngzhe de] II VT (*liter*) 唤醒 [huànxǐng] III VI (*liter*) 醒来 [xǐnglái] ▶ **wide awake** 完全清醒 ▶ **he lay awake all night worrying** 他整晚忧心忡忡地睡不着觉

awakening [ə'weɪknɪŋ] N [C] 觉醒 [juéxǐng] ▶ **a rude awakening** 猛然醒悟

award [ə'wɔːd] I N [C] **1** (*prize*) 奖 [jiǎng] **2** (LAW) (*damages*) 赔偿金 [péichángjīn] II VT **1** [+ *prize*] 授予 [shòuyǔ] **2** (LAW) [+ *damages*] 判给 [pàngěi] **3** [+ *penalty, free kick*] 判罚 [pànfá]

aware [ə'wɛə(r)] ADJ ▶ **politically/socially aware** 有政治/社会意识的 [yǒu zhèngzhì/shèhuì yìshí de] ▶ **to be aware of sth** (*know about*) 意识到某事; (*be conscious of*) 觉察到某事 ▶ **to be aware that...** 知道… ▶ **I am fully** *or* **well aware that...** 我充分意识到…

awareness [ə'wɛənɪs] N [U/s] (*knowledge*) 意识 [yìshí] ▶ **to develop** *or* **raise people's awareness of sth** 增强人们对某事的意识

awash [ə'wɒʃ] ADJ **1** ▶ **awash (with)** (*with water*) (被)淹没的 [(bèi)…yānmò de] **2** ▶ **awash with** (*knee-deep in*) 充斥的 [chōngchì de]

○ **away** [ə'weɪ] I ADV **1** (*move, walk* +) 开 [...kāi] ▷ *He rose and walked slowly away.* 他站起身，慢慢地走开。**2** (*not present*) 不在 [bùzài] ▷ *Jason is away in Germany.* 杰森现在在德国。▷ *She was away at the time of the accident.* 发生意外时她不在。**3** ▶ **to put sth away** 妥善保存某物 [tuǒshàn bǎocún mǒuwù] ▶ **to hide sth away** 藏起某物 **4** [*melt, fade, fall* +] …掉 […diào] ▷ *The snow has already melted away.* 雪已经融化掉了。II ADJ [+ *match, game*] 客场的 [kèchǎng de] ▶ **a week/month away** 还有一个星期/月 ▶ **two kilometres away** 离这里两公里远 ▶ **to play away** 在对方球场比赛 ▶ **it's two hours away by car** 有两小时车程 ▶ **away from** 远离 ▷ *a pleasant spot away from the city* 一个远离城市的宜人之地 ▶ **to work/pedal/scrub away** 连续不断地工作/蹬车/擦洗

awe [ɔː] I N [U] (*respect*) 敬畏 [jìngwèi] II VT ▶ **to be awed by sth/sb** 对某事/某人肃然起敬 [duì mǒushì/mǒurén sùránqǐjìng] ▶ **to be in awe of sb/sth** 敬畏某人/某事

awesome ['ɔːsəm] ADJ **1** (*impressive*) 使人敬畏的 [shǐ rén jìngwèi de] **2** (*inf*) (*amazing*) 令人惊叹的 [lìng rén jīngtàn de]

awful ['ɔːfəl] I ADJ **1** (*frightful*) 糟糕的 [zāogāo de] **2** (*dreadful*) [+ *shock, crime etc*] 可怕的 [kěpà de] **3** ▶ **to look/feel awful** (*ill*) 看起来/感觉很糟糕的 [kàn qǐlái/gǎnjué hěn zāogāo de] II ADV (US: *inf*) (*very*) 十分地 [shífēn de] ▶ **an awful lot (of)** (*amount*) 大量的; (*number*) 非常多的

awfully ['ɔːfəlɪ] ADV (*very*) (*used for emphasis*) 非常 [fēicháng] ▶ **would you mind awfully if...?** 你非常介意…吗？

awkward ['ɔːkwəd] ADJ **1** (*clumsy*) [+ *movement*] 笨拙的 [bènzhuó de] **2** (*inconvenient*) [+ *time,*

question] 令人尴尬的 [lìng rén gāngà de]
3 (difficult to use, do, or carry) 不方便的 [bù
fāngbiàn de] **4** (deliberately difficult) [+ person] 不
合作的 [bù hézuò de] ▶ he's at an awkward
age 他正处于爱找别扭的年龄

awoke [ə'wəʊk] PT of awake

awoken [ə'wəʊkən] PP of awake

axe, (US) **ax** [æks] **I** N [C] 斧 [fǔ] **II** VT 大刀阔
斧地削减 [dà dāo kùo fǔ de xuējiǎn] ▶ to have

an axe to grind (inf) 另有企图

axle ['æksl] (AUT) N [C] 轴 [zhóu]

aye [aɪ] (BRIT) **I** INT (yes) 是 [shì] ▶ to vote aye
投赞成票 **II** N ▶ the ayes 投赞成票者 [tóu
zànchéngpiào zhě]

azalea [ə'zeɪlɪə] N [C] 杜鹃花 [dùjuānhuā]

Azerbaijan [æzəbaɪ'dʒɑːn] N 阿塞拜疆
[Āsàibàijiāng]

Bb

B¹, b [bi:] N [c/u] (letter) 英语的第二个字母

B² [bi:] N **1** [c/u] (MUS) C大调音阶中的第七音 **2** [c] (SCOL, UNIV) (mark) 良 [liáng]

B³ (TEXTING) ABBR = **be**

b. ABBR (= born) 出生 [chūshēng]

B4 (TEXTING) ABBR = **before**

BA N ABBR (= Bachelor of Arts) (qualification) 文科学士学位 [wénkē xuéshì xuéwèi]; (person) 文科学士 [wénkē xuéshì]

baby ['beɪbɪ] I N [c] **1** (infant) 婴儿 [yīng'ér] **2** (ESP US: inf) (darling) 宝贝 [bǎobèi] II CPD [复合词] **1** [+ seal, elephant] 幼小动物 [yòuxiǎo dòngwù] **2** [+ vegetable] 嫩菜 [nèncài] ▷ baby sweetcorn 嫩的甜玉米 ▸ **to have a baby** 生孩子 ▸ **to be a baby** (inf) 真是个小孩儿

baby carriage (US) N [c] 婴儿车 [yīng'ér chē] [英 = **pram**]

baby food N [c/u] 婴儿食品 [yīng'ér shípǐn]

babysit ['beɪbɪsɪt] (pt, pp **babysat**) VI 代人照看孩子 [dài rén zhàokàn háizi]

babysitter ['beɪbɪsɪtə(r)] N [c] 代人照看孩子的人 [dài rén zhàokàn háizi de rén]

baby wipe N [c] 婴儿卫生纸 [yīng'ér wèishēngzhǐ]

bachelor ['bætʃələ(r)] N [c] **1** (unmarried man) 单身汉 [dānshēnhàn] **2** ▸ **Bachelor of Arts/Science** (degree) 文/理科学士学位 [wén/lǐ kē xuéshì xuéwèi]; (BRIT) (person) 文/理科学士 [wén/lǐ kē xuéshì]

⊙ **back** [bæk] I N [c] **1** [of person, animal] 背部

[bèibù] **2** (not front) [of hand, neck, legs] 背面 [bèimiàn]; [of house, door, book] 后面 [hòumiàn]; [of car] 后部 [hòubù]; [of train] 尾部 [wěibù]; [of chair] 靠背 [kàobèi] **3** (FOOTBALL) (defender) 后卫 [hòuwèi] II VT **1** (support) [+ candidate, plan] 支持 [zhīchí] ▷ The union will back Mr Green. 工会将支持格林先生。; (financially) 资助 [zīzhù] ▷ The group is backed by big multinationals. 该团体由大型的跨国公司资助。 **2** (bet on) [+ horse, team] 下赌注于 [xià dǔzhù yú] ▷ Did you back the winner? 你是否赌赢家？ **3** (reverse) [+ car] 倒 [dào] ▷ She backed the car a few feet. 她把车向后倒了几英尺。 III VI (reverse) [person, car etc +] 倒着行驶 [dàozhe xíngshǐ] ▷ She backed out of the drive. 她倒着行驶出车道。 IV ADJ **1** [+ garden, door, room, wheels] 后面的 [hòumiàn de] **2** [+ payment, rent] 拖欠的 [tuōqiàn de] V ADV **1** (not forward) 向后 [xiàng hòu] ▷ Charlie glanced back. 查理向后扫了一眼。 **2** (returned) ▸ **to be back** 回来 [huílái] ▷ He's back. 他回来了。 **3** (when returning sth) 还 [huán] ▷ She handed the knife back. 她把刀还回来了。 ▷ Can I have it back? 我能要回它吗？ **4** (repetition) 回 [huí] ▷ He stared back at me. 她回瞪着我。 **5** (in the past) 以前 [yǐqián] ▷ The story starts back in 1950. 故事开始于1950年。 **6** (away) 远离 [yuǎnlí] ▷ Keep back from the edge of the platform. 站在远离站台边缘的地方。 ▸ **to do sth behind sb's back** 背着某人做某事 ▸ **to turn one's back on sb/sth** (fig) 不理睬某人某事 ▸ **to have one's back to the wall** (fig) 陷入困境 ▸ **to break the back of a job** 度过最艰难的时刻 ▸ **to take a back seat** (fig) 把权利让与他人 ▸ **back and forth** 来回 ▸ **at the back (of)** (of crowd, building) 在(…的)后面 ▸ **back to front** (ESP BRIT) 前后倒置 ▷ You've got your T-shirt on back to front. 你把T恤衫前后穿反了。

▸ **back away** VI 向后退 [xiàng hòu tuì]
▸ **back down** VI 做出让步 [zuòchū ràngbù]
▸ **back off** VI (draw back) 退避 [tuìbì]
▸ **back onto** VT FUS [不可拆分] 背靠 [bèikào]
▸ **back out** VI (withdraw) 退出 [tuìchū] ▸ **to back out of sth** [+ deal, agreement etc] 退出某事
▸ **back up** I VT **1** (support) [+ statement, theory etc] 证实 [zhèngshí] ▷ Her views are backed up by an official report on crime. 一份官方犯罪报告证实了她的观点。 **2** (provide alibi for) [+ friend, accomplice] 为…作证 [wèi…zuòzhèng] ▷ The girl denied being there, and the man backed her up. 女孩否定当时在那里，男子为她作了证。 **3** (help) [+ person] 支持 [zhīchí] ▷ His employers backed him up. 他的雇主支持他。 **4** (COMPUT) [+ disk] 备份 [bèifèn] **5** (reverse) [+ car] 倒 [dào] II VI (reverse) [person, car +] 倒行 [dàoxíng]

backache ['bækeɪk] N [c/u] 背痛 [bèitòng]

backbone ['bækbəun] N **1** [c] 脊椎骨 [jǐzhuīgǔ] **2** [u] (courage) 骨气 [gǔqì] **3** [s] (key person) 中坚 [zhōngjiān]

backfire [bæk'faɪə(r)] VI **1** [plan +] 事与愿违
[shì yǔ yuàn wéi] **2** [car, engine +] 回火
[huíhuǒ]

backgammon ['bækgæmən] N [U] 十五子棋
[shíwǔzǐqí]

background ['bækgraund] I N **1** [c] [of
picture, scene, events] 背景 [bèijǐng] **2** [c/U] [of
person] (origins) 出身 [chūshēn]; (experience) 经
验 [jīngyàn] II CPD [复合词] [+ noise, music,
information] 背景 [bèijǐng] ▸ **in the background**
在背后 ▸ **family background** 家庭出身
▸ **background reading** 辅助材料阅读

backing ['bækɪŋ] N **1** [U] (support) 支持
[zhīchí]; (financial) 资助 [zīzhù] **2** [c] (layer) 背
衬 [bèichèn] **3** [c] (MUS) 伴奏音乐 [bànzòu
yīnyuè]

backlog ['bæklɒg] N [c] 积压 [jīyā]

backpack ['bækpæk] N [c] 双肩背包
[shuāngjiān bēibāo]

backpacker ['bækpækə(r)] N [c] 背包旅行者
[bēibāo lǚxíngzhě]

> ■ **BACKPACKER**
>
> **backpacker** 一词指预算紧张的青年旅行
> 者。他们把全部的随身物品放在一个背包
> 里,尽可能地节俭开支,为的是能延长旅
> 行时间多了解一个地区,多看一些地方。

backside ['bæksaɪd] (inf) N [c] 屁股 [pìgu]

backslash ['bækslæʃ] N [c] 后斜线
[hòuxiéxiàn]

backstage [bæk'steɪdʒ] ADV 后台 [hòutái]

backstroke ['bækstrəuk] N [U] (also: the
backstroke) 仰泳 [yǎngyǒng]

backup ['bækʌp] I ADJ **1** [+ staff, services] 备
用的 [bèiyòng de] **2** (COMPUT) [+ copy, file, disk]
备份的 [bèifèn de] II N **1** [U] (support) 支持
[zhīchí] **2** [c] (reserve) 备份 [bèifèn]

backward ['bækwəd] I ADJ **1** [+ glance,
movement] 向后的 [xiàng hòu de] **2** (pej)
[+ country] 落后的 [luòhòu de]; [+ person] 迟钝
的 [chídùn de] II ADV (ESP US) = **backwards** ▸ **a
backward step** (fig) 倒退

backwards ['bækwədz] ADV **1** [move, look +] 向
后地 [xiàng hòu de] **2** (in reverse) [count, work +]
倒着地 [dàozhe de] **3** (fig) 倒退地 [dàotuì de]
▷ Technologically, this is a step backwards. 技术上
这是个退步。 **4** (in time) 向后地 [xiàng hòu
de] ▸ **to move backwards and forwards** 来
回移动 ▸ **to know sth backwards backward
and forward** or (US) **backward and forward** 极
熟悉某事

backyard [bæk'jɑːd] N [c] [of house] 后院
[hòuyuàn]

bacon ['beɪkən] N [U] 腌猪肉 [yān zhūròu]

bacteria [bæk'tɪərɪə] NPL 细菌 [xìjūn]

◑ bad [bæd] ADJ **1** (not good) [+ weather, health,
conditions, temper] 坏的 [huài de]; [+ actor, driver]
不胜任的 [bù shèngrèn de]; [+ behaviour, habit]
不良的 [bùliáng de] **2** (wicked) [+ person] 恶的 [è
de] **3** (naughty) [+ child] 不听话的 [bù tīnghuà
de] **4** (serious) [+ mistake, accident, headache] 严重
的 [yánzhòng de] **5** (injured) [+ back, arm] 有病的
[yǒubìng de] **6** (rotten) [+ fruit, meat etc] 腐烂的
[fǔlàn de] ▸ **to be bad for sth/sb** 对某事/某物
有害 ▸ **to be bad at sth/at doing sth** 不擅长某
事/做某事 ▸ **to feel bad about sth** (guilty) 对某
事感到愧疚 ▸ **to feel bad that...** (guilty) 因…而
感到愧疚 ▸ **to go bad** [food, milk +] 变质 ▸ **to
go from bad to worse** 每况愈下 ▸ **not bad** 不
错 ▷ The wine wasn't bad. 这葡萄酒不错。 ▸ **too
bad!** 那没办法!

bade [bæd] PT of **bid**

badge [bædʒ] N [c] **1** (BRIT) (metal, cloth) 徽章
[huīzhāng] [美= **button**] **2** (fig) [of power etc] 象
征 [xiàngzhēng]

badger ['bædʒə(r)] I N [c] 獾 [huān] II VT 纠
缠 [jiūchán]

bad language N [U] 粗话 [cūhuà]

badly ['bædlɪ] ADV **1** (poorly) [work, play +] 不
令人满意地 [bù lìng rén mǎnyì de]; [+ dressed]
不得体地 [bù détǐ de] **2** (seriously) [+ damaged,
injured] 严重地 [yánzhòng de] ▸ **to think badly
of sb/sth** 认为某人/某事不好 ▸ **to reflect
badly on sb/sth** 对某人/某事有坏影响 ▸ **to
want/need sth badly** 非常想要/需要某物
▸ **to be badly off** (in a bad situation) 境况不好;
(financially) 穷困

badminton ['bædmɪntən] N [U] 羽毛球
[yǔmáoqiú]

bad-tempered [bæd'tɛmpəd] ADJ (by nature)
脾气坏的 [píqi huài de]; (on one occasion) 发脾
气的 [fā píqi de]
  ■用法参见 **angry**

baffle ['bæfl] VT (puzzle) 使困惑 [shǐ kùnhuò]

baffled ['bæfld] ADJ [+ expression] 困惑的
[kùnhuò de] ▸ **to be baffled (by sth)** (被某
事)困惑

bag [bæg] I N [c] **1** (made of paper, plastic,
with handle) 袋 [dài] **2** (suitcase) 行李箱
[xínglǐxiāng] **3** (handbag) 手袋 [shǒudài] **4** (pej,
inf) (woman) 讨厌的女人 [tǎoyàn de nǚrén]
II VT (BRIT: inf) (claim) 抢占 [qiǎngzhàn]
▸ **bags of** (BRIT: inf) (lots of) 许多 ▸ **to pack
one's bags** 准备离开 ▸ **to have bags under
one's eyes** 有眼袋 ▸ **it's in the bag** (inf) 稳
操胜券

baggage ['bægɪdʒ] N [U] **1** (luggage) 行李
[xíngli] **2** (fig) 累赘 [léizhuì]

baggage allowance N [c] (at airport) 行李限
重 [xíngli xiànzhòng]

baggage (re)claim N [U] (at airport) 行李领
取 [xíngli lǐngqǔ]

baggy ['bægɪ] ADJ [+ suit, trousers, sweater] 宽松
的 [kuānsōng de]

bagpipes ['bægpaɪps] NPL 风笛 [fēngdí]

● **BAGPIPES**

● **bagpipes**，风笛，是一种您能让人联想起
苏格兰的古老乐器。演奏者，即 **pipers**，
通过一根管子把气吹到一个袋子里，然后
挤压袋子把气送出其他管子，使发出嗡
嗡的响声。风笛能制造出浓郁的婚礼和
官方庆典活动的气氛。乐手们盛装起来，
身着代表苏格兰不同家族图案的传统褶皱
短裙。现场观看这样的风笛军乐队演奏
蔚为壮观。

bail [beɪl] I N [U] (LAW) (payment) 保释金
[bǎoshìjīn]; (release) 保释 [bǎoshì] II VT
[+ prisoner] 准许保释 [zhǔnxǔ bǎoshì] III VI
(also: **bail out**) (on boat) 舀出 [yǎochū] ▸ grant
bail (to) [+ prisoner] 准许保释 ▸ on bail
[+ prisoner] 保释中 ▸ to be released on bail 被
保释
▸ **bail out** VT 1 [+ prisoner] 保释 [bǎoshì]
2 (fig) [+ firm, industry] 使摆脱困境 [shǐ bǎituō
kùnjìng]; [+ friend] 帮助…摆脱困境 [bāngzhù…
bǎituō kùnjìng]

bait [beɪt] I N [U/S] 1 (for fish) 鱼饵 [yú'ěr]
2 (for animal) 诱饵 [yòu'ěr] 3 (fig) (for criminal
etc) 引诱物 [yǐnyòu wù] II VT 1 [+ hook, trap] 放
诱饵于 [fàng yòu'ěr yú] 2 (tease) [+ person] 侮
弄 [wǔnòng]

bake [beɪk] I VT 1 [+ potatoes, cake, bread] 烤
[kǎo] 2 [+ clay] 烤硬 [kǎo yìng] II VI 1 [+ bread,
cake etc +] 烤 [kǎo] 2 (make cakes etc) [person +]
烘烤食品 [hōngkǎo shípǐn]
▨用法参见 **cook**

baked beans [beɪkt-] NPL (BRIT) (beans) 烘豆
[hōngdòu]; (US) (with pork) 有肉的烘豆 [yǒu ròu
de hōngdòu]

baked potato N [C] 烤土豆 [kǎo tǔdòu]

baker ['beɪkə(r)] N [C] 1 (person) 面包师
[miànbāoshī] 2 (shop) (also: **baker's**) 面包店
[miànbāodiàn]

bakery ['beɪkərɪ] N [C] 面包房 [miànbāofáng]

baking ['beɪkɪŋ] I N [U] 1 (activity) 烤食品 [kǎo
shípǐn] 2 (cakes, bread) 烘烤的面食 [hōngkǎo
de miànshí] II ADJ (inf) (hot) 灼热的 [zhuórè
de] ▸ **baking hot** 炎热

baking powder N [U] 发酵粉 [fājiàofěn]

balance ['bæləns] I N 1 [U] (equilibrium) [of
person, object] 平衡 [pínghéng] 2 [U/S] (fig) (in
situation) 平衡 [pínghéng] 3 [C] (in bank account)
余额 [yú'é] 4 [S] (remainder to be paid) 余欠之数
[yúqiàn zhī shù] II VT 1 [+ object] 使平衡 [shǐ
pínghéng] 2 [+ budget, account] 使收支平衡
[shǐ shōuzhī pínghéng] 3 [+ pros and cons] 权
衡 [quánhéng] 4 (compensate for) 弥补 [míbǔ]
5 (make equal) 等量齐观 [děng liàng qí guān]
III VI [person, object +] 保持平衡 [bǎochí

pínghéng] ▸ to keep/lose one's balance 保
持/失去平衡 ▸ off balance 失去平衡 ▸ to
hang in the balance 悬而未决 ▸ on balance
总的来看 ▸ balance of payments 国际收
支差额 ▸ balance of trade 进出口贸易差
额 ▸ balance carried forward 余额转下页
▸ balance brought forward 余额承前页 ▸ to
balance the books 平衡收支

balanced ['bælənst] ADJ 1 (unbiased) [+ report]
不偏不倚的 [bù piān bù yǐ de] 2 [+ diet] 均
衡的 [jūnhéng de] 3 (calm) [+ person] 平和的
[pínghé de]

balance sheet N [C] 资产负债表 [zīchǎn
fùzhài biǎo]

balcony ['bælkənɪ] N [C] 1 [of building] (open) 露
台 [lùtái]; (covered) 阳台 [yángtái] 2 (in cinema,
theatre) 楼座 [lóuzuò]

bald [bɔːld] ADJ 1 [+ head, person] 秃的 [tū de]
2 [+ tyre] 严重磨损的 [yánzhòng mósǔn de]
3 [+ statement] 直截了当的 [zhíjié-liǎodàng de]
▸ to go bald 变秃

ball [bɔːl] I N [C] 1 (football, golf ball etc) 球 [qiú]
2 [of wool, string] 团 [tuán] 3 (sphere) 球状
[qiúzhuàng] 4 (dance) 舞会 [wǔhuì] 5 [of foot,
thumb] 球形部分 [qiúxíng bùfen] II VT (also:
ball up) [+ paper, cloth] 把…抟成团 [bǎ…tuán
chéng tuán] ▸ to start or get or set the ball
rolling 开始 ▸ to play ball (with sb) (inf) (fig)
(与某人) 协作 ▸ to be on the ball 敏锐 ▸ the
ball is in your court 轮到你了 ▸ to have a ball
(inf) 过得愉快

ballerina [bælə'riːnə] N [C] 芭蕾舞女演员
[bāléiwǔ nǚ yǎnyuán]

ballet ['bæleɪ, US bæ'leɪ] N 1 [U] (art form) 芭
蕾舞 [bāléiwǔ] 2 [C] (particular work) 芭蕾舞剧
[bāléiwǔ jù]

ballet dancer N [C] 芭蕾舞演员 [bāléiwǔ
yǎnyuán]

balloon [bə'luːn] I N [C] 1 (child's) 气球 [qìqiú]
2 (also: **hot-air balloon**) 热气球 [rèqìqiú] II VI
(increase in size) 膨胀 [péngzhàng]

ballot ['bælət] I N [C] (vote) 无记名投票
[wújìmíng tóupiào] II VT [+ group] 使投票表决
[shǐ tóupiào biǎojué]

ballpoint (pen) ['bɔːlpɔɪnt(-)] N [C] 圆珠笔
[yuánzhūbǐ]

ballroom ['bɔːlrum] N [C] 舞厅 [wǔtīng]

ballroom dancing N [U] 交际舞 [jiāojìwǔ]

Baltic ['bɔːltɪk] N ▸ the Baltic (Sea) 波罗的海
[Bōluódì Hǎi]

bamboo [bæm'buː] N [U] 1 (plant) 竹子 [zhúzi]
2 (material) 竹 [zhú]

bamboo shoots NPL 竹笋 [zhúsǔn]

ban [bæn] I N [C] (prohibition) 禁止 [jìnzhǐ]
II VT (prohibit) 禁止 [jìnzhǐ] ▸ to be banned
from driving 被禁止开车

banana [bə'nɑːnə] N [C] 香蕉 [xiāngjiāo]

band [bænd] I N [C] 1 (group) [of supporters,

helpers, rebels etc] 群 [qún] **2** (MUS) (jazz, rock etc) 乐队 [yuèduì]; (military) 军乐队 [jūnyuèduì] **3** (strip) [of cloth] 带子 [dàizi]; [of light, land] 条 纹 [tiáowén] **4** (loop) [of metal, material] 箍 [gū] **5** (range) 幅度 [fúdù] II VT (BRIT) [+ tax] 划分级 别 [huàfēn jíbié] 〔美=**bracket**〕
▶ **band together** VI 联合 [liánhé]

bandage ['bændɪdʒ] I N [c] 绷带 [bēngdài] II VT [+ wound, leg] 用绷带包扎 [yòng bēngdài bāozhā]

Band-Aid® ['bændeɪd] (US) N [c] 邦迪创可贴 [Bāngdí chuàngkětiē] 〔英=**plaster**〕

B & B N ABBR = **bed and breakfast**

bandit ['bændɪt] N [c] 强盗 [qiángdào]

bang [bæŋ] I N [c] **1** (noise) [of door] 砰的一 声 [pēng de yīshēng]; [of gun, exhaust] 爆炸 声 [bàozhà shēng] **2** (blow) 撞击 [zhuàngjī] II INT 砰 [pēng] III VT **1** [+ door] 砰地一声 关上 [pēng de yīshēng guānshang] **2** (also: **bang on**) [+ wall, drum etc] 大声撞击 [dàshēng zhuàngjī] **3** [+ one's head, elbow etc] 撞 [zhuàng] IV VI **1** [door +] 砰地关上 [pēng de guānshang] **2** [firework, engine +] 砰砰作响 [pēng pēng zuò xiǎng] V ADV ▶ **to be bang on time/in the middle** (inf) 正准时/当中 [zhèng zhǔnshí/ dāngzhōng] VI **bangs** NPL (US) (fringe) 刘海 [liúhǎi] 〔英=**fringe**〕 ▶ **to bang into sth/sb** 猛 撞某物/某人

Bangladesh [bæŋglə'dɛʃ] N 孟加拉国 [Mèngjiālāguó]

bangle ['bæŋgl] N [c] (bracelet) 镯 [zhuó]

banish ['bænɪʃ] VT (exile) 放逐 [fàngzhú]

banister(s) ['bænɪstə(z)] NPL 楼梯扶手 [lóutī fúshǒu]

banjo ['bændʒəu] (pl **banjoes** or **banjos**) N [c] 班卓琴 [bānzhuóqín]

⊙ **bank** [bæŋk] N [c] **1** (FIN) (building, institution) 银行 [yínháng] **2** [of data] 库 [kù] **3** [of river, lake] 岸 [àn] **4** [of earth] 斜坡 [xiépō] **5** [of fog] 一堆 [yī duī] **6** [of switches, dials] 排 [pái] II VI **1** [plane +] 倾斜飞行 [qīngxié fēixíng] **2** (COMM) ▶ **to bank with** 在…有银行账户 [zài…yǒu yínháng zhànghù]
▶ **bank on** VT FUS [不可拆分] (rely on) 指望 [zhǐwang]

bank account N [c] 银行账户 [yínháng zhànghù]

bank balance N [c] 银行存款余额 [yínháng cúnkuǎn yú'é]

bank card N [c] **1** (BRIT) (for cash machine) 银行 卡 [yínhángkǎ] 〔美=**ATM card**〕 **2** (US) (credit card) 银行信用卡 [yínháng xìnyòngkǎ]

banker ['bæŋkə(r)] N [c] 银行家 [yínhángjiā]

bank holiday (BRIT) N [c] 法定假期 [fǎdìng jiàqī] 〔美=**national holiday**〕

banking ['bæŋkɪŋ] N [U] 银行业 [yínhángyè]

banknote ['bæŋknəut] N [c] 纸币 [zhǐbì]

bankrupt ['bæŋkrʌpt] I ADJ **1** [+ person,

company] 破产的 [pòchǎn de] **2** (fig) ▶ **morally bankrupt** 道德沦丧的 [dàodé lúnsàng de] II N [c] [+ person] 破产者 [pòchǎnzhě] III VT [+ person, organization] 使破产 [shǐ pòchǎn] ▶ **to go bankrupt** 破产 ▶ **to be made bankrupt** 宣 告破产

bankruptcy ['bæŋkrʌptsɪ] N **1** [U] (lit) 破 产 [pòchǎn] **2** [c] (particular instance) 破产 [pòchǎn] **3** [U] (fig) 完全缺乏 [wánquán quēfá]

bank statement N [c] 银行结单 [yínháng jiédān]

banner ['bænə(r)] N [c] **1** (for decoration, advertising) 横幅 [héngfú] **2** (carried in a demonstration) 横幅标语 [héngfú biāoyǔ]

bannister(s) ['bænɪstə(z)] NPL = **banister(s)**

banquet ['bæŋkwɪt] N [c] 盛宴 [shèngyàn]

baptism ['bæptɪzəm] N [c/U] 洗礼 [xǐlǐ]

⊙ **BAPTISM**

baptism，洗礼，是一种基督教仪式。牧 师把水浇在受洗人额头上，或把受洗人浸 在水中，以示其罪已得到原谅，或已成为 该教堂的一员。实际上，这种仪式与新生 儿正式命名 (**christened**) 同时进行。

baptize [bæp'taɪz] VT 给…施行洗礼 [gěi…shīxíng xǐlǐ]

⊙ **bar** [bɑ:(r)] I N [c] **1** (place for drinking) 酒吧 [jiǔbā] **2** (counter) (in pub) 吧台 [bātái] **3** (rod) [of metal etc] 条 [tiáo] **4** (on window, in prison) 铁 栏杆 [tiě lángān] **5** (tablet) [of soap, chocolate] 块 [kuài] **6** (fig) (obstacle) 障碍 [zhàng'ài] **7** (ESP BRIT: MUS) 小节线 [xiǎojiéxiàn] 〔美= **measure**〕 **8** (LAW) ▶ **the Bar** (profession) 律师 业 [lùshīyè] II VT **1** [+ way, road] 阻挡 [zǔdǎng] **2** [+ door, window] 闩上 [shuānshang] **3** [+ person, activity] 禁止 [jìnzhǐ] ▶ **to be behind bars** [prisoner +] 坐牢 ▶ **no holds barred** 竭尽全力 ▶ **bar none** 无例外

barbaric [bɑ:'bærɪk] ADJ 野蛮的 [yěmán de]

barbecue ['bɑ:bɪkju:] I N [c] **1** (cooking device) 烤肉架 [kǎoròu jià] **2** (meal, party) 烧烤聚会 [shāokǎo jùhuì] II VT 烧烤 [shāokǎo]

barbed wire ['bɑ:bd-] N [U] 有刺铁丝 [yǒu cì tiěsī]

barber ['bɑ:bə(r)] N [c] **1** (person) 男理发师 [nán lǐfàshī] **2** (BRIT) (shop) ▶ **barber's** 男子理发店 [nánzǐ lǐfàdiàn] 〔美=**barber shop**〕

barber shop N [c] 男子理发店 [nánzǐ lǐfà diàn]

bar code N [c] 条形码 [tiáoxíngmǎ]

bare [bɛə(r)] I ADJ **1** (naked) [+ body, feet] 裸露 的 [luǒlù de] **2** (not covered) [+ rock, floor] 光秃的 [guāngtū de] **3** (empty) [+ cupboard, shelf, room] 空的 [kōng de] **4** [+ minimum, essentials] 基本 的 [jīběn de] II VT (reveal) [+ one's body, teeth] 露 出 [lùchū] ▶ **with one's bare hands** 赤手空拳

▶ **to bare one's soul** 诉说衷肠

barefoot(ed) ['bɛəfʊt(ɪd)] I ADJ 赤脚的 [chìjiǎo de] II ADV 赤脚地 [chìjiǎo de]

barely ['bɛəlɪ] ADV (scarcely) 几乎不 [jīhū bù]

bargain ['bɑːgɪn] I N [c] **1** (good buy) 廉价品 [liánjiàpǐn] **2** (deal, agreement) 协议 [xiéyì] II VI **1** (negotiate) ▶ **to bargain (with sb)** (与某人) 谈判 [(yǔ mǒurén) tánpàn] **2** (haggle) (与某人) 讨价还价 [(yǔ mǒurén) tǎo jià huán jià] ▶ **to drive a hard bargain** 极力讨价还价 ▶ **into the bargain** 此外
　▶ **bargain for, bargain on** VT FUS [不可拆分] 预料 [yùliào]

barge [bɑːdʒ] N [c] (boat) 驳船 [bóchuán]
　▶ **barge in** (inf) VI **1** (enter) 闯进 [chuǎng jìn] **2** (interrupt) 打断 [dǎduàn]
　▶ **barge into** (inf) VT FUS [不可拆分] **1** [+ room] 闯入 [chuǎng rù] **2** (bump into) [+ person] 碰撞 [pèngzhuàng]

bark [bɑːk] I N **1** [U] [of tree] 树皮 [shùpí] **2** [c] [of dog] 犬吠声 [quǎnfèishēng] II VI [dog +] 叫 [jiào] ▶ **she's barking up the wrong tree** (inf) 她搞错了对象

barley ['bɑːlɪ] N [U] 大麦 [dàmài]

barmaid ['bɑːmeɪd] (ESP BRIT) N [c] 酒吧女侍 [jiǔbā nǚshì] [美= **bartender**]

barman ['bɑːmən] (pl **barmen**) (ESP BRIT) N [c] 酒吧男侍 [jiǔbā nánshì] [美= **bartender**]

barn [bɑːn] N [c] 仓房 [cāngfáng]

barometer [bə'rɒmɪtə(r)] N [c] 晴雨表 [qíngyǔbiǎo]

baron ['bærən] N [c] 男爵 [nánjué] ▶ **press/ drug baron** 报业/毒品大王

baroness ['bærənɪs] N [c] (wife of baron) 男爵夫人 [nánjué fūrén]; (in own right) 女男爵 [nǚ nánjué]

barracks ['bærəks] (pl **barracks**) N [c] 营房 [yíngfáng]

barrage ['bærɑːʒ] N [c] **1** (MIL) 火力网 [huǒlìwǎng] **2** (dam) 拦河坝 [lánhébà] **3** (fig) [of criticism, questions etc] 连珠炮 [liánzhūpào]

barrel ['bærəl] N [c] **1** (cask) [of wine, beer] 桶 [tǒng]; [of oil] 琵琶桶 [pípátǒng] **2** [of gun] 枪管 [qiāngguǎn]

barren ['bærən] ADJ **1** (infertile) [+ land] 不毛的 [bùmáo de] **2** (bare) [+ landscape] 贫瘠的 [pínjí de] **3** (fig) [+ spell, patch] 无成效的 [wú chéngxiào de]

barricade ['bærɪkeɪd] I N [c] 路障 [lùzhàng] II VT [+ road, entrance] 在…设路障 [zài…shè lùzhàng] ▶ **to barricade oneself in** 把自己关在里面

barrier ['bærɪə(r)] N [c] **1** (at frontier, entrance) 关口 [guānkǒu] **2** (BRIT) (also: **crash barrier**) 护栏 [hùlán] **3** (to progress, communication etc) 障碍 [zhàng'ài]

barring ['bɑːrɪŋ] PREP 除非 [chúfēi]

barrister ['bærɪstə(r)] (BRIT) N [c] 律师 [lùshī]

barrow ['bærəu] N [c] **1** (also: **wheelbarrow**) 手推车 [shǒutuīchē] **2** (BRIT) (for selling fruit, vegetables etc) 手推双轮车 [shǒu tuī shuānglúnchē]

bartender ['bɑːtɛndə(r)] (US) N [c] 酒吧侍者 [jiǔbā shìzhě] [英= **barman, barmaid**]

⊙ **base** [beɪs] I N [c] **1** (bottom) [of post, tree] 底部 [dǐbù] ▷ the base of the cliffs 悬崖的底部; [of cup, vase] 底座 [dǐzuò] **2** (layer) [of paint, make up] 底 [dǐ] ▷ Use this paint as a base before you varnish. 在你上清漆前，先用这种漆作为底漆。 **3** (BASEBALL) 垒 [lěi] **4** (basis) 根基 [gēnjī] **5** (centre) (military) 基地 [jīdì] ▷ an army base 军事基地; (for individual, organization) 总部 [zǒngbù] ▷ The company has its base in London. 该公司的总部设在伦敦。 II VT ▶ **to base sth on or upon sth** 以某物作为某物的根据 [yǐ mǒuwù zuòwéi mǒuwù de gēnjù] III ADJ (liter) [+ mind, thoughts] 卑鄙的 [bēibǐ de] ▶ **to be based on sth** 以某物为根据 ▶ **to be based at** [troops, employee +] 以…为基地 ▶ **I'm based in London** 我长驻伦敦

baseball ['beɪsbɔːl] N **1** [U] (sport) 棒球 [bàngqiú] ▷ He likes baseball. 他喜欢棒球。 **2** [c] (ball) 棒球 [bàngqiú] ▷ Each box contains five baseballs. 每个盒子里装有5个棒球。

basement ['beɪsmənt] I N [c] 地下室 [dìxiàshì] II ADJ [+ flat, apartment, kitchen etc] 地下室的 [dìxiàshì de]

bases¹ ['beɪsɪz] N PL of **base**

bases² ['beɪsiːz] N PL of **basis**

bash [bæʃ] (inf) I VT (hit) 猛击 [měngjī] II VI (crash) ▶ **to bash into/against sth/sb** 猛撞某物/某人 [měngzhuàng mǒuwù/mǒurén] III N [c] **1** (party) 聚会 [jùhuì] **2** (BRIT) (try) ▶ **to have a bash (at sth/at doing sth)** 尝试(某事/做某事) [chángshì (mǒushì/zuò mǒushì)]
　▶ **bash up** VT (BRIT) (beat up) 痛打 [tòngdǎ]

basic ['beɪsɪk] ADJ **1** [+ principle, rule, right] 基本的 [jīběn de] **2** (primitive) [+ facilities] 根本的 [gēnběn de] see also **basics**

basically ['beɪsɪklɪ] ADV **1** (fundamentally) 基本上 [jīběnshang] **2** (in fact, put simply) 简而言之 [jiǎn ér yán zhī]

basics ['beɪsɪks] N PL ▶ **the basics** 基本点 [jīběndiǎn]

basil ['bæzl] N [U] 罗勒属植物 [luólè shǔ zhíwù]

basin ['beɪsn] N [c] **1** (bowl) 盆 [pén] **2** (also: **wash basin**) 洗脸盆 [xǐliǎnpén] **3** [of river, lake] 流域 [liúyù]

basis ['beɪsɪs] (pl **bases**) N [c] **1** (starting point) 基础 [jīchǔ] **2** (foundation) 根据 [gēnjù] ▶ **on a voluntary basis** 基于自愿 ▶ **on a regular basis** 定期 ▶ **on the basis of what you've said** 根据你所说的话

basket ['bɑːskɪt] N [c] **1** (container) 筐 [kuāng] **2** (in basketball) 球篮 [qiúlán]

basketball ['bɑːskɪtbɔːl] N **1** [U] (sport) 篮球

[lánqiú] **2** [c] (ball) 篮球 [lánqiú]

bass [beɪs] (MUS) N **1** [c] (singer) 男低音 [nándīyīn] **2** [U] (part) 低音部 [dīyīnbù] **3** [c/U] (also: **bass guitar**) 低音吉他 [dīyīn jítā] **4** [U] (on radio, music system etc) 低音 [dīyīn]

bastard ['bɑːstəd] N [c] **1** (inf!) 王八蛋 [wángbā dàn] **2** (o.f.) (illegitimate offspring) 私生子 [sīshēngzǐ]

bat [bæt] I N [c] **1** (animal) 蝙蝠 [biānfú] **2** (for cricket, baseball) 球板/棒 [qiúbǎn/bàng] **3** (BRIT) (for table tennis) 球拍 [qiúpāi] [美= **paddle**] II VI (CRICKET, BASEBALL) 用板/棒 击球 [yòngbǎn bàng jīqiú] III VT ▸ **he didn't bat an eyelid** or (US) **eye** 他未露声色 [tā wèilù shēngsè] ▸ **off one's own bat** (BRIT) 独立地 做某事

batch [bætʃ] N [c] (of letters, papers, applicants, goods) 批 [pī]

bath [bɑːθ] I N [c] **1** (BRIT) (bathtub) 浴缸 [yùgāng] [美= **bathtub**] **2** (act of bathing) 洗 澡 [xǐzǎo] II VT (BRIT) (+ baby, patient) 给…洗 澡 [gěi…xǐzǎo] [美= **bathe**] III **baths** NPL (swimming pool) 室内公共游泳池 [shìnèi gōnggòng yóuyǒngchí] ▸ **to have** or **take a bath** 洗澡

bathe [beɪð] I VI **1** (ESP BRIT) (frm) (swim) 戏 水 [xìshuǐ] **2** (ESP US) (have a bath) 洗澡 [xǐzǎo] II VT **1** (+ wound) 清洗 [qīngxǐ] **2** (US) (+ baby, patient) 给…洗澡 [gěi…xǐzǎo] [英= **bath**] **3** (fig) (in light, warmth) 笼罩 [lǒngzhào]

bathing ['beɪðɪŋ] (ESP BRIT) (frm) N [U] 游泳 [yóuyǒng]

bathing costume (BRIT) N = **bathing suit**

bathing suit N [c] 游泳衣 [yóuyǒngyī]

bathrobe ['bɑːθrəub] N [c] 浴衣 [yùyī]

bathroom ['bɑːθrum] N [c] **1** (in house) 卫生间 [wèishēngjiān] **2** (US) (toilet) 厕所 [cèsuǒ] [英= **toilet**] ▸ **to go to the bathroom** (US) 去卫生间

bath towel N [c] 浴巾 [yùjīn]

bathtub ['bɑːθtʌb] (US) N [c] 浴缸 [yùgāng] [英= **bath**]

baton ['bætən, US bə'tɑːn] N [c] **1** (MUS) 指挥棒 [zhǐhuībàng] **2** (in athletics) 接力棒 [jiēlìbàng] **3** (BRIT) (truncheon) 警棍 [jǐnggùn]

batter ['bætə(r)] I VT **1** (+ child, wife) 连续猛打 [liánxù měngdǎ] **2** (wind, rain +) 吹打 [chuīdǎ] II N [U] (CULIN) 奶蛋面糊 [nǎidàn miànhú]

battered ['bætəd] ADJ **1** (+ wife, child) 受虐的 [shòunüè de] **2** (+ suitcase, car) 破旧不堪的 [pòjiù bùkān de]

battery ['bætərɪ] N [c] **1** (for torch, radio etc) 电 池 [diànchí] **2** (in car) 电瓶 [diànpíng] **3** [of tests] 一连串 [yīliánchuàn] **4** [of cameras, lights] 电池 组 [diànchízǔ]

battle ['bætl] I N [c] **1** (MIL) 战役 [zhànyì] **2** (fig) (struggle) 斗争 [dòuzhēng] II VI **1** (fight) 交战 [jiāozhàn] **2** (struggle) ▸ **to battle for sth/ to do sth** 力争某事/做某事 [lìzhēng mǒushì/

zuò mǒushì] **3** (compete) ▸ **to battle (with sb) for sth/to do sth** (与某人)争夺某物/争做某 事 [(yǔ mǒurén) zhēngduó mǒuwù/zhēngzuò mǒushì] ▸ **that's half the battle** 那是成功的 一半 ▸ **it's a** or **we're fighting a losing battle** 这/我们注定要失败 ▸ **to do battle (with sb)** (fight) (与某人)交战; (compete) (与某人)争 高下

battlefield ['bætlfiːld] N [c] 战场 [zhànchǎng]

bay [beɪ] I N [c] **1** (GEO) 湾 [wān] **2** (for loading, parking etc) 隔间 [géjiān] II ADJ (+ horse) 红棕 色的 [hóngzōngsè de] ▸ **to hold** or **keep sb/sth at bay** 不让某人/某物接近

bazaar [bə'zɑː(r)] N [c] **1** (market) 市场 [shìchǎng] **2** (fete) 义卖市场 [yìmài shìchǎng]

BBC N ABBR (= **British Broadcasting Corporation**) ▸ **the BBC** 英国广播公司 [Yīngguó Guǎngbō Gōngsī]

BC ADV ABBR (= **before Christ**) 公元前 [gōngyuán qián]

○

be [biː] (pt **was, were**, pp **been**) I VI **1** (with complement) 是 [shì] ▸ **I'm English/Chinese** 我是英国人/中国人 ▸ **she's tall/pretty** 她 长得高/漂亮 ▸ **I'm tired/hot** 我累了/很 热 ▸ **she's hungry/thirsty** 她饿了/渴了 ▸ **your hair's wet** 你的头发湿了 ▸ **he's a doctor** 他是医生 ▸ **this is my mother** 这 是我妈妈 ▸ **who is it?** 是谁啊? ▸ **it's only me/the postman** 是我/邮递员啊 ▸ **it was Diana who paid the bill** 是黛安娜付 的账单 ▸ **2 and 2 are 4** 2加2等于4 ▸ **be careful/quiet!** 当心/安静!

2 (referring to time, date) 是 [shì] ▸ **it's 5 o'clock** 现在是5点钟 ▸ **it's the 28th of April, it's April 28th** 今天是4月28日

3 (describing weather) ▸ **it's hot/cold** 天 热/冷 [tiān rè/lěng] ▸ **it's foggy/wet** 天有 雾/天气潮湿 ▸ **it's windy today** 今天有风

4 (talking about health) ▸ **how are you?** 你身 体怎么样? [nǐ shēntǐ zěnmeyàng?] ▸ **I'm fine, thanks** 我很好, 谢谢 ▸ **I'm better now** 我现在好多了

5 (talking about age) 有 [yǒu] ▸ **how old are you?** 你多大了? ▸ **I'm 16 (years old)** 我 16(岁) ▸ **I'll be 18 on Friday** 星期五我就 18岁了

6 (talking about place) 在 [zài] ▸ **Madrid is in Spain** 马德里在西班牙 ▸ **it's on the table** 在桌上 ▸ **the supermarket isn't far from here** 超市离这儿不远 ▸ **I won't be here tomorrow** 我明天不在这儿 ▸ **have you been to Beijing?** 你去过北京吗? ▸ **we've been here for ages** 我们已经在这里好久 了 ▸ **where have you been?** 你去哪儿了? ▸ **has the postman been yet?** 邮递员来过 了吗? ▸ **the meeting will be in the canteen**

会议将在食堂举行

7 (*referring to distance*) 有 [yǒu] ▶ **it's 10 km to the village** 这儿离村庄有10公里 ▶ **it's 20 miles from here to London** 从这儿到伦敦有20英里

8 (*cost*) 花 [huā] ▶ **how much was the meal?** 这顿饭花了多少钱? ▶ **that'll be £5 please** 请付5英镑 ▶ **these trousers are only £30** 这条裤子仅仅30英镑

9 (*linking clauses*) 是 [shì] ▶ **the problem is that...** 问题是… ▶ **the fact is that...** 事实是…

10 (*exist, occur etc*) 存在 [cúnzài] ▶ **the best singer that ever was** 曾经有过的最好的歌手 ▶ **is there a God?** 存在上帝吗? ▶ **be that as it may** 即使如此

11 (*assessing a situation*) ▶ **it is likely that he'll resign** 很可能他将辞职 [hěn kěnéng tā jiāng cízhí] ▶ **it is difficult for me to complain** 我很难抱怨

II AUX VB **1** (*forming continuous tenses*) ▶ **what are you doing?** 你在干什么? [nǐ zài gàn shénme?] ▶ **it is raining** 天下着雨 ▶ **people are using their cars too much** 人们正在过多地使用汽车 ▶ **they're coming tomorrow** 他们明天来

2 (*forming passives*) ▶ **to be murdered** 被谋杀 [bèi móushā] ▶ **he was killed in a car crash** 他在一场车祸中丧生 ▶ **the building was designed by a famous architect** 这座建筑由一位著名的建筑师设计 ▶ **the box had been opened** 盒子已被打开了

3 (*with "to" infinitive*) ▶ **the house is to be sold** 房子将要出售 [fángzi jiāng yào chūshòu] ▶ **what is to be done?** 我们该怎么办? ▶ **these flowers are to be found all over the country** 这些花在全国都能看到 ▶ **the thief was nowhere to be seen** 小偷不知去向

4 (*in tag questions*) ▶ **it was fun, wasn't it?** 有意思, 是不是? [yǒu yìsi, shì bù shì?] ▶ **it wasn't good timing, was it?** 时间选得不太好, 是不是? ▶ **he's good-looking, isn't he?** 他长得不错, 是不是? ▶ **so you're back again, are you?** 所以你又回来了, 是不是?

5 (*in short answers*) ▶ **"was it where I said?" - "yes, it was/no, it wasn't"** "就在我说的地方吗?""是/不是" [jiù zài wǒ shuō de dìfang ma?" "shì/bù shì"] ▶ **"you're all right, aren't you?" - "yes, I am/no, I'm not"** "你还好, 是不是?""是的, 我还好/不, 我不好"

beach [biːtʃ] **I** N [c] 海滩 [hǎitān] **II** VT [+ *boat*] 使靠岸 [shǐ kào'àn]

beacon [ˈbiːkən] N [c] **1** (*signal*) 信号灯 [xìnhàodēng] **2** (*fig*) 指路明灯 [zhǐlù]

míngdēng]

bead [biːd] **I** N [c] **1** (*glass, plastic etc*) 小珠子 [xiǎo zhūzi] **2** [*of sweat*] 滴 [dī] **II beads** NPL (*necklace*) 项链 [xiàngliàn]

beak [biːk] N [c] 鸟嘴 [niǎohuì]

beam [biːm] **I** N [c] **1** [*of wood, metal*] 梁 [liáng] **2** [*of light*] 束 [shù] **3** (RAD, PHYS) 射线 [shèxiàn] **II** VI **1** (*smile*) 喜形于色 [xǐ xíng yú sè] **2** (*shine*) 发光 [fāguāng] **III** VT [+ *signals, pictures*] 播送 [bōsòng] ▶ **to drive on full** *or* **main** *or* (US) **high beam** 驾车时, 前大灯都开着

bean [biːn] N [c] 豆 [dòu] ▶ **coffee/cocoa beans** 咖啡/可可豆

bean sprouts NPL 豆芽 [dòuyá]

bear [bɛə(r)] (*pt* **bore**, *pp* **borne**) **I** N [c] (*animal*) 熊 [xióng] **II** VT **1** (*liter*) (*carry*) [+ *object*] 携带 [xiédài] **2** (*support*) [+ *weight*] 支撑 [zhīchēng] **3** [+ *responsibility*] 承担 [chéngdān] **4** [+ *cost*] 负担 [fùdān] **5** (*tolerate*) [+ *person*] 容忍 [róngrěn] **6** (*endure*) 忍受 [rěnshòu] **7** (*show*) [+ *traces, signs*] 留有 [liúyǒu] **8** (*stand up to*) [+ *examination, scrutiny*] 经得起 [jīng de qǐ] **9** (*frm*) [+ *malice, ill will*] 心怀 [xīnhuái] **10** (COMM) [+ *interest, dividend*] 产生 [chǎnshēng] **11** (*o.f.*) [*woman* +] [+ *children*] 生育 [shēngyù] **12** [*plant* +] [+ *fruit*] 结出 [jiéchū] **III** VI ▶ **to bear right/left** (AUT) 向右/左转 [xiàng yòu/zuǒ zhuǎn] ▶ **to bear no resemblance/relation to** 与…无相似之处/没有关联 ▶ **to bring pressure/influence to bear on sb** 对某人施加压力/影响

▶ **bear down on** VT FUS [不可拆分] **1** (*move towards*) 冲向 [chōng xiàng] ▷ *The girl flashed a smile at the television crew and cameras bearing down on her.* 女孩冲着涌过来的电视工作人员和相机镜头微笑。 **2** (*press*) 压 [yā]

▶ **bear out** VT [+ *person, suspicions, claims*] 证实 [zhèngshí]

▶ **bear up** VI [*person* +] 挺得住 [tǐng de zhù] ▷ *He bore up well.* 他咬紧牙关坚持下来。

▶ **bear with** VT FUS [不可拆分] [+ *person*] 容忍 [róngrěn]

beard [bɪəd] N [c] 胡须 [húxū]

bearded [ˈbɪədɪd] ADJ 有胡须的 [yǒu húxū de]

bearer [ˈbɛərə(r)] N [c] **1** [*of letter, news*] 送信人 [sòngxìnrén] **2** (*frm*) [*of cheque, passport*] 持有人 [chíyǒurén]

bearing [ˈbɛərɪŋ] N **1** [U] (*frm*) (*posture*) 举止 [jǔzhǐ] **2** (*connection*) ▶ **to have a bearing on sth** 与某事有关系 [yǔ mǒushì yǒu guānxi] **3** [c] (TECH) 轴承 [zhóuchéng] ▶ **to get** *or* **find one's bearings** 确定自己的位置; (*fig*) 确定自己的方向 ▶ **to take a bearing** 判明位置

beast [biːst] N [c] **1** (*liter*) (*animal*) 野兽 [yěshòu] **2** (*o.f., inf*) (*person*) 野蛮的人 [yěmán de rén]

○ **beat** [biːt] (*pt* **beat**, *pp* **beaten**) **I** N [c] **1** [*of heart*] 跳动 [tiàodòng] **2** (MUS) (*rhythm*) 节拍 [jiépāi] **3** [*of policeman*] 巡逻区域 [xúnluó qūyù]

▷ *on the beat* 在巡逻 **II** VT **1** (*strike*) [+ *wife, child*] 打 [dǎ] ▷ *She was beaten to death.* 她被打死了。 **2** [+ *eggs, cream*] 搅 [jiǎo] **3** (*defeat*) [+ *opponent, record*] 击败 [jībài] ▷ *Arsenal beat Oxford United 5-1.* 阿森纳以5比1击败了牛津联合队。 **III** VI **1** [*heart* +] 跳动 [tiàodòng] **2** (*strike*) 拍打 [pāidǎ] ▷ *The rain beat against the window.* 雨水打在窗户上。 ▷ *Somebody was beating at the door.* 有人在用力敲门。 ▶ **to beat time** (MUS) 打拍子 ▶ **beat it!** (*inf*) 走开！ ▶ **you can't beat it** 什么也比不上它 ▶ **off the beaten track** 在人迹罕至之处
▶ **beat down I** VI **1** [*rain* +] 瓢泼而下 [piáopō ér xià] **2** [*sun* +] 曝晒 [pùshài] **II** VT [+ *seller*] 迫使…压低价格 [pòshǐ…yādī jiàgé]
▶ **beat off** VT [+ *attack, attacker*] 打退 [dǎtuì]
▶ **beat up** VT [+ *person*] 狠打 [hěn dǎ] ▶ **to beat oneself up about sth** (*inf*) 因某事而折磨自己

beaten ['bi:tn] PP *of* **beat**

beating ['bi:tɪŋ] N [c] (*physical*) 痛打 [tòngdǎ]
▶ **to take a beating** (*in contest*) 惨败 ▶ **that will take some beating** (*inf*) 难以超越

beautiful ['bju:tɪful] ADJ **1** [+ *woman, day, place, weather*] 美丽的 [měilì de] **2** [+ *shot, performance*] 精彩的 [jīngcǎi de]

当描写男人的外表时，女人、女孩和婴儿用 **beautiful** 和 **pretty** *one of the most beautiful women in the world…She's a very pretty little girl.*，**beautiful** 比 **pretty** 程度更深。与之相对，描写男人的词是 **handsome**。*He is still very handsome.* **good-looking** 和 **attractive** 可用于两性。

beautifully ['bju:tɪflɪ] ADV **1** [*play, sing etc* +] 极好地 [jíhǎo de] **2** [+ *quiet, written etc*] 令人满意地 [lìng rén mǎnyì de]

beauty ['bju:tɪ] **I** N **1** [U] (*quality*) 美 [měi] **2** [c] (*beautiful woman*) 美人 [měirén] **3** [c] (*fig*) (*attraction*) ▶ **the beauty of it is that…** 好处在于… [hǎochù zàiyú…] **II beauties** NPL (*liter*) 魅力 [mèilì]

beauty parlour, (US) **beauty parlor** N [c] 美容院 [měiróngyuàn]

beauty salon N = **beauty parlour**

beaver ['bi:və(r)] N [c] 海狸 [hǎilí]
▶ **beaver away** VI 勤奋工作 [qínfèn gōngzuò]
▶ **to beaver away at sth** 孜孜不倦地做某事

became [bɪ'keɪm] PT *of* **become**

○ **because** [bɪ'kɔz] CONJ 因为 [yīnwéi] ▷ *He did it because he was angry.* 他因为生气才那么做的。
▶ **because of** 因为

我们在解释一件事发生的原因时，可以使用 **because、as** 或 **since**。**because** 最为常用，并且是唯一可以回答以 **why** 提出的问题。*"Why can't you come?" – "Because I'm too busy."* 在引出含有原因的从句时，尤其是在书面语中，我们可以用 **as** 或 **since** 代替 **because**。*I was rather nervous, as I hadn't seen her for a long time…Since the juice is quite strong, you should always dilute it.*

beckon ['bekən] **I** VT [+ *person*] 招手 [zhāoshǒu] **II** VI **1** (*signal*) ▶ **to beckon (to sb)** (向某人)招手 [(xiàng mǒurén) zhāoshǒu] **2** (*fig*) 吸引 [xīyǐn]

○ **become** [bɪ'kʌm] (*pt* **became,** *pp* **become**) VI **1** (*noun*) 成为 [chéngwéi] ▷ *He became a professional footballer.* 他成了一名职业足球运动员。 **2** (*adj*) 变 [biàn] ▷ *The smell became stronger.* 气味变浓了。 ▶ **what has become of him?** 他的情况怎么样了？

BEd N ABBR (= *Bachelor of Education*) (*qualification*) 教育学学士学位 [jiàoyùxué xuéshì xuéwèi]; (*person*) 教育学学士 [jiàoyùxué xuéshì]

bed [bed] N [c] **1** (*piece of furniture*) 床 [chuáng] **2** (*bottom*) [*of river, sea*] 底部 [dǐbù] **3** [*of flowers*] 坛 [tán] ▷ *beds of strawberries and rhubarb* 一小片一小片的草莓和大黄 **4** [*of coal, clay*] 层 [céng] ▶ **to go to bed** 去睡觉 ▶ **to go to bed with sb** 与某人发生性关系
▶ **bed down** VI [*person* +] 过夜 [guòyè]

bed and breakfast N **1** [U] (*service*) 住宿加早餐 [zhùsù jiā zǎocān] **2** [c] (*guest house*) 兼包早餐的旅馆 [jiān bāo zǎocān de lǚguǎn]

bedclothes ['bedkləʊðz] NPL 床上用品 [chuángshang yòngpǐn]

bedding ['bedɪŋ] N [U] 床上用品 [chuángshang yòngpǐn]

bed linen N [U] 床单和枕套 [chuángdān hé zhěntào]

bedroom ['bedrum] N [c] 卧室 [wòshì]

bedside ['bedsaɪd] N ▶ **at sb's bedside** 在床前护理某人 [zài chuángqián hùlǐ mǒurén]

bedside lamp N [c] 床头灯 [chuángtóudēng]

bedside table N [c] 床头柜 [chuángtóuguì]

bedsit(ter) ['bedsɪt(ə(r))] (BRIT) N [c] 卧室兼起居室 [wòshì jiān qǐjùshì]

bedspread ['bedspred] N [c] 床罩 [chuángzhào]

bedtime ['bedtaɪm] N [U] 就寝时间 [jiùqǐn shíjiān] ▶ **at bedtime** 睡前 ▶ **it's past my bedtime** 已经过了我的就寝时间 ▶ **a bedtime story** 睡前讲的故事

bee [bi:] N [c] 蜜蜂 [mìfēng] ▶ **to have a bee in one's bonnet (about sth)** 总想着(某事)

beech [bi:tʃ] N **1** [c] (*tree*) 山毛榉 [shānmáojǔ] **2** [U] (*wood*) 山毛榉木 [shānmáojǔ mù]

beef [bi:f] N [U] 牛肉 [niúròu] ▶ **roast beef** 烤牛肉
▶ **beef up** VT (*inf*) [+ *security etc*] 加强 [jiāqiáng]

beefburger ['bi:fbə:gə(r)] (BRIT) N [c] 牛肉汉堡包 [niúròu hànbǎobāo]

Beefeater ['bi:fi:tə(r)] N [c] 伦敦塔守卫

beehive ['bi:haɪv] N [c] 蜂房 [fēngfáng]

been [bi:n] PP *of* **be**

beer [bɪə(r)] N [U] (*substance*) 啤酒 [píjiǔ]

▶ **would you like a beer?** 你想喝一瓶啤酒吗？

beet [biːt] N **1** [U] (crop) 甜菜 [tiáncài] **2** [C] (US) (red vegetable) 甜菜根 [tiáncàigēn] [英=**beetroot**]

beetle ['biːtl] N [C] 甲虫 [jiǎchóng]

beetroot ['biːtruːt] (BRIT) N [C/U] 甜菜根 [tiáncàigēn] [美=**beet**]

○ **before** [bɪ'fɔː(r)] I PREP **1** (in time) 之前 [zhīqián] ▷ just before Christmas 就在圣诞节前 **2** (frm) (in front of, ahead of) 在···前面 [zài···qiánmian] ▷ They stopped before a large white house. 他们在一座大白房子前面停了下来。▷ the duty which lay before me 摆在我面前的职责 II CONJ (in time) 在···之前 [zài···zhīqián] ▷ Can I see you before you leave? 你走之前，我去看你，好吗？ III ADV (time) 以前 [yǐqián] ▷ Have you been to Greece before? 你以前去过希腊吗？ ▶ **before doing sth** 在做某事之前 ▶ **the day/week before** 前一天/上一个星期 ▶ **I've never seen it before** 我以前从没见过

beforehand [bɪ'fɔːhænd] ADV 事先 [shìxiān]

beg [bɛg] I VI [beggar +] 乞讨 [qǐtǎo] II VT **1** [+ food, money] 讨 [tǎo] **2** [+ favour] 请求 [qǐngqiú] **3** [+ forgiveness, mercy etc] 乞求 [qǐqiú] ▶ **to beg for sth** 乞求某物 ▶ **to beg sb to do sth** 恳求某人做某事 ▶ **I beg your pardon** (apologizing) 对不起；(not hearing) 请再说一遍 ▶ **to beg the question (as to) whether** 令人质疑 ▶ **beg off** VI 请求免除 [qǐngqiú miǎnchú]

began [bɪ'gæn] PT of **begin**

beggar ['bɛgə(r)] I N [C] 乞丐 [qǐgài] II VT (impoverish) 使贫穷 [shǐ pínqióng]

○ **begin** [bɪ'gɪn] (pt **began**, pp **begun**) I VT 开始 [kāishǐ] ▷ He had begun his career as a painter. 他开始了他的画家生涯。II VI 开始 [kāishǐ] ▷ The concert begins at 5 p.m. 音乐会于下午5点开始。▶ **to begin doing or to do sth** 开始做某事 ▶ **I can't begin to thank you** 我真不知道怎样感谢你 ▶ **beginning (from) Monday** (从)星期一开始 ▶ **to begin with...** 首先··· ▷ To begin with, I was sceptical, but I was soon convinced. 起初我持怀疑态度，但很快就相信了。▷ You should invite your closest friends to begin with, and then see if there's room for anybody else. 你首先应该邀请最亲近的朋友，然后再看是否有位置给其他人。

> begin、start 和 commence 的意思相同，但 begin 比 start 稍正式一些，而 commence 则很正式，并且通常不用于口语。*The meeting is about to begin...He tore the list up and started a fresh one...The academic year commences at the beginning of October.* 当谈及起动车辆和机器时用 start。*I couldn't start the car.* 当谈及创办一项业务或其他组织时，也要用 start。*He's started his own printing business.* 注意 begin、start 和 commence 后面都可以跟动

词的 -ing 形式或名词，但只有 begin 和 start 可以跟由 to 引导的不定式。

beginner [bɪ'gɪnə(r)] N [C] 初学者 [chūxuézhě]

beginning [bɪ'gɪnɪŋ] I N [C] (of event, period, book) 开始 [kāishǐ] II **beginnings** NPL 征兆 [zhēngzhào] ▶ **at the beginning** 开始时 ▶ **right from the beginning** or **from the very beginning** 从一开始

begun [bɪ'gʌn] PP of **begin**

behalf [bɪ'hɑːf] N ▶ **on behalf of,** (US) **in behalf of** (as representative of) 代表 [dàibiǎo]; (for benefit of) 为···的利益 [wèi···de lìyì] ▶ **on my/his behalf** 代表我/他

behave [bɪ'heɪv] VI **1** [person +] 表现 [biǎoxiàn] **2** [object +] 运转 [yùnzhuǎn] **3** (behave well) 行为得体 [xíngwéi détǐ] ▶ **to behave oneself** 守规矩

behaviour, (US) **behavior** [bɪ'heɪvjə(r)] N **1** [U] 举止 [jǔzhǐ] **2** [C/U] (PSYCH, SOCIOL) 行为 [xíngwéi]

○ **behind** [bɪ'haɪnd] I PREP **1** (at the back of) 在···后面 [zài···hòumian] ▷ Behind the cottage was a shed. 在小屋的后面是一个棚子。**2** (supporting) 支持 [zhīchí] ▷ The country is behind the President. 整个国家都支持总统。**3** (in race, career etc) 落后于 [luòhòu yú] **4** (responsible for) 对···负责 [duì···fùzé] ▷ It is not clear who is behind the killing. 谁是这次谋杀的幕后策划者，目前尚不清楚。II ADV **1** (at/towards the back) 在/向后面 [zài/xiàng hòumian] ▷ I sat in the front row and Mick sat behind. 我坐在前排，米克坐在后面。**2** (stay, wait +) 留在原处 [liúzài yuánchù] ▷ Afterwards Ian asked me to stay behind. 后来，伊恩叫我留在原处。III N (inf) (buttocks) 屁股 [pìgu] ▶ **to be behind** (schedule) 落后于(计划) ▶ **we're behind (them) in technology** 在技术方面，我们没有(他们)那么好 ▶ **to get behind** 落后 ▶ **to leave sth behind** (forget) 落下 ▶ **to get left behind** [person +] 被甩掉

beige [beɪʒ] ADJ 灰棕色的 [huīzōngsè de]

Beijing ['beɪ'dʒɪŋ] N 北京 [Běijīng]

being ['biːɪŋ] N **1** [U] (existence) 存在 [cúnzài] **2** [C] (creature) 生物 [shēngwù] ▶ **to come into being** 形成 ▶ **to bring sth into being** 使某事物出现

belated [bɪ'leɪtɪd] ADJ [+ thanks, welcome] 来迟的 [láichí de]

belch [bɛltʃ] I VI **1** [person +] 打嗝 [dǎgé] **2** (also: **belch out**) [smoke, steam etc +] 喷出 [pēnchū] II VT (also: **belch out**) [+ smoke, steam etc] 喷出 [pēnchū] III N [C] 打嗝 [dǎgé]

Belgian ['bɛldʒən] I ADJ 比利时的 [Bǐlìshí de] II N [C] (person) 比利时人 [Bǐlìshírén]

Belgium ['bɛldʒəm] N 比利时 [Bǐlìshí]

belief [bɪ'liːf] N **1** [U/S] (opinion) 看法 [kànfǎ] **2** [C/U] (trust, faith) 信仰 [xìnyǎng] ▶ **contrary to popular belief** 与普遍观点相反的是 ▶ **beyond belief** 难以置信 ▶ **in the belief that**

相信

⊙**believe** [bɪ'liːv] I VT [+ person, story] 相信 [xiāngxìn] ▷ I didn't believe him. 我不相信他。 II VI ▶ **to believe in** [+ God, ghosts] 信 [xìn]; [+ honesty, discipline] 坚信 [jiānxìn] ▷ I believe in being truthful. 我相信诚实是好的。 ▶ **to believe that...** 认为… ▷ Experts believe that the drought will be extensive. 专家们认为干旱的波及面会很广。 ▶ **he is believed to be abroad** 人们认为他在国外 ▶ **I don't believe in corporal punishment** 我不相信体罚有益处 ▶ **to believe in sb/oneself** 对某人/自己有信心

如果你 **believe** 某事，你认为那是真的，即使你不能合理地证明。你可以 **believe a claim, believe that** 某事将要发生，或者 **believe that** 某事应该被完成。No one ever believes the official answer... I believed that I was at the beginning of a great adventure... The government believes that such powers are essential. 如果你 **believe in** 上帝，你认为上帝是存在的。如果你 **believe in** 鬼，你认为世上有鬼。如果你 **believe in** 某事，诸如一个系统，你认为它能正常运转。如果你 **believe in** 做某事，你觉得这么做是对的。Elaine believes in love... The Kirks are a modern couple, and believe in dividing all tasks equally between them.

believer [bɪ'liːvə(r)] N [c] 1 (in idea, activity) 笃信者 [dǔxìnzhě] 2 (REL) 信徒 [xìntú]

bell [bɛl] N [c] 1 (of church) 钟 [zhōng] 2 (also: **handbell**) 摇铃 [yáolíng] 3 (on door) 门铃 [ménlíng] ▶ **that rings a bell** (inf) 那使人想起某事

bellow ['bɛləʊ] I VI 1 (person +) 大声叫喊 [dàshēng jiàohǎn] 2 (bull +) 吼叫 [hǒujiào] II VT [+ orders] 大声叫 [dàshēng jiào] III N [c] (sound) 大吼 [dàhǒu]

belly ['bɛlɪ] N [c] (of person, animal) 腹部 [fùbù]

belly button (inf) N [c] 肚脐 [dùqí]

belong [bɪ'lɒŋ] VI ▶ **to belong to** [+ person] 属于 [shǔyú]; [+ club, society etc] 是…的成员 [shì…de chéngyuán] ▶ **this book belongs here** 这本书应该在这里 ▶ **which category does it belong in?** 它是属于哪个范畴的?

belongings [bɪ'lɒŋɪŋz] NPL 所有物 [suǒyǒuwù]

beloved [bɪ'lʌvɪd] I ADJ [+ person, thing, place] 心爱的 [xīn'ài de] II N [c] (o.f.) 心爱的人 [xīn'ài de rén]

below [bɪ'ləʊ] I PREP 1 (beneath) 在…之下 [zài…zhīxià] 2 (less than) [+ level, rate] 低于 [dīyú] II ADV 1 (beneath) 下面 [xiàmian] 2 (less) 以下 [yǐxià] ▶ **below zero** 零度以下 ▶ **below sea level** 在海平面以下 ▶ **temperatures below normal** or **average** 低于正常{或}平均温度 ▶ **see below** (in piece of writing) 见下

belt [bɛlt] I N [c] 1 (clothing) 腰带 [yāodài] 2 (of land, sea, air) 地带 [dìdài] 3 (TECH) 传动带 [chuándòngdài] II VT (inf) (hit) 抽打 [chōudǎ] III VI (inf) ▶ **to belt along/down/into** etc 迅速去/下/入 {等} [xùnsù qù/xià/rù {děng}] ▶ **to tighten one's belt** (fig) 节衣缩食 ▶ **to have sth under one's belt** 完成某事

▶ **belt out** VT (inf) [+ song] 大声唱 [dàshēng chàng]

▶ **belt up** (BRIT: inf) VI 住口 [zhùkǒu]

beltway ['bɛltweɪ] (US) N [c] (ring road) 环城公路 [huánchéng gōnglù] [英= ring road]

bemused [bɪ'mjuːzd] ADJ [+ person, expression] 迷惑的 [míhuò de]

bench [bɛntʃ] N [c] 1 (seat) 长椅 [chángyǐ] 2 (table) (in factory, laboratory etc) 工作台 [gōngzuòtái] 3 (BRIT: POL) 议员席 [yìyuánxí] 4 (LAW) ▶ **the Bench** 法官席 [fǎguānxí] ▶ **to be on the bench** (SPORT) (substitute) 候补

bend [bɛnd] (pt, pp **bent**) I VT [+ leg, arm, bar, wire] 使弯曲 [shǐ wānqū] II VI 1 (person +) 屈身 [qūshēn] 2 [leg, arm, bar, wire +] 弯曲 [wānqū] 3 [road, river +] 转弯 [zhuǎnwān] III N [c] 1 (in road, river) 弯 [wān] 2 (in pipe) 弯曲部分 [wānqū bùfen] IV **bends** NPL ▶ **the bends** 潜水员病 [qiánshuǐyuán bìng] ▶ **to bend the rules** 变通

▶ **bend down** VI 弯腰 [wānyāo]

▶ **bend over** I VI 俯身 [fǔshēn] ▶ **to bend over backwards (to do sth)** (fig) 竭力(做某事) II VT [+ table, wall] 弯腰靠近

beneath [bɪ'niːθ] I PREP 1 (in position) 在…之下 [zài…zhīxià] 2 (in status) ▶ **beneath him/her** 有失他/她的身份 [yǒushī tā/tā de shēnfèn] II ADV 在下面 [zài xiàmian]

beneficial [bɛnɪ'fɪʃəl] ADJ [+ effect, influence] 有益的 [yǒuyì de] ▶ **beneficial to** 有益于

benefit ['bɛnɪfɪt] I N 1 [c/u] (advantage) 好处 [hǎochù] 2 [c/u] (money) 救济金 [jiùjìjīn] 3 [c] (also: **benefit concert/dinner**) 募捐 [mùjuān] II VT 有益于 [yǒuyì yú] III VI ▶ **to benefit from sth** 从某事中获益 [cóng mǒushì zhōng huòyì] ▶ **to have the benefit of sth** 受益于某事 ▶ **to be of benefit (to sb)** (对某人)有益 ▶ **to give sb the benefit of the doubt** 在证据不足的情况下，假定某人无辜

benevolent [bɪ'nɛvələnt] ADJ 1 [+ person] 仁慈的 [réncí de] 2 (BRIT) [+ organization, fund] 慈善的 [císhàn de]

benign [bɪ'naɪn] ADJ 1 [+ person, attitude] 仁慈的 [réncí de] 2 (MED) 良性的 [liángxìng de]

bent [bɛnt] I PT, PP of **bend** II N [inclination] 天赋 [tiānfù] III ADJ 1 [+ wire, pipe] 弯曲的 [wānqū de] 2 (BRIT: inf) (dishonest) 贪污受贿的 [tānwū shòuhuì de] ▶ **to be bent on (doing) sth** 决心做某事

bereaved [bɪ'riːvd] I ADJ 丧失亲友的 [sàngshī qīnyǒu de] II NPL ▶ **the bereaved** 丧

失亲人的人 [sàngshī qīnrén de rén]

beret [ˈbɛreɪ] N [c] 贝雷帽 [bèiléimào]

berry [ˈbɛrɪ] N [c] 浆果 [jiāngguǒ]

berth [bəːθ] N [c] **1** (bed) (on boat, train) 卧铺 [wòpù] **2** (NAUT) (mooring) 泊位 [bówèi] II VI [ship +] 停泊 [tíngbó] ▶ **to give sb/sth a wide berth** 躲开某人/某物

beside [bɪˈsaɪd] PREP (next to) 在…旁边 [zài…pángbiān] ▶ **to be beside oneself with rage/excitement** 愤怒/兴奋得发狂 ▶ **that's beside the point** 那是离题了 see also **besides**

besides [bɪˈsaɪdz] I ADV **1** (also: **beside**) (in addition) 另外 [lìngwài] **2** (in any case) 而且 [érqiě] II PREP (also: **beside**) (in addition to, as well as) 除…之外 [chú…zhīwài]

besides 引出的事物包括在我们所谈 及的事情之内。She is very intelligent besides being very beautiful. 不过，当我 们说 **the only person besides** 另外某人 时，或 **the only thing besides** 另外某 物时，我们指在某一特定场合或上下 文中的惟一其他人或物。There was only one person besides me who knew where the money was hidden. 介词 **except** 后面 通常用于我们的陈述中惟独不包括的那 些物、人、事的名词或代词形式。She spoke to everyone except me... I never take any drugs, except aspirin for colds. **except** 也可作连词，引导从句和副词短语。 There was nothing to do now except wait... Travelling was impossible except in the cool of the morning. **except** 还可以引 出由连词 that、when 或 if 引导的从 句。The house stayed empty, except when we came for the holidays. **except for** 是 用在名词前的介词短语，用来引出某人 或某物，说明要不是有某人或某物，所 陈述的便为全部事实。Everyone was late except for Richard. **unless** 是连词，后面 的从句表示某事不会发生或不会成为事 实。Unless you really want to lose weight, it will be hard to stick to a diet.

◆best [bɛst] I ADJ (in quality, suitability, extent) 最 好的 [zuìhǎo de] ▷ It's one of the best films I've seen. 这是我看过的最好的电影之一。II ADV 最 [zuì] ▷ He is best known as an actor. 他是位家 喻户晓的演员。▷ What music do you like best? 你 最喜欢什么样的音乐? III N ▶ **the best 1** (in quality etc) 最好的事物 [zuìhǎo de shìwù] ▷ We offer only the best to our clients. 我们只为客户提 供最上乘的产品。**2** (in achievement) 最大努力 [zuìdà nǔlì] ▷ He knows how to get the best out of his students. 他懂得如何发挥学生的最大潜力。 ▶ **the best thing to do is...** 最好是… ▶ **the best part of** (most of) 大部分 ▶ **you'd best leave early** 你最好早点离开 ▶ **at best** 至多 ▶ **to be at one's best** 处于最佳状态 ▶ **to make the best of sth** 既来之则安之 ▶ **to do** or **try one's**

best 尽某人最大的努力 ▶ **to the best of my knowledge** 尽我所知 ▶ **to the best of my ability** 尽我能力所及 ▶ **it's for the best** 是一 件好事 ▶ **he's not exactly patient at the best of times** 即使在最好的情况下，他也不怎么耐 心 ▶ **to have the best of both worlds** 两全其美

best-before date [ˈbɛstbɪˈfɔː(r)-] N [c] (on food etc) 保质日期 [bǎozhì rìqī]

best man N [c] 男傧相 [nán bīnxiàng]

bestow [bɪˈstəu] (frm) VT ▶ **to bestow sth on sb** [+ honour, title] 赠与某人某物 [zèngyǔ mǒurén mǒuwù]

bestseller [ˈbɛstˈsɛlə(r)] N [c] (book) 畅销书 [chàngxiāoshū]

bet [bɛt] (pt, pp **bet**, or **betted**) I N [c] (wager) 赌注 [dǔzhù] II VT **1** (wager) ▶ **to bet sb 100 pounds that...** 就…和某人赌100英镑 [jiù…hé mǒurén dǔ yībǎi yīngbàng] **2** (expect, guess) ▶ **to bet (that)** 断定 [duàndìng] III VI (wager) ▶ **to bet on** [+ horse, result] 下赌注于 [xià dǔzhù yú] ▶ **it's a good** or **safe bet that...** 非常有可 能… ▶ **I wouldn't bet on it** (inf) 我不敢打包票 ▶ **you bet** or **you bet your life** (inf) 那还用说

betray [bɪˈtreɪ] VT **1** [+ friend, country, comrade] 背叛 [bèipàn] **2** [+ sb's trust, confidence] 辜负 [gūfù] **3** (reveal) [+ emotion] 流露 [liúlù]

◆better [ˈbɛtə(r)] I ADJ **1** (comparative of good) 更 好的 [gènghǎo de] ▷ The results were better than expected. 结果比预期的更好。**2** (after an illness or injury) 好转的 [hǎozhuǎn de] ▷ Are you better now? 你现在好点了吗? II ADV **1** (comparative of well) 更好地 [gènghǎo de] ▷ Some people can ski better than others. 一些人比其他人滑雪 滑得好。**2** (more) [like +] 更 [gèng] ▷ I always liked you better than Sandra. 与桑德拉相比，我 总是更喜欢你。III VT [+ score, record] 提高 [tígāo] ▷ We have bettered last year's figures. 我们 比去年的数字又有了提高。IV N ▶ **to get the better of** [curiosity etc +] 占…的上风 [zhàn…de shàngfēng] ▷ My curiosity got the better of me. 我 的好奇心占了上风。▶ **to get better** (improve) 变得更好 或 [sick person +] 渐愈 ▶ **to feel better** 感觉好一些 ▶ **that's better!** 那就好多了! ▶ **it would be better to...** 不如… ▶ **you're better waiting till tomorrow** 你最好等到明天 ▶ **I'd better go** or **I had better go** 我得走了 ▶ **you'd better do it** or **you had better do it** 你最好做这 件事 ▶ **he thought better of it** 他重新考虑后 决定不做 ▶ **to better oneself** 提高自己 ▶ **to change for the better** 有好转

better off ADJ **1** ▶ **to be better off** (wealthier) 较 富裕的 [jiào fùyù de] **2** (more comfortable etc) 情 况更好的 [qíngkuàng gènghǎo de] ▶ **you'd be better off without him** 不和他在一起，你会 过得更好

betting [ˈbɛtɪŋ] N [U] **1** (gambling) 赌博 [dǔbó] **2** (odds) 差距 [chājù]

betting shop (BRIT) N [c] 彩票经营店

[cǎipiào jīngyíngdiàn]

⊙between [bɪ'twiːn] I PREP **1** (in space) 在⋯中间 [zài⋯zhōngjiān] ▷ He was sitting between two old ladies. 他坐在两个老妇人中间。 **2** (in time) 介于⋯之间 [jièyú⋯zhījiān] ▷ between 9 and 10 tomorrow 在明天9点至10点之间 **3** (in amount, age etc) 介于⋯之间 [jièyú⋯zhījiān] ▷ people aged 18 and 30 年龄在18至30之间的人们 ▷ It weighs between 30 and 40 kilos. 它重约30至40公斤。 **4** (among) 之间 [zhījiān] ▷ the relationship between doctors and patients 医生与患者之间的关系 **5** (fig) 之间 [zhījiān] ▷ the obstacles that lay between him and success 摆在他和成功之间的障碍 II ADV ▸ in between (in space) 在⋯中间 [zài⋯zhōngjiān] ▷ Court Road and all the little side streets in between 考特路及所有那些夹在中间的小街道; (in time) 期间 [qijiān] ▷ He had to make two flights, with a 5-hour wait in between. 他得坐两次航班，期间要等5个小时。 ▸ to choose between [+ two things] 从中选一个 ▸ to be shared/divided between people 由大家一起分享/分用 ▸ the road between here and London 这里和伦敦之间的道路 ▸ we only had 5 pounds between us 我们俩一共只有5英镑 ▸ between you and me, between ourselves 私下

▐用法参见 **among**

beverage ['bevərɪdʒ] (frm) N [c] 饮料 [yǐnliào]

beware [bɪ'weə(r)] VI ▸ beware! 注意！[zhùyì!] ▸ to beware of (doing) sth 留神（做）某事 ▸ "beware of the dog" "当心狗"

bewildered [bɪ'wɪldəd] ADJ (stunned, confused) 困惑的 [kùnhuò de]

beyond [bɪ'jɒnd] I PREP **1** (on the other side of) [+ house, line] 在⋯的另一边 [zài⋯de lìng yībiān] **2** (fig) 超出⋯的范围 [chāochū⋯de fànwéi] **3** (after) [+ time, date, age] 迟于 [chíyú] **4** (past) [+ understanding, recognition] 超过 [chāoguò] **5** (exceeding) 超出 [chāochū] II ADV **1** (in space) 在另一边 [zài lìng yībiān] **2** (in time) 在⋯之后 [zài⋯zhīhòu] ▸ beyond doubt 毫无疑问 ▸ to be beyond repair 无法修理 ▸ it's beyond me 我不能理解

Bhutan [buː'tɑːn] N 不丹 [Bùdān]

bias ['baɪəs] N **1** [U] (prejudice) 成见 [chéngjiàn] **2** [c] (preference) 偏向 [piānxiàng]

bias(s)ed ['baɪəst] ADJ [+ jury, judgement, reporting] 有偏见的 [yǒu piānjiàn de] ▸ to be bias(s)ed against 对⋯有偏见 ▸ to be bias(s)ed towards 偏向于

bib [bɪb] N (for baby) 围嘴 [wéizuǐ]

Bible ['baɪbl] (REL) N [c] ▸ the Bible 圣经 [Shèngjīng]

bibliography [bɪblɪ'ɒgrəfɪ] N [c] (in text) 参考书目 [cānkǎo shūmù]

bicarbonate of soda [baɪ'kɑːbənɪt-] N [U] **1** (for baking) 小苏打 [xiǎosūdá] **2** (medicinal) 碳酸氢钠 [tànsuānqīngnà]

biceps ['baɪseps] (pl **biceps**) N [c] 二头肌 [èrtóujī]

bicker ['bɪkə(r)] VI (squabble) 口角 [kǒujiǎo] ▸ to bicker with sb 与某人口角

bicycle ['baɪsɪkl] N [c] 自行车 [zìxíngchē] ▸ to ride a bicycle 骑自行车

bicycle pump N [c] 自行车打气筒 [zìxíngchē dǎqìtǒng]

bid [bɪd] (pt **bade** or **bid**, pp **bid** or **bidden**) I N [c] **1** (attempt) 尝试 [chángshì] **2** (at auction) 出价 [chūjià] **3** (to buy a company) 投标 [tóubiāo] II VI (at auction) 出价竞买 [chūjià jìngmǎi] III VT (offer) 出价 [chūjià] ▸ to bid sb farewell/goodnight (frm) 向某人道别/说晚安

bidder ['bɪdə(r)] N [c] 投标人 [tóubiāorén] ▸ the highest bidder 出价最高的人

bidet ['biːdeɪ] N [c] 坐浴盆 [zuòyùpén]

⊙big [bɪg] ADJ **1** (in size) [+ man, country, object] 大的 [dà de] **2** (inf) [+ person] (important) 有影响的 [yǒu yǐngxiǎng de] ▷ Their father was very big in the army. 他们的父亲在军中很有影响。 **3** [+ ideas] 远大的 [yuǎndà de] ▷ He's got a lot of big ideas about how to change the system. 就如何改变体制，他有一些远大的想法。 **4** (major) [+ change, increase, problem] 大的 [dà de] ▷ The biggest problem is unemployment. 最大的问题是失业问题。 ▸ big brother/sister 哥哥/姐姐 ▸ big words (inf) 深奥的词语 ▸ in a big way (inf) 大张旗鼓

bigheaded ['bɪg'hedɪd] (inf) ADJ 自大的 [zìdà de]

big toe N [c] 大脚趾 [dàjiǎozhǐ]

bike [baɪk] N [c] **1** (bicycle) 自行车 [zìxíngchē] **2** (motorcycle) 摩托车 [mótuōchē]

bikini [bɪ'kiːnɪ] N [c] 比基尼 [bǐjíní]

bilingual [baɪ'lɪŋgwəl] ADJ [+ dictionary, secretary] 双语的 [shuāngyǔ de] ▸ to be bilingual 能讲两国语言的

bill [bɪl] I N [c] **1** (requesting payment) 账单 [zhàngdān] **2** (BRIT) (in restaurant) 账单 [zhàngdān] [美=check] **3** (POL) 法案 [fǎ'àn] **4** (US) (banknote) 钞票 [chāopiào] [英=note] **5** [of bird] 鸟喙 [niǎohuì] **6** (THEAT) 节目单 [jiémùdān] II VT **1** [+ customer] 给⋯开账单 [gěi⋯kāi zhàngdān] **2** (advertise) 宣传 [xuānchuán] ▸ to fit or fill the bill 合乎要求 ▸ bill of fare (o.f.) 菜单 ▸ "post no bills" "禁止张贴" ▸ bill of exchange 汇票 ▸ bill of lading 提单 ▸ bill of sale 卖据

billboard ['bɪlbɔːd] N [c] 广告牌 [guǎnggàopái]

billfold ['bɪlfəʊld] (US) N [c] 钱夹 [qiánjiā] [英=wallet]

billiards ['bɪljədz] N [U] 台球 [táiqiú]

⊙billion ['bɪljən] N [c] 十亿 [shíyì]

bin [bɪn] I N [c] **1** (BRIT) (for rubbish) 垃圾箱 [lājīxiāng] [美= garbage can or trash can] **2** (container) 箱 [xiāng] II VT (BRIT: inf) (throw *away*) 扔掉 [rēngdiào]

bind [baɪnd] (*pt, pp* **bound**) I VT 1 (*tie*) 捆 [kǔn]
2 (*tie together*) [+ *hands, feet*] 绑 [bǎng] 3 (*connect*)
使联合 [shǐ liánhé] 4 (*oblige*) 约束 [yuēshù]
5 [+ *book*] 装订 [zhuāngdìng] II N (BRIT: *inf*)
(*nuisance*) 麻烦 [máfan]
▶ **bind over** VT (LAW) ▶ **to bind sb over** (**to keep
the peace**) 保证某人遵守法纪 [bǎozhèng
mǒurén zūnshǒu fǎjì]

binder ['baɪndə(r)] N [c] (*file*) 文件夹
[wénjiànjiá]

binding ['baɪndɪŋ] I ADJ [+ *agreement, contract*]
具有约束力的 [jùyǒu yuēshùlì de] II N [c] [*of
book*] 装订 [zhuāngdìng]

binge [bɪndʒ] (*inf*) I N ▶ **to go on a binge** 狂
欢作乐 [kuánghuān zuòlè] II VI ▶ **to binge on
chocolate/whisky** 无节制地吃巧克力/喝威士
忌酒 [wú jiézhì de chī qiǎokèlì/hē wēishìjìjiǔ]

bingo ['bɪŋɡəʊ] N [U] 宾戈 (一种赌博游戏)

binoculars [bɪ'nɔkjʊləz] NPL 双筒望远镜
[shuāngtǒng wàngyuǎnjìng]

biochemistry [baɪə'kemɪstrɪ] N [U] 生物化学
[shēngwù huàxué]

biodegradable ['baɪəʊdɪ'ɡreɪdəbl] ADJ 可由
生物降解的 [kě yóu shēngwù jiàngjiě de]

biography [baɪ'ɔɡrəfɪ] N [c] 传记 [zhuànjì] ▶ **a
biography of Dylan Thomas** 迪兰·托马斯传

biological [baɪə'lɔdʒɪkl] ADJ 1 [+ *process, weapon,
warfare, washing powder*] 生物的 [shēngwù de]
2 [+ *research, science*] 生物学的 [shēngwùxué
de]

biology [baɪ'ɔlədʒɪ] N [U] 生物学 [shēngwùxué]

birch [bə:tʃ] N 1 [c] (*tree*) 桦树 [huàshù] 2 [U]
(*wood*) 桦木 [huàmù]

bird [bə:d] N [c] 1 (ZOOL) 鸟 [niǎo] 2 (BRIT: *inf*)
(*woman*) 姑娘 [gūniang] ▶ **a bird in the hand**
已到手的东西 ▶ **to kill two birds with one
stone** 一举两得

bird of prey N [c] 猛禽 [měngqín]

bird-watching ['bə:dwɔtʃɪŋ] N [U] 野鸟习性
观察 [yěniǎo xíxíng guānchá]

Biro® ['baɪərəʊ] (BRIT) N [c] 圆珠笔 [yuánzhūbǐ]

birth [bə:θ] N 1 [c/U] [*of baby, animal*] 出生
[chūshēng] 2 [s] (*fig*) 开始 [kāishǐ] ▶ **to give
birth (to)** [+ *child, animal*] 分娩; [+ *idea*] 促成

birth certificate N [c] 出生证明 [chūshēng
zhèngmíng]

birth control N [U] 节育 [jiéyù]

birthday ['bə:θdeɪ] I N [c] 生日 [shēngrì]
II CPD (复合词) [+ *cake, card, present etc*] 生日
[shēngrì]

birthplace ['bə:θpleɪs] N 1 出生地
[chūshēngdì] 2 (*fig*) 发祥地 [fāxiángdì]

biscuit ['bɪskɪt] N [c] 1 (BRIT: *cookie*) 饼干
[bǐnggān] [美= **cookie**] 2 (US) (*cake*) 小圆饼
[xiǎoyuánbǐng]

bishop ['bɪʃəp] N [c] 1 (REL) 主教 [zhǔjiào]
2 (CHESS) 象 [xiàng]

bistro ['bi:strəʊ] N [c] 小餐馆 [xiǎo cānguǎn]

○ **bit** [bɪt] I PT *of* **bite** II N [c] 1 (ESP BRIT) (*piece*)
少许 [shǎoxǔ] ▶ **a bit of string** 一小段绳子
2 (ESP BRIT) (*part*) 部分 [bùfen] ▷ Now comes
the really important bit. 现在要说的是最重要的
部分。3 (*tool*) 钻头 [zuàntóu] 4 (COMPUT) 比
特 [bǐtè] 5 [*of horse*] 嚼子 [jiáozi] 6 (US) (*coin*)
12.5美分的硬币 ▶ **to come** *or* **fall to bits** (*break*)
破碎 ▶ **bits and pieces** *or* **bits and bobs** (*inf*) 零
碎儿 ▶ **a bit of** 有点 ▷ I'm sorry, the room's in
a bit of a mess. 对不起，房间有点乱。▶ **a bit
mad/dangerous** 有点疯狂/危险 ▶ **it's/that's
a bit much** (*inf*) 有点过分 ▶ **bit by bit** 一点
一点 ▶ **to do one's bit** 尽自己的一份力量
▶ **every bit as good/interesting as** 与…同
样好/有趣 ▶ **for a bit** (*inf*) 一会儿 ▶ **quite a
bit** 不少

bitch [bɪtʃ] I N [c] 1 (*dog*) 母狗 [mǔgǒu] 2 (*inf!*)
(*woman*) 恶毒的女人 [èdú de nǚrén] II VI (*inf*)
(*complain*) 埋怨 [mǎnyuàn]

○ **bite** [baɪt] (*pt* **bit**, *pp* **bitten** [bɪtn]) I VT [*person,
dog, snake, mosquito* +] 咬 [yǎo] II VI 1 [*dog
etc* +] 咬人 [yǎo rén] 2 (*fig*) (*take effect*) [*action,
policy* +] 生效 [shēngxiào] III N [c] 1 (*act of
biting*) ▷ He took another bite of his apple. 他又咬
了一口苹果。2 (*mouthful*) 口 [kǒu] ▷ I enjoyed
every bite. 我每一口吃得都很香。3 (*from dog*)
咬伤 [yǎoshāng] 4 (*from snake, mosquito*) 咬痕
[yǎohén] ▶ **to bite one's nails** 咬指甲 ▶ **to
bite one's lip** *or* **tongue** (*inf*) 保持沉默 ▶ **to
have a bite to eat** (*inf*) 吃点东西

bitter ['bɪtə(r)] I ADJ 1 [+ *person, experience*] 充
满怨恨的 [chōngmǎn yuànhèn de] 2 [+ *taste*]
苦的 [kǔ de] 3 [+ *disappointment, blow*] 难以忍受
的 [nányǐ rěnshòu de] 4 [+ *wind, weather*] 严寒
的 [yánhán de] 5 [+ *argument, fighting*] 激烈的
[jīliè de] II N [U] (BRIT) (*beer*) 苦啤酒 [kǔpíjiǔ]
▶ **to the bitter end** 坚持到底

bitterly ['bɪtəlɪ] ADV [*say, laugh* +] 怨恨地
[yuànhèn de]; [*regret* +] 惨痛地 [cǎntòng de];
[*resent* +] 十分地 [shífēn de]; [*weep, complain* +]
强烈地 [qiángliè de]; [+ *jealous, disappointed,
ashamed*] 非常地 [fēicháng de]; [*oppose,
criticize* +] 刻薄地 [kèbó de] ▶ **it's bitterly cold**
天气寒冷刺骨

bitterness ['bɪtənɪs] N [U] 1 [*of person*] 怨恨
[yuànhèn] 2 [*of conflict, dispute*] 怀恨 [huáihèn]

bizarre [bɪ'zɑ:(r)] ADJ [+ *story, contraption*] 稀奇
古怪的 [xīqí gǔguài de]

○ **black** [blæk] I ADJ 1 (*in colour*) [+ *paint, jacket, cat*]
黑色的 [hēisè de] 2 [+ *person*] 黑人的 [hēirén
de] 3 [+ *tea, coffee*] 不加牛奶的 [bù jiā niúnǎi
de] 4 [+ *humour*] 黑色的 [hēisè de] ▷ a black
comedy 黑色喜剧 5 (*grim*) 暗淡的 [àndàn de]
▷ one of the blackest days of his political career 他政
治生涯中最暗淡的一个日子 II N 1 [U] (*colour*)
黑色 [hēisè] 2 [c] (*person*) 黑人 [hēirén] ▷ the
first black to be elected to Congress 第一个被选入

国会的黑人 **III** VT (BRIT) 抵制 [dǐzhì] ▷ *The Union blacked incoming goods at the docks.* 工会抵制了进入码头的货物。▶ **to give sb/to have a black eye** 把某人眼睛打青/眼睛青了 ▶ **black and blue** (bruised) 青一块，紫一块的 ▶ **there it is in black and white** 白纸黑字清清楚楚地写着 ▶ **to be in the black** (in credit) 有赢余 ▶ **black out** VI (faint) 暂时失去知觉 [zànshí shīqù zhījué]

blackberry ['blækbərɪ] N [c] 黑莓 [hēiméi]

blackbird ['blækbə:d] N [c] 乌鸫 [wūdōng]

blackboard ['blækbɔ:d] N [c] 黑板 [hēibǎn]

blackcurrant ['blæk'kʌrənt] (BRIT) N [c] 黑醋栗 [hēicùlì]

blacken ['blækn] VT **1** (lit) 使变黑 [shǐ biànhēi] **2** (fig) [+ sb's name, reputation] 败坏 [bàihuài]

black ice N [u] 薄冰 [bóbīng]

blackmail ['blækmeɪl] **I** N [u] 敲诈 [qiāozhà] **II** VT 敲诈 [qiāozhà]

black market N [c] 黑市 [hēishì] ▶ **on the black market** 在黑市上

blackout ['blækaut] N [c] **1** (in wartime) 灯火管制 [dēnghuǒ guǎnzhì] **2** (power cut) 停电 [tíngdiàn] **3** (TV, RAD) 封锁 [fēngsuǒ] **4** (MED) 暂时性昏迷 [zànshíxìng hūnmí] ▶ **to have a blackout** (MED) 暂时性昏迷

black pepper N [u] 黑胡椒 [hēihújiāo]

black pudding (BRIT) N [c/u] 黑香肠 [hēixiāngcháng]

◉ **BLACK PUDDING**

● **black pudding**，黑香肠，是英国传统早餐中的一种食品，因表皮颜色而得名。成分主要为猪油和猪血，切成厚圆片，炸食。

Black Sea N ▶ **the Black Sea** 黑海 [Hēi Hǎi]

bladder ['blædə(r)] (ANAT) N [c] 膀胱 [pángguāng]

blade [bleɪd] N [c] **1** [of knife, sword] 刃 [rèn] **2** [of oar] 桨叶 [jiǎngyè] **3** [of propeller] 螺旋桨翼 [luóxuánjiǎng yì] ▶ **a blade of grass** 一片草叶

blame [bleɪm] **I** N [u] (for mistake, crime) 责备 [zébèi] **II** VT ▶ **to blame sb for sth** 为某事责备某人 [wèi mǒushì zébèi mǒurén] ▶ **to take the blame** (for sth) (对某事)负责 ▶ **to be to blame** (for sth) 该(为某事)负责任 ▶ **to blame sth on sb** 把某事归咎于某人 ▶ **you can't blame him for trying** 你不能怪他去尝试 ▶ **who's to blame?** 是谁的责任? ▶ **I'm not to blame** 责任不在我

bland [blænd] ADJ **1** [+ personality, building, film] 枯燥乏味的 [kūzào fáwèi de] **2** [+ taste, food] 平淡无味的 [píngdàn wúwèi de]

blank [blæŋk] **I** ADJ **1** [+ paper, cassette] 空白的 [kòngbái de] **2** [+ expression] 茫然的 [mángrán de] **II** N [c] **1** (on form) 空白处 [kòngbáichù] **2** (cartridge) 空弹 [kōngdàn] ▶ **my mind went blank** or **was a blank** 我的大脑一片空白 ▶ **we drew a blank** (inf) 我们白费心机了

blanket ['blæŋkɪt] **I** N [c] **1** (for bed) 毛毯 [máotǎn] **2** [of snow, fog] 层 [céng] **II** ADJ (comprehensive) 全面的 [quánmiàn de] **III** VT [snow +] 覆盖 [fùgài]

blast [blɑ:st] **I** N [c] **1** [of wind, air, whistle, horn] 一阵 [yīzhèn] **2** (explosion) 爆炸 [bàozhà] **II** VT **1** (blow up) 炸掉 [zhàdiào] **2** (shoot) 枪击 [qiāngjī] **III** INT (inf) 该死 [gāisǐ] ▶ **(at) full blast** [play music etc +] 最大限度地 ▶ **blast off** VI (SPACE) 发射上天 [fāshè shàngtiān]

blatant ['bleɪtənt] ADJ [+ discrimination, attempt] 公然的 [gōngrán de]

blatantly ['bleɪtəntlɪ] ADV [lie +] 极明显地 [jí míngxiǎn de]; [+ untrue] 显然地 [xiǎnrán de]; [+ sexist] 明显地 [míngxiǎn de] ▶ **it's blatantly obvious** 显而易见

blaze [bleɪz] **I** N [c] **1** (fire) 大火 [dàhuǒ] **2** [of colour, light] 强烈 [qiángliè] **3** [of glory, publicity] 大量 [dàliàng] **II** VI **1** [fire +] 熊熊燃烧 [xióngxióng ránshāo] **2** (also: **blaze away**) [guns +] 连连开枪 [liánlián kāiqiāng] **3** (liter) [eyes +] 放光彩 [fàng guāngcǎi] **III** VT ▶ **to blaze a trail** 开辟新路 [kāipì xīnlù] ▶ **in a blaze of publicity** 在公众瞩目之下 ▶ **to blaze with colour** [garden etc +] 鲜艳夺目

blazer ['bleɪzə(r)] N [c] [of school, team etc] 上装 [shàngzhuāng]

bleach [bli:tʃ] **I** N [u] (chemical) 漂白剂 [piǎobáijì] **II** VT **1** [+ fabric, foodstuff etc] 漂白 [piǎobái] **2** [+ hair] 漂淡颜色 [piǎo dàn yánsè]

bleachers ['bli:tʃəz] (US: SPORT) NPL 露天看台 [lùtiān kàntái]

bleak [bli:k] ADJ **1** [+ place] 凄凉的 [qīliáng de] **2** [+ weather] 阴冷的 [yīnlěng de] **3** [+ future, outlook] 暗淡的 [àndàn de] **4** [+ expression, voice] 冷酷的 [lěngkù de]

bleed [bli:d] (pt, pp **bled** [bled]) **I** VI **1** (MED) [person, arm, wound etc +] 流血 [liúxuè] **2** (run) [colour +] 渗色 [shènsè] **II** VT [+ brakes, radiator] 抽出…的液体/气体 [chōuchū...de yètǐ/qìtǐ] ▶ **my nose is bleeding** 我流鼻血了 ▶ **to bleed to death** 流血而死

blemish ['blemɪʃ] **I** N [c] **1** (on skin, fruit) 瑕疵 [xiácī] **2** (fig) 缺陷 [quēxiàn] **II** VT (fig) [+ reputation] 损害 [sǔnhài]

blend [blend] **I** N [c] [of tea, whisky] 混合物 [hùnhéwù] **II** VT **1** [+ ingredients] 混合 [hùnhé] **2** [+ ideas, styles, policies etc] 融合 [rónghé] **III** VT (also: **blend in**) [colours, sounds +] 调和 [tiáohé] ▶ **to blend in with sth** 与某物融为一体

blender ['blendə(r)] N [c] 搅拌器 [jiǎobànqì]

bless [bles] VT (REL) 赐福 [cìfú] ▶ **to be blessed with** 具有 ▶ **bless you!** (after sneeze) 上帝保

佑！: (inf) (expressing affection) 愿上帝保佑你 14世纪时，黑死病席卷欧洲。人们相信打喷嚏是得病的前兆，不久就会死。当一个人打喷嚏后，身旁的人就会说 Bless you!，希望上帝能保佑这个人的灵魂。

blessing ['blɛsɪŋ] N [c] **1** (approval) 应允 [yìngyún] **2** (godsend) 幸事 [xìngshì] **3** (REL) 赐福 [cìfú] ▶ to count one's blessings 看自己有多幸运 ▶ it was a blessing in disguise 因祸得福 ▶ a mixed blessing 优劣参半

blew [blu:] PT of blow

blight [blaɪt] I VT [+ career, life etc] 损害 [sǔnhài] II N **1** [c] (fig) 损害 [sǔnhài] **2** [U] [of plants] 枯萎病 [kūwěibìng]

blind [blaɪnd] I ADJ **1** (MED) 失明的 [shīmíng de] **2** [+ faith, panic, obedience] 盲目的 [mángmù de] **3** [+ corner] 看不见另一头的 [kànbùjiàn lìngyìtóu de] II N (for window) 向上卷的帘子 [xiàng shàng juǎn de liánzi] III VT **1** (MED) 使⋯失明 [shǐ⋯shīmíng] **2** (dazzle) 使晕眩 [shǐ yūnxuàn] **3** (fig) (make insensitive) 使意识不到 [shǐ yìshi bùdào] IV the blind NPL (blind people) 盲人 [mángrén] ▶ to go blind 失明 ▶ to be blind to sth 对某事意识不到 ▶ blind in one eye 一只眼睛失明 ▶ to turn a blind eye (to sth) (对某事)视而不见

blind alley N [c] **1** (US) (without exit) 死胡同 [sǐhútong] [英=cul-de-sac] **2** (fig) 无出路 [wú chūlù]

blindfold ['blaɪndfəʊld] I N [c] 蒙眼的布 [méngyǎn de bù] II ADJ (also: blindfolded) 蒙住眼睛的 [méngzhù yǎnjing de] III VT 蒙住眼睛 [méngzhù yǎnjing] ▶ I could do it blindfold 我闭着眼睛都能做

blindly ['blaɪndlɪ] ADV **1** (without seeing) 看不见地 [kànbùjiàn de] **2** (without thinking) 盲目地 [mángmù de]

blindness ['blaɪndnɪs] N [U] **1** (disability) 失明 [shīmíng] **2** (fig) 意识不到 [yìshí bùdào]

blink [blɪŋk] I VI **1** [person, animal +] 眨眼睛 [zhǎ yǎnjing] **2** [light +] 闪烁 [shǎnshuò] II VT ▶ to blink one's eyes 眨眼睛 [zhǎ yǎnjing] III N [c] [of eyes] 一眨 [yī zhǎ] ▶ in the blink of an eye 转眼之间 ▶ the TV's on the blink (inf) 电视出毛病了

bliss [blɪs] N [U] 巨大的幸福 [jùdà de xìngfú]

blister ['blɪstə(r)] I N [c] **1** (on skin) 水泡 [shuǐpào] **2** (in paint, rubber) 气泡 [qìpào] II VI **1** [skin +] 起泡 [qǐpào] **2** [paint +] 呈气泡状 [chéng qìpàozhuàng]

blizzard ['blɪzəd] N [c] 暴风雪 [bàofēngxuě]

bloated ['bləʊtɪd] ADJ **1** (swollen) [+ face, stomach, body] 肿胀的 [zhǒngzhàng de] **2** (full) ▶ to feel bloated 觉得饱 [juéde bǎo]

blob [blɔb] (inf) N [c] **1** [of glue, paint] 一滴 [yīdī] **2** (something indistinct) 模糊不清的东西 [móhu bùqīng de dōngxi]

block [blɔk] I N [c] **1** (group of buildings) 街区 [jiēqū] **2** (toy) 积木 [jīmù] **3** [of stone, wood, ice] 块 [kuài] II VT **1** [+ entrance, road] 堵塞 [dǔsè] **2** [+ view] 挡住 [dǎngzhù] **3** [+ activity, agreement] 阻止 [zǔzhǐ] ▶ block of flats or (US) apartment block 公寓楼 ▶ 3 blocks from here 离这里有3个街区那么远 ▶ to have a (mental) block about sth 对某事感到(脑子)一片空白 ▶ block and tackle (TECH) 滑轮组 ▶ block off VT [+ door, window] 堵住 [dǔzhù] ▶ block out VT [+ thought, memory] 尽可能不想 [jìn kěnéng bùxiǎng] ▶ block up I VT [+ sink, pipe etc] 堵塞 [dǔsè] II VI [sink, pipe +] 堵 [dǔ]

blockade [blɔ'keɪd] I N [c] 封锁 [fēngsuǒ] II VT 封锁 [fēngsuǒ]

blockage ['blɔkɪdʒ] N [c] (in pipe, tube) 堵塞 [dǔsè]

blockbuster ['blɔkbʌstə(r)] (inf) N [c] (film, book) 风靡一时的事物 [fēngmí yīshí de shìwù]

block capitals NPL 大写字母 [dàxiě zìmǔ] ▶ in block capitals 用大写字母

block letters NPL = block capitals

bloke [bləʊk] (BRIT: inf) N [c] 家伙 [jiāhuo]

blond(e) [blɔnd] I ADJ **1** [+ hair] 金色的 [jīnsè de] **2** [+ person] 金发的人 [jīnfà de rén] II N [c] ▶ blonde (woman) 金发女子 [jīnfà nǚzǐ]

blood [blʌd] N [U] **1** (BIO) 血液 [xuèyè] **2** (referring to person's ancestry) 血统 [xuètǒng] ▶ in cold blood 残忍地 ▶ new or fresh or young blood (fig) 新生力量

blood donor N [c] 献血者 [xiànxuèzhě]

blood group N [c] 血型 [xuèxíng]

blood poisoning N [U] 血中毒 [xuè zhòngdú]

blood pressure N [U] 血压 [xuèyā] ▶ to have high/low blood pressure 有高/低血压 ▶ to take sb's blood pressure 量某人的血压

bloodshed ['blʌdʃed] N [U] 流血 [liúxuè]

bloodshot ['blʌdʃɔt] ADJ [+ eyes] 充血的 [chōngxuè de]

bloodstream ['blʌdstri:m] N [c] 血流 [xuèliú]

blood test N [c] 验血 [yànxuè] ▶ to have a blood test 验血

blood transfusion N [c] 输血 [shūxuè]

blood type N = blood group

blood vessel N [c] 血管 [xuèguǎn]

bloody ['blʌdɪ] I ADJ **1** [+ battle, riot] 血腥的 [xuèxīng de] **2** [+ knife, nose etc] 血淋淋的 [xuèlínlín de] **3** (BRIT: inf!) ▶ this bloody... 这个该死的⋯ [zhège gāisǐ de⋯] II VT [+ nose, hands] 使流血 [shǐ liúxuè] ▶ bloody heavy/good (BRIT: inf!) 重/好极了

bloom [blu:m] I N [c] (flower) 花 [huā] II VI **1** [tree, flower +] 开花 [kāihuā] **2** (fig) [talent etc +] 得以发展 [déyǐ fāzhǎn] ▶ to be in bloom [plant +] 盛开

blossom ['blɔsəm] I N [c/u] 花 [huā] II VI 开花 [kāihuā] ▶ to blossom (into sth) (fig) 成长

（为某事）

blot [blɔt] I N [C] **1** (on text) 污迹 [wūjì] **2** (fig) (on name etc) 损坏 [sǔnhuài] II VT **1** (with blotting paper) 吸干 [xīgān] **2** (with towel) 吸干 [xīgān] ▶ **a blot on the landscape** 有碍观瞻的物体 ▶ **to blot one's copybook** 损坏自己的名誉
▶ **blot out** VT **1** [+ view] 遮挡 [zhēdǎng] **2** [+ memory] 清除 [qīngchú]

blotchy ['blɔtʃi] ADJ [+ complexion] 斑斑点点的 [bānbān diǎndiǎn de]

blouse [blauz, US blaus] N [C] (woman's garment) 女士衬衫 [nǚshì chènshān]

> **shirts** 男女都可以穿，但 **blouses** 只是女装。

blow [bləu] (pt **blew**, pp **blown**) I N [C] **1** (punch) 拳打 [quándǎ] **2** (fig) (setback) 打击 [dǎjī] II VI **1** [wind, sand, dust etc +] 吹 [chuī] **2** [person +] 吹气 [chuīqì] **3** [whistle, horn +] 响 [xiǎng] III VT **1** [+ wind] 吹 [chuī] **2** [+ whistle, horn] 吹 [chuī] **3** (destroy) (by explosion) 炸毁 [zhàhuǐ] **4** (inf) [+ chance] 失去 [shīqù] **5** (inf) (spend) [+ money] 挥霍 [huīhuò] ▶ **to come to blows** 互相殴打 ▶ **a fuse has blown** 保险丝烧断了 ▶ **to blow one's nose** 擤鼻子 ▶ **you've blown it!** 你把事情弄糟了！
▶ **blow away** I VT 吹走 [chuīzǒu] II VI 刮跑 [guāpǎo]
▶ **blow down** VT [+ tree, house] 刮倒 [guādǎo]
▶ **blow off** I VT [+ hat etc] 吹走 [guāzǒu] II VI [hat etc +] 刮跑 [guāpǎo] ▶ **to be blown off course** [ship +] 被吹得偏离了航向
▶ **blow out** VT [+ flame, candle] 吹灭 [chuīmiè]
▶ **blow over** VI [trouble, crisis +] 平息 [píngxī]
▶ **blow up** I VI (explode) 爆炸 [bàozhà] II VT **1** (destroy) [+ bridge etc] 使爆炸 [shǐ bàozhà] **2** (inflate) [+ balloon, tyre] 冲气 [chōngqì] **3** (PHOT) (enlarge) 放大 [fàngdà]

blow-dry ['bləudraɪ] I VT [+ hair] 吹干 [chuīgān] II N [C] (hairstyle) 吹风定型 [chuīfēng dìngxíng]

blown [bləun] PP of **blow**

○ **blue** [blu:] I ADJ **1** (in colour) 蓝色的 [lánsè de] **2** (inf) (depressed) 抑郁的 [yìyù de] ▷ There's no reason for me to feel so blue. 我不知道为什么感到这么抑郁。II N [U] 蓝色 [lánsè] III **blues** NPL **1** (MUS) ▶ **the blues** 蓝调 [lándiào] **2** (inf) (depression) ▶ **to have the blues** 感到抑郁 [gǎndào yìyù] ▶ **blue movie/joke** 色情电影/笑话 ▶ **(only) once in a blue moon** (仅是) 难得的一次 ▶ **out of the blue** 意料之外

bluebell ['blu:bɛl] N [C] 风铃草 [fēnglíngcǎo]

blueberry ['blu:bɛrɪ] N [C] 越橘 [yuèjú]

blue cheese N [C/U] 蓝奶酪 [lánnǎilào]

blueprint ['blu:prɪnt] N **1** ▶ **a blueprint (for)** (fig) (…的) 蓝图 [(…de)lántú] **2** [C] (ARCHIT) (…的) 设计图 [(…de) shèjìtú]

blue tit N [C] 蓝山雀 [lánshānquè]

bluff [blʌf] I VI (pretend, threaten) 虚张声势 [xū zhāng shēngshì] II N **1** [C/U] (deception) 虚张声势 [xū zhāng shēngshì] **2** [C] (GEO) (steep cliff or bank) 峭壁 [qiàobì] III ADJ [+ man] 直截了当的 [zhíjié-liǎodàng de] ▶ **to call sb's bluff** 叫某人摊牌

blunder ['blʌndə(r)] I N [C] (mistake) 失策 [shīcè] II VI (bungle) 犯愚蠢的错误 [fàn yúchǔn de cuòwù] ▶ **to blunder into sb/sth** 笨手笨脚地撞倒人/某物

blunt [blʌnt] I ADJ **1** (not sharp) [+ pencil, knife] 钝的 [dùn de] **2** [+ person, remark] 直率的 [zhíshuài de] II VT **1** [+ scissors, chisel etc] 弄钝 [nòng dùn] **2** [+ appetite, emotion] 使减弱 [shǐ jiǎnruò] ▶ **blunt instrument** (LAW) 钝器 ▶ **to be blunt…** 坦率地说…

blur [blə:(r)] I N [C] (in vision, memory) 模糊不清 [móhu bùqīng] II VT **1** [+ vision, image] 模糊 [móhu] **2** [+ distinction] 使模糊不清 [shǐ móhu bùqīng] III VI [image +] 变模糊 [biàn móhu]

blush [blʌʃ] I VI (with shame, embarrassment) 脸红 [liǎnhóng] II N [C] 脸红 [liǎnhóng] ▶ **to spare** or **save sb's blushes** 不让某人感到脸红

blusher ['blʌʃə(r)] N [C/U] 胭脂 [yānzhi]

Blvd. ABBR (= boulevard) 大街 [dàjiē]

B.O. N ABBR (BRIT: inf) (= body odour) 狐臭 [húchòu]

board [bɔ:d] I N **1** [C] (piece of wood) 木板 [mùbǎn] **2** [C] (also: noticeboard) 公告板 [gōnggàobǎn] **3** [C] (also: blackboard) 黑板 [hēibǎn] **4** [C] (for chess etc) 盘 [pán] **5** [C] (committee) 委员会 [wěiyuánhuì] **6** [C] (in firm) 董事会 [dǒngshìhuì] **7** [U] (at hotel) 膳食 [shànshí] II VT (frm) [+ ship, train, plane] 上 [shàng] III VI (frm) (on ship, train, plane) 登上 [dēngshang] ▶ **full/half board** (BRIT) 全日/部分膳食供应 ▶ **board and lodging** 食宿 ▶ **on board** 在船/车/飞机上 ▶ **to take sth on board** [+ idea, suggestion] 接受某事物 ▶ **above board** 光明正大 ▶ **across the board** (as adv) 全面地; (as adj) 全面的 ▶ **to go by the board** 被忽略
▶ **board up** VT [+ door, window] 用板覆盖 [yòng bǎn fùgài]

board game N [C] 棋盘游戏 [qípán yóuxì]

boarding card ['bɔ:dɪŋ-] N [C] 登机卡 [dēngjīkǎ]

boarding pass N = **boarding card**

boarding school N [C/U] 寄宿学校 [jìsù xuéxiào]

boardroom ['bɔ:dru:m] N [C] 董事会议室 [dǒngshì huìyìshì]

boast [bəust] I VI ▶ **to boast (about** or **of)** 说 (关于某事的) 大话 [shuō (guānyú mǒushì de) dàhuà] II VT (possess, have) 夸耀 [kuāyào] III N [C] 自夸 [zìkuā] ▶ **to boast that…** 夸耀说…

boat [bəut] N [C] **1** (small vessel) 船 [chuán] **2** (ship) 轮船 [lúnchuán] ▶ **to go by boat** 乘

船去 ▶ **to be in the same boat** 处境相同 ▶ **to rock the boat** 捣乱

bob [bɒb] VI (also: **bob up and down**) [boat, cork +] 上下浮动 [shàngxià fúdòng] ▶ **bob up** VI 浮现 [fúxiàn]

bode [bəʊd] VI ▶ **to bode well/ill (for)** (为⋯)预示着好运/厄运 [(wèi⋯) yùshìzhe hǎoyùn/èyùn]

⊙ **body** ['bɒdɪ] N 1 [C] (ANAT) 身体 [shēntǐ] ▷ *My whole body hurt.* 我的整个身体都在痛。 2 [c] (torso, trunk) 躯干 [qūgàn] 3 [C] (corpse) 尸体 [shītǐ] ▷ *Police later found a body.* 警方后来找到了一具尸体。 4 [S] (main part) [of building] 主体 [zhǔtǐ] ▷ *the main body of the church* 教堂的主体; [of speech, document] 正文 [zhèngwén] 5 [c] [of car] 身 [shēn] 6 [c] (organization) 团体 [tuántǐ] ▷ *public bodies such as local authorities* 像地方当局这样的公共团体 7 [c] (quantity) [of evidence] 许多 [xǔduō] ▷ *There is a growing body of evidence pointing to these effects.* 越来越多的证据表明了这些后果。 8 [U] [of wine etc] 粘稠 [niánchóu]

bodybuilding ['bɒdɪ'bɪldɪŋ] N [U] 健身 [jiànshēn]

bodyguard ['bɒdɪɡɑːd] N [c] (of statesman, celebrity) 保镖 [bǎobiāo]

bodywork ['bɒdɪwɜːk] (AUT) N [U] 车身 [chēshēn]

bog [bɒg] I N [c] (marsh) 沼泽 [zhǎozé] II VT ▶ **to get bogged down** 被缠住 [bèi chánzhù]

bogus ['bəʊgəs] ADJ [+ claim, evidence etc] 伪造的 [wěizào de]

bohemian [bəʊ'hiːmɪən] I ADJ (writer, lifestyle) 放荡不羁的 [fàngdàng bùjī de] II N [c] (unconventional person) 放荡不羁的人 [fàngdàng bùjī de rén]

boil [bɔɪl] I VT 1 [+ water] 烧开 [shāokāi] 2 [+ eggs, potatoes etc] 煮 [zhǔ] II VI [liquid +] 沸腾 [fèiténg] III N (MED) 疖子 [jiēzi] ▶ **to boil a kettle** 烧开水 ▶ **to be boiling with anger** or **rage** 气愤至极 ▶ **to come to the** or (US) **a boil** 开始沸腾 ▶ **to bring a liquid to the boil** 把液体烧至沸腾

⬛用法参见 **cook**

▶ **boil down to** VT FUS [不可拆分] 归根结底 [guīgēn jiédǐ]

▶ **boil over** VI [kettle, milk +] 沸腾至溢出 [fèiténg zhì yìchū]

boiled egg ['bɔɪld-] N [C] 煮鸡蛋 [zhǔjīdàn]

boiled potatoes NPL 煮土豆 [zhǔtǔdòu]

boiler ['bɔɪlə(r)] N [c] (device) 锅炉 [guōlú]

boiling (hot) ['bɔɪlɪŋ-] (inf) ADJ ▶ **I'm boiling (hot)** 我太热了 [wǒ tài rè le] ▶ **it's boiling (hot)** 太热了

⬛用法参见 **hot**

boiling point N [U] [of liquid] 沸点 [fèidiǎn]

boisterous ['bɔɪstərəs] ADJ (noisy, excitable) [+ person, crowd] 喧闹的 [xuānnào de]

bold [bəʊld] I ADJ 1 (brave) [+ person, action] 大

胆的 [dàdǎn de] 2 [+ pattern, colours] 突出的 [tūchū de] II N [U] (TYP) 粗体字 [cūtǐzì] ▶ **in bold** (TYP) 用粗体字 [yòng cūtǐzì] ▶ **if I may be so bold** 恕我冒昧

bollard ['bɒləd] N [c] 1 (BRIT: AUT) 护柱 [hùzhù] 2 (NAUT) 系缆柱 [jì lǎn zhù]

bolt [bəʊlt] I N [c] 1 (to lock door) 插销 [chāxiāo] 2 (used with nut) 螺钉 [luódīng] II VT 1 [+ door] 闩 [shuān] 2 (fasten) ▶ **to bolt sth to sth** 把某物栓在某物上 [bǎ mǒuwù shuānzài mǒuwù shang] 3 [+ food] 囫囵吞下 [húlún tūnxià] III VI (run very fast) [horse +] 迅速跑开 [xùnsù pǎokāi]; [person +] 跑开 [pǎokāi] IV ADV ▶ **bolt upright** 笔直 [bǐzhí] ▶ **a bolt of lightning** 一道闪电 ▶ **a bolt from the blue** 晴天霹雳

bomb [bɒm] I N [c] 炸弹 [zhàdàn] II VT 轰炸 [hōngzhà]

bombard [bɒm'bɑːd] VT (MIL) 连续炮击 [liánxù pàojī] ▶ **to bombard sb with questions/ requests** 连珠炮似地向某人提问题/要求

bomber ['bɒmə(r)] N [c] 1 (AVIAT) 轰炸机 [hōngzhàjī] 2 (terrorist) 投放炸弹的人 [tóufàng zhàdàn de rén]

bombing ['bɒmɪŋ] N [C/U] 轰炸 [hōngzhà]

bombshell ['bɒmʃel] N [C] (revelation) 爆炸性事件 [bàozhàxìng shìjiàn]

bond [bɒnd] I N [c] 1 (link) [of affection etc] 纽带 [niǔdài] 2 (FIN) 公债 [gōngzhài] II VI 1 ▶ **to bond (with)** [mother + / child +] (与)⋯联结 [(yǔ)⋯liánjié] 2 [material +] 黏合 [niánhé] III **bonds** (liter) NPL (ties) 约束 [yuēshù]

bone [bəʊn] I N 1 [C/U] (in body of human, animal: ANAT) 骨头 [gǔtou] 2 [C] (in fish) 刺 [cì] II VT [+ meat, fish] 剔除骨刺 [tìchú gǔcì] ▶ **I've got a bone to pick with you** 我对你有怨言 ▶ **to make no bones about sth** 公开承认某事

bone marrow N [U] 骨髓 [gǔsuǐ]

bonfire ['bɒnfaɪə(r)] N [c] 1 (as part of a celebration) 篝火 [gōuhuǒ] 2 (to burn rubbish) 火堆 [huǒduī]

Bonfire Night (BRIT) N [U] 篝火之夜

⬛用法参见 **Guy Fawkes night**

bonnet ['bɒnɪt] N [c] 1 (BRIT) [of car] 引擎罩 [yǐnqíngzhào] [美 = **hood**] 2 (hat) 在颌下系带的帽子 [zài hé xià jì dài de màozi]

bonus ['bəʊnəs] N [c] 1 (extra payment) (on wages) 红利 [hónglì] 2 (additional benefit) 额外收获 [éwài shōuhuò]

bony ['bəʊnɪ] ADJ 1 [+ arm, face, fingers, person] 瘦的 [shòu de] 2 (ANAT) 骨的 [gǔ de] 3 [+ fish] 多刺的 [duō cì de]

boo [buː] I INT 1 (as joke) 在吓唬别人时发出的声音哇 2 (as criticism) 在表示批评时发出的声音:呸 II VT 为⋯喝倒彩 [wèi⋯hè dàocǎi] III VI 发嘘声表示不满 IV N [c] 嘘声 [xū shēng]

⊙ **book** [buk] I N [c] 1 (novel etc) 书 [shū] 2 [of

stamps, tickets] 册 [cè] II VT 1 [+ ticket, table, seat, room] 预订 [yùdìng] 2 [traffic warden, police officer +] 登记 [dēngjì] ▷ I was booked for speeding. 我因超速驾车而被记名。3 (FOOTBALL) 记名 警告 [jìmíng jǐnggào] III **books** NPL (COMM) (accounts) 账目 [zhàngmù] ▶ **by the book** 照 章办事 ▶ **to throw the book at sb** 重罚某人 ▶ **fully booked** 预订一空 ▶ **to keep the books** 作簿记

▶ **book in** (BRIT) VI (at hotel) 登记入住 [dēngjì rùzhù] [美= **check in**]

▶ **book into** (BRIT) VT FUS [不可拆分] [+ hotel] 登 记入住 [dēngjì rùzhù] [美= **check into**]

▶ **book up** VI 预订 [yùdìng] ▶ **all seats are booked up** 所有座位都被预订了 ▶ **the hotel is booked up** 这个宾馆已经订满了

bookcase ['bukkeɪs] N [c] 书橱 [shūchú]

booking ['bukɪŋ] N [c] 预订 [yùdìng]

booking office (BRIT: RAIL, THEAT) N [c] 售票 处 [shòupiàochù] [美= **ticket office**]

bookkeeping ['buk'kiːpɪŋ] N [U] 簿记 [bùjì]

booklet ['buklɪt] N [c] 小册子 [xiǎocèzi]

bookmaker ['bukmeɪkə(r)] N [c] 赌注登记人 [dǔzhù dēngjìrén]

bookmark ['bukmɑːk] I N [c] 书签 [shūqiān] II VT (COMPUT) 放书签 [fàng shūqiān]

bookseller ['bukselə(r)] N [c] 书商 [shūshāng]

bookshelf ['bukʃelf] N [c] 书架 [shūjià]

bookshop ['bukʃɒp] (BRIT) N [c] 书店 [shūdiàn] [美= **bookstore**]

bookstore ['bukstɔː(r)] (ESP US) N = **bookshop**

boom [buːm] I N [c] 1 (noise) 轰轰声 [hōnghōngshēng] 2 (ECON) 繁荣 [fánróng] 3 (in prices, popularity) 兴盛 [xīngshèng] II VI 1 (also: **boom out**) [guns, thunder +] 发出隆隆的 响声 [fāchū lónglóng de xiǎngshēng]; [voice +] 发出低沉有力的声音 [fāchū dīchén yǒulì de shēngyīn] 2 [sales, business, economy +] 繁荣 [fánróng]

boost [buːst] I N [c] 1 (to sales, economy etc) 促进 [cùjìn] 2 (to confidence, morale) 增强 [zēngqiáng] II VT 1 [+ sales, economy etc] 促进 [cùjìn] 2 [+ confidence, morale] 增强 [zēngqiáng]

boot [buːt] I N [c] 1 (footwear) (for winter) 靴子 [xuēzi]; (for football, walking etc) 鞋 [xié] 2 (BRIT) [of car] 车后行李箱 [chē hòu xínglǐxiāng] [美= **trunk**] II VT (inf) (kick) 猛踢 [měng tī] ▶ **... to boot** (in addition) 再者… ▶ **to get** or be **given the boot** (inf) 被解雇

▶ **boot up** (COMPUT) I VT 使运行 [shǐ yùnxíng] II VI 开始运行 [kāishǐ yùnxíng]

booth [buːð] N [c] 1 (for telephoning) 隔开的 小间 [gékāi de xiǎojiān] 2 (for voting) 投票站 [tóupiàozhàn] 3 (at fair) 摊子 [tānzi]

booze [buːz] (inf) I N [U] 酒 [jiǔ] II VI 饮酒 [yǐnjiǔ]

border ['bɔːdə(r)] I N [c] 1 [of country] 边界 [biānjiè] 2 (in garden) 花坛 [huātán] 3 (band,

edge) (on cloth etc) 饰边 [shìbiān] II VT 1 [+ road] 环绕 [huánrào] 2 [+ another country] 与···接壤 [yǔ...jiērǎng] III **Borders** N (BRIT: GEO) ▶ **the Borders** 英格兰与苏格兰交界区

▶ **border on** VT FUS [不可拆分] (fig) [+ insanity, brutality] 近于 [jìnyú]

borderline ['bɔːdəlaɪn] N [c] 边境线 [biānjìngxiàn] ▶ **to be on the borderline** (in exam etc) 两可之间

bore [bɔː(r)] I PT of **bear** II VT 1 [+ hole] 钻 [zuàn] 2 [+ oil well, tunnel] 开凿 [kāizáo] 3 [+ person] 使厌烦 [shǐ yànfán] III N 1 ▶ **12-bore shotgun** 12膛径的猎枪 [shí'èr tángjìng de lièqiāng] 2 [+ a bore [person +] 令人讨 厌的人 [lìng rén tǎoyàn de rén]; [situation +] 令 人厌烦的事 [lìng rén yànfán de shì] ▶ **it's a bore** 令人讨厌 ▶ **it/he bores me to tears** or **to death** or **stiff** 它/他把我烦死了 ▶ **to be bored (with sth)** (对某事) 不感兴趣 ▶ **to be bored to tears** or **bored to death** or **bored stiff** (inf) 厌 烦得要死

> 如果你感觉 **bored**，是因为你对所做 的事情不感兴趣，或没有你所感兴趣 的事情去做。If you're bored, we could go for a walk. 当你觉得某人、某地或某物 没意思而使你感觉乏味时，就可以用 **boring** 来形容。a boring job...a boring little mining town... He can be a bit boring sometimes.

boredom ['bɔːdəm] N [U] 1 (state of being bored) 厌烦 [yànfán] 2 (boring quality) 乏味 [fáwèi]

boring ['bɔːrɪŋ] ADJ (tedious) [+ person, job, film] 乏味的 [fáwèi de]

born [bɔːn] ADJ ▶ **to be born** [baby +] 出生 [chūshēng] ▶ **to be born of** or **to sb** (frm) 是某 人的孩子 ▶ **a born comedian** 天生的喜剧演 员 ▶ **born and bred** 土生土长

borne [bɔːn] PP of **bear**

borough ['bʌrə, US 'bʌroʊ] N [c] 自治城市 [zìzhì chéngshì]

borrow ['bɒrəʊ] VT (from sb, from library) 借 [jiè] ▶ **can I borrow a pen please?** 我能不能 借枝笔？

bosom ['buzəm] I N 1 [c] (o.f.) (also: **bosoms**) [of woman] 乳房 [rǔfáng] 2 [s] (liter) [of family, community] 中间 [zhōngjiān] II ADJ [+ friend] 亲 密的 [qīnmì de]

boss [bɒs] I N [c] 1 (employer) 老板 [lǎobǎn] 2 (inf) (leader) 领导 [lǐngdǎo] II VT 支配 [zhīpèi] ▶ **to be one's own boss** 一切由自己 作主

▶ **boss around, boss about** VT 对某人呼来唤 去 [duì mǒurén hū lái huàn qù]

bossy ['bɒsɪ] ADJ 霸道的 [bàdào de]

botany ['bɒtənɪ] N [U] 植物学 [zhíwùxué]

○ **both** [bəʊθ] I ADJ 两者都 [liǎngzhě dōu] ▷ Both policies make good sense. 两项政策都很 有道理。II PRON 1 (things) 两者 [liǎngzhě]

▷ *Most of them speak English or German or both.* 他们大部分会说英语或者德语，或者两种语言都会。**2** *(people)* ▷ *He's fond of you both.* 你们两个他都喜欢。**III** CONJ ▶ **both A and B** A和B两者都 [A hé B liǎngzhě dōu] ▶ **both (of them)** （他们）两个都 ▶ **both of us went** *or* **we both went** 我们两个都去了 ▶ **they saw both of us** 我们两个他们都看见了

bother ['bɔðə(r)] **I** VT **1** *(worry)* 烦扰 [fánrǎo] **2** *(disturb)* 打扰 [dǎrǎo] **II** VI 在乎 [zàihū] **III** N **1** [U] *(trouble)* 麻烦 [máfan] **2** [U] *(difficulty)* 费力 [fèilì] **3** [S] *(nuisance)* 麻烦事 [máfanshì] **IV** INT *(also: bother it)* (ESP BRIT: *o.f.*) 真讨厌 [zhēn tǎoyàn] ▶ **to bother doing sth** *or* **to do sth** 费心做某事 ▶ **I can't be bothered to go** *(it's unnecessary)* 我没必要去; *(I'm too lazy)* 我没劲去 ▶ **don't bother** 不用了 ▶ **it's no bother** 不麻烦 ▶ **it's a bother** 是件麻烦事

bottle ['bɔtl] **I** N **1** [C] *(glass etc container) (for milk, wine, perfume)* 瓶子 [píngzi] **2** [C] *(amount contained)* 瓶 [píng] **3** [C] *(baby's)* 奶瓶 [nǎipíng] **4** [U] (BRIT: *inf) (courage)* 胆量 [dǎnliàng] **II** VT **1** [+ *beer, wine*] 装瓶 [zhuāngpíng] **2** [+ *fruit*] 装罐储藏 [zhuāngguàn chǔcáng] ▶ **a bottle of wine/milk** 一瓶葡萄酒/牛奶 ▶ **a wine/milk bottle** 葡萄酒/牛奶瓶 ▶ **bottled beer** 瓶装啤酒 ▶ **bottled water** 瓶装水
▶ **bottle up** VT [+ *emotion*] 抑制 [yìzhì]

bottle bank (BRIT) N [C] 旧瓶回收处 [jiùpíng huíshōuchù]

bottle opener N [C] 开瓶器 [kāipíngqì]

bottom ['bɔtəm] **I** N **1** [C] *(of container, sea)* 底部 [dǐbù] **2** [C] *(of page, list)* 下端 [xiàduān] **3** [U/S] *(of class, league)* 最后一名 [zuìhòu yīmíng] **4** [S] *(of organization, company)* 最底层 [zuìdǐcéng] **5** [C] *(of hill, tree, stairs)* 最底部 [zuìdǐbù] **6** [C] *(buttocks)* 臀部 [túnbù] **7** [C] *(also: bottoms)* [*of bikini, tracksuit*] 下装 [xiàzhuāng] **II** ADJ **1** *(lowest)* 最下面的 [zuì xiàmian de] **2** *(least important)* [+ *rung, position*] 最低的 [zuì dī de] ▶ **at the bottom of** 在…的底部 ▶ **to get to the bottom of sth** 彻底查明某事
▶ **bottom out** VI [*recession etc* +] 降到最低点 [jiàng dào zuìdīdiǎn]

bought [bɔːt] PT, PP *of* **buy**

boulder ['bəʊldə(r)] N [C] 巨石 [jùshí]

bounce [bauns] **I** VI **1** [*ball* +] 弹起 [tánqǐ] **2** [*hair* +] 跳动 [tiàodòng] **3** [*cheque* +] 退回 [tuìhuí] **II** VT **1** [+ *ball*] 拍 [pāi] **2** [+ *cheque*] 拒付 [jùfù] **III** N [C/U] [*of ball*] 弹起 [tánqǐ] ▶ **to bounce on** [+ *bed etc*] 蹦跳上 ▶ **to bounce up and down** 上下跳动 ▶ **to bounce in/out etc** [*person* +] 蹦跳地进来/出去 {等}

bouncer ['baunsə(r)] (*inf*) N [C] *(at dance, club)* 保安 [bǎo'ān]

bound [baund] **I** PT, PP *of* **bind** **II** N [C] *(liter) (leap)* 跳 [tiào] **III** VI *(leap)* 大步快走

[dàbù kuàizǒu] **IV** VT *(border)* 接壤 [jiērǎng] **V** ADJ ▶ **bound by** [+ *law, regulation*] 被…约束 [bèi…yuēshù] **VI bounds** NPL *(limit)* 限制 [xiànzhì] ▶ **to be bound to do sth** *(certain)* 一定做某事; *(obliged)* 有义务做某事 ▶ **bound for** (NAUT, AUT, RAIL) 开往 ▶ **to be bound up in sth** 忙于某事 ▶ **to be bound up with sth** 与某事密切相关 ▶ **out of bounds** [+ *place*] 不准进入 ▶ **to know no bounds** 无可限量

boundary ['baundrı] N [C] *(border, limit)* 边界 [biānjiè]

bouquet ['bukeɪ] N **1** [C] *(of flowers)* 束 [shù] **2** [C/U] *(of wine)* 芳香 [fāngxiāng]

bourbon ['buəbən] (US) N [U] 波旁威士忌 [bōpáng wēishìjì]

bourgeois ['buəʒwɑ:] ADJ *(pej)* 资产阶级的 [zīchǎn jiējí de]

bout [baut] N [C] **1** [*of illness*] 发作 [fāzuò] **2** [*of activity*] 次 [cì] **3** (BOXING ETC) 场 [chǎng]

boutique [bu:'ti:k] N [C] 小型精品店 [xiǎoxíng jīngpǐndiàn]

bow¹ [bəu] N [C] **1** *(knot)* 蝴蝶结 [húdiéjié] **2** *(weapon)* 弓 [gōng] **3** (MUS) 琴弓 [qíngōng]

bow² [bau] **I** N [C] **1** [*of head, body*] 鞠躬 [jūgōng] **2** (NAUT) *(also: bows)* 船首 [chuánshǒu] **II** VI *(with head, body)* 鞠躬 [jūgōng] **III** VT [+ *head*] 低头 [dītóu] ▶ **to bow to** [+ *pressure, sb's wishes*] 服从 ▶ **to bow to the inevitable** 向命运低头
▶ **bow out** VI ▶ **to bow out (of sth)** 退出 (某事) [tuìchū (mǒushì)]

bowels ['bauəlz] NPL **1** (ANAT) 肠 [cháng] **2** *(liter)* [*of the earth etc*] 深处 [shēnchù]

bowl [bəul] **I** N [C] **1** *(container for eating)* 碗 [wǎn] **2** *(contents)* 一碗的量 [yī wǎn de liàng] **3** *(for washing clothes/dishes)* 盆 [pén] **4** [*of toilet*] 马桶 [mǎtǒng] **5** (SPORT) *(ball)* 木球 [mùqiú] *see also* **bowls** **6** [*of pipe*] 烟斗 [yāndǒu] **7** (ESP US) *(stadium)* 体育场 [tǐyùchǎng] **II** VI (CRICKET) 投球 [tóuqiú]
▶ **bowl over** VT **1** *(knock over)* 撞倒 [zhuàngdǎo] **2** *(impress)* 使大吃一惊 [shǐ dàchī yìjīng]

bowler ['bəulə(r)] N [C] **1** (CRICKET) 投球员 [tóuqiúyuán] **2** (BRIT) = **bowler hat**

bowler hat (BRIT) N [C] 圆顶硬礼帽 [yuándǐng yìng lǐmào]

bowling ['bəulıŋ] N [U] *(game)* 保龄球 [bǎolíngqiú] ▶ **to go bowling** 打保龄球

bowling alley N [C] *(building)* 保龄球球道 [bǎolíngqiú qiúdào]

bowling green N [C] 地滚球草地球场 [dìgǔnqiú cǎodì qiúchǎng]

bowls [bəulz] (BRIT) N [U] *(game)* 地滚球戏 [dìgǔnqiúxì] [美 = **lawn bowling**]

bow tie [bəu-] N [C] 蝶形领结 [diéxíng lǐngjié]

box [bɔks] **I** N [C] **1** *(container)* 盒子 [hézi] **2** *(contents)* 盒 [hé] ▷ *a box of chocolates/tissues* 一盒巧克力/纸巾 **3** *(also: cardboard box)* 纸

箱 [zhǐxiāng] **4** (crate) 箱 [xiāng] **5** (THEAT, SPORT) 包厢 [bāoxiāng] **6** ▶ **the box** (BRIT: inf) (television) 电视 [diànshì] **7** ▶ **the box** (FOOTBALL) (penalty area) 罚球区 [fáqiúqū] **8** (BRIT) (road marking) 十字路口路面的方格标记 **9** (on form) 方框 [fāngkuàng] **II** VT (put in a box) 装箱 [zhuāngxiāng] **III** VI (SPORT) 拳击 [quánjī]
▶ **box in** VT [+ car, person] 围困 [wéikùn]

boxer ['bɔksə(r)] N [c] **1** (person) 拳击运动员 [quánjī yùndòngyuán] **2** (dog) 斗拳狗 [dòuquángǒu]

boxer shorts, boxers NPL 平角裤 [píngjiǎokù]

boxing ['bɔksɪŋ] (SPORT) N [U] 拳击 [quánjī]

Boxing Day (BRIT) N [c/U] 圣诞节后的第一天，是公共假日

boxing gloves NPL 拳击手套 [quánjī shǒutào]

boxing ring N [c] 拳击台 [quánjītái]

box office N **1** [c] (in theatre/cinema) 售票处 [shòupiàochù] **2** [s] (fig) 票房 [piàofáng] ▶ **a box office success** 非常卖座

○ boy [bɔɪ] N [c] **1** (male child) 男孩 [nánhái] **2** (young man) 男青年 [nán qīngnián] ▷ the age when girls get interested in boys 女孩子开始对男青年感兴趣的年龄 **3** (inf) (son) 儿子 [érzi]

boycott ['bɔɪkɔt] **I** N [c] 联合抵制 [liánhé dǐzhì] **II** VT [+ product, place, event] 联合抵制 [liánhé dǐzhì]

boyfriend ['bɔɪfrɛnd] N [c] 男朋友 [nánpéngyou]

boyish ['bɔɪʃ] ADJ **1** [+ man, looks, smile] 男孩子气的 [nánháizi qì de] **2** [+ woman] 男孩式的 [nánhái shì de]

bra [brɑ:] N [c] 胸罩 [xiōngzhào]

brace [breɪs] **I** N [c] **1** (on teeth) 牙箍 [yágū] **2** (on leg, neck) 支架 [zhījià] **II** **braces** NPL **1** (BRIT) 背带 [bēidài] [美 = suspenders] **2** (US: TYP) (also: curly braces) 大括弧 [dà kuòhú] [英 = curly brackets] **III** VT [+ knees, shoulders] 绷紧 [bēngjǐn] ▶ **to brace oneself** (in order to steady oneself) 使自己紧撑; (fig) (for shock) 稳定情绪

bracelet ['breɪslɪt] N [c] 手镯 [shǒuzhuó]

bracing ['breɪsɪŋ] ADJ [+ air, climate, walk, swim] 令人振奋的 [lìng rén zhènfèn de]

bracket ['brækɪt] **I** N [c] **1** (group, range) 类别 [lèibié] **2** (TECH) 托架 [tuōjià] **3** (also: round bracket) 圆括号 [yuánkuòhào] **4** (also: square bracket) 方括号 [fāngkuòhào] **II** VT **1** (also: bracket together) (fig) 把…归入同类 [bǎ…guīrù tónglèi] **2** [+ word, phrase] 把…括在括号内 [bǎ…kuò zài kuòhào nèi] ▶ **income bracket** 收入阶层 ▶ **in brackets** 括号内

brag [bræg] VI ▶ **to brag (about)** 吹嘘 [chuīxū]

braid [breɪd] **I** N **1** [U] (on clothes, curtains) 穗带 [suìdài] **2** [c] (US) (plait) 辫子 [biànzi]

[英 = plait] **II** VT (US) [+ hair] 把…编成辫子 [bǎ…biānchéng biànzi] [英 = plait]

Braille [breɪl] N [U] 布莱叶盲文 [Bùláiyè mángwén]

brain [breɪn] **I** N **1** [c] (ANAT) 脑 [nǎo] **2** [U] (fig) 大脑 [dànǎo] **II** **brains** NPL **1** (CULIN) 脑髓 [nǎosuǐ] **2** (intelligence) 智力 [zhìlì] ▶ **he's got brains** 他很聪慧 ▶ **he's the brains of the organization** (inf) 他是该组织的中枢人物 ▶ **to pick sb's brains** (inf) 问某人的意见 ▶ **to rack one's brains** 绞尽脑汁

brainwash ['breɪnwɔʃ] VT 给…洗脑 [gěi…xǐnǎo]

brainy ['breɪnɪ] ADJ (inf) [+ child, person] 聪明的 [cōngming de]

braise [breɪz] VT 炖 [dùn]

brake [breɪk] **I** N [c] **1** (AUT) 刹车 [shāchē] **2** (fig) 阻碍 [zǔ'ài] **II** VI [driver, vehicle +] 刹车 [shāchē] **III** VT [+ vehicle] 刹 [shā]

brake light N [c] 刹车灯 [shāchēdēng]

bran [bræn] N [U] 麸 [fū]

branch [brɑ:ntʃ] N [c] **1** [of tree] 树枝 [shùzhī] **2** [of shop] 分店 [fēndiàn]; [of bank, company etc] 分支机构 [fēnzhī jīgòu] **3** [of family, organization] 支系 [zhīxì] **4** [of subject] 分科 [fēnkē]
▶ **branch off** VI **1** [road, path +] 分叉 [fēnchà] **2** [person +] 转向 [zhuǎnxiàng]
▶ **branch out** VI ▶ **to branch out into** 向新的方向发展 [xiàng xīn de fāngxiàng fāzhǎn]

brand [brænd] **I** N [c] **1** (make) 牌子 [páizi] **2** (fig) (type) 模式 [móshì] **II** VT **1** (fig) ▶ **to brand sb a racist** etc 给某人栽上种族主义者{等}的恶名 [gěi mǒurén zāishang zhǒngzúzhǔyìzhě {děng} de èmíng] **2** [+ cattle] 打烙印于 [dǎ làoyìn yú]

brand-new ['brænd'nju:] ADJ 全新的 [quánxīn de]

brandy ['brændɪ] N [c/U] 白兰地酒 [báilándìjiǔ]

brash [bræʃ] ADJ (forward, cheeky) 恭撞的 [mǎngzhuàng de]

brass [brɑ:s] N [U] (metal) 铜 [tóng] ▶ **the brass (section)** (MUS) 铜管乐器

brass band N [c] 铜管乐队 [tóngguǎn yuèduì]

brassiere ['bræsɪə(r)] (o.f.) N [c] 胸罩 [xiōngzhào]

brat [bræt] (pej) N [c] (child) 臭小孩儿 [chòu xiǎoháir]

brave [breɪv] **I** ADJ **1** [+ person] 勇敢的 [yǒnggǎn de] **2** [+ attempt, smile, action] 英勇的 [yīngyǒng de] **II** N [c] (o.f.) (warrior) 北美印第安勇士 [Běiměi Yìndì'ān Yǒngshì] **III** VT (face up to) 勇敢面对 [yǒnggǎn miànduì] ▶ **to put a brave face on sth** 面对某事时显示出勇气

bravery ['breɪvərɪ] N [U] 英勇 [yīngyǒng]

brawl [brɔ:l] **I** N [c] (in pub, street) 打闹 [dǎnào] **II** VI 打架 [dǎjià]

Brazil [brə'zɪl] N 巴西 [Bāxī]

breach [briːtʃ] I VT 1 [+ agreement, law] 违反 [wéifǎn] 2 [+ security, defences] 突破 [tūpò] 3 (frm) [+ wall, barrier] 冲破 [chōngpò] II N [c] 1 [of agreement, law] 违反 [wéifǎn] 2 (gap) (in wall, barrier) 缺口 [quēkǒu] 3 (frm) (rupture) (between people, groups) 破裂 [pòliè] ▶ breach of the peace (LAW) 扰乱治安罪 ▶ breach of security 冲破重围 ▶ breach of contract 违背合同

bread [brɛd] N [U] 面包 [miànbāo]

breadbin ['brɛdbɪn] (BRIT) N [c] 面包箱 [miànbāoxiāng] [美=breadbox]

breadbox ['brɛdbɒks] (US) N = breadbin

breadcrumbs ['brɛdkrʌmz] NPL 面包屑 [miànbāoxiè]

breadth [brɛtθ] N [U] 1 (width) 宽度 [kuāndù] 2 (fig) [of experience, knowledge] 丰富 [fēngfù]

○ **break** [breɪk] (pt **broke**, pp **broken**) I VT 1 [+ cup, window etc] 打碎 [dǎsuì] 2 [+ leg, arm] 弄断 [nòngduàn] 3 [+ equipment] 损坏 [sǔnhuài] 4 [+ promise, contract] 违背 [wéibèi] 5 [+ law, rule] 违反 [wéifǎn] 6 [+ record] 打破 [dǎpò] 7 [+ habit, pattern etc] 改变 [gǎibiàn] 8 [+ person] 毁掉 [huǐdiào] ▷ He never let his jailers break him. 他是永远不会让他的监狱看守弄垮的。 9 [+ fall, impact] 减弱 [jiǎnruò] ▷ The trees broke his fall. 树丛使他下落的坠势稍缓。 10 [+ news] 透露 [tòulù] ▷ Then Louise broke the news that she was leaving me. 然后路易丝向我透露她要和我分手。 11 [+ code] 破译 [pòyì] 12 (TENNIS) [+ sb's serve] 破发成功 [pòfā chénggōng] II VI 1 [cup, window etc +] 破碎 [pòsuì] 2 [storm, weather +] 突然发生 [tūrán fāshēng] 3 [dawn, day +] 破晓 [pòxiǎo] 4 [story, news +] 传开 [chuánkāi] 5 (pause, rest) 暂停 [zhàntíng] ▷ They broke for lunch. 他们暂停去吃午餐了。 6 [wave +] 冲击 [chōngjī] 7 [voice +] (of boy) 变声 [biànshēng] III N 1 [c] (rest) 休息 [xiūxi] ▷ I'm going to have a break. 我要休息一下。 2 [c] (pause, interval) 间歇 [jiànxiē] ▷ There was a break in the middle of the day's events. 那天的活动中有一次间歇。 3 [c] (fracture) 骨折 [gǔzhé] 4 [U] (BRIT: SCOL) 课间休息 [kèjiān xiūxi] [美=recess] 5 [c] (inf) (chance) 运气 [yùnqi] ▷ Her big break came when she appeared on TV. 上电视的机会给她带来了好运气。 6 [c] (holiday) 休假 [xiūjià] ▶ to break the news to sb 委婉地向某人透露消息 ▶ to break even (COMM) 收支持平 ▶ to break with sb/sth 与某人绝交/放弃某事 ▶ to break free or loose (of sb/sth) [person, animal +] 摆脱(某人/某事) ▶ to take a break (for a few minutes) 休息一下; (have a holiday) 休假 ▶ without a break 连续不断 ▶ a lucky break 好运气
  ▶ **break away** VI (from pursuer etc) 逃脱
  ▶ **break down** I VI 1 [machine, car +] 坏掉 [huàidiào] 2 (CHEM) 分解 [fēnjiě] 3 [person +] 情绪失控 [qíngxù shīkòng] 4 [talks +] 破裂

[pòliè] II VT 1 [+ figures, data] 把…分类 [bǎ… fēnlèi] 2 [+ door etc] 捣毁 [dǎohuǐ] 3 (CHEM) 分解 [fēnjiě] 4 (fig) [+ barriers, prejudices] 解除 [jiěchú]
  ▶ **break in** I VI 1 [burglar +] 破门而入 [pòmén ér rù] 2 (interrupt) 打断 [dǎduàn] II VT [+ new shoes, engine etc] 使合用 [shǐ héyòng]
  ▶ **break into** VT FUS [不可拆分] 1 [+ house] 强行进入 [qiángxíng jìnrù] 2 [+ new activity] 开始进入 [kāishǐ jìnrù] ▷ She finally broke into films after an acclaimed stage career. 继一段成功的舞台生涯之后她最终投身电影业。 ▶ to break into song/a run 突然唱起来/跑了起来
  ▶ **break off** I VI 1 [branch +] 折断 [zhéduàn] 2 [speaker +] 突然打住 [tūrán dǎzhù] II VT 1 [+ branch, piece of chocolate] 折断 [zhéduàn] 2 [+ talks] 突然终止 [tūrán zhōngzhǐ] 3 [+ engagement, relationship] 断绝 [duànjué] ▶ to break it off with sb 同某人分手
  ▶ **break open** VT [+ door, window etc] 用力打开 [yònglì dǎkāi]
  ▶ **break out** VI 1 (begin) [war, fight +] 爆发 [bàofā] 2 (escape) [prisoner +] 逃脱 [táotuō] ▶ to break out in spots/a rash/a sweat 突然出了一身红点/疹子/汗
  ▶ **break through** I VI [sun +] 显现 [xiǎnxiàn] II VT FUS [不可拆分] [+ defences, barrier] 突破 [tūpò]
  ▶ **break up** I VI 1 [ship +] 碎裂 [suìliè] 2 [couple, marriage +] 破裂 [pòliè] 3 [meeting, party +] 纷纷离去 [fēnfēn líqù] 4 (BRIT) 学期结束 [xuéqí jiéshù] II VT 1 [rocks, biscuit etc] 弄碎 [nòngsuì] 2 [+ journey, day] 使有间歇 [shǐ yǒu jiànxiē] 3 [+ fight etc] 调停 [tiáotíng] 4 [+ meeting, demonstration] 驱散 [qūsàn] 5 [+ marriage] 使破裂 [shǐ pòliè] ▶ to break up with sb 同某人分手

breakdown ['breɪkdaun] N [c] 1 (AUT) 故障 [gùzhàng] 2 [of system, talks] 中断 [zhōngduàn] 3 [of marriage] 破裂 [pòliè] 4 (MED) (also: nervous breakdown) 精神崩溃 [jīngshén bēngkuì] 5 [of costs, figures] 分类细目 [fēnlèi xìmù] ▶ to have a breakdown 精神崩溃

breakfast ['brɛkfəst] I N [c/U] 早餐 [zǎocān] II VI 吃早餐 [chī zǎocān]
▓▓用法参见 meal

break-in ['breɪkɪn] N [c] 闯入 [chuǎngrù]

breakthrough ['breɪkθruː] N [c] 1 (achievement) 重要成果 [zhòngyào chéngguǒ] 2 (progress) 突破性进展 [tūpòxìng jìnzhǎn]

breast [brɛst] N 1 [c] [of woman] 乳房 [rǔfáng] 2 [c] (liter) (chest) 胸部 [xiōngbù] 3 [c/U] (CULIN) (of chicken, lamb) 胸脯肉 [xiōngpúròu] 4 [c] [of bird] 前胸 [qiánxiōng] ▶ to make a clean breast of sth 坦白承认某事

breast-feed ['brɛstfiːd] (pt, pp **breast-fed**) I VT 母乳哺养 [mǔrǔ bǔyǎng] II VI 母乳哺养 [mǔrǔ bǔyǎng]

breaststroke ['brɛststrəʊk] N [U] (also: **the breaststroke**) 蛙泳 [wāyǒng]

breath [brɛθ] N 1 [C/U] (intake of air) 呼吸 [hūxī] **2** [U] (air from mouth) 口气 [kǒuqì] ▶ **out of breath** 上气不接下气 ▶ **under one's breath** 低声说 ▶ **bad breath** 口臭 ▶ **to get one's breath back** (BRIT) 恢复正常呼吸 ▶ **to go out for a breath of (fresh) air** 出去呼吸 (新鲜) 空气 ▶ **a breath of fresh air** (fig) 新意 ▶ **there wasn't a breath of wind** 一丝风都没有 ▶ **to catch one's breath** 喘口气 ▶ **to hold one's breath** 屏住呼吸 ▶ **don't hold your breath!** (fig) (inf) 别太指望了！ ▶ **to be short of breath** 呼吸短促 ▶ **to take a deep breath** 深呼一口气 ▶ **it takes your breath away** 使人心醉神迷

Breathalyzer®, Breathalyser® ['brɛθəlaɪzə(r)] N [C] 测醉器 [cèzuìqì]

breathe [bri:ð] I VT 1 [+ air] 呼吸 [hūxī] **2** (liter) (whisper) 低语 [dīyǔ] II VI 呼吸 [hūxī] ▶ **I won't breathe a word about it** 我不会透露一点儿风声的 ▶ **to breathe life into sth** 给某事带来活力
▶ **breathe in** I VI 吸入 [xīrù] II VT [+ air, smoke] 吸入 [xīrù]
▶ **breathe out** VI 呼出 [hūchū]

breathing ['bri:ðɪŋ] N [U] 呼吸 [hūxī]

breathless ['brɛθlɪs] ADJ (from exertion) 气喘吁吁的 [qìchuǎn xūxū de] ▶ **breathless with excitement** 激动地透不过气来

breathtaking ['brɛθteɪkɪŋ] ADJ [+ speed, view] 惊人的 [jīngrén de]

breath test N [C] 呼吸测醉分析 [hūxī cèzuì fēnxī]

breed [bri:d] (pt, pp **bred** [brɛd]) I VT **1** [+ animals] 繁殖 [fánzhí] **2** [+ plants] 培植 [péizhí] **3** (fig) (give rise to) [+ situation, quality, hate, suspicion] 引起 [yǐnqǐ] II VI (ZOOL) 繁殖 [fánzhí] III N [C] **1** (ZOOL) 品种 [pǐnzhǒng] **2** (type, class) 类型 [lèixíng]

breeze [bri:z] I N [C] 微风 [wēifēng] II VI ▶ **to breeze in/out** 飘然而至/去 [piāorán ér zhì/qù] ▶ **it was a breeze** (inf) 这是小事一桩

breezy ['bri:zɪ] ADJ **1** [+ manner, tone] 轻松活泼的 [qīngsōng huópō de] **2** [+ weather] 惠风和畅的 [huìfēng héchàng de]

brew [bru:] I VT **1** [+ tea, coffee] 冲泡 [chōngpào] **2** [+ beer] 酿造 [niàngzào] II VI **1** [crisis +] 酝酿 [yùnniàng] **2** [storm +] 即将来临 [jíjiāng láilín] **3** [tea, coffee +] 煮 [zhǔ] **4** [beer +] 酿制 [niàngzhì] III N [C] (of tea, coffee) (drink) 饮料 [yǐnliào]; (type) 茶或咖啡的种类 [chá huò kāfēi de zhǒnglèi]

brewery ['bru:ərɪ] N [C] 啤酒厂 [píjiǔchǎng]

bribe [braɪb] I N [C] 贿赂 [huìlù] II VT [+ person, witness] 行贿 [xínghuì] ▶ **to bribe sb to do sth** 贿赂某人去做某事

bribery ['braɪbərɪ] N [U] (with money, favours) 行贿 [xínghuì]

bric-a-brac ['brɪkəbræk] N [U] 小摆设 [xiǎobǎishè]

brick [brɪk] N [C/U] (for building) 砖 [zhuān] ▶ **brick up** VT [+ door, window] 用砖填砌 [yòng zhuān tiánqì]

bricklayer ['brɪkleɪə(r)] N [C] 砌砖工 [qìzhuāngōng]

bride [braɪd] N [C] 新娘 [xīnniáng]

bridegroom ['braɪdgru:m] N [C] 新郎 [xīnláng]

bridesmaid ['braɪdzmeɪd] N [C] 伴娘 [bànniáng]

bridge [brɪdʒ] I N **1** [C] (ARCHIT) 桥 [qiáo] **2** [C] (NAUT) 舰桥 [jiànqiáo] **3** [C] (of nose) 鼻梁 [bíliáng] **4** [C/U] (CARDS) 桥牌 [qiáopái] **5** [C] (fig) 桥梁作用 [qiáoliáng zuòyòng] II VT (fig) [+ gap, gulf] 跨越 [kuàyuè]

bridle ['braɪdl] I N [C] 马笼头 [mǎlóngtóu] II VT [+ horse] 给…套笼头 [gěi…tào lóngtóu] III VI ▶ **to bridle (at)** (liter) [+ memory, comment etc] 表示愤怒 [biǎoshì fènnù]

brief [bri:f] I ADJ **1** [+ period, visit, appearance] 短暂的 [duǎnzhàn de] **2** [+ description, speech] 简短的 [jiǎnduǎn de] II N [C] (ESP BRIT: frm) (task) 任务 [rènwu] III VT (inform) 对…作任务指示 [duì…zuò rènwù zhǐshì] IV **briefs** NPL **1** (for men) 男式三角内裤 [nánshì sānjiǎo nèikù] **2** (for women) 女式三角内裤 [nǚshì sānjiǎo nèikù] ▶ **in brief…** 简而言之… ▶ **I'll try to be brief** 我尽量简单地说

briefcase ['bri:fkeɪs] N [C] 公事包 [gōngshìbāo]

briefing ['bri:fɪŋ] N [C/U] 发布会 [fābùhuì]

briefly ['bri:flɪ] ADV [smile, talk, explain, say +] 简短地 [jiǎnduǎn de]

brigadier [brɪgə'dɪə(r)] N [C] 准将 [zhǔnjiàng]

bright [braɪt] ADJ **1** [+ light] 亮的 [liàng de] **2** [+ weather, day] 晴朗的 [qínglǎng de] **3** [+ room] 明亮的 [míngliàng de] **4** (clever) [+ person] 聪明的 [cōngmíng de]; [+ idea] 巧妙的 [qiǎomiào de] **5** (lively) [+ person] 愉快的 [yúkuài de] **6** [+ colour] 鲜亮的 [xiānliàng de] **7** [+ clothes] 鲜艳的 [xiānyàn de] **8** [+ outlook, future] 光明的 [guāngmíng de] ▶ **to look on the bright side** 抱着乐观的态度

brilliance ['brɪljəns] N [U] **1** [of light, sun] 光辉 [guānghuī] **2** [of person, talent] 才华横溢 [cáihuá héngyì]

brilliant ['brɪljənt] ADJ **1** [+ person, mind] 才华横溢的 [cáihuá héngyì de] **2** [+ idea, performance] 出色的 [chūsè de] **3** [+ sunshine, light, colour] 光彩夺目的 [guāngcǎi duómù de] **4** (successful) [+ career, future] 辉煌的 [huīhuáng de] **5** (ESP BRIT: inf) (wonderful) 棒极了的 [bàngjíle de]

brim [brɪm] I N [C] (of hat) 帽边 [màobiān] II VI ▶ **to be brimming with** [+ confidence, love] 洋溢 [yángyì] ▶ **her eyes were brimming with tears** 她的眼里溢满了泪水 ▶ **to be full to the**

brim 满到边

brine [braɪn] N [U] 盐水 [yánshuǐ]

○ **bring** [brɪŋ] (pt, pp **brought**) VT **1** [+ thing, person] (with you) 带来 [dàilái] ▷ He brought Judy with him. 他把朱迪带来了。; (to sb) 拿来 [nálái] ▷ Would you bring me a glass of water? 请给我拿杯水来, 好吗? **2** (move) 移 [yí] ▷ She brought her hands up to her face. 她将手移到脸上。 **3** [+ satisfaction, trouble] 带来 [dàilái] ▷ Her three children brought her joy. 她的3个孩子给她带来欢乐。 **4** (cause to come) 使来到 [shǐ láidào] ▷ What brought you to this town in the first place? 究竟是什么使你来到这个城市的呢? ▶ **to bring sth to a stop/an end** 使某事停止/结束 ▶ **I can't bring myself to fire him** 我不忍心解雇他

▶ **bring about** VT (cause) 造成 [zàochéng]

▶ **bring along** VT 随身携带 [suíshēn xiédài]

▶ **bring around** VT = **bring round**

▶ **bring back** VT **1** (return) 带回来 [dài huílái] ▷ She brought my book back. 她把我的书带回来了。 **2** (restore) [+ hanging etc] 恢复 [huīfù] ▷ Some people want to bring back the death penalty. 一些人想恢复死刑。 **3** [+ memory] 使人回忆起 [shǐ rén huíyì qǐ] ▷ Your article brought back sad memories for me. 你的文章使我回忆起一些难过的往事。

▶ **bring down** VT **1** [+ government] 使···倒台 [shǐ···dǎotái] **2** [+ price] [competition, circumstances +] 降低 [jiàngdī] ▷ The discovery of new oilfields brought the price down. 新油田的发现使油价有所降低。; [company, government +] 调低 [tiáodī] ▷ They brought down income taxes. 他们调低了所得税。

▶ **bring forth** VT (frm) 取出 [qǔchū]

▶ **bring forward** VT **1** [+ meeting] 提前 [tíqián] **2** [+ argument, proposal] 提出 [tíchū] **3** (BOOKKEEPING) 承前 [chéngqián]

▶ **bring in** VT **1** [+ law, system, object, person] 引进 [yǐnjìn] ▷ It would be a mistake to bring in an outsider. 引一个局外人进来会是一个错误。 **2** [+ money] 挣得 [zhèngdé] **3** (LAW) [+ verdict] 宣判 [xuānpàn]

▶ **bring off** VT [+ attempt, plan] 完成 [wánchéng]

▶ **bring on** VT [+ illness, pain] 导致 [dǎozhì]

▶ **bring out** VT (publish, produce) [+ book, album] 出版 [chūbǎn] ▶ **to bring out the best/worst in sb** 使某人最好/最坏的一面显示出来

▶ **bring round** VT [+ unconscious person] 使苏醒 [shǐ sūxǐng]

▶ **bring up** VT **1** (rear) [+ child] 抚养 [fǔyǎng] **2** [+ question, subject] 提出 [tíchū] **3** (inf) (vomit) [+ food] 呕出 [ǒuchū]

brink [brɪŋk] N ▶ **to be on the brink of** [+ disaster, war etc] 在···的边缘 [zài···de biānyuán]

brisk [brɪsk] ADJ **1** (abrupt) [+ tone, person] 简捷直接的 [jiǎnjié zhíjiē de] **2** [+ pace] 轻快的 [qīngkuài de] **3** [+ trade, business] 兴旺的 [xīngwàng de] **4** [+ breeze, weather] 清新的 [qīngxīn de] ▶ **to go for a brisk walk** 快步走路

bristle ['brɪsl] I N [c] **1** (animal hair, of beard) 毛发楂儿 [máofà chár] **2** [of brush] 硬毛 [yìngmáo] II VI **1** [person +] (in anger) 愤怒 [fènnù] **2** [hairs +] 竖起 [shùqǐ] ▶ **to bristle with sth** 布满某物

Brit [brɪt] N [c] 英国人 [Yīngguórén]

Britain ['brɪtən] N (also: **Great Britain**) 英国 [Yīngguó] ▶ **in Britain** 在英国

⊙ **BRITAIN**

● **Britain** 或 **Great Britain** 由英格兰、威尔士、苏格兰和北爱尔兰组成。如指整个不列颠, 应慎用 **England** 和 **English**, 以免引起苏格兰和北爱尔兰人的不满。**United Kingdom** 作为王国的官方称谓, 常简略为 **the UK**, 覆盖大不列颠及北爱尔兰。**British Isles** 包括大不列颠、北爱尔兰、爱尔兰共和国 (不隶属 **the UK**) 和四周岛屿。

British ['brɪtɪʃ] I ADJ 英国的 [Yīngguó de] II NPL ▶ **the British** 英国人 [Yīngguórén]

British Isles [-aɪlz] NPL ▶ **the British Isles** 不列颠群岛 [Bùlièdiān Qúndǎo]

brittle ['brɪtl] ADJ (fragile) [+ glass, bones etc] 脆弱的 [cuìruò de]

B-road ['biːrəʊd] (BRIT) N [c] 辅路 [fǔlù]

broad [brɔːd] I ADJ **1** [+ street, shoulders] 宽的 [kuān de] **2** [+ smile] 明显的 [míngxiǎn de] **3** [+ range] 广泛的 [guǎngfàn de] **4** (general) [+ outlines, distinction etc] 概略的 [gàiluè de]; [+ sense] 广义的 [guǎngyì de] **5** [+ accent] 浓重的 [nóngzhòng de] II N [c] (US: inf) (woman) 女人 [nǚrén] ▶ **in broad daylight** 光天化日之下 ▶ **a broad hint** 明显的暗示

broadband ['brɔːdbænd] (COMPUT) I ADJ 宽带的 [kuāndài de] II N 宽带 [kuāndài]

broad bean (ESP BRIT) N [c] 蚕豆 [cándòu] [美= **fava bean**]

broadcast ['brɔːdkɑːst] (pt, pp **broadcast**) I N [c] 广播 [guǎngbō] II VT 播送 [bōsòng] III VI 广播 [guǎngbō]

broaden ['brɔːdn] I VT [+ scope, appeal] 扩大 [kuòdà] II VI **1** [river, smile +] 变宽 [biànkuān] **2** [scope, appeal +] 扩大影响 [kuòdà yǐngxiǎng] ▶ **to broaden the/sb's mind** 拓宽思想/拓宽某人的思想

broadly ['brɔːdlɪ] ADV **1** (in general terms) 大体上 [dàtǐshang] **2** [smile +] ▶ **to smile broadly** 咧嘴笑 [liězuǐxiào] ▶ **broadly speaking** 广义地说

broadminded ['brɔːd'maɪndɪd] ADJ 宽宏大量的 [kuānhóng dàliàng de]

broccoli ['brɒkəlɪ] N [U] 花椰菜 [huāyēcài]

brochure ['brəʊʃʊə(r), US brəʊ'ʃʊr] N [c] (booklet) 小册子 [xiǎocèzi]

broil [brɔɪl] (US) VT 烤 [kǎo] [英=**grill**] ▪用法参见 **cook**

broke [brəʊk] I PT of **break** II ADJ (inf) (penniless) 身无分文的 [shēn wú fēnwén de] ▸ **to go broke** (inf) [company, person +] 破产

broken ['brəʊkn] I PP of **break** II ADJ **1** [+ window, cup etc] 破碎的 [pòsuì de] **2** [+ machine] 坏损的 [huàisǔn de] **3** [+ promise, vow] 背弃的 [bèiqì de] **4** [+ line] ▸ **broken line** 虚线 [xūxiàn] ▸ **a broken leg** 折断的腿 ▸ **a broken marriage** 破裂的婚姻 ▸ **a broken home** 破裂的家庭 ▸ **in broken English/French** 用蹩脚的英语/法语

broker ['brəʊkə(r)] I N [c] (in shares etc) 经纪人 [jīngjìrén] II VT (POL) [+ agreement, ceasefire] 斡旋 [wòxuán]

bronchitis [brɔŋ'kaɪtɪs] N [U] 支气管炎 [zhīqìguǎnyán]

bronze [brɔnz] I N **1** [U] (metal) 青铜 [qīngtóng] **2** [c] (sculpture) 青铜像 [qīngtóngxiàng] **3** [c] (SPORT) (also: **bronze medal**) 铜牌 [tóngpái] II ADJ (in colour) 古铜色的 [gǔtóngsè de]

brooch [brəʊtʃ] N [c] 胸针 [xiōngzhēn]

brood [bru:d] I N [c] **1** (baby birds) 同窝幼鸟 [tóngwō yòuniǎo] **2** [of children] 同一个家庭的一群孩子 [tóngge jiātíng de yīqún háizi] II VI ▸ **to brood on** or **over** or **about sth** 沉思某事 [chénsī mǒushì]

broom [brum] N [c] (for cleaning) 扫帚 [sàozhou]

Bros. (COMM) ABBR (= **brothers**) 兄弟 [xiōngdì]

broth [brɔθ] N [c/U] 清汤 [qīngtāng]

brothel ['brɔθl] N [c] 妓院 [jìyuàn]

○ **brother** ['brʌðə(r)] N [c] **1** (in family) 兄弟 [xiōngdì]; (elder) 哥哥 [gēge]; (younger) 弟弟 [dìdi] **2** (REL) 教友 [jiàoyǒu] **3** (fig) 哥们儿 [gēmenr]

brother-in-law ['brʌðərɪnlɔ:] N [c] (older sister's husband) 姐夫 [jiěfu]; (younger sister's husband) 妹夫 [mèifu]; (husband's older brother) 大伯子 [dàbózi]; (husband's younger brother) 小叔子 [xiǎoshūzi]; (wife's older brother) 内兄 [nèixiōng]; (wife's younger brother) 内弟 [nèidì]

brought [brɔ:t] PT, PP of **bring**

brow [braʊ] N [c] **1** (forehead) 额 [é] **2** (eyebrow) 眉毛 [méimáo] **3** ▸ **brow of a hill** 山顶 [shāndǐng]

○ **brown** [braʊn] I ADJ **1** (in colour) [+ object] 褐色的 [hèsè de]; [+ hair, eyes] 棕色的 [zōngsè de] **2** (tanned) [+ skin, person] 晒黑的 [shàihēi de] II N [U] (colour) 褐色 [hèsè] III VI (CULIN) 变成褐色 [biànchéng hèsè] IV VT (CULIN) 烧至金黄 [shāo zhì jīnhuáng]

brown bread N [U] 黑面包 [hēimiànbāo]

Brownie ['braʊnɪ] I N [c] 幼年女童军队员 [yòunián nǚtóngjūn duìyuán] II **Brownies** NPL ▸ **the Brownies** 幼年女童军 [yòunián nǚtóngjūn]

brown rice N [U] 糙米 [cāomǐ]

brown sugar N [U] 红糖 [hóngtáng]

browse [braʊz] I VI **1** 浏览 [liúlǎn] **2** (in shop) 随意翻阅 [suíyì fānyuè] **3** (cow etc +) 吃草 [chīcǎo] II N ▸ **to have a browse (around)** 随意逛逛 [suíyì guàngguàng]

browser ['braʊzə(r)] (COMPUT) N [c] 浏览器 [liúlǎnqì]

bruise [bru:z] I N [c] **1** (on face etc) 青瘀 [qīngyū] **2** (on fruit) 伤处 [shāngchù] II VT **1** [+ person, fruit] 碰伤 [pèngshāng] **2** [+ arm, leg etc] (one's own) 挫伤 [cuòshāng]; (other person's) 弄伤 [nòngshāng] III VI **1** [person +] 显出瘀痕 [xiǎnchū yūhén] **2** [fruit +] 被碰伤 [bèi pèngshāng]

Brunei ['bru:naɪ] N 文莱 [Wénlái]

brunette [bru:'nɛt] N [c] 棕发女子 [zōngfà nǚzǐ]

brush [brʌʃ] I N [c] **1** (tool) (for cleaning, for decorating) 刷子 [shuāzi]; (for hair) 发刷 [fàshuā]; [artist's] 画笔 [huàbǐ] **2** (unpleasant encounter) 遭遇 [zāoyù] II VT **1** (sweep) [+ carpet etc] 刷 [shuā]; (with hands) 拂拭 [fúshì] **2** (groom) [+ hair] 梳 [shū] **3** (also: **brush against**) [+ person, object] 轻拂 [qīngfú] ▸ **a brush with death** 差点丢命的经历 ▸ **a brush with the police** 与警察的小摩擦 ▸ **to brush one's teeth** 刷牙

▸ **brush aside**, **brush away** VT [+ protest, criticism] 漠视 [mòshì]

▸ **brush off** VT [+ person] 怠慢 [dàimàn]

▸ **brush past** VT [+ person, object] 擦过 [cāguò]

▸ **brush up (on)** VT [+ subject, language] 复习 [fùxí]

Brussels sprout ['brʌslz-] N [c] 芽甘蓝 [yágānlán]

brutal ['bru:tl] ADJ **1** [+ person, killing] 残忍的 [cánrěn de] **2** [+ honesty, frankness] 直率的 [zhíshuài de]

brute [bru:t] I N [c] (person) 畜牲 [chùsheng] II ADJ [+ strength, force] 蛮力的 [mánlì de] ▸ **by brute force** 凭蛮力

BS (US) N ABBR = **BSc**

BSc N ABBR (= *Bachelor of Science*) (*qualification*) 理科学士学位 [lǐkē xuéshì xuéwèi]; (*person*) 理科学士 [lǐkē xuéshì]

BST N ABBR (= *British Summer Time*) 英国夏令时 [Yīngguó Xiàlìngshí]

BTW ABBR (= *by the way*) 顺便说一句 [shùnbiàn shuō yī jù]

bubble ['bʌbl] I N [c] 1 (*in liquid*) 泡 [pào] 2 (*also*: soap bubble) 肥皂泡 [féizàopào] II VI [*liquid +*] 起泡 [qǐ pào] ▶ **to be bubbling (over) with confidence/ideas** 充满信心/想法

bubble bath N [U] (*liquid*) 泡泡浴液 [pàopào yùyè]

bubble gum N [U] 泡泡糖 [pàopàotáng]

buck [bʌk] I N [c] 1 (US: *inf*) (*dollar*) 元 [yuán] 2 (*rabbit*) 雄兔 [xióngtù] 3 (*deer*) 雄鹿 [xiónglù] II VI [*horse +*] 弓背跳跃 [gōngbèi tiàoyuè] ▶ **to make a fast** *or* **quick buck** (*inf*) 很快地捞一笔 ▶ **to pass the buck** (*inf*) 推卸责任 ▶ **buck up** (BRIT: *inf*) I VI 振作精神 [zhènzuò jīngshén] II VT (*cheer up*) [+ *person, sb's spirits*] 使振奋精神 [shǐ zhènfèn jīngshén] ▶ **to buck one's ideas up** 振奋某人的精神

bucket ['bʌkɪt] I N [c] 1 (*pail*) 桶 [tǒng] 2 (*contents*) 一桶 [yītǒng] II VI (BRIT: *inf*) ▶ **it** *or* **the rain is bucketing down** 大雨倾盆而下 [dàyǔ qīngpén ér xià]

buckle ['bʌkl] I N [c] (*on shoe, belt*) 扣环 [kòuhuán] II VT 1 [+ *shoe, belt*] 扣住 [kòuzhù] 2 (*distort*) [+ *object*] 使变形 [shǐ biànxíng] III VI 1 [*object +*] 变形 [biànxíng] 2 [*legs, knees +*] 腿软 [tuǐruǎn] ▶ **buckle down** VI ▶ **to buckle down (to sth)** (*inf*) 开始认真地做(某事) [kāishǐ rènzhēn de zuò (mǒushì)]

bud [bʌd] I N [c] (*on tree, plant*) (*leaf bud*) 芽 [yá]; (*flower bud*) 蓓蕾 [bèilěi] II VI 1 (*produce leaves*) 萌芽 [méngyá] 2 (*produce flowers*) 出花苞 [chū huābāo] ▶ **to nip sth in the bud** (*inf*) 把某事消灭在萌芽状态

Buddhism ['budɪzəm] N [U] 佛教 [Fójiào]

Buddhist ['budɪst] I ADJ 佛教的 [Fójiào de] II N [c] 佛教徒 [Fójiàotú]

budding ['bʌdɪŋ] ADJ 1 [+ *actor, writer*] 初露头角的 [chūlù tóujiǎo de] 2 [+ *romance, democracy*] 开始发展的 [kāishǐ fāzhǎn de]

buddy ['bʌdɪ] (*inf*) N [c] 1 (ESP US) (*friend*) 朋友 [péngyou] 2 (US) (*form of address*) 老兄 [lǎoxiōng]

budge [bʌdʒ] I VT 1 [+ *object*] 稍微移动 [shāowēi yídòng] 2 (*fig*) [+ *person*] 动摇 [dòngyáo] II VI 1 [*object +*] 移动 [yídòng] 2 (*fig*) [*person +*] 改变立场 [gǎibiàn lìchǎng]

budgerigar ['bʌdʒərɪgɑ:(r)] N [c] 小长尾鹦鹉 [xiǎo chángwěi yīngwǔ]

budget ['bʌdʒɪt] I N [c] (*of person, government*) 预算 [yùsuàn] II VT [+ *sum of money*] 预算出 [yùsuàn chū] III VI ▶ **to budget for sth** 为某

事做预算 [wèi mǒushì zuò yùsuàn] IV ADJ (*economy*) [+ *travel agents etc*] 廉价的 [liánjià de] ▶ **I'm on a tight budget** 我经济拮据

budgie ['bʌdʒɪ] (*inf*) N = **budgerigar**

buff [bʌf] I N [c] (*inf*) (*enthusiast*) 爱好者 [àihàozhě] II ADJ (*in colour*) 暗黄色的 [ànhuángsè de] III VT (*polish*) 擦亮 [cāliàng]

buffalo ['bʌfələu] (*pl* **buffalo** *or* **buffaloes**) N [c] 1 (BRIT) 水牛 [shuǐniú] 2 (US) (*bison*) 野牛 [yěniú]

buffer ['bʌfə(r)] I N [c] 1 (ESP BRIT: RAIL) 缓冲器 [huǎnchōngqì] 2 (COMPUT) 缓冲存储器 [huǎnchōng cúnchǔqì] 3 (*fig*) (*against harm, shortage etc*) 缓冲储备 [huǎnchōng chǔbèi] II VT (*protect*) 保护 [bǎohù]

buffet[1] ['bufeɪ, US bu'feɪ] N [c] 1 (*in station*) 餐厅 [cāntīng] 2 (*food*) 自助餐 [zìzhùcān] 3 (BRIT: RAIL) (*also*: buffet car) 餐车 [cānchē] [美= dining car]

buffet[2] ['bʌfɪt] VT [*wind, sea +*] 冲击 [chōngjī]

bug [bʌg] I N [c] 1 (ESP US) (*insect*) 虫子 [chóngzi] 2 (COMPUT) (*in program*) 病毒 [bìngdú] 3 (*inf*) (*virus*) 病菌 [bìngjūn] 4 (*hidden microphone*) 窃听器 [qiètīngqì] II VT 1 (*inf*) (*annoy*) 烦扰 [fánrǎo] 2 [+ *room, telephone etc*] 窃听 [qiètīng] ▶ **I've got** *or* **been bitten by the travel bug** (*inf*) 我迷上了旅游

buggy ['bʌgɪ] (BRIT) N [c] (*for baby*) 婴儿车 [yīng'érchē] [美= **stroller**]

⊙**build** [bɪld] (*pt, pp* **built**) I N [c/U] (*of person*) 体格 [tǐgé] ▷ *He is of medium build.* 他中等体格。 II VT 1 [+ *house, machine*] 建造 [jiànzào] 2 (*fig*) [+ *organization, relationship*] 建立 [jiànlì] ▷ *I wanted to build a relationship with my team.* 我想同我的团队建立起关系。 III VI 建设 [jiànshè] ▶ **build into** VT 1 [+ *wall, ceiling*] 固定在 [gùdìng zài] ▷ *The TV was built into the ceiling.* 电视被固定在天花板上。 2 (*fig*) [+ *policy, system, product*] 纳入 [nàrù] ▷ *We have to build computers into the school curriculum.* 我们必须将计算机纳入学校课程安排中。 ▶ **build on, build upon** VT FUS [不可拆分] (*fig*) [+ *success etc*] 建基于 [jiànjī yú] ▷ *We must build on the success of these industries.* 我们必须依靠这些企业的成功。 ▶ **build up** I VT 1 [+ *business, collection*] 发展起来 [fāzhǎn qǐlái] 2 [+ *confidence, morale*] 激励 [jīlì] II VI (*accumulate*) 积累 [jījù] ▶ **don't build your hopes up (too soon)** 不要(这么早)期望这么高

builder ['bɪldə(r)] N [c] (*worker*) 建筑工人 [jiànzhù gōngrén]

⊙**building** ['bɪldɪŋ] N 1 [c] (*house, office etc*) 建筑物 [jiànzhùwù] 2 [U] (*industry, construction*) 建设 [jiànshè] ▷ *Building has stopped while the dispute is being resolved.* 在解决分歧期间建设工作暂停。

building site N [c] 建筑工地 [jiànzhù gōngdì]

building society (BRIT) N [c] 建屋互助

会 [jiànwū hùzhùhuì] [美= **savings and loan association**]

built [bɪlt] I PT, PP of build II ADJ ▸ well-/heavily-built [+ person] 体态优美/粗笨的 [tǐtài yōuměi/cūbèn de]

built-in ['bɪlt'ɪn] ADJ 1 [+ device] 内置式的 [nèizhìshì de] 2 [+ safeguards] 内在的 [nèizài de]

built-up ['bɪltʌp] ADJ [+ area] 被建筑物覆盖的 [bèi jiànzhùwù fúgài de]

bulb [bʌlb] N [c] 1 (ELEC) 电灯泡 [diàndēngpào] 2 (BOT) 球茎 [qiújīng]

Bulgaria [bʌl'gɛərɪə] N 保加利亚 [Bǎojiālìyà]

bulge [bʌldʒ] I N [c] 1 (bump) 凸起 [tūqǐ] 2 (in birth rate, sales) 激增 [jīzēng] II VI [eyes, muscles, stomach etc +] 凸出 [tūchū] ▸ to be bulging with 塞满

bulimia [bə'lɪmɪə] N [U] (also: bulimia nervosa) 暴食症 [bàoshízhèng]

bulimic [bə'lɪmɪk] ADJ 患有暴食症的 [huànyǒu bàoshízhèng de]

bulk [bʌlk] N 1 [S/U] [of person] 肥硕的身躯 [féishuò de shēnqū] 2 [S] [of object] 庞然大物 [pángrán dà wù] ▸ to buy/sell in bulk (COMM) 批量购买/销售 ▸ the bulk of (most of) 大部分的

bulky ['bʌlkɪ] ADJ [+ equipment, parcel] 笨重的 [bènzhòng de]

bull [bul] N [c] 1 (ZOOL) 公牛 [gōngniú] 2 (male elephant/whale) 雄兽 [xióngshòu] 3 (REL) 教皇诏书 [jiàohuáng zhàoshū]

bulldozer ['buldəuzə(r)] N [c] 推土机 [tuītǔjī]

bullet ['bulɪt] N [c] 子弹 [zǐdàn]

bulletin ['bulɪtɪn] N [c] 1 (TV ETC) (news update) 公告 [gōnggào] 2 (journal) 会刊 [huìkān]

bulletin board N [c] 1 (COMPUT) 公共留言板 [gōnggòng liúyánbǎn] 2 (US) (noticeboard) 布告栏 [bùgàolán] [英= **noticeboard**]

bullfighting ['bulfaɪtɪŋ] N [U] 斗牛 [dòuniú]

bully ['bulɪ] I N [c] 恃强凌弱者 [shìqiáng língruò zhě] II VT 欺侮 [qīwǔ] ▸ to bully sb into (doing) sth 胁迫某人 (做) 某事

bum [bʌm] (inf) N [c] 1 (BRIT) (backside) 屁股 [pìgu] 2 (ESP US) (tramp) 流浪汉 [liúlànghàn] ▸ bum around (inf) VI 闲荡 [xiándàng]

bumblebee ['bʌmblbiː] N [c] 大黄蜂 [dàhuángfēng]

bump [bʌmp] I N [c] 1 (swelling) (on head) 肿包 [zhǒngbāo] 2 (jolt) 重击 [zhòngjī] 3 (inf) (in car) (minor accident) 碰撞 [pèngzhuàng] 4 (on road) 隆起物 [lóngqǐwù] II VT (strike) 碰 [pèng] III VI (jolt) [car +] 颠簸 [diānbǒ] ▸ bump into VT FUS [+ obstacle, person] 撞到 [zhuàngdào] 2 (inf) (meet) [+ person] 碰见 [pèngjiàn]

bumper ['bʌmpə(r)] I N [c] (AUT) 保险杠 [bǎoxiǎngàng] II ADJ ▸ bumper crop/harvest 大丰收 [dà fēngshōu]

bumpy ['bʌmpɪ] ADJ [+ road] 崎岖不平的

[qíqū bùpíng de] 2 [+ flight, ride] 颠簸的 [diānbǒ de]

bun [bʌn] N [c] 1 (CULIN) 小圆面包 [xiǎoyuán miànbāo] 2 (hair style) 圆髻 [yuánjì]

bunch [bʌntʃ] I N [c] 1 [of flowers] 束 [shù] 2 [of keys, bananas, grapes] 串 [chuàn] 3 (inf) [of people] 群 [qún] II bunches NPL (BRIT) (in hair) 双辫 [shuāngbiàn]

▸ bunch up, bunch together I VI 挤在一起 [jǐ zài yīqǐ] II VT 聚集 [jùjí]

bundle ['bʌndl] I N [c] (parcel) [of clothes] 包裹 [bāoguǒ]; [of papers] 捆 [kǔn] II VT (put) ▸ to bundle sth/sb into 匆匆忙忙地把某事/某人塞进 [cōngcōng mángmáng de bǎ mǒushì/mǒurén sāijìn] ▸ a bundle of fun/laughs 非常好玩/风趣 ▸ he was a bundle of nerves 他感到非常紧张

▸ bundle off VT [+ person] 匆忙送走 [cōngmáng sòngzǒu]

▸ bundle up VT 捆扎 [kǔnzhā]

bungalow ['bʌŋgələu] N [c] 平房 [píngfáng]

bungee jumping ['bʌndʒiː'dʒʌmpɪŋ] N [U] 蹦极跳 [bèngjítiào]

bungle ['bʌŋgl] VT 搞糟 [gǎozāo]

bunion ['bʌnjən] N [c] 拇囊炎肿 [mǔnáng yánzhǒng]

bunk [bʌŋk] N [c] (bed) 铺位 [pùwèi] ▸ to do a bunk (BRIT: inf) 逃走

▸ bunk off (BRIT: inf) I VI (from school, work) 擅自走掉 [shànzì zǒudiào] II VT [+ school, work] 擅自离开 [shànzì líkāi]

bunk beds NPL 双层床 [shuāngcéngchuáng]

bunker ['bʌŋkə(r)] N [c] 1 (MIL) 掩体 [yǎntǐ] 2 (GOLF) 沙坑 [shākēng] 3 (coal store) 煤箱 [méixiāng]

bunny ['bʌnɪ] (inf) N [c] (also: bunny rabbit) 小兔子 [xiǎotùzi]

buoy [bɔɪ, US 'buːɪ] N [c] 浮标 [fúbiāo] ▸ buoy up VT [+ person] 鼓舞 [gǔwǔ]

buoyant ['bɔɪənt] ADJ 1 (able to float) 有浮力的 [yǒu fúlì de] 2 (COMM) [+ economy, market] 繁荣的 [fánróng de]; [+ prices, currency] 上涨的 [shàngzhǎng de] 3 [+ person, mood] 愉快的 [yúkuài de]

burden ['bəːdn] I N [c] 1 (responsibility, worry) 负担 [fùdàn] 2 (frm) (load) 负荷 [fùhè] II VT ▸ to burden sb with [+ problem, news] 使某人负担某事 [shǐ mǒurén fùdān mǒushì] ▸ to be a burden on sb 成为某人的累赘

bureau ['bjuərəu] (pl bureaux or bureaus) N [c] 1 (office) (for travel, information etc) 办事处 [bànshìchù] 2 (BRIT) (writing desk) 书桌 [shūzhuō] 3 (US) (chest of drawers) 五斗橱 [wǔdǒuchú]

bureaucracy [bjuə'rɔkrəsɪ] N [c] 1 (usually pej) 官僚作风 [guānliáo zuòfēng] 2 (system) 官僚体系 [guānliáo tǐxì]

bureaucrat ['bjuərəkræt] (usually pej) N [c] 官

僚 [guānliáo]

bureaux ['bjuərəuz] NPL *of* bureau

burger ['bə:gə(r)] N [C] 汉堡包 [hànbǎobāo]

burglar ['bə:glə(r)] N [C] 窃贼 [qièzéi]

用法参见 thief

burglar alarm N [C] 防盗铃 [fángdàolíng]

burglary ['bə:glərɪ] N **1** [C] (*act*) 盗窃 [dàoqiè] **2** [U] (*crime*) 盗窃罪 [dàoqièzuì]

burial ['bɛrɪəl] N [C/U] 葬礼 [zànglǐ]

burn [bə:n] (*pt, pp* burned *or* BRIT **burnt**) I VT **1** [+ *papers etc*] 焚烧 [fénshāo] **2** [+ *fuel*] 燃烧 [ránshāo] **3** [+ *toast, rice*] 烧焦 [shāojiāo] II VI **1** (*fire, flame* +) 燃烧 [ránshāo] **2** (*house, car* +) 烧着 [shāozháo] **3** [*food* +] 烧糊了 [shāo húle] **4** [*person, skin* +] (*in sun*) 晒伤 [shàishāng] **5** (*sting*) [*eyes, throat* +] 灼痛 [zhuótòng] III N [C] 烧伤 [shāoshāng] ▶ **I've burnt myself!** 我把自己烫伤了！▶ **the cigarette burnt a hole in her dress** 香烟在她的连衣裙上烫了个洞 ▶ **to be burning with impatience/ambition** 充满极度的不耐/野心
▶ **burn down** I VT [+ *house etc*] 烧毁 [shāohuǐ] II VI (*house etc* +) 烧毁 [shāohuǐ]
▶ **burn out** VI [*writer etc* +] 精疲力竭 [jīng pí lì jié] ▶ **to burn oneself out** 累垮自己
▶ **burn up** I VI [*spacecraft* +] 烧毁 [shāohuǐ] II VT [+ *fuel, energy*] 消耗 [xiāohào]

burning ['bə:nɪŋ] ADJ **1** [+ *house, car*] 着火的 [zháohuǒ de] **2** (*also:* **burning hot**) [+ *sand, desert*] 灼热的 [zhuórè de] **3** [+ *ambition, desire*] 强烈的 [qiángliè de] **4** [+ *issue, question*] 激烈的 [jīliè de]

burnt [bə:nt] PT, PP *of* burn

burp [bə:p] (*inf*) I N [C] 打嗝声 [dǎgéshēng] II VI 打嗝 [dǎgé]

burrow ['bʌrəu] I N [C] [*of rabbit etc*] 地洞 [dìdòng] II VI **1** (*dig*) 打洞 [dǎdòng] **2** (*rummage*) 搜寻 [sōuxún]

burst [bə:st] (*pt, pp* burst) I VT **1** [+ *bag, balloon etc*] 爆炸 [bàozhà] **2** [*river* +] [*banks etc*] 溃决 [kuìjué] II VI [*pipe, tyre* +] 爆裂 [bàoliè] III N [C] [*of gunfire, applause, laughter*] 一阵 [yīzhèn] ▶ **to burst into flames** 突然着火 ▶ **to burst into tears** 突然大哭起来 ▶ **to burst out laughing** 突然大笑起来 ▶ **to be bursting with** (*full of*) 挤满; [+ *pride, curiosity*] 充满 ▶ **to be bursting to do sth** (*inf*) 急于做某事 ▶ **to burst open** [*door etc* +] 猛然打开 ▶ **a burst of energy/activity** 一股劲/一阵行动 ▶ **a burst pipe** 破裂的水管 ▶ **a burst blood vessel** 爆裂的血管
▶ **burst in on** VT FUS [不可拆分] [+ *person*] 突然出现 [tūrán chūxiàn]
▶ **burst into** VT FUS [不可拆分] [+ *room etc*] 闯入 [chuǎngrù]
▶ **burst out of** VT FUS [不可拆分] [+ *room etc*] 冲出 [chōngchū]

bury ['bɛrɪ] VT **1** (*in ground*) 掩埋 [yǎnmái] **2** [+ *dead person*] 埋葬 [máizàng] **3** (*fig*) (*under rubble, debris*) 埋 [mái] ▶ **to bury oneself in one's work** 埋头工作 ▶ **to bury one's face in one's hands** 双手掩面 ▶ **to bury one's head in the sand** 逃避现实 ▶ **to bury the hatchet** 言归于好

bus [bʌs] N [C] 公共汽车 [gōnggòng qìchē]

bus driver N [C] 公共汽车司机 [gōnggòng qìchē sījī]

bush [buʃ] N **1** [C] (*plant*) 灌木 [guànmù] **2** [U] (*scrubland*) 荒野 [huāngyě] ▶ **to beat about the bush** 拐弯抹角

bushy ['buʃɪ] ADJ **1** [+ *tail, hair, eyebrows*] 浓密的 [nóngmì de] **2** [+ *plant*] 茂密的 [màomì de]

busily ['bɪzɪlɪ] ADV 忙碌地 [mánglù de]

○ **business** ['bɪznɪs] N **1** [U/S] (*matter, question*) 事情 [shìqíng] ▷ *I've some important business to discuss.* 我有重要事情要进行讨论。**2** [C] (*firm*) 公司 [gōngsī] ▷ *a small business* 一家小公司 **3** [U] (*occupation*) 商业 [shāngyè] ▷ *a career in business* 从商生涯 **4** [U] (*trade*) 生意 [shēngyì] ▷ *Companies would lose business.* 公司生意将下滑。▶ **to be away on business** 出差 ▶ **he's in the insurance/transport business** 他在做保险/运输业务 ▶ **to do business with sb** 和某人做生意 ▶ **to go out of business** 破产 ▶ **to get down to business** 开始干正事 ▶ **to make it one's business to do sth** 主动承担办某事 ▶ **he means business** (*inf*) 他是认真的 ▶ **to have no business doing sth** 无权做某事 ▶ **it's none of your business** 别多管闲事 ▶ **that's my business** 那是我自己的事

business class (*on aircraft*) I N [U] 公务舱 [gōngwùcāng] II ADV 乘公务舱 [chèng gōngwùcāng]

businesslike ['bɪznɪslaɪk] ADJ 高效率的 [gāo xiàolù de]

businessman ['bɪznɪsmən] (*pl* **businessmen**) N [C] 商人 [shāngrén]

business trip N [C] 出差 [chuchāi]

businesswoman ['bɪznɪswumən] (*pl* **businesswomen**) N [C] 女商人 [nǚ shāngrén]

busker ['bʌskə(r)] (BRIT) N [C] **1** (*singer*) 街头艺人 [jiētóu yìrén] **2** (*musician*) 街头音乐家 [jiētóu yīnyuèjiā]

BUSKER

buskers 指在街上或其他公共场所演奏乐器或歌唱的街头艺人。住在英美城市里的人可以经常得到来自他们自己也们的娱乐。过路人可以停下来听，然后在他们放在身边地上的帽子或琴盒里放上些零钱。buskers 还有可能跳上你所乘坐的火车或公共汽车，为你演奏几站地。

bus pass N [C] 公交车通票 [gōngjiāochē tōngpiào]

bus shelter N [C] 公交车候车亭 [gōngjiāochē hòuchētíng]

bus station N [C] 公共汽车车站 [gōnggòng qìchē chēzhàn]

bus stop N [C] 公共汽车站 [gōnggòng qìchē zhàn]

bust [bʌst] I VT 1 (inf) (break) 打破 [dǎpò] 2 (inf) (arrest) 逮捕 [dàibǔ] II N [C] 1 (breasts) 胸部 [xiōngbù] 2 (sculpture) 胸像 [xiōngxiàng] III ADJ (inf) (broken) 坏 [huài] ▶ to go bust (inf) [company +] 破产

bustle ['bʌsl] I VI (person +) 忙碌 [mánglù] II N [U] (activity) 繁忙 [fánmáng]

bustling ['bʌslɪŋ] ADJ [+ town, place] 喧嚷的 [xuānrǎng de] ▶ to be bustling with people/activity 到处是人群/活动

busy ['bɪzi] I ADJ 1 [+ person] 忙的 [máng de] 2 [+ shop, street] 繁忙的 [fánmáng de] 3 [+ schedule, time, day] 忙碌的 [mánglù de] 4 (ESP US: TEL) [+ line] 占线的 [zhànxiàn de] [英=engaged] II VT ▶ to busy oneself (with sth) 忙于做 (某事) [mángyú zuò (mǒushì)] ▶ he's a very busy man 他是个大忙人 ▶ I'm busy 我正忙着呢

busy signal (US) N [C] 忙音 [mángyīn] [英=engaged tone]

but [bʌt] I CONJ 1 (yet, however) 但是 [dànshì] ▶ I'd love to come, but I'm busy 我想来，但是有事 ▶ he may not be very bright, but he is hard-working 他可能不是很聪明，但很努力 ▶ but then 不过 ▶ she isn't English but American 她不是英国人而是美国人 ▶ enjoyable but tiring 很开心但也很累 ▶ not only... but also 不但…而且 2 (showing disagreement, surprise etc) ▶ but that's far too expensive! 但是那太贵了！[dànshì nà tài guì le!] ▶ but it does work! 但那确实奏效! II PREP (apart from, except) 除了 [chú le] ▶ nothing but 仅仅 ▶ anything but 决不 ▶ they've got no-one but themselves to blame 他们只有责备自己 ▶ who but...? 除了…还有谁? III ADV 1 (just, only) 只 [zhǐ] ▶ to name but two 只提两个 ▶ had I but known 要是我知道的话 ▶ I can but try 我只能试一下 ▶ you cannot (help) but be impressed 你不能不产生深刻印象 ▶ she's but a child 她只不过是个孩子 2 ▶ but for (without) 若不是 [ruò bù shì]; (except for) 除了 [chú le] ▶ but for his help/him, we wouldn't have finished the job 没有他的帮助/他，我们还没有完成工作呢 ▶ the box was empty but for a small piece of paper 除了一张小纸片外，盒子里空空如也

> **but** 主要用作连词。I was going to stay till tomorrow but I've changed my mind. **however** 主要用作副词，多用于书面语。Most of the crops failed. The cotton did quite well, however.

butcher ['bʊtʃə(r)] I N [C] 1 (person) 肉商 [ròushāng] 2 (tyrant, murderer) 刽子手 [guìzishǒu] 3 (shop) (also: **butcher's**) 肉铺 [ròupù] II VT 1 [+ prisoners, children] 屠杀 [túshā] 2 [+ meat, animal] 屠宰 [túzǎi]

butler ['bʌtlə(r)] N [C] 男管家 [nán guǎnjiā]

butt [bʌt] I N [C] 1 [of gun, tool] 柄 [bǐng] 2 [of cigarette] 烟蒂 [yāndì] 3 (BRIT) (fig) (target) [of teasing, criticism etc] 对象 [duìxiàng] 4 (barrel) 大桶 [dàtǒng] 5 (US: inf) (backside) 屁股 [pìgu] II VT [goat, person +] 顶撞 [dǐngzhuàng] ▶ **butt in** VI (interrupt) 插嘴 [chāzuǐ]

butter ['bʌtə(r)] I N [U] 黄油 [huángyóu] II VT [+ bread] 涂黄油于 [tú huángyóu yú]

buttercup ['bʌtəkʌp] N [C] 金凤花 [jīnfènghuā]

butterfly ['bʌtəflaɪ] N 1 [C] (insect) 蝴蝶 [húdié] 2 [U] (also: **the butterfly**) (in swimming) 蝶泳 [diéyǒng]

buttocks ['bʌtəks] NPL 臀部 [túnbù]

button ['bʌtn] I N [C] 1 (on clothes) 纽扣 [niǔkòu] 2 (on machine) 按钮 [ànniǔ] 3 (US) (badge) 徽章 [huīzhāng] [英=badge] ▶ on the button (inf) 准确 II VT (also: **button up**) 扣钮扣 [kòu niǔkòu]

buy [baɪ] (pt, pp **bought**) I VT 1 买 [mǎi] 2 (COMM) [+ company] 收购 [shōugòu] 3 (fig) [+ time, freedom] 赢得 [yíngdé] ▷ It was a risky operation, but might buy more time. 这样做有风险，但可能会赢得更多的时间。II N [C] (purchase) 所买之物 [suǒ mǎi zhī wù] ▷ Other good buys include cameras and toys. 其他买来的好东西还包括相机和玩具。▶ to buy sb sth 给某人买某物 ▶ to buy sb a drink 请某人喝一杯 ▶ to buy sth from a shop 从店里购买某物 ▶ to buy sth off or from sb 从某人处购买某物 ▶ **buy back** VT 回买 [huímǎi] ▶ **buy in** (BRIT) VT [+ goods] 买进 [mǎijìn] ▶ **buy into** (BRIT: COMM) VT FUS (不可拆分) 入股 [rùgǔ] ▶ **buy off** VT (bribe) 贿赂 [huìlù] ▶ **buy out** VT [+ business partner] 全部通吃 [quánbù tōngchī] ▶ **buy up** VT [+ land, property] 全部买进 [quánbù mǎijìn]

buyer ['baɪə(r)] N [C] 1 (purchaser) 买主 [mǎizhǔ] 2 (for store) 采购员 [cǎigòuyuán]

buzz [bʌz] I N 1 [C] (noise) 嗡嗡声 [wēngwēngshēng] 2 (inf) (phone call) ▶ to give sb a buzz 给某人打电话 [gěi mǒurén dǎ diànhuà] II VI [insect, machine +] 发出嗡嗡声 [fāchū wēngwēngshēng] III VT (inf) (call on

intercom etc) 用蜂音器传呼 [yòng fēngyīnqì chuánhū] ▶ **to be buzzing with activity/ conversation** 充斥着活动/谈论
▶ **buzz off** (ESP BRIT: *inf*) VI 走开 [zǒukāi]
buzzer ['bʌzə(r)] N [C] 蜂鸣器 [fēngmíngqì]

by [baɪ] I PREP **1** (*referring to cause, agent*) 被 [bèi] ▶ **he was struck by a football** 他被足球打中了 ▶ **a painting by Picasso** 毕加索的画 ▶ **surrounded by a fence** 由篱笆围着
2 (*referring to method, manner, means*) ▶ **by bus/car/train** 乘公共汽车/汽车/火车 [chéng gōnggòng qìchē/qìchē/huǒchē] ▶ **to pay by cheque** 以支票支付 ▶ **she grabbed him by the arm** 她抓住了他的胳膊 ▶ **by moonlight/candlelight** 借助月光/烛光 ▶ **by saving hard, you can...** 通过使劲攒钱，你能…
3 (*via, through*) 经由 [jīngyóu] ▶ **he came in by the back door** 他从后门进来
4 (*close to, beside*) 靠近 [kào jìn] ▶ **he was standing by the door** 他正站在门边 ▶ **the house by the river** 河边的房子
5 (*past*) 经过 [jīngguò] ▶ **she rushed by me** 她急匆匆地从我身边过去
6 (*with times, dates, years*) 以前 [yǐqián]
▶ **by 4 o'clock** 4点以前 ▶ **by April 7** 4月7号以前 ▶ **by 2005** 2005年以前 ▶ **by this time tomorrow** 到明天这个时候 ▶ **by the time I got here** 到我到这儿的时候 ▶ **by now/then** 到如今/那时
7 (*during*) ▶ **by day/night** 在白天/晚上 [zài báitiān/wǎnshang]
8 (*specifying number, quantity, rate*) 按 [àn]
▶ **sold by the kilo/metre** 按公斤/米卖
▶ **paid by the hour** 按小时付酬 ▶ **parcels arrived by the dozen** 按打发来的包裹
▶ **little by little, bit by bit** 一点一点地
9 (*specifying degree of change*) 相差 [xiāngchā] ▶ **crime has increased by 10 per cent** 犯罪率上升了10%
10 (*in measurements*) ▶ **a room 3 metres by 4** 一间长3米宽4米的房间 [yī jiān cháng sān mǐ kuān sì mǐ de fángjiān] ▶ **it's broader by a metre** 宽了1米

11 (MATH) ▶ **to divide/multiply by 3** 被3除/乘 [bèisān chú/chéng]
12 (*according to*) ▶ **by law** 按照法律 [ànzhào fǎlù] ▶ **to play by the rules** 按规则玩游戏 ▶ **it's all right by me** 对我来说没问题
▶ **by profession/birth/nature** 就职业/祖籍/天性而言
13 ▶ **by myself/himself** *etc* (*unaided*) 我/他{等}自己 [wǒ/tā {děng} zìjǐ]; (*alone*) 我/他{等}单独 [wǒ/tā {děng} dāndú]
II ADV **1** *see* **go by, pass by** *etc*
2 ▶ **by and by** (*in the past*) 不久以后 [bùjiǔ yǐhòu]; (*in the future*) 不久 [bùjiǔ]
3 ▶ **by and large** 大体说来 [dàtǐ shuō lái]

如果你说 *I'll be home by ten o'clock*，你的意思是你要在10点或10点以前到家，但绝不会晚于10点。如果你说 *I'll be home before ten o'clock*，你的意思是10点是你到家的最晚时间，你可能9点以前就到家了。如果你说 *I'll be at home until ten o'clock*，你的意思是10点以前你会在家里，但10点以后就不在了。当我们谈论某人写了一本书或剧本、导演了一部电影、作了一部乐曲或画了一幅画时，我们说一部作品是 **by** 那个人或是 **written by** 那个人。*...three books by Jane Austen...a collection of piano pieces by Mozart...a painting by Picasso* 当我们谈到某人给你写信或留言时，我们说信或留言是 **from** 那个人。*He received a letter from his brother...It's a message from your boss.*

bye(-bye) ['baɪ'baɪ] (*inf*) INT 再见 [zàijiàn]
by-election ['baɪɪlɛkʃən] (BRIT) N [C] 补缺选举 [bǔquē xuǎnjǔ]
bypass ['baɪpɑːs] I N [C] **1** (AUT) 旁道 [pángdào] **2** (MED) (*operation*) 分流术 [fēnliúshù] II VT **1** [+ *town*] [*road, driver* +] 饶过 [ràoguò] **2** (*ignore*) [+ *person, problem etc*] 避开 [bìkāi]
by-product ['baɪprɔdʌkt] N [C] **1** [*of industrial process*] 副产品 [fùchǎnpǐn] **2** [*of situation*] 附带结果 [fùdài jiēguǒ]
byte [baɪt] (COMPUT) N [C] 字节 [zìjié]

C¹, c [si:] N [C/U] **1** (letter) 英语的第三个字母 **2** (SCOL, UNIV) (mark) 中等 [zhōngděng]

C² [si:] **I** N [C/U] (MUS) C大调音阶中的第一音 **II** ABBR (= Celsius, centigrade) 摄氏 [shèshì]

c. ABBR **1** (= circa) 大约 [dàyuē] **2** (= cents) 分 [fēn]

cab [kæb] N [C] **1** (taxi) 出租车 [chūzūchē] **2** [of truck, tractor, train] 驾驶室 [jiàshǐ shì] **3** (horse-drawn) 轻便两轮马车 [qīngbiàn liǎnglún mǎchē]

cabaret ['kæbəreɪ] **I** N **1** [U] (live entertainment) 餐馆、夜总会里的歌舞表演 [cānguǎn yèzǒnghuìlǐ de gēwǔ biǎoyǎn] **2** [C] (show) 餐馆、夜总会里的歌舞表演 [cānguǎn yèzǒnghuìlǐ de gēwǔ biǎoyǎn] **II** CPD [复合词] [+ act, singer] 餐馆、夜总会里的歌舞表演的 [cānguǎn yèzǒnghuìlǐ de gēwǔ biǎoyǎn de]

cabbage ['kæbɪdʒ] N [C/U] 卷心菜 [juǎnxīncài]

cabin ['kæbɪn] N [C] **1** (on ship) 船舱 [chuáncāng] **2** (on plane) 机舱 [jīcāng] **3** (house) 小木屋 [xiǎo mùwū]

cabin crew N [C] 机组人员 [jīzǔ rényuán]

cabinet ['kæbɪnɪt] N [C] **1** (cupboard) 贮藏橱 [zhùcáng chú]; (display cabinet) 陈列柜 [chénliè guì] **2** (POL) 内阁 [nèigé]

cabinet minister N [C] 内阁大臣 [nèigé dàchén]

cable ['keɪbl] **I** N **1** [C/U] (rope) 缆绳 [lǎnshéng] **2** [C/U] (ELEC) 电缆 [diànlǎn] **3** [U] (also: **cable television**) 有线电视 [yǒuxiàn diànshì] **II** VT **1** [+ person] 发电报 [fā diànbào]; [+ message, money] 用电报拍发 [yòng diànbào pāifā] **2** [+ city, building] (for cable TV) 配备电缆 [pèibèi diànlǎn]

cable car N [C] 缆车 [lǎnchē]

cable television N [U] 有线电视 [yǒuxiàn diànshì]

cactus ['kæktəs] (pl **cactuses** or **cacti** ['kæktaɪ]) N [C] 仙人掌 [xiānrénzhǎng]

café ['kæfeɪ] N [C] 咖啡店 [kāfēi diàn]

cafeteria [kæfɪ'tɪərɪə] N [C] 自助餐厅 [zìzhù cāntīng]

caffeine ['kæfi:n] N [U] 咖啡因 [kāfēiyīn]

cage [keɪdʒ] N [C] 笼子 [lóngzi]

cagoule [kə'gu:l] N [C] 连帽防雨长夹克衫 [liánmào fángyǔ cháng jiákèshān]

cake [keɪk] N **1** [C/U] (sponge, fruitcake etc) (large) 蛋糕 [dàngāo]; (small) 糕点 [gāodiǎn] **2** [C] [of soap] 块 [kuài] **3** [C] (savoury) ▶ **crab/rice/potato cake** 蟹/米/土豆饼 [xiè/mǐ/tǔdòubǐng] ▶ **it's a piece of cake** (inf) 太容易了 ▶ **he wants to have his cake and eat it** 他想两者兼得

calcium ['kælsɪəm] N [U] 钙 [gài]

calculate ['kælkjuleɪt] VT **1** (work out) [+ number, amount] 计算 [jìsuàn] **2** (estimate) [+ effect] 预测 [yùcè] ▶ **to calculate (that)...** (using maths) 计算···; (judge) 判断··· **3** ▶ **to be calculated to do sth** 使适合某种目的 [shǐ shìhé mǒuzhǒng mùdì]

calculation [kælkju'leɪʃən] N **1** [C/U] (MATH) 计算 [jìsuàn] **2** [C/U] (estimate) 预测 [yùcè] **3** [U] (selfishness) 自私的打算 [zìsī de dǎsuàn]

calculator ['kælkjuleɪtə(r)] N [C] 计算器 [jìsuànqì]

calendar ['kæləndə(r)] N [C] **1** (showing date) 日历 [rìlì] **2** (schedule) (for organization) 日程表 [rìchéng biǎo]; (for person) 日程安排 [rìchéng ānpái] **3** (system) 历法 [lìfǎ]

calf [kɑ:f] (pl **calves**) N [C] **1** 小牛 [xiǎoniú] **2** (ZOOL) (elephant) 幼兽 [yòushòu]; (whale) 崽 [zǎi] **3** (ANAT) 腿肚 [tuǐdù]

caliber ['kælɪbə(r)] (US) N = **calibre**

calibre, (US) **caliber** ['kælɪbə(r)] N **1** [U] [of person, skill, work] 质量 [zhìliàng] **2** [C] [of gun] 口径 [kǒujìng]

○ call [kɔːl] **I** VT **1** (name) 为···取名 [wèi···qǔmíng] ▷ **We called our son Ian.** 我们为儿子取名为伊恩。 **2** (address as) 称呼 [chēnghū] ▷ **What did you call him?** 你称呼他什么？ ▷ **Her name's Elizabeth but everyone calls her Liz.** 她名叫伊丽莎白，但每个人都称呼她莉兹。 **3** (describe as) 说成是 [shuōchéng shì] ▷ **They called him a traitor.** 他们把他说成是叛徒。 **4** (shout) 喊 [hǎn] ▷ **I heard someone calling my name.** 我听见有人大声喊我的名字。 **5** (TEL) 打电话 [dǎ diànhuà] ▷ **Call me when you get home.** 你回家后打电话给我。 **6** (summon) [+ person] 召唤

[zhāohuàn] ▷ *I think we should call the doctor.* 我认为我们应该请医生。; [+ *witness*] 传唤 [chuánhuàn] ▷ *I was called as an expert witness.* 我被作为专家证人传唤。**7** (*arrange*) [+ *meeting*] 召集 [zhàojí] ▷ *He called a press conference.* 他召集了一场记者招待会。; [+ *strike*] 下令举行 [xiàlìng jǔxíng] **8** (*announce*) [+ *flight*] 广播 [guǎngbō] ▷ *They've just called our flight.* 他们刚刚广播我们的班机即将起飞。**II** VI **1** (*shout*) 喊 [hǎn] **2** (*telephone*) 打电话 [dǎ diànhuà] ▷ *May I ask who's calling?* 请问您是哪位？**3** (*also:* **call in, call round**) 访问 [fǎngwèn] ▷ *Good night. Do call again.* 晚安。请再次光临。▷ *Do call round the college again.* 欢迎再次访问我校。**4** (*stop*) [*ship, train, bus* +] 停靠 [tíngkào] **III** N **1** [c] (*shout*) [*of person*] 大喊 [dà hǎn] ▷ *a call for help* 求救声 ▷ *He gave a loud call.* 他大喊了一声。**2** [c] (TEL) 电话 [diànhuà] ▷ *Were there any calls while I was out?* 我不在时有人打电话来吗？**3** [c] (*demand*) 对某事的要求 [duì mǒushì de yāoqiú] ▷ *MPs renewed their call for electoral reform.* 议员们重申他们对选举改革的要求。**4** [c] [*of bird, animal*] 鸟兽的叫声 [niǎoshòu de jiàoshēng] **5** [c] (*visit*) 探访 [tànfǎng] ▷ *The doctor made three calls to sick patients.* 医生3次探访病人。**6** [c] (*summons*) (*for flight*) 呼叫 [hūjiào] ▷ *That's the call for our flight.* 刚刚广播我们的飞机要起飞。**7** [s] (*fig*) (*lure*) 召唤 [zhāohuàn] ▷ *All his life he had felt the call of the sea.* 他一生中都感到大海的召唤。

▸ **to be called sth** [*person* +] 被叫某名 ▷ *She's called Susan.* 她叫苏姗。; [*object* +] 被称为某物 ▷ *A dictionary of synonyms is called a thesaurus.* 同义词字典称为类属词典。▸ **who's calling?** (TEL) 请问是谁？▸ **to be on call** [+ *nurse, doctor*] 值班 ▸ **to make a phone call** 打电话 ▸ **a long-distance call** 长途电话 ▸ **a local call** 本地电话 ▸ **to give sb a call** 打电话给某人 ▸ **to pay a call on sb** 拜访某人 ▸ **there's not much call for these items** 对这些东西没什么需求 ▸ **a call for sb to do sth** 要求某人做某事

▸ **call back** VI **1** (*return*) 回来 [huílái] **2** (TEL) 再打电话 [zài dǎ diànhuà] **II** VT (TEL) 给…回电话 [gěi…huí diànhuà]

▸ **call for** VT FUS [不可拆分] **1** (*fetch*) [+ *person*] 去接 [qùjiē]; [+ *parcel*] 去取 [qùqǔ] ▷ *I'll call for you at seven o'clock.* 我7点来接你。**2** (*demand*) 要求 [yāoqiú] ▷ *They are calling for your resignation.* 他们要求你辞职。**3** (*require*) 需要 [xūyào] ▷ *Does the situation call for military intervention?* 当前的形势是否需要军事干涉？▸ **to call for sb to do sth** 要求某人做某事

▸ **call in I** VT **1** [+ *doctor, expert, police*] 召来 [zhāolái] **2** (*request return of*) [+ *loan*] 下令收回 [xiàlìng shōuhuí]; [+ *books*] 要求退回 [yāoqiú tuìhuí] **II** VI 访问 [fǎngwèn]

▸ **call off** VT [+ *deal, event*] 取消 [qǔxiāo]

▸ **call on** VT FUS [不可拆分] (*visit*) 拜访 [bàifǎng]

▸ **to call on sb to do sth** 呼吁某人做某事

▸ **call out I** VI 叫喊 [jiàohǎn] **II** VT **1** (*shout*) 喊 [hǎn] ▷ *He called out my name.* 他喊出我的名字。**2** (*summon*) [+ *police, doctor, fire service*] 召唤 [zhāohuàn] **3** (*order out*) [+ *troops*] 命令 [mìnglìng]

▸ **call up** VT **1** (MIL) 征召 ▷ 入伍 [zhēngzhào… rùwǔ] **2** (TEL) 给…打电话 [gěi…dǎ diànhuà]

▸ **call up** VT FUS [不可拆分] = **call on**

callbox ['kɔːlbɔks] (BRIT: TEL) N [c] 电话亭 [diànhuà tíng]

call centre, (US) **call center** N [c] (TEL) 电话中心 [diànhuà zhōngxīn]

caller ['kɔːlə(r)] N [c] **1** (*visitor*) 来访者 [láifǎngzhě] **2** (TEL) 打电话者 [dǎ diànhuàzhě]

▸ **hold the line, caller!** 请别挂线！

callous ['kæləs] ADJ [+ *person*] 麻木不仁的 [mámù bùrén de]; [+ *act, attitude*] 冷酷无情的 [lěngkù wúqíng de]

calm [kɑːm] **I** ADJ **1** [+ *person*] 冷静的 [lěngjìng de]; [+ *voice*] 镇静的 [zhènjìng de]; [+ *place*] 安宁的 [ānníng de] **2** (*not stormy*) [+ *sea*] 平静的 [píngjìng de]; [+ *weather*] 平静无风的 [píngjìng wúfēng de] **II** N [U/S] (*tranquillity*) 平静 [píngjìng] **III** VT [+ *person, child, animal*] 使平静 [shǐ píngjìng]; [+ *nerves, fears*] 平息 [píngxī]

▸ **calm down I** VT [+ *person, animal*] 使平静 [shǐ píngjìng] **II** VI [*person* +] 平静下来 [píngjìng xiàlái]

calmly ['kɑːmlɪ] ADV [*say, react* +] 平静地 [píngjìng de]

Calor gas® ['kælə(r)-] N [U] 罐装煤气 [guànzhuāng méiqì]

calorie ['kælərɪ] N [c] 卡路里 [kǎlùlǐ]

calves [kɑːvz] NPL *of* **calf**

Cambodia [kæm'bəʊdɪə] N 柬埔寨 [Jiǎnpǔzhài]

Cambodian [kæm'bəʊdɪən] **I** ADJ 柬埔寨的 [Jiǎnpǔzhài de] **II** N [c] (*person*) 柬埔寨人 [Jiǎnpǔzhàirén]

camcorder ['kæmkɔːdə(r)] N [c] 摄像放像机 [shèxiàng fàngxiàng jī]

came [keɪm] PT *of* **come**

camel ['kæməl] N [c] 骆驼 [luòtuo]

camera ['kæmərə] N [c] **1** (PHOT) 照相机 [zhàoxiàngjī] **2** (CINE, TV) 摄影机 [shèyǐngjī] ▸ **on camera** 在电视摄像机前 ▸ **in camera** (LAW) 在法官的私室里

cameraman ['kæmərəmæn] (*pl* **cameramen**) N [c] 摄影师 [shèyǐngshī]

Cameroon [kæmə'ruːn] N 喀麦隆 [Kāmàilóng]

camomile ['kæməʊmaɪl] N [U] 黄春菊 [huángchūnjú]

camouflage ['kæməflɑːʒ] **I** N **1** [U] (MIL) 伪装 [wěizhuāng] **2** [U/S] (ZOOL) 保护色 [bǎohùsè] **II** VT (MIL) 伪装 [wěizhuāng]

camp [kæmp] **I** N **1** [c] (*for refugees, prisoners,*

soldiers) 营 [yíng] **2** [C/U] (encampment) 临时
居住的帐篷 [línshí jūzhù de zhàngpeng] **3** [C]
(faction) 阵营 [zhènyíng] **II** VI 扎营 [zhāyíng]
III ADJ (inf) 娘娘腔的 [niángniangqiāng de]
▶ **to go camping** 外出露营

⊙**campaign** [kæm'peɪn] **I** N [C] **1** (for change)
运动 [yùndòng] **2** (MIL) 战役 [zhànyì] **II** VI
[pressure group +] 发起运动 [fāqǐ yùndòng] ▶ **to**
campaign for/against sth 为/反对某事参加
运动

campaigner [kæm'peɪnə(r)] N [C] 参加活动
的人 [cānjiā huódòng de rén] ▶ **campaigner**
for/against sth 为提倡/反对某事而参加某
事的人

camp bed (BRIT) N [C] 折叠床 [zhédiéchuáng]
[美=**cot**]

camper ['kæmpə(r)] N [C] **1** (person) 野营
者 [yěyíngzhě] **2** (also: **camper van**) 野营车
[yěyíngchē]

campfire ['kæmp'faɪə] N [C] 营火 [yínghuǒ]

camping ['kæmpɪŋ] N [U] 野营 [yěyíng]

campsite ['kæmpsaɪt] N [C] 营地 [yíngdì]

campus ['kæmpəs] N [C] 校园 [xiàoyuán] ▶ **to**
live on campus 住校

⊙**can¹** [kæn] **I** N [C] **1** (for food, drinks) 罐头
[guàntou]; (with lid) 容器 [róngqì]; (for petrol, oil)
罐 [guàn] ▷ I had to take a can to the garage to get
some petrol. 我不得不带个罐去加油站买汽油。
2 (contents) 一听所装的量 [yītīng suǒ zhuāng
de liàng] **3** (contents and container) 一罐 [yīguàn]
II VT [+ food, drink] 罐装 [guànzhuāng] ▶ **to**
carry the can (BRIT: inf) 承担责任

○**can²** [kæn] (negative **cannot, can't**; conditional,
pt **could**) AUX VB **1** (be able to) 能 [néng]
▶ **can I help you?** (in shop) 您要买点儿什
么? ; (in general) 我能帮你吗? ▶ **you can**
do it if you try 如果试试的话你是能够
的 ▶ **I can't hear/see anything** 我什么也
听/我不见 ▶ **I can't remember** 我不记得
了 ▶ **she can't sleep** 她不能入睡 ▶ **you**
can always try telephoning him at home
你可以试着让他家里打电话 ▶ **as you can**
imagine... 就如你能想像的那样… ▶ **how**
can I ever thank you? 我该怎么谢你才好
呢? ▶ **I can't understand why...** 我不能理
解为什么…
2 (know how to) 会 [huì] ▶ **I can swim/drive**
我会游泳/开车 ▶ **can you play a musical**
instrument? 你会一种乐器吗?
3 (permission, requests) 可以 [kěyǐ] ▶ **can I**
use your phone? 我可以用你的电话吗?
▶ **can you help me?** 你可以帮我一下吗?
▶ **can't you leave me alone?** 你就不能
让我单独呆一会儿吗? ▶ **this cannot be**
allowed to continue 不能再这样下去了
4 (disbelief, puzzlement) ▶ **it can't be true!** 这

不可能是真的! [zhè bù kěnéng shì zhēn
de!] ▶ **you can't be serious!** 你不是认真
的吧! ▶ **it can't have been them!** 不可
能是他们! ! ▶ **what can he want?** 他究竟
想要什么?
5 (possibility) 可能 [kěnéng] ▶ **the illness**
can last for up to six months 病情可能持
续长达6个月 ▶ **he can be very unpleasant** 他
有时会非常不高兴 ▶ **can she have finished**
already? 她有可能已经完成了吗? ▶ **how**
can millions of dollars disappear? 成百万的
美金怎么可能消失呢?

> **can**、**could** 和 **be able to** 都是用来
> 表示某人有能力做某事，后接原形动
> 词。**can** 或 **be able to** 的现在式都可
> 以指现在，但 **can** 更为常用。They
> can all read and write...The snake is able
> to catch small mammals. **could** 或 **be**
> **able to** 的过去式可用来指过去。
> **will** 或 **shall** 加 **be able to** 则用于
> 表示将来。指在某一特定时间能够做
> 某事，用 **be able to**。After treatment
> he was able to return to work. **can** 和
> **could** 用于表示可能性。**could** 指
> 的是某个特定情况下的可能性，而
> **can** 则表示一般情况下的可能性。
> Many jobs could be lost...Too much salt
> can be harmful. 在谈论过去的时候，
> 使用 **could have** 加过去分词形式。It
> could have been much worse. 在谈论规
> 则或表示许可的时候，用 **can** 表示
> 现在，用 **could** 表示过去。They can
> leave at any time. 注意，当表示请求
> 时，**can** 和 **could** 两者都可。Can I
> have a drink?...Could we put the fire on?
> 但表示建议时只能使用 **could**。You
> could phone her and ask.

Canada ['kænədə] N 加拿大 [Jiānádà]

Canadian [kə'neɪdɪən] **I** ADJ 加拿大
的 [Jiānádà de] **II** N [C] (person) 加拿大人
[Jiānádàrén]

canal [kə'næl] N [C] **1** (for ships, barges) 运河
[yùnhé] **2** (for irrigation) 水渠 [shuǐqú] **3** (ANAT)
管 [guǎn]

Canaries [kə'nɛərɪz] NPL ▶ **the Canaries** 加那
利群岛 [Jiānàlì qúndǎo]

canary [kə'nɛərɪ] N [C] 金丝雀 [jīnsìquè]

Canary Islands [kə'nɛərɪ 'aɪləndz] NPL ▶ **the**
Canary Islands 加那利群岛 [Jiānàlì qúndǎo]

cancel ['kænsəl] VT [+ meeting, visit, reservation,
flight] 取消 [qǔxiāo]; [+ contract, order] 撤销
[chèxiāo]; [+ document] 废除 [fèichú]; [+ debt] 注
销 [zhùxiāo]; [+ cheque, stamp etc] 盖销 [gàixiāo]
▶ **cancel out** VT 抵消 [dǐxiāo] ▶ **they cancel**
each other out 他们相互抵消

cancellation [kænsə'leɪʃən] N **1** [C/U] [of
meeting, visit, flight] 取消 [qǔxiāo]; [of debt] 注
销 [zhùxiāo] **2** [C] (cancelled seat, holiday) 退票

[tuìpiào]

cancer ['kænsə(r)] N 1 [C/U] (MED) 癌症 [áizhèng] 2 (ASTROL) ► **Cancer** [U] (sign) 巨蟹座 [Jùxiè Zuò] [C] (person) 巨蟹座的人 [Jùxiè Zuò de rén] ► **to be (a) Cancer** 是巨蟹座的人

candidate ['kændɪdeɪt] N [C] 1 (for job) 候选人 [hòuxuǎnrén] 2 (in exam) 报考者 [bàokǎozhě] 3 (POL) 候选人 [hòuxuǎnrén] ► **he's a prime candidate for a heart attack** 他很容易患心脏病

candle ['kændl] N [C] 蜡烛 [làzhú] ► **to burn the candle at both ends** 操劳过度 ► **he can't hold a candle to you** 他比不上你

candlestick ['kændlstɪk] N [C] 烛台 [zhú tái]

candy ['kændɪ] (US) N [C/U] 糖果 [tángguǒ] ► **piece of candy** 一块糖果 [英=**sweet**]

candy bar (US) N [C] 条形巧克力 [tiáoxíng qiǎokèlì]

candyfloss ['kændɪflɔs] (BRIT) N [U] 棉花糖 [miánhuā táng] [美=**cotton candy**]

cane [keɪn] I N 1 [C/U] (BOT) 茎 [jīng] 2 [U] (for furniture, baskets) 藤条 [téngtiáo] 3 [C] (stick) 手杖 [shǒuzhàng] II VT (SCOL) 用笞杖打 [yòng chīzhàng dǎ] ► **to get** or **be given the cane** (SCOL) 被笞

canister ['kænɪstə(r)] N [C] (of gas, chemicals) 霰弹筒 [xiàndàn tǒng]; (for tea, sugar) 罐 [guàn]; (CINE, PHOT) 匣子 [xiázi]

cannabis ['kænəbɪs] N [U] 大麻 [dàmá]

canned [kænd] ADJ 1 [+ fruit, vegetables] 罐装的 [guànzhuāng de] 2 (inf) [+ music, laughter] 预先录制的 [yùxiān lùzhì de]

cannon ['kænən] (pl **cannon** or **cannons**) N [C] 1 (artillery piece) 大炮 [dàpào] 2 (automatic gun) 机关炮 [jīguān pào]

cannot ['kænɔt] = **can not**

canoe [kə'nu:] I N [C] 独木船 [dúmùchuán] II VI ► **to go canoeing** 去划独木船 [qù huá dúmùchuán]

canoeing [kə'nu:ɪŋ] N [U] 划独木船 [huá dúmùchuán]

canon ['kænən] N [C] 1 (clergyman) 大教堂教士 [dàjiàotáng jiàoshì] 2 (frm) (rule) 准则 [zhǔnzé]

can opener [-'əupnə(r)] N [C] 开罐器 [kāi guànqì]

can't [ka:nt] = **can not**

canteen [kæn'ti:n] N [C] 1 (in workplace, school) 食堂 [shítáng] 2 (BRIT) [for cutlery] 餐具柜 [cānjùguì] 3 (flask) 水壶 [shuǐhú]

canter ['kæntə(r)] I VI (horse +) 慢跑 [mànpǎo] II N [C] 慢跑 [mànpǎo]

Cantonese [kæntə'ni:z] I ADJ 广东的 [Guǎngdōng de] II N 1 [C] (person) 广东人 [Guǎngdōngrén] 2 [U] (language) 广东话 [Guǎngdōnghuà]

canvas ['kænvəs] N 1 [U] (fabric) 帆布 [fānbù] 2 [C] (painting) 油画 [yóuhuà] ► **under canvas** (in a tent) 在帐篷里

canvass ['kænvəs] I VI (seeking support) 游说 [yóushuì] II VT 1 (for research) [+ opinions, views, people] 征求意见 [zhēngqiú yìjiàn] 2 (seeking support) [+ electorate] 拉选票 [lāxuǎnpiào] ► **to canvass for sb** 为某人拉选票 ► **to canvass opinion** 征求意见

canyon ['kænjən] N [C] 峡谷 [xiágǔ]

cap [kæp] I N [C] 1 (hat) 帽 [mào] 2 (top) [of pen] 套子 [tàozi]; [of bottle] 盖 [gài] 3 (for toy gun) 火药帽 [huǒyào mào] 4 (for swimming) 游泳帽 [yóuyǒng mào] 5 (BRIT: FOOTBALL, CRICKET) 国家运动队队员 [guójiā yùndòng duì duìyuán] II VT 1 (complete) 达到顶峰 [dádào dǐngfēng] 2 (POL) (put limit on) 给…定限额 [gěi…dìng xiàn'é] 3 (BRIT: FOOTBALL, CRICKET) 选…入国家队 [xuǎn…rù guójiā duì] 4 [+ tooth] 包 [bāo] ► **capped with sth** 被某物覆盖 ► **and to cap it all, he said...** 更有甚者, 他说… ► **to have a tooth capped** 包牙

capability [keɪpə'bɪlɪtɪ] N [C/U] 1 (competence) 能力 [nénglì] 2 (military, nuclear etc) 能力 [nénglì] ► **to be beyond sb's capabilities** 超出某人的能力范围 ► **to have the capability to do sth** 有做某事的能力; (MIL) 有做某事的能力

capable ['keɪpəbl] ADJ (able) [+ person] 有能力的 [yǒu nénglì de] ► **to be capable of sth** [+ speed, output] 有做某事的能力 ► **to be capable of doing sth** 有做某事的能力

capacity [kə'pæsɪtɪ] N 1 [S] [of container, ship] 容量 [róngliàng]; [of stadium, theatre] 可容纳人数 [kě róngnà rénshù]; [of lift] 可装载人数 [kě zhuāngzài rénshù] 2 [U] [of factory] 产量 [chǎnliàng] 3 [C/U] (capability) 能力 [nénglì] 4 [S] (role) 职位 [zhíwèi] ► **filled to capacity** 没有位置 ► **a capacity crowd** 座无虚席 ► **to work at full capacity** 以最大限度工作 ► **capacity for sth/to do sth** 某事/做某事的能力 ► **in his capacity as...** 以他作为…的身份 ► **in an advisory capacity** 以顾问的身份

cape [keɪp] N [C] 1 (headland) 海角 [hǎijiǎo] 2 (cloak) 斗篷 [dǒupéng] 3 ► **the Cape** 好望角 [Hǎowàngjiǎo]

caper ['keɪpə(r)] N [C] 1 (CULIN) 续随子花蕾 [xùsuízǐ huālěi] 2 (inf) (frolic) 恶作剧 [èzuòjù]; (pej) 胡闹 [húnào]

capital ['kæpɪtl] I N 1 [C] (city) 首都 [shǒudū] ▷ *the Danish capital, Copenhagen* 丹麦的首都, 哥本哈根 2 [U] (money) 资本 [zīběn] ▷ *He provided most of the capital.* 他提供了大部分的资本。 3 [C] (also: **capital letter**) 大写字母 [dàxiě zìmǔ] II ADJ (LAW) [+ offence, crime] 死刑 [sǐxíng] ► **in capitals** 用大写字母 ▷ *The name was written in capitals.* 名字是用大写的。► **capital R/L etc** 大写字母R/L [等]

capitalism ['kæpɪtəlɪzəm] N [U] 资本主义 [zīběn zhǔyì]

capitalist ['kæpɪtəlɪst] I ADJ [+ system, society] 资本主义的 [zīběn zhǔyì de] II N [C] 资本家

[zīběnjiā]

capitalize ['kæpɪtəlaɪz] I VI ▸ **to capitalize on sth** 利用某事 [lìyòng mǒushì] II VT (COMM) 为…提供资本 [wèi…tígōng zīběn]

capital punishment N [U] 死刑 [sǐxíng]

Capricorn ['kæprɪkɔːn] N 1 [U] (sign) 摩羯座 [Mójié Zuò] 2 [c] (person) 摩羯座的人 [Mójié Zuò de rén] ▸ **I'm (a) Capricorn** 我是摩羯座的

caps [kæps] NPL ABBR (= capital letters) 大写字母 [dàxiě zìmǔ]

capsize [kæp'saɪz] I VT 使倾覆 [shǐ qīngfù] II VI 倾覆 [qīngfù]

capsule ['kæpsjuːl] N [c] 1 [of medicine] 胶囊 [jiāonáng] 2 (spacecraft) 太空舱 [tàikōngcāng]

captain ['kæptɪn] I N [c] 1 [of ship] 船长 [chuánzhǎng] 2 [of plane] 机长 [jīzhǎng] 3 [of team] 队长 [duìzhǎng] 4 (in army) 上尉 [shàngwèi] 5 (in navy) 上校 [shàngxiào] 6 (US: POLICE) 副巡官 [fù xúnguān] II VT 1 [+ship] 当船长 [dāng chuánzhǎng] 2 [+team] 当队长 [dāng duìzhǎng]

caption ['kæpʃən] N [c] 标题 [biāotí]

captivity [kæp'tɪvɪtɪ] N [U] 监禁 [jiānjìn] ▸ **in captivity** 被监禁

capture ['kæptʃə(r)] I VT 1 (catch) [+animal] 捕获 [bǔhuò]; [+person] 俘虏 [fúlǔ] 2 [+town, country] 攻占 [gōngzhàn] 3 (COMM) [+share of market] 占有 [zhànyǒu] 4 (reflect) [+mood, atmosphere, spirit] 反映 [fǎnyìng] II N [U] 1 [of person] 被捕 [bèibǔ] 2 [of town] 占领 [zhànlǐng] ▸ **to capture sb's imagination** 使某人为之神往

car [kɑː(r)] N [c] 1 (AUT) 汽车 [qìchē] 2 (US: RAIL) 车厢 [chēxiāng] [英=carriage, coach] ▸ **by car** 乘汽车 ▸ **the dining/buffet car** (BRIT: RAIL) 餐车

carafe [kə'ræf] N [c] [of wine, water] 精美的盛葡萄酒或水的玻璃容器 [jīngměi de chéng pútáo jiǔ huò shuǐ de bōlí róngqì]

caramel ['kærəməl] (CULIN) N 1 [c] (piece of confectionery) 太妃糖 [tàifēi táng] 2 [U] (burnt sugar) 焦糖 [jiāotáng]

carat ['kærət] N [c] 1 [of diamond] 克拉 [kèlā] 2 [of gold] 开 [kāi] ▸ **18-carat gold** 18开金

caravan ['kærəvæn] N [c] 1 (BRIT) (vehicle) 活动住房 [huódòng zhùfáng] [美=trailer] 2 (in desert) 旅行队 [lǚxíng duì]

caravan site (BRIT) N [c] 活动住房停放处 [huódòng zhùfáng tíngfàngchù]

carbohydrate [kɑːbəu'haɪdreɪt] N [c/U] 碳水化合物 [tànshuǐ huàhéwù]

carbon ['kɑːbən] N [U] 碳 [tàn]

carbonated ['kɑːbəneɪtɪd] ADJ [+drink] 带气的 [dàiqì de]

carbon dioxide [-daɪ'ɒksaɪd] N [U] 二氧化碳 [èryǎnghuàtàn]

carbon monoxide [-mɒ'nɒksaɪd] N [U] 一氧化碳 [yīyǎnghuàtàn]

car boot sale (BRIT) N [c] 将不要的物品放在汽车行李箱中出售 [jiāng bù yào de wùpǐn fàngzài xínglixiāng zhōng chūshòu]

carburettor, (US) **carburetor** [kɑːbju'retə(r)] N [c] 汽化器 [qìhuàqì]

card [kɑːd] N 1 [c] (record card, index card etc) 卡片 [kǎpiàn] 2 [c] (also: playing card) 扑克牌 [pūkèpái] 3 [c] (greetings card) 贺卡 [hèkǎ] 4 [c] (also: business card) 名片 [míngpiàn] 5 [c] (bank card, credit card etc) 信用卡 [xìnyòngkǎ] 6 [c] (membership card) 会员卡 [huìyuánkǎ] 7 [U] (material) 厚纸板 [hòuzhǐbǎn] ▸ **to play cards** 打牌

cardboard ['kɑːdbɔːd] N [U] 硬纸板 [yìng zhǐbǎn]

card game N [c] 纸牌游戏 [zhǐpái yóuxì]

cardigan ['kɑːdɪgən] N [c] 开襟毛衣 [kāijīn máoyī]

cardinal ['kɑːdɪnl] I ADJ [+rule, principle] 基本的 [jīběn de] II N [c] (REL) 红衣主教 [hóngyī zhǔjiào]

care [kɛə(r)] I N 1 [U] (attention) 照顾 [zhàogù] ▷ **She needed a lot of care at home.** 她在家需要不少照顾。2 [c] (worry) 烦恼 [fánnǎo] II VI 关心 [guānxīn] ▸ **with care** 小心 ▸ **in sb's care** 由某人照顾 ▸ **take care!** (saying goodbye) 慢走！▸ **to take care to do sth** 确保做某事 ▸ **to take care of sb** 照顾某人 ▸ **to take care of sth** [+possession, clothes] 保管某物; [+problem, situation] 处理某物 ▸ **to be in care** (BRIT) 由福利院抚养 ▸ **the child has been taken into care** 这个孩子被送入福利院抚养 ▸ **not to have a care in the world** 无忧无虑 ▸ **would you care to join us?** (frm) 你想和我们一起去吗？▸ **would you care for some tea?** 你想喝点茶吗？▸ **I don't care for it/him** (o.f.) 我不喜欢它/他 ▸ **I don't care to remember** (choose) 我不想去记住 ▸ **"care of...", "in care of..."** (US) (on letter) "由…转交" ▸ **I don't care** 我不在乎 ▸ **who cares!** (inf) 谁管呢！▸ **I couldn't care less** (US: inf) ▸ **I could care less** 我才不在乎呢 ▸ **care about** VT FUS [不可拆分] [+person, thing, idea] 关心 [guānxīn] ▸ **care for** VT FUS [不可拆分] 1 (look after) 照顾 [zhàogù] 2 (like) 喜欢 [xǐhuan]

career [kə'rɪə(r)] I N [c] 1 (job, profession) 事业 [shìyè] 2 (working life) 生涯 [shēngyá] II VI ▸ **to career off a road/into a tree** 冲出路面/撞到树上 [chōngchū lùmiàn/zhuàngdào shùshang] ▸ **his school/university career** 他的学校/大学生涯

carefree ['kɛəfriː] ADJ [+person] 无忧无虑的 [wúyōu wúlǜ de]; [+period] 轻松愉快的 [qīngsōng yúkuài de]

careful ['kɛəful] ADJ 1 (cautious) 小心的 [xiǎoxin de] 2 (thorough) [+work, thought, analysis] 仔细的 [zǐxì de] ▸ **(be) careful!** 小心！▸ **to be careful with sth** [+money] 谨慎地

使用某物; [+ fragile object] 小心对待某物 ▶ **to be careful (not) to do sth** 小心(别)做某事

carefully ['kɛəfəlɪ] ADV **1** (cautiously) 小心地 [xiǎoxīn de] **2** (methodically) 用心地 [yòngxīn de]

caregiver ['kɛəgɪvə(r)] (US) N [c] 照顾者 [zhàogùzhě] [英=**carer**]

careless ['kɛəlɪs] ADJ **1** (negligent) [+ person, worker] 粗心的 [cūxīn de]; [+ driving] 疏忽的 [shūhu de]; [+ mistake] 疏忽造成的 [shūhu zàochéng de] ▶ **how careless of me!** 我真是太不小心了! ▶ **it was careless of him to let the dog out** 他真不当心，把狗放了出去 ▶ **to be careless with sth** [+ money, resources] 对某物很随便 ▶ **to be careless of sth** (frm) (heedless) 不顾某物

carelessness ['kɛəlɪsnɪs] N [U] (negligence) 粗心大意 [cūxīn dàyì]

carer ['kɛərə(r)] (BRIT) N [c] 照顾者 [zhàogùzhě] [美=**caregiver, caretaker**]

caress [kə'rɛs] I VT 爱抚 [àifú] II N [c] 爱抚 [àifú]

caretaker ['kɛəteɪkə(r)] N [c] **1** (BRIT) [of building] 看门人 [kānménrén] [美=**janitor**] **2** (US) [of person] 照顾者 [zhàogùzhě] [英=**carer**]

car ferry N [c] 汽车渡轮 [qìchē lúndù]

cargo ['kɑːgəʊ] (pl **cargoes**) N [c/U] 货物 [huòwù]

car hire (BRIT) N [U] 汽车出租 [qìchē chūzū] [美=**car rental**]

Caribbean [kærɪ'biːən] I N ▶ **the Caribbean (Sea)** 加勒比海 [Jiālèbǐhǎi] II ADJ 加勒比海的 [Jiālèbǐhǎi de]

caring ['kɛərɪŋ] ADJ [+ person, society, organization] 有爱心的 [yǒu àixīn de]

car keys NPL 车钥匙 [chē yàoshi]

carnation [kɑː'neɪʃən] N [c] 康乃馨 [kāngnǎixīn]

carnival ['kɑːnɪvl] N **1** [c/U] (festival) 狂欢节 [kuánghuānjié] **2** [c] (US) 游艺团 [yóuyìtuán] [英=**fair, funfair**]

carol ['kærəl] N [c] ▶ **(Christmas) carol** 圣诞颂歌 [shèngdàn sònggē]

car park (BRIT) N [c] 停车场 [tíngchēchǎng] [美=**parking lot**]

carpenter ['kɑːpɪntə(r)] N [c] 木匠 [mùjiàng]

carpentry ['kɑːpɪntrɪ] N [U] **1** 木工业 [mùgōngyè] **2** (at school, college etc) 木工手艺 [mùgōng shǒuyì]

carpet ['kɑːpɪt] I N [c] **1** (fitted) 地毯 [dìtǎn]; (rug) 小地毯 [xiǎo dìtǎn] **2** (liter) [of leaves, snow] 厚厚的一层 [hòuhòu de yīcéng] II VT [+ room, stairs] 铺地毯于 [pū dìtǎn yú]

car rental N [U] 汽车出租 [qìchē chūzū]

carriage ['kærɪdʒ] N **1** [c] (BRIT: RAIL) 车厢 [chēxiāng] [美=**car**] **2** [c] (horse-drawn) 马车 [mǎchē] **3** [U] (COMM) (delivery) 运费 [yùnfèi] ▶ **carriage free** (COMM) 运费免付 ▶ **carriage**

paid (COMM) 运费已付

carriageway ['kærɪdʒweɪ] (BRIT) N [c] 车道 [chēdào]

carrier ['kærɪə(r)] N [c] **1** (airline) 航空公司 [hángkōng gōngsī] **2** (freight company) 运输公司 [yùnshū gōngsī] **3** (MED) 带菌者 [dàijūnzhě]

carrier bag (BRIT) N [c] 购物袋 [gòuwùdài] [美=**shopping bag**]

carrot ['kærət] N **1** [c/U] 胡萝卜 [húluóbo] **2** [c] (incentive) 诱饵 [yòu'ěr] ▶ **a carrot and stick approach** 软硬兼施的做法

◐ carry ['kærɪ] I VT **1** [+ person] 抱 [bào]; (by hand with the arm down) 提 [tí]; (on one's back) 背 [bēi]; (by hand) 拿 [ná] ▷ *She carried her son to the car.* 她把儿子抱到车上。**2** (take) [+ message] 传递 [chuándì] ▷ *He was carrying a message of thanks to the President.* 他代人向总统表达了谢意。**3** (have on person) 带着 [dàizhe] ▷ *He always carried a gun.* 他总是带着枪。**4** (transport) [ship, plane+] 运载 [yùnzài] ▷ *The ship could carry seventy passengers.* 这只船能载70名乘客。**5** (pass) [+ motion, bill] 通过 [tōngguò] ▷ *The motion was carried by 259 votes to 162.* 这项提案以259对162票通过。**6** (involve) [+ risk, responsibility, penalty] 带来 [dàilái] **7** (MED) [+ disease, virus] 传染 [chuánrǎn] ▷ *Rats carry nasty diseases.* 老鼠传染严重的疾病。**8** (have) [+ picture, slogan] 刊登 [kāndēng] II VI [sound+] 传播 [chuánbō] ▷ *Sound seems to carry better in the evening air.* 声音好像在傍晚空气中传播得远些。▶ **to get carried away** (by enthusiasm, idea) 失去自制力 ▶ **to carry sth further/to extremes** 进一步做某事/把某事做到极至

▶ **carry forward** VT (in book-keeping) [+ balance] 结转 [jiézhuǎn]

▶ **carry off** VT ▶ **to carry it off** (succeed) 顺利完成 [shùnlì wánchéng]

▶ **carry on** I VI **1** (continue) 继续 [jìxù] **2** (inf) (make a fuss) 吵吵闹闹 [chǎochǎo-nàonào] II VT **1** (conduct) [+ conversation, research] 继续进行 [jìxù jìnxíng] **2** (continue) [+ work, tradition] 继续 [jìxù] ▶ **to carry on with sth** 继续做某事 [jìxù zuò mǒushì] ▶ **to carry on doing sth** 继续做某事

▶ **carry out** VT [+ order, instruction] 执行 [zhíxíng]; [+ investigation, attack] 进行 [jìnxíng]; [+ plan, threat] 实行 [shíxíng]

▶ **carry over** VT 延续 [yánxù]

▶ **carry through** VT 成功地完成 [chénggōng de wánchéng]

cart [kɑːt] I N [c] **1** (for people, goods) 大车 [dàchē] **2** (US) (motorized) 轻便小车 [qīngbiàn xiǎochē] **3** (US) = **shopping cart** 手推车 [shǒutuīchē] [英=**trolley**] **4** (handcart) 手推车 [shǒutuīchē] II VT (inf) ▶ **to cart sb/sth away/around** 费力地运送/随身携带某人/某物 [fèilì de yùnsòng/suíshēn xiédài mǒurén/mǒuwù]

carton ['kɑːtən] N [c] **1** (ESP US) (cardboard box) 纸箱 [zhǐxiāng] **2** [of milk, juice, yoghurt] 容器

[róngqì] **3** [of cigarettes] 一条 [yìtiáo]

cartoon [kɑ:ˈtu:n] N [c] **1** (drawing) 漫画 [mànhuà] **2** (BRIT) (comic strip) 系列幽默画 [xìliè yōumò huà] **3** (animated) 卡通片 [kǎtōngpiàn]

cartridge [ˈkɑ:trɪdʒ] N [c] **1** (for gun) 弹壳 [dànké] **2** [of ink] (for pen) 笔芯 [bǐxīn]; (for printer) 墨盒 [mòhé] **3** (for camera) 胶卷盒 [jiāojuǎn hé] **4** (TECH) 匣子 [xiázi]

carve [kɑ:v] VT **1** (CULIN) [+ meat] 把…切片 [bǎ…qiēpiàn] **2** [+ wood, stone, figure] 雕刻 [diāokè]; [+ initials, design] 刻 [kè] ▶ **to carve (out) a career for o.s.** 为自己创业
▶ **carve up** VT [+ land, property] 划分 [huàfēn]

carving [ˈkɑ:vɪŋ] N **1** [c] (object) 雕刻品 [diāokèpǐn] **2** [c/u] (design) 雕刻 [diāokè] **3** [u] (technique) 雕刻术 [diāokèshù]

car wash N [c] 汽车擦洗 [qìchē cāxǐ]

○ **case** [keɪs] N **1** [c] (instance) 情况 [qíngkuàng] ▷ This causes problems in some cases. 这在某些情况下引起了问题。 **2** [c] [of doctor, social worker, solicitor etc] 个案 [gè'àn] **3** [c] (before judge, tribunal etc, for investigation) 案件 [ànjiàn] ▷ a murder case 一桩谋杀案 ▷ one of Sherlock Holmes's most famous cases 夏洛克·福尔摩斯最出名的案件之一 **4** [c] (container) 盒子 [hézi] **5** [c] (BRIT) (also: **suitcase**) 行李箱 [xínglixiāng] **6** [c] (quantity) [of wine, whisky] 一箱 [yìxiāng] ▷ a case of champagne 一箱香槟酒 **7** [c/u] (LING) 格 [gé] ▶ **lower/upper case** 小/大写 ▶ **to have a good case** (argument) 有充足的论证 ▶ **there's a strong case for/against reform** 有强烈支持/反对改革的理由 ▶ **it's a case of trying to get fit** 需要保持健康 ▶ **in case of** [+ fire, emergency] 如果发生 ▶ **in case he comes** 以防万一他会来 ▶ **in case you hadn't noticed** 如果你还没注意到的话 ▶ **in any case** 无论如何 ▶ **just in case** 以防万一 ▶ **in that case** 既然是那样 ▶ **if that is the case** 如果是这样的话 ▶ **a case in point** 恰当的例子

cash [kæʃ] N **1** [u] (notes and coins) 现金 [xiànjīn] **2** (money) 现款 [xiànkuǎn] II VT [+ cheque, money order] 兑现 [duìxiàn] ▶ **to pay (in) cash** 付现金 ▶ **cash on delivery** 货到交款 ▶ **cash down** 即刻付款
▶ **cash in** VT [+ insurance policy, shares] 把…兑为现金 [bǎ…duìwéi xiànjīn]
▶ **cash in on** VT FUS [不可拆分] 从…中获利 [cóng…zhōng huòlì]

cashback [kæʃbæk] N [u] **1** (discount) 现金折扣 [xiànjīn zhékòu] **2** (with debit card) 取现金 [qǔxiànjīn]; (system) 现金支取，即在用银行卡付款时要求提取一定数额现金

cash card (BRIT) N [c] 提款卡 [tíkuǎn kǎ]

cash desk (BRIT) N [c] 收款台 [shōukuǎntái]

cash dispenser (BRIT) N [c] 自动取款机 [zìdòng qǔkuǎn jī] [美＝**ATM**]

cashew [kæˈʃu:] N [c] (also: **cashew nut**) 腰果

[yāoguǒ]

cashier [kæˈʃɪə(r)] N [c] (in bank) 出纳员 [chūnàyuán]; (in shop, restaurant) 收银员 [shōuyínyuán]

cashmere [ˈkæʃmɪə(r)] I N [u] 山羊绒 [shānyángróng] II ADJ 山羊绒的 [shānyángróng de]

cashpoint [ˈkæʃpɔɪnt] (BRIT) N [c] 自动取款机 [zìdòng qǔkuǎn jī] [美＝**ATM**]

cash register N [c] 出纳机 [chūnàjī]

casino [kəˈsi:nəu] N [c] 赌场 [dǔchǎng]

casket [ˈkɑ:skɪt] N [c] **1** (US) (coffin) 棺材 [guāncai] **2** (liter) (for jewellery) 小盒 [xiǎohé]

casserole [ˈkæsərəul] N [c] **1** (food) 沙锅 [shāguō] **2** (container) (also: **casserole dish**) 炖锅 [dùnguō] II VT 炖 [dùn]

cassette [kæˈset] N [c] 磁带 [cídài]

cassette player N [c] 放音机 [fàngyīnjī]

cassette recorder N [c] 录音机 [lùyīnjī]

cast [kɑ:st] (pt, pp **cast**) I VT **1** (throw) [+ light, shadow] 投射 [tóushè]; [+ net, fishing line] 投 [tóu] **2** [+ statue] 铸造 [zhùzào] **3** (THEAT) ▶ **to cast sb as sth** 分配某人扮演某个角色 [fēnpèi mǒurén bànyǎn mǒuge juésè] II VI (in fishing) 抛 [pāo] III N [c] **1** (THEAT) 演员表 [yǎnyuánbiǎo] **2** (mould) 模子 [múzi] **3** (also: **plaster cast**) 石膏 [shígāo] ▶ **to cast one's vote** 投票 ▶ **to cast doubt on sth** 对某事产生怀疑 ▶ **to cast a glance** 瞄一瞄 ▶ **to cast an eye** or **one's eye(s) over sth** 看一眼某物 ▶ **to cast a spell on sb** [witch, fairy etc +] 施咒于某人; (fig) 迷住某人 ▶ **to cast sb/sth into sth** (liter) 将某人/某物扔入某处
▶ **cast about, cast around** VI ▶ **to cast about for sth** 想方设法寻找 [xiǎng fāng shè fǎ xúnzhǎo]
▶ **cast aside** VT (reject) 抛弃 [pāoqì]
▶ **cast off** I VT (liter) (get rid of) 抛弃 [pāoqì] II VI **1** (NAUT) 解船缆 [jiěchuánlǎn] **2** (in knitting) 收针 [shōuzhēn]
▶ **cast on** (in knitting) I VI 起针 [qǐzhēn] II VT [+ stitch] 开始编织 [kāishǐ biānzhī]
▶ **cast out** VT (get rid of) 驱除 [qūchú]

caster sugar, (BRIT) **castor sugar** [ˈkɑ:stə-] N [u] 精白砂糖 [jīngbáishātáng]

cast-iron [ˈkɑ:staɪən] ADJ **1** (metal) 铸铁制的 [zhùtiězhì de] **2** (certain) [+ guarantee, alibi] 无可质疑的 [wú kě zhìyí de]

castle [ˈkɑ:sl] N [c] **1** 城堡 [chéngbǎo] **2** (CHESS) 车 [chē]

castor sugar N = **caster sugar**

casual [ˈkæʒjul] ADJ **1** (chance) [+ remark] 漫不经心的 [màn bù jīngxīn de]; [+ observer] 偶然的 [ǒurán de] **2** (non-permanent) [+ work, workers] 临时的 [línshí de] **3** (unconcerned) 随便的 [suíbiàn de] **4** (informal) [+ clothes] 非正式的 [fēizhèngshì de] ▶ **casual wear** 便服 ▶ **casual sex** 随便的性行为

casually ['kæʒjʊlɪ] ADV 1 (in a relaxed way) 漫不经心地 [màn bù jīngxīn de] 2 [dress, say, mention+] 随便地 [suíbiàn de] 3 (by chance) 偶然地 [ǒurán de]

casualty ['kæʒjʊltɪ] N [c] 1 [of war, accident] (injured) 伤病员 [shāngbìngyuán]; (dead) 伤亡人员 [shāngwáng rényuán] 2 [c] [of situation, event] 牺牲品 [xīshēngpǐn] 3 [U] (BRIT) (in hospital) 急诊室 [jízhěnshì] [美=emergency room, ER] ► heavy casualties (MIL) 伤亡惨重

cat [kæt] N [c] 1 猫 [māo] 2 (lion, tiger etc) 猫科动物 [māokē dòngwù] ► (a game of) cat and mouse 猫捉老鼠 (的游戏)

catalogue, (US) **catalog** ['kætəlɒg] I N [c] 1 (for mail order) 目录 [mùlù] 2 [of exhibition] 目录 [mùlù] 3 [of series] 书目 [shūmù] 4 (series) [of events, faults] 一系列 [yīxìliè] II VT 1 [+objects] 把…编入目录 [bǎ…biānrù mùlù] 2 [+events, faults] 列举 [lièjǔ]

catalytic converter [kætə'lɪtɪkkən'vɜːtə(r)] (AUT) N [c] 催化转化器 [cuīhuà zhuǎnhuà qì]

cataract ['kætərækt] (MED) N [c] 白内障 [báinèizhàng]

catarrh [kə'tɑː(r)] N [U] 黏膜炎 [niánmóyán]

catastrophe [kə'tæstrəfɪ] N [c] 大灾难 [dàzāinàn]

catch [kætʃ] (pt, pp **caught**) I VT 1 [+animal, fish] 捕获 [bǔhuò]; [+thief, criminal] 抓获 [zhuāhuò] 2 [+ball] 接 [jiē] 3 [+bus, train, plane] 赶上 [gǎnshang] 4 (discover) [+person] 发现 [fāxiàn] 5 (causing damage) 打 [dǎ]; (snag) 钩住 [gōuzhù] 6 (hear) 听清楚 [tīng qīngchu] 7 [+flu, illness] 染上 [rǎnshang] ▷ I caught a cold. 我感冒了。 II VI (on branches, door etc) 被钩住 [bèi gōuzhù] III N [c] 1 [of ball etc] 接住 [jiēzhù] 2 [of fish] 捕获量 [bǔhuò liàng] 3 (downside) 蹊跷 [qīqiāo] 4 (on door, window, bag) [of shuān] 5 (game) ► to play catch 玩掷球游戏 [wán zhìqiú yóuxì] ► to catch sb doing sth 撞见某人做某事 ► to catch sb's attention or eye 引起某人的注意 ► to catch the light 反光 ► to be or get caught in sth [+storm] 遇到某事; [+traffic jam] 不巧碰到某事; [+crossfire] 遭到某事
  ► **catch on** VI 1 (understand) 理解 [lǐjiě] 2 (become popular) 流行起来 [liúxíng qǐlái] ► to **catch on to sth** 理解某事
  ► **catch out** (BRIT) VT 证明有错 [zhèngmíng yǒucuò]
  ► **catch up** VI 1 (walking, driving) 追上 [zhuīshang] 2 (in standard) 赶上 [gǎnshang] ► to be caught up in sth 被卷入某事
  ► **catch up on** VT FUS [不可拆分] [+work, sleep] 弥补 [míbǔ]
  ► **catch up with** VT FUS [不可拆分] (walking, driving, in standard) 赶上 [gǎnshang] ► the law caught up with him yesterday 昨天警方发现他做了违法的事 ► his past caught up with him 他的过去阴影不散

catching ['kætʃɪŋ] ADJ (inf) (infectious) 传染性的 [chuánrǎnxìng de]

categorize ['kætɪgəraɪz] VT 把…分类 [bǎ…fēnlèi] ► to categorize sb/sth as 认定某人/某事为

category ['kætɪgərɪ] N [c] 种类 [zhǒnglèi]

cater ['keɪtə(r)] VI 1 ► to cater for (supply food for) [+occasion, wedding, party] 承办 [chéngbàn] 2 ► to cater for or (US) to sth [+sb's needs, tastes] 迎合某事 [yínghé mǒushì] 3 ► to cater for or (US) to sb [+readers, consumers] 迎合某人 [yínghé mǒurén]

caterer ['keɪtərə(r)] N [c] 酒席承办人 [jiǔxí chéngbànrén]

catering ['keɪtərɪŋ] N [U] 1 (industry) 饮食业 [yǐnshíyè] 2 (for specific occasion) 酒席承办 [jiǔxí chéngbàn] ► to do the catering 承办饮食

caterpillar ['kætəpɪlə(r)] N [c] 毛虫 [máochóng]

cathedral [kə'θiːdrəl] N [c] 大教堂 [dàjiàotáng]

Catholic ['kæθəlɪk] I ADJ 天主教的 [Tiānzhǔjiào de] II N [c] 天主教徒 [Tiānzhǔjiào tú]

Catseye® ['kætsˈaɪ] (BRIT: AUT) N [c] 反光灯 [fǎnguāngdēng]

cattle ['kætl] NPL 牛 [niú]

catwalk ['kætwɔːk] N [c] 1 (for models) T型台 [T xíngtái] 2 (bridge) 狭窄通道 [xiázhǎi tōngdào]

caught [kɔːt] PT, PP of catch

cauliflower ['kɒlɪflauə(r)] N [c/U] 菜花 [càihuā]

○ **cause** [kɔːz] I N 1 [c] [of event] 起因 [qǐyīn] ▷ Nobody knew the cause of the explosion. 没有人知道这次爆炸的起因。 2 [U] (reason) 理由 [lǐyóu] 3 [c] (aim, principle) 事业 [shìyè] ▷ He is sympathetic to our cause. 他支持我们的事业。 II VT (produce, lead to) 导致 [dǎozhì] ▷ Does smoking cause cancer? 吸烟是否导致癌症? ► to have cause for sth/to do sth 某事/做某事有原因 ► there is no cause for concern 没有理由担心 ► to cause sb to do sth 促使某人做某事 ► to cause sth to happen 导致某事发生

caution ['kɔːʃən] I N 1 [U] (prudence) 谨慎 [jǐnshèn] 2 [c] (BRIT: POLICE) 警告 [jǐnggào] II VT (BRIT: POLICE) 警告 [jǐnggào] ► to caution sb that... 警告某人… ► to caution sb against sth/against doing sth 警告某人某事/防止某人做某事

cautious ['kɔːʃəs] ADJ 谨慎的 [jǐnshèn de] ► to be cautious about doing sth 对做某事持谨慎的态度

cave [keɪv] I N [c] 山洞 [shāndòng] II VI ► to go caving 探察洞穴 [tànchá dòngxué]
  ► **cave in** VI 1 [roof, wall+] 倒塌 [dǎotā] 2 [person+] (to demands, pressure) 屈服 [qūfú] ► to cave in to sth/sb 屈服于某事/某人

caviar(e) ['kævɪɑː(r)] N [U] 鱼子酱 [yúzǐjiàng]

cavity ['kævɪtɪ] N [C] (frm) (in wall, tooth) 洞 [dòng]; (in body) 腔 [qiāng]

cc ABBR **1** (= cubic centimetres) 立方厘米 [lìfāng límǐ] **2** (= carbon copy) 抄送 [chāosòng]

CD N ABBR (= compact disc) 激光唱片 [jīguāng chàngpiàn]

CDC (US) N ABBR (= Center for Disease Control) 疾病控制中心 [Jíbìng Kòngzhì Zhōngxīn]

CD player N [C] 激光唱机 [jīguāng chàngjī]

CD-ROM N ABBR (= compact disc read-only memory) 光盘只读存储器 [guāngpán zhǐdú cúnchǔ qì] ▸ **on CD-ROM** 光盘版

CDT (US) ABBR (= Central Daylight Time) 中部夏令时 [Zhōngbù Xiàlìngshí]

cease [si:s] (frm) I VI **1** 停止 [tíngzhǐ] II VT [+ production, operations, work] 停止 [tíngzhǐ] ▸ **to cease doing sth** 停止做某事 ▸ **to cease trading** 停止营业 ▸ **to cease to do sth** 停止做某事 ▸ **he never ceases to amaze me** 他不停地使我惊讶

ceasefire ['si:sfaɪə(r)] N [C] 停火 [tínghuǒ]

cedar ['si:də(r)] N **1** [C] (tree) 雪松 [xuěsōng] **2** [U] (wood) 雪松木材 [xuěsōng mùcái]

ceiling ['si:lɪŋ] N [C] **1** (in room) 天花板 [tiānhuābǎn] **2** (limit) (on amount, salaries etc) 最高限度 [zuìgāo xiàndù] ▸ **to put a ceiling on sth** 给某物制定上限

celebrate ['sɛlɪbreɪt] I VT **1** [+ success, birthday] 庆祝 [qìngzhù] **2** (REL) [+ mass] 主持 [zhǔchí] II VI 庆祝 [qìngzhù]

celebrated ['sɛlɪbreɪtɪd] ADJ [+ author, film] 著名的 [zhùmíng de]

celebration [sɛlɪ'breɪʃən] N [C/U] 庆祝 [qìngzhù]

celebrity [sɪ'lɛbrɪtɪ] N **1** [C] (person) 名人 [míngrén] **2** [U] (fame) 名望 [míngwàng]

celery ['sɛlərɪ] N [U] 芹菜 [qíncài] ▸ **a stick of celery** 一根芹菜

cell [sɛl] N [C] **1** (BIO) 细胞 [xìbāo] **2** (in prison) 牢房 [láofáng]; (in monastery) 单人小室 [dānrén xiǎoshì] **3** (group) 小组 [xiǎozǔ]

cellar ['sɛlə(r)] N [C] 地下室 [dìxiàshì]; (for wine) 酒窖 [jiǔjiào]

cellist ['tʃɛlɪst] N [C] 大提琴手 [dàtíqínshǒu]

cello ['tʃɛləʊ] N [C] 大提琴 [dàtíqín]

cellophane® ['sɛləfeɪn] N [U] 玻璃纸 [bōlizhǐ]

cellphone ['sɛlfəʊn] N [C] 手机 [shǒujī]

cellular phone ['sɛljʊlə-] N = **cellphone**

Celsius ['sɛlsɪəs] ADJ 摄氏的 [Shèshì de]

Celt [kɛlt, sɛlt] N [C] 凯尔特人 [Kǎi'ěrtèrén]

Celtic ['kɛltɪk, 'sɛltɪk] ADJ 凯尔特的 [Kǎi'ěrtè de]

cement [sə'mɛnt] I N [U] **1** (powder) 黏固剂 [niángùjì] **2** (concrete) 水泥 [shuǐní] **3** (glue) 胶接剂 [jiāojiējì] II VT **1** (stick, glue) 胶合 [jiāohé] **2** [+ relationship, agreement] 巩固 [gǒnggù] ▷ *Nothing cements a friendship between countries so much as trade.* 没有什么能像贸易一样如此这般地巩固两国之间的友谊。**3** [+ path, floor] 铺水泥于 [pū shuǐní yú]

cemetery ['sɛmɪtrɪ] N [C] 墓地 [mùdì]

censor ['sɛnsə(r)] I VT [+ newspaper report, book, play etc] 审查 [shěnchá] II N [C] 审查员 [shěncháyuán]

censorship ['sɛnsəʃɪp] N [U] [of book, play etc] 审查制度 [shěnchá zhìdù]; [of news] 审查 [shěnchá]

census ['sɛnsəs] N [C] 人口调查 [rénkǒu diàochá]

cent [sɛnt] N [C] 分 [fēn]

centenary [sɛn'ti:nərɪ] (BRIT) N [C] 一百周年 [yībǎi zhōunián] [美= **centennial**]

centennial [sɛn'tɛnɪəl] (US) N [C] 一百周年 [yībǎi zhōunián] [英= **centenary**]

center ['sɛntə(r)] (US) N = **centre**

centigrade ['sɛntɪgreɪd] ADJ 摄氏的 [Shèshì de]

centimetre, (US) centimeter ['sɛntɪmi:tə(r)] N [C] 厘米 [límǐ]

centipede ['sɛntɪpi:d] N [C] 蜈蚣 [wúgōng]

◇ **central** ['sɛntrəl] ADJ **1** (in the centre) 中心的 [zhōngxīn de] ▷ *central London* 伦敦中心 ▷ *The cafe was near Oxford Street, very central for her.* 这家咖啡店靠近牛津街，对她来说很近。**2** [+ committee, government] 中央的 [zhōngyāng de] ▷ *the central committee of the Cuban communist party* 古巴共产党中央委员会 **3** (most important) [+ idea, figure] 最关键的 [zuì guānjiàn de] ▷ *the central character in the film* 电影主角 ▷ *She is the central person in this project.* 她是这个工程中最关键的人物。

Central America N 中美洲 [Zhōngměizhōu]

central heating N [U] 中央供暖系统 [zhōngyāng gōngnuǎn xìtǒng]

central reservation (BRIT: AUT) N [C] 中央分车带 [zhōngyāng fēnchēdài] [美= **median strip**]

◇ **centre, (US) center** ['sɛntə(r)] I N **1** [C] [of circle, line, town, activity] 中心 [zhōngxīn] ▷ *the centre of the room* 房间当中 ▷ *the city centre* 市中心 ▷ *London is the major international insurance centre.* 伦敦是重要的国际保险中心。**2** [C] (building) 中心 [zhōngxīn] **3** [S] (POL) 中间派 [zhōngjiānpài] II VT (TYP) (on page) 使…居中 [shǐ…jūzhōng]; [+ object] 把…放在中央 [bǎ…fàngzài zhōngyāng]; (PHOT) 将…放在中心位置 [jiāngfàngzài zhōngxīn wèizhì] ▷ *It's a lovely shot – just a pity it isn't a bit better centred.* 照得很好，可惜有点偏了。; (FOOTBALL) [+ ball] 将…传至球场中央 [jiāng…chuánzhì qiúchǎng zhōngyāng] ▸ **to be at the centre of sth** 是某事的关键 ▸ **to be the centre of attention** or **interest** 注意 (或) 兴趣的焦点 ▸ **to centre** or **be centred on** (focus on) 集中于 ▸ **to be centred in London/Rome** 集中于伦敦/罗马

◇ **century** ['sɛntjʊrɪ] N [C] **1** (period) 世纪 [shìjì]

2 (CRICKET) 百分 [bǎifēn] ► **the 21st century** 21世纪 ► **in the twenty-first century** 在21世纪

CEO N ABBR (= *chief executive officer*) 首席执行官 [Shǒuxí Zhíxíngguān]

ceramic [sɪˈræmɪk] ADJ 陶瓷的 [táocí de]

cereal [ˈsiːrɪəl] N **1** [c] (*plant, crop*) 谷类植物 [gǔlèi zhíwù] **2** [c/u] (*also:* **breakfast cereal**) 谷类食品 [gǔlèi shípǐn]

ceremonial [sɛrɪˈməʊnɪəl] **I** ADJ 礼节性的 [lǐjiéxìng de] **II** N [u] 礼仪 [lǐyí]

ceremony [ˈsɛrɪmənɪ] N **1** [c] (*event*) 典礼 [diǎnlǐ]; (*ritual*) 礼仪 [lǐyí] **2** [u] (*formality*) 仪式 [yíshì] ► **to stand on ceremony** 拘于礼节

certain [ˈsɜːtən] ADJ **1** (*sure*) [+ *person*] 肯定的 [kěndìng de] **2** [+ *defeat, success, victory, death*] 一定的 [yīdìng de] **3** (*some*) [+ *times, people, days*] 某些 [mǒuxiē] ► **to be certain that...** [*person* +] 肯定… ► **it is certain that...** 肯定… ► **he is certain to be there** 他肯定在那儿 ► **to make certain that...** 证实… ► **to be certain of** 肯定 ► **a certain coldness/pleasure** 有点冷淡/高兴 ► **a certain amount of sth** 一定量的某物 ► **to know sth for certain** 确定某事

certainly [ˈsɜːtənlɪ] ADV **1** (*undoubtedly*) 无疑地 [wúyí de] **2** (*of course*) 当然 [dāngrán] ► **certainly not** 绝对不行

certainty [ˈsɜːtəntɪ] N **1** [u] (*assurance*) 确定 [quèdìng] **2** [c/u] (*inevitability*) 必然的事 [bìrán de shì] ► **all that can be said with certainty is that...** 惟一确定无疑的是… ► **there is no certainty that...** 不能肯定… ► **there are never any certainties** 从来都没有必然的事

certificate [səˈtɪfɪkɪt] N [c] **1** [*of birth, marriage etc*] 证 [zhèng] **2** (*diploma*) 结业证书 [jiéyè zhèngshū]

certified mail [ˈsɜːtɪfaɪd-] (US) N [u] 挂号信 [guàhào xìn]

certify [ˈsɜːtɪfaɪ] VT **1** (*attest to*) 证实 [zhèngshí] ▷ *The National Election Council is supposed to certify the results.* 国家选举委员会应该证实这些结果。 **2** (*award diploma to*) 发证书给 [fā zhèngshū gěi] **3** (*declare insane*) 确诊为精神失常 [quèzhěnwéi jīngshén shīcháng] ► **to certify that...** 证明… ► **to certify sb dead** 确证某人死亡

cf. ABBR (= *confer*) 比较 [bǐjiào]

CFC N ABBR (= *chlorofluorocarbon*) 氟氯化炭 [fúlùhuàtàn]

ch. ABBR (= *chapter*) 章 [zhāng]

Chad [tʃæd] N 乍得 [Zhàdé]

chain [tʃeɪn] **I** N **1** [c/u] 链条 [liàntiáo] **2** [c] (*piece of jewellery*) 链子 [liànzi] **3** [c] [*of islands, mountains*] 一系列 [yīxìliè] **4** [c] [*of shops, hotels*] 连锁 [liánsuǒ] **5** [c] [*of events, circumstances*] 一连串 [yīliánchuàn] **II** VT ► **to chain sb/sth to sth** 用链条将某人/某物拴在某物上 [yòng liàntiáo jiāng mǒurén/mǒuwù shuānzài

mǒuwùshang] ► **in chains** 用枷锁锁着 ► **to pull the chain** 冲厕所
► **chain up** VT [+ *prisoner, dog*] 用链条拴住 [yòng liàntiáo shuānzhù]

chair [tʃeə(r)] **I** N [c] **1** 椅子 [yǐzi]; (*armchair*) 扶手椅 [fúshǒuyǐ] **2** (BRIT: UNIV) 大学教授职位 [dàxué jiàoshòu zhíwèi] **3** (*chairperson*) 主席 [zhǔxí] **4** (US) (*electric chair*) ► **the chair** 电椅 [diànyǐ] **II** VT [+ *meeting*] 主持 [zhǔchí]

chair lift N [c] 架空吊椅 [jiàkōng diàoyǐ]

chairman [ˈtʃeəmən] (*pl* **chairmen**) N [c] [*of committee, company, meeting*] 主席 [zhǔxí]

chairperson [ˈtʃeəpəːsn] N [c] 主席 [zhǔxí]

chairwoman [ˈtʃeəwumən] (*pl* **chairwomen**) N [c] 女主席 [nǚ zhǔxí]

chalet [ˈʃæleɪ] N [c] 小木屋 [xiǎomùwū]

chalk [tʃɔːk] **I** N **1** [u] 白垩 [bái'è] **2** [c/u] (*for writing*) 粉笔 [fěnbǐ] **II** VT 用粉笔写 [yòng fěnbǐ xiě] ► **a piece of chalk** (*for blackboard*) 一支粉笔
► **chalk up** VT [+ *success, victory*] 取得 [qǔdé]

challenge [ˈtʃælɪndʒ] **I** N [c/u] **1** (*hard task*) 挑战 [tiǎozhàn] **2** (*to authority, ideas*) 异议 [yìyì]; (*to rival, competitor*) 挑战 [tiǎozhàn] **II** VT [+ *authority, right, idea*] 质疑 [zhìyí]; [+ *rival, competitor*] 向…挑战 [xiàng…tiǎozhàn] ► **to rise to the challenge** 迎接挑战 ► **to challenge sb to do sth** 向某人提出挑战做某事 ► **to challenge sb to a fight/game** 挑战某人打架/比赛

challenging [ˈtʃælɪndʒɪŋ] ADJ **1** [+ *job, task*] 具有挑战性的 [jùyǒu tiǎozhànxìng de] **2** [+ *tone, look etc*] 挑衅的 [tiǎoxìn de]

chamber [ˈtʃeɪmbə(r)] **I** N [c] **1** (*meeting room*) 会议室 [huìyì shì]; (*room for particular purpose*) 房间 [fángjiān] **2** (POL) (*section of parliament*) 议院 [yìyuàn] **II** **chambers** NPL (LAW) (*for judges*) 法官办公室 [fǎguān bàngōngshì]; (*for barristers*) 律师事务所 [lùshī shìwùsuǒ] ► **chamber of commerce** 商会 ► **the Upper/Lower Chamber** (POL) 上/下议院

chambermaid [ˈtʃeɪmbəmeɪd] N [c] (*in hotel*) 旅馆女服务员 [lǚguǎn nǚ fúwùyuán]

champagne [ʃæmˈpeɪn] N [c/u] 香槟酒 [xiāngbīn jiǔ]

champion [ˈtʃæmpɪən] **I** N [c] **1** [*of league, contest*] 冠军 [guànjūn] **2** [*of cause, person, underdog*] 拥护者 [yōnghùzhě] **II** VT [+ *cause, principle, person*] (*support*) 支持 [zhīchí]; (*defend*) 捍卫 [hànwèi]

championship [ˈtʃæmpɪənʃɪp] N **1** [c] (*contest*) 锦标赛 [jǐnbiāo sài] **2** [s] (*title*) 冠军称号 [guànjūn chēnghào]

⊘ chance [tʃɑːns] **I** N **1** [c/u] (*likelihood, possibility*) 可能性 [kěnéngxìng] **2** [s] (*opportunity*) 机会 [jīhuì] **3** [u] (*luck*) 运气 [yùnqì] ▷ *It all depends on chance.* 全靠运气。 **II** VT **1** (*risk*) ► **to chance it** 碰碰运气 [pèngpeng yùnqì] **2** ► **to chance to do**

sth (frm) 碰巧做某事 [pèngqiǎo zuò mǒushì] **III** ADJ [+ meeting, discovery] 偶然的 [ǒurán de] ▶ he hasn't much chance of winning 他赢的机会不大 ▶ to stand a chance of (doing) sth 有 (做) 某事的机会 ▶ there is little chance of his coming 他来的机会很小 ▶ the chances are that... 很可能… ▶ the chance to do sth 做某事的机会 ▷ She left before I had the chance to reply. 她在我有机会回答前就离开了。▶ to give sb the chance to do sth 给某人做某事的机会 ▶ it's the chance of a lifetime 一生难得的机会 ▶ to take a chance (on sth) 冒险 (做某事) ▶ by chance 偶然 ▶ by any chance 有没有可能 ▷ Are they by any chance related? 他们是否有可能有联系?

▶ chance (up)on (frm) VT FUS [不可拆分] [+ person, thing] 偶然遇到 [ǒurán yùdào]

chancellor ['tʃɑːnsələ(r)] N [c] **1** (head of government) 总理 [zǒnglǐ] **2** (BRIT) [of university] 校长 [xiàozhǎng] **3** (BRIT) = Chancellor of the Exchequer

Chancellor of the Exchequer (BRIT) N [c] 财政大臣 [cáizhèng dàchén]

chandelier [ʃændə'lɪə(r)] N [c] 枝形吊灯 [zhīxíng diàodēng]

○ **change** [tʃeɪndʒ] **I** VT **1** (alter) 改变 [gǎibiàn] ▷ You can't change human nature. 你不可能改变人的本性。**2** (replace) [+ wheel, battery etc] 换 [huàn] ▷ Try changing the battery. 试试换电池。**3** [+ trains, buses etc] 换 [huàn] ▷ At Glasgow I changed trains for Greenock. 我在格拉斯哥换火车去格林诺克。**4** [+ clothes] 换 [huàn] ▷ I'll just change my shirt. 我要换衬衫。**5** [+ bed, sheets] 更换 [gēnghuàn] **6** [+ job, address] 更改 [gēnggǎi] ▷ His doctor advised him to change his job. 他的医生建议他换工作。▷ He has changed his address. 他更改了他的地址。**7** (put fresh nappy on) [+ baby] 更换 [gēnghuàn] **8** (replace) [+ nappy] 换 [huàn] ▷ She fed the baby and changed its nappy. 她给婴儿喂了饭,换了尿布。**9** (exchange) [+ money] 兑换 [duìhuàn] ▷ These places charge exorbitant rates for changing money. 这些地方对换汇收取极高的手续费。**10** (transform) ▶ to change sb/sth into sth 将某人/某物变成某物 [jiāng mǒurén/mǒuwù biànchéng mǒuwù]; (by magic) 将某人/某物变成某物 [jiāng mǒurén/mǒuwù biànchéng mǒuwù] ▷ The witch changed him into a frog. 女巫把他变成了一只青蛙。**II** VI **1** (alter) 变化 [biànhuà] ▷ Little has changed since then. 从那时至今没什么变化。**2** (change clothes) 换衣 [huànyī] ▷ They allowed her to shower and change. 他们允许她冲澡和换衣服。**3** [traffic lights +] 变色 [biànsè] ▷ The lights changed to green. 交通灯变绿了。**4** (on bus, train etc) 换车 [huànchē] **5** (be transformed) ▶ to change into sth 变成某物 [biànchén mǒuwù] **III** N **1** [c/u] (alteration) 转变 [zhuǎnbiàn] ▷ I dislike change of any kind. 我不喜欢任何方式的转变。**2** [s]

(novelty) 变化 [biànhuà] ▷ It's a change to finally win a match. 最后赢一场也是个变化。**3** [c] [of government, climate, job] 更换 [gēnghuàn] ▷ A change of leadership alone will not be enough. 更换领导本身是不够的。**4** [U] (referring to money) (coins) 零钱 [língqián] ▷ I haven't got any change. 我没零钱。; (money returned) 找头 [zhǎotou] ▷ The shopkeeper handed Hooper his change. 店主递给了胡珀他的找头。▶ to change sth for sth 将某物换成某物 ▶ to change one's mind 改变主意 ▶ to change gear (BRIT: AUT) 换挡 [美 = to shift gear] ▶ to change hands (be sold) 转手买卖 ▶ she changed into an old skirt 她换上了一条旧裙子 ▶ it makes a change 换换花样 ▶ for a change 为了改变一下 ▶ a change of clothes/underwear 一套换洗的衣服/内衣 ▶ a change of scene 换换环境 ▶ small change 零钱 ▶ to give sb change for or of 10 pounds 给某人10英镑的零钱 ▶ keep the change! 不用找了!

▶ change over VI ▶ to change over to sth 改变成某事 [gǎibiàn chéng mǒushì]

changeable ['tʃeɪndʒəbl] ADJ [+ weather] 多变的 [duōbiàn de]; [+ person] 变化无常的 [biànhuà wúcháng de]

change machine N [c] 零钱兑换机 [língqián duìhuàn jī]

changing ['tʃeɪndʒɪŋ] ADJ [+ world, attitudes, role] 日新月异的 [rì xīn yuè yì de]

changing room (BRIT) N [c] **1** (in shop) 试衣室 [shìyīshì] **2** (SPORT) 更衣室 [gēngyīshì]

channel ['tʃænl] **I** N [c] **1** (TV) 频道 [píndào] **2** (for water) 沟渠 [gōuqú] **3** (for shipping) 水道 [shuǐdào] **4** (groove) 凹槽 [āocáo] **5** (fig) (means) 途径 [tújìng] **II** VT ▶ to channel sth into [+ money, resources] 调拨某物于 [diàobō mǒuwù yú]; [+ energies] 引导某物于 [yǐndǎo mǒuwù yú] ▶ through the usual/normal channels 经过通常的/一般的渠道 ▶ the (English) Channel 英吉利海峡

Channel Tunnel N ▶ the Channel Tunnel 英法海底隧道 [Yīngfǎ Hǎidǐ Suìdào]

chant [tʃɑːnt] **I** N [c] **1** (from crowd) 反复喊叫 [fǎnfù hǎnjiào] **2** (REL) 赞美诗 [zànměi shī] **II** VT **1** [+ word, name, slogan] 反复喊 [fǎnfù hǎn] **2** (REL) 唱 [chàng] **III** VI **1** [supporters, demonstrators +] 反复喊 [fǎnfù hǎn] **2** (REL) 唱歌 [chànggē] ▶ the demonstrators chanted their disapproval 示威者反复抗议

chaos ['keɪɔs] N [U] 混乱 [hùnluàn]

chaotic [keɪ'ɔtɪk] ADJ [+ mess, jumble etc] 紊乱的 [wěnluàn de]; [+ situation, life etc] 混乱的 [hùnluàn de]

chap [tʃæp] (BRIT: inf) N [c] **1** (man) 家伙 [jiāhuo] **2** ▶ old chap (o.f.) (term of address) 老兄 [lǎoxiōng]

chapel ['tʃæpl] N **1** [c] (in church) 小教堂 [xiǎo jiàotáng] **2** [c] (in hospital, prison, school) 附属

教堂 [fùshǔ jiàotáng] **3** [C/U] (non-conformist chapel) 非国教教堂 [fēi guójiào jiàotáng] **4** [C] [of union] 职工会 [zhígōng huì]

chapped [tʃæpt] ADJ [+ skin, lips] 皲裂的 [jūnliè de]

chapter ['tʃæptə(r)] N [C] **1** [of book] 章 [zhāng] **2** (in life, history) 时期 [shíqī] ▷ a new chapter in the history of international relations 国际关系史上新的一页 [guójì guānxì shǐ shàng xīn de yī yè]

character ['kærɪktə(r)] N **1** [C] (nature) [of person, place] 特性 [tèxìng]; [of object, idea] 性质 [xìngzhì] **2** [C/U] (reputation) 名誉 [míngyù] **3** [C] (in novel, film) 角色 [juésè] **4** [U] (moral strength) 毅力 [yìlì] **5** [C] (inf) (eccentric) 怪人 [guàirén] **6** [C] (letter, symbol etc) 字母 [zìmǔ] ▶ a strange/sad character (inf) 一个古怪/可悲的人 ▶ a person of good character 道德高尚的人 ▶ to behave in/out of character 行为与自身特性相符/不相符

characteristic [kærɪktə'rɪstɪk] I ADJ 特有的 [tèyǒu de] II N [C] 特征 [tèzhēng] ▶ to be characteristic of sb/sth 反映某人/某物的特性

characterize ['kærɪktəraɪz] (frm) VT **1** (typify) 以⋯为特征 [yǐ… wéi tèzhēng] **2** (describe the character of) 描绘 [miáohui] ▶ to characterize sb/sth as 把某人/某物描绘 成

charcoal ['tʃɑːkəul] N [U] (for fuel) 木炭 [mùtàn]; (for drawing) 炭笔 [tànbǐ] ▶ a piece of charcoal 一块木炭

○**charge** [tʃɑːdʒ] I N [C] **1** (fee) 费用 [fèiyòng] ▷ No charge is made for repairs. 免费修理。 **2** (accusation) 指控 [zhǐkòng] ▷ a murder charge 一项谋杀指控 **3** (attack) 猛攻 [měnggōng] **4** (explosive) (in cartridge) 炸药量 [zhàyàoliàng] **5** (ELEC) 电荷 [diànhé] ▷ an electrical charge 一个电荷 II VT **1** [+ sum of money] 要价 [yàojià]; [+ customer, client] 收费 [shōufèi] ▷ They charged fifty cents admission. 他们收了50美分的入场费。 **2** (POLICE) ▶ to charge sb (with sth) 控告某人 (犯某罪) [kònggào mǒurén (fàn mǒuzuì)] **3** (attack) [+ enemy] 猛攻 [měnggōng] ▷ an order to charge enemy positions 猛攻敌人阵地的命令 **4** (also: charge up) [+ battery] 使充电 [shǐ chōngdiàn] III VI **1** (animal +) 向前冲 [xiàngqián chōng] **2** (MIL) (attack) 冲锋 [chōngfēng] IV charges NPL (bank charges, telephone charges etc) 费 [fèi] ▶ is there a charge? 要收费吗? ▶ there's no charge 免费 ▶ at no extra charge 不额外收费 ▶ free of charge 免费 ▶ in/under sb's charge (responsibility) 在某人照管下 ▷ My first concern is for the people under my charge. 我首先考虑的是由我照管的人。 ▶ to take charge of sb 管理某人 ▶ to take charge of sth 掌管某物 ▶ to be in charge (of sth/sb) (of person, machine) 主管 (某事/某人); (of business) 负责 (某事/某人)

▶ how much do you charge? 你收费多少? ▶ to charge sb £20 for sth 因某物收某人20英镑 ▶ to charge an expense to sb's account 将某项消费记到某人账上 ▶ to charge in/out/off etc 急速进来/出去/离开 {等} ▶ to charge into a room/down the road etc 跑进房间/跑上马路 {等}

charge card N [C] **1** (BRIT) (for particular shop) 记账卡 [jìzhàngkǎ] **2** (US) (credit card) 信用卡 [xìnyòngkǎ]

charger ['tʃɑːdʒə(r)] N [C] **1** (also: battery charger) 充电器 [chōngdiàn qì] **2** (o.f.) (warhorse) 战马 [zhànmǎ]

charismatic [kærɪs'mætɪk] ADJ 极有性格魅力的 [jí yǒu xìnggé mèilì de]

charity ['tʃærɪtɪ] N **1** [C] (organization) 慈善机构 [císhàn jīgòu] **2** [U] (money, gifts) 赈济 [zhènjì] **3** [U] (kindness, generosity) 仁慈 [réncí] ▶ to give money to charity 把钱捐给慈善团体 ▶ to raise money for charity 为慈善团体募捐

charity shop (BRIT) N [C] 慈善商店 [císhàn shāngdiàn] [美=thrift shop]

◉ **CHARITY SHOP**

charity shops (美国称之为 thrift shops) 是廉价品追求者的快乐之源。人们把闲置的衣服、书籍、玩具和其他物品送到慈善商店。慈善商店的存在离不开人们的捐赠。慈善商店的全部收入归特定的慈善机构所有,比如,Oxfam (救济发展中国家人民的机构) 或 Barnados (帮助英国贫困儿童的机构)。

charm [tʃɑːm] I N **1** [C/U] [of place, thing] 魅力 [mèilì]; [of person] 迷人的特性 [mírén de tèxìng] **2** [C] (for good luck) 护身符 [hùshēnfú] **3** [C] (spell) 符咒 [fúzhòu] **4** [C] (on bracelet, necklace) 坠儿 [zhuìr] II VT 迷住 [mízhù]

charming ['tʃɑːmɪŋ] ADJ [+ person] 迷人的 [mírén de]; [+ place, custom] 吸引人的 [xīyǐn rén de]

chart [tʃɑːt] I N [C] **1** (graph, diagram) 图表 [túbiǎo] **2** (map) 海图 [hǎitú] II VT **1** [+ progress, development] 详述 [xiángshù] **2** [+ land, sea, stars] 绘制 [huìzhì] III the charts NPL (MUS) 流行音乐排行榜 [liúxíng yīnyuè páihángbǎng] ▶ to be in the charts [record, pop group +] 在排行榜上

charter ['tʃɑːtə(r)] I VT 包租 [bāozū] II N [C] 宪章 [xiànzhāng]

charter flight N [C] 包机 [bāojī]

chase [tʃeɪs] I VT **1** (pursue) 追赶 [zhuīgǎn] **2** ▶ to chase sb off one's land/away from a place 将某人赶出某人的土地/从某处赶走 [jiāng mǒurén gǎnchū mǒurén de tǔdì/cóng mǒuchù gǎnzǒu] **3** (seek) [+ job, money, opportunity] 寻找 [xúnzhǎo] II N [C] (pursuit) 追逐 [zhuīzhú]

▶ **chase down** VT **1** (US) (run after) 追上 [zhuīshang] **2** (track down) [+ person] 寻觅到 [xúnmì dào]; [+ information] 设法寻找 [shèfǎ xúnzhǎo]

▶ **chase up** VT [+ person] 催 [cuī]; [+ information] 寻找 [xúnzhǎo]

chat [tʃæt] **I** VI (also: **have a chat**) 聊天 [liáotiān] **II** N [C] (conversation) 聊天 [liáotiān]

▶ **chat up** (BRIT: inf) VT 与…调情 [yǔ… tiáoqíng]

chat room (COMPUT) N [C] 聊天室 [liáotiānshì]

chat show (BRIT) N [C] 访谈节目 [fǎngtán jiémù] ［美=**talk show**］

chatter [ˈtʃætə(r)] **I** VI **1** [person +] 喋喋不休 [diédiébùxiū] **2** (liter) [bird, animal +] 唧唧叫 [jījijiào] **3** [teeth +] 打战 [dǎzhàn] **II** N [U] **1** [of people] 喋喋不休 [diédiébùxiū] **2** (liter) [of birds, animals] 唧唧声 [jījīshēng]

chauffeur [ˈʃəufə(r)] **I** N [C] 司机 [sījī] **II** VT ▶ **to chauffeur sb around** 开车载某人到处转 [kāichē zài mǒurén dàochù zhuàn]

chauvinist [ˈʃəuvɪnɪst] N [C] **1** 沙文主义者 [shāwénzhǔyìzhě] **2** (also: **male chauvinist**) 大男子主义者 [dànánzǐzhǔyìzhě]

cheap [tʃi:p] **I** ADJ **1** (inexpensive) 便宜的 [piányi de] **2** (reduced) [+ ticket] 降价的 [jiàngjià de]; [+ fare, rate] 廉价的 [liánjià de] **3** (poor quality) 劣质的 [lièzhì de] **4** [+ remark, joke] 粗鄙的 [cūbǐ de] **II** ADV ▶ **to buy/sell sth cheap** 廉价买/卖某物 [liánjià mǎi/mài mǒuwù] ▶ **that was a cheap shot** 那可真够低级的

cheaply [ˈtʃi:plɪ] ADV 便宜地 [piányi de]

cheat [tʃi:t] **I** VI (in game, exam) 作弊 [zuòbì] **II** VT 欺骗 [qīpiàn] **III** N [C] (in games, exams) 作弊者 [zuòbìzhě]; (in business) 骗子 [piànzi]; (sexually) 不忠的人 [bùzhōng de rén] ▶ **to feel cheated** 感到受骗当上 ▶ **to cheat sb out of sth** 骗取某人的某物

▶ **cheat on** (inf) VT FUS [不可拆分] [+ husband, girlfriend, etc] 不忠实于 [bù zhōngshí yú]

check [tʃɛk] **I** VT **1** (examine, verify) [+ bill, progress, facts, figures] 核对 [héduì]; [+ passport, ticket] 检查 [jiǎnchá] **2** (also: **check in**) [+ luggage] (at airport) 托运 [tuōyùn] **3** (halt) [+ advance, disease] 制止 [zhìzhǐ] **4** (restrain) [+ impulse] 抑制 [yìzhì]; [+ person] 使突然停止 [shǐ tūrán tíngzhǐ] **II** VI **1** (investigate) 检查 [jiǎnchá] **2** (tally) 符合 [fúhé] **III** N [C] **1** (inspection) 检查 [jiǎnchá] **2** (curb) 制止 [zhìzhǐ] **3** (US) (in restaurant etc) 账单 [zhàngdān] ［英=**bill**］ **4** (US: ECON) = **cheque 5** (pattern) (gen pl) 方格图案 [fānggé tú'àn] **6** (US) (mark) 勾号 [gōuhào] ［英=**tick**］ **IV** ADJ (also: **checked**) [+ pattern, cloth] 方格图案的 [fānggé tú'àn de] ▶ **to check that...** 检查… ▶ **to check sth against sth** 将某物与某物相比较 ▶ **to check on sb/sth** 察看某人/某物 ▶ **to check with sb** 向某人证实 ▶ **to keep a check on sb/sth** (watch) 监视某人/某物 ▶ **to**

▶ **hold** or **keep sb/sth in check** 控制某人/某物

▶ **"check"** (CHESS) "将军"

▶ **check in I** VI (at hotel, clinic) 登记 [dēngjì]; (at airport) 办理登机手续 [bànlǐ dēngjì shǒuxù] **II** VT 托运 [tuōyùn]

▶ **check into** VT [+ hotel, clinic] 登记入住 [dēngjì rùzhù]

▶ **check off** VT 核对 [héduì]

▶ **check out I** VI (of hotel) 结账离开 [jiézhàng líkāi] **II** VT (investigate) [+ story] 证实 [zhèngshí]; [+ person] 查对 [cháduì]

▶ **check up** VI 检查 [jiǎnchá]

▶ **check up on** VT FUS [不可拆分] (investigate) 追查 [zhuīchá]

checkbook [ˈtʃɛkbuk] (US) N = **cheque book**

checked [tʃɛkt] ADJ see **check**

checkers [ˈtʃɛkəz] (US) NPL 西洋跳棋 [xīyáng tiàoqí] ［英=**draughts**］

check-in [ˈtʃɛkɪn] (also: **check-in desk**) N [C] (at airport) 旅客验票台 [lǚkè yànpiào tái]

checking account [ˈtʃɛkɪŋ-] (US) N [C] (ECON) 活期存款账户 [huóqī cúnkuǎn zhànghù] ［英=**current account**］

checklist [ˈtʃɛklɪst] N [C] 一览表 [yīlǎnbiǎo]

checkout [ˈtʃɛkaut] N [C] (in shop) 付款台 [fùkuǎntái]

checkpoint [ˈtʃɛkpɔɪnt] N [C] (on border) 边防检查站 [biānfáng jiǎnchá zhàn]

checkroom [ˈtʃɛkrum] (US) N [C] (left-luggage office) 行李寄存处 [xíngli jìcúnchù]

check-up [ˈtʃɛkʌp] N [C] (by doctor) 体检 [tǐjiǎn]; (by dentist) 牙科检查 [yákē jiǎnchá] ▶ **to have a check-up** (by doctor) 进行体检; (by dentist) 进行牙科检查

cheddar [ˈtʃɛdə(r)] N [U] 切达干酪 [qièdágānlào]

cheek [tʃi:k] N **1** [C] (on face) 面颊 [miànjiá] **2** [U] (inf) (impudence) 厚颜无耻 [hòuyánwúchǐ] ▶ **to have the cheek to do sth** 居然有脸做某事

cheekbone [ˈtʃi:kbəun] N [C] 颧骨 [quángǔ]

cheeky [ˈtʃi:kɪ] (ESP BRIT) ADJ 恬不知耻的 [tián bù zhī chǐ de]

cheer [tʃɪə(r)] **I** VT **1** [+ team, speaker] 用欢呼声激励 [yòng huānhūshēng jīlì] **2** (gladden) 使高兴 [shǐ gāoxìng] **II** VI 欢呼 [huānhū] **III** N [C] 喝彩 [hècǎi] ▶ **cheers!** (ESP BRIT) (toast) 干杯!; (BRIT: inf) (thanks) 多谢

▶ **cheer on** VT 为…鼓气 [wèi…gǔqì]

▶ **cheer up I** VI [person +] 振作起来 [zhènzuò qǐlái] **II** VT [+ person] 使…高兴起来 [shǐ…gāoxìng qǐlái]

cheerful [ˈtʃɪəful] ADJ **1** [+ wave, smile, person] 兴高彩烈的 [xìnggāocǎiliè de] **2** [+ place, object] 使人感到愉快的 [shǐ rén gǎndào yúkuài de]

cheerio [tʃɪərɪˈəu] (BRIT: o.f., inf) INT 再见 [zàijiàn]

cheerleader [ˈtʃɪəliːdə(r)] N [C] 拉拉队长 [lālāduìzhǎng]

cheese [tʃiːz] N [c/U] 干酪 [gānlào]

cheeseburger ['tʃiːzbə:gə(r)] N [c] 干酪汉堡包 [gānlào hànbǎobāo]

cheesecake ['tʃiːzkeɪk] N [c/U] 干酪饼 [gānlàobǐng]

chef [ʃɛf] N [c] 厨师 [chúshī]

chemical ['kɛmɪkl] I ADJ 1 [+reaction, composition] 化学的 [huàxué de] 2 (MIL) [+warfare, weapon] 化学的 [huàxué de] II N [c] 化学剂 [huàxué jì]

chemist ['kɛmɪst] N [c] 1 (BRIT) (also: **chemist's**) 药商 [yàoshāng] [美= **pharmacy**] 2 (BRIT) (in shop) 药剂师 [yàojìshī] [美= **druggist, pharmacist**] 3 (scientist) 化学家 [huàxuéjiā]

> 在英式英语中，售药或者配药的商店通常叫做 **chemist** 或者 **chemist's**。*She went into a chemist's and bought some aspirin.* **pharmacy** 也表示同样的意思，但不常用。在美式英语中，也使用 **pharmacy**。另一个同义词是 **druggist**。**drugstore** 也表示同样意思，但通常是指除了药品以外还兼售饮料、小吃和其他小商品的商店。*At the drugstore I bought a can of Coke and the local papers.*

chemistry ['kɛmɪstrɪ] N [U] 化学 [huàxué]

cheque, (US) **check** [tʃɛk] N [c] 支票 [zhīpiào]
▶ **to pay by cheque** 用支票付款

cheque book, (US) **checkbook** ['tʃɛkbuk] N [c] 支票簿 [zhīpiào bù]

cheque card (BRIT) N [c] (also: **cheque guarantee card**) 支票保付卡 [zhīpiào bǎofù kǎ]

cherish ['tʃɛrɪʃ] VT [+person, object] 爱护 [àihù]; [+right, freedom] 珍惜 [zhēnxī]; [+hope] 抱有 [bàoyǒu]; [+memory] 怀念 [huáiniàn]

cherry ['tʃɛrɪ] N [c] 1 (fruit) 樱桃 [yīngtáo] 2 (also: **cherry tree**) 樱桃树 [yīngtáo shù]

chess [tʃɛs] N [U] 象棋 [xiàngqí]

chest [tʃɛst] N [c] 1 (part of body) 胸部 [xiōngbù] 2 (box) 箱子 [xiāngzi] ▶ **to get sth off one's chest** (inf) 倾诉积存已久的话

chestnut ['tʃɛsnʌt] I N [c] 1 (nut) 栗子 [lìzi] 2 (also: **chestnut tree**) 栗子树 [lìzi shù] II ADJ [+hair] 栗色的 [lìsè de] ▶ **old chestnut** 老掉牙的论调

chest of drawers N [c] 五斗橱 [wǔdǒu chú]

chew [tʃuː] I VT [+food, gum] 嚼 [jiáo]; [+pen, fingernails] 咬 [yǎo] II VI 咀嚼 [jǔjué]

chewing gum ['tʃuːɪŋ-] N [U] 口香糖 [kǒuxiāngtáng]

chic [ʃiːk] ADJ [+clothes] 雅致的 [yǎzhì de]; [+person, place] 时髦的 [shímáo de]

chick [tʃɪk] N [c] 1 (young bird) 小鸟 [xiǎodǎo] 2 (inf) (girl) 妞 [niū]

chicken ['tʃɪkɪn] N 1 [c] (bird) (young) 小鸡 [xiǎojī]; (grown) 鸡 [jī] 2 [c/U] (meat) 鸡肉 [jīròu] 3 [c] (inf) (coward) 胆小鬼 [dǎnxiǎoguǐ]

▶ **chicken out** (inf) VI 因胆怯而放弃 [yīn dǎnqiè ér fàngqì] ▶ **to chicken out of (doing) sth** 因胆怯而放弃(做)某事

chickenpox ['tʃɪkɪnpɒks] N [U] 水痘 [shuǐdòu]

chick pea N [c] 鹰嘴豆 [yīngzuǐdòu]

○ **chief** [tʃiːf] I N [c] [of organization, department] 首领 [shǒulǐng] ▷ *the police chief* 警长; [of tribe] 酋长 [qiúzhǎng] II ADJ 首要的 [shǒuyào de] ▷ *one of his chief rivals* 他的首要竞争对手之一

chief executive (officer) N [c] 首席执行官 [Shǒuxí Zhíxíngguān]

chiefly ['tʃiːflɪ] ADV 主要 [zhǔyào]

○ **child** [tʃaɪld] (pl **children**) N [c] 1 儿童 [értóng] 2 (son, daughter) 孩子 [háizi] ▷ *Their children are all married.* 他们的孩子都结婚了。▷ *a father and his two teenage children* 一位父亲和他的两个十几岁的孩子 ▶ **she's just had her second child** 她刚生了第二个孩子

childbirth ['tʃaɪldbə:θ] N [U] 分娩 [fēnmiǎn]

childcare ['tʃaɪldkeə(r)] N [U] 儿童托管服务 [értóng tuōguǎn fúwù]

childhood ['tʃaɪldhud] I N [U] 童年 [tóngnián] II CPD [复合词] [+disease, memory, friend] 童年期 [tóngnián qī]

childish ['tʃaɪldɪʃ] ADJ 1 (pej) [+person, behaviour] 幼稚的 [yòuzhì de] 2 [+games, enthusiasm] 孩子般的 [háizi bān de]

child minder (BRIT) N [c] 保姆 [bǎomǔ]

children ['tʃɪldrən] NPL of child

child seat (AUT) N [c] 儿童座 [értóng zuò]

Chile ['tʃɪlɪ] N 智利 [Zhìlì]

Chilean ['tʃɪlɪən] I ADJ 智利的 [Zhìlì de] II N [c] (person) 智利人 [Zhìlìrén]

chill [tʃɪl] I N [c] 1 (in air, water) 寒气 [hánqì] 2 (illness) 着凉 [zháoliáng] II ADJ [+wind, air] 凉飕飕的 [liángsōusōu de] III VT 1 (cool) [+food, drinks] 使冷冻 [shǐ lěngdòng] 2 (liter) (frighten) 使⋯害怕 [shǐ⋯hàipà] ▶ **to catch a chill** 着凉 ▶ **it sent a chill down my spine** 这使我胆战心惊 ▶ **I'm chilled to the bone** or **marrow** 我感到寒气刺骨 ▶ "**serve chilled**" "冰镇食用" ▶ **chill out** (inf) VI 放松一下 [fàngsōng yīxià]

chilli, (US) **chili** ['tʃɪlɪ] N [c/U] 辣椒 [làjiāo]

chilly ['tʃɪlɪ] ADJ 1 [+weather, day] 相当冷的 [xiāngdāng lěng de] 2 [+response, welcome] 冷淡的 [lěngdàn de] ▶ **to feel** or **be chilly** [person +] 感到寒冷 ▶ **it's a bit chilly today** 今天有点冷 ▮▮用法参见 cold

chimney ['tʃɪmnɪ] N [c] 烟囱 [yāncōng]

chimpanzee [tʃɪmpæn'ziː] N [c] 黑猩猩 [hēixīngxing]

chin [tʃɪn] N [c] 下巴 [xiàba] ▶ (**keep your**) **chin up!** 振作精神！ ▶ **to take sth on the chin** 勇敢地忍受某事

China ['tʃaɪnə] N 中国 [Zhōngguó]

china ['tʃaɪnə] I N [U] 1 (also: **china clay**) 陶瓷 [táocí] 2 (crockery) 瓷器 [cíqì] II CPD [复合词] [+cup, plate] 瓷 [cí]

Chinese [tʃaɪˈniːz] (pl **Chinese**) I ADJ 中国的 [Zhōngguó de] II N 1 [c] (person) 中国人 [Zhōngguórén] 2 [U] (language) 汉语 [Hànyǔ]

chip [tʃɪp] I N [c] 1 (BRIT) 薯条 [shǔtiáo] [美= (French) fry] 2 (US) (snack) 薯片 [shǔpiàn] [英= crisp] 3 [of wood] 屑片 [xièpiàn] 4 [of glass, stone] 碎片 [suìpiàn] 5 (in glass, cup etc) 缺口 [quēkǒu] 6 (for gambling) 筹码 [chóumǎ] 7 (COMPUT) (also: **microchip**) 集成电路片 [jíchéng diànlù piàn] II VT [+ cup, plate] 碰出缺口 [pèngchū quēkǒu] ▶ to have a chip on one's shoulder (inf) 持寻衅的态度 ▶ he's a chip off the old block (inf) 他和他老子一样 ▶ when the chips are down (inf) 当危急关头
▶ chip in (inf) VI 1 (financially) 捐助 [juānzhù] 2 (interrupt) 插嘴 [chāzuǐ]

chip shop (BRIT) N [c] 薯条店 [shǔtiáo diàn]

⬤ CHIP SHOP

⬤ chip shop，也叫 fish and chip shops 或
⬤ 俗称 chippies，是专卖外卖食品的小店，
⬤ 不仅出售炸鱼排和薯条 (另见 fish and
⬤ chips)，还出售肉饼、香肠和其他英国传
⬤ 统食品。如果要带回家吃，你可以让店员
⬤ 打包; 如果你要在街上吃，也可以不包。
⬤ 为了保温，店员还会用纸包好。

chiropodist [kɪˈrɒpədɪst] (BRIT) N [c] 足医 [zúyī]

chisel [ˈtʃɪzl] I N [c] 凿子 [záozi] II VT [+ wood, stone] 凿 [záo]

chives [tʃaɪvz] NPL 细香葱 [xìxiāngcōng]

chlorine [ˈklɔːriːn] N [U] 氯气 [lùqì]

chocolate [ˈtʃɒklɪt] I N 1 [U] 巧克力 [qiǎokèlì] 2 [c/U] (drinking chocolate) 巧克力饮料 [qiǎokèlì yǐnliào] 3 [c] (piece of confectionery) 巧克力糖 [qiǎokèlì táng] II CPD [复合词] [+ cake, pudding, mousse] 巧克力 [qiǎokèlì] ▶ bar of chocolate 巧克力条 ▶ piece of chocolate 一块巧克力

choice [tʃɔɪs] I N 1 [c/U] (between items) 选择 [xuǎnzé] 2 [c] (option) 选择 [xuǎnzé] 3 [c] (item chosen, preference) 被选中的东西 [bèi xuǎnzhòng de dōngxi] II ADJ (frm) (quality) 优质的 [yōuzhì de] ▶ a wide choice 多种多样 ▶ it's available in a choice of colours 有各种颜色供选择 ▶ to make a choice 作出选择 ▶ to have no/little choice 没有/没有太多选择 ▶ the book/film of your choice 你所选择的书/电影

choir [ˈkwaɪə(r)] N [c] 1 合唱团 [héchàngtuán] 2 (area of church) 唱诗班的席位 [chàngshībān de xíwèi]

choke [tʃəʊk] I VI (on food, drink etc) 噎住 [yēzhù]; (with smoke, dust) 呛 [qiàng] II VT 1 (strangle) [rope etc +] 使窒息 [shǐ zhìxī] ▶ to choke sb 扼某人的脖子 [qiā mǒurén de bózi] 2 (block) ▶ to be choked with sth 塞满某物

[sāimǎn mǒuwù] III N [c] (AUT) 阻塞门 [zǔsāi mén] ▶ to choke on sth 被某物噎了 ▶ to choke to death 呛死
▶ choke back VT [+ tears] 忍住 [rěnzhù]

cholesterol [kəˈlɛstərɒl] N [U] 胆固醇 [dǎngùchún]

choose [tʃuːz] (pt **chose**, pp **chosen**) I VT [+ clothes, profession, candidate etc] 挑选 [tiāoxuǎn] ▶ to choose between 在…之间作出选择 [zài…zhījiān zuòchū xuǎnzé] ▶ to choose from 从…中选择 ▶ to choose to do sth 选择做某事

chop [tʃɒp] I VT 1 [+ wood] 劈 [pī] 2 (also: **chop up**) [+ vegetables, fruit, meat] 切 [qiē] II N [c] (CULIN) 排骨 [páigǔ] ▶ to get the chop (BRIT: inf) [project +] 被终止; [person +] 被解雇
▶ chop down VT [+ tree] 砍倒 [kǎndǎo]
▶ chop off VT [+ arm, leg] 砍 [kǎn]
▶ chop up VT 切 [qiē]

chopsticks [ˈtʃɒpstɪks] NPL 筷子 [kuàizi]

chord [kɔːd] N [c] 1 (MUS) 和弦 [héxián] 2 (MATH) 弦 [xián]

chore [tʃɔː(r)] I N [c] (unpleasant task) 琐碎烦人的杂务 [suǒsuì fánrén de záwù] II **the chores** NPL 家庭杂务 [jiātíng záwù] ▶ household chores 家务

chorus [ˈkɔːrəs] N [c] 1 (refrain) 齐唱 [qíchàng] 2 (song) 合唱曲 [héchàngqǔ] 3 (choir, not soloists) 合唱队 [héchàngduì] 4 [of complaints, criticism] 异口同声 [yìkǒutóngshēng] 异口同声地说 [yìkǒutóngshēng de shuō] ▶ in chorus 一齐

chose [tʃəʊz] PT of choose

chosen [ˈtʃəʊzn] PP of choose

Christ [kraɪst] I N 耶稣 [Yēsū] II INT (infl) 耶稣 [Yēsū]

christen [ˈkrɪsn] VT 1 [+ baby] 洗礼时给…命名 [xǐlǐ shí gěi…mìngmíng] 2 (with nickname) 取绰号为 [qǔ chuòhào wéi]

christening [ˈkrɪsnɪŋ] N [c] 洗礼 [xǐlǐ]

Christian [ˈkrɪstɪən] I ADJ 基督教的 [Jīdūjiào de] II N [c] 基督徒 [Jīdūjiào]

Christianity [krɪstɪˈænɪtɪ] N [U] 基督教 [Jīdūjiào]

Christian name N [c] 教名 [jiàomíng]

Christmas [ˈkrɪsməs] N [c/U] 1 (REL) (festival) 圣诞节 [Shèngdàn Jié] 2 (period) 圣诞节期间 [Shèngdàn Jié qījiān] ▶ Happy or Merry Christmas! 圣诞快乐！ ▶ at Christmas 在圣诞节 ▶ for Christmas 为了圣诞节

Christmas card N [c] 圣诞卡 [Shèngdàn kǎ]

Christmas Day N [c/U] 圣诞日 [Shèngdàn Rì]

Christmas Eve N [c/U] 圣诞夜 [Shèngdàn Yè]

Christmas tree N [c] 圣诞树 [Shèngdàn shù]

chrome [krəʊm] N [U] 铬黄 [gèhuáng]

chronic [ˈkrɒnɪk] ADJ 1 (MED) [+ illness] 慢性的 [mànxìng de] 2 [+ liar, smoker, etc] 积习难改的 [jīxí nánggǎi de] 3 (serious) [+ problem, shortage]

严重的 [yánzhòng de]

chrysanthemum [krɪ'sænθəməm] (BOT) N [C] 菊花 [júhuā]

chubby ['tʃʌbɪ] ADJ [+ cheeks, child] 肥胖的 [féipàng de]
🔳用法参见 **fat**

chuck [tʃʌk] (inf) VT 1 (throw) [+ object] 扔 [rēng] 2 [+ job, hobby] 放弃 [fàngqì] 3 [+ boyfriend, girlfriend] 抛弃 [pāoqì]
▶ **chuck away** VT see **chuck out**
▶ **chuck out** VT 1 [+ person] 撵走 [niǎnzǒu] 2 (also: **chuck away**) [+ rubbish] 扔掉 [rēngdiào]

chuckle ['tʃʌkl] I VI 暗笑 [ànxiào] II N [C] 轻声笑 [qīngshēngxiào] ▶ **to have a chuckle about sth** 因某事发笑

chunk [tʃʌŋk] N [C] 1 [of ice, food etc] 大块 [dàkuài] 2 (inf) [of land, income] 相当大的部分 [xiāngdāng dà de bùfen]

church [tʃə:tʃ] N 1 [C/U] (building) 教堂 [jiàotáng] 2 [C] (denomination) 教会 [jiàohuì]
▶ **the Church of England** 英国国教会

churchyard ['tʃə:tʃjɑ:d] N [C] 教堂墓地 [jiàotáng mùdì]

churn [tʃə:n] I N [C] 1 (for butter) 搅拌器 [jiǎobànqì] 2 (also: **milk churn**) 大桶 [dàtǒng] II VT (also: **churn up**) [+ mud, water, dust] 剧烈搅动 [jùliè jiǎodòng] III VI [stomach +] 翻腾 [fānténg]
▶ **churn out** I VT [+ objects, books] 粗制滥造 [cūzhìlànzào]

chute [ʃu:t] N [C] 1 (slide) 滑道 [huádào] 2 (for rubbish, coal, parcels, laundry) 倾卸槽 [qīngxiècáo] 3 (inf) (parachute) 降落伞 [jiàngluòsǎn]

chutney ['tʃʌtnɪ] N [C/U] 酸辣酱 [suānlàjiàng]

CID (BRIT) N ABBR (= **Criminal Investigation Department**) ▶ **the CID** 刑事调查部 [xíngshì diàochá bù]

cider ['saɪdə(r)] N [C/U] 1 (BRIT) (alcoholic) 苹果酒 [píngguǒ jiǔ] 2 (US) (non-alcoholic) 苹果汁 [píngguǒ zhī]

cigar [sɪ'gɑ:(r)] N [C] 雪茄烟 [xuějiā yān]

cigarette [sɪgə'ret] N [C] 香烟 [xiāngyān]

cinema ['sɪnəmə] N 1 [C] (BRIT) (place) 电影院 [diànyǐng yuàn] [美=**movie theater**] 2 [U] (film-making) 电影业 [diànyǐng yè]

cinnamon ['sɪnəmən] N [U] 肉桂 [ròuguì]

circle ['sə:kl] I N 1 [C] 圆圈 [yuánquān] 2 [C] [of friends] 圈子 [quānzi] ▷ He has a small circle of friends. 他有一小圈朋友。 3 [S] (in cinema, theatre) 楼厅 [lóutīng] II VI [bird, plane +] 盘旋 [pánxuán] III VT (move round, surround) 环绕 [huánrào]

circuit ['sə:kɪt] N [C] 1 (ELEC) 电路 [diànlù] 2 (BRIT) (track) 赛车道 [sàichē dào] 3 (lap) 环道 [huándào] ▶ **the lecture circuit** 巡回讲学

circular ['sə:kjulə(r)] I ADJ 1 [+ shape] 圆形的 [yuánxíng de]; [+ movement, motion] 环形

的 [huánxíng de] 2 [+ argument] 循环论证的 [xúnhuán lùnzhèng de] 3 [+ journey, route] 绕圈的 [ràoquān de] II N [C] 1 (letter) 供传阅的函件 [gōng chuányuè de hánjiàn] 2 (advertisement) 传单 [chuándān]

circulate ['sə:kjuleɪt] I VI [traffic, blood +] 循环 [xúnhuán]; [news, rumour +] 散播 [sànbō]; [person +] (at party) 交际 [jiāojì] II VT [+ report] 传阅 [chuányuè]

circulation [sə:kju'leɪʃən] N 1 [U] [of air] 流通 [liútōng]; [of blood] 循环 [xúnhuán]; [of document] 传阅 [chuányuè] 2 [C] [of newspaper, magazine] 发行量 [fāxíng liàng] ▶ **in circulation** 在流通中

circumstances ['sə:kəmstənsɪz] NPL 1 (conditions, state of affairs) 情况 [qíngkuàng] 2 [of accident, death] 事实 [shìshí] 3 (financial condition) 状况 [zhuàngkuàng] ▶ **in** or **under the circumstances** 在这种情况下 ▶ **under no circumstances** 决不

circus ['sə:kəs] N 1 [C] (show) 马戏团 [mǎxì tuán] 2 [C] (fig) 乱哄哄 [luànhōnghōng] 3 (BRIT) (in street names) ▶ **Circus** 广场 [guǎngchǎng]

cite [saɪt] VT 1 (quote) [+ example] 引用 [yǐnyòng] 2 (LAW) [+ person] 传讯 [chuánxùn]; [+ fact] 引证 [yǐnzhèng]

citizen ['sɪtɪzn] N [C] [of country] 公民 [gōngmín]; [of town, area] 居民 [jūmín]

citizenship ['sɪtɪznʃɪp] N [U] 公民身份 [gōngmín shēnfèn]

citrus fruit ['sɪtrəs-] N [C/U] 柑橘属果实 [gānjú shǔ guǒshí]

❍city ['sɪtɪ] N [C] 城市 [chéngshì] ▶ **the City** (BRIT : FIN) 英国伦敦商业区

city centre (ESP BRIT) N [C] 市中心 [shì zhōngxīn] [美=**downtown**]

civic ['sɪvɪk] ADJ 1 [+ leader, authorities] 城市的 [chéngshì de] 2 [+ duties, pride] 公民的 [gōngmín de]

civil ['sɪvɪl] ADJ 1 [+ unrest] 国内的 [guónèi de] 2 (not military) 民用的 [mínyòng de] 3 (not religious) [+ ceremony] 非宗教的 [fēi zōngjiào de] 4 (not criminal) [+ case] 民事的 [mínshì de] 5 (polite) ▶ **to be civil (to sb)** 礼貌地 (对某人) [lǐmào de (duì mǒurén)]

civilian [sɪ'vɪlɪən] I N [C] 平民 [píngmín]

II ADJ [+ *population, casualties, life*] 平民的 [píngmín de]

civilization [sɪvɪlaɪ'zeɪʃən] N [C/U] (*society*) 文明 [wénmíng]

civilized ['sɪvɪlaɪzd] ADJ **1** (*socially advanced*) [+ *society, people*] 文明的 [wénmíng de] **2** (*polite*) [+ *person, behaviour*] 有教养的 [yǒu jiàoyǎng de]

civil law N [U] 民法 [mínfǎ]

civil rights NPL 公民权 [gōngmín quán]

civil servant N [C] 公务员 [gōngwù yuán]

Civil Service N ▶ the Civil Service 行政机关 [xíngzhèng jīguān]

civil war N [C/U] 内战 [nèizhàn]

cl ABBR (= *centilitres*) 厘升 [líshēng]

⊙ **claim** [kleɪm] I VT **1** (*allege*) 声称 [shēngchēng] **2** (*for o.s.*) [+ *responsibility, credit*] 声称 [shēngchēng]; [+ *success rate*] 自称 [zìchēng] ▷ *The terrorists claimed responsibility for the bombing.* 恐怖分子声称对这起爆炸事件负责。**3** (*demand*) [+ *expenses, rights, inheritance*] 要求 [yāoqiú] ▷ *Voluntary workers can claim travelling expenses.* 义工可以申请回交通费。**4** [+ *compensation, damages, benefit*] 索取 [suǒqǔ] **5** (*frm*) (*take*) ▶ **the disease claimed millions of lives** 此病使上百万人丧生 [cǐbìng shǐ shàngbǎiwàn rén sàngshēng] II VT (*for insurance*) 提出索赔 [tíchū suǒpéi] III N [C] **1** (*assertion*) 声称 [shēngchēng] **2** (*application*) (*for pension, wage rise, compensation*) 索赔 [suǒpéi] **3** (*to inheritance, land*) 要求 [yāoqiú] **4** (*right to demand*) 权利 [quánlì] ▶ **to claim that...** 声称… [shēngchēng] ▷ *a man claiming to be a journalist* 一位声称是记者的人 ▶ **to claim** *or* **make a claim on one's insurance** 提出保险索赔的要求 ▶ **insurance claim** 保险索赔要求 ▶ **to put in a claim for** [+ *expenses*] 就…提出索赔要求 ▶ **to have a claim on sb** 对某人有要求权 ▶ **his claim to fame** 他出名的来由 ▶ **to lay claim to sth** 对某物提出所有权要求

clam [klæm] (ZOOL, CULIN) N [C] 蛤蜊 [géchú] ▶ **clam up** (*inf*) VI 沉默不语 [chénmò bùyǔ]

clamber ['klæmbə(r)] VI ▶ **to clamber up a hill/over a wall** 攀登山坡/费劲地爬墙 [pāndēng shānpō/fèijìn de páqiáng]

clamp [klæmp] I N [C] **1** (*device*) 夹具 [jiājù] **2** (BRIT) (*also*: **wheel clamp**) 车轮固定夹 [chēlún gùdìngjiā] [美= **Denver boot**] II VT **1** (*attach*) ▶ **to clamp sth to sth** 将某物与某物紧夹在一起 [jiāng mǒuwù yǔ mǒuwù jǐnjiā zài yīqǐ] **2** (*put*) ▶ **to clamp sth on/round sth** 将某物固定在某物上 [jiāng mǒuwù gùdìng zài mǒuwùshang] **3** (BRIT) [+ *wheel, car*] 锁 [suǒ] [美= **boot**]
▶ **clamp down** VI 强行限制 [qiángxíng xiànzhì]
▶ **clamp down on** VT FUS [不可拆分] [+ *people, activities*] 压制 [yāzhì]

clan [klæn] N [C] (*family*) 家族 [jiāzú]

clap [klæp] I VI [*audience* +] 鼓掌 [gǔzhǎng] II VT ▶ **to clap one's hands** 拍手 [pāishǒu] III N **1** ▶ **to give sb a clap** 向某人鼓掌 [xiàng mǒurén gǔzhǎng] **2** ▶ **a clap of thunder** 一声霹雳 [yīshēng pīlì] ▶ **to clap a hand over sth** 突然用手将某物捂住 ▶ **to clap sb on the back** 拍某人的背

claret ['klærət] N [C/U] (*wine*) 波尔多红葡萄酒 [Bōěrduō hóng pútao jiǔ]

clarify ['klærɪfaɪ] VT 澄清 [chéngqīng]

clarinet [klærɪ'nɛt] (MUS) N [C] 单簧管 [dānhuángguǎn]

clarity ['klærɪtɪ] N [U] 清晰度 [qīngxī dù]

clash [klæʃ] I N [C] **1** (*fight, disagreement*) 冲突 [chōngtū]; [*of personalities* +] 矛盾 [máodùn] **2** (*liter*) (*metallic noise*) 撞击声 [zhuàngjī shēng] II VI **1** (*fight*) [*rival gangs* +] 发生冲突 [fāshēng chōngtū] **2** (*disagree*) [*political opponents etc* +] 有重大分歧 [yǒu zhòngdà fēnqí] **3** (*be in conflict*) [*beliefs, ideas, views* +] 不一致 [bù yīzhì] **4** (*colours, styles* +) 不协调 [bù xiétiáo] **5** [*events, dates, appointments* +] 有冲突 [yǒu chōngtū] **6** (*liter*) [*weapons, pans etc* +] 撞击 [zhuàngjī]

clasp [klɑːsp] I N [C] **1** (*of necklace, bag*) 扣子 [kòuzi] **2** (*hold, embrace*) 紧握 [jǐnwò] II VT (*hold, embrace*) 紧抱 [jǐnbào] ▶ **he clasped her to him** 他紧紧地抱住她

⊙ **class** [klɑːs] I N **1** [C] (SCOL) (*group of pupils*) 班级 [bānjí]; (*lesson*) 课 [kè] **2** [C/U] (*social*) 阶级 [jiējí] **3** [C] (*type, group*) 种类 [zhǒnglèi] ▷ *We can identify several classes of fern.* 我们可以识别几种蕨类植物。**4** [U] (*sophistication*) 风度 [fēngdù] ▷ *His performance showed enormous class.* 他的表现显示出极好的风度。II CPD [复合词] [+ *structure, conflict, struggle*] 阶级 [jiējí] III VT (*categorize*) ▶ **to class sb/sth as** 将某人/某物分类为 [jiāng mǒurén/mǒuwù fēnlèi wéi] ▷ *At nineteen you're still classed as a teenager.* 即使十九岁，你仍被定为十几岁的青少年。▶ **in class** (SCOL) 上课时 ▶ **to be in a class of one's own** 独一无二

classic ['klæsɪk] I ADJ **1** [+ *example*] 典型的 [diǎnxíng de] **2** [+ *film, work etc*] 经典的 [jīngdiǎn de] **3** [+ *style, dress etc*] 传统式样的 [chuántǒng shìyàng de] II N [C] (*film, novel etc*) 经典 [jīngdiǎn] ▶ **to be a classic** 典范

classical ['klæsɪkl] ADJ **1** (*traditional*) 传统的 [chuántǒng de] **2** (MUS) 古典的 [gǔdiǎn de] **3** (*Greek, Roman*) 古希腊或古罗马文明的 [gǔ Xīlà huò gǔ Luómǎ wénmíng de]

Classics ['klæsɪks] N [U] 古典学 [gǔdiǎn xué]

classification [klæsɪfɪ'keɪʃən] N **1** [U] (*process*) 分类 [fēnlèi] **2** [C] (*category*) 类别 [lèibié]

classified ad ['klæsɪfaɪd-] (*also*: **classified advertisement**) N [C] 分类广告栏 [fēnlèi guǎnggào lán]

classify ['klæsɪfaɪ] VT [+ *books, fossils etc*] 分类

[fēnlèi] ▶ **to classify sb/sth as sth** 将某人/某物归类为某物

classmate ['klɑ:smeɪt] N [C] 同学 [tóngxué]

classroom ['klɑ:srum] N [C] 教室 [jiàoshì]

classy ['klɑ:sɪ] (inf) ADJ 1 [+ person] 时髦的 [shímáo de]; [+ restaurant, hotel] 奢华的 [shēhuá de]; [+ neighbourhood] 高级的 [gāojí de]; [+ performance] 出色的 [chūsè de]

clatter ['klætə(r)] I VI (liter) [dishes, pots etc+] 发出喀嗒声 [fāchū kādā shēng] II N [S] (liter) 喀嗒声 [kādā shēng] ▶ **to clatter around** 乒乒乓乓地乱动 ▶ **he clattered down the stairs** 他乒乒乓乓地下了楼梯

clause [klɔ:z] N [C] 1 (LAW) 条款 [tiáokuǎn] 2 (LING) 从句 [cóngjù] ▶ **main/subordinate clause** (LING) 主/从句

claustrophobic [klɔ:strə'fəubɪk] ADJ 1 [+ place, situation] 导致幽闭恐怖的 [dǎozhì yōubì kǒngbù de] 2 ▶ **to be/feel claustrophobic** 患/感到幽闭恐怖 [huàn/gǎndào yōubì kǒngbù]

claw [klɔ:] N [C] [of cat, tiger, bird] 爪子 [zhuǎzi]; [of lobster, crab] 钳子 [qiánzi]
▶ **claw at** VT FUS [不可拆分] 1 (scratch) 挠 [náo] 2 (grab) 抓 [zhuā] ▶ **to claw at the air** 抓空

clay [kleɪ] N [U] 黏土 [niántǔ]

clean [kli:n] I ADJ 1 [+ place, surface, clothes etc] 干净的 [gānjìng de]; [+ water] 清洁的 [qīngjié de] 2 (in habits) [+ person, animal] 爱清洁的 [ài qīngjié de] 3 (fair) [+ fight, contest] 公正的 [gōngzhèng de] 4 (not offensive) [+ joke, story] 纯净的 [chúnjìng de] 5 (spotless) [+ record, reputation] 清白的 [qīngbái de] 6 (well-defined) [+ edge, line] 平整的 [píngzhěng de] 7 (MED) [+ fracture] 边缘整齐的 [biānyuán zhěngqí de] II VT [+ car, cooker etc] 弄干净 [nòng gānjìng]; [+ room] 打扫 [dǎsǎo] III ADV ▶ **he clean forgot** 他忘得一干二净 [tā wàngde yīgān'èrjìng] IV N ▶ **to give sth a clean** 把某物清理干净 [bǎ mǒuwù qīnglǐ gānjìng] ▶ **to come clean about sth** (inf) 全盘招供某事 ▶ **a clean driving licence** or (US) **record** 未有违章记录的驾照 ▶ **a clean sheet of paper** 一张白纸 ▶ **to make a clean break** or **start** 重新开始 ▶ **to clean one's teeth** (BRIT) 刷牙 ▶ **the thief got clean away** (inf) 小偷逃得无影无踪
▶ **clean out** VT 1 [+ cupboard, drawer] 清理干净 [qīnglǐ gānjìng] 2 (inf) [+ person] 耗尽…的钱财 [hàojìn…de qiáncái]
▶ **clean up** I VT 1 [+ room, place] 打扫干净 [dǎsǎo gānjìng]; [+ mess] 整理 [zhěnglǐ] 2 (fig) (remove crime from) 整治 [zhěngzhì] II VI 1 打扫干净 [dǎsǎo gānjìng] 2 (inf) (make profit) 发大财 [fā dàcái]

cleaner ['kli:nə(r)] N 1 [C] (person) 清洁工 [qīngjié gōng] 2 [C/U] (substance) 清洁剂 [qīngjié jì]

cleaning ['kli:nɪŋ] N [U] [of house etc] 扫除 [sǎochú] ▶ **to do the cleaning** 做扫除

cleanse [klɛnz] VT 1 [+ face, cut] 清洗 [qīngxǐ] 2 [+ mind, organization] 净化 [jìnghuà] ▶ **to cleanse sth of sth** 使某物不再受某物的污染

cleanser ['klɛnzə(r)] N [C/U] (for face) 洁肤霜 [jiéfū shuāng]

○**clear** [klɪə(r)] I ADJ 1 (understandable) [+ explanation, account] 明确的 [míngquè de] 2 (visible) [+ footprint, photograph] 清晰的 [qīngxī de] 3 (audible) [+ voice, echo] 清晰的 [qīngxī de] ▷ He called out my name in a clear voice. 他清楚地叫出我的名字。▷ His voice was very clear. 他的声音非常清晰。4 (obvious) 无疑的 [wúyí de] ▷ a clear case of homicide 确信无疑的谋杀案 5 (definite) [+ choice, commitment] 明确的 [míngquè de] ▷ The letter contained a clear commitment to reopen talks. 这封信明确承诺要重新开始谈判。6 [+ profit, majority] 绝对的 [juéduì de] ▷ They won the vote by a clear majority. 他们赢得绝对多数选票。7 (transparent) [+ glass, plastic, water] 透明的 [tòumíng de] ▷ a clear glass panel 一张透明玻璃板 8 (unobstructed) [+ road, way, floor etc] 畅通的 [chàngtōng de] ▷ The runway is clear, go ahead and land. 跑道畅通无阻，可以降落。9 (untroubled) [+ conscience] 清白的 [qīngbái de] 10 (cloudless) [+ day, sky] 晴朗的 [qínglǎng de] 11 (healthy) [+ skin, eyes] 明亮的 [míngliàng de] II VT 1 [+ place, room] 清空 [qīngkōng] ▷ The police cleared the building following a bomb alert. 收到炸弹警告后，警察清空了那幢建筑。2 ▶ **to clear sth from sth** [+ rubbish, weeds] 从某处清理出某物 [cóng mǒuchù qīnglǐ chū mǒuwù] ▷ Firemen were still clearing rubble from apartments. 消防队员还在从单元房里清理出瓦砾。3 [+ slums] 拆除 [chāichú] 4 (LAW) [+ suspect] 宣告无罪 [xuāngào wúzuì] 5 (jump) [+ fence, wall] 跳过 [tiàoguò] 6 (authorize) 允许 [yǔnxǔ] ▷ The helicopter was cleared for take-off. 直升机被允许起飞。7 [+ cheque] 兑现 [duìxiàn] ▷ The bank cleared the cheque in three days. 银行在3天内兑现了支票。8 (COMM) ▶ **"half price to clear"** "半价清仓" [bànjià qīngcāng] III VI 1 [weather, sky+] 变睛 [biànqíng]; [fog, smoke+] 消散 [xiāosàn] ▷ We're expecting this weather to clear soon. 我们期望很快就会天晴。▷ The fog had cleared a little. 雾已经散开一点了。2 [cheque+] 兑现 [duìxiàn] ▷ Allow time for the cheque to clear. 要等支票兑现。IV ADV ▶ **clear of sth** [+ place, ground] 不接触某物 [bù jiēchù mǒuwù] V N ▶ **to be in the clear** (free of suspicion) 不被怀疑 [bùbèi huáiyí]; (free of danger) 安然无事 [ānránwúshì] ▶ **to be clear about sth** 很明确某事 ▶ **to make o.s. clear** 表达清楚 ▶ **to make sth clear to sb** 使某人明确某事 ▶ **to keep** or **stay** or **steer clear of sb/sth** 避开某人/某物 ▶ **to have a clear head** 头脑清醒 ▶ **to clear the table** 收拾饭桌 ▶ **to clear** one's throat 清嗓咙 ▶ **to clear sb of doing sth** [+ *suspect*] 洗刷某人某罪 ▶ **to clear a profit** 获得一笔净利 ▶ **to be in the clear** (*out of danger*) 无危险

▶ **clear away I** VT [+ *plates etc*] 清除 [qīngchú] **II** VI (*remove plates etc*) 收拾 [shōushi]

▶ **clear off** (*inf*) VI (*leave*) 走开 [zǒukāi] ▷ *Clear off and leave me alone.* 快走开，别烦我。

▶ **clear out I** VI (*leave*) 走开 [zǒukāi] **II** VT [+ *cupboard, room*] 清除 [qīngchú]

▶ **clear up I** VT **1** [+ *room, mess*] 清理 [qīnglǐ] **2** [+ *mystery, problem*] 澄清 [chéngqīng] **II** VI **1** (*tidy up*) 清理 [qīnglǐ] **2** [*illness +*] 痊愈 [quányù] **3** [*rain +*] 转晴 [zhuǎnqíng]

clearance ['klɪərəns] N [C/U] **1** (*removal*) [*of trees, mines etc*] 清除 [qīngchú]; [*of slums*] 拆除 [chāichú] **2** [*of place*] 清理 [qīnglǐ] **3** (*authorization*) 许可 [xǔkě] **4** [*of bridge*] 净空 [jìngkōng] ▶ **to get** *or* **be given clearance to land** 得到降落许可

clear-cut ['klɪə'kʌt] ADJ [+ *case, issue*] 黑白分明的 [hēibái fēnmíng de]

clearing ['klɪərɪŋ] N [C] (*in wood*) 林中空地 [línzhōng kòngdì]

clearly ['klɪəlɪ] ADV **1** (*with vb*) [*explain +*] 明确地 [míngquè de]; [*think +*] 清醒地 [qīngxǐng de]; [*see +*] 清楚地 [qīngchu de]; [*speak, hear +*] 清晰地 [qīngxī de] **2** (*with adj*) [+ *visible, audible*] 清楚地 [qīngchu de] **3** (*obviously*) 显然 [xiǎnrán]

clench [klentʃ] VT [+ *fist*] 捏紧 [niējǐng]; [+ *teeth*] 咬紧 [yǎojǐn]

clergy ['klɜːdʒɪ] NPL 神职人员 [shénzhí rényuán]

clerk [klɑːk, US klɜːrk] N [C] **1** (*office worker*) 职员 [zhíyuán] **2** (US) (*sales person*) 售货员 [shòuhuòyuán]

clever ['klevə(r)] ADJ **1** (*intelligent*) 聪明的 [cōngmíng de] **2** (*sly, crafty*) 耍小聪明的 [shuǎ xiǎocōngmíng de] **3** (*ingenious*) [+ *device, arrangement*] 巧妙的 [qiǎomiào de]

cliché ['kliːʃeɪ] N [C] 陈词滥调 [chéncí làndiào]

click [klɪk] **I** VI **1** [*device, switch, camera +*] 发出喀嗒声 [fāchū kādā shēng] **2** (COMPUT) 按 [àn] **3** (*inf*) (*get on*) ▶ **to click (with sb)** (和某人)一见如故 [(hé mǒurén) yījiànrúgù] **4** (*inf*) (*become clear*) 豁然开朗 [huòrán kāilǎng] **II** VT (*make sound with*) 使…发出喀嗒声 [shǐ…fāchū kādā shēng] **2** (COMPUT) ▶ **with a click of one's mouse** 按一下鼠标 [àn yīxià shǔbiāo] ▶ **to click on sth** (COMPUT) 点击某处 [diǎnjī mǒuchù] ▶ **to click one's tongue** 咂咂舌头 ▶ **to click one's heels** 喀嚓一声立正

client ['klaɪənt] N [C] [*of lawyer*] 委托人 [wěituōrén]; [*of company, restaurant, shop*] 顾客 [gùkè]

cliff [klɪf] N [C] 悬崖 [xuányá]

climate ['klaɪmɪt] N **1** [C/U] (*weather*) 气候 [qìhòu] **2** [C] [*of opinion etc*] 气候 [qìhòu]

climax ['klaɪmæks] **I** N **1** [C] [*of event, career*] 高峰 [gāofēng] **2** [C/U] (*sexual*) 高潮 [gāocháo] **II** VI 达到高潮 [dádào gāocháo]

climb [klaɪm] **I** VT (*also:* **climb up**) [+ *tree etc*] 爬 [pá]; [+ *mountain, hill*] 攀登 [pāndēng]; [+ *ladder*] 登 [dēng]; [+ *stairs, steps*] 上 [shàng] **II** VI **1** [*sun +*] 徐徐上升 [xúxú shàngshēng] **2** [*plane +*] 爬升 [páshēng] **3** [*prices, shares +*] 上涨 [shàngzhǎng] **4** [*person +*] (*on frame, up mountain etc*) 攀爬 [pānpá] **5** (*move with effort*) ▶ **to climb into/onto/over sth** 爬入/上/过某物 [pàrù/shàng/guò mǒuwù] **III** N [C] [*of mountain, hill*] 攀登 [pāndēng] ▶ **to go climbing** 去爬山

▶ **climb down** VI (*in argument, dispute*) 退让 [tuìràng]

climber ['klaɪmə(r)] N [C] **1** (*mountaineer*) 登山者 [dēngshānzhě] **2** (*plant*) 攀缘植物 [pānyuán zhíwù]

climbing ['klaɪmɪŋ] N [U] 攀登 [pāndēng]

clinch [klɪntʃ] VT [+ *argument, contest*] 拿下 [náxià]; [+ *deal*] 达成 [dáchéng]

cling [klɪŋ] (*pt, pp* **clung**) VI **1** ▶ **to cling (on) to** [+ *person, object*] 紧紧抓住 [jǐnjǐn zhuāzhù]; [+ *idea, belief*] 坚持 [jiānchí] **2** ▶ **to cling to sb's body** [*clothes, dress +*] 紧紧地贴在身上 [jǐnjǐn de tiē zài shēnshang]

clingfilm ['klɪŋfɪlm] (BRIT) N [U] 保鲜纸 [bǎoxiān zhǐ] [美= **plastic wrap**]

clinic ['klɪnɪk] (MED) N [C] (*place*) 诊所 [zhěnsuǒ]; (*session*) 门诊 [ménzhěn]

clinical ['klɪnɪkl] ADJ **1** (MED) [+ *tests, trials*] 临床的 [línchuáng de] **2** (*fig*) (*dispassionate*) 客观的 [kèguān de]

clip [klɪp] **I** N [C] **1** (*for papers etc*) 回形针 [huíxíng zhēn]; (*for hair*) 发夹 [fàjiā] **2** (TV, CINE) 剪辑 [jiǎnjí] **II** VT **1** (*fasten*) 夹住 [jiāzhù] **2** (*cut*) [+ *hedge, nails*] 修剪 [xiūjiǎn] ▶ **to clip papers together** 将纸张夹在一起

clipping ['klɪpɪŋ] N [C] (*from newspaper*) 剪报 [jiǎnbào]

cloak [kləuk] **I** N [C] (*cape*) 斗篷 [dǒupeng] **II** VT (*liter*) (*in mist, secrecy*) 掩藏 [yǎncáng]

cloakroom ['kləukrum] N [C] **1** (*for coats*) 衣帽间 [yīmàojiān] **2** (BRIT) (*bathroom*) 厕所 [cèsuǒ]

clock [klɔk] N [C] 钟 [zhōng] ▶ **around the clock** [*work, guard +*] 日夜不停 ▶ **to turn** *or* **put the clock back** (*fig*) 回到过去 ▶ **to work against the clock** 争分夺秒地工作 ▶ **30,000 miles on the clock** (BRIT: AUT) 里程计上记有3万英里行程

▶ **clock in** VI (*for work*) 打卡上班 [dǎkǎ shàngbān]

▶ **clock off** VI (*from work*) 打卡下班 [dǎkǎ xiàbān]

▶ **clock on** VI = **clock in**

▶ **clock out** VI = **clock off**

▶ **clock up** (BRIT) VT [+ *hours, miles*] 达到 [dádào]

clockwise ['klɔkwaɪz] I ADV 顺时针地 [shùn shízhēn de] II ADJ [+ direction] 顺时针的 [shùn shízhēn de]

clockwork ['klɔkwəːk] I N ▸ **to go like clockwork** 顺利地进行 [shùnlì de jìnxíng] II ADJ [+ model, toy] 机械的 [jīxiè de]

clog [klɔg] I N [c] (shoe) 木屐 [mùjī] II VT (also: **clog up**) [+ drain, pipe, skin, pores] 堵塞 [dǔsè]; [+ roads] 阻塞 [zǔsè] III VI (also: **clog up**) [drain, pipe +] 堵塞 [dǔsè]

clone [kləun] I N [c] 1 [of animal, plant] 克隆 [kèlóng] 2 (fig) (object) 复制品 [fùzhìpǐn]; (person) 几乎一模一样的人 [jīhū yīmúyīyàng de rén] II VT [+ animal, plant] 无性繁殖 [wúxìng fánzhí]

⊙ **close¹** [kləus] I ADJ 1 (near) 近的 [jìn de] 2 (devoted) 亲密的 [qīnmì de] ▷ She and Linda were very close. 她和琳达很亲密。3 [+ relative] 直系的 [zhíxì de] ▷ the death of a close relative 一位直系亲属的死亡 4 [+ contact, ties] 密切的 [mìqiè de]; [+ connection, resemblance] 严密的 [yánmì de] ▷ He keeps in close contact with his sons. 他和儿子们保持密切的联系。▷ There is a close connection between pain and tension. 疼痛与紧张是息息相关的。5 [+ examination, look] 彻底的 [chèdǐ de] ▷ She took a closer look at the car. 她更彻底地检查了那辆车。6 [+ contest] 势均力敌的 [shìjūnlìdí de] ▷ It is close but we are going to win. 双方势均力敌但我们会赢。7 (oppressive) [+ weather, atmosphere] 闷热的 [mēnrè de] ▷ It's very close today, isn't it? 今天很闷热，是不是？II ADV (near) 紧紧地 [jǐnjǐn de] ▷ The children followed close behind them. 孩子们紧紧地跟着他们。▸ **close to** (near) 近 ▷ The museum is quite close to the port. 博物馆离港口相当近。▸ **how close is** Edinburgh to Glasgow? 爱丁堡距离格拉斯哥有多近？▸ **a close friend** 一位密友 ▸ **she's very close to her brother** 她和她兄弟很亲近 ▸ **it was a close shave** or **call** or **thing** 这真是死里逃生 ▸ **at close quarters** 很接近 ▸ **to see sth close up** or **to** 从近处看看某事 ▸ **close by, close at hand** 在近旁 ▸ **close to** or **on 30 years** 近30年 ▸ **she was close to tears** 她几乎要哭了

⊙ **close²** [kləuz] I VT 1 [+ door, window, lid] 关 [guān] ▷ He closed the door behind him. 他走前把门关上了。2 [+ shop, factory] 关闭 [guānbì] ▷ They closed the local college. 他们关闭了当地的学院 3 (finalize) [+ sale, deal] 结束 [jiéshù] ▷ He needs another $30,000 to close the deal. 他还需要3万美元来完结这个交易。4 (end) [+ case, conversation] 结束 [jiéshù] II VI 1 [+ door, window, lid +] 关 [guān] ▷ She heard the door close. 她听见门关了。2 [shop, library +] 关门 [guānmén] ▷ Many libraries close on Saturdays at 1 p.m. 很多图书馆星期六下午一点关门。3 (end) [film, book +] 收尾 [shōuwěi] ▷ The film closes with a scene of sickening violence. 这部电影以一个令人作呕

的暴力镜头收尾。III N [s] (end) 结束 [jiéshù] ▷ the close of the day 黄昏时分 ▸ **to bring sth to a close** 结束某事 ▸ **to draw to a close** 接近尾声

▸ **close down** I VI [factory, business +] 关闭 [guānbì] II VT [+ factory, business] 使关闭 [shǐ guānbì]

▸ **close in** VI 1 [hunters, police +] 包围 [bāowéi] 2 [winter, darkness +] 渐渐缩短 [jiànjiàn suōduǎn] ▸ **the days are closing in** 白天渐渐变短

▸ **close off** VT [+ area] 封锁 [fēngsuǒ]

▸ **close on** VT FUS [不可拆分] (in race, pursuit) 渐渐赶上 [jiànjiàn gǎnshàng]

closed [kləuzd] ADJ 1 (lit) [+ door, window] 关着的 [guānzhe de]; [+ shop, library] 关着门的 [guānzhe mén de]; [+ road] 封锁着的 [fēngsuǒzhe de] 2 (fig) [+ society, community] 闭关自守的 [bìguānzìshǒu de]

closely ['kləusli] ADV 1 [examine, watch +] 仔细地 [zǐxì de] 2 [+ connected] 密切地 [mìqiè de] 3 [resemble +] 非常 [fēicháng] 4 [follow +] 紧紧地 [jǐnjǐn de] 5 [work +] 密切地 [mìqiè de] ▸ **we are closely related** 我们是近亲 ▸ **a closely guarded secret** 一个严格保守的秘密

closet ['klɔzɪt] I N [c] (US) 壁橱 [bìchú] [英= **cupboard**] II ADJ 隐蔽的 [yǐnbì de] ▸ **to come out of the closet** (fig) 从隐蔽状态转为公开

close-up ['kləusʌp] (PHOT) N [c] 特写 [tèxiě]

closing time ['kləuzɪŋ-] N [c/u] (in shop, pub) 关门时间 [guānmén shíjiān]

closure ['kləuʒə(r)] N 1 [c/u] [of factory, business] 倒闭 [dǎobì] 2 [c] [of road, border] 封锁 [fēngsuǒ]

clot [klɔt] I N [c] [(blood) +] (also: **blood clot**) 凝块 [níngkuài] II VI [blood +] 凝固 [nínggù]

cloth [klɔθ] N 1 [c/u] (fabric) 布料 [bùliào] 2 [c] (for cleaning, dusting) 布 [bù] 3 [c] (tablecloth) 桌布 [zhuōbù] ▸ **piece of cloth** 一块布

clothe [kləuð] VT (provide with clothes) 供给…衣服 [gōngjǐ…yīfu] ▸ **clothed in green** 穿绿色衣服

clothes [kləuðz] NPL 衣服 [yīfu] ▸ **to put one's clothes on** 穿衣服 ▸ **to take one's clothes off** 脱衣服

clothesline ['kləuðzlaɪn] N [c] 晾衣绳 [liàngyīshéng]

clothes peg (BRIT) N [c] 晾衣夹 [liàngyījiā] [美= **clothespin**]

clothespin [kləuðzpɪn] (US) N [c] 晾衣夹 [liàngyījiā] [英= **clothes peg**]

clothing ['kləuðɪŋ] N [U] 衣服 [yīfu] ▸ **an item** or **a piece of clothing** 一件衣服

> **clothing** 是不可数名词。不能用 **clothings** 或 **a clothing**。He took off his wet clothing. 可以说 **an item of clothing**，**a piece of clothing** 或者 **an article of clothing**。

clotted cream ['klɔtɪd-] (BRIT) N [U] 浓缩奶油 [nóngsuō nǎiyóu]

cloud [klaʊd] I N 1 [C/U] (in sky) 云 [yún] 2 [c] [of smoke, dust] 雾 [wù] II VT [+ judgement, view] 使模糊 [shǐ móhu]; [+ outlook, atmosphere] 使暗淡 [shǐ àndàn] ▶ **every cloud has a silver lining** 黑暗中总有一线光明
▶ **cloud over** VI 1 [sky +] 阴云密布 [yīnyún mìbù] 2 [face, eyes +] 阴沉下来 [yīnchén xiàlái] ▶ **it's clouding over** 天阴了

cloudy ['klaʊdɪ] ADJ 1 [+ day, sky, weather] 多云的 [duōyún de] 2 [+ liquid] 混浊的 [húnzhuó de] ▶ **it's cloudy** 天阴

clove [kləʊv] N [C] 1 (spice) 丁香 [dīngxiāng] 2 [of garlic] 瓣 [bàn]

clown [klaʊn] I N [C] (in circus) 小丑 [xiǎochǒu] II VI (also: **clown about, clown around**) 胡闹 [húnào]

○ **club** [klʌb] I N [C] 1 (society, place) 俱乐部 [jùlèbù] ▷ a chess club 象棋俱乐部 ▷ I'll see you at the club. 我在俱乐部见你。 2 (SPORT) 俱乐部 [jùlèbù] ▷ Liverpool football club 利物浦足球俱乐部 3 (nightclub) 夜总会 [yèzǒnghuì] 4 (weapon) 大头棒 [dàtóubàng] 5 (stick) (also: **golf club**) 球棒 [qiúbàng] II VT (hit) 用棒棍打 [yòng bànggùn dǎ] III VI ▶ **to club together** (BRIT) (for gift, card) 凑钱 [còuqián] IV **clubs** NPL (CARDS) 梅花 [méihuā] ▶ **to club sb to death** 用棍棒将某人打死

club class N [U] 会员级 [huìyuán jí]

clue [klu:] N [C] 1 (in investigation) 线索 [xiànsuǒ] 2 (in crossword, game) 提示 [tíshì] 3 (fig) (indication) 线索 [xiànsuǒ] ▶ **I haven't a clue** (inf) 我一无所知

clump [klʌmp] N [C] [of trees, grass] 丛 [cóng]; [of hair] 绺 [liǔ]

clumsy ['klʌmzɪ] ADJ 1 [+ person] 笨手笨脚的 [bènshǒubènjiǎo de] 2 [+ effort, attempt] 笨拙的 [bènzhuō de] 3 [+ object] 不好使用的 [bùhǎo shǐyòng de]

clung [klʌŋ] PT, PP of **cling**

cluster ['klʌstə(r)] I N [C] [of people] 群 [qún]; [of things, cases] 组 [zǔ] II VT ▶ **to be clustered around sth** 聚集在某物的周围 [jùjí zài mǒuwù de zhōuwéi]
▶ **cluster around** VT FUS [不可拆分] 聚集 [jùjí]
▶ **cluster together** VI [people +] 成群 [chéngqún]; [things +] 成簇 [chéngcù]

clutch [klʌtʃ] I VT 紧抓 [jǐnzhuā] II N [C] (AUT) 离合器 [líhéqì] III **clutches** NPL ▶ **to fall into sb's clutches** 陷入某人的控制中 [xiànrù mǒurén de kòngzhì zhōng]
▶ **clutch at** VT FUS [不可拆分] (lit) 抓住 [zhuāzhù]

clutter ['klʌtə(r)] I VT (also: **clutter up**) 使凌乱 [shǐ língluàn] II N [U] 杂乱的东西 [záluàn de dōngxi]

cm ABBR (= centimetres) 厘米 [límǐ]

Co. ABBR 1 (= company) 公司 [gōngsī] 2 (= county) 郡 [jùn]

c/o ABBR (= care of) 由···转交 [yóu···zhuǎnjiāo]

coach [kəʊtʃ] I N [C] 1 (BRIT) 长途汽车 [chángtú qìchē] [美= **bus**] 2 (horse-drawn) 大马车 [dàmǎchē] [美= **car**] 3 (BRIT) [of train] 车厢 [chēxiāng] [美= **car**] 4 (SPORT) (trainer) 教练 [jiàoliàn] 5 (tutor) 私人教师 [sīrén jiàoshī] II VT 1 (SPORT) 训练 [xùnliàn] 2 (SCOL) 辅导 [fǔdǎo]

coach trip (BRIT) N [C] 长途汽车旅行团 [chángtú qìchē lǚxíng tuán] ▶ **to go on a coach trip** 参加长途汽车旅行团

coal [kəʊl] N 1 [U] (substance) 煤 [méi] 2 [c] (piece of coal) 煤块 [méikuài]

coalition [kəʊə'lɪʃən] N [C/U] 1 (government) 联合 [liánhé] 2 (with same aim) 联盟 [liánméng]

coal mine N [C] 煤矿 [méikuàng]

coarse [kɔ:s] ADJ 1 [+ cloth, salt, sand] 粗的 [cū de] 2 (vulgar) [+ person, remark] 粗俗的 [cūsú de]

coast [kəʊst] I N [C] 海岸 [hǎi'àn] II VI 1 [car, bicycle +] 滑行 [huáxíng] 2 (in school, competition) 毫不费力地进行 [háobùfèilì de jìnxíng] ▶ **to coast to success/to a victory** 轻松取胜

coastal ['kəʊstl] ADJ [+ area, town, waters] 沿海的 [yánhǎi de]

coastguard ['kəʊstgɑ:d] (ESP BRIT) N 1 [C] (person) 海岸警卫队队员 [hǎi'àn jǐngwèi duì duìyuán] 2 ▶ **the coastguard** (service) 海岸警卫队 [hǎi'àn jǐngwèiduì]

coastline ['kəʊstlaɪn] N [C] 海岸线 [hǎi'àn xiàn]

coat [kəʊt] I N [C] 1 (overcoat) 外套 [wàitào] 2 [of animal] 皮毛 [pímáo] 3 [of paint, varnish] 层 [céng] II VT 撒满 [sǎnmǎn]

coat hanger N [C] 衣架 [yījià]

coating ['kəʊtɪŋ] N [C] [of chocolate, sugar, oil] 一层 [yīcéng]; [of dust] 外层 [wàicéng]

coax [kəʊks] VT ▶ **to coax sb into doing sth** 哄某人做某事 [hǒng mǒurén zuò mǒushì]

cob [kɔb] N see **corn**

cobbled ['kɔbld] ADJ [+ street] 用大卵石铺的 [yòng dàluǎnshí pū de]

cobweb ['kɔbwɛb] N [C] 蜘蛛网 [zhīzhū wǎng]

cocaine [kə'keɪn] N [U] 可卡因 [kěkǎyīn]

cock [kɔk] I N [C] 1 (BRIT) 公鸡 [gōngjī] [美= **rooster**] 2 (BRIT) (male bird) 雄禽 [xióngqín] 3 (inf!) (penis) 阴茎 [yīnjīng] II VT 1 [+ head, ear] 翘起 [qiàoqǐ] 2 [+ gun] 扳起···的扳机 [bānqǐ···de bānjī]

cockerel ['kɔkərəl] (ESP BRIT) N [C] 小公鸡 [xiǎo gōngjī]

cockpit ['kɔkpɪt] N [C] (in aircraft) 驾驶舱 [jiàshǐ cāng]; (in racing car) 驾驶座 [jiàshǐ zuò]

cockroach ['kɔkrəʊtʃ] N [C] 蟑螂 [zhāngláng]

cocktail ['kɔkteɪl] N [C] 1 (drink) 鸡尾酒 [jīwěi jiǔ] 2 (fig) 合成物 [héchéngwù]

cocoa ['kəʊkəʊ] N [U] 可可 [kěkě]

coconut ['kəʊkənʌt] N 1 [C] (nut) 椰子 [yēzi] 2 [U] (flesh) 椰肉 [yēròu]

COD ABBR (= cash on delivery, (US) = collect on delivery) 货到付款 [huòdào fùkuǎn]

cod [kɔd] (pl **cod** or **cods**) N 1 [C] (fish) 鳕鱼 [xuěyú] 2 [U] (as food) 鳕鱼 [xuěyú]

code [kəʊd] N 1 [C] [of practice, behaviour] 准则 [zhǔnzé] 2 [C] (cipher) 密码 [mìmǎ] 3 [C] (as reference) 标记 [biāojì] 4 [C] (TEL) 区号 [qūhào] 5 [C/U] (COMPUT, SCI) 编码 [biānmǎ] ▶ **code of conduct** 行为准则 ▶ **code of practice** 实践准则 ▶ **in code** 用密码

co-ed ['kəʊ'ɛd] I ADJ ABBR (SCOL) (= coeducational) 男女同校的 [nánnǚ tóngxiào de] II N ABBR (US) (female student) 男女同校的女生 [nánnǚ tóngxiào de nǚshēng]

coffee ['kɔfɪ] N 1 [U] 咖啡 [kāfēi] 2 [C] (cup of coffee) 一杯咖啡 [yībēi kāfēi] ▶ **black coffee** 黑咖啡 ▶ **white coffee** 牛奶咖啡 ▶ **coffee with cream** 加奶油的咖啡

coffee bar N [C] 咖啡馆 [kāfēi guǎn]

coffee bean N [C] 咖啡豆 [kāfēi dòu]

coffee break N [C] 工间休息时间 [gōngjiān xiūxi shíjiān]

coffee pot N [C] 咖啡壶 [kāfēi hú]

coffee shop N [C] 咖啡店 [kāfēi diàn]

coffee table N [C] 咖啡桌 [kāfēi zhuō]

coffin ['kɔfɪn] N [C] 棺材 [guāncai]

cog [kɔg] (TECH) N [C] 轮齿 [lúnchǐ]

cognac ['kɔnjæk] N 1 [C/U] (liquid) 法国白兰地 [Fǎguó báilándì] 2 [C] (glass of cognac) 一杯法国白兰地 [yībēi Fǎguó báilándì]

cognitive ['kɔgnɪtɪv] (frm) ADJ 认识的 [rènshi de]

coherent [kəʊ'hɪərənt] ADJ 1 [+ strategy, policy] 连贯的 [liánguàn de] 2 [+ person] 条理清楚的 [tiáolǐ qīngchu de]

coil [kɔɪl] I N [C] 1 [of rope, wire] 卷 [juǎn] 2 (loop) 圈 [quān] 3 (AUT, ELEC) 线圈 [xiànquān] 4 (contraceptive) 子宫节育环 [zǐgōng jiéyù huán] II VT (also: **coil up**) [+ rope etc] 卷 [juǎn] III VI [rope etc +] 盘绕 [pánrào]

coin [kɔɪn] I N [C] 硬币 [yìngbì] II VT [+ word, slogan] 创造 [chuàngzào]

coincide [kəʊɪn'saɪd] VI 1 [events +] 同时发生 [tóngshí fāshēng] 2 [ideas, views +] 相一致 [xiāngyīzhì] ▶ **to coincide with sth** [event +] 和某事同时发生

coincidence [kəʊ'ɪnsɪdəns] N [C/U] 巧合 [qiǎohé]

Coke® [kəʊk] N [U] (drink) 可口可乐 [Kěkǒu Kělè]

coke [kəʊk] N [U] 1 (fuel) 焦炭 [jiāotàn] 2 (inf) (cocaine) 可卡因 [kěkǎyīn]

cola ['kəʊlə] N [C/U] 可乐 [kělè]

colander ['kɔləndə(r)] N [C] 滤器 [lùqì]

cold [kəʊld] I ADJ 1 [+ water, object] 凉的 [liáng de]; [+ weather, room, meat] 冷的 [lěng de] 2 [+ person] (unemotional) 冷淡的 [lěngdàn de]; (unfriendly) 不友好的 [bùyǒuhǎo de] II N 1 [U] (weather) **the cold** 寒冷天气 [hánlěng tiānqì] 2 [C] (illness) 感冒 [gǎnmào] ▷ I've got a cold. 我感冒了。 ▶ **it's cold** 天气寒冷 ▶ **to be** or **feel cold** [person +] 感到冷 ▶ **to catch (a) cold** 患感冒 ▶ **in cold blood** [kill etc +] 残忍地 ▶ **to have/get cold feet (about sth)** (在某事上) 临阵畏缩

freezing 可用于强调天气很冷，尤其是有霜冻的严冬。夏季如果气温低于平均温度，可以用 **cool**。通常，**cold** 表示的温度比 **cool** 低。**cool** 表示温度适宜、凉爽。A cool breeze swept off the sea; it was pleasant out there. 如果非常 **cool**，或太 **cool**，可以用 **chilly**。

coldly ['kəʊldlɪ] ADV [speak, behave +] 冷漠地 [lěngmò de]

cold sore (BRIT: MED) N [C] 唇疱疹 [chúnchuāngzhěn]

coleslaw ['kəʊlslɔː] (CULIN) N [U] 酸卷心菜丝 [suānjuǎnxīncàisī]

colic ['kɔlɪk] (MED) N [U] 急腹痛 [jífùtòng]

collaborate [kə'læbəreɪt] VI 1 (on book, research) 合作 [hézuò] 2 (with enemy) 勾结 [gōujié] ▶ **to collaborate (with sb) on sth** (与某人) 合作做某事

collaboration [kələbə'reɪʃən] N 1 [C/U] (on book, research) 合作 [hézuò] 2 [U] (with enemy) 勾结 [gōujié] ▶ **in collaboration with** 与…合作

collapse [kə'læps] I VI [building, table +] 倒坍 [dǎotān]; [system, company +] 瓦解 [wǎjiě]; (from hunger, weakness etc) [person +] 倒下 [dǎoxià] II N [S/U] [of building, table] 倒塌 [dǎotān]; [of system, company] 瓦解 [wǎjiě]; (from hunger, weakness etc) 垮掉 [kuǎdiào]

collar ['kɔlə(r)] I N [C] 1 [of coat, shirt] 领子 [lǐngzi] 2 [of dog, cat] 颈圈 [jǐngquān] II VT (inf) [+ person] 抓住 [zhuāzhù]

collarbone ['kɔləbəʊn] N [C] 锁骨 [suǒgǔ]

colleague ['kɔliːg] N [C] 同事 [tóngshì]

collect [kə'lɛkt] I VT 1 [+ wood, litter etc] 采集 [cǎijí] 2 (as hobby) 收集 [shōují] 3 (BRIT) (fetch) [+ person] 接 [jiē]; [+ object] 取 [qǔ] 4 [+ money, donations] 募捐 [mùjuān] 5 [+ debts, taxes etc] 收 [shōu] 6 [+ mail] 取 [qǔ] II VI 1 [dust, dirt +] 积聚 [jījù] 2 (for charity, gift) 募捐 [mùjuān] ▶ **to call collect, make a collect call** (US: TEL) 打对方付款的电话 [英= **to reverse the charges**] ▶ **to collect o.s.** or **one's thoughts** 使自己镇定下来 ▶ **collect on delivery** (US: COMM) 货到付款

collection [kə'lɛkʃən] N 1 [C] [of art, stamps etc] 收藏品 [shōucáng pǐn] 2 [C] [of poems, stories etc] 文集 [wénjí] 3 [U] (picking up) [of goods, mail] 收取 [shōuqǔ]; [of data] 收集 [shōují] 4 [C] (for charity, gift) 募捐 [mùjuān]

collective [kə'lɛktɪv] I ADJ 集体的 [jítǐ de]
II N [c] 合作社 [hézuò shè]

collector [kə'lɛktə(r)] N [c] 1 [of art, stamps etc]
收藏家 [shōucáng jiā] 2 ▸ **tax/debt collector**
收税员/讨债员 [shōushuì/tǎozhàiyuán] ▸ **a
collector's item** 一件收藏品

college ['kɔlɪdʒ] N 1 [c/u] (for further education)
学院 [xuéyuàn] 2 [c] (of university) 学院
[xuéyuàn] ▸ **to go to college** 上大学 ▸ **college
of education** (BRIT) 师范学院

collide [kə'laɪd] VI (cars, people +) 碰撞
[pèngzhuàng] ▸ **to collide with sth/sb** 与某
物/某人碰撞

collision [kə'lɪʒən] N [c/u] (of vehicles) 碰撞
[pèngzhuàng] ▸ **to be on a collision course** (lit)
必然相撞; (fig) 必然发生冲突

cologne [kə'ləun] N [c/u] (also: **eau de cologne**)
科隆香水 [kēlóng xiāngshuǐ]

Colombia [kə'lɔmbɪə] N 哥伦比亚 [Gēlúnbǐyà]

Colombian [kə'lɔmbɪən] I ADJ 哥伦比亚的
[Gēlúnbǐyà de] II N [c] (person) 哥伦比亚人
[Gēlúnbǐyàrén]

colon ['kəulən] N [c] 1 (punctuation mark) 冒号
[màohào] 2 (ANAT) 结肠 [jiécháng]

colonel ['kə:nl] N [c] 上校 [shàngxiào]

colonial [kə'ləunɪəl] ADJ 殖民地的 [zhímíndì
de]

colony ['kɔlənɪ] N [c] 1 (country) 殖民地
[zhímíndì] 2 [of animals] 群体 [qúntǐ]

color etc ['kʌlə(r)] (US) = **colour** etc

colour, (US) **color** ['kʌlə(r)] I N 1 [c] 颜色
[yánsè] 2 [c] (skin colour) 肤色 [fūsè] ▷ South
Africans of all colours 各种肤色的南非人 3 [u]
(interest) 生动 [shēngdòng] II VT 1 (with paint,
crayons, dye) 给…着色 [gěi…zhuósè] ▷ Does
she colour her hair? 她染头发吗? 2 (affect)
[+ judgement, account] 影响 [yǐngxiǎng] III VI
(blush) 脸红 [liǎnhóng] IV CPD (复合词) [+ film,
photograph, television] 彩色 [cǎisè] ▸ **in colour**
[+ film, illustrations] 彩色
▸ **colour in** VT [+ picture] 给…着色 [gěi…zhuósè]

colour-blind, (US) **color-blind** ['kʌləblaɪnd]
ADJ 色盲的 [sèmáng de]

coloured, (US) **colored** ['kʌləd] ADJ
1 [+ illustration etc] 有色的 [yǒusè de] 2 (o.f.)
[+ person] 有色的 [yǒusè de] ▸ **brightly
coloured** 色泽鲜艳

colour film, (US) **color film** N [c/u] 彩色胶
卷 [cǎisè jiāojuǎn]

colourful, (US) **colorful** ['kʌləful] ADJ
1 (brightly coloured) 色泽鲜艳的 [sèzé
xiānyàn de] 2 [+ account, history] 丰富多彩的
[fēngfùduōcǎi de] 3 [+ personality] 引人注目的
[yǐnrénzhùmù de]

colouring, (US) **coloring** ['kʌlərɪŋ] N 1 [u]
(complexion) 面色 [miànsè] 2 [c/u] (in food) 色
素 [sèsù]

colour television, (US) **color television** N

[c/u] 彩色电视 [cǎisè diànshì]

column ['kɔləm] N [c] 1 (ARCHIT) 支柱 [zhīzhù]
2 [of smoke] 柱形物 [zhùxíngwù] 3 [of people,
tanks] 纵队 [zòngduì] 4 (in newspaper etc) 专栏
[zhuānlán]

coma ['kəumə] (MED) N [c/u] 昏迷 [hūnmí]
▸ **to be in a coma** 处于昏迷状态

comb [kəum] I N [c] 梳子 [shūzi] II VT
1 [+ hair] 梳理 [shūlǐ] 2 (search) [+ area] 彻底搜
寻 [chèdǐ sōuxún]

combat ['kɔmbæt] I N (MIL) [u/c] 战斗
[zhàndòu] II VT (oppose) [+ drugs, crime etc]
与…斗争 [yǔ…dòuzhēng]

combination [kɔmbɪ'neɪʃən] N [c] 1 (mixture)
混合 [hùnhé] 2 (for lock, safe etc) 密码 [mìmǎ]

combine [vb kəm'baɪn, n 'kɔmbaɪn] I VT 1 ▸ **to
combine sth with sth** 将某物与某物结合起
来 [jiāng mǒuwù yǔ mǒuwù jiéhé qǐlái] II VI
[qualities, situations +] 结合 [jiéhé]; [people,
groups +] 组合 [zǔhé]; (CHEM) 化合 [huàhé]
III N (ECON) 联合公司 [liánhé gōngsī] ▸ **a
combined effort** 协力

○

come [kʌm] (pt **came**, pp **come**) VI 1 (move
towards, arrive) 来 [lái] ▸ **come here!** 到
这儿来! ▸ **I'm just coming!** 我这就来!
▸ **can I come too?** 我也能来吗? ▸ **come
with me** 跟我来 ▸ **a girl came into the
room** 一个女孩进了房间 ▸ **he came to a
door** 他到了门口 ▸ **why don't you come
to lunch on Saturday?** 何不星期六过来吃
午饭呢? ▸ **to come to/and do sth** 来做某
事 ▸ **he's come here to work** 他已经到了
这儿工作
2 ▸ **to come to** (reach) 到达 [dàodá];
(amount to) 达到 [dádào] ▸ **her hair came
to her waist** 她的头发长到腰的位置了
▸ **to come to a decision** 做出决定 ▸ **the
bill came to £40** 账单共计40英镑
3 (occur) ▸ **an idea came to me** 我想到了
一个主意 [wǒ xiǎngdàole yīgè zhǔyì] ▸ **it
suddenly came to me that...** 我突然想
到…
4 (in inheritance, as payment etc) ▸ **to come to
sb** 留给某人 [liúgěi mǒurén]
5 (be, become) ▸ **to come first/second/
last etc** (in series) 排在第一/第二/最后
{等} [páizài dìyī/dì'èr/zuìhòu{děng}]; (in
competition, race) 位居第一/第二/最后
{等} [wèijū dìyī/dì'èr/zuìhòu{děng}] ▸ **to
come loose/undone etc** 松了/解开了{等}
▸ **I've come to like him** 我开始喜欢上他了
▸ **how did you come to meet him?** 你是怎
么遇到他的?
6 (be available) ▸ **it comes in blue or green**
蓝色或绿色的有现货 [lánsè huò lùsè de
yǒu xiànhuò]

7 (in expressions) ▶ **when you come down to it, when it comes down to it** 归根结底 [guīgēnjiédǐ] ▶ **come to think of it** 再想想 ▷ You know, when you come to think of it, this is very odd. 再想想的话，当这样是很奇怪的。
▶ **when it comes to...** 当谈到…
▶ **come about** VI [discovery, solution +] 发生 [fāshēng]
▶ **come across** I VT FUS [不可拆分] (find) 偶然发现 [ǒurán fāxiàn]
II VI ▶ **to come across well/badly** [person +] 留下好/坏印象 [liúxià hǎo/huài yìnxiàng]; [idea, meaning +] 表达清楚/不清楚 [biǎodá qīngchu/bùqīngchu]
▶ **come along** VI **1** 来 [lái]
2 (arrive) 不期而至 [bùqī'érzhì] ▶ **it was lucky you came along** 真幸运你来了
3 (come on the scene) 出现 [chūxiàn] ▶ **when an exciting new author comes along...** 当一个令人兴奋的新作家出现时…
4 (make progress) 进展 [jìnzhǎn] ▶ **come along!** (encouraging) 快一点！
▶ **come apart** VI 裂成碎片 [lièchéng suìpiàn]
▶ **come around** VI **1** (visit) 来访 [láifǎng]
2 (agree) 改变态度 [gǎibiàn tàidù]
3 (reoccur) 来到 [láidào] ▷ I can't believe Christmas has come around again so fast! 我不能相信这么快又是圣诞节了！
4 (regain consciousness) 苏醒过来 [sūxǐng guòlái]
▶ **come at** VT FUS [不可拆分] 扑向 [pūxiàng] ▶ **he came at me with a knife** 他拿着刀扑向我
▶ **come away** VI **1** (depart) 离开 [líkāi]
2 (become detached) 脱落 [tuōluò]
▶ **come back** VI **1** (return) 回来 [huílái]
▶ **I'm coming back to that** (in discussion etc) 我过会儿再回到那个问题 ▶ **can I come back to you on that one?** 我能过会儿再跟你讨论那个问题吗？ ▶ **to come back into fashion** 重新又流行起来
2 (come to mind) ▶ **it will come back to you** 你会回想起来的 [nǐ huì huíxiǎng qǐlái de]
▶ **it all came back** 全都想起来了
▶ **come between** VT FUS [不可拆分] 离间 [líjiàn]
▶ **come by** VT FUS [不可拆分] (acquire) 得到 [dédào] ▶ **jobs were hard to come by** 很难找到工作
▶ **come down** VI **1** [price +] 降低 [jiàngdī]
2 (fall to ground) [plane +] 坠落 [zhuìluò]; [tree +] 倒下 [dǎoxià]; [building +] 倒塌 [dǎotā]
3 (descend) 降下 [jiàngxià]
▶ **come down on** VT FUS [不可拆分] (declare support for) ▶ **to come down on the side of sth** 声明支持某事的一方 [shēngmíng zhīchí mǒushì de yīfāng]
▶ **come down to** VT FUS [不可拆分] 归结为 [guījié wéi]
▶ **come down with** VT FUS [不可拆分] [+ illness] 染上 [rǎnshang]
▶ **come forward** VI (volunteer) 自告奋勇 [zìgàofènyǒng]
▶ **come from** VT FUS [不可拆分] [+ place, source] 来自 [láizì] ▶ **I come from London** 我来自伦敦 ▶ **where do you come from?** 你是哪里人？ ▶ **the feeling of elation that comes from winning** 来自胜利的得意感
▶ **come in** VI **1** (to room, house etc) 进入 [jìnrù] ▶ **come in!** 进来！ ▶ **the tide is coming in** 潮水正在上涨
2 [report, mail, phone call +] 收到 [shōudào]
3 [money, salary +] 进账 [jìnzhàng]
4 (on deal etc) 参与 [cānyǔ]
5 (become common) [system +] 普遍起来 [pǔbiàn qǐlái]; [idea, fashion +] 流行起来 [liúxíng qǐlái]
6 (fit in) 起作用 [qǐ zuòyòng]
▶ **come in for** VT FUS [不可拆分] [+ criticism] 受到 [shòudào]
▶ **come into** VT FUS [不可拆分] **1** (inherit) 继承 [jìchéng]
2 (be involved in) 起作用 [qǐ zuòyòng]
3 (play a role) ▶ **money doesn't come into it** 钱不是问题 [qián bùshì wèntí]
4 (enter) ▶ **to come into operation/force** 开始运行/生效 [kāishǐ yùnxíng/shēngxiào]
▶ **to come into fashion** 开始流行
▶ **come of** VT FUS [不可拆分] (result from) 是…的结果 [shì…de jiéguǒ] ▶ **nothing came of it** 没有任何结果 ▶ **no good will come of it** 这不会产生任何好处
▶ **come off** I VI **1** [button, handle +] 脱落 [tuōluò]
2 (succeed) [event, attempt, plan +] 成功 [chénggōng] ▶ **to come off best/worst** etc 表现最佳/最差 {等}
II VT FUS [不可拆分] **1** [+ drug, medicine] 戒掉 [jièdiào]
2 (inf) ▶ **come off it!** 别胡扯了！ [bié húchě le!]
▶ **come on** VI **1** (progress) [pupil, work, project +] 进展 [jìnzhǎn] ▶ **come on!** (giving encouragement) 来！; (hurry up) 快一点！
2 [lights, heating, electricity +] 接通 [jiētōng]
▶ **come on to** VT FUS [不可拆分] 开始讨论 [kāishǐ tǎolùn]
▶ **come out** VI **1** [person +] (out of house, for evening etc) 出去 [chūqù]
2 (appear) [sun +] 出现 [chūxiàn]
3 (become known) 为人所知 [wéirénsuǒzhī]
4 (become available) [book +] 出版 [chūbǎn]; [film +] 上映 [shàngyìng]
5 (be printable) [photograph +] 冲洗得出

[chōngxǐ de chū]

6 (as homosexual) 公开承认是同性恋 [gōngkāi chéngrèn shì tóngxìngliàn]

7 (fig) (emerge) 显得 [xiǎn de]

8 (be erased) [stain +] 除去 [chúqù]

9 [workers +] ▶ **to come out (on strike)** 罢工 [bàgōng]

10 (declare o.s.) ▶ **to come out against/in favour of sth** 宣布反对/支持某事 [xuānbù fǎnduì/zhīchí mǒushì]

▶ **come out in** VT FUS [不可拆分] ▶ **to come out in spots/in a rash** 起满小包/疹子 [qǐmǎn xiǎobāo/zhěnzǐ]

▶ **come out with** VT FUS [不可拆分] [+ remark] 说出 [shuōchū]

▶ **come over** I VT FUS [不可拆分] [feeling +] 牢牢控制 [láoláo kòngzhì] ▶ **I don't know what's come over him!** 我不知道他是怎么了!

II VI **1** (appear) 表现 [biǎoxiàn] ▶ **to come over as** 表现为

2 (visit) 顺便拜访 [shùnbiàn bàifǎng] ▶ **I'll come over later** 我一会儿过来

▶ **come round** VI = **come around**

▶ **come through** I VT FUS [不可拆分] (survive) [+ crisis, illness] 经历⋯而幸存 [jīnglì⋯ér xìngcún]

II VI **1** (be obvious) 清晰可辨 [qīngxīkěbiàn]

2 (arrive) [call, news, money +] 传来 [chuánlái]

▶ **come to** VI (regain consciousness) 苏醒 [sūxǐng]

▶ **come under** VT FUS [不可拆分]

1 [+ criticism, pressure, attack] 受到 [shòudào]

2 [+ heading] 归入 [guīrù]

3 [+ authority] 受⋯支配 [shòu⋯zhīpèi]

▶ **come up** VI **1** (approach) 走近 [zǒujìn]

2 (arise) [problem, opportunity +] 突然出现 [tūrán chūxiàn]

3 (be about to happen) 即将发生 [jíjiāng fāshēng]

4 (be mentioned) 被提到 [bèi tídào]

5 (rise) [sun +] 升起 [shēngqǐ]

▶ **come up against** VT FUS [不可拆分] [+ resistance, difficulties] 碰到 [pèngdào]

▶ **come upon** VT FUS [不可拆分] (find) 偶然碰到 [ǒurán pèngdào]

▶ **come up to** VT FUS [不可拆分] **1** (get on for) 接近 [jiējìn] ▶ **it's coming up to 11 o'clock** 快到11点钟了

2 (approach) 走近 [zǒujìn]

3 (meet) ▶ **the film didn't come up to our expectations** 电影没有我们预期的那么好 [diànyǐng méiyǒu wǒmen yùqī de nàme hǎo]

▶ **come up with** VT FUS [不可拆分] [+ idea, suggestion] 提出 [tíchū]; [+ money] 设法弄到 [shèfǎ nòngdào]

comeback ['kʌmbæk] N **1** ▶ **to make a**

comeback [pop star, sportsperson +] 东山再起 [dōngshān zàiqǐ]; [fashion +] 重新流行 [chóngxīn liúxíng] **2** ▶ **to have no comeback** 得不到补偿 [débùdào bǔcháng]

comedian [kə'miːdɪən] (THEAT, TV) N [c] 喜剧演员 [xǐjù yǎnyuán]

comedy ['kɒmɪdɪ] N **1** [U] (humour) 幽默 [yōumò] **2** [c] (play, film) 喜剧 [xǐjù]

comet ['kɒmɪt] N [c] 彗星 [huìxīng]

comfort ['kʌmfət] I N **1** [U] (physical, material) 舒适 [shūshì] **2** [c/U] (solace, relief) 安慰 [ānwèi] II VT (console) 安慰 [ānwèi] III **comforts** NPL 使生活舒适的东西 [shǐ shēnghuó shūshì de dōngxi] ▶ **to live in comfort** 过着舒适的生活

comfortable ['kʌmfətəbl] ADJ **1** [person +] ▶ **to be comfortable** (physically) 舒服的 [shūfu de]; (financially) 富足的 [fùzú de] **2** [furniture, room, clothes] 使人舒服的 [shǐ rén shūfu de] **3** (MED) [+ sick person] 情况良好的 [qíngkuàng liánghǎo de] **4** [life, job etc] 轻松的 [qīngsōng de] **5** [+ victory, majority] 不费力的 [bù fèilì de] ▶ **to make o.s. comfortable** 自在点 ▶ **I don't feel very comfortable about it** 我对这件事感到不自在 ▶ **to be/feel comfortable with sth/sb** 对某事/某人感到舒坦

comfortably ['kʌmfətəblɪ] ADV **1** [sit, settle +] 舒服地 [shūfu de] **2** [live +] 宽裕地 [kuānyù de] **3** ▶ **to be comfortably off** 生活宽裕 [shēnghuó kuānyù]

comfort station (US) N [c] 公共厕所 [gōnggòng cèsuǒ]

comic ['kɒmɪk] I ADJ **1** (also: **comical**) 滑稽的 [huájī de] **2** [+ actor, opera] 喜剧的 [xǐjù de] II N [c] **1** (comedian) 喜剧演员 [xǐjǔ yǎnyuán] **2** (BRIT) (magazine) 连环漫画 [liánhuán mànhuà] [美= **comic book**]

comic book (US) N [c] 连环漫画 [liánhuán mànhuà] [英= **comic**]

○ **coming** ['kʌmɪŋ] ADJ [+ event, attraction] 即将到来的 [jíjiāng dàolái de] ▷ the coming election 即将到来的选举 ▶ **in the coming months** 下几个月

comma ['kɒmə] N [c] 逗号 [dòuhào]

command [kə'mɑːnd] I N **1** [c] (order) 命令 [mìnglìng] **2** [U] (MIL) (authority) 指挥 [zhǐhuī] **3** [U] (mastery) [of subject] 运用能力 [yùnyòng nénglì] **4** [c] (COMPUT) 指令 [zhǐlìng] II VT **1** (liter) ▶ **to command sb to do sth** 命令某人做某事 [mìnglìng mǒurén zuò mǒushì]

2 [+ troops] 指挥 [zhǐhuī] **3** [+ respect, attention, obedience] 博得 [bódé] ▶ **to be in command** [person, government +] 处于指挥地位 ▶ **to be in command of sth** (MIL) 指挥某事 ▶ **to have/ take command of sth** [+ situation] 控制/取得控制某事; (MIL) [squadron etc] 指挥某事 ▶ **at sb's command** (frm) [+ money, resources etc] 可自由支配

commander [kə'mɑːndə(r)] (MIL) N [c] 指挥

官 [zhǐhuī guān]

commemorate [kə'mɛməreɪt] VT [+ *person, event*] 纪念 [jìniàn]

commence [kə'mɛns] (*frm*) VT, VI 开始 [kāishǐ]

commencement [kə'mɛnsmənt] N 1 [U] (*frm*) 开始 [kāishǐ] 2 [C/U] (US: UNIV) 学位授予典礼 [xuéwèi shòuyǔ diǎnlǐ] [英 = graduation]

commend [kə'mɛnd] (*frm*) VT (*praise*) 表扬 [biǎoyáng] ▶ **to commend sb for sth/for doing sth** 表扬某人某事/做某事 ▶ **to commend sth/sb to sb** (*recommend*) 向某人推荐某物/某人

comment ['kɔmɛnt] I N 1 [C/U] (*written, spoken*) 评论 [pínglùn] 2 [S] (*reflection*) (*on situation, development etc*) 写照 [xiězhào] II VI ▶ **to comment (on sth)** (对某事)发表意见 [(duì mǒushì) fābiǎo yìjiàn] ▶ **"no comment"** "无可奉告" ▶ **to comment that...** 评论… **comment on** 或 **make a comment about** 某个情形，即对该情形发表意见。*Mr Cook has not commented on these reports... I was wondering whether you had any comments.* **mention** 某事，表示简要地提及未谈到的话题。*He mentioned that he might go to New York.* **remark on** 或 **make a remark about** 某事，表示把你的想法或所见到的事情说出来，通常是以一种比较随意的方式。*Visitors have remarked on how well the children look...General Smith's remarks about the conflict.*

commentary ['kɔmɛntərɪ] N 1 [C/U] (*on match, proceedings*) 实况报道 [shíkuàng bàodào] 2 [C] (*book, article*) 集注 [jízhù]

commentator ['kɔmɛnteɪtə(r)] N [C] 1 (*describing match, proceedings*) 解说员 [jiěshuōyuán] 2 (*expert*) 评论者 [pínglùnzhě]

commerce ['kɔmə:s] N [U] 贸易 [màoyì]

commercial [kə'mə:ʃəl] I ADJ [+ *organization, activity*] 商业的 [shāngyè de]; [+ *success, failure*] 从盈利角度出发 [cóng yínglì jiǎodù chūfā]; [+ *television, radio*] 商业性的 [shāngyè xìng de] II N [C] (*advertisement*) 广告 [guǎnggào] ▶ **Christmas has become too commercial** 圣诞节已经变得太商业化了

commission [kə'mɪʃən] I N 1 [C/U] (*to artist, musician etc*) 委托 [wěituō] 2 [C] (*piece of work*) 委托项目 [wěituō xiàngmù] 3 [C/U] (*money*) 佣金 [yōngjīn] 4 [C] (*committee*) 委员会 [wěiyuánhuì] 5 [C] (MIL) 授衔令 [shòuxiánlìng] II VT 1 [+ *study, book, painting etc*] 委托人做 [wěituō rén zuò] 2 (MIL) 任命 [rènmìng] ▶ **out of commission** (*not working*) 不能使用 ▷ *His car is out of commission.* 他的车坏了。▶ **I get 10% commission** 我得到10%的佣金 ▶ **to commission sb to do sth** 委托某人做某事 ▶ **to commission sth from sb** 委托某人做某事

commissioner [kə'mɪʃənə(r)] N [C] 1 (*in organization, government*) 长官 [zhǎngguān] 2 (*also*: **police commissioner**) 警察局长 [jǐngchá júzhǎng]

commit [kə'mɪt] VT 1 [+ *crime, offence*] 犯 [fàn]; [+ *sin, adultery*] 做 [zuò] 2 (*pledge*) [+ *money, resources*] 调配 [tiáopèi] 3 ▶ **to commit sb to** [+ *hospital, prison*] 把某人关进 [bǎ mǒurén guānjìn] ▶ **to commit suicide** 自杀 ▶ **to commit sth to sth** (*pledge*) 调配某物用于某事 ▶ **to commit o.s. (to doing sth)** 承诺(做某事) ▶ **to commit sth to writing** 书面记录某事 ▶ **to commit sb for trial** (BRIT) 将某人送交刑事法庭受审

commitment [kə'mɪtmənt] N 1 [U] (*to ideology, system*) ▶ **commitment (to sth)** 献身(于某事) [xiànshēn (yú mǒushì)] 2 [C] (*obligation*) 义务 [yìwù] ▶ **to make a commitment (to do sth)** 作出承诺(做某事)

committed [kə'mɪtɪd] ADJ [+ *writer, politician*] 忠诚的 [zhōngchéng de]; [+ *Christian*] 虔诚的 [qiánchéng de] ▶ **to be committed to sth/ doing sth** 尽忠于某事/做某事

○**committee** [kə'mɪtɪ] N [C] 委员会 [wěiyuánhuì] ▶ **to be on a committee** 任委员会委员

commodity [kə'mɔdɪtɪ] N [C] 商品 [shāngpǐn]

○**common** ['kɔmən] I ADJ 1 (*usual*) 常见的 [chángjiàn de] ▷ *Jones is a common name there.* 琼斯在那儿是个常见的名字。2 (*shared*) 共同的 [gòngtóng de] ▷ *Our countries share a common frontier.* 我们的国家有共同的边界线。3 (*not special*) 普通的 [pǔtōng de] ▷ *the common man* 普通人 4 (*vulgar*) [+ *person, manners*] 粗俗的 [cūsú de] ▷ *She's a little common at times.* 她有时有点俗气。II N [C] (*area*) 公用地 [gōngyòng dì] ▶ **common to** 常见于 ▶ **in common use** 常用 ▶ **it's common knowledge that...** 大家都知道… ▶ **for the common good** 为了大家的利益 ▶ **the idea has become common currency** 这观点已是众所周知的了 ▶ **common ground** 共同点 ▶ **to have sth in common** [+ *people*] 有某些共同点; [*things +*] 有共同的某种特征 ▶ **to have sth in common with sb/sth** 与某人/某物有某共同点 ▶ **not to have anything in common (with sb/sth)** (与某人/某物)没有任何共同点

commonly ['kɔmənlɪ] ADV 通常地 [tōngcháng de]

commonplace ['kɔmənpleɪs] I ADJ 普通的 [pǔtōng de] II N [C] 寻常的事 [xúncháng de shì]

Commons ['kɔmənz] (BRIT) N ▶ **the Commons** (*also*: **House of Commons**) 下议院 [xiàyìyuàn]

common sense N [U] 常识 [chángshí]

Commonwealth ['kɔmənwɛlθ] N ▶ **the Commonwealth** 英联邦 [Yīngliánbāng]

commotion [kə'məuʃən] N [C/U] 混乱

[hùnluàn]

communal ['kɒmjuːnl] ADJ 1 (shared) [+ area,
room, kitchen] 公用的 [gōngyòng de] 2 (between
communities) [+ tension, violence] 小群体间的
[xiǎo qúntǐ jiān de]

commune [n 'kɒmjuːn, vb kə'mjuːn] I N [C]
(group) 公社 [gōngshè] II VI (liter) ▶ to
commune with sth 与某物沟通 [yǔ mǒuwù
gōutōng] ▷ to commune with nature 与大自然
交融

communicate [kə'mjuːnɪkeɪt] I VI 1 (by
writing, speaking etc) 联络 [liánluò] 2 (talk openly)
沟通 [gōutōng] II VT [+ idea, decision, feeling] 表
达 [biǎodá] ▶ to communicate with sb (by
writing, speaking etc) 与某人联络 (talk openly to)
与某人沟通

communication [kəmjuːnɪ'keɪʃən] I N 1 [U]
交流 [jiāoliú] 2 [C] (frm) (message) 信息 [xìnxī]
II communications NPL 通讯 [tōngxùn]

communion [kə'mjuːnɪən] N [U] (also: Holy
Communion) 圣餐仪式 [Shèngcān yíshì] ▶ to
take communion 领圣餐 ▶ communion with
nature 与大自然的交融

communism ['kɒmjunɪzəm] N [U] 共产主义
[gòngchǎnzhǔyì]

communist ['kɒmjunɪst] I ADJ 共产主义
的 [gòngchǎnzhǔyì de] II N [C] 共产主义者
[gòngchǎnzhǔyìzhě]

○**community** [kə'mjuːnɪtɪ] N [C]
1 (neighbourhood) 社区 [shèqū] 2 ▶ the
business/black/Jewish community 商业界/黑
人/犹太人 [shāngyèjiè/hēirén/yóutàirén] ▶ a
sense of community 社区感

community centre, (US) **community
center** N [C] 社区活动中心 [shèqū huódòng
zhōngxīn]

community service (LAW) N [U] 社区服务
[shèqū fúwù]

commute [kə'mjuːt] I VI 乘车上下班
[chéchē shàngxiàbān] II VT ▶ to be
commuted (to life imprisonment) 减刑 (为终
生监禁) [jiǎnxíng (wéi zhōngshēng jiānjìn)]
III N [C] (journey) 乘车上下班的路程 [chéngchē
shàngxiàbān de lùchéng] ▶ to commute
to/from London/Brighton 去/从伦敦/布赖
顿乘车上下班 ▶ to commute between Oxford
and Birmingham 乘车上下班往返于牛津与
伯明翰之间

commuter [kə'mjuːtə(r)] N [C] 乘车上下班的
人 [chéngchē shàngxiàbān de rén]

compact [adj, vb kəm'pækt, n 'kɒmpækt] I ADJ
1 [+ camera, cassette, car] 袖珍的 [xiùzhēn de];
[+ size, design, shape] 小巧的 [xiǎoqiǎo de] II VT
将…压紧在一起 [jiāng… yājǐn zài yīqǐ] III N
[C] (also: powder compact) 粉盒 [fěnhé]

compact disc N [C] 激光唱片 [jīguāng
chàngpiàn] 〔美= also compact disk〕

compact disc player N [C] 激光唱机

[jīguāng chàngpiàn] 〔美= also compact disk
player〕

companion [kəm'pænjən] N [C] 同伴
[tóngbàn]

companionship [kəm'pænjənʃɪp] N [U] 陪伴
[péibàn]

○**company** ['kʌmpənɪ] N 1 [C] (firm) 公司
[gōngsī] 2 [C] (THEAT) 剧团 [jùtuán] 3 [C] (MIL)
连 [lián] 4 [U] (companionship) 交往 [jiāowǎng]
▶ Smith and Company 史密斯公司 ▶ he's
good company 他是个好伙伴 ▶ we have
company 我们有客人 ▶ to keep sb company
陪伴某人 ▶ to part company (with sb) (when
walking etc) (与某人) 分手; (in work, relationship)
(与某人) 断绝联系

company car N [C] 单位公车 [dānwèi
gōngchē]

company director N [C] 公司董事 [gōngsī
dǒngshì]

comparable ['kɒmpərəbl] ADJ [+ size, quality]
类似的 [lèisì de]; [+ place, situation, job] 可比较
的 [kě bǐjiào de] ▶ comparable to 比得上

comparative [kəm'pærətɪv] I ADJ 1 (relative)
[+ ease, safety, freedom, peace] 比较而言的
[bǐjiào'éryán de] 2 [+ study] 用比较方法的
[yòng bǐjiào fāngfǎ de] 3 [+ adjective, adverb,
literature, religion] 比较的 [bǐjiào de] II N ▶ the
comparative 比较级 [bǐjiàojí]

comparatively [kəm'pærətɪvlɪ] ADV (relatively)
[+ easy, safe, peaceful] 相对地 [xiāngduì de]

compare [kəm'pɛə(r)] I VT 比较 [bǐjiào de]
II VI ▶ to compare favourably/unfavourably
(with sth/sb) 比得上/比不上 (某物/某人)
[bǐdeshang/bǐbùshang (mǒuwù/mǒurén)]
III N ▶ beyond or without compare (liter) 无
与伦比 [wúyǔlúnbǐ] ▶ to compare sth with
or to sth (contrast) 将某人/某物与某物相比较
▶ to compare sb/sth to (liken to) 把某人/某物
比作 ▶ compared with or to 与…相比 ▶ you
can't compare… 你不能将…相比 ▶ how does
he compare with his predecessor? 和他前任
比起来他怎么样? ▶ her garden can't compare
with ours 她的花园没法和我们的相比

comparison [kəm'pærɪsn] N [C/U] 比较
[bǐjiào] ▶ it is an unfair comparison 这样比
较是不公平的 ▶ for comparison 以作比较
▶ in or by comparison (with) (与…) 比较起来
▶ (there's) no comparison 不能相提并论

compartment [kəm'pɑːtmənt] N [C] 1 (RAIL)
隔间 [géjiān] 2 [of wallet, fridge etc] 格 [gé]

compass ['kʌmpəs] N [C] 1 (for finding direction)
指南针 [zhǐnánzhēn] 2 (also: pair of compasses)
(for drawing circles) 圆规 [yuánguī] ▶ beyond/
within the compass of (frm) 超出/在…的范围

compassion [kəm'pæʃən] N [U] 同情
[tóngqíng] ▶ sb's compassion for sb 某人对
某人的同情

compassionate [kəm'pæʃənɪt] ADJ [+ person,

look] 有同情心的 [yǒu tóngqíngxīn de] ▶ **on compassionate grounds** 出于特殊照顾

compatible [kəm'pætɪbl] ADJ [+ *people*] 意气相投的 [yìqì xiāngtóu de]; [+ *ideas, activities*] 协调的 [xiétiáo de]; (COMPUT) 兼容的 [jiānróng de] ▶ **to be compatible with sb** 与某人意气相投 [yǔ mǒurén yìqì xiāngtóu]; [*activity, idea* +] 与某物一致; (COMPUT) 与某物兼容

compel [kəm'pɛl] VT ▶ **to compel sb to do sth** 强制某人做某事 [qiángzhì mǒurén zuò mǒushì] ▶ **to feel compelled to do sth** 感到不得不做某事

compelling [kəm'pɛlɪŋ] ADJ [+ *evidence, reason*] 令人信服的 [lìng rén xìnfú de]

compensate ['kɔmpənseɪt] I VT ▶ **to compensate sb (for sth)** (由于某事) 赔偿某人 [(yóuyú mǒushì) péicháng mǒurén] II VI ▶ **to compensate (for sth)** 弥补 (某事) [míbǔ (mǒushì)]

compensation [kɔmpən'seɪʃən] N 1 [U] (*money*) 赔偿金 [péicháng jīn] 2 [C/U] (*fig*) (*for disappointment etc*) 补偿 [bǔcháng] 3 [C/U] (*adjustment*) 补偿 [bǔcháng] ▶ **compensation for sth** (*money*) 因某事而获得的赔偿金; (*fig*) (*for disappointment etc*) 因某事而得到的补偿 ▶ **in compensation (for sth)** (*money*) 作为 (某事的) 赔偿金

compete [kəm'piːt] VI [*companies, rivals* +] 竞争 [jìngzhēng]; (*in contest, game*) 比赛 [bǐsài] ▶ **to compete for sth** [*companies, rivals* +] 争夺某物; (*in contest, game*) 争夺某物 ▶ **to compete with sb/sth (for sth)** [*companies, rivals* +] 与某人/某物竞争 (以得到某物); (*in contest, game*) 与某人/某物竞争 (以获得某奖项)

competence ['kɔmpɪtəns] N [U] 能力 [nénglì]

competent ['kɔmpɪtənt] ADJ [+ *person*] 称职的 [chènzhí de]; [+ *piece of work*] 合格的 [hégé de]

competition [kɔmpɪ'tɪʃən] N 1 [U] (*rivalry*) (*for job, position, between companies*) 竞争 [jìngzhēng] 2 [C] (*contest*) 竞赛 [jìngsài] ▶ **in competition with** 与…竞争

competitive [kəm'pɛtɪtɪv] ADJ 1 [+ *industry, society*] 竞争性的 [jìngzhēngxìng de] 2 [+ *person*] 求胜心切的 [qiúshèngxīnqiè de] 3 [+ *price, product*] 有竞争力的 [yǒu jìngzhēnglì de] 4 [+ *sport*] 竞技性的 [jìngjìxìng de]

competitor [kəm'pɛtɪtə(r)] N [C] 1 (*in business*) 竞争对手 [jìngzhēng duìshǒu] 2 (*participant*) 参赛者 [cānsàizhě]

complacent [kəm'pleɪsnt] ADJ 自满的 [zìmǎn de] ▶ **to be complacent about sth** 对某事疏忽大意

complain [kəm'pleɪn] VI 1 ▶ **to complain (about sth)** (*to relevant person*) (就某事) 投诉 [jiù mǒushì) tóusù]; (*grumble*) (就某事) 诉苦 [(jiù mǒushì) sùkǔ] 2 (MED) ▶ **to complain of sth** 诉说某病痛 [sùshuō mǒu bìngtòng] ▶ **to complain to sb (about sth)** (就某事) 向某人投

诉 ▶ **to complain that...** 抱怨…

complaint [kəm'pleɪnt] N 1 [U] (*criticism*) 抱怨 [bàoyuàn] 2 [U] (*complaining*) 投诉 [tóusù] 3 [C] (*reason for complaining*) 抱怨的原因 [bàoyuàn de yuányīn] 4 [C] (*illness*) 疾病 [jíbìng] ▶ **to make a complaint (to sb)** (向某人) 投诉

complement [n 'kɔmplɪmənt, vb 'kɔmplɪmɛnt] I N [C] 1 ▶ **a complement (to sth)** (*enhancement*) (与某物) 互补的东西 [(yǔ mǒuwù) hùbǔ de dōngxi]; (*supplement*) (某物的) 补充 [(mǒuwù de) bǔchōng] 2 [*of staff, things*] 需要/允许的数额 [xūyào/yǔnxǔ de shù'é] 3 (LING) 补语 [bǔyǔ] II VT 1 (*enhance*) 与…相辅相成 [yǔ…xiāngfǔxiāngchéng] 2 (*supplement*) 与…配套 [yǔ…pèitào] 3 (*combine well with*) 互补 [hùbǔ] ▶ **to have a full complement of** …都齐全了

请勿将 **complement** 和 **compliment** 混淆。**complement** 指使某事物变得完整、良好或者有效。例如，如果一种食物 **complement** 另一种食物，或是另一种食物的 **complement**，表示这两种食物搭配得很好。如果两个人彼此 **complement**，表示他们的个性相符。*Rice is a good complement to curry...He complements his wife perfectly.* 如果你 **compliment** 某人，或者 **pay them a compliment**，表示你欣赏他们或对他们赞赏有加。*I always compliment her cooking skills...She blushed every time he paid her a compliment.*

complementary [kɔmplɪ'mɛntərɪ] ADJ [+ *approaches, skills*] 互补的 [hùbǔ de]; [+ *medicine, therapies*] 非传统的 [fēi chuántǒng de]

○ complete [kəm'pliːt] I ADJ 1 (*total*) 完全的 [wánquán de] 2 (*whole*) 完整的 [wánzhěng de] 3 (*finished*) 完成的 [wánchéng de] II VT 1 (*finish*) [+ *piece of work, building*] 完成 [wánchéng] [+ *collection, set etc*] [*person* +] 使完整 [shǐ wánzhěng]; [*thing* +] 使完美 [shǐ wánměi] 3 (*fill in*) [+ *form, coupon*] 填写 [tiánxiě] ▶ **complete with** 附带

completely [kəm'pliːtlɪ] ADV [+ *different, satisfied, untrue etc*] 完全 [wánquán]; [*forget, destroy etc* +] 彻底 [chèdǐ]

completion [kəm'pliːʃən] N [U] [*of project, piece of work, building*] 完成 [wánchéng]; [*of sale*] 正式完成 [zhèngshì wánchéng] ▶ **to be nearing completion** 接近尾声 [chèdǐ] ▶ **on completion of sth** 某物完成后

complex ['kɔmplɛks] I ADJ 复杂的 [fùzá de] II N [C] 1 (*group of buildings*) 综合性建筑 [zōnghéxìng jiànzhù] 2 (PSYCH) 情绪 [qíngjié] ▶ **to have a complex about sth** 对某事有强烈的情绪反应

complexion [kəm'plɛkʃən] N [C] 1 (*colouring*) 面色 [miànsè] 2 (*frm*) [*of event etc*] 性质 [xìngzhì]

compliance [kəmˈplaɪəns] N [U] 遵从
[zūncóng] ▶ **compliance with sth** 遵守某事
▶ **in compliance with...** 服从…

complicate [ˈkɒmplɪkeɪt] VT 使复杂化 [shǐ
fùzá huà] ▶ **to complicate matters** or **things
further,...** 更加复杂的是…

complicated [ˈkɒmplɪkeɪtɪd] ADJ 复杂的
[fùzá de]

complication [kɒmplɪˈkeɪʃən] N 1 [C/U]
(problem) 问题 [wèntí] 2 [C] (MED) 并发症
[bìngfāzhèng]

compliment [n ˈkɒmplɪmənt, vb
ˈkɒmplɪment] I N [C] 1 (remark) 赞美 [zànměi]
2 (action) 荣幸 [róngxìng] II VT 赞美 [zànměi]
▶ **to pay sb a compliment** 赞美某人 ▶ **to take
sth as a compliment** 把某事当作是对自己的
肯定 ▶ **(my) compliments to the chef!** 向厨师
致意！ ▶ **to compliment sb on sth** 为某事赞美
某某人 ▶ **to compliment sb for doing sth** 因为
做某事赞美某人
▉用法参见 **complement**

complimentary [kɒmplɪˈmentərɪ] ADJ
1 (approving) [+ remark] 赞美的 [zànměi de];
[+ person] 赞不绝口的 [zànbùjuékǒu de] 2 (free)
[+ ticket, seat, copy] 赠送的 [zèngsòng de] ▶ **to
be complimentary about sb/sth** 对某人/某事
赞不绝口

comply [kəmˈplaɪ] VI ▶ **to comply (with sth)**
[person +] 遵从 (某事) [zūncóng (mǒushì)];
[thing +] 遵守 (某事) [zūnshǒu (mǒushì)]

component [kəmˈpəʊnənt] I N [C] [of plan]
组成部分 [zǔchéng bùfen]; [of weapon, body,
substance] 成分 [chéngfèn]; (IND, COMM) (for
machinery etc) 部件 [bùjiàn] II ADJ [+ parts,
elements] 组成的 [zǔchéng de]

compose [kəmˈpəʊz] VT 1 ▶ **to be composed
of** 由…组成 [yóu... zǔchéng] 2 (write) [+ music]
创作 [chuàngzuò]; (frm) [+ poem, letter] 写 [xiě]
▶ **to compose o.s.** 使自己镇定下来

composed [kəmˈpəʊzd] ADJ (calm) 沉着的
[chénzhuó de]

composer [kəmˈpəʊzə(r)] N [C] 作曲家
[zuòqǔjiā]

composition [kɒmpəˈzɪʃən] N 1 [U] (make-up)
[of thing] 组成 [zǔchéng]; [of substance] 构成
成分 [gòuchéng chéngfèn]; [of group] 结构
[jiégòu] 2 [C] (essay) 作文 [zuòwén] 3 [C/U]
(MUS) 作品 [zuòpǐn]

composure [kəmˈpəʊʒə(r)] N [U] [of person] 镇
静 [zhènjìng] ▶ **to keep/lose one's composure**
保持/不失镇静 ▶ **to regain one's composure**
恢复镇静

compound [n, adj ˈkɒmpaʊnd, vb kəmˈpaʊnd]
I N [C] 1 (CHEM) 化合物 [huàhéwù]
2 (enclosure) 场地 [chǎngdì] 3 (LING) 复合词
[fùhé cí] II ADJ 1 [+ structure, eye, leaf etc] 复合的
[fùhé de] 2 (LING) 复合的 [fùhé de] III VT (frm)
[+ problem, tragedy] 使…更糟 [shǐ...gèngzāo]

comprehend [kɒmprɪˈhend] (frm) VT 理解
[lǐjiě]

comprehension [kɒmprɪˈhenʃən] N 1 [U]
(understanding) 理解 [lǐjiě] 2 [C/U] (SCOL) 理
解力练习 [lǐjiělì liànxí] ▶ **it's beyond my
comprehension** 我无法理解

comprehensive [kɒmprɪˈhensɪv] I ADJ
1 [+ review, list] 全面的 [quánmiàn de] 2 [+ of
insurance] 综合的 [zōnghé de] II N [C] (BRIT)
(also: **comprehensive school**) 综合性中学
[zōnghéxìng zhōngxué]

compress [vb kəmˈpres, n ˈkɒmpres] I VT
1 [+ gas, material etc] 压缩 [yāsuō] ▷ Moira
compressed her lips and looked away. 莫伊拉紧抿着
嘴，朝别处看去。2 (summarize) [+ text, information]
概括 [gàikuò] 3 (COMPUT) [+ data, file] 压缩
[yāsuō] II N [C] (MED) 敷布 [fūbù]

comprise [kəmˈpraɪz] (frm) VT 1 (consist of) (also:
be comprised of) 包括 [bāokuò] 2 (constitute)
构成 [gòuchéng]

compromise [ˈkɒmprəmaɪz] I N [C/U] 妥协
[tuǒxié] II VI 妥协 [tuǒxié] III VT [+ beliefs,
principles] 损害 [sǔnhài] IV CPD [复合词]
[+ decision, solution] 折中 [zhézhōng] ▶ **to
compromise with sb** 与某人妥协

compulsion [kəmˈpʌlʃən] N 1 [C] (desire,
impulse) 强烈的欲望 [qiángliè de yùwàng]
2 [U] (pressure) 强制 [qiángzhì]

compulsive [kəmˈpʌlsɪv] ADJ [+ liar, gambler]
强迫性的 [qiángpòxìng de] ▶ **it's compulsive
reading/viewing** 这是本/部令人着迷的
书/片子

compulsory [kəmˈpʌlsərɪ] ADJ 必须的 [bìxū
de]; [+ course] 必修的 [bìxiū de] ▷ compulsory
military service 义务兵役 ▶ **to make sth
compulsory** 使某事强制化 ▶ **it is compulsory
to wear a seat belt** 必须系安全带

computer [kəmˈpjuːtə(r)] I N [C] 计算机
[jìsuànjī] II CPD [复合词] [+ language, program,
system, technology etc] 电脑 [diànnǎo] ▶ **it was
designed by computer** 这是由电脑设计的

computer game N [C] 电脑游戏 [diànnǎo
yóuxì]

computer programmer N [C] 电脑编程员
[diànnǎo biānchéngyuán]

computer programming [-ˈprəʊɡræmɪŋ] N
[U] 电脑编程 [diànnǎo biānchéng]

computer science N [U] 计算机科学
[jìsuànjī kēxué]

computer studies N [U] 计算机学
[jìsuànjīxué]

computing [kəmˈpjuːtɪŋ] I N [U] 计算机运
用 [jìsuànjī yùnyòng]; (also: **computing studies**)
计算机学 [jìsuànjīxué] II CPD [复合词] [+ course,
skills] 电脑 [diànnǎo]

con [kɒn] (inf) I VT 1 (deceive) 欺骗 [qīpiàn]
2 (cheat) ▶ **to con sb (out of sth)** 骗取某人 (某
物) [piànqǔ mǒurén (mǒuwù)] II N [C] (trick)

骗局 [piànjú] ▶ **to con sb into doing sth** 骗某人去做某事

conceal [kən'siːl] VT [+ object] 隐藏 [yǐncáng]; [+ secret, emotion] 掩饰 [yǎnshì] ▶ **to conceal sth from sb** 对某人隐瞒某事

concede [kən'siːd] I VT (admit) 承认 [chéngrèn] II VI 让步 [ràngbù] ▶ **to concede that...** 承认…

conceited [kən'siːtɪd] ADJ 自高自大的 [zì gāo zì dà de]

conceive [kən'siːv] I VT 1 [+ child] 怀上 [huáishang] 2 [+ idea, plan] 构想出 [gòuxiǎngchū] II VI 1 [woman, female animal +] 怀孕 [huáiyùn] 2 (imagine) ▶ **I cannot conceive of...** 我不能想象… ▶ **I cannot conceive how/why...** 我不能想像怎么/为什么…

concentrate ['kɔnsəntreɪt] I VI 集中精力 [jízhōng jīnglì] II VT 1 ▶ **to be concentrated in** [+ place] 集中在 [jízhōngzài] 2 ▶ **to concentrate one's energies/attention on sth** 集中精力/注意力于某事 [jízhōng jīnglì/zhùyìlì yú mǒushì] ▶ **to concentrate on sth** (keep attention on) 全神贯注于某事; (focus on) 集中注意力于某事 ▶ **to concentrate on doing sth** 集中精力于做某事

concentrated ['kɔnsəntreɪtɪd] ADJ 1 [+ juice, solution] 浓缩的 [nóngsuō de] 2 [+ effort, attempt] 集中的 [jízhōng de]

concentration [kɔnsən'treɪʃən] N 1 [U] (ability to concentrate) 专心 [zhuānxīn] 2 [U] (focus) ▶ **concentration on sth/on doing sth** 集中于某事/做某事 [jízhōng yú mǒushì/zuò mǒushì] 3 [C/U] (in one area, space) 集中 [jízhōng] 4 [C/U] (CHEM) 浓度 [nóngdù]

concept ['kɔnsɛpt] N [C] 概念 [gàiniàn]

⊙ concern [kən'səːn] I N 1 [U] (anxiety) 担忧 [dānyōu] ▷ There is no cause for concern. 没必要担忧。 2 [C] (cause of anxiety) 关切的事 [guānqiè de shì] ▷ Unemployment was the electorate's main concern. 失业是选民最关切的事。 3 [U/S] (care) 关心 [guānxīn] 4 [S] (affair) 事务 [shìwù] ▷ That's your concern. 那是你的事。 5 [C] (firm) 公司 [gōngsī] ▷ It's a family concern. 这是个家族公司。 II VT 1 (worry) 使担忧 [shǐ dānyōu] ▷ One of the things that concerns me is the rise in vandalism. 令我担忧的问题之一是蓄意破坏案件的上升。 2 (be about) 关于 [guānyú] ▷ The book concerns two middle-aged men. 这本书是有关两位中年男性的。 3 (involve) 关系到 [guānxì dào] ▷ That doesn't concern you. 这跟你没关系。 ▶ **that's none of your concern** 这不关你事儿 ▶ **concern for sb** 为某人担心 ▶ **it concerns me that...** 令我担心的是… ▶ **to concern o.s. with** 关心 ▶ **as far as I'm concerned** 据我看来 ▶ **as far as his career is concerned** 就他的事业来说 ▶ **"to whom it may concern"** "致有关人士" ▶ **the people concerned** (in question) 有关人士; (involved) 相关人士

concerned [kən'səːnd] ADJ (worried) 担心的 [dānxīn de] ▶ **to be concerned about sb/sth** 担心某人/某事 ▶ **to be concerned that...** 担心… ▶ **we're concerned for her** 我们为她担忧 ▶ **to be concerned with sth** (be worried about) 关心某事; (be about) 关于某事

concerning [kən'səːnɪŋ] PREP 关于 [guānyú]

concert ['kɔnsət] N [C] 音乐会 [yīnyuèhuì] ▶ **in concert** (MUS) 现场表演; (frm) (together) 合作

concerted [kən'səːtɪd] ADJ [+ effort, action] 一致的 [yīzhì de]

concert hall N [C] 音乐厅 [yīnyuètīng]

concession [kən'sɛʃən] N [C] 1 (compromise) 让步 [ràngbù] 2 (right) 特许权 [tèxǔquán] 3 (BRIT) (reduced price) 减价 [jiǎnjià] [美 = reduction]

concise [kən'saɪs] ADJ [+ description, text] 简洁的 [jiǎnjié de]

conclude [kən'kluːd] I VT 1 (finish) 结束 [jiéshù] 2 (frm) [+ treaty, deal, agreement] 缔结 [dìjié] II VI ▶ **to conclude with sth** [event +] 以某物而告终 [yǐ mǒuwù ér gàozhōng]; [speaker +] 以某物收尾 [yǐ mǒuwù shōuwěi] ▶ **I'd like to conclude by saying...** 我想讲的最后一句话是… ▶ **to conclude that...** 断定… ▶ **"that," he concluded, "is why we did it"** "那," 他断定说, "就是我们这样做的原因"

conclusion [kən'kluːʒən] N 1 [S] (end) [of speech, chapter] 结尾 [jiéwěi] 2 [S] (frm) [of treaty, deal, agreement] 缔结 [dìjié] 3 [C] (deduction) 结论 [jiélùn] ▶ **to come to the conclusion that...** 得出的结论是… ▶ **in conclusion** 总之

conclusive [kən'kluːsɪv] ADJ [+ evidence, proof] 确凿的 [quèzáo de]

concrete ['kɔnkriːt] I N [U] 混凝土 [hùnníngtǔ] II ADJ 1 (lit) [+ block, floor] 混凝土的 [hùnníngtǔ de] 2 (fig) [+ proposal, evidence] 确实的 [quèshí de]

concussion [kən'kʌʃən] N [U] 脑震荡 [nǎozhèndàng]

condemn [kən'dɛm] VT 1 (denounce) 谴责 [qiǎnzé] 2 (sentence) ▶ **to condemn sb to death/life imprisonment** etc 判处某人死刑/无期徒刑[等] [pànchǔ mǒurén sǐxíng/wúqī túxíng [děng]] 3 (declare unsafe) [+ building] 宣告…不适于居住 [xuāngào...bù shìyú jūzhù]

condemnation [kɔndɛm'neɪʃən] N [C/U] 谴责 [qiǎnzé]

condensation [kɔndɛn'seɪʃən] N [U] 凝结的小水珠 [níngjié de xiǎoshuǐzhū]

condense [kən'dɛns] I VT [+ report, book] 使简缩 [shǐ jiǎnsuō] II VI [vapour +] 凝结 [níngjié]

⊙ condition [kən'dɪʃən] I N 1 [S] (state) 状态 [zhuàngtài] ▷ You can't go home in that condition. 在那种状态下你不能回家。 2 [C] (stipulation) 条件 [tiáojiàn] ▷ the conditions of our release 我们释放的条件 3 [C] (illness) 疾病 [jíbìng]

▷ *Hypothermia is an extremely complex condition.* 体温过低是种非常复杂的疾病。 II VT 1 ▸ **to condition sb (to do sth)** 训练某人（做某事）[xùnliàn mǒurén (zuò mǒushì)] ▷ *We are conditioned to think that way.* 我们被训练成那样思考。 2 [+ *hair, skin*] 使状况良好 [shǐ zhuàngkuàng liánghǎo] III **conditions** NPL 环境 [huánjìng] ▷ *People are living in appalling conditions.* 人们的居住环境糟糕透了。 ▸ **in good/poor condition** 状况良好/不好 ▸ **out of condition** 健康状况欠佳 ▸ **a heart condition** 心脏病 ▸ **weather conditions** 天气形势 ▸ **on condition that...** 在…条件下

conditional [kən'dɪʃənl] I ADJ 有条件的 [yǒu tiáojiàn de] II N (LING) ▸ **the conditional** 条件从句 [tiáojiàn cóngjù] ▸ **to be conditional on** or **upon sth** 视某事而定

conditioner [kən'dɪʃənə(r)] N [C/U] 1 (*for hair*) 护发素 [hùfàsù] 2 (*for fabric*) 柔顺剂 [róushùnjì]

condo ['kɔndəu] (US: *inf*) N [C] 1 (*apartment*) 产权归住户者所有的公寓套房 2 (*building*) 产权归住房者所有的公寓楼

condom ['kɔndəm] N [C] 安全套 [ānquán tào]

condominium [kɔndə'mɪnɪəm] (US) N [C] 1 (*apartment*) 产权归住房者所有的公寓套房 2 (*building*) 产权归住房者所有的公寓楼

condone [kən'dəun] VT [+ *misbehaviour, crime*] 容忍 [róngrěn]

conduct [*n* 'kɔndʌkt, *vb* kən'dʌkt] I N 1 [U] [*of person*] 行为 [xíngwéi] 2 [S] [*of task, activity*] 方式 [fāngshì] II VT 1 [+ *survey, research, experiment etc*] 进行 [jìnxíng] 2 [+ *life*] 表现 [biǎoxiàn] 3 [+ *orchestra, choir etc*] 指挥 [zhǐhuī] 4 [+ *heat, electricity*] 传导 [chuándǎo] ▸ **to conduct o.s.** (*behave*) 表现

conducted tour [kən'dʌktɪd-] N [C] 1 [*of area*] 有导游解说的旅游 [yǒu dǎoyóu jièshuō de lǚyóu] 2 [*of building*] 有导游解说的参观 [yǒu dǎoyóu jièshuō de cānguān]

conductor [kən'dʌktə(r)] N [C] 1 [*of orchestra*] 指挥家 [zhǐhuījiā] 2 (US) (*on train*) 列车员 [lièchēyuán] [英= **guard**] 3 (*on bus*) 售票员 [shòupiàoyuán] 4 (ELEC) 导体 [dǎotǐ]

cone [kəun] N [C] 1 (*shape*) 圆锥体 [yuánzhuītǐ] 2 (also: **traffic cone**) 锥形路标 [zhuīxíng lùbiāo] 3 (*on tree*) 球果 [qiúguǒ] 4 (also: **ice cream cone**) 锥形蛋卷冰淇淋 [zhuīxíng dànjuǎn bīngqílín] 5 (*ice cream*) 蛋筒 [dàntǒng]

confectioner's sugar [kən'fɛkʃənəz-] (US) N [U] 糖粉 [tángfěn] [英= **icing sugar**]

confectionery [kən'fɛkʃənrɪ] (*frm*) N [U] 甜食 [tiánshí]

confer [kən'fə:(r)] I VT (*frm*) ▸ **to confer sth (on sb)** [+ *power, authority, status*] 授予（某人）某物 [shòuyǔ (mǒurén) mǒuwù]; [+ *advantage, benefit*] （给某人）带来某利 [(gěi mǒurén) dàilái mǒuwù]; [+ *degree*] 授予（某人）某物 [shòuyǔ (mǒurén) mǒuwù] II VI ▸ **to confer (with sb**

about sth) （就某事和某人）商议 [(jiù mǒushì hé mǒurén) shāngyì]

conference ['kɔnfərəns] N [C] (*meeting*) 会议 [huìyì] ▸ **to be in conference** 在开会

confess [kən'fɛs] I VI (*to sin, crime*) 坦白 [tǎnbái] II VT [+ *sin, guilt, crime*] 坦白 [tǎnbái]; [+ *weakness, ignorance*] 承认 [chéngrèn] ▸ **to confess to sth/to doing sth** 承认某事/做了某事 ▸ **to confess sth to sb** 向某人坦白某事 ▸ **I must confess that...** 我得承认…

confession [kən'fɛʃən] N 1 [C/U] (*admission*) 坦白 [tǎnbái] 2 [C] (*written*) 供认状 [gòngrèn zhuàng] 3 [C/U] (REL) 忏悔 [chànhuǐ] ▸ **to make a confession** 坦白 ▸ **to go to confession** (REL) 作忏悔

confide [kən'faɪd] I VI ▸ **to confide in sb** 向某人吐露秘密 [xiàng mǒurén tǔlù mìmì] II VT ▸ **to confide sth to sb** 向某人倾吐某事 [xiàng mǒurén qīngtǔ mǒushì] ▸ **to confide to sb that...** 向某人吐露…

confidence ['kɔnfɪdns] N 1 [U] (*faith*) 信赖 [xìnlài] 2 [U] (*self-assurance*) 自信 [zìxìn] 3 [C] (*secret*) 秘密 [mìmì] ▸ **to have (every) confidence in sb/sth** 对某人/某事（很）有信心 ▸ **to have (every) confidence that...** 对（很）有信心… ▸ **to take sb into one's confidence** 把某人作为知心人 ▸ **in confidence** [*speak, say, write etc* +] 秘密地

confident ['kɔnfɪdənt] ADJ (*self-assured*) 自信的 [zìxìn de] ▸ **to be confident that...** 有信心… ▸ **to be confident of sth/of doing sth** 对某事/做某事充满信心 ▸ **to be confident about sth** 对某事充满信心

confidential [kɔnfɪ'dɛnʃəl] ADJ [+ *report, information*] 机密的 [jīmì de]; [+ *tone*] 表示信任的 [biǎoshì xìnrèn de]

confine [kən'faɪn] VT 1 (*imprison*) ▸ **to confine sb to sth** 将某人限制在某处 [jiāng mǒurén xiànzhì zài mǒuchù] 2 (*limit*) ▸ **to confine sth (to sth)** 控制某物（在某物之内）[kòngzhì mǒuwù (zài mǒuwù zhī nèi)] ▸ **to confine o.s. to sth/to doing sth** 只局限于某事/做某事

confined [kən'faɪnd] ADJ [+ *space, area*] 狭小的 [xiáxiǎo de] ▸ **to be confined to** [+ *place, group*] 仅限于…

confines ['kɔnfaɪnz] NPL (*boundaries*) [*of area*] 范围 [fànwéi]; (*limitations*) [*of situation*] 界限 [jièxiàn]

confirm [kən'fə:m] VT 1 (*verify*) [+ *statement, report, story etc*] 肯定 [kěndìng]; [+ *appointment, date*] 确认 [quèrèn] 2 (*bear out*) [+ *suspicion, fear*] 证实 [zhèngshí] 3 (REL) 给…施坚信礼 [gěi…shī jiānxìnlǐ] ▸ **to confirm that...** [*person, data* +] 证实…

confirmation [kɔnfə'meɪʃən] N [C/U] 1 (*verification*) [*of belief, statement, report etc*] 证实 [zhèngshí] 2 [*of appointment, date*] 确认 [quèrèn] 3 (REL) 坚信礼 [jiānxìn lǐ]

confiscate ['kɒnfɪskeɪt] VT 没收 [mòshōu]
▶ **to confiscate sth from sb** 没收某人的某物

conflict [n 'kɒnflɪkt, vb kən'flɪkt] I N 1 [U] (disagreement, fighting) 冲突 [chōngtū] **2** [C/U] (difference) [of interests, loyalties etc] 矛盾 [máodùn] II VI 1 ▶ **to conflict with sth** [opinions, research etc +] 与某事截然不同 [yǔ mǒushì jiéránbùtóng] III N ▶ **to be in conflict (with sb)** (与某人) 发生冲突 [(yǔ mǒurén) fāshēng chōngtū]

conform [kən'fɔːm] VI 循规蹈矩 [xúnguīdǎojǔ] ▶ **to conform to sth** [+ expectations, regulations etc] 与某事物相符

confront [kən'frʌnt] VT 1 [+ opponent, enemy] 面对 [miànduì] **2** (fig) [problem, task +] 面对 [miànduì] ▶ **to be confronted with sth** [+ problem, task] 面临某事

confrontation [kɒnfrən'teɪʃən] N [C/U] (dispute) 对抗 [duìkàng]; (fight) 冲突 [chōngtū]

confuse [kən'fjuːz] VT 1 (perplex) 把…弄糊涂 [bǎ…nòng hútu] **2** (mix up) 混淆 [hùnxiáo] **3** (complicate) 搞乱 [gǎoluàn] ▶ **to confuse sb/sth with sb/sth** 把某人/某物与某人/某物搞混

confused [kən'fjuːzd] ADJ 1 (bewildered) 困惑的 [kùnhuò de] **2** (disordered) 混乱的 [hùnluàn de] ▶ **to get confused** [+ person] 糊涂

confusing [kən'fjuːzɪŋ] ADJ 含混不清的 [hánhùn bùqīng de]

confusion [kən'fjuːʒən] N 1 [C/U] (uncertainty) 惶惑 [huánghuò] **2** [U] (mix-up) 混淆 [hùnxiáo] **3** [C/U] (perplexity) 困惑 [kùnhuò] **4** [U] (disorder) 混乱 [hùnluàn]

congested [kən'dʒɛstɪd] ADJ 1 [+ road, area] 拥挤不堪的 [yōngjǐbùkān de] **2** (frm) [+ nose, arteries] 不通的 [bùtòng de]

congestion [kən'dʒɛstʃən] N [U] 1 (of road) 堵塞 [dǔsè] **2** (in nose, throat) 堵塞 [dǔsè]; (in lungs) 充血 [chōngxuè]

Congo ['kɒŋgəʊ] N 刚果 [Gāngguǒ]

congratulate [kən'grætjuleɪt] VT 祝贺 [zhùhè] ▶ **to congratulate sb on sth/on doing sth** 祝贺某人某事/做某事

congratulations [kəngrætjʊ'leɪʃənz] NPL 祝贺 [zhùhè] ▶ **congratulations!** 恭喜 [gōngxǐ] ▶ **congratulations on your engagement!** 祝贺你订婚了!

congregation [kɒŋgrɪ'geɪʃən] N [C] 教堂会众 [jiàotáng huìzhòng]

congress ['kɒŋgrɛs] N [C] 1 (conference) 代表大会 [dàibiǎo dàhuì] **2** (US) ▶ **Congress** 国会 [guóhuì]

congressman ['kɒŋgrɛsmən] (pl **congressmen**) (US) N [C] 国会议员 [guóhuì yìyuán]

congresswoman ['kɒŋgrɛswʊmən] (pl **congresswomen**) (US) N [C] 女国会议员 [nǔ guóhuì yìyuán]

conifer ['kɒnɪfə(r)] N [C] 针叶树 [zhēnyèshù]

conjunction [kən'dʒʌŋkʃən] (LING) N [C] 连词 [liáncí] ▶ **in conjunction with** 与…一道

conjure ['kʌndʒə(r)] VI [magician +] 变魔术 [biàn móshù]
▶ **conjure up** VT [+ memory, image] 使…浮现于脑际 [shǐ…fúxiàn yú nǎojì]

connect [kə'nɛkt] VT 1 (join) 连接 [liánjiē] **2** (TEL) [+ caller] 给…接通 [gěi…jiētōng]; [+ telephone, subscriber] 接通 [jiētōng] **3** (fig) (associate) 将…联系起来 [jiāng…liánxì qǐlái] II VI ▶ **to connect with** [+ train, plane etc] 与…联运 [yǔ…liányùn] ▶ **to connect sth to sth** (join) 将某物与某物连接起来; (to electricity supply etc) 将某物与某物接通 ▶ **to connect sth with sth** (join) 将某物与某物连接起来 ▶ **to connect sb/sth with sb/sth** (associate) 将某人/某物与某人/某物联系起来 ▶ **to be connected with sth** (associated) 与某事有关系

connection [kə'nɛkʃən] I N 1 [C/U] (link) 联系 [liánxì] **2** [C] (ELEC) 接头 [jiētóu] **3** [C] (train, plane etc) 联运 [liányùn] **4** [C] (TEL) (for caller, new subscriber) 接通 [jiētōng] II **connections** NPL (people) 熟人 [shúrén] ▶ **what is the connection between them?** 他们之间有什么关系? ▶ **to have a connection with or to sb/sth** 与某人/某物有联系 ▶ **in connection with** 与…有关 ▶ **to miss/get one's connection** 误了/赶上要换的交通工具

conquer ['kɒŋkə(r)] VT 1 [+ country, enemy] 征服 [zhēngfú] **2** [+ fear, feelings, problem] 克服 [kèfú]

conquest ['kɒŋkwɛst] N 1 [C/U] [of country, space etc] 征服 [zhēngfú] **2** [C] (sexual) 俘虏 [fúlǔ]

cons [kɒnz] NPL 1 = **conveniences** see **mod cons 2** see **pro**

conscience ['kɒnʃəns] N 1 [C] (sense of morality) 是非感 [shìfēi gǎn] **2** [U] (belief) 良心 [liángxin] ▶ **to have a guilty/clear conscience** 感到内疚/问心无愧 ▶ **to have sth on one's conscience** 因某事而感到内疚 ▶ **in all** or **good conscience** (frm) 凭良心

conscientious [kɒnʃɪ'ɛnʃəs] ADJ 认真的 [rènzhēn de] ▶ **to be conscientious about sth/about doing sth** 认真地对待某事/做某事

conscious ['kɒnʃəs] ADJ 1 (awake) 清醒的 [qīngxǐng de] **2** (deliberate) [+ decision, effort] 蓄意的 [xùyì de] ▶ **to be conscious of sth** 意识到某事 ▶ **to be conscious that…** 意识到… ▶ **to be politically conscious/health-conscious** 有政治/健康意识 ▶ **to become conscious of/that** 意识到

consciousness ['kɒnʃəsnɪs] N 1 [U] (MED) 知觉 [zhījué] **2** [C/U] (mind) 脑海 [nǎohǎi] **3** [U] (mentality) [of group, society etc] 意识 [yìshi] ▶ **to lose consciousness** 失去知觉 ▶ **to regain consciousness** 恢复知觉

consecutive [kən'sɛkjutɪv] ADJ 连续的 [liánxù de]

consensus [kən'sɛnsəs] N [S] 一致 [yīzhì]

▶ the consensus (of opinion) is that... 一致的(意见)是…

consent [kən'sɛnt] I N [U] 许可 [xǔkě] II VI ▶ to consent (to do sth) 同意(做某事) [tóngyì (zuò mǒushì)] ▶ to consent to sth 同意(某事) ▶ to give one's consent 同意 ▶ by common or mutual consent 经一致同意

consequence ['kɔnsɪkwəns] N 1 [c] (result) 后果 [hòuguǒ] 2 (importance) ▶ of consequence 重要性 [zhòngyàoxìng] ▶ in consequence 因而 ▶ it's of little/no consequence 这是无关紧要的

consequently ['kɔnsɪkwəntlɪ] ADV 所以 [suǒyǐ]

conservation [kɔnsə'veɪʃən] N [U] (of environment) 环保 [huánbǎo]; (of energy etc) 节约 [jiéyuē]; (of paintings, books, buildings, species) 保护 [bǎohù]

conservative [kən'sə:vətɪv] I ADJ 1 (traditional) [+ person, attitude] 保守的 [bǎoshǒu de] 2 (cautious) [+ estimate] 保守的 [bǎoshǒu de] 3 (right-wing) 右派的 [yòupài de] 4 (BRIT: POL) ▶ Conservative 保守党的 [bǎoshǒudǎng de] II N [c] 1 (right-wing) 保守主义者 [bǎoshǒuzhǔyìzhě] 2 (BRIT: POL) ▶ Conservative 保守党人士 [bǎoshǒudǎng rénshì]

Conservative Party (BRIT) N ▶ the Conservative Party 保守党 [bǎoshǒudǎng]

conservatory [kən'sə:vətrɪ] N [c] 1 (on house) 暖房 [nuǎnfáng] 2 (MUS) 音乐学院 [yīnyuè xuéyuàn]

conserve [vb kən'sə:v, n 'kɔnsə:v] I VT [+ resources, supplies, energy] 保存 [bǎocún]; [+ forest, building, species] 保护 [bǎohù] II N [C/U] (jam) 果酱 [guǒjiàng]

○ consider [kən'sɪdə(r)] VT 1 (think about) 考虑 [kǎolù] ▷ They are having a meeting to consider the report. 他们在开会考虑这份报告。 2 (take into account) 考虑到 [kǎolù dào] ▷ You have to consider the feelings of others. 你需要考虑到其他人的感觉。 3 (believe) ▶ to consider sb (to be) an idiot/a coward etc 认为某人是傻子/胆小鬼{等} [rènwéi mǒurén shì shǎzi/dǎnxiǎoguǐ {děng}] ▶ to consider doing sth 考虑做某事 ▶ all things considered 考虑到各个方面 ▶ they consider themselves (to be) superior/happy 他们认为自己高人一等/开心 ▶ she considered it a disaster 她认为这是个灾难

considerable [kən'sɪdərəbl] ADJ 相当的 [xiāngdāng de]

considerably [kən'sɪdərəblɪ] ADV [improve, vary +] 在很大程度上 [zài hěndà chéngdùshang]; [+ bigger, smaller etc] 相当地 [xiāngdāng de]

considerate [kən'sɪdərɪt] ADJ 体贴的 [tǐtiē de]

consideration [kənsɪdə'reɪʃən] N 1 [U] (deliberation) 考虑 [kǎolù] 2 [c] (factor) 要

考虑的因素 [yào kǎolù de yīnsù] 3 [U] (thoughtfulness) 考虑周到 [kǎolù zhōudào] ▶ consideration (for) (对…的) 顾及 [(duì…de) gùjí] ▶ to take sth into consideration 考虑到某事 ▶ under consideration 在考虑中 ▶ out of consideration for sb/sth 顾及到某人/某事

considering [kən'sɪdərɪŋ] I PREP 考虑到 [kǎolù dào] II CONJ ▶ considering (that)... 考虑到…[kǎolù dào…]

consignment [kən'saɪnmənt] N [c] 托运 [tuōyùn]

consist [kən'sɪst] VI ▶ to consist of 由…组成 [yóu… zǔchéng]

consistency [kən'sɪstənsɪ] N [U] 1 (in actions, policies etc) 连贯性 [liánguànxìng] 2 (of yoghurt, cream etc) 粘稠度 [niánchóudù]

consistent [kən'sɪstənt] ADJ [+ person] 一贯的 [yīguàn de]; [+ argument, theory, ideas] 一致的 [yīzhì de] ▶ to be consistent with 与…相符

consolation [kɔnsə'leɪʃən] N [C/U] 安慰 [ānwèi]

consolation prize N [c] 1 (in competition) 安慰奖 [ānwèi jiǎng] 2 (fig) 安慰表示 [ānwèi biǎoshì]

console [vb kən'səul, n 'kɔnsəul] I VT 安慰 [ānwèi] II N [c] 操纵台 [cāozòng tái]

consolidate [kən'sɔlɪdeɪt] VT [+ position, power, success] 巩固 [wěngù]

consommé [kən'sɔmeɪ] N [C/U] 清炖肉汤 [qīngdùn ròutāng]

consonant ['kɔnsənənt] N [c] 辅音 [fǔyīn]

conspicuous [kən'spɪkjuəs] ADJ [+ person, feature] 惹人注目的 [rěrén zhùmù de] ▶ to make o.s. conspicuous 引人注目 ▶ he was conspicuous by his absence 他因缺勤而引人注目

conspiracy [kən'spɪrəsɪ] N [C/U] ▶ conspiracy (to do sth) (做某事的) 阴谋 [(zuò mǒushì de) yīnmóu]

constable ['kʌnstəbl] (BRIT) N [c] (最低等级的) 警员 [(zuìdī děngjí de) jǐngyuán]

constant ['kɔnstənt] ADJ 1 (ever-present) [+ threat, pressure, pain, reminder etc] 不断的 [bùduàn de] 2 (repeated) [+ interruptions, demands etc] 重复的 [chóngfù de] 3 (fixed) [+ temperature, speed etc] 恒定的 [héngdìng de]

constant、continual 和 continuous 都可以表示某事持续发生或一直存在。constant 表示某种事情总是发生或从未消失过。*He was in constant pain... Jane's constant criticism...* continual 表示某事在一段时间内经常发生，尤其指人们不愿看到的情况。*...his continual drinking...continual demands to cut costs...* continuous 表示某事一直延续而不停止或毫无停止的迹象。*...days of continuous rain...a continuous background noise...*

constantly ['kɒnstəntlɪ] ADV **1** (repeatedly) 不断地 [bùduàn de] **2** (uninterruptedly) 持续地 [chíxù de]

constipated ['kɒnstɪpeɪtɪd] ADJ 便秘的 [biànmì de]

constipation [kɒnstɪ'peɪʃən] N [U] 便秘 [biànmì]

constituency [kən'stɪtjuənsɪ] N [C] **1** (area) 选区 [xuǎnqū] **2** (people) 选民 [xuǎnmín]

constitute ['kɒnstɪtjuːt] VT **1** (represent) 是 [shì] **2** (comprise) 组成 [zǔchéng]

constitution [kɒnstɪ'tjuːʃən] N [C] **1** [of country] 宪法 [xiànfǎ]; [of club, organization] 章程 [zhāngchéng] **2** (health) 体质 [tǐzhì] **3** (formation) 组成 [zǔchéng] ▶ **she's got the constitution of an ox** 她健壮得像头公牛

constitutional [kɒnstɪ'tjuːʃənl] ADJ [+ right, crisis, reform] 宪法的 [xiànfǎ de]

constraint [kən'streɪnt] N **1** [C] (restriction) 限制 [xiànzhì] **2** [U] (restraint) 约束 [yuēshù] **3** [U] (strain) 约束感 [yuēshù gǎn] ▶ **to do sth under constraint** 受逼迫而做某事

construct [vb kən'strʌkt, n 'kɒnstrʌkt] I VT **1** [+ building, road, machine] 建造 [jiànzào] **2** [+ theory, argument] 构思 [gòusī] II N [C] (idea) 观念 [guānniàn]

construction [kən'strʌkʃən] N **1** [U] [of building, road, machine] 建造 [jiànzào] **2** [C] (structure) 建筑 [jiànzhù] **3** [C] (interpretation) 解释 [jiěshì] ▶ **to be under construction** [building, road etc +] 建造中

constructive [kən'strʌktɪv] ADJ [+ criticism, suggestion, discussion etc] 建设性的 [jiànshèxing de]; [+ person] 有助益的 [yǒu zhùyì de]

consul ['kɒnsl] N [C] 领事 [lǐngshì]

consulate ['kɒnsjʊlɪt] N [C] 领事馆 [lǐngshì guǎn]

consult [kən'sʌlt] VT [+ doctor, lawyer, friend] 咨询 [zīxún]; [+ book, map] 查阅 [cháyuè] ▶ **to consult sb about sth** 就某事向某人咨询

consultant [kən'sʌltənt] I N [C] **1** (ESP BRIT) (doctor) 会诊医师 [huìzhěn yīshī] [美= **specialist**] **2** (adviser) 顾问 [gùwèn] II CPD [复合词] [+ paediatrician, surgeon, psychiatrist] 顾问 [gùwèn] ▶ **a consultant to sb** 某人的顾问

consultation [kɒnsəl'teɪʃən] N **1** [C] (meeting) 磋商会议 [cuōshāng huìyì] **2** [C] (ESP BRIT) (session) (with doctor) 会诊 [huìzhěn]; (with lawyer) 咨询 [zīxún] **3** [U] (discussion) 磋商 [cuōshāng] **4** [U] (ESP BRIT) (obtaining advice) (with doctor) 会诊 [huìzhěn]; (with lawyer) 咨询 [zīxún] ▶ **in consultation with** 与…磋商

consulting room [kən'sʌltɪŋ-] (BRIT: MED) N [C] 诊室 [zhěnchá shì] [美= **doctor's office**]

consume [kən'sjuːm] VT **1** [+ food] 吃 [chī]; [+ drink] 喝 [hē] **2** [+ fuel, energy, time] 消耗 [xiāohào] **3** [fire +] 烧毁 [shāohuǐ] **4** (liter) [emotion, idea +] 充满 [chōngmǎn] ▷ **He was consumed by rage.** 他生气得不得了。

consumer [kən'sjuːmə(r)] N [C] [of goods, services] 消费者 [xiāofèizhě]; [of resources] 使用者 [shǐyòngzhě]

consumption [kən'sʌmpʃən] N [U] **1** (act of consuming) [of food] 进食 [jìnshí]; [of drink] 饮用 [yǐnyòng]; [of fuel, energy etc] 消耗 [xiāohào] **2** (amount consumed) [of food, drink, fuel, energy, etc] 消耗量 [xiāohàoliàng] **3** (buying) 消费 [xiāofèi] **4** (o.f.) (tuberculosis) 肺结核 [fèijiéhé] ▶ **unfit for human consumption** 不适于人类使用

cont. ABBR (= continued) 转至 [zhuǎnzhì]

contact ['kɒntækt] I N **1** [C/U] (communication) 联络 [liánluò] **2** [U] (touch) 接触 [jiēchù] **3** [C] (person) 熟人 [shúrén] II VT 联系 [liánxì] ▶ **to be in contact with sb** 与某人有联络 ▶ **to come into contact with sb/sth** 与某人/某物有接触 ▶ **to make contact (with sb)** (和某人)取得联络 ▶ **to lose contact (with sb)** (与某人)失去联系

contact lenses NPL 隐形眼镜 [yǐnxíng yǎnjìng]

contagious [kən'teɪdʒəs] ADJ **1** [+ disease] 接触传染的 [jiēchù chuánrǎn de] **2** [+ laughter, enthusiasm] 感染性的 [gǎnrǎnxìng de]

contain [kən'teɪn] VT **1** (hold) [+ objects] 装有 [zhuāngyǒu]; [+ component, ingredient etc] 含有 [hányǒu]; [+ letter, report, film +] 包含 [bāohán] **2** (control) [+ growth, spread] 控制 [kòngzhì]; [+ fire, violence] 阻止…的蔓延 [zǔzhǐ…de mànyán]; [+ curiosity, delight] 抑制 [yìzhì] ▶ **I could hardly contain myself** 我几乎不能控制自己

container [kən'teɪnə(r)] N [C] **1** (box, jar etc) 容器 [róngqì] **2** (for transport) 集装箱 [jízhuāngxiāng]

contaminate [kən'tæmɪneɪt] VT [+ water, food, soil etc] 污染 [wūrǎn]

cont'd ABBR (= continued) 转至 [zhuǎnzhì]

contemplate ['kɒntəmpleɪt] VT **1** (consider) [+ course of action] 仔细考虑 [zǐxì kǎolù] **2** (think about) [+ idea, subject] 慎重考虑 [shènzhòng kǎolù] **3** (regard) [+ person, painting etc] 凝视 [níngshì] ▶ **to contemplate doing sth** 想做某事

contemporary [kən'tempərərɪ] I ADJ **1** (present-day) [+ art, music, society, artist etc] 当代的 [dāngdài de] **2** (of the same time) [+ account, writer, artist etc] 同一时代的 [tóngyī shídài de] II N [C] (person) 同代人 [tóngdàirén] ▶ **Shakespeare and his contemporaries** 莎士比亚和他的同代人

contempt [kən'tempt] N [U] 轻视 [qīngshì] ▶ **to have contempt for sb/sth** 瞧不起某人/某物 ▶ **to hold sb in contempt** 藐视某人 ▶ **to be beneath contempt** 实在是不值一顾

▶ **contempt of court** 蔑视法庭

contend [kən'tɛnd] I VI 1 ▶ **to contend with** [+ *problem, difficulty*] 对付 [duìfù] 2 ▶ **to contend for** [+ *power, title, medal, prize*] 争夺 [zhēngduó] II VT ▶ **to contend that…** 争辩道… [zhēngbiàn dào…] ▶ **he has a lot to contend with** 他有许多问题要处理

content¹ ['kɔntɛnt] I N [U] 1 [*of speech, book, film*] 内容 [nèiróng] 2 ▶ **fat/moisture content** 脂肪/水分含量 [zhīfáng/shuǐfèn hánliàng] II **contents** NPL [*of bottle, packet*] 所含之物 [suǒhán zhī wù]; [*of letter, speech*] 内容 [nèiróng] ▶ **(table of) contents** 目录

content² [kən'tɛnt] I ADJ (*satisfied*) 满足的 [mǎnzú de] II VT (*satisfy*) ▶ **to content o.s. with sth/with doing sth** 满足于某事/做某事 [mǎnzú yú mǒushì/zuò mǒushì] ▶ **to be content with sth** 满足于某事 ▶ **to be content to do sth** 乐于做某事

contented [kən'tɛntɪd] ADJ 心满意足的 [xīn mǎn yì zú de]

contentment [kən'tɛntmənt] N [U] 心满意足 [xīnmǎnyìzú]

contest [*n* 'kɔntɛst, *vb* kən'tɛst] I N [C] 1 (*competition*) 比赛 [bǐsài] 2 (*for control, power etc*) 竞争 [jìngzhēng] II VT 1 [+ *statement, decision*] 反驳 [fǎnbó] 2 (ESP BRIT) [+ *election, competition*] 角逐 [juézhú] 3 ▶ **to contest sb's will** 对某人的遗嘱提出质疑 [duì mǒurén de yízhǔ tíchū zhìyí]

contestant [kən'tɛstənt] N [C] 参赛者 [cānsàizhě]

context ['kɔntɛkst] N [C/U] 1 [*of events, ideas etc*] 环境 [huánjìng] 2 [*of word, phrase*] 上下文 [shàngxiàwén] ▶ **in context** 纵观全局 ▶ **out of context** 断章取义

continent ['kɔntɪnənt] N [C] 大陆 [dàlù] ▶ **the Continent** (BRIT) (*mainland Europe*) 欧洲大陆 ▶ **on the Continent** (BRIT) 在欧洲大陆

continental [kɔntɪ'nɛntl] I ADJ 1 (BRIT) (*of the European continent*) [+ *country, Europe*] 欧洲大陆的 [Ōuzhōu dàlù de]; (*typical of European continent*) [+ *person, place, thing*] 欧式的 [Ōushì de] 2 (US) (*on mainland*) 北美大陆的 [běiměi dàlù de] II N [C] (BRIT: *inf*) 欧洲大陆人 [Ōuzhōu dàlùrén]

continental breakfast N [C] 欧洲大陆式早餐 [Ōuzhōu dàlù shì zǎocān]

continual [kən'tɪnjuəl] ADJ 1 (*repeated*) [+ *harassment, demands, changes etc*] 频频的 [pínpín de] 2 (*ceaseless*) [+ *pressure, pain, struggle etc*] 连续不断的 [liánxùbùduàn de]
🔲 用法参见 **constant**

continually [kən'tɪnjuəlɪ] ADV 1 (*repeatedly*) [*change, interrupt, try etc*] 一再地 [yīzài de] 2 (*ceaselessly*) [*evolve, grow, sob etc*] 不停地 [bùtíng de]

continuation [kəntɪnju'eɪʃən] N 1 [U] [*of war, situation etc*] 持续 [chíxù] 2 [C] (*extension*) 继续

[jìxù] 3 [C] [*of story*] 续篇 [xùpiān]

◎continue [kən'tɪnjuː] I VI 1 (*carry on uninterrupted*) [*situation, event etc +*] 继续 [jìxù] 2 (*after interruption*) [*event +*] 继续 [jìxù]; [*speaker +*] 继续说 [jìxù shuō] II VT 1 (*carry on uninterrupted*) 继续 [jìxù] 2 (*after interruption*) 继续 [jìxù]; [*speaker +*] 继续说 [jìxù shuō] ▷ *He arrived in Norway, where he continued his campaign.* 他到达了挪威，继续进行他的运动。▷ "*OK,*" *she continued after a pause.* "好"，她停了一下后继续说。▶ **to continue to do sth** *or* **doing sth** 持续做某事 ▶ **to continue with sth** 继续某事 ▶ **to continue up/along/through sth** 继续上/沿着/走过某处 ▶ **"to be continued"** "未完待续" ▶ **"continued on page 10"** "转至第10页"

continuity [kɔntɪ'njuːɪtɪ] N 1 [C/U] (*in policy, management etc*) 连贯性 [liánguàn xìng] 2 [U] (TV, CINE) 各场景的串联 [gè chǎngjǐng de chuànlián]

continuous [kən'tɪnjuəs] ADJ 1 [+ *process, growth etc*] 连续不停的 [liánxù bù tíng de] 2 [+ *line, surface*] 不断延伸的 [bùduàn yánshēn de] 3 (LING) [+ *tense*] 进行时的 [jìnxíng shí de]
🔲 用法参见 **constant**

continuous assessment (BRIT) N [U] 连续性评估 [liánxù xìng pínggū]

continuously [kən'tɪnjuəslɪ] ADV 持续不断地 [chíxùbùduàn de]

contour ['kɔntuə(r)] N [C] 1 (*shape, outline*) 轮廓 [lúnkuò] 2 (*also:* **contour line**) (*on map*) 地形线 [dìxíng xiàn]

contraception [kɔntrə'sɛpʃən] N [U] 避孕 [bìyùn]

contraceptive [kɔntrə'sɛptɪv] I N [C] (*drug*) 避孕药 [bìyùn yào]; (*device*) 避孕工具 [bìyùn gōngjù] II ADJ [+ *device, method, pill*] 避孕的 [bìyùn de]

contract [*n* 'kɔntrækt, *vb* kən'trækt] I N [C] 合同 [hétong] II VI 1 (*become smaller*) [*metal, muscle +*] 收缩 [shōusuō] 2 ▶ **to contract (with sb) to do sth** （和某人）订做某事的合同 [(hé mǒurén) dìngzuò mǒushì de hétong] III VT [+ *illness*] 感染 [gǎnrǎn] IV CPD [复合词] [+ *work*] 合同 [hétong] ▶ **contract of employment** 工作合同
▶ **contract out** (BRIT) I VT [+ *work*] 把…包出去 [bǎ…bāochūqù] II VI 退出和约 [tuìchū héyuē]

contractor [kən'træktə(r)] N [C] 承包商 [chéngbāoshāng]

contradict [kɔntrə'dɪkt] VT 1 (*challenge*) [+ *person, statement etc*] 驳斥 [bóchì] 2 (*be contrary to*) 与…相悖 [yǔ xiāngbèi]

contradiction [kɔntrə'dɪkʃən] N [C/U] 矛盾 [máodùn] ▶ **a contradiction in terms** 措辞矛盾

contrary¹ ['kɔntrərɪ] I ADJ (*opposite, different*) 相反的 [xiāngfǎn de] II N [C/U] ▶ **the contrary**

相反 [xiāngfǎn] ▶ on the contrary 正相反 ▶ contrary to popular opinion 与公众看法相反 ▶ to the contrary 相反的

请勿将 on the contrary 和 in contrast 混淆。on the contrary 用于驳斥某人或某事,指出他们是错误的。'People just don't do things like that.' – 'On the contrary, they do them all the time.' in contrast 用来表示你现在谈论的内容与先前所说的内容是截然不同的。The company said yesterday that in contrast with much of the rest of the industry, it is currently enjoying rapid growth.

contrary² [kən'trɛərɪ] ADJ (argumentative) 好与人作对的 [hào yǔrén zuòduì de]

contrast [n 'kɒntrɑːst, vb kən'trɑːst] I N [C/U] **1** 明显的差异 [míngxiǎn de chāyì] **2** ▶ to be a contrast to sth 与某物截然不同 [yǔ mǒuwù jiérán bùtóng] II VT 对比 [duìbǐ] III VI ▶ to contrast with sth 与某事形成对照 [yǔ mǒushì xíngchéng duìzhào] ▶ by or in contrast 对比之下 ▶ in contrast to... 与…形成对比 ▶ to contrast sth with sth 将某物与某物进行对比

用法参见 contrary

contribute [kən'trɪbjuːt] I VI ▶ to contribute (to sth) (help) (为某事) 做出贡献 [(wèi mǒushì) zuò gòngxiàn]; (with money) (给某事) 捐助 [(gěi mǒushì) juānzhù]; (write articles) (为某刊) 撰稿 [(wèi mǒukān) zhuàngǎo]; (be a cause) 造成 (某事) [zàochéng (mǒushì)] II VT ▶ to contribute 10 pounds (to sth) (给某事) 捐献10英镑 [(gěi mǒushì) juānxiàn shí yīngbàng] ▶ to contribute an article to sth 给某刊投稿

contribution [kɒntrɪ'bjuːʃən] I N [C] **1** (donation) 捐献 [juānxiàn] **2** (help) 贡献 [gòngxiàn] **3** (article) 稿件 [gǎojiàn] II contributions NPL (BRIT) 定期扣缴 [dìngqí kòujiǎo]

contributor [kən'trɪbjutə(r)] N [C] **1** (to appeal, fund) 捐献者 [juānxiànzhě] **2** (to magazine) 投稿人 [tóugǎorén]

○ **control** [kən'trəul] I VT [+ country, organization] 统治 [tǒngzhì]; [+ person, emotion, disease, fire] 控制 [kòngzhì]; [+ machine, process] 操纵 [cāozòng]; [+ wages, prices] 管制 [guǎnzhì] II N [U] [of country, organization] 控制权 [kòngzhì quán]; [of people] 指挥能力 [zhǐhuī nénglì]; [of vehicle, machine] 控制 [kòngzhì] III controls NPL **1** [of vehicle, machine, TV] 操纵装置 [cāozòng zhuāngzhì] **2** ▶ price/planning etc controls 价格/规划 [等] 管制 [jiàgé/guīhuà {děng} guǎnzhì] ▶ to control o.s. 克制自己 [kèzhì zìjǐ] ▶ to take control (of sth) 控制住 (某事) ▶ to lose control (of sth) (emotionally) 克制不住 (某事); (in vehicle, on machine) 失去 (对某物的) 控制 ▶ to keep control (of sth) 保持 (对某物的) 控制 ▶ to keep control of o.s. 控制自己 ▶ to be in control (of sth) (of situation, car etc) 控制着 (某事) ▶ to be under control [fire, situation +]

处于控制之下 ▶ to be out of control [fire, situation +] 失去控制 ▶ the car went out of control 那辆车失控了 ▶ circumstances beyond our control 不在我们控制之中的情况 ▶ to be at the controls 操纵

control tower N [C] 指挥调度台 [zhǐhuī diàodùtái]

controversial [kɒntrə'vəːʃl] ADJ [+ decision, issue, person] 有争议的 [yǒu zhēngyì de]; [+ book, film] 引起争论的 [yǐnqǐ zhēnglùn de]

controversy ['kɒntrəvəːsɪ] N [C/U] 辩论 [biànlùn]

convene [kən'viːn] (frm) I VT [+ meeting, conference] 召集 [zhāojí] II VI [parliament, inquiry +] 正式开始 [zhèngshì kāishǐ]; [people +] 开会 [kāihuì]

convenience [kən'viːnɪəns] I N **1** [U] (ease, suitability) 方便 [fāngbiàn] **2** [C] (useful thing) 便利设施 [biànlì shèshī] II conveniences NPL 方便的用具 [fāngbiàn de yòngjù] ▶ at sb's convenience 在某人方便的时候 ▶ at your earliest convenience 在你方便时尽早

convenient [kən'viːnɪənt] ADJ [+ method, system, time] 方便的 [fāngbiàn de]; [+ place] 近便的 [jìnbiàn de] ▶ to be convenient for [+ person] 适合于; [+ place] 容易到达

convent ['kɒnvənt] N [C] 女修道院 [nǚ xiū dàoyuàn]

convention [kən'vɛnʃən] N **1** [C] (custom) 社会习俗 [shèhuì xísú] **2** [C] (conference) [of organization, group] 大会 [dàhuì]; (political) 代表大会 [dàibiǎo dàhuì] **3** [C] (agreement) 协定 [xiédìng]

conventional [kən'vɛnʃənl] ADJ [+ person, behaviour] 符合习俗的 [fúhé xísú de]; [+ method, product] 传统的 [chuántǒng de]; [+ war, weapons] 常规的 [chángguī de]

conversation [kɒnvə'seɪʃən] N [C/U] 交谈 [jiāotán] ▶ to have a conversation (about sth/with sb) (和某人) 谈 (某事) ▶ to make conversation 说应酬话

conversely [kɒn'vəːslɪ] ADV 正相反 [zhèng xiāngfǎn]

conversion [kən'vəːʃən] N **1** [C/U] (transformation) [of substance] 转化 [zhuǎnhuà]; [of building] 改建 [gǎijiàn] **2** [C/U] [of quantity, money] 换算 [huànsuàn] **3** [C/U] [of person] (to belief) 改变信仰 [gǎibiàn xìnyǎng]; (to religion) 皈依 [guīyī] **4** [C] (RUGBY) 触地得分后再射门得的分 ▶ the conversion of sth into sth 从某物到某物的转变 ▶ sb's conversion to sth [+ Islam, Christianity] 某人对某教的皈依; [+ belief] 某人转而对某事的信仰

convert [vb kən'vəːt, n 'kɒnvəːt] I VT **1** (transform) [+ substance] 使转化 [shǐ zhuǎnhuà]; [+ building] 改建 [gǎijiàn]; [+ vehicle, equipment] 改装 [gǎizhuāng] **2** [+ person] (to belief) 使…改变信仰 [shǐ…gǎibiàn xìnyǎng];

(to religion) 使…皈依 [shǐ…guīyī] **3** [+ quantity, money] 把…折合 [bǎ…zhéhé] **4** (RUGBY) 触地得分后再射中球门获得附加分 **II** VI (REL) 皈依 [guīyī] **III** N [C] (to belief) 改变信仰的人 [gǎibiàn xìnyǎng de rén]; (to religion) 皈依者 [guīyīzhě] ▶ **to convert sth into sth** [+ substance] 将某物转化成某物; [+ building] 将某建筑改建成某建筑 ▶ **to convert sth to sth** [+ equipment] 将某物改装成某物 ▶ **to convert to sth** [person +] (to belief) 改为信仰某物; (to religion) 皈依某教

convertible [kən'və:təbl] **I** N [C] (car) 折篷汽车 [zhépéng qìchē] **II** ADJ [+ currency] 可兑换的 [kě duìhuàn de]

convey [kən'veɪ] (frm) VT **1** ▶ **to convey sth (to sb)** [+ information, idea, thanks] (向某人)传达某事 [(xiàng mǒurén) chuándá mǒushì] **2** ▶ **to convey sb/sth to sth** [+ cargo, traveller] 将某人/某物运送至某处 [jiāng mǒurén/mǒuwù yùnsòng zhì mǒuchù]

conveyor belt [kən'veɪə-] N [C] 传送带 [chuánsòng dài]

convict [vb kən'vɪkt, n 'kɒnvɪkt] **I** VT ▶ **to convict sb (of sth)** 宣判某人有(…)罪 [xuānpàn mǒurén yǒu (…) zuì] **II** N [C] (person) 囚犯 [qiúfàn]

conviction [kən'vɪkʃən] N **1** [C] (belief) 坚定的信仰 [jiāndìng de xìnyǎng] **2** [U] (certainty) 坚信 [jiānxìn] **3** [C/U] (LAW) 定罪 [dìngzuì]

convince [kən'vɪns] VT **1** (cause to believe) 使信服 [shǐ xìnfú] **2** (ESP US) (persuade) 说服 [shuōfú] ▶ **to convince sb of sth** 使某人相信某事 ▶ **to convince sb that...** 说服某人… ▶ **to convince sb to do sth** (ESP US) 说服某人去做某事

convinced [kən'vɪnst] ADJ ▶ **to be convinced that...** 坚信… [jiānxìn…] ▶ **to be/become convinced of sth** 确信/开始相信某事

convincing [kən'vɪnsɪŋ] ADJ 令人信服的 [lìng rén xìnfú de]

convoy ['kɒnvɔɪ] N [C] 车/船队 [chē/chuánduì] ▶ **in convoy** 由…护送

COO N ABBR (= chief operating officer) 首席营运官 [Shǒuxí Yíngyùnguān]

cook [kuk] **I** VT [+ food, meat, vegetables] 烹调 [pēngtiáo]; [+ meal] 做 [zuò] **II** VI **1** [person +] 做饭 [zuòfàn] **2** [food +] 烧 [shāo] **III** N [C] 厨师 [chúshī] ▶ **a good cook** 会做饭的人
▶ **cook up** (inf) VT [+ scheme] 策划 [cèhuà]; [+ excuse, story] 捏造 [niēzào]

> 表示烹调的具体方法时，通常会使用比 **cook** 更具体的词。比如，用烤箱烤肉用 **roast**，烤面包或蛋糕则用 **bake**。用水煮蔬菜用 **boil**，隔水蒸食物则用 **steam**。用油炒肉类或蔬菜用 **fry**。用火烤食物可以用 **grill**，或在美式英语中用 **broil**。烤面包一般不用 **grill**，而用 **toast**。

cookbook ['kukbuk] N [C] 菜谱 [càipǔ]

cooker ['kukə(r)] (BRIT) N [C] 厨灶 [chúzào] [美 = stove]

cookery ['kukərɪ] N [U] 烹饪 [pēngrèn]

cookery book (BRIT) N = cookbook

cookie ['kukɪ] N [C] **1** (US) (for eating) 小甜饼 [xiǎotiánbǐng] [英 = biscuit] **2** (COMPUT) 记忆块 [jìyì kuài]

cooking ['kukɪŋ] **I** N [U] **1** (activity) 烹调 [pēngtiáo] **2** (food) 饭菜 [fàncài] **II** CPD [复合词] [+ apples, chocolate] 烹调用 [pēngtiáo yòng]; [+ utensils] 用于烹饪 [yòngyú pēngrèn]

cool [ku:l] **I** ADJ **1** [+ water, breeze, evening, place] 凉的 [liáng de] **2** (light) [+ clothes] 凉爽的 [liángshuǎng de] **3** (calm, unemotional) 冷静的 [lěngjìng de] **4** (unfriendly) 冷淡的 [lěngdàn de] **5** (inf) (good) 顶呱呱的 [dǐngguāguā de]; (fashionable) 酷的 [kù de] **II** VT 使变凉 [shǐ biànliáng] **III** VI 冷下来 [lěngxiàlái] **IV** N ▶ **to keep/lose one's cool** (inf) 保持冷静/失去自制而激动起来 [bǎochí lěngjìng/shīqù zìzhì 'ér jīdòng qǐlái] ▶ **it's quite cool today** 今天挺凉 ▶ **to keep sth cool** 保持某物的凉度 ▶ **(that's) cool!** (inf) (fine) 再好不过! ▶ **a cool two million dollars** (inf) 整整两百万美元
▶ **cool down I** VI **1** (become colder) 变凉 [biànliáng] **2** (fig) [person, situation +] 平息 [píngxī] **II** VT **1** (decrease heat of) 冷却 [lěngquè] **2** (fig) [+ person, situation] 使冷静下来 [shǐ lěngjìng xiàlái]
▶ **cool off I** VI (after heat) 变凉 [biànliáng] **II** VT 使变凉 [shǐ biànliáng]
■ 用法参见 cold

co-operate [kəu'ɒpəreɪt] VI **1** (collaborate) 合作 [hézuò] **2** (be helpful) 配合 [pèihé] ▶ **to co-operate with sb** (collaborate with) 与某人合作 (be helpful to) 配合某人

co-operation [kəuɒpə'reɪʃən] N [U] **1** (collaboration) 合作 [hézuò] **2** (help) 配合 [pèihé]

co-operative [kəu'ɒpərətɪv] **I** ADJ [+ person, attitude] 乐意合作的 [lèyì hézuò de]; [+ effort] 合作的 [hézuò de] **II** N [C] (factory, business) 合作社 [hézuòshè]

co-ordinate [vb kəu'ɔ:dɪneɪt, n kəu'ɔ:dɪnət] **I** VT [+ activity, work, effort, limbs, movement] 协调 [xiétiáo] **II** N [C] (MATH, GEO) 坐标 [zuòbiāo]

co-ordination [kəuɔ:dɪ'neɪʃən] N [U] **1** (of activity, work, efforts) 协作 [xiézuò] **2** (of movements) 协调 [xiétiáo]

cop [kɒp] (inf) N [C] 警察 [jǐngchá]

cope [kəup] VI 对付 [duìfù] ▶ **to cope with sth/with doing sth** [+ problem, situation, task] 妥善地处理某事/做某事

copper ['kɒpə(r)] **I** N **1** [U] (metal) 铜 [tóng] **2** [C] (BRIT: inf) (policeman/woman) 警察 [jǐngchá] **II** **coppers** NPL (small change, coins) 铜板 [tóngbǎn] **III** CPD [复合词] [+ pipe, bracelet etc] 铜 [tóng]

copy ['kɒpɪ] I N **1** [c] (duplicate) 复制品 [fùzhìpǐn] **2** [c] (issue) [of book, record, newspaper] 本/张/份 [běn/zhāng/fèn] **3** [U] (PUBLISHING) (text) 文字稿 [wénzì gǎo] II VT **1** (imitate) [+ person, idea etc] 模仿 [mófǎng] **2** (also: **copy out**) 抄写 [chāoxiě] ▶ **to make a copy of sth** 复印某物 ▶ **to make a good copy** (PUBLISHING) 成为好材料 ▶ **to copy sth into a notebook** 将某事写入笔记本里
▶ **copy down** VT 记下来 [jìxiàlái]

copyright ['kɒpɪraɪt] N [U] 版权 [bǎnquán]

coral ['kɒrəl] N [U] (substance) 珊瑚 [shānhú]

cord [kɔːd] I N [c/U] **1** (string) 绳 [shéngzi] **2** (ELEC) 电线 [diànxiàn] II CPD (复合词) (corduroy) 灯心绒的 [dēngxīnróng de] III **cords** NPL (trousers) 灯心绒裤子 [dēngxīnróng kùzi]

cordial ['kɔːdɪəl] I ADJ 热烈诚挚的 [rèliè chéngzhì de] II N [c/U] **1** (BRIT) (fruit drink) 甜饮料 [tián yǐnliào] **2** (US) (alcoholic drink) 香甜酒 [xiāngtián jiǔ] [英= **liqueur**]

cordless ['kɔːdlɪs] ADJ [+ phone, kettle etc] 无绳的 [wúshéng de]

cordon ['kɔːdn] N [c] (MIL, POLICE) 警戒线 [jǐngjiè xiàn]
▶ **cordon off** VT [+ area] 封锁 [fēngsuǒ]

corduroy ['kɔːdərɔɪ] I N [U] 灯心绒 [dēngxīnróng] II CPD (复合词) [+ jacket, trousers etc] 灯心绒 [dēngxīnróng]

core [kɔː(r)] I N [c] [of fruit] 核 [hé]; [of building, place] 中心 [zhōngxīn]; [of earth] 地核 [dìhé]; [of nuclear reactor] 活性区 [huóxìng qū]; [of problem, issue] 核心 [héxīn] II VT [+ apple, pear etc] 去掉…的果核 [qùdiào…de guǒhé] ▶ **to be a Republican/royalist to the core** 是个十足的共和主义者/保皇主义者

coriander [kɒrɪ'ændə(r)] N [U] 香菜 [xiāngcài]

cork [kɔːk] I N **1** [c] (stopper) 瓶塞 [píngsāi] **2** [U] (material) 软木 [ruǎnmù] II CPD (复合词) [+ mat, tile etc] 软木制 [ruǎnmù zhì]

corkscrew ['kɔːkskruː] N [c] 瓶塞钻 [píngsāizuàn]

corn [kɔːn] N **1** [U] (BRIT) (cereal crop) 谷物 [gǔwù] [美= **grain**] **2** [U] (US) (maize) 玉米 [yùmǐ] [英= **maize**] **3** [c] (on foot) 鸡眼 [jīyǎn]
▶ **corn on the cob** 玉米 (棒子)

corned beef ['kɔːnd-] N [U] 腌牛肉 [yānniúròu]

corner ['kɔːnə(r)] N [c] **1** 角落 [jiǎoluò] **2** [of road] 街角 [jiējiǎo] **3** (FOOTBALL) (also: **corner kick**) 角球 [jiǎoqiú] **4** (BOXING) 场角 [chǎngjiǎo] II VT [+ person, animal] 使走投无路 [shǐ zǒutóu wúlù] III VI [car, driver +] 拐弯 [guǎiwān] ▶ **to cut corners** (fig) 走捷径 ▶ **to be (just) round** or **around the corner** (fig) 即将发生 ▶ **to turn the corner** (fig) 渡过难关 ▶ **to corner the market** 垄断市场

cornflakes ['kɔːnfleɪks] NPL 玉米片 [yùmǐ piàn]

cornflour ['kɔːnflauə(r)] (BRIT) N [U] 玉米面 [yùmǐ miàn] [美= **cornstarch**]

cornstarch ['kɔːnstɑːtʃ] (US) N [U] 玉米面 [yùmǐ miàn] [英= **cornflour**]

coronary ['kɒrənərɪ] (MED) I N [c] (also: **coronary thrombosis**) 冠心病 [guànxīnbìng] II ADJ [+ artery] 冠状动脉的 [guànzhuàng dòngmài de] ▶ **to have a coronary** 患冠心病

coronation [kɒrə'neɪʃən] N [c] 加冕典礼 [jiāmiǎn diǎnlǐ]

coroner ['kɒrənə(r)] N [c] 验尸官 [yànshīguān]

Corp. ABBR (= corporation) 股份有限公司 [gǔfèn yǒuxiàn gōngsī]

corporal ['kɔːpərəl] N [c] 下士 [xiàshì]

corporal punishment N [U] 体罚 [tǐfá]

corporate ['kɔːpərɪt] ADJ [+ executive, culture, earnings, image] 公司的 [gōngsī de]; [+ client] 集团的 [jítuán de]; [+ responsibility] 共同的 [gòngtóng de]

corporation [kɔːpə'reɪʃən] N [c] **1** (COMM) 股份有限公司 [gǔfèn yǒuxiàn gōngsī] **2** (BRIT) [of town] 市政当局 [shìzhèng dāngjú]

corps [kɔː(r)] (pl **corps**) N [c] **1** (MIL) 特种部队 [tèzhǒng bùduì] **2** [of diplomats, journalists] 团 [tuán]

corpse [kɔːps] N [c] 死尸 [sǐshī]

correct [kə'rɛkt] I ADJ **1** [+ answer, details, amount, spelling] 正确的 [zhèngquè de]; [+ decision, means, procedure] 适当的 [shìdàng de] **2** (socially) [+ person, behaviour] 得体的 [détǐ de] II VT **1** (put right) [+ mistake, fault, person] 纠正 [jiūzhèng] **2** (mark) [+ exam] 批改 [pīgǎi] ▶ **you are correct** 你是对的

correction [kə'rɛkʃən] N **1** [c] (correcting) 修改 [xiūgǎi] **2** [U] (correcting) 改正 [gǎizhèng]

correspond [kɒrɪs'pɒnd] VI **1** (be equivalent) ▶ **to correspond (to sth)** (与某物) 相符合 [(yǔ mǒuwù) xiāng fúhé] **2** (write) ▶ **to correspond (with sb)** (和某人) 通信 [(hé mǒurén) tōngxìn]

correspondence [kɒrɪs'pɒndəns] N **1** [U] (letter-writing) 通信 [tōngxìn] **2** [U] (letters) 信件 [xìnjiàn] **3** [c] (relationship) 一致 [yízhì]

correspondent [kɒrɪs'pɒndənt] N [c] (reporter) 记者 [jìzhě]

corresponding [kɒrɪs'pɒndɪŋ] ADJ 相应的 [xiāngyìng de]

corridor ['kɒrɪdɔː(r)] N [c] (in house, building) 走廊 [zǒuláng]; (on train) 车厢过道 [chēxiāng guòdào]

corrode [kə'rəud] I VI [metal +] 受腐蚀 [shòu fúshí] II VT [+ metal] 腐蚀 [fúshí]

corrupt [kə'rʌpt] I ADJ **1** [+ person] 腐败的 [fǔbài de] **2** [+ data] 破坏的 [pòhuài de] II VT **1** [+ person] 使堕落 [shǐ duòluò] **2** [+ data] 破坏 [pòhuài] ▶ **corrupt practices** 贪赃舞弊的行为

corruption [kə'rʌpʃən] N [U] 贪赃舞弊

[tānzāng wǔbì]

'cos [kɔz] (BRIT: inf) CONJ 因为 [yīnwèi]

cosmetic [kɔz'mɛtɪk] I N [c] (beauty product) 化妆品 [huàzhuāng pǐn] II ADJ [+ measure, improvement] 表面的 [biǎomiàn de]

cosmetic surgery N [U] 整容手术 [zhěngróng shǒushù]

cosmic ['kɔzmɪk] ADJ 宇宙的 [yǔzhòu]

cosmopolitan [kɔzmə'pɔlɪtn] ADJ [+ place, person, outlook] 世界性的 [shìjiè xìng de]

○ **cost** [kɔst] (pt, pp **cost**) I N 1 [c] 价格 [jiàgé] ▷ the cost of a loaf of bread 一条面包的价格 2 [C/U] (fig) (loss, damage etc) 代价 [dàijià] ▷ The cost in human life was enormous. 付出了巨大的生命代价。II VT 1 (be priced at) 价格为 [jiàgé wéi] ▷ It cost five thousand dollars. 价格为5000美元。2 (COMM) (work out cost of) [+ project, purchase etc] (pt, pp **costed**) 估价 [gūjià] III **costs** NPL 1 (overheads) 成本 [chéngběn] 2 (LAW) 诉讼费用 [sùsòng fèiyòng] ▶ how much does it cost? 这多少钱？▶ it cost me fifty pounds 这花了我50英镑 ▶ it costs 5 pounds/too much 价格为5英镑/太高 ▶ what will it cost to have it repaired? 修理它要多少钱？▶ it cost him his life/job 这让他付出了生命/失去工作的代价 ▶ the cost of living 生活费用 ▶ at all costs 不惜一切代价

co-star ['kəʊstɑː(r)] (TV, CINE) I N [c] 合演者 [héyǎnzhě] II VI ▶ to co-star (with sb) (与某人)联袂主演 [(yǔ mǒurén) liánmèi zhǔyǎn]

Costa Rica ['kɔstə'riːkə] N 哥斯达黎加 [Gēsīdálíjiā]

costly ['kɔstlɪ] ADJ 1 (expensive) 昂贵的 [ángguì de] 2 (fig) 代价惨重的 [dàijià cǎnzhòng de]

costume ['kɔstjuːm] N 1 [C/U] [of actor, artist] 戏装 [xìzhuāng] 2 [U] (style of dress) 服装式样 [fúzhuāng shìyàng]

cosy, (US) cozy ['kəʊzɪ] ADJ 1 [+ room, house] 温暖舒适的 [wēnnuǎn shūshì de] 2 [+ person] ▶ to be/feel cosy 感到舒适安逸 [gǎndào shūshì 'ānyì] 3 [+ chat, evening, atmosphere] 亲切友好的 [qīnqiè yǒuhǎo de]

cot [kɔt] N [c] 1 (BRIT) (child's) 幼儿床 [yòu'ér chuáng] [美= **crib**] 2 (US) (bed) 帆布床 [fānbù chuáng] [英= **camp bed**]

cottage ['kɔtɪdʒ] N [c] 村舍 [cūnshè]

cottage cheese N [U] 农家鲜干酪 [nóngjiā xiān gānlào]

cottage pie (BRIT) N [C/U] 农家馅饼 [nóngjiā xiànbǐng]

cotton ['kɔtn] I N [U] 1 (fabric) 棉布 [miánbù] 2 (plant) 棉树 [miánshù] 3 (thread) 棉线 [miánxiàn] II CPD [复合词] [+ dress, sheets etc] 棉布 [miánbù]
▶ **cotton on** (BRIT: inf) VI ▶ to cotton on (to sth) 明白 (某事) [míngbai (mǒushì)]

cotton candy (US) N [U] 棉花糖 [miánhuā táng] [英= **candy floss**]

cotton wool (BRIT) N [U] 脱脂棉 [tuōzhī mián] [美= **absorbent cotton**]

couch [kautʃ] I N [c] 1 长沙发 [cháng shāfā] 2 (doctor's, psychiatrist's) 诊察台 [zhěnchátái] II VT ▶ to be couched in polite language/legal terms 以礼貌的语言/法律措辞表达 [yǐ lǐmào de yǔyuán/fǎlǜ cuòcí biǎodá]

cough [kɔf] I VI 1 [person +] 咳嗽 [késou] 2 [engine +] 喀喀作响 [kākāzuòxiǎng] II N [c] (noise, illness) 咳嗽 [késou] III VT [+ blood] 咳 [ké] ▶ to have a cough 咳嗽
▶ **cough up** I VT 1 [+ blood] 咳出 [kéchū] 2 (inf) [+ money] 不情愿地支付 [bù qíngyuàn de zhīfù] II VI (inf) 出钱 [chūqián]

cough mixture (BRIT) N [U] 咳嗽糖浆 [késou tángjiāng]

O

could [kud] AUX VB 1 (referring to past) ▶ we couldn't go to the party 我们没能去参加聚会 [wǒmen méi néng qù cānjiā jùhuì] ▶ last year we couldn't afford a holiday 去年我们度不起假 ▶ he could be very unkind 他可能会很刻薄 ▶ he couldn't read or write 他不会读也不会写 ▶ we could hear him whistling 我们能听到他正在吹口哨 ▶ she said she couldn't hear me 她说听不见我说的话
2 (possibility) ▶ he could be in the library 他可能在图书馆 [tā kěnéng zài túshūguǎn] ▶ I couldn't be happier 我再高兴不过了 ▶ he could be released next year 他明年可能被释放 ▶ you could have been killed! 可能你连命都没了！▶ the accident could have been caused by an oil leak 事故可能是由石油泄漏引起的
3 (in conditionals with "if") ▶ if we had more time, I could finish this 如果有更多时间，我能够完成的 [rúguǒ yǒu gèngduō shíjiān, wǒ nénggòu wánchéng de] ▶ we could have a holiday, if we could afford it 如果能支付得起的话，我们就去度假了
4 (in offers, suggestions, requests) 可以 [kěyǐ] ▶ I could call a doctor 我可以叫个医生 ▶ we could always go to the cinema 我们还是可以去看电影 ▶ couldn't you give him a call? 你可不可以给他打个电话？▶ could I borrow the car? 我可以借一下车吗？▶ if I could just interrupt you for a minute 我是否可以打扰你一小会儿 ▶ he asked if he could make a phone call 他问是否可以打个电话
5 (emphatic) ▶ you could at least be polite! 你至少可以礼貌点儿！[nǐ zhìshǎo kěyǐ lǐmàodiǎnr!] ▶ you could have told me! 你早该告诉我！▶ I could scream! 我真想大叫！▶ how could you have lied to me? 你怎么能向我撒谎呢？

couldn't ['kʊdnt] = **could not**

○ **council** ['kaʊnsl] N [c] **1** (*of city, county*) 议会 [yìhuì] **2** (*in names*) 理事会 [lǐshìhuì] ▷ *the Arts Council* 艺术理事会

council estate (BRIT) N [c] 由市政经营的房产

council house (BRIT) N [c] 地方当局建造的简易住宅

councillor ['kaʊnslə(r)] N [c] 地方议员 [dìfāng yìyuán]

council tax (BRIT) N [U] 市政税，由英国地方政府根据房屋价值而征收并自由支配的税种

counsel ['kaʊnsl] I N **1** [U] (*advice*) 劝告 [quàngào] **2** [c] (*lawyer*) 讼务律师 [sòngwù lùshī] II VT **1** (*advise*) [+ *person*] 给…提建议 [gěi...tí jiànyì] **2** [+ *caution, patience*] 建议 [jiànyì] ▶ **to keep one's own counsel** 将自己的意见保密 ▶ **counsel for the defence, defence counsel** 辩护律师 ▶ **counsel for the prosecution, prosecuting counsel** 公诉律师 ▶ **to counsel sb to do sth** (*frm*) 劝告某人做某事

counselling, (US) **counseling** ['kaʊnsəlɪŋ] N [U] 辅导 [fǔdǎo]

counsellor, (US) **counselor** ['kaʊnslə(r)] N [c] **1** (*advisor*) 顾问 [gùwèn] **2** (US) (*lawyer*) 律师 [lùshī]

count [kaʊnt] I VT **1** (*also*: **count up**) 数 [shǔ] **2** (*include*) 把…计算在内 [bǎ... jìsuàn zàinèi] II VI **1** (*add*) 数 [shǔ] **2** (*enter into consideration*) 认可 [rènkě] **3** (*matter*) 有价值 [yǒu jiàzhí] III N [c] **1** (*total*) [*of things, people, votes*] 数目 [shùmù] **2** (*level*) [*of pollen, alcohol etc*] 计数 [jìshù] **3** (*nobleman*) 伯爵 [bójué] ▶ **to count (up) to 10** 数到10 ▶ **to count the cost of sth** 计算某事的成本 ▶ **not counting the children** 儿童不算在内 ▶ **10 counting him** 算上他10个 ▶ **count yourself lucky** 你应该感到幸运 ▶ **to count as sth** 算得上某事 ▶ **it counts for little/a lot** 没用/有用 ▶ **to keep/lose count of sth** 知道/不知道某事的数目
▶ **count against** VT FUS [不可拆分] 对…不利 [duì...bùlì]
▶ **count down** VT FUS [不可拆分] [+ *seconds, minutes*] 倒数 [dàozhe shǔ] ▶ **to be counting down the days to sth** 迫切期待着某事的到来
▶ **count down to** VT FUS [不可拆分] **1** (*lit*) [+ *midnight, blast-off*] 倒读数至 [dàodú shùzhì] **2** (*fig*) [+ *Christmas, anniversary, etc*] 迫切期待着 [pòqiè qídàizhe]
▶ **count in** VT [+ *person*] 把…算在内 [bǎ... suàn zàinèi]
▶ **count on, count upon** VT FUS [不可拆分] [+ *support, help*] 指望 [zhǐwàng]; [+ *person*] 依靠 [yīkào] ▶ **to count on doing sth** 指望做某事
▶ **count out** VT FUS [不可拆分] **1** [+ *coins, notes*] 清点 [qīngdiǎn] **2** (*exclude*) [+ *person*] 不把…算入 [bù bǎ... suànrù]

countdown ['kaʊntdaʊn] N [c] (*to launch*) 倒

counter ['kaʊntə(r)] I N [c] **1** (*desk*) (*in shop, café, bank, post office*) 柜台 [guìtái] **2** (*in game*) 筹码 [chóumǎ] **3** (*for keeping count*) 计数器 [jìshùqì] **4** ▶ **a counter to sth** 对某事物的反作用 [duì mǒu shìwù de fǎn zuòyòng] II VT **1** (*offset*) 反击 [fǎnjī] **2** (*respond to*) 反驳 [fǎnbó] III ADV ▶ **to run or be counter to sth** 违背某事 [wéibèi mǒushì] ▶ **to buy/sell sth under the counter** 私下买/卖某物 ▶ **to counter with sth/by doing sth** 用某事/通过做某事来反对

counteract ['kaʊntər'ækt] VT [+ *effect, tendency*] 对抗 [duìkàng]

counterclockwise ['kaʊntə'klɒkwaɪz] (US) I ADV 逆时针方向地 [nì shízhēn fāngxiàng de] [英=**anticlockwise**] II ADJ 逆时针方向的 [nì shízhēn fāngxiàng de] [英=**anticlockwise**]

counterfeit ['kaʊntəfɪt] I ADJ [+ *money, goods, document*] 伪造的 [wěizào de] II N [c] 仿制品 [fǎngzhì pǐn] III VT 伪造 [wěizào]

counterpart ['kaʊntəpɑːt] N [c] [*of person, company etc*] 相对应的人/物 [xiāng duìyìng de rén/wù]

countertop ['kaʊntətɒp] (US) N [c] 厨房里做饭的平台 [chúfáng lǐ zuòfàn de píngtái] [英=**worktop**]

countess ['kaʊntɪs] N [c] (*in own right*) 女伯爵 [nǚ bójué]; (*wife of count/earl*) 伯爵夫人 [bójué fūrén]

countless ['kaʊntlɪs] ADJ 无数的 [wúshù de]

○ **country** ['kʌntrɪ] I N **1** [c] (*nation*) 国家 [guójiā] **2** [s] (*population*) 全国人民 [quánguó rénmín] **3** [c] (*native land*) 家乡 [jiāxiāng] ▷ *He loved his country.* 他热爱自己的家乡。 **4** [U] (*area*) 地区 [dìqū] ▷ *mountainous country* 山区 **5** (*countryside*) ▶ **the country** 乡下 [xiāngxià] ▷ *a healthy life in the country* 乡下的健康生活 II CPD [复合词] (*also*: **country and western**) [+ *music, singer*] 西部乡村 [xībù xiāngcūn] ▶ **in the country** 在乡下

country house (BRIT) N [c] 乡间别墅 [xiāngjiān biéshù]

countryside ['kʌntrɪsaɪd] N [U] 农村 [nóngcūn]

county ['kaʊntɪ] N [c] 郡 [jùn]

coup [kuː] N [c] **1** (*also*: **coup d'état**) 政变 [zhèngbiàn] **2** (*achievement*) 意外而成功的行动 [yìwài ér chénggōng de xíngdòng]

couple ['kʌpl] I N [c] **1** (*married*) 夫妻 [fūqī]; (*living together*) 情侣 [qínglǚ] **2** (*twosome*) 对 [duì] **3** ▶ **a couple of** (*two*) 两个 [liǎnggè]; (*a few*) 几个 [jǐgè] II VT (*combine*) 配上某事物 [pèishang mǒuwù] ▶ **to couple sth to sth** [+ *machinery*] 将某物与某物连接起来

coupon ['kuːpɒn] N [c] **1** (*voucher*) 折价券 [zhéjià quàn] **2** (*form*) 索取单 [suǒqǔ dān]

courage ['kʌrɪdʒ] N [U] 勇气 [yǒngqì] ▶ **to have the courage to do sth** 有勇气做某事

courageous [kəˈreɪdʒəs] ADJ 勇敢的 [yǒnggǎn de]

courgette [kuəˈʒet] (BRIT) N [C/U] 密生西葫芦 [mìshēng xīhúlu] [美= **zucchini**]

courier [ˈkurɪə(r)] N [C] **1** (messenger) 信使 [xìnshǐ] **2** (rep) 旅游团的服务员 [lǚyóutuán de fúwùyuán]

◎ **course** [kɔːs] I N **1** [C] (educational) 课程 [kèchéng] **2** [C] [of injections, antibiotics] 疗程 [liáochéng] **3** [C] (direction) [of life, events, time etc] 进程 [jìnchéng]; [of ship, aircraft] 航向 [hángxiàng]; [of river] 流向 [liúxiàng] **4** [C] (also: **course of action**) 做法 [zuòfǎ] **5** [of meal] ▸ **first/next/last course** 第一/下一/最后一道菜 [dìyī/xiàyī/zuìhòu yīdào cài] **6** [C] (for golf, horse-racing) 场 [chǎng]; (for cycling) 道 [dào] II VI (liter) ▸ **to course down/through sth** 在某物上/中迅速流动 [zài mǒuwù shang/zhōng xùnsù liúdòng] ▸ **of course** (naturally) 自然 (certainly) 当然 ▷ That is of course true. 自然是真的。▷ Of course you should accept. 你当然应该接受。▸ **of course!** 没问题！▸ **of course not!** 当然不行！▸ **in the course of the next few days** 在今后几天期间 ▸ **to be on course for...** 在迈向…的正确方向上 ▸ **to run** or **take its course** 听其自然发展 ▸ **a course of action** 做法 ▸ **a course of treatment** 一个疗程 ▸ **a course of lectures** 系列讲座

◎ **court** [kɔːt] I N [C] **1** (LAW) (place) 法庭 [fǎtíng]; (people) 全体审判员 [quántǐ shěnpànyuán] **2** (for tennis, badminton etc) 球场 [qiúchǎng] **3** (royal) 宫廷 [gōngtíng] II VT **1** (seek) [+ publicity, popularity] 试图获得 [shìtú huòdé] **2** (risk) [+ disaster, unpopularity] 招致 [zhāozhì] **3** (o.f.) [+ man, woman] 与…谈恋爱 [yǔ tánliàn'ài] III VI [couple +] 恋爱 [liàn'ài] ▸ **to take sb to court** 起诉某人 ▸ **to settle sth out of court** 庭外和解 ▸ **to go to court** (LAW) 起诉 ▸ **to hold court** 接待仰慕者

courteous [ˈkəːtɪəs] ADJ 谦恭有礼的 [qiāngōng yǒulǐ de]

courtesy [ˈkəːtəsɪ] I N [U] (politeness) 谦恭有礼 [qiāngōng yǒulǐ] II CPD [复合词] [+ bus, car etc] 免费 [miǎnfèi] ▸ **(by) courtesy of...** (thanks to) 承蒙…

courthouse [ˈkɔːthaus] (US) N [C] 法院 [fǎyuàn] [英= **court**]

courtroom [ˈkɔːtruːm] N [C] 法庭 [fǎtíng]

courtyard [ˈkɔːtjɑːd] N [C] 庭院 [tíngyuàn]

cousin [ˈkʌzn] N [C] (older male on father's side) 堂兄 [tángxiōng]; (younger male on father's side) 堂弟 [tángdì]; (older female on father's side) 堂姐 [tángjiě]; (younger female on father's side) 堂妹 [tángmèi]; (older male on mother's side) 表兄 [biǎoxiōng]; (younger male on mother's side) 表弟 [biǎodì]; (older female on mother's side) 表姐 [biǎojiě]; (younger female on mother's side) 表妹 [biǎomèi] ▸ **first cousin** 嫡堂或表兄弟姐妹

▸ **second cousin** 远房堂或表兄弟姐妹

◎ **cover** [ˈkʌvə(r)] I VT **1** ▸ **to cover sth (with sth)** (用某物) 盖着某物 [(yòng mǒuwù) gàizhe mǒuwù] ▷ She covered her face with her hands. 她用手蒙着自己的脸。**2** (travel) [+ distance] 行 [xíng] ▷ We covered twenty kilometres a day. 我们每天行20公里。**3** (in insurance) ▸ **to cover sb (against sth)** 给某人保(某事的)险 [gěi mǒurén bǎo (mǒushì de) xiǎn] ▷ We're not covered against accidental damage. 我们没有保意外损害险。**4** (deal with) [law, regulation +] 适用于 [shìyòngyú] ▷ The law covers four categories of experiments. 这条法则适用于4种试验。; [speaker, writer, course +] 讨论 [tǎolùn] ▷ We've covered a wide range of subjects today. 我们今天讨论了一系列广泛的课题。; [journalist, reporter +] 报道 [bàodào] ▷ My editor asked me to cover the elections. 编辑叫我报道这些选举。**5** (be sufficient money for) 足够支付 [zúgòu zhīfù] ▷ £1.50 to cover postage 1英镑50便士用来支付邮资 II N **1** [C] (for furniture, machinery etc) 套子 [tàozi] **2** [C] (jacket) [of book, magazine] 封面 [fēngmiàn] **3** [U] (insurance) 保险 [bǎoxiǎn] **4** [U] (shelter) 掩蔽物 [yǎnbìwù] ▷ They ran for cover. 他们向可以躲避的地方跑去。**5** [C] (for illegal activities) 幌子 [huǎngzi] III **covers** NPL (on bed) 铺盖 [pūgài] ▸ **to be covered in** or **with sth** [+ mud, blood, dust etc] 被某物覆盖 ▸ **to take cover** 隐蔽 ▸ **under cover** 躲起来 ▸ **under cover of darkness** 在黑夜的掩护下 ▸ **under separate cover** 在另函内

▸ **cover for** VT FUS [不可拆分] **1** [+ wrongdoer] 为…隐瞒 [wèi…yǐnmán] **2** [+ absent colleague] 代替 [dàitì]

▸ **cover up** VT **1** ▸ **to cover sth up (with sth)** [+ person, object] (用某物) 将某物盖住 [(yòng mǒuwù) jiāng mǒuwù gàizhù] **2** [+ facts, feelings, mistakes] (用某事) 掩饰某事 [(yòng mǒushì) yǎnshì mǒushì] II VI ▸ **to cover up for sb** 替某人掩饰 [tì mǒurén yǎnshì]

coverage [ˈkʌvərɪdʒ] N [U] (TV, PUBLISHING) 报道 [bàodào] ▸ **television coverage of the conference** 大会的电视报道 ▸ **to give full coverage of** 全面报道

covering [ˈkʌvərɪŋ] N [C] (layer, around sth) 层 [céng] ▸ **floor/wall covering** 地板/墙壁覆盖物

covert [ˈkəuvət] ADJ [+ operation, action, support] 秘密的 [mìmì de]

cover-up [ˈkʌvərʌp] N [C] 掩盖 [yǎngài]

cow [kau] I N [C] **1** (farm animal) 奶牛 [nǎiniú] **2** (ZOOL) [of elephant, whale] 雌兽 [císhòu] **3** (inf!) (woman) 婆娘 [póniáng] II VT (intimidate) 胁迫 [xiépò]

coward [ˈkauəd] N [C] 胆小鬼 [dǎnxiǎoguǐ]

cowardly [ˈkauədlɪ] ADJ [+ act] 怯懦的 [qiènuò de]; [+ person] 胆小的 [dǎnxiǎo de]

cowboy [ˈkaubɔɪ] N [C] **1** (in US) 牛仔 [niúzǎi]

2 (BRIT: *inf*) (*tradesman*) 奸滑之辈 [jiānhuá zhī bèi]

cozy ['kəʊzɪ] (US) ADJ = **cosy**

CPA (US) N ABBR (= *certified public accountant*) 会计师 [kuàijìshī]

crab [kræb] N **1** [c] (*creature*) 螃蟹 [pángxiè] **2** [U] (*meat*) 蟹肉 [xièròu]

crack [kræk] I N **1** [c] (*in bone, dish, glass, wall*) 裂缝 [lièfèng] **2** [s] (*gap*) 缝隙 [fèngxì] **3** [c] (*noise*) 噼啪声 [pīpāshēng]; [+ *of whip*] 噼啪声 [pīpāshēng] **4** [c] (*inf*) (*joke*) 挖苦话 [wākǔ huà] **5** (*inf*) (*attempt*) ▶ **to have a crack (at sth)** 尝试 (某事) [chángshì (mǒushì)] **6** [U] (*drug*) 纯可卡因 [chún kěkǎyīn] II VT **1** (*break*) [+ *dish, glass, mirror*] 使开裂 [shǐ kāiliè]; [+ *bone*] 使骨折 [shǐ gǔzhé]; [+ *nut, egg*] 打破 [dǎpò] **2** (*noisily*) [+ *whip, twig*] 使噼啪作响 [shǐ pīpā zuòxiǎng] **3** (*solve*) [+ *problem, code*] 解决 [jiějué] III VI **1** (*dish, mirror, pipe* +] 开裂 [kāiliè] **2** (*inf*) [*person* +] (*lose control*) 垮掉 [kuǎdiào] IV ADJ [+ *soldier, athlete*] 技艺高超的 [jìyì gāochāo de] ▶ **to crack one's head/knee on sth** 头/膝盖在某物上撞了一下 ▶ **to crack an egg into a bowl** 打一个鸡蛋在碗里 ▶ **to crack a joke** 讲笑话 ▶ **to get cracking** (BRIT: *inf*) 开始大干起来
▶ **crack down on** VT FUS [不可拆分] [+ *drug dealers, crime etc*] 对…严惩不贷 [duì… yánchéng bùdài]
▶ **crack up** VI (*inf*) (*mentally*) 精神崩溃 [jīngshén bēngkuì]

cracked [krækt] ADJ **1** [+ *dish, glass, mirror*] 破裂的 [pòliè de] **2** (*inf*) (*mad*) 疯狂的 [fēngkuáng de]

cracker ['krækə(r)] N [c] **1** (*biscuit*) 薄脆饼干 [báozuì bǐngbān] **2** (*also*: **Christmas cracker**) 圣诞爆竹 [shèngdàn bàozhú] ▶ **she's a cracker** (BRIT: *inf*) 她棒极了 ▶ **it was a cracker of a match** (BRIT: *inf*) 那场比赛棒极了 ▶ **he's crackers** (BRIT: *inf*) 他疯了

crackle ['krækl] I VI (*fire, radio, telephone* +] 发噼啪声 [fā pīpāshēng] II N [c] [*of fire, radio, telephone*] 噼啪声 [pīpāshēng]

cradle ['kreɪdl] I N [c] (*baby's*) 摇篮 [yáolán] II VT [+ *child, object*] 抱 [bào] ▶ **the cradle of civilization** 文明的发源地

craft [krɑ:ft] I N **1** (pl **craft**) (*boat*) 船舶 [chuánbó]; (*plane*) 飞机 [fēijī] **2** (*weaving, pottery etc*) 工艺 [gōngyì] **3** (*trade*) 行业 [hángyè] II VT 精工制作 [jīnggōng zhìzuò]

craftsman ['krɑ:ftsmən] (pl **craftsmen**) N [c] 手艺人 [shǒuyìrén]

craftsmanship ['krɑ:ftsmənʃɪp] N [U] 工艺技巧 [gōngyì jìqiǎo]

cram [kræm] I VT **1** ▶ **to cram sth into sth** 将某物塞入某物 [jiāng mǒuwù sāirù mǒuwù] ▶ **to cram sb into sth** 将某人挤入某物 [jiāng mǒurén jǐrù mǒuwù] **2** (*fill*) [+ *place*] 挤满 [jǐmǎn] II VI **1** ▶ **to cram into sth** [+ *building,*

vehicle] 挤进某处 [jǐjìn mǒuchù] **2** (*for exam*) 临时抱佛脚 [línshí bào fójiǎo] ▶ **to cram sth with or full of sth** 用某物将某物塞得满满的

cramp [kræmp] I N [c/U] (*muscular*) 抽筋 [chōujīn] II VT ▶ **to cramp sb's style** (*inf*) 使某人不能放开手脚 [shǐ mǒurén bùnéng fàngkāi shǒujiǎo] ▶ **to have cramp (in one's leg)** (腿) 抽筋

cramped [kræmpt] ADJ [+ *room, building*] 狭小的 [xiáxiǎo de]; [+ *conditions*] 受限制的 [shòu xiànzhì de]

cranberry ['krænbərɪ] I N [c] 越橘 [yuèjú] II CPD [复合词] [+ *juice*] 越橘 [yuèjú]

crane [kreɪn] I N [c] **1** (*machine*) 起重机 [qǐzhòngjī] **2** (*bird*) 鹤 [hè] II VT ▶ **to crane one's neck** 伸长脖子 [shēncháng bózi] III VI ▶ **to crane forward** 向前伸长脖子 [xiàngqián shēncháng bózi]

cranefly ['kreɪnflaɪ] N [c] 大蚊 [dàwén]

crap [kræp] (*inf!*) I ADJ 糟糕的 [zāogāo de] II N [U] **1** (*faeces*) 屎 [shǐ] **2** (*nonsense*) 胡扯 [húchě] III VI 拉屎 [lāshǐ] ▶ **to have a crap** 拉屎

crash [kræʃ] I N [c] **1** [*of car*] 撞击 [zhuàngjī]; [*of plane*] 坠机 [zhuìjī] **2** [*of stock market, business*] 暴跌 [bàodiē] **3** (*noise*) 哗啦声 [huālā shēng] II VT [+ *car, plane etc*] 使撞毁 [shǐ zhuànghuǐ] III VI **1** [*car, driver* +] 撞击 [zhuàngjī]; [*plane* +] 坠毁 [zhuìhuǐ] **2** [*market, firm* +] 突然倒台 [tūrán dǎotái] **3** (COMPUT) 死机 [sǐjī] **4** (*clatter*) 轰然猛撞 [hōngrán měngzhuàng] ▶ **a car/plane crash** 撞车/飞机失事 ▶ **to crash into sth** 猛地撞上某物 ▶ **he crashed the car into a wall** 他把车撞到了墙上

crash helmet N [c] 安全帽 [ānquán mào]

crate [kreɪt] N [c] **1** (*box*) 装货箱 [zhuānghuò xiāng]; (*for bottles*) 装瓶箱 [zhuāngpíng xiāng] ▶ **a crate of oranges/beer** 一箱桔子/啤酒

cravat [krə'væt] N [c] 男用领结 [nányòng lǐngjié]

crave [kreɪv] VT (*also*: **crave for**) [+ *attention, affection*] 渴望得到 [kěwàng dédào]; [+ *food, drink*] 渴求 [kěqiú]

crawfish ['krɔ:fɪʃ] (pl **crawfish**) (US) N [c/U] 淡水鳌虾 [dànshuǐ áoxiā] [英= **crayfish**]

crawl [krɔ:l] I VI **1** [*adult, child, insect* +] 爬 [pá]; [*vehicle* +] 徐缓而行 [xúhuǎn ér xíng] **2** (*inf*) (*grovel*) ▶ **to crawl to sb** 拍 (某人) 的马屁 [pāi (mǒurén de) mǎpì] II N [U] (*also*: **the crawl**) (*in swimming*) 自由泳 [zìyóu yǒng] ▶ **to do the crawl** 游自由泳 ▶ **to be crawling with** (*inf*) [+ *people, things*] 充满了 ▶ **to drive along at a crawl** 缓慢地行进

crayfish ['kreɪfɪʃ] (pl **crayfish**) N [c/U] 淡水鳌虾 [dànshuǐ áoxiā]

crayon ['kreɪən] N [c] **1** (*coloured pencil*) 彩色铅笔 [cǎisè qiānbǐ] **2** (*wax crayon*) 彩色蜡笔 [cǎisè làbǐ]

craze [kreɪz] N [c] (*fashion*) 一时的狂热 [yīshí

de kuángrè] ▶ **a craze for sth** 狂热地爱好某物

crazy ['kreɪzɪ] (inf) ADJ (mad) 发疯的 [fāfēng de] ▶ **to be crazy about sth/doing sth** 对某事/做某事着迷 ▶ **to be crazy about sb** 对某人神魂颠倒 ▶ **to go crazy** 发疯 ▶ **to make** or **drive sb crazy** 使某人心烦意乱 ▶ **like crazy** 拼命

creak [kri:k] I VI [floorboard, door +] 嘎吱嘎吱作响 [gāzhī gāzhī zuòxiǎng] II N [c] (sound) 嘎吱嘎吱声 [gāzhī gāzhī shēng]

cream [kri:m] I N 1 [U] (dairy cream) 奶油 [nǎiyóu] 2 [c/U] (for skin) 乳霜 [rǔshuāng] 3 (élite) ▶ **the cream** 精华 [jīnghuá] II ADJ (in colour) 乳白色的 [rǔbáisè de] ▶ **cream off** VT [+ people] 选拔 [xuǎnbá]; [+ money, profits] 提取并挪为私用 [tíqǔ bìng nuówéi sīyòng]

cream cheese N [U] 奶油干酪 [nǎiyóu gānlào]

creamy ['kri:mɪ] ADJ 1 (containing cream) 含大量奶油的 [hán dàliàng nǎiyóu de] 2 (smooth) 光滑细腻的 [guānghuá xìnì de]

crease [kri:s] I N [c] (in cloth, paper) (fold) 折痕 [zhéhén]; (wrinkle) 皱纹 [zhòuwén]; (in trousers) 折缝 [zhéfèng] II VT (wrinkle) 使起皱 [shǐ qǐzhòu] III VI [cloth, paper +] 起皱 [qǐzhòu]; [face +] 皱起来 [zhòuqǐlái]

○ **create** [kri:'eɪt] VT [+ job, situation, wealth, problem etc] 创造 [chuàngzào]; [+ feeling] 引起 [yǐnqǐ]

creation [kri:'eɪʃən] N 1 [U] (act) 创造 [chuàngzào] 2 [c] (work) 作品 [zuòpǐn] 3 [U] (REL) (also: **the creation**) 创世 [chuàngshì]

creative [kri:'eɪtɪv] ADJ 1 [+ person] 有创造力的 [yǒu chuàngzàolì de] 2 [+ use, manner] 创造性的 [chuàngzàoxìng de]

creator [kri:'eɪtə(r)] N [c] 创造者 [chuàngzàozhě]

creature ['kri:tʃə(r)] N 1 (animal) 动物 [dòngwù] 2 (person) 人 [rén]

crèche [krɛʃ] (BRIT) N [c] 托儿所 [tuō'érsuǒ]

credentials [krɪ'dɛnʃlz] NPL 1 (qualifications) 资格 [zīgé] 2 (references) 证明书 [zhèngmíngshū] 3 (identifying papers) 证件 [zhèngjiàn]

credibility [krɛdɪ'bɪlɪtɪ] N [U] (of person, organization) 信誉 [xìnyù]; (of candidate, policy, idea) 可靠性 [kěkàoxìng]; (of statement, claim) 可信性 [kěxìnxìng] ▶ **to lose one's credibility** 失去信誉

credible ['krɛdɪbl] ADJ [+ person, organization] 可靠的 [kěkào de]; [+ candidate, policy, idea] 有希望的 [yǒu xīwàng de]; [+ statement, claim] 可信的 [kěxìn de]

credit ['krɛdɪt] I N 1 [U] (financial) 贷款 [dàikuǎn] 2 [U] (recognition) 赞扬 [zànyáng] 3 [c] (SCOL, UNIV) 学分 [xuéfēn] II VT 1 ▶ **the money will be credited to you/your account** 钱会记入你的账户 [qián huì jìrù nǐ de

zhànghù] 2 (believe) 相信 [xiāngxìn] III **credits** NPL 片尾字幕 [piànwěi zìmù] ▶ **to be in credit** (ESP BRIT) [person, bank account +] 有余额 ▶ **on credit** 赊账 ▶ **it's to his credit that...** 他值得赞扬的是… ▶ **to have sth to one's credit** 完成某事 ▶ **to take the credit for sth** 把某事归功于自己 ▶ **it does you credit** 你值得为此受到称赞 ▶ **he's a credit to his family** 他是他家庭的骄傲 ▶ **would you** or **can you credit it!** 难以置信！ ▶ **to credit sb with sth** 将某事归功于某人 ▷ I used to credit you with a bit of common sense. 我曾认为你有点常识。

credit card N [c] 信用卡 [xìnyòng kǎ]

creek [kri:k] N [c] 1 (BRIT) (inlet) 小海湾 [xiǎo hǎiwān] 2 (US) (stream) 小溪 [xiǎoxī] ▶ **to be up the creek (without a paddle)** (inf) 处于困境

creep [kri:p] (pt, pp **crept**) I VI 1 [person, animal +] ▶ **to creep up/down/into sth** 蹑手蹑脚地走上/下/进某处 [nièshǒu nièjiǎo de zǒushàng/xià/jìn mǒuchù] 2 [mist +] ▶ **to creep in** 不知不觉地到来 [bùzhī bùjué de dàolái] 3 [inflation, rate, price +] ▶ **to creep up** 渐渐上升 [jiànjiàn shàngshēng] 4 [mistakes, complacency, doubts +] ▶ **to creep in** 渐渐产生 [jiànjiàn chǎnshēng] 5 (inf) (person) 马屁精 [mǎpìjīng] ▶ **it makes my flesh creep** 使我毛骨悚然 ▶ **to creep up on sb** [person +] 悄悄靠近某人; [feeling +] 不知不觉地降临到某人身上 ▶ **it gives me the creeps** (inf) 这使我毛骨悚然

creepy ['kri:pɪ] ADJ [+ story, place, person] 令人毛骨悚然的 [lìng rén máo gǔ sǒngrán de]

cremate [krɪ'meɪt] VT 火化 [huǒhuà]

crematorium [krɛmə'tɔ:rɪəm] (pl **crematoria** [krɛmə'tɔ:rɪə]) N [c] 火化场 [huǒhuà chǎng]

crepe [kreɪp] I N 1 [U] (fabric) 绉织物 [zhòuzhīwù] 2 [c] (pancake) 薄煎饼 [báojiānbǐng] 3 [U] (rubber) 绉胶 [zhòujiāo] II CPD [复合词] [+ dress, jacket etc] 绉织的 [zhòuzhī de]

crept [krɛpt] PT, PP of **creep**

crescent ['krɛsnt] N [c] 1 (shape) 月牙形 [yuèyáxíng] 2 (ESP BRIT) (in street names) 新月形街道 [xīnyuèxíng jiēdào]

cress [krɛs] N [U] 水芹 [shuǐqín]

crest [krɛst] N [c] 1 (top) [of hill] 峰 [fēng]; [of wave] 波峰 [bōfēng] 2 [of bird] 羽冠 [yǔguān] 3 (coat of arms) 饰章 [shìzhāng]

crew [kru:] N 1 [c] [of ship, aircraft, spacecraft] 全体工作人员 [quántǐ gōngzuò rényuán] 2 [c] (TV) 组 [zǔ] 3 [s] (inf) (gang) 一帮 [yìbāng]

crew neck N [c] (also: **crew neck sweater**) 圆式紧衣领 [yuánshì jǐn yīlǐng]

crib [krɪb] I N 1 [c] 1 (US) (for baby) 有围栏的童床 [yǒu wéilán de tóngchuáng] [英= cot] 2 (nativity scene) 耶稣诞生的情景雕像 II VI (inf, o.f.) (copy) 抄袭 [chāoxí]

cricket ['krɪkɪt] N 1 [U] (sport) 板球 [bǎnqiú] 2 [c] (insect) 蟋蟀 [xīshuài]

CRICKET

在大英帝国时代，cricket（板球）做为一种夏季运动引入印度、巴基斯坦和澳大利亚等国。如今，板球在这些国家依然十分盛行。两队各11名队员，通常为男性。队员通常穿传统的白色运动服。板球的规则以复杂著称。两队轮流击球。击球的队尽力争取最多次数的 run（跑垒），其打击手在两组称为 stump（三门柱）的柱子间跑。另一队争取在击球手跑到门柱前用球击中门柱，还可以在球触地前接住球将该击球手淘汰出局。

cricketer ['krɪkɪtə(r)] N [c] 板球运动员 [bǎnqiú yùndòngyuán]

crime [kraɪm] N **1** [c] (illegal act) 罪行 [zuìxíng] **2** [U] (illegal activities) 犯罪活动 [fànzuì huódòng] **3** [c] (fig) 罪过 [zuìguò]

criminal ['krɪmɪnl] I N [c] 罪犯 [zuìfàn] II ADJ **1** (LAW) [+ offence, activity, record] 犯罪的 [fànzuì de]; [+ law, court] 刑事的 [xíngshì de] **2** (fig) (wrong) 应受责备的 [yīng shòu zébèi de]

crimson ['krɪmzn] ADJ 深红色的 [shēn hóngsè de]

cringe [krɪndʒ] VI (in embarrassment) 畏缩 [wèisuō] ▶ **to cringe with embarrassment/ horror** 由于尴尬/恐惧而畏缩

cripple ['krɪpl] I VT **1** [+ person] 使…变跛 [shǐ biànbǒ] **2** [+ ship, plane] 严重损坏 [yánzhòng sǔnhuài] **3** [+ organization, system] 使陷于瘫痪 [shǐ xiànyú tānhuàn] II N [c] (o.f.) 残废 [cánfèi] ▶ **crippled with arthritis** 因关节炎而残疾

crisis ['kraɪsɪs] (pl **crises** ['kraɪsi:z]) N [c/U] 危机 [wēijī]

crisp [krɪsp] I ADJ **1** [+ bacon, biscuit] 松脆的 [sōngcuì de]; [+ lettuce, apple] 新鲜而脆生的 [xīnxiān ér cuìsheng de] **2** [+ weather, day] 清新凉爽的 [qīngxīn liángshuǎng de] **3** [+ tone, manner] 干脆的 [gāncuì de] **4** [+ cotton, shirt, paper] 挺括的 [tǐngkuò de] II N [c] (BRIT) (potato crisp) 薯片 [shǔpiàn] [美= **chip, potato chip**]

crispy ['krɪspɪ] ADJ 松脆的 [sōngcuì de]

criterion [kraɪ'tɪərɪən] (pl **criteria** [kraɪ'tɪərɪə]) N [c] 标准 [biāozhǔn]

critic ['krɪtɪk] N [c] **1** [of person, system, policy] 批评家 [pīpíngjiā] **2** (reviewer) 评论员 [pínglùnyuán]

critical ['krɪtɪkl] ADJ **1** (crucial) 关键的 [guānjiàn de] **2** (serious) 危急的 [wēijí de] **3** (seriously ill) 病危的 [bìngwēi de] **4** (negative) [+ person, remark] 吹毛求疵的 [chuīmáoqiúcī de] **5** (analytical) [+ examination, analysis, study etc] 一丝不苟的 [yīsībùgǒu de] **6** (from critics) [+ acclaim, success] 评论的 [pínglùn de] ▶ **in a critical condition** 情况危急 ▶ **to be critical of**

critically ['krɪtɪklɪ] ADV **1** (crucially) [+ important] 极其 [jíqí] **2** (seriously) [+ low, ill, injured] 严重地 [yánzhòng de] **3** (negatively) [speak, say +] 以批评的态度 [yǐ pīping de tàidù] **4** (analytically) [examine, think, study +] 一丝不苟地 [yīsībùgǒu de] **5** (by critics) [acclaimed, successful +] 根据评论家判断 [gēnjù pínglùnjiā pànduàn]

criticism ['krɪtɪsɪzəm] N **1** [U] (censure) 批评 [pīping] **2** [c] (complaint) 指责 [zhǐzé] **3** [U] [of book, play etc] 评论 [pínglùn]

criticize ['krɪtɪsaɪz] VT 批评 [pīping] ▶ **to criticize sb for (doing) sth** 批评某人(做)某事

Croat ['krəuæt] N **1** [c] (person) 克罗地亚人 [Kèluódìyàrén] **2** [U] (language) 克罗地亚语 [Kèluódìyà yǔ]

Croatia [krəu'eɪʃə] N 克罗地亚 [Kèluódìyà]

Croatian [krəu'eɪʃən] I ADJ 克罗地亚的 [Kèluódìyà de] II N = **Croat**

crochet ['krəuʃeɪ] I N [U] 钩针编织 [gōuzhēn biānzhī] II VI, VT 用钩针编织 [yòng gōuzhēn biānzhī]

crockery ['krɔkərɪ] N [U] 陶器 [táoqì]

crocodile ['krɔkədaɪl] N [c] 鳄鱼 [èyú]

crocus ['krəukəs] N [c] 番红花 [fānhónghuā]

croissant ['kwæsnt] N [c] 羊角面包 [yángjiǎo miànbāo]

crook [kruk] N [c] **1** (inf) (criminal) 坏蛋 [huàidàn] **2** (stick) [of shepherd, bishop] 手杖 [shǒuzhàng] ▶ **the crook of one's arm/leg** 臂弯/膝弯

crooked ['krukɪd] ADJ **1** (twisted) [+ nose, teeth] 变形的 [biànxíng de]; [+ line] 弯曲的 [wānqū de] **2** (off-centre) [+ picture, tie] 歪的 [wāi de] **3** (inf) (dishonest) 不老实的 [bùlǎoshí de]

crop [krɔp] I N **1** [c] (plant) 庄稼 [zhuāngjia] **2** [c] (amount produced) 收成 [shōuchéng] **3** [S] (fig) (batch) 一批 [yīpī] **4** [c] (hairstyle) 平头 [píngtóu] **5** [c] (also: **riding crop**) 短马鞭 [duǎn mǎbiān] II VT **1** [+ hair] 剪短 [jiǎnduǎn] **2** [animal +] [+ grass] 啃吃 [kěnchī] ▶ **crop up** VI **1** (appear unexpectedly) 意外地出现 [yìwài de chūxiàn] **2** (appear) 被提到 [bèi tídào]

cross [krɔs] I N [c] **1** (x shape) 交叉符号 [jiāochā fúhào] (showing disagreement) 叉号 [chāhào] **2** (crucifix shape) 十字 [shízì] **3** (REL) 十字架 [shízìjià] **4** (mixture) ▶ **a cross between sth and sth** 某物和某物的混合物 [mǒuwù hé mǒuwù de hùnhéwù] **5** (crossbreed) 杂交品种 [zájiāo pǐnzhǒng] **6** (FOOTBALL) 横传 [héngchuán] II VT **1** [+ person +] [+ street, room etc] 横穿 [héngchuān] [+ road, railway, bridge +] [+ river, land etc] 横跨 [héngkuà] **3** [+ arms, legs, fingers] 交叉 [jiāochā] **4** [smile, expression +] [+ face] 显露在 [xiǎnlù zài] **5** (BRIT) [+ cheque] 在支票上画两条平行线，只可转账无法兑现 **6** (crossbreed) ▶ **to cross sth with sth** 将

某物与某物交配 [jiāng mǒuwù yǔ mǒuwù jiāopèi] **7** (FOOTBALL) [+ *ball*] 横传 [héngchuán] **8** (*oppose*) [+ *person*] 阻挠 [zǔnáo] **III** **VI** **1** [*roads, lines +*] 相交 [xiāngjiāo] **2** ▶ **to cross from ... to ...** (*walking*) 从…走到… [cóng…zǒudào…]; (*on ferry*) 从…横渡到… [cóng…héngdùdào…] **IV** **ADJ** (*angry*) 生气的 [shēngqì de] ▶ **the thought never crossed my mind** 我从来都没这么想过 ▶ **to cross o.s.** (REL) 划十字祈求上帝保佑 ▶ **we have a crossed line** (BRIT) (*on telephone*) 我们的电话串线了 ▶ **they've got their lines** *or* **wires crossed** (*fig*) 他们相互误会了 ▶ **to be/get cross with sb** 生某人的气 ▶ **to be/get cross about sth** 因为某事生气 ▶ **it makes me very cross** 这令我很生气
　▶ **cross off** **VT** (*delete*) 取消 [qǔxiāo]
　▶ **cross out** **VT** (*delete*) 取消 [qǔxiāo]
　▶ **cross over** **VI** (*cross the street*) 过马路 [guò mǎlù] ▶ **to cross over from ... to ...** 从…到…去

cross-country [krɔs'kʌntrɪ] **I** **N** [U] (*running*) 越野赛跑 [yuèyě sàipǎo] **II** **ADJ** [+ *running, race, skier, journey etc*] 越野的 [yuèyě de] **III** **ADV**
　▶ **to go cross-country** 走小路 [zǒu xiǎolù]

crossing ['krɔsɪŋ] **N** [C] **1** (*voyage*) 横渡 [héngdù] **2** (BRIT) (*also*: **pedestrian crossing**) 人行横道 [rénxíng héngdào] [美 = **crosswalk**]

crossing guard (US) **N** [C] 为保证儿童安全过马路手持暂停指挥牌的交通管理员 [英 = **lollipop man, lollipop lady**]

crossroads ['krɔsrəudz] (*pl* **crossroads**) **N** [C] (*junction, decisive point*) 十字路口 [shízì lùkǒu]

cross section **N** [C] **1** [*of*] (*population*) 典型 [diǎnxíng] **2** [*of object*] 横截面 [héngjiémiàn]

crosswalk ['krɔswɔːk] (US) **N** [C] 人行横道 [rénxíng héngdào] [英 = **(pedestrian) crossing**]

crossword ['krɔswɜːd] **N** [C] (*also*: **crossword puzzle**) 填字游戏 [tiánzì yóuxì]

crotch [krɔtʃ], **crutch** [krʌtʃ] **N** [C] **1** (*groin*) 胯部 [kuàbù] **2** [*of garment*] 裤裆 [kùdāng]

crouch [krautʃ] **VI** (*also*: **crouch down**) 蹲 [dūn]
　▶ **to be crouching** 蹲着 [dūnzhe] ▶ **to crouch over sth** 蹲在某物上

crouton ['kruːtɔn] **N** [C] 烤的/炸的面包丁 [kǎo de/zhá de miànbāodīng]

crow [krəu] **I** **N** [C] (*bird*) 乌鸦 [wūyā] **II** **VI** **1** [*cockerel +*] 啼叫 [tíjiào] **2** (*boast*) ▶ **to crow about** *or* **over sth** 因某事得意洋洋 [yīn mǒushì déyìyángyáng]

crowd [kraud] **I** **N** [C] [*of people, fans etc*] 人群 [rénqún] **II** **VT** (*cram*) 挤满 [jǐmǎn] **III** **VI** **1** (*gather*) ▶ **to crowd around sb/sth** 聚集在某人/某处周围 [jùjí zài mǒurén/mǒuchù zhōuwéi] **2** (*cram*) ▶ **to crowd into sth** 大批涌入某处 [dàpī yǒngrù mǒuchù] ▶ **the/our crowd** [*of friends etc*] 一伙人/我们这伙人
　▶ **crowds of people** 大批人群 ▶ **don't crowd me** 别挤我
　▶ **crowd in** **VI** 大批涌入 [dàpī yǒngrù]

crowded ['kraudɪd] **ADJ** **1** (*full*) [+ *room, ship, train*] 拥挤的 [yōngjǐ de] **2** (*densely populated*) [+ *area*] 人口众多的 [rénkǒu zhòng duō de]; [+ *conditions*] 拥挤的 [yōngjǐ de] ▶ **to be crowded with** [+ *people*] 挤满了; [+ *things*] 满是

crown [kraun] **I** **N** [C] **1** [*of monarch*] 皇冠 [huángguān] **2** ▶ **the Crown** (*monarchy*) 君主立宪政府 [jūnzhǔ lìxiàn zhèngfǔ] **3** (*top*) [*of head*] 头顶 [tóudǐng]; [*of hat*] 帽顶 [màodǐng] **4** (*on tooth*) 假齿冠 [jiǎchǐ guān] **II** **VT** **1** [+ *monarch*] 为…加冕 [wèi…jiāmiǎn] **2** (*liter*) [+ *hill, cliff*] 覆盖…的顶端 [fùgài…de dǐngduān] **3** (*fig*) [+ *event, career*] 圆满地结束 [yuánmǎn de jiéshù] ▶ **to crown sb king** 加冕某人为国王

crown jewels **NPL** ▶ **the Crown Jewels** 御宝 [yùbǎo]

crucial ['kruːʃl] **ADJ** 关键性的 [guānjiàn xìng de] ▶ **to be crucial to sth** 对某事是至关重要的

crucifix ['kruːsɪfɪks] **N** [C] 耶稣十字架 [yēsū shízìjià]

crude [kruːd] **ADJ** **1** (*simple*) 简陋的 [jiǎnlòu de] **2** (*vulgar*) 粗俗的 [cūsú de] **3** (*not processed*) 未加工的 [wèi jiāgōng de]

crude oil **N** [U] 原油 [yuányóu]

cruel ['kruəl] **ADJ** **1** (*unkind*) [+ *person*] 残忍的 [cánrěn de]; [+ *treatment, behaviour*] 恶毒的 [èdú de] **2** (*tough*) [+ *situation, action, world*] 残酷的 [cánkù de] ▶ **to be cruel to sb** 残酷地对待某人

cruelty ['kruəltɪ] **N** [U] [*of person*] 残忍 [cánrěn]; [*of situation, action*] 残酷性 [cánkùxìng]
　▶ **cruelty to animals** 对动物的虐待

cruise [kruːz] **I** **N** [C] 游船 [yóuchuán] **II** **VI** **1** (*go on cruise*) 坐游船 [zuò yóuchuán] **2** [*car, ship, aircraft +*] 以中等速度航行 [yǐ zhōngděng sùdù hángxíng] **3** [*taxi +*] 漫无目的地行驶 [mànwú mùdì de xíngshǐ] ▶ **to be/go on a cruise** 乘游船旅行 ▶ **world cruise** 环球游船旅行 ▶ **to cruise up** *or* **along a road** 在路上缓慢行驶

crumb [krʌm] **N** [C] **1** [*of bread, cake*] 碎屑 [suìxiè] **2** [*of information, comfort*] 一点点 [yīdiǎndiǎn]

crumble ['krʌmbl] **I** **VI** **1** [*plaster, earth etc +*] 破碎 [pòsuì] **2** (*also*: **crumble away**) [*building, cliff etc +*] 碎裂 [suìliè] **3** [*system, relationship, hope +*] 崩溃 [bēngkuì] **II** **VT** [+ *bread, biscuit etc*] 弄碎 [nòngsuì]

crumpet ['krʌmpɪt] **N** **1** [C] (ESP BRIT: CULIN) 烤面饼 [kǎo miànbǐng] **2** [U] (BRIT: *infl*) (*attractive women*) 性感女人 [xìnggǎn nǚrén]

crumple ['krʌmpl] **VT** (*also*: **crumple up**) [+ *paper, clothes*] 弄皱 [nòngzhòu] **II** **VI** [*face +*] 皱起来 [zhòuqǐlái]

crunch [krʌntʃ] **I** **VT** **1** (*with teeth*) 嘎吱嘎吱地咬嚼 [gāzhīgāzhī de yǎojiáo] **2** (*underfoot*) 使发出刺耳的碎裂声 [shǐ fāchū cìěr de suìliè shēng] II VI [gravel, wheels +] 发出嘎吱声 [fāchū gāzhī shēng] III N 1 [c] (sound) 嘎吱声 [gāzhī shēng] 2 (moment of truth) ► the crunch 关键时刻 [guānjiàn shíkè] ► if/when it comes to the crunch 如果/当必须得做点什么的时候

crunchy ['krʌntʃi] ADJ [+ salad, vegetables, cornflakes, nuts] 脆的 [cuì de]

crush [krʌʃ] I VT 1 [+ tin, box] 压坏 [yāhuài] 2 (break up) [+ garlic] 压碎 [yāsuì]; [+ ice] 碾碎 [niǎnsuì] 3 (squeeze) [+ person] 使挤在一起 [shǐ jǐzài yīqǐ] 4 (defeat) [+ army, opposition] 镇压 [zhènyā] 5 (devastate) [+ hopes, person] 使意气消沉 [shǐ yìqì xiāochén] II N [c] 1 (crowd) 拥挤的人群 [yōngjǐ de rénqún] 2 (inf) ► to have a crush on sb 迷恋某人 [míliàn mǒurén] ► to be crushed to death 被压死

crust [krʌst] N [c] (on bread, pastry) 皮 [pí]; (on snow, ice) 硬表层 [yìng biǎocéng] ► the earth's crust 地壳

crusty ['krʌsti] ADJ [+ loaf, bread] 有脆皮的 [yǒu cuìpí de]

crutch [krʌtʃ] N [c] 1 (stick) 拐杖 [guǎizhàng] 2 (fig) (support) 支持 [zhīchí] 3 (ESP BRIT) = crotch ► on crutches 拄拐杖

cry [kraɪ] I VI (weep) 哭 [kū] II VI (also: cry out) 叫喊 [jiàohǎn] III N [c] 1 (shriek) (human) 尖叫 [jiānjiào]; [of bird, animal] 大叫 [dàjiào] 2 (shout) 叫喊 [jiàohǎn] ► what are you crying about? 你哭什么？ ► to cry for help 呼救 ► a cry for help 呼救声 ► to have a good cry 痛哭一场 ► it's a far cry from... 和⋯大相径庭
► **cry off** VI 打退堂鼓 [dǎ tuìtánggǔ]
► **cry out** VI, VT 叫喊 [jiàohǎn]
► **cry out for** VT FUS [不可拆分] (need) 迫切需要 [pòqiè xūyào]

cryptic ['krɪptɪk] ADJ [+ remark, clue] 有隐义的 [yǒu yǐnyì de]

crystal ['krɪstl] I N 1 [c] (mineral) 结晶体 [jiéjīngtǐ] 2 [c/u] (in jewellery) 水晶 [shuǐjīng] 3 [u] (glass) 晶质玻璃制品 [jīngzhì bōli zhìpǐn] II CPD [复合词] [+ glass, vase] 水晶 [shuǐjīng]

CTC (BRIT) N ABBR (= city technology college) 城市科技学院 [Chéngshì Kējì Xuéyuàn]

CU (TEXTING) ABBR (= see you) 再见！[zàijiàn]

cub [kʌb] I N [c] 1 (young lion, wolf, fox, bear) 幼兽 [yòushòu] 2 (also: cub scout) 幼童军 [yòutóngjūn] II the Cubs NPL (also: the Cub Scouts) 幼童军 [yòutóngjūn]

Cuba ['kjuːbə] N 古巴 [Gǔbā]

Cuban ['kjuːbən] I ADJ 古巴的 [Gǔbā de] II N [c] (person) 古巴人 [Gǔbārén]

cube [kjuːb] I N [c] 1 (shape) 立方体 [lìfāngtǐ] 2 (MATH) [of number] 立方 [lìfāng] II VT (MATH) 使自乘两次 [shǐ zìchéng liǎngcì]

cubicle ['kjuːbɪkl] N [c] 小室 [xiǎoshì]

cuckoo ['kuku:] N [c] 杜鹃 [dùjuān]

cucumber ['kjuːkʌmbə(r)] N [c/u] 黄瓜 [huángguā]

cuddle ['kʌdl] I VT, VI 搂抱 [lǒubào] II N [c] 拥抱 [yōngbào] ► to have a cuddle 拥抱 ► to give sb a cuddle 拥抱某人

cue [kjuː] N [c] 1 (in theatre) 提示 [tíshì] 2 (stick) 球杆 [qiúgān] 3 (fig) ► a cue for sth/to do sth 某事/做某事的暗示 [mǒushì/zuò mǒushì de 'ànshì] ► to take one's cue from sb (fig) 以某人为榜样 ► on cue (at the expected time) 就在这时

cuff [kʌf] I N [c] 1 [of sleeve] 袖口 [xiùkǒu] 2 (US) [of trousers] 翻边 [fānbiān] [英= turn-up] 3 (blow) 轻轻的一拍 [qīngqīng de yīpāi] II VT (hit) 用掌轻拍 [yòngzhǎng de qīngpāi] ► off the cuff 未经准备

cufflinks ['kʌflɪŋks] NPL 袖扣 [xiùkòu]

cuisine [kwɪˈziːn] N [u] [of country, region] 烹饪 [pēngrèn]

CUL8R (TEXTING) ABBR (= see you later) 一会儿见 [yīhuìr jiàn]

cul-de-sac ['kʌldəsæk] (ESP BRIT) N [c] (road) 死胡同 [sǐ hútòng] [美= dead end]

culinary ['kʌlɪnəri] (frm) ADJ 烹饪的 [pēngrèn de]

cull [kʌl] I VT 1 [+ animals] 杀掉⋯中的一部分以减少其数量 [shādiào...zhōng de yībùfen yǐ jiǎnshǎo qí shùliàng] 2 ► to cull sth from sth [+ story, idea] 从某物中精选出某物 [cóng mǒuwù zhōng jīngxuǎnchū mǒuwù] II N [c] [of animals] 剔除 [tíchú]

culminate ['kʌlmɪneɪt] VI ► to culminate in or with sth 终于获得某物 [zhōngyú huòdé mǒuwù]

culprit ['kʌlprɪt] N [c] 1 (perpetrator) 罪犯 [zuìfàn] 2 (cause) 原因 [yuányīn]

cult [kʌlt] I N [c] 1 (REL) 异教 [yìjiào] 2 (fashion) 时尚 [shíshàng] II CPD [复合词] [+ status] 狂热崇拜的 [kuángrè chóngbài de]; [+ film] 风靡一时的 [fēngmíyīshí de] ► cult figure 崇拜偶像

cultivate ['kʌltɪveɪt] VT 1 [+ land] 耕作 [gēngzuò]; [+ crop] 种植 [zhòngzhí] 2 (fig) [+ attitude, image, skill] 培养 [péiyǎng]; [+ person] 结交 [jiéjiāo]; [+ relationship] 建立 [jiànlì]

cultivation [kʌltɪˈveɪʃən] N [u] 1 [of land] 耕种 [gēngzhòng]; [of crop] 种植 [zhòngzhí] 2 (fig) [of attitude, image, skill] 培养 [péiyǎng]

cultural ['kʌltʃərəl] ADJ [+ heritage, tradition, exchange] 文化的 [wénhuà de]

culture ['kʌltʃə(r)] N 1 [c/u] 文化 [wénhuà] 2 [c] (BIO) 培养的细菌 [péiyǎng de xìjūn]

cultured ['kʌltʃəd] ADJ 1 [+ person] 有修养的 [yǒu xiūyǎng de] 2 [+ pearl] 人工养殖的 [réngōng yǎngzhí de]

cumin ['kʌmɪn] N [u] 小茴香 [xiǎohuíxiāng]

cunning ['kʌnɪŋ] I ADJ [+ person, plan, idea] 狡猾的 [jiǎohuá de] II N [u] 狡诈 [jiǎozhà]

○ **cup** [kʌp] I N [c] 1 (for drinking) 杯子 [bēizi] 2 (trophy) 奖杯 [jiǎngbēi] 3 (quantity) 杯 [bēi] 4 [of bra] 罩杯 [zhàobēi] II VT ► to cup sth in one's hands 用手捧拢着某物 [yòngshǒu qūlǒngzhe mǒuwù] ▸ **a cup of tea** 一杯茶 ▸ **to cup one's hands** 捧起手

cupboard ['kʌbəd] N [C] **1** (piece of furniture) 柜子 [guìzi] **2** (BRIT) (room) 小储藏室 [xiǎo chǔcángshì] [美= closet]

cup final N [C] 优胜杯决赛 [yōushèng bēi juésài]

curate ['kjuərɪt] N [C] 助理牧师 [zhùlǐ mùshī]

curator [kjuə'reɪtə(r)] N [C] (of museum, gallery) 馆长 [guǎnzhǎng]

curb [kə:b] I VT [+ powers, expenditure] 约束 [yuēshù]; [+ emotion, behaviour] 抑制 [yìzhì] II N [C] **1** (restraint) ▸ **curb on sth** 对某事的管制 [duì mǒushì de guǎnzhì] **2** (US) = **kerb**

curdle ['kə:dl] I VI 凝结 [níngjié] II VT 使凝结 [shǐ níngjié]

cure [kjuə(r)] I VT **1** (MED) [+ illness] 治好 [zhìhǎo]; [+ patient] 治愈 [zhìyù] **2** (solve) [+ problem] 解决 [jiějué] **3** (preserve) [+ meat, fish] 熏 [xūn]; [+ skin, hide] 腌 [yán] II N [C] **1** (MED) 疗法 [liáofǎ] **2** (solution) 对策 [duìcè] ▸ **to be cured of sth** 被治好了某病

curfew ['kə:fju:] N [C/U] 宵禁令 [xiāojìnlìng] ▸ **to put** or **place sth/sb under curfew** 对某处/某人实行宵禁 ▸ **to impose a curfew on sth/sb** 对某处/某人实行宵禁

curiosity [kjuərɪ'ɔsɪti] N **1** [U] (inquisitiveness) 好奇心 [hàoqíxīn] **2** [C] (unusual thing) 奇物 [qíwù]

curious ['kjuərɪəs] ADJ **1** (inquisitive) 好奇的 [hàoqí de] **2** (strange) 奇特的 [qítè de] ▸ **to be curious about sb/sth** 对某人/某物感到好奇 ▸ **to be curious to know/see…** 好奇地想知道/看…

curl [kə:l] I N [C] (of hair) 卷发 [juǎnfà]; (of smoke) 缕 [lǚ] II VT [+ hair] 使变卷 [shǐ biànjuǎn] III VI **1** [hair +] 卷曲 [juǎnqū] **2** [smoke +] 盘绕 [pánrào] ▸ **curl up** VI [person, animal +] 蜷作一团 [quánzuò yītuán]

curler ['kə:lə(r)] N [C] 卷发夹 [juǎnfà jiā]

curly ['kə:lɪ] ADJ [+ hair, leaves, tail] 卷曲的 [quánqū de]

currant ['kʌrnt] N [C] **1** (dried grape) 无子葡萄干 [wúzǐ pútɑo gān]; (also: **blackcurrant**) 黑加仑 [hēijiālún]; (also: **redcurrant**) 红加仑 [hóngjiālún] **2** (bush) (also: **blackcurrant**) 黑加仑灌木 [hēijiālún guànmù]; (also: **redcurrant**) 红加仑灌木 [hóngjiālún guànmù]

currency ['kʌrnsɪ] N [C/U] **1** 货币 [huòbì] **2** ▸ **to gain currency** 流行起来 [liúxíng qǐlái] ▸ **to have currency** 流行

◎**current** ['kʌrnt] I N [C] **1** [of air, water] 流 [liú] **2** (ELEC) 电流 [diànliú] **3** [of opinion, thought etc] 趋势 [qūshì] II ADJ **1** (present) [+ situation, tendency, policy etc] 目前的 [mùqián de] ▷ *The current situation is very different.* 目前的情况很不同。**2** (accepted) [+ idea, thought, custom] 流行的 [liúxíng de] ▷ *This custom was still current in the 1960s.* 这个习俗在20世纪60年代还是很流行。▸ **the current issue** [of magazine] 最近一期

current account (BRIT) N [C] 活期存款账户 [huóqī cúnkuǎn zhànghù] [美= checking account]

current affairs NPL 时事 [shíshì] ▸ **a current affairs programme** 时事讨论节目

currently ['kʌrntlɪ] ADV 现在 [xiànzài]

curriculum [kə'rɪkjuləm] (pl **curriculums** or **curricula** [kə'rɪkjulə]) N [C] **1** (for all subjects) 全部课程 [quánbù kèchéng] **2** (for particular subject) 课程 [kèchéng]

curriculum vitae [-'vi:taɪ] (ESP BRIT) N [C] 简历 [jiǎnlì] [美= résumé]

curry ['kʌrɪ] I N [C/U] (dish) 咖哩 [gālí] II VT ▸ **to curry favour with sb** 拍某人的马屁 [pāi mǒurén de mǎpì]

curry powder N [U] 咖喱粉 [gālí fěn]

curse [kə:s] I VI (swear) 诅咒 [zǔzhòu] II VT **1** (swear at) 诅咒 [zǔzhòu] **2** (complain about) 咒骂 [zhòumà] III N [C] **1** (spell) 诅咒 [zǔzhòu] **2** (swearword) 咒骂的话 [zhòumà de huà] **3** (scourge) 灾祸 [zāihuò] ▸ **to curse sb for sth/for doing sth** 因某事/做某事而咒骂某人

cursor ['kə:sə(r)] (COMPUT) N [C] 光标 [guāngbiāo]

curt [kə:t] ADJ [+ reply, tone, person] 唐突无礼的 [tángtūwúlǐ de]

curtain ['kə:tn] N [C] **1** (ESP BRIT) (at window) 窗帘 [chuānglián] [美= **drape**] **2** (in theatre) 帷幕 [wéimù] ▸ **to draw the curtains** (together) 拉上窗帘; (apart) 拉开窗帘

curve [kə:v] I N [C] 曲线 [qūxiàn]; (in road) 弯曲部分 [wānqū bùfen] II VI [road, line +] 弯曲 [wānqū]; [structure, spine etc +] 成曲线形 [chéng qūxiàn xíng]

curved [kə:vd] ADJ 弯曲的 [wānqū de]

cushion ['kuʃən] I N [C] **1** (on sofa, chair) 靠垫 [kàodiàn] **2** (fig) [of air] 垫状物 [diànzhuàng wù] II VT **1** [+ impact, fall] 对…起缓冲作用 [duì…qǐ huǎnchōng zuòyòng] **2** [+ shock, effect] 缓和…的影响 [huǎnhé…de yǐngxiǎng]

custard ['kʌstəd] N [U] (for pouring) 蛋奶沙司 [dànnǎi shāsī]; (set) 蛋奶糕 [dànnǎigāo]

custody ['kʌstədɪ] N [U] **1** [of child] 监护权 [jiānhù quán] **2** (for offenders) 拘留 [jūliú] ▸ **to be remanded in custody** 拘留候审 ▸ **to take sb into custody** 拘捕某人

custom ['kʌstəm] I N **1** [C/U] (tradition) 传统 [chuántǒng] **2** [C/U] (convention) 惯例 [guànlì] **3** [C] (habit) 习惯 [xíguàn] **4** [U] (BRIT) [of shop] 光顾 [guānggù] II **customs** NPL 海关 [hǎiguān] ▸ **to go through customs** 过海关

customer ['kʌstəmə(r)] N [C] (in shop) 顾客 [gùkè] ▸ **he's a cool customer** (inf) 他是个很酷的家伙

customize ['kʌstəmaɪz] VT [+ product, car, software etc] 按顾客的具体要求制造 [àn gùkè de jùtǐ yāoqiú zhìzào]

customs officer N [C] 海关官员 [hǎiguān guānyuán]

○ **cut** [kʌt] (pt, pp **cut**) I VT 1 [+ bread, meat] 切 [qiē] 2 (injure) ▸ **to cut one's hand/knee** 割破手/膝盖 [gēpò shǒu/xīgài] 3 (shorten) [+ grass, hair, nails] 修剪 [xiūjiǎn] 4 (remove) [+ scene, episode, paragraph] 删剪 [shānjiǎn] 5 (reduce) [+ prices, spending] 削减 [xiāojiǎn] 6 (stop) [+ supply] 中断 [zhōngduàn] 7 (shape) [+ clothes] 剪裁 [jiǎncái] 8 (ESP US: inf) (miss) [+ class, school] 逃避 [táobì] II VI (take shortcut) ▸ **to cut across** or **through a place** 穿过某处抄近路 [chuānguò mǒuchù chāo jìnlù] III N 1 [C] (injury) 伤口 [shāngkǒu] 2 [C] (reduction) (in salary, spending etc) 削减 [xuējiǎn] 3 [C] (interruption) (in supply) 中断 [zhōngduàn] 4 [C] of meat) 切下的肉块 [qiēxià de ròukuài] 5 [S] of garment) 款式 [kuǎnshì] ▸ **to cut sth in half** [+ food, object] 将某物切成两半; [+ line, path] 将某物分成两部分 ▸ **to cut o.s.** 割破自己 ▸ **to cut a hole in sth** 在某物上打个洞 ▸ **to cut a tooth** 长牙 ▸ **to get** or **have one's hair cut** 剪发 ▸ **to cut a visit short** 缩短访问时间 ▸ **to make a cut in sth** 在某物上划一下 ▸ **a cut and blow-dry** 剪发吹干 ▸ **to be a cut above...** 比…高一等 ▸ **cut across** VT FUS [不可拆分] [issue, problem +] [+ groups, generations] 影响到 [yǐngxiǎng dào] ▸ **cut back** VT 1 [+ plants, foliage] 修剪 [xiūjiǎn] 2 (also: **cut back on**) [+ production, expenditure] 削减 [xuējiǎn] ▸ **cut down** VT 1 [+ tree] 砍倒 [kǎndǎo] 2 (reduce) [+ consumption etc] 减少 [jiǎnshǎo] ▸ **to cut sb down to size** (inf) 使某人摆正自己的位置 ▸ **cut down on** VT FUS [不可拆分] [+ alcohol, coffee, cigarettes etc] 减少 [jiǎnshǎo] ▸ **cut in** VI 1 (interrupt) ▸ **to cut in (on sb)** 打断 (某人) [dǎduàn (mǒurén)] 2 [car, driver +] 超车抢道 [chāochē qiǎngdào] ▸ **cut off** I VT 1 [+ part of sth] 切掉 [qiēdiào] 2 [+ person, village] 使隔绝 [shǐ géjué] 3 [+ supply] 停止供应 [tíngzhǐ gōngyìng] 4 (TEL) (during conversation) 中断…的通话 [zhōngduàn…de tōnghuà] ▸ **to get cut off** (TEL) 通话中断 ▸ **cut out** I VT 1 [+ coupon, newspaper article] 剪下 [jiǎnxià] 2 (stop) [+ activity] 停止 [tíngzhǐ] 3 (remove) [+ scene, episode, paragraph] 删去 [shānqù] 4 (keep out) [+ light] 遮蔽 [zhēbì] II VI [engine +] 不再起作用 [bùzài qǐzuòyòng] ▸ **cut up** VT 1 [+ paper, food] 切碎 [qiēsuì] 2 [+ driver, car] 超车抢道 [chāochē qiǎngdào] ▸ **to be cut up about sth** (ESP BRIT: inf) 因某事伤心

cutback ['kʌtbæk] N [C] ▸ **cutback (in sth)** 减少(某物) [jiǎnshǎo]

cute [kjuːt] ADJ 1 (inf) (sweet) [+ child, dog, house] 可爱的 [kě'ài de] 2 (ESP US: inf) (attractive) 迷

人的 [mírén de] 3 (US: esp inf) (clever) 小聪明的 [xiǎocōngmíng de]

cutlery ['kʌtlərɪ] (BRIT) N [U] 餐具 [cānjù]

cutlet ['kʌtlɪt] N [C] 炸肉饼 [zhá ròubǐng] ▸ **vegetable/nut cutlet** 蔬菜/坚果炸饼

cut-price ['kʌtˈpraɪs] (BRIT) ADJ 削价的 [xuējià de] [美= **cut-rate**]

cut-rate ['kʌtˈreɪt] (US) ADJ 削价的 [xuējià de] [英= **cut-price**]

cutting ['kʌtɪŋ] I N [C] 1 (BRIT) (from newspaper) 剪报 [jiǎnbào] [美= **clipping**] 2 (BRIT: RAIL) 路基 [lùjī] [美= **cut**] 3 (from plant) 插条 [chātiáo] II ADJ [+ remark] 尖刻的 [jiānkè de] ▸ **at the cutting edge of sth** 在某事的前沿

CV N ABBR (= curriculum vitae) 简历 [jiǎnlì] [美= **résumé**]

cyanide ['saɪənaɪd] N [U] 氰化物 [qínghuàwù]

cybercafé ['saɪbəkæfeɪ] N [C] 网吧 [wǎngbā]

cyberspace ['saɪbəspeɪs] N [U] 电脑空间 [diànnǎo kōngjiān]

cycle ['saɪkl] I N [C] 1 (of events, seasons etc) 周期 [zhōuqī]; (of songs, poems) 组 [zǔ] 2 (bicycle) 自行车 [zìxíngchē] 3 (TECH) (movement) 循环 [xúnhuán] II VI 骑自行车 [qí zìxíngchē] III CPD [复合词] [+ shop, helmet, route] 自行车 [zìxíngchē] ▸ **to go cycling** 骑自行车

cycle hire N [U] 自行车出租 [zìxíngchē chūzū]

cycle lane N [C] 自行车道 [zìxíngchēdào]

cycle path N [C] 自行车道 [zìxíngchēdào]

cycling ['saɪklɪŋ] N [U] 骑自行车 [qí zìxíngchē] ▸ **to go on a cycling holiday** (BRIT) 骑自行车旅行度假

cyclist ['saɪklɪst] N [C] 骑自行车的人 [qí zìxíngchē de rén]

cyclone ['saɪkləʊn] N [C] 龙卷风 [lóngjuǎnfēng]

cylinder ['sɪlɪndə(r)] N [C] 1 (shape) 圆柱体 [yuánzhùtǐ] 2 [of gas] 罐 [guàn] 3 (in engine, machine etc) 汽缸 [qìgāng]

cymbal ['sɪmbl] N [C] 钹 [pō]

cynic ['sɪnɪk] N [C] 愤世嫉俗者 [fènshìjísúzhě]

cynical ['sɪnɪkl] ADJ [+ person, attitude] 愤世嫉俗的 [fènshìjísú de] ▸ **to be cynical about sth** 不信任某事

cynicism ['sɪnɪsɪzəm] N [U] 愤世嫉俗 [fènshìjísú] ▸ **cynicism (about sth/sb)** (对某事/某人的)不信任感

Cypriot ['sɪprɪət] I ADJ 塞浦路斯的 [Sàipǔlùsī de] II N [C] (person) 塞浦路斯人 [Sàipǔlùsīrén]

Cyprus ['saɪprəs] N 塞浦路斯 [Sàipǔlùsī]

cyst [sɪst] N [C] 囊肿 [nángzhǒng]

cystitis [sɪsˈtaɪtɪs] N [U] 膀胱炎 [pángguāngyán]

Czech [tʃɛk] I ADJ 捷克的 [Jiékè de] II N 1 [C] (person) 捷克人 [Jiékèrén] 2 [U] (language) 捷克语 [Jiékè yǔ]

Czech Republic N ▸ **the Czech Republic** 捷克共和国 [Jiékègònghéguó]

Dd

D¹, d [di:] N [C/U] (letter) 英语的第四个字母

D² [di:] I N **1** [C/U] (MUS) C大调音阶中的第二音 **2** [C] (SCOL, UNIV) (mark) 差 [chà] II (US: POL) ABBR = **democrat(ic)**

d. ABBR (= died) 死亡 [sǐwáng]

D.A. (US) N ABBR (= district attorney) 地方检察官 [dìfāng jiǎncháguān]

dab [dæb] I VT **1** [+ eyes, lips] 轻擦 [qīngcā] **2** [+ paint, cream] 轻而快地涂 [qīng ér kuài de tú] II N [C] (inf) ▶ **a dab (of sth)** [of paint, glue] 少量(的某物) [shǎoliàng (de mǒuwù)] ▶ **to dab a wound with sth** 用某物轻擦伤口 ▶ **to be a dab hand at sth/doing sth** (BRIT: inf) 是某方面的能手/擅长做某事
▶ **dab at** VT FUS [不可拆分] [+ mouth, eyes, paper] 轻轻地按 [qīngqīng de àn]

dabble ['dæbl] VI ▶ **to dabble in sth** [+ politics, antiques etc] 涉猎某事 [shèliè mǒushì] ▶ **she dabbled with drugs** 她染上了毒品

dad [dæd] (inf) N [C] 爸爸 [bàba]

daddy ['dædɪ] (inf) N = **dad**

daffodil ['dæfədɪl] N [C] 黄水仙 [huángshuǐxiān]

daft [dɑ:ft] (BRIT: inf) ADJ (silly) 傻的 [shǎ de] ▶ **to be daft about sb/sth** 酷爱某人/某事

dagger ['dægə(r)] N [C] 匕首 [bǐshǒu] ▶ **to be at daggers drawn with sb** (BRIT) 与某人势不两立 ▶ **to look daggers at sb** 对某人怒目而视

daily ['deɪlɪ] I ADJ 每日的 [měirì de] II N [C] (newspaper) 日报 [rìbào] III ADV 每日 [měirì]
▶ **twice daily** 每天两次 ▶ **daily life** 日常生活

dairy ['dɛərɪ] I N [C] **1** (company) 牛奶及乳品店 [niúnǎi jí rǔpǐn diàn] **2** (on farm) 牛奶场 [niúnǎichǎng] II ADJ **1** (made from milk) [+ products, produce] 乳制品的 [rǔzhìpǐn de] **2** (producing milk) [+ cattle, cow, herd] 产乳的 [chǎnrǔ de]; [+ industry, farming] 生产乳品的 [shēngchǎn rǔpǐn de]

daisy ['deɪzɪ] N [C] 雏菊 [chùjú]

dam [dæm] I N [C] (on river) 水坝 [shuǐbà] II VT [+ river] 建水坝于 [jiàn shuǐbà yú]

damage ['dæmɪdʒ] I N [U] **1** (harm) 损坏 [sǔnhuài] **2** (dents, scratches etc) 损伤 [sǔnshāng] **3** (to sb's reputation etc) 损害 [sǔnhài] II VT **1** (spoil, break) [+ object, building] 毁坏 [huǐhuài] **2** (harm) [+ reputation, economy] 破坏 [pòhuài] III **damages** NPL (LAW) 损害赔偿金 [sǔnhuài péichángjīn] ▶ **to pay 5,000 pounds in damages** 支付5,000英镑赔偿金 ▶ **to cause/inflict damage** (physically) 造成损失; (fig) 造成破坏

damn [dæm] I ADJ (inf) (also: **damned**) 该死的 [gāisǐ de] II ADV (inf) (also: **damned**) 非常地 [fēicháng de] III N (inf) ▶ **I don't give a damn** 我根本不在乎 [wǒ gēnběn bù zàihu] IV VT (condemn) 指责 [zhǐzé] ▶ **damn (it)!** (inf) 该死!

damned [dæmd] I ADJ = **damn** II ADV = **damn**

damning ['dæmɪŋ] ADJ [+ evidence, report] 非常不利的 [fēicháng bùlì de]

damp [dæmp] I ADJ [+ building, air, cloth] 潮湿的 [cháoshī de] II N [U] (in air, in walls) 湿气 [shīqì] III VT (also: **dampen**) [+ cloth] 使潮湿 [shǐ cháoshī]; [+ enthusiasm, spirits etc] 打击 [dǎjī]
▶ **damp down** VT FUS [不可拆分] (calm) 减轻 [jiǎnqīng]

dampen ['dæmpən] VT **1** [+ enthusiasm, spirits] 使减弱 [shǐ jiǎnruò] **2** (make wet) 弄湿 [nòngshī]

dance [dɑ:ns] I N **1** [C] (e.g. waltz, tango) 舞蹈 [wǔdǎo] **2** [C] (social event) 舞会 [wǔhuì] **3** [U] (dancing) 舞蹈 [wǔdǎo] II VI 跳舞 [tiàowǔ]
▶ **to dance the tango** 跳探戈 ▶ **to dance with sb** 和某人跳舞 ▶ **to dance about/off** (liter) 欢呼雀跃

dance floor N [C] 舞池 [wǔchí]

dancer ['dɑ:nsə(r)] N [C] **1** (professional) 舞蹈演员 [wǔdǎo yǎnyuán] **2** (person who is dancing) 跳舞者 [tiàowǔzhě] ▶ **to be a good/bad dancer** 舞跳得好/不好

dancing ['dɑ:nsɪŋ] N [U] 跳舞 [tiàowǔ] ▶ **to go dancing** 去跳舞

dandelion ['dændɪlaɪən] N [C] 蒲公英 [púgōngyīng]

dandruff ['dændrəf] N [U] 头皮屑 [tóupíxiè]

Dane [deɪn] N [C] 丹麦人 [Dānmàirén]

danger ['deɪndʒə(r)] N **1** [U] (unsafe situation) 危

险 [wēixiǎn] **2** [C] (hazard, risk) 威胁 [wēixié]
▶ **there is a danger of/that...** 有…的危险
▶ **"danger!"** (on sign) "危险！" ▶ **your life
is/you are in danger** 你有生命危险/你有危险
▶ **to put sb/sb's life in danger** 危及某人/某人
的生命 ▶ **to be in danger of doing sth** 有…的
危险 ▶ **out of danger** [+ patient] 脱离危险 ▶ **to
be a danger to sb/sth** 是对某人/某物的威胁

dangerous ['deɪndʒrəs] ADJ 危险的 [wēixiǎn
de] ▶ **it's dangerous to...** …是危险的

dangle ['dæŋgl] I VI ▶ **to dangle from sth**
[earrings, keys +] 某处悬吊着 [mǒuchù xuándiào
zhe] II VT (swing) [+ keys, toy] 摇晃 [yáohuang];
[+ arms, legs] 晃荡 [huàngdang]

Danish ['deɪnɪʃ] I ADJ 丹麦的 [Dānmài de]
II N [U] (language) 丹麦语 [Dānmàiyǔ]

dare [dɛə(r)] I VT ▶ **to dare sb to do sth** 激某人
做某事 [jī mǒurén zuò mǒushì] II VI ▶ **to dare
(to) do sth** 敢做某事 [gǎn zuò mǒushì] III N [C]
激将 [jījiàng] ▶ **I daren't tell him** (BRIT) 我不敢
告诉他 ▶ **I dare say** (I suppose) 我相信 ▶ **don't
you dare** 你竟敢 ▶ **how dare you!** 你怎敢！
▶ **to do sth for a dare** 因为受到激将而做某事

daring ['dɛərɪŋ] I ADJ **1** (audacious) [+ escape,
rescue, person] 勇敢的 [yǒnggǎn de] **2** (bold)
[+ film, question, artist] 大胆的 [dàdǎn de]
II N [U] (courage) 勇敢 [yǒnggǎn]

dark [dɑːk] I ADJ **1** (in brightness) [+ room, night]
黑暗的 [hēi'àn de] **2** (in complexion) [+ eyes,
hair, skin] 黑色的 [hēisè de]; [+ person] 头发
和皮肤深色的 [tóufa hé pífū shēnsè de] **3** (in
colour) [+ suit, fabric etc] 深色的 [shēnsè de]
4 (unpleasant) [+ time] 黑暗的 [hēi'àn de]; [+ look]
阴郁的 [yīnyù de]; [+ remark] 悲观的 [bēiguān
de]; [+ rumour] 恶毒的 [èdú de] II N ▶ **the dark**
黑暗 [hēi'àn] ▶ **dark blue/green** 深蓝色/绿
色 ▶ **dark chocolate** (plain chocolate) 黑巧克力
▶ **it is/is getting dark** 天黑了 ▶ **after dark** 天
黑以后 ▶ **to be in the dark about sth** 对某事
一无所知

darken [dɑːkn] I VT 使变黑 [shǐ biànhēi] II VI
1 (become darker) [+ sky, clouds] 变黑 [biànhēi]
2 (liter) [+ face] 阴沉 [yīnchén]

darkness ['dɑːknɪs] N [U] 黑暗 [hēi'àn]

darkroom ['dɑːkrum] N [C] 暗房 [ànfáng]

darling ['dɑːlɪŋ] I N **1** (as address) (dear) 亲爱
的 [qīn'àide] **2** (kind, helpful person) 好人
[hǎorén] II ADJ 心爱的 [xīn'ài de] ▶ **to be the
darling of sb, to be sb's darling** (favourite) 受到
某人的宠爱

dart [dɑːt] I VI **1** [person, animal +] 急冲
[jíchōng] **2** (liter) [eyes +] 飞快地瞥一眼 [fēikuài
de piē yīyǎn] II VT (liter) [+ look, glance] 瞥 [piē]
III N [C] **1** (in game) 飞镖 [fēibiāo] **2** (weapon)
镖 [biāo] IV **darts** NPL 投镖游戏 [tóubiāo
yóuxì]

dartboard ['dɑːtbɔːd] N [C] 镖靶 [biāobǎ]

dash [dæʃ] I N **1** [C] (in punctuation) 破折号

[pòzhéhào] **2** ▶ **a dash of sth** [of lemon juice, milk
etc] 少量的某物 [shǎoliàng de mǒuwù] **3** ▶ **to
make a dash for somewhere** (rush) 冲向某地
[chōngxiàng mǒudì] **4** [C] (dashboard) 仪表板
[yíbiǎobǎn] **5** [C] (US) (race) 短跑 [duǎnpǎo] II VI
▶ **to dash in/out/upstairs** 猛冲进来/出去/上
楼 [měngchōng jìnlai/chūqu/shàng lóu] III VT
1 (liter) (throw) 扔向 [rēngxiàng] **2** [+ hopes] 使
破灭 [shǐ pòmiè] ▶ **a dash of soda** 少量苏打
▶ **to make a dash for it** 得赶紧走了 ▶ **I must
dash** (inf) 我得赶紧走了
▶ **dash away** VI = **dash off**
▶ **dash off** I VI 赶 [gǎn] II VT (write, compose)
匆忙完成 [cōngmáng wánchéng]

dashboard ['dæʃbɔːd] N [C] 仪表板
[yíbiǎobǎn]

data ['deɪtə] NPL 数据 [shùjù]

database ['deɪtəbeɪs] N [C] 数据库 [shùjùkù]

data processing [-'prəusesɪŋ] N [U] 数据处
理 [shùjù chǔlǐ]

date [deɪt] I N [C] **1** (particular day) 日期 [rìqī]
2 (meeting with friend) 约会 [yuēhuì] **3** (friend)
约会对象 [yuēhuì duìxiàng] **4** (fruit) 海枣
[hǎizǎo] II VT **1** (establish date of) [+ event,
object] 确定…的年代 [quèdìng…de niándài]
2 (write date on) [+ letter, cheque] 给…注明日
期 [gěi…zhùmíng rìqī] **3** (go out with) [+ person]
和…约会 [hé…yuēhuì] III VI **1** (go out with
sb) 约会 [yuēhuì] **2** (become old-fashioned) 过
时 [guòshí] ▶ **what's the date today?, what's
today's date?** 今天几号？▶ **date of birth** 出
生日期 ▶ **to date** (until now) 迄今 ▶ **to be out
of date** (old-fashioned) 落伍; (expired) 过期 ▶ **to
be up to date** (modern) 时新 ▶ **to bring sth up
to date** [+ correspondence, information] 更新某
物 ▶ **to bring sb up to date** 告知某人最新动
态 ▶ **to keep up to date** 紧随形势 ▶ **to keep
sb up to date (with sth)** 告知某人(某事)的最
新动态 ▶ **it was dated 5th July** [+ letter] 信上的
日期是7月5日
▶ **date back** VI ▶ **date back (to)** 回溯(至…)
[huíshù (zhì…)]
▶ **date from** VI (自…)存在至今 [(zì…) cúnzài
zhìjīn]

dated ['deɪtɪd] ADJ [+ expression, style] 过时的
[guòshí de]

◊ **daughter** ['dɔːtə(r)] N [C] 女儿 [nǚ'ér]

daughter-in-law ['dɔːtərɪnlɔː] (pl **daughters-
in-law**) N [C] 媳妇 [xífu]

daunting ['dɔːntɪŋ] ADJ [+ task, prospect] 吓人
的 [xiàrén de]

dawdle ['dɔːdl] VI 磨蹭 [móceng] ▶ **to dawdle
over (doing) sth** 慢吞吞做某事

dawn [dɔːn] I N **1** [C/U] (of day) 黎明 [límíng]
2 ▶ **the dawn of sth** 某事的开端 [mǒushì de
kāiduān] II VI **1** [day +] 开始 [kāishǐ] **2** (liter)
[period, age +] 开始 [kāishǐ] ▶ **from dawn to
dusk** 从早到晚

▶ **dawn on, dawn upon** VT FUS [不可拆分] ▶ **it dawned on me/him that...** 我/他逐渐意识到… [wǒ/tā zhújiàn yìshí dào]

day [deɪ] N **1** [C] (period of 24 hours) 天 [tiān] ▷ **three days ago** 3天前 **2** [C/U] (daylight hours) 白天 [báitiān] ▷ **during the day** 在白天 **3** [C/U] (working day) 工作日 [gōngzuòrì] ▷ **The office is only open during the day.** 办公室只在工作日开放。 **4** [C] (heyday) 时代 [shídài] ▷ **The days of the silent film are long gone.** 无声电影的时代早已过去。 ▶ **the day before/after** 前/后一天 ▶ **the day after tomorrow** 后天 ▶ **the day before yesterday** 前天 ▶ **these days** (nowadays) 现在 ▶ **day in, day out** 日复一日 ▶ **to the day** 一天也不差 ▶ **the following day** 第二天 ▶ **the day that I...** 我…的那一天 ▶ **day by day/from day to day** 一天天地 ▶ **one day a week** 每周一天 ▶ **one day/some day/one of these days** 有一天 ▶ **the other day** 在不久前某天 ▶ **by day** 在白天 ▶ **all day (long)** 一天到晚 ▶ **day and night** 日日夜夜地 ▶ **to work an 8 hour day** 每天工作8小时 ▶ **to call it a day** 停工

daybreak ['deɪbreɪk] N [U] 黎明 [límíng] ▶ **at daybreak** 拂晓时

day-care centre, (US) **day-care center** ['deɪkɛə-] N [C] **1** (for children) 日托托儿所 [rìtuō tuō'érsuǒ] **2** (for old people) 日间看护中心 [rìjiān kānhù zhōngxīn]

daydream ['deɪdriːm] **I** VI 做白日梦 [zuò báirìmèng] **II** N [C] 白日梦 [báirìmèng]

daylight ['deɪlaɪt] N [U] 白昼 [báizhòu]

day nursery N [C] 托儿所 [tuōérsuǒ]

day return (BRIT) N [C] (ticket) 当天来回的车票 [dāngtiān láihuí de chēpiào] [美=**round trip ticket**]

daytime ['deɪtaɪm] **I** N ▶ **in the daytime** 在白天 [zài báitiān] **II** ADJ [+ television] 日间的 [rìjiān de]; [+ telephone number] 白天的 [báitiān de]

day-to-day ['deɪtə'deɪ] ADJ [+ life, routine] 日常的 [rìcháng de] ▶ **on a day-to-day basis** 一天天地

day trip N [C] 当天来回的旅行 [dāngtiān láihuí de lǚxíng]

daze [deɪz] N ▶ **in a daze** (confused) 茫然地 [mángrán de]

dazed [deɪzd] ADJ (confused) 头晕眼花的 [tóuyūn yǎnhuā de]

dazzle ['dæzl] **I** VT **1** (blind) 使目眩 [shǐ mùxuàn] **2** (impress) 使惊奇 [shǐ jīngqí] **II** N **1** ▶ **the dazzle of sth** (attraction) 某物的魅力 [mǒuwù de mèilì] **2** [U] (glare) 强光 [qiángguāng]

dazzling ['dæzlɪŋ] ADJ **1** [+ light, sun] 耀眼的 [yàoyǎn de] **2** [+ smile] 迷人的 [mírén de] **3** [+ display, performance] 精彩的 [jīngcǎi de]

D/D ABBR (= direct debit) 直接借记 [jíjiē jièjì]

dead [dɛd] **I** ADJ **1** (not alive) [+ person, animal, plant] 死的 [sǐ de] **2** (not working) [+ phone, line] 坏的 [huài de]; [battery] 不能再用的 [bùnéng zài yòng de] **3** (finished) [+ cigarette, drink] 用完了的 [yòng wán le de] **4** (total, absolute) 正 [zhèng]; [+ silence] 完全的 [wánquán de] **II** ADV **1** (inf) (very) 非常地 [fēicháng de] **2** ▶ **dead against** (completely) 绝对反对 [juéduì fǎnduì] **III** NPL ▶ **the dead** 死者 [sǐzhě] ▶ **to drop (down) dead** 暴毙 [bàobì] ▶ **to stop dead** 突然停止 [tūrán tíngzhǐ] ▶ **dead tired** 精疲力竭 ▶ **dead on time** 完全准时 ▶ **dead ahead** 正前方 ▶ **dead on target** 正中目标 ▶ **dead centre/in the middle** 正中央 ▶ **over my dead body!** (inf) 绝对不行！ ▶ **the line has gone dead** (TEL) (interrupted conversation) 通话断了; (on picking up the receiver) 线路不通 ▶ **my leg/arm has gone dead** (numb) 我的腿/胳膊麻了 ▶ **at/in the dead of night** 夜深人静时 ▶ **at/in the dead of winter** (liter) 在隆冬

请勿将 **dead** 与 **died** 混淆。**died** 是动词 **die** 的过去式和过去分词，表示动作。*She died in 1934...Two men have died since the rioting broke out.* **died** 不能用作形容词，要表达形容词词性时应该使用 **dead**。*More than 2,200 dead birds have been found...My parents are dead. They died a long time ago.*

dead end N [C] **1** (street) 死路 [sǐlù] **2** (impasse) 僵局 [jiāngjú]

deadline ['dɛdlaɪn] N [C] 截止日期 [jiézhǐ rìqī] ▶ **to work to a deadline** 根据截止日期工作 ▶ **to meet a deadline** 如期

deadly ['dɛdlɪ] **I** ADJ **1** [+ poison, disease, dose, weapon] 致命的 [zhìmìng de] **2** (devastating) [+ logic, insult] 恶毒的 [èdú de] **II** ADV **1** ▶ **deadly dull** 极其枯燥 [jíqí kūzào] **2** ▶ **deadly serious** 极其严肃 [jíqí yánsù]

Dead Sea N ▶ **the Dead Sea** 死海 [Sǐ Hǎi]

deaf [dɛf] **I** ADJ **1** (totally) 聋的 [lóng de]; (partially) 耳背的 [ěrbèi de] **2** ▶ **deaf to sth** 不听某事 [bùtīng mǒushì] **II** NPL ▶ **the deaf** 耳聋者 [ěrlóngzhě] ▶ **to turn a deaf ear to sth** 对某事充耳不闻

deafen ['dɛfn] VT 使聋 [shǐ lóng]

deafening ['dɛfnɪŋ] ADJ [+ noise] 震耳欲聋的 [zhèn ěr yù lóng de]

deafness ['dɛfnɪs] N [U] 耳聋 [ěrlóng]

deal [diːl] (pt, pp **dealt**) **I** N [C] (agreement) 协议 [xiéyì] ▷ **a business deal** 买卖协议 **II** VT **1** ▶ **to deal (out)** [+ card] 发给 [fāgěi] ▷ **He dealt each player a card.** 他发给每个打牌的人一张牌。**2** (sell) [+ drugs] 出售 [chūshòu] ▶ **to do/make/strike a deal with sb** 和某人做买卖 ▶ **it's a deal!** (inf) 成交！ ▶ **a good/fair/bad deal** 好的/公平的/不公的待遇 ▶ **a good** or **great deal (of)** 大量(的…) ▶ **to deal a (severe/heavy) blow to sb/sth** (严重/沉重地) 打击某人/某事 ▶ **deal in** (COMM) VT FUS [不可拆分] 经营

[jīngyíng]

▶ **deal out** VT [+ punishment, criticism] 使遭受 [shǐ zāoshòu]

▶ **deal with** VT FUS [不可拆分] **1** [+ criminal, wrongdoer etc] 惩处 [chéngchǔ] ▷ Criminals should be dealt with severely. 罪犯应该被严厉惩处。 **2** [+ company] 和…有往来 [hé…yǒu wǎnglái] **3** [+ problem] 处理 [chǔlǐ] **4** [book, film +] [+ subject] 论述 [lùnshù]

dealer ['di:lə(r)] N [c] **1** (in goods, services) 商人 [shāngrén] **2** (in drugs) 毒品贩子 [dúpǐn fànzi] **3** (in card game) 发牌人 [fāpáirén]

dealings ['di:lɪŋz] NPL **1** (transactions) 往来 [wǎnglái] **2** (relations) 交往 [jiāowǎng]

dealt [dɛlt] PT, PP of **deal**

dean [di:n] N [c] **1** [of church, cathedral] 教长 [jiàozhǎng] **2** (BRIT) [of university, college] 系主任 [xìzhǔrèn] **3** (US) [of school, college] 教务长 [jiàowùzhǎng]

dear [dɪə(r)] I ADJ **1** [+ friend, house, car] 亲爱的 [qīn'ài de] **2** ▶ **to be dear to sb** 对某人很珍贵 [duì mǒurén hěn zhēnguì] **3** (ESP BRIT) (expensive) 昂贵的 [ángguì de] II N ▶ **(my) dear** 亲爱的 [qīn'ài de] III INT ▶ **oh dear/dear dear/dear me!** 呵/哎呀！ [hè/āiyā!] ▶ **Dear Sir/Madam** (in letter) 亲爱的先生/女士 ▶ **Dear Mr/Mrs X** 亲爱的X先生/夫人 ▶ **Dear Peter/Jane** 亲爱的彼得/简 ▶ **to be dear to sb's heart** 在某人心目中非常重要

dearly ['dɪəlɪ] ADV **1** ▶ **to love sb dearly** 深爱某人 [shēn'ài mǒurén] **2** ▶ **I would dearly love to...** 我很想… [wǒ hěnxiǎng…] **3** ▶ **to pay dearly (for sth)** (为某事) 付出沉重代价 [(wèi mǒushì) fùchū chénzhòng dàijià]

death [dɛθ] N **1** [c/u] [of person, animal] 死亡 [sǐwáng] **2** [s] (end) [of way of life, tradition] 消亡 [xiāowáng] **3** [c] (fatality) 死亡 [sǐwáng] ▶ **(to die) a horrible/lonely death** 恐怖地/孤独地死去 ▶ **(a matter of) life and death** 生死攸关(的事情) ▶ **to put sb to death** 处死某人 ▶ **to be stabbed/beaten to death** 被刺死/打死 ▶ **to scare/bore sb to death** 吓死某人/使某人感到无聊之极

death penalty N ▶ **the death penalty** 死刑 [sǐxíng]

death sentence (LAW) N [c] 死刑判决 [sǐxíng pànjué]

debatable [dɪ'beɪtəbl] ADJ 可争辩的 [kě zhēngbiàn de] ▶ **it is debatable whether...** 是否…尚未决定

debate [dɪ'beɪt] I N **1** [c/u] (discussion) 讨论 [tǎolùn] **2** [c] (formal discussion) 辩论 [biànlùn] II VT **1** [+ topic, issue, motion] 讨论 [tǎolùn] **2** [+ course of action] 考虑 [kǎolù] ▶ **to debate whether...** 盘算是否…

debit ['dɛbɪt] I N [c] 记入借方的款项 [jìrù jièfāng de kuǎnxiàng] II VT 将…记入某人的借方 [jiāng…jìrù mǒurén de jièfāng]

debit card N [c] 借记卡 [jièjìkǎ]

debris ['dɛbri:] N [u] **1** (rubble) 碎片 [suìpiàn] **2** (mess) (after meal, party etc) 杯盘狼藉 [bēipán lángjí] **3** (things lying about) 废物 [fèiwù]

debt [dɛt] N **1** [c] (sum of money owed) 债务 [zhàiwù] **2** [u] (state of owing money) 欠债 [qiànzhài] ▶ **to be in/get into debt** 负债 ▶ **to be/get out of debt** 不欠债 ▶ **bad debt** 坏账 ▶ **to be in sb's debt/owe sb a debt** (frm) 欠某人的人情债

debtor ['dɛtə(r)] N [c] 债务人 [zhàiwùrén]

debut ['deɪbju:] I N [c] 首次亮相 [shǒucì liàngxiàng] II CPD [复合词] [+ album, match, performance] 首次问世 [shǒucì wènshì]

Dec. ABBR (= December) 十二月 [shí'èryuè]

decade ['dɛkeɪd] N [c] 十年 [shínián]

decaffeinated [dɪ'kæfɪneɪtɪd] ADJ [+ coffee] 不含咖啡因的 [bù hán kāfēiyīn de]

decay [dɪ'keɪ] I VI **1** (rot) [body, leaves, teeth +] 腐烂 [fǔlàn] **2** [society, system etc +] 腐朽 [fǔxiǔ] II N [u] **1** [of body, tooth] 腐烂 [fǔlàn] **2** [of society, system etc] 腐朽 [fǔxiǔ]

deceased [dɪ'si:st] (frm) I ADJ 已故的 [yǐgù de] II N ▶ **the deceased** 死者 [sǐzhě]

deceit [dɪ'si:t] N [u] 欺骗 [qīpiàn]

deceitful [dɪ'si:tful] ADJ 骗人的 [piànrén de]

deceive [dɪ'si:v] VT (fool) 欺骗 [qīpiàn] ▶ **to deceive sb into doing sth** 骗某人去做某事 ▶ **to deceive o.s.** 自欺

December [dɪ'sɛmbə(r)] N [c/u] 十二月 [shí'èryuè] see also **July**

decency ['di:sənsɪ] N [u] 正派 [zhèngpài] ▶ **he didn't have the decency to...** 他没有…的礼数

decent ['di:sənt] ADJ **1** (proper) [+ education, wages, English etc] 体面的 [tǐmiàn de]; [+ interval, behaviour] 适当的 [shìdàng de] **2** (honest) [+ person] 受尊重的 [shòu zūnzhòng de] ▶ **to do the decent thing** 识时务 ▶ **they were very decent about it** 他们对此很公正 ▶ **that was very decent of him** 他那么做真是个好人 ▶ **are you decent?** (inf) (dressed) 你穿戴像样吗？

deception [dɪ'sɛpʃən] N **1** [u] (deceiving) 欺骗 [qīpiàn] **2** [c] (deceitful act) 诡计 [guǐjì]

deceptive [dɪ'sɛptɪv] ADJ [+ appearance, impression] 骗人的 [piànrén de]

○ decide [dɪ'saɪd] I VT **1** (settle) [+ question, argument] 解决 [jiějué] **2** (persuade) [+ person] 使下决心 [shǐ xià juéxīn] ▷ I don't know what decided me to come. 我不知道什么使我下决心来这儿。 II VI 决定 [juédìng] ▶ **to decide to do sth** 决定做某事 ▶ **to decide on or upon sth** (choose) 决定某事 ▶ **to decide in favour of/against (doing) sth** 决定(做)某事/反对(做)某事 ▶ **to decide that...** 决定… ▶ **I can't decide whether...** 我无法决定是否…

decidedly [dɪ'saɪdɪdlɪ] ADV 明显地 [míngxiǎn de]

decimal ['dɛsɪməl] I ADJ [+ system, currency] 十进位的 [shíjìnwèi de] II N [c] 小数 [xiǎoshù]
▶ to three decimal places 保留到小数点后3位

⊙**decision** [dɪ'sɪʒən] N 1 [c] (choice) 决定 [juédìng] ▷ The government has announced its decision. 政府已经宣布了决定。 2 [u] (act of choosing) 决心 [juéxīn] ▷ The moment of decision can't be delayed. 下决心的时刻不能拖了。 3 [u] (decisiveness) 决断力 [juéduànlì] ▶ to make a decision 作出决定

decisive [dɪ'saɪsɪv] ADJ 1 [+ battle, phase] 决定性的 [juédìngxìng de] 2 [+ person] 果断的 [guǒduàn de] 3 [+ manner, reply] 坚定果断的 [jiāndìng guǒduàn de]

deck [dɛk] N [c] 1 (on ship) (floor) 舱面 [cāngmiàn]; (top deck) 甲板 [jiǎbǎn] 2 [of bus] 层面 [céngmiàn] 3 (also: tape deck, record deck, cassette deck) 磁带录音机的走带装置 [cídài lùyīnjī de zǒudài zhuāngzhì] 4 (ESP US) [of cards] 一副 [yīfù] [= pack] ▶ (to go up) on deck (上到) 在甲板上 ▶ below deck(s) 甲板下 ▶ deck out VT 用…装扮 [yòng…zhuāngbàn]

deckchair ['dɛktʃeə(r)] N [c] 折叠式躺椅 [zhédiéshì tǎngyǐ]

declaration [dɛklə'reɪʃən] N [c] 1 (statement) 宣布 [xuānbù] 2 (public announcement) 宣言 [xuānyán]

declare [dɪ'kleə(r)] I VT 1 (state) [+ intention, attitude] 宣布 [xuānbù]; [+ support] 表明 [biǎomíng]; [+ income] 申报 [shēnbào] 2 (at customs) [+ goods] 报关 [bàoguān] II VI 宣称 [xuānchēng] ▶ to declare sb innocent/insane 宣布某人无罪/精神失常 ▶ to declare war (on sb) (向某人)宣战

decline [dɪ'klaɪn] I N ▶ a decline in sth 某物的下降 [mǒuwù de xiàjiàng] II VT (turn down) [+ invitation, offer] 谢绝 [xièjué] III VI [strength, health +] 衰退 [shuāituì]; [business, population +] 萎缩 [wěisuō] ▶ to be on the decline/in decline 正在衰落 ▶ to fall into decline 衰弱 ▶ to decline to do sth 婉言拒绝做某事

decor ['deɪkɔː(r)] N [u] [of house, room] 装饰 [zhuāngshì]

decorate ['dɛkəreɪt] VT 1 (adorn) ▶ to decorate (with) (用…)装饰 [(yòng…)zhuāngshì] 2 (paint etc) [+ room, house] 装潢 [zhuānghuáng] ▶ to be decorated (awarded medal) 被授予勋章 [bèi shòuyǔ xūnzhāng]

decoration [dɛkə'reɪʃən] N 1 [c/u] (adornment) 装饰 [zhuāngshì] 2 [u] [of room, building] 装饰 [zhuāngshì] 3 [c] (medal) 勋章 [xūnzhāng] ▶ for decoration 用于装饰

decorator ['dɛkəreɪtə(r)] N [c] 1 (BRIT) (painter) 粉刷工 [fěnshuāgōng] 2 (US) 室内装潢家 [shìnèi zhuānghuángjiā] [英= interior decorator]

decrease [n 'diːkriːs, vb diːkriːs] I N [c] (reduction, drop) ▶ decrease (in sth) (某物的)减少 [(mǒuwù de) jiǎnshǎo] II VT, VI 减少

[jiǎnshǎo] ▶ to be on the decrease 正在减少

decree [dɪ'kriː] I N [c] 1 (by ruler) 法令 [fǎlìng] 2 (US) (in law court) 判决 [pànjué] II VT 颁布 [bānbù] ▶ to decree that... 下令…

dedicate ['dɛdɪkeɪt] VT 1 ▶ to dedicate one's time/life to (doing) sth 把时间/一生奉献给(做)某事 [bǎ shíjiān/yīshēng fèngxiàn gěi (zuò) mǒushì] 2 [+ book, song] 把…献给 [bǎ…xiàn gěi] ▶ to dedicate o.s. to sth 致力于某事

dedicated ['dɛdɪkeɪtɪd] ADJ 1 [+ person] 专心致志的 [zhuān xīn zhì zhì de] 2 (specialized) [+ word processor, software] 专门的 [zhuānmén de] ▶ to be dedicated to sth/doing sth [+ person] 专心致志于/做某事; [+ book, museum] 专门关于某物/做某事的

dedication [dɛdɪ'keɪʃən] N 1 [u] (devotion) 献身 [xiànshēn] 2 [c] (in book) 题献 [tíxiàn]; (on radio) 献辞 [xiàncí]

deduce [dɪ'djuːs] VT 推断 [tuīduàn] ▶ to deduce that... 推断…

deduct [dɪ'dʌkt] VT ▶ to deduct sth (from sth) (从某物中)减去某物 [(cóng mǒuwùzhōng) jiǎnqù mǒuwù]

deduction [dɪ'dʌkʃən] N 1 [c] (conclusion) 推论 [tuīlùn] 2 [u] (deductive reasoning) 演绎 [yǎnyì] 3 [u] (subtraction) 扣除 [kòuchú] 4 [c] (amount deducted) 扣除额 [kòuchú'é]

deed [diːd] N [c] 1 (liter) (feat) 行为 [xíngwéi] 2 (document) 契约 [qìyuē]

deem [diːm] (frm) VT (judge, consider) 认为 [rènwéi] ▶ to deem it wise/unnecessary 认为是明智的/没必要的

deep [diːp] I ADJ 1 [+ water, hole, cut, breath] 深的 [shēn de] 2 [+ voice, sound] 低沉的 [dīchén de] 3 [+ sleep] 酣睡的 [hānshuì de] 4 (profound) [+ person] 高深莫测的 [gāoshēn mòcè de]; [+ thoughts, ideas] 深刻的 [shēnkè de]; [+ love, sympathy etc] 深厚的 [shēnhòu de] 5 (serious) [+ trouble, concern] 严重的 [yánzhòng de] 6 [+ colour] 浓重的 [nóngzhòng de] II ADV 深 [shēn] ▶ it is 1 m deep [+ water, pool] 它有1米深 [+ shelf] 它有1米厚 ▶ to be deep in thought/conversation 沉思/深谈 ▶ to take a deep breath 深呼吸 ▶ in deepest sympathy 最深切的同情 ▶ ankle-/knee-deep (in water) (水深)及脚踝/及膝 ▶ deep down/inside 在内心深处 ▶ to go/run deep 加重 ▶ to stand three deep 围了3层

deepen ['diːpn] I VT 1 [+ hole] 加深 [jiāshēn] 2 (extend) [+ knowledge, awareness etc] 加深 [jiāshēn] 3 [+ gloom, recession] 使增烈 [shǐ qiángliè] II VI 1 [crisis, feelings +] 深化 [shēnhuà] 2 [sound, voice +] 变低沉 [biàn dīchén] 3 [river, sea etc +] 变深 [biàn shēn]

deep end N ▶ the deep end [of swimming pool] 深水区 [shēnshuǐqū] ▶ to be thrown in at the deep end 被免为其难

deep freeze N [C] 冷藏箱 [lěngcángxiāng]

deep-fried ['di:p'fraɪd] ADJ 油炸的 [yóuzhá de]

deep-fry ['di:p'fraɪ] VT 油炸 [yóuzhá]

deeply ['di:plɪ] ADV 1 [*breathe, sigh +*] 深深地 [shēnshēn de] 2 (*profoundly*) [+ *depressed, moved, religious*] 非常地 [fēicháng de] 3 [*sleep +*] 沉沉地 [chénchén de]

deer [dɪə(r)] (*pl* **deer**) N [C] 鹿 [lù] ▶ **red deer** 赤鹿 ▶ **roe deer** 牝鹿

default [dɪ'fɔ:lt] I N [C] 1 (*in computing*) ▶ **default (value/setting)** 默认(值/设置) [mòrèn (zhí/shèzhì)] 2 ▶ **to be in default (on/of sth)** [+ *loan, debt*] 拖欠(某物) [tuōqiàn (mǒuwù)] II VI ▶ **to default on a debt** 拖欠借款 [tuōqiàn jièkuǎn] ▶ **to win by default** 因对手未出场而赢得比赛

defeat [dɪ'fi:t] I N [C/U] 1 [*of army*] 战败 [zhànbài] 2 [*of team*] 击败 [jībài] 3 (*failure*) 失败 [shībài] II VT 1 [+ *enemy, opposition*] 战胜 [zhànshèng] 2 [+ *team*] 击败 [jībài] 3 [+ *plan, proposal etc*] 否决 [fǒujué] 4 (*be too difficult for*) [*task, challenge +*] 难住 [nánzhù]

defect [*n* 'di:fɛkt, *vb* dɪ'fɛkt] I N [C] (*flaw*) 缺点 [quēdiǎn] II VI ▶ **to defect (to/from)** 背叛(投奔于/了) [bèipàn (tóubèn yú/le)] ▶ **hearing defect** 听觉缺陷

defective [dɪ'fɛktɪv] ADJ 有缺点的 [yǒu quēdiǎn de]

defence, (US) defense [dɪ'fɛns] I N 1 [U] (*protection*) 防御 [fángyù] 2 [U] (MIL) 国防措施 [guófáng cuòshī] 3 [C] ▶ **defence (of sth)** (*justification*) (为某事的)辩护 [(wèi mǒushì de) biànhù] 4 [C] (*in court*) 辩护 [biànhù] 5 ▶ **the defence** (*in court*) 被告方 [bèigàofāng] 6 [S/PL] (*in sport*) 守方 [shǒufāng] II CPD [复合词] [+ *spending, cuts, minister*] 国防开支 [guófáng kāizhī] III **defences** NPL 1 (MIL) 军事能力 [jūnshì nénglì] 2 [*of body*] 抵抗力 [dǐkànglì] ▶ **to come to sb's defence** 上前为某人辩护 ▶ **in defence of sth/sb** 为某事/某人辩护 ▶ **to use a knife in defence** 用匕首防身 ▶ **a defence against sth** 对某物的抵抗力 ▶ **the Ministry of Defence, (US) the Department of Defense** 国防部 ▶ **witness for the defence** 被告方证人

defenceless [dɪ'fɛnslɪs] ADJ 无自卫能力的 [wú zìwèi nénglì de]

defend [dɪ'fɛnd] VT 1 (*protect*) 防御 [fángyù] 2 (*justify*) 为…辩护 [wèi…biànhù] 3 (*in court*) 为…辩护 [wèi…biànhù] 4 (*in sport*) [+ *goal, record, title*] 防守 [fángshǒu] ▶ **to defend o.s.** 自卫

defendant [dɪ'fɛndənt] N [C] 被告 [bèigào]

defender [dɪ'fɛndə(r)] N [C] 1 [*of view, policy*] 拥护者 [yōnghùzhě] 2 (*in team*) 防守队员 [fángshǒu duìyuán]

defense [dɪ'fɛns] (US) N = **defence**

defensive [dɪ'fɛnsɪv] I ADJ 1 [+ *weapons, measures*] 防御的 [fángyù de] 2 [+ *behaviour, manner*] 防卫的 [fángwèi de] II N ▶ **on the defensive** 采取守势 [cǎiqǔ shǒushì]

defer [dɪ'fə:(r)] I VT (*postpone*) 推迟 [tuīchí] II VI ▶ **to defer to sb** 遵从某人的意见 [zūncóng mǒurén de yìjiàn]

defiance [dɪ'faɪəns] N [U] 蔑视 [miǎoshì] ▶ **in defiance of sth** [+ *the rules, sb's orders etc*] 无视某事

defiant [dɪ'faɪənt] ADJ [+ *tone, reply, person*] 蔑视的 [miǎoshì de]

deficiency [dɪ'fɪʃənsɪ] N 1 [C/U] (*lack*) 缺乏 [quēfá] 2 [C/U] (*inadequacy*) 缺陷 [quēxiàn]

deficient [dɪ'fɪʃənt] (*frm*) ADJ (*inadequate*) 缺乏的 [quēfá de] ▶ **to be deficient in sth** (*lacking*) 缺乏某物

deficit ['dɛfɪsɪt] N [C] 赤字 [chìzì]

define [dɪ'faɪn] VT 1 [+ *limits, boundaries, role*] 限定 [xiàndìng] 2 [+ *expression, word*] 解释 [jiěshì]

definite ['dɛfɪnɪt] ADJ 1 [+ *plan, answer, views*] 明确的 [míngquè de] 2 (*distinct*) [+ *improvement, possibility, advantage*] 肯定的 [kěndìng de] 3 (*certain*) [+ *proof, evidence, information*] 确切的 [quèqiè de] ▶ **is that definite?** 肯定吗? ▶ **he was definite about it** 他对此很肯定

definitely ['dɛfɪnɪtlɪ] ADV 确定地 [quèdìng de]

definition [dɛfɪ'nɪʃən] N 1 [C] [*of word*] 定义 [dìngyì] 2 [U] (*clarity*) [*of thought, expression*] 明确性 [míngquèxìng] 3 [U] [*of photograph, features*] 清晰度 [qīngxīdù] ▶ **by definition** 就本身而言

definitive [dɪ'fɪnɪtɪv] ADJ 1 (*conclusive*) [+ *answer*] 确定的 [quèdìng de] 2 (*authoritative*) [+ *version, account*] 权威性的 [quánwēixìng de]

deflate [di:'fleɪt] VT 1 [+ *tyre, balloon*] 放出…的气 [fàngchū…de qì] 2 [+ *person, hopes*] 使泄气 [shǐ xièqì] II VI [*tyre, dinghy +*] 放气 [fàngqì]

deflect [dɪ'flɛkt] VT [+ *attention, criticism, shot, blow*] 使转向 [shǐ zhuǎnxiàng] ▶ **to deflect sb (from...)** 使某人转变(…)

defraud [dɪ'frɔ:d] VT ▶ **to defraud sb (of sth)** 从某人处骗取(某物) [cóng mǒurén chù piànqǔ (mǒuwù)]

defrost [di:'frɒst] I VT 1 [+ *fridge, freezer*] 除去…的冰霜 [chúqù…de bīngshuāng] 2 [+ *food*] 使解冻 [shǐ jiědòng] II VI 1 [*fridge, freezer +*] 除霜 [chúshuāng] 2 [*food +*] 解冻 [jiědòng]

defuse [di:'fju:z] VT 1 [+ *bomb*] 拆除…的引信 [chāichú…de yǐnxìn] 2 [+ *crisis, situation*] 使缓和 [shǐ huǎnhé]

defy [dɪ'faɪ] VT 1 (*refuse to obey*) [+ *person*] 公然反抗 [gōngrán fǎnkàng]; [+ *law, ban*] 蔑视 [miǎoshì] 2 [+ *description, comprehension*] 使不能 [shǐ bùnéng] 3 ▶ **to defy sb to do sth** (*dare*) 看某人敢不敢做某事 [kàn mǒurén gǎn bù gǎn zuò mǒushì]

degree [dɪ'griː] N [C] **1** ▶ **degree (of sth)**
(level) (某事的)程度 [(mǒushì de chéngdù)]
2 (measure of temperature, angle, latitude) 度 [dù]
3 (at university) 学位 [xuéwèi] ▶ **with varying
degrees of success** 不同程度的成功 ▶ **to
some degree/a certain degree** 从某种/一定程
度上来说 ▶ **10 degrees below (zero)** 零下10度
▶ **a degree in maths** 数学学位 ▶ **by degrees**
(gradually) 逐渐地

dehydrated [diːhaɪ'dreɪtɪd] ADJ 脱水的
[tuōshuǐ de]

delay [dɪ'leɪ] I VT **1** (postpone) [+ decision,
ceremony] 推迟 [tuīchí] **2** (make late) [+ person]
耽搁 [dāngé]; [+ plane, train] 延误 [yánwù] II VI
耽搁 [dāngé] III N [U] (delay) 延误 [yánwù] ▶ **to be
delayed** [person, flight, departure etc +] 被耽搁了
▶ **without delay** 立即

delegate [n 'dɛlɪgɪt, vb 'dɛlɪgeɪt] I N [C] 代表
[dàibiǎo] II VT **1** ▶ **to delegate sb to do sth** 委
派某人做某事 [wěipài mǒurén zuò mǒushì]
2 ▶ **to delegate sth (to sb)** [+ task] 委托某事(给
某人) [wěituō mǒushì (gěi mǒurén)]

delete [dɪ'liːt] VT **1** (cross out) 删除 [shānchú]
2 (COMPUT) (remove) [+ file, folder, message] 删除
[shānchú]

deli ['dɛlɪ] N [C] 熟食店 [shúshídiàn]

deliberate [adj dɪ'lɪbərɪt, vb dɪ'lɪbəreɪt] I ADJ
1 (intentional) 故意的 [gùyì de] **2** (careful) 审慎
的 [shěnshèng de] II VI (think) 仔细考虑 [zǐxì
kǎolù] ▶ **it wasn't deliberate** 那不是故意的

deliberately [dɪ'lɪbərɪtlɪ] ADV **1** (intentionally)
故意地 [gùyì de] **2** (carefully) 审慎地
[shěnshèng de]

delicacy ['dɛlɪkəsɪ] N **1** [U] (fragility) [of material]
娇嫩 [jiāonèn] **2** [C] (choice food) 珍馐美味
[zhēnxiū měiwèi] **3** [U] (sensitivity) [of problem,
situation] 微妙 [wēimiào]

delicate ['dɛlɪkɪt] ADJ **1** (fine) [+ features,
hands, flower] 柔软的 [róuruǎn de] **2** (fragile)
[+ object, material] 易碎的 [yìsuì de] **3** (sensitive)
[+ problem, situation, issue etc] 微妙的 [wēimiào
de] **4** (frail) [+ person, health] 脆弱的 [cuìruò de]
5 (subtle) [+ colour, flavour, smell] 清淡可口的
[qīngdàn kěkǒu de]

delicatessen [dɛlɪkə'tɛsn] N [C] 熟食店
[shúshídiàn]

delicious [dɪ'lɪʃəs] ADJ **1** [+ food, smell] 美味的
[měiwèi de] **2** [+ feeling] 美妙的 [měimiào de]

delight [dɪ'laɪt] I N **1** [U] (feeling) 快乐 [kuàilè]
2 [C] (person, experience) 令人开心的人/事 [lìng
rén kāixīn de rén/shì] II VT (please) 使快乐 [shǐ
kuàilè] III VI ▶ **to delight in sth** 以某事为乐
[yǐ mǒushì wéi lè] ▶ **to my delight...** 令我高兴
的是… ▶ **to take (a) delight in sth/doing sth**
以某事/做某事为乐 ▶ **she was a delight to
interview** 采访她是一件乐事

delighted [dɪ'laɪtɪd] ADJ ▶ **delighted (at or
with sth)** (对某事)感到高兴 [(duì mǒushì)

gǎndào gāoxìng] ▶ **to be delighted to do sth**
乐意做某事 ▶ **I'd be delighted** 我十分乐意

delightful [dɪ'laɪtful] ADJ 使人快乐的 [shǐ rén
kuàilè de]

delinquent [dɪ'lɪŋkwənt] I ADJ [+ teenager,
child] 违法的 [wéifǎ de] II N [C] 违法者
[wéifǎzhě]

deliver [dɪ'lɪvə(r)] VT **1** (bring) [+ letter, parcel etc]
传送 [chuánsòng] **2** (frm) ▶ **to be delivered into
sb's hands/care** (handed over) 移交到某人手
中/给某人照看 [yíjiāo dào mǒurén shǒuzhōng/
gěi mǒurén zhàokàn] **3** [+ baby] 接生 [jiēshēng]
4 [+ speech, lecture etc] 发表 [fābiǎo] **5** (come up
with) 履行诺言 [lǚxíng nuòyán] **6** (frm) [+ verdict,
judgement] 宣告 [xuāngào] **7** (frm) [+ warning,
ultimatum] 发出 [fāchū] **8** (frm) [+ blow] 给予
[gěiyǔ] **9** (frm) ▶ **to deliver sb from sth** (release)
将某人从某事中解救出来 [jiāng mǒurén cóng
mǒushì zhōng jiějiù chūlái]

delivery [dɪ'lɪvərɪ] I N **1** [U] (distribution)
[of goods, mail] 传送 [chuánsòng] **2** [C]
(consignment) 递送的货物 [dìsòng de huòwù]
3 [U] [of speaker] 讲演 [jiǎngyǎn] **4** [C/U] (MED)
分娩 [fēnmiǎn] II CPD [复合词] [+ man, service]
送到某物 [sòngdào] ▶ **to take delivery of sth** 收
到某物 ▶ **allow 28 days for delivery** 交货期
为28天

delusion [dɪ'luːʒən] N [C/U] 错觉 [cuòjué]
▶ **to be under a/the delusion that...** 有…的
错觉 [yǒu…de cuòjué] ▶ **to have delusions of
grandeur** 自大狂想症

deluxe [də'lʌks] ADJ 豪华的 [háohuá de]

delve [dɛlv] VI ▶ **to delve into sth** [+ subject, past]
探究某事 [tànjiū mǒushì]; [+ cupboard, handbag]
翻找某物 [fānzhǎo mǒuwù]

Dem. (POL) ABBR = **democrat(ic)**

● **demand** [dɪ'mɑːnd] I VT **1** (ask for) [+ apology,
explanation, pay rise] 要求 [yāoqiú] **2** (require)
[+ patience, attention] 需要 [xūyào] II N **1** [C]
(request) 要求 [yāoqiú] ▷ There have been
demands for improved services. 一直以来都有
改进服务的要求。 **2** [U] (for product) 需求
量 [xūqiúliàng] ▷ Demand for this product is
increasing. 对这种产品的需求量越来越大。
III **demands** NPL (requirements) 要求 [yāoqiú]
▷ the demands of a new job 新工作的要求 ▶ **to
demand to do sth** 要求做某事 ▶ **to demand
sth from or of sb** 要求某人某事 ▶ **I have many
demands on my time** 我有许多工作要花时
间去做 ▶ **to make demands on sb/sth** 对某
人/某事提出要求 ▶ **to be in demand** 受欢迎
▶ **on demand** 随时地

demanding [dɪ'mɑːndɪŋ] ADJ **1** [+ work] 高要
求的 [gāo yāoqiú de] **2** [+ boss, child] 苛求的
[kēqiú de]

demented [dɪ'mɛntɪd] ADJ **1** (frm) (ill) 发狂的
[fākuáng de] **2** (inf) (crazed) 发狂的 [fākuáng
de]

demise [dɪ'maɪz] (frm) N [U] **1** (end) 结束 [jiéshù] **2** (death) 死亡 [sǐwáng]

demo ['dɛməʊ] (BRIT: inf) N ABBR [C] (= *demonstration*) 示威 [shìwēi]

democracy [dɪ'mɔkrəsɪ] N **1** [U] (system) 民主 [mínzhǔ] **2** [C] (country) 民主国 [mínzhǔ guó]

democrat ['dɛməkræt] N [c] **1** (believer in democracy) 民主主义者 [mínzhǔ zhǔyìzhě] **2** ▶ **Democrat** 民主党人 [mínzhǔdǎngrén]

democratic [dɛmə'krætɪk] ADJ 民主的 [mínzhǔ de] ▶ **Democratic** 民主党的 [mínzhǔdǎng de]

Democratic Party (US) N ▶ **the Democratic Party** 民主党 [mínzhǔdǎng]

demolish [dɪ'mɔlɪʃ] VT **1** [+ building] 拆毁 [chāihuǐ] **2** [+ argument] 推翻 [tuīfān]

demolition [dɛmə'lɪʃən] N [C/U] [of building] 拆毁 [chāihuǐ]

demon ['diːmən] I N [C] (evil spirit) 恶魔 [èmó] II ADJ (skilled, enthusiastic) 胜人一筹的 [shèng rén yīchóu de]

demonstrate ['dɛmənstreɪt] I VT **1** (make clear) [+ theory] 表明 [biǎomíng] **2** (show) [+ skill, appliance] 演示 [yǎnshì] **3** (prove) 证实 [zhèngshí] II VI ▶ **to demonstrate (for/against sth)** 示威(支持/反对某事) [shìwēi (zhīchí/fǎnduì mǒushì)] ▶ **to demonstrate that…** 证实… ▶ **to demonstrate how to do sth** 演示如何做某事

demonstration [dɛmən'streɪʃən] N [C] **1** (protest march) 示威 [shìwēi] **2** (proof) 证实 [zhèngshí] **3** [of appliance, cooking etc] 演示 [yǎnshì] ▶ **to hold/stage a demonstration** 举行示威

demonstrator ['dɛmənstreɪtə(r)] N [C] **1** (protester) 示威者 [shìwēizhě] **2** (sales person) 向顾客演示产品的推销员

demote [dɪ'məʊt] VT **1** [+ employee] 使降级 [shǐ jiàngjí] **2** (BRIT) (relegate) [+ team] 使降级 [shǐ jiàngjí]

den [dɛn] N [C] **1** [of fox, lion] 兽穴 [shòuxué] **2** (ESP US) (room) 私室 [sīshì] **3** ▶ **drinking/gambling den** 饮酒/赌博秘室 [yǐnjiǔ/dǔbó mìshì] ▶ **a den of iniquity/vice** 藏污纳垢之处

denial [dɪ'naɪəl] N **1** [C/U] (refutation) 否定 [fǒudìng] **2** [U] (refusal) 拒绝 [jùjué] **3** ▶ **to be in denial** 拒绝接受 [jùjué jiēshòu]

denim ['dɛnɪm] I N [U] (fabric) 斜纹粗棉布 [xiéwén cū miánbù] II **denims** NPL (jeans) 工装裤 [gōngzhuāngkù]

Denmark ['dɛnmɑːk] N 丹麦 [Dānmài]

denomination [dɪnɔmɪ'neɪʃən] N [C] **1** (religious) 宗派 [zōngpài] **2** [of money] 货币单位 [huòbì dānwèi]

denounce [dɪ'naʊns] VT [+ person, action] 谴责 [qiǎnzé] ▶ **to denounce sb as a traitor/impostor** 痛斥某人是叛徒/骗子

dense [dɛns] ADJ **1** [+ crowd, forest] 稠密的 [chóumì de] **2** [+ smoke, fog] 浓厚的 [nónghòu de] **3** (inf) (stupid) 愚钝的 [yúdùn de]

densely ['dɛnslɪ] ADV ▶ **densely populated** 人口稠密的 [rénkǒu chóumì de] ▶ **densely wooded** 丛林密布的

density ['dɛnsɪtɪ] N [C/U] 密度 [mìdù]

dent [dɛnt] I N [C] (in metal, box) 凹部 [āobù] II VT **1** [+ metal, box] 使…凹陷 [shǐ…āoxiàn] **2** [+ pride, ego, confidence] 削弱 [xuēruò] ▶ **to make a dent in sth** [+ car] 在某物上弄个小凹痕; [+ savings] 削弱某物

dental ['dɛntl] ADJ [+ treatment, hygiene etc] 牙齿的 [yáchǐ de]

dentist ['dɛntɪst] N [C] **1** (person) 牙医 [yáyī] **2** ▶ **the dentist('s)** 牙医诊所 [yáyī zhěnsuǒ]

dentures ['dɛntʃəz] NPL 假牙 [jiǎyá]

Denver boot ['dɛnvə(r)-] (US) N 车轮固定夹 [chēlún gùdìng jiā] [英= **clamp, wheel clamp**]

deny [dɪ'naɪ] VT **1** [+ charge, allegation, accusation] 否定 [fǒudìng] **2** [+ permission, chance, access] 拒绝某人某事 [jùjué mǒurén mǒushì] **3** (frm) (disown) [+ country, religion, person] 否认…与己有关 [fǒurèn…yǔ jǐ yǒuguān] ▶ **he denies having said it** 他否认这样说过 ▶ **to deny that…** 否认…

deodorant [diː'əʊdərənt] N [C/U] 除臭剂 [chúchòujì]

depart [dɪ'pɑːt] VI **1** ▶ **to depart (from/for somewhere)** [traveller, visitor +] (从某地)出发/出发(赶往某地) [(cóng mǒudì) chūfā/chūfā (gǎnwǎng mǒudì)]; [bus, plane, train +] 出发 [chūfā] **2** ▶ **to depart from sth** (stray from) 不合某事 [bùhé mǒushì]

○ department [dɪ'pɑːtmənt] N [C] **1** (in shop) 部[bù] **2** (in school or college) 系[xì] **3** (in government) 部[bù] ▶ **that's not my department** 那不是我的专责 ▶ **Department of State** (US) 国务院 ▶ **Department of Health/the Environment** (BRIT) 卫生/环境部

department store N [C] 百货商店 [bǎihuò shāngdiàn]

departure [dɪ'pɑːtʃə(r)] N **1** [C/U] [of visitor, traveller, plane etc] 出发 [chūfā] **2** [C] (scheduled journey) 离去 [líqù] **3** [C/U] (frm) [of employee, colleague] 离去 [líqù] **4** ▶ **a departure from sth** 背离某事 [bèilí mǒushì] ▶ **a new departure** 新起点

departure lounge N [C] 候机厅 [hòujītīng]

depend [dɪ'pɛnd] VI **1** ▶ **to depend on sth** (be decided by) 依某物而定 [yī mǒuwù ér dìng] **2** ▶ **you can depend on me/him** (rely on, trust) 你可以信赖我/他 [nǐ kěyǐ xìnlài wǒ/tā] **3** ▶ **to depend on sb/sth** (for survival) 依靠某人/某物为生 [yīkào mǒurén/mǒuwù wéishēng] ▶ **it (all) depends** 要看情况而定 ▶ **depending on the result…** 根据结果…

dependable [dɪ'pɛndəbl] ADJ 可靠的 [kěkào de]

dependant, dependent [dɪ'pɛndənt] N [C]
(person) 受赡养者 [shòu shànyǎngzhě]

dependence [dɪ'pɛndəns] N [U] 依赖 [yīlài]

dependent [dɪ'pɛndənt] I ADJ ▶ to be
dependent on sb/sth [+ person, decision] 依
赖某人/某物 [yīlài mǒurén/mǒuwù] II N =
dependant

depict [dɪ'pɪkt] VT 1 (in picture) 描绘 [miáohuì]
2 (describe) 描述 [miáoshù]

deplete [dɪ'pli:t] VT (frm) 大量消耗 [dàliàng
xiāohào]

deport [dɪ'pɔ:t] VT ▶ to deport sb (from
somewhere) [+ criminal, illegal immigrant] 将某
人(从某地)逐出 [jiāng mǒurén (cóng mǒudì)
zhúchū]

deposit [dɪ'pɒzɪt] I N [C] 1 (money) (in
account) 储蓄 [chǔxù]; (on goods) 保证金
[bǎozhèngjīn]; (on house, bottle, when hiring) 押
金 [yājīn] 2 (residue) (from chemical process) 沉
淀物 [chéndiànwù] 3 [of ore, oil, minerals etc]
沉积 [chénjī] II VT 1 [+ money] 把…存入
[bǎ…cúnrù] 2 (put, leave) 寄存 [jìcún] 3 (from
chemical or geological process) 沉积 [chénjī] ▶ to
put down a deposit of 50 pounds 支付50英镑
的保证金

depot ['dɛpəʊ] N [C] 1 (storehouse) 仓库
[cāngkù] 2 (for vehicles) 车库 [chēkù] 3 (US)
(station) 车站 [chēzhàn] [英=station]

depreciate [dɪ'pri:ʃɪeɪt] VI [currency, property,
value etc +] 贬值 [biǎnzhí]

depress [dɪ'prɛs] VT 1 [+ person] 使沮丧 [shǐ
jǔsàng] 2 [+ price, wages] 使跌价 [shǐ diējià]
3 (press down) [+ accelerator, lever] 压下 [yāxià]

depressed [dɪ'prɛst] ADJ 1 [+ person] 沮丧
的 [jǔsàng de] 2 [+ prices] 降低的 [jiàngdī de]
3 [+ industry] 萧条的 [xiāotiáo de] 4 [+ area] 不
景气的 [bù jǐngqì de] ▶ to feel depressed 感到
沮丧 ▶ to get depressed 心情沮丧

depressing [dɪ'prɛsɪŋ] ADJ [+ place, situation etc]
令人沮丧的 [lìng rén jǔsàng de]

depression [dɪ'prɛʃən] N 1 [U] [of person] 抑郁
症 [yìyùzhèng] 2 [C] (slump) (in economy) 萧条
[xiāotiáo] 3 [C] (weather system) 低气压 [dīqìyā]
4 [C] (hollow) 凹陷 [āoxiàn]

deprivation [dɛprɪ'veɪʃən] N [C/U] 1 (poverty)
穷困 [qióngkùn] 2 (loss) 丧失 [sàngshī]
▶ sleep deprivation 失眠

deprive [dɪ'praɪv] VT ▶ to deprive sb of sth 剥
夺某人某物 [bōduó mǒurén mǒuwù] ▶ to
deprive o.s. (of sth) (对某物) 自我克制

deprived [dɪ'praɪvd] ADJ [+ area, background,
child, region] 贫困的 [pínkùn de]

dept. ABBR (= department) 部系 [bùxì]

depth [dɛpθ] N 1 [C/U] (from top to bottom)
[of hole, water] 深 [shēn] 2 [C/U] (from front to
back) [of cupboard, shelf etc] 厚度 [hòudù] 3 [U]
[of emotion, feeling] 深厚 [shēnhòu] 4 [U] [of
knowledge] 渊博 [yuānbó]; [of understanding etc]

5 **the depths** (liter) [of ocean,
earth] 深处 [shēnchù] ▶ at/to/from a depth
of 3 metres 在/到/从3米深处 ▶ 18 metres
in depth 深18米 ▶ to be/go out of one's
depth (in water) 水深没顶处 ▶ to be/feel out
of one's depth (in situation) 力所不及 ▶ to
study/analyse sth in depth 深入研究/分析某
事 ▶ an in-depth investigation/analysis 深入
的调查/分析 ▶ the depths of the forest/
countryside 森林深处/乡郊野外 ▶ in the
depths of despair/recession/winter 深深陷入
绝望/衰退中/在隆冬

deputy ['dɛpjʊtɪ] I N [C] 1 (second in command)
副 [fù] 2 (elected member) 下院议员 [xiàyuàn
yìyuán] 3 (US) (also: deputy sheriff) 县助
理司法行政长官 [xiàn zhùlǐ sīfǎ xíngzhèng
zhǎngguān] II ADJ ▶ deputy chairman/
director 副主席/总监 [fù zhǔxí/zǒngjiān]
▶ deputy head (BRIT) (in school) 学监

derail [dɪ'reɪl] I VT ▶ to be derailed [train +] 出
轨 [chūguǐ] 2 [+ plan, negotiations] 使离开原定
进程 [shǐ líkāi yuándìng jìnchéng]

derelict ['dɛrɪlɪkt] I ADJ [+ building] 弃置的
[qìzhì de] II N [C] (frm) (vagrant) 无家可归者
[wú jiā kě guī zhě]

derive [dɪ'raɪv] I VT ▶ to derive sth (from sth)
[+ pleasure, benefit] (从某事中) 取得某事 [(cóng
mǒushì zhōng) qǔdé mǒushì] II VI ▶ to derive
from/be derived from sth (originate in) [word +]
从某物中派生出 [cóng mǒuwù zhōng pàishēng
chū]; [situation +] 来自某物 [láizì mǒuwù]

derogatory [dɪ'rɒgətərɪ] ADJ [+ remark,
comment] 贬低的 [biǎndī de]

descend [dɪ'sɛnd] I VT (frm) [+ stairs, hill] 下
[xià] II VI 1 (frm) (go down) 下来 [xiàlai] 2 ▶ to
descend (on/upon sb/sth) [calm, hush, gloom +]
向 (某人/某物) 袭来 [xiàng (mǒurén/mǒuwù)
xílái]; [visitors, tourists +] 突然涌向 (某人/某
地) [tūrán yǒngxiàng (mǒurén/mǒuwù)] ▶ to
be descended from [person +] 是…的后裔;
[animal +] 由…演变而来 ▶ to descend to sth/
to doing sth [+ lying, begging etc] 屈尊于某事/做
某事 ▶ in descending order 按递减的顺序

descendant [dɪ'sɛndənt] N [C] 后裔 [hòuyì]

descent [dɪ'sɛnt] N 1 [C/U] [of mountain, hill etc]
下坡 [xiàpō] 2 [C/U] (by aircraft) 下降 [xiàjiàng]
3 [U] (origin) 血统 [xuètǒng] 4 [C] (slope) 斜
坡 [xiépō] ▶ of African/European descent 非
洲/欧洲血统

⊙ **describe** [dɪs'kraɪb] VT 描述 [miáoshù] ▶ to
describe sth/sb/o.s. as... 把某事/某人/自
己描述成… ▷ ▶ a man described by the police as
extremely dangerous 一个被警察描述为极为危
险的人 ▶ to describe sb/sth to sb 向某人描
述某人/某事

description [dɪs'krɪpʃən] N [C/U] 描述
[miáoshù] ▶ of some/any description 某/任
何一种

desert [n 'dɛzət, vb dɪ'zəːt] I N 1 [c/u] (GEO) 沙漠 [shāmò] 2 [c] (fig) (wasteland) 荒地 [huāngdì] II VT (leave) [+ place] 离弃 [líqì]; [+ person] 遗弃 [yíqì] III VI (MIL) 逃跑 [táopǎo]

deserted [dɪ'zəːtɪd] ADJ 被舍弃的 [bèi shěqì de]

deserve [dɪ'zəːv] VT 应受 [yīng shòu] ▶ to deserve to do sth 应该获得某事

deserving [dɪ'zəːvɪŋ] ADJ 应得的 [yīngdé de]

○ **design** [dɪ'zaɪn] I N 1 [u] (art, process, layout, shape) 设计 [shèjì] 2 [c] (drawing) 图样 [túyàng] ▷ a design for a new office block 新办公楼区的图样 3 [c] (pattern) 图案 [tú'àn] II VT [+ kitchen, product, test, system] 设计 [shèjì] ▶ to be designed for sb/to do sth 专门为某人/做某事设计 ▶ by design (on purpose) 故意地 ▶ to have designs on sb/sth 对某人/某事抱不良企图

designate [vb 'dɛzɪɡneɪt, adj 'dɛzɪɡnɪt] I VT 1 (nominate) 指定 [zhǐdìng] ▶ to be designated for/as sth 专门用于某事 [zhuānmén yòngyú mǒushì] II ADJ ▶ chairman/prime minister designate 已受委任的主席/首相 [yǐ shòu wěirèn de zhǔxí/shǒuxiàng] ▶ in designated areas 在指定区域

designer [dɪ'zaɪnə(r)] I N [c] 设计者 [shèjìzhě] II CPD [复合词] [+ clothes, label, jeans etc] 名师设计的 [míngshī shèjì de]

desirable [dɪ'zaɪərəbl] ADJ 1 (attractive) 称心如意的 [chènxīn rúyì de] 2 (sexually attractive) 性感的 [xìnggǎn de] 3 (proper) 值得想要的 [zhídé xiǎngwàng de] ▶ it is desirable that... ···是合乎要求的

desire [dɪ'zaɪə(r)] I N 1 [c] (frm) (urge) 愿望 [yuànwàng] 2 [u] (sexual) 情欲 [qíngyù] II VT 1 (frm) (want) 想望 [xiǎngwàng] 2 (sexually) 想要 [xiǎngyào] ▶ to desire to do sth 想要做某事 ▶ the desired effect/result 期望的效果/结果

desk [dɛsk] N [c] 1 (in office) 办公桌 [bàngōngzhuō] 2 (for pupil) 书桌 [shūzhuō] 3 (in hotel, at airport, hospital etc) 服务台 [fúwùtái] 4 ▶ news/fashion desk (department) 新闻/时装部 [xīnwén/shízhuāng bù]

desk clerk (US) N [c] 接待员 [jiēdàiyuán] [英 = receptionist]

desktop publishing ['dɛsktɔp-] N [u] 桌面出版 [zhuōmiàn chūbǎn]

desolate ['dɛsəlɪt] ADJ 1 [+ place] 荒凉的 [huāngliáng de] 2 [+ person] 孤寂的 [gūjì de]

despair [dɪs'pɛə(r)] I N [u] 绝望 [juéwàng] II VI 绝望 [juéwàng] ▶ in despair 绝望地 ▶ to despair of doing sth 丧失做某事的信心 ▶ to despair at sb/sth 对某人/某事绝望

despatch [dɪs'pætʃ] N, VT = dispatch

desperate ['dɛspərɪt] ADJ 1 [+ person] 绝望的 [juéwàng de] 2 [+ attempt, effort] 铤而走险的 [tǐng ér zǒu xiǎn de] 3 [+ situation] 危急

的 [wēijí de] 4 [+ criminal, person] 不顾死活的 [bùgù sǐhuó de] ▶ to be desperate for sth/to do sth 极想某事/做某事

desperately ['dɛspərɪtlɪ] ADV 1 (frantically) [struggle, shout etc +] 拼命地 [pīnmìng de] 2 (terribly, awfully) [+ ill, unhappy etc] 极度地 [jídù de] ▶ desperately trying to escape 拼命逃窜 ▶ he desperately needs help 他极度需要帮助

desperation [dɛspə'reɪʃən] N [u] 绝望 [juéwàng] ▶ in or out of (sheer) desperation 处于/出于（完全的）绝望

despise [dɪs'paɪz] VT 鄙视 [bǐshì]

despite [dɪs'paɪt] PREP 尽管 [jǐnguǎn]

dessert [dɪ'zəːt] N [c/u] 饭后甜点 [fànhòu tiándiǎn]

dessert spoon N [c] 1 (object) 点心匙 [diǎnxīnchí] 2 (quantity) 一点心匙的量 [yī diǎnxīnchí de liàng]

destination [dɛstɪ'neɪʃən] N [c] [of traveller, mail, supplies etc] 目的地 [mùdìdì]

destined ['dɛstɪnd] ADJ 1 (bound) ▶ to be destined to do sth/for sth 注定做某事/某事 [zhùdìng zuò mǒushì/zuò mǒushì] 2 ▶ to be destined for sth [goods +] 指定送到某地 [zhǐdìng sòngdào mǒudì]; [person +] 指定送到某地 [zhǐdìng sòngdào mǒudì]

destiny ['dɛstɪnɪ] N 1 [c] (future) 命运 [mìngyùn] 2 [u] (fate) 缘分 [yuánfèn]

destroy [dɪs'trɔɪ] VT 1 [+ building, object] 破坏 [pòhuài] 2 [+ faith, confidence] 打破 [dǎpò] 3 [+ animal] 杀死 [shāsǐ]

destruction [dɪs'trʌkʃən] N [u] 1 (act of destroying) 破坏 [pòhuài] 2 (state of being destroyed) 毁灭 [huǐmiè]

destructive [dɪs'trʌktɪv] ADJ 1 [+ capacity, force] 破坏性的 [pòhuàixìng de] 2 [+ child, person] 有危害的 [yǒu wēihài de]

detach [dɪ'tætʃ] (frm) I VT 分开 [fēnkāi] II VI 分离 [fēnlí]

detached [dɪ'tætʃt] ADJ [+ person, attitude] 客观的 [kèguān de] ▶ detached house 独立式住房

detail ['diːteɪl] I N 1 [c] (individual feature, minor point) 细节 [xìjié] 2 [u] (in picture, work etc) 细节 [xìjié] II VT (frm) (list) 详述 [xiángshù] III details NPL 详情 [xiángqíng] ▶ in detail 详细地 ▶ to (not) go into details (usually negative) （没有）详细叙述

detailed ['diːteɪld] ADJ [+ account, description] 详细的 [xiángxì de]

detain [dɪ'teɪn] VT 1 (frm) (keep, delay) 耽搁 [dānge] 2 [police +] 扣留 [kòuliú] 3 (in hospital) 留下 [liúxià]

detect [dɪ'tɛkt] VT 1 (sense) 察觉 [chájué] 2 [+ illness, disease] 发现 [fāxiàn] 3 [+ enemy, pollution] 侦查 [zhēnchá]

detection [dɪ'tɛkʃən] N [u] 1 [of illness, disease] 发现 [fāxiàn] 2 [of criminal, secret] 侦查 [zhēnchá] ▶ to escape/avoid detection [*criminal* +] 逃之夭夭; [*mistake* +] 未被察觉

detective [dɪˈtɛktɪv] N [c] **1** (*in police*) 侦探 [zhēntàn] **2** (BRIT) ▶ **detective inspector/ constable/sergeant** 刑侦警察 [xíngzhēn jǐngchá] **3** (US) 侦探 [zhēntàn] ▶ **(private) detective** 私家侦探

detective story, detective novel N [c] 侦探小说 [zhēntàn xiǎoshuō]

detention [dɪˈtɛnʃən] N **1** [U] (*arrest*) 扣留 [kòuliú] **2** [C/U] (*at school*) 课后留校 [kèhòu liúxiào] ▶ **to be in detention** 被课后留校

deter [dɪˈtəː(r)] VT (*discourage*) [+ *person*] 吓住 [xiàzhù]; [+ *crime*] 威慑 [wēishè] ▶ **to deter sb from doing sth** 威慑某人不做某事

detergent [dɪˈtəːdʒənt] N [C/U] 清洁剂 [qīngjiéjì]

deteriorate [dɪˈtɪərɪəreɪt] VI 恶化 [èhuà]

determination [dɪtəːmɪˈneɪʃən] N **1** [U] (*resolve*) 决心 [juéxīn] **2** [C/U] (*establishment*) 确定 [quèdìng]

determine [dɪˈtəːmɪn] VT **1** (*frm*) (*discover*) [+ *facts*] 确定 [quèdìng] **2** (*decide on*) [+ *budget, amount*] 确定 [juédìng] **3** (*frm*) (*dictate*) 决定 [juédìng] ▶ **to determine that...** (*frm*) (*decide*) 决定⋯; (*establish*) 确定⋯ ▶ **to determine to do sth** (*frm*) 决定做某事

determined [dɪˈtəːmɪnd] ADJ **1** [+ *person*] 坚定的 [jiāndìng de] **2** [+ *effort, attempt*] 坚决的 [jiānjué de] ▶ **to be determined to do sth** 决心做某事

deterrent [dɪˈtɛrənt] I N [c] **1** (*nuclear*) 威慑因素 [wēishè yīnsù] **2** (LAW) 威慑手段 [wēishè shǒuduàn] II ADJ [+ *effect*] 威慑的 [wēishè de] ▶ **to act as a deterrent** 发挥威慑作用

detest [dɪˈtɛst] VT 嫌恶 [xiánwù]

detour [ˈdiːtuə(r)] N [c] **1** ▶ **to make a detour** 绕道 [ràodào] **2** (US) (*on road*) 绕行道路 [ràoxíng dàolù] [英= **diversion**]

detract [dɪˈtrækt] VI ▶ **to detract from sth** [+ *effect, achievement, pleasure etc*] 减损某物 [jiǎnsǔn mǒuwù]

detrimental [dɛtrɪˈmɛntl] ADJ ▶ **detrimental (to sth)** (对某事)不利的 [(duì mǒushì) bùlì de] ▶ **to have a detrimental effect (on sb/sth)** (对某人/某事)有不利影响

devastate [ˈdɛvəsteɪt] VT **1** (*destroy*) 破坏 [pòhuài] **2** (*shock*) ▶ **to be devastated (by sth)** (被某事)震惊 [(bèi mǒushì) zhènjīng]

devastating [ˈdɛvəsteɪtɪŋ] ADJ **1** [+ *weapon, storm*] 破坏性的 [pòhuàixìng de] **2** [+ *news, effect*] 惊人的 [jīngrén de]

○**develop** [dɪˈvɛləp] I VT **1** (*change and improve*) [+ *business, idea, relationship*] 发展 [fāzhǎn]; [+ *land, resource*] 开发 [kāifā] **2** (*produce*) [+ *product, weapon*] 开发 [kāifā] **3** (PHOT) 冲洗 [chōngxǐ] **4** (*begin to have*) [+ *fault, engine trouble*] 逐步显现 [zhúbù xiǎnxiàn]; [+ *disease*] 显现⋯的症状 [xiànshì...de zhēngzhuàng] II VI **1** (*evolve*)

[*person* +] 成长 [chéngzhǎng]; [*country, situation, friendship, skill* +] 发展 [fāzhǎn] **2** (*appear*) [*facts, symptoms* +] 逐步产生 [zhúbù chǎnshēng]; [*problem, difficulty* +] 逐步显现 [zhúbù xiǎnxiàn] ▶ **to develop a taste for sth** 逐步形成对某物的喜好 ▶ **to develop into sth** 发展成为某物

developing country [dɪˈvɛləpɪŋ-] N [c] 发展中国家 [fāzhǎnzhōng guójiā]

○**development** [dɪˈvɛləpmənt] N **1** [U] (*growth*) 成长 [chéngzhǎng] ▷ *the development of the embryo* 胚胎的成长; (*political, economic*) 发展 [fāzhǎn] **2** [c] (*event*) 新形势 [xīn xíngshì] ▷ *the latest developments in Moscow* 莫斯科最近的形势 **3** [U] (*of land, area*) 开发 [kāifā] **4** [c] (*building complex*) 新开发地 [xīn kāifādì] ▷ *an industrial development* 新开发的工业园区 ▷ *an unexpected development* 出乎意料的新事件

device [dɪˈvaɪs] N [c] **1** (*apparatus*) 设备 [shèbèi] **2** (*ploy, stratagem*) 手法 [shǒufǎ] ▶ **explosive device** (*bomb*) 引爆装置 ▶ **to leave sb to their own devices** 听任某人自行其是

devil [ˈdɛvl] N **1** [c] (*evil spirit*) 魔鬼 [móguǐ] **2** [c] ▶ **poor/lucky devil** 可怜/幸运的家伙 [kělián/xìngyùn de jiāhuo] **3** ▶ **the Devil** 撒旦 [Sādàn] ▶ **go on, be a devil!** (*inf*) 来，怕什么！ ▶ **talk of the devil!** 说到某人，某人就到！ ▶ **what/how/why the devil...?** (*inf*) (*used for emphasis*) 究竟什么/如何/为什么⋯？

devious [ˈdiːvɪəs] ADJ **1** [+ *person, mind*] 不光明正大的 [bù guāngmíng zhèngdà de] **2** [+ *route, path*] 迂回的 [yúhuí de]

devise [dɪˈvaɪz] VT **1** [+ *plan, scheme*] 想出 [xiǎngchū] **2** [+ *machine*] 设计 [shèjì]

devoid [dɪˈvɔɪd] ADJ ▶ **devoid of sth** (*lacking*) 毫无某物 [háowú mǒuwù]

devote [dɪˈvəut] VT ▶ **to devote time/energy to sth** 为某事付出时间/精力 [wèi mǒushì fùchū shíjiān/jīnglì] ▶ **to devote o.s. to sth** 致力于某事

devoted [dɪˈvəutɪd] ADJ **1** (*enthusiastic*) 热中的 [rèzhōng de] **2** (*loving*) [+ *husband, daughter etc*] 忠诚的 [zhōngchéng de] **3** ▶ **devoted to sth** (*specialising in*) 致力于某事的 [zhìlì yú mǒushì de] ▶ **to be devoted to sb** 深爱某人 ▶ **Horace is devoted to his garden** 霍勒斯热中于园艺

devotion [dɪˈvəuʃən] N [U] (*to person*) 热爱 [rè'ài] **2** (*to duty, job etc*) 献身 [xiànshēn]

devour [dɪˈvauə(r)] VT **1** (*eat*) 狼吞虎咽似地吃 [láng tūn hǔ yàn shìde chī] **2** (*read*) 贪婪地读 [tānlán de dú]

devout [dɪˈvaut] ADJ [+ *person*] 虔诚的 [qiánchéng de] ▶ **a devout Catholic/Muslim etc** 虔诚的天主教/穆斯林〔等〕

dew [djuː] N [U] 露水 [lùshuǐ]

diabetes [daɪəˈbiːtiːz] N [U] 糖尿病 [tángniàobìng]

diabetic [daɪəˈbɛtɪk] I ADJ **1** [+ *person, patient*] 患糖尿病的 [huàn tángniàobìng de] **2** [+ *coma*]

糖尿病的 [tángniàobìng de] **3** [+ *chocolate, jam*] 糖尿病患者食用的 [tángniàobìng huànzhě shíyòng de] **II** N [c] 糖尿病患者 [tángniàobìng huànzhě]

diagnose [daɪəg'nəʊz] VT [+ *illness, problem*] 诊断 [zhěnduàn] ▸ **to be diagnosed as...** [*person* +] 被诊断为患了…; [*illness* +] 被诊断为… ▸ **to be diagnosed as suffering from/having...** 被诊断为患有…

diagnosis [daɪəg'nəʊsɪs] (*pl* **diagnoses** [daɪə g'nəʊsi:s]) N [c/u] 诊断 [zhěnduàn]

diagonal [daɪ'ægənl] **I** ADJ [+ *line*] 斜的 [xié de] **II** N [c] **1** (*in geometry*) 对角线 [duìjiǎoxiàn] **2** (*in pattern or design*) 斜纹 [xiéwén]

diagonally [daɪ'ægənəlɪ] ADV 倾斜地 [qīngxié de]

diagram ['daɪəgræm] N [c] 图解 [tújiě]

dial ['daɪəl] **I** N [c] **1** (*on clock or meter*) 标度盘 [biāodùpán] **2** (*on radio*) 调谐度盘 [tiáoxiédùpán] **3** (*on telephone*) 拨号盘 [bōhàopán] **II** VT [+ *number*] 拨 [bō] **III** VI 拨号 [bōhào] ▸ **can I dial London direct?** 我可以直接往伦敦打电话吗？

dialect ['daɪəlɛkt] N [c/u] 方言 [fāngyán]

dialling code ['daɪəlɪŋ-] (BRIT) N [c] 电话区号 [diànhuà qūhào] [美= **area code**]

dialling tone (BRIT) N [c] 拨号音 [bōhàoyīn] [美= **dial tone**]

dialogue, (US) **dialog** ['daɪəlɒg] N [c/u] **1** (*conversation*) 对话 [duìhuà] **2** (*discussions*) 交换意见 [jiāohuàn yìjiàn] **3** (*in play, film, novel etc*) 对白 [duìbái]

dial tone (US) N = **dialling tone**

diameter [daɪ'æmɪtə(r)] N [c] 直径 [zhíjìng] ▸ **15 cm in diameter** 直径为15厘米

diamond ['daɪəmənd] **I** N [c] **1** (*gem*) 钻石 [zuànshí] **2** (*shape*) 菱形 [língxíng] **II diamonds** NPL (*on playing cards*) 方块 [fāngkuài] ▸ **the six/king of diamonds** 方块6/K

diaper ['daɪəpə(r)] (US) N [c] 尿布 [niàobù] [英= **nappy**]

diarrhoea, (US) **diarrhea** [daɪə'riːə] N [u] 腹泻 [fùxiè] ▸ **to have diarrhoea** 腹泻

diary ['daɪərɪ] N [c] **1** (*engagements book*) 日记簿 [rìjìbù] **2** (*daily account*) 日记 [rìjì] ▸ **to keep a diary** 记日记 ▸ **video/tape diary** 录像带/磁带日记

dice [daɪs] (*pl* **dice**) **I** N **1** [c] (*in game*) 骰子 [shǎizi] **2** [u] (*game*) 掷骰赌博 [zhì shǎi dǔbó] **II** VT (*in cooking*) 将…切成丁 [jiāng…qiē chéng dīng]

dictate [*vb* dɪk'teɪt, *n* 'dɪkteɪt] **I** VT **1** [+ *letter, memo etc*] 口述 [kǒushù] **2** (*determine*) [+ *conditions*] 规定 [guīdìng] **II** VI ▸ **to dictate to sb** (*order about*) 命令某人 [mìnglìng mǒurén] **III** N [c] (*order*) 命令 [mìnglìng] ▸ **the dictates of one's conscience** 某人的做人原则

▸ **common sense dictates that...** 依据常识…

dictation [dɪk'teɪʃən] N **1** [u] (*of letter*) 口述 [kǒushù] **2** [c/u] (*at school, college*) 听写 [tīngxiě]

dictator [dɪk'teɪtə(r)] (*pej*) N [c] **1** (*ruler*) 独裁者 [dúcáizhě] **2** (*overbearing person*) 霸道的人 [bàdào de rén]

dictatorship [dɪk'teɪtəʃɪp] N **1** [c/u] (*government*) 独裁政府 [dúcái zhèngfǔ] **2** [c] (*country*) 独裁国家 [dúcái guójiā]

dictionary ['dɪkʃənrɪ] N [c] 词典 [cídiǎn]

did [dɪd] PT *of* **do**

didn't ['dɪdnt] = **did not**

⊙ **die** [daɪ] **I** VI **1** [*person, animal, plant* +] 死 [sǐ] **2** [*love, hope* +] 消失 [xiāoshī] **3** [*engine* +] 熄灭 [xīmiè] **II** N [c] (*pl* **dice**) (*for games*) 骰子 [shǎizi] ▸ **to die of or from sth** 死于某事 ▸ **to die a natural/violent death** 自然死亡/惨死 ▸ **to be dying** [*person, plant, animal* +] 奄奄一息 ▸ **old habits die hard** 积习难改 ▸ **I'm dying of thirst/boredom** 我渴死了/无聊死了 ▸ **to be dying for sth/to do sth** 渴望某事/做某事
▸ **die away** VI [*sound, light* +] 逐渐消失 [zhújiàn xiāoshī]
▸ **die down** VI **1** [*wind* +] 停止 [tíngzhǐ] **2** [*fire* +] 熄灭 [xīmiè] **3** [*excitement, controversy, laughter* +] 平息 [píngxī]
▸ **die out** VI **1** [*custom, way of life* +] 灭亡 [mièwáng] **2** [*species* +] 灭绝 [mièjué]

▦ 用法参见 **dead**

在需要解释某人的死亡原因时，可以说他们 **die of** 或 **die from** 某个具体原因。*Both he and my mother died of cancer... He died from brain injuries five days later.* 还可以用 **be dying of thirst**，**hunger**，**boredom** 或者 **curiosity** 来强调非常口渴、饥饿、厌倦或好奇的状态。这是非正式用法。*Order a pot of tea, I'm dying of thirst.*

diesel ['diːzl] N **1** [u] (*also*: **diesel oil**) 柴油 [cháiyóu] **2** [c] (*vehicle*) 柴油机驱动的车辆 [cháiyóujī qūdòng de chēliàng]

diet ['daɪət] **I** N **1** [c/u] (*food intake*) 饮食 [yǐnshí] **2** [c] (*restricted food*) (*medical*) 特种饮食 [tèzhǒng yǐnshí]; (*slimming*) 减肥饮食 [jiǎnféi yǐnshí] **3** ▸ **a diet of mindless pop songs/soap operas** 多得令人腻烦的无聊的流行歌曲/肥皂剧 **II** VI 节食 [jiéshí] **III** CPD [复合词] 特制的 [tèzhì de] ▸ **to be on a diet** 实行减肥节食 ▸ **to go on a diet** 开始减肥节食 ▸ **to live on a diet of fish and rice** 以鱼和米为主食

differ ['dɪfə(r)] VI **1** (*be different*) ▸ **to differ (from sth)** (与某物)不同 [(yǔ mǒuwù) bùtóng] **2** (*disagree*) ▸ **to differ (on sth)** (就某事)意见不同 [(jiù mǒushì) yìjiàn bùtóng] ▸ **to agree to differ** 同意保留各自不同意见

difference ['dɪfrəns] N **1** [c] (*between things, people*) 差异 [chāyì] **2** [s] (*between two quantities*)

差 [chā] **3** [c] (*disagreement*) 分歧 [fēnqí] ▶ the difference in size/colour 尺寸/颜色上的差异 ▶ to make a/no difference (to sb/sth) (对某人/某事) 有/无影响 ▶ I can't tell the difference between them 我看不出他们的区别 ▶ to settle/resolve one's differences 消除分歧

○ **different** ['dɪfrənt] ADJ **1** (*not the same*) 不同的 [bùtóng de] **2** (*unusual*) 不同寻常的 [bùtóng xúncháng de] ▶ different from 与…不同 ▶ different to or (US) than 与…不同

differentiate [dɪfə'renʃieɪt] I VI ▶ to differentiate between one thing and another 区分一事与另一事 [qūfēn yīshì yǔ lìng yīshì] II VT ▶ to differentiate sth from sth (*distinguish*) 把某物与某物区分开 [bǎ mǒuwù yǔ mǒuwù qūfēn kāi]; (*set apart*) 使某物与某物有区别 [shǐ mǒuwù yǔ mǒuwù yǒu qūbié]

differently ['dɪfrəntlɪ] ADV **1** [*feel, think etc +*] 不同地 [bùtóng de] **2** [*treat, regard +*] 有差异地 [yǒu chāyì de] **3** [*+ shaped, designed*] 不同地 [bùtóng de]

○ **difficult** ['dɪfɪkəlt] ADJ **1** [*+ task, problem, decision*] 困难的 [kùnnán de] **2** [*+ person, child*] 执拗的 [zhíniù de] ▷ Don't be difficult! 别那么执拗! ▶ I found it difficult to... 我认为…很难 ▶ it is difficult being a parent 为人父母很难 ▶ it is difficult for us to understand her 我们很难理解她 ▶ it is difficult to save 省钱是件难事

difficulty ['dɪfɪkəltɪ] N **1** [c] (*problem*) 困难 [kùnnán] **2** [c] [*of question, exam*] 难度 [nándù] ▶ to have difficulty/difficulties 有困难 ▶ to be in difficulty 陷入困境 ▶ he stood up with difficulty 他艰难地站了起来

dig [dɪg] (*pt, pp* **dug**) I VT **1** [*+ hole*] 挖 [wā] **2** [*+ garden*] 掘土 [juétǔ] **3** ▶ to dig sth into sth (*sink*) 将某物伸进某物 [jiāng mǒuwù shēnjìn mǒuwù] II VI **1** (*with spade*) 挖掘 [wājué] **2** ▶ to dig into sth (*sink*) 戳进 [chuōjìn] III N **1** (*prod*) ▶ to give sb a dig in the ribs 戳了某人肋部一下 [chuōle mǒurén lèibù yīxià] **2** [c] (*also*: archaeological dig) (*excavation*) 考古挖掘 [kǎogǔ wājué] **3** (*inf*) ▶ to have/take a dig at sb (*criticism*) 挖苦某人 [wākǔ mǒurén]

▶ **dig in** (*also*: dig o.s. in) I VI [*soldiers +*] 挖壕固守 [wāháo gùshǒu] II VT [*+ compost*] 翻土时把…混入泥土中 [fāntǔshí bǎ…hùnrù nítǔ zhōng] ▶ to dig one's heels in (*fig*) 坚持自己的立场

▶ **dig into** VT FUS [不可拆分] [*+ savings*] 动用 [dòngyòng]

▶ **dig out** VT **1** [*+ survivors, car*] 发掘出 [fājuéchū] **2** (*inf*) (*find*) 找寻到 [zhǎoxúndào]

▶ **dig up** VT **1** [*+ plant, body*] 挖出 [wāchū] **2** [*+ land, area*] 掘起 [juéqǐ] **3** (*discover*) [*+ information, evidence*] 搜集 [sōují]

digest [*vb* daɪ'dʒɛst, *n* 'daɪdʒɛst] I VT **1** [*+ food, meal*] 消化 [xiāohuà] **2** [*+ facts, information etc*]

领会 [lǐnghuì] II VI [*food, meal +*] 消化 [xiāohuà] III N [c] (*book*) 摘要 [zhāiyào]

digestion [dɪ'dʒɛstʃən] N **1** [U] (*process*) 消化 [xiāohuà] **2** [c] (*system*) 消化能力 [xiāohuà nénglì]

digit ['dɪdʒɪt] N [c] **1** (*number*) 0到9之间的任何一个数字 **2** (*frm*) (*finger*) 手指 [shǒuzhǐ]; (*toe*) 足趾 [zúzhǐ]

digital ['dɪdʒɪtl] ADJ **1** [*+ clock, watch etc*] 数字的 [shùzì de] **2** [*+ recording, technology*] 数码的 [shùmǎ de]

digital camera N [c] 数码相机 [shùmǎ xiàngjī]

digital television N [U] 数字电视 [shùzì diànshì]

dignified ['dɪgnɪfaɪd] ADJ [*+ person, manner*] 高贵的 [gāoguì de]

dignity ['dɪgnɪtɪ] N [U] **1** (*composure*) 庄严 [zhuāngyán] **2** (*worth*) 尊严 [zūnyán] **3** (*self-respect*) 高贵 [gāoguì]

digs [dɪgz] (BRIT: *inf, o.f.*) NPL (*lodgings*) 住宿处 [zhùsùchù]

dilemma [daɪ'lɛmə] N [c] (*political, moral*) 进退两难 [jìn tuì liǎng nán] ▶ to be in a dilemma 处在进退两难的境地

diligent ['dɪlɪdʒənt] ADJ **1** [*+ worker*] 勤奋的 [qínfèn de] **2** [*+ research, work*] 细致的 [xìzhì de]

dilute [daɪ'luːt] I VT **1** [*+ liquid*] 冲淡 [chōngdàn] **2** [*+ belief, principle*] 削弱 [xuēruò] II ADJ [*+ liquid, solution*] 稀释的 [xīshì de]

dim [dɪm] I ADJ **1** (*not bright*) [*+ light*] 暗淡的 [àndàn de]; [*+ room, place*] 昏暗的 [hūn'àn de] **2** (*unclear*) [*+ outline, figure*] 模糊的 [móhu de] **3** (*faint*) [*+ memory, sight*] 模糊的 [móhu de] **4** [*+ future, prospects*] 暗淡的 [àndàn de] **5** (*inf*) (*stupid*) 迟钝的 [chídùn de] II VT **1** [*+ light*] 使变淡 [shǐ biàndàn] **2** (US: AUT) ▶ to dim one's lights 打近光灯 [dǎ jìnguāngdēng] [英=dip] III VI [*light +*] 变暗 [biàn'àn] ▶ to take a dim view of sth 对某事持不赞成的态度

dime [daɪm] (US) N [c] 一角银币 [yījiǎo yínbì] ▶ a dime a dozen 多得很

dimension [daɪ'mɛnʃən] I N [c] **1** (*aspect*) 方面 [fāngmiàn] **2** (*in maths, science*) 维 [wéi] II **dimensions** NPL **1** (*measurements*) 面积 [miànjī] **2** (*scale, size*) 尺寸 [chǐcùn]

diminish [dɪ'mɪnɪʃ] VI, VT 减小 [jiǎnxiǎo]

dimple ['dɪmpl] N [c] 酒窝 [jiǔwō]

din [dɪn] N [s] [*+ row, racket*] 喧闹声 [xuānnàoshēng]

dine [daɪn] (*frm*) VI 进餐 [jìncān] ▶ dine out VI 外出吃饭 [wàichū chīfàn]

diner ['daɪnə(r)] N **1** (*person*) 就餐者 [jiùcānzhě] **2** (US) (*restaurant*) 廉价餐馆 [liánjià cānguǎn]

dinghy ['dɪŋgɪ] N [c] **1** (*inflatable*) (*also*: **rubber dinghy**) 橡皮筏 [xiàngpífá] **2** (*also*: **sailing dinghy**) 小船 [xiǎochuán]

dingy ['dɪndʒɪ] ADJ **1** [+ *street, room*] 阴暗的 [yīn'àn de] **2** [+ *clothes, curtains etc*] 邋遢的 [lāta de]

dining car ['daɪnɪŋ-] (BRIT) N [c] 餐车 [cānchē]

dining room N [c] **1** (*in house*) 饭厅 [fàntīng] **2** (*in hotel*) 餐厅 [cāntīng]

dining table N [c] 餐桌 [cānzhuō]

dinner ['dɪnə(r)] N **1** [c/u] (*evening meal*) 晚餐 [wǎncān] **2** [c/u] (*lunch*) 午餐 [wǔcān] **3** [c] (*formal meal*) 正餐 [zhèngcān]
　■用法参见 **meal**

dinner jacket (BRIT) N [c] 男用晚礼服 [nán yòng wǎnlǐfú] [美=**tuxedo**]

dinner party N [c] 宴会 [yànhuì]

dinner time N [c/u] **1** (*in evening*) 晚饭时间 [wǎnfàn shíjiān] **2** (*at midday*) 午饭时间 [wǔfàn shíjiān]

dinosaur ['daɪnəsɔ:(r)] N [c] **1** 恐龙 [kǒnglóng] **2** (*pej*) 庞然大物 [pángrán dà wù]

dip [dɪp] I VT **1** (*into liquid*) [+ *bread, spoon, finger*] 蘸 [zhàn] **2** (*into container*) [+ *hand*] 伸进 [shēnjìn] **3** (BRIT) [+ *headlights*] 使···变暗 [shǐ···biàn'àn] [美=**dim**] II VI **1** (*ground, road +*) 倾斜 [qīngxié] **2** (*boat +*) 下降 [xiàjiàng] **3** ▸ **to dip into sth** [+ *container*] 伸进某物 [shēnjìn mǒuwù]; [+ *book*] 翻阅某物 [fānyuè mǒuwù]; [+ *savings*] 动用某物 [dòngyòng mǒuwù] **4** (*decrease, fall*) 下降 [xiàjiàng] III N [c] **1** (*slope*) 斜坡 [xiépō] **2** (*swim*) ▸ **to take a dip/go for a dip** 下水 [xiàxiàshuǐ] **3** [c/u] (*sauce*) 奶油沙司 [nǎiyóu shāsī] **4** [c] (*decrease*) 下降 [xiàjiàng]

diploma [dɪ'pləumə] N [c] 毕业文凭 [bìyè wénpíng]

diplomacy [dɪ'pləuməsɪ] N [u] **1** (*between governments*) 外交 [wàijiāo] **2** (*tact*) 外交手腕 [wàijiāo shǒuwàn]

diplomat ['dɪpləmæt] N [c] 外交官 [wàijiāoguān]

diplomatic [dɪplə'mætɪk] ADJ **1** [+ *mission, solution etc*] 外交上的 [wàijiāo shàng de] **2** (*tactful*) [+ *person*] 老练的 [lǎoliàn de]; [+ *answer, letter*] 圆滑的 [yuánhuá de] ▸ **to break off/resume diplomatic relations (with sb)** (与某人)断绝/恢复外交关系

dipstick ['dɪpstɪk] (BRIT) N [c] 量油尺 [liángyóuchǐ]

dire [daɪə(r)] ADJ **1** [+ *consequences, poverty*] 极端的 [jíduān de] **2** (*inf*) (*terrible*) 可怕的 [kěpà de] ▸ **to be in dire straits** (*financially*) 捉襟见肘 ▸ **to be in dire need of sth** 极需某物

⊙ **direct** [daɪ'rɛkt] I ADJ **1** [+ *route, flight*] 直达的 [zhídá de] **2** [+ *sunlight, contact, experience, challenge*] 直接的 [zhíjiē de] ▷ *"keep out of direct sunlight"* "避免阳光直接照射" ▷ *She died as a direct result of this injection.* 注射这支针剂是导致她死亡的直接原因。▷ *He avoided giving a direct answer.* 他避免作出直截了当的回答。

3 [+ *descendant*] 直系的 [zhíxì de] II VT **1** (*show*) 给···指路 [gěi···zhǐlù] ▷ *Could you direct them to my office, please?* 请您告诉他们如何到我的办公室,好吗? ▷ *I directed the way for the stranger.* 我给那个陌生人指路。**2** (*send*) [+ *letter*] 寄往 [jìwǎng] ▷ *His mail is being directed to his new address.* 他的信件正寄往他的新住处。**3** (*focus*) [+ *attention, remark*] 集中于 [jízhōngyú] **4** (*manage*) [+ *company, project etc*] 管理 [guǎnlǐ] **5** [+ *play, film, programme*] 导演 [dǎoyǎn] **6** (*frm*) (*order*) ▸ **to direct sb to do sth** 指引某人做某事 [zhǐyǐn mǒurén zuò mǒushì] III ADV (*directly*) [*go, write, fly +*] 直接地 [zhíjiē de] ▷ *You can fly direct to Amsterdam from Liverpool.* 你可以从利物浦直接飞往阿姆斯特丹。▸ **to direct one's attention to sth** 把注意力集中于某物

direct debit (BRIT) N [c/u] 直接借记 [zhíjiē jièjì]

direction [dɪ'rɛkʃən] I N **1** [c] (*way*) (*for travelling*) 方向 [fāngxiàng]; (*of development*) 趋势 [qūshì] **2** [u] (*of film, play etc*) 导演 [dǎoyǎn] II **directions** NPL **1** (*to get somewhere*) 指路说明 [zhǐlù shuōmíng] **2** (*for doing something*) 用法说明 [yòngfǎ shuōmíng] ▸ **sense of direction** 方向感 ▸ **in the direction of** (*towards*) 朝 ▸ **in all directions** (*everywhere*) 向四面八方 ▸ **to ask for directions** 问路 ▸ **directions for use** 使用说明

directly [dɪ'rɛktlɪ] ADV **1** ▸ **directly above/below/in front** *etc* 正上/下/前方{等} [zhèngshàng/xià/qiánfāng {děng}] **2** (*straight*) [*go, fly +*] 径直地 [jìngzhí de] **3** (*at once*) 立即 [lìjí] **4** (*as a direct result*) 直接地 [zhíjiē de]

⊙ **director** [dɪ'rɛktə(r)] N [c] **1** [*of company*] 经理 [jīnglǐ] **2** [*of organization, public authority*] 主任 [zhǔrèn] **3** [*of play, film etc*] 导演 [dǎoyǎn]

directory [dɪ'rɛktərɪ] N [c] **1** (*also:* **telephone directory**) 电话号码簿 [diànhuà hàomǎbù] **2** (*list of names, addresses etc*) 姓名地址录 [xìngmíng dìzhǐ lù] **3** (*on computer*) 文件名录 [wénjiàn mínglù]

directory enquiries [-ɪn'kwaɪərɪz] (BRIT) N [u] 查号台 [cháhàotái] [美=**information, directory assistance**]

dirt [də:t] N [u] **1** 污物 [wūwù] **2** (*earth*) 泥土 [nítǔ] ▸ **to treat sb like dirt** 视某人如草芥

dirty ['də:tɪ] I ADJ **1** [+ *clothes, face etc*] 脏的 [zāng de] **2** [+ *joke, magazine*] 黄色的 [huángsè de] II VT [+ *clothes, face etc*] 弄脏 [nòngzāng]

dirty trick N [c] 卑鄙伎俩 [bēibǐ jiliǎng] ▸ **a dirty tricks campaign** 大骗局

disability [dɪsə'bɪlɪtɪ] N **1** [c] (*physical*) 伤残 [shāngcán] **2** [c] (*mental*) 残疾 [cánjí] **3** [u] (*state of being disabled*) 残废 [cánfèi]

disabled [dɪs'eɪbld] I ADJ **1** (*physically*) 伤残的 [shāngcán de] **2** (*mentally*) 残疾的 [cánjí de] II NPL ▸ **the disabled** 残疾人 [cánjírén]

disadvantage [dɪsəd'vɑ:ntɪdʒ] N [c/u]

(*drawback*) 不利 [bùlì] ► **to be** *or* **work to sb's disadvantage** 对某人不利 ► **to be at a disadvantage** 处于不利地位

disagree [dɪsə'ɡriː] VI 1 ► **to disagree (with sb)** 不同意(某人的观点) [bù tóngyì (mǒurén de guāndiǎn)] ► **to disagree (with sth)** (对某事表示)不同意 [(duì mǒushì biǎoshì) bù tóngyì] 2 (ESP BRIT) ► **to disagree with sth** (*oppose*) 反对某事 [fǎnduì mǒushì] ► **I disagree with you** 我不同意你的看法 ► **garlic disagrees with me** 大蒜不对我的口味

disagreeable [dɪsə'ɡriːəbl] ADJ 1 [+ *encounter, experience, smell*] 令人不快的 [lìng rén bùkuài de] 2 [+ *person*] 难相处的 [nán xiāngchǔ de]

disagreement [dɪsə'ɡriːmənt] N 1 [U] (*objection*) 反对 [fǎnduì] 2 [c] (*argument*) 争执 [zhēngzhí] ► **to have a disagreement (with sb)** (与某人)意见不统一

disappear [dɪsə'pɪə(r)] VI 1 (*from view*) [*person, vehicle, object +*] 消失 [xiāoshī] 2 (*go missing*) 失踪 [shīzōng] 3 (*cease to exist*) 消失 [xiāoshī] ► **to disappear from view** 不见

disappearance [dɪsə'pɪərəns] N 1 [C/U] [*of person*] 失踪 [shīzōng] 2 [c] (*loss, theft*) [*of vehicle, object*] 失窃 [shīqiè] 3 [U] [*of custom, species*] 消失 [xiāoshī]

disappoint [dɪsə'pɔɪnt] VT [+ *person*] 使失望 [shǐ shīwàng]

disappointed [dɪsə'pɔɪntɪd] ADJ 失望的 [shīwàng de] ► **to be disappointed in sb** 对某人失望 ► **to be disappointed that...** 令人失望的是…

> 请勿将 **disappointed** 与 **disappointing** 混淆。如果你 **disappointed**，表示你由于某事没有发生或某事不如期望的那么好而感到沮丧。*Helen was disappointed that he hadn't called...I know that my dad will be very disappointed when he hears my exam results.* 某事物 **disappointing** 表示该事物没有达到你的期望值，令你感到失望。*The food at the restaurant was disappointing.*

disappointing [dɪsə'pɔɪntɪŋ] ADJ [+ *result, book, performance*] 使人失望的 [shǐ rén shīwàng de]

用法参见 **disappointed**

disappointment [dɪsə'pɔɪntmənt] N 1 [U] (*emotion*) 失望 [shīwàng] 2 [c] (*cause*) 令人失望的人/事 [lìng rén shīwàng de rén/shì] ► **to my disappointment** 令我失望的是

disapproval [dɪsə'pruːvəl] N [U] 不赞成 [bù zànchéng]

disapprove [dɪsə'pruːv] VI ► **to disapprove (of sb/sth)** 不同意(某人/某事) [bù tóngyì (mǒurén/mǒushì)]

disarm [dɪs'ɑːm] I VT 1 [+ *soldier, terrorist*] 解除…的武装 [jiěchú…de wǔzhuāng] 2 (*win over*) 消除 [xiāochú] II VI (*give up weapons*) 放下武器 [fàngxià wǔqì]

disarmament [dɪs'ɑːməmənt] N [U] 裁军 [cáijūn]

disaster [dɪ'zɑːstə(r)] N [C/U] 1 (*earthquake, flood etc*) 灾难 [zāinàn] 2 (*accident, crash etc*) 灾祸 [zāihuò] 3 (*fiasco*) 惨败 [cǎnbài] 4 (*serious situation*) 灾难 [zāinàn]

disastrous [dɪ'zɑːstrəs] ADJ 1 (*catastrophic*) 灾难性的 [zāinànxìng de] 2 (*unsuccessful*) 惨败的 [cǎnbài de]

disbelief ['dɪsbə'liːf] N [U] 怀疑 [huáiyí] ► **in disbelief** 怀疑地

disc [dɪsk] N [c] 1 (*round, flat object*) 圆盘 [yuánpán] 2 (*in backbone*) 椎间盘 [zhuījiānpán] 3 (*o.f.*) (*record*) 唱片 [chàngpiàn] 4 (COMPUT) = **disk**

discard [dɪs'kɑːd] VT [+ *unwanted object*] 丢弃 [diūqì]; [+ *idea, plan, system*] 抛弃 [pāoqì]

discern [dɪ'sɜːn] (*frm*) VT 1 (*see*) 隐约看见 [yǐnyuē kànjiàn] 2 (*identify*) 看出 [kànchū]

discharge [vb dɪs'tʃɑːdʒ, n 'dɪstʃɑːdʒ] I VT 1 [+ *waste, water, blood*] 排出 [páichū] 2 (*from hospital*) 允许…离开 [yǔnxǔ…líkāi] 3 (*from armed services*) 使…离开 [shǐ…líkāi] 4 (*from court/prison*) 释放 [shìfàng] 5 [+ *duties*] 使免除 [shǐ miǎnchú] 6 (*frm*) (*settle*) [+ *debt*] 清偿 [qīngcháng] 7 (*o.f.*) (*fire*) [+ *gun, weapon*] 射出 [shèchū] II N 1 [C/U] (*frm*) [*of waste, gas*] 排放 [páifàng] 2 [C/U] (*frm*) (*from eye, wound*) 分泌物 [fēnmìwù] 3 [U] (*dismissal*) [*of patient*] 出院证明 [chūyuàn zhèngmíng]; [*of soldier*] 退役 [tuìyì]; [*of defendant*] 释放 [shìfàng]

discipline ['dɪsɪplɪn] I N 1 [U] [*of children, pupils*] 纪律 [jìlǜ] 2 [U] (*self-control*) 约束 [yuēshù] 3 [c] (*branch of knowledge*) 学科 [xuékē] II VT 1 (*train*) ► **to discipline o.s. (to do sth)** 训练自己(做某事) [xùnliàn zìjǐ (zuò mǒushì)] 2 (*punish*) 惩处 [chéngchǔ]

disc jockey N [c] 简称为DJ，意为广播电台或迪斯科舞厅流行音乐唱片播放及介绍人

disclose [dɪs'kləuz] VT [+ *information*] 透露 [tòulù] ► **to disclose that...** (*reveal*) 透露…

disco ['dɪskəu] N 1 (*nightclub*) 迪斯科舞厅 [dísīkē wǔtīng] 2 (*event*) 迪斯科 [dísīkē]

discoloured, (US) **discolored** [dɪs'kʌləd] ADJ 褪色的 [tuìsè de]

discomfort [dɪs'kʌmfət] I N [U] 1 (*in body*) 不舒服 [bù shūfu] 2 (*unease*) 不安 [bù'ān] II **discomforts** NPL 不舒服的事 [bù shūfu de shì]

disconnect [dɪskə'nɛkt] VT 1 [+ *pipe, tap, hose etc*] 拆开 [chāikāi] 2 [+ *computer, cooker, TV etc*] 断开 [duànkāi] 3 ► **to be disconnected** (*for non-payment of bill*) 被切断 [bèi qiēduàn]; (*during telephone conversation*) 被中断 [bèi zhōngduàn]

discontent [dɪskən'tɛnt] N [c] 不满意 [bù mǎnyì]

discontented [dɪskən'tɛntɪd] ADJ 不满的 [bùmǎn de]

discontinue [dɪskən'tɪnju:] VT 1 (frm) [+ visits, treatment] 停止 [tíngzhǐ] 2 (frm) [+ payments] 中止 [zhōngzhǐ] 3 ▸ to be discontinued [product +] 停产 [tíngchǎn]

discount [n 'dɪskaunt, vb dɪs'kaunt] I N [c/u] 折扣 [zhékòu] II VT 1 [+ goods] 打折扣 [dǎ zhékòu] 2 (ignore, reject) 不理会 [bù lǐhuì] ▸ to give sb a discount on sth 给予某人某物的折扣 ▸ at a discount (cheaply) 在打折出售

discourage [dɪs'kʌrɪdʒ] VT 1 (dishearten) [+ person] 使泄气 [shǐ xièqì] 2 (dissuade) ▸ to discourage sb from doing sth 劝阻某人不做某事 [quàn mǒurén bù zuò mǒushì] 3 [+ activity] 设法阻止 [shèfǎ zǔzhǐ] ▸ to be discouraged 感到气馁

discover [dɪs'kʌvə(r)] VT 发现 [fāxiàn] ▸ to discover that... (find out) 发现… ▸ to discover how to do sth 发现如何做某事

> discover、find 和 find out 都可以表示"发现"。He discovered the whole school knew about it...The young child finds that noise attracts attention...We found out that she was wrong. discover 比 find 更正式，多用于科研文章或正式的调查报告中，比如 discover 某种疾病的治疗方法。还可以用 discover 表示意外地发现某物。This well-known flower was discovered in 1903. 如果你看不到你想找的东西，可以说你无法 find 它，而不能用 discover 或 find out。I'm lost – I can't find the bridge. 可以说某人 find out 某个事实，而不能用 find 和 discover。I found out the train times.

discovery [dɪs'kʌvərɪ] N 1 [c/u] (of treasure, cure) 发现 [fāxiàn] 2 [c] (thing found) 被发现的事物 [bèi fāxiàn de shìwù] ▸ to make a discovery 发现 ▸ the discovery that... …的发现

discredit [dɪs'krɛdɪt] VT 1 [+ person, group] 使丧失名誉 [shǐ sàngshī míngyù] 2 [+ claim, idea] 使不可信 [shǐ bù kěxìn]

discreet [dɪs'kri:t] ADJ 1 (diplomatic) [+ person, remark] 谨慎的 [jǐnshèn de] 2 (quiet, secretive) 悄声的 [qiāoshēng de] 3 [+ decor, appearance, place] 精巧的 [jīngqiǎo de] ▸ at a discreet distance 保持一定恭敬的距离

discrepancy [dɪs'krɛpənsɪ] N [c/u] ▸ discrepancy (between two things) (inconsistency) （两者间的）差异 [liǎngzhě jiān de chāyì] ▸ a discrepancy in sth 在某事上存在的差异

discretion [dɪs'krɛʃən] N [u] (tact) 谨慎 [jǐnshèn] ▸ at the discretion of sb (frm) 由某人自行处理 ▸ to have the discretion to do sth (frm) 有做某事的决定权 ▸ to use one's discretion (frm) 由某人自行决定

discriminate [dɪs'krɪmɪneɪt] VI 1 ▸ to discriminate between two things 区别

两种事物 [qūbié liǎngzhǒng shìwù] 2 ▸ to discriminate against/in favour of sb 歧视/特别优待某人 [qíshì/tèbié yōudài mǒurén]

discrimination [dɪskrɪmɪ'neɪʃən] N [u] 1 (bias) 歧视 [qíshì] 2 (discernment) 辨别力 [biànbiélì] ▸ racial/sexual discrimination 种族/性别歧视

discuss [dɪs'kʌs] VT 1 (talk over) 讨论 [tǎolùn] 2 (analyse) 论述 [lùnshù] ▸ to discuss what/how/who... 讨论做什么/如何做/谁做…

discussion [dɪs'kʌʃən] N [c/u] 1 (talk) 讨论 [tǎolùn] 2 (debate) (in article, lecture etc) 论述 [lùnshù] ▸ under discussion 正在讨论中

disdain [dɪs'deɪn] I N [u] 蔑视 [mièshì] II VT 蔑视 [mièshì] III VI ▸ to disdain to do sth 不屑做某事 [bùxiè zuò mǒushì]

disease [dɪ'zi:z] N 1 [c/u] (illness) 病 [bìng] 2 [c] (liter) (affliction) 弊病 [bìbìng]

disembark [dɪsɪm'bɑ:k] (frm) VI [passengers +] 离船/下飞机/下车 [líchuán/xià fēijī/xiàchē]

disgrace [dɪs'greɪs] I N [u] (shame, dishonour) 耻辱 [chǐrǔ] II VT [+ one's family, country] 使受耻辱 [shǐ shòu chǐrǔ] ▸ it's a disgrace! 这是件丢人的事! ▸ to be a disgrace to sb (cause of shame) 是某人的耻辱

disgraceful [dɪs'greɪsful] ADJ [+ behaviour, condition, state] 可耻的 [kěchǐ de]

disgruntled [dɪs'grʌntld] ADJ [+ person, tone] 不满的 [bùmǎn de]

disguise [dɪs'gaɪz] I N [c] (make-up, costume) 伪装品 [wěizhuāngpǐn] 2 [u] (art) 乔装打扮 [qiáozhuāng dǎbàn] II VT 1 ▸ (to be) disguised (as sth/sb) [+ person] 假扮成（某物/某人）[jiǎbànchéng (mǒuwù/mǒurén)] 2 [+ fact, emotions] 掩饰 [yǎnshì] 3 [+ voice] 伪装 [wěizhuāng] ▸ in disguise 乔装着 ▸ there's no disguising the fact that... 毫无隐瞒事实真相… ▸ to disguise o.s. (as sb) 把自己假扮（成某人）

disgust [dɪs'gʌst] I N [u] 厌恶 [yànwù] II VT 使厌恶 [shǐ yànwù] ▸ she walked off in disgust 她厌恶地走开了

disgusted [dɪs'gʌstɪd] ADJ 感到厌恶的 [gǎndào yànwù de]

disgusting [dɪs'gʌstɪŋ] ADJ 1 (revolting) [+ food, habit] 令人作呕的 [lìng rén zuò'ǒu de] 2 (disgraceful) [+ behaviour, situation] 讨厌的 [tǎoyàn de]

dish [dɪʃ] I N [c] 1 (piece of crockery) (for serving) 盘 [pán]; (for eating) 碟 [dié] 2 (contents) 盘 [pán] 3 (recipe, food) 一道菜 [yī dào cài] 4 (also: satellite dish) 盘形物 [pánxíngwù] II dishes N PL 碗碟 [wǎndié] ▸ to do or wash the dishes 刷洗碗碟
▸ dish out VT 1 (serve) [+ food] 分配 [fēnpèi] 2 (give out) [+ money, books, drugs] 分发 [fēnfā]; [+ advice, criticism] 施加 [shījiā]
▸ dish up (inf) I VT [+ food] 把…盛在盘中端上

[bǎ…shèng zài pán zhōng duān shàng] II VI
装盘上菜 [zhuāngpán shàngcài]

dishcloth ['dɪʃklɒθ] N [c] (for drying dishes) 擦
碗布 [cāwǎnbù]; (for washing dishes) 洗碗布
[xǐwǎnbù]

dishonest [dɪs'ɒnɪst] ADJ 1 [+ person] 不诚实的
[bù chéngshí de] 2 [+ behaviour] 不正直的 [bù
zhèngzhí de]

dishonourable, (US)**dishonorable**
[dɪs'ɒnərəbl] ADJ [+ person, behaviour] 不光彩的
[bù guāngcǎi de]

dish soap (US) N [U] 洗洁剂 [xǐjiéjì]
[英=**washing-up liquid**]

dishtowel ['dɪʃtauəl] (US) N [c] 擦碗布
[cāwǎnbù] [英=**tea towel**]

dishwasher ['dɪʃwɒʃə(r)] N [c] 洗碗机
[xǐwǎnjī]

dishwashing liquid ['dɪʃwɒʃɪŋ-] (US) N [U] 洗
洁剂 [xǐjiéjì] [英=**washing-up liquid**]

disillusioned [dɪsɪ'luːʒənd] ADJ (to become)
disillusioned (with sth) (变得) (对某事) 不抱
幻想 [(biànde) (duì mǒushì) bù bào huànxiǎng]

disinfect [dɪsɪn'fɛkt] VT [+ object, wound, water]
给…消毒 [gěi…xiāodú]

disinfectant [dɪsɪn'fɛktənt] N [c/U] 消毒剂
[xiāodújì]

disintegrate [dɪs'ɪntɪɡreɪt] VI 1 [object +] 支离
破碎 [zhīlí pòsuì] 2 [marriage, partnership +] 崩溃
[bēngkuì] 3 [organization +] 瓦解 [wǎjiě]

disk [dɪsk] N [c] (COMPUT) (hard) 硬盘 [yìngpán];
(floppy) 软盘 [ruǎnpán]

disk drive N [c] 磁盘驱动器 [cípán qūdòngqì]

diskette [dɪs'kɛt] N (COMPUT) =**disk**

dislike [dɪs'laɪk] I N 1 (feeling) ▶ dislike (of
sb/sth) 讨厌 (某人/某物) [tǎoyàn (mǒurén/
mǒuwù)] 2 [c] (object of dislike) 不喜欢的东
西 [bù xǐhuān de dōngxi] II VT 不喜欢 [bù
xǐhuān] ▶ to take a dislike to sb/sth 厌恶某
人/某事 ▶ one's likes and dislikes 某人的爱好
和厌恶 ▶ I dislike the idea 我不喜欢这个主意
▶ to dislike doing sth 不喜欢做某事

dislocate ['dɪsləkeɪt] VT [+ finger, shoulder, jaw etc]
使…脱臼 [shǐ…tuōjiù] ▶ he has dislocated his
shoulder 他的肩膀脱臼了

disloyal [dɪs'lɔɪəl] ADJ (to country, family, friend)
不忠诚的 [bù zhōngchéng de]

dismal ['dɪzml] ADJ 1 (depressing) [+ weather,
place, mood] 阴沉的 [yīnchén de] 2 (very bad)
[+ prospects, record, failure] 令人忧郁的 [lìng rén
yōuyù de]

dismantle [dɪs'mæntl] VT 1 [+ machine,
structure] 拆卸 [chāik;xiè] 2 [+ organization,
system] 废除 [fèichú]

dismay [dɪs'meɪ] I N [U] 气馁 [qìněi] II VT 使
气馁 [shǐ qìněi] ▶ much to my dismay 颇令
我失望

dismiss [dɪs'mɪs] VT 1 [+ worker] 解雇 [jiěgù]
2 (send away) 让…离开 [ràng…líkāi] 3 [+ case,

charge] 驳回 [bóhuí] 4 [+ possibility, problem, idea]
不考虑 [bù kǎolù]

dismissal [dɪs'mɪsl] N [c/U] (sacking) 解雇
[jiěgù] 2 (disregard) 不予考虑 [bùyǔ kǎolù]

disobedience [dɪsə'biːdɪəns] N [U] 不服从
[bù fúcóng]

disobedient [dɪsə'biːdɪənt] ADJ 不服从的 [bù
fúcóng de]

disobey [dɪsə'beɪ] VT 1 [+ person] 不顺从 [bù
shùncóng] 2 [+ order] 不服从 [bù fúcóng]

disorder [dɪs'ɔː(r)] N 1 [U] (untidiness) 杂乱
[záluàn] 2 [U] (rioting) 动乱 [dòngluàn] 3 [c]
(illness) 失调 [shītiáo] ▶ civil/public disorder
市民动乱

disorganized [dɪs'ɔːɡənaɪzd] ADJ 1 [+ person]
缺乏条理的 [quēfá tiáolǐ de] 2 [+ event] 无序
的 [wúxù de]

disown [dɪs'əun] VT 1 [+ action, comment] 否
认同…有关系 [fǒurèn tóng…yǒu guānxi]
2 [+ child] 不认 [bùrèn]

dispatch, despatch [dɪs'pætʃ] I VT
1 (send) [+ message, goods, mail] 发送 [fāsòng];
[+ messenger, soldiers] 派遣 [pàiqiǎn] 2 (o.f.) (deal
with) [+ business] 迅速办理 [xùnsù bànlǐ] 3 (o.f.)
(kill) [+ person, animal] 杀死 [shāsǐ] II VT
(sending) 派遣 [pàiqiǎn] 2 [c] (report) 报告
[bàogào]

dispel [dɪs'pɛl] VT [+ idea, fear] 消除 [xiāochú]

dispense [dɪs'pɛns] VT 1 [+ medicines] 配 [pèi]
2 [+ advice, justice] 施与 [shīyǔ] 3 [machine +]
[+ product] 售出 [shòuchū]
▶ **dispense with** VT FUS [不可拆分] 1 (get
rid of) 摆脱 [bǎituō] 2 (do without) 用不着
[yòngbùzháo]

dispenser [dɪs'pɛnsə(r)] N [c] (machine) 自动售
货机 [zìdòng shòuhuòjī]

disperse [dɪs'pəːs] VT 1 VT [+ smoke, leaflets, crowd]
驱散 [qūsàn] II VI 1 [oil, smoke, fog, cloud +] 散去
[sànqù] 2 [crowd +] 散开 [sànkāi]

displace [dɪs'pleɪs] VT 1 (supplant) 取代 [qǔdài]
2 ▶ to be displaced [+ people] 背井离乡 [bèi jǐng
lí xiāng]

display [dɪs'pleɪ] I N 1 [c] (in shop, at exhibition)
陈列 [chénliè] 2 [c] (exhibition) 展览 [zhǎnlǎn]
3 [c/U] (show) [of feeling] 表现 [biǎoxiàn] 4 [c]
(information on screen) 显示 [xiǎnshì] 5 [c]
(screen) 显示屏 [xiǎnshìpíng] II VT 1 (show)
[+ exhibits] 陈列 [chénliè]; [+ feelings, courage]
表现 [biǎoxiàn]; (proudly) 炫耀 [xuànyào]
2 [+ results, information] 显示 [xiǎnshì] ▶ **on
display** [+ exhibits, goods, work] 正在展览的

displease [dɪs'pliːz] VT (offend, annoy) 使不高
兴 [shǐ bù gāoxìng]

disposable [dɪs'pəuzəbl] ADJ [+ lighter, nappy,
razor] 一次性的 [yīcìxìng de] ▶ **disposable
income** 可支配的收入

disposal [dɪs'pəuzl] N [U] 清理 [qīnglǐ] ▶ **to
have sth at one's disposal** 手边有某物 ▶ **to**

put sth at sb's disposal 把某事交某人自由处理

dispose [dɪs'pəuz] ▶ **to dispose of** VT FUS [不可拆分] **1** (get rid of) [+ body, unwanted goods] 把…处理掉 [bǎ…chùlǐdiào] **2** (deal with) [+ problem, task] 处理 [chùlǐ] **3** (frm) (kill) 干掉 [gàndiào]

disposed [dɪs'pəuzd] ADJ (frm) (inclined, willing) ▶ **to be disposed to do sth** 倾向于做某事 [qīngxiàng yú zuò mǒushì] ▶ **to be well/favourably/ill disposed towards sb** 认为…很好/不好

disposition [dɪspə'zɪʃən] N **1** [c] (nature) 性情 [xìngqíng] **2** (frm) ▶ **a disposition to do sth** (inclination) 做某事的倾向 [zuò mǒushì de qīngxiàng] ▶ **of a nervous disposition** 生性紧张的

disproportionate [dɪsprə'pɔːʃənət] ADJ [+ amount, effect] 不相称的 [bù xiāngchèn de] ▶ **disproportionate to sth** 与某事不相称的

disprove [dɪs'pruːv] VT [+ belief, theory] 证明…不成立 [zhèngmíng…bù chénglì]

dispute [dɪs'pjuːt] I N [c/u] **1** (between people) 争论 [zhēnglùn] **2** (industrial) 争执 [zhēngzhí] **3** (between countries, organizations) 争端 [zhēngduān] II VT [+ fact, statement] 对…提出质疑 [duì…tíchū zhìyí]; [+ ownership, rights] 争夺 [zhēngduó] ▶ **to be in dispute** [+ people, countries] 有纠纷; [+ issue] 有争论 ▶ **I don't dispute that…** 我毫不怀疑…

disqualify [dɪs'kwɔlɪfaɪ] VT [+ team, competitor] 取消…的资格 [qǔxiāo…de zīgé] ▶ **to disqualify sb from (doing) sth** 取消某人(做)某事的资格 ▶ **to be disqualified from driving** (BRIT) 被取消驾驶的资格

disregard [dɪsrɪ'gɑːd] I VT (ignore) 不理 [bùlǐ] II N [u] ▶ **disregard (for sth)** 忽视(某事) [hūshì (mǒushì)]

disrupt [dɪs'rʌpt] VT **1** (interrupt) [+ conversation, meeting] 扰乱 [rǎoluàn] **2** (disturb) [+ plan, process] 妨碍 [fáng'ài]

disruption [dɪs'rʌpʃən] N [c/u] **1** (interruption) 扰乱 [rǎoluàn] **2** (disturbance) 混乱 [hùnluàn]

dissatisfaction [dɪssætɪs'fækʃən] N [u] 不满 [bùmǎn]

dissatisfied [dɪs'sætɪsfaɪd] ADJ ▶ **dissatisfied (with sth)** (对某事)不满 [(duì mǒushì) bùmǎn]

dissect [dɪ'sɛkt] VT **1** [+ animal, body] 解剖 [jiěpōu] **2** (scrutinize) [+ theory, work] 仔细分析 [zǐxì fēnxi]

dissent [dɪ'sɛnt] I N [u] (disagreement) 异议 [yìyì] II VI (disagree) 不同意 [bù tóngyì]

dissertation [dɪsə'teɪʃən] N [c] 学位论文 [xuéwèi lùnwén]

dissolve [dɪ'zɔlv] I VT **1** (in liquid) 溶解 [róngjiě] **2** ▶ **to be dissolved** [+ organization, marriage] 终结 [zhōngjié]; [+ parliament] 被解散

[bèi jiěsàn] II VI [material +] 溶解 [róngjiě] ▶ **to dissolve in(to) tears/laughter** 情不自禁地流泪/大笑起来

distance ['dɪstns] I N **1** [c/u] (between two places) 距离 [jùlí] **2** [u] (remoteness) 遥远 [yáoyuǎn] **3** [u] (frm) (reserve) 冷淡 [lěngdàn] II VT ▶ **to distance o.s. (from sb/sth)** 逐渐疏远(某人/某物) [zhújiàn shūyuǎn (mǒurén/mǒuwù)] ▶ **in the distance** 在远处 ▶ **from a distance** 从远处 ▶ **what's the distance to London?** 到伦敦的距离有多远? ▶ **to be some distance/quite a distance/a fair distance from sth** (far) 距离某物相当远 ▶ **within walking distance** 步行可到 ▶ (at) **a distance of 2 metres** 相距两米的距离 ▶ **keep your distance!** 保持距离!

distant ['dɪstnt] ADJ **1** [+ place] 远的 [yuǎn de] **2** [+ future, past] 久远的 [jiǔyuǎn de] **3** [+ relative, cousin] 远房的 [yuǎnfáng de] **4** (aloof) [+ person, manner] 冷淡的 [lěngdàn de] **5** (absent) [+ person, look] 茫然的 [mángrán de]

distil, (US) distill [dɪs'tɪl] VT **1** [+ water, whisky] 蒸馏 [zhēngliú] **2** (extract) [+ information, ideas etc] ▶ **distilled from sth** 提取某物的精华 [tíqǔ mǒuwù de jīnghuá]

distillery [dɪs'tɪləri] N [c] 酒厂 [jiǔchǎng]

distinct [dɪs'tɪŋkt] ADJ **1** (different) 截然不同的 [jiérán bùtóng de] **2** (clear) [+ smell, flavour etc] 明显的 [míngxiǎn de] **3** (unmistakable) [+ advantage, change] 明确的 [míngquè de] ▶ **as distinct from** (in contrast to) 不同于

distinction [dɪs'tɪŋkʃən] N [c] (difference) 区别 [qūbié] **2** (honour) ▶ **to have the distinction of being sth** 具有成就某事的杰出表现 [jùyǒu chéngjiù mǒushì de jiéchū biǎoxiàn] **3** [c] (in exam) (honour, award) 优秀 [yōuxiù] ▶ **to draw or make a distinction (between two things)** 区分(两事物) ▶ **a writer/wine of distinction** 知名作家/葡萄酒

distinctive [dɪs'tɪŋktɪv] ADJ 与众不同的 [yǔ zhòng bù tóng de]

distinguish [dɪs'tɪŋgwɪʃ] I VT **1** (frm) (identify) [+ details, sounds] 辨别 [biànbié] **2** ▶ **to distinguish one thing from another** (differentiate) 将一事物与另一事物区别开来 [jiāng yīshìwù yǔ lìngyī shìwù qūbié kāilái] **3** ▶ **to distinguish sb/sth from others** (set apart) 使某人/某物显得与众不同 [shǐ mǒurén/mǒuwù xiǎnde yǔ zhòng bù tóng] II VI ▶ **to distinguish between truth and fiction** 分清事实和虚构 [fēnqīng shìshí hé xūgòu] ▶ **to distinguish o.s.** 出名

distinguished [dɪs'tɪŋgwɪʃt] ADJ **1** (eminent) 杰出的 [jiéchū de] **2** (in appearance) 高贵的 [gāoguì de]

distinguishing [dɪs'tɪŋgwɪʃɪŋ] ADJ ▶ **distinguishing feature/characteristic** 明显的特征 [míngxiǎn de tèzhēng]

distort [dɪs'tɔːt] VT 1 [+ *statement, fact, idea*] 歪曲 [wāiqū] 2 [+ *sound, shape, image*] 使失真 [shǐ shīzhēn]

distract [dɪs'trækt] VT [+ *person*] 使分心 [shǐ fēnxīn] ▸ **to distract sb's attention** 分散某人的注意力

distracted [dɪs'træktɪd] ADJ 心烦意乱的 [xīnfán yìluàn de]

distraction [dɪs'trækʃən] N 1 [C/U] (*diversion*) 精神涣散 [jīngshén huànsàn] 2 [C] (*amusement*) 消遣 [xiāoqiǎn] ▸ **to drive sb to distraction** 使某人发狂

distraught [dɪs'trɔːt] ADJ 心烦意乱的 [xīnfán yìluàn de]

distress [dɪs'trɛs] I N [U] (*anguish*) 极度忧伤 [jídù yōushāng] II VT (*cause anguish to*) 使忧伤 [shǐ yōushāng] ▸ **in distress** [+ *ship, aircraft etc*] 遭难的; [+ *person*] 处于危难中

distressing [dɪs'trɛsɪŋ] ADJ [+ *experience, time*] 使人痛苦的 [shǐ rén tòngkǔ de]

distribute [dɪs'trɪbjuːt] VT 1 (*hand out*) [+ *food, leaflets*] 分发 [fēnfā] 2 (*share out*) [+ *resources, profits, work etc*] 分配 [fēnpèi] 3 (*supply*) [+ *goods (to shops)*] 配送 [pèisòng]

distribution [dɪstrɪ'bjuːʃən] N 1 [U] [*of food, supplies, newspaper*] 分发 [fēnfā] 2 [C/U] [*of resources, wealth, power*] 分布 [fēnbù] 3 [U] [*of films*] 发行 [fāxíng]

distributor [dɪs'trɪbjutə(r)] N [C] 1 (*in business*) 批发商 [pīfāshāng] 2 (*in car engine*) 配电盘 [pèidiànpán]

district [dɪstrɪkt] N [C] 1 [*of country, town*] 地区 [dìqū] 2 (*official area*) 行政区 [xíngzhèngqū] 3 (*in titles*) 区 [qū]

district attorney (US) N [C] 地方检察官 [dìfāng jiǎncháguān]

distrust [dɪs'trʌst] I N [U] 怀疑 [huáiyí] II VT 不信任 [bù xìnrèn]

disturb [dɪs'tɜːb] VT 1 (*interrupt*) 打扰 [dǎrǎo] 2 (*upset*) 使心烦 [shǐ xīnfán] 3 (*rearrange*) [+ *belongings, papers etc*] 弄乱 [nòngluàn] ▸ **sorry to disturb you** 对不起，打扰您了

请勿将 **interrupt** 与 **disturb** 混淆。如果你 **interrupt** 某个正在讲话的人，表示你说或做某事打断他们讲话。*He tried to speak, but she interrupted him.* 如果想要表示打断正在讲话或开会的人谈话，正确的表达是 *Sorry to interrupt.* 如果 **interrupt** 某个过程或者活动，就意味着使它中断一段时间。*The match took nearly three hours and was interrupted at times by rain.* 如果 **disturb** 某人，就是使他们停止了正在做的事情并且令他们感到不快。*Find a quiet, warm, comfortable room where you won't be disturbed.*

disturbance [dɪs'tɜːbəns] N 1 [C/U] (*upheaval, upset*) 干扰 [gānrǎo] 2 [C] (*violent incident*) 骚乱 [sāoluàn] 3 [C/U] (*emotional, psychological*) 失调 [shītiáo] ▸ **to cause a disturbance** 引起混乱

disturbed [dɪs'tɜːbd] ADJ 1 (*worried, anxious*) 不安的 [bù'ān de] 2 (*unhappy*) [+ *childhood, relationship etc*] 有问题的 [yǒu wèntí de] 3 (*traumatised, damaged*) 精神失常的 [jīngshén shīcháng de] ▸ **mentally disturbed** 精神受困扰的 ▸ **emotionally disturbed** 情绪失常的

disturbing [dɪs'tɜːbɪŋ] ADJ [+ *experience, situation, aspect*] 令人不安的 [lìng rén bù'ān de]

disused [dɪs'juːzd] ADJ [+ *building*] 废弃的 [fèiqì de]

ditch [dɪtʃ] I N [C] 1 (*at roadside, in field*) 沟 [gōu] 2 (*also*: **irrigation ditch**) 沟渠 [gōuqú] II VT (*inf*) [+ *partner*] 同…断绝关系 [tóng…duànjué guānxi]; [+ *car, sofa etc*] 丢弃 [diūqì]; [+ *plan, policy*] 抛弃 [pāoqì]

dither ['dɪðə(r)] (*pej*) VI 犹豫不决 [yóuyù bùjué]

ditto ['dɪtəu] ADV 同样地 [tóngyàng de]

dive [daɪv] I VI 1 [*swimmer +*] (*into water*) 跳水 [tiàoshuǐ]; (*under water*) 潜水 [qiánshuǐ] 2 [*bird +*] 俯冲 [fúchōng] 3 [*fish, submarine +*] 潜入水中 [qián rù shuǐ zhōng] 4 ▸ **to dive into/under sth** (*leap*) 钻入某物中/下 [zuān rù mǒuwù zhōng/xià] 5 ▸ **to dive into sth** [+ *bag, drawer etc*] 把手伸进某物 [bǎ shǒu shēnjìn mǒuwù] II N [C] 1 (*into water*) 跳水 [tiàoshuǐ] 2 (*underwater*) 潜水 [qiánshuǐ] 3 (*inf, pej*) (*place*) 下等娱乐场所 [xiàděng yúlè chǎngsuǒ] 4 (*in football*) ▸ **to take a dive** 假摔 [jiǎshuāi]

diver ['daɪvə(r)] N [C] 潜水员 [qiánshuǐyuán]

diverse [daɪ'vɜːs] ADJ 多种多样的 [duōzhǒng duōyàng de]

diversion [daɪ'vɜːʃən] N 1 [C] (BRIT) (*for traffic*) 临时改道 [línshí gǎidào] [美 = **detour**] 2 [C/U] (*distraction*) 注意力的转移 [zhùyìlì de zhuǎnyí] 3 [C/U] [*of profits, funds*] 转移 [zhuǎnyí] 4 [C/U] [*of ship*] 转向 [zhuǎnxiàng] ▸ **to create a diversion** 转移注意力

diversity [daɪ'vɜːsɪtɪ] N 1 [U] (*variety*) 多样性 [duōyàngxìng] 2 (*range*) ▸ **a diversity of** 各种各样的 [gèzhǒng gèyàng de]

divert [daɪ'vɜːt] VT 1 (*re-route*) [+ *traffic, plane*] 使绕道行驶 [shǐ ràodào xíngshǐ] 2 [+ *money, resources*] 转移 [zhuǎnyí] 3 (*amuse*) 使欢娱 [shǐ huānyú] ▸ **to divert (sb's) attention from sth** 转移（某人）对某事的注意力

divide [dɪ'vaɪd] I VT 1 ▸ **to divide (up)** (*separate*) (*into groups, areas*) 划分 [huàfēn] 2 (*in maths*) 除 [chú] 3 ▸ **to divide sth between/among sb/sth** (*share*) 在两个/3个以上的人/物之间分配某物 [zài liǎnggè/sāngè yǐshàng de rén/wù zhījiān fēnpèi mǒuwù] 4 ▸ **to divide sth (from sth)** (*keep separate*) [*road, frontier +*] 将某物（与某物）分隔 [jiāng mǒuwù (yǔ mǒuwù) fēngé] 5 (*split*) 使有分歧 [shǐ yǒu fēnqí] II VI 1 [*people +*] (*into groups*) 分开 [fēnkāi] 2 [*cells +*] 分裂 [fēnliè] III N [C] (*gulf, rift*) 分水

岭 [fēnshuǐlíng] ▶ **to divide sth in half** 将某物一分为二 ▶ **40 divided by 5** 40除以5 ▶ **divide 7 into 35** 7除35

divided highway [dɪ'vaɪdɪd-] (US) N [C] 有隔离带的高速公路 [yǒu gélídài de gāosù gōnglù] [英= **dual carriageway**]

divine [dɪ'vaɪn] I ADJ **1** (from God) [+ inspiration, punishment] 神的 [shén de] **2** (o.f.) (wonderful) 极好的 [jíhǎo de] II VI ▶ **to divine for sth** [+ water, metal] 勘探某物 [kāntàn mǒuwù]

diving ['daɪvɪŋ] N [U] **1** (underwater) 潜水 [qiánshuǐ] **2** (from board) 跳水 [tiàoshuǐ]

diving board N [C] 跳水板 [tiàoshuǐbǎn]

divinity [dɪ'vɪnɪtɪ] N **1** [U] (quality of being divine) 神性 [shénxìng] **2** [C] (god, goddess) 神 [shén] **3** [U] (theology) 神学 [shénxué]

division [dɪ'vɪʒən] N **1** [U] (splitting up) 分开 [fēnkāi] **2** [U] (MATH) 除法 [chúfǎ] **3** [U] (sharing out) [of labour, resources] 分配 [fēnpèi] **4** [C/U] (gulf) 分歧 [fēnqí] **5** [C] (department) 部门 [bùmén] **6** [C] (military unit) 师 [shī] **7** [C] (in sport, especially football) 级 [jí] **8** [C] (BRIT) (in parliament) 分组表决 [fēnzǔ biǎojué]

divorce [dɪ'vɔːs] I N [C/U] 离婚 [líhūn] II VT **1** [+ spouse] 与…离婚 [yǔ…líhūn] **2** (frm) (dissociate) ▶ **to divorce sth from sth** 将某事与某事脱离 [jiāng mǒushì yǔ mǒushì tuōlí] III VI 离婚 [líhūn]

divorced [dɪ'vɔːst] ADJ 离异的 [líyì de] ▶ **to be divorced from sb** 与某人离婚 ▶ **to get divorced** 离婚

divorcee [dɪvɔː'siː] N [C] 离了婚的人 [lí le hūn de rén]

DIY (BRIT) N ABBR (= *do-it-yourself*) 自己动手的活计 [zìjǐ dòngshǒu de huójì] ▶ **to do DIY** 自己动手做

● **DIY**
英国人对 DIY 很上瘾，有时幽默地称其为一种全民性消遣。DIY 意为 do-it-yourself，是指自己动手制作和修理东西，尤其是在家里。房主不雇佣专业的建筑工人、木匠或油漆匠，这样不仅省钱，还能从自己动手改造家里的设备、环境中得到莫大的满足感。专门的 DIY 商店销售工具、油漆和其他能满足 DIY 爱好者嗜好的用品。

dizzy ['dɪzɪ] ADJ **1** ▶ **to feel dizzy** 感到头晕 [gǎndào tóuyūn] **2** [+ turn, spell] 头晕的 [tóuyūn de] **3** [+ woman, blonde] 傻乎乎的 [shǎhūhū de] ▶ **the dizzy heights of...** 使人晕乎乎的…高度 ▶ **to make sb dizzy** 使人头晕目眩

DJ N ABBR **1** (= *disc jockey*) 简称为DJ，意为广播电台或迪斯科舞厅流行音乐唱片播放及介绍人 **2** (BRIT) (= *dinner jacket*) 男用晚礼服 [nányòng wǎnlǐfú] [美= **tuxedo**]

DNA N ABBR (= *deoxyribonucleic acid*) 脱氧核糖核酸 [tuōyǎng hétáng hésuān]

○

do [duː] (pt **did**, pp **done**) I VT **1** (be engaged in, achieve) 做 [zuò] ▶ **what are you doing?** 你在做什么呢？ ▶ **what is he doing here?** 他怎么在这儿？ ▶ **are you doing anything tomorrow evening?** 你明晚有什么打算？ ▶ **what you should do is...** 你应该做的是… ▶ **we must do everything possible to help them** 我们必须想尽一切办法帮助他们 ▶ **what did you do with the money?** (how did you spend it) 你怎么用这笔钱的？; (where did you put it) 你把钱放哪儿了？ ▶ **what are you going to do about this?** 你打算对此怎么办？ **2** (for a living) ▶ **what do you do?** 你做什么工作？ [nǐ zuò shénme gōngzuò?] **3** (with noun) ▶ **to do the cooking** 做饭 [zuòfàn] ▶ **to do one's teeth/hair** 刷牙/做头发 ▶ **we're doing "Othello" at school** (studying it) 我们正在学校里学习《奥赛罗》; (performing it) 我们正在学校里排演《奥赛罗》 **4** (referring to speed, distance) ▶ **the car was doing 100** 汽车以100英里的时速行进 [qìchē yǐ yìbǎi yīnglǐ de shísù xíngjìn] ▶ **we've done 200 km already** 我们的时速已达到了200公里 **5** (cause) ▶ **the explosion did a lot of damage** 爆炸造成了很大损失 [bàozhà zàochéng le hěndà sǔnshī] ▶ **a holiday will do you good** 休次假会对你有好处 II VI **1** (act, behave) 做 [zuò] ▶ **do as I do** 跟我做 ▶ **do as I tell you** 按我告诉你的做 **2** (get on) 进展 [jìnzhǎn] ▶ **he's doing well/badly at school** 他的学习成绩很好/很差 ▶ **the firm is doing well** 这个公司业绩良好 ▶ **"how do you do?" – "how do you do?"** "你好" "你好" **3** (suit) 行 [xíng] ▶ **will it do?** 行吗？ ▶ **it doesn't do to upset her** 不可以让她心烦意乱 **4** (be sufficient) 足够 [zúgòu] ▶ **will £15 do?** 15镑够吗？ ▶ **that'll do** 足够了 ▶ **that'll do!** (in annoyance) 够了！ III AUX VB **1** (in negative constructions) ▶ **I don't understand** 我不懂 [wǒ bùdǒng] ▶ **she doesn't want it** 她不想要这个 ▶ **he didn't seem to care** 他看起来并不在乎 ▶ **don't be silly!** 别傻了！ **2** (to form questions) ▶ **do you like jazz?** 你喜欢爵士乐吗？ [nǐ xǐhuān juéshìyè ma?] ▶ **what do you think?** 你怎么想？ ▶ **where does she live?** 她住在哪里？ ▶ **didn't you know?** 你难道不知道吗？ ▶ **why didn't you come?** 你为什么没来？

3 (*for emphasis, in polite expressions*) ▶ **people do make mistakes sometimes** 有时人们的确会犯一些错误 [yǒushí rénmen díquè fàn yīxiē cuòwù] ▶ **she does seem rather late** 看来她的确是晚了 ▶ **do sit down/help yourself** 赶快坐啊/千万别客气 ▶ **do take care!** 千万保重! ▶ **oh do shut up!** 噢，赶快闭嘴吧!

4 (*used to avoid repeating vb*) 用于避免动词的重复 ▶ **I make more money than he does** 我比他挣得钱多 ▶ **they say they don't care, but they do** 他们说不在乎，但实际是在乎的 ▶ **he asked me to help him and I did** 他让我帮一下忙，我照做了 ▶ **(and) so do I** 我也是 ▶ **and neither did we** 我们也不 ▶ **better than I do** 比我做得好 ▶ **"who made this mess?" – "I did"** 是谁弄得乱七八糟的?" "是我" ▶ **"do you have a metal detector?" – "no, I don't"** "你有金属探测器吗?" "不，我没有"

5 (*in question tags*) ▶ **I don't know him, do I?** 我不认识他，是吗? [wǒ bù rènshi tā, shì ma?] ▶ **you like him, don't you?** 你喜欢他，不是吗? ▶ **she lives in London, doesn't she?** 她住在伦敦，不是吗?

IV N (BRIT: *inf*)(*party etc*) 聚会 [jùhuì] ▶ **we're having a little do on Saturday** 我们星期六有个小型聚会 ▶ **it was quite a do** 那是个相当大型的聚会

▶ **do away with** VT FUS [不可拆分] (*get rid of*) 处理掉 [chǔlǐdiào]

▶ **do for** (*inf*) VT FUS [不可拆分] ▶ **to be done for** 完蛋 [wándàn] ▶ **if I can't finish this report, I'm done for** 如果完不成这份报告，我就完蛋了

▶ **do in** (*inf*) VT (*kill*) 干掉 [gàndiào]

▶ **do out of** (*inf*) VT (*deprive of*) 夺去 [duóqù] ▶ **he did me out of my share** 他把我那份儿夺去了

▶ **do up** VT FUS [不可拆分] **1** (*fasten*) [+ *laces*] 系紧 [jìjǐn]; [+ *dress, coat, buttons*] 扣上 [kòu shàng]

2 (ESP BRIT) (*renovate*) [+ *room, house*] 装修 [zhuāngxiū]

▶ **do with** VT FUS [不可拆分] **1** (*need*) ▶ **I could do with a drink/some help** 我想喝一杯/需要帮助 [wǒ xiǎng hē yībēi/xūyào bāngzhù]

2 (*be connected*) ▶ **to have to do with** 与…有关 [yǔ…yǒuguān] ▶ **what has it got to do with you?** 这跟你有什么关系? ▶ **I won't have anything to do with it** 我跟这事毫不相干 ▶ **it has to do with money** 这跟钱有关 ▶ **it was something to do with football** 这是与足球有关的

▶ **do without** VT FUS [不可拆分] 没有…也行 [méiyǒu…yě xíng]

II VI 不用也行 [bùyòng yě xíng]

d.o.b. ABBR (= *date of birth*) 出生日期 [chūshēng rìqí]

dock [dɔk] **I** N **1** [C] (NAUT) 船坞 [chuánwù] **2** ▶ **the dock** (*in law court*) 刑事法庭的被告席 [xíngshì fǎtíng de bèigàoxí] **3** [C/U] (BOT) 一种阔叶野草，名为酸模 **II** VI **1** [*ship* +] 入船坞 [rù chuánwù] **2** [*spacecraft* +] 对接 [duìjiē] **III** VT **1** [+ *salary, wages*] 扣减 [kòujiǎn] **2** [+ *ship*] 靠码头 [kào mǎtóu] **3** [+ *spacecraft*] 使对接 [shǐ duìjiē] **IV docks** NPL (NAUT) 港区 [gǎngqū]

dockyard [ˈdɔkjɑːd] N [C] 船舶修造厂 [chuánbó xiūzàochǎng]

doctor [ˈdɔktə(r)] **I** N [C] **1** (*medic*) 医生 [yīshēng] **2** ▶ **the doctor's** 诊所 [zhěnsuǒ] **3** (PhD etc) 博士 [bóshì] **II** VT [+ *food, drink*] 下药 [xià yào]; [+ *figures, photograph*] 窜改 [cuàngǎi] ▶ **doctor's office** (US) 诊所 [英= surgery]

document [n ˈdɔkjʊmənt, vb ˈdɔkjʊment] **I** N [C] **1** (*gen*) 文件 [wénjiàn] **2** (COMPUT) 文档 [wéndàng] **II** VT 记录…事实 [jìlù…shìshí]

documentary [dɔkjʊˈmentəri] **I** N [C] 纪录片 [jìlùpiàn] **II** ADJ [+ *evidence*] 书面的 [shūmiàn de]

documentation [dɔkjʊmənˈteɪʃən] N [U] 证件 [zhèngjiàn]

dodge [dɔdʒ] **I** VT **1** [+ *blow, ball, car*] 躲开 [duǒkāi] **2** [+ *tax, military service*] 逃避 [táobì] **3** [+ *question, issue etc*] 搪塞 [tángsè] **II** VI 躲闪 [duǒshǎn] **III** N (*trick*) 诡计 [guǐjì] ▶ **to dodge out of the way** 躲开

dodgy [ˈdɔdʒi] (*inf*) ADJ **1** (*suspect*) [+ *person, deal*] 狡猾的 [jiǎohuá de] **2** (*risky, unsafe*) 冒险的 [màoxiǎn de]

does [dʌz] VB *see do*

doesn't [ˈdʌznt] = **does not**

dog [dɔg] **I** N [C] **1** 狗 [gǒu] **2** (*male*) 雄兽 [xióngshòu] **II** VT [*problems, injuries* +] 缠住 [chánzhù] ▶ **to go to the dogs** 大不如前

do-it-yourself [ˈduːɪtjɔːˈself] **I** N [U] 自己动手的活计 [zìjǐ dòngshǒu de huójì] **II** ADJ [+ *store*] 出售供购买者自行装配物品的 [chūshòu gòng gòumǎizhě zìxíng zhuāngpèi wùpǐn de]

dole [dəʊl] (*inf*) N [U] (BRIT) ▶ **(the) dole** (*payment*) 失业救济金 [shīyè jiùjìjīn] [美= welfare] ▶ **(to be) on the dole** (BRIT) 靠失业救济金生活 [美= on welfare]

▶ **dole out** VT **1** [+ *food*] 发放 [fāfàng] **2** [+ *money*] 施舍 [shīshě]

doll [dɔl] N [C] (*toy*) 娃娃 [wáwa]

◇ **dollar** [ˈdɔlə(r)] N [C] 元 [yuán]

dolphin [ˈdɔlfɪn] N [C] 海豚 [hǎitún]

dome [dəʊm] N [C] 圆屋顶 [yuán wūdǐng]

domestic [dəˈmestɪk] ADJ **1** [+ *flight, politics, news*] 国内的 [guónèi de] **2** [+ *appliances*] 家用的 [jiāyòng de] **3** [+ *chores, violence*] 家庭的 [jiātíng de] **4** [+ *animal*] 驯养的 [xúnyǎng de]

domesticated [dəˈmɛstɪkeɪtɪd] ADJ
1 [+ *animal*] 驯化的 [xúnhuà de] **2** [+ *person*] 居家型的 [jūjiāxíng de]

dominant [ˈdɒmɪnənt] ADJ [+ *position, role, figure*] 占主导地位的 [zhàn zhǔdǎo dìwèi de]

dominate [ˈdɒmɪneɪt] VT **1** [+ *discussion, place*] 在⋯中占首要地位 [zài⋯zhōng zhàn shǒuyào dìwèi] **2** [+ *person*] 支配 [zhīpèi]

Dominican Republic [dəˈmɪnɪkən-] N
▶ **the Dominican Republic** 多米尼加共和国 [Duōmǐníjiā Gònghéguó]

domino [ˈdɒmɪnəu] (*pl* **dominoes**) N [C] 多米诺骨牌 [duōmǐnuò gǔpái] ▶ **domino effect** 多米诺效应

dominoes [ˈdɒmɪnəuz] N [U] 多米诺骨牌游戏 [duōmǐnuò gǔpái yóuxì]

donate [dəˈneɪt] VT **1** ▶ **to donate (to sb)** [+ *money, clothes*] 捐赠 (给某人) [juānzèng (gěi mǒurén)] **2** [+ *blood, organs*] 捐献 [juānxiàn]

donation [dəˈneɪʃən] N **1** [U] (*act of giving*) 捐赠 [juānzèng] **2** [C] (*contribution*) 捐赠物 [juānzèngwù] **3** [C/U] [*of blood, organs*] 捐献 [juānxiàn]

done [dʌn] PP *of* **do**

donkey [ˈdɒŋkɪ] N [C] 驴 [lú]

donor [ˈdəunə(r)] N [C] **1** [*of blood, heart, kidney etc*] 捐献者 [juānxiànzhě] **2** (*to charity*) 捐赠者 [juānzèngzhě]

donor card N [C] 器官捐献卡 [qìguān juānxiànkǎ]

don't [dəunt] = **do not**

donut [ˈdəunʌt] (US) N = **doughnut**

doodle [ˈduːdl] I N [C] 涂鸦 [túyā] II VI 涂鸦 [túyā]

doom [duːm] I N [U] **1** (*ruin*) 毁灭 [huǐmiè] **2** (*fate*) 厄运 [èyùn] **3** (*feeling of depression*) 悲观 [bēiguān] II VT ▶ **to be doomed to failure** 注定要失败 [zhùdìng yào shībài]

☉ **door** [dɔː(r)] N [C] **1** [*of house, room, railway carriage*] 门 [mén] **2** (*doorway*) 门口 [ménkǒu] ▶ **to answer the door** 应门 ▶ **out of doors** 在门外 ▶ **from door to door** 挨家挨户地

doorbell [ˈdɔːbɛl] N [C] 门铃 [ménlíng]

door handle N [C] 门把手 [mén bǎshǒu]

doorknob [ˈdɔːnɒb] N [C] 门上的球形把手 [mén shang de qiúxíng bǎshǒu]

doorstep [ˈdɔːstɛp] N [C] 门前台阶 [ménqián táijiē] ▶ **on one's doorstep** 很近

doorway [ˈdɔːweɪ] N [C] 门口 [ménkǒu] ▶ **in the doorway** 在门口

dope [dəup] I N **1** [U] (*cannabis*) 麻醉品 [mázuìpǐn] **2** [U] (*illegal drug*) 毒品 [dúpǐn] **3** [C] (*person*) 呆子 [dāizi] **4** [U] (*information*) 内部消息 [nèibù xiāoxi] II VT [+ *horse, person*] 给⋯服麻醉品 [gěi⋯fú mázuìpǐn]

dormitory [ˈdɔːmɪtrɪ] N [C] **1** (*room*) 宿舍 [sùshè] **2** (US) (*building*) 宿舍楼 [sùshèlóu]

[英= **hall of residence**]

dosage [ˈdəusɪdʒ] N [C] 用药计量 [yòngyào jìliàng]; (*on label*) 用量 [yòngliàng]

dose [dəus] N [C] **1** [*of medicine*] 一剂 [yījì] **2** (BRIT) (*bout*) [*of flu*] 一次 [yīcì] II VT ▶ **to dose sb/o.s. (up) with aspirin** *etc* 给某人/自己服阿斯匹灵 [等] [gěi mǒurén/zìjǐ fú āsīpīlíng {děng}]

dot [dɒt] N [C] **1** (*small round mark*) 圆点 [yuándiǎn] **2** (*speck, spot*) (*in the distance*) 小点 [xiǎodiǎn] II VT [+ *area, landscape*] 星罗棋布于 [xīng luó qí bù yú] ▶ **on the dot** (*punctually*) 准时地 ▶ **dotted with** 密布着

dot-com [dɒtˈkɒm] N [C] 网络公司 [wǎngluò gōngsī]

dotted line [ˈdɒtɪd-] N [C] 虚线 [xūxiàn] ▶ **to sign on the dotted line** 签字画押

double [ˈdʌbl] I ADJ **1** [+ *doors, tracks*] 双的 [shuāng de] **2** [+ *murder, wedding*] 成双的 [shuāng de] **3** [+ *helping, share, whisky, garage*] 双份的 [shuāngfèn de] **4** (*for two*) [+ *room, sheet*] 双人的 [shuāngrén de] II N **1** ▶ **to be sb's double** 酷似某人 [kùsì mǒurén] **2** [C] (*drink*) 双份 [shuāngfèn] III VT [+ *offer, size*] 使⋯增至两倍 [shǐ⋯zēng zhì liǎngbèi] IV VT [*population, size +*] 变成两倍 [biànchéng liǎngbèi] ▶ **double five two six** (BRIT) (5526) 五五二六 ▶ **it's spelt with a double "M"** 它的拼写中有两个"M" ▶ **double the size/number (of sth)** (是某物) 大小/数量的两倍 ▶ **double in size/weight** 两倍大/重 ▶ **to double as sth** 兼做某事 ▶ **at** or **on the double** (*inf*) (*immediately*) 迅速地
▶ **double back** VI [*person +*] 原路折回 [yuánlù zhé huí]
▶ **double up** I VI **1** (*bend over*) 直不起腰 [zhí bù qǐ yāo] **2** (*share room*) 共用 [gòngyòng] II VT 使⋯身体弯曲 [shǐ⋯shēntǐ wānqū] ▶ **to be doubled up with pain/laughter** 痛得/笑得弯下了身

double bass N [C/U] 低音提琴 [dīyīn tíqín]

double bed N [C] 双人床 [shuāngrénchuáng]

double-check [ˈdʌblˈtʃɛk] I VT 再检查 [zài jiǎnchá] II VI 复查 [fùchá]

double-click [ˈdʌblˈklɪk] VI 双击 [shuāngjī]

double-decker [ˈdʌblˈdɛkə(r)] (ESP BRIT) N [C] (*bus*) 双层公共汽车 [shuāngcéng gōnggòng qìchē]

double glazing [-ˈgleɪzɪŋ] (BRIT) N [U] 双层玻璃 [shuāngcéng bōlí]

double room N [C] 双人房 [shuāngrénfáng]

doubles [ˈdʌblz] (TENNIS) N [U] 双打 [shuāngdǎ]

doubly [ˈdʌblɪ] ADV 加倍地 [jiābèi de]

doubt [daut] I N [C/U] (*uncertainty*) 怀疑 [huáiyí] II VT **1** (*disbelieve*) [+ *person*] 怀疑 [huáiyí]; [+ *person's word*] 不信 [bùxìn] **2** (*mistrust, suspect*) 怀疑 [huáiyí] ▶ **without (a) doubt** 无疑地 ▶ **to be in doubt** 不确定 ▶ **beyond doubt** 毫

无疑问地 ► **no doubt** 无疑地 ► **to doubt if** or **whether...** 拿不准是否… ► **I doubt it (very much)** 我(很)怀疑 ► **I don't doubt that...** 我毫不怀疑

doubtful ['dautful] ADJ **1** (questionable) ► **it is doubtful that/whether...** 不能确定…/是否… [bùnéng quèdìng.../shìfǒu...] **2** (unconvinced) [+person] ► **to be doubtful that/whether...** 怀疑…/是否… [huáiyí.../shìfǒu...] ► **to be doubtful about sth** 对某事有怀疑 ► **I'm a bit doubtful** 我有点怀疑

doubtless ['dautlɪs] ADV 无疑地 [wúyí de]

dough [dəu] N [U] **1** 生面团 [shēngmiàntuán] **2** (inf) (money) 钱 [qián]

doughnut, (US) **donut** ['dəunʌt] N [C] 炸面饼圈 [zhà miànbǐngquān]

dove [dʌv] N [C] (bird) 鸽子 [gēzi]

○**down** [daun] I N [U] (soft feathers) 绒毛 [róngmáo] II ADV **1** (downwards) 向下 [xiàngxià] ▷ She looked down. 她向下看。**2** (in a lower place) 在下面 [zài xiàmian] ▷ They're down on the ground floor. 他们在下面底层。**3** (in or towards the south) 在南方 [zài nánfāng] ▷ They live down in London. 他们住在伦敦。▷ They've gone down south to London. 他们南下去伦敦。III PREP **1** (towards lower level) 沿着…往下 [yánzhe...wǎng xià] ▷ They walked down the steps. 他们沿着台阶往下走。**2** (at lower part of) 在下面 [zài xiàmian] ▷ She lives down the street. 她住在街那边。▷ a ledge 40ft down the rock face 在岩石表面以下40英尺处的岩石架 **3** (along) 沿着 [yánzhe] ▷ He walked down the road. 他沿街走去。IV VT (inf) [+drink] 喝下 [hēxià] ► **down there** 在那儿 ► **down here** 在这儿 ► **the price of meat is down** (lower) 肉的价格下降了 ► **I've got it down in my diary** 我已把它写进了日记里 ► **to pay 5 pounds down** (ESP US) 现付5英镑 ► **England are two goals down** (behind) 英格兰落后两球 ► **I'm down to my last five pounds** 我就剩最后5英镑了 ► **five down, two to go** 完成了5项，还剩两项 ► **to be down for sth** 被安排做某事 ► **down with X!** 打倒X！► **it's all down to hard work** 都是由于工作太辛苦的缘故 ► **to down tools** (BRIT) 停工

down-and-out ['daunəndaut] N [C] (tramp) 穷困潦倒的人 [qióngkùn liáodǎo de rén]

downfall ['daunfɔːl] N [C] **1** (failure) 垮台 [kuǎtái] **2** (cause of failure) ► **to be sb's downfall** 是某人垮台的原因 [shì mǒurén kuǎtái de yuányīn]

downhill ['daun'hɪl] I ADV **1** (go, drive, walk +) 向坡下 [xiàng pōxià] **2** (face, look +) 往山下 [wǎng shānxià] II N [C] (also: downhill race) (in skiing) 下坡滑雪比赛 [xiàpō huáxuě bǐsài] ► **to go downhill** (fig) [business, person +] 每况愈下

Downing Street ['daunɪŋ-] (BRIT) N ► **10 Downing Street** 唐宁街10号 [Tángníng jiē shí hào]

● **DOWNING STREET**

● Downing Street 在伦敦威斯敏斯特区，是英国首相和财政部大臣的官邸所在，分别为10号和11号。媒体常用唐宁街来指首相或政府。

download ['daunləud] VT 下载 [xiàzǎi]

downright ['daunraɪt] I ADJ (used for emphasis) 彻头彻尾的 [chètóu chèwěi de] II ADV (used for emphasis) 十分地 [shífēn de]

Down's syndrome [daunz-] N [U] 唐氏综合征 [Tángshì zōnghézhèng]

downstairs ['daun'stɛəz] I ADV **1** (on or to floor below) 楼下 [lóuxià] **2** (on or to ground level) 在一层 [zài yī céng] II ADJ 楼下的 [lóuxià de]

down-to-earth ['dauntu'əːθ] ADJ [+person, manner] 务实的 [wùshí de]

downtown ['daun'taun] (US) I ADV **1** (be, work +) 在市中心 [zài shì zhōngxīn] **2** (go +) 去市中心 [qù shì zhōngxīn] II ADJ ► **downtown Chicago** 芝加哥的市中心 [Zhījiāgē de shì zhōngxīn]

down under (BRIT: inf) ADV (in Australia or New Zealand) 澳大利亚和新西兰 [Àodàlìyà hé Xīnxīlán]

downward ['daunwəd] I ADJ 向下的 [xiàngxià de] II ADV = **downwards** ► **a downward trend** 没落的趋势

downwards ['daunwədz] ADV 向下 [xiàngxià]

doz. ABBR (= dozen) 一打 [yīdǎ]

doze [dəuz] I VI 打瞌睡 [dǎ kēshuì] II N [S] 瞌睡 [kēshuì] ► **to have a doze** 打个瞌睡 ► **doze off** VI 打盹 [dǎdǔn]

dozen ['dʌzn] N [C] 一打 [yīdǎ] ► **a dozen books** 一打书 ► **two dozen eggs** 两打鸡蛋 ► **dozens of** 许多

Dr, Dr. (ESP US) ABBR **1** (= doctor) 医生 [yīshēng] **2** (= Drive) 私家车道 [sījiā chēdào]

drab [dræb] ADJ [+building, clothes] 单调的 [dāndiào de]

draft [drɑːft] I N **1** [C] (first version) 草稿 [cǎogǎo] **2** [C] [of bill] 草案 [cǎo'àn] **3** [C] (bank draft) 汇票 [huìpiào] **4** ► **the draft** (US: MIL) 征兵 [zhēngbīng] [英=conscription] II VT **1** [+letter, book, speech] 起草 [qǐcǎo] **2** (MIL) ► **to be drafted** 应征入伍 [yìngzhēng rùwǔ] **3** ► **to draft sb in** (to do a job) 选派某人 [xuǎnpài mǒurén] see also **draught**

drag [dræg] I VT **1** (pull) [+large object, body] 拖 [tuō] **2** (force) ► **to drag sb out of a car/upstairs** 把某人从车里拖出来/拖到楼上 [bǎ mǒurén cóng chē lǐ tuō chū lái/tuō dào lóushàng] **3** (fig) ► **it's impossible to drag him out of bed/out of the house** 让他下床/离开房子是不可能的

[ràng tā xiàchuáng/líkāi fángzi shì bù kěnéng de] **4** (*search*) [+*river, lake*] 打捞 [dǎlāo] **II** VI [*time, film +*] 拖沓 [tuōtà] **III** N **1** (*inf*) ▸ **a drag** 累赘 [léizhuì] **2** (*women's clothing*) ▸ **in drag** 男人穿着女子服装 [nánrén chuānzhe nǚzi fúzhuāng] **3** [U] (NAUT, AVIAT) 阻力 [zǔlì] ▸ **to drag your feet** or **heels** 故意拖沓 ▸ **to drag sth out of sb** 逼某人交待某事

▸ **drag away** VT ▸ **to drag sb away (from sth)** 迫使某人离开(某物) [pòshǐ mǒurén líkāi (mǒuwù)] ▸ **to drag o.s. away (from sth)** 迫使自己离开(某物)

▸ **drag on** VI [*meeting, concert, war +*] 拖延 [tuōyán]

▸ **drag out** VT (*prolong*) 拖长 [tuōcháng]

dragon ['drægn] N [c] 龙 [lóng]

dragonfly ['drægənflaɪ] N [c] 蜻蜓 [qīngtíng]

drain [dreɪn] **I** N **1** [c] (*in street*) 排水沟 [páishuǐgōu] **2** ▸ **to be a drain on sth** [+*resources, funds*] 某物的大量消耗 [mǒuwù de dàliàng de xiāohào] **II** VT **1** [+*land, marsh, pond*] 排去…的水 [páiqù…de shuǐ] **2** [+*vegetables*] 使…流干 [shǐ…liúgān] **3** [+*liquid*] 排掉 [páidiào] **4** [+*glass, cup*] 喝干 [hē gān] **5** (*exhaust*) [+*person*] 使…精疲力竭 [shǐ…jīngpí lìjié] **III** VI [*liquid +*] 流入 [liúrù] ▸ **to feel drained (of energy** or **emotion)** 感到(精力(或)感情)耗尽 ▸ **(to go) down the drain** (*inf*) 白费

drainage ['dreɪnɪdʒ] **I** N [U] 排水 [páishuǐ] **II** CPD [复合词] [+*ditch, system*] 排水系统 [páishuǐ xìtǒng]

drainpipe ['dreɪnpaɪp] N [c] 排水管 [páishuǐguǎn]

drama ['drɑːmə] N **1** [U] (*theatre*) 戏剧 [xìjù] **2** [c] (*play*) 一出戏剧 [yīchū xìjù] **3** [c/U] (*excitement*) 戏剧性 [xìjùxìng]

dramatic [drə'mætɪk] **I** ADJ **1** (*marked, sudden*) 戏剧性的 [xìjùxìng de] **2** (*exciting, impressive*) 激动人心的 [jīdòng rénxīn de] **3** (*theatrical*) 戏剧的 [xìjù de] **II** CPD [复合词] [+*society, group*] 戏剧的 [xìjù de]

dramatics [drə'mætɪks] N [U] 业余的戏剧活动 [yèyú de xìjù huódòng]

drank [dræŋk] PT of **drink**

drape [dreɪp] VT [+*cloth, flag, clothing*] 披上 [pīshang]

drapes [dreɪps] (US) NPL 窗帘 [chuānglián] [英=**curtains**]

drastic ['dræstɪk] ADJ **1** [+*measure, step etc*] 严厉的 [yánlì de] **2** [+*change, reduction*] 剧烈的 [jùliè de]

draught, (US) **draft** [drɑːft] **I** N [c] [*of air*] 气流 [qìliú] **II** ADJ [+*beer, bitter etc*] 散装的 [sǎnzhuāng de] ▸ **on draught** [+*beer*] 散装的

draughts [drɑːfts] (BRIT) N [U] 西洋跳棋 [xīyáng tiàoqí] [美=**checkers**]

○ **draw** [drɔː] (*pt* **drew**, *pp* **drawn**) **I** VT **1** [+*picture, map*] 画 [huà] **2** (*pull*) [+*cart*] 拖 [tuō]

3 [+*curtains, blinds*] (*close*) 拉上 [lāshang]; (*open*) 拉开 [lākāi] **4** ▸ **to draw sth/sb somewhere** (*move*) 把某人/某物拉到某地 [bǎ mǒurén/mǒuwù lā dào mǒudì] ▷ *He drew his chair nearer the fire.* 他把椅子拉到炉火旁。**5** (*takeout*) [+*gun, knife, sword*] 拔出 [báchū] **6** (*attract*) [+*response*] 引起 [yǐnqǐ] **7** [+*breath*] 吸 [xī] **8** ▸ **to draw (out) money from a bank/an account** 从银行/帐户上取钱 [cóng yínháng/zhànghù shang qǔ qián] ▷ *He drew fifty pounds from his savings account.* 他从活期帐户上取走了50英镑。**9** [+*wages, salary*] 领取 [lǐngqǔ] **10** [+*water*] 汲取 [jíqǔ] **11** ▸ **to draw a conclusion (from sth)** (从某事中)得出结论 [(cóng mǒushì zhōng) déchū jiélùn] **12** ▸ **to draw a comparison/distinction (between two things)** (在两事物之间)作比较 [(zài liǎng shìwù zhī jiān) zuò bǐjiào] **II** VI **1** (*with pen, pencil etc*) 画画 [huàhuà] **2** ▸ **to draw near/close/away** (*move*) 走近/开 [zǒujìn/kāi] **3** ▸ **to draw (with/against sb)** (ESP BRIT: SPORT) (与某人)打成平局 [(yǔ mǒurén) dǎ chéng píngjú] ▷ *Brazil drew against Spain.* 巴西队与西班牙队战平。[美=**tie**] **III** N [c] **1** (ESP BRIT: SPORT) 平局 [píngjú] ▷ *The match ended in a draw.* 比赛以平局告终。[美=**tie**] **2** (*lottery*) 抽奖 [chōujiǎng] ▷ *She won 200 pounds in a prize draw.* 她在一次抽奖中赢了200英镑。▸ **to draw (sb's) attention (to sth)** 吸引(某人)的注意力(到某物) ▸ **to draw near** or **close** (*approach*) [*person, event +*] 临近 ▸ **to draw level/alongside** 慢慢接近 ▸ **to draw to a close** 结束

▸ **draw in I** VI (BRIT) [*nights +*] 变长 [biàncháng] ▷ *The nights draw in and the mornings get darker.* 黑夜变长，早晨天色变得昏暗。**II** VT (*also:* **draw into**) (*involve*) 使参与 [shǐ cānyù] ▷ *She's the perfect hostess, drawing everyone into the conversation.* 她是位完美的女主人，能使每个人都参与到谈话中来。

▸ **draw on I** VT FUS [不可拆分] (*also:* **draw upon**) [+*resources*] 凭借 [píngjiè] ▷ *The company drew on its vast resources to fund the project.* 公司凭借其大量的资源为这个项目提供资金。; [+*imagination, knowledge*] 靠 [kào] ▷ *He drew on his imagination to write about Moscow.* 他靠想像力描写莫斯科。**II** VI (*pass*) 临近 [línjìn] ▷ *As the afternoon drew on, we got impatient.* 随着下午的临近，我们变得不耐烦起来。

▸ **draw out** VI ▸ **draw out (of)** [*train, bus +*] (*leave*) 离开 [líkāi] ▷ *The train drew out of the station.* 火车驶离车站。

▸ **draw up I** VI (*stop*) [*car, bus etc +*] 停下来 [tíngxiàlái] ▷ *Just before eleven a bus drew up.* 就在11点前，一辆公共汽车停了下来。**II** VT **1** [+*document, plan*] 草拟 [cǎonǐ] ▷ *I drew up plans for the new course.* 我为新课程草拟了计划。**2** [+*chair etc*] 拉近 [lājìn] ▷ *He drew up a chair and sat down.* 他把椅子拉近坐了下来。

drawback ['drɔːbæk] N [c] 欠缺 [qiànquē]

drawer [drɔː(r)] I N [c] [of desk etc] 抽屉
[chōuti] II **drawers** NPL (o.f.) (knickers) 内裤
[nèikù]

drawing ['drɔːɪŋ] N 1 [c] (picture) 素描
[sùmiáo] 2 [U] (skill, discipline) 绘画 [huìhuà]

drawing pin (BRIT) N [c] 图钉 [túdīng]
[美=**thumbtack**]

drawing room (o.f.) N [c] 客厅 [kètīng]

drawn [drɔːn] I PP of **draw** II ADJ (haggard) 憔
悴的 [qiáocuì de]

dread [drɛd] I N [U] ▸ dread (of) (对…的)畏
惧 [(duì…de) wèijù] II VT (fear) 惧怕 [jùpà]

dreadful ['drɛdful] ADJ [+ weather, day, person etc]
糟透的 [zāotòu de] ▸ I feel dreadful! (ill) 我觉
得很不舒服! ; (ashamed) 我感到心里不好受!

dream [driːm] (pt, pp **dreamed** or **dreamt**)
I N [c] 1 (when asleep) 梦 [mèng] 2 (ambition) 梦
想 [mèngxiǎng] II VI ▸ to dream about (when
asleep) 梦到 [mèngdào] ▸ to have a dream
about sb/sth (when asleep) 梦到某人/某事
▸ sweet dreams! (sleep well!) 睡个好觉!
▸ to dream that... (when asleep) 梦见…; (when
wishing for sth) 渴望… ▸ to dream of doing sth
(fantasize) 梦想着做某事 ▸ I wouldn't dream
of... 我永远不…
▸ dream up VT [+ plan, idea etc] 凭空想出
[píngkōng xiǎngchū]

dreamer ['driːmə(r)] N [c] 空想家
[kōngxiǎngjiā]

dreamt [drɛmt] PT, PP of **dream**

dreamy ['driːmɪ] ADJ 1 (faraway) [+ expression]
心不在焉的 [xīn bù zài yān de] 2 (gorgeous)
[+ music, picture] 梦幻般的 [mènghuàn bān de]

dreary ['drɪərɪ] ADJ [+ place, time etc] 沉闷的
[chénmèn de]

drench [drɛntʃ] VT (soak) 使湿透 [shǐ shītòu]
▸ drenched to the skin (used for emphasis) 浑
身湿透

dress [drɛs] I N 1 [c] (frock) 连衣裙 [liányīqún]
2 [U] (clothing) 服装 [fúzhuāng] II VT 1 (child)
给…穿衣 [gěi…chuān yī] 2 [+ wound] 敷裹
[fūguǒ] 3 [+ salad] 拌 [bàn] III VI 穿衣 [chuān
yī] ▸ to dress o.s., get dressed 穿好衣服
▸ she dresses in jeans 她身穿牛仔服
▸ dress down VI 穿上便装 [chuānshang
biànzhuāng]
▸ dress up VI 1 (wear best clothes) 穿上盛装
[chuānshang shèngzhuāng] 2 ▸ to dress up as
(in fancy dress) 化装成 [huàzhuāng chéng]

dress circle (BRIT) N [c] (in theatre) 二楼正座
[èr lóu zhèngzuò]

dresser ['drɛsə(r)] N [c] 1 (BRIT) (cupboard) 碗
橱 [wǎnchú] 2 (US) (chest of drawers) 梳妆台
[shūzhuāngtái] 3 ▸ a smart dresser 穿着利索
的人 [chuānzhuó lìsuo de rén]

dressing ['drɛsɪŋ] N 1 [c] (on a wound) 敷料
[fūliào] 2 [c/U] ▸ (salad) dressing 调料
[tiáoliào]

dressing gown N [c] 晨衣 [chényī]

dressing room N [c] 1 (in a theatre) 化装室
[huàzhuāngshì] 2 (in a sports stadium) 更衣室
[gēngyīshì]

dressing table N [c] 梳妆台 [shūzhuāngtái]

dressmaker ['drɛsmeɪkə(r)] N [c] 做女服童装
的裁缝 [zuò nǚfú tóngzhuāng de cáiféng]

drew [druː] PT of **draw**

dribble ['drɪbl] I VI 1 (trickle) [liquid +] 一滴滴
地流 [yīdīdī de liú] 2 [baby, person +] 流口水 [liú
kǒushuǐ] 3 (in football, basketball) 运球 [yùnqiú]
II VT 1 (in football, basketball) [+ ball] 运 [yùn]
2 [+ liquid] 使一滴滴地流 [shǐ yīdīdī de liú]

dried [draɪd] ADJ [+ fruit, herbs] 干的 [gān de];
[+ eggs, milk] 粉状的 [fěnzhuàng de]

drier ['draɪə(r)] N = **dryer**

drift [drɪft] I VI 1 [boat +] 漂流 [piāoliú] 2 [sand,
snow, mist +] 飘散 [piāosàn] II N 1 [c] [snow] 吹
积物 [chuījīwù] 2 [S/U] (movement) [of people] 迁
移 [qiānyí] 3 [S] (meaning) 大意 [dàyì] ▸ to drift
away [crowd, people +] 散去 ▸ to drift apart
[friends, couple +] 疏远 ▸ to drift into [+ crime,
prostitution] 不知不觉地陷入 ▸ to get or follow
sb's drift 明白某人的大意 ▸ to get or follow
the drift of sth 明白某事的大意
▸ drift off VI ▸ to drift off (to sleep) 慢慢睡着
[mànmàn shuìzháo]

drill [drɪl] I N 1 [c] (tool, machine) (for DIY etc) 钻
[zuàn]; [of dentist] 钻头 [zuàntóu]; (for mining
etc) 钻孔器 [zuànkǒngqì] 2 [U] (fabric) 斜纹
布 [xiéwénbù] 3 [c] [(for fire, air raid)] 演习
[yǎnxí] II VT 1 [+ hole] 在…上钻孔 [zài…shang
zuàn kǒng] 2 (train) [+ troops] 训练 [xùnliàn]
3 [+ pupils] (in grammar, maths, singing etc) 训练
[xùnliàn] III VI 1 ▸ to drill (into) [wall, floor etc +]
(在…)钻孔 [(zài…)zuàn kǒng] 2 ▸ to drill
(for) [oil, water, gas +] 钻(探某物) [zuàn (tàn
mǒuwù)]

drink [drɪŋk] (pt **drank**, pp **drunk**) I N 1 [c] (tea,
water etc) 饮料 [yǐnliào] 2 [c] (alcoholic) 酒 [jiǔ]
3 [U] (alcohol) 饮酒 [yǐnjiǔ] II VT [+ tea, water etc]
喝 [hē] III VI (drink alcohol) 喝酒 [hējiǔ] ▸ to
have a drink 喝一杯; (alcoholic) 喝酒 ▸ to take
or have a drink of... 喝… ▸ a drink of water 一
杯水 ▸ would you like something to drink? 你
想喝点什么吗?
▸ drink in VT [+ sight] 陶醉于 [táozuì yú];
[+ words] 听…听得出神 [tīng…tīng de
chūshén]
▸ drink to VT FUS [不可拆分] 为…干杯
[wèi…gānbēi]
▸ drink up VT, VI 喝光 [hē guāng]

drink-driving ['drɪŋk'draɪvɪŋ] (BRIT) N [U] 酒
后驾车 [jiǔhòu jiàchē] [美=**drunk driving**]

drinker ['drɪŋkə(r)] N [c] 1 ▸ tea/coffee/beer
drinker 喝茶/咖啡/啤酒的人 [hē chá/kāfēi/
píjiǔ de rén] 2 (of alcohol) 酗酒者 [xùjiǔzhě] ▸ a
heavy/moderate/habitual drinker (of alcohol)

过度/适度/习惯性饮酒者

drinking water ['drɪŋkɪŋ-] N [U] 饮用水 [yǐnyòngshuǐ]

drip [drɪp] I N [c] **1** (drop) 一滴 [yīdī] **2** (sound) 水滴声 [shuǐdīshēng] **3** (MED) 滴液 [dīyè] **4** (inf) (person) 讨厌鬼 [tǎoyànguǐ] II VI **1** [water, rain +] 滴下 [dīxià] **2** [tap +] 漏水 [lòushuǐ] **3** [washing, clothes etc +] 滴水 [dīshuǐ] III VT (spill, trail) 使滴下 [shǐ dīxià]

○ drive [draɪv] (pt **drove**, pp **driven**) I N **1** [c] (journey) 车程 [chēchéng] ▷ It's a thirty mile drive. 有30英里的车程。 **2** [c] (also: **driveway**) 私家车道 [sījiā chēdào] ▷ A private drive leads up to the palace. 一条私家车道通往宫殿。 **3** (in road names) ▷ **15 Alexander Drive** 亚历山大大道15号 [Yàlìshāndà dàdào shíwǔ hào] **4** [U] (energy) 干劲 [gànjìng] **5** [c] (campaign) 运动 [yùndòng] ▷ a drive to recruit more staff 征召更多成员的运动 **6** [c] (in golf) 猛击 [měngjī] **7** [c] (also: **CD ROM/disk drive**) 驱动器 [qūdòngqì] II VT [+ vehicle] 驾驶 [jiàshǐ] ▷ It's her turn to drive the car. 该她驾驶了。 **2** ▶ **to drive sb to the station/airport** 驱车送某人去车站/飞机场 [qūchē sòng mǒurén qù chēzhàn/fēijīchǎng] **3** (run) [+ machine, motor, wheel] 推动 [tuīdòng] **4** [+ nail, stake etc] ▶ **to drive sth into sth** 把某物钉入某物 [bǎ mǒuwù dìng rù mǒuwù] **5** [+ animal] 驱赶 [qūgǎn] **6** [+ people] 迫使 [pòshǐ] ▷ The war drove thousands of people into Thailand. 战争迫使成千上万的人进入泰国。 **7** [+ ball] 猛击 [měngjī] ▷ Tom drove the ball into the net. 汤姆将球击入网内。 **8** (incite, encourage) 驱使 [qūshǐ] ▷ a man driven by greed and envy 受到贪欲和嫉妒驱使的男人 III VI **1** (at controls of vehicle) 开车 [kāichē] ▷ They have never learned to drive. 他们从未学过开车。 **2** (travel) 开车 [kāichē] ▶ **to go for a drive** 开车兜风 ▶ **it's a 3-hour drive from London** 到伦敦要3个小时的车程 ▶ **left-/right-hand drive** 左/右手座驾驶 ▶ **front-/rear-wheel drive** 前/后轮驱动 ▶ **he drives a taxi/lorry** 他开出租车/卡车 ▶ **to drive sb mad/to desperation** 逼得某人发疯/绝望 ▶ **to drive sb to (do) sth** 迫使某人做某事 ▶ **to drive at 50 km an hour** 以每小时50公里的速度驾车 ▶ **what are you driving at?** 你是什么意思？

▶ **drive away** VT 赶走 [gǎnzǒu] ▷ Increased crime is driving away customers. 不断增长的犯罪赶走了顾客。

▶ **drive off** I VT (repel) 击退 [jītuì] ▷ The government drove the guerrillas off using infantry. 政府出动步兵围击退了游击队员。 II VI [car, driver +] 驱车离开 [qūchē líkāi] ▷ He drove off without saying goodbye. 他没道别就驱车离开了。

▶ **drive on** VI 一直不停地开 [yīzhí bùtíng de kāi] ▷ We drove on for a few miles. 我们一直不停地开了几英里。

▶ **drive out** VT (force to leave) 逐出 [zhúchū] ▷ He cut his prices to drive out rivals. 为了逐出竞争对手，他降低了价格。

drive-in ['draɪvɪn] (US) I N [c] (restaurant) 免下车餐馆 [miǎn xiàchē cānguǎn]; (movie theater) 免下车电影院 [miǎn xiàchē diànyǐngyuàn] II ADJ [+ restaurant, movie theater] 免下车的 [miǎn xiàchē de]

driven ['drɪvn] PP of drive

driver ['draɪvə(r)] N [c] **1** [of own car] 驾驶员 [jiàshǐyuán] **2** [of taxi, bus, lorry, train] 司机 [sījī] **3** (chauffeur) 司机 [sījī]

driver's license ['draɪvəz-] (US) N [c] 驾驶执照 [jiàshǐ zhízhào] [英= **driving licence**]

driveway ['draɪvweɪ] N [c] 车道 [chēdào]

driving ['draɪvɪŋ] I N [U] (motoring) 驾驶 [jiàshǐ] II ADJ ▶ **driving rain/snow/wind** 瓢泼大雨/暴雪/暴风 [piáopō dàyǔ/bàoxuě/bàofēng]

driving instructor N [c] 驾驶教练 [jiàshǐ jiàoliàn]

driving lesson N [c] 驾驶课 [jiàshǐ kè]

driving licence (BRIT) N [c] 驾驶执照 [jiàshǐ zhízhào] [美= **driver's license**]

driving test N [c] 驾驶执照考试 [jiàshǐ zhízhào kǎoshì]

drizzle ['drɪzl] I N [S/U] 蒙蒙细雨 [méngméng xìyǔ] II VI ▶ **it is drizzling** 下着毛毛雨 [xiàzhe máomáoyǔ]

droop [druːp] VI **1** [flower +] 发蔫 [fā'niān] **2** [shoulders, head +] 垂下 [chuíxià]

drop [drɒp] I N **1** [c] [of liquid] 滴 [dī] **2** (reduction) ▶ **a drop in sth** 某物的下降 [mǒuwù de xiàjiàng] **3** (vertical distance) ▶ **a 300m drop/a drop of 300m** 300米的落差 [sānbǎi mǐ de luòchā] **4** [c] (also: **air drop**) (delivery) (by parachute etc) 空投 [kōngtóu] II VT **1** (accidentally) 失手落下 [shīshǒu luòxià]; (deliberately) 放 [fàng] **2** (lower) [+ arm, leg, hand etc] 垂下 [chuíxià] **3** [+ voice] 降低 [jiàngdī] **4** (reduce) [+ price] 降低 [jiàngdī] **5** (drop off) (set down from car) 车…送到 [jiāng…sòng dào] **6** (abandon) [+ idea, case etc] 丢弃 [diūqì] **7** (from team) 解雇 [jiěgù] III VI **1** (fall) [amount, level +] 下降 [xiàjiàng]; [object +] 落下 [luòxià] **2** (flop) 倒下 [dǎoxià] **3** (die down) [wind +] 减弱 [jiǎnruò] **4** (fall) [voice +] 压低 [yādī] IV drops N PL (medicine) 滴剂 [dījì] ▶ **a drop of 10%** 10%的下降 ▶ **chocolate/fruit drops** 巧克力/水果球形糖 ▶ **to drop sb a line** 给某人留言 ▶ **to drop a hint** 随便暗示一下

▶ **drop by** VI 顺便拜访 [shùnbiàn bàifǎng]

▶ **drop in** (inf) VI (visit) ▶ **to drop in (on sb)** 顺便拜访(某人) [shùnbiàn bàifǎng (mǒurén)]

▶ **drop off** I VI (fall asleep) 睡着 [shuìzháo] II VT [+ passenger] 将…送到 [jiāng…sòng dào]

▶ **drop out** VI **1** (withdraw) 退出 [tuìchū] **2** (of college, university etc) 辍学 [chuòxué]

drought [draʊt] N [C/U] 旱灾 [hànzāi]

drove [drəʊv] I PT of **drive** II ▶ **droves of people** 一群群的人 [yī qún qún de rén] ▶ **they came in (their) droves** 他们成群结队地进来

drown [draʊn] I VT 1 (deliberately) [+ person, animal] 使淹死 [shǐ yānsǐ] 2 ▶ **to be drowned** 被淹死 [bèi yānsǐ] 3 (also: **drown out**) [+ sound, voice] 淹没 [yānmò] II VI [person, animal +] 溺死 [nìsǐ]

drowsy ['draʊzɪ] ADJ 昏昏欲睡的 [hūn hūn yù shuì de]

○ **drug** [drʌg] I N [C] 1 (prescribed) 药 [yào] ▷ This drug is prescribed to treat hay fever. 开的这种药是用来治疗花粉热的。 2 (recreational) 毒品 [dúpǐn] ▷ Cocaine is a highly addictive drug. 可卡因是一种极为容易上瘾的毒品。 II VT (sedate) [+ person, animal] 使麻醉 [shǐ mázuì] ▶ **to be on drugs** 吸毒 ▶ **to take drugs** 吸毒 ▶ **hard/soft drugs** 硬/软毒品

drug addict N [C] 吸毒成瘾者 [xīdú chéngyǐnzhě]

drug dealer N [C] 毒品贩子 [dúpǐn fànzi]

druggist ['drʌgɪst] (US) N [C] 1 (pharmacist) (person) 药剂师 [yàojìshī] [英= **chemist**] 2 ▶ **druggist('s)** (shop) 药店 [yàodiàn] ▆▆用法参见 **chemist**

drugstore ['drʌgstɔː(r)] (US) N [C] 杂货店 [záhuòdiàn] [英= **chemist**] ▆▆用法参见 **chemist**

drum [drʌm] I N [C] 1 (instrument) 鼓 [gǔ] 2 (container) 圆桶 [yuántǒng] II VI 1 [rain +] 发出敲击声 [fāchū qiāojīshēng] 2 (with fingers) 敲击 [qiāojī] III VT [+ fingers] 敲打 [qiāodǎ] IV **drums** NPL (kit) 鼓 [gǔ] ▶ **drum into** VT 反复灌输 [fǎnfù guànshū] ▶ **drum up** VT [+ enthusiasm, support] 竭力争取 [jiélì zhēngqǔ]

drummer ['drʌmə(r)] N [C] 鼓手 [gǔshǒu]

drunk [drʌŋk] I PP of **drink** II ADJ 醉的 [zuì de] III N [C] (drunkard) 醉汉 [zuìhàn] ▶ **to get drunk** 喝醉了

drunk driving ['drʌŋk'draɪvɪŋ] (US) N [U] 酒后驾车 [jiǔhòu jiàchē] [英= **drink-driving**]

drunken ['drʌŋkən] ADJ [+ laughter, party, sleep] 酒醉引起的 [jiǔzuì yǐnqǐ de]; [+ person] 醉的 [zuì de]

dry [draɪ] I ADJ 1 [+ ground, clothes, paint] 干的 [gān de] 2 [+ climate, weather, day] 干燥的 [gānzào de] 3 [+ skin, hair] 干枯的 [gānkū de] 4 (empty) [+ lake, riverbed, well] 干涸的 [gānhé de] 5 [+ wine, sherry] 不甜的 [bù tián de] 6 [+ humour, account] 装成正经的 [zhuāngchéng zhèngjīng de] 7 (uninteresting) [+ lecture, subject, style] 枯燥无味的 [kūzào wúwèi de] II VT [+ clothes, hair] 把…弄干 [bǎ…nòng gān] III VI [paint, washing +] 变干 [biàn gān] ▶ **on dry land** 在陆地上 ▶ **to dry (up) the dishes** 擦干碗碟 ▶ **to dry one's hands/hair** 擦干手/头发 ▶ **to**

▶ **dry one's eyes** 擦干眼泪

▶ **dry off** I VI 变干 [biàn gān] II VT 把…弄干 [bǎ…nòng gān]

▶ **dry out** VI 干透 [gān tòu]

▶ **dry up** VI 1 [river, well +] 干涸 [gānhé] 2 (stop) [supply, flow etc +] 停滞 [tíngzhì] 3 (during speech) 忘词 [wàng cí]

dry-clean ['draɪ'kliːn] VT 干洗 [gānxǐ]

dry-cleaner ['draɪ'kliːnə(r)] N [C] 1 (also: **dry cleaner's**) 干洗店 [gānxǐdiàn] 2 (person) 干洗商 [gānxǐshāng]

dryer ['draɪə(r)] N [C] 1 (= tumble dryer, spin-dryer) 干衣机 [gānyījī] 2 (hair dryer) 吹风机 [chuīfēngjī]

dryness ['draɪnɪs] N [U] 1 [of ground] 干涸 [gānhé] 2 [of climate, weather] 干燥 [gānzào] 3 [of skin] 干枯 [gānkū]

DST (US) N ABBR (= Daylight Saving Time) 夏令时 [Xiàlìngshí]

DTP N ABBR (= desktop publishing) 桌面出版系统 [zhuōmiàn chūbǎn xìtǒng]

dual ['djuəl] ADJ 双的 [shuāng de]

dual carriageway (BRIT) N [C] 双行道 [shuāngxíngdào] [美= **divided highway**]

dub [dʌb] VT 1 [+ film, TV programme] 为…配音 [wèi…pèiyīn] 2 (nickname) ▶ **a man dubbed "the terminator"** 被冠以"终结者"绰号的人 [bèi guàn yǐ "zhōngjiézhě" chuòhào de rén] ▶ **dubbed into Spanish/French** 用西班牙语/法语译配

dubious ['djuːbɪəs] ADJ [+ claim, reputation, company] 可疑的 [kěyí de] ▶ **to have the dubious honour/pleasure/distinction of...** 令人怀疑的…的荣誉/愉快/区别 ▶ **to be dubious about sth** 对某事半信半疑

duck [dʌk] I N [C] (bird) 鸭 [yā] 2 [U] (as food) 鸭肉 [yāròu] II VI (also: **duck down**) 急忙弯下身子 [jímáng wānxià shēnzi] III VT 1 [+ blow] 急忙避开 [jímáng bìkāi] 2 [+ duty, responsibility] 逃避 [táobì]

due [djuː] I ADJ 1 ▶ **to be due** [person, train, bus +] 应到 [yīng dào]; [baby +] 预期 [yùqī]; [rent, payment +] 应支付 [yīng zhīfù] 2 ▶ **to be due (to sb)** (owed) [+ money, holidays] 应给 (某人) [yīng gěi (mǒurén)] 3 (proper) [+ consideration] 适当的 [shìdàng de] II N ▶ **to give sb his** (or **her) due** 公平对待他/她 [gōngpíng de duìdài tā/tā] III ADV ▶ **due north/south** 正北方/南方 [zhèng běifāng/nánfāng] IV **dues** NPL (for club, union) 应付款 [yīngfùkuǎn] ▶ **due to...** (because of) 由于… [yóuyú] ▶ **to be due to sth/sb** 由于某事/某人 ▶ 由于某物 ▶ **I am due 6 days' leave** 我应有6天的休假 ▶ **I am due 5 pounds** 我应得5英镑 ▶ **she's due next week** (inf) (to give birth) 她下星期临产 ▶ **in due course** (eventually) 在适当的时候

duel ['djuəl] N [C] 1 (formal fight) 决斗 [juédòu] 2 (ongoing dispute) 争辩 [zhēngbiàn]

duet [dju:'ɛt] N [C] 二重唱曲/奏曲 [èr chóng chàng qǔ/zòu qǔ]

dug [dʌg] PT, PP of dig

duke [dju:k] N [C] 公爵 [gōngjué] ▸ **the Duke of Edinburgh** 爱丁堡公爵

dull [dʌl] I ADJ **1** (not bright) [+ weather, day] 阴沉的 [yīnchén de]; [+ light, colour] 暗淡的 [àndàn de] **2** (boring) [+ event, place, person, book] 单调乏味的 [dāndiào fáwèi de] **3** (sluggish) 迟钝的 [chídùn de] **4** [+ sound, pain] 隐约的 [yǐnyuē de] II VT **1** [+ pain, grief] 减轻 [jiǎnqīng] **2** [+ mind, senses] 使迟钝 [shǐ chídùn] III VI [eyes, expression etc +] 变得呆滞 [biàn de dāizhì]

duly ['dju:lɪ] ADV **1** (as expected) 如期地 [rúqī de] **2** (correctly) 适当地 [shìdàng de]

dumb [dʌm] ADJ **1** (mute, silent) 哑的 [yǎ de] **2** (pej) (stupid, foolish) 愚蠢的 [yúchǔn de] **3** (US: inf) (silly, annoying) [+ idea] 傻的 [shǎ de] ▸ **to be struck dumb** 哑口无言

dummy ['dʌmɪ] I N [C] **1** (BRIT) (for baby) 橡皮奶头 [xiàngpí nǎitóu] [美= **pacifier**] **2** (mannekin) 人体模型 [réntǐ móxíng] **3** (inf) (idiot) 笨蛋 [bèndàn] **4** (in cards) (also: **dummy hand**) 明手牌 [míngshǒupái] II ADJ (false) 假的 [jiǎ de] ▸ **a dummy run** (BRIT) (test run) 试演

dump [dʌmp] I N [C] **1** (tip) (for rubbish) 垃圾场 [lājīchǎng] **2** (inf) (pigsty, tip) 脏乱的地方 [zāngluàn de dìfang] **3** (store) (for ammunition, arms) 临时存放处 [língshí cúnfàngchù] II VT **1** (put down) 扔下 [diūxià] **2** (get rid of) 倾倒 [qīngdào] **3** [+ computer data] 转储 [zhuǎn chǔ] ▸ **to be down in the dumps** (inf) 神情沮丧 ▸ **"no dumping"** "严禁乱倒垃圾"

dumpling ['dʌmplɪŋ] N [C] 饺子 [jiǎozi]

Dumpster® ['dʌmpstə(r)] (US) N [C] (用以装运工地废料的无盖) 废料筒 [(yòngyǐ zhuāngyùn gōngdì fèiliào de wú gài) fèiliàotǒng] [英= **skip**]

dune [dju:n] N [C] (also: **sand dune**) 沙丘 [shāqiū]

dung [dʌŋ] N [U] 粪 [fèn]

dungarees [dʌŋɡə'ri:z] NPL (for work) 工装裤 [gōngzhuāngkù]; (for child, woman) 背带裤 [bèidàikù]

dungeon ['dʌndʒən] N [C] 地牢 [dìláo]

dunk [dʌŋk] VT 把…浸一浸 [bǎ…jìn yī jìn]

duplex ['dju:plɛks] (US) N [C] **1** (house) 供两家居住的房屋 **2** (apartment) 跨两层楼的公寓套房

duplicate [n, adj 'dju:plɪkət, vb 'dju:plɪkeɪt] I N [C] [of document, key] 复制品 [pùzhǐpǐn] II ADJ [+ key, copy] 复制的 [fùzhì de] III VT **1** (repeat) [+ success, result] 重复 [chóngfù] **2** (copy) [+ document, tape] 复制 [fùzhì] **3** (reuse, rehash) 重做 [chóngzuò]

durable ['djuərəbl] ADJ [+ goods, materials] 耐用的 [nàiyòng de]

duration [djuə'reɪʃən] N [U] [of process, course, film] 持续时间 [chíxù shíjiān] ▸ **for the duration of the holiday/his stay** 假期/他停留期间 ▸ **for the duration** 在接下去的时期内 ▸ **of 8 months' duration** 长达8个月

○ **during** ['djuərɪŋ] PREP **1** (throughout) 在…期间 [zài…qījiān] ▷ Snowstorms are common during winter. 暴风雪在冬天是常见的。▷ Many soldiers died during the war. 在战争期间许多战士阵亡了。**2** (at some point in) 在…时候 [zài…shíhou] ▷ During the night the fence blew down. 在夜里的时候篱笆给吹倒了。

dusk [dʌsk] N [U] 黄昏 [huánghūn] ▸ **at dusk** 黄昏时刻

dust [dʌst] I N [U] (dirt) (outdoors) 尘土 [chéntǔ]; (indoors) 灰尘 [huīchén] II VT **1** [+ furniture] 拭去…上的灰尘 [shìqù…shang de huīchén] **2** ▸ **to dust sth with sth** [+ cake] (with flour, sugar) 把某物撒在某物上 [bǎ mǒuwù sǎ zài mǒuwù shang] ▸ **dust off, dust down** VT **1** ▸ **to dust o.s. off** 重新振作起来 [chóngxīn zhènzuò qǐlái] **2** (reuse) 重新使用 [chóngxīn shǐyòng]

dustbin ['dʌstbɪn] (BRIT) N [C] 垃圾箱 [lājīxiāng] [美= **garbage can**]

duster ['dʌstə(r)] N [C] (cloth) 抹布 [mābù]

dustman ['dʌstmən] (BRIT) (pl **dustmen**) N [C] 清洁工 [qīngjiégōng] [美= **garbage man**]

dusty ['dʌstɪ] ADJ 满是尘土的 [mǎn shì chéntǔ de]

Dutch [dʌtʃ] I ADJ 荷兰的 [Hélán de] II N [U] (language) 荷兰语 [Hélányǔ] III ADV ▸ **to go Dutch (on sth)** (inf) 各人自己付 (某物的) 钱 [gèrén zìjǐ fù (mǒuwù de) qián] IV **the Dutch** NPL (people) 荷兰人 [Hélánrén]

Dutchman ['dʌtʃmən] (pl **Dutchmen**) N [C] 荷兰人 [Hélánrén]

Dutchwoman ['dʌtʃwumən] (pl **Dutchwomen**) N [C] 荷兰妇女 [Hélán fùnǔ]

duty ['dju:tɪ] I N [C/U] **1** (responsibility) 责任 [zérèn] **2** (tax) 税 [shuì] II **duties** NPL (tasks) 任务 [rènwù] ▸ **it is my duty to…** …是我的职责 ▸ **to pay duty on sth** 支付某物的税 ▸ **to report for duty** 求职 ▸ **to be on/off duty** 上/下班 ▸ **duty chemist/ officer/doctor** 值班药剂师/官员/医生

duty-free ['dju:tɪ'fri:] ADJ [+ drink, cigarettes] 免税的 [miǎnshuì de] ▸ **duty-free shop** 免税商店

duvet ['du:veɪ] (BRIT) N [C] 羽绒被 [yǔróngbèi]

DVD player N [C] DVD播放器 [DVD bōfàngqì]

dwarf [dwɔ:f] (pl **dwarves** [dwɔ:vz]) I N [C] **1** (in stories) 小矮人 [xiǎo'ǎirén] **2** (o.f., offensive) (small person) 矮子 [ǎizi] II ADJ [+ shrub, plant etc] 矮小的 [ǎixiǎo de] III VT 使相形见绌 [shǐ xiāng xíng jiàn chù]

dwell [dwɛl] (pt, pp **dwelt** [dwɛlt]) VI (frm) 住 [zhù] ▸ **dwell on** VT FUS [不可拆分] 详述 [xiángshù]

dwindle ['dwɪndl] VI [*resources, supplies, strength +*] 缩小 [suōxiǎo]

dye [daɪ] I N [C/U] (*for hair, cloth*) 染料 [rǎnliào] II VT 染色 [rǎnsè] ▶ **to dye sth red/black** 把某物染成红色/黑色

dying ['daɪɪŋ] I ADJ 1 [*+ person, animal*] 垂死的 [chuísǐ de] 2 (*final*) [*+ wishes, words, breath*] 临终的 [língzhōng de]; [*+ days, moments etc*] 行将完结的 [xíngjiāng wánjié de] 3 (*fading*) [*+ tradition, industry*] 行将消失的 [xíngjiāng xiāoshī de] II NPL ▶ **the dying** 垂死的人 [chuísǐ de rén]

dynamic [daɪ'næmɪk] ADJ 生气勃勃的

[shēngqì bóbó de]

dynamite ['daɪnəmaɪt] I N [U] 1 (*explosive*) 甘油炸药 [gānyóu zhàyào] 2 (*something controversial*) 具有爆炸性的事/物 [jùyǒu bàozhàxìng de shì/wù] 3 (*inf*) (*sensational*) 轰动的事/物 [hōngdòng de shì/wù] II VT 炸毁 [zhàhuǐ]

dyslexia [dɪs'lɛksɪə] N [U] 诵读困难 [sòngdú kùnnan]

dyslexic [dɪs'lɛksɪk] ADJ 诵读有困难的 [sòngdú yǒu kùnnan de]

Ee

E¹, e [iː] [c/u] (*letter*) 英语的第五个字母
E² [iː] I N [c/u] (MUS) C大调音阶中的第三音
II ABBR 1 (*direction*) = east 2 (*inf*) (*drug*) = ecstasy

○ **each** [iːtʃ] I ADJ [+*thing, person, idea*] 每 [měi]
II PRON (*each one*) 每个 [měigè] ▷ *two bedrooms, each with three beds* 两间卧室, 每间有3张床 ► **each one of them** 他们中的每一个 ► **each other** 互相 ► **they have 2 books each** 他们每人有两本书 ► **they cost 5 pounds each** 每个售价5镑 ► **each of us** 我们每个人

each 表示一个群体中的每一个人或物, 强调的是每一个个体。every 指由两个以上的个体组成的群体中的所有的人或物, 强调的是整体。*He listened to every news bulletin…an equal chance for every child…* 注意 each 指两个当中的任何一个。*Each apartment has two bedrooms…We each carried a suitcase.* each 和 every 后面都只能跟名词单数形式。

eager [ˈiːgə(r)] ADJ (*keen*) 热切的 [rèqiè de] ► **eager to do** 急于做 ► **eager for** 渴望
eagle [ˈiːgl] N [c] 鹰 [yīng]
ear [ɪə(r)] N [c] 1 (ANAT) 耳朵 [ěrduo] 2 [*of wheat*] 穗 [suì] ► **to have an ear for language/music** 有语言/音乐欣赏能力 ► **to be up to one's ears in debt/work** 深陷入债务/工作 ► **we'll play it by ear** (*fig*) 我们会见机行事
earache [ˈɪəreɪk] N [c/u] 耳朵痛 [ěrduo tòng]
eardrum [ˈɪədrʌm] N [c] 鼓膜 [gǔmó]

earl [əːl] (BRIT) N [c] 伯爵 [bójué]
earlier [ˈəːlɪə(r)] I ADJ 1 [+*date, time etc*] 较早的 [jiàozǎo de] 2 [+*edition, idea*] 以前的 [yǐqián de] II ADV [*leave, go etc* +] 提早 [tízǎo] ► **earlier this year** 本年初 ► **she left earlier than us** 她比我们早离开 ► **I can't come any earlier** 我不能来得再早了

○ **early** [ˈəːlɪ] I ADV 1 (*in day, month etc*) 在初期 [zài chūqī] ▷ *early this morning* 今天一大早 ▷ *early last week* 上星期初 2 (*before usual time*) [*get up, go to bed, arrive, leave* +] 早 [zǎo] ▷ *I usually get up early.* 我通常早起床。II ADJ 1 (*near the beginning*) [+*stage, career*] 早期的 [zǎoqī de] ▷ *the early stages of pregnancy* 怀孕早期 ▷ *Shakespeare's early works* 莎士比亚的早期著作 2 (*in history*) [+*Christians, settlers*] 早期的 [zǎoqī de] 3 (*premature*) [+*death, departure*] 提早的 [tízǎo de] 4 (*quick*) [+*reply*] 很快的 [hěnkuài de] ▷ *We look forward to your early reply.* 我们期待您及早的答复。► **early on** 在初期 ► **early in the morning** 清早 ► **in the early** *or* **early in the spring/19th century** 早春/19世纪初期 ► **she's in her early forties** 她40出头 ► **in the early hours of the morning** 凌晨 ► **you're early!** 你怎么这么早! ► **to take the early train** 坐早班火车 ► **to have an early night** 早上床 ► **at your earliest convenience** (COMM, ADMIN) 在您尽早方便时

early retirement N ► **to take early retirement** 提前退休 [tíqián tuìxiū]
earmark [ˈɪəmɑːk] VT ► **to earmark (for)** [+*funds, site etc*] 指定…用途 [zhǐdìng…yòngtú]
earn [əːn] VT 1 [+*salary, money*] 挣得 [zhèngdé] 2 (COMM) [+*interest*] 生利 [shēnglì] 3 [+*praise, hatred, reputation*] 博得 [bódé] ► **to earn one's** *or* **a living** 谋生 ► **he's earned a rest/reward** 他应得休息/奖励
earnest [ˈəːnɪst] ADJ 1 [+*person, manner*] 认真的 [rènzhēn de] 2 [+*wish, effort*] 诚挚的 [chéngzhì de] ► **to do sth in earnest** 认真地做某事 ► **to be in earnest** (*frm*) 认真地
earnings [ˈəːnɪŋz] NPL 收入 [shōurù]
earphones [ˈɪəfəunz] NPL 耳机 [ěrjī]
earplugs [ˈɪəplʌgz] NPL (*to keep out sound, water*) 耳塞 [ěrsāi]
earring [ˈɪərɪŋ] N [c] 耳环 [ěrhuán]
earshot [ˈɪəʃɒt] N ► **within earshot (of sb/sth)** 在(某人/某物)的听力所及范围内 [zài (móurén/mǒuwù) de tīnglì suǒjí fànwéi nèi] ► **out of earshot of sb/sth** 不在(某人/某物)的听力范围之内
earth [əːθ] I N 1 [u/s] (*also*: **the Earth**) (*planet*) 地球 [dìqiú] 2 [u] (*land surface*) 陆地 [lùdì] 3 [u] (*soil*) 泥土 [nítǔ] 4 [c] (BRIT: ELEC) 接地 [jiēdì] [美=**ground**] II VT (BRIT: ELEC) 把…接地 [bǎ…jiēdì] [美=**ground**] ► **what/where/why on earth…?** 究竟什么/在哪/为什么…? ► **to bring sb/come down to**

earth 使某人回到现实中来

earthquake ['əːθkweɪk] N [C] 地震 [dìzhèn]

ease [iːz] I N [U] 1 (easiness) 容易 [róngyì] 2 (comfort) 安适 [ānshì] II VT (reduce) [+ pain, problem] 减轻 [jiǎnqīng]; [+ tension] 缓和 [huǎnhé] III VI 1 (lessen) [tension +] 缓和 [huǎnhé] 2 [pain, grief +] 减轻 [jiǎnqīng] 3 [rain, snow +] 减弱 [jiǎnruò] ▶ to be/feel at ease 放松 ▶ (stand) at ease! (MIL) 稍息! ▶ with ease 不费吹灰之力 ▶ to ease sth in/out 将某物慢慢挪入/挪出
  ▶ **ease off, ease up** VI (lessen) [wind, rain +] 减弱 [jiǎnruò]; [pressure, tension +] 缓和 [huǎnhé]
  ▶ **ease up** VI 1 = ease off 2 (reduce one's effort) 放松 [fàngsōng]

easily ['iːzɪlɪ] ADV 1 (without difficulty) 不费力地 [bù fèilì de] 2 (for emphasis) 很可能 [hěn kěnéng] 3 (quickly) 容易地 [róngyì de] 4 (in a relaxed way) 从容自在地 [cóngróng zìzài de]

○ **east** [iːst] I N 1 [S/U] 东方 [dōngfāng] ▷ The sun rises in the east. 太阳从东方升起。 2 ▶ the East (the Orient) 东方国家 [dōngfāng guójiā]; (o.f.: POL) (Iron Curtain) 东方集团 [Dōngfāng Jítuán] II ADJ 东部的 [dōngbù de] III ADV 向东方 [xiàng dōngfāng] ▶ the east of Spain 西班牙东部 ▶ to the east 以东 ▶ the east wind 东风 ▶ east of ... 以东 ▷ It's 15 miles or so east of Manchester. 它位于曼彻斯特以东15英里左右。

Easter ['iːstə(r)] N [U] 复活节 [Fùhuó Jié] ▶ the Easter holidays 复活节假期 ▶ Happy Easter! 复活节快乐!

Easter egg N [C] 复活节彩蛋 [Fùhuó Jié cǎidàn]

eastern ['iːstən] ADJ 1 (GEO) 东部的 [dōngbù de] 2 ▶ Eastern (oriental) 东方的 [dōngfāng de] ▶ Eastern Europe 东欧

Easter Sunday N [C/U] 复活主日 [Fùhuó Zhǔrì]

○ **easy** ['iːzɪ] I ADJ 1 (simple) 容易的 [róngyì de] 2 (relaxed) 畅谈 [zìzài de] ▷ an easy conversation 畅谈 ▷ Everyone wants a free and easy life. 每个人都想过自由自在的生活。 3 (comfortable) [+ life, time] 安逸的 [ānyì de] 4 [+ target, prey] 易上当的 [yì shàngdàng de] ▷ Tourists have become easy prey. 旅客成了容易受害的人。 II ADV ▶ to take it or things easy (relax) 放松一点 [fàngsōng yīdiǎn]; (go slowly) 不慌不忙 [bù huāng bù máng]; (not worry) 不急 [bù jí] ▶ dogs are easy to train 狗很容易训练 ▷ The shower is easy to install. 这个淋浴很容易安装。 ▶ it's easy to train dogs 训狗是容易的 ▷ It's easy to get lost in this part of town. 在镇子的这边容易迷路。 ▶ it's easy for sb to do sth 对于某人来说，做某事是容易的 ▷ That's easy for you to say! 你说得轻松! ▶ to make life easier 使生活更方便 ▶ to feel or be easy about sth 对某事感到安心 ▶ I'm easy (inf) 我随便 ▶ payment on easy terms (COMM) 分期

付款 ▶ that's easier said than done 说时容易做时难

easy-going ['iːzɪ'gəuɪŋ] ADJ 脾气随和的 [píqì suíhé de]

eat [iːt] (pt ate, pp eaten ['iːtn]) I VT [+ food, breakfast, lunch, etc] 吃 [chī] II VI 1 (consume food) 吃 [chī] 2 (have a meal) 吃饭 [chīfàn]
  ▶ **eat away** (also: **eat away at**) VT 1 [sea, rust +] 侵蚀 [qīnshí] 2 = eat into
  ▶ **eat into** VT FUS [不可拆分] [+ time, savings, resources] 吞噬 [tūnshì]
  ▶ **eat out** VI 下馆子吃饭 [xià guǎnzi chīfàn]
  ▶ **eat up** I VT 1 [+ food] 把⋯吃光 [bǎ⋯chī guāng] 2 (fig) [+ money, time] 消耗 [xiāohào] II VI 吃光 [chī guāng]

eavesdrop ['iːvzdrɔp] VI ▶ to eavesdrop (on sb/sth) 偷听(某人/某事) [tōutīng (mǒurén/mǒushì)]

ebony ['ɛbənɪ] N [U] (wood) 乌木 [wūmù]

e-business ['iːbɪznɪs] N 1 [C] (company) 电子商务公司 [diànzǐ shāngwù gōngsī] 2 [U] (commerce) 电子商务 [diànzǐ shāngwù]

EC N ABBR (= European Community) ▶ the EC 欧洲共同市场 [Ōuzhōu Gòngtóng Shìchǎng]

eccentric [ɪk'sɛntrɪk] I ADJ 1 [+ person] 怪僻的 [guàipì de] 2 [+ behaviour, views, ideas] 古怪的 [gǔguài de] II N [C] 古怪的人 [gǔguài de rén]

ECG N ABBR (= electrocardiogram) 心电图 [xīndiàntú] [美= EKG]

echo ['ɛkəu] (pl echoes) I N [C] 1 [of sound] 回音 [huíyīn] 2 [of opinion, attitude] 共鸣 [gòngmíng] II VT (fig) (repeat) 重复 [chóngfù] III VI 1 [sound +] 发出回声 [fāchū huíshēng] 2 [cave, room +] 产生回响 [chǎnshēng huíxiǎng]

eclipse [ɪ'klɪps] I N [C] [of sun, moon] 食 [shí] II VT [+ achievement] 使失色 [shǐ shīsè]

eco-friendly ['iːkəu'frɛndlɪ] ADJ 有益于生态的 [yǒuyì yú shēngtài de]

ecological [iːkə'lɔdʒɪkəl] ADJ [+ damage, disaster] 生态的 [shēngtài de]; [+ group, movement] 主张生态保护的 [zhǔzhāng shēngtài bǎohù de]

ecology [ɪ'kɔlədʒɪ] N [U] 1 (environment) 生态 [shēngtài] 2 (subject) 生态学 [shēngtàixué]

e-commerce ['iːkɔmɜːs] N = e-business

○ **economic** [iːkə'nɔmɪk] ADJ 1 [+ system, history, reform] 经济的 [jīngjì de] 2 (profitable) [+ business etc] 有利可图的 [yǒulì kětú de]

economical [iːkə'nɔmɪkl] ADJ 1 [+ system, car, machine] 节约的 [jiéyuē de] 2 [+ person] 节省的 [jiéshěng de]

economics [iːkə'nɔmɪks] N 1 [U] (SCOL, UNIV) 经济学 [jīngjìxué] 2 [PL] [of project, situation] 经济意义 [jīngjì yìyì]

economist [ɪ'kɔnəmɪst] N [C] 经济学家 [jīngjì xuéjiā]

economize [ɪ'kɔnəmaɪz] VI (make savings) 节约 [jiéyuē] ▶ to economize on sth 节约用某物

○ **economy** [ɪ'kɔnəmɪ] N 1 [C] [of country] 经济

[jīngjì] **2** [U] (thrift) 节约 [jiéyuē] ▶ **economies of scale** 规模经济

economy class I ADJ 经济舱的 [jīngjìcāng de] II ADV 经济舱地 [jīngjìcāng de] III N [U] 经济舱 [jīngjìcāng]

ecstasy ['ɛkstəsɪ] N **1** [C/U] (rapture) 狂喜 [kuángxǐ] **2** [U] (drug) 迷幻药 [míhuànyào] ▶ **to be in ecstasy** 兴奋极了 ▶ **to go into ecstasies over** 对…发狂

ecstatic [ɛks'tætɪk] ADJ [+ welcome, reaction, person] 欣喜若狂的 [xīnxǐ ruò kuáng de]

Ecuador ['ɛkwədɔː(r)] N 厄瓜多尔 [Èguāduō'ěr]

eczema ['ɛksɪmə] N [U] 湿疹 [shīzhěn]

edge [ɛdʒ] I N [C] **1** (border) [of road, town] 边缘 [biānyuán]: [of lake] 边 [biān] ▷ She was standing at the water's edge. 她站在水边。 **2** [of table, chair etc] 棱 [léng] **3** [of knife, sword etc] 刃 [rèn] II VI ▶ **to edge forward** 一点一点地向前移动 [yīdiǎn yīdiǎn de xiàngqián yídòng] ▶ **on edge** 紧张不安 ▶ **to have the** or **an edge (over sb)** 胜过(某人) ▶ **to edge past** 缓缓通过 ▶ **to edge away from** 悄悄离开
▶ **edge out** VT (in contest) 小胜 [xiǎoshèng]

edgy ['ɛdʒɪ] (inf) ADJ (nervous, agitated) 紧张的 [jǐnzhāng de]

edible ['ɛdɪbl] ADJ [+ mushroom, plant] 可食用的 [kě shíyòng de]

edit ['ɛdɪt] VT **1** [+ text, report] 校订 [jiàodìng] **2** [+ book] 编辑 [biānjí] **3** [+ film, broadcast] 剪辑 [jiǎnjí] **4** [+ newspaper, magazine] 主编 [zhǔbiān]
▶ **edit out** VT (of book, film) 删去 [shānqù]

edition [ɪ'dɪʃən] N [C] **1** [of book, newspaper, magazine] 版 [bǎn] **2** (TV, RAD) 集 [jí]

editor ['ɛdɪtə(r)] N [C] **1** [of newspaper, magazine, book] 编辑 [biānjí] **2** [of text, report] 校订者 [jiàodìngzhě] **3** 剪辑者 [jiǎnjízhě] **4** (TV, RAD) 编辑 [biānjí] ▶ **foreign/literary editor** 外文/文学编辑

editorial [ɛdɪ'tɔːrɪəl] I ADJ [+ staff, meeting, policy] 编辑的 [biānjí de] II N [C] [of newspaper] 社论 [shèlùn]

EDT (US) ABBR (= Eastern Daylight Time) 东部夏令时 [Dōngbù Xiàlìngshí]

educate ['ɛdjʊkeɪt] VT **1** (teach) 教育 [jiàoyù] **2** (instruct) 使懂得 [shǐ dǒngdé] ▶ **she was educated at...** 她在…受的教育

educated ['ɛdjʊkeɪtɪd] ADJ [+ person] 受过教育的 [shòuguò jiàoyù de]

education [ɛdjʊ'keɪʃən] N [U/S] (schooling, teaching) 教育 [jiàoyù]

educational [ɛdjʊ'keɪʃənl] ADJ **1** [+ institution, policy, needs] 教育的 [jiàoyù de] **2** (instructive) [+ experience] 有教育意义的 [yǒu jiàoyù yìyì de]

eel [iːl] N [C/U] 鳗鱼 [mànyú]

eerie ['ɪərɪ] ADJ (strange) 令人恐惧的 [lìng rén kǒngjù de]

○**effect** [ɪ'fɛkt] I N **1** [C/U] (result, consequence) 影响 [yǐngxiǎng] ▷ the effect of divorce on children 离婚对儿童产生的影响 **2** [C] (impression) [of speech, picture etc] 效果 [xiàoguǒ] ▷ Don't move, or you'll destroy the effect. 别动，不然你会破坏效果的。 II VT (frm) [+ repairs, savings etc] 完成 [wánchéng] ▷ Production was halted until repairs could be effected. 在修理完成之前停止生产。 III **effects** NPL **1** (frm) (belongings) 财物 [cáiwù] **2** (CINE) 特别效果 [tèbié xiàoguǒ] ▶ **to come into** or **take effect** [law +] 生效 ▶ **to take effect** [drug +] 见效 ▶ **to put** or **bring** or **carry sth into effect** 实施某事 ▶ **to have an effect on sb/sth** 对某人/某事产生影响 ▶ **in effect** 实际上 ▶ **his letter is to the effect that...** 他信的大意是… ▶ **to good/no effect** 有/无效
▇ 用法参见 **affect**

effective [ɪ'fɛktɪv] ADJ **1** (successful) 有效的 [yǒuxiào de] **2** (actual) [+ leader, command] 事实上的 [shìshí shang de] ▶ **to become effective** (LAW) 生效

effectively [ɪ'fɛktɪvlɪ] ADV **1** (successfully) 有效地 [yǒuxiào de] **2** (in reality) 事实上 [shìshí shang]

efficiency [ɪ'fɪʃənsɪ] N [U] [of person, organization] 效率 [xiàolù]

efficient [ɪ'fɪʃnt] ADJ [+ person, organization, system] 效率高的 [xiàolù gāo de]

efficiently [ɪ'fɪʃntlɪ] ADV 效率高地 [xiàolù gāo de]

○**effort** ['ɛfət] N **1** [U] (energy) 努力 [nǔlì] ▷ a waste of effort 白费力气 **2** [C] (attempt) 尝试 [chángshì] ▷ It was a good effort. 这是个很好的尝试。 **3** [U/S] (physical/mental exertion) 费力 [fèilì] ▷ It was an effort to concentrate. 费劲须集中精力。 ▶ **to make an effort to do sth** 努力做某事 ▶ **with an effort** 费力地

effortless ['ɛfətlɪs] ADJ (movement, style) 不费劲的 [bù fèijìn de]

e.g. ADV ABBR (= exempli gratia) (for example) 举例来说 [jǔlì lái shuō]

egg [ɛg] N **1** [C] [of bird, turtle etc] 蛋 [dàn] **2** [C/U] (for eating) 蛋 [dàn] **3** [C] (BIO) 卵子 [luǎnzǐ]
▶ **egg on** VT (in fight etc) 怂恿 [sǒngyǒng]

eggcup ['ɛgkʌp] N [C] 蛋杯 [dànbēi]

eggplant ['ɛgplɑːnt] (US) N [C/U] 茄子 [qiézi] [英=aubergine]

eggshell ['ɛgʃɛl] I N [C/U] 蛋壳 [dànké] II ADJ [+ paint] 淡黄褐色的 [dàn huánghèsè de]

egg white N [C/U] 蛋白 [dànbái]

egg yolk N [C/U] 蛋黄 [dànhuáng]

ego ['iːgəu] N [C] (self-esteem) 自尊 [zìzūn]

Egypt ['iːdʒɪpt] N 埃及 [Āijí]

Egyptian [ɪ'dʒɪpʃən] I ADJ 埃及的 [Āijí de] II N [C] (person) 埃及人 [Āijírén]

○**eight** [eɪt] NUM 八 [bā] see also **five**

○**eighteen** [eɪ'tiːn] NUM 十八 [shíbā] see also **fifteen**

eighteenth [eɪ'tiːnθ] NUM 第十八 [dì shíbā]

see also **fifth**

eighth [eɪtθ] NUM **1** 第八 [dì bā] **2** *(fraction)* 八分之一 [bā fēn zhī yī] *see also* **fifth**

eightieth ['eɪtɪəθ] NUM 第八十 [dì bāshí]

⊙ **eighty** ['eɪtɪ] NUM 八十 [bāshí] *see also* **fifty**

Eire ['ɛərə] N 爱尔兰共和国 [Ài'ěrlán Gònghéguó]

⊙ **either** ['aɪðə(r)] I ADJ **1** *(one or other)* 两者任一的 [liǎngzhě rènyī de] ▷ *Either bus will take you there.* 两路公共汽车之中任一辆都会把你带到那儿。**2** *(both, each)* 两者中每一方的 [liǎngzhě zhōng měiyìfāng de] ▷ *In either case the answer is the same.* 两者答案是一样的。II PRON **1** *(after negative)* 两者之中任何一个 [liǎngzhě zhī zhōng rènhé yígè] ▷ *There was no sound from either of the flats.* 两个单元都没声音。**2** *(after interrogative)* 两者之中任何一个 [liǎngzhě zhī zhōng rènhé yígè] ▷ *"Which one?" – "Either of them."* "哪一个?" "哪个都行。" III ADV *(in negative statements)* 也 [yě] ▷ *His singing is hopeless and he can't act either.* 他唱歌不行,表演也不行。IV CONJ ▶ **either... or...** 要么…要么… [yàome...yàome...] ▶ **on either side** 在两边 [zài liǎngbiān] ▶ **I don't like either of them** 两个我都不喜欢 ▶ **no, I don't either** 不,我也不 ▶ **I haven't seen either one or the other** 我两个都没看见

eject [ɪ'dʒɛkt] I VT **1** [+ *object*] 喷射 [pēnshè] ▷ *He fired a shot, then ejected the spent cartridge.* 他开了一枪,然后倒出了用过的弹夹。**2** [+ *tenant, gatecrasher*] 驱逐 [qūzhú] II VI [*pilot +*] 弹射出来 [tánshè chūlai]

EKG (US) N ABBR = **ECG**

elaborate [*adj* ɪ'læbərɪt, *vb* ɪ'læbəreɪt] I ADJ *(complex)* [+ *network, plan*] 复杂的 [fùzá de]; [+ *ritual, ceremony*] 精心制作的 [jīngxīn zhìzuò de] II VT *(develop)* [+ *plan, policy*] 仔细制订 [zǐxì zhìdìng] III VI ▶ **to elaborate (on sth)** [+ *idea, plan etc*] 详述(某事) [xiángshù (mǒushì)]

elastic [ɪ'læstɪk] I N [U] *(material)* 橡皮 [xiàngpí] II ADJ **1** *(stretchy)* 有弹性的 [yǒu tánxìng de] **2** *(fig)* *(adaptable)* 灵活的 [línghuó de]

elastic band (BRIT) N [C] 橡皮筋 [xiàngpíjīn] [美 = **rubber band**]

elbow ['ɛlbəu] I N [C] **1** (ANAT) 肘 [zhǒu] **2** [*of sleeve*] 肘部 [zhǒubù] II VT [+ *person*] 用肘打 [yòng zhǒu dǎ] ▶ **to elbow one's way through the crowd** 挤过人群 ▶ **to elbow sb aside** 把某人挤到一旁

elder ['ɛldə(r)] I ADJ [+ *brother, sister etc*] 年龄较大的 [niánlíng jiào dà de] ▷ *He had none of his elder brother's charm.* 他没有他哥哥的魅力。II N [C] **1** *(frm)* *(older person)* 长者 [zhǎngzhě]; *(in tribe etc)* 头人 [tóurén] **2** *(tree)* 接骨木 [jiēgǔmù]

elderly ['ɛldəlɪ] I ADJ *(old)* 年长的 [niánzhǎng de] II NPL ▶ **the elderly** 老人家 [lǎorénjiā]

eldest ['ɛldɪst] I ADJ [+ *child, daughter*] 年龄最

大的 [niánlíng zuìdà de] II N [S/PL] 年龄最大的孩子 [niánlíng zuìdà de háizi]

elect [ɪ'lɛkt] I VT [+ *government, councillor, spokesman etc*] 选举 [xuǎnjǔ] II ADJ ▶ **the president elect** *(frm)* 当选的总统 [dāngxuǎn de zǒngtǒng] ▶ **to elect to do sth** *(frm)* *(choose)* 选择做某事

⊙ **election** [ɪ'lɛkʃən] N **1** [C] *(ballot)* 选举 [xuǎnjǔ] **2** [S] [*of person, government*] 当选 [dāngxuǎn] ▶ **to hold an election** 举行选举

electoral [ɪ'lɛktərəl] ADJ [+ *system*] 选举的 [xuǎnjǔ de]

electorate [ɪ'lɛktərɪt] N [C] 选民 [xuǎnmín]

electric [ɪ'lɛktrɪk] ADJ **1** [+ *lawnmower, toothbrush*] 电动的 [diàndòng de] **2** [+ *current, charge, socket*] 电的 [diàn de] **3** *(fig)* [+ *mood, atmosphere*] 高度刺激的 [gāodù cìjī de]

electrical [ɪ'lɛktrɪkl] ADJ **1** [+ *appliance, equipment*] 电动的 [diàndòng de] **2** [+ *system*] 电的 [diàn de] **3** [+ *industry, failure*] 电力的 [diànlì de] ▷ *a blackout resulting from an electrical failure* 断电造成的黑暗

electric blanket N [C] 电热毯 [diànrètǎn]

electric fire (BRIT) N [C] 电热炉 [diànrèlú]

electric guitar N [C/U] 电吉他 [diànjítā]

electrician [ɪlɛk'trɪʃən] N [C] 电工 [diàngōng]

electricity [ɪlɛk'trɪsɪtɪ] I N [U] **1** *(energy)* 电 [diàn] **2** *(supply)* 供电 [gòngdiàn] II CPD [复合词] **1** [+ *company*] 电力 [diànlì] **2** [+ *bill, meter*] 电 [diàn]

electric razor N [C] 电动剃须刀 [diàndòng tìxūdāo]

electric shock N [C] 触电 [chùdiàn]

electrify [ɪ'lɛktrɪfaɪ] VT **1** [+ *rail network*] 使电气化 [shǐ diànqìhuà] **2** *(fig)* *(thrill)* 使震惊 [shǐ zhènjīng]

electrocute [ɪ'lɛktrəkju:t] VT 使触电死亡 [shǐ chùdiàn sǐwáng] ▶ **to electrocute o.s.** 电死自己

electronic [ɪlɛk'trɔnɪk] ADJ 电子的 [diànzǐ de]

electronics [ɪlɛk'trɔnɪks] I N [U] *(technology)* 电子学 [diànzǐxué] II NPL [*of machine*] 电子仪器 [diànzǐ yíqì]

elegance ['ɛlɪgəns] N [U] **1** [*of person, building*] 雅致 [yǎzhì] **2** [*of piece of writing*] 典雅 [diǎnyǎ]

elegant ['ɛlɪgənt] ADJ **1** [+ *person, building*] 优雅的 [yōuyǎ de] **2** [+ *idea, prose*] 上乘的 [shàngchéng de]

element ['ɛlɪmənt] I N [C] **1** *(part)* [*of job, process, plan*] 要素 [yàosù] **2** (CHEM) 元素 [yuánsù] **3** [*of heater, kettle etc*] 电热丝 [diànrèsī] II NPL ▶ **the elements** *(weather)* 自然力 [zìránlì] ▶ **the story contains an element of truth** 这个故事有真实的成分 ▶ **criminal elements** 为非作歹的人 ▶ **to be in one's element** 各得其所

elementary [ɛlɪ'mɛntərɪ] ADJ 初级的 [chūjí de]

elementary school (US) N [C/U] 小学

[xiǎoxué] [英=**primary school**]

elephant ['ɛlɪfənt] N [C] 大象 [dàxiàng]

elevate ['ɛlɪveɪt] (frm) VT **1** (in rank) 提升…的职位 [tíshēng…de zhíwèi] **2** (in amount, intensity) 提高 [tígāo] **3** (physically) 使上升 [shǐ shàngshēng]

elevator ['ɛlɪveɪtə(r)] (US) N [C] 电梯 [diàntī] [英=**lift**]

◊**eleven** [ɪ'lɛvn] NUM 十一 [shíyī] see also **five**

eleventh [ɪ'lɛvnθ] NUM 第十一 [dì shíyī] ▶ **at the eleventh hour** 在最后时刻 see also **fifth**

elicit [ɪ'lɪsɪt] VT **1** [+ response, reaction] 引导出 [yǐndǎo chū] **2** (frm) [+ information] 推导出 [tuīdǎo chū]

eligible ['ɛlɪdʒəbl] ADJ **1** [+ man, woman] 合意的 [héyì de] ▶ **to be eligible for sth** 符合某事的条件 ▶ **to be eligible to do sth** 合格做某事

eliminate [ɪ'lɪmɪneɪt] VT **1** [+ poverty] 消除 [xiāochú]; [+ smoking] 戒除 [jièchú] **2** [+ team, contestant, candidate] 淘汰 [táotài]

élite [eɪ'liːt] I N [C] 精英 [jīngyīng] II ADJ 精锐的 [jīngruì de]

elm [ɛlm] N **1** [C] (also: **elm tree**) 榆树 [yúshù] **2** [U] (wood) 榆木 [yúmù]

eloquent ['ɛləkwənt] ADJ **1** [+ speech, description] 有说服力的 [yǒu shuōfúlì de] **2** [+ person] 能言善辩的 [néng yán shàn biàn de]

El Salvador [ɛl'sælvədɔː(r)] N 萨尔瓦多 [Sà'ěrwǎduō]

◊**else** [ɛls] ADV ▶ **or else** (otherwise) 否则 [fǒuzé]; (threatening) 要不然 [yàobùrán] ▷ Don't talk to me like that again, or else! 别这么跟我说话，要不够你受的！ ▶ **something else, anything else** 其他东西，任何其他东西 ▶ **where else?** 别的什么地方？ ▶ **what else?** 其他什么？ ▶ **somewhere else** 其他地方 ▶ **everywhere else** 其他任何地方 ▶ **everyone else** 其他人 ▶ **nobody else** 没有其他人 ▶ **little else** 其他什么都没有 ▶ **if nothing else** 起码

elsewhere [ɛls'wɛə(r)] ADV **1** [be+] 在别处 [zài biéchù] **2** [go+] 到别处去 [dào biéchù]

elusive [ɪ'luːsɪv] ADJ **1** [+ person, animal] 不易找到的 [bùyì zhǎodào de] **2** [+ quality] 难以捉摸的 [nányǐ zhuōmō de]

e-mail ['iːmeɪl] I N [C/U] 电子邮件 [diànzǐ yóujiàn] II VT **1** [+ person] 给…发电子邮件 [gěi…fā diànzǐ yóujiàn] **2** [+ file, document] 用电子邮件寄 [yòng diànzǐ yóujiàn jì]

e-mail account N [C] 电子邮件账号 [diànzǐ yóujiàn zhànghào]

e-mail address N [C] 电子邮件地址 [diànzǐ yóujiàn dìzhǐ]

embankment [ɪm'bæŋkmənt] N [C] [of road, railway, river] 堤 [dī]

embargo [ɪm'baːgəu] (pl **embargoes**) I N [C] 限制贸易令 [xiànzhì màoyì lìng] II VT [+ goods] 禁运 [jìnyùn] ▶ **to impose** or **place an embargo on sth** 对某物实行禁运 ▶ **to lift an embargo** 解禁

embark [ɪm'baːk] VI (NAUT) ▶ **to embark (on)** 登上 [dēngshang]
▶ **embark on** VT FUS [不可拆分] [+ task, course of action] 着手 [zhuóshǒu]

embarrass [ɪm'bærəs] VT **1** (emotionally) 使不好意思 [shǐ bùhǎo yìsi] **2** [+ politician, government] 使陷入困境 [shǐ xiànrù kùnjìng]

embarrassed [ɪm'bærəst] ADJ [+ laugh, silence] 尴尬的 [gāngà de] ▶ **to be embarrassed** 不好意思的

embarrassing [ɪm'bærəsɪŋ] ADJ **1** [+ statement, situation] 令人尴尬的 [lìng rén gāngà de] **2** (to politician, government) 令人难堪的 [lìng rén nánkān de]

embarrassment [ɪm'bærəsmənt] N **1** [U] (feeling) 难堪 [nánkān] **2** [C] (situation, problem) 令人为难的事情 [lìng rén wéinán de shìqíng] **3** [C] (person) 使人为难的人 [shǐ rén wéinán de rén] ▶ **to be an embarrassment to sb** 是令某人困窘的人/事

embassy ['ɛmbəsɪ] N [C] 大使馆 [dàshǐguǎn]

embody [ɪm'bɔdɪ] VT **1** [+ idea, quality] 体现 [tǐxiàn] **2** (include, contain) 包含 [bāohán]

embrace [ɪm'breɪs] I VT **1** (hug) 拥抱 [yōngbào] **2** (fig) (welcome) [+ new idea, system etc] 欣然接受 [xīnrán jiēshòu] **3** (include) [+ group of people, things] 包括 [bāokuò] II VI (hug) 拥抱 [yōngbào] III N [C] (hug) 拥抱 [yōngbào]

embroider [ɪm'brɔɪdə(r)] VT **1** [+ cloth] 在…上刺绣 [zài…shang cìxiù] **2** (fig) [+ a story, the truth] 渲染 [xuānrǎn]

embroidery [ɪm'brɔɪdərɪ] N **1** [C/U] (cloth) 绣制品 [xiùzhìpǐn] **2** [U] (activity) 刺绣 [cìxiù]

embryo ['ɛmbrɪəu] N [C] (BIO) 胚胎 [pēitāi] ▶ **in embryo** (fig) 在酝酿中

emerald ['ɛmərəld] N [C] (gem) 祖母绿 [zǔmǔlǜ]

emerge [ɪ'məːdʒ] VI **1** (come out) [person +] 出来 [chūlái] **2** (become known) [evidence, facts +] 暴露 [bàolù] **3** (come into existence) [new idea, movement, society +] 兴起 [xīngqǐ] ▶ **to emerge from sth** (from room, building) 从某物中出现; (from crisis, recession) 摆脱某种状况; (from discussion, investigation) 从某物中暴露出 ▶ **it emerged that...** 事实显现

emergence [ɪ'məːdʒəns] N [U] [of new idea, nation] 出现 [chūxiàn]

emergency [ɪ'məːdʒənsɪ] I N [C] (crisis) 紧急情况 [jǐnjí qíngkuàng] II CPD [复合词] [+ repair, talks, supplies, aid] 紧急 [jǐnjí] ▶ **in an emergency** 在紧急情况下 ▶ **a state of emergency** (POL) 紧急状况

emergency brake (US: AUT) N [C] 紧急刹车 [jǐnjí shāchē] [英=**handbrake**]

emergency exit N [C] 安全出口 [ānquán chūkǒu]

emergency landing N [C] 紧急着陆 [jǐnjí

zhuólù] ▶ **to make an emergency landing** 进行紧急着陆

emergency room (US) N [C] 急诊室 [jízhěnshì] 〔英 = **accident and emergency**〕

emergency services NPL ▶ **the emergency services** (fire, police, ambulance) 紧急服务 [jǐnjí fúwù]

emigrate ['ɛmɪgreɪt] VI 移居外国 [yíjū wàiguó]

emigration [ɛmɪ'greɪʃən] N [U] 移居外国 [yíjū wàiguó]

eminent ['ɛmɪnənt] ADJ [+ scientist, writer] 卓越的 [zhuōyuè de]

emission [ɪ'mɪʃən] (frm) I N [C/U] [of radiation, gas] 散发 [sànfā] II **emissions** NPL 废物 [fèiwù]

emit [ɪ'mɪt] VT [+ heat, light, smell, sound] 发出 [fāchū]

emotion [ɪ'məuʃən] N 1 [C/U] (feeling) 感情 [gǎnqíng] 2 [U] (as opposed to reason) 情感 [qínggǎn]

emotional [ɪ'məuʃənl] ADJ 1 [+ support, problems] 感情的 [gǎnqíng de]; [+ stress] 情绪的 [qíngxù de] 2 [+ person] 易动感情的 [yì dòng gǎnqíng de] 3 [+ scene, issue] 令人情绪激动的 [lìng rén qíngxù jīdòng de] 4 [+ speech, plea] 动人的 [dòngrén de] ▶ **to get emotional** 动感情 [dòng gǎnqíng]

emperor ['ɛmpərə(r)] N [C] 皇帝 [huángdì]

emphasis ['ɛmfəsɪs] (pl **emphases** ['ɛmfəsiːz]) N [C/U] 1 (on word, syllable) 重音 [zhòngyīn] 2 (fig) 重点 [zhòngdiǎn] ▶ **to put** or **place emphasis on sth** (fig) 把重点放在某事上 ▶ **the emphasis is on reading** 着重于阅读

emphasize ['ɛmfəsaɪz] VT 1 [+ word, point] 强调 [qiángdiào] 2 (make conspicuous) 使明显 [shǐ míngxiǎn] ▶ **I must emphasize that...** 我必须强调…

emphatic [ɛm'fætɪk] ADJ 1 [+ statement, denial] 断然的 [duànrán de] 2 [+ person, manner] 强硬的 [qiángyìng de] 3 [+ victory] 令人瞩目的 [lìng rén zhǔmù de]

empire ['ɛmpaɪə(r)] N [C] 1 (group of countries) 帝国 [dìguó] 2 (fig) (group of companies) 王国 [wángguó] ▶ **a business/publishing empire** 商业/出版王国

employ [ɪm'plɔɪ] I VT 1 [+ person, workforce] 雇用 [gùyòng] 2 (use) [+ methods, materials] 使用 [shǐyòng] II N ▶ **to be in sb's employ** (frm) 受雇于某人 [shòugù yú mǒurén] ▶ **he was employed as a technician** 他受雇做技师

employee [ɪmplɔɪ'iː] N [C] 雇员 [gùyuán]

employer [ɪm'plɔɪə(r)] N [C] 雇主 [gùzhǔ]

employment [ɪm'plɔɪmənt] N [U] (work) 工作 [gōngzuò] ▶ **to find employment** 找到工作 ▶ **to be in employment** 有工作 ▶ **place of employment** 工作地点

employment agency N [C] 职业介绍所 [zhíyé jièshàosuǒ]

empower [ɪm'pauə(r)] VT 1 ▶ **to empower sb to do sth** (frm) 授权某人做某事 [shòuquán mǒurén zuò mǒushì] 2 [+ women, minority] 授予…权利 [shòuyǔ…quánlì]

empress ['ɛmprɪs] N [C] (woman ruling empire) 女皇 [nǔhuáng]; (wife of emperor) 皇后 [huánghòu]

emptiness ['ɛmptɪnɪs] N [U] 1 [of area, region etc] 空旷 [kōngkuàng] 2 [of life etc] 空虚 [kōngxū]

empty ['ɛmptɪ] I ADJ 1 [+ glass, container] 空的 [kōng de] 2 [+ place, street] 无人的 [wúrén de] 3 [+ house, room] 空的 [kōng de] 4 [+ threat, gesture] 虚张声势的 [xū zhāng shēngshì de] II VT 1 [+ bin, ashtray] 倒空 [dào kōng] 2 [+ room, house etc] 使空 [shǐ kōng] III VI [room, building +] 成为空的 [chéngwéi kōng de] ▶ **on an empty stomach** 空着肚子 ▶ **to empty sth into sth** (pour out) 将某物全部倒入某物中 ▶ **to empty into** [river +] 流入

empty-handed ['ɛmptɪ'hændɪd] ADJ ▶ **to go away empty-handed** 一无所获地离开 [yī wú suǒ huò de líkāi] ▶ **he returned empty-handed** 他空手回来

emulsion [ɪ'mʌlʃən] N [C/U] 1 (also: **emulsion paint**) 乳状油漆 [rǔzhuàng yóuqī] 2 (PHOT) 感光乳剂 [gǎnguāng rǔjì]

enable [ɪ'neɪbl] VT 1 ▶ **to enable sb to do sth** (make possible) 使某人能够做某事 [shǐ mǒurén nénggòu zuò mǒushì] 2 (permit, allow) [law +] 批准 [pīzhǔn]

enamel [ɪ'næməl] N 1 [C/U] (for decoration) 搪瓷 [tángcí] 2 [C/U] (also: **enamel paint**) 瓷漆 [cíqī] 3 [U] (on tooth) 珐琅质 [fǎlángzhì]

enc. ABBR (= enclosed, enclosure) 附 [fù]

enchant [ɪn'tʃɑːnt] VT (delight) 使入迷 [shǐ rùmí]

enchanting [ɪn'tʃɑːntɪŋ] ADJ [+ place, child] 迷人的 [mírén de]

encl. ABBR (= enclosed, enclosure) = **enc.**

enclose [ɪn'kləuz] VT 1 [+ garden, space] 围住 [wéizhù] 2 [+ object in wrapping etc] 包住 [bāozhù] 3 (in letter) [+ cheque] 附入 [fùrù] ▶ **enclosed by sth** 被某物围住 ▶ **please find enclosed** 兹附上

enclosure [ɪn'kləuʒə(r)] N [C] 1 (area of land) 围场 [wéichǎng] 2 (in letter) 附件 [fùjiàn]

encompass [ɪn'kʌmpəs] VT (include) 包含 [bāohán]

encore [ɔŋ'kɔː(r)] (THEAT) I N [C] 加演的节目 [jiāyǎn de jiémù] ▷ The Stone Roses have never played an encore. Stone Roses乐队从不应观众要求而加演节目。II INT 再来一个 [zài lái yīgè]

encounter [ɪn'kauntə(r)] I N 1 (meeting) 相遇 [xiāngyù] 2 (experience) 遭遇 [zāoyù] II VT 1 (frm) [+ person] 意外遇见 [yìwài yùjiàn]

2 [+ *difficulty, problem*] 遭到 [zāodào]

encourage [ɪnˈkʌrɪdʒ] VT **1** [+ *person*] 鼓励 [gǔlì] **2** [+ *activity, attitude*] 支持 [zhīchí] **3** [+ *growth, industry*] 助长 [zhùzhǎng] ▶ **to encourage sb to do sth** 鼓励某人去做某事 ▶ **to be encouraged by sth** 由于某事受到鼓励

encouragement [ɪnˈkʌrɪdʒmənt] N [U] (*support*) 鼓励 [gǔlì]

encouraging [ɪnˈkʌrɪdʒɪŋ] ADJ [+ *meeting, news*] 令人鼓舞的 [lìng rén gǔwǔ de]

encyclop(a)edia [ɛnsaɪkləuˈpiːdɪə] N [c] 百科全书 [bǎikē quánshū]

 end [ɛnd] I N **1** [s] [*of period, event*] 末期 [mòqī] ▷ *at the end of August* 在8月末 **2** [s] [*of film, book*] 末尾 [mòwěi] **3** [c] [*of street, queue, rope, table*] 尽头 [jìntóu] **4** [c] [*of town*] 端 [duān] **5** [c] [*of pencil, finger etc*] 末梢 [mòshāo] **6** [c] (*purpose*) 目的 [mùdì] ▷ *for political ends* 为了政治目的 II VT (*finish, stop*) [+ *fighting, strike*] 终止 [zhōngzhǐ] III VI **1** [*meeting, film, book* +] 结束 [jiéshù] **2** [*journey, road, river* +] 终结 [zhōngjié] ▶ **at the end of the day** (*fig*) 到头来 ▶ **to come to an end** 完结 ▶ **to be at an end** 结束 ▶ **in the end** 最终 ▶ **at the end of the street** 在街的尽头 ▶ **from end to end** 从头到尾 ▶ **to make sb's hair stand on end** 使某人毛骨悚然 ▶ **no end** (*inf*) (*a lot*) 许多 ▶ **for hours on end** 连续几个小时 ▶ **to bring sth to an end, put an end to sth** 使某事终止 ▶ **to this end, with this end in view** 为了达到这个目的 ▶ **to make ends meet** 勉强维持生活 ▶ **to end in tragedy/disaster** 以悲剧/大祸收尾
▶ **end up** VI ▶ **to end up in/at** [+ *place*] 最终到了 [zuìzhōng dào le]; [+ *trouble, a mess etc*] 结束于 [jiéshù yú] ▶ **to end up doing sth** 以做某事告终

endanger [ɪnˈdeɪndʒə(r)] VT [+ *lives, prospects*] 危害 [wēihài] ▶ **an endangered species** 一个濒于灭绝的物种

endearing [ɪnˈdɪərɪŋ] ADJ [+ *personality, smile*] 使人喜爱的 [shǐ rén xǐ'ài de]

endeavour, (US) **endeavor** [ɪnˈdɛvə(r)] (*frm*) I N **1** [c] (*attempt*) 尝试 [chángshì] **2** [U] (*effort*) 努力 [nǔlì] II VI ▶ **to endeavour to do sth** 尝试做某事 [chángshì zuò mǒushì]

ending [ˈɛndɪŋ] N [c] **1** [*of book, film, play etc*] 结局 [jiéjú] **2** (LING) 词尾 [cíwěi] ▶ **a happy ending** 美满结局

endless [ˈɛndlɪs] ADJ **1** (*very lengthy*) [+ *drought, war, speech*] 没完没了的 [méiwán méiliǎo de] **2** (*interminable*) [+ *arguments, meetings*] 无休止的 [wú xiūzhǐ de] **3** (*very long, very large*) [+ *forest, beach*] 无穷尽的 [wú qióngjìn de] **4** [+ *possibilities*] 无限的 [wúxiàn de]

endorse [ɪnˈdɔːs] VT **1** (*approve*) [+ *proposal, plan, candidate*] 赞同 [zàntóng] **2** (COMM) [+ *product, company*] 为⋯做广告 [wèi⋯zuò guǎnggào] **3** [+ *cheque*] 在⋯背后签字 [zài⋯bèihòu qiānzì]

▶ **to have one's driving licence endorsed** (BRIT) 执照被注上违章记录

endorsement [ɪnˈdɔːsmənt] N **1** [c/U] (*approval*) 赞同 [zàntóng] **2** [c] (BRIT) (*on driving licence*) 违章记录 [wéizhāng jìlù] **3** [c] (COMM) (*for product, company*) 商业广告 [shāngyè guǎnggào]

endurance [ɪnˈdjuərəns] N [U] 忍耐 [rěnnài]

endure [ɪnˈdjuə(r)] I VT (*bear*) [+ *pain, suffering*] 忍耐 [rěnnài] II VI (*last*) [*relationship, work of art* +] 持续 [chíxù]

enemy [ˈɛnəmɪ] I N **1** [c] (*opponent*) 敌人 [dírén] **2** [s] (*army*) 敌军 [díjūn] II CPD [复合词] [+ *forces, strategy, aircraft*] 敌方的 [dífāng de] ▶ **to make an enemy of sb** 使某人与自己为敌

energetic [ɛnəˈdʒɛtɪk] ADJ **1** [+ *person*] 精力充沛的 [jīnglì chōngpèi de] **2** [+ *activity*] 生机勃勃的 [shēngjī bóbó de]

energy [ˈɛnədʒɪ] I N [U] **1** (*strength*) 力量 [lìliàng] **2** (*power*) 能源 [néngyuán] II **energies** NPL 精力 [jīnglì]

enforce [ɪnˈfɔːs] VT [+ *law, rule*] 执行 [zhíxíng]

engage [ɪnˈgeɪdʒ] I VT **1** (*frm*) [+ *attention, interest*] 吸引 [xīyǐn] **2** (*frm*) (*employ*) [+ *consultant, lawyer, sb's services*] 雇用 [gùyòng] **3** (AUT) [+ *clutch*] 接合 [jiēhé] **4** (MIL) [+ *enemy*] 与⋯交战 [yǔ⋯jiāozhàn] II VI (TECH) 啮合 [nièhé] ▶ **to engage in** [+ *commerce, research etc*] 从事于 ▶ **to engage sb in conversation** 使某人参加谈话

engaged [ɪnˈgeɪdʒd] ADJ **1** (*to be married*) 已订婚的 [yǐ dìnghūn de] **2** (BRIT: TEL) 被占用的 [bèi zhànyòng de] [美= **busy**] **3** (BRIT) [+ *toilet*] 被占用的 [bèi zhànyòng de] [美= **occupied**] ▶ **to get engaged (to)** (与⋯)订婚 ▶ **he is engaged in research** (*frm*) 他正从事研究

engaged tone (BRIT: TEL) N [c] 忙音 [mángyīn]

engagement [ɪnˈgeɪdʒmənt] N **1** [c] (*frm*) (*appointment*) 约会 [yuēhuì] **2** [c] (*to marry*) 婚约 [hūnyuē] **3** [c/U] (MIL) (*battle*) 交战 [jiāozhàn] **4** [c] (*employment*) 受聘期 [shòupìnqī] ▶ **I have a previous engagement** 我有个前约

engagement ring N [c] 订婚戒指 [dìnghūn jièzhǐ]

engaging [ɪnˈgeɪdʒɪŋ] ADJ [+ *personality, smile*] 有吸引力的 [yǒu xīyǐnlì de]

engine [ˈɛndʒɪn] N [c] **1** (AUT) 发动机 [fādòngjī] **2** (RAIL) 机车 [jīchē]

engineer [ɛndʒɪˈnɪə(r)] I N [c] **1** (*who designs machines, bridges etc*) 工程师 [gōngchéngshī] **2** (*who repairs machines, phones etc*) 机械师 [jīxièshī] **3** (US) (*train driver*) 火车司机 [huǒchē sījī] **4** (*on ship*) 轮机员 [lúnjīyuán] II VT **1** [+ *bridge, building etc*] 设计 [shèjì] **2** (*fig*) [+ *situation, event*] 策划 [cèhuà]

engineering [ɛndʒɪˈnɪərɪŋ] N [U] **1** (*design,*

construction) (*of roads, bridges, machinery*) 工程 [gōngchéng] **2** (*science*) 工程学 [gōngchéngxué] ► **engineering works** or **factory** 机械工厂

England ['ɪŋɡlənd] N 英格兰 [Yīnggélán]

English ['ɪŋɡlɪʃ] **I** ADJ 英国的 [Yīngguóde] **II** N (*language*) 英语 [Yīngyǔ] **III the English** NPL (*people*) 英国人 [Yīngguórén] ► **an English speaker** 一个讲英语的人

English Channel N ► **the English Channel** 英吉利海峡 [Yīngjílì Hǎixiá]

Englishman ['ɪŋɡlɪʃmən] (*pl* **Englishmen**) N [C] 英格兰男人 [Yīnggélán nánrén]

Englishwoman ['ɪŋɡlɪʃwumən] (*pl* **Englishwomen**) N [C] 英格兰女人 [Yīnggélán nǚrén]

engrave [ɪn'ɡreɪv] VT 雕刻 [diāokè]

engraving [ɪn'ɡreɪvɪŋ] N [C] (*picture, print*) 雕刻品 [diāokèpǐn]

engrossed [ɪn'ɡrəust] ADJ ► **engrossed in** [+ *book, programme*] 全神贯注于 [quán shén guàn zhù yú]

enhance [ɪn'hɑːns] VT **1** [+ *enjoyment, beauty, value*] 增加 [zēngjiā] **2** [+ *reputation*] 提高 [tígāo]

enjoy [ɪn'dʒɔɪ] VT **1** (*take pleasure in*) [+ *life, marriage*] 享受…的乐趣 [xiǎngshòu…de lèqù] **2** (*frm*) (*have benefit of*) [+ *good health, privilege*] 享有 [xiǎngyǒu] ► **to enjoy doing sth** (*like doing*) 喜欢做某事 ► **to enjoy o.s.** 过得快活 ► **enjoy your meal!** 吃好！

enjoyable [ɪn'dʒɔɪəbl] ADJ 有乐趣的 [yǒu lèqù de]

enjoyment [ɪn'dʒɔɪmənt] N [U] 乐趣 [lèqù]

enlarge [ɪn'lɑːdʒ] **I** VT **1** (*make bigger*) 扩大 [kuòdà] **2** (PHOT) 放大 [fàngdà] **II** VI 增大 [zēngdà] ► **to enlarge on** or **upon** (*frm*) [+ *subject*] 详述

enlargement [ɪn'lɑːdʒmənt] N **1** [U] (*expansion*) 扩大 [kuòdà] **2** [C] (PHOT) 放大的照片 [fàngdà de zhàopiàn]

enlightened [ɪn'laɪtnd] ADJ [+ *person, policy, system*] 开明的 [kāimíng de]

enlist [ɪn'lɪst] **I** VI (MIL) 应募 [yìngmù] **II** VT **1** (MIL) 征募 [zhēngmù] **2** [+ *support, help*] 赢得 [yíngdé] ► **enlisted man** (US: MIL) 士兵

enormous [ɪ'nɔːməs] ADJ **1** (*in size or amount*) [+ *room, dog*] 庞大的 [pángdà de] **2** (*in degree or extent*) [+ *pleasure, success, disappointment*] 巨大的 [jùdà de]

◐ **enough** [ɪ'nʌf] **I** ADJ [+ *time, books, people*] 足够的 [zúgòu de] ▷ *They had enough cash for a one-way ticket.* 他们有足够的现金支付单程票。 **II** PRON (*sufficient, more than desired*) 足够的东西 [zúgòu de dōngxi] ▷ *I've got five thousand dollars, I hope it's enough.* 我有5000美金，希望足够了。▷ *I only met him once, and that was enough.* 我只见过他一次，足已了。 **III** ADV

1 ► **big/old/tall enough** 足够大/到年龄了/足够高 [zúgòu dà/dào niánlíng le/zúgòu gāo] **2** (*reasonably*) ► **it's nice/interesting enough** 相当好/相当有趣 [xiāngdāng hǎo/xiāngdāng yǒuqù] ► **enough time/money to do sth** 有足够的时间/金钱去做某事 [yǒu zúgòu de shíjiān/jīnqián qù zuò mǒushì] ► **he has not worked enough** 他工作不够努力 ► **have you got enough?** 你够吗？ ► **enough to eat** 够吃 ► **will 5 be enough?** 5个够吗？ ► **I've had enough!** 我受够了！ ► **it's hot/difficult enough as it is** 已经够热/难的了 ► **he was kind enough to lend me the money** 他很仁慈，借钱给我 ► **(that's) enough!** 够了！ ► **I've had enough of him** 我已经受够他了 ► **that's enough, thanks** 足已，谢谢 ► **funnily/interestingly enough...** 说来也奇怪/有趣…

enquire [ɪn'kwaɪə(r)] VT, VI = **inquire**

enquiry [ɪn'kwaɪərɪ] N = **inquiry**

enrage [ɪn'reɪdʒ] VT 激怒 [jīnù]

enrich [ɪn'rɪtʃ] VT **1** (*improve*) 使丰富 [shǐ fēngfù] **2** (*financially*) 使富裕 [shǐ fùyù]

enrol, (US) **enroll** [ɪn'rəul] **I** VT **1** (*at school, university*) 招…入学 [zhāo…rùxué] **2** (*on course, in club*) 注册 [zhùcè] **II** VI (*at school, university, on course, in club*) 注册 [zhùcè]

enrolment, (US) **enrollment** [ɪn'rəulmənt] N [U] (*registration*) 注册 [zhùcè]

en route [ɔn'ruːt] ADV (*on the way*) 在途中 [zài túzhōng] ► **en route to/from** 在去/从…来的途中

en suite ['ɔnswiːt] (BRIT) ADJ **1** [+ *bathroom*] 接连的 [jiēlián de] **2** [+ *bedroom*] 带浴室的 [dài yùshì de]

ensure [ɪn'ʃuə(r)] (*frm*) VT [+ *success, safety*] 保证 [bǎozhèng] ► **to ensure that...** 保证…

entail [ɪn'teɪl] VT (*involve*) 牵涉 [qiānshè]

enter ['ɛntə(r)] **I** VT **1** (*frm*) [+ *room, building*] 进入 [jìnrù] **2** [+ *army, profession, Parliament*] 入 [rù] **3** [+ *race, competition*] 参加 [cānjiā] **4** [+ *new phase, period*] 开始进入 [kāishǐ jìnrù] **5** (*write down*) (*in book*) 登录 [dēnglù] **6** (COMPUT) [+ *data*] 输入 [shūrù] **II** VI (*frm*) (*come or go in*) 进来 [jìnlái] ► **to enter sb for sth** (*for competition, race*) 给某人报名参加某事 ► **as the war enters its second month** 当战争进入第2个月时
► **enter for** VT FUS [不可拆分] [+ *race, competition*] 报名参加 [bàomíng cānjiā]
► **enter into** (*frm*) VT FUS [不可拆分] **1** [+ *agreement, talks*] 开始进入 [kāishǐ jìnrù] **2** (*be relevant to*) 构成…的一部分 [gòuchéng…de yībùfen]

enterprise ['ɛntəpraɪz] N **1** [C] (*company, business*) 企业 [qǐyè] **2** [C] (*venture*) 事业 [shìyè] **3** [U] (*initiative*) 事业心 [shìyèxīn] ► **free enterprise** 自由企业 ► **private enterprise** 私营企业

enterprising [ˈɛntəpraɪzɪŋ] ADJ 有进取心的 [yǒu jìnqǔxīn de]

entertain [ɛntəˈteɪn] I VT **1** (amuse) 给…娱乐 [gěi…yúlè] **2** (invite) [+ guest] 招待 [zhāodài] **3** (frm) (consider idea, suggestion) 考虑 [kǎolǜ] II VI 款待 [kuǎndài]

entertainer [ɛntəˈteɪnə(r)] N [c] 表演者 [biǎoyǎnzhě]

entertaining [ɛntəˈteɪnɪŋ] I ADJ 引人入胜的 [yǐn rén rù shèng de] II N [U] 招待 [zhāodài]

entertainment [ɛntəˈteɪnmənt] N **1** [U] (amusement) 娱乐活动 [yúlè huódòng] **2** [c] (show) 表演会 [biǎoyǎnhuì]

enthusiasm [ɪnˈθuːzɪæzəm] N **1** [U] (eagerness) 热情 [rèqíng] **2** [c] (interest) 兴趣 [xìngqù] ▶ **enthusiasm for sth** 对某事的热情

enthusiast [ɪnˈθuːzɪæst] N [c] (fan) 爱好者 [àihàozhě] ▶ **a jazz enthusiast** 爵士乐爱好者

enthusiastic [ɪnθuːzɪˈæstɪk] ADJ (excited, eager) [+ person] 极感兴趣的 [jí gǎn xìngqù de]; [+ response, reception] 热情的 [rèqíng de] ▶ **to be enthusiastic about sth** 对某事满怀热情

entire [ɪnˈtaɪə(r)] ADJ 整个的 [zhěnggè de]

entirely [ɪnˈtaɪəlɪ] ADV 完全地 [wánquán de]

entitle [ɪnˈtaɪtl] VT ▶ **to entitle sb to sth** 给某人获得某物的资格 [gěi mǒurén huòdé mǒuwù de zīgé] ▶ **to entitle sb to do sth** 给某人做某事的权利 ▶ **to be entitled to sth** 有资格获得某物 ▶ **to be entitled to do sth** 有资格做某事

entitled [ɪnˈtaɪtld] ADJ [+ book, film etc] ▶ **entitled "The Next Generation"** 题为"下一代" [tí wéi "xiàyīdài]

entity [ˈɛntɪtɪ] (frm) N [c] 实体 [shítǐ]

entrance[1] [ˈɛntrns] N [c] **1** (way in) 入口 [rùkǒu] **2** (arrival) 到场 [dàochǎng] ▶ **the entrance to sth** 某处的入口 ▶ **to gain entrance to** [+ university, profession etc] 加入; (frm) [+ place] 能够进入 ▶ **to deny sb entrance** 拒绝让某人入场

entrance[2] [ɪnˈtrɑːns] VT (enchant) 使入迷 [shǐ rùmí]

entrance examination N [c] 入学考试 [rùxué kǎoshì]

entrance fee N [c] 入场费 [rùchǎngfèi]

entrance ramp (US: AUT) N [c] 通向高速公路的岔道 [tōngxiàng gāosù gōnglù de chàdào] [英= **slip road**]

entrant [ˈɛntrnt] N [c] **1** (in competition) 参赛者 [cānsàizhě] **2** (BRIT: SCOL, UNIV) 新学员 [xīn xuéyuán]

entrepreneur [ˈɔntrəprəˈnəː(r)] N [c] 企业家 [qǐyèjiā]

entrust [ɪnˈtrʌst] VT ▶ **to entrust sth to sb** 交托某事给某人 [jiāotuō mǒushì gěi mǒurén] ▶ **to entrust sb with sth** 把某事委托给某人

entry [ˈɛntrɪ] N **1** [c] (way in) 入口 [rùkǒu] **2** [c] (in competition) 登记 [dēngjì] **3** [c] (item) (in diary) 项目 [xiàngmù]; (COMPUT) 输入 [shūrù];

(in reference book) 条目 [tiáomù] **4** [U] (arrival) (in country) 进入权 [jìnrùquán]; (in room) 入场 [rùchǎng]; (in institution) 加入 [jiārù] ▶ **"no entry"** (to land, room) "禁止入内"; (AUT) "禁止通行" ▶ **single/double entry book-keeping** (COMM) 单/复式记账

envelope [ˈɛnvələup] N [c] 信封 [xìnfēng]

envious [ˈɛnvɪəs] ADJ [+ person, glance] 羡慕的 [xiànmù de] ▶ **to be envious of sth/sb** 羡慕某物/某人

environment [ɪnˈvaɪrnmənt] N [c/U] (surroundings) 环境 [huánjìng] ▶ **the environment** (natural world) 自然环境

environmental [ɪnvaɪərnˈmɛntl] ADJ **1** (of the natural world) 环境保护的 [huánjìng bǎohù de] **2** (of surroundings) 有关环境的 [yǒuguān huánjìng de] ▶ **environmental studies** (SCOL) 环境学

environmentalist [ɪnvaɪərnˈmɛntlɪst] N [c] 环境保护论者 [huánjìng bǎohùlùn zhě]

environmentally [ɪnvaɪərnˈmɛntlɪ] ADV ▶ **environmentally sound/harmful** etc 环境上有利/有害〔等〕的 [huánjìng shang yǒulì/yǒuhài {děng} de]

environmentally friendly ADJ 不污染环境的 [bù wūrǎn huánjìng de]

envisage [ɪnˈvɪzɪdʒ] VT (foresee) 设想 [shèxiǎng] ▶ **I envisage that...** 我设想…

envision [ɪnˈvɪʒn] (US) VT = **envisage**

envoy [ˈɛnvɔɪ] N [c] (diplomat) 使者 [shǐzhě]

envy [ˈɛnvɪ] I N [U] (jealousy) 羡慕 [xiànmù] II VT (be jealous of) 羡慕 [xiànmù] ▶ **to envy sb sth** 羡慕某人的某物

epic [ˈɛpɪk] I N [c] (book, film, poem) 史诗 [shǐshī] II ADJ [+ journey] 英雄的 [yīngxióng de]

epidemic [ɛpɪˈdɛmɪk] I N [c] (of disease) 流行 [liúxíng] II ADJ 流行性的 [liúxíngxing de]

epilepsy [ˈɛpɪlɛpsɪ] N [U] 癫痫 [diānxián]

epileptic fit [ɛpɪˈlɛptɪk-] N [c] 癫痫发作 [diānxián fāzuò]

episode [ˈɛpɪsəud] N [c] **1** (period, event) 插曲 [chāqǔ] **2** (TV, RAD) (instalment) 集 [jí]

epitomize [ɪˈpɪtəmaɪz] VT 集中体现 [jízhōng tǐxiàn]

equal [ˈiːkwl] I ADJ **1** [+ size, number, amount] 相等的 [xiāngděng de] **2** [+ intensity, importance] 同样的 [tóngyàng de] II N [c] (peer) 相仿的人 [xiāngfǎng de rén] III VT **1** [+ number, amount] 等于 [děngyú] **2** (match, rival) 比得上 [bǐdéshàng] ▶ **they are roughly equal in size** 它们大小差不多 ▶ **to be equal to** (the same as) 与…相同 ▶ **to be equal to a task/demand** 胜任一项任务/要求 ▶ **79 minus 14 equals 65** 79减14等于65

equality [iːˈkwɔlɪtɪ] N [U] 平等 [píngděng] ▶ **equality of opportunity** 机会均等

equalize [ˈiːkwəlaɪz] I VI (BRIT: FOOTBALL ETC) 拉平比分 [lāpíng bǐfēn] II VT (balance) [+ society, *opportunities*] 使平等 [shǐ píngděng]

equally ['iːkwəlɪ] ADV 1 [*share, divide etc +*] 平等地 [píngděng de] 2 [*good, important etc*] 同样地 [tóngyàng de] ▶ **they are equally clever** 他们同样聪明 ▶ **equally,...** (*introducing clause*) 同时，…

equation [ɪ'kweɪʒən] (MATH) N [C] 等式 [děngshì]

equator [ɪ'kweɪtə(r)] N ▶ **the equator** 赤道 [chìdào]

Equatorial Guinea [ɛkwə'tɔːrɪəl'gɪnɪ] N 赤道几内亚 [Chìdào Jǐnèiyà]

equilibrium [iːkwɪ'lɪbrɪəm] N 1 [C/U] (*balance*) 平衡 [pínghéng] 2 [U] (*composure*) 心境的安宁 [xīnjìng de ānníng]

equip [ɪ'kwɪp] VT 1 ▶ **to equip (with)** [*+ person, army*] 装备 [zhuāngbèi] 2 [*+ room, car etc*] 配备 [pèibèi] ▶ **to equip sb for sth/to do sth** (*prepare*) 为某事/做某事使某人做好准备 ▶ **to be well equipped** 装备充分的

equipment [ɪ'kwɪpmənt] N [U] 设备 [shèbèi]

equivalent [ɪ'kwɪvələnt] I ADJ 相同的 [xiāngtóng de] II N [C] (*equal*) 相当的人/物 [xiāngdāng de rén/wù] ▶ **the equivalent of** (*amount etc*) …的等值物 ▶ **to be equivalent to** 与…相等

ER I N ABBR (US: MED) (= *emergency room*) 急诊室 [jízhěnshì] [英= A & E *or* casualty] II ABBR (BRIT) (= *Elizabeth Regina*) 伊丽莎白女王 [Yīlìshābái nǚwáng]

era ['ɪərə] N [C] 时代 [shídài] ▶ **the post-war era** 战后年代

erase [ɪ'reɪz] VT 1 [*+ words, mark*] 擦掉 [cādiào] 2 [*+ sound from tape etc*] 抹掉 [mǒdiào] 3 (*fig*) [*+ thought, memory*] 消除 [xiāochú]

eraser [ɪ'reɪzə(r)] (ESP US) N 橡皮 [xiàngpí] [英= rubber]

erect [ɪ'rɛkt] I ADJ 1 [*+ person, posture*] 挺直的 [tǐngzhí de] 2 [*+ tail, ears*] 竖起的 [shùqǐ de] 3 [*+ penis*] 勃起的 [bóqǐ de] II VT (*frm*) (*build*) [*+ building, bridge*] 架设 [jiàshè]; (*assemble*) [*+ barrier*] 设置 [shèzhì] ▶ **to hold o.s. erect** 把身子挺直

erection [ɪ'rɛkʃən] N 1 [U] (*of building, statue*) 建造 [jiànzào] 2 [U] (*of tent, fence etc*) 架设 [jiàshè] 3 [C] (PHYSIOL) 勃起 [bóqǐ]

Eritrea [ɛrɪ'treɪə] N 厄立特里亚 [Èlìtèlǐyà]

erode [ɪ'rəud] I VT 1 [*+ soil, rock*] 侵蚀 [qīnshí] 2 (*frm*) [*+ confidence, authority*] 削弱 [xuēruò] II VI 1 [*soil, rock +*] 遭侵蚀 [zāo qīnshí] 2 (*frm*) [*confidence, authority +*] 削弱 [xuēruò]

erosion [ɪ'rəuʒən] N [U] 1 [*of soil, rock*] 侵蚀 [qīnshí] 2 (*frm*) [*of confidence, authority, freedom*] 削弱 [xuēruò]

erotic [ɪ'rɔtɪk] ADJ 1 [*+ experience, dream*] 引起性欲的 [yǐnqǐ xìngyù de] 2 [*+ books, films*] 色情的 [sèqíng de]

errand ['ɛrənd] N [C] 差事 [chāshì] ▶ **to run**

errands 跑腿 ▶ **to go on an errand** 跑腿 ▶ **an errand of mercy** 仁慈之行

erratic [ɪ'rætɪk] ADJ [*+ behaviour, progress*] 不规则的 [bù guīzé de]

error ['ɛrə(r)] N [C/U] 差错 [chācuò] ▶ **to make an error** 犯错误 ▶ **typing/mathematical error** 打字/算术差错 ▶ **in error** 错误地

erupt [ɪ'rʌpt] VI 1 [*volcano +*] 喷发 [pēnfā] 2 [*war, crisis +*] 爆发 [bàofā]

eruption [ɪ'rʌpʃən] N 1 [C/U] [*of volcano*] 喷发 [pēnfā] 2 [C] [*of conflict, violence*] 爆发 [bàofā]

escalate ['ɛskəleɪt] I VI [*conflict, crisis +*] 逐步升级 [zhúbù shēngjí] II VT [*+ conflict, crisis*] 使逐步升级 [shǐ zhúbù shēngjí]

escalator ['ɛskəleɪtə(r)] N [C] 自动扶梯 [zìdòng fútī]

escape [ɪs'keɪp] I N 1 [C/U] (*from prison*) 逃跑 [táopǎo] 2 (*from accident*) ▶ **a narrow/lucky escape** 九死一生 [jiǔ sǐ yī shēng] 3 [C] (*from person*) 逃脱 [táotuō] 4 [C] (*fig*) 逃避 [táobì] II VI 1 (*get away*) 逃走 [táozǒu] 2 (*from jail*) 逃跑 [táopǎo] 3 (*from accident*) ▶ **to escape unhurt** 安然逃脱 [ānrán táotuō] 4 (*leak*) [*gas, liquid, heat +*] 漏出 [lòuchū] III VT [*+ injury*] 避免 [bìmiǎn] ▶ **to escape from** [*+ place*] 从…逃跑; [*+ person*] 逃离 ▶ **to escape to** (*another place*) 逃往 (某处) ▶ **to escape to safety** 安全逃走 ▶ **his name escapes me** 我想不起他的名字 ▶ **to escape sb's attention** 避开某人的注意

escort [n 'ɛskɔːt, vb ɪs'kɔːt] I N [C] 1 (MIL) 护卫 [hùwèi] 2 (*companion*) 陪同 [péitóng] II VT [*+ person*] 护送 [hùsòng] ▶ **under escort** 被护送 ▶ **to escort sb to the door** 送某人到门口

Eskimo ['ɛskɪməu] N [C] (*person*) 爱斯基摩人 [Àisījīmórén]

esp. ABBR (= *especially*) 尤其 [yóuqí]

especially [ɪs'pɛʃlɪ] ADV 1 (*particularly*) 尤其 [yóuqí] 2 (*more than usually*) [*+ happy, gifted, fond of sb*] 特别 [tèbié]

espionage ['ɛspɪənɑːʒ] (POL, MIL, COMM) N [U] 间谍活动 [jiàndié huódòng]

essay ['ɛseɪ] N 1 (SCOL) 论文 [lùnwén] 2 (*paper, discussion*) 散文 [sǎnwén]

essence ['ɛsns] N 1 [U] (*true nature*) 本质 [běnzhì] 2 [C/U] (CULIN) 香精 [xiāngjīng] ▶ **in essence** (*frm*) 基本上 ▶ **speed is of the essence** (*frm*) 速度是至关重要的

essential [ɪ'sɛnʃl] I ADJ 1 (*necessary, vital*) 必要的 [bìyào de] 2 (*basic*) 基本的 [jīběn de] II **essentials** NPL (*necessities*) 必需品 [bìxūpǐn] ▶ **it is essential that...** …是必要的 ▶ **it is essential to...** 必须…

essentially [ɪ'sɛnʃəlɪ] (*frm*) ADV 1 (*basically*) 基本来说 [jīběn lái shuō] 2 (*mainly*) 大致上 [dàzhì shang]

EST (US) ABBR (= *Eastern Standard Time*) 东部标准时间 [Dōngbù Biāozhǔn Shíjiān]

establish [ɪs'tæblɪʃ] VT 1 (*set up*) [*+ company,*

relations, contact] 建立 [jiànlì] **2** (find out) [+ facts, cause] 证实 [zhèngshí] **3** (acquire) [+ reputation] 确立 [quèlì] ▶ **to establish that...** (frm) 证实⋯

established [ɪs'tæblɪʃt] ADJ **1** [+ organization] 已被确认的 [yǐ bèi quèrèn de] ▷ the established church 国教 **2** [+ custom, practice] 历时已久的 [lìshí yǐjiǔ de]

establishment [ɪs'tæblɪʃmənt] N **1** [U] (frm) [of organization, company etc] 建立 [jiànlì] **2** [C] (frm) (shop, restaurant etc) 机构 [jīgòu] **3** ▶ **the Establishment** 领导集团 [lǐngdǎo jítuán]

estate [ɪs'teɪt] N [C] **1** (land) 庄园 [zhuāngyuán] **2** (BRIT) (also: housing estate) 住宅区 [zhùzháiqū] **3** (LAW) (money and property) 遗产 [yíchǎn]

estate agent (BRIT) N [C] 房地产经纪人 [fángdìchǎn jīngjìrén] [美= **realtor** or **real estate agent**]

estate car (BRIT) N [C] 旅行车 [lǚxíngchē] [美= **station wagon**]

esthetic [ɪs'θetɪk] (US) ADJ = **aesthetic**

estimate [n 'estɪmət, vb 'estɪmeɪt] I N [C] **1** (calculation) 估计 [gūjì] **2** (assessment) 评估 [pínggū] **3** (COMM) [of price] 估价 [gūjià] II VT (reckon, calculate) 估计 [gūjì] ▶ **the damage was estimated at 300 million pounds** 估计损失为 3亿英镑 ▶ **I estimate that...** 我估计⋯

Estonia [es'təʊnɪə] N 爱沙尼亚 [Àishāníyà]

Estonian [es'təʊnɪən] I ADJ 爱沙尼亚的 [Àishāníyà de] II N **1** [C] (person) 爱沙尼亚人 [Àishāníyàrén] **2** [U] (language) 爱沙尼亚语 [Àishāníyàyǔ]

ETA N ABBR (= estimated time of arrival) 估计到达 时间 [gūjì dàodá shíjiān]

etc, (ESP US) **etc.** ABBR (= et cetera) 等等 [děngděng]

eternal [ɪ'tə:nl] ADJ **1** (everlasting) [+ youth, life] 永久的 [yǒngjiǔ de] **2** (unchanging) [+ truths, questions, values] 永恒的 [yǒnghéng de]

eternity [ɪ'tə:nɪtɪ] (REL) N [U] 永生 [yǒngshēng] ▶ **it seemed to last for an eternity** (inf) 时间长得似乎无穷无尽

ethical [ˈɛθɪkl] ADJ **1** (relating to ethics) [+ question, problem] 伦理的 [lúnlǐ de] **2** (morally right) 合乎 道德的 [héhū dàodé de]

ethics [ˈɛθɪks] I N [U] (study of moral philosophy) 伦理学 [lúnlǐxué] II NPL (morality) 道德准则 [dàodé zhǔnzé]

Ethiopia [iː'θɪəupɪə] N 埃塞俄比亚 [Àisài'ébǐyà]

Ethiopian [iː'θɪəupɪən] I ADJ 埃塞俄比亚的 [Àisài'ébǐyà de] II N [C] (person) 埃塞俄比亚人 [Àisài'ébǐyàrén]

ethnic [ˈɛθnɪk] ADJ **1** [+ population] 种族的 [zhǒngzú de] **2** [+ music, culture etc] 具有民族特 色的 [jùyǒu mínzú tèsè de]

ethnic minority N [C] 少数民族 [shǎoshù mínzú]

etiquette [ˈɛtɪkɛt] N [U] 礼节 [lǐjié]

EU N ABBR (= European Union) ▶ **the EU** 欧洲共 同体 [Ōuzhōu Gòngtóngtǐ]

euro [ˈjuərəu] (pl **euros**) N [C] 欧元 [Ōuyuán]

Europe [ˈjuərəp] N 欧洲 [Ōuzhōu]

European [juərə'piːən] I ADJ 欧洲的 [Ōuzhōu de] II N [C] (person) 欧洲人 [Ōuzhōurén]

European Community (formerly) N ▶ **the European Community** 欧洲共同市场 [Ōuzhōu Gòngtóng Shìchǎng]

European Union N ▶ **the European Union** 欧洲共同体 [Ōuzhōu Gòngtóngtǐ]

evacuate [ɪ'vækjueɪt] VT **1** [+ people] 疏散 [shùsàn] **2** [+ place] 撤离 [chèlí]

evade [ɪ'veɪd] VT **1** [+ tax] 逃避 [táobì] **2** [+ question, issue] 回避 [huíbì] **3** [+ duty, responsibility] 规避 [guībì] **4** (elude) [+ person] 逃 脱 [táotuō]; (liter) [happiness, love +] 回避 [huíbì] ▶ **to evade capture** 逃脱擒拿

evaluate [ɪ'væljueɪt] VT [+ situation, importance] 评估 [pínggū]

evaporate [ɪ'væpəreɪt] VI **1** [liquid +] 挥发 [huīfā] **2** (fig) [anger, fear, hopes +] 消失 [xiāoshī]

eve [iːv] N ▶ **on the eve of** 在⋯的前夕 [zài⋯de qiánxī]

◐ even [ˈiːvn] I ADV 甚至 [shènzhì] ▷ He didn't even hear what I said. 他甚至根本没听见我的 话。II ADJ **1** (flat) 平坦的 [píngtǎn de] ▷ The road isn't very even. 路很不平坦。**2** (constant) [+ temperature, rate] 平稳的 [píngwěn de] **3** (equal) [+ contest, score] 势均力敌的 [shì jūn lì dí de] ▷ It was an even contest. 这是一场势均 力敌的较量。; [+ distribution] 均等的 [jūnděng de] ▷ a more even distribution of wealth 更加均 等的财富分配 **4** [+ number] 偶数的 [ǒushù de] ▷ houses with even numbers 带偶数门牌号的房子 ▶ **even more** 甚至更多 ▶ **even better/faster** 甚至更好/快 ▶ **even if** 即使 ▶ **even though** 尽管 ▶ **even so** 虽然如此 ▶ **not even** 连⋯也 不 ▶ **even as** (liter) 正当 ▶ **even he was there** 连他都在那儿 ▶ **even on Sundays** 甚至星期 天 ▶ **to break even** 不盈不亏 ▶ **now we're even** (inf) 现在我们两清了 ▶ **to get even with sb** (inf) 报复某人
▶ **even out** I VI 拉平 [lāpíng] II VT 使均匀 [shǐ jūnyún]

evening [ˈiːvnɪŋ] N [C/U] **1** (early) 傍 晚 [bàngwǎn] **2** (late) 晚上 [wǎnshang] **3** (whole period, event) 晚上 [wǎnshang] ▶ **in the evening** 在晚上 ▶ **this evening** 今晚 ▶ **tomorrow/yesterday evening** 明/昨晚

evening class N [C] 夜校 [yèxiào]

evening dress N **1** [C] (gown) 女装晚礼服 [nǚzhuāng wǎnlǐfú] **2** [U] (formal clothing) 晚礼 服 [wǎnlǐfú]

evenly [ˈiːvnlɪ] ADV [distribute, spread, breathe +] 均匀地 [jūnyún de]; [divide +] 均等地 [jūnděng de]

○**event** [ɪ'vent] N [C] **1** (occurrence) 事件 [shìjiàn] **2** (SPORT) 比赛项目 [bǐsài xiàngmù] ▶ **in the normal course of events** 按照事情自然发展的进程 ▶ **in the event of/that...** 如果···发生 ▶ **in the event** (BRIT) 到头来 ▶ **in any event** 不管怎样

eventful [ɪ'ventful] ADJ [+ day, life, game, journey] 丰富多彩的 [fēngfù duōcǎi de]

eventual [ɪ'ventʃuəl] ADJ [+ outcome, aim] 最终的 [zuìzhōng de]

eventually [ɪ'ventʃuəlɪ] ADV **1** (finally) 终于 [zhōngyú] **2** (ultimately) 最终 [zuìzhōng]

请勿将 **eventually** 和 **finally** 混淆。如果某事拖延了很久，或者经历了相当复杂的过程后终于发生了，可以说它 **eventually** 发生了。Eventually, they got to the hospital...I found Victoria Avenue eventually. **eventually** 还可以表示发生的一系列事情中的最后一件事，通常这最后的一件事是前面一系列事情的结果。Eventually, they were forced to return to England. 在经历了长期等待或期盼后，某事终于发生了，可以说它 **finally** 发生了。Finally, I went to bed...The heat of the sun finally became too much for me. **finally** 还可以表示发生的一系列事情当中最后的一件事。The sky turned red, then purple, and finally black.

○**ever** ['evə(r)] ADV **1** (at any time) 从来 [cónglái] ▷ Neither of us has ever been to Japan. 我们俩都从来没去过日本。▷ I forbid you ever to use that word! 我不允许你在任何时候用那个字眼！**2** (always) 总是 [zǒngshì] ▷ Ever hopeful, he continued to apply for jobs. 他总是满怀希望，又继续申请工作了。▶ **have you ever seen it/been there** etc? 你曾经见过它/去过那儿{等}吗？▶ **ever since** (adv) 从···以来 ▷ We have been friends ever since. 我们从那时以来一直是朋友。; (conj) 自从 [zìcóng] ▷ Jack has loved trains ever since he was a boy. 杰克自小就喜爱火车。▶ **why ever not?** 究竟为什么不呢？▶ **who ever would do such a thing?** 究竟谁会做这样的事？▶ **the best ever** 迄今最佳 ▶ **hardly ever** 几乎不 ▶ **better than ever** 前所未有的好 ▶ **she's ever so pretty** (BRIT: inf) 她非常漂亮 ▶ **I like him ever so much.** (BRIT: inf) 我很喜欢他。▶ **he's ever such a good dancer** (BRIT: inf) 他跳舞跳得很好 ▶ **thank you ever so much** 非常感谢你 ▶ **yours ever** (BRIT: o.f.) (in letters) 你永久的朋友 ▶ **as ever** 照常

evergreen ['evəgri:n] **I** N [C] 常绿植物 [chánglù zhíwù] **II** ADJ 常绿的 [chánglù de]

everlasting [evə'lɑ:stɪŋ] ADJ [+ love, life] 永恒的 [yǒnghéng de]

○**every** ['evrɪ] ADJ **1** (each) 每个 [měigè] ▶ **every village should have a post office** 每个村庄都应该有一个邮局 ▶ **every one of them** (people) 他们中的每个人; (objects) 每个 [měigè] **2** (all possible) 一切可能的 [yīqiè kěnéng de] ▶ **there is every chance that...** 很有可能··· ▶ **recipes for every occasion** 各个场合均适用的菜谱 ▶ **I have every confidence in him** 我对他有十足的信心 ▶ **I gave you every assistance** 我给你各种可能的援助 **3** (with time words) 每 [měi] ▶ **every day/week** 每天/周 ▶ **every Sunday** 每个星期天 ▶ **every other week** 每隔一周 ▶ **every other/third day** 每隔一天/每三天 ▶ **every few days/minutes** 每隔几天/分钟 ▶ **every now and then** or **again** 不时地 **4** (statistics) ▶ **one in every five people** 每五人中有一人 [měi wǔ rén zhōng yǒu yī rén]

用法参见 **each**

everybody ['evrɪbɒdɪ] PRON 每人 [měirén] ▶ **everybody knows about it** 谁都知道 ▶ **everybody else** 其他所有人

everyday ['evrɪdeɪ] ADJ **1** (daily) [+ life, routine] 日常的 [rìcháng de] **2** (usual, common) [+ problem, occurrence] 平常的 [píngcháng de]

everyone ['evrɪwʌn] PRON = **everybody**

请勿将 **everyone** 和 **every one** 混淆。**everyone** 总是指人，并且用作单数名词。Everyone likes him...On behalf of everyone in the school, I'd like to thank you... 在短语 **every one** 中，**one** 是代词，在不同的上下文当中，它能够指代任何人或事物。其后经常紧随单词 **of**, We've saved seeds from every one of our plants...Every one of them phoned me. 在这些例子当中，**every one** 是表达 **all** 的含义，而且语气更强烈。

○**everything** ['evrɪθɪŋ] PRON 所有事物 [suǒyǒu shìwù] ▶ **is everything OK?** 都还好吧？▶ **everything is ready** 所有都准备就绪 ▶ **he did everything possible** 他尽了最大努力

everywhere ['evrɪweə(r)] **I** ADV 各处 [gèchù] **II** PRON 所有地方 [suǒyǒu dìfang] ▶ **there's rubbish everywhere** 到处都是垃圾 ▶ **everywhere you go** 无论你去哪里

evict [ɪ'vɪkt] VT [+ squatter, tenant] 逐出 [zhúchū]

evidence ['evɪdns] N [U] **1** (proof) 根据 [gēnjù] **2** (LAW) (information) 证据 [zhèngjù]; (objects) 物证 [wùzhèng]; (testimony) 证言 [zhèngyán] **3** (signs, indications) 迹象 [jìxiàng] ▶ **to produce sth as evidence** (LAW) 提供某物作为证据 ▶ **to give evidence** (LAW) 作证 ▶ **to show evidence of sth** 表明某事 ▶ **to be in evidence** [quality +] 明显的; [soldiers, tourists etc +] 可看见的

evident ['evɪdnt] ADJ 明显的 [míngxiǎn de] ▶ **to be evident (to sb/that...)** (对某人来说/···) 显而易见

evidently ['evɪdntlɪ] ADV **1** (obviously) 明显地

[míngxiǎn de] **2** (apparently) 显然地 [xiǎnrán de]

evil ['iːvl] I ADJ 1 [+ person, system] 邪恶的 [xié'è de] II N 1 [U] (wickedness) 邪恶 [xié'è] 2 [c] (curse, scourge) 祸害 [huòhài] ► **the evils of alcohol** 酗酒的害处 ► **a necessary evil** 不可避免的邪恶

evoke [ɪ'vəuk] (frm) VT [+ feeling, memory] 引起 [yǐnqǐ]

evolution [iːvə'luːʃən] N [U] 1 (BIO) 进化 [jìnhuà] 2 (development) 演变 [yǎnbiàn]

evolve [ɪ'vɒlv] I VI 1 [animal, plant etc +] 演化 [yǎnhuà] 2 [plan, style, organization +] 逐步形成 [zhúbù xíngchéng] II VT [+ scheme, style] 发展 [fāzhǎn] ► **to evolve from sth** 从某物演化而来 ► **to evolve into sth** 演化成某物

ewe [juː] N [c] 母羊 [mǔyáng]

ex- [ɛks] PREFIX (former) [+ husband, president etc] 前 [qián] ► **my ex-wife** 我的前妻

exact [ɪg'zækt] I ADJ 1 (precise) [+ time, number, word etc] 确切的 [quèqiè de] 2 [+ person, worker] 严谨的 [yánjǐn de] 3 (used for emphasis) 恰恰 [qiàqià] II VT ► **to exact sth (from sb)** (frm) (向某人) 索取某物 [(xiàng mǒurén) suǒqǔ mǒuwù] ► **astrology is not an exact science** 占星术并不是一门精确的科学 ► **to be exact** 准确来说

exactly [ɪg'zæktlɪ] ADV 1 (precisely) 确切地 [quèqiè de] ▷ **It was exactly ten metres in height.** 一座正好10米高的塔。**2** (indicating emphasis) 正是 [zhèngshì] **3** (indicating agreement) 一点不错 [yīdiǎn bùcuò] ► **at 5 o'clock exactly** 在5点整时 ► **not exactly** (indicating disagreement) 不完全是 ► **he's not exactly rich/poor** 他一点也算不上富/穷

exaggerate [ɪg'zædʒəreɪt] I VI 夸张 [kuāzhāng] II VT 1 (overemphasize) [+ situation, effects] 夸大 [kuādà] 2 (draw attention to) [+ feature, quality +] 使扩大 [shǐ kuòdà]

exaggeration [ɪgzædʒə'reɪʃən] N [C/U] 夸张 [kuāzhāng]

exam [ɪg'zæm] N 测验 [cèyàn]

examination [ɪgzæmɪ'neɪʃən] N 1 [C/U] (inspection) [of object, plan, accounts] 检查 [jiǎnchá] 2 [c] (SCOL, UNIV) (exam) 考试 [kǎoshì] 3 [C/U] (MED) 体检 [tǐjiǎn] ► **the matter is under examination** 这件事尚在审查中

examine [ɪg'zæmɪn] VT 1 (inspect) [+ object, plan, accounts] 检查 [jiǎnchá] 2 (SCOL, UNIV) 对…进行测验 [duì…jìnxíng cèyàn] 3 (MED) 检查 [jiǎnchá]

examiner [ɪg'zæmɪnə(r)] (SCOL, UNIV) N [c] **1** (setting exam) 主考官 [zhǔkǎoguān] **2** (marking exam) 判卷官 [pànjuànguān]

⊙**example** [ɪg'zɑːmpl] N [c] 1 (typical illustration) 例子 [lìzi] 2 (model) (of good behaviour etc) 榜样 [bǎngyàng] ▷ **Their example shows us what we**

are all capable of. 他们树立的榜样显示出我们也都能做到些什么。► **for example** 例如 ► **an example of sth** 某物的例子 ► **to set an example** 树立榜样 ► **to follow sb's example** 学习某人的榜样 ► **he is an example to us all** 他是我们每一个人的楷模 ► **to make an example of sb** 惩罚某人以儆戒他人

exasperated [ɪg'zɑːspəreɪtɪd] ADJ ► **exasperated (at or by or with sth)** (被某事)搞得恼火 [(bèi mǒushì) gǎodé nǎohuǒ]

excavate ['ɛkskəveɪt] VT 1 [archaeologist +] 发掘 [fājué] 2 (frm) (dig) 挖掘 [wājué]

exceed [ɪk'siːd] (frm) VT 1 (be greater than) [+ number, amount, expectations] 超出 [chāochū] 2 (go beyond) [+ speed limit, budget] 超过 [chāoguò]; [+ powers, duties] 超越 [chāoyuè]

exceedingly [ɪk'siːdɪŋlɪ] (o.f.) ADV 极其 [jíqí]

excel [ɪk'sɛl] I VI ► **to excel (in/at)** [+ sports, business etc] 擅长 [shàncháng] II VT ► **to excel o.s.** 出类拔萃 [chūlèi bácuì]

excellence ['ɛksələns] N [U] 卓越 [zhuóyuè]

excellent ['ɛksələnt] I ADJ 极好的 [jíhǎo de] II INT ► **excellent!** 太好了! [tài hǎo le!]

except [ɪk'sɛpt] PREP (apart from) 除了 [chúle] ► **except for** 除了…外 ► **except that...** 除了… ► **except if/when** …时例外

exception [ɪk'sɛpʃən] N [c] (special case) 例外 [lìwài] ► **to make an exception** 破例 ► **with the exception of** 除…外 ► **to take exception (to sth)** (对某事) 不悦

exceptional [ɪk'sɛpʃənl] ADJ 1 (outstanding) [+ person, talent] 杰出的 [jiéchū de] 2 (frm) (unusual) [+ situation, circumstances] 独特的 [dútè de]

exceptionally [ɪk'sɛpʃənlɪ] ADV 格外 [géwài]

excerpt ['ɛksəːpt] N [c] (from text, film) 选录 [xuǎnlù]

excess [n ɪk'sɛs, 'ɛksɛs, adj 'ɛksɛs] I N 1 ► **an excess of** 过多 [guòduō] ▷ **Inflation results from an excess of demand over supply.** 通货膨胀是供过于求的结果。**2** [c] (BRIT: INSURANCE) 保险押金 [bǎoxiǎn yājīn] II ADJ [+ water, fat] 过多的 [guòduō de] III **excesses** NPL (of person, war) 过分的行为 [guòfèn de xíngwéi] ► **in excess of** 超过 ► **to do sth to excess** 过度做某事

excess baggage N [U] 超重行李 [chāozhòng xíngli]

excessive [ɪk'sɛsɪv] ADJ [+ amount, force] 过分的 [guòfèn de]

exchange [ɪks'tʃeɪndʒ] I VT 1 [+ gifts, addresses] 交换 [jiāohuàn] 2 [+ greetings, glances] 互换 [hùhuàn] ► **to exchange sth (for sth)** [+ goods] 用某物交换 (某物) [yòng mǒuwù jiāohuàn (mǒuwù)] II N 1 [C/U] (giving and receiving) [of information, views, gifts, prisoners] 交换 [jiāohuàn]; [of students, sportspeople etc] 交流 [jiāoliú] 2 [c] (frm) (conversation) 交锋 [jiāofēng] 3 [c] (also: **telephone exchange**) 电

话局 [diànhuàjú] ▶ **in exchange (for)** 作为 (对…的) 交换

exchange rate N [C] 汇率 [huìlǜ]

Exchequer [ɪks'tʃɛkə(r)] (BRIT) N ▶ **the Exchequer** 财政部 [cáizhèngbù]

excite [ɪk'saɪt] VT 1 [+ person] 刺激 [cìjī] 2 [+ enthusiasm, curiosity] 引起 [yǐnqǐ] 3 (sexually) 使兴奋 [shǐ xīngfèn]

excited [ɪk'saɪtɪd] ADJ 兴奋的 [xīngfèn de] ▶ **to be excited about sth/about doing sth** 对某事/做某事感到激动 ▶ **to get excited** 激动兴奋

excitement [ɪk'saɪtmənt] N [U] (exhilaration) 兴奋 [xīngfèn]

exciting [ɪk'saɪtɪŋ] ADJ [+ time, event, place] 令人兴奋的 [lìng rén xīngfèn de]

excl. ABBR (= excluding, exclusive of) 不含 [bùhán]

exclaim [ɪks'kleɪm] I VI 大声叫嚷 [dàshēng jiàorǎng] II VT ▶ **to exclaim that...** 叫喊… [jiàohǎn…]

exclamation [ɛksklə'meɪʃən] N [C] 惊叫 [jīngjiào]

exclamation mark (BRIT), **exclamation point** (US) N [C] 感叹号 [gǎntànhào]

exclude [ɪks'kluːd] VT 1 (leave out) [+ person] 把…排斥在外 [bǎ…páichì zàiwài]; [+ substance, fact] 不包括 [bù bāokuò] 2 (rule out) [+ possibility] 排除 [páichú] 3 [+ child] (from school) 开除 [kāichú] ▶ **to exclude sb from sth** (place, activity) 拒绝某人做某事 ▶ **to exclude sth from sth** 将某物排除于某物之外

excluding [ɪks'kluːdɪŋ] PREP 不包括 [bù bāokuò]

exclusion [ɪks'kluːʒən] N [C/U] 1 [of person, fact, possibility] 排除在外 [páichú zàiwài] 2 [of child] (from school) 开除 [kāichú] ▶ **to the exclusion of sth** 把某事除外

exclusive [ɪks'kluːsɪv] I ADJ 1 [+ club, district] 高级的 [gāojí de] 2 (PUBLISHING) [+ story, interview] 独家的 [dújiā de] II N [C] (PUBLISHING) 独家报道 [dújiā bàodào] ▶ **have exclusive use of sth** 有使用某物的专有权 ▶ **to be exclusive to sth** 只有某处才有的 ▶ **mutually exclusive** 互不相容 ▶ **exclusive of postage/tax** 不含邮费/税

exclusively [ɪks'kluːsɪvlɪ] ADV (only) 仅仅 [jǐnjǐn] (entirely) 完全 [wánquán]

excruciating [ɪks'kruːʃɪeɪtɪŋ] ADJ 1 [+ pain] 极其的 [jíqí de] 2 [+ boredom, embarrassment] 难以忍受的 [nányǐ rěnshòu de]

excursion [ɪks'kəːʃən] N [C] (trip) (by tourists) 游览 [yóulǎn]; (shopping etc) 短途旅行 [duǎntú lǚxíng] ▶ **to go on an excursion** 去旅行 ▶ **an excursion into** (fig) (venture) 涉猎于

excuse [n ɪks'kjuːs, vb ɪks'kjuːz] I N [C/U] (justification) 借口 [jièkǒu] II VT 1 (justify) [+ person, behaviour] 是…的正当理由 [shì…de zhèngdàng lǐyóu] 2 (forgive) [+ person, behaviour]

原谅 [yuánliàng] ▶ **an excuse to do/not to do sth** 做/不做某事的借口 ▶ **to make an excuse** 找借口 ▶ **to make excuses for sb** 给某人找借口 ▶ **there's no excuse for such behaviour** 没有理由这样表现 ▶ **to be excused from (doing) sth** 被免除 (做) 某事 ▶ **to excuse sb for sth/for doing sth** 原谅某人某事/做某事 ▶ **excuse me!** (attracting attention) 劳驾！; (as apology) 对不起！ ▶ **excuse me, please** 请原谅 ▶ **excuse me?** (US) 对不起，你说什么？ [英=pardon? or sorry?] ▶ **he excused himself and left the room** 他说了声"请原谅"就离开了房间 ▶ **if you'll excuse me** 请见谅

ex-directory ['ɛksdɪ'rɛktərɪ] (BRIT: TEL) ADJ [+ number] 未列入电话簿的 [wèi lièrù diànhuàbù de] [美=unlisted] ▶ **she's ex-directory** 她的电话未列入电话簿

execute ['ɛksɪkjuːt] VT 1 [+ person] 将…处死 [jiāng…chǔsǐ] 2 (frm) [+ plan, order] 实行 [shíxíng] 3 [+ manoeuvre] 完成 [wánchéng]

execution [ɛksɪ'kjuːʃən] N 1 [C/U] [of person] 处死刑 [chǔ sǐxíng] 2 [U] (frm) [of plan, order] 实施 [shíshī] 3 [U] [of manoeuvre] 完成 [wánchéng]

executive [ɪg'zɛkjutɪv] I N 1 [C] (person) 主管人员 [zhǔguǎn rényuán] 2 (committee) 执行委员会 [zhíxíng wěiyuánhuì] 3 (POL) ▶ **the executive** 政府行政部门 [zhèngfǔ xíngzhèng bùmén] II ADJ 1 [+ committee] 执行的 [zhíxíng de]; [+ role, decision] 行政的 [xíngzhèng de] 2 (for executives) [+ car] 豪华的 [háohuá de]; [+ plane] 专用的 [zhuānyòng de] ▶ **executive briefcase** 密码公文箱 ▶ **executive toy** 办公室的小玩意儿

exempt [ɪg'zɛmpt] I ADJ ▶ **exempt from** [+ duty, obligation] 免除的 [miǎnchú de] II VT ▶ **to exempt sb from sth** [+ duty, obligation] 免除某人某事 [miǎnchú mǒurén mǒushì]

exercise ['ɛksəsaɪz] I N 1 [U] (physical exertion) 运动 [yùndòng] 2 [C] (series of movements) 练习 [liànxí] 3 [C] (SCOL, MUS) 练习 [liànxí] 4 [C] (MIL) 演习 [yǎnxí] 5 [S] (frm) [of authority etc] 行使 [xíngshǐ] II VT 1 (use) [+ right, authority etc] 行使 [xíngshǐ]; [+ patience, restraint, care etc] 运用 [yùnyòng] 2 [+ muscles] 锻炼 [duànliàn]; [+ mind] 运用 [yùnyòng] 3 [+ dog] 遛 [liù] III VI (person +) 锻炼 [duànliàn] ▶ **to take or get exercise** 做健身活动 ▶ **to do exercises** (SPORT) 锻炼身体

exercise book (BRIT: SCOL) N [C] 练习本 [liànxíběn] [美=notebook]

exert [ɪg'zəːt] VT (frm) [+ influence, pressure] 施加 [shījiā] ▶ **to exert o.s.** 尽力

exertion [ɪg'zəːʃən] N [U] 尽力 [jìnlì]

exhale [ɛks'heɪl] (frm) I VI (breathe out) 呼气 [hūqì] II VT [+ air, smoke] 呼出 [hūchū]

exhaust [ɪg'zɔːst] I N (ESP BRIT) 1 [C] (also: exhaust pipe) 排气管 [páiqìguǎn] 2 [U] (fumes) 废气 [fèiqì] II VT 1 [+ person] 使精疲力竭 [shǐ jīng pí lì jié] 2 [+ money, resources etc] 耗尽

[hàojìn] **3** [+ topic] 详尽无遗地论述 [xiángjìn wú yí de lùnshù] ▶ **to exhaust o.s.** 精力力竭

exhausted [ɪgˈzɔːstɪd] ADJ (tired) 精疲力竭的 [jīng pí lì jié de]

exhaustion [ɪgˈzɔːstʃən] N [U] (tiredness) 精疲力竭 [jīng pí lì jié]

exhibit [ɪgˈzɪbɪt] I N [C] **1** (ART) 展览品 [zhǎnlǎnpǐn] **2** (LAW) 物证 [wùzhèng] II VT **1** [+ quality, emotion] 显示 [xiǎnshì] **2** [+ paintings] 展出 [zhǎnchū] III VI (ART) 展出作品 [zhǎnchū zuòpǐn]

exhibition [ɛksɪˈbɪʃən] N **1** [C] [of paintings etc] 展览会 [zhǎnlǎnhuì] **2** [S] (display) [of skill, talent etc] 表演 [biǎoyǎn] ▶ **to make an exhibition of o.s.** 出洋相

exhilarating [ɪgˈzɪləreɪtɪŋ] ADJ [+ experience, feeling] 使人兴奋的 [shǐ rén xīngfèn de]

exile [ˈɛksaɪl] I N **1** [U] (condition, state) 流亡 [liúwáng] **2** [C] (person) 流亡者 [liúwángzhě] II VT 使流亡 [shǐ liúwáng] ▶ **in exile** 在流亡中

exist [ɪgˈzɪst] VI **1** (be present) 存在 [cúnzài] **2** (live, subsist) 生存 [shēngcún] ▶ **to exist on sth** 靠某物生存

existence [ɪgˈzɪstəns] N **1** [U] (reality) 存在 [cúnzài] **2** [C] (life) 生活 [shēnghuó] ▶ **to be in existence** 存在的

existing [ɪgˈzɪstɪŋ] ADJ (present, actual) 现有的 [xiànyǒu de]

exit [ˈɛksɪt] I N [C] **1** (from room, building, motorway etc) 出口 [chūkǒu] **2** (departure) ▶ **to make a hasty/quick exit** 急速离去 [jísù líqù] II VT **1** (frm) [+ room, building] 离开 [líkāi] **2** (COMPUT) 退出 [tuìchū] III VI (THEAT) 退场 [tuìchǎng] ▶ **to exit from sth** (frm) [+ room, motorway etc] 离开某处

exit ramp (US: AUT) N [C] 离开高速公路的岔道 [líkāi gāosù gōnglù de chàdào] [英= **slip road**]

exotic [ɪgˈzɒtɪk] ADJ [+ food, place] 有异国情调的 [yǒu yìguó qíngdiào de]

expand [ɪksˈpænd] I VT **1** [+ business, staff, numbers] 扩展 [kuòzhǎn] **2** [+ area] 拓展 [tuòzhǎn] II VI **1** [business +] 扩展 [kuòzhǎn] **2** [gas, metal +] 膨胀 [péngzhàng] ▶ **to expand on sth** [+ notes, story, comments] 详述某事

expanse [ɪksˈpæns] N [C] [of sea, sky, land] 广阔 [guǎngkuò]

expansion [ɪksˈpænʃən] N **1** [C/U] [of business, population, economy] 扩展 [kuòzhǎn] **2** [U] [of gas, metal] 膨胀 [péngzhàng]

○ **expect** [ɪksˈpɛkt] I VT **1** (anticipate) 预料 [yùliào] ▷ I expect it will rain. 我预计会下雨。**2** (await) 期待 [qídài] ▷ I am expecting an important letter. 我正在等一封重要的信。**3** [+ baby] 怀有 [huáiyǒu] ▷ She was expecting her second child. 她正怀着她的第2个孩子。**4** (require) 期望 [qīwàng] ▷ They expect a good

tip. 他们期望得到不少小费。**5** (suppose) 料想 [liàoxiǎng] ▷ I expect you're tired. 我想你一定累了吧。II VI **1** ▶ **to be expecting** (be pregnant) 怀孕 [huáiyùn] ▶ **to expect sth to happen** 预期某事将会发生 ▶ **to expect sb to do sth** (anticipate) 期望某人做某事 ▷ I expected him to turn down the invitation. 我想他会谢绝这个邀请。; (require) 指望某人做某事 ▷ I wasn't expecting you to help. 我并没有指望你帮忙。▶ **to expect to do sth** 预计要做某事 ▶ **I expect so** 我想会的 ▶ **as expected** 如所预料的

expectation [ɛkspɛkˈteɪʃən] N [C/U] **1** (hope) 期望 [qīwàng] **2** (belief) 预计 [yùjì] ▶ **against or contrary to all expectation(s)** 出乎意料 ▶ **to live up to sb's expectations** 不负某人的期望 ▶ **in the expectation that…** 预计…

expedition [ɛkspəˈdɪʃən] N [C] **1** (to explore) 探险 [tànxiǎn] **2** (to go shopping, fishing) 出行 [chūxíng]

expel [ɪksˈpɛl] VT **1** [+ child] (from school) 把…开除 [bǎ…kāichù] **2** [+ person] (from place) 赶走 [gǎnzǒu] **3** [+ gas, liquid] 排出 [páichū]

expend [ɪksˈpɛnd] (frm) VT [+ money, time, energy] 花费 [huāfèi]

expenditure [ɪksˈpɛndɪtʃə(r)] N [C/U] [of money] 开支 [kāizhī] **2** [U] [of energy, time] 消耗 [xiāohào]

expense [ɪksˈpɛns] I N [C/U] (cost) 费用 [fèiyòng] II **expenses** NPL 经费 [jīngfèi] ▶ **to go to the expense of doing sth** 花钱于做某事 ▶ **at great expense** 以很大代价 ▶ **to do sth at one's own expense** 自己花钱做某事 ▶ **at the expense of** 以…为代价 ▶ **to make a joke at sb's expense** 说笑话让某人出丑

expense account N [C] 支出账 [zhīchūzhàng]

expensive [ɪksˈpɛnsɪv] ADJ **1** [+ article] 昂贵的 [ángguì de] **2** [+ mistake] 代价高的 [dàijià gāo de]; [+ tastes] 奢华的 [shēhuá de]

○ **experience** [ɪksˈpɪərɪəns] I N **1** [U] (in job) 经验 [jīngyàn] ▷ He has managerial experience. 他有管理经验。**2** [U] (of life) 阅历 [yuèlì] **3** [C] (individual event) 经历 [jīnglì] ▷ The funeral was a painful experience. 那次追悼会是个痛苦的经历。II VT [+ feeling, problem] 体验 [tǐyàn] ▶ **to know from experience** 根据经验知道 ▶ **to learn from experience** 从经验中学到

experienced [ɪksˈpɪərɪənst] ADJ 有经验的 [yǒu jīngyàn de]

experiment [n ɪksˈpɛrɪmənt, vb ɪksˈpɛrɪmɛnt] I N [C] **1** (SCI) 实验 [shíyàn] **2** (trial) 试用 [shìyòng] II VI **1** ▶ **to experiment (with/on)** (SCI) (用…) 做实验 [(yòng…) zuò shíyàn] **2** (fig) 试验 [shìyàn] ▶ **to perform or conduct or carry out an experiment** 做实验 ▶ **as an experiment** 作为实验 ▶ **an experiment in sth** 在某事上的试点

experimental [ɪkspɛrɪˈmɛntl] ADJ **1** (innovative) [+ methods, ideas, art forms] 实验

性的 [shíyànxìng de] **2** (SCI) [+ tests, results] 根据实验的 [gēnjù shíyàn de] ▶ **at the experimental stage** 处于试验阶段

expert ['ɛkspəːt] I N [C] (specialist) 专家 [zhuānjiā] II ADJ [+ opinion, help, advice] 专家 的 [zhuānjiā de] ▶ **an expert on sth** 某事的专 家 ▶ **expert in** or **at doing sth** 做某事的高手 ▶ **expert witness** (LAW) 专家证人

expertise [ɛkspəː'tiːz] N [U] 专门知识 [zhuānmén zhīshí]

expire [ɪks'paɪə(r)] VI **1** [passport, licence etc +] 过 期 [guòqī] **2** (liter) (die) 逝世 [shìshì]

expiry date N [C] [of credit card, passport, visa, contract etc] 到期日 [dàoqīrì]; (on drug, medicine) 有效期 [yǒuxiàoqī]

explain [ɪks'pleɪn] VT **1** (make understandable) [+ situation, contract] 解释 [jiěshì] **2** (give reasons for) [+ decision, actions] 阐明 [chǎnmíng] ▶ **to explain why/how** etc 解释为什么/如何{等} ▶ **to explain sth to sb** 向某人解释某事 ▶ **to explain that…** 解释… ▶ **explain away** VT [+ mistake, situation] 把…解 释过去 [bǎ…jiěshì guòqù]

explanation [ɛksplə'neɪʃən] N **1** [C/U] (reason) ▶ **explanation (for)** (对…的) 解释 [(duì…de) jiěshì] **2** [C] (description) ▶ **explanation (of)** (…的) 说明 [(…de) shuōmíng]

explanatory [ɪks'plænətrɪ] (frm) ADJ [+ statement, comment] 说明的 [shuōmíng de]

explicit [ɪks'plɪsɪt] ADJ **1** (clear) [+ support, permission] 明确的 [míngquè de] **2** (blatant) [+ sex, violence] 显然可见的 [xiǎnrán kě jiàn de] ▶ **to be explicit about sth** (frank) 对某事 直言不讳

explode [ɪks'pləud] I VI **1** [bomb +] 爆炸 [bàozhà] **2** [population +] 猛增 [měngzēng] **3** [person +] (with rage etc) 迸发 [bèngfā] ▷ Simon exploded with anger. 西蒙勃然大怒。 II VT **1** [+ bomb, tank] 使爆炸 [shǐ bàozhà] **2** [+ myth, theory] 戳穿 [chuōchuān]

exploit [n 'ɛksplɔɪt, vb ɪks'plɔɪt] I N (deed, feat) 英勇业绩 [yīngyǒng yèjì] II VT (make use of) [+ opportunity, talent] 利用 [lìyòng]; [+ resources] 开发 [kāifā]; (unfairly) [+ person, idea] 剥削 [bōxuē]

exploitation [ɛksplɔɪ'teɪʃən] N [U] [of person, idea] 剥削 [bōxuē] [of resources] 开发 [kāifā]

explore [ɪks'plɔː(r)] I VT **1** [+ place, space] 探索 [tànsuǒ] **2** (with hands) 探察 [tànchá] **3** [+ idea, suggestion] 探究 [tànjiū] II VI (look around) 探 险 [tànxiǎn] **2** ▶ **to explore for oil** 勘探石油 [kāntàn shíyóu]

explorer [ɪks'plɔːrə(r)] N [C] 探险者 [tànxiǎnzhě]

explosion [ɪks'pləuʒən] N [C] **1** [of bomb] 爆炸 [bàozhà] **2** (increase) [of population] 激增 [jīzēng] **3** (outburst) [of rage, laughter etc] 迸发 [bèngfā]

explosive [ɪks'pləusɪv] I ADJ **1** [+ device, effect] 爆炸的 [bàozhà de] **2** (fig) [+ situation, issue] 爆 炸性的 [bàozhàxìng de]; [+ person, temper] 暴躁 的 [bàozào de] II N [C/U] (substance, device) 炸 药 [zhàyào]

export [vb ɛks'pɔːt, n 'ɛkspɔːt] I VT [+ goods, ideas, problems, file] 输出 [shūchū] II N **1** [U] (process) 出口 [chūkǒu] **2** [C] (product) 出口 物 [chūkǒuwù] III CPD (复合词) [+ duty, permit, licence] 出口 [chūkǒu]

exporter [ɛks'pɔːtə(r)] N [C] 出口商 [chūkǒushāng]

expose [ɪks'pəuz] VT (reveal) [+ object] 显露 [xiǎnlù]; [+ impostor, scandal] 揭穿 [jiēchuān] ▶ **to expose sb to sth** (radiation, virus etc) 使某人 接触某物 ▶ **to expose o.s.** (LAW) 性暴露

exposed [ɪks'pəuzd] ADJ **1** [+ house, place etc] 无 遮蔽的 [wú zhēbì de] **2** (ELEC) [+ wire] 裸露的 [luǒlù de]

exposure [ɪks'pəuʒə(r)] N **1** [U] (to poison, radiation) ▶ **exposure (to)** 暴露 (在…中) [bàolù (zài…zhōng)] **2** [U] (MED) 冻伤 [dòngshāng] **3** [U] (publicity) 公开露面 [gōngkāi lòumiàn] **4** [U] [of wrongdoing, impostor] 揭露 [jiēlù] **5** [C] (PHOT) (shot) 软片 [ruǎnpiàn] ▷ a camera capable of taking a hundred exposures 能拍100张 照片的照相机; (amount of light) [C/U] 曝光量 [pùguāngliàng] ▶ **to die from** or **of exposure** (MED) 死于冻馁

express [ɪks'prɛs] I VT **1** [+ idea, view, concern] 表达 [biǎodá] **2** (frm) [+ quantity, number] ▶ **expressed as a percentage/fraction** etc 用 百分比/分数{等}表示的 [yòng bǎifēnbǐ/ fēnshù {děng} biǎoshì de] II ADJ **1** (frm) (clear) [+ command, wishes etc] 明确的 [míngquè de] **2** (deliberate) [+ purpose, intention] 专门的 [zhuānmén de] III N [C] (train, coach) 快车 [kuàichē] **IV** ADV [send +] 用快递 [yòng kuàidì] ▶ **to express o.s.** 表达自己的意思 ▶ **how does this attitude express itself?** 这个态度如何体 现出?

expression [ɪks'prɛʃən] N **1** [C] (word, phrase) 言辞 [yáncí] **2** [C/U] (on face) 表情 [biǎoqíng] **3** [C/U] [of idea, emotion] 表达 [biǎodá] **4** [U] (feeling) [of actor, singer etc] 感情 [gǎnqíng]

expressive [ɪks'prɛsɪv] ADJ [+ face] 富于表情 的 [fùyú biǎoqíng de] ▶ **expressive of** (frm) 表 达…的

expressway [ɪks'prɛsweɪ] (AUT) N [C] 高速公 路 [gāosù gōnglù]

exquisite [ɛks'kwɪzɪt] ADJ **1** (beautiful) [+ lace, workmanship] 精致的 [jīngzhì de] [+ taste] 高雅 的 [gāoyǎ de] **2** (liter) (keenly felt) [+ pleasure, relief] 极其的 [jíqí de]

ext. (TEL) ABBR (= extension) 分机 [fēnjī]

extend [ɪks'tɛnd] I VT **1** [+ visit] 延长 [yáncháng] **2** [+ building] 扩展 [kuòzhǎn] **3** [+ contract, deadline] 给…延期 [gěi…yánqī]

4 [+ *arm, hand*] 伸出 [shēnchū] **5** [+ *welcome, invitation*] 发出 [fāchū] **6** (COMM) [+ *credit*] 提供 [tígòng] **II** VI **1** [*land, road* +] 延伸 [yánshēn] **2** [*period* +] 延续 [yánxù] **3** [*influence, power etc* +] 延及 [yánjí] ▷ *His influence extends beyond the TV viewing audience.* 他的影响超出了电视观众的范围。▶ **to extend from** (*protrude*) 从…中伸出 ▶ **to extend to** (*include*) 涉及

extension [ɪksˈtɛnʃən] N [C] **1** [*of building*] 扩建部分 [kuòjiàn bùfen] **2** [*of contract, visa*] 延期 [yánqī] **3** [*of rights, campaign, idea*] 扩展 [kuòzhǎn] **4** (ELEC) 延长部分 [yáncháng bùfen] **5** [*of road, railway*] 附加部分 [fùjiā bùfen] **6** (*to wire, table*) 延伸部分 [yánshēn bùfen] **7** (TEL) 分机 [fēnjī] ▶ **extension 3718** (TEL) 3718分机

extensive [ɪksˈtɛnsɪv] ADJ **1** [+ *area, grounds*] 广阔的 [guǎngkuò de] **2** [+ *damage*] 巨大的 [jùdà de] **3** [+ *inquiries, discussion*] 广泛的 [guǎngfàn de] **4** [+ *use*] 大量的 [dàliàng de]

extent [ɪksˈtɛnt] N [U/S] **1** [*of area, land etc*] 大小 [dàxiǎo] **2** [*of problem, damage etc*] 程度 [chéngdù] ▶ **to a certain extent** 在一定程度上 ▶ **to a large extent** 在很大程度上 ▶ **to the extent of...** 到了…地步 ▶ **to some extent** 在某种程度上 ▶ **to such an extent that...** 到这样的程度，以至于… ▶ **to what extent?** 到什么程度？

exterior [ɛksˈtɪərɪə(r)] **I** ADJ (*external*) [+ *drain, wall*] 外部的 [wàibù de] **II** N [C] **1** (*outside*) [*of building, vehicle*] 外部 [wàibù] **2** (*appearance*) [*of person*] 外表 [wàibiǎo]

external [ɛksˈtəːnl] **I** ADJ **1** [+ *wall, surface*] 外部的 [wàibù de] **2** (ESP BRIT) [+ *examiner, auditor*] 外界的 [wàijiè de] **II externals** NPL 外表 [wàibiǎo] ▶ **for external use only** (MED) 只供外用 ▶ **external affairs** (POL) 外交事务

extinct [ɪksˈtɪŋkt] ADJ **1** [+ *animal, plant*] 灭绝的 [mièjué de] **2** [+ *volcano*] 熄灭的 [xīmiè de]

extinction [ɪksˈtɪŋkʃən] N [U] [*of species*] 灭绝 [mièjué] ▶ **to face extinction** 面临灭绝

extinguish [ɪksˈtɪŋgwɪʃ] VT **1** (*frm*) [+ *fire*] 扑灭 [pūmiè]; [+ *light, cigarette*] 熄灭 [xīmiè] **2** (*liter*) [+ *hope, memory*] 使破灭 [shǐ pòmiè]

extra [ˈɛkstrə] **I** ADJ [+ *thing, person, amount*] 额外的 [éwài de] **II** ADV **1** (*in addition*) 额外地 [éwài de] **2** (*inf*) (*particularly*) 特别地 [tèbié de] **III** N [C] **1** (*luxury*) 额外的事物 [éwài de shìwù] **2** (*surcharge*) 另外的收费 [lìngwài de shōufèi] **3** (CINE, THEAT) 配角 [pèijué] ▶ **wine will cost extra** 酒另外收钱 ▶ **there are no hidden extras** (*on bill*) 没有隐含的额外费用

extract [*vb* ɪksˈtrækt, *n* ˈɛkstrækt] **I** VT **1** (*liter*) (*take out*) [+ *object*] 取出 [qǔchū] **2** [+ *money, promise, information*] 逼取 [bīqǔ] **3** [+ *tooth*] 拔出 [báchū] **4** [+ *substance, mineral etc*] 提取 [tíqǔ] **II** N **1** [C] (*from novel, recording*) 摘录 [zhāilù] **2** [C/U] [*of substance*] 萃取物 [cuìqǔwù]

▶ **lemon extract, extract of lemon** 柠檬精

extradite [ˈɛkstrədaɪt] (*frm*) VT 引渡 [yǐndù] ▶ **to be extradited to Britain** 被引渡到英国

extraordinary [ɪksˈtrɔːdnrɪ] ADJ **1** (*exceptional*) 非凡的 [fēifán de] **2** (*frm*) [+ *meeting*] 特别的 [tèbié de] ▶ **the extraordinary thing is that...** 令人惊奇的是…

extravagance [ɪksˈtrævəgəns] N **1** [U] (*spending*) 奢侈 [shēchǐ] **2** [C] (*luxury*) 奢侈品 [shēchǐpǐn]

extravagant [ɪksˈtrævəgənt] ADJ **1** (*lavish*) [+ *person, tastes*] 奢侈的 [shēchǐ de] **2** (*wasteful*) 浪费的 [làngfèi de] **3** (*exaggerated*) [+ *praise, generosity*] 过度的 [guòdù de] **4** (*unrealistic*) [+ *ideas, claim*] 过分的 [guòfèn de]

extreme [ɪksˈtriːm] **I** ADJ **1** [+ *poverty, caution*] 极度的 [jídù de] **2** [+ *opinions, methods etc*] 极端的 [jíduān de] **3** [+ *point, edge*] 末端的 [mòduān de] **II** N [C] 极端 [jíduān] ▶ **the extreme right/left** (POL) 极右/左 ▶ **extremes of temperature** 冷热气温悬殊 ▶ **in the extreme** (*frm*) 极度 ▶ **to go to extremes** 走极端 ▶ **to go from one extreme to the other** 从一个极端到另一个极端

extremely [ɪksˈtriːmlɪ] ADV **1** (*with adj*) [+ *useful, hot, heavy*] 非常 [fēicháng] **2** (*with adv*) [*carefully, well, hard* +] 非常 [fēicháng]

extremist [ɪksˈtriːmɪst] **I** N [C] 过激分子 [guòjī fènzǐ] **II** ADJ [+ *views, group*] 极端主义的 [jíduān zhǔyì de]

extrovert [ˈɛkstrəvəːt] **I** ADJ (ESP BRIT) 外向的 [wàixiàng de] [美 = **extroverted**] **II** N [C] 性格外向者 [xìnggé wàixiàngzhě]

○ **eye** [aɪ] **I** N **1** [C] (ANAT) 眼睛 [yǎnjing] **2** [C] (*fig*) 眼光 [yǎnguāng] ▷ *He scrutinised the pages with a critical eye.* 他以挑剔的眼光细看了几页。**3** [C] [*of needle*] 孔 [kǒng] **4** [S] [*of tornado, hurricane*] 风眼 [fēngyǎn] **II** VT (*look at*) 审视 [shěnshì] ▷ *We eyed each other thoughtfully.* 我们仔细地审视了对方。▶ **to keep an eye on sb/sth** 密切注意某人/某事 ▶ **before** *or* **in front of** *or* **under one's eyes** 在某人的眼皮底下 ▶ **to catch sb's eye** [*action, movement* +] 被某人看到; [*person* +] (*deliberately*) 引起某人的注意 ▶ **to clap** *or* **lay** *or* **set eyes on sb/sth** (*inf*) 看见某人/某事 ▶ **to have one's eye on sth** (*inf*) (*want*) 想要某物 ▶ **to keep one's eyes open for** *or* **to keep an eye out for sb/sth** 留意某人/某事 ▶ **to look sb in the eye** *or* **to meet sb's eyes** 正视某人 ▶ **to see sth through sb's eyes** 从某人的角度看 ▶ **as far as the eye can see** 视力所及的范围 ▶ **in the public eye** 广为人知 ▶ **to see eye to eye (with sb)** (与某人)看法完全一致 ▶ **to have an eye for sth** 具有对某物的鉴赏力 ▶ **there's more to this than meets the eye** 并不像看到的那么简单

eyeball [ˈaɪbɔːl] N [C] 眼球 [yǎnqiú]

eyebrow [ˈaɪbrau] N [C] 眉毛 [méimáo] ▶ **his**

behaviour raised a few eyebrows 他的行为颇
令某些人瞠目

eyedrops ['aɪdrɔps] NPL 眼药水 [yǎnyàoshuǐ]

eyelash ['aɪlæʃ] N [c] 眼睫毛 [yǎnjiémáo]

eyelid ['aɪlɪd] N [c] 眼皮 [yǎnpí]

eyeliner ['aɪlaɪnə(r)] N [c/U] 眼线笔

[yǎnxiànbǐ]

eyeshadow ['aɪʃædəu] N [c/U] 眼影 [yǎnyǐng]

eyesight ['aɪsaɪt] N [U] 视力 [shìlì]

eye witness N [c] (to crime, accident) 目击者
[mùjīzhě]

Ff

F¹, f [ɛf] **I** N [C/U] (letter) 英语的第六个字母 **II** ABBR (= female) 女性 [nǚxìng]

F² [ɛf] **I** N [C/U] (MUS) C大调音阶中的第四个音符 **II** ABBR (= Fahrenheit) 华氏温度计 [huáshì wēndùjì]

fable ['feɪbl] N **1** [C] (story) 寓言 [yùyán] **2** [C/U] (myth) 传说 [chuánshuō]

fabric ['fæbrɪk] N **1** [C/U] (cloth) 织物 [zhīwù] **2** [S] (of society) 结构 [jiégòu] **3** [S] (frm) (of building) 结构 [jiégòu]

fabricate ['fæbrɪkeɪt] VT **1** [+ evidence, story] 编造 [biānzào] **2** [+ parts, equipment] 制造 [zhìzào]

fabulous ['fæbjuləs] ADJ **1** (inf) (fantastic) [+ person, looks, mood] 极好的 [jíhǎo de] **2** (extraordinary) [+ beauty, wealth, success] 格外的 [géwài de] **3** (mythical) 传说中的 [chuánshuōzhōng de]

○ face [feɪs] **I** N **1** [C] (ANAT) 脸 [liǎn] ▷ She had a beautiful face. 她的脸很漂亮。 **2** [C] (expression) 表情 [biǎoqíng] ▷ He looked at her with a puzzled face. 他用疑惑的表情看着她。 **3** [C] (of clock) 正面 [zhèngmiàn] **4** [C] (of mountain, cliff) 陡面 [dǒumiàn] ▷ the north face of Mount Tai 泰山朝北的陡面; (of building) 面 [miàn] **5** [C] (side) (of cube, dice etc) 面 [miàn] **6** [S] (aspect) (of belief, system) 一面 [yīmiàn] ▷ the ugly face of capitalism 资本主义的丑恶的一面; (of city, institution) 面貌 [miànmào] ▷ The face of a city can change completely in a year. 城市的面貌一年一个样。 **II** VT **1** [+ direction] [person +] 面向 [miànxiàng]; [building, seat, car +] 朝 [cháo] **2** (confront) 面临 [miànlín] ▷ We are faced with a serious problem. 我们正面临一个严重的问题。 **3** [+ unpleasant situation] 面对 [miànduì]; [+ truth, facts] 正视 [zhèngshì] ▷ Williams faces life in prison if convicted. 如果被定罪的话，威廉姆斯将面对终生监禁。 ▷ We simply must face facts. 我们显然必须得正视现实。 **III** VI [person +] 面向 [miànxiàng]; [building, seat, car +] 朝 [cháo] ▷ He was facing forwards. 他面向前方。 ▷ The garden faces south. 这座花园朝南。 ▶ **I can't** or **couldn't face it** 我应付不了 ▶ **to be** or **lie face down/up** [person +] 俯卧/仰卧 [fǔwò/yǎngwò]; [card +] 正面 [zhèngmiàn] ▶ **to lose/save face** 丢/挽回面子 ▶ **to make** or (BRIT) **pull a face (at sb)** (对某人)做鬼脸 ▶ **in the face of** [+ difficulties, opposition] 面对 ▶ **on the face of it** (superficially) 表面看来 ▶ **to come face to face with** [+ person] 与…面对面; [+ problem] 正视 [zhèngshì] ▶ **face up to** VT FUS [不可拆分] **1** [+ truth, facts] 接受 [jiēshòu] **2** [+ responsibilities, duties] 承担 [chéngdān]

face cloth (BRIT) N [C] 洗脸毛巾 [xǐliǎn máojīn] [美 = **washcloth**]

facelift ['feɪslɪft] N [C] **1** [of person] 面部拉皮整容手术 [miànbù lāpí zhěngróng shǒushù] **2** [of place, building] 翻新 [fānxīn] ▶ **to have a facelift** 做面部拉皮整容手术 ▶ **to give a room a facelift** 翻修房间

face pack (BRIT) N [C] 面膜 [miànmó]

facet ['fæsɪt] N [C] **1** [of question, personality] 方面 [fāngmiàn] **2** [of gem] 琢面 [zhuómiàn]

face value N **1** [C] [of coin, banknote, ticket] 票面价值 [piàomiàn jiàzhí] **2** ▶ **to take sth at face value** (accept unquestioningly) 认为真如其显示的那样 [rènwéi zhēn rúqí xiǎnshì de nàyàng]

facial ['feɪʃl] **I** ADJ **1** [+ hair, expression] 面部的 [miànbù de] **II** N [C] 面部按摩 [miànbù ànmó] ▶ **to have a facial** 做面部按摩

facilitate [fə'sɪlɪteɪt] VT [+ action, process] 使容易 [shǐ róngyì]

facility [fə'sɪlɪtɪ] N **1** (feature) 设施 [shèshī] **2** (service) 设施 [shèshī] ▶ **to have a facility for sth** (skill, aptitude) 有做某事的天分

○ fact [fækt] N **1** [C] (piece of information) 真相 [zhēnxiàng] ▷ It may help you to know the full facts of the case. 了解本案的全部真相会对你有所帮助。 **2** [U] (truth) 事实 [shìshí] ▷ I don't know whether the rumour was based on fact or not. 我不知道这个传闻是否基于事实。 ▶ **in (actual) fact** or **as a matter of fact** (for emphasis) 实际上; (when disagreeing) 其实 ▷ In fact, I'm not at all sure that Freud was correct. 其实，我一点儿也不肯定弗洛伊德是正确的。; (when qualifying statement) 事实上 ▷ It was terribly cold weather, a blizzard in fact. 天气异常冷，事实上，是暴风雪。 ▶ **to know for a fact (that)…** 肯定… ▶ **the fact (of the matter) is (that)…** 事实是… ▶ **the facts**

of life 性知识 ▶ **a fact of life** 无法改变的事实 ▶ **facts and figures** 精确的资料

faction ['fækʃən] (REL, POL) N [c] **1** (group) 派别

factor ['fæktə(r)] N [c] **1** [of problem, decision etc] 因素 [yīnsù] **2** (MATH) 因数 [yīnshù] ▶ **factor in** VT [+ cost] 把···作为因素考虑 [bǎ···zuòwéi yīnsù kǎolǜ]

factory ['fæktərɪ] N [c] 工厂 [gōngchǎng]

factual ['fæktjʊəl] ADJ [+ account, error] 事实的 [shìshí de]

faculty ['fækəltɪ] N **1** [c] (sense, ability) 官能 [guānnéng] **2** [c/u] (BRIT) [of university] 学院 [xuéyuàn] **3** [c/u] (US) (teaching staff) 全体教师 [quántǐ jiàoshī]

fad [fæd] N [c] (craze) 时尚 [shíshàng]

fade [feɪd] I VI **1** [colour, wallpaper, photograph +] 褪色 [tuìsè]; [sound, light +] 渐弱 [jiànruò]; **2** [memory, interest +] 逐渐消失 [zhújiàn xiāoshī]; [hope +] 破灭 [pòmiè] ▷ Hopes are fading for the success of the cease-fire. 停火协议能够成功的希望即将破灭。; [prospects +] 暗淡 [àndàn]; [possibilities +] 减少 [jiànshǎo] II VT [+ colour] 使褪色 [shǐ tuìsè]
▶ **fade away** VI **1** [music, sound +] 慢慢减弱 [mànmàn jiǎnruò] **2** [image +] 变模糊 [biàn móhu] **3** (fig) 逐渐消失 [zhújiàn xiāoshī]
▶ **fade in** VT [+ picture, sound] 使淡入 [shǐ dànrù]
▶ **fade out** VI **1** [+ light, image, sound] 逐渐减弱 [zhújiàn jiǎnruò] **2** (fig) 逐渐消失 [zhújiàn xiāoshī]

faeces, (US) **feces** ['fiːsiːz] (frm) NPL 粪便 [fènbiàn]

fag [fæg] (inf) N [c] **1** (BRIT) (cigarette) 香烟 [xiāngyān] **2** (US: inf!) (homosexual) 男同性恋 [nán tóngxìngliàn]

Fahrenheit ['færənhaɪt] I ADJ 华氏的 [huáshì de] II N 华氏温度计 [huáshì wēndùjì]

○**fail** [feɪl] I VT **1** [+ exam, test] 没有通过 [méiyǒu tōngguò] ▷ I failed my driving test twice. 我两次驾驶考试都没合格。 **2** [+ candidate] 评定···不及格 [píngdìng···bù jígé] ▷ One of the examiners wanted to fail him. 其中一位考官想要评定他不及格。 **3** [leader, system +] 使失望 [shǐ shīwàng] ▷ Our leaders have failed us. 我们的领导使我们失望。 **4** [courage, memory +] 失去 [shīqù] ▷ At the last minute his courage failed him. 在关键时刻，他失去了勇气。 II VI **1** [candidate +] 没通过 [méi tōngguò] ▷ "Did you pass?" - "No, I failed." "你过了吗？" "没过。" **2** [attempt, plan, remedy +] 失败 [shībài] ▷ The attempt to bribe the clerk had failed. 贿赂职员的尝试失败了。 **3** [brakes +] 失灵 [shīlíng] ▷ The brakes failed and his car crashed into a tree. 由于刹车失灵，他的车撞坏上了。 **4** [eyesight, health +] 衰退 [shuāituì] ▷ They go and read to people whose sight is failing. 他们给那些视力衰退的人读书听。 **5** [light +] 变暗 [biàn'àn] ▷ In a few hours the light will fail. 几个小时以后，天色

就会变暗。▶ **to fail to do sth** (not succeed) 未能做某事 ▷ The England team failed to win a place in the finals. 英格兰队未能进入决赛。; (neglect) 没有做某事 ▷ The bomb failed to explode. 炸弹没有爆炸。▶ **without fail** (definitely) 一定 ▷ Don't worry, I'll be there without fail. 别担心，我一定会去。; (without exception) 毫无例外 ▷ He attended every meeting without fail. 他每次会议都参加，没有例外的。

failing ['feɪlɪŋ] I N [c] (weakness) 缺陷 [quēxiàn] II PREP ▶ **failing that** 不然的话 [bùrán de huà]

failure ['feɪljə(r)] N **1** [c/u] (lack of success) 失败 [shībài] **2** [c] (person) 废物 [fèiwù] **3** [c/u] (mechanical, electrical) 故障 [gùzhàng] **4** [c/u] [of crops] 歉收 [qiànshōu] ▶ **failure to do sth** 没有做某事 ▶ **heart/kidney failure** 心力/肾衰竭 ▶ **it was a (complete) failure** 那是个（彻底的）失败

faint [feɪnt] I ADJ **1** [+ sound, light, smell, hope] 微弱的 [wēiruò de] **2** [+ recollection, smile] 淡淡的 [dàndàn de] **3** [+ mark, trace] 隐约的 [yǐnyuē de] **4** [+ breeze] 轻柔的 [qīngróu de] II N [c] (MED) 昏厥 [hūnjué] III VI (MED) 晕倒 [yūndǎo] ▶ **to feel faint** 感到眩晕

faintest ['feɪntɪst] N ▶ **I haven't the faintest (idea)** 我一点儿也不知道 [wǒ yīdiǎnr bù zhīdào]

faintly ['feɪntlɪ] ADV **1** (slightly) 有些 [yǒu xiē] **2** (weakly) 微弱地 [wēiruò de]

fair [fɛə(r)] I ADJ **1** (just, right) [+ person, decision, trial] 公平的 [gōngpíng de] **2** (quite large) [+ size, number, distance, amount] 相当的 [xiāngdāng de] **3** (quite good) [+ chance, guess, idea] 大体的 [dàtǐ de] **4** [+ skin, complexion] 白皙的 [báixī de]; [+ hair] 金色的 [jīnsè de] **5** (frm) (fine) 晴朗的 [qínglǎng de] II ADV ▶ **to play fair** 公平行事 [gōngpíng xíngshì] III N [c] **1** (trade fair) 交易会 [jiāoyìhuì] **2** (BRIT) (also: **funfair**) 游乐场 [yóulèchǎng] [美= **carnival**] ▶ **it's not fair!** 太不公平了！▶ **a fair amount of** 不少

fairground ['fɛəɡraʊnd] N [c] 游乐场 [yóulèchǎng]

fair-haired [fɛə'hɛəd] ADJ [+ person] 金色毛发的 [jīnsè máofà de]

fairly ['fɛəlɪ] ADV **1** (justly) [share, distribute +] 公平地 [gōngpíng de] **2** (quite) [+ heavy, fast, good] 相当 [xiāngdāng]

fairness ['fɛənɪs] N [u] (justice, impartiality) 公正 [gōngzhèng] ▶ **in all fairness** 公正地说

fairway ['fɛəweɪ] (GOLF) N [c] 球座与终点间经过修整的草地

fairy ['fɛərɪ] N [c] 仙女 [xiānnǚ]

fairy tale N [c] 童话 [tónghuà]

faith [feɪθ] N **1** [u] (trust) 信任 [xìnrèn] **2** [c] (specific religion) 宗教 [zōngjiào] **3** [u] (religious belief) 信仰 [xìnyǎng] ▶ **to have faith in sb/sth** 相信某人/某事 ▶ **in good faith** 真心实意的

faithful ['feɪθful] ADJ **1** (loyal) [+ service, supporter, friend] 忠实的 [zhōngshí de] **2** (sexually) [+ husband, wife, lover] 忠诚的 [zhōngchéng de] **3** (accurate) [+ account, version, copy] 真实的 [zhēnshí de] ▶ **to be faithful to** [+ book, film] 忠实于; (sexually) [+ husband, wife] 忠诚于

faithfully ['feɪθfəlɪ] ADV **1** (loyally) [serve, promise, follow+] 忠实地 [zhōngshí de] **2** (accurately) [restore, repeat, copy+] 精确地 [jīngquè de] ▶ **Yours faithfully** (BRIT) 您忠实的 [美 = Sincerely yours]

fake [feɪk] I N [C] **1** (painting, antique, document) 赝品 [yànpǐn] **2** (person) 骗子 [piànzi] II ADJ **1** [+ painting, antique, document] 假的 [jiǎ de] III VT **1** [+ painting, antique, document] 伪造 [wěizào] **2** [+ emotion, reaction] 假装 [jiǎzhuāng]; [+ death, injury] 佯装 [yángzhuāng]

falcon ['fɔːlkən] N [C] 猎鹰 [lièyīng]

○**fall** [fɔːl] (pt **fell**, pp **fallen**) I VI **1** [person, object+] 掉 [diào] ▷ Bombs fell in the town. 炸弹掉进城里。 ▷ Her father fell into the sea. 她父亲掉到海里了。 **2** (fall over) [person, building+] 倒下 [dǎoxià] ▷ She gripped his shoulders to stop herself from falling. 她抓住他的肩膀以防自己倒下。 **3** [snow, rain+] 下 [xià] ▷ An inch of rain fell within 15 minutes. 15分钟内下了1英寸的雨。 **4** [price, temperature, currency+] 下降 [xiàjiàng] ▷ Oil prices fell by 0.2 per cent. 油价下降了0.2%。 **5** [government, leader, country+] 下台 [xiàtái] ▷ The prime minister fell from power. 首相下台。 **6** [night, darkness+] 降临 [jiànglín] ▷ as darkness fell 当黑暗降临时 **7** [light, shadow+] 投射 [tóushè] ▷ A shadow fell over her book. 一道阴影投射到她的书上。 **8** [silence, sadness, tiredness+] 降临 [jiànglín] ▷ Silence fell on the passengers as the police checked identity cards. 警察检查身份证的时候, 沉默降临到每个乘客身上。 II N **1** [C] [of person] 摔倒 [shuāidǎo] ▷ He had a nasty fall. 他摔得不轻。 **2** [C] (in price, temperature) 下降 [xiàjiàng] ▷ There has been a sharp fall in the value of the pound. 英镑值急剧下降。 **3** [S] [of government, leader] 垮台 [kuǎtái] ▷ a debate which led to the Government's fall 一场导致政府垮台的辩论 **4** [C] [of rain, snow] 场 [chǎng] ▷ a heavy fall of snow 一场大雪 **5** [C/U] (US) (autumn) 秋天 [qiūtiān] ▷ in the fall of 1991 1991年秋天 [英 = autumn] III **falls** NPL (waterfall) 瀑布 [pùbù] ▷ Niagara Falls 尼亚加拉大瀑布 ▶ **Christmas falls on a Sunday** 圣诞节适逢星期天 ▶ **to fall in love (with sb/sth)** 爱上(某人/某事) ▶ **to fall flat** [joke+] 毫无效果 ▶ **to fall short of the required amount** 达不到要求的数量 ▶ **to fall ill/pregnant** 生病/怀孕 ▶ **which group do you fall into?** 你属于哪一组?

▶ **fall apart** VI **1** [building, structure+] 破碎 [pòsuì] **2** [system, organization+] 瓦解 [wǎjiě] **3** (inf) (emotionally) 崩溃 [bēngkuì]

▶ **fall back** VI (retreat) 撤退 [chètuì]

▶ **fall back on** VT FUS [不可拆分] (resort to) 依靠 [yīkào]

▶ **fall behind** VI 落后 [luòhòu] ▶ **to fall behind with one's payments** 逾期不付款

▶ **fall down** VI **1** [person+] 摔倒 [shuāidǎo] **2** [building+] 倒塌 [dǎotā]

▶ **fall for** VT FUS [不可拆分] **1** [+ trick, story, lie] 上…的当 [shàng…de dàng] **2** [+ person] 爱上 [àishang]

▶ **fall in** VI **1** [roof, ceiling+] 塌陷 [tāxiàn] **2** (MIL) 集合 [jíhé]

▶ **fall in with** VT FUS [不可拆分] [sb's plans+] 赞成 [zànchéng]

▶ **fall off** VI **1** [person, object+] 掉下 [diàoxià] **2** (diminish) [takings, attendance+] 减少 [jiǎnshǎo]

▶ **fall out** VI **1** [hair, teeth+] 掉 [diào] **2** [friends+] 争吵 [zhēngchǎo] ▶ **to fall out with sb** 与某人争吵

▶ **fall over** I VI [person, object+] 跌倒 [diēdǎo] II VT FUS [不可拆分] ▶ **to fall over o.s. to do sth** (inf) 想方设法做某事 [xiǎngfāng shèfǎ zuò mǒushì]

▶ **fall through** VI [plan+] 落空 [luòkōng]

▶ **fall to** VT FUS [不可拆分] ▶ **to fall to sb to do sth** [responsibility+] 做某事的责任落在某人身上 [zuò mǒushì de zérèn luòzài mǒurén shēnshang]

fallacy ['fæləsɪ] N [C/U] (misconception) 谬论 [miùlùn]

fallen ['fɔːlən] PP of **fall**

fallout ['fɔːlaut] N [U] (radiation) 放射尘 [fàngshèchén]

false [fɔːls] ADJ **1** (artificial) 假的 [jiǎ de] **2** (untrue) [+ statement, accusation, name] 假的 [jiǎ de] **3** (mistaken) [+ impression] 错误的 [cuòwù de] **4** (insincere) [+ person, smile, promise] 假装的 [jiǎzhuāng de] ▶ **under false pretences** (LAW) 以欺诈手段 ▶ **false negative/positive** (MED) 误诊阴性/阳性

false alarm N [C] 虚惊 [xūjīng]

false teeth (BRIT) NPL 假牙 [jiǎ yá]

falter ['fɔːltə(r)] VI **1** (be unsteady) [voice+] 颤抖 [chàndǒu]; [person+] 犹豫 [yóuyù]; [steps+] 蹒跚 [pánshān] **2** (weaken) [person+] 迟疑 [chíyí]; [demand+] 下降 [xiàjiàng]; [interest+] 减少 [jiǎnshǎo]

fame [feɪm] N [U] 声誉 [shēngyù]

familiar [fə'mɪlɪə(r)] ADJ **1** (well-known) [+ face, voice, name] 熟悉的 [shúxī de] **2** (intimate) [+ behaviour, tone] 亲密的 [qīnmì de] ▶ **to be familiar with** [+ subject] 对…熟悉 ▶ **to be on familiar terms (with sb)** (与某人)交情好

familiarize [fə'mɪlɪəraɪz] VT ▶ **to familiarize o.s. with sth** 熟悉某事 [shúxī mǒushì]

○**family** ['fæmɪlɪ] I N [C] **1** (relations) 家庭 [jiātíng] ▷ the Adams Family 亚当斯一家

2 (children) 孩子 [háizi] ▷ couples with large families 有很多孩子的夫妇们 **3** (ancestors) 祖先 [zǔxiān] ▷ Her family came to Los Angeles at the turn of the century. 她的祖先在世纪初时来到洛杉矶。 **II** CPD [复合词] [+ members, home, life, business] 家庭 [jiātíng]

family doctor (BRIT) N [C] 家庭医生 [jiātíng yīshēng]

family planning N [U] 计划生育 [jìhuà shēngyù] ▶ **family planning clinic** 计划生育诊所

famine ['fæmɪn] N [C/U] 饥荒 [jīhuāng] ▶ **famine relief** 赈济饥荒

famous ['feɪməs] ADJ 著名的 [zhùmíng de] ▶ **to be famous for sth** 因某事而闻名

famous 的人或事物比 **well-known** 的人或事物更出名。**notorious** 的人或事物是因为不好的名声而出名，即臭名昭著。**infamous** 不是 **famous** 的反义词，词义和 **notorious** 相近，但语气更强。**notable** 的人或事物是重要的或让人感兴趣的人或事物。

fan [fæn] **I** N [C] **1** (admirer) [of pop star] 迷 [mí]; (SPORT) 球迷 [qiúmí] **2** (ELEC) 风扇 [fēngshàn] **3** (handheld) 扇子 [shànzi] **II** VT **1** [+ face, person] 扇 [shàn] **2** [+ fire] 煽 [shān] **3** (fig) [+ fears, hatred] 煽动 [shāndòng] ▶ **fan out** VI (spread out) 散开 [sànkāi]

fanatic [fə'nætɪk] N [C] **1** (extremist) 狂热者 [kuángrè zhě] **2** (enthusiast) 迷恋…的人 [míliàn…de rén]

fan belt (AUT) N [C] 风扇皮带 [fēngshàn pídài]

fanciful ['fænsɪful] ADJ **1** (unrealistic) [+ notion, idea] 不切实际的 [bùqiè shíjì de] **2** (elaborate) [+ design, name] 新颖奇特的 [xīnyǐng qítè de]

fan club N [C] …迷俱乐部 [...mí jùlèbù]

fancy ['fænsɪ] **I** ADJ **1** (elaborate) [+ jewellery, clothes, hat] 别致的 [biézhì de] **2** (high-quality, expensive) [+ school, hotel, food] 高档的 [gāodàng de] **II** VT **1** (ESP BRIT: inf) (feel like, want) 想要 [xiǎngyào] **2** (think, imagine) 认为 [rènwéi] **3** (inf) [+ person] 喜欢 [xǐhuan] **III** N **1** [C/U] (imagination) 想象力 [xiǎngxiàng lì] **2** [C] (whim) 幻想 [huànxiǎng] **3** [C/U] (fantasy) 幻想 [huànxiǎng] ▶ **to fancy o.s.** (pej) 高估自己 ▶ **to take a fancy to sb/sth** 喜欢上某人/某事 ▶ **when the fancy takes him** 当他突发奇想时 ▶ **a passing fancy** 心血来潮 ▶ **to take or tickle sb's fancy** 吸引某人 ▶ **fancy seeing you here!** 真想不到在这见到你！

fancy dress N [U] 奇装异服 [qízhuāng yìfú]

fancy-dress party ['fænsɪdrɛs-] N [C] 化装舞会 [huàzhuāng wǔhuì]

fang [fæŋ] N [C] [of snake, wolf etc] 獠牙 [liáoyá]

fanlight ['fænlaɪt] N [C] 气窗 [qìchuāng]

fantasize ['fæntəsaɪz] VI ▶ **to fantasize about (doing) sth** 幻想(做)某事 [huànxiǎng (zuò) mǒushì] ▶ **to fantasize that…** 幻想…

fantastic [fæn'tæstɪk] ADJ **1** (wonderful)

[+ person, film, meal] 极好的 [jíhǎo de] **2** (enormous) [+ sum, amount, profit] 巨大的 [jùdà de] **3** (also: **fantastical**) (strange, incredible) 荒诞的 [huāngdàn de]

fantasy ['fæntəsɪ] N **1** [C] (dream) 幻想 [huànxiǎng] **2** [C/U] (film, story) 虚构 [xūgòu] **3** [U] (imagination) 想像 [xiǎngxiàng]

fanzine ['fænziːn] N [C] 迷友杂志 [míyǒu zázhì]

FAO ABBR (= for the attention of) 请…亲自处理 [qǐng…qīnzì chǔlǐ]

FAQ N ABBR (= frequently asked question) 常见问题 [chángjiàn wèntí]

⚬**far** [fɑː(r)] **I** ADJ **1** (distant) 远的 [yuǎn de] ▷ Yes, it's quite far. 是的，是挺远。 **2** (extreme) ▶ **the far end/side** 尽头的 [jìntóu de] **II** ADV **1** (a long way) (in space) 远 [yuǎn] ▷ He didn't hit the ball very far. 他没把球打得很远。 ; (in time) 久远地 [jiǔyuǎn de] ▷ if we look far into the future 如果我们展望久远的未来 **2** (much, greatly) 得多 […de duō] ▷ His new house is far bigger. 他的新房子要大得多。 ▶ **as far as…** 一直到… ▷ Go as far as the church. 一直走到教堂。 ▶ **as far as possible** 尽可能 ▶ **as far as I know** 据我所知 ▶ **by far** 得多 ▷ She was by far the best swimmer. 她显然是最好的游泳者。 ▶ **so far** 迄今为止 ▶ **far from** 一点也不 ▷ His hands were far from clean. 他的手一点也不干净。 ▷ Far from speeding up, the tank came to a halt. 坦克不但没有加速，反而停了下来。 ▶ **is it far to London?** 离伦敦远吗？ ▶ **it's not far from here** 离这里不远 ▶ **how far?** (in distance) 多远？ ▷ How far is the Great Wall from here? 长城离这里有多远？ ; (in degree) 到什么程度 [dào shénme chéngdù] ▷ How far can he be trusted? 他的可信度有多少？ ; (in progress) 进展如何 [jìnzhǎn rúhé] ▷ How far have you got with the work? 你工作进展如何？ ▶ **far away** 遥远 ▷ He sat as far away from the others as possible. 他坐在尽可能远离他人的地方。 ▶ **far off** (in time) 遥远 ▶ **far better** 好得多 ▶ **at the far end (of)** (of table) 在(…的)另一边、(of room, theatre) 在(…的)那一边；(of field) 在(…的)对面 ▶ **at the far side (of)** 在(…的)那一边 ▶ **as far back as the 13th century** 早在13世纪 ▶ **to go too far** (fig) 做得过分 ▶ **he went so far as to resign** 他甚至辞职了 ▶ **far and away** 无疑 ▷ This is far and away the most important point. 这无疑是最重要的一点。 ▶ **from far and wide** 从四面八方 ▶ **far from it** 远非如此 ▶ **far be it from me to criticize** 我并不想指责谁 ▶ **the far left/right** (POL) 极左/右

faraway ['fɑːrəweɪ] ADJ **1** [+ place] 遥远的 [yáoyuǎn de] **2** [+ look, smile, voice] 恍惚的 [huǎnghū de]

farce [fɑːs] N **1** (THEAT) 滑稽剧 [huájī jù] **2** (fig) 闹剧 [nàojù]

fare [fɛə(r)] **I** N **1** [C] (price) (on train, bus) 票价

[piàojià]; *(in taxi)* 乘客 [chéngkè] **2** [U] *(frm)* *(food)* 食物 [shíwù] **II** VI 进展[jìnzhǎn] ▶ **how did you fare?** 你过得怎么样？ ▶ **half/full fare** 半/全价

Far East N ▶ **the Far East** 远东 [Yuǎndōng]

farewell [fɛə'wɛl] *(o.f., liter)* **I** INT 再见 [zàijiàn] ▶ **to bid sb farewell** 向某人告别 **II** N [c] 告别 [gàobié] **III** CPD [复合词] [+ *party, gift*] 送别 [sòngbié]

farm [fɑ:m] **I** N [c] 农场 [nóngchǎng] **II** VT [+ *land*] 耕种[gēngzhòng] **III** VI 务农 [wùnóng] ▶ **farm out** VT [+ *work etc*] 招人承包 [zhāorén chéngbāo]

farmer ['fɑ:mə(r)] N [c] 农民 [nóngmín]

farmhouse ['fɑ:mhaʊs] N [c] 农舍 [nóngshè]

farming ['fɑ:mɪŋ] N [U] *(agriculture)* 农业 [nóngyè] ▶ **sheep farming** 养羊

farmland ['fɑ:mlænd] N [U] *(being farmed)* 耕地 [gēngdì]; *(suitable for farming)* 适于耕种的土地 [shìyú gēngzhòng de tǔdì]

farmyard ['fɑ:mjɑ:d] N [c] 农家的庭院 [nóngjiā de tíngyuàn]

far-reaching ['fɑ:'ri:tʃɪŋ] ADJ [+ *reforms, effects, implications*] 意义深远的 [yìyì shēnyuǎn de]

far-sighted ['fɑ:'saɪtɪd] (US) ADJ 远视的 [yuǎnshì de] [英=**long-sighted**]

fart [fɑ:t] *(infl)* **I** VI 放屁 [fàngpì] **II** N [c] **1** 屁 [pì] **2** *(fig) (person)* ▶ **old fart** 讨厌的老家伙 [tǎoyàn de lǎo jiāhuo]

farther ['fɑ:ðə(r)] **I** ADV **1** *(in distance, time)* 更远地 [gèngyuǎn de] **2** *(in degree)* 更多 [gèngduō] **II** ADJ *(liter)* [+ *shore, side*] 更远的 [gèngyuǎn de]

> farther 和 further 都是 'far' 的比较级形式，并且两者都可以用作形容词和副词。farther 和 further 都可用来表示距离和时间。*Birds were able to find food by flying farther and farther...He must have found a window open further along the balcony...The use of animals by man stretches farther back in time than we had previously imagined.* 只有 further 可以用来表示事物的程度或者范围。如果进行 further discussions，就是进行 more discussions。若某情况 further worsened，表示某个本已糟糕的情况 becomes worse。*It was agreed to call a further meeting on the 10th...The government announced further changes to the scheme...aspects of advanced technology which complicate the world further...*

farthest ['fɑ:ðɪst] **I** ADV **1** *(in distance)* 最远地 [zuìyuǎn de] **2** *(in time)* 最久远地 [zuì jiǔyuǎn de] **3** *(in degree)* 最多 [zuìduō] **II** ADJ [+ *point, extent*] 最远的 [zuìyuǎn de]

fascinate ['fæsɪneɪt] VT *(intrigue, interest)* 使着迷 [shǐ zháomí]

fascinated ['fæsɪneɪtɪd] ADJ 入迷的 [rùmí de]

fascinating ['fæsɪneɪtɪŋ] ADJ [+ *story, person, place*] 迷人的 [mírén de]

fascination [fæsɪ'neɪʃən] N [U/s] 着迷 [zháomí]

fascist ['fæʃɪst] **I** N [c] **1** (POL) 法西斯主义者 [fǎxīsīzhǔyìzhě] **2** *(fig)* 极端分子 [jíduānfènzǐ] **II** ADJ (POL) 法西斯主义的 [fǎxīsīzhǔyì de]

fashion ['fæʃən] **I** N **1** [U/s] *(trend)* *(in clothes, thought, behaviour)* 流行的式样 [liúxíng de shìyàng] **2** [c] *(clothes)* 时装 [shízhuāng] **3** [s] *(manner)* 方式 [fāngshì] **II** VT *(frm) (make)* 制作 [zhìzuò] ▶ **in fashion** 流行 ▶ **to be/go out of fashion** 过时 ▶ **after a fashion** [*finish, manage* +] 勉强算是

fashionable ['fæʃnəbl] ADJ [+ *clothes, restaurant, resort*] 流行的 [liúxíng de]; [+ *writer, director*] 受欢迎的 [shòuhuānyíng de]

fast [fɑ:st] **I** ADJ **1** [+ *runner, car, progress*] 快的 [kuài de] ▷ *He was a very fast driver.* 他开车很快。 **2** [+ *dye, colour*] 不褪色的 [bù tuìsè de] **II** ADV **1** [*run, act, think* +] 快 [kuài] **2** [*stick, hold* +] 紧紧地 [jǐnjǐn de] **III** N [c] (REL) 禁食 [jìnshí] **IV** VI (REL) 禁食 [jìnshí] ▶ **to be fast** [*clock, watch* +] 快 ▷ *my watch is 5 minutes fast* 我的表快5分钟。 ▶ **fast asleep** 酣睡 ▶ **to hold fast to sth** *(fig)* 坚持某事 ▶ **to stand fast** *(fig)* 不让步 ▶ **as fast as I can** 我尽快 ▶ **to make a boat fast** (BRIT) 把船拴牢

fasten ['fɑ:sn] **I** VT **1** *(tie, join)* 固定 [gùdìng] **2** [+ *coat, jacket, belt*] 系 [xì] **II** VI [*coat, jacket* +] 扣上 [kòushang] ▶ **fasten (up)on** VT FUS [不可拆分] [+ *idea, scheme*] 集中在… [jízhōng zài…]

fastener ['fɑ:snə(r)] N [c] *(button, clasp, zip etc)* 紧固物 [jǐngù wù]

fast food **I** N [U] *(burger etc)* 快餐 [kuàicān] **II** CPD [复合词] [+ *restaurant, industry etc*] 快餐 [kuàicān]

fastidious [fæs'tɪdɪəs] ADJ *(fussy)* 挑剔的 [tiāoti de]

fat [fæt] **I** ADJ **1** [+ *person*] 肥胖的 [féipàng de]; [+ *animal*] 肥的 [féi de] **2** [+ *book*] 厚的 [hòu de]; [+ *wallet*] 装得满满的 [zhuāng de mǎnmǎn de] **3** *(inf)* [+ *profit, fee*] 大量的 [dàliàng de] **II** N **1** [U] *(on person, animal, meat)* 脂肪 [zhīfáng] **2** [c/U] *(for cooking)* 食用油 [shíyòng yóu] **3** (CHEM) 脂肪 [zhīfáng] ▶ **to live off the fat of the land** 锦衣玉食 ▶ **that's a fat lot of good** or **help** *(inf)* 这有什么屁用

> 用 fat 形容某人胖，显得过于直接，甚至有些粗鲁。比较礼貌而又含蓄的说法是 plump 或 chubby，后者更为正式。overweight 和 obese 暗示某人因为肥胖而有健康问题。obese 是医学术语，表示某人极度肥胖或超重。一般而言，应尽量避免当面使用任何代表示肥胖的词语。

fatal ['feɪtl] ADJ **1** [+ accident, injury, illness] 致命的 [zhìmìng de] **2** (fig) [+ mistake] 严重的 [yánzhòng de]

fatality [fə'tælɪtɪ] N [c] (death, victim) 死亡 [sǐwáng]

fatally ['feɪtəlɪ] ADV **1** [+ wounded, injured] 致命地 [zhìmìng de] **2** (fig) 严重地 [yánzhòng de]

fate [feɪt] N **1** [U] (destiny) 天意 [tiānyì] **2** [c] [of person, company, plan] 命运 [mìngyùn]

fateful ['feɪtful] ADJ [+ moment, decision] 决定命运的 [juédìng mìngyùn de]

◊ **father** ['fɑːðə(r)] N [c] **1** (parent) 父亲 [fùqīn] **2** (fig) (originator) 鼻祖 [bízǔ] ▷ the father of modern photography 现代摄影艺术的鼻祖 **3** (REL) 神父 [shénfù] ▷ Father William 神父威廉

Father Christmas (BRIT) N 圣诞老人 [Shèngdàn lǎorén] [美= **Santa Claus**]

father-in-law ['fɑːðərɪnlɔː] (pl **fathers-in-law**) N [c] [of woman] 公公 [gōnggong]; [of man] 岳父 [yuèfù]

Father's Day N [c/U] 父亲节 [Fùqīn Jié]

fathom ['fæðəm] I N [c] (NAUT) 英寻 [yīngxún] II VT (also: **fathom out**) [+ meaning, mystery, reason] 领悟 [lǐngwù]

fatigue [fə'tiːg] I N [U] (tiredness) 疲劳 [píláo] II **fatigues** NPL (MIL) 制服 [zhìfú] ▶ **metal fatigue** 金属疲劳

fattening ['fætnɪŋ] ADJ 容易让人长胖的 [róngyì ràngrén zhǎngpàng de]

fatty ['fætɪ] I ADJ **1** [+ food] 含脂肪多的 [hán zhīfáng duō de] **2** [+ acids, tissue] 脂肪的 [zhīfáng de] II (inf) (man, woman) 胖子 [pàngzi]

faucet ['fɔːsɪt] (US) N [c] 水龙头 [shuǐlóngtou] [英= **tap**]

fault [fɔːlt] I N **1** [s] (mistake) 错误 [cuòwù] **2** [c] (defect) (in person) 缺点 [quēdiǎn]; (in machine) 故障 [gùzhàng] **3** [c] (GEO) (crack) 断层 [duàncéng] **4** [c] (TENNIS) 失误 [shīwù] II VT (criticize) 挑剔 [tiāotī] ▶ **it's my fault** 是我的错 ▶ **at fault** 有责任 ▶ **to find fault with sb/sth** 找某人/某事的错 ▶ **through no fault of one's own** 不是自身的过失 ▶ **generous/modest to a fault** 过分慷慨/谦虚

faultless ['fɔːltlɪs] ADJ (perfect) 无懈可击的 [wúxiè kějī de]

faulty ['fɔːltɪ] ADJ [+ machine] 有故障的 [yǒu gùzhàng de]

fauna ['fɔːnə] N [U/PL] 动物群 [dòngwùqún]

fava bean ['fɑːvə-] (US) N [c] 蚕豆 [cándòu] [英= **broad bean**]

favour, (US) **favor** ['feɪvə(r)] I N **1** [U] (approval) 赞成 [zànchéng] **2** [c] (act of kindness) 恩惠 [ēnhuì] II VT **1** (prefer) [+ solution] 赞成 [zànchéng]; [+ person] 偏爱 [piān'ài] **2** (be advantageous to) 对…有利 [duì…yǒulì] ▶ **to ask a favour of sb** 请求某人帮忙 ▶ **to do sb a favour** 帮某人的忙 ▶ **to be in favour of sth/**

doing sth 赞成某事/做某事 ▶ **to be in/out of favour** 得到/失去赞同 ▶ **to reject sth in favour of sth else** 拒绝某事转而选择另外某事 ▶ **to rule in sb's favour** (LAW) 裁决对某人有利 ▶ **biased in favour of** 偏袒 ▶ **to find favour with sb** [suggestion, plan +] 受到某人的青睐 ▶ **to win sb's favour** 赢得某人的好感

favourable, (US) **favorable** ['feɪvrəbl] ADJ **1** [+ comment, reaction, impression] 赞成的 [zànchéng de] **2** [+ comparison] 好的 [hǎode] **3** [+ terms, conditions] 有利的 [yǒulì de] ▶ **to be favourable to sth** 赞同某事 ▶ **to be favourable to sb** 对某人有利

favourite, (US) **favorite** ['feɪvrɪt] I ADJ [+ author, film, food, colour] 最喜欢的 [zuì xǐhuan de] II N [c] **1** (thing, person) 偏爱 [piān'ài] **2** (in race) 最有希望的获胜者 [zuì yǒu xīwàng de huòshèngzhě]

fawn [fɔːn] I N [c] (young deer) 幼鹿 [yòulù] II ADJ (also: **fawn-coloured**) 浅黄褐色的 [qiǎn huánghèsè de] III VI ▶ **to fawn over** or **(up)on sb** 巴结某人 [bājie mǒurén]

fax [fæks] I N [c] **1** (document) 传真 [chuánzhēn] **2** (also: **fax machine**) 传真机 [chuánzhēnjī] II VT [+ document] 用传真发送 [yòng chuánzhēn fāsòng]

FBI (US) N ABBR (= Federal Bureau of Investigation) 联邦调查局 [Liánbāng Diàochájú]

FDA (US) N ABBR (= Food and Drug Administration) ▶ **the FDA** 食品及药物管理局 [Shípǐn Jí Yàowù Guǎnlǐjú]

◊ **fear** [fɪə(r)] I N **1** [c/U] (terror) 害怕 [hàipà] ▷ I stood there crying and shaking with fear. 我站在那里，因为害怕而哭泣着，颤抖着。▷ She was brought up with no fear of animals. 她从小到大都不怕动物。**2** [c/U] (anxiety) 焦虑 [jiāolǜ] ▷ My worst fears were quickly realized. 最令我焦虑的事情很快就发生了。II VT **1** (be scared of) 害怕 [hàipà] ▷ a woman whom he disliked and feared 一个他不喜欢而且害怕的女人 **2** (be worried about) 担心 [dānxīn] ▷ An epidemic of plague was feared. 人们担心将会流行瘟疫。III VI ▶ **to fear for sb/sth** 为某人/某事担忧 [wèi mǒurén/mǒushì dānyōu] ▶ **fear of heights/the dark** 怕高/黑 ▶ **for fear of doing sth** 以免做某事 ▷ They did not mention it for fear of offending him. 他们没有提那件事以免触犯了他。▶ **to fear that…** … 恐怕…

fearful ['fɪəful] ADJ **1** (frightened) 害怕的 [hàipà de] **2** (frm) (dreadful) [+ risk, accident] 可怕的 [kěpà de] **3** (inf, o.f.) (terrible) [+ sight, noise] 极坏的 [jíhuài de] ▶ **to be fearful of sth** 害怕某事

fearless ['fɪəlɪs] ADJ [+ person] 无所畏惧的 [wú suǒ wèijù de]

feasible ['fiːzəbl] ADJ [+ proposal, idea] 可行的 [kěxíng de]

feast [fiːst] I N [c] **1** (banquet) 宴会 [yànhuì] **2** (REL) (festival) 节日 [jiérì] II VI (liter) 宴饮 [yànyǐn] ▶ **a feast of** (fig) 许许多多的 ▶ **to**

feast on sth 尽情地享用某物 ▶ **to feast one's eyes (up)on sb/sth** 尽情观赏某人/某物

feat [fiːt] N [c] (achievement) 技艺 [jìyì] ▶ **a brilliant feat of engineering** 工程上的高超技艺

feather ['fɛðə(r)] I N [c] (of bird) 羽毛 [yǔmáo] II CPD [复合词] [+ mattress, bed, pillow] 羽绒 [yǔróng] III VT ▶ **to feather one's nest** 中饱私囊 [zhōngbǎo sīnáng] ▶ **a feather in one's cap** 引以为豪的成就

feature ['fiːtʃə(r)] I N [c] 1 (characteristic) 特点 [tèdiǎn] ▷ This is a common feature of modern life. 这是现代生活的共同特点。▷ safety features 安全装置 2 (PUBLISHING, TV) 专题 [zhuāntí] 3 (CINE) (also: feature film) 故事片 [gùshìpiàn] II VT [film, exhibition +] 由…主演 [yóu…zhǔyǎn] III VI ▶ **to feature in** [+ situation, exhibition, magazine] 被包括在…内 [bèi bāokuò zài…nèi] IV features NPL [of face] 五官 [wǔguān]

feature film N [c] 故事片 [gùshìpiàn]

Feb. ABBR (= February) 二月 [èryuè]

February ['fɛbruərɪ] N [c/u] 二月 [èryuè] see also July

feces ['fiːsiːz] (US) NPL = **faeces**

fed [fɛd] PT, PP of **feed**

federal ['fɛdərəl] ADJ [+ country, system] 联邦制的 [liánbāngzhì de]; [+ government, judge] 联邦的 [liánbāng de]

federation [fɛdə'reɪʃən] N [c] (association) 联合会 [liánhéhuì]

fed up (inf) ADJ ▶ **to be fed up** 厌倦 [yànjuàn]

fee [fiː] N [c] (payment) 费 [fèi]; [+ of doctor, lawyer] 费用 [fèiyòng]; (for examination, registration) 费 [fèi] ▶ **school fees** 学费 ▶ **entrance fee** 门票费 ▶ **membership fee** 会员费 ▶ **for a small fee** 收少许费用

feeble ['fiːbl] ADJ 1 (weak) [+ person, animal, voice] 虚弱的 [xūruò de] 2 (ineffectual) [+ attempt, excuse, argument] 无力的 [wúlì de]; [+ joke] 不好笑的 [bù hǎoxiào de]

feed [fiːd] (pt, pp **fed**) I VT 1 [+ baby, invalid, dog] 喂 [wèi] 2 [+ family, guests] 供给…食物 [gōngjǐ…shíwù] II VI 1 [baby +] 喝奶 [hēnǎi] 2 [animal +] 吃 [chī] III N 1 [u] [of animal] 饲料 [sìliào] 2 [c] [of baby] 喂奶 [wèinǎi] ▶ **to feed sth into** [+ document, tape] 把某事放进…里; [+ data, information] 把某物输入…; [+ coins, money] 把某物放入…
▶ **feed on** VT FUS [不可拆分] 1 (live on) 以…为食 [yǐ…wéi shí] ▷ Not all bats feed on insects. 不是所有的蝙蝠都以昆虫为食物。2 (fig) 助长 [zhùzhǎng]

feedback ['fiːdbæk] N [u] 1 (information) 反馈 [fǎnkuì] 2 (noise) 噪声 [zàoshēng]

○ **feel** [fiːl] (pt, pp **felt**) I VT 1 (touch) [+ object, face] 摸 [mō] ▷ Eric felt his face. "Am I bleeding?" 埃里克摸着自己的脸。"我在流血吗？" 2 (experience) [+ desire, anger, grief] 觉得 [juéde] ▷ Mrs Oliver

felt a sudden desire to burst out crying. 奥利弗夫人突然觉得很想哭出来。; [+ pain] 感到 [gǎndào] ▷ He felt a sudden pain in his leg. 他突然感到一阵腿疼。3 (be aware of) 发觉 [fājué] ▷ He felt her leg against his. 他发觉她的腿正抵着他的腿。4 (sense) 感觉到 [gǎnjué dào] 5 (think, believe) 认为 [rènwéi] ▷ We felt she would win. 我们认为她会赢。▷ She knew how I felt about the subject. 她知道我对这事的看法。III N [s] 1 [of substance, cloth] 摸上去的感觉 [mōshangqù de gǎnjué] ▷ He remembered the feel of her skin. 他记得她皮肤摸上去的感觉。2 (impression) 感觉 [gǎnjué] ▷ The room has a warm, cosy feel. 这个房间有种温暖舒适的感觉。▶ **to feel that...** 感到…▷ I feel I'm neglecting my duty. 我感到我失职了。
▶ **to feel hungry** 觉得饿 ▶ **to feel cold** 觉得冷 ▶ **to feel the cold/the heat** 怕冷/热 ▶ **to feel lonely/better** 感到孤独/感觉好多了 ▶ **I don't feel well** 我觉得身体不适 ▶ **to feel sorry for sb** 同情某人 ▶ **it feels soft** 这摸上去软软的 ▶ **it feels colder here** 这儿感觉更冷些 ▶ **it feels like velvet** 它摸上去像天鹅绒 ▶ **to feel like** (want) 想要 ▷ I feel like a stroll. 我想散散步。; (consider o.s.) 觉得自己像 ▷ I felt like a murderer. 我觉得自己像是杀人犯。▶ **it feels like or it feels as if...** 仿佛觉得… ▶ **to have a feel of sth** 摸一摸某物 ▶ **to get the feel of sth** 开始熟悉某事 ▶ **to have the feel of sth** (impression) 有种好似某事的感觉 ▶ **I'm still feeling my way** 我仍然在摸索前进 ▶ **I don't feel myself** 我觉得身体不舒服
▶ **feel about, feel around** VI (in pocket, bag, the dark) 摸索
▶ **feel for** VT FUS [不可拆分] 1 (grope for) 摸索着找 [mōsuǒ zhe zhǎo] ▷ I felt for my wallet. 我摸索着找我的钱包。2 (sympathize with) 同情 ▷ I really feel for you. 我真的同情你。

feeling ['fiːlɪŋ] I N 1 [c] (emotion) 感受 [gǎnshòu] 2 [c] (physical sensation) 感觉 [gǎnjué] 3 [u] (sense of touch) 触觉 [chùjué] 4 [s] (impression) 感觉 [gǎnjué] 5 [u] (sympathy) 同情 [tóngqíng] II feelings NPL 1 (attitude) 看法 [kànfǎ] 2 (emotions) 情感 [qínggǎn] ▶ **feelings were running high** 群情激愤 ▶ **what are your feelings about the matter?** 你对这事的看法是什么？▶ **I have a feeling that...** 我有种感觉… ▶ **my feeling is that...** 我的感觉是… ▶ **bad or ill feeling** 反感 ▶ **to hurt sb's feelings** 伤害某人的感情

feet [fiːt] NPL of **foot**

feign [feɪn] VT (frm) [+ illness, interest] 假装 [jiǎzhuāng]

fell [fɛl] I PT of **fall** II VT 1 [+ tree] 砍倒 [kǎndǎo] 2 [+ opponent] 打倒 [dǎdǎo] III the fells NPL (BRIT) (moorland) 沼泽地 [zhǎozédì] IV ADJ ▶ **in one fell swoop** 一下子 [yīxiàzi]

fellow ['fɛləu] I N [c] 1 (o.f., inf) (man) 小伙子 [xiǎohuǒzi] 2 (frm) (comrade) 同事 [tóngshì]

3 [of learned society] 会员 [huìyuán] **4** [of university] 研究员 [yánjiūyuán] **II** CPD [复合词] ▶ their fellow prisoners/students 他们的狱友/同学 [tāmen de yùyǒu/tóngxué] ▶ her fellow workers 她的同事们

fellowship ['fɛləʊʃɪp] N **1** [c] (society) 团体 [tuántǐ] **2** [c] (UNIV) 研究员职位 [yánjiūyuán zhíwèi] **3** [U] (comradeship) 友谊 [yǒuyì]

felony ['fɛlənɪ] (LAW) N [c] 重罪 [zhòngzuì]

felt [fɛlt] **I** PT, PP of **feel** **II** N [U] (fabric) 毛毡 [máozhān]

felt-tip pen, felt-tip ['fɛlttɪp-] N [c] 毡头墨水笔 [zhāntóu mòshuǐbǐ]

female ['fiːmeɪl] **I** N [c] **1** (ZOOL) 雌兽 [císhòu] **2** (woman) 女性 [nǚxìng] **II** ADJ **1** (ZOOL) 雌性的 [cíxìng de] **2** [+ sex, character, child] 女性的 [nǚxìng de] **3** (relating to women) 妇女的 [fùnǚ de] ▶ male and female students 男女学生

feminine ['fɛmɪnɪn] ADJ **1** [+ clothes, behaviour] 女性的 [nǚxìng de] **2** (LING) 阴性的 [yīnxìng de]

feminist ['fɛmɪnɪst] **I** N [c] 女权主义者 [nǚquán zhǔyìzhě] **II** ADJ 女权主义的 [nǚquán zhǔyì de]

fence [fɛns] **I** N [c] (barrier) 篱笆 [líba] **II** VT **1** (also: **fence in**) [+ land] 把…用篱笆围起 [bǎ…yòng líba wéiqǐ] **2** (also: **fence off**) 把…用篱笆圈起 [bǎ…yòng líba quānqǐ] **III** VI (SPORT) 击剑 [jījiàn] ▶ to sit on the fence (fig) 持观望态度

fencing ['fɛnsɪŋ] N [U] **1** (SPORT) 击剑 [jījiàn] **2** (material for fences) 筑栅栏的材料 [zhù zhàlán de cáiliào]

fend [fɛnd] VI ▶ to fend for o.s. 自谋生计 [zìmóu shēngjì]
▶ **fend off** VT **1** (physically) [+ attack, attacker, blow] 挡开 [dǎngkāi] **2** (verbally) [+ questions, requests, person] 回避 [huíbì]

fender ['fɛndə(r)] N [c] **1** [of fireplace] 围栏 [wéilán] **2** (US) [of car] 挡泥板 [dǎngníbǎn] [英=**wing**] **3** (US) [of car] 保险杠 [bǎoxiǎn gàng] [英=**bumper**] **4** (on boat) 护舷物 [hùxiánwù]

fennel ['fɛnl] N [U] 茴香 [huíxiāng]

ferment [vb fə'mɛnt, n 'fəːmɛnt] **I** VI [beer, dough, fruit +] 发酵 [fājiào] **II** VT [+ beer, dough, fruit] 使发酵 [shǐ fājiào] **III** N [U] (unrest) 骚动 [sāodòng] ▶ to be in ferment 处于动荡不安中

fern [fəːn] N [c] 蕨 [jué]

ferocious [fə'rəʊʃəs] ADJ **1** [+ animal, assault] 凶猛的 [xiōngměng de] **2** [+ battle, competition, argument] 激烈的 [jīliè de]

ferret ['fɛrɪt] N [c] 雪貂 [xuědiāo]
▶ **ferret about, ferret around** VI (BRIT: inf) [person, animal +] 到处搜寻 [dàochù sōuxún]
▶ **ferret out** (inf) VT [+ information] 查出 [cháchū]

ferry ['fɛrɪ] **I** N [c] (small) 摆渡 [bǎidù];

(large) (also: **ferryboat**) 渡船 [dùchuán] **II** VT (transport) (by sea, air, road) 运送 [yùnsòng] ▶ **to ferry sth/sb across** or **over** 载某物/某人渡过

fertile ['fəːtaɪl] ADJ **1** [+ land, soil] 肥沃的 [féiwò de]; [+ woman] 能生育的 [néng shēngyù de] **2** [+ imagination, mind] 丰富的 [fēngfù de] ▶ **fertile ground** (fig) 沃土

fertilize ['fəːtɪlaɪz] VT **1** (BIO) 使受精 [shǐ shòujīng] **2** (AGR) [+ land] 施肥于 [shīféiyú]

fertilizer ['fəːtɪlaɪzə(r)] N [c/U] (for plants, land) 肥料 [féiliào]

fervent ['fəːvənt] ADJ [+ admirer, supporter] 强烈的 [qiángliè de]; [+ belief, hope] 热切的 [rèqiè de]

fervour, (US) fervor ['fəːvə(r)] N [U] 热情 [rèqíng]

fester ['fɛstə(r)] VI (liter) **1** [sore, wound +] 化脓 [huànóng] **2** (fig) [resentment +] 加剧 [jiājù]

festival ['fɛstɪvəl] N [c] **1** (REL) 节日 [jiérì] **2** (THEAT, MUS) 艺术节 [yìshù jié]

festive ['fɛstɪv] ADJ **1** [+ mood, atmosphere] 喜庆的 [xǐqìng de] **2** (relating to Christmas) 节日的 [jiérì de] ▶ **the festive season** 节日期

festoon [fɛs'tuːn] VT ▶ **to be festooned with** 给…饰以花饰 [gěi…shìyǐ huāshì]

fetch [fɛtʃ] VT **1** (bring) 去拿来 [qù nálái] **2** (sell for) 卖得 [màidé] ▶ **to fetch sth for sb, fetch sb sth** 去给某人拿来某物 ▶ **how much did it fetch?** 这个卖多少钱?
▶ **fetch up** (inf) VI 到达 [dàodá]

fête [feɪt] **I** N [c] (at church, school) 游园会 [yóuyuán huì] **II** VT 特别款待 [tèbié kuǎndài]

feud [fjuːd] **I** N [c] (quarrel) 长期不和 [chángqī bùhé] **II** VI 长期不和 [chángqī bùhé] ▶ **to feud with sb** 与某人结怨 ▶ **a family feud** 家族世仇

feudal ['fjuːdl] ADJ [+ system, society, lord] 封建的 [fēngjiàn de]

fever ['fiːvə(r)] N **1** [c/U] (MED) 发烧 [fāshāo] **2** (fig) (frenzy) ▶ **a fever of excitement/anxiety** 激动若狂/极度不安 [jīdòng ruòkuáng/jídù bù'ān] ▶ **he has a fever** 他发烧了

fever blister (US: MED) N [c] 疱疹 [chuāngzhěn] [英=**cold sore**]

feverish ['fiːvərɪʃ] ADJ **1** (MED) 发烧的 [fāshāode] **2** (fig) [+ emotion, activity] 狂热的 [kuángrè de]

○**few** [fjuː] **I** ADJ **1** (not many) 少数的 [shǎoshù de] ▷ She has few friends. 她的朋友不多。 **2** ▶ **a few** (some) 几个 [jǐge] ▷ She has a few friends. 她有几个朋友。 **II** PRON **1** ▶ **a few** (some) 几个 [jǐge] ▷ Many of us tried and a few succeeded. 我们中的许多人都试了,只有几个成功了。;(not many) 很少几个 [hěnshǎo jǐge] ▷ Many of us tried but few succeeded. 我们中的许多人都试了,但很少几个成功了。 **2** ▶ **in the next few days** 在接下来的几天里 [zài jiēxiàlái de jǐtiān lǐ] ▶ **in the past few days** 在过去的几天里 ▶ **every few days/months** 每几天/几

个月 ▶ **a few of us/them** 我们/他们中的几个 ▶ **a few more** 再多几个 ▶ **very few survive** 极少幸存 ▶ **a good few** or **quite a few** 相当多 ▶ **as few as** 竟少至 ▶ **they are few and far between** 他们简直是凤毛麟角

> **few** 和 **a few** 都用在可数名词的复数形式之前，但意义不同。例如，I have a few friends 表示肯定含义，表示你有一些朋友。然而，I have few friends 表示否定含义，即你几乎没有朋友。

fewer ['fjuːə(r)] ADJ 较少的 [jiàoshǎo de] ▶ **no fewer than** 不少于 ▶ **there are fewer buses on Sundays** 星期天公共汽车比较少

用法参见 **less**

fewest ['fjuːɪst] ADJ 最少的 [zuìshǎo de]

fiancé [fɪ'ɒnseɪ] N [c] 未婚夫 [wèihūnfū]

fiancée [fɪ'ɒnseɪ] N [c] 未婚妻 [wèihūnqī]

fiasco [fɪ'æskəʊ] (pl **fiascos**) N [c] (disaster) 惨败 [cǎnbài]

fib [fɪb] (inf) I N [c] (lie) 小谎 [xiǎohuǎng] II VI 撒小谎 [sā xiǎohuǎng]

fibre, (US) **fiber** ['faɪbə(r)] N 1 [c] (thread) 纤维 [xiānwéi] 2 [c/U] (cloth) 纤维制品 [xiānwéi zhìpǐn] 3 [U] (roughage) 纤维质 [xiānwéizhì] 4 [c] (ANAT) (tissue) 纤维 [xiānwéi]

fibreglass, (US) **fiberglass** ['faɪbəglɑːs] N [U] 玻璃纤维 [bōli xiānwéi]

fickle ['fɪkl] ADJ [+ person] 易变的 [yìbiàn de]; [+ weather] 无常的 [wúcháng de]

fiction ['fɪkʃən] N 1 [U] (novels, stories) 小说 [xiǎoshuō] 2 [U] (invention) 虚构的事 [xūgòu de shì] 3 [c] (lie) 杜撰 [dùzhuàn]

fictional ['fɪkʃənl] ADJ [+ character, event] 虚构的 [xūgòude]

fictitious [fɪk'tɪʃəs] ADJ 1 (non-existent) 杜撰的 [dùzhuàn de] 2 (imaginary) [+ character, event] 虚构的 [xūgòu de]

fiddle ['fɪdl] I N [c] 1 (MUS) 小提琴 [xiǎo tíqín] 2 (BRIT: inf) (fraud, swindle) 诓骗 [kuāngpiàn] II VT (BRIT: inf) [+ books, accounts, taxes] 篡改 [cuàngǎi] ▶ **tax fiddle** 骗税
▶ **fiddle with** VT FUS [不可拆分] 不停拨弄 [bùtíng bōnòng]

fiddler ['fɪdlə(r)] N [c] (MUS) 小提琴手 [xiǎo tíqínshǒu]

fidelity [fɪ'dɛlɪtɪ] N [U] (frm) 1 [of spouse, dog] 忠诚 [zhōngchéng] 2 (accuracy) [of report, translation] 精确 [jīngquè]

field [fiːld] I N [c] 1 (grassland) 草地 [cǎodì] 2 (cultivated) 田地 [tiándì] 3 (SPORT) (pitch) 场地 [chǎngdì] 4 (subject, area of interest) 领域 [lǐngyù] 5 (range) [of gravitation, magnetism] 场 [chǎng] 6 (MIN) 矿区 [kuàngqū] 7 (COMPUT) 字段 [zìduàn] II VI (CRICKET) 接球 [jiēqiú] III CPD [复合词] [+ study, trip] 实地 [shídì] ▶ **the field** (competitors, entrants) 全体出场参赛者 ▶ **to lead the field** (SPORT) 领头; (fig) 一马当先 ▶ **field of vision** 视野 ▶ **to have a field**

day 忙得不亦乐乎

fielder ['fiːldə(r)] (CRICKET, BASEBALL) N [c] 外野手 [wàiyěshǒu]

field marshal N [c] 陆军元帅 [lùjūn yuánshuài]

fieldwork ['fiːldwɜːk] N [U] (research) 实地考察 [shídì kǎochá]

fierce [fɪəs] ADJ 1 [+ animal] 凶猛的 [xiōngměng de]; [+ warrior, enemy] 凶恶的 [xiōng'è de]; [+ battle] 猛烈的 [měngliè de] 2 [+ loyalty, resistance, competition] 强烈的 [qiángliè de]; [+ wind, heat, storm] 强劲的 [qiángjìn de]

fiery ['faɪərɪ] ADJ 1 (lit) 着火的 [zháohuǒ de]; [+ red, orange] 如火的 [rúhuǒ de] 2 (fig) [+ person, temper, speech] 火爆的 [huǒbào de]

⊙fifteen [fɪf'tiːn] NUM 十五 [shíwǔ] ▶ **that will be fifteen pounds, please** 请付15英镑 ▶ **she's fifteen (years old)** 她15岁了 ▶ **there are fifteen of us** 我们有15个人 ▶ **all fifteen of them** 他们15个人都

fifteenth [fɪf'tiːnθ] NUM 第十五 [dì shíwǔ] see also **fifth**

fifth [fɪfθ] I NUM 1 (in series) 第五 [dìwǔ] 2 (fraction) 五分之一 [wǔfēnzhīyī] II N (AUT) (also: **fifth gear**) 第五挡 [dìwǔdǎng] III ADV ▶ **to come fifth** (in race, competition) 名列第五名 [mínglièdìwǔ míng] ▶ **on July fifth, on the fifth of July** 在7月5日 ▶ **Charles the fifth** 查尔斯五世

⊙fifty ['fɪftɪ] NUM 五十 [wǔshí] ▶ **he's in his fifties** 他50多岁 ▶ **during the fifties** 在50年代

fifty-fifty ['fɪftɪ'fɪftɪ] (inf) I ADJ 各半的 [gèbàn de] II ADV [divide, share, split +] 各半地 [gèbàn de] ▶ **to have a fifty-fifty chance (of success)** 有百分之五十 (成功) 的机会

fig [fɪg] N [c] 1 (fruit) 无花果 [wúhuāguǒ] 2 (also: **fig tree**) 无花果树 [wúhuāguǒ shù] ▶ **I don't care** or **give a fig** (inf, o.f.) 我毫不在意

⊙fight [faɪt] (pt, pp **fought**) I N [c] 1 (lit) 斗殴 [dòu'ōu] ▷ There were sometimes fights between the workers. 有时工人之间会发生斗殴。 2 (BOXING) 拳击赛 [quánjī sài] 3 (fig) (against disease, alcoholism, prejudice) 斗争 [dòuzhēng] ▷ the fight against drug abuse 与滥用毒品所作的斗争 4 (quarrel) 争吵 [zhēngchǎo] ▷ He had a big fight with his dad. 他和他的父亲大吵了一架。 II VT 1 [+ person, enemy, army] 与…对打 [yǔ…duìdǎ] ▷ I fought him, and I won. 我跟他对打，我赢了。 2 [+ battle] 与…战斗 [yǔ…zhàndòu] ▷ Police fought a gun battle with the gang. 警察与歹徒展开一场枪击战。 3 [+ disease, prejudice etc] 与…斗争 [yǔ…dòuzhēng] ▷ She devoted her life to fighting poverty. 她一生都与贫穷作斗争。 4 [+ fire] 与…搏斗 [yǔ…bódòu] ▷ They fought the fire for three days. 他们与大火搏斗了3天。 5 [+ urge, impulse] 抑制 [yìzhì] ▷ He fought the urge to cry. 他抑制住了想哭的冲动。 6 (LAW)

[+ case] 为…极力争辩 [wèi…jílì zhēngbiàn] ▷ He fought his case in various courts. 他在各个法庭为他的案子据理力争。**7** [+ election] 力争 ▷ the parties fighting the election 力争获选的各个政党 **8** (BOXING) 与…进行拳击赛 [yǔ…jìnxíng quánjī sài] ▷ I'd like to fight him for the title. 我想与他进行拳击赛争夺冠军头衔. **III** VI **1** [people, enemies, armies +] 战斗 [zhàndòu] ▷ He fought in the war. 他在战争中作战. **2** (quarrel) 争吵 [zhēngchǎo] ▷ They fight about who pays the bills. 他们为谁付账而争吵. **3** (struggle) 奋斗 [fèndòu] ▷ We had fought to hold on to the company. 我们曾经为保住公司而奋斗. ▶ **to put up a fight** 开展斗争 ▶ **to fight with sb** 跟某人打架 ▶ **to fight for/against sth** 为支持/反对某事而斗争 ▶ **to fight one's way through a crowd/the undergrowth** 费力地穿过人群/丛林

▶ **fight back I** VI 回击 [huíjī] **II** VT [+ tears, fear] 抑制住 [yìzhì zhù]

▶ **fight down** VT [+ urge] 努力抑制 [nǔlì yìzhì]

▶ **fight off** VT **1** [+ attacker] 击退 [jītuì] **2** [+ disease] 消除 [xiāochú] **3** [+ sleep, urge] 克制 [kèzhì]

▶ **fight out** VT ▶ **to fight it out** 一决雌雄 [yījué cíxióng]

fighter ['faɪtə(r)] N [C] **1** (boxer etc) 拳击手 [quánjīshǒu] **2** (also: **fighter plane**) 战斗机 [zhàndòu jī] **3** (courageous person) 勇士 [yǒngshì]

fighting ['faɪtɪŋ] N [U] (battle, violence) 搏斗 [bódòu]

figurative ['fɪɡjʊrətɪv] ADJ [+ painting, style] 华美的 [huáměi de] ▶ **in a figurative sense** 用比喻义

○ **figure** ['fɪɡə(r)] **I** N [C] **1** (DRAWING, GEOM) 图形 [túxíng] ▷ A hexagon is a six-sided figure. 六边形是有6个边的图形. **2** (number, statistic) 统计数字 [tǒngjì shùzì] ▷ unemployment figures 失业统计数字 **3** (digit) 数字 [shùzì] ▷ The second figure looks like a five. 第二个数字看起来像5. **4** (body, shape) 身材 [shēncái] ▷ She's got a fabulous figure. 她的身材棒极了. **5** (person) 轮廓 [lúnkuò] ▷ the figure of a man silhouetted against the skyline 被天际衬托着的男人轮廓 **6** (ART) 画像 [huàxiàng] ▷ a life-size figure of a woman 真人同样大小的女人画像 **7** (personality) 人物 [rénwù] ▷ He's a controversial figure. 他是一个颇有争议的人物. **II** VT (ESP US: inf) (reckon) 估计 [gūjì] ▷ They figured it was better to stay where they were. 他们估计最好还是待在原处。 **III** VI (feature) 出现 [chūxiàn] ▷ Loneliness figures a lot in his conversation. 孤独在他的谈话中出现了好几次. ▶ **in single/double figures** 以单位数/双位数 ▶ **I couldn't put a figure on it** 我说不出它的确切数字 ▶ **public figure** 公众人物 ▶ **a hero/mother** etc **figure** 英雄/母亲(等)式的人物 ▶ **that figures** (inf)

那不足为怪

▶ **figure out** (inf) VT (work out) 弄清楚 [nòng qīngchu] ▷ She had not yet figured out what she was going to do. 她还没有弄清楚她要做什么。

figurehead ['fɪɡəhed] N [C] **1** [of organization] 傀儡 [kuílěi] **2** (NAUT) 船头雕饰 [chuántóu diāoshì]

file [faɪl] **I** N [C] **1** (dossier) 档案 [dàng'àn] **2** (folder) 文件夹 [wénjiànjiā] **3** (for loose leaf) 卷宗 [juànzōng] **4** (COMPUT) 文件 [wénjiàn] **5** (tool) 锉刀 [cuòdāo] **II** VT **1** (also: **file away**) [+ papers, document] 把…归档 [bǎ…guīdàng] **2** (LAW) [+ accusation, complaint, request] 把…备案 [bǎ…bèi'àn] **3** [+ wood, metal, fingernails] 把…锉平 [bǎ…cuòpíng] **III** VI ▶ **to file in/out/past** 鱼贯而入/出/过 [yúguàn érrù/chū/guò] ▶ **to file for divorce** 申请离婚

filing cabinet ['faɪlɪŋ-] N [C] 档案柜 [dàng'ànguì]

Filipino [fɪlɪ'piːnəu] (pl **Filipinos**) **I** ADJ 菲律宾的 [Fēilùbīn de] **II** N [C] (person) 菲律宾人 [Fēilùbīn rén]

fill [fɪl] **I** VT **1** [+ container] 装满 [zhuāngmǎn] **2** [+ space, area] 占满 [zhànmǎn] **3** [+ crack, hole] 塞满 [sāimǎn] **4** [+ tooth] 补 [bǔ] **5** [+ role, position] 担任 [dānrèn] **6** [+ job vacancy] [company +] 选人补上 [xuǎnrén bǔshang]; [candidate +] 补上 [bǔshang] **7** [+ gap, need] 弥补 [míbǔ] **II** VI [room, hall +] 挤满 [jīmǎn] **III** N ▶ **to have had one's fill of sth** 已经受够了某事 [yǐjīng shòugòu le mǒushì] ▶ **to eat/drink one's fill** 吃个饱/喝个够 ▶ **to fill sth with sth** 用某物填满某物 ▶ **to be filled with anger/resentment** 满腔怒火/憎恨

▶ **fill in I** VT **1** [+ hole, crack] 填满 [tiánmǎn] **2** (ESP BRIT) [+ form, questionnaire] 填写 [tiánxiě] [美= **fill out**] ▶ **to fill sb in on sth** (inf) 给某人提供关于某事的详情 **II** VI ▶ **to fill in for sb** 临时补某人的缺 [línshí bǔ mǒurén de quē]

▶ **fill out** VT [+ form] 填写 [tiánxiě]

▶ **fill up I** VT **1** [food +] [+ person] 使…有饱胀的感觉 [shǐ…yǒu bǎozhàng de gǎnjué] **2** (occupy) [+ container, space] 占满 [zhànmǎn] **3** [+ cup, saucepan] 倒满 [dàomǎn] ▶ **fill it** or **her up, please** (AUT) 请加满油 **II** VI [room, stadium +] 挤满 [jīmǎn]

filler ['fɪlə(r)] N [C/U] (for wood, plaster) 填充物 [tiánchōngwù]

fillet ['fɪlɪt] **I** N [C/U] [of meat, fish] 片 [piàn] **II** VT [+ fish, meat] 把…切成片 [bǎ…qiēchéng piàn]

fillet steak N [C/U] 牛肉片 [niúròu piàn]

filling ['fɪlɪŋ] **I** N **1** [C/U] (in tooth) 填补物 [tiánbǔ wù] **2** [C/U] [of cake, pie, sandwich] 馅 [xiàn] **II** ADJ [+ food] 易使人饱的 [yì shǐrén bǎo de]

filling station (ESP BRIT) N [C] 加油站 [jiāyóu zhàn] [美= **gas station**]

○ **film** [fɪlm] **I** N **1** [C] (ESP BRIT: TV) 影片

[yǐngpiàn] [美=**movie**] **2** [C/U] (PHOT) 胶卷 [jiāojuǎn] ▷ *a roll of film* 一卷胶卷 **3** [C] [*of dust, tears, grease*] 薄层 [báocéng] ▷ *A film of dust covered every surface.* 薄薄的一层灰尘覆盖了每一处表面。 **4** [U] (BRIT) (*also*: **clingfilm**) 薄膜 [bómó] **II** VT [+ *scene, person, book*] 把…拍成影片 [bǎ…pāichéng yǐngpiàn] **III** VI 拍摄 [pāishè] ▷ *The TV crews couldn't film at night.* 电视剧组人员晚上无法拍摄。

film star N [C] (ESP BRIT) 影星 [yǐngxīng]

filter [ˈfɪltə(r)] **I** N [C] **1** (*for water, oil*) 过滤器 [guòlù qì] **2** (PHOT) 滤器 [lùqì] **II** VT [+ *water, soil etc*] 过滤 [guò lù]

▶ **filter into** VT FUS [不可拆分] [*sound, light +*] 微微透入 [wēiwēi tòurù]

▶ **filter through** VI [*news, information +*] 慢慢传开 [mànmàn chuánkāi]

filter lane (BRIT: AUT) N [C] 转弯车道 [zhuǎnwān chēdào]

filth [fɪlθ] N [U] **1** (*dirt*) 污物 [wūwù] **2** (*smut*) 污秽内容 [wūhuì nèiróng]

filthy [ˈfɪlθɪ] ADJ **1** (*dirty*) [+ *object, person*] 污秽的 [wūhuì de] **2** (*disgusting*) [+ *language, book, habit*] 污秽的 [wūhuì de]

fin [fɪn] N [C] **1** [*of fish*] 鳍 [qí] **2** [*of aircraft*] 翼 [yì]

○**final** [ˈfaɪnl] **I** ADJ **1** (*last*) 最后的 [zuìhòu de] ▷ *Astronauts will make a final attempt to rescue the satellite.* 宇航员将做出最后的努力抢救卫星。 **2** (*definitive*) [+ *decision, offer*] 不可变更的 [bùkě biàngēng de] ▷ *The judges' decision is final.* 法官的决定是不可变更的。 **3** (*ultimate*) [+ *irony, humiliation*] 莫大的 [mòdà de] ▷ *Being sacked was the final humiliation.* 被解雇是莫大的羞辱。 **II** N [C] (SPORT) 决赛 [juésài] **III** finals NPL **1** (UNIV) 期末考试 [qīmò kǎoshì] **2** (SPORT) 决赛 [juésài] ▶ **to sit one's finals** 参加大学毕业考试

finale [fɪˈnɑːlɪ] N [C] **1** (THEAT) 最后一幕 [zuìhòu yīmù]; (MUS) 终曲 [zhōngqǔ] **2** (*fig*) 收场 [shōuchǎng]

finalist [ˈfaɪnəlɪst] N [C] 决赛选手 [juésài xuǎnshǒu]

finalize [ˈfaɪnəlaɪz] VT [+ *plans, deal, arrangements*] 最终确定 [zuìzhōng quèdìng]

finally [ˈfaɪnəlɪ] ADV **1** (*eventually*) 终于 [zhōngyú] **2** (*lastly*) 最后 [zuìhòu] **3** (*in conclusion*) 总之 [zǒngzhī] **4** (*irrevocably*) 确定地 [quèdìng de]

用法参见 **eventually**

finance [faɪˈnæns] **I** N [U] **1** (*money, backing*) 资金 [zījīn] **2** (*money management*) 财政 [cáizhèng] **II** VT (*back, fund*) 为…提供资金 [wèi…tígōng zījīn] **III** ˈn**ances** NPL 财力 [cáilì]

○**financial** [faɪˈnænʃəl] ADJ [+ *difficulties, adviser*] 财政的 [cáizhèng de] ▷ *The company is in financial difficulties.* 公司正处于财政困难时期。

financial year N [C] 财政年度 [cáizhèng niándù]

financier [faɪˈnænsɪə(r)] N [C] 出资人 [chūzīrén]

○**find** [faɪnd] (*pt, pp* **found**) **I** VT **1** (*locate*) [+ *person, object, exit*] 找到 [zhǎodào] ▷ *The police found a pistol at his home.* 警察在他家里找到一支手枪。; [+ *lost object*] 找回 [zhǎohuí] ▷ *He eventually found the book under his bed.* 他终于在床下找回了那本书。 **2** (*discover*) [+ *answer, solution*] 找出 [zhǎochū] ▷ *There is a genuine effort to find a solution.* 人们真心实意地努力寻找一条解决的途径。; [+ *object, person*] 发现 [fāxiàn] ▷ *When she got home she found a six-page letter from Tom.* 她到家时发现了一封汤姆写给她的6页的信。 **3** (*consider*) 认为 [rènwéi] ▷ *I don't find that funny at all.* 我认为那一点都没什么好玩的。 **4** (*get*) [+ *work, job*] 得到 [dédào] ▷ *He cannot find work.* 他没能得到工作。; [+ *money*] 筹集 [chóují] ▷ *Some families cannot even find enough money for basic needs.* 有些家庭甚至筹不到满足基本需要的钱。; [+ *time*] 有 [yǒu] ▷ *How do you find time to write these books?* 你怎么有时间写这些书? **II** N [C] (*discovery*) 难得之才 [nándé zhī cái] ▷ *They've got a new singer, and she's a real find.* 他们已经找到了一位新歌手，她是一个真正的难得之才。 ▶ **to find sb guilty/not guilty** 判决某人有罪/无罪 ▶ **to find one's way** 认得路 ▶ **many exotic species are found there** 那儿有许多奇异的物种 ▶ **I found myself starting to laugh** 我不由自主地笑了起来 ▶ **to find that…** 发现… ▷ *When I woke up, I found I couldn't move my legs.* 醒来时，我发觉腿动不了了。 ▶ **to find sth easy/difficult** 觉得某事容易/难

用法参见 **discover**

▶ **find out I** VT **1** [+ *fact, truth*] 查明 [chámíng] ▷ *You'll have to wait next week to find out what happens.* 让你们等到下周看看会怎样。 **2** [+ *person*] (*in wrongdoing*) 发现 [fāxiàn] ▷ *I wondered for a moment if she'd found me out.* 我一度想知道她是否已经发现我了。 **II** VI ▶ **to find out about sth** (*deliberately*) 获知某事 [huòzhī mǒushì]; (*by chance*) 偶然发现某物 [ǒurán fāxiàn mǒuwù]

findings [ˈfaɪndɪŋz] NPL [*of report*] 调查结果 [diàochá jiéguǒ]; [*of court, committee*] 裁决 [cáijué]

fine [faɪn] **I** ADJ **1** (*satisfactory*) 还不错的 [hái bùcuò de] **2** (*excellent*) [+ *object, person*] 好的 [hǎo de] **3** (*in texture*) [+ *hair, thread, powder, sand*] 细的 [xì de] **4** (*pleasant*) [+ *weather, day*] 晴朗的 [qínglǎng de] **5** (*subtle*) [+ *adjustment, detail, distinction*] 细微的 [xìwēi de] **II** ADV **1** (*well*) 不错地 [bùcuò de] **2** (*thinly*) 细地 [xì de] **III** N [C] (LAW) 罚款 [fákuǎn] **IV** VT (LAW) 处…以罚金 [chǔ…yǐ fájīn] ▶ **(I'm) fine** (我) 很好 ▶ **(that's) fine** (那) 好吧 ▶ **to cut it fine** (*in time*) 扣得紧 ▶ **you're doing fine** 你做得很好

fine art N [U] (*also*: **fine arts**) 美术 [měishù]

▶ **he's got it down to a fine art** 他对此游刃有余

finger ['fɪŋgə(r)] I N [c](ANAT) 手指 [shǒuzhǐ] II VT(touch) 触摸 [chùmō] ▶ **to keep one's fingers crossed** (fig) 祈愿好运 ▶ **to cross one's fingers** 食指与中指交叉重叠 ▶ **to point the finger at sb** (fig) 指责某人 ▶ **to put one's finger on sth** (fig) 对某事有充分把握

fingernail ['fɪŋgəneɪl] N [c] 指甲 [zhǐjia]

fingerprint ['fɪŋgəprɪnt] I N [c] 指纹 [zhǐwén] II VT[+ person] 取…的指纹 [qǔ…de zhǐwén] ▶ **to take sb's fingerprints** 取下某人的指纹

fingertip ['fɪŋgətɪp] N [c] 指尖 [zhǐjiān] ▶ **to have sth at one's fingertips** (at one's disposal) 轻而易举地得到某物; (know well) 对某事了如指掌

finish ['fɪnɪʃ] I N 1 [s](end) 结束 [jiéshù] 2 [c] (SPORT) 终点 [zhōngdiǎn] 3 [c](appearance, texture) 末道漆 [mòdào qī] II VT[+ work] 结束 [jiéshù]; [+ task, report, book] 完成 [wánchéng]; [+ drink] 喝完 [hēwán]; [+ sandwich] 吃完 [chīwán]; [+ cigarette] 吸完 [xīwán] III VI 1 [course, event +] 结束 [jiéshù] 2 [person +] 说完 [shuōwán] ▶ **a close finish** (SPORT) 扣人心弦的终场 ▶ **to finish doing sth** 做完某事 ▶ **to finish third** (in race, competition) 最后得了第三名 ▶ **to put the finishing touches to sth** 最后完结某事 ▶ **she's finished with him** (inf) 她已经跟他分手了
▶ **finish off** VT 1 [+ job, report] 完成 [wánchéng]; [+ dinner, wine] 吃/喝光 [chī/hēguāng] 2 (inf) (kill) 干掉 [gàndiào]
▶ **finish up** I VI (end up) 告终 [gàozhōng] II VT 1 [+ meal] 吃完 [chīwán]; [+ drink] 喝完 [hēwán] 2 (US) (finish off) 完成 [wánchéng]

finite ['faɪnaɪt] ADJ 1 [+ number, amount] 有限的 [yǒuxiàn de] 2 [+ verb] 限定的 [xiàndìng de]

Finland ['fɪnlənd] N 芬兰 [Fēnlán]

Finn [fɪn] N [c] 芬兰人 [Fēnlánrén]

Finnish ['fɪnɪʃ] I ADJ 芬兰的 [Fēnlán de] II N [U](language) 芬兰语 [Fēnlán yǔ]

fir [fə:(r)] N (also: **fir tree**) 冷杉 [lěngshān]

fire ['faɪə(r)] I N 1 [U](flames) 火 [huǒ] 2 [c] (in fireplace, hearth etc) 炉火 [lúhuǒ] 3 [c/U] (accidental) 火灾 [huǒzāi] 4 [U](shots) 射击 [shèjī] II VT 1 (shoot) [+ gun, bullet, shot, arrow] 射出 [shèchū] 2 (stimulate) [+ imagination, enthusiasm] 激起 [jīqǐ] 3 (inf) (dismiss) [+ employee] 解雇 [jiěgù] III VI (shoot) 开火 [kāihuǒ] ▶ **on fire** 起火 ▶ **to set fire to sth, set sth on fire** 放火烧某物 ▶ **electric/gas fire** (ESP BRIT) 电/煤气炉 [美=**heater**] ▶ **to come/be under fire (from)** 遭到(来自…的)射击 ▶ **to catch fire** 着火 ▶ **to open fire (on sb)** (向某人)开火 ▶ **to fire questions at sb** 向某人急速地连续发问

fire alarm N [c] 火警警报 [huǒjǐng jǐngbào]

firearm ['faɪərɑ:m] N [c] 枪支 [qiāngzhī]

fire brigade N [c] 消防队 [xiāofáng duì]

fire department (US) N [c] 消防部门 [xiāofáng bùmén] [英=**fire service**]

fire engine (BRIT) N [c] 救火车 [jiùhuǒchē] [美=**fire truck**]

fire escape N [c] 太平梯 [tàipíngtī]

fire exit N [c] 安全出口 [ānquán chūkǒu]

fire extinguisher N [c] 灭火器 [mièhuǒqì]

fireman ['faɪəmən] (pl **firemen**) N [c] 消防队员 [xiāofáng duìyuán]

fireplace ['faɪəpleɪs] N [c] 壁炉 [bìlú]

fire service (BRIT) N [c] 消防部门 [xiāofáng bùmén]

fire station N [c] 消防站 [xiāofángzhàn]

fire truck (US) N [c] 救火车 [jiùhuǒchē] [英=**fire engine**]

firewall ['faɪəwɔ:l] (COMPUT) N [c] 防火墙 [fánghuǒqiáng]

firewood ['faɪəwʊd] N [U] 木柴 [mùchái]

firework ['faɪəwɜ:k] N [c](explosive) 烟火 [yānhuǒ] II **'reworks** NPL (display) 烟火表演 [yānhuǒ biǎoyǎn]

firing line ['faɪərɪŋ-] N ▶ **to be in the firing line** (fig) 在第一线 [zài dìyīxiàn]

○**firm** [fə:m] I ADJ 1 [+ mattress, ground] 硬实的 [yìngshí de] 2 [+ person] 坚定的 [jiāndìng de] 3 [+ grasp, hold, grip] (lit) 稳定而有力的 [wěndìng ér yǒulì de] ▷ I took a firm hold on the rope. 我牢牢地抓着绳子。; (fig) 毫不动摇的 [háobù dòngyáo de] ▷ He has a firm grasp of the principles. 他毫不动摇地坚持原则。4 [+ views, leadership] 强有力的 [qiángyǒulì de] 5 [+ offer] 确定的 [quèdìng de] 6 [+ decision, opinion] 坚决的 [jiānjué de] ▷ He made a firm decision to leave. 他作出坚决的决定要离开。7 [+ evidence, news, information] 确凿的 [quèzáo de] ▷ We have no firm evidence. 我们没有确凿的证据。II N [c] (company) 公司 [gōngsī] ▶ **to be firm with sb** 严格对待某人 ▶ **to stand firm** 立场坚定 ▶ **to be a firm believer in sth** 是某事坚定的信仰者

firmly ['fə:mlɪ] ADV 1 [rest, stand +] 牢牢地 [láoláo de]; [push, pull, hold +] 紧紧地 [jǐnjǐn de] 2 [believe +] 坚定地 [jiāndìng de] 3 [say, tell +] 坚决地 [jiānjué de]

○**first** [fə:st] I ADJ 1 (in series) 第一的 [dìyī de] ▷ For the first time in our lives… 我们生命中的第一次… 2 (initial) [+ reaction, impression] 最初的 [zuìchū de] ▷ My first reaction was one of horror. 我最初的反应是害怕。3 (top) [+ prize, division] 头等的 [tóuděng de] ▷ She won first prize. 她得了头等奖。4 (front) [+ row] 第一的 [dìyī de] ▷ We had seats in the first row. 我们的座位在第一排。5 (main) [+ duty, responsibility] 首要的 [shǒuyào de] ▷ My first duty is to my patients. 我首先要对病人负责。II ADV 1 (before anyone else) [speak, arrive +] 首先 [shǒuxiān] ▷ Jenny spoke first. 詹妮首先发言。2 (before other things) 首先

[shǒuxiān] ▷ But first I had to get a visa. 但是首先我得先拿到签证。**3** (when listing reasons) 第一 [dìyī] ▷ There were several reasons for this. First, four submarines had been sighted. 这有几个原因。第一，发现了4艘潜水艇。**4** (for the first time) 第一次 [dìyīcì] ▷ Sophie and Dave first met in the summer of 1910. 索菲和戴夫第一次是在1910年夏天相遇。**5** (in race, competition) [come, finish +] 第一名 [dìyīmíng] ▷ Johnson came first in the one hundred metres. 约翰逊在一百米跑比赛中获得第一名。**III** N **1** [U] (AUT) (also: **first gear**) 一挡 [yīdǎng] ▷ I changed down into first. 我换到了一挡。**2** [C] (BRIT: UNIV) 甲等 [jiǎděng] ▷ He got a first in French. 他的法语得了甲等。**3** [C] (event) 首次 [shǒucì] ▷ The meeting between financial analysts was a first for the company. 金融分析家之间的会议在公司里是首次。▶ **at first** 起先 ▶ **first of all** 首先 ▶ **the first of January** 1月1号 ▶ **in the first instance** 起初 ▶ I'll do it first thing tomorrow 明天我首先做这件事 ▶ **from the (very) first** 从(最)一开始 ▶ **to put sb/sth first** 把某人/某事放在第一位 ▶ **at first hand** 直接地 ▶ **the first I heard/knew of it** 最初我所听到的/所知道的

first aid N [U] 急救 [jíjiù]

first-aid kit [fə:st'eɪd-] N [C] 急救包 [jíjiùbāo]

first-class I ADJ **1** (excellent) [+ worker, piece of work] 第一流的 [dìyīliú de] **2** [+ carriage, ticket, stamp] 一类的 [yīlèi de] **II** ADV [travel, send +] 作为一类 [zuòwéi yīlèi]

first-hand [fə:st'hænd] ADJ [+ knowledge, experience] 第一手的 [dìyīshǒu de]

first lady N [C] 第一夫人 [dìyī fūrén] ▶ **the first lady of jazz** 爵士乐之后

firstly ['fə:stlɪ] ADV 首先 [shǒuxiān]

first name N [C] 名 [míng] ▶ **to be on first-name terms (with sb)** (与某人) 关系亲密

first-rate [fə:st'reɪt] ADJ [+ actor, swimmer, performance] 第一流的 [dìyīliú de]

fiscal ['fɪskl] ADJ [+ year, policy] 财政的 [cáizhèng de]

fish [fɪʃ] I N **1** [C] (ZOOL) 鱼 [yú] **2** [U] (food) 鱼肉 [yúròu] **II** VT [+ river, area] 捕 [bǔ] **III** VI **1** (commercially) 捕鱼 [bǔyú]; (as sport, hobby) 钓鱼 [diàoyú] ▶ **to go fishing** 去钓鱼
▶ **fish out** (inf) VT (from water) 打捞 [dǎlāo]; (from box, bag etc) 掏出 [tāochū]

fish and chips (BRIT) N [U] 炸鱼排加炸薯条

◆ **FISH AND CHIPS**

● **fish and chips** 是一种英国传统的外卖食
● 品，由卷着面糊的大块炸鱼排和炸薯条组
● 成，用醋或辣酱调味。**fish and chips** 可以
● 在 **chip shop** [参见 **chip shop**] 里买
● 到。你可以买回家吃，也可以在街上吃。
● 鱼一般用鳕鱼、黑斑鳕鱼或鲽鱼。

fisherman ['fɪʃəmən] (pl **fishermen**) N [C] 渔民 [yúmín]

fishery ['fɪʃərɪ] N [C] **1** (fishing grounds) 渔场 [yúchǎng] **2** (fish farm) 养鱼场 [yǎngyúchǎng]

fish fingers (BRIT) NPL 炸鱼条 [zháyú tiáo]

fishing ['fɪʃɪŋ] N [U] 钓鱼 [diàoyú]

fishing boat N [C] 渔船 [yúchuán]

fishing line N [C] (line) 钓丝 [diàosī]

fishing rod N [C] 钓竿 [diàogān]

fishmonger ['fɪʃmʌŋgə(r)], **fishmonger's** (ESP BRIT) N [C] 鱼贩 [yúfàn]

fish sticks (US) NPL 炸鱼条 [zháyú tiáo] [英= **fish fingers**]

fishy ['fɪʃɪ] ADJ **1** [+ taste, smell] 鱼味的 [yúwèi de] **2** (inf) (suspicious) 可疑的 [kěyí de]

fist [fɪst] N [C] 拳 [quán]

fit [fɪt] I ADJ **1** (suitable) 合适的 [héshì de] **2** (healthy) 健康的 [jiànkāng de] **II** VT **1** [clothes, shoes +] 合…的身 [hé…de shēn] **2** (attach) [+ lock, wheels] 安装 [ānzhuāng] **3** (be suitable for) [+ needs, aims] 与…相协调 [yǔ…xiāng xiétiáo] **4** (match) [+ facts, theory, description] 与…相符 [yǔ…xiāngfú] **III** VI **1** [clothes, shoes +] 合身 [héshēn] **2** (in space, gap) 适合 [shìhé] **IV** N [C] (MED) 发作 [fāzuò] ▶ **to be fit to** (inf) (about to) 马上就 ▶ **to be fit for** (suitable for) 适于 ▶ **to keep fit** 保持健康 ▶ **to see fit to do sth** 认为做某事合适 ▶ **a fit of rage** 一阵怒火 ▶ **a fit of giggles** 一阵咯咯的笑 ▶ **a fit of hysterics** 一阵歇斯底里的发作 ▶ **to have a fit** (MED) 癫痫病发作; (fig) 震惊 ▶ **to be a good fit** 很合身 ▶ **in or by fits and starts** 一阵一阵的 ▶ **to fit sth with sth** 给某物安装某物
▶ **fit in** I VI **1** (lit) [person, object +] 容纳 [róngnà] **2** (fig) [person +] 接纳 [jiēnà] **II** VT (fig) [+ appointment, visitor] 定时用于 [dìng shíjiān yú] ▶ **to fit in with sb's plans** 正合某人的计划
▶ **fit into** VT **1** [+ hole, gap] 刚好放下 [gānghǎo fàngxià] **2** [+ suitcase, room] 放得下 [fàngdexià] **3** [person +] [+ group] 合群 [héqún]
▶ **fit out, fit up** VT (equip) 提供装备 [tígōng zhuāngbèi]

fitment ['fɪtmənt] N [C] (furnishing) 家具 [jiājù]; (equipment) 设备 [shèbèi]

fitness ['fɪtnɪs] N [U] **1** (MED) 健康 [jiànkāng] **2** (suitability) 适合 [shìhé]

fitted ['fɪtɪd] ADJ [+ jacket] 合身的 [héshēn de]; [+ carpet, wardrobe] 定做的 [dìngzuò de] ▶ **fitted with** 配备…的

fitted carpet N [C] 按照房间尺寸铺好的地毯

fitted kitchen (BRIT) N [C] 有固定设备的厨房

fitted sheet N [C] 四角缝紧兜住床垫的床单 [sìjiǎo féngjǐn dōuzhù de chuángdān]

fitter ['fɪtə(r)] N [C] (person) 装备工 [zhuāngbèi gōng]

fitting ['fɪtɪŋ] I ADJ (appropriate) [+ tribute, conclusion] 恰当的 [qiàdàng de] II N [C] **1** (for *clothes*) 试穿 [shìchuān] **2** (*handle, tap*) 配件 [pèijiàn] **III 'ttings** NPL (*in building*) 装置 [zhuāngzhì]

fitting room N [c] (*in shop*) 试衣间 [shìyījiān]

○**five** [faɪv] NUM 五 [wǔ] ▸ **that will be five pounds, please** 请付5镑 ▸ **she's five (years old)** 她5岁了 ▸ **it's five o'clock** 5点了 ▸ **no later than five (o'clock)** 不迟于5点 ▸ **there are five of us** 有5个人 ▸ **all five of them** 他们5个人都 ▸ **five hundred/thousand children** 五百/千名儿童

fiver ['faɪvə(r)] (BRIT: *inf*) N [c] 五镑钞票 [wǔbàng chāopiào]

fix [fɪks] I VT **1** (*set*) [+ *date, price, meeting*] 确定 [quèdìng] **2** (*mend*) [+ *machine, leak, fault*] 修理 [xiūlǐ] **3** (*resolve*) [+ *problem*] 解决 [jiějué] **4** (*prepare*) [+ *meal, drink*] 准备 [zhǔnbèi] **5** (*inf*) [+ *game, election, result*] 操纵 [cāozòng] **II** N (*inf*) **1** ▸ **to be in a fix** 陷入进退维谷的境地 [xiànrù jìn tuì wéi gǔ de jìngdì] **2** [c] (*injection*) 毒品注射 [dúpǐn zhùshè] ▸ **a fix of coffee/chocolate** (*inf*) 我每天需要定量的咖啡/巧克力 ▸ **to fix sth to/on sth** (*attach*) 把某物安装在某物上 ▸ **to fix one's eyes on sb/sth** 盯着某人/某事 ▸ **to fix one's attention on sb/sth** 将注意力集中于某人/某物 ▸ **the fight was a fix** 这场拳击赛受到了操纵
▸ **fix up** VT (*arrange*) [+ *meeting, appointment*] 安排 [ānpái] ▸ **to fix sb up with sth** 给某人提供某物

fixed [fɪkst] ADJ **1** [+ *price, amount, intervals*] 固定的 [gùdìng de] **2** [+ *ideas*] 固执的 [gùzhí de] **3** [+ *smile*] 呆板的 [dāibǎn de] ▸ **there's a fixed charge** 收费固定 ▸ **how are you fixed for money/time?** 经济情况如何/有时间吗？ ▸ **of no fixed address** or (BRIT: *frm*) **abode** 没有固定的住所

fixture ['fɪkstʃə(r)] N [c] **1** (*bath, sink, cupboard*) 固定装置 [gùdìng zhuāngzhì] **2** (BRIT: SPORT) 预定日期的比赛项目 [yùdìng rìqī de bǐsài xiàngmù] ▸ **she is a fixture in New York's nightclubs** 她是纽约夜总会的常客 ▸ **sold with fixtures and fittings** 连同家具和设备一同出售的

fizzy ['fɪzɪ] (BRIT) ADJ [+ *drink*] 带气的 [dàiqì de] [美= **carbonated**]

flag [flæg] N [c] **1** 旗 [qí] **2** (*also*: **flagstone**) 石板 [shíbǎn] **II** VI [*person +*] 疲倦 [píjuàn]; [*spirits, enthusiasm +*] 衰退 [shuāituì] ▸ **to fly the flag** (*fig*) 表示拥护和支持
▸ **flag down** VT [+ *taxi, car*] 挥手示意…停下 [huīshǒu shìyì…tíngxià]

flagpole ['flægpəʊl] N [c] 旗杆 [qígān]

flair [flεə(r)] N **1** ▸ **to have a flair for sth** 对某事有天分 [duì mǒushì yǒu tiānfèn] **2** [U] (*panache*) 气派 [qìpài]

flak [flæk] N [U] **1** (MIL) 高射炮 [gāoshè pào] **2** (*fig*) (*criticism*) 批评 [pīpíng]

flake [fleɪk] I N [c] **1** (*of rust, paint*) 薄片 [báopiàn] **2** (*of snow*) 片 [piàn] **II** VI (*also*: **flake off**) [*paint, enamel +*] 剥落 [bōluò]
▸ **flake out** (*inf*) VI [*person +*] 累得瘫倒 [lèidé tāndǎo]

flamboyant [flæm'bɔɪənt] ADJ [+ *clothes, style*] 艳丽的 [yànlìde]; [+ *person*] 派头十足的 [pàitóu shízúde]

flame [fleɪm] N [c/U] (*of fire*) 火焰 [huǒyán] ▸ **to burst into flames** 烧起来 ▸ **in flames** 燃烧着 ▸ **an old flame** (*inf*) 老情人

flamingo [flə'mɪŋgəʊ] (*pl* **flamingos** or **flamingoes**) N [c] 火烈鸟 [huǒliè niǎo]

flammable ['flæməbl] ADJ [+ *gas, fabric*] 易燃的 [yìrán de]

flan [flæn] N [c] 果酱饼 [guǒjiàng bǐng]

flank [flæŋk] I N [c] **1** (*of animal*) 胁腹 [xiéfù] **2** (*of army*) 侧翼 [cèyì] **II** VT ▸ **to be flanked by sb/sth** 某人/某物在…的旁边 [mǒurén/mǒuwù zài…de pángbiān]

flannel ['flænl] I N **1** [U] (*fabric*) 法兰绒 [fǎlánróng] **2** [c] (BRIT) (*also*: **face flannel**) 面巾 [miànjīn] [美= **washcloth**] **3** [U] (BRIT: *inf*) (*waffle*) 兜圈子 [dōuquānzi] **II** ,**annels** NPL (*o.f.*) 法兰绒裤子 [fǎlánróng kùzi]

flap [flæp] I N [c] (*of pocket, envelope, skin*) 盖 [gài] **II** VT [+ *arms, wings*] 摆动 [bǎidòng] **III** VI [*sail, flag +*] 摆动 ▸ **to be in a flap (about** or **over sth)** (*inf*) （对某事）慌作一团

flare [flεə(r)] I N [c] (*signal*) 信号弹 [xìnhàodàn] **II** VI **1** [*fire, match +*] 火焰突然变旺 [huǒyàn tūrán biànwàng] **2** (*also*: **flare up**) [*fighting, violence, trouble +*] 突然爆发 [tūrán bàofā] **3** [*tempers +*] 突然发怒 [tūrán fānù] **4** [*nostrils +*] 鼓起 [gǔqǐ] ▸ **flare up** VI [*disease, injury +*] 突然发作 [tūrán fāzuò] **III** ,**ares** NPL (*trousers*) 喇叭裤 [lǎbakù]

flash [flæʃ] I VT **1** [+ *light*] 使闪光 [shǐ shǎnguāng] **2** (*send*) [+ *news, message*] 传送 [chuánsòng] **3** [+ *look, smile*] 闪过 [shǎnguò] **II** VI **1** [*lightning, light +*] 闪光 [shǎnguāng] **2** (*liter*) [*eyes +*] 闪烁 [shǎnshuò] **III** N [c] **1** (*of light, lightning*) 闪光 [shǎnguāng] **2** (PHOT) 闪光灯 [shǎnguāngdēng] **3** (US: *inf*) (*also*: **flashlight**) 闪光信号灯 [shǎnguāng xìnhàodēng] [英= **torch**] **IV** ADJ (*inf*) [+ *restaurant, car*] 浮华的 [fúhuá de] ▸ **in a flash** 一刹那间 ▸ **quick as a flash** 极快 ▸ **a flash of inspiration/anger** 突如其来的灵感/怒气 ▸ **to flash one's headlights** 亮起车头灯 ▸ **the thought flashed through his mind** 一个想法在他脑子里突然闪现 ▸ **to flash by** or **past** 一闪而过

flashback ['flæʃbæk] N [c] **1** (CINE) 闪回 [shǎnhuí] **2** (PSYCH) 回想 [huíxiǎng]

flashbulb ['flæʃbʌlb] N [c] 闪光灯泡 [shǎnguāng dēngpào]

flashlight ['flæʃlaɪt] (ESP US) N [c] 手电筒

▶ **flecks of dust/blood** 尘粒/血斑

flashy ['flæʃɪ] (inf, pej) ADJ 华丽而俗气的 [huálì ér súqì de]

flask [flɑːsk] N [c] 1 (also: **vacuum flask**) 保温瓶 [bǎowēnpíng] 2 (bottle) 携带式酒瓶 [xiédàishì jiǔpíng] 3 (CHEM) 烧瓶 [shāopíng]

flat [flæt] I ADJ 1 (level) [+ ground, surface] 平的 [píng de] 2 (shallow) 浅的 [qiǎn de] 3 [+ tyre, ball] 气不足的 [qì bùzú de] 4 (BRIT) [+ battery] 没电的 [méidiàn de] [美=**dead**] 5 [+ beer, champagne] 跑了气的 [pǎole qì de] 6 [+ refusal, rejection, denial] 断然的 [duànrán de] 7 (MUS) [+ singing, instrument] 降音的 [jiàngyīn de] 8 [+ rate, fee] 统一的 [tǒngyī de] 9 (without emotion) [+ voice] 无精打采的 [wújīngdǎcǎi de] II N [c] 1 (BRIT) (in building) 公寓 [gōngyù] [美=**apartment**] 2 (AUT) 漏气车胎 [lòuqì chētāi] 3 (MUS) 降号 [jiànghào] III ADV 1 [lie +] 平地 [píngdì] 2 (MUS) [sing, play +] 降音地 [jiàngyīn de] ▶ **to work flat out** (BRIT) 全力工作 ▶ **in 10 minutes flat** 就10分钟 ▶ **to fall flat** [joke, attempt +] 毫无效果 ▶ **the flat of one's hand** 手掌 ▶ **B/A flat** (MUS) 降B/A音

flatten ['flætn] I VT 1 (also: **flatten out**) 使变平 [shǐ biànpíng] 2 (destroy) [+ building, crop, city] 夷平 [yípíng] II VI (also: **flatten out**) 平展 [píngzhǎn] ▶ **to flatten o.s. against a wall** 自己平倚着墙

flatter ['flætə(r)] VT 1 (praise) 奉承 [fèngchéng] 2 (dress, photograph +) 使更漂亮 [shǐ gèng piàoliàng] ▶ **to be flattered (that...)** (对于…)感到荣幸 ▶ **to flatter o.s. (that...)** (对…)自我感觉良好

flattering ['flætərɪŋ] ADJ 1 [+ comment] 奉承的 [fèngchéng de] 2 [+ dress, photograph] 使美过其实的 [shǐ měiguo qíshí de]

flaunt [flɔːnt] VT [+ wealth, possessions] 炫耀 [xuànyào]

flavour, (US) flavor ['fleɪvə(r)] I N [c/u] [of food, drink] 味 [wèi] II VT [+ food, drink] 给…调味 [gěi...tiáowèi] ▶ **strawberry-flavoured** 草莓味的 ▶ **music with an African flavour** 具有非洲风情的音乐

flavoured, (US) flavored ['fleɪvəd] ADJ 经调味的 [jīng tiáowèi de] ▶ **flavoured with** 加了…调味的

flavouring, (US) flavoring ['fleɪvərɪŋ] N [c/u] 调味品 [tiáowèipǐn]

flaw [flɔː] N [c] (in argument, theory) 缺陷 [quēxiàn]; (in character) 缺点 [quēdiǎn]; (in cloth, pattern) 瑕疵 [xiácī]

flawless ['flɔːlɪs] ADJ [+ performance, complexion] 完美无瑕的 [wánměi wúxiá de]

flea [fliː] N [c] 跳蚤 [tiàozǎo]

fleck [flek] I N [c] 1 (of mud, paint, colour) 斑点 [bāndiǎn] 2 (pattern) 点 [diǎn] II VT ▶ **to be flecked with mud/blood** etc 溅有泥点/血斑 {等} [jiànyǒu nídiǎn/xuèbān{děng}] ▶ **brown flecked with white** 夹杂白色斑点的褐色

flee [fliː] (pt, pp **fled** [fled]) I VT [+ danger, famine, country] 逃离 [táolí] II VI (refugees, escapees +) 逃走 [táozǒu]

fleece [fliːs] I N [c] 1 (sheep's wool) 羊毛 [yángmáo]; (sheep's coat) 羊的皮毛 [yángde pímáo] 2 (garment) 毛呢衣物 [máoní yīwù] II VT (inf) (cheat) 诈取 [zhàqǔ]

fleet [fliːt] N [c] [of ships, lorries, buses] 队 [duì]

fleeting ['fliːtɪŋ] ADJ [+ glimpse, visit, happiness] 短暂的 [duǎnzàn de]

Flemish ['flemɪʃ] I ADJ 佛兰芒的 [Fólánmáng de] II N [u] (language) 佛兰芒语 [Fólánmáng yǔ]

flesh [fleʃ] N [u] 1 (ANAT) 肉 [ròu] 2 (skin) 肉体 [ròutǐ] 3 [of fruit, vegetable] 果肉 [guǒròu] ▶ **in the flesh** 亲自 ▶ **she's my own flesh and blood** 她是我的亲骨肉
▶ **flesh out** VT [+ proposal, account] 充实 [chōngshí]

flew [fluː] PT of **²fly**

flex [fleks] I N [c/u] (BRIT) [of appliance] 电线 [diànxiàn] [美=**cord**] II VT [+ muscles, fingers] 屈曲 [qūqū]

flexibility [fleksɪ'bɪlɪtɪ] N [u] 1 [of object, material] 柔韧性 [róurènxìng] 2 [of ideas, approach] 灵活性 [línghuóxìng]

flexible ['fleksəbl] ADJ 1 [+ material] 柔韧的 [róurèn de] 2 [+ response, policy] 灵活的 [línghuó de] 3 [+ person, schedule] 机动的 [jīdòng de]

flexitime ['fleksɪtaɪm] (BRIT) N [u] 弹性工作制 [tánxìng gōngzuò zhì] ▶ **to work flexitime, be on flexitime** 按弹性工作制工作 [美=**flextime**]

flick [flɪk] I VT (with fingers) 轻弹 [qīngtán]; [+ whip, towel] 轻拂 [qīngfú]; [+ cigarette ash] 弹去 [tánqù]; [+ switch] 拨 [bō] II VI 快而轻地移动 [kuài ér qīng de yídòng] III N [c] [of finger, hand] 轻拂 [qīngfú]; [of whip] 轻打 [qīngdǎ]; (through book, pages) 快速翻阅 [kuàisù fānyuè] IV **the icks** NPL (BRIT: inf) 电影院 [diànyǐngyuàn]
▶ **flick through** VT FUS [不可拆分] [+ book, pages] 快速翻阅 [kuàisù fānyuè]

flicker ['flɪkə(r)] I VI 1 [light, candle +] 闪烁 [shǎnshuò] 2 [smile, look +] 闪过 [shǎnguò] II N [c] 1 [of light, flames] 闪烁 [shǎnshuò] 2 [of pain, fear] 一丝 [yīsī] 3 [of smile] 闪现 [shǎnxiàn]

flight [flaɪt] N 1 [u] (action) [of plane] 飞行 [fēixíng]; [of birds] 飞翔 [fēixiáng] 2 [c] (AVIAT) (journey) 航班 [hángbān]; (plane) 班机 [bānjī] 3 [u] (escape) 逃逸 [táoyì] 4 [c] ▶ **flight of stairs, flight of steps** 一段楼梯 [yīduàn lóutī] ▶ **to take flight** 逃跑 ▶ **a flight of fancy** 异想天开

flight attendant N [c] (male) 男空服人员 [nán kōngfú rényuán]; (female) 空姐 [kōngjiě]

flight deck N [C] **1** (AVIAT) 驾驶舱 [jiàshǐ cāng] **2** (NAUT) 飞行甲板 [fēixíng jiǎbǎn]

flimsy ['flɪmzɪ] ADJ **1** [+ structure, door, lock] 不结实的 [bù jiēshi de]; [+ clothes, shoes] 轻薄的 [qīngbó de] **2** [+ excuse, evidence] 不足信的 [bùzúxìn de]

flinch [flɪntʃ] VI (in pain) 退缩 [tuìsuō] ▶ **to flinch from** [+ unpleasant duty, decision] 逃避

fling [flɪŋ] (pt, pp **flung**) I VT [+ ball, stone, hat] 掷 [zhì]; [+ one's arms, oneself] 猛然移动 [měngrán yídòng] II N (inf) **1** (love affair) 一时的行乐 [yìshí de xínglè] **2** [S] (spree) 放纵 [fàngzòng]

flint [flɪnt] N **1** [U] (stone) 燧石 [suìshí] **2** [U] (in cigarette lighter) 打火石 [dǎhuǒshí]

flip [flɪp] I VT **1** [+ lights, switch] 捻 [niǎn] **2** (also: **flip over**) 快速地翻转 [kuàisù de fānzhuǎn] II VI 一下翻转 [yíxià fānzhuǎn] ▶ **to flip a coin** 抛硬币 ▶ **to flip a pancake** 翻烙饼
▶ **flip through** VT FUS [不可拆分] [+ book, pages] 快速翻阅 [kuàisù fānyuè]

flip-flops ['flɪpflɔps] (ESP BRIT) NPL 夹趾拖鞋 [jiāzhǐ tuōxié] [美=**thongs**]

flipper ['flɪpə(r)] N [C] **1** [of seal, penguin] 鳍状肢 [qízhuàngzhī] **2** [for swimming] 脚蹼 [jiǎopǔ]

flirt [flə:t] I VI (with person) 调情 [tiáoqíng] II N [C] 调情者 [tiáoqíngzhě] ▶ **to flirt with an idea** 对某个想法只是想想而已

flit [flɪt] VI **1** [person +] 换来换去 [huànlái huànqù]; [bird, butterfly +] 飞来飞去 [fēilái fēiqù] **2** [expression, smile +] 掠过 [lüèguò]

float [fləʊt] I VI **1** (on water) [object +] 漂浮 [piāofú] **2** (through air) [paper, feather +] 飘浮 [piāofú] **3** (liter) [sound, smell +] 飘散 [piāosàn] **4** (stay afloat) [swimmer, object +] 浮着 [fúzhe] **5** (COMM) [currency +] 浮动 [fúdòng] II VT **1** (COMM) [+ currency] 使浮动 [shǐ fúdòng] **2** (COMM) [+ company] 首次公开发行公司股票 [shǒucì gōngkāi fāxíng gōngsī gǔpiào] **3** [+ idea, plan] 提出 [tíchū] III N [C] **1** (for fishing) 鱼漂 [yúpiāo] **2** (for swimming) 浮板 [fúbǎn] **3** (in carnival) 彩车 [cǎichē] **4** (BRIT) (money) 周转零款 [zhōuzhuǎn língkuǎn]
▶ **float around** VI [idea, rumour +] 广为流传 [guǎngwéiliúchuán]

flock [flɔk] I N [C] **1** [of sheep, birds] 群 [qún] **2** (o.f.: REL) 同一牧师管辖下的全体教徒 II VI [people +] 成群结队 [chéngqúnjiéduì] ▶ **flocks of journalists** 众多的新闻记者

flog [flɔg] VT **1** (whip) 抽打 [chōudǎ] **2** (BRIT: inf) (sell) 卖 [mài]

flood [flʌd] N **1** [C/U] [of water] 洪水 [hóngshuǐ] **2** [C] [of letters, requests, imports] 大量 [dàliàng] II VT **1** (through forces of nature) 淹没 [yānmò] **2** (intentionally) 浇灌 [jiāoguàn] **3** (AUT) [+ engine] 使…溢流 [shǐ…yìliú] III VI **1** [place +] 为水所淹 [wéishuǐ suǒyān] **2** [people, goods +] ▶ **to flood into** 洪水般涌入 [hóngshuǐ bān yǒngrù] ▶ **to flood the market** (COMM) 充斥市场 ▶ **in flood** 泛滥

flooding ['flʌdɪŋ] N [U] 泛滥 [fànlàn]

floodlight ['flʌdlaɪt] I N [C] 泛光灯 [fànguāng dēng] II VT 用泛光灯照亮 [yòng fànguāngdēng zhàoliàng]

floor [flɔ:(r)] N I **1** [C] [of room] 地板 [dìbǎn] **2** [C] (storey) 楼层 [lóucéng] **3** [S] [of sea, valley] 底 [dǐ] II VT **1** (knock down) 把…打翻在地 [bǎ…dǎfān zàidì] **2** (surprise) [question, remark +] 使惊得无以应付 [shǐ jīngde wúyǐ yìngfu] ▶ **on the floor** 在地板上 ▶ **ground floor** (BRIT) 一楼 ▶ **first floor** (BRIT) 二楼; (US) 一楼 ▶ **top floor** 顶层 ▶ **to take the floor** [speaker +] 开始发言

在英式英语中，建筑的 **ground floor** 是指紧贴地面的那个楼层。它上面的一层叫 **first floor**。在美式英语中，**first floor** 是指紧贴地面的楼层，它上面的一层是 **second floor**。

floorboard ['flɔ:bɔ:d] N [C] 地板块 [dìbǎn kuài]

flooring ['flɔ:rɪŋ] N [U] 地板材料 [dìbǎn cáiliào]

floor show N [C] 夜总会的文娱表演

flop [flɔp] I VI **1** (into chair, onto floor etc) 猛落 [měngluò] **2** (inf) (fail) 失败 [shībài] II N [C] (inf) (failure) 失败 [shībài]

floppy ['flɔpɪ] I ADJ [+ hat, bow] 松垂的 [sōngchuí de] II N [C] (also: **floppy disk**) 软盘 [ruǎnpán]

flora ['flɔ:rə] N [U/PL] 植物群 [zhíwù qún]

floral ['flɔ:rl] ADJ [+ dress, pattern] 花卉的 [huāhuì de] ▶ **a floral arrangement** 花饰

florist ['flɔrɪst] N [C] **1** (shopkeeper) 花商 [huāshāng] **2** (also: **florist's**) 花店 [huādiàn]

flotation [fləʊ'teɪʃən] N [C/U] [of company] 股票发行 [gǔpiào fāxíng]

flounder ['flaʊndə(r)] (pl **flounder**) I VI **1** [swimmer +] 挣扎 [zhēngzhá] **2** [career, economy +] 垂死挣扎 [chuísǐ zhēngzhá]; [person, speaker +] 漫无目的 [mànwú mùdì] II N [C/U] (ZOOL) 鲆鲽 [píngdié]

flour ['flaʊə(r)] N [U] 面粉 [miànfěn]

flourish ['flʌrɪʃ] I VI **1** [business, economy, arts +] 繁荣 [fánróng] **2** [plant, animal +] 兴旺 [xīngwàng] II VT [+ document, handkerchief] 挥舞 [huīwǔ] III N ▶ **with a flourish** 用花哨的动作 [yòng huāxiao de dòngzuò]

flout [flaʊt] VT [+ law, convention] 蔑视 [mièshì]

flow [fləʊ] I VI **1** [liquid, gas, electricity +] 流动 [liúdòng] **2** [traffic, people +] 川流不息 [chuānliú bùxī] **3** [money, information +] 流通 [liútōng] **4** (liter) [clothes, hair +] 飘垂 [piāochuí] II N [C/U] **1** [of liquid, gas, electricity] 流动 [liúdòng] **2** [of traffic] 川流不息 [chuānliú bùxī] **3** [of money, information] 流通 [liútōng] **4** [of tide] 涨潮 [zhǎngcháo] **5** [of thought, speech] 流畅 [liúchàng]

flower ['flaʊə(r)] I N [c] 花 [huā] II VI 1 [plant, tree +] 开花 [kāihuā] 2 (fig) (blossom) 成熟 [chéngshú] ▶ **in flower** 正开着花

flower bed N [c] 花坛 [huātán]

flowerpot ['flaʊəpɒt] N [c] 花盆 [huāpén]

flown [fləʊn] PP of ²**y**

flu [fluː] N [U] 流感 [liúgǎn]

fluctuate ['flʌktjʊeɪt] VI [price, rate, temperature +] 波动 [bōdòng]; [opinions, attitudes +] 动摇 [dòngyáo]

fluent ['fluːənt] ADJ [+ speech, reading, writing] 流畅的 [liúchàng de] ▶ **he's a fluent speaker/ reader** 他是个说话/阅读流利的人 ▶ **to speak fluent French, be fluent in French** 讲流利的法语

fluff [flʌf] I N [U] 1 (on clothes, carpet) 绒毛 [róngmáo] 2 (fur) [of kitten, chick] 绒毛 [róngmáo] II VT 1 (inf) [+ speech, interview] 将…搞糟 [jiāng…gǎozāo] 2 (also: fluff up) [+ hair, pillow, feathers] 抖松 [dǒu sōng]

fluffy ['flʌfɪ] ADJ 1 [+ towel, sweater] 蓬松的 [péngsōng de] 2 [+ cake] 松软的 [sōngruǎn de] ▶ **fluffy toy** 绒毛玩具

fluid ['fluːɪd] I N [c/U] (liquid) 流体 [liútǐ] II ADJ 1 [+ movement] 流畅的 [liúchàng de] 2 (fig) [+ situation, arrangement] 易变的 [yìbiàn de]

fluke [fluːk] (inf) N [c] 侥幸 [jiǎoxìng]

flung [flʌŋ] PT, PP of ²**ing**

fluorescent [fluə'rɛsnt] ADJ [+ material, colour] 发荧光的 [fā yíngguāng de]; [+ light] 荧光的 [yíngguāng de]

fluoride ['fluəraɪd] N [U] 氟化物 [fúhuàwù]

flurry ['flʌrɪ] N [c] [of snow, wind] 一阵 [yīzhèn] ▶ **a flurry of activity** 一阵活动 ▶ **a flurry of excitement** 一阵激动

flush [flʌʃ] I N [c] 1 (on face) 红晕 [hóngyùn] 2 [of toilet] 冲水 [chōngshuǐ] 3 (CARDS) 同花 [tónghuā] II VT ▶ **to flush the toilet** 冲厕所 [chōng cèsuǒ] III VI 1 (become red) 脸红 [liǎnhóng] 2 [toilet +] 冲水 [chōngshuǐ] IV ADJ ▶ **flush with** 与…齐平的 [yǔ…qípíng de] ▶ **in the first flush of freedom** 获得自由的最初兴奋期 ▶ **in the first flush of youth** 在风华正茂的青春时期
▶ **flush out** VT [+ animals, birds] 赶出 [gǎnchū]; [+ criminal] 逐出 [zhúchū]

flute [fluːt] N [c] 长笛 [chángdí]

flutter ['flʌtə(r)] I VI 1 [bird +] 拍翅 [pāichì]; [flag, clothes +] 飘动 [piāodòng] 2 [heart, stomach +] 悸动 [jìdòng] II VT [+ wings] 拍 [pāi] III N [s] 1 [of wings] 拍动 [pāidòng]; [of cloth] 飘动 [piāodòng] 2 [of panic, excitement] 一阵心绪不宁 [yīzhèn xīnxùbùníng]

flux [flʌks] N ▶ **in a state of flux** 处于不断变化之中 [chǔyú bùduàn biànhuà zhīzhōng]

○fly [flaɪ] (pt flew, pp flown) I VT 1 [+ plane] 驾驶 [jiàshǐ] ▷ He flew a small plane to Cuba. 他驾驶一

架小飞机去古巴了。2 [+ passengers, cargo] 空运 [kōngyùn] ▷ The supplies are being flown from Pisa. 补给品正从比萨空运过来。3 [+ distance] 飞行 [fēixíng] ▷ He flew thousands of miles just to be with her. 他飞行数千英里，只是为了和她在一起。4 [+ kite] 放 [fàng] II VI 1 [bird, insect, plane +] 飞 [fēi] ▷ No other creature can fly as far as birds. 没有比鸟飞得更远的动物。▷ The planes flew through the clouds. 飞机飞过云层。2 [passengers +] 乘飞机 [chéng fēijī] ▷ He flew back to London. 他乘飞机回伦敦了。3 [pilot +] 驾驶飞机 [jiàshǐ fēijī] ▷ She is learning to fly. 她在学习驾驶飞机。4 (rush) 飞奔 [fēibēn] ▷ I flew downstairs. 我飞奔到楼下。5 (dash away) 快走 [kuàizǒu] ▷ I'm sorry, I must fly. 对不起，我得赶快走。6 (liter) (flee) 逃跑 [táopǎo] ▷ By the time they returned, their prisoner had flown. 等他们回来时，他们的囚犯已经逃跑了。7 [flag, hair +] 飘动 [piāodòng] ▷ A red flag was flying from the balcony. 一面红旗在阳台上飘动着。III N [c] 1 (insect) 苍蝇 [cāngying] 2 (also: flies) (on trousers) 有拉锁/纽扣的开口 [yǒu lāsuǒ/niǔkòu de kāikǒu] ▷ His flies were undone. 他裤子的拉锁没拉上。▶ **to fly open** 猛地突然打开 ▶ **to fly off the handle** 发火 ▶ **to go flying** 横飞出去 ▶ **to send sb flying** 将某人抛了出去 ▶ **she came flying into the room** 她飞快地跑进房间 ▶ **her glasses flew off** 她的眼镜突然跌落 ▶ **to fly into a rage** 勃然大怒
▶ **fly away** VI [bird, insect +] 飞走 [fēizǒu]
▶ **fly in** VI 1 [plane +] 降落 [jiàngluò] 2 [person +] 飞抵 [fēidǐ]
▶ **fly off** VI = fly away
▶ **fly out** VI 1 [plane +] 飞离 [fēilí] 2 [person +] 乘机离开 [chéngjī líkāi]

fly-drive ['flaɪdraɪv] ADJ ▶ **fly-drive holiday** 空陆联程的旅游方式，即乘飞机到达目的地机场后，驾驶租用的汽车前往其他地方

flyer ['flaɪə(r)] N [c] 1 (notice) 传单 [chuándān] 2 (AVIAT) (passenger) 乘客 [chéngkè]

flying ['flaɪɪŋ] I N [U] (activity) 飞行 [fēixíng]; (going by plane) 乘飞机 [chéng fēijī] II ADJ [+ insect, animal] 会飞的 [huìfēi de] ▶ **a flying visit** 短暂的访问 ▶ **to get off to a flying start** 开端良好 ▶ **he doesn't like flying** 他不喜欢坐飞机 ▶ **with flying colours** 大获全胜地

flying saucer (o.f.) N [c] 飞碟 [fēidié]

flyover ['flaɪəʊvə(r)] (BRIT) N [c] 立交桥 [lìjiāoqiáo] [美 = overpass]

FM ABBR (RAD) (= frequency modulation) 调频 [tiáopín]

foal [fəʊl] N [c] 驹子 [jūzi]

foam [fəʊm] I N [U] 1 (on liquid, soap, beer, coffee) 泡沫 [pàomò] 2 (also: foam rubber) 泡沫橡胶 [pàomò xiàngjiāo] II VI [soapy water, champagne +] 起泡沫 [qǐ pàomò] ▶ **to be foaming at the mouth** (fig) 大怒 [dànù]

fob [fɒb] I VT ▶ **to fob sb off** 搪塞某人 [tángsāi

mǒurén] **II** N [C](*also*: **watch fob**) 怀表链 [huáibiǎo liàn]

focal point ['fəʊkl-] N [C](*of room, activity, lens*) 焦点 [jiāodiǎn]

focus ['fəʊkəs] (*pl* **focuses**) **I** N **1** [U](PHOT) 聚焦 [jùjiāo] **2** [C] (*fig*) (*subject*) 重点 [zhòngdiǎn] **3** [c] (*fig*) (*attention*) 关注点 [guānzhùdiǎn] **II** VT **1** [+ *camera, telescope*] 调节⋯的焦距 [tiáojié⋯de jiāojù] **2** [+ *light rays*] 使聚焦 [shǐ jùjiāo] **3** [+ *eyes*] 使注视 [shǐ zhùshì] **III** VI ▸ **to focus (on)** (*with camera*) 聚焦(于) [jùjiāo (yú)]; [*eyes* +] 注视(于) [zhùshì (yú)]; (*fig*)(*concentrate on*) 集中(于) [jízhōng (yú)] ▸ **in focus/out of focus** 焦点对准/没对准 ▸ **to be the focus of attention** 为关注的焦点 ▸ **to focus (one's) attention on sb/sth** 把精力集中于某人/某事

fodder ['fɒdə(r)] N [U] (*food*) 饲料 [sìliào]

foe [fəʊ] (*liter*) N [C] (*enemy*) 敌人 [dírén]

foetus, (US) **fetus** ['fiːtəs] N [C] 胎儿 [tāi'ér]

fog [fɒg] N [C/U] 雾 [wù]

foggy ['fɒgɪ] ADJ [+ *day, climate*] 有雾的 [yǒuwù de] ▸ **it's foggy** 今天有雾 ▸ **I haven't the foggiest (idea)** (*inf*) 我一点也不知道

fog lamp, (US) **fog light** N [C] 雾灯 [wùdēng]

foil [fɔɪl] **I** VT [+ *attempt, plan*] 阻止 [zǔzhǐ] **II** N **1** [U] (*also*: **kitchen foil**) 箔纸 [bózhǐ] **2** [C] (*fig*) (*complement*) 陪衬 [péichèn] **3** [C] (FENCING) 花剑 [huājiàn] ▸ **to act as a foil to** (*fig*) 作⋯的陪衬 [zuò⋯de péichèn]

fold [fəʊld] **I** N **1** [C] (*in paper, cloth*) 折叠 [zhédié] **2** [C] (*in dress*) 褶 [zhě] **3** [C] (*for sheep*) 羊栏 [yánglán] **4** (REL) ▸ **the fold** 信徒 [xìntú] **II** VT **1** (*also*: **fold up**) [+ *cloth, clothes, paper, map*] 折叠 [zhédié] **2** (*also*: **fold up**) [+ *chair, table*] 折 [zhé] **3** [+ *one's arms, hands*] 交叠 [jiāodié] **III** VI **1** (ESP BRIT) [*business, organization* +] 关停 [guāntíng] **2** (*also*: **fold up**) [*map, chair, table* +] 折叠起来 [zhédié qǐlái]

folder ['fəʊldə(r)] N [C] (*for papers*) 文件夹 [wénjiàn jiā]

folding ['fəʊldɪŋ] ADJ [+ *chair, bed*] 折叠的 [zhédié de]

foliage ['fəʊlɪɪdʒ] N [U] 叶子 [yèzi]

folk [fəʊk] **I** NPL (*also*: **folks**) (*people*) 人们 [rénmen] **II** CPD [复合词] [+ *art, tales, medicine*] 民间 [mínjiān] **III** ▸ **my folks** NPL (*inf*) 我的家人

folklore ['fəʊklɔː(r)] N [U] 民俗 [mínsú]

folk music N [U] 民间音乐 [mínjiān yīnyuè]

folk song N [C] 民歌 [míngē]

○ **follow** ['fɒləʊ] **I** VT **1** [+ *person, car*] (*go behind*) 跟随 [gēnsuí] ▸ *We followed him up the steps.* 我们跟随他上了台阶。 **2** [+ *person*] (*join later*) 跟着到来 [gēnzhe dàolái] ▸ *He followed Julie to New York.* 他跟着朱莉到了纽约。 **3** (*come after*) [+ *event, activity, time*] 继之而来 [jìzhī'érlái] ▷ *the rioting that followed the verdict* 裁定后继之而来的暴乱 **4** (*take heed of*) [+ *example, advice,*

instructions] 遵循 ▷ *She promised to follow his advice.* 她承诺要遵循他的忠告。 **5** [+ *route, path*] 沿着⋯行进 [yánzhe⋯xíngjìn] ▷ *We followed a path along the creek.* 我们沿着小溪边的一条小路行进。 **6** (*understand*) [+ *event, story*] 领会 [lǐnghuì] ▷ *They were having some difficulty in following the plot.* 他们在理解情节上有困难。 **7** (*take an interest in*) [+ *sport, TV serial*] 对⋯感兴趣 [duì⋯gǎnxìngqù] ▷ *Millions of people follow football.* 成百上万的人对足球感兴趣。 **8** (*with eyes*) 追随 [zhuīsuí] ▷ *Suzy's eyes followed a police car as it drove slowly past.* 苏西的眼睛追随着一辆慢慢驶过的警车。 **II** VI **1** [*person* +] 跟随 [gēnsuí] ▷ *They took him into a small room and I followed.* 他们把他带进一间小屋里,我跟了进去。 **2** [*event, activity, time* +] 接下来 [jiēxiàlái] ▷ *He was arrested in the confusion which followed.* 他在接下来的一片混乱中被捕了。 **3** (*result*) [*conclusion, benefit* +] 必然发生 [bìrán fāshēng] ▷ *If the explanation is right, two things follow...* 如果这一解释正确的话,两件事情必然发生⋯ ▸ **to follow in sb's footsteps** 步某人后尘 ▸ **I don't quite follow you** 我不太理解你的意思 ▸ **it follows that...** 一定是⋯ ▸ **as follows** (*when listing*) 如下 [rúxià] ▷ *The winners are as follows:...* 获奖者如下:⋯; (*in this way*) 按如下方式 [àn rúxià fāngshì] ▷ *The sum will be calculated as follows...* 总额将按如下方式计算⋯ ▸ **to follow suit** (*fig*) 照样去做 [zhàoyàngqùzuò] ▸ **to follow one thing (up) with another thing** 紧接着一件事做另一件事 ▸ **followed by** 接着是

▸ **follow on** VI (*continue*) 继续下去 [jìxùxiàqù]

▸ **follow through** VT [+ *plan, idea*] 将⋯进行到底 [jiāng⋯jìnxíng dàodǐ]

▸ **follow up** VT **1** [+ *letter, offer*] 对⋯采取进一步行动 [duì⋯cǎiqǔ jìnyībù xíngdòng] ▷ *I followed up an advertisement for a second-hand Volkswagen.* 看了广告后,我对二手的大众车作了进一步了解。 **2** [+ *idea, suggestion*] 把⋯探究到底 [bǎ⋯tànjiūdàodǐ] ▷ *The police are following up several leads.* 警方正顺着几个线索追查到底。

follower ['fɒləʊə(r)] N [C] (*of person, belief*) 拥护者 [yōnghùzhě]

following ['fɒləʊɪŋ] **I** PREP (*after*) 在⋯之后 [zài⋯zhīhòu] **II** ADJ **1** (*next*) [+ *day, week*] 接着的 [jiēzhe de] **2** (*next-mentioned*) [+ *way, list etc*] 下述的 [xiàshù de] **III** N [C] (*of party, religion, group*) 一批拥护者 [yīpī yōnghùzhě]

follow-on call ['fɒləʊɒn-] (TEL) N [C] 继续拨叫电话 [jìxù bōjiào diànhuà]

follow-up ['fɒləʊʌp] **I** N [C] 后续 [hòuxù] **II** ADJ [+ *treatment, survey, programme*] 后续的 [hòuxù de]

folly ['fɒlɪ] N **1** [C/U] (*foolishness*) 愚蠢 [yúchǔn] **2** [C] (*building*) 装饰性建筑 [zhuāngshìxìng jiànzhù]

fond [fɒnd] ADJ **1** ▸ **to be fond of** [+ *person*] 喜

爱 [xǐ'ài]; [+ food, walking etc] 喜欢 [xǐhuan]
2 [+ memory] 美好的 [měihǎo de]; [+ smile, look]
深情的 [shēnqíng de]; [+ hope, wish] 不切实际
的 [bùqiè shíjì de]

○ **food** [fu:d] N [C/U] 食物 [shíwù] ▸ **food for thought** 引人深思的事

food mixer N [C] 食物搅拌器 [shíwù jiǎobànqì]

food poisoning N [U] 食物中毒 [shíwù zhòngdú]

food processor [-prəusɛsə(r)] N [C] 食品加工机 [shípǐn jiāgōngjī]

food stamp N [C] (US) 政府发给低收入者的食品券，可用于换取食物

fool [fu:l] I N **1** (idiot) 白痴 [báichī] **2** [C/U] (BRIT: CULIN) 奶油拌果子泥甜点 II VT (deceive) 欺骗 [qīpiàn] III VI ▸ **to fool with sb/sth** 戏弄某人/摆弄某物 [xìnòng mǒurén/bǎinòng mǒuwù] ▸ **to make a fool of sb** (ridicule) 嘲弄某人 ▸ **to make a fool of o.s.** 使己出丑 ▸ **you can't fool me** 你骗不了我
▸ **fool about, fool around** (pej) VI (behave foolishly) 做蠢事 [zuò chǔnshì]

foolish ['fu:lɪʃ] ADJ **1** (ridiculous) 愚蠢的 [yúchǔn de] **2** (unwise) 不明智的 [bù míngzhì de]

foolproof ['fu:lpru:f] ADJ [+ plan etc] 万无一失的 [wànwúyīshī de]

○ **foot** [fut] (pl **feet**) I N **1** [C] (measure) 英尺 [yīngchǐ] ▷ a man over 6 feet tall 一个6英尺多高的男子 **2** [C] [of person] 脚 [jiǎo] **3** [C] [of animal] 蹄 [tí] **4** [C] [of bed] 放脚的一头 [fàngjiǎo de yītóu] **5** [S] [of cliff, hill, stairs] 最底部 [zuì dǐbù] II VT ▸ **to foot the bill** 付账 [fùzhàng] ▸ **on foot** 步行 ▸ **to be on one's feet** (standing) 站起来 ▸ **to get or rise to one's feet** 站起来 ▸ **to get back on one's feet** (after illness, bad experience) 恢复元气 ▸ **to find one's feet** (fig) 适应 ▸ **to put one's foot down** (in car) (accelerate) 踩油门; (say no) 坚决反对 ▸ **to put one's feet up** (relax) 双脚搁起来休息 ▸ **to set foot somewhere** 去某处 ▸ **to stand on one's own two feet** 自力更生 ▸ **at the foot of the page** 在页脚

footage ['futɪdʒ] (CINE) N [U] 镜头 [jìngtóu]

football ['futbɔ:l] N **1** [C] (ball) 足球 [zúqiú] **2** [U] (sport) (BRIT) 足球 [zúqiú] [美= soccer] (US) 美式足球 [měishì zúqiú] [英= American football]

football boots (BRIT) NPL 足球鞋 [zúqiú xié]

footballer ['futbɔ:lə(r)] (BRIT) N [C] 足球运动员 [zúqiú yùndòngyuán]

football match (BRIT) N [C] 足球赛 [zúqiú sài]

footbrake ['futbreɪk] N [C] 脚刹车 [jiǎoshāchē]

footbridge ['futbrɪdʒ] N [C] 步行桥 [bùxíng qiáo]

foothills ['futhɪlz] NPL 山麓小丘 [shānlù xiǎoqiū]

foothold ['futhəuld] N [C] **1** (CLIMBING) 立足处 [lìzúchù] **2** (fig) 立足点 [lìzúdiǎn]

footing ['futɪŋ] N [C] (basis) ▸ **on a more formal/scientific footing** 在更正式/科学的基础上 [zài gèng zhèngshì/kēxué de jīchǔ shàng] ▸ **to lose one's footing** 失去平衡 ▸ **on an equal footing** 在平等的基础上

footnote ['futnəut] N [C] (in book) 脚注 [jiǎozhù]

footpath ['futpa:θ] N [C] 人行小径 [rénxíng xiǎojìng]

footprint ['futprɪnt] N [C] [of person, animal] 足迹 [zújì]

footstep ['futstɛp] N [C] (sound) 脚步声 [jiǎobùshēng]

footwear ['futwɛə(r)] N [U] 鞋类 [xiélèi]

○

for [fɔ:(r)] I PREP **1** (recipient) 为 [wèi] ▸ **is this for me?** 这是为我准备的吗？ ▸ **a table for two** 供两人用的桌子 ▸ **it's meant for children rather than adults** 专门用于儿童而非成人 ▸ **skiing is not for me** 滑雪不适合我
2 (purpose) 为了 [wèile] ▸ **what's it for?** 它有什么用途？ ▸ **it's time for lunch** 该吃午饭了 ▸ **what for?** 为什么？ ▸ **a knife for chopping vegetables** 用于切菜的刀 ▸ **have you got time for a coffee?** 你有时间喝杯咖啡吗？ ▸ **a tricycle designed for use on the road** 公路专用三轮车
3 (time) ▸ **he was away for two years** 他离开两年了 [tā líkāi liǎngnián le] ▸ **she will be away for a month** 她将离开一个月 ▸ **can you do it for tomorrow?** 你能明天前做完吗？ ▸ **it hasn't rained for three weeks** 已经有3周没下雨了 ▸ **the trip is scheduled for June 5** 旅行安排在6月5日
4 (in exchange for) ▸ **I sold it for £50** 我以五十镑卖掉了它 [wǒ yǐ wǔshí bàng màidiào le tā] ▸ **to pay 50 pence for a ticket** 花50便士买张票 ▸ **pound for pound/dollar for dollar** 物有所值
5 (reason) 因为 [yīnwèi] ▸ **for this reason** 由于这个原因 ▸ **for lack of sth** 由于缺乏某物 ▸ **our reasons for doing this** 我们这么做的原因
6 (on behalf of, representing) 为 [wèi] ▸ **he works for a local firm** 他为一家当地公司工作 ▸ **the MP for...** 代表…的国会议员 ▸ **I'll do it for you** 我会替你做的 ▸ **G for George** George中的G
7 (destination) 前往 [qiánwǎng] ▸ **the train for London** 开往伦敦的火车 ▸ **he left for Rome** 他前往罗马
8 (with infinitive clause) ▸ **it is not for me to decide** 这不是由我来决定的 [zhè bùshì yóu wǒ lái juédìng de] ▸ **it would be best**

for you to leave 你最好离开 ▶ **there is still time for you to do it** 你还有时间去做 **9** (to get) 欲知 [yùzhī] ▶ **for further information, see...** 欲知进一步的信息，见… ▶ **he went for the paper** 他去找报纸了 **10** (in spite of) 尽管 [jǐnguǎn] ▶ **for all his complaints, he is very fond of her** 尽管他牢骚满腹，他还是很喜欢她 **11** (with regard to) 就…而言 [jiù…éryán] ▶ **it's cold for July** 对7月而言这算冷天了 ▶ **he's mature for his age** 对他的年龄而言他算是成熟的 ▶ **for scientists, this is less important** 对于科学家来说，这不太重要 ▶ **another word for this is...** 对于这个的另一种说法是… ▶ **what's the French for "flower"?** "flower"用法语怎么说？ **12** (in favour of) 赞成 [zànchéng] ▶ **are you for or against us?** 你是赞成还是反对我们？ ▶ **I'm all for it** 我完全赞成 ▶ **vote for X** 投票赞成X **13** (referring to distance) 达 [dá] ▶ **there are roadworks for 50 km** 长跑练习长达50公里 ▶ **we walked for miles** 我们走了几英里 **14** (with "if") ▶ **I wouldn't be alive today, if it weren't for him** 若不是由于他，我不会活到今天的 [ruò bùshì yóuyú tā, wǒ bùhuì huódào jīntiān de] ▶ **had it not been for Bill, we'd have been late** 若不是比尔，我们一定迟到了 **II** CONJ (liter) (since, as) 因为 [yīnwèi] ▶ **she was very angry, for he was late again** 她非常生气，因为他又迟到了

▌用法参见 **since**

for 和 **to** 都可用于表示某人的目的，但后接不同的语言结构。**for** 用于表示目的时，后面必须跟名词。*Occasionally I go to the pub for a drink.* **for** 通常不用在动词前面。不能说 *I go to the pub for to have a drink*。**for** 用在 *-ing* 形式前表示某物的用途。*...a small machine for weighing the letters...* 与动词连用时，不定式前不加 **for**。*She went off to fetch help.*

forage ['fɒrɪdʒ] **I** VI (search) (for food) 觅食 [mìshí] **II** N [U] 饲料 [sìliào] ▶ **to forage for sth** [person, animal +] 搜寻某物

foray ['fɒreɪ] N [c] **1** (MIL) (raid) 偷袭 [tōuxí] **2** (venture) 冒险 [màoxiǎn] ▶ **to make a foray into** (MIL) 对…进行袭击; (fig) 对…进行初步尝试

forbid [fə'bɪd] (pt **forbade**, pp **forbidden**) VT (prohibit) [+ sale, marriage, event] 禁止 [jìnzhǐ]; (make impossible) 阻止 [zǔzhǐ] ▶ **to forbid sb to do sth** (prohibit) 禁止某人做某事; (make impossible) 阻止某人做某事

forbidden [fə'bɪdn] **I** PP of **forbid II** ADJ [+ subject] 被禁止的 [bèi jìnzhǐ de] ▶ **forbidden**

fruit (fig) 禁果

○**force** [fɔːs] **I** N **1** [U] (violence) 武力 [wǔlì] ▷ *We have renounced the use of force to settle our disputes.* 我们摒弃使用武力解决我们的争端。**2** [U] (strength) 力量 [lìliàng] ▷ *The force of the explosion shattered the windows.* 爆炸的力量击碎了窗玻璃。**3** [c] (power, influence) 势力 [shìlì] ▷ *the forces of evil* 邪恶势力 **4** [c/U] (PHYS) 力 [lì] ▷ *the earth's gravitational force* 地球的重力 **II** VT **1** (drive, compel) 强迫 [qiǎngpò] ▷ *Ought he to be forced out of the Presidency?* 应该强迫他离任总统一职吗？**2** (push) 用力推 [yònglì tuī] ▷ *I forced his head back.* 我用力把他的头往后推开了。**3** (break open) [+ lock, door] 强行打开 [qiángxíng dǎkāi] ▷ *They had to force the lock on the trunk.* 他们不得不强行打开箱子上的锁。**III** **forces** NPL (MIL) **1** 部队 [bùduì] ▷ *the deployment of American forces in the region* 美国部队在该地区的部署 **2** ▶ **the Forces** (BRIT) 军队 [jūnduì] ▶ **in force** (in large numbers) 大批地 ▷ *Animal rights campaigners turned up in force.* 动物权利运动参与者大批涌现。▶ **to be in force** [law, system +] 正在施行中 ▶ **to come into force** [law, system +] 生效 ▶ **to join forces (with sb)** (与某人)联合 ▶ **a force 5 gale** 5级风 ▶ **the sales force** (COMM) 推销人员 ▶ **from or through force of habit** 出于习惯 ▶ **to force o.s. to do sth** 强迫自己做某事 ▶ **to force sb to do sth** 强迫某人做某事 ▶ **to force sth (up)on sb** 将某事强加于某人 ▶ **to force o.s. (up)on sb** 试图强暴某人 ▶ **to force a smile/laugh** 强作笑脸/强颜欢笑 ▶ **force back** VT [+ tears, urge] 强忍住 [qiáng rěnzhù]

forced [fɔːst] ADJ **1** [+ labour] 强迫的 [qiángpò de]; [+ landing] 被迫的 [bèipò de] **2** [+ smile, gesture] 勉强的 [miǎnqiǎng de]

forceful ['fɔːsful] ADJ [+ person] 坚定有力的 [jiāndìng yǒulì de]; [+ impression, reminder] 有力的 [yǒulì de]

ford [fɔːd] **I** N [c] (in river) 浅滩 [qiǎntān] **II** VT [+ river, stream] 涉过 [shèguò]

fore [fɔː(r)] **I** N [c] ▶ **to come to the fore** 涌现出来 [yǒngxiàn chūlái] **II** ADJ (NAUT, AVIAT) 在前部的 [zài qiánbù de] **III** ADV (NAUT, AVIAT) 在前部 [zài qiánbù]

forearm ['fɔːrɑːm] N [c] 前臂 [qiánbì]

forecast ['fɔːkɑːst] (pt, pp **forecast** or **forecasted**) **I** N [c] **1** [of weather] 预报 [yùbào] **2** [of profits, prices] 预测 [yùcè] **II** VT [+ predict] 预测 [yùcè] ▶ **to forecast that...** 预测到…

forecourt ['fɔːkɔːt] (ESP BRIT) N [c] [of garage] 前院 [qiányuàn]

forefinger ['fɔːfɪŋɡə(r)] N [c] 食指 [shízhǐ]

forefront ['fɔːfrʌnt] N [c] ▶ **at the forefront of** [+ industry, campaign] 在…的最前锋 [zài…de zuì qiánfēng]

foregone ['fɔːɡɒn] ADJ ▶ **it's a foregone conclusion** 这是个预料之中的必然结局 [zhè shì gè yùliào zhīzhōng de bìrán jiéjú]

foreground ['fɔːgraund] N [C/U] *(of painting)* 前景 [qiánjǐng] ▶ **to be in/come to the foreground** *(fig)* 处于/取得突出地位

forehead ['fɔrɪd] N [C] 额 [é]

⊙**foreign** ['fɒrɪn] ADJ 1 [+ *country, holiday, language*] 外国的 [wàiguó de] 2 [+ *trade, policy*] 对外的 [duìwài de] ▶ **foreign to** 对⋯陌生

foreign currency N [C/U] 外币 [wàibì]

foreigner ['fɒrɪnə(r)] N [C] 外国人 [wàiguórén]

foreign exchange N 1 [C] *(system)* 国际汇兑 [guójì huìduì] 2 [U] *(money)* 外汇 [wàihuì]

Foreign Office (BRIT) N [C] ▶ **the Foreign Office** 外交部 [Wàijiāo Bù]

Foreign Secretary (BRIT) N [C] 外交部长 [wàijiāo bùzhǎng]

foreman ['fɔːmən] *(pl* **foremen***)* N [C] 1 *[of factory, building site]* 领班 [lǐngbān] 2 *[of jury]* 陪审长 [péishěn zhǎng]

foremost ['fɔːməust] I ADJ *(most important)* 首屈一指的 [shǒuqū yīzhǐ de] II ADV ▶ **first and foremost** 首要地 [shǒuyào de]

forename ['fɔːneɪm] N [C] 名 [míng]

forensic [fə'rɛnsɪk] ADJ [+ *expert, test, evidence*] 法庭的 [fǎtíng de]

forerunner ['fɔːrʌnə(r)] N [C] ▶ **the forerunner of** ⋯的前身 [⋯de qiánshēn]

foresee [fɔː'siː] *(pt* **foresaw***, pp* **foreseen***)* VT [+ *problem, development*] 预见 [yùjiàn]

foreseeable [fɔː'siːəbl] ADJ ▶ **in the foreseeable future** 在可预见的未来 [zài kě yùjiàn de wèilái]

foresight ['fɔːsaɪt] N [U] 先见之明 [xiānjiàn zhī míng]

forest ['fɒrɪst] N [C/U] *(science)* 森林 [sēnlín]

forestall [fɔː'stɔːl] VT [+ *person*] 抢在⋯之前行动 [qiǎngzài⋯zhīqián xíngdòng]; [+ *event*] 阻止 [zǔzhǐ]

forestry ['fɒrɪstrɪ] N [U] *(science)* 林学 [línxué]; *(skill)* 造林术 [zàolín shù]

forever [fə'rɛvə(r)] ADV 1 *(permanently)* 永远 [yǒngyuǎn] 2 *(always)* 一直 [yīzhí] ▶ **it has gone forever** 它已经一去不复返了 ▶ **it will last forever** 它会一直持续下去的 ▶ **you're forever finding difficulties** 你总是自寻烦恼

foreword ['fɔːwəːd] N [C] 前言 [qiányán]

forfeit ['fɔːfɪt] I N [C] *(price, fine)* 罚金 [fájīn] II VT *(lose)* [+ *right, chance, privilege*] 丧失 [sàngshī]; *(give up)* [+ *one's happiness, health, income*] 放弃 [fàngqì]

forgave [fə'geɪv] PT OF **forgive**

forge [fɔːdʒ] I VT 1 *(fraudulently)* [+ *signature, banknote*] 伪造 [wěizào] 2 *(create)* [+ *alliance, relationship, links*] 创建 [chuàngjiàn] 3 [+ *wrought iron*] 锻造 [duànzào] II N [C] *(smithy)* 铁匠铺 [tiějiàng pù]

▶ **forge ahead** VI ▶ **forge ahead with sth** 在某方面稳步前进 [zài mǒu fāngmiàn wěnbù

qiánjìn]

forger ['fɔːdʒə(r)] N [C] 伪造者 [wěizàozhě]

forgery ['fɔːdʒərɪ] N 1 [U] *(crime)* 伪造罪 [wěizào zuì] 2 [C] *(document, painting etc)* 伪造品 [wěizàopǐn]

forget [fə'gɛt] *(pt* **forgot***, pp* **forgotten***)* I VT 1 [+ *fact, face, skill, appointment*] 忘记 [wàngjì] 2 *(leave behind)* [+ *object*] 忘带 [wàng dài] 3 *(put out of mind)* [+ *quarrel, person*] 忘掉 [wàngdiào] II VI *(fail to remember)* 忘记 [wàngjì] ▶ **to forget to do sth** 忘记做某事 ▶ **to forget how to do sth** 忘记如何做某事 ▶ **to forget that...** 忘记⋯ ▶ **to forget o.s.** 忘乎所以

forgetful [fə'gɛtful] ADJ [+ *person*] 健忘的 [jiànwàng de]

forgive [fə'gɪv] *(pt* **forgave***, pp* **forgiven** [fə'gɪvn]*)* VT *(pardon)* 原谅 [yuánliàng] ▶ **to forgive sb for sth** 原谅某人某事 ▶ **forgive my ignorance, but...** 请原谅我的无知，但是⋯ ▶ **they could be forgiven for thinking that...** 他们认为⋯也不为过 ▶ **to forgive and forget** 不记前嫌

forgiveness [fə'gɪvnɪs] N [U] 宽恕 [kuānshù] ▶ **to ask** *or* **beg for forgiveness** 请求〔或〕乞求原谅

forgot [fə'gɒt] PT OF **forget**

forgotten [fə'gɒtn] PP OF **forget**

fork [fɔːk] I N [C] 1 *(for eating)* 餐叉 [cānchā] 2 *(for gardening)* 耙子 [pázi] 3 *(in road, river, railway)* 岔路 [chàlù] II VI *(road, river +)* 岔开 [chàkāi]

▶ **fork out** *(inf)* I VI *(pay)* 支付 [zhīfù] II VT 花费 [huāfèi]

forlorn [fə'lɔːn] ADJ *(liter)* 1 [+ *person*] 孤苦伶仃的 [gūkǔ língdīng de] 2 [+ *attempt, hope*] 几乎无望的 [jīhū wúwàng de] 3 [+ *place*] 荒凉的 [huāngliáng de]

⊙**form** [fɔːm] I N 1 [C] *(type)* 类型 [lèixíng] ▷ *The symptoms take various forms.* 症状有多种类型。 ▷ *a rare form of cancer* 一种罕见的癌症类型 2 [C] *(manner)* 形式 [xíngshì] ▷ *She didn't like the form in which the questions were written.* 她不喜欢这些问题的书写形式。 3 [C] *(body)* 体态 [tǐtài] ▷ *She gazed at his slumbering form.* 她注视着他沉睡时的体态。 4 [C] *(BRIT: SCOL)* *(class)* 年级 [niánjí] ▷ *the sixth form* 六年级 5 [C] *(document)* 表格 [biǎogé] ▷ *You will be asked to fill in a form.* 你需要填一份表格。 6 [U] *(SPORT)* 竞技状态 [jìngjì zhuàngtài] ▷ *His form this season has been brilliant.* 他本季的竞技状态极佳。 II VT 1 *(make)* [+ *shape, queue, object*] 组成 [zǔchéng] ▷ *Form a circle please, children.* 孩子们，请组成一个圈。 2 *(cause to exist)* 形成 [xíngchéng] ▷ *The islands were formed comparatively recently.* 这些岛屿是在比较近的年代形成的。 3 *(comprise)* 构成 [gòuchéng] ▷ *Cereals form their staple diet.* 谷物构成了他们的主食。 4 *(create)* [+ *group, organization, company*] 成立 [chénglì] ▷ *The*

League was formed in 1959. 该俱乐部是于1959年成立的。**5** [+ *idea, impression*] 形成 [xíngchéng] ▷ *the impression I'd formed of Jack* 我对杰克形成的印象 **6** [+ *habit*] 养成 [yǎngchéng] ▷ *He formed the habit of taking long solitary walks.* 他养成了独自长途徒步走的习惯。**7** [+ *relationship*] 建立 [jiànlì] ▷ *He is wary of forming another close relationship.* 他对再与人建立密切关系非常谨慎。**III** VI **1** [*shape, queue* +] 产生 [chǎnshēng] ▷ *That's why this natural phenomenon forms.* 那就是这个自然现象产生的原因。▷ *A scab had formed on his knee.* 他的膝盖上结了个痂。**2** (*begin to exist*) [*stars, mountains* +] 形成 [xíngchéng] ▷ *The stars must have formed around 10 billion years ago.* 星星一定是在大约一百亿年前形成的。▶ **in the form of** 通过…方式 ▷ *She is taking lots of exercise in the form of walks or swimming.* 她正通过走路或者游泳的方式作大量的锻炼。▶ **to take the form of** 以…形式 ▷ *The broadcast took the form of an interview.* 这个节目是以采访的形式进行的。▶ **to form part of sth** 构成某事的一部分 ▶ **to be in good** or **top form** (SPORT) 处于良好的竞技状态 [或] 巅峰状态; (BRIT) (*fig*) 处于良好的精神状态 ▶ **to be on/off form** (SPORT) 竞技状态良好/不好; (BRIT) (*fig*) 能/不能发挥正常水平

formal ['fɔːməl] ADJ **1** [+ *offer, approval, occasion, dinner*] 正式的 [zhèngshì de] **2** [+ *speech, behaviour*] 合礼仪的 [hé lǐyí de] **3** [+ *education, qualifications*] 正规的 [zhèngguī de] **4** [+ *approach, style*] 有条理的 [yǒu tiáolǐ de] ▶ **formal dress** (*evening dress*) 礼服 [lǐfú] ▶ **formal gardens** 官方公园

formality [fɔː'mælɪtɪ] I N **1** [c] 形式 [xíngshì] **2** [U] (*politeness*) 礼节 [lǐjié] II **formalities** NPL (*procedures*) 手续 [shǒuxù]

formally ['fɔːməlɪ] ADV [*announce, approve, dress, behave* +] 正式地 [zhèngshì de] ▶ **to be formally invited** 受到正式邀请

format ['fɔːmæt] I N [c] **1** (*form, style*) 形式 [xíngshì] **2** [*of software, recording*] 格式 [géshì] II VT (COMPUT) [+ *disk*] 将…格式化 [jiāng…géshìhuà]

formation [fɔː'meɪʃən] N **1** [U] [*of organization, business*] 组成 [zǔchéng]; [*of idea, relationship, rocks, clouds*] 形成 [xíngchéng] **2** [c] (*pattern*) 结构 [jiégòu] ▶ **to fly in formation** (AVIAT) 编队飞行

formative ['fɔːmətɪv] ADJ [+ *influence, experience*] 形成的 [xíngchéng de] ▶ **one's formative years** 性格形成时期

○**former** ['fɔːmə(r)] I ADJ **1** [+ *husband, president etc*] 前任的 [qiánrèn de] ▷ *He's a former army officer.* 他是位前任军官。**2** (*earlier*) [+ *power, authority*] 以前的 [yǐqián de] ▷ *They have lost much of their former authority.* 他们失去了许多以前的权利。II PRON ▶ **the former** 前者 [qiánzhě] ▷ *The former believe in a strong*

centralized government. 前者信仰强有力的中央集权制的政府。▶ **in former times/years** 以前请勿将 **former** 和 **previous** 混淆。**former** 是指某人曾经拥有的某个特定的工作、职位或角色，或者指某个曾经存在，但现已消失的状况。…*former President Bill Clinton…He murdered his former wife.* **previous** 用来指先前，即说话者前所发生的事情或存在的事物。*She has a teenage daughter from a previous marriage… Crime increased in 2001 compared with the previous year.*

formerly ['fɔːməlɪ] ADV (*previously*) 从前 [cóngqián]

formidable ['fɔːmɪdəbl] ADJ [+ *task*] 艰巨的 [jiānjù de]; [+ *opponent*] 难以对付的 [nányǐ duìfu de]

formula ['fɔːmjulə] (*pl* **formulae** ['fɔːmjuliː] or **formulas**) N **1** [c] (MATH) 公式 [gōngshì] **2** [c] (CHEM) 分子式 [fēnzǐ shì] **3** [c] (*plan*) 方案 [fāng'àn] **4** [U] (*also:* **formula milk**) 配方奶粉 [pèifāng nǎifěn] ▶ **Formula One** (AUT) 一级方程式赛车

formulate ['fɔːmjuleɪt] VT **1** [+ *plan, proposal*] 构想出 [gòuxiǎng chū] **2** (*express*) [+ *thought, opinion*] 表达 [biǎodá]

formulation [fɔːmju'leɪʃən] N **1** [C/U] [*of medicine, cosmetic*] 配制 [pèizhì] **2** [U] [*of policy, plan*] 制订 [zhìdìng] **3** [C/U] (*frm*) (*form of words*) 表达方式 [biǎodá fāngshì]

fort [fɔːt] N [c] 堡垒 [bǎolěi] ▶ **to hold the fort** or (US) **hold down the fort** (*fig*) 暂时代人维持现状

forth [fɔːθ] ADV (*liter*) ▶ **to go forth** 向前 [xiàngqián] ▶ **back and forth** 来回 ▶ **to go back and forth** 来来回回 ▶ **to bring forth** (*liter*) 提出 ▶ **and so forth** 等等

forthcoming [fɔːθ'kʌmɪŋ] ADJ **1** [+ *event*] 临近的 [línjìn de] **2** (*frm*) [+ *help, money, information*] 随要随到的 [suíyào suídào de] **3** [+ *person*] 乐于助人的 [lèyú zhùrén de]

forthright ['fɔːθraɪt] ADJ [+ *person, language*] 直率的 [zhíshuài de]; [+ *condemnation, opposition*] 直言不讳的 [zhíyán bùhuì de]

fortieth ['fɔːtɪɪθ] NUM 第四十 [dì sìshí]

fortify ['fɔːtɪfaɪ] VT **1** [+ *place*] 设防于 [shèfángyú] **2** [+ *food, drink*] 使…加强 [shǐ…jiāqiáng] **3** [+ *person*] [*food, drink* +] 使精力旺盛 [shǐ jīnglì wàngshèng]

fortnight ['fɔːtnaɪt] (BRIT) N [c] 两星期 [liǎng xīngqī] ▶ **it's a fortnight since…** 自从…已经过了两个星期了

fortnightly ['fɔːtnaɪtlɪ] (BRIT) I ADJ [+ *meeting, magazine*] 每两星期一次的 [měi liǎng xīngqī yīcì de] II ADV [*meet, publish* +] 每两星期一次地 [měi liǎng xīngqī yīcì de]

fortress ['fɔːtrɪs] N [c] 堡垒 [bǎolěi]

fortunate ['fɔːtʃənɪt] ADJ [+ *person, coincidence,*

escape] 幸运的 [xìngyùn de] ▶ **he was fortunate to survive** 他幸运地活了下来 ▶ **it is fortunate that...** 幸亏…

fortunately ['fɔ:tʃənɪtlɪ] ADV 幸运的是 [xìngyùn de shì]

fortune ['fɔ:tʃən] I N 1 [U] (also: **good fortune**) (luck) 好运 [hǎoyùn] 2 [c] (wealth) 大笔钱 [dàbǐqián] II **fortunes** NPL 时运 [shíyùn] ▶ **to make a fortune** 发大财 ▶ **to tell sb's fortune** 给某人算命

fortune-teller ['fɔ:tʃəntelə(r)] N [c] 算命者 [suànmìngzhě]

○**forty** ['fɔ:tɪ] NUM 四十 [sìshí]

forum ['fɔ:rəm] N [c] 1 (for discussion) 论坛 [lùntán] 2 (Roman square) 公共集会场所 [gōnggòng jíhuì chǎngsuǒ]

forward ['fɔ:wəd] I ADJ 1 (in position) 前部的 [qiánbù de] 2 (in movement) 向前的 [xiàngqián de] 3 (not shy) 冒失的 [màoshi de] II N [c] (SPORT) 前锋 [qiánfēng] III VT 1 [+ letter, goods] 转递 [zhuǎndì] 2 [+ career, plans] 促进 [cùjìn] ▶ **"please forward"** "请转交" IV ADV = **forwards** ▶ **forward planning** 预先计划

forwards ['fɔ:wədz] ADV (in space, time) 向前 [xiàngqián]

fossil ['fɒsl] N [c] 化石 [huàshí]

foster ['fɒstə(r)] I VT 1 [+ child] 领养 [lǐngyǎng] 2 [+ idea, activity, feeling] 培养 [péiyǎng] II CPD [复合词] [+ parent, mother, child] 寄养 [jìyǎng]

fought [fɔ:t] PT, PP of **fight**

foul [faul] I ADJ 1 (filthy) [+ state, taste, smell] 令人作呕的 [lìngrénzuò'ǒu de]; [+ place] 污秽的 [wūhuì de] 2 (dreadful) [+ temper, mood] 坏透的 [huàitòu de]; [+ day, time, luck] 糟透的 [zāotòu de]; [+ weather] 恶劣的 [èliè de] 3 (obscene) [+ language] 下流的 [xiàliú de] II N (SPORT) 犯规 [fànguī] III VT 1 (dirty) 弄脏 [nòngzāng] 2 (dog +) 弄脏 [nòngzāng] 3 (SPORT) 对…犯规 [duì…fànguī] 4 (entangle) [+ anchor, propeller] 缠住 [chánzhù] ▶ **to fall foul of sb** (ESP BRIT) 与某人发生冲突

foul play N [U] 1 (LAW) 暴力行径 [bàolì xíngjìng] 2 (SPORT) 犯规行为 [fànguī xíngwéi]

found [faund] I PT, PP of **find** II VT [+ organization, company] 创办 [chuàngbàn]

foundation [faun'deɪʃən] I N 1 [U] (of organization, company, city) 成立 [chénglì] 2 [c] (basis) [of belief, way of life] 基础 [jīchǔ] 3 [U] (substance) (fig) 根据 [gēnjù] 4 [c] (organization) 基金会 [jījīnhuì] 5 [U/c] (also: **foundation cream**) 粉底霜 [fěndǐshuāng] II **foundations** NPL [of building] 地基 [dìjī] ▶ **without foundation** 没有根据 ▶ **to lay the foundations of sth** 为某事奠定基础

founder ['faundə(r)] I N [c] [of institution, organization] 创始人 [chuàngshǐrén] II VI 1 (ship +) 沉没 [chénmò] 2 (plan, project +) 失

败 [shībài]

founding ['faundɪŋ] ADJ ▶ **founding father** (HIST) (in US) 开国者 [kāiguózhě]; (fig) [of institution, organization] 创始人 [chuàngshǐrén]

fountain ['fauntɪn] N [c] 1 (lit) 喷泉 [pēnquán] 2 (liter) (fig) [of liquid] 大量 [dàliàng]

fountain pen N [c] 自来水笔 [zìláishuǐ bǐ]

○**four** [fɔ:(r)] NUM 四 [sì] ▶ **on all fours** 爬着地 see also **five**

four-letter word ['fɔ:lɛtə-] N [c] (swear word) 脏话 [zānghuà]

four-poster ['fɔ:'pəustə(r)] N [c] (also: **four-poster bed**) 有四根帷柱的床

○**fourteen** ['fɔ:'ti:n] NUM 十四 [shísì] see also **fifteen**

fourteenth ['fɔ:'ti:nθ] NUM 第十四 of see also see also **fifth**

fourth ['fɔ:θ] I NUM 1 第四 [dìsì] 2 (US) (quarter) 四分之一 [sìfēnzhīyī] [英= **quarter**] II N [c] (AUT) (also: **fourth gear**) 第四挡 [dìsì dǎng] see also **fifth**

four-wheel drive ['fɔ:wi:l-] N [c] (AUT) 四轮驱动 [sìlún qūdòng]

fowl [faul] N [c] 禽 [qín]

fox [fɒks] I N [c] 狐狸 [húlí] II VT (BRIT) (baffle) 使迷惑 [shǐ míhuò]

foyer ['fɔɪeɪ] N [c] [of hotel, theatre, cinema] 门厅 [méntíng]

Fr. (REL) ABBR (= **father**) 神父 [shénfù]

fraction ['frækʃən] N [c] 1 (portion) 小部分 [xiǎo bùfen] 2 (MATH) 分数 [fēnshù]

fracture ['fræktʃə(r)] I N [c] [of bone] 断裂 [duànliè] II VT [+ bone] 折断 [zhéduàn] III VI [bone +] 断裂 [duànliè]

fragile ['frædʒaɪl] ADJ 1 [+ object, structure] 易损的 [yìsǔn de] 2 [+ economy, peace] 薄弱的 [bóruò de] 3 (delicate) 纤巧的 [xiánqiǎo de] 4 (unwell) [+ person] 虚弱的 [xūruò de]

fragment [n 'frægmənt, vb fræg'mɛnt] I N [c] 1 [of bone, glass etc] 碎片 [suìpiàn] 2 [of conversation, poem etc] 片断 [piànduàn] II VI 1 (lit) 裂成碎片 [liè chéng suìpiàn] 2 (fig) 分裂 [fēnliè] III VT 分裂 [fēnliè]

fragrance ['freɪgrəns] N [c/U] (smell) 香气 [xiāngqì]

fragrant ['freɪgrənt] ADJ 芳香的 [fāngxiāng de]

frail [freɪl] ADJ 1 [+ person, invalid] 虚弱的 [xūruò de] 2 [+ structure] 易破碎的 [yì pòsuì de]

frame [freɪm] I N [c] 1 [of building, structure] 框架 [kuàngjià] 2 [of body] 骨架 [gǔjià] 3 [of picture, mirror, door, window] 框 [kuàng] 5 (also: **frames**) [of spectacles] 眼镜架 [yǎnjìngjià] 6 (CINE) 画面 [huàmiàn] II VT 1 [+ picture, photograph] 给…镶框 [gěi…xiāngkuàng] 2 [+ reply, law, theory] 表达 [biǎodá] 3 (inf) (incriminate) 诬陷 [wūxiàn]

frame of mind (pl **frames of mind**) N [c] 心

境 [xīnjìng]

framework ['freɪmwɜːk] N [C] **1** (structure) 结构 [jiégòu] **2** (fig) 框架 [kuàngjià]

France [frɑːns] N 法国 [Fǎguó]

franchise ['fræntʃaɪz] **I** N [C] **1** (COMM) 特许经营 [tèxǔ jīngyíng] **2** (POL) 选举权 [xuǎnjǔ quán] **II** VT (COMM) 授予…特许权 [shòuyǔ…tèxǔ quán]

frank [fræŋk] ADJ **I 1** [+ person] 坦率的 [tǎnshuài de] **2** [+ discussion, admission] 坦诚的 [tǎnchéng de] **II** VT [+ letter] 盖邮资已付戳于 [gài yóuzī yǐfù chuō yú]

frankly ['fræŋklɪ] ADV **1** (honestly) [say, admit +] 坦白地 [tǎnbái de] **2** (introducing statement) 说实话 [shuō shíhuà]

frantic ['fræntɪk] ADJ **1** [+ person] 发疯的 [fāfēngde] **2** [+ rush, pace, search] 狂乱的 [kuángluàn de]

fraternity [frə'tɜːnɪtɪ] N **1** [U] (feeling) 友爱 [yǒu'ài] **2** [C] (group of people) 同人 [tóngrén] **3** [C] (US: UNIV) 联谊会 [liányìhuì]

fraud [frɔːd] N **1** [C/U] (crime) 诈骗 [zhàpiàn] **2** [C] (person) 骗子 [piànzi]

fraudulent ['frɔːdjʊlənt] ADJ [+ scheme, claim] 欺骗的 [qīpiàn de]

fraught [frɔːt] ADJ **1** ▶ **fraught with danger/problems** 充满危险/问题 [chōngmǎn wēixiǎn/wèntí] **2** (tense, anxious) [+ situation, evening, meeting] 令人焦虑的 [lìngrén jiāolǜ de]

fray [freɪ] **I** VI [cloth, rope +] 磨损 [mósǔn] **II** N [C] ▶ **to join or enter the fray** 参加角逐 [cānjiā juézhú] ▶ **tempers were frayed** 发火了 ▶ **her nerves were frayed** 她神经非常紧张

freak [friːk] **I** N [C] **1** (person) (in attitude, behaviour) 怪人 [guàirén]; (in appearance) 怪物 [guàiwù] **2** (inf) (fanatic) ▶ **health/fitness freak** 健康/健身狂 [jiànkāng/jiànshēn kuáng] **II** CPD [复合词] [+ accident, storm] 反常 [fǎncháng] **III** VI (inf) (also: **freak out**) 躁动不安 [zàodòng bù'ān] **IV** VT (inf) (also: **freak out**) 使躁动不安 [shǐ zàodòng bù'ān]

freckle ['frekl] N [C] 雀斑 [quèbān]

○ **free** [friː] **I** ADJ **1** (costing nothing) [+ meal, ticket etc] 免费的 [miǎnfèi de] ▷ The coffee was free. 咖啡是免费的。 **2** [+ person] 自由的 [zìyóu de] ▷ The slave escaped and became a free man. 奴隶逃跑了，成了自由人。 **3** [+ time] 空闲的 [kòngxián de] ▷ They don't have much free time. 他们没有多少空闲时间。 **4** [+ seat, table] 空余的 [kòngyú de] ▷ Is that seat free? 那个座位是空的吗? **5** (unrestricted) [+ choice, press, speech, elections] 自由的 [zìyóu de] ▷ It's their free choice. 那是他们的自由选择。 ▷ We can't do that if we haven't got a free press. 如果没有自由的新闻界，我们根本做不到。; [+ passage, movement] 畅通的 [chàngtōng de] **6** [+ hand, arm] 闲着的 [xiánzhe de] ▷ He buttoned his overcoat with his free hand. 他用闲着的那只手扣上了外衣

的扣子。 **II** VT **1** (release) [+ prisoner, slave] 释放 [shìfàng] ▷ They were freed by their kidnappers unharmed. 他们被绑匪释放了，并没有受到伤害。 [+ injured person] 解救 [jiějiù] ▷ Firemen tried to free the injured. 消防队员尽力解救受伤人员。; [+ jammed object] 使脱开 [shǐ tuōkāi] ▷ He used a screwdriver to free the lock. 他用螺丝刀打开了锁。 **2** [+ person] (from responsibility, duty) 摆脱 [bǎituō] ▷ His contract will run out shortly, freeing him to pursue his own projects. 他的合同很快就要到期了，这样他得以摆脱来发展自己的项目。 ▶ **free (of charge), for free** 免费 ▶ **to give sb a free hand** 给某人自主权 ▶ **admission free** 免费进入 ▶ **to be free of or from sth** 没有某物 ▷ The area will be free of pollution by the year 2006. 到2006年，这个地区将没有污染。 ▶ **to be free to do sth** 随意做某事 ▷ Women should be free to dress as they please. 女性应该任其喜好随意穿戴。 ▶ **free and easy** 自由自在的 ▶ **to feel free** 随便 ▶ **to free sb of sth** 使某人摆脱某物

freedom ['friːdəm] N [U] **1** (liberty) 自由 [zìyóu] **2** [of prisoner, slave, movement] 自由 [zìyóu] **3** (political) 自由 [zìyóu] **4** (from poverty, disease, hunger) 免受 [miǎnshòu]

Freefone® ['friːfəun] (BRIT) N [C] ▶ **call Freefone 0800** 拨打免费电话0800 [bōdǎ miǎnfèi diànhuà líng bā líng líng] [美=**toll-free**]

free gift N [C] 赠品 [zèngpǐn]

free kick (FOOTBALL) N [C] 任意球 [rènyì qiú]

freelance ['friːlɑːns] **I** ADJ [+ journalist, photographer, work] 自由职业的 [zìyóu zhíyè de] **II** ADV ▶ **to work freelance** 做自由职业工作 [zuò zìyóu zhíyè gōngzuò]

freely ['friːlɪ] ADV **1** (without restriction) [move +] 自由地 [zìyóu de]; [talk +] 无拘束地 [wú jūshù de] **2** (liberally) [spend, give +] 大手大脚地 [dàshǒudàjiǎo de]; [perspire +] 大量地 [dàliàng de] **3** (willingly) [share, admit +] 自愿地 [zìyuàn de] ▶ **to be freely available** 随意获得

Freepost® ['friːpəust] (BRIT) N [U] 免费邮寄 [miǎnfèi yóujì]

free-range ['friː'reɪndʒ] ADJ [+ eggs, chickens] 放养的 [fàngyǎng de]

freeway ['friːweɪ] (US) N [C] 高速公路 [gāosù gōnglù] [英=**motorway**]

free will N [C] ▶ **of one's own free will** 自觉自愿地 [zìjuézìyuàn de]

freeze [friːz] (pt **froze**, pp **frozen**) **I** VI **1** [liquid, weather +] 结冰 [jiébīng] **2** [pipe +] 冻住 [dòngzhù] **3** [person +] (with cold) 冻僵 [dōngjiāng] **4** (fig) (from fear, shock) 呆住 [dāizhù] **II** VT **1** [+ water, lake] 使结冰 [shǐ jiébīng] **2** [+ food] 冷冻 [lěngdòng] **3** [+ wages, prices, bank account, assets] 冻结 [dòngjié] **III** N [C] **1** (cold weather) 霜冻 [shuāngdòng] **2** (on wages, prices) 冻结 [dòngjié] ▶ **it may freeze tonight** 今晚可能会结冰

▶ **freeze out** VT ▶ **to freeze sb out of sth** 把某人从某处挤走 [bǎ mǒurén cóng mǒuchù jǐzǒu]
▶ **freeze over** VI 1 [*river, lake+*] 结冰 [jiébīng] 2 [*windscreen, windows+*] 结霜 [jiéshuāng]

freezer ['friːzə(r)] N [c] 冰柜 [bīngguì]

freezing ['friːzɪŋ] ADJ (*also:* **freezing cold**) [+ *day, weather*] 极冷的 [jílěng de]; [+ *water, place, room*] 冰冷的 [bīnglěng de]; [+ *person, hands*] 冰凉的 [bīngliáng de] ▶ **I'm freezing** 冻死我了 ▶ **it's freezing outside** 外面特别冷 ▶ **3 degrees below freezing** 零下3度
■用法参见 **cold**

freezing point N [c/u] 冰点 [bīngdiǎn]

freight [freɪt] N [u] (*goods*) 货物 [huòwù] ▶ **by air/sea freight** 通过空/海运

freight train N [c] 货运列车 [huòyùn lièchē]

French [frɛntʃ] I ADJ 法国的 [Fǎguó de] II N [u] (*language*) 法语 [Fǎyǔ] III **the French** NPL (*people*) 法国人 [Fǎguórén]

French bean (BRIT) N [c] 菜豆 [càidòu] [美= **string bean**]

French bread N [u] 法式棍子面包 [Fǎshì gùnzi miànbāo]

French dressing N [u] 法式色拉调料 [Fǎshì sèlā tiáoliào]

French fries [-fraɪz] (ESP US) NPL 炸薯条 [zhá shǔtiáo] [英= **chips**]

Frenchman ['frɛntʃmən] (*pl* **Frenchmen**) N [c] 法国男人 [Fǎguó nánrén]

French stick N [c] 法式棍子面包 [Fǎshì gùnzi miànbāo]

French window N [c] 落地窗 [luòdì chuāng]

Frenchwoman ['frɛntʃwumən] (*pl* **Frenchwomen**) N [c] 法国女人 [Fǎguó nǚrén]

frenzy ['frɛnzɪ] N [c/u] 狂热 [kuángrè] ▶ a **frenzy of activity/excitement** 活动的/兴奋得狂乱 ▶ **to drive sb into a frenzy** 把某人逼得发狂 ▶ **to be in a frenzy** 发狂地

frequency ['friːkwənsɪ] N 1 [u] (*of event*) 频繁性 [pínfánxìng] 2 [c/u] (RAD) 频率 [pínlǜ] ▶ **to increase in frequency** 频率增加

frequent [*adj* 'friːkwənt, *vb* frɪ'kwɛnt] I ADJ [+ *occurrence, visitor*] 频繁的 [pínfán de] II VT (*frm*) [+ *pub, restaurant*] 常去 [chángqù]

frequently ['friːkwəntlɪ] ADV 时常地 [shícháng de]

fresh [frɛʃ] ADJ 1 [+ *food, bread, vegetables*] 新鲜的 [xīnxiān de] 2 [+ *paint, footprints*] 新的 [xīn de] 3 [+ *water*] 淡的 [dàn de] 4 (*new*) [+ *approach, way*] 新颖的 [xīnyǐng de] 5 (*recent*) [+ *instructions, inquiries*] 附加的 [fùjiā de]; [+ *memories*] 鲜明的 [xiānmíng de] 6 (*cheeky*) [+ *person*] 冒失的 [màoshi de] ▶ **fresh air** 新鲜空气 ▶ **to make a fresh start** 重新开始 ▶ **he's fresh from** *or* **out of university** 他刚刚大学毕业 ▶ **to be fresh out of sth** (*inf*) 刚用完某物

freshen ['frɛʃən] VI [*wind+*] 变强 [biànqiáng]
▶ **freshen up** VI [*person+*] 梳洗一番

fresher ['frɛʃə(r)] (BRIT: UNIV) (*inf*) N [c] 大学一年级新生 [dàxué yīniánjí xīnshēng]

freshly ['frɛʃlɪ] ADV [+ *made, cooked, painted*] 刚刚 [gānggāng]

freshman ['frɛʃmən] (*pl* **freshmen**) (US) N [c] 大学一年级学生 [dàxué yīniánjí xuéshēng]

freshwater ['frɛʃwɔːtə(r)] ADJ [+ *lake, fish*] 淡水的 [dànshuǐ de]

fret [frɛt] VI (*worry*) 担心 [dānxīn]

Fri. ABBR (= **Friday**) 星期五 [xīngqīwǔ]

friar ['fraɪə(r)] N [c] 修道士 [xiūdàoshì]

friction ['frɪkʃən] N 1 [u] (PHYS) (*resistance*) 摩擦力 [mócālì] 2 (*rubbing*) 摩擦 [mócā] 3 (*fig*) (*conflict*) (*also:* **frictions**) 冲突 [chōngtū]

Friday ['fraɪdɪ] N [c/u] 星期五 [xīngqīwǔ] *see also* **Tuesday**

fridge [frɪdʒ] (BRIT) N [c] 冰箱 [bīngxiāng] [美= **refrigerator**]

fried [fraɪd] I PT, PP *of* **fry** II ADJ [+ *food*] 炒的 [chǎo de]

○ **friend** [frɛnd] N [c] 朋友 [péngyou] ▶ **to be friends** 是朋友 ▶ **to be friends with sb** 是某人的朋友 ▶ **to make friends** 交朋友 ▶ **to make friends with sb** 与某人交朋友 ▶ **the friends of Birmingham Royal Ballet** 伯明翰皇家芭蕾舞团的赞助者

friendly ['frɛndlɪ] I ADJ 1 [+ *person*] 友善的 [yǒushàn de]; [+ *tone, hug, atmosphere, government*] 友好的 [yǒuhǎo de] 2 (BRIT: SPORT) [+ *game, match*] 友谊的 [yǒuyì de] II N [c] (BRIT: SPORT) 友谊比赛 [yǒuyì bǐsài] ▶ **to be friendly with** 跟…友好 ▶ **to be friendly to** 对…友好

friendship ['frɛndʃɪp] N 1 (*relationship*) 友情 [yǒuqíng] 2 (*state*) 友爱 [yǒu'ài]

frieze [friːz] N 中楣 [zhōngméi]

frigate ['frɪgɪt] N [c] 护卫舰 [hùwèijiàn]

fright [fraɪt] N 1 [u] (*terror*) 恐惧 [kǒngjù] 2 [c] (*shock*) 惊吓 [jīngxià] ▶ **to take fright** 受惊 ▶ **to give sb a fright** 吓唬某人一下 ▶ **to look a fright** (*inf*) 看起来怪得吓人

frighten ['fraɪtn] VT 使惊恐 [shǐ jīngkǒng]
▶ **frighten away** VT 1 [+ *birds, children etc*] 吓跑 [xiàpǎo] 2 (*fig*) (*deter*) 使踌躇 [shǐ chóuchú]
▶ **frighten into** VT ▶ **to frighten sb into doing sth** 吓得某人去做某事 [xiàde mǒurén qù zuò mǒushì]
▶ **frighten off** VT = **frighten away**

frightened ['fraɪtnd] ADJ 1 [+ *person, animal*] ▶ **to be frightened** 被吓倒 [bèi xiàdǎo] 2 [+ *eyes, expression*] 恐惧的 ▶ **to be frightened of sth/of doing sth** *or* **to do sth** 害怕某事/做某事

请勿将 **frightened** 和 **frightening** 混淆。如果你感到 **frightened**，表示你感到恐惧或紧张。*I think he was truly frightened of me at times…I was more frightened than I had ever been in my life.*

如果某事物 frightening，表示它让人感到恐惧。Do you ever have frightening dreams?… It was a strange, rather frightening place.

frightening ['fraɪtnɪŋ] ADJ [+experience, prospect] 令人恐惧的 [lìngrén kǒngjù de]

■用法参见 **frightened**

frightful ['fraɪtful] (o.f.) ADJ **1** (dreadful) [+smell, mistake] 可怕的 [kěpà de] **2** (inf) (emphatic use) 极大的 [jídà de]

frill [frɪl] N [c] (on dress, shirt) 褶边 [zhěbiān]
► **with no** or **without frills** 毫无虚饰的

fringe [frɪndʒ] N [c] **1** (BRIT) (hair) 刘海 [liúhǎi] [美= **bangs**] **2** (on shawl, lampshade) 流苏 [liúsū] **3** (edge) (of town, forest) 外围 [wàiwéi] **4** (fig) [of activity, organization] 次要部分 [cìyào bùfen]

Frisbee® ['frɪzbɪ] N [c] 飞盘 [Fēipán]

fritter ['frɪtə(r)] N [c] 油煎饼 [yóujiānbǐng]
► **fritter away** VT [+time, money] 浪费掉 [làngfèi diào]

frivolous ['frɪvələs] ADJ [+conduct, person] 轻浮的 [qīngfú de]; [+activity] 无所谓的 [wúsuǒwèi de]

fro [frəu] ADV see **to**

frock [frɔk] (o.f.) N [c] (dress) 女服 [nǚfú]

frog [frɔg] (ZOOL) N [c] 青蛙 [qīngwā] ► **to have a frog in one's throat** 声音嘶哑

frogman ['frɔgmən] (pl **frogmen**) N [c] 蛙人 [wārén]

frolic ['frɔlɪk] VI [animals, children +] 嬉戏 [xìxì]

from [frɔm] PREP **1** (indicating starting place) 来自 [láizì] ► **where are you from?** 你来自哪里？► **to run away from home** 离家出走 ► **from London to Glasgow** 从伦敦到格拉斯哥 ► **to be back from Spain/Paris** etc 从西班牙/巴黎[等]回来 ► **viewed from above** 从上鸟瞰 ► **a light bulb hung from the ceiling** 从天花板上垂下的灯泡 **2** (indicating origin) 来自 [láizì] ► **a present/telephone call/letter from sb** 来自某人的礼物/电话/信 ► **to take sth from sb/sth** 从某人/某物处拿某物 **3** (with time, distance, price, numbers) 从 [cóng] ► **from January (on)** 从1月 (开始) ► **from one o'clock to** or **until two** 从1点到2点 ► **it's 1 km from the beach** 从海滩到这儿有1公里 ► **a long way from home** 离家很远 ► **prices starting from £10** 从10镑起价 ► **unemployment has fallen from 7.5% to 7.2%** 失业率已经从7.5%降到7.2% ► **six from ten leaves four** 10减去6还剩4 **4** (because of, on the basis of) 根据 [gēnjù] ► **from what he says** 根据他所说的 ► **from what I understand** 据我所了解 **5** (out of) ► **made from** 用…做成 [yòng…zuòchéng]

○front [frʌnt] I N **1** [c] [of house, dress] 前面 [qiánmiàn] ► **jackets with buttons down the front** 前面有纽扣的上衣; [of coach, train, car] 前部 [qiánbù] ► **The cop searched the front of the car.** 警方搜查了汽车的前部。**2** [c] (MIL) 前线 [qiánxiàn] ► **Her husband is fighting at the front.** 她的丈夫在前线打仗。**3** [c] (MET) 锋 [fēng] ► **a cold/warm front** 冷/暖锋 **4** [s] (also: **sea front**) 海滨人行道 [hǎibīn rénxíngdào] ► **a stroll along the front** 沿海滨人行道的散步 **5** [c] (pretence) 模样样 [zhuāngmúyàng] ► **Richard kept up a brave front.** 理查德一直装作一副勇敢的样子。**6** [c] (disguise) 幌子 [huǎngzi] ► **The organization was used as a front for drug trafficking.** 该组织被用作毒品贩运的幌子。**II** ADJ **1** [+seat, garden, entrance etc] 前面的 [qiánmiàn de] **2** [+tooth] 前部的 [qiánbù de] **III** VI ► **to front onto sth** (house +) 面向某物 [miànxiàng mǒuwù] ► **houses that front directly onto little courtyards** 直接面向小庭院的房子 **IV** VT **1** (BRIT) [+organization] 当…的头儿 [dāng…de tóur] [美= **head**] **2** [+pop group] 做…的主唱 [zuò…de zhǔchàng] ► **in front** (in moving line) 在前面 ► **He was driving too close to the car in front.** 他车开得离前面的车太近。; (in race, distance) 领先 ► **David is in front in the jockeys' title race.** 大卫在马术冠军赛中居领先位置。► **in front of** (facing) 在…前面 ► **A car drew up in front of the house.** 一辆汽车在房子前面停了下来。; (in the presence of) 在…面前 ► **They never argued in front of their children.** 他们从来不在孩子面前吵架。► **on the political/economic front** 在政治/经济方面 ► **to put on a front** 装腔作势

front door N [c] 前门 [qiánmén]

frontier ['frʌntɪə(r)] N [c] **1** (BRIT) (between countries) 国界 [guójiè] [美= **border**] **2** (fig) 界限 [jièxiàn]

front page (PUBLISHING) N [c] 头版 [tóubǎn]
► **to make the front page** 成为头条新闻

frost [frɔst] N [c] **1** [c] (weather) 霜 [shuāng] **2** [u] (ice) 冰霜 [bīngshuāng]

frostbite ['frɔstbaɪt] N [u] 冻伤 [dòngshāng]

frosting ['frɔstɪŋ] N [u] (on cake) 糖霜 [tángshuāng] [英= **icing**]

frosty ['frɔstɪ] ADJ **1** [+day, night, weather] 有霜冻的 [yǒu shuāngdòng de]; [+grass, window] 结霜的 [jiéshuāng de] **2** [+reception, look] 冷淡的 [lěngdàn de]

froth [frɔθ] I N [u] (on liquid) 泡沫 [pàomò] II VI [liquid +] 起泡沫 [qǐ pàomò]

frown [fraun] I N [c] 皱眉 [zhòuméi] II VI 皱眉 [zhòuméi]
► **frown (up)on** VT FUS [不可拆分] (fig) 不赞成 [bù zànchéng]

froze [frəuz] PT of **freeze**

frozen ['frəuzn] I PP of **freeze** II ADJ **1** [+food] 冷冻的 [lěngdòng de]; [+ground, lake] 结冰的 [jiébīng de] **2** [+person, fingers] 冰冷的

[bīnglěng de] **3** (COMM) [+ *assets*] 冻结的 [lěngdòng de]

frugal ['fru:gl] ADJ [+ *person*] 节俭的 [jiéjiǎn de]; [+ *meal*] 廉价的 [liánjià de]

fruit [fru:t] (*pl* **fruit** *or* **fruits**) N [C/U] **1** 水果 [shuǐguǒ] **2** (*fig*) (*results*) 成果 [chéngguǒ] ▸ **to bear fruit** (*fig*) 取得成果

fruitful ['fru:tful] ADJ [+ *meeting, discussion*] 富有成效的 [fùyǒu chéngxiào de]

fruition [fru:'ɪʃən] N [C] ▸ **to come to fruition** (*frm*) 得以实现 [déyǐ shíxiàn]

fruit juice N [C/U] 果汁 [guǒzhī] ▸ **I'd like a fruit juice** 我想要杯果汁

fruit machine (BRIT) N [C] 吃角子老虎机 [chījiǎozi lǎohǔjī] [美= **slot machine**]

fruit salad N [C/U] 水果色拉 [shuǐguǒ sèlā]

frustrate [frʌs'treɪt] VT **1** [+ *person*] 使沮丧 [shǐ jǔsàng] **2** [+ *plan, attempt*] 阻碍 [zǔ'ài]

frustrated [frʌs'treɪtɪd] ADJ 泄气的 [xièqì de]

fry [fraɪ] (*pt, pp* **fried**) I VT (CULIN) 油煎 [yóujiān] II **fries** NPL (CULIN) = **French fries** 用法参见 **cook**

frying pan ['fraɪɪŋ-] N [C] 平底煎锅 [píngdǐ jiānguō]

ft. ABBR (= *foot, feet*) 英尺 [yīngchǐ]

fudge [fʌdʒ] I N [U] (CULIN) 软糖 [ruǎntáng] II VT [+ *issue, problem*] 规避 [guībì]

fuel ['fjuəl] I N [C/U] (*for heating etc*) 燃料 [ránliào] II VT **1** [+ *furnace, aircraft*] 由⋯作燃料 [yóu⋯zuò ránliào] **2** (*fig*) [+ *rumours, dispute*] 加剧 [jiājù]

fugitive ['fju:dʒɪtɪv] N [C] 逃亡者 [táowángzhě]

fulfil, (US) **fulfill** [ful'fɪl] VT **1** [+ *function, role, task*] 完成 [wánchéng]; [+ *condition, requirement*] 满足 [mǎnzú] **2** (*satisfy*) [+ *person*] 令⋯满足 [lìng⋯mǎnzú]

fulfilment, (US) **fulfillment** [ful'fɪlmənt] N [U] **1** (*satisfaction*) 满足 [mǎnzú] **2** [*of promise, threat, request*] 实行 [shíxíng]; [*of hope, dream, ambition*] 实现 [shíxiàn]

○**full** [ful] I ADJ **1** [+ *container, cup*] 满的 [mǎn de] ▷ *The bucket is almost full.* 桶要满了。; [+ *cinema, car, restaurant*] 满的 [mǎn de] ▷ *All the car parks are full.* 所有的停车场都满了。**2** (*complete*) [+ *use, volume, force*] 最大限度的 [zuìdà xiàndù de] ▷ *The radio was playing at full volume.* 收音机以最大音量播放着。**3** (*complete*) [+ *details*] 全部的 [quánbù de] ▷ *Full details will be sent to you.* 全部的具体情况会发给你。; [+ *information, name*] 完全的 [wánquán de] ▷ *I haven't got his full name.* 我没有他的全名。**4** [+ *flavour*] 醇厚的 [chúnhòu de] **5** [+ *skirt, sleeves*] 肥大的 [féidà de] **6** [+ *life*] 充实的 [chōngshí de] ▷ *a very full and interesting life* 非常充实而有趣的生活 **7** [+ *impact, implication*] 所有的 [suǒyǒu de] ▷ *I paused to allow the full impact of this to register.*

我停下来，以便仔细感受这一切带来的所有影响。II ADV ▸ **to know full well that...** 完全清楚地了解 [wánquán qīngchu de liǎojiě] ▸ **full up** [*hotel etc*] 爆满 ▸ **I'm full (up)** 我吃饱了 ▸ **a full week/month** 整整一个星期/月 ▷ *For a full week we did not eat.* 整整一个星期，我们没吃东西。▸ **in full view of sb** 完全看得见某人 ▸ **full marks** (BRIT: SCOL) 满分 ▸ **at full speed** 以全速 ▸ **full of** [+ *objects, people*] 充满 ▷ *His office was full of policemen.* 他的办公室里满是警察。; [+ *confidence, hope*] 充满 ▷ *I was full of confidence.* 我充满了信心。▸ **in full** [*reproduce, quote, pay* +] 全部地 ▷ *The bill has been paid in full.* 账单已被付清了。▸ **to write one's name in full** 写出自己的全名 ▸ **to strike sb full in the face** 正打在某人的脸上 ▸ **to do sth to the full** 充分地做某事

full employment N [U] 充分就业 [chōngfèn jiùyè]

full-length ['ful'leŋθ] I ADJ **1** [+ *book, film*] 未删节的 [wèi shānjié de] **2** [+ *coat, skirt*] 长及脚踝的 [chángjíjiǎohuái de] **3** [+ *portrait, mirror*] 全身的 [quánshēn de] II ADV [*lie* +] 直直地 [zhízhí de]

full moon N [S] 满月 [mǎnyuè]

full-scale ['fulskeɪl] ADJ **1** [+ *war, search, inquiry*] 全面的 [quánmiàn de] **2** [+ *model, drawing*] 与原物同样大的 [yǔ yuánwù tóngyàng dà de]

full stop (BRIT) N [C] 句号 [jùhào] [美= **period**] ▸ **to come to a full stop** (*fig*) 完全停止

full-time ['ful'taɪm] I ADJ [+ *work, study*] 全职的 [quánzhí de]; [+ *student, staff*] 全日制的 [quánrìzhì de] II ADV [*work, study* +] 全日地 [quánrì de]

fully ['fulɪ] ADV **1** (*completely*) [*understand, recover* +] 完全地 [wánquán de]; [+ *automatic*] 完全地 [wánquán de]; [+ *trained, qualified*] 全面地 [quánmiàn de] **2** (*in full*) [*answer, describe* +] 充分地 [chōngfèn de] **3** (*as many as*) 整整 [zhěngzhěng]

fully-fledged ['fulɪ'fledʒd] ADJ [+ *member, atheist etc*] 完全的 [wánquán de]

fully-licensed ['fulɪ'laɪsnst] (BRIT) ADJ [+ *hotel, restaurant*] 可以售酒的 [kěyǐ shòujiǔ de]

fumble ['fʌmbl] VI ▸ **to fumble for** 笨手笨脚地摸索 [bènshǒu bènjiǎo de mōsuǒ] ▸ **fumble with** VT FUS [不可拆分] [+ *key, pen*] 笨手笨脚地抓住 [bènshǒu bènjiǎo de zhuāzhù]

fume [fju:m] VI (*rage*) 大怒 [dànù]

fumes [fju:mz] NPL [*of fire, fuel, car*] 浓烈的烟气 [nóngliè de yānqì]

fumigate ['fju:mɪgeɪt] VT [+ *house, clothes*] 烟熏 [yānxūn]

fun [fʌn] N [U] 乐趣 [lèqù] ▸ **to have fun** 玩得开心 ▸ **to get a lot of fun out of sth** 从某事得到许多乐趣 ▸ **he's good fun (to be with)** 跟他(在一起)很有趣 ▸ **it was a lot of fun** 非常开心 ▸ **it's not much fun** 没什么劲儿 ▸ **to do**

sth for fun 为找乐而做某事 ▸ to do sth in fun 开玩笑地做某事 ▸ to make fun of sb/sth 取笑某人/某物

function ['fʌŋkʃən] I N [c] 1 (role) 作用 [zuòyòng] 2 (frm) (product) ▸ to be a function of sth 取决于某物 [qǔjué yú mǒuwù] 3 (social occasion) 社交聚会 [shèjiāo jùhuì] II VI [system, process +] 运行 [yùnxíng]; [device +] 运转 [yùnzhuǎn] ▸ to function as 起…的作用

functional ['fʌŋkʃənl] ADJ 1 (practical) [+ furniture, design etc] 实用的 [shíyòng de] 2 [+ working equipment, device] 在运转的 [zài yùnzhuǎn de]

⚪**fund** [fʌnd] I N [c] 1 [of money] 基金 [jījīn] ▷ the disaster fund 救灾基金 2 (source, store) [of knowledge, experience] 储备 [chǔbèi] ▷ a large fund of scientific knowledge 大量科学知识的储备 II VT 资助 [zīzhù] ▷ The work is funded by private industry. 这项工作是由私人企业资助的。 III funds NPL (money) 资金 [zījīn]

fundamental [fʌndə'mentl] ADJ 1 (essential) [+ principle, concept] 根本的 [gēnběn de] 2 (basic) [+ change, difference, error] 基本的 [jīběn de] ▸ fundamental to 对…是必要的

funeral ['fju:nərəl] N [c] 葬礼 [zànglǐ]

funeral home N = funeral parlour

funeral parlour (BRIT) N [c] 殡仪馆 [bìnyí guǎn]

funfair ['fʌnfeə(r)] (BRIT) N [c] 露天游乐场 [lùtiān yóulèchǎng] 〔美= carnival〕

fungus ['fʌŋgəs] (pl fungi ['fʌŋgaɪ]) N 1 [c] (plant) 真菌 [zhēnjūn] 2 [U] (mould) 霉 [méi]

funnel ['fʌnl] I N [c] 1 (for pouring) 漏斗 [lòudǒu] 2 [of ship] 烟囱 [yāncōng] II VI [water, wind +] 汇集 [huìjí] III VT 1 [+ water, wind] 使汇集 [shǐ huìjí] 2 (fig) [+ money, resources] 汇集 [huìjí]

funny ['fʌni] ADJ 1 (amusing) 可笑的 [kěxiào de] 2 (strange) 奇怪的 [qíguài de] ▸ to feel funny (inf) (unwell) 稍感不适

fur [fə:(r)] I N 1 [c/U] [of animal] 毛 [máo] 2 [c] (garment) 毛皮大衣 [máopí dàyī] 3 [U] (BRIT) (in kettle) 水锈 [shuǐxiù] II CPD [复合词] [+ hat, collar etc] 毛皮 [máopí]

fur coat N [c] 毛皮大衣 [máopí dàyī]

furious ['fjuərɪəs] ADJ 1 [+ person] 大发雷霆的 [dà fā léitíng de] 2 [+ row, argument] 激烈的 [jīliè de] 3 [+ effort, speed] 强劲的 [qiángjìn de] ▸ to be furious with sb 对某人大发雷霆
　　用法参见 angry

furlong ['fə:lɔŋ] N [c] 长度单位弗隆，相当于 201.167米

furnace ['fə:nɪs] N [c] 熔炉 [rónglú]

furnish ['fə:nɪʃ] VT 1 [+ room, building] 布置 [bùzhì] 2 (frm) (supply) 提供 [tígōng] ▸ to furnish sb with sth (frm) 给某人提供某物 ▸ furnished flat or (US) apartment 带家具的公寓

furnishings ['fə:nɪʃɪŋz] NPL 陈设 [chénshè]

furniture ['fə:nɪtʃə(r)] N [U] 家具 [jiājù] ▸ a piece of furniture 一件家具

furrow ['fʌrəu] I N [c] 1 (in field) 垄沟 [lǒnggōu] 2 (in skin) 皱纹 [zhòuwén] II VT [+ brow] 使起皱纹 [shǐ qǐ zhòuwén] III VI [brow +] 起皱纹 [qǐ zhòuwén]

furry ['fə:rɪ] ADJ [+ animal, tail, toy] 毛茸茸的 [máoróngróng de]; [+ coat, hat] 毛皮的 [máopí de]

⚪**further** ['fə:ðə(r)] I ADJ [+ additional] 进一步的 [jìnyībù de] ▷ Doctors are carrying out further tests. 医生们在做进一步的检查。 II ADV 1 (farther) (in distance, time) 更远地 [gèngyuǎn de] ▷ further along the beach 沿着海滨更远处 ▷ It has its origins much further back in time. 它的起源在时间上要追溯得更远。; (in degree) 更深地 [gèngshēn de] ▷ He sank further into debt. 他更加深陷债务中。; (in development) 进一步地 [jìnyībù de] ▷ He did not develop that idea any further. 他没有再进一步发展那个设想。 2 (frm) (furthermore) 此外 [cǐwài] III VT [+ career, project, cause] 促进 [cùjìn] ▷ a plot by Morris to further his career 莫里斯促进其事业的一个计划 ▸ to further one's/sb's interests 增进自己/某人的利益 ▸ until further notice 直到另行通知 ▸ how much further is it? 还有多远？ ▸ further to your letter of... (BRIT: frm): COMM 鉴于你…的来信
　　用法参见 farther

further education N [U] 继续教育 [jìxù jiàoyù]

furthermore [fə:ðə'mɔ:(r)] ADV 此外 [cǐwài]

furthest ['fə:ðɪst] I SUPERL of far II ADV (farthest) (in distance) 最远地 [zuìyuǎn de]; (in time) 最久远地 [zuì jiǔyuǎn de]; (in degree) 最大程度地 [zuìdà chéngdù de] III ADJ 最远的 [zuìyuǎn de]

furtive ['fə:tɪv] ADJ [+ glance, manner] 鬼鬼祟祟的 [guǐguǐsuìsuì de]

fury ['fjuərɪ] N [U/S] 狂怒 [kuángnù] ▸ in a fury 勃然大怒地

fuse, (US) **fuze** [fju:z] I N [c] 1 (ELEC) (in plug, circuit) 保险丝 [bǎoxiǎnsī] 2 (for bomb, firework) 导火线 [dǎohuǒ xiàn] II VT 1 (BRIT: ELEC) 使短路 [shǐ duǎnlù] 2 (join together) [+ substances, metals] 熔合 [rónghé] 3 [+ ideas, systems] 结合 [jiéhé] III VI 1 (BRIT: ELEC) 短路 [duǎnlù] 2 (join together) [substances, metals +] 熔合 [rónghé] 3 [ideas, systems +] 结合 [jiéhé] ▸ a fuse has blown 保险丝烧断了

fuse box N [c] 保险丝盒 [bǎoxiǎnsī hé]

fuselage ['fju:zəla:ʒ] N [c] 机身 [jīshēn]

fusion ['fju:ʒən] N 1 [c/U] [of ideas, qualities] 融合 [rónghé] 2 [U] (PHYS) (also: nuclear fusion) 核聚变 [hé jùbiàn]

fuss [fʌs] I N 1 [S/U] (bother) 大惊小怪 [dàjīng xiǎoguài] 2 [c] (disturbance) 慌乱 [huāngluàn]

II VI (*fret*) 大惊小怪 [dàjīng xiǎoguài] ▶ to make *or* kick up a fuss (about sth) (*inf*) （对某事）小题大做 ▶ to make a fuss of sb (BRIT) 对某人过分关心

▶ fuss over VT FUS [不可拆分] 1 [+ *person*] 娇宠 [jiāochǒng] 2 [+ *health, appearance, details*] 过分注意 [guòfén zhùyì]

fussy ['fʌsɪ] ADJ 1 [+ *person*] 挑剔的 [tiāoti de] 2 [+ *clothes, decorations*] 过分装饰的 [guòfèn zhuāngshì de] ▶ I'm not fussy (*I don't mind*) 我无所谓

futile ['fjuːtaɪl] ADJ [+ *attempt, gesture, search*] 无效的 [wúxiào de]

○**future** ['fjuːtʃə(r)] I ADJ 将来的 [jiānglái de] ▷ *at some future date* 在将来的某一天；[+ *president, spouse*] 未来的 [wèilái de] ▷ *She met her future husband at the party.* 她是在那个晚会上认识她未来的丈夫的。II N 1 (*time to come*) ▶ the future 未来 [wèilái] ▷ *We will have to see what the future holds.* 我们还得看未来的发展如何。2 [C] (*prospects*) 前途 [qiántú] ▷ *I decided that my future lay in medicine.* 我决心把我的前途放在医学方面。3 (LING) (*also:* future tense) ▶ the future 将来时 [jiāngláishí] III futures NPL (FIN) 期货交易 [qīhuò jiāoyì] ▶ in (the) future (*from now on*) 从今以后 ▶ in the future (*not now*) 将来 ▶ in the near/foreseeable future 在不久/可预见的未来 ▶ there's no future in this idea 这个设想没有前途

fuze [fjuːz] (US) N [C] VT, VI = fuse

fuzzy ['fʌzɪ] ADJ 1 (*blurred*) [+ *photo, image*] 模糊的 [móhu de] 2 [+ *hair*] 毛茸茸的 [máoróngróng de] 3 (*confused*) [+ *thoughts, ideas*] 含糊不清的 [héhu bùqīng de]

fuzzy logic (COMPUT) N [U] 模糊逻辑 [móhu luójí]

FYI ABBR (= *for your information/interest*) 供参考 [gòng cānkǎo]

G¹, g¹ [dʒiː] N [C/U] *(letter)* 英语的第七个字母

G² [dʒiː] I N [C/U] (MUS) C大调音阶中的第五音 II N ABBR **1** (BRIT: SCOL) (= *good*) 优 [yōu] **2** (US: CINE) (= *general audience*) 各种年龄段都可观看

g² ABBR **1** (= *gram*) 克 [kè] **2** (PHYS) (= *gravity*) 重力 [zhònglì]

gable ['geɪbl] N [C] *[of building]* 三角墙 [sānjiǎoqiáng]

gadget ['gædʒɪt] N [C] 小装置 [xiǎozhuāngzhì]

Gaelic ['geɪlɪk] I ADJ 盖尔人的 [Gài'ěrrén de] II N [U] *(language)* 盖尔语 [Gài'ěryǔ]

○ **GAELIC**

○ 爱尔兰和苏格兰西北部的一部分人说
○ **Gaelic** (盖尔语)。爱尔兰盖尔语和苏格兰
○ 盖尔语稍有差别,但是两者都和威尔士语
○ 有关。100多万人说爱尔兰盖尔语,爱尔兰
○ 宪法将其定为第一官方语言。在苏格兰,
○ 说盖尔语的人数在急速下降,近来降到了
○ 5万人以下。

gag [gæg] I N [C] **1** *(on mouth)* 塞口物 [sāikǒuwù] **2** *(joke)* 笑话 [xiàohua] II VT **1** [+ *prisoner*] 塞住…的嘴 [sāizhù…de zuǐ] **2** *(fig)* 使缄默 [shǐ jiānmò] III VI *(choke)* 作呕 [zuò'ǒu] ▶ **to gag on sth** 被某物卡住喉咙

gain [geɪn] I VT **1** [+ *speed, weight, confidence*] 增加 [zēngjiā] **2** *(obtain)* 获得 [huòdé] II VI [*clock, watch* +] 走快 [zǒukuài] III N [C/U] *(increase, improvement)* 获益 [huòyì] ▶ **to gain in value/popularity** 增值/提高声望 ▶ **to gain ground** [*idea* +] 开始被人接受 ▶ **to gain on sb** 赶上某人 ▶ **weight gain** 体重增加 ▶ **to gain 3lbs (in weight)** (体重)增加3磅 ▶ **to do sth for gain** *(for profit)* 为获利而做某事 ▶ **to gain from sth** [+ *money*] 从某事中获利; [+ *knowledge*] 从某事中获益 ▶ **a gain in efficiency/productivity** 效率/生产力的提高 ▶ **a gain of 10%** 10%的增长

gal. ABBR (= *gallon*) 加仑 [jiālún]

gala ['gɑːlə] N [C] *(festival)* 盛会 [shènghuì] ▶ **a swimming/sports gala** 游泳/体育大赛

galaxy ['gæləksɪ] N **1** [C] 星系 [xīngxì] **2** ▶ **the Galaxy** 银河系 [Yínhéxì]

gale [geɪl] N [C] *(wind)* 大风 [dàfēng] ▶ **to be blowing a gale** 刮大风 ▶ **gale force 10 or force 10 gale** 10级大风 ▶ **gales of laughter** 阵阵笑声

gale-force wind [geɪlfɔːs-] N [C] 7至10级大风

gall. ABBR (= *gallon*) 加仑 [jiālún]

gallant ['gælənt] ADJ **1** *(brave)* [+ *person, fight, effort*] 英勇的 [yīngyǒng de] **2** *(polite)* (o.f.) 献殷勤的 [xiàn yīnqín de]

gall bladder [gɔːl-] N [C] 胆囊 [dǎnnáng]

gallery ['gælərɪ] N [C] **1** (also: **art gallery**) *(public)* 美术馆 [měishùguǎn]; *(private)* 画廊 [huàláng] **2** *(in hall, church, theatre)* 廊台 [lángtái]

galley ['gælɪ] N [C] **1** *(kitchen)* [*of ship, aircraft*] 厨房 [chúfáng] **2** *(ship)* 大型划船 [dàxíng huáchuán]

gallon ['gæln] N [C] (= *8 pints*; BRIT = 4.5*l*; US = 3.8*l*) 加仑 [jiālún]

gallop ['gæləp] I VI [*horse* +] 飞跑 [fēipǎo]; [*rider* +] 骑马驰驱 [qí mǎ bēnchí] II N [C] **1** *(ride)* 骑马奔驰 [qí mǎ bēnchí] **2** [*of horse*] 飞跑 [fēipǎo] ▶ **at a gallop** 飞奔

gallstone ['gɔːlstəun] N [C] 胆石 [dǎnshí]

galore [gə'lɔː(r)] ADJ ▶ **bargains/prizes galore** 大量的便宜货/奖品 [dàliàng de piányihuò/jiǎngpǐn]

Gambia ['gæmbɪə] N 冈比亚 [Gāngbǐyà]

gamble ['gæmbl] I VI **1** *(bet)* 赌博 [dǔbó] **2** *(take a risk)* 投机 [tóujī] II VT [+ *money*] 赌 [dǔ] III N [C] *(risk)* 冒险 [màoxiǎn] ▶ **to gamble on sth** 对某事打赌; [+ *horses, race*] 对某物下赌注; [+ *success, outcome*] 对某事冒险 ▶ **to take a gamble** 冒险行事

▶ **gamble away** VT [+ *money*] 输光 [shūguāng]

gambler ['gæmblə(r)] N [C] **1** *(person who bets)* 赌博者 [dǔbózhě] **2** *(risk-taker)* 投机者 [tóujīzhě]

gambling ['gæmblɪŋ] N [U] 赌博 [dǔbó]

○ **game** [geɪm] I N **1** [C] *(sport)* 运动 [yùndòng] ▷ *the wonderful game of football* 精彩的足球运动 **2** [C] *(activity)* (children's) 游戏 [yóuxì] ▷ *This is a great game for children's parties.* 这是孩子们聚会上的一个绝妙的游戏。 **3** [C] (also: **board game**)

棋盘游戏 [qípán yóuxì] ▷ *a box of toys, games, and books* 一箱玩具、游戏器具和书; (also: **computer game**) 电脑游戏 [diànnǎo yóuxì] **4** [c] (*match*) 比赛 [bǐsài] ▷ *a game of cricket against Birkenhead School* 一场对伯肯黑德学校的板球比赛 **5** [c] 一局 [yī jú] ▷ *Sampras leads by four games to one.* 桑普拉斯在局数上以4比1领先 **6** [c] (*strategy, scheme*) 花招 [huāzhāo] ▷ *The government is playing a very shrewd political game.* 政府在玩弄一出非常狡猾的政治花招。**7** [U] (*animals, birds*) 猎物 [lièwù] **II** ADJ (*willing*) ► **game for** 敢作敢为的 [gǎnzuò gǎnwéi de] ▷ *I'm game for anything!* 我什么都敢干! **III games** NPL(BRIT: SCOL) 体育活动 [tǐyù huódòng] ▷ *I was hopeless at games.* 我对学校的体育活动都不在行。► **a game of football/tennis** 一场足球/网球赛 ► **big game** (*animals*) 大猎物 ► **to give the game away** 露出马脚 ► **to beat sb at his own game** 将计就计地战胜某人 ► **the name of the game** 头等大事 ► **to be on the game** (BRIT: inf) 从事卖淫嫖娼活动 ► **to play games (with sb)** (fig) (对某人)耍花招

games console ['geɪmz-] (COMPUT) N [c] 游戏机 [yóuxìjī]

game show I N [c] 电视竞赛游戏 [diànshì jìngsài yóuxì] **II** CPD [复合词] [+ *host, contestant*] 电视竞赛游戏 [diànshì jìngsài yóuxì]

gammon ['gæmən] (BRIT) N [U] 熏猪腿 [xūnzhūtuǐ]

gang [gæŋ] N [c] **1** (*of criminals, hooligans*) 一帮 [yī bāng] **2** (*of friends, colleagues*) 一伙 [yī huǒ] **3** (*of workmen*) 一组 [yī zǔ]
► **gang up** VI ► **to gang up on sb** 联合起来对付某人 [liánhé qǐlái duìfu mǒurén]

gangster ['gæŋstə(r)] N [c] 歹徒 [dǎitú]

gaol [dʒeɪl] (BRIT) N, VT = **jail**

gap [gæp] N [c] **1** (*in space*) 缝隙 [fèngxì] **2** (*in time*) 间隔 [jiàngé] **3** (*in knowledge, coverage, records*) 空白 [kòngbái] **4** (*difference*) 差距 [chājù] ► **a gap in the market** 市场空白

gape [geɪp] VI **1** (*stare*) 目瞪口呆地凝视 [mùdèng kǒudāi de níngshì] **2** [*shirt, hole +*] 裂开 [lièkāi]

gaping ['geɪpɪŋ] ADJ [+ *hole, wound*] 裂开的 [lièkāi de]

gap year (BRIT) N [c] 高中和大学之间的空隙年

● **GAP YEAR**

● 在高中毕业以后，进入大学继续接受高等教育之前，学生可以休息一年，这一年被称为 **gap year**。在 **gap year** 其间，很多人选择去旅游或去国外生活，也有人更愿意工作。无论如何选择，他们都能从学校学习生活之外获得宝贵的生活经验。

garage ['gærɑ:ʒ] N [c] **1** (*of private house*) 车库 [chēkù] **2** (*for car repairs*) 汽车修理厂 [qìchē xiūlǐchǎng] **3** (BRIT) (*petrol station*) 加油站 [jiāyóuzhàn]

garbage ['gɑ:bɪdʒ] N [U] **1** (ESP US) (*rubbish*) 垃圾 [lājī] **2** (*nonsense*) 废话 [fèihuà] **3** (*bad film, book etc*) 拙劣作品 [zhuōliè zuòpǐn]

garbage bag (US) N [c] 垃圾袋 [lājīdài]

garbage can (US) N [c] 垃圾箱 [lājīxiāng] [英 = **dustbin**]

garbage man (pl **garbage men**) (US) N [c] 清洁工 [qīngjiégōng] [英 = **dustman**]

garden ['gɑ:dn] **I** N [c] 花园 [huāyuán] **II** VI 收拾花园 [shōushí huāyuán] **III gardens** NPL **1** (*public park*) 公园 [gōngyuán] **2** (*private, in street names*) 花园 [huāyuán]

garden centre, (US) **garden center** N [c] 园艺中心 [yuányì zhōngxīn]

gardener ['gɑ:dnə(r)] N [c] (*professional*) 园丁 [yuándīng]; (*amateur*) 园艺爱好者 [yuányì àihàozhě]

gardening ['gɑ:dnɪŋ] N [U] (*non-professional*) 园艺 [yuányì]; (*professional*) 园艺学 [yuányìxué] ► **to do the gardening** 侍弄花草

garish ['gɛərɪʃ] ADJ [+ *colour, clothing, decor*] 俗艳的 [súyàn de]

garland ['gɑ:lənd] N [c] (*of flowers*) 花环 [huāhuán]

garlic ['gɑ:lɪk] **I** N [U] 大蒜 [dàsuàn] **II** CPD [复合词] [+ *puree, salt*] 大蒜 [dàsuàn]; [+ *mayonnaise*] 有大蒜味的 [yǒu dàsuàn wèi de]

garment ['gɑ:mənt] N [c] 衣服 [yīfu]

garnish ['gɑ:nɪʃ] **I** VT [+ *food*] 加饰菜于 [jiāshìcài yú] **II** N [c/U] 装饰菜 [zhuāngshìcài]

garrison ['gærɪsn] N [c] (*soldiers*) 卫戍部队 [wèishù bùduì]; (*building*) 卫戍区 [wèishùqū]

garters ['gɑ:təz] NPL 吊袜带 [diàowàdài] [英 = **suspenders**]

gas [gæs] **I** N **1** [c/U] (CHEM) 气体 [qìtǐ] **2** [U] (*for cooking, heating*) 煤气 [méiqì] **3** [U] (US: inf) (also: **gasoline**) 汽油 [qìyóu] [英 = **petrol**] **4** [U] (*anaesthetic*) 麻醉气 [mázuìqì] **II** VT (*kill*) 用毒气处死 [yòng dúqì chǔsǐ]

gas cooker (BRIT) N [c] 煤气炉 [méiqìlú]

gas cylinder N [c] 煤气罐 [méiqìguàn]

gas fire (BRIT) N [c] 煤气取暖器 [méiqì qǔnuǎnqì]

gash [gæʃ] **I** N [c] (*wound, tear*) 深长的伤口 [shēncháng de shāngkǒu] **II** VT (*wound*) 在⋯上划深长切口 [zài⋯shang huá shēncháng qiēkǒu]

gasket ['gæskɪt] N [c] 垫圈 [diànquān]

gasoline ['gæsəli:n] (US) N [U] 汽油 [qìyóu] [英 = **petrol**]

gasp [gɑ:sp] **I** N [c] **1** (*breath*) 喘息 [chuǎnxī] **2** (*of pain, astonishment, in surprise*) 上气不接下气 [shàngqì bùjiē xiàqì] **II** VI **1** (*pant*) 喘息 [chuǎnxī] **2** (*in surprise*) 猛地吸口气 [měng de xī kǒu qì] ▶ to gasp for breath/air 气喘 ▶ to be gasping for a drink/cigarette (BRIT: inf) 口渴/烟瘾难熬

gas pedal (ESP US) N [C] 油门 [yóumén]

gas station (US) N [C] 加油站 [jiāyóuzhàn] [英=filling or petrol station]

gas tank (US) N [C] 汽油罐 [qìyóuguàn] [英=petrol tank]

gate [geɪt] N [C] 1 (of garden, field) 门 [mén]; (of building) 大门 [dàmén] 2 (at airport) 登机口 [dēngjīkǒu] 3 (at level-crossing) 栅门 [shānmén] 4 (at sporting event) 观众数 [guānzhòngshù]

gateau ['gætəu] (pl **gateaux** ['gætəuz]) (ESP BRIT) N [C] 奶油蛋糕 [nǎiyóu dàngāo]

gatecrash ['geɪtkræʃ] I VT [+ party] 擅自进入 [shànzì jìnrù] II VI 不请自来 [bù qǐng zì lái]

gateway ['geɪtweɪ] N [C] (entrance) 门口 [ménkǒu] ▶ the gateway to the continent 通向大陆的门户 ▶ a gateway to success/ stardom 成功/成名之道

gather ['gæðə(r)] I VT 1 (pick, collect) [+ flowers, fruit, wood] 采集 [cǎijí] 2 (also: gather up) (put together) [+ papers, clothes] 收拢 [shōulǒng] 3 (assemble) [+ information, evidence] 搜集 [sōují] 4 (understand) ▶ to gather (that)... 获悉… [huòxī…] II VI 1 (assemble) 聚集 [jùjí] 2 [dust +] 积聚 [jījù] 3 [clouds +] 密集 [mìjí] ▶ to gather speed 逐渐加速 ▶ to gather momentum/ force 势头渐猛/逐渐加强力量 ▶ to gather one's thoughts 集中思想 ▶ as far as I can gather 据我推测 ▶ to gather dust (fig) 束之高阁

gathering ['gæðərɪŋ] N [C] 集会 [jíhuì] ▶ family gathering 家庭聚会

gauge [geɪdʒ] I N [C] 1 (measuring device) 量表 [liángbiǎo] 2 (RAIL) 轨距 [guǐjù] II VT [+ distance, speed] 测量 [cèliáng]; [+ feelings, reaction] 揣测 [chuǎicè] ▶ pressure/ temperature gauge 压力/温度仪 ▶ fuel or petrol gauge or (US) gas gauge 燃料表

gaunt [gɔːnt] ADJ 1 (haggard) [+ person, face, appearance] 憔悴的 [qiáocuì de] 2 (grim, desolate) [+ place, outline] 荒凉的 [huāngliáng de]

gave [geɪv] PT of give

gay [geɪ] I ADJ 1 (homosexual) 同性恋的 [tóngxìngliàn de] 2 (cheerful) [+ person] 欢快的 [huānkuài de]; [+ colour, music, dress] 明快的 [míngkuài de] II N [C] (homosexual) 同性恋 [tóngxìngliàn]

gaze [geɪz] I VI ▶ to gaze at sth/sb 凝视着某物/某人 [níngshìzhe mǒuwù/mǒurén] II N [C] (stare) 凝视 [níngshì]

GB ABBR (= Great Britain) 大不列颠 [Dàbùlièdiān]

GCSE (BRIT) N ABBR (= General Certificate of Secondary Education) 普通中等教育证书 [Pǔtōng Zhōngděng Jiàoyù Zhèngshū]

Gdns. ABBR (= Gardens) 花园 [huāyuán]

GDP N ABBR (= gross domestic product) 国内生产总值 [guónèi shēngchǎn zǒngzhí]

gear [gɪə(r)] I N 1 [C] (TECH) [of machine] 齿轮 [chǐlún]; [of car, bicycle] 排挡 [páidǎng] 2 [U] (equipment) 装备 [zhuāngbèi] 3 [U] (clothing) 服装 [fúzhuāng] II VT ▶ to be geared to or towards 使适应 [shǐ shìyìng] ▶ to be in first/ second etc gear 第一/二{等}挡 ▶ to leave the car in gear 摘挡停车 ▶ to change or (US) shift gear 换挡
▶ **gear up** VI ▶ to gear (o.s.) up to do sth (自己)作好做某事的心理准备 [(zìjǐ) zuòhǎo zuò mǒushì de xīnlǐ zhǔnbèi] ▶ to gear o.s. up for sth (自己)为某事做好心理准备

gearbox ['gɪəbɔks] N [C] 变速箱 [biànsùxiāng]

gear lever, gear stick (BRIT) N [C] 换挡杆 [huàndǎnggān] [美=gearshift]

gearshift ['gɪəʃɪft] (US) N [C] 换挡杆 [huàndǎnggān] [英=gear lever, gear stick]

geese [giːs] NPL of goose

gel [dʒɛl] I N [C/U] (for hair, washing, shaving) 啫喱 [zhēlí] II VI 1 [people +] 凝聚 [níngjù] 2 [thought, idea +] 变得明朗 [biàn de mínglǎng] ▶ to gel with sb 与某人配合融洽 ▶ bath/ shower gel 浴液

gem [dʒɛm] N [C] 1 (stone) 宝石 [bǎoshí] 2 (fig) 难能可贵的人 [nánnéng kěguì de rén]

Gemini ['dʒɛmɪnaɪ] N 1 [U] (sign) 双子座 [Shuāngzǐ Zuò] 2 [C] (person) 属双子座的人 [shǔ Shuāngzǐ Zuò de rén] ▶ I'm (a) Gemini 我是双子座的

gen. ABBR = general, generally

gender ['dʒɛndə(r)] N [C/U] 1 (sex) 性 [xìng] 2 (LING) 性 [xìng]

gene [dʒiːn] N [C] 基因 [jīyīn]

general ['dʒɛnərl] I ADJ 1 (overall) [+ situation] 总的 [zǒng de]; [+ decline, standard] 一般的 [yībān de] ▷ the general standard of education in England 英格兰教育的一般标准; [+ performance] 总体的 [zǒngtǐ de] 2 (widespread) [+ interest, awareness, feeling] 普遍的 [pǔbiàn de] ▷ a topic of general interest 普遍感兴趣的话题 ▷ a general feeling of optimism 普遍的乐观情绪 3 (non-specific) [+ terms, outline, idea] 笼统的 [lǒngtǒng de] ▷ principles that are stated in very general terms 非常笼统地注明的原则 4 (miscellaneous) [+ expenses, details] 常规的 [chángguī de] ▷ general expenses such as meals and phone calls 常规消费例如饭费和电话费 II N [C] (MIL) 将军 [jiāngjūn] ▷ General Montgomery 蒙哥马利将军 ▶ in general (as a whole) 总的来说 ▷ Teachers in general are pleased with the new scheme. 总的来说教师们对新方案比较满意。; (on the whole) 一般来说 ▷ In general, it was the young who voted in the election. 一般来说是年轻人在选举中投票。▶ as a general rule 一般而言 ▶ in general terms 大致上说 ▶ the general public 广大公众

general anaesthetic, (US) general

anesthetic N [C/U] 全身麻醉 [quánshēn mázuì] ▸ **to have a general anaesthetic** 被全身麻醉

general election N [C] (in Britain, United States) 大选 [dàxuǎn]

generalize ['dʒɛnrəlaɪz] VI 笼统概括 [lǒngtǒng gàikuò]

generally ['dʒɛnrəlɪ] ADV **1** (on the whole) 大体上 [dàtǐshang] **2** (widely) 普遍地 [pǔbiàn de] **3** (usually) 通常 [tōngcháng] ▷ He generally gets up very early. 他通常很早起床。 ▸ **generally speaking** 一般说来

generate ['dʒɛnəreɪt] VT **1** [+ power, electricity] 产生 [chǎnshēng] **2** [+ income, profits, jobs] 创造 [chuàngzào]; [+ interest] 引起 [yǐnqǐ]

generation [dʒɛnə'reɪʃən] N **1** [C] (of people, family) 一代人 [yīdàirén] **2** [C] (period of time) 代 [dài] **3** (series) [of computers, mobile phones] 代 [dài] **4** [U] (production) (of electricity, power) 产生 [chǎnshēng]

generator ['dʒɛnəreɪtə(r)] (ELEC) N [C] 发电机 [fādiànjī]

generosity [dʒɛnə'rɒsɪtɪ] N [U] 慷慨 [kāngkǎi]

generous ['dʒɛnərəs] ADJ **1** [+ person] 大方的 [dàfāng de] **2** (sizeable) [+ measure, gift] 大量的 [dàliàng de]

genetic [dʒɪ'nɛtɪk] ADJ 遗传的 [yíchuán de]

genetically modified [dʒɪ'nɛtɪklɪ'mɒdɪfaɪd] ADJ 转基因的 [zhuǎn jīyīn de]

genetics [dʒɪ'nɛtɪks] N [U] (science) 遗传学 [yíchuánxué]

genial ['dʒiːnɪəl] ADJ [+ person] 和蔼可亲的 [hé'ǎi kěqīn de]; [+ face, personality] 亲切的 [qīnqiè de]

genitals ['dʒɛnɪtlz] NPL 生殖器 [shēngzhíqì]

genius ['dʒiːnɪəs] N **1** [C] (person) 天才 [tiāncái] **2** [U] (ability, skill) 天赋 [tiānfù] ▸ **a stroke of genius** 天才之举

gent [dʒɛnt] (BRIT: inf) N [C] 绅士 [shēnshì] see also **gents**

gentle ['dʒɛntl] ADJ **1** [+ person, nature] 温和的 [wēnhé de] **2** (light) [+ movement, breeze, shake] 轻柔的 [qīngróu de] **3** [+ slope, curve] 平缓的 [pínghuǎn de] **4** (CULIN) [+ heat] 文 [wén] **5** [+ soap] 柔和的 [róuhé de] ▸ **to give sb a gentle hint/reminder** 给某人一个善意的暗示/提醒

gentleman ['dʒɛntlmən] (pl **gentlemen**) N [C] **1** (man) 先生 [xiānsheng] **2** (well-mannered man) 绅士 [shēnshì] **3** (referring to social position) 有身份的人 [yǒu shēnfèn de rén] ▸ **a real gentleman** 一位真正的绅士 ▸ **gentleman's agreement** 君子协定

gently ['dʒɛntlɪ] ADV **1** [touch, move +] 温柔地 [wēnróu de]; [say, smile +] 温和地 [wēnhé de] **2** [slope, curve +] 平缓地 [pínghuǎn de] **3** (CULIN) [cook, heat +] 用文火炖 [yòng wénhuǒ dè]

gentry ['dʒɛntrɪ] NPL ▸ **the gentry** (aristocracy) 贵族 [guìzú]

gents [dʒɛnts] N ▸ **the gents** (BRIT: inf) (men's toilet) 男厕 [náncè]

genuine ['dʒɛnjuɪn] ADJ **1** (real) [+ antique, leather] 真正的 [zhēnzhèng de] **2** (sincere) [+ person] 真诚的 [zhēnchéng de]; [+ emotion, interest] 实实在在的 [shíshí zàizài de]

genuinely ['dʒɛnjuɪnlɪ] ADV [+ interested, concerned] 真地 [zhēn de]

geographical [dʒɪə'græfɪkl] ADJ 地理的 [dìlǐ de]

geography [dʒɪ'ɔgrəfɪ] N [U] **1** [of country, region] 地理 [dìlǐ] **2** (school/university subject) 地理学 [dìlǐxué]

geological [dʒɪə'lɔdʒɪkl] ADJ 地质的 [dìzhì de]

geology [dʒɪ'ɔlədʒɪ] N [U] **1** [of area, rock] 地质 [dìzhì] **2** (university subject) 地质学 [dìzhìxué]

geometric [dʒɪə'mɛtrɪk] ADJ **1** (mathematical) [+ law, problem] 几何的 [jǐhé de] **2** (regular) [+ shape, design, pattern] 几何图形的 [jǐhé túxíng de]

geometry [dʒɪ'ɔmətrɪ] N [U] **1** (science) 几何学 [jǐhéxué] **2** (shape, proportions) 几何图形 [jǐhé túxíng]

geranium [dʒɪ'reɪnɪəm] N [C] 天竺葵 [tiānzhúkuí]

geriatric [dʒɛrɪ'ætrɪk] ADJ [+ patient, hospital, medicine] 老年病学的 [lǎonián bìngxué de]

germ [dʒəːm] (BIO) N [C] 细菌 [xìjūn] ▸ **the germ of an idea** 一个想法的萌芽

German ['dʒəːmən] I ADJ 德国的 [Déguó de] II N **1** [C] (person) 德国人 [Déguórén] **2** [U] (language) 德语 [Déyǔ]

German measles (BRIT) N [U] (rubella) 风疹 [fēngzhěn]

Germany ['dʒəːmənɪ] N 德国 [Déguó]

gesture ['dʒɛstjə(r)] I N [C] **1** (movement) 表情动作 [biǎoqíng dòngzuò] **2** (symbolic) 姿态 [zītài] II VI (wave, point) 用动作表示 [yòng dòngzuò biǎoshì] ▸ **to make a gesture** (lit) 做手势 ▸ **a gesture of goodwill/support** 善意/支持的姿态

○

get [ɡɛt] (pt, pp **got**, (US) pp **gotten**) I VT **1** ▸ **to have got** see also **have, got**
2 (obtain, find) [+ money, permission, results, information] 获得 [huòdé]; [+ job, flat, room] 得到 [dédào] ▸ **he got a job in London** 他在伦敦得到一份工作 ▸ **we can get something to eat on the train** 我们可以在火车上弄点儿吃的 ▸ **to get a look at sth/sb** 看看某物/某人
3 (fetch) [+ person, doctor, object] 去拿 [qùná] ▸ **to get sth for sb** 为某人去拿某物 ▸ **could you get me my coat please?** 请你把我的外套拿来好吗？ ▸ **can I get you a**

coffee? 要我给你拿杯咖啡吗？▶ **I'll come and get you** 我会来接你的
4 (receive) [+ present, letter, prize, TV channel] 收到 [shōudào]; [+ price] 得到 [dédào] ▷ He got a good price for the car. 他把车卖了个好价钱。▶ **what did you get for your birthday?** 你生日时得到了什么礼物？▶ **how much did you get for the painting?** 你这幅画卖了多少钱？▶ **he gets a lot of pleasure from music** 他从音乐中得到了很大乐趣
5 (board) [+ plane, bus etc] 乘坐 [chéngzuò] ▶ **I'll get the bus** 我会乘坐公共汽车
6 (prepare) [+ meal] 准备 [zhǔnbèi] ▶ **I'll get lunch** 我来准备午餐
7 (cause to be/become) ▶ **to get sth/sb ready** 使某事/某人准备就绪 [shǐ mǒurén/mǒushì zhǔnbèi jiùxù] ▶ **to get sb drunk/into trouble** 使某人喝醉/陷入麻烦 ▶ **did you get the answer right?** 你的答案正确吗？
8 (seize, catch) 抓住 [zhuāzhù] ▶ **get him!** 抓住他！▶ **the police will get him eventually** 警察最终会抓住他的
9 (hit) [+ target etc] 击中 [jīzhòng]
10 (take, move) 把…送到 [bǎ…sòngdào] ▶ **we must get him to hospital** 我们必须把他送到医院 ▶ **I'll get you there somehow** 我会设法让你到那儿 ▶ **do you think we'll get it through the door?** 你觉得我们能把它弄进门吗？▶ **to get sth to sb** 为某人取得某物
11 (buy) 买 [mǎi]; (regularly) 买到 [mǎidào] ▶ **I'll get some milk from the supermarket** 我要去超市买牛奶 ▶ **we don't get a newspaper** 我们小没买到报纸 ▶ **let me get you a drink** 让我给你来杯喝的吧
12 (be infected by) [+ cold, measles etc] 染上 [rǎnshang] ▶ **you'll get a cold** 你会得感冒的
13 (understand) [+ joke, point] 领会 [lǐnghuì]
14 (hear) 听见 [tīngjiàn] ▶ **I didn't get your name** 我没听见你的名字
15 (have) [+ time, opportunity] 有 [yǒu] ▶ **I get the impression that...** 我有…的印象 ▶ **I got a shock when I saw him** 当我看见他时我惊呆了
16 ▶ **to get sth done** (do oneself) 做某事 [zuò mǒushì]; (have done) 完成某事 [wánchéng mǒushì] ▶ **to get the washing/dishes done** 洗好衣物/餐具 ▶ **to get one's hair cut** 理发 ▶ **to get the car going** or **to go** 使汽车发动起来 ▶ **to get sb to do sth** 让某人做某事
17 (inf) (annoy) 使…恼火 [shǐ…nǎohuǒ] ▶ **what gets me is his attitude** 是他的态度让我恼火
II VI **1** (become, be) (adj) 变得 [biàn de] ▶ **to get old/tired/cold/dirty** 变老/变得疲倦/变冷/变脏 ▶ **to get drunk** 喝醉了 ▶ **to**

get bored 变得无聊 ▶ **it's getting late** 不早了
2 (go) ▶ **to get to work/the airport/Beijing etc** 到办公室/到达机场/到达北京 {等} [dào bàngōngshì/dàodá jīchǎng/dàodá Běijīng {děng}] ▶ **how did you get here?** 你是怎么到这儿的？▶ **he didn't get home till 10pm** 他直到晚上10点才到家 ▶ **how long does it take to get from London to Paris?** 从伦敦到巴黎需要多久？▶ **the talks are getting nowhere** 会谈毫无进展
3 (begin) ▶ **to get to know sb** 开始了解某人 [kāishǐ liǎojiě mǒurén] ▶ **let's get going** or **started!** 开始吧！
4 (manage) ▶ **how often do you get to see him?** 你多久见他一次？[nǐ duōjiǔ jiàn tā yī cì?]
5 (in expressions) ▶ **don't let it get to you** 别受它的影响 [bié shòu tā de yǐngxiǎng] ▶ **get lost!** 走开！▶ **how crazy/stupid can you get?** 你怎么变得这样疯狂/愚蠢呢？
III AUX VB **1** ▶ **to have got to** see also **have, got**
2 (passive use) 作为构成被动语态的助动词 ▶ **to get killed** 被杀 ▶ **to get paid** 拿薪水
▶ **get about** VI **1** (person +) (travel) 旅行 [lǚxíng]; (move about) 各处走动 [gèchù zǒudòng] ▶ **I can't get about as much as I used to** 我不能再像我过去那样到处走动了
2 (ESP BRIT) [news, rumour +] 流传 [liúchuán]
▶ **get across** VT [+ message, meaning, idea] 使…被理解 [shǐ…bèi lǐjiě]
▶ **get along** VI **1** (be friends) 相处 [xiāngchǔ] ▶ **to get along well with sb** 与某人相处融洽
2 (manage) 过活 [guòhuó]
3 (depart) 离开 [líkāi] ▶ **I'd better be getting along soon** 我最好尽快离开
▶ **get around** I VT FUS [不可拆分] [+ problem] 克服 [kèfú]; [+ law, rule] 规避 [guībì]; [+ person] 说服 [shuōfú]
II VI 传开来 [chuánkāilái]
▶ **get around to** VT FUS [不可拆分] ▶ **to get around to sth/to doing sth** 终于有时间做某事 [zhōngyú yǒu shíjiān zuò mǒushì]
▶ **get at** (BRIT: inf) VT FUS [不可拆分]
1 (attack, criticize) 不断指责 [bùduàn zhǐzé]
▶ **you're always getting at me** 你总是数落我
2 (reach) 够着 [gòuzháo] ▷ We want to get at the truth. 我们想了解真相。
3 (insinuate) ▶ **what are you getting at?** 你讲这话什么意思？[nǐ jiǎng zhèhuà shénme yìsi?]
▶ **get away** VI (leave) 脱身 [tuōshēn]; (on holiday) 去度假 [qù dùjià]; (escape) 逃跑 [táopǎo]

▶ **get away with** VT FUS [不可拆分] 不因⋯而受惩罚 [bù yīn⋯ér shòu chéngfá] ▶ **to get away with doing sth** 不因做某事而受惩罚 ▶ **he'll never get away with it!** 他决不会逃脱干系的！

▶ **get back** I VI **1** (*return*) 回来 [huílái]

2 (*move away*) ▶ **get back!** 快回来！ [kuài huílái!]

II VT (*reclaim*) 重新得到 [chóngxīn dédào] ▷ *All he wanted was to get his girlfriend back.* 他所想的一切都是让女朋友再回到身边。

▶ **get back at** VT FUS [不可拆分] ▶ **to get back at sb (for sth)** （因某事）对某人进行报复 [(yīn mǒushì) duì mǒurén jìnxíng bàofù]

▶ **get back to** VT FUS [不可拆分] **1** (*return to*) [+ *activity, work*] 回到 [huídào]; [+ *normality*] 恢复 [huīfù]; [+ *subject*] 重新回到 [chóngxīn huídào] ▶ **to get back to sleep** 重又睡着

2 (*contact again*) 再与⋯联络 [zài yǔ⋯liánluò]

▶ **get by** VI **1** (*manage*) 过得去 [guò de qù] ▶ **I can get by in Dutch** 我的荷兰语还凑合 ▶ **to get by on a small salary** 靠微薄的薪水勉强度日

2 (*pass*) 过去 [guòqù]

▶ **get down** I VI **1** 趴下 [pāxià]

II VT **1** (*depress*) [+ *person*] 使⋯沮丧 [shǐ⋯jǔsàng]

2 (*write*) 记下来 [jìxiàlái]

3 (*swallow*) [+ *food, pill*] 吞下 [tūnxià]

▶ **get down to** VT FUS [不可拆分] [+ *work*] 开始认真处理 [kāishǐ rènzhēn chǔlǐ] ▶ **to get down to business** (*fig*) 安心处理事务

▶ **get in** I VI **1** (*be elected*) [*candidate, party* +] 当选 [dāngxuǎn]

2 (*arrive*) [*train, bus, plane* +] 抵达 [dǐdá]

3 (*arrive home*) 到家 [dàojiā]

II VT **1** (*bring in*) [+ *shopping, supplies*] 购买 [gòumǎi]; [+ *harvest*] 收获 [shōuhuò]

2 ▶ **I couldn't get a word in** 我一句话也插不进 [wǒ yī jù huà yě chā bù jìn]

▶ **get into** VT FUS [不可拆分] **1** (*become part of*) [+ *conversation, argument, fight*] 进行 [jìnxíng]; [+ *sphere of activity*] 开始从事 [kāishǐ cóngshì]; [+ *university, school*] 进入 [jìnrù]

2 [+ *vehicle*] 乘坐 [chéngzuò]

3 [+ *clothes*] 穿上 [chuānshang]

4 (*in expressions*) ▶ **to get into bed** 上床 [shàngchuáng] ▶ **I don't know what has got into him** 我不知道他是怎么回事

▶ **get off** I VI **1** (*from train, bus*) 下车 [xiàchē]

2 (*leave*) 离开 [líkāi]

3 (*escape*) 从轻处罚 [cóngqīng chǔfá] ▶ **he got off with a £50 fine** 他只被罚了50英镑而已

4 ▶ **to get off to a good start** 开头顺利

[kāitóu shùnlì]

II VT **1** (*remove*) [+ *clothes*] 脱下 [tuōxià]; [+ *stain*] 消除 [xiāochú]

2 (*as holiday*) [+ *day, week*] 放假 [fàngjià] ▶ **we get three days off at Christmas** 圣诞节时我们放了3天假

III VT FUS [不可拆分] (*leave*) [+ *train, bus*] 从⋯下来 [cóng⋯xiàlái]; [+ *bed, table*] 从⋯起身 [cóng⋯qǐshēn]

▶ **get off with** (BRIT: *inf*) VT FUS [不可拆分] 与⋯有染 [yǔ⋯yǒurǎn]

▶ **get on** I VI **1** (*be friends*) 和睦相处 [hémù xiāngchǔ] ▶ **to get on well with sb** 与某人相处融洽

2 (*progress*) 进展 [jìnzhǎn] ▶ **how are you getting on?** 你过得怎么样？ ▶ **to get on well with sth** 在某方面进展顺利 ▶ **time is getting on** 不早了

II VT FUS [不可拆分] [+ *bus, train*] 上 [shàng]

▶ **get on to** VT FUS [不可拆分] **1** [+ *subject, topic*] 开始涉及 [kāishǐ shèjí]

2 (ESP BRIT) (*contact*) [+ *person*] 与⋯联系 [yǔ⋯liánxì]

▶ **get on with** VT FUS [不可拆分] **1** (*be friends with*) [+ *person*] 与⋯和睦相处 [yǔ⋯hémù xiāngchǔ]

2 (*continue, start*) [+ *meeting, work etc*] 开始继续做 [kāishǐ jìxù zuò]

▶ **get out** I VI [*person* +] (*of place*) 离开 [líkāi]; (*of vehicle*) 下车 [xiàchē]; (*to enjoy o.s.*) 尽情享乐 [jìnqíng xiǎnglè]; [*news etc* +] 泄露 [xièlòu]

II VT **1** (*take out*) [+ *book, object etc*] 拿出 [náchū]

2 (*remove*) [+ *stain*] 消除 [xiāochú]

▶ **get out of** I VT FUS [不可拆分] **1** [+ *vehicle*] 从⋯下来 [cóng⋯xiàlái]

2 (*avoid*) [+ *duty etc*] 摆脱 [bǎituō] ▶ **to get out of doing sth** 逃避做某事

II VT (*from bank*) [+ *money*] 提取 [tíqǔ] ▶ **I need to get some money out of the bank** 我需要去银行取些钱

2 (*extract*) [+ *confession, details etc*] 打探出 [dǎtànchū] ▶ **we finally got the name out of him** 我们终于从他那里打探出了名字

3 (*derive*) [+ *pleasure, benefit*] 获得 [huòdé]

▶ **get over** I VT FUS [不可拆分] [+ *illness, shock*] 从⋯中恢复过来 [cóng⋯zhōng huīfù guòlái]

II VT **1** (*communicate*) [+ *idea etc*] 使⋯明白 [shǐ⋯míngbai]

2 ▶ **to get it over with** 尽快从⋯中解脱 [jìnkuài cóng⋯zhōng jiětuō]

▶ **get round** = **get around**

▶ **get through** I VI (TEL) 接通 [jiētōng]

II VT FUS [不可拆分] **1** (*finish*) [+ *work, book*] 完成 [wánchéng]

2 (ESP BRIT) (*use up*) 用完 [yòngwán]

3 (survive) 捱过 [áiguò]
▶ **get through to** VT FUS [不可拆分] **1** (TEL) 接通 [jiētōng]
2 (make understand) 使…理解 [shǐ…lǐjiě]
▶ **get together** I VI [people +] 聚在一起 [jùzài yīqǐ]
II VT **1** (amass) [+ money] 积累 [jīlěi]
2 (gather up) 把…收拾起来 [bǎ…shōushi qǐlái]
3 (organize) [+ project, plan etc] 组织筹备 [zǔzhī chóubèi]
▶ **get up** I VI (rise) (from chair, sofa) 站起来 [zhànqǐlái]; (out of bed) 起床 [qǐchuáng]
II VT ▶ **to get up enthusiasm for sth** 对某事产生热情 [duì mǒushì chǎnshēng rèqíng]
▶ **get up to** (ESP BRIT) VT FUS [不可拆分] [+ prank etc] 搞 [gǎo] ▷ **What has he been getting up to?** 他在搞什么花样？

getaway ['gɛtəweɪ] N ▶ **to make a** or **one's getaway** 逃跑 [táopǎo]

Ghana ['gɑːnə] N 加纳 [Jiānà]

Ghanaian [gɑː'neɪən] I ADJ 加纳的 [Jiānà de] II N [C] (person) 加纳人 [Jiānàrén]

ghastly ['gɑːstlɪ] ADJ [+ person, behaviour] 糟透的 [zāotòu de]; [+ event, crime] 可怕的 [kěpà de]

ghetto ['gɛtəʊ] (pl **ghettos** or **ghettoes**) N [C] 贫民窟 [pínmínkū]

ghost [gəʊst] I N [C] (spirit) 鬼神 [guǐshén] II VT 为…捉刀 [wèi…zhuōdāo] ▶ **to give up the ghost** (person) 绝望; (machine) 停止运转 ▶ **the ghost of a chance (of doing sth)** 只有很少机会 (做某事)

giant ['dʒaɪənt] I N [C] **1** (in stories) 巨人 [jùrén] **2** (large company) 巨头 [jùtóu] II ADJ (huge) 巨大的 [jùdà de] ▶ **an opera/a football giant** 歌剧/足球巨星

giddy ['gɪdɪ] ADJ ▶ **to be** or **feel giddy** (faint, dizzy) 感到头晕 [gǎndào tóuyūn] ▶ **to feel giddy with excitement/delight** 激动/高兴得晕头转向

gift [gɪft] N [C] **1** (present) 礼物 [lǐwù] **2** (talent) 天赋 [tiānfù] ▶ **to have a gift for sth** (talent) 对某事有天赋

gifted ['gɪftɪd] ADJ [+ person] 有天赋的 [yǒu tiānfù de] ▶ **gifted children** 天资聪颖的孩子

gift shop, (US) **gift store** N [C] 礼品店 [lǐpǐndiàn]

gift token, **gift voucher** N [C] 礼品券 [lǐpǐnquàn]

gig [gɪg] N [C] (show) 现场演出 [xiànchǎng yǎnchū]

gigabyte ['dʒɪgəbaɪt] (COMPUT) N [C] 千兆字节 [qiānzhào zìjié] ▶ **a ten-gigabyte hard drive** 10千兆字节硬盘

gigantic [dʒaɪ'gæntɪk] ADJ 庞大的 [pángdà de]

giggle ['gɪgl] I VI 咯咯地笑 [gēgē de xiào]

II N [C] 咯咯笑 [gēgēxiào]

gills [gɪlz] NPL 鳃 [sāi]

gilt [gɪlt] I ADJ [+ frame, jewellery] 镀金的 [dùjīn de] II N [U] 镀金 [dùjīn]

gimmick ['gɪmɪk] N [C] 花招 [huāzhāo]

gin [dʒɪn] N [U] (alcohol) 杜松子酒 [dùsōngzǐjiǔ]
▶ **a gin and tonic** 杜松子酒加奎宁水

ginger ['dʒɪndʒə(r)] I N [U] (spice) 姜 [jiāng] II ADJ (colour) [+ hair, moustache] 姜色的 [jiāngsè de]
▶ **ginger up** VT (liven up) 使有活力 [shǐ yǒu huólì]

gingerly ['dʒɪndʒəlɪ] ADV (cautiously) 小心翼翼地 [xiǎoxīn yìyì de]

gipsy ['dʒɪpsɪ] N = **gypsy**

giraffe [dʒɪ'rɑːf] N [C] 长颈鹿 [chángjǐnglù]

◐ **girl** [gəːl] N [C] **1** (child) 女孩 [nǚhái]; (young woman, woman) 姑娘 [gūniang] ▷ **She's a good-looking girl.** 她是个漂亮的姑娘。 **2** (daughter) 女儿 [nǚ'ér] ▷ **She has two girls and a boy.** 她有两个女儿和一个儿子。

girlfriend ['gəːlfrɛnd] N **1** [C] (of girl) 女性朋友 [nǚxìng péngyǒu] **2** (of boy) 女朋友 [nǚ péngyǒu]

Girl Scout (US) N **1 the Girl Scouts** (organization) 女童子军 [Nǚ Tóngzǐjūn] **2** (person) 女童子军成员 [Nǚ Tóngzǐjūn Chéngyuán]

gist [dʒɪst] N ▶ **the gist of his speech/article** 他讲话/文章的主旨 [tā jiǎnghuà/wénzhāng de zhǔzhǐ]

○

give [gɪv] (pt **gave**, pp **given**) I VT **1** (hand over) ▶ **to give sb sth, to give sth to sb** 给某人某物 [gěi mǒurén mǒuwù]; (as gift) 送给某人某物 [sònggěi mǒurén mǒuwù] ▶ **I gave David the book, I gave the book to David** 我把这本书送给了戴维 ▶ **give it to him** 把它送给他
2 (provide) [+ advice, details] 提供 [tígōng]
▶ **to give sb sth** [+ opportunity, surprise, shock, job] 给某人某物 ▶ **I gave him the chance to deny it** 我给他机会拒绝 ▶ **you'll need to give me more time** 你需要给我更多的时间 ▶ **to give sb the impression that...** 给某人…的印象
3 (deliver) ▶ **to give a speech/a lecture** 做演讲/讲座 [zuò yǎnjiǎng/jiǎngzuò]
4 (organize) ▶ **to give a party/dinner party etc** 做东办一个聚会/宴会 {等} [zuòdōng bàn yī gè jùhuì/yànhuì {děng}]
5 (used with noun to replace a verb) ▶ **to give a sigh/cry/shout** etc 叹了口气/哭了出来/大叫了一声 {等} [tànle kǒu qì/kūle chūlái/dàjiàole yī shēng {děng}] ▶ **to give a shrug/push** 耸了耸肩/推了一把
II VI **1** (also: **give way**) (break, collapse) 支

撑不住 [zhīchēng bù zhù] ► **his legs gave beneath him** 他腿软了 ► **the roof/floor gave as I stepped on it** 我刚一踩上去屋顶/地板就塌了

2 (stretch) [fabric, shoes +] 变松 [biànsōng]

► **give away** VT **1** [+ money, object, prize] 赠送 [zèngsòng]

2 (betray) [+ secret, information, person] 泄露 [xièlòu]

3 [+ bride] 在婚礼上把新娘交给新郎

► **give back** VT [+ money, book etc] 交还 [jiāohuán] ► **to give sth back to sb** 把某物交还给某人

► **give in** I VI (yield) 屈服 [qūfú] ► **to give in to sth** 屈服于某事

II VT [+ essay etc] 上交 [shàngjiāo]

► **give off** VT [+ heat, smoke, smell] 散发 [sànfā]

► **give out** I VT (distribute) [+ prizes, books, drinks etc] 分发 [fēnfā]

II VI **1** (run out) [supplies +] 用完 [yòngwán]

2 (fail) 出故障 [chū gùzhàng]

► **give up** I VI (stop trying) 放弃 [fàngqì]

II VT **1** [+ job] 辞掉 [cídiào]; [+ hobby] 抛弃 [pāoqì]; [+ hope, right, territory] 放弃 [fàngqì] ► **to give up smoking** 戒烟

2 (surrender) ► **to give o.s. up** 投案自首 [tóu'àn zìshǒu]

given ['gɪvn] I PP of **give** II ADJ (fixed) [+ time, amount] 一定的 [yídìng de] III PREP (taking into account) ► **given the circumstances...** 考虑到当时的情况… [kǎolùdào dāngshí de qíngkuàng…] ► **given that...** 考虑到…

glacier ['glæsɪə(r)] N [c] 冰川 [bīngchuān]

glad [glæd] ADJ (happy, pleased) 高兴的 [gāoxìng de] ► **to be glad about sth** 对某事高兴 ► **to be glad that...** 很高兴… ► **to be glad of sth** 因某事而高兴 ► **I'm glad to see you** 我非常高兴见到你 ► **I'd be glad to help you** 我很愿意帮助你

gladly ['glædlɪ] ADV **1** (happily) 高兴地 [gāoxìng de] **2** (willingly) 乐意地 [lèyì de]

glamor ['glæmə(r)] (US) N = **glamour**

glamorous ['glæmərəs] ADJ 富有魅力的 [fùyǒu mèilì de]

glamour, (US) **glamor** ['glæmə(r)] N [U] 魅力 [mèilì]

glance [glɑːns] I N [c] (look) 扫视 [sǎoshì] II VI 瞥 [piē] ► **to glance at sb/sth** 看某人/某物一眼 ► **at a glance** 一瞥之下 ► **at first glance** 乍一看

► **glance off** VT FUS [不可拆分] 擦过 [cāguò]

gland [glænd] N [c] 腺 [xiàn]

glare [gleə(r)] I N **1** [U] [of light] 强光 [qiángguāng] **2** [c] (angry look) 怒视 [nùshì] II VI **1** [light +] 眩目地照射 [xuànmù de zhàoshè] **2** [person +] 怒目而视 [nùmù ér shì] ► **the glare of publicity** 众目睽睽 ► **to glare at**

sb 怒视某人

glaring ['gleərɪŋ] ADJ [+ error, example, omission] 明显的 [míngxiǎn de]

glass [glɑːs] I N **1** [U] (substance) 玻璃 [bōlí] **2** [c] (container) 玻璃杯 [bōlíbēi] **3** [c] (glassful) 一杯 [yì bēi] II **glasses** NPL (spectacles) 眼镜 [yǎnjìng] ► **a pair of glasses** 一副眼镜

glaze [gleɪz] I VT **1** [+ pottery] 上釉于 [shàngyòu yú] **2** [+ bread, pastry] 浇在…上 [jiāo zài…shang] II N [c/U] (on pottery) 釉 [yòu]

► **glaze over** 显得呆滞 [xiǎn de dāizhì]

gleam [gliːm] I VI **1** [light, eyes +] 闪烁 [shǎnshuò] **2** [polished surface +] 发光 [fāguāng] II N [c] (from polished surface) 亮光 [liàngguāng] ► **a gleam in sb's eye** 某人眼里闪烁的光芒

gleaming ['gliːmɪŋ] ADJ (shiny) 闪闪发亮的 [shǎnshǎn fāliàng de]

glean [gliːn] VT [+ information, ideas] 搜集 [sōují]

glee [gliː] N [U] (joy) 欣喜 [xīnxǐ]

glen [glɛn] N [c] 峡谷 [xiágǔ]

glide [glaɪd] VI **1** [person, snake +] 滑行 [huáxíng] **2** [bird, aeroplane +] 滑翔 [huáxiáng]

glider ['glaɪdə(r)] N [c] (aircraft) 滑翔机 [huáxiángjī]

gliding ['glaɪdɪŋ] N (in aircraft) 滑翔运动 [huáxiáng yùndòng] ► **to go gliding** 去滑翔

glimmer ['glɪmə(r)] I N [c] [of light] 微光 [wēiguāng] II VI [light +] 发微光 [fā wēiguāng] ► **a glimmer of hope/interest** 一线希望/一丝兴趣

glimpse [glɪmps] I N ► **a glimpse of** [person, place, object] 一瞥 [yì piē] II VT [+ person, place, object] 瞥见 [piējiàn] ► **to catch a glimpse of sb/sth** 瞥见某人/某事

glint [glɪnt] I VI **1** [light, shiny surface +] 闪闪发光 [shǎnshǎn fāguāng] **2** [eyes +] 闪烁 [shǎnshuò] II N [c] **1** [of metal, light] 反光 [fǎnguāng] **2** (in eyes) 光芒 [guāngmáng]

glisten ['glɪsn] VI (with sweat, rain, oil etc) 闪闪发光 [shǎnshǎn fāguāng] ► **to glisten with sth** 某物晶莹发亮

glitter ['glɪtə(r)] I VI **1** [light, shiny surface +] 闪闪发光 [shǎnshǎn fāguāng]; [eyes +] 闪烁 [shǎnshuò] II N [U] (decoration) 小发光物 [xiǎo fāguāng wù]

gloat [gləut] VI 幸灾乐祸 [xìng zāi lè huò] ► **to gloat over** or **about sth** 对某事幸灾乐祸

global ['gləubl] ADJ **1** (worldwide) 全球的 [quánqiú de] **2** (overall) 综合的 [zōnghé de]

global warming [-'wɔːmɪŋ] N [U] 全球变暖 [quánqiú biànnuǎn]

globe [gləub] N **1** ► **the globe** (the world) 世界 [shìjiè] **2** [c] (model) 地球仪 [dìqiúyí] ► **around the globe** 全世界

gloom [gluːm] N **1** (dark) ► **the gloom** 黑暗 [hēi'àn] **2** [U] (sadness) 忧郁 [yōuyù]

► **economic gloom** 经济萧条

gloomy ['gluːmɪ] ADJ **1** (dark) [+ place, weather]

黑暗的 [hēi'àn de] **2** (sad) [+ person, situation, news] 忧郁的 [yōuyù de]

glorify ['glɔːrɪfaɪ] VT (glamorize) 颂扬 [sòngyáng]

glorious ['glɔːrɪəs] ADJ **1** [+ sunshine, day, weather] 灿烂的 [cànlàn de] **2** [+ victory, occasion, career] 光荣的 [guāngróng de]

glory ['glɔːrɪ] I N **1** [U] (prestige) 荣誉 [róngyù] **2** [C/U] (splendour) 壮观 [zhuàngguān] II VI ▶ to glory in 自豪于 [zìháo yú] ▶ moment of glory 光荣时刻

gloss [glɒs] N **1** [S/U] (shine) 光泽 [guāngzé] **2** [C/U] (also: gloss paint) 光泽涂料 [guāngzé túliào]
▶ gloss over VT FUS [不可拆分] [+ problem, error] 掩饰 [yǎnshì]

glossary ['glɒsərɪ] N [C] 词汇表 [cíhuìbiǎo]

glossy ['glɒsɪ] ADJ **1** [+ hair, surface] 有光泽的 [yǒu guāngzé de] **2** [+ magazine, brochure] 光纸印刷的 [guāngzhǐ yìnshuā de]

glove [glʌv] N [C] 手套 [shǒutào] ▶ a pair of gloves 一副手套 ▶ to fit like a glove 正合适

glove compartment N [C] 汽车仪表板上的小贮藏箱

glow [gləʊ] I VI **1** [embers, stars +] 发光 [fāguāng] **2** [face, skin, cheeks +] 发红 [fāhóng] II N [S] **1** [of embers, stars] 光亮 [guāngliàng] **2** [of face, cheeks, skin] 红润 [hóngrùn] ▶ a glow of pride/satisfaction 自豪/满意的心情 ▶ to glow with pleasure/pride 洋溢着喜悦/自豪之情

glowing ['gləʊɪŋ] ADJ **1** [+ fire] 红彤彤的 [hóngtōngtōng de] **2** [+ complexion] 容光焕发的 [róngguāng huànfāde] **3** (excellent) [+ tribute, report, description] 热烈的 [rèliè de]

glucose ['gluːkəʊs] N [U] 葡萄糖 [pútáotáng]

glue [gluː] I N [C/U] 胶 [jiāo] II VT 粘贴 [zhāntiē] ▶ to glue sth together 把某物粘在一起 ▶ to glue sth to sth 把某物粘在某物上 ▶ to be glued to the television 紧盯着电视

glum [glʌm] ADJ (miserable) [+ person, face, expression] 忧郁的 [yōuyù de]

glut [glʌt] I N [C] 供应过剩 [gōngyìng guòshèng] II VT ▶ to be glutted (with...) [market, economy +] 充斥着 (⋯) [chōngchìzhe (⋯)] ▶ a glut of oil/fruit 油/水果供应过剩

GM ADJ ABBR (= genetically modified) 转基因的 [zhuǎn jīyīn de]

gm (pl **gm** or **gms**) ABBR (= gram) 克 [kè]

GMT ABBR (= Greenwich Mean Time) 格林尼治标准时间 [Gélínnízhì Biāozhǔn Shíjiān]

gnaw [nɔː] I VT [+ bone] 啃 [kěn] II VI ▶ to gnaw at [+ guilt, doubt] 折磨 [zhémó]

GNP N ABBR (= Gross National Product) 国民生产总值 [guómín shēngchǎn zǒngzhí]

GNVQ (BRIT: SCOL) N ABBR (= general national vocational qualification) 国家职业技能综合考试 [Guójiā Zhíyè Jìnéng Zònghé Kǎoshì]

○

go [gəʊ] (pt **went**, pp **gone**, pl **goes**) I VI **1** (travel, move) 去 [qù] ▶ he's going to New York 他要去纽约 ▶ where's he gone? 他去哪儿了? ▶ shall we go by car or train? 我们开车去还是坐火车去? ▶ to go to do sth, go and do sth (BRIT) 去做某事 **2** (depart) 离开 [líkāi] ▶ let's go 我们走吧 ▶ I must be going 我必须得走了 ▶ they came at eight and went at nine 他们8点来9点走的 ▶ our plane goes at 11pm 我们的飞机晚上11点起飞 **3** (disappear) 消失 [xiāoshī] ▶ all her jewellery had gone 她所有的珠宝首饰都不见了 ▶ where's the tea gone? 茶怎么不见了? **4** (attend) ▶ to go to school/university 上学/上大学 [shàngxué/shàng dàxué] ▶ to go to evening classes 去上夜校 **5** (with activity) ▶ to go for a walk 去散步 [qù sànbù] ▶ to go on a trip 去旅行 ▶ to go swimming 去游泳 **6** (work) [clock, video etc +] 运转 [yùnzhuàn] ▷ I can't believe your watch is still going after all these years. 我真不能相信你的表这么多年后还在走。; [bell +] 敲响 [qiāoxiǎng] **7** (become) ▶ to go pale/mouldy/bald 变得苍白/发霉/秃顶 [biàn de cāngbái/fāméi/tūdǐng] ▶ she went red 她脸红了 **8** (be sold) ▶ to go for £10 卖10镑 [mài shí bàng] **9** (be about to, intend to) ▶ are you going to come? 你要来吗? [nǐ yào lái ma?] ▶ I think it's going to rain 我想天要下雨了 ▶ I'm going to be a doctor when I grow up 我长大后想成为一名医生 **10** (progress) [time, event, activity +] 进行 [jìnxíng] ▶ time went very slowly/quickly 时间过得很慢/很快 ▶ how did it go? 这事进展如何? **11** (be placed) ▶ where does this cup go? 把这个茶杯放在哪儿? [bǎ zhège chábēi fàng zài nǎr?] ▶ the milk goes in the fridge 牛奶放在冰箱里 ▶ it won't go in 放不进去 **12** (lead) [road, path +] 通向 [tōngxiàng] **13** (pass) 归 [guī] ▶ the job is to go to someone else 这份工作将归别人所得 ▶ and the prize goes to... 奖品归⋯ **14** (fail) [sight, hearing +] 减退 [jiǎntuì]; [clutch, battery +] 衰竭 [shuāijié] ▶ the battery's going 电池没电了 **15** (be removed) [object +] 被丢弃 [bèi diūqì]; [jobs +] 被取消 [bèi qǔxiāo]; [employee +] 被辞退 [bèi cítuì] ▶ more jobs are to go at the factory 这家工厂会有更多的工作被取消

16 (combine well) [colours, clothes, foods +] 相配 [xiāngpèi]

17 (say) [story, poem, saying +] 正如…所说 [zhèngrú…suǒshuō] ▶ **as the story goes** 如故事中所讲的

18 (be available) ▶ **there's a flat going downstairs** 楼下有间空的公寓 [lóuxià yǒu jiān kòng de gōngyù] ▶ **I'll take whatever's going** 无论什么样的我都要

19 (to take away) ▶ **a hamburger and fries to go** (US) 汉堡包和炸薯条外卖 [hànbǎobāo hé zhá shǔtiáo wàimài]

20 (in other expressions) ▶ **there's still a week to go before the exams** 考试前还有一个星期的时间 [kǎoshì qián háiyǒu yī gè xīngqī de shíjiān] ▶ **he has a lot going for him** 他有很多有利条件 ▶ **to get going** 走 ▷ Give me the keys. I've got to get going. 给我钥匙。我得走了。 ▶ **to keep going** 继续下去

II VT (travel) [+ distance] 走 [zǒu]

III N **1** [c] (try) 尝试 [chángshì] ▶ **to have a go (at sth/at doing sth)** 试一下(某事/做某事) [shì yīxià (mǒushì/zuò mǒushì)]

2 [c] (turn) 轮流 [lúnliú] ▶ **whose go is it?** 轮到谁了？▶ **it's your go** 轮到你了

3 ▶ **to have sth on the go** 手头上正忙着某事 [shǒutóushang zhèng mángzhe mǒushì]

4 (ESP BRIT: inf) (move) ▶ **to be on the go** 忙忙碌碌的 [mángmáng lùlù de]

▶ **go about** **I** VT FUS [不可拆分] (tackle) 处理 [chǔlǐ] ▶ **how do I go about doing this?** 我该怎样着手做这事呢？**II** VI **1** [rumour +] 传开 [chuánkāi] ▶ **there's a rumour going about that...** 一条关于…的谣言正流传开来 **2** (manner) ▶ **he goes about in a white suit** 他总是穿着白西装 [tā zǒngshì chuānzhe bái xīzhuāng]

▶ **go after** VT FUS [不可拆分] **1** (pursue) [+ person] 追赶 [zhuīgǎn] **2** (try to get) [+ job] 设法得到 [shèfǎ dédào]; [+ record] 设法打破 [shèfǎ dǎpò]

▶ **go against** VT FUS [不可拆分] **1** (be unfavourable to) 不利于 [bù lìyú] **2** (disregard) [+ advice, wishes etc] 违背 [wéibèi]

▶ **go ahead** VI **1** (take place) [event +] 发生 [fāshēng] **2** (press on) ▶ **to go ahead with sth** 着手做某事 [zhuóshǒu zuò mǒushì] ▶ **go ahead!** (encouraging) 干吧！

▶ **go along** VI 去 [qù]

▶ **go along with** VT FUS [不可拆分] (agree with) [+ plan, idea, decision] 赞同 [zàntóng]; [+ person] 同意 [tóngyì]

▶ **go around** VI **1** (circulate) [news, rumour +] 传播 [chuánbō] **2** (revolve) 转动 [zhuàndòng]

3 (ESP BRIT) (visit) ▶ **to go around (to sb's)** 拜访(某人的家) [bàifǎng (mǒurén de jiā)] **4** (suffice) 够每人一份 [gòu měirén yī fèn] **5** (as a habit) 习惯于 [xíguàn yú] ▶ **he goes around in an orange baseball cap** 他总是戴着一顶橘黄色的棒球帽 [tā zǒngshì dàizhe yī dǐng júhuángsè de bàngqiúmào]

▶ **go away** VI **1** (leave) 离开 [líkāi] **2** (on holiday) 外出 [wàichū]

▶ **go back** VI (return) 返回 [fǎnhuí]

▶ **go back on** VT FUS [不可拆分] [+ promise, agreement] 背弃 [bèiqì]

▶ **go back to** VT FUS [不可拆分] [+ activity, work, school] 回到 [huídào]

▶ **go by** **I** VI [vehicle, years, time +] 过去 [guòqu] **II** VT FUS [不可拆分] [+ rule etc] 遵照 [zūnzhào]

▶ **go down** **I** VI **1** (fall) [price, level, amount +] 下降 [xiàjiàng] **2** (set) [sun +] 落下 [luòxià] **3** (sink) [ship +] 沉没 [chénmò] **4** (crash) [computer +] 死机 [sǐjī]; [plane +] 坠毁 [zhuìhuǐ] **5** (SPORT) (lose) 输掉 [shūdiào]; (be relegated) 降级 [jiàngjí] ▶ **we went down to Newcastle** 我们输给了纽卡斯尔队 **6** ▶ **to go down well/badly** [speech, remark, idea +] 受到/不受欢迎 [shòudào/bù shòu huānyíng] **7** ▶ **to go down with flu** 得流感 [dé liúgǎn] **II** VT FUS [不可拆分] [+ stairs, ladder] 从…下来 [cóng…xiàlái]

▶ **go for** VT FUS [不可拆分] **1** (fetch) 去取 [qùqǔ] **2** (opt for) 选择 [xuǎnzé] **3** (be attracted by) 喜欢 [xǐhuan] **4** (attack) 攻击 [gōngjī] **5** (apply to) 适用于 [shìyòng yú] ▶ **that goes for me too** 那也适用于我

▶ **go in** VI (enter) 进去 [jìnqù]

▶ **go in for** VT FUS [不可拆分] **1** [+ competition] 参加 [cānjiā] **2** (like) 爱好 [àihào] ▶ **he doesn't go in for compliments** 他不喜欢恭维

▶ **go into** VT FUS [不可拆分] **1** (enter) [+ building, room] 进入 [jìnrù] **2** (examine) [+ subject, details] 探究 [tànjiū] **3** (embark on) [+ career] 从事 [cóngshì]

▶ **go off** **I** VT FUS [不可拆分] (ESP BRIT) (begin to dislike) [+ person, place, idea etc] 不再喜欢 [bù zài xǐhuan] **II** VI **1** (leave) 离去 [líqù] ▶ **he's gone off to work** 他已经去上班了 **2** (explode) [bomb, gun +] 爆炸 [bàozhà] **3** (sound) [alarm +] 响起 [xiǎngqǐ] **4** (pass off) [event +] 进行 [jìnxíng] ▶ **the wedding went off without a hitch** 婚礼进

行得非常顺利

5 (switch off) [lights etc +] 熄灭 [xīmiè]

6 (ESP BRIT) [food, milk, meat +] 变质 [biànzhì]

▶ **go off with** VT FUS [不可拆分] **1** (run away with) [+ lover] 同…私奔 [tóng…sībēn]

2 (take) [+ object] 抢走 [qiǎngzǒu]

▶ **go on** I VI **1** (continue) 继续 [jìxù] ▶ **to go on with one's work** 继续自己的工作

▶ **we have enough to be going on with** (ESP BRIT) 目前我们够了 ▶ **to go on doing sth** 继续做某事

2 (happen) 发生 [fāshēng] ▶ **what's going on here?** 这里发生什么事了？

3 (come on) [lights etc +] 打开 [dǎkāi]

4 ▶ **to go on to do sth** 接着做某事 [jiēzhe zuò mǒushì]

II VT FUS [不可拆分] **1** (be guided by) [+ evidence etc] 把…作为依据 [bǎ…zuòwéi yījù] ▶ **there isn't much to go on** 没有太多可以依据的东西

2 (approach) ▶ **he's going on 50** 他马上就要50岁了 [tā mǎshàng jiùyào wǔshí suì le]

▶ **go on about** VT FUS [不可拆分] 对…唠唠叨叨 [duì…láolao dāodao]

▶ **go on at** (BRIT: inf) VT FUS [不可拆分] (nag) 向…唠唠叨叨 [xiàng…láolao dāodao]

▶ **she's always going on at me to tidy my room** 她总是唠唠叨叨地要我清理房间

▶ **go out** VI **1** [person +] (to party, club etc) 出去消遣 [chūqù xiāoqiǎn]

▶ **to go out of** 离开 ▶ **are you going out tonight?** 你今晚出去吗？

2 [couple +] 和…交往 [hé…jiāowǎng]

▶ **they've been going out for 3 years and have just got engaged** 他们已经交往3年了，并且刚刚订婚 ▶ **to go out with sb** 和某人交往

3 (be extinguished) [light, fire +] 熄灭 [xīmiè]

▶ **go over** I VI 过去 [guòqù]

II VT (check) 仔细检查 [zǐxì jiǎnchá] ▶ **to go over sth in one's mind** 在脑子里过一遍

▶ **go round** VI = **go around**

▶ **go through** VT FUS [不可拆分] **1** [+ place, town] 路过 [lùguò]

2 (undergo) 经历 [jīnglì] ▶ **he's going through a difficult time** 他正经历着困难时期

3 (search through) 翻遍 [fānbiàn]

4 (run through) [+ list, book, story] 仔细查看 [zǐxì chákàn]

5 (perform) [+ routine, procedure, exercise] 履行 [lǚxíng]

▶ **go through with** VT FUS [不可拆分] [+ plan, crime] 做到 [zuòdào] ▶ **I couldn't go through with it** 我无法把它做完

▶ **go together** VI [colours, clothes, foods +] 相配 [xiāngpèi]

▶ **go towards** VT FUS [不可拆分] [money +] 作为…的部分付款 [zuòwéi…de bùfen fùkuǎn]

▶ **go under** VI **1** (sink) [ship, person +] 沉没 [chénmò]

2 [business, project +] 失败 [shībài]

▶ **go up** VI **1** (rise) [price, level, value +] 上涨 [shàngzhǎng]

2 (go upstairs) 上楼 [shànglóu]

▶ **go up to** VT FUS [不可拆分] 向…走过去 [xiàng…zǒuguòqù]

▶ **go with** VT FUS [不可拆分] **1** (combine well with) [colours, clothes, foods +] 与…协调 [yǔ…xiétiáo]

2 (accompany) 与…相伴共存 [yǔ…xiāngbàn gòngcún]

▶ **go without** VT FUS [不可拆分] [+ food, treats] 没有 [méiyǒu…]

go-ahead ['gəʊəhɛd] I N ▶ **the go-ahead** (for project) 许可 [xǔkě] ▶ **to give sb/sth the go-ahead** 准许某人做某事/某事得以进行 II ADJ [+ person, firm] 有进取心的 [yǒu jìnqǔ xīn de]

goal [gəʊl] N [c] **1** (SPORT) (point scored) 进球得分 [jìnqiú défēn]; (on pitch) 球门 [qiúmén]

2 (aim) 目标 [mùbiāo] ▶ **to score a goal** 进一球

goalkeeper ['gəʊlkiːpə(r)] N [c] 守门员 [shǒuményuán]

goalpost ['gəʊlpəʊst] N [c] 门柱 [ménzhù]

▶ **to move or shift the goalposts** 改变规则

goat [gəʊt] N [c] 山羊 [shānyáng]

gobble ['gɔbl] VT 狼吞虎咽 [láng tūn hǔ yàn]

▶ **gobble down** VT 大口吞下 [dàkǒu tūnxià]

God [gɔd] I N 上帝 [Shàngdì] II INT 天啊 [tiān'ā] ▶ **to play God** (pej) 以上帝自居

god [gɔd] N [c] 天神 [tiānshén] ▶ **the god of thunder** 雷神

godchild ['gɔdtʃaɪld] (pl **godchildren**) N [c] (male) 教子 [jiàozǐ]; (female) 教女 [jiàonǚ]

goddaughter ['gɔddɔːtə(r)] N [c] 教女 [jiàonǚ]

goddess ['gɔdɪs] N [c] (lit) 女神 [nǚshén] ▶ **the moon goddess** 月神 ▶ **sex/screen goddess** 性感/银屏女神

godfather ['gɔdfɑːðə(r)] N [c] **1** (male godparent) 教父 [jiàofù] **2** (gangster) 帮头 [bāngtóu]

godmother ['gɔdmʌðə(r)] N [c] 教母 [jiàomǔ]

godparent ['gɔdpɛərənt] N [c] 教父教母 [jiàofù jiàomǔ]

godson ['gɔdsʌn] N [c] 教子 [jiàozǐ]

goggles ['gɔglz] NPL 护目镜 [hùmùjìng]

○**going** ['gəʊɪŋ] I PRESENT PARTICIPLE of **go** II ADJ ▶ **the going rate/price** 现行率/时价 [xiànxínglù/shíjià] III N ▶ **the going** (progress) 进展 [jìnzhǎn] ▷ The going was becoming easier as the talks progressed. 随着对话的进行进展变得更加顺利。; (conditions) 路况 [lùkuàng] ▷ The going became more difficult as the rain became

heavier. 雨越下越大，路况变得更差了。
▶ **when the going gets tough** 当情况艰难
时 ▶ **while the going is good** 趁情况顺利时
▶ **it was hard** or **tough** or **heavy going** 困难重
重 ▶ **that's good** or **not bad going** 还不错 ▶ **a
going concern** 运作正常的公司

gold [gəʊld] I N **1** (U) (metal) 黄金 [huángjīn]
2 (U) (jewellery) 金饰品 [jīnshìpǐn] **3** (U) (colour)
金色 [jīnsè] **4** (C) (SPORT) (inf) (also: **gold medal**)
金牌 [jīnpái] II ADJ **1** (made of gold) [+ ring, watch,
tooth] 金的 [jīn de] **2** (gold-coloured) 金色的
[jīnsè de] ▶ **as good as gold** 很乖

golden ['gəʊldən] ADJ **1** (made of gold) 金
制的 [jīnzhì de] **2** (colour) 金色的 [jīnsè de]
3 (wonderful) [+ opportunity, future] 绝妙的
[juémiào de]

goldfish ['gəʊldfɪʃ] (pl **goldfish**) N (C) 金鱼
[jīnyú]

goldmine ['gəʊldmaɪn] N (S) (fig) 金矿
[jīnkuàng]

gold-plated ['gəʊld'pleɪtɪd] ADJ 包金的
[bāojīn de]

golf [gɒlf] N (U) 高尔夫球 [gāo'ěrfūqiú] ▶ **to
play golf** 打高尔夫球

golf ball N (C) 高尔夫球 [gāo'ěrfūqiú]

golf club N (C) **1** (stick) 高尔夫球棍
[gāo'ěrfūqiúgùn] **2** (organization) 高尔夫球俱
乐部 [gāo'ěrfūqiú jùlèbù]

golf course N (C) 高尔夫球场
[gāo'ěrfūqiúchǎng]

golfer ['gɒlfə(r)] N (C) 高尔夫球运动员
[gāo'ěrfūqiú yùndòngyuán]

gone [gɒn] I PP of **go** II ADJ 离去的 [líqù de]
III PREP (BRIT: inf) (after) 过 [guò] ▶ **the food's
all gone** 食物都没了

gong [gɒŋ] N (C) 锣 [luó]

✪**good** [gʊd] I ADJ **1** (pleasant) 令人愉快的 [lìng
rén yúkuài de] ▷ They had a really good time. 他
们玩得很开心。 **2** (high quality) [+ food, school,
job] 好的 [hǎo de] ▷ She speaks very good English.
她英语说得很好。 **3** (well-behaved) [+ boy, girl,
dog] 乖的 [guāi de] ▷ Were the kids good? 孩子
们乖吗？ **4** (sensible) [+ idea, reason, advice] 好的
[hǎo de] ▷ It was a good idea to bring a torch. 带
手电筒是个好主意。 **5** (skilful) 好的 [hǎo de]
▷ He's a good footballer. 他是个很好的足球运动
员。 **6** (positive) [+ news, luck, example] 好的 [hǎo
de] ▷ a piece of good news 一条好消息 **7** (cheerful)
[+ mood, temper] 愉快的 [yúkuài de] ▷ She had a
good time in Italy. 她在意大利度过了一段快乐
的时光。 ▷ She's in a good mood! 她心情很好！
8 (morally correct) 公正的 [gōngzhèng de] ▷ The
president is a good man. 总统是个公正的人。
II N (U) (right) 善 [shàn] ▷ the battle between
good and evil 善恶之争 ▶ **good!** 好！ ▶ **to be
good at (doing) sth** 精于(做)某事 ▶ **to be
no good at (doing) sth** 不擅长(做)某事 ▶ **to
be good for doing sth** (useful) 对做某事有帮

助 ▶ **it's no good doing...** 做…没有用 ▶ **it
didn't do any good** 没什么用处 ▶ **to be up to
no good** 不怀好意 ▶ **it's good for you** (healthy,
beneficial) 对你有益 ▶ **to be good to sb** (kind)
对某人很好 ▷ He's always been very good to me. 他
总是对我很好。 ▶ **to be good with people/with
figures** 擅长与人/数字打交道 ▶ **to be good
with one's hands** 手很灵巧 ▶ **is it any good?**
(will it do?) 这行吗？ ; (what's it like?) 怎
么样？ ▷ Is her new novel any good? 她的新小
说怎么样？ ▶ **it's good to see you** 很高兴见
到你 ▶ **it's a good thing you were there, it's
a good job you were there** (BRIT) 幸亏你在
那儿 ▶ **that's very good of you** 你实在太好
了 ▶ **would you be good enough to...?** 可不
可以请您…？ ▶ **good morning/afternoon!**
早上/下午好！ ▶ **good evening!** 晚上好！
▶ **good night!** (before going home) 再见！ ; (before
going to bed) 晚安！ ▶ **to feel good** (happy) 感
到高兴 ▶ **to make good** [+ damage, loss] 弥补
▷ Three years was a short time in which to make good
the deficiencies. 弥补这些不足，3年的时间是
很短的。 ; (succeed) 成功 ▶ **to take a good look**
好好看一看 ▶ **as good a while ago** 很久以前
▶ **as good as** (almost) 几乎相当于 ▶ **for good**
(forever) 永久地 ▶ **for the good of sb** 为了某人
的利益 ▶ **it's for your own good** 是为了你自
己好 ▶ **to do sb good** 对某人有益 ▶ **not until
I'm good and ready** 直到我彻底准备好时才
see also **goods**

请勿将 **be good for** 和 **be good to** 混
淆。若某事 **be good for** 某个个人或组
织，即它有益于该人或组织。The policy
is good for company morale. 如果某人 **be
good to** 你，表示对你很友好，很体
贴。Phil cannot replace my dad but he has
been very good to me.

goodbye [gʊd'baɪ] INT 再见 [zàijiàn] ▶ **to say
goodbye** 告别

Good Friday N (U) 耶稣受难日，即复活节前
的星期五

good-looking ['gʊd'lʊkɪŋ] ADJ 好看的
[hǎokàn de]

good-natured ['gʊd'neɪtʃəd] ADJ [+ person] 性
情温和的 [xìngqíng wēnhé de]; [+ discussion] 和
善的 [héshàn de]

goodness ['gʊdnɪs] I N (U) (of person) 善
良 [shànliáng] II INT ▶ **(my) goodness!** (我
的) 天哪！ [(wǒde) tiānna!] ▶ **for goodness
sake!** 看在老天爷的份上！ ▶ **goodness
gracious!** 天哪！ ▶ **thank goodness!** 谢天谢
地！ ▶ **out of the goodness of his heart** 出于
他的好心

goods ['gʊdz] NPL **1** (COMM) 商品 [shāngpǐn]
2 (possessions) 动产 [dòngchǎn] ▶ **to come up
with** or **deliver the goods** 达到要求

goods train (BRIT) N (C) 货物列车 [huòwù

lièchē)[美=freight train]

goodwill [gud'wɪl] N [U] 善意 [shànyì] ▶ a gesture of goodwill 善意的表示

goose [guːs] (pl geese) N [C] 鹅 [é]

gooseberry ['guzbərɪ] N [C] (fruit) 醋栗 [cùlì] ▶ to play gooseberry (BRIT) 当电灯泡

goose bumps NPL 鸡皮疙瘩 [jīpí gēda] ▶ to get goose bumps 起鸡皮疙瘩

gooseflesh ['guːsfleʃ] N [U] = goose bumps

goose pimples NPL = goose bumps

gorge [gɔːdʒ] I N [C] (valley) 峡谷 [xiágǔ] II VT ▶ to gorge o.s. (on sth) 狼吞虎咽(吃某物) [láng tūn hǔ yàn (chī mǒuwù)]

gorgeous ['gɔːdʒəs] ADJ 1 [+ necklace, dress] 华丽的 [huálì de]; [+ weather, day] 宜人的 [yírén de] 2 [+ person] 光彩夺目的 [guāngcǎi duó mù de]

gorilla [gə'rɪlə] N [C] (animal) 大猩猩 [dàxīngxing]

gory ['gɔːrɪ] ADJ 血淋淋的 [xuèlínlín de] ▶ the gory details 令人毛骨悚然的细节

gosh [gɒʃ] INT 啊呀![āyā]

gospel ['gɒspl] N 1 [C] (REL) 福音书 [fúyīnshū] 2 [C] (doctrine) 信条 [xìntiáo] 3 [U] (also: **gospel music**) 福音音乐 [fúyīn yīnyuè] 4 [U] (also: **gospel truth**) 绝对真理 [juéduì zhēnlǐ] ▶ the **gospel** (Christ's teachings) 福音书

gossip ['gɒsɪp] I N 1 [U] (rumours) 流言蜚语 [liúyán fēiyǔ] 2 [C] (chat) 闲谈 [xiántán] 3 [C] (busybody) 爱飞短流长的人 [ài fēi duǎn liú cháng de rén] II VI (chat) 闲谈 [xiántán] ▶ to **gossip with sb** 和某人闲谈

○ **got** [gɒt] PT, PP of **get** ▶ have you got your umbrella? 你有伞吗? ▶ he has got to accept the situation 他只得接受现状 ▶ he's got to be guilty 他肯定有罪

gotten ['gɒtn] (US) PP of **get**

gourmet ['guəmeɪ] I N [C] (person) 美食家 [měishíjiā] II ADJ [+ food, cooking] 精美的 [jīngměi de]

govern ['gʌvən] I VT 1 [+ country] 统治 [tǒngzhì] 2 [+ event, conduct] 控制 [kòngzhì] II VI 统治 [tǒngzhì]

○ **government** ['gʌvnmənt] I N 1 [C] (institution) 政府 [zhèngfǔ] ▷ The Government is in the wrong. 是政府的错误。2 [U] (act of governing) 执政 [zhízhèng] ▷ He had no previous experience of government. 他以前没有执政的经验。II CPD [复合词] [+ grant, report, official, policy] 政府 [zhèngfǔ]

governor ['gʌvənə(r)] N [C] 1 [of state] 州长 [zhōuzhǎng]; [of colony] 总督 [zǒngdū] 2 [of bank, school, hospital] 董事 [dǒngshì] ▷ the Board of Governors 理事会 3 (BRIT) [of prison] 狱长 [yùzhǎng]

Govt ABBR (= **government**) 政府 [zhèngfǔ]

gown [gaun] N [C] 1 (dress) 礼服 [lǐfú] 2 (BRIT) [of teacher, judge] 礼袍 [lǐpáo]

GP N ABBR [C] (= general practitioner) 家庭医生 [jiātíng yīshēng]

GR8 ABBR = **great** 太好了 [tàihǎo le]

grab [græb] I VT 1 (seize) 抓住 [zhuāzhù] 2 [+ food, drink, sleep] 抓紧做 [zhuājǐn zuò] 3 [+ chance, opportunity] 抓住 [zhuāzhù] 4 [+ attention] 吸引 [xīyǐn] II VI ▶ to **grab at sth** 抢某物 [qiǎng mǒuwù] III N ▶ to **make a grab for sth** 向某物抓去 [xiàng mǒuwù zhuāqù] ▶ to **grab hold of sth/sb** 抓住某物/某人

grace [greɪs] I N [U] 1 (gracefulness) 优雅 [yōuyǎ] 2 (dignified behaviour) 体面 [tǐmiàn] II VT (adorn) 使增光 [shǐ zēngguāng] ▶ his fall from grace 他的不得势 ▶ to **fall from grace** 不得势 ▶ 5 days' grace 5天的宽限 ▶ with (a) good/bad grace 欣然地/勉强地 ▶ to **say grace** 谢恩祈祷

graceful ['greɪsful] ADJ 1 [+ animal, athlete, movement, style] 优美的 [yōuměi de] 2 (polite) 得体的 [détǐ de]

gracious ['greɪʃəs] I ADJ 1 (courteous) [+ person] 有礼的 [yǒulǐ de]; [+ speech, smile] 亲切的 [qīnqiè de] 2 (elegant) [+ era, lifestyle] 高雅的 [gāoyǎ de] II INT ▶ (good or goodness) gracious! 天哪![tiānna!]

grade [greɪd] I N [C] 1 (quality) [of goods, product] 等级 [děngjí] 2 (rank) (in company, organization) 级别 [jíbié] 3 (school mark) 分数 [fēnshù] 4 (US) (school class) 年级 [niánjí] 5 (US) (gradient) 坡 [pō] II VT (rank, class) 按等次分 [fēn děngcì] ▶ to **make the grade** 达到标准

grade crossing (US) N [C] 铁路线与公路交叉处 [英 = level crossing]

grade school (US) N [C/U] 小学 [xiǎoxué] [英 = primary school]

gradient ['greɪdɪənt] (BRIT) N [C] [of road, slope] 坡度 [pōdù] [美 = grade]

gradual ['grædjuəl] ADJ [+ change, process, improvement] 逐渐的 [zhújiàn de]

gradually ['grædjuəlɪ] ADV 逐渐地 [zhújiàn de]

graduate [n 'grædjuɪt, vb 'grædjueɪt] I N [C] 1 (person with degree) 毕业生 [bìyèshēng] 2 (US) ▶ high school/elementary school graduate 中学/小学毕业生 [zhōngxué/xiǎoxué bìyèshēng] II VI 1 (from university) 毕业 [bìyè]; (US) (from high school/elementary school etc) 毕业 [bìyè] 3 (progress) 发展 [fāzhǎn] ▶ a philosophy graduate, a graduate in philosophy (BRIT) 哲学专业毕业生

graduation [grædju'eɪʃən] N 1 [U] (from university) 毕业 [bìyè] 2 [U] (US) (from high school, elementary school etc) 毕业 [bìyè] 3 [C/U] (also: **graduation ceremony**) (after degree) 毕业典礼 [bìyè diǎnlǐ]; (US) (after high school, elementary school etc) 毕业典礼 [bìyè diǎnlǐ]

graffiti [grə'fiːtɪ] N [U] 涂鸦 [túyā]

graft [grɑːft] I N 1 [c] (of skin, bone) 移植物 [yízhíwù] 2 [U] (BRIT: inf) (hard work) 苦差 [kǔchāi] 3 [U] (US) (bribery) 贿赂 [huìlù] II VT ▸ **to graft (onto)** [+ skin, bone] 移植 (到) [yízhí (dào)]; [+ plant] 嫁接 (到) [jiàjiē (dào)] ▸ **skin/bone graft** 皮肤/骨移植

grain [greɪn] N 1 [c] (of wheat, rice) 谷粒 [gǔlì] 2 [c/U] (cereals) 谷物 [gǔwù] 3 [U] (US) (corn) 玉米 [yùmǐ] 4 [c] [of sand, salt, sugar] 颗粒 [kēlì] 5 ▸ **the grain** [of wood] 纹理 [wénlǐ] ▸ **it goes against the grain** 格格不入 ▸ **a grain of truth** 一点真实性

gram [græm] N [c] 克 [kè]

grammar ['græmə(r)] N [U] 1 (rules of language) 语法 [yǔfǎ] 2 (use of rules) 语法运用 [yǔfǎ yùnyòng]

grammar school (BRIT) N [c] 文法学校，11到18岁孩子就学的公立学校，学生成绩一般都比较优秀

gramme [græm] (BRIT) N = **gram**

gran [græn] N [c] (on mother's side) 外婆 [wàipó]; (on father's side) 奶奶 [nǎinai]

grand [grænd] I ADJ 1 (impressive) [+ building, landscape] 壮丽的 [zhuànglì de]; [+ scheme, design] 宏伟的 [hóngwěi de] 2 (wonderful) 美好的 [měihǎo de] II N (a thousand pounds/dollars) 1000英镑/美元 [yī qiān yīngbàng/měiyuán] ▸ **grand total** 总数

grandad, granddad ['grændæd] N [c] (on mother's side) 外公 [wàigōng]; (on father's side) 爷爷 [yéye]

grandchild ['græntʃaɪld] (pl **grandchildren**) N [c] (male on father's side) 孙子 [sūnzi]; (female on father's side) 孙女 [sūnnǚ]; (male on mother's side) 外孙 [wàisūn]; (female on mother's side) 外孙女 [wàisūnnǚ]

granddaughter ['grændɔːtə(r)] N [c] (on father's side) 孙女 [sūnnǚ]; (on mother's side) 外孙女 [wàisūnnǚ]

grandfather ['grændfɑːðə(r)] N [c] (on mother's side) 外公 [wàigōng]; (on father's side) 爷爷 [yéye]

grandiose ['grændɪəus] ADJ 浮夸的 [fúkuā de]

grandma ['grænmɑː] N [c] (on mother's side) 外婆 [wàipó]; (on father's side) 奶奶 [nǎinai]

grandmother ['grænmʌðə(r)] N [c] (on mother's side) 外婆 [wàipó]; (on father's side) 奶奶 [nǎinai]

grandpa ['grænpɑː] N [c] (on mother's side) 外公 [wàigōng]; (on father's side) 爷爷 [yéye]

grandparents ['grændpɛərənts] NPL (on mother's side) 外公外婆 [wàigōng wàipó]; (on father's side) 爷爷奶奶 [yéye nǎinai]

grand piano N [c] 大钢琴 [dàgāngqín]

Grand Prix ['grɑːn'priː] (pl **Grands Prix** or **Grand Prix**) N (motor racing) 国际汽车大奖赛 [Guójì Qìchē Dàjiǎngsài]

grandson ['grænsʌn] N [c] (on father's side) 孙子 [sūnzi]; (on mother's side) 外孙 [wàisūn]

granite ['grænɪt] N [U] 花岗石 [huāgāngshí]

granny, grannie ['grænɪ] N [c] (on mother's side) 外婆 [wàipó]; (on father's side) 奶奶 [nǎinai]

grant [grɑːnt] I VT + request, visa, permission) 授予 [shòuyǔ] II N (award) 拨款 [bōkuǎn] ▸ **to take sb for granted** 认为某人做的事情是理所当然 ▸ **to take sth for granted** 想当然地认为某事 ▸ **to take it for granted that...** 认为…是理所当然 ▸ **to grant that...** 承认… ▸ I **grant (you) that...** 我 (向你) 承认…

grape [greɪp] N [c] 葡萄 [pútáo] ▸ **a bunch of grapes** 一串葡萄 ▸ **sour grapes** 酸葡萄

grapefruit ['greɪpfruːt] N [c/U] 葡萄柚 [pútáo yòu]

graph [grɑːf] N [c] 图表 [túbiǎo]

graphic ['græfɪk] ADJ 1 [+ account, description, scene] 生动的 [shēngdòng de] 2 [+ art, design] 绘画艺术的 [huìhuà yìshù de] see also **graphics**

graphic designer N [c] 平面造型设计师 [píngmiàn zàoxíng shèjìshī]

graphics ['græfɪks] I N [U] (design) 制图学 [zhìtúxué] II NPL (images) 图形 [túxíng]

grapple ['græpl] VI 1 ▸ **to grapple with sb** 与某人搏斗 [yǔ mǒurén bódòu] 2 ▸ **to grapple with** [+ problem] 设法解决 [shèfǎ jiějué]

grasp [grɑːsp] I VT 1 (hold, seize) 抓住 [zhuāzhù] 2 (understand) 理解 [lǐjiě] II N [s] 1 (grip) 紧握 [jǐnwò] 2 (understanding) 理解力 [lǐjiělì] ▸ **to slip from sb's grasp** 从某人手中溜掉 ▸ **within/beyond sb's grasp** 为某人力所能及/力所不及 ▸ **to grasp at...** [+ rope, handle] 向…抓去

grass [grɑːs] I N 1 [c/U] (BOT) 草 [cǎo] 2 [c] (BRIT: inf) (informer) 告密者 [gàomìzhě] 3 [U] (marijuana) 大麻 [dàmá] II VI ▸ **to grass on sb** (BRIT: inf) 告某人的密 [gào mǒurén de mì] ▸ **the grass** (the lawn) 草坪

grasshopper ['grɑːshɒpə(r)] N [c] 蚱蜢 [zhàměng]

grass roots ['grɑːsruːts] I NPL ▸ **the grass roots** 基层 [jīcéng] II CPD [复合词] [+ level, opinion, support] 基层群众 [jīcéng qúnzhòng]

grate [greɪt] I VI 1 ▸ **to grate (on sth)** (scrape) (磨到某物) 发出刮擦声 [(módào mǒuwù) fāchū guācāshēng] 2 ▸ **to grate on sb** (annoy) 使某人烦躁 [shǐ mǒurén fánzào] II VT [+ food] 磨碎 [mósuì] III N [c] (for fire) 炉栅 [lúshān]

grateful ['greɪtful] ADJ [+ person] 感激的 [gǎnjī de] ▸ **to be grateful to sb** 感激某人 ▸ **to be grateful for** [+ help, opportunity] 感激… ▸ **to be grateful to sb for sth** 为某事感激某人

grater ['greɪtə(r)] N [c] 磨碎器 [mósuìqì] ▸ **cheese/nutmeg grater** 奶酪/肉豆蔻磨碎器

gratifying ['grætɪfaɪɪŋ] ADJ (pleasing, satisfying) 令人满意的 [lìng rén mǎnyì de] ▸ **it is gratifying to...** …是令人满足的 ▸ **it is gratifying that...** 令人满足的是…

gratitude ['grætɪtjuːd] N [U] 感激 [gǎnjī]

grave [greɪv] I N [c] (*tomb*) 坟墓 [fénmù]
II ADJ 1 [+ *situation, crisis*] 严重的 [yánzhòng
de]; [+ *concern, danger*] 重大的 [zhòngdà de]
2 [+ *expression, person*] 严肃的 [yánsù de]

gravel ['grævl] N [U] 砾石 [lìshí]

gravestone ['greɪvstəun] N [c] 墓碑 [mùbēi]

graveyard ['greɪvjɑːd] N [c] 墓地 [mùdì]

gravity ['grævɪtɪ] N [U] 1 (PHYS) 重力 [zhònglì]
2 (*seriousness*) 严重性 [yánzhòngxíng]

gravy ['greɪvɪ] N [U] (*sauce*) 肉卤 [ròulǔ]

gray [greɪ] (US) ADJ = **grey**

graze [greɪz] I VI [*animal +*] 吃青草 [chī cǎo]
II VT 1 (*scrape*) [+ *arm, leg, knee*] 擦伤 [cāshāng]
2 (*touch lightly*) 擦过 [cāguò] III N (*wound*) 擦
伤 [cāshāng]

grease [griːs] I N [U] 1 (*lubricant*) 润滑油
[rùnhuáyóu] 2 (*fat*) 油脂 [yóuzhī] 3 (*dirt*) 油污
[yóuwū] II VT 1 (*lubricate*) 上润滑油于 [shàng
rùnhuáyóu yú] 2 [+ *cooking dish*] 给…涂油脂
[gěi…tú yóuzhī]

greasy ['griːsɪ] ADJ 1 [+ *tools, hands*] 油污
的 [yóuwū de] 2 [+ *food*] 油腻的 [yóunì de]
3 [+ *skin, hair*] 多油脂的 [duō yóuzhīde]

◎great [greɪt] I ADJ 1 (*large*) [+ *area, amount,
number*] 巨大的 [jùdà de] ▷ *a great black cloud of
smoke* 一团巨大的黑烟 ▷ *a great number of people*
很多人 2 (*considerable*) [+ *success, achievement*] 重
大的 [zhòngdà de]; [+ *pleasure, difficulty, value*]
极大的 [jídà de]; [+ *risk*] 超乎寻常的 [chāohū
xúncháng de] 3 (*intense*) [+ *heat, pain*] 强烈的
[qiánglìe de] ▷ *David had a great desire to live in
the countryside.* 大卫有住在乡下的强烈愿望。
▷ *The heat was so great I took off my shirt.* 实在太
热了，于是我脱下了我的衬衫。; [+ *love*] 深
的 [shēn de] 4 (*important, famous*) [+ *city, person,
work of art*] 伟大的 [wěidà de] ▷ *the great
novels of the 19th century* 19世纪的伟大小说
▷ *Shakespeare was a great man.* 莎士比亚是个伟
人。5 (*terrific*) [+ *person, place*] 好极了的 [hǎojíle
de]; [+ *idea*] 棒极了的 [bàngjíle de] ▷ *It's a
great idea.* 这是个棒极了的主意。6 (*ardent*)
[+ *believer, supporter*] 十足的 [shízú de] II INT
▶ **great!** (*enthusiastically*) 太好了！[tàihǎole!];
(*sarcastically*) 天啊！[tiān'ǎ!] III N [c] (*success*)
(*person*) 伟人 [wěirén] ▷ *She is one of the greats
of modern cinema.* 她是当今电影界的巨星之
一。; (*work of art, film, literature*) 巨作 [jùzuò]
▷ *the greats of feminist literature* 女权文学的巨作
▶ **I feel great** 我感觉好极了 ▶ **they're great
friends** 他们是挚友 ▶ **we had a great time** 我
们玩得很快活

Great Britain N 大不列颠 [Dàbùlièdiān]

great-grandfather [greɪt'grænfɑːðə(r)]
N [c] 曾祖父 [zēng zǔfù]

great-grandmother [greɪt'grænmʌðə(r)]
N [c] 曾祖母 [zēng zǔmǔ]

greatly ['greɪtlɪ] ADV [+ *surprised, amused,
honoured*] 非常 [fēicháng]; [*benefit, improve,*
increase, reduce +] 大大地 [dàdà de]

Greece [griːs] N 希腊 [Xīlà]

greed [griːd] N [U] 贪婪 [tānlán] ▶ **greed for
sth** 对某物贪得无厌

greedy ['griːdɪ] ADJ 贪心的 [tānxīn de] ▶ **to
be greedy for** [+ *money, power*] 贪图; [+ *affection*]
渴望

Greek [griːk] I ADJ 希腊的 [Xīlà de] II N 1 [c]
(*person*) 希腊人 [Xīlàrén] 2 [U] (*modern language*)
希腊语 [Xīlàyǔ] 3 [U] (*also*: **ancient Greek**) 古希
腊语 [gǔ Xīlàyǔ]

◎green [griːn] I ADJ 1 (*colour*) 绿色的 [lǜsè de]
2 (*inexperienced*) 缺乏经验的 [quēfá jīngyàn
de] ▷ *He was very green, straight out of college.* 他
刚毕业，没什么经验。3 (*environmental*) 环保
的 [huánbǎo de] ▷ *green activists* 环保分子 II N
1 [c/U] (*colour*) 绿色 [lǜsè] ▷ *The walls were a
bright green.* 墙是鲜绿色的。2 [c] (GOLF) 球穴
区 [qiúxuéqū] 3 [c] (*also*: **village green**) 村庄公
共绿地 [cūnzhuāng gōnggòng lǜdì] III **greens**
NPL 1 (*vegetables*) 绿叶菜 [lǜyècài] 2 (POL)
▶ **the Greens** 绿党成员 [lǜdǎng chéngyuán]
▶ **to have green fingers** *or* (US) **a green thumb**
擅长侍弄花草 ▶ **to give sb/sth the green light**
准许某人做某事/某事的发生 ▶ **to be green
with envy** 十分妒忌

green card (US) N [c] (*work permit*) 绿卡 [lùkǎ]

greenery ['griːnərɪ] N [U] 绿色植物
[lùsèzhíwù]

greengage ['griːngeɪdʒ] N [c] (*fruit*) 西洋李子
[xīyáng lǐzi]

greengrocer ['griːngrəusə(r)] (ESP BRIT)
N [c] 1 (*person*) 蔬菜水果商 [shūcài shuǐguǒ
shāng] 2 (*shop*) (*also*: **greengrocer's**) 果蔬店
[guǒshūdiàn]

greenhouse ['griːnhaus] I N [c] 暖房
[nuǎnfáng] II CPD [复合词] [+ *gas, emissions*] 温
室 [wēnshì]

greenhouse effect N ▶ **the greenhouse
effect** 温室效应 [wēnshì xiàoyìng]

Greenland ['griːnlənd] N 格陵兰岛
[Gélínglándǎo]

Greenlander ['griːnləndə(r)] N [c] 格陵兰岛
人 [Gélínglándǎorén]

green salad N [c/U] 蔬菜色拉 [shūcài sèlā]

greet [griːt] VT 1 (*welcome*) [+ *person*] 欢迎
[huānyíng] 2 (*receive*) [+ *announcement, news*] 回
应 [huíyìng]

greeting ['griːtɪŋ] N [c] (*welcome*) 问候
[wènhòu] ▶ **Christmas/birthday greetings** 圣
诞节/生日祝福 ▶ **Season's greetings** 节日
问候

greetings card, greeting card N [c] 贺
卡 [hèkǎ]

grew [gruː] PT *of* **grow**

grey, (US) **gray** [greɪ] I ADJ 1 (*colour*) 灰色的
[huīsè de]; [+ *hair*] 灰白的 [huībái de] 2 (*dull*)
[+ *weather, day*] 阴沉的 [yīnchén de] 3 (*fig*)

(faceless) 了无生趣的 [liǎowú shēngqù de] **II** **N**
[c/u] *(colour)* 灰白 [huībái] ▸ **to go grey** *[person, hair+]* 变灰白

grey-haired [greɪˈheəd] **ADJ** 灰白头发的
[huībái tóufa de]

grid [grɪd] **N 1** [c] *(pattern)* 网格状
[wǎnggézhuàng] **2** ▸ **the (National) Grid** （国
家）输电网 [(guójiā) shūdiànwǎng] **3** [c]
(cover for drain) 阴沟铁栅 [yīngōu tiězhà] **4** [c]
(diagram) 坐标方格 [zuòbiāo fānggé]

gridlock [ˈgrɪdlɒk] **I** **N** [u] **1** *(traffic jam)* 大堵
塞 [dàdǔsè] **2** *(stalemate)* 僵局 [jiāngjú] **II** **VT**
▸ **to be gridlocked** *[roads+]* 陷入交通大堵塞
[xiànrù jiāotōng dàdǔsè]; *[talks, process+]* 陷入
僵局 [xiànrù jiāngjú]

grief [griːf] **N** [u] *(distress, sorrow)* 悲痛 [bēitòng]
▸ **to come to grief** *[plan+]* 归于失败; *[person+]*
遭到不幸 ▸ **good grief!** 哎呀！

grievance [ˈgriːvəns] **N** [c/u] *(complaint)* 抱怨
[bàoyuàn]

grieve [griːv] **I** **VI** *(feel sad)* 伤心 [shāngxīn]
II **VT** *(sadden)* 使伤心 [shǐ shāngxīn] ▸ **to
grieve for sb** 因某人亡故而伤心 ▸ **to grieve
over sth** 因某事伤心

grievous [ˈgriːvəs] **ADJ** *[+ loss, mistake, blow]* 沉
痛的 [chéntòng de] ▸ **grievous bodily harm**
(LAW) 严重的人身伤害

grill [grɪl] **I** **N** [c] (BRIT) *(on cooker)* 烤架
[kǎojià] [美=**broiler**] **II** **VT 1** (BRIT) *[+ food]* 烤
[kǎo] [美=**broil**] **2** *(question)* 严厉盘问 [yánlì
pánwèn]

grille [grɪl] **N** [c] *(screen)* *(on window, counter)* 格
栅 [gézhà] ▸ **radiator grille** *(on car)* 散热器
护栅

grim [grɪm] **ADJ 1** *(unpleasant)* *[+ situation, news]*
严酷的 [yánkù de] **2** *(unattractive)* *[+ place]* 阴
森的 [yīnsēn de] **3** *(serious, stern)* *[+ person,
expression]* 令人生畏的 [lìng rén shēng wèi de]
▸ **grim reality** 严酷的现实

grime [graɪm] **N** [u] *(dirt)* 污垢 [wūgòu]

grin [grɪn] **I** **N** [c] *(smile)* 露齿的笑 [lòuchǐ de
xiào] **II** **VI** 露齿而笑 [lòuchǐ ér xiào] ▸ **to grin
and bear it** 逆来顺受

grind [graɪnd] *(pt, pp* **ground**) **I** **VT 1** *(crush)*
[+ coffee, pepper] 磨碎 [mósuì] **2** *(squash)* 碾
[niǎn] **3** (US) *[+ meat]* 绞碎 [jiǎosuì] **4** *(sharpen)*
[+ knife, blade] 磨快 [mókuài] **II** **VI** *(vehicle,
gears+]* 轰鸣着缓慢行进 [hōngmíngzhe
huǎnmàn xíngjìn] **III** **N** ▸ **the grind** *(work)* 苦
差 [kǔchāi] ▸ **to grind one's teeth** 咬牙切齿
▸ **to grind to a halt** *[vehicle+]* 嘎嘎作响地慢慢
停下; *[talks, process+]* 逐渐停滞
▸ **grind down** *(fig)* **VT** *[+ person]* 消磨…的意志
[xiāomó…de yìzhì]
▸ **grind out** **VT** *(churn out)* 费心劳力地做出
[fèixīn láolì de zuòchū]

grip [grɪp] **I** **N 1** [c] *(hold)* 紧握 [jǐnwò] **2** [s]
(control) 支配 [zhīpèi] **3** [u/s] *(of tyre, shoe)* 抓
力 [zhuālì] **II** **VT 1** *[+ object]* 紧握 [jǐnwò]
2 *[+ audience, attention]* 吸引住 [xīyǐnzhù] ▸ **to
come or get to grips with** *[+ problem, difficulty]* 认
真对付 ▸ **to lose one's grip (on)** *(fig)* 失去控制
▸ **to get a grip on** 把握住 ▸ **in the grip of** 笼
罩在…中

gripping [ˈgrɪpɪŋ] **ADJ** *[+ story, film]* 扣人心弦的
[kòurén xīnxuán de]

grisly [ˈgrɪzlɪ] **ADJ** *[+ death, murder]* 恐怖的
[kǒngbù de]

grit [grɪt] **I** **N** [u] **1** *(sand, gravel)* 沙粒 [shālì]
2 *(determination)* 勇气 [yǒngqì] **II** **VT** *[+ road]* 用
沙子覆盖 [yòng shāzi fùgài] **III** **grits** **NPL** (US:
CULIN) 粗玉米粉 [cūyùmǐfěn] ▸ **to grit one's
teeth** *(lit)* 咬紧牙；*(fig)* 咬紧牙关

groan [grəun] **I** **N** [c] *(of pain)* 呻吟 [shēnyín];
(of unhappiness) 哼声 [hēngshēng]; *(of
disappointment, disapproval)* 嘘声 [xūshēng]
II **VI 1** *(in pain)* 呻吟 [shēnyín]; *(with disapproval)*
嘟囔 [dūnang] **2** *(tree, floorboard+)* 发出嘎吱
声 [fāchū gāzhīshēng] **III** **VT** ▸ **"not again!"**
he groaned "够了！"他抱怨道 ["gòule!" tā
bàoyuàndào]

grocer [ˈgrəusə(r)] **N** [c] **1** *(person)* 食品杂货商
[shípǐn záhuòshāng] **2** *(shop)* *(also:* **grocer's**) 食
品杂货店 [shípǐn záhuòdiàn]

grocery [ˈgrəusərɪ] **I** **N** [c] *(also:* **grocery shop**)
(BRIT) *(also:* **grocery store**) (ESP US) 食品杂
货店 [shípǐn záhuòdiàn] **II** **groceries** **NPL**
(provisions) 食品杂货 [shípǐn záhuò]

groin [grɔɪn] **N** [c] 腹股沟 [fùgǔgōu]

groom [gruːm] **I** **N** [c] **1** *(for horse)* 马夫 [mǎfū]
2 *(also:* **bridegroom**) 新郎 [xīnláng] **II** **VT**
[+ horse] 给…刷毛 [gěi…shuāmáo] ▸ **to be
groomed for sth** 接受做某事的培养 ▸ **well-
groomed** *[+ person]* 服饰整洁的

groove [gruːv] **N** [c] **1** *(in record, surface)* 槽 [cáo]
2 *(rhythm)* 节奏 [jiézòu]

grope [grəup] **VI 1** ▸ **to grope for** *(lit)* *(feel for)* 摸
索 [mōsuǒ]; *(fig)* *(try to think of)* *[+ word, phrase]* 搜
寻 [sōuxún] **2** *(molest)* 性骚扰 [xìng sāorǎo]
▸ **to grope one's way through/towards sth** 摸
索着通过/走向某物

gross [grəus] **I** **ADJ 1** *(extreme)* *[+ misconduct,
indecency, negligence]* 严重的 [yánzhòng de]
2 *(horrible)* 粗俗的 [cūsú de] **3** (COMM) *[+ weight]*
毛的 [máo de]; *[+ income, profit, interest]* 总的
[zǒng de] **II** **NPL** *(twelve dozen)* 罗 [luó] **III** **VT**
(COMM) ▸ **to gross £500,000** 获得50万英镑的
总收入 [huòdé wǔshí wàn yīngbàng de zǒng
shōurù] **IV** **ADV** (COMM) 税前地 [shuìqián de]

grossly [ˈgrəuslɪ] **ADV** *(greatly)* *[+ unfair,
exaggerated, inadequate]* 十分地 [shífēn de]

grotesque [grəˈtɛsk] **ADJ 1** *(shocking)* 荒唐的
[huāngtáng de] **2** *(ugly)* 丑陋的 [chǒulòu de]

○ **ground** [graund] **I** **PT, PP** of **grind** **II** **N 1** *(floor)*
▸ **the ground** 地面 [dìmiàn] ▷ *He picked his
coat up from the ground.* 他从地上拾起大衣。

2 (earth, soil, land) ▸ **the ground** 土地 [tǔdì] ▷ The ground was very wet and soft. 土地非常潮湿松软。 ▷ a rocky piece of ground 一块多岩石的土地 **3** [c] (SPORT) 场 [chǎng] ▷ Manchester United's football ground 曼联队的足球场 **4** [c] (US: ELEC) 接地装置 [jiēdì zhuāngzhì] [英=earth] **III grounds** NPL **1** (gardens etc) 庭园 [tíngyuán] ▷ the palace grounds 宫殿庭园 **2** (reasons, basis) 理由 [lǐyóu] **3** (also: **coffee grounds**) 咖啡渣 [kāfēizhā] **IV** VT **1** [+ plane] 使停飞 [shǐ tíngfēi] **2** [+ child] 限制出门 [xiànzhì chūmén] ▷ His father grounded him for a month. 他爸爸整个月都限制他出门。 **3** (US: ELEC) 使接地 [shǐ jiēdì] [英=earth] **V** ADJ **1** [+ coffee, almonds, spice, pepper] 磨碎的 [mósuì de] **2** (US) [+ meat] 绞碎的 [jiǎosuì de] **VI** VI [ship +] 搁浅 [gēqiǎn] ▷ the rocks where the ship had grounded 船搁浅处的礁石 ▸ **on the ground** 在地面上 ▸ **the facilities on the ground** 地面设备 ▸ **below/above ground** 地下/上 ▸ **common ground** 共同点 ▸ **to gain/lose ground** (fig) 越来越有利/渐失优势 ▸ **to get off the ground** (fig) 开始进行 ▸ **to stand** or **hold one's ground** 坚持立场 ▸ **to be thin on the ground** (BRIT) 为数不多 ▸ **to break new ground** 开辟新天地 ▸ **to burn/raze sth to the ground** 把某物烧成平地/夷为平地 ▸ **to go to ground** 躲了起来 ▸ **to find the middle ground** 找到中间立场 ▸ **to prepare the ground for sth** 为某事铺平道路 ▸ **to shift** or **change one's ground** 改变立场 ▸ **it suits him down to the ground** (BRIT: inf) 这完全适合他 ▸ **grounds for** [+ optimism, hope, concern] …的原因; [+ divorce, appeal, complaint] …的理由 ▸ **grounds for doing sth** 做某事的根据 ▸ **on (the) grounds of** 以…为理由 ▸ **on the grounds that...** 以…为理由 ▸ **on medical/humanitarian grounds** 基于人道主义/健康状况 ▸ **burial/hunting ground(s)** 坟地/猎场

groundcloth ['graundklɔθ] (US) N [c] 铺地防潮布 [pūdì fángcháobù] [英=groundsheet]

ground floor N [c] 一楼 [yīlóu] [美=first floor]

grounding ['graundɪŋ] N (foundation) ▸ **a grounding in** …的基础 […de jīchǔ]

groundsheet ['graundʃi:t] (BRIT) N [c] 铺地防潮布 [pūdì fángcháobù] [美=groundcloth]

groundwork ['graundwə:k] N [U] (preparation) 基础 [jīchǔ] ▸ **to lay the groundwork for sth** 为某事打下基础

○ **group** [gru:p] **I** N [c] **1** (of people, buildings etc) 组 [zǔ] ▷ A group of experts on the case. 一组专家正在解决问题。 ▷ dinner with a small group of friends 和几个朋友吃的晚饭 **2** (organization) 团体 [tuántǐ] ▷ members of an environmental group 一个环保团体的成员 **3** (also: **pop group, rock group**) 组合 [zǔhé] **4** (COMM) (of businesses) 集团 [jítuán] **II** VT (organize, arrange) 把…分组 [bǎ...fēnzǔ] ▸ **in groups** 成组地 ▸ **age/**

income group 年龄/收入组 ▸ **newspaper/property group** 报纸/房地产集团 ▸ **group together** VI (band together) 团结起来 [tuánjié qǐlái] ▷ They encouraged the workers to group together. 他们鼓励工人们团结起来。

grouse [graus] **I** N **1** [c/u] (game bird) 松鸡 [sōngjī] **2** [c] (complaint) 牢骚 [láosāo] **II** VI (complain) 发牢骚 [fā láosāo]

grovel ['grɔvl] VI **1** (be humble) 奴颜婢膝 [nú yán bì xī] **2** (crawl about) 爬行 [páxíng] ▸ **to grovel to sb** 向某人卑躬屈膝

○ **grow** [grəu] (pt **grew**, pp **grown**) **I** VI **1** [plant, tree +] 生长 [shēngzhǎng] ▷ the oak tree growing at the end of the lane 在小巷尽头的橡树; [person, animal +] 长大 [zhǎngdà] ▷ He's grown a lot since I last saw him. 自从我上次见他，他长大了许多。; [hair, nails +] 留 [liú] **2** (increase) [amount, feeling, problem +] 扩大 [kuòdà] ▷ Their influence is steadily growing. 他们的影响在稳步扩大。; [economy, business +] 发展 [fāzhǎn] **II** VT [+ flowers, vegetables] 栽种 [zāizhòng] ▷ I'm growing leeks in my garden. 我在花园里种韭葱。; [+ beard, hair] 留 [liú] ▷ I've decided to grow my hair. 我决定留头发。 ▸ **to grow (by) 20cm** 长了20厘米 ▸ **to grow by 10%** 增长10% ▸ **to grow rich/old/impatient** 变富/变老/变得不耐烦 ▸ **grow apart** VI 变得有隔阂 [biàn de yǒu géhé] ▸ **grow into** VT FUS [不可拆分] (become) 变成 [biànchéng] ▸ **grow on** VT FUS [不可拆分] ▸ **to grow on sb** 越来越为某人喜欢 [yuèláiyuè wéi mǒurén xǐhuan] ▷ That painting is growing on me. 我越来越喜欢那幅画。 ▸ **grow out of** VT FUS [不可拆分] [+ clothes] 长得穿不下 [zhǎng de chuān bù xià]; [+ habit] 逐渐放弃 [zhújiàn fàngqì] ▷ He grew out of his late night coffee habit. 他逐渐放弃了晚上喝咖啡的习惯。 ▷ Many children suck their thumbs. Most of them grow out of it. 很多孩子嗓大拇指，但大多数大了就不会了。 ▸ **grow up** VI (be brought up) 长大 [zhǎngdà] ▷ She grew up in Japan. 她在日本长大。; (be mature) 成熟 [chéngshú] ▷ It's time you grew up. 你到了应该成熟的时候了。

grower ['grəuə(r)] N [c] ▸ **fruit/vegetable growers** 果/菜农 [guǒ/càinóng]

growing ['grəuɪŋ] ADJ **1** [+ number] 日趋增多的 [rìqū zēngduō de]; [+ concern, pressure, demand] 越来越多的 [yuèláiyuè duō de]; [+ interest, awareness] 日益增强的 [rìyì zēngqiáng de]; [+ problem, evidence] 日趋严重的 [rìqū yánzhòng de] **2** [+ child, plant] 生长中的 [shēngzhǎng zhōng de] ▸ **fast-growing** [+ business, market] 高速发展的

growl [graul] **I** VI **1** [dog, bear, lion +] 嗥叫 [háojiào] **2** [person +] 咆哮 [páoxiào] **II** VT [person +] 低吼 [dīhǒu] **III** N [c] **1** (of dog, bear, *lion*] 嗥叫 [háojiào] **2** [*of person*] 低吼 [dīhǒu]

grown [grəun] **I** PP *of* grow **II** ADJ [+ *man, woman*] 成年的 [chéngnián de]

grown-up [grəun'ʌp] **I** N [c] (*adult*) 成年人 [chéngniánrén] **II** ADJ **1** (*fully grown*) 成人的 [chéngrén de] **2** (*mature*) 成熟的 [chéngshú de]

growth [grəuθ] **I** N **1** [U/s] [*of economy, industry*] 发展 [fāzhǎn] **2** [U] [*of child, animal, plant*] 生长 [shēngzhǎng] **3** [c] (*tumour*) 肿块 [zhǒngkuài] ▶ **a growth in sth** 某方面的发展 ▶ **population/earnings/sales growth** 人口/收入/销售量的增长 **II** CPD [复合词] [+ *industry, area*] 成长型 [chéngzhǎngxíng]

grub [grʌb] N **1** [c] (*larva*) 蛴螬 [qícáo] **2** [U] (*food*) 食物 [shíwù]

grubby ['grʌbɪ] ADJ **1** (*dirty*) [+ *person, clothes*] 肮脏的 [āngzāng de] **2** (*sordid*) [+ *business, tactics*] 卑鄙的 [bēibǐ de]

grudge [grʌdʒ] (*grievance*) 积怨 [jīyuàn] ▶ **to have** or **bear a grudge (against sb)** 对(某人)怀恨在心

grudging ['grʌdʒɪŋ] ADJ [+ *respect, admiration, acceptance*] 勉强的 [miǎnqiǎng de]

gruelling, (US) **grueling** ['gruəlɪŋ] ADJ [+ *experience, activity, schedule*] 折磨人的 [zhémórén de]

gruesome ['gruːsəm] ADJ [+ *murder, discovery, details*] 令人毛骨悚然的 [lìng rén máo gǔ sǒngrán de]

grumble ['grʌmbl] **I** VI (*complain*) 抱怨 [bàoyuàn] **II** VT (*complain*) 表示不满 [biǎoshì bùmǎn] ▶ **to grumble that...** 抱怨… **III** N [c] (*complaint*) 抱怨 [bàoyuàn]

grumpy ['grʌmpɪ] ADJ 脾气坏的 [píqí huài de]

grunt [grʌnt] **I** VI (*person* +] 发哼哼声 [fā hēnghēngshēng]; [*pig, bear* +] 发出呼噜声 [fāchū hūlūshēng] **II** VT 咕哝着表示 [gūnongzhe biǎoshì] **III** N [c] [*of person*] 咕哝声 [gūnongshēng]; [*of pig, bear*] 呼噜声 [hūlūshēng]

GSOH ABBR (= *good sense of humour*) 有幽默感 [yǒu yōumògǎn]

guarantee [gærən'tiː] **I** N [c] **1** (*assurance*) 保证 [bǎozhèng] **2** (COMM) (*warranty*) 质保承诺 [zhìbǎo chéngnuò] **II** VT **1** (*promise*) [+ *success, safety, happiness*] 确保 [quèbǎo] **2** (*ensure*) 保证 [bǎozhèng] **3** (COMM) [+ *product, work*] 担保 [dānbǎo] ▶ **a/no guarantee that...** 有/没有…的保证 ▶ **to guarantee (that)...** 保证… ▶ **to guarantee to do sth** 保证做某事

guaranteed [gærən'tiːd] ADJ [+ *income, price, rate*] 有保证的 [yǒu bǎozhèng de]; [+ *success, satisfaction*] 确保的 [quèbǎo de]

guard [gɑːd] **I** N **1** [c] (*sentry*) 警卫 [jǐngwèi] **2** [U] (*squad*) 保卫队 [bǎowèiduì] **3** [c] (BRIT: RAIL) 列车员 [lièchēyuán] **4** [c] (*protective cover*) 防护装置 [fánghù zhuāngzhì] **II** VT [+ *building, entrance, door*] 守卫 [shǒuwèi]; [+ *person*] 保护

[bǎohù]; [+ *prisoner*] 看守 [kānshǒu] ▶ **to be on one's guard (against)** 提防 ▶ **to lower** or **drop one's guard** 放松警惕 ▶ **to catch sb off (their) guard** 乘某人不备 ▶ **to be on guard** 值班 ▶ **to stand guard** 站岗 ▶ **I will guard it with my life** 我将尽最大努力保护它

▶ **guard against** VT FUS [不可拆分] [+ *disease, damage*] 防止 [fángzhǐ]; [+ *complacency*] 警惕 [jǐngtì]

guarded ['gɑːdɪd] ADJ [+ *person, statement*] 谨慎的 [jǐnshèn de]; [+ *optimism*] 有保留的 [yǒu bǎoliú de] ▶ **a closely guarded secret** 一个严格保守的秘密 ▶ **the entrance was heavily guarded** 入口处戒备森严

guardian ['gɑːdɪən] N [c] **1** (LAW) [*of minor*] 监护人 [jiānhùrén] **2** (*defender*) 保护者 [bǎohùzhě]

Guatemala [gwɑːtɪ'mɑːlə] N 危地马拉 [Wēidìmǎlā]

Guatemalan [gwɑːtɪ'mɑːlən] **I** ADJ 危地马拉的 [Wēidìmǎlā de] **II** N [c] 危地马拉人 [Wēidìmǎlārén]

guerrilla [gə'rɪlə] **I** N [c] 游击队员 [yóujī duìyuán] **II** CPD [复合词] [+ *group, war*] 游击队 [yóujīduì]

guess [gɛs] **I** VT, VI **1** (*conjecture*) 猜测 [cāicè] **2** (*work out*) 推测 [tuīcè] **II** N [c] 猜测 [cāicè] ▶ **I guess so** 我想是吧 ▶ **to guess (that)...** (*conjecture*) 猜测…; (*work out*) 推测…; (*suppose*) 想… ▶ **to keep sb guessing** 让某人捉摸不定 ▶ **guess what** 猜猜到 ▶ **guess what I did last night** 猜猜我昨晚干什么了 ▶ **you're right, I guess** 我想你是对的 ▶ **my guess is (that)...** 我的猜测是… ▶ **to take** or **have** or **make a guess** 猜猜看 ▶ **I'll give you three guesses** 我让你猜3次 ▶ **why it happened is anyone's** or **anybody's guess** 没人拿得准究竟是怎么回事 ▶ **best guess** 最佳猜测

▶ **guess at** VT FUS [不可拆分] (*estimate*) 估计 [gūjì]

guesswork ['gɛswəːk] N [U] (*speculation*) 猜测 [cāicè] ▶ **to take the guesswork out of sth** 排除某事中的不定因素

guest [gɛst] **I** N [c] (*at home*) 客人 [kèrén]; (*on TV, radio show*) 特邀嘉宾 [tèyāo jiābīn]; (*at special event*) 宾客 [bīnkè]; (*in hotel*) 房客 [fángkè] **II** VI 作特邀嘉宾 [zuò tèyāo jiābīn] ▶ **be my guest** 请便 **III** CPD [复合词] [+ *speaker, appearance*] 特邀 [tèyāo]

guest house ['gɛsthaus] (BRIT) N [c] 招待所 [zhāodàisuǒ]

guest room N [c] 客房 [kèfáng]

guidance ['gaɪdəns] N [U] (*advice*) 指导 [zhǐdǎo] ▶ **guidance on (doing) sth** (做)某事的指导

guide [gaɪd] **I** N [c] **1** (*tour guide*) 导游 [dǎoyóu] **2** (*local guide*) 向导 [xiàngdǎo] **3** (*also:* **guide book**) 指南 [zhǐnán] **4** ▶ **Guide** (BRIT) (*group member*) 女童子军成员 [Nǚ Tóngzǐjūn

Chéngyuán] **II Guides** NPL (BRIT) (youth group)
女童子军 [Nǚ Tóngzǐjūn] ［美=**Girl Scouts**］
III VT **1** (round city, museum etc) 给…导游
[gěi…dǎoyóu] **2** (lead) 给…领路 [gěi…lǐnglù]
3 (with advice) ▶ **to guide sb through sth** 指
引某人做某事 [zhǐyǐn mǒurén zuò mǒushì]
4 (influence) [conscience, principles +] 指引 [zhǐyǐn]
5 (direct) 引导 [yǐndǎo]

⊙ GUIDES

⊙ **Guides** （女童子军）是英国的 **Girl Guides**
⊙ 或美国的 **Girl Scouts** 的成员，年龄一般
⊙ 在10到15岁之间（美国为10到14岁之间）。
⊙ 她们分成小组活动，培养实践能力和提
⊙ 高独立性。她们帮助社区其他成员，保护
⊙ 环境并了解不同的文化。活动主要围绕运
⊙ 动、户外技能、急救和看护动物等展开。

guidebook ['gaɪdbʊk] N [C] 旅游指南 [lǚyóu
zhǐnán]
guided tour ['gaɪdɪd-] N [C] 有导游的游览
[yǒu dǎoyóu de yóulǎn]
guide dog (BRIT) N [C] 导盲犬 [dǎomángquǎn]
［美=**seeing-eye dog**］
guidelines ['gaɪdlaɪnz] NPL 指导方针 [zhǐdǎo
fāngzhēn]
guild [gɪld] N [C] (association) 协会 [xiéhuì]
guilt [gɪlt] N [U] **1** (remorse) 内疚 [nèijiù]
2 (responsibility) 有罪 [yǒu zuì]
guilty ['gɪltɪ] ADJ **1** (remorseful) [+ person, feelings]
内疚的 [nèijiù de] **2** [+ expression, smile] 心虚
的 [xīnxū de]; [+ secret, conscience] 自知有过错
的 [zìzhī yǒu guòcuò de] **3** (responsible) 有过
失的 [yǒu guòshī de] **4** (LAW) 有罪的 [yǒuzuì
de] ▶ **guilty of murder/manslaughter** 谋
杀/误杀罪
Guinea ['gɪnɪ] N ▶ **Republic of Guinea** 几内
亚 [Jǐnèiyà]
guinea pig ['gɪnɪ-] N **1** (animal) 豚鼠 [túnshǔ]
2 (person) 实验品 [shíyànpǐn]
guise [gaɪz] N ▶ **in** or **under the guise of** 在…的
幌子下 [zài…de huǎngzi xià] ▶ **in a different
guise** 在不同的伪装下
guitar [gɪ'tɑː(r)] N [C] 吉他 [jítā]
gulf [gʌlf] N **1** [C] (bay) 海湾 [hǎiwān] **2** [C]
(difference) 鸿沟 [hónggōu] **3** ▶ **the Gulf** 海湾地
区 [Hǎiwān Dìqū] **II** CPD [复合词] ▶ **Gulf** [+ war,
crisis] 海湾 [Hǎiwān]
gull [gʌl] N [C] (seagull) 海鸥 [hǎiōu]
gullible ['gʌlɪbl] ADJ 易上当的 [yì shàngdàng
de]
gully ['gʌlɪ] N [C] (ravine) 隘谷 [àigǔ]
gulp [gʌlp] **I** VT (also: **gulp down**) [+ food] 狼吞
虎咽地吞下 [láng tūn hǔ yàn de tūnxià]; [+ drink]
大口地饮 [dàkǒu de yǐn] **II** VI (from nerves,
excitement) 哽住 [gěngzhù] **III** N [C] (of air) 一
大口 [yī dà kǒu]; (of drink, food) 吞咽 [tūnyàn]

▶ **to swallow sth in one gulp** (food) 将某物一口
吞下; (drink) 将某物一饮而尽
gum [gʌm] N [C] (ANAT) 牙床 [yáchuáng]
2 [U] (glue) 胶 [jiāo] **3** [U] (also: **chewing gum/
bubblegum**) 口香糖 [kǒuxiāngtáng] **4** [C] (also:
gumdrop) (sweet) 胶姆糖 [jiāomǔtáng]
▶ **gum up** VT 使出毛病 [shǐ chū máobìng]
gun [gʌn] N [C] (small, medium-sized) 枪 [qiāng];
(large) 炮 [pào] ▶ **to stick to one's guns** 固执
己见
▶ **gun down** VT 枪杀 [qiāngshā]
▶ **gun for** VT FUS [不可拆分] 伺机攻击 [sìjī
gōngjī]
gunfire ['gʌnfaɪə(r)] N [U] 炮火 [pàohuǒ]
gunman ['gʌnmən] (pl **gunmen**) N 持枪歹
徒 [chíqiāng dǎitú]
gunpoint ['gʌnpɔɪnt] N ▶ **at gunpoint** 在枪口
威胁下 [zài qiāngkǒu wēixié xià]
gunpowder ['gʌnpaʊdə(r)] N [U] 火药
[huǒyào]
gunshot ['gʌnʃɔt] **I** N [C] (act, sound) 射击
[shèjī] **II** CPD [复合词] [+ wound] 枪击 [qiāngjī]
gurney ['gəːnɪ] (US) N [C] 有轮子的病床 [yǒu
lúnzi de bìngchuáng] ［英=**trolley**］
gush [gʌʃ] **I** VI **1** [blood, water, oil +] 喷出
[pēnchū] **2** [person +] 表现过火 [biǎoxiàn
guòhuǒ] **II** N [S] [of water] 涌流 [yǒngliú]
gust [gʌst] **I** N [C] [of wind] 一阵 [yī zhèn] **II** VI
[wind +] 狂风大作 [kuángfēng dàzuò]
gut [gʌt] **I** N **1** [C] (intestine) 肠子 [chángzi]
2 [U] (MUS, SPORT) (also: **catgut**) 羊肠
线 [yángchángxiàn] **3** [C] (pot belly) 肚子
[dùzi] **II** VT **1** [+ animal, fish] 取出…的内脏
[qǔchū…de nèizàng] **2** [+ building] 损毁…的内
部 [sǔnhuǐ…de nèibù] **III** guts NPL **1** (ANAT)
[of person, animal] 内脏 [nèizàng] **2** (courage) 勇
气 [yǒngqì] ▶ **to hate sb's guts** 对某人恨之入
骨 **IV** CPD [复合词] [+ feeling, reaction, instinct]
直觉 [zhíjué]
gutter ['gʌtə(r)] N [C] **1** (in street) 阴沟 [yīngōu]
2 (of roof) 檐槽 [yáncáo] ▶ **to end up in the
gutter** 最终落得一无所有 [zuìzhōng luò dé yī
wú suǒ yǒu]
guy [gaɪ] N [C] **1** (man) 家伙 [jiāhuo] **2** (BRIT)
(effigy) 盖·福克斯肖像 [gài fúkèsī xiàng] **3** (also:
guy rope) 支索 [zhīsuǒ] ▶ **(you) guys** 伙计们
Guy Fawkes Night [gaɪ'fɔːks-] (BRIT) N [U]
篝火之夜

⊙ GUY FAWKES NIGHT

⊙ 每年的11月5日，是英国人纪念揭穿
⊙ 盖·福克斯（**Guy Fawkes**）**Gunpowder
Plot**（火药阴谋）的日子－1605年11月
⊙ 5日，盖·福克斯企图引爆英国国会两
⊙ 院。孩子们用旧衣服做成盖·福克斯的
⊙ 头像（称为 **guys**），并向过路人要钱，用
⊙ 以在 **Guy Fawkes Night** 购买烟花。这个

节日也被叫做 **Bonfire Night**，人们在公园和花园里点燃篝火，并在篝火上焚烧盖·福克斯的头像。

Guyana [gaɪ'ænə] N 圭亚那 [Guīyànà]

guzzle ['gʌzl] VT [+ *drink*] 狂饮 [kuángyǐn]; [+ *food*] 大吃 [dàchī]

gym [dʒɪm] N **1** [c] (*also:* **gymnasium**) 健身房 [jiànshēnfáng] **2** [U] (*also:* **gymnastics**) 体操 [tǐcāo]

gymnast ['dʒɪmnæst] N [c] 体操运动员 [tǐcāo yùndòngyuán]

gymnastics [dʒɪm'næstɪks] N [U] 体操 [tǐcāo]

gym shoes NPL 体操鞋 [tǐcāoxié]

gynaecologist, (US) **gynecologist** [gaɪnɪ'kɔlədʒɪst] N [c] 妇科医生 [fùkē yīshēng]

gypsy ['dʒɪpsɪ] N [c] 吉卜赛人 [Jípǔsàirén]

H, h [eɪtʃ] N [C/U] (letter) 英语的第八个字母

habit ['hæbɪt] N 1 [C/U] (custom, practice) 习惯 [xíguàn] 2 [C] (also: **drug habit**) 瘾 [yǐn] 3 [C] (REL) (costume) 宗袍 [zōngpáo] ▶ to be in the habit of doing sth 有做某事的习惯 ▶ to have a habit of doing sth 习惯做某事 ▶ to get out of/into the habit of doing sth 改掉/养成做某事的习惯 ▶ to do sth out of habit 出于习惯做某事 ▶ don't make a habit of it 别经常这么做 ▶ a bad habit 坏习惯

habitat ['hæbɪtæt] N [C/U] 栖息地 [qīxīdì]

habitual [hə'bɪtjuəl] ADJ 1 [+ action] 通常的 [tōngcháng de] 2 [+ drinker, criminal, liar] 积习已深的 [jīxí yǐshēn de]

habitually [hə'bɪtjuəlɪ] ADV [+ late, untidy etc] 习惯性地 [xíguànxìng de]

hack [hæk] I VT, VI 砍 [kǎn] II N [C] (pej) (writer) 雇佣文人 [gùyōng wénrén] 3 [C] ▶ to hack (away) at sth with a knife 用刀乱砍某物 ▶ to hack (one's way/a path) through the jungle 从丛林中开出条路来 ▶ to hack sb to death 乱刀砍死某人 ▶ to hack sb/sth to pieces 把某人/某物砍碎 ▶ he can't hack it as a singer (inf) 他没本事做歌手
▶ **hack into** VT FUS [不可拆分] [+ computer system] 窃入 [qièrù]
▶ **hack off** VT 砍下 [kǎnxià]

hacker ['hækə(r)] (COMPUT) N [C] 黑客 [hēikè]

had [hæd] PT, PP of **have**

haddock ['hædək] N [C/U] (pl **haddock**) 黑线鳕 [hēixiànxuě] ▶ **smoked haddock** 熏鳕鱼

hadn't ['hædnt] = **had not**

haemorrhage, (US) **hemorrhage** ['hemərɪdʒ] I N [C/U] 出血 [chūxiě] II VI 出血 [chūxiě] ▶ to have a brain haemorrhage 大脑内出血

haemorrhoids, (US) **hemorrhoids** ['hemərɔɪdz] NPL 痔疮 [zhìchuāng]

haggle ['hægl] VI 1 (bargain) 讨价还价 [tǎojià huánjià] 2 (argue) 争论 [zhēnglùn] ▶ to haggle over the price of sth 就某物讨价还价

hail [heɪl] I N [U] 冰雹 [bīngbáo] II VT [+ taxi] 招手叫停 [zhāoshǒu jiàotíng]; (liter) [+ person] 招呼 [zhāohu] III VI 下雹 [xiàbáo] ▶ he died in a hail of bullets 他死于一阵弹雨 ▶ the meeting was hailed as a triumph 会议被认为是一大成功 ▶ he hails from Scotland 他来自苏格兰

hailstone ['heɪlstəun] N [C] 冰雹 [bīngbáo]

hair [heə(r)] N 1 (human) [U] (on head) 头发 [tóufa]; [U] (on body) 汗毛 [hànmáo]; [C] (single strand) 毛发 [máofà] 2 [C/U] (animal) (on body, single strand) 毛毛 [máomao] 3 [C] (on plants and insects) 绒毛 [róngmáo] ▶ to do one's hair 梳头 ▶ to have or get one's hair done (styled) 打理头发 ▶ to have or get one's hair cut 剪头发 ▶ by a hair's breadth (fig) 极端的距离 ▶ to let one's hair down (fig) 放松一点 ▶ to make sb's hair stand on end (fig) 使某人毛骨悚然 ▶ not a hair out of place 衣着一丝不乱 ▶ he didn't turn a hair (inf) 泰然处之 ▶ to get in sb's hair 惹恼某人

hairbrush ['heəbrʌʃ] N [C] 发刷 [fàshuā]

haircut ['heəkʌt] N [C] 1 (at hairdresser's etc) 理发 [lǐfà] 2 (hairstyle) 发型 [fàxíng] ▶ to have or get a haircut 剪头发

hairdo ['heəduː] (inf) N [C] 发型 [fàxíng]

hairdresser ['heədresə(r)] N [C] 1 (person) 美发师 [měifàshī] 2 (also: **hairdresser's**) 发廊 [fàláng]

hairdryer ['heədraɪə(r)] N [C] 吹风机 [chuīfēngjī]

hair gel N [U] 发胶 [fàjiāo]

hairspray ['heəspreɪ] N [U] 喷发定型剂 [pēnfà dìngxíngjì]

hairstyle ['heəstaɪl] N [C] 发型 [fàxíng]

hairy ['heərɪ] ADJ 1 [+ person, arms, animal] 多毛的 [duōmáo de] 2 [+ leaf, stem] 毛茸茸的 [máoróngróng de] 3 (inf) [+ situation] 惊险的 [jīngxiǎn de]

Haiti ['heɪtɪ] N 海地 [Hǎidì]

hake [heɪk] (pl **hake**) N [C/U] 狗鳕 [gǒuxuě]

○half [hɑːf] (pl **halves**) I N, PRON [C] 1 [of amount, object] 一半 [yībàn] ▷ Just give me half (of) that, please. 请给我一半。 ▷ We ate half (of) the cake. 我们吃了蛋糕的一半。 ▷ The bridge was re-built in two halves. 桥是分开两半重建的。 2 (BRIT) [of beer etc] 半品脱 [bàn pǐntuō] ▷ a half of lager

半品脱贮藏啤酒 **3** (BRIT) (*child's ticket*) 半票 [bànpiào] ▷ *A half to Oxford Street, please.* 请给 一张到牛津街的半价票。 **II** ADJ [*+ bottle*] 一半 的 [yíbàn de] ▷ *a half bottle of wine* 半瓶葡萄酒 **III** ADV (*inf*) [*+ empty, closed, open, asleep*] 半 [bàn] ▷ *By the end of his speech the room was half empty.* 他讲完话时，人已走了一半了。 ▶ **the two halves of the brain** 左右脑 ▶ **the first/second half** (SPORT) 上/下半场 ▶ **to cut sth in half** 把某物切成两半 ▶ **two/three** *etc* **and a half** 二/三{等}点五 ▶ **half a pound/kilo/mile** *etc* 半磅/公斤/英里{等} ▶ **half a pint** 半品脱 ▶ **a day/week/pound** *etc* **and a half** 一天/星 期/磅{等}半 ▶ **half an hour** 半小时 ▶ **half past three/four** *etc* 三/四 {等}点半 ▶ **half three/four** *etc* (BRIT: *inf*) 三/四{等}点半 ▶ **he was drunk half the time** (*inf*) 他大部分时候都是喝醉的 ▶ **to be half German/Irish** *etc* 有一半德国/爱尔兰{等}血 统的 ▶ **half as much (as)** …的一半 ▶ **to go halves (with sb on sth)** (与某人)平摊(某物的 费用) ▶ **she never does things by halves** 她做 事总是很彻底的 ▶ **she's half his age** 她的年 龄是他的一半 ▶ **he's too clever by half!** 他聪 明过头了!

half board (ESP BRIT) N [U] 半膳宿 [bàn shànsù]

half-brother ['haːfbrʌðə(r)] N [c] (*same mother, different father*) 同母异父的兄弟 [tóngmǔ yìfù de xiōngdì]; (*same father, different mother*) 同父 异母的兄弟 [tóngfù yìmǔ de xiōngdì]

half day N [c] 半日 [bànrì]

half fare N [c] (*on bus, train etc*) 半票 [bànpiào]

half-hearted ['haːf'haːtɪd] ADJ [*+ attempt, apology*] 心不在焉的 [xīn bù zài yān de]

half-hour [haːf'auə(r)] **I** N [c] 半小时 [bàn xiǎoshí] **II** CPD [复合词] [*+ programme, film, drive*] 半小时 [bàn xiǎoshí]

half price ['haːf'praɪs] **I** ADJ 半价的 [bànjià de] **II** ADV 半价地 [bànjià de] **III** N [U] ▶ **we sold them at half price** 我们把它们半价卖了 [wǒmen bǎ tāmen bànjià mài le] ▶ **we got it for half price** 我们半价买的

half-sister ['haːf'sɪstə(r)] N [c] (*same mother, different father*) 同母异父的姐妹 [tóngmǔ yìfù de jiěmèi]; (*same father, different mother*) 同父异 母的姐妹 [tóngfù yìmǔ de jiěmèi]

half-term [haːf'təːm] (BRIT: SCOL) N [c/U] 期 中假 [qīzhōng jià] ▶ **at half-term** 期中假时

half-time [haːf'taɪm] (SPORT) N [U] 半场 [bànchǎng] ▶ **at half-time** 半场时

halfway ['haːf'weɪ] ADV (*between two points*) 到 一半 [dào yíbàn] ▶ **to meet sb halfway** (*fig*) 和 某人折中妥协 ▶ **halfway through sth** 在某事 过了一半时 ▶ **the halfway point** *or* **stage of a race** 比赛中点时

halibut ['hælɪbət] (*pl* **halibut**) N [c/U] 大比目 鱼 [dà bǐmùyú]

hall [hɔːl] N **1** [c] (ESP BRIT) (*entrance*) 门厅 [méntīng] [美= **entrance hall**] **2** [c] (*room*) 礼 堂 [lǐtáng] **3** (UNIV) ▶ **to live in hall** (BRIT), **to live in a hall** (US) 住宿舍 [zhù sùshè]

hallmark ['hɔːlmɑːk] N [c] **1** (*on metal*) 纯度 印记 [chúndù yìnjì] **2** [*of writer, artist, style*] 特 征 [tèzhēng]

hallo [hə'ləu] INT = **hello**

hall of residence (BRIT) (*pl* **halls of residence**) N [c] 宿舍 [sùshè]

Halloween ['hæləu'iːn] N [U] 万圣节 [Wànshèng Jié]

○ **HALLOWEEN**

很早以前，人们相信在 **Halloween** (10月 31日万圣节)的夜晚，死人的灵魂会重返 人间。如今，万圣节为孩子们装扮成巫婆 和鬼魂提供了一个好机会。孩子们去敲 邻居的门，问邻居是要给 **treat** 还是要 **trick**。如果没有糖果或钱 (即 **treat**)， 孩子们就会威胁要玩把戏 (即 **trick**) 来 捉弄你。

hallucination [həluːsɪ'neɪʃən] N [c/U] 幻觉 [huànjué]

hallway ['hɔːlweɪ] (BRIT) N [c] (*vestibule*) 门厅 [méntīng]

halo ['heɪləu] N [c] [*of saint, angel*] 光轮 [guānglún]; (*around object, planet*) 晕 [yùn]

halt [hɔːlt] **I** VT [*+ person, vehicle, movement*] 使 停止 [shǐ tíngzhǐ]; [*+ progress, activity, growth*] 阻 止 [zǔzhǐ] **II** VI [*person, vehicle +*] 停止 [tíngzhǐ]; [*progress, activity, growth +*] 阻止 [zǔzhǐ] ▶ **to call a halt to sth** 命令停止 ▶ **to come to a halt** 停 了下来 ▶ **to bring sth to a halt** 制止某事

halve [haːv] **I** VT **1** (*reduce*) 将…减半 [jiāng…jiǎnbàn] **2** (*divide in two*) 将…分成两 半 [jiāng…fēnchéng liǎngbàn] **II** VI (*decrease by half*) 减半 [jiǎnbàn]

halves [haːvz] PL *of* **half**

ham [hæm] **I** N **1** (*meat, joint*) 火腿 [huǒtuǐ] **2** (*inf*) (*actor*) 蹩脚演员 [biéjiǎo yǎnyuán] **II** CPD [复合词] [*+ sandwich, roll, salad*] 火腿 [huǒtuǐ]

hamburger ['hæmbəːgə(r)] N [c] 汉堡包 [hànbǎobāo]

hamlet ['hæmlɪt] N [c] 小村庄 [xiǎo cūnzhuāng]

hammer ['hæmə(r)] **I** N [c] (*tool*) 锤子 [chuízi] **II** VT **1** [*+ nail*] 锤击 [chuíjī] **2** (ESP BRIT: *inf*) (*attack*) 严厉批评 [yánlì pīpíng] **3** (BRIT: *inf*) (*beat*) 击败 [jībài] **III** VI (*on door, table, surface*) 接连捶打 [jiēlián chuídǎ] ▶ **to hammer an idea into sb** *or* **across to sb** 反复地向某人灌输一个 观点 ▶ **to hammer away at sth** [*+ subject, theme*] 不断地致力于某事

▶ **hammer in** VT [*+ nail*] 锤击 [chuíjī]

▶ **hammer out** VT (fig) [+ solution, agreement] 推敲出 [tuīqiāo chū]

hammock ['hæmək] N [C] 吊床 [diàochuáng]

hamper ['hæmpə(r)] I VT [+ person, movement, effort] 阻碍 [zǔ'ài] II N [C] 食品篮 [shípǐn lán]

hamster ['hæmstə(r)] N [C] 仓鼠 [cāngshǔ]

hamstring ['hæmstrɪŋ] I N [C] 腱 [jiàn] II VT [+ person, development] 使受挫 [shǐ shòucuò]

⊙ **hand** [hænd] I N 1 [C] (ANAT) 手 [shǒu] 2 [C] (of clock) 指针 [zhǐzhēn] 3 [C] (worker) 工人 [gōngrén] 4 [U] (liter) (handwriting) 手迹 [shǒujì] ▷ The manuscripts were written in Bach's own hand. 这些手稿是巴赫本人的手迹。5 [C] (of cards) 一手牌 [yīshǒu pái] 6 [C] (measurement) 一手之宽 [yīshǒu zhī kuān] II VT (pass, give) 递 [dì] ▷ He handed me a piece of paper. 他递给我一张纸。▶ **to do sth by hand** 手工制作 ▶ **"hands off!"** "别碰!" ▶ **in sb's hands** 在某人照管下 ▶ **to be in safe hands/the wrong hands** 在可靠/不可靠的人手中 ▶ **to get or lay one's hands on sth** (inf) 找到某物 ▶ **to join hands** 手拉手 ▶ **hand in hand** (holding hands) 手拉手 ▶ **to go hand in hand (with sth)** (和某事)密切关联地 ▶ **to have one's hands full (with sth)** 手头忙于(某事) ▶ **to give or lend sb a hand (with sth)** 帮某人(做某事) ▶ **to have a hand in sth** 参与某事 ▶ **to be (near or close) at hand** 在附近 ▶ Hughes finished with 15 seconds in hand (BRIT) 休斯完成时还剩下15秒 ▶ **the job in hand** 我们手工的工作 ▶ **we have the matter in hand** 我们控制了局势 ▶ **to be on hand** [person, services etc +] 在近处 ▶ **to reject/dismiss sth out of hand** 不假思索地拒绝/抛弃某事 ▶ **to have sth to hand** [+ information etc] 手头有某物 ▶ **on the one hand..., on the other hand...** 一方面···,另一方面···

▶ **hand around** VT (distribute) 传递 [chuándì]
▶ **hand down** VT [+ knowledge, possessions] 传下去 [chuán xiàqù]
▶ **hand in** VT 上交 [shàngjiāo]
▶ **hand out** VT 分配 [fēnpèi]
▶ **hand over** VT [+ object, present, letter] 交给 [jiāogěi]; [+ prisoner, hostage] 移交 [yíjiāo]
▶ **hand over to** VT 移交 [yíjiāo]
▶ **hand round** (BRIT) VT = **hand around**

handbag ['hændbæg] (BRIT) N [C] 手包 [shǒubāo] [美= **purse**]

hand baggage N [U] 手提行李 [shǒutí xínglǐ]

handbook ['hændbuk] N [C] 手册 [shǒucè]

handbrake ['hændbreɪk] (ESP BRIT) N [C] 手闸 [shǒuzhá] [美= **emergency brake**]

handcuffs ['hændkʌfs] NPL 手铐 [shǒukào] ▶ **in handcuffs** 带手铐

handful ['hændful] N [C] (of soil, stones, sand) 一把 [yībǎ] ▶ **a handful of** [+ people, places etc] 少数 ▶ **she's quite a handful** (inf) 她真难管

handicap ['hændɪkæp] I N [C] 1 (disability) 残疾 [cánjí] 2 (disadvantage) 不利条件 [bùlì tiáojiàn] 3 (GOLF) 差点 [chàdiǎn] II VT (hamper) 妨碍 [fáng'ài]

handicapped ['hændɪkæpt] ADJ 有残疾的 [yǒu cánjí de] ▶ **mentally/physically handicapped** 心理/身体残疾的

handkerchief ['hæŋkətʃɪf] N [C] 手帕 [shǒupà]

handle ['hændl] I N [C] (of bag) 提手 [bǎshǒu]; [of cup, knife, paintbrush, broom, spade] 柄 [bǐng]; [of door, window] 拉手 [lāshǒu] II VT 1 [+ object, ornament] 拿 [ná]; [+ baby] 抱 [bào] 2 (operate) [+ gun, car] 操纵 [cāozòng] 3 (deal with) [+ problem, job, responsibility] 处理 [chǔlǐ]; [+ people] 对付 [duìfu] III VI (perform) 操作 [cāozuò] ▶ **to fly off the handle** (inf) 勃然大怒 ▶ **to get a handle on a problem** (inf) 控制某个问题 ▶ **"handle with care"** "小心轻放"

handlebars ['hændlbɑː(z)] NPL 把手 [bǎshǒu]

hand luggage N [U] 手提行李 [shǒutí xínglǐ]

handmade ['hænd'meɪd] ADJ 手工制作的 [shǒugōng zhìzuò de]

handout ['hændaut] N [C] (money, clothing, food etc) 接济物 [jiējìwù]; (notes) (at lecture, meeting etc) 讲义 [jiǎngyì]; (publicity leaflet) 传单 [chuándān]

hands-free kit ['hændz'friː-] N [C] 手机车载免提套件 [shǒujī chēzài miǎntí tàojiàn]

handsome ['hænsəm] ADJ 1 (attractive) [+ man] 英俊的 [yīngjùn de]; [+ woman] 健美的 [jiànměi de]; [+ building] 堂皇的 [tánghuáng de] 2 (good) [+ profit, return] 可观的 [kěguān de] ▷ They made a handsome profit on the sale of the flat. 他们从卖房中获得可观的利润。; [+ victory] 出色的 [chūsè de]

handwriting ['hændraɪtɪŋ] N [U] 笔迹 [bǐjì]

handy ['hændɪ] ADJ 1 (useful) 方便的 [fāngbiàn de] 2 (close at hand) 手边的 [shǒubiān de] 3 ▶ **to be handy with sth** 巧于某事 [qiǎoyú mǒushì] ▶ **to come in handy** 迟早有用 ▶ **to be handy for doing sth** 对做某事有用

hang [hæŋ] (pt, pp **hung**) I VT 1 [+ clothes, light, picture] 挂 [guà] 2 (execute) [+ criminal] (pt, pp **hanged**) 吊死 [diàosǐ] II VI 1 (be suspended) [clothes, light, picture +] 悬挂 [xuánguà]; [breath, smoke, smell +] 飘浮 [piāofú] 2 (fall) [clothing, fabric, hair +] 垂 [chuí] ▶ **to hang one's head (in shame)** (羞愧得)低下头 ▶ **the walls are hung with old pictures** 墙上挂着旧画 ▶ **to hang loose** [hair +] 披散; [arms +] 轻松下垂 ▶ **to hang open** [door, mouth +] 开着 III N ▶ **to get the hang of sth** (inf) 掌握某事的方法 [zhǎngwò mǒushì de fāngfǎ]

▶ **hang about** VI = **hang around**
▶ **hang around** (inf) I VI 闲荡 [xiándàng] II VT FUS [不可拆分] 闲荡 [xiándàng]
▶ **hang back** VI (hesitate) 踌躇不前 [chóuchú bùqián]
▶ **hang down** VI 吊下来 [diào xiàlái]

▶ **hang on I** VI (wait) 稍等 [shāoděng] **II** VT FUS [不可拆分] (depend on) 有赖于 [yǒulài yú]

▶ **hang onto, hang on to** VT FUS [不可拆分] **1** (grasp) 紧紧抓住 [jǐnjǐn zhuāzhù] **2** (inf) (fig) (keep) 保留 [bǎoliú]

▶ **hang out I** VT [+ washing] 晾 [liàng] **II** VI **1** [washing +] 晾 [liàng] **2** (inf) (go) 闲荡 [xiándàng]

▶ **hang round** (BRIT) VI = **hang around**

▶ **hang together** VI [argument, story +] 一致 [yīzhì]

▶ **hang up I** VI (TEL) 挂断电话 [guàduàn diànhuà] **II** VT [+ coat, hat, clothes] 挂起 [guàqǐ]

▶ **hang up on** VT FUS [不可拆分] (TEL) 挂断···电话 [guàduàn···diànhuà]

hanger ['hæŋə(r)] N [c] (also: **coat hanger**) 衣架 [yījià]

hang-gliding ['hæŋɡlaɪdɪŋ] N [U] 悬挂式滑翔运动 [xuánguàshì huáxiáng yùndòng] ▶ **to go hang-gliding** 做悬挂式滑翔运动

hangover ['hæŋəʊvə(r)] N [c] (after drinking) 宿醉 [sùzuì] ▶ **a hangover from the past** 遗留物

hankie ['hæŋkɪ] (inf) N = **hanky**

hanky ['hæŋkɪ] (inf) N 手帕 [shǒupà]

haphazard [hæp'hæzəd] ADJ [+ system, arrangement] 杂乱的 [záluàn de]

◐ **happen** ['hæpən] VI (occur, result) [incident, accident +] 发生 [fāshēng] ▷ What's happening? 发生什么事? ▶ **what will happen if...?** 如果···会怎么样? ▶ **tell me what happened** 告诉我发生了什么事 ▶ **to happen to do sth** 刚巧做某事 ▶ **as it happens** 碰巧 ▶ **it's the best thing that ever happened to me** 我从未遇上这么好的事情

▶ **happen (up)on** VT FUS [不可拆分] 偶然发现 [ǒurán fāxiàn]

happily ['hæpɪlɪ] ADV **1** (fortunately) 幸运地 [xìngyùn de] **2** (cheerfully) 愉快地 [yúkuài de] ▶ **happily married** 婚姻幸福 ▶ **I will happily do it for you** 我很高兴帮你做这件事 ▶ **and they all lived happily ever after** 他们永远幸福地生活下去

happiness ['hæpɪnɪs] N [U] 幸福 [xìngfú]

happy ['hæpɪ] ADJ **1** (contented) [+ person, mood] 高兴的 [gāoxìng de]; [+ face] 愉快的 [yúkuài de] ▷ I was happy to hear that you passed your exams. 非常高兴听到你考试通过了。 **2** (cheerful) [+ life, childhood, marriage, place] 美满的 [měimǎn de] **3** (fortunate) [+ coincidence] 幸运的 [xìngyùn de] ▶ **to be happy with sth** (satisfied) 对某事满意 ▶ **to be happy to do sth** (willing) 乐意做某事 ▶ **to be happy for sb to do sth** 乐意让某人做某事 ▶ **to be happy for sb** (delighted) 为某人高兴 ▶ **to have a happy ending** [story +] 有个美满的结局; [incident +] 有个圆满的结局 ▶ **happy birthday!** 生日快乐! ▶ **happy Christmas!** 圣诞快乐! ▶ **happy Easter!** 复活节快乐! ▶ **happy anniversary!** 周年纪念日快乐!

harass ['hærəs] VT (annoy, pester) 骚扰 [sāorǎo]

harassment ['hærəsmənt] N [U] 骚扰 [sāorǎo] ▶ **sexual harassment** 性骚扰

harbour, (US) **harbor** ['hɑːbə(r)] **I** N [c] (NAUT) 港口 [gǎngkǒu] **II** VT **1** [+ hope, fear] 心怀 [xīnhuái] **2** [+ criminal, fugitive] 藏匿 [cángnì] ▶ **to harbour a grudge against sb** 对某人心怀怨恨

◐ **hard** [hɑːd] **I** ADJ **1** (not soft) [+ surface, object] 硬的 [yìng de] ▷ the hard wooden floor 硬木地板 **2** (not easy) [+ question, problem] 困难的 [kùnnan de] ▷ That is a very hard question to answer. 那个问题很难回答。; [+ work] 费力的 [fèilì de] ▷ Their work is hard and dangerous. 他们的工作既费力又危险。; [+ life, time] 艰辛的 [jiānxīn de] ▷ He's had a very hard life. 他的生活很艰难。 **3** (violent) [+ push, punch, kick] 用力的 [yònglì de] **4** (severe) [+ person, expression] 苛刻的 [kēkè de] **5** (CHEM) [+ water] 硬的 [yìng de] **6** (cold) [+ winter, frost] 寒冷的 [hánlěng de] **II** ADV **1** [work, try, think +] 努力地 [nǔlì de] ▷ I've been working hard all day. 我已努力地工作了一整天。 **2** [laugh, rain, snow +] 猛烈地 [měngliè de] ▷ I've never seen Terry laugh so hard. 我从没见过特里笑得那么么厉害。 ▷ The wind is blowing hard. 风猛烈地刮着。 **3** (violently) [hit, punch, kick +] 用力地 [yònglì de] ▶ **it is hard to understand what is happening** 很难理解现在发生了什么事情 ▶ **it's hard to tell/say/know** 很难讲/说/知道 ▶ **such events are hard to understand** 这种事很难理解 ▶ **to be hard to please** 难以取悦 ▶ **to find it hard to do sth** 觉得做某事困难 ▶ **it's hard work serving in a shop** 商店工作很难做 ▶ **hard luck!** 真倒霉! ▶ **to be hard on sb** [person +] 对某人过分严厉; [situation +] 对某人来说有害 ▶ **no hard feelings!** 别记仇! ▶ **to be hard of hearing** 听力不佳 ▶ **to feel hard done by** (BRIT) 觉得受到不公平待遇 ▶ **hard evidence/facts** 铁证/客观的事实 ▶ **be hard put or pushed to do sth** 难以做某事 ▶ **to look hard at** [stare at +]; (consider) [+ idea, problem, situation] 认真考虑

hardback ['hɑːdbæk] N [c] (book) 精装本 [jīngzhuāngběn] ▶ **it's only available in hardback** 只有精装本

hard-boiled egg ['hɑːd'bɔɪld-] N [c] 煮老了的鸡蛋 [zhǔ lǎo le de jīdàn]

hard disk (COMPUT) N [c] 硬盘 [yìngpán]

hard drugs NPL 烈性毒品 [lièxìng dúpǐn]

harden ['hɑːdn] **I** VT **1** [+ wax, glue etc] 使变硬 [shǐ biànyìng] **2** [person, attitude, resolve] 使变得冷酷无情 [shǐ biànde lěngkù wúqíng] **II** VI **1** [wax, glue etc +] 变硬 [biànyìng] **2** [person, attitude, resolve +] 变得冷酷无情 [biànde lěngkù wúqíng] ▶ **to harden one's heart** 使心肠变硬

hardly ['hɑːdlɪ] ADV **1** (scarcely) 几乎不 [jīhū bù] **2** (no sooner) ▶ **he had hardly sat down when the door burst open** 他一坐下门就被猛地打开

了 [tā yī zuòxià mén jiù bèi měng de dǎkāi le]
▶ **hardly ever/any/anyone** 几乎从不/没有/没有任何人 ▶ **I can hardly believe it** 我简直不能相信 ▶ **it's hardly surprising** 并不出奇

hardship ['hɑːdʃɪp] N [C/U] 困难 [kùnnan]

hard shoulder (ESP BRIT) N [C] 高速公路紧急停车带 [gāosù gōnglù jǐnjí tíngchēdài] [美= **shoulder**]

hard up (inf) ADJ 拮据的 [jiéjū de]

hardware ['hɑːdwɛə(r)] N [U] 1 (ironmongery) 五金制品 [wǔjīn zhìpǐn] 2 (COMPUT) 硬件 [yìngjiàn] 3 (MIL) 重武器 [zhòng wǔqì]

hardware store N [C] 五金商店 [wǔjīn shāngdiàn]

hardworking [hɑːd'wəːkɪŋ] ADJ [+ employee, student] 勤奋的 [qínfèn de]

hardy ['hɑːdɪ] ADJ [+ animal, person] 能吃苦的 [néng chīkǔ de]; [+ plant] 耐寒的 [nàihán de]

hare [hɛə(r)] N 1 [C] (animal) 野兔 [yětù] 2 [U] (meat) 野兔肉 [yětù ròu]
▶ **hare off** (BRIT: inf) VI 飞跑 [fēipǎo]

harm [hɑːm] I VT 1 (damage) 损坏 [sǔnhuài] 2 (injure) 伤害 [shānghài] II N [U] 1 (damage) 损害 [sǔnhài] 2 (injury) 伤害 [shānghài] ▶ **to mean no harm** 没有恶意 ▶ **out of harm's way** 在安全的地方 ▶ **there's no harm (in) trying** 试一试也无妨 ▶ **to come to no harm** 平安无事 ▶ **to do more harm than good** 得不偿失 ▶ **it wouldn't do any harm (for you) to get an answerphone** 买个录音电话(对你)没什么害处

harmful ['hɑːmful] ADJ [+ effect, chemical, influence] 有害的 [yǒuhài de] ▶ **to be harmful to sb/sth** 对某人/某物有害

harmless ['hɑːmlɪs] ADJ 1 (safe) 无害的 [wúhài de] 2 (inoffensive) [+ person, joke, pleasure, activity] 无恶意的 [wú èyì de]

harmonica [hɑː'mɔnɪkə] N [C] 口琴 [kǒuqín]

harmonious [hɑː'məunɪəs] ADJ 1 [+ discussion, relationship] 和睦的 [hémù de] 2 [+ balance, layout, design] 协调的 [xiétiáo de] 3 [+ sound, tune] 悦耳的 [yuè'ěr de]

harmony ['hɑːmənɪ] N [U] 1 (accord) 和睦 [hémù] 2 (MUS) 和声 [héshēng] ▶ **in harmony (with)** [work, live+] 与…协调一致

harness ['hɑːnɪs] I N [C] 1 (for horse, dog etc) 挽具 [wǎnjù] 2 (safety harness) 安全带 [ānquándài] II VT 1 [+ resources, energy] 利用 [lìyòng] 2 [+ horse, dog] 套上 [tàoshàng]

harp [hɑːp] I N [C] (MUS) 竖琴 [shùqín] II VI ▶ **to harp on (about sth)** (pej) (对某事) 唠唠叨叨叨叨 [(duì mǒushì) láoláodāodāo]

harrowing ['hærəuɪŋ] ADJ [+ film, experience] 令人伤心的 [lìngrén shāngxīn de]

harsh [hɑːʃ] ADJ 1 [+ criticism, sentence, treatment] 严酷的 [yánkù de] 2 [+ conditions, climate, winter] 恶劣的 [èliè de] 3 [+ sound, light] 刺耳的 [cì'ěr de]; [+ chemical] 刺激性的 [cìjīxìng de]

harvest ['hɑːvɪst] I N 1 [C/U] (harvest time) 收获 [shōuhuò] 2 [c] (crop) 收成 [shōucheng] II VT [+ wheat, fruit, potatoes] 收割 [shōugē]

has [hæz] VB see **have**

hasn't ['hæznt] = **has not**

hassle ['hæsl] (inf) I N [C/U] (bother) 麻烦 [máfan] II VT [+ person] 打扰 [dǎrǎo]

haste [heist] N [U] 仓促 [cāngcù] ▶ **in haste** 匆忙地 ▶ **to make haste (to)** (o.f.) 赶快

hasten ['heisn] I VT [+ decision, downfall, process etc] 加速 [jiāsù] II VI (liter) 赶快 [gǎnkuài] ▶ **to hasten to do sth** 赶快做某事 ▶ **I hasten to add...** 我急忙补充说… ▶ **to hasten to say...** 忙不迭地说…

hastily ['heistɪlɪ] ADV 1 (hurriedly) 赶快地 [gǎnkuài de] 2 (rashly) 仓促地 [cāngcù de]

hasty ['heistɪ] ADJ 1 (hurried) [+ departure, return] 仓促的 [cāngcù de] 2 (rash) [+ decision, reply] 草率的 [cǎoshuài de] ▶ **don't be hasty** 别性急

hat [hæt] N [C] 帽子 [màozi] ▶ **to keep sth under one's hat** 对某事保守秘密 ▶ **at the drop of a hat** 毫不迟疑地 ▶ **that's old hat now** 那已经过时了 ▶ **to take one's hat off to sb** 向某人表示赞赏 ▶ **to talk through one's hat** 胡说

hatch [hætʃ] I N [C] 1 (NAUT) 舱口 [cāngkǒu] 2 (ESP BRIT) (also: **serving hatch**) 小窗口 [xiǎo chuāngkǒu] II VI 1 [bird+] 出壳 [chūké] 2 [egg+] 孵化 [fūhuà] III VT 1 [+ egg] 孵 [fū] 2 [+ plot, scheme] 策划 [cèhuà] ▶ **to be hatched** 孵出

hatchback ['hætʃbæk] N [C] 有仓门式后背的汽车 [yǒu cāngménshì hòubèi de qìchē]

hate [heit] I VT [+ person] 恨 [hèn]; [+ food, activity, sensation] 讨厌 [tǎoyàn] II N [U] 仇恨 [chóuhèn] ▶ **to hate doing/to do sth** 不喜欢做某事 ▶ **I hate to trouble you, but...** 我本不愿意麻烦你，但是… ▶ **I hate to tell you this, but...** 我抱歉地告诉你…

hatred ['heitrɪd] N [U] 仇恨 [chóuhèn]

haul [hɔːl] I VT 1 ▶ **to haul sth/sb up/out etc** 用力拉某物/某人起来/出来 {等} [yònglì lā mǒuwù/mǒurén qǐlái/chūlái {děng}] II N [C] [+ stolen goods] 被窃物 [bèiqièwù] ▶ **to haul o.s. out of sth** 把自己硬拉出某物 ▶ **to be hauled (up) before the court** 被送上法庭 ▶ **a long haul** 长久战

haunt [hɔːnt] I VT 1 [ghost, spirit+] 常出没于 [cháng chūmò yú] 2 [problem, memory, fear+] 萦绕在心头 [yíngrào zài xīntóu] II N [C] 常去的地方 [chángqù de dìfang]

haunted ['hɔːntɪd] ADJ 1 [+ house, building] 闹鬼的 [nàoguǐ de] 2 [+ expression] 愁容满面的 [chóuróng mǎnmiàn de]

have [hæv] (pt, pp **had**) I VT 1 (possess) 有 [yǒu] ▶ **he has** or **he has got blue eyes/dark**

hair 他长着蓝眼睛/黑头发 ► **do you have or have you got a car/phone?** 你有车/电话吗? ► **I have** or **I have got an idea** 我有个主意 ► **to have** or **have got sth to do** 有必须得做的事 ► **she had her eyes closed** 她闭上了眼睛

2 (*with meals, drinks*) ► **to have breakfast** 吃早饭 [chī zǎofàn] ► **to have a drink/a cigarette** 喝一杯/抽支烟

3 (*with activity*) ► **to have a swim/bath** 游泳/洗澡 [yóuyǒng/xǐzǎo] ► **to have a meeting/party** 开会/开派对

4 (*receive, obtain*) 得到 [dédào] ► **can I have a packet of sugar, please?** 请给我一包糖, 好吗? ► **can I have your address?** 能告诉我你的地址吗? ► **you can have it for £5** 付5英磅它就是你的了 ► **I must have it by tomorrow** 明天以前我必须得到它

5 (*give birth to*) ► **to have a baby** 生孩子 [shēng háizi]

6 (*allow*) 容忍 [róngrěn] ► **I won't have it!** 我绝不允许! ► **we can't have that** 我们绝不允许那样

7 ► **to have sth done** 指使/安排做某事 [zhǐshǐ/ānpái zuò mǒushì] ► **to have one's hair cut** 理发

8 (*experience, suffer*) ► **to have a headache** 头痛 [tóutòng] ► **to have a cold/flu/ diabetes** 得感冒/流感/糖尿病 ► **to have a heart attack** 心脏病发作 ► **to have an operation** 动手术 ► **she had her bag stolen/her arm broken** 她的包被偷了/她的胳膊断了

9 (*inf*) (*dupe*) ► **to be had** 被骗 [bèipiàn] ► **you've been had!** 你被骗了!

10 (*inf*) ► **to have had it** (*be in trouble*) 没希望了 [méi xīwàng le]

II AUX VB **1** ► **to have arrived/gone** 已到了/走了 [yǐ dàole/zǒule] ► **has he told you?** 他已经告诉你了吗? ► **when she had dressed, she went downstairs** 穿好衣服后, 她下了楼 ► **having lived abroad for years, I wasn't familiar with...** 已在国外呆了多年, 我都对···不熟悉了 ► **I haven't seen him for ages/since July** 我已经很久/自7月以来就没见过他了

2 (*in tag questions*) ► **you've done it, haven't you?** 你已经做了, 是不是? [nǐ yǐjing zuò le, shì bùshì?] ► **he hasn't done it, has he?** 他还没做, 是吗?

3 (*in short answers and questions*) ► **yes, I have** 是的, 我有/已做了 [shìde, wǒ yǒu/yǐ zuò le] ► **no I haven't!** 不, 我还没有/没做呢! ► **so have I!** 我也一样! ► **neither have I** 我也没有过 ► **"I've seen this movie before" "oh have you?"** "我以前看过这部电影" "噢, 是吗?" ► **"we haven't been there before" "oh haven't you?"** "我们

以前没去过那儿" "噢, 是吗?" ► **I've finished, have you?** 我已经完成了, 你呢?

4 (*be obliged*) ► **to have (got) to do sth** 不得不做某事 [bùdébù zuò mǒushì] ► **she has (got) to do it** 她必须得这么做 ► **this has (got) to be a mistake** 这一定是个错误 ► **he had to go away** 他必须得走

► **have in** (*inf*) VT ► **to have it in for sb** 对某人怀恨在心 [duì mǒurén huáihèn zàixīn]

► **have on** VT **1** [+ *clothes*] 穿着 [chuānzhe] ► **he didn't have anything on** 他什么都没穿 ► **I don't have any money on me** 我一点钱都没带

2 (BRIT: *inf*) (*tease*) 逗 [dòu] ► **you're having me on!** 你在逗我!

3 ► **to have sth on** 已安排了某事 [yǐ ānpái le mǒushì] ► **do you have anything on tomorrow?** 你明天有事吗?

► **have out** VT ► **to have it out with sb** 同某人辩个明白 [tóng mǒurén biàn gè míngbai]

haven ['heɪvn] N [c] 避难处 [bìnànchù]

haven't ['hævnt] = **have not**

havoc ['hævək] N [U] 大破坏 [dà pòhuài] ► **to cause havoc** 使混乱 ► **to play havoc with** or **wreak havoc on sth** 扰乱某事

Hawaii [hə'waɪiː] N 夏威夷 [Xiàwēiyí]

Hawaiian [hə'waɪjən] **I** ADJ 夏威夷的 [Xiàwēiyí de] **II** N **1** [c] (*person*) 夏威夷人 [Xiàwēiyírén] **2** [U] (*language*) 夏威夷语 [Xiàwēiyíyǔ]

hawk [hɔːk] **I** N [c] **1** (*bird*) 鹰 [yīng] **2** (*person*) 主战分子 [zhǔzhàn fènzǐ] **II** VT (*pej*) (*sell*) 硬卖 [yìngmài] ► **to watch sb like a hawk** 看某人看得很紧

hawthorn ['hɔːθɔːn] N [c/U] 山楂 [shānzhā]

hay [heɪ] N [U] 干草 [gāncǎo]

hay fever N [U] 花粉病 [huāfěnbìng]

haystack ['heɪstæk] N [c] 大干草垛 [dà gāncǎoduò]

hazard ['hæzəd] **I** N [c] 危险 [wēixiǎn] **II** VT ► **to hazard a guess that...** 试着猜猜··· [shìzhe cāicai···] ► **to be a hazard to sb** 对某人构成危险 ► **to be a health/fire hazard** 健康/火灾上的危害

hazardous ['hæzədəs] ADJ (*dangerous*) 危险的 [wēixiǎn de]

hazard (warning) lights (AUT) NPL 警报灯 [jǐngbào dēng]

haze [heɪz] N [S/U] 薄雾 [bówù] ► **a haze of cigarette smoke** 香烟的烟雾

hazel ['heɪzl] **I** N [c] (*tree*) 榛树 [zhēnshù] **II** ADJ [+ *eyes*] 淡褐色的 [dàn hèsè de]

hazelnut ['heɪzlnʌt] N [c] 榛子 [zhēnzi]

hazy ['heɪzɪ] ADJ **1** (*indistinct*) [+ *sky, day, sunshine*] 雾蒙蒙的 [wùméngméng de]; [+ *outline, view*] 朦胧的 [ménglóng de] **2** (*vague*) [+ *idea, memory*] 模

糊的 [móhu de] ▸ **he's rather hazy about the details** 他对细节有点遮遮掩掩

he [hi:] PRON **1** (man, boy) 他 [tā] ▷ He didn't do it. I did. 他没做，我做了。**2** (male animal) 它 [tā] ▷ He's a good dog. 它是只好狗。

head [hɛd] I N [c] **1** (ANAT) 头 [tóu] **2** (mind) 头脑 [tóunǎo] **3** [of company, organization, department] 领导 [lǐngdǎo] **4** (BRIT) (head teacher) 校长 [xiàozhǎng] **5** [of table] 首 [shǒu] **6** [of queue, list] 最前面 [zuì qiánmiàn] **7** (on tape recorder, video) 磁头 [cítóu] **8** (on beer) 泡沫 [pàomò] II VT **1** [+ list, group] 以…打头 [yǐ…dǎtóu] ▷ The list of most polluted cities is headed by London. 污染最严重的城市列表以伦敦打头。**2** [+ group, organization] 领导 [lǐngdǎo] ▷ The firm is headed by John Murray. 公司是由约翰·麦瑞领导的。**3** (FOOTBALL) [+ ball] 用头顶 [yòng tóu dǐng] ▸ **he fell head first into the river** 他头向下地栽到水里 ▸ **to go** or **fall head over heels** (lit) 头朝下跌倒 ▸ **to fall head over heels (in love)** (fig) 神魂颠倒地坠入（情网） ▸ **10 pounds a** or **per head** 每人10英磅 ▸ **she's got a head for figures/heights** 她有算术才能/能登高 ▸ **I have no head for heights/figures** 我登高/算数不灵 ▸ **to come to a head/to be brought to a head** (situation +) 到了紧要关头 ▸ **let's put our heads together** 咱们共同商量 ▸ **off the top of my head** 我估计 ▸ **on your own head be it!** 由你自负后果！ ▸ **to bite** or **snap sb's head off** 对某人大发脾气 ▸ **it went to his head** [alcohol +] 喝得他晕头转向；[success, power +] 冲昏了他的头脑 ▸ **to keep one's head** 保持镇定 ▸ **to lose one's head** 仓皇失措 ▸ **I can't make head** or **nor tail of this** (inf) 我对这件事一点也摸不着头脑 ▸ **to go/be off one's head** (ESP BRIT: inf) 发疯了 ▸ **to be off** or **out of one's head** (on drink, drugs) 神志不清 ▸ **to have got it into one's head that...** (be under impression that) 固执地认为…；(have understood that) 明白了… ▸ **from head to foot** or **toe** 从头到脚 ▸ **to laugh/scream one's head off** 狂笑/狂呼不已 ▸ **to go over sb's head** 令某人不能理解 ▸ **heads or tails?** 正面还是反面？ ▸ **it's heads** 硬币正面

▸ **head for** VT FUS [不可拆分] [+ place] 前往 [qiánwǎng] ▷ What's the name of the place we're heading for? 我们要去的地方叫什么？ ▷ They are heading for the airport. 他们正前往机场。 ▸ **to be heading** or **headed for Glasgow** 正前往格拉斯哥 ▸ **to be heading** or **headed for disaster** 快要碰到灾祸

▸ **head off** I VT **1** [+ person, vehicle] 上前拦住 [shàngqián lánzhù] **2** [+ threat, danger] 防止 [fángzhǐ] ▷ They did this in order to head off a strike. 他们这样做是为了防止罢工的发生。 II VI (leave) 出发 [chūfā] ▷ I think we'd better be heading off. 我们该出发了。

▸ **head up** VT [+ organization, investigation] 领

导 [lǐngdǎo] ▷ Judge Samuel Evans headed up the investigation. 塞缪尔·爱文斯法官领导这项调查。

headache ['hɛdeɪk] N [c] **1** (pain) 头痛 [tóutòng] **2** (problem) 令人头疼的问题 [lìngrén tóuténg de wèntí] ▸ **to have a headache** 头痛 ▸ **to be a headache (for sb)** [(problem) +] 是件（令某人）头痛的事

heading ['hɛdɪŋ] N [c] [of chapter, article] 标题 [biāotí]

headlamp ['hɛdlæmp] (BRIT) N = **headlight**

headlight ['hɛdlaɪt] N [c] 前灯 [qiándēng]

headline ['hɛdlaɪn] N [c] 标题 [biāotí] ▸ **the headlines** (PUBLISHING) 头条新闻；(TV, RAD) 内容提要 ▸ **to hit the headlines** 成为头条新闻 ▸ **it was headline news** 是头条新闻

headmaster [hɛd'mɑːstə(r)] (BRIT) N [c] 校长 [xiàozhǎng]

headmistress [hɛd'mɪstrɪs] (BRIT) N [c] 女校长 [nǚ xiàozhǎng]

head office N [c/u] [of company] 总部 [zǒngbù]

head of state (pl **heads of state**) N [c] 元首 [yuánshǒu]

headphones ['hɛdfəunz] NPL 耳机 [ěrjī]

headquarters ['hɛdkwɔːtəz] NPL **1** [of company, organization] 总部 [zǒngbù] **2** (MIL) 指挥部 [zhǐhuī bù]

headroom ['hɛdrum] N [u] (in car, under bridge) 净空高度 [jìngkōng gāodù] ▸ **"Max. Headroom: 3.4 metres"** "高度限制：3.4米"

headscarf ['hɛdskɑːf] (pl **headscarves**) N [c] (BRIT) 头巾 [tóujīn]；(worn by Muslim women) 包头巾 [bāo tóujīn]

headset ['hɛdsɛt] N [c] 耳机 [ěrjī]

head teacher (BRIT) N [c] 校长 [xiàozhǎng]

headway ['hɛdweɪ] N ▸ **to make headway** 取得进展 [qǔdé jìnzhǎn]

heal [hi:l] I VT **1** [+ injury] 愈合 [yùhé]；[+ sick person] 治愈 [zhìyù] **2** (emotionally) 治愈 [zhìyù] **3** [+ rift, disagreement] 调解 [tiáojiě] II VI **1** (physically) 痊愈 [quányù] **2** (emotionally) 愈合 [yùhé]

health [hɛlθ] N [u] **1** 健康 [jiànkāng] ▷ Her health has never been very good. 她的健康从来都不好。**2** (prosperity) 发达 [fādá] ▸ **to be good/bad for one's health** 对某人的健康有益/不利 ▸ **to be in good/poor health** 身体健康/不好 ▸ **to drink (to) sb's health** 举杯祝某人健康

health care I N [u] 保健 [bǎojiàn] II CPD [复合词] [+ system, worker, services] 保健 [bǎojiàn]

health centre, (US) **health center** N [c] 医疗中心 [yīliáo zhōngxīn]

health food N [c/u] 保健食品 [bǎojiàn shípǐn]

Health Service (BRIT) N ▸ **the (National) Health Service** 英国国民医疗服务制度 [Yīngguó Guómín Yīliáo Fúwù Zhìdù]

healthy ['hɛlθɪ] ADJ **1** [+ person, teeth, organ, skin] 健康的 [jiànkāng de] **2** (hearty) [+ appetite] 好的

[hǎo de] **3** (health-promoting) [+ diet, lifestyle] 对
健康有益的 [duì jiànkāng yǒuyì de] **4** (good)
[+ profit, turnover] 相当大的 [xiāngdāng dà de]
5 (successful) [+ economy, company, account] 兴旺
发达的 [xīngwàng fādá de]

heap [hi:p] **I** N [c] (pile) [of clothes, papers] 堆
[duī] **II** VT ▶ **to heap sth on sth** [+ sand, earth,
clothes] 将某物堆在某物上 [jiāng mǒuwù
duīzài mǒuwù shang]; (food) 将某物装满某物
[jiāng mǒuwù zhuāngmǎn mǒuwù] ▶ **heaps**
or **a heap of** (inf) [+ time, work, money etc] 大量
▶ **to heap praise/criticism on sb** 对某人大加
赞赏/批评
▶ **heap up** VT [+ stones, sand] 堆起 [duīqǐ]

○ **hear** [hɪə(r)] (pt, pp **heard** [hɜːd]) VT **1** [+ sound,
voice, music] 听见 [tīngjiàn] ▷ He heard voices
in the garden. 他听见从花园里传来的声音。
2 (listen to) [+ news, lecture, concert] 听 [tīng] ▷ I
heard the news on the radio this morning. 我今天早
上听了新闻广播。▷ We went to hear the Berlin
Philharmonic. 我们去听了柏林交响乐团。
3 (LAW) [+ case, evidence] 审理 [shěnlǐ] ▶ **to hear
sb doing sth** 听见某人做某事 ▶ **to hear that...**
听说… ▶ **I've heard it all before** 我早就听了多
少遍了 ▶ **to hear about sth/sb** 听说某事/某
人 ▶ **to hear from sb** 得到某人的消息 ▶ **have
you heard of Damien Hirst?** 你有没有听说过
戴米安·赫斯特? ▶ **I've never heard of him**
我从来没听说过他 ▶ **I wouldn't** or **won't hear
of it!** 我坚决不同意! ▶ **hear, hear** (BRIT: frm)
说的好, 说的好
▶ **hear out** VT ▶ **to hear sb out** 听某人讲完
[tīng mǒurén jiǎngwán]

hearing [ˈhɪərɪŋ] N **1** [U] (sense) 听力 [tīnglì]
2 [c] (LAW) 开审 [kāishěn] ▶ **in** or **within sb's
hearing** 在某人听得到的范围内 ▶ **to give sb a
(fair) hearing** (BRIT) (公正地)听取某人的申诉

hearing aid N [c] 助听器 [zhùtīngqì]

hearse [hɜːs] N [c] 灵车 [língchē]

heart [hɑːt] **I** N **1** [c] (ANAT) 心脏 [xīnzàng]
2 [c] (emotions) 情感 [gǎnqíng] **3** [c/U]
(character, attitude) 心灵 [xīnlíng] **4** [c] (shape)
心形物 [xīnxíng wù] **5** [c] [of lettuce] 菜心
[càixīn] **II hearts** NPL (CARDS) 红桃 [hóngtáo]
▶ **to learn/know sth (off) by heart** 背诵某事
▶ **I knew in my heart (of hearts) it was true** 在
我内心深处我知道这是对的 ▶ **at the heart of
the problem/debate** (在)问题/争论的
实质 ▶ **the heart of London** 伦敦中心 ▶ **at
heart** (basically) 本质上 ▶ **to have a soft/hard
heart** 心肠软/硬 ▶ **to lose heart** 失去信心
▶ **to take heart (from sth)** (从某事)受到鼓舞
▶ **she set her heart on being a lawyer** 她一心
想当律师 ▶ **the heart of the matter** 问题的
关键 ▶ **my heart went out to them** 我非常同
情他们 ▶ **matters** or **affairs of the heart** 感情
问题 ▶ **with all one's heart** [believe +] 全心全
意地; [love +] 真心实意地 ▶ **to break sb's heart**

使某人伤心 ▶ **to have a broken heart** 心碎
了 ▶ **to have a change of heart** 改变主意 ▶ **be
close** or **dear to one's heart** 是某人所关心的
▶ **I thanked him from the bottom of my heart**
我从心底里感激他 ▶ **my heart sank** 我心头
一沉 ▶ **to take sth to heart** 对某事耿耿于怀
▶ **to one's heart's content** 尽情地

heart attack N [c] 心脏病发作 [xīnzàngbìng
fāzuò] ▶ **to have a heart attack** 心脏病发作

heartbeat [ˈhɑːtbiːt] N **1** [s] (beating) 心跳
[xīntiào] **2** [c] (single beat) 心跳 [xīntiào]

heartbreaking [ˈhɑːtbreɪkɪŋ] ADJ [+ news,
story] 令人伤心的 [lìngrén shāngxīn de] ▶ **it
was heartbreaking to watch** 看着真让人心碎

heartbroken [ˈhɑːtbrəukən] ADJ 心碎的
[xīnsuì de]

heartburn [ˈhɑːtbɜːn] N [U] 胃灼热
[wèizhuórè] ▶ **I've got heartburn** 我有胃灼热

heart disease N [U] 心脏病 [xīnzàngbìng]

hearth [hɑːθ] N [c] (fireplace) 壁炉炉床 [bìlú
lúchuáng]

heartily [ˈhɑːtɪlɪ] ADV **1** [laugh +] 起劲地 [qǐjìn
de] **2** [eat, drink +] 尽情地 [jìnqíng de] **3** [agree,
dislike +] 非常 [fēicháng]; [+ glad, sick, sorry] 非
常 [fēicháng]

heartless [ˈhɑːtlɪs] ADJ [+ person, attitude] 无情
的 [wúqíng de]

hearty [ˈhɑːtɪ] ADJ **1** (cheerful) [+ person, laugh]
开心快活的 [kāixīn kuàihuó de] **2** (satisfying)
[+ meal] 丰盛的 [fēngshèng de] **3** [+ appetite] 大
的 [dà de] **4** (strong) [+ agreement, dislike] 强烈的
[qiángliè de]

heat [hiːt] **I** N **1** [U] (warmth) 热 [rè] **2** [U]
(temperature) 热度 [rèdù] **3** [U] (hob, flame etc) 热
源 [rèyuán] **4** [c] (SPORT) (also: qualifying heat)
预赛 [yùsài] **II** VT [+ water, food] 加热 [jiārè];
[+ room, house] 取暖 [qǔnuǎn] ▶ **in the heat of
the election campaign** 在选举竞争的白热阶
段 ▶ **in the heat of the moment** 一时激动之下
▶ **to be on** or (US) **in heat** (ZOOL) 正在发情 ▶ **I
find the heat unbearable** 热得我实在受不了
▶ **heat up** **I** VI [water, room +] 热起来 [rè qǐlái]
II VT [+ food] 加热 [jiārè]

heated [ˈhiːtɪd] ADJ **1** [+ pool, room] 加热的
[jiārè de] **2** [+ argument, debate] 激烈的 [jīliè de]

heater [ˈhiːtə(r)] N [c] (electric heater, gas heater)
供暖装置 [gōngnuǎn zhuāngzhì]; (in car) 暖气
设备 [nuǎnqì shèbèi]

heather [ˈhɛðə(r)] N [U] 石南属植物
[shínánshǔ zhíwù]

heating [ˈhiːtɪŋ] N [U] **1** (process) 供暖
[gòngnuǎn] **2** (system) 暖气 [nuǎnqì]

heatwave [ˈhiːtweɪv] N [c] 酷暑时期 [kùshǔ
shíqī]

heave [hiːv] **I** VT ▶ **to heave sth/sb onto
sth** 将某物/某人用力移动到某物上 [jiāng
mǒuwù/mǒurén yònglì yídòngdào mǒuwù
shang] **II** VI **1** [chest, sea +] 起伏 [qǐfú] **2** (retch)

[*person, stomach +*] 恶心 [ěxīn] **III** N [C] (*pull*) 拉 [lā]; (*push*) 推 [tuī]; (*lift*) 举 [jǔ] ▶ **to heave o.s. up** 拉自己起来 ▶ **to heave a sigh** 叹了一口气 ▶ **to heave a sigh of relief** 松了一口气 ▶ **heave to** (*pt, pp* **hove**) (NAUT) VI 停航 [tínghángǐ]

heaven ['hɛvn] **I** N [U] (REL) (*inf*) 天堂 [tiāntáng] **II heavens** NPL ▶ **the heavens** (*liter*) 天空 [tiānkōng] ▶ **the heavens opened** 下了一场倾盆大雨 ▶ **to move heaven and earth to do sth** 竭尽全力做某事 ▶ **heaven forbid!** 千万不要!

heavenly ['hɛvnlɪ] ADJ **1** (REL) (*celestial*) 天堂的 [tiāntáng de] **2** (*inf*) (*wonderful*) [+ *day, place, occasion*] 无比快乐的 [wúbǐ kuàilè de]

heavily ['hɛvɪlɪ] ADV **1** [*land, fall, sigh +*] 沉重地 [chénzhòng de] **2** (*a lot*) [*drink, smoke +*] 大量地 [dàliàng de]; [*rain, snow +*] 大 [dà] **3** [+ *armed, guarded*] 大量 [dàliàng]; [+ *sedated*] 厉害地 [lìhài de] **4** [*criticize +*] 严厉地 [yánlì de] ▶ **to be heavily made up** 浓妆艳抹的 ▶ **heavily pregnant** 怀孕后期 ▶ **to rely heavily on** *or* **be heavily reliant on sb/sth** 过分依赖某人/某物 ▶ **he was very heavily built** 他身材庞大

heavy ['hɛvɪ] ADJ **1** (*in weight*) [+ *load, suitcase*] 重的 [zhòng de] **2** (*well-built*) [+ *person*] 壮实的 [zhuàngshí de] **3** (*thick*) [+ *material, door etc*] 厚的 [hòu de] **4** (*in amount, number etc*) [+ *responsibility, commitment*] 重大的 [zhòngdà de]; [+ *casualties*] 大量的 [dàliàng de]; [+ *fighting*] 激烈的 [jīliè de]; [+ *traffic*] 拥挤的 [yōngjǐ de]; [+ *fine, penalty, sentence*] 重的 [zhòng de]; [+ *drinking, smoking, gambling*] 过度的 [guòdù de]; [+ *rain, snow*] 大的 [dà de]; [+ *blow, fall*] 沉重有力的 [chénzhòng yǒulì de]; [+ *breathing*] 沉重的 [chénzhòng de] **5** (*schedule, week*) 繁忙的 [fánmáng de] **5** (*physically demanding*) 繁重的 [fánzhòng de] **6** (*rich*) [+ *food, meal*] 难消化的 [nán xiāohuà de] **7** (*inf*) (*difficult*) [+ *situation*] 难办的 [nánbàn de]; [+ *discussion*] 沉重的 [chénzhòng de] ▶ **how heavy are you/is it?** 你/它有多重? ▶ **it's ten times heavier than** *or* **ten times as heavy as we estimated** 比我们预计的要重10倍 ▶ **a heavy drinker/smoker** 酒/烟鬼 ▶ **to make heavy weather of sth** 对某事小题大做 ▶ **with a heavy heart** (*liter*) 沉重的心情 ▶ **tanks are very heavy on fuel** 坦克很耗油 ▶ **the air was heavy with moisture** (*liter*) 空气湿度很大

Hebrew ['hi:bru:] **I** ADJ 希伯来的 [Xībólái de] **II** N [U] (*language*) 希伯来语 [Xībóláiyǔ]

hectare ['hɛktɑ:(r)] N [C] 公顷 [gōngqǐng]

hectic ['hɛktɪk] ADJ [+ *schedule, pace, life etc*] 繁忙的 [fánmáng de]

he'd [hi:d] = **he would, he had**

hedge [hɛdʒ] **I** N [C] 树篱 [shùlí] **II** VI (*stall*) 闪烁其词 [shǎnshuò qící] ▶ **a hedge against inflation** 防止通货膨胀的手段 ▶ **to hedge**

one's bets 两面下注

hedgehog ['hɛdʒhɒg] N [C] 刺猬 [cìwei]

heed [hi:d] VT (*frm*) [+ *advice, warning*] 听从 [tīngcóng] ▶ **to pay (no) heed to** *or* **take (no) heed of** (不)听取

heel [hi:l] **I** N [C] **1** [*of foot*] 脚后跟 [jiǎohòugēn] **2** [*of shoe*] 鞋跟 [xiégēn] **II heels** NPL (*also:* **high heels**) 高跟鞋 [gāogēnxié] ▶ **to bring sb to heel** 使某人屈服 ▶ **to take to one's heels** (*liter*) 逃跑 ▶ **to turn on one's heel** 急转身

hefty ['hɛftɪ] (*inf*) ADJ **1** [+ *person*] 强壮的 [qiángzhuàng de] **2** [+ *push*] 有力的 [yǒulì de] **3** [+ *profit, fine*] 可观的 [kěguān de]

height [haɪt] **I** N **1** [*of person, tree, building*] 高度 [gāodù] **2** [*C*] (*altitude*) 高处 [gāochù] **II heights** NPL (*altitude*) 高 [gāo]; (*high ground*) 高地 [gāodì] ▶ **of average/medium height** 平均/中等高度 ▶ **what height are you?** 你有多高? ▶ **the cliff is 100m in height** 悬崖有100米高 ▶ **to gain/lose height** 升高/降低高度 ▶ **flying at a height of 5000 m** 在5000米的高空飞行 ▶ **at knee/waist/shoulder height** 齐膝盖/腰/肩膀 ▶ **from a (great) height** 从(很)高处 ▶ **at the height of the summer** 在盛夏之际 ▶ **a writer at the height of his powers** 一名处于巅峰状态的作家 ▶ **it is the height of fashion/good taste** 那是最时髦/最有品位的 ▶ **at its height,...** 在鼎盛时期,…

heighten ['haɪtn] VT [+ *awareness, tension, fears, interest*] 增加 [zēngjiā]

heir [ɛə(r)] N [C] 继承人 [jìchéngrén] ▶ **to be (the) heir to sth** 是某物的继承人 ▶ **the heir to the throne** 王位的继承人

heiress ['ɛərɛs] N [C] 女继承人 [nǚ jìchéngrén]

held [hɛld] PT, PP *of* **hold**

helicopter ['hɛlɪkɒptə(r)] N [C] 直升飞机 [zhíshēng fēijī]

hell [hɛl] **I** N **1** [U] (REL) 地狱 [dìyù] **2** [C/U] (*fig*) (*life, situation*) 活受罪 [huó shòuzuì] **II** INT (*inf!*) 天啊 [tiān a] ▶ (*just*) **for the hell of it** (*inf*) 仅为取乐 ▶ **to give sb hell** (*inf*) (*tell off*) 狠狠数落某人; (*cause pain*) 使某人吃苦头; (*cause trouble for*) 给某人找麻烦 ▶ **all hell broke loose** (*inf*) 突然之间闹翻天 ▶ **a** *or* **one hell of a job/time etc** (*inf*) 一份艰难的工作/一段难熬的时光 ▶ **a** *or* **one hell of a lot of** (*inf*) 好多 ▶ **to go to hell** (REL) 下地狱; (*fig*) (*inf!*) 见鬼去吧 ▶ **it was hell** (*inf*) 糟糕极了 ▶ **the babysitter/neighbour from hell** (*inf*) 糟透了的保姆/邻居 ▶ **what/where/who the hell** (*inf*) 究竟什么/哪里/谁 ▶ **to run like hell** (*inf*) 拼命地跑 ▶ **oh, to hell with it!** 见鬼吧!

he'll [hi:l] = **he will, he shall**

hello [hə'ləʊ] INT (*as greeting*) 你好 [nǐhǎo]; (TEL) 喂 [wèi]; (*to attract attention*) 劳驾 [láojià]; (*expressing surprise*) 嘿 [hēi]

helmet ['hɛlmɪt] N [C] [*of motorcyclist, cyclist,*

astronaut] 头盔 [tóukuī]; [of soldier, policeman, fireman] 钢盔 [gāngkuī]

○ **help** [hɛlp] I N [U] 帮助 [bāngzhù] ▷ Thanks for your help. 多谢你的帮助。; (when in danger) 救命 [jiùmìng] ▷ He was screaming for help. 他大叫救命。II VT 1 [+ person] 帮助 [bāngzhù] ▷ His car wouldn't start, so I helped him. 他的车起动不了，所以我帮助了他。2 (improve) 改善 [gǎishàn] ▷ The new law does little to help the environment. 新法律在改善环境方面没起什么作用。III VI 1 (assist) 帮忙 [bāngmáng] ▷ Can I help? 我能帮忙吗？2 (be useful) 有用 [yǒuyòng] ▷ The right style of swimsuit can help by hiding bulges. 款式适当的游泳衣有助于掩饰肥胖部位。▷ Does that help? 那有用吗？ ▶ she needs help to get up the stairs 她需要帮助才能上楼梯 ▶ the book wasn't much help 这本书没什么用 ▶ thanks, you've been a great help 谢谢，你帮了很大忙 ▶ with the help of sb/sth 在某人/某物的帮助下 ▶ to be of help (to sb) (对某人)有所帮助 ▶ I helped him (to) fix his car 我帮助他修了他的车 ▶ I helped her to her feet 我帮她站起来 ▶ help! 救命！ ▶ can I help you? (in shop) 我能为您效劳吗？ ▶ people who can help themselves (be independent) 能自立的人 ▶ to help o.s. to sth (serve oneself) 随意用某物; (inf) (steal) 顺手牵羊拿某物 ▶ he can't help it 他毫无办法 ▶ I can't help feeling sorry for him 我情不自禁地同情他 ▶ it can't be helped 没办法

▶ help out I VI 帮忙 [bāngmáng] ▶ help out with sth 帮忙做某事 ▷ I help out with the secretarial work. 我帮忙做秘书工作。II VT 帮忙 [bāngmáng] ▷ I had no money, but my mum helped me out. 我没钱，但我妈妈帮了我的忙。

helper ['hɛlpə(r)] N [c] 帮手 [bāngshǒu]

helpful ['hɛlpful] ADJ [+ person] 有用的 [yǒuyòng de]; [+ advice, suggestion] 有建设性的 [yǒu jiànshèxìng de]

helping ['hɛlpɪŋ] N [c] [of food] 一份 [yīfèn]

helpless ['hɛlplɪs] ADJ (defenceless) 无依无靠的 [wúyīwúkào de] ▶ he was helpless to resist 他无法抵制

helpline ['hɛlplaɪn] N [c] (for emergencies, information) 热线 [rèxiàn]

hem [hɛm] I N [c] [of skirt, dress] 褶边 [zhěbiān] II VT [+ skirt, dress etc] 给…缝边 [gěi…féngbiān]
▶ hem in VT 包围 [bāowéi]

hemisphere ['hɛmɪsfɪə(r)] N 1 (GEO) 半球 [bànqiú] 2 [of brain] 大脑半球 [dànǎo bànqiú]
▶ the northern/southern hemisphere 北/南半球

hemorrhage ['hɛmərɪdʒ] (US) N = haemorrhage

hemorrhoids ['hɛmərɔɪdz] (US) NPL = haemorrhoids

hen [hɛn] N 1 (chicken) 母鸡 [mǔjī] 2 (of other species) 雌禽 [cíqín] ▶ a hen pheasant/

chaffinch etc 一只雌雉/花鸡{等}

hence [hɛns] ADV (therefore) 因此 [yīncǐ] ▶ 2 years hence 今后两年

henceforth [hɛns'fɔ:θ] ADV 今后 [jīnhòu]

hen night (BRIT) N [c] 婚礼前新娘与女伴们的聚会

hepatitis [hɛpə'taɪtɪs] N [U] 肝炎 [gānyán]

○ **her** [hə:(r)] I PRON 1 (of woman, girl) 她 [tā] ▷ I haven't seen her. 我还没见到她。▷ They gave her the job. 他们给了她那份工作。▷ Tell her that I'll be late. 告诉她我会晚到。▷ You could write her a letter. 你可以给她写封信。▷ "It's her again," said Peter. 彼得说：“又是她。” ▷ I was at school with her. 我和她是同学。2 (of female animal) 它 [tā] ▷ You'll have to take her to the vet. 你得带它去看兽医。II ADJ 1 (of woman, girl) 她的 [tā de] ▷ Her face was very red. 她的脸很红。2 (referring to female animal) 它的 [tā de] ▷ a cow and her calf 母牛和它的小牛

herb [hə:b, US ə:rb] N [c] 草本植物 [cǎoběn zhíwù]

herbal ['hə:bl, US ə:rbl] ADJ [+ medicine, remedy] 药草的 [yàocǎo de]

herbal tea N [c/U] 药茶 [yàochá]

herd [hə:d] I N [c] [of cattle, goats] 牧群 [mùqún] II VT (drive) [+ animals] 牧放 [mùfàng]; [+ people] 驱赶 [qūgǎn]

○ **here** [hɪə(r)] ADV 1 (in/to this place) 在这里 [zài zhèlǐ] 2 (near me) 到这里 [dào zhèlǐ] 3 (at this point) 这时 [zhèshí] ▶ "here!" (present) “在这儿！” ▶ here's my phone number 你的电话号码 ▶ here's your taxi 你的出租车来了 ▶ here he is (he's just arrived) 他到了 ▶ here you are (take this) 给你 ▶ here we are! (found it!) 找到了！ ▶ here and there 各处 ▶ "here's to…" (toast) “为…干杯” ▶ I'm here to help you 我是来帮你的 ▶ OK here goes, I'll try it 好，来吧，我来试试 ▶ here we go (again) (inf) 噢，(又)来了 ▶ (in the) here and now 现在

hereditary [hɪ'rɛdɪtrɪ] ADJ 1 [+ disease] 遗传的 [yíchuán de] 2 [+ title] 世袭的 [shìxí de]

heritage ['hɛrɪtɪdʒ] I N [U/s] 遗产 [yíchǎn] II CPD [复合词] (BRIT) [+ centre, industry, site] 文化遗产 [wénhuà yíchǎn]

hernia ['hə:nɪə] N [c] 疝 [shàn]

hero ['hɪərəu] (pl heroes) N [c] 1 [in book, film] 男主人公 [nán zhǔréngōng] 2 [of battle, struggle etc] 英雄 [yīngxióng] ▶ Clint Eastwood is my hero 克林特·伊斯特伍德是我崇拜的偶像

heroic [hɪ'rəuɪk] ADJ 英勇的 [yīngyǒng de]

heroin ['hɛrəuɪn] N [U] 海洛因 [hǎiluòyīn]

heroine ['hɛrəuɪn] N [c] 1 [in book, film] 女主人公 [nǚ zhǔréngōng] 2 [of battle, struggle etc] 女英雄 [nǚ yīngxióng] ▶ Elizabeth Taylor was my heroine 伊丽莎白·泰勒是我崇拜的偶像

heroism ['hɛrəuɪzəm] N [U] 英勇 [yīngyǒng] ▶ an act of heroism 英雄行为

heron ['hɛrən] N [c] 鹭 [lù]

herring ['hɛrɪŋ] (pl **herring** or **herrings**) N [c/u]
鲱鱼 [fēiyú]

hers [hə:z] PRON **1** (of woman, girl) 她的 [tā de]
▷ This is hers. 这是她的。 **2** (of female animal) 它
的 [tā de] ▷ Which bowl is hers? 哪个食盆是它
的？ ▶ **a friend of hers** 她的一个朋友

○**herself** [hə:'sɛlf] PRON **1** 她自己 [tā zìjǐ] ▷ She
hurt herself. 她伤了自己。 ▷ She made the dress
herself. 她自己做的这件连衣裙。 ▷ She'll have
to try it out for herself. 她必须得自己试试。
2 (emphatic) 她本人 [tā běnrén] ▷ She herself
lives in London. 她本人住在伦敦。 ▶ **by herself**
(unaided) 她独立地 ▷ She painted the house by
herself. 她自己一个人粉刷了房子。 ; (alone) 她
独自地 ▷ She lives by herself. 她独自一人住。

he's [hi:z] = **he is, he has**

hesitant ['hɛzɪtənt] ADJ [+ smile, reaction] 迟疑
不决的 [chíyí bùjué de] ▶ **to be hesitant about
doing** or **to do sth** 对于做某事犹豫不决

hesitate ['hɛzɪteɪt] VI 犹豫 [yóuyù] ▶ **I would
hesitate to say yes at this stage** 我目前还不太
想给肯定的答复 ▶ **he did not hesitate to take
action** 他毫不迟疑地采取了行动 ▶ **don't
hesitate to contact me** 请务必和我联系

hesitation [hɛzɪ'teɪʃən] N [c/u] **1** (delay)
犹豫 [yóuyù] **2** (in speech) 迟疑 [chíyí]
3 (unwillingness) 不愿意 [bù yuànyì] ▶ **I have
no hesitation in agreeing with him** 我毫不犹
豫地同意了他的意见 ▶ **he accepted without
hesitation** 他毫不犹豫地接受了

heterosexual ['hɛtərəu'sɛksjuəl] I ADJ
[+ person, relationship] 异性的 [yìxìng de] II N
[c] 异性恋者 [yìxìngliànzhě]

hexagon ['hɛksəgən] N [c] 六角形 [liùjiǎoxíng]

hey [heɪ] INT **1** (to attract attention) 喂 [wèi]
2 (showing surprise, interest, anger) 嘿 [hēi]

heyday ['heɪdeɪ] N ▶ **the heyday of the
railways** 铁路的黄金时代 [tiělù de huángjīn
shídài] ▶ **in its heyday,...** 在最兴旺发达的时
候,...

HGV (BRIT) N ABBR (= heavy goods vehicle) 载重车
辆 [zàizhòng chēliàng]

hi [haɪ] INT (as greeting) 嘿 [hēi] ; (in e-mail) 你
好 [nǐhǎo]

hibernate ['haɪbəneɪt] VI 冬眠 [dōngmián]

hiccough ['hɪkʌp] VI = **hiccup**

hiccup ['hɪkʌp] I N **1** 打嗝 [dǎgé] II N [c]
(problem) 小问题 [xiǎo wèntí] III **hiccups** NPL
▶ **to have/get (the) hiccups** 打嗝 [dǎgé]

hid [hɪd] PT of **hide**

hidden ['hɪdn] I PP of **hide** II ADJ [+ feelings,
dangers, facts] 暗藏的 [àncáng de] ; [+ place,
camera, microphone] 隐秘的 [yǐnmì de] ▶ **there
are no hidden charges** 没有变相的额外费用
▶ **hidden agenda** 隐藏的动机

hide [haɪd] (pt **hid**, pp **hidden**) I N [c/u] (skin)
兽皮 [shòupí] II VT **1** (conceal) [+ object, person]
隐藏 [yǐncáng] ; [+ feeling, information] 隐瞒

[yǐnmán] **2** (obscure) [+ sun, view] 遮挡 [zhēdǎng]
III VI 藏起来 [cáng qǐlái] ▶ **to hide from sb** 躲
着某人 ▶ **to hide o.s.** 躲起来 ▶ **to hide sth
from sb** (lit) 让某人找不到某物 ; (fig) 对某人隐
瞒某事 ▶ **he hid his face in his hands** 他用手
遮住自己的脸 ▶ **I have nothing to hide** 我没
什么可隐瞒的

hideous ['hɪdɪəs] ADJ [+ painting, face] 极丑的
[jíchǒu de] ; [+ conditions, mistake] 令人惊骇的
[lìngrén jīnghài de]

hiding ['haɪdɪŋ] N **1** ▶ **to give sb/get a (good)
hiding** (inf) (痛)打某人/被(痛)打一顿
[(tòng)dǎ mǒurén/bèi (tòng)dǎ yī dùn] **2** ▶ **go
into/be in hiding** 躲藏起来 [duǒcáng qǐlái]
▶ **to come out of hiding** 从躲藏处出来

hi-fi ['haɪfaɪ] N [c] 高保真音响设备
[gāobǎozhēn yīnxiǎng shèbèi]

○**high** [haɪ] I ADJ **1** (tall) [+ mountain, building, wall,
heel etc] 高的 [gāo de] ▷ the high walls of the
prison 监狱的高墙 **2** (not low down) [+ ceiling, shelf,
sun, collar] 高的 [gāo de] **3** (in degree, quantity)
[+ level, price, speed, temperature etc] 高的 [gāo
de] ; [+ risk] 极大的 [jídà de] ▷ a high risk of failure
极高的失败的风险 ; [+ wind] 强烈的 [qiángliè
de] ▷ High winds have damaged the power lines. 强
风已毁坏了电缆。 **4** (high-pitched) [+ voice, note]
尖锐的 [jiānruì de] **5** (high-ranking) [+ person]
高级的 [gāojí de] ▷ someone very high in the
government 在政府里地位极高的某人 **6** (good)
[+ principles, standards, morals] 高的 [gāo de]
▷ He was a man of the highest principles. 他是个
非常有原则的人。 ▷ The standard was very high.
标准很高。 ; [+ quality, standard] 高的 [gāo de]
▷ The standard of university education is very high. 大
学教育的标准是非常高的。 **7** (inf) (on drugs) 醉
的 [zuì de] **8** (CULIN) [+ meat, game] 略微腐坏
的 [lüèwēi fǔhuài de] II ADV (reach, throw+] 高
高地 [gāogāo de] ▷ He threw the ball high in the
air. 他把球高高地扔到空中。 ; [fly, climb+] 高
[gāo] III N [c] 最高记录 [zuìgāo jìlù] ▷ Exports
have reached a new high. 出口已创一个新记录。
▶ **it is 20 m high** 有20米高 ▶ **how high is the
door?** 门有多高？ ▶ **foods that are high in fat**
脂肪含量高的食品 ▶ **the temperature was in
the high eighties** 气温高达85到90度 ▶ **safety
has always been our highest priority** 安全一
直是我们最重视的问题 ▶ **I have a very high
opinion of him** 我对他的评价很高 ▶ **to have
high expectations (of sb/sth)** (对某人/某
事)有很高的期望 ▶ **to be in high spirits** 情绪
很高 ▶ **to be high on** [+ drug] 因…而神情恍惚
▶ **sales of vodka have reached an all-time high**
伏特加酒的销售量创历史最高记录 ▶ **to pay a
high price for sth** (fig) 为某事付出很高的代价
▶ **it's high time you learned how to do it** 这是
你该学怎么做的时候了 ▶ **to aim high** (fig) 力
争上游 ▶ **plates piled high with food** 碟子里
高高地堆着食物 ▶ **economic reform is high on**

our agenda or list 经济改革是我们的日程表
上非常重要的问题 ▶ **high up** (above the ground)
离地面高的; (in rank) 居高位的 ▶ **to search** or
look high and low for sth 到处寻找某物

high 不能用于描写人、动物和植物,
而应用 tall。She was rather tall for a
woman. tall 还可以用来描写建筑物,
如摩天大楼等, 以及其他高度大于宽
度的东西。…tall pine trees…a tall glass
vase…

high chair N [C] 高脚椅 [gāojiǎoyǐ]

high-class ['haɪ'klɑːs] ADJ [+ performer, service]
第一流的 [dì yīliú de]; [+ shop, neighbourhood,
hotel] 高级的 [gāojí de]

higher education ['haɪə(r)-] N [U] 高等教育
[gāoděng jiàoyù]

high heels N PL (shoes) 高跟鞋 [gāogēnxié]

high jump N (SPORT) ▶ **the high jump** 跳高
[tiàogāo] ▶ **you'll be for the high jump** (fig) 你
将受到严厉惩罚

highlands ['haɪləndz] N PL 高原地区
[gāoyuán dìqū] ▶ **the Highlands (of Scotland)**
(苏格兰) 高地

highlight ['haɪlaɪt] I N [C] (best part) 最精彩
的部分 [zuì jīngcǎi de bùfèn] II VT [+ problem,
need] 强调 [qiángdiào] III **highlights**
N PL **1** (TV) 最精彩的场面 [zuì jīngcǎi de
chǎngmiàn] **2** (in hair) 挑染 [tiǎorǎn]

highlighter ['haɪlaɪtə(r)] N [C] (pen) 荧光记号
笔 [yíngguāng jìhào bǐ]

highly ['haɪlɪ] ADV (extremely) [+ unlikely, critical,
confidential, successful] 非常 [fēicháng] ▶ **highly
paid** 高薪 ▶ **highly skilled** [+ person] 技巧非常
熟练的; [+ job] 熟练 ▶ **to speak/think highly of
sb** 赞扬/尊重某人 ▶ **to be highly regarded** or
thought of 倍受尊重的

highness ['haɪnɪs] N ▶ **His/Your Highness** 殿
下 [diànxià]

high-rise ['haɪraɪz] I ADJ [+ flats, offices] 高层
的 [gāocéng de] II N [C] 高层建筑 [gāocéng
jiànzhù]

high school N [C/U] **1** (BRIT) (for students aged
11-18) 中学 [zhōngxué] **2** (US) (for students aged
14-18) 中学 [zhōngxué]

high season (BRIT) N ▶ **the high season** 旺
季 [wàngjì]

high street (ESP BRIT) I N [C] 大街 [dàjiē]
[美=**main street**] II ADJ (ESP BRIT) 大街的
[dàjiē de]

high-tech, hi-tech ['haɪ'tɛk] ADJ [+ industry,
company, equipment] 高科技的 [gāokējì de]

highway ['haɪweɪ] (ESP US) N [C] 公路 [gōnglù]

Highway Code (BRIT) N ▶ **the Highway Code**
公路法规 [gōnglù fǎguī]

hijack ['haɪdʒæk] I VT [+ plane, idea, event] 劫持
[jiéchí] II N 劫持 [jiéchí]

hijacker ['haɪdʒækə(r)] N [C] 劫持者 [jiéchízhě]

hike [haɪk] I VI (go walking) 步行 [bùxíng]

II VT (inf) (raise) 突然提高 [tūrán tígāo] III N
[C] **1** (walk) 徒步旅行 [túbù lǚxíng] **2** (inf) (in
prices etc) 突然上涨 [tūrán shàngzhǎng] ▶ **to
go for a hike** 做徒步旅行 ▶ **to go hiking** 做
徒步旅行
▶ **hike up** VT (inf) **1** (pull up) [+ trousers, skirt] 提
起 [tíqǐ] **2** (raise) 急剧提高 [jíjù tígāo]

hiker ['haɪkə(r)] N [C] 徒步旅行者 [túbù
lǚxíngzhě]

hiking ['haɪkɪŋ] N [U] 步行 [bùxíng]

hilarious [hɪ'lɛərɪəs] ADJ [+ account, adventure]
滑稽的 [huájī de]

hill [hɪl] N [C] (hillock) 小山 [xiǎoshān]; (slope) 坡
[pō] ▶ **to be over the hill** (inf) 过了巅峰时期

hillside ['hɪlsaɪd] N [C] 山坡 [shānpō]

hill-walking ['hɪlwɔːkɪŋ] N [U] 登山
[dēngshān] ▶ **to go hill-walking** 登山

hilly ['hɪlɪ] ADJ [+ country, area] 多小山的 [duō
xiǎoshān de]

⊙ him [hɪm] PRON **1** (of man, boy) 他 [tā] ▷ I
haven't seen him. 我还没看见他。▷ They gave him
the job. 他们给了他那份工作。▷ Not him again!
又是他! ▷ I was at school with him. 我和他是
同学。▷ I gave the bag to him. 我把包给了他。
2 (male animal) 它 [tā] ▷ You'll have to take him to
the vet. 你得带它去看兽医。

⊙ himself [hɪm'sɛlf] PRON **1** 他自己 [tā zìjǐ] ▷ He
hurt himself. 他伤了自己。▷ He prepared the supper
himself. 他自己准备了晚餐。▷ He'll have to try it
out for himself. 他必须得自己试试。**2** (emphatic)
他本人 [tā běnrén] ▷ He himself lives in London.
他本人住在伦敦。▶ **by himself** (unaided) 他独
立地 ▷ He painted the house by himself. 他自己一
个人粉刷了房子。; (alone) 他独自地 ▷ He lives
by himself. 他独自一人住。

hind [haɪnd] I ADJ (rear) [+ legs, quarters] 后面的
[hòumiàn de] II N (female deer) 雌鹿 [cílù]

hinder ['hɪndə(r)] VT [+ progress, movement,
person] 阻碍 [zǔ'ài] ▶ **to hinder sb from doing
sth** 妨碍某人做某事

hindsight ['haɪndsaɪt] N ▶ **with hindsight,
we'd have done it differently** 事后想来, 我们
本该换个方法 [shìhòu xiǎnglái, wǒmen běngāi
huàn gè fāngfǎ] ▶ **in hindsight, this was a
mistake** 事后想来, 这是个错误

Hindu ['hɪnduː] I N [C] 印度教信徒 [Yìndùjiào
xìntú] II ADJ 与印度教有关的 [yǔ Yìndùjiào
yǒuguān de]

Hinduism ['hɪnduːɪzəm] N [U] 印度教
[Yìndùjiào]

hinge [hɪndʒ] N [C] 铰链 [jiǎoliàn]
▶ **hinge on** VT FUS [不可拆分] (depend on) 取决
于 [qǔjué yú]

hint [hɪnt] I N **1** [C] (suggestion) 暗示 [ànshì]
2 [C] (advice) 建议 [jiànyì] **3** [S] (sign, trace) 迹
象 [jìxiàng] II VT ▶ **to hint that…** (suggest) 暗
示… [ànshì…] ▶ **to give a hint that…** 暗示…
▶ **to take a hint** 理会了暗示

▸ **hint at** VT FUS [不可拆分] 暗示 [ànshì]

hip [hɪp] I N [C] (ANAT) 髋部 [kuānbù] II ADJ (inf) (trendy) 赶时髦的 [gǎn shímáo de]

hippie ['hɪpɪ] N [C] 嬉皮士 [xīpíshì]

hippo ['hɪpəʊ] (inf) N [C] 河马 [hémǎ]

hippopotamus [hɪpə'pɒtəməs] (pl **hippopotamuses** or **hippopotami** [hɪpə'pɒtə maɪ]) N [C] 河马 [hémǎ]

hippy ['hɪpɪ] N = hippie

hire ['haɪə(r)] I VT (ESP BRIT) [+ car, equipment, hall] 租用 [zūyòng] [美=rent]; [+ worker] 雇用 [gùyòng] II N [U] (BRIT) [of car, hall etc] 租用 [zūyòng] [美=rental] ▸ **for hire** (ESP BRIT) [+ car, boat, building] 供出租; [+ taxi] 空车 ▸ **the car is on hire** 这辆车已被租用
▸ **hire out** VT [+ cars, equipment, hall] 出租 [chūzū]; [+ cleaners, security guards] 出雇 [chūgù]

hire car (BRIT) N [C] 租的车 [zū de chē] [美= rental car]

○**his** [hɪz] I ADJ 1 (of man, boy) 他的 [tā de] ▷ His face was very red. 他的脸很红。2 (of animal) 它的 [tā de] ▷ The dog is having his dinner. 狗正在吃晚餐。II PRON 1 (of man, boy) 他的 [tā de] ▷ These are his. 这些是他的。2 (of male animal) 它的 [tā de] ▷ Which bowl is his? 哪个食盆是它的? ▸ **a friend of his** 他的一个朋友

Hispanic [hɪs'pænɪk] I ADJ 拉丁裔美国人的 [Lādīngyì Měiguórén de] II N [C] 拉丁裔美国人 [Lādīngyì Měiguórén]

hiss [hɪs] I VI [snake, cat, steam, fat in pan etc +] 发出嘶嘶声 [fāchū sīsī shēng]; [person, audience +] 发尖利的嘘声 [fā jiānlì de xūshēng] II VT 压低嗓门地说 [yādī sǎngmén de shuō] ▷ "Be quiet!" she hissed. "别说话!" 她压低了嗓门斥责道。III N [C] [of snake, steam, fat etc] 嘶嘶声 [sīsī shēng]; [of person, audience] 嘘声 [xūshēng] ▸ **to hiss at sb/sth** (in disapproval) 对某人/某物发嘘声

historian [hɪ'stɔːrɪən] N [C] 历史学家 [lìshǐxuéjiā]

historic [hɪ'stɔrɪk] ADJ (important) [+ change, achievement, moment] 历史性的 [lìshǐxìng de]

historical [hɪ'stɔrɪkl] ADJ [+ figure, event, novel, film] 历史的 [lìshǐ de]

○**history** ['hɪstərɪ] N 1 [U] [of town, country, person] 历史 [lìshǐ] ▷ one of the most dramatic moments in Polish history 波兰历史上最激动人心的时刻之一 2 [U] (SCOL) 历史 [lìshǐ] 3 [C] (record) 历史 [lìshǐ] ▷ a college with a tremendous sporting history 一家有了不起的体育史的学院 ▸ **to have a history of sth/doing sth** 有某事/做某事的前科 ▸ **that's history** 那已成为历史了 ▸ **the rest is history** 后来的事就众所周知了 ▸ **to make history** 创造历史

○**hit** [hɪt] (pt, pp **hit**) I VT 1 (strike) [+ person, thing] 打 [dǎ] ▷ He hit me on the head. 他打了我的头。2 (collide with) [+ car, tree, wall] 碰撞 [pèngzhuàng] ▷ The truck had hit a wall. 卡车撞

了墙。3 [+ target] (bomb, bullet +] 击中 [jīzhòng] ▷ a missile that could hit its target with deadly accuracy 一个命中率极高的导弹; [bomber, gunner +] 命中 [mìngzhòng] ▷ He hit the bull's eye and won the prize. 他命中了靶心，赢了奖。4 (appear in) [+ news, newspapers] 登出 [dēngchū] 5 (affect) [+ person, services, event etc] 打击 [dǎjī] ▷ Consumers will be hit hard by the rise in prices. 物价上涨对消费者打击重大。6 (occur to) 想出 [xiǎngchū] ▷ Then the answer hit me. 我一下子想出了答案。II N [C] 1 (knock) 击 [jī] 2 (on website) 点击 [diǎnjī] 3 (hit song) 成功而流行一时的事物 [chénggōng ér fēngxíng yìshí de shìwù] ▸ **to be/become a hit** [song, film, play +] 是/成为成功而风行一时的
▸ **hit back** I VI 1 (lit) (strike) 回击 [huíjī] 2 (fig) (counterattack) ▸ **to hit back (at sb)** 回击(某人) [huíjī(mǒurén)] II VT 回击 [huíjī]
▸ **hit off** VT ▸ **to hit it off (with sb)** (inf) (与某人)很合得来 [(yǔ mǒurén)xiāngchǔ hěnhǎo]
▸ **hit out at** (ESP BRIT) VT FUS [不可拆分] 1 (lit) 猛打 [měngdǎ] ▷ Ralph hit out at his assailant. 拉尔夫猛打攻击他的人。2 (fig) ▸ **to hit out at sb** 猛烈抨击某人 [měngliè pēngjī mǒurén] ▷ The Prime Minister hit out at his colleagues. 首相猛烈抨击他的同事。
▸ **hit (up)on** VT FUS [不可拆分] [+ solution] 灵机一动地想出 [língjīyīdòng de xiǎngchū]

hitch [hɪtʃ] I VI (inf) (hitchhike) 搭便车旅行 [dā biànchē lǚxíng] II N [C] (difficulty) 障碍 [zhàng'ài] ▸ **to hitch a ride** or **lift** (inf) 搭便车 [dā biànchē] ▸ **to hitch sth (on) to sth** (fasten) 将某物拴在某物上 ▸ **to get hitched (to sb)** (inf) (与某人)结婚 ▸ **technical hitch** 技术故障
▸ **hitch up** VT 1 [+ trousers, skirt] 急速拉起 [jísù lāqǐ] 2 [+ horse and cart] 套车 [tàochē]

hitchhike ['hɪtʃhaɪk] VI 搭便车旅行 [dā biànchē lǚxíng] ▸ **to hitchhike to New York** 搭便车到纽约去

hitchhiker ['hɪtʃhaɪkə(r)] N [C] 搭便车旅行者 [dā biànchē lǚxíngzhě]

hitchhiking ['hɪtʃhaɪkɪŋ] N [U] 搭便车旅行 [dā biànchē lǚxíng]

hi-tech ['haɪtek] ADJ = high-tech

hitman ['hɪtmæn] (pl **hitmen**) (inf) N 职业杀手 [zhíyè shāshǒu]

HIV N ABBR (= human immunodeficiency virus) 艾滋病病毒 [àizībìng bìngdú] ▸ **to be HIV positive/negative** 携带艾滋病病毒/未受艾滋病病毒感染

hive [haɪv] N [C] (beehive) 蜂箱 [fēngxiāng] ▸ **a hive of activity/industry** 紧张繁忙的场所/喧闹的工业区
▸ **hive off** (ESP BRIT: inf) VT [+ company] 使分立出来 [shǐ fēnlì chūlái]

HMS (BRIT) ABBR (= His/Her Majesty's Ship) 英国皇家海军舰艇 [Yīngguó Huángjiā Hǎijūn Jiàntǐng]

HNC (BRIT) N ABBR (= Higher National Certificate) 国家高等合格证书 [Guójiā Gāoděng Hégé Zhèngshū]

HND (BRIT) N ABBR (= Higher National Diploma) 国家高等技术学校毕业证书 [Guójiā Gāoděng Jìshù Xuéxiào Bìyè Zhèngshū]

hoard [hɔːd] I N [c] (of food, money, treasure) 秘藏物 [mìcángwù] II VT [+ food, money, treasure] 储藏 [chǔcáng] III VI 积聚 [jījù]

hoarse [hɔːs] ADJ [+ person, voice, whisper] 嘶哑的 [sīyǎ de]

hoax [həuks] N [c] 戏弄 [xìnòng]

hob [hɔb] (BRIT) N [c] (on cooker, stove) 炉盘 [lúpán]

hobble ['hɔbl] VI 跛行 [bǒxíng]

hobby ['hɔbɪ] N [c] 爱好 [àihào]

hobo ['həubəu] (US) N [c] 流浪汉 [liúlànghàn]

hockey ['hɔkɪ] N [U] 1 (BRIT) (on grass) 曲棍球 [qūgùnqiú] [美= field hockey] 2 (US) (on ice) 冰球 [bīngqiú] [英= ice hockey]

hockey stick N [c] 曲棍球球棍 [qǔgùnqiú qiúgùn]

hog [hɔg] I N [c] 1 (BRIT) (boar) 阉公猪 [yān gōngzhū] 2 (US) (pig) 猪 [zhū] II VT [+ road, telephone etc] 霸占 [zhànyòng] ▶ to go the whole hog (inf) 彻底地干

Hogmanay [hɔgmə'neɪ] N [U] 新年前夜 [Xīnnián Qiányè]

● **HOGMANAY**

○ **New Year's Eve**（新年前夜）是即将过去
○ 的一年的最后一天，在苏格兰被称为
○ **Hogmanay**。在苏格兰，除夕的庆典尤为
○ 重要。全家和朋友们汇聚一堂，一起聆听
○ 午夜的钟声，然后争当 **first-foot**（第一
○ 个拜年的人）。在拜访友人和邻居时，人们
○ 会随身带上酒（一般是威士忌），还有一块
○ 煤，据说这样能为来年带来好运气。

hoist [hɔɪst] I N [c] (apparatus) 起重机 [qǐzhòngjī] II VT [+ heavy object] 举起 [jǔqǐ]; [+ flag, sail] 升起 [shēngqǐ] ▶ to hoist o.s. onto a table 自己爬到桌子上了

▶ **hoist up** VT [+ person, thing] 举起 ▶ to hoist o.s. up 往上爬

○ **hold** [həuld] (pt, pp **held**) I VT 1 (grip) [+ bag, umbrella, box etc] 拿 [ná] ▷ Hold the baby while I load the car. 我装车时帮我抱着婴儿。▷ I held the box tightly. 我紧紧地拿着盒子。2 (keep) [+ hand, arm, head etc] 保持 [bǎochí] ▷ Hold your hands in front of your face. 把你的双手举在面前。▷ Hold your arms still. 胳膊保持不动。3 (contain) [room, box, bottle etc +] 容纳 [róngnà] ▷ Each bottle will hold a litre. 每个瓶子有一升的容量。4 (have) [+ office, power] 担任 [dānrèn] ▷ She has never held ministerial office. 她从来没有担任过部长级职位。; [+ ticket, licence, opinion]

持有 [chíyǒu] ▷ He did not hold a firearms licence. 他没有持枪执照。▷ I myself hold the view that... 我本人持有的观点是…; [+ meeting, interview, election] 举行 [jǔxíng] ▷ The government said it would hold an investigation. 政府表示将会进行一项调查。5 (detain) 拘留 [jūliú] ▷ I was held overnight in a cell. 我整个晚上被拘留在牢房。II VI 1 (withstand pressure) 支持得住 [zhīchí de zhù] ▷ How long will the roof hold? 屋顶能支持多久？2 (be valid) [argument, theory +] 有根据 [yǒu gēnjù] ▷ Your argument doesn't hold. 你的论点立不住。3 (stay same) [offer, invitation +] 有效 [yǒuxiào] ▷ Will you tell her the offer still holds. 你能告诉她邀请仍然有效吗？; [luck, weather, ceasefire +] 持续 [chíxù] ▷ If my luck continues to hold, I think I've got a fair chance. 如果我继续走运，我想我的机会不小。4 (TEL) 等着 [děngzhe] ▷ The line's engaged: will you hold? 电话占线，你能等一下吗？III N [c] 1 (grasp) 握 [wò] ▷ He released his hold on the camera. 他撒手放开照相机。2 (of ship, plane) 货舱 [huòcāng]

▶ to hold one's head up 抬起头; (fig) 保持信心
▶ to hold sb responsible/liable/accountable 要求某人负责 ▶ hold the line! (TEL) 别挂线！
▶ to hold one's breath 屏息 ▶ don't hold your breath! (inf) 别指望！▶ to hold one's own (against sb) (fig) （和某人）不相上下 ▶ to hold sth shut/open 使某物保持关着的/开着的状态 ▶ to hold sb prisoner/hostage 扣留某人作为囚犯/人质 ▶ I don't hold with all this modern art 我不赞同现代艺术 ▶ hold it! 别动！▶ to hold sb's interest or attention 保持某人的兴趣{或}注意力 ▶ hold still or hold steady 静止不动 ▶ to have a hold over sb 影响某人 ▶ to get/grab/take hold of sb/sth 紧紧拿着/抓着/握着某人/某物 ▶ I need to get hold of Bob 我需要找到鲍勃 ▶ to take hold of sb (overwhelm) 征服某人 ▶ to put sth on hold 暂时不做某事

▶ **hold against** VT ▶ to hold sth against sb 因某事对某人记仇 [yīn mǒushì duì mǒurén jìchóu] ▷ He lost the case, but never held it against me. 他输了这场官司，但从未因此而记恨过我。

▶ **hold back** VT 1 [+ person, progress] 阻拦 [zǔlán] ▷ She's very ambitious, so don't try to hold her back. 她很有野心，别阻拦她。2 [+ secret, information] 隐瞒 [yǐnmán] ▷ I want the truth, now, with nothing held back. 我现在要的是真相，没有一点隐瞒。

▶ **hold down** VT 1 (restrain) [+ person] 把⋯按倒在地上 [bǎ⋯àndào zài dìshang] ▷ It took three men to hold him down. 要3个男人才把他按在地上。2 (manage) [+ job] 保持住 [bǎochí zhù] ▷ He could never hold down a regular job. 他从来都保不住一份稳定的工作。

▶ **hold forth** VI 滔滔不绝地讲 [tāotāo bùjué de jiǎng] ▷ Jenkins was there, holding forth on his *favourite subject.* 詹金斯在那儿，滔滔不绝地讲述他最喜欢的话题。

▶ **hold off** I VT [+ *challenge*] 使不能接近 [shǐ bùnéng jiējìn] ▷ *Alesi drove magnificently, holding off the challenge from Berger.* 阿勒西开得棒极了，使勃克不能接近。 II VI 拖延 [tuōyán] ▷ *They threatened military action but have held off until now.* 他们以军事行动相威胁，但一直拖到现在。; [*rain +*] 不下 [bùxià] ▶ **to hold off doing sth** 推迟做某事

▶ **hold on** VI **1** (*keep hold*) 抓牢 [zhuāláo] ▷ *The rope was wet, but Nancy held on.* 绳子湿了，但南希仍然牢牢地抓着。 **2** (*inf*) (*wait*) 等一会儿 [děng yīhuìr] ▷ *Hold on a moment, please.* 请等一会儿。

▶ **hold on to** VT FUS [不可拆分] **1** (*grasp*) 抓住 [zhuāzhù] ▷ *He had to hold on to the chair to steady himself.* 他不得不抓住椅子使自己站稳。 **2** (*keep*) 保留 [bǎoliú] ▷ *Will you hold on to this for me for a couple of days?* 这个你能帮我保留几天吗？

▶ **hold out** I VT **1** [+ *hand*] 伸出 [shēnchū] ▷ *Sam held out his hand for the briefcase.* 山姆伸手拿公文包。 **2** [+ *hope, prospect*] 带来 [dàilái] ▷ *Science may hold out some prospect of feeding the hungry.* 科学为解决饥饿问题带来了希望。 II VI ▶ **to hold out (for sth)** 坚决要求 (某物) [jiānjué yāoqiú (mǒuwù)] ▷ *I should have held out for a better deal.* 我本该要求更好的待遇。

▶ **hold over** VT (*postpone*) 推迟 [tuīchí]

▶ **hold up** VT **1** (*lift up*) 举起 [jǔqǐ] ▷ *The Englishman held up the rifle.* 英国人举起了手枪。 **2** (*support*) 支撑 [zhīchēng] ▷ *These books hold the bed up.* 这些书支撑着床。 **3** (*delay*) 阻碍 [zǔ'ài] ▷ *Why were you holding everyone up?* 你为什么要阻碍其他人？ **4** (*rob*) [+ *person, bank*] 抢劫 [qiǎngjié] ▷ *He held me up at gunpoint.* 他持枪抢劫了我。

holder ['həʊldə(r)] N [C] **1** (*container*) 容器 [róngqì] **2** (*owner*) [*of ticket, licence*] 持有者 [chíyǒuzhě]; [*of title, record*] 保持者 [bǎochízhě]

hold-up ['həʊldʌp] N [C] **1** (*robbery*) 持械抢劫 [chíxiè qiǎngjié] **2** (*delay*) 延搁 [yángē]; (*in traffic*) 交通阻塞 [jiāotōng zǔsè]

hole [həʊl] I N [C] **1** (*space, gap*) 洞 [dòng] **2** (*tear*) (*in clothing, pocket, bag*) 破洞 [pòdòng] **3** (*for rabbit, mouse etc*) 洞穴 [dòngxué] **4** (*inf*) (*unpleasant place*) 陋室 [lòushì] **5** (GOLF) 球洞 [qiúdòng] II VT [+ *ship, building etc*] 打洞 [dǎdòng] ▶ **hole in the heart** (MED) 心脏穿孔 ▶ **to pick holes (in sth)** (*inf*) (*fig*) 挑某物(中)的漏洞 ▶ **a hole in one** 一击入洞

▶ **hole up** VI 躲藏 [duǒcáng]

holiday ['hɒlɪdeɪ] (BRIT) N [C/U] 假期 [jiàqī] [美 = **vacation**] ▶ **public holiday** 公共假期 ▶ **the school/summer/Christmas holidays** (BRIT: SCOL) 学校/暑/圣诞假期 [美 = **vacation**] ▶ **to be on holiday** 在度假

holidaymaker ['hɒlɪdeɪmeɪkə(r)] (BRIT) N [C] 度假者 [dùjiàzhě]

holiday resort N [C] 旅游胜地 [lǚyóu shèngdì]

Holland ['hɒlənd] N 荷兰 [Hélán]

hollow ['hɒləʊ] I ADJ **1** (*not solid*) [+ *container, log, tree*] 空的 [kōng de] **2** (*sunken*) [+ *cheeks, eyes*] 凹陷的 [āoxiàn de] **3** (*empty*) [+ *claim, threat*] 空洞的 [kōngdòng de] **4** (*dull*) [+ *sound, laugh*] 沉闷的 [chénmèn de] II N [C] (*in ground*) 凹地 [āodì]

▶ **hollow out** VT 挖空 [wākōng]

holly ['hɒlɪ] N [U] 冬青 [dōngqīng]

Hollywood ['hɒlɪwʊd] I N 好莱坞 [Hǎoláiwū] II CPD [复合词] [+ *studio, star, film*] 好莱坞 [Hǎoláiwū]

holocaust ['hɒləkɔːst] N [C] 大屠杀 [dàtúshā] ▶ **the Holocaust** (HIST) 第二次世界大战期间纳粹对犹太人的大屠杀

holy ['həʊlɪ] ADJ [+ *picture, place, water*] 神圣的 [shénshèng de]; [+ *person*] 圣洁的 [shèngjié de]

homage ['hɒmɪdʒ] N [U] 敬意 [jìngyì] ▶ **to pay homage to sb/sth** 向某人/某物表示敬意

⊙ **home** [həʊm] I N **1** [C/U] (*house*) 家 [jiā] ▷ *His home is in Hampstead.* 他家在汉姆斯塔德。 **2** [C/U] (*country, area*) 家乡 [jiāxiāng] ▷ *Jack often dreamed of home from his prison cell.* 杰克在监狱牢房里常常梦见家乡。 **3** [C] (*institution*) 收容院 [shōuróngyuàn] ▷ *a home for handicapped children* 残疾儿童收容院 II ADJ **1** (*made at home*) 家庭的 [jiātíng de] ▷ *home cooking* 家庭式烹调 **2** (ECON, POL) (*domestic*) 国内的 [guónèi de] ▷ *the expansion of the home market* 国内市场的扩大 **3** (SPORT) [+ *team, game*] 主场的 [zhǔchǎng de] ▷ *They are Celtic fans, and attend all home games.* 他们是凯尔特人队的球迷，观看所有的主场比赛。 III ADV [*be, go, get etc +*] 在家 [zàijiā] ▷ *I want to go home.* 我想回家。 ▷ *I'll phone you as soon as I get home.* 我一回家就给你电话。 ▶ **at home** (*in house*) 在家 ▷ *She went out to work, while he stayed at home to care for the children.* 她出去工作，而他则在家照顾孩子。; (SPORT) 在主场 ▷ *Our team are at home this weekend.* 这个周末我们的球队是主场。; (*comfortable*) 自在 ▷ *I felt at home at once, because I recognized familiar faces.* 我立即感到自在，因为我见到熟悉的面孔。 ▶ **make yourself at home** 请不要拘束 ▶ **the home of free enterprise/the blues** 自由企业/蓝调音乐的起源地 ▶ **home and dry** (BRIT) or **home free** (US) 大功告成 ▶ **a home from** or (US) **away from home** 像家一样舒适的地方 ▶ **to bring sth home to sb** 使某人认识到某事 ▶ **to drive/hammer sth home** (*fig*) 强调某事; (*lit*) 全部碰进去

▶ **home in on** VT FUS [不可拆分] **1** (*locate*) [*missile, equipment +*] 自动追击 [zìdòng zhuījī] ▷ *The Sidewinder missile can home in on its target with pinpoint accuracy.* 响尾蛇导弹能非常准确

地追击目标。**2** (concentrate on) 把注意力集中于[bǎ zhùyìlì jízhōng yú] ▷ Critics immediately homed in on the group's greatest weakness. 评论家立即针对该团体最薄弱环节进攻。▷ He homed in on the details. 他把注意力集中于细节方面。

home address N [C] 家庭地址 [jiātíng dìzhǐ]

home economics N [U] 家政学 [jiāzhèngxué]

homeland ['hǝumlænd] N [C] 祖国 [zǔguó]

homeless ['hǝumlɪs] I ADJ [+ family, refugee] 无家可归的 [wújiā kěguī de] II NPL ▸ **the homeless** 无家可归的人 [wújiā kěguī de rén] ▸ **to be made homeless** 被弄成无家可归

homely ['hǝumlɪ] ADJ **1** (BRIT) (comfortable) 令人感到舒适的 [lìng rén gǎndào shūshì de] [美= homey] **2** (US) (in looks) 相貌平平的 [xiàngmào píngpíng de]

home-made [hǝum'meɪd] ADJ [+ bread, bomb] 自制的 [zìzhì de]

Home Office (BRIT) N ▸ **the Home Office** 内政部 [Nèizhèngbù]

homeopathic [hǝumɪǝu'pæθɪk] ADJ 顺势疗法的 [shùnshì liáofǎ de]

homeowner ['hǝumǝunǝ(r)] N [C] 房产主 [fángchǎnzhǔ]

homepage ['hǝumpeɪdʒ] (COMPUT) N [C] 主页 [zhǔyè]

Home Secretary (BRIT) N ▸ **the Home Secretary** 内政部长 [Nèizhèng Bùzhǎng]

homesick ['hǝumsɪk] ADJ 想家的 [xiǎngjiā de]

home town N [C] 家乡 [jiāxiāng]

homework ['hǝumwǝːk] N [U] 家庭作业 [jiātíng zuòyè] ▸ **to do one's homework** (lit) 做家庭作业; (fig) 做必要的准备工作

homey ['hǝumɪ] (US) ADJ 舒适的 [shūshì de] [英= homely]

homicide ['hɒmɪsaɪd] (US) N [C/U] 杀人 [shārén] [英= murder]

homoeopathic [hǝumɪǝu'pæθɪk] (BRIT) ADJ = homeopathic

homosexual [hɒmǝu'sɛksjuǝl] I ADJ [+ person, relationship] 同性恋的 [tóngxìngliàn de] II N [C] (man, woman) 同性恋者 [tóngxìngliànzhě]

Honduras [hɒn'djuǝrǝs] N 洪都拉斯 [Hóngdūlāsī]

honest ['ɒnɪst] I ADJ **1** (truthful) 诚实的 [chéngshí de] **2** (trustworthy) 可信的 [kěxìn de] II ADV (inf) (honestly) 老实说 [lǎoshí shuō] ▸ **to be honest,...** 说实话，…

honestly ['ɒnɪstlɪ] ADV **1** (with integrity) 正直地 [zhèngzhí de] **2** (bluntly) 坦白地 [tǎnbái de] **3** (emphasizing sth) 真的 [zhēn de] ▸ **I honestly don't know** 我真的不知道 ▸ **oh, honestly!** 真是的！

honesty ['ɒnɪstɪ] N [U] **1** (integrity) 诚实 [chéngshí] **2** (bluntness) 坦白 [tǎnbái] ▸ **in all honesty** 说实话

honey ['hʌnɪ] N [U] **1** (food) 蜂蜜 [fēngmì]

2 (ESP US: inf) (darling) 宝贝 [bǎobèi]

honeymoon ['hʌnɪmuːn] N [C] **1** 蜜月 [mìyuè] **2** (fig) 早期的和谐时期 [zǎoqī de héxié shíqī] ▸ **to be on (one's) honeymoon** [couple +] 在度蜜月 ▸ **the honeymoon period is over** 初期的和谐时期已经过去了

honeysuckle ['hʌnɪsʌkl] N [U] 金银花 [jīnyínhuā]

Hong Kong ['hɒŋ'kɒŋ] N 香港 [Xiānggǎng]

honor ['ɒnǝ(r)] (US) VT, N = honour

honorable ['ɒnǝrǝbl] (US) ADJ = honourable

honorary ['ɒnǝrǝrɪ] ADJ **1** [+ job, secretary] 名誉的 [míngyù de] **2** [+ title, degree] 荣誉的 [róngyù de]

honour, (US) **honor** ['ɒnǝ(r)] I VT **1** [+ hero, leader] 向…表示敬意 [xiàng…biǎoshì jìngyì] **2** [+ commitment, promise] 遵守 [zūnshǒu] II N **1** [U] (pride, self-respect) 自尊 [zìzūn] **2** [C] (tribute) 荣誉 [róngyù] ▸ **I would be honoured to accept** 我将非常荣幸地接受 ▸ **a festival in honour of David Hockney** 为了对大卫•霍克尼表示敬意而举行的庆祝活动 ▸ **it is an honour to work with her** 和她一起工作是很光荣的 ▸ **the honour of hosting the Olympic Games** 主办奥林匹克运动会的光荣 ▸ **to do the honours** (inf) 尽主人之道 ▸ **on my honour** 用我的名誉担保 ▸ **your/his honour** (LAW) 阁下

honourable, (US) **honorable** ['ɒnǝrǝbl] ADJ **1** [+ person, action, defeat] 高尚的 [gāoshàng de] **2** (in parliament) 尊敬的 [zūnjìng de]

honours degree N [C] 优等成绩学位 [yōuděng chéngjì xuéwèi]

hood [hud] N [C] **1** [of coat etc] 兜帽 [dōumào] **2** (mask, blindfold) 面罩 [miànzhào] **3** (US: AUT) 发动机罩 [fādòngjī zhào] [英= bonnet] **4** (cover) 罩 [zhào] **5** [of cooker] 排油烟机 [páiyóuyānjī]

hoof [huːf] (pl hooves) N 蹄 [tí]

hook [huk] I N [C] (for coats, fishing, curtains etc, on dress) 钩 [gōu] II VT **1** (fasten) 钩住 [gōuzhù] **2** ▸ **to hook one's arm around sth** 用胳膊钩住某物 [yòng gēbo gōuzhù mǒuwù] III VI (fasten) ▸ **to hook onto sth** 挂在某物上 [guàzài mǒuwù shang] ▸ **left/right hook** 左/右钩拳 ▸ **to get sb off the hook** 使某人脱离困境 ▸ **to be off the hook** 脱身 ▸ **to take the phone off the hook** 不把电话听筒挂上 ▸ **hook up** VT (RAD) 联机 [liánjī]

hooligan ['huːlɪgǝn] N [C] 流氓 [liúmáng]

hoop [huːp] N [C] **1** (ring) 圈 [quān] **2** (in basketball) 篮圈 [lánquān] **3** (for croquet) 拱门 [gǒngmén] ▸ **to jump through a hoop** or **hoops** 受磨炼

hooray [huː'reɪ] INT 好哇 [hǎo wa]

hoot [huːt] I VI **1** [driver, car, siren +] 鸣响 [míngxiǎng]; [owl +] 鸣叫 [míngjiào] **2** (laugh, jeer) 哈哈大笑 [hāhā dàxiào] II VT [+ horn] 按 [àn] III N [C] [of horn] 汽车喇叭声 [qìchē lǎbā shēng]; [of owl] 猫头鹰的叫声 [māotóuyīng de jiàoshēng] ▶ **to hoot with laughter** 呵呵大笑 ▶ **a hoot of laughter** 呵呵大笑 ▶ **it's/he's a hoot** (inf) 这是滑稽的/他是个滑稽的人

Hoover® ['huːvə(r)] (BRIT) I N [C] 吸尘器 [xīchénqì] II VT [+ carpet] 用吸尘器吸 [yòng xīchénqì xī]

hooves [huːvz] NPL of **hoof**

hop [hɒp] I VI 1 (jump) [person+] 单脚跳 [dānjiǎo tiào]; [bird+] 双脚跳 [shuāngjiǎo tiào] 2 (inf) (move quickly) 飞奔 [fēibēng] ▷ I hopped out of bed. 我跳下床。 II N [C] (by person) 单脚跳 [dānjiǎo tiào]; (by bird) 双爪跳 [shuāngzhuǎ tiào] ▶ **to be hopping mad** (inf) 气得暴跳如雷 ▶ **to catch sb on the hop** (BRIT: inf) 使某人措手不及 see also **hops**

○**hope** [həup] I VT 希望 [xīwàng] ▷ I sat down, hoping to remain unnoticed. 我坐下，希望没有被人注意到。 ▷ They hope that a vaccine will be available soon. 他们希望很快能有疫苗。 II VI 盼望 [pànwàng] ▷ Nothing can be done except to wait, hope, and pray. 除了等待、期望和祈祷外，什么都没用。 III N 1 [U] 希望 [xīwàng] ▷ She never completely gave up hope. 她从来没有完全放弃希望。 2 [C] (aspiration) 期望 [qīwàng] ▷ the hopes and dreams of reformers 改革者的期望和梦想 ▶ **I hope so/not** 希望是这样/希望不会 ▶ **to hope that...** 希望… ▶ **I hope you don't mind** 希望你不介意 ▶ **to hope to do sth** 希望能做某事 ▶ **to hope for the best** 保持乐观 ▶ **to have no hope of sth/doing sth** 对某事/做某事不抱希望 ▶ **in the hope of/that...** 希望… ▶ **to hope against hope that...** 抱有一线希望…

hopeful ['həupful] I ADJ 1 (optimistic) [+ person] 乐观的 [lèguān de] 2 (promising) [+ situation, sign] 鼓舞人心的 [gǔwǔ rénxīn de] II N [C] 有前途的人 [yǒu qiántú de rén] ▶ **to be hopeful that...** 对…抱有希望 ▶ **surgeons are hopeful of saving her** 外科医生对挽救她抱有希望

hopefully ['həupfulɪ] ADV (expectantly) 怀着希望地 [huáizhe xīwàng de] ▶ **hopefully,...** 如果运气好，…

hopeless ['həuplɪs] ADJ 1 (in despair) 绝望的 [juéwàng de] 2 (dismal) [+ situation, position] 糟糕的 [zāogāo de] 3 (inf) (useless) [+ teacher, driver, service] 无能的 [wúnéng de] ▶ **to be hopeless at doing sth** 实在不会做某事 ▶ **I'm hopeless at cooking** 我做饭实在不行

hops [hɒps] NPL 啤酒花 [píjiǔ huā]

horizon [hə'raɪzn] I N (skyline) ▶ **the horizon** 地平线 [dìpíngxiàn] II **horizons** NPL 眼界 [yǎnjiè] ▶ **on the horizon** (fig) 即将发生的

horizontal [hɒrɪ'zɒntl] ADJ 水平的 [shuǐpíng de]

hormone ['hɔːməun] N [C] 激素 [jīsù]

horn [hɔːn] N 1 [C] [of animal] 角 [jiǎo] 2 [U] (substance) 角质物 [jiǎozhìwù] 3 [C] (MUS) 号 [hào] 4 [C] (AUT) 喇叭 [lǎba]

horoscope ['hɒrəskəup] N [C] 占星术 [zhānxīngshù]

horrendous [hə'rɛndəs] ADJ [+ crime, error] 恐怖的 [kǒngbù de]

horrible ['hɒrɪbl] ADJ [+ colour, food, mess] 糟透的 [zāotòu de]; [+ accident, crime] 可怕的 [kěpà de]; [+ experience, moment, situation, dream] 令人恐惧的 [lìng rén kǒngjù de]

horrid ['hɒrɪd] ADJ [+ person, place, thing] 极糟的 [jízāo de] ▶ **to be horrid to sb** 对某人极不友好

horrific [hɒ'rɪfɪk] ADJ [+ injury, accident, crime] 极其可怕的 [jíqí kěpà de]

horrified ['hɒrɪfaɪd] ADJ 受惊吓的 [shòu jīngxià de] ▶ **to be horrified at sth** 对某事感到震惊

horrifying ['hɒrɪfaɪɪŋ] ADJ [+ experience, crime] 极其恐怖的 [jíqí kǒngbù de]

horror ['hɒrə(r)] N [U] (alarm) 恐怖 [kǒngbù] ▶ **to have a horror of sth** 痛恨某事 ▶ **the horrors of war** 战争的恐怖

horror film N [C] 恐怖片 [kǒngbù piān]

hors d'oeuvre [ɔː'dəːvrə] N [C/U] 餐前的开胃小吃 [cānqián de kāiwèi xiǎochī]

horse [hɔːs] N [C] 马 [mǎ]

horseback ['hɔːsbæk] N ▶ **on horseback** 骑着马 [qízhe mǎ]

horse chestnut N [C] 1 (tree) 七叶树 [qīyèshù] 2 (conker) 七叶树坚果 [qīyèshù jiānguǒ]

horsepower ['hɔːspauə(r)] N [U] [of engine, car etc] 马力 [mǎlì]

horse racing N [U] 赛马 [sàimǎ]

horseradish ['hɔːsrædɪʃ] N [C/U] 辣根 [làgēn]

horse riding N [U] 骑马 [qímǎ]

hose [həuz] N [C] (also: **hosepipe**) 输水软管 [shūshuǐ ruǎnguǎn] ▶ **hose down** VT 用软管输水冲洗 [yòng ruǎnguǎn shūshuǐ chōngxǐ]

hospitable ['hɒspɪtəbl] ADJ 1 [+ person, behaviour] 好客的 [hàokè de] 2 [+ climate] 宜人的 [yírén de]

○**hospital** ['hɒspɪtl] N [C/U] 医院 [yīyuàn] ▶ **to be in hospital** or (US) **in the hospital** 住院

hospitality [hɒspɪ'tælɪtɪ] N [U] 1 [of host, welcome] 好客 [hàokè] 2 (COMM) (food, drink) 招待 [zhāodài]

○**host** [həust] I N [C] 1 (at party, dinner) 主人 [zhǔrén] 2 (TV, RAD) [of television programme] 主持人 [zhǔchírén] 3 (for festival, conference etc) 东道主 [dōngdàozhǔ] II ADJ [+ country, organization] 东道的 [dōngdào de] III VT 1 [+ party, dinner] 举行 [jǔxíng] 2 (TV, RAD) [+ show] 主持 [zhǔchí] 3 [+ festival, conference] 主办 [zhǔbàn] ▶ **a whole host of problems** 许多问题 ▶ **the host** (REL) 圣饼

hostage ['hɒstɪdʒ] N [C] (prisoner) 人质 [rénzhì] ▶ **to be taken/held hostage** 被绑架/扣押做人质

hostel ['hɒstl] (ESP BRIT) N [C] (for homeless etc)

招待所 [zhāodàisuǒ]

hostess ['həustɪs] N [c] **1** (at party, dinner etc) 女主人 [nǚ zhǔrén] **2** (in night club) 女招待 [nǚ zhāodài]

hostile ['hɒstaɪl] ADJ **1** (aggressive) [+ person, attitude] 不友好的 [bù yǒuhǎo de]
2 [+ conditions, environment] 恶劣的 [èliè de]
3 (enemy) 敌方的 [dífāng de] ▶ to be hostile to or towards sb 对某人不友善

hostility [hɒ'stɪlɪtɪ] I N [U] (aggression) 敌意 [díyì] II **hostilities** NPL (fighting) 交战 [jiāozhàn]

hot [hɒt] ADJ **1** [+ object] 烫的 [tàng de]; [+ weather, person] 热的 [rè de] **2** (spicy) [+ food] 辣的 [là de] **3** (inf) (up-to-the-moment) 热门的 [rèmén de] **4** (fierce) [+ temper] 暴躁的 [bàozào de] ▶ he's not so hot on physics (inf) 他物理不怎么好 ▶ hot and bothered 焦躁不安的
▶ **hot up** (BRIT: inf) I VI [situation, party +] 热闹起来 [rènao qǐlái] II VT [+ pace] 使增加 [shǐ zēngjiā]

> 在非正式英语中，**boiling** 或 **scorching** 可用于强调天气非常炎热。在冬天，如果气温比平均气温要高，可以用 **mild**。一般而言，**hot** 所表达的气温要高于 **warm**。warm 的东西是热得令人感到舒服的东西。...a warm evening...

hot chocolate N [U] 热巧克力 [rè qiǎokèlì]

hot dog N [c] 热狗 [règǒu]

hotel [həu'tɛl] N [c] 旅馆 [lǚguǎn] ▶ to stay at a hotel 住旅馆

hotline ['hɒtlaɪn] N [c] 热线 [rèxiàn]

hotly ['hɒtlɪ] ADV **1** [speak +] 生气地 [shēngqì de] **2** [contest, pursue +] 激烈地 [jīliè de] ▶ a claim which he has hotly denied 他极力否认的说法

hot-water bottle [hɒt'wɔːtə(r)-] N [c] 热水袋 [rèshuǐdài]

hound [haund] I N [c] (dog) 猎狗 [liègǒu] II VT (harass, persecute) 不断烦扰 [bùduàn fánrǎo]

hour ['auə(r)] I N **1** [c] 小时 [xiǎoshí] **2** [s] (frm) (time) 时间 [shíjiān] ▷ The hour of his execution was approaching. 处决他的时间快到了。 II **hours** NPL **1** (ages) 很长时间 [hěncháng shíjiān] ▷ Getting there would take hours. 去那儿要花很长时间。 **2** (in job) 工作时间 [gōngzuò shíjiān] ▷ I worked quite irregular hours. 我的工作时间很不固定。 ▶ office/visiting hours 办公/参观时间 ▶ the buses leave on the hour 每小时正点有一班公共汽车 ▶ in the early or small hours 凌晨 ▶ after hours 工作结束后 ▶ at all hours of the day and night 白天和晚上任何时候 ▶ for three/four hours 三/四个小时 ▷ They slept for two hours. 他们睡了两个小时。
▶ (at) 60 kilometres/miles an or per hour 每小时60公里/英里 ▶ to pay sb by the hour 按小时付费给某人 ▶ lunch hour 午餐时间

hourly ['auəlɪ] I ADV (once each hour) 每小时 [měi xiǎoshí] II ADJ **1** (once each hour) 每小时一次的 [měi xiǎoshí yīcì de] **2** (per hour) [+ rate, income] 每小时的 [měi xiǎoshí de]

○ **house** [n haus, vb hauz] I N **1** [c] (home) 家 [jiā] **2** [s] (household) 全家 [quánjiā] ▷ The noise woke the whole house. 那个声音吵醒了全家。 **3** [c] (company) ▶ publishing house/steak house 出版社/牛肉馆 [chūbǎnshè/niúròuguǎn]
4 [c] (POL) 议院 [yìyuàn] **5** [c] (THEAT) 观众 [guānzhòng] **6** [c] (dynasty) 王室 [wángshì] ▷ the House of Windsor 英国王室 II VT **1** [+ person] 提供住房 [tígōng zhùfáng] ▷ Too many married couples are waiting to be housed. 太多已婚夫妻正等着提供住房。 **2** [+ collection] 储藏 [chǔcáng] ▷ This is the building which houses the library. 这就是藏书的那个建筑。 ▶ at/to my house 在/到我家 ▶ to get or put or set one's house in order 把自己的事情处理妥当 ▶ to bring the house down (inf) 博得全场喝彩 ▶ to get on like a house on fire (inf) 意气相投 ▶ drinks are on the house 饮料免费 ▶ to keep house 料理家务

household ['haushəuld] N [c] **1** (family) 家庭 [jiātíng] **2** (home) 家 [jiā] ▶ to be a household name 是家喻户晓的名字

housekeeper ['hauskiːpə(r)] N [c] 管家 [guǎnjiā]

housekeeping ['hauskiːpɪŋ] N [U] **1** (work) 管理家务 [guǎnlǐ jiāwù] **2** (BRIT) (money) 持家费 [chíjiāfèi]

House of Commons N ▶ the House of Commons 下议院 [xiàyìyuàn]

House of Lords N ▶ the House of Lords 上议院 [shàngyìyuàn]

House of Representatives N ▶ the House of Representatives 众议院 [zhòngyìyuàn]

Houses of Parliament NPL ▶ the Houses of Parliament 议院 [yìyuàn]

housewife ['hauswaɪf] (pl **housewives**) N [c] 家庭主妇 [jiātíng zhǔfù]

house wine N [C/U] 饭馆、酒吧提供的最便宜的葡萄酒 [fànguǎn jiǔbā tígōng de zuì piányi de pútáojiǔ]

housework ['hauswəːk] N [U] 家务劳动 [jiāwù láodòng]

housing ['hauzɪŋ] I N [U] **1** (houses) 房屋 [fángwū] **2** (provision) 住房 [zhùfáng] II CPD [复合词] [+ problem, shortage] 住房 [zhùfáng]

housing estate (BRIT) N [c] 住宅区 [zhùzhái qū]

housing project (US) N [c] 安居工程 [ānjū gōngchéng]

hove [həuv] PT, PP of heave to

hover ['hɒvə(r)] VI **1** [bird, insect +] 翱翔 [áoxiáng]; [helicopter +] 盘旋 [pánxuán] **2** [person +] 徘徊 [páihuái]

hovercraft ['hɒvəkrɑːft] (pl **hovercraft**) N [c] 气垫船 [qìdiàn chuán]

○

how [hau] **I** ADV **1** (*in questions*) 怎样 [zěnyàng] ▶ **how did you do it?** 你是怎么做的？ ▶ **how was the film?** 电影怎么样？ ▶ **how are you?** 你好吗？ ▶ **how can you be so unkind?** 你怎么能如此刻薄呢？ ▶ **"how do you do?" "how do you do?"** "你好！" "你好！" ▶ **how long have you lived here?** 你在这儿住了多久了？ ▶ **how much milk/many people?** 有多少奶/人？ ▶ **how old are you?** 你多大了？ ▶ **how tall is he?** 他有多高？ ▶ **how well do you know her?** 你对她了解有多少？
2 (*in exclamations*) ▶ **how lovely/awful!** 太可爱/糟了！ [tài kě'ài/zāo le!]
3 (*in suggestions*) ▶ **how about a cup of tea/a walk** *etc*? 来杯茶/去散步〔等〕好吗？ [lái bēi chá/qù sànbù 〔děng〕 hǎo ma?] ▶ **how about going to the cinema?** 去看电影好吗？ ▶ **how would you like to eat out tonight?** 今天晚上出去吃好吗？
4 (*avoiding repetition*) ▶ **how about you?** 你呢？ [nǐ ne?]
II CONJ 怎么 [zěnme] ▶ **I know how you did it** 我知道你怎么做的 ▶ **to know how to do sth** 知道如何做某事 ▶ **it's amazing how he always seems to understand** 他总是如此善解人意真是太了不起了

○**however** [hau'evə(r)] **I** ADV **1** (*but*) 但是 [dànshì] ▷ *I hoped he might offer me a job. However, he didn't.* 我希望他能给我一份工作。但是他并没有这么做。 **2** (*with adj, adv*) 不管怎样 [bùguǎn zěnyàng] ▷ *However hard she tried, nothing seemed to work.* 不管她怎样努力，都不行。 **3** (*in questions*) 究竟怎样 [jiūjìng zěnyàng] ▷ *However did you find me?* 你究竟怎样找到我的？ **II** CONJ (*no matter how*) 无论 [wúlùn] ▷ *Wear your hair however you want.* 你想梳什么型都行。 ▷ *I will wait for you however late you are.* 无论多晚我都会等你。

howl [haul] **I** VI (*animal* +) 嗥叫 [háojiào]; (*baby, person* +) 嚎哭 [háokū]; (*laugh*) 狂笑 [kuángxiào]; (*wind* +) 呼啸 [hūxiào] **II** N [c] [(*of animal*)] 嗥叫 [háojiào]; [(*of baby, person*)] 嚎哭 [háokū]; [(*of laughter*)] 狂笑 [kuángxiào]

hp (AUT) ABBR (= *horsepower*) 马力 [mǎlì]

HQ ABBR (= *headquarters*) 总部 [zǒngbù]

HRH (BRIT) ABBR (= *His/Her Royal Highness*) 殿下 [diànxià]

hr(s) ABBR (= *hours*) 小时 [xiǎoshí]

HST (US) ABBR (= *Hawaiian Standard Time*) 夏威夷标准时间 [Xiàwēiyí Biāozhǔn Shíjiān]

hubcap [ˈhʌbkæp] N [c] 毂盖 [gǔgài]

huddle [ˈhʌdl] **I** VI 蜷缩 [quánsuō] **II** N [c] 挤作一团 [jǐzuò yìtuán] ▶ **to huddle together** 挤作一团 ▶ **to huddle around sth** 围着某物

huff [hʌf] N ▶ **to be in a huff** 发怒 [fānù]

hug [hʌg] **I** VT **1** [+ *person*] 拥抱 [yōngbào]

2 [+ *object*] 紧抱 [jǐnbào] **II** N [c] 拥抱 [yōngbào] ▶ **to give sb a hug** 拥抱某人

huge [hjuːdʒ] ADJ [+ *crowd, skyscraper, wardrobe*] 巨大的 [jùdà de]; [+ *amount, profit, debt*] 巨额的 [jù'é de]; [+ *task*] 庞大的 [pángdà de]

hull [hʌl] **I** N [c] **1** (NAUT) 船体 [chuántǐ]; [*of nut*] 壳 [ké] **2** [*of strawberry etc*] 花萼 [huā'è] **II** VT [+ *fruit*] 除去…花萼 [chúqù…huā'è]

hum [hʌm] **I** VT [+ *tune, song*] 哼 [hēng] **II** VI [*person* +] 哼 [hēng]; [*machine, insect* +] 发出嗡嗡声 [fāchū wēngwēng shēng] **III** N [s] [*of traffic, machines, voices*] 嗡嗡声 [wēngwēng shēng]

○**human** [ˈhjuːmən] **I** ADJ [+ *body, behaviour*] 人的 [rén de] ▷ *the human body* 人体; [+ *weakness, emotion*] 有人性的 [yǒu rénxìng de] **II** N [c] (*also*: **human being**) 人 [rén] ▷ *Could a computer ever beat a human at chess?* 下象棋电脑能打败人吗？ ▶ **the human race** 人类 ▶ **human nature** 人性 ▶ **human error** 人为错误 ▶ **we're only human** 我们只是普通人

humane [hjuːˈmeɪn] ADJ [+ *treatment, slaughter*] 人道的 [réndào de]

humanitarian [hjuːmænɪˈtɛəriən] ADJ [+ *aid, principles*] 人道主义的 [rédào zhǔyì de] ▶ **on humanitarian grounds** 以人道主义的原则

humanity [hjuːˈmænɪtɪ] **I** N [u] **1** (*mankind*) 人类 [rénlèi] **2** (*kindness*) 博爱 [bó'ài] **3** (*humanness*) 人性 [rénxìng] **II the humanities** NPL 人文学科 [rénwén xuékē]

human rights NPL 人权 [rénquán]

humble [ˈhʌmbl] **I** ADJ **1** (*modest*) [+ *person*] 谦虚的 [qiānxū de] **2** (*lowly*) [+ *background*] 卑贱的 [bēijiàn de] **II** VT (*humiliate, crush*) 使谦卑 [shǐ qiānbēi] ▶ **to humble sb's pride** 打掉某人的傲气

humid [ˈhjuːmɪd] ADJ [+ *atmosphere, climate*] 潮湿的 [cháoshī de]

humidity [hjuːˈmɪdɪtɪ] N [u] [*of atmosphere, climate*] 湿度 [shīdù]

humiliate [hjuːˈmɪlɪeɪt] VT [+ *rival, person*] 羞辱 [xiūrǔ]

humiliating [hjuːˈmɪlɪeɪtɪŋ] ADJ [+ *experience, defeat*] 丢脸的 [diūliǎn de]

humiliation [hjuːmɪlɪˈeɪʃən] **N 1** [u] (*feeling*) 羞辱 [xiūrǔ] **2** [c] (*situation, experience*) 丢脸 [diūliǎn]

humility [hjuːˈmɪlɪtɪ] N [u] (*modesty*) 谦恭 [qiāngōng]

humor [ˈhjuːmə(r)] (US) N = humour

humorous [ˈhjuːmərəs] ADJ [+ *remark, book, person*] 幽默的 [yōumò de]

humour, (US) **humor** [ˈhjuːmə(r)] **I** N [u] 幽默 [yōumò] **II** VT 迎合 [yínghé] ▶ **sense of humour** 幽默感 ▶ **to be in good/bad humour** 情绪好/不好

hump [hʌmp] **I** N [c] (*in ground*) 丘陵 [qiūlíng]; (*to restrict speed*) 凸面 [tūmiàn]; [*of camel*] 峰 [fēng]; (*deformity*) 驼背 [tuóbèi] **II** VT 扛

[káng] ▶ **to get the hump** (BRIT: *inf*) 闷闷不乐

hunch [hʌntʃ] I N [c] (*intuition*) 直觉 [zhíjué]
▶ **I have a hunch that…** 我的直觉是… II VT
▶ **to hunch one's shoulders** 耸起双肩 [sǒngqǐ shuāngjiān]

◉ **hundred** ['hʌndrəd] I NUM 百 [bǎi]
II **hundreds** NPL 几百 [jǐbǎi] ▷ *He handed me hundreds of forms.* 他递给我几百张表格。 ▶ **a or one hundred books/people/dollars** 一百本书/个人/美元 ▶ **a or one hundred per cent** 百分之百

hundredth ['hʌndrədθ] I ADJ 第一百的 [dì yībǎi de] II N ▶ **a hundredth (of a)** 百分之一 [bǎifēn zhī yī]

hung [hʌŋ] I PT, PP *of* **hang** II ADJ ▶ **a hung parliament** 各党势均力敌的议院 [gèdǎng shìjūn lìdí de yìyuàn]

Hungarian [hʌŋ'gɛərɪən] I ADJ 匈牙利的 [Xiōngyálì de] II N 1 [c] (*person*) 匈牙利人 [Xiōngyálìrén] 2 [U] (*language*) 匈牙利语 [Xiōngyálìyǔ]

Hungary ['hʌŋgərɪ] N 匈牙利 [Xiōngyálì]

hunger ['hʌŋgə(r)] I N [U] 1 (*lack of food*) 饿 [è] 2 (*starvation*) 饥饿 [jī'è] II VI ▶ **they hunger for adventure** 他们渴望冒险 [tāmen kěwàng màoxiǎn] ▶ **his hunger for adventure** 他想冒险的强烈期望

hungry ['hʌŋgrɪ] ADJ 饥饿的 [jī'è de] ▶ **to be hungry** 饿了 ▶ **to be hungry for success** 渴望成功 ▶ **to go hungry** 挨饿

hunt [hʌnt] I VT 1 (*for food, sport*) 打猎 [dǎliè] 2 [+ *criminal, fugitive*) 追捕 [zhuībǔ] II VI 1 (*for food, sport*) 打猎 [dǎliè] 2 (BRIT) (*for foxes*) 猎狐 [lièhú] III N [c] 1 (*for food, sport*) 狩猎 [shòuliè] 2 (BRIT) (*group of fox hunters*) 猎狐队 [lièhú duì] 3 (*for missing person*) 搜寻 [sōuxún] 4 (*for criminal*) 追捕 [zhuībǔ] ▶ **detectives are hunting for clues** 刑警们在寻找线索
▶ **hunt down** VT 追捕到 [zhuībǔ dào]

hunter ['hʌntə(r)] N [c] (*for food, sport*) 猎手 [lièshǒu] ▶ **bargain/house hunter** 寻便宜货/屋者

hunting ['hʌntɪŋ] N [U] (*for food, sport*) 打猎 [dǎliè] ▶ **job/house/bargain hunting** 到处找工作/住房/便宜货

hurdle ['hə:dl] I N [c] (*difficulty*) 障碍 [zhàng'ài] II **hurdles** NPL (SPORT) 跳栏 [tiàolán]

hurl [hə:l] VT 1 [+ *object*) 用力投掷 [yònglì tóuzhì] 2 [+ *insult, abuse*) 叫嚷 [jiàorǎng]

hurrah [hu'rɑ:] INT = **hooray**

hurray [hu'reɪ] INT = **hooray**

hurricane ['hʌrɪkən] N [c] 飓风 [jùfēng]
▶ **hurricane Charley/Tessa** 查理/特萨号台风

hurriedly ['hʌrɪdlɪ] ADV 匆忙地 [cōngmáng de]

hurry ['hʌrɪ] I VI 赶紧 [gǎnjǐn] II VT [+ *person*) 催 [cuī] III N ▶ **to be in a hurry (to do sth)** 急于(做某事) [jí yú (zuò mǒushì)] ▶ **to hurry in/off/home** 赶着进来/走/回家 ▶ **they hurried to help him** 他们赶紧去帮他 ▶ **to do**

sth in a hurry 匆忙地做某事 ▶ **there's** *or* **I'm in no hurry** 不着急〔或〕我不着急 ▶ **what's the hurry?** 着什么急?
▶ **hurry along** VT 加速 [jiāsù]
▶ **hurry up** I VI 赶快 [gǎnkuài] II VT 使赶紧 [shǐ gǎnjǐn]

hurt [hə:t] (*pt, pp* **hurt**) I VT 1 (*cause pain to*) 弄痛 [nòngtòng] 2 (*injure*) [+ *arm, leg, finger etc*) 使受伤 [shǐ shòushāng] 3 (*emotionally*) 使伤心 [shǐ shāngxīn] II VI (*be painful*) 痛 [tòng] III ADJ 1 (*injured*) 受伤的 [shòushāng de] 2 (*emotionally*) 受委屈的 [shòu wěiqū de]
▶ **to hurt o.s.** 伤了自己 ▶ **I didn't want to hurt your feelings** 我并不想伤害你的感情
▶ **where does it hurt?** 哪儿疼?

hurtful ['hə:tful] ADJ [+ *remark*) 刻薄的 [kèbó de]

◉ **husband** ['hʌzbənd] I N [c] 丈夫 [zhàngfu]
II VT (*liter*) [+ *resources*) 节省 [jiéshěng]

hush [hʌʃ] I INT 嘘 [xū] II VI (*be quiet*) 安静下来 [ānjìng xiàlái] III VT (*quieten*) 使安静 [shǐ ānjìng] IV N ▶ **a hush fell over the crowd** 人群顿时一片寂静 [rénqún dùnshí yīpiàn jìjìng]
▶ **hush up** VT [+ *scandal etc*) 不让张扬 [bùràng zhāngyáng]

husky ['hʌskɪ] I ADJ [+ *voice*) 嘶哑的 [sīyǎ de] II N [c] (*dog*) 爱斯基摩狗 [Àisījīmó gǒu]

hut [hʌt] N [c] 1 (*house*) 简陋的小屋 [jiǎnlòu de xiǎowū] 2 (*shed*) 木棚 [mùpéng]

hyacinth ['haɪəsɪnθ] N [c] 风信子 [fēngxìnzǐ]

hydrofoil ['haɪdrəfɔɪl] N [c] (*boat*) 水翼船 [shuǐyì chuán]

hydrogen ['haɪdrədʒən] (CHEM) N [U] 氢 [qīng]

hygiene ['haɪdʒi:n] N [U] 卫生 [wèishēng]

hygienic [haɪ'dʒi:nɪk] ADJ 卫生的 [wèishēng de]

hymn [hɪm] N [c] 赞美诗 [zànměi shī]

hype [haɪp] (*inf*) I N [U] 炒作 [chǎozuò] II VT 炒作 [chǎozuò]

hyphen ['haɪfn] N [c] 连字符 [liánzìfú]

hypnosis [hɪp'nəusɪs] N [U] 1 (*state*) 催眠状态 [cuīmián zhuàngtài] 2 (*hypnotism*) 催眠术 [cuīmián shù] ▶ **under hypnosis** 处于被催眠状态

hypnotize ['hɪpnətaɪz] VT 1 (*lit*) 使进入催眠状态 [shǐ jìnrù cuīmián zhuàngtài] 2 (*fig*) (*fascinate*) 使着迷 [shǐ zháomí]

hypocrite ['hɪpəkrɪt] N [c] 伪君子 [wěijūnzǐ]

hypocritical [hɪpə'krɪtɪkl] ADJ [+ *person, behaviour*) 虚伪的 [xūwěi de]

hypothesis [haɪ'pɔθɪsɪs] (*pl* **hypotheses** [haɪ'pɔθɪsi:z]) (*frm*) N [c] (*theory*) 假设 [jiǎshè]

hysterical [hɪ'stɛrɪkl] ADJ 1 [+ *person, laughter*) 歇斯底里的 [xiēsīdǐlǐ de] 2 (*inf*) (*hilarious*) 歇斯底里的 [xiēsīdǐlǐ de]

hysterics [hɪ'stɛrɪks] (*inf*) NPL ▶ **to be in/have hysterics** (*panic, be angry*) 歇斯底里发作 [xiēsīdǐlǐ fāzuò]; (*laugh loudly*) 不可控制的狂笑 [bùkě kòngzhì de kuángxiào]

I¹, i [aɪ] N [C/U] (letter) 英语的第九个字母

I² [aɪ] PRON 我 [wǒ]

I³ ABBR (= island, isle) 岛 [dǎo]

IC (TEXTING) ABBR (= I see) 知道了 [zhīdàole]

ice [aɪs] I N 1 [U] (on lake, river, road) 冰 [bīng]; (for drink) 冰块 [bīngkuài] 2 [C] (BRIT: o.f.) (ice cream) 冰淇淋 [bīngqílín] II VT [+ cake] 在…撒上糖霜 [zài…sǎshàng tángshuāng] III VI (also: **ice over, ice up**) [road, window +] 结冰 [jiēbīng] ▶ **to put sth on ice** (fig) 搁置某事 ▶ **to break the ice** (fig) 使气氛活跃起来 ▶ **to cut no ice (with sb)** (fig) (对某人)不起作用 ▶ **to be (skating) on thin ice** (fig) 如履薄冰

iceberg ['aɪsbəːg] N [C] 冰山 [bīngshān] ▶ **the tip of the iceberg** (fig) 冰山一角

ice cream N [C/U] 冰淇淋 [bīngqílín]

ice cube N [C] 冰块 [bīngkuài]

iced [aɪst] ADJ 1 [+ drink] 冰的 [bīng de] 2 [+ cake] 有糖霜的 [yǒu tángshuāng de]

ice hockey (ESP BRIT) N [U] 冰球 [bīngqiú] [美= **hockey**]

Iceland ['aɪslənd] N 冰岛 [Bīngdǎo]

Icelander ['aɪsləndə(r)] N [C] 冰岛人 [Bīngdǎorén]

Icelandic [aɪs'lændɪk] I ADJ 冰岛的 [Bīngdǎo de] II N [U] (language) 冰岛语 [Bīngdǎoyǔ]

ice lolly (BRIT) N [C] 冰棍 [bīnggùn] [美= **Popsicle®**]

ice rink N [C] 溜冰场 [liūbīngchǎng]

ice-skating ['aɪsskeɪtɪŋ] N [U] 溜冰 [liūbīng];

(figure skating) 花样滑冰 [huāyàng huábīng] ▶ **to go ice-skating** 去溜冰

icing (CULIN) N [U] 糖霜 [tángshuāng] ▶ **the icing on the cake** (fig) 锦上添花

icing sugar (BRIT) N [U] 糖粉 [tángfěn] [美= **confectioners' sugar**]

icon ['aɪkɔn] N [C] 1 (religious) 圣像 [shèngxiàng] 2 (COMPUT) 图符 [túfú] 3 (fig) (symbol) 偶像 [ǒuxiàng]

ICT (BRIT) N ABBR (= Information and Communication Technology) 通信技术 [tōngxìn jìshù]

icy ['aɪsɪ] ADJ [+ air, water, temperature] 冰冷的 [bīnglěng de]; [+ road] 结冰的 [jiēbīng de]

ID N ABBR (= identification) 身份证明 [shēnfèn zhèngmíng] ▶ **do you have any ID?** 你有证件吗?

I'd [aɪd] = I would, I had

ID card [aɪ'diː-] N = identity card

◇idea [aɪ'dɪə] N 1 [C] (scheme) 主意 [zhǔyì] ▷ I had a brilliant idea. 我有个绝妙主意。 2 [C] (opinion, theory) 看法 [kànfǎ] ▷ People had some odd ideas about us. 人们对我们有些古怪的看法。 3 [C/U] (notion) 概念 [gàiniàn] ▷ Do you have any idea how big the project is going to be? 你对项目规模有概念吗? ▷ Have you any idea how much it would cost? 你知道大概是多少钱吗? 4 [S] (objective) 目的 [mùdì] ▷ The idea is to try and avoid further expense. 目的是尽量避免更多的开销。 ▶ **once you get the idea** 一旦你明白了 ▶ **(what a) good idea!** (真是个)好主意! ▶ **to have a good/clear idea of sth** 非常了解某事 ▶ **I haven't the slightest** or **faintest idea** 我根本就不知道 ▶ **that's not my idea of fun** 那不是我的兴趣所在

ideal [aɪ'dɪəl] I ADJ [+ person, world] 理想的 [lǐxiǎng de] II N 1 [C] (principle) 理想 [lǐxiǎng] 2 [S] (epitome) 完美典范 [wánměi diǎnfàn]

ideally [aɪ'dɪəlɪ] ADV 1 [+ suited, located, qualified] 理想地 [lǐxiǎng de] 2 (preferably) 按理想说 [àn lǐxiǎng shuō]

identical [aɪ'dɛntɪkl] ADJ 完全相同的 [wánquán xiāngtóng de] ▶ **identical to** 和…完全相同

identification [aɪdɛntɪfɪ'keɪʃən] N [U] 1 (pinpointing) 识别 [shíbié] 2 (of person, dead body, disease) 确认 [quèrèn] 3 (proof of identity) 身份证明 [shēnfèn zhèngmíng] 4 (association) 关联 [guānlián] 5 (empathy) 息息相通感 [xī xī xiāng tōng gǎn]

identify [aɪ'dɛntɪfaɪ] VT (recognize) 识别 [shíbié] ▶ **to identify with sb/sth** (empathize) 与某人/某物认同 ▶ **to identify sb/sth with** (associate) 与某人/某物相关联

identity [aɪ'dɛntɪtɪ] N [C/U] 1 [of person, culprit] 身份 [shēnfèn] 2 [of group, culture, nation, place] 特性 [tèxìng]

identity card N [C] 身份证 [shēnfènzhèng]

ideological [aɪdɪə'lɒdʒɪkl] ADJ 思想上的 [sīxiǎngshang de]

ideology [aɪdɪ'ɒlədʒɪ] N [C/U] (beliefs) 意识形态 [yìshí xíngtài]

idiom ['ɪdɪəm] N **1** [C] (saying) 习语 [xíyǔ] **2** [C/U] (frm) (style) 风格 [fēnggé]

idiot ['ɪdɪət] N [c] 傻子 [shǎzi]

idle ['aɪdl] **I** ADJ **1** (inactive) 闲散的 [xiánsǎn de] **2** (lazy) 懒惰的 [lǎnduò de] **3** [+conversation, curiosity] 无用的 [wúyòng de] **4** [+threat, boast] 虚张声势的 [xū zhāng shēngshì de] ▷ This is no idle threat. 这不是随便说说吓唬人的。 **5** [+machinery, factory] 闲置的 [xiánzhì de] **6** [+worker] 无所事事的 [wú suǒ shì shì de] **II** VI [machine, engine +] 闲置 [xiánzhì] ▸ **to lie** or **stand idle** [factory, machinery +] 被搁置不用 ▸ **idle away** VT ▸ **to idle away the time** 虚度光阴 [xūdù guāngyīn]

idol ['aɪdl] N [c] **1** (hero) 偶像 [ǒuxiàng] **2** (religious) 圣像 [shèngxiàng]

idyllic [ɪ'dɪlɪk] ADJ [+place, situation, childhood] 质朴宜人的 [zhìpǔ yírén de]

i.e. ABBR (= id est) 也就是 [yě jiùshì]

if [ɪf] CONJ **1** (conditional use) 如果 [rúguǒ] ▸ **I'll go if you come with me** 如果你和我一起的话我就去 ▸ **if anyone comes in...** 如果有人来… ▸ **if I were you** 如果我是你的话 ▸ **if necessary** 如有必要 ▸ **if so** 如果是这样的话 ▸ **if not** 如果不行的话 **2** (stating facts) 即使 [jíshǐ] ▸ **she understood his meaning if not his words** 虽然不懂他的话，她明白他的意思 **3** (whenever) 无论何时 [wúlùn héshí] ▸ **if we are in Hong Kong, we always go to see her** 我们无论何时去香港，都会去看她 **4** (also: even if) 即使 [jíshǐ] ▸ **I'll get this sorted if it's the last thing I do!** 无论怎样我都会这事解决好！ **5** (whether) 是否 [shìfǒu] ▸ **I don't know if he's in** 我不知道他是否会在 ▸ **ask him if he can come** 问他是否能来 **6** (in requests) 请 [qǐng] ▸ **if you could sign here, please** 请在这儿签名，好吗 **7** (in expressions) ▸ **if ever** 要是有 [yàoshì yǒu] ▷ If ever a man needed help, it was I. 要是有人需要帮助的话，那就是我。 ▸ **if only** (giving reason) 即使只是; (expressing wish) 要是…就好了 ▸ **let's invite her here, if only to find out what she's doing** 我们邀请她来这儿吧，即使只是问问她在忙些什么 ▸ **if only we had more time!** 要是我们再多点时间就好了！

ignite [ɪg'naɪt] **I** VT **1** (cause to burn) [+explosive, petrol] 点燃 [diǎnrán]; [+fire] 点 [diǎn] **2** (fig) [+interest, passion] 使激动 [shǐ jīdòng]; [+war, debate] 激起 [jīqǐ] **II** VI 着火 [zháohuǒ]

ignition [ɪg'nɪʃən] (AUT) N **1** [U] (process) 发火 [fāhuǒ] **2** [C] (mechanism) 发火装置 [fāhuǒ zhuāngzhì] ▸ **turn the ignition on/off** 开/关点火装置

ignorance ['ɪgnərəns] N [U] (lack of knowledge) 无知 [wúzhī] ▸ **to keep sb in ignorance of sth** 不让某人知道某事

ignorant ['ɪgnərənt] ADJ **1** (uninformed, unaware) 无知的 [wúzhī de] **2** (rude) 粗鲁无礼的 [cūlǔ wúlǐ de] ▸ **to be ignorant of** [+subject, events] 不知道的

ignore [ɪg'nɔː(r)] VT **1** (pay no attention to) [+person] 不理 [bù lǐ]; [+advice, event] 不顾 [bù gù] **2** (overlook) [+fact] 忽视 [hūshì]

I'll [aɪl] = I will, I shall

ill [ɪl] **I** ADJ **1** (sick) 有病的 [yǒubìng de] **2** (harmful) [+effects, luck, fortune] 坏的 [huài de] **II** N (liter) (evil) 恶意 [èyì] **III** ▸ **the ill** NPL ▸ **the mentally/terminally ill** 精神/晚期病人 [jīngshén/wǎnqí bìngrén] **IV** N PL [+troubles] 弊病 [bìbìng] **V** ADV (frm) ▸ **to speak/think ill of sb** 讲某人坏话/认为某人坏 [jiǎng mǒurén huàihuà/rènwéi mǒurén huài] ▸ **to fall** or **be taken ill** 生病

单词 ill 和 sick 在语意上很相近，但使用方法略有不同。ill 通常不用在名词前，但可用在动词词组中，比如 fall ill 和 be taken ill。He fell ill shortly before Christmas...One of the jury members was taken ill. sick 经常用在名词前。...sick children... 在英式英语中，ill 比 sick 更为文雅和委婉。sick 常常指实际的身体病痛，例如晕船或呕吐。I spent the next 24 hours in bed, groaning and being sick. 美式英语中，sick 经常用在英国人说 ill 的地方。Some people get hurt in accidents or get sick.

illegal [ɪ'liːgl] ADJ 非法的 [fēifǎde] ▸ **it is illegal to...** 做…是非法的

illegible [ɪ'lɛdʒɪbl] ADJ [+writing] 难以辨认的 [nányǐ biànrèn de]

illegitimate [ɪlɪ'dʒɪtɪmət] ADJ **1** [+child] 私生的 [sīshēng de] **2** [+activity] 违法的 [wéifǎ de]

ill health N [U] 健康状况不佳 [jiànkāng zhuàngkuàng bù jiā]

illiterate [ɪ'lɪtərət] ADJ **1** [+person] 文盲的 [wénmáng de] **2** [+letter, writing] 语言错误的 [yǔyán cuòwù de]

illness ['ɪlnɪs] N [C/U] 病 [bìng]

illuminate [ɪ'luːmɪneɪt] VT **1** [+room, street, building] 照明 [zhàomíng] **2** (explain) 解释 [jiěshì]

illuminated [ɪ'luːmɪneɪtɪd] ADJ **1** [+sign, building] 被照明的 [bèi zhàomíng de] **2** [+manuscript] 加了彩饰的 [jiāle cǎishì de]

illusion [ɪ'luːʒən] N [C] **1** (false idea) 幻想 [huànxiǎng] **2** (false appearance) 错觉 [cuòjué] ▸ **to have no illusions about sth** 对某事不抱有

幻想 ▶ to be under the illusion that... 对…存有幻想

illustrate ['ɪləstreɪt] VT **1** (demonstrate) 显示 [xiǎnshì] **2** [+ point, argument] 说明 [shuōmíng] **3** [+ book] 用插图装饰 [yòng chātú zhuāngshì]

illustration [ɪlə'streɪʃən] N **1** [c] (picture) 插图 [chātú] **2** [c/u] (example) 实例 [shílì]

I'm [aɪm] = I am

image ['ɪmɪdʒ] N [c] **1** (mental picture) 印象 [yìnxiàng] **2** (picture) 图像 [túxiàng] **3** (reflection) 映像 [yìngxiàng] **4** (public face) 形象 [xíngxiàng] **5** (in poem, novel) 意象 [yìxiàng] ▶ to project an or the image of... 给人的印象是…

imaginary [ɪ'mædʒɪnərɪ] ADJ **1** [+ danger] 虚构的 [xūgòu de] **2** [+ being, place] 想象中的 [xiǎngxiàng zhōng de]

imagination [ɪmædʒɪ'neɪʃən] N **1** [c/u] 想象力 [xiǎngxiànglì] **2** [c] (mind's eye) 想象 [xiǎngxiàng] ▶ a lack of imagination 缺乏想象力 ▶ it's just your imagination 只是你的想象而已

imaginative [ɪ'mædʒɪnətɪv] ADJ **1** [+ person] 富于想象的 [fù yú xiǎngxiàng de] **2** [+ idea, approach, solution] 新颖的 [xīnyǐng de]

imagine [ɪ'mædʒɪn] VT **1** (envisage) 想象 [xiǎngxiàng] **2** (dream) 幻想 [huànxiǎng] **3** (suppose) 设想 [shèxiǎng]

imbalance [ɪm'bæləns] N [c/u] 不平衡 [bù pínghéng]

IMF N ABBR (= International Monetary Fund) ▶ the IMF 国际货币基金组织 [Guójì Huòbì Jījīn Zǔzhī]

imitate ['ɪmɪteɪt] VT **1** (copy) 效仿 [xiàofǎng] **2** (mimic) [+ person, sound, gesture] 模仿 [mófǎng]

imitation [ɪmɪ'teɪʃən] **I** N **1** [u] (act) 模仿 [mófǎng] **2** [c] (copy) 仿制品 [fǎngzhìpǐn] **II** ADJ 仿制的 [fǎngzhì de] ▶ to do an imitation of sb 模仿某人

immaculate [ɪ'mækjʊlət] ADJ **1** [+ room, appearance] 无瑕疵的 [wú xiácī de] **2** [+ performance] 完美的 [wánměi de] ▶ the Immaculate Conception 圣灵怀胎说

immature [ɪmə'tjʊə(r)] ADJ **1** [+ organ, organism] 发育未全的 [fāyù wèi quán de] **2** (childish) [+ person, behaviour] 不成熟的 [bù chéngshú de]

immediate [ɪ'miːdɪət] ADJ **1** [+ reaction, effect, result] 立即的 [lìjí de] **2** (urgent) [+ need, problem] 当前的 [dāngqián de] **3** (nearest) [+ family, superior, vicinity] 最近的 [zuìjìn de]

immediately [ɪ'miːdɪətlɪ] **I** ADV **1** (at once) 立即地 [lìjí de] **2** [+ apparent, obvious] 直接地 [zhíjiē de] **3** (directly) 紧接地 [jǐnjiē de] **II** CONJ ▶ immediately he had said it, he regretted it 他刚一说完马上就后悔了 [tā gāng yī shuōwán mǎshàng jiù hòuhuǐle] ▶ immediately next to 紧靠着 ▶ immediately before/after 紧接着…之前/后

immense [ɪ'mɛns] ADJ 巨大的 [jùdà de]

immensely [ɪ'mɛnslɪ] ADV [like, help +] 非常 [fēicháng]; [+ popular, grateful] 非常 [fēicháng]

immerse [ɪ'məːs] VT (submerge) 浸没 [jìnmò] ▶ to immerse sth in water etc 把某物浸没在水{等}里 ▶ to immerse o.s. in sth [+ work, thought, subject] 沉浸于某事之中

immigrant ['ɪmɪgrənt] N [c] 移民 [yímín]

immigration [ɪmɪ'greɪʃən] **I** N [u] **1** (process) 移民 [yímín] **2** (also: immigration control) (at airport, port, border) 移民局检查 [yímínjú jiǎnchá] **II** CPD [复合词] [+ authorities, policy, controls, officer] 移民 [yímín]

imminent ['ɪmɪnənt] ADJ [+ danger, death, arrival, departure] 逼近的 [bījìn de]

immoral [ɪ'mɒrəl] ADJ [+ person, behaviour, idea] 不道德的 [bù dàodé de] ▶ it is immoral to... …是不道德的

immortal [ɪ'mɔːtl] **I** ADJ **1** [+ god, being] 不朽的 [bù xiǔ de] **2** [+ poetry, words] 流芳百世的 [liúfāng bǎishì de] **II** N **1** 不朽者 [bùxiǔzhě] **2** (famous person) 流芳百世的人 [liúfāng bǎishì de rén]

immune [ɪ'mjuːn] ADJ ▶ immune to **1** [+ disease] 对…有免疫力 [duì…yǒu miǎnyìlì] **2** [+ flattery, criticism, attack] 不受…影响的 [bù shòu…yǐngxiǎng de] ▶ immune from [+ prosecution, scandal] 免除…

immune system N [c] 免疫系统 [miǎnyì xìtǒng]

immunize ['ɪmjʊnaɪz] VT 使免疫 [shǐ miǎnyì] ▶ to immunize sb against sth 使某人免患某病

impact [n 'ɪmpækt, vb ɪm'pækt] **I** N **1** [c/u] [of collision, blow] 冲击 [chōngjī] **2** [c] [of law, change, situation] 影响 [yǐngxiǎng] **II** VI ▶ to impact (up)on sb/sth 冲击某人/某物 [chōngjī mǒurén/mǒuwù] ▶ to have an impact (up)on sb/sth 对某人/某物产生影响 ▶ to make an impact 产生影响 ▶ (up)on impact 在碰撞时

impair [ɪm'pɛə(r)] VT [+ faculties, vision, judgement] 削弱 [xuēruò]

impartial [ɪm'pɑːʃl] ADJ [+ judge, observer] 公正的 [gōngzhèng de]; [+ advice] 不偏不倚的 [bù piān bù yǐ de]

impasse ['ɪm'pɑːs] N [s] (in war, negotiations) 僵局 [jiāngjú] ▶ to reach an impasse 陷入僵局

impatience [ɪm'peɪʃəns] N [u] **1** (annoyance at waiting) 急躁 [jízào] **2** (irritation) 不耐烦 [bù nàifán] **3** (eagerness) 急切 [jíqiè]

impatient [ɪm'peɪʃənt] ADJ **1** (at waiting) 急躁的 [jízào de] **2** (irritable) 不耐烦的 [bù nàifán de] ▶ to get impatient (at or with sth) (对某事)不耐烦 ▶ to be impatient for sth/to do sth 渴望某事/做某事

impeccable [ɪm'pɛkəbl] ADJ [+ dress, manners, taste] 无瑕疵的 [wú xiácī de]; [+ credentials, reputation] 勿容置疑的 [wù róng zhìyí de]

impede [ɪm'piːd] VT [+ progress, development,

movement] 妨碍 [fáng'ài]

impending [ɪmˈpɛndɪŋ] ADJ [+ war, marriage] 即将来临的 [jíjiāng láilín de]; [+ doom, disaster] 逼近的 [bījìn de]

imperative [ɪmˈpɛrətɪv] I ADJ 绝对必要的 [juéduì bìyào de] II N [C] 1 (frm) (necessity) 要务 [yàowù] 2 (LING) 祈使语气 [qíshǐ yǔqì] ▶ it is imperative to stick to your budget 绝对不能超过预算 ▶ it is imperative for us to act quickly 我们必须要立即行动 ▶ it is imperative that... …是非常重要的 ▶ in the imperative (LING) 用祈使语气

imperfect [ɪmˈpəːfɪkt] I ADJ [+ goods] 有瑕疵的 [yǒu xiácī de]; [+ system, understanding, world] 不完美的 [bù wánměi de] II N (also: imperfect tense) ▶ the imperfect 未完成时态 [wèi wánchéng shítài] ▶ in the imperfect 用未完成时态

imperial [ɪmˈpɪərɪəl] ADJ 1 [+ palace, family] 皇帝的 [huángdì de]; [+ power] 帝国的 [dìguó de] 2 (BRIT) [+ measure] 英制的 [yīngzhì de]

impersonal [ɪmˈpəːsənl] ADJ 1 [+ place, organization] 没人情味的 [méi rénqíngwèi de] 2 (objective) [+ basis] 客观的 [kèguān de]

impersonate [ɪmˈpəːsəneɪt] VT 1 (fraudulently) 冒充 [màochōng] 2 (for entertainment) 模仿 [mófǎng]

impetus [ˈɪmpətəs] N [U/S] 动力 [dònglì]

implant [vb ɪmˈplɑːnt, n ˈɪmplɑːnt] I VT 1 [+ embryo, tissue, cells] 植入 [zhírù] 2 [+ idea, principle] 灌输 [guànshū] II N [C] 植入物 [zhírùwù]

implement [vb ˈɪmplɪmɛnt, n ˈɪmplɪmənt] I VT [+ plan, regulation] 实施 [shíshī] II N [C] (tool) 器具 [qìjù]

implicate [ˈɪmplɪkeɪt] VT 牵连 [qiānlián] ▶ to be implicated in sth 牵连在某事中

implication [ɪmplɪˈkeɪʃən] N 1 [C] (possible consequence) 牵扯的后果 [qiānchě de hòuguǒ] 2 [C/U] (inference) 含意 [hányì] 3 [U] (involvement) 牵连 [qiānlián] ▶ by implication 含蓄地

implicit [ɪmˈplɪsɪt] ADJ 1 (implied) [+ threat, meaning, criticism] 含蓄的 [hánxù de] 2 (absolute) [+ belief, trust] 绝对的 [juéduì de] 3 (inherent) 内含的 [nèihán de]

imply [ɪmˈplaɪ] VT 1 (person +) (suggest) 暗示 [ànshì] ▶ to imply that... 暗示… 2 (fact +) (mean) 意味 [yìwèi]

impolite [ɪmpəˈlaɪt] ADJ 没礼貌的 [méi lǐmào de] ▶ it would be impolite to refuse the invitation 拒绝邀请将会是没礼貌的

import [vb ɪmˈpɔːt, n, cpd ˈɪmpɔːt] I VT [+ goods] 进口 [jìnkǒu] II N 1 [C] (sth imported) 进口商品 [jìnkǒu shāngpǐn] 2 [U] (importation) 进口 [jìnkǒu] 3 [S] (significance) 重要性 [zhòngyàoxìng] III CPD [复合词] [+ duty, licence, restrictions] 进口 [jìnkǒu] ▶ of little/no import

无关紧要

importance [ɪmˈpɔːtns] N [U] 1 (significance) 重要性 [zhòngyàoxìng] 2 (influence) 影响 [yǐngxiǎng] ▶ of importance 有影响的 ▶ of great/little importance 至关重要/无关紧要

○**important** [ɪmˈpɔːtənt] ADJ 1 (significant) [+ thing, factor, decision] 重要的 [zhòngyào de] ▷ That is a very important point that you've raised. 你提的问题是很重要的。2 (influential) 有影响的 [yǒu yǐngxiǎng de] ▷ a very important criminal lawyer 一个非常有影响的刑事辩护律师 ▷ the list of important people who are coming 到场的要人名单 ▶ it is important to eat sensibly 合理进食是很重要的 ▶ it is important for them to understand that... 他们一定要懂得… ▶ it is important that... …是非常重要的 ▶ it's not important 不重要的

importer [ɪmˈpɔːtə(r)] N [C] 进口商 [jìnkǒushāng]

impose [ɪmˈpəʊz] I VT [+ sanctions, restrictions, fine] 施加 [shījiā] II VI ▶ to impose on sb 强加于某人 [qiángjiā yú mǒurén]

imposing [ɪmˈpəʊzɪŋ] ADJ [+ building] 壮观的 [zhuàngguān de]; [+ person, manner] 威严的 [wēiyán de]

impossible [ɪmˈpɒsɪbl] ADJ 1 [+ task, demand] 不可能的 [bù kěnéng de] 2 (difficult) [+ situation, position] 无法忍受的 [wúfǎ rěnshòu de]; [+ person] 难以对付的 [nányǐ duìfu de] ▶ it is impossible to understand what's going on 不可能了解事情的进展情况 ▶ these feelings are impossible to ignore 不能忽视这些情感 ▶ it's impossible for me to leave now 我现在走不了 ▶ the impossible 不可能的事

impotent [ˈɪmpətənt] ADJ 1 (frm) (powerless) [+ person, group] 无力的 [wúlì de]; [+ rage] 不起作用的 [bù qǐ zuòyòng de] 2 (sexually) 阳萎的 [yángwěi de]

impoverished [ɪmˈpɒvərɪʃt] ADJ [+ country, area, person] 贫困的 [pínkùn de]

impractical [ɪmˈpræktɪkl] ADJ 1 [+ idea, plan] 不切实际的 [bù qiè shíjì de] 2 [+ person] 实践能力差的 [shíjiàn nénglì chà de]

impress [ɪmˈprɛs] VT [+ person] 给…极深的印象 [gěi…jíshēn de yìnxiàng] ▶ to be impressed by or with sb/sth 对某人/某物印象深刻 ▶ to impress sth (up)on sb 使某人铭记某事

impression [ɪmˈprɛʃən] N 1 [of place, situation, person] 印象 [yìnxiàng] 2 (mark) [of stamp, seal, foot] 印记 [yìnjì] 3 (imitation) 滑稽模仿 [huájī mófǎng] ▶ to be under the impression that... 以为… ▶ first impressions 第一印象 ▶ to make or create a good/bad impression 留下好/不良印象 ▶ to give the impression of/that... 给人的印象是…

impressive [ɪmˈprɛsɪv] ADJ [+ reputation, achievement, performance] 给人深刻印象的 [gěi rén shēnkè yìnxiàng de]

imprison [ɪmˈprɪzn] VT 监禁 [jiānjìn]

imprisonment [ɪmˈprɪznmənt] N [U] 监禁 [jiānjìn]

improbable [ɪmˈprɒbəbl] ADJ 1 (unlikely) [+ outcome, explanation, story] 不大可能的 [bù dà kěnéng de] 2 (strange) [+ event, story] 未必可信的 [wèibì kěxìn de] ▸ it is improbable that... …是不大可能的

improper [ɪmˈprɒpə(r)] ADJ 1 (unsuitable) [+ procedure] 不适当的 [bù shìdàng de] 2 (dishonest) [+ activities] 不正当的 [bù zhèngdàng de] 3 (o.f.) (rude) 不合适的 [bù héshì de] ▸ It would be improper to... …是不适当的

improve [ɪmˈpruːv] I VT [+ quality, conditions, situation] 改进 [gǎijìn] II VI [weather, situation +] 改善 [gǎishàn]; [pupil, performance +] 进步 [jìnbù]; [patient, health +] 改善 [gǎishàn] ▸ **improve on** VT FUS [不可拆分] 改进 [gǎijìn]

improvement [ɪmˈpruːvmənt] N [C/U] 改进 [gǎijìn] ▸ **improvement in** [+ person, thing] 进步 ▸ to be an improvement (on sb/sth) 比(某人/某物)有进步 ▸ to make improvements to sth 改进某物

improvise [ˈɪmprəvaɪz] I VI 1 (make do) 临时凑合 [línshí còuhe] 2 (THEAT, MUS) 即兴创作 [jíxìng chuàngzuò] II VT 1 [+ bed, meal, shelter] 临时凑成 [línshí còuchéng] 2 (THEAT, MUS) 即兴创作 [jíxìng chuàngzuò]

impulse [ˈɪmpʌls] N 1 [C/U] (urge) 冲动 [chōngdòng] 2 [C] (ELEC) 脉冲 [màichōng] ▸ to have an impulse to do sth 有做某事的冲动 ▸ to do sth on impulse 一时冲动做某事 ▸ to act on impulse 凭一时冲动行事

impulsive [ɪmˈpʌlsɪv] ADJ [+ person] 冲动的 [chōngdòng de]; [+ purchase, decision] 凭冲动的 [píng chōngdòng de]

in [ɪn] I PREP 1 (indicating place, position) 在…里 [zài…lǐ] ▸ it's in the house/garden/box 它在房子/花园/盒子里 ▸ put it in the house/garden/box 把它放在房子/花园/盒子里 ▸ in here/there 在这儿/那儿 ▸ there's a crack in the wall 墙上有个裂缝 2 (with place names) 在 [zài] ▸ in London/England 在伦敦/英格兰 3 (time) (during) 在 [zài]; (within) (referring to future) 在…之后 [zài…zhīhòu]; (referring to past) 在…之内 [zài…zhīnèi] ▸ in 1988/May 在1988年/5月 ▸ in spring/summer 在春天/夏天 ▸ in the morning/afternoon 在上午/下午 ▸ in term time/the holidays 在学期/假期中 ▸ in the nineties 在90年代 ▸ I'll see you in two weeks' time or in two weeks 我两周后见你 ▸ I did it in 3 hours/days 我花了3小时/天完成 ▸ most people can do this in half an hour 大多数

人能够在半小时内完成 4 (indicating manner, style etc) 以 [yǐ] ▸ in a loud/soft voice 大声地/用柔和的声音 ▸ in pencil/ink 用铅笔/墨水笔 ▸ the boy in the blue shirt 穿蓝衬衫的男孩儿 ▸ a tall woman, dressed in blue 一位身穿蓝衣的高个女子 ▸ in the sun/rain 在阳光下/雨中 5 (with languages) 用 [yòng] ▸ in English/French 用英语/法语 6 (mood, state) 处于 [chǔyú] ▸ he looked up in surprise 他吃惊地往上看 ▸ to be in a mood/a bad temper 心情/脾气不好 ▸ in good condition 状况良好地 7 (with ratios, numbers) 每 [měi] ▸ one in ten people 十分之一的人 ▸ 20 pence in the pound 每1英镑中的20便士 ▸ they lined up in twos 他们排成两排 ▸ people came in their thousands 数以千计的人们涌了进来 8 (in book, film, activity) 在 [zài] ▸ I read it in a newspaper 我在报纸上看到的 ▸ in (the works of) Dickens 在狄更斯的(作品)中 ▸ to be in teaching/publishing 从事教育/出版业 9 (amongst) [+ group, collection] 在…中 [zài…zhōng] ▸ the best athlete in the team 该队中最好的运动员 ▸ the disease is common in children 这种病在儿童中是常见的 10 (with present participle) 通过 [tōngguò] ▸ in saying this 通过这么一说 II ADV 1 ▸ to be in (at home, work etc) 在 [zài] ▷ My flatmate was in at the time. 我寓友那时候在家。; (in fashion) 流行地 [liúxíng de]; (in station, port) 到达 [dàodá] ▸ miniskirts are in again this year 迷你裙今年又流行了 ▸ the train isn't in yet 火车还没到站 ▸ to ask sb in 把某人请到家中 2 ▸ to be in for sth [+ shock, surprise] 即将体验到某事 [jíjiāng tǐyàn dào mǒushì] III N ▸ the ins and outs (of proposal, situation etc) 来龙去脉 [láilóng qùmài]

in. (pl in. or ins) ABBR (= inch) 英寸 [yīngcùn]

inability [ɪnəˈbɪlɪtɪ] N ▸ my/his inability (to do sth) 我/他没能力(做某事) [wǒ/tā méi nénglì (zuò mǒushì)]

inaccurate [ɪnˈækjurət] ADJ 不准确的 [bù zhǔnquè de]

inadequacy [ɪnˈædɪkwəsɪ] N [C/U] 1 [of system, preparations] 不充分 [bù chōngfèn] 2 [of person] 不胜任 [bù shèngrèn]

inadequate [ɪnˈædɪkwət] ADJ 1 [+ income, amount, supply] 不充分的 [bù chōngfèn de] 2 [+ person] 不能胜任的 [bù néng shèngrèn de]

inadvertently [ɪnədˈvəːtntlɪ] ADV 漫不经心地 [màn bù jīngxīn de]

inappropriate [ɪnəˈprəuprɪət] ADJ 1 (unsuitable)

不适当的 [bù shìdàng de] **2** (*improper*) [+ *remark, behaviour*] 不相宜的 [bù xiāngyí de] ▶ **it would be inappropriate to comment** 进行评论将是不恰当的 ▶ **it would be inappropriate for me to interfere** 我干涉将是不恰当的 ▶ **to be inappropriate to sth** 对某事不相宜

inaugurate [ɪˈnɔːɡjʊreɪt] VT **1** [+ *president, official*] 为…举行就职典礼 [wèi…jǔxíng jiùzhí diǎnlǐ] **2** [+ *system, measure*] 开创 [kāichuàng]

Inc. (ESP US) ABBR (= *incorporated*) 有限公司 [yǒuxiàn gōngsī]

inc. ABBR (= *including*) 包括 [bāokuò]

incapable [ɪnˈkeɪpəbl] ADJ ▶ **to be incapable of sth/doing sth** 不会某事/做某事 [bù huì mǒushì/zuò mǒushì]

incense [*n* ˈɪnsɛns, *vt* ɪnˈsɛns] I N [U] (*perfume*) 香 [xiāng] II VT (*enrage*) 激怒 [jīnù]

incentive [ɪnˈsɛntɪv] I N [C/U] 刺激 [cìjī] II CPD [复合词] (COMM) [+ *payment, plan*] 激励 [jīlì] ▶ **tax incentives** 税收鼓励

inch [ɪntʃ] I N [C] 英寸 [yīngcùn] II VI ▶ **to inch forward/up** 一点一点地向前/上 [yīdiǎn yīdiǎn de xiàngqián/shàng] III VT ▶ **to inch sth forward/up** 一点一点地使某物向前/上 [yīdiǎn yīdiǎn de shǐ mǒuwù xiàngqián/shàng] ▶ **we searched every inch of the house** 我们彻底地搜查了那间房子 ▶ **he didn't give an inch** (*back down, yield*) 他寸步不让

incidence [ˈɪnsɪdns] N [C/U] [*of crime, disease*] 发生率 [fāshēnglǜ]

incident [ˈɪnsɪdnt] N [C] (*event*) 事件 [shìjiàn]

incidentally [ɪnsɪˈdɛntəlɪ] ADV (*by the way*) 顺便提一句 [shùnbiàn tí yī jù]

incl. ABBR = **inc.**

inclination [ɪnklɪˈneɪʃən] N [C/U] (*desire*) 倾向 [qīngxiàng]

incline [*n* ˈɪnklaɪn, *vb* ɪnˈklaɪn] I N [C] (*slope*) 斜坡 [xiépō] II VT (*bend*) [+ *head*] 低 [dī] III VI [*surface* +] 倾斜 [qīngxié] ▶ **I incline to the view that…** (*frm*) 我倾向于…的观点

inclined [ɪnˈklaɪnd] ADJ ▶ **to be inclined to do sth** (*tend to*) 倾向于做某事 [qīngxiàng yú zuò mǒushì]; (*want to*) 想做某事 [xiǎng zuò mǒushì] ▶ **to be mathematically/artistically inclined** 在数学/艺术方面有天赋

⊙**include** [ɪnˈkluːd] VT 包括 [bāokuò] ▷ *The four-man crew included one Briton.* 四人小组包括一个英国人。▷ *Carpets and curtains are included in the purchase price.* 地毯和窗帘包括在购物价格里。

included [ɪnˈkluːdɪd] ADJ 包括在内的 [bāokuò zàinèi de] ▶ **myself included** 包括我在内 ▶ **service is not included** 不含小费 ▶ **included in the price** 包括在价格内

⊙**including** [ɪnˈkluːdɪŋ] PREP 包括 [bāokuò] ▶ **it costs £15.50, including postage and packing** 价格15英镑50便士，邮资和包装费包括在内 ▶ **nine people were injured, including two Britons** 九个人受了伤，包括两个英国人

▶ **up to and including** 直到并包括 ▶ **including service charge** 内含小费

inclusion [ɪnˈkluːʒən] N [U] 包括 [bāokuò]

inclusive [ɪnˈkluːsɪv] I ADJ **1** [+ *price*] 一切费用包括在内的 [yīqiè fèiyòng bāokuò zàinèi de] **2** [+ *organization, society*] 包罗广泛的 [bāoluó guǎngfàn de] II ADV 包括一切费用在内地 [bāokuò yīqiè fèiyòng zàinèi de] ▶ **inclusive of tax** 含税 ▶ **Monday to Friday inclusive** 从周一到周五，包括首尾两天

income [ˈɪnkʌm] N [C/U] 收入 [shōurù] ▶ **gross/net income** 总/净收入 ▶ **income bracket** 收入类别

income tax N [U] 所得税 [suǒdéshuì]

incoming [ˈɪnkʌmɪŋ] ADJ **1** [+ *flight, call, tide*] 进来的 [jìnlái de]; [+ *missile*] 正袭来的 [zhèng xílái de] **2** [+ *government, president*] 即将就任的 [jíjiāng jiùrèn de]

incompatible [ɪnkəmˈpætɪbl] ADJ **1** [+ *lifestyles, systems, aims*] 不相容的 [bù xiāngróng de]; [+ *people*] 合不来的 [hébùlái de] **2** [+ *computers, software*] 不兼容的 [bù jiānróng de] ▶ **incompatible with** 与…不相容

incompetence [ɪnˈkɒmpɪtns] N [U] 不胜任 [bù shèngrèn]

incompetent [ɪnˈkɒmpɪtnt] ADJ 不胜任的 [bù shèngrèn de]

incomplete [ɪnkəmˈpliːt] ADJ **1** (*unfinished*) [+ *book, painting, process*] 未完成的 [wèi wánchéng de] **2** (*partial*) [+ *success, achievement*] 不彻底的 [bù chèdǐ de]

inconsistent [ɪnkənˈsɪstnt] ADJ **1** [+ *behaviour, action, person*] 反复无常的 [fǎnfù wúcháng de] **2** [+ *statements*] 前后矛盾的 [qiánhòu máodùn de] ▶ **inconsistent with** 与…不一致

inconvenience [ɪnkənˈviːnjəns] I N [C/U] 不便 [bùbiàn] II VT 打扰 [dǎrǎo]

inconvenient [ɪnkənˈviːnjənt] ADJ [+ *time, moment*] 不合时宜的 [bùhé shíyí de]; [+ *journey, place*] 不方便的 [bù fāngbiàn de] ▶ **that's very inconvenient for me** 那对我来说是很不方便的

incorporate [ɪnˈkɔːpəreɪt] VT (*include*) 包含 [bāohán]

Incorporated [ɪnˈkɔːpəreɪtɪd] ADJ (US: COMM) 组成公司的 [zǔchéng Gōngsī de]

incorrect [ɪnkəˈrɛkt] ADJ **1** [+ *information, answer*] 错误的 [cuòwù de] **2** [+ *posture, diet*] 不适当的 [bù shìdàng de]

⊙**increase** [*n* ˈɪnkriːs, *vb* ɪnˈkriːs] I N [C] 增长 [zēngzhǎng] ▷ *a sharp increase in productivity* 生产率的急剧增长 ▷ *an increase of 2 per cent in the volume of sales* 销售量增长了百分之二 II VI [*price, level, productivity* +] 增长 [zēngzhǎng] ▷ *The population continues to increase.* 人口不断增长。III VT [+ *price, number, level*] 提高 [tígāo] ▷ *The company has increased the price of its cars.* 公司提高了汽车价格。▶ **a 5% increase, an**

increase of 5% 百分之五的增长 ▶ a tax/price
increase 加税/价 ▶ to be on the increase 在
增加中 ▶ to increase by 3% 增长了百分之三

increasingly [ɪnˈkriːsɪŋlɪ] ADV (with adj) 越来
越 [yuèláiyuè]; (with verb) 日益 [rìyì]

incredible [ɪnˈkrɛdɪbl] ADJ 1 (amazing,
wonderful) 不可思议的 [bùkě sīyì de]
2 (unbelievable) 难以置信的 [nányǐ zhìxìn de]
3 (enormous) 惊人的 [jīngrén de]

incredibly [ɪnˈkrɛdɪblɪ] ADV 1 (surprisingly) 难
以置信地 [nányǐ zhìxìnde] 2 (extremely) 非常地
[fēicháng de]

incur [ɪnˈkəː(r)] (frm) VT [+ expenses, loss, debt]
遭受 [zāoshòu]; [+ disapproval, anger] 招致
[zhāozhì]

indecent [ɪnˈdiːsnt] ADJ 1 [+ behaviour,
suggestion, photo] 下流的 [xiàliú de] 2 [+ haste]
不合适的 [bù héshì de]

indeed [ɪnˈdiːd] ADV 1 (certainly) 确实 [quèshí]
2 (as a reply) 是的 [shì de] 3 (as intensifier) 实
在 [shízài] 4 (in fact) 实际上 [shíjìshang] ▶ yes
indeed! 的确如此！

indefinitely [ɪnˈdɛfɪnɪtlɪ] ADV [postpone,
continue, wait +] 无限期地 [wú xiànqī de]

independence [ɪndɪˈpɛndns] N [U] 独立
[dúlì] ▶ to declare independence 宣布独
立 ▶ independence of mind/spirit 思想/精
神独立

Independence Day N [C/U] 独立纪念日
[Dúlì Jìniànrì]

●**independent** [ɪndɪˈpɛndnt] ADJ 1 [+ country,
person, inquiry, organization] 独立的 [dúlì
de] ▷ Two independent studies came to the
same conclusions. 两个独立的研究得出了相
同的结论。 2 (BRIT) [+ school] 私立的 [sīlì
de] ▶ financially independent 经济自立的
▶ independent of each other 相互独立

index [ˈɪndɛks] (pl indexes) I N [C] 1 (in book,
library etc) 索引 [suǒyǐn] 2 (sign) 指数 [zhǐshù]
II VT [+ book, information] 编索引 [biān suǒyǐn]

India [ˈɪndɪə] N 印度 [Yìndù]

Indian [ˈɪndɪən] I ADJ 印度的 [Yìndù de]
II N [C] 1 (person from India) 印度人
[Yìndùrén] 2 (o.f.) (Native American) 印第安人
[Yìndì'ānrén]

indicate [ˈɪndɪkeɪt] I VT 1 (show) 表明
[biǎomíng] 2 (point to) 指向 [zhǐxiàng]
3 (mention) 暗示 [ànshì] II VI (BRIT) (in car)
▶ to indicate left/right 打左/右转向灯 [dǎ
zuǒ/yòu zhuǎnxiàngdēng] [美= signal]

indication [ɪndɪˈkeɪʃən] N [C/U] (sign) 迹象
[jìxiàng] ▶ to give an/no indication that... 显
示/不显示出… ▶ all the indications are that...
所有的迹象显示…

indicator [ˈɪndɪkeɪtə(r)] N [C] 1 (BRIT) [on
car] 指示器 [zhǐshìqì] [美= turn signal]
2 (measurement) 指标 [zhǐbiāo] ▶ an indicator
of health/economic activity 健康/经济活动
指标

indict [ɪnˈdaɪt] (ESP US: LAW) VT 控告
[kònggào] ▶ to be indicted for murder 被控
谋杀罪

indictment [ɪnˈdaɪtmənt] N 1 [C]
(condemnation) 谴责 [qiǎnzé] 2 [C/U] (ESP US:
LAW) 起诉 [qǐsù]

indifference [ɪnˈdɪfrəns] N [U] (lack of interest)
冷淡 [lěngdàn]

indifferent [ɪnˈdɪfrənt] ADJ 1 (uninterested) 没
兴趣的 [méi xìngqù de] 2 (mediocre) 平庸的
[píngyōng de] ▶ to be indifferent to sth 不关
心某事

indigestion [ɪndɪˈdʒɛstʃən] N [U] 消化不良
[xiāohuà bù liáng]

indignant [ɪnˈdɪgnənt] ADJ ▶ indignant
(at sth/that...) (对某事/…) 感到气愤 [(duì
mǒushì/…)gǎndào qìfèn]

indirect [ɪndɪˈrɛkt] ADJ 1 [+ result, effect] 间接的
[jiànjiē de] 2 [+ route, journey] 迂回的 [yūhuí de]
3 [+ answer, reference] 非直截了当的 [fēi zhíjié
liǎodàng de]

indirectly [ɪndɪˈrɛktlɪ] ADV 1 [+ responsible] 间
接地 [jiànjiē de] 2 [refer to, cause +] 间接地
[jiànjiē de]

indispensable [ɪndɪsˈpɛnsəbl] ADJ 必不可
少的 [bìbù kěshǎo de] ▶ indispensable to/for
对…必需的

●**individual** [ɪndɪˈvɪdjuəl] I N (single person) 个
人 [gèrén] II ADJ 1 (personal) 个人的 [gèrén de]
2 (particular) 单个的 [dāngè de] 3 (unique) 独特
的 [dútè de] ▶ he is an unpleasant/interesting
individual 他是个讨厌的/有趣的人

individuality [ɪndɪvɪdjuˈælɪtɪ] N [U] 个性
[gèxìng]

individually [ɪndɪˈvɪdjuəlɪ] ADV 1 (by oneself)
单独地 [dāndú de] 2 (separately) 个别地 [gèbié
de]

Indonesia [ɪndəˈniːzɪə] N 印度尼西亚
[Yìndùníxīyà]

Indonesian [ɪndəˈniːzɪən] I ADJ 印度尼西亚
的 [Yìndùníxīyà de] II N 1 [C] (person) 印度尼
西亚人 [Yìndùníxīyàrén] 2 [U] (language) 印度
尼西亚语 [Yìndùníxīyàyǔ]

indoor [ˈɪndɔː(r)] ADJ 室内的 [shìnèi de] ▪ indoor
请勿将 indoor 和 indoors 混淆。indoor
是形容词，用在名词之前。它可以描述
存在于建筑物内部的东西或者发生在建
筑物内的事情。…an indoor swimming
pool…Table tennis, chess and cards are all
indoor games. indoors 是副词。如果去
indoors，就是去建筑物的内部。如果某
事发生在indoors，表示它发生在建筑物
内部。He ran indoors and up the stairs to
pack his bag…On a rainy day, the children
were forced to play indoors.

indoors [ɪnˈdɔːz] ADV 在室内 [zài wū nèi]
▪ 用法参见 indoor

induce [ɪn'djuːs] VT **1** (cause) 导致 [dǎozhì] **2** [+ birth, labour] 人工引导 [réngōng yǐndǎo] ▸ **to induce sb to do sth** 引诱某人做某事

indulge [ɪn'dʌldʒ] I VT **1** [+ desire, passion] 纵情享受 [zòngqíng xiǎngshòu] **2** [+ person, child] 纵容 [zòngróng] II VI ▸ **to indulge (in)** [+ luxury, hobby, vice] 沉湎(于) [chénmiǎn (yú)] ▸ **to indulge o.s.** 纵情享受

indulgence [ɪn'dʌldʒəns] N **1** [U] (leniency) 纵容 [zòngróng] **2** [C] (pleasure) 嗜好 [shìhào]

indulgent [ɪn'dʌldʒənt] ADJ [+ parent] 溺爱的 [nì'ài de]; [+ smile] 宽容的 [kuānróng de]

industrial [ɪn'dʌstrɪəl] ADJ [+ equipment, production, waste, society] 工业的 [gōngyè de]; [+ accident] 因工的 [yīngōng de]

industrial estate (BRIT) N [C] 工业区 [gōngyè qū] [美= **industrial park**]

industrialist [ɪn'dʌstrɪəlɪst] N [C] 工业家 [gōngyèjiā]

industrialized [ɪn'dʌstrɪəlaɪzd] ADJ 工业化的 [gōngyèhuà de]

industrial park (US) N [C] 工业区 [gōngyè qū] [英= **industrial estate**]

○**industry** ['ɪndəstrɪ] N **1** [U] (manufacturing) 工业 [gōngyè] ▷ Industry is making increasing use of robots. 工业生产越来越多地利用机器人。 **2** [C] (business) 行业 [hángyè] ▷ the film industry 电影业 **3** [U] (diligence) 勤劳 [qínláo] ▷ No one doubted his industry. 没人怀疑他的勤劳。

ineffective [ɪnɪ'fɛktɪv] ADJ [+ policy, system] 无效的 [wúxiào de]

inefficiency [ɪnɪ'fɪʃənsɪ] N [U] [of person, machine, system] 无效率 [wúxiàolǜ]

inefficient [ɪnɪ'fɪʃənt] ADJ [+ person, machine, system] 效率低的 [xiàolǜ dī de]

inept [ɪ'nɛpt] ADJ [+ politician, management] 无能的 [wúnéng de] ▸ **to be inept at sth** 不擅长某事

inequality [ɪnɪ'kwɔlɪtɪ] N [C/U] 不平等 [bù píngděng]

inevitable [ɪn'ɛvɪtəbl] I ADJ [+ outcome, result, consequence] 不可避免的 [bùkě bìmiǎn de] II N ▸ **the inevitable** 不可避免的事情 [bùkě bìmiǎn de shìqing]

inevitably [ɪn'ɛvɪtəblɪ] ADV 必然地 [bìrán de]

inexpensive [ɪnɪk'spɛnsɪv] ADJ 便宜的 [piányi de]

inexperienced [ɪnɪk'spɪərɪənst] ADJ 无经验的 [wújīngyàn de]

inexplicable [ɪnɪk'splɪkəbl] ADJ [+ decision, mistake] 莫名其妙的 [mòmíng qímiào de]

infamous ['ɪnfəməs] ADJ [+ crime, murderer] 臭名昭著的 [chòumíng zhāozhù de]
■用法参见 **famous**

infancy ['ɪnfənsɪ] N [U] [of person] 婴儿期 [yīng'érqī] ▸ **to die in infancy** 夭折 ▸ **to be in its infancy** [research, organization +] 处于初创阶段

infant ['ɪnfənt] I N [C] **1** (baby) 婴儿 [yīng'ér] **2** (young child) 幼儿 [yòu'ér] II CPD [复合词] **1** [+ food, seat] 婴儿 [yīng'ér] **2** [+ son, daughter] 年幼 [niányòu]

infantry ['ɪnfəntrɪ] (MIL) N ▸ **the infantry** 步兵 [bùbīng]

infect [ɪn'fɛkt] VT **1** [+ person, animal, plant] 感染 [gǎnrǎn] **2** [vice, enthusiasm +] 感染 [gǎnrǎn] ▸ **to become infected** [wound +] 感染了; [person +] 染上了

infection [ɪn'fɛkʃən] N **1** [C] (disease) 感染 [gǎnrǎn] **2** [U] (contagion) 传染 [chuánrǎn] ▸ **to have an ear/throat infection** 耳朵/咽喉感染

infectious [ɪn'fɛkʃəs] ADJ **1** [+ disease] 传染的 [chuánrǎn de] **2** [+ enthusiasm, laughter] 有感染力的 [yǒu gǎnrǎnlì de]

infer [ɪn'fəː(r)] VT **1** (deduce) 推断 [tuīduàn] **2** (imply) 暗示 [ànshì]

inferior [ɪn'fɪərɪə(r)] I ADJ **1** (lower in hierarchy) 低等的 [dīděng de] **2** (in worth) [+ work, person] 差的 [chà de]; [+ goods] 次的 [cì de] II N [C] **1** (in hierarchy) 下级 [xiàjí] **2** (in worth) 低下的人 [dīxià de rén] ▸ **to be inferior to** 比…低一等 ▸ **to feel inferior (to)** 感到(比…)低一等

infertile [ɪn'fəːtaɪl] ADJ **1** [+ man, woman, animal] 不能生育的 [bùnéng shēngyù de] **2** [+ soil, land] 贫瘠的 [pínjí de]

infertility [ɪnfəː'tɪlɪtɪ] N **1** [U] **1** [of man, woman, animal] 不育症 [bùyùzhèng] **2** [of soil] 贫瘠 [pínjí] II CPD [复合词] [+ clinic, specialist] 不育症 [bùyùzhèng]

infested [ɪn'fɛstɪd] ADJ [+ plant, animal] 被侵扰的 [bèi qīnrǎo de] ▸ **to be infested with** 被…侵扰

infinite ['ɪnfɪnɪt] ADJ **1** (very great) [+ variety, patience] 极大的 [jídà de] **2** (limitless) [+ universe, number] 无限的 [wúxiàn de]

infinitely ['ɪnfɪnɪtlɪ] ADV (with adj) 非常地 [fēicháng de]; (with comparative) …得多 […de duō]

infirmary [ɪn'fəːmərɪ] N [C] 医院 [yīyuàn]

inflame [ɪn'fleɪm] VT [+ situation, passions] 使火上浇油 [shǐ huǒshàng jiāoyóu]

inflamed [ɪn'fleɪmd] ADJ [+ throat, appendix, joint] 发炎的 [fāyán de] ▸ **to become inflamed** 发炎了

inflammation [ɪnflə'meɪʃən] N [U] 发炎 [fāyán]

inflatable [ɪn'fleɪtəbl] ADJ [+ life jacket, dinghy, ball] 充气的 [chōngqì de]

inflate [ɪn'fleɪt] I VT **1** [+ tyre, balloon] 使充气 [shǐ chōngqì] **2** [+ price] 抬高 [táigāo] **3** (exaggerate) [+ amount, effect] 夸大 [kuādà] II VI [tyre, balloon +] 膨胀 [péngzhàng]

inflated [ɪn'fleɪtɪd] ADJ [+ price] 飞涨的 [fēizhǎng de]; [+ opinion, idea] 夸大的 [kuādà de]

inflation [ɪn'fleɪʃən] N [U] 通货膨胀 [tōnghuò péngzhàng]

inflexible [ɪnˈflɛksɪbl] ADJ **1** [+ *rule, system*] 固定的 [gùdìng de] **2** [+ *person*] 不灵活的 [bù línghuó de] **3** [+ *object, material*] 不可弯曲的 [bùkě wānqū de]

inflict [ɪnˈflɪkt] VT ▸ **to inflict sth on sb** [+ *damage, suffering*] 使某人遭受某事 [shǐ mǒurén zāoshòu mǒushì]

influence [ˈɪnfluəns] **I** N **1** [C/U] (*power*) 权势 [quánshì] **2** [C] (*effect*) 影响 [yǐngxiǎng] **II** VT [+ *person, situation, choice*] 影响 [yǐngxiǎng] ▸ **to be/have an influence on sb** 对某人有影响 ▸ **to be a good/bad influence on sb** 对某人有好/坏的影响 ▸ **to have a good/bad influence on sb** 对某人有好/坏的影响 ▸ **under the influence of alcohol/drugs** 在酒精/毒品的作用下

influential [ˌɪnfluˈɛnʃl] ADJ [+ *politician, critic*] 有权势的 [yǒu quánshì de] ▸ **to be influential in doing sth** 对做某事有影响

influx [ˈɪnflʌks] N [C] (*of people*) 涌入 [yǒngrù]; (*of funds, goods*) 流入 [liúrù]

info [ˈɪnfəʊ] (*inf*) N [U] 信息 [xìnxī]

inform [ɪnˈfɔːm] **I** VT **1** (*tell*) 告诉 [gàosù] **2** (*frm*) (*give form to*) 贯穿 [guànchuān] **II** VI ▸ **to inform on sb** (*to police, authorities*) 告发某人 [gàofā mǒurén] ▸ **to inform sb of sth** 把某事通知某人 ▸ **to inform sb that...** 告诉某人…

informal [ɪnˈfɔːml] ADJ **1** (*relaxed*) [+ *person, speech, behaviour*] 不拘礼节的 [bùjù lǐjié de] **2** (*casual*) [+ *clothes, party*] 日常的 [rìcháng de] **3** (*unofficial*) [+ *meeting, discussions, agreement*] 非正式的 [fēizhèngshì de]

⊙ **information** [ˌɪnfəˈmeɪʃən] N [U] 信息 [xìnxī] ▷ *If you have any new information, please let us know.* 如果有任何新信息，请告诉我们。 ▷ *For further information, contact the number below.* 如需详情，请打以下电话。 ▸ **a piece of information** 一条信息 ▸ **for your information** 供参考

information technology N [U] 信息技术 [xìnxī jìshù]

informative [ɪnˈfɔːmətɪv] ADJ [+ *report, article*] 增长见闻的 [zēngzhǎng jiànwén de]

informed [ɪnˈfɔːmd] ADJ [+ *person*] 有见识的 [yǒu jiànshì de] ▸ **to be well/poorly informed** 见多识广的/孤陋寡闻的 ▸ **an informed guess/choice** 有根据的猜测/选择

infra-red [ˌɪnfrəˈrɛd] ADJ [+ *rays, light, equipment*] 红外线的 [hóngwàixiàn de]

infrastructure [ˈɪnfrəstrʌktʃə(r)] N [C/U] (*of country, organization*) 基础结构 [jīchǔ jiégòu]

infrequent [ɪnˈfriːkwənt] ADJ [+ *buses*] 稀少的 [xīshǎo de]; [+ *visits*] 不经常的 [bù jīngcháng de]

infuriate [ɪnˈfjʊərɪeɪt] VT [+ *person*] 激怒 [jīnù]

infuriating [ɪnˈfjʊərɪeɪtɪŋ] ADJ 令人讨厌的 [lìng rén tǎoyàn de]

ingenious [ɪnˈdʒiːnjəs] ADJ [+ *idea, solution*] 有独创性的 [yǒu dúchuàngxìng de]; [+ *invention, device*] 精巧的 [jīngqiǎo de]

ingredient [ɪnˈgriːdɪənt] N [C] **1** (*in food*) 配料 [pèiliào] **2** (*in situation*) 要素 [yàosù]

inhabit [ɪnˈhæbɪt] VT 居住 [jūzhù]

inhabitant [ɪnˈhæbɪtnt] N [C] 居民 [jūmín]

inhale [ɪnˈheɪl] **I** VT [+ *smoke, gas*] 吸入 [xīrù] **II** VI **1** 吸气 [xīqì] **2** (*when smoking*) 吸入肺部 [xīrù fèibù]

inhaler [ɪnˈheɪlə(r)] N [C] 吸入器 [xīrùqì]

inherent [ɪnˈhɪərənt] ADJ (*danger, problem, qualities*) 内在的 [nèizài de] ▸ **to be inherent in** or **to sth** 某物内在固有的

inherit [ɪnˈhɛrɪt] VT **1** [+ *property, money*] 继承 [jìchéng] **2** [+ *characteristic, disease*] 由遗传而得 [yóu yíchuán ér dé] **3** [+ *situation*] 接手 [jiēshǒu]

inheritance [ɪnˈhɛrɪtəns] N **1** [C/U] (*property, money*) 继承 [jìchéng] **2** [U/S] (*genetic*) 遗传 [yíchuán] **3** [U/S] (*fig*) (*legacy*) 遗产 [yíchǎn]

inhibit [ɪnˈhɪbɪt] VT **1** (*slow down, stop*) 阻止 [zǔzhǐ] **2** ▸ **to inhibit sb from doing sth** (*discourage*) 阻止某人做某事 [zǔzhǐ mǒurén zuò mǒushì]

inhibited [ɪnˈhɪbɪtɪd] ADJ 拘束的 [jūshù de]

inhibition [ˌɪnhɪˈbɪʃən] N **1** [C] (*hang-up*) 抑制 [yìzhì] **2** [U] (*restraint*) 约束 [yuēshù]

initial [ɪˈnɪʃl] **I** ADJ [+ *stage, reaction, meeting*] 初步的 [chūbù de] **II** N [C] (*letter*) 首字母 [shǒuzìmǔ] **III** VT [+ *document*] 草签 [cǎoqiān] **IV initials** NPL (*of name*) 首字母 [shǒuzìmǔ]

initially [ɪˈnɪʃəlɪ] ADV 最初 [zuìchū]

initiate [ɪˈnɪʃɪeɪt] **I** VT (*begin*) [+ *talks, process*] 发动 [fādòng] **II** N (*member*) 新入会的人 [xīn rùhuì de rén] ▸ **to initiate sb into** [+ *religion, mysteries, secrets*] 把…传授给某人; [+ *society, organization*] 接纳某人加入 ▸ **to initiate proceedings against sb** 开始提起对某人的诉讼

initiation [ɪˌnɪʃɪˈeɪʃən] N [C/U] **1** (*start*) 开创 [kāichuàng] **2** (*into group, organization*) 加入仪式 [jiārù yíshì]

initiative [ɪˈnɪʃətɪv] N **1** [C] (*idea, measure*) 倡议 [chàngyì] **2** [U] (*resourcefulness*) 主动性 [zhǔdòng xìng] ▸ **to take the initiative** 采取主动 ▸ **to act on one's own initiative** 主动采取行动 ▸ **to have the initiative** 掌握主动权 ▸ **to have the initiative to do sth** 有做某事的主动性

inject [ɪnˈdʒɛkt] **I** VT **1** [+ *drugs, poison*] 注射 [zhùshè] **2** ▸ **to inject fun/interest into sth** 给某物注入乐趣/兴趣 [gěi mǒuwù zhùrù lèqù/xìngqù] ▸ **to inject money into sth** 把资金投入某事 **II** VI [*drug user*+] 注射 [zhùshè] ▸ **to inject sb with sth** 给某人注射某物

injection [ɪnˈdʒɛkʃən] N [C] **1** (MED) 注射 [zhùshè] **2** [*of money*] 投入 [tóurù] ▸ **to give sb an injection** 给某人注射 ▸ **to have an injection** 打针

injure ['ɪndʒə(r)] VT [+ person] 伤害 [shānghài]; [+ leg, arm, hand] 伤 [shāng] ▶ **to injure o.s.** 伤害自己 ▶ **he was badly injured in the attack** 他在进攻中受了重伤

injured ['ɪndʒəd] I ADJ **1** [+ person, part of body] 受伤的 [shòushāng de] **2** [+ pride, feelings] 受伤的 [shòushāng de] II NPL ▶ **the injured** 受伤者 [shòushāngzhě] ▶ **the injured party** (LAW) 受害方

injury ['ɪndʒərɪ] N [C/U] (wound) 伤害 [shānghài] ▶ **to do o.s. an injury** 伤害自己 ▶ **to escape without injury** 安然脱险

injustice [ɪn'dʒʌstɪs] N [C/U] 不公正 [bù gōngzhèng] ▶ **you do me an injustice** 你让我受委屈了

ink [ɪŋk] I N [C/U] (in pen) 墨水 [mòshuǐ]; (in printing) 油墨 [yóumò] II VT 涂墨于 [túmò yú]

inland [adj 'ɪnlənd, adv ɪn'lænd] I ADJ [+ lake, sea, waterway] 内陆的 [nèilù de] II ADV [travel, live +] 在内陆 [zài nèilù]

Inland Revenue (BRIT) N ▶ **the Inland Revenue** 国内税收部 [Guónèi Shuìshōubù] [美= **Internal Revenue Service, IRS**]

in-laws ['ɪnlɔːz] NPL 姻亲 [yīnqīn]

inmate ['ɪnmeɪt] N [C] [of prison, psychiatric hospital] 同住者 [tóngzhùzhě]

inn [ɪn] N [C] 小旅馆 [xiǎo lǚguǎn]

innate [ɪ'neɪt] ADJ [+ skill, quality, characteristic] 天生的 [tiānshēng de]

inner ['ɪnə(r)] ADJ **1** [+ office, courtyard] 内部的 [nèibù de] **2** [+ calm, feelings] 内心的 [nèixīn de]

inner city N [C] 旧城区，尤其指社会和经济问题较严重的市中心

inner-city ['ɪnəsɪtɪ] ADJ 旧城区的 [jiùchéngqū de]

inning ['ɪnɪŋ] (BASEBALL) N [C] 局 [jú]

innings ['ɪnɪŋz] (pl **innings**) (CRICKET) N [C] 局 [jú] ▶ **he's had a good innings** (fig) 他一生幸福而长寿

innocence ['ɪnəsns] N [U] **1** (LAW) 清白 [qīngbái] **2** (naivety) 单纯 [dānchún]

innocent ['ɪnəsnt] I ADJ **1** (not guilty) 清白的 [qīngbái de] **2** (naive) [+ child, person] 单纯的 [dānchún de] **3** (not involved) 无辜的 [wúgūde] **4** [+ remark, question] 无恶意的 [wúyì de] II N [C] (naive person) 幼稚的人 [yòuzhì de rén] ▶ **to be innocent of a crime** 无罪 ▶ **to play the innocent** 假装无知

innocently ['ɪnəsntlɪ] **1** ADV (trustingly) 天真地 [tiānzhēn de] **2** (feigning innocence) [say, act +] 假装无心地 [jiǎzhuāng wúxīn de]

innovation [ɪnəʊ'veɪʃən] N [C/U] 创新 [chuàngxīn]

innovative ['ɪnəvɪtɪv] ADJ **1** [+ product, design] 新颖的 [xīnyǐng de] **2** [+ person] 富有创新精神的 [fùyǒu chuàngxīn jīngshén de]

innuendo [ɪnjuˈɛndəʊ] (pl **innuendoes** or **innuendos**) N [C/U] 影射 [yǐngshè] ▶ **sexual**

innuendo 性暗示

in-patient ['ɪnpeɪʃənt] N [C] 住院病人 [zhùyuàn bìngrén]

input ['ɪnpʊt] I N **1** [C/U] [of resources] 投入 [tóurù] **2** [U] (COMPUT) 输入 [shūrù] II VT (COMPUT) 输入 [shūrù]

inquest ['ɪnkwɛst] N [C] **1** (on sb's death) 审讯 [shěnxùn] **2** (fig) (into defeat, failure) 调查 [diàochá]

inquire [ɪn'kwaɪə(r)] VT, VI 询问 [xúnwèn] ▶ **to inquire about** [+ person, fact] 打听 ▶ **to inquire where/what/whether** 询问哪里/什么/是否 ▶ **inquire after** VT FUS [不可拆分] ▶ **to inquire after sb/sb's health** 问起某人/某人的健康情况 [wènqǐ mǒurén/mǒurén de jiànkāng qíngkuàng] ▶ **inquire into** VT FUS [不可拆分] [+ death, circumstances] 调查 [diàochá]

inquiry [ɪn'kwaɪərɪ] N **1** [C] (question) 询问 [xúnwèn]; (about advertisement) 咨询 [zīxún] **2** [C] (investigation) 调查 [diàochá] **3** [U] (POLICE) 质询 [zhìxún] ▶ **to make inquiries** 进行调查 ▶ **public inquiry** 公开调查 ▶ **to hold an inquiry into sth** 对某事进行调查 ▶ **a court of inquiry** 调查庭

ins ABBR (= inches) 英寸 [yīngcùn]

insane [ɪn'seɪn] I ADJ **1** (clinically) [+ person] 精神错乱的 [jīngshén cuòluàn de] **2** (foolish) [+ idea, scheme] 愚蠢的 [yúchǔn de] II NPL ▶ **the insane** 精神病患者 [jīngshénbìng huànzhě] ▶ **to go insane** 疯了

insanity [ɪn'sænɪtɪ] N [U] **1** (clinical) 精神病 [jīngshénbìng] **2** (of idea, decision, action) 荒谬 [huāngmiù]

insect ['ɪnsɛkt] N [C] 昆虫 [kūnchóng]

insect repellent N [C/U] 杀虫剂 [shāchóngjì]

insecure [ɪnsɪ'kjʊə(r)] ADJ **1** [+ person] 缺乏自信的 [quēfá zìxìn de] **2** [+ job, system] 无保障的 [wú bǎozhàng de]

insecurity [ɪnsɪ'kjʊərɪtɪ] N **1** [C/U] [of person] 不安全感 [bù ānquángǎn] **2** [U] [of job, finances] 无保障 [wú bǎozhàng]

insensitive [ɪn'sɛnsɪtɪv] ADJ (uncaring) [+ person] 不敏感的 [bù mǐngǎn de]; [+ remark] 麻木不仁的 [mámù bùrén de]

insert [vb ɪn'sə:t, n 'ɪnsə:t] I VT **1** [+ object] (into sth) 插入 [chārù]; (between two things) 夹 [jiá] **2** [+ word] (into text) 插入 [chārù] II N [C] (in magazine, book) 插页 [chāyè]

inside [ɪn'saɪd] I N [C] 内部 [nèibù] II ADJ **1** [+ wall, surface] 内部的 [nèibù de]; [+ lavatory] 室内的 [shì nèi de]; [+ pocket] 里面的 [lǐmiàn de] **2** [+ knowledge, information, story] 内幕的 [nèimù de] III ADV **1** [go +] 里面 [lǐmiàn]; [be +] 在里面 [zài lǐmiàn] **2** (indoors) 在屋内 [zài wū nèi] IV PREP **1** [+ place, container] 在…的里面 [zài…de lǐmiàn] **2** [+ time] 在…之内 [zài…

zhīnèi] **3** [+ organization] 在内部 [zài…nèibù]
V **insides** NPL (inf) (stomach) [+ of person, animal]
内脏 [nèizàng]

inside lane N [C] 里道 [lǐdào]

inside out ADV 里面朝外地 [lǐmiàn cháowài
de] ▶ **to know sth/sb inside out** 透彻了解某
事/某人 ▶ **to turn sth inside out** (lit) 把某物的
里面翻到外面; (fig) 彻底查看某物

insider [ɪn'saɪdə(r)] N [C] 内部人士 [nèibù
rénshì]

insight ['ɪnsaɪt] N **1** [C/U] (into situation, problem)
见识 [jiànshi] **2** [U] (understanding) 洞察力
[dòngcháli] ▶ **to gain/give an insight into sth**
对某事了解/使了解某事

insignificant [ɪnsɪg'nɪfɪknt] ADJ 无足轻重的
[wú zú qīng zhòng de]

insincere [ɪnsɪn'sɪə(r)] ADJ [+ person] 不诚恳
的 [bù chéngkěn de]; [+ words, flattery] 虚假的
[xūjiǎ de]; [+ smile] 虚伪的 [xūwěi de]

insist [ɪn'sɪst] VI, VT 坚持 [jiānchí] ▶ **to insist
that...** (claim) 坚持…; (demand) 坚决要求…
▶ **to insist on sth/doing sth** 坚持要求某事/做
某事

insistence [ɪn'sɪstəns] N [U] 坚决主张 [jiānjué
zhǔzhāng] ▶ **at his insistence** 经他坚决要求
▶ **his insistence on sth/doing sth** 他坚决主张
某事/做某事

insistent [ɪn'sɪstənt] ADJ **1** (determined)
[+ person] 坚持的 [jiānchí de] **2** (continual)
[+ noise, rhythm] 不断的 [bùduàn de] ▶ **to be
insistent that...** 一再坚持

insomnia [ɪn'sɒmnɪə] N [U] 失眠 [shīmián]

inspect [ɪn'spɛkt] VT **1** (examine) 检查 [jiǎnchá]
2 (officially) [+ premises, equipment, troops] 视察
[shìchá]

inspection [ɪn'spɛkʃən] N [C/U] **1** (examination)
检查 [jiǎnchá] **2** (official) [of premises, equipment,
troops] 视察 [shìchá] ▶ **to carry out an
inspection (of sth)** 检查(某物)

inspector [ɪn'spɛktə(r)] N [C] **1** (official) 检
查员 [jiǎncháyuán] **2** (BRIT: POLICE) 巡官
[xúnguān] **3** (BRIT) (also: ticket inspector) 查票
员 [chápiàoyuán]

inspiration [ɪnspə'reɪʃən] N **1** [U]
(encouragement) 鼓舞 [gǔwǔ] **2** [S] (stimulus) 灵
感 [línggǎn] **3** [S] (inspiring person, action) 鼓舞人
心的人/物 [gǔwǔ rénxīn de rén/wù] **4** [C] (idea)
妙想 [miàoxiǎng] ▶ **to be the inspiration for
sth** 是某事的灵感起源 ▶ **to be an inspiration
to sb** 是对某人的鼓舞

inspirational [ɪnspə'reɪʃənl] ADJ 激发灵感的
[jīfā línggǎn de]

inspire [ɪn'spaɪə(r)] VT **1** [+ person] 激励 [jīlì]
2 [+ work of art] 给予灵感 [gěiyǔ línggǎn]
3 [+ confidence, hope, respect] 唤起 [huànqǐ] ▶ **to
inspire sb to do sth** 鼓舞某人做某事

inspiring [ɪn'spaɪərɪŋ] ADJ 鼓舞人心的 [gǔwǔ
rénxīn de]

instability [ɪnstə'bɪlɪtɪ] N [U] [of place, situation,
person] 不稳定性 [bù wěndìngxìng]

install, instal [ɪn'stɔːl] VT **1** [+ equipment,
software] 安装 [ānzhuāng] **2** [+ official] 使…就
职 [shǐ…jiùzhí]

installation [ɪnstə'leɪʃən] N **1** [U] [of machine,
equipment] 安装 [ānzhuāng] **2** [C] (place) 设施
[shèshī]

instalment, (US) **installment** [ɪn'stɔːlmə
nt] N [C] **1** (payment) 分期付款 [fēnqī fùkuǎn]
2 [of story, TV serial] 连载的一部分 [liánzǎi de
yī bùfen] ▶ **in instalments** [pay, receive +] 分
期付款

instance ['ɪnstəns] N [C] (example) 例子 [lìzi]
▶ **for instance** 例如 ▶ **in many instances** 很
多情况下 ▶ **in the first instance** 首先

instant ['ɪnstənt] **I** N [C] (moment) 瞬息
[shùnxī] **II** ADJ **1** [+ reaction, success] 立即的
[lìjí de] **2** [+ coffee, soup, noodles] 速食的 [sùshí
de] ▶ **she called the police the instant he left**
他一走，她就叫警察了 ▶ **at that instant** 在
那一瞬间 ▶ **for an instant** 一瞬间 ▶ **in an
instant** 立即

instantly ['ɪnstəntlɪ] ADV (with verb) 立即 [lìjí];
(with adjective) 即刻 [jíkè]

instead [ɪn'stɛd] ADV 代替 [dàitì] ▶ **instead
of** 而不是

instinct ['ɪnstɪŋkt] N [C/U] **1** (biological) 本
能 [běnnéng] **2** (inclination) 直觉 [zhíjué]
▶ **survival/killer instinct** 求生本能/嗜杀本性

instinctive [ɪn'stɪŋktɪv] ADJ [+ reaction, feeling]
本能的 [běnnéng de]

institute ['ɪnstɪtjuːt] **I** N [C] **1** (research
or teaching organization) 学院 [xuéyuàn]
2 (professional body) [of architects, planners etc] 协
会 [xiéhuì] **II** VT [+ system, rule, measure] 设
立 [shèlì]; [+ inquiry] 着手 [zhuóshǒu] ▶ **to
institute proceedings against sb** 对某人提
出诉讼

institution [ɪnstɪ'tjuːʃən] N **1** [C] (custom,
tradition) 风俗 [fēngsú] **2** [C] (organization) 公
共机构 [gōnggòng jīgòu] **3** [C] (mental hospital,
children's home) 收容所 [shōuróngsuǒ] **4** [U]
(putting in place) [of system, rule] 设立 [shèlì]

institutional [ɪnstɪ'tjuːʃənl] ADJ 机构性的
[jīgòuxìng de] ▶ **to be in institutional care** 在
慈善机构的收容照顾下

instruct [ɪn'strʌkt] VT **1** (tell) ▶ **to instruct sb
to do sth** 命令某人做某事 [mìnglìng mǒurén
zuò mǒushì] **2** (teach) ▶ **to instruct sb in sth** 教
某人某事 [jiāo mǒurén mǒushì]

instruction [ɪn'strʌkʃən] **I** N [U] (teaching) 教
育 [jiàoyù] **II** CPD [复合词] [+ manual, leaflet] 说
明 [shuōmíng] **III** **instructions** NPL **1** (orders)
指示 [zhǐshì] **2** (directions) (on label, in manual) 说
明 [shuōmíng]

instructor [ɪn'strʌktə(r)] N [C] (for skiing,
swimming, driving) 教员 [jiàoyuán]

instrument ['ɪnstrumənt] N [C] **1** (tool, device) 器械 [qìxiè] **2** (MUS) 乐器 [yuèqì] ▸ an instrument of diplomacy/repression 外交/镇压手段

instrumental [ɪnstru'mɛntl] **I** ADJ [+ music, piece] 乐器的 [yuèqì de] **II** N [C] (piece of music) 器乐 [qìyuè] ▸ to be instrumental in (doing) sth 在(做)某事中起到关键作用

insufficient [ɪnsə'fɪʃənt] ADJ [+ funds, evidence] 不足的 [bùzú de]

insulate ['ɪnsjuleɪt] VT **1** [+ house, body] (against cold) 使…隔热 [shǐ...gérè] **2** [+ room, studio] (against sound) 使…隔音 [shǐ...géyīn] **3** [+ equipment] (against electricity) 使绝缘 [shǐ juéyuán] **4** (fig) ▸ to insulate sb/o.s. from or against sth 使某人/自己与某物隔离 [shǐ mǒurén/zìjǐ yǔ mǒuwù gélí] ▸ to insulate sth from or against [+ cold] 使某物不受…；[+ sound] 使某物与…隔离

insulation [ɪnsju'leɪʃən] N [U] **1** (against cold) (action) 防寒 [fánghán]; (material) 防寒材料 [fánghán cáiliào] **2** (fig) [of person, group] 隔绝 [géjué]

insulin ['ɪnsjulɪn] N [U] 胰岛素 [yídǎosù] ▸ to be on insulin 用胰岛素

insult [n 'ɪnsʌlt, vb ɪn'sʌlt] **I** N [C] 侮辱 [wǔrǔ] **II** VT 侮辱 [wǔrǔ] ▸ to be an insult to sth 对某物的亵渎 ▸ to add insult to injury 雪上加霜

insulting [ɪn'sʌltɪŋ] ADJ [+ attitude, remark] 侮辱的 [wǔrǔ de]; [+ person] 无礼的 [wúlǐ de]

insurance [ɪn'ʃuərəns] N [U] 保险 [bǎoxiǎn] ▸ fire/life/health insurance 火/人寿/健康险 ▸ to take out insurance (against) 买(防备…的)保险 ▸ as (an) insurance against (fig) 作为预防…的措施

insurance policy N [C] **1** (lit) 保险单 [bǎoxiǎndān] **2** (fig) 保险措施 [bǎoxiǎn cuòshī] ▸ life/health/travel insurance policy 人寿/健康/旅行保险单 ▸ to take out an insurance policy 买保险

insure [ɪn'ʃuə(r)] VT [+ house, car] 给…保险 [gěi...bǎoxiǎn] ▸ to be insured for 5000 pounds 上了5000英磅保险 ▸ to be insured against fire 保火险

insurer [ɪn'ʃuərə(r)] N [C] 承保人 [chéngbǎorén]

intact [ɪn'tækt] ADJ **1** (whole) 完整的 [wánzhěng de] **2** (unchanged) 完好无损的 [wánhǎo wúsǔn de]

intake ['ɪnteɪk] N **1** [S] [of food, water, air] 摄取 [shèqǔ] **2** [C] [of students, recruits] 招收 [zhāoshōu]

integral ['ɪntɪɡrəl] ADJ 构成整体所必需的 [gòuchéng zhěngtǐ suǒ bìxū de] ▸ an integral part of …的组成部分 ▸ integral to 对…是不可缺的

integrate ['ɪntɪɡreɪt] **I** VT **1** [+ newcomer] ▸ to

integrate sb into sth 使某人与某物融为一体 [shǐ mǒurén yǔ mǒuwù róng wéi yītǐ] **2** [+ ideas, systems] 使结合 [shǐ jiéhé] **II** VI [groups, individuals +] 融成一体 [róngchéng yītǐ]

integrity [ɪn'tɛɡrɪtɪ] N [U] **1** (honesty) 刚正不阿 [gāngzhèng bù'ē] **2** (purity) [of culture, group] 完整 [wánzhěng]

intellect ['ɪntəlɛkt] N [C/U] **1** (thinking) 智力 [zhìlì] **2** (intelligence) 才智 [cáizhì]

intellectual [ɪntə'lɛktjuəl] **I** ADJ **1** [+ activity, interest, pursuit] 智力的 [zhìlì de] **2** (clever) 高智商的 [gāo zhìshāng de] **II** N [C] (person) 知识分子 [zhīshi fènzǐ]

intelligence [ɪn'tɛlɪdʒəns] N [U] **1** (intellect) 才智 [cáizhì] **2** (understanding) 理解力 [lǐjiělì] **3** (MIL) (service) 情报机构 [qíngbào jīgòu] **4** (MIL) (information) 情报 [qíngbào]

intelligent [ɪn'tɛlɪdʒənt] ADJ **1** [+ person] 聪明的 [cōngmíng de] **2** [+ decision, conversation] 明智的 [míngzhì de] **3** [+ machine, life] 智能的 [zhìnéng de]

intend [ɪn'tɛnd] VT ▸ to intend to do sth 打算做某事 [dǎsuàn zuò mǒushì] ▸ to intend doing sth 打算做某事 ▸ to intend that... 打算… ▸ to be intended to do sth 用来做某事 ▸ to be intended for sb/sth [gift, money +] 专门用于某人/某事 ▸ to be intended as sth [announcement, declaration +] 被有意作为某物

intense [ɪn'tɛns] ADJ **1** (great) [+ heat, pain] 剧烈的 [jùliè de]; [+ anger, joy, desire] 强烈的 [qiángliè de]; [+ competition] 激烈的 [jīliè de] **2** [+ person] 认真的 [rènzhēn de]

intensely [ɪn'tɛnslɪ] ADV (extremely) 非常地 [fēicháng de]

intensify [ɪn'tɛnsɪfaɪ] **I** VT [+ efforts, pressure] 加强 [jiāqiáng] **II** VI [efforts, pressure +] 加剧 [jiājù]

intensity [ɪn'tɛnsɪtɪ] N [U] [of heat, anger, desire] 强度 [qiángdù]; [of debate, attack] 激烈 [jīliè]

intensive [ɪn'tɛnsɪv] ADJ [+ training, study, talks] 深入细致的 [shēnrù xìzhì de]; [+ efforts] 集中的 [jízhōng de]; [+ treatment, therapy] 强化的 [qiánghuà de]

intensive care N ▸ to be in intensive care 接受重病特别护理 [jiēshòu zhòngbìng tèbié hùlǐ]

intent [ɪn'tɛnt] **I** N [U] (frm) 意图 [yìtú] **II** ADJ **1** ▸ to be intent on sth (absorbed in) 专心致志于某事 [zhuānxīn zhìzhì yú mǒushì] **2** ▸ to be intent on doing sth (determined) 一心想做某事 [yīxīn xiǎngzuò mǒushì] ▸ to all intents (and purposes) 实际上

intention [ɪn'tɛnʃən] N [C/U] 打算 [dǎsuàn] ▸ with the best (of) intentions 好心好意地 ▸ to have no/every intention of doing sth 根本没有做某事的意图/打定主意做某事

intentional [ɪn'tɛnʃənl] ADJ 故意的 [gùyì de]

intentionally [ɪn'tɛnʃnəlɪ] ADV 故意地 [gùyì de]

interact [ɪntər'ækt] VI 互相影响 [hùxiāng yǐngxiǎng] ▸ **to interact with** 与…接合

interaction [ɪntər'ækʃən] N [C/U] **1** [of people] 互相联系 [hùxiāng liánxì] **2** [of ideas, objects] 相互影响 [xiānghù yǐngxiǎng]

interactive [ɪntər'æktɪv] ADJ **1** [+television, computer, game] 交互的 [jiāohù de] **2** [+group, teaching] 互动的 [hùdòng de]

intercept [ɪntə'sεpt] VT [+person, car] 截住 [jiézhù]; [+message, supplies] 截取 [jiéqǔ]; [+plane, missile] 截获 [jiéhuò]

interchange [n 'ɪntətʃeɪndʒ, vb ɪntə'tʃeɪndʒ] **I** N **1** [C/U] (exchange) [of ideas, information] 交换 [jiāohuàn] **2** [C] (on motorway, freeway) 立体交叉道 [lìtǐ jiāochādào] **II** VT 交换 [jiāohuàn]

intercourse ['ɪntəkɔːs] N [U] **1** (frm) (also: **sexual intercourse**) 性交 [xìngjiāo] **2** ▸ **social intercourse** (o.f.) 社交 [shèjiāo] ▸ **to have (sexual) intercourse** 性交

○**interest** ['ɪntrɪst] **I** N **1** [U/S] (in subject, idea, person) 兴趣 [xìngqù] ▷ There has been a lively interest in the elections. 大家对选举兴致颇高。 **2** [C] (pastime, hobby) 爱好 [àihào] ▷ His interests include cooking and photography. 他的爱好是烹调和摄影。 **3** [C] (advantage, profit) 利益 [lìyì] ▷ They would protect the interests of their members. 他们将保护成员的利益。 **4** [U] (on loan, savings) 利息 [lìxī] ▷ Does your current account pay interest? 你的活期存款账户付利息吗？ ▷ the interest you pay on your mortgage 你付贷款的利息 **II** interests NPL (COMM) (in a company) 股权 [gǔquán] ▷ Her business interests include a theme park. 她的公司股权包括一个主题公园。 **III** VT [work, subject, idea +] 使感兴趣 [shǐ gǎnxìngqù] ▷ These are the stories that interest me. 这些是使我感兴趣的故事。 ▸ **to take an interest in sth/sb** 对某事/某人感兴趣 ▸ **to show an interest in sth/sb** 显露对某事/某人的兴趣 ▸ **to lose interest (in sth/sb)** 对(某事/某人)失去兴趣 ▸ **controlling interest** (COMM) 控股权益 ▸ **to be in sb's interests** 对某人有益 ▸ **in the interests of stability/security** 为稳定/安全起见 ▸ **to interest sb in sth** 使某人对某事发生兴趣

interested ['ɪntrɪstɪd] ADJ **1** ▸ **to be interested (in sth/doing sth)** 对(某事/做某事)有兴趣 [duì (mǒushì/zuò mǒushì) yǒu xìngqù] **2** [+party, body] 有关的 [yǒuguān de]

请勿将 **interested** 和 **interesting** 混淆。如果你 **interested** 在某事，说明你对它感兴趣，很想了解或知道更多关于它的事情，或者想花更多的时间来做这件事。Not all of the children were interested in animals...She asked him how he became interested in politics. 如果你发现某事 **interesting**，表示它令人感兴趣，引人注意，使你乐于更多地了解这件事或者去做这件事。It must be

an awfully interesting job...The interesting thing is that this is exactly the answer we got before.

interesting ['ɪntrɪstɪŋ] ADJ [+idea, place, person] 有趣的 [yǒuqù de] ▸ **it is interesting that...** 令人关注的是… ▸ **it will be interesting to see how he reacts** 看他怎么反应会是很有趣的 ▓用法参见 **interested**

interestingly ['ɪntrɪstɪŋlɪ] ADV 有趣的是 [yǒuqù de shì]

interest rate N [C] 利率 [lìlǜ]

interface ['ɪntəfeɪs] **I** N [C] **1** (COMPUT) 界面 [jièmiàn] **2** (area of contact) 接合处 [jiēhéchù] **II** VI (frm) (interact) ▸ **to interface (with sth)** (与某物) 互相影响 [(yǔ mǒuwù) hùxiāng yǐngxiǎng]

interfere [ɪntə'fɪə(r)] VI **1** (meddle) (in situation, sb's affairs) 干涉 [gānshè] **2** (disrupt) 妨碍 [fáng'ài] ▸ **to interfere in sth** 干预某事 ▸ **to interfere with sth** [+plans, career, duty] 妨碍某事

interference [ɪntə'fɪərəns] N [U] **1** (meddling) 干涉 [gānshè] **2** (RAD, TV) 干扰 [gānrǎo]

interim ['ɪntərɪm] **I** ADJ [+agreement, report] 临时的 [línshí de]; [+results, profits] 中期的 [zhōngqī de]; [+government] 过渡的 [guòdù de] **II** N ▸ **in the interim** 在此期间 [zài cǐ qījiān]

interior [ɪn'tɪərɪə(r)] **I** N **1** [C] [of building, car, box] 内部 [nèibù] **2** [S] [of country] 内地 [nèidì] **II** ADJ **1** [+door, window, room] 内部的 [nèibù de] **2** [+minister, department] 内政的 [nèizhèng de] ▸ **Minister/Ministry of the Interior** 内政部长/部

interior design N [U] 室内设计 [shìnèi shèjì]

intermediate [ɪntə'miːdɪət] ADJ **1** [+stage, position] 中间的 [zhōngjiān de] **2** [+student, course, level] 中级的 [zhōngjí de]

intermission [ɪntə'mɪʃən] N [C] (CINE) 休息时间 [xiūxi shíjiān]; (US: THEAT, MUS) 幕间休息 [mùjiān xiūxi] [英=interval]

intern [vb ɪn'tɜːn, n 'ɪntɜːn] **I** VT (imprison) 拘留 [jūliú] **II** N [C] (US: MED, POL) 实习生 [shíxíshēng]

internal [ɪn'tɜːnl] ADJ **1** [+wall, dispute, reform, mail] 内部的 [nèibù de] **2** [+bleeding, injury, examination] 内的 [nèi de] **3** [+security, politics] 国内的 [guónèi de]

internally [ɪn'tɜːnəlɪ] ADV **1** (within) 在内部 [zài nèibù] **2** (MED) 在体内 [zài tǐnèi] **3** (within a company) 从内部 [cóng nèibù] ▸ **"not to be taken internally"** "切勿内服"

Internal Revenue Service (US) N ▸ **the Internal Revenue Service** 国税局 [Guóshuìjú] [英=Inland Revenue]

○**international** [ɪntə'næʃənl] **I** ADJ 国际的 [guójì de] **II** N [C] (BRIT: SPORT) **1** (match) 国际比赛 [guójì bǐsài] **2** (player) 国际比赛选手 [guójì bǐsài xuǎnshǒu]

international relations NPL 国际关系

[guójì guānxì]

Internet ['ɪntənɛt] N ▸ **the Internet** 因特网 [yīntèwǎng]

Internet café N [c] 网吧 [wǎngbā]

Internet service provider N [c] 因特网服务提供者 [yīntèwǎng fúwù tígōngzhě]

interpret [ɪn'tə:prɪt] I VT 1 (explain) [+ message, poem] 把…理解为 [bǎ…lǐjiě wéi]; [+ behaviour, statement] 阐释 [chǎnshì] 2 (translate) 口译 [kǒuyì] II VI (translate) 口译 [kǒuyì] ▸ to interpret sth as sth 把某事理解为某事

interpretation [ɪntə:prɪ'teɪʃən] N 1 [c/u] (explanation, understanding) 解释 [jiěshì] 2 [c] (THEAT, MUS) 艺术表现 [yìshù biǎoxiàn]

interpreter [ɪn'tə:prɪtə(r)] N [c] 口译者 [kǒuyìzhě]

interrogate [ɪn'tɛrəʊgeɪt] VT [+ witness, prisoner, suspect] 审问 [shěnwèn]

interrogation [ɪntɛrəʊ'geɪʃən] N 1 [u] (activity) 审问 [shěnwèn] 2 [c] (period of questioning) 审讯期 [shěnxùnqī]

interrupt [ɪntə'rʌpt] I VT 1 [+ speaker, conversation] 打断 [dǎduàn] 2 [+ activity] 中断 [zhōngduàn] II VI (in conversation) 打岔 [dǎchà] ▩用法参见 disturb

interruption [ɪntə'rʌpʃən] N [c/u] 打扰 [dǎrǎo]

intersection [ɪntə'sɛkʃən] N [c] [of roads] 交叉口 [jiāochākǒu]

interstate ['ɪntəsteɪt] I ADJ 州与州之间的 [zhōu yǔ zhōu zhījiān de] II N (US) 州际公路 [zhōujì gōnglù]

interval ['ɪntəvl] N [c] 1 (break, pause) 间隔 [jiàngé] 2 (BRIT: THEAT, MUS, SPORT) 幕间休息 [mùjiān xiūxi] [美 = **intermission**] ▸ at intervals (in time) 不时; (in space) 每隔一定距离 ▸ sunny intervals 偶尔出太阳

intervene [ɪntə'vi:n] VI 1 [person +] 干预 [gānyù] 2 [event +] 介入 [jièrù] 3 [time +] 介于 [jièyú] 4 (in speech) 打断 [dǎduàn]

intervention [ɪntə'vɛnʃən] N [c/u] (by person) 干预 [gānyù]; (military) 干涉 [gānshè]

interview ['ɪntəvju:] I N [c/u] 1 (for job) 面试 [miànshì] 2 (PUBLISHING, RAD, TV) 采访 [cǎifǎng] II VT 1 (for job) 面试 [miànshì] 2 (PUBLISHING, RAD, TV) 采访 [cǎifǎng] 3 (POLICE) 盘问 [pánwèn] ▸ to go for/have an interview 参加面试 ▸ to give an interview 接受采访

interviewer ['ɪntəvjuə(r)] N [c] 1 (RAD, TV) 采访者 [cǎifǎngzhě] 2 [of job applicant] 面试者 [miànshìzhě]

intimacy ['ɪntɪməsɪ] N [u] 1 (mental) 亲密 [qīnmì] 2 (physical) 亲昵 [qīnnì]

intimate [adj 'ɪntɪmət, vb 'ɪntɪmeɪt] I ADJ 1 (very close) [+ friend, relationship] 亲密的 [qīnmì de] 2 (sexual) [+ relationship] 暧昧的 [àimèi de] 3 (private) [+ conversation, details] 私人的

[sīrén de] 4 (cosy) [+ restaurant, atmosphere] 惬意的 [qièyì de] 5 (thorough) [+ knowledge] 精通的 [jīngtōng de] II VT (frm) (hint at) 暗示 [ànshì] ▸ to be intimate (with sb) (sexually) 和(某人)关系暧昧 ▸ to have an intimate knowledge of sth 对某事造诣很深 ▸ to intimate that... (frm) 暗示…

intimidate [ɪn'tɪmɪdeɪt] VT 恐吓 [kǒnghè] ▸ to intimidate sb into doing sth 胁迫某人做某事

intimidated [ɪn'tɪmɪdeɪtɪd] ADJ 被胁迫的 [bèi xiépò de]

intimidating [ɪn'tɪmɪdeɪtɪŋ] ADJ [+ atmosphere, place, experience] 恐怖的 [kǒngbù de]; [+ person] 可怕的 [kěpà de]

○ **into** ['ɪntu] PREP (indicating motion, direction) 到…里面 [dào…lǐmiàn] ▸ **come into the house/garden** 走进房子/花园里 ▸ **get into the car** 进入车子 ▸ **he threw some socks into his case** 他把几只袜子扔进了箱子里 ▸ **let's go into town** 我们进城吧 ▸ **she poured some tea into the cup** 她把一些茶倒进了杯子里 ▸ **to translate Chinese into French** 把汉语翻译成法语 ▸ **it broke into pieces** 它碎成一片片的了 ▸ **research into cancer** 对癌症的深入研究 ▸ **he worked late into the night** 他工作到深夜 ▸ **they got into trouble** 他们陷入麻烦之中 ▸ **I'd like to change some dollars into euros** 我想把一些美元换成欧元

intolerable [ɪn'tɔlərəbl] ADJ [+ behaviour, situation, burden] 无法忍受的 [wúfǎ rěnshòu de]

intolerant [ɪn'tɔlərnt] ADJ [+ person, society] 偏狭的 [piānxiá de]; [+ attitude] 不容忍的 [bù róngrěn de] ▸ to be intolerant of sth/sb 不能容忍某事/某人

intranet ['ɪntrənɛt] N [c] 内联网 [nèilián wǎng]

intricate ['ɪntrɪkət] ADJ [+ pattern, design] 复杂的 [fùzá de]

intrigue [ɪn'tri:g, vb ɪn'tri:g] I N [c/u] 阴谋 [yīnmóu] II VT (fascinate) 使…感兴趣 [shǐ…gǎnxìngqù]

intrigued [ɪn'tri:gd] ADJ 被迷住的 [bèi mízhù de] ▸ **I would be intrigued to hear more** 我有兴趣接着听

intriguing [ɪn'tri:gɪŋ] ADJ 引人入胜的 [yǐn rén rù shèng de]

introduce [ɪntrə'dju:s] VT 1 [+ new idea, measure, technology] 引进 [yǐnjìn] 2 [+ speaker, TV show, radio programme] 介绍 [jièshào] 3 ▸ to introduce sb (to sb) 给某人介绍(某人) [gěi mǒurén jièshào (mǒurén)] 4 ▸ to introduce sb to sth [+ pastime, technique] 引导某人做某事 [yǐndǎo mǒurén zuò mǒushì] ▸ **may I introduce you (to...)?** 让我介绍你(认识…)好吗?

introduction [ɪntrə'dʌkʃən] N 1 [u] [of new idea, measure, technology] 引进 [yǐnjìn] 2 [c] [of person]

介绍 [jièshào] **3** [C] (beginning) [of book, talk] 引言 [yǐnyán] **4** (first experience of sth) ▸ China's introduction to British ballet 中国首次接触英国芭蕾 [Zhōngguó shǒucì jiēchù Yīngguó bāléi] **5** (presentation of basic facts) ▸ an introduction to linguistics 语言学入门 [yǔyánxué rùmén] ▸ letter of introduction 介绍信

introductory [ɪntrə'dʌktərɪ] ADJ **1** [+ remarks, course] 介绍性的 [jièshàoxìng de] **2** [+ offer, price] 试销的 [shìxiāo de]

intrude [ɪn'truːd] VI **1** (person +) 侵入 [qīnrù] **2** ▸ to intrude on [person, thing +] [+ conversation, grief, party] 打扰 [dǎrǎo] ▸ am I intruding? 我没有打扰吧?

intruder [ɪn'truːdə(r)] N [C] 闯入者 [chuǎngrùzhě]

intuition [ɪntjuː'ɪʃən] N [C/U] 直觉 [zhíjué]

inundate ['ɪnʌndeɪt] VT ▸ to be inundated with [+ calls, letters, requests] …多得应接不暇 […duō de yìngjiē bù xiá]

invade [ɪn'veɪd] VT **1** (MIL) 侵略 [qīnlüè] **2** (fig) [people, animals +] 涌入 [yǒngrù]

invalid [n 'ɪnvəlɪd, adj ɪn'vælɪd] **I** N [C] 病弱者 [bìngruòzhě] **II** ADJ [+ procedure, document, argument] 无效的 [wúxiào de]

invaluable [ɪn'væljuəbl] ADJ [+ experience, advice] 无价的 [wújià de]

> 特别注意,请勿将单词 invaluable, priceless 和 worthless 混淆。某事物 invaluable,表示该事物非常有价值。Their advice to me was invaluable at that stage of my work. priceless 表示事物非常珍贵,是无价之宝。...priceless masterpieces by Van Gogh... 与之相反 worthless 表示某事物没有什么价值。I'm afraid your shares are now worthless.

invariably [ɪn'vɛərɪəblɪ] ADV 不变地 [bùbiàn de]

invasion [ɪn'veɪʒən] N [C/U] **1** (MIL) 入侵 [rùqīn] **2** (fig) 侵袭 [qīnxí] **3** ▸ an invasion of privacy 对隐私的侵犯 [duì yǐnsī de qīnfàn]

invent [ɪn'vɛnt] VT **1** [+ machine, system, game, word] 发明 [fāmíng] **2** [+ lie, excuse] 捏造 [niēzào]

invention [ɪn'vɛnʃən] N **1** [C] (machine, system) 发明 [fāmíng] **2** [C] (untrue story) 捏造 [niēzào] **3** [U] (act of inventing) [of machine, system] 发明 [fāmíng]

inventive [ɪn'vɛntɪv] ADJ [+ person, mind, idea] 有发明才能的 [yǒu fāmíng cáinéng de]

inventor [ɪn'vɛntə(r)] N [C] [of machine, system] 发明家 [fāmíngjiā]

inventory ['ɪnvəntrɪ] N **1** [C] [of house, ship] 清单 [qīngdān] **2** [C/U] (US) (supply, stock) 库存 [kùcún]

inverted commas [ɪn'vəːtɪd-] (BRIT) NPL 引号 [yǐnhào] ▸ in inverted commas (lit) 用引号标志;(fig) 所谓的 [美=quotation marks]

invest [ɪn'vɛst] **I** VT **1** [+ money] 投资 [tóuzī] **2** [+ time, energy] 投入 [tóurù] **II** VI ▸ invest in (COMM) 投资于 [tóuzī yú];(fig) [+ product, system] 购买 [gòumǎi] ▸ to invest sb with rights/responsibilities (frm) 授予某人权利/责任 ▸ by the powers invested in me (frm) 根据授予我的权力

investigate [ɪn'vɛstɪgeɪt] VT 调查 [diàochá]

investigation [ɪnvɛstɪ'geɪʃən] N [C/U] 调查 [diàochá] ▸ to be under investigation (for sth) (由于某事)接受调查

investigator [ɪn'vɛstɪgeɪtə(r)] N [C] 调查员 [diàocháyuán]

investment [ɪn'vɛstmənt] N **1** [U] (activity) 投资 [tóuzī] **2** [C] (amount of money) 投资额 [tóuzī'é] **3** [C] (property, painting etc) 投资 [tóuzī] ▷ I bought a flat as an investment. 我买了一套公寓作为投资。**4** [U/S] (fig) 投资 [tóuzī]

investor [ɪn'vɛstə(r)] (FIN) N [C] 投资者 [tóuzīzhě]

invisible [ɪn'vɪzɪbl] ADJ **1** 看不见的 [kànbùjiàn de] **2** [+ problem, situation] 被忽略的 [bèi hūlüè de] **3** [+ exports, earnings, assets] 无形的 [wúxíng de]

invitation [ɪnvɪ'teɪʃən] N **1** [C] 邀请 [yāoqǐng] **2** [C] (card) 请柬 [qǐngjiǎn] **3** ▸ an invitation to disaster/crime 招致灾难/犯罪的诱因 [zhāozhì zāinàn/fànzuì de yòuyīn] ▸ by invitation only 凭柬入场 ▸ at sb's invitation 应某人的邀请

invite [vb ɪn'vaɪt, n 'ɪnvaɪt] **I** VT **1** 邀请 [yāoqǐng] **2** (encourage) [+ trouble, criticism] 招致 [zhāozhì] **II** N [C] (inf) (invitation) 邀请 [yāoqǐng] ▸ to invite sb to do sth 邀请某人做某事 ▸ to invite sb to dinner 请某人赴宴 ▸ invite out VT 将…请去

inviting [ɪn'vaɪtɪŋ] ADJ 吸引人的 [xīyǐnrén de]

invoice ['ɪnvɔɪs] **I** N [C] 发票 [fāpiào] **II** VT [+ person] 开发票 [kāi fāpiào] ▸ to invoice sb for goods 给某人开物品发票

invoke [ɪn'vəuk] VT **1** [+ law, saying, famous person] 援引 [yuányǐn] **2** (evoke) [+ feelings, memories] 唤起 [huànqǐ]

involve [ɪn'vɒlv] VT **1** (entail) 包含 [bāohán] **2** (concern, affect) 使卷入 [shǐ juǎnrù] ▸ to involve sb (in sth) 使某人参与(某事)

involved [ɪn'vɒlvd] ADJ **1** (complicated) 复杂的 [fùzá de] **2** ▸ to be involved in (take part in) 参与 [cānyù];(be engrossed in) 专心于 [zhuānxīn yú] **3** (be entailed by) …所需的 […suǒxū de] ▸ to feel involved in sth 感到成为某事的一部分 ▸ to be involved with sb 和某人关系亲密

involvement [ɪn'vɒlvmənt] N **1** [U] (participation) 参与 [cānyù] **2** [U] (concern, enthusiasm) 眷顾 [juàngù] **3** [C/U] (relationship) 牵连 [qiānlián]

inward ['ɪnwəd] **I** ADJ **1** [+ movement] 向内的 [xiàngnèi de] **2** [+ thoughts, feelings] 内心的

[nèixīn de] **II** ADV = **inwards**

inwards ['ɪnwədz] ADV [*move, face +*] 向内 [xiàngnèi]

iodine ['aɪəudiːn] N [U] 碘 [diǎn]

IOU N ABBR (= *I owe you*) 借条 [jiètiáo]

IQ N ABBR (= *intelligence quotient*) 智商 [zhìshāng]

IRA N ABBR **1** (= *Irish Republican Army*) 爱尔兰共和军 [Ài'ěrlán Gònghéjūn] **2** (US) (= *individual retirement account*) 个人退休帐户 [gèrén tuìxiū zhànghù]

Iran [ɪ'rɑːn] N 伊朗 [Yīlǎng]

Iranian [ɪ'reɪnɪən] **I** ADJ 伊朗的 [Yīlǎng de] **II** N **1** [c] (*person*) 伊朗人 [Yīlǎngrén] **2** [U] (*language*) 伊朗语 [Yīlǎngyǔ]

Iraq [ɪ'rɑːk] N 伊拉克 [Yīlākè]

Iraqi [ɪ'rɑːkɪ] **I** ADJ 伊拉克的 [Yīlākè de] **II** N [c] (*person*) 伊拉克人 [Yīlākèrén]

Ireland ['aɪələnd] N 爱尔兰 [Ài'ěrlán] ▶ **the Republic of Ireland** 爱尔兰共和国

iris ['aɪrɪs] N [c] **1** (*of eye*) 虹膜 [hóngmó] **2** (*flower*) 蝴蝶花 [húdiéhuā]

Irish ['aɪrɪʃ] **I** ADJ 爱尔兰的 [Ài'ěrlán de] **II** N [U] (*language*) 爱尔兰语 [Ài'ěrlányǔ] **III** **the Irish** NPL 爱尔兰人 [Ài'ěrlánrén]

Irishman ['aɪrɪʃmən] (*pl* **Irishmen**) N [c] 爱尔兰男人 [Ài'ěrlán nánrén]

Irishwoman ['aɪrɪʃwumən] (*pl* **Irishwomen**) N [c] 爱尔兰女人 [Ài'ěrlán nǚrén]

iron ['aɪən] **I** N **1** [U] (*metal*) 铁 [tiě] **2** [c] (*for clothes*) 熨斗 [yùndǒu] **II** ADJ **1** [+ *bar, railings*] 铁的 [tiě de] **2** (*fig*) [+ *will, discipline*] 刚强的 [gāngqiáng de] **III** VT [+ *clothes*] 熨 [yùn] **IV** **irons** NPL (*chains*) 镣铐 [liàokào] ▶ **to clap sb in irons** 给某人戴上镣铐
▶ **iron out** VT [+ *problems*] 消除 [xiāochú]

ironic [aɪ'rɔnɪk] ADJ **1** [+ *remark, smile*] 挖苦的 [wākǔ de] **2** [+ *situation*] 令人啼笑皆非的 [lìng rén tí xiào jiē fēi de] ▶ **it is ironic that...** 具有讽刺性的是…

ironically [aɪ'rɔnɪklɪ] ADV **1** (*say +*) 挖苦地 [wākǔ de] **2** ▶ **ironically (enough)...** (极) 具有讽刺性的是… [(jí) jùyǒu fěngcìxìng de shì…]

ironing ['aɪənɪŋ] N [U] **1** (*activity*) 熨烫 [yùntàng] **2** (*clothes*) 要熨烫的衣服 [yào yùntàng de yīfu] ▶ **to do the ironing** 熨衣服

ironing board N [c] 熨衣板 [yùnyībǎn]

irony ['aɪrənɪ] N **1** [U] (*in speech*) 讽刺 [fěngcì] **2** [c/U] (*of situation*) 讥讽 [jīfěng]

irrational [ɪ'ræʃənl] ADJ [+ *feelings, behaviour*] 无理性的 [wúlǐxìng de]

irregular [ɪ'rɛgjulə(r)] ADJ **1** [+ *surface, pattern*] 不整齐的 [bù zhěngqí de] **2** (*not set*) [+ *hours, times*] 不定期的 [bù dìngqíde]; [+ *meals, periods*] 不规律的 [bù guīlǜ de]; [+ *heartbeat, pulse*] 不规则的 [bù guīzé de] **3** (*not acceptable*) [+ *behaviour*] 不正当的 [bù zhèngdàng de] **4** (LING) [+ *verb, noun, adjective*] 不规则的 [bù guīzé de] ▶ **at irregular intervals** 不定时的间隔

irrelevant [ɪ'rɛləvənt] ADJ 不相干的 [bù xiānggān de] ▶ **irrelevant to sb/sth** 与某人/某事无关

irresistible [ɪrɪ'zɪstɪbl] ADJ **1** [+ *urge, desire*] 压不住的 [yābùzhù de] **2** [+ *person, charm, food*] 无法抗拒的 [wúfǎ kàngjù de] **3** [+ *force, pressure*] 不可抗拒的 [bùkě kàngjù de]

irrespective [ɪrɪ'spɛktɪv] ▶ **irrespective of** PREP 不论 [bùlùn]

irresponsible [ɪrɪ'spɔnsɪbl] ADJ [+ *person, driver*] 无责任感的 [wúzérèngǎn de]; [+ *attitude, behaviour*] 不负责任的 [bù fù zérèn de] ▶ **it is irresponsible to drive when tired** 疲劳驾车是很不负责任的

irreversible [ɪrɪ'vəːsəbl] ADJ [+ *damage, change*] 不可扭转的 [bùkě niǔzhuǎn de]

irrigation [ɪrɪ'geɪʃən] N [U] 灌溉 [guàngài]

irritable ['ɪrɪtəbl] ADJ [+ *person*] 易激怒的 [yì jīnù de]
　　用法参见 **angry**

irritate ['ɪrɪteɪt] VT **1** [+ *person*] 使烦躁 [shǐ fánzào] **2** [+ *skin, eyes*] 使不舒服 [shǐ bù shūfu]

irritating ['ɪrɪteɪtɪŋ] ADJ [+ *person, habit, noise*] 烦人的 [fánrén de]

irritation [ɪrɪ'teɪʃən] N **1** [U] (*feeling of annoyance*) 恼怒 [nǎonù] **2** [c] (*annoying thing*) 恼人的事 [nǎorén de shì] **3** [c/U] (*of skin, eyes*) 刺激 [cìjī]

IRS (US) N ABBR (= *Internal Revenue Service*) ▶ **the IRS** 国税局 [Guóshuìjú]

is [ɪz] VB *of* **be**

Islam ['ɪzlɑːm] N [U] 伊斯兰教 [Yīsīlánjiào]

Islamic [ɪz'læmɪk] ADJ [+ *law, faith*] 伊斯兰教的 [Yīsīlánjiào de]; [+ *country*] 伊斯兰的 [Yīsīlán de]

island ['aɪlənd] N [c] **1** (GEO) 岛 [dǎo] **2** (*also*: **traffic island**) 交通岛 [jiāotōngdǎo]

islander ['aɪləndə(r)] N [c] 岛上居民 [dǎoshang jūmín]

isle [aɪl] N [c] 岛 [dǎo]

isn't ['ɪznt] = **is not**

isolate ['aɪsəleɪt] VT **1** [+ *person, country*] 孤立 [gūlì] **2** [+ *substance, sick person, animal*] 隔离 [gélí]

isolated ['aɪsəleɪtɪd] ADJ **1** [+ *place*] 孤零零的 [gūlínglíng de] **2** [+ *person*] 孤立的 [gūlì de] **3** (*single*) [+ *incident, case, example*] 个别的 [gèbié de]

isolation [aɪsə'leɪʃən] N [U] **1** (*of person*) 孤立 [gūlì] **2** ▶ **to consider sth in isolation** 孤立地看待某事 [gūlì de kàndài mǒushì]

ISP N ABBR (= *Internet service provider*) 因特网服务提供者 [yīntèwǎng fúwù tígōngzhě]

Israel ['ɪzreɪl] N 以色列 [Yǐsèliè]

Israeli [ɪz'reɪlɪ] **I** ADJ 以色列的 [Yǐsèliè de] **II** N [c] (*person*) 以色列人 [Yǐsèlièrén]

○ **issue** ['ɪʃuː] **I** N **1** [c] (*problem, subject*) 问题 [wèntí] ▷ *the issue of human rights* 人权问题 **2** ▶ **the issue** (*most important part*) 要点

[yàodiǎn] ▷ *That's not the issue.* 那不是问题所在。**3** [c] [*of magazine, newspaper*] 期[qī] ▷ *the latest issue of the magazine* 最新一期杂志 **4** [c] (*pl* **issue**) (*o.f.*) (*offspring*) 子女 [zǐnǚ] ▷ *He died without issue.* 他死后无子女。**II** VT **1** [+ *rations, equipment, documents*] 发给 [fāgěi] ▷ *Who issued the travel documents?* 谁签发旅行证件？ **2** [+ *statement*] 发表 [fābiǎo] ▷ *We need to issue some sort of statement.* 我们要发表某种声明。 **III** VI (*frm*) ▶ **to issue (from)** [*liquid, sound, smell* +] （从…）出来 [(cóng…) chūlái] ▶ **to avoid the issue** 回避问题 ▶ **to confuse** *or* **cloud the issue** 混淆问题 ▶ **to take issue with sb** 与某人争论 ▶ **to make an issue of sth** 把某事看得极为重要 ▶ **to be at issue** 在争议中的 ▶ **to issue sth to sb** 给某人发放某物 ▶ **to issue sb with sth** 给某人发放某物

IT N ABBR (= *Information Technology*) 信息技术 [xìnxī jìshù]

○**it** [ɪt] PRON **1** (*object or animal*) 它 [tā] ▷ "*Where's my pen?*" – "*It's on the table.*" "我的钢笔在哪儿呢？" "在桌子上。" ▷ *I can't find it.* 我找不到。 ▷ *Give it to me.* 把它给我。▷ *I spoke to him about it.* 我跟他说了这事儿。 ; (*referring to baby*) 他/她 [tā/tā] ▷ *Is it a boy or a girl?* 是男孩儿还是女孩儿？ **2** (*weather, date, time*) ▷ *It's raining.* 正在下雨。▷ *It's very cold in winter here.* 这里的冬天很冷。▷ *It's Friday.* 今天星期五。▷ *It's 6 o'clock.* 现在6点。▷ *It's August 10th.* 今天是8月10日。 **3** (*impersonal*) ▷ *It doesn't matter.* 没关系。▷ *It's easy to see why you left.* 你离开的原因显而易见。 ▷ *It was John who spoke to them.* 是约翰告诉他们的。▶ **what is it?** (*thing*) 是什么东西？; (*what's the matter?*) 怎么了？▶ "**who is it?**" – "**it's me**" "是谁？" "是我。"

Italian [ɪˈtæljən] **I** ADJ 意大利的 [Yìdàlì de] **II** N **1** [c] (*person*) 意大利人 [Yìdàlìrén] **2** [U] (*language*) 意大利语 [Yìdàlìyǔ]

italics [ɪˈtælɪks] NPL 斜体字 [xiétǐzì] ▶ **in italics** 用斜体

Italy [ˈɪtəlɪ] N 意大利 [Yìdàlì]

itch [ɪtʃ] **I** N [c] (*on skin*) 痒 [yǎng] **II** VI [*person, part of body* +] 发痒 [fāyǎng] ▶ **to be itching to do sth** (*inf*) 渴望做某事

itchy [ˈɪtʃɪ] ADJ [+ *skin, nose, eyes, scalp etc*] 发痒的 [fāyǎng de]; [+ *piece of clothing*] 使人发痒的 [shǐ rén fāyǎng de] ▶ **to have itchy feet** 渴望漫游

it'd [ˈɪtd] = it would, it had

item [ˈaɪtəm] N [c] **1** (*on list, agenda*) 项目 [xiàngmù]; (*on bill*) 项 [xiàng]; (*in collection,*) (*object*) 物品 [wùpǐn] **2** (*in newspaper, on TV*) 新闻 [xīnwén] ▶ **items of clothing** 几件衣服

itinerary [aɪˈtɪnərərɪ] N [c] 旅行计划 [lǚxíng jìhuà]

it'll [ˈɪtl] = it will

○**its** [ɪts] ADJ **1** (*of animal*) 它的 [tā de] ▷ *The horse lifted its head.* 马抬起头来。**2** (*of baby*) 他/她的 [tā/tā de] ▷ *The baby was sucking its thumb.* 宝宝吮着大拇指。

请勿将 its 和 it's 混淆。its 意为"它的"。it's 是 it is 或者 it has 的缩略形式。*The dog wagged its tail...It's hot in here... It's stopped raining.*

it's [ɪts] = it is, it has

用法参见 its

○**itself** [ɪtˈsɛlf] PRON **1** (*reflexive*) 它自己 [tāzìjǐ] ▷ *It switches itself on automatically.* 它自动接通。 **2** (*emphatic*) 本身 [běnshēn] ▷ *I think life itself is a learning process.* 我认为生活本身是个学习的过程。▶ **the baby can hold the toy itself** 宝宝自己能拿住玩具 ▶ **she is kindness/politeness itself** 她是仁慈/礼貌的化身 ▶ **in itself** 本身 ▷ *Stress in itself is not necessarily harmful.* 压力本身并不一定是有害的。▶ **by itself** (*unaided*) 自己独立地 ▷ *The cat managed to climb down the tree by itself.* 猫自己设法爬下了树。▷ *The wound will heal by itself.* 伤口会自己愈合的。; (*alone*) 单独地 ▷ *The dog shouldn't have been left at home by itself.* 狗不该被单独留在家里。

ITV (BRIT: TV) N ABBR (= *Independent Television*) 独立电视台 [Dúlì Diànshìtái]

IUD N ABBR (= *intra-uterine device*) 避孕环 [bìyùnhuán]

I've [aɪv] = I have

ivory [ˈaɪvərɪ] N [U] **1** (*substance*) 象牙 [xiàngyá] **2** (*colour*) 乳白色 [rǔbáisè]

ivy [ˈaɪvɪ] N [U] 常春藤 [chángchūnténg]

Ivy League N 常春藤盟校 [chángchūnténg méngxiào]

● **IVY LEAGUE**

美国东北部的 8 所一流大学被称作 **Ivy League**（常青藤盟校）。哈佛大学、耶鲁大学、宾夕法尼亚大学、普林斯顿大学、哥伦比亚大学、布朗大学、达特莫斯大学和康奈尔大学最初常聚到一起举行体育比赛。这个名字据称是取之于爬满了老楼墙壁的常青藤。另一种说法是，最初只有4所大学，罗马数字的4是 IV，发音近似于 **ivy**。

Jj

J, j [dʒeɪ] N [C/U] (letter) 英语的第十个字母

jab [dʒæb] I VT ▸ **to jab sb (in the arm/back/eye) with sth** 用某物戳某人 (的胳膊/背部/眼睛) [yòng mǒuwù chuō mǒurén de (gēbo/bèibù/yǎnjing)] II VI ▸ **to jab at sb with sth** 用某物戳某人 [yòng mǒuwù chuō mǒurén] III N [C] (BRIT: inf) (injection) 注射 [zhùshè] ▸ **to jab one's finger/stick at sb** 用手指/棍子戳某人 ▸ **to jab sth into sth/sb** 把某物刺向某物/某人 ▸ **to have a flu/tetanus jab** (BRIT: inf) 打感冒/破伤风预防针 ▸ **to give sb a jab** (BRIT: inf) 给某人打针

jack [dʒæk] N 1 (AUT) 千斤顶 [qiānjīndǐng] 2 (CARDS) 勾儿 [gōur] 3 (BOWLS) 靶子球 [bǎziqiú]
▸ **jack in** (inf) VT 放弃 [fàngqì]
▸ **jack up** VT 1 (AUT) 用千斤顶顶起 [yòng qiānjīndǐng dǐng qǐ] 2 (inf) [+ price, amount] 提高 [tígāo]

jacket ['dʒækɪt] N [C] 1 (garment) 夹克 [jiākè] 2 (ESP US) (also: **dust jacket**) 护封 [hùfēng]
▸ **potatoes in their jackets, jacket potatoes** (BRIT) 带皮的马铃薯 [美= baked potatoes]

jackpot ['dʒækpɒt] N [C] 头彩 [tóucǎi] ▸ **to hit the jackpot** (inf) (fig) 获得最大成功

Jacuzzi® [dʒə'ku:zɪ] N [C] 一种用于涡流式沐浴或用于在浴池中产生旋涡的装置的商标

jade [dʒeɪd] I N [U] (stone) 玉 [yù] II ADJ (also: **jade green**) 碧绿的 [bìlǜ de] III CPD [复合词] [+ necklace, ornament] 玉的 [yù de]

jagged ['dʒægɪd] ADJ [+ outline, edge, rocks] 参差不齐的 [cēncī bùqí de]

jail [dʒeɪl] I N [C/U] 监狱 [jiānyù] II VT 监禁 [jiānjìn] ▸ **in jail** 在监狱 ▷ *He was sentenced to two years in jail.* 他被判两年监禁。▸ **to go to jail** 入狱

jail sentence N [C] 监狱刑期 [jiānyù xíngqī]

jam [dʒæm] I N 1 [C/U] (BRIT) (preserve) 果酱 [guǒjiàng] [美= jelly] 2 [C] (also: **traffic jam**) 交通堵塞 [jiāotōng dǔsè] II VT 1 ▸ **to jam sth into/on sth** 将某物塞进/扣住某物 [jiāng mǒuwù sāijìn/kòuzhù mǒuwù] 2 (fill) [+ road, square etc] 拥塞 [yōngsāi] 3 (immobilize) [+ mechanism, drawer etc] 使卡住 [shǐ qiǎzhù] 4 (inundate) [+ switchboard, phone lines] 使塞满 [shǐ sāimǎn] 5 (RAD) (prevent from broadcasting) 干扰 [gānrǎo] III VI 1 (get stuck) [drawer, mechanism, gun +] 卡住 [qiǎzhù] 2 ▸ **to jam into a stadium/hall etc** 涌进体育馆/大厅 {等} [yǒngjìn tǐyùguǎn/dàtīng {děng}] 3 (inf: MUS) 即兴演奏 [jíxìng yǎnzòu] ▸ **to be in a jam** (inf) (in difficulty) 陷入困境 ▸ **to get sb out of a jam** (inf) 使某人摆脱困境

Jamaica [dʒə'meɪkə] N 牙买加 [Yámǎijiā]

Jamaican [dʒə'meɪkən] I ADJ 牙买加的 [Yámǎijiā de] II N [C] (person) 牙买加人 [Yámǎijiārén]

jammed [dʒæmd] ADJ 1 [+ roads] 堵塞的 [dǔsè de] 2 [+ mechanism, machine] 卡住的 [qiǎzhù de] 3 [+ switchboard, phone lines] 应接不暇的 [yìngjiē bù xiá de] ▸ **to be jammed with people/cars** 挤满了人/汽车

Jan. ABBR (= January) 一月 [yīyuè]

janitor ['dʒænɪtə(r)] N [C] 看门人 [kānménrén]

January ['dʒænjuərɪ] N [C/U] 一月 [yīyuè] see also **July**

Japan [dʒə'pæn] N 日本 [Rìběn]

Japanese [dʒæpə'ni:z] (pl **Japanese**) I ADJ 日本的 [Rìběn de] II N 1 [C] (person) 日本人 [Rìběnrén] 2 [U] (language) 日语 [Rìyǔ]

jar [dʒɑ:(r)] I N [C] 1 (container) 广口瓶 [guǎngkǒupíng] 2 (contents) 罐装物 [guànzhuāngwù] II VI 1 ▸ **to jar (on sb)** [sound, remark +] 给 (某人) 不愉快的感觉 [gěi (mǒurén) bù yúkuài de gǎnjué] 2 (move) 颠簸 [diānbǒ] III VT 1 (shake, knock) 使震伤 [shǐ zhènshāng] 2 (grate on) [sound, remark +] 刺激 [cìjī]

jargon ['dʒɑ:gən] N [U] 行话 [hánghuà]

javelin ['dʒævlɪn] N [C] 1 (spear) 标枪 [biāoqiāng] 2 (competition) ▸ **the javelin** 标枪赛 [biāoqiāngsài]

jaw [dʒɔ:] (ANAT) I N [C] [of person] 颌 [hé] II **jaws** NPL [of person, animal] 嘴巴 [zuǐba] ▸ **his jaw dropped** 他大吃一惊

jazz [dʒæz] N [U] (MUS) 爵士乐 [juéshìyuè] ▸ **and all that jazz** (inf) 诸如此类的事情 ▸ **jazz up** VT (inf) [+ food, party, one's image] 使有趣 [shǐ yǒuqù]

jealous ['dʒɛləs] ADJ 1 (possessive) [+ husband,

wife etc] 爱妒忌的 [ài dùjì de] **2** (*envious*) 妒忌的 [dùjì de] ▶ **to be jealous of sb/sth** 忌妒某人/某事

jealousy ['dʒɛləsɪ] N [U] **1** (*possessiveness*) [*of husband, wife etc*] 嫉妒 [jídù] **2** (*envy*) 妒忌 [dùjì]

jeans [dʒiːnz] NPL 牛仔裤 [niúzǎikù] ▶ **a pair of jeans** 一条牛仔裤

jeep® [dʒiːp] N [C] 吉普车 [jípǔchē]

jelly ['dʒɛlɪ] N [C/U] **1** (BRIT) (*dessert*) 果冻 [guǒdòng] [美=**Jell-O®**] **2** (US) (*preserve*) 果酱 [guǒjiàng] [英=**jam**]

Jell-O® ['dʒɛləu] (US) N [U] 果冻 [guǒdòng] [英=**jelly**]

jellyfish ['dʒɛlɪfɪʃ] (*pl* **jellyfish**) N [C] 海蜇 [hǎizhé]

jeopardize ['dʒɛpədaɪz] VT [+ *job, relationship, outcome*] 危害 [wēihài]

jerk [dʒəːk] I VT (*pull*) ▶ **to jerk sth up/away/back** 将某物猛地拉上/开/回 [jiāng mǒuwù měng de lāshang/kāi/huí] II VI ▶ **to jerk up/back** 猛然向上/后一动 [měngrán xiàng shàng/hòu yī dòng] III N [C] **1** (*jolt*) 急动 [jídòng] **2** (*inf*) (*idiot*) 呆子 [dāizi] ▶ **the bus jerked to a halt** 巴士猛地停住了 ▶ **the train started with a jerk** 火车颠簸着起动了 ▶ **with a jerk of his head** 扭动一下他的头 ▶ **to give a jerk** 抖了一下

jersey ['dʒəːzɪ] N **1** [C] (*o.f.*) (*pullover*) 针织毛衫 [zhēnzhī máoshān] **2** [U] (*fabric*) 细毛纱 [xìmáoshā] II CPD [复合词] [+ *dress, top*] 针织紧身衣 [zhēnzhī jǐnshēnyī]

Jesus ['dʒiːzəs] N (REL) 耶稣 [Yēsū] ▶ **Jesus Christ** 耶稣基督 ▶ **Jesus!** (*inf*) 天哪!

jet [dʒɛt] I N **1** [C] [*of gas, liquid*] 喷射流 [pēnshèliú] **2** [C] (*aeroplane*) 喷气式飞机 [pēnqìshì fēijī] **3** [U] (*stone*) 黑玉 [hēiyù] II VI ▶ **to jet off to Paris/on holiday** 飞往巴黎/度假 [fēiwǎng Bālí/dùjià] III CPD [复合词] [+ *earring, necklace*] 黑玉 [hēiyù]

jet engine N [C] 喷气发动机 [pēnqì fādòngjī]

jet lag N [U] 时差反应 [shíchā fǎnyìng]

jetty ['dʒɛtɪ] N [C] 码头 [mǎtóu]

Jew [dʒuː] N [C] 犹太人 [Yóutàirén]

jewel ['dʒuːəl] N [C] **1** (*gem*) 宝石 [bǎoshí] **2** (*fig*) 珍宝 [zhēnbǎo] ▶ **it's the jewel in the/sb's crown** 是/某人的宝中之宝

jeweller, (US) **jeweler** ['dʒuːələ(r)] N [C] **1** (*person*) 珠宝商 [zhūbǎoshāng] **2** (*also*: **jeweller's**) 珠宝店 [zhūbǎodiàn]

jewellery, (US) **jewelry** ['dʒuːəlrɪ] N [U] 首饰 [shǒushì]

Jewish ['dʒuːɪʃ] ADJ 犹太的 [Yóutài de]

jigsaw ['dʒɪgsɔː] N **1** (*also*: **jigsaw puzzle**) 拼图玩具 [pīntú wánjù] **2** (*fig*) 错综复杂的局势 [cuòzōng fùzá de júshì] **3** (*tool*) 竖锯 [shùjù]

○**job** [dʒɔb] N [C] **1** (*position*) 工作 [gōngzuò] ▷ *Gladys got a job as a secretary.* 格拉迪斯找到了一份秘书工作。 **2** (*task*) 任务 [rènwù] ▷ *We managed to finish the entire job in three months.* 我们花了3个月的时间完成了全部任务。 **3** (*function*)

职责 [zhízé] ▷ *It's not my job to look after your children.* 给你看孩子不是我的职责。 ▶ **it's a good job that...** 幸好… ▶ **to do or (BRIT) make a good job of sth** 把事情做好 ▶ **I had a job finding it** 我好不容易才找到 ▶ **on the job** [*learn, teach* +] 工作着 ▶ **a part-time/full-time job** 半职/全职工作 ▶ **he's only doing his job** 他只是在履行职责 ▶ **it's just the job** (BRIT: *inf*) 正是想要的 ▣用法参见 **position**

job centre (BRIT) N [C] 职业介绍所 [zhíyè jièshàosuǒ]

jobless ['dʒɔblɪs] I ADJ 失业的 [shīyè de] II NPL ▶ **the jobless** 失业者 [shīyèzhě]

jockey ['dʒɔkɪ] I N [C] (SPORT) 赛马骑师 [sàimǎ qíshī] II VI ▶ **to jockey for position** [*rivals, competitors* +] 运用手段谋取利益 [yùnyòng shǒuduàn móuqǔ lìyì]

jog [dʒɔg] I VT 轻碰 [qīngpèng] II VI 慢跑 [mànpǎo] III N ▶ **to go for a jog** 去慢跑 [qù mànpǎo] ▶ **to jog sb's memory** 唤起某人的记忆 ▶ **to go jogging** 去慢跑

jogging ['dʒɔgɪŋ] N [U] 慢跑 [mànpǎo]

○**join** [dʒɔɪn] I VT **1** (*become member of*) [+ *club, party, army, navy, queue*] 加入 [jiārù] ▷ *We both joined the Labour Party.* 我们俩都加入了工党。 **2** (*connect*) [+ *things, places*] 连接 [liánjiē] ▷ *Draw a straight line joining these two points.* 画一直线，将这两点连接起来。 **3** (*meet*) [+ *person*] 会面 [huìmiàn] ▷ *She flew out to join him in Africa.* 她飞往非洲与他会面。 **4** [+ *road, river*] 汇合 [huìhé] ▷ *This road joins the motorway at junction 16.* 这条路在16号岔路口与高速公路汇合。 II VI [*roads, rivers* +] 汇合 [huìhé] ▷ *The two streams join and form a river.* 两条小溪汇合，形成河流。 III N [C] 接缝 [jiēfèng] ▶ **to join forces (with sb)** (与某人) 通力合作 ▶ **will you join us for dinner?** 你想不想和我们一起吃晚饭? ▶ **I'll join you later** 我一会儿过来
▶ **join in** I VI 参与 [cānyù] II VT FUS [不可拆分] [+ *work, discussion etc*] 参加 [cānjiā]
▶ **join up** I VI (MIL) 参军 [cānjūn] **2** (*meet*) ▶ **to join up (with sb)** (与某人) 联合起来 [(yǔ mǒurén) liánhé qǐlái]

joiner ['dʒɔɪnə(r)] (BRIT) N [C] 细木工人 [xìmù gōngrén]

joint [dʒɔɪnt] I N [C] **1** (ANAT) 关节 [guānjié] **2** (TECH) (*in woodwork, pipe etc*) 连接处 [liánjiēchù] **3** (BRIT: CULIN) [*of beef, lamb*] 大块肉 [dàkuàiròu] [美=**roast**] **4** (*inf*) (*bar, club*) 低级场所 [dījí chǎngsuǒ] **5** (*inf*: DRUGS) 含大麻的香烟 [hán dàmá de xiāngyān] II ADJ **1** (*shared*) [+ *effort, decision*] 共同的 [gòngtóng de]; [+ *owners*] 联合的 [liánhé de] ▶ **to be out of joint** 不协调的

joint account N [C] 共有帐户 [gòngyǒu zhànghù]

jointly ['dʒɔɪntlɪ] ADV [*own, run, fund, produce* +] 共同地 [gòngtóng de]; [+ *responsible*] 共同地 [gòngtóng de]

joke [dʒəʊk] I N [c] **1** (*funny story*) 笑话 [xiàohuɑ] **2** (*prank*) 玩笑 [wánxiào] II VI 开玩 笑 [kāi wánxiào] ▶ **the decision was a joke** (*inf*) 这个决定真是荒唐 ▶ **it's no joke** (*inf*) 不是闹 着玩儿的 ▶ **to play a joke on sb** 开某人的玩笑 ▶ **to joke about sth** 以某事为笑柄 ▶ **you're joking** or **you must be joking!** (*inf*) 你在开玩笑 〔或〕你一定在开玩笑吧！

joker ['dʒəʊkə(r)] N [c] **1** (*CARDS*) 王 [wáng] **2** (*person*) 爱开玩笑的人 [ài kāiwánxiào de rén]

jolly ['dʒɒlɪ] I ADJ **1** (*merry*) [+ *person, laugh*] 愉 快的 [yúkuài de] **2** (*enjoyable*) [+ *time, party*] 欢 乐的 [huānlè de] II ADV (BRIT: o.f., inf) 非常 [fēicháng] III VT (BRIT) ▶ **to jolly sb along** 哄 某人开心 [hǒng mǒurén kāixīn] ▶ **jolly good** (BRIT) 太好了

jolt [dʒəʊlt] I N [c] **1** (*jerk*) 颠簸 [diānbǒ] **2** (*shock*) 震惊 [zhènjīng] II VT **1** (*physically*) 摇晃 [yáohuàng] **2** (*emotionally*) 使震惊 [shǐ zhènjīng] III VI 颠簸 [diānbǒ] ▶ **to give sb a jolt** (*emotionally*) 使某人震惊 ▶ **I realized with a jolt that...** 我猛然意识到…

Jordan ['dʒɔːdən] N **1** (*country*) 约旦 [Yuēdàn] **2** ▶ **the (River) Jordan** 约旦河 [Yuēdànhé]

Jordanian [dʒɔːˈdeɪnɪən] I ADJ 约旦的 [Yuēdàn de] II N [c] 约旦人 [Yuēdànrén]

journal ['dʒəːnl] N [c] **1** (*publication*) 报刊 [bàokān] **2** (*diary*) 日记 [rìjì] ▶ **to keep a journal (of sth)** 记(关于某事的)日记

journalism ['dʒəːnəlɪzəm] N [u] (*profession*) 新闻业 [xīnwényè] ▶ **piece of journalism** 报导

journalist ['dʒəːnəlɪst] N [c] 新闻工作者 [xīnwén gōngzuòzhě]

journey ['dʒəːnɪ] I N [c] 旅程 [lǚchéng] II VI (*frm*) 旅行 [lǚxíng] ▶ **a 5-hour journey** 5个小 时的路程 ▶ **to go on a journey** 去旅行

请勿将 **journey**、**voyage** 和 **trip** 混 淆。**journey** 是指从一地搭乘车船或飞 机到另一地的过程。…*a journey of over 2000 miles…* 如果你 **journey** to 某 地，你就是去那里。这是书面的用法。 *The nights became colder as they journeyed north.* **voyage** 是指从一地到另一地的 长途行程，通常指乘船旅行或者太空 旅行。…*the voyage to the moon in 1972…* **trip** 是指从一地到另一地的旅行过程， 在目的地做短暂的停留后返回。…*a business trip to Milan…*

joy [dʒɔɪ] N **1** [u] (*happiness*) 快乐 [kuàilè] **2** [c] (*delight*) 愉悦 [yúyuè]

joyrider ['dʒɔɪraɪdə(r)] N [c] 开偷来的车去兜 风的人

joystick ['dʒɔɪstɪk] N [c] **1** (*AVIAT*) 操纵杆 [cāozònggǎn] **2** (*COMPUT*) 控制杆 [kòngzhìgǎn]

JP (BRIT) N ABBR (= *Justice of the Peace*) 地方执法 官 [dìfāng zhífǎguān]

Jr, (US)**Jr.** ABBR (*in names*) (= *junior*) 小 [Xiǎo]

judge [dʒʌdʒ] I N [c] **1** (*LAW*) 法官 [fǎguān] **2** (*in competition*) 裁判 [cáipàn] II VT **1** [+ *exhibits, competition etc*] 评定 [píngdìng] **2** (*evaluate*) [+ *effect, impact*] 评估 [pínggū]; [+ *person*] 评判 [píngpàn] **3** (*estimate*) [+ *age, weight, size*] 判断 [pànduàn] **4** (*frm*) (*consider*) 断定 [duàndìng] III VI (*form opinion*) 判断 [pànduàn] ▶ **I'll be the judge of that** 这由我说 了算 ▶ **judging by** or **from his expression** 从他 的表情上判断 ▶ **as** or **so far as I can judge** 依我 看 ▶ **to be a good judge of sth** 很会判断某事

judg(e)ment ['dʒʌdʒmənt] N **1** [c/u] (*view, opinion*) 看法 [kànfǎ] **2** [u] (*discernment*) 判断力 [pànduànlì] **3** [c/u] (*LAW*) 审判 [shěnpàn] ▶ **in my judgment** 依我来看 ▶ **to pass judgment (on sb/sth)** (*LAW*) (对某人/某事) 作出判决; (*fig*) 评论(某人/某事) ▶ **an error of judgment** 判断失误

judo ['dʒuːdəʊ] N [u] 柔道 [róudào]

jug [dʒʌg] N [c] **1** (*container*) 壶 [hú] **2** (*contents*) 壶中物 [húzhōngwù]

juggle ['dʒʌgl] I VI 玩杂耍 [wán záshuǎ] II VT **1** (*lit*) 连续抛接 [liánxù pāo jiē] **2** (*fig*) [+ *demands, priorities*] 同时兼顾 [tóngshí jiāngù] ▶ **to juggle with sth** [+ *balls, plates etc*] 连续抛接 某物;[+ *figures, numbers*] 窜改数据

juggler ['dʒʌglə(r)] N [c] 杂耍演员 [záshuǎ yǎnyuán]

juice [dʒuːs] I N **1** [c/u] (*from fruit*) 汁 [zhī] **2** [u] (*inf*) (*petrol*) 汽油 [qìyóu] II **juices** NPL **1** [of meat] 汁 [zhī] **2** (*digestive*) 液 [yè]

juicy ['dʒuːsɪ] ADJ **1** [+ *fruit, steak*] 多汁液的 [duō zhīyè de] **2** (*inf*) (*scandalous*) [+ *details, rumours, gossip*] 绘声绘色的 [huì shēng huì sè de]

Jul. ABBR (= *July*) 七月 [qīyuè]

July [dʒuːˈlaɪ] N [c/u] 七月 [qīyuè] ▶ **the first of July** 七月一日 ▶ (**on**) **the eleventh of July** (在)七月十一日 ▶ **in the month of July** 在 七月份 ▶ **at the beginning/end of July** 在七 月初/末 ▶ **in the middle of July** 在七月中旬 ▶ **during July** 在七月份期间 ▶ **in July of next year** 在明年七月 ▶ **each** or **every July** 每年 七月 ▶ **July was wet this year** 今年七月份多雨

jumble ['dʒʌmbl] I N **1** [s] (*muddle*) 杂乱 [záluàn] **2** [u] (BRIT) (*items for sale*) 义卖的旧杂 物 [yìmài de jiù záwù] [美= **rummage**] II VT (*also*: **jumble up**) 使混乱 [shǐ hùnluàn]

jumble sale (BRIT) N [c] 杂物义卖 [záwù yìmài] [美= **rummage sale**]

◈ Jumble sale

在学校或教堂里举行 **jumble sale** (杂物拍 卖)可以为慈善机构、学校(例如，为了购 买电脑)或教会(或许为了修葺屋顶)筹措 资金。人们捐出不需要的衣物、玩具、图 书和其他家庭用品，有意者前来观看，以 期"掏到"便宜的二手货。

jumbo ['dʒʌmbəʊ] I N [c] (also: **jumbo jet**) 大型喷气式客机 [dàxíng pēnqìshì kèjī] II ADJ (also: **jumbo-sized**) 特大的 [tèdà de]

jump [dʒʌmp] I VI 1 (into air) 跳 [tiào] 2 (from seat etc) 跳起来 [tiào qǐlái] 3 (with fear, surprise) 突然跃起 [tūrán yuèqǐ] 4 (increase) 暴涨 [bàozhǎng] II VT [+ fence, stream] 跳过 [tiàoguò] III N [c] 1 (leap) 跳 [tiào] 2 (increase) 猛增 [měngzēng] ▶ to jump over sth 跳过某物 ▶ to jump out of a window 从窗户跳下 ▶ to jump on/off sth 跳上/下某物 ▶ to jump to one's feet 噌地站起来 ▶ to jump the queue (BRIT) 加塞儿 ▶ to get a or (US) the jump on sb/sth 抢在某人/某事之前行动
▶ **jump at** VT FUS [+ chance, offer] 欣然接受 [xīnrán jiēshòu]
▶ **jump up** VI 突然站立 [tūrán zhànlì]

jumper ['dʒʌmpə(r)] N [c] 1 (BRIT) (sweater) 毛衣 [máoyī] [美 = **sweater**] 2 (US) (dress) 无袖连衣裙 [wúxiù liányīqún] [英 = **pinafore**] 3 (SPORT) ▶ a long/high jumper 跳远/跳高运动员 [tiàoyuǎn/tiàogāo yùndòngyuán]

Jun. ABBR (= **June**) 六月 [liùyuè]

junction ['dʒʌŋkʃən] (BRIT) N [c] 1 [of roads] 交叉点 [jiāochādiǎn] [美 = **intersection**] 2 (RAIL) 联轨点 [liánguǐdiǎn]

June [dʒuːn] N [c/u] 六月 [liùyuè] see also **July**

jungle ['dʒʌŋgl] N 1 [c/u] 丛林 [cónglín] 2 [s] (fig) 混乱 [hùnluàn] ▶ the law of the jungle 弱肉强食的原则

junior ['dʒuːnɪə(r)] I ADJ 级别低的 [jíbié dī de] II N [c] 1 (subordinate) 下级 [xiàjí] 2 (BRIT: SCOL) 小学生 [xiǎoxuésheng] ▶ he's my junior by 2 years, he's 2 years my junior 他比我小两岁 ▶ to be junior to sb 是某人的下属 ▶ George Bush Junior (US) 小乔治·布什

junior high, (US) **junior high school** N [c/u] 初中 [chūzhōng]

junior school (BRIT) N [c/u] 小学 [xiǎoxué]

junk [dʒʌŋk] I N 1 [u] (inf) (rubbish) 废旧杂物 [fèijiù záwù] 2 [u] (antiques) 古董 [gǔdǒng] 3 [c] (ship) 平底帆船 [píngdǐ fānchuán] II VT (inf) 扔掉 [rēngdiào]

junk food N [u] 垃圾食品 [lājī shípǐn]

junkie ['dʒʌŋkɪ] (inf) N [c] 吸毒者 [xīdúzhě]

junk mail N [u] 垃圾邮件 [lājī yóujiàn]

Jupiter ['dʒuːpɪtə(r)] N [u] (planet) 木星 [Mùxīng]

jurisdiction [dʒʊərɪs'dɪkʃən] N [u] 司法权 [sīfǎquán] ▶ to have jurisdiction over 对…有管辖权 ▶ it falls or comes within/outside my jurisdiction 这件事在我的权限之内/之外

jury ['dʒʊərɪ] N [c] 1 (LAW) 陪审团 [péishěntuán] 2 (in competition) 评审团 [píngshěn tuán] ▶ the jury is (still) out 陪审团 (仍) 在合议

just [dʒʌst] I ADJ 1 (frm) (fair) [+ decision, punishment, reward] 公平的 [gōngpíng de]
▷ Was Pollard's life sentence just or was it too severe? 判波拉德无期徒刑公平呢，还是太重了?; [+ society, cause] 公正的 [gōngzhèng de] ▷ a just and civilized society 一个公正文明的社会 II ADV 1 (exactly) 正好 [zhènghǎo] ▷ That's just what I wanted to hear. 那正好是我想要听的。 2 (merely) 仅仅 [jǐnjǐn] ▷ It's not true, it's just a story. 不是真的，仅仅是个故事。 3 (barely) 刚刚 [gānggāng] ▷ Her hand was just visible. 刚刚能看见她的手。 4 (for emphasis) 简直 [jiǎnzhí] ▷ She just won't relax. 她就是无法放松。 5 (in instructions, requests) (only) 只是 [zhǐshì] ▷ I just want some information on ferries, please. 劳驾，我只是想要一些有关渡船的信息。 ▶ it's just right 正合适 ▶ I'm just finishing this 我马上就做完了 ▶ we were just going 我们正要走 ▶ I was just about to phone or I was just going to phone 我正要打电话 ▶ to have just done sth 刚刚做完某事 ▷ He has just left. 他刚走。 ▶ just now (a moment ago) 刚才 ; (at the present time) 现在 ▶ just about everything/everyone 差不多所有东西/所有人 ▶ it's just about big enough 差不多够大了 ▶ we can just about get there in time 我们可能刚刚能准时赶到那里 ▶ it's just that… 不过… ▶ she's just as clever as you 她跟你一样聪明 ▶ just as I expected 正如我所预料的那样 ▶ just as he was leaving 就在他要离开时 ▶ just before/after… 就在…以前/以后 ▶ just enough time/money 时间/钱正好够 ▶ he just missed (failed to hit target) 他差点就打中目标 ▶ he just missed the wall (avoided crashing into) 他差点撞到墙上 ▶ not just now 不是现在 ▶ just a minute, just one moment (asking someone to wait) 等一下; (interrupting) 慢着

justice ['dʒʌstɪs] N 1 [u] (LAW) (system) 司法 [sīfǎ] 2 [u] (fairness) 正义 [zhèngyì] 3 [u] (legitimacy) [of cause, complaint] 正当 [zhèngdàng] 4 [c] (US) (judge) 法官 [fǎguān] ▶ Lord Chief Justice (BRIT: LAW) 首席大法官 ▶ to do justice to sb/sth 使某人/某事达到最佳效果 ▷ The photograph I had seen didn't do her justice. 照片没有她本人好看。 ▶ she didn't do herself justice 她没有充分发挥自己的才能 ▶ to bring sb to justice 把某人缉拿归案

justifiable [dʒʌstɪ'faɪəbl] ADJ 有理的 [yǒulǐ de]

justification [dʒʌstɪfɪ'keɪʃən] N [c/u] 正当理由 [zhèngdàng lǐyóu]

justify ['dʒʌstɪfaɪ] VT 1 [+ action, decision] 证明…是有理由的 [zhèngmíng…shì yǒu lǐyóu de] ▷ he is justified in doing it 他的做法是有理由的 ▶ to justify o.s. 为自己辩护

jut [dʒʌt] VI (also: **jut out**) 突出 [tūchū]

juvenile ['dʒuːvənaɪl] I ADJ 1 [+ crime, offender, court] 青少年的 [qīngshàonián de] 2 (pej) [+ humour, mentality, person] 幼稚的 [yòuzhì de] II N [c] (frm) 青少年 [qīngshàonián]

Kk

K¹, k [keɪ] N [C/U] (letter) 英语的第十一个字母

K² ABBR **1** (inf) (= **thousands**) 千 [qiān]
2 (COMPUT) (= **kilobytes**) 千字节 [qiānzìjié]

kabob [kəˈbɒb] (US) N [C] **1** (on stick) 烤肉
串 [kǎoròuchuàn] **2** (in bread) 夹烤肉饼
[jiākǎoròubǐng] [英= kebab]

Kampuchea [kæmpuˈtʃɪə] (formerly) N 柬埔寨
[Jiǎnpǔzhài]

Kampuchean [kæmpuˈtʃɪən] (formerly) ADJ 柬
埔寨的 [Jiǎnpǔzhài de]

kangaroo [kæŋgəˈruː] N [C] 袋鼠 [dàishǔ]

karaoke [kɑːrəˈəʊkɪ] N [U] 卡拉OK [kǎlā ōukèi]

karate [kəˈrɑːtɪ] N [U] 空手道 [kōngshǒudào]

Kazakhstan [kæzækˈstɑːn] N 哈萨克斯坦
[Hāsàkèsītǎn]

kebab [kəˈbæb] N [C] **1** (on stick) 烤肉串
[kǎoròuchuàn] **2** (in bread) 夹烤肉饼
[jiākǎoròubǐng] [英= kabob]

keel [kiːl] N [C] (NAUT) 龙骨 [lónggǔ] ▶ **to keep
sb/sth on an even keel** 使某人/某物保持稳
定 ▶ **to get** or **put sth back on an even keel** 使
某物恢复稳定
▶ **keel over** (inf) VI [person +] 倒下 [dǎoxià]

keen [kiːn] ADJ **1** (enthusiastic) 热衷的 [rèzhōng
de] **2** [+ interest, desire] 强烈的 [qiángliè de]
3 [+ sense, mind, intelligence] 敏锐的 [mǐnruì de]
4 [+ competition] 激烈的 [jīliè de] ▶ **to have a
keen eye for detail** 对细节有敏锐的观察力 ▶ **to
be keen to do sth** 渴望做某事 ▶ **to be keen
for sb to do sth** 极力要求某人做某事 ▶ **to be**

keen that... 积极主张⋯ ▶ **to be keen on sth**
热衷于某事 ▶ **to be keen on doing sth** (enjoy
doing) 喜欢做某事; (eager to do) 很想做某事
▶ **to be keen on sb** 喜爱某人

Ⓞ **keep** [kiːp] (pt, pp **kept**) I VT **1** (retain) [+ receipt,
money, job] 保留 [bǎoliú] ▷ Make sure you always
keep your receipts. 记住留着收据。 **2** (store) 保存
[bǎocún] ▷ Keep your card in a safe place. 把你的
卡保存好。 ▷ The rubbish is kept in the basement.
垃圾是放在地下室的。 **3** (detain) 留 [liú] ▷ They
kept her in hospital overnight. 他们留她在医院
过夜。 **4** (hold) 保持 [bǎochí] ▷ Keep your back
straight. 别驼背。 ▷ Keep costs to a minimum. 尽
量减低费用。 **5** (manage) [+ shop, guest house] 经
营 [jīngyíng] ▷ My aunt kept a sweetshop. 我姨
妈经营糖果店。 **6** (look after) [+ chickens, bees etc]
饲养 [sìyǎng] **7** [+ accounts, diary] 记 [jì] ▷ As a
young girl I used to keep a diary. 当我是小女孩时我
常记日记。 **8** (support) [+ family] 养 [yǎng] II VI
1 (stay) 保持 [bǎochí] ▷ It's not always easy to
keep warm. 保暖并不总是那么容易。 **2** (last)
[food +] 保鲜 [bǎoxiān] ▷ Homemade muesli keeps
for ages. 自己作的穆兹利可以保鲜很长时间。
▷ Fish doesn't keep well, even in the fridge. 就算把鱼
放在冰箱里也不容易保鲜。 III N **1** [S] (expenses)
生活费 [shēnghuófèi] ▷ I need to give my parents
money for my keep. 我需要给父母我的生活费。
2 [C] [of castle] 要塞 [yàosài] ▶ **to keep doing
sth** (repeatedly) 总是做某事; (continuously) 不停
做某事 ▶ **to keep sb happy** 让某人高兴 ▶ **to
keep sb waiting** 让某人等着 ▶ **to keep the
room tidy** 保持房间整洁 ▶ **to keep sth to o.s.**
保守秘密 ▶ **to keep an appointment** 守约
▶ **to keep a promise** 履行诺言 ▶ **to keep one's
word** 履行诺言 ▶ **can you keep a secret?** 你
能保守秘密吗？ ▶ **to keep a record (of sth)** 记
录(某事) ▶ **to keep o.s.** 供养自己 ▶ **to keep
(good) time** [clock +] 准时 ▶ **what kept you?** 怎
么会晚了？ ▶ **how are you keeping?** (inf) 你还
好吗？ ▶ **to keep at it** (persevere) 坚持干

▶ **keep away** I VT ▶ **to keep sth/sb away
(from sth)** 使某物/某人不要来(某处) [shǐ
mǒuwù/mǒurén bùyào lái (mǒuchù)] ▷ Keep
animals away from the kitchen. 别让动物到厨房
里。 II VI ▶ **to keep away (from sth)** 不接近(某
处) [bù jiējìn (mǒuchù)] ▷ They kept away from
the forest. 他们不接近森林。

▶ **keep back** I VT **1** (reserve) [+ paint, ingredients]
保留 [bǎoliú] ▷ Keep back enough juice to make
the sauce. 留足够的汁做调味汁。 **2** (conceal)
[+ information] 隐瞒 [yǐnmán] ▷ I can't help feeling
he's keeping something back. 我总觉得他在隐瞒着
什么。 II VI 不靠近 [bù kàojìn] ▷ Keep back or
I'll shoot. 别向前，不然我就开枪了。

▶ **keep down** VT **1** (control) [+ prices, spending] 控
制 [kòngzhì] ▷ We want to try and keep costs down.
我们想尽量压缩费用。 **2** (not vomit) [+ food] 咽
下 [yànxià] ▷ I can't keep anything down, not even

water. 我什么都咽不下，连水都不行。
▶ **keep from I** VT FUS [不可拆分] ▶ **to keep from doing sth** 克制 [kèzhì] ▶ *to keep from crying*. 她咬着嘴唇克制着自己不要哭。**II** VT ▶ **to keep sb/sth from doing sth** 不让某人/某物做某事 [bù ràng mǒurén/mǒuwù zuò mǒushì] ▷ *Can't you keep your children from stealing my apples?* 你不能不让你孩子偷我的苹果吗？
▶ **keep in** VT [+ *invalid, child*] 不让外出 [bù ràng wàichū]; (*as punishment*) 关禁闭 [guānjìnbì]
▶ **keep in with** (ESP BRIT) VT FUS [不可拆分] 搞好关系 [gǎohǎo guānxì] ▷ *Now he is getting old he wishes he had kept in with his family.* 他年纪大了，后悔当初没有多亲近家人。
▶ **keep off I** VT 使不接近 [shǐ bù jiējìn] ▷ *a bamboo shelter to keep the rain off* 挡雨的竹棚 ▷ *Keep your dog off my lawn!* 别让你的狗接近我的草坪！▶ **Keep your hands off me!** 别碰我！**II** VT FUS [不可拆分] ▶ **keep off the grass!** 请勿进入草坪！[qǐng wù jìnrù cǎopíng!] **III** VI [*rain +*] 不下(雨) [bù xià(yǔ)] ▷ *Luckily the rain kept off.* 幸好没有下雨。
▶ **keep on** VI ▶ **to keep on doing sth** 继续做某事 [jìxù zuò mǒushì] ▷ *They kept on walking for a while in silence.* 他们继续走了一会儿，谁都没说话。
▶ **keep out** VT [+ *intruder, unwelcome visitor*] 阻拦 [zǔlán] ▷ *a guard dog to keep out intruders* 阻止闯入者的看家狗
▶ **keep to** VT FUS [不可拆分] (*observe*) [+ *agreement*] 遵守 [zūnshǒu]; [+ *limit*] 局限于 [júxiànyú] ▷ *You've got to keep to the speed limit.* 你绝对不能超速。
▶ **keep up I** VT **1** (*maintain*) [+ *standards*] 维持 [wéichí] ▷ *It's important to keep up our standards.* 维持水准是很重要的。**2** (*continue*) [+ *payments, diet*] 继续 [jìxù] ▷ *He was unable to keep up the payments.* 他没能力继续付款。**3** (*prevent from sleeping*) (使)熬夜 [(shǐ) áoyè] ▷ *We were kept up by the noise from next door.* 隔壁的噪音使我们睡不着觉。▶ **to keep up appearances** 撑场面 **II** VI ▶ **to keep up** (*with walker, vehicle*) 跟上 [gēnshang]; (*with demand, inflation*) 跟上 [gēnshang]; (*in work*) 跟上 [gēnshang] ▶ **to keep up with sb** (*walking, moving*) 跟上某人; (*in work*) 跟上某人 ▶ **to keep up with demand/inflation** 跟上需求/通货膨胀

keeper ['ki:pə(r)] N [c] **1** (*at zoo*) 饲养员 [sìyǎngyuán] **2** [c] (BRIT: *inf*) (*goalkeeper*) 守门员 [shǒuményuán]

keep fit (ESP BRIT) N [U] 健身运动 [jiànshēn yùndòng]

keep-fit [ki:p'fit] CPD [复合词] [+ *class, session, course*] 健身 [jiànshēn]

keeping ['ki:pɪŋ] N [U] ▶ **in keeping with** [+ *image, surroundings*] 与…协调 [yǔ…xiétiáo]; [+ *regulation, law*] 与…一致 [yǔ…yīzhì] ▶ **out of**

keeping with 与…不协调

kennel ['kɛnl] N [c] (BRIT) (*dog house*) 狗窝 [gǒuwō] **II** (*also*: **kennels**) NPL (*establishment*) 养狗场 [yǎnggǒuchǎng]

Kenya ['kɛnjə] N 肯尼亚 [Kěnníyà]

Kenyan ['kɛnjən] **I** ADJ 肯尼亚的 [Kěnníyà de] **II** N (*person*) 肯尼亚人 [Kěnníyàrén]

kept [kɛpt] PT, PP *of* **keep**

kerb, (US) **curb** [kə:b] N [c] 路缘 [lùyuán]

kerosene ['kɛrəsi:n] N [U] **1** (*aviation fuel*) 航空燃料 [hángkōng ránliào] **2** (US) (*for heater, lamp*) 煤油 [méiyóu] [英 = **paraffin**]

ketchup ['kɛtʃəp] N [U] 番茄酱 [fānqiéjiàng]

kettle ['kɛtl] N [c] 水壶 [shuǐhú] ▶ **to put the kettle on** 烧水 ▶ **the kettle's boiling** 水开了

key [ki:] N [c] **1** (*for lock, mechanism*) 钥匙 [yàoshi] **2** [*of computer, typewriter, piano*] 键 [jiàn] **3** (MUS) 调 [diào] **4** ▶ **the key (to sth)** (*to success, victory, peace, mystery*) (某事的)关键 [(mǒushì de) guānjiàn] **II** ADJ [+ *issue, factor etc*] 关键的 [guānjiàn de] **III** VT (*also*: **key in**) 输入 [shūrù] ▶ **to hold the key to sth** 掌握某事的关键 ▶ **the key to doing sth** 做某事的关键

keyboard ['ki:bɔ:d] **I** N [c] [*of computer, typewriter, piano*] 键盘 [jiànpán] **II keyboards** NPL (*instrument*) 键盘乐器 [jiànpán yuèqì]

keyhole ['ki:həʊl] N [c] 钥匙孔 [yàoshikǒng]

key ring N [c] 钥匙环 [yàoshihuán]

kg ABBR (= **kilograms**) 公斤 [gōngjīn]

khaki ['kɑ:kɪ] **I** N [U] **1** (*colour*) 土黄色 [tǔhuángsè] **2** (*material*) 卡其布 [kǎqíbù] **II** ADJ **1** (*colour*) 土黄色的 [tǔhuángsè de] **2** (*material*) 卡其布的 [kǎqíbù de]

kHz ABBR (= **kilohertz**) 千赫兹 [qiānhèzī]

kick [kɪk] **I** VT [+ *person, ball*] 踢 [tī] **II** VI [*person, horse +*] 踢 [tī] **III** N [c] **1** (*blow from person, animal*) 踢 [tī] **2** (SPORT) 踢 [tī] **3** [*of rifle*] 反冲 [fǎnchōng] ▶ **to give sb a kick** 踢某人 ▶ **to get a kick out of sth** 从某事中获得乐趣 ▶ **to do sth for kicks** (*inf*) 为刺激而做某事 ▶ **to kick the habit** (*inf*) 戒除恶习 ▶ **to kick the bucket** (*inf*) 翘辫子 ▶ **I could have kicked myself!** (*inf*) 我真后悔！
▶ **kick about** VT, VI = **kick around**
▶ **kick around** (*inf*) **I** VI 在 [zài] **II** VT [+ *ideas*] 随便谈一谈 [suíbiàn tányìtán]
▶ **kick in** VI (*take effect*) [*electrical device +*] 开启 [kāiqǐ]; [*medicine +*] 起作用 [qǐ zuòyòng]
▶ **kick off I** VI **1** (SPORT) 开赛 [kāisài] **2** (*inf*) (*begin*) 开始 [kāishǐ] **II** VT 开始 [kāishǐ]
▶ **kick up** VT FUS [不可拆分] ▶ **to kick up a fuss** (*about sth*) (为某事)大发牢骚 [(wèi mǒushì) dàfā láosāo]

kick-off ['kɪkɔf] (SPORT) N [s] 开场时间 [kāichǎng shíjiān]

kid [kɪd] **I** N [c] **1** (*inf*) (*child*) 小孩 [xiǎohái]; (*teenager*) 年轻人 [niánqīngrén] **2** (*goat*) 小山羊 [xiǎoshānyáng] **II** VI (*inf*) (*joke*) 开玩笑

[kāi wánxiào] ▶ **you're kidding!** 你一定是在开玩笑吧！ ▶ **kid brother** (inf) 弟 ▶ **kid sister** (inf) 妹

kidnap ['kɪdnæp] I VT 绑架 [bǎngjià] II N [C/U] 绑架 [bǎngjià]

kidnapping ['kɪdnæpɪŋ] N [C/U] 绑架 [bǎngjià]

kidney ['kɪdnɪ] N 1 [C] (ANAT) 肾脏 [shènzàng] 2 [C/U] (CULIN) 腰子 [yāozi]

kidney bean N [C] 云豆 [yúndòu]

◎ **kill** [kɪl] I VT 1 [+person, animal, plant] 致死 [zhìsǐ] ▷ Her mother was killed in a car crash. 她母亲死于车祸。 2 (murder) 谋杀 [móushā] ▷ She killed him with a hammer. 她用锤子杀死了他。 3 (fig) [+rumour, hope, idea] 扼杀 [èshā] 4 (inf) [+lights, motor] 关掉 [guāndiào] 5 [+pain] 止痛 [zhǐtòng] ▷ I'll give you something to kill the pain. 我给你点止痛的药。 II N [S] (after hunt) 捕杀 [bǔshā] ▶ **my back's killing me** (inf) 我的背疼死了 ▶ **to kill time** 消磨时间 ▶ **he certainly hasn't been killing himself** (inf) (fig) 他肯定没有竭尽全力 ▶ **to kill o.s. (laughing or with laughter)** (inf) (fig) 笑得前仰后合 ▶ **to go or move in for the kill** (fig) 出致命的一击
▶ **kill off** VT 1 [+bacteria, species] 灭绝 [mièjué] 2 [+hope, idea] 扼杀 [èshā]

有几个词和 **kill** 语意相近。**murder** 是蓄意谋杀。**assassinate** 是指出于政治目而暗杀某重要人物。**slaughter** 和 **massacre** 表示大屠杀，**slaughter** 还可以指宰杀动物用以供食。

killer ['kɪlə(r)] N [C] 1 (murderer) 凶手 [xiōngshǒu] 2 (disease, activity) 杀灭物 [shāmièwù] ▶ **learning English vocabulary is a killer** 学习英文单词真是难死人了

killing ['kɪlɪŋ] N [C] 谋杀 [móushā] ▶ **to make a killing** (inf) 发大财

kiln [kɪln] N [C] 窑 [yáo]

kilo ['kiːləʊ] N [C] 公斤 [gōngjīn]

kilobyte ['kɪləbaɪt] (COMPUT) N [C] 千字节 [qiānzìjié]

kilogram(me) ['kɪləʊɡræm] N [C] 公斤 [gōngjīn]

kilometre, (US) **kilometer** ['kɪləmiːtə(r)] N [C] 公里 [gōnglǐ]

kilowatt ['kɪləʊwɒt] N [C] 千瓦 [qiānwǎ]

kilt [kɪlt] N [C] 苏格兰短裙 [Sūgélán duǎnqún]

kin [kɪn] (o.f.) NPL 亲属 [qīnqi]

◎ **kind** [kaɪnd] I ADJ [+person, action, smile, voice] 友好的 [yǒuhǎo de] ▷ They are all extremely kind and helpful. 他们都很友好，乐于助人。 ▷ Thank you. You've been very kind. 谢谢，你太好心了。 II N [C] (type, sort) 种类 [zhǒnglèi] ▷ an opportunity to meet all kinds of people 与各种各样的人见面的机会 ▶ **it was kind of them to help** 他们来帮忙真是太好了 ▶ **would you be kind enough to or so kind as to close the window?** 麻烦你把窗户关上好吗？ ▶ **he's a kind of**

explorer 他可以说是个探险者 ▶ **she's kind of cute** (inf) 她还算可爱 ▶ **in kind** (similarly) 以牙还牙; (not in money) 以物偿付 ▶ **payment in kind** 以货代款 ▶ **to be two/three/four of a kind** 两/三/四个都属同一类

kindergarten ['kɪndəɡɑːtn] N [C] 幼儿园 [yòu'éryuán]

kindly ['kaɪndlɪ] I ADJ [+person, tone, interest] 友善的 [yǒushàn de]; [agree, offer+] 亲切地 [qīnqiè de]; II ADV [say, smile, treat+] 友善地 [yǒushàn de] ▶ **will you kindly stop shouting at me!** 请别冲着我大喊大叫！ ▶ **he doesn't take kindly to criticism/people criticizing him** 他不乐意接受批评

kindness ['kaɪndnɪs] N 1 [U] (quality) 仁慈 [réncí] 2 [C] (act) 友好的行为 [yǒuhǎo de xíngwéi]

king [kɪŋ] N [C] 1 国王 [guówáng] 2 (CARDS) 老K [lǎokèi] 3 (CHESS) 王 [wáng] ▶ **the king of the jungle/rock'n'roll** 森林/摇滚乐之王

kingdom ['kɪŋdəm] N [C] 王国 [wángguó] ▶ **the animal/plant kingdom** 动/植物王国

kingfisher ['kɪŋfɪʃə(r)] N [C] 翠鸟 [cuìniǎo]

king-size(d) ['kɪŋsaɪz(d)] ADJ 特大的 [tèdà de]

kiosk ['kiːɒsk] N [C] 1 (shop) 售货亭 [shòuhuòtíng] 2 (BRIT) (phone box) 电话亭 [diànhuàtíng]

kipper ['kɪpə(r)] N [C] 熏制鲱鱼 [xūnzhì fēiyú]

kiss [kɪs] I N [C] 吻 [wěn] II VT 吻 [wěn] III VI 接吻 [jiēwěn] ▶ **to give sb a kiss** 吻某人一下 ▶ **to kiss sb goodbye/goodnight** 与某人吻别/吻某人一下，道晚安

kiss of life (BRIT) N [S] 口对口人工呼吸 [kǒu duì kǒu réngōng hūxī]

kit [kɪt] N 1 [U] (ESP BRIT) (equipment) 成套用品 [chéngtào yòngpǐn]; (clothing) 服装 [fúzhuāng]; (MIL) 装备 [zhuāngbèi] 2 [C] (set) 用品包 [yòngpǐnbāo] 3 [C] (for assembly) 配套元件 [pèitào yuánjiàn]
▶ **kit out** (BRIT: inf) VT ▶ **to kit sb out (with/in sth)** (用某物) 装备某人 [(yòng mǒuwù) zhuāngbèi mǒurén] ▶ **to be kitted out with/in sth** 全副武装地穿着某物 ▶ **to kit o.s. out with/in sth** 全副武装地穿着某物

kitchen ['kɪtʃɪn] N [C] 厨房 [chúfáng]

kitchen sink N [C] 厨房洗涤池 [chúfáng xǐdíchí]

kite [kaɪt] N [C] 1 (toy) 风筝 [fēngzheng] 2 (ZOOL) 鸢 [yuān] ▶ **as high as a kite** 晕乎乎的

kitten ['kɪtn] N [C] 小猫 [xiǎomāo]

kiwi fruit ['kiːwiː-] N [C] 猕猴桃 [míhóutáo]

Kleenex® ['kliːnɛks] N [C] (pl **Kleenex**) 纸巾 [zhǐjīn]

km ABBR (= kilometres) 公里 [gōnglǐ]

km/h ABBR (= kilometres per hour) 每小时…公里 [měi xiǎoshí…gōnglǐ]

knack [næk] N [c] ▶ **to have the knack of doing sth** 掌握做某事的诀窍 [zhǎngwò zuò mǒushì de juéqiào] ▶ **there's a knack to doing this** 干这个是有诀窍的

knee [ni:] I N [c] 膝盖 [xīgài] II VT 用膝盖撞击 [yòng xīgài zhuàngjī] ▶ **to bring sb to his/her knees** 迫使某人屈服 ▶ **(to sit/be) on sb's knee** (坐) 在某人的膝上 ▶ **to be on one's knees** 跪着 ▶ **to fall to one's knees** 跪倒

kneecap ['ni:kæp] I N [c] 膝盖骨 [xīgàigǔ] II VT 用枪击穿膝盖骨 [yòng qiāng jīchuān xīgàigǔ]

kneel [ni:l] (pt, pp **knelt**) VI (also: **kneel down**) 跪下 [guìxià] ▶ **to be kneeling** 跪着

knelt [nɛlt] PT, PP OF **kneel**

knew [nju:] PT OF **know**

knickers ['nɪkəz] (BRIT) NPL 女式内裤 [nǚshì nèikù] [美= **panties**] ▶ **a pair of knickers** 一条女式内裤 ▶ **to get one's knickers in a twist** (BRIT: inf) 恼火

knife [naɪf] (pl **knives**) I N [c] 刀 [dāo] II VT 用刀刺 [yòng dāo cì] ▶ **knife and fork** 刀叉 ▶ **to go under the knife** 动手术 ▶ **the knives are out for him** (BRIT) 他成为众矢之的

knight [naɪt] I N [c] 1 (HIST) 骑士 [qíshì] 2 (CHESS) 马 [mǎ] II VT 封…为爵士 [fēng…wéi juéshì]

knit [nɪt] I VT [+ garment] 织 [zhī] II VI 1 (with wool) 织 [zhī] 2 [bones +] 愈合 [yùhé]

knitted ['nɪtɪd] ADJ [+ garment] 针织的 [zhēnzhī de]

knitting ['nɪtɪŋ] N [U] 1 (activity) 织 [zhī] 2 (garments) 编织物 [biānzhīwù] ▶ **to do one's knitting** 织东西

knitting needle N [c] 编织针 [biānzhīzhēn]

knitwear ['nɪtwɛə(r)] N [U] 针织品 [zhēnzhīpǐn]

knives [naɪvz] NPL OF **knife**

knob [nɔb] N [c] 1 [on door] 球形把手 [qiúxíng bǎshǒu] 2 (on radio, TV etc) 旋钮 [xuánniǔ] 3 [on gatepost, stick, umbrella] 圆把儿 [yuánbàr] ▶ **a knob of butter** (BRIT) 一小块黄油

knock [nɔk] I VT 1 (strike) 碰撞 [pèngzhuàng] 2 (inf) (criticize) 批评 [pīpíng] II VI 1 (on door, window) 敲 [qiāo] 2 [engine +] 发出爆震声 [fāchū bàozhènshēng]; [pipes +] 嘭嘭作响 [pēngpēng zuòxiǎng] III N [c] 1 (blow, bump) 碰撞 [pèngzhuàng] 2 (on door) 敲门声 [qiāoménshēng] ▶ **to knock a nail into sth** 在某处钉钉子 ▶ **to knock a hole in sth** 在某处打个洞 ▶ **he knocked the drink out of my hand** 他碰掉了我手里的饮料 ▶ **to knock sb to the ground/floor** [blow, blast, person +] 把某人击倒在地 ▶ **to knock sb unconscious** [blow, blast +] 把某人打昏; [person +] 打昏某人 ▶ **to knock some sense into sb** 让某人明事理 ▶ **knock it off!** (inf) 别胡闹了！ ▶ **he knocked on or at the door** 他敲了门

▶ **knock about** (inf) I VT [+ person] 不断打 [bùduàn dǎ] II VI ▶ **knock about with sb** 和某人厮混 [hé mǒurén sīhùn]

▶ **knock around** (inf) VI = **knock about**

▶ **knock back** (inf) VT [+ drink] 一饮而尽 [yìyǐn érjìn]

▶ **knock down** VT 1 (run over) 撞倒 [zhuàngdǎo] 2 (demolish) 拆除 [chāichú] 3 (ESP US) [+ price] 减 [jiǎn]

▶ **knock off** I VI (inf) (finish work) 下班 [xiàbān] II VT 1 [+ percentage, amount] 减价 [jiǎnjià] 2 (BRIT: inf) (steal) 偷 [tōu]

▶ **knock out** VT 1 (make unconscious) [blow, person +] 打昏 [dǎhūn]; [drug +] 使丧失知觉 [shǐ sàngshī zhījué]; (cause to sleep) [sedative +] 使入睡 [shǐ rùshuì] 2 (BOXING) 击昏 [jīhūn] 3 (eliminate) (in game, competition) 淘汰 [táotài]

▶ **knock over** VT 撞倒 [zhuàngdǎo]

knockout ['nɔkaut] I N [c] 1 (BOXING) 击倒对手获胜 [jīdǎo duìshǒu huòshèng] 2 (inf) (sensation) (person) 令人倾倒的人 [lìng rén qīngdǎo de rén]; (thing) 引人注目的东西 [yǐn rén zhùmù de dōngxi] II ADJ (BRIT) [+ competition] 淘汰赛 [táotàisài]

knot [nɔt] N [c] 1 (in rope, string) 结 [jié]; (in hair) 髻 [jì] 2 (in wood) 节瘤 [jiéliú] 3 (NAUT) 节 [jié] II VT 将…打个结 [jiāng…dǎ gè jié] ▶ **to tie a knot** 打个结 ▶ **to tie the knot** (get married) 结婚 ▶ **to have a knot in one's stomach** 感到心里一阵紧张

○ **know** [nəu] (pt **knew**, pp **known**) VT 1 [+ facts, dates etc] 知道 [zhīdào] ▷ *I don't know her address.* 我不知道她的地址。 2 [+ language] 懂 [dǒng] ▷ *I don't know Chinese very well.* 我不怎么懂汉语。 3 (be acquainted with) [+ person, place, subject] 认识 [rènshi] ▷ *I've known David for years.* 我认识戴维很多年了。 ▷ *He didn't know London very well.* 他不怎么熟悉伦敦。 4 (recognize) 识别 [shíbié] ▷ *He knew a good bargain when he saw one.* 他很会识别便宜货。 ▶ **to know that...** 知道… ▷ *I knew that he lived in Glasgow.* 我知道他住在格拉斯哥。 ▷ *I knew at once that something was wrong.* 我马上就知道有点不对头。 ▶ **to know where/when** 知道何处/何时… ▶ **do you know how to swim?** 你会游泳吗？ ▶ **everyone knew him as Robert** 每个人都叫他罗伯特 ▶ **to get to know sb** 逐渐开始了解某人 ▶ **to let it be known that...** 使人们间接了解到… ▶ **to know sth about sb/sth** 知道某人/某事的情况 ▷ *She didn't know anything about music.* 她对音乐一窍不通。 ▶ **to know about sth** 听说过某事 ▶ **I don't know about that** 我不这么认为 ▶ **yes, I know** 对，的确如此 ▶ **you never know** 很难讲 ▶ **to know of sth/sb** 听说过某事/某人 ▶ **you know** (used for emphasis) 你得知道 ▷ *The conditions in there are awful, you know.* 你得知道，那里的条件很差。; (in explanations) 你知道的 ▷ *the white*

dress, you know, the one with the short sleeves 白色
连衣裙，你知道的，就是短袖的那件 ▸ **to
know better (than to do sth)** 明白而不至于
(做某事) [míngbái ér bù zhì yú (zuò mǒu shì)] ▸ **you should know better than to
do that** 你应该知道不该那样做 ▸ **to be in the
know** 知情

know-all ['nəuɔːl] (BRIT: *inf, pej*) N [C] 自以为
无所不知的人 [zì yǐwéi wú suǒ bù zhī de rén]
[美= **know-it-all**]

know-how ['nəuhau] (*inf*) N [U] 技能 [jìnéng]

knowing ['nəuɪŋ] ADJ [+ *smile, look*] 心照不宣
的 [xīnzhào bùxuān de]

knowingly ['nəuɪŋlɪ] ADV **1** (*intentionally*) 蓄意
地 [xùyì de] **2** [*smile, look* +] 会意地 [huìyì de]

know-it-all ['nəuɪtɔːl] (US: *inf, pej*) N [C] 自以
为无所不知的人 [zì yǐwéi wú suǒ bù zhī de rén]
[英= **know-all**]

knowledge ['nɔlɪdʒ] N [U] 知识 [zhīshi] ▸ **to
(the best of) my knowledge** 据我所知 ▸ **it
is common knowledge that...** 众所周知…
▸ **safe in the knowledge that...** 对…心中有数

knowledgeable ['nɔlɪdʒəbl] ADJ 知识渊博
的 [zhīshi yuānbó de] ▸ **to be knowledgeable
about sth** 对某事在行

known [nəun] **I** PP *of* know **II** ADJ [+ *criminal,
cure*] 已知的 [yǐzhī de] ▸ **to be known for sth**
因某事而出名

knuckle ['nʌkl] N [C] 指节 [zhǐjié]
▸ **knuckle down** (*inf*) VI 开始认真工作 [kāishǐ
rènzhēn gōngzuò] ▸ **to knuckle down to sth**
埋头做某事
▸ **knuckle under** (*inf*) VI 屈服 [qūfú]

koala [kəu'ɑːlə] N [C] 树袋熊 [shùdàixióng]

Koran [kɔ'rɑːn] N ▸ **the Koran** 《古兰经》
[Gǔlánjīng]

Korea [kə'rɪə] N *see also* **North Korea, South
Korea**

Korean [kə'rɪən] **I** ADJ (GEO) 朝鲜的 [Cháoxiǎn
de] **II** N **1** (*person*) 朝鲜人 [Cháoxiǎnrén]
2 (*language*) 朝鲜语 [Cháoxiǎnyǔ]

kosher ['kəuʃə(r)] ADJ **1** (*lit*) [+ *meat, restaurant*]
按犹太教规的 [àn Yóutài jiàoguī de] **2** (*inf*) (*fig*)
正确的 [zhèngquè de]

Kremlin ['krɛmlɪn] N ▸ **the Kremlin** (*building*)
克里姆林宫 [Kèlǐmǔlín Gōng]; (*government*) 俄
罗斯政府 [Éluósī zhèngfǔ]

Kurd [kəːd] N 库尔德人 [Kù'ěrdérén]

Kuwait [ku'weɪt] N 科威特 [Kēwēitè]

Kuwaiti [ku'weɪtɪ] **I** ADJ 科威特的 [Kēwēitè
de] **II** N (*person*) 科威特人 [Kēwēitèrén]

kW, KW ABBR (= *kilowatt*) 千瓦 [qiānwǎ]

Kyrgyzstan [kə:gɪs'tɑːn] N 吉尔吉斯斯坦
[Jí'ěrjísīsītǎn]

Ll

L¹, l [ɛl] N *(letter)* 英语的第十二个字母

L² ABBR **1** (BRIT: AUT) (= *learner*) 驾驶学员 [jiàshǐ xuéyuán] **2** (= *large*) 大的 [dà de]

L., l. ABBR **1** (= *lake*) 湖 [hú] **2** (= *left*) 左的 [zuǒ de]

l ABBR (= *litres*) 升 [shēng]

L8R (TEXTING) ABBR = **later**

lab [læb] (*inf*) N *(laboratory)* 试验室 [shìyànshì]

label ['leɪbl] I N [c] **1** *(lit) (on suitcase, clothing, bottle, tin etc)* 标签 [biāoqiān] **2** *(fig)* 绰号 [chuòhào] **3** (MUS) *[of record]* 原指贴在唱片上的标签，现专指唱片公司 II VT **1** *(lit) [+ object]* 用标签贴标明 [yòng biāoqiān biāomíng] **2** *(fig) [+ person]* 把…称为 [bǎ…chēngwéi]

labor ['leɪbə(r)] (US) N = **labour**

laboratory [lə'bɔrətərɪ] N [c] **1** *(for analysis, research)* 研究室 [yánjiūshì] **2** *(in school)* 实验室 [shíyànshì]

Labor Day (US) N [U] 劳动节 [Láodòngjié]

laborious [lə'bɔ:rɪəs] ADJ 艰苦的 [jiānkǔ de]

labor union (US) N [c] 工会 [gōnghuì] [英= **trade union**]

Ⓞ **labour,** (US) **labor** ['leɪbə(r)] I N [U] **1** *(hard work)* 劳动 [láodòng] ▷ *the culmination of fifteen months' labour* 15个月劳动的终结 **2** *(manpower)* 劳动力 [láodònglì] ▷ *a shortage of skilled labour* 熟练劳动力的缺乏 **3** (IND) *(work done by work force)* 工作 [gōngzuò] ▷ *They are threatening a withdrawal of labour.* 他们威胁要撤回完成的工作。 **4** (MED) 分娩 [fēnmiǎn] **5** ▶ **Labour** (*Labour*

Party) 工党 [Gōngdǎng] II ADJ ▶ **Labour** [+ *politician, voter*] 工党 [Gōngdǎng] III VI ▶ **to labour to do sth** 不辞辛劳地做某事 [bùcí xīnláo de zuò mǒushì] IV VT ▶ **to labour a point** 一再重复 [yīzài chóngfù] ▶ **to labour under a delusion/an illusion** 抱着错觉不放 ▶ **to be in labour** (MED) 处于阵痛期 ▶ **to vote Labour** 投工党的票

labo(u)rer ['leɪbərə(r)] N [c] 劳动者 [láodòngzhě]

Labour Party (BRIT) N 工党 [Gōngdǎng]

lace [leɪs] I N **1** [U] *(fabric)* 花边 [huābiān] **2** [c] *(of shoe etc)* 系带 [jìdài] II ADJ [+ *curtains, handkerchief, garment*] 有花边的 [yǒu huābiān de] III VT **1** *(also:* **lace up**) [+ *shoe etc*] 系紧 [jìjǐn] **2** ▶ **to lace sth with** [+ *alcohol, poison*] 搀某物于 [chān mǒuwù yú]

lack [læk] I N [S/U] *(absence)* 缺乏 [quēfá] II VT [+ *means, skills, experience, confidence*] 缺乏 [quēfá] ▶ **through** *or* **for lack of sth** 因缺乏某物 ▶ **to be lacking** 不足 ▶ **to be lacking in sth** [+ *confidence, imagination, talent*] 缺乏某物

lacquer ['lækə(r)] N [c/U] **1** *(finish)* 漆 [qī] **2** (BRIT) (*also:* **hair lacquer**) 发胶 [fàjiāo] [美= **hairspray**]

lacy ['leɪsɪ] ADJ [+ *dress, nightdress, tights etc*] 花边的 [huābiān de]; [+ *flowers, pattern*] 花边似的 [huābiān sì de]

lad [læd] (*inf*) N [c] *(boy)* 小伙子 [xiǎohuǒzi]; *(young man)* 青年男子 [qīngnián nánzǐ]

ladder ['lædə(r)] I N [c] **1** *(for climbing)* 梯子 [tīzi] **2** (BRIT) *(in tights)* 抽丝 [chōusī] [美= **run**] II VT, VI (BRIT) [+ *tights*] 抽丝 [chōusī] ▶ **the social/career ladder** *(fig)* 社会/事业阶梯

ladle ['leɪdl] I N [c] 长柄勺子 [chángbǐng sháozi] II VT ▶ **to ladle sth into/onto sth** 把某物舀到某物里/上 [bǎ mǒuwù yǎodào mǒuwù lǐ/shàng] ▶ **ladle out** VT *(fig)* [+ *advice, money etc*] 慷慨地提供 [kāngkǎi de tígōng]

lady ['leɪdɪ] N [c] **1** *(woman)* 女士 [nǚshì] **2** *(educated woman)* 淑女 [shūnǚ] **3** (BRIT) *(title)* 夫人 [fūrén] ▶ **Our Lady** (REL) 圣母 ▶ **ladies and gentlemen...** 女士们，先生们... ▶ **young lady** 小姐 ▶ **the ladies'** (BRIT) ▶ **the ladies' room** (US) 女厕所

ladybird ['leɪdɪbə:d] (BRIT) N [c] 瓢虫 [piáochóng] [美= **ladybug**]

ladybug ['leɪdɪbʌɡ] (US) N [c] 瓢虫 [piáochóng] [英= **ladybird**]

lag [læɡ] (ESP BRIT) VT [+ *pipes etc*] 给…加上外套 [gěi…jiāshang wàitào] ▶ **lag behind** I VI 落后 [luòhòu] II VT FUS [不可拆分] ▶ **to lag behind sb** *(in league tables, studies, technology)* 落后于某人 [luòhòu yú mǒurén]

lager ['lɑ:ɡə(r)] (BRIT) N [c/U] 淡啤酒 [dànpíjiǔ]

lagoon [lə'ɡu:n] N [c] 泻湖 [xièhú]

laid [leɪd] PT, PP *of* lay

laid-back [leɪd'bæk] *(inf)* ADJ 松弛的 [sōngchí de]

lain [leɪn] PP *of* lie

lake [leɪk] N [C] 湖 [hú] ▶ **the wine/milk lake** 欧盟储备的多余葡萄酒/牛奶

lamb [læm] N **1** [C] *(animal)* 羔羊 [gāoyáng] **2** [U] *(meat)* 羔羊肉 [gāoyángròu]

lame [leɪm] ADJ **1** [+ *person, animal*] 跛的 [bǒ de] **2** *(weak)* [+ *excuse, argument*] 站不住脚的 [zhànbùzhù jiǎo de] ▶ **to go lame** [*horse +*] 变成瘸子

lament [lə'ment] *(frm)* I N [C] *(complaint)* 悲伤 [bēishāng] II VT *(regret)* 为…而痛惜 [wèi…ér tòngxī]; [+ *sb's death*] 哀悼 [āidào] ▶ **to lament (the fact) that...** 哀叹…(的事实) ▷ "prices have dropped," he lamented "价格下跌了," 他哀叹道

lamp [læmp] N [C] 灯 [dēng]

lamp-post ['læmppəʊst] *(BRIT)* N [C] 路灯柱 [lùdēngzhù] [美= street lamp, street light]

lampshade ['læmpʃeɪd] N [C] 灯罩 [dēngzhào]

○ **land** [lænd] I N **1** [U] *(area of open ground)* 土地 [tǔdì] ▷ *agricultural land* 田地 **2** [U] *(property, estate)* 田产 [tiánchǎn] ▷ *Their home is on his father's land.* 他们的屋宅也列在父亲的田产中。 **3** [U] *(not sea)* 陆地 [lùdì] ▷ *We turned away from land and headed out to sea.* 我们离开陆地, 向海洋进发。 **4** [C] *(liter)* *(country, nation)* 国家 [guójiā] ▷ *a foreign land* 外国 II **lands** NPL *(liter)* 地产 [dìchǎn] III VI **1** *(fall)* 落下 [luòxià] ▷ *Three shells had landed close to a crowd of people.* 3颗炮弹在人群附近落下。 **2** *(AVIAT, SPACE)* 降落 [jiàngluò] ▷ *His plane lands at six-thirty.* 他的飞机于6点30分降落。 **3** *(from ship)* 登陆 [dēnglù] ▷ *Three divisions of troops landed in Malaysia.* 3个师的部队在马来西亚登陆。 **4** *(fig)* *(arrive unexpectedly)* [*object, item +*] 不期而至 [bù qī ér zhì] ▷ *The report landed on his desk.* 那份报告不期然地落到他的办公桌上。 IV VT **1** [+ *plane, spacecraft*] 使降落 [shǐ jiàngluò]; [+ *ship*] 使登陆 [shǐ dēnglù] **2** *(ESP BRIT)* [+ *goods, fish*] 卸 [xiè] ▷ *The catch was landed at Liverpool.* 捕获物在利物浦即上岸。 **3** [+ *job, place*] 捞到 [lāo dào] ▷ *He landed a place on the graduate training scheme.* 他在毕业生培训项目中捞到一个位置。 **4** [+ *blow, punch*] 打 [dǎ] ▷ *He landed a blow on the Italian's chin.* 他在那个意大利人的下颌上打了一拳。 ▶ **to own land** 拥有田产 ▶ **to go/travel by land** 从陆路去/陆路旅行 ▶ **on dry land** 陆地上 ▶ **to land sb with sth/sb** *(BRIT: inf)* 把某事/某人硬推给某人 ▶ **to land sb in trouble** *(BRIT: inf)* 使某人陷入麻烦

▶ **land up** *(ESP BRIT: inf)* VI 落得 [luòde] ▷ *You'll land up in jail if you aren't careful.* 如果你不小心的话, 你就会落得个入狱的下场。

landing ['lændɪŋ] N **1** [C] *(on stairs)* 楼梯平台 [lóutī píngtái] **2** [C/U] *(AVIAT)* 降落 [jiàngluò]

landing card *(AVIAT, NAUT)* N [C] 入境登记卡 [rùjìng dēngjìkǎ]

landlady ['lændleɪdɪ] N [C] **1** *(of rented house, flat, room)* 女房东 [nǚfángdōng] **2** *(BRIT)* [*of pub*] 女店主 [nǚdiànzhǔ]

landlord ['lændlɔːd] N [C] **1** *(of rented house, flat, room)* 男房东 [nánfángdōng] **2** *(BRIT)* [*of pub*] 男店主 [nándiànzhǔ]

landmark ['lændmɑːk] N [C] **1** *(building, hill etc)* 界标 [jièbiāo] **2** *(fig)* 里程碑 [lǐchéngbēi]

landowner ['lændəʊnə(r)] N [C] 土地所有者 [tǔdì suǒyǒuzhě]

landscape ['lændskeɪp] I N **1** [C/U] 风景 [fēngjǐng] **2** [C] *(ART)* 风景画 [fēngjǐnghuà] II VT 使自然美化 [shǐ zìrán měihuà]

landslide ['lændslaɪd] N **1** *(lit)* 塌方 [tāfāng] **2** *(fig)* *(electoral)* 竞选选票的一面倒 [jìngxuǎn xuǎnpiào de yī miàn dǎo] ▶ **to win by a landslide** 大获全胜

lane [leɪn] N [C] **1** *(in country)* 小路 [xiǎolù] **2** *(in town)* 巷 [xiàng] **3** [C] [*of road*] 车道 [chēdào] **4** [*of athletics track, swimming pool*] 道 [dào]

language ['læŋgwɪdʒ] N **1** [C] *(English, Russian etc)* 语言 [yǔyán] **2** [U] *(speech)* 语言表达能力 [yǔyán biǎodá nénglì] **3** [U] *(specialized terminology)* 术语 [shùyǔ] **4** [U] *(style)* [*of writing, speech*] 措辞 [cuòcí]

language laboratory N [C] 语言实验室 [yǔyán shíyànshì]

lantern ['læntən] N [C] 灯笼 [dēnglóng]

Laos [laʊs] *(GEO)* N 老挝 [Lǎowō]

Laotian [laʊʃn] *(GEO)* I ADJ 老挝的 [Lǎowō de] II N **1** [C] *(person)* 老挝人 [Lǎowōrén] **2** [U] *(language)* 老挝语 [Lǎowōyǔ]

lap [læp] I N [C] **1** [*of person*] 大腿的上方 [dàtuǐ de shàngfāng] **2** *(in race)* 圈 [quān] II VT **1** *(also: lap up)* [+ *milk etc*] 舔 [tiǎn] **2** *(also: lap against)* [+ *shore, cliff, pier*] 拍打 [pāidǎ] **3** [+ *competitor*] *(in race)* 领先…一圈 [lǐngxiān…yī quān] III VI ▶ **to lap against sth** [*waves, water +*] 拍打某物 [pāidǎ mǒuwù]

▶ **lap up** VT *(lit)* [+ *milk etc*] 舔 [tiǎn]; *(fig)* [+ *flattery, news story*] 欣然接受 [xīnrán jiēshòu]

lapel [lə'pel] N [C] 翻领 [fānlǐng]

Lapland ['læplænd] *(GEO)* N 拉普兰 [Lāpǔlán]

Lapp [læp] I ADJ *(GEO)* 拉普的 [Lāpǔ de] II N **1** [C] *(person)* 拉普人 [Lāpǔrén] **2** [U] *(language)* 拉普语 [Lāpǔyǔ]

lapse [læps] I N [C] **1** *(bad behaviour)* 差错 [chācuò] **2** [*of memory, concentration*] 丧失 [sàngshī] **3** [*of time*] 流逝 [liúshì] II VI **1** [*time +*] 流逝 [liúshì] **2** *(expire)* [*contract +*] 失效 [shīxiào]; [*membership +*] 丧失 [sàngshī] **3** *(REL)* [*person +*] 背离 [bèilí] ▶ **to lapse into silence** 陷入沉默

laptop ['læptɒp] N [C] *(also: laptop computer)* 笔记本电脑 [bǐjìběn diànnǎo]

lard [lɑːd] N [U] 猪油 [zhūyóu]

larder ['lɑːdə(r)] *(ESP BRIT)* N [C] 食品室 [shípǐnshì]

large [lɑːdʒ] ADJ **1** (big) [+ house, person etc] 大的 [dà de]; [+ number, amount] 大量的 [dàliàng de] ▷ We are facing a large number of problems. 我们面临大量的问题。▷ a large number of people 许多人 **2** (serious) [+ problem, question] 重大的 [zhòngdà de] ▶ **at large** (as a whole) 整个 ▷ their attitude to the world at large 他们对整个世界的态度 ▶ **to be at large** 逍遥自在 ▷ There were three convicts still at large. 3名囚犯仍逍遥法外。▶ **by and large** 总的来说

largely ['lɑːdʒlɪ] ADV (mostly) 大体上 [dàtǐshang] ▶ **largely because of** 主要是因为

large-scale ['lɑːdʒ'skeɪl] ADJ **1** [+ action, event] 大规模的 [dàguīmó de] **2** [+ map, diagram] 大比例的 [dàbǐlì de]

lark [lɑːk] N [C] **1** (bird) 云雀 [yúnquè] **2** (BRIT: inf) (fun) 戏谑 [xìxuè] ▶ **to do sth for a lark** (BRIT) 为闹着玩而做某事
▶ **lark around, lark about** VI 胡闹 [húnào]

larva ['lɑːvə] (pl larvae ['lɑːviː]) N [C] 幼虫 [yòuchóng]

laryngitis [lærɪn'dʒaɪtɪs] (MED) N [U] 喉炎 [hóuyán]

laser ['leɪzə(r)] N **1** [C/U] (beam) 激光 [jīguāng] **2** [C] (machine) 激光器 [jīguāngqì]

lash [læʃ] I VT **1** (tie) ▶ **to lash sth to sth** 把某物紧紧系在某物上 [bǎ mǒuwù jǐnjǐn jì zài mǒuwù shang] **2** (liter) [rain, wind +] 抽打 [chōudǎ] **3** (whip) 鞭打 [biāndǎ] II N [C] (blow of whip) 鞭打 [biāndǎ] III **lashes** NPL (eyelashes) 睫毛 [jiémáo]
▶ **lash down** I VT (tie) 捆紧 [kǔnjǐn] II VI [rain +] 猛烈冲击 [měngliè chōngjī]
▶ **lash out** VI ▶ **to lash out** (at sb) (strike out) 痛打 (某人) [tòngdǎ (mǒurén)] ▶ **to lash out at sb** (verbally) 严厉斥责某人

lass [læs] (BRIT: inf) N [C] 少女 [shàonǚ]

last [lɑːst] I ADJ **1** (most recent) [+ visit, trip, letter] 最近的 [zuìjìn de] ▷ Much had changed since my last visit. 自我最近一次拜访以后，那里发生了很大的变化。; [+ Monday, July, weekend etc] 上个 [shàng gè] ▷ last Monday 上个星期一 **2** (final) [+ bus, hope etc] 最后的 [zuìhòu de] ▷ He missed the last bus home. 他错过了回家的最后一班车。; (of series, row) 最后的 [zuìhòu de] ▷ the last classroom along the passage 走廊里的最后一个教室 ▷ the last three pages of the chapter 这一章的最后3页 **3** (remaining) [+ traces, piece etc] 剩下的 [shèngxià de] ▷ the last piece of pizza 剩下的一块比萨饼 **4** (for emphasis) 最不的 [zuìbù de] ▷ The last thing I wanted to do was teach. 我最不想做的事就是教书了。▷ You are the last person I'd confide in! 你是我最不信任的人！ II PRON **1** (previous one) 上一个 [shàng yī gè] ▷ The next tide would be even higher than the last. 下一次的潮水要比上一次的还高。**2** (final ones) 最后一个 [zuìhòu yī gè] ▷ Which address is the last on your list? 你单子上的最后一

个地址是哪一个？▷ The trickiest bits are the last on the list. 最棘手的是单子上的最后一个。**3** (for emphasis) 最后一个 [zuìhòu yī gè] ▷ He is the last person I would think of. 他是我最不会考虑的一个人。▷ I would be the last to say that science has explained everything. 我绝对不觉得科学已经解释了所有事情。**4** (remainder) 剩下的 [shèngxià de] ▷ He finished off the last of the wine. 他把剩下的葡萄酒喝完了。▷ We've eaten the last of the pineapples. 我们把剩下的菠萝都吃了。 III ADV **1** (most recently) 最近 [zuìjìn] ▷ They last saw their homeland nine years ago. 他们最近一次看到故乡是9年以前了。**2** (at the end) 最后 [zuìhòu] ▷ He added the milk last. 他最后把牛奶加进去。**3** (in final position) 最后 [zuìhòu] IV VI **1** (continue) 持续 [chíxù] ▷ Their marriage only lasted six months. 他们的婚姻只持续了6个月。▷ The war in Croatia lasted until January 1992. 克罗地亚的战争一直持续到1992年1月。**2** (stay fresh) 保鲜 [bǎoxiān] ▷ A fresh pepper lasts about three weeks. 新鲜的辣椒能保鲜约3个星期。**3** (be sufficient) [money, commodity +] 够用 [gòu yòng] ▷ The curry lasted for two nights. 这些咖喱饭够两个晚上用了。▶ **last week** 上个星期 ▷ I had lunch with him last week. 我上个星期跟他一起吃的午饭。▶ **last night** (yesterday evening) 昨晚; (during the night) 昨天夜里 ▶ **the last time** (the final time) 最后一次; (the previous time) 上一次 ▶ **at (long) last** (finally) 终于 ▶ **the last I heard** 最近一次我听到的是 ▶ **I'm always the last to find out** 我总是最后一个知道 ▶ **the night/Christmas before last** 前天晚上/前年圣诞节 ▶ **our house is the last but one** 我们的房子是倒数第二个 ▶ **the last president but one** 倒数第二个总统 ▶ **last but not least** 最后一个，但不是不重要的 ▶ **it lasts (for) 2 hours** 持续了两个小时 ▶ **it can't/won't last** 它不会持久

last-ditch ['lɑːst'dɪtʃ] ADJ ▶ **a last-ditch attempt** 孤注一掷 [gū zhù yī zhì]

lasting ['lɑːstɪŋ] ADJ [+ impression, solution] 持久的 [chíjiǔ de]

lastly ['lɑːstlɪ] ADV 最后 [zuìhòu]

last-minute ['lɑːstmɪnɪt] ADJ [+ decision, appeal etc] 最后一刻的 [zuìhòu yīkè de]

last name N [C] 姓 [xìng]

latch [lætʃ] N [C] (on door, gate) 闩 [shuān]
▶ **on/off the latch** 上/没上闩
▶ **latch on to** VT FUS (不可拆分) **1** (inf) (take interest in) [+ person] 缠住不放 [chánzhù bù fàng]; [+ idea] 关注 [guānzhù] **2** (attach to) [+ object] 附着 [fùzhuó]

late [leɪt] I ADJ **1** (at an advanced point of) 晚的 [wǎn de] ▷ in the late afternoon 傍晚 **2** (not on time) 迟的 [chí de] ▷ I apologize for my late arrival. 真抱歉，我迟到了。**3** (after the usual time) 稍晚的 [shāowǎn de] ▷ They had a late lunch. 他们午餐吃得比较晚。**4** (deceased) ▶ **the late**

Mr Parkin 已故的帕金先生 [yǐgù de Pàjīn Xiānsheng] **II** ADV **1** (at an advanced point of) 晚 [wǎn] ▷ The case is expected to end late next week. 该案可望于下周晚些时候结束。**2** (not on time) 迟 [chí] ▷ Steve arrived late. 斯蒂夫迟到了。**3** (after the usual time) 晚 [wǎn] ▷ We went to bed very late. 我们很晚才睡觉。▶ **we're late** 我们迟到了 ▶ **sorry I'm late** 对不起，我迟到了 ▶ **to be 10 minutes late** 迟到10分钟 ▶ **it's late** 太迟了 ▶ **to be in one's late thirties/forties** 接近40/50岁 ▶ **late of** (frm) (until recently of) 直到最近 ▷ Jane Smith, late of Bristol 简·史密斯，直到最近一直住在布里斯托尔 ▶ **to work late** 工作到很晚 ▶ **late in life** 晚年 ▶ **of late** (frm) (recently) 近来 ▶ **in late May** 5月下旬 ▶ **late in the day** (fig) 为时已晚

latecomer ['leɪtkʌmə(r)] N [c] 迟到者 [chídàozhě]

lately ['leɪtlɪ] ADV (recently) 最近 [zuìjìn]

latent ['leɪtnt] ADJ [+ energy, skill, ability] 潜在的 [qiánzài de]

⊙ later ['leɪtə(r)] **I** ADJ [+ time, date, meeting etc] 较晚的 [jiàowǎn de] ▷ An inquest will be held at a later date. 审讯将于再晚些时候进行。; [+ version, edition] 以后的 [yǐhòu de] ▷ He changed his approach in later editions. 在以后的版本中，他改变了方法。**II** ADV 以后 [yǐhòu] ▷ I'll join you later. 我一会儿就来。▶ **in later life** 在晚年 ▶ **some time/weeks/years later** 一些时候/几个星期/几年以后 ▶ **later on** 以后

用法参见 after

latest ['leɪtɪst] ADJ **1** (most recent) [+ book, film, news etc] 最新的 [zuìxīn de] **2** (most up-to-date) [+ fashion] 最新式的 [zuì xīnshì de] ▶ **at the latest** 最迟

lather ['lɑːðə(r)] **I** N [s/u] (soapy) 泡沫 [pàomò] **II** VT [+ hair, fabric] 涂泡沫于 [tú pàomò yú] **III** VI [soap etc +] 起泡沫 [qǐ pàomò] ▶ **to get in a lather** or **to work o.s. up into a lather (over** or **about sth)** （对某事）过分焦躁不安

Latin ['lætɪn] **I** N **1** [u] (language) 拉丁语 [Lādīngyǔ] **2** [c] (person) 拉丁人 [Lādīngrén] **II** ADJ 拉丁的 [Lādīng de]

Latin America N 拉丁美洲 [Lādīngměizhōu]

Latin American I ADJ 拉丁美洲的 [Lādīngměizhōu de] **II** N [c] (person) 拉丁美洲人 [Lādīngměizhōurén]

latitude ['lætɪtjuːd] N **1** [c/u] (GEO) 纬度 [wěidù] **2** [u] (freedom) 自由 [zìyóu]

latter ['lætə(r)] **I** ADJ **1** (not former) 后者的 [hòuzhě de] **2** (later) [+ part, half] 后半的 [hòubàn de] **II** N ▶ **the latter** 后者 [hòuzhě]

Latvia ['lætvɪə] (GEO) N 拉脱维亚 [Lātuōwéiyà]

Latvian ['lætvɪən] **I** ADJ 拉脱维亚的 [Lātuōwéiyà de] **II** N **1** [c] (person) 拉脱维亚人 [Lātuōwéiyàrén] **2** [u] (language) 拉脱维亚语 [Lātuōwéiyàyǔ]

⊙ laugh [lɑːf] **I** N [c] 笑 [xiào] **II** VI 笑 [xiào] ▶ **to give a laugh** 发笑 ▶ **to do sth for a laugh** or **for laughs** 做某事取乐 ▶ **to have the last laugh** 取得最后胜利
▶ **laugh at** VT FUS [不可拆分] **1** (lit) 对…发笑 [duì…fāxiào] **2** (fig) (mock) 嘲笑 [cháoxiào]
▶ **laugh off** VT [+ criticism, problem] 对…一笑置之 [duì…yī xiào zhì zhī]

laughable ['lɑːfəbl] ADJ [+ attempt, idea, proposition] 可笑的 [kěxiào de]

laughter ['lɑːftə(r)] N [u] 笑声 [xiàoshēng]

launch [lɔːntʃ] **I** VT **1** (NAUT) (on maiden voyage) [+ ship, liner] 使下水 [shǐ xiàshuǐ]; (for rescue) [+ lifeboat] 放下 [fàngxià] **2** (SPACE) [+ rocket, missile, satellite] 发射 [fāshè] **3** (fig) [+ product, publication] 推出 [tuīchū]; [+ campaign] 发起 [fāqǐ] **II** N [c] **1** (NAUT) [of ship] 下水 [xiàshuǐ]; [of lifeboat] 放下 [fàngxià] **2** (SPACE) [of rocket, missile, satellite] 发射 [fāshè] **3** (fig) [+ of product, publication] 首次推出 [shǒucì tuīchū]; [of campaign] 发起 [fāqǐ] **4** (motorboat) 汽艇 [qìtǐng]
▶ **launch into** VT FUS [不可拆分] [+ speech, activity] 开始 [kāishǐ]

launder ['lɔːndə(r)] VT **1** (o.f.) [+ clothes, sheets] 洗熨 [xǐyùn] **2** (fig) [+ money] 洗 [xǐ] ▷ banks that launder drug money 洗毒品赃款的银行

Launderette® [lɔːnˈdrɛt], (US) **Laundromat®** ['lɔːndrəmæt] N [c] 自助洗衣店 [zìzhù xǐyīdiàn]

laundry ['lɔːndrɪ] N **1** [u] (dirty washing) 待洗的衣物 [dàixǐ de yīwù]; (clean washing) 洗好的衣物 [xǐhǎo de yīwù] **2** [c] (business) 洗衣店 [xǐyīdiàn] **3** [c] (also: **laundry room**) 洗衣房 [xǐyīfáng] ▶ **to do the laundry** 洗涤衣物

laundry detergent (US) N [u/c] 洗衣粉 [xǐyīfěn] [英=**washing powder**]

lava ['lɑːvə] N [u] 熔岩 [róngyán]

lavatory ['lævətərɪ] (BRIT: o.f.) N [c] 卫生间 [wèishēngjiān] [美=**bathroom**]

lavender ['lævəndə(r)] **I** N [u] **1** (plant) 薰衣草 [xūnyīcǎo] **2** (colour) 淡紫色 [dànzǐsè] **II** ADJ (lavender-coloured) 淡紫色的 [dànzǐsè de] **III** CPD [复合词] [+ oil] 薰衣草 [xūnyīcǎo]

lavish ['lævɪʃ] **I** ADJ **1** (grand) [+ meal] 丰盛的 [fēngshèng de]; [+ party] 盛大的 [shèngdà de] [+ production] 大量的 [dàliàng de] **2** (generous) [+ lifestyle, spending, gift] 奢华的 [shēhuá de]; [+ praise] 慷慨的 [kāngkǎi de] **II** VT ▶ **to lavish sth on sb** [+ gifts, praise] 将某物慷慨赠予某人 [jiāng mǒuwù kāngkǎi zèngyǔ mǒurén] ▷ The prince lavished gifts on his guests. 王子将礼物赠予到访客人。; [+ time, attention] 将某物花在某人身上 ▶ **to be lavish with sth** 在某物上非常大方 ▶ **to be lavish in one's praise of sth** 对某物赞不绝口

⊙ law [lɔː] **I** N **1** [s/u] (legal system) 法律 [fǎlù] ▷ Changes in the law are needed. 有必要修改

法律。**2** [U] (*profession*) 司法界 [sīfǎjiè] ▷ *a career in law* 在司法界的事业 **3** [U] (UNIV) 法学 [fǎxué] ▷ *a degree in law* 法学学位 **4** [C] (*regulation*) 法规 [fǎguī] ▷ *Britain's blasphemy laws* 英国的有关亵渎神的法规 **5** [C] (*code*) 规范 [guīfàn] ▷ *inflexible moral laws* 固定的道德规范 **6** [C] (*of nature, science*) 定律 [dìnglǜ] ▷ *the law of gravity* 引力定律 **II laws** NPL (*rules*) [*of organization, activity*] 规则 [guīzé] ▶ **against the law** 违法 ▶ **to break the law** 违法 ▶ **by law** 依照法律 ▶ **to be above the law** 凌驾于法律之上 ▶ **criminal/company law** 刑/公司法 ▶ **to take the law into one's own hands** 越过法律权限擅自处理 ▶ **to study law** 学习法律 ▶ **to go to law** (ESP BRIT) 诉诸法律 ▶ **law and order** 治安

lawful ['lɔːful] ADJ [+ *activity, organization*] 合法的 [héfǎ de]

lawless ['lɔːlɪs] ADJ [+ *action*] 不法的 [bùfǎ de]

lawn [lɔːn] N [C] 草坪 [cǎopíng]

lawn bowling (US) N [U] 草地保龄球 [cǎodì bǎolíngqiú] [英=**bowls**]

lawnmower ['lɔːnməʊə(r)] N [C] 割草机 [gēcǎojī]

law school (US) N [C/U] 法律学校 [fǎlǜ xuéxiào] ▶ **to go to law school** 进法律学校

lawsuit ['lɔːsuːt] N [C] (*frm*) 诉讼 [sùsòng]

lawyer ['lɔːjə(r)] N [C] 律师 [lǜshī]

lax [læks] ADJ [+ *behaviour, standards*] 不严格的 [bù yángé de]

laxative ['læksətɪv] **I** N [C] 泻药 [xièyào] **II** ADJ 缓泻的 [huǎnxiè de]

lay [leɪ] (*pt, pp* **laid**) **I** PT OF **lie II** VT **1** (*put*) 放 [fàng] **2** (*put down*) [+ *carpet, cable etc*] 铺 [pū] **3** (*set*) [+ *trap*] 设置 [shèzhì] **4** [+ *egg*] 产 [chǎn] **III** ADJ **1** (*secular*) [+ *preacher*] 非神职的 [fēi shénzhí de] ▶ **to lay the table** 摆放餐具 ▶ **to lay the blame for sth on sb** 因某事责怪某人 ▶ **to lay charges** 提出指控 ▶ **to lay the foundations/basis for sth** 为某事奠定基础 ▶ **to lay a trap for sb** 为某人设置圈套 ▶ **to get laid** (*inf*) 性交 ▶ **the lay person** 外行
  ▶ **lay aside** VT **1** [+ *object*] 把⋯放在一边 [bǎ⋯fàng zài yī biān] **2** [+ *feeling, belief*] 放弃 [fàngqì]
  ▶ **lay down** VT **1** (*put down*) 放下 [fàngxià] **2** [+ *rules, laws etc*] 制定 [zhìdìng] ▶ **to lay down the law** 定下规矩 ▶ **to lay down one's life for sb** (*liter*) (*in war etc*) 为某人而牺牲自己的生命
  ▶ **lay in** VT [+ *supply*] 储存 [chǔcún]
  ▶ **lay into** VT FUS (不可拆分) **1** (*attack physically*) 痛打 [tòngdǎ] **2** (*criticize*) 斥责 [chìzé]
  ▶ **lay off I** VT [+ *workers*] 解雇 [jiěgù] **II** VI (*inf*) 住手 [zhùshǒu]
  ▶ **lay on** VT [+ *meal, entertainment etc*] 提供 [tígōng] ▷ *Mrs Kaul had laid on dinner.* 考尔太太设了宴席。
  ▶ **lay out** VT **1** (*spread out*) [+ *objects*] 摊开 [tānkāi]

2 (*present*) [+ *ideas, plans*] 陈述 [chénshù]
3 (*design*) [+ *land, building*] 设计 [shèjì] **4** (*inf*) (*spend*) 耗费 [hàofèi] **5** (*corpse*) 为⋯做殡葬准备 [wèi⋯zuò bìnzàng zhǔnbèi]
  ▶ **lay up** VT ▶ **to be laid up (with sth)** (*inf*) (*with illness*) (因⋯而)卧床 [(yīn⋯ér) wòchuáng]

lay-by ['leɪbaɪ] (BRIT) N [C] 路侧停车处 [lùcè tíngchēchù] [美=**pull-off**]

layer ['leɪə(r)] N [C] **1** [*of substance, material*] 层 [céng] **2** (*fig*) [*of system, idea*] 层 [céng] **II** VT 把⋯分层 [bǎ⋯fēncéng]

layman ['leɪmən] (*pl* **laymen**) N [C] 外行 [wàiháng] ▶ **in layman's terms** 用非专业的语言

lay-off ['leɪɔf] (IND) N [C] 下岗 [xiàgǎng]

layout ['leɪaʊt] N [C] **1** [*of building, garden*] 布局 [bùjú] **2** [*of report, article*] 设计 [shèjì]

lazy ['leɪzɪ] ADJ **1** [+ *person*] 懒惰的 [lǎnduò de] **2** (*relaxed*) [+ *day, lunch*] 懒散的 [lǎnsǎn de]; [+ *movement, drawl*] 缓慢的 [huǎnmàn de]

lb ABBR (= *pound*) 磅 [bàng]

LCD N ABBR (= *liquid crystal display*) 液晶显示屏 [yèjīng xiǎnshìpíng]

○ **lead**¹ [liːd] (*pt, pp* **led**) **I** N **1** [s] (*in race, competition*) (*front position*) 领先 [lǐngxiān] **2** [C] (*fig*) (*example*) 榜样 [bǎngyàng] **3** [C] (*clue*) 线索 [xiànsuǒ] ▷ *The police were following up several leads.* 警方顺着几条线索进一步调查。 **4** [C] (CINE, THEAT) (*part*) 主角 [zhǔjué] ▷ *Richard is to play the lead in their new film.* 理查德将在他们的新片中扮演主角。; (*actor, actress*) 主演 [zhǔyǎn] **5** [C] (ESP BRIT) (*for dog*) 皮带 [pídài] [美=**leash**] **6** [C] (ELEC) 导线 [dǎoxiàn]; (*to battery*) 导线 [dǎoxiàn] **II** VT **1** (*guide*) 带领 [dàilǐng] ▷ *The nurse led me to a large room.* 护士把我带到一个大房间。 **2** (*be at the head of*) [+ *group, party, organization*] 领导 [lǐngdǎo] ▷ *He led the country between 1949 and 1984.* 他于1949至1984年领导这个国家。; [+ *march, demonstration, parade*] 带领 [dàilǐng] ▷ *He led a demonstration through the city.* 游行队伍在他的带领下穿过市区。 **3** (*spearhead*) [+ *campaign, activity*] 指挥 [zhǐhuī]; (*start*) [+ *move*] 发起 [fāqǐ] ▷ *The educated middle class led the move towards independence.* 受过教育的中产阶级发起了走向独立的运动。 **4** (*direct*) [+ *discussion, conversation*] 引向 [yǐnxiàng] ▷ *After a while I led the conversation around to her job.* 过了一会，我把谈话内容引向了她的工作。 **III** VI **1** (*walker, rider, driver +*) 领路 [lǐnglù] ▷ *Tom was leading; I followed behind.* 汤姆领路，我跟在后面。 **2** (*in race, competition*) 领先 [lǐngxiān] ▷ *Spurs lead by four goals to two.* 斯帕思队以4比2领先。 **3** [*road, pipe, wire etc +*] 通往 [tōngwǎng] ▷ *A path leads straight to Stonehenge.* 一直通往巨石阵的小径。
  ▶ **to be in the lead** (*in race, competition, poll*) 领先 ▶ **to go into the lead** 进入领先位置 ▶ **to take the lead** (SPORT) 领先; (*fig*) 起带头作用 ▷ *They*

took the lead in the development of naval aviation. 他们在海军航空学的发展中起了带头作用。▸ **to have a lead of 5 points** (SPORT) 领先5分 ▸ **to follow sb's lead** 仿效某人的做法 ▷ Many others followed his lead. 许多人效仿了他的做法。▸ **to lead a busy/active life** 过着繁忙/活跃的生活 ▸ **to lead the way** (lit) 引路；(fig) 率先 ▸ **to lead sb to believe that...** 使某人相信… ▸ **to lead sb to do sth** 促使某人做某事 ▷ What led you to do this work? 什么促使你做这项工作？

▸ **lead away** VT [+ prisoner etc] 带走 [dàizǒu]

▸ **lead back** VI 带回 [dàihuí]

▸ **lead off** I VI (in game, conversation, meeting etc) 开始 [kāishǐ] ▷ She led off with a few of her old hit songs. 她以她的几首流行的旧歌开始了演出。II VT FUS [不可拆分] (also: **lead off from**) [road, room, door +] 由…通向 [yóu…tōngxiàng]

▸ **lead on** VT (deceive) [+ person] 劝诱 [quànyòu] ▷ I bet she led him on. 我想她一定引诱他了。

▸ **lead on to** (ESP BRIT) VT FUS [不可拆分] (result in) 引起 [yǐnqǐ]

▸ **lead to** VT FUS [不可拆分] (result in) 导致 [dǎozhì]

▸ **lead up to** VT FUS [不可拆分] 1 (culminate in) [+ situation] 导致 [dǎozhì] ▷ the events that led up to her death 导致她死亡的事件 2 (precede) [+ time, event] 临近 [línjìn] ▷ the weeks leading up to Christmas 临近圣诞节前的几个星期 3 (in conversation) 渐渐引到 [jiànjiàn yǐndào] ▷ Since you came in you've been leading up to this question. 自你进来后，一直在渐渐引向这个问题。

○**lead²** [lɛd] I N 1 [U] (metal) 铅 [qiān] 2 [C/U] (in pencil) 铅笔心 [qiānbǐxīn] II CPD [复合词] [+ pipe, roof] 铅 [qiān]

leaded ['lɛdɪd] ADJ 1 [+ petrol] 含铅的 [hánqiān de] 2 [+ window, glass] 铅框的 [qiānkuàng de]

○**leader** ['liːdə(r)] N [C] 1 [of group, organization] 领导人 [lǐngdǎorén] 2 (SPORT) 领先者 [lǐngxiānzhě] 3 (BRIT) (in newspaper) 社论 [shèlùn] [美= editorial] 4 ▸ **Leader of the House of Commons/Lords** (BRIT: PARL) 下/上议院议长 [xià/shàng yìyuàn yìzhǎng]

leadership ['liːdəʃɪp] N [U] 1 (leading people) 领导人 [lǐngdǎorén] 2 (position) 领导 [lǐngdǎo] 3 (quality) 领导能力 [lǐngdǎo nénglì]

lead-free ['lɛdfriː] ADJ [+ petrol, paint] 无铅的 [wúqiān de]

leading ['liːdɪŋ] ADJ 1 (most important) [+ person, thing] 主导的 [zhǔdǎo de] 2 (THEAT, CINE) [+ role, part] 主要的 [zhǔyào de] 3 (front) 引领的 [yǐnlǐng de]

lead singer [liːd-] N [C] (in pop group) 主唱 [zhǔchàng]

leaf [liːf] (pl **leaves**) N [C] 1 [of tree, plant] 叶 [yè] 2 [of table] 活动桌板 [huódòng zhuōbǎn] ▸ **to turn over a new leaf** 翻开新的篇章 ▸ **to take a leaf out of sb's book** 模仿某人

▸ **leaf through** VT FUS [不可拆分] [+ book, magazine] 翻阅 [fānyuè]

leaflet ['liːflɪt] I N [C] (booklet) 小册子 [xiǎocèzi]; (single sheet) 传单 [chuándān] II VT [+ place] 向…散发传单 [xiàng…sànfā chuándān]

league [liːg] N [C] 1 (like-minded group) 联盟 [liánméng] 2 (SPORT) 联赛 [liánsài] ▸ **to be in league with sb** 与某人勾结 ▸ **to be in the same league** (comparing) 与某人同类 ▸ **out of sb's league** (fig) 与某人不是一类人

leak [liːk] I N [C] 1 [of liquid, gas] 裂隙 [lièxì] 2 (hole) (in roof, pipe etc) 漏洞 [lòudòng] 3 [of document, information] 泄露 [xièlù] II VI [shoes, pipe, liquid, gas +] 漏 [lòu] III VT 1 [+ liquid, gas] 漏 [lòu] 2 [+ document, information] 泄露 [xièlòu]

▸ **leak out** VI [news, information +] 泄露 [xièlòu]

lean [liːn] I VT ▸ **to lean sth on/against sth** 把某物靠在某物上 [bǎ mǒuwù kàozài mǒuwù shang] II VI (slope) 倾斜 [qīngxié] III ADJ 1 [+ person] 精瘦的 [jīngshòu de] 2 [+ meat] 瘦的 [shòu de] 3 [+ period of time] 不景气的 [bù jǐngqì de] ▸ **to lean against sth** [person +] 靠在某物上 ▸ **to lean forward/back** 向前/后倾

▸ **lean on** VT FUS [不可拆分] 1 (rest against) [+ person, object] 倚 [yǐ] 2 (fig) [+ person] 依赖 [yīlài] 3 (inf) (threaten) 威胁 [wēixié]

▸ **lean towards** VT FUS [不可拆分] [+ idea, belief, right, left] 倾向于 [qīngxiàngyú]

leaning ['liːnɪŋ] N [C] 倾向 [qīngxiàng]

leant [lɛnt] PT, PP of **lean**

leap [liːp] (pt, pp **leaped** or **leapt**) I N [C] 1 (jump) 跳 [tiào] 2 (increase) (in price, number etc) 激增 [jīzēng] II VI 1 (jump) 跳 [tiào] 2 ▸ **to leap into/onto sth** 迅速跳进/上某物 [xùnsù tiàojìn/shàng mǒuwù] 3 (increase) [price, number etc +] 激增 [jīzēng] ▸ **to take a leap of faith** 碰运气 ▸ **by** or **in leaps and bounds** 突飞猛进地 ▸ **my heart leapt** (with happiness) 我的心狂跳不已；(with fear) 我的心突突直跳

▸ **leap at** VT FUS [不可拆分] [+ offer, chance] 迫不及待地接受 [pò bù jí dài de jiēshòu]

▸ **leap up** VI 1 [person +] 一跃而起 [yīyuè ér qǐ] 2 (increase) [price, amount +] 激增 [jīzēng]

leapt [lɛpt] PT, PP of **leap**

leap year N [C] 闰年 [rùnnián]

○**learn** [ləːn] (pt, pp **learned** or **learnt**) I VT 1 (study) [+ skill] 学 [xué] ▷ Children learn foreign languages very easily. 孩子学外语非常容易。; [+ poem, song] 背 [bèi] ▷ We have to learn the whole poem by heart. 我们得把整首诗背下来。2 (find out) [+ news, fact] 得知 [dézhī] ▷ I remember when I learned the terrible news. 我还记得什么时候得知这条坏消息的。II VI 学 [xué] ▷ Experienced teachers help you learn quickly. 经验丰富的老师帮你学得快。▸ **to learn about sth** (study) 学到某物 ▸ **to learn to do sth/how to do sth** (by studying) 学做某事/怎样做某事

▷ *He is learning to play the piano.* 他在学弹钢琴。; (*through experience*) 学做某事/学习如何做某事 ▷ *He learned to conceal his views.* 他学会了隐瞒观点。▶ **to learn of sth** (*find out*) 获悉某事 ▶ **to learn that...** (*find out*) 获悉… ▶ **to learn from one's mistakes** 从错误中吸取教训

learned ['lə:nɪd] ADJ **1** [+ *person*] 博学的 [bóxué de] **2** [+ *book, paper*] 学术性的 [xuéshùxìng de]

learner ['lə:nə(r)] N [c] **1** (*student*) 学习者 [xuézhě] **2** (BRIT) (*also:* **learner driver**) 驾驶学员 [jiàshǐ xuéyuán]

learning ['lə:nɪŋ] N [U] (*study*) 学习 [xuéxí]

learnt [lə:nt] PT, PP of **learn**

lease [li:s] **I** N [c] (*legal agreement, contract*) (*on flat, car*) 租约 [zūyuē] **II** VT [+ *flat, car*] 租 [zū] ▶ **on lease (to)** 被租给 ▶ **to give sb a new lease of life** 给某人注入新的活力 ▶ **to lease sth to sb** [+ *flat, car, land*] 把某物租给某人

leash [li:ʃ] N [c] 皮带 [pídài] ▶ **on a leash** 拴在链条上

○ **least** [li:st] **I** ADJ (*noun*) 最少的 [zuìshǎo de] ▷ *the area where there is least unemployment* 失业率最低的地区 **II** ADV **1** (*adjective*) ▶ **the least expensive/attractive/interesting** 最便宜/没有魅力/没趣的 [zuì piányi/méiyǒu mèilì/méi qù de] ▷ *the least interesting of all his theories* 他所有理论中最没趣的 **2** (*verb*) 最不 [zuìbù] ▷ *He came out when I least expected it.* 在我最意想不到的时候,他出现了。▷ *those who need help the least* 最不需要帮助的那些人 **III** PRON ▶ **the least** 最少 [zuìshǎo] ▷ *the gap between those earning the most and those earning the least* 收入最多的人与收入最少的人之间的差距 ▶ **at least** (*in expressions of quantity, comparisons*) 至少 ▷ *I must have slept twelve hours at least.* 我一定至少睡了12个小时。; (*still*) 无论如何 ▷ *It looks difficult but at least it is not dangerous.* 看起来很困难,但无论如何没有什么危险。; (*or rather*) 起码 ▷ *I spotted my ex-wife; at least I thought I did.* 我看见我前妻了;起码我认为是的。; (*at the very minimum*) 你至少应该写信吧。▷ *You could at least have written.* 你至少应该写信吧。▶ **not in the least** 一点也不 ▶ **it was the least I could do** 是我力所能及的 ▶ **not least because** 尤其是因为 ▶ **to say the least** 至少可以说 ▶ **least of all** 尤其

leather ['lɛðə(r)] **I** N [U] 皮革 [pígé] **II** CPD [复合词] [+ *jacket, shoes, chair*] 皮 [pí]

○ **leave** [li:v] (*pt, pp* **left**) **I** VT **1** (*depart from*) [+ *place*] 离开 [líkāi] ▷ *They left the house after tea.* 吃过茶点后,他们离开了家。**2** (*give up*) [+ *school, job, group*] 放弃 [fàngqì] ▷ *He left school with no qualifications.* 他弃学了,没有拿到任何文凭。**3** (*take leave of*) [+ *person*] 与…分开 [yǔ...fēnkāi] ▷ *I simply couldn't bear to leave my little girl.* 我就是忍受不了与我的小女儿分开。**4** (*abandon*) [+ *wife, family*] 抛弃 [pāoqì] ▷ *My husband left me for another woman.* 我丈夫为了另一个女人抛弃了我。**5** (*cause*) [+ *mark, stain,*

impression] 留下 [liúxià] ▷ *Coffee leaves a stain.* 咖啡会留下污迹。**6** (*leave behind*) (*deliberately*) 留下 [liúxià] ▷ *Leave your key with a neighbour.* 把钥匙留给邻居。; (*accidentally*) 落下 [luò] ▷ *I had left my raincoat in the restaurant.* 我把雨衣落在饭店里了。**7** [+ *message*] 留 [liú] ▷ *Can I leave a message for Jim?* 我能不能给吉姆留个口信? **8** (*keep back*) [+ *food, space, time*] 留 [liú] ▷ *Leave some of the stew for the boys.* 把炖菜给那几个男孩留一些。**9** (*waste*) [+ *food, drink*] 剩 [shèng] **II** VI **1** (*depart*) [*person +*] 离开 [líkāi]; [*bus, train +*] 出发 [chūfā] ▷ *My train leaves at 11.30.* 我坐的火车11点30分出发。**2** (*give up school*) 辍学 [chuòxué]; (*give up job*) 辞职 [cízhí] ▷ *He hated his job, so he left.* 他憎恶他的工作,所以辞职了。**III** N [U] (*time off maternity/sick etc leave*) 休假 [xiūjià] ▷ *Why don't you take a few days' leave?* 你为什么不休几天假? ; (MIL) 假期 [jiàqī] ▷ *How much leave do you get?* 你有多少探亲假? ▶ **to leave sth to sb** [+ *money, property etc*] 把某物留给某人 ▶ **to leave sth until later** 把某事往后拖延 ▶ **to leave sb/sth alone** 不理会某人/某物 ▶ **to leave sb to do sth** 让某人做某事 ▶ **the accident left four people dead** 该事故造成4人死亡 ▶ **he leaves a wife and two children** 他死后留下了妻子和两个孩子 ▶ **to be left with sth** 被赠予某物 ▷ *When their mother died they were left with nothing.* 母亲死后没有留给他们任何遗产。▶ **to leave for** [+ *destination*] 前往 ▷ *My plan was to leave for the seaside.* 我的计划是前往海边。▶ **to take one's leave (of sb)** (*frm*) (向某人)告别 ▶ **to be on leave** 在休假 ▶ **leave behind** VT **1** (*forget*) 忘带 [wàngdài] **2** (*decide not to take*) 留下 [liúxià] **3** (*say goodbye to*) [+ *person, place*] 永别 [yǒngbié] **4** (*leave in one's wake*) [+ *situation*] 留下 [liúxià] **5** (*advance beyond*) [+ *country, organization*] 超过 [chāoguò] ▶ **leave off I** VT **1** [+ *cover, lid*] 敞开 [chǎngkāi] **2** [+ *heating, light*] 关掉 [guāndiào] **3** (*omit*) (*from list*) 遗漏 [yílòu] **II** VI (*inf*) (*stop*) 别… [bié...] ▷ *Just leave off, will you?* 别烦了,行不行! ▶ **leave on** VT [+ *light, heating*] 开着 [kāizhe] ▶ **leave out** VT 删掉 [shāndiào] ▷ *One or two scenes in the play were left out.* 剧中的一两个场景被删掉了。▶ **to leave sb/sth out of sth** 不把某人/某物包括在某物内

leaves [li:vz] NPL of **leaf**

Lebanese [lɛbə'ni:z] (*pl* **Lebanese**) **I** ADJ 黎巴嫩的 [Líbānèn de] **II** N (*person*) 黎巴嫩人 [Líbānènrén]

Lebanon, the Lebanon ['lɛbənən] N 黎巴嫩 [Líbānèn]

lecture ['lɛktʃə(r)] **I** N [c] (*talk*) 讲座 [jiǎngzuò] **II** VI 做讲座 [zuò jiǎngzuò] **III** VT (*scold*) ▶ **to lecture sb on or about sth** 告诫某人有关某事 [gàojiè mǒurén yǒuguān mǒushì] ▶ **to give a lecture (on sth)** 作(某方面的)讲座 ▶ **to give sb a lecture (on or about sth)** (*telling off*) (就某

事)斥责某人

lecture hall (US) N [C] 讲演厅 [jiǎngyǎntīng] [英= **lecture theatre**]

lecturer ['lɛktʃərə(r)] N [C] 讲师 [jiǎngshī]

lecture theatre (BRIT) N [C] 讲演厅 [jiǎngyǎntīng] [美= **lecture hall**]

LED N ABBR (= *light-emitting diode*) 发光二极管 [fāguāng èrjíguǎn]

led [lɛd] PT, PP of **lead**[1]

ledge [lɛdʒ] N [C] **1** [of mountain] 岩石突出部 [yánshí tūchūbù] **2** [of window] 台 [tái]

leek [liːk] N [C] 韭葱 [jiǔcōng]

leer [lɪə(r)] I VI ▶ **to leer at sb** 色迷迷地看某人 [sèmímí de kàn mǒurén] II N [C] 斜眼一瞥 [xiéyǎn yī piē]

⊙left[1] [lɛft] I ADJ (not right) 左的 [zuǒ de] ▷ *his left eye* 他的左眼 II N ▶ **the left** 左侧 [zuǒcè] ▷ *There was a strong light coming from the left.* 有一道强光从左侧射来。 III ADV [turn, go, look +] 向左 [xiàng zuǒ] ▷ *Turn left at the traffic lights.* 在红绿灯处向左拐。 ▶ **on the left** 在左边 ▶ **to the left** 靠左边 ▶ **the Left** (POL) 左翼

⊙left[2] [lɛft] I PT, PP of **leave** II ADJ ▶ **to be left** (remain) 剩下 [shèngxià] ▷ *Is there any gin left?* 剩没剩杜松子酒？ ▶ **to be left over** [food, money etc +] 剩下

left-hand ['lɛfthænd] ADJ [+ side, corner] 左侧的 [zuǒcè de]

left-handed [lɛft'hændɪd] ADJ 左撇子的 [zuǒpiězi de]

left-luggage [lɛft'lʌgɪdʒ] (BRIT) N [U] ▶ **left-luggage locker** 行李寄存柜 [xínglǐ jìcún guì] ▶ **left-luggage office** 行李寄存处

leftovers ['lɛftəuvəz] NPL [of meal] 剩饭 [shèngfàn]

left-wing ['lɛft'wɪŋ] (POL) I ADJ [+ person, ideas] 左翼的 [zuǒyì de] II N ▶ **the left wing** 左翼 [zuǒyì]

leg [lɛg] N **1** [C] [of person, bird, table, chair] 腿 [tuǐ] **2** [C] [of trousers, shorts] 腿部 [tuǐbù] ▶ **trouser legs** 裤腿 **3** [C/U] (CULIN) [of lamb, chicken] 腿 [tuǐ] ▶ **he doesn't have a leg to stand on** (inf) 他完全站不住脚 ▶ **the first/second/last leg** [of journey] 第一/第二/最后一段行程; (ESP BRIT: SPORT) 一段赛程

legacy ['lɛgəsɪ] N [C] (in will) 遗产 [yíchǎn] ▶ **the legacy of** [+ event, historical period] …的后果

legal ['liːgl] ADJ **1** (relating to law) [+ system, requirement] 法律的 [fǎlǜ de] **2** (allowed by law) [+ action, situation] 合法的 [héfǎ de] ▶ **to take legal action/proceedings against sb** 对某人采取法律行动/提出诉讼

legal holiday (US) N [C] 法定假期 [fǎdìng jiàqī] [英= **bank holiday, public holiday**]

legalize ['liːgəlaɪz] VT 使合法化 [shǐ héfǎhuà]

legally ['liːgəlɪ] ADV **1** (as regards the law) 在法律上 [zài fǎlǜ shang] **2** (according to law) 依照法律地 [yīzhào fǎlǜ de] ▶ **legally binding** 受法律约束

legend ['lɛdʒənd] N **1** [C/U] (story) 传奇 [chuánqí] **2** [C] (fig) (person) 传奇人物 [chuánqí rénwù]

legendary ['lɛdʒəndərɪ] ADJ **1** (from legend) 传奇的 [chuánqí de] **2** (fig) (very famous) 传奇般的 [chuánqíbān de]

leggings ['lɛgɪŋz] NPL **1** (woman's) 裤袜 [kùwà] **2** (protective) 绑腿 [bǎngtuǐ]

legible ['lɛdʒəbl] ADJ 易读的 [yìdú de]

legislate ['lɛdʒɪsleɪt] VI 立法 [lìfǎ] ▶ **to legislate on sth** 就某事立法 ▶ **to legislate against sth** 立法禁止某事

legislation [lɛdʒɪs'leɪʃən] N [U] 立法 [lìfǎ]

legislative ['lɛdʒɪslətɪv] ADJ [+ assembly, power, reform] 立法的 [lìfǎ de]

legitimate [lɪ'dʒɪtɪmət] ADJ **1** (reasonable) [+ fear, claim, excuse] 合理的 [hélǐ de] **2** (legal) 合法的 [héfǎ de] **3** [+ child] 婚生的 [hūnshēng de]

leisure ['lɛʒə(r), US 'liːʒə(r)] N [U] (free time) 闲暇 [xiánxiá] ▶ **at (one's) leisure** 在闲暇的时候

leisure centre (BRIT) N [C] 娱乐中心 [yúlè zhōngxīn]

leisurely ['lɛʒəlɪ] ADJ [+ pace, walk] 悠闲的 [yōuxián de]

lemon ['lɛmən] I N [C] 柠檬 [níngméng] II ADJ (also: **lemon yellow**) 柠檬黄色的 [níngménghuáng sè de]

lemonade [lɛmə'neɪd] N [U] 柠檬汽水 [níngméng qìshuǐ]

lend [lɛnd] (pt, pp **lent**) VT **1** ▶ **to lend sth to sb** 把某物借给某人 [bǎ mǒuwù jiègěi mǒurén] **2** (loan) [bank etc +] 贷 [dài] **3** (frm) ▶ **to lend dignity to sth** 显示对某事的尊重 [xiǎnshì duì mǒushì de zūnzhòng] ▶ **it lends itself to...** 适宜于…

length [lɛŋθ] N **1** [C/U] (size) [of object, animal] 长度 [chángdù]; [of sentence, article] 篇幅 [piānfú] **2** [C] (piece) [of wood, string, cloth etc] 一段 [yī duàn] **3** [C] (in swimming pool) 长度 [chángdù] **4** [C/U] (duration) 期间 [qījiān] ▶ **at length** (for a long time) 详尽地; (liter) (at last) 最后 ▶ **it is 10 metres in length** 10米长 ▶ **to go to great lengths to do sth** 竭尽全力做某事 ▶ **they travelled the length of the island** 他们走遍了整个岛屿

lengthen ['lɛŋθən] I VT 使延长 [shǐ yáncháng] II VI 变长 [biàncháng]

lengthways ['lɛŋθweɪz], **lengthwise** ['lɛŋθwaɪz] ADV [slice, fold, lay +] 纵向地 [zòngxiàng de]

lengthy ['lɛŋθɪ] ADJ **1** [+ process, procedure, meeting] 漫长的 [màncháng de] **2** [+ report, book, document] 冗长的 [rǒngcháng de]

lenient ['liːnɪənt] ADJ [+ person, attitude, punishment] 宽大的 [kuāndà de]

lens [lɛnz] N [C] [of spectacles] 镜片 [jìngpiàn]; [of

telescope, camera] 镜头 [jìngtóu]

Lent [lɛnt] N [U] 大斋节 [Dàzhāijié]

lent [lɛnt] PT, PP *of* **lend**

lentil ['lɛntɪl] N [C] 小扁豆 [xiǎobiǎndòu]

Leo ['liːəu] N **1** [U] (*sign*) 狮子座 [Shīzi Zuò] **2** [C] (*person*) 狮子座的人 [Shīzi Zuò de rén] ▶ **I'm (a) Leo** 我是狮子座的

leopard ['lɛpəd] N [C] 豹 [bào]

leotard ['liːətɑːd] N [C] 紧身衣 [jǐnshēnyī]

leprosy ['lɛprəsɪ] N [U] 麻风病 [máfēngbìng]

lesbian ['lɛzbɪən] I ADJ 女同性恋的 [nǚ tóngxìngliàn de] II N [C] 女同性恋者 [nǚ tóngxìngliànzhě]

Lesotho [lɪ'suːtuː] N 莱索托 [Láisuǒtuō]

◇ **less** [lɛs] I ADJ (*noun*) 更少的 [gèng shǎo de] ▷ *A shower uses less water than a bath.* 淋浴比盆浴用的水要少。II ADV **1** (*adjective/adverb*) 较少地 [jiàoshǎo de] ▷ *Malaria is less common in Britain.* 疟疾在英国较少见。但还是吃奶酪，但不像以前那么频繁了。**2** (*verb*) 较少 [jiàoshǎo] ▷ *I visit him less than I should.* 我应该多去看他。▷ *He goes out less than he used to.* 他比以前出去得少了。III PRON 较少的东西 [jiàoshǎo de dōngxi] ▷ *I've got less than you.* 我的比你的少。IV PREP ▶ **less tax/10% discount** 去掉税/10%的折扣 [qùdiào shuì/bǎifēnzhīshí de zhékòu] ▶ **less of the money/time** 较少的钱/时间 ▶ **I see less of them now they've moved** 他们搬家了，我与他们见面的机会少了 ▶ **less than half** 不到一半 ▶ **no less than 45% of the electorate** 不少于45%的全体选民 ▶ **less than ever** 不比从前 ▶ **less than perfect/helpful** 决不完美/决没有帮助 ▶ **less and less** (*as adj*) 越来越少的; (*as adv*) 越来越少地 ▶ **the less he works, the more he complains** 他做的越少，抱怨的越多 ▶ **the Prime Minister, no less** 居然是首相

> **less** 可以修饰不可数名词。…*less meat…* 修饰可数名词应该使用 **fewer**。…*fewer potatoes…*

lessen ['lɛsn] I VI 减少 [jiǎnshǎo] II VT 使减少 [shǐ jiǎnshǎo]

lesser ['lɛsə(r)] ADJ (*smaller*) (in degree, importance, amount) 次要的 [cìyào de] ▶ **to a lesser extent or degree** 在较小程度上

lesson ['lɛsn] N [C] **1** (*class*) (in history, dancing etc) 课 [kè] **2** (*fig*) 教训 [jiàoxùn] ▶ **to teach sb a lesson** (fig) 给某人一个教训

lest [lɛst] (*frm*) CONJ 以免 [yǐmiǎn]

◇ **let** [lɛt] (pt, pp **let**) VT **1** ▶ **to let sb do sth** (*give permission*) 允许某人做某事 [yǔnxǔ mǒurén zuò mǒushì] ▷ *My parents wouldn't let me go out with boys.* 我父母不许我与男孩子们一起交往。**2** ▶ **to let sth happen** 让某事发生 [ràng mǒushì fāshēng] ▷ *People here let everyone else do the work.* 这里的人让别人做工作。**3** (BRIT) (*also:* **let out**) (lease) 出租 [chūzū] ▷ *She is thinking of letting her house to an American serviceman.* 她

在想把房子租给一个美国军人。[美= **rent**] ▶ **to let sb know that...** 告诉某人… **4** ▶ **to let sb in/out** 让某人进去/出去 [ràng mǒurén jìnqù/chūqù] ▷ *I'm bored. Let's go home.* 我觉得无聊，我们回家吧。▶ **let me explain/help** 让我来解释/帮忙 ▶ **he can't afford his rent, let alone a holiday** 他付不起房租，更别提度假了 ▶ **"to let"** "现房待租" ▶ **let go** (*release one's grip*) 松开 [sōngkāi] ▶ **let go of** (*stop holding*) 松开 ▶ **to let sb/sth go** (*release*) 放走某人/某物 ▷ *Eventually I let the frog go.* 最后，我放走了青蛙。▶ **to let o.s. go** (*relax*) 放得开; (*neglect o.s.*) 不修边幅

▶ **let down** VT **1** (*fail*) [+ *person*] 令…失望 [lìng...shīwàng] ▷ *Charlie's never let me down yet.* 查理从来没有令我失望过。**2** (ESP BRIT) [+ *tyre etc*] 给…放气 [gěi...fàngqì] **3** [+ *dress, hem etc*] 放长 [fàngcháng]

▶ **let in** VT **1** [+ *water, air*] 允许进来 [yǔnxǔ jìnlái] **2** (*open door for*) [+ *person*] 给…开门 [gěi...kāimén] ▶ **to let sb in on a secret** 让某人知道一个秘密

▶ **let off** VT **1** [+ *culprit*] 放过 [fàngguò] ▷ *He let me off with a warning.* 他给我一个警告就放过我了。**2** (*excuse*) ▶ **to let sb off sth** 允许某人不用做某事 [yǔnxǔ mǒurén bù yòng zuò mǒushì] **3** [+ *firework, gun, bomb*] 放 [fàng]

▶ **let on** VI ▶ **not to let on that...** 不泄漏出去… [bù xièlòu chūqù...]

▶ **let out** VT **1** VT [+ *water, air, breath*] 放掉 [fàngdiào] **2** [+ *scream, cry*] 发出 [fāchū] ▷ *She let out a terrible shriek.* 她发出一声可怕的尖叫。**3** (BRIT) (*lease*) 出租 [chūzū] ▷ *She is thinking of letting out her house to an American serviceman.* 她在想把她的房子租给一个美国军人。[美= **rent**]

▶ **let up** VI **1** (*cease*) 停止 [tíngzhǐ] ▷ *We thought the rain would let up soon.* 我们觉得雨不久会停。**2** (*diminish*) 减缓 [jiǎnhuǎn] ▷ *Still the heat didn't let up.* 炎热依旧没有减缓。

lethal ['liːθl] ADJ [+ *weapon, chemical etc*] 致命的 [zhìmìng de]

◇ **letter** ['lɛtə(r)] N [C] **1** (*note*) 信 [xìn] **2** (*of alphabet*) 字母 [zìmǔ] ▷ *the letter E* 字母E ▶ **to the letter** 不折不扣地

letterbox ['lɛtəbɔks] (BRIT) N [C] (in door) 信箱 [xìnxiāng] [美= **mailbox**]

lettuce ['lɛtɪs] N [C/U] 生菜 [shēngcài]

leukaemia, (US) **leukemia** [luː'kiːmɪə] N [U] 白血病 [báixuèbìng]

◇ **level** ['lɛvl] I ADJ **1** (*flat*) 平的 [píng de] ▷ *The floor is quite level.* 地板很平。**2** (CULIN) [+ *spoonful*] 平的 [píng de] **3** (*at same height*) 一样高的 [yīyàng gāo de] ▷ *The tree tops are level with the roof.* 树冠与屋顶一样高。▷ *Amy knelt down so that their eyes were level.* 艾米蹲下身子，这样他们可以平视对方。**4** (in points, goals etc) 平的 [píng de] ▷ *The teams were level at the end of extra time.* 加时赛结束时，两队比分平了。II ADV

to draw level with (ESP BRIT) [+ person, vehicle] 与…平齐 [yǔ…píngqí]; [+ team, opponent] 与…比分拉平 [yǔ…bǐfēn lāpíng] **III** N [C] **1** (amount, degree) (on scale) 程度 [chéngdù] ▷ The lowest level of inflation for years 多年来最低程度的通货膨胀率 **2** (standard) 水平 [shuǐpíng] ▷ The general level of training was not high. 培训的总体水平不高。 **3** (height) [of lake, river] 水位 [shuǐwèi] ▷ The level of the lake continues to rise. 湖水的水位继续上升。 **IV** VT (flatten) [+ building, forest etc] 把…弄平 [bǎ…nòngpíng] ▷ Tractors levelled more than 1000 acres of forest. 拖拉机将1000多英亩的森林夷为平地。 **V** VI ▶ **to level with sb** (inf) 对某人开诚布公 [duì mǒurén kāi chéng bù gōng] ▶ **to be level with** (ESP BRIT) [+ person, vehicle] 与…平齐; [+ team, opponent] 与…并驾齐驱 ▶ **at eye/waist** etc **level** 在与眼/腰(等)平齐的位置 ▷ He held the gun at waist level. 他把枪端与腰平齐的位置上。 ▶ **to be on the level** (inf) [plan etc +] 真实可信; [person +] 诚恳 ▶ **to level the score** (SPORT) 扳平比分 ▶ **to level an accusation/a criticism at** or **against sb** 指控/批评某人 ▶ **to level a gun at sb** 把枪对准某人 ▶ **to do one's level best** 全力以赴
▶ **level off** VI **1** [prices etc +] 稳定 [wěndìng] **2** [plane +] 平飞 [píngfēi]
▶ **level out** VI = **level off**

level crossing (BRIT) N [C] 平交道口 [píngjiāodàokǒu] [美= **railroad crossing**]

lever ['li:və(r), US 'levə(r)] **I** N [C] **1** (to operate machine) 杆 [gān] **2** (to provide leverage) 杠杆 [gànggǎn] **3** (fig) 手段 [shǒuduàn] **II** VT ▶ **to lever sth open** 撬开某物 [qiàokāi mǒuwù] ▶ **to lever o.s. up** 把自己支撑起来

leverage ['li:vərɪdʒ, US 'levərɪdʒ] N [U] **1** (using bar, lever) 杠杆作用 [gànggǎn zuòyòng] **2** (fig) (influence) 影响 [yǐngxiǎng]

levy ['levi] **I** N (tax, charge) 税款 [shuìkuǎn] **II** VT [+ tax, charge] 征收 [zhēngshōu]

liability [laɪə'bɪlətɪ] **I** N **1** [C] (burden, risk) 负担 [fùdān] **2** [U] (responsibility) 责任 [zérèn] **II liabilities** NPL (COMM) 债务 [zhàiwù]

liable ['laɪəbl] ADJ ▶ **to be liable to sth/to do sth** [person +] 有…/做某事的倾向 [yǒu…/zuò mǒushì de qīngxiàng]; [thing +] 可能会…/做某事 [kěnéng huì…/zuò mǒushì] ▶ **to be liable (for sth)** [for damages, debt] 负(某事的)责任

liaise [li:'eɪz] VI ▶ **to liaise (with sb)** (initiate contact) (与某人)联络 [(yǔ mǒurén) liánluò]; (maintain contact) (与某人)保持联系 [(yǔ mǒurén) bǎochí liánxì]

liar ['laɪə(r)] N [C] 说谎者 [shuōhuǎngzhě]

liberal ['lɪbərl] **I** ADJ **1** (tolerant) [+ person, attitude] 开明的 [kāimíng de] **2** (generous) [+ use, amount] 大方的 [dàfang de] **3** (POL) ▶ **Liberal** 自由党 [Zìyóudǎng] **II** N [C] **1** (tolerant person) 开明的人 [kāimíng de rén] **2** (POL) ▶ **Liberal** 自由党党员 [Zìyóudǎng dǎngyuán] ▶ **to be**

liberal with sth (generous) 慷慨提供某物

Liberal Democrat (BRIT) N [C] 自由民主党党员 [Zìyóu Mínzhǔdǎng Dǎngyuán] ▶ **the Liberal Democrat Party** 自由民主党

liberate ['lɪbəreɪt] VT [+ city, country] 解放 [jiěfàng]; [+ oppressed people etc] 使获自由 [shǐ huò zìyóu]; [+ hostage, prisoner] 释放 [shìfàng]

liberation [lɪbə'reɪʃən] N [U] [of country, oppressed group] 解放 [jiěfàng]

Liberia [laɪ'bɪərɪə] N 利比里亚 [Lìbǐlǐyà]

Liberian [laɪ'bɪərɪən] **I** ADJ 利比里亚的 [Lìbǐlǐyà de] **II** N [C] (person) 利比里亚人 [Lìbǐlǐyàrén]

liberty ['lɪbətɪ] N [C/U] 自由 [zìyóu] ▶ **to be at liberty** [criminal +] 自由的 ▶ **to be at liberty to do sth** 有权做某事 ▶ **to take the liberty of doing sth** 冒昧地做某事

Libra ['li:brə] N **1** [U] (sign) 天秤座 [Tiānchèng Zuò] **2** [C] (person) 天秤座的人 [Tiānchèng Zuò de rén] ▶ **I'm (a) Libra** 我是天秤座的

librarian [laɪ'brɛərɪən] N [C] 图书管理员 [túshū guǎnlǐyuán]

library ['laɪbrərɪ] N [C] **1** (public) 图书馆 [túshūguǎn] **2** (in private house) 书斋 [shūzhāi] **3** (private collection) 收藏 [shōucáng]

Libya ['lɪbɪə] N 利比亚 [Lìbǐyà]

Libyan ['lɪbɪən] **I** ADJ 利比亚的 [Lìbǐyà de] **II** N [C] (person) 利比亚人 [Lìbǐyàrén]

lice [laɪs] NPL of **louse**

licence, (US) **license** ['laɪsns] N **1** [C] (permit) 许可证 [xǔkězhèng] **2** (also: **driving licence**) 驾驶执照 [jiàshǐ zhízhào] **3** [C] (COMM) 特许 [tèxǔ] **4** [U] (pej) ▶ **licence to do sth** 放肆地做某事 [fàngsì de zuò mǒushì] ▶ **under licence** (COMM) 经特许

▮▮用法参见 **license**

license, (US) ['laɪsns] **I** N (US) = **licence** **II** VT ▶ **to license sb/sth (to do sth)** 许可某人/某组织(做某事) [xǔkě mǒurén/mǒuzǔzhī (zuò mǒushì)]

┃请勿将 **licence** 和 **license** 混淆。在英式英语中,以 **-ce** 结尾的 **licence** 是名词。...a driver's licence. 以 **-se** 结尾的 **license** 是动词。The restaurant was licensed to serve alcohol. 在美式英语中,后一种拼写也可用作名词。

licensed ['laɪsnst] ADJ **1** [+ car, gun] 领有许可证的 [lǐngyǒu xǔkězhèng de] **2** (BRIT) [+ restaurant, hotel] (to sell alcohol) 领有卖酒许可证的 [lǐngyǒu màijiǔ xǔkězhèng de]

license number (US) N [C] 车牌号 [chēpáihào] [英= **registration number**]

license plate (US) N [C] 车牌照 [chēpáizhào] [英= **number plate**]

lick [lɪk] **I** VT **1** [+ stamp, fingers, lolly etc] 舔 [tiǎn] **2** (inf) (defeat) 击败 [jībài] **II** N [C] 舔 [tiǎn] ▶ **to lick one's lips** (lit) 舔嘴唇; (fig) 垂涎欲滴 ▶ **a lick of paint** (inf) 少许涂料

lid [lɪd] N [C] **1** (of box, case, pan) 盖 [gài] **2** (eyelid) 眼睑 [yǎnjiǎn] ▸ **to keep a/the lid on sth** (fig) 隐瞒某事

lie¹ [laɪ] (pt **lay**, pp **lain**) VI **1** (be horizontal) [person +] 躺 [tǎng] **2** (be situated) [place +] 位于 [wèiyú]; [object +] 平放 [píngfàng] **3** (fig) [problem, cause etc +] 在于 [zàiyú] **4** (BRIT) (be placed) (in race, league etc) 处于 [chǔyú] **5** ▸ **to lie hidden/forgotten** 被遗忘 [bèi yíwàng] ▸ **to lie ahead** 摆在面前 ▸ **to lie low** (fig) 隐藏
▸ **lie about** (BRIT) VI = **lie around**
▸ **lie around** VI **1** [things +] 乱放 [luànfàng] **2** [people +] 懒懒散散 [lǎnlǎnsǎnsǎn]
▸ **lie back** VI [person +] 向后靠 [xiànghòu kào]
▸ **lie behind** VI FUS [不可拆分] (cause) 是…的缘由 [shì…de yuányóu]
▸ **lie down** VI [person +] 躺下 [tǎngxià] ▸ **to take sth lying down** 对某事俯首屈服

lie² [laɪ] I VI (tell lies) 说谎 [shuōhuǎng] II N [C] 谎言 [huǎngyán] ▸ **to tell lies** 说谎 ▸ **to live a lie** 过着虚伪的生活

Liechtenstein ['lɪktənstaɪn] (GEO) N 列支敦士登 [Lièzhīdūnshìdēng]

lie-in ['laɪɪn] (BRIT: inf) N ▸ **to have a lie-in** 睡懒觉 [shuì lǎnjiào]

lieutenant [lɛf'tɛnənt, US luː'tɛnənt] N [C] 中尉 [zhōngwèi]

○**life** [laɪf] (pl **lives**) N **1** [C/U] (living, existence) 生命 [shēngmìng] ▷ her last hours of life 她生命的最后时刻 **2** [U] (living things) 生物 [shēngwù] ▷ Is there life on Mars? 火星上有生物吗? ▷ Your life is in danger. 你的生命处于危险之中。 **3** [C] (lifespan) [of person] 一生 [yīshēng] ▷ People spend their lives worrying about money. 人的一生都在为钱而担忧。; [of machine, organization] 寿命 [shòumìng] ▷ The repairs did not increase the life of the equipment. 维修并没有增加设备的使用寿命。 **4** [U] (events, experience) 生活 [shēnghuó] ▷ Life had not been kind to her. 生活没有善待她。 **5** [U] (vitality) [of person, place] 活力 [huólì] ▷ The town was full of life. 这座城市充满了活力。 **6** [U] (inf) value: **life imprisonment** 无期徒刑 [wúqī túxíng] ▷ He could get life, if convicted. 如果定罪, 他会被判无期徒刑。 ▸ **to paint from life** 写生 ▸ **to fight for one's life** 与生命抗争 ▸ **to be jailed/scarred for life** 遭受终生监禁/创伤 ▸ **his personal/working life** 他的个人/工作生活 ▸ **to come to life** [person, party etc +] 苏醒过来 ▸ **to take sb's life/one's own life** (frm) 杀害某人/自杀

lifebelt ['laɪfbɛlt] N [C] 救生带 [jiùshēngdài]

lifeboat ['laɪfbəut] N [C] 救生船 [jiùshēngchuán]

lifeguard ['laɪfgɑːd] N [C] (at beach, swimming pool) 救生员 [jiùshēngyuán]

life insurance N [U] 人寿保险 [rénshòu bǎoxiǎn]

life jacket N [C] 救生衣 [jiùshēngyī]

lifelike ['laɪflaɪk] ADJ **1** (+ model, dummy etc) 逼真的 [bīzhēn de] **2** (realistic) (+ painting, character) 栩栩如生的 [xǔxǔ rú shēng de]

life preserver [-prɪ'zəːvə(r)] (US) N [C] (lifebelt) 救生用具 [jiùshēng yòngjù]; (life jacket) 救生衣 [jiùshēngyī]

life sentence N [C] 无期徒刑 [wúqī túxíng]

lifestyle ['laɪfstaɪl] N [C/U] 生活方式 [shēnghuó fāngshì]

lifetime ['laɪftaɪm] N **1** [C] (of person) 一生 [yīshēng] **2** [S] (of product, organization) 寿命 [shòumìng] ▸ **the chance of a lifetime** 千载难逢的机会

lift [lɪft] I VT **1** (raise) (+ thing, part of body) 举起 [jǔqǐ] **2** (end) (+ ban, sanctions, embargo) 解除 [jiěchú] **3** (increase) (+ rate, price) 提高 [tígāo] **4** (inf) (copy) 抄袭 [chāoxí] II VI [fog +] 消散 [xiāosàn] III N [C] (BRIT) 电梯 [diàntī] [美= **elevator**] ▸ **to give sb a lift** (ESP BRIT: AUT) 让某人搭便车
▸ **lift off** VI [rocket, aircraft +] 起飞 [qǐfēi]
▸ **lift up** VT [+ person, thing] 举起 [jǔqǐ]

lift-off ['lɪftɔf] N [C/U] (of rocket) 起飞 [qǐfēi]

light [laɪt] I N **1** [U] (from sun, moon, lamp, fire) 光 [guāng] **2** [C] (ELEC, AUT) 灯 [dēng] **3** [S] (for cigarette etc) 打火机 [dǎhuǒjī] II VT **1** (set alight) (+ candle, fire, cigarette) 点燃 [diǎnrán] **2** (+ room) 照亮 [zhàoliàng] III ADJ **1** (pale) (+ colour) 淡的 [dàn de] **2** (bright) (+ building, room) 明亮的 [míngliàng de] **3** (not dark) (+ evening, morning) 亮的 [liàng de] **4** (not heavy) (+ object) 轻的 [qīng de] **5** (not intensive) (+ rain, traffic, sleep) 小量的 [xiǎoliàng de] **6** (not strenuous) (+ work) 容易做的 [róngyì zuò de] **7** (graceful, gentle) (+ movement, action) 轻快的 [qīngkuài de] **8** (lenient) (+ sentence) 从轻的 [cóngqīng de] **9** (not serious) (+ book, music) 轻松的 [qīngsōng de]; (+ discussion etc) 轻松的 [qīngsōng de] IV ADV (travel +) 轻装地 [qīng zhuāng de] V **lights** NPL **1** (AUT) (also: **traffic lights**) 交通指示灯 [jiāotōng zhǐshìdēng] ▸ **to turn or switch the light on/off** 开/关灯 ▸ **to cast** or **shed** or **throw light on sth** (fig) 使某事清楚明白地显示出来 ▸ **to present sth in a favourable/an unfavourable light** 表现某物宜人/不宜人之处 ▸ **to set light to sth** (ESP BRIT) 点燃某物 [美= **set fire to**] ▸ **to come** or **be brought to light** [fact, information +] 暴露 ▸ **in the light of** [+ discussions, new evidence etc] 鉴于 ▸ **to make light of sth** 对某事不以为意
▸ **light up** I VI **1** (illuminate) 变亮 [biànliàng] **2** [face, eyes +] 放光彩 [fàng guāngcǎi] II VT (illuminate) 照亮 [zhàoliàng]

light bulb N [C] 灯泡 [dēngpào]

lighten ['laɪtn] I VT **1** (make less heavy) 使变轻 [shǐ biànqīng] **2** (make less difficult) (+ load, burden) 减轻 [jiǎnqīng] **3** (make less serious) (+ situation, atmosphere, mood) 使轻松 [shǐ qīngsōng] **4** (make less dark) 使变浅 [shǐ biàn qiǎn] **II** VI **1** (become more cheerful) [mood +] 变得愉快 [biànde yúkuài] **2** (become less dark) 变浅 [biàn qiǎn]

lighter ['laɪtə(r)] N [c] (also: cigarette lighter) 打火机 [dǎhuǒjī]

light-hearted [laɪt'hɑ:tɪd] ADJ [+ person] 轻松愉快的 [qīngsōng yúkuài de]; [+ question, remark etc] 轻松的 [qīngsōng de]

lighthouse ['laɪthaʊs] N [c] 灯塔 [dēngtǎ]

lighting ['laɪtɪŋ] N [U] (on roads, in theatre) 照明设备 [zhàomíng shèbèi]

lightly ['laɪtlɪ] ADV **1** (gently) [kiss, touch +] 轻轻地 [qīngqīng de] **2** (not heavily) [sleep, eat +] 轻微地 [qīngwēi de] **3** (CULIN) [cook, brown, steam +] 稍微地 [shāowēi de] **4** (not seriously) 轻率地 [qīngshuài de] ▶ **to get off lightly** 从轻发落

lightning ['laɪtnɪŋ] **I** N [U] (in sky) 闪电 [shǎndiàn] **II** ADJ ▶ **with lightning speed** 闪电般的 [shǎndiànbān de]

lightweight ['laɪtweɪt] **I** ADJ **1** [+ fabric, product] 重量轻的 [zhòngliàng qīng de] **2** (fig) [+ person] 无足轻重的 [wú zú qīng zhòng de] **II** N [c] **1** (BOXING) 轻量级运动员 [qīngliàngjí yùndòngyuán] **2** (fig) (person) 无足轻重的人 [wú zú qīng zhòng de rén]

⊙ **like¹** [laɪk] PREP **1** (similar to) 像 [xiàng] ▷ a house like ours 像我们这样的房子 **2** (in similes) 像…一样 [xiàng…yīyàng] ▷ I was trembling like a leaf. 我抖得像片叶子一样。 **3** (such as) 如 [rú] ▷ big countries like Australia and India 如澳大利亚和印度这样的大国 ▶ **something like that** 差不多 ▶ **to be like sth/sb** 像某物/某人 ▶ **what's he/the weather like?** 他/天气怎么样? ▶ **to look like** [+ person] 长得像; [+ thing] 类似 ▶ **to sound/taste like** 听/尝起来像 ▶ **what does sth/sb taste like?** 看/听/尝起来怎么样? ▶ **he was acting like an idiot** 他做事像白痴一样 ▶ **there's nothing like...** 什么也比不上… ▶ **that's just like him** 他就是这样 ▶ **like this** 像这样 ▶ **and the like** 诸如此类

⊙ **like²** [laɪk] **I** VT **1** (find attractive, enjoyable) [+ person, thing] 喜欢 [xǐhuan] ▷ I can't think why Grace doesn't like me. 我不明白格雷丝为什么不喜欢我。 **2** (approve of) [+ action, behaviour] 赞同 [zàntóng] **II** N ▶ **his likes and dislikes** 他的好恶 [tā de hàowù] ▶ **to like doing sth** 喜欢做某事 ▶ **to like to do sth** 喜欢做某事 ▷ I like to go to bed early during the week. 不是周末的时候，我喜欢早点上床休息。 ▷ She doesn't like him working so hard. 她不愿意他工作得那么辛苦。 ▷ His wife didn't like him drinking so much. 他妻子不愿意他喝这么多酒。 ▶ **I would** or **I'd like an ice-cream/to go for a walk** 我想吃个冰淇淋/去散步 ▶ **would you like a coffee?** 你想来杯咖啡? ▶ **if you like** (in offers, suggestions) 如果你愿意的话 ▷ You can stay here if you like. 如果你愿意的话，你可以呆在这里。; (in other

words) 换句话说

likeable ['laɪkəbl] ADJ [+ person] 可爱的 [kě'ài de]

likelihood ['laɪklɪhʊd] N [U/s] 可能性 [kěnéngxìng] ▶ **there is every likelihood that...** 非常有可能… ▶ **in all likelihood** 十有八九

⊙ **likely** ['laɪklɪ] ADJ **1** (probable) 很可能的 [hěn kěnéng de] ▷ A "yes" vote is still the likely outcome. 结果仍很有可能是赞成票。 **2** [+ person, place, thing] 合适的 [héshì de] ▷ He seemed a likely candidate to become Prime Minister. 他似乎是成为首相的合适人选。 ▶ **it is likely that...** 有可能… ▶ **to be likely to do sth** 很可能做某事 ▶ **not likely!** (inf) 太不可能!

likeness ['laɪknɪs] N [s] (similarity) 相似 [xiāngsì] ▶ **that's a good likeness** (photo, portrait) 那张像本人

likewise ['laɪkwaɪz] ADV (similarly) 同样地 [tóngyàng de] ▶ **to do likewise** 照样做

liking ['laɪkɪŋ] N ▶ **to have a liking for sb/sth** 喜爱某人/某物 [xǐ'ài mǒurén/mǒuwù] ▶ **to be to sb's liking** 合某人意 ▶ **it's too big for my liking** 对我来说太大了 ▶ **to take a liking to sb** 对某人产生好感

lilac ['laɪlək] **I** N **1** [c] (BOT) 丁香树 [dīngxiāngshù] **2** [c] (flower) 丁香花 [dīngxiānghuā] **3** [U] (colour) 淡紫色 [dàn zǐsè] **II** ADJ 淡紫色的 [dàn zǐsè de]

lily ['lɪlɪ] N [c] (plant) 百合属 [bǎihéshǔ]; (flower) 百合花 [bǎihéhuā]

limb [lɪm] N [c] **1** (ANAT) 四肢 [sìzhī] **2** (liter) [of tree] 大枝 [dàzhī] ▶ **to go out on a limb** (fig) 惹是生非

limbo ['lɪmbəʊ] N ▶ **to be in limbo** 处于不定状态 [chǔyú bùdìng zhuàngtài]

lime [laɪm] N **1** [c] (fruit) 酸橙 [suānchéng] **2** [c] (also: **lime tree**) (linden) 椴树 [duàn shù]; (bearing limes) 酸橙树 [suānchéng shù] **3** [c/U] (also: **lime juice**) 酸橙汁 [suānchéng zhī] **4** [U] (for soil) 石灰 [shíhuī]

limelight ['laɪmlaɪt] N ▶ **to be in the limelight** 为公众所瞩目 [wéi gōngzhòng suǒ zhǔmù]

limestone ['laɪmstəʊn] N [U] 石灰岩 [shíhuīyán]

limit ['lɪmɪt] **I** VT [+ production, expense etc] 限制 [xiànzhì] **II** N [c] **1** (maximum point) 限度 [xiàndù] **2** [of area, city] 界线 [jièxiàn] **3** (restriction) (on time, money etc) 限定 [xiàndìng] ▶ **to limit o.s. to sth** 自我限定某物 ▶ **to be off limits (to sb)** 禁止(某人)入内 ▶ **to be over the limit** (BRIT) 饮酒过量 ▶ **within limits** 适度地

limitation [lɪmɪ'teɪʃən] **I** N [U] (control) 限制 [xiànzhì] **II** **limitations** NPL (shortcomings) 局限 [júxiàn] ▶ **a limitation on sth** 对某事的限额

limited ['lɪmɪtɪd] ADJ [+ choice, resources etc] 有限的 [yǒuxiàn de] ▶ **to be limited to sth/sb** 只限于某物/某人

limousine ['lɪməzi:n] N [c] 豪华轿车 [háohuá

jiàochē]

limp [lɪmp] I N [C] 跛行 [bǒxíng] II VI [person, animal +] 跛行 [bǒxíng] III ADJ [+ body, material etc] 柔软的 [róuruǎn de] ▶ **to have a limp** 腿瘸 ▶ **to walk with a limp** 一瘸一拐地走

⊙ **line** [laɪn] I N [C] 1 (long thin mark) 线 [xiàn] 2 (wrinkle) 皱纹 [zhòuwén] 3 (row) (of people, things) 排 [pái] ▷ a line of women queueing for bread 一排妇女在排队等面包 ▷ long lines of trees 长排的树木 4 [+ of words] (written, printed) 行 [háng] ▷ I only read the first few lines. 我只读了前几行。; (in poem, song) 句 [jù] ▷ the most famous line in English poetry 英语诗歌中最有名的一句 5 (THEAT, CINE) 台词 [táicí] ▷ He's learning his lines for the school play. 他在为学校里的一出剧背台词。6 (rope, cord) 线 [xiàn]; (also: **washing line**) 晾衣绳 [liàngyīshéng] ▷ She hung her washing on the line. 她把衣服挂到晾衣绳上。; (also: **fishing line**) 钓鱼线 [diàoyúxiàn]; (ELEC) (wire) 电线 [diànxiàn] ▷ High winds had brought the lines down. 猛烈的风把电线刮断了。; (TEL) 线路 [xiànlù] ▷ The line was dead. 线路不通。7 (railway track) 铁路线路 [tiělù xiànlù] ▷ repairs to the line 对铁路线路的维修 8 (bus, coach, train route) 路线 [lùxiàn] ▷ They had taken the wrong line on the London Tube. 他们在伦敦地铁坐错了线。9 (boundary) 界线 [jièxiàn] ▷ just across the state line in Nevada 刚刚越过内华达州的界线 10 (liter) (edge, contour) 曲线 [qūxiàn] ▷ an evening dress that follows the lines of the body 显现身体曲线的晚礼服 11 (attitude, policy) 方针 [fāngzhēn] ▷ the official line of the Labour Party 工党的方针 12 (also: **line of business, line of work**) 生产线 [shēngchǎnxiàn] ▷ What line are you in? 你在哪一条生产线上？13 (COMM) (of product) 种 [zhǒng] ▷ a new line of computer printers 一种新的电脑打印机 II VT 1 (form rows along) [people, trees +] 沿…排成行 [yán…pái chéng háng] ▷ Crowds lined the route. 一群人沿路排成一行。2 (form layer inside) 覆盖…的里层 [fùgài…de lǐcéng] ▷ Moisture lined the walls of the cave. 湿气覆盖洞穴内壁。▷ the muscles that line the intestines 肠内壁的肌肉 3 (put lining in) [+ clothing] 加里衬于 [jiā lǐchèn yú]; [+ container] 放在…的内壁 [fàng zài…de nèibì] ▶ **to line sth with sth** 把某物放在某物的内壁 ▶ **hold the line please!** (TEL) 请稍等！▶ **to stand** or **wait in line** (ESP US) 排队等候 [英= **queue**] ▶ **in line with** (according to) 与…一致 ▶ **to be in line for sth** 即将获得某事物 ▶ **somewhere along** or **down the line** 在某个时期 ▶ **to bring sth into line with sth** 使某物与某物一致 ▶ **to be on the line** 面临威胁 ▶ **on the right lines** 大体正确 ▶ **to be/step out of line** (fig) 越轨 ▶ **to draw the line at doing sth** 拒绝做某事 ▶ **to take a hard line on sth** 对某事态度强硬

▶ **line up** I VI (form queue) 排队 [páiduì] II VT

1 [+ people, objects] 使排队 [shǐ páiduì] ▷ The men were lined up against a wall. 这些男子们被靠墙排成排。2 (organize) [+ event, celebration] 安排 [ānpái] ▷ A formal party was lined up. 人们正在安排一场正式的晚会。3 ▶ **to line sb up (for sth)** (为某事) 安排组织好某人 [(wèi mǒushì) ānpái zǔzhī hǎo mǒurén] ▷ I had lined up a wonderful cast. 我已经安排好一组优秀的演员到场。▶ **to have sb/sth lined up** 安排某人/某事

linear [ˈlɪnɪə(r)] ADJ 1 [+ process, sequence] 线性的 [xiànxìng de] 2 [+ shape, form] 直线的 [zhíxiàn de]

lined [laɪnd] ADJ 1 [+ face, skin] 褶皱的 [zhězhòu de] 2 [+ paper] 带横格的 [dài hénggé de] 3 [+ skirt, jacket etc] 带衬里的 [dài chènlǐ de]

linen [ˈlɪnɪn] I N [U] 1 (cloth) 亚麻布 [yàmábù] 2 (tablecloths, sheets etc) 亚麻制品 [yàmá zhìpǐn] II CPD [复合词] [+ jacket, sheets, etc] 亚麻料 [yàmáliào]

liner [ˈlaɪnə(r)] N [C] (ship) 班轮 [bānlún]

line-up [ˈlaɪnʌp] N [C] 1 (chosen group): SPORT) 阵容 [zhènróng]; (at concert, festival) 演出名单 [yǎnchū míngdān] 2 (identity parade) 等待检查的一排人 [děngdài jiǎnchá de yī pái rén]

linger [ˈlɪŋɡə(r)] VI [smell, tradition, feelings +] 继续存留 [jìxù cúnliú]; [person +] 逗留 [dòuliú]

lingerie [ˈlænʒəriː] N [U] 女内衣 [nǚ nèiyī]

lingering [ˈlɪŋɡərɪŋ] ADJ [+ sense, feeling, doubt] 继续存在的 [jìxù cúnzài de]; [+ death] 拖久的 [tuōjiǔ de]

linguist [ˈlɪŋɡwɪst] N [C] 1 (knowing languages) 通晓数国语言的人 [tōngxiǎo shùguó yǔyán de rén] 2 (knowing linguistics) 语言学家 [yǔyánxuéjiā]

linguistic [lɪŋˈɡwɪstɪk] ADJ [+ ability, awareness, studies etc] 语言学的 [yǔyánxué de]

linguistics [lɪŋˈɡwɪstɪks] N [U] 语言学 [yǔyánxué]

lining [ˈlaɪnɪŋ] N 1 [C/U] (of garment) 衬里 [chènlǐ] 2 [C] (ANAT) (of stomach etc) 膜 [mó]

link [lɪŋk] I N [C] 1 (relationship) 关系 [guānxì] 2 (connection) (between people, organizations) 联系 [liánxì] 3 (COMPUT) (also: **hyperlink**) 超链接 [chāoliànjiē] 4 (means of transport/communication) 线路 [xiànlù] 5 (of chain) 环节 [huánjié] II VT 1 (join) [+ places, objects] 连接 [liánjiē] 2 (relate) [+ people, situations] 联系 [liánxì] 3 [+ arms, hands] 挽住 [wǎnzhù] III **links** NPL (GOLF) 球场 [qiúchǎng]

▶ **link up** I VT [+ machines, systems] 联接 [liánjiē] II VI [people, groups +] 联合 [liánhé]

lion [ˈlaɪən] N [C] 狮子 [shīzi] ▶ **the lion's share of sth** 某物的最大一部分

lioness [ˈlaɪənɪs] N [C] 母狮 [mǔshī]

lip [lɪp] N 1 [C] (ANAT) 唇 [chún] 2 [C] (of cup, jug etc) 边缘 [biānyuán] 3 [U] (inf) (insolence) 唐突无礼的话 [tángtū wúlǐ de huà]

lip-read [ˈlɪpriːd] VI 唇读 [chúndú]

lipstick ['lɪpstɪk] N [C/U] 口红 [kǒuhóng]

liqueur [lɪ'kjuə(r), US lɪ'kɜː(r)] N [C/U] 饭后饮用的甜的烈性酒

liquid ['lɪkwɪd] I N [C/U] 液体 [yètǐ] II ADJ 液体的 [yètǐ de]

liquidize ['lɪkwɪdaɪz] (CULIN) VT 使液化 [shǐ yèhuà]

liquidizer ['lɪkwɪdaɪzə(r)] (ESP BRIT: CULIN) N [C] 榨汁机 [zhàzhǐjī]

liquor ['lɪkə(r)] (US) N [U] 酒 [jiǔ] ▶ **hard liquor** 烈性酒 [英= **spirits**]

liquor store (US) N [C] 酒店 [jiǔdiàn] [英= **off-licence**]

lisp [lɪsp] I N [C] 咬舌 [yǎoshé] II VI 咬着舌说 [yǎozhe shé shuō] ▶ **to speak with a lisp** 口齿不清地说

⊙ **list** [lɪst] I N [C] 单子 [dānzi] ▷ *There were six names on the list.* 单子上有6个名字。II VT **1** (record) [person+] 列出 [lièchū] ▷ *The pupils listed their favourite sports.* 小学生们把他们最喜好的运动列了出来。**2** (show) [document, label+] 标明 [biāomíng] ▷ *There was a label on each case listing its contents.* 每个箱子都有一个标签标明箱内东西。**3** (COMPUT) 列出 [lièchū] ▷ *Have you tried listing your other directories?* 你有没有试着把其他的目录列出来？**4** (include on list) 列在…之内 [liè zài…zhīnèi] ▷ *He is not listed in the phone book.* 他的名字没列在电话簿内。III VI [ship+] 倾斜 [qīngxié]

listen ['lɪsn] VI **1** (try to hear) (to sound, music) 听 [tīng]; (to speaker) 听…说 [tīng…shuō] **2** (follow advice) 听从 [tīngcóng] ▶ **to listen to sb** (pay attention to) 留神听某人说话; (follow advice of) 听从某人 ▶ **to listen to sth** 听某事 ▶ **listen!** (to a sound) 你听!; (pay attention to me) 听着! ▶ **to listen for** (also: **listen out for**) (BRIT) 注意听
▶ **listen in** VI ▶ **listen in on** or **to** (eavesdrop) 偷听 [tōutīng]

listener ['lɪsnə(r)] (RAD) N [C] 听众 [tīngzhòng] ▶ **to be a good listener** 会倾听的人

lit [lɪt] PT, PP of **light**

liter ['liːtə(r)] (US) N = **litre**

literacy ['lɪtərəsɪ] N [U] 读写能力 [dúxiě nénglì]

literal ['lɪtərəl] ADJ [+ sense, meaning] 字面的 [zìmiàn de]; [+ translation] 直译的 [zhíyì de]

literally ['lɪtrəlɪ] ADV **1** (used for emphasis) 确实地 [quèshí de] **2** [translate+] 逐字地 [zhúzì de]

literary ['lɪtərərɪ] ADJ [+ work, criticism, theory] 文学的 [wénxué de]; [+ word, expression, language] 书面的 [shūmiàn de]

literate ['lɪtərət] ADJ (able to read and write) 有读写能力的 [yǒu dúxiě nénglì de]; (well-educated) 有文化修养的 [yǒu wénhuà xiūyǎng de]

literature ['lɪtrɪtʃə(r)] N [U] **1** (novels, plays, poetry) 文学 [wénxué] **2** (printed information) 印刷品 [yìnshuāpǐn] **3** (publications) 文献 [wénxiàn]

Lithuania [lɪθju'eɪnɪə] (GEO) N 立陶宛 [Lìtáowǎn]

Lithuanian [lɪθju'eɪnɪən] I ADJ 立陶宛的 [Lìtáowǎn de] II N **1** [C] (person) 立陶宛人 [Lìtáowǎnrén] **2** [U] (language) 立陶宛语 [Lìtáowǎnyǔ]

litre, (US) liter ['liːtə(r)] N [C] 升 [shēng]

litter ['lɪtə(r)] I N **1** [U] (rubbish) 垃圾 [lājī] **2** [C] [+ of dogs, cats, pigs etc] 一窝 [yī wō] II VT 使…布满杂乱东西 [shǐ…bùmǎn záluàn dōngxi]

litter bin (BRIT) N [C] 垃圾箱 [lājīxiāng] [美= **trash can**]

littered ['lɪtəd] ADJ ▶ **littered with** [+ papers, debris] 胡乱堆满 [húluàn duīmǎn]; [+ mistakes, references] 布满 [bùmǎn]

⊙ **little** ['lɪtl] I ADJ **1** (small) [+ thing, person] 小的 [xiǎo de] ▷ *a little house* 小房子 **2** (young) [+ child] 小的 [xiǎo de] ▷ *a little boy of 8* 一个8岁的小男孩 **3** (younger) ▶ **little brother/sister** 弟弟/妹妹 [dìdi/mèimei] **4** (short) [+ distance, time, event] 短的 [duǎn de] ▷ *a little while longer* 过一段时间 ▷ *There is very little time left.* 只剩下很短的时间了。**5** (trivial) 琐碎的 [suǒsuì de] ▷ *Harry would often get angry over little things.* 哈利总是为琐事动怒。**6** (quantifier) ▶ **to have little time/money** 没有多少时间/金钱 [méiyǒu duōshao shíjiān/jīnqián] II ADV 少 [shǎo] ▷ *I have seen him very little recently.* 最近我很少见到他。▷ *We tried to interfere as little as possible.* 我们尽可能不干预。▶ **a little** (small amount) 一点 [yīdiǎn]; [sleep, eat+] 一点 ▷ *Try to persuade her to eat a little.* 试着劝她吃点东西。▶ **a little bit** (adj) 有点 ▶ **little by little** 逐渐地

> **little** 和 **a little** 都用在不可数名词前，但是意义不同。例如，如果说 **I have a little money**，这是一个肯定的表达，说明你有钱。然而，如果说 **I have little money**，它就是一个否定的表达，意思是基本上没钱。

little finger N [C] 小指 [xiǎozhǐ]

⊙ **live¹** [lɪv] I VI **1** (reside) (in house, town, country) 住 [zhù] ▷ *I used to live in Grange Road.* 我曾经住在格兰治山路。**2** (lead one's life) 生活 [shēnghuó] ▷ *people who live in poverty* 生活在贫困中的人们 **3** (survive) 活着 [huózhe] ▷ *Do you work to live or live to work?* 你是为活着而工作还是为工作而活着？▷ *We need water to live.* 我们需要水来维持生命。II VT [+ life] 过 [guò] ▷ *We can start living a normal life again.* 我们可以重新开始过正常的生活。▶ **to live by hunting/fishing** 以狩猎/捕鱼为生
▶ **live down** VT [+ defeat, error, failure] 使人淡忘 [shǐ rén dànwàng]
▶ **live for** VT FUS [不可拆分] [+ work, pleasure] 为…而生活 [wèi…ér shēnghuó]
▶ **live in** VI [student+] 住学校公寓 [zhù xuéxiào gōngyù]; [maid, nurse etc+] 住在雇主家里 [zhù

zài gùzhǔ jiāli]

▶ **live off** VT FUS [不可拆分] **1** [+ money] 靠…生活 [kào…shēnghuó] **2** [+ food] 以…为主食 [yǐ…wéi zhǔshí] ▷ We lived off fruit for a week. 我们一个星期都以水果为主食。**3** [+ parents etc] 依靠…生活 [yīkào…shēnghuó] ▷ I was living off my parents. 我依靠父母生活。

▶ **live on** Ⅰ VT FUS [不可拆分] **1** [+ money] 靠…维持生活 [kào…wéichí shēnghuó] ▷ I don't have enough money to live on. 我的钱不够维持生活。**2** [+ food] 以…为主食 [yǐ…wéi zhǔshí] ▷ The children live on chips. 孩子们把薯条当主食。Ⅱ VI (survive) (in memory, history) 留下印记 [liúxià yìnjì]

▶ **live out** VT **1** ▶ to live out one's days or life 度过一生 [dùguò yīshēng] **2** [+ dream, fantasy] 付诸实践 [fù zhū shíjiàn]

▶ **live through** VT FUS [不可拆分] [+ war, crisis etc] 历经 [lìjīng]

▶ **live together** VI 同居 [tóngjū]

▶ **live up** VT ▶ to live it up (inf) 狂欢 [kuánghuān]

▶ **live up to** VT FUS [不可拆分] [+ expectations] 符合 [fúhé]

▶ **live with** VT FUS [不可拆分] [+ partner] 与…同居 [yǔ…tóngjū]

○ **live²** [laɪv] Ⅰ ADJ **1** [+ animal, plant] 活的 [huó de] **2** [+ pictures, broadcast] 实况的 [shíkuàng de]; [+ performance] 现场的 [xiànchǎng de] **3** (ELEC) [+ wire] 带电的 [dàidiàn de] **4** [+ bullet] 未爆炸的 [wèi bàozhà de] Ⅱ ADV **1** [broadcast +] 实况地 [shíkuàng de] **2** [perform, play +] 现场地 [xiànchǎng de]

livelihood ['laɪvlɪhud] N [c/u] (source of income) 生计 [shēngjì]

lively ['laɪvlɪ] ADJ [+ person] 活泼的 [huópo de]; [+ place, event, discussion] 活跃的 [huóyuè de] ▶ to take a lively interest in sth (enthusiastic) 对某物有浓厚的兴趣

liven up ['laɪvn-] Ⅰ VT [+ place, discussion, evening etc] 使有生气 [shǐ yǒu shēngqì]; [+ person] 使活跃 [shǐ huóyuè] Ⅱ VI [place, discussion, evening, person etc +] 活跃起来 [huóyuè qǐlái]

liver ['lɪvə(r)] N [c] (ANAT) 肝脏 [gānzàng] **2** [c/u] (CULIN) 肝 [gān]

lives [laɪvz] NPL of life

livestock ['laɪvstɔk] N [u] 家畜 [jiāchù]

living ['lɪvɪŋ] Ⅰ ADJ [+ author, relative] 在世的 [zàishì de] Ⅱ N [u] (life) 生活 [shēnghuó] Ⅲ the living NPL 活着的人们 [huózhe de rénmen] ▶ for a living 作为谋生之道 ▶ to earn or make a/one's living 谋生 ▶ within living memory 就当今人们所能记住的

living room N [c] 起居室 [qǐjūshì]

lizard ['lɪzəd] N [c] 蜥蜴 [xīyì]

LMT (US) ABBR (= Local Mean Time) 地方平均时 [Dìfāng Píngjūnshí]

load [ləud] Ⅰ N [c] **1** (thing carried) [of person,

animal] 负荷 [fùhè]; [of vehicle] 装载量 [zhuāngzàiliàng] **2** (weight) 负重 [fùzhòng] **3** (ELEC) 负荷 [fùhè] **4** (workload) 工作量 [gōngzuòliàng] Ⅱ VT **1** (also: load up) [+ vehicle, ship etc] 装 [zhuāng] **2** (COMPUT) [+ program, data] 下载 [xiàzǎi] **3** [+ gun] 给…上子弹 [gěi…shàng zǐdàn]; [+ camera] 把胶卷装入 [bǎ jiāojuǎn zhuāngrù] ▶ loads of or a load of money/people (inf) 很多钱/人 ▶ a load of nonsense (inf) 一派胡言

loaded ['ləudɪd] ADJ **1** [+ gun] 装有子弹的 [zhuāngyǒu zǐdàn de] **2** [+ question, word] 别有用意的 [biéyǒu yòngyì de] **3** (inf) (rich) 很有钱的 [hěn yǒuqián de] ▶ to be loaded in favour of/against sb (biased) 一味地偏袒/反对某人 ▶ to be loaded with sth [+ goods] 满载某物 **4** [+ humour, irony] 充满某事 [chōngmǎn mǒushì]

loaf [ləuf] (pl loaves) Ⅰ N [c] (of bread) 一条(面包) [yītiáo (miànbāo)] Ⅱ VI (also: loaf about, loaf around) 闲逛 [xiánguàng] ▶ use your loaf! (BRIT: inf) 动动脑筋!

loan [ləun] Ⅰ N **1** [c] (sum of money) 贷款 [dàikuǎn] **2** [s] [of book, car, house etc] 借出 [jièchū] Ⅱ VT ▶ to loan sth (out) to sb [+ money, thing] 把某物借给某人 [bǎ mǒuwù jiègěi mǒurén] ▶ to be on loan (to/from sb/sth) (从某人/某处)借来 ▶ to give/offer sb the loan of sth 主动提出借给某人某物

loathe [ləuð] VT 憎恨 [zēnghèn] ▶ to loathe doing sth 极讨厌做某事

loaves [ləuvz] NPL of loaf

lobby ['lɔbɪ] Ⅰ N [c] **1** [of building] 大厅 [dàtīng] **2** (POL) (pressure group) 游说团 [yóushuìtuán] Ⅱ VT [+ MP, councillor] 游说 [yóushuì] Ⅲ VI ▶ to lobby for sth 为某事而游说 [wèi mǒushì ér yóushuì]

lobster ['lɔbstə(r)] N **1** [c] (ZOOL) 龙虾 [lóngxiā] **2** [c/u] (CULIN) 龙虾肉 [lóngxiāròu]

○ **local** ['ləukl] Ⅰ ADJ **1** [+ council, newspaper, library] 当地的 [dāngdì de]; [+ residents] 本地的 [běndì de] **2** (TEL) [+ call] 本地的 [běndì de] Ⅱ N [c] (BRIT: inf) (pub) 当地酒店 [dāngdì jiǔdiàn] Ⅲ the locals NPL (people) 当地人 [dāngdìrén]

local anaesthetic N [c/u] 局部麻醉 [júbù mázuì]

local authority (BRIT) N [c] 地方当局 [dìfāng dāngjú] [美= local government]

local government N **1** [u] (system) 地方政府 [dìfāng zhèngfǔ] **2** [c] (US) (organization) 地方当局 [dìfāng dāngjú] [英= local authority]

locally ['ləukəlɪ] ADV **1** (not nationally) 在地方 [zài dìfāng] **2** (in the neighbourhood) 在附近 [zài fùjìn]

local time N [u] 当地时间 [dāngdì shíjiān]

locate [ləu'keɪt] VT (frm) (find) [+ person, thing] 找到 [zhǎodào] ▶ to be located (frm) (situated) 位于

location [ləuˈkeɪʃən] N 1 [c] (place) 地点
[dìdiǎn] 2 [C/U] (CINE) 外景 [wàijǐng] 3 [C/U]
(setting) 位置 [wèizhi] 4 [c] (whereabouts) 位置
[wèizhi] ▶ on location (CINE) 外景拍摄

loch [lɒx] N [c] 湖 [hú]

lock [lɒk] I N [c] 1 [of door, drawer, suitcase] 锁
[suǒ] 2 (on canal) 水闸 [shuǐzhá] 3 (also: **lock
of hair**) 一绺头发 [yī liǔ tóufa] II VT 1 [+ door,
drawer, suitcase] 锁 [suǒ] 2 [+ screen]
锁 [suǒ] III VI 1 [door etc +] 锁得上 [suǒ de
shàng] 2 (jam) [wheels, knee, mechanism +] 卡住
[qiǎzhù] 3 ▶ **to lock (into place)** 挤住 [jǐzhù]
IV **locks** NPL (liter) (hair) 头发 [tóufa] ▶ **lock,
stock and barrel** 全部地
▶ **lock away** VT 1 [+ valuables] 将…锁藏起来
[jiāng…suǒcáng qǐlái] 2 [+ criminal] 把…关起
来 [bǎ…guān qǐlái]
▶ **lock in** VT [+ person, object] (in room, safe)
把…锁起来 [bǎ…suǒ qǐlái] ▶ **to lock sb in** 把
某人锁在屋里
▶ **lock out** VT 1 [+ person] (deliberately) 把…锁在
外面 [bǎ…suǒ zài wàimian] ▶ **to lock o.s. out**
把自己锁在外面 2 (IND) 不准工人进厂以威胁
工人接受条件
▶ **lock up** I VT 1 [+ house, car] 锁好 [suǒhǎo]
2 [+ criminal] 把…监禁起来 [bǎ…jiānjìn
qǐlái]; [+ mental patient] 把…关进精神病院
[bǎ…guānjìn jíngshénbìngyuàn] II VI 锁好门
窗 [suǒhǎo ménchuāng]

locked [lɒkt] ADJ 上了锁的 [shàngle suǒ de]

locker [ˈlɒkə(r)] N [c] 小柜 [xiǎoguì]

locksmith [ˈlɒksmɪθ] N [c] 锁匠 [suǒjiàng]

locomotive [ləukəˈməutɪv] N [c] (frm) 机车
[jīchē]

lodge [lɒdʒ] I VI 1 (person +) ▶ **to lodge (with)**
寄宿 [jìsù] 2 (get stuck) [bullet +] 射入 [shèrù]
II VT [+ complaint, protest, appeal] 提出 [tíchū]
III N [c] 1 (at entrance) 小屋 [xiǎowū] 2 (hunting
lodge) 小屋 [xiǎowū]

lodger [ˈlɒdʒə(r)] N [c] 房客 [fángkè]

lodging [ˈlɒdʒɪŋ] I N 1 [U] (accommodation)
宿处 [sùchù] II **lodgings** NPL 租住的房子
[zūzhù de fángzi]

loft [lɒft] N [c] 1 (attic) 阁楼 [gélóu]
2 (apartment) 顶楼公寓 [dǐnglóu gōngyù]

log [lɒg] I N [c] 1 (from tree) (trunk) 原木
[yuánmù]; (for fuel etc) 木柴 [mùchái] 2 (diary)
日志 [rìzhì] II N ABBR (= logarithm) (MATH) 对
数 [duìshù] III VT [+ event, fact] 记录 [jìlù] ▶ **to
keep a log (of sth)** 登记某事
▶ **log in, log on** (COMPUT) VI 登录 [dēnglù]
▶ **log into** (COMPUT) VT FUS [不可拆分] 登入
[dēngrù]
▶ **log out, log off** (COMPUT) VI 退出系统
[tuìchū xìtǒng]

logic [ˈlɒdʒɪk] N [U] 1 (PHILOSOPHY) 逻辑 [luójí]
2 (judgment) 逻辑性 [luójíxìng]

logical [ˈlɒdʒɪkl] ADJ [+ argument, analysis] 逻辑

的 [luójí de]; [+ conclusion, result] 合逻辑的 [hé
luójí de]; [+ course of action] 合乎情理的 [héhū
qínglǐ de] ▶ **it is logical to assume that...** 假
定…是合乎情理的

logistics [lɒˈdʒɪstɪks] NPL 后勤 [hòuqín]

logo [ˈləugəu] N [c] [of firm, organization] 标识
[biāozhì]

lollipop [ˈlɒlɪpɒp] N [c] 棒棒糖 [bàngbàngtáng]

lollipop lady (BRIT) N [c] 为保证儿童安全过
马路手持暂停指挥牌的女交通管理员

lollipop man (BRIT) (pl **lollipop men**) N [c] 为
保证儿童安全过马路手持暂停指挥牌的男交
通管理员

lolly [ˈlɒlɪ] (BRIT: inf) N [c] (lollipop) 棒棒糖
[bàngbàngtáng] see also **ice lolly**

London [ˈlʌndən] N 伦敦 [Lúndūn]

Londoner [ˈlʌndənə(r)] N [c] 伦敦人
[Lúndūnrén]

lone [ləun] ADJ [+ person, thing] 孤独的 [gūdú de]
▶ **a lone voice** 自持一个观点

loneliness [ˈləunlɪnɪs] N [U] 孤独 [gūdú]

lonely [ˈləunlɪ] ADJ 1 (sad) [+ person] 孤独的
[gūdú de]; [+ situation, period] 孤寂的 [gūjì de]
2 (unfrequented) [+ place] 人迹罕至的 [rénjì hǎn
zhì de]

loner [ˈləunə(r)] N [c] 喜独处的人 [xǐ dúchǔ
de rén]

⊙ **long** [lɒŋ] I ADJ 1 (in distance) [+ rope, hair, table,
tunnel etc] 长的 [cháng de] 2 (in time) [+ meeting,
discussion, film, time] 长的 [cháng de] ▷ It was a
long meeting. 这个会议很长。 3 (in words) [+ book,
poem] 长的 [cháng de] II ADV (time) 长久
[chángjiǔ] ▷ Have you been here long? 你在这
里时间长吗？ III VI ▶ **to long for sth/to do
sth** 渴望某物/做某事 [kěwàng mǒuwù/zuò
mǒushì] ▶ **how long is the tunnel?** 这个隧道
有多长？ ▶ **how long is the lesson?** 这节课多
长时间？ ▶ **6 metres long** 6米长 ▶ **the film is
three hours long** 这部电影长达3个小时 ▶ **all
day/night long** 整天/夜 ▶ **so** or **as long as**
(provided) 只要; (while) 在…同时 ▷ You can't
turn the heat off as long as the system is on. 在系统
开着的同时，不能中断供暖。 ▶ **he no longer
comes** or **he doesn't come any longer** 他不再来
了 ▶ **long ago** 很久以前 ▶ **long before/after**
很久以前/以后 ▶ **before long** (future) 不久
▷ They're bound to catch him before long. 不久，他
们一定会抓到他。; (past) 很快 ▷ Before long
we were all safely back home. 很快，我们就都安
全到家了。 ▶ **for long** 很久 ▶ **it won't take
long** 这不需花很多时间 ▶ **it won't be long
before/until...** 很快就… ▶ **I won't be long** 我
很快就来 ▶ **at long last** 终于 ▶ **a long way** 很
远 ▶ **so long!** (inf) 再见！ ▶ **the long and the
short of it is that...** 总而言之…

long-distance [lɒŋˈdɪstəns] I ADJ [+ journey,
phone call] 长途的 [chángtú de]; [+ race, runner]
长跑的 [chángpǎo de] II ADV [phone +] 通过长

途电话 [tōngguò chángtú diànhuà]

long-haul [ˈlɒŋhɔːl] ADJ [*flight, route*+] 长途的 [chángtú de]

longing [ˈlɒŋɪŋ] N [C/U] ▶ **longing (for)** (对…的) 渴望 [(duì…de) kěwàng]

longitude [ˈlɒŋgɪtjuːd] N [C/U] 经度 [jīngdù]
▶ **250 degrees longitude** 经度250度

long jump (SPORT) N ▶ **the long jump** 跳远 [tiàoyuǎn]

long-life [ˈlɒŋlaɪf] ADJ [+*milk*] 可长久保存的 [kě chángjiǔ bǎocún de]; [+*batteries, bulb*] 耐用的 [nàiyòng de]

long-sighted [ˈlɒŋˈsaɪtɪd] (BRIT) ADJ 远视的 [yuǎnshì de] [美=**far-sighted**]

long-standing [ˈlɒŋˈstændɪŋ] ADJ [+*tradition, problem, dispute*] 长期存在的 [chángqī cúnzài de]; [+*relationship*] 长久的 [chángjiǔ de]

long-term [ˈlɒŋtɜːm] ADJ [+*effects, prospects, future*] 长远的 [chángyuǎn de]; [+*plan, project, solution*] 长久的 [chángjiǔ de]; [+*memory*] 长期的 [chángqī de] ▶ **the long-term unemployed** 长期失业

long wave N [U] 长波 [chángbō]

loo [luː] (BRIT) *inf* N [C] 厕所 [cèsuǒ] [美=**bathroom**]

⊙look [lʊk] I VI 1 (*glance, gaze*) 看 [kàn] 2 (*search*) 找 [zhǎo] ▷ *Have you looked behind the sofa?* 你有没找沙发后面？ 3 (*seem, appear*) 看起来 [kànqǐlái] ▷ *He looked scared.* 他看起来害怕了。▷ *It looks all right to me.* 我看可以。II N 1 (*expression*) 表情 [biǎoqíng] ▷ *There was a worried look on his face.* 他脸上有一种担忧的表情。2 (*appearance*) 装扮 [zhuāngbàn] ▷ *the punk look* 朋克式装扮 III **looks** NPL (*appearance*) 外表 [wàibiǎo]; (*good looks*) 美貌 [měimào] ▶ **to look out of the window** 望向窗外 ▶ **to look south/onto the sea** [*building, window, garden*+] 面向南方/大海 ▶ **look (here)!** (*expressing annoyance etc*) 喂！ ▶ **look!** (*expressing surprise*) 看！ ▶ **look out!** 当心！ ▶ **to look like sb** (*in appearance*) 长得像某人 ▶ **it looks like Jim** (*it may be him*) 看起来像吉姆 ▶ **to look like sth** (*in appearance*) 看起来像某物 ▶ **it looks like rain** 看来要下雨了 ▶ **it looks as if...** 看来… ▷ *It looks about 4 metres long.* 看起来约4米长。 ▶ **to have** or **take a look at** (*examine*) 看一看; (*consider*) 细看 ▶ **to give sb a quizzical/puzzled look** 揶揄地/疑惑地看某人一眼 ▶ **to have a look for sth/sb** 找某物/某人 ▶ **by the look** or **looks of it** 根据外表来判断 ▶ **I don't like the look of it/him** 看它/他的样子就不舒服
▶ **look after** VT FUS [不可拆分] 1 (*care for*) 照顾 [zhàogù] 2 (*deal with*) 照管 [zhàoguǎn]
▶ **look ahead** VI (*in time*) 向前看 [xiàng qián kàn]
▶ **look around** = **look round**
▶ **look at** VT FUS [不可拆分] 1 (*gaze at*) 看一看 [kàn yī kàn] 2 (*consider*) [+*problem, subject etc*] 考

虑 [kǎolǜ]
▶ **look back** VI 1 (*think back*) 回顾 [huígù] ▷ *The past always seems better when you look back on it.* 当你回顾往事的时候，过去总是那么美好。 2 (*glance back*) 回头看 [huítóu kàn] ▶ **to look back at sth/sb** 回头看某物/某人 ▶ **looking back,...** 回想起来，…
▶ **look down on, look down upon** VT FUS [不可拆分] 轻视 [qīngshì]
▶ **look for** VT FUS [不可拆分] (*seek*) [+*person, thing*] 寻找 [xúnzhǎo]
▶ **look forward to** VT FUS [不可拆分] 盼望 [pànwàng] ▶ **to look forward to doing sth** 盼望做某事 ▶ **we look forward to hearing from you** 我们盼望收到你的回音
▶ **look in** VI ▶ **to look in on sb** 顺便看望某人 [shùnbiàn kànwàng mǒurén]
▶ **look into** VT FUS [不可拆分] (*investigate*) 调查 [diàochá] ▶ **to look into doing sth** 为做某事作调查准备
▶ **look on** I VI (*watch*) 旁观 [pángguān] II VT FUS [不可拆分] (*also:* **look upon**) (*consider*) 看待 [kàndài] ▷ *Employers look favourably on applicants who have work experience.* 雇主对有工作经验的申请者另眼看待。 ▶ **to look on sb as sth** 把某人当作某物看待
▶ **look out for** VT FUS [不可拆分] (*pay attention to*) 留心 [liúxīn]
▶ **look over** VT (*examine*) [+*document, essay*] 检查 [jiǎnchá]; [+*building*] 查看 [chákàn]
▶ **look round, look around** I VI 1 (*turn head*) 环顾 [huángù] 2 (*in building etc*) 看看 [kànkan] II VT FUS [不可拆分] [+*place, building*] 游览 [yóulǎn]
▶ **look through** VT FUS [不可拆分] [+*book, magazine, papers*] 翻阅 [fānyuè]
▶ **look to** VT FUS [不可拆分] ▶ **to look to sb for sth/to do sth** 指望某人提供某事/做某事 [zhǐwàng mǒurén tígōng mǒushì/zuò mǒushì]
▶ **look up** I VI 1 (*raise eyes*) 抬眼看 [tái yǎn kàn] 2 (*inf*) ▶ **things are looking up** 事情有好转了 [shìqíng yǒu hǎozhuǎn le] II VT 1 [+*information, meaning etc*] 查 [chá] 2 [+*person*] 看望 [kànwàng]
▶ **look upon** = **look on**
▶ **look up to** VT FUS [不可拆分] [+*hero, idol*] 敬佩 [jìngpèi]

lookout [ˈlʊkaʊt] I N [C] 1 (*person*) 看守 [kānshǒu] 2 (*place*) 瞭望台 [liàowàngtái] II CPD [复合词] [+*post, tower, point*] 瞭望 [liàowàng] ▶ **to be on the lookout for sth** 留心某事 ▶ **to keep a lookout (for sb/sth)** 密切注视(某人/某事)

loom [luːm] I VI 1 (*also:* **loom up**) [*object, shape*+] 隐隐出现 [yǐnyǐn chūxiàn] 2 [*event*+] 逼近 [bījìn] II N [C] (*for weaving*) 织布机 [zhībùjī] ▶ **to loom large** 赫然显现

loony [ˈluːnɪ] (*inf*) I ADJ 发疯的 [fāfēng de]

II N [c] 疯子 [fēngzi]

loop [lu:p] **I** N [c] **1** (in string, ribbon etc) 圈 [quān] **2** (COMPUT) 重复指令 [chóngfù zhǐlìng] **II** ▸ **to loop sth around/over sth** 把某物缠绕在某物上 [bǎ mǒuwù chánrào zài mǒuwù shang] **III** VI 环绕 [huánrào]

loophole ['lu:phəul] N [c] (in law) 漏洞 [lòudòng]

loose [lu:s] **I** ADJ **1** (not firm) [+ screw, connection, tooth] 松动的 [sōngdòng de] **2** (not tied back) [+ hair] 散开的 [sǎnkāi de] **3** (not tight) [+ clothes, trousers etc] 宽松的 [kuānsōng de]; [+ coalition, arrangement] 松散的 [sōngsǎn de] **4** (vague) [+ definition, translation] 不精确的 [bù jīngquè de] **5** (o.f.) (promiscuous) [+ woman, morals] 放荡的 [fàngdàng de] **II** N ▸ **to be on the loose** [prisoner, animal +] 行动不受限制 [xíngdòng bùshòu xiànzhì] **III** VT **1** (frm) (free) [+ animal, prisoner] 把…放开 [bǎ…fàngkāi] ▸ **to set sb/ sth loose** 释放某人/某物 ▸ **to let sb loose on sth** 放任某人做某事 ▸ **to break loose** 挣脱出来

loosely ['lu:slɪ] ADV **1** (hold, hang, tie +] 松散地 [sōngsǎn de] **2** [+ organized, arranged] 不周密地 [bù zhōumì de] **3** [define, translate +] 粗略地 [cūlüè de] ▸ **loosely speaking** 笼统地说

loosen ['lu:sn] VT **1** (undo) [+ screw, nuts] 拧松 [nǐngsōng]; [+ clothing, belt, tie etc] 松开 [sōngkāi] **2** (relax) [+ restrictions, laws] 放松 [fàngsōng] ▸ **to loosen one's grip on sth** [+ object] 对紧抓的某物稍稍松手; [+ power, people] 放松对某物的掌控

▸ **loosen up** VI **1** (exercise) 放松 [fàngsōng] **2** (relax) 松弛下来 [sōngchí xiàlái]

loot [lu:t] **I** VT [+ shops, homes] 洗劫 [xǐjié] **II** N [U] (inf) 掠夺品 [lüèduópǐn]

lopsided ['lɔp'saɪdɪd] ADJ (crooked) 歪斜的 [wāixié de]

lord [lɔːd] (BRIT) N [c] (peer) 贵族 [guìzú] ▸ **Lord Smith** 史密斯阁下 ▸ **the Lord** (REL) 上帝 ▸ **my lord** (BRIT) (to bishop, noble) 大人; (to judge) 阁下 ▸ **good Lord!** 我的天！ ▸ **the Lords** (BRIT) 上议院

lorry ['lɔrɪ] (BRIT) N [c] 卡车 [kǎchē] [美= **truck**]

lorry driver (BRIT) N [c] 卡车司机 [kǎchē sījī] [美= **truck driver**]

○ **lose** [lu:z] (pt, pp **lost**) **I** VT **1** (mislay) [+ keys, pen etc] 丢失 [diūshī] ▷ I lost my keys. 我把钥匙丢了。 **2** (not win) [+ contest, fight, argument] 输 [shū] **3** (be dismissed from) [+ job, place] 丢掉 [diūdiào] ▷ He lost his place in the team. 他丢掉了在队里的位置。 **4** (through death) [+ relative, wife etc] 失去 [shīqù] ▷ He had just lost his wife. 他刚刚失去了妻子。 **5** (waste) [+ time, opportunity] 浪费 [làngfèi] **6** (COMM) [+ money] 亏损 [kuīsǔn] ▷ The company was losing a million pounds a week. 该公司一个星期亏损100万英镑。 **7** (through injury, disease) [+ blood, tooth, leg] 失掉 [shīdiào]; [+ voice, sight etc] 丧失 [sàngshī] **8** (run out of)

[+ confidence, control etc] 丧失 [sàngshī] **9** (shake off) [+ pursuers] 摆脱 [bǎituō] ▷ He managed to lose his pursuers in the maze of streets. 在繁杂的街道上，他竭力摆脱了跟踪者。 **II** VI (in competition, argument) 输 [shū] ▸ **to lose o.s. in sth** 沉湎于某事 ▸ **to lose weight** 减重 ▸ **to lose no time in doing sth** 马上着手做某事 ▷ Bill lost no time in telling me about his idea. 比尔赶紧和我讲他的想法。 ▸ **to lose sight of sth** (no longer see) 看不见某物; (forget) 忽略某事

▸ **lose out** VI 受损失 [shòu sǔnshī]

loser ['lu:zə(r)] N [c] **1** (in game, contest) 失败者 [shībàizhě] **2** (inf) (failure) 不成器的人 [bù chéngqì de rén] ▸ **to be a good/bad loser** 输得起/不起的人

loss [lɔs] **I** N [c/u] **1** 丧失 [sàngshī] **2** [c/u] (death) 失去 [shīqù] **II losses** NPL (MIL) 伤亡 [shāngwáng] ▸ **loss of life** 丧生 ▸ **to make a loss** [company +] 亏损 ▸ **to sell sth at a loss** 亏本卖某物 ▸ **to cut one's losses** 赶紧罢手以免更大损失 ▸ **to be at a loss (as to how/why etc...)** (对如何/为何{等}…)不知所措

lost [lɔst] **I** PT, PP of **lose II** ADJ [+ object] 丢失的 [diūshī de]; [+ person, animal] 走失的 [zǒushī de] ▸ **to be lost** (having lost one's way) 迷路 ▸ **to get lost** (lose one's way) 迷路 ▸ **to feel lost** 不知所措 ▸ **get lost!** (inf) (go away) 走开！ ▸ **to be lost in thought** 陷入沉思 ▸ **to be lost on sb** [advice, words +] 对某人不起作用

lost and found (US) N = **lost property**

lost property N [U] **1** (things) 招领的失物 [zhāolǐng de shīwù] **2** (BRIT) (office) 失物招领处 [shīwù zhāolǐngchù] [美= **lost and found**]

○ **lot** [lɔt] N [c] **1** (set, group) (of papers, books, people etc) 批 [pī] ▷ We've just sacked one lot of builders. 我们刚刚解雇了一批建筑工人。 **2** (US) (land) 地皮 [dìpí] see also **parking lot 3** (at auction) 批件 [pījiàn] ▷ lot no. 359 批件号为359 **4** (destiny) 命运 [mìngyùn] ▷ attempts by the workers to improve their lot 工人为改变自身命运所做的努力 ▸ **a lot** (many) [of books etc] 许多 ▷ Have one of mine, I've got a lot. 给你一个吧，我有很多。; (much) [of money etc] 很多 ▷ We still owe quite a lot. 我们还是欠很多钱。 ▸ **a lot of** (many, much) 许多 ▷ a lot of people 许多人 ▷ I drink a lot of coffee. 我喝许多咖啡。 ▸ **lots of** [+ things, people] 许多 ▷ he reads/smokes a lot 他非常喜欢你 ▸ **the lot** (inf) (everything) 全部 ▷ She's taken the lot! 她全部都拿走了！ ▸ **they're a boring/friendly lot** (inf) 他们这些人很无聊/友好 ▸ **to draw lots** 抽签

lotion ['ləuʃən] N [c/u] 洗液 [xǐyè]

lottery ['lɔtərɪ] N [c] **1** (game) 彩票 [cǎipiào] **2** (fig) 难料的事 [nánliào de shì]

loud [laud] **I** ADJ **1** [+ noise, voice, laugh] 响亮的 [xiǎngliàng de] **2** (gaudy) [+ clothes] 俗艳的 [súyàn de] **II** ADV (speak etc +] 大声地 [dàshēng de] ▸ **out loud** [read, laugh etc +] 出声地 ▸ **to be**

loud in one's support/condemnation of sth 大力支持/强烈谴责某事

loudly ['laʊdlɪ] ADV 大声地 [dàshēng de]

loudspeaker [laʊd'spiːkə(r)] N [C] 1 扬声器 [yángshēngqì]

lounge [laʊndʒ] I N [C] 1 (in hotel) 休息室 [xiūxíshì] 2 (at airport, station) 等候室 [děnghòushì] 3 (ESP BRIT) (in house) 起居室 [qǐjūshì] 4 (BRIT) (also: **lounge bar**) 豪华酒吧 [háohuá jiǔbā] II VI 懒洋洋地倚靠着 [lǎnyángyáng de yǐkàozhe]
▶ **lounge about,** (BRIT) **lounge around** VI 闲逛 [xiánguàng] ▶ **to lounge around the house/pool** 在家/游泳池消磨时间

louse [laʊs] (pl **lice**) N [C] 虱子 [shīzi]
▶ **louse up** (inf) VT 搞糟 [gǎozāo]

lousy ['laʊzɪ] (inf) ADJ [+ show, meal, weather etc] 糟糕的 [zāogāo de]; [+ cook, singer, teacher etc] 蹩脚的 [biéjiǎo de] ▶ **to feel lousy** (ill) 感觉不舒服

lout [laʊt] N [C] 粗人 [cūrén]

lovable ['lʌvəbl] ADJ 可爱的 [kě'ài de]

○ **love** [lʌv] I N [U] 1 (for partner, sweetheart) 爱情 [àiqíng]; (for child, pet) 爱 [ài] ▷ my love for my children 我对孩子的爱 2 (BRIT: inf) (term of address) 对不相识者的客气称呼 ▷ Are you OK, love? 你没事吧? II VT [+ partner, child, pet] 爱 [ài] ▷ I love you. 我爱你。; [+ thing, food, activity] 热爱 [rè'ài] ▶ **sb's love for sb** 某人对某人的爱 ▶ **to be in love (with sb)** (与某人)恋爱 ▶ **to fall in love (with sb)** 爱上(某人) ▶ **to make love** 做爱 ▶ **love at first sight** 一见钟情 ▶ **love (from) Anne** (on letter) 爱你的, 安妮 ▶ **to send one's love to sb** 向某人问候 ▶ **a love of music/football/animals** 对音乐/足球/动物的热爱 ▶ "**15 love**" (TENNIS) 15比0 ▶ **to love doing/to do sth** 喜爱做某事 ▶ **I'd love to come** 我非常想来 ▶ **I'd love you to come** or **I'd love it if you came** 你要是来真是太好了

   ▦用法参见 **nought**

love affair N [C] 风流韵事 [fēngliú yùnshì]

love life N [C/U] 爱情生活 [àiqíng shēnghuó]

lovely ['lʌvlɪ] (ESP BRIT) ADJ 1 (beautiful) [+ place, person, music etc] 漂亮的 [piàoliang de] 2 (delightful) [+ holiday, meal, present] 令人愉快的 [lìng rén yúkuài de]; [+ person] 可爱的 [kě'ài de] ▶ **how lovely to see you!** 见到你真是高兴!

lover ['lʌvə(r)] N [C] 1 (sexual partner) 情人 [qíngrén] 2 (liter) (person in love) 情侣 [qínglǚ] ▶ **a lover of art** or **an art lover** 钟爱艺术的人

loving ['lʌvɪŋ] ADJ [+ person] 表示爱的 [biǎoshì ài de]; [+ relationship] 充满爱的 [chōngmǎn ài de]; [+ care, support] 细心周到的 [xìxīn zhōudào de] ▶ **in loving memory of...** 充满爱意地追念…

○ **low** [ləʊ] I ADJ 1 (not tall) [+ wall, hill, heel etc] 矮的 [ǎi de] 2 (not high up) [+ ceiling, shelf, sun,

neckline] 低的 [dī de] 3 (deep) [+ bow, curtsey] 深的 [shēn de] 4 (in degree) [+ temperature, price, level, speed etc] 低的 [dī de] 5 (in intensity) [+ heat, light, volume] 低的 [dī de] 6 (poor) [+ standard, quality] 低劣的 [dīliè de] ▷ work of very low quality 质量低劣的工作 ▷ The standard of child care is very low in many homes. 在许多家庭里, 对孩子的照顾是不足的。 7 (low-pitched) [+ voice, note] 低音的 [dīyīn de] ▷ a long low note 长长的低音音调 8 (quiet) [+ voice, whisper, murmur] 低声的 [dīshēng de] 9 (depressed) [+ person, morale] 情绪低落的 [qíngxù dīluò de] ▷ I was really low after my father died. 我父亲去世以后, 我的情绪非常低落。 II ADV [fly+] [低] ▷ I asked him to fly low over the beach. 我让他在海滩上方低飞。 III N [C] 1 (MET) 低气压区 [dīqìyāqū] 2 (low point) 低点 [dīdiǎn] ▶ **to be/run low on sth** 快用完某物 ▶ **low in calories/salt/fat** 低卡路里/盐/脂肪

low-alcohol ['ləʊ'ælkəhɒl] ADJ [+ wine, beer] 低度酒的 [dīdùjiǔ de]

low-calorie ['ləʊ'kælərɪ] ADJ [+ food] 低卡路里的 [dī kǎlùlǐ de]

lower ['ləʊə(r)] I VT 1 ▶ **to lower sth into/to/onto sth** 把某物向下移到某物里/上 [bǎ mǒuwù xiàngxià yídào mǒuwù lǐ/shang] 2 (reduce) [+ rate, level, price etc] 降低 [jiàngdī] 3 (make less loud) [+ voice] 放低 [fàngdī]; [+ volume] 减弱 [jiǎnruò] 4 (bow) [+ head, eyes] 低垂 [dīchuí] II ADJ 1 (bottom) [+ deck, lip] 下层的 [xiàcéng de] 2 (less important) [+ court, rank] 下级的 [xiàjí de] ▶ **the lower sixth** (BRIT: SCOL) 中学六年级 ▶ **to lower o.s. into a chair/onto a bed** 屈身坐在椅子/躺在床上

low-fat ['ləʊ'fæt] ADJ [+ food, yogurt, diet] 低脂肪的 [dī zhīfáng de]

loyal ['lɔɪəl] ADJ [+ friend, supporter, customer etc] 忠实的 [zhōngshí de] ▶ **to be/remain loyal to sb** 对某人保持忠诚

loyalty ['lɔɪəltɪ] N [U] 忠诚 [zhōngchéng] ▶ **sb's loyalty to sb** 对某人的忠诚 ▶ **out of loyalty to sb** 出于对某人的忠诚 ▶ **to have strong/divided loyalties** 非常忠诚/部分的忠诚

LP N ABBR (= **long-playing record**) 慢转密纹唱片 [mànzhuǎn mìwén chàngpiàn]

L-plates ['ɛlpleɪts] (BRIT: AUT) NPL L车牌(以提示其他司机该车由学员驾驶员驾驶)

   ● **L-PLATES**

按照英国法律, 学员驾驶员在未通过考试以前, 要在他驾驶的任何车辆前后贴上 **L-plate** 标志。**L-plate** 是塑料或金属的方形牌子、白底、带有一个大大的红色 **L**(意为 **learner**)。学员驾驶员驾驶车辆时, 必须有合格的司机陪同。在通过考试前, 驾车上高速公路是违法的。

LSAT (US) N ABBR (= *Law School Admissions Test*) 法学院入学考试 [Fǎxuéyuàn Rùxué Kǎoshì]

Ltd (COMM) ABBR (= *limited company*) 股份有限公司 [gǔfèn yǒuxiàn gōngsī]

lubricate ['lu:brɪkeɪt] VT [+ *part of machine, chain etc*] 给…上油 [gěi…shàngyóu]

luck [lʌk] N [U] **1** (*chance*) 运气 [yùnqì] **2** (*good fortune*) 幸运 [xìngyùn] ▶ **good luck** 好运 ▶ **good luck!** or **best of luck!** 祝你好运! ▶ **bad luck** 不走运 ▶ **bad** or **hard** or **tough luck!** (*showing sympathy*) 真不走运! ▶ **hard** or **tough luck!** (*not showing sympathy*) 活该倒霉! ▶ **to be in luck** 走运 ▶ **to be out of luck** 不走运 ▶ **to have no luck (doing sth)** 没有(做某事的)运气 ▶ **to try one's luck (at sth/at doing sth)** 碰碰(某事/做某事的)运气 ▶ **with (any) luck** 如果幸运的话

luckily ['lʌkɪlɪ] ADV 幸运地 [xìngyùn de shì] ▶ **luckily for me/us** 我/我们挺运气的

lucky ['lʌkɪ] ADJ **1** [+ *person*] 幸运的 [xìngyùn de] **2** [+ *charm, number*] 吉祥的 [jíxiáng de] ▶ **to be lucky** [*person* +] 走运 ▶ **I'm lucky to be alive** 我很庆幸我活着 ▶ **to be lucky enough to do sth** 有幸做某事 ▶ **it is lucky that...** 侥幸的是… ▶ **today's your lucky day** 今天是你的吉日 ▶ **to have a lucky escape** 侥幸逃脱 ▶ **lucky break** 命运的转机 ▶ **you'll be lucky!** (*inf*) 你会有好运的! ▶ **you'll be lucky if...** (*inf*) 如果…就算你走运了

lucrative ['lu:krətɪv] ADJ [+ *contract, business, market*] 有利的 [yǒulì de]

ludicrous ['lu:dɪkrəs] ADJ (*ridiculous*) [+ *situation, idea, price etc*] 荒唐的 [huāngtáng de] ▶ **it is ludicrous to suggest that...** 建议…真是荒唐 ▶ **it's ludicrous that...** …真是荒唐

luggage ['lʌgɪdʒ] N [U] 行李 [xíngli] ▶ **piece of luggage** 一件行李

luggage rack N [C] **1** (*in train, coach*) 行李架 [xínglijià] **2** (US) (*on car*) 车顶架 [chēdǐngjià] [英= **roof rack**]

lukewarm ['lu:kwɔ:m] ADJ **1** (*tepid*) 微温的 [wēiwēn de] **2** (*unenthusiastic*) [+ *reaction, welcome*] 冷淡的 [lěngdàn de] ▶ **to be lukewarm about sth/doing sth** 对某事/做某事热情不高 ▶ **to be lukewarm towards sb** 对某人不冷不热

lull [lʌl] **I** N [C] (*break*) (*in conversation, fighting etc*) 间歇 [jiànxiē] **II** VT ▶ **to lull sb to sleep** [*sound, motion* +] 哄某人睡觉 [hǒng mǒurén shuìjiào] ▶ **to be lulled into sth/doing sth** 被哄得产生某事/被哄得做某事

lullaby ['lʌləbaɪ] N [C] 催眠曲 [cuīmiánqǔ]

lumber ['lʌmbə(r)] **I** N [U] **1** (ESP US) (*wood*) 木材 [mùcái] [英= **timber**] **2** (BRIT: *o.f.*) (*junk*) 废旧杂物 [fèijiù záwù] **II** VI ▶ **to lumber into view/across the square** [*person, animal* +] 笨重缓慢地走进视野/通过广场

[bènzhòng huǎnmàn de zǒujìn shìyě/tōngguò guǎngchǎng]; [*truck, tank* +] 缓缓地移动进入视野/穿过广场 [huǎnhuǎn de yídòng jìnrù shìyě/chuānguò guǎngchǎng]
▶ **lumber with** VT (BRIT: *inf*) ▶ **to be/get lumbered with sb/sth** 为某人/某事所累 [wèi mǒurén/mǒushì suǒlěi] ▶ **to be/get lumbered with doing sth** 苦于无奈做某事

luminous ['lu:mɪnəs] ADJ **1** [+ *hands, dial, paint, etc*] 发光的 [fāguāng de] ▷ *the luminous dial on the clock* 钟表上的夜光指针 **2** (*bright*) 明亮的 [míngliàng de]

lump [lʌmp] **I** N [C] **1** (*piece*) [*of clay, butter, wood, sugar etc*] 块 [kuài] **2** (*protrusion*) (*on body*) 肿块 [zhǒngkuài] **II** VT ▶ **to lump together** (*inf*) [+ *things, places*] 杂凑在一起 [zácòu zài yìqǐ]; [+ *people*] 混在一起 [hùn zài yìqǐ]

lump sum N [C] 一次性付的钱 [yīcìxìng fù de qián]

lumpy ['lʌmpɪ] ADJ [+ *rice, sauce*] 多块的 [duōkuài de]; [+ *bed, mattress*] 凹凸不平的 [āotū bùpíng de]

lunar ['lu:nə(r)] ADJ [+ *landscape, module, landing etc*] 月的 [yuè de]

lunatic ['lu:nətɪk] **I** N [C] **1** (*inf*) (*fool*) 疯子 [fēngzi] **2** (*o.f.*) (*mentally ill*) 精神失常者 [jīngshén shīchángzhě] **II** ADJ [+ *behaviour*] 疯的 [fēng de]

lunch [lʌntʃ] **I** N **1** [C/U] (*meal*) 午餐 [wǔcān] **2** [U] (*lunchtime*) 午餐时间 [wǔcān shíjiān] **II** VI (*frm*) 吃午饭 [chī wǔfàn] ▶ **to have lunch (with sb)** (与某人)共进午餐 ▶ **to have sth for lunch** 午餐吃某物 ▶ **to invite sb to lunch** 邀请某人共进午餐
用法参见 **meal**

lunch break N [C] 午休时间 [wǔxiū shíjiān] ▶ **to be on one's lunch break** 在午休

lunch hour N [C] = **lunch break**

lunchtime ['lʌntʃtaɪm] N [C/U] 午餐时间 [wǔcān shíjiān] ▶ **at lunchtime** 午休时候

lung [lʌŋ] N [C] 肺 [fèi]

lure [luə(r)] **I** VT (*entice, tempt*) ▶ **to lure sb into/to sth** 引诱某人进入某处/做某事 [yǐnyòu mǒurén jìnrù mǒuchù/zuò mǒushì] **II** N [C] **1** (*attraction*) 魅力 [mèilì] **2** (FISHING, HUNTING) 饵 [ěr] ▶ **lure away** VT 诱惑 [yòuhuò]

lurk [lə:k] VI **1** [*animal, person* +] 暗藏 [àncáng] **2** (*fig*) [*danger, suspicion, doubt* +] 潜伏 [qiánfú]

lush [lʌʃ] ADJ [+ *fields, gardens*] 茂盛的 [màoshèng de]; [+ *grass, vegetation*] 繁茂的 [fánmào de]

lust [lʌst] **I** N **1** [U] (*sexual*) 性欲 [xìngyù] **2** [U/S] ▶ **lust for money/power/revenge** 金钱/权力/复仇欲 [jīnqián/quánlì/fùchóu yù] **II** VI **1** ▶ **to lust after sb** 贪恋某人 [tānliàn mǒurén] **2** ▶ **to lust for** or **after sth** [+ *power, money*] 对某物有强烈的欲望 [duì mǒuwù yǒu qiángliè de yùwàng]

Luxembourg ['lʌksəmbəːg] (GEO) N 卢森堡 [Lúsēnbǎo]

luxurious [lʌg'zjuərɪəs] ADJ [+ hotel, surroundings, lifestyle] 豪华的 [háohuá de]

luxury ['lʌkʃərɪ] I N 1 [U] (comfort) 奢华 [shēhuá] 2 [C] (extra) 奢侈品 [shēchǐpǐn] 3 [S] (pleasure) 奢侈享受 [shēchǐ xiǎngshòu] II CPD [复合词] [+ hotel, car, goods etc] 豪华 [háohuá] ▶ to live in luxury 过奢华的生活 ▶ it's a

luxury (for me/us) to be able to lie in (对我/我们来说) 睡懒觉简直是一种奢侈

LW (RAD) ABBR (= long wave) 长波 [chángbō]

Lycra® ['laɪkrə] I N [U] 莱卡 [Láikǎ] II CPD [复合词] [+ clothes, shorts] 莱卡 [Láikǎ]

lying ['laɪɪŋ] I VB see lie¹ see lie² II N [U] 说谎 [shuōhuǎng] III ADJ 好说谎的 [hào shuōhuǎng de]

lyric ['lɪrɪk] I ADJ [+ poetry] 抒情的 [shūqíng de] II lyrics NPL [of song] 词句 [cíjù]

Mm

M¹, m¹ [ɛm] **I** N (letter) 英语的第十三个字母 **II** ABBR (= male) 男性 [nánxìng]

M² **I** ABBR (= medium) 中等的 [zhōngděng de] **II** N ABBR (BRIT) (= motorway) ▶ the M1 1号高速公路 [yīhào gāosù gōnglù]

m² ABBR **1** (= metres) 米 [mǐ] **2** (= million) 百万 [bǎiwàn]

MA N ABBR (= Master of Arts) (qualification) 文学硕士学位 [wénxué shuòshì xuéwèi]; (person) 文学硕士 [wénxué shuòshì]

ma [mɑ:] (inf) N [c] 妈 [mā]

mac [mæk] (BRIT) N [c] 雨衣 [yǔyī]

macaroni [mækə'rəunɪ] N [U] 通心粉 [tōngxīnfěn] ▶ macaroni cheese or (US) macaroni and cheese 干酪通心粉布丁

Macedonia [mæsɪ'dəunɪə] N 马其顿 [Mǎqídùn]

Macedonian [mæsɪ'dəunɪən] **I** ADJ 马其顿的 [Mǎqídùn de] **II** N **1** [c] (person) 马其顿人 [Mǎqídùnrén] **2** [U] (language) 马其顿语 [Mǎqídùnyǔ]

machine [mə'ʃi:n] **I** N [c] **1** 机器 [jīqì] **2** (system) [party, war, propaganda] 机构 [jīgòu] **3** (automaton) 自动装置 [zìdòng zhuāngzhì] **II** VT **1** (TECH) 机械加工 [jīxiè jiāgōng] **2** [+ dress etc] 用缝纫机制作 [yòng féngrènjī zhìzuò] ▶ by machine 用机器制造

machine gun N 机关枪 [jīguānqiāng]

machinery [mə'ʃi:nərɪ] N [U] **1** 机器 [jīqì] **2** (of government) 体系 [tǐxì]

machine washable [-'wɔʃəbl] ADJ 可机洗的 [kě jīxǐ de]

macho ['mætʃəu] ADJ [+ man, attitude, approach] 大男子气概的 [dànánzǐ qìgài de]

mackerel ['mækrl] N [c/U] (pl mackerel) 鲭鱼 [qīngyú]

mackintosh ['mækɪntɔʃ] (BRIT) N [c] 雨衣 [yǔyī]

mad [mæd] ADJ **1** (insane) 精神失常的 [jīngshén shīcháng de] **2** (foolish) 愚蠢的 [yúchǔn de] **3** (wild) 疯狂的 [fēngkuáng de] **4** (inf) (angry) 恼怒的 [nǎonù de] ▶ to go mad (inf) (go insane) 发疯; (= get angry) 发火 ▶ you are/must be mad (to do that) 你(那么做)准是犯傻了 ▶ to drive sb mad (inf) 逼得某人发疯 ▶ to be mad at sb (inf) 对某人很恼火 ▶ to be mad about or on sth (inf) 狂热地爱好某物 ▶ to be mad about or on sb (inf) 迷恋某人 ▶ like mad (inf) 拼命

Madagascar [mædə'gæskə(r)] N 马达加斯加 [Mǎdájiāsījiā]

madam ['mædəm] N **1** (form of address) 女士 [nǚshì] **2** [c] (ESP BRIT) (child) 任性的大小姐 [rènxìngde dàxiǎojiě] ▶ Madam Chairman/Speaker 主席/议长女士 ▶ Dear Madam 尊敬的女士

mad cow disease (ESP BRIT) N [U] (BSE) 疯牛病 [fēngniúbìng]

made [meɪd] **I** PT, PP of make **II** ADJ ▶ a British-made car 一辆英国制造的汽车 [yīliàng Yīngguó zhìzào de qìchē]

made-to-measure ['meɪdtə'mɛʒə(r)] (BRIT) ADJ 量身定做的 [liángshēn dìngzuò de]

made-up ['meɪdʌp] ADJ **1** (wearing make-up) 化了妆的 [huàlezhuāng de] [word, name, story] **2** (invented) 编造的 [biānzào de]

madly ['mædlɪ] ADV **1** (frantically) [grin, scream, rush +] 疯狂地 [fēngkuáng de] **2** (extremely) [+ jealous, angry] 极其地 [jíqí de] ▶ madly in love 深深地爱恋

madman ['mædmən] (pl madmen) N [c] 疯子 [fēngzi] ▶ like a madman 像个疯子一样

madness ['mædnɪs] N [U] **1** (insanity) 疯狂 [fēngkuáng] **2** (foolishness) 愚蠢 [yúchǔn] ▶ it would be madness to do that 那么做真是愚蠢之极

Mafia ['mæfɪə] N ▶ the Mafia 黑手党 [Hēishǒudǎng]

mag [mæg] (BRIT: inf) N (magazine) 杂志 [zázhì]

magazine [mægə'zi:n] N [c] **1** (PUBLISHING, RAD, TV) 杂志 [zázhì] **2** (of firearm) 弹匣 [dànxiá] **3** (MIL) (store) 弹药库 [dànyàokù]

maggot ['mægət] N [c] 蛆 [qū]

magic ['mædʒɪk] **I** N [U] **1** (supernatural power) 魔法 [mófǎ] **2** (wonder) 魔力 [mólì] **3** (conjuring) 魔术 [móshù] **II** ADJ **1** [+ formula, solution, cure] 神奇的 [shénqí de] **2** (special) [+ place, moment, experience] 迷人的 [mírén de] **3** (supernatural)

魔法的 [mófǎ de] ▶ **as if by/like magic** 不可思议 ▶ **the magic number/word** 神奇数字/咒语

magical ['mædʒɪkl] ADJ **1** (supernatural) 魔力的 [mólì de] **2** (wonderful) 迷人的 [mírén de]

magician [mə'dʒɪʃən] N [c] (wizard, conjurer) 魔术师 [móshùshī]

magistrate ['mædʒɪstreɪt] N [c] 地方法官 [dìfāng fǎguān]

magnet ['mægnɪt] N [c] **1** 磁铁 [cítiě] **2** ▶ **a magnet for** (attraction) 吸引物 [xīyǐnwù]

magnetic [mæg'nɛtɪk] ADJ **1** (PHYS) 有磁性的 [yǒu cíxìng de] **2** [+ tape, strip, disk] 磁的 [cí de] **2** [+ personality] 有魅力的 [yǒu mèilì de]

magnificent [mæg'nɪfɪsnt] ADJ (excellent) [+ book, painting] 极棒的 [jíbàng de]; (impressive) [+ work, performance] 出色的 [chūsè de]; (beautiful) [+ building, view, costume] 华丽的 [huálì de]

magnify ['mægnɪfaɪ] VT **1** (enlarge) [+ object] 放大 [fàngdà] **2** (amplify) [+ sound] 扩大 [kuòdà] **3** (increase) 加强 [jiāqiáng]

magnifying glass ['mægnɪfaɪɪŋ-] N [c] 放大镜 [fàngdàjìng]

magpie ['mægpaɪ] N [c] 喜鹊 [xǐquè]

mahogany [mə'hɔgənɪ] I N [u] 红木 [hóngmù] II CPD [复合词] [+ table, desk] 红木 [hóngmù]

maid [meɪd] N [c] (servant) 女仆 [nǚpú]

maiden name ['meɪdn-] N [c] 娘家姓 [niángjiā xìng]

mail [meɪl] I N [u] **1** ▶ **the mail** (the post) 邮政 [yóuzhèng] **2** (letters) 邮件 [yóujiàn] **3** (e-mail) 电子邮件 [diànzǐ yóujiàn] II VT **1** (ESP US) (post) 寄出 [jìchū] [英= **post**] **2** (e-mail) 发电邮给 [fā diànyóu gěi] ▶ **your cheque is in the mail** 你的支票已寄出 ▶ **by mail** 以邮寄方式

mailbox ['meɪlbɔks] N [c] **1** (US) (for letters etc) 信箱 [xìnxiāng] [英= **letterbox**] **2** (US) 邮筒 [yóutǒng] [英= **post box**] **3** (COMPUT) 电子信箱 [diànzǐ xìnxiāng]

mailing list ['meɪlɪŋ-] N [c] 邮寄名单 [yóujì míngdān]

mailman ['meɪlmæn] (pl **mailmen**) (US) N [c] 邮差 [yóuchāi] [英= **postman**]

mail order I N [u] (system) 邮购 [yóugòu] II CPD [复合词] ▶ **mail-order** [+ firm, catalogue] 邮购的

mailwoman ['meɪlwumən] (pl **mailwomen**) (US) N [c] 女邮递员 [nǚ yóudìyuán] [英= **postwoman**]

⊙ **main** [meɪn] I ADJ [+ reason, place, entrance, meal] 主要的 [zhǔyào de] ▷ My main concern is to protect the children. 保护孩子们是我主要关心的事。▷ Mrs Foster hurried through the main entrance. 福斯特太太匆匆忙忙地从主入口进来了。II N [c] (pipe) [+ water, gas] 总管道 [zǒng guǎndào] ▷ A bulldozer has severed a gas main. 推土机切断了一条煤气总管道。▶ **in the main** (in general) 大体上

main course N [c] 主菜 [zhǔcài]

mainland ['meɪnlənd] I N ▶ **the mainland** 大陆 [dàlù] II ADJ 大陆的 [dàlù de]

mainly ['meɪnlɪ] ADV 主要地 [zhǔyào de]

main road N [c] 主干道 [zhǔ gàndào]

mains [meɪnz] I NPL (ELEC) 总输送网 [zǒng shūsòng wǎng] II CPD [复合词] [+ electricity, water, drainage] 干线 [gànxiàn]

mainstream ['meɪnstriːm] I N ▶ **the mainstream** 主流 [zhǔliú] II ADJ [+ cinema, politics etc] 主流的 [zhǔliú de]

main street (US) N [c] 大街 [dàjiē] [英= **high street**]

maintain [meɪn'teɪn] VT **1** (preserve) [+ friendship, peace] 保持 [bǎochí] **2** (keep up) [+ momentum, output] 维持 [wéichí] **3** (look after) [+ building, equipment] 保养 [bǎoyǎng] **4** (affirm) [+ belief, opinion, innocence] 坚持 [jiānchí] **5** (provide for) [+ dependant] 赡养 [shànyǎng] ▶ **to maintain that...** 坚称… ▶ **to maintain o.s.** 养活自己

maintenance ['meɪntənəns] N [u] **1** (running) [of building, equipment] 保养 [bǎoyǎng] **2** (preservation) [of peace, system] 维持 [wéichí] **3** (LAW) (alimony) 赡养费 [shànyǎng fèi]

maize [meɪz] (ESP BRIT) N [u] 玉米 [yùmǐ] [美= **corn**]

majestic [mə'dʒɛstɪk] ADJ 壮观的 [zhuàngguān de]

majesty ['mædʒɪstɪ] N **1** (title) ▶ **Your/His/Her Majesty** 陛下 [bìxià] **2** (u) (splendour) 雄伟 [xióngwěi]

⊙ **major** ['meɪdʒə(r)] I ADJ **1** (important, significant) [+ event, factor] 重要的 [zhòngyào de] ▷ Exercise has a major part to play in preventing disease. 锻炼对于预防疾病有重要作用。**2** (MUS) [+ key, scale] 大调 [dàdiào] II N [c] **1** (MIL) 少校 [shàoxiào] **2** (US: SCOL) (main subject) 专业 [zhuānyè] **3** ▶ **a history major** (US: SCOL) (student) 历史专业学生 [lìshǐ zhuānyè xuéshēng] III VI ▶ **to major in sth** (US: SCOL) 主修某专业 [zhǔxiū mǒu zhuānyè] ▷ I decided to major in French. 我决定主修法语。▶ **(symphony/concerto) in C major** C大调（交响乐/协奏曲）

majority [mə'dʒɔrɪtɪ] I N **1** [s + PL VB] [of people, things] 大多数 [dàduōshù] **2** (margin) [of votes] 多数票 [duōshù piào] **3** (u) (adulthood) 成年 [chéngnián] II CPD [复合词] [+ verdict, holding] 多数 [duōshù] ▶ **to be in a or the majority** 占多数 ▶ **the (vast) majority of...** （绝）大多数…

⊙ **make** [meɪk] (pt, pp **made**) I VT **1** (produce, form) [+ object, clothes, cake] 做 [zuò] ▷ Sheila makes her own bread. 希拉自己做面包。; [+ noise] 制造 [zhìzào] ▷ We made a terrible racket as we came out of the club. 我们大声喧哗着走出了夜总会。; [+ speech] 发表 [fābiǎo] ▷ He made a speech about the need for unity. 他发表了有关统一之必

要的演讲。; [+ *remark, suggestion*] 提出 [tíchū] ▷ *May I make a suggestion?* 我能提个建议吗?; [+ *mistake*] 犯 [fàn] ▷ *You have made a terrible mistake.* 你犯了个严重的错误。**2** (*manufacture*) [+ *goods*] 生产 [shēngchǎn] ▷ *The firm makes a wide range of electrical goods.* 这家公司生产各种电器产品。**3** (*cause to be*) ► **to make sb sad** 使某人难过 [shǐ mǒurén nánguò] ▷ *The whole business makes me really angry.* 整件事使我实在恼火。**4** ► **to make sb famous** 使某人成名 [shǐ mǒurén chéngmíng] ▷ *James Bond, the role that made Sean Connery a star* 詹姆士·邦德,这个使肖恩·康纳利成名的角色 **5** ► **to make sth into sth** 将某物改成某物 [jiāng mǒuwù gǎichéng mǒuwù] ▷ *a disused factory that was made into an art gallery* 一座废弃的工厂被改成了美术馆 **6** (*force*) ► **to make sb do sth** 促使某人做某事 [cùshǐ mǒurén zuò mǒushì] **7** (*earn*) [+ *money*] 挣 [zhèng] ▷ *He was making nine hundred dollars a week.* 他一周挣900美元。**8** (*equal*) ► **2 and 2 make 4** 2加2等于4 [èrjiā'èr děngyú sì] **9** [+ *friend, enemy*] 结交 [jiéjiāo] ▷ *I made some good friends at the conference.* 我在会上结交了一些好朋友。▷ *On his first day at school he made friends with a girl called Janet.* 他上学的头一天结交了一位叫珍妮特的女孩。**10** (*cause to be successful*) 使成功 [shǐ chénggōng] ▷ *What really makes the book are the illustrations.* 真正使这本书成功的是它的插图。▷ *Meeting you has really made my day!* 能认识你实在是我今天最高兴的事! **11** (*be, constitute*) 成为 [chéngwéi] ▷ *She'll make a good teacher.* 她将会成为一名好老师。**II** N [c] (*brand*) 牌子 [páizi] ▷ *She couldn't tell what make of car he was driving.* 她看不出他开的是辆什么牌子的车。► **to make a profit/loss** 赢利/赔钱 ► **to make one's bed** 铺床 ► **to make a fool of sb** 愚弄某人 ► **to make it** (*arrive*) 及时抵达; (*succeed*) 达成目标; (*in life*) 成功 ► **what time do you make it?** 你表几点了? ► **to make good** (*succeed*) 有成就 ▷ *He was born poor but made good and went to the States.* 他出身贫苦,但后来颇有成就并去了美国。; (*carry out*) [+ *threat, promise*] 履行 ▷ *Arkoff made good his promise.* 阿考夫履行了他的诺言。; (*put right*) [+ *damage, loss*] 弥补 ▷ *Three years was a short time in which to make good the deficiencies.* 用3年时间弥补亏空是很短的。► **to make do with sth** 将就某事 ► **it's made (out) of glass** 是玻璃做的 ► **to have (got) it made** (*inf*) 有成功的把握 ► **make for** VT FUS [不可拆分] [+ *place*] 走向 [zǒuxiàng] ▷ *He rose from his seat and made for the door.* 他从座位上起身,向门走去。► **make of** VT FUS [不可拆分] 看待 [kàndài] ▷ *What did you make of the Prime Minister's speech last night?* 你怎么看待昨晚首相的讲话? ► **make off** VI 逃走 [táozǒu] ► **make off with** VT FUS [不可拆分] 偷走 [tōuzǒu]

► **make out** VT **1** (*understand*) 明白 [míngbai] ▷ *It's difficult to make out what he says.* 他说的话很难让人明白。**2** (*see*) 看出 [kànchū] ▷ *I could just make out the outline of the house.* 我只能看出房子的轮廓。**3** (*write*) [+ *cheque*] 开出 [kāichū] ▷ *I made a cheque out for 300 pounds.* 我开出一张300英镑的支票。**4** (*pretend*) ► **to make out that...** 假装… [jiǎzhuāng] **5** (*claim, imply*) ► **to make sb out to be rich/talented** 把某人说成很富有/有才华 [bǎ mǒurén shuōchéng hěn yǒu cáihuá] ▷ *He's not as hard as people make out.* 他并不像人们说的那么强硬。► **to make out a case for sth** 提出理由证实某事 ► **make over** VT (*assign*) ► **to make sth over (to sb)** 把某物的所有权转让(给某人) [bǎ mǒuwù de suǒyǒuquán zhuǎnràng (gěi mǒurén)] ▷ *The land was made over to the Council for building purposes.* 这块地的所有权已转让给市议会作为建筑用地。► **make up I** VT **1** (*constitute*) 构成 [gòuchéng] ▷ *Women make up two-fifths of the British labour force.* 妇女构成英国劳动力人数的五分之二。► **to be made up of** 由…组成 **2** (*invent*) [+ *story, excuse*] 捏造 [niēzào] ▷ *He was very good at making up excuses.* 他对捏造借口很在行。**3** (*prepare*) [+ *bed*] 准备 [zhǔnbèi] **4** (*with cosmetics*) 化妆 [huàzhuāng] ▷ *She spent too much time making herself up.* 她花太多的时间来化妆。**II** VI (*after quarrel*) 和好 [héhǎo] ▷ *She came back and they made up.* 她回来了,他们和好如初。► **to make up one's mind** 下定决心 ► **to make it up to sb** 对某人作出补偿 ▷ *I'll make it up to you, I promise.* 我保证对你作出补偿。► **to make o.s. up** 化妆 ► **make up for** VT FUS [不可拆分] [+ *deficiency*] 弥补 [míbǔ] ▷ *What the country lacks in natural resources it makes up for in bright ideas.* 国家在自然资源方面的缺乏由明智的决策加以弥补; [+ *loss, disappointment*] 补偿 [bǔcháng] ▷ *I'm sorry I broke your vase I'll make up for it.* 我抱歉打碎了你的花瓶,我会做出补偿的。

makeover ['meɪkəʊvə(r)] N [c] **1** (*facelift*) [*of person*] 整容 [zhěngróng]; [*of room*] 翻新 [fānxīn] **2** (*improvement*) 革新 [géxīn]

maker ['meɪkə(r)] N [c] **1** (*person*) [*of programme, film etc*] 制作者 [zhìzuòzhě] **2** (*manufacturer*) 制造商 [zhìzàoshāng]

makeshift ['meɪkʃɪft] ADJ (*temporary*) 临时凑合的 [línshí còuhe de]

make-up ['meɪkʌp] N **1** [U] (*cosmetics*) 化妆品 [huàzhuāngpǐn] **2** [s] (*personality*) 性格 [xìnggé] **3** [s] (*composition*) 组成 [zǔchéng]

making ['meɪkɪŋ] N [U] 制作 [zhìzuò] ► **a star in the making** 一个成长中的明星 ► **to have (all) the makings of** 具备…的(所有)素质 ► **of one's own making** 自作自受 ► **to be the making of sb/sth** 某人/某事成功的因素

malaria [mə'lɛərɪə] N [U] 疟疾 [nüèji]

Malawi [məˈlɑːwɪ] N 马拉维 [Mǎlāwéi]

Malaysia [məˈleɪzɪə] N 马来西亚 [Mǎláixīyà]

Malaysian [məˈleɪzɪən] I ADJ 马来西亚的 [Mǎláixīyà de] II N [c] (person) 马来西亚人 [Mǎláixīyàrén]

Maldives [ˈmɔːldaɪvz] NPL ▸ **the Maldives** 马尔代夫群岛 [Mǎ'ěrdàifū Qúndǎo]

male [meɪl] I N [c] **1** (man) 男子 [nánzǐ] **2** (BIO) 雄性动物 [xióngxìng dòngwù] II ADJ **1** (in gender) [+ animal, insect, plant, tree etc] 雄性的 [xióngxìng de]; [+ animal, insect, plant, tree etc] 雄性的 [xióngxìng de] **2** (relating to men) [+ role, characteristic, behaviour] 男性的 [nánxìng de]

male nurse N [c] 男护士 [nán hùshi]

malfunction [mælˈfʌŋkʃən] I N [c] [of computer, machine] 故障 [gùzhàng] II VI [computer, machine +] 发生故障 [fāshēng gùzhàng]

Mali [ˈmɑːlɪ] N 马里 [Mǎlǐ]

malicious [məˈlɪʃəs] ADJ [+ person, gossip] 恶意的 [èyì de]

malignant [məˈlɪɡnənt] ADJ **1** (MED) [+ tumour, growth] 恶性的 [èxìng de] **2** (harmful, cruel) [+ behaviour, intention] 恶毒的 [èdú de]

mall [mɔːl] N [c] (also: **shopping mall**) 大型购物中心 [dàxíng gòuwù zhōngxīn]

mallet [ˈmælɪt] N [c] 木槌 [mùchuí]

malnutrition [mælnjuːˈtrɪʃən] N [u] 营养不良 [yíngyǎng bùliáng]

malpractice [mælˈpræktɪs] N [c/u] 渎职 [dúzhí]

malt [mɔːlt] N **1** [u] (grain) 麦芽 [màiyá] **2** [c/u] (also: **malt whisky**) 麦芽威士忌酒 [màiyá wēishìjìjiǔ]

Malta [ˈmɔːltə] N 马耳他 [Mǎ'ěrtā]

Maltese [mɔːlˈtiːz] (pl **Maltese**) I ADJ 马耳他的 [Mǎ'ěrtā de] II N **1** [c] (person) 马耳他人 [Mǎ'ěrtārén] **2** [u] (language) 马耳他语 [Mǎ'ěrtāyǔ]

mammal [ˈmæml] N [c] 哺乳动物 [bǔrǔ dòngwù]

mammoth [ˈmæməθ] I ADJ (enormous) [+ task] 巨大的 [jùdà de] II N [c] (ZOOL) 猛犸 [měngmǎ]

⚬ **man** [mæn] (pl **men**) I N **1** [c] (person) 男人 [nánrén] ▷ Larry was a handsome man in his early fifties. 50刚出头的拉里是个帅气的男人。**2** [u] (mankind) 人类 [rénlèi] ▷ the most dangerous substance known to man 人类所知的最危险的物质 **3** (form of address) 老兄 [lǎoxiōng] ▷ Hey man, where d'you get those boots? 嗨，老兄，你从哪儿搞来的这些靴子？**4** [c] (in board game) (piece) 棋子 [qízǐ] ▷ Both players begin with the same number of men. 双方选手以同样数目的棋子开始比赛。II VT (staff) 在…值班 [zài…zhíbān] ▷ The station is seldom manned in the evening. 这个车站晚上很少有人值班。III **men** NPL (troops, workers) 雇员 [gùyuán] ▷ The men

voted to accept the pay offer. 雇员们投票决定接受工资条件。▸ **a betting/outdoors man** 好赌博/户外活动的人 ▸ **man and wife** 夫妻

manage [ˈmænɪdʒ] I VT (run, control) [+ business, shop, time, money] 管理 [guǎnlǐ] II VI (cope) 应付 [yìngfù] ▸ **to manage to do sth** 设法做到某事 ▸ **to manage without sb/sth** 在没有某人/某物的情况下设法对付过去 ▸ **he managed a smile** 他勉强一笑

manageable [ˈmænɪdʒəbl] ADJ [+ task, number, problem] 易处理的 [yì chǔlǐ de]

management [ˈmænɪdʒmənt] N **1** [u] (managing) 管理 [guǎnlǐ] **2** [u/s] (managers) 管理人员 [guǎnlǐ rényuán] ▸ **under new management** 在新的领导下

manager [ˈmænɪdʒə(r)] N [c] **1** [of business, department etc] 经理 [jīnglǐ] **2** [of entertainer] 经纪人 [jīngjìrén] **3** (SPORT) 球队经理 [qiúduì jīnglǐ] ▸ **sales manager** 销售经理

manageress [mænɪdʒəˈrɛs] N [c] 女经理 [nǔ jīnglǐ]

managerial [mænɪˈdʒɪərɪəl] ADJ [+ position, role, skills] 管理的 [guǎnlǐ de] ▸ **managerial staff** 管理人员

managing director [ˈmænɪdʒɪŋ-] N [c] 总裁 [zǒngcái]

mandarin [ˈmændərɪn] N **1** [u] ▸ **Mandarin (Chinese)** 普通话 [Pǔtōnghuà] **2** [c] (Chinese official) 官人 [guānrén] **3** [c] (BRIT) (civil servant) 内务官员 [nèiwù guānyuán] **4** [c] (also: **mandarin orange**) 柑橘 [gānjú]

mandate [ˈmændeɪt] I N [c] **1** (POL) 委任 [wěirèn] **2** (authority) 授权 [shòuquán] II VT ▸ **to be mandated to do sth** 被授权做某事 [bèi shòuquán zuò mǒushì]

mandatory [ˈmændətərɪ] ADJ (obligatory) 强制的 [qiángzhì de]

mane [meɪn] N [c] **1** [of horse] 马鬃 [mǎzōng] **2** [of lion] 狮鬣 [shīliè] **3** [of person] 厚密的头发 [hòumì de tóufa]

maneuver [məˈnuːvə(r)] (US) VT, VI, N = **manoeuvre**

mangetout [ˈmɒnʒˈtuː] (BRIT) N [c] 可连荚吃的豆 [kě liánjiáchī de dòu]

mangle [ˈmæŋɡl] VT (twist, crush) 压损 [yāsǔn]

mango [ˈmæŋɡəu] (pl **mangoes**) I N [c] (fruit) 芒果 [mángguǒ] II CPD (复合词) [+ juice, yoghurt] 芒果 [mángguǒ]

manhole [ˈmænhəul] N [c] 检修孔 [jiǎnxiū kǒng] ▸ **manhole cover** 窨井盖

manhood [ˈmænhud] N [u] **1** (adulthood) 成年 [chéngnián] **2** (masculinity) 男子气概 [nánzǐ qìgài]

mania [ˈmeɪnɪə] N **1** [c] (craze) 狂热 [kuángrè] **2** [u] (illness) 躁狂症 [zàokuángzhèng]

maniac [ˈmeɪnɪæk] N [c] **1** (lunatic) 疯子 [fēngzi] **2** (idiot) 傻子 [shǎzi] **3** (freak) ▸ **a baseball/religious maniac** 棒球迷/宗教狂

[bàngqiú mí/zōngjiào kuáng]

manic ['mænɪk] ADJ [+ behaviour, activity] 疯狂
的 [fēngkuáng de]

manicure ['mænɪkjʊə(r)] I N [c] 修指甲
[xiū zhǐjiǎ] II VT 修 [xiū zhǐjiǎ] ▶ **to have a
manicure** 修指甲

manifest ['mænɪfɛst] (frm) I VT (show, display)
表明 [biǎomíng] II ADJ (evident, obvious) [+ failure,
injustice] 明显的 [míngxiǎn de] III N [c] (AVIAT,
NAUT) 舱单 [cāngdān] ▶ **it manifests itself** 显
现出来 ▶ **to be/become** or **be made manifest**
明了/变得明了

manifesto [mænɪ'fɛstəʊ] N [c] 宣言 [xuānyán]

manipulate [mə'nɪpjʊleɪt] VT 1 (influence)
[+ person, situation, events] 操纵 [cāozòng];
[+ nature] 控制 [kòngzhì] 2 (handle) [+ object,
substance] 熟练使用 [shúliàn shǐyòng] 3 (MED)
[+ joint] 推拿 [tuīná] 4 (operate) [+ machine,
controls] 操作 [cāozuò]

manipulation [mənɪpjʊ'leɪʃən] N [c/U]
1 (influencing) [of person, situation, events] 操
纵 [cāozòng]; [of nature] 调控 [tiáokòng]
2 (handling) [of object, substance] 使用 [shǐyòng]
3 (MED) 推拿 [tuīná] 4 (operation) [of machine,
controls] 操作 [cāozuò]

mankind [mæn'kaɪnd] N [U] (human beings) 人
类 [rénlèi]

manly ['mænlɪ] ADJ [+ quality, feeling] 男子气
的 [nánzǐqì de]; [+ activity] 适合男子的 [shìhé
nánzǐ de]; [+ person, appearance] 男子汉的
[nánzǐhàn de]

man-made ['mæn'meɪd] ADJ 人造的 [rénzào
de]

manner ['mænə(r)] I N [S] 1 (way) 方式
[fāngshì] 2 (behaviour) 举止 [jǔzhǐ] II **manners**
N PL (polite behaviour) 礼貌 [lǐmào] ▶ **in a
manner of speaking** 在某种意义上 ▶ **all
manner of objects/things** 各种各样的东西
▶ **to have good/bad manners** 有礼貌/无礼
▶ **it's good/bad manners to arrive on time** 准
时是有礼貌/无礼的表现

manoeuvre, (US) **maneuver** [mə'nu:və(r)]
I VT 1 (move) [+ vehicle, bulky object] 设法移动
[shèfǎ yídòng] 2 (manipulate) [+ person, things]
操纵 [cāozòng] II VI (move) [driver, vehicle +] 驶
[shǐ] III N [c] 1 (movement) 动作 [dòngzuò]
2 (move) 策略 [cèlüè] IV **manoeuvres** N PL
(MIL) 演习 [yǎnxí] ▶ **room for manoeuvre** 回
旋的余地

manpower ['mænpaʊə(r)] N [U] 人力 [rénlì]

mansion ['mænʃən] N [c] 宅第 [zháidì]

manslaughter ['mænslɔ:tə(r)] N [U] 过失杀
人 [guòshī shārén]

mantelpiece ['mæntlpi:s] N [c] 壁炉台 [bìlú
tái]

manual ['mænjʊəl] I ADJ 1 [+ work, worker] 手
工的 [shǒugōng de] 2 (hand-operated) [+ controls,
car, gearbox] 手动的 [shǒudòng de] 3 (relating

to hands) [+ dexterity] 手的 [shǒu de] II N [c]
(handbook) 手册 [shǒucè de]

manually ['mænjʊəlɪ] ADV [operate +] 人工地
[réngōng de]

manufacture [mænjʊ'fæktʃə(r)] I VT 1 (make,
produce) [+ goods] 生产 [shēngchǎn] 2 (fabricate)
[+ information] 捏造 [niēzào] II N [U] (making)
生产 [shēngchǎn]

manufacturer [mænjʊ'fæktʃərə(r)] N [c] 制
造商 [zhìzàoshāng]

manure [mə'njʊə(r)] N [U] 粪肥 [fèn féi]

manuscript ['mænjʊskrɪpt] N [c] 1 [of book,
report] 底稿 [dǐgǎo] 2 (old document) 手稿
[shǒugǎo]

○**many** ['mɛnɪ] I ADJ (a lot of) [+ people, things,
ideas] 许多的 [xǔduō de] ▷ Many people have
been killed. 许多人被害害。▷ Not many films are
made in Finland. 芬兰出品的电影不是很多。
II PRON 许多的 [xǔduō de] ▷ Some find jobs, but
many are forced to beg. 一些人找到了工作，但许
多人被迫去乞讨。▶ **how many** (direct question)
多少 ▷ How many cigarettes do you smoke a day? 你
一天抽多少支香烟？; (indirect question) 多少
▷ No-one knows how many people were killed. 没有
人知道有多少人被害害。▶ **as many as you can**
(maximum amount) 尽可能多 ▶ **twice as many
(as)** (comparison) (是…的)两倍 ▷ We produce
ten times as many tractors as the United States. 我
们生产的拖拉机是美国的10倍。▶ **as many
as ten thousand people** (emphatic) 一万人之
多 ▶ **a good** or **great many** 相当多 ▶ **many a
time** 许多次

map [mæp] I N [c] 地图 [dìtú] II VT (make a
map of) 绘制…的地图 [huìzhì…de dìtú]
▶ **map out** VT 1 [+ plan, task] 筹划 [chóuhuà]
2 [+ career] 安排 [ānpái]

maple ['meɪpl] I N 1 [c/U] (tree) 枫树 [fēngshù]
2 [U] (wood) 枫木 [fēngmù] II CPD [复合词]
[+ wood, tree, leaf] 枫 [fēng]

Mar. ABBR (= March) 三月 [sānyuè]

mar [ma:(r)] VT (spoil) 毁坏 [huǐhuài]

marathon ['mærəθən] I N [c] (race) 马拉松长
跑 [mǎlāsōng chángpǎo] II ADJ 马拉松式的
[mǎlāsōngshì de]

marble ['ma:bl] I N 1 [U] (stone) 大理石
[dàlǐshí] 2 [c] (glass ball) 弹子 [dànzǐ] II CPD [复
合词] [+ tiles, statue, fireplace] 大理石 [dàlǐshí]
III **marbles** N PL (game) 弹子游戏 [dànzǐ yóuxì]
▶ **to lose one's marbles** (inf) 丧失理智

○**March** [ma:tʃ] N [c/U] 三月 [sānyuè] see also
July

march [ma:tʃ] I VI 1 (MIL) [soldiers +] 行军
[xíngjūn] 2 [protesters +] 行进 [xíngjìn] 3 (walk
briskly) 快步走 [kuàibù zǒu] II VT 1 使行军 [shǐ
xíngjūn] 2 迫使前进 [pòshǐ qiánjìn] III N [c]
1 (MIL) 行军 [xíngjūn] 2 (demonstration) 游行示
威 [yóuxíng shìwēi] 3 ▶ **the march of progress**
事情的进展 [shìqíng de jìnzhǎn]

Mardi Gras [mɑːdɪˈgrɑː] N [U] 参见下文

⊙ **MARDI GRAS**

Mardi Gras 是在基督教的 **Shrove Tuesday**（忏悔星期二）举行的狂欢节，即在 **Lent**（大斋节）开始的前一天。复活节之前的40天为 **Lent**，基督徒有在这个期间斋戒的传统。Mardi Gras 的名称来自法语，原意为 **fat Tuesday**，因为在这一天，人们在斋戒前要吃掉所有油腻的食物。在某些地方，比如，美国新奥尔良的南部城市，这天是人们纵情狂欢的时刻，人们穿上五颜六色的盛装，在街头载歌载舞。

mare [mɛə(r)] N [c] 母马 [mǔmǎ]

margarine [mɑːdʒəˈriːn] N [U] 人造黄油 [rénzào huángyóu]

margin [ˈmɑːdʒɪn] N [c] **1** (difference) (of votes, points) 差数 [chāshù] **2** (extra amount) (for safety, error etc) 余地 [yúdì] **3** (space) (of page) 页边空白 [yèbiān kòngbái] **4** (edge) 边缘 [biānyuán] ▶ **(on) the margins (of sth)** (在) (某事物的) 边缘

marginal [ˈmɑːdʒɪnl] I ADJ **1** (minor) [+ increase, improvement] 微小的 [wēixiǎo de] **2** [+ person, group] (socially excluded) 边缘的 [biānyuán de] II (BRIT) N [c] (also: **marginal seat**) 边座 [biānzuò]

marginally [ˈmɑːdʒɪnəlɪ] ADV [+ different, better etc] 稍许 [shāoxǔ]; [improve, increase, etc +] 稍微 [shāowēi]

marigold [ˈmærɪɡəʊld] N [c] 金盏花 [jīnzhǎnhuā]

marijuana [mærɪˈwɑːnə] N [U] 大麻 [dàmá]

marina [məˈriːnə] N [c] 小艇船坞 [xiǎotǐng chuánwù]

marinade [ˈmærɪneɪd] I N [c] 腌泡汁 [yānpàozhī] II VT, VI = **marinate**

marinate [ˈmærɪneɪt] I VT 使浸泡 [shǐ jìnpào] II VI 腌泡 [yānpào]

marine [məˈriːn] I ADJ **1** [+ life, plant, biology] 海洋的 [hǎiyáng de] **2** (maritime) [+ engineering, law, insurance] 海事的 [hǎishì de] II N [c] (soldier) 海军陆战队士兵 [hǎijūn lùzhànduì shìbīng]

marital [ˈmærɪtl] ADJ 婚姻的 [hūnyīn de]

marital status N [U] 婚姻状况 [hūnyīn zhuàngkuàng]

maritime [ˈmærɪtaɪm] ADJ [+ nation, museum] 海洋的 [hǎiyáng de] ▶ **maritime law** 海事法

marjoram [ˈmɑːdʒərəm] N [U] 墨角兰 [mòjiǎolán]

mark [mɑːk] I N **1** [c] (cross, tick etc) 记号 [jìhao] **2** [c] (stain) 污点 [wūdiǎn] **3** [c] (trace) [of shoes, fingers, tyres] 印迹 [yìnjì] **4** [s] (token) 特征 [tèzhēng] **5** [c] (BRIT) (grade, score) 分数 [fēnshù] **6** (level, stage) ▶ **the halfway mark** 中点标志 [zhōngdiǎn biāozhì] **7** (version, model) ▶ **Mark 3 Ford Escort** 福特护卫者3型 [Fútè Hùwèizhě Sānxíng] II VT **1** (with word, symbol) 标明 [biāomíng] **2** (stain, damage) [+ clothes, furniture] 留痕迹于 [liú hénjì yú] **3** (indicate) [+ place] 标示 [biāoshì] **4** (signal) [+ event] 标志 [biāozhì] **5** (characterize) 以…为特征 [yǐ…wéi tèzhēng] **6** (BRIT: SCOL) 评分 [píngfēn] **7** (ESP BRIT: SPORT) [+ player] 盯住 [dīngzhù] III VI (stain) 留下痕迹 [liúxià hénjì] ▶ **to leave your or a mark** 留下你的/一个深远影响 ▶ **to make one's mark** 成名 ▶ **"on your marks** or (US) **mark"** (SPORT) "各就各位" ▷ On your marks, get set, go! 各就各位, 预备, 跑！ ▶ **to be up to the mark** 达到要求的标准 ▶ **to be quick/slow off the mark (in doing sth)** 不失时机地/慢吞吞地开始 (做某事) ▶ **to be wide of the mark** [claim, estimate +] 毫不相干 ▶ **to mark time** 原地踏步
▶ **mark down** VT **1** (reduce) [+ prices, goods] 削价 [xuējià] **2** (write down) 记下 [jìxià]
▶ **mark off** VT (tick off) 标记画出 [biāojì chū]
▶ **mark out** VT **1** [+ area, road] 划出 [huàchū] **2** [+ person, place] 区别 [qūbié]
▶ **mark up** VT (increase) [+ price, goods] 标高 [biāogāo]

marked [mɑːkt] ADJ (obvious) 显著的 [xiǎnzhù de] ▶ **in marked contrast to...** 与…形成鲜明对照 ▶ **he is a marked man** 他被盯上了

marker [ˈmɑːkə(r)] N [c] **1** (sign) 标识 [biāoshí] **2** (also: **marker pen**) 记号笔 [jìhàobǐ]

⊙ **market** [ˈmɑːkɪt] I N [c] **1** (in town, village etc) (place) 市场 [shìchǎng]; (event) 集市 [jíshì] **2** (demand) 市场 [shìchǎng] ▷ The foreign market was increasingly important. 国外市场日益重要起来。II VT 销售 [xiāoshòu] ▶ **to be on/come onto the market** 在市场上出售 ▶ **on the open market** 在开放的市场上 ▶ **to play the market** (ECON) 投机倒把

marketing [ˈmɑːkɪtɪŋ] I N [U] 市场营销 [shìchǎng yíngxiāo] II CPD [复合词] [+ campaign, director] 销售 [xiāoshòu]

marketplace [ˈmɑːkɪtpleɪs] N [c] **1** (COMM) ▶ **the marketplace** 市场 [shìchǎng] **2** (area, site) 集市场 [jíshìchǎng]

market research N [U] 市场调查 [shìchǎng diàochá]

marmalade [ˈmɑːməleɪd] N [C/U] 橘子酱 [júzi jiàng]

maroon [məˈruːn] I ADJ (colour) 褐红色的 [hèhóngsè de] II VT ▶ **to be marooned** (stranded) 被困 [bèi kùn]

marquee [mɑːˈkiː] N [c] 大帐篷 [dà zhàngpeng]

marriage [ˈmærɪdʒ] N **1** [C/U] (relationship, institution) 婚姻 [hūnyīn] **2** [c] (wedding) 婚礼 [hūnlǐ] ▶ **marriage of convenience** 权宜婚姻

marriage certificate N [c] 结婚证书 [jiéhūn

zhèngshū]

married ['mærɪd] ADJ **1** [+ man, woman] 已婚的 [yǐhūn de] **2** [+ life] 婚姻的 [hūnyīn de] ▶ **a married man/woman** 有妇之夫/有夫之妇 ▶ **to be married to sb** 和某人结婚 ▶ **to get married** 结婚

marrow ['mærəʊ] N **1** [C/U] (vegetable) 西葫芦 [xīhúlu] **2** [U] (bone marrow) 骨髓 [gǔsuǐ]

marry ['mærɪ] I VT **1** [man, woman +] 和…结婚 [hé…jiéhūn] **2** [priest, registrar +] 为…主持婚礼 [wèi…zhǔchí hūnlǐ] II VI 结婚 [jiéhūn]

Mars [mɑːz] N (planet) 火星 [Huǒxīng]

marsh [mɑːʃ] N [C/U] (bog) 沼泽 [zhǎozé]

marshal ['mɑːʃl] N **1** (official) (at sports meeting etc) 典礼官 [diǎnlǐguān] **2** (US: POLICE) 执法官 [zhífǎguān] **3** (MIL) (also: **field marshal, air marshal**) 元帅 [yuánshuài] II VT **1** (organize) [+ resources, support] 聚集 [jùjí] **2** [+ soldiers] 集结 [jíjié]

martial art ['mɑːʃl-] N [C] 武术 [wǔshù] ▶ **the martial arts** 武术

martyr ['mɑːtə(r)] I N [C] 殉道者 [xùndàozhě] II VT (kill) 使成为殉道者 [shǐ chéngwéi xùndàozhě]

marvel ['mɑːvl] I N [C] (wonder) 奇迹 [qíjì] II VI ▶ **to marvel at sth** 对某事感到大为惊讶 [duì mǒushì gǎndào dàwéi jīngyà]

marvellous, (US) **marvelous** ['mɑːvləs] ADJ 极好的 [jíhǎo de]

Marxism ['mɑːksɪzəm] N 马克思主义 [Mǎkèsīzhǔyì]

Marxist ['mɑːksɪst] I ADJ 马克思主义的 [Mǎkèsīzhǔyì de] II N [C] 马克思主义者 [Mǎkèsīzhǔyìzhě]

marzipan ['mɑːzɪpæn] N [U] 杏仁蛋白糊 [xìngrén dànbái hú]

mascara [mæsˈkɑːrə] N [U] 睫毛膏 [jiémáogāo]

mascot ['mæskət] N [C] 吉祥物 [jíxiángwù]

masculine ['mæskjʊlɪn] ADJ **1** (of men) [+ characteristic, value etc] 男性的 [nánxìng de] **2** (manly) [+ man, woman, image] 男子气的 [nánzǐqì de]; [+ room, clothes] 男性化的 [nánxìnghuà de] **3** (LING) [+ pronoun etc] 阳性的 [yángxìng de]

mash [mæʃ] (CULIN) I VT (also: **mash up**) 把…捣成糊状 [bǎ…dǎochéng húzhuàng] II N [U] (BRIT: inf) (mashed potato) 土豆泥 [tǔdòuní]

mashed potato [mæʃt-] N [C/U] 土豆泥 [tǔdòuní]

mask [mɑːsk] I N [C] **1** (disguise) 面罩 [miànzhào] **2** (protection) 口罩 [kǒuzhào] **3** (concealing emotions) 伪装 [wěizhuāng] II VT (hide) [+ feelings] 掩饰 [yǎnshì]; [+ object] 遮住 [zhēzhù] ▶ **a masked man** (robber etc) 戴面具的人

mason ['meɪsn] N [C] **1** (also: **stone mason**) 石

匠 [shíjiàng] **2** (also: **freemason**) 共济会会员 [gòngjìhuì huìyuán]

masonry ['meɪsnrɪ] N [U] (stonework) 砖石结构 [zhuānshí jiégòu]

mass [mæs] I N **1** [C] (large amount, number) [of objects, people, substance] 大量 [dàliàng] **2** [C] (area, volume) [of air, water, land] 团 [tuán] **3** [C] (PHYS) [of object] 体积 [tǐjī] **4** [C/U] (REL) ▶ **Mass** 弥撒 [mísa] II CPD [复合词] [+ communication, unemployment etc] 大规模 [dà guīmó] III VI [troops, protesters +] 聚集 [jùjí] IV VT [+ troops] 集结 [jíjié] V **the masses** NPL 群众 [qúnzhòng] ▶ **masses of** (inf) 大量 ▶ **to go to Mass** 去做弥撒

massacre ['mæsəkə(r)] I N [C/U] 大屠杀 [dàtúshā] II VT 大规模屠杀 [dà guīmó túshā] 用法参见 kill

massage ['mæsɑːʒ] I N [C/U] 按摩 [ànmó] II VT **1** 按摩 [ànmó] **2** (manipulate) [+ statistics] 篡改 [cuàngǎi] ▶ **to give sb a massage** 为某人按摩

massive ['mæsɪv] ADJ **1** (huge) [+ amount, increase etc] 巨大的 [jùdà de]; [+ explosion] 大规模的 [dà guīmó de] **2** [+ heart attack, haemorrhage] 严重的 [yánzhòng de] **3** (inf) (emphatic) 极大的 [jídà de]

mass media N ▶ **the mass media** 大众传媒 [dàzhòng chuánméi]

mass-produce ['mæsprə'djuːs] VT [+ goods, cars etc] 批量生产 [pīliàng shēngchǎn]

mass-produced ['mæsprə'djuːst] ADJ 批量生产的 [pīliàng shēngchǎn de]

mast [mɑːst] N [C] **1** (NAUT) 船桅 [chuánwéi] **2** [for radio, television etc] 天线杆 [tiānxiàn gān]

master ['mɑːstə(r)] I N [C] **1** [of servant, dog] 主人 [zhǔrén] **2** [of situation] 主宰者 [zhǔzǎizhě] **3** (o.f.) (teacher) (in secondary school) 男教师 [nán jiàoshī] **4** (o.f.) ▶ **Master Simon** 西蒙少爷 [Xīméng shàoye] **5** (o.f.) (on envelope) ▶ **Master Simon Fisher** 西蒙·费舍先生 [Xīméng Fèishě xiānsheng] **6** (ART) 大师 [dàshī] **7** (also: **master copy**) 母版 [mǔbǎn] **8** ▶ **master's (degree)** 硕士 (学位) [shuòshì (xuéwèi)] II CPD [复合词] [+ baker, craftsman, builder etc] 师傅 [shīfu] III VT **1** (overcome) [+ situation, difficulty, feeling] 控制 [kòngzhì] **2** (learn) [+ skill, language] 掌握 [zhǎngwò]

mastermind ['mɑːstəmaɪnd] I VT 策划 [cèhuà] II N [C] 策划者 [cèhuàzhě]

Master of Arts N [S] **1** (degree) 文学硕士学位 [wénxué shuòshì xuéwèi] **2** (person) 文学硕士 [wénxué shuòshì]

Master of Science N [S] **1** (degree) 理学硕士学位 [lǐxué shuòshì xuéwèi] **2** (person) 理学硕士 [lǐxué shuòshì]

masterpiece ['mɑːstəpiːs] N [C] **1** (great work) 杰作 [jiézuò] **2** (greatest work) ▶ **sb's masterpiece** 某人最杰出的作品 [mǒurén zuì jiéchū de zuòpǐn] **3** (superb example) ▸ **a masterpiece of sth** 某事的典范 [mǒushì de diǎnfàn]

mat [mæt] **I** N [c] **1** (on floor) 席 [xí] **2** (also: **doormat**) 门口地垫 [ménkǒu dìdiàn] **3** (also: **table mat**) 桌垫 [zhuōdiàn] **II** ADJ = matt

⊙ **match** [mætʃ] **I** N **1** [c] (game) [of football, tennis etc] 比赛 [bǐsài] **2** [c] (for lighting fire etc) 火柴 [huǒchái] **3** (combination) ▸ **to be a good/perfect match** [colours, clothes +] 很/非常相称 [hěn/fēicháng xiāngchèn] ▷ Helen's choice of lipstick was a good match for her skin-tone. 海伦选的唇膏和她的肤色非常相称。**II** VT **1** (go well with) [colours, clothes +] 和…相配 [hé…xiāngpèi] ▷ The lampshades matched the curtains. 灯罩和窗帘很相配。**2** ▸ **to match sth to** or **with sth** (coordinate) 使某物和某物相配 [shǐ mǒuwù hé mǒuwù xiāngpèi] ▷ She likes to match her lipstick with her outfit. 她喜欢用和她的服饰相配的口红。; (put together) 使某物和某物相匹配 [shǐ mǒuwù hé mǒuwù xiāngpǐpèi] ▷ an organization which matches job seekers with vacancies 把求职者安排在相应空缺岗位上的机构 **3** (also: **match up**) [+ socks, gloves etc] 配成对 [pèichéngduì] ▷ She was trying to match all the odd socks that were lying about. 她正试着将散落四处的单只袜子配成对。**4** (equal) 比得上 [bǐdeshàng] ▷ efforts to match ever-increasing demand by building new schools 建立新学校以努力满足不断增长的需求 **5** (correspond to) 和…一致 [hé…yīzhì] ▷ to check that the buyer's name matches the name on the credit card 检查一下买主姓名是否和信用卡上的姓名一致 **III** VI **1** (go together) [colours, materials +] 相配 [xiāngpèi] ▷ All the chairs matched. 所有的椅子都很搭配。**2** (correspond) 相符合 [xiāngfúhé] ▷ The sale will only go ahead if the serial numbers match. 只有当序号都相符合时，销售才能继续进行。▸ **to be no match for sb/sth** 同某人/某物没法相比 ▸ **to be** or **make a good match** [couple +] 很般配的一对 ▷ Don't they make a good match! 他们真是很般配的一对！▸ **to meet one's match** 遇到对手 ▸ **with shoes to match** 配以合适的鞋子 ▸ **match up to** VT FUS [不可拆分] 配得上 [pèideshàng]

matchbox ['mætʃbɒks] N [c] 火柴盒 [huǒcháihé]

matching ['mætʃɪŋ] ADJ [+ clothes, curtains etc] 相称的 [xiāngchèn de]

mate [meɪt] **I** N [c] **1** (BRIT: inf) (friend) 伙伴 [huǒbàn] **2** (animal) 配偶 [pèi'ǒu] **3** (NAUT) (also: **first mate**) 大副 [dàfù]; (MIL) (junior officer) 军士 [jūnshì] **4** (assistant) 助手 [zhùshǒu] **II** VI [animals +] 交配 [jiāopèi]

material [mə'tɪərɪəl] **I** N **1** [c/u] (substance) 材料 [cáiliào] **2** [c/u] (cloth) 衣料 [yīliào] **3** [U] (information, data) 资料 [zīliào] **II** ADJ **1** (physical) 物质的 [wùzhì de] **2** (frm) (relevant)

[+ evidence] 决定性的 [juédìngxìng de] **III materials** NPL (equipment) 用具 [yòngjù]

materialize [mə'tɪərɪəlaɪz] VI **1** (happen) [problem, event +] 出现 [chūxiàn] **2** (suddenly appear) 突然出现 [tūrán chūxiàn]

maternal [mə'tɜːnl] ADJ **1** [+ feelings, role] 母亲的 [mǔqīn de] **2** [+ grandfather, aunt etc] 母系的 [mǔxì de]

maternity [mə'tɜːnɪtɪ] **I** N [U] (motherhood) 母亲身份 [mǔqīn shēnfèn] **II** CPD [复合词] [+ clothes, ward, care] 孕产妇 [yùnchǎnfù]

maternity hospital N [c] 产科医院 [chǎnkē yīyuàn]

maternity leave N [U] 产假 [chǎnjià] ▸ **to be on maternity leave** 休产假

math [mæθ] (US) N = maths

mathematical [mæθə'mætɪkl] ADJ **1** [+ formula, calculation] 数学的 [shùxué de] **2** [+ mind, abilities] 数学方面的 [shùxué fāngmiàn de]

mathematician [mæθəmə'tɪʃən] N [c] **1** (by career) 数学家 [shùxuéjiā] **2** (mathematically gifted person) 数学好的人 [shùxué hǎo de rén]

mathematics [mæθə'mætɪks] (frm) N [U] 数学 [shùxué]

maths [mæθs] (BRIT) N [U] 数学 [shùxué] [美 = math]

matinée ['mætɪneɪ] **I** N [c] 午后的演出 [wǔhòu de yǎnchū] **II** CPD [复合词] [+ performance] 下午场 [xiàwǔchǎng]

matron ['meɪtrən] (BRIT) N [c] **1** (in nursing home, hospital) 护士长 [hùshìzhǎng] **2** (in school) 女舍监 [nǚ shèjiān]

matt, matte, mat [mæt] ADJ [+ colour, finish, paint] 无光泽的 [wú guāngzé de]

matted ['mætɪd] ADJ [+ hair] 缠结的 [chánjié de]

⊙ **matter** ['mætə(r)] **I** N **1** [c] (affair, situation, problem) 事件 [shìjiàn] ▷ Will you report the matter to the authorities? 你会将该事件报告给当局吗？**2** [U] (PHYS) 物质 [wùzhì] ▷ An atom is the smallest indivisible particle of matter. 原子是最小的不可分的物质微粒。**3** [U] ▸ **waste/ vegetable matter** 废物/植物 [fèiwù/zhíwù] **II** VI (be important) 要紧 [yàojǐn] ▷ Your happiness is the only thing that matters. 你的幸福是惟一要紧的事。**III matters** NPL 事态 [shìtài] ▷ It is hard to see how this would improve matters. 很难看出这会对事态有怎样的改善。▸ **what's the matter (with…)?** (…)怎么了？▸ **in a matter of days/weeks** 仅几天/几周 ▸ **as a matter of urgency** or **priority** 作为紧急〔或〕优先考虑的事情 ▸ **no matter what** (whatever happens) 不管发生什么 ▸ **another** or **a different matter** 另一回事 ▸ **it is only a matter of time** 这仅仅是时间问题 ▸ **as a matter of course** 理所当然的事 ▸ **as a matter of fact** 事实上 ▸ **for that matter** (used for *emphasis*) 而且 ▸ **no matter how/what/who** 不管怎样/什么/无论谁 ▸ **it doesn't matter** 没关系

matter-of-fact ['mætərəv'fækt] ADJ [+ *person, voice, attitude etc*] 不带感情的 [bù dài gǎnqíng de]

mattress ['mætrɪs] N [C] 床垫 [chuángdiàn]

mature [mə'tjuə(r)] I ADJ 1 (*not childlike*) 成熟的 [chéngshú de] 2 (*fully grown*) 成年的 [chéngnián de] 3 (*ripe*) [+ *cheese, wine*] 酿熟的 [niàngshú de] II VI 1 (*grow up*) [*person +*] 长成 [zhǎngchéng] 2 (*develop*) [*artist, style +*] 成熟 [chéngshú] 3 (*ripen, age*) [*cheese, wine etc +*] 酿熟 [niàngshú] 4 (FIN) 到期 [dàoqī] III VT [+ *wine, cheese*] 使酿熟 [shǐ niàngshú] ▸ **mature cheddar (cheese)** 浓味切达干酪

mature student (BRIT) N [C] 成年学生 [chéngnián xuéshēng]

maturity [mə'tjuərɪtɪ] N [U] (*adulthood, wisdom*) 成熟 [chéngshú]

maul [mɔːl] VT 1 [*lion, bear, dog etc +*] 伤害 [shānghài] 2 (*criticize*) 抨击 [pēngjī]

Mauritania [mɔːrɪ'teɪnɪə] N 毛里塔尼亚 [Máolǐtǎníyà]

Mauritius [mə'rɪʃəs] N 毛里求斯 [Máolǐqiúsī]

mauve [məuv] ADJ 淡紫色的 [dàn zǐsè de]

maverick ['mævrɪk] I N [C] 自行其是的人 [zìxíng qíshì de rén] II ADJ 自行其是的 [zìxíng qíshì de]

max. ABBR = **maximum**

maximize ['mæksɪmaɪz] VT 1 [+ *profit, output, efficiency etc*] 使增至最大限度 [shǐ zēngzhì zuìdà xiàndù] 2 (COMPUT) 使…最大化 [shǐ… zuìdàhuà] ▷ *Click on the square icon to maximize the window.* 点击方形图标使窗口最大化。

maximum ['mæksɪməm] I ADJ 1 (*highest, greatest*) [+ *speed, height*] 最高的 [zuìgāo de]; [+ *weight*] 最重的 [zuìzhòng de]; [+ *sentence*] 最严厉的 [zuìyánlì de] 2 (*great*) 最大的 [zuìdà de] II N [C] 最大量 [zuìdàliàng] ▸ **a maximum of two years** 至多两年 ▸ **six weeks maximum** 6星期的最大极限

Ⓞ **May** [meɪ] N [C/U] 五月 [wǔyuè] *see also* **July**

Ⓞ

may [meɪ] AUX VB 1 (*possibility*) ▸ **it may rain later** 等会儿可能要下雨 [děnghuì'r kěnéng yào xiàyǔ] ▸ **we may not be able to come** 我们可能来不了 ▸ **he may be out** 他可能出去了 ▸ **he may have hurt himself** 他可能伤了自己 ▸ **the coat may be worn with or without the hood** 外套可以连帽穿也可以不连帽穿

2 (*permission*) ▸ **may I come in?** 我可以进来吗? [wǒ kěyǐ jìnlái ma?] ▸ **may I offer you a glass of wine?** 给你来一杯酒好吗? ▸ **you may go now** 你现在可以走了

3 (*conceding*) ▸ **I may be old, but I'm not**

stupid 我也许是老了，但绝不愚蠢 [wǒ yěxǔ shì lǎole, dàn juébù yúchǔn]; (*expressing wishes*) 祝愿 [zhùyuàn] ▸ **may you be very happy together!** 祝愿你们百年好合!

4 (*in expressions*) ▸ **you may as well go** 你不妨也去 [nǐ bùfáng yěqù] ▸ **come what may** 无论发生什么事

maybe ['meɪbiː] ADV 1 (*indicating uncertainty, concession*) 可能 [kěnéng] 2 (*making suggestions*) 也许 [yěxǔ] 3 (*estimating*) 大概 [dàgài] ▸ **maybe so/not** 可能如此/不是

May Day N [U] 五一节 [wǔyījié]

mayhem ['meɪhɛm] N [U] 混乱 [hùnluàn]

mayonnaise [meɪə'neɪz] N [U] 蛋黄酱 [dànhuángjiàng] ▸ **egg/tuna mayonnaise** 蛋黄酱鸡蛋/金枪鱼

mayor [mɛə(r)] N [C] 市长 [shìzhǎng]

mayoress ['mɛərɛs] (BRIT) N [C] 1 (*female mayor*) 女市长 [nǚshìzhǎng] 2 (*wife of mayor*) 市长夫人 [shìzhǎng fūrén]

maze [meɪz] N [C] 1 (*puzzle*) 迷宫 [mígōng] 2 ▸ **maze of streets/corridors** 迷宫似的街道/走廊 [mígōngshì de jiēdào/zǒuláng] 3 ▸ **maze of rules/jargon** 错综复杂的规则/术语 [cuòzōng fùzá de guīzé/shùyǔ]

MBA N ABBR (= *Master of Business Administration*) (*qualification*) 工商管理硕士学位 [gōngshāng guǎnlǐ shuòshì xuéwèi]; (*person*) 工商管理硕士 [gōngshāng guǎnlǐ shuòshì]

MD N ABBR 1 (= *Doctor of Medicine*) (*with doctorate*) 医学博士 [yīxué bóshì]; (US) (*with degree*) 医学博士 [yīxué bóshì] 2 (ESP BRIT: COMM) (= *Managing Director*) 总经理 [zǒngjīnglǐ] 3 = MiniDisc®

MDT (US) ABBR (= *Mountain Daylight Time*) 山区时间 [Shānqū Shíjiān]

Ⓞ **me** [miː] PRON 我 [wǒ] ▷ *He loves me.* 他爱我。 ▷ *Give me the key.* 把钥匙给我。 ▸ **it's me** 是我

meadow ['mɛdəu] N [C] 草地 [cǎodì]

meagre, (US) **meager** ['miːgə(r)] ADJ 微薄的 [wēibó de]

meal [miːl] N 1 [C] (*occasion*) 一餐 [yīcān] 2 [C] (*food*) 膳食 [shànshí] 3 [U] (*flour*) 粗磨粉 [cūmófěn] ▸ **to go out for a meal** 出去吃饭 ▸ **to make a meal of sth** (BRIT: *inf*) 对某事做得太过分

每天的第一顿饭叫做 **breakfast**。午餐最常用的表达法是 **lunch**，但是在英国的某些地方，或在某些场合下，也可以用 **dinner**。*He seldom has lunch at all…school dinners… Christmas dinner.* **dinner** 通常用来指晚餐。在英式英语里，它还可以指正式的或特殊的一餐。*In the evening they had a dinner to celebrate.* **supper** 和 **tea** 有时也被用来表示晚餐，但是有人用 **supper** 表示夜宵，用 **tea** 表示下午小餐。

mealtime ['mi:ltaɪm] N [C/U] 吃饭时间 [chīfàn shíjiān]

◊ mean [mi:n] (pt, pp **meant**) I VT 1 (signify) 表示…意思 [biǎoshì…yìsi] ▷ What does "imperialism" mean? "imperialism" 是什么意思? ▷ In modern Welsh, "glas" means "blue". 在现代威尔士语中, "glas" 表示的意思是蓝色。 2 (refer to) 意指 [yìzhǐ] ▷ I thought you meant her, not me. 我想你所指的是她, 不是我。 3 (involve) 意味着 [yìwèizhe] ▷ Becoming a millionaire didn't mean an end to his money worries. 成为百万富翁并不意味着他不再被钱困扰。 4 (intend) ▸ to mean to do sth 意欲做某事 [yìyù zuò mǒushì] 5 ▸ a film meant for adults 针对成人的电影 [zhēnduì chéngrén de diànyǐng] II ADJ 1 (not generous) 吝啬的 [lìnsè de] 2 (unkind) [+ person] 刻薄的 [kèbó de] 3 (US: inf)(cruel) [+ person, animal] 残忍的 [cánrěn de] 4 (shabby) [+ street, lodgings] 破旧的 [pòjiù de] ▸ I mean it, I mean what I say 我是当真的 ▸ what do you mean? 你什么意思? ▸ do you mean it? 你当真吗? ▸ to mean a lot to sb 对某人很重要 ▸ I mean 我是说 ▸ he's meant to be an expert (reputed) 他被公认为专家 ▸ to be mean with sth (ungenerous) 在某事上很吝啬 ▸ to be mean to sb (unkind) 对某人刻薄 ▸ he plays a mean guitar (inf) 他弹吉他很出色 ▸ he's no mean pianist/footballer 他是位很好的钢琴家/足球运动员 see also **means**

meaning ['mi:nɪŋ] N 1 [C/U] (sense, signification) [of word, expression] 意思 [yìsi]; [of symbol, dream, gesture] 含义 [hányì] 2 [U] (purpose, value) 意义 [yìyì]

meaningful ['mi:nɪŋful] ADJ 1 [+ result, explanation] 有意义的 [yǒu yìyì de] 2 [+ glance, remark] 意味深长的 [yìwèi shēncháng de] 3 [+ relationship, occasion] 有意义的 [yǒu yìyì de]

meaningless ['mi:nɪŋlɪs] ADJ 1 (nonsensical) 无意义的 [wú yìyì de] 2 (pointless) 无目的的 [wú mùdì de]

means [mi:nz] (pl **means**) I N [C] (method) 方法 [fāngfǎ] II NPL (frm)(money) 财富 [cáifù] ▸ by means of 通过 ▸ by all means! 当然! ▸ by no means 决不

meant [mɛnt] PT, PP of **mean**

meantime ['mi:ntaɪm] I N ▸ in the meantime 同时 [tóngshí] II ADV (US) 在此期间 [zài cǐ qījiān]

meanwhile ['mi:nwaɪl] ADV 同时 [tóngshí]

measles ['mi:zlz] N [U] 麻疹 [mázhěn]

measure ['mɛʒə(r)] I VT 1 [+ size, distance, temperature etc] 测量 [cèliáng] 2 (evaluate) [+ impact, success, performance] 衡量 [héngliáng] II VI (room, person, object +] 有 [yǒu] III N 1 [C] (step) 措施 [cuòshī] 2 (frm)(degree, amount) ▸ a or some measure of 相当程度的 [xiāngdāng chéngdù de] 3 ▸ a/the measure of [+ achievement, situation] 一定程度的 [yīdìng

chéngdù de] 4 [C] (serving) [of whisky, brandy etc] 固定量 [gùdìngliàng] 5 [C] (US: MUS) 小节 [xiǎojié] [英= **bar**] ▸ to take measures to do sth (frm) 采取措施以应对某事 ▸ for good measure 另外 ▸ beyond measure (used for emphasis) 非常地
▸ **measure up** VI ▸ to measure up (to sth) 符合 (某标准) [fúhé (mǒu biāozhǔn)]

measurement ['mɛʒəmənt] I N 1 [C] (length, width etc) 尺寸 [chǐcùn] 2 [U] (process of measuring) 测量 [cèliáng] II **measurements** NPL [of person] 三围 [sānwéi] ▸ chest/hip measurement 胸围/臀围 ▸ to take measurements 量尺寸

meat [mi:t] I N [U] (food) 肉 [ròu] II CPD [复合词] [+ product, dish, pie] 肉类 [ròulèi] ▸ crab meat 蟹肉

meatball ['mi:tbɔ:l] N [C] 肉丸 [ròuwán]

Mecca ['mɛkə] N 1 (GEO) 麦加 [Màijiā] 2 [C] (fig) ▸ mecca 向往的地方 [xiàngwǎng de dìfang]

mechanic [mɪ'kænɪk] N [C] 机械工 [jīxiègōng]

mechanical [mɪ'kænɪkl] ADJ 1 [+ device, problem, work] 机械的 [jīxiè de] 2 (automatic) [+ gestures] 呆板的 [dāibǎn de]

mechanical engineering N [U] (science) 机械工程 [jīxiè gōngchéng]

mechanics [mɪ'kænɪks] I N [U] (PHYS) 力学 [lìxué] II NPL [of process, system, government] 构成 [gòuchéng]

mechanism ['mɛkənɪzəm] N [C] 1 (device) 机械装置 [jīxiè zhuāngzhì] 2 (procedure) 途径 [tújìng] 3 (reflex) 本能反应 [běnnéng fǎnyìng]

medal ['mɛdl] N [C] (award) 奖章 [jiǎngzhāng]

medallist, (US) **medalist** ['mɛdlɪst] N [C] 奖牌获得者 [jiǎngpái huòdézhě] ▸ gold/silver medallist 金牌/银牌获得者

meddle ['mɛdl] VI ▸ to meddle 干预 [gānyù] ▸ to meddle with or in sth 干预某事

media ['mi:dɪə] I PL of medium II NPL ▸ the media 媒体 [méitǐ] III CPD [复合词] [+ coverage, attention, bias] 媒体 [méitǐ]

mediaeval [mɛdɪ'i:vl] ADJ = medieval

median strip ['mi:dɪən-] (US: AUT) N [C] 中央分车带 [zhōngyāng fēnchē dài] [英= **central reservation**]

mediate ['mi:dɪeɪt] VI 调停 [tiáotíng]

medical ['mɛdɪkl] I ADJ [+ treatment, care] 医疗的 [yīliáo de] II N [C] (examination) 体格检查 [tǐgé jiǎnchá]

medical certificate N [C] 诊断书 [zhěnduànshū]

medical student N [C] 医科学生 [yīkē xuéshēng]

medicated ['mɛdɪkeɪtɪd] ADJ [+ soap, shampoo] 含药物的 [hán yàowù de]

medication [mɛdɪ'keɪʃən] N [C/U] 药物 [yàowù] ▸ to be on medication 进行药物治疗

medicinal [mɛ'dɪsɪnl] ADJ [+ substance] 药用的 [yàoyòng de]; [+ qualities, effects] 药疗的 [yàoliáo de]

medicine ['mɛdsɪn] N 1 [U] (science) 医学 [yīxué] 2 [C/U] (medication) 药 [yào]

medieval, mediaeval [mɛdɪ'i:vl] ADJ 中世纪的 [zhōngshìjì de]

mediocre [mi:dɪ'əukə(r)] ADJ 平庸的 [píngyōng de]

meditate ['mɛdɪteɪt] VI 1 冥想 [míngxiǎng] 2 (reflect) 沉思 [chénsī] ▶ **to meditate on sth** 对某事进行深思

meditation [mɛdɪ'teɪʃən] N 1 [U] (ritual) 冥想 [míngxiǎng] 2 [C] (thought) 沉思 [chénsī]

Mediterranean [mɛdɪtə'reɪnɪən] I N ▶ **the Mediterranean** (sea) 地中海 [Dìzhōnghǎi]; (region) 地中海沿岸地区 [Dìzhōnghǎi yán'àn dìqū] II ADJ [+ climate, diet] 地中海地区的 [Dìzhōnghǎi dìqū de]

medium ['mi:dɪəm] (pl **media** or **mediums**) I ADJ 1 (average) [+ size, height] 中等的 [zhōngděng de] 2 (clothing size) 中码的 [zhōngmǎ de] II N [C] 1 (means) [of communication] 媒介 [méijiè] 2 (substance, material) 传导体 [chuándǎotǐ] 3 (pl **mediums**) (person) 灵媒 [língméi] ▶ **to strike** or **find a happy medium** 找到一种折中办法

medium-sized ['mi:dɪəm'saɪzd] ADJ 中等大小的 [zhōngděng dàxiǎo de]

medium wave (ESP BRIT) N [U] 中波 [zhōngbō]

meek [mi:k] ADJ 温顺的 [wēnshùn de]

◎ **meet** [mi:t] (pt, pp **met**) I VT 1 [+ friend] (accidentally) 遇见 [yùjiàn] ▷ I met Dave this morning while I was out shopping. 今天早晨我出去购物的时候遇见了戴夫。; (by arrangement) 和⋯见面 [hé⋯jiànmiàn] ▷ I could meet you for a drink after work. 我可以下班后和你见面去喝一杯。 2 [+ stranger] (for the first time) 结识 [jiéshí] ▷ I met a Swedish girl on the train from Copenhagen. 我在从哥本哈根开出的火车上结识了一位瑞典女孩。; (be introduced to) 认识 [rènshi] ▷ Hey, Terry, come and meet my Dad. 嗨，特里，来介绍你认识我爸爸。 3 (go and fetch) (at station, airport) 接 [jiē] ▷ Dan came to the airport to meet me. 丹来机场接我。 4 [+ opponent] 对抗 [duìkàng] ▷ Arsenal meet Liverpool in the next round of the Cup. 在足总杯下一轮的比赛中，阿森纳队将和利物浦队对抗。 5 (satisfy) [+ need, condition] 达到 [dádào] ▷ Certain standards must be met by all applicants. 所有的申请者都必须达到这些标准。 6 (deal with) [+ problem, challenge, deadline] 应付 [yìngfù] ▷ It is going to be difficult to meet the deadline. 很难在截止日期前完成。 7 (pay) [+ expenses, bill, cost] 支付 [zhīfù] ▷ The government will meet the cost of any damage. 政府将支付任何损失费用。 8 (join) [line, road, area +] 汇合 [huìhé] ▷ where the Atlantic meets the Indian

Ocean 大西洋和印度洋汇合的地方 9 (touch) 接触 [jiēchù] ▷ The plane jolted as the wheels met the ground. 轮子触地后飞机颠簸前行。 10 [+ eyes, gaze] 正视 [zhèngshì] ▷ Nina's eyes met her sister's across the table. 尼娜和坐在桌子另一边的姐姐互相对视着。 II VI 1 [friends +] (accidentally) 相遇 [xiāngyù] ▷ They met again while walking their dogs in Hyde Park. 他们在海德公园遛狗的时候又相遇了。; (by arrangement) 见面 [jiànmiàn] ▷ After that they met every day. 此后他们天天见面。 2 [strangers +] (for the first time) 认识 [rènshi] ▷ I don't think we've met, have we? 我想我们不认识，对吧？ 3 [club, committee etc +] (for talks, discussion) 开会 [kāihuì] ▷ The committee meets four times a year. 委员会一年开4次会。 4 (join) [lines, roads, areas +] 相交 [xiāngjiāo] ▷ Parallel lines never meet. 平行线永远不会相交。 5 [opponents +] 交手 [jiāoshǒu] ▷ The two women will meet tomorrow in the final. 这两位女选手将在明天的决赛中交手。 6 (touch) 相碰 [xiāngpèng] ▷ Their mouths met. 他们相吻了。 7 [eyes +] 相遇 [xiāngyù] ▷ Our eyes met. 我们的目光相遇了。 III N [C] 1 (BRIT) (in hunting) 集合 [jíhé] 2 (US: SPORT) 比赛 [bǐsài] ▷ a track meet 一场田径比赛 ▶ **pleased to meet you** 见到你很高兴 ▶ **nice to have met you** 很高兴认识你

▶ **meet up** VI (by arrangement) 会面 [huìmiàn] ▷ We meet up for lunch once a week. 我们每周会面一次共进午餐。; (accidentally) 偶遇 [ǒuyù]

▶ **meet up with** VT FUS [不可拆分] 1 (by arrangement) 和⋯会面 [hé⋯huìmiàn]; (accidentally) 和⋯偶遇 [hé⋯ǒuyù]

▶ **meet with** VT FUS [不可拆分] 1 [+ difficulty, success] 经历 [jīnglì] ▷ The strikes met with little success. 罢工不太成功。 2 (have meeting with) [+ person] 与⋯会面 [yǔ⋯huìmiàn]

◎ **meeting** ['mi:tɪŋ] N 1 [C] (assembly) [of club, committee etc] 会议 [huìyì] ▷ There is a different chairman at each meeting. 每次会议都有不同的主席。 2 [S] (people) 与会者 [yùhuìzhě] ▷ The meeting decided that further efforts were needed. 与会者决定要进一步努力。 3 [C] (encounter) 会面 [huìmiàn] ▷ Christopher remembers his first meeting with Alice. 克里斯托弗记得他和艾丽斯的第一次会面。 ▷ a chance meeting on the way to the office 去办公室途中的一次偶遇 ▶ **to call a meeting** 召集一次会议 ▶ **she's in** or **at a meeting** 她在开会

meeting place N [C] 会场 [huìchǎng]

megabyte ['mɛgəbaɪt] N [C] 兆字节 [zhàozìjié]

megaphone ['mɛgəfəun] N [C] 扩音器 [kuòyīnqì]

melancholy ['mɛlənkəlɪ] I ADJ (sad) 忧郁的 [yōuyù de] II N [U] (sadness) 忧郁 [yōuyù]

melody ['mɛlədɪ] N 1 [C] (tune) 旋律 [xuánlǜ] 2 [U] (tunefulness) 抑扬顿挫 [yìyáng dùncuò]

melon ['mɛlən] N [C/U] 瓜 [guā]

melt [mɛlt] I VI 1 [metal, ice, snow, butter,

chocolate +] 融化 [rónghuà] **2** ▸ **melt into**
[+ *darkness, crowd*] 消失 [xiāoshī] **II** vt [+ *metal,
ice, snow, butter, chocolate*] 使融化 [shǐ rónghuà]
III N [c] (US: CULIN:) 烤的奶酪加肉面包 ▸ **my
heart melted** 我的心软了
▸ **melt away** vi **1** [*people* +] 逐渐散去 [zhújiàn
sànqù] **2** [*doubts* +] 消除 [xiāochú]
▸ **melt down** vt 熔毁 [rónghuǐ]

⊙member ['mɛmbə(r)] N [c] **1** [*of family, staff,
public*] 一员 [yīyuán] ▷ *He refused to name the
members of staff involved.* 他拒绝说出职工中参
加者的姓名。**2** [*of club, party*] 成员 [chéngyuán]
▷ *Britain is a member of NATO.* 英国是北大西洋
公约组织的成员。**3** [*of parliament, assembly*] 议
员 [yìyuán] ▷ *He was elected to Parliament as the
Member for Leeds.* 他被选为代表利兹市的议会议
员。▸ **member country/state** 成员国/州
Member of Congress (US) N [c] 国会议员
[Guóhuì Yìyuán]
Member of Parliament (BRIT) N [c] 下院议
员 [Xiàyuàn Yìyuán]
Member of the European Parliament
N [c] 欧洲议会议员 [Ōuzhōu Yìhuì Yìyuán]
membership ['mɛmbəʃɪp] N **1** [u] (*member
status*) 会员身份 [huìyuán shēnfèn] **2** [s + PL
VB] (*members*) 全体会员 [quántǐ huìyuán] **3** [c]
(*number of members*) 会员人数 [huìyuán rénshù]
membership card N [c] 会员证
[huìyuánzhèng]
memento [mə'mɛntəu] (*pl* mementos *or*
mementoes) N [c] 纪念品 [jìniànpǐn]
memo ['mɛməu] N [c] 备忘录 [bèiwànglù]
memorabilia [mɛmərə'bɪlɪə] NPL 纪念品
[jìniànpǐn]
memorable ['mɛmərəbl] ADJ 难忘的
[nánwàng de]
memorandum [mɛmə'rændəm] (*frm*) N [c] 备
忘录 [bèiwànglù]
memorial [mɪ'mɔːrɪəl] **I** N [c] 纪念碑
[jìniànbēi] **II** ADJ [+ *service, prize*] 纪念仪式的
[jìniàn yíshì de]
memorize ['mɛməraɪz] VT 记住 [jìzhù]
memory ['mɛmərɪ] N **1** [c/u] (*ability to
remember*) 记忆力 [jìyìlì] **2** [c] (*thing remembered*)
记忆 [jìyì] **3** [c] [+ *of dead person*] 追忆 [zhuīyì]
4 [c/u] (COMPUT) 存储器 [cúnchǔqì] ▸ **to have
a good/bad memory (for sth)** (对某事)记忆
力好/差 ▸ **to lose one's memory** 丧失记忆
▸ **loss of memory** *or* **memory loss** 失忆 ▸ **to do
sth from memory** 凭记忆做某事 ▸ **in memory
of** 以纪念
men [mɛn] NPL *of* man
menace ['mɛnɪs] **I** N **1** [c] (*source of danger*)
威胁 [wēixié] **2** [u] (*feeling of danger*) 危险
[wēixiǎn] **3** (*inf*) (*nuisance*) ▸ **to be a menace** 讨
厌的东西 [tǎoyànde dōngxi] **II** VT (*threaten*) 威
胁 [wēixié]
menacing ['mɛnɪsɪŋ] ADJ [+ *person, gesture,*

expression] 凶恶的 [xiōng'è de]
mend [mɛnd] VT **1** (*repair*) [+ *object*] 修理 [xiūlǐ]
2 (*heal*) [+ *division, quarrel*] 弥合 [míhé] ▸ **to
mend one's ways** 改善自己的行为方式 ▸ **to
be on the mend** (*inf*) 在好转中
menial ['miːnɪəl] ADJ (*lowly*) [+ *work, tasks*] 卑下
的 [bēixià de]
meningitis [mɛnɪn'dʒaɪtɪs] N [u] 脑膜炎
[nǎomóyán]
menopause ['mɛnəupɔːz] N ▸ **the menopause**
绝经期 [juéjīngqī]
men's room (US) N [c] (*men's toilet*) 男厕所
[nán cèsuǒ]
menstruation [mɛnstru'eɪʃən] N [u] 月经
[yuèjīng]
menswear ['mɛnzwɛə(r)] N [u] 男装
[nánzhuāng]
mental ['mɛntl] ADJ **1** [+ *ability, effort,
development*] 智力的 [zhìlì de] **2** [+ *illness, health*]
精神的 [jīngshén de] **3** (BRIT: *inf*) (*crazy, mad*)
发疯的 [fāfēng de] ▸ **mental arithmetic** 心算
mental hospital N [c] 精神病院
[jīngshénbìngyuàn]
mentality [mɛn'tælɪtɪ] N [c] 心态 [xīntài]
mentally ['mɛntlɪ] ADV [+ *disturbed, unstable,
exhausted*] 精神上 [jīngshén shang] ▸ **to be
mentally handicapped** 智力发育不全 ▸ **to be
mentally ill** 精神失常
menthol ['mɛnθɔl] N [u] 薄荷醇 [bòhechún]
mention ['mɛnʃən] **I** VT 提到 [tídào] **II** N [c/u]
(*reference*) 提及 [tíjí] ▸ **to mention that...** 谈
到… ▸ **don't mention it!** 不客气! ▸ **not to
mention...** 更不必说… ▸ **to make no mention
of sth** 未提及某事
▓用法参见 comment
menu ['mɛnjuː] N [c] **1** (*list of dishes*) 菜单
[càidān] **2** (*also:* **set menu**) (*meal*) 套餐 [tàocān]
3 (COMPUT) 选择菜单 [xuǎnzé càidān]
MEP N ABBR (= *Member of the European Parliament*)
欧洲议会议员 [Ōuzhōu Yìhuì yìyuán]
mercenary ['məːsɪnərɪ] **I** N [c] (*soldier*) 雇佣
兵 [gùyōngbīng] **II** ADJ (*pej*) [+ *person*] 惟利是图
的 [wéilì shìtú de]
merchandise ['məːtʃəndaɪz] N [u] 商品
[shāngpǐn]
merchant ['məːtʃənt] **I** N [c] 商人 [shāngrén]
II ADJ [+ *seaman, ship, fleet*] 商业的 [shāngyè
de]
merchant marine (US) N = merchant navy
merchant navy N ▸ **the merchant navy** 商
船队 [shāngchuánduì]
merciless ['məːsɪlɪs] ADJ 冷酷无情的 [lěngkù
wúqíng de]
mercury ['məːkjurɪ] N **1** [u] 水银 [shuǐyín]
2 ▸ **Mercury** (ASTRON) 水星 [Shuǐxīng]
mercy ['məːsɪ] N [u] 宽恕 [kuānshù] ▸ **to beg
or plead for mercy** 乞求宽恕 ▸ **to have mercy
on sb** 怜悯某人 ▸ **to be at the mercy of sb** 任

凭某人的摆布

mere [mɪə(r)] ADJ **1** (simple) 仅仅的 [jǐnjǐn de]
2 (slightest) 微不足道的 [wēibùzúdào de] ▶ a
mere 2% 仅仅2%

merely ['mɪəlɪ] ADV 只不过 [zhǐbùguò] ▶ not
merely... but... 不仅…而且…

merge [məːdʒ] I VT 合并 [hébìng] II VI
1 (combine) [objects, organizations+] 联合
[liánhé] **2** (blend) [colours, sounds, shapes+] 融合
[rónghé] ▶ to merge sth with sth 将某物和某
物结合 ▶ to merge with sth (combine) [object,
organization+] 和某物结合; (blend) [colour, sound,
shape etc+] 和某物融合

merger ['məːdʒə(r)] N [c] 合并 [hébìng]

meringue [məˈræŋ] N [c/u] 蛋白酥皮饼
[dànbái sūpí bǐng]

merit ['merɪt] I N [u] (worth, value) 价值 [jiàzhí]
II VT (frm) (deserve) 值得 [zhídé] III **merits**
NPL (advantages) 优点 [yōudiǎn] ▶ on merit or
on its/their merits 根据实际功过〔或〕根据
是非曲直

mermaid ['məːmeɪd] N [c] 美人鱼 [měirényú]

merry ['merɪ] ADJ **1** (happy) [+ person, mood] 快
乐的 [kuàilè de] **2** (cheerful) [+ tune] 欢快的
[huānkuài de] **3** (BRIT: inf) (tipsy) 微醉的
[wēizuì de] ▶ **Merry Christmas!** 圣诞快乐!

merry-go-round ['merɪgəuraund] N [c]
1 (roundabout) 旋转木马 [xuánzhuàn mùmǎ]
2 (whirl) 走马灯似的更迭 [zǒumǎdēng shì de
gēngdié]

mesh [meʃ] I N [c/u] (net) 网 [wǎng] II VI 紧
密配合 [jǐnmì pèihé] ▶ to mesh with sth 与某
物协调一致

mess [mes] N **1** (untidiness) 凌乱 [língluàn]
2 [s/u] (chaotic situation) 混乱的局面 [hùnluàn
de júmiàn] **3** [s/u] (filth) 脏东西 [zāng dōngxi]
4 [c] (MIL) 食堂 [shítáng] ▶ **what a mess!**
(house, room) 真是又脏又乱!; (situation) 真是
乱七八糟! ▶ **to be a mess** [room, house+] 又
脏又乱; [life, situation+] 一团糟 ▶ **to be in a
mess** [hair, room+] 乱七八糟地; [organization,
country+] 陷入困境 ▶ **to get o.s. in a mess** 使
自己陷入困境

▶ **mess about, mess around** (inf) I VI **1** (waste
time) 混日子 [hùn rìzi] **2** (joke) ▶ **to be messing
about** 开玩笑 [kāiwánxiào] II VT (ESP BRIT)
(treat unfairly) 玩弄 [wánnòng]

▶ **mess about with, mess around with** (inf) VT
FUS [不可拆分] (interfere with) 干预 [gānyù]

▶ **mess up** (inf) I VT **1** (spoil) [+ plan, system]
毁掉 [huǐdiào] **2** (make untidy) [+ house, room,
things] 弄乱 [nòngluàn] **3** (make dirty) [+ room,
floor] 搞脏 [gǎozāng] II VI (make a mistake) 搞
砸 [gǎozá]

▶ **mess with** (inf) VT FUS [不可拆分] 插手
[chāshǒu]

message ['mesɪdʒ] N [c] **1** (to sb) 消息 [xiāoxi]
2 (meaning) [of play, book etc] 主旨 [zhǔzhǐ] ▶ to

leave (sb) a message (给某人)留个信 ▶ to
get the message (inf) 领会 ▶ to get the/one's
message across 使人理解这个/自己的意思

messenger ['mesɪndʒə(r)] N [c] 通信员
[tōngxìnyuán]

messy ['mesɪ] ADJ **1** (untidy) [+ person, activity] 邋
遢的 [lāta de]; [+ thing, place] 凌乱的 [língluàn
de] **2** (awkward) [+ situation] 棘手的 [jíshǒu de]

met [met] PT, PP of meet

metabolism [meˈtæbəlɪzəm] N [c/u] 新陈代
谢 [xīnchén dàixiè]

metal ['metl] I N [c/u] 金属 [jīnshǔ] II CPD
[复合词] [+ plate, bar, rod] 金属 [jīnshǔ]

metallic [mɪˈtælɪk] ADJ **1** [+ sound] 金属
的 [jīnshǔ de] **2** (made of metal) 金属制的
[jīnshǔzhì de] **3** [+ paint, colour] 像金属的
[xiàngjīnshǔ de] **4** [+ taste] 有金属腥味的 [yǒu
jīnshǔ xīngwèi de]

metaphor ['metəfə(r)] N [c/u] 隐喻 [yǐnyù]

meteor ['miːtɪə(r)] N [c] 流星 [liúxīng]

meteorite ['miːtɪəraɪt] N [c] 陨星 [yǔnxīng]

meteorology [miːtɪəˈrɔlədʒɪ] N [u] 气象学
[qìxiàngxué]

meter ['miːtə(r)] I N [c] **1** (instrument) (for gas,
water, electricity) 仪表 [yíbiǎo]; (also: parking
meter) 停车计时器 [tíngchē jìshíqì] **2** (US)
(unit) = metre II VT [+ gas, water, electricity] 用表
计量 [yòngbiǎo jìliáng]

请勿将 meter 和 metre 混淆。在英式
英语里,以 -er 结尾的meter,是用来
测量或记录某事的工具,而以 –re 结
尾的 metre,是测量单位。在美式英语
中,meter 对于这两个含义都适用

method ['meθəd] N [c/u] (way) 方法 [fāngfǎ]
▶ method of payment or payment method 付
款方式

methodical [mɪˈθɔdɪkl] ADJ 有条不紊的 [yǒu
tiáo bù wěn de]

meths [meθs] (BRIT: inf) N [u] 甲基化酒精
[jiǎjīhuà jiǔjīng]

methylated spirits [meθəleɪtɪd-] (BRIT: frm)
N [u] 甲基化酒精 [jiǎjīhuà jiǔjīng]

meticulous [mɪˈtɪkjuləs] ADJ [+ person, detail]
严谨的 [yánjǐn de]; [+ care] 过度重视细节的
[guòdù zhòngshì xìjié de] ▶ to be meticulous
about sth/about doing sth 对某事/做某事
非常谨慎

metre, (US) **meter** ['miːtə(r)] N [c] (unit) 米
[mǐ]

用法参见 meter

metric ['metrɪk] I ADJ 公制的 [gōngzhì de]
II N ▶ to think/work in metric (inf) 用公制考
虑/工作 [yòng gōngzhì kǎolǜ/gōngzuò] ▶ to go
metric 采用公制

metro ['metrəu] N ▶ the metro 地铁 [dìtiě]

metropolitan [metrəˈpɔlɪtn] ADJ 大都市的
[dàdūshì de]

Mexican ['meksɪkən] I ADJ 墨西哥的 [Mòxīgē

de] II N [c] (person) 墨西哥人 [Mòxīgērén]

Mexico ['mɛksɪkəʊ] N 墨西哥 [Mòxīgē]

mg ABBR (= milligram) 毫克 [háokè]

MHz ABBR (= megahertz) 兆赫 [zhàohè]

mice [maɪs] N PL of mouse

microchip ['maɪkrəʊtʃɪp] N [c] 集成电路块 [jíchéng diànlù kuài]

microphone ['maɪkrəfəun] N [c] 话筒 [huàtǒng]

microscope ['maɪkrəskəup] N [c] 显微镜 [xiǎnwēijìng] ▸ under the microscope (fig) 仔细审查

microwave ['maɪkrəʊweɪv] I N [c] (also: microwave oven) 微波炉 [wēibōlú] II VT 用微波炉烹调 [yòng wēibōlú pēngtiáo]

mid- [mɪd] ADJ 中的 [zhōng de] ▸ he's in his mid-thirties/forties 他大约三十五六/四十五六岁

mid-air ['mɪdɛə(r)] I N ▸ in mid-air 在空中 [zài kōngzhōng] II ADJ 空中的 [kōngzhōng de]

midday [mɪd'deɪ] I N [u] **1** (noon) 正午 [zhèngwǔ] **2** (middle of the day) 中午 [zhōngwǔ] II ADJ 中午的 [zhōngwǔ de] ▸ at midday (at noon) 在正午; (in the middle of the day) 在中午

○ **middle** ['mɪdl] I N **1** [c] (centre) 中央 [zhōngyāng] ▷ Howard stood in the middle of the room. 霍华德站在房间中央。 **2** [s] (half-way point) 中间 [zhōngjiān] ▷ in the middle of the party 舞会中 ▷ in the middle of the morning 上午10点左右 **3** [c] (inf) (waist) 腰部 [yāobù] II ADJ **1** [+ position, event, period] 中间的 [zhōngjiān de] ▷ the middle month of each quarter 每一季的中间那个月份 ▷ She was the middle child of three. 她在3个孩子中排行老二。 **2** (moderate) [+ course, way, path] 中间派的 [zhōngjiānpài de] ▷ a middle course between free enterprise and state intervention 介于自由企业与政府干预之间的中间道路 ▸ in the middle of the night 在半夜 ▸ to be in the middle of sth/of doing sth 正忙于某事/做某事

middle-aged [mɪdl'eɪdʒd] ADJ **1** (neither young nor old) 中年的 [zhōngnián de] **2** (stuffy, boring) 老气的 [lǎoqì de]

Middle Ages N PL ▸ the Middle Ages 中世纪 [zhōngshìjì] ▸ in the Middle Ages 在中世纪时期

middle class I N ▸ the middle class(es) 中产阶级 [zhōngchǎn jiējí] II ADJ (also: middle-class) **1** (sociologically) 中层社会的 [zhōngcéng shèhuì de] **2** (pej) (bourgeois) 中产阶级的 [zhōngchǎn jiējí de]

Middle East N ▸ the Middle East 中东 [Zhōngdōng]

Middle Eastern N ADJ 中东的 [Zhōngdōng de]

middle name N [c] 中间名字 [zhōngjiān míngzi] ▸ trouble is her middle name 麻烦是

她的突出特征

○ **MIDDLE NAME**

first name 是由父母取的名字。last name 或 surname 是家族的姓氏。在说英语的国家中，名在姓之前。在 first name 和 last name 之间，还可能有 middle name (中名)，这是你父母给你取的第二个"名"。middle name 通常只用于正式场合，例如，选课或签署文件时。

midge [mɪdʒ] N [c] 蠓 [měng]

midget ['mɪdʒɪt] I N [c] 矮人 [ǎirén] II ADJ (miniature) 袖珍的 [xiùzhēn de]

midnight ['mɪdnaɪt] I N [u] 半夜 [bànyè] II CPD [复合词] 午夜的 [wǔyè de] ▸ at midnight 在午夜

midst [mɪdst] N ▸ in the midst of [+ situation, event] 在…之际 [zài…zhījì]; [+ crowd, group] 在…中 [zài…zhōng] ▸ to be in the midst of doing sth 正在做某事

midsummer [mɪd'sʌmə(r)] N [u] 仲夏 [zhòngxià]

midway [mɪd'weɪ] I ADJ ▸ the midway point (in space) 中间位置 [zhōngjiān wèizhì]; (in time) 到一半的时候 [dào yībàn de shíhou] II ADV **1** (in space) ▸ midway between sth and sth 某地与某地的中间 [mǒudì yǔ mǒudì de zhōngjiān] **2** (in time) ▸ midway through sth 某事中途 [mǒushì zhōngtú]

midweek [mɪd'wiːk] I ADJ 一周中间的 [yīzhōu zhōngjiān de] II ADV 一周中间 [yīzhōu zhōngjiān]

midwife ['mɪdwaɪf] (pl **midwives**) N [c] 助产士 [zhùchǎnshì]

midwinter [mɪd'wɪntə(r)] N [u] 仲冬 [zhòngdōng]

○ **might** [maɪt] I AUX VB **1** (possibility) ▸ I might get home late 我可能会晚点回家 [wǒ kěnéng huì wǎn huíjiā] ▸ you might be right 你也许是对的 ▸ it might have been an accident 可能是个事故 ▸ you might have been killed! 你差点儿没命了! **2** (suggestions) ▸ you might try the bookshop 你可以试一下书店 [nǐ kěyǐ shìyīxià shūdiàn] **3** (permission) ▸ might I make a suggestion? 我可以提个建议吗? [wǒ kěyǐ tígè jiànyì ma?] **4** (in expressions) ▸ I might have known or guessed 我早就该知道〔或〕猜到 [wǒ zǎojiù gāi zhīdào 〔huò〕 cāidào] ▸ you might as well go 你不妨也去 II N [u] (power) 力量 [lìliàng] ▸ with all one's might 竭尽全力地

mighty ['maɪtɪ] I ADJ (powerful) 强大的 [qiángdà de] II ADV (us: inf) (very) 很 [hěn]

migraine ['miːgreɪn] N [c/u] 偏头痛 [piāntóutòng]

migrant ['maɪgrənt] I N [c] **1** (person) 移民 [yímín] **2** (animal) 迁徙动物 [qiānxǐ dòngwù]

migrate [maɪˈgreɪt] VI 1 [person +] 迁移 [qiānyí] **2** [bird +] 迁徙 [qiānxǐ]

migration [maɪˈgreɪʃən] N [C/U] 1 [+ of people] 移居 [yíjū] **2** [+ of birds] 迁徙 [qiānxǐ]

mike [maɪk] (inf) N (microphone) 麦克风 [màikèfēng]

mild [maɪld] I ADJ 1 (slight) [+ feeling, tone] 温和的 [wēnhé de] **2** (not severe) [+ infection, illness] 轻微的 [qīngwēi de] **3** (gentle) [+ person, nature] 和善的 [héshàn de] **4** (moderate) [+ climate, weather] 温暖的 [wēnnuǎn de] **5** (not harsh) [+ soap, cosmetic] 温和的 [wēnhé de] **6** (not strong) [+ curry, cheese] 淡味的 [dànwèi de] II N [U] (BRIT) (beer) 淡啤酒 [dàn píjiǔ]

▓用法参见 **hot**

mildew [ˈmɪldjuː] N [U] 霉 [méi]

mildly [ˈmaɪldlɪ] ADV 1 (slightly) 稍微 [shāowēi] **2** (gently) [say, remark +] 温和地 [wēnhé de] **3** (not strongly) [+ spiced, flavoured] 适度地 [shìdù de] ▶ **to put it mildly** 说得婉转些

mile [maɪl] I N [C] 英里 [yīnglǐ] II **miles** NPL (inf) (a long way) 很远的距离 [hěnyuǎn de jùlí] ▶ **to do 30 miles to the gallon** 1加仑油可跑30英里 ▶ **70 miles per** or **an hour** 每小时70英里 ▶ **to win by a mile** or **miles** (inf) 远远胜出 ▶ **to be miles away** (inf) (distracted) 心不在焉 ▶ **miles better/slow** (inf) 好得多/过分慢

mileage [ˈmaɪlɪdʒ] N [C/U] 1 (number of miles) 英里里程 [yīnglǐ lǐchéng] **2** (fuel efficiency) 燃油效率 [rányóu xiàolù] **3** ▶ **to get a lot of mileage out of sth** 从某事中获取大量好处 [cóng mǒushì zhōng huòqǔ dàliàng hǎochù]

mileometer, milometer [maɪˈlɒmɪtə(r)] N [C] 计程表 [jìchéngqì]

milestone [ˈmaɪlstəun] N [C] (important event) 里程碑 [lǐchéngbēi]

militant [ˈmɪlɪtənt] I ADJ (politically active) 激进的 [jījìn de] II N [C] (political activist) 激进分子 [jījìn fènzǐ]

Ⓞ**military** [ˈmɪlɪtərɪ] I ADJ [+ leader, action] 军事的 [jūnshì de] II N ▶ **the military** 军队 [jūnduì]

militia [mɪˈlɪʃə] N [C] 民兵 [mínbīng]

milk [mɪlk] I N [U] 奶 [nǎi] II VT 1 [+ cow, goat] 挤⋯的奶 [jǐ⋯de nǎi] **2** (exploit) [+ situation, person] 榨取 [zhàqǔ]

milk chocolate N [U] 牛奶巧克力 [niúnǎi qiǎokèlì]

milkman [ˈmɪlkmæn] (pl **milkmen**) N [C] 送牛奶的人 [sòng niúnǎi de rén]

milkshake [ˈmɪlkʃeɪk] N [C/U] 奶昔 [nǎixī]

milky [ˈmɪlkɪ] ADJ 1 (in colour) 乳白色的 [rǔbái sè de] **2** [+ drink] 掺奶的 [chānnǎi de]

mill [mɪl] I N [C] 1 (for grain) 磨坊 [mòfáng] **2** (for coffee, pepper) 碾磨器 [niǎnmóqì] **3** (factory) 厂 [chǎng] II VT (grind) [+ grain, flour] 磨 [mó]

▶ **mill about, mill around** VI [people, crowd +] 乱转 [luànzhuàn]

millennium [mɪˈlɛnɪəm] (pl **millenniums** or **millennia** [mɪˈlɛnɪə]) N [C] 1 (1000 years) 一千年 [yīqiānnián] **2** ▶ **the Millennium** (year 2000) 千禧年 [qiānxǐnián]

milligram, (BRIT) milligramme [ˈmɪlɪgræm] N [C] 毫克 [háokè]

millilitre, (US) milliliter [ˈmɪlɪliːtə(r)] N [C] 毫升 [háoshēng]

millimetre, (US) millimeter [ˈmɪlɪmiːtə(r)] N [C] 毫米 [háomǐ]

Ⓞ**million** [ˈmɪljən] I NUM 百万 [bǎiwàn] ▷ three million pounds 300万英镑 II **millions** NPL (lit) 数百万 [shùbǎiwàn]; (inf)(fig) 无数 [wúshù] ▶ **a** or **one million books/people/dollars** 100万本书/个人/元 ▶ **millions are starving** 数以百万的人正在忍受饥饿 ▶ **millions of people/things** (loads of) 无数的人/物

millionaire [mɪljəˈnɛə(r)] N [C] 百万富翁 [bǎiwàn fùwēng]

millionth [ˈmɪljənθ] I ADJ 第一百万的 [dì yībǎiwàn de] II N [C] (millionth part) 百万分之一 [bǎiwànfēn zhī yī]

milometer [maɪˈlɒmɪtə(r)] N = **mileometer**

mime [maɪm] I VT 1 假唱 [jiǎchàng] **2** (act out) 模仿 [mófǎng] II VI 1 假装 [jiǎzhuāng] **2** (act) 用手比划表示 [yòngshǒu bǐhuà biǎoshì] III N 1 [U] (art form) 哑剧 [yǎjù] **2** [C] (performance) 哑剧表演 [yǎjù biǎoyǎn] IV CPD [复合词] [+ artist] 哑剧 [yǎjù]

mimic [ˈmɪmɪk] I VT 模仿 [mófǎng] II N [C] 善于模仿的人 [shànyú mófǎng de rén]

min. (pl **min.** or **mins**) N ABBR 1 (= minute) 分钟 [fēnzhōng] **2** = minimum

mince [mɪns] I N [U] (BRIT: CULIN) 肉末 [ròumò] [美 = ground beef] II VT (BRIT) [+ meat] 绞碎 [jiǎosuì] [美 = grind] III VI (in walking) 扭扭捏捏地走 [niǔniǔ-niēniē de zǒu] ▶ **he doesn't mince (his) words** 他直言不讳

mincemeat [ˈmɪnsmiːt] N [U] 1 (fruit) 百果馅 [bǎiguǒxiàn] **2** (BRIT) (meat) 肉末 [ròumò] [美 = ground beef, hamburger meat] ▶ **to make mincemeat of sb** 彻底击败某人

mince pie N [C/U] 百果馅饼 [bǎiguǒ xiànbǐng]

Ⓞ**mind** [maɪnd] I N [C] 1 (thoughts) 脑海 [nǎohǎi] ▷ He couldn't get her out of his mind. 他无法将她从脑海中摆脱。**2** (intellect) 智力 [zhìlì] ▷ Studying stretched my mind and got me thinking. 学习开发了我的智力并让我勤于思考。**3** (mentality) 头脑 [tóunǎo] ▷ Andrew, you have a very suspicious mind. 安德鲁，你有个善猜疑的头脑。**4** (thinker) 有才智的人 [yǒu cáizhì de rén] ▷ a team of the brightest minds available 才智出众的人组成的团队 II VT 1 (BRIT) (look after) [+ child, shop] 照看 [zhàokàn] ▷ My mother is minding the office. 我母亲正照看着办公室。**2** (be careful of) 当心 [dāngxīn] ▷ Mind your head! 当心头！

3 (object to) 介意 [jièyì] ▷ I don't mind walking. 我不介意走路。**4** (have a preference) ▶ I don't mind(what/who...) 我不在乎(什么／谁…) [wǒ bù zàihu (shénme/shéi…)] ▷ I don't mind what we have for dinner. 我不在乎我们晚饭吃什么。**5** ▶ do/would you mind (if...)? (如果…) 你介意吗? [(rúguǒ…) nǐ jièyì ma?] ▷ Would you mind waiting outside for a moment? 你介意在外面等一会儿吗? ▶ to be out of one's mind 发疯 ▶ to have a lot on one's mind 有许多事牵肠挂肚 ▶ to my mind (in my opinion) 据我看来 ▶ to make up one's mind or make one's mind up 下定决心 ▶ to change one's/sb's mind 改变主意 ▶ to be in or (us) of two minds about sth 对某事犹豫不决 ▶ what do you have in mind? 你有什么主意? ▶ to bear or keep sth in mind 记住某事 ▶ it slipped my mind 我忘了 ▶ it never crossed my mind 我从未想过 ▶ in my mind's eye 在我的想象中 ▶ to come or spring to mind 在脑海中闪现 ▶ my mind was on other things 我的心思在其他事情上 ▶ to have or keep an open mind 暂不作决定 ▶ state of mind 精神状况 ▶ to take one's mind off sth 暂时丢开不想 ▶ mind you,... (admittedly) 说真的,… ▶ never mind 不要紧 ▶ I wouldn't mind a coffee 我挺想喝杯咖啡 ▶ mind your own business (inf) 别多管闲事 ▶ mind the step 小心脚下

minder ['maɪndə(r)] N [c] **1** (bodyguard) 保镖 [bǎobiāo] **2** (BRIT) (also: child minder) 保育员 [bǎoyùyuán]

mindful ['maɪndful] (frm) ADJ ▶ mindful of 留神的 [liúshén de]

mindless ['maɪndlɪs] ADJ **1** (senseless) [+ violence] 盲目的 [mángmù de] **2** (stupid) [+ person] 没头脑的 [méi tóunǎo de] **3** (boring) [+ work] 无需动脑的 [wúxū dòngnǎo de]

○ **mine¹** [maɪn] PRON 我的 [wǒ de] ▶ a friend of mine 我的一个朋友 ▶ this is mine 这是我的 ▶ these are mine 这些是我的

○ **mine²** [maɪn] I N [c] **1** (for coal, gold etc) 矿 [kuàng] **2** (bomb) 地雷 [dìléi] II VT **1** (dig out) [+ coal, gold etc] 开采 [kāicǎi] **2** (lay mines in) [+ area] 布雷于 [bùléi yú] ▶ he's a real mine of information 他真是一本活字典

minefield ['maɪnfi:ld] N [c] **1** (area) 雷区 [léiqū] **2** (situation) 危险地带 [wēixiǎn dìdài]

miner ['maɪnə(r)] N [c] 矿工 [kuànggōng]

mineral ['mɪnərəl] I N [c] 矿物 [kuàngwù] II CPD [复合词] [+ deposit, resources] 矿物 [kuàngwù]

mineral water N [U/c] 矿泉水 [kuàngquánshuǐ]

mingle ['mɪŋgl] VI **1** ▶ to mingle (with sth) (mix) [sounds, smells etc +] (和某物) 混杂 [(hé mǒuwù) hùnzá] **2** (person +) (at party) 交往 [jiāowǎng]

miniature ['mɪnətʃə(r)] I ADJ **1** 微型的 [wēixíng de] II N [c] **1** (painting) 微型画 [wēixínghuà]

2 (bottle) 小瓶装的酒 [xiǎopíngzhuāng de jiǔ] ▶ in miniature 缩影的

minibar ['mɪnɪbɑ:(r)] N [c] 客房内酒吧 [kèfángnèi jiǔbā]

minibus ['mɪnɪbʌs] N [c] 小公共汽车 [xiǎo gōnggòng qìchē]

minicab ['mɪnɪkæb] (BRIT) N [c] 必须得事先预定的出租车

MiniDisc®, minidisc ['mɪnɪdɪsk] N **1** [U] (system) MD格式 [MD géshì] **2** [c] (disc) 迷你光碟 [mínǐ guāngdié] **3** [c] (also: MiniDisc®) (also: player) 微型唱片机 [wēixíng chàngpiàn jī]

minimal ['mɪnɪml] ADJ 最低限度的 [zuìdī xiàndù de]

minimize ['mɪnɪmaɪz] VT **1** (reduce) [+ risks, disease] 使…减少到最低 [shǐ…jiǎnshǎo dào zuìdī] **2** (play down) [+ role, weakness] 贬低 [biǎndī] **3** (COMPUT) 把…最小化 [bǎ…zuìxiǎohuà]

minimum ['mɪnɪməm] I ADJ **1** (lowest, smallest) 最低的 [zuìdī de] **2** (little) 最少的 [zuìshǎo de] II N [c] 最少量 [zuìshǎoliàng] ▶ to reduce/keep sth to a minimum 将某物降到/保持在最低限度 ▶ a minimum of... 最少的 ▶ three months minimum 最少3个月

mining ['maɪnɪŋ] I N [U] 矿业 [kuàngyè] II CPD [复合词] [+ village, expert] 采矿 [cǎikuàng]

miniskirt ['mɪnɪskə:t] N [c] 超短裙 [chāoduǎnqún]

○ **minister** ['mɪnɪstə(r)] I N [c] **1** (BRIT: POL) 部长 [bùzhǎng] ▷ the new Defence Minister 新国防部部长 **2** (REL) 牧师 [mùshī] II VI ▶ to minister to [+ people, needs] 照料 [zhàoliào]

ministry ['mɪnɪstrɪ] N **1** [c] (BRIT: POL) 部 [bù] **2** (REL) ▶ the ministry 牧师 [mùshī] ▶ the Ministry of Defence/Agriculture (BRIT) 国防部/农业部

minor ['maɪnə(r)] I ADJ **1** (unimportant) [+ repairs, changes] 不重要的 [bù zhòngyào de] **2** (MUS) [+ key, scale] 小调的 [xiǎodiào de] II N [c] **1** (under-age child) 未成年人 [wèichéngniánrén] **2** (US: SCOL) (subject) 辅修科目 [fǔxiū kēmù] **3** (US: SCOL) (student) ▶ a history minor 历史辅修生 [lìshǐ fǔxiūshēng] III VI (US: SCOL) ▶ to minor in sth 辅修某科 [fǔxiū mǒukē] ▷ Chopin's Scherzo in B flat minor 用降B小调演奏肖邦的谐谑曲

minority [maɪ'nɒrɪtɪ] I N **1** [S + PL VB] [of group, society] 少数 [shǎoshù] **2** [c] (ethnic, cultural, religious) 少数民族 [shǎoshù mínzú] II CPD [复合词] [+ shareholder, verdict] 少数 [shǎoshù] ▶ to be in a or the minority 占少数 ▶ a (small) minority of (极)少数的

mint [mɪnt] I N **1** [U] (plant) 薄荷 [bòhe] **2** (sweet) 薄荷糖 [bòhe táng] **3** ▶ the (Royal) Mint, the Mint (英国皇家)铸币局, (美国)铸币局 [(Yīngguó huángjiā) zhùbìjú,

(Měiguó) zhùbìjú] **II** VT [+ *coins*] 铸造 [zhùzào]
▶ **in mint condition** 状况完好

minus ['maɪnəs] **I** N [C] **1** (*also*: minus sign) 负
号 [fùhào] **2** (*disadvantage*) 不足 [bùzú] **II** PREP
(*inf*) (*without*) 没有 [méiyǒu] ▶ **12 minus 3** (*is or
equals 9*) 12减3(等于9) ▶ **minus 24** (*degrees
C/F*) (*temperature*) 零下24(摄氏/华氏度)
▶ **minus 24** (MATH) 负24 ▶ **B minus** (SCOL) B减

⊙ **minute¹** [maɪ'njuːt] ADJ [+ *amount*] 极小的
[jíxiǎo de] ▶ **in minute detail** 细枝末节

⊙ **minute²** ['mɪnɪt] **I** N [C] **1** (*unit*) 分钟
[fēnzhōng] **2** (*fig*) (*short time*) 一会儿 [yīhuìr]
▷ Will you excuse me if I sit down for a minute? 我可
以坐一会儿吗? **II** minutes NPL [*of meeting*]
会议记录 [huìyì jìlù] ▶ **5 minutes past 3** 3点
过5分 ▶ **wait** *or* **just a minute!** 等一会儿!
▶ **(at) any minute** *or* **any minute (now)** 随
时 ▶ **the minute (that)...** 一…就… ▶ **this
minute** (*inf*) 立刻 ▶ **(at/until) the last minute**
(在/到)最后一刻

miracle ['mɪrəkl] **I** N [C] **1** (REL) 圣迹 [shèngjì]
2 (*marvel*) 奇迹 [qíjì] **II** CPD [复合词] [+ *cure,
drug*] 特效 [tèxiào] ▶ **it's a miracle (that)...**
…真是个奇迹

miraculous [mɪ'rækjuləs] ADJ **1** 奇迹般的
[qíjìbān de] **2** (REL) 圣迹般的 [shèngjìbān de]

mirage ['mɪrɑːʒ] N [C] **1** (*optical illusion*) 海市蜃
楼 [hǎishì shènlóu] **2** (*delusion*) 幻影 [huànyǐng]

mirror ['mɪrə(r)] **I** N [C] 镜子 [jìngzi]; [*in car*] 后
视镜 [hòushìjìng] **II** VT 反映 [fǎnyìng]

misbehave [mɪsbɪ'heɪv] VI 行为无礼 [xíngwéi
wúlǐ]

misc. ABBR = **miscellaneous**

miscalculate [mɪs'kælkjuleɪt] **I** VT 错误估计
[cuòwù gūjì] **II** VI 算错 [suàncuò]

miscarriage ['mɪskærɪdʒ] N [C] (MED) 流产
[liúchǎn] ▶ **to have a miscarriage** 流产
▶ **miscarriage of justice** 误判

miscellaneous [mɪsɪ'leɪnɪəs] ADJ [+ *people,
objects*] 形形色色的 [xíngxíng sèsè de]
▶ **miscellaneous expenses** 各种花销

mischief ['mɪstʃɪf] N [U] **1** (*playfulness, fun*) 顽
皮 [wánpí] **2** (*trouble, harm*) 损害 [sǔnhài] ▶ **to
get into** *or* **up to mischief** 胡闹 ▶ **to do o.s. a
mischief** (*inf*) 使自己受伤

mischievous ['mɪstʃɪvəs] ADJ **1** (*playful, fun-
loving*) 淘气的 [táoqì de] **2** (*malicious*) 恶意的
[èyì de]

misconception ['mɪskən'sɛpʃən] N [C] 误解
[wùjiě]

misconduct [mɪs'kɒndʌkt] N [U] (*misbehaviour*)
行为不端 [xíngwéi bùduān]

miser ['maɪzə(r)] (*pej*) N [C] 守财奴 [shǒucáinú]

miserable ['mɪzərəbl] ADJ **1** (*unhappy*) [+ *person*]
痛苦的 [tòngkǔ de] **2** (*wretched*) [+ *conditions,
place*] 破败的 [pòbài de] **3** (*unpleasant*)
[+ *weather, day*] 恶劣的 [èliè de] **4** (*bad-tempered,
unfriendly*) [+ *person, nature*] 坏脾气的 [huài píqì

de] **5** (*meagre*) [+ *amount*] 少得可怜的 [shǎode
kělián de] **6** (*hopeless*) [+ *failure*] 悲惨的 [bēicǎn
de] ▶ **to feel miserable** 感到痛苦

misery ['mɪzərɪ] N **1** [U] (*unhappiness*) 痛苦
[tòngkǔ] **2** [U] (*wretchedness*) 穷困 [qióngkùn]
3 [C] (ESP BRIT: *inf*) (*person*) 爱发牢骚的人 [ài fā
láosāo de rén] ▶ **to put sb out of their misery**
(*inf*) 解开某人心中的疑团 ▶ **to put sth out
of its misery** 杀死某动物以结束其痛苦 ▶ **to
make sb's life a misery** 使某人日子不好过

misfortune [mɪs'fɔːtʃən] N [C/U] 不幸
[bùxìng]

misgiving [mɪs'gɪvɪŋ] N [C/U] ▶ **to have
misgivings about sth** 对某事感到担心 [duì
mǒushì gǎndào dānxīn] ▶ **to be filled with
misgiving about sth** 对某事疑虑重重

misguided [mɪs'gaɪdɪd] ADJ [+ *opinion, attempt*]
误导的 [wùdǎo de]; [+ *person*] 误入歧途的
[wùrù qítú de]

mishandle [mɪs'hændl] VT [+ *situation, project*]
错误处理 [cuòwù chǔlǐ]

mishap ['mɪshæp] N [C] 小小的不幸 [xiǎoxiǎo
de bùxìng] ▶ **without mishap** 毫无波折

mishear [mɪs'hɪə(r)] (*pt, pp* **misheard** [mɪs'hɜːd])
I VT [+ *person, remark*] 听错 [tīngcuò] **II** VI 听
错 [tīngcuò]

misinterpret [mɪsɪn'tɜːprɪt] VT 曲解 [qūjiě]

misjudge [mɪs'dʒʌdʒ] VT [+ *person, situation*] 错
误判断 [cuòwù pànduàn]

mislay [mɪs'leɪ] (*pt, pp* **mislaid** [mɪs'leɪd]) VT 忘
记把…放在何处 [wàngjì bǎ…fàng zài héchù]

mislead [mɪs'liːd] (*pt, pp* **misled**) VT 误导
[wùdǎo] ▶ **to mislead sb about sth** 在某事上
误导某人

misleading [mɪs'liːdɪŋ] ADJ 使人误解的 [shǐ
rén wùjiě de]

misled [mɪs'lɛd] PT, PP *of* mislead

misplace [mɪs'pleɪs] (*frm*) VT (*mislay*) 误置
[wùzhì]

misprint ['mɪsprɪnt] N [C] 印刷错误 [yìnshuā
cuòwù]

misrepresent [mɪsrɛprɪ'zɛnt] VT [+ *person,
views*] 歪曲 [wāiqū]

Miss [mɪs] N **1** (*before surname*) 小姐 [xiǎojiě]
2 (ESP BRIT) (*as form of address*) 小姐 [xiǎojiě]
▶ **Dear Miss Smith** 亲爱的史密斯小姐 ▶ **Miss
World** (*in beauty contests*) 世界小姐

MISS, MRS, MS

在说英语的国家中，**Mrs** (夫人)用于已
婚女士的姓名前。**Miss** (小姐)用于未婚
女士的姓名前。有些女士认为，让人们知
道她是否结婚并不重要，所以往往用 **Ms**
(女士)称呼自己。与 **Mr** (先生)类似，
Ms 不表明任何婚姻状况。

⊙ **miss** [mɪs] **I** VT **1** (*fail to hit*) 未击中 [wèi

jīzhòng] ▷ *She threw an ashtray across the room, narrowly missing my head.* 她从房间那端扔过来一只烟灰缸，差点击中我的头。**2** (SPORT) [+ *shot, penalty*] 打偏 [dǎpiān] ▷ *He scored four goals but missed a penalty.* 他进了4个球，却踢偏了1个点球。**3** (*fail to catch*) [+ *train, bus, plane*] 错过 [cuòguò] ▷ *Daniel nearly missed his flight.* 丹尼尔差点错过他的航班。**4** (*notice loss of*) [+ *money etc*] 发觉丢失 [fājué diūshī] ▷ *He didn't miss his wallet until he was on the plane.* 直到上了飞机他才发觉丢失了钱包。**5** (*fail to notice*) 忽视 [hūshì] ▷ *Captain Cobbins was an experienced officer and didn't miss much.* 科宾斯上尉是个有经验的军官，不会忽视太多东西。**6** (*feel the absence of*) [+ *person, thing*] 想念 [xiǎngniàn] ▷ *Did you miss me?* 你想念我吗？▷ *If I moved into a flat I'd really miss my garden.* 如果我搬到公寓去住，我肯定会很想念我的花园。**7** (*fail to take*) [+ *chance, opportunity*] 错过 [cuòguò] ▷ *It was too good an opportunity to miss.* 这个机会好得不容错过。**8** (*fail to attend*) [+ *class, meeting*] 缺席 [quēxí] ▷ *I couldn't miss a departmental meeting.* 系里开会我不可以缺席。**II** VI (*fail to hit*) [*person +*] 没打中 [méi dǎzhòng] ▷ *She threw her plate at his head and missed.* 她把盘子朝他的头扔去，但没打中。**III** N [C] **1** (*failure to hit*) 击不中 [jī bùzhòng] ▷ *After more misses, they shot the lion in the chest.* 又有几次没击中后，他们射中了狮子的胸部。**2** (SPORT) 失误 [shīwù] ▷ *Striker Marcus Smith's miss cost them the match.* 前锋马克斯·史密斯的失误使他们输掉了这场比赛。▶ **to just miss sth** 刚好错过某事 ▶ **you can't miss it** 你不会找不到 ▶ **to miss the point** 没领会要点 ▶ *his shirt was missing a button* (inf) 他的衬衫少了一粒纽扣 ▶ **to give sth a miss** (BRIT) 避开某事
▶ **miss out** (BRIT) **I** VT (*accidentally*) 遗漏 [yílòu] ▷ *It's easy to miss out a comma when you're writing quickly.* 在你写快地书写的时候很容易会遗漏一个逗号。[美= **leave out**] **II** VI (*lose out*) 错过机会 [cuòguò jīhuì]
▶ **miss out on** VT FUS [不可拆分] [+ *opportunity, fun*] 错过 [cuòguò]

missile ['mɪsaɪl] N [C] **1** (MIL) 导弹 [dǎodàn] **2** (*object thrown*) 投掷物 [tóuzhìwù]

missing ['mɪsɪŋ] ADJ (*absent, lost*) [+ *person*] 失踪的 [shīzōng de]; [+ *object*] 丢失的 [diūshī de] ▶ **to go missing** 不知去向 ▶ **missing person** 失踪人员 ▶ **missing in action** 作战中失踪

mission ['mɪʃən] N [C] **1** (*task*) 任务 [rènwù] **2** (*mission*) 使命 [shǐmìng] **3** (*official representatives*) 代表团 [dàibiǎotuán] **4** (MIL, AVIAT) (*flight*) 飞行任务 [fēixíng rènwù] **5** (REL) (*campaign*) 传教活动 [chuánjiào huódòng]; (*building*) 教区 [jiàoqū]

missionary ['mɪʃənrɪ] N [C] 传教士 [chuánjiào shì]

misspell ['mɪs'spɛl] (pt, pp **misspelt** (BRIT) or

misspelled) VT 拼错 [pīncuò]

mist [mɪst] N [C/U] 薄雾 [bówù]
▶ **mist over, mist up I** VI [*window, glasses +*] 被蒙上水汽 [bèi méngshàng shuǐqì] ▶ **his eyes misted over** 他泪眼模糊 **II** VT [+ *window, glasses*] 使蒙上水汽 [shǐ méngshàng shuǐqì]

mistake [mɪs'teɪk] (pt **mistook**, pp **mistaken**) **I** N [C] **1** (*error*) (*in calculations, text etc*) 错误 [cuòwù] **2** (*blunder*) 过失 [guòshī] **II** VT (*be wrong about*) 弄错 [nòngcuò] ▶ **to make a mistake** 犯错 ▶ **you're making a big mistake** 你正在犯一个严重的错误 ▶ **to make the mistake of doing sth** 做某事 ▶ **it was a (big) mistake to do that** 那么做是个(严重的)错误 ▶ **there must be some mistake** 一定是搞错了 ▶ **to do sth by mistake** 误做某事 ▶ **to mistake A for B** 把A误认为B ▶ **there is no mistaking...** …不可能被弄错

mistaken [mɪs'teɪkən] **I** PP of **mistake II** ADJ [+ *idea, belief etc*] 错误的 [cuòwù de] ▶ **to be mistaken (about sth)** [*person +*] (把某事)搞错 ▶ **if I'm not** or **unless I'm mistaken** 如果我没弄错的话

mister ['mɪstə(r)] N (inf) 先生 [xiānsheng] see **Mr**

mistletoe ['mɪsltəu] N [U] 槲寄生 [hújìshēng]

▶ **MISTLETOE**

mistletoe 是一种灌木，绿色茎叶和蜡白色浆果。在英国和美国，被用作圣诞节装饰物。根据传统，人们在槲寄生下面亲吻。

mistook [mɪs'tuk] PT of **mistake**

mistress ['mɪstrɪs] N [C] **1** (*lover*) 情妇 [qíngfù] **2** (BRIT: o.f.): SCOL (*teacher*) 女教师 [nǚ jiàoshī] **3** (*owner*) 女主人 [nǚ zhǔrén] **4** [*of house, servant*] 女主人 [nǚ zhǔrén]

mistrust [mɪs'trʌst] **I** N [U] ▶ **mistrust (of sth/sb)** (对某事/某人)不信任 [(duì mǒushì/mǒurén) bù xìnrèn] **II** VT 不相信 [bù xiāngxìn]

misty ['mɪstɪ] ADJ [+ *day, weather*] 有雾的 [yǒuwù de] ▶ **it's misty** 有雾

misunderstand [mɪsʌndə'stænd] (pt, pp **misunderstood**) VT, VI 误解 [wùjiě]

misunderstanding ['mɪsʌndə'stændɪŋ] N **1** [C/U] 误会 [wùhuì] **2** [C] (*disagreement*) 争执 [zhēngzhí]

misunderstood [mɪsʌndə'stud] **I** PT, PP of **misunderstand II** ADJ 被误解的 [bèi wùjiě de]

misuse [n mɪs'juːs, vb mɪs'juːz] **I** N [C/U] 滥用 [lànyòng] **II** VT 误用 [wùyòng]

mitt [mɪt] N [C] **1** (inf) (*mitten*) 连指手套 [liánzhǐ shǒutào] **2** (BASEBALL) (*glove*) 棒球手套 [bàngqiú shǒutào] **3** (inf) (*hand*) 手 [shǒu]

mitten ['mɪtn] N [C] 连指手套 [liánzhǐ shǒutào]

mix [mɪks] I VT 1 (combine) [+ liquids, ingredients, colours] 混合 [hùnhé] 2 (prepare) [+ cake, sauce] 拌和 [bànhuò]; [+ cement] 搅拌 [jiǎobàn] 3 [+ sounds, tracks] 混 [hùn] II VI 1 混合 [hùnhé] 2 (socially) ▶ **to mix (with sb)** (和某人) 相处 [(hé mǒurén) xiāngchǔ] III N 1 [c] (combination) 混合 [hùnhé] 2 [c/U] (powder) 混合料 [hùnhé liào] ▶ **to mix sth with sth** [+ activities] 将某物同某物混淆 ▶ **to mix business with pleasure** 把生意和娱乐相结合 ▶ **to mix sb a drink** 给某人调制一杯饮料 ▶ **politics and sport don't mix** 政治和运动互不相容
 ▶ **mix in** VT [+ eggs etc] 搅拌加入 [jiǎobàn jiārù]
 ▶ **mix up** VT (confuse) [+ people] 分辨不出 [fēnbiàn bùchū]; [+ things] 混淆 [hùnxiáo]

mixed [mɪkst] ADJ 1 (varying) [+ reactions, signals] 复杂的 [fùzá de] 2 (combined) [+ salad, herbs] 什锦的 [shíjǐn de] 3 (diverse) [+ group, community] 形形色色的 [xíngxíng sèsè de] 4 [+ race] 混血的 [hùnxuè de] 5 [+ marriage] 异族的 [yìzú de] 6 (coeducational) [+ school, education] 男女混合的 [nánnǚ hùnhé de] ▶ **to have mixed feelings (about sth)** (对于某事) 百感交集

mixed grill (BRIT: CULIN) N [c] 烤杂排 [kǎozápái]

mixed up ADJ (confused) 糊涂的 [hútu de] ▶ **to get mixed up (about sth)** (把某事) 混淆起来 ▶ **to get sth mixed up** [+ facts, dates] 把某事弄混 ▶ **to be/get mixed up in sth** 被卷入某事

mixer ['mɪksə(r)] N [c] 1 (also: food mixer) 搅拌器 [jiǎobànqì] 2 (drink) 调酒用的饮料 [tiáojiǔ yòng de yǐnliào] 3 (person) ▶ **to be a good mixer** 是交际能手 [shì jiāojì néngshǒu]

mixture ['mɪkstʃə(r)] N [c/U] 混合物 [hùnhéwù]

mix-up ['mɪksʌp] (inf) N [c] 混乱 [hùnluàn]

mm ABBR (= millimetres) 毫米 [háomǐ]

moan [məʊn] I VI 1 (groan) 呻吟 [shēnyín] 2 (inf) (complain) ▶ **to moan (about sth)** 抱怨 (某事) [bàoyuàn (mǒushì)] 3 (say) 呻吟着说 [shēnyínzhe shuō] II N [c] 1 (groan) 呻吟 [shēnyín] 2 (complaint) 抱怨 [bàoyuàn]

moat [məʊt] N [c] 护城河 [hùchénghé]

mob [mɔb] I N 1 [c] (disorderly crowd) 暴民 [bàomín] 2 [c] (inf) (gang, crew) 团伙 [tuánhuǒ] 3 (inf) (mafia) ▶ **the Mob** 黑手党 [Hēishǒudǎng] II VT [+ person] 成群围住 [chéngqún wéizhù] III CPD [复合词] [+ violence, rule] 暴民 [bàomín]

mobile ['məʊbaɪl] I ADJ 1 [+ library, studio, office] 流动的 [liúdòng de] 2 [+ person] (having transport) 有私人的代步工具的 [yǒu sīrén de dàibù gōngjù de]; (able to walk) 能活动的 [néng huódòng de] 3 [+ workforce, population] 流动的 [liúdòng de] II N [c] 1 (BRIT: inf) (mobile phone) 手机 [shǒujī] 2 (decoration) 风动饰物 [fēngdòng shìwù]

mobile home N [c] 活动住房 [huódòng zhùfáng]

mobile phone (BRIT) N [c] 手机 [shǒujī] [美= **cellphone, cellular phone**]

mobility [məʊˈbɪlɪtɪ] N [U] 1 [of person] (through transport) 机动性 [jīdòngxìng]; (ability to walk) 行走能力 [xíngzǒu nénglì] 2 [of workforce, population] 流动性 [liúdòngxìng]

mobilize ['məʊbɪlaɪz] I VT 1 (organize) [+ people, support] 动员 [dòngyuán] 2 (MIL) [+ army] 调动 [diàodòng] II VI (MIL) [country, army +] 动员起来 [dòngyuán qǐlái]

mock [mɔk] I VT (ridicule) 嘲笑 [cháoxiào] II ADJ 1 (artificial, false) [+ style, material] 仿制的 [fǎngzhì de] 2 (pretend) [+ emotion] 假装的 [jiǎzhuāng de] 3 (staged) [+ battle, execution] 模拟的 [mónǐ de] III **mocks** NPL (BRIT) (also: **mock exams, mock examinations**) 模拟考试 [mónǐ kǎoshì]

mockery ['mɔkərɪ] N [U] 嘲弄 [cháonòng] ▶ **to make a mockery of sth** 使某事成为笑柄

mocking ['mɔkɪŋ] ADJ 讥讽的 [jīfěng de]

mod cons (BRIT: inf) NPL ABBR (= modern conveniences) 现代化生活设备 [xiàndàihuà shēnghuó shèbèi]

mode [məʊd] (frm) N [c] 1 (form) 形式 [xíngshì] 2 (setting) 模式 [móshì]

model ['mɔdl] I N [c] 1 [of boat, building etc] 模型 [móxíng] 2 (fashion model) 时装模特 [shízhuāng mótè] 3 [artist's model] 模特 [mótè] 4 (example) ▶ **a model of** …的典范 [...de diǎnfàn] II ADJ 1 (exemplary) [+ teacher, mother, farm etc] 模范的 [mófàn de] 2 (miniature) ▶ **model aircraft/train** 模型飞机/火车 [móxíng fēijī/huǒchē] III VT 1 [+ clothes] 展示 [zhǎnshì] 2 (sculpt) 塑造 [sùzào] IV VI (for designer, photographer etc) 当模特 [dāng mótè] ▶ **to model o.s. on sb** 以某人为榜样

modem ['məʊdɛm] N [c] 调制解调器 [tiáozhì jiětiáo qì]

moderate [adj, n 'mɔdərət, vb 'mɔdəreɪt] I ADJ 1 (not extreme) [+ views, people] 中庸的 [zhōngyōng de] 2 (not big, not small) [+ amount, improvement] 适度的 [shìdù de] II N [c] (POL) 温和派 [wēnhépài] III VT 1 [+ tone of voice, language] 使缓和 [shǐ huǎnhé] 2 [+ demands] 减轻 [jiǎnqīng]; [+ views] 使温和 [shǐ wēnhé] IV VI (abate) [storm, crisis etc +] 变温和 [biàn wēnhé]

moderation [mɔdəˈreɪʃən] N [U] 中庸 [zhōngyōng] ▶ **in moderation** 适度

modern ['mɔdən] ADJ 1 (present-day) [+ world, times, society etc] 现代的 [xiàndài de] 2 (up-to-date) [+ technology, design etc] 新式的 [xīnshì de]

modern languages NPL 现代语言 [xiàndài yǔyán]

modernize ['mɔdənaɪz] VT 使现代化 [shǐ xiàndàihuà]

modest ['mɔdɪst] ADJ 1 (small) [+ amount,

improvement] 少量的 [shǎoliàng de]; [+ *house, flat*] 朴素的 [pǔsù de] **2** (*not boastful*) [+ *person*] 谦虚的 [qiānxū de] **3** (*decent*) [+ *woman, clothes, behaviour*] 端庄的 [duānzhuāng de]

modesty ['mɒdɪstɪ] N [U] **1** (*humility*) 谦逊 [qiānxùn] **2** (*smallness*) 小 [xiǎo] **3** (*simplicity*) 朴实 [pǔshí] **4** (*decency*) 端庄 [duānzhuāng]

modification [mɒdɪfɪ'keɪʃən] N [C/U] (*to machine*) 改装 [gǎizhuāng]; (*to policy, plan*) 修改 [xiūgǎi] ▸ **to make modifications to sth** 对某物进行修改

modify ['mɒdɪfaɪ] VT [+ *machine*] 改装 [gǎizhuāng]; [+ *policy, plan*] 修改 [xiūgǎi]

module ['mɒdju:l] N [C] **1** (SCOL) 单元 [dānyuán] **2** (SPACE) 舱 [cāng] **3** [*of building*] 部件 [bùjiàn] **4** [*of machine*] 组件 [zǔjiàn]

mohair ['məuhɛə(r)] I N [U] 马海毛 [mǎhǎimáo] II CPD [复合词] [+ *jumper, scarf, dress*] 马海毛 [mǎhǎimáo]

Mohammed [mə'hæmɛd] N 穆罕默德 [Mùhǎnmòdé]

moist [mɔɪst] ADJ 潮湿的 [cháoshī de]

moisten ['mɔɪsn] VT 弄湿 [nòngshī]

moisture ['mɔɪstʃə(r)] N [U] 水分 [shuǐfèn]

moisturizer ['mɔɪstʃəraɪzə(r)] N [C/U] 保湿霜 [bǎoshīshuāng]

molasses [mə'læsɪz] N [U] 糖浆 [tángjiāng]

mold *etc* [məuld] (US) N, VT = **mould** *etc*

Moldova [mɒl'dəuvə] N 摩尔多瓦 [Mó'ěrduōwǎ]

Moldovan [mɒl'dəuvən] I ADJ 摩尔多瓦的 [Mó'ěrduōwǎ de] II N **1** [c] (*person*) 摩尔多瓦人 [Mó'ěrduōwǎrén] **2** [U] (*language*) 摩尔多瓦语 [Mó'ěrduōwǎyǔ]

mole [məul] N [C] **1** (*on skin*) 痣 [zhì] **2** (*animal*) 鼹鼠 [yǎnshǔ] **3** (*spy*) 间谍 [jiàndié]

molecule ['mɒlɪkju:l] N [C] 分子 [fēnzǐ]

molest [mə'lɛst] VT (*sexually*) 猥亵 [wěixiè]

molten ['məultən] ADJ [+ *metal, glass, rock*] 熔化的 [rónghuà de]

mom [mɒm] (US: *inf*) N [C] 妈妈 [māma] [英 = **mum**]

○ **moment** ['məumənt] N [C] (*period of time*) 片刻 [piànkè] ▷ *It lasted only a moment.* 只持续了片刻。 **2** [c] (*point in time*) 瞬间 [shùnjiān] ▷ *That was the moment I understood.* 在那一瞬间我明白了。 **3** [U] (*frm*) (*importance*) 重要 [zhòngyào] ▷ *a matter of the greatest moment* 最重要的一件事 ▸ **for a** *or* **one moment** (*showing disbelief*) 一刻 ▷ *I don't for a moment think there'll be a divorce.* 我一刻都没想过会离婚。; (*showing relief*) 有那么一刻 ▷ *For a moment I thought he wasn't going to make it.* 有那么一刻我还以为他不会来了。; (*briefly*) 一会儿 ▷ *She stared at him for a moment, then turned away.* 她盯着他看了一会儿，然后转过身。▸ **for the moment** 暂时 ▸ **in a moment** (*explaining when*) 马上; (*explaining duration*) 一瞬间 ▸ **one moment, please** (*on*

the telephone) 请稍等 ▸ **the moment (that)...** 一…，就… ▸ **at that moment** 当时 ▸ **at the/ this (present) moment** 此刻/当前 ▸ **(at) any moment (now)** 随时 ▸ **at the last moment** 在最后一刻

momentarily ['məuməntrɪlɪ] ADV **1** (BRIT) (*for a moment*) 短暂地 [duǎnzàn de] **2** (US) (*very soon*) 立即 [lìjí]

momentary ['məuməntərɪ] ADJ 短暂的 [duǎnzàn de]

momentous [məu'mɛntəs] ADJ 重大的 [zhòngdà de]

momentum [məu'mɛntəm] N [U] **1** [*of events, change, political movement*] 势头 [shìtóu] **2** (PHYS) 动量 [dòngliàng] ▸ **to gather** *or* **gain momentum** [*process* +] 势头增长; [*object, vehicle* +] 积聚动力

mommy ['mɒmɪ] (US: *inf*) N [C] 妈妈 [māma]

Mon. ABBR (= *Monday*) 星期一 [xīngqīyī]

monarch ['mɒnək] N [C] 君主 [jūnzhǔ]

monarchy ['mɒnəkɪ] N **1** [U] (*system*) 君主制 [jūnzhǔzhì] **2** [C] (*country*) 君主制国家 [jūnzhǔzhì guójiā] **3** ▸ **the monarchy** (*royal family*) 皇室 [huángshì]

monastery ['mɒnəstərɪ] N [C] 寺院 [sìyuàn]

Monday ['mʌndɪ] N [C/U] 星期一 [xīngqīyī] *see also* **Tuesday**

monetary ['mʌnɪtərɪ] ADJ [+ *system, policy, control*] 货币的 [huòbì de]

○ **money** ['mʌnɪ] I N [U] **1** (*cash*) 钱 [qián] ▷ *Do you have any money on you?* 你身边带钱了吗？ **2** (*in the bank*) 存款 [cúnkuǎn] ▷ *I spent all my money on the house.* 我把存款都用来买房子了。 **3** (*currency*) 货币 [huòbì] ▷ *They might not accept British money.* 他们可能不接受英国货币。 II **monies** NPL (*frm*) 款项 [kuǎnxiàng] ▷ *the investment and management of monies by pension funds* 退休基金各款项的投资及管理 ▸ **to make money** [*person, business* +] 赚钱 ▸ **to be in the money** (*inf*) 有钱 ▸ **to get your money's worth** 物有所值

money belt N [C] 腰包 [yāobāo]

money order (US) N [C] 汇票 [huìpiào] [英 = **postal order**]

Mongol ['mɒŋgəl] I N [C] 蒙古人 [Ménggǔ rén] II ADJ 蒙古的 [Ménggǔ de]

Mongolia [mɒŋ'gəulɪə] N 蒙古 [Ménggǔ]

Mongolian [mɒŋ'gəulɪən] I ADJ 蒙古的 [Ménggǔ de] II N **1** [C] (*person*) 蒙古人 [Ménggǔrén] **2** [U] (*language*) 蒙古语 [Ménggǔ yǔ]

mongrel ['mʌŋgrəl] N [C] (*dog*) 杂种狗 [zázhǒng gǒu]

monitor ['mɒnɪtə(r)] I N [C] **1** (*screen*): COMPUT 显示屏 [xiǎnshìpíng]; [*of video, television*] 监视器 [jiānshìqì] **2** (MED) (*machine*) 监控器 [jiānkòngqì] **3** (*observer*) 监察员 [jiāncháyuán] **4** (SCOL) 导生 [dǎoshēng] II VT **1** [+ *progress,*

monk [mʌŋk] N [c] 僧侣 [sēnglǚ]

monkey ['mʌŋkɪ] N [c] **1** (ZOOL) 猴 [hóu] **2** (inf) (scamp) 淘气鬼 [táoqìguǐ]

monologue ['mɒnəlɒg] N **1** [c/u] (speech) 独白 [dúbái] **2** [c] (rant) 长篇大论 [chángpiān dàlùn]

monopoly [mə'nɒpəlɪ] N [c] **1** (control)
▸ **monopoly (over/on sth)** (对某事的) 垄断 [(duì mǒushì de) lǒngduàn] **2** (company) 垄断企业 [lǒngduàn qǐyè] ▸ **to have a monopoly on/over sth** 对某事实行垄断 ▸ **doctors don't have a monopoly on morality** 并非只有医生才有道德规范

monosodium glutamate
[mɒnə'səudɪəm'gluːtəmeɪt] N [u] 味精 [wèijīng]

monotonous [mə'nɒtənəs] ADJ [+ life, job etc, voice, tune] 单调的 [dāndiào de]

monotony [mə'nɒtənɪ] N [u] (of life, job etc) 一成不变 [yīchéng búbiàn]; (of voice, tune) 单调 [dāndiào]

monsoon [mɒn'suːn] N [c] **1** (also: **monsoon season**) ▸ **the monsoon** 季风季节 [jìfēng jìjié] **2** (rainstorm) 季风雨 [jìfēngyǔ]

monster ['mɒnstə(r)] I N [c] **1** (imaginary creature) 怪物 [guàiwu] **2** (large thing) 庞然大物 [pángrán dàwù] **3** (evil person) (cruel, frightening) 恶人 [èrén] II ADJ (inf) (massive) 巨大的 [jùdà de]

○ **month** [mʌnθ] N [c] **1** (calendar month) 月 [yuè] **2** (four-week period) 一个月的时间 [yīgè yuè de shíjiān] ▸ **every month** 每个月 ▸ **300 dollars a month** 一个月300美元

monthly ['mʌnθlɪ] I ADJ 每月的 [měiyuè de] II ADV (every month) 按月 [ànyuè] III N [c] 月刊 [yuèkān]

monument ['mɒnjumənt] N [c] **1** (memorial) 纪念碑 [jìniànbēi] **2** (historical building) 历史遗迹 [lìshǐ yíjì] ▸ **a monument to sb/sth** (structure) 某人/某事的纪念碑; (fig) 某人/某事的典范

mood [muːd] N [c] (of person) 心情 [xīnqíng]; (of crowd, group) 氛围 [fēnwéi] **2** [s] (of place) 气氛 [qìfēn] ▸ **to be in a mood** 心情不好 ▸ **to be in a good/bad/awkward mood** 心情好/坏/不痛快 ▸ **I'm (not) in the mood to do this** 我想做这个(没有心思做这个)

moody ['muːdɪ] ADJ **1** (unpredictable) [+ person] 喜怒无常的 [xǐnù wúcháng de] **2** (atmospheric) [+ film, music] 忧郁的 [yōuyù de]

moon [muːn] I N **1** ▸ **the moon** 月球 [yuèqiú] **2** [c] (of other planets) 卫星 [wèixīng] II VI (BRIT: inf) 亮出光屁股 [liàngchū guāng pìgu] ▸ **to be over the moon** (inf) 非常喜悦 ▸ **once in a blue moon** 千载难逢 ▷ Once in a blue moon you get some problems. 偶尔你也碰到一些麻烦。
▸ **moon about** VI = **moon around**

▸ **moon around** I VI (inf) 闲混 [xiánhùn] II VT FUS [不可拆分] 闲逛 [xiánguàng]

moonlight ['muːnlaɪt] N [u] 月光 [yuèguāng] II VI (inf) (work) 兼职 [jiānzhí] ▸ **in the moonlight** 在月光下

moor [muə(r)] I N [c] (ESP BRIT) (heath) 荒泽 [huāngzé] II VT [+ boat, ship] 系泊 [jìbó] III VI 停泊 [tíngbó]

moose [muːs] (pl **moose**) N 麋 [mí]

mop [mɒp] I N [c] **1** (for floors) 拖把 [tuōbǎ] **2** ▸ **mop (of hair)** 蓬乱的(头发) [péngluàn de (tóufa)] II VT **1** [+ floor] 用拖把擦洗 [yòng tuōbǎ cāxǐ] **2** [+ brow, forehead] 擦 [cā]
▸ **mop up** VT **1** [+ liquid] 擦干净 [cā gānjìng] **2** (inf) (deal with) 处理 [chǔlǐ]

mope [məup] VI 郁闷 [yùmèn]
▸ **mope about** VI, VT = **mope around**
▸ **mope around** I VI 闷闷不乐 [mènmèn bùlè] II VT FUS [不可拆分] [+ house, office] 没精打采地闲逛 [méijīngdǎcǎi de xiánguàng]

moped ['məupɛd] N [c] 机动自行车 [jīdòng zìxíngchē]

moral ['mɒrl] I ADJ **1** [+ issues, values] 道德的 [dàodé de]; [+ courage, duty] 道义的 [dàoyì de]; [+ behaviour, person] 品行端正的 [pǐnxíng duānzhèng de] II N [c] (of story) 寓意 [yùyì] III **morals** NPL (principles, values) 道德规范 [dàodé guīfàn] ▸ **(to give sb) moral support** (encouragement) (给某人以)道义上的支持

morale [mɒ'rɑːl] N [u] (of army, staff) 士气 [shìqì]

morality [mə'rælɪtɪ] N **1** [u] (ethics) 道德伦理 [dàodé lúnlǐ] **2** [c] (system of morals) 道德观 [dàodéguān] **3** [u] (of something) 道德性 [dàodéxìng]

morally ['mɒrəlɪ] ADV **1** (from a moral perspective) [+ right, wrong, justifiable] 从道德观点看 [cóng dàodé guāndiǎn kàn]; [+ superior] 道德上 [dàodé shang] **2** (in a moral way) [live, behave +] 品行端正地 [pǐnxíng duānzhèng de]

morbid ['mɔːbɪd] ADJ [+ person, interest, subject] 病态的 [bìngtài de]

○

more [mɔː(r)] I ADJ **1** (in comparisons with uncount noun, plural noun) 更多的 [gèngduō de] ▸ **I get more money/holidays than you do** 我比你有更多的钱/假期 ▸ **there are more problems than solutions** 问题多于解决方案
2 (additional) (with uncount noun, plural noun) 再一些的 [zài yīxiē de] ▸ **would you like some more tea/peanuts?** 你要再来点茶/花生吗? ▸ **is there any more wine?** 还有酒吗? ▸ **are there any more cakes?** 还有蛋糕吗? ▸ **I have no more** or **I don't have any more milk/pencils** 我没有牛奶/铅笔了 ▸ **a few more weeks** 再几个星期

II PRON **1** (in comparisons) (more in quantity, number) 更多的量 [gèngduō de liàng]
▸ there's/there are more than I thought 比我想得更多 ▸ it cost more than we expected 比我们预料得更贵 ▸ more than 20 大于20 ▸ she's got more than me 她比我得到的多
2 (further, additional) (in quantity) 额外的量 [éwài de liàng] ▸ is there/are there any more? 还有多的吗？ ▸ there isn't/there aren't any more left 没有多余的了 ▸ have you got any more of it/them? 你还有吗？ ▸ a little/a few more 多一点点 ▸ much/many more 多得多
III ADV **1** (to form comparative) 更 [gèng]
▸ more dangerous/difficult (than) (比…) 更危险/难 ▸ more easily/quickly (than) (比…) 更容易/快 ▸ I go out more than I used to 我比过去出去得多了 **2** (in expressions) ▸ more and more 越来越 [yuèláiyuè] ▸ more or less (adj, adv) 差不多; (at end of sentence) 或多或少 ▸ more than ever 空前的多 ▸ once more 再一次 ▸ what's more 更有甚者

moreover [mɔː'rəuvə(r)] ADV 而且 [érqiě]
morgue [mɔːg] N [c] 停尸房 [tíngshīfáng]
○**morning** ['mɔːnɪŋ] **I** N [c/u] (early in the morning) 早晨 [zǎochén]; (later in the morning) 上午 [shàngwǔ] ▷ We spent all morning cleaning the kitchen. 我们花了一上午时间来打扫厨房。 **II** CPD [复合词] [+ paper, sun, walk] (early in the morning) 早晨 [zǎochén]; (later in the morning) 上午 ▸ good morning! 早上好！ ▸ he'll phone back in the morning 他会在明天上午回电话 ▸ at 3 o'clock/7 o'clock in the morning 凌晨3点/早上7点 ▸ this morning 今天上午 ▸ the next morning 第二天早上 ▸ on Monday morning 星期一上午
morning sickness N [u] 孕妇晨吐 [yùnfù chéntù]
Moroccan [mə'rɔkən] **I** ADJ 摩洛哥的 [Móluògē de] **II** N [c] (person) 摩洛哥人 [Móluògērén]
Morocco [mə'rɔkəu] N 摩洛哥 [Móluògē]
moron ['mɔːrɔn] (inf) N [c] 蠢货 [chǔnhuò]
morphine ['mɔːfiːn] N [u] 吗啡 [mǎfēi]
Morse [mɔːs] N (also: Morse code) 莫尔斯电码 [Mò'ěrsī Diànmǎ]
mortal ['mɔːtl] **I** ADJ **1** (not immortal) 终有一死的 [zhōngyǒu yīsǐ de] **2** [+ danger, enemy, combat] 致命的 [zhìmìng de] **II** N ▸ a mere/an ordinary mortal 凡人/普通人 [fánrén/pǔtōng rén]
mortar ['mɔːtə(r)] N **1** [u] (ARCHIT) 砂浆 [shājiāng] **2** [c] (MIL) 迫击炮 [pǎijīpào] **3** [c] (CULIN) (bowl) 研钵 [yánbō] ▸ pestle and mortar 杵和臼
mortgage ['mɔːgɪdʒ] **I** N [c] 抵押贷款 [dǐyā]

dàikuǎn] **II** VT [+ house, property] 抵押 [dǐyā]
▸ to take out a mortgage (on sth) 用抵押贷款 (购置某物)
mortician [mɔː'tɪʃən] (US) N [c] 殡葬业者 [bìnzàngyèzhě]
mortified ['mɔːtɪfaɪd] (inf) ADJ (embarrassed)
▸ to be mortified 感到羞辱 [gǎndào xiūrǔ]
mortuary ['mɔːtjuərɪ] N [c] 太平间 [tàipíngjiān]
mosaic [məu'zeɪɪk] N [c] 镶嵌图案 [xiāngqiàn tú'àn]
Moslem ['mɔzləm] ADJ, N = **Muslim**
mosque [mɔsk] N [c] 清真寺 [qīngzhēnsì]
mosquito [mɔs'kiːtəu] (pl mosquitoes) N [c] 蚊 [wén]
mosquito net N [c] 蚊帐 [wénzhàng]
moss [mɔs] N [c/u] 苔藓 [táixiǎn]

○**most** [məust] **I** ADJ **1** (almost all) (with uncount noun, plural noun) 大部分的 [dàbùfen de]
▸ most people 大多数人
2 (in comparisons) ▸ (the) most (with uncount noun, plural noun) 最 [zuì] ▸ who won the most money/prizes? 谁赢了最多的钱/奖品？ ▸ we see each other most days 我们大多数时间都见面
II PRON (uncount) 大部分 [dàbùfen]; (plural) 大多数 [dàduōshù] ▸ most of it/them 它/他/它们的大部分 ▸ I paid the most 我付了大部分 ▸ to make the most of sth 充分利用某物 ▸ at the (very) most 顶多
III ADV (superlative) **1** (with verb) ▸ (the) most 最 [zuì] ▸ what I miss (the) most is… 我最想念的是…
2 (with adj) ▸ the most comfortable/expensive sofa in the shop 店里最舒服/贵的沙发 [diànlǐ zuì shūfu/guì de shāfā]
3 (with adv) ▸ most efficiently/effectively 最有效率/有效地 [zuì yǒuxiàolǜ/yǒuxiào de] ▸ most of all 最起码的
4 (very) [+ polite, interesting etc] 很 [hěn] ▸ a most interesting book 一本很有趣的书

注意，可以说 Most children love sweets，但不能说 Most of children love sweets。然而，如果后接代词，就可以说 Most of them love sweets。

mostly ['məustlɪ] ADV **1** (chiefly) 主要 [zhǔyào] **2** (usually) 通常 [tōngcháng]
MOT [ɛməu'tiː] (BRIT) N 旧车性能测试 [jiùchē xìngnéng cèshì]
motel [məu'tɛl] N [c] 汽车旅馆 [qìchē lǚguǎn]
moth [mɔθ] N [c] 蛾 [é]
○**mother** ['mʌðə(r)] **I** N **1** [c] (parent) 母亲 [mǔqīn] **2** (as address) ▸ Mother 妈妈 [māma]
II VT **1** (be mother to) 抚养 [fǔyǎng] **2** (pamper, protect) 慈母般照顾 [címǔbān zhàogù] ▷ She mothers all her lodgers. 她慈母般照顾所有的房客。

motherhood ['mʌðəhud] N [U] 母亲身份 [mǔqīn shēnfèn]

mother-in-law ['mʌðərɪnlɔː] (pl **mothers-in-law**) N [C] [of woman] 婆婆 [pópo]; [of man] 岳母 [yuèmǔ]

motherly ['mʌðəlɪ] ADJ [+ feeling, behaviour] 母亲的 [mǔqīn de]; [+ person, figure] 母亲般的 [mǔqīnbān de]

mother-of-pearl ['mʌðərəv'pɜːl] N [U] 珠母层 [zhūmǔcéng]

Mother's Day (BRIT) N [C/U] 母亲节 [Mǔqīn Jié]

mother-to-be ['mʌðətə'biː] (pl **mothers-to-be**) N [C] 孕妇 [yùnfù]

mother tongue N [C] 母语 [mǔyǔ]

motif [məu'tiːf] N [C] **1** (design) 基调 [jīdiào] **2** (theme) 主题 [zhǔtí]

motion ['məuʃən] **I** N **1** [U] 运动 [yùndòng] **2** [C] (gesture) 动作 [dòngzuò] **3** [C] (in meeting) 动议 [dòngyì] **4** [C] (BRIT) (also: **bowel motion**) 大便 [dàbiàn] [美= **movement**] **II** VI ▸ **to motion to sb (to do sth)** (gesture, signal) 示意某人(做某事) [shìyì mǒurén (zuò mǒushì)] ▸ **to be in motion** [process, event +] 在进行中; [vehicle, device +] 在行驶中 ▸ **to set sth in motion** [+ process, event] 使某事开始进行; [+ device] 使某物开始运转 ▸ **to go through the motions** 敷衍了事

motionless ['məuʃənlɪs] ADJ 不动的 [bùdòng de]

motion picture (ESP US) N [C] 电影 [diànyǐng]

motivate ['məutɪveɪt] VT **1** (prompt, drive) ▸ **to be motivated by sth** [act, decision +] 受某事的驱使 [shòu mǒushì de qūshǐ]; [person +] 受到某事的激发 [shòudào mǒushì de jīfā] **2** [+ worker, student etc] 激励 [jīlì] ▸ **to motivate sb to do sth** 激励某人做某事 ▷ What motivates athletes to take drugs? 什么驱使运动员服用禁药? ▸ **a racially motivated attack** 带有种族动机的攻击行动

motivated ['məutɪveɪtɪd] ADJ 士气高涨的 [shìqì gāozhàng de]

motivation [məutɪ'veɪʃən] N [U] **1** (motive) 动机 [dòngjī] **2** (commitment) 动力 [dònglì]

motive ['məutɪv] **I** N [C] (reason) 动机 [dòngjī] **II** ADJ [+ power, force] 产生运动的 [chǎnshēng yùndòng de]

motor ['məutə(r)] **I** N [C] **1** [of machine, vehicle] 发动机 [fādòngjī] **2** (BRIT: inf) (car) 汽车 [qìchē] **II** ADJ [+ industry, trade] 机动车辆的 [jīdòng chēliàng de] **III** VI (o.f.) (drive) 开汽车 [kāi qìchē]

motorbike ['məutəbaɪk] N [C] 摩托车 [mótuōchē]

motorboat ['məutəbəut] N [C] 摩托艇 [mótuōtǐng]

motor car ['məutəkɑː] (BRIT: frm) N [C] 汽车 [qìchē]

motorcycle ['məutəsaɪkl] (frm) N [C] 摩托车 [mótuōchē]

motorcyclist ['məutəsaɪklɪst] N [C] 摩托车手 [mótuōchēshǒu]

motoring ['məutərɪŋ] (ESP BRIT) **I** N [U] (activity) 驾驶汽车 [jiàshǐ qìchē] **II** ADJ [+ offence, organization] 汽车驾驶的 [qìchē jiàshǐ de] [美= **automobile, driving**]

motorist ['məutərɪst] (ESP BRIT) N [C] 开汽车的人 [kāi qìchē de rén] [美= **driver**]

motor racing (BRIT) N [U] 赛车 [sàichē]

motorway ['məutəweɪ] (BRIT) **I** N [C] 高速公路 [gāosù gōnglù] [美= **freeway**] **II** CPD [复合词] [+ traffic, network] 高速公路 [gāosù gōnglù]

motto ['mɔtəu] (pl **mottoes**) N [C] **1** (slogan) [of school, regiment] 格言 [géyán] **2** (principle) [of person] 座右铭 [zuòyòumíng]

mould, (US) mold [məuld] **I** N **1** [C] (cast) (for jelly, metal) 模子 [múzi] **2** [U] (fungus) 霉菌 [méijūn] **II** VT **1** (shape) [+ plastic, clay etc] 使成形 [shǐ chéngxíng] **2** (influence) [+ public opinion, character] 影响 [yǐngxiǎng]

mouldy, (US) moldy ['məuldɪ] ADJ [+ bread, cheese] 发霉的 [fāméi de]

mound [maund] N [C] **1** [of earth] 土堆 [tǔduī] **2** (heap) [of objects] 堆 [duī] **3** (BASEBALL) 投球区土墩 [tóuqiúqū tǔdūn]

mount [maunt] **I** VT **1** (organize) [+ attack, campaign] 发起 [fāqǐ]; [+ exhibition, display] 举办 [jǔbàn] **2** (fix) [+ jewel, picture] 安放 [ānfàng] **3** (get onto) [+ horse, cycle] 骑上 [qíshàng] **4** (climb) [+ staircase, platform] 登上 [dēngshàng] **II** VI **1** (increase) [tension, problems +] 加剧 [jiājù] **2** (pile up) 增加 [zēngjiā] **3** (get onto horse or cycle) 骑 [qí] **III** N **1** (mountain) (in names) ▸ **Mount Rushmore** 拉什莫尔山 [Lāshímò'ěr Shān] **2** [C] (frm) (horse) 坐骑 [zuòqí] **3** [C] (for picture, photograph etc) 框 [kuàng] ▸ **the car mounted the pavement** 汽车轧上人行道 ▸ **mounting debts/bills** 成堆的债务/账单 ▸ **mount up** VI 不断增加 [bùduàn zēngjiā]

mountain ['mauntɪn] **I** N [C] 山 [shān] **II** CPD [复合词] [+ road, stream] 山 [shān] ▸ **a mountain of sth** [+ papers, work] 一大堆某物 ▸ **to make a mountain out of a molehill** 小题大做

mountain bike N [C] 山地自行车 [shāndì zìxíngchē]

mountaineer [mauntɪ'nɪə(r)] N [C] 登山能手 [dēngshān néngshǒu]

mountaineering [mauntɪ'nɪərɪŋ] N [U] 登山运动 [dēngshān yùndòng] ▸ **to go mountaineering** 爬山

mountainous ['mauntɪnəs] ADJ [+ country, area] 多山的 [duōshān de]

mountain range N [C] 山脉 [shānmài]

mountainside ['mauntɪnsaɪd] N [C] 山坡 [shānpō]

mourn [mɔːn] I vt 1 [+ death] 哀悼 [āidào]; [+ person] 悼念 [dàoniàn] 2 [+ loss of something] 为…感到痛心 [wèi…gǎndào tòngxīn] II vi
▸ **to mourn for** [+ person] 悼念 [dàoniàn]; [+ thing, time] 为…感到惋惜 [wèi…gǎndào wǎnxī]

mourner ['mɔːnə(r)] N [c] 送葬者 [sòngzàngzhě]

mourning ['mɔːnɪŋ] N [u] 哀悼 [āidào] ▸ **to be in mourning** 服丧

mouse [maus] (pl **mice**) N [c] 1 (ZOOL) 鼠 [shǔ] 2 (COMPUT) 鼠标 [shǔbiāo]

mouse mat ['mausmæt] N [c] 鼠标垫 [shǔbiāo diàn]

moussaka [muˈsɑːkə] N [u] 碎肉茄子蛋 [suìròu qiézi dàn]

mousse [muːs] N [c/u] 1 (CULIN) 奶油冻 [nǎiyóudòng] 2 (foam) 摩丝 [mósī]

moustache, (US) **mustache** [məsˈtɑːʃ] N [c] 髭 [zī]

mouth [n mauθ, vb mauð] I N [c] 1 [+ of person, animal] 嘴 [zuǐ] 2 (way of talking) 说话方式 [shuōhuà fāngshì] 3 [of river] 河口 [hékǒu] 4 [of cave, tunnel] 口 [kǒu] II vt 1 (mime) 唇语 [chúnyǔ] 2 (trot out) 言不由衷地说 [yán bù yóu zhōng de shuō]

mouthful ['mauθful] N [c] [of food] 一口 [yīkǒu] 2 [s] (inf) (word) 拗口的词 [àokǒu de cí]

mouth organ (ESP BRIT) N [c] 口琴 [kǒuqín]

mouthpiece ['mauθpiːs] N [c] 1 [of telephone] 送话口 [sònghuàkǒu]; [of trumpet etc] 吹口 [chuīkǒu] 2 (spokesman) 代言人 [dàiyánrén]

mouthwash ['mauθwɔʃ] N [c/u] 漱口剂 [shùkǒujì]

○ **move** [muːv] I vi 1 (change position) [vehicle +] 行进 [xíngjìn] ▷ The train began to move. 火车开始开动了。; [person, object +] 动 [dòng] 2 (relocate) 搬家 [bānjiā] ▷ She had often considered moving to London. 她常考虑搬到伦敦去住。 3 (also: **move on**) (from job) 换 [huàn] ▷ Christina moved to another job to get more experience. 克里斯蒂娜换了另一份工作以获得更多的经验。; (from activity) 改换 [gǎihuàn] 4 (shift) ▸ **to move to(wards)** 倾向于 [qīngxiàng yú] ▷ The Labour Party has moved to the right. 工党已倾向于右派立场。 5 (develop) [situation, events +] 进展 [jìnzhǎn] ▷ Events are moving fast. 事情进展迅速。 II vt 1 (change position of) [+ furniture, car etc] 挪动 [nuódòng] ▷ Workmen were moving a heavy wardrobe down the stairs. 工人们正把一个很重的衣橱搬到楼下去。 2 (transfer) [+ worker] 调动 [diàodòng] ▷ His superiors moved him to another department. 他的上司把他调到另一个部门。 3 (change) ▸ **to move sth (to)** [+ event, date] 改(到) [gǎi (dào)] ▷ The club has moved its meeting to January 22nd. 俱乐部已把聚会的日期改到1月22日。 4 (affect emotionally) [+ person] 感动 [gǎndòng]

▷ The whole incident had moved her profoundly. 整个事件深深地感动了她。 5 ▸ **to move sb to do sth** (motivate) 促使某人做某事 [cùshǐ mǒurén zuò mǒushì] ▷ What has moved the President to take this step? 是什么促使总统采取这一举措？ 6 ▸ **to move that...** (POL) 提议… [tíyì…] ▷ She moved that the meeting be adjourned. 她提议休会。 III N [c] 1 (movement) 动作 [dòngzuò] ▷ Daniel's eyes followed her every move. 丹尼尔的眼光紧随她的每一个动作。 2 (act) 行动 [xíngdòng] ▷ A government move to drop the plan could affect share prices. 政府终止这项计划的行动将会影响到股票价格。 3 (change) [of house] 搬家 [bānjiā] ▷ The move to Prague was a daunting prospect. 搬家至布拉格，其前景颇令人沮丧。 4 (change) [of job, belief] 变动 [biàndòng] ▷ His move to the personnel department was no surprise. 他被调到人事部门的变动并不令人吃惊。 5 (in game) (go, turn) 一步 [yībù]; (change of position) 一步棋 [yībùqí] ▸ **to move house/jobs/offices** 搬家/换工作/更换办公地点 ▸ **a good/bad move** 好/糟糕的一步 ▸ **one false move** 不明智的行为 ▸ **to get a move on** (inf) 快点 ▸ **to be on the move** 迁移中 ▸ **to make a move** (take action) (leave) 离去
▸ **move about, move around** vi 1 (change position) 走来走去 [zǒulái zǒuqù] 2 (change residence, job) 不断迁移 [bùduàn qiānyí] ▷ I was born in Fort Worth but we moved about a lot. 我出生在沃思堡，但我们不断在各地迁移。
▸ **move along** I vi 1 (develop) 发展 [fāzhǎn] ▷ Research tends to move along at a slow but orderly pace. 研究趋于缓慢而有序地发展。 2 (keep walking) 走开 [zǒukāi] ▷ Move along there, please. 请走开。 II vt 1 (cause to develop) 使进展 [shǐ jìnzhǎn] ▷ I hope we can move things along without too much delay. 我希望我们能使事情有所进展而不致有太多延误。 2 (order to move) [police +] 命令走开 [mìnglìng zǒukāi] ▷ Our officers are moving them along and not allowing them to gather in large groups. 我们的官员命令他们走开，不允许他们聚众。
▸ **move around** vi = **move about**
▸ **move away** vi (from town, area) 离开 [líkāi] ▷ He moved away and lost contact with the family. 他离开家，和家人失去了联系。; (from window, door) 走开 [zǒukāi] ▷ She moved away from the window. 她从窗户处走开。
▸ **move back** I vi 1 (return) (to town, area) 回来 [huílái] 2 (backwards) [person, troops, vehicle +] 后退 [hòutuì] II vt 1 [+ crowd] 使后退 [shǐ hòutuì]; [+ object] (less far forward) 往后移 [wǎng hòuyí]; (to original position) 使回原位 [shǐ huíyuánwèi]; (in board game) 后退 [hòutuì] ▷ Move back three squares. 后退3格。
▸ **move down** vi 下降 [xiàjiàng]
▸ **move forward** I vi [person, troops, vehicle +] 向前移动 [xiàngqián yídòng]; (in board game)

前进 [qiánjìn] II VT [+ object] 使向前移 [shǐ xiàngqián yí]

▶ **move in** VI 1 (into house) 搬入 [bānrù] ▷ The house wasn't ready when she moved in. 她搬进去的时候房子还没装修好。 2 [+ police, soldiers] 开进来 [kāijìnlái] ▷ The troops moved in to stop the riot. 军队开进来镇压暴乱。

▶ **move in on** VT FUS [不可拆分] 开始参与 [kāishǐ cānyù]

▶ **move into** VT FUS [不可拆分] (house, area) 搬进 [bānjìn]

▶ **move in with** VT FUS [不可拆分] 和…同居 [hé…tóngjū] ▷ Her husband had moved in with a younger woman. 她的丈夫和一个比她年轻的女人同居了。

▶ **move off** VI [car+] 开走 [kāizǒu] ▷ Gil waved his hand and the car moved off. 吉尔挥了挥手，车开走了。

▶ **move on** I VI 1 (leave) 启程前往 [qǐchéng qiánwǎng] ▷ After three weeks in Hong Kong, we moved on to Japan. 在香港逗留了3个星期后，我们启程前往日本。 2 (progress) 进行 [jìnxíng] ▷ Now, can we move on and discuss productivity. 好，让我们进行下一项，讨论生产率问题。 II VT 1 (order to move) 命令走开 [mìnglìng zǒukāi] ▷ I used to busk, but I was always being moved on by the police. 我以前常在街头卖艺，但警察总是命令我走开。 2 (cause to develop) 使有所进展 [shǐ yǒusuǒ jìnzhǎn] ▷ I think we need to move things on a bit. 我认为我们应该使情况略有所进展。

▶ **move out** VI (of house) 搬出去 [bān chūqù] ▷ The guy that lived there moved out a month ago. 以前住在那儿的家伙一个月前搬出去了。

▶ **move over** VI (to make room) 让开些 [ràngkāixiē] ▷ Move over and let me drive. 让开些，让我来开车。

▶ **move up** VI 1 (on sofa etc) 靠拢 [kàolǒng] ▷ Move up, John, and make room for the lady. 靠拢点，约翰，给那位女士挪个地方。 2 [+ employee, pupil] 升级 [shēngjí]

movement ['muːvmənt] I N 1 [c] (REL, POL) (group of people) 团体 [tuántǐ] 2 [c/U] (moving) 动静 [dòngjìng] 3 [c] (gesture) 动作 [dòngzuò] 4 [c/U] (transport, travel) [of goods, people] 运输 [yùnshū] 5 [c/U] (shift) (in attitude, policy) 动向 [dòngxiàng] 6 [c] (MUS) 乐章 [yuèzhāng] 7 [c] (also: bowel movement) 排便 [páibiàn] II **movements** NPL [of person] 活动 [huódòng]

movie ['muːvɪ] (US) N [c] 电影 [diànyǐng] [英=film] ▶ the movies 电影 [英=the cinema]

movie theater (US) N [c] 电影院 [diànyǐngyuàn] [英=cinema]

moving ['muːvɪŋ] ADJ 1 (emotionally) 动人的 [dòngrén de] 2 (not static) 活动的 [huódòng de]

mow [məʊ] (pt **mowed**, pp **mowed** or **mown** [məʊn]) VT [+ grass, lawn] 刈 [yì]

▶ **mow down** VT (kill) [+ person] [driver+] 撞死 [zhuàngsǐ]; [gunman+] 枪杀 [qiāngshā]

mower ['məʊə(r)] N [c] (also: **lawnmower**) 割草机 [gēcǎojī]

Mozambique [məʊzəm'biːk] N 莫桑比克 [Mòsāngbǐkè]

MP N ABBR 1 (BRIT) (= Member of Parliament) 下院议员 [Xiàyuàn Yìyuán] 2 (= Military Police) 军警 [jūnjǐng]

MP3 [ɛmpiːˈθriː] N 1 (format) 一种音频压缩格式 2 (file) 以这种音频压缩格式储存的声音文件

mph ABBR (= miles per hour) 每小时…英里 [měi xiǎoshí…yīnglǐ]

Mr ['mɪstə(r)], (US) **Mr.** ▶ Mr Smith 史密斯先生 [Shǐmìsī xiānsheng]

Mrs ['mɪsɪz], (US) **Mrs.** ▶ Mrs Smith 史密斯太太 [Shǐmìsī tàitai]

MS N ABBR 1 (= Master of Science) = MSc 2 (= multiple sclerosis) 多发性硬化 [duōfāxìng yìnghuà]

Ms [mɪz], (US) **Ms.** N (Miss or Mrs) ▶ Ms Smith 史密斯女士 [Shǐmìsī nǚshì]

MSc N ABBR (= Master of Science) (qualification) 理学硕士学位 [lǐxué shuòshì xuéwèi]; (person) 理学硕士 [lǐxué shuòshì]

MSG I (TEXTING) ABBR = message II N ABBR (= monosodium glutamate) 味精 [wèijīng]

MSP N ABBR (= Member of the Scottish Parliament) 苏格兰下院议员 [Sūgélán Xiàyuàn Yìyuán]

MST (US) N ABBR (= Mountain Standard Time) 山区标准时间 [Shānqū Biāozhǔn Shíjiān]

Mt, Mt. (ESP US) (pl **Mts**) ABBR (= mount) 山 [shān]

○

much [mʌtʃ] I ADJ 大量的 [dàliàng de] ▶ we haven't got much time/money 我们没有多少时间/钱 II PRON 大量 [dàliàng] ▶ there isn't much left 剩下的不多了 ▶ he doesn't do much at the weekends 周末他不做太多事 ▶ much of the time/his life 大多数时间/他人生的大部分 III ADV 1 (a great deal) 许多 [xǔduō] ▶ he hasn't changed much 他没变化多少 ▶ "did you like her?" – "not much" "你喜欢她吗？" "不太喜欢" ▶ much as I like him… 尽管我喜欢他，但是… ▶ however much you may try to forget… 无论你怎么竭力想忘掉都… 2 (far) …得多 […deduō] ▶ I'm much better now 我感觉好多了 ▶ it's much the biggest publishing company in Europe 它是欧洲最大的出版公司 ▶ those trousers are much too big for you 那些裤子对你而言实在太肥了 3 (often) 经常 [jīngcháng] ▶ do you go out

much? 你经常出去吗?

4 (*almost*) 几乎 [jīhū] ▶ **the two books are much the same** 这两本书几乎是一样的 ▶ **"how are you feeling?" – "much the same"** "你感觉怎么样?" "几乎没变"

muck [mʌk] N [U] (*inf*) (*dirt*) 污垢 [wūgòu]
▶ **muck about** (BRIT: *inf*) I VI **1** (*fool about*) 鬼混 [guǐhùn] **2** ▶ **to muck about with sth** 瞎摆弄某物 [xiā bǎinòng mǒuwù] II VT [+ *person*] 耍弄 [shuǎnòng]
▶ **muck around** VI = **muck about**
▶ **muck in** (BRIT: *inf*) VI 一起出力 [yīqǐ chūlì]
▶ **muck out** I VT 清除 [qīngchú] II VI 打扫畜舍 [dǎsǎo chùshè]
▶ **muck up** (BRIT: *inf*) VT [+ *exam, interview etc*] 搞糟 [gǎozāo] [美 = **screw up**]

mucky ['mʌkɪ] (*inf*) ADJ [+ *boots, field*] 肮脏的 [āngzāng de]

mucus ['mju:kəs] N [U] 黏液 [niányè]

mud [mʌd] N [U] 泥 [ní]

muddle ['mʌdl] N **1** [C/U] **1** [*of papers, figures, things*] 混乱状态 [hùnluàn zhuàngtài] **2** (*situation*) 糟糕局面 [zāogāo júmiàn] II VT (*also*: **muddle up**) [+ *things*] 把…弄乱 [bǎ…nòngluàn]; [+ *names, words*] 混淆 [hùnxiáo]; [+ *person*] 使糊涂 [shǐ hútu] ▶ **to be in a muddle** 一片混乱 ▶ **to get in a muddle** [*person* +] 弄糊涂了; [*objects* +] 搞得一团糟 ▶ **to muddle sb/sth (up) with sb/sth** 将某人和某人/某物和某物搞混
▶ **muddle along** VI (*inf*) (*drift*) 混日子 [hùn rìzi]
▶ **muddle through** (*inf*) VI (*get by*) 对付过去 [duìfu guòqù]

muddled ['mʌdld] ADJ (*confused*) [+ *person, thinking, ideas*] 糊涂的 [hútu de]

muddy ['mʌdɪ] ADJ **1** [+ *floor, field*] 沾满烂泥的 [zhānmǎn lànnì de] **2** [+ *colour, green*] 灰暗的 [huī'àn de] II VT (*dirty*) 使沾上烂泥 [shǐ zhānshàng lànnì]

mudguard ['mʌdɡɑ:d] (ESP BRIT) N [C] 挡泥板 [dǎngníbǎn]

muesli ['mju:zlɪ] N [U] 穆兹利, 和干水果混在一起的燕麦早餐

muffin ['mʌfɪn] N [C] **1** 松饼 [sōngbǐng] **2** (BRIT) 英式松饼 [yīngshì sōngbǐng]

muffle ['mʌfl] VT [+ *sound*] 使低沉 [shǐ dīchén]

muffled ['mʌfld] ADJ **1** [+ *sound*] 低沉的 [dīchén de] **2** (*against cold*) 裹住的 [guǒzhù de]

muffler ['mʌflə(r)] N [C] **1** (US: AUT) 消音器 [xiāoyīnqì] **2** (*o.f.*) (*scarf*) 围巾 [wéijīn]

mug [mʌɡ] I N [C] **1** (*large cup*) (*for drinks*) 大杯子 [dà bēizi]; (*for beer*) 啤酒杯 [píjiǔ bēi] **2** (*contents*) 一大杯的量 [yídàbēi de liàng] **3** (*inf*) (*face*) 脸 [liǎn] **4** (BRIT: *inf*) (*fool*) 傻瓜 [shǎguā] II VT (*rob*) 行凶抢劫 [xíngxiōng qiǎngjié] ▶ **it's a mug's game** (BRIT: *inf*) 这是桩无利可图的事
▶ **mug up** (BRIT: *inf*) VT (*also*: **mug up on**) 突击

学习 [tūjī xuéxí]

mugger ['mʌɡə(r)] N [C] 抢劫犯 [qiǎngjiéfàn]

mugging ['mʌɡɪŋ] N [C/U] (*assault*) 行凶抢劫 [xíngxiōng qiǎngjié]

muggy ['mʌɡɪ] ADJ [+ *weather, day*] 闷热而潮湿的 [mēnrè ér cháoshī de] ▶ **it's muggy today** 今天天气很闷热

mule [mju:l] N [C] **1** (ZOOL) 骡 [luó] **2** (*shoe*) 拖鞋 [tuōxié]

multicoloured, (US) **multicolored** ['mʌltɪkʌləd] ADJ 多色的 [duōsè de]

multi-level [mʌltɪ'levl] (US) ADJ [+ *building, car park*] 多层的 [duōcéng de] [英 = **multi-storey**]

multimedia [mʌltɪ'mi:dɪə] I N [U] **1** (COMPUT) 多媒体 [duōméitǐ] **2** (SCOL) 多媒体教学 [duōméitǐ jiàoxué] II ADJ 多媒体的 [duōméitǐ de]

multinational [mʌltɪ'næʃənl] I ADJ **1** [+ *company, corporation*] 跨国的 [kuàguó de] **2** [+ *force*] 多国的 [duōguó de] II N [C] 跨国公司 [kuàguó gōngsī]

multiple ['mʌltɪpl] I ADJ [+ *injuries*] 多次的 [duōcì de]; [+ *collision*] 多重的 [duōchóng de]; [+ *birth*] 多胎的 [duōtāi de] II N [C] (MATH) 倍数 [bèishù]

multiple-choice ['mʌltɪpltʃɔɪs] ADJ [+ *exam, question*] 多项选择的 [duōxiàng xuǎnzé de]

multiple sclerosis [-sklɪ'rəusɪs] N [U] 多发性硬化 [duōfāxìng yìnghuà]

multiplex ['mʌltɪpleks] N [C] (*also*: **multiplex cinema**) 多剧场影剧院 [duōjùchǎng yǐngjùyuàn]

multiplication [mʌltɪplɪ'keɪʃn] N **1** [U] (MATH) 乘法 [chéngfǎ] **2** [S] (*increase*) 倍增 [bèizēng]

multiply ['mʌltɪplaɪ] I VT (MATH) ▶ **to multiply sth (by sth)** (某数)乘以某数 [(mǒushù) chéngyǐ mǒushù] II VI **1** (*increase*) 增加 [zēngjiā] **2** (*reproduce*) 繁殖 [fánzhí] **3** (MATH) 做乘法 [zuò chéngfǎ]

multiracial [mʌltɪ'reɪʃl] ADJ [+ *school, society*] 多种族的 [duōzhǒngzú de]

multi-storey [mʌltɪ'stɔ:rɪ] I ADJ [+ *building, car park*] 多层的 [duōcéng de] II N [C] (*car park*) 多层停车场 [duōcéng tíngchēchǎng]

multitude ['mʌltɪtju:d] N **1** ▶ **a multitude of** [+ *reasons, ideas*] 许多 [xǔduō] **2** (*liter*) (*crowd*) 人群 [rénqún] ▶ **to cover** or **hide a multitude of sins** 掩盖种种罪恶

mum [mʌm] I N (BRIT: *inf*) (*mother*) 妈妈 [māma] [美 = **mom**] II ADJ ▶ **to keep mum** 保密 [bǎomì] ▶ **mum's the word** 别声张

mumble ['mʌmbl] I VT 含糊地说 [hánhude shuō] II VI 咕哝 [gūnong] III N [C] 咕哝 [gūnong]

mummy ['mʌmɪ] N [C] **1** (BRIT: *inf*) (*mother*) 妈妈 [māma] [美 = **mommy**] **2** (*embalmed body*) 木乃伊 [mùnǎiyī]

mumps [mʌmps] N [U] 腮腺炎 [sāixiànyán]

munch [mʌntʃ] I VT 大嚼 [dàjiáo] II VI 出声咀嚼 [chūshēng jǔjué]

municipal [mjuːˈnɪsɪpl] ADJ 市政的 [shìzhèng de]

mural [ˈmjuərl] N [C] 壁画 [bìhuà]

murder [ˈmɜːdə(r)] I N [C/U] (killing) 谋杀 [móushā] II VT 1 (kill) 谋杀 [móushā] 2 (spoil) [+ piece of music, language] 糟蹋 [zāota] ▶ to get away with murder (inf) 为所欲为 ▶ the traffic was murder! (inf) 交通真要命！▶ I could murder him! 我真该杀了他！
▓▓▓用法参见 kill

murderer [ˈmɜːdərə(r)] N [C] 凶手 [xiōngshǒu]

murky [ˈmɜːkɪ] ADJ 1 [+ street, night] 昏暗的 [hūn'àn de] 2 [+ water] 混浊的 [húnzhuó de] 3 (BRIT) (shady, shadowy) 不可告人的 [bùkě gàorén de] 4 (hazy, unclear) 晦涩难懂的 [huìsè nándǒng de]

murmur [ˈmɜːmə(r)] I VT (say quietly) 小声说 [xiǎoshēng shuō] II VI (speak quietly) 小声说话 [xiǎoshēng shuōhuà] III N 1 [C] (voice) 低语 [dīyǔ] 2 [S] (low sound) [of voices] 窃窃低语声 [qièqiè dīyǔshēng]; [of wind, waves] 细声 [xìshēng] 3 [C] (MED) (also: heart murmur) 杂音 [záyīn] ▶ without a murmur 毫无怨言

muscle [ˈmʌsl] N 1 [C/U] (ANAT) 肌肉 [jīròu] 2 [U] (power) 实力 [shílì] ▶ he didn't move a muscle 他一动不动 ▶ to flex one's muscles 显示力量
▶ **muscle in** VI 强行挤入 [qiángxíng jǐrù]
▶ **muscle in on** VT FUS [不可拆分] 强行插足 [qiángxíng chāzú]

muscular [ˈmʌskjulə(r)] ADJ [+ person, body] 肌肉发达的 [jīròu fādá de]; [+ pain, weakness] 肌肉的 [jīròu de]

museum [mjuːˈzɪəm] N [C] 博物馆 [bówùguǎn]

mushroom [ˈmʌʃrum] I N [C] (edible) 蘑菇 [mógu]; (poisonous) 毒蘑菇 [dú mógu] II VI [town, organization +] 迅速发展 [xùnsù fāzhǎn] III CPD [复合词] [+ soup, omelette, pizza] 蘑菇 [mógu]

○ music [ˈmjuːzɪk] N [U] 1 (sound) 音乐 [yīnyuè] ▷ classical music 古典音乐 2 (activity) 音乐艺术 [yīnyuè yìshù] ▷ He plans to make his career in music. 他打算在音乐艺术方面发展。 3 (SCOL, UNIV) 音乐课 [yīnyuè kè] 4 (score) 乐谱 [yuèpǔ] ▷ He's never been able to read music. 他一向不识乐谱。 ▶ to face the music 承担自己行为的后果 ▶ to be music to sb's ears 佳音

musical [ˈmjuːzɪkl] I ADJ 1 (related to music) [+ career, skills] 音乐的 [yīnyuè de] 2 (musically gifted) [+ person] 有音乐天赋的 [yǒu yīnyuè tiānfù de] 3 (resembling music) [+ tone, voice, accent] 悦耳的 [yuè'ěr de] II N [C] (show, film) 音乐剧 [yīnyuèjù]

musical instrument N [C] 乐器 [yuèqì]

musician [mjuːˈzɪʃən] N [C] 音乐家 [yīnyuèjiā]

Muslim, Moslem [ˈmuzlɪm] I N [C] 穆斯林 [Mùsīlín] II ADJ 穆斯林的 [Mùsīlín de]

muslin [ˈmʌzlɪn] N [U] 平纹细布 [píngwén xìbù]

mussel [ˈmʌsl] N [C] 贻贝 [yíbèi]

○ must [mʌst] I AUX VB 1 (expressing importance or necessity) 必须 [bìxū] ▷ The doctor must allow the patient to decide. 医生必须让病人来决定。 2 (expressing intention) 得 [děi] ▷ I really must be getting back. 我真得回去了。 3 (expressing forceful suggestion) 一定要 [yīdìng yào] ▷ You must see my new guitar. 你一定要看看我的新吉他。 4 (expressing anger in question) 偏要 [piānyào] ▷ Must you be so careless? 你偏要这么粗心吗？ 5 (expressing presumption) 一定 [yīdìng] ▷ Russell must be one of the youngest ever Wembley referees. 拉塞尔一定是温布利体育场上历来最年轻的裁判之一。 ▷ He must have forgotten to pick up the tickets. 他一定忘记去取票了。 6 (expressing sympathy) 一定 [yīdìng] ▷ Sit down, you must be exhausted. 坐吧，你一定累坏了。 7 (expressing surprise or shock) ▶ **you must be joking** 你准是在开玩笑 [nǐ zhǔn shì zài kāi wánxiào] ▷ I must be mad! 我准是疯了！ II N (necessity) ▶ **to be a must** 是必备之物 [shì bìbèi zhī wù] ▷ Rubber gloves are a must if your skin is sensitive. 橡胶手套对于敏感皮肤是必备之物。 ▶ **if you must** (expressing reluctant agreement) 如果你坚持要 [rúguǒ nǐ jiānchí yào] ▶ **if you must know** (expressing reluctance to tell sb sth) 如果你一定要知道的话

mustache [ˈmʌstæʃ] (US) N = moustache

mustard [ˈmʌstəd] N [U] 芥末 [jièmo]

mustn't [ˈmʌsnt] = must not

mute [mjuːt] I ADJ (silent) 缄默的 [jiānmò de] II VT (reduce) 抑制 [yìzhì]

mutilate [ˈmjuːtɪleɪt] VT [+ person, corpse] 毁伤 [huǐshāng]

mutiny [ˈmjuːtɪnɪ] I N [C/U] [of soldiers, sailors] 哗变 [huábiàn] II VI [soldiers, sailors +] 反叛 [fǎnpàn]

mutter [ˈmʌtə(r)] I VI 嘟哝 [dūnong] II VT 低声说 [dīshēng shuō] III N [C] 低语 [dīyǔ]

mutton [ˈmʌtn] N [U] (meat) 羊肉 [yángròu] ▶ **mutton dressed (up) as lamb** (BRIT: inf) 老来俏

mutual [ˈmjuːtʃuəl] ADJ (shared) [+ feeling, attraction] 共有的 [gòngyǒu de]; [+ benefit, interest] 共同的 [gòngtóng de] ▶ **a mutual friend** 共同的朋友 ▶ **the feeling is mutual** 有同感

mutually [ˈmjuːtʃuəlɪ] ADV [+ convenient, acceptable] 彼此 [bǐcǐ] ▶ **mutually exclusive** 互不相容

muzzle [ˈmʌzl] I N [C] 1 (restraint) (for dog) 口套 [kǒutào] 2 (nose and mouth) [of dog] 鼻口部分 [bíkǒu bùfen] 3 [of gun] 枪口 [qiāngkǒu] II VT 1 [+ dog] 给…套口套 [gěi…tào kǒutào] 2 (gag)

[+ press, person] 使缄默 [shǐ jiānmò]

MW (RAD) ABBR (= *medium wave*) 中波 [zhōngbō]

🔾**my** [maɪ] ADJ 我的 [wǒ de] ▷ *my parents* 我的父母 ▷ *I've washed my hair.* 我洗了头。

Myanmar, Myanma ['maɪænmɑ:] [mjænmɑ:] N 缅甸 [Miǎndiàn]

myself [maɪ'sɛlf] PRON **1** 我自己 [wǒ zìjǐ] ▷ *I hurt myself.* 我伤了自己。▷ *I prepared the dinner myself.* 我自己做的晚餐。▷ *I bought myself a new CD.* 我给自己买了张新唱片。▷ *I want to try it out for myself.* 我想自己试一下。**2** (emphatic) 我本人 [wǒ běnrén] ▷ *I myself live in London.* 我本人住在伦敦。**3** (me) 我 [wǒ] ▷ *a complete beginner like myself* 像我这样的一个初学者 ► **by myself** (unaided) 我独力地 ▷ *I did it all by myself.* 这都是我自己一个人独力做的。; (alone) 我独自 ▷ *I live by myself.* 我独自一个人住。

mysterious [mɪs'tɪərɪəs] ADJ **1** (strange) 神秘的 [shénmì de] **2** (enigmatic) ► **to be mysterious about sth** 对某事卖弄玄虚 [duì mǒushì màinòng xuánxū]

mystery ['mɪstərɪ] **I** N **1** [c] (puzzle) 谜 [mí] **2** [U] (strangeness) [of place, person] 离奇 [líqí] **3** [c] (story) 推理作品 [tuīlǐ zuòpǐn] **II** ADJ (unknown, mysterious) 神秘的 [shénmì de]

mystical ['mɪstɪkl] ADJ [+ experience, cult, rite] 玄妙的 [xuánmiào de]

mystify ['mɪstɪfaɪ] VT 使困惑 [shǐ kùnhuò]

myth [mɪθ] N [c] **1** (legend, story) 神话 [shénhuà] **2** (fallacy) 谬论 [miùlùn]

mythical ['mɪθɪkl] ADJ **1** [+ beast, monster] 神话中的 [shénhuà zhōng de] **2** [+ jobs, opportunities etc] 虚构的 [xūgòu de]

mythology [mɪ'θɔlədʒɪ] N [C/U] 神话 [shénhuà]

Nn

N¹, n [ɛn] N [C/U] (letter) 英语的第十四个字母

N² ABBR (= north) 北方 [běifāng]

n/a ABBR (= not applicable) 不适用 [bù shìyòng]

nag [næg] I VT (go on at) 唠叨 [láodao] II VI 唠叨 [láodao] III N [C] 1 (inf) (horse) 马 [mǎ] 2 (pej) (person) 喋喋不休的人 [diédié bùxiū de rén] ▶ to nag at sb [worry, doubt, feeling +] 令某人烦恼 ▶ to nag (at) sb to do sth 唠叨某人做某事 ▶ to nag sb into doing sth 非叫某人做某事不可

nagging ['nægɪŋ] I ADJ [+ doubt, suspicion] 挥之不去的 [huī zhī bù qù de]; [+ pain] 令人心烦的 [lìngrén xīnfán de] II [U] 纠缠不休 [jiūchán bùxiū]

nail [neɪl] I N [C] 1 [of finger, toe] 指甲 [zhǐjia] 2 (for hammering) 钉子 [dīngzi] II VT 1 (attach) ▶ to nail sth to/on sth 把某物钉在某物上 [bǎ mǒuwù dìng zài mǒuwù shang] 2 (inf) [+ thief] 抓住 [zhuāzhù] ▶ to be nailed shut 用钉子钉死
▷ **nail down** VT 1 (identify) 确定 [quèdìng] 2 (agree on) 达成 [dáchéng] 3 (attach) 钉牢 [dìngláo] ▶ to nail sb down to a date/price 要某人确定日期/价格

nailfile ['neɪlfaɪl] N [C] 指甲锉 [zhǐjia cuò]

nail polish N [U] 指甲油 [zhǐjia yóu]

nail polish remover N [U] 洗甲水 [xǐjiǎ shuǐ]

nail varnish (BRIT) N = nail polish

naive, naïve [naɪ'iːv] ADJ [+ person, ideas] 天真的 [tiānzhēn de] ▶ it was naive of him to believe her 他真是天真, 竟然相信了她

naked ['neɪkɪd] ADJ 1 [+ person, body] 裸体的 [luǒtǐ de] 2 [+ flame, light] 无遮蔽的 [wúzhēbì de] 3 [+ fear, hatred] 分明的 [fēnmíng de] ▶ visible to the naked eye 肉眼可见的 ▶ to see sth with the naked eye 肉眼可见某物

◐ name [neɪm] I N [C] 1 [of person, thing] 名字 [míngzi] 2 (reputation) 名声 [míngshēng] II VT 1 (give name to) [+ child, ship] 取名 [qǔmíng] ▷ Have they named the baby yet? 他们给孩子取名了吗? 2 (identify) [+ accomplice, victim, criminal] 确定 [quèdìng] ▷ The victims have not been named. 遇难者的身份还没有确定。 3 (specify) [+ date, place, price] 说定 [shuōdìng] ▷ Name the place, we'll be there. 说定个地方, 我们会在那儿。 ▶ what's your name? 你叫什么名字? ▶ my name is Peter 我叫彼得 ▶ to mention sb by name 指名道姓 ▶ in sb's name 以某人的名义 ▶ crimes committed in the name of freedom 以自由为名违法犯罪 ▶ to call sb names 嘲弄某人 ▶ to give one's name and address 留下姓名和地址 ▶ to make a name for o.s. 成名 ▶ to give sb/sth a bad name 损害某人/某事的声誉 ▶ the name of the game (inf) 最要紧的方面 ▶ to be named after or (US) for sb/sth 以某人/某事物的名字命名 ▶ to name sb as sb 确认某人是某人 ▷ The victim was named as John Smith. 遇难者被确认是约翰史密斯。 ▶ to name sb as sth 任命某人某种职务 ▷ McGovern was named as the new chairman. 麦戈文被任命为新的主席。

namely ['neɪmlɪ] ADV 即 [jí] ▶ namely that... 就是说…

nanny ['nænɪ] N [C] 保姆 [bǎomǔ]

nap [næp] I N 1 [C] (sleep) 小睡 [xiǎoshuì] 2 [S] [of fabric] 绒毛 [róngmáo] II VI (inf) ▶ to be caught napping 被察觉有失误之处 [bèi chájué yǒu shīwù zhī chù] ▶ to have a nap 小睡一会儿

napkin ['næpkɪn] N [C] (serviette) 餐巾 [cānjīn]

nappy ['næpɪ] (BRIT) N [C] 尿布 [niàobù] [美= diaper]

narcotic [nɑː'kɔtɪk] I ADJ [+ drug, effects] 麻醉的 [mázuì de] II N [C] (type of drug) 麻醉药 [mázuìyào] III narcotics NPL (ESP US) (illegal drugs) 毒品 [dúpǐn]

narrative ['nærətɪv] N [C/U] 叙述 [xùshù]

narrator [nə'reɪtə(r)] N [C] 1 (in novel, play) 叙述者 [xùshùzhě] 2 (CINE, TV, RAD) 解说员 [jiěshuōyuán]

narrow ['nærəu] I ADJ 1 [+ road, ledge, feet] 窄的 [zhǎi de] 2 [+ majority, victory, defeat] 勉强的 [miǎnqiǎng de] 3 [+ ideas, view] 狭隘的 [xiá'ài de] II VI 1 [road, river +] 变窄 [biànzhǎi] 2 [gap, difference +] 缩小 [suōxiǎo] 3 [eyes +] 眯 [mī] III VT 1 [+ gap, difference] 缩小 [suōxiǎo] 2 [+ eyes] 眯起 [mīqǐ] ▶ to have a narrow escape 勉强逃脱 ▶ in the narrow sense of the

word 就该词的狭义来说
▶ **narrow down** VT [+ choice, possibility] 减少 [jiǎnshǎo] ▶ to narrow the list down (to three) 把名单减少(到3个)

narrowly ['nærəʊlɪ] ADV [avoid, escape, miss +] 勉强地 [miǎnqiǎng de]

narrow-minded [nærəʊ'maɪndɪd] ADJ [+ person] 心胸狭窄的 [xīnxiōng xiázhǎi de]; [+ attitude] 狭隘偏执的 [xiá'ài piānzhí de]

NASA [næsə] (US) N ABBR (= National Aeronautics and Space Administration) 国家航空和宇宙航行局 [Guójiā Hángkōng hé Yǔzhòu Hángxíng Jú]

nasal ['neɪzl] ADJ **1** (ANAT, MED) [+ passage, cavity, congestion] 鼻的 [bí de] **2** [+ voice] 带鼻音的 [dài bíyīn de]

nasty ['nɑːstɪ] ADJ **1** (obnoxious) [+ person] 令人憎恶的 [lìng rén zèngwù de]; [+ remark] 恶意的 [èyì de] **2** (bad) [+ taste, smell] 恶心的 [ěxīn de]; [+ weather, temper, shock] 讨厌的 [tǎoyàn de] **3** (serious) [+ injury, accident, disease] 严重的 [yánzhòng de]; [+ problem] 难的 [nán de] ▶ to be nasty to sb 待某人不好 ▶ to turn nasty [person +] 露出凶相 ▶ a nasty business 令人难受的事

○ **nation** ['neɪʃən] N **1** [c] (country) 国家 [guójiā] **2** ▶ the nation (people) 国民 [guómín]

○ **national** ['næʃənl] I ADJ **1** [+ election, newspaper, interest] 国家的 [guójiā de]; [+ characteristic, hobby] 民族的 [mínzú de] II N [c] (citizen) 公民 [gōngmín]

national anthem N [c] 国歌 [guógē]

national dress N [U] 民族服装 [mínzú fúzhuāng]

National Health Service (BRIT) N ▶ the National Health Service 英国国民医疗服务制度 ▶ on the National Health Service 由国民保健署提供

national holiday (US) N [c] 法定假期 [fǎdìng jiàqī] [英= bank holiday]

National Insurance (BRIT) I N [U] 英国国民保险制度 [Yīngguó guómín bǎoxiǎn zhì dù] II CPD [复合词] [+ contributions, card] 国民保险 [guómín bǎoxiǎn]

nationalism ['næʃnəlɪzəm] N [U] 民族主义 [mínzú zhǔyì]

nationalist ['næʃnəlɪst] I ADJ 民族主义的 [mínzú zhǔyì de] II N [c] 民族主义者 [mínzú zhǔyìzhě]

nationality [næʃə'nælɪtɪ] N [c/U] 国籍 [guójí] ▶ What nationality is he? 他是哪国人?

nationalize ['næʃnəlaɪz] VT 使国有化 [shǐ guóyǒuhuà]

nationally ['næʃnəlɪ] ADV [broadcast, agree +] 全国性地 [quánguóxìng de]; [+ available] 在全国范围内 [zài quánguó fànwéi nèi]

national park N [c] 国家公园 [guójiā gōngyuán]

National Trust (BRIT) N ▶ the National Trust

全国名胜古迹托管协会

nationwide ['neɪʃənwaɪd] I ADJ [+ problem, tour, campaign, search etc] 全国性的 [quánguóxìng de] II ADV [distribute, broadcast, campaign etc +] 全国性地 [quánguóxìng de]; [available +] 在全国范围内 [zài quánguó fànwéi nèi]

native ['neɪtɪv] I ADJ [+ country] 本国的 [běnguó de]; [+ language, tongue] 母语的 [mǔyǔ de]; [+ plant, species] 土生的 [tǔshēng de] II N [c] 当地人 [dāngdìrén] ▶ to be a native of Canada/France [+ person] 加拿大/法国本地人 ▶ to be native to Canada/France [plant, animal +] 加拿大/法国本土的

Native American I N [c] 印第安人 [Yìndì'ānrén] II ADJ 印第安人的 [Yìndì'ānrén de]

◉ **NATIVE AMERICAN**

Native American (美洲印第安人)由许多部族组成，例如，科曼奇族、阿帕契族和苏人族，他们在欧洲人到来之前就一直居住在北美洲。继欧洲人之后，后来非洲人和亚洲人也陆续来到北美大陆。**Native American** 最初被西方人称为 **Indian**，因为人们错误地认为发现者克里斯托弗·哥伦布到达了东印度而不是北美大陆，切不可使用带有种族歧视色彩的字眼 **Red Indian** 或 **redskin** 等。

native speaker N [c] 讲母语的人 [jiǎng mǔyǔ de rén] ▶ a native speaker of English, an English native speaker 以英语为母语的人

NATO ['neɪtəʊ] N ABBR (= North Atlantic Treaty Organization) 北约 [Běiyuē]

natural ['nætʃrəl] ADJ **1** (normal) 正常的 [zhèngcháng de] **2** (instinctive) [+ inclination, instinct] 出于本性的 [chūyú běnxìng de] **3** (innate) [+ flair, aptitude, talent] 天生的 [tiānshēng de] **4** (unaffected) [+ person, manner] 自然的 [zìrán de] **5** (not man-made) [+ material, product, food] 天然的 [tiānrán de]; [+ disaster] 大自然的 [dàzìrán de] **6** (MUS) 本位音的 [běnwèiyīn de] **7** (biological) [+ father, parent, sister] 亲生的 [qīnshēng de] ▶ it's natural to worry about one's children 担心自己的孩子是很自然的 ▶ it is natural for us to want excitement 对我们来说，寻求刺激是很自然的 ▶ to die of natural causes 自然死亡 ▶ Martin is a natural musician 马丁是个天生的音乐家

natural gas N [U] 天然气 [tiānránqì]

natural history N [U] 博物学 [bówùxué]

naturally ['nætʃrəlɪ] ADV **1** (unsurprisingly) 自然地 [zìrán de] **2** [behave, lead, arise, result +] 自然地 [zìrán de] **3** [occur, happen +] 自然而然地 [zìrán ér rán de] **4** (by nature) 天生地

[tiānshēng de] ▶ **"naturally!"** "当然啦！" ▶ **to come naturally (to sb)** (对某人来说)很容易

natural resources NPL 自然资源 [zìrán zīyuán]

nature ['neɪtʃə(r)] N **1** [U] (also: **Nature**) 自然界 [zìránjiè] **2** (character) [of thing] [S/U] 特性 [tèxìng]; [of person] [C/U] 天性 [tiānxìng] ▶ **the protests were political in nature** 那些抗议都是政治性的 ▶ **it was not in her nature to tell lies** 她生性不会说谎 ▶ **I am an optimist by nature** 我天生是个乐天派 ▶ **by its (very) nature** 理所当然 ▶ **documents of a confidential nature** 机密文件 ▶ **or something of that nature** 或者类似性质的事物

naught [nɔːt] N = **nought**

naughty ['nɔːtɪ] ADJ **1** (disobedient) [+ child] 淘气的 [táoqì de] **2** (rude) [+ magazine, film] 低级的 [dījí de]; [+ word] 下流的 [xiàliú de]

nausea ['nɔːsɪə] N [U] 恶心 [ěxīn]

naval ['neɪvl] ADJ [+ uniform, battle, forces] 海军的 [hǎijūn de]

navel ['neɪvl] N [C] 肚脐 [dùqí]

navigate ['nævɪgeɪt] I VT **1** [+ ship, aircraft] 导航 [dǎoháng] **2** [+ river, ocean] 在⋯航行 [zài⋯hángxíng] II VI (in a car) 指路 [zhǐlù]; [birds, fish+] 找到正确的方向 [zhǎodào zhèngquè de fāngxiàng] ▶ **to navigate (one's way) around sth** (lit) 绕过某物 ▶ **to navigate (a path) through sth** (fig) 找到解决的方法

navigation [nævɪ'geɪʃən] N **1** (action) 航行 [hángxíng] **2** (science) 航行学 [hángxíngxué]

navy ['neɪvɪ] I N **1** the navy (service) 海军 [hǎijūn] **2** [c] (ships) 海军舰队 [hǎijūn jiànduì] **3** [U] (also: **navy-blue**) 藏青色 [zàngqīngsè] II ADJ (also: **navy-blue**) 藏青色的 [zàngqīngsè de] ▶ **to be in the navy** 在海军服役 ▶ **to join the navy** 参加海军 ▶ **the Department of the Navy** (US) 海军部

Nazi ['nɑːtsɪ] I N [c] 纳粹分子 [Nàcuì fènzǐ] II CPD [复合词] [+ party, propaganda, sympathizer] 纳粹 [Nàcuì]

NB ABBR (= nota bene) 注意 [zhùyì]

NBA (US) N ABBR (= National Basketball Association) 全国篮球协会 [Quánguó Lánqiú Xiéhuì]

NBC (US) N ABBR (= National Broadcasting Company) 国家广播公司 [Guójiā Guǎngbō Gōngsī]

NE ABBR (= north-east) 东北 [dōngběi]

⊕ **near** [nɪə(r)] I ADJ **1** (physically, in time) 近的 [jìn de] ▷ The nearest shops are 5 km away. 最近的商店离这里有5公里远。 ▷ Christmas is quite near now. 圣诞节很近了。 ▷ My office is quite near. 我的办公室离这儿不远。 **2** (not complete) [+ darkness, tragedy] 几乎 [jīhū] ▷ We were sitting in near darkness. 我们几乎是在黑暗中坐着。 II ADV **1** (close) 近 [jìn] ▷ He must live quite

near. 他一定住得很近。 **2** (almost) [+ disastrous, perfect, impossible, fatal] 几乎 [jīhū] ▷ a near fatal accident 一场几乎致命的事故 III PREP (also: **near to**) **1** (physically) 近 [jìn] ▷ I stood very near them. 我站得离他们很近。 **2** (just before/after) 临近 [línjìn] ▷ It happened near the beginning of the game. 这件事发生在临近比赛的时候。 **3** (bordering on) [+ completion, truth, collapse] 接近 [jiējìn] ▷ Her views were fairly near the truth. 她的观点相当接近真相。 IV VT **1** [+ place, end, age, time] 接近 [jiējìn] ▷ He was nearing the door when the light went on. 他接近门的时候，灯亮了。 ▷ They were nearing the end of their training. 他们的训练接近尾声了。 **2** (border on) 近于 [jìnyú] ▷ The crisis neared a critical point last week. 上星期，危机近于顶点。 ▶ **25,000 pounds or nearest offer** (BRIT) 25,000英镑或者是与之相似的报价 ▶ **in the near future** 在不远的将来 ▶ **to draw near** [event, time+] 临近 [línjìn] ▷ The wedding day drew near. 婚礼快到了。 ▶ **near enough** 将近 ▶ **she's nowhere near ready** 她根本没准备好 ▶ **don't go/come any nearer!** 不许再走！靠近了！ ▶ **don't come near me!** 别走近我 ▶ **he won't (ever) go near a hospital** 他(怎么也)不愿意去医院 ▶ **the building is nearing completion** 这座楼房要竣工了

nearby [nɪə'baɪ] I ADJ 附近的 [fùjìn de] II ADV 在附近 [zài fùjìn]

nearly ['nɪəlɪ] ADV 差不多 [chà bù duō] ▶ **you're nearly as tall as I am** 我跟我差不多了 ▶ **the film isn't nearly as good as the book** 电影拍得没有书好看 ▶ **it's not nearly big enough** 根本不够大 ▶ **I (very) nearly fell over** 我差点摔倒了 ▶ **nearly always** 几乎总是 ▶ **she was nearly in tears** 她差点要哭了

near-sighted [nɪə'saɪtɪd] (US) ADJ (short-sighted) 近视的 [jìnshì de]

neat [niːt] ADJ **1** (tidy) [+ house, desk, pile, clothes] 整洁的 [zhěngjié de]; [+ handwriting] 工整的 [gōngzhěng de] **2** [+ person] (organized) 爱整洁的 [ài zhěngjié de]; (in appearance) 干净得体的 [gānjìng détǐ de] **3** (simple, effective) [+ plan, solution, description] 简明的 [jiǎnmíng de] **4** (ESP BRIT) (undiluted) [+ whisky, gin etc] 纯的 [chún de] ▷ I drink my whisky neat. 我爱喝纯威士忌酒。 **5** (US: inf) (great) 绝妙的 [juémiào de]

neatly ['niːtlɪ] ADV (tidily, conveniently) 整齐地 [zhěngqí de]

necessarily ['nesɪsrɪlɪ] ADV (inevitably) 必然 [bìrán] ▶ **not necessarily** 未必

necessary ['nesɪsrɪ] ADJ **1** (required) [+ skill, quality, item] 必要的 [bìyào de] **2** (inevitable) [+ consequence, connection] 必然的 [bìrán de] ▶ **if/when/where necessary** 如有必要/必要时/在必要处 ▶ **I don't want to stay longer than necessary** 我不想呆得太久 ▶ **it may be necessary (for us) to buy a new cooker** (我们)可能应该买一个新的炊具

necessity [nɪˈsɛsɪtɪ] N 1 [U] (need) 需要
[xūyào] 2 [C] (essential item) 必需品 [bìxūpǐn]
3 [C] (essential measure) 不可避免的事情 [bùkě
bìmiǎn de shìqíng] ▶ there is no necessity for
us to do anything 我们没有必要做什么 ▶ of
necessity (frm) 必定 ▶ out of necessity 迫不
得已 ▶ the necessity of doing sth 做某事的
必要性

neck [nɛk] I N [C] 1 (ANAT) [of person, animal]
颈 [jǐng] 2 (of shirt, dress, jumper) 领子 [lǐngzi]
3 (narrow part) [of bottle] 颈部 [jǐngbù]; (of guitar,
violin) 颈状部位 [jǐngzhuàng bùwèi] II VI (inf)
盘颈亲昵 [pánjǐng qīnnì] ▶ to be breathing
down sb's neck 紧紧盯着某人 ▶ to be neck
and neck 并驾齐驱 ▶ to stick one's neck out
(inf) 担风险

necklace [ˈnɛklɪs] N [C] 项链 [xiàngliàn]

necktie [ˈnɛktaɪ] (US) N [C] 领带 [lǐngdài]
[英=**tie**]

nectarine [ˈnɛktərɪn] N [C] (fruit) 油桃 [yóutáo]

◐**need** [niːd] I VT 1 (require) 需要 [xūyào] ▷ The
animals need food supplements throughout the winter.
动物整个冬天都需要食物补给。 ▷ You need
glasses. 你得戴眼镜。 2 (want) [+ drink, holiday,
cigarette] 想要 [xiǎngyào] ▷ I need a holiday.
我想要去度假。 3 (could do with) [+ a haircut, a
bath, a wash] 得 [děi] ▷ The car needs a wash. 这
车得洗洗了。 II N [S] 1 (demand) 需求 [xūqiú]
▷ These groups are obviously answering a need. 这些
团体显然是在满足一种需求。 2 (necessity) 必
要 [bìyào] ▷ There's a need for more information.
有必要再寻求一些信息。 III needs NPL
(requirements) 需求 [xūqiú] ▷ He had not been
able to satisfy her emotional needs. 他没能满足她
感情上的需求。 ▷ the needs of industry 工业的需
求 ▶ to need to do sth 必须做某事 ▷ You need
to see a doctor. 你必须去看医生。 ▶ the car needs
servicing 这辆车需要修了 ▶ you don't
need (to have) a degree to see what's going on
你很容易就能知道发生了什么 ▶ he doesn't
need to know or he needn't know 他不必知道
▶ "need I stay?" – "no, you needn't" "需要我
留下吗?" "不必了" ▶ to be in need 有困
难 ▶ to be (badly) in need of sth （急）需某物
▶ (there's) no need (it's not necessary) （那）不用
了 ▶ there's no need to shout (please don't)
嚷嚷 ▶ there's no need for us to finish this 我
们没有必要完成 ▶ he has no need to work 他
没有必要工作 ▶ to feel the need to do sth 觉
得应该做某事

needle [ˈniːdl] I N [C] 1 (for sewing) 针 [zhēn]
2 (for knitting) 编织针 [biānzhīzhēn] 3 (for
injections) 注射针 [zhùshèzhēn] 4 (on record
player) 唱针 [chàngzhēn] 5 (on dial) 指针
[zhǐzhēn] 6 (on pine tree) 针叶 [zhēnyè] II VT
(inf) (nag) 刺激 [cìjī]

needless [ˈniːdlɪs] ADJ [+ death, suffering, worry,
risk etc] 不必要的 [bù bìyào de] ▶ needless to

say 不用说

needlework [ˈniːdlwəːk] N [U] 针线活
[zhēnxiànhuó]

needn't [ˈniːdnt] = need not

needy [ˈniːdɪ] I ADJ 贫困的 [pínkùn de] II NPL
▶ the needy 贫困的人 [pínkùn de rén]

negative [ˈnɛɡətɪv] I ADJ 1 [+ effect, news]
负面的 [fùmiàn de] 2 [+ test, result] 阴性的
[yīnxìng de] 3 (gloomy) [+ person, attitude, view]
消极的 [xiāojí de] 4 (not affirmative) [+ answer,
response] 否定的 [fǒudìng de] 5 (ELEC) [+ charge,
current] 负极的 [fùjí de] 6 (MATH) 负的 [fù de]
II N [C] 1 (PHOT) 底片 [dǐpiàn] 2 (LING) 否
定词 [fǒudìngcí] ▶ why do you have to be so
negative about everything? 你怎么对什么都
这么消极呢? ▶ to answer in the negative 作
否定的回答

neglect [nɪˈɡlɛkt] I VT 1 (not care for) [+ child,
area, house, garden] 忽略 [hūlüè] 2 (not pay
attention to) [+ person] 怠慢 [dàimàn]; [+ work,
duty] 疏忽 [shūhu] 3 (overlook) [+ writer, artist] 忽
视 [hūshì] II N [U] 1 [of child] 疏忽 [shūhu] 2 [of
area, house, garden] 疏于照顾 [shū yú zhàogù]
▶ to neglect to do sth 漏做某事

neglected [nɪˈɡlɛktɪd] ADJ 1 (uncared for)
[+ animal, child, garden] 未被妥善照管的 [wèi
bèi tuǒshàn zhàoguǎn de] 2 (ignored) [+ family,
wife] 被冷落的 [bèi lěngluò de] ▷ She's feeling
rather neglected. 她感到倍受冷落。 3 (overlooked)
[+ writer, artist] 被忽视的 [bèi hūshì de];
[+ aspect] 被忽略的 [bèi hūlüè de]

negligence [ˈnɛɡlɪdʒəns] (frm) N [U]
(carelessness) 玩忽职守 [wánhū zhíshǒu]

negligible [ˈnɛɡlɪdʒɪbl] ADJ [+ risk, amount, level]
无足轻重的 [wú zú qīng zhòng de]

negotiate [nɪˈɡəʊʃɪeɪt] I VI 商讨 [shāngtǎo]
II VT 1 [+ treaty, contract] 谈判 [tánpàn]
2 [+ obstacle, hill, bend] 顺利通过 [shùnlì
tōngguò] ▶ to negotiate with sb (for sth) （就
某事)与某人协商

negotiation [nɪɡəʊʃɪˈeɪʃən] I N [U] (bargaining)
谈判 [tánpàn] II negotiations NPL (discussions)
洽谈 [qiàtán]

negotiator [nɪˈɡəʊʃɪeɪtə(r)] N [C] 谈判人
[tánpànrén]

neighbour, (US) **neighbor** [ˈneɪbə(r)] N [C]
1 (person living nearby) 邻居 [línjū] 2 (person next
to you) 旁边的人 [pángbiān de rén]

neighbourhood, (US) **neighborhood**
[ˈneɪbəhud] N [C] 1 (place) 地区 [dìqū] 2 (people)
邻里 [línlǐ] ▶ in the neighbourhood of sth
[+ place] 邻近某处; [+ amount] 大约某数量

neighbouring, (US) **neighboring** [ˈneɪbə
rɪŋ] ADJ [+ town, state, house, building] 邻近的
[línjìn de]

neither [ˈnaɪðə(r)] I PRON (person) 两人都不
[liǎngrén dōu bù]; (thing) 两者都不 [liǎngzhě
dōu bù] II CONJ ▶ I didn't move and neither

did John 我和约翰都没动 [wǒ hé Yuēhàn dōu méi dòng] ▶ **neither do/have I** 我也不/没 ▶ **neither... nor...** 既不…也不… ▶ **that is neither here nor there** 不相干

neither 和 none 作代词的时候用法不同。用 neither 指两个人或事物，表示否定含义。*Neither had close friends at university.* neither of 的用法与之相同，后接代词或名词词组。*Neither of them spoke...Neither of these options is desirable.* 注意，也可以把 neither 用在单数可数名词之前。*Neither side can win.* none 可以指代三个或者三个以上的人或事物，表示否定含义。*None could afford the food.* none of 的用法与之相同，后接代词或名词词组。*None of them had learned anything...None of his companions answered.*

neon ['niːɒn] I N [U] 氖 [nǎi] II CPD [复合词] [+ *light, sign*] 霓虹 [níhóng]

Nepal [nɪ'pɔːl] N 尼泊尔 [Níbó'ěr]

Nepalese [nɛpə'liːz] (*pl* **Nepalese**) I ADJ 尼泊尔的 [Níbó'ěr de] II N 1 [U] (*language*) 尼泊尔语 [Níbó'ěryǔ] 2 [c] (*person*) 尼泊尔人 [Níbó'ěrrén] ▶ **the Nepalese** (*people*) 尼泊尔人

Nepali [nɪ'pɔːli] I ADJ 尼泊尔的 [Níbó'ěr de] II N 1 [U] (*language*) 尼泊尔语 [Níbó'ěryǔ] 2 [c] (*person*) 尼泊尔人 [Níbó'ěrrén]

nephew ['nɛvjuː] N [c] (*brother's son*) 侄子 [zhízi]; (*sister's son*) 外甥 [wàisheng] ▶ **my nieces and nephews** 我的甥侄辈

nerve [nəːv] N 1 [c] (ANAT) 神经 [shénjīng] 2 [U] (*courage*) 勇气 [yǒngqì] 3 **nerves** NPL (*anxiety*) 神经紧张 [shénjīng jǐnzhāng]; (*strength of character*) 精神力量 [jīngshén lìliang] ▶ **to lose one's nerve** 失去勇气 ▶ **to have the nerve to do sth** (*courage*) 有胆量做某事; (*cheek*) 厚颜无耻地做某事 ▶ **you've got a nerve!** (*inf*) 你真有脸! ▶ **what a nerve!** 真有胆量! ▶ **to get on sb's nerves** 使某人心烦

nervous ['nəːvəs] ADJ 1 (*worried*) 紧张的 [jǐnzhāng de] 2 (*by nature*) [+ *person, animal, disposition*] 神经质的 [shénjīngzhì de] 3 (*mental*) [+ *strain, tension, disorder*] 神经的 [shénjīng de] ▶ **to be nervous about sth/about doing sth** 对某事/做某事感到紧张不安 ▶ **to be nervous of sb/sth** 对某事/某人心中不安

nervous breakdown N [c] 精神崩溃 [jīngshén bēngkuì] ▶ **to have a nervous breakdown** 精神崩溃

nervousness ['nəːvəsnɪs] N [U] (*anxiety*) 焦虑 [jiāolù]

nervous system N [c] 神经系统 [shénjīng xìtǒng]

nest [nɛst] I N [c] [*of bird*] 巢 [cháo]; [*of insect, animal*] 穴 [xué] II VI 筑巢 [zhùcháo]

net [nɛt] I N 1 (*for fishing, trapping, in games*) 网 [wǎng] 2 [c] (*for protecting plants, pram*) 网罩 [wǎngzhào] 3 [U] (*fabric*) 网眼织物 [wǎngyǎn zhīwù] 4 (COMPUT) ▶ **the Net** 网络 [wǎngluò] II VT 1 [+ *fish, butterfly*] 用网捕捉 [yòng wǎng bǔ] 2 [+ *sum of money*] 净得 [jìngdé] III ADJ 1 (*also*: **nett**) [+ *assets, income, profit*] 净的 [jìng de] 2 (*final*) [+ *result, effect*] 最终的 [zuìzhōng de] ▶ **to slip through the net** (*escape arrest*) 漏网; (*miss out*) 漏掉 ▶ **to cast/spread one's net wider** 抛开/撒开大网 ▶ **an income/profit of 10,000 pounds net** 纯收入/利润10,000英镑 ▶ **net weight 250g** 净重250克 ▶ **250g net** 净重250克

netball ['nɛtbɔːl] N [U] 无挡板篮球 [wúdǎngbǎn lánqiú]

Netherlands ['nɛðələndz] NPL ▶ **the Netherlands** 荷兰 [Hélán]

nett [nɛt] (BRIT) ADJ = net

nettle ['nɛtl] N [c] 荨麻 [qiánmá] ▶ **to grasp the nettle** (ESP BRIT) 果断处理棘手问题

network ['nɛtwəːk] I N [c] 1 [*of roads, veins etc*] 网状系统 [wǎngzhuàng xìtǒng] 2 [*of people, offices, shops*] 联络网 [liánluòwǎng] 3 (*system*) 网络 [wǎngluò] 4 (TV, RAD) (*company*) 网 [wǎng] II VI 1 (*socialize*) 建立关系 [jiànlì guānxi] 2 ▶ **to be networked** (RAD, TV) 联播 [liánbō]

neurotic [njuə'rɒtɪk] I ADJ [+ *person, behaviour*] 神经质的 [shénjīngzhì de] II N 神经质者 [shénjīngzhìzhě] ▶ **to be/become neurotic about sth** 对某事极为焦虑

neuter ['njuːtə(r)] I VT [+ *male*] 阉割 [yāngē]; [+ *female*] 骟 [shàn] II ADJ (LING) 中性的 [zhōngxìng de]

neutral ['njuːtrəl] I ADJ 1 [+ *person, country, position*] 中立的 [zhōnglì de] 2 (*impassive*) [+ *voice, language, expression*] 不带感情色彩的 [bù dài gǎnqíng sècǎi de] 3 [+ *colour*] 暗淡的 [àndàn de] 4 (ELEC) [+ *wire*] 不带电的 [bù dàidiàn de] II N (*in vehicle*) ▶ **in/into neutral** 处于空挡位置 [chǔyú kōngdǎng wèizhi] ▶ **to remain neutral** 保持中立

○ **never** ['nɛvə(r)] ADV 1 (*not at any time*) 从未 [cóngwèi] ▷ *I never met him.* 我从未见过他。 2 (*emphatic*) 决不 [juébù] ▷ *I would never do anything to hurt him.* 我决不会做任何伤害他的事情。 ▶ **never again!** 下次绝对不许了! ▶ **we never saw him again** 我们再没有见过他 ▶ **never ever** (*inf*) 永不 ▶ **never in my life** 我从未 ▷ *Never in my life have I seen anyone drink as much as you.* 我从未见过任何人有你这么能喝酒。 ▶ **well I never!** (*inf, o.f.*) 真没想到!

never-ending [nɛvər'ɛndɪŋ] ADJ [+ *supply, quest, struggle*] 永无休止的 [yǒng wú xiūzhǐ de]

nevertheless [nɛvəðə'lɛs] ADV (*frm*) 不过 [bùguò]

○ **new** [njuː] ADJ 1 (*brand new*) 崭新的 [zhǎnxīn de] ▷ *We have just bought a new television.* 我们刚买了一台崭新的电视。 ▷ *smart new houses* 漂

亮的新居 **2** (recent) [+ product, system, method etc] 新式的 [xīnshì de] ▷ a new type of bandage 一种新式绷带 **3** (different) [+ job, address, boss, president] 新的 [xīn de] ▷ He's got a new job. 他 找到了一个新工作。 **4** (recently found) [+ star, country, friend, evidence] 新发现的 [xīnfāxiàn de] ▷ New evidence has come to light. 有新的证据出现了。 **5** (inexperienced) [+ mother, member] 无经验的 [wú jīngyàn de] ▷ The society welcomes new members. 协会欢迎新成员。 ▶ **this concept is new to me** 我对这个概念不熟悉 ▶ **I'm new to this way of doing things** 我不熟悉这种做事方式 ▶ **I'm new here** 我是新来的

New Age ADJ 新世纪的 [Xīnshìjì de]

newborn ['nju:bɔ:n] ADJ [+ baby, lamb] 新生的 [xīnshēng de]

newcomer ['nju:kʌmə(r)] N [c] (to area, organization, activity) 新来的人 [xīnlái de rén] ▶ **to be a newcomer to sth** 某领域的新手

newly ['nju:lɪ] ADV [+ formed, discovered, acquired] 新近地 [xīnjìn de]

○**news** [nju:z] N [U] 消息 [xiāoxi] ▷ News travels pretty fast around here. 在这里，消息传得很快。
▶ **a piece of news** 一条消息 ▶ **good/bad news** 好/坏消息 ▶ **to be good/bad news (to/for sb)** 对某人有利/不利 ▶ **the news** (TV, RAD) 新闻 ▶ **to be on the news** 在新闻中播出 ▶ **to be in the news** 被作为新闻报道

> 注意，尽管 **news** 看起来像是复数，事实上它是一个不可数名词。不能说 **a news**，但是可以说 **a piece of news**，指某个具体的事实或消息。*One of my colleagues told me a very exciting piece of news.* 当谈到电视、广播或者报纸新闻的时候，可以把一个独立的故事或报道叫做 **a news item**。

news agency N [c] 通讯社 [tōngxùnshè]

newsagent ['nju:zeɪdʒənt] (BRIT) N [c]
1 (person) 报刊经销人 [bàokān jīngxiāorén] **2** (also: **newsagent's**) 报刊店 [bàokāndiàn]

newscaster ['nju:zkɑ:stə(r)] (US) N [c] 播音员 [bōyīnyuán] [英= **newsreader**]

newsletter ['nju:zletə(r)] N [c] 通讯 [tōngxùn]

newspaper ['nju:zpeɪpə(r)] N **1** [c] (publication) 报纸 [bàozhǐ] **2** [c] (organization) 报社 [bàoshè] **3** [U] (sheets of paper) 报纸 [bàozhǐ] ▶ **in the newspaper** 报上 ▶ **to be in the newspapers** 在报上报道

newsreader ['nju:zri:də(r)] (BRIT) N [c] 播音员 [bōyīnyuán] [美= **newscaster**]

newt [nju:t] N [c] 水螈 [shuǐyuán]

New Year N [U] ▶ **(the) New Year** 新年 [Xīnnián] ▶ **in the New Year** 在新的一年中 ▶ **Happy New Year!** 新年快乐！ ▶ **to wish sb a happy new year** 祝愿某人新年快乐

New Year's Day, (US) **New Year's** N [U] 元旦 [Yuándàn] ▶ **on New Year's Day** 在元旦

那天

New Year's Eve, (US) **New Year's** N [U] 元旦前夜 [Yuándàn qiányè]

New Zealand [-'zi:lənd] I N 新西兰 [Xīnxīlán] II ADJ 新西兰的 [Xīnxīlán de]

New Zealander [-'zi:ləndə(r)] N [c] 新西兰人 [Xīnxīlánrén]

○**next** [nɛkst] I ADJ **1** (in time) 下一个的 [xiàyīgè de] ▷ I've got a meeting next Friday. 下星期五我有个会。 ▷ I'm getting married next year. 明年我结婚。 **2** (adjacent) [+ house, street, room] 旁边的 [pángbiān de] ▷ The telephone was ringing in the next room. 隔壁房间的电话在响。 ▷ He is talking with the next person. 他正在和旁边的人说话。 **3** (in queue, series, list) 下一个的 [xiàyīgè de] ▷ the next person in the queue 队伍中的下一个人 II ADV 接下来地 [jiēxiàlái de] ▷ Allow the sauce to cool. Next, add the parsley. 先冷却调味汁。接下来，放入欧芹。 ▷ The news is next. 接下来是新闻。 III PRON 下一个 [xiàyīgè] ▷ I don't want to be the next to go. 我不想是下一个要走的人。 ▶ **the next day/morning** 第2天/天早晨 ▶ **the next five years/weeks will be very important** 接下来的5年/周将是至关重要的 ▶ **the next five days/weeks were a nightmare** 接下来的5天/周简直是恶梦一场 ▶ **the next flight/prime minister** 下一次航班/下一任首相 ▶ **next time, be a bit more careful** 下一次，要更谨慎些 ▶ **who's next?** 下一位是谁？ ▶ **when next I saw him...** 当我再一次看到他的时候… ▶ **next to nothing** [cost, do, know +] 几乎不 ▶ **the next best thing** 仅次于最好的 ▶ **the next largest category** 第二大范畴 ▶ **the next thing I knew** (inf) 突然发现 ▶ **the week after next** 下下个星期 ▶ **next to** (beside) 旁边 ▶ **next on the right/left** 右/左面第一个 ▶ **next (please)!** (at doctor's etc) 下一位！

next door I ADV (in neighbouring building, room etc) 隔壁 [gébì] II ADJ [+ building, house, flat, room] 隔壁的 [gébì de] ▶ **my next door neighbour** 我的隔壁邻居 ▶ **the people/family next door** 隔壁的人/人家

next of kin ['nɛkstəv'kɪn] (frm) I N [U] (individual) 直系亲属 [zhíxì qīnshǔ] II NPL (family) 家人 [jiārén]

NFL N ABBR (= **National Football League**) 全国橄榄球联盟 [Quánguó Gǎnlǎnqiú Liánméng]

NHS (BRIT) N ABBR (= **National Health Service**) ▶ **the NHS** 英国国民医疗服务制度

nibble ['nɪbl] VT **1** (bite) 轻咬 [qīng yǎo] **2** (eat) 啃 [kěn] ▶ **to nibble (away) on** or **at sth** 一点一点地咬某物

Nicaragua [nɪkə'ræɡjuə] N 尼加拉瓜 [Níjiālāguā]

Nicaraguan [nɪkə'ræɡjuən] I ADJ 尼加拉瓜的 [Níjiālāguā de] II N [c] 尼加拉瓜人 [Níjiālāguārén]

nice [naɪs] ADJ **1** (good) [+ time, holiday, meal,

weather etc] 好的 [hǎo de] **2** [+ person] (likeable) 和蔼的 [hé'ǎi de]; (friendly) 友好的 [yǒuhǎo de] **3** (kind) [+ remark, act] 善意的 [shànyì de] **4** (adj) (lovely) 宜人的 [yírén de] ▶ to look nice [person, place +] 看上去不错 ▶ it's nice to see you 很高兴见到你 ▶ it's nice that... 太好了… ▶ to be nice to sb 对某人好 ▶ it's nice of you to ask... 谢谢你问起… ▶ it's nice and warm/bright in here 这里真好, 挺温暖/明亮的

nicely ['naɪslɪ] ADV **1** (satisfactorily) [work, run +] 令人满意地 [lìng rén mǎnyì de] **2** (attractively) [dress, arrange +] 好看地 [hǎokàn de] ▶ you can have a biscuit if you ask nicely 如果你好好问的话, 你可以吃一块饼干 ▶ that will do nicely 对我来说就够了 ▶ she's doing (very) nicely 她过得(很)好

niche [niːʃ] N [C] **1** (for statue) 壁龛 [bìkān] **2** (in market, organization, field) 空白 [kòngbái] ▶ to find one's niche 找到自己合适的位置 ▶ to carve a niche for o.s. 为自己寻求发展的空间

nick [nɪk] I VT **1** (BRIT: inf) (steal) 偷 [tōu] **2** (BRIT: inf) (arrest) 抓获 [zhuāhuò] **3** (cut) 刮破 [guāpò] II N [C] (scratch) 小伤口 [xiǎoshāngkǒu] ▶ to be nicked for doing sth (BRIT: inf) 因做某事而被捕 ▶ in good nick (BRIT: inf) 状况良好 ▶ the nick (BRIT: inf) 监狱 ▶ in the nick of time 正当紧要关头

nickel ['nɪkl] N [C] **1** (metal) 镍 [niè] **2** (US) (coin) 5美分硬币 [wǔ měifēn yìngbì]

nickname ['nɪkneɪm] I N [C] 绰号 [chuòhào] II VT ▶ to nickname sb sth 给某人起某个绰号 [gěi mǒurén qǐ mǒugè chuòhào]

nicotine ['nɪkətiːn] N [U] 尼古丁 [nígǔdīng]

niece [niːs] N [C] (brother's daughter) 侄女 [zhínǚ]; (sister's daughter) 甥女 [shēngnǚ] ▶ my nieces and nephews 我的甥侄辈

Niger N **1** [niːʒeə(r)] (country) 尼日尔 [Nírì'ěr] **2** ['naɪdʒə(r)] (river) 尼日河 [Nírì'ěrhé]

Nigeria [naɪ'dʒɪərɪə] N 尼日利亚 [Nírìlìyà]

Nigerian [naɪ'dʒɪərɪən] I ADJ 尼日利亚的 [Nírìlìyà de] II N [C] 尼日利亚人 [Nírìlìyàrén]

○ **night** [naɪt] N **1** [C/U] (period of darkness) 黑夜 [hēiyè] **2** [C] (evening) 晚上 [wǎnshang] ▶ at night 夜间 ▶ from nine o'clock at night until nine in the morning 从晚上9点到早上9点 ▶ by night 夜里 ▶ They travelled by night to avoid detection. 他们夜间赶路以免被人察觉。 ▶ in/during the night 夜里 ▶ the night before last 前天晚上 ▶ the night before (sth) 前一天晚上 ▶ night and day or day and night 日日夜夜 ▶ night was falling 夜幕降临了

nightclub ['naɪtklʌb] N [C] 夜总会 [yèzǒnghuì]

nightdress ['naɪtdrɛs] (BRIT) N [C] 睡衣 [shuìyī] [美= nightgown]

nightfall ['naɪtfɔːl] N [U] 黄昏 [huánghūn] ▶ at nightfall 在傍晚

nightgown ['naɪtgaun] (ESP US) N [C] 睡衣 [shuìyī] [英= nightdress]

nightie ['naɪtɪ] N = nightdress

nightingale ['naɪtɪŋgeɪl] N [C] 夜莺 [yèyīng]

nightlife ['naɪtlaɪf] N [U] 夜生活 [yèshēnghuó]

nightly ['naɪtlɪ] I ADJ 晚间的 [wǎnjiān de] II ADV 每晚 [měiwǎn]

nightmare ['naɪtmeə(r)] N [C] 恶梦 [èmèng] ▶ to have a nightmare 做恶梦 ▶ the bus journey was a nightmare 乘公共汽车旅行真是一场恶梦

night school N [C/U] 夜校 [yèxiào] ▶ to go to night school 上夜校

night shift N [C] **1** (hours) 夜班 [yèbān] **2** (people) 夜班工作人员 [yèbān gōngzuòrényuán] ▶ to do the night shift 值夜班 ▶ to be on night shift 值夜班

night-time ['naɪttaɪm] I N [U] 夜间 [yèjiān] ▶ at night-time 在晚上 II CPD [复合词] [+ curfew, raid, activity] 夜间 [yèjiān]

nil [nɪl] N **1** [U] (BRIT: SPORT) 零 [líng] ▶ they lost two nil to Italy 他们以0比2输给意大利队 **2** ▶ their chances of survival are nil 他们没有幸存的可能 [tāmen méiyǒu xìngcún de kěnéng]

用法参见 nought

nimble ['nɪmbl] ADJ [+ person, fingers, movements] 灵巧的 [língqiǎo de]; [+ mind] 敏锐的 [mǐnruì de]

○ **nine** [naɪn] NUM 九 [jiǔ] see also five

○ **nineteen** [naɪn'tiːn] NUM 十九 [shíjiǔ] see also fifteen

nineteenth [naɪn'tiːnθ] NUM 第十九 [dì shíjiǔ] see also fifth

ninetieth ['naɪntɪɪθ] NUM 第九十 [dì jiǔshí]

○ **ninety** ['naɪntɪ] NUM 九十 [jiǔshí] see also fifty

ninth [naɪnθ] NUM **1** (in series) 第九 [dì jiǔ] **2** (fraction) 九分之一 [jiǔfēn zhī yī] see also fifth

nip [nɪp] I VT (bite) 咬 [yǎo] II N **1** (bite) ▶ to give sb a nip 轻咬某人 [qīng yǎo mǒurén] **2** (drink) 少量 [shǎoliàng] ▶ to nip to a place (BRIT: inf) 快去某处 ▶ to nip out/down/up (to do sth) (BRIT: inf) 快点去/下去/上去(做某事)

nipple ['nɪpl] N [C] **1** (on body) 乳头 [rǔtóu] **2** (US) (on bottle) 橡皮奶头 [xiàngpí nǎitóu] [英= teat]

nitrogen ['naɪtrədʒən] N [U] 氮 [dàn]

○

no [nəu] (pl noes) I ADV (opposite of "yes") 不 [bù] ▶ "did you see it?" – "no (I didn't)" "你看见了吗?" "不(我没见到)" ▶ no thank you, no thanks 不用, 谢谢你 ▶ oh no! 噢不! ▶ no fewer/more than 不少/多于

II ADJ (not any) 没有 [méiyǒu] ▶ I have no milk/books 我没有牛奶/书 ▶ I've no time 我没时间 ▶ there's no other solution 没有其他办法 ▶ "no entry" "严禁入

内 ▶ "no smoking" "严禁吸烟" ▶ no way! 没门儿!
III N 否决 [fǒujué] ▶ there were 20 noes and one "don't know" 有二十个 说 "不" ，一个说 "不确定" ▶ I won't take no for an answer 我不会接受否定 的答复

no. (pl **nos.**) ABBR (= number) 编号 [biānhào]

nobility [nəu'bɪlɪtɪ] N 1 [U] (quality) 高尚 [gāoshàng] 2 ▶ the nobility 贵族 [guìzú]

noble ['nəubl] I ADJ 1 (admirable) [+ person, character] 高尚的 [gāoshàng de] 2 (aristocratic) [+ family, birth] 贵族的 [guìzú de] II N [c] 贵族 [guìzú]

nobody ['nəubədɪ] PRON 没有人 [méiyǒu rén] ▶ he's a nobody 他是个无名小卒

nod [nɔd] I VI (to show agreement) 点头 [diǎntóu]; (as greeting) 点头打招呼 [diǎntóu dǎ zhāohu]; (indicating sth/sb) 点头示意 [diǎntóu shìyì] II VT ▶ to nod one's head (to show agreement) 点头表示同意 [diǎntóu biǎoshì tóngyì]; (as greeting) 点头招呼 [diǎntóu zhāohu]; (indicating sth/sb) 点头示意 [diǎntóu shìyì] III N [c] (to show agreement) 点头同意 [diǎntóu tóngyì]; (as greeting) 点头打招呼 [diǎntóu dǎ zhāohu]; (indicating sth/sb) 点头示意 [diǎntóu shìyì] ▶ to nod to sb (as greeting) 对某人点头打招呼 ▶ to nod the ball into the net/over the line (BRIT: inf) 把球顶入网/顶过线 ▶ to give a nod (to show agreement) 点头同意; (as greeting) 点头打招呼
▶ nod off (inf) VI (also: nod off to sleep) 打瞌睡 [dǎ kēshuì]

noise [nɔɪz] N 1 [c] (sound) 响声 [xiǎngshēng] 2 [U] (din) 噪音 [zàoyīn] ▶ to make a noise 发出响声 ▶ try not to make so much noise 尽量不要弄出这么多响声

noisy ['nɔɪzɪ] ADJ [+ people, machine] 嘈杂的 [cáozá de]; [+ place] 喧闹的 [xuānnào de]

nominal ['nɔmɪnl] ADJ 1 [+ leader, head, Christian] 名义上的 [míngyìshang de] 2 [+ fee, sum, amount] 微不足道的 [wēi bù zú dào de]

nominate ['nɔmɪneɪt] VT 1 (propose) (for job, award) 提名 [tímíng] 2 (appoint) 任命 [rènmìng] ▶ to nominate sb for sth [+ post, position] 任命某人担任某职位 ▶ to nominate sb/sth for sth [+ award, prize] 提名某人/某事获某某物 ▶ to nominate sb to sth [+ body, organization] 为某团体选任某人

nomination [nɔmɪ'neɪʃən] N 1 [c] (proposal) (for post, award) 提名 [tímíng] 2 [c/U] (appointment) 任命 [rènmìng]

nominee [nɔmɪ'niː] N [c] 被提名者 [bèi tímíngzhě]

non-alcoholic [nɔnælkə'hɔlɪk] ADJ 不含酒精的 [bù hán jiǔjīng de]

none [nʌn] PRON 1 (not one) 没有一个 [méiyǒu yī gè] 2 (not any) 没有一点儿 [méiyǒu yīdiǎnr] ▶ none of us/them 我们/他们谁也没 ▶ I've/there are none left (not one) 我一个也没有了/一个也没剩 ▶ I've/there's none left (not any) 我一点也没有了/一点也没剩 ▶ none at all (not any) 一点儿都没有了; (not one) 根本没有 ▶ I was none the wiser 我还是不明白 ▶ she would have none of it (inf) 她决不接受 ▶ it was none other than Jim Murdoch 不是别人，正是吉姆·默多克 ▶ to be none too pleased about sth 对某事很不高兴 ▶ none but (frm) 只有

▨ 用法参见 **neither**

nonetheless [nʌnðə'lɛs] ADV 不过 [bùguò]

non-existent [nɔnɪg'zɪstənt] ADJ 不存在的 [bù cúnzài de]

non-fiction [nɔn'fɪkʃən] I N [U] 非小说类文学 [fēixiǎoshuōlèi wénxué] II CPD [复合词] [+ book, prize] 写实的 [xiěshí de]

nonsense ['nɔnsəns] N [U] 1 (rubbish) 胡说八道 [hú shuō bādào] 2 (gibberish) 无意义的词语 [wúyìyì de cíyǔ] ▶ nonsense! 胡说！ ▶ to make a nonsense of sth 使某事变得荒谬

non-smoker ['nɔn'sməukə(r)] N [c] 不吸烟的人 [bù xīyān de rén]

non-smoking ['nɔn'sməukɪŋ] ADJ [+ area, carriage] 禁烟的 [jìn yān de]

non-stick ['nɔn'stɪk] ADJ [+ pan, surface] 不粘的 [bù nián de]

non-stop ['nɔn'stɔp] I ADJ [+ activity, music] 不停的 [bù tíng de]; [+ flight] 直达的 [zhídá de] II ADV 1 (ceaselessly) 不断地 [bùduàn de] 2 (without interruption) (fly, drive +) 不停地 [bù tíng de]

noodles ['nuːdlz] NPL 面条 [miàntiáo]

noon [nuːn] I N [U] 中午 [zhōngwǔ] II CPD [复合词] 正午的 [zhōngwǔ de] ▶ at noon 中午

no-one ['nəuwʌn] PRON = nobody

nor [nɔː(r)] CONJ 也不 [yěbù] ▶ nor me! 我也不是！ see also **neither**

norm [nɔːm] N [c] 1 (convention) 规范 [guīfàn] 2 (rule, requirement) 标准 [biāozhǔn] ▶ to be the norm 是正常现象

normal ['nɔːməl] ADJ [+ life, behaviour, circumstances, person] 正常的 [zhèngcháng de] ▶ in normal circumstances... 在正常情况下… ▶ to get back or return to normal 恢复正常 ▶ to continue as normal 照常继续 ▶ more/higher/worse than normal 比正常的多/高/糟糕

normally ['nɔːməlɪ] ADV 1 (usually) 通常地 [tōngcháng de] 2 (conventionally) [act, behave +] 正常地 [zhèngcháng de] ▶ to be working normally 正常运作

○ **north** [nɔːθ] I N [U/S] 北方 [běifāng] II ADJ 北部的 [běibù de] III ADV 向北方 [xiàng běifāng] ▶ the north of France 法国北部 ▶ to the north 以北 ▶ the north wind 北风 ▶ north of …以北 ▷ It's 15 miles or so north of

Oxford. 在牛津以北15英里左右。

North America N 北美 [Běiměi]

North American I ADJ 北美的 [Běiměi de] II N [c] 北美人 [Běiměirén]

north-east [nɔːˈθiːst] I N 东北 [dōngběi] II ADJ 东北的 [dōngběi de] III ADV 向东北 [xiàng dōngběi]

north-eastern [ˈnɔːˈθiːstən] ADJ 东北的 [dōngběi de]

northern [ˈnɔːðən] ADJ 北方的 [běifāng de] ▶ the northern hemisphere 北半球

Northern Ireland N 北爱尔兰 [Běiˈàiˈěrlán]

North Korea N 朝鲜 [Cháoxiǎn]

North Korean I ADJ 朝鲜的 [Cháoxiǎn de] II N [c] 朝鲜人 [Cháoxiǎnrén]

North Pole N ▶ the North Pole 北极 [Běijí]

North Sea N ▶ the North Sea 北海 [Běi Hǎi]

northward(s) [ˈnɔːθwəd(z)] ADV 向北 [xiàng běi]

north-west [nɔːˈθwɛst] I N 西北 [xīběi] II ADJ 西北的 [xīběi de] III ADV 向西北 [xiàng xīběi]

north-western [ˈnɔːˈθwɛstən] ADJ 西北的 [xīběi de]

Norway [ˈnɔːweɪ] N 挪威 [Nuówēi]

Norwegian [nɔːˈwiːdʒən] I ADJ 挪威的 [Nuówēi de] II N 1 [c] (person) 挪威人 [Nuówēirén] 2 [U] (language) 挪威语 [Nuówēiyǔ]

nos. ABBR (= numbers) 编号 [biānhào]

nose [nəuz] I N 1 (on face) 鼻子 [bízi]; (sense of smell) 嗅觉 [xiùjué] 2 [of aircraft] 机头 [jītóu] II VI ▶ to nose forward/out 缓慢前行/驶出 [huǎnmàn qiánxíng/shǐchū] ▶ just follow your nose 凭本能行事 ▶ to get (right) up sb's nose (BRIT: inf) (真是) 使某人恼怒 ▶ to have a (good) nose for sth 善于觉察某事 ▶ to keep one's nose clean (inf) 洁身自好 ▶ to look down one's nose at sb/sth (inf) 小看某人/某事 ▶ to pay through the nose (for sth) (inf) 付出过高价格 (买某物) ▶ to rub sb's nose in sth (inf) 哪壶不开提哪壶 ▶ to turn one's nose up at sth (inf) 对某事不屑一顾 ▶ to be happening/going on under sb's nose 在某人眼皮底下发生/进行 ▶ to poke or stick one's nose into sth (inf) 干预某事

▶ nose around, nose about (inf) I VI 察看 [chákàn] II VT FUS [不可拆分] 考察 [kǎochá]

nosebleed [ˈnəuzbliːd] N [c] 鼻出血 [bí chū xiě] ▶ to have a nosebleed 流鼻血

nosey [ˈnəuzi] (inf) ADJ = nosy

nostalgia [nɔsˈtældʒɪə] N [U] 怀旧 [huáijiù] ▶ nostalgia for 对某事物的怀恋

nostalgic [nɔsˈtældʒɪk] ADJ [+ person] 怀旧的 [huáijiù de]; [+ trip, memory, song, book] 令人怀旧的 [lìng rén huáijiù de] ▶ to be nostalgic about/for sth 怀恋某事物

nostril [ˈnɔstrɪl] N [c] 鼻孔 [bíkǒng]

nosy [ˈnəuzi] (inf) ADJ 爱多管闲事的 [ài duō guǎn xiánshì de]

⊙ not [nɔt] ADV 不 [bù] ▶ he is not or isn't here 他不在这儿 ▶ I do not or don't want to go out tonight 我今晚不想出去 ▶ it's too late, isn't it? 现在太晚了,不是吗? ▶ he asked me not to do it 他叫我不要这么做 ▶ are you coming or not? 你来不来? ▶ not at all (in answer to question) 一点也不; (in answer to thanks) 不客气 ▶ I'm not at all tired 我一点也不累 ▶ not yet/now 还没/现在不 ▶ not really 并不是的 ▶ not everyone has the time to cook 不是所有人都有时间下厨的

notable [ˈnəutəbl] I ADJ [+ success, achievement, example] 显著的 [xiǎnzhù de] II N [c] (frm) 要人 [yàorén] ▶ it is notable for sth 因某事物而著称 ▶ it is notable that... 值得注意的是… ▶ with a few notable exceptions 除了别明显的例外

⬛用法参见 famous

notably [ˈnəutəbli] ADV 1 (particularly) 尤其 [yóuqí] 2 (noticeably) 显著地 [xiǎnzhù de] ▶ most notably 最为显著地

notch [nɔtʃ] N [c] 1 (in wood, blade) 凹口 [āokǒu] 2 (level) 等级 [děngjí]

▶ notch up VT (victory, sales, profit) 取得 [qǔdé]

note [nəut] I N [c] 1 (message) 便条 [biàntiáo] 2 (to remind o.s.) 笔记 [bǐjì] 3 (in book, article) 注释 [zhùshì] 4 (BRIT) (banknote) 纸币 [zhǐbì] [美 = **bill**] 5 (MUS) (sound) 音 [yīn]; (printed, written) 音符 [yīnfú] II VT 1 (observe) 留意 [liúyì] 2 (point out) 指出 [zhǐchū] 3 (also: note down) 记下 [jìxià] III notes NPL (from or for lecture etc) 笔记 [bǐjì] ▶ to make a note of sth 记下某事 ▶ to take notes 记笔记 ▶ to compare notes 交换意见 ▶ the film ends on a positive note 影片以大团圆的结局告终 ▶ to sound/strike a note of caution 听起来有/带着一种警告的语气 ▶ there was a note of triumph in her voice 她说话时带着一种胜利的口吻 ▶ to take note (of sth) 留意到(某事) ▶ of note 有名望 ▶ to note that... 指出… ▶ (please) note that... (请)注意…

notebook [ˈnəutbuk] N [c] 笔记本 [bǐjìběn]

noted [ˈnəutɪd] ADJ (famous) 知名的 [zhīmíng de] ▶ to be noted for sth 以某事物而著名

notepad [ˈnəutpæd] N [c] 1 (pad of paper) 记事本 [jìshìběn] 2 (COMPUT) 记事簿 [jìshìbù]

notepaper [ˈnəutpeɪpə(r)] N [U] 信纸 [xìnzhǐ]

noteworthy [ˈnəutwəːðɪ] (frm) ADJ [+ fact, event] 值得注意的 [zhídé zhùyì de] ▶ it is noteworthy that... 值得注意的是…

⊙ nothing [ˈnʌθɪŋ] PRON 1 (not anything) 什么也没有 [shénme yě méiyǒu] ▷ I pressed the button but nothing happened. 我按了按钮,但什么都没有发生。▷ The man nodded but said nothing. 男子点了点头,但什么也没有说。 2 (something trivial) 无关紧要 [wúguān jǐnyào]

▷ *a fight that started over nothing* 因无关紧要的事而打架 ▶ **nothing new/serious/to worry about** 没有什么新的/要紧的/值得担忧的 ▶ **there's nothing better/worse (than...)** 没有(比…)更好/更糟糕的 ▶ **nothing much** 没有什么 ▶ **nothing else** 没有别的 ▶ **for nothing** *(free)* 免费; *(cheap)* 便宜; *(in vain)* 白白地 ▶ **to be worth nothing** 一文不值 ▶ **nothing at all** 什么也没有 ▷ *"What did you say?" - "Nothing. Nothing at all."* "你说什么?" "没有。什么也没说。" ▶ **nothing but** 只 ▶ **he's nothing if not well-organized** *(frm)* 他条理分明之极 ▶ **it's nothing less than outrageous!** 简直是蛮横无理! ▶ **he's nothing less than a thief!** 他简直是个贼! ▶ **it was nothing of the sort** or **kind** 根本没有那回事

notice ['nəʊtɪs] **I** VT *(observe)* 注意到 [zhùyì dào] **II** N **1** [C] *(sign)* 公告 [gōnggào] **2** [U] *(warning)* 通知 [tōngzhī] **3** [C] *(BRIT)* *(review)* *[of play, film]* 评论 [pínglùn] ▶ **to notice that...** 注意到… ▶ **to bring sth to sb's notice** 引起某人对某事的注意 ▶ **to take no notice of sb/sth** 不理某人/某事 ▶ **to escape sb's notice** 躲过某人的注意 ▶ **it has come to my notice that...** 我察觉到… ▶ **to give sb notice of sth** 事先通知某人有关某事 ▶ **without notice** 不事先通知 ▶ **advance notice** 提前通知 ▶ **at short/a moment's/24 hours' notice** 一经通知就/马上就/24小时内就 ▶ **until further notice** 直到另行通知 ▶ **to hand in** or **give in one's notice** 递交辞呈 ▶ **to be given one's notice** 接到解雇通知

noticeable ['nəʊtɪsəbl] ADJ *[+effect, difference, improvement]* 明显的 [míngxiǎn de] ▶ **it is noticeable that...** 可以明显注意到…

noticeably ['nəʊtɪsəblɪ] ADV 明显地 [míngxiǎn de] ▶ **most noticeably** 最明显地

noticeboard ['nəʊtɪsbɔːd] *(BRIT)* N [C] 布告栏 [bùgàolán] ▶ **on the noticeboard** 在布告栏上 [美= **bulletin board**]

notification [nəʊtɪfɪ'keɪʃən] N [U] 通知 [tōngzhī] ▶ **to be given** or **receive notification of sth** 收到有关某事的通知

notify ['nəʊtɪfaɪ] VT ▶ **to notify sb (of sth)** 将(某事)通知某人 [jiāng (mǒushì) tōngzhī mǒurén] ▶ **to notify sb that...** 告诫某人…

notion ['nəʊʃən] **I** N [C] *(idea)* 概念 [gàiniàn] **II notions** NPL *(US)* 小件针线用品 [xiǎojiàn zhēnxiàn yòngpǐn]

notorious [nəʊ'tɔːrɪəs] ADJ *[+case, criminal, murderer, womanizer]* 声名狼籍的 [shēngmíng lángjí de] ▶ **to be notorious for sth/for doing sth** 因某事/做某事而臭名远扬 ▧ 用法参见 **famous**

notoriously [nəʊ'tɔːrɪəslɪ] ADV *[+unreliable, inefficient]* 人所共知地 [rén suǒ gòng zhī de]

notwithstanding [nɔtwɪθ'stændɪŋ] PREP, ADV 尽管 [jǐnguǎn]

nought [nɔːt] *(ESP BRIT)* NUM 零 [líng] [美= **zero**]

> 在英式英语的口语中, **nought** 比 **zero** 常用得多。*...from nought to 60 miles per hour...* 在科技性内容中, **zero** 通常作为数字使用。当你想显得精确时, 通常也使用 **zero**。在美式英语中, 一般使用 **zero**, 而不用 **nought**。在报电话号码时, 用 **o** ([əu])。在体育评论中, 尤其是表示足球比分时, 多用 **nil**。*England beat Poland two-nil at Wembley*。网球运动中, 通常用 **love** 表示零的含义。*...a two-games-to-love lead...*

noun [naʊn] N [C] 名词 [míngcí]

nourish ['nʌrɪʃ] VT *[+person]* 养育 [yǎngyù]; *[+plant]* 滋养 [zīyǎng]

nourishment ['nʌrɪʃmənt] N [U] *(food)* 营养 [yíngyǎng]

Nov. ABBR (= *November*) 十一月 [shíyīyuè]

novel ['nɔvl] **I** N [C] 小说 [xiǎoshuō] **II** ADJ *[+idea, approach]* 新颖的 [xīnyǐng de]

novelist ['nɔvəlɪst] N [C] 小说家 [xiǎoshuōjiā]

novelty ['nɔvəltɪ] **I** N **1** [U] *(newness)* 新奇 [xīnqí] **2** [C] *(new concept, experience)* 新奇的事物 [xīnqí de shìwù] **II novelties** NPL *(knick-knacks)* 小玩意 [xiǎowányì]

November [nəʊ'vɛmbə(r)] N [C/U] 十一月 [shíyīyuè] *see also* **July**

novice ['nɔvɪs] N [C] **1** *(beginner)* 新手 [xīnshǒu] **2** *(REL)* *(female)* 见习修女 [jiànxí xiūnǚ]; *(male)* 见习修士 [jiànxí xiūshì] ▶ **to be a novice at sth** 对某物不熟悉

◎ **now** [naʊ] **I** ADV **1** *(at the present time)* 现在 [xiànzài] ▷ *It is now just after one o'clock.* 现在刚过入1点钟。▷ *I'm going home now.* 我要回家了。**2** *(these days)* 如今 [rújīn] ▷ *Most schoolchildren now own calculators.* 如今大多数学童都有计算器。**3** *(under the circumstances)* 看来 [kànlái] ▷ *I was hoping to go tomorrow. That won't be possible now.* 我本来想明天走。看来这不可能了。**4** *(specifying length of time)* 到现在为止 [dào xiànzài wéizhǐ] ▷ *They've been married now for 30 years.* 到现在为止, 他们已经结婚30年了。**5** *(introducing new information)* 喂 [wèi] ▷ *Now, I hadn't told him this, so he must have found out for himself.* 喂, 这件事我没告诉他, 他一定是自己发现的。**II** CONJ ▶ **now (that)** 既然 [jìrán] ▷ *Now that he's feeling better, he can go back to work.* 既然他感觉好些了, 就可以去上班了。▶ **right now** 这时 ▷ *What if a shark came along right now?* 这时, 如果来了鲨鱼该怎么办呢? ▶ **by now** 到现在 ▷ *He should be here by now.* 他现在应该到了。▷ *By now he'll be home and in bed.* 现在, 他一定到了家, 上床休息了。▶ **just now** *(at the moment)* 眼下 ▷ *I'm pretty busy just now.* 眼下我很忙。▶ **(every) now and then** or **again** 时而 ▶ **from now on** 从现在起 ▶ **in 3 days from now** 从现在起3天后 ▶ **between now and Monday**

从现在到星期一 ▶ **that's all for now** 就到这里 ▶ **any day/moment/time now** 不日/随时/任何时候 ▶ **now then** 喂(以引起注意)

nowadays ['nauədeɪz] ADV 现今[xiànjīn]

nowhere ['nəuwɛə(r)] ADV (no place) 无处[wúchù]; (emphatic) 没有地方[méiyǒu dìfāng] ▶ **nowhere else** (no place else) 没有其他地方; (emphatic) 不在任何其他地方 ▶ **to come/appear from** or **out of nowhere** 不知从什么地方突然冒出来/出现 ▶ **this is getting us nowhere, we're getting nowhere with this** 这么做我们只能一无所获 ▶ **in the middle of nowhere** 前不着村, 后不着店

nozzle ['nɒzl] N [C] 喷嘴[pēnzuǐ]

nuclear ['nju:klɪə(r)] ADJ [+ fission, physics, weapon, power] 核能的[hénéng de]

nucleus ['nju:klɪəs] (pl **nuclei** ['nju:klɪiː]) N [C] **1** [of atom, cell] 核[hé] **2** [of group] 核心人物[héxīn rénwù]

nude [nju:d] **I** ADJ 裸体的[luǒtǐ de] **II** N [C] (picture) 裸体画[luǒtǐhuà]; (sculpture) 裸体雕像[luǒtǐ diāoxiàng] ▶ **in the nude** (naked) 裸体

nudge [nʌdʒ] **I** VT 用肘轻推[yòng zhǒu qīng tuī] **II** N [C] 轻推[qīng tuī] ▶ **to give sb a nudge** 用肘轻推某人

nudist ['nju:dɪst] **I** N [C] 裸体主义者[luǒtǐ zhǔyìzhě] **II** CPD [复合词] [+ beach] 裸体[luǒtǐ]

nudity ['nju:dɪtɪ] N [U] 裸体[luǒtǐ]

nugget ['nʌgɪt] N [C] **1** [of gold] 小块[xiǎokuài] **2** (CULIN) 碎块[suìkuài] **3** [of information] 有价值的东西[yǒu jiàzhí de dōngxi]

nuisance ['nju:sns] N [C] ▶ **to be a nuisance** [thing +] 讨厌的东西[tǎoyàn de dōngxi]; [person +] 讨厌的人[tǎoyàn de rén] ▶ **it's a nuisance that…** 真是讨厌… ▶ **what a nuisance!** 真讨厌!

numb [nʌm] **I** ADJ **1** [+ fingers, toes, arm etc] 麻木的[mámù de] **2** (through fear, shock) 僵住的[jiāngzhu de] **II** VT (lit) [+ fingers, part of body] 麻痹[mábì] **2** [+ person, senses] 使失去知觉[shǐ shīqù zhījué] ▶ **to go numb** [fingers, toes, arm +] 变麻[biàn má] ▶ **to be numb with shock/fear/grief** 因震惊/恐惧/悲痛而失去知觉 ▶ **to numb the pain** 麻痹疼痛

⊕ **number** ['nʌmbə(r)] **I** N **1** [C] (MATH) 数[shù] ▷ Think of a number between one and ten. 在1至10之间想一个数。 **2** [C] (telephone number) 电话号码[diànhuà hàomǎ] **3** [C] [of house, bank account, bus etc] 号[hào] ▷ He lives at number 3, Argyll Street. 他住在阿盖尔街3号。 **4** [C/U] (quantity) [of things, people] 数量[shùliàng] ▷ The number of traffic accidents has fallen. 交通事故的数量已经减少。 ▷ A surprising number of men never marry. 男性不结婚的人数惊人的多。 **II** VT **1** [+ pages] 给…标号码[gěi…biāo hàomǎ] ▷ Number the pages before you start. 在开始之前, 先把页码标上。 **2** (amount to) 总计[zǒngjì] ▷ The force numbered almost a quarter of a million men. 该部队总计约有25万男子。 ▶ **their album reached number twenty three** 他们的

唱片在排行榜上名列23 ▶ **a number of** (several) 几个 ▶ **a large/small number of** 大量/少数 ▶ **any number of** [+ things, reasons] 许多 ▶ **to be numbered among** (frm) 属于

number one ADJ [+ priority, position, choice, issue] 首要的[shǒuyào de]

number plate (BRIT) N [C] 车号牌[chēhàopái] [美 = **license plate**]

Number Ten (BRIT) N (10 Downing Street) 唐宁街10号是指英国伦敦唐宁街10号, 即英国首相的办公住所。

numerical [nju:'mɛrɪkl] ADJ [+ value] 数字的[shùzì de]; [+ advantage, superiority] 人数的[rénshù de] ▶ **in numerical order** 按数字顺序

numerous ['nju:mərəs] ADJ [+ examples, attempts etc] 许多的[xǔduō de] ▶ **on numerous occasions** 许多次

nun [nʌn] N [C] 修女[xiūnǔ]

nurse [nəːs] **I** N [C] **1** (in hospital) 护士[hùshi] **2** (o.f.) (nanny) 保姆[bǎomǔ] **II** VT **1** [+ patient] 照料[zhàoliào] **2** [+ cold, injury] 护理[hùlǐ] ▶ **to nurse a grudge against sb** 对某人怀恨在心

nursery ['nəːsərɪ] N [C] **1** (kindergarten) 幼儿园[yòu'éryuán] **2** (room) 保育室[bǎoyùshì] **3** (garden) 苗圃[miáopǔ]; (garden centre) 花卉商店[huāhuì shāngdiàn]

nursery rhyme N [C] 儿歌[érgē]

nursery school N [C/U] 幼儿园[yòu'éryuán]

nursing ['nəːsɪŋ] **I** N [U] (profession, care) 护理[hùlǐ] **II** CPD [复合词] **1** [+ staff, profession, care] 护理[hùlǐ] **2** [+ mother] 喂奶[wèinǎi]

nursing home N [C] 私人疗养院[sīrén liáoyǎngyuàn]

nurture ['nəːtʃə(r)] VT [+ child, talent, relationship, new player] 培养[péiyǎng]; [+ plant] 培育[péiyù]; [+ hopes, ambition, dream] 抱有[bàoyǒu]

nut [nʌt] N [C] **1** (BOT, CULIN) 坚果[jiānguǒ] **2** (TECH) 螺母[luómǔ] **3** (inf) (lunatic) 疯子[fēngzi] ▶ **the nuts and bolts of sth** 某事的基本要点 see also **nuts**

nutmeg ['nʌtmɛg] N [U] 肉豆蔻[ròudòukòu]

nutrient ['nju:trɪənt] **I** N [C] 营养[yíngyǎng] **II** ADJ 有营养的[yǒu yíngyǎng de]

nutrition [nju:'trɪʃən] N [U] (nourishment) 营养[yíngyǎng]

nutritious [nju:'trɪʃəs] ADJ [+ food, meal] 有营养的[yǒu yíngyǎng de]

nuts [nʌts] (inf) ADJ ▶ **to be nuts** 发疯的[fāfēng de] ▶ **to be nuts about sth/sb** 迷恋某物/某人 ▶ **to go nuts** (get angry) 暴跳如雷; (become crazed) 发疯 see also **nut**

NVQ (BRIT: SCOL) N ABBR (= national vocational qualification) 国家职业考试[Guójiā Zhíyè Kǎoshì]

NW ABBR (= north-west) 西北[xīběi]

nylon ['naɪlɒn] **I** N [U] 尼龙[nílóng] **II** CPD [复合词] [+ shirt, sheets] 尼龙[nílóng]

NZ ABBR (= New Zealand) 新西兰[Xīnxīlán]

Oo

O, o [əu] N [C/U] **1** (letter) 英语的第十五个字母 **2** (US: SCOL) (outstanding) 优秀 [yōuxiù] **3** (TEL ETC) (number) 零 [líng] ▍▍用法参见 **nought**

oak [əuk] I N **1** [C] (also: **oak tree**) 橡树 [xiàngshù] **2** [U] (wood) 橡木 [xiàngmù] II CPD [复合词] [+ furniture, door] 橡木 [xiàngmù]

OAP (BRIT) N ABBR (= **old-age pensioner**) 拿退休金的人 [ná tuìxiūjīn de rén]

oar [ɔ:(r)] N [C] 桨 [jiǎng] ▶ **to put** or **shove one's oar in** (inf) (interfere) 干预

oasis [əu'eɪsɪs] (pl **oases** [əu'eɪsi:z]) N [C] **1** (in desert) 绿洲 [lùzhōu] **2** (sanctuary) 慰藉 [wèijiè]

oath [əuθ] N [C] **1** (promise) 誓言 [shìyán] **2** (o. f.) (swearword) 咒骂 [zhòumà] ▶ **on** (BRIT) or **under oath** 在发誓的情况下 ▶ **to take the oath** (LAW) 宣誓

oatmeal ['əutmi:l] N [U] **1** (for cooking) 燕麦粉 [yànmài fěn] **2** (porridge) 燕麦粥 [yànmài zhōu] [英= **porridge**]

oats [əuts] NPL 燕麦 [yànmài]

obedience [ə'bi:dɪəns] N [U] 服从 [fúcóng] ▶ **in obedience to** 遵从

obedient [ə'bi:dɪənt] ADJ [+ child, dog] 顺从的 [shùncóng de]

obese [əu'bi:s] ADJ 肥胖的 [féipàng de] ▍▍用法参见 **fat**

obesity [əu'bi:sɪtɪ] N [U] 肥胖症 [féipàngzhèng]

obey [ə'beɪ] I VT [+ person, orders] 听从 [tīngcóng]; [+ law, regulations] 服从 [fúcóng] II VI 服从 [fúcóng]

obituary [ə'bɪtjuərɪ] N [C] 讣告 [fùgào]

object [n 'ɔbdʒɛkt, vb əb'dʒɛkt] I N [C] **1** (thing) 物体 [wùtǐ] **2** (aim, purpose) 目的 [mùdì] **3** ▶ **an object of ridicule/the object of his affection** 嘲笑的对象/他爱慕的对象 [cháoxiào de duìxiàng/tā àimù de duìxiàng] **4** (LING) 宾语 [bīnyǔ] II VI 反对 [fǎnduì] ▶ **money/distance is no object** 金钱/距离不成问题 ▶ **to object to sth** 反对某事 ▶ **to object that...** 反对说… ▶ **I object!** 我反对!

objection [əb'dʒɛkʃən] N [C] 异议 [yìyì] ▶ **to make** or **raise an objection** 提出异议 ▶ **to have no objection to sth** 不反对某事

objective [əb'dʒɛktɪv] I ADJ 客观的 [kèguān de] II N [C] (goal) 目标 [mùbiāo]

obligation [ɔblɪ'geɪʃən] N [C/U] 责任 [zérèn] ▶ **to have an obligation to do sth** 有责任做某事 ▶ **to have an obligation to sb (to do sth)** 对某人有(做某事)的责任 ▶ **to be under an obligation to do sth** 有义务做某事 ▶ **to be under an obligation to sb** 对某人有义务

obligatory [ə'blɪgətərɪ] ADJ 强制性的 [qiángzhìxìng de]

oblige [ə'blaɪdʒ] I VT **1** (compel) ▶ **to oblige sb to do sth** 迫使某人做某事 [pòshǐ mǒurén zuò mǒushì] **2** (do a favour for) 施惠于 [shīhuì yú] II VI (cooperate) 帮忙 [bāngmáng] ▶ **to feel obliged to do sth** 感到必须得做某事 ▶ **to be (much) obliged to sb (for sth)** (frm, o.f.) (grateful) (由于某事)(非常)感激某人 ▶ **I would be obliged if...** (frm) 烦请您…

oblique [ə'bli:k] I ADJ **1** (indirect) [+ reference, warning] 间接的 [jiànjiē de] **2** [+ angle] 斜的 [xié de] II N [C] (BRIT: TYP) 斜线 [xiéxiàn] ▶ **at an oblique angle** (与某物) 呈斜角

oblivion [ə'blɪvɪən] N [U] 遗忘 [yíwàng] ▶ **to be consigned to oblivion** 被忘却

oblivious [ə'blɪvɪəs] ADJ ▶ **oblivious of** or **to sth** 忘却某事 [wàngquè mǒushì]

oblong ['ɔblɔŋ] I N [C] 长方形 [chángfāngxíng] II ADJ 长方形的 [chángfāngxíng de]

obnoxious [əb'nɔkʃəs] ADJ [+ behaviour, person, smell] 讨厌的 [tǎoyàn de]

oboe ['əubəu] N [C] 双簧管 [shuānghuángguǎn]

obscene [əb'si:n] ADJ **1** (offensive) [+ gesture, remark, image] 猥亵的 [wěixiè de] **2** (immoral) [+ wealth, income etc] 可憎的 [kězēng de]

obscenity [əb'sɛnɪtɪ] N **1** [U] (behaviour) 淫行 [yínxíng] **2** [C] (swearword) 脏话 [zānghuà]

obscure [əb'skjuə(r)] I ADJ **1** (little-known) [+ place, author etc] 不知名的 [bù zhīmíng de] **2** (difficult to understand) 晦涩的 [huìsè de] II VT (conceal) [+ view, object] 遮蔽 [zhēbì]; [+ truth, meaning etc] 混淆 [hùnxiáo]

observant [əb'zə:vənt] ADJ 观察力敏锐的 [guānchálì mǐnruì de]

observation [ɔbzə'veɪʃən] N **1** (*remark*) 评论 [pínglùn] **2** [U] (*act of observing*) 观察 [guānchá] **3** [U] (MED) 观察 [guānchá] ▶ **powers of observation** 观察力 ▶ **she's under observation** 她受到严密监视

observatory [əb'zə:vətrɪ] N [c] 天文台 [tiānwéntái]

observe [əb'zə:v] VT **1** (*watch*) 观察 [guānchá] **2** (*frm*) (*notice*) 注意到 [zhùyì dào] **3** (*comment*) 评论 [pínglùn] **4** (*abide by*) [+*rule, convention*] 遵守 [zūnshǒu] ▶ **to observe that...** 评述说…

observer [əb'zə:və(r)] N [c] **1** (*onlooker*) 旁观者 [pángguānzhě] **2** (*commentator*) 评论员 [pínglùnyuán]

obsess [əb'sɛs] VT 使着迷 [shǐ zháomí] ▶ **to be obsessed by** *or* **with sb/sth** 被某人/某事迷住心窍

obsession [əb'sɛʃən] N [c] 着迷 [zháomí]

obsessive [əb'sɛsɪv] ADJ [+*person*] 着迷的 [zháomí de]; [+*behaviour, interest*] 着魔的 [zháomó de] ▶ **to be obsessive about sth** 对某物着迷

obsolete ['ɔbsəli:t] ADJ 不再用的 [bùzài yòng de]

obstacle ['ɔbstəkl] N [c] **1** (*physical barrier*) 障碍 [zhàng'ài] **2** (*difficulty*) 阻碍 [zǔ'ài] ▶ **an obstacle to sth/to doing sth** 某事/做某事的障碍

obstinate ['ɔbstɪnɪt] ADJ **1** (*stubborn*) [+*person*] 固执的 [gùzhí de]; [+*resistance, refusal*] 顽固的 [wángù de] **2** (*troublesome*) [+*problem, stain etc*] 难对付的 [nán duìfu de]

obstruct [əb'strʌkt] VT **1** (*block*) [+*road, path*] 堵塞 [dǔsè] **2** (*hinder*) [+*justice, progress*] 阻碍 [zǔ'ài]

obstruction [əb'strʌkʃən] N **1** [c] (*blockage*) 障碍物 [zhàng'àiwù] **2** [U] (*of plan, law*) 阻碍 [zǔ'ài]

obtain [əb'teɪn] (*frm*) **I** VT (*get*) [+*book, information, degree etc*] 获得 [huòdé] **II** VI (*exist, be the case*) 通行 [tōngxíng]

obvious ['ɔbvɪəs] ADJ 明显的 [míngxiǎn de] ▶ **it's obvious that...** 很明显… ▶ **for obvious reasons** 由于显然的理由

obviously ['ɔbvɪəslɪ] ADV **1** (*of course*) 显然地 [xiǎnrán de] **2** (*noticeably*) 明显地 [míngxiǎn de] ▶ **obviously!** 当然! ▶ **obviously not** 显然不是 ▶ **he was obviously not drunk** 很显然,他没醉 ▶ **he was not obviously drunk** 他醉得不明显

occasion [ə'keɪʒən] **I** N [c] **1** (*moment*) 时刻 [shíkè] **2** (*event, celebration*) 场合 [chǎnghé] **3** (*opportunity*) ▶ **an occasion for sth/for doing sth** 某事/做某事的机会 [mǒushì/zuò mǒushì de jīhuì] **II** VT (*frm*) (*cause*) 引起 [yǐnqǐ] ▶ **on occasion(s)** 有时 ▶ **to rise to the occasion** 应付自如 ▶ **a sense of occasion** 隆重感

occasional [ə'keɪʒənl] ADJ 偶尔的 [ǒu'ěr de]

▶ **I like the occasional drink** 我喜欢偶尔喝点酒

occasionally [ə'keɪʒənəlɪ] ADV 偶尔地 [ǒu'ěr de] ▶ **very occasionally** 非常偶然地

occult [ɔ'kʌlt] **I** N ▶ **the occult** 神鬼之事 [shénguǐ zhī shì] **II** ADJ [+*subject, powers*] 玄妙的 [xuánmiào de]

occupant ['ɔkjupənt] N [c] **1** (*long-term*) [*of house*] 占用者 [zhànyòngzhě] **2** (*short-term*) [*of car, room etc*] 使用者 [shǐyòngzhě]

occupation [ɔkju'peɪʃən] N **1** [c] (*job*) 职业 [zhíyè] **2** [c] (*pastime*) 消遣 [xiāoqiǎn] **3** [U] (*annexation*) [*of building, country etc*] 占领 [zhànlǐng]

occupier ['ɔkjupaɪə(r)] (*frm*) N [c] 占用者 [zhànyòngzhě]

occupy ['ɔkjupaɪ] VT **1** (*inhabit*) [+*house, office*] 占用 [zhànyòng] **2** ▶ **to be occupied** [*seat, place etc*+] 被占用 [bèi zhànyòng] **3** (*take possession of*) [+*country etc*] 占领 [zhànlǐng] **4** (*take up*) [+*attention, mind*] 填满 [tiánmǎn]; [+*space*] 占 [zhàn] **5** (*fill*) [+*time*] 占用 [zhànyòng]; [+*position, post*] 担任 [dānrèn] ▶ **to occupy o.s. (with sth/doing sth)** (*to be busy*) 使自己忙于(某事/做某事) ▶ **to be occupied with sth/doing sth** 忙于某事/做某事

occur [ə'kə:(r)] VI **1** (*happen*) 发生 [fāshēng] **2** (*be found*) 出现 [chūxiàn] ▶ **to occur to sb** 某人想到

occurrence [ə'kʌrəns] (*frm*) N [c] **1** (*event*) 事件 [shìjiàn] **2** (*incidence*) 事故 [shìgù] ▶ **an everyday/daily occurrence** 每天/日常发生的事情

ocean ['əuʃən] N [c] 海洋 [hǎiyáng] ▶ **oceans of** (*inf*) 许多 ▶ **it's a drop in the ocean** 沧海一粟

o'clock [ə'klɔk] ADV ▶ **six o'clock** 6点钟 [liùdiǎnzhōng]

Oct. ABBR (= *October*) 十月 [shíyuè]

October [ɔk'təubə(r)] N [c/u] 十月 [shíyuè] *see also* **July**

octopus ['ɔktəpəs] N [c] 章鱼 [zhāngyú]

odd [ɔd] ADJ **1** (*strange*) 奇怪的 [qíguài de] **2** (*not paired*) [+*sock, glove, shoe etc*] 单只的 [dānzhī de] **3** (*assorted, unspecified*) 任意的 [rènyì de] **4** [+*number*] 奇数的 [jīshù de] ▶ **to be the odd man/woman/one out** 落单的男人/女人/一人 ▶ **the odd drink/walk/holiday** 偶尔的饮酒/散步/度假 ▶ **sixty odd** 六十几个 *see also* **odds**

oddly ['ɔdlɪ] ADV **1** (*strangely*) [*behave, dress*+] 古怪地 [gǔguài de] **2** *see also* **enough**

odds [ɔdz] NPL **1** 可能性 [kěnéngxìng] **2** (*in betting*) 赌注赔率 [dǔzhù péilǜ] ▶ **the odds are in favour of/against him** 形势对他有利/不利 ▶ **against all (the) odds** 克服各种不利条件 ▶ **odds and ends** (*inf*) 零碎的东西 ▶ **it makes no odds** (*inf*) 没有区别 ▶ **to be at odds**

(with) (in disagreement)（与）不和；(at variance)
（与）不相称

odometer [ɔ'dɔmɪtə(r)] (US) N [C] 里程表
[lǐchéngbiǎo]

odour, (US) **odor** ['əudə(r)] N [C/U] 气味
[qìwèi]

○ **of** [ɔv, əv] PREP **1** (gen) 的 [de] ▶ the history of
China 中国历史 的 [de] ▶ at the end of the street
在街的尽头 ▶ the president of France 法
国总统 ▶ a friend of ours/mine 我们/我
的一个朋友 ▶ the city of New York 纽约城
▶ south of Madrid 马德里的南部 ▶ how
silly of him not to say anything! 他只字未
提真是太傻了！
2 (expressing quantity, amount) ▶ a kilo of
flour 一公斤面粉 [yī gōngjīn miànfěn] ▶ a
cup of tea/vase of flowers 一杯茶/一瓶
花 ▶ a slice of bread 一片面包 ▶ there
were three of them 他们有3个 ▶ three of
us went 我们3人去了 ▶ can some of you
help? 你们中有人能帮忙吗？ ▶ I'll eat half
of it 我要吃一半 ▶ the number of road
accidents 交通事故的数量 ▶ an annual
income of $30,000 每年3万美元的收入
3 (made of) 由…制成 [yóu…zhìchéng]
▶ made of wood 木制的
4 (in dates) ▶ the 5th of July 7月5日 [qīyuè
wǔrì] ▶ the winter of 2001 2001年的冬天
5 (US) (in times) ▶ at five of three 3点差5分
[sāndiǎn chà wǔfēn]

○ **off** [ɔf] I ADJ **1** (not turned on) [+ machine, light,
engine, tap] 关着的 [guānzhe de]
2 (cancelled) [+ meeting, match, agreement] 取
消的 [qǔxiāo de]
3 (BRIT) [+ milk, cheese, meat etc] 不新鲜的
[bù xīnxiān de] ▶ the milk's off 牛奶变
质了
4 (in expressions) ▶ on the off chance (just in
case) 怀着渺茫的希望 [huáizhe miǎománg
de xīwàng] ▶ to have an off day (inf) 状
态欠佳
II ADV **1** (away) ▶ I must be off 我必须得走了
[wǒ bìxū děi zǒu le] ▶ where are you off
to? 你上哪儿去？ ▶ to go off to Paris/Italy
去巴黎/意大利 ▶ it's a long way off (in
distance) 它在很远的地方；(in time) 它还远
未结束 ▶ the game is three days off 3天
后开赛
2 (not at work) ▶ to be off (on holiday) 在休
假 [zài xiūjià]；(due to illness) 休病假 [xiū
bìngjià] ▶ I'm off on Fridays 我周五不上
班 ▶ to have a day off (as holiday) 休假一
天；(because ill) 休病假一天
3 (COMM) ▶ 10% off 10%的折扣 [bǎifēn zhī

shí de zhékòu]
4 (removed, detached) 脱落/掉 [tuōluò/diào]
▶ there's a button off 一颗扣子掉了
III PREP (indicating motion, removal etc)
▶ to take a picture off the wall 把画像从墙
上取下来 [bǎ huàxiàng cóng qiáng shang
qǔ xiàlái] ▶ to fall/jump off a cliff 摔/跳
下悬崖 ▶ to get off a bus/train 下公共汽
车/火车
2 (distant from) ▶ it's just off the
motorway 它就在高速公路边上 [tā jiù zài
gāosùgōnglù biān shang] ▶ it's 15 km off
the main road 它离主干道15公里远 ▶ an
island off the coast 海岸边的一个小岛
3 (not enjoying) ▶ to be off meat/beer etc 不
想吃肉/喝啤酒｛等｝[bù xiǎng chīròu/hē
píjiǔ｛děng｝]

off-colour ['ɔf'kʌlə(r)] (BRIT) ADJ (ill) 身体不舒
服的 [shēntǐ bù shūfu de] ▶ to feel off-colour
感觉不适

off-duty ['ɔf'djuːtɪ] ADJ 不当班的 [bù dāngbān
de]

offence, (US) **offense** [ə'fens] N **1** [C] (crime)
罪行 [zuìxíng] **2** [U] (hurt feelings) 冒犯 [màofàn]
3 (US: SPORT) ▶ the offense 进攻方 [jìngōng
fāng] ▶ to commit an offence 犯罪 ▶ to give
or cause offence (to sb) 冒犯(某人) ▶ to
take offence (at sth) (因某事而) 生气 ▶ no
offence, but... 不要见怪，但…

offend [ə'fend] I VT (upset) 得罪 [dézuì] II VI
(commit an offence) 犯罪 [fànzuì] ▶ to offend
against [+ law, rule] 违反

offender [ə'fendə(r)] N [C] **1** (criminal) 罪犯
[zuìfàn] **2** (culprit) 作祟的人/物 [zuòsuì de
rén/wù]

offense [ə'fens] (US) N [C] = offence

offensive [ə'fensiv] I ADJ **1** [+ remark, behaviour]
无礼的 [wúlǐ de] **2** (US: SPORT) 攻方的
[gōngfāng de] II N [C] (MIL) 进攻 [jìngōng]
▶ to be offensive to sb 得罪某人 ▶ offensive
weapon 进攻性武器 ▶ to go on the offensive
采取攻势

○ **offer** ['ɔfə(r)] I VT **1** (making invitation) 给 [gěi]
▷ I was offered a place at Harvard University. 哈佛
大学给了我一次入学机会。▷ Meadows stood up
and offered her his chair. 梅多斯站起来把座位让
给了她。**2** (bid) [+ money] 出价 [chūjià] ▷ They
offered Ramon 2,000 pesos an acre for his farm. 他
们向拉蒙出价一英亩2000比索来购买他的农
场。**3** (provide) [+ service, product] 提供 [tígōng]
▷ We are successful because we offer a quality service.
我们的成功在于我们提供优质的服务。**4** (give)
[+ advice, help, congratulations] 提出 [tíchū] ▷ Do
you have any advice to offer parents? 你有什么建议
要向家长提吗？ II N [C] **1** (proposal) 提议 [tíyì]
▷ Anne would not accept Steele's offer. 安妮将不会
接受斯蒂尔的提议。**2** (special deal) 特价 [tèjià]
▷ today's special offer 今天的特价商品 **3** (bid) 报

价 [bàojià] ▸ **to make (sb) an offer (for sth)**
(就某物)向(某人)报价 ▷ *I'll make you one final
offer.* 我将给你一个最终报价。▸ **to be on offer**
(COMM) (*available*) 供出售的

off-hand [ɒf'hænd] I ADJ 随便的 [suíbiàn de]
II ADV 当下 [dāngxià] ▸ **I can't tell you** or **say
off-hand** 我不能即刻告诉你

○ **office** ['ɒfɪs] N 1 [c] (*room*) 办公室 [bàngōngshì]
▷ *He called me into his office.* 他把我叫进他的办
公室。2 [c] (*department*) 部门 [bùmén] 3 [c] (US)
[*of doctor, dentist*] 诊所 [zhěnsuǒ] [英=**surgery**]
4 [U] (*job, position*) 职务 [zhíwù] ▸ **Office of Fair
Trading** (BRIT) 公平贸易部 ▸ **to be in** or **hold
office** 担任要职 ▸ **to run for office** 竞选公职
▸ **to take office** 就职 ▸ **through his good
offices** (*frm*) 通过他的斡旋

office block N [c] 办公大楼 [bàngōng dàlóu]

office building N [c] 办公大楼 [bàngōng
dàlóu]

office hours NPL 1 (COMM) 办公时间
[bàngōng shíjiān] 2 (US: MED) 门诊时间
[ménzhěn shíjiān] ▸ **during/outside office
hours** 上班/下班时间

○ **officer** ['ɒfɪsə(r)] N [c] 1 (MIL) 军官 [jūnguān]
2 (*also*: **police officer**) 警官 [jǐngguān]
3 (*official*) 官员 [guānyuán]

office worker N [c] 职员 [zhíyuán]

○ **official** [ə'fɪʃl] I ADJ 1 (*approved*) 官方的
[guānfāng de] ▷ *the official unemployment figures*
官方的失业统计数据 2 (*job-related*) [+ *residence,
visit*] 公务的 [gōngwù de] ▷ *the Irish President's
official residence* 爱尔兰总统的官邸 ▷ *Tony Blair
is currently on an official visit to Hungary.* 托尼·布
莱尔正在对匈牙利进行正式访问。II N [c] (*in
government, organization etc*) 官员 [guānyuán]

off-licence ['ɒflaɪsns] (BRIT) N [c] (*shop*) 有卖
酒许可的店 [yǒu màijiǔ xǔkě de diàn]
[美=**liquor store**]

offline, off-line [ɒf'laɪn] (COMPUT) I ADJ 1 脱
机的 [tuōjī de] 2 (*switched off*) 关机的 [guānjī
de] II ADV 脱机地 [tuōjī de]

off-peak ['ɒf'pi:k] I ADJ 1 [+ *heating, telephone
calls, train, ticket*] 非高峰时间的 [fēi gāofēng
shíjiān de] II ADV [*call, travel +*] 非高峰时间地
[fēi gāofēng shíjiān de]

off-putting ['ɒfputɪŋ] (BRIT) ADJ 令人讨厌的
[lìng rén tǎoyàn de]

off-season ['ɒf'si:zn] I N ▸ **the off season** 淡
季 [dànjì] II ADJ [+ *holiday, booking, ticket*] 淡季
的 [dànjì de] III ADV [*travel, book etc +*] 淡季地
[dànjì de]

offset ['ɒfsɛt] (*pt, pp* **offset**) VT (*counteract*) 抵
销 [dǐxiāo]

offshore [ɒf'ʃɔ:(r)] I ADJ 1 [+ *rig, wind, fishing*] 离
岸的 [lí'àn de]; [+ *company, bank, investment*] 海
外的 [hǎiwài de] II ADV 近海地 [jìnhǎi de]

offside ['ɒf'saɪd] I ADJ 1 (AUT) (*right*) 右侧的
[yòucè de]; (*left*) 左侧的 [zuǒcè de] 2 (SPORT)

越位的 [yuèwèi de] II ADV (SPORT) 越位地
[yuèwèi de] III N ▸ **the offside** (AUT) (*right*) 右
侧 [yòucè]; (*left*) 左侧 [zuǒcè]

offspring ['ɒfsprɪŋ] (*pl* **offspring**) (*frm*) N [c] 后代
[hòudài]

○ **often** ['ɒfn] ADV 1 (*frequently*) 经常 [jīngcháng]
▷ *She didn't write very often.* 她不经常写信。
▸ **how often do you wash the car?** 你多久洗
一次车？▸ **I wash up twice as often as them**
or **as they do** 我洗碗的次数是他们的两倍
2 ▸ **more often than not** or **as often as not** 往往
[wǎngwǎng] ▸ **every so often** 时常 ▸ **it's not
often that...** 并不经常…

不能用 **often** 来表示在短期内发生
了几次的事情。例如，不能说 *I often
phoned her yesterday*，而是说 *I phoned
her several times yesterday* 或 *I kept
phoning her yesterday*。

oh [əu] INT 1 (*beginning reply*) 哦 [ò] 2 (*expressing
feelings*) 啊 [à]

OHP N ABBR (= *overhead projector*) 高架投影仪
[gāojià tóuyǐngyí]

○ **oil** [ɔɪl] I N [c/U] 油 [yóu] II VT [+ *engine, machine*]
给…加油 [gěi…jiāyóu]; [+ *wood, skin*] 给…涂油
[gěi…túyóu]

oil filter (AUT) N [c] 滤油器 [lùyóuqì]

oil painting N [c] (*picture*) 油画 [yóuhuà]

oil refinery N [c] 炼油厂 [liànyóuchǎng]

oil rig N [c] (*on land*) 石油钻塔 [shíyóu zuàntǎ];
(*at sea*) 钻井平台 [zuànjǐng píngtái]

oil slick N [c] (*granted*) 浮油 [fúyóu]

oil tanker N [c] (*ship*) 油轮 [yóulún]

oil well N [c] 油井 [yóujǐng]

oily ['ɔɪlɪ] ADJ 1 [+ *rag, substance*] 多油的
[duōyóu de] 2 [+ *food*] 油腻的 [yóunì de]

ointment ['ɔɪntmənt] N [c] 油膏 [yóugāo]

OK [əu'keɪ] = **okay**

okay [əu'keɪ] (*inf*) I ADJ 1 (*acceptable*) 可以的
[kěyǐ de] 2 (*safe and well*) 好的 [hǎo de] II ADV
(*acceptably*) 不错 [bùcuò] III INT 1 (*expressing
agreement*) 行 [xíng] 2 (*in questions*) 好吗 [hǎo
ma] 3 (*granted*) 好吧 [hǎo ba] IV VT (*approve*)
批准 [pīzhǔn] V N ▸ **to give sb/sth the okay**
同意某人/某事 [tóngyì mǒurén/mǒushì] ▸ **are
you okay?** 你还好吗？▸ **are you okay for
money?** 你钱够用吗？▸ **it's okay with** or **by
me** 这对我没问题

○ **old** [əuld] ADJ 1 (*aged*) [+ *person*] 年老的 [niánlǎo
de] ▷ *an old lady* 一位年老的女士 2 (*talking
about age*) 岁数的 [suìshù de] ▷ *He wasn't old
enough to understand.* 他还没到能明白的岁数。
3 (*not new, not recent*) 古老的 [gǔlǎo de] ▷ *an old
proverb* 古老的谚语 4 (*worn out*) 破旧的 [pòjiù
de] ▷ *an old toothbrush lying on the window sill* 窗
台上有一把破牙刷 5 (*former*) 以前的 [yǐqián
de] ▷ *his old job at the town hall* 他以前在市政
厅的工作 6 (*long-standing*) [+ *friend, enemy, rival*]
老的 [lǎo de] ▷ *Pete's an old friend of mine.* 彼得

是我的一个老朋友。▸ **how old are you?** 你多
大了？▸ **he's 10 years old** 他10岁了 ▸ **older
brother/sister** 哥哥/姐姐 ▸ **any old thing** (inf)
随便什么东西

old age N [U] **1** (state) 老年 [lǎonián] **2** (time of
life) 晚年 [wǎnnián]

old age pension (BRIT) N [C] (state pension) 退
休金 [tuìxiūjīn] [美= **social security benefit,
social security payment**]

old age pensioner (BRIT) N [C] (senior citizen)
拿退休金的人 [ná tuìxiūjīn de rén] [美= **senior
citizen, retiree**]

old-fashioned ['əʊld'fæʃnd] ADJ [+ object,
custom, idea] 旧式的 [jiùshì de]; [+ person] 守旧
的 [shǒujiù de]

old people's home (ESP BRIT) N [C] 养老院
[yǎnglǎoyuàn]

olive ['ɔlɪv] I N [C] **1** (fruit) 橄榄 [gǎnlǎn]
2 (also: **olive tree**) 橄榄树 [gǎnlǎnshù] II ADJ
(also: **olive-green**) 橄榄绿的 [gǎnlǎnlǜ de] ▸ **to
offer an olive branch to sb** 向某人提出和解
的建议

olive oil N [U] 橄榄油 [gǎnlǎnyóu]

Olympic [əʊ'lɪmpɪk] I ADJ 奥林匹克的
[Àolínpǐkè de] II **the Olympics** NPL 奥林匹克
运动会 [Àolínpǐkè Yùndònghuì]

Olympic Games NPL 奥林匹克运动会
[Àolínpǐkè Yùndònghuì]

Oman [əʊ'mɑːn] N [C] 阿曼 [Āmàn]

omelette, (US) **omelet** ['ɔmlɪt] N [C] 煎蛋饼
[jiāndànbǐng] ▸ **ham/cheese omelet(te)** 火
腿/奶酪煎蛋饼

omen ['əʊmən] N [C] (sign) 预兆 [yùzhào] ▸ **a
good/bad omen** 一个好的/坏的预兆

ominous ['ɔmɪnəs] ADJ [+ sign, event, silence,
warning] 不祥的 [bùxiáng de]; [+ clouds, smoke]
预示的 [yùshì de]

omit [əʊ'mɪt] (frm) VT 删去 [shānqù] ▸ **to omit
to do sth** 忽略做某事

on [ɔn] I PREP **1** (indicating position) 在…上
[zài…shang] ▸ **it's on the table/wall** 它在
桌上/墙上 ▸ **he put the book on the shelf**
他把书放到架子上 ▸ **the house is on the
main road** 房子在主路旁 ▸ **to live on a
farm/an island** 在一个农场/岛上
▸ **on the left/right** 在左边/右边 ▸ **on the
top floor** 在顶楼 ▸ **she was lying on her
back/stomach** 她仰面躺着/俯卧着
2 (indicating means, method, condition etc)
▸ **on foot** 步行 [bùxíng] ▸ **on the train/bus**
[be, sit+] 在火车/公共汽车上；[travel, go+]
乘坐 ▸ **on the television/radio** 在电视上/
广播中 ▸ **she's on the telephone** (engaged)
她正在打电话 ▸ **on the Internet** 在因特网
上 ▸ **to be on antibiotics** 定期服用抗生素
▸ **to be away on business** 出差

3 (referring to time) 在 [zài] ▸ **on Friday** 在
星期五 ▸ **on Fridays** 在每个星期五 ▸ **on
June 20th** 在6月20日 ▸ **on Friday, June
20th** 在6月20日，星期五 ▸ **on Christmas
Day** 在圣诞日 ▸ **a week on Friday** 下个星
期五 ▸ **on arrival** 到了后 ▸ **on seeing this**
看到这个以后
4 (about, concerning) 关于 [guānyú]
▸ **information on train services** 火车服
务信息
II ADV **1** (clothes) ▸ **to have one's coat on**
穿着外套 [chuānzhe wàitào] ▸ **what's she
got on?** 她穿着什么？
2 (covering, lid etc) ▸ **screw the lid on tightly**
把盖子旋紧 [bǎ gàizi xuánjǐn]
3 (onwards, further) ▸ **to walk/read on** 继续
走/读 [jìxù zǒu/dú] ▸ **from now/that day
on** 从此/那一天以后 ▸ **on and on** 不停地
III ADJ **1** (turned on) [+ machine, light, engine,
tap] 打开的 [dǎkāi de]
2 (happening) ▸ **is the meeting still on?** 会
议还在进行吗？[huìyì háizài jìnxíng ma?]
▸ **there's a good film on at the cinema** 电
影院正在上映一部好电影 ▸ **the weather
forecast will be on in a minute** 马上就有
天气预报
3 (inf) ▸ **that's not on!** 那可不行！[nà kě
bùxíng!]

once [wʌns] I ADV **1** (one time only) 一次
[yīcì] **2** (at one time) 曾经 [céngjīng] ▷ Texas
was once ruled by Mexico. 德克萨斯州曾经受
墨西哥管辖。**3** (on one occasion) 有一次 [yǒu
yīcì] ▷ I went to Portugal once. 我去过一次葡
萄牙。II CONJ (as soon as) 一旦 [yīdàn] ▸ **at
once** (immediately) 立刻；(simultaneously) 同
时 ▸ **once a or every month** 每月一次 ▸ **once
more** or **again** 再一次 ▸ **once and for all** 一
劳永逸地 ▸ **once upon a time** (in stories) 很久
以前；(in the past) 从前 ▸ **once in a while** 偶尔
▸ **all at once** (suddenly) 突然 ▸ **for once** 就这
一次 ▸ **just this once** (inf) 就这一次 ▸ **once or
twice** (a few times) 一两次

oncoming ['ɔnkʌmɪŋ] ADJ (approaching)
[+ traffic, car] 迎面而来的 [yíngmiàn ér lái de]

one [wʌn] I ADJ **1** (number) 一 [yī] ▸ **he's one
year old** 他1岁 ▸ **it's one o'clock** 现在
1点 ▸ **one hundred/thousand children**
100/1000个孩子 ▸ **one hundred and fifty**
150 ▸ **we'll go there one day** 总有一天我
们会去那儿的 ▸ **there will be one or two
changes** 会有一两个改动 ▸ **one thing I
don't understand is why...** 我不明白的一
件事是为什么…
2 (sole) 唯一的 [wéiyī de] ▸ **my one hope is
that...** 我唯一的希望是…
3 (instead of "a") 一个 [yīgè]

4 (same) 同一的 [tóngyī de] ▶ shall I put it all on the one plate? 要我把它都放在同一个盘子里吗？

II PRON **1** (number) 一 [yī] ▶ I've already got one 我已经有一个了 ▶ one of them/of the boys 他们中的一个/男孩中的一个 ▶ it's one of the biggest airports in the world 这是世界上最大的飞机场之一 ▶ two coffees, not one 两杯咖啡，而不是一杯 ▶ one by one 一个一个地 ▶ all in one 合为一体的

2 (with adj) 一个 [yīgè] ▶ I've already got a red one. 我已经有一个红的了。▶ you are the only one who can do it 你是唯一可以做这事的人

3 (in generalizations) 人人 [rénrén] ▶ what can one do? 一个人能做什么呢？▶ one's (possessive) 本人的 ▶ to cut one's finger/hair 割破手指/剪头发 ▶ this one 这个 ▶ that one 那个 ▶ one another(us) 相互; (you, them) 彼此 ▶ one never knows 没有人会知道 ▶ to be at one (with sb) (与某人)一致 ▶ to be/get one up on sb 胜某人一筹

III N (numeral) 一 [yī]

one-off [wʌnˈɔf] (ESP BRIT) I ADJ 一次性的 [yīcìxìng de] II N [c] (inf) 一次性事件 [yīcìxìng shìjiàn]

oneself [wʌnˈsɛlf] PRON 自己 [zìjǐ] ▷ It's important to give oneself time to think. 给自己一些时间思考是很重要的。▶ to hurt oneself 伤了自己 ▶ to keep sth for oneself 把某物留给己 ▶ to talk to oneself 自言自语 ▶ by oneself (unaided) 独力地 ▷ One should learn to deal with one's problems by oneself. 每个人应该学会自己独立解决问题。; (alone) 独自 ▷ Living by oneself is very lonely. 独自一个人生活很孤单。

one-sided [wʌnˈsaɪdɪd] ADJ **1** (unequal) [+ contest, relationship] 一边倒的 [yībiāndǎo de] **2** (biased) 片面的 [piànmiàn de]

one-to-one [ˈwʌntəwʌn] I ADJ [+ relationship, tuition] 一对一的 [yīduìyī de] II ADV [+ talk, deal with] 一对一地 [yīduìyī de]

one-way [ˈwʌnweɪ] ADJ **1** [+ street, traffic] 单行的 [dānxíng de] **2** [+ ticket, trip] 单程的 [dānchéng de]

ongoing [ˈɔŋɡəʊɪŋ] ADJ [+ project, situation etc] 持续的 [chíxù de]

onion [ˈʌnjən] I N [c] 洋葱 [yángcōng] II CPD [复合词][+ soup] 洋葱 [yángcōng] ▶ to know one's onions (inf) 精明干练

online, on-line [ˈɔnlaɪn] (COMPUT) I ADJ **1** (connected to the Internet) [+ person, computer] 在线的 [zàixiàn de] **2** (available on the Internet) [+ service] 在线的 [zàixiàn de] II ADV (on the Internet) 网上 [wǎngshang] ▶ to go online (connect to the Internet) [person +] 上网; (become available on the Internet) [person, organization +] 在线

onlooker [ˈɔnlukə(r)] N [c] 旁观者 [pángguānzhě]

only [ˈəʊnlɪ] I ADV **1** (emphasizing one thing) 仅仅 [jǐnjǐn] ▷ I'm only interested in finding out the facts. 我仅仅对找出事实真相有兴趣。▷ The video is to be used for teaching purposes only. 该录像仅供教学使用。**2** (emphasizing sth must happen) 只有 [zhǐyǒu] ▷ The lawyer is paid only if he wins. 律师只有赢了官司才能拿钱。**3** (emphasizing insignificance) 只 [zhǐ] ▷ I was only joking. 我只是在开玩笑。II ADJ (sole) 唯一的 [wéiyī de] ▷ He was the only survivor. 他是唯一的幸存者。III CONJ (but) 可是 [kěshì] ▷ I saw her only last week 我上周才见了她 ▶ I'd be only too pleased or happy to help 我非常乐意来帮忙 ▶ I know only too well... 我太了解… ▶ it's only fair/natural 这很公平/自然 ▶ we asked for her autograph only to be ignored 我们要她的签名却被置之不理 ▶ only just (recently) 刚刚 ▷ I've only just arrived 我刚刚才到; (barely) 勉强 ▷ Farmers have only just managed to survive 农民们只是勉强维持生计 ▶ not only... but (also)... 不但…而且… ▷ Chimps not only use tools but make them. 黑猩猩不但使用而且制造工具。▶ the only one (person) 唯一; (thing) 唯一 ▶ an only child 独生子女

o.n.o. (BRIT) ABBR (= or nearest offer) 或依买方接近售价的出价 [huò yī mǎifāng jiējìn shòujià de chūjià]

on-screen, onscreen [ˈɔnskriːn] I ADJ **1** (COMPUT) 在屏幕上的 [zài píngmù shang de] **2** (TV, CINE) 银屏上的 [yínpíng shang de] **3** (TV, CINE) 银幕的 [yínmù de] II ADV **1** (COMPUT) 在屏幕上 [zài píngmù shang] **2** (TV, CINE) 银幕上 [yínmù shang]

onset [ˈɔnsɛt] N [s] [of war, winter, illness] 开始 [kāishǐ]

onstage [ɔnˈsteɪdʒ] ADV [appear, walk +] 舞台上 [wǔtái shang]

onto, on to [ˈɔntu] PREP 到…上 [dào...shang] ▶ to get onto sth [+ bus, train, plane] 上某交通工具; [+ subject, matter] 开始谈论某事 ▶ to hold/hang/cling onto sth 紧紧抓/握/揪住某物 ▶ to be onto something (inf) 将要揭示某事 ▶ to be onto sb (inf) 追究某人

onward [ˈɔnwəd] I ADJ **1** [+ journey, flight] 延续的 [yánxù de] **2** [+ progress] 前进的 [qiánjìn de] II ADV = onwards

onwards [ˈɔnwədz] ADV **1** (on journey, walk etc) [continue, go +] 向前地 [xiàngqián de] **2** (in development) [move, progress +] 前进地 [qiánjìn de] ▶ from that time onwards 从那一时刻起

oops [ups] (inf) INT 哎呀 [āiya]

ooze [uːz] I VI [mud, water, slime +] 渗出 [shènchū] II VT **1** [+ pus, blood etc] 渗出 [shènchū] **2** [person +] [+ confidence, sex appeal] 散发出 [sànfāchū]

op [ɔp] (inf) N [C] **1** (ESP BRIT: MED) 手术 [shǒushù] **2** (MIL) 行动 [xíngdòng] **3** (opportunity) 机会 [jīhuì] ▶ **photo op** 拍照机会 [pāizhào jīhuì]

opaque [əʊˈpeɪk] ADJ **1** [+ substance, glass, window] 不透明的 [bù tòumíng de] **2** [+ comment, language] 晦涩的 [huìsè de]

OPEC [ˈəʊpɛk] N ABBR (= Organization of Petroleum-Exporting Countries) 石油输出国组织 [Shíyóu Shūchūguó Zǔzhī]

◐ **open** [ˈəʊpn] **I** ADJ **1** (unfastened, unsealed) [+ door, window] 开着的 [kāizhe de] ▷ He climbed through the open window. 他从开着的窗户中爬了进来。; [+ container] 打开的 [dǎkāi de] ▷ an opened packet of cigarettes 一包打开的香烟; [+ mouth, eyes] 张着的 [zhāngzhe de] ▷ Angelica looked at me with her mouth open. 安吉莉卡张着嘴看着我。 **2** (accessible to the public) [+ shop] 营业的 [yíngyè de] ▷ The bank won't be open for another half-hour. 这家银行再过半个小时就不营业了。 **3** [+ countryside, road] 开阔的 [kāikuò de] ▷ The road stretched across open country. 道路穿过开阔地带向前延伸。 **4** (frank) [+ nature, character] 坦率的 [tǎnshuài de] ▷ Judy had an open and trusting nature. 朱迪天性坦率、易信赖他人。 **5** (not reserved) [+ ticket, return] 日期待定的 [rìqī dàidìng de] ▷ I can stay as long as I want, I've got an open ticket. 我想呆多久就呆,我买了张日期待定的票。 **6** (available) [+ offer, vacancy] 可得到的 [kě dédào de] ▷ We should use all the opportunities open to us. 我们应该利用一切可得到的机会。 ▷ I'm afraid the vacancy is no longer open. 我恐怕这个职位空缺没了。 **II** VT **1** (unfasten, unseal) [+ container] 打开 [dǎkāi] ▷ I opened a can of beans. 我打开了一罐豆子。; [+ door, lid] 开 [kāi] ▷ She opened the door with her key. 她用钥匙开了门。; [+ letter] 拆开 [chāikāi] ▷ I'll open the mail after breakfast. 我会在早饭后拆开信件。; [+ book, hand, mouth, eyes] 开 [kāi] ▷ He opened the heavy Bible. 他翻开厚重的圣经。 ▷ He opened his mouth and yawned. 他张开嘴打了个哈欠。 ▷ She opened her eyes and looked around. 她睁开眼睛向四周望了望。 **2** (launch, declare operational) 宣布营业 [xuānbù yíngyè] ▷ The leisure centre was opened by the Queen in 1976. 这个休闲中心是在1976年由女王宣布开业的。 **III** VI **1** (unfastened or unsealed) [door, lid +] 开 [kāi] ▷ The door opened and a tall man entered the room. 门开了,一个高个子男人走进了房间。; [+ container] 开 [kāi] ▷ The box opened and the books fell out. 盒子开了,里面的书掉了出来。 **2** [book, hand, mouth, eye, flower +] 张开 [zhāngkāi] ▷ The officer's mouth opened in astonishment. 这个官员吃惊地张大了嘴。 ▷ Her eyes opened and she woke up. 她的眼睛睁开了,她醒过来了。 **3** [public building +] (each day) 开门 [kāimén] ▷ He was waiting for the bar to open. 他等着酒吧开门。; (for first time) 开始营运 [kāishǐ

yíngyùn] ▷ The original railway station opened in 1854. 最早的火车站于1854年开始营运。 **4** (have first night) [film, play +] 首演 [shǒuyǎn] ▷ The new Spielberg film has opened in New York. 斯皮尔伯格的新电影已在纽约首映。 **IV** N ▶ (out) in the open (not secret) 公开 [gōngkāi] ▶ an open question 容许争论的问题 ▶ an open secret 公开的秘密 ▶ an open fire 未封上的炉火 ▶ in the open (air) 在户外 ▶ the open sea/ocean 远海/洋 ▶ to open one's mouth (speak) 张口说话 ▶ to be open to [+ suggestions, ideas] 乐意接受; [+ criticism, abuse] 容易受到 ▶ open to the public seven days a week 一周向公众开放7天 ▶ to open an account 开立账户

▶ **open onto** VT FUS [不可拆分] [room, door +] 通向 [tōngxiàng]

▶ **open up I** VT **1** [+ country, market, opportunities] 开放 [kāifàng] ▷ If the agreement is to succeed, the EU must open up its markets. 如能达成协议,欧盟必须开放其市场。 **2** (unlock) 打开 [dǎkāi] **II** VI **1** (unlock) 开门 [kāimén] ▷ Open up! It's freezing out here. 开门! 外面很冷。 **2** (confide) 倾诉 [qīngsù] ▷ She was disappointed that he hadn't opened up more. 他未能倾诉更多的情况,为此她很失望。 **3** [country, market, opportunities +] 展现 [zhǎnxiàn] ▷ New opportunities are opening up for investors who want... 新的机会正展现给那些想…的投资者们。

open-air [əʊpnˈɛə(r)] ADJ [+ concert, swimming pool] 户外的 [hùwài de]

opener [ˈəʊpnə(r)] N [C] **1** (also: tin opener, can opener) 开启工具 [kāiqǐ gōngjù] **2** (also: bottle opener) 开瓶器 [kāipíng qì]

opening [ˈəʊpnɪŋ] **I** ADJ (initial) [+ remarks, stages, scene] 开始的 [kāishǐ de] **II** N [C] **1** (gap, hole) 开口 [kāikǒu] **2** (beginning) [of play, book etc] 开头 [kāitóu] **3** (ceremony) [of building, bridge etc] 开放 [kāifàng] **4** (opportunity) 机会 [jīhuì] **5** (job) 空缺 [kòngquē]

opening hours NPL 营业时间 [yíngyè shíjiān]

openly [ˈəʊpnlɪ] ADV [speak, cry +] 公开地 [gōngkāi de] ▶ to be openly gay 公开同性恋

open-minded [əʊpnˈmaɪndɪd] ADJ 开明的 [kāimíng de]

open-necked [ˈəʊpnnɛkt] ADJ [+ shirt] 开领的 [kāilǐng de]

openness [ˈəʊpnnɪs] N [U] **1** (frankness) 坦率 [tǎnshuài] **2** (receptiveness) 开放 [kāifàng]

open-plan [ˈəʊpnˈplæn] ADJ [+ office] 开敞式布置 [kāichǎngshì bùzhì]

Open University (BRIT) N ▶ the Open University 开放大学 [Kāifàng Dàxué]

◉ **OPEN UNIVERSITY**

英国 **Open University** 的学生在家里完成大部分的学业,通过广播和电视节目接受

函授辅导，通过邮件收到作业。他们可以不时地在普通大学中和辅导老师见面，也可以参加夏季学校。**Open University** 又称为 **OU**，使不具备正式资格或无法参加传统课程的人们获得学位。许多成年人报名入学。

opera ['ɔpərə] N [C] (*individual work*) 歌剧 [gējù] **2** [U] (*art form*) 歌剧 [gējù]

opera house N [C] 歌剧院 [gējùyuàn]

opera singer N [C] 歌剧演唱者 [gējù yǎnchàngzhě]

operate ['ɔpəreɪt] I VT (*work*) [+ *machine, vehicle, system*] 操作 [cāozuò]; [+ *company, organization*] 经营 [jīngyíng] II VI **1** (*work*) [*machine, vehicle, system +*] 工作 [gōngzuò] ▷ *Calculators and computers operate on the same principle.* 计算器和计算机是按同样的原理工作的。; [*company, organization +*] 运作 [yùnzuò] ▷ *the multinational companies which operate in their country* 在他们国家做生意的跨国公司; [*laws, forces +*] 生效 [shēngxiào] ▷ *Laws of the same kind operate in nature.* 同样的法则也在自然界起作用。 **2** (MED) 动手术 [dòngshǒushù] ▷ *They operated but it was too late.* 他们动了手术，但已经太迟了。 ▶ **to operate on sb** (MED) 给某人动手术

operating room ['ɔpəreɪtɪŋ-] (US: MED) N [C] 手术室 [shǒushùshì]

operating system (COMPUT) N [C] 操作系统 [cāozuò xìtǒng]

operating table (MED) N [C] 手术台 [shǒushùtái] ▶ **to be on the operating table** 在手术台上

operating theatre (BRIT: MED) N [C] 手术室 [shǒushùshì] [美= operating room]

operation [ɔpə'reɪʃən] N **1** [C] (*procedure*) 实施步骤 [shíshī bùzhòu] ▷ *the risks at each stage of the operation* 各个实施步骤的风险 **2** [C] (MIL) 行动 [xíngdòng] ▷ *the most successful customs operation of the year* 本年度最成功的海关行动 **3** [C] (MED) 手术 [shǒushù] ▷ *a major heart operation* 一次大的心脏手术 **4** [U] (*use*) [*of machine, vehicle etc*] 操作 [cāozuò] ▷ *a guide to the operation of the machine* 机器操作指南 **5** [C] (COMM) (*business*) 企业 [qǐyè] ▷ *The two groups now run their business as a single combined operation.* 两个集团现在作为一个单一的联合企业经营业务。 ▶ **to be in operation** [*law, scheme +*] 在实施中; [*machine, device +*] 运转着 ▶ **to come into operation** 生效 ▶ **to bring** or **put sth into operation** 使某事开始实施 ▶ **to have an operation** (MED) 接受手术 ▶ **to perform** or **carry out an operation** (MED) 施行手术 ▷ *Dr Jones will perform the operation.* 琼斯医生将施行这次手术。

operational [ɔpə'reɪʃənl] ADJ [+ *machine, vehicle, system*] 可使用的 [kě shǐyòng de]

operative ['ɔpərətɪv] I ADJ [+ *machine, measure, system*] 有效的 [yǒuxiào de] II N [C] **1** (*worker*) 工人 [gōngrén] **2** (US) (*government agent*) 特工 [tègōng] ▶ **the operative word** 关键词

operator ['ɔpəreɪtə(r)] N [C] **1** (TEL) 接线员 [jiēxiànyuán] **2** [*of machine*] 操作员 [cāozuòyuán] **3** (*business*) 经营者 [jīngyíngzhě]

opinion [ə'pɪnjən] N **1** [C] (*individual view*) 观点 [guāndiǎn] **2** [U] (*collective view*) 见解 [jiànjiě] ▶ **in my/her opinion** 按我的/她的意见 ▶ **to have a good** or **high opinion of sb** 对某人评价好｛或｝高 ▶ **to have a good** or **high opinion of o.s.** 自视很好｛或｝很高 ▶ **to be of the opinion that...** (frm) 认为…

opinionated [ə'pɪnjəneɪtɪd] ADJ 固执己见的 [gùzhí jǐjiàn de]

opinion poll N [C] 民意测验 [mínyì cèyàn]

opium ['əupɪəm] N [U] 鸦片 [yāpiàn]

opponent [ə'pəunənt] N [C] **1** (*adversary*) (*in competition, fight, election*) 对手 [duìshǒu] **2** (*enemy*) [*of government*] 政敌 [zhèngdí] **3** [*of course of action*] 反对者 [fǎnduìzhě]

opportunity [ɔpə'tjuːnɪtɪ] N [C/U] 机会 [jīhuì] ▶ **to take the opportunity of doing sth** or **to do sth** 趁机会做某事 ▶ **at the first opportunity** 一有机会

oppose [ə'pəuz] VT [+ *person, idea*] 反对 [fǎnduì] ▶ **to be opposed to sth** 反对某事 ▶ **as opposed to** 而不是

opposing [ə'pəuzɪŋ] ADJ **1** [+ *side, team*] 对立的 [duìlì de] **2** [+ *ideas, tendencies*] 相反的 [xiāngfǎn de]

opposite ['ɔpəzɪt] I ADJ **1** (*facing*) [+ *side, house*] 对面的 [duìmiàn de] **2** (*farthest*) [+ *end, corner*] 最远的 [zuìyuǎn de] **3** (*contrary*) [+ *meaning, direction*] 相反的 [xiāngfǎn de] II ADV (*live, work, sit +*) 在对面 [zài duìmiàn] III PREP **1** (*across from*) 在…的对面 [zài…de duìmiàn] **2** (*corresponding to*) (*on list, form etc*) 对应 [duìyìng] IV N ▶ **the opposite** 对立面 [duìlìmiàn] ▶ **the opposite sex** 异性

opposition [ɔpə'zɪʃən] N **1** [U] (*resistance*) 反对 [fǎnduì] **2** ▶ **the opposition** (SPORT) (*opponents*) 对手 [duìshǒu] ▶ **the Opposition** (BRIT: POL) 反对派

oppress [ə'prɛs] VT 压迫 [yāpò]

opt [ɔpt] VI ▶ **to opt for sth** 选择某事 [xuǎnzé mǒushì] ▶ **to opt to do sth** 选择做某事
▶ **opt out** VI ▶ **to opt out (of sth)** 决定退出 (某事) [juédìng tuìchū (mǒushì)]

optician [ɔp'tɪʃən] N [C] **1** (*person*) 眼镜商 [yǎnjìngshāng] **2** (*also*: **optician's**) 眼镜店 [yǎnjìngdiàn]

optimism ['ɔptɪmɪzəm] N [U] 乐观 [lèguān]

optimist ['ɔptɪmɪst] N [C] 乐观主义者 [lèguān zhǔyìzhě]

optimistic [ɔptɪ'mɪstɪk] ADJ 乐观的 [lèguān de]

optimum ['ɔptɪməm] ADJ [+ *conditions, number,*

size etc] 最佳的 [zuìjiā de]

option ['ɔpʃən] N [C] **1** *(choice)* 选择 [xuǎnzé] **2** (SCOL, UNIV) 选修课 [xuǎnxiūkè] **3** (COMM) 买卖权 [mǎimàiquán] ▸ **to keep one's options open** 暂不做决定 ▸ **to have no other option (but to...)** (除…之外)别无选择 ▸ **I'm afraid that's not an option** 我恐怕那样行不通

optional ['ɔpʃənl] ADJ 可选的 [kěxuǎn de] ▸ **optional extras** 选装配件

○ **or** [ɔ:(r)] CONJ **1** *(linking alternatives)* 还是 [háishì] ▷ *Would you like tea or coffee?* 你要茶还是咖啡? **2** *(also:* **or else**) 否则 [fǒuzé] ▷ *Don't put plastic dishes in the oven or they'll melt.* 别把塑料盘子放进烤箱，否则它们会熔化的。**3** *(qualifying previous statement)* 或者说 [huòzhě shuō] ▷ *The man was a fool, or at least incompetent.* 那人是个傻瓜，或者说，至少很无能。**4** *(giving approximate amount)* 大约 [dàyuē] ▸ *five or ten minutes* 大约5到10分钟

oral ['ɔ:rəl] I ADJ **1** *(spoken)* 口头的 [kǒutóu de] **2** *[+ vaccine, medicine, contraceptive]* 口服的 [kǒufú de] II N [C] *(spoken examination)* 口试 [kǒushì] ▸ **oral sex** 口交

orange ['ɔrɪndʒ] I N **1** [C] *(fruit)* 柑橘 [gānjú] **2** [U] *(drink)* 橙汁 [chéngzhī] II ADJ *(in colour)* 橙色的 [chéngsè de]

orange juice ['ɔrɪndʒdʒu:s] N [U] 橘子汁 [júzizhī]

orange squash [ɔrɪndʒ'skwɔʃ] N [U] 浓缩橙汁 [nóngsuō chéngzhī]

orange tree ['ɔrɪndʒtri:] N [C] 橘树 [júshù]

orbit ['ɔ:bɪt] I N [C] *[of planet, satellite etc]* 轨道 [guǐdào] II VT *[+ earth, moon etc]* 环绕…运行 [huánrào...yùnxíng] ▸ **to put a satellite into orbit** 将卫星送入轨道

orchard ['ɔ:tʃəd] N [C] 果园 [guǒyuán]

orchestra ['ɔ:kɪstrə] N **1** [C] *(players)* 管弦乐队 [guǎnxián yuèduì] **2** (US) *(stalls)* ▸ **the orchestra** 剧场正厅前座 [jùchǎng zhèngtīng qiánzuò] [英=stalls]

orchid ['ɔ:kɪd] N [C] 兰花 [lánhuā]

ordeal [ɔ:'di:l] N [C] 煎熬 [jiān'áo]

○ **order** ['ɔ:də(r)] I N **1** [C] *(command)* 命令 [mìnglìng] **2** [C] (COMM) *(from shop, company)* 定货 [dìnghuò]; *(in restaurant)* 点菜 [diǎncài] ▷ *A waiter came to take their order.* 一位服务员过来请他们点菜。**3** [U] *(sequence)* 次序 [cìxù] **4** [U] *(stability)* 常规 [chángguī] **5** [U] *(peace)* 秩序 [zhìxù] ▷ *Troops were sent to the islands to restore order.* 军队被派往岛上以恢复秩序。**6** [S] *(system)* 制度 [zhìdù] ▷ *questioning the existing social order* 质疑现行社会制度 **7** [C] (REL) 修道会 [xiūdàohuì] II VT **1** *(command)* 命令 [mìnglìng] ▷ *Sherman ordered an investigation into the deaths.* 舍曼下令对死亡事件进行调查。**2** (COMM) *(from shop, company)* 定购 [dìnggòu] ▷ *She phoned the shop and ordered a couple of CDs.* 她给商店打电话定购了两张CD。▷ *Davis ordered*

a pizza. 戴维斯定了一份比萨饼。; *(in restaurant)* 点菜 [diǎncài] **3** *(arrange)* 整理 [zhěnglǐ] ▷ *He spent five minutes ordering the notes for his speech.* 他花了5分钟整理演讲稿。III VI *(in restaurant)* 点菜 [diǎncài] ▷ *Are you ready to order?* 可以点菜了吗? ▸ **to be under orders to do sth** 奉命做某事 ▸ **to take orders** 接受命令 ▷ *I'm not taking orders from you or anyone else!* 我不会接受你或其他任何人的命令! ▸ **to place an order for sth with sb** 向某人定购某物 ▷ *She placed an order for a carton of fresh cream with the milkman.* 她向卖牛奶的人定购了一盒新鲜奶油。▸ **made/done to order** (COMM) 定制 ▸ **on order** (COMM) 已定而尚未交货的 ▸ **in order** *(in sequence)* 按顺序; *(correct)* 妥当的 ▷ *Thank you, sir, your papers seem to be in order.* 谢谢您，先生，您的资料看起来都很妥当。▸ **in order of size** 按尺寸大小 ▸ **in alphabetical/numerical order** 按字母/数字顺序 ▸ **in short order** 迅速地 ▸ **in (good) working order** 运转(良好) ▸ **out of order** *(not working)* 已坏停用; *(in the wrong sequence)* 顺序颠倒 ▷ *It's hopeless, the pages are all out of order.* 全完了，所有页码顺序都颠倒了。▸ **in order to do sth** 为了做某事 ▷ *He had to hurry in order to catch his train.* 为了赶上火车他得快点了。▸ **in order for sth to happen** 为了成就某事 ▸ **in order that...** 以便… ▸ **to the order of** (ECON) 面值 ▷ *a cheque to the order of five thousand pounds* 一张面值5000英镑的支票 ▸ **of or in the order of** *(approximately)* 大约 ▸ **to order sb to do sth** 命令某人做某事 ▷ *He ordered me to leave the building.* 他命令我离开大楼。

▸ **order around, order about** VT 支使 [zhīshǐ]

order form N [C] 定货单 [dìnghuòdān]

orderly ['ɔ:dəlɪ] I ADJ *(well-organized)* *[+ manner, sequence, system]* 有秩序的 [yǒu zhìxù de] II N [C] **1** (MED) 勤杂工 [qínzhágōng] **2** (MIL) 勤务兵 [qínwùbīng]

ordinary ['ɔ:dnrɪ] ADJ **1** *(everyday)* 普通的 [pǔtōng de] **2** *(pej)* *(mediocre)* 平常的 [píngcháng de] ▸ **out of the ordinary** *(exceptional)* 非凡的

ore [ɔ:(r)] N [C/U] 矿石 [kuàngshí]

oregano [ɔrɪ'gɑ:nəu, US ə'rɛgənəu] N [U] 牛至 [niúzhì]

organ ['ɔ:gən] N [C] **1** (ANAT) 器官 [qìguān] **2** (MUS) 管风琴 [guǎnfēngqín]

organic [ɔ:'gænɪk] ADJ **1** *[+ food, farming]* 有机的 [yǒujī de] **2** *[+ substance]* 有机物的 [yǒujīwù de]

organism ['ɔ:gənɪzəm] N [C] 生物体 [shēngwùtǐ]

organization [ɔ:gənaɪ'zeɪʃən] N **1** [C] *(business, club, society, arranging)* 组织 [zǔzhī] **2** [U] *(order)* 条理 [tiáolǐ]

organize ['ɔ:gənaɪz] VT **1** *(arrange)* *[+ activity, event]* 组织 [zǔzhī] **2** *(order)* 整理 [zhěnglǐ]

organized ['ɔ:gənaɪzd] ADJ **1** *(structured)* 有

组织的 [yǒu zǔzhī de] **2** (*efficient*) 并然有序的 [jǐngrán yǒuxù de]

organizer ['ɔːɡənaɪzə(r)] N [c] [*of conference, party etc*] 组织者 [zǔzhīzhě]

orgasm ['ɔːɡæzəm] N [c/u] 性高潮 [xìnggāocháo] ▶ **to have an orgasm** 达到性高潮

orgy ['ɔːdʒɪ] N [c] 纵酒狂欢 [zòngjiǔ kuánghuān] ▶ **an orgy of violence/destruction** 极度暴力/破坏

oriental [ɔːrɪ'ɛntl] ADJ 东方的 [dōngfāng de]

orientation [ɔːrɪən'teɪʃən] N [c/u] (*beliefs, preferences*) 定位 [dìngwèi] ▶ **orientation course** 迎新情况介绍

origin ['ɒrɪdʒɪn] N [c/u] **1** (*source*) 起源 [qǐyuán] **2** (*ancestry*) 出身 [chūshēn] ▶ **country of origin** 祖国 ▶ **people of Indian origin** 印度人

original [ə'rɪdʒɪnl] I ADJ **1** (*first, earliest*) 最初的 [zuìchū de] **2** (*authentic*) [+ *art, writing, music*] 原作的 [yuánzuò de] **3** (*imaginative*) [+ *artist, idea*] 独创的 [dúchuàng de] II N [c] (*not a copy*) [*of painting, document etc*] 原作 [yuánzuò]

originally [ə'rɪdʒɪnəlɪ] ADV (*at first*) 起初 [qǐchū]

originate [ə'rɪdʒɪneɪt] VI ▶ **to originate in** [*idea, custom etc* +] 发源于 [fāyuán yú] ▶ **to originate with** or **from** 由…首创

ornament ['ɔːnəmənt] N **1** [c] (*object*) 装饰物 [zhuāngshìwù] **2** [u] (*decorations*) 装饰 [zhuāngshì]

ornamental [ɔːnə'mɛntl] ADJ (*decorative*) [+ *pond, tree*] 装饰的 [zhuāngshì de]

ornate [ɔː'neɪt] ADJ (*highly decorative*) [+ *necklace, design*] 装饰华丽的 [zhuāngshì huálì de]

orphan ['ɔːfn] I N [c] 孤儿 [gū'ér] II VT ▶ **to be orphaned** 成为孤儿 [chéngwéi gū'ér]

orthodox ['ɔːθədɒks] ADJ **1** (*conventional, accepted*) [+ *beliefs, methods*] 正统的 [zhèngtǒng de] **2** (*conservative, traditional*) [+ *person*] 保守的 [bǎoshǒu de] **3** ▶ **Orthodox** (REL) 东正教的 [Dōngzhèngjiào de]

orthopaedic, (US) **orthopedic** [ɔːθə'piːdɪk] ADJ [+ *surgeon, ward, shoes*] 矫形的 [jiǎoxíng de]

ostentatious [ɒstɛn'teɪʃəs] ADJ [+ *building, car etc*] 装饰花哨的 [zhuāngshì huāshao de]; [+ *person*] 卖弄的 [màinòng de]

osteopath ['ɒstɪəpæθ] N [c] 整骨医生 [zhěnggǔ yīshēng]

ostrich ['ɒstrɪtʃ] N [c] 鸵鸟 [tuóniǎo]

○ **other** ['ʌðə(r)] I ADJ **1** (*additional*) 另外的 [lìngwài de] ▷ *May I make one other point?* 我能再另外讲一点吗? **2** (*not this one*) 其他的 [qítā de] ▷ *Calls are cheaper in the evening than at other times.* 晚上打电话比其他时间开便宜。▷ *toys, paints, books and other equipment* 玩具、颜料、书和其他装备 **3** ▶ **the other...** (*of two things or people*) 另一… [lìngyī…] ▷ *the other side of the street* 街道的另一边 **4** (*apart from oneself*) 其他

的 [qítā de] ▷ *She likes to be with other people.* 她喜欢和其他人在一起。II PRON **1** (*additional one, different one*) 其他 [qítā] ▷ *in our family, as in many others* 在我们的家庭, 就像在许多其他家庭一样 ▷ *Some projects are shorter than others.* 某些项目比其他的工期短。▷ *He and two others were sentenced to death.* 他和其他两个人被判死刑。**2** (*of two things or people*) ▶ **the other** 另一个 [lìng yīgè] ▷ *his papers in one hand, his hat in the other* 他一只手拿着报纸, 另一只拿着帽子 **3** ▶ **others** (*other people*) 他人 [tārén] ▷ *a brave man who died helping others* 一个为拯救他人而死的勇士 ▶ **the others** (*people*) 其他人; (*things*) 其余 ▶ **other than** (*apart from*) 除了 ▶ **the other day/week** (*inf*) (*recently*) 几天/星期前 ▶ **somebody/something or other** (*inf*) 某个人/某件事 ▶ **none other than** 不是别人而正是

otherwise ['ʌðəwaɪz] ADV **1** (*if not*) 否则 [fǒuzé] **2** (*apart from that*) 除此以外 [chúcǐ yǐwài] **3** (*differently*) 别样 [biéyàng] ▶ **otherwise known as...** 又以…为人们所熟知

otter ['ɒtə(r)] N [c] 水獭 [shuǐtǎ]

OU (BRIT) N ABBR (= **Open University**) ▶ **the OU** 开放大学 [Kāifàng Dàxué]

ouch [autʃ] INT 哎哟 [āiyō]

ought [ɔːt] (*pt* **ought**) AUX VB **1** (*indicating advisability*) ▶ **you ought to see a doctor** 你应该去看医生 [nǐ yīnggāi qù kàn yīshēng] **2** (*indicating likelihood*) ▶ **he ought to be there now** 他现在应该到那儿了 [tā xiànzài yīnggāi dào nàr le] ▶ **this ought to be easy** (*but it isn't*) 这本该容易的 ▶ **you ought to have been more careful** 你早该更当心点的 ▶ **he ought to have arrived by now** 他这会儿该到了

ounce [auns] N [c] (*unit of weight*) 盎司 [àngsī] ▶ **an** or **every ounce of** 一点 (或) 每一分

○ **our** ['auə(r)] ADJ 我们的 [wǒmen de] ▷ *our apartment* 我们的公寓

ours [auəz] PRON 我们的 [wǒmen de] ▶ **this is ours** 这是我们的 ▶ **a friend of ours** 我们的一个朋友

ourselves [auə'sɛlvz] PRON PL 我们自己 [wǒmen zìjǐ] ▷ *We didn't hurt ourselves.* 我们没伤到自己。▷ *We built the house ourselves.* 我们自己盖了房子。▷ *We ourselves live in London.* 我们本人住在伦敦。▷ *We bought ourselves a new car.* 我们给自己买了辆新车。▶ **by ourselves** (*unaided*) 我们独力地 ▷ *We're learning to play the guitar by ourselves.* 我们在自学吉他。; (*alone*) 我们单独地 ▷ *We were left by ourselves.* 我们单独留了下来。

oust [aust] VT (*forcibly remove*) [+ *government, MP etc*] 驱逐 [qūzhú]

○ **out** [aut] I ADV **1** (*outside*) 在外面 [zài wàimiàn] ▶ **it's sunny/cold out** 外面阳光明媚/冷

▶ **out here/there** 这儿/那儿 ▶ **to pull sth out** 把某物拿开 ▶ **to be/get out and about** 四处走动 **2** (absent, not in) 不在 [bù zài] ▶ **Mr Green is out at the moment** 格林先生这会儿不在 ▶ **to have a day/night out** 外出玩一天/一晚 **3** (indicating distance) 出发地 [chūfā de] ▶ **the boat was 25 km out** 船开出了25公里 ▶ **three days out from Plymouth** 从普利茅斯出发3天的路程 **4** (SPORT) 出界地 [chūjiè de] ▶ **the ball was out** 球出界了 ▶ **out!** 出界！ **II** ADJ **1** ▶ **to be out** (unconscious) 不省人事的 [bùxǐngrénshì de]; (out of game) 出局的 [chūjú de]; (out of fashion) 过时的 [guòshí de]; (in flower) 盛开的 [shèngkāi de]; (known) [news, secret +] 被泄露的 [bèi xièlòu de]; (available) [book, CD +] 有售的 [yǒushòu de]; (extinguished) [fire, light, gas +] 熄灭的 [xīmiè de]; (impossible) 不可行的 [bù kěxíng de]; (inf) (on strike) 在罢工中的 [zài bàgōng zhōng de]; [tide +] 退潮的 [tuìcháo de] ▶ **before the week was out** 在这周结束前 **2** (inf) ▶ **to be out to do sth** (intend) 力求做某事 [lìqiú zuò mǒushì] **3** (wrong) ▶ **to be out in one's calculations** 计算有错误 [jìsuàn yǒu cuòwù] **III** VT [+ homosexual] 揭露…的性倾向 [jiēlù…de xìngqīngxiàng] **IV** ▶ **out of** PREP **1** (outside) (with movement) 出 [chū]; (beyond) 朝…外 [cháo…wài] ▶ **to go/come out of the house** 从房子里走出去/来 ▶ **to take sth out of a box/bag** etc 把某物从盒子/包[等]里拿出来 ▶ **to look out of the window** 向窗外望去 ▶ **to drink sth out of a cup** 用杯子喝某物 ▶ **to copy sth out of a book** 从书中直接摘录某物 ▶ **to be out of danger** 脱离危险 ▶ **to stay out of the sun/rain** 避免日晒/躲雨 **2** (with cause, motive) 出于 [chūyú] ▶ **out of curiosity/fear/greed** 出于好奇/害怕/贪心 **3** (from among) …中的 […zhōng de] ▶ **one out of every three smokers** 每3个烟民中的1个 ▶ **out of 100 cars sold, only one had any faults** 100辆售出的车中，只有1辆有问题 **4** (without) ▶ **to be out of milk/petrol** 牛奶喝完了/汽油用完了 [niúnǎi hē wán le/qìyóu yòng wán le]

outback ['autbæk] N ▶ **the outback** 内地 [nèidì]

outbound ['autbaund] ADJ [+ flight, journey] 开往外地的 [kāiwǎng wàidì de]

outbreak ['autbreɪk] N [C] [of war, disease, violence] 爆发 [bàofā]

outburst ['autbəːst] N [C] **1** (fit) [of rage, temper, joy etc] 爆发 [bàofā] **2** (period) [of violence] 突发 [tūfā]

outcast ['autkɑːst] N [C] 被遗弃的人 [bèi yíqì de rén]

outcome ['autkʌm] N [C] 结果 [jiéguǒ]

outcry ['autkraɪ] N [C] 强烈抗议 [qiángliè kàngyì]

outdated [aut'deɪtɪd] ADJ [+ custom, idea, method] 过时的 [guòshí de]

outdo [aut'duː] (pt **outdid**, pp **outdone**) VT 胜过 [shèngguò] ▶ **not to be outdone** 为了不相形见绌

outdoor [aut'dɔː(r)] ADJ **1** (taking place outdoors) [+ activity] 户外的 [hùwài de] **2** (for use outdoors) [+ swimming pool, toilet] 露天的 [lùtiān de]; [+ clothes] 室外的 [shìwài de] **3** [+ person] 爱好户外活动的 [àihào hùwài huódòng de]

请勿将 **outdoor** 和 **outdoors** 混淆。**outdoor** 是用在名词前面的形容词。它是用来描述发生在或存在于室内而非室外的事情。*David enjoyed outdoor activities, such as sailing, climbing and cycling... In summer when it's really hot, we go swimming at the outdoor pool.* **outdoors** 是副词。如果某事发生或存在于 **outdoors**，它发生在户外而非室内。*It was such a beautiful day that I decided it would do him good to be outdoors...Outdoors, the children played happily, while the adults talked inside the house.*

outdoors [aut'dɔːz] **I** ADV (in the open air) [play, stay, sleep +] 在户外 [zài hùwài] **II** N ▶ **the (great) outdoors** 野外活动 [yěwài huódòng]
用法参见 outdoor

outer ['autə(r)] ADJ 外部的 [wàibù de]

outer space N [U] 太空 [tàikōng]

outfit ['autfɪt] **I** N [C] **1** (clothes and accessories) 全套衣装 [quántào yīzhuāng] **2** (suit of clothes) 套装 [tàozhuāng] **3** (inf) (firm) 组织 [zǔzhī] **II** VT (US) 装备 [zhuāngbèi]

outgoing ['autgəuɪŋ] ADJ **1** (extrovert) 开朗的 [kāilǎng de] **2** (leaving office) [+ president, mayor etc] 将离任的 [jiāng lírèn de] **3** [+ mail, call, flight] 外发的 [wàifā de]

outgoings ['autgəuɪŋz] (BRIT) NPL 开销 [kāixiāo]

outgrow [aut'grəu] (pt **outgrew**, pp **outgrown**) VT **1** [+ clothes] 因长大而穿不下 [yīn zhǎngdà ér chuānbùxià] **2** [+ behaviour, idea, taste] 因成长而不再有 [yīn chéngzhǎng ér bùzài yǒu]

outhouse ['authaus] N [C] **1** (building) 外屋 [wàiwū] **2** (US) (toilet) 户外厕所 [hùwài cèsuǒ]

outing ['autɪŋ] N [C] (excursion) 出游 [chūyóu]

outlaw ['autlɔː] **I** VT [+ activity, organization] 宣布…为非法 [xuānbù…wéi fēifǎ] **II** N [C] 逃犯 [táofàn]

outlay ['autleɪ] (frm) N [C] 支出 [zhīchū]

outlet ['autlet] N [C] **1** (hole, pipe) 排放口

[páifàngkǒu] **2** (US: ELEC) 电源插座 [diànyuán chāzuò] ［英=**socket**］ **3** (COMM) (also: **retail outlet**) 经销店 [jīngxiāodiàn] **4** (for feelings, anger, talents, energy) 发泄途径 [fāxiè tújìng]

outline ['autlaɪn] **I** N[C] **1** (shape) (of object, person, house etc) 轮廓 [lúnkuò] **2** (brief explanation) (of plan, subject) 概要 [gàiyào] **II** VT **1** (explain briefly) 概括 [gàikuò] **2** (silhouette) 衬出轮廓 [chènchū lúnkuò]

outlook ['autluk] N **1** [C] (attitude) 看法 [kànfǎ] **2** [S] (prospects, weather forecast) 前景 [qiánjǐng]

outlying ['autlaɪɪŋ] ADJ 远离中心的 [yuǎnlí zhōngxīn de]

outnumber [aut'nʌmbə(r)] VT 在数量上超过 [zài shùliàng shang chāoguò] ▶ **they outnumbered us (by) five to one** 他们的人数是我们的5倍

out-of-date [autəv'deɪt] ADJ **1** (expired) [+ passport, ticket etc] 过期的 [guòqī de] **2** (old-fashioned) [+ book, object, idea] 过时的 [guòshí de]

out of doors ADV [play, eat, sit +] 在户外 [zài hùwài]

out-of-the-way ['autəvðə'weɪ] ADJ **1** (remote) [+ place] 偏僻的 [piānpì de] **2** (little-known) 不知名的 [bù zhīmíng de]

out-of-town ['autəvtaun] ADJ [+ shop, supermarket] 郊区的 [jiāoqū de]

out-of-work ['autəvwɜːk] ADJ 失业的 [shīyè de]

outpatient ['autpeɪʃənt] N[C] 门诊病人 [ménzhěn bìngrén]

outpost ['autpəust] N[C] **1** (MIL) 前哨 [qiánshào] **2** (COMM) 边远分部 [biānyuǎn fēnbù]

output ['autput] **I** N[C/U] **1** (production) [of factory, mine, writer etc] 产量 [chǎnliàng] **2** (COMPUT) 输出 [shūchū] **II** VT (COMPUT) [program, computer +] 输出 [shūchū]

outrage ['autreɪdʒ] **I** N **1** [C] (scandal) 引起义愤的事 [yǐnqǐ yìfèn de shì] **2** [C] (atrocity) 暴行 [bàoxíng] **3** [U] (anger) 愤慨 [fènkǎi] **II** VT (shock, anger) 使义愤 [shǐ yìfèn]

outrageous [aut'reɪdʒəs] ADJ **1** (appalling) [+ remark, behaviour] 惊人的 [jīngrén de] **2** (daring, flamboyant) [+ clothes] 大胆的 [dàdǎn de]

outright [adv aut'raɪt, adj 'autraɪt] **I** ADV **1** (absolutely) [reject, condemn +] 彻底地 [chèdǐ de] **2** (openly) [ask, deny, refuse +] 直率地 [zhíshuài de] **II** ADJ **1** (absolute) [+ winner, victory] 完全的 [wánquán de] **2** (open) [+ refusal, denial, hostility] 无保留的 [wú bǎoliú de] ▶ **to be killed outright** 当场毙命

outset ['autset] N (start) ▶ **at the outset** 在开始时 [zài kāishǐ shí] ▶ **from the outset** 从一开始

⚙ **outside** [aut'saɪd] **I** N[C] (exterior) [of container] 外面 [wàimiàn]; [of building] 外表 [wàibiǎo]

II ADJ **1** (exterior) [+ wall, surface] 外部的 [wàibù de] ▷ a long wooden shed that stood against the outside wall 紧靠外墙的一个长长的木棚 **2** (outdoor) [+ toilet] 户外的 [hùwài de] ▷ We only had an outside toilet. 我们只有一个户外厕所。 **3** (independent) 外界的 [wàijiè de] ▷ a report prepared by a group of outside consultants 由一组外界顾问准备的报告 **III** ADV **1** [be, wait +] 在外面 [zài wàimiàn] ▷ It was dark outside. 外面很黑。 **2** [go +] 向外面 [xiàng wàimiàn] ▷ Let's go outside. 我们到外面去吧。 **IV** PREP **1** (on the outside of) [+ place] 在…外 [zài…wài] ▷ There was a demonstration outside the embassy. 在大使馆外有示威游行。; [+ organization] 在…以外 [zài…yǐwài] ▷ He is hoping to recruit a chairman from outside the company. 他希望在公司以外招聘一位主席。 **2** (not included in) [+ period] 在…以外 [zài…yǐwài] ▷ You'll have to do it outside office hours. 你得在办公时间以外做这件事。; [+ price range] 超出 [chāochū] ▷ a beautiful guitar, but way outside my price range 是把漂亮的吉他，但超出了我能承受的价格范围 **3** (near to) [+ larger place] 在…附近 [zài…fùjìn] ▷ a small village just outside Birmingham 在伯明翰附近的小村庄 **4** ▶ **an outside chance** 微乎其微的机会 [wēi hū qí wēi de jīhuì] ▷ He's got an outside chance of winning. 他赢的机会微乎其微。 ▶ **at the outside** (at the most) 最多; (at the latest) 最迟 ▶ **the outside world** 外界 ● **outside of** (apart from) 除了

outside lane N[C] (right-hand side of road) 右边车道 [yòubiān chēdào]; (left-hand side of the road) 左边车道 [zuǒbiān chēdào]

outside line (TEL) N[C] 外线 [wàixiàn]

outsider [aut'saɪdə(r)] N[C] **1** (stranger) 外人 [wàirén] **2** (odd man out) 局外人 [júwàirén] **3** (in race etc) 不被看好的选手 [bù bèi kànhǎo de xuǎnshǒu]

outsize ['autsaɪz] (BRIT) ADJ **1** (extra-large) [+ clothes] 特大的 [tèdà de] **2** (huge) 巨大的 [jùdà de]

outskirts ['autskəːts] NPL ▶ **the outskirts** 郊区 [jiāoqū] ▶ **on the outskirts of...** 在…的郊区

outspoken [aut'spəukən] ADJ [+ person, critic] 直言不讳的 [zhíyán bùhuì de]; [+ statement, criticism] 坦率的 [tǎnshuài de]

outstanding [aut'stændɪŋ] ADJ **1** (excellent) 杰出的 [jiéchū de] **2** (remaining) [+ debt] 未付款的 [wèi fùkuǎn de]; [+ work, problem] 未解决的 [wèi jiějué de] **3** (obvious) [+ example] 显著的 [xiǎnzhù de]

outward ['autwəd] ADJ **1** (external) [+ sign, appearances] 外表的 [wàibiǎo de] **2** (outbound) [+ journey] 外出的 [wàichū de]

outwardly ['autwədlɪ] ADV 外表上 [wàibiǎo shang]

outward(s) ['autwəd(z)] ADV 向外 [xiàngwài]

outweigh [aut'weɪ] (frm) VT ▶ **the advantages**

(far) outweigh the disadvantages 利(远远)大于弊 [lì (yuǎnyuǎn) dàyú bì]

oval ['əuvl] I ADJ [+ table, mirror, face] 椭圆形的 [tuǒyuánxíng de] II N [C] 椭圆 [tuǒyuán] ▶ the Oval Office (US) 白宫椭圆形办公室

ovary ['əuvərɪ] N [C] 卵巢 [luǎncháo]

oven ['ʌvn] N [C] 烤箱 [kǎoxiāng]

ovenproof ['ʌvnpruːf] ADJ 耐热的 [nàirè de]

oven-ready ['ʌvnrɛdɪ] ADJ 即可入炉烤制的 [jíkě rùlú kǎozhì de]

over ['əuvə(r)] I ADJ (finished) [+ game, life, relationship etc] 结束的 [jiéshù de] II PREP 1 (more than) 超过 [chāoguò] ▶ over 200 people came 超过二百人来了 2 (indicating position) (above, on top of) 在…上 [zài…shang]; (spanning) 横跨 [héngkuà]; (across) 穿过 [chuānguò]; (on the other side of) 在…对面 [zài…duìmiàn] ▶ there's a picture over the fireplace 壁炉上挂着一幅画 ▶ a bridge over the river 横跨河流的一座桥 ▶ a helicopter flew over the building 一架直升机在大楼上方飞过 ▶ to climb over a wall 爬过一堵墙 ▶ pour the sauce over the mushrooms 把汁浇在蘑菇上 ▶ the pub over the road 街对面的酒吧 3 (during) 在…期间 [zài…qījiān] ▶ we talked about it over dinner 我们边吃晚饭边讨论 ▶ let's discuss it over a drink (invitation) 我们边喝东西边商议吧 ▶ over the weekend 在周末 4 (recovered from) [+ illness, shock, trauma] 康复 [kāngfù] ▶ he's over the flu 他流感好了 5 (about) 关于 [guānyú] ▶ concern over recent events 对最近事态的关心 6 ▶ all over the town/house/floor 全镇/满屋子/满地 [quánzhèn/mǎn wūzi/mǎndì] III ADV 1 (across) [walk, jump, fly etc +] 过 [guò] ▶ to cross over to the other side of the road 穿过马路到另一边 ▶ over here/there 在这里/那里 ▶ to ask or invite sb over (to one's house) 邀请某人来作客 ▶ I'll drive over to her place later 我过会儿会开车去她那儿 2 ▶ to fall/turn over 跌倒/打翻 [diēdǎo/dǎfān] 3 (remaining) (money, food etc) 剩下 [shèngxià] ▶ there are three over 还剩3个 ▶ is there any cake (left) over? 还有蛋糕剩下吗? 4 (more, above) 超过 [chāoguò] ▶ people aged 65 and over 65岁及以上年龄的人 5 (very) [+ clever, rich, generous etc] 过于 [guòyú] ▶ not over intelligent 不太聪明 6 (US) (again) 再 [zài] ▶ if she'd had the chance to do it over 如果她有机会再做一次的话 ▶ twice over 再次

7 (in expressions) ▶ all over (everywhere) 到处 [dàochù] ▶ all over again 重新 ▶ over and over (again) 三番五次

overall [adj, n 'əuvərɔːl, adv əuvər'ɔːl] I ADJ 1 (total) [+ length, cost etc] 全部的 [quánbù de] 2 (general) [+ impression, view] 总体的 [zǒngtǐ de] II ADV 总的说来 [zǒngdeshuōlái] III N [C] (BRIT) (woman's, child's, painter's) 罩衫 [zhàoshān] IV overalls NPL (protective clothing) 工装裤 [gōngzhuāngkù]

overboard ['əuvəbɔːd] (NAUT) ADV 向船外 [xiàng chuánwài] ▶ to go overboard (on sth) (inf) (对某事) 走极端

overbooked [əuvə'bukt] ADJ 超员预订的 [chāoyuán yùdìng de]

overcame [əuvə'keɪm] PT of overcome

overcast ['əuvəkaːst] ADJ 多云的 [duōyún de]

overcharge [əuvə'tʃɑːdʒ] VT, VI 要价太高 [yàojià tàigāo]

overcoat ['əuvəkəut] N [C] 大衣 [dàyī]

overcome [əuvə'kʌm] (pt overcame, pp overcome) VT 1 [+ difficulty, problem, fear] 战胜 [zhànshèng] 2 ▶ to be overcome by sth (emotionally) 因某事而不能自持 [yīn mǒushì ér bùnéng zìchí]; (physically) 受不了某物 [shòubùliǎo mǒuwù] ▶ to be overcome with grief 悲痛不已

overcrowded [əuvə'kraudɪd] ADJ 过度拥挤的 [guòdù yōngjǐ de]

overcrowding [əuvə'kraudɪŋ] N [U] 过度拥挤 [guòdù yōngjǐ]

overdo [əuvə'duː] (pt overdid, pp overdone) VT 1 (take to extremes) [+ exercise] 做得过多 [zuòde guòduō]; [+ whisky, beer, eating] 过度饮食 [guòdù yǐnshí]; [+ praise] 过度使用 [guòdù shǐyòng] ▶ (overcook) 煮得过久 [zhǔde guòjiǔ] ▶ to overdo it (inf) (overtax oneself) 工作过度; (exaggerate) 夸张

overdone [əuvə'dʌn] ADJ [+ food] 煮得过久的 [zhǔde guòjiǔ de]

overdose [əuvə'dəus] I N [C] 过量用药 [guòliàng yòngyào] II VI ▶ to overdose (on sth) 过量用 (某药物) [guòliàng yòng (mǒu yàowù)] ▶ to take an overdose 服药过量

overdraft ['əuvədraːft] N [C] 透支额 [tòuzhī'é]

overdrawn [əuvə'drɔːn] ADJ [+ account, person] 透支的 [tòuzhī de]

overdue [əuvə'djuː] ADJ 1 (late) [+ person, bus, train] 迟到的 [chídào de] 2 (much needed) [+ change, reform] 期待已久的 [qīdài yǐjiǔ de] 3 (late) [+ library book, rented video] 到期的 [dàoqī de] 4 (outstanding) [+ bill, rent] 过期未付的 [guòqī wèifù de] ▶ to be long overdue (reform) 早该实行的 ▶ to be two weeks overdue (library book, rented video) 过期两周的

overestimate [vb əuvər'ɛstɪmeɪt, n əuvər'ɛstɪmət] I VT 过高估计 [guògāo gūjì] II N [C] 过高的估计 [guògāo de gūjì]

overexcited [əuvərɪk'saɪtɪd] ADJ 过度兴奋的 [guòdù xīngfèn de]

overflow [əuvə'fləu] I VI 1 [*sink, bath, jug +*] 满得溢出 [mǎnde yìchū]; [*river +*] 泛滥 [fànlàn] 2 [*liquid +*] 溢出 [yìchū] 3 (*fig*) ► **to be overflowing (with sth/sb)** 挤满 (某物/某人) [jǐmǎn (mǒuwù/mǒurén)] 4 (*become apparent*) [*emotion +*] 爆发 [bàofā] 5 ► **to overflow with sth** [*+ emotion*] 满怀某事 [mǎnhuái mǒushì] II N [C] 1 (*hole, pipe*) 溢流口 [yìliúkǒu] 2 (*excess*) 过剩之物或人 [guòshèng zhī wù huò rén] ► **to be full to overflowing** 满得要溢出来

overgrown [əuvə'grəun] ADJ [*+ garden*] 蔓生的 [mànshēng de] ► **an overgrown child** 思想言行幼稚的成年人

overhaul [*vb* əuvə'hɔːl, *n* 'əuvəhɔːl] I VT 1 [*+ engine*] 大修 [dàxiū] 2 [*+ system, method*] 彻底革新 [chèdǐ géxīn] II N [C] 1 (*of engine etc*) 大修 [dàxiū] 2 [*+ of system*] 检查修正 [jiǎnchá xiūzhèng]

overhead [*adv* əuvə'hɛd, *adj* 'əuvəhɛd] I ADV 1 (*above*) 在头顶上 [zài tóudǐng shang] 2 (*in the sky*) 在空中 [zài kōngzhōng] II ADJ 1 [*+ light, lighting*] 头顶上的 [tóudǐng shang de] 2 (*cables, railway*) 高架的 [gāojià de]

overheads ['əuvəhɛdz] NPL (*expenses*) 经费 [jīngfèi]

overhead projector N [C] 高架投影仪 [gāojià tóuyǐngyí]

overhear [əuvə'hɪə(r)] (*pt, pp* **overheard** [ə uvə'həːd]) VT [*+ person*] 偶然听到 [ǒurán tīngdào]; [*+ conversation*] 无意听到 [wúyì tīngdào]

overheat [əuvə'hiːt] VI 1 [*engine +*] 变得过热 [biànde guòrè] 2 [*economy +*] 发展过热 [fāzhǎn guòrè]

overjoyed [əuvə'dʒɔɪd] ADJ 极度高兴的 [jídù gāoxìng de] ► **to be overjoyed at sth** 因某事而欣喜若狂

overland ['əuvəlænd] I ADJ [*+ journey*] 经由陆路的 [jīngyóu lùlù de] II ADV [*travel +*] 经陆路 [jīng lùlù]

overlap [*vb* əuvə'læp, *n* 'əuvəlæp] I VI 1 (*physically*) [*objects, areas +*] 重叠 [chóngdié] 2 (*coincide*) [*ideas, activities, events +*] 巧合 [qiǎohé] II VT 1 (*go over*) 部分重叠 [bùfen chóngdié] 2 (*put over*) 交搭 [jiāodā] III N [C] 重叠部分 [chóngdié bùfen] ► **overlap with** VT FUS [不可拆分] 与…重叠 [yǔ…chóngdié]

overleaf [əuvə'liːf] ADV 在背面 [zài bèimiàn]

overload [əuvə'ləud] I VT 1 [*+ vehicle*] 使超载 [shǐ chāozài] 2 ► **to overload sb with sth** 使某人负载过多某物 [shǐ mǒurén fùzài guòduō mǒuwù] 3 (ELEC) [*+ circuit*] 使超负荷 [shǐ chāo fùhè] II N [U] (*of information, work*) 过重的负担 [guòzhòng de fùdān] ► **to be overloaded (with sth)** [*vehicle +*] (因某物而) 超载; [*person, system +*]

(因某物而) 负荷过重

overlook [əuvə'luk] VT 1 (*have view over*) 俯瞰 [fǔkàn] 2 (*fail to notice*) 忽略 [hūlüè] 3 (*forgive*) 宽容 [kuānróng]

overnight [*adv* əuvə'naɪt, *adj* 'əuvənaɪt] I ADV 1 (*during the whole night*) [*sleep, stay +*] 一整夜 [yī zhěngyè] 2 (*fig*) (*suddenly*) 一下子 [yī xiàzi] II ADJ (*for a night*) [*+ accommodation*] 过夜的 [guòyè de] ► **an overnight success** 突如其来的成功 ► **overnight stop** or **stay** 过一夜

overnight bag ['əuvənaɪtbæg] N [C] 短途旅行包 [duǎntú lǚxíngbāo]

overpass ['əuvəpɑːs] (*ESP US*) N [C] 立交桥 [lìjiāoqiáo] [英= **flyover**]

overpay [əuvə'peɪ] VT 多付 [duōfù]

overpower [əuvə'pauə(r)] VT (*physically*) [*+ thief, assailant*] 制服 [zhìfú]; [*+ team, opponent*] 打败 [dǎbài]

overpowering [əuvə'pauərɪŋ] ADJ 1 [*+ smell, sound, taste*] 极其强烈的 [jíqí qiángliè de] 2 [*+ desire, urge*] 难以抑制的 [nányǐ yìzhì de] 3 (*imposing*) 强悍的 [qiánghàn de]

overran [əuvə'ræn] PT of **overrun**

overreact [əuvəriː'ækt] VI 反应过火 [fǎnyìng guòhuǒ]

overrule [əuvə'ruːl] VT [*+ person, decision*] 否决 [fǒujué]

overrun [əuvə'rʌn] (*pt* **overran**, *pp* **overrun**) I VT [*army, rebels +*] [*+ area*] 横行于 [hèngxíng yú] II VI ► **to overrun (by 10 minutes)** 超出 (10分钟) [chāochū (shí fēnzhōng)] ► **to be overrun by** or **with sth** 某物泛滥成灾的

oversaw [əuvə'sɔː] PT of **oversee**

overseas [əuvə'siːz] I ADV 向海外 [xiàng hǎiwài] II ADJ (*foreign*) [*+ market, trade*] 海外的 [hǎiwài de]; [*+ student, visitor*] 在国外的 [zài guówài de]

oversee [əuvə'siː] (*pt* **oversaw**, *pp* **overseen**) VT (*supervise*) 监督 [jiāndū]

overshadow [əuvə'fædəu] VT 1 (*cloud*) 给…蒙上阴影 [gěi…méngshang yīnyǐng] 2 (*eclipse*) ► **to be overshadowed by sb/sth** 与某人/某物相比黯然失色 [yǔ mǒurén/mǒuwù xiāngbǐ ànrán shīsè] 3 (*tower over*) 高出 [gāochū]

oversight ['əuvəsaɪt] N [C] 疏忽 [shūhu] ► **due to an oversight** 由于疏忽

oversleep [əuvə'sliːp] (*pt, pp* **overslept**) VI 睡过头 [shuì guòtóu]

overspend [əuvə'spɛnd] (*pt, pp* **overspent**) VI 超支 [chāozhī] ► **we have overspent by 5,000 dollars** 我们超支了5000美元

overt [əu'vəːt] ADJ 公开的 [gōngkāi de]

overtake [əuvə'teɪk] (*pt* **overtook**, *pp* **overtaken**) I VT 1 (ESP BRIT: AUT) 超过 [chāoguò] [美= **pass**] 2 [*event, change +*] [*+ person, place*] 突然降临 [tūrán jiànglín] 3 [*emotion, weakness +*] [*+ person*] 压倒 [yādǎo] II VI (ESP BRIT: AUT) 超车 [chāochē] [美=

pass]

overthrow [vb əuvə'θrəu, n 'əuvəθrəu] (pt **overthrew**, pp **overthrown**) I VT [+ government, leader] 推翻 [tuīfān] II N [S] 推翻 [tuīfān]

overtime ['əuvətaɪm] N [U] **1** 加班时间 [jiābān shíjiān] **2** (US: SPORT) 加时赛 [jiāshísài] ▶ **to do** or **work overtime** 加班 ▶ **to work overtime to do sth** (inf) 加班加点地做某事

overtook [əuvə'tuk] PT of **overtake**

overturn [əuvə'tə:n] I VT **1** [+ glass, chair] 打翻 [dǎfān] **2** (reverse) [+ decision, ruling] 推翻 [tuīfān] **3** [+ government, system] 颠覆 [diānfù] II VI [vehicle +] 翻倒 [fāndǎo]; [boat +] 翻了 [fānle]

overweight [əuvə'weɪt] ADJ [+ person] 超重的 [chāozhòng de]
用法参见 **fat**

overwhelm [əuvə'wɛlm] VT **1** (affect deeply) [feelings, emotions +] 使不知所措 [shǐ bùzhīsuǒcuò] **2** (defeat) [+ opponent, enemy etc] 制服 [zhìfú]

overwhelming [əuvə'wɛlmɪŋ] ADJ **1** [+ desire, sense] 极其强烈的 [jíqí qiángliè de] **2** [+ majority, victory] 压倒性的 [yādǎoxìng de]

overwork [əuvə'wə:k] I N [U] 过分劳累 [guòfèn láolèi] II VT [+ person] 使工作过度 [shǐ gōngzuò guòdù] III VI 工作过度 [gōngzuò guòdù]

overworked [əuvə'wə:kt] ADJ **1** [+ person] 过度劳累的 [guòdù láolèi de] **2** [+ word, expression] 使用过滥的 [shǐyòng guòlàn de]

ow [au] INT 哎哟 [āiyō]

owe [əu] VT [+ money] 欠 [qiàn] ▶ **to owe sb sth** [+ money] 欠某人某物; [+ apology, explanation] 应给予某人某物 ▶ **to owe sth to sb** [+ success, life] 应把某事归功于某人 ▶ **to owe it to sb/o.s. (to do sth)** 该为某人/自己(做某事)

owing to ['əuɪŋ-] PREP (because of) 因为 [yīnwèi]

owl [aul] N [C] 猫头鹰 [māotóuyīng]

◎ **own** [əun] I ADJ (emphasizing possession, individual action) 自己的 [zìjǐ de] ▷ I decided I wanted to have my own shop. 我决定要拥有自己的商店。 ▷ They will be expected to make their own beds. 他们被要求自己铺床。 II PRON (emphasizing possession, individual action) 自己的 [zìjǐ de] ▷ Did she hire skis or take her own? 她是租的滑雪板还是拿的自己的? ▷ There's no

career structure, you have to create your own. 并没有什么职业模式,你得创造出你自己的。 III VT (possess) [+ house, land, car etc] 拥有 [yōngyǒu] ▷ Julie's father owned a pub. 朱莉的父亲拥有一家酒吧。 ▶ **a room of my own** 我自己的房间 ▶ **to get one's own back (on sb)** (ESP BRIT: inf) (take revenge) (向某人)报复 [美 = **get even (with sb)**] ▶ **on one's own** (alone) 独自地 ▷ She lived on her own. 她独自一人住。; (without help) 独立地 ▷ We can't solve this problem on our own. 我们无法独立解决这个问题。 ▶ **a place to call one's own** 一个属于自己的地方 ▶ **to come into one's own** 进入鼎盛时期 ▶ **as if** or **like he owns the place** (inf) 好像他是这儿的主人似的
▶ **own up** VI (confess) 坦白 [tǎnbái] ▷ Come on, own up! Who did it? 得了,坦白吧!是谁干的?
▶ **own up to** VT FUS (不可拆分) 承认 [chéngrèn] ▶ **to own up to having done sth** 承认干了某事

owner ['əunə(r)] N [C] 物主 [wùzhǔ]

ownership ['əunəʃɪp] N [U] 所有权 [suǒyǒuquán]

ox [ɔks] (pl **oxen**) N [C] 公牛 [gōngniú]

Oxbridge ['ɔksbrɪdʒ] (BRIT) N [U] (Oxford and Cambridge universities) 牛津和剑桥大学 [Niújīn hé Jiànqiáo Dàxué]

OXBRIDGE

Oxbridge 是英国两所久副盛名的大学牛津大学和剑桥大学的合称。这两所大学的历史都可以追溯到12世纪。其间任何一所学院中的教育都被认为具备世界一流水平。许多 **Oxbridge** 的毕业生进入政治、商务以及外交领域,开始他们辉煌的职业生涯。

oxen ['ɔksn] NPL of **ox**

oxtail soup ['ɔksteɪl-] N [U] 牛尾汤 [niúwěi tāng]

oxygen ['ɔksɪdʒən] N [U] 氧气 [yǎngqì]

oyster ['ɔɪstə(r)] N [C] 牡蛎 [mǔlì] ▶ **the world is your oyster** 这个世界是你的

oz ABBR (= **ounce**) 盎司 [àngsī]

ozone ['əuzəun] N [U] 臭氧 [chòuyǎng]

ozone-friendly [əuzəun'frɛndlɪ] ADJ 无害臭氧层的 [wúhài chòuyǎngcéng de]

ozone layer N [C] 臭氧层 [chòuyǎngcéng]

Pp

P, p¹ [piː] N [C/U] (letter) 英语的第十六个字母

p² (BRIT) ABBR (= penny/pence) 便士 [biànshì]

p. (pl **pp.**) ABBR (= page) 页 [yè]

PA N ABBR 1 (= personal assistant) 私人助理 [sīrén zhùlǐ] 2 ▶ **PA (system)** (= public address system) 有线广播系统 [yǒuxiàn guǎngbō xìtǒng]

p.a. ABBR (= per annum) 每年 [měinián]

pace [peɪs] I N 1 [S] (speed) [of change, life etc] 速度 [sùdù]; [of walker, runner] 步速 [bùsù] 2 [C] (as measurement) 步 [bù] II VT (also: **pace around**) [+ room] 踱步于 [duóbù yú] ▶ **to set the pace** (in race) 定步速 ▶ **to keep pace with** [+ person] 与…并驾齐驱; [+ events] 与…同步 ▶ **to do sth at one's own pace** 按自己的步调做某事 ▶ **to take a pace forwards/backwards** 进一步/退一步 ▶ **to put sb through his/her paces** 考察某人的能力 ▶ **to pace up and down** 踱来踱去

pacemaker ['peɪsmeɪkə(r)] N [C] 1 (MED) 起搏器 [qǐbóqì] 2 (SPORT) 定步速者 [dìng bùsù zhě]

Pacific [pə'sɪfɪk] N ▶ **the Pacific (Ocean)** 太平洋 [Tàipíngyáng]

pacifier ['pæsɪfaɪə(r)] (US) N [C] (for sucking) 橡皮奶头 [xiàngpí nǎitóu] [英= **dummy**]

pacifist ['pæsɪfɪst] N [C] 和平主义者 [hépíng zhǔyìzhě]

pack [pæk] I VT 1 [+ clothes] 把…打包 [bǎ…dǎbāo] 2 [+ suitcase, bag] 把…装箱 [bǎ…zhuāngxiāng] 3 [+ hole] (with earth, cement) 填塞 [tiánsāi] II VI 打点行装 [dǎdiǎn xíngzhuāng] III N [C] 1 (bundle) [of goods] 捆 [kǔn]; [of documents] 包 [bāo] 2 (US) [of cigarettes] 包 [bāo] 3 (group) [of hounds] 群 [qún]; [of people] 伙 [huǒ] 4 (back pack) 背包 [bēibāo] 5 [of cards] 副 [fù] ▶ **to pack one's bags** (fig) 卷铺盖走人 ▶ **to pack sb/sth into sth** (cram) 把某人/某物塞满某物 ▶ **to pack sth into/around sth** (compress) 把某物塞进某物/在某物周围压紧 ▶ **to send sb packing** (inf) 把某人赶走
▶ **pack in** (BRIT: inf) VT [+ job] 放弃 [fàngqì]
▶ **pack it in!** (stop it!) 停止!
▶ **pack off** (inf) VT ▶ **to pack sb off to school/bed** etc 打发某人上学/上床睡觉 {等} [dǎfa mǒurén shàngxué/shàngchuáng shuìjiào {děng}]
▶ **pack up** I VI 1 (BRIT: inf) (stop working) 停止工作 [tíngzhǐ gōngzuò] 2 (BRIT) (put things away) 打点行装 [dǎdiǎn xíngzhuāng] II VT [+ belongings, clothes] 打包 [dǎbāo]

package ['pækɪdʒ] I N [C] 1 (parcel) 包裹 [bāoguǒ] 2 [of measures, proposals] 一揽子 [yīlǎnzi] 3 (COMPUT) 程序包 [chéngxùbāo] II VT [+ goods] 包装 [bāozhuāng]

package deal N [C] 1 (set of proposals) 一揽子交易 [yīlǎnzi jiāoyì] 2 (holiday) 包价旅游 [bāojià lǚyóu]

package holiday (BRIT) N [C] 包价旅游 [bāojià lǚyóu] [英= **package tour**]

package tour N = **package holiday**

packaging ['pækɪdʒɪŋ] N [U] 包装 [bāozhuāng]

packed [pækt] ADJ 1 (crowded) 拥挤的 [yōngjǐ de] 2 (compacted) [+ snow, earth] 压坚实的 [yā jiānshí de] ▶ **packed solid** (with people) 挤得水泄不通

packed lunch (BRIT) N [C] 盒装午餐 [hézhuāng wǔcān]

packet ['pækɪt] N [C] [of cigarettes, biscuits] 盒 [hé]; [of crisps, sweets, seeds] 袋 [dài]; [of cereals] 包 [bāo] ▶ **to make a packet** (BRIT: inf) 赚大钱

packing ['pækɪŋ] N 1 (act) 打包 [dǎbāo] 2 (wrapping) 包装材料 [bāozhuāng cáiliào] ▶ **to do one's/the packing** 打包

pact [pækt] N [C] 合同 [hétong]

pad [pæd] I N [C] 1 [of paper] 便笺簿 [biànjiānbù] 2 (to prevent friction, damage) 垫 [diàn] 3 (for cleaning) 抹布 [mābù] 4 (inf) (home) 住所 [zhùsuǒ] II VT [+ cushion, shoulders, upholstery] 填塞 [tiánsāi] III VI ▶ **to pad about/out** etc 踱来踱去/踱出 {等} [duólái duóqù/duóchū {děng}] ▶ **elbow/knee pad** 护肘/护膝

padded ['pædɪd] ADJ [+ jacket, shoulder, collar] 加有衬垫的 [jiāyǒu chèndiàn de]

padding ['pædɪŋ] N [U] 1 (material) 填塞物 [tiánsāiwù] 2 (fig) 冗词赘句 [rǒngcí zhuìjù]

paddle ['pædl] I N [C] 1 (for canoe) 短桨 [duǎnjiǎng] 2 (US) (for table tennis) 球拍 [qiúpāi]

〔英=**bat**〕II VT [+ *boat, canoe*] 用桨划 [yòng jiǎng huá] III VI (*at seaside*) 戏水 [xìshuǐ] ▶ **to go for a paddle** 去戏水

paddling pool ['pædlɪŋ-] (BRIT) N [c] 浅水池 [qiǎnshuǐchí] 〔美=**wading pool**〕

paddock ['pædək] N [c] (*field*) 围场 [wéichǎng]; (*at race course*) 马的集中场 [mǎ de jízhōngchǎng]

padlock ['pædlɔk] I N [c] 挂锁 [guàsuǒ] II VT 锁上 [suǒshang]

paedophile, (US) **pedophile** ['piːdəʊfaɪl] I N [c] 恋童癖者 [liàntóngpǐzhě] II ADJ [+ *ring, network, activity*] 恋童癖的 [liàntóngpǐ de]

○ **page** [peɪdʒ] I N [c] **1** [*of book, magazine, newspaper*] 页 [yè] **2** (*also:* **page boy**) (*in hotel*) 男听差 [nán tīngchāi]; (*at wedding*) 小男傧相 [xiǎo nán bīnxiàng] II VT (*in hotel, place of work*) [+ *person*] 广播寻 [guǎngbō zhǎo]

pager ['peɪdʒə(r)] N [c] 寻呼机 [xúnhūjī]

paid [peɪd] I PT, PP *of* **pay** II ADJ [+ *work*] 有薪金的 [yǒu xīnjīn de]; [+ *holiday*] 带薪的 [dàixīn de]; [+ *staff, official*] 受雇用的 [shòu gùyòng de] ▶ **well paid** [+ *person*] 拿高薪的; [+ *job*] 薪金丰厚的 ▶ **badly** *or* **poorly paid** [+ *person*] 拿低薪的; [+ *job*] 低收入的 ▶ **to put paid to sth** (BRIT) 结束某事

pain [peɪn] N **1** [c/u] (*physical*) 疼痛 [téngtòng] **2** [u] (*fig*) (*unhappiness*) 痛苦 [tòngkǔ] **3** (*inf*) (*nuisance*) ▶ **to be a pain (in the neck)** 讨厌的家伙 [tǎoyàn de jiāhuo] ▶ **to have a pain in one's chest/arm** 胸痛/胳膊疼 ▶ **to be in pain** 在苦恼中 ▶ **to take (great) pains to do sth** 尽力做某事 ▶ **to take (great) pains with/over sth** 对某事煞费苦心 ▶ **what a pain!** (*inf*) 真讨厌！▶ **on pain of death/imprisonment** 违者以死/监禁论处

painful ['peɪnfʊl] ADJ **1** (*physically*) [+ *back, joint, swelling etc*] 疼痛的 [téngtòng de]; [+ *treatment, blow, spasm etc*] 痛苦的 [tòngkǔ de] **2** (*upsetting, unpleasant*) [+ *memory, decision, situation, sight*] 讨厌的 [tǎoyàn de] **3** (*inf*) (*embarrassing*) [+ *performance, interview*] 令人难堪的 [lìngrén nánkān de]

painfully ['peɪnfəlɪ] ADV [+ *aware, obvious, shy*] 痛苦地 [tòngkǔ de]; [+ *slow*] 使人心烦地 [shǐ rén xīnfán de]

painkiller ['peɪnkɪlə(r)] N [c] 止痛药 [zhǐtòngyào]

painless ['peɪnlɪs] ADJ **1** [+ *treatment, operation, childbirth*] 无痛的 [wútòng de] **2** (*fig*) [+ *solution, method, process*] 不费力的 [bù fèilì de]

painstaking ['peɪnzteɪkɪŋ] ADJ [+ *work, research, investigation*] 艰苦的 [jiānkǔ de]; [+ *person*] 勤奋努力的 [qínfèn nǔlì de]

paint [peɪnt] I N [c/u] **1** (*decorator's*) 油漆 [yóuqī] **2** (*artist's*) 颜料 [yánliào] II VT **1** (*decorate*) [+ *wall, door, house*] 油漆 [yóuqī] **2** (*portray*) [+ *person, object*] 描绘 [miáohuì] **3** (*create*)

[+ *picture, portrait*] 用颜料画 [yòng yánliào huà] III VI (*creatively*) 绘画 [huìhuà] ▶ **a tin of paint** 一罐颜料 ▶ **to paint sth blue/white** *etc* 把某物涂成蓝色/白色{等} ▶ **to paint a grim/gloomy/vivid picture of sth** 将某物描绘成一副凄凉/灰暗/生动的景象 ▶ **to paint in oils** 画油画

paintbrush ['peɪntbrʌʃ] N [c] **1** (*decorator's*) 漆刷 [qīshuā] **2** (*artist's*) 画笔 [huàbǐ]

painter ['peɪntə(r)] N [c] **1** (*artist*) 画家 [huàjiā] **2** (*decorator*) 油漆工 [yóuqīgōng]

painting ['peɪntɪŋ] N **1** [u] (*activity*) (*artistic*) 绘画 [huìhuà]; (*decorating walls, doors etc*) 上油漆 [shàng yóuqī] **2** [c] (*picture*) 画 [huà]

paintwork ['peɪntwəːk] N [u] 漆面 [qīmiàn]

pair [pɛə(r)] N [c] **1** [*of shoes, gloves, socks*] 双 [shuāng] **2** (*two people*) 对 [duì] ▶ **a pair of scissors** 一把剪刀 ▶ **a pair of trousers** 一条裤子 ▶ **in pairs** 成对地 ▶ **pair off** VI ▶ **to pair off with sb** 与某人成双成对 [yǔ mǒurén chéngshuāng chéngduì]

> 名词 **pair** 后既可跟动词单数形式也可跟动词复数形式，具体用法取决于它所指的两个事物或人是被看作一个整体还是两者的集合。*A good pair of trainers is essential...The pair are still friends and meet regularly.*

pajamas [pə'dʒɑːməz] (US) NPL = **pyjamas**

Pakistan [pɑːkɪ'stɑːn] N 巴基斯坦 [Bājīsītǎn]

Pakistani [pɑːkɪ'stɑːnɪ] I ADJ 巴基斯坦的 [Bājīsītǎn de] II N [c] 巴基斯坦人 [Bājīsītǎn rén]

pal [pæl] (*inf*) N [c] 好友 [hǎoyǒu]

palace ['pæləs] N [c] 宫殿 [gōngdiàn] ▶ **Buckingham Palace** 白金汉宫

pale [peɪl] I ADJ **1** (*light*) [+ *wall, wood*] 灰暗的 [huī'àn de]; [+ *colour*] 淡的 [dàn de] **2** (*milky*) [+ *light, sky*] 昏暗的 [hūn'àn de] **3** (*fair*) [+ *skin, complexion*] 白皙的 [báixī de] **4** (*from sickness, fear*) [+ *face, person*] 苍白的 [cāngbái de] II N [c] ▶ **beyond the pale** 越轨的 [yuèguǐ de] III VI (*cheeks +*) 变苍白 [biàn cāngbái] ▶ **pale blue/pink/green** 淡蓝色/粉红色/绿色 ▶ **to grow** *or* **turn** *or* **go pale** 变得苍白 ▶ **to pale into insignificance (beside sth)** （与某事比）微不足道

Palestine ['pælɪstaɪn] N 巴勒斯坦 [Bālèsītǎn]

Palestinian [pælɪs'tɪnɪən] I ADJ 巴勒斯坦的 [Bālèsītǎn de] II N [c] 巴勒斯坦人 [Bālèsītǎn rén]

palette ['pælɪt] N [c] **1** (*for mixing paints*) 调色盘 [tiáosèpán] **2** (*range of colours*) 一套颜料 [yítào yánliào]

palm [pɑːm] N [c] **1** (*also:* **palm tree**) 棕榈树 [zōnglǘshù] **2** [*of hand*] 手掌 [shǒuzhǎng] ▶ **palm off** (*inf*) VT ▶ **to palm sth off on sb** 把某物硬塞给某人 [bǎ mǒuwù yìngsāi gěi mǒurén]

palmtop ['pɑːmtɔp] N [c] 掌上电脑

[zhǎngshàng diànnǎo]

pamper ['pæmpə(r)] VT [+ child, pet] 纵容
[zòngróng] ▶ **to pamper o.s.** 放纵自己

pamphlet ['pæmflət] N [C] 小册子 [xiǎocèzi]

pan [pæn] I N [C] **1** (also: **saucepan**) 炖锅
[dùnguō] **2** (US) (for baking) 平底锅 [píngdǐguō]
II VI (CINE, TV) 摇镜头 [yáo jìngtóu] III VT
(inf) [+ book, film] 严厉批评 [yánlì pīpíng] ▶ **to
pan for gold** 淘金

Panama ['pænəmɑ:] N 巴拿马 [Bā'námǎ]

pancake ['pænkeɪk] N [C] 薄煎饼 [báo
jiānbǐng]

⊚ **PANCAKE**

如果你要求英国厨师和美国厨师为你做一
张 **pancake**，饼的样子决不会是一模一
样。在这两个国家，**pancake** 都呈扁平
圆形。用水、面粉和鸡蛋打成面糊，油
炸后，趁热吃。英国的饼很薄，经常卷起
来，或者夹有甜味或其他口味的馅儿。很
多人在 **Shrove Tuesday** (忏悔星期二)即
Lent (大斋节)开始前的一天吃饼，这一
天就是人们熟知的 **Pancake Day** (煎饼
节)。(**Lent** 是指复活节前的40天，从前基
督教徒有在这段时间里斋戒的传统。)在
美国，**pancake** 相对较小、较厚，通常在
早餐时，就着黄油和枫糖吃。

panda ['pændə] N [C] 熊猫 [xióngmāo]

pander ['pændə(r)] VI ▶ **to pander to** [+ person,
whim, desire, opinion] 迎合 [yínghé]

p & h (US) ABBR (= postage and handling) = p & p

p & p (BRIT) ABBR (= postage and packing) 邮费及
包装费 [yóufèi jí bāozhuāngfèi] [美 = p & h]

pane [peɪn] N [C] (of glass) 窗格玻璃 [chuānggé
bōli]

panel ['pænl] N [C] **1** (of wood, metal etc) 板 [bǎn]
2 (group of judges, experts) 专门小组 [zhuānmén
xiǎozǔ] ▶ **control** or **instrument panel** 控制板
〔或〕仪表板

panelled, (US) **paneled** ['pænld] ADJ [+ room,
wall, door] 有镶板的 [yǒu xiāngbǎn de]

panelling, (US) **paneling** ['pænəlɪŋ] N [U] 镶
板 [xiāngbǎn]

pang [pæŋ] N [C] (of regret, sadness, guilt,
conscience) 悲痛 [bēitòng] ▶ **hunger pangs** 一
阵饥饿感

panhandler ['pænhændlə(r)] (US: inf) N [C] 乞
丐 [qǐgài] [英 = beggar]

panic ['pænɪk] I N **1** [U] (anxiety) 惊恐
[jīngkǒng] **2** [C] (scare) 恐慌 [kǒnghuāng]
II VI [person, crowd +] 惊慌 [jīnghuāng] III VT
[+ person] 使惊慌 [shǐ jīnghuāng] ▶ **to be in a
panic** 处于焦虑不安中 ▶ **to do sth in a panic**
惊慌失措地做某事 ▶ **to get into a panic** 陷
入恐慌

panorama [pænə'rɑ:mə] N 全景 [quánjǐng]

pansy ['pænzɪ] N [C] (flower) 三色紫罗兰 [sānsè
zǐluólán]

pant [pænt] VI [person +] 喘气 [chuǎnqì];
[animal +] 气喘吁吁 [qìchuǎn xūxū]

panther ['pænθə(r)] N [C] 豹 [bào]

panties ['pæntɪz] (ESP US) NPL 短衬裤 [duǎn
chènkù] [英 = pants, knickers]

pantomime ['pæntəmaɪm] (BRIT) N [C/U] 童
话剧 [tónghuàjù]

⊚ **PANTOMIME**

作为圣诞节期间的特殊节目，英国家长
会带孩子去看一场 **pantomime**，又称为
panto，一种取材于童话传说或传统故事
的戏剧。演员穿着奇特的戏装，还有很多
歌曲和舞蹈表演。观众的参与受到鼓励。
孩子们给反派角色喝倒彩，使劲给男女主
人公鼓劲。男主人公可能会由年轻的女演
员反串，而男演员则反串岁数较大的女性
角色(常常是男主人公的母亲)。

pants [pænts] NPL **1** (BRIT) (underwear) 内裤
[nèikù] [美 = underpants] **2** (US) (trousers) 裤
子 [kùzi] [英 = trousers] ▶ **a pair of pants**
(BRIT) (underwear) (woman's, man's) 一条内裤;
(US) (trousers) 一条裤子

pantyhose ['pæntɪhəʊz] (US) NPL 连裤袜
[liánkùwà] ▶ **a pair of pantyhose** 一条连裤袜
[英 = tights]

⊙ **paper** ['peɪpə(r)] I N **1** [U] 纸 [zhǐ] **2** [C] (also:
newspaper) 报纸 [bàozhǐ] **3** [C] (exam) 试
卷 [shìjuàn] **4** [C] (academic essay) (spoken) 论
文 [lùnwén]; (written) 文章 [wénzhāng] **5** [C]
(official report) 文件 [wénjiàn] **6** [U] (wallpaper)
壁纸 [bìzhǐ] II ADJ [+ hat, aeroplane, cup, plate,
towel] 纸制的 [zhǐzhì de] III VT [+ room] 贴
壁纸于 [tiē bìzhǐ yú] IV **papers** NPL **1** (also:
identity papers) 身份证件 [shēnfèn zhèngjiàn]
2 (documents) 文件 [wénjiàn] ▶ **a piece of
paper** (odd bit) 一张纸; (sheet) 一张纸 ▶ **to put
sth down on paper** 把某事写下来

paperback ['peɪpəbæk] I N [C] 平装书
[píngzhuāng shū] II ADJ ▶ **paperback edition**
平装版 [píngzhuāng bǎn]

paper bag N [C] 纸制购物袋 [zhǐzhì gòuwùdài]

paper clip N [C] 回形针 [huíxíngzhēn]

paper handkerchief N [C] 面巾纸
[miànjīnzhǐ]

paper hanky (inf) N [C] 面巾纸 [miànjīnzhǐ]

paperweight ['peɪpəweɪt] N [C] 压纸器
[yāzhǐqì]

paperwork ['peɪpəwə:k] N [U] 文书工作
[wénshū gōngzuò]

paprika ['pæprɪkə] N [U] 辣椒粉 [làjiāofěn]

pap smear, pap test [pæp-] N [C] 子宫颈涂
片检查 [zǐgōngjǐng túpiàn jiǎnchá] [英 = smear
(test)]

par [pɑː(r)] N [U] **1** (standard) ▸ **to be below par** 一般水平以下 [yìbān shuǐpíng yǐxià] **2** (GOLF) 标准杆数 [biāozhǔn gānshù] ▸ **to be on a par with** 与⋯同等水平 ▸ **to feel below** or **under par** 感觉身体不适 ▸ **under/over par** (GOLF) 低于/高于标准杆数 ▸ **to be par for the course** (fig) 不出所料的

paracetamol [pærə'siːtəmɒl] N [C/U] 扑热息痛 [pūrèxītòng]

parachute ['pærəʃuːt] I N [C] 降落伞 [jiàngluòsǎn] II VI 跳伞 [tiàosǎn] III VT 伞投 [sǎntóu] ▸ **to parachute sb/sth into** [+ country, region] 用降落伞将某人/某物空投到

parade [pə'reɪd] I N [C] 游行 [yóuxíng] II VT **1** [+ prisoners] 使⋯游街 [shǐ⋯yóujiē] **2** (show off) [+ object, person, wealth, knowledge] 炫耀 [xuànyào] III VI 游行 [yóuxíng]

paradise ['pærədaɪs] N **1** [U] (REL) (heaven) 天堂 [tiāntáng] **2** [C/U] (fig) 乐园 [lèyuán]

paradox ['pærədɒks] N [C] **1** (situation) 自相矛盾 [zìxiāng máodùn] **2** (statement) 反论 [fǎnlùn]

paradoxically [pærə'dɒksɪklɪ] ADV 自相矛盾地 [zìxiāng máodùn de]

paraffin ['pærəfɪn] (BRIT) N [U] (also: **paraffin oil**) 石蜡 [shílà] [美= **kerosene**]

paragraph ['pærəgrɑːf] N [C] 段落 [duànluò] ▸ **to begin a new paragraph** 开始一个新的段落

Paraguay ['pærəgwaɪ] N **1** (country) 巴拉圭 [Bālāguī] **2** (river) ▸ **the Paraguay** 巴拉圭河 [Bālāguī Hé]

Paraguayan [pærə'gwaɪən] I ADJ 巴拉圭的 [Bālāguī de] II N [C] 巴拉圭人 [Bālāguīrén]

parallel ['pærəlɛl] I ADJ **1** [+ lines, walls, streets] 平行的 [píngxíng de] **2** (fig) (similar) 相似的 [xiāngsì de]; (simultaneous) 同时的 [tóngshí de] **3** (COMPUT) 并行的 [bìngxíng de] II N [C] **1** (similarity) 相似 [xiāngsì] **2** (GEO) 纬度圈 [wěidùquān] III VT 与⋯相似 [yǔ⋯xiāngsì] ▸ **to be parallel to sth** 与某物平行 ▸ **to run parallel (with** or **to)** (lit) 平行; (fig) (与⋯) 同时发生 ▸ **in parallel (with sth)** (与某事) 同时 ▸ **to draw parallels between/with** 从⋯中/与⋯找到相似之处

paralyse, (US) **paralyze** ['pærəlaɪz] VT **1** (MED) 使瘫痪 [shǐ tānhuàn] **2** [+ airport, organization, production] 使瘫痪 [shǐ tānhuàn] ▸ **to be paralysed with** or **by fear/indecision** 害怕/优柔寡断得不知所措

paralysed, (US) **paralyzed** ['pærəlaɪzd] (MED) ADJ [+ person, limb] 瘫痪的 [tānhuàn de]

paralysis [pə'rælɪsɪs] (MED) N [U] 瘫痪 [tānhuàn]

paralyze ['pærəlaɪz] (US) VT = **paralyse**

paramedic [pærə'mɛdɪk] N [C] 护理人员 [hùlǐ rényuán]

paramount ['pærəmaʊnt] ADJ 最高的 [zuìgāo de] ▸ **of paramount importance** 至

关重要

paranoid ['pærənɔɪd] (inf) ADJ (suspicious) 多疑的 [duōyí de]

parasite ['pærəsaɪt] N [C] **1** (lit) (insect) 寄生虫 [jìshēngchóng]; (plant) 寄生植物 [jìshēng zhíwù] **2** (fig) (person) 寄生虫 [jìshēngchóng]

parcel ['pɑːsl] I N [C] (package) 包裹 [bāoguǒ] [美= **package**] II VT (also: **parcel up**) 打包 [dǎbāo] ▸ **parcel out** [+ land] 瓜分 [guāfēn]

pardon ['pɑːdn] I VT **1** (LAW) [+ prisoner] 赦免 [shèmiǎn] **2** (forgive) [+ sin, error, person] 原谅 [yuánliàng] II N [C] (LAW) 赦免 [shèmiǎn] ▸ **to pardon sb for sth/for doing sth** 原谅某人某事/做某事 ▸ **I beg your pardon!, pardon me!** (I'm sorry!) 对不起！ ▸ **(I beg your) pardon?,** (US) **pardon me?** (what did you say?) 请你原谅刚才说什么？ ▸ **pardon me!** (ESP BRIT) (to get attention) 劳驾！

○**parent** ['pɛərənt] I N [C] **1** (father) 父亲 [fùqīn] **2** (mother) 母亲 [mǔqīn] II **parents** NPL 父母 [fùmǔ]

parental [pə'rɛntl] ADJ [+ guidance, responsibility] 父母的 [fùmǔ de]

parish ['pærɪʃ] N [C] **1** [of church] 教区 [jiàoqū] **2** (civil) 行政堂区 [xíngzhèng tángqū]

park [pɑːk] I N [C] **1** (public garden) 公园 [gōngyuán] **2** (BRIT) (private) 私家庄园 [sījiā zhuāngyuán] II VT 停放 [tíngfàng] III VI 停车 [tíngchē]

parked ['pɑːkt] ADJ [+ driver, car] 停着的 [tíng zhe de]

parking ['pɑːkɪŋ] N [U] 停车 [tíngchē] ▸ **"no parking"** "严禁停车"

parking lights (US) NPL = **sidelights**

parking lot (US) N [C] 停车场 [tíngchēchǎng] [英= **car park**]

parking meter N [C] 停车计时器 [tíngchē jìshíqì]

parking ticket N [C] 违章停车罚款单 [wéizhāng tíngchē fákuǎndān]

parliament ['pɑːləmənt] (BRIT) N [C/U] 议会 [yìhuì]

parliamentary [pɑːlə'mɛntərɪ] ADJ 议会的 [yìhuì de]

parlour, (US) **parlor** ['pɑːlə(r)] N [C] **1** (in house) 起居室 [qǐjūshì] **2** (shop) ▸ **pizza/ice-cream parlour** 比萨饼/冰淇淋店 [bǐsàbǐng/bīngqílín diàn]

Parmesan [pɑːmɪ'zæn] N [U] (also: **Parmesan cheese**) 巴尔马干酪 [Bā'ěrmǎ Gānlào]

parole [pə'rəʊl] I N [U] 假释 [jiǎshì] II VT 假释 [jiǎshì] ▸ **to be on parole** 宣誓后获释

parrot ['pærət] N [C] 鹦鹉 [yīngwǔ]

parsley ['pɑːslɪ] N [U] 欧芹 [ōuqín]

parsnip ['pɑːsnɪp] N [C] 欧洲防风根 [ōuzhōu fángfēnggēn]

parson ['pɑːsn] (o.f.) N [C] (Church of England) 教

区牧师 [jiàoqū mùshī]; (in other church) 牧师 [mùshī]

⚪ **part** [pɑːt] I N 1 [C/U] (section, division) 部分 [bùfen] ▷ She spent the first part of her honeymoon in hospital. 她蜜月的头一部分是在医院里度过的。▷ The exam is divided into two parts. 考试分为两部分。▷ This is still a major problem in some parts of the world. 这仍然是世界上某些地方的一个主要问题。**2** [C] (piece) [of machine, vehicle] 部件 [bùjiàn] ▷ a group of workers who make parts for generators 一组生产发电机部件的工人 **3** [C] (THEAT, CINE, TV, RAD) (role) 角色 [juésè] ▷ King Lear is the most difficult part in the play. 李尔王无疑是这部戏中最难的角色。**4** [S] (involvement) 份儿 [fènr] ▷ If only he could conceal his part in the accident. 但愿他会隐瞒他在事故中也有份儿。**5** [C] (of serialized story, play) 分部 [fēnbù] **6** [C] (US) (in hair) 分缝 [fēnfèng] [英 = **parting**] **7** [C] (MUS) 声部 [shēngbù] II ADV = **partly** III VT 1 (separate) [+ objects] 使分开 [fēnkāi]; [+ couple, family members] 使分开 [shǐ fēnkāi]; [+ fighters] 拉开 [lākāi] **2** (divide) [+ hair] 分 [fēn] IV VI 1 (leave each other) [couple +] 分手 [fēnshǒu] **2** (take one's leave) [people +] 分别 [fēnbié] **3** (divide) [crowd +] 分开 [fēnkāi] ▶ to take part in (participate in) 参加 ▶ to play a part in (be part of) 在⋯中起作用 ▶ to look the part 仪表得体 ▶ to take sth in good part 不因某事而见怪 ▶ to take sb's part 支持某人 ▶ on sb's part 就⋯方面 ▶ for my/his part 就我/他来说 ▶ for the most part (usually, generally) 大抵 ▶ in part 在某种程度上 ▶ for the better or best part of the day 一天中大部分时间 ▶ to be part and parcel of sth 某事物的主要组成部分
▶ **part company** VT FUS [不可拆分] [+ possessions] 放弃 [fàngqì]; [+ money, cash] 花 [huā]

partial ['pɑːʃl] ADJ **1** (incomplete) [+ victory, support, solution] 部分的 [bùfen de] **2** (unjust) 偏袒的 [piāntǎn de] **3** ▶ to be partial to sb/sth 偏爱某人/某事 [piān'ài mǒurén/mǒushì]

partially ['pɑːʃəlɪ] ADV (partly) 部分地 [bùfen de] ▶ **partially sighted/deaf** 半盲/聋

participant [pɑː'tɪsɪpənt] N [C] (in activity, debate, on course etc) 参加者 [cānjiāzhě]

participate [pɑː'tɪsɪpeɪt] VI 参与 [cānyǔ]
▶ **to participate in sth** [+ activity, discussion] 参加某事

participation [pɑːtɪsɪ'peɪʃən] N [U] (in competition, discussion) 参与 [cānyǔ]

particle ['pɑːtɪkl] N [C] [of dust, metal] 微粒 [wēilì]; [of food] 小粒 [xiǎolì]

particular [pə'tɪkjulə(r)] I ADJ **1** (specific) [+ person, thing, time, place] 特定的 [tèdìng de] **2** (special) 特有的 [tèyǒu de] **3** (great) 特别的 [tèbié de] II **particulars** NPL (details) 细节 [xìjié]; (name, address etc) 详情 [xiángqíng] ▶ **in particular** 尤其 ▶ **to be very particular about**

sth (fussy, demanding) 对某事很挑剔

particularly [pə'tɪkjulələɪ] ADV **1** (especially) 尤其 [yóuqí] **2** (really) [+ difficult, good, beautiful, badly] 特别地 [tèbié de]; [like, dislike, want +] 格外地 [géwài de]

parting ['pɑːtɪŋ] I N **1** [C/U] (leave-taking) 分离 [fēnlí] **2** [C/U] (separation) 分界 [fēnjiè] **3** [C] (BRIT) (in hair) 分缝 [fēnfèng] [美 = **part**] II ADJ [+ words, gift, kiss] 临别的 [línbié de]
▶ **parting shot** 临别恶语

partition [pɑː'tɪʃən] I N **1** [C] (wall, screen) 分隔物 [fēngéwù] **2** [U] [of country] 分裂 [fēnliè] II VT **1** [+ room, office] 分隔 [fēngé] **2** [+ country] 分裂 [fēnliè]

partly ['pɑːtlɪ] ADV (to some extent) 部分地 [bùfen de]

partner ['pɑːtnə(r)] I N [C] **1** (wife, husband, girlfriend, boyfriend) 伴侣 [bànlǚ] **2** (in firm) 合伙人 [héhuǒrén] **3** (in treaty, agreement etc) 合作者 [hézuòzhě] **4** (SPORT) 搭档 [dādàng] **5** (for cards, games) 对家 [duìjiā] **6** (at dance) 舞伴 [wǔbàn] II VT [+ person] (at dance) 做⋯的舞伴 [zuò⋯de wǔbàn]; (in card game) 做⋯的对家 [zuò⋯de duìjiā] ▶ **business partner** 生意伙伴

partnership ['pɑːtnəʃɪp] N [C/U] **1** (between people, organizations) 合伙关系 [héhuǒ guānxì] **2** (in firm, business) 合伙人身份 [héhuǒrén shēnfen] ▶ **to go into partnership** or **form a partnership (with sb)** (与某人)合伙做生意

part of speech (pl parts of speech) N [C] 词性 [cíxìng]

partridge ['pɑːtrɪdʒ] N [C] 山鹑 [shānchún]

part-time ['pɑːt'taɪm] I ADJ [+ work, staff, course, student] 兼职的 [jiānzhí de] II ADV [work, study +] 部分时间地 [bùfen shíjiān de]

⚪ **party** ['pɑːtɪ] N [C] **1** (POL) 党 [dǎng] **2** (social event) 聚会 [jùhuì] **3** (group) 群 [qún] **4** (LAW) 一方 [yīfāng] ▶ **birthday party** 生日聚会 ▶ **dinner party** 家宴 ▶ **to give** or **throw** or **have a party** 举行晚会 ▶ **to be (a) party to sth** [+ crime, undertaking] 参与某事

⚪ **pass** [pɑːs] I VT **1** (spend) [+ time] 度过 [dùguò] ▷ The children passed the time playing in the street. 孩子们在街上玩以消磨时间。**2** (hand) ▶ **to pass sb sth** [+ salt, glass, newspaper, tool] 把某物递给某人 [bǎ mǒuwù dìgěi mǒurén] ▷ She passed me her glass. 她把她的玻璃杯递给我。**3** (go past) [+ place, person] 经过 [jīngguò] ▷ We passed the new hotel. 我们经过了那家新旅馆。**4** (move) ▶ **to pass sth through/around/over sth** 将某物穿过/围住/跨过某物 [jiāng mǒuwù chuānguò/wéizhù/kuàguò mǒuwù] **5** (overtake, exceed) [+ vehicle] 超过 [chāoguò] ▷ We got behind a tractor and couldn't pass it. 我们跟在一辆拖拉机后面，没法超过。▷ Contributions for 1986 have already passed the 3 million mark. 1986年的捐款额已超过了300万英镑的数目。**6** [+ exam, test] 通过 [tōngguò] ▷ Kevin has just passed his *driving test.* 凯文刚刚通过驾驶测试。**7** (*approve*) [+*law, proposal*] 批准 [pīzhǔn] ▷ *Many of the laws passed by Parliament are never enforced.* 国会批准的许多法案从未强制执行。**8** (SPORT) ▶ **to pass sb the ball** 把球传给某人 [bǎ qiú chuángěi mǒurén] **II** **1** (*go by*) [*time*+] 过去 [guòqù] ▷ *Several minutes passed.* 几分钟过去了。**2** (*go past*) [*vehicles, people*+] 经过 [jīngguò] ▷ *The ships sounded their hooters as they passed.* 船只经过时鸣汽笛。**3** (*go*) ▶ **to pass through/over/near sth** 穿过/跨过/移近某物 [chuānguò/kuàguò/yíjìn mǒuwù] **4** (*in exam*) 及格 [jígé] ▷ *She told me that I had passed.* 她告诉我我及格了。**5** ▶ **to pass to sb** [*inheritance, estate*+] 传给某人 [chuángěi mǒurén] **III** N [C] **1** (*permit*) 许可证 [xǔkězhèng] **2** (*in mountains*) 隘口 [àikǒu] **3** (SPORT) 传球 [chuánqiú] ▶ **to pass without comment** 默许 ▶ **to pass unnoticed** 被忽略过去 ▶ **to pass for 25** 被认为有25岁 ▶ **to pass as sth/sb** 当作某事/某人 ▶ **I'll pass, thanks** (*inf*) 不用了，谢谢 ▶ **to get a pass (in sth)** (SCOL, UNIV) (某考试) 达到及格标准 ▶ **to make a pass at sb** (*inf*) 向某人调情 ▶ **things have come to a pretty pass** (BRIT: *inf*) 事情到了如此糟糕的境地

▶ **pass around, pass round** VT 传递 [chuándì]
▶ **pass away** VI (*die*) 去世 [qùshì]
▶ **pass by** **I** VI 走过 [zǒuguò] **II** VT [*life, love*+] 漠视 [mòshì]
▶ **pass down** VT [+*customs, inheritance*] 把…往下传 [bǎ…wǎngxià chuán]
▶ **pass off** VI [*event, demonstration*+] 完成 [wánchéng]
▶ **pass off as** VT [+*person, object*] 冒充作 [màochōng zuò] ▷ *She passed him off as her young brother.* 她把他冒充作自己的弟弟。▷ *horse meat passed off as beef* 牛马肉假冒作牛肉 ▶ **to pass o.s. off as sth** 自己冒充作某物
▶ **pass on** **I** VT ▶ **to pass sth on (to sb)** [+*news, information, message*] 把某物传给(某人) [bǎ mǒuwù chuángěi (mǒurén)]; [+*illness*] 把某病传染给(某人) [bǎ mǒubìng chuánrǎn gěi (mǒurén)]; [+*benefits, costs, price rises*] 将某事波及(某人) [jiāng mǒushì bōjí (mǒurén)] **II** VI (*die*) 去世 [qùshì]
▶ **pass out** VI **1** (*faint*) 昏厥 [hūnjué] **2** (BRIT: MIL) 毕业 [bìyè]
▶ **pass over** **I** VT (*ignore*) 不予考虑 [bùyù kǎolù] **II** VI (*die*) 去世 [qùshì]
▶ **pass round** VT = **pass around**
▶ **pass up** VT [+*opportunity, chance*] 放弃 [fàngqì]

passable ['pɑːsəbl] ADJ **1** [+*road*] 可通行的 [kě tōngxíng de] **2** (*acceptable*) [+*restaurant, attempt, quality*] 尚可的 [shàngkě de]

passage ['pæsɪdʒ] N **1** [C] (*corridor*) 走廊 [zǒuláng] **2** [C] (*in book, speech, piece of music*) 段 [duàn] **3** [C] (ANAT) 通道 [tōngdào] **4** [U] (*movement, progress*) 通过 [tōngguò] **5** [C] (*on*

boat) (*journey*) 航行 [hángxíng] ▶ **to clear a passage (through sth)** (从某事物中) 开出一条路 ▶ **the passage of time** 时间的推移

passageway ['pæsɪdʒweɪ] N [C] 走廊 [zǒuláng]

passenger ['pæsɪndʒə(r)] N [C] (*in car, boat, plane etc*) 乘客 [chéngkè]

passer-by [pɑːsə'baɪ] (*pl* **passers-by**) N [C] 过路人 [guòlùrén]

passing ['pɑːsɪŋ] **I** ADJ [+*comment, glimpse, thought*] 短暂的 [duǎnzàn de]; [+*moment*] 飞逝的 [fēishì de] **II** [U] (*of person*) 去世 [qùshì]; (*of era, years, custom*) 消逝 [xiāoshì] ▶ **a passing interest in sb/sth** 对某人/某事短暂的兴趣 ▶ **to bear a passing resemblance to sth/sb** 与某事/某人非常相似 ▶ **in passing** [*mention, note*+] 顺便地

passing place (BRIT) N [C] 窄路会车时车辆的停靠处

passion ['pæʃən] N **1** [U] (*for person*) 情爱 [qíng'ài] **2** [C] (*for cars, sport, politics*) 酷爱 [kù'ài] **3** [U] (*fervour*) 激情 [jīqíng] ▶ **to have a passion for sth** 酷爱某事

passionate ['pæʃənɪt] ADJ **1** [+*person*] (*fervent*) 充满激情的 [chōngmǎn jīqíng de]; (*loving*) 热恋的 [rèliàn de] **2** [+*affair, embrace*] 感情强烈的 [gǎnqíng qiángliè de]

passion fruit (*pl* **passion fruit**) N [C] 西番莲果 [xīfānliánguǒ]

passive ['pæsɪv] **I** ADJ [+*person, attitude*] 消极的 [xiāojí de] **II** N ▶ **the passive** (LING) 被动语态 [bèidòng yǔtài] ▶ **passive resistance** 消极抵抗

passport ['pɑːspɔːt] N **1** [C] 护照 [hùzhào] **2** (*fig*) ▶ **a/the passport to** …的保障 […de bǎozhàng]

passport control N [U] 验照处 [jiǎnzhàochù]

passport office N [C] 护照管理局 [hùzhào guǎnlǐjú]

password ['pɑːswɜːd] N [C] 密码 [mìmǎ]

past [pɑːst] **I** PREP (*in front of, beyond, later than*) 过 [guò] ▷ *He walked past the hat shop.* 他走过了这家帽子店。▷ *The farm was just past the village.* 过了村庄就是农场。▷ *I think we must have gone past the turn.* 我想我们已经过了转弯处。▷ *It's long past bedtime.* 早过了就寝的时间了。**II** ADV (*by*) ▶ **to go/walk/drive past** 经/走/开过 [jīng/zǒu/kāiguò] **III** ADJ (*previous*) [+*life, experience, government*] 过去的 [guòqù de]; [+*week, month, year etc*] 刚过去的 [gāng guòqù de] **IV** N [C] **1** ▶ **the past** 过去 [guòqù]; (*tense*) 过去时 [guòqùshí] **2** [*of person, country*] 过去 [guòqù] ▶ **he ran past me** 他从我身边跑过 ▶ **he's past forty** 他40多岁了 ▶ **it's past midnight** 过了午夜 ▶ **ten/(a) quarter past eight** 8点10/15分 ▶ **I'm past caring** 我已不在乎了 ▶ **to be past it** (BRIT: *inf*) [*person, thing*+] 老而无用了 ▶ **for the past few/3 days** 过去几/3天以来 ▶ **the past**

tense 过去时 ▶ **in the past** (*before now*) 在过去; (*in the past tense*) 用过去时态

pasta ['pæstə] N [U] 意大利面食 [Yìdàlì miànshí]

paste [peɪst] I N **1** [C/U] (*wet mixture*) 浆糊 [jiànghu] **2** [U] (*jewellery*) 人造宝石 [rénzào bǎoshí] **3** [U] (CULIN) ▶ **fish/meat/tomato** *etc* **paste** 鱼/肉/番茄[等]酱 [yú/ròu/fānqié {děng} jiàng] II VT **1** (*stick*) ▶ **to paste sth on/ to sth** [+ *paper, label, poster*] 把某物贴在某物上 [bǎ mǒuwù tiēzài mǒuwù shang] **2** (COMPUT) ▶ **to paste sth into a file** 把某物粘贴在文件里 [bǎ mǒuwù zhāntiē zài wénjiàn lǐ] ▶ **wallpaper paste** 壁纸胶

pastel ['pæstl] I ADJ [+ *colour*] 浅色的 [qiǎnsè de] II N **1** [C/U] (*chalk*) 彩色粉笔 [cǎisè fěnbǐ] **2** [c] (*picture*) 彩色粉笔画 [cǎisè fěnbǐhuà]

pasteurized ['pæstʃəraɪzd] ADJ [+ *milk, cream*] 巴氏杀菌法的 [bāshì shājūnfǎ de]

pastime ['pɑːstaɪm] N [c] 消遣 [xiāoqiǎn]

pastor ['pɑːstə(r)] N [c] 牧师 [mùshī]

past participle [-'pɑːtɪsɪpl] N [c] 过去分词 [guòqù fēncí]

pastry ['peɪstrɪ] N **1** [U] (*dough*) 油酥面团 [yóusū miàntuán] **2** [c] (*cake*) 酥皮糕点 [sūpí gāodiǎn]

pasture ['pɑːstʃə(r)] N **1** [U] (*grazing land*) 牧草 [mùcǎo] **2** [c] (*field*) 牧场 [mùchǎng]

pasty [*n* 'pæstɪ, *adj* 'peɪstɪ] I N [c] (BRIT) 馅饼 [xiànbǐng] II ADJ [+ *complexion, face*] 苍白的 [cāngbái de]

pat [pæt] I VT [+ *hand, shoulder, dog*] 轻拍 [qīngpāi] II N [c] ▶ **to give sb a pat (on the shoulder/arm)** (在某人肩/臂上)轻拍一下 [(zài mǒurén jiān/bì shang) qīngpāi yīxià] III ADJ [+ *answer, remark*] 敷衍了事的 [fūyǎn liǎoshì de] ▶ **to pat sb on the head/arm** 拍拍某人的头/胳膊 ▶ **to give sb/o.s. a pat on the back** (*fig*) 对某人/自己表示赞同 ▶ **he knows it off pat,** (US) **he has it down pat** 他对这了如指掌

patch [pætʃ] I N [c] **1** (*piece of material*) 补钉 [bǔdīng] **2** (*over eye*) 罩 [zhào] **3** (*area*) 斑片 [bānpiàn] II VT [+ *clothes, roof, tyre*] 补 [bǔ] ▶ **vegetable/cabbage** *etc* **patch** 蔬菜/卷心菜{等}地 ▶ **(to go through) a bad/rough patch** 经受不幸/困难时期 ▶ **patch up** VT **1** [+ *clothes, roof, tyre*] 修补 [xiūbǔ] **2** (*fig*) [+ *marriage, relationship*] 弥合 [míhé]; [+ *quarrel*] 平息 [píngxī]

patchy ['pætʃɪ] ADJ **1** (*uneven*) [+ *colour, lawn, fog, rain*] 不均匀的 [bù jūnyún de]; [+ *performance, progress, education*] 杂凑的 [záicòu de] **2** (*incomplete*) [+ *information, knowledge, results*] 不调和的 [bù tiáohé de]

pâté ['pæteɪ] N [C/U] (CULIN) 肉酱 [ròujiàng]

patent ['peɪtnt] I N [c] 专利权 [zhuānlìquán] II VT 取得…的专利权 [qǔdé…de zhuānlìquán]

III ADJ [+ *nonsense, lie*] 显而易见的 [xiǎn ér yì jiàn de]

paternal [pə'tə:nl] ADJ [+ *responsibility, love*] 父亲般的 [fùqīn bān de] ▶ **paternal grandmother/grandfather** 祖母/父

path [pɑːθ] N [c] **1** (*track*) 小路 [xiǎolù]; (*in garden*) 小径 [xiǎojìng] **2** [*of bullet, planet, car, person*] 路线 [lùxiàn] **3** (*fig*) (*way*) 道路 [dàolù] ▶ **garden path** 公园小径

pathetic [pə'θɛtɪk] ADJ **1** (*pitiful*) [+ *person, animal*] 可怜的 [kělián de]; [+ *sight, cries*] 哀怜的 [āilián de] **2** (*very poor*) [+ *excuse, effort, attempt*] 不足道的 [bùzúdào de]

pathway ['pɑːθweɪ] N [c] **1** (*path*) 小路 [xiǎolù] **2** (*fig*) (*to success, good career etc*) 途径 [tújìng]

patience ['peɪʃns] N [U] **1** (*tolerance*) 耐心 [nàixīn] **2** (BRIT: CARDS) 单人纸牌游戏 [dānrén zhǐpái yóuxì] ▶ **to lose (one's) patience** 失去耐心

patient ['peɪʃnt] I N [c] (MED) 病人 [bìngrén] II ADJ [+ *person*] 耐心的 [nàixīn de] ▶ **to be patient with sb** 对某人有耐心

patio ['pætɪəu] N [c] 露台 [lùtái]

patriotic [pætrɪ'ɔtɪk] ADJ [+ *person, song, speech*] 爱国的 [àiguó de]

patrol [pə'trəul] I N **1** [c] (*group*) 巡逻队 [xúnluó duì] **2** [c/u] (*activity*) 巡逻 [xúnluó] II VT [+ *city, streets, area*] 在…巡逻 [zài…xúnluó] ▶ **to be on patrol** 在巡逻中 ▶ **to do a patrol (of sth)** (对某处)进行巡逻

patron ['peɪtrən] N [c] **1** (*customer*) [*of pub, hotel*] 主顾 [zhǔgù] **2** (*benefactor*) [*of charity, campaign, group*] 赞助人 [zànzhùrén] ▶ **patron of the arts** 提倡艺术的人

patronize ['pætrənaɪz] VT **1** (*treat condescendingly*) 居高临下地对待 [jū gāo lín xià de duìdài] **2** (*support*) [+ *artist, writer, musician*] 资助 [zīzhù] **3** (*frm*) [+ *shop, firm, restaurant*] 惠顾 [huìgù]

patronizing ['pætrənaɪzɪŋ] ADJ [+ *person*] 居高临下的 [jū gāo lín xià de]; [+ *tone, comment*] 屈尊俯就的 [qūzūn fǔjiù de]

patter ['pætə(r)] I N **1** [S] (*sound*) [*of feet, rain*] 嗒嗒声 [dādāshēng] **2** [U/S] (*talk*) 珠玑妙语 [zhūjī miàoyǔ] II VI [*footsteps, person +*] 嗒嗒地行走 [dādā de xíngzǒu]; [*rain +*] 发出嗒嗒声 [fāchū dādāshēng]

pattern ['pætən] N [c] **1** (*design*) (*on material, carpet*) 花样 [huāyàng] **2** [*of behaviour, activity*] 方式 [fāngshì] **3** (*for sewing, knitting*) 样式 [yàngshì] **4** (*model*) 模范 [mófàn] ▶ **patterns of behaviour** 行为模式

patterned ['pætənd] ADJ [+ *fabric, carpet*] 有图案的 [yǒu tú'àn de]

pause [pɔːz] I N [c] **1** (*temporary halt*) 停顿 [tíngdùn] **2** (MUS) 延长号 [yánchánghào] II VI (*when speaking*) 停顿 [tíngdùn]; (*when doing sth*) 暂停 [zàntíng] ▶ **to pause for breath** 停下来喘口气

pave [peɪv] VT [+ *street, yard, path*] 铺砌 [pūqì] ▸ **to pave the way for sth** 为某事铺平道路

pavement ['peɪvmənt] N [C] 1 (BRIT) (*for pedestrians*) 人行道 [rénxíngdào] [美= **sidewalk**] 2 (US) (*road surface*) 铺筑过的路面 [pūzhù guò de lùmiàn]

pavilion [pə'vɪliən] (BRIT) N [C] 1 (*building*) 休息处 [xiūxi chù] 2 (*temporary structure*) 搭建物 [dājiànwù]

paving ['peɪvɪŋ] N [U] (*material*) 铺筑材料 [pūzhù cáoliào]

paw [pɔː] I N [C] [*of cat, dog, lion, bear*] 爪子 [zhuǎzi] II VT (*also:* **paw at**) (*with paw*) 抓挠 [zhuānáo]; (*with hoof*) 扒 [bā]; (*pej*) (*touch*) 粗鲁地摸弄 [cūlǔ de mōnòng]

pawn [pɔːn] I N [C] 1 (CHESS) 卒 [zú] 2 (*fig*) 工具 [gōngjù] II VT 典当 [diǎndàng]

pawnbroker ['pɔːnbrəukə(r)] N [C] 当铺老板 [dàngpù lǎobǎn]

○ **pay** [peɪ] (*pt, pp* **paid**) I N [U] (*wage, salary*) 工资 [gōngzī] ▷ *The pay is dreadful.* 工资低微。II VT 1 [+ *debt, bill, tax*] 付 [fù] 2 [+ *person*] (*as wage, salary*) ▸ **to get paid** 发工资 [fā gōngzī]; (*for goods, services*) 付给 [fùgěi] 3 ▸ **to pay sb sth** (*as wage, salary, for goods, services*) 付给某人某物 [fùgěi mǒurén mǒuwù] III VI (*be profitable, beneficial*) 有利 [yǒulì] ▸ **how much did you pay for it?** 你买那个花了多少钱? ▸ **I paid 10 pounds for that record** 我买那张唱片花了10英镑 ▸ **to pay the price** *or* **penalty for sth** (*fig*) 为某事付出代价 ▸ **to pay one's way** 自谋生路 ▸ **it pays to be cautious** 小心谨慎不吃亏
▸ **pay back** VT 1 [+ *money, loan*] 偿还 [chánghuán] 2 [+ *person*] (*with money*) 还给 [huángěi]
▸ **pay for** VT FUS [不可拆分] 1 [+ *purchases*] 买 [mǎi] 2 (*fig*) [+ *mistake*] 为…付出代价 [wèi…fùchū dàijià]
▸ **pay in** VT [+ *money, cheque*] 存入账户 [cúnrù zhànghù]
▸ **pay off** I VT 1 [+ *debt, mortgage*] 还清 [huánqīng] 2 [+ *creditor etc*] 付清 [fùqīng] II VI [*scheme, decision, patience +*] 得益 [déyì]
▸ **pay out** VT 1 [+ *rope*] 松出 [sōngchū] 2 [+ *money*] 付出 [fùchū]
▸ **pay up** VI [*person, company +*] 付清 [fùqīng]

payable ['peɪəbl] ADJ [+ *tax, interest*] 应付的 [yīngfù de] ▸ **to make a cheque payable to sb** 开一张可由某人兑现的支票

pay day N [U] 发薪日 [fāxīn rì]

pay envelope (US) N [C] 工资袋 [gōngzī dài] [英= **pay packet**]

payment ['peɪmənt] N 1 [C] (*sum of money*) 付款额 [fùkuǎn é] 2 [U] (*act of paying*) 支付 [zhīfù] ▸ **advance payment** 预付款 ▸ **monthly payment** 月付 ▸ **on payment of** 在支付…的情况下

payout ['peɪaut] N [C] 支出 [zhīchū]

pay packet (BRIT) N [C] 工资袋 [gōngzī dài] [美= **pay envelope**]

payphone ['peɪfəun] N [C] 公用电话 [gōngyòng diànhuà]

payroll ['peɪrəul] N [C] 工资名单 [gōngzī míngdān] ▸ **to be on the/sb's payroll** 受雇/于某公司

pay slip (BRIT) N [C] 薪水单 [xīnshuǐdān]

PC I N ABBR 1 (= *personal computer*) 个人电脑 [gèrén diànnǎo] 2 (BRIT) (= *police constable*) 普通警员 [pǔtōng jǐngyuán] II ADJ ABBR (= *politically correct*) 不会造成冒犯的 [bù huì zàochéng màofàn de]

pc I ABBR (= *per cent*) 百分之 [bǎifēnzhī] II N ABBR (= *postcard*) 明信片 [míngxìnpiàn]

PDA N ABBR (= *personal digital assistant*) 掌上电脑 [zhǎngshàng diànnǎo]

PDT (US) ABBR (= *Pacific Daylight Time*) 太平洋夏令时间 [Tàipíngyáng Xiàlìng Shíjiān]

PE (SCOL) N ABBR (= *physical education*) 体育 [tǐyù]

pea [piː] N [C] 豌豆 [wāndòu]

○ **peace** [piːs] N [U] 1 (*not war*) 和平 [hépíng] 2 (*calm*) [*of place, surroundings*] 宁静 [níngjìng] ▷ *He chose to return to the relative peace of his childhood village.* 他选择回到相对宁静的童年时的村子来。; (*personal*) 平静 [píngjìng] ▷ *the search for this elusive inner peace* 寻找难得的内心平静 ▸ **to be at peace with sb/sth** 对某人/某事平和处之 ▸ **to keep the peace** (*police +*) 维持治安; [*ordinary person +*] 守规矩

peaceful ['piːsful] ADJ 1 [+ *place, time*] 安静的 [ānjìng de] 2 [+ *person*] 平和的 [pínghé de]

peach [piːtʃ] I N [C] 桃 [táo] II ADJ (*in colour*) 桃色的 [táosè de]

peacock ['piːkɔk] N [C] 孔雀 [kǒngquè]

peak [piːk] I N [C] 1 [*of mountain*] 山顶 [shāndǐng] 2 [*of cap*] 舌 [shé] 3 (*fig*) [*of powers, career, fame etc*] 顶峰 [dǐngfēng] II ADJ [+ *level, times*] 高峰的 [gāofēng de] III VI [*person, temperature, crisis, career +*] 达到顶峰 [dádào dǐngfēng]

peanut ['piːnʌt] N [C] 花生 [huāshēng]

peanut butter N [U] 花生酱 [huāshēng jiàng]

pear [pɛə(r)] N [C] 梨 [lí]

pearl [pəːl] N [C] 珍珠 [zhēnzhū]

peasant ['pɛznt] N [C] 农民 [nóngmín]

peat [piːt] N [U] 泥煤 [níméi]

pebble ['pɛbl] N [C] 卵石 [luǎnshí]

peck [pɛk] I VT (*bird +*) 啄 [zhuó] II VI ▸ **to peck at sth** [*bird +*] 啄某物 [zhuó mǒuwù] III VT 1 [*of bird*] 啄 [zhuó] 2 (*kiss*) 匆匆地吻 [cōngcōng de wěn] ▸ **to peck a hole in sth** 在某物上啄一个洞 ▸ **to peck sb on the cheek, give sb a peck on the cheek** 轻吻某人面颊

peckish ['pɛkɪʃ] (BRIT: *inf*) ADJ ▸ **to be** *or* **feel peckish** 觉得有点饿 [juéde yǒudiǎn è]

peculiar [pɪ'kjuːliə(r)] ADJ (*strange*) [+ *person,*

taste, shape, idea] 奇怪的 [qíguài de] ▶ **peculiar to sth/sb** 为某事/某人所特有

peculiarity [pɪkju:lɪˈærɪtɪ] N [c] **1** (*habit*) [*of person*] 怪癖 [guàipǐ] **2** (*characteristic*) [*of person, place, style*] 特质 [tèzhì]

pedal [ˈpɛdl] I N [c] **1** (*on bicycle*) 脚蹬子 [jiǎodēngzi] **2** (*in car, on piano*) 踏板 [tàbǎn] II vi 踩踏板 [cǎitàbǎn]

pedestal [ˈpɛdəstl] N [c] 基座 [jīzuò] ▶ **to put sb on a pedestal** 把某人当偶像崇拜

pedestrian [pɪˈdɛstrɪən] I N [c] 行人 [xíngrén] II adj **1** [+ *street, traffic*] 步行的 [bùxíng de] **2** (*prosaic*) 乏味的 [fáwèi de]

pedestrian crossing (BRIT) N [c] 人行横道 [rénxíng héngdào]

pedestrianized [pɪˈdɛstrɪənaɪzd] adj 步行的 [bùxíng de]

pedestrian precinct (BRIT) N [c] 步行区 [bùxíngqū]

pedigree [ˈpɛdɪgri:] N [c] **1** [*of animal*] 系谱 [xìpǔ] **2** [*of person*] 门第 [méndì] **3** (*track record*) [*of person, sports team*] 记录 [jìlù] ▶ **pedigree dog/cattle** 纯种狗/牛

pedophile [ˈpi:dəufaɪl] (US) N, adj = **paedophile**

pee [pi:] (*inf*) I vi 撒尿 [sāniào] II N ▶ **to have a pee** 撒尿 [sāniào] ▶ **to need a pee** 要撒尿

peek [pi:k] I vi ▶ **to peek at/over/into** *etc* 向/从上/向里 [等] 窥视 [xiàng/cóngshàng/xiànglǐ {děng} kuīshì] II N ▶ **to have** *or* **take a peek (at sth/sb)** 瞥（某物/某人）一眼 [piē (mǒuwù/mǒurén) yīyǎn]

peel [pi:l] I N [U] [*of orange, potato*] 皮 [pí] II vt [+ *vegetables, fruit*] 削 [xiāo] III vi [*paint, wallpaper* +] 剥落 [bōluò]; (*after sunburn etc*) [*skin, back, person* +] 脱皮 [tuōpí]
▶ **peel back** vt 剥开 [bōkāi]
▶ **peel off** vt [+ *label, wrapping etc*] 剥掉 [bōdiào]

peep [pi:p] I N ▶ **to have** *or* **take a peep (at sth/sb)** 瞥（某物/某人）一眼 [piē (mǒuwù/mǒurén) yīyǎn] II N (*look*) 窥视 [kuīshì] ▶ **I didn't hear a peep from him** (*inf*) 我没有听到他一点声响
▶ **peep out** vi (*be visible*) 慢慢露出 [mànmàn lùchū]

peer [pɪə(r)] I N [c] **1** (BRIT) (*noble*) 贵族 [guìzú] **2** (*equal*) 同等的人 [tóngděng de rén] **3** (*contemporary*) 同龄人 [tónglíngrén] II vi ▶ **to peer at sb/sth** 盯着看某人/某事 [dīngzhe kàn mǒurén/mǒushì]

peg [pɛg] I N [c] **1** (*for coat, hat, bag*) 挂钉 [guàdīng] **2** (BRIT) (*also:* **clothes peg**) 衣夹 [yījiā] **3** (*also:* **tent peg**) 系帐篷的桩 [jì zhàngpeng de zhuāng] II vt ▶ **to peg sth at/to sth** [+ *price, rate, level*] 将某物固定于某物 ▶ **to peg the washing on the line** 把洗好的衣服夹在晾衣绳上

pelican [ˈpɛlɪkən] N [c] 鹈鹕 [tíhú]

pelican crossing (BRIT) N [c] 自控人行横道

[zìkòng rénxínghéngdào]

pellet [ˈpɛlɪt] N [c] **1** [*of paper, mud, dung*] 小团 [xiǎotuán] **2** (*for shotgun*) 小弹丸 [xiǎo dànwán] **3** [*of animal feed*] 丸 [wán]

pelt [pɛlt] I vt ▶ **to pelt sb with sth** 向某人扔某物 [xiàng mǒurén rēng mǒuwù] II vi (*inf*) (*run*) 飞奔 [fēibēn] III N [c] (*animal skin*) 毛皮 [máopí] ▶ **it is** *or* **the rain is pelting down** (*inf*) 大雨倾盆

pelvis [ˈpɛlvɪs] N [c] 骨盆 [gǔpén]

pen [pɛn] I N **1** [c] (*for writing*) 笔 [bǐ]; (*also:* **fountain pen**) 自来水笔 [zìláishuǐbǐ]; (*also:* **ballpoint pen**) 圆珠笔 [yuánzhūbǐ] **2** [c] (*enclosure*) (*for sheep, pigs*) 栏 [lán] **3** (*US:* *inf*) (*prison*) ▶ **the pen** 监狱 [jiānyù] II vt (*frm*) [+ *letter, note, article*] 写 [xiě] ▶ **to put pen to paper** 下笔 ▶ **to be penned in** *or* **up** [*person, animal* +] 被关起来

penalize [ˈpi:nəlaɪz] vt **1** ▶ **to penalize sb (for sth/for doing sth)** (SPORT) (因某事/做某事) 判罚某人 [(yīn mǒushì/zuò mǒushì) pànfá mǒurén]; (*in exam*) (因某事/做某事) 扣某人分 [(yīn mǒushì/zuò mǒushì) kòu mǒurén fēn]; (*disadvantage*) (因某事/做某事) 使某人处不利地位 [(yīn mǒushì/zuò mǒushì) shǐ mǒurén chǔ bùlì dìwèi] **2** [+ *activity, attitude*] 处罚 [chǔfá]

penalty [ˈpɛnltɪ] N [c] **1** (*punishment, fine*) 处罚 [chǔfá] **2** (FOOTBALL, RUGBY) 罚球 [fáqiú]

pence [pɛns] (BRIT) NPL *of* **penny**

pencil [ˈpɛnsl] N [c] 铅笔 [qiānbǐ]
▶ **pencil in** vt [+ *appointment, person*] 暂定为 [zàndìng wéi]

pencil case N [c] 铅笔盒 [qiānbǐhé]

pencil sharpener N [c] 铅笔刀 [qiānbǐdāo]

pendant [ˈpɛndnt] N [c] 垂饰 [chuíshì]

pending [ˈpɛndɪŋ] I prep 直至 [zhízhì] II adj (*frm*) [+ *business, lawsuit, divorce*] 未决的 [wèijué de]

penetrate [ˈpɛnɪtreɪt] vt [*light, water, sound* +] 透过 [tòuguò]; [*person* +] [+ *territory, forest*] 进入 [jìnrù]; [+ *profession, organisation*] 进入 [jìnrù]; [+ *enemy group etc*] 打入 [dǎrù]

penfriend [ˈpɛnfrɛnd] (BRIT) N [c] 笔友 [bǐyǒu] [美= **pen pal**]

penguin [ˈpɛŋgwɪn] N [c] 企鹅 [qǐ'é]

penicillin [pɛnɪˈsɪlɪn] N [U] 青霉素 [qīngméisù]

peninsula [pəˈnɪnsjulə] N [c] 半岛 [bàndǎo]

penis [ˈpi:nɪs] N [c] 阴茎 [yīnjìng]

penitentiary [pɛnɪˈtɛnʃərɪ] (US) N [c] 监狱 [jiānyù]

penknife [ˈpɛnnaɪf] (*pl* **penknives**) N [c] 小刀 [xiǎodāo]

penniless [ˈpɛnɪlɪs] adj [+ *person*] 身无分文的 [shēn wú fēnwén de]

penny [ˈpɛnɪ] (*pl* **pennies** *or* (BRIT) **pence**) N **1** (BRIT) (*after 1971*) 便士 [biànshì] **2** (*US:* *inf*) 分 [fēn] ▶ **it was worth every penny** 那非常值

得 ► **it won't cost you a penny** 这不会花你一分一厘

pen pal (US) N [C] 笔友 [bǐyǒu]〔英=**penfriend**〕

pension ['pɛnʃən] N [C] (from state) 养老金 [yǎnglǎojīn]; (from employer) 退休金 [tuìxiūjīn] ► **pension off** VT 发给…养老金使其退休 [fāgěi…yǎnglǎojīn shǐqí tuìxiū]

pensioner ['pɛnʃənə(r)] (BRIT) N [C] 领养老金的人 [lǐng yǎnglǎojīn de rén]〔美=**retiree**〕

Pentagon ['pɛntəgən] (US) N ► **the Pentagon** 五角大楼 [Wǔjiǎo Dàlóu]

penthouse ['pɛnthaus] N [C] 屋顶公寓 [wūdǐng gōngyù]

penultimate [pɛ'nʌltɪmət] ADJ [+ paragraph, day] 倒数第二的 [dàoshǔ dì'èr de]

⊙ **people** ['piːpl] I NPL 1 (individuals) 人 [rén] ▷ There were 120 people at the lecture. 120人去听了上座。2 (generalizing) 人们 [rénmen] ▷ There has been a complete change in people's ideas on the subject. 人们完全改变了对这个问题的看法。3 ► **the people** (ordinary people) 人民 [rénmín] ▷ a rift between the people and their leadership 人民和领导层的不和; (POL) 国民 [guómín] II N [C] (nation, race) 民族 [mínzú] ▷ the native peoples of Central America 中美洲的土著民族 III VT (populate) 居住于 [jūzhù yú] ► **old people** 老人 ► **young people** 年轻人 ► **many people** 许多人 ► **people say that...** 有人说… ► **a man of the people** 同人民打成一片的人

pepper ['pɛpə(r)] I N 1 (spice) 胡椒粉 [hújiāofěn] 2 [C] (vegetable) 胡椒 [hújiāo] II VT ► **to pepper sth with sth** 将某物接二连三地点缀于某物 [jiāng mǒuwù jiē èr lián sān de diǎnzhuì yú mǒuwù]

peppermint ['pɛpəmɪnt] N 1 [C] (sweet, candy) 薄荷糖 [bòhe táng] 2 [U] (plant) 胡椒薄荷 [hújiāo bòhe]

per [pəː(r)] PREP 每 [měi] ► **per day** 每天 ► **per person** 每人 ► **per hour** 每小时 ► **per kilo** 每公斤 ► **per annum** 每年 ► **per capita** 每人 ► **as per your instructions** (frm) 按照你的指示

perceive [pə'siːv] VT 1 [+ sound, light, difference] 察觉 [chájué] 2 (understand) 理解 [lǐjiě] ► **to perceive sb/sth as being/doing sth** 认为某人/某物为/做某事

⊙ **per cent, percent** [pə'sɛnt] (pl **per cent**) N [c] 百分之… [bǎifēnzhī…] ► **a 20 per cent discount** 优惠百分之20 ► **by 15 per cent** 以百分之15

percentage [pə'sɛntɪdʒ] N [C] (amount) 百分数 [bǎifēnshù] ► **to be paid on a percentage basis** 按百分比支付

perception [pə'sɛpʃən] N 1 [U] (perspicacity) 悟性 [wùxìng] 2 [C] (idea) 看法 [kànfǎ] 3 [C] (way of thinking) 感知 [gǎnzhī]

perceptive [pə'sɛptɪv] ADJ 1 [+ person] 观察敏锐的 [guānchá mǐnruì de] 2 [+ comment, analysis] 富有见地的 [fùyǒu jiàndì de]

perch [pəːtʃ] I N 1 [C] (for bird) 栖息地 [qīxīdì] 2 [C] (pl **perch**) (fish) 鲈鱼 [lúyú] II VI 1 [bird +] 栖息 [qīxī] 2 [person +] 坐 [zuò]

percussion [pə'kʌʃən] N [U] 打击乐器 [dǎjī yuèqì]

perfect [adj, n 'pəːfɪkt, vb pə'fɛkt] I ADJ 1 (faultless) [+ weather, behaviour] 完美的 [wánměi de]; [+ sauce, skin, teeth] 无瑕的 [wúxiá de] 2 (ideal) [+ crime, solution, example] 理想的 [lǐxiǎng de] 3 (complete) [+ sense, nonsense, madness] 完全的 [wánquán de]; [+ idiot, fool, stranger] 绝对的 [juéduì de] II VT [+ technique, skill] 使完善 [shǐ wánshàn] III N ► **the perfect (tense)** 完成(时) [wánchéng(shí)] ► **perfect for sb/sth** 对某人/某事完全合适 ► **he's a perfect stranger to me** 对我来说他完全是个陌生人

perfection [pə'fɛkʃən] N [U] (faultlessness) 完美 [wánměi] ► **to perfection** [+ done, cooked] 恰到好处

perfectly ['pəːfɪktlɪ] ADV 1 [perform, work, do, speak +] 非常好地 [fēicháng hǎo de] 2 [suit, capture +] 完美地 [wánměi de] 3 (emphatic) [+ honest, reasonable, clear] 绝对地 [juéduì de] ► **I'm perfectly happy with the situation** 我对这个情况完全满意 ► **you know perfectly well that...** 你知道得很清楚…

perform [pə'fɔːm] I VT 1 [+ task] 执行 [zhíxíng]; [+ operation] 施行 [shīxíng]; [+ ceremony] 举行 [jǔxíng] 2 [+ piece of music, dance, play] 表演 [biǎoyǎn] II VI 1 (function) [person, organization, business +] 表现 [biǎoxiàn]; [instrument, vehicle +] 运转 [yùnzhuǎn] 2 [actor, musician, singer, dancer +] 演出 [yǎnchū]

performance [pə'fɔːməns] N 1 [C] (THEAT) (by actor, musician, singer, dancer) 表演 [biǎoyǎn]; [of play, show] 演出 [yǎnchū] 2 [U] [of employee, surgeon, athlete, team] 表现 [biǎoxiàn]; [of company, economy] 运作 [yùnzuò]; [of car, engine] 性能 [xìngnéng] ► **the team put up a good performance** 该队表现良好

performer [pə'fɔːmə(r)] N [C] (actor, musician, singer, dancer) 表演者 [biǎoyǎnzhě] ► **to be a good/poor performer** 有造诣/水平差的表演者

perfume ['pəːfjuːm] I N 1 [C/U] 香水 [xiāngshuǐ] 2 [C] (liter) (smell) [of flowers, spices] 芳香 [fāngxiāng] II VT (liter) [+ air, room] 使…散发香味 [shǐ…sànfā xiāngwèi]; (intentionally) 洒香水 [sǎ xiāngshuǐ]

⊙ **perhaps** [pə'hæps] ADV 可能 [kěnéng] ► **perhaps he'll come** 他可能会来 ► **perhaps not** 未必

perimeter [pə'rɪmɪtə(r)] N [C] 周边 [zhōubiān]

period ['pɪərɪəd] I N [C] 1 (interval, stretch) 周期 [zhōuqī] 2 (time) 时期 [shíqī] 3 (era) 时代 [shídài]

4 (SCOL) 课时 [kèshí] **5** (ESP US) (punctuation mark) 句号 [jùhào] ［英=**full stop**］ **6** (also: menstrual period) 月经期 [yuèjīngqī] II ADJ [+ costume, furniture etc] 古式的 [gǔshì de] ▶ **for a period of three weeks** 3周的时间 ▶ **the holiday period** (BRIT) 假期 ▶ **I won't do it. Period.** 我不愿意做。就这样。 ▶ **to have one's period** 来例假

periodic [pɪərɪ'ɒdɪk] ADJ [+ event, occurrence] 周期性的 [zhōuqīxìng de]

periodical [pɪərɪ'ɒdɪkl] I N [C] 期刊 [qīkān] II ADJ 定期的 [dìngqī de]

periodically [pɪərɪ'ɒdɪklɪ] ADV 定期地 [dìngqī de]

peripheral [pə'rɪfərəl] I ADJ **1** [+ issue, activity] 边缘的 [biānyuán de] **2** [+ area, vision] 外围的 [wàiwéi de] II N [C] (COMPUT) 外围设备 [wàiwéi shèbèi] ▶ **to be peripheral to sth** 对某事不重要

perish ['perɪʃ] VI **1** (die) 死亡 [sǐwáng] **2** (ESP BRIT) [rubber, elastic, leather +] 老化 [lǎohuà]

perjury ['pə:dʒərɪ] N [U] 伪证 [wěizhèng] ▶ **to commit perjury** 作伪证

perk [pə:k] (inf) N [C] 好处 [hǎochù] ▶ **perk up** I VI (cheer up) 活跃起来 [huóyuè qǐlai] II VT 使活泼 [shǐ kuàihuo]

perm [pə:m] I N [C] (BRIT) 烫发 [tàngfà] ［美= **permanent**］ II VT ▶ **to have one's hair permed** 烫头发 [tàng tóufa]

permanent ['pə:mənənt] I ADJ [+ relationship, feature, solution] 持久的 [chíjiǔ de]; [+ damage] 永久的 [yǒngjiǔ de]; [+ state, job, position] 长期的 [chángqī de] II N (US) = **perm** ▶ **permanent address** 固定地址 ▶ **I'm not permanent here** 我不会一直呆在这里

permanently ['pə:mənəntlɪ] ADV **1** (for ever) [affect, damage +] 永远地 [yǒngyuǎn de] **2** [stay, live +] 一直地 [yīzhí de]; [+ locked, open, frozen] 长期地 [chángqī de]

permissible [pə'mɪsɪbl] ADJ 容许的 [róngxǔ de]

permission [pə'mɪʃən] N [U] **1** (consent) 准许 [zhǔnxǔ] **2** (official authorization) 批准 [pīzhǔn] ▶ **to give sb permission to do sth** (consent) 许可某人做某事; (official authorization) 批准某人做某事

permit [n 'pə:mɪt, vb pə'mɪt] I N [C] (authorization) 许可证 [xǔkězhèng] II VT (frm) **1** (allow) 允许 [yǔnxǔ] **2** (make possible) 容许 [róngxǔ] ▶ **fishing permit** 捕鱼许可证 ▶ **to permit sb to do sth** (allow) 允许某人做某事; (make possible) 使某人可能做某事 ▶ **weather permitting** 天气许可的话

perpendicular [pə:pən'dɪkjulə(r)] I ADJ [+ line, surface] 垂直的 [chuízhí de] II N [C] ▶ **the perpendicular** (GEOM) 垂直线 [chuízhíxiàn] ▶ **perpendicular to** 与⋯垂直

perplex [pə'plɛks] VT 使⋯迷惑 [shǐ⋯míhuò]

persecute ['pə:sɪkju:t] VT 迫害 [pòhài]

persecution [pə:sɪ'kju:ʃən] N [U] 迫害 [pòhài]

persevere [pə:sɪ'vɪə(r)] VI ▶ **to persevere (with sth)** 百折不挠做(某事) [bǎi zhé bù náo zuò (zuò mǒushì)]

Persian ['pə:ʃən] I ADJ 波斯的 [Bōsī de] II N **1** [U] (language) 波斯语 [Bōsīyǔ] **2** [C] (person) 波斯人 [Bōsīrén]

Persian Gulf N ▶ **the Persian Gulf** 波斯湾 [Bōsīwān]

persist [pə'sɪst] VI [rain, problem, symptom etc +] 持续 [chíxù] ▶ **to persist with sth** 执意坚持某事 ▶ **to persist in doing sth** 坚持不懈地做某事

persistence [pə'sɪstəns] N [U] **1** (determination) 坚持不懈 [jiānchí bùxiè] **2** (continuing existence) 持续 [chíxù]

persistent [pə'sɪstənt] ADJ **1** [+ smell, noise] 不断的 [bùduàn de]; [+ problem, rain, wind] 持续的 [chíxù de]; [+ symptom, cough] 顽固性的 [wángùxìng de]; [+ rumour, report] 连续不断的 [liánxù bùduàn de] **2** [+ person] 坚持不懈的 [jiānchí bùxiè de]

⊙ **person** ['pə:sn] (pl gen **people**) N [C] 人 [rén] ▶ **in person** [appear, collect, sing +] 亲自 ▶ **on or about one's person** 带在身上 ▶ **first/second/third person** 第一/二/三人称

> **person** 的复数形式通常为 **people**。
> They were both lovely, friendly people... There were a lot of people at the party.
> **persons** 只用于正式场合和法律用语中。Persons who wish to adopt a child may contact their local social services department.

personal ['pə:snl] ADJ **1** (individual) [+ telephone number, bodyguard] 私人的 [sīrén de]; [+ opinion, habits] 个人的 [gèrén de]; [+ care, contact, appearance, appeal] 亲自的 [qīnzì de] **2** (private) [+ life, matter, relationship] 私人的 [sīrén de] **3** (against sb) [+ remark, attack] 人身的 [rénshēn de] ▶ **personal belongings or property** 私人物品 ▶ **nothing personal!** 不针对个人！

personal assistant N [C] 私人秘书 [sīrén mìshū]

personal computer N [C] 个人电脑 [gèrén diànnǎo]

personal details NPL 个人信息 [gèrén xìnxī]

personality [pə:sə'nælɪtɪ] N **1** [C/U] (character) 个性 [gèxìng] **2** [C] (famous person) 名人 [míngrén]

personally ['pə:snəlɪ] ADV **1** (for my part) 就我个人来说 [jiù wǒ gèrén láishuō] **2** (in person) 亲自 [qīnzì] **3** [meet, know +] 个人地 [gèrén de] ▶ **to take sth personally** 认为某事是针对个人的

personal organizer N [C] 个人备忘录 [gèrén bèiwànglù]

personal stereo N [C] 随身听 [suíshēntīng]

personify [pə'sɒnɪfaɪ] VT **1** (embody) 是⋯的化身 [shì⋯de huàshēn] **2** (represent) [+ quality] 象征 [xiàngzhēng]

personnel [pɜːsə'nɛl] **I** NPL (staff) 人员 [rényuán] **II** N [U] (department) 人事部门 [rénshì bùmén]

perspective [pə'spɛktɪv] **1** [C] (way of thinking) 视角 [shìjiǎo] **2** [U] (ART) 透视法 [tòushìfǎ] ▶ to put sth into perspective (fig) 正确地看待某事

perspiration [pɜːspɪ'reɪʃən] N [U] 汗 [hàn]

persuade [pə'sweɪd] VT ▶ to persuade sb to do sth 劝说某人做某事 [quànshuō mǒurén zuò mǒushì] ▶ to persuade sb that... 说服某人⋯ ▶ to be persuaded of sth (certain) 确信某事

persuasion [pə'sweɪʒən] N **1** [U] 说服 [shuōfú] **2** [C] (frm) (belief) 信仰 [xìnyǎng] ▶ people of all political persuasions 持各种政见的人们

persuasive [pə'sweɪsɪv] ADJ [+ person] 有说服力的 [yǒu shuōfúlì de]; [+ argument, evidence] 令人信服的 [lìngrén xìnfú de]

Peru [pə'ruː] N 秘鲁 [Bìlǔ]

Peruvian [pə'ruːvjən] **I** ADJ 秘鲁的 [Bìlǔ de] **II** N [C] 秘鲁人 [Bìlǔrén]

perverse [pə'vɜːs] ADJ [+ person] 刚愎的 [gāngbì de]; [+ behaviour, remark] 背理的 [bèilì de]; [+ delight, pleasure] 违反常情的 [wéifǎn chángqíng de]

pervert [n 'pɜːvɜːt, vb pə'vɜːt] **I** N [C] 堕落者 [duòluòzhě] **II** VT (frm) **1** (corrupt) [+ person, mind] 腐蚀 [fǔshí] **2** (distort) [+ truth, custom] 曲解 [qūjiě] ▶ to pervert the course of justice 滥用司法程序

pessimist ['pɛsɪmɪst] N [C] 悲观主义者 [bēiguān zhǔyìzhě]

pessimistic [pɛsɪ'mɪstɪk] ADJ [+ person, attitude] 悲观的 [bēiguān de] ▶ to be pessimistic about sth 对某事感到悲观

pest [pɛst] N [C] **1** (insect) 害虫 [hàichóng] **2** (fig) (inf) (nuisance) (person) 讨厌的人 [tǎoyàn de rén]

pester ['pɛstə(r)] VT 烦扰 [fánrǎo] ▶ to pester sb for sth 缠着某人要某物 ▶ to pester sb to do sth 缠住某人做某事

pesticide ['pɛstɪsaɪd] N [C] 杀虫剂 [shāchóngjì]

pet [pɛt] **I** N [C] **1** (animal) 宠物 [chǒngwù] **II** ADJ [+ theory, subject, project] 特别的 [tèbié de] **III** VT (stroke) [+ person, animal] 抚摸 [fǔmō] **IV** VI (sexually) 爱抚 [àifǔ] ▶ teacher's pet (favourite) 老师的宠儿 ▶ pet dog/rabbit etc 宠物狗/兔{等} ▶ pet hate 特别讨厌的事物

petal ['pɛtl] N [C] 花瓣 [huābàn]

peter out ['piːtə-] VI [road, stream +] 逐渐消失 [zhújiàn xiāoshī]; [conversation, meeting +] 逐渐停息 [zhújiàn tíngxī]

petite [pə'tiːt] ADJ [+ woman] 娇小的 [jiāoxiǎo de]

petition [pə'tɪʃən] **I** N [C] **1** (signed document) 请愿书 [qǐngyuànshū] **2** (LAW) 诉状 [sùzhuàng] **II** VT (LAW) 请愿 [qǐngyuàn] **III** VI (LAW) ▶ to petition for divorce 起诉离婚 [qǐsù líhūn] ▶ to petition to do sth 申请做某事

petrified ['pɛtrɪfaɪd] (fig) ADJ (terrified) 吓呆的 [xiàdāi de] ▶ to be petrified of sth 很害怕某事

petrify ['pɛtrɪfaɪ] ['pɛtrəl] VT (terrify) 使吓呆 [shǐ xiàdāi]

petrol ['pɛtrəl] (BRIT) N [U] 汽油 [qìyóu] [美= gas, gasoline]

petroleum [pə'trəʊlɪəm] N [U] 石油 [shíyóu]

petrol pump (BRIT) N [C] **1** (at petrol station) 加油泵 [jiāyóubèng] [美= gas pump] **2** (in engine) 油泵 [yóubèng]

petrol station (BRIT) N [C] 加油站 [jiāyóuzhàn] [美= gas station]

petrol tank (BRIT) N [C] 汽油罐 [qìyóuguàn] [美= gas tank]

petticoat ['pɛtɪkəʊt] (o.f.) N [C] (full length) 裙子 [qúnzi]; (underskirt) 衬裙 [chènqún]

petty ['pɛtɪ] ADJ **1** (trivial) 琐碎的 [suǒsuì de] **2** (small-minded) 狭隘的 [xiá'ài de] **3** (minor) [+ crime, criminal, theft] 不严重的 [bù yánzhòng de]

pew [pjuː] N [C] (in church) 靠背长凳 [kàobèi chángdèng]

pewter ['pjuːtə(r)] N [U] 白蜡 [báilà]

PG (BRIT: CINE) N ABBR (= parental guidance) 宜在家长指导下观看 [yí zài jiāzhǎng zhǐdǎo xià guānkàn]

PG13 (US: CINE) N ABBR (= parental guidance) 13岁以下儿童宜在家长指导下观看

phantom ['fæntəm] **I** N [C] (ghost) 幽灵 [yōulíng] **II** ADJ (fig) 幻想的 [huànxiǎng de]

pharmacist ['fɑːməsɪst] N [C] **1** (person) 药剂师 [yàojìshī] **2** (shop) (also: pharmacist's) 药店 [yàodiàn]

pharmacy ['fɑːməsɪ] N **1** [C] (shop) 药店 [yàodiàn] **2** [U] (science) 药学 [yàoxué]
▪用法参见 chemist

phase [feɪz] **I** N [C] 阶段 [jiēduàn] **II** VT [+ action, change] 分阶段进行 [fēn jiēduàn jìnxíng]
▶ **phase in** VT 分阶段引进 [fēn jiēduàn yǐnjìn]
▶ **phase out** VT 分阶段结束 [fēn jiēduàn jiéshù]

PhD N ABBR (= Doctor of Philosophy) (qualification) 博士学位 [bóshì xuéwèi]; (person) 博士 [bóshì]

pheasant ['fɛznt] N **1** [C] (bird) 雉 [zhì] **2** [U] (meat) 雉肉 [zhìròu]

phenomena [fə'nɒmɪnə] NPL of phenomenon

phenomenal [fə'nɒmɪnl] ADJ [+ increase, talent, success] 非凡的 [fēifán de]

phenomenon [fə'nɒmɪnən] (pl **phenomena**) N [C] 现象 [xiànxiàng] ▶ a natural phenomenon 自然现象

Philippines ['fɪlɪpiːnz] NPL ▶ the Philippines

(*also:* **Republic of the Philippines**) 菲律宾 [Fēilǜbīn]

philosopher [fɪˈlɒsəfə(r)] N [c] 哲学家 [zhéxuéjiā]

philosophical [fɪləˈsɒfɪkl] ADJ **1** [+ *ideas, discussion, debate*] 哲学的 [zhéxué de] **2** (*calm, resigned*) 达观的 [dáguān de] ▸ **to be philosophical about sth** 对某事泰然处之

philosophy [fɪˈlɒsəfɪ] N **1** [u] (*subject*) 哲学 [zhéxué] **2** [c] (*set of ideas*) [*of philosopher*] 哲学体系 [zhéxué tǐxì] **3** [c] (*personal beliefs*) 人生观 [rénshēngguān]

phlegm [flɛm] N [u] 痰 [tán]

phobia [ˈfəʊbjə] N [c] 恐惧 [kǒngjù] ▸ **a phobia about sth/about doing sth** 对某事/做某事的恐惧症

phone [fəʊn] I N **1** [u] (*system*) (*also:* **the phone**) 电话 [diànhuà] **2** [c] (*object*) 电话 [diànhuà] II VT [+ *person, organization*] 打电话给 [dǎ diànhuà gěi] III VI 打电话 [dǎ diànhuà] ▸ **to be on the phone** (*possess a phone*) 装有电话;(*be calling*) 在通话 ▸ **by phone** 通过电话 ▸ **over the phone** 通过电话
▸ **phone back** I VT **1** (*return call of*) 给…回电话 [gěi…huí diànhuà] **2** (*call again*) 再给…打电话 [zài gěi…dǎ diànhuà] II VI **1** (*return call*) 回电 [huídiàn] **2** (*call again*) 再打电话 [zài dǎ diànhuà]
▸ **phone up** I VT 给…打电话 [gěi…dǎ diànhuà] II VI 打电话 [dǎ diànhuà]

phone bill N [c] 话费单 [huàfèi dān]

phone book N [c] 电话簿 [diànhuà bù]

phone booth (US) N = **phone box**

phone box (BRIT) N [c] 电话亭 [diànhuà tíng] [美= **phone booth**]

phone call N [c] 电话 [diànhuà] ▸ **to make a phone call** 打电话

phonecard [ˈfəʊnkɑːd] N [c] 电话卡 [diànhuà kǎ]

phone number N [c] 电话号码 [diànhuà hàomǎ]

phonetics [fəˈnɛtɪks] N [u] 语音学 [yǔyīnxué]

phoney [ˈfəʊnɪ] (*inf*) I ADJ [+ *address, accent*] 伪造的 [wěizào de]; [+ *person*] 冒充的 [màochōng de] II N [c] 冒充者 [màochōngzhě]

⊙ **photo** [ˈfəʊtəʊ] (*inf*) N [c] 照片 [zhàopiàn] ▸ **to take a photo (of sb/sth)** 给(某人/某物)拍照片

photocopier [ˈfəʊtəʊkɒpɪə(r)] N [c] 影印机 [yǐngyìnjī]

photocopy [ˈfəʊtəʊkɒpɪ] I N [c] 影印本 [yǐngyìnběn] II VT [+ *document, picture*] 影印 [yǐngyìn]

photograph [ˈfəʊtəgræf] I N [c] 照片 [zhàopiàn] II VT [+ *person, object, place*] 给…拍照 [gěi…pāizhào] ▸ **to take a photograph of sb/sth** 给某人/某物拍照

photographer [fəˈtɒgrəfə(r)] N [c] 摄影师 [shèyǐngshī]

photographic [fəʊtəˈgræfɪk] ADJ [+ *equipment, paper, evidence*] 摄影的 [shèyǐng de]

photography [fəˈtɒgrəfɪ] N [u] 摄影 [shèyǐng]

phrase [freɪz] I N [c] **1** (*expression*) 习语 [xíyǔ] **2** (*in phrase book, dictionary*) 短语 [duǎnyǔ] **3** (*not clause*) 词组 [cízǔ] **4** (*quotation*) 警句 [jǐngjù] **5** (MUS) 短句 [duǎnjù] II VT (*word*) (*in speech*) 表达 [biǎodá]; (*in writing*) 措辞 [cuòcí] ▸ **set phrase** 固定词组 ▸ **turn of phrase** 措辞

phrase book N [c] 常用词手册 [chángyòngcí shǒucè]

physical [ˈfɪzɪkl] I ADJ **1** (*not mental*) [+ *needs, harm, exercise, strength*] 生理的 [shēnglǐ de] **2** [+ *geography, properties*] 自然的 [zìrán de] **3** (*material*) [+ *object, world*] 物质的 [wùzhì de] **4** (*scientific*) [+ *law, explanation*] 物理的 [wùlǐ de] **5** (*sexual*) [+ *love, relationship, attraction*] 肉体上的 [ròutǐ shang de] II N [c] 体格检查 [tǐgé jiǎnchá]

physical education N [u] 体育 [tǐyù]

physically [ˈfɪzɪklɪ] ADV [+ *fit, attractive*] 身体上地 [shēntǐ shang de]

physician [fɪˈzɪʃən] (US) N [c] 医生 [yīshēng]

physicist [ˈfɪzɪsɪst] N [c] 物理学家 [wùlǐxué jiā]

physics [ˈfɪzɪks] N [u] 物理学 [wùlǐxué]

physiotherapist [fɪzɪəʊˈθɛrəpɪst] N [c] 理疗师 [lǐliáoshī]

physiotherapy [fɪzɪəʊˈθɛrəpɪ] N [u] 物理疗法 [wùlǐ liáofǎ]

physique [fɪˈziːk] N [c] 体格 [tǐgé]

pianist [ˈpiːənɪst] N [c] (*professional*) 钢琴家 [gāngqínjiā]; (*amateur*) 钢琴演奏者 [gāngqín yǎnzòuzhě]

piano [pɪˈænəʊ] N [c] 钢琴 [gāngqín]

pick [pɪk] I N **1** [c] (*also:* **pickaxe**) 镐 [gǎo] **2** ▸ **the pick of** …的精华 […de jīnghuá] II VT **1** (*choose*) 选择 [xuǎnzé] **2** (*gather*) [+ *fruit, flowers*] 采摘 [cǎizhāi] **3** (*remove, take*) ▸ **to pick sth off/out of/from sth** 把某物从某物中摘下/挑出/拣出 [bǎ mǒuwù cóng mǒuwù zhōng zhāixià/tiāochū/jiǎnchū] **4** [+ *lock*] 拨开 [bōkāi] **5** [+ *scab, spot*] 除掉 [chúdiào] ▸ **take your pick** 随意挑选 ▸ **to pick one's nose** 挖鼻孔 ▸ **to pick one's teeth** 剔牙 ▸ **to pick sb's brains** (*inf*) 向某人请教 ▸ **to pick sb's pocket** 扒窃某人的口袋 ▸ **to pick a fight/argument (with sb)** (向某人)挑起争斗/争论 ▸ **to pick one's way across/through sth** 谨慎地通过某物
▸ **pick at** VT FUS [不可拆分] [+ *food*] 一点点地吃 [yìdiǎndiǎn de chī]
▸ **pick off** VT (*shoot*) [+ *people, aircraft*] 瞄准射击 [miáozhǔn shèjī]
▸ **pick on** (*inf*) VT FUS [不可拆分] 找…的碴 [zhǎo…de chá]
▸ **pick out** VT **1** (*make out*) [+ *person, thing*] 分辨出 [fēnbiàn chū] **2** (*select*) [+ *person, thing*] 挑中 [tiāozhòng]

▶ **pick up I** VI (*improve*) [*health +*] 恢复 [huīfù]; [*economy, business etc +*] 好转 [hǎozhuǎn] **II** VT **1** [+ *object*] (*take hold of*) 拿起 [náqǐ]; (*from floor, ground*) 捡起 [jiǎnqǐ] **2** (*collect*) [+ *person, parcel*] 接 [jiē] **3** (*catch*) [+ *illness*] 获得 [huòdé] **4** [+ *hitchhiker*] 搭载 [dāzài] **5** (*inf*) [+ *person*] (*for sexual encounter*) 随便结识 [suíbiàn jiéshí] **6** (*inf*) (*learn*) [+ *language, skill, idea*] 学会 [xuéhuì] **7** (*arrest*) 收捕 [shōubǔ] **8** (*receive*) [+ *signal, radio station*] 收到 [shōudào] ▶ **to pick up where one left off** 从停下来的地方继续 ▶ **to pick o.s. up** (*after falling*) 自己站起来 ▶ **to pick up speed** 加速

pickle ['pɪkl] **I** N [C/U] (*preserve*) 腌菜 [yāncài] **II** VT (*in vinegar*) 腌渍 [yānzì]; (*in brine*) 腌制 [yānzhì] **III pickles** NPL 腌菜 [yāncài] ▶ **to be/get in a pickle** (*inf*) 处于/进入进退两难的境地

pickpocket ['pɪkpɒkɪt] N [C] 扒手 [páshǒu]

pick-up ['pɪkʌp] N [C] (*also*: **pick-up truck**) 轻型小货车 [qīngxíng xiǎohuòchē]

picnic ['pɪknɪk] **I** N [C] (*meal*) 野餐 [yěcān] **II** VI 去野餐 [qù yěcān] ▶ **to have a picnic** 野餐 ▶ **to go on** *or* **for a picnic** 去野餐

picnic area N [C] 野餐区 [yěcān qū]

picture ['pɪktʃə(r)] **I** N [C] **1** (*painting, drawing, print*) 画 [huà] **2** (*photograph*) 照片 [zhàopiàn] **3** (*TV*) 图像 [túxiàng] **4** (*film, movie*) 电影 [diànyǐng] **5** (*fig*) (*description*) 描绘 [miáohuì]; (*situation*) 局面 [júmiàn] **II** VT (*imagine*) 想象 [xiǎngxiàng] **III the pictures** NPL (BRIT: *inf*) (*the cinema*) 电影院 [diànyǐngyuàn] ［美 = **the movies**］▶ **to take a picture of sb/sth** 给某人/某物拍照 ▶ **to paint a vivid/gloomy/bleak etc picture (of sth)** 描绘了（某事的）一副生动/灰暗/凄凉｛等｝的景象 ▶ **to put sb in the picture** 使某人非常了解情况 ▶ **to get the picture** (*inf*) 了解情况 ▶ **to have a picture of sth** (*mentally*) 非常明白某事 ▶ **to be pictured** 登照片

picture messaging [-'mɛsɪdʒɪŋ] N [U] 彩信 [cǎixìn]

picturesque [pɪktʃə'rɛsk] ADJ [+ *village, building*] 美丽如画的 [měilì rúhuà de]

pie [paɪ] N [C/U] 派 [pài]

piece [piːs] N [C] **1** (*fragment*) 块 [kuài] **2** (*length*) [*of string, ribbon, sticky tape*] 段 [duàn] **3** (*portion*) [*of cake, bread, chocolate*] 块 [kuài] **4** (*article, work of art, composition*) 篇 [piān] **5** (*for game, chess, draughts*) 棋子 [qízǐ] ▶ **in pieces** 破碎 ▶ **to take sth to pieces** (*dismantle*) 把某物全部拆开来 ▶ **to be in one piece** [*object +*] 完整无损; [*person +*] 安然无恙 ▶ **piece by piece** 一点一点地 ▶ **to pick up the pieces** 重新振作起来 ▶ **to go to pieces** (*inf*) 崩溃 ▶ **a piece of paper** 一张纸 ▶ **a piece of clothing** 一块布 ▶ **a piece of furniture** 一件家具 ▶ **a piece of machinery** 一部机器 ▶ **a piece of advice** 一条建议 ▶ **a piece of research** 一项调查 ▶ **a twenty-piece**

dinner service 20人的套餐服务 ▶ **to say one's piece** 吐出心里话 ▶ **a 10p piece** (BRIT) 一枚10便士硬币

▶ **piece together** VT **1** [+ *information, truth*] 搜集 [sōují] **2** [+ *object*] 拼合 [pīnhé]

pie chart N [C] 饼形图 [bǐngxíng tú]

pier [pɪə(r)] N [C] 码头 [mǎtóu]

pierce [pɪəs] VT [+ *surface, material, skin*] 刺 [cì] ▶ **to have one's ears pierced** 扎耳洞

pierced [pɪəst] ADJ [+ *ears, nose, lip*] 穿孔的 [chuānkǒng de]

piercing ['pɪəsɪŋ] **I** ADJ **1** [+ *cry, scream*] 尖锐的 [jiānruì de] **2** [+ *eyes, stare*] 敏锐的 [mǐnruì de] **3** [+ *wind*] 刺骨的 [cìgǔ de] **II** N [C] 人体穿孔 [réntǐ chuānkǒng]

pig [pɪg] N [C] **1** 猪 [zhū] **2** (*inf*) (*person*) (*unkind*) 粗俗的人 [cūsú de rén]; (*greedy*) 贪吃的人 [tānchī de rén]

pigeon ['pɪdʒən] N [C] 鸽子 [gēzi]

piggy bank ['pɪgɪ-] N [C] 储蓄罐 [chǔxùguàn]

pigpen ['pɪgpɛn] (US) N = **pigsty**

pigsty ['pɪgstaɪ] (ESP BRIT) N [C] **1** (*on farm*) 猪圈 [zhūjuàn] ［美 = **pigpen**］**2** (*inf*) (*room, house*) 邋遢的房子 [lātā de fángzi]

pigtail ['pɪgteɪl] N [C] 辫子 [biànzi]

pike [paɪk] (*pl* **pike** *or* **pikes**) N [C] (*fish*) 狗鱼 [gǒuyú]

pilchard ['pɪltʃəd] N [C] 沙丁鱼 [shādīngyú]

pile [paɪl] **I** N [C] **1** [*of earth, leaves, boxes, clothes etc*] 堆 [duī] **2** [*of carpet*] 绒面 [róngmiàn] **3** (*pillar*) 桩 [zhuāng] **II** VT [+ *objects*] 堆起 [duīqǐ] **III piles** NPL (*haemorrhoids*) 痔疮 [zhìchuāng] ▶ **piles of** *or* **a pile of sth** (*inf*) 一大堆某物 ▶ **in a pile** 堆成堆 ▶ **to pile into/out of sth** (*inf*) [+ *vehicle, building*] 一窝蜂地进入/离开某处

▶ **pile on** VT ▶ **to pile it on** (*inf*) 夸张 [kuāzhāng]

▶ **pile up** VI **1** [*papers +*] 堆积 [duījī] **2** [*problems, work +*] 积累 [jīlěi]

pile-up ['paɪlʌp] N [C] 数辆车同时碰撞事件 [shùliàng chē tóngshí pèngzhuàng shìjiàn]

pilgrimage ['pɪlgrɪmɪdʒ] N [C] 朝圣 [cháoshèng] ▶ **to go on** *or* **make a pilgrimage to** 前去朝圣

pill [pɪl] N [C] 药丸 [yàowán] ▶ **the pill** (*contraceptive pill*) 避孕药 ▶ **to be on the pill** 服避孕药

pillar ['pɪlə(r)] N [C] 柱子 [zhùzi] ▶ **a pillar of society/of the community** 社会/社区的支柱

pillow ['pɪləu] N [C] 枕头 [zhěntou]

pillowcase ['pɪləukeɪs] N [C] 枕套 [zhěntào]

pilot ['paɪlət] **I** N [C] **1** (AVIAT) 飞行员 [fēixíngyuán] **2** (NAUT) 领航员 [lǐnghángyuán] **3** (TV) (*also*: **pilot episode**) 试播片断 [shìbō piànduàn] **II** ADJ [+ *scheme, study*] 试验性的 [shìyànxìng de] **III** VT [+ *aircraft*] 驾驶 [jiàshǐ] ▶ **to pilot a scheme/programme** 试行计划/项目

pimple ['pɪmpl] N [C] 粉刺 [fěncì]

PIN [pɪn] N ABBR (= *personal identification number*) (*also:* **PIN number**) 密码 [mìmǎ]

pin [pɪn] I N [C] **1** (*used in sewing*) 大头针 [dàtóuzhēn] **2** (*badge*) 饰针 [shìzhēn] **3** (*in wheel, machine*) 轴钉 [zhóudīng] **4** (*in bone*) 骨钉 [gǔdīng] **5** (*in grenade*) 保险针 [bǎoxiǎnzhēn] **6** (BRIT: ELEC) ▶ **a 3-pin plug** 三相插头 [sānxiàng chātóu] II VT **1** (*on wall, door, board*) 钉住 [dìngzhù]; (*to clothes*) 别住 [biézhù] **2** [+ *person, part of body*] (*in position*) 使不能动 [shǐ bùnéng dòng] ▶ **pins and needles** 发麻 ▶ **to pin sth on sb** 把某事归罪于某人 ▶ **to pin the blame on sb** 推说是某人的责任 ▶ **to pin one's hopes on sth/sb** 寄希望于某事/某人 ▶ **pin down** VT **1** ▶ **to pin sb down (to sth)** 迫使某人履行(某事) [pòshǐ mǒurén lǚxíng (mǒushì)] **2** (*identify*) [+ *date, location, source of problem*] 确定 [quèdìng]

pinafore ['pɪnəfɔː(r)] (ESP BRIT) N [C] **1** (*also:* **pinafore dress**) 无袖女裙 [wúxiù nǚqún] **2** (*apron*) 围裙 [wéiqún]

pinch [pɪntʃ] I N **1** [c] [*of spice, salt, sugar*] 一撮 [yīcuō] **2** ▶ **to give sb a pinch** 捏某人 [niē mǒurén] II VT **1** [+ *person*] (*with finger and thumb*) 捏 [niē] **2** (*inf*) (*steal*) 偷窃 [tōuqiè] III VI [*shoe* +] 夹脚 [jiājiǎo] ▶ **at a pinch** 必要时 ▶ **to feel the pinch** 感到缺钱

pine [paɪn] I N **1** [C] (*also:* **pine tree**) 松树 [sōngshù] **2** [U] (*wood*) 松木 [sōngmù] II VI ▶ **to pine (for sth, place)** [+ *person, place*] 朝思暮想(某人/某物) [zhāosī mùxiǎng (mǒurén/mǒuwù)] ▶ **pine away** VI 憔悴 [qiáocuì]

pineapple ['paɪnæpl] N [C] 菠萝 [bōluó]

ping [pɪŋ] N (*noise*) 砰 [pēng]

ping-pong® ['pɪŋpɒŋ] (*inf*) N [U] 乒乓球 [pīngpāngqiú]

pink [pɪŋk] I ADJ 粉红色的 [fěnhóngsè de] II N [C/U] 粉红色 [fěnhóngsè]

pinpoint ['pɪnpɔɪnt] VT [+ *cause, problem*] 查明 [chámíng]; [+ *position, place*] 指出 [zhǐchū]

pint [paɪnt] N [C] **1** (*measure*) (BRIT) (568 *cc*) 品脱 [pǐntuō]; (US) (473 *cc*) 品脱 [pǐntuō] **2** (BRIT: *inf*) (*beer*) 一品脱啤酒 [yī pǐntuō píjiǔ] ▶ **to go for a pint** (BRIT: *inf*) 去酒吧喝酒

pioneer [paɪə'nɪə(r)] I N [C] **1** [*of scheme, science, method*] 先驱 [xiānqū] **2** (*early settler*) 拓荒者 [tuòhuāngzhě] II VT [+ *technique, invention*] 倡导 [chàngdǎo]

pious ['paɪəs] ADJ **1** (*religious*) 虔诚的 [qiánchéng de] **2** (*sanctimonious*) 虚伪的 [xūwěi de] **3** (*empty*) [+ *hopes, words*] 空洞的 [kōngdòng de]

pip [pɪp] I N [C] [*of apple, orange*] 种子 [zhǒngzi] II VT (BRIT) (*fig*) ▶ **to be pipped at the post** 最后一刻功败垂成 [zuìhòu yīkè bàibèi] III **the pips** NPL (BRIT) (*time signal on radio*) 报时信

号 [bàoshí xìnhào]; (*during phone call*) 嘟嘟声 [dūdū shēng]

pipe [paɪp] I N [C] **1** (*for water, gas*) 管子 [guǎnzi] **2** (*for smoking*) 烟斗 [yāndǒu] **3** (MUS) (*instrument*) 管乐器 [guǎnyuèqì]; [*of organ*] 管 [guǎn] II VT [+ *water, gas, oil*] 管道输送 [guǎndào shūsòng] III **pipes** NPL (*also:* **bagpipes**) 风笛 [fēngdí] ▶ **pipe down** (*inf*) VI (*be quiet*) 安静下来 [ānjìng xiàlái]

pipeline ['paɪplaɪn] N [C] (*for oil, gas*) 管道 [guǎndào] ▶ **to be in the pipeline** 在酝酿中

piper ['paɪpə(r)] N [C] 风笛手 [fēngdíshǒu]

piping ['paɪpɪŋ] I N [U] **1** (*pipes*) 管道 [guǎndào] **2** (*on clothes*) 滚边 [gǔnbiān] II ADV ▶ **piping hot** [+ *water, food, coffee*] 滚烫 [gǔntàng]

pirate ['paɪərət] I N [C] 海盗 [hǎidào] II VT [+ *video, CD, software etc*] 盗版 [dàobǎn]

pirated ['paɪərətɪd] (COMM) ADJ [+ *video, CD, software etc*] 盗版的 [dàobǎn de]

Pisces ['paɪsiːz] N **1** [U] (*sign*) 双鱼座 [Shuāngyú Zuò] **2** [C] (*person*) 双鱼座的人 [Shuāngyú Zuò de rén] ▶ **I'm (a) Pisces** 我是双鱼座的

piss [pɪs] (*inf!*) I VI (*urinate*) 撒尿 [sāniào] II N [U] (*urine*) 尿 [niào] ▶ **it's pissing down** (BRIT) (*raining*) 下大雨 ▶ **piss off!** 滚开！ ▶ **to piss o.s. (laughing)** (BRIT) 大笑不止 ▶ **to be pissed off (with sb/sth)** (*annoyed*) 厌烦(某人/某事) ▶ **to take the piss (out of sb)** (BRIT) 取笑(某人)

pissed [pɪst] (*inf!*) ADJ (*drunk*) 醉的 [zuì de]

pistol ['pɪstl] N [C] 手枪 [shǒuqiāng]

piston ['pɪstən] N [C] 活塞 [huósāi]

pit [pɪt] I N [C] **1** (*coal mine*) 矿井 [kuàngjǐng] **2** (*hole in ground*) (*road*) 坑 [kēng] **3** (US: *gravel pit*) 采石场 [cǎishíchǎng] **4** (US) (*fruit stone*) 核 [hé] **5** (*also:* **orchestra pit**) 乐队池 [yuèduìchí] II VT ▶ **to pit one's wits/skills against sb** 与某人较量才智/技能 [yǔ mǒurén jiàoliàng cáizhì/jìnéng] III **the pits** NPL (AUT) 维修加油站 [wéixiū jiāyóuzhàn] ▶ **in the pit of one's stomach** 在内心深处 ▶ **to be pitted against sb/sth** 与某人/某物较量

pitch [pɪtʃ] I N **1** [C] (BRIT: SPORT) (*field*) 球场 [qiúchǎng] [美= **field**] **2** [S/U] [*of note, sound, voice*] 音高 [yīngāo] **3** [S] (*fig*) (*level, degree*) [*of feeling, situation*] 程度 [chéngdù] **4** [U] (*tar*) 沥青 [lìqīng] **5** [C] (*also:* **sales pitch**) 推销商品的行话 [tuīxiāo shāngpǐn de hánghuà] **6** [U] (NAUT) [*of boat*] 颠簸 [diānbǒ] II VT **1** [+ *tent*] 搭 [dā] **2** (*throw*) [+ *ball, object*] 投 [tóu] **3** (*knock*) [+ *person*] 摔出 [shuāichū] **4** (*set*) [+ *price, message*] 定位 [dìngwèi] III VI **1** (*fall forwards*) 重重倒下 [zhòngzhòng dǎoxià] **2** (NAUT) [*boat* +] 颠簸 [diānbǒ] ▶ **pitch in** (*inf*) VI [*person* +] 起劲地干 [qǐjìn de gàn]

pitch-black ['pɪtʃ'blæk] ADJ [+ *night, place*] 漆

黑的 [qīhēi de]

pitcher ['pɪtʃə(r)] N [C] **1** (ESP US) (jug) 大罐 [dàguàn] **2** (US: BASEBALL) 投手 [tóushǒu]

pitfall ['pɪtfɔːl] N [C] 隐患 [yǐnhuàn]

pith [pɪθ] N [U] **1** (of orange, lemon) 髓 [suǐ] **2** (fig) (of matter, question) 精髓 [jīngsuǐ]

pitiful ['pɪtɪful] ADJ **1** (touching) (+ person, appearance, sight etc) 可怜的 [kělián de] **2** (lamentable) (+ excuse, attempt, effort etc) 可鄙 的 [kěbǐ de]

pity ['pɪtɪ] I N **1** [U] (compassion) 同情 [tóngqíng] **2** (misfortune) ▶ it is a pity that... 真遗憾… [zhēn yíhàn…] II VT (+ person) 同 情 [tóngqíng] ▶ to take pity on sb 怜悯某人 ▶ what a pity! 真可惜!

pizza ['piːtsə] N [C] 比萨饼 [bǐsàbǐng]

placard ['plækɑːd] N [C] (outside shop) 招贴 [zhāotiē]; (in demonstration) 标语牌 [biāoyǔ pái]

placate [plə'keɪt] (frm) VT (+ person) 安慰 [ānwèi]; (+ opposition, anger) 平息 [píngxī]

⊕ **place** [pleɪs] I N **1** [C] (location) 地方 [dìfang] ▷ We were looking for a good place to camp. 我们 寻找露营的地方。▷ The cellar was a very dark place. 地窖是个很黑的地方。▷ They seem to have scheduled the president to be in two places at once. 他们似乎想让总统同时出现在两个不同的地 方。▷ The pain was always in the same place. 总是 在一个地方疼。▷ I keep these cards in a very safe place. 我把卡片放在一个非常安全的地方。**2** [c] (empty) (space) 空位 [kòngwèi] ▷ I found a place to park. 我找到了一个空位停车。; (seat) 座 位 [zuòwèi] ▷ There was only one place left for him to sit. 只有一个座位留给他。; (at university, on course, on committee, in team) 名额 [míng'é] ▷ I got a place at a teachers' training college nearby. 我 得到了附近师范学院的一个名额。**3** [s] (inf) (home) 家 [jiā] ▷ Do you want to meet at your place or mine? 你想在你家还是我家见面? **4** (in street names) 路 [lù] ▷ Laurel Place 劳瑞尔路 **5** [s] (role) (in society, system, world) 地位 [dìwèi] ▷ Britain's place in the world 英国在世界上的地 位 **6** [C] (in competition) 名次 [míngcì] ▷ Britain won third place at the games in Barcelona. 英国 在巴塞罗那奥运会上得了第3名。**7** (US: inf) ▶ some/every/no/any place 某些/每个/没 有/任何地方 [mǒuxiē/měigè/méiyǒu/rènhé dìfang] ▷ The poor guy obviously had no any place to go. 那个可怜的家伙显然没有任何地 方可去。II VT **1** (put) (+ object) 放 [fàng] ▷ She placed the music on the piano and sat down. 她把乐 谱放在钢琴上, 坐了下来。**2** (classify) (+ person, work, drug) 归类 [guīlèi] ▷ Some place him on a par with Einstein. 有人将他归为与爱因斯坦比 肩的人。**3** (identify) (+ person) 记起 [jìqǐ] ▷ She was looking at me as if she could not quite place me. 她看着我好像记不起我是谁了。▶ from place to place 从一个地方到另一个地方 ▶ all over the place (everywhere) 到处 ▶ in places 有几处

▶ in the first place (first of all) 首先; (originally) 原先 ▶ to change places with sb (fig) 与某人 交换位置 ▶ at sb's place (home) 在某人的家 里 ▶ to sb's place 到某人的家里 ▶ he's going places 他正飞黄腾达 ▶ in sb's/sth's place 代 替某人/某物 ▶ to take sb's/sth's place 代替 某人/某物 ▶ it's not my place to do it 我无权 这么做 ▶ to put sb in his/her place (fig) 煞住 他/她的傲气 ▶ to fall into place (become clear) 开始有头绪; (go well) 开始明朗化 ▶ in place (in correct place) 到位; (ready) 就绪 ▶ out of place (in wrong place) 不在应在的地方; (inappropriate) 不适当的 ▶ to feel out of place 感到不自在 的 ▶ to take place (happen) 发生 ▶ to place an order 订购 ▶ to place an advertisement 打广 告 ▶ to be placed third etc (in race, exam) 得第 3名〔等〕 ▶ to place one's faith in/hopes on sth 对某事寄于信任/希望 ▶ how are you placed? 你有什么安排吗?

placement ['pleɪsmənt] N **1** [C] (job) 职位 [zhíwèi] **2** [U] (placing) (of object) 放置 [fàngzhì]; (in home, school) (of person) 安置 [ānzhì]

place of birth N [C] 出生地 [chūshēngdì]

placid ['plæsɪd] ADJ **1** (+ person) 平静的 [píngjìng de] **2** (+ place, river, life) 宁静的 [níngjìng de]

plague [pleɪg] I N **1** [C] (disease) 瘟疫 [wēnyì] **2** (fig) (of locusts, rats) 灾难 [zāinàn]; (of robberies, attacks) 祸患 [huòhuàn] II VT (fig) (problems, difficulties +) 烦扰 [fánráo] ▶ to plague sb with questions 不断向某人发问

plaice [pleɪs] (pl **plaice**) N [C/U] 鲽鱼 [diéyú]

plain [pleɪn] I ADJ **1** (not patterned) 无图案花 纹的 [wú tú'àn huāwén de] **2** (simple) (+ dress, food, design) 简单的 [jiǎndān de] **3** (clear, easily understood) 清楚的 [qīngchǔ de] **4** (not beautiful) (+ girl, woman) 不漂亮的 [bù piàoliàng de] II ADV (+ wrong, stupid, terrible etc) 简直 [jiǎnzhí] III N [C] **1** (area of land) 平原 [píngyuán] **2** (in knitting) ▶ one plain, one purl 一针平织, 一针 反织 [yīzhēn píngzhī yīzhēn fǎnzhī] ▶ in plain clothes (POLICE) 身穿便服 ▶ it is plain that... 显然… ▶ to make it plain to sb that... 对某人 明确表示…

plain chocolate (BRIT) N [U] 纯巧克力 [chún qiǎokèlì] 〔美= **dark chocolate**〕

plainly ['pleɪnlɪ] ADV **1** (obviously) 显然地 [xiǎnrán de] **2** (distinctly) (hear, see, recognize +) 清楚地 [qīngchǔ de]; (state +) 明确地 [míngquè de]

plaintiff ['pleɪntɪf] (LAW) N [C] 原告 [yuángào]

plait [plæt] I N [C] (of hair) 辫子 [biànzi]; (of rope, leather) 辫状物 [biànzhuàng wù] 〔美= **braid**〕 II VT (+ hair, rope, leather) 编 [biān] 〔美= **braid**〕

⊕ **plan** [plæn] I N [C] **1** (scheme, project) 计划 [jìhuà] **2** (drawing) 详图 [xiángtú] II VT **1** (+ crime, holiday, future etc) 计划 [jìhuà] **2** (design) (+ building, garden etc) 设计 [shèjì] III VI (think ahead) 打算 [dǎsuàn] ▷ *We must plan for the future.* 我们必须为将来做打算. **IV plans** NPL (*intentions*) 计划 [jìhuà] ▷ *Do you have any plans for the weekend?* 你周末有什么计划吗？ ▸ **to go according to plan** 按计划进行 ▸ **to plan to do sth** 计划做某事 ▸ **how long do you plan to stay?** 你准备住多久？ ▸ **to plan for** or **on sth** (*expect*) 预先想到某事 ▸ **to plan on doing sth** 意欲做某事

plane [pleɪn] **I** N [c] **1** 飞机 [fēijī] **2** (MATH) 平面 [píngmiàn] **3** (*fig*) (*level*) [*of existence, consciousness*] 水平 [shuǐpíng] **4** (*tool*) 刨子 [bàozi] **5** (*also*: **plane tree**) 悬铃木 [xuánlíngmù] **II** VT [+ *wood*] 刨 [bào]

planet ['plænɪt] N [c] 行星 [xíngxīng]

plank [plæŋk] N [c] **1** [*of wood*] 板 [bǎn] **2** ▸ **the main/central plank** [*of policy, argument*] 主要/中心政纲准则 [zhǔyào/zhōngxīn zhènggāng zhǔnzé]

planning ['plænɪŋ] N [U] **1** (*organization*) 计划 [jìhuà] **2** (*town planning*) 规划 [guīhuà]

⊙**plant** [plɑːnt] **I** N **1** [c] 植物 [zhíwù] **2** [U] (*machinery*) 机器 [jīqì] ▷ *new plant and equipment* 新的机器设备 **3** [c] (*factory, power station*) 工厂 [gōngchǎng] **II** VT **1** [+ *flower, tree, crop etc*] 栽种 [zāizhòng]; [+ *field, garden*] 种植 [zhòngzhí] ▷ *Alongside the road was a field planted with maize.* 路的两边是种了玉米的田地. **2** (*put secretly*) [+ *microphone, bomb*] 安放 [ānfàng] ▷ *They had planted the bomb beneath the house.* 他们在房子下安放了炸弹. ; [+ *incriminating evidence*] 栽赃 [zāizāng] ▷ *I'm convinced the evidence was planted in John's flat.* 我相信在约翰房里发现的证据是栽赃的. **3** (*place*) [+ *object, kiss*] 放置 [fàngzhì]

plantation [plæn'teɪʃən] N [c] **1** (*for tea, rubber, sugar*) 种植园 [zhòngzhíyuán] **2** [*of trees*] 人工林 [réngōng lín]

plaque [plæk] N **1** [c] (*on building, wall*) 饰板 [shìbǎn] **2** [U] (*on teeth*) 斑 [bān]

plaster ['plɑːstə(r)] **I** N **1** [U] (*for walls, ceilings*) 灰泥 [huīní] ; (*also*: **plaster of Paris**) 熟石灰 [shú shíhuī] **3** [c/U] (BRIT) (*also*: **sticking plaster**) 橡皮膏 [xiàngpígāo] [美= **Band-Aid**] **II** VT **1** [+ *wall*] 用灰泥涂抹 [yòng huīní túmǒ] **2** (*cover*) ▸ **to plaster sth with sth** 用某物贴满某物 [yòng mǒuwù tiēmǎn mǒuwù] ▸ **in plaster** (BRIT) 打了石膏的

plaster cast (MED) N [c] 石膏绷带 [shígāo bēngdài]

plastic ['plæstɪk] **I** N [c/U] 塑料 [sùliào] **II** ADJ **1** [+ *bucket, chair, cup*] 塑料的 [sùliào de] **2** (*flexible*) 可塑的 [kěsù de]

plastic bag N [c] 塑料袋 [sùliào dài]

plastic surgery N [U] 整形手术 [zhěngxíng shǒushù]

plastic wrap (US) N [U] 保鲜膜 [bǎoxiān mó] [英= **clingfilm**]

plate [pleɪt] N **1** [c] (*dish*) 碟 [dié] ; (*for serving*)

托盘 [tuōpán] **2** [c] (*on door*) 牌 [pái] **3** [c] (*on machine*) 金属牌 [jīnshǔ pái] **4** [U] (*metal objects*) (*also*: **gold plate**) 镀金餐具 [dùjīn cānjù]; (*also*: **silver plate**) 银餐具 [yín cānjù] **5** [c] (TYP) (*for printing*) 印版 [yìnbǎn] **6** [c] (*picture, photograph*) 整页插图 [zhěngyè chātú] **7** [c] (*number plate*) 牌照 [páizhào] **8** [c] (*dental plate*) 托牙板 [tuōyá bǎn] ▸ **a plate of cakes/biscuits** 一盘蛋糕/饼干

plateau ['plætəu] (*pl* **plateaus** or **plateaux** ['plætəuz] N [c] **1** 高原 [gāoyuán] **2** (*fig*) [*of activity, process*] 稳定状态 [wěndìng zhuàngtài]

platform ['plætfɔːm] N [c] **1** (*stage*) 平台 [píngtái] **2** (*for landing on*) 平台 [píngtái] **3** (RAIL) 站台 [zhàntái] **4** (POL) 政纲 [zhènggāng] **5** (BRIT) [*of bus*] 出入口平台 [chūrùkǒu píngtái] ▸ **the train leaves from platform 7** 火车从7号站台出发

platinum ['plætɪnəm] N [U] 白金 [báijīn]

platoon [plə'tuːn] N [c] 排 [pái]

platter ['plætə(r)] N [c] 大浅盘 [dà qiǎnpán]

plausible ['plɔːzɪbl] ADJ [+ *theory, explanation*] 似乎有理的 [sìhū yǒulǐ de]; [+ *person, rogue, liar*] 花言巧语的 [huāyán qiǎoyǔ de]

⊙**play** [pleɪ] **I** N **1** [c] (THEAT, TV, RAD) 戏剧 [xìjù] **2** [U] (*activity*) (*with toys, games etc*) 游戏 [yóuxì] ; (*sport*) 活动 [huódòng] ▷ *Rain again interrupted play at Wimbledon today.* 温布尔登赛事又受到下雨的干扰. **II** VT **1** [+ *game, chess*] 玩 [wán] ▷ *Let's play a game.* 咱们玩游戏吧. ; [+ *football*] 踢 [tī]; [+ *cricket, tennis*] 玩 [wán] **2** (*compete against*) [+ *team, opponent*] 同…比赛 [tóng…bǐsài] **3** (*in play, film*) [+ *part, role, character*] 扮演 [bànyǎn] **4** (MUS) [+ *instrument, piece of music*] 演奏 [yǎnzòu] **5** (*listen to*) [+ *CD, record, tape*] 播放 [bōfàng] **III** VI **1** [*children +*] 玩耍 [wánshuǎ] ▷ *Polly was playing with her teddy bear.* 波丽在玩她的玩具熊. **2** [*orchestra, band +*] 演奏 [yǎnzòu] **3** [*CD, record, tape, radio +*] 播放 [bōfàng] ▷ *There was classical music playing in the background.* 古典音乐正作为背景音乐播放. ▸ **a play on words** 双关语 ▸ **to bring into play** 调动 ▸ **to play cards** 玩纸牌 ▸ **to play a trick on sb** 对某人耍花招 ▸ **to play a part** or **role in sth** (*fig*) 在某事中起作用 ▸ **to play (it) safe** 谨慎行事 ▸ **to play for time** 为争取时间而拖延 ▸ **to play into sb's hands** 让某人占便宜

▸ **play about with** VT FUS [不可拆分] = **play around with**

▸ **play along with** VT FUS [不可拆分] [+ *person*] 同…合作 [tóng…hézuò]; [+ *idea, charade*] 依照…行事 [yīzhào…xíngshì]

▸ **play around** (*inf*) VI (*be silly*) 胡闹 [húnào]

▸ **play around with, play about with** (*inf*) VT FUS [不可拆分] [+ *idea, problem*] 摆弄 [bǎinòng]

▸ **play at** VT FUS [不可拆分] ▸ **to play at (doing/being) sth** (*do half-heartedly*) 敷衍地做某事 [fūyǎn de zuò mǒushì]; (*as game*) 扮成某

事 [bànchéng mǒushì] ▷ *They played at (being) soldiers.* 他们扮成士兵。 ▶ **what's he playing at?** 他在胡闹些什么?

▶ **play back** VT [+ *recording, message, video*] 回放 [huífàng]

▶ **play down** VT 减低 [jiǎndī]

▶ **play off against** VT 挑拨离间 [tiǎobō líjiàn]

▶ **play on** VT FUS [不可拆分] [+ *sb's feelings, fears*] 利用 [lìyòng] ▶ **to play on sb's mind** 萦绕某人的心头

▶ **play up** (*inf*) VI 1 [*machine, part of body +*] 出毛病 [chū máobìng] 2 [*child +*] 调皮捣乱 [tiáopí dǎoluàn]

○ **player** ['pleɪə(r)] N [c] 1 (SPORT) 选手 [xuǎnshǒu] ▷ *He was a good tennis player.* 他是名优秀的网球选手。 2 (MUS) ▶ **a trumpet/flute/piano player** 小号/长笛/钢琴演奏者 [xiǎohào/chángdí/gāngqín yǎnzòuzhě] 3 (THEAT) 演员 [yǎnyuán] 4 (COMM, POL) (*party involved*) 参与者 [cānyùzhě] ▷ *America is a key player in the negotiations.* 美国是这次谈判的主要参与者。

playful ['pleɪful] ADJ [+ *person, gesture*] 开玩笑的 [kāiwánxiào de]; [+ *animal*] 顽皮的 [wánpí de]

playground ['pleɪgraʊnd] N [c] (*at school*) 运动场 [yùndòng chǎng]; (*in park*) 游戏场 [yóuxì chǎng]

playgroup ['pleɪgruːp] N [c] 幼儿园 [yòu'éryuán]

playing card ['pleɪɪŋ-] N [c] 纸牌 [zhǐpái]

playing field ['pleɪɪŋ-] N [c] 运动场 [yùndòng chǎng] ▶ **a level playing field** (*fig*) 公平竞争

playschool ['pleɪskuːl] N = playgroup

playtime ['pleɪtaɪm] N [u] 游戏时间 [yóuxì shíjiān]

playwright ['pleɪraɪt] N [c] 剧作家 [jùzuòjiā]

plc (BRIT) ABBR (= *public limited company*) 股票上市公司 [gǔpiào shàngshì gōngsī]

plea [pliː] N [c] 1 (*request*) ▶ **plea (for sth)** 恳求(某事) [kěnqiú (mǒushì)] 2 (LAW) (*in court*) 抗辩 [kàngbiàn] 3 (*excuse*) 托词 [tuōcí] ▶ **a plea for help** 请求帮助 ▶ **a plea for sb to do sth** 请求某人做某事

plead [pliːd] I VT 1 (LAW) [+ *case, cause*] 为…辩护 [wèi…biànhù] 2 (*give as excuse*) [+ *ignorance, ill health, poverty*] 以…为借口 [yǐ…wéi jièkǒu] II VI (LAW) (*in court*) 辩护 [biànhù] ▶ **to plead with sb (to do sth)** 恳求某人(做某事) ▶ **to plead for sth** 恳求某物 ▶ **to plead guilty** 服罪 ▶ **to plead not guilty** 不服罪

pleasant ['plɛznt] ADJ 1 (*agreeable*) 令人愉快的 [lìngrén yúkuài de] 2 (*friendly*) 友善的 [yǒushàn de]

pleasantly ['plɛzntlɪ] ADV [+ *warm, tired, relaxed*] 愉快地 [yúkuàide]; [*say, behave, spend time +*] 亲切地 [qīnqiè de] ▶ **to be pleasantly surprised** 感到惊喜的

please [pliːz] I INT 1 (*in polite requests, written instructions*) 请 [qǐng] 2 (*accepting sth*) 好的 [hǎo de] 3 (*to attract attention*) 劳驾 [láojià] II VT (*satisfy*) 使高兴 [shǐ gāoxìng] III VI (*give pleasure, satisfaction*) 满意 [mǎnyì] ▶ **yes, please** 好的 ▶ **my bill, please** 请给我账单 ▶ **please don't cry!** 拜托, 别哭了! ▶ **it pleased them to...** …让他们开心 ▶ **please yourself!** (*inf*) 请便! ▶ **do as you please** 按你喜欢的做

pleased [pliːzd] ADJ (*happy, satisfied*) 开心的 [kāixīn de] ▶ **to be pleased that...** 对…感到高兴 ▶ **to be pleased to help** 乐意相助 ▶ **pleased to meet you** 见到你很高兴 ▶ **pleased with sth** 对某事满意 ▶ **we are pleased to inform you that...** 我们荣幸地告诉你…

pleasing ['pliːzɪŋ] ADJ [+ *situation, picture, person*] 令人愉快的 [lìngrén yúkuài de] ▶ **it's pleasing to see/know that...** 高兴地看到/知道…

pleasurable ['plɛʒərəbl] ADJ [+ *experience, sensation*] 令人愉快的 [lìngrén yúkuài de]

pleasure ['plɛʒə(r)] N 1 [u] (*happiness, satisfaction*) 高兴 [gāoxìng] 2 [u] (*fun*) 享乐 [xiǎnglè] 3 [c] (*enjoyable experience*) 乐事 [lèshì] ▶ **to take pleasure in sth/in doing sth** 乐于某事/做某事 ▶ **to give sb great pleasure** 使某人很高兴 ▶ **"it's a pleasure", "my pleasure"** "乐意效劳" ▶ **with pleasure** 非常愿意 ▶ **is this trip for business or pleasure?** 这趟旅行是出公差还是度假?

pleat [pliːt] N [c] 褶 [zhě]

pleated ['pliːtɪd] ADJ 有褶的 [yǒuzhě de] ▷ *a pleated skirt* 百褶裙

pledge [plɛdʒ] I N [c] (*promise*) 誓言 [shìyán] II VT (*promise*) [+ *money, support, help*] 发誓 [fāshì] ▶ **to pledge that...** 保证… ▶ **to pledge to do sth** 保证做某事 ▶ **to pledge sb to secrecy** 叫某人发誓保密 ▶ **to pledge o.s. to sth** 保证某事

plentiful ['plɛntɪful] ADJ [+ *food, supply, resources*] 大量的 [dàliàng de]

plenty ['plɛntɪ] PRON 1 (*lots*) 大量 [dàliàng] 2 (*sufficient*) 充足 [chōngzú] ▶ **plenty of** [+ *food, money, time*] 很多; [+ *jobs, people, houses*] 许多 ▶ **we've got plenty of time to get there** 我们有充足的时间去那里

pliers ['plaɪəz] NPL 钳子 [qiánzi] ▶ **a pair of pliers** 一把钳子

plight [plaɪt] N [s] [*of person, country*] 困境 [kùnjìng]

plod [plɒd] VI 沉重而缓慢地走 [chénzhòng ér huǎnmàn de zǒu] ▶ **to plod up/down the stairs** 拖着脚步走上/下楼梯

▶ **plod along, plod on** VI [*work, production +*] 缓慢进行 [huǎnmàn jìnxíng]

▶ **plod along with, plod on with** VT FUS [不可拆分] 努力从事 [nǔlì cóngshì]

plonk [plɒŋk] I N [u] (BRIT: *inf*) (*wine*) 劣质酒

[lièzhì jiǔ] **II** VT ▸ **to plonk sth down on sth** 把某物重重地放在某物上 [bǎ mǒuwù zhòngzhòng de fàngzài mǒuwù shang] ▸ **to plonk o.s. down (on sth)** 猛地坐下 (坐在某处)

plot [plɔt] **I** N **1** [C] (secret plan) ▸ **a plot (to do sth)** (做某事的) 阴谋 [(zuò mǒushì de) yīnmóu] **2** [C/U] [of story, play, film] 情节 [qíngjié] **3** [C] (also: plot of land) 小块地皮 [xiǎokuài dìpí] **2** [C] (for gardening) 小块土地 [xiǎokuài tǔdì] **II** VT **1** [+ sb's downfall, overthrow] 密谋 [mìmóu] **2** [+ strategy] 谋划 [móuhuà] **3** (AVIAT, NAUT) [+ position, course] 标绘 [biāohuì] **4** (MATH) [+ point on graph] 绘制 [huìzhì] **III** VI (conspire) 密谋 [mìmóu] ▸ **to plot to do sth** 密谋做某事

plough, (US) **plow** [plau] **I** N [C] 犁 [lí] **II** VT [+ field, land] 耕 [gēng]
▸ **plough back** VT ▸ **to plough sth back (into sth)** [+ profits] 把某事再投资 (于某事) [bǎ mǒushì zài tóuzī (yú mǒushì)]
▸ **plough into I** VT FUS [不可拆分] [+ crowd] 猛力撞入 [měnglì zhuàngrù] **II** VT (invest) ▸ **to plough money into sth** 把钱投资于某事 [bǎ qián tóuzī yú mǒushì]
▸ **plough through** VT FUS [不可拆分] [+ meal, work, meeting] 费力而缓慢地进行 [fèilì ér huǎnmàn de jìnxíng]

ploughman's lunch ['plaumənz-] (BRIT) N [C] 酒吧供应的农夫午餐，包括面包、奶酪、色拉和泡菜

plow [plau] (US) N, VT = **plough**

ploy [plɔɪ] N [C] ▸ **ploy (to do sth)** (做某事的) 花招 [(zuò mǒushì de) huāzhāo]

pls ABBR (= please) 请 [qǐng]

pluck [plʌk] **I** VT **1** [+ fruit, flower, leaf] 采摘 [cǎizhāi] **2** (seize) 扯 [chě] **3** [+ guitar, strings] 拨 [bō] **4** [+ chicken, turkey, goose] 拔…的毛 [bá…de máo] **5** [+ eyebrows] 拔 [bá] **II** N [U] (courage) 勇气 [yǒngqì] ▸ **to be plucked from danger** 脱离危险 ▸ **to be plucked to safety** 转危为安 ▸ **to pluck up (the) courage (to do sth)** 鼓起勇气 (做某事)
▸ **pluck at** VT FUS [不可拆分] 抓住 [zhuāzhù]

plug [plʌg] **I** N [C] **1** (ELEC) (on appliance) 插头 [chātóu]; (inf) (socket) 插座 [chāzuò] **2** (in sink, bath) 塞子 [sāizi] **3** (also: sparking plug) 火花塞 [huǒhuāsāi] **4** [of flush toilet] ▸ **to pull the plug** 冲厕所 [chōng cèsuǒ] **5** (advertisement) ▸ **to give sb/sth a plug** 大肆宣传某人/某物 [dàsì xuānchuán mǒurén/mǒuwù] **II** VT **1** [+ hole, leak] 塞住 [sāizhù] **2** (inf) (advertise) 推销 [tuīxiāo] ▸ **to pull the plug (on sth)** (inf) [+ project, deal] 停止 (某事)
▸ **plug in** (ELEC) **I** VT 插上…的插头 [chāshang…de chātóu] **II** VI 插上插头 [chāshang chātóu]

plughole ['plʌghəul] (BRIT) N [C] 排水孔 [páishuǐ kǒng] ▸ **to go down the plughole** (inf)

付诸东流

plum [plʌm] **I** N [C] (fruit) 梅子 [méizi] **II** ADJ (inf) ▸ **a plum job** 美差 [měichāi]

plumber ['plʌmə(r)] N [C] 管子工 [guǎnzi gōng]

plumbing ['plʌmɪŋ] N [U] **1** (piping) 管道装置 [guǎndào zhuāngzhì] **2** (trade, work) 管道装修 [guǎndào zhuāngxiū]

plummet ['plʌmɪt] VI **1** [price, amount, rate +] 暴跌 [bàodiē] **2** [aircraft, bird etc +] 俯冲 [fǔchōng]

plump [plʌmp] ADJ [+ person, arm, chicken, fruit] 丰满的 [fēngmǎn de]
　用法参见 **fat**
▸ **plump for** (inf) VT FUS [不可拆分] 选定 [xuǎndìng]
▸ **plump up** VT [+ cushion, pillow] 使鼓起 [shǐ gǔqǐ]

plunder ['plʌndə(r)] **I** VT (frm) **1** (steal from) [+ city, tomb] 抢劫 [qiǎngjié] **2** (take) [+ goods] 取得 [qǔdé] **II** N [U] (activity) 抢劫 [qiǎngjié] **2** (stolen things) 赃物 [zāngwù]

plunge [plʌndʒ] **I** N [C] **1** (fall) [of person] 跳入 [tiàorù] **2** [in prices, rates] 猛跌 [měngdiē] **II** VT **1** ▸ **to plunge sth into sth** [+ knife, hand etc] 把某物猛插入另一物 [bǎ mǒuwù měng chārù lìng yī wù] **2** ▸ **to be plunged into darkness/chaos** 陷入黑暗/混乱 [xiànrù hēi'àn/hùnluàn] **III** VI **1** ▸ **to plunge into sth** (fall) 撞入某处 [zhuàngrù mǒuchù]; (leap) 跳入某处 [tiàorù mǒuchù] **2** [economy, interest rates +] ▸ **to plunge into sth** 猛然跌入 (某状态) [měngrán diērù (mǒu zhuàngtài)] **3** [bird +] 俯冲 [fǔchōng] ▸ **to take the plunge** (fig) 采取断然行动 ▸ **to plunge (o.s.)/be plunged into sth** (become involved) 全身心投入某事

plural ['pluərl] **I** ADJ 复数的 [fùshù de] **II** N [C] 复数 [fùshù]

plus [plʌs] **I** CONJ **1** (added to) 加 [jiā] **2** (as well as) 和 [hé] **II** ADJ (positive) [+ number] 正的 [zhèng de] **III** ADV (additionally) 此外 [cǐwài] **IV** N [C] (inf) ▸ **it's a plus** 这是个附加的好处 [zhè shì gè fùjiā de hǎochù] ▸ **ten/twenty plus** 十几/二十多 ▸ **B plus** (SCOL) B加

ply [plaɪ] **I** VT **1** (offer) ▸ **to ply sb with food/drink** 反复给某人食物/饮料 [fǎnfù gěi mǒurén shíwù/yǐnliào] **2** (bombard) ▸ **to ply sb with questions** 向某人问个不休 [xiàng mǒurén wèn ge bùxiū] **3** [+ tool] 使用 [shǐyòng] **4** [ship, aircraft, vehicle +] [+ route] 定期来回 [dìngqí láihuí] **II** VI ▸ **to ply between… and…** [ship, aircraft, vehicle +] 在…和…之间定期来回 [zài…hé…zhījiān dìngqí láihuí] **III** N [C] [of wool, rope] 股 [gǔ] ▸ **to ply one's trade** 从事自己的工作

plywood ['plaɪwud] N [U] 胶合板 [jiāohé bǎn]

PM (BRIT: inf) N ABBR (= Prime Minister) ▸ **the PM** 总理 [Zǒnglǐ]

p.m. ADV ABBR (= post meridiem) 下午 [xiàwǔ]

pneumatic drill [nju:ˈmætɪk-] N [C] 风钻 [fēngzuān]

pneumonia [nju:ˈməunɪə] N [U] 肺炎 [fèiyán]

poach [pəutʃ] I VT 1 (steal) [+ fish, animals, birds] 偷猎 [tōuliè] 2 [+ person] 挖人 [wārén] 3 [+ idea] 窃取 [qièqǔ] 4 (cook) [+ egg] 水煮 [shuǐzhǔ]; [+ fish, chicken, fruit] 炖 [dùn] II VI (steal) 偷猎 [tōuliè]

poached [pəutʃt] ADJ [+ egg, salmon] 煮的 [zhǔ de]

PO Box N ABBR (= Post Office Box) 邮箱 [yóuxiāng]

pocket [ˈpɒkɪt] I N [C] 1 (in jacket, trousers, shirt, skirt) 口袋 [kǒudài] 2 (in suitcase, car door, handbag) 袋子 [dàizi] 3 (fig) (small area) [of air, resistance] 小范围 [xiǎo fànwéi] II CPD [复合词] [+ calculator, dictionary] 袖珍的 [xiùzhēn de] III VT 1 (take) 把…据为己有 [bǎ…jùwéi jǐyǒu] 2 (steal) [+ money, document] 据为己有 [jùwéi jǐyǒu] ▶ to put money in sb's pocket 把钱放入某人腰包 ▶ to be out of pocket (BRIT) 赔钱

pocketbook [ˈpɒkɪtbuk] N [C] 1 (US) (wallet) 皮夹 [píjiā] 2 (US) (handbag) 手提包 [shǒutíbāo] 3 (notebook) 袖珍记事本 [xiùzhēn jìshìběn]

pocket money (ESP BRIT) N [U] 零花钱 [línghuāqián] [美= allowance]

pod [pɒd] N [C] (on plant) 豆荚 [dòujiá]

podgy [ˈpɒdʒɪ] (inf) ADJ [+ person, cheeks, arms etc] 矮胖的 [ǎipàng de]

podiatrist [pəˈdaɪətrɪst] (ESP US) N [C] 足病医生 [zúbìng yīshēng]

podium [ˈpəudɪəm] N [C] 指挥台 [zhǐhuī tái]

poem [ˈpəuɪm] N [C] 诗 [shī]

poet [ˈpəuɪt] N [C] 诗人 [shīrén]

poetic [pəuˈɛtɪk] ADJ 1 [+ drama, language, description] 有诗意的 [yǒu shīyì de] 2 [+ tradition] 诗的 [shī de]

poetry [ˈpəuɪtrɪ] N [U] 1 (poems) 诗 [shī] 2 (form of literature) 诗歌 [shīgē]

poignant [ˈpɔɪnjənt] ADJ 心酸的 [xīnsuān de]

⊙ point [pɔɪnt] I N 1 [C] (in report, lecture, interview) 论点 [lùndiǎn] ▷ The research made some valid points. 研究得出了一些有效的论点。 2 [S] (significant part) [of argument, discussion] 要害 [yàohài] ▷ He came straight to the point. 他切中要害。 3 [S] (purpose) [of action] 目的 [mùdì] ▷ What was the point in getting married? 结婚目的何在？ 4 [C] (aspect) [of report, project, situation] 点 [diǎn] ▷ The most interesting point about the village was its religion. 关于这个村庄最有趣的一点是它的宗教。 5 [C] (place) 位置 [wèizhì] ▷ We were nearing the point where the lane curved round to the right. 我们在道路向右转弯这个位置附近。 6 [S] (moment) 时刻 [shíkè] ▷ At this point the girl slowly sat up on the sofa. 就在这时女孩在沙发上慢慢坐起。 7 [C] (sharp end) [of needle, knife, instrument] 尖端 [jiānduān] 8 [C] (in score, competition, game, sport) 分 [fēn] ▷ New Zealand

have beaten Scotland by 21 points to 18. 新西兰以21分比18分赢了苏格兰。 9 [C] (also: **power point**) 插座 [chāzuò] 10 [C] (also: **decimal point**) 小数点 [xiǎoshùdiǎn] ▷ seven point eight per cent 百分之七点八 II VI (with finger, stick) 指出 [zhǐchū] III VT ▶ to point sth at sb [+ gun, finger, stick] 把某物瞄准某人 [bǎ mǒuwù miáozhǔn mǒurén] IV points NPL 1 (AUT) 接触点 [jiēchùdiǎn] 2 (BRIT: RAIL) 道岔 [dàochà] ▶ there's no point (in doing that) (那样做) 无意义 [wúyìyì] ▶ good/bad points [of person] 优/缺点 ▶ a strong point 长处 ▶ the train stops at Carlisle and all points south 火车停靠卡莱尔及其以南的所有站点 ▶ at that point 那时 ▶ to a point 在某种程度上 ▶ two point five (2.5) 二点五 ▶ to be on the point of doing sth 正要做某事时 ▶ to make a point of doing sth 特意做某事 ▶ to get/miss the point 理解/不理解要点 ▶ to come/get to the point 切中要点 ▶ to make one's point 使他人领会自己的意思 ▶ to prove one's point 证明某人的观点 ▶ that's the whole point! 正是这个意思！ ▶ to be beside the point 不切题的 ▶ you've got a point there! 你言之有理！ ▶ I take your point 我接受/理解你的看法 ▶ in point of fact 事实上 ▶ the points of the compass 罗盘上的罗经点 ▶ to point at sth/sb (with finger, stick) 指着某物/某人 ▶ to point to sth/sb (with finger/stick) 指向某物/某人 ▷ Mr Jones pointed to a chair and asked her to sit down. 琼斯先生指指椅子请她坐下。 ▶ to point to or towards sth [sign, needle, arrow +] 指向某物 ▶ to point to sth [fact +] 暗示某事; [speaker +] 指出 ▷ They pointed proudly to the administration's success in recent years. 他们自豪地指出近年来在管理上的成功。 ▶ to point forwards/north 指向前/北 ▶ to point the way forward 标引前方道路

▶ **point out** VT [+ person, place, mistake, fact] 指出 [zhǐchū] ▶ to point out that... 指出…

▶ **point to** VT FUS [不可拆分] 暗示 [ànshì]

point-blank [ˈpɔɪntˈblæŋk] I ADV 1 [refuse, say, ask +] 直截了当地 [zhíjié liǎodàng de] 2 (also: **at point-blank range**) 短射程 [duǎn shèchéng] II ADJ [+ refusal] 直截了当的 [zhíjié liǎodàng de]

pointed [ˈpɔɪntɪd] ADJ 1 [+ stick, nose, roof, shoes] 尖的 [jiān de] 2 (fig) [+ remark, question] 一针见血的 [yìzhēn jiànxiě de]

pointedly [ˈpɔɪntɪdlɪ] ADV [ask, reply +] 直截了当地 [zhíjié liǎodàng de]

pointer [ˈpɔɪntə(r)] N [C] 1 (tip) 点子 [diǎnzi] 2 (indication) 暗示 [ànshì] 3 (needle) (on machine) 指针 [zhǐzhēn] 4 (stick) 教鞭 [jiàobiān] 5 (dog) 指示犬 [zhǐshì quǎn]

pointless [ˈpɔɪntlɪs] ADJ 无意义的 [wú yìyì de] ▶ it is pointless to complain 抱怨无用

point of view N [C] 观点 [guāndiǎn] ▶ from

the point of view of... 从…的观点来看 ▸ **from a practical point of view** 从现实的角度看

poison ['pɔɪzn] I N [C/U] 毒药 [dúyào] II VT 1 [+ person, animal] 下毒 [xiàdú] 2 [+ relationship, atmosphere] 毒害 [dúhài]

poisoning ['pɔɪznɪŋ] N [U] 下毒 [xiàdú] ▸ **lead/alcohol poisoning** 铅/酒精中毒

poisonous ['pɔɪznəs] ADJ 1 (lit) [+ animal, plant, fumes, chemicals] 有毒的 [yǒudú de] 2 (fig) [+ rumours, comments] 恶毒的 [èdú de]

poke [pəʊk] I VT 1 (jab) (with finger, stick) 戳 [chuō] 2 (put) ▸ **to poke sth in (to) sth** 把某物戳到某物中 [bǎ mǒuwù chuōdào mǒuwù zhōng] II N ▸ **to give sb/sth a poke** 捅捅某人/某物 [tǒngtǒng mǒurén/mǒuwù] ▸ **to poke the fire** 拨火 ▸ **to poke one's head out of the window/around the door** etc 把头探出窗户/门{等} ▸ **to poke fun at sb/sth** 嘲笑某人/某物

▸ **poke about, poke around** (inf) VI (search) ▸ **to poke about (for sth)** 摸索着找 (某物) [mōsuǒzhe zhǎo (mǒuwù)]

▸ **poke at** VT FUS [不可拆分] (prod) 拨弄 [bōnòng]

▸ **poke out** VI (stick out) 露出 [lòuchū]

poker ['pəʊkə(r)] N 1 [U] (CARDS) 扑克牌 [pūkèpái] 2 [C] (for fire) 拨火棒 [bōhuǒ bàng]

Poland ['pəʊlənd] N 波兰 [Bōlán]

polar ['pəʊlə(r)] ADJ [+ ice-cap, region] 地极的 [dìjí de]

polar bear N [C] 北极熊 [běijíxióng]

Pole [pəʊl] N [C] 波兰人 [Bōlánrén]

pole [pəʊl] N [C] 1 (stick) 杆 [gān] 2 (GEO) 地极 [dìjí] 3 (ELEC) 电极 [diànjí] ▸ **to be poles apart** 截然相反 ▸ **to be in pole position** (in motor racing) 在跑道内圈

pole bean (US) N [C] (runner bean) 蔓生菜豆 [mànshēng càidòu]

pole vault N [S] ▸ **the pole vault** 撑杆跳高 [chēnggān tiàogāo]

⊘ **police** [pə'liːs] I N PL 1 (organization) 警方 [jǐngfāng] 2 (members) 警察 [jǐngchá] II VT [+ street, area, event] 维持治安 [wéichí zhì'ān]

police car N [C] 警车 [jǐngchē]

police force N [C] 警力 [jǐnglì]

policeman [pə'liːsmən] (pl **policemen**) N [C] 男警察 [nán jǐngchá]

police officer N [C] 警察 [jǐngchá]

police station N [C] 警察局 [jǐngchá jú]

policewoman [pə'liːswʊmən] (pl **policewomen**) N [C] 女警察 [nǚ jǐngchá]

⊘ **policy** ['pɒlɪsɪ] N 1 [C/U] [of government, council] 政策 [zhèngcè] ▷ What is their policy on nuclear testing? 他们对核试验的政策是什么?; [of company, newspaper] 方针 [fāngzhēn] 2 [C] (also: **insurance policy**) 保单 [bǎodān] ▸ **to take out a policy** (INSURANCE) 买保险

polio ['pəʊlɪəʊ] N [U] 小儿麻痹症 [xiǎo'ér mábìzhèng]

Polish ['pəʊlɪʃ] I ADJ 波兰的 [Bōlán de] II N [U] (language) 波兰语 [Bōlányǔ]

polish ['pɒlɪʃ] I N 1 [C/U] (for shoes, furniture, floor) 上光剂 [shàngguāng jì] 2 [U] (shine) (on shoes, furniture, floor) 光泽 [guāngzé] 3 [U] (fig) (refinement) 优雅 [yōuyǎ] II VT [+ shoes] 擦亮 [cāliàng]; [+ furniture, floor] 上光 [shàngguāng]

▸ **polish off** (inf) VT [+ food, drink] 吃/喝掉 [chī/hē diào]

polished ['pɒlɪʃt] ADJ 1 [+ furniture, floor] 擦亮的 [cāliàng de] 2 (fig) [+ person] 优雅的 [yōuyǎ de]; [+ performance, style] 优美的 [yōuměi de]

polite [pə'laɪt] ADJ 1 (well-mannered) [+ person, behaviour] 有礼貌的 [yǒu lǐmào de] 2 (refined) [+ company, society] 上流的 [shàngliú de] ▸ **to make polite conversation** 谈吐斯文 ▸ **it isn't polite to do that** 那样做是不礼貌的

politeness [pə'laɪtnɪs] N 礼貌 [lǐmào] ▸ **to do sth out of politeness** 出于礼貌做某事

⊘ **political** [pə'lɪtɪkl] ADJ 1 [+ system, party, issue, agenda, crisis etc] 政治的 [zhèngzhì de] 2 [+ person] 从事政治的 [cóngshì zhèngzhì de]

politically [pə'lɪtɪklɪ] ADV [+ motivated, sensitive] 政治上 [zhèngzhì shang] ▸ **politically correct** [+ person, word] 得体的 [détǐ de] ▸ **politically incorrect** 不得体的

politician [pɒlɪ'tɪʃən] N [C] 政治家 [zhèngzhì jiā]

politics ['pɒlɪtɪks] I N [U] 1 (activity) 政治 [zhèngzhì] 2 (subject) 政治学 [zhèngzhì xué] II N PL (beliefs, opinions) 观见 [zhèngjiàn] ▸ **office politics** 人际关系

poll [pəʊl] I N [C] (also: **opinion poll**) 民意调查 [mínyì diàochá] II VT 1 [+ people] (in opinion poll) 向…提问 [xiàng...tíwèn] 2 (number of votes) 获得选票 [huòdé xuǎnpiào] III **polls** N PL (election) 选举投票 [xuǎnjǔ tóupiào] ▸ **to go to the polls** [voters +] 去投票; [government +] 进行选举 ▸ **the polls have closed** 投票结束了

pollen ['pɒlən] N [U] 花粉 [huāfěn]

polling station ['pəʊlɪŋ-] (BRIT) N [C] 投票站 [tóupiào zhàn]

pollute [pə'luːt] VT [+ air, water, land] 污染 [wūrǎn]

polluted [pə'luːtɪd] ADJ [+ river, beach, water] 被污染的 [bèi wūrǎn de]

pollution [pə'luːʃən] N [U] 1 (process) 污染 [wūrǎn] 2 (substances) 污染物 [wūrǎn wù]

polo ['pəʊləʊ] N [U] (SPORT) 马球 [mǎqiú]

polo neck (BRIT) N [C] 圆高领 [yuán gāolǐng]

polo shirt N [C] 短袖有领的运动T恤衫

polyester [pɒlɪ'ɛstə(r)] N [U] 聚酯 [jùzhǐ]

polystyrene [pɒlɪ'staɪriːn] I N [U] 聚苯乙烯 [jùběnyǐxī] II CPD [复合词] [+ cup, tile] 聚苯乙烯 [jùběnyǐxī]

polytechnic [pɒlɪ'tɛknɪk] (BRIT: HIST) N [C] 专科学校 [zhuānkē xuéxiào]

polythene ['pɒlɪθiːn] N [U] 聚乙烯 [jùyǐxī]

polythene bag N [C] 聚乙烯塑料袋 [jùyǐxī sùliàodài]

pomegranate ['pɒmɪgrænɪt] N [C] 石榴 [shíliu]

pompous ['pɒmpəs] (pej) ADJ [+ person] 自大的 [zìdà de]; [+ speech, comment, article, gesture] 浮夸的 [fúkuā de]

pond [pɒnd] N [C] 池塘 [chítáng]

ponder ['pɒndə(r)] I VT (think about) 深思 [shēnsī] II VI 沉思 [chénsī]

pony ['pəʊnɪ] N [C] 小马 [xiǎomǎ]

ponytail ['pəʊnɪteɪl] N [C] 马尾辫 [mǎwěibiàn]
▸ **to have one's hair in a ponytail** 梳成马尾辫

pony trekking [-trɛkɪŋ] (BRIT) N [U] 骑小马出游 [qí xiǎomǎ chūyóu] ▸ **to go pony trekking** 骑小马出游

poodle ['puːdl] N [C] 卷毛狮子狗 [juǎnmáo shīzigǒu]

pool [puːl] I N 1 [C] (pond) 水塘 [shuǐtáng] 2 [C] (also: **swimming pool**) 游泳池 [yóuyǒngchí] 3 (fig) ▸ **pool of light/blood** 一滩亮光/血 [yītān liàngguāng/xiě] 4 [C] (amount, number) [of cash] 公库 [gōngkù]; [of secretaries, workers, vehicles] 储备 [chǔbèi] 5 [C] (CARDS) (kitty) 全部赌注 [quánbù dǔzhù] 6 [U] (game) 美式台球 [měishì táiqiú] II VT [+ money, knowledge, resources, ideas] 集中 [jízhōng] III **pools** NPL (BRIT) (also: **football pools**) 足球彩票 [zúqiú cǎipiào] ▸ **car pool** 合伙用车 ▸ **typing pool**, (US) **secretary pool** 秘书组 ▸ **to do the (football) pools** 赌足球彩票

poor [puə(r)] I ADJ 1 (not rich) [+ person] 贫穷的 [pínqióng de]; [+ country, area] 贫困的 [pínkùn de] 2 (bad) [+ quality, performance] 低水平的 [dī shuǐpíng de]; [+ eyesight, memory, health] 不好的 [bùhǎo de]; [+ swimmer, reader] 糟糕的 [zāogāo de]; [+ wages, conditions, results, attendance] 差的 [chà de] II NPL ▸ **the poor** 穷人 [qióngrén] ▸ **to be poor in sth** [+ resources, vitamins] 缺乏某物 [quēfá mǒuwù] ▸ **to be poor at doing sth** 不善于做某事 ▸ **poor (old) Bill** 可怜的(老)比尔

poorly ['puəlɪ] I ADJ (inf) (ill) 身体不适的 [shēntǐ bùshì de] II ADV [+ designed, paid, furnished, educated etc] 不足地 [bùzú de]; [play, sell, perform +] 糟糕地 [zāogāo de]

pop [pɒp] N 1 [U] (MUS) 流行音乐 [liúxíng yīnyuè] 2 [U] (BRIT: inf) (fizzy drinks) 汽水 [qìshuǐ] [美 = **soda pop**] 3 [C] (US: inf) (father) 爸爸 [bàba] 4 [C] (sound) 爆破声 [bàopò shēng] II VI 1 [balloon, cork +] 爆开 [bàokāi] 2 (inf) [eyes +] 张大 [zhāngdà] III VT (inf) ▸ **to pop sth into/onto sth** 快速地将某物放进某物里/放在某处 [kuàisù de jiāng mǒuwù fàngjìn mǒuwù lǐ/fàng zài mǒuchù] ▸ **to go pop** (inf) 发出爆裂声 ▸ **she popped her head out of the window** 她猛地从窗户里探出头
▸ **pop in** (inf) VI 来/去一会儿 [lái/qù yīhuìr]

▸ **pop out** (inf) VI 出去一会儿 [chūqù yīhuìr]
▸ **pop up** (inf) VI 突然出现 [tūrán chūxiàn]

popcorn ['pɒpkɔːn] N [U] 爆米花 [bàomǐhuā]

pope [pəʊp] N [C] 教皇 [jiàohuáng]

poplar ['pɒplə(r)] N [C] 杨树 [yángshù]

popper ['pɒpə(r)] N [C] 1 (BRIT: inf) (for fastening) 揿扣儿 [qènkòu'r] 2 (ESP US) (for popcorn) 爆爆米花的器皿 [bào bàomǐhuā de qìmǐn]

poppy ['pɒpɪ] N [C] 罂粟 [yīngsù]

Popsicle® ['pɒpsɪkl] (US) N [C] 冰棒 [bīngbàng] [英 = **ice lolly**]

pop star N [C] 明星 [míngxīng]

popular ['pɒpjʊlə(r)] ADJ 1 (well-liked) [+ person, place, thing] 流行的 [liúxíng de] 2 (general) [+ idea, belief, appeal] 普遍的 [pǔbiàn de] 3 (fashionable) [+ name, activity] 时髦的 [shímáo de] 4 (not elitist) [+ books, newspapers, TV programmes] 通俗的 [tōngsú de] 5 (POL) [+ movement, activity] 民众的 [mínzhòng de] ▸ **to be popular with sb** [food, activity etc +] 某人所喜欢的; [person +] 受某人欢迎的

popularity [pɒpjʊ'lærɪtɪ] N [U] [of person] 名望 [míngwàng]; [of thing, activity] 普及 [pǔjí]

popularly ['pɒpjʊləlɪ] ADV [+ called, known as] 一般地 [yībān de]; [+ believed, supposed] 普遍地 [pǔbiàn de]

population [pɒpjʊ'leɪʃən] N [C] 1 (inhabitants) 人口 [rénkǒu] 2 ▸ **the male/civilian/elephant population** 男性/平民/大象的数量 [nánxìng/píngmín/dàxiàng de shùliàng] ▸ **a prison population of 44,000** 44,000名囚犯

porcelain ['pɔːsəlɪn] N [U] 瓷 [cí]

porch [pɔːtʃ] N [C] 1 (entrance) [of house] 门廊 [ménláng]; [of church] 柱廊 [zhùláng] 2 (US) (veranda) 走廊 [zǒuláng]

pore [pɔː(r)] I N [C] 1 (ANAT) 毛孔 [máokǒng] 2 (BOT) 气孔 [qìkǒng] II VI ▸ **to pore over** or **through sth** [+ book, article] 钻研某物 [zuānyán mǒuwù]

pork [pɔːk] N [U] 猪肉 [zhūròu]

pork chop N [C] 猪排 [zhūpái]

porn [pɔːn] (inf) N [U] 色情作品 [sèqíng zuòpǐn]

pornographic [pɔːnə'græfɪk] ADJ [+ film, book, magazine] 色情的 [sèqíng de]

pornography [pɔː'nɒgrəfɪ] N [U] 色情作品 [sèqíng zuòpǐn]

porridge ['pɒrɪdʒ] N [U] 麦片粥 [màipiàn zhōu]

port [pɔːt] I N 1 [C] (harbour) 港口 [gǎngkǒu] 2 [C] (town) 港市 [gǎngshì] 3 [U] (NAUT) (left side) 左舷 [zuǒxián] 4 [U] (wine) 波尔图葡萄酒，一种酒精浓度较高、味甜、供餐后饮用的红葡萄酒 5 [C] (COMPUT) 端口 [duānkǒu] II ADJ (NAUT) [+ side] 左舷的 [zuǒxián de] ▸ **port of call** (NAUT) 停靠港 ▸ **to port** (NAUT) 向左舷

portable ['pɔːtəbl] ADJ [+ television, computer etc] 便携式的 [biànxiéshì de]

porter ['pɔːtə(r)] N [C] 1 (for luggage) 搬运

工 [bānyònggōng] **2** (BRIT) (doorkeeper) 门房 [ménfáng] [美=**doorman**] **3** (BRIT) (in hospital) 勤杂工 [qínzágōng] [美=**orderly**] **4** (US) (on train) 列车员 [lièchēyuán] [英=**attendant**]

portfolio [pɔːtˈfəʊlɪəʊ] N [C] **1** (case) 公事包 [gōngshìbāo] **2** (work) [of artist, student] 文件夹 [wénjiànjiā] **3** (POL) 部长职责 [bùzhǎng zhízé] **4** (FIN) 投资组合 [tóuzī zǔhé]

portion [ˈpɔːʃən] N [C] **1** (part) 部分 [bùfen] **2** (helping of food) 份 [fèn]

portrait [ˈpɔːtreɪt] N [C] (picture) 画像 [huàxiàng]

portray [pɔːˈtreɪ] VT **1** (depict) 描绘 [miáohuì] **2** (play) [actor +] 扮演 [bànyǎn]

portrayal [pɔːˈtreɪəl] N [C] **1** (depiction) 描述 [miáoshù] **2** (actor's) 表演 [biǎoyǎn]

Portugal [ˈpɔːtjʊgəl] N 葡萄牙 [Pútáoyá]

Portuguese [pɔːtjʊˈgiːz] (pl **Portuguese**) **I** ADJ 葡萄牙的 [Pútáoyá de] **II** N **1** [C] (person) 葡萄牙人 [Pútáoyárén] **2** [U] (language) 葡萄牙语 [Pútáoyáyǔ]

pose [pəʊz] **I** N [C] 姿势 [zīshì] **II** VT **1** [+ question] (ask) 问 [wèn]; (raise) 提出 [tíchū] **2** [+ problem, danger] 引发 [yǐnfā] **III** VI ► to pose as sb 摆出某人的样子 [bǎichū mǒurén de yàngzi] ► to pose for sth [+ painting, photograph] 为某事摆姿势 ► to strike a pose 装样子

posh [pɒʃ] (inf) ADJ **1** (smart) [+ hotel, restaurant, car] 豪华的 [háohuá de] **2** (upper-class) [+ person, voice] 上流的 [shàngliú de] ► to talk posh 装腔作势地说话

○ **position** [pəˈzɪʃən] **I** N [C] **1** (place) [of house, person, thing] 位置 [wèizhi] ▷ The house is in a very exposed position. 房子处在一个显眼的位置。; [of sun, stars] 方位 [fāngwèi] **2** (posture) [of person's body] 姿势 [zīshì] ▷ She remained in that position. 她保持那种姿势。 **3** (frm) (job) 职位 [zhíwèi] **4** (role) [in society] 地位 [dìwèi] **5** (in race, competition) 名 [míng] **6** (attitude) 观点 [guāndiǎn] **7** (situation) 处境 [chǔjìng] **II** VT [+ person, thing] 放置 [fàngzhì] ► to be in position 在适当的位置 ► to be in a position to do sth 能做某事

请勿将 **position**、**post** 和 **title** 混淆。某人拥有的固定工作，在正式的英语被称为 **position** 或 **post**。在招聘广告中，工作职位通常被称为 **position** 或 **post**，人们申请工作时，通常可以使用这两者中的任何一个。*He left a career in teaching to take up a position with a charity...She is well qualified for the post.* 在会话中，用 **job** 一词。*He's afraid of losing his job.* 某人的 **title** 是指他在某组织机构中的地位或职位。*"Can you tell me your official job title?" "It's Sales Manager."*

positive [ˈpɒzɪtɪv] ADJ **1** (hopeful, confident) [+ person, attitude] 积极的 [jījí de] **2** (good)

[+ situation, experience] 有益的 [yǒuyì de] **3** (decisive) [+ decision, action, step] 明确的 [míngquè de] **4** [+ response] 正面的 [zhèngmiàn de] **5** (affirmative) [+ test, result] 阳性的 [yángxìng de] **6** (clear) [+ proof, evidence] 确定的 [quèdìng de] **7** (sure) ► to be positive (about sth) 确信 (某事) [quèxìn (mǒushì)] **8** (MATH) 正的 [zhèng de] **9** (ELEC) 正极的 [zhèngjí de] ► positive thinking 乐观的想法 ► to be positive that... (sure) 确信…

positively [ˈpɒzɪtɪvlɪ] ADV **1** (really) 确实地 [quèshí de] **2** (encouragingly) 积极地 [jījí de]

possess [pəˈzɛs] VT **1** (own) [+ car, watch, radio] 拥有 [yōngyǒu] **2** (have) [+ quality, ability] 具有 [jùyǒu] **3** (liter) (take hold of) 支配 [zhīpèi] ► like a man possessed 像着了魔似的人 ► whatever possessed you (to do it)? 什么想法促使你 (去干这事)？

possession [pəˈzɛʃən] **I** N [U] (act, state) 拥有 [yōngyǒu] **II** possessions NPL 财产 [cáichǎn] ► to be in possession of sth (frm) [+ facts, information, documents] 掌握某事 ► to take possession of sth (MIL) 占领某处; [new owner +] 获得某物 ► to be in the possession of sb 被某人所拥有

possessive [pəˈzɛsɪv] **I** ADJ 占有欲强的 [zhànyǒu yù qiáng de] **II** N [U/C] (LING) 所有格 [suǒyǒugé] ► to be possessive about sb 对某人有强烈的占有欲 ► to be possessive about sth 独占某物

possibility [pɒsɪˈbɪlɪtɪ] N [C] **1** (chance) (that sth is true) 可能性 [kěnéngxìng]; (of sth happening) 可能的事 [kěnéng de shì] **2** (option) 可选性 [kěxuǎnxìng]

○ **possible** [ˈpɒsɪbl] ADJ (conceivable) [+ event, reaction, effect, consequence] 可能的 [kěnéng de]; [+ risk, danger] 潜在的 [qiánzài de]; [+ answer, cause, solution] 可接受的 [kě jiēshòu de] ► it's possible (that...) 可能 (…) ► if it's possible to do that 如有可能做的话 ► if possible 如有可能 ► as far as possible 尽可能地 ► to do everything possible 竭尽所能 ► as soon as possible 尽快 ► as much as possible 尽可能多地 ► the best possible/the worst possible time/option etc 再好/再糟不过的时候/选择 {等}

possibly [ˈpɒsɪblɪ] ADV **1** (perhaps) 大概 [dàgài] **2** (conceivably) (expressing surprise) 到底 [dàodǐ] ► to do everything one possibly can 尽最大的能力 ► if you possibly can 你尽可能 ► I can't possibly do that 我无论如何也不会做那事的

post [pəʊst] **I** N **1** (BRIT) ► the post (service, system) 邮政 [yóuzhèng]; (letters, delivery) 邮件 [yóujiàn] [美=**mail**] **2** [C] (pole) 柱子 [zhùzi] **3** [C] (job) 职位 [zhíwèi] **4** [C] (MIL) 岗哨 [gǎngshào] **5** [C] (also: **trading post**) 贸易站 [màoyì zhàn] **6** [C] (also: **goalpost**) 球门柱 [qiúmén zhù] **II** VT **1** (BRIT) [+ letter] 邮

寄 [yóujì] [美=mail] **2** (MIL) 让…站岗
[ràng…zhàngǎng] ▶ **in the post** 邮递中 ▶ **by
post** (BRIT) 以邮件的方式 ▶ **by return of post**
(BRIT) 由下一班回程邮递立即回信 ▶ **to post
sb to Paris/Spain** etc (assign) 派某人到巴黎/西
班牙 [等] ▶ **to keep sb posted (on sth)** 使某人
知情 (某事)
▶ **post up** VT 张贴 [zhāngtiē]
用法参见 **position**

postage ['pəʊstɪdʒ] N [U] (charge) 邮资 [yóuzī]
▶ **postage and packing** 邮费及包装费

postal ['pəʊstl] ADJ [+ charges, service, strike,
worker] 邮政的 [yóuzhèng de]

postal order (BRIT) N [C] 邮政汇票 [yóuzhèng
huìpiào]

postbox ['pəʊstbɒks] (BRIT) N [C] (in street) 邮
筒 [yóutǒng]

postcard ['pəʊstkɑːd] N [C] 明信片
[míngxìnpiàn]

postcode ['pəʊstkəʊd] (BRIT) N [C] 邮政编码
[yóuzhèng biānmǎ] [美=**zip code**]

poster ['pəʊstə(r)] N [C] 海报 [hǎibào]

postgraduate ['pəʊst'grædjʊət] (BRIT) N [C]
研究生 [yánjiūshēng]

postman ['pəʊstmən] (pl **postmen**) (BRIT) N [C]
邮递员 [yóudìyuán] [美=**mailman**]

postmark ['pəʊstmɑːk] N [C] 邮戳 [yóuchuō]

post-mortem [pəʊst'mɔːtəm] N [C] **1** (autopsy)
验尸 [yànshī] **2** (fig) 事后剖析 [shìhòu pōuxī]

post office N **1** [C] (building) 邮局 [yóujú]
2 ▶ **the Post Office** (organization) 邮局 [yóujú]

postpone [pəʊs'pəʊn] VT 推迟 [tuīchí]

posture ['pɒstʃə(r)] I N **1** [C/U] (physical) 姿
势 [zīshì] **2** [C] (frm) (fig) (attitude) 态度 [tàidù]
II VI 摆姿势 [bǎi zīshì]

postwoman ['pəʊstwʊmən] (pl **postwomen**)
(BRIT) N [C] 女邮递员 [nǚ yóudìyuán] [美=
mailwoman]

pot [pɒt] I N **1** [C] (for cooking) 锅 [guō] **2** [C]
(also: **teapot**) 茶壶 [cháhú] **3** [C] (also: **pot of
tea**) 一壶茶 [yīhúchá] **4** [C] (also: **coffeepot**) 咖
啡壶 [kāfēihú] **5** [C] (also: **pot of coffee**) 一壶咖
啡 [yīhú kāfēi] **6** [C] (for paint, jam, marmalade,
honey) 罐 [guàn] **7** [C] (also: **chamber pot**) 尿壶
[niàohú] **8** [C] (also: **flowerpot**) 花盆 [huāpén]
9 [U] (inf) (marijuana) 大麻 [dàmá] II VT [+ plant]
把…栽在盆里 [bǎ…zāi zài pénlǐ] ▶ **pots of
money** [BRIT: inf] 大笔钱 [dà bǐ qián] ▶ **to go to pot** (inf)
[work, performance +] 垮掉

potato [pə'teɪtəʊ] (pl **potatoes**) N [C/U] 马铃薯
[mǎlíngshǔ]；土豆 [tǔdòu]

potato chips (US) NPL 薯片 [shǔpiàn]
[英=**crisps**]

potato peeler [-'piːlə(r)] N [C] 马铃薯削皮器
[mǎlíngshǔ xiāopíqì]

potent ['pəʊtnt] ADJ **1** (powerful) [+ argument,
symbol, mix] 有说服力的 [yǒu shuōfúlì de]；
[+ drug] 有效力的 [yǒu xiàolì de]；[+ drink] 烈

性的 [lièxìng de] **2** [+ man] 有性交能力的 [yǒu
xìngjiāo nénglì de] ▶ **a potent weapon** 强有
力的武器

potential [pə'tɛnʃl] I ADJ [+ sales, advantage,
problem] 潜在的 [qiánzài de] II N [U]
1 (aptitude) ▶ **potential (for sth)** (对某事
的) 可能性 [(duì mǒushì de) kěnéngxìng]
2 (capability) [of person] 潜质 [qiánzhì]
3 (possibilities) [of thing] 潜力 [qiánlì] ▶ **to have
potential** 有潜力 ▶ **to achieve one's potential**
发挥潜力

potentially [pə'tɛnʃəlɪ] ADV 可能地 [kěnéng
de]

pothole ['pɒthəʊl] N [C] **1** (in road) 坑洼
[kēngwā] **2** (cave) 壶穴 [húxué]

pot plant (BRIT) N [C] 盆栽植物 [pénzāi zhíwù]

potter ['pɒtə(r)] I N [C] 陶工 [táogōng] II VI
▶ **to potter around, potter about** (BRIT) 磨磨蹭
蹭地做琐事 [mómó cèngcèng de zuò suǒshì]
▶ **to potter around the house** (BRIT) 在房里
闲逛

pottery ['pɒtərɪ] N **1** [U] (pots, dishes) 陶器
[táoqì] **2** [U] (work, hobby) 陶艺 [táoyì] **3** [C]
(factory, workshop) 制陶厂 [zhìtáo chǎng] ▶ **a
piece of pottery** 一件陶器

potty ['pɒtɪ] (inf) I ADJ (mad) 傻的 [shǎ de]
II N [C] (for child) 尿壶 [niàohú] ▶ **to go potty**
(inf) 发疯

pouch [paʊtʃ] N [C] **1** (for tobacco, coins) 小袋
[xiǎodài] **2** (ZOOL) 育儿袋 [yù'ér dài]

poultry ['pəʊltrɪ] N **1** (birds) 家禽 [jiāqín]
2 (meat) 家禽肉 [jiāqín ròu]

pounce [paʊns] VI **1** (animal, person +) 猛扑 [měngpū] **2** ▶ **to
pounce on sb/sth** [animal, person +] 猛扑向
某人/某物 [měngpū xiàng mǒurén/mǒuwù]
3 ▶ **to pounce on** (criticize) [+ mistake, suggestion,
comment] 抨击 [pēngjī]

○ **pound** [paʊnd] I N [C] **1** (unit of money) 镑
[bàng] **2** (unit of weight) 磅 [bàng] **3** (for dogs,
cats) 认领所 [rènlǐng suǒ]；(for cars) 认领场
[rènlǐng chǎng] II VT **1** (beat) [+ table, wall,
door etc] 猛击 [měngjī] **2** (crush) [+ spice, grain
etc] 捣 [dǎo] III VI **1** [heart +] 剧烈跳动 [jùliè
tiàodòng] **2** [head +] 剧痛 [jùtòng] ▶ **a pound
coin** 1镑硬币 ▶ **a five-pound note** 5镑纸币
▶ **half a pound (of sth)** 半磅 (某物)

pound sterling N [C] 英镑 [yīngbàng]

pour [pɔː(r)] I VT **1** ▶ **to pour sth (into/onto sth)**
[+ liquid] 灌某物 (到某物里/上) [guàn mǒuwù
(dào mǒuwù lǐ/shang)]；[+ powder] 倒某物 (到某
物里/上) [dào mǒuwù (dào mǒuwù lǐ/shang)]
II VI **1** ▶ **to pour (from sth)** [water, blood, smoke +]
(从某物) 涌出 [(cóng mǒuwù) yǒngchū] **2** ▶ **to
pour into/out of sth** [people +] 涌进/出某地
[yǒngjìn/chū mǒudì] ▶ **to pour sb/o.s. a drink**
给某人/自己倒了一杯喝的 ▶ **tears/sweat
poured down his face** 眼泪/汗水顺着他的
面颊流了下来 ▶ **it is pouring (with rain), it is**

pouring down 大雨如注
▸ **pour away** VT [+ *liquid*] 倒掉 [dàodiào]
▸ **pour in** I VI [*news, letters* +] 滚滚而来 [gǔngǔn érlái] II VT [+ *water, milk, eggs*] 倒入 [dàorù]
▸ **pour out** VT **1** [+ *tea, wine etc*] 倒出 [dàochū] **2** (*fig*) [+ *thoughts, feelings, worries*] 倾诉 [qīngsù]
pouring ['pɔ:rɪŋ] ADJ ▸ **pouring rain** 倾盆大雨 [qīngpén dàyǔ]
pout [paut] VI 撅嘴 [juēzuǐ]
poverty ['pɒvətɪ] N [U] 贫穷 [pínqióng] ▸ **to live in poverty** 生活贫困
POW N ABBR (= *prisoner of war*) 战俘 [zhànfú]
powder ['paudə(r)] I N **1** [C/U] 粉 [fěn] **2** [U] (*also*: **face powder**) 扑面粉 [pūmiànfěn] II VT ▸ **to powder one's face** 在脸上擦粉 [zài liǎnshang cāfěn] ▸ **to powder one's nose** 上厕所
powdered milk ['paudəd-] N [U] 奶粉 [nǎifěn]
⊙ **power** ['pauə(r)] I N [U] **1** (*control*) (*over people, activities*) 权力 [quánlì] **2** (*ability*) 能力 [nénglì] **3** (*legal right*) 权限 [quánxiàn] **4** [*of ideas, words*] 影响力 [yǐngxiǎnglì] **5** (*force, energy*) [*of explosion, engine*] 效力 [xiàolì]; [*of person, muscle*] 力量 [lìliàng] **6** (*electricity*) 电力 [diànlì] II VT [+ *machine*] 为…提供动力 [wèi…tígōng dònglì] ▸ **to do everything in one's power to help** 竭尽全力帮助 ▸ **a world power** 世界大国 ▸ **the powers that be** 当权者 ▸ **to be in power** (POL) 掌权 ▸ **to take power** 夺取政权 ▸ **to come to power** 开始执政 ▸ **2 to the power of 3** (MATH) 2的3次幂 ▸ **a power breakfast/lunch** 早/午餐高层汇报会
power cut (BRIT) N [C] 停电 [tíngdiàn] [美 = **outage**]
powered ['pauəd] ADJ ▸ **powered by sth** 由某物提供动力的 [yóu mǒuwù tígōng dònglì de] ▸ **nuclear-powered submarine** 核动力潜艇
power failure N [C] 断电 [duàndiàn]
powerful ['pauəful] ADJ **1** (*influential*) [+ *person, organization*] 有影响力的 [yǒu yǐngxiǎnglì de] **2** (*physically strong*) [+ *person, body, animal*] 强健的 [qiángjiàn de] **3** (*forceful*) [+ *blow, kick*] 有力的 [yǒulì de] **4** [+ *engine, machine*] 大功率的 [dà gōnglù de]; [+ *substance, cleaner, drug*] 强效的 [qiángxiào de] **5** [+ *smell*] 浓的 [nóng de] **6** [+ *voice*] 巨大的 [jùdà de] **7** [+ *argument, evidence*] 令人信服的 [lìngrén xìnfú de]; [+ *writing, speech, work of art, performance*] 有感染力的 [yǒu gǎnrǎnlì de] **8** [+ *emotion*] 强烈的 [qiángliè de]
powerless ['pauəlɪs] ADJ 无力的 [wúlì de] ▸ **to be powerless to do sth** 对做某事无能为力
power point (BRIT) N [C] 电源插座 [diànyuán chāzuò] [美 = **outlet**]
power station N [C] 发电厂 [fādiàn chǎng]
pp ABBR (= *per procurationem*) 以…的名义 [yǐ…de míngyì]

pp. ABBR (= *pages*) 页 [yè]
PR N ABBR **1** (= *public relations*) 公共关系 [gōnggòng guānxì] **2** (= *proportional representation*) 比例代表制 [bǐlì dàibiǎozhì]
practical ['præktɪkl] I ADJ **1** (*not theoretical*) [+ *difficulties, experience*] 实践的 [shíjiàn de] **2** [+ *ideas, methods, advice, suggestions*] 切合实际的 [qièhé shíjì de] **3** (*sensible person, mind*) 有实际经验的 [yǒu shíjì jīngyàn de] **4** (*good with hands*) 动手能力强的 [dòngshǒu nénglì qiáng de] **5** (*functional*) [+ *clothes, things*] 实用的 [shíyòng de] II N [C] **1** (*examination*) 实践考试 [shíjiàn kǎoshì] **2** (*lesson*) 实习课 [shíxí kè]
practical joke N [C] 恶作剧 [èzuòjù]
practically ['præktɪklɪ] ADV **1** (*almost*) 几乎 [jīhū] **2** (*not theoretically*) 实际上 [shíjì shang]
practice ['præktɪs] I N **1** [C] (*custom*) 习俗 [xísú] **2** [C/U] (*way of operating*) 惯例 [guànlì] **3** [U] (*not theory*) 实践 [shíjiàn] **4** [U] (*exercise, training*) 练习 [liànxí] **5** [C] (*training session*) 实习 [shíxí] **6** [U] [*of religion*] 信奉活动 [xìnfèng huódòng] **7** (MED, LAW) (*business*) [C] 从业 [cóngyè]; (*work*) [U] 工作 [gōngzuò] II VT, VI (US) = **practise** ▸ **it's normal** *or* **standard practice** 这是通常 [或] 标准做法 ▸ **in practice** (*in reality*) 实际上 ▸ **to put sth into practice** 应用某事 ▸ **to be out of practice** 荒疏 ▸ **2 hours' piano practice** 2小时的练琴时间
practise, (US) **practice** ['præktɪs] I VT **1** (*work on*) [+ *sport, technique, musical instrument, piece of music*] 练习 [liànxí] **2** (*carry out*) [+ *custom, activity, craft, religion*] 实行 [shíxíng] ▷ *Acupuncture was first practised in China in the third millennium BC.* 公元前3000年中国人首次使用针灸。 **3** [+ *medicine, law*] 从业 [cóngyè] II VI **1** (*train*) (*in music, theatre, sport*) 练习 [liànxí] **2** [*lawyer, doctor, dentist* +] 从业 [cóngyè] ▸ **to practise as a lawyer** 做律师
practising ['præktɪsɪŋ] ADJ [+ *Christian, Jew, Muslim*] 笃信的 [dǔxìn de]; [+ *doctor, dentist, lawyer*] 从业的 [cóngyè de]; [+ *homosexual*] 有实际性行为的 [yǒu shíjìxìng xíngwéi de]
practitioner [præk'tɪʃənə(r)] (*frm*) N [C] (*also*: **general practitioner**) 开业者 [kāiyèzhě] ▸ **alternative practitioner** 使用非传统治疗方式的从业者 ▸ **legal practitioner** 从业律师
pragmatic [præg'mætɪk] ADJ [+ *person, approach etc*] 务实的 [wùshí de]
prairie ['prɛərɪ] N [C] 大草原 [dà cǎoyuán] ▸ **the prairies** 北美洲大草原
praise [preɪz] I N [U] **1** 赞扬 [zànyáng] **2** (*to God*) 赞美 [zànměi] II VT **1** 称赞 [chēngzàn] **2** (REL) [+ *God*] 颂扬 [sòngyáng] ▸ **to sing sb's praises** 称颂某人 ▸ **to praise sb for sth/for doing sth** 因某事赞扬某人/赞扬某人做某事
pram [præm] (BRIT) N [C] 婴儿车 [yīng'érchē] [美 = **baby carriage**]
prank [præŋk] (*o.f.*) N [C] 恶作剧 [èzuòjù]

prawn [prɔːn] (BRIT) N [C] 虾 [xiā] [美=
shrimp]

prawn cocktail (BRIT) N [C/U] 冷盘虾
[lěngpánxiā] [美=shrimp cocktail]

pray [preɪ] VI 祷告 [dǎogào] ▶ to pray for/that
(REL) 为⋯祈祷/祈祷⋯ ▶ I pray that she'll
never find out (inf) (fig) 我祈祷她永远不会
发现

prayer [prɛə(r)] (REL) I N 1 [U] (activity) 祷告
[dǎogào] 2 [C] (words) 祈祷文 [qídǎowén]
II **prayers** NPL (service) 祈祷式 [qídǎoshì] ▶ to
say one's prayers 祈祷

preach [priːtʃ] I VI 1 [priest, vicar +] 布道
[bùdào] 2 (moralize) 说教 [shuōjiào] II VT
1 [+ sermon] 讲道 [jiǎngdào] 2 (advocate) 宣扬
[xuānyáng] ▶ to preach at sb (fig) 对某人说教
▶ to be preaching to the converted (fig) 对人
们宣传他们早已持有的观点 ▶ to preach the
Gospel 传播福音

preacher ['priːtʃə(r)] N [C] 传教士
[chuánjiàoshì]

precarious [prɪ'kɛərɪəs] ADJ 1 (dangerous) 危
险的 [wēixiǎn de] 2 (fig) [+ position, situation, job]
不确定的 [bù quèdìng de]

precaution [prɪ'kɔːʃən] N [C] 预防措施
[yùfáng cuòshī] ▶ as a precaution 以防万一
▶ to take precautions 采取防范措施

precede [prɪ'siːd] VT 1 (in time) [+ event] 早
于 [zǎoyú] 2 (in space) [+ person] 先于 [xiānyú]
3 [words, sentences, section +] 在⋯之前
[zài⋯zhīqián]

precedent ['prɛsɪdənt] (frm) N [C/U] 1 先例
[xiānlì] 2 (LAW) 判例 [pànlì] ▶ to establish or
set a precedent 开创先例;(LAW) 援为判例

preceding [prɪ'siːdɪŋ] ADJ [+ chapter, programme,
day etc] 在前的 [zài qián de]

precinct ['priːsɪŋkt] I N [C] 1 (BRIT) (also:
shopping precinct) 购物区 [gòuwù qū] 2 (US)
(part of city) 管辖区 [guǎnxiá qū] II **precincts**
NPL (frm) [of cathedral, college] 周围地区
[zhōuwéi dìqū] ▶ pedestrian precinct (BRIT)
行人专用区

precious ['prɛʃəs] ADJ 1 (valuable) [+ time,
resource, memories] 宝贵的 [bǎoguì de];
(financially) 贵重的 [guìzhòng de] 2 (important)
▶ precious (to sb) (对某人)珍贵 [(duì mǒurén)
zhēnguì] 3 (pej) [+ person, writing, style] 矫揉造
作的 [jiǎoróu zàozuò de] 4 (inf) (damned) 该死
的 [gāisǐ de] 5 (inf) ▶ precious little/few 极
少 [jíshǎo]

precise [prɪ'saɪs] ADJ 1 [+ time, nature, position,
circumstances] 精确的 [jīngquè de];[+ figure,
definition] 准确的 [zhǔnquè de];[+ explanation]
清晰的 [qīngxī de] 2 (detailed) [+ instructions,
plans] 详尽的 [xiángjìn de] ▶ to be precise (in
fact) 确切地说

precisely [prɪ'saɪslɪ] ADV (exactly) 确切地
[quèqiè de];(referring to time) 正好 [zhènghǎo]

▶ **precisely!** 的确如此!

precision [prɪ'sɪʒən] N [U] 精确 [jīngquè]

precocious [prɪ'kəʊʃəs] ADJ 1 [+ child] 早熟
的 [zǎoshú de];(talented) 过早发展的 [guòzǎo
fāzhǎn de] 2 [+ talent] 早慧的 [zǎohuì de]

predator ['prɛdətə(r)] N [C] 1 (ZOOL) 肉食动物
[ròushí dòngwù] 2 (fig) (person, organization) 掠
夺者 [lüèduózhě]

predecessor ['priːdɪsɛsə(r)] N [C] 1 (person) (in
job) 前任 [qiánrèn] 2 (machine, object) 被替代的
事物 [bèi tìdài de shìwù]

predicament [prɪ'dɪkəmənt] N [C] 困境
[kùnjìng] ▶ to be in a predicament 处于困
境之中

predict [prɪ'dɪkt] VT [+ event, death etc] 预言
[yùyán] ▶ to predict that... 预言⋯

predictable [prɪ'dɪktəbl] ADJ [+ outcome,
behaviour, remark etc] 可预料的 [kě yùliào de];
[+ person] 平庸的 [píngyōng de]

prediction [prɪ'dɪkʃən] N [C] 预言 [yùyán]

predominantly [prɪ'dɔmɪnəntlɪ] ADV 主要
地 [zhǔyào de]

preface ['prɛfəs] I N [C] 序言 [xùyán] II VT
▶ to preface sth with sth [+ speech, action] 以
某物开启某物 [yǐ mǒuwù kāiqǐ mǒuwù] ▶ he
prefaced his remark by saying that... 以说⋯作
为他的开场白 ▶ to be prefaced by sth 以某
事作为开场

prefect ['priːfɛkt] (BRIT) N [C] (in school) 级长
[jízhǎng]

prefer [prɪ'fə:(r)] VT 偏爱 [piān'ài] ▶ to prefer
coffee to tea 喜欢咖啡胜于茶 ▶ to prefer
doing sth 更喜欢做某事 ▶ I'd prefer to go by
train 我宁愿坐火车去 ▶ I'd prefer him to go
to university 我宁可他上大学 ▶ to prefer
charges 提出控告

preferable ['prɛfrəbl] ADJ ▶ preferable (to
sth/to doing sth) (比某事/做某事)更可取
[(bǐ mǒushì/zuò mǒushì) gèng kěqǔ] ▶ it is
preferable to discuss matters openly 公开地
讨论事情会更好

preferably ['prɛfrəblɪ] ADV 最好 [zuìhǎo]

preference ['prɛfrəns] N [C/U] 偏爱 [piān'ài]
▶ to have a preference for sth/for doing sth 偏
爱某物/做某事 ▶ in preference to sth 更倾
向于某事 ▶ to give preference to sb 给某人
以优待

preferential [prɛfə'rɛnʃəl] ADJ [+ treatment,
arrangement] 优待的 [yōudài de]

prefix ['priːfɪks] (LING) N [C] 前缀 [qiánzhuì]

pregnancy ['prɛgnənsɪ] N 1 [U] (condition) 孕
期 [yùnqī] 2 (instance) 怀孕 [huáiyùn]

pregnant ['prɛgnənt] ADJ 1 [+ woman, animal]
怀孕的 [huáiyùn de] 2 (fig) [+ pause, silence] 耐
人寻味的 [nàirén xúnwèi de] ▶ 3 months
pregnant 怀孕3个月 ▶ when I was pregnant
with Stephen 当我怀着史蒂芬的时候 ▶ to
get pregnant 怀孕了

prehistoric ['priː'hɪs'tɔrɪk] ADJ 史前的 [shǐqián de]

prejudice ['predʒʊdɪs] I N [C/U] (bias) 偏见 [piānjiàn] II VT 1 (influence) [+ person, result, case] 使有偏见 [shǐ yǒu piānjiàn] 2 (compromise) [+ situation, health etc] 侵害 [qīnhài] ▶ prejudice against/in favour of sb 对某人有偏见/偏爱某人 ▶ without prejudice to (frm) 无损于 ▶ to prejudice sb against/in favour of sth 使某人对某事抱有偏见/怀有好感

prejudiced ['predʒʊdɪst] ADJ (biased) [+ person] 有偏见的 [yǒu piānjiàn de]; [+ view, opinion, information] 偏颇的 [piānpō de] ▶ to be prejudiced in favour of sb/sth 偏向于某人/某事 ▶ to be prejudiced against sb/sth 对某人/某事存有偏见

preliminary [prɪ'lɪmɪnərɪ] I ADJ [+ talks, results etc] 预备性的 [yùbèixìng de] II N [C] (SPORT) 预赛 [yùsài] ▶ preliminary round (SPORT) 分组预选赛 ▶ as a preliminary to sth/to doing sth 作为某事/做某事的预备

prelude ['preljuːd] N [C] 1 (MUS) 前奏曲 [qiánzòuqǔ] 2 ▶ a prelude to sth/to doing sth 某事/做某事的前奏 [mǒushì/zuò mǒushì de qiánzòu]

premature ['premətʃʊə(r)] ADJ [+ baby] 早产的 [zǎochǎn de]; [+ death, arrival, congratulations] 过早的 [guòzǎo de] ▶ you're being a little premature 你有点草率

premier ['premɪə(r)] I ADJ (best) 首位的 [shǒuwèi de] II N [C](POL) 首相 [shǒuxiàng]

première ['premɪɛə(r)] N [C] [of film, play, musical] 首次公演 [shǒucì gōngyǎn]

Premier League (BRIT: FOOTBALL) N ▶ the Premier League 超级联赛 [Chāojí Liánsài]

premise ['premɪs] (frm) I N [C] 1 [of argument] 前提 [qiántí] II premises NPL [of business, institution, school] 地产 [dìchǎn] ▶ on the premises (in the buildings) 在屋内; (outside) 在房屋周围

premium ['priːmɪəm] I N [C] 1 (COMM) (additional sum) 额外费用 [éwài fèiyòng] 2 (INSURANCE) 保险费 [bǎoxiǎnfèi] II ADJ (also: premium-quality) [+ product, service] 质量一流的 [zhìliàng yīliú de] ▶ to be at a premium (expensive) 稀有而昂贵的; (hard to get) 稀缺的

premonition [premə'nɪʃən] N [C] 预感 [yùgǎn] ▶ to have a premonition that... 预感到…

preoccupied [priː'ɒkjʊpaɪd] ADJ [+ person] 全神贯注的 [quánshén guànzhù de] ▶ to be preoccupied with sth 对某事心事重重

prep [prep] I VT (ESP US) 1 (prepare) 预备 [yùbèi] 2 (MED) [+ patient] 为…作术前准备 [wèi…zuò shù qián zhǔnbèi] II N [U] (BRIT) (homework) 课外作业 [kèwài zuòyè] ▶ to do one's prep 做课外作业

prepaid [priː'peɪd] ADJ [+ fee, activity, funeral] 预付的 [yùfù de]; [+ envelope, phone card] 预先付讫的 [yùxiān fùqì de]

preparation [prepə'reɪʃən] I N 1 [U] (activity) 准备 [zhǔnbèi] 2 [C] (food, medicine, cosmetic) 配制品 [pèizhìpǐn] II preparations NPL (arrangements) ▶ preparations (for sth) (为某事的) 准备工作 [(wèi mǒushì de) zhǔnbèi gōngzuò] ▶ in preparation for sth 为某事而准备的 ▶ to make preparations for sth 为某事做好准备

preparatory school [prɪ'pærətərɪ-] N = prep school

prepare [prɪ'peə(r)] I VT [+ speech, room, report, object etc] 准备 [zhǔnbèi]; [+ food, meal] 预备 [yùbèi] II VI ▶ to prepare (for sth) [+ event, exam, interview] (为某事) 做准备 [(wèi mǒushì) zuò zhǔnbèi] ▶ to prepare o.s. for sth [+ shock, meeting, event] 使自己对某事有所准备 ▶ to prepare to do sth (get ready) 准备好做某事 ▶ to prepare for action 准备战斗

prepared [prɪ'peəd] ADJ ▶ to be prepared to do sth (willing) 有意做某事 [yǒuyì zuò mǒushì] ▶ prepared (for sth) (ready) (对某事) 有所准备的

preposition [prepə'zɪʃən] N [C] 介词 [jiècí]

prep school N [C/U] 1 (BRIT) 只收男生或女生的私立小学 [zhǐshōu nánshēng huò nǚshēng de sīlì xiǎoxué] 2 (US) 预科学校 [yùkē xuéxiào]

prerequisite [priː'rekwɪzɪt] N [C] 先决条件 [xiānjué tiáojiàn]

preschool ['priː'skuːl] ADJ [+ age, child, education] 学龄前的 [xuélíngqián de]

prescribe [prɪ'skraɪb] VT 1 (MED) 开 [kāi] 2 (state) 规定 [guīdìng] ▶ to prescribe sth for sb/sth 给某人/因为某事开某物

prescription [prɪ'skrɪpʃən] N [C] (MED) (slip of paper) 处方 [chǔfāng]; (medicine) 药方 [yàofāng] ▶ to make up a prescription 配方 ▶ to give sb a prescription for sth 给某人开用于某事的处方 ▶ "only available on prescription" "凭处方购买"

presence ['prezns] N 1 [U] (existence, attendance) 到场 [dàochǎng] 2 [U] (fig) (personality) 风度 [fēngdù] 3 [C] (spirit, invisible influence) 存在 [cúnzài] ▶ in sb's presence 当着某人的面 ▶ to make one's presence felt 让人感到自身的存在

present [adj, n 'preznt, vb prɪ'zent] I ADJ 1 (current) 现有的 [xiànyǒu de] 2 (in attendance) 在场的 [zàichǎng de] II N 1 (not past) ▶ the present 目前 [mùqián] 2 [C] (gift) 礼物 [lǐwù] 3 ▶ the present (also: present tense) 现在时态 [xiànzài shítài] III VT 1 (give) ▶ to present sth (to sb) [+ prize, award] 授予 (某人) 某事 [shòuyǔ (mǒurén) mǒushì] 2 (cause, provide) [+ problem, threat] 产生 [chǎnshēng]; [+ challenge, opportunity] 呈现 [chéngxiàn] 3 (introduce)

[+ *information, view*] 表述 [biǎoshù]; [+ *person*] 介绍 [jièshào] **4** (*portray*) [+ *person, thing*] 描述 [miáoshù] **5** (RAD, TV) [+ *programme*] 主持 [zhǔchí] ▶ **the present day** 当今 ▶ **to be present at sth** 出席某事 ▶ **to be present in sth** 存在于某事中 ▶ **all those present** 全体在场人员 ▶ **at present** 现在 ▶ **to give sb a present** 给某人礼物 ▶ **to present sb with sth** [+ *prize, award*] 授予某人某物; [+ *choice, option*] 给予某人某物 ▶ **to present sb with sth** [+ *difficulty, problem, threat*] 给某人带来某物 ▶ **to present o.s. as being...** 将自己表述为… ▶ **to present itself** [*opportunity* +] 出现

presentable [prɪˈzɛntəbl] ADJ [+ *person*] 中看的 [zhōngkàn de]

presentation [prɛznˈteɪʃən] N **1** [C] [*of award, prize*] 授予 [shòuyǔ] **2** [U] (*appearance*) [*of product, food*] 外观 [wàiguān]; [*of essay, report*] 观感 [guāngǎn] **3** [C] (*lecture, talk*) 陈述 [chénshù] **4** [C] (THEAT) (*production*) 演出 [yǎnchū] ▶ **to give a presentation** 做陈述 ▶ **on presentation of...** [+ *voucher, invitation*] 一经出示…

present-day [ˈprɛzntdeɪ] ADJ 当前的 [dāngqián de]

presenter [prɪˈzɛntə(r)] N [C] (*on radio, TV*) 节目主持人 [jiémù zhǔchírén]

presently [ˈprɛzntlɪ] ADV **1** (*after a while*) 一会儿 [yīhuìr] **2** (*shortly*) 马上 [mǎshang] **3** (*currently*) 目前 [mùqián]

present participle [-ˈpɑːtɪsɪpl] N [C] 现在分词 [xiànzài fēncí]

preservation [prɛzəˈveɪʃən] N [U] **1** (*continuation*) [*of peace, standards, life etc*] 保持 [bǎochí] **2** (*maintenance*) [*of building, monument, furniture etc*] 保存 [bǎocún]

preservative [prɪˈzəːvətɪv] N [C/U] (*for food, wood*) 防腐剂 [fángfǔjì]

preserve [prɪˈzəːv] I VT **1** [+ *customs, independence, peace*] 维护 [wéihù]; [+ *building, artefact*] 保存 [bǎocún]; [+ *character, area, forest*] 保护 [bǎohù] **2** (*in salt, syrup, vinegar etc*) [+ *food*] 防腐 [fángfǔ] II N [C/U] (*jam, marmalade, chutney*) 果酱 [guǒjiàng] **2** [C] (*for game, fish*) 私人渔猎区 [sīrén yúliè qū] **3** [C] ▶ **a male/working class preserve** 男性/工人阶级所独有 [nánxìng/gōngrén jiējí suǒ dúyǒu] ▶ **strawberry preserve** 草莓酱

preside [prɪˈzaɪd] VI ▶ **to preside over sth** [+ *meeting, event*] 主持某事 [zhǔchí mǒushì]

○ **president** [ˈprɛzɪdənt] N [C] **1** (POL) 总统 [zǒngtǒng] **2** [+ *of society, club, institution*] 主席 [zhǔxí] **3** (US) [*of company*] 总裁 [zǒngcái]

presidential [prɛzɪˈdɛnʃl] ADJ (POL) [+ *election, candidate*] 总统职位的 [zǒngtǒng zhíwèi de]; [+ *adviser, representative*] 总统的 [zǒngtǒng de]

○ **press** [prɛs] I N **1** (*newspapers, journalists*) ▶ **the press** 新闻界 [xīnwén jiè] **2** [C] (*for wine*) 榨汁机 [zhàzhījī] **3** [C] (*also*: **printing press**) 印

刷机 [yìnshuājī] II VT **1** [+ *button, switch, bell*] 按 [àn]; [+ *accelerator*] 踏 [tà] **2** (*squeeze*) 挤 [jǐ] **3** (*iron*) [+ *clothes, sheets etc*] 熨平 [yùnpíng] **4** (*put pressure on*) ▶ **to press sb for sth/to do sth** 催逼某人某事/做某事 [cuībī mǒurén mǒushì/zuò mǒushì] **5** (*express*) [+ *claim, views, point*] 坚持 [jiānchí] III VI (*squeeze*) 挤 [jǐ] ▶ **to go to press** [*newspaper* +] 付印 ▶ **to give sth a press** [+ *switch, button, bell*] 按某物 ▶ **at the press of a switch** 按了开关后 ▶ **to press sb about sth** 从某人处打探某事 ▶ **to press sb for an answer** 催人回答 ▶ **to press sb into doing sth** (*urge*) 迫切要求某人做某事 ▶ **to press sth (up)on sb** (*force*) 迫使某人接受某事 ▶ **to press charges (against sb)** (LAW) 起诉(某人) ▶ **to be pressed for time/money** 时间紧迫/手头紧 ▶ **to press (down) on sth** (向下) 压某物 ▶ **to press for sth** [+ *changes etc*] 迫切要求某事
▶ **press ahead, press on** VI 勇往直前 [yǒngwǎng zhíqián] ▶ **to press on with sth** 加紧某事

press conference N [C] 新闻发布会 [xīnwén fābùhuì]

pressing [ˈprɛsɪŋ] ADJ [+ *problem, issue*] 紧迫的 [jǐnpò de]

press stud (BRIT) N [C] 摁扣儿 [ènkòur]

press-up [ˈprɛsʌp] (BRIT) N [C] 俯卧撑 [fǔwòchēng]

○ **pressure** [ˈprɛʃə(r)] I N **1** [U] (*physical force*) 压力 [yālì] **2** [U] [*of air, gas, water*] 压强 [yāqiáng] **3** [U] (*fig*) (*coercion*) ▶ **pressure (to do sth)** (做某事的) 压力 [(zuò mǒushì de) yālì] **4** [C/U] (*stress*) 压力 [yālì] II VT ▶ **to pressure sb (to do sth)** 强使某人(做某事) [qiángshǐ mǒurén (zuò mǒushì)] ▶ **high/low pressure** 高/低压 ▶ **to put pressure on sb (to do sth)** 对某人施加压力(去做某事) ▶ **under pressure** (*with stress*) 在压力下 ▶ **to be under pressure to do sth** 被迫做某事 ▶ **to pressure sb into doing sth** 迫使某人做某事

pressure cooker N [C] 高压锅 [gāoyāguō]

pressure group N [C] 压力集团 [yālì jítuán]

prestige [prɛsˈtiːʒ] N [U] [*of person, organization, job*] 威望 [wēiwàng]

prestigious [prɛsˈtɪdʒəs] ADJ [+ *institution, job*] 有威望的 [yǒu wēiwàng de]

presumably [prɪˈzjuːməblɪ] ADV 据推测 [jù tuīcè]

presume [prɪˈzjuːm] VT **1** (*assume*) ▶ **to presume (that...)** 认定 (…) [rèndìng(…)] **2** (*dare*) ▶ **to presume to do sth** 擅自做某事 [shànzì zuò mǒushì] ▶ **I presume so** 我认为是的 ▶ **to be presumed dead** 被认定死亡

pretence, (US) **pretense** [prɪˈtɛns] N [C/U] 假装 [jiǎzhuāng] ▶ **under false pretences** 虚情假意地 ▶ **to make a pretence of doing sth** 假装做某事

pretend [prɪˈtɛnd] I VT ▶ **to pretend to do**

sth/pretend that... (make believe) 假装做某事/假装… [jiǎzhuāng zuò mǒushì/jiǎzhuāng…] ▷ The children were pretending to be pirates. 孩子们扮成海盗。▷ She can sunbathe and pretend she's in Spain. 她能照日光浴，想像着她是在西班牙。II VI 假装 [jiǎzhuāng] ▶ I don't pretend to understand it (claim) 我不会不懂装懂的

pretense [prɪ'tɛns] (US) N = **pretense**

pretentious [prɪ'tɛnʃəs] ADJ [+ person, play, restaurant etc] 矫饰的 [jiǎoshì de]

pretext ['pri:tɛkst] N [C] 借口 [jièkǒu] ▶ on or under the pretext of sth/of doing sth 以某事/做某事为借口

pretty ['prɪtɪ] I ADJ [+ person, face, house, dress] 漂亮的 [piàoliang de] II ADV (inf) (quite) [+ good, happy, soon etc] 相当 [xiāngdāng] ▶ to look pretty 看上去漂亮 ▶ pretty much/pretty well (inf) (more or less) 差不多

prevail [prɪ'veɪl] VI 1 (be current) [custom, belief, conditions, fashion +] 盛行 [shèngxíng] 2 (triumph) ▶ to prevail (over sth) 胜过(某事) [shèngguò (mǒushì)] ▶ to prevail upon sb to do sth 说服某人做某事

prevailing [prɪ'veɪlɪŋ] ADJ 1 [+ wind] 盛行的 [shèngxíng de] 2 (dominant) [+ view, opinion] 主导的 [zhǔdǎo de]

prevalent ['prɛvələnt] ADJ [+ belief, custom, attitude] 普遍的 [pǔbiàn de]

prevent [prɪ'vɛnt] VT [+ war, disease, situation] 阻止 [zǔzhǐ]; [+ accident, fire] 防止 [fángzhǐ] ▶ to prevent sb (from) doing sth 阻止某人做某事 ▶ to prevent sth (from) happening 防止某事发生

preventable [prɪ'vɛntəbl] ADJ [+ disease, death, accident] 可预防的 [kě yùfáng de]

prevention [prɪ'vɛnʃən] N [U] 预防 [yùfáng]

preventive [prɪ'vɛntɪv] ADJ [+ measures, medicine] 预防的 [yùfáng de]

preview ['pri:vju:] N [C] [of film, exhibition] 预演 [yùyǎn]

previous ['pri:vɪəs] ADJ 1 (prior) [+ marriage, relationship, experience, owner] 前的 [qián de] 2 (preceding) [+ chapter, week, day] 以前的 [yǐqián de] ▶ previous to (before) 在…之前
用法参见 **former**

previously ['pri:vɪəslɪ] ADV 1 以前 [yǐqián] 2 10 days previously 10天前 [shí tiān qián]

pre-war [pri:'wɔ:(r)] ADJ 二战前的 [èrzhàn qián de]

prey [preɪ] N [U] 猎物 [lièwù] ▶ to fall prey to sth (fig) 受某事折磨 ▶ to be prey to sth 为某事而受苦
▶ **prey on** VT FUS [不可拆分] [animal +] 捕食 [bǔshí] ▶ to prey on sb's mind 烦扰某人

○ **price** [praɪs] I N [C/U] 价格 [jiàgé] II VT [+ goods] 定价 [dìngjià] ▶ what is the price of...? …多少钱? ▶ to go up or rise in price 涨价 ▶ you can't put a price on friendship/your

health 友谊/健康无价 ▶ to pay a high price for sth (fig) 为某事付出很高代价 ▶ it's a small price to pay for freedom 这是为自由付出的小小代价 ▶ at a price 以很高代价 ▶ what price he'll change his mind? 他改变主意的可能性有多少? ▶ to be priced at 定价为 ▶ to price o.s. out of the market 漫天要价以至无人问津

priceless ['praɪslɪs] ADJ 1 [+ diamond, painting] 无价的 [wújià de] 2 (very useful) [+ experience, skill, assistance] 宝贵的 [bǎoguì de] 3 (inf) (amusing) [+ person, comment] 很有趣的 [hěn yǒuqù de]
用法参见 **invaluable**

price list N [C] 价目表 [jiàmùbiǎo]

prick [prɪk] I N [C] 1 (sting) 刺 [cì] 2 (inf!) (penis) 阴茎 [yīnjīng]; (idiot) 蠢人 [chǔnrén] II VT 1 (scratch) (on thorn, with needle) 刺 [cì] 2 (also: prick holes in) 刺孔于 [cìkǒng yú] ▶ to prick o.s. (on/with sth) 被(某物)刺到 ▶ to prick up one's ears (listen) 侧耳倾听

prickly ['prɪklɪ] ADJ 1 [+ plant, fabric, animal] 多刺的 [duōcì de] 2 (irritable) [+ person] 易怒的 [yì'nù de]

pride [praɪd] I N [U] 1 (satisfaction, dignity, self-respect) 自豪 [zìháo] 2 (arrogance) 傲慢 [àomàn] II VT ▶ to pride o.s. on sth/on doing sth 因某事/做某事而自豪 [yīn mǒushì/zuò mǒushì ér zìháo] ▶ to take (a) pride in sb/sth 因某人/某事而自豪 ▶ to take a pride in doing sth 以做某事为豪 ▶ to have or take pride of place (BRIT) 占据头等重要的位置

priest [pri:st] N [C] 神职人员 [shénzhí rényuán]

primarily ['praɪmərɪlɪ] ADV 主要地 [zhǔyào de]

primary ['praɪmərɪ] I ADJ 1 (principal) [+ reason, aim, cause] 主要的 [zhǔyào de] 2 (BRIT) [+ education, teacher] 小学的 [xiǎoxué de] II N [C] (in US) (also: **primary election**) 初选 [chūxuǎn]

primary school (BRIT) N [C/U] 小学 [xiǎoxué] [美 = **elementary school, grade school**]

prime [praɪm] I ADJ 1 (major) [+ cause, concern, target] 首要的 [shǒuyào de] 2 (best) [+ condition, position] 第一流的 [dìyīliú de] II N [C] ▶ in one's prime 处于黄金时期 [chǔyú huángjīn shíqī] III VT 1 (prepare) ▶ to prime sb (to do sth) 事先使某人准备好(做某事) [shìxiān shǐ mǒurén zhǔnbèi hǎo (zuò mǒushì)] 2 [+ gun] 装[zhuāng] 3 [+ wood] 给…上底漆 [gěi…shàng dǐqī] ▶ of prime importance 最重要 ▶ prime beef 上等牛肉 ▶ a prime example of... …最典型的例子 ▶ in the prime of life 处于壮年时期

Prime Minister N [C] 总理 [Zǒnglǐ]

primitive ['prɪmɪtɪv] ADJ 1 (simple) [+ tribe, society, tool] 原始的 [yuánshǐ de] 2 (early) [+ man, life form, instinct] 早期的 [zǎoqī de] 3 (crude) [+ conditions, technique] 简陋的 [jiǎnlòu de]

primrose ['prɪmrəuz] N [C] 报春花

[bàochūnhuā]

prince [prɪns] N [C] 王子 [wángzǐ]

princess [prɪnˈsɛs] N [C] 公主 [gōngzhǔ]

principal [ˈprɪnsɪpl] I ADJ **1** (main) [+ reason, aim] 主要的 [zhǔyào de] **2** (THEAT) [+ role, part, character] 主要的 [zhǔyào de] II N **1** [C] (head teacher) [of school, college] 校长 [xiàozhǎng] **2** [C] (THEAT) 主角 [zhǔjué] **3** [S] (FIN) (sum) 资本 [zīběn]

principally [ˈprɪnsɪplɪ] ADV 主要地 [zhǔyào de]

principle [ˈprɪnsɪpl] N **1** [C/U] (moral belief) 正直 [zhèngzhí] **2** [C/U] (of philosophy, theory) 原理 [yuánlǐ] **3** [C] (basic law) 原则 [yuánzé] ▶ **in principle** (in theory) 原则上 ▶ **to agree to/approve of sth in principle** 原则上同意/批准某事 ▶ **on principle** 根据原则

print [prɪnt] I N **1** [U] (type) 印刷字体 [yìnshuā zìtǐ] **2** [C] (picture) 图片 [túpiàn] **3** [C] (photograph) 照片 [zhàopiàn] **4** [C] (fabric) 印花布 [yìnhuā bù] II VT **1** (produce) [+ book, newspaper, leaflet] 印刷 [yìnshuā] **2** (publish) [+ story, article] 出版 [chūbǎn] **3** (stamp) [+ word, number, pattern] 印 [yìn] **4** (write) 用印刷体写 [yòng yìnshuātǐ xiě] **5** (COMPUT) 打印 [dǎyìn] III VI (write) 用印刷体写 [yòng yìnshuātǐ xiě] IV **prints** NPL (fingerprints) 指纹 [zhǐwén] ▶ **the fine** or **small print** 小号印刷体 ▶ **to appear in print/get into print** 刊登出 ▶ **to be in print** [book +] 在销售的 ▶ **to be out of print** [book +] 绝版的 ▶ **print out** VT (COMPUT) [+ document, file] 打印出 [dǎyìn chū]

printer [ˈprɪntə(r)] N [C] **1** (machine) 打印机 [dǎyìnjī] **2** (person) 印刷工 [yìnshuā gōng] **3** (firm) (also: **printer's**) 印刷所 [yìnshuā suǒ]

printout [ˈprɪntaut] N [C] 打印输出 [dǎyìn shūchū]

prior [ˈpraɪə(r)] I ADJ **1** (previous) [+ knowledge, engagement, consent] 在先的 [zàixiān de] **2** (more important) [+ duty, commitment] 更重要的 [gèng zhòngyào de] II N [C] (REL) (head monk) 小修道院院长 [xiǎo xiūdàoyuàn yuànzhǎng]; (deputy head monk) 大修道院副长 ▶ **I have a prior engagement** 我有另一个约会在先 ▶ **without prior warning** 没有事先警告 ▶ **prior to sth/to doing sth** 在某事/做某事之前 ▶ **to have a prior claim on sth** 对某事有优先要求权

priority [praɪˈɔrɪtɪ] I N [C] (concern) 重点 [zhòngdiǎn] II **priorities** NPL 优先考虑的事 [yōuxiān kǎolù de shì] ▶ **to take** or **have priority (over sth/sb)** (比某事/某人)具有优先权 ▶ **to give priority to sth/sb** 给某事/某人以优先权

prison [ˈprɪzn] N **1** [C/U] (institution) 监狱 [jiānyù] **2** [U] (imprisonment) 坐牢 [zuòláo] **3** [C] (fig) 束缚 [shùfú] ▶ **in prison** 坐牢

prisoner [ˈprɪznə(r)] N [C] 囚犯 [qiúfàn]; (during

war) 战俘 [zhànfú] ▶ **the prisoner at the bar** (LAW) 被告 ▶ **to take sb prisoner** 俘房某人 ▶ **to hold sb prisoner** 关押某人

prison officer N [C] 狱官 [yùguān]

prisoner of war N [C] 战俘 [zhànfú]

pristine [ˈprɪstiːn] ADJ [+ house, clothes] 纯净的 [chúnjìng de] ▶ **in pristine condition** 一尘不染的

privacy [ˈprɪvəsɪ] N [U] 隐私 [yǐnsī] ▶ **in the privacy of one's own home** 在自家私下里 ▶ **an invasion of privacy** 对隐私的侵犯

private [ˈpraɪvɪt] I ADJ **1** (not public) [+ property, land, plane] 私人的 [sīrén de]; [+ performance, ceremony] 非公开的 [fēi gōngkāi de] **2** (not state-owned) [+ education, housing, health care, industries] 私有的 [sīyǒu de] **3** (confidential) [+ papers, discussion, conversation, meeting] 秘密的 [mìmì de] **4** (not professional) [+ correspondence, life] 个人的 [gèrén de] **5** (personal) [+ life, thoughts, plans, affairs, belongings] 私人的 [sīrén de] **6** (secluded) [+ place] 幽僻的 [yōupì de] **7** (secretive) [+ person] 内敛的 [nèiliǎn de] II N [C] (MIL) 士兵 [shìbīng] ▶ **to be in private practice** (MED) 私人开业行医 ▶ **in (his) private life** 在他的私生活中 ▶ **in private** 私下

privately [ˈpraɪvɪtlɪ] ADV **1** (in private) 私下地 [sīxià de] **2** (secretly) 秘密地 [mìmì de] ▶ **privately owned** 私人所有

private property N [U] 私人财产 [sīrén cáichǎn]

private school N [C/U] (fee-paying) 私立学校 [sīlì xuéxiào]

privatize [ˈpraɪvətaɪz] VT [+ company, industry] 私有化 [sīyǒuhuà]

privilege [ˈprɪvɪlɪdʒ] N **1** [C] (benefit) 优惠 [yōuhuì] **2** [S] (honour) 荣幸 [róngxìng] **3** [U] (due to background) 特权 [tèquán]

privileged [ˈprɪvɪlɪdʒd] ADJ **1** [+ person, position] 享有特权的 [xiǎngyǒu tèquán de] **2** [+ information] 特许的 [tèxǔ de] ▶ **to be/feel privileged to do sth** 有幸做某事

privy [ˈprɪvɪ] (frm) ADJ ▶ **to be privy to sth** [+ information, facts] 私下知悉某事 [sīxià zhīxī mǒushì]

prize [praɪz] I N [C] **1** (in competition, sport) 奖 [jiǎng] **2** (SCOL, UNIV) (for achievement) 奖励 [jiǎnglì] II ADJ 一流的 [yīliú de] III VT 珍藏 [zhēncáng]

prize-giving [ˈpraɪzgɪvɪŋ] N [C] **1** (after competition) 颁奖仪式 [bānjiǎng yíshì] **2** (SCOL) (for achievement) 颁奖 [bānjiǎng]

prizewinner [ˈpraɪzwɪnə(r)] N [C] **1** (in competition) 获奖者 [huòjiǎngzhě] **2** (SCOL, UNIV) (for achievement) 获奖者 [huòjiǎngzhě]

pro [prəu] I N [C] (professional) 职业选手 [zhíyè xuǎnshǒu] **2** ▶ **the pros and cons (of sth/of doing sth)** (某事/做某事的)利弊

[(mǒushì/zuò mǒushì de) lìbì] II PREP (in favour of) 赞成 [zànchéng]

probability [prɔbə'bɪlɪtɪ] N [C/U] ▶ probability (of sth/that…) (某事/…的)可能性 [(mǒushì/…de) kěnéngxìng] ▶ the probability of sth happening 某事发生的可能性 ▶ the probability is that… 可能性是… ▶ in all probability 极有可能

probable ['prɔbəbl] ADJ 可能的 [kěnéng de] ▶ it is/seems probable that… 可能…/似乎可能…

⊙ **probably** ['prɔbəblɪ] ADV 可能 [kěnéng] ▷ You probably won't understand this word. 你可能不理解这个词。 ▶ probably!/probably not! 很可能！/很可能不是！

probation [prə'beɪʃən] N [U] 1 (for criminal) 缓刑 [huǎnxíng] 2 (for employee) 试用期 [shìyòngqī] ▶ to be on probation [criminal +] 在缓刑中；[employee +] 在试用期中 ▶ to put sb on probation [+ criminal] 判某人缓刑

probe [prəʊb] N [C] 1 (MED) 探针 [tànzhēn] 2 (also: space probe) 航天探测器 [hángtiān tàncèqì] 3 (enquiry) (into corruption, illegal practices) 探究 [tànjiū] II VT 1 (investigate) [+ financial situation, practices, mystery, death] 调查 [diàochá] 2 (search) 探查 [tànchá] 3 (MED) (with instrument) [+ wound] 检查 [jiǎnchá] III VI 1 (investigate) ▶ to probe (into sth) 探究 (某事) [tànjiū (mǒushì)] 2 (MED) (with instrument) 探查 [tànchá]

⊙ **problem** ['prɔbləm] N [C] 1 (difficulty) 难题 [nántí] 2 (puzzle) 疑惑 [yíhuò] ▶ to have problems with sth 对某事有疑惑 ▶ what's the problem? 有什么问题吗？ ▶ I had no problem finding her 我要找她不难 ▶ no problem! (inf) 没问题！

problematic(al) [prɔblə'mætɪk(l)] ADJ [+ activity, situation, relationship] 成问题的 [chéng wèntí de]

procedure [prə'si:dʒə(r)] N 1 [C] (process) 步骤 [bùzhòu] 2 [C/U] (customary method) 程序 [chéngxù]

proceed [prə'si:d] VI 1 (continue) 继续 [jìxù] 2 (frm) (go) (on foot) 走 [zǒu]；(in car) 前进 [qiánjìn]；[car, vehicle +] 行进 [xíngjìn] ▶ to proceed with sth 继续某事 ▶ to proceed to do sth 开始做某事

proceedings [prə'si:dɪŋz] NPL 1 (events) 活动 [huódòng] 2 (LAW) 诉讼 [sùsòng] 3 (minutes) [of conference, meeting] 记录 [jìlù]

proceeds ['prəʊsi:dz] NPL 收入 [shōurù]

⊙ **process** ['prəʊsɛs] N [C] 1 (procedure) 过程 [guòchéng] 2 (BIO, CHEM) 过程 [guòchéng] II VT 1 [+ raw materials, food] 加工 [jiāgōng] 2 [+ application] (for job, visa, benefit) 办理 [bànlǐ] 3 (COMPUT) [+ data] 处理 [chǔlǐ] ▶ by a process of elimination 通过一系列的筛选 ▶ in the process 在过程中 ▶ to be in the process of

doing sth 在从事某事的过程中

procession [prə'sɛʃən] N [C] 队伍 [duìwǔ] ▶ wedding/funeral procession 迎亲/送葬队伍

proclaim [prə'kleɪm] VT 宣告 [xuāngào] ▶ to proclaim that… 声明… ▶ to proclaim o.s. sth 公开宣称自己的某立场

prod [prɔd] I VT 1 (push) (with finger, stick, knife) 戳 [chuō] 2 (encourage) ▶ to prod sb into sth/into doing sth 促使某人做某事 [cùshǐ mǒurén zuò mǒushì] II N [C] 1 (with finger, stick, knife) ▶ to give sb/sth a prod 戳某人/某物一下 [chuō mǒurén/mǒuwù yīxià] 2 (reminder) ▶ to give sb a prod 提醒某人一下 [tíxǐng mǒurén yīxià] ▶ to prod sb to do sth 促使某人做某事

prodigy ['prɔdɪdʒɪ] N [C] 天才 [tiāncái] ▶ child prodigy 神童

⊙ **produce** [n 'prɔdju:s, vb prə'dju:s] I N [U] 产品 [chǎnpǐn] ▷ organic produce 绿色产品 II VT 1 (bring about) [+ effect, result etc] 促成 [cùchéng] ▷ All our efforts have failed to produce an agreement. 我们所有的努力都没能促成一致意见。 2 (make) [+ goods, commodity] 生产 [shēngchǎn] ▷ The company produces components for the aerospace industry. 这家公司为航空业生产零部件。 3 (BIO, CHEM) [+ gas, toxins etc] 产生 [chǎnshēng] 4 (provide) [+ evidence, argument] 提出 [tíchū] ▷ Scientists have produced powerful arguments against his ideas. 科学家们提出了辩驳他的想法的有力论据。 5 (show) [+ passport, knife etc] 出示 [chūshì] 6 [+ play, film, programme] 上演 [shàngyǎn]

producer [prə'dju:sə(r)] N [C] 1 (THEAT, CINE, MUS) [of film, play, programme] 制片人 [zhìpiànrén]；[of record] 制作人 [zhìzuòrén] 2 [of food, material] (country) 产地 [chǎndì]；(company) 制造商 [zhìzào shāng]

⊙ **product** ['prɔdʌkt] N [C] 1 产品 [chǎnpǐn] 2 (result) 产物 [chǎnwù]

production [prə'dʌkʃən] N 1 [U] (IND, AGR) (process) 生产 [shēngchǎn]；(amount produced, amount grown) 产量 [chǎnliàng] 2 [U] (BIO) [of cells, hormones etc] 繁殖 [fánzhí] 3 [C] (play, show) 作品 [zuòpǐn] 4 [U] [of film, programme, play] 制作 [zhìzuò] ▶ to go into production [goods +] 投产 ▶ on production of 一经出示

productive [prə'dʌktɪv] ADJ 1 [+ workforce, factory, writer] 多产的 [duōchǎn de] 2 [+ discussion, meeting, relationship] 富有成效的 [fùyǒu chéngxiào de]

productivity [prɔdʌk'tɪvɪtɪ] N [U] 生产力 [shēngchǎnlì]

profession [prə'fɛʃən] N [C] 1 (job) 职业 [zhíyè] 2 (people) (medical, legal etc) 从业人员 [cóngyè rényuán]

professional [prə'fɛʃənl] I ADJ 1 (work-related) [+ activity, context, capacity] 业务的 [yèwù de] 2 (not amateur) [+ photographer, musician, *footballer*] 职业的 [zhíyè de]; [+ *advice, help*] 专业的 [zhuānyè de] **3** (*correct*) [+ *person, attitude*] 内行的 [nèiháng de] **4** (*skilful*) [+ *performance, piece of work*] 专业水平的 [zhuānyè shuǐpíng de] **II** N [C] **1** (*doctor, lawyer, teacher*) 专业人士 [zhuānyè rénshì] **2** (SPORT) 职业运动员 [zhíyè yùndòngyuán] **3** (*competent person*) 内行 [nèiháng] ▶ **professional misconduct** 渎职 ▶ **to seek/take professional advice** 寻求/采纳专家建议

professionally [prəˈfɛʃnəlɪ] ADV **1** (*as a professional*) [*qualified* +] 专业上 [zhuānyè shang]; [*play* +] 职业地 [zhíyè de] **2** (*correctly*) [*behave* +] 内行地 [nèiháng de] **3** (*skilfully*) [*produce, make etc* +] 专业地 [zhuānyè de] ▶ **speaking professionally** 从专业上讲 ▶ **personally and professionally** 从个人生活和工作来说

professor [prəˈfɛsə(r)] N [C] **1** (BRIT) 教授 [jiàoshòu] **2** (US) 教员 [jiàoyuán]

profile [ˈprəufaɪl] N [C] **1** [*of person's face*] 侧面 [cèmiàn] **2** (*fig*) (*biography*) 简介 [jiǎnjiè] ▶ **to keep a low profile** [*person* +] 保持低调 ▶ **a high profile** (*of person, organization*) 引人注目的形象

profit [ˈprɔfɪt] **I** N [C/U] 利润 [lìrùn] **II** VI ▶ **to profit from sth** 从某事中获益 [cóng mǒushì zhōng huòyì] ▶ **to make a profit** 赚钱 ▶ **to sell (sth) at a profit** 出售(某物)而获利

profitable [ˈprɔfɪtəbl] ADJ **1** [+ *business, deal, activity*] 有利润的 [yǒu lìrùn de] **2** [+ *discussion, meeting*] 有益的 [yǒuyì de]

profound [prəˈfaund] ADJ **1** (*great*) [+ *effect, change, implications*] 深远的 [shēnyuǎn de]; [+ *differences*] 极大的 [jídà de]; [+ *shock, sense, feeling, respect*] 深深的 [shēnshēn de] **2** (*intellectual*) [+ *idea, book, mind*] 深刻的 [shēnkè de]

program [ˈprəugræm] **I** N [C] **1** (*also: computer program*) 程序 [chéngxù] **2** (US) = **programme** **II** VT **1** (COMPUT) ▶ **to program sth (to do sth)** 为某物编程(做某事) [wèi mǒuwù biānchéng (zuò mǒushì)] **2** (US) = **programme**

✪ **programme**, (US) **program** [ˈprəugræm] **I** N [C] **1** (RAD, TV) 节目 [jiémù] **2** (*for theatre, concert*) 节目宣传册 [jiémù xuānchuáncè] **3** (*list*) [*of talks, events, performances*] 节目单 [jiémù dān] **4** (*scheme*) 计划 [jìhuà] **II** VT ▶ **to programme sth (to do sth)** [+ *machine, system*] 设定某事(做某事) [shèdìng mǒushì (zuò mǒushì)] *see also* **program**

programmer [ˈprəugræmə(r)] (COMPUT) N [C] 程序员 [chéngxùyuán]

progress [*n* ˈprəugrɛs, *vb* prəˈgrɛs] **I** N [U] **1** (*headway*) 进展 [jìnzhǎn] **2** (*advances*) 进步 [jìnbù] **3** (*development*) [*of event, match, talks, disease*] 发展 [fāzhǎn] **II** VI **1** (*make headway*) 进展 [jìnzhǎn] **2** ▶ **to progress (to sth/to doing sth)** 提高(到某事/到做某事) [tígāo (dào mǒushì/dào zuò mǒushì)] **3** (*move on*) [*career, day, disease* +] 推进 [tuījìn] ▶ **to make progress (with sth)** (对某事)取得进步 ▶ **in progress** (*meeting, battle, match*) 正在进展中

progression [prəˈgrɛʃən] N **1** [U/S] (*advancement*) (*in career, course*) 进展 [jìnzhǎn] **2** [C] (*development*) (*of events, disease, career*) 进程 [jìnchéng] **3** [C] (*series*) 系列 [xìliè]

progressive [prəˈgrɛsɪv] **I** ADJ **1** (*enlightened*) [+ *person, school, policy*] 先进的 [xiānjìn de] **2** (*gradual*) [+ *loss, decline, change*] 逐渐的 [zhújiàn de] **II** N [C] (*person*) 改革派人士 [gǎigépài rénshì]

prohibit [prəˈhɪbɪt] (*frm*) VT 禁止 [jìnzhǐ] ▶ **to prohibit sb from doing sth** 严禁某人做某事 ▶ **"smoking prohibited"** "严禁吸烟"

project [*n* ˈprɔdʒɛkt, *vb* prəˈdʒɛkt] **I** N [C] **1** (*plan, scheme*) 工程 [gōngchéng] **2** (SCOL, UNIV) 课题 [kètí] **II** VT **1** (*plan*) 计划 [jìhuà] **2** (*estimate*) [+ *figure, amount*] 估计 [gūjì] **3** [+ *light, film, picture*] 投射 [tóushè] **4** [+ *feeling, quality, image*] 表露 [biǎolù] **5** ▶ **to project sb/o.s. as sth** 突出某人/自己作为某物的形象 [tūchū mǒurén/zìjǐ zuòwéi mǒuwù de xíngxiàng] **III** VI (*stick out*) 突出 [tūchū]

projection [prəˈdʒɛkʃən] N **1** [C] (*estimate*) 预测 [yùcè] **2** [C] (*overhang*) 凸出物 [tūchū wù] **3** [U] [*of film, movie*] 投影 [tóuyǐng]

projector [prəˈdʒɛktə(r)] N [C] 放映机 [fàngyìngjī]

prolific [prəˈlɪfɪk] ADJ [+ *artist, composer, writer*] 多产的 [duōchǎn de]

prologue, (US) **prolog** [ˈprəulɔg] N [C] [*of play, book*] 序 [xù]

prolong [prəˈlɔŋ] VT 延长 [yáncháng]

prom [prɔm] N [C] **1** (BRIT) (*by sea*) 海滨大道 [hǎibīn dàdào] **2** (US) (*dance*) 学生的正式舞会

> **PROM**
>
> 在英国，**prom**（即 **promenade concert** 的略称）是由一系列古典音乐会组成。每年夏天，由 **Royal Albert Hall** 在伦敦举办的 **prom** 最为著名。每季的最后一场音乐会—**Last Night of the Proms**—通常会有电视转播，并总要演奏一些爱国歌曲。在场的听众一边站着挥舞手中的英国国旗，一边纵情歌唱。美国人对 **prom** 的理解却不大相同，其含义为高中或大学学年末举行的一场正式舞会。**senior prom** 标志着 **high school** 的结束。对于美国年轻人而言，这也是成长历程中一个重要的典礼。

promenade [prɔməˈnɑːd] **I** N [C] 海滨大道 [hǎibīn dàdào] **II** VI [*person* +] 散步 [sànbù]

prominence [ˈprɔmɪnəns] N [U] (*importance*)

卓越[zhuōyuè] ▸ **to give prominence to sth** 重视某事 ▸ **to rise to prominence** 崭露头角

prominent ['prɒmɪnənt] ADJ **1** (*important*) 重要的[zhòngyào de] **2** (*noticeable*) 显著的[xiǎnzhù de]

promiscuous [prə'mɪskjuəs] ADJ [+ *person, behaviour*] 滥交的[lànjiāo de]

promise ['prɒmɪs] I N **1** [c] 许诺 (許諾) [xǔnuò] **2** [U] (*potential*) [*of person*] 有前途[yǒu qiántú]; [*of thing*] 前景[qiánjǐng] **II** VT ▸ **to promise sb sth, promise sth to sb** 保证给某人某物[bǎozhèng gěi mǒurén mǒuwù] ▸ **to make a promise (to do sth)** 保证(做某事) ▸ **to break/keep a promise (to do sth)** 违背/遵守(做某事的)诺言 ▸ **a young man of promise** 有希望的小伙子 ▸ **to promise (sb) that…** (向某人)保证… ▸ **to promise to do sth** 保证做某事 ▸ **it promises to be lively** 这看来很来劲

promising ['prɒmɪsɪŋ] ADJ [+ *person, career*] 有希望的[yǒu xīwàng de]

promote [prə'məʊt] VT **1** [+ *employee*] 晋升[jìnshēng] **2** (*publicize*) [+ *record, film, book, product*] 促销[cùxiāo] **3** (*encourage*) [+ *understanding, peace*] 促进[cùjìn] **4** (*sponsor, organize*) [+ *event*] 赞助[zànzhù] ▸ **the team was promoted to the first division** (BRIT: SPORT) 该队升到第一级别

promoter [prə'məʊtə(r)] N [c] **1** [*of concert, sporting event*] 赞助人[zànzhùrén] **2** [*of cause, idea*] 推广人[tuīguǎngrén]

promotion [prə'məʊʃən] N **1** [c/U] (*at work*) 晋级[jìnjí] **2** [U] (*pushing*) [*of product*] 促销[cùxiāo] **3** [c] (*publicity campaign*) 推广[tuīguǎng] **4** [U] (BRIT: SPORT) 升级[shēngjí]

prompt [prɒmpt] I ADJ **1** (*on time*) 干脆的[gāncuì de] **2** (*rapid*) [+ *action, response*] 迅速的[xùnsù de] **II** N [c] **1** (THEAT) ▸ **to give sb a prompt** 给某人提词[gěi mǒurén tící] **2** (COMPUT) 提示符[tíshì fú] **III** VT **1** (*cause*) [+ *action, plan*] 引发[yǐnfā] **2** (*when talking*) 提示[tíshì] **3** (THEAT) 提词[tící] ▸ **to be prompt to do sth** 立刻做某事 ▸ **at 8 o'clock prompt** 8点整 ▸ **to prompt sb to do sth** 促使某人做某事

promptly ['prɒmptlɪ] ADV **1** (*immediately*) 立刻[lìkè] **2** (*punctually*) 准时地[zhǔnshí de]

prone [prəʊn] ADJ **1** ▸ **to be prone to sth** 易于某事的[yìyú mǒushì de] **2** (*face down*) ▸ **to lie prone** 俯卧[fǔwò] ▸ **she is prone to burst into tears if…** 如果…她动辄就哭 ▸ **accident-/injury-prone** 易出事/受伤的

prong [prɒŋ] N [c] [*of fork*] 尖齿[jiānchǐ]

pronoun ['prəʊnaʊn] N [c] 代词[dàicí]

pronounce [prə'naʊns] I VT **1** [+ *word, name*] 发音[fāyīn] **2** (*frm*) [+ *verdict, sentence*] 宣布[xuānbù] **3** (*frm*) (*opine*) 断言[duànyán] **II** VI (*frm*) ▸ **to pronounce (up)on sth** 就某事发表意见[jiù mǒushì fābiǎo yìjiàn] ▸ **to pronounce sb**

fit/dead 宣布某人康复/死亡 ▸ **to pronounce o.s. satisfied** 表示满意

pronunciation [prənʌnsɪ'eɪʃən] N [c/U] 发音[fāyīn]

proof [pru:f] I N [U] 证据[zhèngjù] II (*frm*) ADJ ▸ **to be proof against sth** 不受某事影响的[bùshòu mǒushì yǐngxiǎng de] III **proofs** NPL (TYP) 校样[jiàoyàng] ▸ **to be 70% proof** [*alcohol* +] 70%的标准酒精度

prop [prɒp] I N [c] **1** (*stick, post*) 支柱[zhīzhù] **2** (*fig*) (*person, thing*) 靠山[kàoshān] II VT (*also:* **prop up**) (*lean*) ▸ **to prop sth (up) against/on sth** 把某物靠在某物上[bǎ mǒuwù kàozài mǒuwù shang] III **props** NPL (THEAT) 道具[dàojù]

▸ **prop up** VT **1** (*lit*) (*lean*) 支撑[zhīchēng] **2** (*fig*) [+ *government, industry, currency*] 支持[zhīchí]

propaganda [prɒpə'gændə] N [U] 宣传[xuānchuán]

propel [prə'pel] VT **1** [+ *vehicle, boat, machine, person*] 推动[tuīdòng] **2** (*fig*) ▸ **to propel sb into sth** 促使某人做某事[cùshǐ mǒurén zuò mǒushì]

propeller [prə'pelə(r)] N [c] 推进器[tuījìn qì]

proper ['prɒpə(r)] ADJ **1** (*genuine*) [+ *job, meal, teacher etc*] 适当的[shìdàng de] **2** (*correct*) [+ *procedure, place, word*] 恰当的[qiàdàng de] **3** (*socially acceptable*) [+ *behaviour, job*] 适宜的[shìyí de] **4** (*inf*) (*real*) [+ *idiot, thug etc*] 十足的[shízú de] ▸ **to go through the proper channels** 通过正当渠道 ▸ **the town/city proper** 城/市区

properly ['prɒpəlɪ] ADV **1** (*adequately*) [*eat, work, concentrate* +] 充分地[chōngfèn de] **2** (*decently*) [*behave* +] 体面地[tǐmiàn de]

proper noun N [c] 专有名词[zhuānyǒu míngcí]

property ['prɒpətɪ] N **1** [U] (*possessions*) 财产[cáichǎn] **2** [c/U] (*buildings and land*) 地产[dìchǎn] **3** [c] (*characteristic*) [*of substance, material*] 特性[tèxìng]

prophecy ['prɒfɪsɪ] N [c] 预言[yùyán]

prophet ['prɒfɪt] N [c] (REL) 先知[xiānzhī] ▸ **prophet of doom** 悲观预言家

proportion [prə'pɔ:ʃən] I N **1** [c] (*frm*) (*part*) [*of group, amount*] 部分[bùfen] **2** [c] (*number*) [*of people, things*] 比例[bǐlì] ▸ **proportion (of sth to sth)** (某物与某物的)比例[(mǒuwù yǔ mǒuwù de) bǐlì] II **proportions** NPL (*dimensions*) [*of building, design*] 比例[bǐlì]; (*fig*) 程度[chéngdù] ▸ **in (direct) proportion to sth** (*at the same rate as*) 与某事成(正)比; (*in relation to*) 与某事相称 ▸ **to keep sth in proportion** 如实对待某事 ▸ **to get sth out of proportion** 无根据地夸大某事 ▸ **to be out of all proportion to sth** 完全全与某事不相称 ▸ **to have a sense of proportion** 具有辨别轻重缓急的能力

proportional [prə'pɔːʃənl] ADJ ▶ **proportional to sth** 与某物成比例的 [yǔ mǒuwù chéng bǐlì de]

proportionate [prə'pɔːʃənɪt] ADJ = **proportional**

proposal [prə'pəuzl] N [c] **1** (plan) 提案 [tí'àn] **2** (also: **proposal of marriage**) 求婚 [qiúhūn]

propose [prə'pəuz] I VT **1** [+ plan, idea] 提出 [tíchū] **2** [+ motion] 提议 [tíyì] II VI (offer marriage) 求婚 [qiúhūn] ▶ **to propose to do** or **doing sth** (intend) 意欲做某事 ▶ **to propose that...** (suggest) 建议…; (in debate) 提出… ▶ **to propose a toast** 提议干杯

proposition [prɔpə'zɪʃən] I N [c] **1** (idea) ▶ **a difficult/attractive proposition** 一个棘手/有趣的问题 [yīgè jíshǒu/yǒuqù de wèntí] **2** (offer, suggestion) 提议 [tíyì] **3** (frm) (statement) 主张 [zhǔzhāng] II VT ▶ **to proposition sb** 向某人提出猥亵的要求 [xiàng mǒurén tíchū wěixiè de yāoqiú] ▶ **to make sb a proposition** 向某人提议

proprietor [prə'praɪətə(r)] N [c] [of hotel, shop, newspaper] 业主 [yèzhǔ]

prose [prəuz] N [U] 散文 [sǎnwén]

prosecute ['prɔsɪkjuːt] I VT **1** ▶ **to prosecute sb (for sth/for doing sth)** (因某事/做某事而)起诉某人 [(yīn mǒushì/zuò mǒushì ér) qǐsù mǒurén] **2** [+ case] 起诉 [qǐsù] II VI 起诉 [qǐsù]

prosecution [prɔsɪ'kjuːʃən] N [c/U] [of person] 起诉 [qǐsù] **2** (accusing side) ▶ **the prosecution** 原告 [yuángào]

prosecutor ['prɔsɪkjuːtə(r)] N [c] 起诉人 [qǐsùrén]

prospect [n 'prɔspɛkt, vb prə'spɛkt] I N **1** [c] (likelihood) 可能 [kěnéng] **2** [s] (thought) 期望 [qīwàng] II VI ▶ **to prospect (for sth)** [+ gold, oil, minerals] 勘探(某物) [kāntàn (mǒuwù)] III **prospects** NPL (for work, marriage) 前景 [qiánjǐng]

prospective [prə'spɛktɪv] ADJ [+ husband, employer, buyer etc] 可能的 [kěnéng de]

prospectus [prə'spɛktəs] N [c] **1** [of university, school] 简介 [jiǎnjiè] **2** [of company] 计划书 [jìhuàshū]

prosper ['prɔspə(r)] (frm) VI [person, business, city +] 兴隆 [xīnglóng]

prosperity [prɔ'spɛrɪtɪ] N [U] 繁荣 [fánróng]

prosperous ['prɔspərəs] ADJ [+ person, business, city] 繁荣的 [fánróng de]

prostitute ['prɔstɪtjuːt] I N [c] (female) 妓女 [jìnǚ] II VT ▶ **to prostitute o.s./one's talents** (fig) 作践自己/自己的才华 [zuòjiàn zìjǐ/zìjǐ de cáihuá] ▶ **a male prostitute** 男妓

protect [prə'tɛkt] VT [+ person, floor, rights, freedom] 保护 [bǎohù] ▶ **to protect sb/sth from** or **against sth** 保护某人/某物不受某物的伤害 ▶ **to protect o.s. from** or **against sth** 保护自己不受某物的伤害

protection [prə'tɛkʃən] N **1** [c/U] ▶ **protection (from** or **against sth)** [of person, floor, plant] (免受某物侵害的)保护 [(miǎnshòu mǒuwù qīnhài de) bǎohù] **2** [U] [of rights, freedom, interests] 保护 [bǎohù] **3** (INSURANCE) ▶ **protection (against sth)** (防止某事的)保险 [(fángzhǐ mǒushì de) bǎoxiǎn] ▶ **to be offered police protection** 被提供了警方保护的

protective [prə'tɛktɪv] ADJ **1** [+ clothing, layer] 保护性的 [bǎohùxìng de] **2** [+ person] 给予保护的 [jǐyǔ bǎohù de] ▶ **protective custody** (LAW) 保护性拘留

protein ['prəutiːn] N [c/U] 蛋白质 [dànbáizhì]

protest [n 'prəutɛst, vb prə'tɛst] I N [c/U] 抗议 [kàngyì] II VI ▶ **to protest about/against/at sth** (BRIT) 抗议某事 [kàngyì mǒushì] III VT **1** (claim) 申辩 [shēnbiàn] **2** (US) (voice opposition to) 示威 [shìwēi] ▶ **to protest that...** 坚决声明…

Protestant ['prɔtɪstənt] I N [c] 新教徒 [Xīnjiàotú] II ADJ 新教的 [Xīnjiào de]

protester [prə'tɛstə(r)] N [c] 抗议者 [kàngyìzhě]

protractor [prə'træktə(r)] N [c] 量角器 [liángjiǎoqì]

proud [praud] ADJ **1** [+ parents, owner] 自豪的 [zìháo de] **2** (arrogant) 骄傲的 [jiāo'ào de] **3** (dignified) [+ person, people] 自尊心强的 [zìzūnxīn qiáng de] ▶ **to be proud of sb/sth** 为某人/某事感到自豪 ▶ **to be proud to do sth** 以做某事为荣 ▶ **to be proud that...** 为…感到自豪 ▶ **to do sb proud** (inf) 盛情款待某人

prove [pruːv] I VT [+ idea, theory] 证明 [zhèngmíng] II VI ▶ **to prove (to be) correct** etc 证明是对的{等} [zhèngmíng shì duì de {děng}] ▶ **to prove that...** [person +] 证明…; [situation, experiment, calculations +] 显示… ▶ **to prove sb right/wrong** 证明某人是对的/错的 ▶ **to prove o.s. (to be) useful** etc 证明自己是有用的{等}

proverb ['prɔvəːb] N [c] 谚语 [yànyǔ]

○ provide [prə'vaɪd] VT **1** [+ food, money, shelter] 供应 [gōngyìng]; [+ answer, opportunity, details] 提供 [tígōng] **2** ▶ **to provide that...** [law, agreement +] 规定… [guīdìng…] ▶ **to provide sb with sth** [+ food, job, resources] 提供某人某物 ▶ **to be provided with** [+ person] 具有; [+ thing] 有 ▶ **provide for** VT FUS [不可拆分] **1** [+ person] 供养 [gōngyǎng] **2** [+ future event] 提前准备 [tíqián zhǔnbèi] ▶ **to be well provided for** 保障生活无忧的 ▶ **to provide for sth (to happen)** [law, agreement +] 规定某事(发生)

provided (that) [prə'vaɪdɪd-] CONJ 假如 [jiǎrú]

providing [prə'vaɪdɪŋ] CONJ ▶ **providing (that)** 假如 [jiǎrú]

province ['prɔvɪns] I N **1** [c] [of country] 省

[shěng] **2** [S] (area of responsibility etc) [of person] 本分 [běnfèn] **II the provinces** NPL 首都以外的地方 [shǒudū yǐwài de dìfāng]

provincial [prə'vɪnʃəl] ADJ **1** [+ town, newspaper etc] 省的 [shěng de] **2** (unsophisticated) 偏狭的 [piānxiá de]

provision [prə'vɪʒən] **I** N **1** [U] [+ of service] 供应 [gōngyìng] **2** [C/U] (arrangement) (for potential need) 准备 [zhǔnbèi] **3** [C] (stipulation) (in contract, agreement) 规定 [guīdìng] **II provisions** NPL (food) 食物 [shíwù] ▶ **to make provision for** [+ sb's future, family] 为…做准备 [+ security, defences] 为…做好安排

provisional [prə'vɪʒənl] ADJ [+ government, agreement, arrangement etc] 临时的 [línshí de]

provocative [prə'vɒkətɪv] ADJ **1** [+ remark, article, behaviour, action] 挑衅的 [tiǎoxìn de] **2** (sexually) [+ clothing, behaviour, gesture] 挑逗的 [tiǎodòu de]

provoke [prə'vəʊk] VT **1** (annoy) [+ person] 激怒 [jīnù] **2** (cause) [+ fight, reaction, anger] 挑起 [tiǎoqǐ] ▶ **to provoke sb into doing sth** 刺激某人做某事

prowl [praʊl] **I** VI [animal, person +] 潜行 [qiánxíng] **II** N **1** (lit) ▶ **to be on the prowl** [animal +] 潜行觅食 [qiánxíng mìshí] **2** (fig) ▶ **to be on the prowl (for sth)** [person +] 来回寻觅 (某物) [láihuí xúnmì (mǒuwù)]

proximity [prɒk'sɪmɪtɪ] N [U] ▶ **proximity (to sth/sb)** 邻近 (某物/某人) [línjìn (mǒuwù/mǒurén)]

proxy ['prɒksɪ] N ▶ **by proxy** 由代理人 [yóu dàilǐrén]

prudent ['pruːdnt] ADJ 慎重的 [shènzhòng de]

prudently ['pruːdntlɪ] ADV [act, behave +] 谨慎地 [jǐnshèn de]

prune [pruːn] **I** N [C] 梅干 [méigān] **II** VT [+ bush, plant, tree] 修剪 [xiūjiǎn]

pry [praɪ] VI ▶ **to pry (into sth)** 刺探 (某事) [cìtàn (mǒushì)] ▶ **safe from prying eyes** 躲开窥视的眼睛

PS ABBR (= postscript) 附言 [fùyán]

pseudonym ['sjuːdənɪm] N [C] 笔名 [bǐmíng] ▶ **under a pseudonym** 以笔名

PST (US) ABBR (= Pacific Standard Time) 太平洋标准时间 [Tàipíngyáng Biāozhǔn Shíjiān]

psychiatric [saɪkɪ'ætrɪk] ADJ 精神病学的 [jīngshénbìng xué de]

psychiatrist [saɪ'kaɪətrɪst] N [C] 精神病医生 [jīngshénbìng yīshēng]

psychic ['saɪkɪk] ADJ [+ person, powers] 特异功能的 [tèyì gōngnéng de] ▶ **I'm not psychic!** 我没有特异功能!

psychoanalysis [saɪkəʊə'nælɪsɪs] N [U] 精神分析学 [jīngshén fēnxī xué]

psychoanalyst [saɪkəʊ'ænəlɪst] N [C] 精神分析学家 [jīngshén fēnxī xuéjiā]

psychological [saɪkə'lɒdʒɪkl] ADJ **1** (mental) [+ effect, problem, disorder] 心理的 [xīnlǐ de] **2** (relating to psychology) [+ test, treatment] 心理学的 [xīnlǐxué de]

psychologist [saɪ'kɒlədʒɪst] N [C] 心理学家 [xīnlǐxué jiā]

psychology [saɪ'kɒlədʒɪ] N **1** [U] (science) 心理学 [xīnlǐxué] **2** [C/U] (character) 心理 [xīnlǐ]

psychotherapist [saɪkəʊ'θɛrəpɪst] N [C] 精神治疗师 [jīngshén zhìliáoshī]

psychotherapy [saɪkəʊ'θɛrəpɪ] N [U] 心理疗法 [xīnlǐ liáofǎ]

PTO ABBR (= please turn over) 请翻过来 [qǐng fān guòlái]

pub [pʌb] (BRIT) N [C] 酒吧 [jiǔbā]

puberty ['pjuːbətɪ] N [U] 青春期 [qīngchūnqī]

○ **public** ['pʌblɪk] **I** ADJ **1** (from people) [+ support, opinion, interest] 公众的 [gōngzhòng de] **2** (for people) [+ building, service, library] 公共的 [gōnggòng de] **3** (not private) [+ announcement, meeting] 公开的 [gōngkāi de] [+ figure, life] 社会的 [shèhuì de] **4** (state) [+ funding, spending, service] 国家的 [guójiā de] **II** N [S + PL VB] **1** ▶ **the (general) public** 民众 [mínzhòng] **2** (audience, fans) ▶ **sb's public** 某人的支持公众 [mǒurén de zhīchí gōngzhòng] ▶ **it's public knowledge** 众所周知 ▶ **in/out of the public eye** 常/不常在公开场合露面的 ▶ **to make sth public** 将某事公布于世 ▶ **to become public** 变得公开的 ▶ **to go public** (COMM) 上市 ▶ **in public** [speak, smoke, drink +] 公开地

publication [pʌblɪ'keɪʃən] N **1** [U] (of book, magazine, article) 出版 [chūbǎn] **2** [C] (book, magazine) 刊物 [kānwù]

public company N [C] 上市公司 [shàngshì gōngsī]

public convenience (BRIT: frm) N [C] 公共厕所 [gōnggòng cèsuǒ]

public holiday N [C] 法定假期 [fǎdìng jiàqī]

public house (BRIT) N = pub

publicity [pʌb'lɪsɪtɪ] N [U] **1** (information, advertising) 宣传 [xuānchuán] **2** (attention) 关注 [guānzhù]

publicize ['pʌblɪsaɪz] VT [+ fact, event, book] 宣传 [xuānchuán]

public limited company N [C] 上市有限公司 [shàngshì yǒuxiàn gōngsī]

publicly ['pʌblɪklɪ] ADV **1** [say, announce, deny +] 公开地 [gōngkāi de] **2** (state) [+ owned, run, funded] 由公众地 [yóu gōngzhòng de]

public opinion N [U] 舆论 [yúlùn]

public relations N [U] 公共关系 [gōnggòng guānxì] ▶ **a public relations exercise** 公关演习

public school N [C/U] **1** (BRIT) (private school) 私立中学 [sīlì zhōngxué] **2** (US) (state school) 公立学校 [gōnglì xuéxiào]

public transport N [U] 公共交通 [gōnggòng jiāotōng]

publish ['pʌblɪʃ] VT **1** [company+] [+ book, magazine] 出版 [chūbǎn] **2** [newspaper, magazine+] [+ letter, article] 刊登 [kāndēng] **3** [writer+] [+ article, story] 发表 [fābiǎo]

publisher ['pʌblɪʃə(r)] N [c] **1** (person) 出版商 [chūbǎnshāng] **2** (company) 出版社 [chūbǎnshè]

publishing ['pʌblɪʃɪŋ] N [U] 出版 [chūbǎn]

pub lunch (BRIT) N [c] 由酒吧提供的午餐

pudding ['pudɪŋ] N **1** [C/U] (type of dessert) 布丁 [bùdīng] **2** [C/U] (BRIT) (dessert in general) 甜点 [tiándiǎn] ▶ rice pudding 米饭布丁 ▶ black pudding, (US) blood pudding 黑血肠

puddle ['pʌdl] N [c] **1** [of rain] 水坑 [shuǐkēng] **2** [of blood, oil] 滩 [tān]

Puerto Rico ['pwɜːtəuˈriːkəu] N 波多黎各 [Bōduōlígè]

puff [pʌf] I N [c] **1** (on cigarette, pipe) ▶ to take a puff 吸一口 [xī yīkǒu] **2** (gasp) 喘息 [chuǎnxī] II VI **1** (pant) 喘气 [chuǎnqì] **2** ▶ to puff on or at sth [+ cigarette, pipe] 吸某物 [xī mǒuwù] **3** ▶ a puff of wind/air/smoke 一阵风/空气/烟 ▶ puff out VT [+ one's chest, cheeks] 鼓起 [gǔqǐ]

puff pastry N [U] 松饼 [sōngbǐng]

pull [pul] I VT **1** [+ rope, hair] 拖 [tuō]; [+ handle, door, cart, carriage] 拉 [lā] **2** (draw) [+ curtain, blind] 拉 [lā] **3** (squeeze) [+ trigger] 扣 [kòu] **4** (inf) (attract) [+ people] 吸引 [xīyǐn]; [+ sexual partner] 勾引 [gōuyǐn] **5** [+ pint of beer] 灌 [guàn] II VI 猛拉 [měnglā] III N **1** [c] (tug) ▶ to give sth a pull 拉一下某物 [lā yìxià mǒuwù] **2** [s] [of moon, magnet, current] 牵引力 [qiānyǐnlì] **3** [s] (fig) [+ of homeland, past] 吸引力 [xīyǐnlì] ▶ to pull sth free/out of sth [+ arm, hand, foot] 将某物从某物中抽出来 ▷ She pulled her feet out of the wet boots. 她把脚从湿靴子中抽了出来。▶ to pull a muscle 扭伤肌肉 ▶ to pull a face 夸张地做表情 ▶ to pull sth to pieces (criticize) 将某事批得体无完肤 ▶ to pull o.s. together 振作起来 ▶ to pull sb's leg (fig) 开某人的玩笑 ▶ to pull strings (for sb) (为某人)暗中操作

▶ pull apart VT **1** (separate) [+ fighters] 拉开 [lākāi] **2** (destroy) 扯坏 [chěhuài]

▶ pull away VI **1** [vehicle, driver+] 开走 [kāizǒu] **2** [person+] (from sb) 疏远 [shūyuǎn]

▶ pull back VI **1** (retreat) [troops+] 撤退 [chètuì] **2** (change mind) ▶ to pull back (from sth/from doing sth) 中止(某事/做某事) [zhōngzhǐ (mǒushì/zuò mǒushì)]

▶ pull down VT [+ building] 拆毁 [chāihuǐ]

▶ pull in I VI **1** (at the kerb) 停了下来 [tíngle xiàlái] **2** [train+] 到站 [dàozhàn] II VT **1** (inf) [+ money] 赚 [zhuàn] **2** [+ crowds, people] 吸引 [xīyǐn] **3** [police+] ▶ to pull sb in (for sth/for doing sth) (为某事/做某事)拘捕某人 [(wèi mǒushì/zuò mǒushì) jūbǔ mǒurén]

▶ pull into VT FUS [不可拆分] [driver, vehicle+] [+ road, drive] 拐入 [guǎirù]

▶ pull off VT **1** (take off) [+ clothes] 脱下 [tuōxià] **2** (fig) [+ plan, deal, trick, victory] 实现 [shíxiàn] ▶ to pull it off 成功

▶ pull out I VI **1** (AUT) (from kerb) 开出 [kāichū]; (when overtaking) 超车 [chāochē] **2** [train+] 离站 [lízhàn] **3** (withdraw) (from agreement, contest) 退出 [tuìchū]; [troops+] 撤离 [chèlí] II VT (extract) [+ file, information] 调出 [diàochū]

▶ pull over I VI (AUT) 靠边停下 [kàobiān tíngxià] II VT ▶ the police pulled him over 警察叫他停车 [jǐngchá jiào tā tíngchē]

▶ pull through VI (from illness) 恢复健康 [huīfù jiànkāng]; (from difficulties) 渡过难关 [dùguò nánguān]

▶ pull together VI 同心协力 [tóngxīn xiélì]

▶ pull up I VI (stop) [driver, vehicle+] 停下 [tíngxià] II VT **1** (raise) [+ socks, trousers] 拉起 [lāqǐ] **2** (uproot) [+ plant, weed] 拔除 [báchú] ▶ to pull up a chair 拖把椅子过来

pulley ['pulɪ] N [c] 滑轮 [huálún]

pull-off ['pu:lɔf] (US) N [c] 路侧停车处 [lùcè tíngchēchù] [英=lay-by]

pullover ['puləuvə(r)] N [c] 套头衫 [tàotóushān]

pulp [pʌlp] I N [c] **1** [of fruit] (inside) 果肉 [guǒròu]; (crushed) 浆 [jiāng] **2** (for paper) 浆 [jiāng] II ADJ (pej) [+ magazine, novel] 低劣的 [dīliè de] III VT [+ paper, documents] 销毁 [xiāohuǐ] ▶ to beat sb to a pulp 把某人打得遍体鳞伤

pulp fiction N [U] 低俗小说 [dīsú xiǎoshuō]

pulpit ['pulpɪt] N [c] 讲坛 [jiǎngtán]

pulse [pʌls] I N [c] **1** (ANAT) 脉搏 [màibó] **2** (rhythm) 节奏 [jiézòu] **3** (TECH) 脉冲 [màichōng] II VI 有节奏地跳动 [yǒu jiézòu de tiàodòng] III PULSES NPL (CULIN) 豆子 [dòuzi] ▶ to take or feel sb's pulse 给某人诊脉 ▶ to have one's finger on the pulse (of sth) 了解(某物)最新动态

puma ['pjuːmə] N [c] (mountain lion) 美洲狮 [měizhōu shī]

pump [pʌmp] I N [c] **1** (for liquid, gas) 泵 [bèng] **2** (for getting water) 抽水机 [chōushuǐjī] **3** (for inflating sth) 打气筒 [dǎqìtǒng] **4** (ESP BRIT) (shoe) 浅口无带皮鞋 [qiǎnkǒu wúdài píxié] II VT **1** (move) ▶ to pump sth into/out of/up from sth [+ liquid, gas] 把某物从某物抽入/抽出/抽上去 [bǎ mǒuwù cóng mǒuwù chōurù/chōuchū/chōu shàngqù] **2** (obtain) [+ oil, water, gas] 用泵抽 [yòng bèng chōu] ▶ water/petrol pump 水/油泵 ▶ to pump money into sth (inf) 不断把钱投入某物 ▶ to have one's stomach pumped 洗胃 ▶ to pump sb for information (inf) 从某人处探出消息

▶ pump out VT (supply) 源源不断供应 [yuányuán bùduàn gōngyìng]

▶ pump up VT (inflate) 打气 [dǎqì]

pumpkin ['pʌmpkɪn] N [c] 南瓜 [nánguā]

pun [pʌn] N [c] 双关 [shuāngguān]

punch [pʌntʃ] I N 1 [c] (blow) 拳打 [quándǎ]
2 [U] (fig) (force) 力量 [lìliàng] 3 [c] (tool) (for making holes) 打孔器 [dǎkǒng qì] 4 [c/U] (drink) 混合饮料 [hùnhé yǐnliào] II VT 1 (hit) 用拳打击 [yòng quán dǎjī] 2 [+ button, keyboard] 敲击 [qiāojī] 3 (make a hole in) [+ ticket, paper] 在…上打孔 [zài…shang dǎkǒng] ▶ he didn't pull his or any punches 他直言不讳 ▶ to punch sb on the nose/in the eye 拳打某人的鼻子/眼睛
▶ to punch a hole in sth 在某物上打孔
▶ punch in VT 敲入 [qiāorù]
▶ punch out (US) VT (hit) 拳打 [quándǎ]

punchline ['pʌntʃlaɪn] N [c] 妙语 [miàoyǔ]

punch-up ['pʌntʃʌp] (BRIT: inf) N [c] 打架 [dǎjià]

punctual ['pʌŋktjuəl] ADJ 准时的 [zhǔnshí de]

punctuation [pʌŋktju'eɪʃən] N [U] 标点 [biāodiǎn]

puncture ['pʌŋktʃə(r)] I N [c] 刺孔 [cìkǒng]
II VT [+ tyre, lung] 戳破 [chuōpò] ▶ to have a puncture 轮胎被扎破了

pundit ['pʌndɪt] N [c] 专家 [zhuānjiā]

punish ['pʌnɪʃ] VT 1 [+ person] 惩罚 [chéngfá]
2 [+ crime] 处罚 [chǔfá] ▶ to punish sb for sth/for doing sth 因某事/做某事而惩罚某人

punishment ['pʌnɪʃmənt] N 1 [U] 惩罚 [chéngfá] 2 [c/U] (penalty) 处罚 [chǔfá] ▶ to take a lot of punishment (fig) [car, machine, person, body+] 受到很大损伤

punk [pʌŋk] N 1 [c] (also: punk rocker) 朋克 [péngkè] 2 [U] (also: punk rock) 朋克摇滚乐 [péngkè yáogǔnyuè] 3 [c] (US: inf) (hoodlum) 小阿飞 [xiǎo āfēi]

punter ['pʌntə(r)] (BRIT: inf) N [c] 1 (gambler) 下赌注的人 [xià dǔzhù de rén] 2 (customer) 顾客 [gùkè]

pup [pʌp] N [c] 1 (young dog) 小狗 [xiǎogǒu]
2 [of seal, otter] 幼兽 [yòushòu]

pupil ['pju:pl] N [c] 1 (student) 学生 [xuéshēng]
2 [of eye] 瞳孔 [tóngkǒng]

puppet ['pʌpɪt] N [c] 1 (on strings) 木偶 [mù'ǒu]
2 (also: glove puppet) 布袋式木偶 [bùdàishì mù'ǒu] 3 (fig) (person, government) 傀儡 [kuǐlěi]

puppy ['pʌpɪ] N [c] 小狗 [xiǎogǒu]

purchase ['pə:tʃɪs] (frm) I VT 购买 [gòumǎi]
II N 1 [U] (act of buying) 购买 [gòumǎi] 2 [c] (item bought) 购买物 [gòumǎi wù] 3 (grip) ▶ to get or gain (a) purchase on sth 牢牢抓住某物 [láoláo zhuāzhù mǒuwù]

pure [pjuə(r)] ADJ 1 [+ silk, gold, wool] 纯的 [chún de] 2 (clean) [+ water, air] 纯净的 [chúnjìng de]
3 (chaste) [+ woman, girl] 纯洁的 [chúnjié de]
4 (theoretical) [+ maths, science, research] 纯理论的 [chún lǐlùn de] 5 (complete) [+ coincidence, luck, joy, speculation] 完全的 [wánquán de] ▶ a pure wool jumper 纯毛衫衣 ▶ this is fraud, pure and simple 这完完全全是欺诈

puree ['pjuəreɪ] N [c/U] 酱 [jiàng]

purely ['pjuəlɪ] ADV (wholly) 完全地 [wánquán de]

purify ['pjuərɪfaɪ] VT [+ air, water, gold] 净化 [jìnghuà]

purity ['pjuərɪtɪ] N [U] 1 [of air, water] 纯净 [chúnjìng] 2 [of woman, girl] 纯洁 [chúnjié]

purple ['pə:pl] I ADJ 紫色的 [zǐsè de] II N [c/U] 紫色 [zǐsè]

purpose ['pə:pəs] N [c] 1 [of person] 目的 [mùdì]
2 [of act, meeting, visit] 意义 [yìyì] ▶ a sense of purpose (in life) 意义感; (in activity) 目标感 ▶ for that purpose 出于那种目的 ▶ for medicinal/propaganda etc purposes 出于医疗/宣传〔等〕的目的 ▶ for all practical purposes, to all intents and purposes 实际上 ▶ to little/no purpose 徒劳无益的 ▶ on purpose 故意地

purposeful ['pə:pəsful] ADJ [+ person, look, gesture] 坚定的 [jiāndìng de]

purr [pə:(r)] I N 1 [cat+] 呜呜叫 [wūwū jiào] 2 [engine, car+] 发出隆隆声 [fāchū lónglóngshēng] 3 [person+] 呢喃 [nínán] II N [c] [of cat] 呜呜声 [wūwūshēng]; [of engine, car] 隆隆声 [lónglóngshēng]

purse [pə:s] I N [c] 1 (BRIT) (for money) 钱包 [qiánbāo] 2 (US) (handbag) 手袋 [shǒudài] 〔英=handbag〕 II VT ▶ to purse one's lips 撅起嘴 [juēqǐ zuǐ]

pursue [pə'sju:] (frm) VT 1 (follow) [+ person, car] 追赶 [zhuīgǎn] 2 (involve o.s. in) [+ activity, interest, policy, career] 继续 [jìxù] 3 (try to obtain) [+ aim, objective] 追求 [zhuīqiú] 4 (follow up) [+ matter, claim] 穷追不舍 [qióngzhuī bùshě]; [+ topic, possibility, idea] 探究 [tànjiū]

pursuit [pə'sju:t] N 1 ▶ the pursuit of [+ happiness, pleasure, excellence] 对…的追求 [duì…de zhuīqiú] 2 [c] (pastime) 消遣 [xiāoqiǎn] ▶ in pursuit of [+ happiness, pleasure] 追求; [+ person, car, animal] 穷追 ▶ in hot pursuit 紧紧追赶

pus [pʌs] N [U] 脓 [nóng]

push [puʃ] I N [c] 1 推 [tuī] 2 (encouragement) 鼓励 [gǔlì] II VT 1 (press) [+ button] 按 [àn]
2 (shove) [+ car, door, person] 推 [tuī] 3 (put pressure on) [+ person] 逼迫 [bīpò] 4 (promote) [+ product, project] 推销 [tuīxiāo]; [+ case, argument] 努力争取 [nǔlì zhēngqǔ] 5 (inf) (sell) [+ drugs] 贩卖 [fànmài] III VI 1 (press) 按 [àn]
2 (shove) 推 [tuī] ▶ to give sth/sb a push (with hand) 推了某物/某人一下 ▶ at the push of a button 只要按一下按钮 ▶ at a push (BRIT: inf) 紧急情况下 ▶ to push one's way through the crowd 挤过人群 ▶ to push sth/sb out of the way 把某物/某人推开 ▶ to push a door open/shut 把门推开/上 ▶ "push" (on door) "推" ▶ to push sb to do sth 促使某人做某事 ▶ to push sb into doing sth 迫使某人做某

事 ▸ **to push o.s. to the limit** 将自己推到极
限 ▸ **to be pushed for time/money** (inf) 赶时
间/缺钱 ▸ **she's pushing fifty** (inf) 她将近50岁
了 ▸ **to push forward/push through the crowd**
挤向/过人群

▸ **push ahead** VI (make progress) ▸ **to push
ahead (with sth)** 推进 (某事) [tuījìn (mǒushì)]
▸ **push around** (inf) VT (bully) 摆布 [bǎibù]
▸ **push aside** VT [+ idea, thought] 忽略 [hūlüè]
▸ **push back** VT [+ chair, hair] 往后推 [wǎnghòu
tuī]
▸ **push down** VT [+ total, prices] 降低 [jiàngdī]
▸ **push for** VT FUS [不可拆分] 迫切要求 [pòqiè
yāoqiú]
▸ **push forward** = **push ahead**
▸ **push in** VI (in queue) 插队 [chāduì]
▸ **push off** (inf) VI (leave) 走开 [zǒukāi] ▸ **push
off!** 滚开！
▸ **push on** VI (continue) ▸ **to push on (with sth)**
加紧 (做某事) [jiājǐn (zuò mǒushì)]
▸ **push over** VT [+ person, wall, furniture] 推倒
[tuīdǎo]
▸ **push through** VT [+ measure, scheme] 促成
[cùchéng]
▸ **push up** VT [+ total, prices] 提高 [tígāo]
pushchair ['pʊʃtʃeə(r)] (BRIT) N [C] 幼儿车
[yòu'érchē] [美= **stroller**]
pusher ['pʊʃə(r)] (inf) N [C] (drug dealer) 毒品贩
子 [dúpǐn fànzi]
push-up ['pʊʃʌp] (US) N [C] 俯卧撑
[fǔwòchēng] ▸ **to do push-ups** 做俯卧撑
pushy ['pʊʃi] (pej) ADJ (assertive) 好胜且好卖弄
的 [hàoshèng jiě hào màinòng de]
pussy ['pʊsi] N [C] (inf) (also: **pussycat**) 小猫咪
[xiǎo māomī]
⊙ **put** [pʊt] (pt, pp **put**) VT **1** (place) [+ thing] 放
[fàng] ▷ I put her suitcase on the table. 我把她的
手提箱放在桌上。; [+ person] (in institution) 安
置 [ānzhì] ▷ They had to put him in an asylum. 他
们只得把他安置在收容所里。▷ He'd been put in
jail. 他被投入了监牢。; [+ confidence, trust, faith]
(in person, thing) 投入 [tóurù] ▷ Are we right to
put our confidence in computers? 我们是否应该对
计算机有信心？**2** (cause to be) [+ person, thing]
(in state, situation) 使处于 [shǐ chǔyú] ▷ It puts
me in a rather difficult position. 这使我处于一个非
常为难的处境。**3** (express) [+ idea, remark] 表达
[biǎodá] ▷ He didn't put it quite as crudely as that.
他表述得并没那么拙劣。**4** (present) ▸ **to put
sth (to sb)** [+ case, view, suggestion] (向某人) 陈
述某事 [(xiàng mǒurén) chénshù mǒushì] ▷ He
should have known how to put his case. 他早该知道
如何陈述他的情况。**5** (classify) 看作 [kànzuò]
▷ I wouldn't put him in the same class as Verdi. 我没
把他看作是与维迪一个级别的。**6** (write, type)
[+ word, information] 写 [xiě] ▸ **to put a lot of
time/energy/effort into sth/into doing sth** 投
入大量的时间/精力/努力于某事/做某事 ▸ **to**

put money on a horse 赌马 ▸ **to stay put** 留
在原处 ▸ **how shall I put it?** 我该怎么说呢？
▸ **let me put it this way** 让我这么说吧 ▸ **to
put a question (to sb)** (向某人) 提问 ▸ **I put
it to you that…** (BRIT: frm) 我认为… ▸ **the cost
is now put at 20 million pounds** 现在成本估计
为20亿英镑

▸ **put about I** VT (BRIT) [+ rumour] 散布 [sànbù]
II VI (NAUT) 改变方向 [gǎibiàn fāngxiàng]
▸ **put across, put over** VT [+ ideas, argument] 讲
清 [jiǎngqīng]
▸ **put aside** VT **1** [+ work, object] 放在一边
[fàngzài yībiān] ▷ My aunt put aside her sewing
and picked up her book. 我舅妈把针线活放在一边
开始看书。**2** (disregard) [+ idea, problem, remark]
置之不理 [zhì zhī bù lǐ] ▷ It's a problem which they
usually put aside. 这是他们通常置之不理的问
题。**3** (save) [+ sum of money] 存 [cún] ▷ She put
aside a small sum every week to pay for her annual
holiday. 她每星期存一点钱用于每年的度假。
▸ **put away** VT **1** (store, unpack) 把…收起
[bǎ…shōuqǐ] ▷ I put away the shopping. 我把买
的东西收起来了。**2** (inf) (imprison) 把…关起
[bǎ…guānqǐ] ▷ They put him away for ten years.
他们把他关了10年。**3** (save) [+ money] 存 [cún]
▷ I've got a thousand pounds put away for a rainy day.
我存了1000镑以备不时之需。**4** (inf) (consume)
(food, drink) 吃喝掉 [chīhē diào]
▸ **put back** VT **1** (replace) 放回 [fànghuí] ▷ I
put the book back on the shelf. 我把书放回书架。
2 (postpone) 推迟 [tuīchí] **3** (delay) 使延误 [shǐ
yánwù] **4** [+ watch, clock] 倒拨 [dàobō]
▸ **put by** VT [+ money, supplies] 存储…备用
[cúnchǔ…bèiyòng]
▸ **put down** VT **1** (on floor, table) 放下 [fàngxià]
2 (in writing) 写下 [xiěxià] **3** [+ money, deposit]
支付 [zhīfù] **4** (quell) [+ riot, rebellion] 镇压
[zhènyā] **5** (inf) (humiliate) [+ person] 羞辱 [xiūrǔ]
6 (put to sleep) [+ animal] 宰杀 [zǎishā]
▸ **put down to** VT (attribute) ▸ **to put sth down
to sth** 把某事归因于某事 [bǎ mǒushì guīyīn
yú mǒushì] ▷ I put it down to arthritis. 我把它归
因于关节炎。
▸ **put forward** VT **1** [+ ideas, proposal, name] 提
出 [tíchū] ▷ These were the arguments which Jenny
put forward. 这些是詹妮提出的论点。**2** [+ watch,
clock] 向前拨 [xiàngqián bō]
▸ **put in I** VT **1** (make) [+ request, complaint,
application] 提出 [tíchū] **2** (dedicate) [+ time, effort,
work] 投入 [tóurù] **3** (install) [+ gas, electricity,
sink] 安装 [ānzhuāng] **II** VI (NAUT) ▸ **to put in
(at)** 进港 [jìngǎng]
▸ **put in for** VT FUS [不可拆分] [+ promotion, leave]
申请 [shēnqǐng]
▸ **put off** VT **1** [+ event] (delay) 推迟 [tuīchí]
2 [+ person] (ask to wait) 使等待 [shǐ děngdài]
▷ They wanted to come this evening but I put them
off until tomorrow. 他们今晚想来，但我让他们

等到明天。; (BRIT) (distract) 使分心 [shǐ fēnxīn]
▷ Every time Peter served, a man in the crowd coughed
and put him off. 每次轮到彼得时，人群中就
有人咳嗽让他分心。; (discourage) 使失去兴
趣 [shǐ shīqù xìngqù] ▷ His personal habits put
her off. 他的个人习惯使她失去了兴趣。▶ to
put off doing sth (postpone) 推迟做某事 ▶ **to
put sb off sth/sb** (alienate from) 使某人摆脱某
事/某人 ▶ **to put sb off doing sth** 使不再喜
欢做某事

▶ **put on** VT **1** [+ clothes, make-up, glasses] 穿
戴 [chuāndài] **2** (switch on) [+ light, TV, radio,
oven] 开 [kāi]; [+ CD, video] 放 [fàng]; [+ dinner]
做 [zuò]; [+ kettle] 用…烧水 [yòng…shāoshuǐ]
3 (organize) [+ play, exhibition] 举行 [jǔxíng];
[+ extra bus, train] 安排 [ānpái] **4** (adopt) [+ look,
accent, act] 假装 [jiǎzhuāng] ▶ **to put on
weight/three kilos** etc 增重/增加了3公斤﹝等﹞
▶ **you're putting it on** (pretending) 你是假装的

▶ **put onto** VT 向
某人引荐某人/某物 [xiàng mǒurén yǐnjiàn
mǒurén/mǒuwù]

▶ **put out** I VT **1** (extinguish) [+ candle, cigarette]
熄灭 [xīmiè]; [+ fire, blaze] 扑灭 [pūmiè] **2** (switch
off) [+ electric light] 关 [guān] **3** (lay out) 摆放
[bǎifàng] **4** (take outside) [+ rubbish, cat] 放出
[fàngchū] **5** [+ one's hand] (to greet, touch, for
help, protection) 伸出 [shēnchū] **6** (make
public) [+ story, statement] 公布 [gōngbù]
7 (BRIT) (dislocate) [+ back, shoulder] 使…脱臼
[shǐ…tuōjiù] **8** (inf) (inconvenience) [+ person] 麻
烦 [máfan] II VI (NAUT) ▶ **to put out to sea** 出
海 [chūhǎi] ▶ **to put out from Plymouth** 从普
利茅斯启航 ▶ **to put out one's tongue** 伸出舌
头 ▶ **to put o.s. out** 难为自己

▶ **put over** VT = **put across**

▶ **put through** VT **1** (TEL) [+ person, phone call] 接
通 [jiētōng] ▷ "Data Room, please." – "I'll put you
through." "请接资料室。" "我给你接通。"
2 (cause to experience) ▶ **to put sb through sth**
使某人经受某事 [shǐ mǒurén jīngshòu mǒushì]
3 (carry out) [+ plan, agreement] 完成 [wánchéng]
▶ **put me through to Miss Blair** 请帮我接布
莱尔小姐

▶ **put together** VT [+ furniture, machine] 装配
[zhuāngpèi]; [+ team, collection] 组成 [zǔchéng];
[+ plan, campaign] 组织 [zǔzhī] ▶ **more than the
rest of them put together** 比其他所有人的
总和都多

▶ **put up** VT **1** [+ fence, building, tent] 建造
[jiànzào]; [+ poster, sign] 张贴 [zhāngtiē]
2 [+ umbrella, hood] 撑起 [chēngqǐ] **3** (provide)
[+ money] 提供 [tígōng] **4** (increase) [+ price, cost]
增加 [zēngjiā] **5** (accommodate) 为…提供住宿
[wèi…tígōng zhùsù] ▶ **to put up one's hand**
举手 ▶ **to put up resistance/a fight** 进行抵
抗/战斗 ▶ **to put sb up to sth/to doing sth**
(incite) 唆使某人做某事 ▶ **to put sth up for
sale** 出售某物

▶ **put upon** VT FUS [不可拆分] ▶ **to be put upon**
被利用 [bèi lìyòng]

▶ **put up with** VT FUS [不可拆分] 容忍 [róngrěn]

putt [pʌt] I VT 轻击 [qīngjī] II N [C] 轻击
[qīngjī]

putting green ['pʌtɪŋ-] N [C] 高尔夫球场中
球洞草坪区

puzzle ['pʌzl] I N **1** [C] (for entertainment) (riddle,
conundrum) 谜 [mí]; (game) 测智游戏 [cèzhì
yóuxì]; (toy) 测智玩具 [cèzhì wánjù] **2** [S]
(mystery) 谜团 [mítuán] II VT (baffle) 使困惑
[shǐ kùnhuò] III VI ▶ **to puzzle over sth** 对某
事冥思苦想 [duì mǒushì míng sī kǔ xiǎng]

puzzled ['pʌzld] ADJ [+ person, expression, frown]
茫然的 [mángrán de] ▶ **to be puzzled by** or
about sth 对某事感到困惑 ▶ **to be puzzled as
to why...** 对于为什么…感到困惑

puzzling ['pʌzlɪŋ] ADJ [+ statement, action,
behaviour] 令人困惑的 [lìngrén kùnhuò de]

PVC N ABBR (= polyvinyl chloride) 聚氯乙烯
[jùlǜyǐxī]

PW (US) N ABBR = **POW**

pyjamas, (US) **pajamas** [pə'dʒɑ:məz] NPL 睡
衣裤 [shuìyīkù] ▶ **a pair of pyjamas** 一套睡衣裤

pylon ['paɪlən] N [C] 电缆塔 [diànlán tǎ]

pyramid ['pɪrəmɪd] N [C] **1** (monument) 金字塔
[jīnzì tǎ] **2** (GEOM) 锥体 [zhuītǐ] **3** (pile of objects)
一堆 [yīduī]

Qq

Q, q [kjuː] N [C/U] (letter) 英语的第十七个字母
QC (BRIT: LAW) N ABBR (= *Queen's Counsel*) 皇室法律顾问 [Huángshì Fǎlù Gùwèn]
quack [kwæk] I N [C] 1 (of duck) 嘎嘎声 [gāgāshēng] 2 (inf, pej) (doctor) 庸医 [yōngyī] II VI 嘎嘎叫 [gāgājiào] III ADJ (inf, pej) [+ remedy] 冒牌的 [màopái de]
quad [kwɔd] N 1 (quadrangle) 四边形 [sìbiānxíng] 2 (quadruplet) ▶ **quads** 四胞胎 [sìbāotāi]
quadruple [kwɔ'druːpl] I VT 使成四倍 [shǐ chéng sìbèi] II VI 成四倍 [chéng sìbèi]
quail [kweɪl] I N [C] (bird) 鹌鹑 [ānchún] II VI (liter) ▶ **to quail (at sth)** (对某事) 感到不寒而栗 [(duì mǒushì) gǎndào bùhán érlì]
quaint [kweɪnt] ADJ 1 [+ house, village] 古雅的 [gǔyǎ de] 2 [+ ideas, customs, times] 离奇的 [líqí de]
quake [kweɪk] I VI (tremble) 战栗 [zhànlì] II N [C] (inf) (also: **earthquake**) 地震 [dìzhèn]
qualification [kwɔlɪfɪ'keɪʃən] N 1 [C] (degree, diploma etc) 资格证明 [zīgé zhèngmíng]; (skill) 素质 [sùzhì] 2 [C/U] (reservation) 条件 [tiáojiàn] 3 [U] (graduation) 取得资格 [qǔdé zīgé]
qualified [ˈkwɔlɪfaɪd] ADJ 1 (trained) [+ doctor, teacher, nurse etc] 合格的 [hégé de] 2 (limited) [+ support, praise] 有保留的 [yǒu bǎoliú de] ▶ **fully qualified** 完全合格的 ▶ **he's not qualified for the job** 他不胜任这项工作 ▶ **to be/feel qualified to do sth** (fit, competent) 有/感

到有资格做某事 ▶ **it was a qualified success** 这是一次有限的胜利
qualify [ˈkwɔlɪfaɪ] I VI 1 (pass examinations) 取得资格 [qǔdé zīgé] 2 (in competition) 具备资格 [jùbèi zīgé] 3 ▶ **to qualify for sth** (be eligible for) 符合某事的条件 [fúhé mǒushì de tiáojiàn] II VT 1 ▶ **to qualify sb for sth/to do sth** 使某人对某事/做某事有资格 [shǐ mǒurén duì mǒushì/zuò mǒushì yǒu zīgé] 2 (modify) [+ statement] 缓和 [huǎnhé] ▶ **to qualify as an engineer/a nurse** etc 取得工程师/护士{等}的资格
quality [ˈkwɔlɪtɪ] I N 1 [U] (standard) [of work, product] 质量 [zhìliàng] 2 [C] (characteristic) [of person] 素质 [sùzhì]; [of wood, stone etc] 特质 [tèzhì] II ADJ [+ goods, product, service] 优质的 [yōuzhì de] ▶ **of good/poor quality** 质量好/坏的 ▶ **quality of life** 生活质量 ▶ **quality time** 休闲时光
qualm [kwɑːm] N [C] 疑虑 [yílù] ▶ **to have no qualms about doing sth** 对于做某事毫无疑虑
quantify [ˈkwɔntɪfaɪ] VT 量化 [liànghuà]
quantity [ˈkwɔntɪtɪ] N 1 [C/U] (amount) 数量 [shùliàng] 2 [U] (volume) 容量 [róngliàng] ▶ **in large/small quantities** 大/少量 ▶ **in quantity** (in bulk) 大批量
quarantine [ˈkwɔrəntiːn] N [U] 检疫 [jiǎnyì] ▶ **in quarantine** 被隔离
quarrel [ˈkwɔrəl] I N [C] 吵架 [chǎojià] II VI 争吵 [zhēngchǎo] ▶ **to have a quarrel with sb** 跟某人争吵 ▶ **I can't quarrel with that** 我对此无可争辩
quarry [ˈkwɔrɪ] I N 1 [C] (for stone, minerals) 采石场 [cǎishí chǎng] 2 [S] (prey) 猎物 [lièwù] II VT [+ stone, minerals] 开采 [kāicǎi]
quart [kwɔːt] (US) N [C] 夸脱 [kuātuō]
quarter [ˈkwɔːtə(r)] I N [C] 1 (fourth part) 四分之一 [sìfēnzhīyī] 2 (three months) 季度 [jìdù] 3 (district) 地区 [dìqū] 4 (US) (coin) 25美分硬币 [èrshíwǔ měifēn yìngbì] II VT 1 (cut into four) 把…切成4片 [bǎ...qiēchéng sìpiàn] 2 (divide by four) 把…4等分 [bǎ...sì děngfēn] 3 ▶ **to be quartered** (accommodated) 被安置 [bèi ānzhì] III ADJ 四分之一的 [sìfēnzhīyī de] IV **quarters** NPL 宿舍 [sùshè] ▶ **to cut/divide sth into quarters** 把某物切/分为4份 ▶ **a quarter of an hour** 一刻钟 ▶ **it's a quarter to three** or (US) **of three** 现在是三点差一刻 ▶ **it's a quarter past three** or (US) **after three** 现在是三点一刻 ▶ **at close quarters** 近距离地
quarter-final [ˈkwɔːtəˈfaɪnl] N [C] 四分之一决赛 [sìfēnzhīyī juésài]
quarterly [ˈkwɔːtəlɪ] I ADJ [+ meeting, payment, report] 季度的 [jìdù de] II ADV [meet, pay +] 季度地 [jìdù de] III N [C] (magazine) 季刊 [jìkān]
quarter-pounder [ˈkwɔːtəˈpaundə(r)] N [C] 四分之一磅重的大汉堡
quartet [kwɔː'tɛt] N [C] 1 (group) 四人表演组

合 [sìrén biǎoyǎn zǔhé] **2** (piece of music) 四声部曲 [sìshēngbù qǔ]

quartz [kwɔːts] **I** N [U] 石英 [shíyīng] **II** CPD [复合词] [+ watch, clock] 石英 [shíyīng]

quay [kiː] N [C] 码头 [mǎtóu]

queasy ['kwiːzɪ] (inf) ADJ (nauseous) ▸ **to feel queasy** 感到恶心 [gǎndào ěxīn]

queen [kwiːn] N [C] **1** (monarch) 女王 [nǚwáng] **2** (king's wife) 王后 [wánghòu] **3** ▸ **the queen of crime fiction** 犯罪小说之冠 [fànzuì xiǎoshuō zhīguàn] **4** (ZOOL) 雌后 [cíhòu] **5** (inf!) (homosexual) 男同性恋者 [nán tóngxìngliànzhě] **6** (CARDS) 皇后 [huánghòu] **7** (CHESS) 王后 [wánghòu] ▸ **Queen Victoria** 维多利亚女王 ▸ **the queen of hearts/spades** 红桃/黑桃皇后

Queen Mother N ▸ **the Queen Mother** 太后 [Tàihòu]

queer [kwɪə(r)] (**I**) ADJ **1** (o.f.) (odd) [+ feeling, story, place] 奇怪的 [qíguài de] **2** (inf, offensive) (homosexual) 同性恋的 [tóngxìngliàn de] **II** N [C] (inf!) (homosexual) 同性恋者 [tóngxìngliànzhě]

quell [kwɛl] VT [+ riot] 镇压 [zhènyā]; [+ unease, fears] 消除 [xiāochú]

quench [kwɛntʃ] VT ▸ **to quench one's thirst** 解渴 [jiěkě]

query ['kwɪərɪ] **I** N [C] (question) 疑问 [yíwèn] **II** VT **1** (check) [+ figures, bill, expenses etc] 询问 [xúnwèn] **2** (ask) ▸ **to query whether/why/what** etc 询问是否/为何/什么 {等} [xúnwèn shìfǒu/wèihé/shénme {děng}]

quest [kwɛst] N [C] ▸ **quest (for sth)** (对某物的) 探寻 [(duì mǒuwù de) tànxún]

✪ question ['kwɛstʃən] **I** N **1** [C] (query) 问题 [wèntí] ▷ A panel of experts attempted to answer our questions. 专家组试图回答我们的问题。 **2** [U] (doubt) 疑问 [yíwèn] ▷ There was no question about the diagnosis: she had lung cancer. 诊断结果已经没有疑问：她患了肺癌。 **3** [C] (issue) 议题 [yìtí] ▷ the nuclear power question 核能源议题 **4** [C] (in written exam) 试题 [shìtí] ▷ You have to answer four questions in two hours. 你得在两小时内回答四道题。 **II** VT **1** (interrogate) 盘问 [pánwèn] ▷ A man is being questioned by police in connection with the attack. 一名与该袭击有关的男子正受到警方盘问。 **2** (doubt) 怀疑 [huáiyí] ▷ It never occurs to them to question the doctor's decisions. 他们从未想过要怀疑医生的决定。 ▸ **to ask sb a question, to put a question to sb** 问某人一个问题，向某人提出问题 ▸ **to be in question** 出问题的 ▸ **to bring** or **call sth into question** 对某事提出质疑 ▸ **to be open to question** 令人怀疑的 ▸ **to be beyond question** 不成问题的 ▸ **without question** (unquestioningly) 毫无异议; (without doubt) 毫无疑问 ▸ **the question is...** 问题是… ▸ **there's no question of a compromise/them agreeing** 妥协/他们同意是不可能的 ▸ **to be out of**

the question 不可能的 ▸ **the person/night in question** 谈及的人/夜晚 ▸ **to question whether...** 询问是否…

questionable ['kwɛstʃənəbl] ADJ [+ value, quality] 可疑的 [kěyí de]; [+ taste] 成问题的 [chéng wèntí de]; [+ motive, behaviour, practice] 靠不住的 [kàobùzhù de]; [+ decision] 不确定的 [bù quèdìng de] ▸ **it is questionable whether...** 是否…还不确定

question mark N [C] 问号 [wènhào]

questionnaire [kwɛstʃə'nɛə(r)] N [C] 问卷 [wènjuàn]

queue [kjuː] (ESP BRIT) **I** N [C] 队 [duì] [美= line] **II** VI (also: queue up) 排队 [páiduì] [美= line up] ▸ **to jump the queue** 加塞儿 ▸ **to queue for sth** 为某事排队 ▸ **to be queueing up for sth/to do sth** (fig) 为某事/做某事排队等候

quiche [kiːʃ] N [C/U] 什锦烘饼 [shíjǐn hōngbǐng]

✪ quick [kwɪk] **I** ADJ **1** (fast) [+ person, movement etc] 快的 [kuài de] ▷ You'll have to be quick. The flight leaves in about three hours. 你得快点。航班大约3小时后起飞。 ▷ He was a very quick learner. 他学东西很快。 **2** (sharp) [+ mind, wit] 敏捷的 [mǐnjié de] **3** (brief) [+ look] 快速的 [kuàisù de]; [+ visit] 短时间的 [duǎn shíjiān de] **4** (swift) [+ reply, response, decision] 迅速的 [xùnsù de] ▷ a quick end to the war 战争的迅速收场 **II** ADV (inf) (quickly) 快地 [kuài de] ▷ Come quick! 快点来！ ▸ **be quick!** 快点！ ▸ **to be quick to do sth** 立马做某事 ▸ **to have a quick temper** 脾气急躁

quicken ['kwɪkən] **I** VT [+ pace, step] 加快 [jiākuài] **II** VI [pace, step, pulse +] 加速 [jiāsù]

quickly ['kwɪklɪ] ADV **1** (at speed) [walk, grow, speak, work +] 快地 [kuài de] **2** (swiftly) [realize, change, react, finish +] 迅速地 [xùnsù de]; [die +] 快速地 [kuàisù de]

quick-witted [kwɪk'wɪtɪd] ADJ 机敏的 [jīmǐn de]

quid [kwɪd] (pl **quid**) (BRIT: inf) N [C] 1英镑 [yī yīngbàng]

quiet ['kwaɪət] **I** ADJ **1** (not noisy) [+ voice, music] 悄声的 [qiāoshēng de]; [+ engine, aircraft] 无噪音的 [wú zàoyīn de]; [+ place] 安静的 [ānjìng de] **2** (tranquil) [+ place, situation, time] 宁静的 [níngjìng de] **3** (reserved) [+ person] 平静的 [píngjìng de] **4** (silent) [+ quiet person +] 沉默的 [chénmò de] **5** (not busy) [+ business, day] 冷清的 [lěngqīng de] **6** (discreet) [+ wedding, celebration] 私下的 [sīxià de] **II** N [U] **1** (peacefulness) 宁静 [níngjìng] **2** (silence) 安静 [ānjìng] **III** VT **1** (US) (silence) 使安静 [shǐ ānjìng] [英= quieten] **2** (US) (calm) [+ fears] 安抚 [ānfǔ] **IV** VI (US) 沉静下来 [chénjìng xiàlái] [英= quieten] ▸ **be quiet!** 请安静！ ▸ **to go quiet** 哑口无言 ▸ **to keep quiet about sth/keep sth quiet** 保守某事的秘密/将某事保

密 ▶ I'll have a quiet word with him 我要私下跟他谈谈 ▶ on the quiet 私下里

quieten ['kwaɪətn] (BRIT) (also: **quieten down**) I VI 1 (grow calm) 平静下来 [píngjìng xiàlái] 2 (grow silent) 安静下来 [ānjìng xiàlái] [美=quiet] II VT [+ person, animal] 使…安静 [shǐ…ānjìng] [美=quiet]

quietly ['kwaɪətlɪ] ADV 1 [speak, play +] 安静地 [ānjìng de] 2 (silently) 默默地 [mòmò de] 3 (calmly) 平静地 [píngjìng de] ▶ quietly confident 沉稳自信

quilt [kwɪlt] N [C] 1 (covering) 被子 [bèizi] 2 (BRIT) (duvet) 羽绒被 [yǔróngbèi]

quirk [kwəːk] N [C] 1 (idiosyncrasy) 怪癖 [guàipǐ] 2 (chance event) 异常的事 [yìcháng de shì] ▶ a quirk of fate 命运灾难

quirky ['kwəːkɪ] ADJ [+ person, humour, film] 怪诞的 [guàidàn de]

quit [kwɪt] (pt, pp **quit** or **quitted**) I VT 1 (ESP US) (give up) [+ habit, activity] 摆脱 [bǎituō] 2 (inf) (leave) [+ job] 辞去 [cíqù]; [+ place, premises] 离开 [líkāi] II VI 1 (give up) 放弃 [fàngqì] 2 (resign) 辞职 [cízhí] ▶ to quit doing sth 戒除做某事 ▶ quit doing that! (US: inf) 别再干那个了! ▶ notice to quit (BRIT) 请辞报告

○ **quite** [kwaɪt] ADV 1 (rather) 相当 [xiāngdāng] ▷ I quite like it. 我相当喜欢它。▷ He's quite young. 他相当年轻。▷ He calls quite often. 他常打电话。2 (completely) 十分 [shífēn] ▷ I stood quite still. 我十分安静地站着。▷ I'm not quite sure. 我不十分肯定。▷ It's quite clear that this won't work. 十分清楚的是，这方法不奏效。▶ I see them quite a lot 我常常见到他们 ▶ it costs quite a lot to go to the States 去美国相当贵 ▶ quite a lot of money 很多钱 ▶ quite a few 相当多 ▶ it's not quite finished 像是还没结束 ▶ it's not quite the same 不十分相同 ▶ there aren't quite enough glasses 杯子不太够 ▶ I can't quite remember 我不太记得了 ▶ I didn't buy quite as many as last time 我没买上次那么多 ▶ I quite understand 我相当

明白 ▶ quite (so)! 的确(是这样)! ▶ it was quite a sight 景色十分了得

quite 可用在 a 或 an 之前，后接形容词加名词结构。例如，可以说 It's quite an old car 或者 The car is quite old，以及 It was quite a warm day 或者 The day was quite warm。如前例所示，quite 应放在不定冠词之前。例如，不能说 It's a quite old car。quite 可以用来修饰形容词和副词，而且程度比 fairly 更强烈，但是比 very 弱。quite 暗示某事物的某种特性超出预料。Nobody here's ever heard of it but it is actually quite common. 注意，不要混淆 quite 和 quiet。

quits [kwɪts] ADJ ▶ we're quits 我们互不相欠了 [wǒmen hùbù xiāngqiàn le] ▶ let's call it quits 让我们就此罢手

quiver ['kwɪvə(r)] VI (tremble) [lip, voice +] 颤抖 [chàndǒu] ▶ to quiver with fear/rage 因恐惧/愤怒而颤抖

quiz [kwɪz] (pl **quizzes**) I N [C] (game) 测验 [cèyàn] II VT (inf) (question) 盘问 [pánwèn]

quota ['kwəʊtə] N [C] 1 (allowance) 定额 [dìng'é] 2 (share) 配额 [pèi'é]

quotation [kwəʊ'teɪʃən] N [C] 1 (from book, play, interview) 引语 [yǐnyǔ] 2 (estimate) 报价 [bàojià]

quotation marks NPL 引号 [yǐnhào] ▶ in quotation marks 带引号

quote [kwəʊt] I VT 1 [+ politician, author etc] 引用 [yǐnyòng]; [+ line] 引述 [yǐnshù]; [+ reference number] 援引 [yuányǐn]; [+ law, statistics] 引证 [yǐnzhèng] 2 ▶ to quote a price/figure for sth 为某事物报出价格/数字 [wèi mǒushìwù bàochū jiàgé/shùzì] II N [C] 1 (from book, play, interview, person) 引语 [yǐnyǔ] 2 (estimate) 报价 [bàojià] III **quotes** (inf) (quotation marks) 引号 [yǐnhào] ▶ to quote sb as saying that... 引用某人的话说… ▶ in quotes 在引号里

Rr

R¹, r [ɑːr(r)] N [C/U] (*letter*) 英语的第十八个字母
R² (US: CINE) ABBR **1** (= *restricted*) 17岁限制级
2 (TEXTING) = are
R.¹ (US: POL) ABBR = republican
R.², r. ABBR **1** (= *river*) 河 [hé] **2** (= *right*) 右边的 [yòubiān de]
rabbi ['ræbaɪ] N [C] 拉比(犹太教教师或法学导师)
rabbit ['ræbɪt] I N **1** [C] (*animal*) 兔子 [tùzi]
2 [U] (*meat*) 兔肉 [tùròu] II VI (BRIT: inf) (*also:* **to rabbit on**) 唠叨 [láodao]
rabies ['reɪbiːz] N [U] 狂犬病 [kuángquǎnbìng]
raccoon [rə'kuːn] N [C] 浣熊 [huànxióng]
○ **race** [reɪs] I N **1** [C] (*speed contest*) 速度竞赛 [sùdù jìngsài] **2** [C] (*for power, control*) 竞赛 [jìngsài] **3** [C/U] (*ethnic group*) 种族 [zhǒngzú] II VI **1** (*compete in races*) 参赛 [cānsài] **2** (*hurry*) 快速行进 [kuàisù xíngjìn] **3** [*pulse, heart* +] 剧烈跳动 [jùliè tiàodòng]; [*mind* +] 飞快地转 [fēikuài de zhuǎn] **4** [*engine* +] 快速运转 [kuàisù yùnzhuǎn] III VT **1** [+ *person*] 与…进行速度竞赛 [yǔ…jìnxíng sùdù jìngsài] **2** (*enter for races*) [+ *horse, dog*] 使参赛 [shǐ cānsài] **3** [+ *car, hand* etc] 赛 [sài] ▶ **a race against time** 抢时间 ▶ **he raced across the road** 他快速穿过马路 ▶ **to race in/out** 快速进/出
race car (US) N = **racing car**
racecourse ['reɪskɔːs] (BRIT) N [C] 赛马场 [sàimǎchǎng] [美 = **racetrack**]
racehorse ['reɪshɔːs] N [C] 赛马 [sàimǎ]

racetrack ['reɪstræk] N [C] (*for cars*) 赛道 [sàidào]; (US) (*for horses*) 赛马场 [sàimǎchǎng] [英 = **racecourse**]
racial ['reɪʃl] ADJ [+ *discrimination, prejudice, equality*] 种族的 [zhǒngzú de]
racing ['reɪsɪŋ] N [U] 比赛 [bǐsài]
racing car (BRIT) N [C] 赛车 [sàichē]
racing driver (BRIT) N [C] 赛车手 [sàichēshǒu]
racism ['reɪsɪzəm] N [U] 种族歧视 [zhǒngzú qíshì]
racist ['reɪsɪst] I ADJ [+ *policy, attack, behaviour, idea*] 种族主义的 [zhǒngzú zhǔyì de]; [+ *person, organization*] 有种族偏见的 [yǒu zhǒngzú piānjiàn de] II N [C] 种族主义者 [zhǒngzú zhǔyìzhě]
rack [ræk] I N [C] **1** (*also:* **luggage rack**) 行李架 [xínglijià] **2** (*for hanging clothes, dishes*) 架 [jià] II VT ▶ **racked by** or **with** [+ *pain, anxiety, doubts*] 被/受折磨 [bèi/shòu zhémó] ▶ **magazine rack** 报刊架 ▶ **to go to rack and ruin** [*building* +] 荒废; [*business, country* +] 衰败 ▶ **to rack one's brains** 绞尽脑汁
racket ['rækɪt] N **1** [C] (*for tennis, squash* etc) 球拍 [qiúpāi] **2** [S] (*noise*) (inf) 吵闹 [chǎonào] **3** [C] (*swindle*) (inf) 非法勾当 [fēifǎ gòudàng]
racquet ['rækɪt] N [C] 球拍 [qiúpāi]
radar ['reɪdɑː(r)] I N [C/U] 雷达 [léidá] II CPD [复合词] [+ *screen, antenna, system*] 雷达 [léidá]
radiant ['reɪdɪənt] ADJ **1** [+ *smile, person*] 容光焕发的 [róngguāng huànfā de] **2** [+ *object*] 光辉灿烂的 [guānghuī cànlàn de] **3** (PHYS) 辐射的 [fúshè de]
radiation [reɪdɪ'eɪʃən] N [U] **1** (*radioactivity*) 辐射 [fúshè] **2** (*radio waves*) 辐射 [shèxiàn]
radiator ['reɪdɪeɪtə(r)] N [C] **1** (*on wall*) 暖气片 [nuǎnqìpiàn] **2** (*in car*) 散热器 [sànrèqì]
radical ['rædɪkl] I ADJ **1** (*fundamental*) [+ *change, reform, disagreement*] 根本的 [gēnběn de] **2** (POL) [+ *person, organization, views*] 激进的 [jījìn de] II N [C] (POL) (*person*) 激进分子 [jījìn fènzǐ]
○ **radio** ['reɪdɪəu] I N **1** [C] (*receiver*) 收音机 [shōuyīnjī] **2** [C] (*two-way*) 无线电收发报机 [wúxiàndiàn shōufābàojī] **3** [U] (*broadcasting*) 广播 [guǎngbō] **4** [U] (*communication system*) 无线通讯 [wúxiàndiàn tōngxùn] II VI 用无线电发送 [yòng wúxiàndiàn fāsòng] III VT **1** (*contact by radio*) [+ *person*] 用无线电联系 [yòng wúxiàndiàn liánxì] **2** (*send by radio*) [+ *information, message*] 广播 [guǎngbō] ▶ **on the radio** 广播中
radioactive ['reɪdɪəu'æktɪv] ADJ 放射性的 [fàngshèxìng de]
radioactive waste N [U] 放射性废物 [fàngshèxìng fèiwù]
radio-controlled ['reɪdɪəukən'trəuld] ADJ 无线电遥控的 [wúxiàndiàn yáokòng de]
radio station N [C] 广播电台 [guǎngbō

diàntái]

radish ['rædɪʃ] N [c] 萝卜 [luóbo]

RAF (BRIT) N ABBR (= *Royal Air Force*) ▶ **the RAF** 皇家空军 [Huángjiā Kōngjūn]

raffle ['ræfl] I N [c] 对奖 [duìjiǎng] II VT [+ *prize*] 抽中 [chōuzhòng]

raft [rɑ:ft] N [c] **1** (*also*: **life raft**) 皮艇 [pítǐng] **2** (*improvised*) 筏 [fá] ▶ **a raft of** 大量

rag [ræg] I N **1** [c/u] (*piece of cloth*) 破布 [pòbù] **2** [c] (*inf, pej*) (*newspaper*) 小报 [xiǎobào] II VT (BRIT) (*tease*) 戏弄 [xìnòng] III **rags** NPL (*torn clothes*) 破旧衣服 [pòjiù yīfu] ▶ **in rags** 衣衫褴褛 ▶ **a rags-to-riches story** 从赤贫到暴富的故事

rage [reɪdʒ] I N [c/u] (*fury*) 盛怒 [shèngnù] II VI **1** (*person +*) 发怒 [fānù] **2** (*storm +*) 肆虐 [sìnüè]; (*debate +*) 持续 [chíxù] ▶ **it's all the rage** (*very fashionable*) 风靡一时 ▶ **to fly into a rage** 勃然大怒

ragged ['rægɪd] ADJ **1** (*untidy*) [+ *clothes, person*] 破烂不堪的 [pòlàn bùkān de] **2** (*uneven*) [+ *edge, line*] 凸凹不平的 [tū'āo bùpíng de]

raid [reɪd] I N [c] (*by soldiers, police*) 突袭 [tūxí]; (*by criminal*) 袭击 [xíjí] II VT [*soldiers, police +*] 突袭 [tūxí]; [*criminal +*] 袭击 [xíjí]

rail [reɪl] I N [c] **1** (*for safety on stairs*) 扶手 [fúshǒu]; (*on bridge, balcony*) 横栏 [hénglán]; (*on ship*) 栏杆 [lángān] **2** (*for hanging clothes*) 横杆 [hénggān] **3** (*also*: **curtain rail**) 窗帘横杆 [chuānglián hénggān] **4** (*for trains*) 铁轨 [tiěguǐ] II CPD [复合词] [+ *travel, transport, strike*] 铁路 [tiělù] ▶ **by rail** (*by train*) 乘火车

railcard ['reɪlkɑ:d] (BRIT) N [c] 火车票优惠卡 [huǒchēpiào yōuhuìkǎ]

railing(s) ['reɪlɪŋ(z)] NPL 围栏 [wéilán]

railroad ['reɪlrəʊd] (US) N [c] = **railway**

railway ['reɪlweɪ] (BRIT) N [c] **1** (*system*) 铁路 [tiělù] **2** (*line*) 铁道 [tiědào] **3** (*company*) 铁路公司 [tiělù gōngsī]

railway line (BRIT) N [c] 铁路线 [tiělùxiàn]

railway station (BRIT) N [c] 火车站 [huǒchēzhàn]

rain [reɪn] I N [u] 雨 [yǔ] II VI 下雨 [xiàyǔ] ▶ **in the rain** 在雨中 ▶ **as right as rain** (*inf*) 完全康复了 ▶ **it's raining** 正在下雨 ▶ **it's raining cats and dogs** 下着倾盆大雨 ▶ **to be rained off** 因雨暂停

rainbow ['reɪnbəʊ] N [c] 彩虹 [cǎihóng]

raincoat ['reɪnkəʊt] N [c] 雨衣 [yǔyī]

raindrop ['reɪndrɒp] N [c] 雨滴 [yǔdī]

rainfall ['reɪnfɔ:l] N [c/u] 降雨量 [jiàngyǔliàng]

rainforest ['reɪnfɒrɪst] N [c/u] 雨林 [yǔlín]

rainy ['reɪnɪ] ADJ [+ *day, night, area*] 多雨的 [duōyǔ de] ▶ **rainy season** 雨季 ▶ **to save sth for a rainy day** 存储某物以备不时之需

○ **raise** [reɪz] I VT **1** (*lift*) [+ *hand, glass*] 举起 [jǔqǐ] [+ *window*] 打开 [dǎkāi] **2** (*increase*) [+ *salary, rate,*

speed limit] 增加 [zēngjiā]; [+ *morale, standards*] 提高 [tígāo] **3** (*bring up*) [+ *subject, question, objection*] 提出 [tíchū]; [+ *doubts, hopes*] 引起 [yǐnqǐ] **4** [+ *money, loan*] 筹集 [chóují] **5** (*rear*) [+ *child, family*] 抚养 [fǔyǎng]; [+ *cattle, chickens*] 饲养 [sìyǎng]; [+ *crop*] 种植 [zhòngzhí] **6** (*end*) [+ *siege, embargo*] 解除 [jiěchú] II N [c] (US) (*payrise*) 加薪 [jiāxīn] [英= raise] ▶ **to raise a glass to sb/sth** 为某人/某事举杯庆贺 ▶ **to raise sb's hopes** 使某人满怀希望 ▶ **to raise a smile/laugh** 引来微笑/大笑 ▶ **to raise one's voice** 提高某人的声音

raisin ['reɪzn] N [c] 葡萄干 [pútáogān]

rake [reɪk] I N **1** (*tool*) 耙 [pá] **2** (*o.f.*) (*person*) 花花公子 [huāhuā gōngzǐ] II VT **1** [+ *soil*] 耙 [pá] **2** [+ *leaves, lawn*] 耙拢 [pálǒng] **3** [*light, gun +*] [+ *area*] 扫射 [sǎoshè] ▶ **he's raking it in** (*inf*) 他发大财了

rally ['rælɪ] I N [c] **1** (*public meeting*) 集会 [jíhuì] **2** (AUT) 拉力赛 [lālìsài] **3** (TENNIS) 连续对打 [liánxù duìdǎ] II VT [+ *support*] 集合 [jíhé] III VI **1** (*unite*) 联合 [liánhé] **2** [*sick person +*] 康复 [kāngfù] **3** [*Stock Exchange +*] 回升 [huíshēng] ▶ **rally round** I VI 团结一致 [tuánjié yīzhì] II VT FUS [不可拆分] 团结在…周围 [tuánjié zài…zhōuwéi]

RAM [ræm] (COMPUT) N ABBR (= *random access memory*) 随机存储器 [suíjī cúnchǔqì]

ram [ræm] I N [c] (*sheep*) 公羊 [gōngyáng] II VT **1** (*crash into*) 撞击 [zhuàngjī] **2** (*push*) [+ *bolt, fist etc*] 捅 [tǒng]

ramble ['ræmbl] I N [c] (*walk*) 散步 [sànbù] II VI **1** (*hike*) 漫步 [mànbù] **2** (*also*: **ramble on**) (*talk*) 闲扯 [xiánchě]

rambler ['ræmblə(r)] N [c] **1** (BRIT) (*walker*) 漫步者 [mànbùzhě] **2** (BOT) 攀缘植物 [pānyuán zhíwù]

rambling ['ræmblɪŋ] I N [u] 散步 [sànbù] II ADJ **1** [+ *speech, letter*] 漫无边际的 [màn wú biānjì de] **2** [+ *house*] 杂乱无章的 [záluàn wúzhāng de] **3** [+ *plant*] 攀缘的 [pānyuán de]

ramp [ræmp] N [c] (*for cars, wheelchairs etc, in garage*) 坡道 [pōdào] ▶ **on/off ramp** (US: AUT) 上/下坡道

rampage [ræm'peɪdʒ] I N ▶ **to go on the rampage** 横冲直撞 [héngchōng zhízhuàng] II VI 横冲直撞 [héngchōng zhízhuàng]

ran [ræn] PT of **run**

ranch [rɑ:ntʃ] N [c] 牧场 [mùchǎng]

rancid ['rænsɪd] ADJ 有腐臭的 [yǒu fǔchòu de]

R & D N ABBR (= *research and development*) 研究与开发 [yánjiū yǔ kāifā]

random ['rændəm] I ADJ **1** [+ *arrangement, selection*] 随机的 [suíjī de] **2** (*haphazard*) 任意的 [rènyì de] II N ▶ **at random** 随意 [suíyì]

rang [ræŋ] PT of **ring**

range [reɪndʒ] I N [c] **1** (*variety*) [*of ages, prices*] 范围 [fànwéi]; [*of subjects, possibilities*]

系列 [xìliè] **2** (COMM) (selection) 范围 [fànwéi]
3 (reach) [of missile, vision] 射程 [shèchéng]
4 (also: **mountain range**) 山脉 [shānmài]
5 (also: **kitchen range**) (BRIT) 炉灶 [lúzào] **II** VT
(place in a line) 排列 [páiliè] **III** VI ▸ **to range
over...** [writing, speech +] 涉及…[shèjí…] ▸ **at
close range** 近距离 ▸ **price range** 价格范围
▸ **within (firing) range** 在(射击)距离内 ▸ **out
of range** 超出范围 ▸ **to range from... to...**
在…到…之间 ▸ **ranged right/left** [text +] 靠
右/左对齐

ranger ['reɪndʒə(r)] N [c] 护林员 [hùlínyuán]

rank [ræŋk] **I** N **1** (row) 行 [háng] **2** [c/U]
(status) 等级 [děngjí] **3** [c] (social class) (frm)
阶层 [jiēcéng] **4** [c] (BRIT) (also: **taxi rank**) 出
租车候客站 [chūzūchē hòukèzhàn] **II** VI ▸ **to
rank as...** 被列为…[bèi lièwéi…] **III** VT ▸ **he
is ranked third in the world** 他在世界上排
名第三 [tā zài shìjièshang páimíng dìsān]
IV ADJ **1** (stinking) 发臭的 [fāchòu de] **2** (utter)
[+ hypocrisy, stupidity etc] 极度的 [jídù de] **V** **the
ranks** NPL **1** (MIL) 士兵 [shìbīng] **2** (group)
行列 [hángliè] ▸ **the rank and file** (ordinary
members) 普通成员 ▸ **to rank among...** 列
入…当中 ▸ **to close ranks** 紧密团结 ▸ **to
break ranks** 打破阶层

ransom ['rænsəm] N [c/U] (money) 赎金
[shújīn] ▸ **to hold to ransom** [+ hostage etc] 勒
取赎金;(fig) [+ nation, company] 要挟

rant [rænt] **I** VI 咆哮 [páoxiào] **II** N [c] 咆哮
[páoxiào] ▸ **to rant and rave** 大嚷大叫

rap [ræp] **I** VT (tap) 敲打 [qiāodǎ] **II** N **1** (tap)
敲击 [qiāojí] **2** (perform rap song) 说唱表演
[shuōchàng biǎoyǎn] **III** N **1** [c] (tap) 敲打声
[qiāodǎshēng] **2** [U] (also: **rap music**) 说唱音乐
[Shuōchàng Yīnyuè] ▸ **to rap sb's knuckles** or **to
rap sb on the knuckles** 斥责某人

rape [reɪp] **I** N **1** [c/U] (crime) 强奸 [qiángjiān]
2 [U] (BOT) (also: **oilseed rape**) 油菜 [yóucài]
II VT 强奸 [qiángjiān]

rapid ['ræpɪd] ADJ [+ growth, development, change]
迅速的 [xùnsù de]; [+ heartbeat, steps] 快的
[kuài de]

rapidly ['ræpɪdlɪ] ADV [grow, change, walk, move +]
迅速地 [xùnsù de]

rapids ['ræpɪdz] NPL 湍流 [tuānliú]

rapist ['reɪpɪst] N [c] 强奸犯 [qiángjiānfàn]

rapport [ræ'pɔː(r)] N [s] 和睦关系 [hémù
guānxi]

rare [reə(r)] ADJ **1** (uncommon) 稀有的 [xīyǒu de]
2 (lightly cooked) [+ steak] 半熟的 [bànshóu de]
▸ **it is rare to find...** 难得找到…

rarely ['reəlɪ] ADV 很少 [hěnshǎo]

rash [ræʃ] **I** N **1** [c] (on skin) 皮疹 [pízhěn] **2** [s]
(spate) [of events, robberies] 一连串 [yīliánchuàn]
II ADJ **1** [+ person] 轻率的 [qīngshuài de]
2 [+ promise, act] 草率的 [cǎoshuài de] ▸ **to
come out in a rash** 出皮疹

rasher ['ræʃə(r)] (BRIT) N [c] 熏肉片
[xūnròupiàn] [美=**slice**]

raspberry ['rɑːzbərɪ] N [c] **1** (fruit) 山莓
[shānméi] ▸ **to blow a raspberry** (inf) 咂舌头
嘲笑某人

rat [ræt] N [c] **1** (ZOOL) 田鼠 [tiánshǔ] **2** (inf)
(person) 卑鄙小人 [bēibǐ xiǎorén]

⊘ **rate** [reɪt] **I** N [c] **1** (speed) 速率 [sùlǜ] **2** (level)
[of interest, taxation, inflation] 率 [lǜ] **3** (ratio)
比率 [bǐlǜ] **II** VT **1** (value) 评价 [píngjià]
2 (estimate) 评估 [pínggū] **3** (price) 对…估
价 [duì…gūjià] **III** **rates** NPL (BRIT: formerly)
(property tax) 房地产税 [fángdìchǎn shuì]
▸ **at a rate of 60 kph** 以每小时60公里的速
度 ▸ **rate of growth** (FIN) 增长率 ▸ **rate of
return** (FIN) 回报率 ▸ **at this/that rate** 照这
种/那种情况继续 ▸ **at any rate** (at least) 无论
如何 ▸ **to rate sb/sth as** 把某人/某事物评价
成 ▸ **to rate sb/sth as sth** 把某人/某事物评为
某事物 ▸ **to rate sb/sth among** 把某人/某事
物归于… ▸ **to rate sb/sth highly** 给某人/某
事物高度评价

⊘ **rather** ['rɑːðə(r)] ADV **1** (somewhat) 相当
[xiāngdāng] **2** (instead) 而 [ér] ▸ **rather a lot**
相当多 ▸ **I would rather go than stay** 我宁
愿走而不愿留下来 ▸ **I'd rather not say** 我
宁可不说 ▸ **rather than** (instead of) 而不是
▸ **or rather** (more accurately) 或者更确切地 ▸ **I
rather think he won't come** 我的确认为他
不会来

rating ['reɪtɪŋ] **I** N [c] **1** (score) 等级 [děngjí]
2 (assessment) 评定 [píngdìng] **3** (BRIT: NAUT)
(sailor) 水兵 [shuǐbīng] **II** **ratings** NPL (RAD)
收听率 [shōutīng lǜ];(TV) 收视率 [shōushìlǜ]

ratio ['reɪʃɪəu] N [c] 比例 [bǐlì] ▸ **a ratio of 5 to
1** 5比1的比例 ▸ **the ratio of... to...** …对…的
比例

ration ['ræʃən] **I** N [c] (allowance) [of food,
petrol etc] 配给限额 [pèijǐ xiàn'é] **II** VT [+ food,
petrol etc] 定量供应 [dìngliàng gōngyìng]
III **rations** NPL (MIL) 口粮 [kǒuliáng]

rational ['ræʃənl] ADJ [+ decision, explanation] 合
理的 [hélǐ de]; [+ person] 理性的 [lǐxìng de]

rationalize ['ræʃnəlaɪz] VT **1** (justify) 使有合理
依据 [shǐ yǒu hélǐ yījù] **2** (streamline) [+ company,
system] 使合理化 [shǐ hélǐ huà]

rattle ['rætl] **I** N [c] **1** (baby's toy) 拨浪鼓
[bōlànggǔ] **2** (noise) [of door, window] 格格
响 [gégéxiǎng]; [of train, car, engine etc] 轰鸣
声 [hōngmíngshēng]; [+ of bottles] 格格响
[gégéxiǎng]; [of chain] 哗啦声 [huālāshēng]
II VI [door, window +] 哐啷哐啷作响 [kuānglāng
kuānglāng zuòxiǎng]; [bottles +] 格格作响
[gégé zuòxiǎng]; [chains +] 哗啦作响 [huālā
zuòxiǎng]; [train, car, engine +] 轰隆作响
[hōnglōng zuòxiǎng] **III** VT **1** (shake) 使颤动
出声 [shǐ zhàndòng chūshēng] **2** (inf) (unsettle)
使不安 [shǐ bù'ān] ▸ **to rattle along** [car, bus +]

轰鸣而过
▶ **rattle off** VT 急促而不假思索地说 [jícù ér bù jiǎ sīsuǒ de shuō]
raucous ['rɔːkəs] ADJ 沙哑的 [shāyǎ de]
rave [reɪv] I VI (talk wildly) 胡言乱语 [húyán luànyǔ] II ADJ (inf) [+ review] 热烈的 [rèliè de] III N [c] (BRIT: inf) (dance) 狂欢舞会 [kuánghuān wǔhuì]
▶ **rave about** VT FUS [不可拆分] (inf) 极力赞美 [jílì zànměi]
raven ['reɪvn] N [c] 渡鸦 [dùyā]
ravine [rə'viːn] N [c] 深谷 [shēngǔ]
raw [rɔː] ADJ 1 (uncooked) [+ meat, vegetables] 生的 [shēng de] 2 (unprocessed) [+ cotton, sugar etc] 未加工的 [wèi jiāgōng de] 3 (sore) 摩擦得疼的 [mócā de téng de] 4 (inexperienced) 生手的 [shēngshǒu de] 5 [+ weather, day] 湿冷的 [shīlěng de] ▶ **to get a raw deal** 受到不公待遇
raw materials NPL 原材料 [yuáncáiliào]
ray [reɪ] N [c] 1 [of light] 光线 [guāngxiàn] 2 [of heat] 辐射 [fúshè] ▶ **a ray of hope** 一线希望
razor ['reɪzə(r)] N [c] 1 (also: **safety razor**) 剃须刀 [tìxūdāo] 2 (also: **electric razor**) 电动剃须刀 [diàndòng tìxūdāo]
razor blade N [c] 剃须刀刀片 [tìxūdāo dāopiàn]
RC ADJ ABBR (= Roman Catholic) 天主教的 [Tiānzhǔjiào de]
Rd, (ESP US) Rd. ABBR (= road) 路 [lù]
RDA N ABBR (= recommended daily amount) 推荐日摄取量 [tuījiàn rì shèqǔliàng]
RE (BRIT: SCOL) N ABBR (= religious education) 宗教教育 [zōngjiào jiàoyù]
re [riː] PREP (with regard to) 关于 [guānyú]
⊙ reach [riːtʃ] I VT 1 (arrive at) [+ place, destination] 到达 [dàodá]; [+ conclusion, agreement, decision] 达成 [dáchéng]; [+ stage, level, age] 达到 [dádào] 2 (be able to touch) 够着 [gòuzháo] 3 (get hold of) 联络 [liánluò] II VI (stretch out one's arm) 伸手 [shēnshǒu] III N [U] (range) [of arm] 伸手可及的范围 [shēnshǒu kějí de fànwéi] IV **reaches** NPL [of river] 游 [yóu] ▶ **within reach** 伸手可及 ▶ **out of reach** 远离 ▶ **within reach of...** 离…近 ▶ **within easy reach of...** 离…很近 ▶ **beyond the reach of sb/sth** (fig) 超出某人/某事能力之外 ▶ **"keep out of the reach of children"** "远离儿童"
▶ **reach out** I VI 伸手 [shēnshǒu] II VT [+ hand] 伸出 [shēnchū] ▶ **to reach out for sth** 伸手拿某物

> **reach** 和 **arrive** 都可以指到达某个地方。**reach** 后可以直接加表示地点的名词或代词，而且强调需要很大努力才能到达。*To reach the capital might not be easy.* **arrive at** 和 **reach** 还可以表示某人最终做了决定或找到了答案。*It took hours to arrive at a decision…They were unable to reach a decision.*

react [riː'ækt] VI 1 (respond) 反应 [fǎnyìng] 2 (rebel) ▶ **to react against sth** 反抗某事 [fǎnkàng mǒushì] 3 (CHEM) ▶ **to react (with)** (和…) 起反应 [(hé…)qǐ fǎnyìng] 4 (MED) (对…) 有反应 [(duì…)yǒu fǎnyìng]
reaction [riː'ækʃən] I N 1 [C/U] (response) 反应 [fǎnyìng] 2 [C] (MED, CHEM) 反应 [fǎnyìng] 3 [U] (conservatism) 极端保守 [jíduān bǎoshǒu] II **reactions** NPL (reflexes) 反应能力 [fǎnyìng nénglì] ▶ **a reaction against sth** 反对某事
reactor [riː'æktə(r)] N [c] 反应器 [fǎnyìngqì]
⊙ read [riːd] (pt, pp **read** [red]) I VI 1 (person +) 阅读 [yuèdú] 2 (piece of writing +) 读起来 [dúqǐlái] II VT 1 [+ book, newspaper etc] 读 [dú] 2 (+ music) 看懂 [kàndǒng] 3 (understand) 了解 [liǎojiě] 4 [+ meter, thermometer etc] 识读 [shídú] 5 (carry stated message) [notice, sign +] 写着 [xiězhe]; [meter, thermometer etc +] 显示 [xiǎnshì] 6 (study at university) (BRIT) 攻读 [gōngdú] III N ▶ **to have a read** 阅读 [yuèdú] ▶ **to read sb's mind** 了解某人的想法 ▶ **to take sth as read** 把某事当作是不容置疑的 ▶ **to read sth into sb's remarks** 从某人的话中读出某种含义 ▶ **it's a good read** 这是本好的读物
▶ **read out** VT 朗读 [lǎngdú]
▶ **read over** VT 细读 [xìdú]
▶ **read through** VT 1 (quickly) 浏览 [liúlǎn] 2 (thoroughly) 仔细阅读 [zǐxì yuèdú]
▶ **read up on** VT FUS [不可拆分] 研读 [yándú]
reader ['riːdə(r)] N [c] 1 [of book, newspaper etc] 读者 [dúzhě] 2 (beginner's book) 初级读本 [chūjí dúběn] 3 (BRIT: UNIV) 高级讲师 [gāojí jiǎngshī]
readily ['redɪlɪ] ADV 1 (without hesitation) 欣然 [xīnrán] 2 (without difficulty) 容易地 [róngyì de]
reading ['riːdɪŋ] N 1 [U] [of books, newspapers etc] (activity) 阅读 [yuèdú] 2 [U] (material read) 阅读材料 [yuèdú cáiliào] 3 [c] (literary event) 朗读会 [lǎngdúhuì] 4 [c] (on meter, thermometer etc) 读数 [dúshù] 5 [c] (interpretation) ▶ **my reading of the situation is that…** 我对于这种情况的理解是… [wǒ duìyú zhèzhǒng qíngkuàng de lǐjiě shì…] 6 [c] (in church) 朗诵会 [lǎngsònghuì] 7 [c] (text from Bible etc) 朗读 [lǎngdú]
ready ['redɪ] I ADJ 1 (prepared, available) 做好准备的 [zuòhǎo zhǔnbèi de] 2 (willing) 乐意的 [lèyì de] 3 (easy, quick) 就绪的 [jiùxù de] II N ▶ **at the ready** 准备好 [zhǔnbèihǎo] III VT 准备 [zhǔnbèi] ▶ **to get ready** (prepare o.s.) 准备好 ▶ **to get sb/sth ready** 使某人/某物准备就绪 ▶ **to be ready to do sth** (prepared) 准备做某事; (willing) 愿意做某事 ▶ **to be ready for sth** (prepared for) 已为某事准备好; (wanting) 想要某物 ▶ **ready for use** 待用
ready-made ['redɪ'meɪd] ADJ 1 [+ clothes] 现成的 [xiànchéng de] 2 (useful) 可用的 [kěyòng de]
⊙ real [rɪəl] I ADJ 1 (not artificial) [+ leather, gold

etc) 真正的 [zhēnzhèng de] **2** (*not feigned*) [+*reason, interest, name*] 真实的 [zhēnshí de] **3** (*not imaginary*) [+*life, feeling*] 真实的 [zhēnshí de] **4** (*for emphasis*) 真的 [zhēn de] ▷ *It's a real shame.* 真是遗憾。II ADV (US: *inf*) (*very*) 很 [hěn] ▸ **for real** 当真 ▸ **the real thing** 真家伙 ▸ **in real life** 现实生活中 ▸ **in real terms** 实际上

real estate I N [U] 不动产 [bùdòngchǎn] II CPD [复合词] (US) [+*agent, business etc*] 房地产 [fángdìchǎn]

realistic [rɪə'lɪstɪk] ADJ **1** (*sensible*) 现实的 [xiànshí de] **2** (*convincing*) [+*book, film, portrayal etc*] 逼真的 [bīzhēn de]

reality [rɪː'ælɪtɪ] N **1** [U] (*real things*) 现实 [xiànshí] **2** [C/U] (*realness*) 真相 [zhēnxiàng] ▸ **in reality** 事实上

reality TV N [U] 真人电视秀 [zhēnrén diànshìxiù]

realization [rɪəlaɪ'zeɪʃən] N **1** [S/U] (*understanding*) 认识 [rènshi] **2** [U] (*fulfilment*) [*of dreams, hopes, fears*] 实现 [shíxiàn] **3** [C/U] (ECON) [*of asset*] 变卖 [biànmài]

realize ['rɪəlaɪz] VT **1** (*understand*) 意识到 [yìshídào] **2** (*fulfil*) [+*dream, ambition, fears*] 实现 [shíxiàn]; [+*design, idea*] 体现 [tǐxiàn] **3** (ECON) [+*amount, profit*] 变卖 [biànmài] ▸ **to realize that...** 意识到…

○ **really** ['rɪəlɪ] ADV **1** (*very*) ▸ **really good/delighted** 真好/真高兴 [zhēnhǎo/zhēn gāoxìng] **2** (*genuinely*) 确实 [quèshí] **3** (*after negative*) 真正地 [zhēnzhèng de] ▸ **really?** (*indicating surprise, interest*) 真的吗? ▸ **really!** (*indicating annoyance*) (BRIT) 哎呀!
▨用法参见 **actually**

realm [rɛlm] N [C] (*domain*) 领域 [lǐngyù]

realtor ['rɪəltɔː(r)] (US) N [C] 房地产商 [fángdìchǎn shāng] [英=**estate agent**]

reappear [riːə'pɪə(r)] VI 重现 [chóngxiàn]

rear [rɪə(r)] I ADJ (*back*) [+*end, entrance*] 后面的 [hòumian de] II N **1** [S] (*back*) 后面 [hòumian] **2** [C] (*buttocks*) (*inf*) 臀部 [túnbù] III VT (*raise*) [+*cattle, chickens*] (ESP BRIT) 饲养 [sìyǎng] [美=**raise**]; [+*family, children*] 抚养 [fǔyǎng] IV VI (*also:* **rear up**) [*horse +*] 用后腿站立 [yòng hòutuǐ zhànlì]

rearrange [riːə'reɪndʒ] VT **1** [+*objects*] 重新安置 [chóngxīn ānzhì] **2** [+*meeting*] 重新安排 [chóngxīn ānpái]

rear-view mirror ['rɪəvjuː-] N [C] 后视镜 [hòushìjìng]

○ **reason** ['riːzn] I N **1** [C] (*cause*) 原因 [yuányīn] **2** [U] (*rationality*) 理性 [lǐxìng] II VI ▸ **to reason with sb** 与某人理论 [yǔ mǒurén lǐlùn] III VT 推理 [tuīlǐ] ▸ **the reason for sth** 某事的动机 ▸ **the reason why** …的原因 ▸ **to have reason to do sth** (*frm*) 有理由做某事 ▸ **by reason of** (*frm*) 因为 ▸ **with good reason** 合乎情理 ▸ **within reason** 在合理的范围内

reasonable ['riːznəbl] ADJ **1** (*moderate, sensible*) [+*person, decision*] 合情合理的 [héqíng hélǐ de]; [+*number, amount*] 相当的 [xiāngdāng de]; [+*price*] 合理的 [hélǐ de] **2** (*not bad*) 凑合的 [còuhe de] **3** (*rational*) [+*explanation, request*] 合理的 [hélǐ de] ▸ **be reasonable!** 理智些!

reasonably ['riːznəblɪ] ADV **1** (*moderately*) 相当地 [xiāngdāng de] **2** (*sensibly*) 明智地 [míngzhì de]

reasoning ['riːznɪŋ] N [U] 推理 [tuīlǐ]

reassurance [riːə'ʃʊərəns] N **1** [U] (*comfort*) 放心 [fàngxīn] **2** [C] (*guarantee*) 保证 [bǎozhèng]

reassure [riːə'ʃʊə(r)] VT 使安心 [shǐ ānxīn]

rebate ['riːbeɪt] N [C] 部分退款 [bùfen tuìkuǎn]

rebel [n 'rɛbl, vb rɪ'bɛl] I N [C] **1** (*against society, parents*) 反叛者 [fǎnpànzhě] **2** (*in uprising*) 起义者 [qǐyìzhě] **3** (*in politics*) 持不同政见者 [chí bùtóng zhèngjiànzhě] II VI **1** (*against society, parents*) 反叛 [fǎnpàn] **2** (*in uprising*) 起义 [qǐyì] **3** (*in politics*) 反对 [fǎnduì]

rebellion [rɪ'bɛljən] N [C/U] (*uprising*) 叛乱 [pànluàn]; (*against society, parents*) 反叛 [fǎnpàn]; (*in politics*) 反抗 [fǎnkàng]

rebellious [rɪ'bɛljəs] ADJ [+*person*] 叛逆的 [pànnì de]; [+*behaviour*] 反叛的 [fǎnpàn de]; [+*politician*] 反对的 [fǎnduì de]

rebuild [riː'bɪld] (*pt, pp* **rebuilt**) VT **1** [+*town, building*] 重建 [chóngjiàn] **2** [+*economy, confidence*] 恢复 [huīfù]

recall [vb rɪ'kɔːl, n 'riːkɔːl] VT **1** (*remember*) 起 [jìqǐ] **2** (*recount*) 回忆起 [huíyìqǐ] **3** (*call back*) [+*parliament, ambassador etc*] 召回 [zhàohuí]; [+*product*] 收回 [shōuhuí] II N **1** [U] (*of memories*) 回忆 [huíyì] **2** [S] (*of ambassador etc*) 召回 [zhàohuí] ▸ **beyond recall** 无法恢复

receding [rɪ'siːdɪŋ] ADJ [+*hair*] 后移的 [hòuyí de]

receipt [rɪ'siːt] I N **1** [C] (*for purchases*) 收据 [shōujù] **2** [C] (*for deposit*) 收条 [shōutiáo] **3** [U] (*act of receiving*) 收到 [shōudào] II **receipts** NPL (*monies received*) 收入 [shōurù] ▸ **on receipt of** (*frm*) 收到…时 ▸ **to be in receipt of sth** (*frm*) 已收到某物

○ **receive** [rɪ'siːv] VT **1** (*get*) [+*money, letter etc*] 收到 [shōudào]; [+*injury, treatment*] 受到 [shòudào]; [+*criticism, acclaim*] 遭受 [zāoshòu] **2** (RAD, TV) 接收 [jiēshōu] **3** (*frm*) (*welcome*) [+*visitor, guest*] 接待 [jiēdài] **4** (*react to*) 接受到 [jiēshòu dào] ▸ **"received with thanks"** (COMM) "钱款已收到,谢谢" ▸ **to be on the receiving end of sth** 遭受某事

receiver [rɪ'siːvə(r)] N [C] **1** (*of telephone*) 听筒 [tīngtǒng] **2** (RAD, TV) 接收器 [jiēshōuqì] **3** (COMM) 破产管理人 [pòchǎn guǎnlǐrén]

○ **recent** ['riːsnt] ADJ [+*event*] 最近的 [zuìjìn de] ▸ **in recent years** *or* **times** 近年来 {或} 近一段时期

recently ['riːsntlɪ] ADV **1** (*lately, not long ago*) 最

近 [zuìjìn] ▶ **until recently** 直到最近

reception [rɪ'sɛpʃən] N 1 [s] (*in public building*) 接待处 [jiēdàichù] 2 [c] (*party*) 欢迎会 [huānyínghuì] 3 [U] (RAD, TV) 接收 [jiēshōu] 4 [c] (*welcome*) 反响 [fǎnxiǎng]

reception desk N [s] 接待处 [jiēdàichù]

receptionist [rɪ'sɛpʃənɪst] (ESP BRIT) N [c] 接待员 [jiēdàiyuán] [美= **desk clerk**]

recession [rɪ'sɛʃən] N [c/U] 衰退 [shuāituì]

recharge [ri:'tʃɑ:dʒ] VT 充电 [chōngdiàn]

recipe ['rɛsɪpɪ] (CULIN) N [c] 食谱 [shípǔ] ▶ **a recipe for disaster/success** 造成灾难的因素/成功的秘诀

recipient [rɪ'sɪpɪənt] N [c] 接受者 [jiēshòuzhě]

recital [rɪ'saɪtl] N [c] 独自表演 [dúzì biǎoyǎn]

recite [rɪ'saɪt] VT 1 [+ *poem*] 背诵 [bèisòng] 2 (*enumerate*) [+ *complaints etc*] 列举 [lièjǔ]

reckless ['rɛkləs] ADJ [+ *person, behaviour*] 鲁莽的 [lǔmǎng de]

reckon ['rɛkən] I VT 1 (*consider*) 认为 [rènwéi] 2 (*calculate*) 计算 [jìsuàn] II VI ▶ **he is somebody to be reckoned with** 他是一个得认真对付的人 [tā shì yī gè děi rènzhēn duìfu de rén] ▶ **to reckon without sb/sth** 未考虑到某人/某事物 ▶ **I reckon that...** (*think*) (*inf*) 我估计... ▶ **reckon on** VT FUS [不可拆分] (*expect*) 期望 [qīwàng]

reclaim [rɪ'kleɪm] VT 1 [+ *luggage, tax etc*] 取回 [qǔhuí] 2 [+ *land*] (*from sea*) 开垦 [kāikěn]

recline [rɪ'klaɪn] I VI 1 [*person +*] 斜倚 [xiéyǐ] 2 [*seat +*] 向后倾斜 [xiànghòu qīngxié] II VT [+ *seat*] 使倾斜 [shǐ qīngxié]

recognition [rɛkəg'nɪʃən] N [U] 1 (*identification*) [*of person, place*] 认出 [rènchū] 2 (*understanding*) [*of problem, fact*] 承认 [chéngrèn] 3 (*approval*) [*of achievement*] 认可 [rènkě] ▶ **to change beyond recognition** 变化得使人认不出来 ▶ **in recognition of** 为酬答…而 ▶ **to gain recognition** 得到承认

recognizable ['rɛkəgnaɪzəbl] ADJ 可辨认的 [kě biànrèn de]

recognize ['rɛkəgnaɪz] VT 1 [+ *person, place, voice*] 认出 [rènchū]; [+ *sign, symptom*] 识别 [shíbié]; [+ *problem, need*] 承认 [chéngrèn] 2 (*accept validity of*) [+ *qualifications*] 认可 [rènkě]; [+ *government*] 承认 [chéngrèn] 3 (*show appreciation of*) [+ *achievement*] 认可 [rènkě] ▶ **to recognize sb by/as** 通过…认出某人/把某人认作…

recollect [rɛkə'lɛkt] VT 想起 [xiǎngqǐ]

recollection [rɛkə'lɛkʃən] N 1 [c] (*memory*) 记忆 [jìyì] 2 [U] (*remembering*) 回忆 [huíyì] ▶ **to the best of my recollection** 如果我没有记错

recommend [rɛkə'mɛnd] VT 1 [+ *book, shop, person*] 推荐 [tuījiàn] 2 [+ *course of action*] 建议 [jiànyì] ▶ **she has a lot to recommend her** 她有许多值得称道的地方 ▶ **to recommend sb**

for promotion 推荐某人升职

recommendation [rɛkəmən'deɪʃən] N [c/U] 推荐 [tuījiàn] ▶ **on the recommendation of** 在…建议下

reconcile ['rɛkənsaɪl] VT 1 [+ *two people*] 和解 [héjiě] 2 [+ *two facts, beliefs*] 调和 [tiáohé] ▶ **to reconcile o.s. to sth** [+ *unpleasant situation etc*] 使自己接受某事

reconsider [ri:kən'sɪdə(r)] VT VI 重新考虑 [chóngxīn kǎolù]

reconstruct [ri:kən'strʌkt] VT 1 (*rebuild*) 重建 [chóngjiàn] 2 (*form picture of*) [+ *event, crime*] 重现 [chóngxiàn]

○ record [n 'rɛkɔ:d, vb rɪ'kɔ:d] I N [c] 1 (*written account*) 记载 [jìzǎi] 2 (*also:* **track record**) 记录 [jìlù] 3 (*sound-recording*) 唱片 [chàngpiàn] 4 (*unbeaten statistic*) 记录 [jìlù] II **records** NPL 记录 [jìlù] III VT 1 (*make record of, document*) 记录 [jìlù] 2 (*show, register*) [*thermometer, clock etc +*] 显示 [xiǎnshì] 3 (*make recording of*) 录制 [lùzhì] IV ADJ [+ *sales, profits, levels*] 创纪录的 [chuàng jìlù de] ▶ **in record time** 破记录地 ▶ **to keep sth on record** 把某事物记录保存下来 ▶ **to have a good/poor record** 有良好/不好的记录 ▶ **to keep a record of sth** 记录某事 ▶ **to set or put the record straight** 澄清事实 ▶ **to be on record** 正式记录的 ▶ **off the record** [*speak +*] 私下里

recorded delivery [rɪ'kɔ:dɪd-] (BRIT) N [U] 挂号邮递 [guàhào yóudì]

recorder [rɪ'kɔ:də(r)] N [c] 1 (MUS) (*instrument*) 八孔竖笛 [bākǒng shùdí] 2 (LAW) 法官 [fǎguān]

recording [rɪ'kɔ:dɪŋ] N 1 [c] (*recorded music, voice etc*) 录音 [lùyīn] 2 [U] (*process of recording*) 录制 [lùzhì]

record player N [c] 唱机 [chàngjī]

recount [rɪ'kaunt] VT [+ *story, event*] 描述 [miáoshù]

recover [rɪ'kʌvə(r)] I VI 1 (*from illness, shock, experience*) 恢复 [huīfù] 2 [*country, economy +*] 复原 [fùyuán] II VT 1 [+ *stolen goods, lost items*] 找回 [zhǎohuí] 2 [+ *body*] 找到 [zhǎodào] 3 [+ *financial loss*] 挽回 [wǎnhuí] 4 [+ *consciousness*] 恢复 [huīfù]

recovery [rɪ'kʌvərɪ] N 1 [c/U] (*from illness, operation*) 康复 [kāngfù] 2 [U] [*of stolen, lost items*] 挽回 [wǎnhuí] 3 [c/U] (*in economy, finances*) 恢复 [huīfù] 4 [U] [*of physical/mental state*] 恢复 [huīfù] ▶ **to be in recovery** (*from addiction etc*) 在恢复中

recreate [ri:krɪ'eɪt] VT 重现 [chóngxiàn]

recreation [rɛkrɪ'eɪʃən] N [U] 消遣 [xiāoqiǎn]

recreational [rɛkrɪ'eɪʃənl] ADJ 娱乐的 [yúlè de]

recruit [rɪ'kru:t] I N [c] 1 (MIL) 新兵 [xīnbīng] 2 (*in company, organization*) 新成员 [xīnchéngyuán] II VT 1 (MIL) 招募 [zhāomù]

2 [+ *staff, new members*] 招收 [zhāoshōu]

recruitment [rɪ'kru:tmənt] N [U] 招收 [zhāoshōu]

rectangle ['rɛktæŋgl] N [C] 长方形 [chángfāngxíng]

rectangular [rɛk'tæŋgjulə(r)] ADJ 长方形的 [chángfāngxíng de]

rectify ['rɛktɪfaɪ] VT 改正 [gǎizhèng]

rector ['rɛktə(r)] N [C] 教区长 [jiàoqūzhǎng]

recur [rɪ'kə:(r)] VI **1** [*error, event* +] 再发生 [zàifāshēng] **2** [*illness, pain* +] 复发 [fùfā]

recurring [rɪ'kə:rɪŋ] **I** ADJ (*recurrent*) [+ *problem, dream*] 重复的 [chóngfù de] **II** ADV (*in decimals*) 循环 [xúnhuán]

recycle [ri:'saɪkl] VT 再生利用 [zàishēng lìyòng]

recycling [ri:'saɪklɪŋ] N [U] 循环利用 [xúnhuán lìyòng]

○ **red** [rɛd] **I** ADJ **1** 红色的 [hóngsè de] **2** [+ *face, person*] 涨红的 [zhànghóng de] **3** [+ *hair*] 红褐色的 [hónghèsè de] **4** [+ *wine*] 红的 [hóng de] **II** N [C/U] 红色 [hóngsè] ▸ **to be in the red** (*inf*) [*bank account, business* +] 负债 ▸ **to see red** (*inf*) 暴怒

Red Cross N ▸ **the Red Cross** 红十字会 [Hóngshízìhuì]

redcurrant ['rɛdkʌrənt] (BRIT: BOT, CULIN) N [C] 小红浆果 [xiǎo hóngjiāngguǒ]; (*also*: **redcurrant bush**) 红浆果树 [hóngjiāngguǒ shù]

redeem [rɪ'di:m] VT **1** [+ *situation*] 挽回 [wǎnhuí] **2** [+ *sth in pawn, loan*] 赎回 [shúhuí] **3** (REL) [+ *person*] 拯救 [zhěngjiù] ▸ **to redeem o.s.** 弥补自己的过失

red-haired [rɛd'hɛəd] ADJ 红棕色头发的 [hóngzōngsè tóufa de]

redhead ['rɛdhɛd] N [C] 有红棕色头发的人 [yǒu hóngzōngsè tóufa de rén]

red-hot [rɛd'hɔt] ADJ **1** (*very hot*) 炽热的 [chìrè de] **2** (*inf*) (*very popular*) 热门的 [rèmén de] **3** (*inf*) (*passionate*) 狂热的 [kuángrè de] ▸ **the red-hot favourite** (*inf*) 大热门

red light N ▸ **to go through a red light** 闯红灯 [chuǎng hóngdēng]

red-light district ['rɛdlaɪt-] N [C] 红灯区 [hóngdēngqū]

red meat N [C/U] 牛羊肉 [niúyángròu]

redo [ri:'du:] VT (*pt* **redid**, *pp* **redone**) 重做 [chóngzuò]

reduce [rɪ'dju:s] VT [+ *spending, numbers, risk etc*] 减少 [jiǎnshǎo] ▸ **to reduce sb to sth** 使某人沦落到某种状态 ▸ **to reduce sth to sth** 使某事陷入某种状态 ▸ **to reduce sth by/to** 将某物减少…/将某物减少到… ▸ **to reduce sb to tears** 使某人伤心流泪 ▸ **to reduce sb to silence** 使某人沉默 ▸ **"reduce speed now"** (AUT) "现在减速"

reduced [rɪ'dju:st] ADJ [+ *goods, ticket etc*] 减

少的 [jiǎnshǎo de] ▸ **"greatly reduced prices"** "大减价"

reduction [rɪ'dʌkʃən] N **1** [C/U] (*decrease*) 减少 [jiǎnshǎo] **2** [C] (*discount*) 减价 [jiǎnjià]

redundancy [rɪ'dʌndənsɪ] (BRIT) N **1** [C] (*dismissal*) 冗员 [rǒngyuán] [美= **layoff**] **2** [U] (*being dismissed*) 裁员 [cáiyuán] ▸ **compulsory redundancy** 强行裁员 ▸ **voluntary redundancy** 自愿裁员

redundant [rɪ'dʌndnt] ADJ (BRIT) **1** (*unemployed*) [+ *worker*] 被裁员的 [bèi cáiyuán de] **2** (*superfluous*) [+ *skills, buildings*] 冗余的 [rǒngyú de] ▸ **to be made redundant** [*worker* +] 被裁员

reed [ri:d] (BOT) N [C] 芦苇 [lúwěi]

reef [ri:f] N [C] 暗礁 [ànjiāo]

reel [ri:l] **I** N [C] **1** [*of thread, cable, film, tape*] 卷轴 [juànzhóu] **2** (CINE) 盘 [pán] **3** (*on fishing-rod*) 钩丝螺旋轮 [gōusī luóxuánlún] **4** (*dance*) 里尔舞(一种轻快的苏格兰或爱尔兰舞) [lǐ'ěrwǔ (yī zhǒng qīngkuài de Sūgélán huò Ài'ěrlán wǔ)] **II** VI **1** (*sway*) 摇晃地移动 [yáohuàng de yídòng] **2** (*from shock*) 眩晕 [xuànyùn] ▸ **my head is reeling** 我头昏脑胀
▸ **reel in** VT [+ *fish*] 收线钓到 [shōuxiàn diàodào]; [+ *line*] 绕[rào]
▸ **reel off** VT (*say*) 一口气说出 [yīkǒuqì shuōchū]

ref [rɛf] (SPORT) (*inf*) N [C] (*referee*) 裁判员 [cáipànyuán]

ref. ABBR (= *reference*) 参考号 [cānkǎohào]

refectory [rɪ'fɛktərɪ] N [C] **1** (*in school, university*) 食堂 [shítáng] **2** (*in monastery*) 斋房 [zhāifáng]

refer [rɪ'fə:(r)] VT ▸ **to refer sb to** [+ *book*] 叫某人参看 [jiào mǒurén cānkàn]; [+ *manager*] 叫某人去…寻求帮助 [jiào mǒurén qù…xúnqiú bāngzhù]; [+ *doctor, hospital*] 将某人交由…治疗 [jiāng mǒurén jiāoyóu…zhìliáo] ▸ **to refer sth to** (*pass on*) [+ *task, problem*] 把某事提交给
▸ **refer to** VT FUS [不可拆分] **1** (*mention*) 提到 [tídào] **2** (*by a name*) 提起 [shuōqǐ] **3** (*relate to*) 指 [zhǐ] **4** (*mean*) 意为 [yìwéi] **5** (*consult*) 参考 [cānkǎo]

referee [rɛfə'ri:] **I** N [C] **1** (SPORT) 裁判员 [cáipànyuán] **2** (BRIT) (*for job application*) 证明人 [zhèngmíngrén] [美= **reference**] **II** VT [+ *football match etc*] 当裁判 [dāng cáipàn]

reference ['rɛfrəns] N [C] **1** (*mention*) 提到 [tídào] **2** (*in book, article*) 参考 [cānkǎo] **3** (*number, name*) 参考号 [cānkǎohào] ▷ *a map reference* 地图图例 **4** (*for job application*) (*letter*) 证明人 [zhèngmíngrén] ▸ **with reference to** or **in reference to** (*in letter*) 关于… ▸ **"please quote this reference"** (COMM) "请注明此编号"

reference number N [C] 参考号 [cānkǎohào]

refill [*vb* ri:'fɪl, *n* 'ri:fɪl] **I** VT 再装满 [zàizhuāngmǎn] **II** N [C] **1** [*of ink*] 替芯 [tìxīn];

[of detergent] 替换装 [tìhuànzhuāng] **2** [of drink] 续杯 [xùbēi]

refine [rɪ'faɪn] VT **1** (purify) [+ substance] 精炼 [jīngliàn]; **2** (improve) [+ theory, method] 改良 [gǎiliáng]

refined [rɪ'faɪnd] ADJ **1** (cultured) [+ person, taste] 有教养的 [yǒu jiàoyǎng de] **2** (purified) [+ substance] 精炼的 [jīngliàn de]

refinery [rɪ'faɪnərɪ] N [c] 精炼厂 [jīngliànchǎng]

reflect [rɪ'flɛkt] I VT **1** (bounce back) [+ image] 映出 [yìngchū]; [+ light, heat] 反射 [fǎnshè] **2** (mirror) [+ situation, attitude] 反映 [fǎnyìng] II VI (think) 沉思 [chénsī]
▶ **reflect on** VT FUS [不可拆分] 带来 [dàilái]

reflection [rɪ'flɛkʃən] I N **1** [c] (image) 影像 [yǐngxiàng] **2** [U] [of light, heat] 反射 [fǎnshè] **3** [c] (indication) [of situation, attitude] 反映 [fǎnyìng] **4** [U] (thought) 沉思 [chénsī]
II reflections NPL 考虑 [kǎolǜ] ▶ on reflection 再经考虑 ▶ to be a reflection on sb/sth (criticism) 有损于某人/某事

reflex ['riːflɛks] I N [c] **1** (PHYSIOL) (action, movement) 反射动作 [fǎnshè dòngzuò] **2** (habit) 反射作用 [fǎnshè zuòyòng] II ADJ [+ action, movement] (also: **reflex action**) 反射动作的 [fǎnshè dòngzuò de] III reflexes NPL (speed of reaction) 反应 [fǎnyìng]

reform [rɪ'fɔːm] I N **1** [U] [of law, system] 改革 [gǎigé] **2** [c] (process, result) 改革 [gǎigé] II VT [+ law, system] 改革 [gǎigé] III VI (criminal, alcoholic +) 改过 [gǎiguò]

refrain [rɪ'freɪn] I VI 克制 [kèzhì] II N [c] [of song] 叠句 [diéjù] ▶ to refrain from doing sth 克制而不做某事

refresh [rɪ'frɛʃ] VT [sleep, drink, rest +] 使恢复 [shǐ huīfù] ▶ to refresh sb's memory 唤起某人的记忆

refreshing [rɪ'frɛʃɪŋ] ADJ **1** [+ drink, sleep] 提神的 [tíshén de] **2** [+ fact, idea etc] 令人耳目一新的 [lìng rén ěr mù yī xīn de]

refreshments [rɪ'frɛʃmənts] NPL 饮料及小吃 [yǐnliào jí xiǎochī]

refrigerator [rɪ'frɪdʒəreɪtə(r)] N [c] 冰箱 [bīngxiāng]

refuel [riː'fjuəl] I VI [aircraft, car +] 加燃料 [jiā ránliào] II VT [+ aircraft, car] 给…加燃料 [gěi…jiā ránliào]

refuelling [riː'fjuəlɪŋ] N [U] 加燃料 [jiā ránliào]

refuge ['rɛfjuːdʒ] N **1** [U] (source of protection) 庇护 [bìhù] **2** [c] (hut) 庇护所 [bìhùsuǒ] **3** [c] (safe house) 避难所 [bìnànsuǒ] ▶ to seek or take refuge in silence/drink 从缄默/饮酒中寻求慰藉

refugee [rɛfju'dʒiː] N [c] 难民 [nànmín] ▶ a political refugee 政治难民

refund [n 'riːfʌnd, vb rɪ'fʌnd] I N [c] 退款

[tuìkuǎn] II VT [+ money] 偿还 [chánghuán]

refurbish [riː'fəːbɪʃ] VT 重新装饰 [chóngxīn zhuāngshì]

refusal [rɪ'fjuːzəl] N [c/U] 拒绝 [jùjué] ▶ to give/offer sb first refusal (option) 给某人优先取舍权

refuse¹ [rɪ'fjuːz] VT, VI 拒绝 [jùjué] ▶ to refuse to do sth 拒绝做某事 ▶ to refuse sb sth 拒绝给某人某物 ▶ to refuse sb permission 不批准某人

refuse² ['rɛfjuːs] N [U] 垃圾 [lājī]

refuse collection N [c/U] 垃圾收集 [lājī shōují]

regain [rɪ'geɪn] VT [+ power, control] 重新取得 [chóngxīn qǔdé]; [+ health, confidence] 恢复 [huīfù]

regard [rɪ'gɑːd] I VT (consider, view) 认为 [rènwéi] II N [U] (esteem) 尊敬 [zūnjìng] ▶ to give one's regards to 向…表示问候 ▶ "with kindest regards" "谨此致候" ▶ as regards, with regard to, in regard to (frm) 关于 ▶ in this/that regard 在这/那方面

regarding [rɪ'gɑːdɪŋ] PREP (frm) 关于 [guānyú]

regardless [rɪ'gɑːdlɪs] ADV [carry on, continue +] 无论如何 [wúlùn rúhé] ▶ regardless of 不管

regenerate [rɪ'dʒɛnəreɪt] I VT 复兴 [fùxīng] II VI (BIO) 再生 [zàishēng]

reggae ['rɛgeɪ] N [U] 西印度群岛的节奏很强的流行音乐和舞蹈

regime [reɪ'ʒiːm] N [c] **1** (system of government) 政体 [zhèngtǐ] **2** (diet, exercise) 养生法 [yǎngshēngfǎ]

regiment [n 'rɛdʒɪmənt, vb 'rɛdʒɪment] I N [c] (MIL) 团 [tuán] II VT [+ people] 严格控制 [yángé kòngzhì]

region ['riːdʒən] N [c] **1** (area) 区域 [qūyù] **2** (administrative division) 地区 [dìqū] ▶ in the region of (frm) (approximately) 大约

regional ['riːdʒənl] ADJ 地区的 [dìqū de]

register ['rɛdʒɪstə(r)] I N [c] **1** (at hotel) 登记 [dēngjì] **2** (in school) 注册 [zhùcè] **3** (official record) 记录 [jìlù] II VT **1** [+ birth, death, marriage] 登记 [dēngjì] **2** [+ letter] 挂号邮寄 [guàhào yóujì] **3** (indicate) [+ amount, measurement] 显示为 [xiǎnshìwéi]; [+ feeling, opinion] 流露出 [liúlùchū] III VI **1** (sign up) (at hotel) 登记 [dēngjì]; (at doctor's, dentist's, for work, class) 注册 [zhùcè] **2** (show) [amount, measurement +] 显示 [xiǎnshì] **3** (make impression) 留有印象 [liúyǒu yìnxiàng] ▶ to register a protest 以示抗议

registered ['rɛdʒɪstəd] ADJ **1** (POST) [+ letter, mail] 挂号的 [guàhào de] **2** [+ drug addict] 有记录的 [yǒu jìlù de] **3** [+ child minder etc] 注册的 [zhùcè de]

registrar ['rɛdʒɪstrɑː(r)] N [c] **1** (in registry office) 登记员 [dēngjìyuán] **2** (BRIT) (in hospital) 专科住院医师 [zhuānkē zhùyuàn yīshī] **3** (in college, university) 大学中主管招生、考试等事务的

负责人

registration [rɛdʒɪs'treɪʃən] N [C/U] [*of birth, death, students etc*] 登记 [dēngjì]

registration number (BRIT) N [C] 牌照号码 [páizhào hàomǎ] [美= **license number**]

registry office ['rɛdʒɪstrɪ-] (BRIT) N [C] 户籍登记处 [hùjí dēngjìchù] ▸ **to get married in a registry office** 在户籍登记处公证结婚

regret [rɪ'grɛt] I N [C/U] 遗憾 [yíhàn] II VT 1 [+ *one's action*] 后悔 [hòuhuǐ] 2 [+ *event*] 对…表示遗憾 [duì…biǎoshì yíhàn] ▸ **with regret** 遗憾地 ▸ **to have no regrets** 没有遗憾 ▸ **to regret that...** 对…感到后悔 ▸ **we regret to inform you that...** 我们遗憾地通知您…

regrettable [rɪ'grɛtəbl] ADJ (*frm*) 令人遗憾的 [lìng rén yíhàn de]

regrettably [rɪ'grɛtəblɪ] ADV (*frm*) 可惜地 [kěxī de]

regular ['rɛgjulə(r)] I ADJ 1 (*even*) [+ *breathing, intervals*] 有规律的 [yǒu guīlǜ de]; [+ *features, shape etc*] 匀称的 [yúnchèn de] 2 (*frequent*) [+ *event*] 有规律的 [yǒu guīlǜ de]; [+ *visitor*] 经常的 [jīngcháng de] 3 (*usual*) 固定的 [gùdìng de] 4 (*normal*) 正常的 [zhèngcháng de] 5 [+ *soldier*] 正规的 [zhèngguī de] 6 (LING) [+ *verb etc*] 规则的 [guīzé de] II N [C] (*client etc*) (*in bar, restaurant, shop*) 常客 [chángkè]

regularly ['rɛgjuləlɪ] ADV 1 (*frequently*) 经常 [jīngcháng] 2 (*at set intervals*) 定期地 [dìngqī de] 3 (*smoothly, evenly*) [+ *spaced, distributed*] 均匀地 [jūnyún de] 4 (*symmetrically*) [+ *shaped etc*] 匀称地 [yúnchèn de]

regulate ['rɛgjuleɪt] VT 1 (*control*) 管制 [guǎnzhì] 2 (*adjust*) [+ *machine, oven*] 调整 [tiáozhěng]

regulation [rɛgju'leɪʃən] N 1 [C] (*rule*) 规章 [guīzhāng] 2 [U] (*control*) [*of process, expenditure, speed*] 法规 [fǎguī]

rehabilitation ['ri:əbɪlɪ'teɪʃən] N [U] [*of criminal, drug addict, invalid*] 康复 [kāngfù]

rehearsal [rɪ'hə:səl] N [C/U] 排练 [páiliàn]

rehearse [rɪ'hə:s] VT, VI 排练 [páiliàn]

reign [reɪn] I N [C] [*of monarch*] 统治 [tǒngzhì] II VI 1 [*monarch*+] 统治 [tǒngzhì] 2 [*peace, calm, silence etc*+] 笼罩 [lǒngzhào] ▸ **a reign of terror** 恐怖时期 ▸ **to reign supreme** 占绝对优势

reimburse [ri:ɪm'bə:s] VT 偿还 [chánghuán]

rein [reɪn] N [C] (*for horse*) 缰绳 [jiāngshéng] ▸ **to give sb free rein** 给予某人充分自由 ▸ **to keep a tight rein on sth** 严密地控制某事 ▸ **rein in** VT 控制 [kòngzhì]

reincarnation [ri:ɪnkɑ:'neɪʃən] N 1 [U] (*belief*) 转世 [zhuǎnshì] 2 [C] (*reincarnated being*) 转世化身 [zhuǎnshì huàshēn]

reindeer ['reɪndɪə(r)] (*pl* **reindeer**) N 驯鹿 [xùnlù]

reinforce [ri:ɪn'fɔ:s] VT 1 (*strengthen*) 加固 [jiāgù] 2 (*back up*) [+ *idea, statement, prejudice*] 加强 [jiāqiáng]

reinforcement [ri:ɪn'fɔ:smənt] I N [C/U] 1 (*strengthening*) 加固 [jiāgù] 2 (*backing up*) [*of attitude, prejudice*] 加强 [jiāqiáng] II **reinforcements** NPL (MIL) 增援 [zēngyuán]

reinstate [ri:ɪn'steɪt] VT 1 [+ *tax, law, practice*] 恢复 [huīfù] 2 [+ *employee*] 恢复职位 [huīfù zhíwèi]

reject [*vb* rɪ'dʒɛkt, *n* 'ri:dʒɛkt] I VT 1 [+ *plan, belief, idea, goods*] 拒绝接受 [jùjué jiēshòu] 2 [+ *applicant, admirer*] 拒绝 [jùjué] 3 [*machine*+] [+ *coin*] 不接受 [bù jiēshòu] 4 (MED) [+ *heart, kidney*] 排斥 [páichì] II N [C] 退货产品 [tuìhuò chǎnpǐn]

rejection [rɪ'dʒɛkʃən] N [C/U] 1 [*of plan, belief etc*] 拒绝接受 [jùjué jiēshòu] 2 [*of applicant*] 拒绝 [jùjué] 3 (*feeling*) 拒绝 [jùjué] 4 (MED) [*of heart, kidney*] 排斥 [páichì]

rejoice [rɪ'dʒɔɪs] VI ▸ **to rejoice at** or **over sth** 因某事感到高兴 [yīn mǒushì gǎndào gāoxìng]

relate [rɪ'leɪt] I VI ▸ **to relate to** (*empathize with*) [+ *person*] 与…交往 [yǔ…jiāowǎng]; (*concern*) [+ *subject*] 与…有关 [yǔ…yǒuguān] II VT 1 (*tell*) [+ *story etc*] 讲述 [jiǎngshù] 2 (*connect*) 将…联系起来 [jiāng…liánxì qǐlái]

related [rɪ'leɪtɪd] ADJ 1 [+ *questions, issues*] 有联系的 [yǒu liánxì de] 2 [+ *people*] 有亲缘关系的 [yǒu qīnyuán guānxì de] 3 [+ *species, languages*] 属同一种类的 [shǔ tóngyī zhǒnglèi de] ▸ **to be related to sb** 和某人有关连 ▸ **to be related to sth** [*species, language*+] 和某事有关连

relating to [rɪ'leɪtɪŋ-] PREP 关于 [guānyú]

relation [rɪ'leɪʃən] I N [C] 1 (*relative*) 亲戚 [qīnqi] 2 (*connection*) 关系 [guānxì] II **relations** NPL (*rapport*) 关系 [guānxì] ▸ **diplomatic/international relations** 外交/国际关系 ▸ **to bear no relation to** 和…无关 ▸ **in relation to** 与…相比

relationship [rɪ'leɪʃənʃɪp] N [C] 1 (*connection*) 关系 [guānxì] 2 (*rapport*) (*between two people, countries*) 关系 [guānxì] 3 (*affair*) 亲密的关系 [qīnmì de guānxì] ▸ **to have a good relationship** 关系亲密

relative ['rɛlətɪv] I N [C] (*member of family*) 亲戚 [qīnqi] II ADJ (*comparative*) 相对的 [xiāngduì de] ▸ **relative to** 相对于 ▸ **it's all relative** 都是相对而言

relatively ['rɛlətɪvlɪ] ADV 相对 [xiāngduì]

relax [rɪ'læks] I VI 1 [*person*+] (*unwind*) 放松 [fàngsōng] 2 [*body, muscle*+] 松弛 [sōngchí] II VT 1 [+ *person, mind*] 使放松 [shǐ fàngsōng] 2 [+ *one's grip, muscles*] 使松弛 [shǐ sōngchí] 3 [+ *rule, control*] 放宽 [fàngkuān]

relaxation [ri:læk'seɪʃən] N [U] 1 (*rest*) 消遣 [xiāoqiǎn] 2 [*of rule, control etc*] 放宽 [fàngkuān]

relaxed [rɪ'lækst] ADJ [+ *person*] 放松的 [fàngsōng de]; [+ *discussion, atmosphere*] 轻松的 [qīngsōng de]

relaxing [rɪˈlæksɪŋ] ADJ 令人放松的 [lìng rén fàngsōng de]

relay [n ˈriːleɪ, vb rɪˈleɪ] I N [c] (also: **relay race**) 接力赛 [jiēlìsài] II VT **1** [+ message, news] 转述 [zhuǎnshù] **2** [+ programme, broadcast] 转播 [zhuǎnbō]

⊙ **release** [rɪˈliːs] I N **1** [c] (of prisoner) 释放 [shìfàng] **2** [c] (of documents, funds etc) 公开 [gōngkāi] **3** [c] (of gas, water etc) 排放 [páifàng] **4** [U] (from obligation, situation) 免除 [miǎnchú] **5** [U] (of film, record) 发行 [fāxíng] **6** [c] (record, film) 发行 [fāxíng] **7** [c] (TECH) (device) 释放器 [shìfàngqì] II VT **1** [+ person] (from captivity) 释放 [shìfàng]; (from wreckage etc) 解救 [jiějiù]; (from obligation, responsibility) 免除 [miǎnchú] **2** [+ gas etc] 排放 [páifàng] **3** (let go of) 放开 [fàngkāi] **4** (TECH) [+ catch, spring etc] 放开 [fàngkāi]; (AUT) [+ clutch, brake] 松开 [sōngkāi] **5** [+ record, film] 发行 [fāxíng] **6** [+ report, news, figures] 发表 [fābiǎo] ▶ "**on general release**" [film +] "公开上映"

relegate [ˈrɛləgeɪt] VT **1** (BRIT: SPORT) ▶ **to be relegated** 被降级 [bèi jiàngjí] **2** (downgrade) ▶ **to relegate sth to...** 把某物降级到…[bǎ mǒuwù jiàngjí dào...]

relent [rɪˈlɛnt] VI 让步 [ràngbù]

relentless [rɪˈlɛntlɪs] ADJ **1** [+ heat, noise, pressure] 不断的 [bùduàn de] **2** [+ tyrant, enemy] 残忍的 [cánrěn de]

relevant [ˈrɛləvənt] ADJ **1** [+ fact, information, question] 切题的 [qiètí de] **2** [+ chapter, area] 相关的 [xiāngguān de] ▶ **relevant to** 和…有关的

reliable [rɪˈlaɪəbl] ADJ [+ person, firm, news, information] 可靠的 [kěkào de]; [+ method, machine] 可信赖的 [kěxìnlài de]

relic [ˈrɛlɪk] N [c] **1** (of the past) 遗物 [yíwù] **2** (historical object) 纪念物 [jìniànwù] **3** (REL) 圣者遗物 [shèngzhě yíwù]

relief [rɪˈliːf] I N **1** [U] (alleviation) 缓解 [huǎnjiě] **2** [U] (gladness) 如释重负 [rú shì zhòng fù] **3** [U] (aid) (to country etc) 救援 [jiùyuán] **4** [c] (ART) 浮雕 [fúdiāo] **5** [U] (GEO) 地势起伏 [dìshì qǐfú] II CPD [复合词] [+ bus, driver] 后备 [hòubèi] ▶ **in relief** (ART) 浮雕

relieve [rɪˈliːv] VT **1** (alleviate) [+ pain, worry] 减轻 [jiǎnqīng] **2** (take over from) [+ colleague] 换班 [huànbān] ▶ **to relieve sb of sth** [+ load] 替某人拿某物; [+ duties, post] 免除 ▶ **to relieve o.s.** (euphemism) 解大小便

relieved [rɪˈliːvd] ADJ 宽慰的 [kuānwèi de] ▶ **to be relieved that...** 对…感到放心 ▶ **I'm relieved to hear it** 听到这么说我感到宽慰

religion [rɪˈlɪdʒən] N **1** [U] (belief) 宗教信仰 [zōngjiào xìnyǎng] **2** [c] (set of beliefs) 宗教 [zōngjiào]

religious [rɪˈlɪdʒəs] ADJ **1** [+ activities, faith] 宗教的 [zōngjiào de] **2** [+ person] 笃信宗教的 [dǔxìn zōngjiào de] **3** [+ book] 有关宗教的 [yǒuguān zōngjiào de]

religious education N [U] 宗教教育 [zōngjiào jiàoyù]

relinquish [rɪˈlɪŋkwɪʃ] VT [+ authority, control, claim] 放弃 [fàngqì]

relish [ˈrɛlɪʃ] I N **1** [c/U] (CULIN) 调味品 [tiáowèipǐn] **2** [U] (enjoyment) 乐趣 [lèqù] II VT (enjoy) [+ challenge, competition] 享受 [xiǎngshòu]; [+ idea, thought, prospect] 喜欢 [xǐhuan] ▶ **to relish doing sth** 乐于做某事

relocate [riːləʊˈkeɪt] I VT [+ business, staff] 调动 [diàodòng] II VI 迁往别处 [qiānwǎng biéchù]

reluctance [rɪˈlʌktəns] N [U] 不情愿 [bùqíngyuàn]

reluctant [rɪˈlʌktənt] ADJ (unwilling) 不情愿的 [bùqíngyuàn de] ▶ **to be reluctant to do sth** 不愿做某事

reluctantly [rɪˈlʌktəntlɪ] ADV 不情愿地 [bùqíngyuàn de]

rely on [rɪˈlaɪ-] VT FUS [不可拆分] **1** (be dependent on) 依赖 [yīlài] **2** (trust) 信赖 [xìnlài]

⊙ **remain** [rɪˈmeɪn] **1** (continue to be) 仍然是 [réngrán shì] **2** (stay) 逗留 [dòuliú] **3** (survive) 遗留 [yíliú] ▶ **to remain silent/in control** 保持沉默/仍然控制局面 ▶ **much remains to be done** 还有许多事情要做 ▶ **the fact remains that...** 事实上情况是…… ▶ **it remains to be seen whether...** 是否…，以后可见分晓

remainder [rɪˈmeɪndə(r)] I N [s] (rest) 剩余部分 [shèngyú bùfen] II VT (COMM) 清仓抛售 [qīngcāng pāoshòu]

remaining [rɪˈmeɪnɪŋ] ADJ 剩下的 [shèngxià de]

remains [rɪˈmeɪnz] NPL **1** (remnants) [of object, building, meal] 剩余物 [shèngyúwù] **2** (relics) 遗迹 [yíjì] **3** (of dead person) 遗体 [yítǐ]

remand [rɪˈmɑːnd] I N ▶ **to be on remand** 被还押 [bèi huányā] II VT **1** ▶ **to be remanded in custody** 被还押 [bèi huányā] **2** ▶ **to be remanded on bail** 被保释候审 [bèi bǎoshì hòushěn]

remark [rɪˈmɑːk] I N [c] (comment) 评论 [pínglùn] II VT (comment) 评论 [pínglùn] ▶ **to remark that...** 说… ▶ **to remark on sth** 谈论某事

用法参见 **comment**

remarkable [rɪˈmɑːkəbl] ADJ 不寻常的 [bù xúncháng de]

remarkably [rɪˈmɑːkəblɪ] ADV 极其地 [jíqí de]

remarry [riːˈmærɪ] VI 再婚 [zàihūn]

remedy [ˈrɛmədɪ] I N [c] **1** (for illness) 治疗法 [zhìliáofǎ] **2** (for situation) 补救的方法 [bǔjiù de fāngfǎ] II VT **1** [+ mistake, injustice] 改正 [gǎizhèng] **2** [+ situation] 补救 [bǔjiù]

⊙ **remember** [rɪˈmɛmbə(r)] VT **1** (still have in mind) [+ person, name, event etc] 记住 [jìzhù] **2** (bring back to mind) 回想起 [huíxiǎngqǐ] **3** (*bear in mind*) 牢记 [láojì] ▶ **remember me to him** (*send greetings*) 代我向他问候 ▶ **to remember doing sth** or **having done sth** 记得做过某事 ▶ **she remembered to do it** 她记得要做某事

remembrance [rɪ'membrəns] N **1** (*memory*) ▶ **in remembrance of** 纪念 [jìniàn] **2** [C/U] (*souvenir*) [*of place, event*] 纪念物 [jìniànwù]

Remembrance Day, Remembrance Sunday (BRIT) N 阵亡将士纪念日

REMEMBRANCE SUNDAY

Remembrance Sunday 是最接近11月11日的那个星期天，在这一天人们纪念在两次世界大战中阵亡的将士。

remind [rɪ'maɪnd] VT 提醒 [tíxǐng] ▶ **to remind sb to do sth** 提醒某人做某事 ▶ **to remind sb that…** 提醒某人… ▶ **to remind sb of sth** (*issue reminder*) 提醒某人某事 ▶ **to remind sb of sb/sth** (*be reminiscent of*) 使某人想起某人/某事 ▶ **that reminds me!** 我记起来了！

reminder [rɪ'maɪndə(r)] N [C] **1** [*of person, place, event*] 唤起记忆的事物 [huànqǐ jìyì de shìwù] **2** (*aide-memoire*) 提醒物 [tíxǐngwù] **3** (*official letter*) 催缴单 [cuījiǎodān]

reminiscent [rɛmɪ'nɪsnt] ADJ ▶ **to be reminiscent of sth** 使人想起某事 [shǐ rén xiǎngqǐ mǒushì]

remnant ['rɛmnənt] N [C] **1** (*relic*) 残余 [cányú] **2** (COMM) [*of cloth*] 碎布头 [suìbùtóu]

remorse [rɪ'mɔːs] N [U] 悔恨 [huǐhèn]

remote [rɪ'məut] ADJ **1** (*isolated*) [*place*] 遥远的 [yáoyuǎn de] **2** (*distant*) [*person*] 冷淡的 [lěngdàn de] **3** (*slight*) [*possibility, chance*] 微小的 [wēixiǎo de] ▶ **in the remote past** 在遥远的过去 ▶ **there is a remote possibility that…** …的可能性极小 ▶ **to be remote from** 与…无关

remote control N **1** [C] (*device*) (*for TV etc*) 遥控器 [yáokòngqì] **2** [U] (*system*) 遥控 [yáokòng]

remotely [rɪ'məutlɪ] ADV (*slightly*) 丝毫 [sīháo]

removal [rɪ'muːvəl] N **1** [U] (*of object, stain*) 去除 [qùchú] **2** [U] [*of threat, suspicion*] 排除 [páichú] **3** [C/U] (BRIT) (*from building*) 搬迁 [bānqiān] **4** [U] (*dismissal*) (*from office*) 免职 [miǎnzhí]

removal man (*pl* **removal men**) (BRIT) N [C] 搬运工 [bānyùngōng]

removal van (BRIT) N [C] 搬迁专用车 [bānqiān zhuānyòngchē]

remove [rɪ'muːv] VT **1** [+ *object, organ*] 移走 [yízǒu] **2** [+ *clothing, bandage etc*] 脱下 [tuōxià] **3** [+ *stain*] 清除 [qīngchú] **4** [+ *obstacle, problem, suspicion, threat*] 消除 [xiāochú] **5** [+ *official*] 免职 [miǎnzhí] **6** [+ *name*] (*from list*) 删除

[shānchú] ▶ **my first cousin once removed** 我堂亲/表亲的子女

rename [riː'neɪm] VT 重新命名 [chóngxīn mìngmíng]

render ['rɛndə(r)] (*frm*) VT **1** (*give*) [+ *service, aid*] 提供 [tígōng] **2** ▶ **to render sth harmless/worthless** 使某物无害/一文不值 [shǐ mǒuwù wúhài/yī wén bù zhí] **3** (*submit*) [+ *account*] 翻译 [fānyì]

rendezvous ['rɔndɪvuː] (*pl* **rendezvous** ['rɔndɪvuːz]) I N [C] **1** (*meeting*) 约会 [yuēhuì] **2** (*place*) 约会地点 [yuēhuì dìdiǎn] II VI **1** [*people, spacecraft +*] 会合 [huìhé] ▶ **to rendezvous with sb** 与某人在约定地点相会

renew [rɪ'njuː] VT **1** [+ *efforts, attack, talks*] 重新开始 [chóngxīn kāishǐ] **2** [+ *loan, contract*] 延长 [yáncháng] **3** [+ *acquaintance, relationship*] 重建 [chóngjiàn]

renewal [rɪ'njuːəl] N [C/U] (*of licence, contract etc*) 更新 [gēngxīn] **2** [S] (*of hostilities, conflict*) 重新开始 [chóngxīn kāishǐ]

renewed [rɪ'njuːd] ADJ 复兴的 [fùxīng de]

renovate ['rɛnəveɪt] VT 修复 [xiūfù]

renowned [rɪ'naund] ADJ 著名的 [zhùmíng de] ▶ **to be renowned for sth** 由于某事而知名

rent [rɛnt] I N [C/U] (*for building, room, land*) 租金 [zūjīn] II VT **1** (*hire*) [+ *building, room, land, car*] 租用 [zūyòng] **2** (*also*: **rent out**) [+ *house, room*] 出租 [chūzū]

rental ['rɛntl] I N **1** [C] (*charge*) 租金 [zūjīn] **2** [U] (*act of renting*) 租赁 [zūlìn] II ADJ 出租的 [chūzū de]

rental car (US) N [C] 租的车 [zū de chē] [英= **hire car**]

reorganize [riː'ɔːgənaɪz] VT 重组 [chóngzǔ]

rep [rɛp] N **1** (*representative*) (*for group*) 代表 [dàibiǎo]; (*also*: **sales rep**) 商品经销代理 [shāngpǐn jīngxiāo dàilǐ] **2** (THEAT) (*repertory*) 仓库 [cāngkù]

Rep. (US: POL) ABBR **1** (= *representative*) 众议院议员 [Zhòngyìyuàn Yìyuán] **2** (= *republican*) 共和党的 [Gònghédǎng de]

repair [rɪ'peə(r)] I N [C/U] 修理 [xiūlǐ] II VT **1** [+ *object, building*] 修补 [xiūbǔ] **2** [+ *damage*] 维修 [wéixiū] ▶ **in good/bad repair** 维修良好/不善 ▶ **to be beyond repair** 无法修复 ▶ **under repair** (*road etc*) 在修理中

repair kit N [C] 成套维修工具 [chéngtào wéixiū gōngjù]

repay [riː'peɪ] (*pt, pp* **repaid**) VT **1** [+ *loan, debt, person*] 偿还 [chánghuán] **2** [+ *favour*] 报答 [bàodá] **3** [+ *sb's efforts, attention*] 值得 [zhídé]

repayment [riː'peɪmənt] N **1** [C] (*sum of money*) 还款 [huánkuǎn] **2** [U] (*action of repaying*) 偿还 [chánghuán]

repeat [rɪ'piːt] I VT **1** [+ *statement, question*] 重复 [chóngfù] **2** [+ *action, mistake*] 重做 [chóngzuò] **3** (RAD, TV) 重播 [chóngbō]

4 (SCOL) [+ *class, course*] 重修 [chóngxiū]
5 [+ *pattern*] 重复 [chóngfù] II VI ▶ **I repeat** 我
重申 [wǒ chóngshēn] III N [C] **1** (RAD, TV) 重
播 [chóngbō] **2** [*of event*] 重演 [chóngyǎn] ▶ **to**
repeat o.s. 一再重述 ▶ **to repeat itself** 再
次发生

repeatedly [rɪ'piːtɪdlɪ] ADV 反复地 [fǎnfù de]

repeat prescription N [C] 同样药方
[tóngyàng yàofāng]

repellent [rɪ'pɛlənt] ADJ 令人厌恶的 [lìng rén
yànwù de]

repetition [rɛpɪ'tɪʃən] N [C/U] (*repeat occurrence*)
重复 [chóngfù]

repetitive [rɪ'pɛtɪtɪv] ADJ [+ *movements, work,*
music] 反复的 [fǎnfù de]

replace [rɪ'pleɪs] VT **1** (*put back*) 将⋯放回
[jiāng...fànghuí] **2** (*supply replacement for*) [+ *sth*
damaged, lost, worn out] 替换 [tìhuàn] **3** (*take the*
place of) 代替 [dàitì] ▶ **to replace sth with sth**
else 用某物代替某物

replacement [rɪ'pleɪsmənt] N **1** [C] (*substitute*
person) 代替人 [dàitì rén] **2** [C] (*substitute object*)
代替物 [dàitìwù] **3** [U] (*act of replacing*) 代替
[dàitì]

replay [*n* 'riːpleɪ, *vb* riː'pleɪ] I N [C] **1** (TV) (*repeat*
showing) 重放 [chóngfàng] **2** [*of match*] 重新
比赛 [chóngxīn bǐsài] II VT [+ *track, song*] (*on*
tape) 重新播放 [chóngxīn bōfàng] ▶ **to replay**
a match 重新比赛

replica ['rɛplɪkə] I N [C] **1** 复制品 [fùzhìpǐn]
II ADJ 复制的 [fùzhì de]

reply [rɪ'plaɪ] I N [C] **1** (*answer*) 回答 [huídá]
2 (*retaliation*) 反应 [fǎnyìng] II VI **1** (*to question,*
letter) 答复 [dáfù] **2** (*retaliation*) (*to attack etc*) 回
应 [huíyìng] ▶ **in reply to your question…** 就
你的问题而言⋯ ▶ **"in reply to your letter..."**
"对您来信的回复⋯" ▶ **there's no reply** (TEL)
无人接听

○ **report** [rɪ'pɔːt] I N [C] **1** (*account*) 报告
[bàogào] **2** (PUBLISHING, TV) (*bulletin*) 报道
[bàodào] **3** (BRIT: **also: school report**) 成绩单
[chéngjìdān] **4** [*of gun*] 爆炸声 [bàozhàshēng]
II VT **1** (*state*) 汇报 [huìbào] **2** (PUBLISHING,
TV) 报道 [bàodào] **3** (*bring to notice*) [+ *theft,*
accident, death] 报案 [bào'àn]; [+ *person*] 告
发 [gàofā] III VI (*make a report*) 汇报 [huìbào]
▶ **to report to sb** (*present o.s. to*) 向某人报到;
(*be responsible to*) 对某人负责 ▶ **to report on**
sth 报告某事 ▶ **to report sick** 报病 ▶ **it is**
reported that... 据报道⋯

report card (US) N [C] 学生成绩报告单
[xuéshēng chéngjì bàogàodān] [英=**report**]

reportedly [rɪ'pɔːtɪdlɪ] ADV 据说 [jùshuō]

reporter [rɪ'pɔːtə(r)] N [C] 记者 [jìzhě]

represent [rɛprɪ'zɛnt] VT **1** (*act on behalf of*)
[+ *person, nation*] 代表 [dàibiǎo] **2** (*reflect*) [+ *view,*
belief] 体现 [tǐxiàn] **3** (*stand for*) [+ *word, object*]
表示 [biǎoshì] **4** (*constitute*) 体现 [tǐxiàn] ▶ **to**

represent sb/sth as (*describe*) 把某人/某事描
绘成

representation [rɛprɪzɛn'teɪʃən] I N **1** [U]
(*representatives*) 代表 [dàibiǎo] **2** [C] (*depiction*)
描绘 [miáohuì] II **representations** NPL
(*protest*) 抗议 [kàngyì]

representative [rɛprɪ'zɛntətɪv] I N [C]
1 [*of person, nation*] 代表 [dàibiǎo] **2** (COMM)
代理 [dàilǐ] **3** (US: POL) 众议院议员
[zhòngyìyuàn yìyuán] II ADJ [+ *group, survey,*
cross-section] 有代表性的 [yǒu dàibiǎoxìng de]
▶ **representative of** 典型的

repress [rɪ'prɛs] VT [+ *people, revolt*] 压制 [yāzhì];
[+ *feeling, impulse*] 压抑 [yāyì]

repression [rɪ'prɛʃən] N **1** [C/U] [*of people,*
country] 镇压 [zhènyā] **2** [C] [*of feelings*] 压抑
[yāyì]

reprimand ['rɛprɪmɑːnd] I N [C] 训斥
[xùnchì] II VT 训斥 [xùnchì]

reproduce [riːprə'djuːs] I VT 复制 [fùzhì]
II VI (*breed*) 繁殖 [fánzhí]

reproduction [riːprə'dʌkʃən] N **1** [C] (*copy*)
[*of document*] 拷贝件 [kǎobèijiàn]; [*of painting,*
furniture] 复制品 [fùzhìpǐn] **2** [U] (*copying*) 复
印 [fùyìn] **3** [U] (*breeding*) 繁殖 [fánzhí] **4** [U] [*of*
sound] 录制 [lùzhì]

reptile ['rɛptaɪl] N [C] 爬行动物 [páxíng
dòngwù]

republic [rɪ'pʌblɪk] N [C] 共和国 [gònghéguó]

republican [rɪ'pʌblɪkən] I ADJ **1** [+ *system,*
government etc] 共和政体的 [gònghé zhèngtǐ
de] **2** (US: POL) ▶ **Republican** 共和党的
[Gònghédǎng de] II N [C] **1** (*anti-monarchist*)
共和主义者 [gònghé zhǔyìzhě] **2** (US: POL)
▶ **Republican** 共和党党员 [Gònghédǎng
Dǎngyuán]

reputable ['rɛpjutəbl] ADJ 声誉好的 [shēngyù
hǎo de]

reputation [rɛpju'teɪʃən] N [C] 名声
[míngshēng] ▶ **to have a reputation for**
因⋯而闻名

reputed [rɪ'pjuːtɪd] ADJ 据说的 [jùshuō de]

request [rɪ'kwɛst] I N [C] **1** (*polite demand*) 要
求 [yāoqiú] **2** (RAD) 点播 [diǎnbō] II VT 要
求 [yāoqiú] ▶ **on request** 应要求 ▶ **at the**
request of 应⋯的要求 ▶ **Mr and Mrs X**
request the pleasure of your company... (*frm*)
X先生和夫人敬请您的大驾光临⋯

require [rɪ'kwaɪə(r)] VT **1** (*need*) 需要 [xūyào]
2 (*demand*) 要求 [yāoqiú] ▶ **to be required**
[*approval, permission* +] 必须有 ▶ **to require sb**
to do sth 要求某人做某事 ▶ **if required** 如有
需要 ▶ **required by law** 法律规定

requirement [rɪ'kwaɪəmənt] N [C] **1** (*need*)
需要的事物 [xūyào de shìwù] **2** (*condition*)
必备条件 [bìbèi tiáojiàn] ▶ **to meet sb's**
requirements 符合某人的要求

rescue ['rɛskjuː] I N [C/U] **1** 营救 [yíngjiù]

II VT 解救 [jiějiù] ▸ **to go/come to sb's rescue** 前往/来营救某人 ▸ **to rescue sb from sth** 从某事中解救某人

○ **research** [rɪ'sɜːtʃ] **I** N [U] 研究 [yánjiū] **II** VT [+ *story, subject*] 研究 [yánjiū] **III** VI ▸ **to research into sth** 研究某事 [yánjiū mǒushì] ▸ **to do research** 从事研究 ▸ **a piece of research** 一个研究课题 ▸ **research and development** 研究与开发

resemblance [rɪ'zembləns] N [C/U] (*likeness*) 相似 [xiāngsì] ▸ **to bear a strong resemblance to** 与⋯极其相似 ▸ **it bears no resemblance to...** 与⋯毫无相似之处

resemble [rɪ'zembl] VT 与⋯相似 [yǔ⋯ xiāngsì]

resent [rɪ'zent] VT [+ *attitude, treatment*] 憎恶 [zēngwù]; [+ *person*] 怨恨 [yuànhèn]

resentful [rɪ'zentful] ADJ 憎恨的 [zēnghèn de]

resentment [rɪ'zentmənt] N [C/U] 憎恨 [zēnghèn]

reservation [rezə'veɪʃən] N **1** [C] (*booking*) 预定 [yùdìng] **2** [C/U] (*doubt*) 保留 [bǎoliú de] **3** [C] (*land*) 保留地 [bǎoliú de] ▸ **with reservation(s)** (*doubts*) 持保留意见 ▸ **to make a reservation** (*in hotel, restaurant, on train*) 预定

reservation desk (US) N [C] (*in hotel*) 预定台 [yùdìngtái]

reserve [rɪ'zɜːv] **I** VT **1** [+ *seat, table, ticket etc*] 预定 [yùdìng] **2** (*keep*) 保留 [bǎoliú] **II** N [C] **1** (*store*) [*of food, fuel, energy, talent etc*] 储备 [chǔbèi] **2** [C] (BRIT: SPORT) 候补队员 [hòubǔ duìyuán] **3** [C] (*also*: **nature reserve**) 自然保护区 [zìrán bǎohùqū] **4** [U] (*restraint*) 矜持 [jīnchí] **II reserves** NPL (MIL) 后备军 [hòubèijūn] ▸ **in reserve** 备用

reserved [rɪ'zɜːvd] ADJ **1** (*unavailable*) [+ *seat*] 已预定的 [yǐ yùdìng de] **2** (*restrained*) 矜持的 [jīnchí de]

reservoir ['rezəvwɑː(r)] N [C] **1** [*of water*] 水库 [shuǐkù] **2** [*of talent etc*] 储备 [chǔbèi]

residence ['rezɪdəns] N **1** [C] (*frm*) (*home*) 居所 [jūsuǒ] **2** [U] (*length of stay*) 居住 [jūzhù] ▸ **to take up residence** 开始居住 ▸ **to be in residence** (*queen etc*) 居住 ▸ **writer/artist in residence** 常驻作家/艺术家 ▸ **place of residence** (*frm*) 居住地

residence permit (BRIT) N [C] 居留许可 [jūliú xǔkě]

resident ['rezɪdənt] **I** N [C] **1** [*of country, town, house*] 居民 [jūmín] **2** [*of hotel*] 房客 [fángkè] **II** ADJ **1** (*frm*) (*residing*) 居住的 [jūzhù de] **2** [+ *population*] 居住的 [jūzhù de]

residential [rezɪ'denʃəl] ADJ **1** [+ *area*] 住宅的 [zhùzhái de] **2** [+ *course*] 寄宿制的 [jìsùzhì de] **3** [+ *staff*] 住宿的 [zhùsù de] **4** [+ *home*] 居住的 [jūzhù de]

residue ['rezɪdjuː] (CHEM) N [C] 残余 [cányú]

resign [rɪ'zaɪn] **I** VT [+ *one's job*] 辞去 [cíqù]

II VI 辞职 [cízhí] ▸ **to resign o.s. to sth** [+ *situation, fact*] 听任某事

resignation [rezɪg'neɪʃən] N **1** [C/U] (*from job*) 辞呈 [cíchéng] **2** [U] (*state of mind*) 达观 [dáguān] ▸ **to tender one's resignation** 宣布辞职

resilient [rɪ'zɪliənt] ADJ **1** [+ *material*] 有弹性的 [yǒu tánxìng de] **2** [+ *person*] 适应力强的 [shìyìnglì qiáng de]

resin ['rezɪn] N [C/U] **1** (*natural*) 树脂 [shùzhī] **2** (*synthetic*) 合成树脂 [héchéng shùzhī]

resist [rɪ'zɪst] VT **1** (*withstand*) [+ *change, demand*] 抗拒 [kàngjù]; [+ *enemy, attack, damage, cold*] 抵抗 [dǐkàng]; [+ *temptation, urge*] 克制 [kèzhì] **2** (*withstand temptation of*) 抗拒 [kàngjù]

resistance [rɪ'zɪstəns] N **1** [S/U] (*opposition*) (*to change, demand*) 抵制 [dǐzhì] **2** [S/U] (MED) (*to illness, infection*) 抵抗力 [dǐkànglì] **3** [S/U] (MIL) 抵抗 [dǐkàng] **4** [U] (ELEC) 电阻 [diànzǔ]

resistant [rɪ'zɪstənt] ADJ **1** (*to change etc*) 抵制的 [dǐzhì de] **2** (*to chemical, disease, antibiotics*) 有抵抗力的 [yǒu dǐkànglì de]

resit [riː'sɪt] (BRIT) **I** VT [+ *exam*] 补考 [bǔkǎo] **II** N [C] 补考 [bǔkǎo]

resolute ['rezəluːt] ADJ [+ *person*] 坚定的 [jiāndìng de]; [+ *refusal, action*] 果断的 [guǒduàn de]

resolution [rezə'luːʃən] N **1** [C/U] (*vow, determination*) 决心 [juéxīn] **2** [C] (*formal decision*) 决议 [juéyì] **3** [U] (*of problem, difficulty*) 解决 [jiějué] ▸ **to make a resolution** 下决心 ▸ **New Year's resolution** 新年决心

resolve [rɪ'zɒlv] **I** VT [+ *problem, difficulty*] 解决 [jiějué] **II** VI ▸ **to resolve to do sth** 下决心去做某事 [xiàjuéxīn qù zuò mǒushì] **III** N [U] (*determination*) 决心 [juéxīn]

resort [rɪ'zɔːt] **I** N **1** [C] (*also*: **holiday resort**) 度假胜地 [dùjià shèngdì] **2** (*recourse*) ▸ **without resort to** 不诉诸于 [bù sù zhū yú] **II** VI ▸ **to resort to sth** 最终诉诸于某事 [zuìzhōng sù zhū yú mǒushì] ▸ **a seaside/winter sports resort** 海边/冬季运动胜地 ▸ **as a last resort** 作为最后手段 ▸ **in the last resort** 最终还得

resource [rɪ'zɔːs] **I** N [C] (*raw material*) 资源 [zīyuán] **II resources** NPL (*coal, iron, oil etc*) 资源 [zīyuán] **2** (*money*) 财力 [cáilì] **III** VT (BRIT) ▸ **to be adequately/poorly resourced** 设备充足/不足 [shèbèi chōngzú/bùzú] ▸ **natural resources** 自然资源

resourceful [rɪ'zɔːsful] ADJ 机敏的 [jīmǐn de]

respect [rɪs'pekt] **I** N [U] (*consideration, esteem*) 尊敬 [zūnjìng] **II** VT [+ *person*] 尊敬 [zūnjìng]; [+ *sb's wishes, beliefs*] 考虑到 [kǎolùdào]; [+ *custom, tradition*] 尊重 [zūnzhòng] **III respects** NPL (*regards*) 问候 [wènhòu] ▸ **to have respect for sb/sth** 对某人/某事怀有敬意 ▸ **to show sb/sth respect** 对某人/某事表示尊敬 ▸ **with respect to** or **in respect of** (*frm*) 关于

▶ **in this respect** 就此而言 ▶ **in some/many respects** 在某些/许多方面 ▶ **with (all due) respect** 尊重您的意见, 但是 ▶ **to pay one's respects** (frm) 表示某人的敬意

respectable [rɪsˈpɛktəbl] ADJ **1** [+ area, background] 体面的 [tǐmiàn de] **2** [+ person] 受人尊敬的 [shòurén zūnjìng de] **3** (adequate) [+ amount, income] 过得去的 [guòdéqù de]; [+ standard, mark etc] 相当好的 [xiāngdāng hǎo de]

respectful [rɪsˈpɛktful] ADJ 恭敬的 [gōngjìng de]

respective [rɪsˈpɛktɪv] ADJ 分别的 [fēnbié de]

respectively [rɪsˈpɛktɪvlɪ] ADV 分别 [fēnbié] ▶ **France and Britain were 3rd and 4th respectively** 法国和英国分别名列第3和第4

respite [ˈrɛspaɪt] N [S/U] (rest) 暂缓 [zànhuǎn]

respond [rɪsˈpɒnd] VI **1** (answer) 回应 [huíyìng] **2** (react) (to pressure, criticism) 回应 [huíyìng]; (to treatment) 反应 [fǎnyìng]

response [rɪsˈpɒns] N [C] **1** (answer) (to question, remark) 回答 [huídá] **2** (reaction) (to situation, event) 反应 [fǎnyìng] ▶ **in response to** 作为回应

responsibility [rɪspɒnsɪˈbɪlɪti] I N **1** [U] (liability) 责任 [zérèn] **2** [S] (duty) 职责 [zhízé] **3** [U] (obligation) 义务 [yìwù] II **responsibilities** NPL 责任 [zérèn] ▶ **to take responsibility for sth/sb** 对某事/某人负责

responsible [rɪsˈpɒnsɪbl] ADJ **1** (at fault) 负有责任的 [fùyǒu zérèn de] **2** (in charge) 负责的 [fùzé de] **3** (sensible, trustworthy) [+ person] 可靠的 [kěkào de]; [+ job] 责任重大的 [zérèn zhòngdà de] ▶ **to be responsible for sth/doing sth** 为某事/做某事负责 ▶ **to be responsible to sb** 对某人负责

> 请勿将 **responsible for** 和 **responsible to** 混淆。如果你 **responsible for** 某事物, 表示你有责任处理此事, 并做出与之有关的决定。*We cannot be responsible for delays between sending and receipt of e-mails.* **responsible for** 也可表示某人是导致某事发生的原因, 或应对此承担责任。*He still felt responsible for her death.* 如果你 **responsible to** 某个人或某个组织, 表明他们是你的上级, 你需要向他们进行汇报。*I'm responsible to my board of directors.*

responsibly [rɪsˈpɒnsɪblɪ] ADV 明事理地 [míng shìlǐ de]

responsive [rɪsˈpɒnsɪv] ADJ **1** (receptive) 积极响应的 [jījí xiǎngyìng de] **2** (to sb's needs, interests etc) 反应灵敏的 [fǎnyìng língmǐn de]

rest [rɛst] I N **1** [U] (relaxation) 休息 [xiūxi] **2** [c] (break) 休息 [xiūxi] **3** [S] (remainder) 剩余 [shèngyú] **4** [c] (support) 支架 [zhījià] II VI **1** (relax) 休息 [xiūxi] **2** (be supported) 依靠 [yīkào] III VT (relax) [+ eyes, legs, muscles] 休息

[xiūxi] ▶ **to rest sth on/against sth** (lean) 把某物靠在某物上 ▶ **to rest on sth** (lean on) 靠在某物上; (be based on) 依据某物 ▶ **the rest** (of them) (people, objects) (他们当中) 其余的 ▶ **and the rest/all the rest of it** 以及其余/其余所有的 ▶ **to put or set sb's mind at rest** 使某人免于忧虑 ▶ **to rest one's eyes** or **gaze on sth** 将目光停留在某物上 ▶ **to come to rest** [object +] 停下来 ▶ **to lay sb to rest** 安葬某人 ▶ **to let the matter rest** 使事情到此为止 ▶ **I won't rest until…** 直到…我才会停止 ▶ **I rest my case** (hum) 我无需多说了

rest area (US) N [C] 路边服务站 [lùbiān fúwùzhàn] [英= **service station**]

restaurant [ˈrɛstərɒn] N [C] 餐馆 [cānguǎn]

restaurant car (BRIT) N [C] 餐车 [cānchē] [美= **dining car**]

restful [ˈrɛstful] ADJ [+ music, lighting, atmosphere] 令人放松的 [lìng rén fàngsōng de]

restless [ˈrɛstlɪs] ADJ **1** (dissatisfied) 焦躁不安的 [jiāozào bù'ān de] **2** (fidgety) 坐立不安的 [zuòlì bù'ān de]

restoration [rɛstəˈreɪʃən] N **1** [C/U] [of painting, church etc] 修复 [xiūfù] **2** [U] [of rights, of law and order] 恢复 [huīfù] **3** [U] [of land] 复原 [fùyuán] **4** [U] [of health, sight, etc] 恢复 [huīfù] **5** (HIST) ▶ **the Restoration** 1660年英国查理二世王权复辟

restore [rɪˈstɔː(r)] VT **1** [+ painting, building etc] 修复 [xiūfù] **2** [+ law and order] 恢复 [huīfù] **3** [+ faith, confidence] 重建 [chóngjiàn] **4** (to power, former state) 使…复位 [shǐ…fùwèi] **5** [+ land] 恢复 [huīfù] **6** (return) (frm) 归还 [guīhuán] **7** [+ health, sight] 恢复 [huīfù]

restrain [rɪsˈtreɪn] VT **1** [+ person] 阻止 [zǔzhǐ] **2** [+ curiosity, anger] 抑制 [yìzhì] **3** [+ growth, inflation] 遏制 [èzhì] ▶ **to restrain sb from doing sth** 阻止某人做某事 ▶ **to restrain o.s. from doing sth** 克制自己做某事

restraint [rɪsˈtreɪnt] N **1** [C/U] (restriction) 约束 [yuēshù] **2** [U] (moderation) 克制 [kèzhì] ▶ **wage restraint** 工资限额政策

restrict [rɪsˈtrɪkt] VT **1** [+ growth, membership, privilege] 限制 [xiànzhì] **2** [+ vision, movements] 阻碍 [zǔ'ài] **3** [+ activities] 约束 [yuēshù]

restriction [rɪsˈtrɪkʃən] N [C] 限制 [xiànzhì]

rest room (US) N [C] 洗手间 [xǐshǒujiān] [英= **toilet, lavatory**]

restructure [riːˈstrʌktʃə(r)] VT **1** [+ organization, system] 改组 [gǎizǔ] **2** [+ debt] 重组 [chóngzǔ]

● **result** [rɪˈzʌlt] I N [C] [of event, action] 后果 [hòuguǒ]; [of match, election, exam, competition] 结果 [jiéguǒ]; [of calculation] 答案 [dá'àn] II VI 产生 [chǎnshēng] ▶ **to result in** 导致 ▶ **as a result of** 由于 ▶ **to result from** 因…而产生 ▶ **as a result it is…** 因此是…

resume [rɪˈzjuːm] I VT [+ work, journey] 继续 [jìxù] II VI (start again) 继续 [jìxù] ▶ **to resume**

one's seat (*frm*) 回到原座

résumé ['reɪzju:meɪ] N [c] **1** (*summary*) 摘要 [zhāiyào] **2** (US) (CV) 简历 [jiǎnlì] [英=CV]

resuscitate [rɪ'sʌsɪteɪt] VT **1** (MED) 使…苏醒 [shǐ…sūxǐng] **2** [+*plan, idea*] 重新启动 [chóngxīn qǐdòng]

retail ['ri:teɪl] **I** ADJ [+*trade, sales*] 零售的 [língshòu de] **II** ADV 零卖地 [língmài de] **III** VT (*sell*) 零售 [língshòu] **IV** VI ▶ **to retail at** *or* **for…** 以…价格零售 [yǐ…jiàgé língshòu]

retailer ['ri:teɪlə(r)] N [c] 零售商 [língshòushāng]

retail price N [c] 零售价 [língshòujià]

retain [rɪ'teɪn] VT [+*independence, humour, heat*] 保持 [bǎochí]; [+*ticket, souvenir*] 保留 [bǎoliú]

retaliate [rɪ'tælɪeɪt] VI 报复 [bàofù]

retaliation [rɪtælɪ'eɪʃən] N [U] 报复 [bàofù] ▶ **in retaliation for** 为…复仇

retarded [rɪ'tɑ:dɪd] ADJ **1** [+*child*] 智力迟缓的 [zhìlì chíhuǎn de] **2** [+*development, growth*] 发育迟缓的 [fāyù chíhuǎn de] ▶ **mentally retarded** 智力迟缓的

retire [rɪ'taɪə(r)] VI **1** (*give up work*) 退休 [tuìxiū] **2** (*frm*) (*withdraw*) 离开 [líkāi] **3** (*frm*) (*go to bed*) 就寝 [jiùqǐn]

retired [rɪ'taɪəd] ADJ 退休的 [tuìxiū de]

retiree [rɪtaɪə'ri:] (US) N [c] 领养老金的人 [lǐng yǎnglǎojīn de rén] [英=pensioner]

retirement [rɪ'taɪəmənt] N [c/U] 退休 [tuìxiū]

retort [rɪ'tɔ:t] **I** VI 反驳 [fǎnbó] **II** N [c] (*reply*) 反驳 [fǎnbó]

retreat [rɪ'tri:t] **I** N **1** [c] (*place*) 隐居处 [yǐnjūchù] **2** [c/U] (*act*) 退避 [tuìbì] **3** [c/U] (MIL) 撤退 [chètuì] **II** VI **1** (*from danger, enemy*) 退避 [tuìbì] **2** (*from promise etc*) 放弃 [fàngqì] **3** (MIL) 撤退 [chètuì] ▶ **to beat a hasty retreat** 迅速逃离

retrieve [rɪ'tri:v] VT **1** [+*object*] 取回 [qǔhuí] **2** (*put right*) [+*situation, error*] 挽回 [wǎnhuí] **3** (COMPUT) 检索 [jiǎnsuǒ]

retrospect ['retrəspɛkt] N ▶ **in retrospect** 回顾 [huígù]

return [rɪ'tɜ:n] **I** VI [*person +*] 返回 [fǎnhuí] ▷ *I returned to my hotel.* 我返回到我住的酒店。; [*situation, symptom +*] 再出现 [zàichūxiàn] ▷ *If the pain returns, repeat the treatment.* 如果疼痛再出现，则重复疗程。 **II** VT **1** [+*something borrowed or stolen*] 归还 [guīhuán] ▷ *He returned her passport.* 他归还了她的护照。 **2** [+*favour, feeling, greeting*] 回 [huí] **3** (LAW) [+*verdict*] 裁决 [cáijué] **4** (POL) [+*candidate*] 当选 [dāngxuǎn] **5** [+*ball*] 回传 [huíchuán] **III** N **1** [S] [*of person*] 返回 [fǎnhuí] **2** [S] [*of something borrowed or stolen*] 归还 [guīhuán] **3** [S] (*to activity, to a state*) 回到 [huídào] **4** [c/U] (ECON) (*from land, shares, investment*) 盈利 [yínglì] **5** [S] [*of merchandise*] 退货 [tuìhuò] **6** [U] (COMPUT) (*key*) 回车键 [huíchējiàn] **IV** **returns** NPL (COMM) 利润

[lìrùn] ▶ **in return (for)** 作为 (对…) 的回报 ▶ **by return of post** 请即赐复 ▶ **many happy returns (of the day)!** 生日快乐! **V** CPD [复合词] **1** (BRIT) [+*journey, ticket*] 往返 [wǎngfǎn] **2** [+*match*] (BRIT) 回访 [huífǎng] ▶ **return to** VT FUS (不可拆分) **1** [+*consciousness, power*] 恢复 [huīfù] **2** [+*subject, activity*] 回到 [huídào]

reunion [ri:'ju:nɪən] N [c] [*of family, school, class etc*] 团聚 [tuánjù] **2** [c/U] [*of two people*] 重聚 [chóngjù]

reunite [ri:ju:'naɪt] VT **1** [+*people*] 重聚 [chóngjù] **2** [+*organization, country etc*] 使…重新团结 [shǐ…chóngxīn tuánjié]

rev [rɛv] (AUT) N ABBR (= *revolution*) 旋转 [xuánzhuǎn]

revamp [ri:'væmp] VT 更新 [gēngxīn]

rev counter (BRIT: AUT) N [c] 转速计数器 [zhuǎnsù jìshùqì]

Rev(d). (REL) ABBR = **reverend**

reveal [rɪ'vi:l] VT **1** (*make known*) 透露 [tòulù] **2** (*make visible*) 展现 [zhǎnxiàn]

revealing [rɪ'vi:lɪŋ] ADJ **1** [+*comment, action*] 揭露事实的 [jiēlù shìshí de] **2** [+*clothes*] 暴露的 [bàolù de]

revel ['rɛvl] VI ▶ **to revel in sth** 尽情享受某事物 [jìnqíng xiǎngshòu mǒushìwù]

revelation [rɛvə'leɪʃən] **I** N **1** [c] (*fact*) 透露出来的事 [tòulù chūlái de shì] **2** [S] (*surprise*) 揭露 [jiēlù] **3** [c/U] (*disclosure*) [*of fact*] 揭露 [jiēlù] **II** **Revelations** NPL (*in Bible*) 启示录 [Qǐshìlù]

revenge [rɪ'vɛndʒ] **I** N [U] 复仇 [fùchóu] **II** VT [+*defeat, injustice*] 报复 [bàofù] ▶ **to get one's revenge (for sth)** (为某事) 进行报复 ▶ **to take (one's) revenge (on sb)** (对某人) 进行报复 ▶ **to revenge o.s. (on sb)** (向某人) 进行报复

revenue ['rɛvənju:] N [c/U] 岁入 [suìrù]

Reverend ['rɛvərənd] ADJ (*in titles*) ▶ **the Reverend John Smith** (*Catholic*) 约翰史密斯神父 [Yuēhànshǐmìsī shénfù]; (*Protestant*) 约翰史密斯牧师 [Yuēhànshǐmìsī mùshī]; (*Anglican*) 约翰史密斯会长 [Yuēhànshǐmìsī huìzhǎng]

reversal [rɪ'vɜ:sl] N [c] **1** (*turnaround*) 翻转 [fānzhuǎn] **2** (*setback*) 挫败 [cuòbài]

reverse [rɪ'vɜ:s] **I** N **1** [S] (*opposite*) 相反 [xiāngfǎn] **2** [U] (AUT) (*also:* **reverse gear**) 倒退挡 [dàotuìdǎng] **3** [S] (*back*) [*of cloth, coin, medal*] 反面 [fǎnmiàn]; [*of paper*] 背面 [bèimiàn] **4** [c] (*setback, defeat*) 挫败 [cuòbài] **II** ADJ **1** [+*process, effect*] 相反的 [xiāngfǎn de] **2** [+*side*] 反面的 [fǎnmiàn de] **III** VT **1** [+*order, position, direction*] 使反转 [shǐ fǎnzhuǎn] **2** [+*process, decision, trend*] 彻底转变 [chèdǐ zhuǎnbiàn] **3** (LAW) [+*judgement, verdict*] 撤销 [chèxiāo] **4** [+*roles*] 互换 [hùhuàn] **5** [+*car*] (ESP BRIT) 倒退行驶 [dàotuì xíngshǐ] [美=back up] **IV** VI (BRIT: AUT) 倒退行驶 [dàotuì xíngshǐ] [美=back up] ▶ **in reverse** (*action, process*) 顺序相反; (AUT)

挂倒挡 ▶ **in reverse order** 逆序 ▶ **to go into reverse** [*trend +*] 逆转; (*in car*) 挂倒挡

reverse-charge call [rɪ'vɜːstʃɑːdʒ-] (BRIT) N [c] 受话人付费电话 [shòuhuàrén fùfèi diànhuà] [美= **collect call**]

reversing lights [rɪ'vɜːsɪŋ-] (BRIT) NPL 倒车灯 [dàochēdēng]

revert [rɪ'vɜːt] VI 1 ▶ **to revert to** [*+ former state*] 回到 [huídào] 2 (LAW) [*money, property +*] 物归原主 [wù guī yuánzhǔ]

review [rɪ'vjuː] I N [c] 1 (*evaluation*) [*of book, film etc*] 评论 [pínglùn] 2 (*examination*) [*of situation, policy etc*] 审查 [shěnchá] 3 (*magazine*) 评论刊物 [pínglùn kānwù] 4 (MIL) 检阅 [jiǎnyuè] II VT 1 [*+ book, film etc*] 评论 [pínglùn] 2 [*+ situation, policy etc*] 审查 [shěnchá] 3 (MIL) [*+ troops*] 检阅 [jiǎnyuè] ▶ **to be/come under review** 受到审查

reviewer [rɪ'vjuːə(r)] N [c] 评论家 [pínglùnjiā]

revise [rɪ'vaɪz] I VT (*alter, adapt*) [*+ manuscript, article*] 修改 [xiūgǎi]; [*+ opinion, attitude*] 修正 [xiūzhèng]; [*+ procedure*] 改进 [gǎijìn]; (*study*) 复习 [fùxí] II VI (*study*) (BRIT) 复习 [fùxí] ▶ **revised edition** 修订本

revision [rɪ'vɪʒən] N 1 [c/u] (*alteration, adaptation*) 修改 [xiūgǎi] 2 [u] (BRIT) (*studying*) 复习 [fùxí]

revival [rɪ'vaɪvəl] N [c] 1 (*renewed popularity*) 复兴 [fùxīng] 2 (*economic*) 复苏 [fùsū] 3 (THEAT) 重新上演 [chóngxīn shàngyǎn]

revive [rɪ'vaɪv] I VT 1 [*+ person*] 使苏醒 [shǐ sūxǐng] 2 [*+ economy, industry*] 复苏 [fùsū] 3 [*+ custom*] 复兴 [fùxīng] 4 [*+ hope, courage, interest etc*] 唤起 [huànqǐ] 5 [*+ play*] 重演 [chóngyǎn] II VI 1 [*person +*] 苏醒 [sūxǐng] 2 [*activity, economy, faith, interest etc +*] 复苏 [fùsū]

revolt [rɪ'vəult] I N [c/u] 1 (*rebellion*) 造反 [zàofǎn] 2 (*rejection*) 反叛 [fǎnpàn] II VI 起义 [qǐyì] III VT 使憎恶 [shǐ zēngwù] ▶ **to revolt against sb/sth** 反抗某人/某物

revolting [rɪ'vəultɪŋ] ADJ 令人厌恶的 [lìng rén yànwù de]

revolution [rɛvə'luːʃən] N 1 [c/u] (POL) 革命 [gémìng] 2 [c] (*change*) (*in industry, education etc*) 变革 [biàngé] 3 [c/u] (*rotation*) 旋转一周 [xuánzhuǎn yī zhōu]

revolutionary [rɛvə'luːʃənrɪ] I ADJ 1 [*+ method, idea, concept*] 创新的 [chuàngxīn de] 2 (POL) [*+ leader, army, movement*] 革命的 [gémìng de] II N [c] (POL) 革命者 [gémìngzhě]

revolutionize [rɛvə'luːʃənaɪz] VT 彻底改变 [chèdǐ gǎibiàn]

revolve [rɪ'vɔlv] VI (*wheel, propeller etc +*) 旋转 [xuánzhuǎn] ▶ **to revolve (a)round sth** 1 [*earth, moon +*] 围绕某物旋转 [wéirào mǒuwù xuánzhuǎn] 2 [*life, discussion +*] 以某物为中心 [yǐ mǒuwù wéi zhōngxīn]

revolver [rɪ'vɔlvə(r)] N [c] 左轮手枪 [zuǒlún shǒuqiāng]

reward [rɪ'wɔːd] I N [c] 1 (*for service, merit, work*) 奖励 [jiǎnglì] 2 (POLICE) (*for capture of criminal, information*) 赏金 [shǎngjīn] 3 (*satisfaction*) 回报 [huíbào] II VT 1 [*+ person*] 奖赏 [jiǎngshǎng] 2 [*+ patience, determination etc*] 报偿 [bàocháng]

rewarding [rɪ'wɔːdɪŋ] ADJ (*worthwhile*) [*+ experience, job etc*] 值得做的 [zhídé zuò de] ▶ **financially rewarding** 报酬丰厚

rewind [riː'waɪnd] (*pt, pp* **rewound**) VT 倒带 [dàodài]

rewrite [riː'raɪt] (*pt* **rewrote**, *pp* **rewritten**) VT 改写 [gǎixiě]

rheumatism ['ruːmətɪzəm] N [u] 风湿病 [fēngshībìng]

rhinoceros [raɪ'nɔsərəs] N [c] 犀牛 [xīniú]

rhubarb ['ruːbɑːb] N [u] 大黄 [dàhuáng]

rhyme [raɪm] I N 1 [c] (*sound, word*) 同韵词 [tóngyùncí] 2 [c] (*verse*) 押韵诗 [yāyùnshī] 3 [u] (*technique*) 押韵 [yāyùn] II VI 押韵 [yāyùn] ▶ **without rhyme or reason** 毫无道理 ▶ **to rhyme with sth** 与某词押韵

rhythm ['rɪðm] N 1 [c/u] [*of drums, music*] 节奏 [jiézòu] 2 [c] [*of body, tides, seasons*] 周期 [zhōuqī]

RI N ABBR (= *religious instruction*) (BRIT: SCOL) 宗教教育 [zōngjiào jiàoyù]

rib [rɪb] I N [c] (ANAT) 肋骨 [lèigǔ] II VT (*mock*) (*inf*) 逗弄 [dòunong]

ribbon ['rɪbən] N 1 [c/u] (*for hair*) 饰带 [shìdài]; (*for decoration*) 捆扎带 [kǔnzādài] 2 [c] [*of typewriter*] 色带 [sèdài] ▶ **in ribbons** (*torn*) 破烂不堪

rice [raɪs] N [c/u] 1 (*grain*) 大米 [dàmǐ] 2 (*when cooked*) 米饭 [mǐfàn]

rice pudding N [c/u] 米饭布丁 [mǐfàn bùdīng]

rich [rɪtʃ] I ADJ 1 [*+ person, country*] 富有的 [fùyǒu de] 2 [*+ food, diet*] 油腻的 [yóunì de] 3 [*+ soil*] 肥沃的 [féiwò de] 4 [*+ colour*] 深的 [shēn de] 5 [*+ voice*] 深沉的 [shēnchén de] 6 [*+ experience, life, history*] 丰富的 [fēngfù de] 7 [*+ tapestries, silks*] 贵重的 [guìzhòng de] II NPL ▶ **the rich** 富人 [fùrén] ▶ **rich in** [*+ minerals, resources etc*] 富含

riches ['rɪtʃɪz] NPL 财富 [cáifù]

richly ['rɪtʃlɪ] ADV 1 [*+ decorated, carved*] 华丽地 [huálì de] 2 [*+ coloured, flavoured*] 浓厚地 [nónghòu de] 3 [*reward, benefit +*] 丰厚地 [fēnghòu de] 4 [*+ deserved, earned*] 完全地 [wánquán de]

rid [rɪd] (*pt, pp* **rid**) VT ▶ **to rid sb/sth of sth** 使某人/某物摆脱某事物 [shǐ mǒurén/mǒuwù bǎituō mǒushìwù] ▶ **to get rid of sth/sb** [*+ smell, dirt, car etc*] 摆脱某事物/某人 ▶ **to be rid of sth/sb** 摆脱某事物/某人

riddle ['rɪdl] N [c] 1 (*conundrum*) 谜语 [míyǔ]

2 (mystery) 谜 [mí]

riddled ['rɪdld] ADJ ► **to be riddled with**
1 [+ guilt, doubts, errors] 充斥着 [chōngchìzhe]
2 [+ holes, bullets] 被弄得千疮百孔 [bèi nòng de qiān chuāng bǎi kǒng]

ride [raɪd] (pt **rode**, pp **ridden** ['rɪdn]) **I** N [c]
1 (in car, on bicycle) 兜风 [dōufēng] **2** (on horse, bus, train) 出行 [chūxíng] **3** (track, path) 供骑马用的小径 [gōng qímǎ yòng de xiǎojìng]
II VI (travel) (on horse) 骑马 [qímǎ]; (on bicycle) 骑车 [qíchē]; (in car) 乘坐 [chéngzuò] **III** VT
1 [+ horse, bicycle, motorcycle] 骑 [qí] **2** [+ distance] 行进 [xíngjìn] ► **a horse/car ride** 骑马/乘车出游 [qímǎ/chéngchē chūyóu] ► **to go for a ride** 出游 ► **to give sb a ride** (US) 让某人搭车 ► **to take sb for a ride** (fig) 欺骗某人 ► **to be riding high** 声明显赫 ► **a rough ride** (inf) 艰难的处境
► **ride out** VT ► **to ride out the storm** 安然度过 [ānrán dùguò]

rider ['raɪdə(r)] N [c] **1** (on horse) 骑师 [qíshī]; (on bicycle) 骑自行车的人 [qí zìxíngchē de rén]; (on motorcycle) 骑手 [qíshǒu] **2** (addendum) 附加意见 [fùjiā yìjiàn]

ridge [rɪdʒ] N [c] **1** 隆起 [lóngqǐ] **2** [of hill] 脊 [jǐ]

ridicule ['rɪdɪkjuːl] **I** VT (mock) [+ person, proposal] 嘲讽 [cháofěng] **II** N [U] 嘲笑 [cháoxiào] ► **to be the object of ridicule** 成为嘲笑的对象

ridiculous [rɪ'dɪkjuləs] ADJ 荒谬的 [huāngmiù de]

riding ['raɪdɪŋ] N [U] 骑马 [qímǎ] ► **to go riding** 去骑马

rife [raɪf] ADJ [corruption, superstition, disease etc +] 普遍的 [pǔbiàn de] ► **to be rife with** [+ rumours, fears etc] 充斥着

rifle ['raɪfl] **I** N [c] (gun) 步枪 [bùqiāng] **II** VT (also: **rifle through**) [+ papers, clothing, bag etc] 搜劫 [sōujié]

rift [rɪft] N [c] **1** (split) (in ground) 裂缝 [lièfèng] **2** (disagreement) 裂痕 [lièhén]

rig [rɪg] **I** N [c] (also: **oil rig**) 钻井台 [zuànjǐngtái] **II** VT [+ election, game etc] 暗箱操纵 [ànxiāng cāozòng]
► **rig out** (BRIT: inf) VT ► **to rig sb out as/in** 将某人打扮成/使某人穿戴着 [jiāng mǒurén dǎbànchéng/shǐ mǒurén chuāndàizhe]
► **rig up** VT [+ device, net] 拼凑做成 [pīncòu zuòchéng]

○**right** [raɪt] **I** ADJ **1** (not left) 右边的 [yòubiān de] ▷ her right hand 她的右手 **2** (correct) [+ answer, size, person] 正确的 [zhèngquè de] ▷ the right answer 正确答案; (appropriate) [+ person, place, clothes] 合适的 [héshì de]; [+ decision, direction, time] 最适宜的 [zuì shìyí de] **3** (proper, fair) 恰当的 [qiàdàng de] **4** [+ side] (of material) 正面的 [zhèngmiàn de] **5** (socially acceptable) 适当的 [shìdàng de] **6** (emphasizing) (BRIT: inf) 不折不扣的 [bù zhé bù kòu de]

II N **1** [s] (not left) 右边 [yòubiān] **2** [U] (what is morally right) 正确 [zhèngquè] **3** [c] (entitlement) 权利 [quánlì] **III** ADV **1** (correctly) 正确地 [zhèngquè de] **2** (properly, fairly) 恰当 [qiàdàng] **3** (not to/on the left) 右边地 [yòubiān de] **4** (directly, exactly) 就 [jiù] **IV** VT **1** (put right way up) [+ ship, car etc] 使…回到正确的位置 [shǐ…huídào zhèngquè de wèizhi] **2** (correct) [+ fault, situation, wrong] 纠正 [jiūzhèng] **V** INT 好 [hǎo] **VI** **rights** NPL (PUBLISHING) 版权 [bǎnquán] ► **this is not the right time for…** 这时间不合适做… ► **do you have the right time?** 你的表几点了? ► **the Right** (POL) 右派; [+ answer, fact +] 对; [clock +] 准确 ► **to get sth right** 做对某事 ► **let's get it right this time!** 这次别再出错了! ► **you did the right thing** 你做得对 ► **to put sth right** [+ mistake, injustice etc] 纠正某事 ► **right now** (inf) 当即 ► **right before/after** 刚好在之前/之后 ► **right against the wall** 正好靠墙 ► **right in the middle** 正中间 ► **right ahead** 正前方 ► **by rights** 按道理 ► **to or on the right** (position) 靠{或}在右侧 ► **to the right** (movement) 向右 ► **to be in the right** 有道理 ► **right away or right off** (immediately) 立刻 ► **to be within one's rights** 不超越权限 ► **in his/her own right** 依靠他/她自身的能力 ► **to go right to the end of sth** 一直走到某物的尽头 ► **film rights** 电影拍摄权

right angle N [c] 直角 [zhíjiǎo] ► **at right angles** 垂直

rightful ['raɪtful] ADJ [+ heir, owner, place, share] 合法的 [héfǎ de]

right-hand drive [raɪthænd-] **I** N [U] 右侧驾驶 [yòucè jiàshǐ] **II** ADJ [+ vehicle] 右侧驾驶的 [yòucè jiàshǐ de]

right-handed [raɪt'hændɪd] ADJ 惯用右手的 [guànyòng yòushǒu de]

right-hand side N [s] 右侧 [yòucè]

rightly ['raɪtlɪ] ADV (with reason) 恰当地 [qiàdàng de] ► **if I remember rightly** (BRIT) 如果我没记错

right of way N [c] **1** (public path) 通行权 [tōngxíngquán] **2** (AUT) (priority) 先行权 [xiānxíngquán]

right-wing [raɪt'wɪŋ] **I** ADJ 右翼的 [yòuyì de] **II** N [s] (of political party) 右翼势力 [yòuyì shìlì]

rigid ['rɪdʒɪd] ADJ **1** [+ structure, back etc] 坚硬的 [jiānyìng de] **2** [+ attitude, principle, views etc] 僵化的 [jiānghuà de] **3** [+ control] 严格的 [yángé de]

rigorous ['rɪgərəs] ADJ [+ control, test, training] 严格的 [yángé de]

rim [rɪm] N [c] **1** [of glass, dish] 边缘 [biānyuán] **2** [of wheel] 辋圈 [wǎngquān]

rind [raɪnd] N [c/U] [of bacon, fruit, cheese] 皮 [pí]

ring [rɪŋ] (pt **rang**, pp **rung**) **I** N [c] **1** (on finger) 戒指 [jièzhi] **2** [of people, objects, light, smoke

etc] 圈 [quān] **3** [*of spies, drug-dealers etc*] 团
伙 [tuánhuǒ] **4** (*for boxing*) 拳击台 [quánjítái]
5 [*of circus*] 马戏场 [mǎxìchǎng] **6** (*bullring*) 斗
牛场 [dòuniúchǎng] **7** (*sound of telephone, bell*)
铃声 [língshēng] **8** (*on cooker*) (ESP BRIT) 灶
眼 [zàoyǎn] **II** VI **1** [*bell +*] 鸣响 [míngxiǎng]
2 [*telephone +*] 响 [xiǎng] **3** (BRIT: TEL) (*call*) 打
电话 [dǎ diànhuà] [美=**call**] **4** (*also*: **ring out**)
[*voice, words, shot +*] 鸣响 [míngxiǎng] **III** VT
1 [*+ bell, doorbell*] 使…响 [shǐ…xiǎng] **2** (BRIT:
TEL) 给…打电话 [gěi…dǎ diànhuà] **3** (*circle*)
圈出 [quānchū] **4** (*surround*) 环绕 [huánrào]
▶ there was a ring at the door, the doorbell
rang 有人按门铃 ▶ to give sb a ring (BRIT:
TEL) 给某人打电话 ▶ that has a ring of truth
about it 那听上去是真的 ▶ to run rings
(a)round sb (*inf*) 远远胜过某人 ▶ my ears are
ringing 我耳中嗡嗡作响 ▶ to ring true/false
听起来正确/错误
  ▶ ring back (BRIT: TEL) **I** VT 回电话 [huí
  diànhuà] [美=**call back**] **II** VI 再打电话 [zài
  dǎ diànhuà] [美=**call back**]
  ▶ ring off (BRIT: TEL) VI 挂断电话 [guàduàn
  diànhuà] [美=**hang up**]
  ▶ ring up (BRIT: TEL) VT 给…打电话 [gěi…dǎ
  diànhuà]
ringing ['rɪŋɪŋ] **I** ADJ [*+ crash*] 清脆的
[qīngcuì de] **II** N [U] **1** [*of telephone, bell*] 鸣响
[míngxiǎng] **2** (*in ears*) 嗡嗡作响 [wēngwēng
zuòxiǎng]
ringing tone (BRIT) N [C] 铃声 [língshēng]
ring road (BRIT: AUT) N [C] 环路 [huánlù]
  [美=**beltway**]
rink [rɪŋk] N [C] **1** (*also*: **ice rink**) 溜冰场
[liūbīngchǎng] **2** (*also*: **roller skating rink**) 旱冰
场 [hànbīngchǎng]
rinse [rɪns] **I** N [C] (*of dishes, clothes*) 漂洗
[piǎoxǐ]; (*of hair, hands*) 冲洗 [chōngxǐ]; (*hair dye*)
染发剂 [rǎnfàjì] **II** VT [*+ dishes, clothes*] 漂洗
[piǎoxǐ]; [*+ hair, hands etc*] 冲洗 [chōngxǐ]; (*also*:
rinse out) [*+ mouth*] 漱 [shù]
riot ['raɪət] **I** N [C] (*disturbance*) 暴乱 [bàoluàn]
II VI 闹事 [nàoshì] ▷ They rioted in protest
against the Government. 他们在反对政府的抗议
中闹事。 ▶ to run riot [*children, football fans etc +*]
撒野 ▶ a riot of colour(s) 五彩缤纷
RIP ABBR (= *rest in peace*) 愿灵安眠 [yuàn líng
ān mián]
rip [rɪp] **I** N [C] 裂口 [lièkǒu] **II** VT 撕裂 [sīliè]
III VI 裂开 [lièkāi]
  ▶ rip off VT **1** [*+ clothes*] 迅速脱掉 [xùnsù
  tuōdiào] **2** (*inf*) (*swindle*) 欺骗 [qīpiàn]
  ▶ rip up VT 把…撕成碎片 [bǎ…sīchéng
  suìpiàn]
ripe [raɪp] ADJ [*+ fruit, corn*] 成熟的 [chéngshú
de]; [*+ cheese*] 发酵好的 [fājiào hǎo de] ▶ to be
ripe for sth 某事的时机已成熟 ▶ the time is
ripe 时机已成熟 ▶ he lived to a ripe old age

他活到高龄
ripen ['raɪpn] **I** VI [*sun +*] [*+ fruit, crop*] 成
熟 [chéngshú] **II** VT [*fruit, crop +*] 使…成熟
[shǐ…chéngshú]
rip-off ['rɪpɔf] (*inf*) N [C] **1** 敲竹杠 [qiāo
zhúgàng] **2** (*copy*) [*of song, film*] 抄袭 [chāoxí]
ripple ['rɪpl] **I** N [C] **1** (*on water*) 涟漪 [liányī]
2 [*of laughter, applause*] 微弱的一阵 [wēiruò
de yī zhèn] **II** VI **1** [*water +*] 起涟漪 [qǐ liányī]
2 [*muscles +*] 凸起 [tūqǐ] **III** VT [*+ surface*]
使…泛起涟漪 [shǐ…fànqǐ liányī]
◎ rise [raɪz] (*pt* **rose**, *pp* **risen** [rɪzn]) **I** N **1** [C]
(*incline*) 斜坡 [xiépō] **2** [C] (BRIT) (*salary increase*)
加薪 [jiāxīn] **3** [C] (*in prices, temperature, crime
rate etc*) 上升 [shàngshēng] **4** [S] (*to power,
fame etc*) 兴起 [xīngqǐ] **II** VI **1** (*move upwards*)
上升 [shàngshēng] **2** [*prices, numbers +*] 上升
[shàngshēng] **3** [*water +*] 上涨 [shàngzhǎng]
4 [*sun, moon +*] 升起 [shēngqǐ] **5** [*wind +*] 刮
起来 [guāqǐlái] **6** (*frm*) [*person +*] (*get up*) 起
床 [qǐchuáng] **7** (*from chair*) 起身 [qǐshēn]
8 [*sound, voice +*] (*in pitch*) 提高 [tígāo] **9** [*land +*]
隆起 [lóngqǐ] **10** (*also*: **rise up**) [*tower, building +*]
矗立 [chùlì] **11** (*revolt*) 反抗 [fǎnkàng] **12** (*in
rank*) 升职 [shēngzhí] ▶ to rise to power 掌权
▶ to rise above sth 不受某事的影响 ▶ to give
rise to sth 引起某事
rising ['raɪzɪŋ] ADJ **1** (*increasing*) 增加的
[zēngjiā de] **2** [*+ tide*] 上涨的 [shàngzhǎng de]
3 (*up-and-coming*) [*film star, politician etc*] 崭露
头角的 [zhǎnlù tóujiǎo de]
risk [rɪsk] **I** N **1** [C/U] (*danger*) 危险 [wēixiǎn]
2 [C] (*possibility, chance*) 风险 [fēngxiǎn]
3 [C] (*dangerous person or thing*) 危险事物
[wēixiǎn shìwù] **II** VT **1** (*endanger*) 冒…危险
[mào…wēixiǎn] **2** (*take the chance of*) 冒险做
[màoxiǎn zuò] ▶ to take a risk 担风险 ▶ to
run the risk of sth/doing sth 冒着某事/做某事
的危险 ▶ at risk 处于危险 ▶ at one's own risk
风险自负 ▶ to risk it (*inf*) 冒险一试
risky ['rɪskɪ] ADJ 有风险的 [yǒu fēngxiǎn de]
rite [raɪt] N [C] 仪式 [yíshì] ▶ rite of passage
人生大事
ritual ['rɪtjʊəl] **I** ADJ [*+ dance, murder*] 仪式上的
[yíshì shang de] **II** N [C/U] **1** (REL) 仪式程序
[yíshì chéngxù] **2** (*procedure*) 程序 [chéngxù]
rival ['raɪvl] **I** N [C] **1** (*in competition, election,
business*) 竞争对手 [jìngzhēng duìshǒu] **2** (*in
love*) 情敌 [qíngdí] **II** ADJ **1** [*+ firm, newspaper
etc*] 竞争的 [jìngzhēng de] **2** [*+ teams, groups,
supporters etc*] 对立的 [duìlì de] **III** VT (*match*)
与…匹敌 [yǔ…pǐdí]
rivalry ['raɪvlrɪ] N [C/U] 竞争 [jìngzhēng]
river ['rɪvə(r)] **I** N [C/U] **1** 河 [hé] **2** [*of blood etc*] 涌
出 [yǒngchū] **II** CPD [复合词] [*+ port, traffic*] 河
[hé] ▶ up/down river 河流上游/下游
river bank N [C] 河岸 [hé'àn]
river bed N [C] 河床 [héchuáng]

rivet ['rɪvɪt] **I** N [c] (bolt) 铆钉 [mǎodīng] **II** VT [+ person, attention] 吸引 [xīyǐn]

○ **road** [rəud] **I** N [c] **1** (in country) 公路 [gōnglù] **2** (in town) 路 [lù] **3** (fig) 道路 [dàolù] **II** CPD [复合词] [+ accident, sense] 交通 [jiāotōng] ▶ it takes four hours by road 要花4小时的车程 ▶ let's hit the road (inf) 我们启程吧 ▶ to be on the road [person +] 在旅途中; [pop group +] 在巡回演出中 ▶ on the road to success/recovery 在获得成功/康复的过程中 ▶ major/minor road 主干道/非主干道

roadblock ['rəudblɔk] N [c] 路障 [lùzhàng]

road map N [c] 道路图 [dàolùtú]

road rage N [U] 行车纠纷 [xíngchē jiūfēn]

road safety N [U] 道路安全 [dàolù ānquán]

roadside ['rəudsaɪd] **I** N [c] 路边 [lùbiān] **II** CPD [复合词] [+ building, sign etc] 路边 [lùbiān] ▶ at or by the roadside 在路边

road sign N [c] 交通标志 [jiāotōng biāozhì]

roadway ['rəudweɪ] N [c] 车行道 [chēxíngdào]

roadworks ['rəudwə:ks] NPL 道路施工 [dàolù shīgōng]

roam [rəum] **I** VI 漫无目的地走动 [màn wú mùdì de zǒudòng] **II** VT [+ streets, countryside] 漫步 [mànbù]

roar [rɔ:(r)] **I** N [c] **1** [of animal] 吼叫声 [hǒujiàoshēng] **2** [of crowd] 喧哗 [xuānhuá] **3** [of traffic, storm] 喧闹声 [xuānnàoshēng] **II** VI **1** [animal +] 吼叫 [hǒujiào] **2** [person, crowd +] 大喊大叫 [dàhǎn dà jiào] **3** [engine, wind etc +] 咆哮 [páoxiào] ▶ to roar with laughter 哈哈大笑 ▶ roar of laughter 大笑声

roast [rəust] **I** N [c] (meat dish) 烤肉 [kǎoròu] **II** VT **1** [+ food] 烤 [kǎo] **2** [+ coffee] 烘焙 [hōngbèi]
用法参见 **cook**

roast beef N [U] 烤牛肉 [kǎoniúròu]

rob [rɔb] VT [+ person, house, bank] 抢劫 [qiǎngjié] ▶ to rob sb of sth 剥夺某人的某物
用法参见 **steal**

robber ['rɔbə(r)] N [c] 强盗 [qiángdào]
用法参见 **thief**

robbery ['rɔbərɪ] N [C/U] 抢劫 [qiǎngjié]

robe [rəub] N [c] **1** (for ceremony etc) 礼袍 [lǐpáo] **2** (also: **bath robe**) 浴袍 [yùpáo] **3** (US) (dressing-gown) 睡袍 [shuìpáo]

robin ['rɔbɪn] N [c] 知更鸟 [zhīgēngniǎo]

robot ['rəubɔt] N [c] 机器人 [jīqìrén]

robust [rəu'bʌst] ADJ **1** [+ person] 强健的 [qiángjiàn de] **2** [+ object, machine] 结实的 [jiēshí de] **3** [+ appetite, health, economy] 旺盛的 [wàngshèng de]

rock [rɔk] **I** N **1** [U] (substance) 岩 [yán] **2** [c] (boulder) 巨石 [jùshí] **3** [c] (ESP US) (small stone) 小石子 [xiǎoshízǐ] **4** [U] (MUS) (also: **rock music**) 摇滚乐 [yáogǔnyuè] **5** [U] (BRIT) (candy) 硬棒糖 [yìngbàngtáng] **II** VT **1** (swing gently) [+ cradle] 摇晃 [yáohuàng]; [+ child] 轻摇 [qīngyáo]

2 (shake) [explosion +] 使剧烈震动 [shǐ jùliè zhèndòng]; (shock) [news, crime +] 使震惊 [shǐ zhènjīng] **III** VI **1** [object +] 摇晃 [yáohuàng] **2** [person +] 轻轻摇摆 [qīngqīng yáobǎi] ▶ on the rocks (inf) [drink +] (with ice) 加冰块的; [marriage +] (in difficulties) 濒于破裂; [business +] (in difficulties) 濒临破产

rock and roll N [U] 摇滚乐 [yáogǔnyuè]

rock-bottom ['rɔk'bɔtəm] **I** N ▶ to reach or touch or hit rock-bottom [person +] 处于最糟的境地 [chǔyú zuì zāo de jìngdì]; [prices +] 降至最低点 [jiàng zhì zuìdīdiǎn] **II** ADJ [+ prices] 最低的 [zuìdī de]

rock climbing N [U] 攀岩运动 [pānyán yùndòng]

rocket ['rɔkɪt] **I** N [c] **1** (SPACE) 火箭 [huǒjiàn] **2** (MIL) 火箭式导弹 [huǒjiànshì dǎodàn] **3** (firework) 火箭式礼花 [huǒjiànshì lǐhuā] **II** VI (also: **sky-rocket**) 剧增 [jùzēng]

rocking chair ['rɔkɪŋ-] N [c] 摇椅 [yáoyǐ]

rocking horse N [c] 木马 [mùmǎ]

rocky ['rɔkɪ] ADJ **1** [+ path, shore, ground] 岩石的 [yánshí de] **2** (inf) [+ business, marriage] 不稳定 [bù wěndìng]

rod [rɔd] N [c] **1** (pole) 杆 [gān] **2** (also: **fishing rod**) 钓鱼竿 [diàoyúgān]

rode [rəud] PT of **ride**

rodent ['rəudnt] N [c] 啮齿目动物 [nièchǐmù dòngwù]

rogue [rəug] N [c] 无赖 [wúlài]

○ **role** [rəul] N [c] **1** (function) [of person, country, organization] 作用 [zuòyòng] **2** (THEAT) (part) 角色 [juésè]

role model N [c] 榜样 [bǎngyàng]

roll [rəul] **I** N [c] **1** [of paper, cloth, film etc] 一卷 [yī juǎn] **2** [of banknotes] 一叠 [yī dié] **3** (also: **bread roll**) 小圆面包 [xiǎoyuánmiànbāo] **4** (register, list) 花名册 [huāmíngcè] **5** (sound) [of drums, thunder] 持续而平稳的振动声 [chíxù ér píngwěn de zhèndòngshēng] **II** VT **1** [+ ball, stone, dice etc] 使滚动 [shǐ gǔndòng] **2** (also: **roll up**) [+ carpet, string] 绕 [rào]; [+ sleeves, cigarette] 卷 [juǎn] **3** [+ eyes] 转动 [zhuàndòng] **4** (also: **roll out**) [+ pastry] 擀 [gǎn] **5** (flatten) [+ lawn, road, surface] 碾平 [niǎnpíng] **III** VI **1** [ball, stone etc +] 滚动 [gǔndòng] **2** [drums, thunder +] 发出隆隆声 [fāchū lónglóngshēng] **3** [vehicle +] 缓行 [huǎnxíng] **4** [ship +] 左右摇晃 [zuǒyòu yáohuàng] **5** [tears, sweat +] 滚落 [gǔnluò] **6** [camera, printing press +] 运转 [yùnzhuǎn] ▶ cheese/ham roll 奶酪/火腿面包卷 ▶ to be rolling in it (inf) 赚大笔的钱 ▶ on a roll (inf) 好运连连 ▶ rolled into one (inf) 合为一体的 ▶ roll about, roll around VI 打滚 [dǎgǔn] ▶ roll in VI (inf) [money, invitations +] 滚滚而来 [gǔngǔn ér lái] ▶ roll over VI 翻滚 [fāngǔn] ▶ roll up I VT [+ carpet, newspaper, string] 卷起

[juǎnqǐ] II vɪ (inf) (arrive) 到达 [dàodá]

roll call N [c/u] 点名 [diǎnmíng]

roller ['rəulə(r)] N [c] **1** (in machine) 滚筒 [gǔntǒng] **2** (for moving heavy object) 滚轮 [gǔnlún] **3** (for lawn) 辗草坪机 [niǎn cǎopíng jī] **4** (for road) 轧路机 [yàlùjī] **5** (for hair) 卷发筒 [juǎnfàtǒng]

rollerblades ['rəuləbleɪdz] NPL 直排轮溜冰鞋 [zhípáilún liūbīngxié]

roller coaster [-'kəustə(r)] N [c] (at funfair) 过山车 [guòshānchē] ▶ **on a roller coaster** 急转突变

roller skates NPL 旱冰鞋 [hànbīngxié]

roller skating N [u] 穿旱冰鞋滑行 [chuān hànbīngxié huáxíng]

rolling pin ['rəulɪŋ-] N [c] 擀面杖 [gǎnmiànzhàng]

ROM [rɔm] N ABBR (= read-only memory) 只读存储器 [zhǐdú cúnchǔqì]

Roman ['rəumən] I ADJ **1** (of ancient Rome) 古罗马的 [gǔ Luómǎ de] **2** (of modern Rome) 罗马的 [Luómǎ de] II N [c] (in ancient Rome) 古罗马人 [gǔ Luómǎrén]

Roman Catholic I ADJ 天主教的 [Tiānzhǔjiào de] II N [c] 天主教教徒 [Tiānzhǔjiào Jiàotú]

romance [rə'mæns] N **1** [c] (affair) 恋情 [liànqíng] **2** [u] (romantic actions, feelings) 浪漫 [làngmàn] **3** [u] (charm, excitement) 迷人之处 [mírén zhī chù] **4** [c] (novel) 爱情小说 [àiqíng xiǎoshuō]

Romania [rə'meɪnɪə] N 罗马尼亚 [Luómǎníyà]

Romanian [rə'meɪnɪən] I ADJ 罗马尼亚的 [Luómǎníyà de] II N **1** [c] (person) 罗马尼亚人 [Luómǎníyàrén] **2** [u] (language) 罗马尼亚语 [Luómǎníyàyǔ]

Roman numeral N [c] 罗马数字 [Luómǎ Shùzì]

romantic [rə'mæntɪk] ADJ **1** [+ person] 浪漫的 [làngmàn de] **2** (connected with love) [+ play, story etc] 爱情的 [àiqíng de] **3** (charming, exciting) [+ setting, holiday, dinner etc] 浪漫的 [làngmàn de] **4** (naive, idealized) [+ view, idea] 理想主义的 [lǐxiǎng zhǔyì de]

rompers ['rɔmpəz] NPL 幼儿连衫裤 [yòu'ér liánshānkù]

romper suit ['rɔmpə-] N [c] 幼儿连衫裤 [yòu'ér liánshānkù]

roof [ru:f] N [c] **1** [of building] 屋顶 [wūdǐng] **2** [of cave, mine, vehicle] 顶 [dǐng] ▶ **to go through the roof** (inf) [level, price +] 突飞猛涨 ▶ **to hit the roof** or **to go through the roof** (inf) (lose one's temper) 怒火冲天

roof rack (BRIT: AUT) N [c] 车顶架 [chēdǐng jià] [美= luggage rack]

rook [ruk] N [c] **1** (bird) 秃鼻乌鸦 [tūbí wūyā] **2** (CHESS) 车 [jū]

○ **room** [ru:m] I N **1** [c] (in house) 室 [shì] **2** [c] (also: bedroom) 卧室 [wòshì] **3** [u] (space) 空间 [kōngjiān] II vɪ ▶ **to room with sb** (ESP US) 和某人一起租住 [hé mǒurén yīqǐ zūzhù] ▶ **single/double room** 单人／双人间 ▶ **to make room for sb** 给某人让出地方

roommate ['ru:mmeɪt] N [c] 室友 [shìyǒu]

room service N [u] 客房送餐服务 [kèfáng sòngcān fúwù]

roomy ['ru:mɪ] ADJ 宽敞的 [kuānchǎng de]

rooster ['ru:stə(r)] (ESP US) N [c] 公鸡 [gōngjī] [英= **cock**]

root [ru:t] I N [c] **1** (BOT) 根 [gēn] **2** (MATH) 方根 [fānggēn] **3** [of hair, tooth] 根 [gēn] **4** [of problem, belief] 根源 [gēnyuán] II vɪ [plant +] 生根 [shēnggēn] III vT ▶ **to be rooted in** [ideas, attitudes +] 根源于 [gēnyuányú] IV **roots** NPL (family origins) 祖先 [zǔxiān] ▶ **to take root** [plant +] 生根 [shēnggēn]; [idea +] 扎根
▶ **root about** vɪ (fig) (search) 翻寻 [fānxún]
▶ **root for** vT FUS [不可拆分] (support) 给…加油 [gěi…jiāyóu]
▶ **root out** vT 不遗余力地寻找 [bù yí yú lì de xúnzhǎo]

rope [rəup] I N [c/u] 绳子 [shéngzi] II vT **1** (tie) 将…拴在 [jiāng…shuān zài] **2** (also: **rope together**) [+ climbers etc] 用绳捆绑 [yòng shéng kǔnbǎng] ▶ **to know the ropes** 掌握诀窍
▶ **rope in** vT (inf) [+ person] 说服…参加 [shuōfú…cānjiā]
▶ **rope off** vT [+ area] 用绳围起 [yòng shéng wéiqǐ]

rop(e)y ['rəupɪ] (BRIT: inf) ADJ 劣质的 [lièzhì de]

rosary ['rəuzərɪ] N [c] (beads) 念珠 [niànzhū]

rose [rəuz] I PT of **rise** II N [c] (flower) 玫瑰 [méigui] III ADJ (pink) 玫瑰色的 [méiguīsè de]

rosé ['rəuzeɪ] N [c/u] 玫瑰红葡萄酒 [méiguīhóng pútáojiǔ]

rosemary ['rəuzmərɪ] N [u] 迷迭香 [mídiéxiāng]

rosy ['rəuzɪ] ADJ **1** (pink) 红扑扑的 [hóngpūpū de] **2** [+ situation] 令人鼓舞的 [lìng rén gǔwǔ de] ▶ **a rosy future** 美好的未来

rot [rɔt] I N [u] **1** (decay) 腐烂 [fǔlàn] **2** (BRIT: inf, o.f.) (rubbish) 蠢话 [chǔnhuà] II vT (cause to decay) 使腐坏 [shǐ fǔhuài] III vɪ (decay) [teeth, wood, fruit etc +] 腐烂 [fǔlàn] ▶ **to stop the rot** (BRIT) 力挽狂澜
▶ **rot away** vɪ 朽烂 [xiǔlàn]

rota ['rəutə] N [c] 勤务轮值表 [qínwù lúnzhíbiǎo] ▶ **on a rota basis** 轮流当值

rotate [rəu'teɪt] I vT **1** (spin) 转动 [zhuàndòng] **2** (change round) [+ crops] 轮种 [lúnzhòng] II vɪ **1** (revolve) 旋转 [xuánzhuǎn] **2** (take turns) 轮换 [lúnhuàn]

rotating [rəu'teɪtɪŋ] ADJ **1** [+ movement] 旋转的 [xuánzhuǎn de] **2** [+ drum, mirror] 可旋转的 [kě xuánzhuǎn de]

rotation [rəu'teɪʃən] N 1 [c/u] [of planet, drum etc] 旋转 [xuánzhuǎn] 2 [u] [of crops] 轮种 [lúnzhòng] 3 [u] [of jobs] 轮流 [lúnliú] ▸ **in rotation** 轮流地

rotten ['rɒtn] ADJ 1 (decayed) [+food] 腐烂的 [fǔlàn de]; [+wood] 朽烂的 [xiǔlàn de]; [+teeth] 蛀烂的 [zhùlàn de] 2 (inf) (awful) 糟透的 [zāotòu de] ▸ **to feel rotten** (ill) (inf) 感觉不适

rouble, ruble ['ru:bl] N [c] 卢布 [lúbù]

rough [rʌf] I ADJ 1 [+skin, surface, cloth] 粗糙的 [cūcāo de] 2 [+terrain] 崎岖的 [qíqū de] 3 [+sea, crossing] 波涛汹涌的 [bōtāo xiōngyǒng de] 4 (violent) [+person] 粗鲁的 [cūlǔ de]; [+town, area] 治安混乱的 [zhì'ān hùnluàn de]; [+treatment, handling] 粗暴的 [cūbào de] 5 (hard) [+life, conditions, journey] 艰难的 [jiānnán de] 6 (approximate) [+outline, plan, idea] 粗略的 [cūlüè de]; [+sketch, drawing] 初步的 [chūbù de] II VT ▸ **to rough it** (inf) 将就着过 [jiāngjiuzhe guò] ▸ **to have a rough time** 处境艰难 ▸ **to sleep rough** (BRIT) [homeless person +] 露宿街头 ▸ **to feel rough** (BRIT: inf) 感觉不适

▸ **rough out** VT [+drawing] 勾勒 [gōulè]; [+idea, article] 拟出…的草案 [nǐchū…de cǎo'àn]

roughly ['rʌflɪ] ADV 1 (violently) [handle, grab, push etc +] 粗暴地 [cūbào de] 2 (aggressively) [speak +] 粗鲁地 [cūlǔ de] 3 [make, construct +] 粗糙地 [cūcāo de] 4 (approximate) 大约 [dàyuē] ▸ **roughly speaking** 粗略地说

roulette [ru:'lɛt] N [u] 轮盘赌 [lúnpándǔ]

round [raund] I ADJ 1 (circular) 圆的 [yuán de] 2 (spherical) 球形的 [qiúxíng de] 3 (approximate) [+figure, sum] 不计尾数的 [bù jì wěishù de] II N [c] 1 (journey) [of milkman, paper boy] (ESP BRIT) 投递路线 [tóudì lùxiàn]; [of doctor] 查房 [cháfáng] 2 (stage) (in competition) 一轮 [yī lún] 3 [of drinks] 一轮 [yī lún] 4 (GOLF) 一场 [yī chǎng] 5 [of ammunition] 一发 [yī fā] 7 [of talks] 一轮 [yī lún] III VT [+corner, bend] 绕过 [ràoguò] IV PREP 1 (surrounding) 围绕 [wéirào] 2 (near) 在…附近 [zài…fùjìn] 3 (on or from the other side of) 绕过 [ràoguò] 4 (indicating circular movement)

▸ **to move round the room/sail round the world** 绕房间一周/环球航行 [rào fángjiān yī zhōu/huánqiú hángxíng] ▸ **all round** 在…周围 ▸ **to go round** (rotate) 转动 ▸ **to go round (sth)** 绕过 (某物) ▸ **to get round sth** [+problem, difficulty] 绕过某事 ▸ **to go round to sb's (house)** 造访某人 (的家) ▸ **enough to go round** 够每个人分的 ▸ **to go round the back** 绕到背面 ▸ **to come/go the long way round** 绕远路来/去 ▸ **all (the) year round** 一年到头 ▸ **the wrong way round** 反了 ▸ **in round figures** 用约整数表示 ▸ **to ask sb round** 邀

请某人来家 ▸ **I'll be round at 6 o'clock** 我会在6点钟到你家 ▸ **round about** (ESP BRIT) (approximately) 大约 ▸ **round the clock** (inf) 连续24小时 ▸ **the daily round** (fig) 每天例行的公事 ▸ **a round of applause** 掌声雷动 ▸ **a round of toast/sandwiches** (BRIT) 一份土司/三明治

▸ **round down** VT 把…调低为整数 [bǎ…tiáodī wéi zhěngshù]

▸ **round off** VT 1 [+meal, evening etc] 圆满结束 [yuánmǎn jiéshù] 2 [+price, figure] 把…四舍五入 [bǎ…sìshě wǔrù]

▸ **round on** (BRIT) VT FUS [不可拆分] 责骂 [zémà] [美=**turn on**]

▸ **round up** VT 1 [+cattle, sheep] 驱拢 [qūlǒng] 2 [+people] 围捕 [wéibǔ] 3 [+price, figure] 把…调高为整数 [bǎ…tiáogāo wéi zhěngshù]

roundabout ['raundəbaut] I N [c] (BRIT) 1 (AUT) 环形交叉路 [huánxíng jiāochālù] [美=**traffic circle**] 2 (at funfair) 旋转木马 [xuánzhuǎn mùmǎ] 3 (in playground) 旋转盘 [xuánzhuǎnpán] II ADJ 1 [+route] 绕道的 [ràodào de] 2 [+way, means] 拐弯抹角的 [guǎiwān mò jiǎo de]

round trip I N [c] 往返旅行 [wǎngfǎn lǚxíng] II ADJ (US) 往返的 [wǎngfǎn de] [英=**return**]

roundup ['raundʌp] N [c] 1 [of news, information] 综述 [zōngshù] 2 [of criminals] 搜捕 [sōubǔ]

rouse [rauz] VT 1 (wake up) (frm) 叫醒 [jiàoxǐng] 2 (stir up) 使激动 [shǐ jīdòng] ▸ **to rouse o.s.** 醒来 ▸ **to rouse sb to anger** 激怒某人

route [ru:t] I N [c] 1 (path, journey) 路 [lù] 2 [of bus, train] 路线 [lùxiàn]; [of ship] 航线 [hángxiàn] 3 (means) 途径 [tújìng] II VT 按路线发送 [àn lùxiàn fāsòng] ▸ **"all routes"** (AUT) "所有车辆按路线行驶"

routine [ru:'ti:n] I ADJ 1 [+work, job] 常规的 [chángguī de]; [+check, inquiries] 例行的 [lìxíng de] II N 1 [c/u] (procedure) 例行公事 [lìxíng gōngshì] 2 [c/u] (drudgery) 日常琐事 [rìcháng suǒshì] 3 [c] (THEAT) 保留节目 [bǎoliú jiémù]

row¹ [rəu] I N [c] 1 (line) [of people, houses, etc] 一排 [yī pái] 2 [of seats in theatre, cinema] 一排 [yī pái] II VI (in boat) 划船 [huáchuán] III VT [+boat] 划 [huá] ▸ **in a row** 连续

row² [rau] I N 1 [s] (noise) (BRIT: inf) 吵闹声 [chǎonàoshēng] 2 [c] (noisy quarrel) 吵架 [chǎojià] 3 [c] (dispute) 争执 [zhēngzhí] II VI (argue) 争吵 [zhēngchǎo] ▸ **to have a row** 吵架

rowboat ['rəubəut] (US) N [c] 划艇 [huátǐng] [英=**rowing boat**]

rowing ['rəuɪŋ] (SPORT) N [u] 赛艇运动 [sàitǐng yùndòng]

rowing boat (BRIT) N [c] 划艇 [huátǐng] [美=**rowboat**]

royal ['rɔɪəl] ADJ 皇家的 [huángjiā de] ▸ **the**

royal family 王室

● **ROYAL FAMILY**

○ **royal family** (英国王室)以伊丽莎白女
○ 王二世为首。女王于1953年登基。她的
○ 丈夫是菲利普亲王，即爱丁堡公爵。
○ 他们育有四名成年子女：查尔斯王子、
○ 安妮公主、安德鲁王子和爱德华王子。
○ 查尔斯王子，即威尔士亲王是王位的
○ 继承人。他有两个孩子，威廉王子和哈
○ 利王子。他们的母亲是已故的威尔士王
○ 妃戴安娜。

Royal Air Force (BRIT) N ▸ **the Royal Air
Force** 皇家空军 [Huángjiā Kōngjūn]

royalty ['rɔɪəltɪ] I N [U] (royal persons) 王室成
员 [wángshì chéngyuán] II **royalties** NPL (to
author) 版税 [bǎnshuì]; (to inventor) 专利权使
用费 [zhuānlìquán shǐyòngfèi]

RRP (BRIT) N ABBR (= recommended retail price) 建
议零售价 [jiànyì língshòujià]

RSI (MED) N ABBR (= repetitive strain injury) 肢体
重复性劳损 [zhītǐ chóngfùxìng láosǔn]

RSVP ABBR (= répondez s'il vous plaît) 请赐复
[qǐng cìfù]

RU (TEXTING) ABBR = **are you**

rub [rʌb] VT (with hand, fingers) 揉 [róu]; (with
cloth, substance) 擦 [cā] ▸ **to rub sth with sth**
将某物涂抹在某物上 ▸ **to rub sth onto** or **into
sth** 用某物揉擦某物 ▸ **to rub one's hands
(together)** 搓手 ▸ **to rub sb up** or (US) **rub sb
the wrong way** (inf) 惹恼某人
▸ **rub down** VT [+ body] 擦干 [cāgān]; [+ horse]
擦刷干净 [cāshuā gānjìng]
▸ **rub in** VT [+ ointment] 将…揉搓进…
[jiāng…róucuō jìn…] ▸ **don't rub it in!** (inf) 别
老提了！
▸ **rub off** I VI [paint +] 被擦掉 [bèi cādiào]
II VT [+ paint, mark etc] 擦掉 [cādiào]
▸ **rub off on** (inf) VT FUS [不可拆分] 影响
[yǐngxiǎng]
▸ **rub out** VT (erase) 擦掉 [cādiào]

rubber ['rʌbə(r)] N 1 [U] (substance) 橡胶
[xiàngjiāo] 2 [C] (BRIT) 橡皮擦 [xiàngpícā]
[美=**eraser**] 3 [C] (US: inf) 安全套 [ānquántào]
[英=**condom**]

rubber band N [C] 橡皮筋 [xiàngpíjīn]

rubber boot (US) N [C] 橡胶长统靴 [xiàngjiāo
chángtǒngxuē] [英=**wellington**]

rubbish ['rʌbɪʃ] (BRIT) I N [U] 1 (refuse) 垃圾
[lājī] [美=**garbage, trash**] 2 (inferior material)
垃圾 [lājī] 3 (nonsense) 废话 [fèihuà] II ADJ
(BRIT: inf) ▸ **I'm rubbish at golf** 我高尔夫球打
得很糟糕 [wǒ gāo'ěrfūqiú dǎde hěn zāogāo]
III VT 贬低 [biǎndī] ▸ **rubbish!** 胡说！

rubbish bin (BRIT) N [C] 垃圾箱 [lājīxiāng]

rubbish dump (BRIT) N [C] 垃圾堆存处 [lājī

duīcúnchù]

rubble ['rʌbl] N [U] 碎石 [suìshí]

ruby ['ruːbɪ] I N [C] (gem) 红宝石 [hóngbǎoshí]
II ADJ (red) 深红色的 [shēnhóngsè de]

rucksack ['rʌksæk] N [C] 背包 [bèibāo]

rudder ['rʌdə(r)] N [C] 1 [of ship] 舵 [duò] 2 [of
plane] 方向舵 [fāngxiàngduò]

rude [ruːd] ADJ 1 [+ person, behaviour, remark] 无
礼的 [wúlǐ de] 2 (vulgar) [+ word, joke, noise] 粗
鄙的 [cūbǐ de] 3 (brutal) [+ shock, surprise] 突然
的 [tūrán de] 4 (crude) [+ table, shelter etc] 简陋
[jiǎnlòu] ▸ **to be rude to sb** 对某人无礼

rudely ['ruːdlɪ] ADV [interrupt, say, push +] 无礼
地 [wúlǐ de]

ruffle ['rʌfl] I VT 1 [+ hair] 抚弄 [fǔnòng]
2 [+ water] 吹皱 [chuīzhòu] 3 [bird +] [+ feathers]
竖起 [shùqǐ] 4 [+ person] 使心烦意乱 [shǐ
xīnfán yìluàn] II **ruffles** NPL 皱边 [zhòubiān]

rug [rʌg] N [C] 1 (carpet) 小地毯 [xiǎodìtǎn]
2 (BRIT) [blanket] 小毛毯 [xiǎomáotǎn]

rugby ['rʌgbɪ] N [U] (also: **rugby football**) 英式
橄榄球 [yīngshì gǎnlǎnqiú]

rugged ['rʌgɪd] ADJ 1 [+ man, features, face] 粗
野的 [cūyě de] 2 [+ piece of equipment] 结实的
[jiēshi de] 3 [+ landscape] 崎岖多岩的 [qíqū
duōyán de] 4 [+ determination, independence] 坚
强的 [jiānqiáng de] 5 [+ character] 坚忍的
[jiānrěn de]

ruin ['ruːɪn] I N 1 [U] (destruction) [of building] 毁
坏 [huǐhuài]; [of hopes, plans etc] 破灭 [pòmiè]
2 [U] (downfall) [of person] 落泊 [luòbó] 3 [U]
(bankruptcy) 破产 [pòchǎn] 4 [C] (old building)
废墟 [fèixū] II VT 1 (spoil) [+ clothes, carpet
etc] 毁坏 [huǐhuài]; [+ plans, prospects etc] 葬
送 [zàngsòng]; [+ eyesight, health] 损害 [sǔnhài]
2 (bankrupt) [+ person] 使破产 [shǐ pòchǎn]
III **ruins** NPL [of building, castle etc] 废墟 [fèixū]
▸ **to be in ruins** [building, town +] 破败不堪; [life,
plans etc +] 严重受损

● **rule** [ruːl] I N 1 [C] (regulation) 规则 [guīzé] 2 [S]
(norm) 惯例 [guànlì] 3 [C] [of language, science]
规则 [guīzé] 4 [U] (government) 统治 [tǒngzhì]
5 [C] (for measuring) 尺 [chǐ] II VT [+ country,
people] 统治 [tǒngzhì] III VI 1 [leader, monarch
etc +] 统治 [tǒngzhì] 2 (on subject) 作出裁决
[zuòchū cáijué] ▸ **to rule in favour of/against/
on** (LAW) 判定…/否决…/对…作出裁决 ▸ **to
rule that…** [umpire, judge etc +] 裁决… ▸ **it's
against the rules** 这是不合规定的 ▸ **as a rule
of thumb** 凭经验行事 ▸ **under British rule** 在
英国的统治下 ▸ **to bend the rules** 通融一下
▸ **to rule over** [+ country, people] 统治 某
人/某地 ▸ **as a rule** 通常
▸ **rule out** VT [+ idea, possibility etc] 排除
[páichú]; [+ situation, competition] 使成为不可能
[shǐ chéngwéi bù kěnéng] ▸ **murder cannot be
ruled out** 不排除他杀的可能性

ruler ['ruːlə(r)] N [C] 1 (for measuring) 直尺

[zhíchǐ] **2** (*sovereign*) 统治者 [tǒngzhìzhě]

ruling ['ruːlɪŋ] I ADJ [+ *party, body*] 执政的 [zhízhèng de] II N [U] (LAW) 裁决 [cáijué]
▸ **the ruling class** 统治阶级

rum [rʌm] N [U] 朗姆酒 [lǎngmǔjiǔ]

Rumania etc [ruːˈmeɪnɪə] N = **Romania** etc

rumble ['rʌmbl] I N [c] [*of thunder, traffic, guns*] 隆隆声 [lónglóngshēng] II VI [*stomach +*] 咕噜作响 [gūlū zuòxiǎng] **2** [*thunder, guns, traffic +*] 发隆隆声 [fā lónglóngshēng] **3** (*also:* **rumble along**) 隆隆地行进 [lónglóng de xíngjìn]

rummage ['rʌmɪdʒ] I N [U] 翻找 [fānzhǎo] II VI (*search*) 翻找 [fānzhǎo]

rumour, (US) **rumor** ['ruːmə(r)] I N [c/u] 谣言 [yáoyán] II VT ▸ **it is rumoured that...** 据谣传… [jù yáochuán…]

rump steak [rʌmp-] N [c/u] 后腿部牛排 [hòutuǐbù niúpái]

⊙ **run** [rʌn] (*pt* **ran**, *pp* **run**) I N [c] **1** (*as exercise, sport*) 跑步 [pǎobù] **2** (*in car*) 旅行 [lǚxíng] **3** (*regular journey*) [*of train, bus etc*] 路线 [lùxiàn] **4** (*series*) [*of victories, defeats etc*] 连续 [liánxù] **5** (CRICKET, BASEBALL) 跑动得分 [pǎodòng défēn] **6** (THEAT) 持续的演出 [chíxù de yǎnchū] **7** (*in tights, stockings*) 抽丝 [chōusī] II VT **1** [+ *race, distance*] 跑 [pǎo] **2** (*operate*) [+ *business, shop, country*] 经营 [jīngyíng]; [+ *competition, course*] 开办 [kāibàn]; [+ *country*] 治理 [zhìlǐ] **3** (*pass*) [+ *water, bath*] 流 [liú] [+ *hand, fingers*] 移动 [yídòng] **5** (*operate*) [+ *machine*] 使运转 [shǐ yùnzhuǎn] **6** (*perform*) [+ *program, test*] 进行 [jìnxíng]; (*own, maintain*) [+ *car, machine*] 使用 [shǐyòng] **7** (PUBLISHING) [+ *feature, article*] 刊登 [kāndēng] III VI **1** [*person, animal +*] 跑 [pǎo] **2** (*flee*) 逃跑 [táopǎo] **3** (*work*) [*machine +*] 运转 [yùnzhuǎn] **4** (*operate*) [*system, organization, etc +*] 运作 [yùnzuò] **5** [*bus, train +*] (*operate*) 行驶 [xíngshǐ] **6** (*continue*) [*play, show etc +*] 连续上演 [liánxù shàngyǎn]; [*contract +*] 有效 [yǒuxiào] **7** (*flow*) [*river, tears, nose +*] 流 [liú] **8** (US) (*in election*) 竞选 [jìngxuǎn] [英 = **stand**] **9** [*road, railway etc +*] 伸展 [shēnzhǎn] **10** [*colours, washing +*] 掉色 [diàosè] **11** (*in combination*) 变得 [biàndé] ▸ **to go for a run** (*as exercise*) 跑步锻炼 ▸ **to break into a run** 突然奔跑起来 ▸ **a run of good/bad luck** 接二连三的好运/厄运 ▸ **to have the run of sb's house** 被允许随意进出某人的住宅 ▸ **there was a run on...** [+ *meat, tickets*] 有…的需求 ▸ **in the long run** 终究 ▸ **in the short run** 从短期看 ▸ **on the run** [*fugitive +*] 逃跑 ▸ **I'll run you to the station** 我开车送你去车站 ▸ **to make a run for it** (*inf*) 试图迅速逃跑 ▸ **to run on** *or* **off petrol/batteries** 以汽油/电池为能源 ▸ **to run for president** 竞选总统 ▸ **to run dry** [*well etc +*] 干涸 ▸ **tempers were running high** 情绪变得激动起来 ▸ **unemployment is running at 20 per cent** 失业率为20% ▸ **it runs**

in the family 这是家族遗传 ▸ **to be run off one's feet** (BRIT) 忙碌不堪

▸ **run across** VT FUS [不可拆分] (*find*) 不期而遇 [bù qī ér yù]

▸ **run after** VT FUS [不可拆分] (*chase*) 追赶 [zhuīgǎn]

▸ **run away** VI (*from home, situation*) 出走 [chūzǒu]

▸ **run away with** VT FUS [不可拆分] 不受…控制 [bù shòu…kòngzhì]

▸ **run by** VT ▸ **to run sth by sb** (*inf*) 看某人对某事的反应 [kàn mǒurén duì mǒushì de fǎnyìng]

▸ **run down** I VT **1** (ESP BRIT) [+ *production, factory*] 逐渐停止 [zhújiàn tíngzhǐ] **2** (AUT) [+ *person*] 撞伤 [zhuàngshāng] **3** (*criticize*) 诋毁 [dǐhuǐ] II VI [*battery +*] 耗尽 [hàojìn] ▸ **to be run down** [*person +*] (*tired*) 筋疲力尽

▸ **run in** (BRIT) VT [+ *car*] 小心试用 [xiǎoxīn shìyòng]

▸ **run into** VT FUS [不可拆分] **1** (*meet*) [+ *person*] 偶然碰见 [ǒurán pèngjiàn]; [+ *trouble, problems*] 遭遇 [zāoyù] **2** (*collide with*) 撞上 [zhuàngshang] ▸ **to run into debt** 陷入债务 ▸ **their losses ran into millions** 他们的损失达到数百万

▸ **run off** I VI **1** [*person, animal +*] 跑掉 [pǎodiào] **2** (*with sb*) 私奔 [sībēn] II VT **1** [+ *liquid*] 使流掉 [shǐ liúdiào] **2** [+ *copies*] 复印一下 [fùyìn yī xià]

▸ **run out** VI **1** [*time, money, luck +*] 用完 [yòngwán] ▷ **Time is running out.** 快没时间了。 **2** [*lease, passport +*] 到期 [dàoqī]

▸ **run out of** VT FUS [不可拆分] 耗尽 [hàojìn]

▸ **run over** I VT (AUT) [+ *person*] 撞倒 [zhuàngdǎo] II VT FUS [不可拆分] (*repeat*) 再来一遍 [zài lái yī biàn] III VI [*bath, sink, water +*] 溢出 [yìchū]

▸ **run through** VT FUS [不可拆分] **1** [+ *instructions*] 扫视 [sǎoshì] **2** (*rehearse*) [+ *scene, lines*] 排练 [páiliàn]

▸ **run up** VT [+ *debt*] 积欠 [jīqiàn]

▸ **run up against** VT FUS [不可拆分] [+ *difficulties*] 遇到 [yùdào]

runaway ['rʌnəweɪ] I ADJ [+ *truck, train*] 失控的 [shīkòng de]; [+ *horse*] 脱缰的 [tuōjiāng de]; [+ *inflation, success*] 势不可挡的 [shì bù kě dǎng de] II N [c] (*child*) 离家出走者 [líjiā chūzǒuzhě]

rung [rʌŋ] I PP *of* **ring** II N [c] **1** [*of ladder*] 横档 [héngdàng] **2** (*in organization*) 级别 [jíbié]

runner ['rʌnə(r)] N [c] **1** (*in race*) (*person*) 赛跑者 [sàipǎozhě]; (*horse*) 赛马 [sàimǎ] **2** (*on sledge, etc*) 滑板 [huábǎn] **3** (*on drawer*) 滑槽 [huácáo] ▸ **drugs/gun runner** 毒品/枪支走私者

runner bean (BRIT) N [c] 红花菜豆 [hónghuācàidòu]

runner-up [rʌnərˈʌp] N [c] 亚军 [yàjūn]

running ['rʌnɪŋ] I N **1** [U] (*sport*) 赛跑 [sàipǎo] **2** [S] [*of business, organization*] 管理 [guǎnlǐ] **3** [S]

[of machine etc] 维修保养 [wéixiū bǎoyǎng]
II ADJ [+ water, stream] 流动的 [liúdòng de] ▶ to
be in the running for sth 有希望得到某物 ▶ to
be out of the running for sth 没有希望得到
某物 ▶ 6 days running 连续6天 ▶ to give a
running commentary on sth 对某事做连续报
导 ▶ to have a running battle with sb 和某人
不断争吵 ▶ a running total 累积总计 ▶ to be
up and running [system etc +] 运作正常

runny ['rʌnɪ] ADJ **1** [+ egg, butter] 流质的 [liúzhì
de] **2** [+ nose] 流鼻涕的 [liú bítì de]; [+ eyes] 流
泪的 [liú lèi de]

run-up ['rʌnʌp] N **1** ▶ the run-up to... [+ election
etc] …的前期 […de qiánqī] **2** [c] (before a jump)
助跑 [zhùpǎo]

runway ['rʌnweɪ] N [c] 跑道 [pǎodào]

rupture ['rʌptʃə(r)] **I** N [c] **1** (MED) 破裂 [pòliè]
2 (conflict) 决裂 [juéliè] **II** VT **1** [+ part of body]
使破裂 [shǐ pòliè] **2** [+ relations] 破坏 [pòhuài]
3 ▶ to rupture o.s. (MED) 发疝气 [fā shànqì]

rural ['ruərl] ADJ **1** [+ area, accent] 乡村的
[xiāngcūn de] **2** [+ economy, problems] 农村的
[nóngcūn de]

rush [rʌʃ] **I** N [s] (hurry) 匆忙 [cōngmáng]; [of
water, air] 冲 [chóng]; [of feeling, emotion] 突
发 [tūfā]; (sudden demand) ▶ a rush (on) 抢购
[qiǎnggòu] **II** VT (hurry) [+ lunch, job etc] 赶紧做
[gǎnjǐn zuò]; [+ person] (to hospital etc) 急速赶往
[jísù gǎnwǎng]; [+ supplies, order] (to person, place)
急速发送 [jísù fāsòng] **III** VI **1** [person +] 急速
前往 [jísù qiánwǎng] ▷ Russian banks rushed to
buy as many dollars as they could. 俄国银行赶紧买

入尽可能多的美元。**2** [air, water +] 急泻 [jíxiè]
▶ don't rush me! 别催我！▶ to rush sth off
(send) 紧急发送某物 ▶ what's the rush? 什么
事那么急？▶ to be in a rush (to do sth) 仓促
(地做某事) ▶ to rush sb into doing sth 催促
某人做某事
▶ rush through VT [+ order, application] 赶紧处
理 [gǎnjǐn chǔlǐ]

rush hour N [c] 高峰时间 [gāofēng shíjiān]

Russia ['rʌʃə] N 俄罗斯 [Éluósī]

Russian ['rʌʃən] **I** ADJ 俄罗斯的 [Éluósī de]
II N **1** [c] (person) 俄罗斯人 [Éluósīrén] **2** [U]
(language) 俄语 [Éyǔ]

Russian Federation N ▶ the Russian
Federation 俄罗斯联邦 [Éluósī Liánbāng]

rust [rʌst] **I** N [U] 铁锈 [tiěxiù] **II** VI [iron, car
etc +] 生锈 [shēngxiù] **III** VT [+ iron, car etc] 使
生锈 [shǐ shēngxiù]

rusty ['rʌstɪ] ADJ **1** [+ surface, object] 生锈的
[shēngxiù de] **2** [+ skill] 荒疏的 [huāngshū de]

rutabaga [ru:tə'beɪgə] (US) N [c/U] 芜菁甘蓝
[wújīnggānlán] [英= swede]

ruthless ['ru:θlɪs] ADJ [+ person] 冷酷的 [lěngkù
de]; [+ determination, efficiency] 坚决的 [jiānjué
de]

RV (US) N ABBR (= recreational vehicle) 娱乐车
[yúlèchē]

Rwanda [ru'ændə] N 卢旺达 [Lúwàngdá]

Rwandan [ru'ændən] **I** ADJ 卢旺达的
[Lúwàngdá de] **II** N [c] (person) 卢旺达人
[Lúwàngdárén]

rye [raɪ] N [U] (cereal) 黑麦 [hēimài]

Ss

S¹, s [ɛs] N [C/U] **1** (letter) 英语的第十九个字母 **2** (US: SCOL) (satisfactory) 成绩 "满意" [chéngjì "mǎnyì"]

S² ABBR **1** (= south) 南方 [nánfāng] **2** (= small) 小的 [xiǎo de] **3** (pl **SS**) (= saint) 圣徒 [shèngtú]

Sabbath ['sæbəθ] N [C] 安息日 [ānxīrì]

sabotage ['sæbətɑːʒ] **I** N [U] (act) 蓄意破坏 [xùyì pòhuài] **II** VT [+ machine, bridge etc] 破坏 [pòhuài]; [+ plan, meeting, relationship etc] 毁 [huǐ] ▶ **an act of sabotage** 破坏行为

saccharin ['sækərɪn] N [U] 糖精 [tángjīng]

sachet ['sæʃeɪ] N [C] [of shampoo, sugar etc] 小袋 [xiǎodài]

sack [sæk] **I** N [C] (bag) 麻袋 [mádài] **II** VT **1** (dismiss) 解雇 [jiěgù] **2** (plunder) 洗劫 [xǐjié] ▶ **to get the sack** 被解雇 ▶ **to give sb the sack** 解雇某人 ▶ **to sack sb for sth/for doing sth** 因某事/做某事解雇某人

sacred ['seɪkrɪd] ADJ **1** (religious) [+ music, art] 宗教的 [zōngjiào de] ▷ sacred songs or music 圣歌或圣乐 **2** (holy) [+ animal, place, writings] 神圣的 [shénshèng de] **3** (fig) (sacrosanct) 神圣不可侵犯的 [shénshèng bùkě qīnfàn de]

sacrifice ['sækrɪfaɪs] **I** N **1** [C] (REL) [of animal, person] 献祭 [xiànjì] **2** [C/U] (fig) 牺牲 [xīshēng] **II** VT **1** (REL) [+ animal] 用⋯祭祀 [yòng⋯jìsì] **2** (forfeit) [+ health, career, human lives] 牺牲 [xīshēng] ▶ **to make sacrifices (for sb/sth)** (为某人/某事) 做出牺牲 ▶ **to sacrifice sth for sb/sth** 为某人/某事牺牲某物

sad [sæd] ADJ **1** (unhappy) 伤心的 [shāngxīn de] **2** (distressing) 令人悲伤的 [lìngrén bēishāng de] **3** (regrettable) 令人遗憾的 [lìngrén yíhàn de] **4** (inf) (pathetic) 可悲的 [kěbēi de] ▶ **to be sad about sth** 因某事难过 ▶ **I'm sad that...** ⋯使我伤心 ▶ **he was sad to see her go** 看着她走, 他很伤心 ▶ **it is sad that...** 很遗憾⋯

sadden ['sædn] VT [+ person] 使伤心 [shǐ shāngxīn] ▶ **I was saddened to learn of his death** 得知他去世令我很悲痛

saddle ['sædl] **I** N [C] (for horse) 马鞍 [mǎ'ān]; (on bike, motorbike) 车座 [chēzuò] **II** VT **1** (also: **saddle up**) 给⋯装鞍 [gěi⋯zhuāng'ān] **2** ▶ **to saddle sb with sth** 使某人承担某项责任 [shǐ mǒurén chéngdān mǒuxiàng zérèn] ▶ **in the saddle** (on horse) 骑着马; (in control) 掌权 ▶ **saddle up** VT 给⋯装鞍 [gěi⋯zhuāng'ān]

sadistic [sə'dɪstɪk] ADJ 施虐狂的 [shīnüè kuáng de]

sadly ['sædlɪ] ADV **1** (unhappily) 难过地 [nánguò de] **2** (unfortunately) 可惜地 [kěxī de] **3** (seriously) [+ mistaken, neglected] 完全地 [wánquán de] ▷ If you think I'm going to leave, you are sadly mistaken. 如果你以为我会离开, 你就完全错了。 ▶ **to be sadly lacking (in sth)** 丝毫没有(某物) ▶ **he will be sadly missed** 大家会很想他的

sadness ['sædnɪs] N [U] 悲痛 [bēitòng]

s.a.e. (BRIT) ABBR (= stamped addressed envelope) 贴有邮票并写好地址的信封 [tiēyǒu yóupiào bìng xiěhǎo dìzhǐ de xìnfēng] [美= SASE]

safari [sə'fɑːrɪ] N [C] 游猎 [yóuliè] ▶ **to go on safari** 去游猎

safe [seɪf] **I** ADJ **1** (not dangerous) 安全的 [ānquán de] **2** (out of danger) 脱险的 [tuōxiǎn de] **3** (secure) [+ place] 保险的 [bǎoxiǎn de] **4** (trouble-free) [+ journey, delivery] 无损的 [wúsǔn de] **5** (without risk) [+ option, action] 无风险的 [wú fēngxiǎn de] **6** (pej) (tame) 沉闷的 [chénmèn de] **II** N [C] 保险箱 [bǎoxiǎnxiāng] ▶ **safe from sth** 不受到某事的攻击 ▶ **safe and sound** 安然无恙 ▶ **safe journey!** 一路平安! ▶ **(just) to be on the safe side** 为谨慎起见 ▶ **it is safe to say that...** 可以有把握地说⋯ ▶ **in safe hands** 在可靠的人手中

safeguard ['seɪfgɑːd] **I** N [C] 保护措施 [bǎohù cuòshī] **II** VT 保护 [bǎohù]

safely ['seɪflɪ] ADV **1** (without harm) [drive, arrive etc +] 安全地 [ānquán de] **2** (securely) [lock up, hide +] 万无一失地 [wànwúyīshī de] **3** (reliably) ▶ **I can safely say/assume that...** 我可以有把握地说/认为⋯ [wǒ kěyǐ yǒu bǎwò de shuō/rènwéi⋯]

safe sex N [U] 安全性交 [ānquán xìngjiāo]

safety ['seɪftɪ] **I** N [U] **1** [of plane, roads, factory] 安全 [ānquán] **2** (wellbeing) [of person, crew] 平安 [píng'ān] **3** (harmful potential) [of object, substance] 安全性 [ānquánxìng] **4** (safe place) 安全场所

[ānquán chǎngsuǒ] II CPD [复合词] [+ features, measures] 安全 [ānquán]

safety pin N [C] 安全别针 [ānquán biézhēn]

saffron ['sæfrən] I N [U] (spice) 藏红花 [zànghóng huā] II ADJ (in colour) 橘黄的 [júhuáng de]

sag [sæg] VI 1 [bed, roof +] 下陷 [xiàxiàn]; [breasts, bottom +] 松弛而下垂 [sōngchí ér xiàchuí] 2 (fig) [spirits +] 萎靡不振 [wěimíbùzhèn]; [demand +] 下跌 [xiàdiē]

sage [seɪdʒ] I N 1 [U] (herb) 鼠尾草 [shǔwěicǎo] 2 [C] (liter) (wise man) 圣贤 [shèngxián] II ADJ (liter) 贤明的 [xiánmíng de]

Sagittarius [sædʒɪ'tɛərɪəs] N 1 [U] (sign) 人马座 [Rénmǎ Zuò] 2 [C] (person) 人马座的人 [Rénmǎ Zuò de rén] ▶ I'm (a) Sagittarius 我是人马座的

Sahara [sə'hɑːrə] N ▶ the Sahara (Desert) 撒哈拉(大沙漠) [Sāhālā (Dà Shāmò)]

said [sɛd] PT, PP OF **say**

sail [seɪl] I N [C] [of boat, yacht] 帆 [fān] II VT [+ boat, yacht] 驾驶 [jiàshǐ] III VI 1 (travel) [ship +] 航行 [hángxíng]; [sailor +] 扬帆行驶 [yángfān xíngshǐ]; [passenger +] 乘船航行 [chèngchuán hángxíng] 2 (begin voyage) 启航 [qǐháng] 3 (fly) ▶ to sail over/across/up to sth 飞过/飞越/上升到某处 [fēiguò/fēiyuè/ shàngshēng dào mǒuchù] ▶ to set sail 起航 ▶ to sail for or to set sail for 起航前往 ▶ to go sailing 去航行
▶ sail through VT FUS [不可拆分] [+ exams, interview etc] 顺利地通过 [shùnlì de tōngguò]

sailboat ['seɪlbəʊt] (US) N [C] 帆船 [fānchuán] [英 = sailing boat]

sailing ['seɪlɪŋ] N 1 [U] (SPORT) 帆船运动 [fānchuán yùndòng] 2 [C] (departure) 轮船航班 [lúnchuán hángbān] ▶ it wasn't all plain sailing 并不都是一帆风顺

sailing boat (BRIT) N [C] 帆船 [fānchuán] [美 = sailboat]

sailor ['seɪlə(r)] N [C] 水手 [shuǐshǒu]

saint [seɪnt] N [C] 1 (REL) 圣徒 [shèngtú] 2 (good person) 圣人 [shèngrén] ▶ he's no saint 他并不是十全十美

sake [seɪk] N ▶ for the sake of [+ health, career, person etc] 为了 [wèile] ▶ do it for my sake! 看在我的情份上做吧！ ▶ for its own sake 为此而已 ▶ he enjoys talking for talking's sake 他喜欢为了说话而说话 ▶ for argument's sake, for the sake of argument 为了便于讨论 ▶ for goodness or heaven's sake! (inf) 看在上帝分上

salad ['sæləd] N [C/U] 色拉 [sèlā] ▶ green/tomato salad 蔬菜/西红柿色拉 ▶ ham/chicken/cheese salad 火腿/鸡肉/干酪色拉 ▶ potato/pasta/rice salad 土豆/意大利粉/米饭色拉

salad cream (BRIT) N [U] 色拉酱 [sèlā jiàng]

salad dressing N [C/U] 色拉调味料 [sèlā tiáowèiliào]

salami [sə'lɑːmɪ] N [C/U] 萨拉米香肠 [sàlāmǐ xiāngcháng]

salary ['sælərɪ] N [C/U] 薪水 [xīnshuǐ] ▶ to be on a good/modest salary 拿高薪/适中的薪水

○ **sale** [seɪl] I N 1 [S] (selling) 出售 [chūshòu] ▷ new laws to control the sale of guns 控制枪支出售的新法律 2 [C] (with reductions) 贱卖 [jiànmài] 3 [C] (auction) 拍卖 [pāimài] ▷ a cattle sale 牛拍卖 II sales NPL 1 (quantity sold) 销售量 [xiāoshòuliàng] ▷ Car sales are down. 小汽车销售量有所下降。2 (department) 销售部 [xiāoshòubù] 3 ▶ the sales 降价期 [jiàngjià qī] 4 (in compounds) [+ campaign, drive, figures, target] 销售 [xiāoshòu]; [+ conference, meeting] 与销售有关的 [yǔ xiāoshòu yǒuguān de] ▶ to be (up) for sale 待售 ▶ to be on sale (BRIT) (available) 上市; (US) (reduced) 廉价出售 ▶ (on) sale or return 卖不出去可以退货 ▶ closing-down or (US) liquidation sale 清仓大甩卖

sales assistant (BRIT) N [C] 售货员 [shòuhuò yuán] [美 = sales clerk]

sales clerk (US) N [C] 售货员 [shòuhuò yuán] [英 = sales assistant]

salesman ['seɪlzmən] (pl salesmen) N [C] 1 (representative) 推销员 [tuīxiāo yuán] 2 (in shop, showroom) 售货员 [shòuhuò yuán]

salesperson ['seɪlzpəːsn] (pl salespeople) N [C] 1 (representative) 推销员 [tuīxiāo yuán] 2 (in shop, showroom) 售货员 [shòuhuò yuán]

sales rep N [C] 推销员 [tuīxiāo yuán]

saleswoman ['seɪlzwʊmən] (pl saleswomen) N [C] 1 (representative) 女推销员 [nǔ tuīxiāo yuán] 2 (in shop, showroom) 女售货员 [nǔ shòuhuò yuán]

saline ['seɪlaɪn] I ADJ [+ water, solution] 含盐的 [hányán de] II N [U] 生理盐水 [shēnglǐ yánshuǐ]

saliva [sə'laɪvə] N [U] 唾液 [tuòyè]

salmon ['sæmən] (pl salmon) N [C/U] 大马哈鱼 [dà mǎhā yú] ▶ smoked salmon 熏制的大马哈鱼

salon ['sælɔn] N [C] 1 (also: hairdressing salon) 美发廊 [měifà láng] 2 (also: beauty salon) 美容院 [měiróngyuàn]

saloon [sə'luːn] N [C] 1 (US) (bar) 酒吧 [jiǔbā]; (BRIT: o.f.) (lounge bar) (also: saloon bar) 雅座酒吧 [yǎzuò jiǔbā] 2 (BRIT: AUT) 可容纳4至7位乘客的轿车 [美 = sedan]

salt [sɔːlt] I N [U] 盐 [yán] II VT 1 (flavour) 加盐于 [jiāyán yú] 2 (preserve) 用盐腌 [yòng yán yān] III CPD [复合词] [+ lake, deposits] 盐 [yán] ▶ to take sth with a pinch or grain of salt 对某事半信半疑 ▶ the salt of the earth 社会中坚分子 ▶ worth one's salt 称职

salt cellar (BRIT) N [C] 盐瓶 [yánpíng] [美 = salt shaker]

salt shaker [-'ʃeɪkə(r)] (US) N [c] 盐瓶 [yánpíng] [英 = **salt cellar**]

saltwater ['sɔːltˈwɔːtə(r)] ADJ [+ fish, lake] 咸水 的 [xiánshuǐ de]

salty ['sɔːltɪ] ADJ [+ food] 咸的 [xián de]; [+ air] 有海洋气息的 [yǒu hǎiyáng qìxī de]

salute [sə'luːt] I N [c] **1** (with hand) 敬礼 [jìnglǐ] **2** (with guns) 礼炮 [lǐpào] **3** (in greeting) 致意 [zhìyì] **4** (expressing admiration) ▶ **a salute to** 向⋯的致敬 [xiàng⋯de zhìjìng] II VT **1** [+ officer, flag] 向⋯行军礼 [xiàng⋯xíng jūnlǐ] **2** (praise) 祝贺 [zhùhè] III VI (with hand) 行礼 [xínglǐ] ▶ **to salute sb for sth** (fig) 因某事对某人表示赞赏

salvage ['sælvɪdʒ] I N [U] **1** (saving) 抢救 [qiǎngjiù] **2** (things saved) 抢救出的财物 [qiǎngjiù chū de cáiwù] II VT (from ship, building) 抢救 [qiǎngjiù]; [+ pride, reputation] 挽救 [wǎnjiù] ▶ **to salvage sth (from sth)** (从某事中)挽回某物

salvation [sæl'veɪʃən] N [U] **1** (REL) 拯救 [zhěngjiù] **2** (fig) [of person, institution] 救星 [jiùxīng] ▶ **to be beyond salvation** 无可救药

Salvation Army N ▶ **the Salvation Army** 救世军 [Jiùshìjūn]

⊛ **same** [seɪm] I ADJ **1** (similar) [+ size, colour, age etc] 相同的 [xiāngtóng de] ▷ He and Tom were the same age. 他和汤姆年龄相同。 **2** (very same) [+ place, person, time etc] 同一个的 [tóngyīgè de] ▷ We stay in the same hotel every year. 我们每年总是住在同一个旅馆。 **3** (aforementioned) 上述的 [shàngshù de] ▷ I had the same experience myself. 我自己也有上述的经历。 II PRON ▶ **the same 1** (similar) 一样 [yīyàng] ▷ The houses were all the same. 房子都一样。 **2** (unchanged) 一成不变的状况 [yīchéngbùbiàn de zhuàngkuàng] ▷ Nothing ever stays the same. 事情不可能是一成不变的。 **3** (also: **the same thing**) 同样 [tóngyàng] ▷ We like him very much and he says the same about us. 我们很喜欢他，他说他也同样喜欢我们。 ▶ **the same as** 与⋯一样 ▶ **the same book/place as** 与⋯一样的书/地方 ▶ **on the same day** 在同一天 ▶ **at the same time** (simultaneously) 同时 ▷ They started moving at the same time. 他们同时开始移动。; (paradoxically) 同时 ▷ They want to stay but at the same time they want to go. 他们想留下，但同时又想走。; (notwithstanding) 尽管如此 ▷ At the same time, I'd like to be sure it's true. 尽管如此，我还是想证实它的真实性。 ▶ **all** or **just the same** 仍然 ▶ **to do the same (as sb)** 也(像某人)那么做 ▶ **(the) same to you!** (after greeting) 祝你也一样！; (after insult) 你也是！ ▶ **same here!** (inf) 我也一样！ ▶ **they're one and the same** 他们完全一样 ▶ **(the) same again** 同样的再来一份 ▷ "Do you want some tea?" – "No, but thanks all the same." "你要茶吗？" "不，但还是要谢谢。"

sample ['sɑːmpl] I N [c] [of work, merchandise] 样品 [yàngpǐn]; (MED) [of blood, urine] 采样 [cǎiyàng]; [of people, things] 抽样 [chōuyàng] II VT [+ food, wine] 品尝 [pǐncháng]; [+ place, situation, way of life] 体验 [tǐyàn] ▶ **free sample** 免费赠样

sanction ['sæŋkʃən] I N **1** [c] (punishment) 制裁 [zhìcái] **2** [U] (approval) 批准 [pīzhǔn] II VT (give approval to) 批准 [pīzhǔn] III **sanctions** N PL (POL) 国际制裁 [guójì zhìcái] ▶ **sanctions against** 对⋯的制裁 ▶ **to impose sanctions (on** or **against)** (对⋯)实施制裁

sanctuary ['sæŋktjuərɪ] N **1** [c] (for birds, animals) 禁猎区 [jìnlièqū] **2** [c] (place of safety) 避难所 [bìnànsuǒ] **3** [U] (safety) 避难 [bìnàn]

sand [sænd] I N [U] 沙子 [shāzi] II VT (also: **sand down**) 打磨 [dǎmó] III **sands** N PL (beach) 沙滩 [shātān]

▶ **sand down** VT 打磨 [dǎmó]

sandal ['sændl] N [c] 凉鞋 [liángxié]

sandbox ['sændbɒks] (US) N [c] (for children) 沙坑 [shākēng] [英 = **sandpit**]

sand castle N [c] 沙堡 [shābǎo]

sand dune N [c] 沙丘 [shāqiū]

sandpaper ['sændpeɪpə(r)] N [U] 砂纸 [shāzhǐ]

sandpit ['sændpɪt] (BRIT) N [c] (for children) 沙坑 [shākēng] [美 = **sandbox**]

sandstone ['sændstəun] I N [U] 砂岩 [shāyán] II CPD [复合词] [+ building, wall, cliff] 砂岩质 [shāyán zhì]

sandwich ['sændwɪtʃ] I N [c] 三明治 [sānmíngzhì] II VT ▶ **to be sandwiched between** 被夹在⋯之间 [bèi jiázài⋯zhījiān] ▶ **a cheese/ham/jam sandwich** 奶酪/火腿/果酱三明治

sandy ['sændɪ] ADJ **1** [+ beach] 覆盖着沙的 [fùgài zhe shā de] **2** (in colour) [+ hair] 沙色的 [shāsè de]

sane [seɪn] ADJ **1** (not crazy) 神志正常的 [shénzhì zhèngcháng de] **2** (reasonable) [+ action, policy, idea] 明智的 [míngzhì de]

sang [sæŋ] PT of **sing**

sanitary napkin ['sænɪtərɪ-] (US) N [c] 卫生巾 [wèishēng jīn] [英 = **sanitary towel**]

sanitary towel (BRIT) N [c] 卫生巾 [wèishēng jīn] [美 = **sanitary napkin**]

sanity ['sænɪtɪ] N [U] **1** (mental health) 精神健全 [jīngshén jiànquán] **2** (sense) 明智 [míngzhì]

sank [sæŋk] PT of **sink**

Santa (Claus) ['sæntə('klɔːz)] N 圣诞老人 [Shèngdàn Lǎorén]

sap [sæp] I N [U] [of plants] 汁 [zhī] II VT ▶ **to sap sb's strength/confidence** 使某人筋疲力尽/挫伤某人的自信心 [shǐ mǒurén jīnpí lìjìn/cuòshāng mǒurén de zìxìnxīn]

sapphire ['sæfaɪə(r)] N [c/U] 蓝宝石 [lán bǎoshí]

sarcasm ['sɑːkæzm] N [U] 讽刺 [fěngcì]

sarcastic [sɑː'kæstɪk] ADJ [+person] 尖刻的 [jiānkè de]; [+remark] 讽刺的 [fěngcì de]

sardine [sɑː'diːn] N [C] 沙丁鱼 [shādīng yú]

SARS [sɑːz] N ABBR (= severe acute respiratory syndrome) 非典型性肺炎 [fēi diǎnxíngxìng fèiyán]

SASE (US) N ABBR (= self-addressed stamped envelope) 贴足邮资写明发信人自己的姓名地址的回信信封 [tiēzú yóuzī xiěmíng fāxìn rén zìjǐ de xìngmíng dìzhǐ de huíxìn xìnfēng] [英 = s.a.e.]

sash [sæʃ] N [C] **1** (around waist) 腰带 [yāodài]; (over shoulder) 肩带 [jiāndài] **2** [of window] 窗框 [chuāngkuàng]

SAT N ABBR **1** (US) (= Scholastic Aptitude Test) 学业能力倾向测试 [Xuéyè Nénglì Qīngxiàng Cèshì] **2** (BRIT) (= Standard Assessment Task) 小学标准评估 [Xiǎoxué Biāozhǔn Pínggū]

sat [sæt] PT, PP of **sit**

Sat. ABBR (= Saturday) 星期六 [xīngqīliù]

satchel ['sætʃl] N [C] 书包 [shūbāo]

satellite ['sætəlaɪt] N **1** [C] (for communications) 人造卫星 [rénzào wèixīng] **2** [U] (also: satellite television) 卫星电视 [wèixīng diànshì] **3** [C] (ASTRON) (moon) 卫星 [wèixīng] **4** [C] (POL) (also: satellite state) 卫星国 [wèixīng guó] ▸ on satellite 在卫星电视上

satellite dish N [C] 圆盘式卫星电视接收器 [yuánpánshì wèixīng diànshì jiēshōuqì]

satellite television N [U] 卫星电视 [wèixīng diànshì]

satin ['sætɪn] I N [U] 缎子 [duànzi] II CPD [复合词] [+ribbon, dress] 缎子 [duànzi] ▸ with a satin finish 有缎子光泽

satire ['sætaɪə(r)] N **1** [U] (humour) 讽刺 [fěngcì] **2** [C] (novel, play) 讽刺作品 [fěngcì zuòpǐn]

satisfaction [sætɪs'fækʃən] N [U] **1** (contentment) 满足感 [mǎnzú gǎn] **2** (for wrong, injustice) ▸ to get satisfaction (from sb) (从某人那里)得到赔偿 [(cóng mǒurén nàlǐ) dédào péicháng] ▸ satisfaction with 对⋯的满意 ▸ has it been done to your satisfaction? 您对此满意吗?

satisfactory [sætɪs'fæktərɪ] ADJ 令人满意的 [lìngrén mǎnyì de] ▸ in a satisfactory condition (MED) 病情稳定

satisfied ['sætɪsfaɪd] ADJ **1** (pleased) 满足的 [mǎnzú de] **2** (convinced) 确信的 [quèxìn de] ▸ to be satisfied with sth (pleased) 对某事满意 ▸ to be satisfied that... 确信⋯

satisfy ['sætɪsfaɪ] VT **1** (please) [+person] 使满足 [shǐ mǎnzú] **2** [+curiosity] 满足 [mǎnzú] **3** [+demand] 满足 [mǎnzú]; [+requirements, conditions] 符合 [fúhé] **4** (convince) ▸ to satisfy sb that... 使人相信⋯ [shǐrén xiāngxìn⋯] ▸ to satisfy o.s. that... 使自己确信⋯

satisfying ['sætɪsfaɪɪŋ] ADJ [+task] 令人满意的 [lìngrén mǎnyì de]; [+meal] 令人心满意足的

[lìngrén xīnmǎn yìzú de]

Saturday ['sætədɪ] N [C/U] 星期六 [xīngqīliù] see also **Tuesday**

sauce [sɔːs] N [C/U] (savoury) 酱 [jiàng]; (sweet) 汁 [zhī]

saucepan ['sɔːspən] N [C] 深平底锅 [shēn píngdǐ guō]

saucer ['sɔːsə(r)] N [C] 茶杯碟 [chábēi dié]

Saudi ['saudɪ] I ADJ (also: Saudi Arabian) 沙特阿拉伯的 [Shātè Ālābó de] II N [C] (person) (also: Saudi Arabian) 沙特阿拉伯人 [Shātè Ālābórén]

Saudi Arabia [saudɪə'reɪbɪə] N 沙特阿拉伯 [Shātè Ālābó]

sauna ['sɔːnə] N [C] **1** (act) 桑拿浴 [sāngná yù] **2** (room) 桑拿浴室 [sāngná yùshì] ▸ to have a sauna 洗桑拿

sausage ['sɔsɪdʒ] N [C/U] 香肠 [xiāngcháng]

sausage roll (BRIT) N [C] 香肠卷 [xiāngcháng juǎn]

sauté ['səuteɪ] I VT 快炒 [kuàizhá] II ADJ (also: sautéed) [+potatoes, mushrooms] 炸的 [zhá de]

savage ['sævɪdʒ] I ADJ [+animal] 凶猛的 [xiōngměng de]; [+attack] 恶毒的 [èdú de] II N [C] (o.f., pej) 野蛮人 [yěmán rén] III VT **1** (maul) 凶猛地攻击 [xiōngměngde gōngjī] **2** (criticize) 猛烈抨击 [měngliè pēngjī] ▸ he was savaged to death 他被残害致死

save [seɪv] VT **1** (rescue) [+person] 救 [jiù] **2** (preserve) [+job, marriage, environment] 保全 [bǎoquán] **3** (put by) [+money] 积攒 [jīzǎn] **4** (economize on) [+money, time] 节省 [jiéshěng] **5** (keep) [+receipts etc] 保存 [bǎocún]; [+food, drink etc] 留着 [liuzhe]; [+seat] 保留 [bǎoliú] **6** (COMPUT) 存储 [cúnchǔ] **7** (SPORT) 救球 [jiùqiú] II VI (also: save up) 积攒 [jīzǎn] III N [C] 救球 [jiùqiú] IV PREP (frm) (also: save for) 除⋯外 [chú⋯wài] ▸ to save sb from sth 挽救某人免于某事 ▸ to save sb's life 挽救某人的生命 ▸ to save (up) for sth 为某物储蓄 ▸ to save sb/o.s. some work/time/expense 对某人/自己来说省事/节省时间/节省开支 ▸ to save sth for sth 为某事留某物 ▸ to save sb from doing sth 使某人免于做某事 ▸ God save the Queen! 上帝保佑女王! ▸ to make a save (SPORT) 救球 ▸ save up VI 积攒 [jīzǎn]

saving ['seɪvɪŋ] I N [C] [of time, money] 节约 [jiéyuē] II **savings** NPL (money) 存款 [cúnkuǎn] ▸ to make a saving (on sth) (在某物上)节省

savings account N [C] 储蓄账户 [chǔxù zhànghù]

savings and loan association (US) N [C] 房屋储蓄借贷联合会 [fángwū chǔxù liánhéhuì] [英 = building society]

saviour, (US) **savior** ['seɪvjə(r)] N [C] **1** 救星

[jiùxīng] **2 ▶ the Saviour** 救世主 [Jiùshìzhǔ]

savoury, (US) **savory** ['seɪvərɪ] I ADJ [+ *food, dish*] 咸辣的 [xiánlà de] II **savouries** NPL (BRIT) 小吃 [xiǎochī]

saw [sɔː] (*pt* **sawed**, *pp* **sawed** *or* **sawn**) I PT *of* **see** II VT 锯 [jù] III VI **▶ to saw through sth** 锯断某物 [jùduàn mǒuwù] IV N [C] 锯子 [jùzi] **▶ to saw sth in half** 将某物锯成两半 **▶ saw up** VT 把…锯成小块 [bǎ…jùchéng xiǎokuài]

sawdust ['sɔːdʌst] N [U] 锯末 [jùmò]

sawn [sɔːn] PP *of* **saw**

sax [sæks] (*inf*) N [C] 萨克斯管 [sàkèsī guǎn]

saxophone ['sæksəfəun] N [C] 萨克斯管 [sàkèsī guǎn]

○ **say** [seɪ] (*pt, pp* **said**) I VT **1** (*utter*) 说 [shuō] ▷ *I couldn't understand what they were saying.* 我不明白他们在说什么。**2** (*indicate*) [*clock, watch, barometer +*] 表明 [biǎomíng] ▷ *My watch says 3 o'clock.* 我的手表3点了。; [*sign +*] 写着 [xiězhe] II N **▶ to have one's say** 表达个人的意见 [biǎodá gèrén de yìjiàn] **▶ to say that...** (*in speech*) 说… ▷ *He said that he'd broken his arm.* 他说他的手臂断了。▷ *She said that I was to give you this.* 她叫我把这个给你。; (*in writing*) [*person +*] 说…; [*book, article +*] 写明… **▶ to say sth to sb** 告诉某人某事 **▶ to say sth to o.s.** 暗自思量某事 **▶ to say yes/no** 同意/不同意 **▶ to say goodbye/sorry (to sb)** (向某人)告别/道歉 **▶ when all is said and done** 归根结底 **▶ there is something/a lot to be said for it** 有一些/很多优点 **▶ it says something/a lot about her state of mind** 这在某种/很大程度上显露了她的想法 **▶ you can say that again!** (*inf*) 我太同意你说的了! **▶ that is to say** 就是说 **▶ that goes without saying** 那自不消说 ▷ *I can't say I'm sorry* 我并不感到内疚 **▶ I must say that...** 依我看… **▶ to say nothing of** 更不用说 **▶ that says it all** 不言自明 **▶ say that...** (*suppose*) 假设… ▷ *Say you won a million pounds.* 假设你赢了100万英镑。**▶ come for dinner at, say, 8 o'clock** 来吃晚饭吧, 比定8点吧 **▶ shall we say Tuesday?** 星期二好吗? **▶ to have a** *or* **some say in sth** 对某事有发言权

saying ['seɪɪŋ] N [C] 格言 [géyán]

scab [skæb] N [C] **1** (*on wound*) 痂 [jiā] **2** (*inf, pej*) (*strike-breaker*) 工贼 [gōngzéi]

scaffolding ['skæfəldɪŋ] N [U] 脚手架 [jiǎoshǒu jià]

scald [skɔːld] I VT 烫伤 [tàngshāng] II N [C] 烫伤 [tàngshāng] **▶ to scald o.s.** 烫伤自己

scale [skeɪl] I N **1** [C] (*size, extent*) 规模 [guīmó] **2** [C] (*measuring system*) (*for temperature etc*) 刻度 [kèdù] **3** [C] (BRIT) [*of salaries, fees etc*] 级别 [jíbié] **4** [C] [*of map, model*] 比例 [bǐlì] **5** [C] (MUS) 音阶 [yīnjiē] **6** [C] [*of fish, reptile*] 鳞 [lín] II CPD [复合词] [+ *model, drawing*] 按比例制作的 [àn bǐlì zhìzuò de] III VT (*climb*) 攀登

[pāndēng] IV **scales** NPL (*for weighing*) (*also:* **bathroom scales, kitchen scales**) 秤 [chèng] (*for heavier things*) 磅秤 [bàngchèng] **▶ a pair** *or* **set of scales** 一架天平 **▶ on a scale of 1 to 10** 从1到10各等级地 **▶ to scale** 按比例 **▶ on a large/small scale** 以大/小规模 **▶ scale down** VT 相应缩减 [xiāngyìng suōjiǎn]

scallion ['skæljən] (US: CULIN, BOT) N [C] 葱 [cōng] [英 = **spring onion**]

scallop ['skɒləp] N [C] (*shellfish*) 扇贝 [shànbèi]

scalp [skælp] I N [C] 头皮 [tóupí] II VT 削下…的头皮 [xuēxià…de tóupí]

scalpel ['skælpl] N [C] (*for surgery*) 手术刀 [shǒushù dāo]; (*for artwork*) 雕刻刀 [diāokè dāo]

scam [skæm] (*inf*) N [C] 骗局 [piànjú]

scampi ['skæmpɪ] (BRIT) NPL 大虾 [dàxiā]

scan [skæn] I VT **1** (*examine closely*) [+ *area, room, horizon, group*] 仔细察看 [zǐxì chákàn] **2** (*glance quickly over*) [+ *newspaper, article, page*] 浏览 [liúlǎn] **3** [*radar +*] 扫描 [sǎomiáo] **4** (COMPUT) [+ *document, picture*] 扫描 [sǎomiáo] **5** (*with x-ray, ultrasound etc*) [+ *luggage*] 查验 [cháyàn]; (MED) 扫描检查 [sǎomiáo jiǎnchá] II VI [*poem +*] 符合格律 [fúhé gélǜ] III N [C] (MED) 扫描检查 [sǎomiáo jiǎnchá]; (*of pregnant woman*) 超声波检查 [chāoshēngbō jiǎnchá] **▶ to scan sth into a computer** 将某物扫描入电脑

scandal ['skændl] N **1** [C] (*shocking event*) 丑闻 [chǒuwén] **2** [U] (*gossip*) 流言飞语 [liúyán fēiyǔ] **3** [C] (*disgrace*) 耻辱 [chǐrǔ] **▶ it is a scandal that...** …真是个耻辱

Scandinavia [skændɪˈneɪvɪə] N 斯堪的纳维亚 [Sīkāndìˈnà wéiyà]

Scandinavian [skændɪˈneɪvɪən] I ADJ 斯堪的纳维亚的 [Sīkāndìˈnà wéiyà de] II N [C] (*person*) 斯堪的纳维亚人 [Sīkāndìˈnà wéiyàrén]

scanner ['skænə(r)] N [C] **1** (*in hospital*) 扫描器 [sǎomiáoqì] **2** (*for security*) 扫描检测装置 [sǎomiáo jiǎncè zhuāngzhì] **3** (COMPUT) 扫描仪 [sǎomiáo yí]

scapegoat ['skeɪpgəut] I N [C] 替罪羊 [tìzuì yáng] II VT **▶ to scapegoat sb (for sth)** 使某人(成为某事的)替罪羊 [shǐ mǒurén (chéngwéi mǒushì de) tìzuì yáng] **▶ to make sb a scapegoat (for sth)** 使某人成为(某事的)替罪羊

scar [skɑː] I N [C] **1** (*on skin*) 伤疤 [shāngbā] **2** (*mental, emotional*) 创伤 [chuàngshāng] II VT **1** (*skin*) 给…留下伤痕 [gěi…liúxià shānghén] **2** [+ *mind*] 给…留下创伤 [gěi…liúxià chuàngshāng] **3** [+ *place*] 在…留下痕迹 [zài…liúxià hénjì] **▶ to scar sb for life** (*physically*) 给某人留下终生的伤疤; (*emotionally*) 给某人留下终生的创伤

scarce [skeəs] ADJ 短缺的 [duǎnquē de] **▶ to make o.s. scarce** (*inf*) 溜走

scarcely ['skɛəslɪ] ADV **1** (barely) 几乎
不 [jīhūbù] **2** (certainly not) 决不 [juébù]
▶ **scarcely anybody** 几乎没人 ▶ **I can scarcely
believe it** 我简直不能相信 ▶ **scarcely had I
arrived when the phone rang** 我刚到电话就
响了

scare [skɛə(r)] **I** VT 使害怕 [shǐ hàipà] **II** N [C]
1 (fright) ▶ **to give sb/have a scare** 把某人吓了
一跳/吓了一跳 [bǎ mǒurén xiàle yītiào/xiàle
yītiào] **2** (public panic) 恐慌 [kǒnghuāng] ▶ **a
bomb/security scare** 炸弹/安全恐慌
▶ **scare away, scare off** VT **1** (+ intruder, visitor,
animal etc) 把…吓跑 [bǎ…xiàpǎo] **2** (put off)
(+ boyfriend, voter etc) 吓跑 [xiàpǎo]

scarecrow ['skɛəkrəʊ] N [C] 稻草人 [dàocǎo
rén]

scared ['skɛəd] ADJ **1** (frightened) ▶ **to be
scared (of sb/sth)** 害怕(某人/某物) [hàipà
(mǒurén/mǒuwù)] **2** (worried) ▶ **to be scared of
sth/that…** 担心某事/… [dānxīn mǒushì/…]
▶ **to be scared of doing sth** (frightened of) 害怕
做某事; (worried about) 担心做某事 ▶ **to be
scared to do sth** 害怕做某事 ▶ **to be scared
stiff** or **scared to death** 吓得要命

scarf [skɑːf] (pl **scarfs** or **scarves**) N [C] (long) 围
巾 [wéijīn]; (square) 头巾 [tóujīn]

scarlet ['skɑːlɪt] ADJ 鲜红的 [xiānhóng de]

scarves [skɑːvz] NPL of **scarf**

scary ['skɛərɪ] (inf) ADJ 令人害怕的 [lìngrén
hàipà de]

scatter ['skætə(r)] **I** VT **1** (drop) ▶ **to scatter
sth over/on sth** 将某物撒在某处 [jiāng
mǒuwù sǎzài mǒuchù] **2** (untidily) 乱放
[luànfàng] **3** (disperse) 驱散 [qūsàn] **II** VI 分
散 [fēnsàn]

scenario [sɪ'nɑːrɪəʊ] N [C] **1** (development) 局
面 [júmiàn] **2** (CINE, THEAT) 剧本提纲 [jùběn
tígāng]

scene [siːn] N [C] **1** (in play, film, book) 一场
[yīchǎng] **2** (of crime, accident) 现场 [xiànchǎng]
3 (picture) 景象 [jǐngxiàng] **4** (event) 场
面 [chǎngmiàn] **5** (inf) (fuss) 当众吵闹
[dāngzhòng chǎonào] ▶ **behind the scenes** 秘
密地 ▶ **to appear on the scene** 到场 ▶ **the
political scene** 政治舞台 ▶ **to set the scene for
sth** 为某事的发生做准备 ▶ **to make a scene**
(inf) (fuss) 大吵大闹

scenery ['siːnərɪ] N [U] **1** (landscape) 风景
[fēngjǐng] **2** (THEAT) 舞台布景 [wǔtái bùjǐng]

scenic ['siːnɪk] ADJ (+ location etc) 风景优美
的 [fēngjǐng yōuměi de] ▶ **to take the scenic
route** 走风景优美的那条路

scent [sɛnt] **I** N **1** [C] (of flowers, herbs etc) 香味
[xiāngwèi] **2** [C/U] (used for tracking) (of person,
animal) 气味 [qìwèi] **3** [C/U] (BRIT) (perfume) 香
水 [xiāngshuǐ] [美=perfume] **II** VT (catch
smell of) 嗅到 [xiùdào] ▶ **to put** or **throw sb off
the scent** 使某人失去线索

scented ['sɛntɪd] ADJ (+ flower, candle, soap etc)
芳香的 [fāngxiāng de]

sceptical, (US) **skeptical** ['skɛptɪkl] ADJ 怀疑
的 [huáiyí de] ▶ **to be sceptical about sth** 对某
事持怀疑态度

schedule ['ʃɛdjuːl, US 'skɛdjuːl] **I** N [C]
1 (agenda) 日程安排 [rìchéng ānpái] **2** (US) (of
trains, buses) 时间表 [shíjiān biǎo]
[英=timetable] **3** (list of prices, details etc) 清单
[qīngdān] ▶ **to be scheduled to do sth** 安
排做某事 [ānpái zuò mǒushì] ▶ **on schedule**
准时 ▶ **to be ahead of/behind schedule** 提前
/落后于计划 ▶ **we are working to a very tight
schedule** 我们的工作日程很紧 ▶ **everything
went according to schedule** 所有事情都按
预定计划进行了 ▶ **to be scheduled for next
week/2 o'clock** 被排在下星期/两点钟进行

scheduled flight ['ʃɛdjuːld-, US 'skɛdjuːld-]
N [C] 定期航班 [dìngqī hángbān]

scheme [skiːm] **I** N [C] **1** (ESP BRIT) 计划
[jìhuà] [美=program] **2** (plan) 方案 [fāng'àn]
II VI 图谋 [túmóu]

schizophrenic [skɪtsə'frɛnɪk] **I** ADJ 精神分
裂的 [jīngshén fēnliè de] **II** N [C] 精神分裂症
患者 [jīngshén fēnliè zhèng huànzhě]

scholar ['skɒlə(r)] N [C] (learned person) 学者
[xuézhě]

scholarship ['skɒləʃɪp] N **1** [C] (grant) 奖学
金 [jiǎngxué jīn] **2** [U] (knowledge) 学术成就
[xuéshù chéngjiù]

school [skuːl] **I** N **1** [C/U] (place) 学校
[xuéxiào]; (pupils and staff) 全体师生 ▷ The
whole school's going to hate you. 全体师生都会
恨你的。 **2** [U] (school time, experience) 上学
[shàngxué] **3** [C/U] (university department) 学
院 [xuéyuàn] ▷ the art school 艺术学院 **4** [C/U]
(US: university) (university) 大学 [dàxué] **5** [C] (specialist
academy) ▶ **riding/driving school** 骑术/驾驶学
校 [qíshù/jiàshǐ xuéxiào] **6** [C] (of fish, dolphins)
群 [qún] **II** CPD [复合词] (+ uniform, shoes, year)
学校的 [xuéxiào de] ▶ **to go to school** (child +)
上学; (US: university) 上大学 ▶ **to leave school**
(child +) 结束义务教育 ▶ **to be at law/medical
school** 攻读法律/医学 ▶ **to go to law/medical
school** 上法/医学院

school book N [C] 教科书 [jiàokēshū]

schoolboy ['skuːlbɔɪ] N [C] 男生 [nánshēng]

schoolchildren ['skuːltʃɪldrən] NPL 学童
[xuétóng]

schoolgirl ['skuːlgəːl] N [C] 女生 [nǚshēng]

schooling ['skuːlɪŋ] N [U] 学校教育 [xuéxiào
jiàoyù]

schoolteacher ['skuːltiːtʃə(r)] N [C] 教师
[jiàoshī]

science ['saɪəns] N **1** [U] (scientific study) 科学
[kēxué] **2** [C/U] (branch of science, school subject)
学科 [xuékē] ▶ **the sciences** 理科

science fiction N [U] 科幻小说 [kēhuàn

xiǎoshuō]

scientific [saɪən'tɪfɪk] ADJ **1** (*relating to science*) 科学的 [kēxué de] **2** (*methodical*) 符合科学定律的 [fúhé kēxué dìnglǜ de]

scientist ['saɪəntɪst] N [c] 科学家 [kēxué jiā]

sci-¹ ['saɪfaɪ] N ABBR (= *science fiction*) 科幻小说 [kēhuàn xiǎoshuō]

scissors ['sɪzəz] NPL 剪刀 [jiǎndāo] ▶ **a pair of scissors** 一把剪刀

scold [skəʊld] VT 责骂 [zémà]

scone [skɒn] (ESP BRIT) N [c] 烤饼 [kǎobǐng]

scoop [sku:p] I N [c] **1** (*implement*) 球形勺 [qiúxíng sháo] **2** (*portion*) ▶ **a scoop (of sth)** 一勺(的某物) [yīsháo (de mǒuwù)] **3** (PUBLISHING) 独家新闻 [dújiā xīnwén] II VT **1** (*lift*) ▶ **to scoop sb/sth into one's arms** 把某人/某物揽在怀里 [bǎ mǒurén/mǒuwù lǎnzài huáilǐ] **2** (*with spoon, hands*) ▶ **to scoop sth into sth** 把某物舀入某物中 [bǎ mǒuwù yǎorù mǒuwù zhōng] **3** [+ *prize, award*] 赢得 [yíngdé]
▶ **scoop out** VT 舀出 [yǎochū]
▶ **scoop up** VT 捞起 [lāoqǐ]

scooter ['sku:tə(r)] N [c] **1** (*also:* **motor scooter**) 小型摩托车 [xiǎoxíng mótuō chē] **2** (*child's*) 踏板车 [tàbǎn chē]

scope [skəʊp] N **1** [U] (*opportunity, potential*) ▶ **scope (for sth/to do sth)** (某事/做某事的)余地 [(mǒushì/zuò mǒushì de) yúdì] **2** [s] (*range*) 范围 [fànwéi] ▶ **there is plenty of scope for improvement** (BRIT) 还有很大的改进余地

scorching ['skɔːtʃɪŋ] (*inf*) ADJ (*also:* **scorching hot**) [+ *day, weather*] 炎热的 [yánrè de] ▶ **it's scorching today** 今天是个大热天
用法参见 **hot**

score [skɔː(r)] I N [c] **1** (*points*) 比分 [bǐfēn] **2** (MUS) 配乐 [pèiyuè] **3** (*liter*) (*twenty*) 二十 [èrshí] II VT **1** [+ *goal, point*] 得 [dé] **2** (*achieve*) [+ *success, victory*] 取得 [qǔdé] **3** (*cut*) [+ *card, leather*] 划 [huá]; [+ *line, mark*] 刻 [kè] **4** (*inf*) [+ *drug*] 非法取得 [fēifǎ qǔdé] III VI (*in game, sport*) 得分 [défēn] ▶ **scores (of)** 许多 ▶ **a score of** 几个 ▶ **on that/this score** 在那/这一点上 ▶ **to score 6 out of 10** 10分中得6分 ▶ **to score a point over sb/score points off sb** (*fig*) 驳倒某人 ▶ **to score a hit** 命中 ▶ **to score low/high** 获低/高分

scoreboard ['skɔːbɔːd] N [c] 记分牌 [jìfēn pái]

scorer ['skɔːrə(r)] N [c] **1** [*of goal, point, run etc*] 得分者 [défēn zhe] **2** (*person keeping score*) 记分员 [jìfēn yuán]

scorn [skɔːn] I N [U] 鄙视 [bǐshì] II VT **1** (*despise*) 瞧不起 [qiáobùqǐ] **2** (*reject*) 拒绝 [jùjué]

Scorpio ['skɔːpɪəʊ] N **1** [U] (*sign*) 天蝎座 [Tiānxiē Zuò] **2** [c] (*person*) 天蝎座的人 [Tiānxiē Zuò de rén] ▶ **I'm (a) Scorpio** 我是天蝎座的

scorpion ['skɔːpɪən] N [c] 蝎子 [xiēzi]

Scot [skɒt] N [c] 苏格兰人 [Sūgélánrén]

Scotch [skɒtʃ] N **1** [U] (*also:* **Scotch whisky**) 苏格兰威士忌 [Sūgélán wēishìjì] **2** [c] (*measure of whisky*) 一杯威士忌 [yībēi wēishìjì]

Scotch tape® (US) N [U] 透明胶带 [tòumíng jiāodài]

Scotland ['skɒtlənd] N 苏格兰 [Sūgélán]

Scots [skɒts] I ADJ 苏格兰的 [Sūgélán de] II N [U] (*dialect*) 苏格兰英语 [Sūgélán yīngyǔ]

Scotsman ['skɒtsmən] (*pl* **Scotsmen**) N [c] 苏格兰男人 [Sūgélán nánrén]

Scotswoman ['skɒtswʊmən] (*pl* **Scotswomen**) N [c] 苏格兰女人 [Sūgélán nǚrén]

Scottish ['skɒtɪʃ] ADJ 苏格兰的 [Sūgélán de]

scout [skaʊt] I N **1** (*also:* **boy scout**) 男童子军成员 [nán tóngzǐjūn chéngyuán] **2** (MIL) 侦察员 [zhēnchá yuán] II VT ▶ **to scout an area (for sth)** 搜索某个地区(寻找某物) [sōusuǒ mǒugè dìqū (xúnzhǎo mǒuwù)] III VI ▶ **to scout for sth** 物色某物 [wùsè mǒuwù] IV **the Scouts** NPL 童子军 [tóngzǐjūn]
▶ **scout around**, (BRIT) **scout round** VI 到处找 [dàochù zhǎo]

scowl [skaʊl] I VI 横眉怒目 [héngméi nùmù] II N [c] 怒容 [nùróng] ▶ **to scowl at sb** 怒视某人

scramble ['skræmbl] I VI (*clamber*) ▶ **to scramble up/down/over sth** 爬上/下/过某物 [páshàng/xià/guò mǒuwù] ▶ **to scramble into/out of sth** 仓促进入/出某处 [cāngcù jìnrù/chū mǒuchù] ▶ **to scramble for sth/to do sth** (*compete*) 争抢某物/做某事 [zhēngqiǎng mǒuwù/zuò mǒushì] II VT [+ *eggs*] 炒 [chǎo] III N [c] **1** ▶ **scramble (for sth)** (*struggle, rush*) 争夺(某物) [zhēngduó (mǒuwù)] **2** (*climb*) 攀登 [pāndēng] ▶ **he scrambled to his feet** 他费劲站起来 ▶ **to go scrambling** (BRIT: SPORT) 参加摩托车越野赛

scrambled egg ['skræmbld-] N [c/U] 炒鸡蛋 [chǎo jīdàn]

scrap [skræp] I N **1** [c] [*of paper, cloth*] 碎屑 [suìxiè]; [*of truth, evidence*] 一丁点 [yīdīngdiǎn] **2** [U] (*also:* **scrap metal**) 废铜烂铁 [fèitóng làntiě] **3** [c] (*inf*) (*quarrel*) 争吵 [zhēngchǎo]; (*fight*) 打架 [dǎjià] II VT **1** [+ *car, ship*] 报废 [bàofèi] **2** [+ *project, idea, system, tax*] 废弃 [fèiqì] III VI (*quarrel*) 争吵 [zhēngchǎo]; 打架 [dǎjià] IV **scraps** NPL [*of food*] 残羹剩饭 [cángēng shèngfàn] ▶ **to sell sth for scrap** 把某物作为废品出售

scrapbook ['skræpbʊk] N [c] 剪贴簿 [jiǎntiē bù]

scrape [skreɪp] I VT **1** (*clean*) 擦净 [cājìng] **2** (*hurt*) 擦伤 [cāshāng] **3** (*damage*) 刮坏 [guāhuài] II VI 刮 [guā] III N **1** [s] (*sound*) 刮擦声 [guācā shēng] **2** [c] (*inf, o.f.*) (*difficulty*) 窘境 [jiǒngjìng] ▶ **to scrape sth off/from sth** 从某物刮掉/刮去某物

▶ **scrape through** VT FUS [不可拆分], VI 勉强通过 [miǎnqiǎng tōngguò]

▶ **scrape together** VT 凑集 [còují]

scrap paper N [U] 废纸 [fèizhǐ] ▶ **a piece of scrap paper** 一张废纸

scratch [skrætʃ] I N [c] **1** (on car, furniture etc) 刮痕 [guāhén] **2** (on body) 擦伤 [cāshāng] II VT **1** (damage) [+ car, furniture, etc] 划破 [huápò] **2** (because of itch) 搔 [sāo] **3** (claw) 抓 [zhuā] III VI 搔痒 [sāoyǎng] ▶ **to do sth from scratch** 白手起家做某事 ▶ **to be up to scratch** 合格 ▶ **to scratch the surface (of sth)** (对某事)浅尝辄止 ▶ **to scratch o.s.** 挠自己

scratch card (BRIT) N [c] 刮卡 [guākǎ]

scrawl [skrɔ:l] I VT 潦草地写 [liáocǎo de xiě] II N [c/U] 潦草的笔迹 [liáocǎo de bǐjì]

scream [skri:m] I N [c] 尖叫声 [jiānjiào shēng] II VI 尖声喊叫 [jiānshēng hǎnjiào] III VT ▶ **to scream sth (at sb)** (冲着某人)大喊某事 [(chòngzhe mǒurén) dàhǎn mǒushì] ▶ **to let out a scream** 发出尖叫 ▶ **he's/it's a scream** (inf) 他/这滑稽透顶了 ▶ **to scream at sb** 大骂某人 ▶ **to scream at sb to do sth** 大声喝叫某人去做某事

screech [skri:tʃ] I VI **1** [car, tyres, brakes +] 发出刺耳的声音 [fāchū cì'ěr de shēngyīn] **2** [bird +] 尖叫 [jiānjiào] **3** [person +] ▶ **to screech (at sb)** (冲某人)尖叫 [(chòng mǒurén) jiānjiào] II VT 尖声喊出 [jiānshēng hǎnchū] III N [c] **1** [of car, tyres, brakes] 刺耳的声音 [cì'ěr de shēngyīn] **2** [of bird, person] 尖叫 [jiānjiào] ▶ **to screech to a halt** 嘎然刹住

screen [skri:n] I N [c] **1** (at cinema) 银幕 [yínmù] **2** [of television, computer] 屏幕 [píngmù] **3** (partition) 屏风 [píngfēng] **4** (for illegal activity) 掩护 [yǎnhù] II VT **1** (conceal) 遮蔽 [zhēbì] **2** [+ film] (in the cinema) 上映 [shàngyìng]; (on television) 播放 [bōfàng] **3** (check) [+ candidates] 筛选 [shāixuǎn] ▶ **to screen sb for sth** (for disease) 对某人进行某病的检查; (for security reasons) 对某人进行某安全事项检查 ▶ **to screen sth from sth** 把某物与某物挡开

screening ['skri:nɪŋ] N [c] **1** [of film] (in the cinema) 上映 [shàngyìng]; (on television) 播放 [bōfàng] **2** [c/U] (MED) 检查 [jiǎnchá] **3** [U] (for security) 审查 [shěnchá]

screenplay ['skri:npleɪ] N [c] 电影剧本 [diànyǐng jùběn]

screensaver ['skri:nseɪvə(r)] N [c] 屏幕保护 [píngmù bǎohù]

screw [skru:] I N [c] 螺丝 [luósī] II VT **1** (fasten) ▶ **to screw sth on/to sth** [+ shelf etc] 用螺丝把某物固定在某物上 [yòng luósī bǎ mǒuwù gùdìngzài mǒuwù shang] **2** (twist into position) ▶ **to screw sth on/into sth** 将某物拧在/入某物 [jiāng mǒuwù nǐngzài/rù mǒuwù] **3** (inf!) (have sex with) 与⋯性交 [yǔ⋯xingjiāo] ▶ **to put the screw(s) on** (inf) 威逼 ▶ **to turn or**

tighten the screw(s) on sb (inf) 对某人增加压力 ▶ **to screw one's eyes/face into a grimace** 眯起双眼/皱起面孔做怪相 ▶ **to screw sth out of sb** (ESP BRIT: inf) 逼迫某人拿出某物 ▶ **to have one's head screwed on** (inf) 保持头脑清醒

▶ **screw down** VT 用螺丝固定 [yòng luósī gùdìng]

▶ **screw in** VT 拧入 [níngrù]

▶ **screw up** I VT **1** (BRIT) [+ paper] 把⋯揉成一团 [bǎ⋯róuchéng yituán] [美 = **crush**] **2** (inf) (ruin) 把⋯弄得一团糟 [bǎ⋯nòngde yituánzāo] II VI (inf) (fail) 弄糟 [nòngzāo] ▶ **to screw up one's eyes/face** 眯起眼睛/皱起眉头

screwdriver ['skru:draɪvə(r)] N [c] 螺丝起子 [luósīqǐzi]

scribble ['skrɪbl] I VT [+ note] 潦草书写 [liáocǎo shūxiě] II VI **1** (write quickly) 潦草书写 [liáocǎo shūxiě] **2** (make marks) 乱涂 [luàntú] III N [c/U] **1** (note) 草草写成的便条 [cǎocǎo xiěchéng de biàntiáo] **2** (drawing) 涂鸦之作 [túyāzhīzuò]

▶ **scribble down** VT 草草写下 [cǎocǎo xiěxià]

script [skrɪpt] N **1** [c] [of play, film] 剧本 [jùběn] **2** [c/U] (writing) 文字体系 [wénzì tǐxì]

scroll [skrəʊl] I N **1** [c] [of paper, parchment] 卷轴 [juǎnzhóu] **2** (decoration) 涡卷形装饰 [wōjuǎn xíng zhuāngshì] II VI ▶ **to scroll up/down** 逐渐上移/下移 [zhújiàn shàngyí/xiàyí]

scrounge [skraʊndʒ] (inf) I VT ▶ **to scrounge sth (off sb)** (从某人处)乞讨某物 [(cóng mǒurén chù) qǐtǎo mǒuwù] II VI ▶ **to scrounge (off sb)** (向某人)乞讨 [(xiàng mǒurén) qǐtǎo] III N ▶ **to be on the scrounge** 在行骗 [zài xíngpiàn]

scrub [skrʌb] I VT **1** [+ floor, pan, clothes] 擦洗 [cāxǐ]; [+ vegetables, one's hands] 刷洗 [shuāxǐ] II VI 用力擦洗 [yònglì cāxǐ] III N **1** [U] (land) 低矮丛林地 [dī'ǎi cónglín dì] **2** [s] (wash) 擦洗 [cāxǐ] ▶ **to scrub sth clean** 将某物擦净 ▶ **to give sth a scrub** 刷净某物

▶ **scrub off** VT 擦掉 [cādiào]

scruffy ['skrʌfɪ] ADJ [+ person, appearance] 邋遢的 [lātà de]; [+ clothes, house] 不整洁的 [bù zhěngjié de]

scrum ['skrʌm] N [c] 橄榄球赛中两队前锋并排用肩膀相抵，用腿争夺抛进中间空隙中的球

scrutiny ['skru:tɪnɪ] N [U] 仔细检查 [zǐxì jiǎnchá] ▶ **to come under scrutiny** 受到密切注意

scuba diving ['sku:bə-] N [U] 带水下呼吸器潜水 [dài shuǐxià hūxīqì qiánshuǐ] ▶ **to go scuba diving** 带水下呼吸器去潜水

scuffle ['skʌfl] I N [c] 混战 [hùnzhàn] II VI 扭打 [niǔdǎ] ▶ **to scuffle with sb** 与某人混战

sculptor ['skʌlptə(r)] N [c] 雕塑家 [diāosù jiā]

sculpture ['skʌlptʃə(r)] N **1** [U] (art) 雕塑

[diāosù] **2** [c] (object) 塑像 [sùxiàng]

scum [skʌm] N **1** [U] (on liquid) 浮渣 [fúzhā] **2** [PL] (inf) (people) 渣滓 [zhāzi]

scurry ['skʌrɪ] ▸ **scurry around** VI 奔忙 [bēnmáng] ▸ **scurry off** VI 匆忙离开 [cōngmáng líkāi]

scythe [saɪð] N [c] 长柄大镰刀 [chángbǐng dà liándāo]

SE ABBR (= south-east) 东南部 [dōngnán bù]

sea [siː] I N **1** ▸ **the sea** 海洋 [hǎiyáng] **2** (in names) ▸ **the North/Irish/Dead Sea** 北/爱尔兰/死海 [Běi/ài'ěrlán/Sǐ Hǎi] II CPD [复合词] [+ breeze, air] 海 [hǎi] ▸ **beside** or **by the sea** 在海边 ▸ **by sea** 由海路 ▸ **at sea** (lit) 在海上 ▸ **to be all at sea** (with sth) (对某事) 不知所措 ▸ **to be swept out to sea** 被大海卷走 ▸ **to look out to sea** 望大海 ▸ **heavy** or **rough sea(s)** 波涛汹涌 ▸ **a sea of faces/glasses** 数不清的面孔/玻璃杯

seafood ['siːfuːd] N [U] 海味 [hǎiwèi]

seafront ['siːfrʌnt] N ▸ **the seafront** 滨海区 [bīnhǎi qū]

seagull ['siːgʌl] N [c] 海鸥 [hǎi'ōu]

seal [siːl] I N [c] **1** (animal) 海豹 [hǎibào] **2** (official stamp) 印章 [yìnzhāng] **3** (in fridge, machine) 密封装置 [mìfēng zhuāngzhì] **4** (sealed condition) 密封 [mìfēng] II VT **1** (close) [+ envelope] 封讫 [fēngqì]; [+ container, opening] 密封 [mìfēng] **2** (finalize) [+ agreement] 使定局 [shǐ dìngjú] ▸ **to give sth one's seal of approval** 正式认可某物 ▸ **to seal sb's fate** 注定某人的命运 ▸ **seal off** VT 封锁 [fēngsuǒ]

sea level N [U] 海平面 [hǎipíngmiàn] ▸ **100 metres above/below sea level** 海拔/低于海平面100米

seam [siːm] N [c] **1** (stitches) 缝 [fèng] **2** [of coal etc] 层 [céng] ▸ **to be bursting at the seams** 拥挤不堪

search [səːtʃ] I N [c] **1** (for missing person) 搜寻 [sōuxún] **2** [of place] 搜查 [sōuchá] **3** (COMPUT) 检索 [jiǎnsuǒ] II VT [+ place, suitcase, person] 搜查 [sōuchá] III VI ▸ **to search (for sb/sth)** 寻找 (某人/某物) [xúnzhǎo (mǒurén/mǒuwù)] ▸ **a search for** [+ object, person] 寻找; [+ solution, settlement] 寻求 ▸ **in search of** 寻找 ▸ **to search sb/sth for sth** 为找某物搜查某人/某物 ▸ **to search one's mind for sth** 绞尽脑汁想某事 ▸ **search through** VT FUS [不可拆分] 彻底搜查 [chèdǐ sōuxún]

search engine (COMPUT) N [c] 搜索引擎 [sōusuǒ yǐnqíng]

search party N [c] 搜索队 [sōusuǒ duì] ▸ **to send out a search party (for sb)** 派搜索队 (寻找某人)

seashore ['siːʃɔː(r)] N [c] 海岸 [hǎi'àn] ▸ **on the seashore** 在海边

seasick ['siːsɪk] ADJ 晕船的 [yūnchuán de] ▸ **to be** or **feel seasick** 感到晕船恶心 ▸ **to be seasick** (vomit) 晕船呕吐

seaside ['siːsaɪd] (BRIT) N ▸ **the seaside** 海边 [hǎibiān] ▸ **at the seaside** 在海边 ▸ **to go to the seaside** 去海边

Ⓢ **season** ['siːzn] I N [c] **1** [of year] 季节 [jìjié] **2** (for activity) 时节 [shíjié] ▷ the planting season 种植时节 ▷ the football season 足球赛季 ▷ the rainy season 雨季 **3** (series) [of films etc] 上映期 [shàngyìngqī] ▷ a new season of horror films 恐怖片新的上映期 II VT ▸ **to season sth (with sth)** (用某物) 给某物调味 [(yòng mǒuwù) fěi mǒuwù tiáowèi] ▸ **raspberries are in season/out of season** 红莓正当令/下市

seasonal ['siːznl] ADJ [+ factors, variations] 季节性的 [jìjiéxìng de]; [+ staff] 节令性的 [jiélìngxìng de]

seasoning ['siːznɪŋ] N [c/U] 调味品 [tiáowèipǐn]

season ticket N [c] 季票 [jìpiào]

seat [siːt] I N [c] **1** (chair) 椅子 [yǐzi]; (in car, theatre, cinema) 座 [zuò] **2** (place) (in theatre, bus, train) 座位 [zuòwèi] **3** [of MP] 议席 [yìxí] **4** (on committee) 席位 [xíwèi] **5** (part) [of chair] 座部 [zuòbù]; [of trousers] 臀 [tún]; (buttocks) 臀部 [túnbù] **6** (centre) [of government, learning etc] 中心 [zhōngxīn] II VT **1** (put) 使就座 [shǐ jiùzuò] **2** (have room for) 容纳 [róngnà] ▸ **are there any seats left?** 还有位子吗? ▸ **to take a/one's seat** 就座 ▸ **to be in the driver's** or **driving seat** 处于控制地位 ▸ **to seat o.s.** 坐下 ▸ **to be seated** (be sitting) 坐下 ▸ **please be seated** (frm) 请坐

seat belt N [c] 安全带 [ānquán dài]

seating ['siːtɪŋ] N [U] 座位 [zuòwèi]

sea turtle (US) N [c] 海龟 [hǎiguī] [英 = **turtle**]

sea water N [U] 海水 [hǎishuǐ]

seaweed ['siːwiːd] N [c/U] 海草 [hǎicǎo]

sec [sek] (inf) N ▸ **a sec** 一会儿 [yīhuǐr] ▸ **I'll just be a sec** 我只要一会儿

sec., sec N ABBR (= seconds) 秒 [miǎo]

secluded [sɪ'kluːdɪd] ADJ [+ place, life] 僻静的 [pìjìng de]

Ⓢ **second** ['sekənd] I ADJ 第二的 [dì'èr de] ▷ his second marriage 他的第二次婚姻 II ADV **1** (after someone else) [perform +] 第二地 [dì'èr de]; (in race, contest) [come, finish +] 第二名地 [dì'èrmíng de] **2** (secondly) 再者 [zàizhě] III N **1** [c] (unit of time) 秒 [miǎo] **2** (short time) ▸ **seconds/a second** 片刻 [piànkè] ▷ Wait a second! 稍等片刻! ▷ It'll only take a second. 一会儿就行。 **3** [U] (also: **second gear**) 第二挡 [dì'èrdǎng] **4** [c] (imperfect product) 次品 [cìpǐn] ▷ Some of the articles are seconds. 有些东西是次品。 IV VT **1** (in formal meeting) [+ motion, nomination] 附议 [fùyì] **2** (back) [+ call] 赞同 [zàntóng] **3** (BRIT:

SCOL) ► upper/lower second 中上/中下 [zhōngshàng/zhōngxià] ► second floor (BRIT) 三层; (US) 二层 ► to be second nature to sb 某人的第二天性 ► to be second to none 首 届一指的 ► to be second only to sth/sb 仅次 于某物/某人 ► Charles the Second 查理二世 ► just a second! 就一会儿!

secondary ['sɛkəndərɪ] I ADJ 1 (less important) [+ issue, role] 次要的 [cìyào de]; [+ road] 支路的 [zhīlù de] 2 (subsequent) [+ effect] 随后的 [suíhòu de]; [+ infection, tumour] 继发性的 [jìfāxìng de] II CPD [复合词] [+ pupil, curriculum] 中学 [zhōngxué] ► of secondary importance 次 要的

secondary school N [C/U] 中学 [zhōngxué]

second-class ['sɛkənd'klɑ:s] I ADJ 1 [+ citizen, education etc] 二等的 [èrděng de] 2 [+ stamp, letter] 第二级的 [dì'èrjí de] 3 [+ ticket, carriage] 二等的 [èrděng de] II ADV 1 [travel +] 乘坐二 等 [chéngzuò èrděng] 2 [send, post +] 作为第 二级邮件 [zuòwéi dì'èrjí yóujiàn] III N [U] 二 等 [èrděng]

second-hand ['sɛkənd'hænd] I ADJ 1 [+ car, books, clothes] 二手的 [èrshǒu de] 2 [+ information, opinions] 间接的 [jiànjiē de] II ADV [buy +] 作为二手货 [zuòwéi 'èrshǒuhuò] ► to hear sth (at) second-hand 间接地得知某 事 III CPD [复合词] [+ shop, bookshop] 经营旧货 [jīngyíng jiùhuò]

secondly ['sɛkəndlɪ] ADV 其次 [qícì]

second-rate ['sɛkənd'reɪt] ADJ 平庸的 [píngyōng de]

second thought N ► to have second thoughts about sth/about doing sth 重新考 虑某事/做某事 [chóngxīn kǎolǜ/zuò mǒushì] ► without a second thought 不加思索地 ► on second thoughts or (US) thought 经重新考 虑后

Second World War N ► the Second World War 第二次世界大战 [dì'èrcì shìjiè dàzhàn]

secrecy ['si:krəsɪ] N [U] 保密 [bǎomì] ► in secrecy 秘密地

secret ['si:krɪt] I ADJ [+ plan, activity, place etc] 秘密的 [mìmì de] II N [C] 秘密 [mìmì] ► to keep sth secret (from sb) (对某人) 保密某事 ► a secret admirer (romantic) 暗恋者 ► can you keep a secret? 你能保守秘密吗? ► to make no secret of sth 不隐瞒某事 ► in secret 暗 地里 ► the secret of (sb's) success (某人) 成 功的秘诀

secretarial [sɛkrɪ'tɛərɪəl] ADJ [+ work, assistance] 秘书的 [mìshū de]; [+ course] 有关秘书事务的 [yǒuguān mìshū shìwù de]; [+ staff] 秘书处的 [mìshū chù de]

○ **secretary** ['sɛkrətərɪ] N [C] 1 (in office) 秘书 [mìshū] 2 (of organization) (committee member) 书 记 [shūjì]; (manager) 干事 [gànshì] 3 (company secretary) 文书 [wénshū] ► Secretary of State (for sth) (BRIT) (某部) 部长 ► Secretary of State (US) 国务卿 ► the Transport/Health Secretary (BRIT) 交通/卫生大臣

secretive ['si:krətɪv] ADJ 爱保密的 [ài bǎomì de] ► to be secretive about sth 对某事守口 如瓶

secretly ['si:krɪtlɪ] ADV [act +] 秘密地 [mìmì de]; [hope +] 暗自地 [ànzì de]

secret service N [C] 情报机关 [qíngbào jīguān]

sect [sɛkt] N [C] 派别 [pàibié]

section ['sɛkʃən] N [C] 1 (part) 部分 [bùfen] 2 (department) 部门 [bùmén] 3 [of document] 节 [jié] 4 (cross-section) 剖面图 [pōumiàn tú] ► the business section 商业版

sector ['sɛktə(r)] N [C] 1 部分 [bùfen] 2 (MIL) 防御地段 [fángyù dìduàn] ► the public/ private sector 政府机构/私营部门

secular ['sɛkjulə(r)] ADJ 非宗教的 [fēi zōngjiào de]

secure [sɪ'kjuə] I ADJ 1 (impregnable) [+ house, windows] 紧闭的 [jǐnbì de]; [+ prison, hospital] 拘留性的 [jūliú xìng de]; [+ border] 固若金汤 的 [gùruò jīntāng de]; [+ data, communication, transaction] 安全的 [ānquán de] 2 (dependable) [+ job, future] 稳定的 [wěndìng de] 3 (firmly fixed) 牢固的 [láogù de] 4 (emotionally) 无 忧虑的 [wúyōulǜ de] II VT 1 (fasten) [+ rope, shelf] 缚牢 [fúláo] 2 (get) [+ contract, votes] 获 得 [huòdé] 3 (make safe) [+ place] 使安全 [shǐ ānquán] 4 ► to secure a loan against sth 用某 物担保贷款 [yòng mǒuwù dānbǎo dàikuǎn] ► to be financially secure 经济上无忧无虑 ► to secure sth to sth 将某物缚在某物上 ► to secure sth for sb 为某人弄到某物

○ **security** [sɪ'kjuərɪtɪ] I N [U] 1 (precautions) 保 安措施 [bǎo'ān cuòshī] ▷ The Queen's visit was marked by tight security. 女王的到访以保安严 密著称。 2 [of country, border, building, person] 安全 [ānquán]; [of data, transaction] 妥善保 管 [tuǒshàn bǎoguǎn] 3 [of job etc] 稳定性 [wěndìng xìng] ▷ fears about job security 对工作 稳定性的担忧 4 (emotional) 安全感 [ānquán gǎn] ▷ a sense of security 安全感 5 (for loan) 抵 押品 [dǐyā pǐn] II securities NPL (ECON) 证 券 [zhèngquàn] ► to increase/tighten security 增加/加强保安

security guard N [C] (at building) 保安人员 [bǎo'ān rényuán]; (transporting money) 押钞人 员 [yāchāo rényuán]

sedan [sə'dæn] (US: AUT) N [C] 箱式小客车 [xiāngshì xiǎo kèchē] [英= saloon]

sedate [sɪ'deɪt] I ADJ 1 [+ person] 安详的 [ānxiáng de]; [+ life] 平静的 [píngjìng de]; [+ pace] 稳健的 [wěnjiàn de] II VT 给⋯服镇 静剂 [gěi⋯fú zhènjìng jì]

sedative ['sɛdɪtɪv] N [C] 镇静剂 [zhènjìng jì]

seduce [sɪ'dju:s] VT (sexually) 勾引 [gōuyǐn];

(tempt) 引诱 [yǐnyòu]; (delight) 吸引 [xīyǐn]
▶ **to seduce sb into doing sth** 引诱某人做某事
seductive [sɪˈdʌktɪv] ADJ [+ person] 性感的 [xìnggǎn de]; [+ offer, argument] 诱惑的 [yòuhuò de]
⊘ **see** [siː] (pt **saw**, pp **seen**) I VT 1 看见 [kànjiàn] ▷ Did you see what happened? 你看见发生的事了吗？2 (meet) [+ person] 见 [jiàn] ▷ I'll see you at the cinema. 我在电影院见你。▷ You need to see a doctor. 你需要去看医生。3 (watch) [+ film, play etc] 看 [kàn] ▷ the best film I've ever seen 我看过的最好的电影 4 (look at) [+ letter, document, picture etc] 看 [kàn] ▷ Did you see the article by Professor Gray? 你看了格雷教授的文章了吗？5 (understand) 明白 [míngbái] ▷ I see what you mean. 我明白你的意思了。6 (notice) 意识到 [yìshí dào] 7 (find out) 查明 [chámíng] 8 (imagine) 想像 [xiǎngxiàng] 9 (regard) 把…当作 [bǎ…dàngzuò] ▷ He saw her as a rival. 他把她当成一个对手。10 (witness) [+ change, event] 目睹 [mùdǔ] ▷ Yesterday saw the resignation of the disgraced Minister. 昨天威望扫地的部长辞职了。II VI 看见 [kànjiàn] ▷ It's dark and I can't see. 太黑了，我看不见。▶ **I can see something** 我能看见某物 ▶ **to see sb doing/do sth** 看见某人做某事 ▶ **there was nobody to be seen** 看不见任何人 ▶ **have you seen my glasses?** 你看见我的眼镜了吗？▶ **I don't know what she sees in him** 我不知道她看中他哪一点 ▶ **to go and see sb** 去见某人 ▶ see Chapter 6 见第6章 ▶ **to see that…** (realize, notice) 意识到… ▷ I could see she was lonely. 我察觉到她很孤独。; (ensure) 确保 ▶ **to see if** (find out if) 查看…是否 ▷ I'll see if she's available. 我去看看她是否有空。▶ **I can see him doing really well** (envisage) 我可以想像他将干得不错 ▶ **see you (soon)!** (inf) 再见！▶ **see you later!** 一会儿见！▶ **to see sb to the door** 送某人出门 ▶ **I'll see what I can do** 我会看看能做些什么 ▶ **let me see, let's see** (show me) 让我看看吧; (let me think) 我明白一点 ▶ **I see** (in explanations) 你知道 ▶ **we'll see** 看看再说 ▶ **see for yourself** 你自己看看 ▶ **as far as I can see** 就我看来
▶ **see about** VT FUS [不可拆分] (deal with) 处理 [chǔlǐ]
▶ **see off** VT 1 (say goodbye to) 向…告别 [xiàng…gàobié] 2 (BRIT) (defeat) [+ opponent, challenge] 击败 [jībài]
▶ **see out** VT (see to the door) 送 [sòng] ▶ **I'll see myself out** 不用送了
▶ **see through** I VT (help) [+ person] 帮助…渡过难关 [bāngzhù…dùguò nánguān] ▷ $50 should see you through. 50美金应该能够帮你渡过难关。▷ He saw me through the hard times. 他曾帮我度过艰难岁月。II VT FUS [不可拆分] (understand) [+ person] 看穿 [kànchuān]; [+ plan] 识破 [shípò] ▷ The jailers saw through my scheme.

看守们识破了我的计划。
▶ **see to** VT FUS [不可拆分] (deal with) 处理 [chǔlǐ] ▷ Franklin saw to the luggage. 福兰克林负责照管行李。▶ **to see to it that…** 确保…
seed [siːd] I N 1 [C/U] [of plant, fruit] 籽 [zǐ] 2 [C] (beginning) 萌芽 [méngyá] 3 [C] (TENNIS) 种子选手 [zhǒngzi xuǎnshǒu] II VT ▶ **to be seeded nine/fifteenth** etc 第9/15 (等) 号种子选手 [dìjiǔ/shíwǔ (děng) hào zhǒngzi xuǎnshǒu] ▶ **to plant** or **sow a seed** (in ground) 播种; (in sb's mind) 播下…的种子 ▶ **to go** or **run to seed** [plant +] 花谢结籽; [person, institution +] 走下坡路
seeing [ˈsiːɪŋ] CONJ ▶ **seeing as** or **that** 鉴于 [jiànyú]
seeing-eye dog [siːɪŋˈaɪ-] (US) N [C] 导盲犬 [dǎo mángquǎn] [英 = guide dog]
seek [siːk] (pt, pp **sought**) VT 1 [+ truth, revenge, shelter, compensation] 寻求 [xúnqiú] 2 [+ work, job] 寻找 [xúnzhǎo] ▶ **to seek advice/help (from sb)** (向某人) 求教/求助 ▶ **to seek to do sth** 试图做某事
▶ **seek out** VT 搜寻出 [sōuxún chū]
⊘ **seem** [siːm] VI 似乎 [sìhū] ▷ Everyone seems busy. 每个人似乎都挺忙。▶ **it seems that…** 看起来像是… ▶ **it seems like…** ▶ **to seem as if…** 好像 ▶ **to seem (to be) happy/interested** 好像 (是) 高兴/感兴趣 ▶ **to seem to do sth** 好像做某事 ▶ **how did she seem to you?** 你觉得她看起来怎么样？▶ **there seems to be…** 好像有… ▶ **it seems that…** 看来… ▶ **it seems to me that…** 我觉得… ▶ **she couldn't seem to stop crying** 她看来是哭不停了 ▶ **I seem to have mislaid it** 我好像忘记把它放在哪里了
seemingly [ˈsiːmɪŋlɪ] ADV 表面上 [biǎomiàn shang]
seen [siːn] PP of see
seesaw [ˈsiːsɔː] I N [C] 跷跷板 [qiāoqiāo bǎn] II VI 反复多变 [fǎnfù duōbiàn]
seethe [siːð] VI 1 [person +] 怒火中烧 [nùhuǒ zhōngshāo] 2 ▶ **to be seething (with)** (crowded) 拥挤不堪 [yōngjǐ bùkān] ▶ **to seethe at sth** 对某事发怒 ▶ **to seethe with anger** 火冒三丈
see-through [ˈsiːθruː] ADJ [+ blouse, dress] 薄如蝉翼的 [bórú chányì de]
segment [ˈsɛgmənt] N [C] [of population, society] 阶层 [jiēcéng]; [of market, economy etc] 部分 [bùfen]; [of orange] 瓣 [bàn]
segregate [ˈsɛgrɪgeɪt] VT (divide) 使隔离 [shǐ gélí]; (isolate) 使孤立 [shǐ gūlì] ▶ **to segregate sb from sth** 将某人与某事分开
seize [siːz] VT 1 [+ person, object, opportunity] 抓住 [zhuāzhù] 2 [+ power, control] 夺取 [duóqǔ]; [+ building, territory] 占据 [zhànjù] 3 [+ hostage] 俘获 [fúhuò] 4 [+ property] 没收 [mòshōu]
▶ **seize up** VI [engine +] 卡住 [kǎzhù]; [part of body +] 僵住 [jiāngzhù]
▶ **seize (up)on** VT FUS [不可拆分] 大肆利用

[dàsì lìyòng]

seizure ['siːʒə(r)] N [C] **1** (MED) 发作 [fāzuò]
2 (taking) [of power, land] 夺取 [duóqǔ]
3 (confiscation) [of drugs etc] 没收 [mòshōu]

seldom ['sɛldəm] ADV 不常 [bùcháng]

select [sɪ'lɛkt] I VT 挑选 [tiāoxuǎn] II ADJ 第
一流的 [dìyīliú de] ▸ **a select group** 精选的一
群 ▸ **a select few** 精选的几个

selection [sɪ'lɛkʃən] N **1** [U] (being chosen) 挑
选 [tiāoxuǎn] **2** [C] (COMM) (range) 供选择的范
围 [gōng xuǎnzéde fànwéi] **3** [C] (collection) 选
集 [xuǎnjí]

selective [sɪ'lɛktɪv] ADJ **1** (discerning) 精挑细
选的 [jīngtiāo xìxuǎn de] **2** (based on selection)
[+ education, school, breeding etc] 选择性的
[xuǎnzé xìng de]

self [sɛlf] (pl **selves**) N ▸ **the self** (ego) 自身
[zìshēn] ▸ **I feel my old or normal self again** 我
感到和以前一模一样

self-assured [sɛlfə'ʃʊəd] ADJ 自信的 [zìxìn de]

self-catering [sɛlf'keɪtərɪŋ] (BRIT) ADJ
[+ holiday, accommodation] 自供伙食的 [zìgōng
huǒshí de]

self-centred, (US) **self-centered** [sɛlf'sɛntə
d] ADJ 以自我为中心的 [yǐ zìwǒ wéi zhōngxīn
de]

self-confidence [sɛlf'kɒnfɪdns] N [U] 自信
心 [zìxìn xīn]

self-conscious [sɛlf'kɒnʃəs] ADJ 容易难为
情的 [yóngyì nánwéiqíng de] ▸ **to be self-
conscious about sth** 极为在意某事

self-contained [sɛlfkən'teɪnd] ADJ [+ flat] 有
独立设施的 [yǒu dúlì shèshī de]; [+ person] 不与
他人往来的 [bùyù tārén wǎnglái de]

self-control [sɛlfkən'trəʊl] N [U] 自制力
[zìzhìlì]

self-defence, (US) **self-defense** [sɛlfdɪ'fɛns]
N [U] 自卫 [zìwèi] ▸ **in self-defence** 出于自卫

self-discipline [sɛlf'dɪsɪplɪn] N [U] 自我约束
[zìwǒ yuēshù]

self-drive [sɛlf'draɪv] (BRIT) ADJ ▸ **a self-drive
car** 由承租人驾驶的车 [yóu chéngzūrén jiàshǐ
de chē] ▸ **a self-drive holiday** 自己租车驾驶
的旅行

self-employed [sɛlfɪm'plɔɪd] I ADJ 个体的
[gètǐ de] II NPL ▸ **the self-employed** 个体户
[gètǐ hù]

self-esteem [sɛlfɪs'tiːm] N [U] 自尊心 [zìzūn
xīn] ▸ **to have low/high self-esteem** 自尊心
差/强

self-indulgent [sɛlfɪn'dʌldʒənt] ADJ 放纵自
己的 [fàngzòng zìjǐ de]

self-interest [sɛlf'ɪntrɪst] N [U] 自身利益
[zìshēn lìyì]

selfish ['sɛlfɪʃ] ADJ [+ person, reason, behaviour] 自
私的 [zìsì de] ▸ **it was a selfish decision** 这是
一个自私的决定

selfless ['sɛlfɪs] ADJ [+ person, act, behaviour] 无

私的 [wúsì de]

self-pity [sɛlf'pɪtɪ] N [U] 自怜 [zìlián]

self-raising [sɛlf'reɪzɪŋ] (BRIT) ADJ ▸ **self-
raising flour** 自发面粉 [zìfā miànfěn] [美 =
self-rising]

self-respect [sɛlfrɪs'pɛkt] N [U] 自尊心 [zìzūn
xīn]

self-rising [sɛlf'raɪzɪŋ] (US) ADJ ▸ **self-rising
flour** 自发面粉 [zìfā miànfěn] [英 = **self-
raising**]

self-service [sɛlf'sɜːvɪs] ADJ [+ shop, restaurant,
garage] 自助的 [zìzhù de]

⊙ **sell** [sɛl] (pt, pp **sold**) I VT **1** 卖 [mài] ▷ **I sold
the house for 80,000 pounds.** 我的房子卖了8万
英镑。▷ **Do you sell flowers?** 你们这儿卖花吗?
▷ **We sell rubber products.** 我们经销橡胶制品。
2 (fig) [+ idea] 使接受 [shǐ jiēshòu] ▷ **She is
hoping she can sell the idea to clients.** 她希望能够
让客户接受这个主意。II VI [goods, product +]
有销路 [yǒu xiāolù] ▷ **I'm not sure if it will sell.**
我不能肯定是否有销路。▸ **to sell at or for 10
pounds** 售价10英镑 ▸ **to sell sb sth, sell sth to
sb** 将某物卖给某人 ▸ **to sell o.s.** 自我推销
▸ **sell off** VI **1** (lit) [shop +] 卖光存货 [màiguāng
cúnhuò]; [book, tickets etc +] 卖光 [màiguāng]
▷ **The tickets have sold out.** 票卖光了。**2** (fig)
(betray principles) 放弃原则 [fàngqì yuánzé]
3 (US) (sell everything) 出售所有财物 [chūshòu
suǒyǒu cáiwù] ▸ **to sell out of sth** 卖光某物
▷ **The shop had sold out of ice creams.** 那家商店的
冰淇淋卖光了。
▸ **sell up** (BRIT) VI 出售所有财物 [chūshòu
suǒyǒu cáiwù]

sell-by date ['sɛlbaɪ-] (BRIT) N [C] 商品必须
售出的截止日期 [shāngpǐn bìxū shòuchū de
jiézhǐ rìqī]

seller ['sɛlə(r)] N [C] (person, company) 销售者
[xiāoshòu zhě] ▸ **to be a big seller** 畅销品
▸ **it's a seller's market** 这是卖方市场

Sellotape® ['sɛləʊteɪp] (BRIT) I N [U] 透明
胶带 [tòumíng jiāodài] [美 = **Scotch tape**]
II VT ▸ **to sellotape sth to sth** 用透明胶带
将某物粘贴在某物上 [yòng tòumíng jiāodài
jiāng mǒuwù zhāntiēzài mǒuwù shang] ▸ **to
sellotape things together** 用透明胶带将东西
粘在一起 [美 = **tape**]

selves [sɛlvz] PL of **self**

semester [sɪ'mɛstə(r)] (ESP US) N [C] 学期
[xuéqī]

semicircle ['sɛmɪsəːkl] N [C] 半圆 [bànyuán]

semi-colon [sɛmɪ'kəʊlən] N [C] 分号 [fēnhào]

semi-detached [sɛmɪdɪ'tætʃt] (BRIT) ADJ 半
独立式的 [bàn dúlì shì de]

semi-final [sɛmɪ'faɪnl] N [C] 半决赛 [bàn
juésài]

seminar ['sɛmɪnɑː(r)] N [C] 专题讨论会
[zhuāntí tǎolùn huì]

semi-skimmed (milk) [sɛmɪˈskɪmd(-)] (BRIT) N [U] 半脱脂奶 [bàn tuōzhīnǎi] 〔美 = **two-percent milk**〕

Sen. (US) ABBR **1** (= *senator*) 参议院议员 [cānyì yuàn yìyuán] **2** (*in names*) (= *senior*) 老 [lǎo]

senate [ˈsɛnɪt] N **1** (POL) ▶ **the Senate** 参议院 [cānyì yuàn] **2** (UNIV) (*also*: **the Senate**) 理事会 [lǐshì huì]

senator [ˈsɛnɪtə(r)] (US) N [C] 参议院议员 [cānyì yuàn yìyuán]

○send [sɛnd] (*pt, pp* **sent**) VT **1** ▶ **to send sth (to sb)** [+ *letter, money etc*] 将某物发送(给某人) [jiāng mǒuwù fāsòng (gěi mǒurén)] ▷ *I promised I would send her the money.* 我答应会将钱给她送去的。 **2** [+ *person*] 派遣 [pàiqiǎn] ▷ *The government sent troops to the region.* 政府派遣军队去那个地区。 **3** (*transmit*) [+ *signal, picture*] 传送 [chuánsòng] ▷ *the pictures that the satellite sent back* 卫星传送回来的照片 ▶ **to send sth by post** *or* (US) **mail** 邮寄某物 ▶ **to send sb for** [+ *check-up, scan etc*] 叫某人去; [+ *bread, water etc*] 差某人去送 ▶ **he was sent there to fight terrorists** 他被派到那儿去对付恐怖分子 ▶ **to send word that…** 捎信说… ▶ **she sends (you) her love** 她(向你)问候 ▶ **to send sb to sleep** 使某人入睡 ▶ **to send sth flying** 把某物撞飞

▶ **send away** VT [+ *unwelcome visitor*] 把⋯打发走 [bǎ⋯dǎfā zǒu]

▶ **send away for** VT FUS [不可拆分] 函购 [hángòu]

▶ **send back** VT [+ *goods*] 退还 [tuìhuán]

▶ **send for** VT FUS [不可拆分] **1** (*also*: **send away for, send off for**) (*by post*) 函购 [hángòu] **2** [+ *doctor, police*] 差人去叫 [chāirén qùjiào]

▶ **send in** VT [+ *report, application etc*] 寄送 [jìsòng]

▶ **send off** VT **1** ▶ **to send sth off (to sb)** [+ *goods, parcel*] 将某物邮寄(给某人) [jiāng mǒuwù yóujì (gěi mǒurén)] **2** (SPORT) [+ *player*] 将⋯罚出场 [jiāng⋯fá chūchǎng]

▶ **send off for** VT FUS [不可拆分] 函购 [hángòu]

▶ **send on** VT [+ *letter*] 转送 [zhuǎnsòng]; [+ *luggage etc*] (*in advance*) 先行发走 [xiānxíng fāzǒu]; (*afterwards*) 转送 [zhuǎnsòng]

▶ **send out** I VT **1** [+ *invitation, leaflet*] 发出 [fāchū] **2** (*emit*) [+ *light, heat, signal*] 发送 [fāsòng chū] II VI ▶ **to send out for sth** [+ *pizza, curry*] 电话订购某物 [diànhuà dìnggòu mǒuwù]

▶ **send round** VT ▶ **to send sth round (to sb)** [+ *letter, document etc*] 分发某物(给某人) [fēnfā mǒuwù (gěi mǒurén)]

▶ **send up** VT **1** (*raise*) [+ *price, blood pressure*] 使上升 [shǐ shàngshēng] **2** (BRIT: *inf*) (*parody*) 通过模仿取笑 [tōngguò mófǎng qǔxiào]

sender [ˈsɛndə(r)] N [C] [*of letter, package, radio message*] 发送人 [fāsòngrén]

send-off [ˈsɛndɔf] (*inf*) N ▶ **to give sb a good**

send-off 为某人饯行 [wèi mǒurén jiànxíng]

Senegal [sɛnɪˈɡɔːl] N 塞内加尔 [Sàinèijiā'ěr]

Senegalese [sɛnɪɡəˈliːz] (*pl* **Senegalese**) I ADJ 塞内加尔的 [Sàinèijiā'ěr de] II N [C] (*person*) 塞内加尔人 [Sàinèijiā'ěrrén]

senile [ˈsiːnaɪl] ADJ 老态龙钟的 [lǎotài lóngzhōng de]

senior [ˈsiːnɪə(r)] ADJ [+ *staff, manager, officer*] 高级的 [gāojí de]; [+ *job, position*] 上级的 [shàngjí de] ▶ **to be senior to sb, be sb's senior** (*in company*) 是某人的上级 ▶ **she is 15 years his senior** 她比他年长15岁 ▶ **Jones Senior** (ESP US) 老琼斯

senior citizen N [C] 已届退休年龄的公民 [yǐjiè tuìxiū niánlíng de gōngmín]

senior high, (US) **senior high school** N [C] 高中 [gāozhōng]

sensation [sɛnˈseɪʃən] N **1** [C] (*physical, mental*) 感觉 [gǎnjué] **2** [U] (*sense of touch*) 触觉 [chùjué] **3** (*great success*) ▶ **to be a sensation** 轰动一时的人物/事件 [hōngdòng yīshí de rénwù/shìjiàn] ▶ **to cause a sensation** 引起轰动

sensational [sɛnˈseɪʃənl] ADJ **1** (*wonderful*) 极好的 [jíhǎo de] **2** (*surprising*) [+ *event*] 轰动性的 [hōngdòng xìng de] **3** (*exaggerated*) [+ *story, report*] 耸人听闻的 [sǒngrén tīngwén de]

○sense [sɛns] I N **1** [C] (*of sight, smell, taste etc*) 感觉官能 [gǎnjué guānnéng] ▷ *the five senses* 5种感觉官能 ▷ *a keen sense of smell* 嗅觉灵敏 **2** [s] (*feeling*) [*of guilt, shame etc*] 感觉 [gǎnjué] ▷ *I was overcome by a sense of failure.* 我被失败感所压倒。 **3** [U] (*good sense*) 明智 [míngzhì] **4** [C] (*meaning*) [*of word*] 释义 [shìyì] ▷ *a noun which has two senses* 一个有两种释义的名词 II VT (*become aware of*) 觉察到 [juéchá dào] ▶ **to have the sense to do sth** 明智地做某事 ▷ *They sometimes have the sense to seek help.* 他们有时很明智，知道求助。 ▶ **it makes sense** (*can be understood*) 讲得通; (*is sensible*) 合情合理 ▶ **there is no sense in doing that** 那么做是不明智的 ▶ **to come to one's senses** (*become reasonable*) 恢复理智 ▶ **to take leave of one's senses** 发疯 ▶ **to talk sense** 说话有道理 ▶ **to make sense of sth** 理解某事 ▶ **in a sense** 从某种意义上说 ▶ **to sense that…** 察觉到⋯ ▷ *He sensed that she did not like him.* 他察觉到她不喜欢他。

senseless [ˈsɛnslɪs] ADJ **1** (*pointless*) 毫无意义的 [háowú yìyì de] **2** (*unconscious*) 不省人事的 [bù xǐng rénshì de] ▶ **to be beaten senseless** 被打得失去知觉

sense of humour N [s] 幽默感 [yōumò gǎn]

sensible [ˈsɛnsɪbl] ADJ [+ *person*] 通情达理的 [tōngqíng dálǐ de]; [+ *decision, suggestion*] 明智的 [míngzhì de]; [+ *shoes, clothes*] 实用耐穿的 [shíyòng nàichuān de] ▶ **it would be sensible to go to bed early** 早上床睡觉是明智的

sensitive [ˈsɛnsɪtɪv] ADJ **1** [+ *person*]

(understanding) 善解人意的 [shànjiě rényì de];
(over-sensitive) 过于敏感的 [guòyú mǐngǎn de]
2 [+ subject] 棘手的 [jíshǒu de] **3** [+ skin] 敏感
的 [mǐngǎn de] **4** [+ instrument] 灵敏的 [língmǐn
de] ▶ **to be sensitive to sth** [+ sb's needs, feelings,
heat, light etc] 对某物敏感 ▶ **to be sensitive
about sth** 对某事敏感

sensitivity [sɛnsɪ'tɪvɪtɪ] **I** N **1** [C/U] [of person]
(to sb's feelings, needs) 敏感性 [mǐngǎn xìng];
(over-sensitive nature) 神经过敏 [shénjīng
guòmǐn] **2** [U] [of device, organism etc] (to heat,
light etc) 灵敏性 [língmǐn xìng] **3** [U] [of issue]
棘手 [jíshǒu] **II sensitivities** NPL 感情
[gǎnqíng]

sensual ['sɛnsjʊəl] ADJ **1** [+ pleasure, experience]
感官的 [gǎnguān de] **2** [+ person] 性感的
[xìnggǎn de]

sensuous ['sɛnsjʊəs] ADJ **1** [+ experience,
pleasure, fabric] 给感官以快感的 [gěi gǎnguān
yǐ kuàigǎn de] **2** [+ person, voice, lips] 性感的
[xìnggǎn de]

sent [sɛnt] PT, PP of send

sentence ['sɛntns] **I** N **1** [C] (LING) 句子
[jùzi] **2** [C/U] (LAW) 刑罚 [xíngfá] **II** VT ▶ **to
sentence sb to death/to 5 years in prison** 判某
人死刑/5年囚禁 [pàn mǒurén sǐxíng/wǔnián
qiújìn] ▶ **to pass sentence on sb** 宣布对某人
的判决

sentiment ['sɛntɪmənt] N **1** [C] (opinion) 观点
[guāndiǎn] **2** [U] (emotion) 多愁善感 [duōchóu
shàngǎn]

sentimental [sɛntɪ'mɛntl] ADJ [+ person] 多
愁善感的 [duōchóu shàngǎn de]; [+ song, story]
充满柔情的 [chōngmǎn róuqíng de]; [+ value,
reasons] 情感的 [qínggǎn de]

separate [adj 'sɛprɪt, vb 'sɛpəreɪt] **I** ADJ
[+ section, piece, pile] 分开的 [fēnkāi de];
[+ occasion, incident] 不同的 [bùtóng de];
[+ existence, organization, species, entity] 独立的
[dúlì de]; [+ rooms] 单独的 [dāndú de]; [+ issue,
question] 不相关的 [bù xiāngguān de] **II** VT
1 (split up) [+ people, things] 分开 [fēnkāi] **2** (make
a distinction between) [+ ideas, facts] 区分 [qūfēn]
3 (exist between) 分隔 [fēngé] **III** VI **1** (move
apart) 分开 [fēnkāi] **2** (split up) [parents, couple +]
分居 [fēnjū] **3** (also: **separate out**) [mixture,
sauce, colours +] 分离 [fēnlí] **IV separates**
NPL (clothes) 单件衣物 [dānjiàn yīwù] ▶ **they
went their separate ways** (to different places) 他
们分道扬镳了; (ended their relationship) 他们
分手了 ▶ **to keep sth separate from** 将某物
与⋯分开 ▶ **to remain separate from** 保持
与⋯分开; [+ husband, wife] 分居 ▶ **to separate
sth from sth** (move apart) 把某物与某物分开;
(make a distinction between) 把某物从某物中
识别出来; (make different) 将某物与某物区分;
(form a barrier between) 把某物与某物分隔 ▶ **to**

be separated [couple +] 分居 ▶ **to separate
(people/things) into groups** 将(人/物)分成组

separated ['sɛpəreɪtɪd] ADJ (not divorced) 分居
的 [fēnjū de]

separately ['sɛprɪtlɪ] ADV 开开地 [fēnkāi de]

separation [sɛpə'reɪʃən] N [C/U] **1** [of things,
groups] 分开 [fēnkāi]; (process of separating) 分离
[fēnlí] **2** (division) (into smaller parts) 分隔 [fēngé]
3 (time apart) (from loved ones) 分离 [fēnlí]
4 (split-up) [of couple] 分居 [fēnjū]

Sept. ABBR (= September) 九月 [jiǔyuè]

September [sɛp'tɛmbə(r)] N [C/U] 九月
[jiǔyuè] see also **July**

septic ['sɛptɪk] ADJ [+ wound, finger etc] 脓毒性
的 [nóngdú xìng de] ▶ **to go septic** 化脓

sequel ['siːkwl] N [C] **1** (to film, story) 续集 [xùjí]
2 (aftermath) 后果 [hòuguǒ]

sequence ['siːkwəns] N [C] **1** (series) 一连串
[yīliánchuàn] **2** (order) 顺序 [shùnxù] **3** (CINE)
连续镜头 [liánxù jìngtóu] ▶ **sequence of
events** 一连串事件 [yīliánchuàn shìjiàn] ▶ **in sequence** 按顺序

sequin ['siːkwɪn] N [C] 装饰性亮片
[zhuāngshìxìng liàngpiàn]

Serb [səːb] ADJ, N = **Serbian**

Serbia ['səːbɪə] N 塞尔维亚 [Sài'ěrwéiyà]

Serbian ['səːbɪən] **I** ADJ 塞尔维亚的 [Sài'ěr
wéiyà de] **II** N **1** (person) 塞尔维亚人
[Sài'ěrwéiyàrén] **2** [U] (language) 塞尔维亚语
[Sài'ěrwéiyàyǔ]

serene [sɪ'riːn] ADJ [+ person, smile] 安祥的
[ānxiáng de]; [+ place] 宁静的 [níngjìng de]

sergeant ['saːdʒənt] N [C] **1** (MIL) 中士
[zhōngshì] **2** (BRIT: POLICE) 小队长 [xiǎo
duìzhǎng]; (US) 巡佐 [xúnzuǒ]

serial ['sɪərɪəl] **I** N [C] (on TV, radio) 连续剧
[liánxùjù]; (in magazine) 连载 [liánzǎi] **II** ADJ
[+ rapist, adulterer, murder etc] 连续的 [liánxù de]

serial killer N [C] 连环杀手 [liánhuán
shāshǒu]

serial number N [C] 编号 [biānhào]

series ['sɪərɪz] (pl **series**) N [C] **1** [of events, things]
一系列 [yīxìliè] **2** (on TV, radio) 系列节目 [xìliè
jiémù]

○ **serious** ['sɪərɪəs] ADJ **1** [+ problem, accident,
illness] 严重的 [yánzhòng de] **2** (not frivolous)
[+ matter] 严肃的 [yánsù de] ▷ I think this is
a serious point. 我认为这是个严肃的问题。;
[+ thought, consideration] 认真的 **3** [+ person]
(sincere) 当真的 [dàngzhēn de] ▷ You really are
serious about this, aren't you? 你是当真的，是不
是？▷ I hope you're not serious. 我希望你不是当
真的。; (solemn) 严肃的 ▶ **are you serious?** 你
是认真的吗？

seriously ['sɪərɪəslɪ] ADV **1** [injure, ill, damage +]
严重地 [yánzhòng de] **2** [talk, think +] 认真地
[rènzhēn de]; [deal with +] 严肃地 [yánsù de]
3 (sincerely) [hope, believe +] 真诚地 [zhēnchéng
de] **4** (truth to tell) 说真的 [shuōzhēn de] ▶ **to**

take sb/sth **seriously** 认真对待某人/某事
▶ **seriously rich** (inf) 极其富有的

seriousness ['sɪərɪəsnɪs] N [U] **1** [of problem, situation] 严重性 [yánzhòng xìng] **2** [of person] 严肃 [yánsù] ▶ **in all seriousness** 说实在的

sermon ['sə:mən] N [C] **1** (REL) 布道 [bùdào] **2** (fig) 说教 [shuōjiào]

servant ['sə:vənt] N [C] **1** (worker) 佣人 [yōngrén] **2** (fig) 工具 [gōngjù]

serve [sə:v] **I** VT **1** [+ country, community, organization] 供职于 [gòngzhíyú] **2** [+ people, area] [hospital, business, library etc +] 为…服务 [wèi…fúwù] **3** (in shop, bar etc) 招待 [zhāodài] **4** [+ food, drink, meal] 端上 [duānshang] **5** (satisfy) [+ purpose] 达到 [dádào] **6** [+ apprenticeship] 当 [dāng]; [+ prison term] 服 [fú] **II** VI **1** (at table) 侍奉用餐 [shìfèng yòngcān] **2** (TENNIS) 发球 [fāqiú] **3** (do duty) [official +] 供职 [gòngzhí]; [soldier +] 服役 [fúyì] **4** (function) ▶ **to serve as sth** 当作某物用 [dàngzuò mǒuwù] **III** N [C] (TENNIS) 发球 [fāqiú] ▶ **are you being served?** 有人接待您吗? ▶ **it serves you right** 你活该 ▶ **to serve on a committee/jury** 是委员会/陪审团的成员 ▶ **to serve to do sth** 有助于做某事
▶ **serve out** VT [+ contract] 做到期满 [zuòdào qīmǎn]; [+ term] 供职到任期结束 [gòngzhí dào rènqí jiéshù]; [+ prison sentence] 服满 [fúmǎn]
▶ **serve up** VT [+ food] 端上 [duānshang]

server ['sə:və(r)] N [C] **1** (COMPUT) 服务器 [fúwù qì] **2** (TENNIS) 发球员 [fāqiú yuán]

○ **service** ['sə:vɪs] **I** N **1** [C] (facility) 服务 [fúwù] ▷ a one hour dry-cleaning service 一小时干洗服务 **2** [U] (in hotel, restaurant) 服务 [fúwù] ▷ The service isn't very good. 服务不怎么好。 **3** [C] (train/bus service) 火车/公共汽车营运 [huǒchē/gōnggòng qìchē yíngyùn] ▷ The service is better than it used to be. 营运服务比以前好。 **4** [U] (employment) 任职 [rènzhí] ▷ Pat is leaving the company after 12 years service. 在任职12年后，帕特将离开公司。 **5** [C] (organization, system) 公共服务业务 [gōnggòng fúwù yèwù] ▷ the postal service 邮政服务 **6** [C] (REL) (ceremony) 仪式 [yíshì] ▷ A religious service is currently underway. 一场宗教仪式正在进行中。▷ the Sunday evening service 星期日的晚祷仪式 **7** [C] (AUT) 维修 [wéixiū] ▷ The car is due for a service. 这车该维修了。 **8** [C] (TENNIS) (serve) 轮到的发球权 [lúndào de fāqiúquán] **9** ▶ **a dinner/tea service** 整套餐/茶具 [zhěngtào cān/chájù] **II** VT [+ vehicle, machine] 检修 [jiǎnxiū] **III** **services** NPL (help) 帮助 [bāngzhù] ▷ Their services are no longer required. 不再需要他们的帮助了。 **IV** **the Services** NPL (MIL) 三军 [sānjūn]
▶ **military** or (ESP BRIT) **national service** 义务兵役 ▶ **service included/not included** (on menu) 含/不含小费 ▶ **to be of service to sb** 为某人效劳 ▶ **to do sb a service** 帮某人的忙 ▶ **to**

be in/out of service [machine, vehicle +] 在使用中/停止使用 ▶ **to have one's car serviced** 把某人的车送去维修 see also **services**

service area (BRIT) N [C] (on motorway) 路边服务区 [lùbiān fúwù qū]

service charge N [C] 服务费 [fúwùfèi]

serviceman ['sə:vɪsmən] (pl **servicemen**) N [C] 军人 [jūnrén]

services ['sə:vɪsɪz] (pl **services**) (BRIT) N [C] (on motorway) 路边服务站 [lùbiān fúwù zhàn]

service station N [C] **1** (petrol station) 加油站 [jiāyóu zhàn] **2** (BRIT) (on motorway) 路边服务站 [lùbiān fúwù zhàn] [美= **rest area**]

serviette [sə:vɪ'ɛt] (BRIT) N [C] 餐巾 [cānjīn] [美= **napkin**]

serving ['sə:vɪŋ] N [C] 一份 [yīfèn]

sesame ['sɛsəmɪ] **I** N [C] 芝麻 [zhīma] **II** CPD [复合词] [+ seeds, oil] 芝麻 [zhīma]

session ['sɛʃən] N [C] **1** (period of activity) 一段时间 [yīduàn shíjiān] ▷ a recording session 录制时间 **2** (sitting) [of court] 开庭 [kāitíng]; [of parliament] 会议 [huìyì] **3** (US) (academic year) 学年 [xuénián]; (term) 学期 [xuéqī] ▶ **to be in session** (at court) 开庭; (in council, parliament) 开会; (over period of months, weeks etc) 开会期

○ **set** [sɛt] (pt, pp **set**) **I** N **1** [C] [of problems, questions] 系列 [xìliè] ▷ a new set of problems 一系列新问题; [of cutlery, saucepans, books, keys] 套 [tào]; [of golf clubs, spanners] 成套 [chéngtào] **2** [C] (TV, RAD) (also: **television set**) 电视机 [diànshìjī] **3** [C] (TENNIS) 局 [jú] **4** [C] (group of people) 群 [qún] ▷ the yachting set 一群快艇爱好者 **5** [C] (also: **film set**) 摄影场 [shèyǐng chǎng] **6** [C] (THEAT, CINE) (stage) 舞台 [wǔtái]; (scenery) 布景 [bùjǐng] **7** [C] (at hairdresser's) 做头发 [zuò tóufa] ▷ a shampoo and set 洗头和做头发 **8** [C] (MATH) 集 [jí] **II** ADJ (fixed) [+ routine, time, price] 规定的 [guīdìng de] ▶ **Meals are at set times.** 在规定时间进餐。 **III** VT **1** (put) 放 [fàng] ▷ He set the glass on the counter. 他把玻璃杯放在柜台上。 **2** (lay) [+ table] 摆放 [bǎifàng] ▶ **Shall I set the table for supper?** 要我为晚餐摆放餐具吗? **3** (fix) [+ time, price, rules etc] 确定 [quèdìng] ▷ They haven't yet set a date for the wedding. 他们还没确定婚礼的日期。 **4** (establish) [+ record] 创造 [chuàngzào] ▷ She set a new world record in the 400 metres. 她创造了新的400米世界记录。; [+ precedent] 开创 [kāichuàng]; [+ example] 树立 [shùlì] **5** (adjust) [+ alarm] 设定 [shèdìng] ▷ He set his alarm clock for four a.m. 他把闹钟设定在早晨4点。; [+ heating, volume etc] 调整 [tiáozhěng] **6** (BRIT) (make up) [+ exam] 出试题 [chūshìtí] **7** (impose) [+ task, challenge, target, deadline] 规定 [guīdìng] ▷ We have set ourselves an ambitious target. 我们为自己制定了一个雄心勃勃的目标。 **8** (typeset) 排版 [páibǎn] ▷ the deadline for setting the text 文字排版的最后期限 **IV** VI **1** [sun +] 落山

[luòshān] **2** [*jam, jelly, concrete, glue+*] 凝固 [nínggù] ▷ *He held the board in place while the glue set.* 他举着板子等着胶水干。**3** [*bone+*] 接合 长好 [jiēhé zhǎnghǎo] ▷ *It'll take six weeks for the bone to set.* 骨头接合长好要用6个星期。▶ **a set of false teeth** 一副假牙 ▶ **a set of dining-room furniture** 一套饭厅家具 ▶ **these chairs are only available as a set** 这些椅子只成套出 售 ▶ **a chess set** 一副国际象棋 ▶ **to be set in one's ways** 习惯难改 ▶ **a set phrase** 一个固 定词组 ▶ **to be set on doing sth** 决心做某事 ▶ **to be set to do sth** (*likely to*) 很有可能做某 事; (*about to*) 将做某事 ▶ **all set for sth/to do sth** (*ready*) 为某事做好准备 ▶ **a house set in parkland** 座落在开阔草坪上的房屋 ▶ **a novel set in Rome** 以罗马为背景的小说 ▶ **a gate set into the wall** 嵌在墙里的大门 ▶ **to set sth to music** 为…谱曲 ▶ **to set the scene** *or* **stage for sth** 为某事创造条件 ▶ **to set sb free** 给 某人自由
▶ **set about** VT FUS [不可拆分] (*embark on*) ▶ **to set about sth/doing sth** 着手某事/做某事 [zhuóshǒu mǒushì/zuò mǒushì]
▶ **set against** VT **1** ▶ **to set sth against sth** [*+argument, fact*] 把某事和某事作比较 [bǎ mǒushì hé mǒushì zuòbǐjiào] **2** ▶ **to set sb against sb** 使某人反对某人 [shǐ mǒurén fǎnduì mǒurén]
▶ **set apart** VT 使显得与众不同 [shǐ xiǎnde yǔzhòng bùtóng]
▶ **set aside** VT **1** [*+money, time*] 留出 [liúchū] **2** [*+belief, emotion*] 不理会 [bùlǐhuì]
▶ **set back** VT **1** (*cost*) ▶ **to set sb back 5 pounds** (*inf*) 花了某人5英镑 [huāle mǒurén wǔ yīngbàng] **2** (*delay*) ▶ **to set sb/sth back** 耽 搁某人/某事 [dānge mǒurén/mǒushì] ▷ *Bad weather set us back by about three weeks.* 恶劣的天 气耽搁了我们3个星期。**3** (*situate*) ▶ **a house set back from the road** 远离公路的一幢房子 [yuǎnlí gōnglù de yīzhuàng fángzi]
▶ **set down** VT [*+rules, guidelines*] 制定 [zhìdìng]
▶ **set forth** (*frm*) VT [*+argument, case*] 陈述 [chénshù]
▶ **set in** VI [*winter, bad weather+*] 到来 [dàolái]; [*panic, infection+*] 开始并持续 [kāishǐ bìng chíxù] ▶ **the rain has set in for the day** 今天雨 会下一整天
▶ **set off** I VI (*depart*) ▶ **to set off (for)** 启程 (前往) [qǐchéng (qiánwǎng)] II VT **1** (*start*) [*+bomb*] 使爆炸 [shǐ bàozhà]; [*+alarm*] 触发 [chùfā]; [*+chain of events*] 导致 [dǎozhì] **2** (*show up well*) [*colour, flavour+*] 衬托出 [chèntuō chū] ▷ *a red dress that set off her marvellous complexion* 一 件衬托出她绝好气色的红色连衣裙
▶ **set out** I VI (*depart*) 出发 [chūfā] II VT **1** (*arrange*) [*+chairs, plates, goods etc*] 摆放 [bǎifàng] **2** (*state*) [*+argument, theory etc*] 阐述 [chǎnshù] ▶ **to set out to do sth** 开始做某事

▶ **to set out from home** 从家里出发
▶ **set up** I VT **1** (*start*) [*+organization, service*] 设 立 [shèlì] **2** (*erect*) [*+tent*] 搭 [dā]; [*+roadblock*] 设置 [shèzhì] II VI (*in business*) 成立 [chénglì] ▶ **to set o.s. up** (*in business*) 开业 ▶ **to set up shop/home** 开店/定居
setback ['setbæk] N [c] (*hitch*) 挫折 [cuòzhé]; (*in health*) 复发 [fùfā]
set menu N [c] 套餐 [tàocān]
settee [sɛ'ti:] N [c] 长沙发椅 [cháng shāfāyǐ]
setting ['setɪŋ] N [c] **1** [*of controls*] 挡 [dǎng] **2** (*location*) 环境 [huánjìng] **3** [*of jewel*] 底座 [dǐzuò]
settle ['setl] I VT **1** [*+argument, question*] 解 决 [jiějué]; [*+affairs*] 料理 [liàolǐ] **2** (*pay*) [*+bill, account, debt*] 支付 [zhīfù] II VI **1** [*sand, dust+*] 沉积 [chénjī]; [*+sediment+*] 沉淀 [chéndiàn] **3** ▶ **to settle on sth** [*insect, bird+*] 停落在某物 上 [tíngluòzài mǒuwù shang] **4** (*go to live*) 定居 [dìngjū] **5** = **settle down** ▶ **they have settled their differences** 他们已经解决了他们之间 的分歧 ▶ **to settle a score** *or* **an old score (with sb)** (与某人)算旧账 ▶ **that's settled then!** 那 么事情就这样定了！▶ **to settle o.s. (into...)** (在…)坐下来 ▶ **it'll settle your stomach** 这 会使你的胃舒服一点 ▶ **to wait for the dust to settle** (*fig*) 等到尘埃落定
▶ **settle down** I VI **1** (*live stable life*) 开始过安 稳的日子 [kāishǐ guò ānwěn de rìzi] **2** (*make o.s. comfortable*) 舒舒服服地歇下来 [shūshu fúfu de xiēxiàlái] **3** (*become calm*) [*person+*] 适应 [shìyìng]; (*situation+*) 平静下来 [píngjìng xiàlái] ▶ **to settle down to sth** 定下心来做某事
▶ **settle for** VT FUS [不可拆分] 勉强认可 [miǎnqiáng rènkě]
▶ **settle in** VI 适应 [shìyìng]
▶ **settle into** VT FUS [不可拆分] **1** [*+school, job etc*] 习惯于 [xíguànyú] **2** [*+chair*] 舒舒服服地 坐下 [shūshufúfu de zuòxià]
▶ **settle on** VT FUS [不可拆分] (*decide on*) [*+object*] 决定 [juédìng]; [*+action, name*] 选定 [xuǎndìng]
▶ **settle up** VI ▶ **to settle up (with sb)** 付清欠 (某人的)账 [fùqīng qiàn (mǒurén de) zhàng]
settlement ['setlmənt] N **1** [c] (*agreement*) 协 议 [xiéyì] **2** [U] (*payment*) 清偿 [qīngcháng] **3** [c] (*village, town*) 定居点 [dìngjūdiǎn] **4** [U] (*colonization*) 殖民地的开拓 [zhímín dì de kāituò] ▶ **in settlement of our account** 结清 我们的账务
setup ['setʌp] (*inf*) N [c] (*organization*) 机构 [jīgòu]; (*system, situation*) 组织情况 [zǔzhī qíngkuàng]
⊙ **seven** ['sevn] NUM 七 [qī] *see also* **five**
⊙ **seventeen** [sevn'ti:n] NUM 十七 [shíqī] *see also* **fifteen**
seventeenth [sevn'ti:nθ] NUM 第十七 [dì shíqī] *see also* **fifth**
seventh ['sevnθ] NUM 第七 [dìqī] *see also* **fifth**

seventieth ['sɛvntɪɪθ] NUM 第七十 [dì qīshí]

○ **seventy** ['sɛvntɪ] NUM 七十 [qīshí] see also **fifty**

sever ['sɛvə(r)] VT 1 [+ limb, pipe] 切断 [qiēduàn] 2 [+ links, relations] 断绝 [duànjué]

○ **several** ['sɛvərl] ADJ, PRON 几个 [jǐgè]
▷ several hours later 几个小时后 ▶ **several times** 几次 ▶ **several of us** 我们中的几个

severe [sɪ'vɪə(r)] ADJ 1 [+ pain, damage, shortage] 严重的 [yánzhòng de] 2 [+ punishment, criticism] 严厉的 [yánlì de]; [+ winter, climate] 严酷的 [yánkù de] 4 (stern) [+ person, expression] 严肃的 [yánsù de] 5 (austere) [+ architecture, dress] 简朴的 [jiǎnpǔ de]

severity [sɪ'vɛrɪtɪ] N [U] 1 [of pain, damage, shortage, injury, illness] 严重 [yánzhòng] 2 [of punishment] 严厉 [yánlì]; [of winter, weather] 严酷 [yánkù] 3 (sternness) [of manner, voice] 严肃 [yánsù] 4 (austerity) [of architecture, dress] 简朴 [jiǎnpǔ]

sew [səu] (pt **sewed**, pp **sewn**) VI, VT 缝 [féng]
▶ **to sew sth together** 缝合某物
▶ **sew up** VT 1 [+ garment] 把…缝起来 [bǎ…féngqǐlái] 2 (inf) [+ deal, contest] 顺利完成 [shùnlì wánchéng]

sewage ['su:ɪdʒ] N [U] 污物 [wūwù]

sewer ['su:ə(r)] N [C] 排污管 [páiwū guǎn]

sewing ['səuɪŋ] N [U] 1 (activity) 缝纫 [féngrèn] 2 (items being sewn) 缝制品 [féngzhìpǐn]

sewing machine N [C] 缝纫机 [féngrèn jī]

sewn [səun] PP of **sew**

sex [sɛks] N 1 [C] (gender) 性别 [xìngbié] 2 [U] (lovemaking) 性交 [xìngjiāo] ▶ **to have sex (with sb)** (和某人)性交

sex education N [U] 性教育 [xìng jiàoyù]

sexism ['sɛksɪzəm] N [U] 性别歧视 [xìngbié qíshì]

sexist ['sɛksɪst] I ADJ [+ person, attitude, behaviour] 性别歧视的 [xìngbié qíshì de] II N [C] (person) 性别歧视者 [xìngbié qíshì zhě]

sexual ['sɛksjuəl] ADJ [+ attraction, relationship, health] 性的 [xìng de]; [+ differences, discrimination] 性别的 [xìngbié de]; [+ reproduction, maturity] 生殖的 [shēngzhí de]

sexuality [sɛksju'ælɪtɪ] N [U] 1 (sexual feelings) 性欲 [xìngyù] 2 (sexual orientation) 性倾向 [xìng qīngxiàng]

sexy ['sɛksɪ] ADJ 性感的 [xìnggǎn de]

Seychelles [seɪ'ʃɛl(z)] NPL ▶ **the Seychelles** 塞舌尔群岛 [Sàishé'ěr Qúndǎo]

Sgt., (ESP US) **Sgt.** ABBR (= sergeant) (in army) 中士 [zhōngshì]; (BRIT) (in police) 巡佐 [xúnzuǒ]

shabby ['ʃæbɪ] ADJ 1 [+ clothes, place] 破旧的 [pòjiù de]; [+ person] 衣衫褴褛的 [yīshān lánlǚ de] 2 [+ treatment, behaviour] 不公正的 [bù gōngzhèng de]

shack [ʃæk] N [C] 棚屋 [péngwū]
▶ **shack up** (inf) VI ▶ **to shack up (with sb)** (与某人)同居 [(yǔ mǒurén) tóngjū]

shade [ʃeɪd] I N 1 [U] (shelter) 阴凉处 [yīnliáng chù] 2 [U] (in painting, photo) 阴影 [yīnyǐng] 3 [C] (hue) [of colour] 色度 [sèdù] 4 [C] (also: **lampshade**) 灯罩 [dēngzhào] 5 [C] (US) (on window) 遮阳窗帘 [zhēyáng chuānglián] [英 = **blind**] II VT [+ place] 遮蔽 [zhēbì]; [+ eyes] 为…挡光 [wèi…dǎngguāng] III **shades** NPL (inf) 太阳镜 [tàiyáng jìng] ▶ **in the shade** 在阴凉处 ▶ **a shade...** 有点… ▶ **shades of meaning/opinion** 有细微差别的意思/意见 ▶ **to shade sth from the light/sun** 遮住某物以使不受光线/阳光照射
▶ **shade into** VT FUS [不可拆分] 逐渐变成 [zhújiàn biànchéng]

shadow ['ʃædəu] I N 1 [C] 影子 [yǐngzi] 2 [U] (shade) 阴影 [yīnyǐng] II VT 跟踪 [gēnzōng] III (BRIT) CPD [复合词] (POL) [+ minister, chancellor] 影子 [yǐngzi] ▶ **in shadow** 在阴影中 ▶ **in the shadow of sth** 在某物的影子下 ▶ **in sb's shadow** 在某人的阴影下 ▶ **without or beyond a shadow of (a) doubt** 毫无疑问

shadow cabinet (BRIT) N ▶ **the Shadow Cabinet** 影子内阁 [yǐngzi nèigé]

shady ['ʃeɪdɪ] ADJ 1 [+ place] 背阴的 [bèiyīn de]; [+ tree] 成荫的 [chéngyīn de] 2 (dishonest) [+ person] 不正当的 [bùzhèngdàng de]; [+ activity, deal] 见不得人的 [jiànbùdé rén de]

shaft [ʃɑ:ft] N [C] 1 [of mine, lift] 井状通道 [jǐngzhuàng tōngdào] 2 [of axe, club, spear etc] 柄 [bǐng] 3 (in machine) 轴 [zhóu] 4 [of light] 束 [shù]

shaggy ['ʃægɪ] ADJ [+ hair, sweater, dog etc] 蓬乱的 [péngluàn de]

shake [ʃeɪk] (pt **shook**, pp **shaken** ['ʃeɪkn]) I VT 1 [+ dice, rug, person] 猛摇 [měngyáo]; [+ bottle, cocktail, medicine] 摇晃 [yáohuàng]; [+ buildings, ground] 使震动 [shǐ zhèndòng] 2 (affect) [+ person] 使震惊 [shǐ zhènjīng] 3 (undermine) [+ belief, confidence] 使动摇 [shǐ dòngyáo] II VI [person, part of the body +] 发抖 [fādǒu]; [voice +] 颤抖 [chàndǒu]; [building, table +] 震动 [zhèndòng]; [ground +] 震颤 [zhènchàn] III N 1 ▶ **to give sth/sb a shake** 猛摇一下某物/某人 [měngyáo yíxià mǒuwù/mǒurén] 2 [C] (also: **milkshake**) 奶昔 [nǎixī] ▶ **to shake one's head** (in refusal) 摇头拒绝; (in dismay) 摇摇头 ▶ **to shake one's fist (at sb)** (朝某人)挥拳 ▶ **to shake hands (with sb)** (和某人)握手 ▶ **to shake with fear/rage/laughter** [person +] 怕/气/笑得发抖; [voice +] 怕/气/笑得颤抖
▶ **he declined with a shake of his head** 他摇摇头拒绝了
▶ **shake down** (US) VT [+ person] 勒索 [lèsuǒ]
▶ **shake off** VT 1 [+ person, sb's hand] 摆脱 [bǎituō] 2 [+ pursuer] 甩掉 [shuǎidiào] 3 [+ illness, habit] 克服 [kèfú]
▶ **shake up** VT 1 (reorganize) 重组 [chóngzǔ] 2 (upset) 使受惊吓 [shǐ shòujīngxià]

shaky ['ʃeɪkɪ] ADJ 1 [+ hand] 发抖的 [fādǒu de]; [+ voice] 颤抖的 [chàndǒu de] 2 (weak) [+ situation, start, economy] 不稳定的 [bù wěndìng de] 3 (unreliable) [+ memory] 不可靠的 [bù kěkào de]; [+ knowledge, understanding] 成问题的 [chéng wèntí de]

shall [ʃæl] AUX VB 1 (indicating future in 1st person) ▶ I shall go 我要走了 [wǒ yào zǒule] 2 (in 1st person questions) ▶ shall I/we open the door? 我/我们把门打开好吗？[wǒ/wǒmen bǎ mén dǎkāi hǎoma?] 3 (in 1st person tag questions) ▶ I'll get some, shall I? 我去拿一些，好吗？[wǒ qù ná yīxiē, hǎoma?] 4 (indicating inevitability) 一定 [yīdìng] ▶ the president shall hold office for five years (frm) 总统要任职5年

shallow ['ʃæləʊ] I ADJ 1 [+ water, ditch, grave] 浅的 [qiǎn de]; [+ container] 浅口的 [qiǎnkǒu de]; [+ breathing] 浅的 [qiǎn de] 2 (superficial) [+ person, argument, idea] 肤浅的 [fūqiǎn de] II shallows NPL ▶ the shallows 浅水处 [qiǎnshuǐchù]

sham [ʃæm] I N [c] 假象 [jiǎxiàng] II CPD [复合词] [+ marriage, fight] 假 [jiǎ]

shambles ['ʃæmblz] N ▶ to be a shambles [place +] 乱七八糟 [luànqībāzāo]; [event, situation +] 一塌糊涂 [yītāhútú] ▶ what a shambles! 真是一团糟！

shame [ʃeɪm] I N [U] 1 (embarrassment) 羞耻 [xiūchǐ] 2 (disgrace) 耻辱 [chǐrǔ] II VT 使感到羞耻 [shǐ gǎndào xiūchǐ] ▶ it is a shame that... …真遗憾 ▶ it would be a shame to waste this 把这浪费掉太可惜了 ▶ what a shame! 太遗憾了！▶ to put sb/sth to shame 使某人/某事相形见绌 ▶ it shamed him to admit... 他羞愧地承认… ▶ to shame sb into sth/into doing sth 使某人羞愧地做某事

shameful ['ʃeɪmful] ADJ [+ action, episode] 可耻的 [kěchǐ de] ▶ it is shameful that... …是可耻的

shameless ['ʃeɪmlɪs] ADJ [+ person, behaviour] 无耻的 [wúchǐ de]

shampoo [ʃæm'puː] I N [c/U] (substance) 洗发液 [xǐfàyè] II VT 用洗发液洗 [yòng xǐfàyè xǐ]

shandy ['ʃændɪ] (BRIT) N 1 [U] (type of drink) 搀柠檬汁的啤酒 [chān níngméngzhī de píjiǔ] 2 [c] (glass) 一杯搀柠檬汁的啤酒 [yībēi chān níngméngzhī de píjiǔ]

shan't [ʃɑːnt] = shall not

shape [ʃeɪp] I N 1 [c] (form, circle, triangle etc) 形状 [xíngzhuàng] 2 [s] (fig) [of plan, organization] 模式 [móshì] II VT 1 (lit) (fashion, form) 塑造 [sùzào] 2 (determine) [+ ideas, life] 决定 [juédìng] ▶ to take shape [idea, plan etc +] 成形 ▶ in the shape of a heart 呈心形 ▶ I can't bear gardening in any shape or form 我受不了任何形式的园艺 ▶ to be in (good) shape [person +] 体形好 ▶ to be out of shape [person +] 体质差 ▶ to get (o.s.) into shape 锻炼身体

▶ **shape up** VI (progress) [events +] 进展 [jìnzhǎn]; [person +] 表现 [biǎoxiàn]

shapeless ['ʃeɪplɪs] ADJ 不成形的 [bùchéngxíng de]

○ **share** [ʃɛə(r)] I N [c] 1 (part) 一份 [yīfèn] 2 (COMM, ECON) (in company) 股票 [gǔpiào] ▷ The firm's shares jumped to 114p. 公司的股票涨到114便士。II VT 1 (have in common) [+ room, bed, taxi] 合用 [héyòng]; [+ feature, quality] 共有 [gòngyǒu] ▷ two tribes who share a common language 说同一种语言的两个部落 2 (be jointly responsible for) [+ job, cooking, task] 分担 [fēndān] 3 (divide) ▶ to share sth among/between 把某物分给… [bǎ mǒuwù fēngěi…] ▷ Share the sweets between the children. 把糖分给孩子们吃。▶ to do one's share 尽自己的责任 ▷ It helps when a father does his share at home. 父亲在家中尽自己的责任会有很大帮助。▶ to get one's share 得到自己应得的一份 ▶ to share sth with sb [+ room, bed, taxi] 和某人合用某物 ▷ the huge house that he shared with his sisters 他和姊妹们合住的大房子; [+ feature, quality] 和某人共有某特性; [+ cost] 和某人分摊开销; [+ job, cooking, task] 和某人分担某事; (allow to use) 和某人分享某物 ▶ to share in [+ success, profits, benefits] 分享: [+ responsibility, work] 分担

▶ **share out** VT 平均分配 [píngjūn fēnpèi]

shareholder ['ʃɛəhəʊldə(r)] N [c] 股东 [gǔdōng] [美 = stockholder]

shark [ʃɑːk] N 1 [c/U] (fish) 鲨鱼 [shāyú] 2 [c] (inf) (person) 骗子 [piànzi]

sharp [ʃɑːp] I ADJ 1 [+ knife, teeth] 锋利的 [fēnglì de]; [+ point, edge] 尖锐的 [jiānruì de] 2 (pointed) [+ nose, chin] 尖的 [jiān de] 3 (abrupt) [+ increase, change] 急剧的 [jíjù de]; [+ curve, bend] 急转的 [jízhuǎn de] 4 (clear) [+ image, distinction] 清晰的 [qīngxī de] 5 (acute) [+ pain, cold] 剧烈的 [jùliè de] 6 (severe) [+ reply, criticism] 严厉的 [yánlì de] 7 (strong) [+ taste, smell] 浓烈的 [nóngliè de] 8 (quick-witted) [+ person] 机敏的 [jīmǐn de] 9 (MUS) 升半音的 [shēng bànyīn de] II ADJ (MUS) 升半音 [bànshēngyīn] III ADV (precisely) ▶ at 2 o'clock sharp 两点整 [liǎng diǎn zhěng] ▶ turn sharp left 向左急转弯 ▶ to be sharp with sb 对某人刻薄 ▶ C sharp/F sharp 升C调/升F调 ▶ sharp practice 不正当的手段

sharpen ['ʃɑːpn] VT 1 (lit) [+ stick, pencil] 削尖 [xiāojiān]; [+ knife] 磨快 [mókuài] 2 (fig) [+ skill, understanding] 磨练 [móliàn]

sharpener ['ʃɑːpnə(r)] N [c] (also: **pencil sharpener**) 卷笔刀 [juǎnbǐdāo]; (also: **knife sharpener**) 磨具 [mójù]

sharply ['ʃɑːplɪ] ADV 1 (abruptly) [turn +] 突然地 [tūrán de] 2 (steeply) [rise, fall +] 急剧地 [jíjù de] 3 (greatly) [contrast +] 鲜明地 [xiānmíng de] 4 (severely) [speak +] 严厉地 [yánlì de]

shatter ['ʃætə(r)] VT, VI 1 (break) 粉碎 [fěnsuì]

2 (fig) (ruin) [+ hopes, confidence] 粉碎 [fěnsuì]

shattered ['ʃætəd] ADJ **1** (overwhelmed, grief-stricken) 感到震骇的 [gǎndào zhènhài de] **2** (inf) (exhausted) 筋疲力尽的 [jīnpílìjìn de]

shave [ʃeɪv] I VT [+ head, legs] 剃毛发 [tìmáofà]; [+ person] 剃须 [tìxū] II VI 刮脸 [guāliǎn] III N ▸ **to have a shave** 刮脸 [guāliǎn] ▸ **shave off** VT [+ beard] 剃去 [tìqù]

shaver ['ʃeɪvə(r)] N [c] (also: **electric shaver**) 电动剃刀 [diàndòng tìdāo]

shaving ['ʃeɪvɪŋ] I N [U] (action) 剃须 [tìxū] II CPD [复合词] [+ gel, things] 剃须 [tìxū] III **shavings** NPL 刨花 [bàohuā]

shaving cream N [U] 剃须膏 [tìxūgāo]

shaving foam N [U] 泡沫剃须膏 [pàomò tìxūgāo]

shawl [ʃɔ:l] N [c] 披肩 [pījiān]

○ **she** [ʃi:] PRON **1** (woman, girl) 她 [tā] ▷ She didn't do it. I did. 她没做。是我做的。**2** (animal) 它 [tā] ▷ She's a good dog. 它是只好狗。

sheath [ʃi:θ] N [c] **1** (for knife) 鞘 [qiào] **2** (BRIT) (condom) 避孕套 [bìyùntào]

shed [ʃɛd] (pt, pp **shed**) I N [c] **1** (in garden) 棚 [péng] **2** (by railway, factory) 棚式外廊 [péngshì wàiláng] II VT **1** (naturally) [+ skin, leaves, hair] 脱落 [tuōluò] **2** (get rid of) 摆脱 [bǎituō] ▸ **to shed tears** 流泪 ▸ **to shed blood** 杀人 ▸ **to shed jobs** 裁员 ▸ **a lorry has shed its load** (BRIT) 一辆大卡车掉落了货物

she'd [ʃi:d] = **she had, she would**

sheep [ʃi:p] (pl **sheep**) N [c] 绵羊 [miányáng]

sheepdog ['ʃi:pdɔg] N [c] **1** (for controlling sheep) 牧羊犬 [mùyángquǎn] **2** (type of dog) 牧羊犬 [mùyángquǎn]

sheepskin ['ʃi:pskɪn] I N [c/U] 绵羊皮 [miányángpí] II CPD [复合词] [+ coat, gloves] 绵羊皮 [miányángpí]

sheer [ʃɪə(r)] ADJ **1** [+ joy, delight, beauty] 纯粹的 [chúncuì de]; [+ determination, brilliance] 绝对的 [juéduì de]; [+ terror, desperation] 彻底的 [chèdǐ de]; [+ size, scale, volume] 巨大的 [jùdà de] **2** (steep) [+ cliff, drop] 陡峭的 [dǒuqiào de] **3** (thin) 纤薄的 [xiānbó de] ▸ **by sheer chance** 纯属偶然 ▸ **it was sheer luck** 这纯粹是运气

sheet [ʃi:t] N [c] **1** (on bed) 床单 [chuángdān] **2** [of paper] 一张 [yīzhāng]; [of glass, metal, wood, ice] 一片 [yīpiàn]

sheik(h) [ʃeɪk, US ʃi:k] N [c] 酋长 [qiúzhǎng]

shelf [ʃɛlf] (pl **shelves**) N [c] (bookshelf) 架子 [jiàzi]; (in cupboard) 搁板 [gēbǎn]; (in oven) 层 [céng] ▸ **a set of shelves** 一整套架子 ▸ **to be left on the shelf** (inf) [+ person] 嫁不出去的

shell [ʃɛl] I N [c] **1** (on beach) 贝壳 [bèiké] **2** [of tortoise, snail, crab, egg, nut] 壳 [ké] **3** (explosive) 炮弹 [pàodàn] **4** (frame) [of building, boat, car] 框架 [kuàngjià] II VT **1** (prepare) [+ nuts, peas, prawns] 去壳 [qùké] **2** (fire shells at) 炮击 [pàojī] ▸ **shell out** (inf) I VT FUS [不可拆分] ▸ **to shell**

out money (for sth/on sth/to do sth) (为某物/就某物/为做某事) 破费 [(wèi mǒuwù/jiù mǒuwù/wèi zuò mǒushì) pòfèi] II VI ▸ **to shell out** (for sth/on sth/to do sth) (为某物/就某物/为做某事) 花钱 [(wèi mǒuwù/jiù mǒuwù/wèi zuò mǒushì) huāqián]

she'll [ʃi:l] = **she will**

shellfish ['ʃɛlfɪʃ] (pl **shellfish**) I N [c/U] 贝类海产 [bèilèi hǎichǎn] II NPL (as food) 贝类海鲜 [bèilèi hǎixiān]

shelter ['ʃɛltə(r)] I N **1** [c] (building) (against bad weather) 遮蔽处 [zhēbìchù]; (against bombs) 防空洞 [fángkōngdòng]; (for homeless) 收容所 [shōuróngsuǒ] **2** [U] (protection) [from rain] 躲避 [duǒbì]; (from danger) 避难 [bìnàn] II VT **1** (protect) (from wind and rain) 遮蔽 [zhēbì] **2** (give lodging to) [+ fugitive] 收容 [shōuróng] III VI 躲避 [duǒbì] ▸ **to take shelter (from sth)** 躲避 (某事)

sheltered ['ʃɛltəd] ADJ **1** [+ bay, harbour] 遮风避雨的 [zhēfēng bìyǔ de] **2** [+ life, upbringing] 受庇护的 [shòu bìhù de] ▸ **sheltered housing** or **accommodation** 福利院

shelves [ʃɛlvz] NPL of **shelf**

shepherd ['ʃɛpəd] I N [c] 牧羊人 [mùyángrén] II VT ▸ **to shepherd sb towards/onto** etc **sth** 护送某人去/上 {等} 某处 [hùsòng mǒurén qù/shàng {děng} mǒuchù]

shepherd's pie (BRIT) N [c/U] 肉馅土豆泥饼 [ròuxiàn tǔdòuní bǐng]

sheriff ['ʃɛrɪf] (US) N [c] **1** (modern) 县治安官 [xiàn zhì'ānguān] **2** (in Wild West) 镇上警长 [zhènshang jǐngzhǎng]

sherry ['ʃɛrɪ] N **1** [c/U] (substance) 雪利酒 [xuělìjiǔ] **2** [c] (also: **glass of sherry**) 一杯雪利酒 [yībēi xuělìjiǔ]

she's [ʃi:z] = **she is, she has**

shield [ʃi:ld] I N [c] **1** (soldier's) 盾牌 [dùnpái] **2** (trophy) 盾形锦标 [dùnxíng jǐnbiāo] **3** (TECH) (protective device) 防护板 [fánghùbǎn] **4** ▸ **a shield against sth** 免受某物侵害的屏障 [miǎnshòu mǒuwù qīnhài de píngzhàng] II VT ▸ **to shield sb/sth (from sth)** (physically) 把某人/某物 (与某物) 遮挡开 [bǎ mǒurén/mǒuwù (yǔ mǒuwù) zhēdǎngkāi]; (fig) 保护某人/某物 (免于某事) [bǎohù mǒurén/mǒuwù (miǎnyú mǒushì)]

shift [ʃɪft] I N [c] **1** (change) 转变 [zhuǎnbiàn] **2** (period of work) 轮班 [lúnbān] **3** (group of workers) 轮班职工 [lúnbān zhígōng] II VT **1** (move) 移动 [yídòng] **2** (change) [+ opinion, policy, emphasis] 改变 [gǎibiàn] **3** (remove) [+ stain] 去除 [qùchú] III VI **1** (move) [cargo, load +] 移动 [yídòng]; [wind +] 转向 [zhuǎnxiàng]; [person, eyes +] 转移 [zhuǎnyí] **2** (change) [opinion, policy +] 改变 [gǎibiàn] ▸ **to shift gears** (US: AUT) 换挡 [英 = **change gears**] ▸ **to shift up/down** (US: AUT) 升一挡/降一挡

[英 = **change**]

shift work N [U] 轮班工作 [lúnbān gōngzuò]
▶ **to do shift work** 做轮班工作

shin [ʃɪn] I N [C] 胫部 [jìngbù] II VI ▶ **to shin up a tree** 爬上树 [páshàng shù]

shine [ʃaɪn] (pt, pp **shone**) I VI 1 (sun, light +) 照耀 [zhàoyào] 2 (eyes, hair +) 发光 [fāguāng] 3 (excel) ▶ **to shine (at sth)** (在某方面) 很出色 [(zài mǒu fāngmiàn) hěn chūsè] II VT 1 [+ torch, headlight] 照 [zhào] ▶ **to shine a light on sth** 用…照 [yòng…zhào] 2 (pt, pp **shined**) (polish) [+ shoes, furniture etc] 擦亮 [cāliàng] III N [S/U] (of surface) 光泽 [guāngzé]

shingles ['ʃɪŋlz] N [U] 带状疱疹 [dàizhuàng pàozhěn]

shiny ['ʃaɪnɪ] ADJ 闪闪发光的 [shǎnshǎnfāguāng de]

ship [ʃɪp] I N [C] 船 [chuán] II VT ▶ **to ship sb/sth to** 运送某人/某物到 [yùnsòng mǒurén/mǒuwù dào] ▶ **to be on board ship** 在船上

shipment ['ʃɪpmənt] N [C] (of goods) (by ship) 船运货物 [chuányùn huòwù]; (by train, plane etc) 运输的货物 [yùnshū de huòwù]

shipping ['ʃɪpɪŋ] N [U] 1 (business) 航运业 [hángyùnyè] 2 (cost of transport) 船运费 [chuányùn fèi] 3 (ships) 船舶 [chuánbó]

shipwreck ['ʃɪprɛk] I N 1 [C/U] (event) 海难 [hǎinàn] 2 [C] (ship) 失事的船只 [shīshì de chuánzhī] II VT ▶ **to be shipwrecked** 遭遇海难 [zāo hǎinàn]

shipyard ['ʃɪpjɑːd] N [C] 船坞 [chuánwù]

shirt [ʃəːt] N [C] 衬衫 [chènshān]

shit [ʃɪt] (inf!) I INT 该死 [gāisǐ] II N [U] 1 (faeces) 粪便 [fènbiàn] 2 (rubbish, nonsense) 狗屎 [gǒushǐ]

shiver ['ʃɪvə(r)] I N [C] 颤抖 [chàndǒu] II VI 发抖 [fādǒu] ▶ **to shiver with fear/cold** 怕得/冷得发抖

shoal [ʃəʊl] N [C] (of fish) 群 [qún]

shock [ʃɔk] I N 1 [C] (unpleasant surprise) 震骇 [zhènhài] 2 [C] (surprise) 震惊 [zhènjīng] 3 [U] (condition) (emotional) 令人震惊的状况 [lìngrén zhènjīng de zhuàngkuàng]; (MED) 休克 [xiūkè] 4 [C/U] (impact) 震动 [zhèndòng] 5 [C] (also: **electric shock**) 触电 [chùdiàn] II VT 1 (upset) 使震惊 [shǐ zhènjīng] 2 (offend, scandalize) 使厌恶 [shǐ yànwù] ▶ **it came as a shock (to hear that...)** (听到…) 令人震惊 ▶ **to be in shock** (MED) 处于休克状态

shocked [ʃɔkt] ADJ 1 (upset) 受到打击的 [shòudào dǎjī de] 2 (offended, scandalized) 感到不快的 [gǎndào bùkuài de] ▶ **I was shocked to learn that...** 听说…我很震惊

shocking ['ʃɔkɪŋ] ADJ 1 (outrageous) 骇人听闻的 [hàiréntīngwén de] 2 (inf) (very bad) 糟透的 [zāotòu de] ▶ **it is shocking that...** 令人吃惊的是…

shoe [ʃuː] (pt, pp **shod** [ʃɔd]) I N [C] 1 (for person) 鞋 [xié] 2 (for horse) 马蹄铁 [mǎtítiě] II VT 钉

马蹄铁 [dìng mǎtítiě] ▶ **a pair of shoes** 一双鞋 ▶ **I wouldn't want to be in his shoes** 我不想处于他的境地

shoelace ['ʃuːleɪs] N [C] 鞋带 [xiédài] ▶ **to do up or tie or fasten one's shoelaces** 系鞋带

shoe polish N [U] 鞋油 [xiéyóu]

shoe shop N [C] 鞋店 [xiédiàn]

shone [ʃɔn] PT, PP of **shine**

shook [ʃʊk] PT of **shake**

shoot [ʃuːt] (pt, pp **shot**) I N [C] 1 (on branch, seedling) 嫩芽 [nènyá] 2 (CINE, PHOT) 拍摄 [pāishè] II VT 1 (kill) [+ person, animal] 向…开枪 [xiàng…kāiqiāng] 2 (BRIT) (hunt) 射猎 [shèliè] [美 = **hunt**] 3 (execute) 枪决 [qiāngjué] 4 [+ film] 拍摄 [pāishè] III VI 1 (with gun, bow) 射击 [shèjī] ▶ **to shoot (at sb/sth)** (朝某人/某物) 射击 [(cháo mǒurén/mǒuwù) shèjī] 2 (FOOTBALL ETC) 射门 [shèmén] ▶ **to shoot sb in the back/leg etc** 射中某人的背部/腿{等} ▶ **to shoot o.s.** 射中自己 ▶ **to shoot o.s. in the head/leg etc** 射中自己的头/腿{等} ▶ **to shoot past/into/through sth etc** (move) 飞快经过/进入/穿过某物{等} ▶ **shoot down** VT 1 [+ plane] 击落 [jīluò] 2 (fig) [+ person] 批驳 [pībó]; [+ idea, rumour etc] 驳倒 [bódǎo] ▶ **shoot up** VI 1 (increase) 暴涨 [bàozhǎng] 2 (inject drugs) 注射毒品 [zhùshè dúpǐn]

shooting ['ʃuːtɪŋ] N [C] 1 (attack, murder, shots) 枪击 [qiāngjī] 2 (of film) 拍摄 [pāishè] 3 (BRIT) (hunting) 射猎 [shèliè] [美 = **hunting**]

shop [ʃɔp] I N [C] 1 (ESP BRIT) 商店 [shāngdiàn] [美 = **store**] 2 (workshop) 车间 [chējiān] II VI 购物 [gòuwù] III VT (BRIT: inf) [+ person] 告发 [gàofā] ▶ **to talk shop** 三句话不离本行 ▶ **to go shopping** 去买东西 ▶ **shop around** VI 仔细选购 [zǐxì xuǎngòu] ▶ **to shop around for sth** 到处物色某物

shop assistant (BRIT) N [C] 店员 [diànyuán] [美 = **sales clerk**]

shopkeeper ['ʃɔpkiːpə(r)] (BRIT) N [C] 店主 [diànzhǔ] [美 = **storekeeper**]

shoplifting ['ʃɔplɪftɪŋ] N [U] 商店货物扒窃 [shāngdiàn huòwù páqiè]

shopper ['ʃɔpə(r)] N [C] 购物者 [gòuwùzhě]

shopping ['ʃɔpɪŋ] N [U] 1 (activity) 购物 [gòuwù] 2 (goods) 所购之物 [suǒgòu zhī wù] ▶ **to do the shopping** 买东西 see also **shop**

shopping bag N [C] 购物袋 [gòuwùdài]

shopping cart (US) N [C] 购物手推车 [gòuwù shǒutuīchē] [英 = **shopping trolley**]

shopping centre, (US) **shopping center** N [C] 购物中心 [gòuwù zhōngxīn]

shopping list N [C] 1 (for purchases) 购物单 [gòuwùdān] 2 (wish list) 心愿表 [xīnyuànbiǎo]

shopping mall N [C] 购物大厦 [gòuwù dàshà]

shopping trolley (BRIT) N [C] 购物手推车 [gòuwù shǒutuīchē] [美 = **shopping cart**]

shop window N [C] 商店橱窗 [shāngdiàn

chúchuāng]

shore [ʃɔː(r)] N [C] 岸 [àn] ► **the shore(s) of...**
…的岸边 ► **on shore** 在陆上
► **shore up** VT [+ wall] 支撑 [zhīchēng]; [+ system]
加强 [jiāqiáng]

○ **short** [ʃɔːt] I ADJ 1 (in time) 短暂的 [duǎnzàn
de] ▷ We had a short meeting. 我们的会面很短
暂。2 (in length) 短的 [duǎn de] ▷ His black hair
was very short. 他的黑头发很短。3 (not tall) 矮
的 [ǎi de] ▷ I'm tall and thin and he's short and fat.
我又高又瘦，他又矮又胖。4 (scarce) 短缺
的 [duǎnquē de] ▷ Money is short. 钱不够。
5 (curt) ► **to be short (with sb)** (对某人) 粗
暴无礼 [(duì mǒurén cūbào wúlǐ)] ▷ I'm sorry
I was so short with you. 对不起，我对你太短
暴无礼了。II [C] 1 (BRIT) (drink) 少量烈
酒 [shǎoliàng lièjiǔ] 2 (film) 短片 [duǎnpiàn]
III **shorts** NPL 1 (short trousers) 短裤 [duǎnkù]
2 (ESP US) (underpants) 男用短衬裤 [nányòng
duǎnchènkù] ► **a short time ago** 不久以前
► **at short notice** 临时通知 ► **in short** 简而
言之 ► **to have a short temper** 脾气暴躁 ► **to
be short of sth** 缺乏某物 ► I'm 3 **short** 我还
缺3个 ► **Fred is short for Frederick** 弗雷德是
弗雷德里克的简称 ► **a pair of shorts** 一条短
裤 ► **to cut short** 缩短 ► **to run short of sth** 所
剩不多了 ► **to fall short of** 未达到 ► **short of
doing...** 除了做…外 ► **nothing/little short
of...** 不亚于/简直就是… ► **to stop short** 突
然停住 ► **to stop short of doing sth** 差点儿就
要做某事

shortage ['ʃɔːtɪdʒ] N [C/U] 短缺 [duǎnquē]

shortbread ['ʃɔːtbrɛd] N [C/U] 白脱甜酥饼
[báituō tiánsūbǐng]

short-circuit [ʃɔːt'səːkɪt] I VI 发生短路
[fāshēng duǎnlù] II VT 1 (ELEC) 使短路 [shǐ
duǎnlù] 2 (fig) [+ process, system] 避开 [bìkāi]
III N [C] 短路 [duǎnlù]

shortcoming ['ʃɔːtkʌmɪŋ] N [C] 缺点
[quēdiǎn]

shortcrust pastry ['ʃɔːtkrʌst-] (BRIT) N [U] 松
脆馅饼底盘 [sōngcuì xiànbǐng dǐpán]

short cut N [C] 1 (route) 近路 [jìnlù] 2 (method)
捷径 [jiéjìng]

shorten ['ʃɔːtn] I VT 1 [+ holiday, life, book, letter]
缩短 [suōduǎn] 2 [+ clothes, plank etc] 截短
[jiéduǎn] II VI 变短 [biànduǎn]

shortfall ['ʃɔːtfɔːl] N [C] 赤字 [chìzì]

shorthand ['ʃɔːthænd] N [U] 1 (system) 速记
[sùjì] 2 (quick name) 简略表达 [jiǎnlüè biǎodá]
► **in shorthand** 用速记记 录

shortlist ['ʃɔːtlɪst] I N [C] 最后一轮候选名
单 [zuìhòu yīlún hòuxuǎn míngdān] II VT (ESP
BRIT) 进入最后一轮候选名单 [jìnrù zuìhòu
yīlún hòuxuǎn míngdān]

short-lived [ʃɔːt'lɪvd] ADJ 短暂的 [duǎnzàn
de]

shortly ['ʃɔːtlɪ] ADV 马上 [mǎshàng] ► **shortly**

after/before sth 某事后/前不久 ► **shortly
after/before doing sth** 做某事后/前不久

short-sighted [ʃɔːt'saɪtɪd] ADJ 1 (BRIT) 近视
的 [jìnshì de] [美 = near-sighted] 2 (misguided)
目光短浅的 [mùguāng duǎnqiǎn de]

short-sleeved ['ʃɔːtsliːvd] ADJ 短袖的
[duǎnxiù de]

short story N [C] 短篇小说 [duǎnpiān
xiǎoshuō]

short-tempered [ʃɔːt'tɛmpəd] ADJ 易怒的
[yìnù de]

short-term ['ʃɔːttəːm] ADJ [+ solution, gain] 短
期的 [duǎnqī de]; [+ memory] 短暂的 [duǎnzàn
de]

short wave N [U] 短波 [duǎnbō]

shot [ʃɒt] I PT, PP of shoot II N 1 [C] (from
gun) 射击 [shèjī] 2 [U] (shotgun pellets) 铅沙弹
[qiānshādàn] 3 [C] (FOOTBALL) 射门 [shèmén]
4 [C] (injection) 皮下注射 [píxià zhùshè] 5 [C]
(CINE, PHOT) 镜头 [jìngtóu] ► **to fire a shot (at
sb/sth)** (朝某人/某物) 开枪 ► **a good/poor
shot** (person) 一位神枪手/不高明的射手 ► **a
shot in the arm** (fig) 起鼓舞作用的事物 ► **to
have a shot at sth/at doing sth** (inf) 尝试某
事/做某事 ► **to give sth one's best shot** (inf)
对某事尽自己最大的努力 ► **to do sth like a
shot** (inf) 立刻做某事 ► **to call the shots** 发号
施令 ► **it's a long shot** 这是大胆的尝试 ► **to
get shot of sb/sth** (inf) 摆脱某人/某物

shotgun ['ʃɒtɡʌn] N [C] 霰弹枪 [sǎndànqiāng]

○ **should** [ʃud] AUX VB 1 (indicating advisability) ► I
should go now 我现在应该走了 [wǒ xiànzài
yīnggāi zǒule] 2 (indicating obligation) 应当
[yīngdāng] 3 (indicating likelihood) ► **he should
be there by now/he should get there soon** 他
现在该到那儿了/他该很快就到那儿了 [tā
xiànzài gāi dào nàrle/tā gāi hěnkuài jiù dào
nàrle] 4 (frm) (would) ► I **should go if he asked
me** 如果他要求，我会走的 [rúguǒ tā yāoqiú,
wǒ huì zǒude] 5 (after 'that') ► **it's not right that
we should be fined** 我们竟会被罚款，这是不
对的 [wǒmen jìnghuì bèi fákuǎn, zhèshì bùduì
de] ► **you should have been more careful** 你本
该更加小心 ► **he should have arrived by now**
他现在应该到了 ► I **should go if I were you** 我
要是你就走了 ► I **should like to** 我很乐意
► I **should like to invite them to dinner** 我想
要请他们吃晚餐 ► I **should like a strawberry
ice cream** 我想要一份草莓冰淇淋 ► **should
he phone** or **if he should phone...** 如果他打电
话来…

shoulder ['ʃəuldə(r)] I N [C] 肩膀 [jiānbǎng]
II VT [+ responsibility, blame] 承担 [chéngdān]
► **to look over one's shoulder** (feel anxious) 焦虑
不安 ► **to rub shoulders with sb** (mix with) 和
某人有交往 ► **to work shoulder to shoulder**
(co-operate) 齐心协力地工作 ► **we will stand
shoulder to shoulder with our allies** 我们将与

我们的同盟并肩协力

shoulder blade N [c] 肩胛骨 [jiānjiǎgǔ]

shouldn't ['ʃʊdnt] = should not

shout [ʃaut] I N [c] 喊叫声 [hǎnjiàoshēng]
II VT (also: **shout out**) 呼喊 [hūhǎn] III VI (also:
shout out) 喊叫 [hǎnjiào] ▶ **to give sb a shout**
(inf) 让某人知道
▶ **shout down** VT [+ speaker] 用叫喊声压倒
[yòng jàohǎnshēng yādǎo]

shouting ['ʃautɪŋ] N [U] (quarrelling) 叫喊
[jiàohǎn]

shove [ʃʌv] I VT 撞 [zhuàng] II N [c] ▶ **to
give sb/sth a shove** 猛推某人/某物 [měng tuī
mǒurén/mǒuwù] ▶ **to shove sth into/under sth**
(inf) (put) 把某物塞进某物/塞到某物下 ▶ **he
shoved me out of the way** 他把我推到一边
▶ **shove off** (inf) VI 走开 [zǒukāi]

shovel ['ʃʌvl] I N [c] 铲 [chǎn] II VT 1 [+ snow,
coal, earth] 铲 [chǎn] 2 (push) 把…胡乱塞入
[bǎ…húluàn sāirù]

☉ show [ʃəu] (pt **showed**, pp **shown**) I N [c]
1 (display) [of emotion, support, strength] 表示
[biǎoshì] ▷ Miners gathered in a show of support
for the government. 矿工们聚集在一起以表示
对政府的支持。2 (exhibition) 展览 [zhǎnlǎn]
3 (THEAT) 演出 [yǎnchū] 4 (TV, RAD) 节目
[jiémù] II VT 1 (indicate) 表明 [biǎomíng] ▶ **to
show sb sth** or **to show sth to sb** 给某人看某物
〔或〕把某物给某人看 [gěi mǒurén kàn mǒuwù
{huò} bǎ mǒuwù gěi mǒurén kàn] ▷ Cut out
this article and show it to your bank manager. 剪
下这篇文章，把它给你的银行经理看一
下。2 (demonstrate) 展示 [zhǎnshì] 3 (display)
[+ signs] 显示 [xiǎnshì]; [+ respect, interest etc] 表
示 [biǎoshì] ▷ The peace talks showed signs of
progress. 和平谈判显示出进展的迹象。4 (put
on) [+ programme, film etc] 播映 [bōyìng] ▷ The
ceremony was shown on BBC1. 典礼在BBC1台
播映。5 (illustrate, depict) [picture, graph, film
etc +] 描述 [miáoshù] ▷ Figure 4.1 shows the
respiratory system. 图4.1显示的是呼吸系
统。6 ▶ **to show sb in/out** 带某人进来/出去
[dài mǒurén jìnlái/chūqù] 7 (exhibit) [+ painting
etc] 展出 [zhǎnchū] III VI 1 (be evident) 显而
易见 [xiǎn'éryìjiàn] ▷ Ferguson was unhappy
and it showed. 弗格森不太高兴，这是显而易
见的。2 (be visible) 看得见 [kàndejiàn] 3 (ESP
US) (arrive, appear) 露面 [lòumiàn] ▶ **a show of
hands** 举手表决 ▶ **who's running the show
here?** 谁在这儿掌管一切？▶ **for show** 为装
门面 ▶ **on show** (exhibits etc) 在展览中 ▶ **to
show that...** 表明… ▷ The post-mortem shows
that death was due to natural causes. 验尸情况证
实死亡是由于自然原因造成的。▶ **to show
sb how to do sth** 示范某人如何做某事 ▶ **to
show a profit/loss** (COMM) 赢利/亏损 ▶ **to
show sb to his seat/to the door** 领某人到他
的座位/门口 ▶ **to have something/nothing**

▶ **to show for sth** 在某方面有所建树/毫无成果
▶ **it just goes to show that...** 这证明…
▶ **show around** VT [+ person] 带…参观
[dài…cānguān]
▶ **show off** I VI 卖弄 [màinòng] II VT 炫耀
[xuànyào]
▶ **show up** I VI 1 (be visible, noticeable) 显露
[xiǎnlù] 2 (arrive, appear) 露面 [lòumiàn] II VT
1 (make visible, noticeable) [+ imperfections etc] 使
显现 [shǐ xiǎnxiàn] 2 (embarrass) 使难堪 [shǐ
nánkān]

show business N [U] 娱乐界 [yúlèjiè]

shower ['ʃauə(r)] I N [c] 1 (rain) 阵雨 [zhènyǔ]
2 [of stones, sparks etc] 一阵 [yīzhèn] 3 (for
washing) 淋浴器 [línyùqì] 4 (US) (party) 送礼
会 [sònglǐhuì] II VI 洗淋浴 [xǐ línyù] III VT
▶ **to shower sb with sth** [+ confetti, rice] 把某
物撒向某人 [bǎ mǒuwù sǎxiàng mǒurén];
[+ gifts, kisses] 送某人大量的某物 [sòng mǒurén
dàliàng de mǒuwù] ▶ **to have** or **take a shower**
洗淋浴

shower cap N [c] 浴帽 [yùmào]

shower gel N [U] 沐浴露 [mùyùlù]

showing ['ʃəuɪŋ] N [c] [of film] 放映 [fàngyìng]

show jumping [-dʒʌmpɪŋ] N [U] 赛马中的障
碍赛 [sàimǎzhōng de zhàng'àisài]

shown [ʃəun] PP of **show**

show-off ['ʃəuɔf] N [c] 爱卖弄的人 [ài
màinòng de rén]

showroom ['ʃəurum] N [c] 陈列室 [chénlièshì]

shrank [ʃræŋk] PT of **shrink**

shred [ʃred] I N [c] 1 (piece) 细条 [xìtiáo]
2 ▶ **not a shred of evidence/truth** 无丝毫证
据/事实 [wú sīháo zhèngjù/shìshí] II VT [+ food]
切碎 [qiēsuì]; [+ paper, documents] 撕碎 [sīsuì]

shrewd [ʃru:d] ADJ [+ person] 精明的 [jīngmíng
de]; [+ investment] 高明的 [gāomíng de]

shriek [ʃri:k] I VI 尖叫 [jiānjiào] II N [c] 尖叫
声 [jiānjiào shēng] ▶ **to shriek with laughter**
尖声大笑

shrimp [ʃrɪmp] N [c] (small) 小虾 [xiǎoxiā]; (US)
(bigger) 虾 [xiā] [英 = **prawn**]

shrimp cocktail N [c] (US) 冷盘虾
[lěngpánxiā] [英 = **prawn cocktail**]

shrine [ʃraɪn] N [c] 1 (religious) 圣坛 [shèngtán]
2 (to sb's memory) 圣地 [shèngdì]

shrink [ʃrɪŋk] (pt **shrank**, pp **shrunk**) I VI
1 [cloth +] 缩水 [suōshuǐ] 2 [forests, profits,
audiences etc +] 减少 [jiǎnshǎo] 3 ▶ **to shrink
away/back** 退缩/畏缩 [tuìsuō/wèisuō] II VT
[+ cloth] 使皱缩 [shǐ zhòusuō] III N [c] (inf, pej)
精神病医生 [jīngshénbìng yīshēng] ▶ **not to
shrink from sth** 不回避某事

shrivel ['ʃrɪvl] (also: **shrivel up**) I VI 枯萎
[kūwěi] II VT 使干枯 [shǐ gānkū]

shroud [ʃraud] I N [c] 裹尸布 [guǒshībù]
II VT 1 ▶ **to be shrouded in mist/smoke** etc 被
雾/烟〔等〕笼罩 [bèi wù/yān {děng} lǒngzhào]

2 ▶ **to be shrouded in mystery** 笼罩着神秘色彩 [lǒngzhàozhe shénmì sècǎi]

shrub [ʃrʌb] N [c] 灌木 [guànmù]

shrug [ʃrʌg] I vi 耸肩 [sǒngjiān] II vt ▶ **to shrug one's shoulders** 耸耸肩 [sǒngsǒngjiān] III N [c] 耸肩 [sǒngjiān]
  ▶ **shrug off** vt [+ criticism, problem, illness] 对…不予理会 [duì…bùyǔ lǐhuì]

shrunk [ʃrʌŋk] pt of **shrink**

shudder [ˈʃʌdə(r)] I vi [person +] 颤抖 [chàndǒu]; [vehicle, machine +] 剧烈摇晃 [jùliè yáohuàng] II N [c] 颤抖 [chàndǒu] ▶ **to shudder with fear/cold** etc 吓得/冷得{等}发抖 ▶ **to shudder to a halt** 随着一阵颤动停了下来 ▶ **I shudder to think what would have happened if...** 我不敢设想如果…将会发生什么 ▶ **to give a shudder** 浑身颤抖

shuffle [ˈʃʌfl] I vi **1** ▶ **to shuffle along/in/out** etc 拖着脚走来走去/走进来/走出去{等} [tuōzhe jiǎo zǒulái zǒuqù/zǒujìnlái/zǒuchūqù {děng}] **2** (fidget) ▶ **to shuffle around** 坐立不安 [zuò lì bù'ān] II vt **1** [+ cards] 洗 [xǐ] **2** [+ papers] 乱翻 [luànfān] **3** ▶ **to shuffle one's feet** 来回地挪动双脚 [láihuí de nuódòng shuāngjiǎo] III N [s] 曳足而行 [yèzúérxíng]

shun [ʃʌn] vt [+ publicity, neighbours etc] 回避 [huíbì]

shut [ʃʌt] (pt, pp **shut**) I vt [+ door, drawer] 关上 [guānshang]; [+ shop] 关门 [guānmén]; [+ mouth, eyes] 闭上 [bìshang] II vi [door, drawer +] 关上 [guānshang]; [shop +] 打烊 [dǎyàng]; [mouth, eyes +] 闭上 [bìshang] III ADJ [+ door, drawer] 关闭的 [guānbì de]; [+ shop] 打烊的 [dǎyàng de]; [+ mouth, eyes] 闭着的 [bìzhe de]
  ▶ **shut away** vt ▶ **to shut o.s. away** 把自己关起来 [bǎ zìjǐ guānqǐlái]
  ▶ **shut down** I vt [+ factory etc] 使停业 [shǐ tíngyè] **2** [+ machine] 关闭 [guānbì] II vi [factory etc +] 停业 [tíngyè]
  ▶ **shut in** vt 把…关起来 [bǎ…guānqǐlái]
  ▶ **shut off** vt [+ supply, water, engine] 切断 [qiēduàn]
  ▶ **shut out** vt **1** [+ person] 把…关在外面 [bǎ…guānzài wàimiàn]; [+ cold, noise etc] 把…隔绝在外 [bǎ…géjué zàiwài] **2** (block) [+ view] 挡住 [dǎngzhù]; [+ thought, memory] 排除 [páichú]
  ▶ **shut up** I vi (inf) 住口 [zhùkǒu] II vt [+ person] 使住口 [shǐ zhùkǒu] ▶ **shut up!** (inf) 闭嘴!

shutter [ˈʃʌtə(r)] N [c] **1** (on window) 百叶窗 [bǎiyèchuāng] **2** (on camera) 快门 [kuàimén]

shuttle [ˈʃʌtl] I N [c] **1** (plane, bus etc) 穿梭班机/班车 [chuānsuō bānjī/bānchē] **2** (also: **space shuttle**) 航天飞机 [hángtiān fēijī] **3** (for weaving) 梭 [suō] II vi [vehicle, person +] ▶ **to shuttle back and forth between** 在…间穿梭往返 [zài…jiān chuānsuō wǎngfǎn] III vt 穿梭 [chuānsuō]

shuttlecock [ˈʃʌtlkɔk] (BADMINTON) N [c] 羽毛球 [yǔmáoqiú]

shy [ʃaɪ] I ADJ [+ person] 害羞的 [hàixiū de]; [+ animal] 易受惊的 [yì shòujīng de] II vi [horse +] 惊退 [jīngtuì] ▶ **to be shy of doing sth** 对做某事有顾忌
  ▶ **shy away from** vt FUS [不可拆分] ▶ **to shy away from sth/from doing sth** 因顾忌而回避某事/做某事 [yīn gùjì 'ér huíbì mǒushì/zuò mǒushì]

Siberia [saɪˈbɪərɪə] N 西伯利亚 [Xībólìyà]

sibling [ˈsɪblɪŋ] (frm) N [c] 兄弟姐妹 [xiōngdì jiěmèi] ▶ **sibling rivalry** 手足相争

Sicilian [sɪˈsɪlɪən] I ADJ 西西里的 [Xīxīlǐ de] II N [c] (person) 西西里人 [Xīxīlǐrén]

Sicily [ˈsɪsɪlɪ] N 西西里岛 [Xīxīlǐdǎo]

sick [sɪk] I ADJ **1** (physically) 患病的 [huànbìng de]; (mentally) 令人厌烦的 [lìngrén tǎoyàn de] **2** ▶ **to be sick** (vomit) 呕吐 [ǒutù] **3** [+ humour, joke] 病态的 [bìngtài de] II N [U] (BRIT) (vomit) 呕吐物 [ǒutùwù] III NPL ▶ **the sick** 病人 [bìngrén] ▶ **to feel sick** 感觉恶心 ▶ **to fall sick** 患病 ▶ **to be off sick** 因病缺勤 ▶ **to make sb sick** (inf) 使某人感到厌恶 ▶ **to be sick of sth/of doing sth** (inf) 讨厌某事/做某事
  ▣ 用法参见 ill

sicken [ˈsɪkn] vt (disgust) 使作呕 [shǐ zuò'ǒu]

sickening [ˈsɪknɪŋ] ADJ 令人作呕的 [lìngrén zuò'ǒu de]

sick leave N [U] 病假 [bìngjià] ▶ **to be on sick leave** 休病假

sickly [ˈsɪklɪ] ADJ **1** [+ child, plant] 多病的 [duōbìng de] **2** [+ smell, taste] 令人作呕的 [lìngrén zuò'ǒu de]

sickness [ˈsɪknɪs] N [U] **1** (illness) 患病 [huànbìng] **2** (vomiting) 呕吐 [ǒutù] ▶ **radiation/altitude/motion sickness** 放射病/高空病/晕动病

♻ side [saɪd] I N [c] **1** 边 [biān] ▷ **on both sides of the border** 边境两边 **2** (surface) [of cube] 面 [miàn] **3** (not back or front) [of building, vehicle] 侧面 [cèmiàn] ▷ **a van with his name on the side** 侧面写有他名字的货车; [of body] 体侧 [tǐcè] **4** (half) [of paper, face, brain etc] 一面 [yīmiàn] ▷ **on the other side of the page** 这页纸的另一面上; [of tape, record] 面 [miàn] ▷ **We want to hear side A.** 我们想听A面。 **5** (edge) [of road, bed etc] 边缘 [biānyuán] ▷ **Park on the side of the road.** 把车停在路边。 **6** [of hill, valley] 坡 [pō] ▷ **narrow valleys with steep sides** 两面陡坡的狭窄山谷 **7** (aspect) 方面 [fāngmiàn] ▷ **Anxiety has a mental and a physical side.** 焦虑有精神方面的因素也有身体方面的因素。 **8** (BRIT) (team) 队 [duì] ▷ **the Scottish First Division side** 苏格兰甲级队 [美 = **team**] **9** (in conflict, contest) 一方 [yīfāng] ▷ **They sold arms to both sides.** 他们向双方出售军火。 **10** [of argument, debate] 派 [pài] ▷ **people on both sides of the issue** 针对该议题的两

派人 II ADJ [+ door, entrance] 旁边的 [pángbiān de] III VI ▶ **to side with sb** 支持某人 [zhīchí mǒurén] ▶ **on either side of sth** 在某物的任一边 ▶ **on the other side of sth** 在某物的另一边 ▶ **the right/wrong side of sth** 某物正确的/错误的一边 ▶ **from side to side** 从一边到另一边 ▶ **to lie on one's side** [person +] 侧卧; [thing +] 侧放 ▶ **by the side of** 在…旁边 ▶ **side by side** 肩并肩 ▶ **she never left my side** 她从没离开过我身边 ▶ **to be at** or **by sb's side** 在某人身旁 ▶ **to get on the right/wrong side of sb** (fig) 讨某人喜欢/不讨某人喜欢 ▶ **they are on our side** 他们站在我们这边 ▶ **to take sides** 偏袒 ▶ **to put sth to one side** 把某事暂搁一边 ▶ **to earn some money on the side** 赚额外的收入 ▶ **a side of beef** 牛的胁肉

sideboard ['saɪdbɔːd] I N [c] 餐具柜 [cānjùguì] II **sideboards** NPL (BRIT) = **sideburns**

sideburns ['saɪdbəːnz] NPL 连鬓胡子 [liánbìn húzi]

side-effect ['saɪdɪfɛkt] N [c] **1** [of drug] 副作用 [fù zuòyòng] **2** [of situation] 意外后果 [yìwài hòuguǒ]

sidelight ['saɪdlaɪt] N [c] **1** (BRIT) (on front of vehicle) 示宽灯 [shìkuāndēng] [美= **parking light**] **2** (US) (side of vehicle) 边灯 [biāndēng]

sideline ['saɪdlaɪn] I N [c] **1** (extra job) 副业 [fùyè] **2** (SPORT) 边线 [biānxiàn] II VT **1** (keep back) [+ person, policy] 使靠边 [shǐ kàobiān] **2** [+ player] 使…退出比赛 [shǐ…tuìchū bǐsài] ▶ **on the sidelines** (not involved) 当局外人

side order N [c] 与主菜同时上的附加菜 [yǔ zhǔcài tóngshí shàng de fùjiācài]

side street N [c] 小街 [xiǎojiē]

sidetrack ['saɪdtræk] VT 使…转移目标 [shǐ…zhuǎnyí mùbiāo]

sideview mirror ['saɪdvjuː-] (US) N [c] 后视镜 [hòushì jìng] [英= **wing mirror**]

sidewalk ['saɪdwɔːk] (US) N [c] 人行道 [rénxíngdào] [英= **pavement**]

sideways ['saɪdweɪz] I ADV [move +] 向一边 [xiàng yībiān]; [look, face +] 斜侧 [xiécè] II ADJ [+ glance, movement] 向一侧的 [xiàng yīcè de]

siege [siːdʒ] N [c] 围困 [wéikùn] ▶ **to lift a siege** 解围 ▶ **to be under siege** 被围困 ▶ **to lay siege to** [police, soldiers +] 围攻; [journalists +] 包围

Sierra Leone [sɪˈɛrəlɪˈəun] N 塞拉利昂 [Sàilālì'áng]

sieve [sɪv] I N [c] (for flour etc) 筛子 [shāizi]; (for liquid) 滤器 [lùqì]; (garden sieve) 筛网 [shāiwǎng] II VT [+ flour, soil etc] 筛 [shāi]; [+ liquid] 滤 [lù] ▶ **to have a memory** or **mind like a sieve** 记性极差

sift [sɪft] VT 筛 [shāi]
▶ **sift through** VT FUS [不可拆分] [+ evidence, wreckage] 详查 [xiángchá]

sigh [saɪ] I N [c] 叹息 [tànxī] II VI 叹气 [tànqì] ▶ **to breathe** or **heave a sigh of relief** 松一口气

sight [saɪt] I N **1** [u] (faculty) 视力 [shìlì] **2** [c] (spectacle) 景象 [jǐngxiàng] **3** [c] (on gun) 瞄准器 [miáozhǔn qì] II **sights** NPL (places of interest) ▶ **the sights** 景点 [jǐngdiǎn] III VT 看见 [kànjiàn] ▶ **to catch sight of sb/sth** 瞧见某人/某物 ▶ **to lose sight of sth** (fig) 忽略某事 ▶ **the sight of sth** 一看见某物 ▶ **to set one's sights on sth** 立志拥有某物 ▶ **in sight** (lit) 看得见 ▶ **out of sight** 看不见 ▶ **to be in** or **within sight** (fig) 在望 ▶ **at first sight** 乍一看 ▶ **I know her by sight** 我看到她就知道她是谁 ▶ **on sight** [shoot, arrest +] 一看见就… ▶ **a sight better/worse** (inf) 好/坏得多

sightseeing ['saɪtsiːɪŋ] N [u] 观光 [guānguāng] ▶ **to go sightseeing** 观光游览

○**sign** [saɪn] I N **1** [c] (notice) 指示牌 [zhǐshìpái] ▷ **a sign saying "No Exit"** 一块写着"禁止入内"的指示牌 **2** [c] (also: road sign) 路标 [lùbiāo] **3** [c] (gesture) (with hand etc) 手势 [shǒushì] ▷ **the V-for-victory sign** 代表胜利的V字手势 **4** [c] (MATH, MUS) (symbol) 符号 [fúhào] ▷ **an equals sign** 一个等于号 **5** [c/u] (indication, evidence) 迹象 [jìxiàng] ▷ **The sky is clear and there's no sign of rain.** 天空晴朗，丝毫没有要下雨的迹象。 **6** [c] (ASTROL) 星座 [xīngzuò] II VT **1** [+ document] 签署 [qiānshǔ] **2** [+ TV programme] (for deaf people) 用手语演播 [yòng shǒuyǔ yǎnbō] **3** (FOOTBALL) [+ player] 与…签约 [yǔ…qiānyuē] III VI **1** (use sign language) 打手势 [shǒuyǔ shǒuyǔ] **2** (FOOTBALL) [player +] 签约 [qiānyuē] ▶ **to make a sign** 做手势 ▶ **a plus/minus sign** 正/负号 ▶ **there's no sign of her changing her mind** 她没有任何要改变主意的表示 ▶ **he was showing signs of improvement** 他的身体有好转的迹象 ▶ **a sign of the times** 时代的特征 ▶ **it's a good/bad sign** 这是个好/坏兆头
▶ **to sign one's name** 签名
▶ **sign away** VT [+ rights etc] 签字放弃 [qiānzì fàngqì]
▶ **sign for** VT FUS [不可拆分] [+ goods] 签收 [qiānshōu]
▶ **sign in** VI (at hotel etc) 签到 [qiāndào]
▶ **sign off** VI **1** (RAD, TV) 结束播放 [jiéshù bōfàng] **2** (in letter) 就此搁笔 [jiùcǐ gēbǐ] **3** (BRIT) (as unemployed) 退出失业救济 [tuìchū shīyè jiùjì]
▶ **sign on** (BRIT) VI (as unemployed) 申请失业救济 [shēnqǐng shīyè jiùjì] ▶ **to sign on for sth** [+ course] 签约做某事
▶ **sign out** VI (from hotel etc) 签名离开 [qiānmíng líkāi]
▶ **sign over** VT ▶ **to sign sth over to sb** 将某物签约转让给某人 [jiāng mǒuwù qiānyuē zhuǎnràng gěi mǒurén]
▶ **sign up** I VI (for job, course, trip etc) 签约受雇

[qiānyuē shòugù] II VT [+ player, recruit] 签约雇用 [qiānyuē gùyòng] ▶ **to sign up for** [+ job, course, trip etc] 签约从事

signal ['sɪɡnl] I N [C] 1 (to do sth) 信号 [xìnhào] 2 (indication) 暗示 [ànshì] 3 (RAIL) 信号机 [xìnhàojī] 4 (ELEC) 信号 [xìnhào] II VI 1 (with gesture, sound) ▶ **to signal (to sb)** (向某人)示意 [(xiàng mǒurén) shìyì] 2 (AUT) (with indicator) 开信号灯示意 [kāi xìnhàodēng shìyì] III VT 1 [+ message] 用信号示意 [yòng xìnhào shìyì]; [+ person] 向…打手势示意 [xiàng…dǎ shǒushì shìyì] 2 (indicate) 标志着 [biāozhìzhe] IV ADJ (frm) [+ triumph, failure] 显著的 [xiǎnzhù de]

signature ['sɪɡnətʃə(r)] N [C] 签名 [qiānmíng]

significance [sɪɡ'nɪfɪkəns] N [U] 重要性 [zhòngyàoxìng] ▶ **of no/some significance** 毫无/有一定重要意义

significant [sɪɡ'nɪfɪkənt] ADJ 1 (important) 重要的 [zhòngyào de] 2 (considerable) [+ amount, number, effect] 相当大的 [xiāngdāng dà de] 3 (meaningful) [+ look, glance etc] 意味深长的 [yìwèi shēncháng de] ▶ **it is significant that…** 值得注意的是…

signify ['sɪɡnɪfaɪ] VT 1 (represent) [symbol, number+] 表示 [biǎoshì] 2 (indicate) [event+] 意味 [yìwèi] 3 (make known) [person+] 示意 [shìyì] ▶ **to signify that…** 意味着…

sign language N [C/U] 手势语 [shǒushìyǔ]; (for deaf people) 手语 [shǒuyǔ]

signpost ['saɪnpəʊst] N [C] 1 (road sign) 路标 [lùbiāo] 2 (indicator) 指标 [zhǐbiāo]

Sikh [si:k] I N [C] 锡克教信徒 [Xīkèjiào xìntú] II ADJ 锡克教的 [Xīkèjiào de]

silence ['saɪləns] I N [C/U] 寂静 [jìjìng] II VT [+ person] 使安静 [shǐ ānjìng]; [+ opposition] 压制 [yāzhì] ▶ **in silence** 鸦雀无声 ▶ **to break one's silence** 开口讲话

silent ['saɪlənt] ADJ [+ person] (on particular occasion) 沉默的 [chénmò de]; (as character trait) 沉默寡言的 [chénmòguǎyán de]; [+ place, object] 安静的 [ānjìng de]; [+ prayer, emotion] 默默的 [mòmò de]; [+ film] 无声的 [wúshēng de] ▶ **to fall silent** (stop talking) 不作声; (stop making noise) 安静下来 ▶ **to be/remain silent about sth** 对某事守口如瓶

silhouette [sɪluː'ɛt] I N [C] 黑色轮廓 [hēisè lúnkuò] II VT ▶ **to be silhouetted against sth** 某物衬出…的轮廓 [mǒuwù chènchu…de lúnkuò]

silicon ['sɪlɪkən] N [U] 硅 [guī]

silicon chip N [C] 硅片 [guīpiàn]

silicone ['sɪlɪkəʊn] I N [U] 硅酮 [guītóng] II CPD [复合词] [+ implant, coating] 硅酮 [guītóng]

silk [sɪlk] I N [C/U] 丝绸 [sīchóu] I CPD [复合词] [+ scarf, shirt etc] 丝绸 [sīchóu]

silky ['sɪlkɪ] ADJ [+ material] 丝质的 [sīzhì de]; [+ skin] 柔软光洁的 [róuruǎn guāngjié de]

silly ['sɪlɪ] ADJ [+ person] 愚蠢的 [yúchǔn de]; [+ idea, object] 可笑的 [kěxiào de] ▶ **he's silly to be upset** 他这么难过真是太傻了 ▶ **it would be silly to waste it** 把它浪费了就太愚蠢了

silver ['sɪlvə(r)] I N [U] 1 银 [yín] 2 (silverware) 银器 [yínqì] 3 (coins) 银币 [yínbì] II ADJ 1 (in colour) [+ hair] 银白色的 [yínbáisè de] 2 (made of silver) [+ spoon, necklace etc] 银的 [yín de] ▶ **silver-grey** 银灰色

silver-plated [sɪlvə'pleɪtɪd] ADJ 镀银的 [dùyín de]

SIM card ['sɪm-] N [C] 手机智能卡 [shǒujī zhìnéngkǎ]

similar ['sɪmɪlə(r)] ADJ 相似的 [xiāngsì de] ▶ **to be similar to sth** 和某事物类似

similarity [sɪmɪ'lærɪtɪ] N 1 (U) (resemblance) 相似 [xiāngsì] 2 [C] (similar feature) 相似之处 [xiāngsì zhīchù]

similarly ['sɪmɪləlɪ] ADV 1 (in a similar way) 类似地 [lèisì de] 2 (likewise) 同样地 [tóngyàng de]

simmer ['sɪmə(r)] I VI 炖 [dùn] II VT 煨 [wēi] ▶ **simmer down** VI (calm down) 安静下来 [ānjìng xiàlái]; [situation+] 平静下来 [píngjìng xiàlái]

simple ['sɪmpl] ADJ 1 (easy) 简单的 [jiǎndān de] 2 (basic) [+ meal, life, cottage etc] 简朴的 [jiǎnpǔ de] 3 (mere) 纯粹的 [chúncuì de] 4 (LING) [+ tense] 简单的 [jiǎndān de] 5 (o.f.) (not intelligent) 智能低的 [zhìnéngdī de] ▶ **it would be simpler to move house** 搬家会更容易些

simplicity [sɪm'plɪsɪtɪ] N [U] 1 (lack of complexity) 简易 [jiǎnyì] 2 [of design, style etc] 朴素 [pǔsù]

simplify ['sɪmplɪfaɪ] VT 简化 [jiǎnhuà]

simply ['sɪmplɪ] ADV 1 (merely) 仅仅 [jǐnjǐn] 2 (live, say, dress etc) 简单地 [jiǎndānde] 3 (absolutely) 完全 [wánquán]

simulate ['sɪmjuleɪt] VT [+ action, feeling] 假装 [jiǎzhuāng]; [+ substance, noise] 模仿 [mófǎng]

simultaneous [sɪməl'teɪnɪəs] ADJ 同时的 [tóngshí de]; [+ translation] 同声的 [tóngshēng de]; [+ broadcast] 同步的 [tóngbù de]

sin [sɪn] I N [C/U] 罪孽 [zuìniè] II VI 有罪 [yǒuzuì]

since [sɪns] I ADV 1 (from then onwards) 此后 [cǐhòu] ▷ They went to college together and have done business together since. 他们一起上的大学并从此后一起做生意。 2 (latterly) 后来 [hòulái] ▷ 6,000 people were arrested, several hundred of whom have since been released. 6000人被逮捕，其中几百人后来被释放。 II PREP 1 (from) 自…以来 [zì…yǐlái] ▷ I've been here since the end of June. 我自6月底以来一直在这儿。 2 (after) 从…以后 [cóng…yǐhòu] ▷ I haven't seen powdered eggs since the war. 自战后我从未见过蛋粉。 III CONJ 1 (from when) 自从 [zìcóng] ▷ I've been wearing glasses since I was three. 我从3岁起就戴眼镜。**2** (after) 从⋯以后 [cóng⋯yǐhòu] ▷ So much has changed in the sport since I was a teenager. 自我十几岁起，这项运动已经改变了很多。**3** (as) 因为 [yīnwèi] ▷ Since it was Saturday, he stayed in bed an extra hour. 因为是星期六，他在床上多呆了一小时。▶ since then or ever since 从那时起 ▶ long since 很久以前

> **for** 表示过去、现在或将来某事持续的时间的长短，或未发生某事的时间的长短。She slept for eight hours…He will be away for three weeks…I hadn't seen him for four years. 表示某个时间段开始时，用 **since**。She has been with the group since it began…the first civilian president since the coup 17 years ago… **since** 还可以表示某事发生的最后时间，或者未发生某事的时间的长短。She hadn't eaten since breakfast…It was a long time since she had been to church.

sincere [sɪn'sɪə(r)] ADJ [+ person] 真诚的 [zhēnchéng de]; [+ belief, apology] 诚挚的 [chéngzhì de]

sincerely [sɪn'sɪəlɪ] ADV 由衷地 [yóuzhōng de] ▶ Yours sincerely or US Sincerely yours 谨上

sing [sɪŋ] (pt **sang**, pp **sung**) I VI [person +] 唱歌 [chànggē]; [bird +] 鸣 [míng] II VT [+ song] [person +] 唱 [chàng]; [bird +] 鸣唱 [míngchàng] ▶ to sing sb sth, sing sth to sb 为某人唱某歌 ▶ sing along VI ▶ to sing along (with/to) (和着⋯) 一起唱 [(hézhe⋯) yìqǐ chàng]

Singapore [sɪŋgə'pɔː(r)] N 新加坡 [Xīnjiāpō]

singer ['sɪŋə(r)] N [c] 歌手 [gēshǒu]

singing ['sɪŋɪŋ] N [U] (activity) 唱歌 [chànggē]; (sounds) 歌声 [gēshēng]

single ['sɪŋgl] I ADJ **1** (solitary) 单个的 [dāngè de] ▷ We heard a single shot. 我们听到一声枪响。**2** (individual) 惟一的 [wéiyī de] ▷ the world's single most important source of oil 世界上惟一最重要的石油来源 **3** (unmarried) 单身的 [dānshēn de] ▷ a single woman 一位单身女子 **4** (for one person, car etc) 单人的 [dānrén de] II N [c] (BRIT) **1** (also: single ticket) 单程票 [dānchéngpiào] [美 = one-way ticket] **2** (record) 单曲唱片 [dānqǔ chàngpiàn] ▶ not a single one was left 一个都没剩 ▶ every single day 每一天 ▶ single spacing (TYP) 单倍行距 ▶ single out VT (choose) 选出 [xuǎnchū] ▶ to single sb out for sth 为某事选出某人

single bed N [c] 单人床 [dānrén chuáng]

single file N ▶ in single file 一列纵队 [yíliè zòngduì]

single-handed [sɪŋgl'hændɪd] ADV 独自一人地 [dúzì yìrén de]

single-minded [sɪŋgl'maɪndɪd] ADJ 一心一意的 [yīxīnyīyì de]

single parent N [c] 单亲 [dānqīn]

single room N [c] 单人房 [dānrén fáng]

singles ['sɪŋglz] (TENNIS) N [U] 单打比赛 [dāndǎ bǐsài]

singular ['sɪŋgjulə(r)] I ADJ **1** (LING) 单数的 [dānshù de] **2** (remarkable) 非凡的 [fēifán de] **2** (o.f.) (strange) 奇怪的 [qíguài de] II N ▶ the singular 单数形式 [dānshù xíngshì] ▶ in the singular 用单数

sinister ['sɪnɪstə(r)] ADJ [+ event, figure, reason] 邪恶的 [xié'è de]

sink [sɪŋk] (pt **sank**, pp **sunk**) I N [c] 洗涤槽 [xǐdí cáo] II VT **1** [+ ship] 使下沉 [shǐ xiàchén] **2** [+ well, mine] 挖掘 [wājué] III VI **1** (in water) [ship +] 沉没 [chénmò]; [object +] 下沉 [xiàchén] **2** (subside) [ground, building, foundation +] 下陷 [xiàxiàn] **3** (drop) [level, price +] 下跌 [xiàdié] ▶ to sink sth into sth [+ teeth, claws, knife, needle] 将某物插入某物 ▶ to sink to… [prices, pay increases etc +] 下降至⋯ ▶ the sun was sinking 太阳落山了 ▶ she sank to her knees 她跪下了 ▶ to sink into a chair 瘫在椅子上 ▶ to sink into depression/a coma 陷入消沉/昏迷 ▶ my heart sank 我心头一沉 ▶ her voice sank to a whisper 她的声音减小成耳语 ▶ sink in VI [words +] 被理解 [bèi lǐjiě]

sinus ['saɪnəs] N [c] 鼻窦 [bídòu]

sip [sɪp] I N [c] 一小口 [yìxiǎokǒu] II VT 抿 [mǐn] III VI 小口地喝 [xiǎokǒude hē] ▶ to take or have a sip (of sth) 抿一口 (某饮料)

sir [sə(r)] N (as address) 先生 [xiānsheng] ▶ yes, sir 是，先生 ▶ Dear Sir 亲爱的先生 ▶ Dear Sirs 诸位先生 ▶ Dear Sir or Madam 亲爱的先生或女士 ▶ Sir John Smith 约翰．史密斯爵士

siren ['saɪərn] N [c] 警报器 [jǐngbàoqì]

sirloin ['sə:lɔɪn] N [c/U] (also: **sirloin steak**) 牛腰上部的肉 [niúyāo shàngbù de ròu]

sister ['sɪstə(r)] I N [c] **1** 姐妹 [jiěmèi]; (elder) 姐姐 [jiějie]; (younger) 妹妹 [mèimei] **2** (nun) 修女 [xiūnǔ] **3** (BRIT) (nurse) 护士长 [hùshìzhǎng] II CPD (复合词) ▶ sister organization/ship 姐妹组织/船 [jiěmèi zǔzhī/chuán] ▶ my brothers and sisters 我的兄弟姐妹们

sister-in-law ['sɪstərɪnlɔː] (pl **sisters-in-law**) N [c] (husband or wife's older sister) 姑子 [gūzi]; (husband or wife's younger sister) 姨子 [yízi]; (older brother's wife) 嫂子 [sǎozi]; (younger brother's wife) 弟媳 [dìxí]

sit [sɪt] (pt, pp **sat**) I VI **1** (also: **sit down**) 坐下 [zuòxià] ▷ A woman came and sat next to her. 一位女子进来，紧挨她坐下。**2** (be sitting) 坐 [zuò] ▷ She was sitting on the edge of the bed. 她正坐在床沿上。**3** [parliament, court +] 开会 [kāihuì] ▷ Parliament sits for only 28 weeks out of 52. 议会一年52周里只开28周的会。**4** (for painter) 当模特 [dāng mótè] ▷ She had sat for famous painters like Rossetti. 她为罗塞蒂等著名画家当过模特。II VT **1** (position) 使坐 [shǐ zuò] ▷ He used to sit me on his lap. 他以前常让我坐在他膝上。**2** (invite to sit) 使就座 [shǐ jiùzuò] **3** (BRIT)

[+*exam*] 参加 [cānjiā] ［美 = **take**］ ▶ **to sit on a committee** 成为委员会成员 ▶ **sit tight! I'll be right back** 等一下！我马上就回来
  ▶ **sit about**(BRIT: *inf*) VI = **sit around**
  ▶ **sit around**(*inf*) VI 闲坐着 [xián zuòzhe]
  ▶ **sit back**(*inf*) VI (*fig*) 在一旁闲着 [zài yīpáng xiánzhe]
  ▶ **sit down** VI (*from standing*) 坐下 [zuòxià] ▶ **to be sitting down** 就座
  ▶ **sit in on** VT FUS [不可拆分] [+*meeting, lesson*] 旁听 [pángtīng]
  ▶ **sit on** (*inf*) VT FUS [不可拆分] (*keep to oneself*) [+*report etc*] 搁置 [gēzhì]
  ▶ **sit out** VT [+*event*] 挨到…结束 [āidào…jiéshù]
  ▶ **sit through** VT [+*film, lecture etc*] 耐着性子到…结束 [nàizhe xìngzi dào…jiéshù]
  ▶ **sit up** VI **1** (*from lying*) 坐起来 [zuòqǐlái] **2** (*straighten*) 坐直 [zuòzhí] **3** (*stay up late*) 熬夜 [áoyè]

sitcom ['sɪtkɔm] N [c] 情景喜剧 [qíngjǐng xǐjù]

site [saɪt] I N [c] **1** (*of event*) 地点 [dìdiǎn] **2** (*building site*) 工地 [gōngdì] **3** (*archaeological*) 遗址 [yízhǐ] **4** (*also:* **website**) 网址 [wǎngzhǐ] II VT [+*factory, missiles*] 设置 [shèzhì]

sitting ['sɪtɪŋ] N [c] **1** [*of assembly etc*] 开会 [kāihuì] **2** (*in canteen*) 分批就餐 [fēnpī jiùcān]
  ▶ **to do sth at a single sitting** 一口气做完某事

sitting room (BRIT) N [c] 起居室 [qǐjūshì] ［美 = **living room**］

situated ['sɪtjueɪtɪd] ADJ ▶ **to be situated in/on/near sth** 位于某物中/上/旁 [wèiyú mǒuwù zhōng/shang/páng]

○**situation** [sɪtju'eɪʃən] N [c] **1** (*circumstances*) 情况 [qíngkuàng] ▷ *It's an impossible situation.* 这情况真是难以应付。**2** (*location*) 环境 [huánjìng] ▷ *The city is in a beautiful situation.* 这座城市环境优美。**3** (*o.f.*) (*job*) 工作 [gōngzuò] ▷ *It's not so easy to find another situation.* 另找份工作并不那么容易。▶ **"situations vacant"** (BRIT) "招聘" ［美 = **Employment**］

○**six** [sɪks] NUM 六 [liù] *see also* **five**

○**sixteen** [sɪks'ti:n] NUM 十六 [shíliù] *see also* **fifteen**

sixteenth [sɪks'ti:nθ] NUM 第十六 [dì shíliù] *see also* **fifth**

sixth ['sɪksθ] NUM **1** (*in series*) 第六 [dìliù] **2** (*fraction*) 六分之一 [liùfēnzhī yī] ▶ **the upper/lower sixth** (BRIT: SCOL) 高级/初级六年级，英国中学教育的最后两年，在此期间学生准备A level考试，以取得大学入学资格 *see also* **fifth**

sixth form (BRIT) N ▶ **the sixth form** 六年级，英国中学教育的最后两年，在此期间学生准备A level考试，以取得大学入学资格

sixth form college (BRIT) N [c] 第六级学校，为16岁以上的学生提供A level考试及相关的课程

sixtieth ['sɪkstɪɪθ] NUM 第六十 [dì liùshí]

○**sixty** ['sɪkstɪ] NUM 六十 [liùshí] *see also* **fifty**

size [saɪz] N **1** [c/u] [*of object*] 大小 [dàxiǎo]; [*of clothing, shoes*] 尺码 [chǐmǎ] **2** [c/u] [*of loan, business*] 多少 [duōshǎo] **3** [u] [*of area, building, task, loss etc*] 大 [dà] ▶ **I take size 12** (*dress, shirt etc*) 我穿12号 ▶ **what size shoes do you take?** 你穿几号的鞋？ ▶ **it's the size of...** 相当于…的大小 ▶ **to cut sth to size** 将某物改至一定大小
  ▶ **size up** (*inf*) VT [+*person, situation*] 评估 [pínggū]

sizeable ['saɪzəbl] ADJ [+*amount, number*] 相当大的 [xiāngdāngdà de]; [+*problem, operation*] 大的 [dà de]; [+*object, company, estate*] 颇大的 [pōdà de]; [+*majority, minority*] 相当数量的 [xiāngdāng shùliàng de]

sizzle ['sɪzl] VI 哗哗作响 [sīsīzuòxiǎng]

skate [skeɪt] I N **1** [c] (*ice skate*) 溜冰鞋 [liūbīngxié] **2** [c] (*roller skate*) 旱冰鞋 [hàn bīngxié] **3** [c/u] (*pl* **skate**) (*fish*) 鳐鱼 [yáoyú] II VI **1** (*ice skate*) 溜冰 [liūbīng] **2** (*roller skate*) 溜旱冰 [liūhànbīng] ▶ **to go skating** (*on ice skates*) 去溜冰; (*on roller skates*) 去溜旱冰
  ▶ **skate around, skate over, skate round** VT FUS [不可拆分] [+*problem, issue*] 一带而过 [yídài'érguò]

skateboard ['skeɪtbɔ:d] N [c] 滑板 [huábǎn]

skateboarding ['skeɪtbɔ:dɪŋ] N [u] 滑板运动 [huábǎn yùndòng]

skater ['skeɪtə(r)] N [c] 滑冰者 [huábīngzhě]

skating ['skeɪtɪŋ] N [u] (*ice-skating*) 冰上运动 [bīngshang yùndòng] *see also* **skate**

skating rink N [c] (*ice rink*) 溜冰场 [liūbīngchǎng]

skeleton ['skelɪtn] N [c] **1** (*bones*) 骨骼 [gǔgé] **2** (*frame*) [*of building*] 框架 [kuàngjià] **3** (*framework*) [*of plan*] 提纲 [tígāng]

skeptical ['skeptɪkl] (US) ADJ = **sceptical**

sketch [sketʃ] I N [c] **1** (*drawing*) 素描 [sùmiáo] **2** (*outline*) 概述 [gàishù] **3** (THEAT, TV, RAD) 诙谐短剧 [huīxié duǎnjù] II VT **1** [+*drawing, landscape, figure, map*] 给…画速写 [gěi…huà sùxiě] **2** (*also:* **sketch out**) [+*ideas, plan*] 概述 [gàishù]

sketchy ['sketʃɪ] ADJ 粗略的 [cūlüè de]

skewer ['skju:ə(r)] I N [c] 串肉扦 [chuànròuqiān] II VT 刺穿 [cìchuān]

skid [skɪd] I VI ▶ **to skid** (**into/across** *etc* **sth**) [*person*+] 滑着 (冲向/穿过 {等} 某物) [huázhe (chōngxiàng/chuānguò {děng} mǒuwù)]; [*car, driver*+] 打滑 [dǎhuá] II N [c] ▶ **to go into a skid** 打滑 [dǎhuá]

skier ['ski:ə(r)] N [c] 滑雪者 [huáxuězhě]

skiing ['ski:ɪŋ] N [u] **1** (*activity*) 滑雪 [huáxuě]

2 (competition) 滑雪比赛 [huáxuě bǐsài] see also **ski**

skilful, (US) **skillful** ['skɪlful] ADJ [+ person, player] 老练的 [lǎoliàn de]; [+ use, choice, management] 技巧娴熟的 [jìqiǎo xiánshú de]
▶ **to be skilful at doing sth** 能熟练地做某事

ski lift N [C] 载送滑雪者上坡的装置

skill [skɪl] N **1** [U] (ability) 技巧 [jìqiǎo] **2** [C] (acquired) 技能 [jìnéng]

skilled [skɪld] ADJ [+ person] 熟练的 [shúliàn de]; [+ work] 技术性的 [jìshùxìng de]

skillful ['skɪlful] (US) ADJ = **skilful**

skim [skɪm] VT **1** ▶ **to skim sth from** or **off sth** [+ fat, cream] 从某物上撇去某物 [cóng mǒuwù shang piēqù mǒuwù] **2** (also: **skim over**) [+ ground, water, wave] 掠过 [lüèguò] **3** (also: **skim through**) [+ book, article] 浏览 [liúlǎn]

skim milk (US) N [U] 脱脂牛奶 [tuōzhī niúnǎi] [英 = **skimmed milk**]

skimmed milk [skɪmd-] (BRIT) N [U] 脱脂牛奶 [tuōzhī niúnǎi] [美 = **skim milk**]

skimpy ['skɪmpɪ] ADJ **1** [+ meal] 不足的 [bùzú de] **2** [+ clothes] 用料少的 [yòngliàoshǎo de]

skin [skɪn] I N **1** [C/U] [of person] 皮肤 [pífū]; [of animal] 皮 [pí]; (complexion) 肤色 [fūsè] **2** [C/U] [of fruit, vegetable] 外皮 [wàipí] **3** [S] (on liquid) 薄层 [báocéng] II VT [+ fruit] 剥去⋯的皮 [bōqù⋯de pí] ▶ **to be soaked** or **drenched to the skin** 全身都湿透了

skin cancer N [C/U] 皮肤癌 [pífū'ái]

skinhead ['skɪnhed] (BRIT) N [C] 留平头的人 (一般被认为有暴力倾向)

skinny ['skɪnɪ] (inf) ADJ [+ person] 极瘦的 [jíshòu de]; [+ arms, legs] 皮包骨的 [píbāogǔ de]

skip [skɪp] I VI **1** (hop) 蹦跳 [bèngtiào] **2** (ESP BRIT) (with rope) 跳绳 [tiàoshéng] [美 = **skip rope**] II VT **1** (miss) [+ lunch, lecture] 故意不做 [gùyì bùzuò]; [+ school] 逃学 [táoxué] **2** (also: **skip over**) [+ boring parts] 略过 [lüèguò] III N [C] **1** (movement) 蹦跳 [bèngtiào] **2** (BRIT) (container) 无盖用以装运工地废料的废料桶 [美 = **Dumpster®**]

ski pass N [C] 滑雪证 [huáxuězhèng]

skipper ['skɪpə(r)] I N [C] [of ship] 船长 [chuánzhǎng]; [of team] 队长 [duìzhǎng] II VT [+ boat] 当⋯的船长 [dāng⋯de chuánzhǎng]; [+ team] 当⋯的队长 [dāng⋯de duìzhǎng]

skipping rope ['skɪpɪŋ-] (BRIT) N [C] 跳绳 [tiàoshéng] [美 = **skip rope**]

skip rope (US) N [C] 跳绳 [tiàoshéng] [英 = **skipping rope**]

skirt [skəːt] I N [C] 裙子 [qúnzi] II VT **1** [+ area, path, road etc +] 环绕 [huánrào]; [person +] 绕⋯的边缘走 [rào⋯de biānyuán zǒu] **2** [+ problem, question] 避而不谈 [bì'érbùtán]
▶ **skirt around, skirt round** VT FUS [不可拆分] = **skirt**

skirting board ['skəːtɪŋ-] (BRIT) N [C/U] 踢脚

板 [tījiǎobǎn] [美 = **baseboard**]

ski slope N [C] 滑雪坡 [huáxuěpō]

skive [skaɪv] (BRIT: inf) VI 逃避劳动 [táobì láodòng]
▶ **skive off** (BRIT: inf) I VT FUS [不可拆分] [+ school, work] 逃避 [táobì] II VI 逃避劳动 [táobì láodòng]

skull [skʌl] N [C] 颅骨 [lúgǔ]

skunk [skʌŋk] N [C] 臭鼬 [chòuyòu]

sky [skaɪ] N [C/U] 天空 [tiānkōng] ▶ **to praise sb to the skies** 把某人捧上了天

skyscraper ['skaɪskreɪpə(r)] N [C] 摩天大厦 [mótiān dàshà]

slab [slæb] N [C] [of stone, concrete] 厚板 [hòubǎn]; [of meat] 厚片 [hòupiàn]

slack [slæk] I ADJ **1** [+ rope, skin] 松弛的 [sōngchí de] **2** [+ market, demand, business] 不景气的 [bù jǐngqì de]; [+ period] 萧条的 [xiāotiáo de] **3** [+ worker] 懈怠的 [xièdài de] **4** [+ security, discipline] 马虎的 [mǎhu de] II N [U] (in rope etc) 松弛部分 [sōngchí bùfen] III **slacks** NPL (o.f.) (trousers) 宽松的裤子 [kuānsōng de kùzi]

slacken ['slækn] I VI **1** [rope +] 变松 [biànsōng] **2** (also: **slacken off**) [speed +] 放慢 [fàngmàn]; [demand, situation +] 减缓 [jiǎnhuǎn]; [rain +] 变小 [biànxiǎo] II VT [+ grip] 放松 [fàngsōng]; [+ speed] 放慢 [fàngmàn]

slain [sleɪn] PP of **slay**

slam [slæm] I VT **1** [+ door] 使劲关 [shǐjìn guān] **2** (throw) ▶ **to slam sth down** 砰地放下某物 [pēng de fàngxià mǒuwù] **3** (criticize) 猛烈抨击 [měngliè pēngjī] II VI [door +] 砰地关上 [pēng de guānshang] ▶ **to slam sth against/into sth** 用某物猛击某物/将某物使劲扔进某物 ▶ **to slam on the brakes** 猛踩刹车 ▶ **to slam into sth** 猛然撞上某物

slander ['slɑːndə(r)] I N [C/U] (LAW) 诽谤 [fěibàng] II VT 诋毁 [dǐhuǐ]

slang [slæŋ] N [U] 俚语 [lǐyǔ] ▶ **military/prison slang** 军队/监狱俚语

slant [slɑːnt] I VI [floor, ceiling, handwriting +] 倾斜 [qīngxié]; [sunlight +] 斜照 [xiézhào] II VT [+ information, programme] 有倾向性地报导 [yǒu qīngxiàngxìng de bàodǎo] III N [S] **1** [of eyes, shoulders, handwriting, hill] 倾斜 [qīngxié] **2** (fig) (approach) 有偏向性的观点 [yǒu piānxiàngxìng de guāndiǎn]

slap [slæp] I N [C] 掌击 [zhǎngjī] II VT [+ child, face, bottom] 掴 [guó] III ADV (inf) (directly) 直接地 [zhíjiēde] ▶ **to give sb a slap** 打某人一巴掌 ▶ **a slap in the face** (fig) 污辱 ▶ **to slap sb on the back** 拍拍某人的后背 ▶ **to slap sth (down) on sth** 啪的一声把某物扔到某物上 ▶ **to slap some paint on a wall** 往墙上涂些油漆 ▶ **slap-bang** or **slap in the middle of sth** (BRIT: inf) 在某物的正中央

slash [slæʃ] I VT **1** [+ tyres, face] 划破 [huápò] **2** [+ prices, costs] 大幅削减 [dàfú xuējiǎn] II N

[c] **1** (slit) 划口 [huákǒu] **2** (also: forward slash) 斜线号 [xiéxiànhào] ▶ **to slash one's wrists** 割腕 ▶ **to slash at sb/sth** 朝某人/某物猛砍

slate [sleɪt] **I** N **1** [U] (rock) 板岩 [bǎnyán] **2** [c] (on roof) 石板瓦 [shíbǎnwǎ] **II** VT (BRIT) (criticize) 严厉批评 [yánlì pīpíng]

slaughter ['slɔːtə(r)] **I** N [U] [of people] 屠杀 [túshā]; [of wildlife] 杀戮 [shālù]; [of cows, sheep, pigs etc] 屠宰 [túzǎi] **II** VT [+people] 屠杀 [túshā]; [+wildlife] 杀戮 [shālù]; [+cows, sheep, pigs etc] 屠宰 [túzǎi]
用法参见 **kill**

slaughterhouse ['slɔːtəhaus] N [c] 屠宰场 [túzǎichǎng]

Slav [slɑːv] N [c] 斯拉夫人 [Sīlāfūrén]

slave [sleɪv] N [c] 奴隶 [núlì] ▶ **to work like a slave** 像奴隶般工作 ▶ **a slave to sth** 受某物掌控
▶ **slave away** VI 苦干 [kǔgàn]
▶ **slave over** VT FUS [不可拆分] 拼命地干 [pīnmìng de gàn] ▶ **to slave over a hot stove** 在灼热的炉子前忙碌

slavery ['sleɪvərɪ] N [U] 奴隶制 [núlìzhì]

slay [sleɪ] (pt **slew**, pp **slain**) VT **1** (liter) [+dragon] 杀死 [shāsǐ]; [+person] 杀害 [shāhài] **2** (ESP US) (murder) 谋杀 [móushā]

sleazy ['sliːzɪ] (inf) ADJ [+place] 肮脏的 [āngzāng de]; [+magazine, person] 淫秽的 [yínhuì de]

sled [slɛd] (US) **I** N [c] 雪橇 [xuěqiāo] [英 =**sledge**] **II** VI ▶ **to go sledding** 乘雪橇 [chéng xuěqiāo] [英 =**go sledging**]

sledge [slɛdʒ] (BRIT) **I** N [c] 雪橇 [xuěqiāo] [美 =**sled**] **II** VI ▶ **to go sledging** 乘雪橇 [chéng xuěqiāo] [美 =**go sledding**]

sleek [sliːk] ADJ **1** [+hair, fur] 油亮的 [yóuliàng de] **2** [+car, boat etc] 锃亮的 [zèngliàng de] **3** [+person] 考究的 [kǎojiù de]

sleep [sliːp] (pt, pp **slept**) **I** N **1** [U] 睡眠 [shuìmián] **2** [c] (nap) 睡觉 [shuìjiào] **II** VI (be asleep) 睡 [shuì]; (fall asleep) 入睡 [rùshuì]; (spend the night) 过夜 [guòyè] **III** VT ▶ **the house sleeps 4** 这个房子可供4个人睡 [zhège fángzi kěgōng sìgerén shuì] ▶ **to go to sleep** 去睡觉 ▶ **to have a good night's sleep** 睡个好觉 ▶ **to put a cat/dog etc to sleep** 把猫/狗〔等〕人道地杀死 ▶ **I didn't lose any sleep over it** (fig) 我并没有为这事忧虑过
▶ **sleep around** (inf) VI 乱搞男女关系 [luàngǎo nánnǚ guānxi]
▶ **sleep in** (BRIT) VI 睡懒觉 [shuì lǎnjiào]
▶ **sleep off** VT 以睡眠消除 [yǐ shuìmián xiāochú]
▶ **sleep through** VT FUS [不可拆分] [+noise] 不被…吵醒 [bùbèi…chǎoxǐng]
▶ **sleep together** VI 有性关系 [yǒu xìngguānxi]
▶ **sleep with** VT FUS [不可拆分] 和…有性关系 [hé…yǒu xìngguānxi]

sleeper ['sliːpə(r)] N [c] **1** (BRIT) (train) 卧车 [wòchē]; (carriage) 卧铺车厢 [wòpù chēxiāng]; (berth) 卧铺 [wòpù] **2** (BRIT) (on track) 枕木 [zhěnmù] **3** ▶ **I'm a light/heavy sleeper** 我是个睡觉警醒/沉的人 [wǒ shìge shuìjiào jǐngxǐng/chén de rén]

sleeping bag ['sliːpɪŋ-] N [c] 睡袋 [shuìdài]

sleeping car N [c] 火车卧铺车厢 [huǒchē wòpù chēxiāng]

sleeping pill N [c] 安眠药 [ānmiányào]

sleepless ['sliːplɪs] ADJ [+person] 失眠的 [shīmián de] ▶ **to have a sleepless night** 过了个无眠之夜

sleepwalk ['sliːpwɔːk] VI 梦游 [mèngyóu]

sleepy ['sliːpɪ] ADJ **1** [+person] 瞌睡的 [kēshuì de] **2** [+village, town] 冷清的 [lěngqīng de]

sleet [sliːt] N [U] 雨夹雪 [yǔjiāxuě]

sleeve [sliːv] N [c] **1** [of jacket, sweater etc] 袖子 [xiùzi] **2** [of record] 唱片套 [chàngpiàn tào] [美 =**jacket**] ▶ **with long/short sleeves** 长袖/短袖 ▶ **to have sth up one's sleeve** (fig) 暗藏某物以备不时之需

sleeveless ['sliːvlɪs] ADJ 无袖的 [wúxiù de]

sleigh [sleɪ] N [c] 雪橇 [xuěqiāo]

slender ['slɛndə(r)] ADJ **1** [+person, legs] 修长的 [xiūcháng de] **2** [+chance, means, majority] 微弱的 [wēiruò de]

slept [slɛpt] PT, PP OF **sleep**

slew [sluː] **I** PT OF **slay** **II** VI [vehicle+] 旋转 [xuánzhuàn] **III** VT [+vehicle] 使旋转 [shǐxuánzhuàn] **IV** N (ESP US) ▶ **a slew of** 大量 [dàliàng]

slice [slaɪs] **I** N [c] **1** [of meat, bread, lemon] 片 [piàn] **2** [share] 份额 [fèn'é] **II** VT 把…切成片 [bǎ…qiēchéng piàn] **III** VI ▶ **to slice through sth** 切开某物 [qiēkāi mǒuwù] ▶ **sliced bread** 切片面包 ▶ **it's the best thing since sliced bread** 这是极好的东西

slick [slɪk] **I** ADJ **1** [+performance, advertisement] 巧妙的 [qiǎomiào de]; [+movement, gear change] 娴熟的 [xiánshú de]; (pej) (clever) 圆滑的 [yuánhuá de] **II** N [c] 浮油 [fúyóu]

slide [slaɪd] (pt, pp **slid**) **I** N [c] **1** (in playground) 滑梯 [huátī] **2** (PHOT) 幻灯片 [huàndēngpiàn] **3** (BRIT) (also: hair slide) 发夹 [fàjiā] **4** (microscope slide) 载物片 [zàiwù piàn] **5** (in prices, earnings) 下滑 [xiàhuá] **II** VT 使…滑动 [shǐ…huádòng] **III** VI **1** (slip) ▶ **to slide down/off/into sth** 滑下/离/进某物 [huáxià/lí/jìn mǒuwù] **2** (quietly) ▶ **to slide into/out of sth** 悄悄溜进/出某处 [qiāoqiāo liūjìn/chū mǒuchù] ▶ **to slide into chaos/a depression** 渐渐陷入混乱/消沉 ▶ **to let standards/things slide** 听任标准下降/事情变糟
▶ **slide away** VI 溜走 [liūzǒu]

sliding ['slaɪdɪŋ] ADJ [+door] 滑动的 [huádòng de]

slight [slaɪt] I ADJ 1 [+ *increase, problem*] 微小的 [wēixiǎo de] 2 (*slim*) [+ *person*] 娇小的 [jiāoxiǎo de] 3 (*insubstantial*) 无足轻重的 [wúzú qīngzhòng de] II VT (*insult*) 怠慢 [dàimàn] III N [C] (*insult*) 污辱 [wūrǔ] ▶ **the slightest noise/problem** *etc* 极轻微的声响/极小的问题 {等} ▶ **not the slightest bit** 一点也不 ▶ **not in the slightest** 一点也不

slightly ['slaɪtlɪ] ADV (*a bit*) 略微地 [lüèwēi de] ▶ **slightly built** 体格纤弱

slim [slɪm] I ADJ 1 [+ *figure*] 苗条的 [miáotiáo de]; [+ *book, wallet*] 薄的 [báo de] 2 [+ *chance*] 小的 [xiǎo de] II VI (*lose weight*) 节食减肥 [jiéshí jiǎnféi] ▶ **slim down** I VI (*company +*) 精简机构 [jīngjiǎn jīgòu] II VT [+ *company*] 精简 [jīngjiǎn]

slimming ['slɪmɪŋ] N [U] 减肥 [jiǎnféi]

slimy ['slaɪmɪ] ADJ 1 [+ *substance*] 泥浆的 [níjiāng de]; (*object*) 有泥浆的 [yǒu níjiāng de] 2 (BRIT) [+ *person*] 谄媚的 [chǎnmèi de]

sling [slɪŋ] (*pt, pp* **slung**) I N [C] 1 (*for arm*) 悬带 [xuándài] 2 (*for baby*) 背带 [bēidài] II VT 1 (*throw*) 扔 [rēng] 2 (*suspend*) 悬挂 [xuánguà] ▶ **to have one's arm in a sling** 胳膊用悬带吊着 ▶ **to sling sth over sth** 将某物挂在某物上

slip [slɪp] I VT (*put*) ▶ **to slip sth into/under sth** 将某物悄悄塞入某物/到某物下面 [jiāng mǒuwù qiāoqiāo sāirù mǒuwù/dào mǒuwù xiàmian] II VI 1 (*slide*) [*person +*] 滑跤 [huájiāo]; [*object +*] 滑落 [huáluò] 2 (*decline*) 下降 [xiàjiàng] III N [C] 1 (*fall*) 滑倒 [huádǎo] 2 (*mistake*) 差错 [chācuò] 3 [*of paper*] 细条 [xìtiáo] 4 (*underskirt*) 衬裙 [chènqún]; (*with top part*) 连身衬裙 [liánshēn chènqún] ▶ **to slip sth on/off** [+ *clothes, shoes*] 迅速穿上/脱下某物 ▶ **to slip sth to sb, slip sb sth** 偷偷将某物塞给某人 ▶ **it slipped my mind** 我忘了 ▶ **to slip into/out of sth** [+ *room, house*] 悄悄溜进/出某处; [+ *clothes, shoes*] 迅速穿上/脱下某物 ▶ **to slip into a habit/routine** 逐渐养成习惯/规律 ▶ **to let slip that...** 无意中透露… ▶ **a slip of the tongue** 口误 ▶ **to give sb the slip** (*inf*) 甩掉某人 ▶ **slip away** VI (*go*) 悄悄溜走 [qiāoqiāo liūzǒu] ▶ **slip out** VI (*go out*) 出去一下 [chūqù yīxià] ▶ **slip up** VI (*make mistake*) 出差错 [chūchācuò]

slipper ['slɪpə(r)] N [C] 拖鞋 [tuōxié]

slippery ['slɪpərɪ] ADJ 1 [+ *surface*] 滑的 [huá de] 2 [+ *person*] 狡猾的 [jiǎohuá de] ▶ **to be on a slippery slope to ruin/anarchy** 将导致毁灭/混乱

slip road (BRIT) N [C] (*to motorway*) 连接高速公路的岔道 [美 = **entrance ramp, exit ramp**]

slit [slɪt] (*pt, pp* **slit**) I N [C] 1 (*cut*) 划口 [huákǒu] 2 (*opening*) 缝 [fèng] II VT (*make a cut in*) 切开 [qiēkāi] ▶ **to slit sb's throat** 割开某人的喉咙

slog [slɔg] (BRIT: *inf*) I VI (*also:* **slog away**) 勤恳

地工作 [qínkěn de gōngzuò] II N [S] 1 (*effort*) (*also:* **hard slog**) 艰辛的事 [jiānxīn de shì] 2 (*journey*) 长途跋涉 [chángtú báshè]

slogan ['sləugən] N [C] 口号 [kǒuhào]

slope [sləup] I N [C] 1 (*gentle hill*) 斜坡 [xiépō] 2 (*side of mountain*) 坡 [pō] 3 (*slant*) 坡度 [pōdù] 4 (*ski slope*) 滑雪坡 [huáxuěpō] II VI ▶ **to slope down** 向下倾斜 [xiàngxià qīngxié] ▶ **on a slope** 在斜坡上 ▶ **to slope to the right/left** 向右/左倾斜

sloping ['sləupɪŋ] ADJ [+ *ground, roof*] 斜的 [xié de]

sloppy ['slɔpɪ] ADJ 1 (*careless*) 马虎的 [mǎhu de] 2 (*sentimental*) 感伤的 [gǎnshāng de]

slot [slɔt] I N [C] 1 (*in machine*) 狭槽 [xiácáo] 2 (*fig*) (*in timetable*) 时段 [shíduàn]; (RAD, TV) 档期 [dàngqī] II VT ▶ **to slot sth into sth** [+ *money, card, cassette*] 把某物放入某处 [bǎ mǒuwù fàngrù mǒuchù] III VI ▶ **to slot into sth** 放入某物 [fàngrù mǒuwù] ▶ **slot in** I VT [+ *money, card, cassette*] 把…放入 [bǎ…fàngrù] ▶ **to slot sb in** 把某人安插进去 II VI 安放 [ānfàng]

slot machine N [C] 投币机 [tóubìjī]; (*for gambling*) 吃角子老虎机 [chījiǎozi lǎohǔjī]

slouch [slautʃ] I VI 1 (*have poor posture*) ▶ **to slouch (over sth)** 无精打采地靠着(某物) [wújīng dǎcǎi de kàozhe (mǒuwù)] 2 (*walk*) ▶ **to slouch in/out** 没精打采地走进/走出 [méijīng dǎcǎi de zǒujìn/zǒuchū] II N [S] 低头垂肩的姿态 [dītóu chuíjiān de zītài] ▶ **she was slouched in a chair** 她没精打采地坐在椅子上 ▶ **slouch around** VI 懒散地闲逛 [lǎnsǎn de xiánguàng]

Slovak ['sləuvæk] I ADJ 斯洛伐克的 [Sīluòfákè de] II N 1 [C] (*person*) 斯洛伐克人 [Sīluòfákèrén] 2 [U] (*language*) 斯洛伐克语 [Sīluòfákèyǔ] ▶ **the Slovak Republic** 斯洛伐克共和国

Slovakia [sləu'vækɪə] N 斯洛伐克 [Sīluòfákè]

Slovakian [sləu'vækɪən] ADJ, N = **Slovak**

Slovene [sləu'viːn] I ADJ 斯洛文尼亚的 [Sīluòwénníyà de] II N 1 [C] (*person*) 斯洛文尼亚人 [Sīluòwénníyàrén] 2 [U] (*language*) 斯洛文尼亚语 [Sīluòwénníyàyǔ]

Slovenia [sləu'viːnɪə] N 斯洛文尼亚 [Sīluòwénníyà]

Slovenian [sləu'viːnɪən] ADJ, N = **Slovene**

slow [sləu] I ADJ 1 [+ *music, journey, process, speed etc*] 慢的 [màn de]; [+ *driver, swimmer, learner*] 迟钝的 [chídùn de] 2 (*not clever*) [+ *person*] 愚钝的 [yúdùn de] 3 (*not exciting*) [+ *place, activity*] 乏味的 [fáwèi de] II ADV (*inf*) 缓慢地 [huǎnmàn de] III VT (*also:* **slow down, slow up**) [+ *vehicle, driver, business*] 放慢 [fàngmàn] IV VI (*also:* **slow down, slow up**) [*vehicle, driver, business +*] 减速 [jiǎnsù] ▶ **to be slow to act/decide** 行动/决定迟了 ▶ **to be slow** [*watch +*]

慢了 ▸ **my watch is 20 minutes slow** 我的表慢了20分钟 ▸ **business is slow** 生意清淡 ▸ **I began to walk slower and slower** 我开始越走越慢 ▸ **"slow"** (road sign) "缓行"
▸ **slow down I** vi (become less active) [person +] 放松 [fàngsōng] **II** vt (make less active) [+ person] 使放松 [shǐ fàngsōng]

slowly ['sləʊlɪ] ADV **1** [walk, move +] 慢慢地 [mànmàn de] **2** (gradually) 逐渐地 [zhújiàn de]

slow motion N ▸ **in slow motion** 以慢动作 [yǐ màn dòngzuò]

slug [slʌg] N [c] **1** 鼻涕虫 [bítìchóng] **2** (US: inf) (bullet) 子弹 [zǐdàn]

sluggish ['slʌgɪʃ] ADJ [+ circulation, stream] 迟缓的 [chíhuǎn de]; [+ economy, growth] 萧条的 [xiāotiáo de]

slum [slʌm] **I** N [c] (house) 陋室 [lòushì]; (area) 贫民窟 [pínmínkū] **II** vt, vi ▸ **to be slumming** (it) 过贫穷的生活 [guò pínqióng de shēnghuó]

slump [slʌmp] **I** N [c] **1** (drop) (in sales, demand etc) 暴跌 [bàodiē] **2** (ECON) (recession) 经济萧条 [jīngjì xiāotiáo] **II** vi **1** [person +] ▸ **to slump (into/onto sth)** 猛地倒 (在某物里/上) [měng de dǎo (zài mǒuwù lǐ/shang)] **2** [sales, demand etc +] 暴跌 [bàodiē] ▸ **he was slumped over the wheel** 他猛地倒在方向盘上

slung [slʌŋ] PT, PP of **sling**

slur [slə:(r)] **I** N (insult) ▸ **a slur (on sb/sth)** (对某人/某物的) 诽谤 [(duì mǒurén/mǒuwù de) fěibàng] **II** vt ▸ **to slur one's speech** 说话含糊 [shuōhuà hánhu]

sly [slaɪ] ADJ [+ smile, expression, remark] 会意的 [huìyì de]; [+ person] 狡诈的 [jiǎozhà de] ▸ **on the sly** (inf) 秘密地

smack [smæk] **I** N [c] 巴掌 [bāzhǎng] **II** vt [+ face, person] 掴 [guó]; (as punishment) 打 [dǎ] **III** vi ▸ **to smack of sth** 带有某事的意味 [dàiyǒu mǒushì de yìwèi] **IV** ADV (inf) ▸ **smack in the middle** 在正中间 [zài zhèng zhōngjiān] ▸ **to smack one's lips** 咂嘴

✪ **small** [smɔ:l] **I** ADJ **1** [+ person, object, quantity, number] 小的 [xiǎo de] ▷ **the smallest church in England** 英格兰最小的教堂 ▷ **a small amount of money** 一小笔钱 **2** (young) [+ child] 年幼的 [niányòu de] ▷ **She had two small children.** 她有两个年幼的孩子。 **3** (minor) [+ mistake, problem, change] 微不足道的 [wēibùzúdào de] ▷ **He made a lot of small mistakes.** 他犯过很多小错。 **II** N [c] ▸ **the small of the** or **one's back** 后腰 [hòuyāo] ▸ **to get** or **grow smaller** [thing +] 变小; [population, number +] 变少 ▸ **to make sth smaller** [+ object, garment] 使某物变小些 ▸ **a small business/businessman** 小本生意/商人 ▸ **to make sb look/feel small** 使某人显得/觉得渺小

smart [sma:t] **I** ADJ **1** (ESP BRIT) (neat, tidy) [+ person, clothes] 漂亮的 [piàoliang de]; [+ place] 整洁的 [zhěngjié de] **2** (fashionable) [+ house, area,

party] 时髦的 [shímáo de] **3** (clever) [+ person, idea] 聪明的 [cōngmíng de] **4** (MIL) [+ bomb, weapon] 精确制导的 [jīngquè zhìdǎo de] **II** vi **1** (sting) [eyes, wound +] 感到刺痛 [gǎndào cìtòng] **2** (feel upset) ▸ **to smart from sth** or **over sth** 对某事感到痛苦 [duì mǒushì gǎndào tòngkǔ] ▸ **the smart set** 时髦的阔人 ▸ **don't get smart with me!** 别对我耍小聪明！

smart card N [c] 智能卡 [zhìnéngkǎ]

smarten up ['sma:tn-] **I** vt [+ place] 整理 [zhěnglǐ] **II** vi [person +] 打扮起来 [dǎbàn qǐlái] ▸ **to smarten o.s. up** 打扮自己

smash [smæʃ] **I** N [c] **1** (inf) (car crash) 撞车 [zhuàngchē] **2** (also: **smash hit**) (song, play, film) 轰动的演出 [hōngdòng de yǎnchū] **3** (TENNIS) 高压球 [gāoyāqiú] **II** vt **1** [+ bottle, window etc] 打碎 [dǎsuì] **2** (beat) [+ record] 打破 [dǎpò] **3** (destroy) [+ life, hope] 破灭 [pòmiè]; [+ organization, system] 消灭 [xiāomiè] **III** vi (break) [bottle, window etc +] 打碎 [dǎsuì] ▸ **to smash sth into/against sth** 用某物猛击某物 ▸ **to smash sth (in)to pieces** or **bits** 将某物击成碎片 ▸ **to smash through sth** 撞穿某物
▸ **smash up** vt [+ room, furniture, car etc] 撞毁 [zhuànghuǐ]

smashing ['smæʃɪŋ] (BRIT: inf) ADJ (wonderful) 极好的 [jíhǎo de]

smear [smɪə(r)] **I** N [c] **1** (mark) 污迹 [wūjì] **2** (insult) 诽谤 [fěibàng] **3** (BRIT) (also: **smear test**) 子宫颈涂片检查 [zǐgōngjǐng túpiàn jiǎnchá] [美 = **pap smear**] **II** vt **1** (spread) [+ cream, ointment, paint etc] 涂抹 [túmǒ] **2** (make dirty with) 弄脏 [nòngzāng] **3** (insult) 诽谤 [fěibàng] ▸ **his hands were smeared with oil/ink** 他的手上沾满了油/墨水

smell [smel] (pt, pp **smelled** or **smelt**) **I** N [c] (aroma, odour) 气味 [qìwèi] **2** [u] (sense) 嗅觉 [xiùjué] **II** vt **1** (notice the smell of) 闻到 [wéndào] **2** (sniff) 嗅 [xiù] **3** (have instinct for) 察觉 [chájué] **III** vi **1** (have unpleasant odour) 发臭 [fāchòu] **2** ▸ **to smell nice/delicious/spicy etc** 闻起来香/好吃/辣 {等} [wén qǐlái xiāng/hǎochī/là {děng}] ▸ **sense of smell** 嗅觉 ▸ **to smell of** 有…气味 [yǒu…qìwèi]

smelly ['smelɪ] (pej) ADJ (not fragrant) 难闻的 [nánwén de]; [+ cheese] 气味强烈的 [qìwèi qiángliè de]

smelt [smelt] **I** PT, PP of **smell** **II** vt [+ ore] 熔炼 [róngliàn]

smile [smaɪl] **I** N [c] 微笑 [wēixiào] **II** vi ▸ **to smile (at sb)** (对某人) 微笑 [(duì mǒurén) wēixiào] **III** vt 用微笑表示 [yòng wēixiào biǎoshì]

smiling ['smaɪlɪŋ] ADJ [+ face, person] 微笑的 [wēixiào de]

smirk [smə:k] (pej) **I** N [c] 傻笑 [shǎxiào] **II** vi 傻笑 [shǎxiào]

smog [smɔg] N [u] 烟雾 [yānwù]

smoke [sməuk] I N [U] 烟 [yān] II VI
1 [person +] 吸烟 [xīyān] **2** [chimney +] 冒烟
[màoyān] III VT **1** [+cigarette, cigar, pipe] 抽
[chōu] **2** [+fish, meat] 熏制 [xūnzhì] ▶ **to
have a smoke**/**go for a smoke** 抽根烟/去抽根烟 ▶ **to
go up in smoke** [house etc +] 被烧光；(fig) 突然
破灭 ▶ **do you smoke?** 你抽烟吗?

smoke alarm N [C] 烟雾报警器 [yānwù
bàojǐngqì]

smoked [sməukt] ADJ [+bacon, salmon] 熏制的
[xūnzhì de]；[+glass] 烟雾过的 [yān xūnguò de]

smoker ['sməukə(r)] N [C] (person) 吸烟者
[xīyānzhě]

smoking ['sməukɪŋ] I N [U] 吸烟 [xīyān]
II ADJ [+area, compartment] 吸烟的 [xīyān de]
▶ **"no smoking"** "禁止吸烟"

smoky ['sməukɪ] ADJ [+atmosphere, room] 烟
雾弥漫的 [yānwù mímàn de]；[+taste] 烟熏的
[yānxūn de]

smooth [smu:ð] I ADJ **1** (not rough) [+surface,
skin] 光滑的 [guānghuá de] **2** (not lumpy)
[+sauce, mixture] 无颗粒的 [wú kēlì de] **3** (not
harsh) [+flavour, whisky] 醇和的 [chúnhé de]
4 (not jerky) [+movement] 流畅的 [liúchàng de]
5 (not bumpy) [+landing, take-off, flight] 平稳的
[píngwěn de] **6** (successful) [+transition, running,
process] 顺利的 [shùnlì de] **7** (pej) [+man] 圆
滑的 [yuánhuá de] II VT (also: **smooth out,
smooth down**) [+skirt, piece of paper etc] 使平滑
[shǐ pínghuá] ▶ **to smooth the path** or **way (for
sth)** (为某事) 铺平道路
▶ **smooth over** VT [+difficulties] 消除 [xiāochú]
▶ **smooth over** VT = **smooth out**

smother ['smʌðə(r)] VT **1** [+fire, flames] 把…闷
熄 [bǎ…mènxī] **2** (suffocate) [+person] 使窒
息 [shǐ zhìxī] **3** (over-protect) [+person] 溺爱
[nì'ài] **4** (repress) [+emotions] 抑制 [yìzhì] ▶ **to
smother sth/sb with sth** (cover) 用某物将某
物/某人覆盖 ▶ **smothered with** or **in sth** 以
（或）被某物覆盖

SMS N ABBR (= short message service) 短信息服务
[duǎn xìnxī fúwù]

smudge [smʌdʒ] I N [C] 污迹 [wūjì] II VT 弄
脏 [nòngzāng]

smug [smʌg] (pej) ADJ [+person, expression] 沾沾
自喜的 [zhānzhān zìxǐ de]

smuggle ['smʌgl] VT [+goods, drugs, refugees] 走
私 [zǒusī] ▶ **to smuggle sth in/out** 走私进
口/出口某物

smuggler ['smʌglə(r)] N [C] 走私者 [zǒusīzhě]

smuggling ['smʌglɪŋ] N [U] 走私 [zǒusī]

snack [snæk] I N [C] 小吃 [xiǎochī] II VI 吃
零食 [chī língshí] ▶ **to have a snack** 吃点零食

snack bar N [C] 小吃部 [xiǎochībù]

snag [snæg] I N [C] (problem) 麻烦 [máfan]
II VT [+clothes] 钩破 [gōupò]

snail [sneɪl] N [C] 蜗牛 [wōniú] ▶ **at a snail's
pace** 极慢地

snake [sneɪk] I N [C] 蛇 [shé] II VI (liter) ▶ **to
snake (through sth)** 蜿蜒 (穿过某物) [wānyán
(chuānguò mǒuwù)]

snap [snæp] I N **1** [S] (sound) 劈啪声
[pīpāshēng] **2** [C] (inf) (photograph) 照片
[zhàopiàn] II ADJ [+decision, judgement] 仓促
的 [cāngcù de] III VT **1** [+rope, stick etc] 把…啪
地拉断 [bǎ…pāde lāduàn] **2** (inf) (photograph)
给…拍照 [gěi…pāizhào] IV VI **1** [rope, stick
etc +] 啪地绷断 [pāde bēngduàn] **2** (fig) (lose
control) 崩溃 [bēngkuì] ▶ **a cold snap** 寒潮
▶ **to snap one's fingers** (lit) 打响指; (fig) 轻而
易举 ▷ I can get anything I want just by snapping
my fingers. 我可以轻而易举地得到任何想要的
东西。 ▶ **to snap open/shut** [trap, jaws, bag etc +]
啪地一声打开/合上
▶ **snap at** VT FUS [不可拆分] **1** [dog +] 一下咬住
[yīxià yǎozhù] **2** [person +] 厉声对…说 [lìshēng
duì…shuō]
▶ **snap off** I VT 折断 [zhéduàn] II VI 断掉
[duàndiào]
▶ **snap out of** VT FUS [不可拆分] ▶ **to snap out
of sth** 很快摆脱某心境 [hěnkuài bǎituō mǒu
xīnjìng] ▶ **to snap out of it** 摆脱沮丧的情绪
▶ **snap up** VT [+bargain] 抢购 [qiǎnggòu]

snapshot ['snæpʃɔt] N [C] **1** (photo) 快照
[kuàizhào] **2** (impression) 简单印象 [jiǎndān
yìnxiàng]

snarl [snɑ:l] I VI [animal +] 嗥叫 [háojiào]
II VT [person +] 咆哮道 [páoxiào dào] III N [C]
[of animal] 嗥叫 [háojiào]
▶ **snarl up** VT [+plan or scheme] 搅乱 [jiǎoluàn]

snatch [snætʃ] I N [C] [of conversation, song
etc] 片段 [piànduàn] II VT **1** (grab) 抢夺
[qiǎngduó] **2** (seize) [+child, hostage] 劫 [jié]
3 (steal) [+handbag etc] 抢走 [qiǎngzǒu] **4** (take)
[+opportunity, some time etc] 抓住 [zhuāzhù]
III VI ▶ **don't snatch!** 别抢！[biéqiǎng!] ▶ **to
snatch a sandwich** 抓紧时间吃个三明治 ▶ **to
snatch some sleep** 抓紧时间睡会儿觉
▶ **snatch up** VT 一把抓住 [yībǎ zhuāzhù]

sneak [sni:k] (pt, pp (US) also **snuck**) I VI ▶ **to
sneak in/out** 偷偷溜进/出 [tōutōu liūjìn/chū]
II VT ▶ **to sneak a look at sth** 偷看一眼某物
[tōukàn yīyǎn mǒuwù] ▶ **to sneak sb/sth into
a place** 将某人/某物偷带进一个地方 III N [C]
(inf) (telltale) 告密者 [gàomìzhě]
▶ **sneak up** VI ▶ **to sneak up on sb** 悄悄地接近
某人 [qiāoqiāo de jiējìn mǒurén]

sneakers ['sni:kəz] (US) NPL 胶底运动鞋
[jiāodǐ yùndòngxié] [英=**trainers**]

sneaky ['sni:kɪ] (inf) ADJ [+person, action] 鬼鬼
祟祟的 [guǐguǐsuìsuì de]

sneer [snɪə(r)] I VI 讥笑 [jīxiào] II N [C] 嘲
讽 [cháofěng] ▶ **to sneer at sb/sth** (mock) 嘲
笑某人/某事

sneeze [sni:z] I VI 打喷嚏 [dǎ pēntì] II N [C]
喷嚏 [pēntì] ▶ **it's not to be sneezed at** (inf) 这

可不应被轻视

sniff [snɪf] I N [c] 1 (from cold, crying) 抽鼻子 [chōu bízi]; (disapproving) 嗤之以鼻 [chīzhǐyǐbí] II VI 抽鼻子 [chōu bízi] III VT [+ perfume, air] 嗅 [xiù]; [+ glue] 吸入 [xīrù] ▶ to take a sniff of sth (smell) 闻一下某物
▶ sniff out I VT 1 [+ drugs etc] 嗅出 [xiùchū] 2 (inf) [+ scandal, bargain] 找出 [zhǎochū]

snigger ['snɪɡə(r)] VI 窃笑 [qièxiào]

snip [snɪp] I VT 剪断 [jiǎnduàn] II VI ▶ to snip at sth 剪某物 [jiǎn mǒuwù] III N 1 [c] 剪 [jiǎn] 2 [s] (BRIT: inf) (bargain) 便宜货 [piányihuò]

sniper ['snaɪpə(r)] N [c] 狙击手 [jūjīshǒu]

snob [snɔb] (pej) N [c] 势利小人 [shìli xiǎorén]

snooker ['snuːkə(r)] I N [U] (SPORT) 英式台球 [yīngshì táiqiú] II VT (BRIT: inf) ▶ to be snookered 处于困境 [chùyú kùnjìng]

snoop [snuːp] VI ▶ to snoop around 到处窥探 [dàochù kuītàn] ▶ to snoop on sb 窥探某人

snooze [snuːz] (inf) I N [c] 小睡 [xiǎoshuì] II VI 打盹 [dǎdǔn] ▶ to have a snooze 打个盹

snore [snɔː(r)] I VI 打鼾 [dǎhān] II N [c] 鼾声 [hānshēng]

snorkel ['snɔːkl] I N [c] 潜水通气管 [qiánshuǐ tōngqìguǎn] II VI 戴潜水通气管潜泳 [dài qiánshuǐ tōngqìguǎn qiányǒng] ▶ to go snorkelling 去潜泳

snort [snɔːt] I N [c] (of person) 哼的一声 [hēngde yīshēng]; (of animal) 喷鼻息的声音 [bíxí] II VI [person +] 哼一声 [hēng yīshēng]; [animal +] 喷鼻息 [pēn bíxí] III VT (inf) [+ cocaine] 从鼻孔吸入 [cóng bíkǒng xīrù]

snow [snəu] I N [U] 雪 [xuě] II VI 下雪 [xiàxuě] III VT ▶ to be snowed under with work (inf) 忙得不可开交 [mángde bùkěkāijiāo] ▶ it's snowing 下雪了

snowball ['snəubɔːl] I N [c] 雪球 [xuěqiú] II VI [problem, campaign +] 滚雪球般地扩大 [gǔn xuěqiú bān de kuòdà]

snowboard ['snəubɔːd] I N [c] 滑雪板 [huáxuěbǎn] II VI 用滑雪板滑雪 [yòng huáxuěbǎn huáxuě] ▶ to go snowboarding 去滑滑雪板

snowboarding ['snəubɔːdɪŋ] N [U] 滑雪板运动 [huáxuěbǎn yùndòng] see also snowboard

snub [snʌb] I VT [+ person] 怠慢 [dàimàn] II N [c] 怠慢 [dàimàn]

snuck [snʌk] (US) PT, PP of sneak

snug [snʌɡ] ADJ 1 [+ place] 温暖舒适的 [wēnnuǎn shūshì de]; [+ person] 安适的 [ānshì de] 2 (well-fitting) [+ garment] 紧身的 [jǐnshēn de] ▶ a snug fit 合体

so [səu] I ADV 1 (thus, likewise) 这样 [zhèyàng] ▶ they do so because... 他们这样做是因为… ▶ if you don't want to go, say so 如果你不想去，就说你不想去 ▶ if so 如果这样 ▶ "it's five o'clock" "so it is!" "5点了。" "的确是！" ▶ I hope/think so 我希望/认为如此 ▶ so far (up to now) 迄今为止; (up to then) 到那时为止 ▶ and so on 等等 2 (also) ▶ so do I/so am I 我也一样 [wǒ yě yīyàng] 3 (in comparisons) (to such a degree) 如此 [rúcǐ] ▶ so quickly/big (that) 如此快/大 (以至于) ▶ not so clever (as) 不(如…)那么聪明 4 (very) 非常 [fēicháng] ▶ we were so worried 我们非常担心 ▶ so much 那么多 ▶ there's so much work to do 有那么多工作要做 ▶ I love you so much 我非常爱你 ▶ so many 那么多 ▶ I've got so many things to do 我有那么多事情要做 5 (linking events) 于是 [yúshì] ▶ so I was right after all 我终究还是对的 ▶ so how was your day? 那你今天过得怎么样？ 6 (inf) ▶ so (what)? 那又怎么样？ [nà yòu zěnmeyàng?] 7 (in approximations) ▶ ten or so 10个左右 [shíge zuǒyòu] 8 (inf) ▶ so long! 再见！ [zàijiàn!] II CONJ 1 (expressing purpose) ▶ so (that) 为的是 [wèi de shì] ▶ I brought it so (that) you could see it 我带过来给你看 ▶ so as to 以便 2 (expressing result) 因此 [yīncǐ] ▶ he didn't come so I left 他没来，因此我走了

soak [səuk] I VT 1 (drench) 使湿透 [shǐ shītòu] 2 (leave in water) 浸泡 [jìnpào] II VI 1 [dirty washing, dishes +] 浸泡 [jìnpào] 2 [person +] (in bath) 泡一泡 [pàoyīpào] ▶ to soak through sth 浸透某物 ▶ to have a soak (in bath) 泡一泡
▶ soak in VI [liquid +] 吸收 [xīshōu]
▶ soak up VT [+ liquid] 吸收 [xīshōu]

soaked [səukt] ADJ (also: soaked through) [+ person, clothes] 湿透的 [shītòu de]

soaking ['səukɪŋ] ADJ (also: soaking wet) [+ person] 湿透的 [shītòu de]; [+ clothes] 湿淋淋的 [shīlínlín de]

so-and-so ['səuənsəu] (inf) N [c] (somebody) 某某人 [mǒumǒurén]; (something) 某某事 [mǒumǒushì] ▶ Mr/Mrs So-and-so 某某先生/太太 ▶ the little so-and-so! (pej) 讨厌的家伙！

soap [səup] N [c/U] 1 肥皂 [féizào] 2 = soap opera

soap opera N [c] 肥皂剧 [féizào jù]

soap powder N [c/U] 皂粉 [zàofěn]

soar [sɔː(r)] VI 1 [bird +] 翱翔 [áoxiáng]; [aircraft +] 升入 [shēngrù] 2 [temperature, price +] 骤升 [zhòushēng] 3 [building, tree etc +] 高耸 [gāosǒng]

sob [sɔb] I N [c] 啜泣 [chuòqì] II VI 啜泣

[chuòqì]

sober ['səubə(r)] ADJ **1** 未醉的 [wèizuìde] **2** (serious) [+person] 郑重的 [zhèngzhòng de]; [+attitude] 清醒的 [qīngxǐng de]; [+colours, clothes] 素净的 [sùjìng de] ▸ **to stay sober** 保持清醒
▸ **sober up** I VI 清醒起来 [qīngxǐng qǐlái] II VT 使醒酒 [shǐ xǐngjiǔ]

so-called [ˌsəʊˈkɔːld] ADJ **1** (before name, title) 号称的 [hàochēng de] **2** (falsely named) 所谓的 [suǒwèi de]

soccer ['sɔkə(r)] N [U] 足球 [zúqiú] [英 = **football**]

sociable ['səʊʃəbl] ADJ 好交际的 [hào jiāojì de]

○social ['səʊʃl] I ADJ **1** [+problems, injustice, change, structure] 社会的 [shèhuì de] **2** [+event, function] 社交的 [shèjiāo de] ▷ We ought to organize more social events. 我们应该组织更多的社交活动. **3** [+animals, insects] 群居的 [qúnjū de] II N [C] (o.f.) 社交聚会 [shèjiāo jùhuì]

socialism ['səʊʃəlɪzəm] N [U] 社会主义 [shèhuì zhǔyì]

socialist ['səʊʃəlɪst] I ADJ [+party, state] 社会主义的 [shèhuì zhǔyì de] II N [C] 社会主义者 [shèhuì zhǔyìzhě]

socialize ['səʊʃəlaɪz] VI 参加社交 [cānjiā shèjiāo] ▸ **to socialize with** 与…交往

social life N [C] 社交生活 [shèjiāo shēnghuó]

socially ['səʊʃəlɪ] ADV [meet, know+] 社会上 [shèhuì shang] ▸ **socially acceptable** 社会上可以接受的 ▸ **socially deprived/disadvantaged** 在全社会中贫困的/处于社会不利地位的

social security (BRIT) N [U] (payment) 社会保障 [shèhuì bǎozhàng] [美 = **welfare**]
▸ **Department of Social Security** 社会保障部 ▸ **to be on social security** 靠社会救济金为生的 [美 = **to be on welfare**]

social services NPL 社会福利事业 [shèhuì fúlì shìyè]

social work N [U] 社会福利工作 [shèhuì fúlì gōngzuò]

social worker N [C] 社会福利工作者 [shèhuì fúlì gōngzuòzhě]

○society [sə'saɪətɪ] I N **1** (people in general) 社会 [shèhuì] ▷ Women must have equal status in society. 妇女在社会上必须有平等的地位. **2** [C/U] (community) 社会 [shèhuì] ▷ a multi-racial society 多种族社会 **3** [C] (club) 社团 [shètuán] ▷ the local film society 当地影视协会 II CPD [复合词] [+wedding] 社交界 [shèjiāo jiè]

sociology [ˌsəʊsɪ'ɔlədʒɪ] N [U] 社会学 [shèhuì xué]

sock [sɔk] I N [C] 袜子 [wàzi] II VT (inf) ▸ **to sock sb in the mouth/on the jaw** 猛击某人的嘴巴/下巴 [měngjī mǒurén de zuǐbā/xiàbā]
▸ **to pull one's socks up** (fig) 加紧努力

socket ['sɔkɪt] N [C] **1** (BRIT: ELEC) 插座 [chāzuò] [美 = **outlet**] **2** (also: **eye socket**) 眼窝 [yǎnwō]; (also: **hip socket** etc) 髋关节{等} [kuānguānjié {děng}]

soda ['səʊdə] N [U] **1** (also: **soda water**) 苏打水 [sūdá shuǐ] **2** (US) (also: **soda pop**) 汽水 [qìshuǐ]

sodium ['səʊdɪəm] N [U] 钠 [nà]

sofa ['səʊfə] N [C] 沙发 [shāfā]

sofa bed N [C] 沙发床 [shāfā chuáng]

soft [sɔft] ADJ **1** [+food] 松软的 [sōngruǎn de]; [+skin] 柔滑的 [róuhuá de] **2** [+bed, paste] 柔软的 [róuruǎn de] **3** [+voice, music] 轻柔的 [qīngróu de] **4** [+light, colour] 柔和的 [róuhé de] **5** (lenient) 宽和的 ▸ **to have a soft spot for sb** 对某人有好感 ▸ **to be soft on sb** 对某人宽厚

soft drink N [C] 软性饮料 [ruǎnxìng yǐnliào]

soft drugs NPL 软毒品 [ruǎn dúpǐn]

soften ['sɔfn] I VT **1** [+food] 使变软 [shǐ biànruǎn] **2** [+impact, blow] 使缓和 [shǐ huǎnhé] **3** [+position, attitude] 使软化 [shǐ ruǎnhuà] **4** [+voice, expression] 使柔和 [shǐ róuhé] II VI **1** (also: **soften up**) [food, material+] 变软 [biànruǎn] **2** [position, attitude+] 变缓和 [biàn huǎnhé] **3** [voice, expression+] 变温和 [biàn wēnhé]
▸ **soften up** I VT (fig) [+person] 使软化 [shǐ ruǎnhuà] II VI [food, material+] 变软 [biànruǎn]

softly ['sɔftlɪ] ADV **1** (gently) 轻轻地 [qīngqing de] **2** (quietly) 温柔地 [wēnróu de]

softness ['sɔftnɪs] N [U] [of hair, skin] 柔性 [róuxìng]

software ['sɔftwɛə(r)] N [U] 软件 [ruǎnjiàn]

soggy ['sɔgɪ] ADJ [+food] 水份太多的 [shuǐfèn tàiduō de]; [+clothes] 湿透的 [shītòu de] ▸ **to go soggy** 受潮

soil [sɔɪl] I N **1** [C/U] (earth) 土壤 [tǔrǎng] **2** [U] (territory) 领土 [lǐngtǔ] II VT (make dirty) 弄脏 [nòngzāng]

solar ['səʊlə(r)] ADJ 太阳的 [tàiyáng de]

solar power N [U] 太阳能 [tàiyáng néng]

solar system N [C] 太阳系 [tàiyáng xì]

sold [səʊld] PT, PP of **sell**

soldier ['səʊldʒə(r)] N [C] 士兵 [shìbīng]
▸ **soldier on** VI 顽强地坚持下去 [wánqiáng de jiānchí xiàqù]

sold out ADJ [+tickets] 卖光的 [màiguāng de]; [+concert, show] 客满的 [kèmǎn de] ▸ **to be sold out of sth** 某物全部卖光了

sole [səʊl] I N [C] [of foot, shoe] 底 [dǐ] **2** [C/U] (pl **sole**) (fish) 鳎鱼 [tǎyú] II ADJ **1** (only) [+aim, purpose, reason] 惟一的 [wéiyī de] **2** (exclusive) [+ownership, responsibility] 专有的 [zhuānyǒu de]

solely ['səʊllɪ] ADV 惟一地 [wéiyī de] ▸ **I will hold you solely responsible** 我要你个人负责

solemn ['sɔləm] ADJ **1** [+person, expression] 一本正经的 [yīběn zhèngjīng de] **2** [+music] 庄严的 [zhuāngyán de] **3** [+promise, agreement] 郑重的 [zhèngzhòng de]

solicitor [sə'lɪsɪtə(r)] (BRIT) N [C] 律师 [lùshī]

solid ['sɒlɪd] I ADJ 1 (not soft) 坚实的 [jiānshí de] 2 (without gaps) 紧密的 [jǐnmì de] 3 (not liquid) 固体的 [gùtǐ de] 4 (reliable) [+ person] 可信赖的 [kě xìnlài de]; [+ advice, experience] 确实的 [quèshí de]; [+ evidence, information] 有根据的 [yǒu gēnjù de] 5 (strong) [+ structure] 牢固的 [láogù de] 6 (unbroken) [+ months, years] 整整的 [zhěngzhěng de] 7 (pure) [+ gold, oak etc] 纯质的 [chúnzhì de] II ADV ▸ I read for 2 hours solid 我阅读了整整两个小时 [wǒ yuèdúle zhěngzhěng liǎngge xiǎoshí] III N [C] 固体 [gùtǐ] IV solids NPL (food) 非流食 [fēi liúshí]

solidarity [sɒlɪ'dærɪtɪ] N [U] 团结一致 [tuánjié yīzhì] ▸ **to show solidarity (with sb)** 显示(同某人)站在一起

solitary ['sɒlɪtərɪ] ADJ 1 [+ person, animal, life] 孤僻的 [gūpì de] 2 [+ activity] 单独的 [dāndú de] 3 (single) 无伴的 [wúbàn de]

solitude ['sɒlɪtjuːd] N [U] 独处 [dúchǔ] ▸ **to live in solitude** 离群索居

solo ['səʊləʊ] I N [C] (piece of music) 独奏 [dúzòu]; (song) 独唱 [dúchàng]; (dance) 独舞 [dúwǔ] II ADJ (flight, album, career) 单独的 [dāndú de] III ADV (fly, play, perform +) 单独地 [dāndú de]

soloist ['səʊləʊɪst] N [C] (instrumentalist) 独奏演员 [dúzòu yǎnyuán]; (singer) 独唱演员 [dúchàng yǎnyuán]

soluble ['sɒljʊbl] ADJ 可溶的 [kěróng de]

solution [sə'luːʃən] N [C] 1 (to problem) 解决方案 [jiějué fāng'àn] 2 (to crossword, riddle) 答案 [dá'àn] 3 (liquid) 溶液 [róngyè]

solve [sɒlv] VT 1 [+ mystery, case] 破解 [pòjiě] 2 [+ problem] 解决 [jiějué] 3 [+ puzzle, riddle] 解答 [jiědá]

solvent ['sɒlvənt] I ADJ (COMM) 有偿付能力的 [yǒu chángfù nénglì de] II N [C/U] (CHEM) 溶剂 [róngjì]

Somali [sə'mɑːlɪ] I ADJ 索马里的 [Suǒmǎlǐ de] II N [C] (person) 索马里人 [Suǒmǎlǐrén]

Somalia [sə'mɑːlɪə] N 索马里 [Suǒmǎlǐ]

sombre, (US) somber ['sɒmbə(r)] ADJ 1 [+ colour, place] 暗淡的 [àndàn de] 2 [+ person, mood, expression] 忧郁的 [yōuyù de]

○

some I ADJ 1 (a little, a few) 一些 [yīxiē]
▸ **some milk/books** 一些牛奶/书 ▸ **would you like some wine?** 你来点葡萄酒吗？
▸ **we've got some time but not much** 我们还有些时间，但不太多了 ▸ **there must be some steps we can take** 我们一定能采取些什么措施

2 (certain, in contrasts) 某些 [mǒuxiē]
▸ **some people say that...** 有些人说…
▸ **some people hate fish, while others love it** 有些人讨厌鱼，而有些人喜欢

3 (unspecified) ▸ **some (or other)** 某一 [mǒuyī] ▸ **he was asking for some book (or other)** 他要某本书 ▸ **some woman was asking for you** 有位女士找你 ▸ **some day** 某天 ▸ **we'll meet again some day** 有一天我们会再见面的 ▸ **shall we meet some day next week?** 我们在下个星期的某天见面好吗？

4 (considerable) 相当的 [xiāngdāng de]

5 (inf) (emphatic) 了不得的 [liǎobudé de]
▸ **that was some party!** 那个聚会好棒！

II PRON (a certain amount, certain number) 一些 [yīxiē] ▸ **I've got some** 我有一些
▸ **there was/were some left** 还剩下一些 ▸ **some of it/them** 它的一部分/他们中的一些 ▸ **some of the play was good** 戏剧中的某些部分是好的 ▸ **could I have some of that cheese?** 给我点儿那种奶酪好吗？
▸ **I've read some of the book** 那本书我读了一些

III ADV 1 (approximately) ▸ **some 10 people** 大约10人 [dàyuē shírén]

2 (US) (to a degree) 一点儿 [yīdiǎnr] ▸ **we can walk some** 我们可以走一走

somebody ['sʌmbədɪ] PRON = **someone**

somehow ['sʌmhaʊ] ADV (in some way) 不知怎样地 [bùzhī zěnyàng de]

someone ['sʌmwʌn] PRON 某人 [mǒurén]
▸ **there's someone coming** 有人来了 ▸ **I saw someone in the garden** 我看见花园里有人 ▸ **someone else** 别人

someplace ['sʌmpleɪs] (US) ADV = **somewhere**

○**something** ['sʌmθɪŋ] PRON 某事物 [mǒushìwù] ▸ **let's do something nice for your birthday** 咱们得好好过过你的生日 ▸ **there was obviously something wrong** 显然有些事情不对劲 ▸ **something to do** 有事要做 ▸ **something else** 其他事情 ▸ **would you like a sandwich or something?** 你要来点三明治或其他什么东西？ ▸ **it's something of a mystery** 这是件神秘的事 ▸ **they make up something like two-thirds of the population** 他们占了差不多三分之二的人口

sometime ['sʌmtaɪm] ADV 某个时候 [mǒugè shíhòu]

请勿将 sometime 和 sometime 混淆。sometimes 表示某事物只发生在某些时候，而不是总是发生。*Do you visit your sister? – Sometimes. ... Sometimes I wish I still lived in Australia.* sometimes 表示某事物发生在特定情况下，而不是在任何情况下都会发生。*Sometimes they stay for a week, sometimes just for the weekend.* sometime 表示未来或过去某个不确定或未指明的时间。*(Can I come and see you sometime? ...He started his new job sometime last month.)*

sometimes ['sʌmtaɪmz] ADV 有时 [yǒushí]
▷ 用法参见 **sometime**

somewhat ['sʌmwɔt] ADV 有点 [yǒudiǎn]
▶ **somewhat to my surprise** 让我有点奇怪
的是

somewhere ['sʌmwɛə(r)] ADV (place) 在
某处 [zài mǒuchù] ▶ **I need somewhere to
live** 我需要找个地方住 ▶ **I must have lost it
somewhere** 我一定把它丢在哪儿了 ▶ **it's
somewhere in Italy** 这是意大利的某个地方
▶ **let's go somewhere quiet** 我们去个安静的
地方吧 ▶ **somewhere else** 别的地方 ▶ **to be
getting somewhere** (making progress) 有些进展
▶ **he's somewhere between 65 and 70** 他的年
纪大约在65至70之间

○ **son** [sʌn] N [c] 儿子 [érzi]

song [sɔŋ] N **1** [c] 歌曲 [gēqǔ] **2** [c] (of bird) 鸣
叫 [míngjiào] **3** [u] (singing) 唱歌 [chànggē]
▶ **to be on song** (BRIT) [sportsperson +] 处于良
好竞技状态

son-in-law ['sʌnɪnlɔ:] (pl **sons-in-law**) N [c] 女
婿 [nǚxu]

○ **soon** [su:n] ADV **1** (in a short time) 不久 [bùjiǔ]
▷ **It will soon be Christmas.** 不久圣诞节就要到
了。**2** (a short time later) 很快 [hěnkuài] ▷ **I soon
forgot about our conversation.** 我很快就忘了我们
的谈话内容。**3** (early) 早 [zǎo] ▷ **It's too soon to
talk about leaving.** 谈离开的事还太早。▶ **soon
afterwards** 不久后 ▶ **as soon as** 一…就…
▶ **quite soon** 很快 ▶ **how soon?** 多快？▶ **see
you soon!** 再见！

sooner ['su:nə(r)] ADV ▶ **I would sooner...** 我
宁愿…[wǒ nìngyuàn…] ▶ **sooner or later** 迟
早 ▶ **the sooner the better** 越快越好 ▶ **no
sooner said than done** 说到做到 ▶ **no sooner
had we left than...** 我们一离开就…

soothe [su:ð] VT **1** [+ person, animal] 使…平
静 [shǐ…píngjìng] **2** [+ pain] 使…缓和
[shǐ…huǎnhé]

soothing ['su:ðɪŋ] ADJ **1** [+ ointment] 镇痛的
[zhèntòng de] **2** [+ words, manner] 令人安慰的
[lìngrén ānwèi de] **3** [+ music, bath] 令人心旷神
怡的 [lìngrén xīnkuàng shényí de]

sophisticated [sə'fɪstɪkeɪtɪd] ADJ **1** [+ person]
老于世故的 [lǎoyú shìgù de]; [+ lifestyle, taste]
高雅时髦的 [gāoyǎ shímáo de] **2** [+ machinery,
system] 精密的 [jīngmì de]

sophomore ['sɔfəmɔ:(r)] (US) N [c] 二年级学
生 [èr niánjí xuéshēng]

soprano [sə'prɑ:nəu] N [c] (woman, girl) 女高音
歌手 [nǚ gāoyīn gēshǒu]; (boy) 男童声最高音
歌手 [nán tóngshēng zuì gāoyīn gēshǒu]

sorbet ['sɔ:beɪ] (BRIT) N [c/u] 果汁冰糕 [guǒzhī
bīnggāo]

sordid ['sɔ:dɪd] ADJ **1** [+ place] 污秽的 [wūhuì
de] **2** [+ behaviour] 卑鄙的 [bēibǐ de]

sore [sɔ:(r)] I ADJ **1** (painful) 痛的 [tòng de]
2 (US: inf) (angry) 恼火的 [nǎohuǒ de] II N [c]

痛处 [tòngchù] ▶ **it's a sore point (with him)**
这是(他的一个)痛处 ▶ **to be sore about sth**
(US: inf) 因某事生气 ▶ **to be sore at sb** (US: inf)
生某人的气

sorely ['sɔ:lɪ] ADV **1** ▶ **to be sorely tempted (to
do sth)** 极想(做某事) [jíxiǎng (zuò mǒushì)]
2 ▶ **he'll be sorely missed** 人们会非常想念他
[rénmen huì fēicháng xiǎngniàn tā]

sorrow ['sɔrəu] I N [c] 悲伤 [bēishāng]
II **sorrows** NPL 烦恼 [fánnǎo]

sorry ['sɔrɪ] ADJ **1** (regretful) 懊悔的 [àohuǐ de]
2 (wretched) [+ condition, excuse] 拙劣的 [zhuōliè
de] ▶ **(I'm) sorry!** (apology) 对不起！▶ **sorry?**
(pardon?) 请再讲一遍 ▶ **to feel sorry for sb** 对
某人表示同情 ▶ **to be sorry about sth** 对某
事表示歉意 ▶ **I'm sorry if I offended you** 如
果我冒犯了你，我很抱歉 ▶ **I'm sorry to hear
that...** 听到…我really很伤心 ▶ **a sorry sight** 悲
惨景象

○ **sort** [sɔ:t] I N **1** [c] (sort (of)) 种类 [zhǒnglèi]
▷ **What sort of school did you go to?** 你去了哪种学
校？▷ **What sort do you want?** 你要哪一种？**2** [c]
(make, brand) [of coffee, car etc] 品牌 [pǐnpái] **3** [s]
(person) 人 [rén] ▷ **He seemed to be just the right
sort for the job.** 他看起来是做这份工作的合适
人选。II VT **1** [+ papers, mail, belongings]
把…分类 [bǎ…fēnlèi] ▷ **Minnie was alone in the
post office, sorting mail.** 明妮独自在邮局，将
邮件分类。**2** (separate) 分开 [fēnkāi] ▷ **The
students are sorted into three ability groups.** 将学生
按能力分成3个组。**3** (inf) (solve) [+ problem] 解
决 [jiějué] ▷ **These problems have now been sorted.**
这些问题已经被解决了。**4** (COMPUT) 整理
[zhěnglǐ] ▶ **sort of** (inf) 有点儿 ▷ **It's a sort of
yellowish colour.** 有点儿发黄的颜色。▶ **all sorts
of** 各种不同的 ▷ **a career/an education of
sorts** 不怎么样的职业/教育
▶ **sort out** VT **1** (separate) 区别 [qūbié] ▷ **the
difficulty of trying to sort out fact from fiction** 区别
事实与虚构的困难 **2** (solve) [+ problem] 解决
[jiějué]

SOS [esəu' ɛs] N 紧急求救 [jǐnjí qiújiù]

so-so ['səusəu] (inf) I ADJ (in quality) 马马虎虎
的 [mǎmǎ hūhū de] II ADV ▶ **"How are you?"
"So-so."** "你好吗？""还凑合。" ["nǐ hǎo
ma?" "hái còuhe."]

sought [sɔ:t] PT, PP of **seek**

soul [səul] N **1** [c] (REL) 灵魂 [línghún] **2** [s] (fig)
精力 [jīnglì] **3** [c] (person) 人 [rén] **4** [u] (MUS)
爵士灵歌 [juéshì línggē] ▶ **I didn't see a soul**
我一个人都没看见 ▶ **poor soul** 可怜的人

○ **sound** [saund] I ADJ **1** (healthy) 健康的
[jiànkāng de] ▷ **My heart is basically sound.** 我
的心脏基本上是健康的。**2** (not damaged)
[+ building] 完好无损的 [wánhǎo wúsǔn
de] ▷ **The house was surprisingly sound after the
explosion.** 爆炸发生后，这所房子令人吃惊地完
好无损。**3** (sensible) [+ advice] 明智的 [míngzhì

de] **4** (safe) [+ investment] 可靠的 [kěkào de]
5 (reliable, thorough) 牢固的 [láogù de] ▷ a
sound theoretical foundation 牢固的理论基础
6 (valid) [+ argument, policy, claim] 合理的 [hélǐ
de] ▷ His argument is basically sound. 他的论点
基本上是合理的。**II** ADV ▶ **sound asleep** 酣
睡 [hānshuì] **III** N **1** [C] (noise) 声音 [shēngyīn]
▷ the sound of footsteps 脚步声 **2** [S] (volume) (on
TV, radio etc) 音量 [yīnliàng] ▷ Morris turned
down the sound. 莫里斯把音量调小了。**3** [U]
(PHYS) 声 [shēng] ▷ twice the speed of sound 声
速的两倍 **IV** VT [+ alarm, bell] 敲响 [qiāoxiǎng]
▷ Sound the alarm! 敲警钟！**V** VI **1** [alarm, bell +]
响 [xiǎng] ▷ The buzzer sounded in Daniel's office.
丹尼尔办公室的门铃响了。**2** (seem) 听起来
[tīng qǐlái] ▷ She sounded a bit worried. 她听起
来有点担心。▶ **to be of sound mind** 心理健
康的 ▶ **to make a sound** 出声 ▶ **I don't like
the sound of that** 我不喜欢那种语气 ▶ **that
sounds like an explosion** 听起来像是爆炸声的
▶ **she sounds like the Queen** (in voice, manner)
她的语气听上去像是女皇 ▶ **that sounds like
a great idea** 这主意听起来妙极了 ▶ **it sounds
as if...** 听起来似乎…
  ▶ **sound off** (inf) VI ▶ **to sound off (about sth)**
(就某事) 夸夸其谈 [(jiù mǒushì) kuākuāqítán]
  ▶ **sound out** VT [+ person] 试探 [shìtàn]
soundly ['saʊndlɪ] ADV **1** [sleep +] 酣畅地
[hānchàng de] **2** [be based +] 稳固地 [wěngù de]
3 [defeat +] 彻底地 [chèdǐ de]
soundtrack ['saʊndtræk] N [C] 声道
[shēngdào]
soup [suːp] N [C/U] 汤 [tāng]
sour ['saʊə(r)] **I** ADJ **1** (bitter-tasting) 酸
的 [suān de] **2** [+ milk] 酸的 [suān de]
3 (bad-tempered) 愠怒的 [yùnnù de] **II** VT
[+ relationship, attitude] 使恶化 [shǐ èhuà] **III** VI
[relationship, attitude +] 变坏 [biànhuài] ▶ **to go
or turn sour** [milk, wine +] 变馊 [relationship +] 变
糟 ▶ **it's sour grapes** 这是酸葡萄
source [sɔːs] N [C] **1** (of money, resources, energy)
来源 [láiyuán] **2** (person) 消息提供者 [xiāoxi
tígōngzhě] **3** (book) 原始资料 [yuánshǐ zīliào]
4 (of river) 源头 [yuántóu] **5** [of problem, anxiety]
根源 [gēnyuán]
Ⓞ**south** [saʊθ] **I** N [S/U] 南方 [nánfāng] **II** ADJ
南部的 [nánbù de] **III** ADV 向南方 [xiàng
nánfāng] ▶ **the south of France** 法国南部
▶ **to the south** 以南 ▶ **the south wind** 南风
▶ **south of...** 在…以南 ▷ It's 15 miles or so south
of Glasgow. 它位于格拉斯哥以南15英里左右。
South Africa N 南非 [Nánfēi]
South African **I** ADJ 南非的 [Nánfēi de] **II** N
[C] (person) 南非人 [Nánfēirén]
South America N 南美洲 [Nán měizhōu]
South American **I** ADJ 南美洲的 [Nán
měizhōu de] **II** N [C] (person) 南美洲人 [Nán
měizhōurén]

south-east [saʊθ'iːst] **I** N 东南 [dōngnán]
II ADJ 东南的 [dōngnán de] **III** ADV 向东南
[xiàng dōngnán]
South-East Asia N 东南亚 [Dōngnán yà]
south-eastern [saʊθ'iːstən] ADJ 东南的
[dōngnán de]
southern ['sʌðən] ADJ 南方的 [nánfāng de]
▶ **the southern hemisphere** 南半球
South Korea N 韩国 [Hánguó]
South Pole N ▶ **the South Pole** 南极 [Nánjí]
southward(s) ['saʊθwəd(z)] ADV 向南
[xiàngnán]
south-west [saʊθ'wɛst] **I** N [S/U] 西南
[xīnán] **II** ADJ 西南的 [xīnán de] **III** ADV 向
西南 [xiàng xīnán]
south-western [saʊθ'wɛstən] ADJ 西南的
[xīnán de]
souvenir [suːvə'nɪə(r)] N [C] 纪念品 [jìniàn
pǐn]
sovereign ['sɔvrɪn] **I** N [C] (frm) (king, queen) 君
主 [jūnzhǔ] **II** ADJ **1** [+ state, country] 独立自主
的 [dúlì zìzhǔ de] **2** [+ power, right] 拥有最高权
力的 [yōngyǒu zuìgāo quánlì de]
sow [saʊ] (pt **sowed**, pp **sown** [saʊn]) VT
1 [+ seeds] 播种 [bōzhǒng] **2** [+ suspicion, doubts
etc] 传播 [chuánbō]
soy [sɔɪ] (US) N [U] 黄豆 [huángdòu] [英 = soya]
soya ['sɔɪə] (BRIT) N [U] 黄豆 [huángdòu]
[美 = soy]
soya bean (BRIT) N [C] 黄豆 [huángdòu]
[美 = soybean]
soybean ['sɔɪbiːn] (US) N [C] 黄豆 [huángdòu]
[英 = soya bean]
soy sauce N [U] 酱油 [jiàngyóu]
spa [spɑː] N [C] **1** (town) 矿泉胜地 [kuàngquán
shèngdì] **2** (US) (also: health spa) 美容健身院
[měiróng jiànshēn yuàn]
Ⓞ**space** [speɪs] **I** N **1** [C/U] (gap, place) 空隙
[kòngxì] **2** [C/U] (room) 空间 [kōngjiān] **3** [U]
(beyond Earth) 太空 [tàikōng] **II** CPD [复合词]
太空 [tàikōng] **III** VT (also: space out) [+ text,
visits] 把…分隔开 [bǎ…fēngé kāi]; [+ payments]
把…均匀分配 [bǎ…jūnyún fēnpèi] ▶ **to clear
a space for sth** 为某物腾地方 ▶ **in a short
space of time** (from now) 片刻后; (in past) 很快
▶ **(with)in the space of an hour** 在一小时内
spacecraft ['speɪskrɑːft] (pl **spacecraft**) N [C]
宇宙飞船 [yǔzhòu fēichuán]
spaceship ['speɪsʃɪp] N = **spacecraft**
spacious ['speɪʃəs] ADJ 宽敞的 [kuānchǎng de]
spade [speɪd] **I** N [C] **1** (tool) 锹 [qiāo] **2** (child's)
小铲 [xiǎochǎn] **II spades** NPL (CARDS) 黑桃
[hēitáo]
spaghetti [spə'gɛtɪ] N [U] 意大利面 [yìdàlì
miàn]
Spain [speɪn] N 西班牙 [Xībānyá]
spam [spæm] (COMPUT) N [U] 垃圾邮件 [lājī
yóujiàn]

span [spæn] I VT 1 [+ *river, lake*] 横跨 [héngkuà] 2 [+*time*] 跨越 [kuàyuè] II N [C] 1 (*of wings*) 翼展 [yìzhǎn] 2 (*of arch*) 跨度 [kuàdù] 3 (*in time*) 一段时间 [yīduàn shíjiān]

Spaniard ['spænjəd] N [C] 西班牙人 [Xībānyá rén]

Spanish ['spænɪʃ] I ADJ 西班牙的 [Xībānyá de] II N [U] (*language*) 西班牙语 [Xībānyáyǔ] III **the Spanish** NPL 西班牙人 [Xībānyárén]

spank [spæŋk] VT [+ *person, bottom*] 打 [dǎ]

spanner ['spænə(r)] (BRIT) N [C] 扳钳 [bānqián] [美 = **wrench**]

spare [spɛə(r)] I ADJ 1 (*free*) 多余的 [duōyú de] 2 (*extra*) 备用的 [bèiyòng de] II N [C] = **spare part** III VT 1 **to spare sb the trouble/pain/details** 避免某人的麻烦/让某人知道详情 [bìmiǎn mǒurén de máfan/ràng mǒurén zhīdào xiángqíng] 2 (*make available*) 抽出 [chōuchū] 3 (*afford to give*) 出让 [chūràng] 4 (*not harm*) 幸免 [xìngmiǎn] ▸ **these two are going spare** 这两个是闲着的 ▸ **to have time/money to spare** 有剩余的时间/金钱 ▸ **to spare no expense** 不惜工本 ▸ **I can spare (you) 5 minutes** 我能（为你）抽出5分钟

spare part N [C] 备件 [bèijiàn]

spare time N [U] 业余时间 [yèyú shíjiān]

spark [spɑːk] I N [C] 1 (*from fire, electricity*) 火花 [huǒhuā] 2 [*of wit, interest, imagination*] 一点儿 [yīdiǎnr] II VT (*also:* **spark off**) 触发 [chùfā]

spark plug N [C] 火花塞 [huǒhuā sāi]

sparkle ['spɑːkl] I N [U] 光亮 [guāngliàng] II VI 1 [*diamonds +*] 闪耀 [shǎnyào] 2 [*water +*] 闪闪发光 [shǎnshǎn fāguāng] 3 [*eyes +*] 发亮 [fāliàng]

sparkling water ['spɑːklɪŋ-] N [U] 苏打水 [sūdáshuǐ]

sparkling wine N [U] 汽酒 [qìjiǔ]

sparrow ['spærəu] N [C] 麻雀 [máquè]

sparse [spɑːs] ADJ 1 [+ *vegetation, traffic*] 稀少的 [xīshǎo de] 2 [+*hair*] 稀疏的 [xīshū de]

spasm ['spæzəm] N 1 [C/U] (MED) 抽搐 [chōuchù] 2 [C] [*of anger etc*] 一阵 [yīzhèn]

spat [spæt] I PT, PP of **spit** II N [C] (US) (*quarrel*) 争端 [zhēngduān]

spate [speɪt] N ▸ **a spate of** 大量 [dàliàng] ▸ **to be in spate** [*river +*] 猛涨

spatula ['spætjulə] N 1 (CULIN) 刮刀 [guādāo] 2 (MED) 压舌板 [yāshébǎn]

○ **speak** [spiːk] (*pt* **spoke**, *pp* **spoken**) I VT 1 [+ *language*] 讲 [jiǎng] ▷ *They both spoke English.* 他们两个都讲英语。 2 ▸ **to speak the truth** [shuō shíhuà] II VI 1 讲话 [jiǎnghuà] ▷ *Simon opened his mouth to speak.* 西蒙开口讲话了。 2 (*make a speech*) 演说 [yǎnshuō] ▷ *The Prime Minister spoke to the nation on television.* 总理在电视上向全国人民作演说。 ▸ **they're not speaking** 他们不再讲话了 ▸ **she's not speaking to me** 她不再和我讲话了

▸ **to speak of** *or* **about sb/sth** 提到某人/某事 ▸ **to speak to sb about sth** 和某人谈某事 ▸ **to speak well** *or* **highly of sb** 赞扬某人 ▸ **to speak ill of sb** 说某人的坏话 ▸ **no food/money to speak of** 不值一提的食物/金钱 ▸ **so to speak** 也就是说 ▸ **generally/technically** *etc* **speaking** 总的/从技术上（等）来说 ▸ **speaking of...** 提到… ▸ **speaking as a parent/teacher,...** 作为家长/老师来说…

▸ **speak for** VT FUS [不可拆分] [+ *other people*] 代表…讲话 [dàibiǎo…jiǎnghuà] ▷ *I think I can speak for everyone here when I express my sincere apologies.* 我想我能够代表这里的所有人表示由衷的歉意。 ▸ **it speaks for itself** 这不言而喻 ▸ **speak for yourself!** (*inf*) 谈你自己的意见！ ▸ **that picture is already spoken for** (*reserved*) 那幅画已经有人要了

▸ **speak out** VI 畅所欲言 [chàngsuǒyùyán]

▸ **speak up** VI ▸ **speak up!** 大声点儿！ [dàshēngdiǎnr]

speaker ['spiːkə(r)] N [C] 1 (*in debate etc*) 演讲者 [yǎnjiǎngzhě] 2 (*also:* **loudspeaker**) 扬声器 [yángshēngqì] 3 ▸ **the Speaker** (*in UK House of Parliament*) 下议院议长 [xiàyìyuàn yìzhǎng]; (*in US House of Representatives*) 众议院议长 [zhòngyìyuàn yìzhǎng] ▸ **a French/Russian speaker** 讲法语/俄语的人

speaking ['spiːkɪŋ] I N [U] (*in debate, meeting*) 演讲 [yǎnjiǎng] II ADJ ▸ **Italian-speaking people** 讲意大利语的人士 [jiǎng Yìdàlìyǔ de rénshì] ▸ **to be on speaking terms (with sb)** (和某人)关系好

spear [spɪə(r)] I N [C] (*weapon*) 矛 [máo] II VT [+ *person*] 用矛刺 [yòngmáo cì]; [+ *object*] 叉 [chā]

○ **special** ['spɛʃl] I ADJ 1 (*important*) 特别的 [tèbié de] ▷ *We only use these plates on special occasions.* 我们只在特别场合才用这些碟子。 2 (*different*) 异常的 [yìcháng de] ▷ *Did you notice anything special about him?* 你有没有注意到他有什么异常的地方？ 3 (*particular*) 专门的 [zhuānmén de] ▷ *To marry a foreigner, special permission has to be obtained.* 与外国人结婚，须经专门许可。 4 (*extra*) [+ *effort, favour*] 额外的 [éwài de] ▷ *a law which provides special assistance to those with large families* 为大家庭提供额外帮助的一项法律 II N [C] 1 (*in restaurant*) 特色菜 [tèsè cài] 2 (TV, RAD) 特别节目 [tèbié jiémù] 3 (*train*) 专列 [zhuānchē] ▸ **to take special care** 格外小心 ▸ **it's nothing special** 没什么特别的

special delivery N ▸ **by special delivery** 用特快专递 [yòng tèkuài zhuāndì]

special effects (CINE) NPL 特技效果 [tèjì xiàoguǒ]

specialist ['spɛʃəlɪst] N [C] 1 (*expert*) ▸ **a specialist in** *or* **on** 一位…方面的专家 [yīwèi…fāngmiàn de zhuānjiā] 2 (MED) 专科医生 [zhuānkē yīshēng]

speciality [spɛʃɪ'ælɪtɪ], (US) **specialty** ['spɛʃəltɪ] N [C] **1** (food) 特制品 [tèzhìpǐn]; (product) 特产 [tèchǎn] **2** (subject area) 专业 [zhuānyè]

specialize ['spɛʃəlaɪz] VI ▸ **to specialize in** [+ subject] 专攻 [zhuāngōng]; [+ food] 擅长于 [shàncháng yú]

specially ['spɛʃlɪ] ADV **1** (specifically) 专门地 [zhuānmén de] **2** (inf) (particularly) 尤其 [yóuqí]

special needs NPL ▸ **children with special needs** (BRIT) 有特殊需要的儿童 [yǒu tèshū xūyào de értóng]

special offer (COMM) N [C] 特价品 [tèjiàpǐn]

specialty ['spɛʃəltɪ] (US) N = **speciality**

species ['spiːʃiːz] N [C] 种 [zhǒng]

specific [spə'sɪfɪk] ADJ **1** (fixed) 特定的 [tèdìng de] **2** (exact) 具体的 [jùtǐ de] **3** ▸ **to be specific to** 对…特有的 [duì…tèyǒu de]

specifically [spə'sɪfɪklɪ] ADV **1** (specially) 特别地 [tèbié de]; (exclusively) 特定的 [tèdìng de] **2** (exactly) 明确的 [míngquè de] ▸ **(more) specifically** (更) 具体地说

specify ['spɛsɪfaɪ] VT 指定 [zhǐdìng] ▸ **unless otherwise specified** 除非额外注明

specimen ['spɛsɪmən] N [C] **1** [of plant, animal] 标本 [biāoběn] **2** [of handwriting, signature] 实例 [shílì] **3** [of blood, urine] 抽样 [chōuyàng]

speck [spɛk] N [C] [of dirt, dust] 斑点 [bāndiǎn] ▷ **a tiny speck of dust** 一小粒灰尘

spectacle ['spɛktəkl] N **1** [C] (scene) 奇观 [qíguān] **2** [C] (event, performance) 场面 [chǎngmiàn] **II spectacles** NPL (glasses) 眼镜 [yǎnjìng]

spectacular [spɛk'tækjulə(r)] **I** ADJ [+ view, scenery] 壮丽的 [zhuànglìde]; [+ rise, growth] 惊人的 [jīngrénde] ▷ **a spectacular rise in house prices** 房价的暴涨; [+ success, result] 引人注目的 [yǐnrén zhùmù de] **II** N [C] (performance) 场面浩大的表演 [chǎngmiàn hàodà de biǎoyǎn]

spectator [spɛk'teɪtə(r)] N [C] 观众 [guānzhòng]

spectrum ['spɛktrəm] (pl **spectra** ['spɛktrə]) N [C] **1** (of colours, radio waves) 谱 [pǔ] **2** [of opinion, emotion etc] 范围 [fànwéi]

speculate ['spɛkjuleɪt] VI **1** (FIN) 投机 [tóujī] **2** ▸ **to speculate (about)** 猜测(关于…) [cāicè (guānyú…)] ▸ **to speculate that...** 推测… [tuīcè…]

speech [spiːtʃ] N **1** [C] (formal talk) 演说 [yǎnshuō] **2** [U] (faculty) 说话能力 [shuōhuà nénglì] **3** [S] (manner of speaking) 说话方式 [shuōhuà fāngshì] **4** [U] (spoken language) 口语 [kǒuyǔ] **5** [C] (THEAT) 台词 [táicí]

speechless ['spiːtʃlɪs] ADJ 讲不出话的 [jiǎngbùchū huà de] ▸ **to be speechless with rage/astonishment** 气/惊讶得讲不出话来

speed [spiːd] (pt, pp **sped** [spɛd]) **I** N **1** [C/U] (rate, promptness) 速度 [sùdù] **2** [U] (fast movement) 快速 [kuàisù] **3** [C] (rapidity) 迅速 [xùnsù] **4** [C] (of typing, shorthand) 速度 [sùdù] **II** VI **1** ▸ **to speed along/by** etc 沿着{等}…迅速行进 [yánzhe {děng}…xùnsù xíngjìn] **2** (drive too fast) 超速行驶 [chāosù xíngshǐ] ▸ **at full or top speed** 以最高速度 ▸ **at a speed of 70km/h** 以时速70公里 ▸ **a five-speed gearbox** 5速变速箱

▸ **speed up** (pt, pp **speeded up**) **I** VI **1** [car, runner etc +] 加快速度 [jiākuài sùdù] **2** [process +] 加速 [jiāsù] **II** VT 加快…的速度 [jiākuài…de sùdù]

speedboat ['spiːdbəut] N [C] 快艇 [kuàitǐng]

speeding ['spiːdɪŋ] (LAW) N [U] 超速行驶 [chāosù xíngshǐ]

speed limit (LAW) N [C] 速度极限 [sùdù jíxiàn]

speedy ['spiːdɪ] ADJ [+ recovery, return, conclusion] 迅速的 [xùnsù de]; [+ sale, trial] 快的 [kuài de]

spell [spɛl] (pt, pp **spelled** or **spelt**) **I** N [C] **1** (period) 一段时间 [yíduàn shíjiān] **2** (also: **magic spell**) 咒语 [zhòuyǔ] **II** VT **1** [+ word] 用字母拼 [yòng zìmǔ pīn] **2** [+ disaster, trouble] 招致 [zhāozhì] ▸ **to cast a spell on sb** [witch +] 用咒语迷惑某人; (fig) 迷住某人 ▸ **to be/fall under sb's spell** 被某人迷住 ▸ **he can't spell** 他不会拼写

▸ **spell out** VT **1** [+ feelings, intentions etc] 详细说明 [xiángxì shuōmíng] **2** [+ word] 把…的字母拼写出 [bǎ…de zìmǔ pīnxiě chū]

spelling ['spɛlɪŋ] N **1** [C] [of word] 拼法 [pīnfǎ] **2** [U] (ability to spell) 拼写 [pīnxiě] ▸ **spelling mistake** 拼写错误

spelt [spɛlt] PT, PP of **spell**

○ **spend** [spɛnd] (pt, pp **spent**) VT **1** [+ money] 花费 [huāfèi] ▷ **I spent a hundred pounds on clothes.** 我花了100英镑买衣服。 **2** [+ time, life] 度过 [dùguò] ▷ **I have spent all my life in this town.** 我在这个镇上度过了一生。 ▸ **to spend time/energy on sth** 在某事上花时间/精力 ▸ **to spend time/energy doing sth** 花时间/精力做某事 ▸ **to spend the night in a hotel** 在旅馆度过一晚

spending ['spɛndɪŋ] N [U] 开支 [kāizhī]

spent [spɛnt] **I** PT, PP of **spend** **II** ADJ **1** [+ cartridge, bullets] 失去效能的 [shīqù xiàonéng de] **2** [+ matches] 已用过的 [yǐ yòngguò de]

sperm [spəːm] N **1** [C] (cell) 精子 [jīngzi] **2** [U] (fluid) 精液 [jīngyè]

sphere [sfɪə(r)] N [C] **1** (area) 球体 [qiútǐ] **2** (area) 领域 [lǐngyù]

spice [spaɪs] N [C/U] 香料 [xiāngliào] **II** VT ▸ **to spice sth (up) with** (fig) 用…为某物增添趣味 [yòng…wèi mǒuwù zēngtiān qùwèi]

spicy ['spaɪsɪ] ADJ [+ food] 辛辣的 [xīnlà de]

spider ['spaɪdə(r)] N [C] 蜘蛛 [zhīzhū] ▸ **spider's web** 蜘蛛网

spike [spaɪk] **I** N [C] **1** (of metal) 尖钉 [jiāndīng] **2** (fig) 尖状物 [jiānzhuàng wù] **II spikes**

NPL (SPORT) (shoes) 钉鞋 [dīngxié] III VT (inf) [+drink] 搀拥 [chānjiā]

spike heels (US) NPL 细高跟鞋 [xì gāogēn xié] [英 = stilettos]

spill [spɪl] (pt, pp **spilt** or **spilled**) I VT [+ liquid] 使溢出 [shǐ yìchū] II VI [liquid +] 溢出 [yìchū]
▸ to spill sth on/over sth 将某物洒在某物上
▸ **spill out** VI 1 [people +] 蜂拥 [fēngyōng]
2 [things +] 流出 [liúchū] 3 (from container) 散落 [sǎnluò]
▸ **spill over** VI 1 [liquid +] 溢出 [yìchū] 2 ▸ spill over into [conflict, tension +] 发展成 [fāzhǎn chéng]

spin [spɪn] (pt, pp **spun**) I N 1 [C/U] (of wheel etc) 旋转 [xuánzhuǎn] 2 [S] (in car) 兜风 [dōufēng] 3 [S] (AVIAT) 急剧下降 [jíjù xiàjiàng] 4 [S] (interpretation) 添油加醋 [tiānyóu jiācù] 5 [U] (pej: POL) 添油加醋 [tiānyóujiācù] 6 [C/U] (of ball) 旋转 [xuánzhuàn] II VT 1 [+ wheel, ball, coin] 使…旋转 [shǐ…xuánzhuǎn] 2 [+ wool, cotton] 纺 [fǎng] 3 (BRIT) (also: **spin-dry**) 甩干 [shuǎigān] III VI 1 [person +] 转身 [zhuǎnshēn] 2 [wheel, ball etc +] 打转 [dǎzhuàn] 3 (make thread) 纺纱 [fǎngshā] ▸ my head's spinning 我头昏脑胀 ▸ to spin a yarn 编造奇闻轶事
▸ **spin out** VT [+ speech etc] 拖长时间 [tuōcháng shíjiān]

spinach [ˈspɪnɪtʃ] N [U] 菠菜 [bōcài]

spinal [ˈspaɪnl] ADJ 脊柱的 [jǐzhù de]

spine [spaɪn] N [C] 1 (backbone) 脊柱 [jǐzhù] 2 (on plant, animal) 刺 [cì] 3 [of book] 书脊 [shūjǐ]

spiral [ˈspaɪərl] I N [C] 螺旋 [luóxuán] II VI 1 ▸ to spiral (upwards) [smoke +] 盘旋 (上升) [pánxuán (shàngshēng)] 2 [prices etc +] 不断急剧上升 [búduàn jíjù shàngshēng] 3 ▸ to spiral downwards [prices, rates +] 不断急剧下降 [búduàn jíjù xiàjiàng]; [person +] 每况愈下 [měikuàng yùxià] ▸ a spiral of debt 一连串债务 ▸ a downward spiral 一连串的倒霉事

spire [ˈspaɪə(r)] N [C] 塔尖 [tǎjiān]

spirit [ˈspɪrɪt] I N 1 [C] (soul) 精神 [jīngshén] 2 [c] (ghost) 幽灵 [yōulíng] 3 [U] (energy, courage) 勇气 [yǒngqì] 4 [S] (of law, agreement) 精神实质 [jīngshén shízhì] 5 [S] (frame of mind) 心态 [xīntài] ▸ to be spirited away 被迅速而神秘地带走 [bèi xùnsù ér shénmì de dàizǒu] III **spirits** NPL 1 (BRIT) (whisky etc) 烈酒 [lièjiǔ] [美 = liquor] 2 (frame of mind) 情绪 [qíngxù] ▸ community spirit 社区精神 ▸ in good spirits 心境良好的

spiritual [ˈspɪrɪtjuəl] I ADJ 1 (of the spirit) 精神上的 [jīngshénshang de] 2 (religious) 宗教的 [zōngjiào de] II N [c] (song) 灵歌 [línggē]

spit [spɪt] (pt, pp **spat**) I N 1 [C] (for roasting) 烤肉叉 [kǎoròu chā] 2 [U] (saliva) 唾液 [tuòyè] II VI 1 [person, animal +] 吐唾液 [tǔ tuòyè] 2 [fire, cooking food +] 乱崩 [luàn bēng] 3 ▸ it's

spitting (BRIT) 天正下着毛毛雨 [tiān zhèng xiàzhe máomáoyǔ] [美 = sprinkle] III VT [+ water, food] 吐出 [tǔchū]
▸ **spit out** VT 吐出 [tǔchū]

spite [spaɪt] I N [U] 恶意 [èyì] II VT 激怒 [jīnù] ▸ in spite of 尽管 ▸ to do sth in spite of o.s. 不由自主地做某事

spiteful [ˈspaɪtful] ADJ [+ person, behaviour] 怀有恶意的 [huáiyǒu èyì de]

splash [splæʃ] I N [c] 1 (sound) 溅泼声 [jiànpō shēng] 2 [of liquid] 少许 [shǎoxǔ] 3 [of colour] 斑点 [bāndiǎn] II INT 扑通 [pūtōng] III VT 溅 [jiàn] IV VI 1 (also: **splash about**) (in sea) 嬉水 [xīshuǐ] 2 [water, rain +] 噼噼啪啪落下 [pīpīpāpā luòxià] ▸ to splash paint on the floor 把油漆泼在地板上 ▸ to make a splash (inf) (fig) 引起轰动
▸ **splash out** (BRIT: inf) VI ▸ to splash out (on) 大手大脚地花钱 (在) [dàshǒu dàjiǎo de huāqián (zài)]

splendid [ˈsplendɪd] ADJ 1 (excellent) [+ idea, work] 极好的 [jíhǎo de] 2 (impressive) [+ architecture, work of art] 辉煌的 [huīhuáng de]

splendour, (US) **splendor** [ˈsplendə(r)] I N [U] 壮观 [zhuàngguān] II **splendours** NPL 辉煌 [huīhuáng]

splinter [ˈsplɪntə(r)] I N [C] 1 [of wood] 刺 [cì] 2 [of glass] 碎片 [suìpiàn] II VI 裂成碎片 [lièchéng suìpiàn]

split [splɪt] (pt, pp **split**) I N 1 [C] (crack, tear) 裂缝 [lièfèng] 2 [S] (division) 划分 [huàfēn] 3 [c] (disagreement) 分裂 [fēnliè] II VT 1 (divide) 把…划分 [bǎ…huàfēn] 2 (cause to divide) [+ party, group] 使分裂 [shǐ fēnliè] 3 (share equally) [+ work, profits] 平分 [píngfēn] III VI 1 ▸ to split (into) (divide) 划分 (成) [huàfēn (chéng)] 2 [party, group +] 分裂 [fēnliè] 3 (crack, tear) [wood, garment +] 裂开 [lièkāi] ▸ to do the splits 劈叉 ▸ let's split the difference 让我们分担差额吧 ▸ to split hairs 在鸡毛蒜皮上争辩
▸ **split up** VI 1 [+ couple, group] 分手 [fēnshǒu] II VT 把…分割 [bǎ…fēngē]

splutter [ˈsplʌtə(r)] VI 1 [engine, flame +] 发噼啪声 [fā pīpā shēng] 2 [person +] 结结巴巴地说 [jiéjie bābā de shuō] 3 (sound angry) 急促而含糊地说 [jícù ér hánhu de shuō]

spoil [spɔɪl] (pt, pp **spoiled** or **spoilt**) I VT 1 (damage) 损害 [sǔnhài] 2 [+ child] 溺爱 [nì'ài] 3 (indulge) [+ person] 宠爱 [chǒng'ài] 4 (BRIT) [+ ballot paper] 作废 [zuòfèi] II VI ▸ to be spoiling for a fight 一心想打架 [yìxīn xiǎng dǎjià] ▸ to spoil o.s. 犒劳自己

spoilt [spɔɪlt] I PT, PP of **spoil** II ADJ 1 [+ child] 宠坏的 [chǒnghuài de] 2 (BRIT) [+ ballot paper] 作废的 [zuòfèi de]

spoke [spəʊk] I PT of **speak** II N [c] [of wheel] 辐条 [fútiáo]

spoken [ˈspəʊkn] PP of **speak**

spokesman ['spəʊksmən] (pl **spokesmen**) N [c] 男发言人 [nán fāyánrén]

spokesperson ['spəʊkspɜːsn] (pl **spokespeople**) N [c] 发言人 [fāyánrén]

spokeswoman ['spəʊkswʊmən] (pl **spokeswomen**) N [c] 女发言人 [nǚ fāyánrén]

sponge [spʌndʒ] I N **1** [u] (substance man-made, natural) 海绵 [hǎimián] **2** [c] (for washing) 海绵擦 [hǎimián cā] **3** [c/u] (also: **sponge cake**) 松糕 [sōnggāo] II VT (wipe) 用海绵擦 [yòng hǎimián cā] III VI ▶ to **sponge off** or **on sb** (inf) 白吃白喝某人 [báichī báihē mǒurén]

sponsor ['spɒnsə(r)] I N [c] **1** [of player, event, TV programme] 赞助者 [zànzhùzhě] **2** (BRIT) (for charity) 出资者 [chūzīzhě] **3** (for application, bill in parliament etc) 倡议者 [chàngyìzhě] II VT **1** [+ player, event, TV programme] 赞助 [zànzhù] **2** (BRIT) (for charity) 赞助 [zànzhù] **3** [+ proposal, bill etc] 倡议 [chàngyì]

sponsorship ['spɒnsəʃɪp] N [u] 资助 [zīzhù]

spontaneous [spɒn'teɪnɪəs] ADJ **1** (unplanned) 自然而然的 [zìrán érrán de] **2** [+ explosion, miscarriage] 自然的 [zìrán de]

spooky ['spuːkɪ] (inf) ADJ 阴森森的 [yīnsēnsēn de]

spoon [spuːn] I N [c] 匙 [chí] II VT ▶ to **spoon sth into/onto/over** 用匙将某物放入/放在…上/浇在…上 [yòng chí jiāng mǒuwù fàngrù/fàngzài…shang/jiāozài…shang]

spoonful ['spuːnfʊl] N [c] ▶ a **spoonful of** 一匙 [yīchí]

sport [spɔːt] I N **1** [c] (particular game) 运动 [yùndòng] **2** [u] (generally) 体育 [tǐyù] II VT [+ clothes] 穿着 [chuānzhe]; [+ jewellery] 戴着 [dàizhe] ▶ she's a (good) **sport** (o.f.) 她是一个大度的人

sporting ['spɔːtɪŋ] ADJ **1** [+ event etc] 体育运动的 [tǐyù yùndòng de] **2** (o.f.) (generous) [+ act, gesture] 大度的 [dàdù de] ▶ to **have a sporting chance of doing sth** 有可能做某事

sport jacket (US) N [c] 粗呢夹克 [cūní jiákè] [英 = **sports jacket**]

sports car N [c] 跑车 [pǎochē]

sports jacket (BRIT) N [c] 粗呢夹克 [cūní jiákè] [美 = **sport jacket**]

sportsman ['spɔːtsmən] (pl **sportsmen**) N [c] 男运动员 [nán yùndòngyuán]

sportswear ['spɔːtsweə(r)] N [u] 运动服 [yùndòngfú]

sportswoman ['spɔːtswʊmən] (pl **sportswomen**) N [c] 女运动员 [nǚ yùndòngyuán]

sporty ['spɔːtɪ] ADJ **1** [+ person] 爱运动的 [ài yùndòng de] **2** [+ car] 像赛车的 [xiàng sàichē de]

spot [spɒt] I N [c] **1** (mark) 斑点 [bāndiǎn] **2** (dot) 点 [diǎn] **3** (pimple) 疱点 [cídiǎn] **4** [of rain] 一滴 [yīdī] **5** (place) 地点 [dìdiǎn] **6** (RAD, TV) 短小节目 [duǎnxiǎo jiémù] **7** ▶ a **spot of** (ESP BRIT) (small amount) [+ lunch, activity] 少量 [shǎoliàng]; [+ trouble, bother] 处境 [chǔjìng] II VT (notice) 发现 [fāxiàn] ▶ **on the spot** (in that place) 在现场; (immediately) 当场 ▶ to **be in a tight spot** (inf) 处于困境中 ▶ to **put sb on the spot** 使某人处于难堪地位

spotless ['spɒtlɪs] ADJ 一尘不染的 [yīchén bùrǎn de]

spotlight ['spɒtlaɪt] I N [c] **1** (on stage) 聚光灯 [jùguāngdēng] **2** (in room) 照明灯 [zhàomíngdēng] II VT 使突出醒目 [shǐ tūchū xǐngmù]

spouse [spaʊs] N [c] 配偶 [pèi'ǒu]

sprain [spreɪn] I VT ▶ to **sprain one's ankle/wrist** 扭伤脚踝/手腕 [niǔshāng jiǎohuái/shǒuwàn] II N [c] 扭伤 [niǔshāng]

sprang [spræŋ] PT of **spring**

sprawl [sprɔːl] I VI **1** [person +] 伸开四肢躺/坐 [shēnkāi sìzhī tǎng/zuò] **2** [place +] 扩展 [kuòzhǎn] II N [u] ▶ **urban sprawl** 城镇漫无计划地扩展 [chéngzhèn mànwú jìhuà kuòzhǎn] ▶ to **send sb sprawling** 把某人摔趴在地上

spray [spreɪ] I N **1** [c/u] [of water] 水花 [shuǐhuā] **2** [c/u] (in can) 喷剂 [pēnjì] **3** [c] (in garden) 喷雾器 [pēnwù qì] **4** [c] [of flowers] 小枝 [xiǎozhī] II VT **1** (sprinkle) [+ liquid] 喷 [pēn]; [+ glass etc] 向…溅射 [xiàng…jiànshè] **2** (with pesticide) [+ crops] 向…喷杀虫剂 [xiàng…pēn shāchóng jì] **3** (with paint) 喷涂 [pēntú] **4** [+ bullets] 向…扫射 [xiàng…sǎoshè] III VI **1** [liquid +] 溅散 [jiànsàn] **2** (with pesticide) 喷杀虫剂 [pēn shāchóng jì]

spread [sprɛd] (pt, pp **spread**) I N **1** [s] (increase) 扩展 [kuòzhǎn] **2** [s] (range, distribution) 各种 [gèzhǒng] **3** [c/u] (on bread) 涂抹酱 [túmǒ jiàng] **4** [c] (inf) (meal) 盛宴 [shèngyàn] **5** [c] (PUBLISHING, TYP) 横贯两版的篇幅 [héngguàn liǎngbǎn de piānfú] II VT **1** ▶ to **spread sth on/over** 把某物摊在…上 [bǎ mǒuwù tānzài…shang] **2** [+ butter, jam etc] 涂 [tú] **3** [+ wings, arms, sails] 张开 [zhāngkāi] **4** (scatter) 撒 [sǎ] **5** (distribute) [+ workload, wealth] 分摊 [fēntān] **6** (distribute) [+ repayments, job losses] 把…分期 [bǎ…fēnqī] **7** [+ disease] 传播 [chuánbō] **8** [+ news +] 不胫而走 [bùjìng érzǒu]; [disease +] 传播 [chuánbō] **2** [liquid, gas, fire +] 蔓延 [mànyán] ▶ to **spread bread/toast with butter** 把黄油抹在面包/烤面包上
▶ **spread out** I VI **1** (move apart) [people, animals, vehicles +] 散开 [sànkāi] **2** (stretch out) [person +] 伸开四肢 [shēnkāi sìzhī] II VT (arrange) 摊开 [tānkāi]

spreadsheet ['sprɛdʃiːt] N [c] 电子表格 [diànzǐ biǎogé]

spree [spriː] N [c] ▶ to **go on a spending/drinking spree** 无节制地花钱/酗酒 [wú jiézhì de huāqián/xùjiǔ]

spring [sprɪŋ] (*pt* **sprang**, *pp* **sprung**) I N
1 [c/u] (*season*) 春季 [chūnjì] **2** [c] (*wire coil*) 弹
簧 [tánhuáng] **3** [c] (*of water*) 泉 [quán] II VI
1 (*leap*) 跳 [tiào] **2** (*move suddenly*) 弹 [tán]
III VT ▶ **to spring a leak** [*pipe etc* +] 出现裂缝
[chūxiàn lièfèng] ▶ **in (the) spring** 在春季
▶ **to walk with a spring in one's step** 轻快有
力地走路 ▶ **to spring into action** 迅速行动起
来 ▶ **to spring from** 起源于 ▶ **he sprang the
news on me** 他突然向我宣布了这条消息
▶ **spring up** VI (*suddenly appear*) 突然出现 [tūrán
chūxiàn]

spring onion (BRIT) N [c] 小葱 [xiǎocōng]
[美 = **scallion**]

sprinkle ['sprɪŋkl] I VT **1** (*with liquid*) 洒 [sǎ]
2 (*with powder*) 撒 [sǎ] ▶ **to sprinkle water on
sth, sprinkle sth with water** 把水洒在某物
上 II VI ▶ **it's sprinkling** (US) 天正下着毛毛雨
[tiān zhèng xiàzhe máomáoyǔ] [英 = **spit**]

sprint [sprɪnt] I N **1** (*race*) 短跑 [duǎnpǎo]
II VI 全速奔跑 [quánsù bēnpǎo] ▶ **to break
into a sprint** 突然开始奔跑

sprinter ['sprɪntə(r)] N [c] 短跑运动员
[duǎnpǎo yùndòngyuán]

sprout [spraut] I VI **1** (*produce shoots*) 发芽
[fāyá] **2** (*grow*) 长出 [zhǎngchū] II VT [+ *hair,
wings*] 长出 [zhǎngchū] III **sprouts** NPL 球芽
甘蓝 [qíuyá gānlán]

sprung [sprʌŋ] PP *of* **spring**

spun [spʌn] PT, PP *of* **spin**

spur [spə:(r)] I N **1** ▶ **a spur to sth** 某物的刺激
物 [mǒuwù de cìjīwù] **2** [c] (*on rider's boot*) 靴
刺 [xuēcì] II VT ▶ **to spur sb into (doing) sth**
激励某人去(做)某事 [jīlì mǒurén qù (zuò)
mǒushì] ▶ **on the spur of the moment** 一时
冲动之下
▶ **spur on** VT 激励 [jīlì]

spurt [spə:t] I N [c] **1** (*of blood etc*) 喷射
[pēnshè] **2** (*of energy*) 迸发 [bèngfā] II VI
1 ▶ **to spurt from sth** [*blood, flame* +] 从某物中
喷出 [cóng mǒuwùzhōng pēnchū] **2** ▶ **to spurt
up/along** (*person, thing* +) 突然加速 [tūrán jiāsù]
▶ **to put on a spurt** (*in race*) 全力冲刺; (*in work*)
全力以赴

spy [spaɪ] I N [c] 间谍 [jiàndié] II VI **1** ▶ **to spy
on** (*watch*) 暗中监视 [ànzhōng jiānshì] **2** (*get
information about*) 刺探 [cìtàn] III VT (*liter*)
(*notice*) 发现 [fāxiàn] IV CPD [复合词] **1** [+ *film,
story*] 间谍 [jiàndié] **2** [+ *satellite, plane*] 侦探
[zhēntàn] ▶ **to spy for** 为⋯充当间谍

spying ['spaɪɪŋ] N [u] 当间谍 [dāng jiàndié]

Sq. (ESP US) **Sq.** ABBR (= **square**) (*in addresses*) 广
场 [guǎngchǎng]

sq. ABBR = **square** 平方 [píngfāng]

squabble ['skwɔbl] I VI 发生口角 [fāshēng
kǒujiǎo] II N [c] 口角 [kǒujiǎo] ▶ **to squabble
with sb** 与某人发生口角

squad [skwɔd] N [c] **1** (MIL, POLICE) 班 [bān]

2 (SPORT) 队 [duì]

squadron ['skwɔdrən] N [c] **1** (*in air force, navy*)
中队 [zhōngduì] **2** (*in army*) 连 [lián]

squander ['skwɔndə(r)] VT [+ *money, resources*]
浪费 [làngfèi]

square [skwɛə(r)] I N [c] **1** 正方形 [zhèngfāng
xíng] **2** (*in town*) 广场 [guǎngchǎng] **3** (MATH)
平方 [píngfāng] **4** (US) (*block of houses*) 街区
[jiēqū] **5** (*inf, o.f.*) (*person*) 老古板 [lǎo gǔbǎn]
II ADJ (*in shape*) 正方形的 [zhèngfāng xíng
de] III VT **1** (MATH) 使自乘 [shǐ zìchéng]
2 (*arrange*) 调正 [tiáozhèng] **3** ▶ **to square sth
with sth** 使某事与某事一致 [shǐ mǒushì yǔ
mǒushì yīzhì] **4** ▶ **to square sth with sb** (*inf*)
就某事获得某人的许可 [jiù mǒushì huòdé
mǒurén de xǔkě] IV VI ▶ **to square with** 符
合 [fúhé] ▶ **we're back to square one** 我们又
得从头来过 ▶ **to be all square** (*inf*) [*people* +] 扯
平; [*match* +] 打平 ▶ **a square meal** 一顿丰盛
的饭菜 ▶ **2 metres square** 2米见方 ▶ **2 square
metres** 2平方米
▶ **square up** (BRIT) VI (*settle bill, debt*) 结清
[jiéqīng] ▶ **to square up with sb** 和某人结清账

squarely ['skwɛəlɪ] ADV **1** (*directly*) [*fall, land
etc* +] 正对着地 [zhèngduìzhe de] **2** (*fully*) [*face,
confront* +] 直面地 [zhímiàn de]

square root N [c] 平方根 [píngfāng gēn]

squash [skwɔʃ] I N **1** [u] (BRIT) ▶ **orange
squash** 浓缩橙汁,需加水再喝 [nóngsuō
chéngzhī, xū jiāshuǐ zài hē] **2** [c/u] (US)
(*vegetable*) 南瓜 [nánguā] **3** [u] (SPORT) 壁球
[bìqiú] II VT **1** (*crush*) 把⋯压碎 [bǎ⋯yāsuì]
2 ▶ **to squash sb/sth into** 将某人/某物硬塞入
[jiāng mǒurén/mǒuwù yìng sāirù] ▶ **to squash
sb/sth against** 将某人/某物挤到 ▶ **to squash
sth flat** 将某物压扁

squat [skwɔt] I VI **1** (*also:* **squat down**) 蹲
下 [dūnxià] **2** (*be sitting*) 蹲坐 [dūnzuò] **3** (*on
property*) 擅自占用 [shànzì zhànyòng] II N [c]
(*illegally occupied building*) 擅自占用的建筑
[shànzì zhànyòng de jiànzhù] III ADJ [+ *person*]
矮胖的 [ǎipàng de]; [+ *shape*] 低矮的 [dī'ǎi de]

squatter ['skwɔtə(r)] N [c] 擅自占地者 [shànzì
zhàndì zhě]

squeak [skwi:k] I VI **1** [*door* +] 嘎吱作响 [gāzhī
zuòxiǎng] **2** [*mouse* +] 吱吱叫 [zhīzhī jiào] II N
[c] **1** [*of hinge*] 嘎吱声 [gāzhī shēng] **2** [*of mouse*]
吱吱声 [zhīzhī shēng]
▶ **squeak by, squeak through** (*inf*) VI 勉强通
过 [miǎnqiáng tōngguò]

squeal [skwi:l] I N [c] **1** [*of person* +] 发出长而尖
的叫声 [fāchū cháng ér jiān de jiàoshēng]
2 [*brakes, tyres* +] 发出尖锐刺耳声 [fāchū
jiānruì cì'ěr shēng] II N [c] **1** [*of person*] 尖叫
声 [jiānjiào shēng] **2** [*of brakes, tyres*] 刺耳声
[cì'ěr shēng]

squeeze [skwi:z] I N [c] **1** [*of hand etc*] 紧握
[jǐnwò] **2** (ECON) 银根紧缩 [yíngēn jǐnsuō]

II VT **1** 用力捏 [yònglì niē] **2 ▸ to squeeze sth under/through sth** 将某物硬挤到某物下面/过某物 [jiāng mǒuwù yìngjǐdào mǒuwù xiàmiàn/guò mǒuwù] **III** VI **6 ▸ to squeeze under/through sth** 硬挤到某物下面/过某物 [yìng jǐdào mǒuwù xiàmiàn/guò mǒuwù] **▸ to give sth a squeeze** 用力捏了捏某物 **▸ a squeeze of lemon** 一点榨出的柠檬汁 **▸ squeeze out** VT **1** [+ *juice, paste etc*] 榨出 [zhà] **2** (*fig*) (*exclude*) [+ *person*] 排挤出 [páijǐ chū]

squid [skwɪd] N [C/U] 鱿鱼 [yóuyú]

squint [skwɪnt] **I** VI 眯着眼看 [mīzhe yǎn kàn] **II** N [C] (MED) 斜视 [xiéshì]

squirm [skwə:m] VI **1** (*wriggle*) 扭动 [niǔdòng] **2** (*fig*) (*with embarrassment*) 局促不安 [júcù bù'ān]

squirrel ['skwɪrəl] N [C] 松鼠 [sōngshǔ]

squirt [skwə:t] **I** VI **▸ to squirt out** 喷射出 [pēnshè chū] **II** VT **▸ to squirt sth into/onto sth** 将某物喷入某物/到某物上 [jiāng mǒuwù pēnrù mǒuwù/dào mǒuwù shang] **III** N [C] [*of liquid*] 喷流 [pénliú]

Sr, (ESP US) **Sr.** ABBR (= *senior*) 老 [lǎo]

Sri Lanka [srɪ'læŋkə] N 斯里兰卡 [Sīlǐlánkǎ]

St, (ESP US) **St.** ABBR **1** (= *street*) 街 [jiē] **2** (*pl* **SS**) (= *saint*) 圣人 [shèngrén]

stab [stæb] **I** VT [+ *person*] 刺 [cì] **II** VI 戳 [chuō] **III** N **1** [C] (*with knife etc*) 刺 [cì] **2 ▸ a stab of pain/pity/jealousy** 一阵疼痛/怜悯/嫉妒 [yīzhèn téngtòng/liánmǐn/jìdù] **3 ▸ to have a stab at (doing) sth** (*inf*) 试图(做)某事 [shìtú (zuò) mǒushì] **▸ to stab sb to death** 刺死某人 **▸ to stab sb in the back** (*fig*) 暗箭伤人 **▸ to stab sth with sth** 用某物戳某物

stability [stə'bɪlɪtɪ] N [U] **1** [*of government, economy etc*] 稳定 [wěndìng] **2** [*of object*] 稳定性 [wěndìng xìng]

stabilize ['steɪbɪlaɪz] **I** VT [+ *prices, rates*] 保持…的稳定 [bǎochí…de wěndìng] **II** VI [*prices, rates, patient's condition +*] 稳定 [wěndìng]

stable ['steɪbl] **I** ADJ **1** [+ *prices, relationship, personality, condition*] 稳定的 [wěndìng de] **2** [+ *object*] 稳固的 [wěngù de] **II** N [C] (*also:* **stables**) **1** (*for horse*) 马厩 [mǎjiù] **2** (*in horse-racing*) 赛马训练场 [sàimǎ xùnliàn chǎng] **III** VT [+ *horse*] 把…拴进马厩 [bǎ…shuānjìn mǎjiù]

stack [stæk] **I** N [C] (*pile*) 堆 [duī] **II** VT (*also:* **stack up**) [+ *chairs, books etc*] 把…堆起来 [bǎ…duī qǐlai] **▸ to be stacked with...** 堆满了… **▸ stacks of time/money** (BRIT: *inf*) 大量时间/钱 **▸ the odds are stacked against them** 他们的胜算不大

stadium ['steɪdɪəm] (*pl* **stadia** ['steɪdɪə]) N [C] 体育场 [tǐyùchǎng]

○**staff** [stɑ:f] **I** N [C] **1** (*workforce*) 职员 [zhíyuán] ▷ *an error by one of his staff* 他的一名职员犯的过失 **2** (*liter*) (*stick*) 棍棒 [gùnbàng] **II** VT 为…配

备职员 [wèi…pèibèi zhíyuán] ▷ *It was staffed by engineers.* 为其配备了工程师。

stag [stæg] N [C] 牡鹿 [mǔlù]

○**stage** [steɪdʒ] **I** N [C] **1** (*in theatre*) 舞台 [wǔtái] **2** (*platform*) 平台 [píngtái] **3** (*period*) 阶段 [jiēduàn] ▷ *the final stage of a world tour* 环球旅行的最后阶段 **II** VT **1** [+ *play*] 上演 [shàngyǎn] **2** [+ *demonstration, strike*] 举行 [jǔxíng] **▸ to do sth in stages** 分期做某事 **▸ the stage** (THEAT) 剧坛 **▸ in the early/final stages** 在早/晚期 **▸ he staged a remarkable recovery** 他奇迹般地康复了

stagger ['stægə(r)] **I** VI 跌跌撞撞 [diēdiē zhuàngzhuàng] **II** VT **1** (*amaze*) 使震惊 [shǐ zhènjīng] **2** [+ *hours, holidays*] 使错开 [shǐ cuòkāi]

staggering ['stægərɪŋ] ADJ 令人吃惊的 [lìngrén chījīng de]

stagnant ['stægnənt] ADJ **1** [+ *economy, business*] 萧条的 [xiāotiáo de] **2** [+ *water*] 停滞的 [tíngzhì de]

stag night N [C] 婚礼前新郎与男伴们的聚会

stain [steɪn] **I** N [C] (*mark*) 污迹 [wūjì] **II** VT **1** (*mark*) 沾污 [zhānwū] **2** [+ *wood*] 给…染色 [gěi…rǎnsè]

stained glass [steɪnd-] N [U] 彩色玻璃 [cǎisè bōli]

stainless steel ['steɪnlɪs-] N [U] 不锈钢 [bùxiù gāng]

stair [steə(r)] **I** N [C] (*step*) 梯级 [tījí] **II** **stairs** NPL (*flight of steps*) 楼梯 [lóutī]

staircase ['steəkeɪs] N [C] 楼梯 [lóutī]

stairway ['steəweɪ] N [C] 楼梯 [lóutī]

stake [steɪk] **I** N [C] **1** (*post*) 桩 [zhuāng] **2** (*interest*) 股份 [gǔfèn] **3** (*in gambling*) 赌注 [dǔzhù] **4** (*in risky situation*) 利害关系 [lìhài guānxi] **II** VT **▸ to stake money on sth** 对某事押赌注 [duì mǒushì yā dǔzhù] **▸ to stake one's reputation on sth** 把某人的声誉押在某事上 **▸ to stake a claim to sth** 声明对某物拥有所有权 **▸ to have a stake in sth** 与某事有利害关系 **▸ to raise the stakes** (*fig*) 冒更大的风险 **▸ there's a lot at stake** 很多事情可能受到很大影响 **▸ I wouldn't stake my life on it** 我并不肯定 **▸ stake out** VT [+ *position, claim*] 申明 [shēnmíng]

stale [steɪl] ADJ **1** [+ *bread, food*] 陈的 [chén de] **2** [+ *smell, air*] 污浊的 [wūzhuó de] **3** (*fig*) [+ *relationship, person, ideas*] 乏味的 [fáwèi de]

stalk [stɔ:k] **I** N [C] [*of flower, leaf*] 梗 [gěng]; [*of fruit*] 柄 [bǐng] **II** VT **1** [+ *animal*] 潜步追踪 [qiánbù zhuīzōng] **2** [+ *person*] 骚扰 [sāorǎo] **III** VI **▸ to stalk out/off** 昂首阔步地走出/离开 [ángshǒu kuòbù de zǒuchū/líkāi]

stall [stɔ:l] **I** N [C] **1** (*in street, market etc*) 货摊 [huòtān] **2** (*in stable*) 牲畜棚 [shēngchù péng] **II** VT **1** [+ *car*] 使熄火 [shǐ xīhuǒ]

2 (delay) [+ person] 拖住 [tuōzhù]; [+ process] 拖延 [tuōyán] **III** VI **1** [engine, car +] 熄火 [xīhuǒ] **2** [person +] 拖延 [tuōyán] **IV the stalls** NPL (BRIT) (in cinema, theatre) 正厅前座 [zhèngtīng qiánzuò]

stamina ['stæminə] N [U] 耐力 [nàilì]

stammer ['stæmə(r)] **I** N [c] 结巴 [jiēba] **II** VI 结巴地说话 [jiēbā de shuōhuà]

stamp [stæmp] **I** N [c] **1** 邮票 [yóupiào] **2** (rubber stamp) 图章 [túzhāng] **3** (in passport etc) 章 [zhāng] **II** VI (with foot) 踩脚 [duòjiǎo] **III** VT [+ passport, visa etc] 盖章于 [gàizhāng yú] ▶ **to bear the stamp of sth** (fig) 有某物的特征 [yǒu mǒuwù de tèzhēng] ▶ **to stamp one's foot** 踩脚 [duòjiǎo] ▶ **to stamp a mark/word on sth** 在某物上盖印/字 ▶ **stamp out** VT [+ bullying, discrimination etc] 消灭 [xiāomiè]

stampede [stæm'piːd] **I** N [c] **1** [of animals] 惊跑 [jīngpǎo] **2** [of people] 蜂拥 [fēngyōng] **II** VI **1** [animals +] 惊跑 [jīngpǎo] **2** [people +] 蜂拥 [fēngyōng]

stance [stæns] N [c] **1** (posture) 站立姿势 [zhànlì zīshì] **2** (attitude) 态度 [tàidù]

○ **stand** [stænd] (pt, pp **stood**) **I** N [c] **1** (stall) 摊子 [tānzi] ▷ a newspaper stand 报摊 **2** (at exhibition) 展台 [zhǎntái] **3** (BRIT) (in stadium, arena) 看台 [kàntái] **4** (for holding things) 架子 [jiàzi] ▷ A number of hats hung from a stand. 架子上挂了几顶帽子。 **II** VI **1** (be upright) 站立 [zhànlì] ▷ She was standing at the bus stop. 她站在公共汽车站。 **2** (rise) 站起来 [zhàn qǐlái] ▷ The judge asked us all to stand. 法官让我们都站起来。 **3** (be situated) [object, building +] 耸立 [sǒnglì] ▷ The house stands alone on top of a hill. 那幢房子傲然耸立在山顶上。 **4** (remain) [decision, offer +] 保持有效 [bǎochí yǒuxiào] ▷ Our original offer stands. 我们当初的提议仍然有效。 **5** (BRIT) (in election) 当候选人 [dāng hòuxuǎn rén] ▷ She was invited to stand as the Liberal candidate. 她被邀请做自由党候选人。 [美 = **run**] **6** ▶ **to stand aside/back** 让开/退后 [ràngkāi/tuìhòu] **7** ▶ **where or how does he stand on...?** 他对…持什么态度？ [tā duì...chí shénme tàidù?] **III** VT **1** ▶ **to stand sth on/in sth** 将某物竖放在某物上/中 [jiāng mǒuwù shùfàngzài mǒuwùshang/zhōng] **2** (withstand, tolerate) 经受住 [jīngshòu zhù] ▷ The economy will not stand another rise in interest rates. 经济将经受不起利息的再次上升。 **3** ▶ **I can't stand him/it** 我无法容忍他/它 [wǒ wúfǎ róngrěn tā/tā] ▶ **to take the stand** (US: LAW) 出庭作证 ▶ **to make a stand against sth** 反抗某物 ▶ **to take a stand on sth** 对某事表明立场 ▶ **sb's last stand** 某人的最后一搏 ▶ **to stand at** [value, level, score etc +] 处于 ▷ Unemployment now stands at 20%. 目前失业率处于20%的水平。 ▶ **as things stand** 照这种样子 ▶ **it stands to reason** 那是显而易见的 ▶ **to stand to gain/lose sth** 很可能会获得/失

去某物 ▶ **to stand for parliament** (BRIT) 竞选议员 ▶ **to stand sb a drink/meal** (inf) 请某人喝一杯/吃一顿 ▶ **to stand trial** 受审判 ▶ **stand by I** VI **1** (be ready) 作好准备 [zuòhǎo zhǔnbèi] **2** (fail to help) 袖手旁观 [xiùshǒu pángguān] ▷ We cannot stand by and watch while our allies are attacked. 我们不能袖手旁观，眼睁睁看着盟军遭到进攻。 **II** VT FUS [不可拆分] **1** [+ promise, decision] 遵守 [zūnshǒu] **2** [+ person] 支持 [zhīchí] ▶ **stand down** VI 辞职 [cízhí] ▶ **stand for** VT FUS [不可拆分] **1** (signify) 主张 [zhǔzhāng] ▷ He hates us and everything we stand for. 他恨我们以及我们主张的一切。 **2** (abbreviation +) 代表 [dàibiǎo] ▷ What does CSE stand for? CSE代表什么？ **3** ▶ **I will not stand for it** 我不会容忍这个 [wǒ bùhuì róngrěn zhège] ▶ **stand in for** VT FUS [不可拆分] [+ teacher etc] 代替 [dàitì] ▶ **stand out** VI (be prominent) 醒目 [xǐngmù] ▷ The name on the van stood out clearly. 货车上的名字非常醒目。 ▶ **stand up** VI **1** [person +] (rise) 起立 [qǐlì] ▷ I put down my glass and stood up. 我把玻璃杯放下，站起来。 **2** [person +] (on one's feet) 站立 [zhànlì] ▷ a shop assistant who has to stand up all day 整天都得站着的售货员 **3** [claim, evidence +] 站得住脚 [zhàndézhù jiǎo] ▷ He made wild accusations that did not stand up. 他做了无根无据、根本站不住脚的指控。 ▶ **stand up for** VT FUS [不可拆分] [+ person] 坚持 [jiānchí]; [+ one's rights] 维护 [wéihù] ▶ **stand up to** VT FUS [不可拆分] **1** (withstand) 经得起 [jīngdeqǐ] ▷ Will this building stand up to the gales? 这座建筑会经得起狂风吗？ **2** [+ person] 勇敢地面对 [yǒnggǎn de miànduì] ▷ He's too weak to stand up to her. 他太软弱了，根本无法面对她。

standard ['stændəd] **I** N [c] **1** (level) 水平 [shuǐpíng] **2** (norm, criterion) 标准 [biāozhǔn] **3** (flag) 旗子 [qízi] **II** ADJ **1** [+ size etc] 普通的 [pǔtōng de] **2** [+ procedure, practice] 标准的 [biāozhǔn de] **3** [+ model, feature] 规范的 [guīfàn de] **4** [+ textbook, work] 权威性的 [quánwēixìng de] **III standards** NPL 规范 [guīfàn] ▶ **to be up to standard** 达到标准

standardize ['stændədaɪz] VT 标准化 [biāozhǔn huà]

standard of living N [c] 生活水平 [shēnghuó shuǐpíng]

stand-by, standby ['stændbaɪ] **I** N [c] 后备 [hòubèi] **II** CPD [复合词] [+ ticket, seat] 剩余 [shèngyú] ▷ on stand-by [doctor, crew, firemen etc +] 待命

standing ['stændɪŋ] **I** N **1** [U] (status) 身份 [shēnfèn] **2** [c] (reputation) 声誉 [shēngyù] **II** ADJ **1** ▶ **a standing invitation** 长期有效的邀请 [chángqí yǒuxiào de yāoqǐng] ▷ Remember *that you have a standing invitation to stay with us.* 记住你随时可以来我们这里住。**2** [+ *army*] 常备的 [chángbèi de] ▸ **of many years' standing** 持续多年的 ▸ **a standing ovation** 起立长时间鼓掌

standing order (BRIT: ECON) N [c] 长期有效委托书 [chángqī yǒuxiào wěituō shū]

standpoint ['stændpɔɪnt] N ▸ **from a military/economic standpoint** 从军事/经济的立场出发 [cóng jūnshì/jīngjì de lìchǎng chūfā]

standstill ['stændstɪl] N ▸ **to be at a standstill** [*traffic, negotiations* +] 停滞不前的 [tíngzhì bùqián de] ▸ **to come** or **be brought to a standstill** [*traffic* +] 停滞下来; [*production, progress* +] 被迫停顿

stank [stæŋk] PT of **stink**

staple ['steɪpl] I N [c] **1** (*for fastening paper*) 订书钉 [dìngshūdīng] **2** (*food*) 主食 [zhǔshí] II ADJ [+ *diet, goods*] 基本的 [jīběn de] III VT (*fasten*) 用订书钉钉 [yòng dìngshūdīng dìng] ▸ **to be a staple of sth** [*product, activity* +] 为某物的一个主要成分

○ **star** [stɑː(r)] I N [c] **1** (*in sky*) 星 [xīng] **2** (*shape*) 星形物 [xīngxíng wù] **3** (*celebrity*) 明星 [míngxīng] II VT [*play, film* +] [+ *actor, actress*] 使主演 [shǐ zhǔyǎn] ▷ *The movie starred Lana Turner.* 莱娜·特纳担任那部电影的主角。III VI ▸ **to star (in)** [+ *play, film*] (在…中) 主演 [(zài…zhōng) zhǔyǎn] IV **the stars** NPL (*inf*) (*horoscope*) 星象 [xīngxiàng] ▸ **a 4-star hotel** 4星级旅馆

starboard ['stɑːbəd] ADJ [+ *side*] 右舷的 [yòuxián de] ▸ **to starboard** 距离右舷

starch [stɑːtʃ] N **1** [c/u] (*in food*) 淀粉 [diànfěn] **2** [u] (*for stiffening clothes*) 淀粉浆 [diànfěn jiāng]

stardom ['stɑːdəm] N [u] 明星地位 [míngxīng dìwèi]

stare [stɛə(r)] I VI ▸ **to stare (at sb/sth)** 盯着 (某人/某物) [dīngzhe (mǒurén/mǒuwù)] II N [c] 凝视 [níngshì] ▸ **to give sb a stare** 盯某人一眼

stark [stɑːk] I ADJ **1** [+ *room, object, landscape*] 光秃秃的 [guāng tūtū de] **2** [+ *warning, choice*] 严峻的 [yánjùn de] **3** ▸ **to be in stark contrast to sth** 和某物形成鲜明对比 [hé mǒuwù xíngchéng xiānmíng duìbǐ] II ADV ▸ **stark naked** 一丝不挂地 [yīsī bùguà de]

○ **start** [stɑːt] I N [c] **1** 开始 [kāishǐ] ▷ *the start of the project* 项目的开始 ▷ *the start of the year* 年初 **2** (*departure*) 开端 [kāiduān] ▷ *We need a fresh start.* 我们要有个新的开端。**3** (*sudden movement*) 惊跳 [jīngtiào] ▷ *He awoke with a start.* 他猛然惊醒。**4** (*lead*) 先行 [xiānxíng] ▷ *You must give me fifty metres start.* 你一定要让我先行50米。II VT **1** (*begin*) 开始 [kāishǐ] ▷ *My father started work when he was ten.* 我父亲

10岁时开始工作。**2** (*cause*) [+ *fire, panic*] 使产生 [shǐ chǎnshēng] ▷ *I started a fire.* 我生了火。**3** (*found*) [+ *business etc*] 创建 [chuàngjiàn] ▷ *He raised the money to start a restaurant.* 他筹资金建了一家餐馆。**4** [+ *engine, car*] 启动 [qǐdòng] III VI **1** (*begin*) 开始 [kāishǐ] ▷ *The meeting starts at 7.* 会议7点开始。**2** (*with fright*) 惊起 [jīngqǐ] ▷ *It caused her to start back in terror.* 她被惊吓得往后退了一下。**3** [*engine, car* +] 启动 [qǐdòng] ▷ *The car wouldn't start.* 那辆车启动不了。**4** ▸ **start as sth** 从做某事发迹 [cóng zuò mǒushì fājì] ▷ *Mr. Dunbar started as an assistant.* 邓伯先生从当助理起家。▸ **at the start** (*at first*) 一开始 ▸ **for a start** (*firstly*) 首先 ▸ **from the start** 从一开始 ▸ **to get off to a good/bad start** 开头顺利/开头不顺利 ▸ **to make an early start** 一早出发 ▸ **from start to finish** 从头至尾 ▸ **to start doing** or **to do sth** 开始做某事 ▸ **to start (off) with** (*initially*) 开始时

▸ **start off** VI **1** (*begin*) 开始从事 [kāishǐ cóngshì] ▷ *He started off as an assistant.* 他从助理做起。**2** (*begin moving*) 动身 [dòngshēn] ▸ **to start off by doing sth** 首先做某事

▸ **start on** VT FUS [不可拆分] 开始 [kāishǐ]

▸ **start out** VI (*begin*) 开始 [kāishǐ] ▷ *It started out as fun, but it became hard work.* 开始很好玩，但后来变得很费劲。▸ **to start out by doing sth** 最先做某事

▸ **start over** (US) VI, VT 重新开始 [chóngxīn kāishǐ]

▸ **start up** I VT **1** [+ *business etc*] 创办 [chuàngbàn] **2** [+ *engine, car*] 发动 [fādòng] II VI [*engine, car* +] 发动 [fādòng]

starter ['stɑːtə(r)] N [c] **1** (*in car*) 起动装置 [qǐdòng zhuāngzhì] **2** (*race official*) 发令员 [fālìngyuán] **3** (*horse, athlete*) 参赛者 [cānsàizhě] **4** (BRIT) (*in meal*) 开胃菜 [kāiwèi cài] ▸ **for starters** (*inf*) 首先

starting point ['stɑːtɪŋ-] N [c] **1** (*for journey*) 起始点 [qǐshǐ diǎn] **2** (*for discussion, idea*) 开端 [kāiduān]

startle ['stɑːtl] VT 使吓一跳 [shǐ xiàyītiào]

startling ['stɑːtlɪŋ] ADJ 惊人的 [jīngrén de]

starvation [stɑːˈveɪʃən] N [u] 饥饿 [jīˈè] ▸ **to die of** or **from starvation** 饿死

starve [stɑːv] I VI **1** (*be very hungry*) 挨饿 [áiˈè] **2** (*die*) 饿死 [èsǐ] II VT [+ *person, animal*] 使挨饿 [shǐ áiˈè] ▸ **I'm starving** (*inf*) 我饿极了 ▸ **to starve to death** 饿死 ▸ **to be starved of...** [+ *investment, love*] 匮乏…的

○ **state** [steɪt] I N **1** [c] (*condition*) 状态 [zhuàngtài] ▷ *They are concerned about the state of the house.* 他们对房子的状态有所担心。**2** [c] (*country*) 国家 [guójiā] ▷ *Europe's only remaining communist state* 欧洲惟一尚存的共产主义国家 **3** [c] (*part of country*) 州 [zhōu] ▷ *the Southern states* 美国南部各州 **4** [s] (*government*) 政府 [zhèngfǔ] ▷ *The state does not collect enough* revenue to cover its expenditure. 政府征收的税收不能满足支出。**II** CPD [复合词] **1** (government-controlled) 政府 [zhèngfǔ] ▷ the state social-security system 政府社会保障系统 **2** (involving head of state) 国事 [guóshì] ▷ a state visit to India 对印度的国事访问 **III** VT (say, declare) 申明 [shēnmíng] ▷ Please state your name. 请申明您的姓名。**IV the States** NPL (inf) 美国 [Měiguó] ▶ **to be in a state** 处于焦虑状态 ▶ **to get into a state** 陷入紧张不安的状态 ▶ **to lie in state** 受公众瞻仰 ▶ **a state of emergency** (POL) 紧急状态 ▶ **state of affairs** 事态 ▶ **state of mind** 心情 ▶ **to state that...** 声明…

stately ['steɪtlɪ] ADJ **1** [+ building] 宏伟的 [hóngwěi de] **2** [+ pace] 庄重的 [zhuāngzhòng de]

statement ['steɪtmənt] N [c] **1** (declaration) 声明 [shēngmíng] **2** (also: **bank statement**) 银行结单 [yínháng jiédān]

state school (BRIT) N [c] 公立学校 [gōnglì xuéxiào] [美 = **public school**]

statesman ['steɪtsmən] (pl **statesmen**) N [c] 政治家 [zhèngzhìjiā]

static ['stætɪk] **I** N [U] **1** (on radio, TV) 静电干扰 [jìngdiàn gānrǎo] **2** (also: **static electricity**) 静电 [jìngdiàn] **II** ADJ 静止的 [jìngzhǐ de] ▶ **to remain static** [numbers, prices etc +] 保持稳定

station ['steɪʃən] **I** N [c] **1** (railway station) 车站 [chēzhàn] **2** (police station) 警察局 [jǐngchá jú] **3** (on radio) 电台 [diàntái] **II** VT **1** (position) 安置 [ānzhì] **2** (MIL) (base) 驻扎 [zhùzhā] ▶ **to marry/be educated above one's station** (o.f.) 与高于本人地位的人结婚/受到高于本人地位的教育 ▶ **to station o.s. somewhere** 呆在某处

stationary ['steɪʃnərɪ] ADJ 停滞的 [tíngzhì de]

stationery ['steɪʃnərɪ] N [U] 文具 [wénjù]

station wagon (US) N [c] 旅行车 [lǚxíng chē] [英 = **estate car**]

statistic [stə'tɪstɪk] N [c] 统计资料 [tǒngjì zīliào]

statistical [stə'tɪstɪkl] ADJ [+ analysis, evidence, information] 统计的 [tǒngjì de]

statistics [stə'tɪstɪks] N [U] (subject) 统计学 [tǒngjì xué]

statue ['stætjuː] N [c] 塑像 [sùxiàng]

stature ['stætʃə(r)] N [U] **1** (height) 身高 [shēngāo] **2** (reputation) 名望 [míngwàng]

status ['steɪtəs] N [U] **1** (position) 地位 [dìwèi] **2** (official classification) 身份 [shēnfèn] **3** (importance) 重要地位 [zhòngyào dìwèi]

status quo [-'kwəu] (frm) N ▶ **the status quo** 现状 [xiànzhuàng]

statutory ['stætjutrɪ] (frm) ADJ 法定的 [fǎdìng de]

staunch [stɔːntʃ] **I** ADJ [+ supporter, ally] 坚定的 [jiāndìng de] **II** (frm) VT **1** [+ flow] 阻止 [zǔzhǐ] **2** [+ blood, wound] 使止住 [shǐ zhǐzhù]

⊘ **stay** [steɪ] **I** N [c] **1** 逗留 [dòuliú] ▷ We want to make your stay as enjoyable as possible. 我们想

尽量令你的逗留愉快。**2** (in institution) 暂住 [zànzhù] ▷ an overnight stay in hospital 在医院里暂住的一夜 **II** VI **1** (in place, position) 呆 [dāi] ▷ "Stay here, Kate said. "I'll bring the car." "呆在这里," 凯特说, "我把车开过来。" **2** (in town, hotel, someone's house) 逗留 [dòuliú] ▷ How long can you stay in Brussels? 你能在布鲁塞尔逗留多长时间? **3** (in state, situation) 保持 [bǎochí] ▷ information on how to stay healthy 有关如何保持健康的资料 **III** VT ▶ **to stay the night** 过夜 [guòyè] ▶ **to stay with sb** 在某人家暂住 ▶ **computers are here to stay** 电脑将深深扎下根来 ▶ **to stay put** 固定不动 ▶ **to stay ahead of sth/sb** 领先于某物/某人

▶ **stay away** VI **1** (from place) 不接近 [bù jiējìn] **2** (from person, activity) 远离 [yuǎnlí]

▶ **stay behind** VI 留在后面 [liúzài hòumiàn]

▶ **stay in** VI 呆在家里 [dāizài jiālǐ]

▶ **stay on** VI (in place, job) 继续留下 [jìxù liúxià]

▶ **stay out** VI 夜不归宿 [yèbù guīsù] ▷ She stayed out all night. 她彻夜未归。▶ **stay out of it!** 别介入这件事!

▶ **stay up** VI 不去睡 [bùqùshuì]

steadily ['stɛdɪlɪ] ADV **1** (continuously) 不断地 [bùduàn de] **2** (calmly) [look, stare +] 镇定地 [zhèndìng de]

steady ['stɛdɪ] **I** ADJ **1** (continuous) [+ progress, increase, fall] 稳定的 [wěndìng de] **2** (regular) [+ job, income] 固定的 [gùdìng de] **3** (uniform) [+ speed] 规律的 [guīlǜ de] **4** (stable) [+ relationship] 稳定的 [wěndìng de] **5** (reliable) [+ person] 踏踏实实的 [tātā shíshí de] **6** (firm) [+ object, hand etc] 稳的 [wěn de] **7** (calm) [+ look, voice] 镇定的 [zhèndìng de] **II** VT (stabilize) 使平稳 [shǐ píngwěn] **III** VI (stabilize) 稳定下来 [wěndìng xiàlái] ▶ **to steady o.s.** (mentally) 使自己镇定下来; (physically) 使自己不摇晃 ▶ **to steady one's nerves** 稳定自己的情绪

steak [steɪk] N **1** [c/U] (beef) 牛排 [niúpái] **2** [c] (fish, pork etc) 厚片 [hòupiàn]

steal [stiːl] (pt **stole**, pp **stolen**) **I** VT 偷窃 [tōuqiè] **II** VI 行窃 [xíngqiè] **2** ▶ **to steal away/out** 悄悄溜走 [qiāoqiāo liūzǒu] ▶ he stole it from me 他从我这里把它偷走了

请勿将 rob 和 steal 混淆。如果你 steal 某物, 例如钱或车, 你未经允许就将他人的东西据为己有, 并且不打算归还。My car was stolen on Friday evening. 注意, 不能说某人 steal 某人, 只能说 steal from 某人。某人 rob 某人或某个地方, 即使用暴力将他人或某个地方的东西据为己有, 并且不打算归还。They planned to rob an old woman...They joined forces to rob a factory. rob 后可以跟 of 加被强占的物品。The two men were robbed of more than £700. 注意, rob 后可以直接跟被抢劫的对象, 即可以说 rob 某人。

steam [stiːm] I N [U] 1 蒸汽 [zhēngqì] 2 *(on window)* 水汽 [shuǐqì] II CPD [复合词] 蒸汽 [zhēngqì] III VT 蒸 [zhēng] IV VI 冒蒸汽 [màozhēngqì] ▶ **to run out of steam** 失去劲头 ▶ **under one's own steam** 靠自己的力量 ▶ **to let off steam** 发泄
▶ **steam up** VI *[window, mirror, spectacles +]* 蒙上 水汽 [méngshang shuǐqì] ▶ **to get steamed up about sth** *(inf)* 因某事而恼火
用法参见 **cook**

steamy ['stiːmɪ] ADJ 1 *[+ room]* 蒸汽弥漫的 [zhēngqì mímàn de] 2 *(inf)* *[+ film, book, scene]* 色情的 [sèqíng de]

steel [stiːl] I N [U] 钢铁 [gāngtiě] II CPD [复合词] 1 *(made from steel)* 钢制 [gāngzhì] 2 *(producing steel)* 钢铁生产 [gāngtiě shēngchǎn] III VT ▶ **to steel o.s. (to do sth)** 狠 下心 (做某事) [hěnxià xīn (zuò mǒushì)]

steep [stiːp] I ADJ 1 *[+ hill, staircase]* 陡的 [dǒu de] 2 *[+ increase, rise]* 急剧的 [jíjù de] 3 *(inf)* *(expensive)* 过高的 [guògāo de] II VT ▶ **to steep sth in liquid** 将某物浸泡在液体中 [jiāng mǒuwù jìnpào zài yètǐ zhōng] ▶ **to be steeped in history** 充满历史气息

steeple ['stiːpl] N [c] 尖塔 [jiāntǎ]

steer [stɪə(r)] I VT 1 *[+ car, boat, plane]* 驾驶 [jiàshǐ] 2 ▶ **to steer sb to/towards** 带领某人 去/向···方向发展 [dàilǐng mǒurén qù/xiàng··· fāngxiàng fāzhǎn] II VI *[car, boat, plane +]* 行 驶 [xíngshǐ] ▶ **to steer clear of sb/sth** 避开某 人/某事

steering ['stɪərɪŋ] N [U] *(in car etc)* 转向装置 [zhuǎnxiàng zhuāngzhì]

steering wheel N [c] 方向盘 [fāngxiàng pán]

stem [stɛm] I N [c] 1 *[of plant]* 茎 [jīng] 2 *[of leaf, fruit]* 梗 [gěng] 3 *[of glass]* 柄脚 [bǐngjiǎo] 4 *[of pipe]* 柄 [bǐng] II VT 1 *(stop)* *[+ flow, tide]* 堵住 [dǔzhù]; *[+ illegal drugs, violence]* 遏制 [èzhì] 2 *[+ bleeding]* 止住 [zhǐzhù]
▶ **stem from** VT FUS [不可拆分] 起源于 [qǐyuán yú]

stench [stɛntʃ] N [c] 恶臭 [èchòu]

○ **step** [stɛp] I N 1 [c] *(footstep)* 脚步 [jiǎobù]
▷ *He heard steps in the corridor.* 他听见走廊里 的脚步声。 2 [c] *(in dance)* 舞步 [wǔbù] 3 [c] *(action)* 步骤 [bùzhòu] ▷ *the first step towards peace* 通向和平的第一步 4 [c] *(stage)* *[of process]* 阶段 [jiēduàn] ▷ *The next step is to put the theory into practice.* 下一阶段是将理论付诸 于实践。 5 [c] *[of stairs]* 梯级 [tījí] ▷ *She was sitting on the top step.* 她坐在最高的一级楼梯 上。 6 [c] *(outside door)* 台阶 [táijiē] 7 [U] *(also:* **step aerobics**) 阶梯健身运动 [jiētī jiànshēn yùndòng] II VI 1 ▶ **to step forward/backward etc** 向前/后 {等} 迈步 [xiàngqián/hòu {děng} màibù] 2 ▶ **to step on/over sth** *(tread)* 踩在某 物上/跨过某物 [cǎizài mǒuwù shang/kuàguò mǒuwù] III **steps** NPL *(BRIT)* = **stepladder**

▶ **step by step** 逐步地 ▶ **to stay** *or* **keep one step ahead of sb/sth** 保持比某人/某物领先 一步 ▶ **to take a step** *(lit)* 迈一步 ▶ **to take steps to do sth** *(fig)* 采取措施做某事 ▶ **to be in step/out of step with sb** *(fig)* 与某人一致/不一 致 ▶ **to walk in step/out of step (with sb)** (与 某人)步伐一致/不一致
▶ **step aside** = **step down**
▶ **step back** VI ▶ **to step back (from sth)** *(fig)* 跳 出 (某事) 来看 [tiàochū (mǒushì) láikàn]
▶ **step down, step aside** VI 辞职 [cízhí]
▶ **step in** VI *(intervene)* 介入 [jièrù]
▶ **step off** VT FUS [不可拆分] *[+ plane, platform]* 走下来 [zǒu xiàlái]
▶ **step up** VT *(increase)* *[+ efforts, pace etc]* 增加 [zēngjiā]

stepbrother ['stɛpbrʌðə(r)] N [c] *(with shared father)* 异母兄弟 [yìmǔ xiōngdì]; *(with shared mother)* 异父兄弟 [yìfù xiōngdì]

stepchild ['stɛptʃaɪld] *(pl* **stepchildren**) N [c] *(of woman)* 丈夫与前妻所生的子女 [zhàngfu yǔ qiánqī suǒ shēng de zǐnǚ]; *(of man)* 妻子与前夫 所生的子女 [qīzi yǔ qiánfū suǒ shēng de zǐnǚ]

stepdaughter ['stɛpdɔːtə(r)] N [c] 继女 [jìnǚ]

stepfather ['stɛpfɑːðə(r)] N [c] 继父 [jìfù]

stepladder ['stɛplædə(r)] N [c] 活梯 [huótī]

stepmother ['stɛpmʌðə(r)] N [c] 继母 [jìmǔ]

stepsister ['stɛpsɪstə(r)] N [c] *(with shared father)* 异母姐妹 [yìmǔ jiěmèi]; *(with shared mother)* 异父姐妹 [yìfù jiěmèi]

stepson ['stɛpsʌn] N [c] 继子 [jìzǐ]

stereo ['stɛrɪəu] I N [c] 立体声装置 [lìtǐ shēng zhuāngzhì] II ADJ 立体声的 [lìtǐ shēng de]
▶ **in stereo** 用立体声

stereotype ['stɛrɪətaɪp] I N [c] 老套 [lǎotào] II VT 使模式化 [shǐ móshì huà]

sterile ['stɛraɪl] ADJ 1 *[+ bandage, needle]* 消过毒 的 [xiāoguò dú de] 2 *[+ person, animal]* 不育的 [bùyù de] 3 *[+ debate, ideas]* 枯燥乏味的 [kūzào fáwèi de]

sterilize ['stɛrɪlaɪz] VT 1 *[+ object]* 消毒 [xiāodú] 2 *[+ person, animal]* 使绝育 [shǐ juéyù]

sterling ['stəːlɪŋ] I N [U] *(currency)* 英国货币 [Yīngguó huòbì] II ADJ 1 *[+ silver]* 纯的 [chún de] 2 *[+ efforts, character]* 优秀的 [yōuxiù de]
▶ **one pound sterling** 一英镑

stern [stəːn] I ADJ 1 *[+ warning, measures]* 严 厉的 [yánlì de] 2 *[+ person]* 严格的 [yángé de] II N [c] *[of boat]* 船尾 [chuánwěi]

steroid ['stɪərɔɪd] N [c] 类固醇 [lèigùchún]

stew [stjuː] I N [c/u] 炖的食物 [dùn de shíwù] II VT, VI 1 *[+ meat, vegetables]* 炖 [dùn] 2 *[+ fruit]* 煨 [wēi] ▶ **stewed tea** 泡过久的茶

steward ['stjuːəd] N [c] 1 *(on ship, plane, train)* 乘务员 [chéngwù yuán] 2 *(at race, march, in club)* 干事 [gànshì]

stewardess ['stjuːədɛs] N [c] 女乘务员 [nǚ chéngwù yuán]

stick [stɪk] (*pt, pp* **stuck**) I N [C] **1** [*of wood*] 枯枝 [kūzhī] **2** (*as weapon*) 棍棒 [gùnbàng] **3** (*walking stick*) 拐杖 [guǎizhàng] **4** [*of chalk, dynamite, celery*] 条 [tiáo] II VT **1** ▸ **to stick sth on** *or* **to sth** (*with glue etc*) 将某物粘贴在某物上 [jiāng mǒuwù zhāntiē zài mǒuwù shang] **2** ▸ **to stick sth in/through sth** (*inf*) (*put*) 随手将某物戳进/放进某物中 [suíshǒu jiāng mǒuwù chuōjìn/fàngjìn mǒuwù zhōng] **3** ▸ **to stick sth in** *or* **into sth** (*push*) 将某物刺入某物中 [jiāng mǒuwù cìrù mǒuwùzhōng] **4** (BRIT: *inf*) (*tolerate*) 忍受 [rěnshòu] III VI **1** ▸ **to stick (to sth)** [*stamp, sticker+*] 粘贴(在某物上) [zhàntiē zài mǒuwù shang] **2** [*substance, paste+*] 粘在 [zhānzài] **3** (*remain*) [*name+*] 长久保留 [chángjiǔ bǎoliú] ▷ *I nicknamed him "Rex", a name which stuck.* 我给他起了个外号叫Rex，一直叫到现在。**4** (*get jammed*) [*door, lift+*] 卡住 [kǎzhù] ▸ **to get (hold of) the wrong end of the stick** (*inf*) 误解 ▸ **to stick in one's mind** [*thought etc+*] 铭记在某人的心中

▸ **stick around** (*inf*) VI 呆在附近 [dāizài fùjìn]
▸ **stick by** VT FUS [不可拆分] [*+person*] 忠于 [zhōngyú]
▸ **stick out** I VI (*protrude*) 伸出 [shēnchū] II VT **1** (*extend*) [*+tongue, hand*] 伸出 [shēnchū] **2** ▸ **to stick it out** (*inf*) 坚持到底 [jiānchí dàodǐ]
▸ **stick to** VT FUS [不可拆分] **1** [*+one's word, agreement*] 信守 [xìnshǒu] **2** [*+the truth, facts*] 紧扣 [jǐnkòu] **3** (*continue on*) [*+road*] 沿着 [yánzhe] **4** [*+job*] 坚持 [jiānchí]
▸ **stick together** VI [*people+*] 团结一致 [tuánjié yīzhì]
▸ **stick up** I VI (*extend upwards*) 竖起 [shùqǐ] II VT [*+picture, notice*] 张贴 [zhāntiē]
▸ **stick up for** VT FUS [不可拆分] [*+person, idea*] 为…辩护 [wèi…biànhù]
▸ **stick with** VT FUS [不可拆分] [*+person, job*] 忠于 [zhōngyú]

sticker ['stɪkə(r)] N [C] 不干胶标签 [bù gānjiāo biāoqiān]

sticky ['stɪkɪ] ADJ **1** [*+substance*] 黏的 [nián de] **2** [*+bottle, tube etc*] 胶黏的 [jiāonián de] **3** (*adhesive*) [*+tape, paper*] 黏性的 [niánxìng de] **4** [*+weather, day*] 湿热的 [shīrè de] **5** (*inf*) (*difficult*) 棘手的 [jíshǒu de]

stiff [stɪf] I ADJ **1** [*+brush, trousers*] 硬挺的 [yìngtǐng de] **2** [*+paste*] 稠的 [chóu de] **3** (*with aching muscles*) [*+person*] 酸痛的 [suāntòng de]; [*+neck, arm etc*] 僵硬的 [jiāngyìng de] **4** [*+door, drawer, zip etc*] 紧的 [jǐn de] **5** [*+manner, smile*] 生硬的 [shēngyìng de] **6** [*+competition*] 激烈的 [jīliè de]; [*+sentence, law*] 严厉的 [yánlì de] **7** [*+whisky, brandy*] 烈性的 [lièxìng de]; [*+breeze*] 强劲的 [qiángjìn de] II ADV ▸ **to be bored/scared stiff** 讨厌/害怕极了 [tǎoyàn/hàipà jíle] ▸ **to keep a stiff upper lip** (BRIT) 感情不外露

stiffen ['stɪfn] I VI **1** [*person, body+*] 变僵直 [biàn jiāngzhí] **2** (*also*: **stiffen up**) [*muscles, joints+*] 变僵硬 [biàn jiāngyìng] **3** [*attitudes, behaviour+*] 变得坚定 [biàn de jiāndìng] II VT **1** [*+cloth*] 使变挺 [shǐ biàntǐng] **2** [*+attitude, behaviour*] 加强 [jiāqiáng]

stifle ['staɪfl] VT **1** [*+yawn, laugh*] 忍住 [rěnzhù] **2** [*+debate, creativity*] 抑制 [yìzhì]

stifling ['staɪflɪŋ] ADJ **1** [*+heat*] 令人窒息的 [lìngrén zhìxī de] **2** (*fig*) [*+situation*] 沉闷的 [chénmèn de]

stigma ['stɪgmə] N **1** [C/U] (*disgrace*) 耻辱 [chǐrǔ] **2** [C] (BOT) [*of flower*] 柱头 [zhùtóu]

stilettos [stɪ'lɛtəuz] (BRIT) NPL 细高跟鞋 [xì gāogēn xié] 〔美 = **spike heels**〕

○ **still** [stɪl] I ADJ **1** (*motionless*) [*person, hands, etc*] 不动的 [bùdòng de] ▷ *He sat very still for several minutes.* 他一动也不动地坐了几分钟。 ▷ *His hands were never still.* 他双手从不停歇。 **2** (*tranquil*) [*+place, water, air*] 平静的 [píngjìng de] ▷ *a still lake* 平静的湖 ▷ *The night air was very still.* 夜空非常寂静。 **3** (BRIT) (*not fizzy*) 无气泡的 [wúqì de] ▷ *a bottle of still water* 一瓶无气泡的水 II ADV **1** (*up to the present*) 仍然 [réngrán] ▷ *She still lives in London.* 她仍住在伦敦。 **2** (*possibly*) 还是 [háishì] ▷ *We could still make it if we rush.* 如果我们快点，还能赶上。 **3** (*even*) 更 [gèng] ▷ *They could delay the flight still further.* 他们可能将航班拖延得更久。 **4** (*yet*) 还 [hái] ▷ *There are ten weeks still to go.* 还有10个星期呢。 **5** (*nonetheless*) 尽管如此 [jǐnguǎn rúcǐ] ▷ *I didn't win. Still, it was fun.* 我没赢。尽管如此，却玩得很开心。 **6** (*for emphasis*) 还是 [háishì] ▷ *Despite the ruling, he was still found guilty.* 尽管有那个裁决，他还是被定了罪。 III N [C] (CINE) 剧照 [jùzhào] ▸ **to stand/keep still** 站着别动/别动 ▸ **he still hasn't arrived** 他还没到 ▸ **better still** 更好

stimulate ['stɪmjuleɪt] VT **1** [*+economy, interest, demand*] 激励 [jīlì] **2** [*+person*] 激发 [jīfā] **3** [*+part of body*] 促进 [cùjìn]

stimulus ['stɪmjuləs] (*pl* **stimuli** ['stɪmjulaɪ]) N **1** [C/U] (*incentive*) 刺激 [cìjī] **2** [C] (BIO, PSYCH) 刺激因素 [cìjī yīnsù]

sting [stɪŋ] (*pt, pp* **stung**) I N [C] **1** (*pain, bite*) 刺 [cì] **2** (*part*) [*of insect*] 螫刺 [áocì] **3** (*inf*) (*by police*) 精心设置的圈套 [jīngxīn shèzhì de quāntào] II VT **1** [*insect, nettle+*] 刺 [cì] **2** [*substance+*] 灼痛 [zhuótòng] **3** [*wind, remarks+*] 刺痛 [cìtòng] III VI **1** [*insect, nettle+*] 叮 [dīng] **2** [*ointment+*] 引起刺痛 [yǐnqǐ cìtòng] **3** [*skin+*] 感到灼痛 [gǎndào zhuótòng]

stink [stɪŋk] (*pt* **stank**, *pp* **stunk**) I N [C] 恶臭 [èchòu] II VI 发臭 [fāchòu] ▸ **to stink of sth** 有某物的气味 ▸ **that idea stinks!** (*inf*) 那个主意糟透了！

stint [stɪnt] I N [C] (*time*) 时间 [shíjiān] II VI ▸ **don't stint on...** 别舍不得…[bié shěbude…]

stir [stə:(r)] I N [S] (*fuss*) 轰动 [hōngdòng] II VT **1** [*+tea, sauce etc*] 搅动 [jiǎodòng] **2** (*move*)

[+ *person*] 打动 [dǎdòng]; [+ *emotion*] 激起 [jīqǐ]
III VI (*move slightly*) [*leaves etc* +] 微动 [wēidòng];
[*person* +] 挪动 [nuódòng] ▶ **to give sth a stir**
搅动某物
▶ **stir up** VT **1** [+ *trouble*] 挑起 [tiǎoqǐ] **2** [+ *dust,
mud*] 扬起 [yángqǐ]

stir-fry ['stə:'fraɪ] **I** VT 煸 [biān] **II** N [C] 炒
菜 [chǎocài]

stitch [stɪtʃ] **I** N **1** [C] (*in sewing*) 针脚 [zhēnjiǎo]
2 [C] (*in knitting*) 针 [zhēn] **3** [C] (MED) 缝针
[féngzhēn] **4** [S] (*pain*) 突然剧痛 [tūrán jùtòng]
II VT **1** ▶ **to stitch sth together/to stitch sth to
sth** 将某物缝起来/将某物缝在某物上 [jiāng
mǒuwù féngqǐlái/jiāng mǒuwù féngzài mǒuwù
shang] **2** (MED) (*also:* **stitch up**) [+ *wound*] 缝合
[fénghé]
▶ **stitch up** VT **1** (MED) [+ *wound*] 缝合 [fénghé]
2 (BRIT: *inf*) (*trick, frame*) 诬陷 [wūxiàn]

stock [stɒk] **I** N **1** [C] (*supply*) 供应物 [gōngyìng
wù] **2** [U] (*in shop*) 库存 [kùcún] **3** [C/U] (ECON)
股票 [gǔpiào] **4** [U] (*gravy*) 汤汁 [tāngzhī] **5** [U]
(*frm*) (*origin*) 血统 [xuètǒng] **II** NPL (*livestock*)
牲畜 [shēngchù] **III** ADJ [+ *answer, response*] 老
一套的 [lǎoyītào de] **IV** VT [*shop* +] [+ *goods*]
储备 [chǔbèi] ▶ **in/out of stock** 有/无存货
▶ **stocks and shares** 股票 ▶ **to take stock (of
sth)** 斟酌 (某事) ▶ **well-stocked** 储备丰富
▶ **stock up** VI ▶ **to stock up (on *or* with sth)** 储
备 (某物) [chǔbèi (mǒuwù)]

stockbroker ['stɒkbrəukə(r)] N [C] 股票经纪
人 [gǔpiào jīngjì rén]

stock exchange N [C] 股票交易所 [gǔpiào
jiāoyì suǒ]

stockholder ['stɒkhəuldə(r)] (US) N [C] 股东
[gǔdōng] [英 = **shareholder**]

stocking ['stɒkɪŋ] N [C] 长统袜 [chángtǒng
wà]

stock market N [C] 股票市场 [gǔpiào
shìchǎng]

stoke [stəuk] VT **1** (*also:* **stoke up**) [+ *fire, furnace*]
添燃料 [tiān ránliào] **2** (*also:* **stoke up**) [+ *feeling*]
煽动 [shāndòng]

stole [stəul] **I** PT *of* **steal II** N [C] (*shawl*) 披
肩 [pījiān]

stolen ['stəuln] PP *of* **steal**

stomach ['stʌmək] **I** N **1** [C] (*organ*) 胃 [wèi]
2 (*abdomen*) 腹部 [fùbù] **II** VT 容忍 [róngrěn]

stomach ache N [C/U] 胃痛 [wèitòng]

stone [stəun] **I** N **1** [U] 石头 [shítou] **2** [C]
(*pebble*) 石子 [shízǐ] **3** [C] (*gem*) 宝石 [bǎoshí]
4 [C] (BRIT) (*in fruit*) 核 [hé] [美 = **pit**] **5** [C]
(BRIT) (*weight*) 英石, 等于14磅或6.35公
斤 **II** CPD (复合词) (*made of stone*) 石制
[shízhì] **III** VT **1** (*throw stones at*) 向…扔石
头 [xiàng…rēng shítou] **2** (BRIT) [+ *fruit*] 去核
[qùhé] [美 = **pit**] ▶ **within a stone's throw of**
与…只有一箭之遥

stood [stud] PT, PP *of* **stand**

stool [stu:l] N [C] **1** (*chair*) 凳子 [dèngzi] **2** (MED)
(*faeces*) 大便 [dàbiàn]

stoop [stu:p] **I** VI **1** (*also:* **stoop down, stoop
over**) (*bend*) 弯腰 [wānyāo] **2** (*walk with a stoop*)
驼背 [tuóbèi] **II** N 驼背 [tuóbèi] ▶ **to stoop to
(doing) sth** 堕落到 (做出) 某事

☉ **stop** [stɒp] **I** VT **1** 停止 [tíngzhǐ] ▷ *Stop the car
and let me out.* 停车让我下车。 **2** (*prevent*) 阻止
[zǔzhǐ] ▷ *Does putting people in prison stop crime?*
把人关在监狱里能阻止犯罪吗? **3** [+ *cheque*]
停止兑现 [tíngzhǐ duìxiàn] **II** VI **1** [*person,
vehicle* +] 停下来 [tíng xiàlái] ▷ *She stopped and
stared at the poster.* 她停下来盯着海报看。
2 (*stop working*) [*watch, engine, heart* +] 停 [tíng]
▷ *My watch has stopped.* 我的手表停了。 **3** [*rain,
noise, activity* +] 停 [tíng] ▷ *The rain had stopped.*
雨停了。 **4** (*also:* **stop off**) (*on journey*) 逗留
[dòuliú] **III** N [C] **1** (*on journey*) (*place*) 站 [zhàn];
(*time*) 停留 [tíngliú] ▷ *Their first stop was a hotel
outside Paris.* 他们旅程中的第一站是巴黎郊外
的一家旅馆。 **2** (*for bus, train*) 车站 [chēzhàn]
▷ *We'll get off at the next stop.* 我们将在下一站下
车。 ▶ **to stop doing sth** 停止做某事 ▶ **to stop
sb (from) doing sth** 阻止某人做某事 ▶ **stop it!**
住手! ▶ **to come to a stop** [*car, train etc* +] 停
下来 ▶ **to put a stop to sth** 使某事停止
▶ **stop by I** VI 顺便访问 [shùnbiàn guòfǎng]
II VT FUS [不可拆分] [+ *place*] 顺道去 [shùndào
qù]
▶ **stop up** VT [+ *hole, leak*] 堵塞 [dǔsāi]

stoplight ['stɒplaɪt] N [C] **1** (*in road*) 交通
信号灯 [jiāotōng xìnhào dēng] [英 = **traffic
light**] **2** (*on vehicle*) 刹车灯 [shāchē dēng]

stopover ['stɒpəuvə(r)] N [C] **1** (*on journey*) 中
途停留 [zhōngtú tíngliú] **2** (*on plane journey*) 转
机停留 [zhuǎnjī tíngliú]

stoppage ['stɒpɪdʒ] N [C] **1** (*strike*) 停工
[tínggōng] **2** (BRIT: SPORT) 暂停 [zàntíng]
[美 = **time out**] **3** (*from salary*) 扣除 [kòuchú]

storage ['stɔːrɪdʒ] N [U] **1** 贮藏 [zhùcáng]
2 (COMPUT) 存储 [cúnchǔ]

store [stɔː(r)] **I** N [C] **1** (*of food etc*) 储备
[chǔbèi] **2** [*of knowledge, jokes etc*) 丰富 [fēngfù]
3 (*depot*) 仓库 [cāngkù] **4** (BRIT) (*large shop*)
大商店 [dà shāngdiàn] **5** (US) (*shop*) 店铺
[diànpù] [英 = **shop**] **II** VT **1** (*also:* **store away**)
[+ *provisions, information etc*] 存放 [cúnfàng]
2 [*computer, brain* +] [+ *information*] 存储 [cúnchǔ]
III **stores** NPL (*provisions*) 补给品 [bǔjǐ pǐn]
▶ **to be** *or* **lie in store (for sb)** 等待着 (某人)
▶ **to set great/little store by sth** (*frm*) 重视/轻
视某物
▶ **store up** VT [+ *food, money*] 储备 [chǔbèi];
[+ *memories*] 积聚 [jījù]

storekeeper ['stɔːkiːpə(r)] (US) N [C] 店主
[diànzhǔ] [英 = **shopkeeper**]

storey, (US) **story** ['stɔːrɪ] N [C] 层 [céng]

storm [stɔːm] **I** N [C] **1** 暴风雨 [bàofēngyǔ]

2 [of criticism, protest] 爆发 [bàofā] **II** VI ▶ **to storm in/out** 猛冲而入/出 [měngchōng' érrù/chū] **III** VT (attack) [+ place] 猛攻 [měnggōng]
▶ **to take sth by storm** 轰动

stormy ['stɔːmɪ] ADJ **1** [+ weather] 有暴风雨的 [yǒu bàofēngyǔ de] **2** [+ relationship] 多风波的 [duō fēngbō de]; [+ debate] 激烈的 [jīliè de]

○ **story** ['stɔːrɪ] N [c] **1** (account) 描述 [miáoshù]
▷ I told her the story of my life. 我向她描述了我的生活。▷ the story of the women's movement in Ireland 对于爱尔兰妇女运动的描述 **2** (tale) 故事 [gùshì] ▷ a ghost story 一个鬼故事 **3** (in newspaper, on news broadcast) 报道 [bàodào] ▷ Those are some of the top stories in the news. 那些是新闻中最重要的报道。**4** (lie) 谎话 [huǎnghuà] ▷ He invented some story about a friend. 他编造了个有关一个朋友的谎话。**5** (US) [of building] = **storey** ▶ **it's a different story** 那是另一回事 ▶ **the (same) old story** 老一套 ▶ **that's only part of or not the whole story** 那不是事实的全部 ▶ **my side of the story** 我的叙述

stout [staut] **I** ADJ **1** [+ shoes] 耐穿的 [nàichuān de]; [+ branch] 粗大的 [cūdà de] **2** [+ person] 肥胖的 [féipàng de] **3** [+ resistance, defence] 顽强的 [wánqiáng de] **II** N [c/u] (BRIT) (beer) 黑啤酒 [hēi píjiǔ]

stove [stəuv] N [c] **1** (for cooking) 炉子 [lúzi] **2** (for heating) 加热器 [jiārè qì] **3** (US) (top of cooker) 炉 [lú]

straddle ['strædl] VT **1** [+ chair, fence etc] (sitting) 跨坐 [kuàzuò]; (standing) 跨立 [kuàlì] **2** [bridge, town +] [+ border, road] 横跨 [héngkuà] **3** [+ period, activity] 跨越 [kuàyuè]

straight [streɪt] **I** ADJ **1** (not curving) 笔直的 [bǐzhí de] **2** [+ hair] 直的 [zhí de] **3** (honest) [+ answer] 直截了当的 [zhíjié liǎodàng de] **4** (simple) [+ fight, choice] 非此即彼的 [fēicǐ jíbǐ de] **5** (uninterrupted) [+ hours, victories] 连续的 [liánxù de] **6** (THEAT) (serious) [+ role, play] 朴实无华的 [pǔshí wúhuá de] **7** (inf) (heterosexual) 异性恋的 [yìxìngliàn de] **8** [+ whisky etc] 纯的 [chún de] **II** ADV **1** [walk, stand, look +] 直 [zhí] **2** (immediately) 直接地 [zhíjiē de] **3** (without an interval) 连续不断地 [liánxù bùduàn de] **III** N [c] (on racetrack) 直道 [zhídào] ▶ **to be straight with sb** (honest) 坦诚地对待某人 ▶ **to put sth straight** (make it clear) 澄清某事 ▶ **to get sth straight** 彻底了解某事 ▶ **let's get this straight** 让我们把事情搞清楚 ▶ **straight away, straight off** 马上 ▶ **to tell sb sth straight (out)** 坦率地告诉某人某事

straighten ['streɪtn] **I** VT (also: straighten out) [+ picture, hair] 弄直 [nòngzhí] **II** VI (also: straighten out) [road etc +] 变直 [biànzhí]
▶ **straighten out** **I** VI = straighten **II** VT **1** = straighten **2** [+ problem, situation] 弄清楚 [nòng qīngchu]

▶ **straighten up** VI (stand straight) 直起身子 [zhíqǐ shēnzi]

straightforward [streɪt'fɔːwəd] ADJ **1** (simple) 简单的 [jiǎndān de] **2** (honest) [+ person, behaviour] 直截了当的 [zhíjié liǎodàng de]

strain [streɪn] **I** N **1** [c/u] (pressure) 负担 [fùdān] **2** [c/u] (tension) 紧张 [jǐnzhāng] **3** [u] (TECH) 作用力 [zuòyòng lì] **4** [c] [of virus, plant] 系 [xì] **5** [c/u] ▶ **back/muscle strain** 背部/肌肉扭伤 [bèibù/jīròu niǔshāng] **II** VT **1** [+ back, muscle] 扭伤 [niǔshāng] **2** (overload) [+ resources, system] 使超过负荷 [shǐ chāoguò fùhè] **3** [+ food] 过滤 [guòlù] **III** VI ▶ **to strain to do sth** 尽力去做某事 [jìnlì qùzuò mǒushì] **IV strains** NPL (liter) [of music] 乐曲 [yuèqǔ] ▶ **to be under great strain** [person +] 处于极度紧张之中; [organization +] 负担过重 ▶ **to put a strain on sth/sb** 给某事/某人增加负担

strained [streɪnd] ADJ **1** [+ back, muscle] 劳损的 [láosǔn de] **2** [+ voice, laugh etc] 勉强的 [miǎnqiǎng de] **3** [+ relations] 紧张的 [jǐnzhāng de]

strainer ['streɪnə(r)] N [c] 滤网 [lùwǎng]

strait [streɪt] **I** N [c] (GEO) (also: straits) 海峡 [hǎixiá] **II straits** NPL ▶ **to be in dire or desperate straits** 处于艰难的境地 [chǔyú jiānnán de jìngdì]

strand [strænd] N [c] **1** [of wire, wool] 股 [gǔ] **2** [of hair] 缕 [lǚ] **3** [of plan, theory, story] 一个组成部分 [yīgè zǔchéng bùfen]

stranded ['strændɪd] ADJ **1** [+ traveller] 受困无援的 [shòukùn wúyuán de] **2** [+ ship, animal] 搁浅的 [gēqiǎn de]

strange [streɪndʒ] ADJ **1** (odd) 奇怪的 [qíguài de] **2** (unfamiliar) [+ person, place] 陌生的 [mòshēng de]

strangely ['streɪndʒlɪ] ADV 奇怪地 [qíguài de]
▶ **strangely (enough)** 奇怪的是

stranger ['streɪndʒə(r)] N [c] **1** (unknown person) 陌生人 [mòshēng rén] **2** (from another area) 异乡人 [yìxiāng rén] ▶ **they are strangers** 他们互相不认识 ▶ **to be a stranger to sth** 很不习惯某事

strangle ['stræŋgl] VT **1** (kill) 扼死 [èsǐ] **2** (fig) (stifle) 压制 [yāzhì]

strap [stræp] **I** N [c] **1** [of watch, bag] 带 [dài] **2** [of slip, dress] 肩带 [jiāndài] **II** VT ▶ **to strap sb/sth in/on** 用带子将某人/某物捆在···里/上 [yòng dàizi jiāng mǒurén/mǒuwù kǔnzài···lǐ/shang]

strategic [strə'tiːdʒɪk] ADJ **1** [+ position] 关键的 [guānjiàn de] **2** [+ plan, site] 有战略意义的 [yǒu zhànlüè yìyì de] **3** [+ weapons, arms] 战略的 [zhànlüè de]

strategy ['strætɪdʒɪ] N **1** [c/u] (plan) 行动计划 [xíngdòng jìhuà] **2** [u] (MIL) 战略 [zhànlüè]

straw [strɔː] N **1** [u] 稻草 [dàocǎo] **2** [c] (drinking straw) 吸管 [xīguǎn] ▶ **that's the last**

straw! 那是最后的极限！

strawberry ['strɔ:bəri] I N [c] 草莓 [cǎoméi] II CPD [复合词] 草莓 [cǎoméi]

stray [streɪ] I ADJ 1 [+ cat, dog] 迷失的 [míshī de] 2 [+ bullet, hair] 零星的 [língxīng de] 3 (scattered) 偶尔发生的 [ǒu'ěr fāshēng de] II VI 1 ▶ to stray into/onto 误入 [wùrù] 2 (fig) [thoughts, mind +] 走神 [zǒushén]; [eyes +] 不由自主地移动 [bùyóu zìzhǔ de yídòng] III N [c] (dog, cat) 走失的动物 [zǒushīde dòngwù]

streak [stri:k] I N [c] 1 (stripe) 条纹 [tiáowén] 2 (in hair) 缕 [lǚ] 3 [of madness, jealousy etc] 个性特征 [gèxìng tèzhēng] II VT 在…上留下条纹 [zài…shang liúxià tiáowén] III VI 1 ▶ to streak past 划过 [huáguò] 2 ▶ to have streaks in one's hair 头发有不同颜色的条缕 ▶ a winning/losing streak 接连赢/失败 ▶ to be streaked with sth 夹杂着某物

stream [stri:m] I N [c] 1 (small river) 溪流 [xīliú] 2 (current) 水流 [shuǐliú] 3 (series) [of people, vehicles] 川流不息 [chuānliú bùxī]; [of questions, insults etc] 一连串 [yīliánchuàn] 4 (BRIT: SCOL) 能力小组 [nénglì xiǎozǔ] II VT (BRIT: SCOL) 把学生分成能力小组 [bǎ xuéshēng fēnchéng nénglì xiǎozǔ] III VI 1 [water, oil, blood +] 涌流 [yǒngliú] ▶ to come on stream [factory etc +] 投入生产 ▶ to stream in/out [people +] 涌入/出

○ **street** [stri:t] N [c] 街道 [jiēdào] ▶ on the street(s) (homeless) 无家可归的 (outdoors) 户外 ▶ the man in the street 普通人

streetcar ['stri:tkɑ:(r)] (US) N [c] 有轨电车 [yǒuguǐ diànchē] [英 = tram]

strength [streŋθ] N 1 (U) (physical) 力气 [lìqi] 2 (U) [of object, material] 强度 [qiángdù] 3 (U) (power, influence) [of person, organization, country] 实力 [shílì] 4 (U) (courage, determination) 勇气 [yǒngqì] 5 [c/U] (quality, ability) 长处 [chángchù] 6 (U) (intensity) [of feeling, opinion, belief] 力量 [lìliàng] 7 (U) (number of people) 人数 [rénshù] 8 [c/U] [of drink, chemical] 浓度 [nóngdù] ▶ on the strength of 依凭 ▶ to go from strength to strength 不断取得成功 ▶ at full strength (fully staffed) 全体 ▶ below strength [+ staff, army, team] 人手不足 ▶ strength of mind/character 充足的信心/坚强的性格

strengthen ['streŋθən] VT 1 [+ building, machine] 加固 [jiāgù] 2 [+ muscle] 使…有力 [shǐ…yǒulì] 3 [+ economy, currency, relationship] 加强 [jiāqiáng] 4 [+ argument] 增强 [zēngqiáng]

strenuous ['strenjuəs] ADJ 1 [+ exercise, walk] 激烈的 [jīliè de] 2 [+ efforts] 努力的 [nǔlì de]

stress [stres] I N [c/U] 1 (mental strain) 压力 [yālì] 2 (force, pressure) 重压 [zhòngyā] 3 (on word, syllable) 重音 [zhòngyīn] 4 (emphasis) 强调 [qiángdiào] II VT 1 [+ point, importance] 强调 [qiángdiào] 2 [+ word, syllable] 重读 [zhòngdú] ▶ to be under stress 有压力 ▶ to lay great stress on sth 极其强调某物 ▶ to stress that… 强调…

stressed [strest] ADJ (tense) 紧张的 [jǐnzhāng de]

stressful ['stresful] ADJ [+ job, situation] 紧张的 [jǐnzhāng de]

stretch [stretʃ] I N [c] 1 [of road, sand, water] 连绵的一片 [liánmián de yīpiàn] 2 (period) 一段时间 [yīduàn shíjiān] II VI 1 [person, animal +] 伸懒腰 [shēn lǎnyāo] 2 (extend) [land, area +] 延伸 [yánshēn] 3 (be flexible) [elastic, garment etc +] 伸缩 [shēnsuō] III VT 1 [+ arm, leg] 伸直 [shēnzhí] 2 (pull) [+ elastic, garment] 拉 [lā] 3 (over-extend) [+ resources] 使紧张 [shǐ jǐnzhāng] [lā] 4 [job, task +] [+ person] 使倾注全力 [shǐ qīngzhù quánlì] ▶ for several days/weeks at a stretch 连续几天/星期 ▶ by no/any stretch of the imagination 无论怎样/任凭如何异想天开 ▶ to stretch one's legs 散散步 ▶ stretch out I VI 舒展着身子躺 [shūzhǎnzhe shēnzi tǎng] II VT [+ arm, leg] 伸出 [shēnchū] ▶ to stretch o.s. out 舒展着身子躺 ▶ stretch to VT FUS [不可拆分] [money, food +] 支付得起 [zhīfùde qǐ]

stretcher ['stretʃə(r)] I N [c] 担架 [dānjià] II VT 用担架抬 [yòng dānjià tái]

strict [strɪkt] ADJ 1 [+ rule, instruction] 严格的 [yángé de] 2 [+ person] 严厉的 [yánlì de] ▶ in the strict(est) sense of the word 就某字精确的意义而言 ▶ a strict vegetarian 绝对的素食主义者 ▶ to tell sb sth in the strictest confidence 极秘密地将某事告诉某人

strictly ['strɪktlɪ] ADV 1 (severely) 严格地 [yángé de] 2 (exactly) 完全地 [wánquán de] 3 (exclusively) 绝对地 [juéduì de] ▶ strictly confidential 绝密 ▶ strictly speaking 严格地说 ▶ strictly between ourselves 只有我们两个人知道

stride [straɪd] (pt, pp strode) I N [c] 大步 [dàbù] II VI ▶ to stride across/off 大步流星地穿过/走开 [dàbù liúxīng de chuānguò/zǒukāi] ▶ to take sth in one's stride or (US) in stride 从容处理某事 ▶ to make strides 取得进步

strike [straɪk] (pt, pp struck) I N [c] 1 [of workers] 罢工 [bàgōng] 2 (MIL) 袭击 [xíjī] II VT 1 (frm) (hit) [+ person, thing] 打 [dǎ] 2 (frm) (collide with) 碰撞 [pèngzhuàng] 3 (affect) 侵袭 [qīnxí] 4 [idea, thought +] 突然想到 [tūrán xiǎngdào] 5 [+ oil, gold] 发现 [fāxiàn] 6 [+ bargain, deal] 达成 [dáchéng] 7 [+ match] 擦 [cā] 8 ▶ to strike fear/terror into people (liter) 引起人们的恐惧/惊恐 [yǐnqǐ rénmen de kǒngjù/jīngkǒng] III VI 1 (go on strike) 罢工 [bàgōng] 2 [illness, disaster +] 降临 [jiànglín] 3 [clock +] 报时 [bàoshí] 4 [killer +] 袭击 [xíjī]; [snake +] 咬 [yǎo] ▶ to be on strike 在罢工

▶ **to go on strike** 参加罢工 ▶ **to call a strike** 号召罢工 ▶ **to be struck by lightning** 遭到雷击 ▶ **to be struck by sth** 某事给…印象深刻 ▶ **it struck me that...** 我突然想到… ▶ **he struck me as very serious/clever** 我感到他很严肃/聪明 ▶ **the clock struck nine** 钟敲了9点 ▶ **to strike a balance (between two things)** (把两者)折中

▶ **strike back** VI 1 (MIL) 反击 [fǎnjī] 2 [person +] (retaliate) 回击 [huíjī]

▶ **strike down** VT (kill) 打倒 [dǎdǎo]; (injure) 使病得厉害 [shǐ bìngdé lìhài]

▶ **strike off** VT 1 (from list) 除名 [chúmíng] 2 [+ doctor, lawyer] 取消从业资格 [qǔxiāo cóngyè zīgé]

▶ **strike out** I VI 1 (speak out) 抨击 [pēngjī] 2 (hit out) 猛力打击 [měnglì dǎjī] 3 (become independent) 独闯新路 [dúchuǎng xīnlù] 4 (liter) (in particular direction) 行进 [xíngjìn] 5 (BASEBALL) 使三击不中出局 [shǐ sānjī bùzhòng chūjú] 6 (US: inf) (fail) 失败 [shībài] II VT [+ word, sentence] 删去 [shānqù]

▶ **strike up** VT 1 [+ conversation] 开始 [kāishǐ] 2 [+ friendship] 开始建立 [kāishǐ jiànlì] 3 [band, orchestra +] [+ music] 开始演奏 [kāishǐ yǎnzòu]

striker ['straɪkə(r)] N [c] 1 (person on strike) 罢工者 [bàgōng zhě] 2 (FOOTBALL) 前锋 [qiánfēng]

striking ['straɪkɪŋ] ADJ 1 (noticeable) 突出的 [tūchū de] 2 (attractive) 出众的 [chūzhòng de]

string [strɪŋ] (pt, pp **strung**) I N 1 [c/u] 细绳 [xìshéng] 2 [of beads, onions] 串 [chuàn] 3 [c] [of islands] 一系列 [yīxìliè] 4 [c] [of disasters, excuses] 一连串 [yīliánchuàn] 5 [c] (COMPUT) 字符串 [zìfú chuàn] 6 [c] (on guitar, violin) 弦 [xián] II VT ▶ **to string sth across sth** 把某物挂在某物上 [bǎ mǒuwù guàzài mǒuwù shang] III **the strings** NPL (in orchestra) 弦乐器 [xiányuèqì] ▶ **to pull strings** 运用影响以达目的 ▶ **with no strings (attached)** 不加附带条件

▶ **string along** VT [+ person] 愚弄 [yúnòng]

▶ **string together** VT [+ words etc] 把…连接在一起 [bǎ…liánjiē zài yīqǐ]

string bean (US) N [c] 菜豆 [càidòu] 〔英 = **French bean**〕

strip [strɪp] I N [c] 1 [of paper, cloth] 狭条 [xiátiáo] 2 [of metal, wood] 条 [tiáo] 3 [of land, water] 带状 [dàizhuàng] 4 (SPORT) (team colours) 彩条球衣 [cǎitiáo qiúyī] 5 (US) (comic strip) 连环画 [liánhuánhuà] II VT 1 (undress) 脱光…的衣服 [tuōguāng…de yīfu] 2 [+ bed] 取下 [qǔxià] 3 [+ paint] 刮去 [guāqù] 4 [+ engine, machine] 拆开 [chāikāi] 5 ▶ **to strip sb of** [+ property, rights, title] 剥夺某人的 [bōduó mǒurén de] III VI (undress) 脱光衣服 [tuōguāng yīfu]; (as entertainer) 表演脱衣舞 [biǎoyǎn tuōyī wǔ]

▶ **strip away** VT (fig) 揭除 [jiēchú]

▶ **strip off** I VI (undress) 脱光衣服 [tuōguāng

yīfu] II VT [+ clothes] 脱下 [tuōxià]

stripe [straɪp] I N [c] 条纹 [tiáowén] II **stripes** NPL (on uniform) 制服上表示军衔或服役时间的条纹

striped [straɪpt] ADJ 有条纹的 [yǒu tiáowén de]

stripper ['strɪpə(r)] N [c] (strip-tease artist) 脱衣舞表演者 [tuōyīwǔ biǎoyǎnzhě]

strip-search ['strɪpsəːtʃ] I N [c] 光身搜查 [guāngshēn sōuchá] II VT 对…进行光身搜查 [duì…jìnxíng guāngshēn sōuchá]

strive [straɪv] (pt **strove**, pp **striven** ['strɪvn]) VI ▶ **to strive for sth/to do sth** 力争某事/做某事 [lìzhēng mǒushì/zuò mǒushì]

strode [strəud] PT OF **stride**

stroke [strəuk] I N [c] 1 (blow) 击 [jī] 2 (in swimming) (single movement) 两臂划水一周 [liǎngbì huáshuǐ yīzhōu]; (style) 泳姿 [yǒngzī] 4 (MED) 中风 [zhòngfēng] 5 (TENNIS, CRICKET, GOLF) 击球 [jīqiú] 6 [of clock] 鸣响 [míngxiǎng] 7 [of paintbrush, pen] 笔划 [bǐhuà] II VT [+ person, animal etc] 抚摸 [fǔmō] ▶ **at a stroke, in one stroke** 一下子 ▶ **a stroke of luck** 好运 ▶ **on the stroke of midnight** 子时 ▶ **a 2-stroke engine** 双冲程发动机

stroll [strəul] I N 散步 [sànbù] II VI 散步 [sànbù] ▶ **to go for a stroll** 去散步 ▶ **to have or take a stroll** 去散步

stroller ['strəulə(r)] (US) N [c] 婴儿小推车 [yīng'ér xiǎo tuīchē] 〔英 = **pushchair**〕

○ **strong** [strɒŋ] I ADJ 1 [+ person, arms, grip] 有力的 [yǒulì de] 2 (healthy) 强健的 [qiángjiàn de] ▷ He was very strong when he was young. 他年轻时身体很强壮。▷ Next week you may travel, when you are a little stronger. 下星期你身体稍稍好一些就可以出去旅行了。 3 [+ object, material] 牢固的 [láogù de] 4 [+ wind, current] 强劲的 [qiángjìng de] 5 [+ drug] 强劲的 [qiángjìng de]; [+ alcoholic drink] 烈性的 [lièxìng de]; [+ chemical, non-alcoholic drink] 浓的 [nóng de] 6 [+ impression, influence] 感染力强的 [gǎnrǎnlì qiáng de] 7 [+ opinion, viewer, supporter] 坚定的 [jiāndìng de] 8 [+ smell, taste, flavour] 浓郁的 [nóngyù de] 9 [+ protest, measures] 激烈的 [jīliè de] 10 [+ personality] 强的 [qiáng de] 11 [+ desire, reaction] 强烈的 [qíngliè de] 12 (likely to succeed) 强有力的 [qiáng yǒulì de] ▷ She is a strong contender for the team. 她是入选队伍强有力的竞争者。 II ADV ▶ **to be going strong** [place, activity +] 状态良好 [zhuàngtài liánghǎo] [person +] 身体硬朗 [shēntǐ yìnglǎng] ▶ **strong language** 激烈的措辞 ▶ **his/her strong point(s)** 他/她的长处 ▶ **they were 50 strong** 他们多达50人

stronghold ['strɒŋhəuld] N [c] [of attitude, belief] 坚固据点 [jiāngù jùdiǎn]

strongly ['strɒŋlɪ] ADV 1 [+ made, built] 牢固 [láogù] 2 [defend, advise, argue +] 坚决 [jiānjué]

3 [*feel, believe +*] 坚定 [jiāndìng] **4** [*impress, influence +*] 强大 [qiángdà] **5** [*taste, smell +*] 浓重 [nóngzhòng] ▶ **I feel strongly about it** 我对此有强烈的看法

strove [strəʊv] PT *of* **strive**

struck [strʌk] PT, PP *of* **strike**

structural ['strʌktʃrəl] ADJ [+ *changes, damage*] 结构的 [jiégòu de]

structural engineer N [c] 房产检视员 [fángchǎn jiǎnshìyuán]

structure ['strʌktʃə(r)] I N **1** [c/u] [*of organization, society, book etc*] 体系 [tǐxì] **2** [c] (*building*) 建筑物 [jiànzhù wù] II VT 安排 [ānpái]

struggle ['strʌgl] I N **1** [c] (*fight*) 搏斗 [bódòu] **2** [c/u] (*attempt to do sth*) 斗争 [dòuzhēng] **3** [c] (*difficulty*) 难事 [nánshì] II VI **1** (*try hard*) 尽力 [jìnlì] **2** (*fight*) 搏斗 [bódòu] **3** (*try to free o.s.*) 挣扎 [zhēngzhá] **4** (*have difficulty*) 艰难地应付 [jiānnán de yìngfù] ▶ **to have a struggle to do sth** 艰难地做某事

strung [strʌŋ] PT, PP *of* **string**

stub [stʌb] I N [c] [*of cheque, ticket etc*] 存根 [cúngēn] ▶ **pencil stub** 铅笔头 ▶ **cigarette stub** 烟蒂 II VT ▶ **to stub one's toe** 踢到了脚趾 [tīdàole jiǎozhǐ]
▶ **stub out** VT [+ *cigarette*] 捻熄 [niǎnxī]

stubble ['stʌbl] N [u] **1** (*on chin*) 胡子茬 [húzi chá] **2** (*in field*) 残株 [cánzhū]

stubborn ['stʌbən] ADJ **1** [+ *person*] 倔强的 [juéjiàng de]; [+ *resistance*] 顽强的 [wánqiáng de] **2** [+ *stain, illness*] 难对付的 [nán duìfu de]

stuck [stʌk] I PT, PP *of* **stick** II ADJ ▶ **to be stuck** (*unable to move*) [*object +*] 卡住 [qiǎzhù]; [*person +*] 陷于 [xiànyú]; (*unable to continue*) 卡住了 [kǎzhù le] ▶ **to get stuck** (*physically*) 被卡住; (*with work*) 被难住

stud [stʌd] I N [c] **1** (*on clothing etc*) 饰钉 [shìdīng] **2** (*earring*) 耳钉 [ěrdīng] **3** (BRIT) (*on soles of boots*) 鞋钉 [xiédīng] **4** (*stud farm*) 种马场 [zhǒngmǎ chǎng] **5** (*inf*) (*man*) 性欲旺盛的男子 [xìngyù wàngshèng de nánzǐ] II VT ▶ **studded with** 镶有 [xiāngyǒu]

○ **student** ['stjuːdənt] I N [c] **1** (*at university*) 大学生 [dà xuéshēng] **2** (*at school*) 中学生 [zhōng xuéshēng] II CPD [复合词] [+ *life, pub*] 学生 [xuéshēng]; [+ *friends*] 同学 [tóngxué] ▶ **a law/medical student** 一名法律/医学学生
▶ **a student nurse/teacher** 一名实习护士/教师

student driver (US) N [c] 见习司机 [jiànxí sījī] [英 = **learner driver**]

studio ['stjuːdɪəʊ] N [c] **1** (TV, RAD, MUS) 摄影室 [shèyǐng shì] **2** [*of artist*] 画室 [huàshì]; [*of photographer*] 摄影室

studio apartment (US) N [c] 带有厨房和卫生间的小型套房 [英 = **studio flat**]

studio flat (BRIT) N [c] 带有厨房和卫生间的小型套房 [美 = **studio apartment**]

○ **study** ['stʌdɪ] I N **1** [u] (*activity*) 学习 [xuéxí] ▷ **rooms set aside for study** 专供学习的房间 **2** [c] (*piece of research*) 研究 [yánjiū] ▷ **the first study of the drug's effects** 第一项探讨药物作用的研究 **3** [c] (*room*) 书房 [shūfáng] II VT **1** [+ *subject*] 攻读 [gōngdú] **2** [+ *sb's face, evidence*] 仔细察看 [zǐxì chákàn] III VI 学习 [xuéxí] IV **studies** NPL 学业 [xuéyè] ▶ **to make a study of sth** 研究某事 ▶ **business/European studies** 商务/欧洲研究

stuff [stʌf] I N [u] **1** (*things*) 物品 [wùpǐn] **2** (*substance*) 东西 [dōngxi] II VT **1** ▶ **to stuff sth in/under sth** 把某物塞入某物内/塞到某物下面 [bǎ mǒuwù sāirù mǒuwù nèi/sāidào mǒuwù xiàmiàn] **2** ▶ **to stuff sth with sth** 用某物装满某物 [yòng mǒuwù zhuāngmǎn mǒuwù] **3** (CULIN) [+ *peppers, mushrooms*] 给…装馅 [gěi...zhuāngxiàn]; [+ *chicken, turkey*] 把填料塞入 [bǎ tiánliào sāirù] **4** [+ *toy, pillow*] 填塞 [tiánsāi] **5** [+ *dead animal*] 制成标本 [zhìchéng biāoběn] **6** ▶ **my nose is stuffed up** 我鼻子堵了 [wǒ bízi dǔ le] ▶ **get stuffed!** (BRIT: *inf!*) 去你的!

stuffing ['stʌfɪŋ] N [u] (*in sofa, chicken etc*) 填料 [tiánliào]

stuffy ['stʌfɪ] ADJ **1** [+ *room*] 闷热的 [mēnrè de] **2** [+ *person, ideas*] 古板的 [gǔbǎn de]

stumble ['stʌmbl] VI **1** (*while moving*) 绊脚 [bànjiǎo] **2** (*while speaking*) 结巴 [jiēba]
▶ **stumble across, stumble on** VT FUS [不可拆分] 偶然遇到 [ǒurán yùdào]

stump [stʌmp] I N [c] **1** [*of tree*] 树桩 [shùzhuāng] **2** [*of limb*] 残肢 [cánzhī] II VT ▶ **to be stumped** 被难倒 [bèi nándǎo] ▶ **stump up** VT (BRIT: *inf*) [+ *money*] 付清 [fùqīng]

stun [stʌn] VT **1** (*shock*) 使震惊 [shǐ zhènjīng] **2** (*daze*) 使昏迷 [shǐ hūnmí]

stung [stʌŋ] PT, PP *of* **sting**

stunk [stʌŋk] PP *of* **stink**

stunned [stʌnd] ADJ (*shocked*) 目瞪口呆的 [mùdèng kǒudāi de] ▶ **a stunned silence** 哑口无言

stunning ['stʌnɪŋ] ADJ **1** (*impressive*) 惊人的 [jīngrén de] **2** (*beautiful*) [+ *person, dress etc*] 极漂亮的 [jí piàoliàng de]

stunt [stʌnt] I N [c] **1** (*in film*) 惊险动作 [jīngxiǎn dòngzuò] **2** (*publicity stunt*) 噱头 [xuétóu] II VT [+ *growth, development*] 阻碍…的正常发育 [zǔài...de zhèngcháng fāyù]

stupid ['stjuːpɪd] ADJ **1** [+ *person*] 笨的 [bèn de] **2** [+ *question, idea, mistake*] 愚蠢的 [yúchǔn de] **3** (*inf*) 乏味的 [fáwèi de]

stupidity [stjuː'pɪdɪtɪ] N [u] 愚蠢 [yúchǔn]

sturdy ['stəːdɪ] ADJ **1** [+ *object*] 结实的 [jiēshi de] **2** [+ *person*] 健壮的 [jiànzhuàng de]

stutter ['stʌtə(r)] I N [c] 口吃 [kǒuchī] II VI

结结巴巴地说 [jiējie bābā de shuō] ▶ **to have a stutter, speak with a stutter** 结结巴巴地说

style [staɪl] I N **1** [c] (type) 方式 [fāngshì] **2** [U] (elegance) 风度 [fēngdù] **3** [C/U] (design) 样式 [yàngshì] II VT **1** [+ hair] 打理 [dǎlǐ] **2** [+ clothes] 使符合特定款式 [shǐ fúhé tèdìng kuǎnshì] ▶ **in the latest style** 最新式样

stylish ['staɪlɪʃ] ADJ 时髦的 [shímáo de]

stylist ['staɪlɪst] N [c] **1** (hair stylist) 发型师 [fàxíng shī] **2** (literary) 文体家 [wéntǐjiā]

sub... [sʌb] PREFIX **1** (under) 下 [xià] **2** (subordinate) 分支 [fēnzhī] **3** (inferior) 次于 [cìyú]

subconscious [sʌb'kɔnʃəs] I N [s] 潜意识 [qián yìshí] II ADJ 潜意识的 [qián yìshí de]

subdued [səb'dju:d] ADJ **1** [+ person] 闷闷不乐的 [mènmèn bùlè de] **2** [+ light] 柔和的 [róuhé de]

subject [n 'sʌbdʒɪkt, vb səb'dʒɛkt] I N [c] **1** (matter) 主题 [zhǔtí] **2** (SCOL) 科目 [kēmù] **3** [of country] 国民 [guómín] **4** (GRAM) 主语 [zhǔyǔ] II VT ▶ **to subject sb to sth** 使某人经受某事 [shǐ mǒurén jīngshòu mǒushì] III ADJ ▶ **to be subject to** 遭到 [zāodào] ▶ **to change the subject** 改变话题 ▶ **subject to availability** 以可取得为准 ▶ **prices may be subject to alteration** 价格可能会有变动

subjective [səb'dʒɛktɪv] ADJ 主观的 [zhǔguān de]

subject matter N [U] 题材 [tícái]

submarine [sʌbmə'ri:n] N [c] 潜水艇 [qiánshuǐtǐng]

submerge [səb'mə:dʒ] I VT 使淹没 [shǐ yānmò] II VI [submarine +] 潜入水中 [qiánrù shuǐzhōng] ▶ **to submerge o.s. in sth** (fig) 献身于某事

submission [səb'mɪʃən] N **1** [U] (subjection) 屈服 [qūfú] **2** [U] (frm) [of document] 提交 [tíjiāo] **3** [c] (proposal) 呈递材料 [chéngdì cáiliào]

submit [səb'mɪt] I VT [+ proposal, application, claim etc] 提交 [tíjiāo] II VI ▶ **to submit to sth** 屈服于某物 [qūfú yú mǒuwù]

subordinate [n, adj sə'bɔ:dɪnət, vb sə'bɔ:dɪneɪt] I N [c] 下属 [xiàshǔ] II ADJ **1** [+ officer, position, role] 下级的 [xiàjí de] **2** ▶ **to be subordinate to sb** 是某人的下属 [shì mǒurén de xiàshǔ] **3** ▶ **to be subordinate to sth** 从属于某事物 [cóngshǔyú mǒuwù] III VT ▶ **to subordinate sth to sth** 使某物服从某物 [shǐ mǒuwù fúcóng mǒuwù]

subordinate clause N 从句 [cóngjù]

subscribe [səb'skraɪb] VI ▶ **to subscribe (to sth)** [+ magazine, service] 订阅 [dìngyuè]; [+ fund, charity] 定期捐款 [dìngqī juānkuǎn] ▶ **I don't subscribe to that view** 我不赞成那个看法

subscriber [səb'skraɪbə(r)] N [c] **1** (to magazine, newspaper) 订阅者 [dìngyuè zhě] **2** (to service) 用户 [yònghù]

subscription [səb'skrɪpʃən] N [c] **1** (to magazine, service) 订阅 [dìngyuè] **2** (money paid) 订阅费 [dìngyuè fèi] **3** (membership dues) 注册费 [zhùcè fèi] **4** (to charity) 捐赠 [juānzèng] ▶ **to take out a subscription to** [+ organization] 注册; [+ magazine etc] 订阅

subsequent ['sʌbsɪkwənt] (frm) ADJ **1** (later) [+ events, generations] 随后的 [suíhòu de] **2** (further) [+ research, investigations] 进一步的 [jìnyíbù de] ▶ **subsequent to** 在···之后

subsequently ['sʌbsɪkwəntlɪ] (frm) ADV 后来 [hòulái]

subside [səb'saɪd] VI **1** [feeling +] 平息 [píngxī] **2** [flood, river +] 减退 [jiǎntuì] **3** [earth, building +] 下陷 [xiàxiàn]

subsidiary [səb'sɪdɪərɪ] I ADJ **1** [+ question, role] 次要的 [cìyào de] **2** (BRIT: UNIV) [+ subject] 辅助的 [fǔzhù de] II N [c] **1** (subsidiary company) 子公司 [zǐ gōngsī] **2** (BRIT: UNIV) (subsidiary subject) 辅助科目 [fǔzhù kēmù]

subsidize ['sʌbsɪdaɪz] VT 给···补助金 [gěi···bǔzhùjīn]

subsidy ['sʌbsɪdɪ] N [c] 补助金 [bǔzhù jīn]

substance ['sʌbstəns] N **1** [c] (matter) 物质 [wùzhì] **2** [s] (frm) [of speech, article etc] 要旨 [yàozhǐ] **3** [U] (frm) (truth) 根据 [gēnjù] **4** [U] (importance, significance) 实质 [shízhì] ▶ **a man of substance** (frm) 要人 ▶ **to lack substance** [speech, article etc +] 缺乏实质性内容

substantial [səb'stænʃl] ADJ **1** [+ building] 牢固的 [láogù de] **2** [+ meal] 丰盛的 [fēngshèng de]; [+ improvement] 重大的 [zhòngdà de]; [+ reward, amount] 相当数额的 [xiāngdāng shù'é de]

substantially [səb'stænʃəlɪ] (frm) ADV **1** (by a large amount) 在很大程度上 [zài hěndà chéngdù shang] **2** (in essence) 基本上 [jīběn shang]

substitute ['sʌbstɪtju:t] I N [c] **1** (person) 代替者 [dàitì zhě] **2** (thing) 代用品 [dàiyòngpǐn] **3** (FOOTBALL) 替补队员 [tìbǔ duìyuán] II VT ▶ **to substitute sth (for sth)** 用某物代替(某物) [yòng mǒuwù dàitì mǒuwù] III VI ▶ **to substitute for** [person +] 接替 [jiētì]; [thing +] 代替 [dàitì]

substitution [sʌbstɪ'tju:ʃən] N [C/U] 代替 [dàitì]; (FOOTBALL) 替换 [tìhuàn]

subtitles ['sʌbtaɪtlz] NPL 字幕 [zìmù]

subtle ['sʌtl] ADJ **1** [+ change, difference] 细微的 [xìwēi de] **2** [+ smell, sound, etc] 隐约的 [yǐnyuē de]; [+ scent] 淡雅的 [dànyǎ de] **3** (indirect) [+ person] 敏锐的 [mǐnruì de]

subtlety ['sʌtltɪ] N **1** [c] (nuance) 细微差别 [xìwēi chābié] **2** [U] (indirect methods) 含蓄的方式 [hánxù de fāngshì] **3** [U] (art of being subtle) 微妙之处 [wēimiào zhīchù]

subtract [səb'trækt] VT ▶ **to subtract sth (from sth)** (从某数中)减去某数 [(cóng mǒushù zhōng) jiǎnqù mǒushù]

suburb ['sʌbə:b] I N [C] 郊区 [jiāoqū] II **the suburbs** NPL 郊区 [jiāoqū]

suburban [sə'bə:bən] ADJ **1** [+ shopping centre, train etc] 郊区的 [jiāoqū de] **2** (pej) [+ clothes, lifestyle] 古板的 [gǔbǎn de]

subway ['sʌbweɪ] N [C] **1** (US) (underground railway) 地铁 [dìtiě] [英 = underground] **2** (BRIT) (underpass) 地下通道 [dìxià tōngdào] [美 = underpass]

succeed [sək'si:d] I VI [plan, person +] 成功 [chénggōng]; [marriage +] 美满 [měimǎn] II VT **1** [+ person] (in job) 接替 [jiētì] **2** (follow) 继…之后 [jì…zhīhòu] ▶ to succeed in doing sth 成功地做某事 ▶ to succeed to the throne 继承王位

success [sək'sɛs] N [U/C] 成功 [chénggōng] ▶ without success 一无所成

successful [sək'sɛsful] ADJ **1** [+ attempt, film, product] 成功的 [chénggōng de] **2** [+ writer, lawyer] 有成就的 [yǒu chéngjiù de] ▶ the successful candidate 获胜的候选人 ▶ to be successful in doing sth 在做某事方面成功

successfully [sək'sɛsfəlɪ] ADV 成功地 [chénggōng de]

succession [sək'sɛʃən] N **1** [S] (series) 一连串 [yī liánchuàn] **2** [U] (to throne etc) 继承 [jìchéng] ▶ for the third year in succession 连续3年 ▶ in quick succession 紧接着

successive [sək'sɛsɪv] ADJ [+ governments, years, attempts] 接连的 [jiēlián de] ▶ on 3 successive days 接连3天

successor [sək'sɛsə(r)] N [C] 继任者 [jìrènzhě] ▶ to be the successor to sb 做某人的接班人

succumb [sə'kʌm] (frm) VI ▶ to succumb (to) (to temptation) 抵挡不住 [dǐdǎng bùzhù] ▶ to succumb to illness 屈服疾病压弯

○ **such** [sʌtʃ] ADJ **1** (of this kind) 此类的 [cǐlèi de] ▷ Such a book should be praised, not banned. 此类书应该得到赞扬，而不应被禁止。**2** (emphasizing similarity) 诸如此类 [zhūrú cǐlèi] ▷ It was in Brighton or Bournemouth or some such place. 是在布赖顿或伯恩茅斯，或诸如此类的地方。**3** (so much) 这等 [zhèděng] ▷ He showed such courage in the face of adversity. 他在厄运面前显示出这等勇气。▶ such a(n) 那么 ▷ It was such a lovely day. 那一天天气那么好。▶ such a lot of 那么多 ▷ such a way that… 以致于… ▶ such as (like) 像 ▷ countries such as France, Germany, and Italy 像法国、德国、意大利等国家 ▶ you're welcome to borrow such books as I have 我只有这些书，但是你尽管借 ▶ I said no such thing 我没有这样讲 ▶ such as it is 尽管价值不过尔尔 ▶ as such (exactly) 如所指的 ▷ I am not a learner as such: I used to ride a bike years ago. 我并不完全是个初学者:许多年前也常常骑自行车。▷ He's not lazy as such: he just lacks energy. 他并不像所说的那样懒：他只是缺少活力。; (on its own) 就其本身而言 ▷ He is not

very interested in politics as such. 他对政治本身并不大感兴趣。

such 修饰单数可数名词时，后面跟 a 或 an。…such a pleasant surprise…such an old car… 修饰名词复数或不可数名词时，后面不加 a 或 an。…such beautiful girls…such power… 不能用 such 指代当场的某事物或说话人所在地，而要用 like that 或 like this。例如，你称赞某人的手表时，不能说 I'd like such a watch，而应说 I'd like a watch like that。同样，谈到目前你所居住的城镇时，不能说 There's not much to do in such a town，而应说 There's not much to do in a town like this.

such-and-such ['sʌtʃənsʌtʃ] ADJ 某某 [mǒumǒu]

suck [sʌk] I VT **1** [+ ice-lolly, sweet] 含在嘴里舔吃 [hánzài zuǐlǐ tiǎnchī]; [+ dummy, thumb] 吮 [shǔn] **2** [pump, machine +] 抽吸 [chōuxī] II VI ▶ to suck (on/at sth) 吮(某物) [shǔn (mǒuwù)]

Sudan [su'dɑ:n] N 苏丹 [Sūdān]

Sudanese [su:də'ni:z] I ADJ 苏丹的 [Sūdān de] II N [C] (person) 苏丹人 [Sūdānrén]

sudden ['sʌdn] ADJ 意外的 [yìwài de] ▶ all of a sudden 出乎意料

suddenly ['sʌdnlɪ] ADV 突然 [tūrán]

sue [su:] I VT 起诉 [qǐsù] II VI 提起诉讼 [tíqǐ sùsòng] ▶ to sue sb for damages 控告某人要求赔偿

suede [sweɪd] I N [U] 仿麂皮 [fǎng jǐpí] II CPD [复合词] [+ shoes, handbag] 仿麂皮 [fǎng jǐpí]

suffer ['sʌfə(r)] I VT **1** [+ blow, setback] 遭受 [zāoshòu] **2** [+ pain, illness] 承受 [chéngshòu] II VI **1** (due to pain, illness poverty etc) [activity +] 受损失 [shòu sǔnshī] **2** (be badly affected) [person +] 受苦难 [shòu kǔnàn] ▶ to suffer from shock/diarrhoea 受惊吓/患腹泻

sufferer ['sʌfərə(r)] N [C] 患者 [huànzhě]

suffering ['sʌfərɪŋ] N [C/U] 痛苦 [tòngkǔ]

suffice [sə'faɪs] (frm) VI 足够 [zúgòu] ▶ suffice it to say that… 只要说…就够了

sufficient [sə'fɪʃənt] ADJ **1** 足够的 [zúgòu de] **2** (frm) [+ condition, cause] 充足的 [chōngzú de] ▶ to be sufficient for sth 对某事来说足够了 ▶ to be sufficient to do sth 足够做某事 ▶ sufficient money to do sth/for sth 足够的资金来做某事/付某笔费用

sufficiently [sə'fɪʃəntlɪ] ADV **1** [recover, provide +] 充分地 [chōngfèn de] **2** [+ large, powerful] 足够地 [zúgòu de]

suffocate ['sʌfəkeɪt] I VI **1** (die) 闷死 [mēnsǐ] **2** (have difficulty breathing) 呼吸困难 [hūxī kùnnán] II VT 使窒息 [shǐ zhìxí]

sugar ['ʃʊɡə(r)] I N [U/C] 糖 [táng] II VT [+ tea etc] 加糖 [jiātáng]

○ **suggest** [sə'dʒɛst] VT 1 (propose) 建议 [jiànyì] ▷ We have to suggest possible topics for next term's class. 我们需要就下学期的课题提些建议。2 (indicate) 显示出 [xiǎnshì chū] ▷ His expression suggested some pleasure at the fact that I had come. 他的表情显示出他对我的到来有些好感。▶ to suggest that... (propose) 建议··· ▷ I suggested that we walk to the park. 我建议走路去公园。; (indicate) 显示出··· ▷ Early reports suggested that he would lose heavily. 早期报告显示出他会惨败。; (imply) 暗示 ▷ I'm not suggesting (that) that is what is happening. 我并未暗示说现在就是这样。

suggestion [sə'dʒɛstʃən] N [C] 1 (proposal) 建议 [jiànyì] 2 (indication) 暗示 [ànshì] 3 (association) 联想 [liánxiǎng] ▶ a suggestion of sth 细微的迹象 ▶ to make a suggestion 提建议

suggestive [sə'dʒɛstɪv] ADJ [remark] 挑逗的 [tiǎodòu de] ▶ to be suggestive of sth 使人联想起某物

suicide ['suɪsaɪd] I N 1 [C/U] 自杀 [zìshā] 2 [U] (harmful action) 自取灭亡 [zìqǔ mièwáng] 3 [C] (person) 自杀者 [zìshāzhě] II CPD [复合词] [+ attack, mission] 自杀性 [zìshā xìng] ▷ a suicide bomber 人肉炸弹 ▶ to commit suicide 自杀

suit [su:t] I N [C] 1 (man's, woman's) 西装 [xīzhuāng] 2 (for particular activity) 套装 [tàozhuāng] 3 (LAW) 诉案 [sòng àn] 4 (CARDS) 一组同样花色的纸牌 [yīzǔ tóngyàng huāsè de zhǐpái] II VT 1 (be convenient, appropriate) 对··· 合适 [duì···héshì] 2 (colour, clothes +) [+ person] 适合 [shìhé] ▶ to file or bring a suit against sb (US: LAW) 起诉某人 ▶ to follow suit (do the same) 跟着做 ▶ to suit sth to sb/sth (adapt) 使某物适合于某人/某物 ▶ to be suited to doing sth 适宜于做某事 ▶ to suit o.s. 随自己的意愿行事 ▶ suit yourself! 自便! ▶ to be well suited (to each other) (互相)很搭配

suitable ['su:təbl] ADJ 1 (convenient) [+ time, place] 合适的 [héshì de] 2 (appropriate) [+ person, clothes etc] 适合的 [shìhé de]

suitably ['su:təblɪ] ADV 1 [+ dressed, qualified] 适当地 [shìdàng de] 2 [+ impressed, amazed] 适宜地 [shìyí de]

suitcase ['su:tkeɪs] N [C] 手提箱 [shǒutíxiāng]

suite [swi:t] N [C] 1 (in hotel, large building) 套间 [tàojiān] see also en suite 2 (furniture) 一套家具 [yītào jiājù] ▶ a bedroom/dining room suite 一套卧室/饭厅家具 ▶ a bathroom suite 一套浴具

sulfur ['sʌlfə(r)] (US) N = sulphur

sulk [sʌlk] I N [C] 生闷气 [shēng mènqì] II VI 生闷气 [shēng mènqì] ▶ to be in a sulk 生闷气

sulphur, (US) **sulfur** ['sʌlfə(r)] N [U] 硫磺 [liúhuáng]

sultana [sʌl'tɑ:nə] (BRIT) N [C] 无核小葡萄干 [wúhé xiǎo pútáo gān]

sum [sʌm] I N [C] 1 (amount) 数额 [shù'é] 2 (calculation) 算术题 [suànshù tí] 3 (MATH) (total) 总数 [zǒngshù] ▶ to do a sum 算术 ▶ in sum (frm) 简而言之
▶ **sum up** I VT 1 (describe briefly) 概括 [gàikuò] 2 (epitomize) 代表 [dàibiǎo] II VI 总结 [zǒngjié]

summarize ['sʌmaraɪz] I VT 概括 [gàikuò] II VI 总结 [zǒngjié]

summary ['sʌmərɪ] I N [C] 1 摘要 [zhāiyào] II ADJ (frm) [+ justice, execution] 草率的 [cǎoshuài de] ▶ in summary 概括地说

summer ['sʌmə(r)] I N [C/U] 夏季 [xiàjì] II CPD [复合词] [+ dress, weather, sunshine] 夏季 [xiàjì] ▶ in (the) summer 在夏季

summertime ['sʌmətaɪm] N [U] 夏季 [xiàjì]

summit ['sʌmɪt] N [C] 1 [of mountain] 峰顶 [fēngdǐng] 2 (POL) (meeting) 高峰会议 [gāofēng huìyì]

summon ['sʌmən] VT 1 [+ person, police, help] 召唤 [zhàohuàn] 2 (LAW) 传讯 [chuánxùn] 3 (also: summon up) [+ strength, courage] 鼓起 [gǔqǐ]

Sun. ABBR (= Sunday) 星期天 [xīngqītiān]

sun [sʌn] N 1 [S/C] (in the sky) 太阳 [tàiyáng] 2 [U] (heat) 太阳的光和热 [tàiyáng de guāng hé rè]; (light) 阳光 [yángguāng] ▶ to sit/lie in the sun 坐/躺在阳光下 ▶ to catch the sun 被晒黑 ▶ everything under the sun 世上万物

sunbathe ['sʌnbeɪð] VI 晒日光浴 [shài rìguāngyù]

sunblock ['sʌnblɒk] N [C/U] 防晒霜 [fángshài shuāng]

sunburn ['sʌnbə:n] N [U] 晒斑 [shàibān]

sunburnt ['sʌnbə:nt] ADJ = sunburned

sunburned ['sʌnbə:nd], **sunburnt** ADJ 晒伤的 [shàishāng de]

Sunday ['sʌndɪ] N [C/U] 星期天 [xīngqītiān] see also **Tuesday**

⊙ **SUNDAY LUNCH**

● 英国传统的 **Sunday lunch** 以大块烤肉
● 为主菜, 如牛肉、猪肉、羊肉或鸡肉。
● 除肉类之外, 还配有烤土豆、蔬菜, 可
● 能还有 **Yorkshire pudding**——一种用加
● 牛奶、鸡蛋的面糊做成的脆皮可口的
● 饼, 要在炉里烤到表层胀起才算好。
● **gravy**（调味肉汁）也会在餐桌上见到。
● 自己不想做也没关系, 许多酒吧和餐馆
● 提供 **Sunday lunch**。

sunflower ['sʌnflauə(r)] N [C] 向日葵 [xiàngrìkuí]

sung [sʌŋ] PP of sing

sunglasses ['sʌnglɑ:sɪz] NPL 墨镜 [mòjìng]

sunk [sʌŋk] PP of sink

sunlight ['sʌnlaɪt] N [U] 阳光 [yángguāng]

sunny ['sʌnɪ] ADJ **1** [+ weather, day] 晴朗的 [qínglǎng de] **2** [+ place] 阳光充足的 [yángguāng chōngzú de] **3** [+ disposition, person] 乐观的 [lèguān de] ▶ **it is sunny** 天气晴朗

sunrise ['sʌnraɪz] N **1** [U] (time) 拂晓 [fúxiǎo] **2** [c] (sky) 日出 [rìchū] ▶ **at sunrise** 拂晓时分

sun roof N [c] (on car) 遮阳篷顶 [zhēyáng péngdǐng]

sun screen N [C/U] 遮光屏 [zhēguāng píng]

sunset ['sʌnsɛt] N **1** [U] (time) 傍晚 [bàngwǎn] **2** [c] (sky) 日落 [rìluò] ▶ **at sunset** 傍晚时

sunshine ['sʌnʃaɪn] N [U] 阳光 [yángguāng]

suntan ['sʌntæn] I N [c] 晒黑 [shàihēi] II CPD [复合词] [+ lotion, cream] 防晒 [fángshài] ▶ **to get a suntan** 皮肤晒黑

super ['suːpə(r)] (BRIT: inf) ADJ 极好的 [jíhǎo de]

superb [suː'pəːb] ADJ 极好的 [jíhǎo de]

superficial [suːpə'fɪʃl] ADJ **1** [+ wound, injury, damage] 表皮的 [biǎopí de] **2** [+ knowledge, analysis] 表面性的 [biǎomiàn xìng de] **3** (pej) [+ person] 肤浅的 [fūqiǎn de]

superintendent [suːpərɪn'tɛndənt] N [c] **1** (POLICE) (BRIT) 警督 [jǐngdū]; (US) 警长 [jǐngzhǎng] **2** [of place, activity] 主管人 [zhǔguǎn rén] **3** (US) [of building, school] 看门人 [kānménrén] 〔英=**caretaker**〕

superior [suː'pɪərɪə(r)] I ADJ **1** (better) 优秀的 [yōuxiù de] **2** (more senior) 上级的 [shàngjí de] **3** (pej) (smug) 高傲的 [gāo'ào de] II N [c] (in rank) 上级 [shàngjí] ▶ **superior to** 优于

superiority [suːpɪərɪ'ɔrɪtɪ] N [U] 优势 [yōushì]

supermarket ['suːpəmaːkɪt] N [U] 超级市场 [chāojí shìchǎng]

supernatural [suːpə'nætʃərəl] I ADJ [+ creature, powers] 神奇的 [shénqí de] II N ▶ **the supernatural** 超自然事物 [chāo zìrán shìwù]

superpower ['suːpəpauə(r)] (POL) N [c] 超级大国 [chāojí dàguó]

superstition [suːpə'stɪʃən] N [C/U] 迷信 [míxìn]

superstitious [suːpə'stɪʃəs] ADJ [+ person, fear, belief] 迷信的 [míxìn de]

supervise ['suːpəvaɪz] VT [+ person, activity] 监督 [jiāndū]

supervision [suːpə'vɪʒən] N [U] [of person] 管理 [guǎnlǐ]; [of activity] 监督 [jiāndū] ▶ **under medical supervision** 遵循医嘱

supervisor ['suːpəvaɪzə(r)] N [c] **1** [of workers] 监工 [jiāngōng] **2** [of student] 导师 [dǎoshī]

supper ['sʌpə(r)] N [C/U] **1** (early evening) 晚餐 [wǎncān] **2** (late evening) 夜宵 [yèxiāo] ▶ **to have supper** 吃晚餐

用法参见 **meal**

supple ['sʌpl] ADJ **1** [+ object, material] 柔韧的 [róurèn de] **2** [+ person, body] 轻盈的 [qīngyíng de]

supplement [n 'sʌplɪmənt, vb sʌplɪ'mɛnt] I N [c] **1** (additional amount) [of vitamins, money etc] 补充 [bǔchōng] **2** [of book] 补编 [bǔbiān] **3** [of newspaper, magazine] 增刊 [zēngkān] II VT 补充 [bǔchōng]

supplier [sə'plaɪə(r)] N [c] 供应商 [gōngyìng shāng]

supply [sə'plaɪ] I VT **1** (provide) 提供 [tígōng] **2** (COMM) (deliver) 送货 [sònghuò] II N **1** [C/U] (stock) 供应量 [gōngyìng liàng] **2** [U] (supplying) 供应 [gōngyìng] III **supplies** NPL **1** (food) 供给 [gōngjǐ] **2** (MIL) 军需品 [jūnxū pǐn] ▶ **to supply sth to sb** 为某人提供某物 ▶ **to supply sb/sth with sth** 为某人/某物提供某物 ▶ **it comes supplied with an adaptor** 内含变压器 ▶ **food is in short supply** 食品供应不足 ▶ **the electricity/gas supply** 电力/煤气供应 ▶ **supply and demand** (ECON) 供求

○ support [sə'pɔːt] I N **1** [U] (moral) 支持 [zhīchí] ▷ The minister gave his full support to the reforms. 首相对改革给予大力支持。 **2** [U] (financial) 资助 [zīzhù] ▷ the proposal to cut agricultural support by 15% 削减15%的农业资助的提议 **3** [U] (kindness, help) 帮助 [bāngzhù] ▷ mentally ill people in need of support 患心理疾病的人士需要帮助 **4** [c] (for object, structure) 支承 [zhīchéng] **5** [U] (balance) 支撑物 [zhīchēng wù] ▷ Alice was leaning against him for support. 艾丽斯把他当支撑物靠着。 **6** [U] (evidence) (for theory, statement) 依据 [yījù] ▷ History offers some support for this view. 历史为此观点提供了某些依据。 II VT **1** (morally) [+ policy, strike etc] 支持 [zhīchí] ▷ He thanked everyone who had supported the strike. 他对支持罢工的所有人士表示感谢。 **2** (financially) 供养 [gōngyǎng] ▷ He has a wife and three children to support. 他需要养妻子和3个孩子。 **3** (hold up) [+ object, structure] 支承 [zhīchéng] ▷ the girders that supported the walkway 支承着人行道的大梁 **4** (hold up) [+ person] 撑着 [chēngzhe] ▷ Let your baby sit on the floor with cushions to support him. 让你的婴儿坐在地上，用坐垫撑着他。 **5** (substantiate) [+ theory, statement] 证实 [zhèngshí] ▷ There was no evidence to support such a theory. 没有证据来证实这一理论。 **6** [+ football team] 支持 [zhīchí] ▷ Tim supports Manchester United. 蒂姆支持曼联队。 ▶ **in support of** 支持 ▶ **to support o.s.** (financially) 养活自己

supporter [sə'pɔːtə(r)] N [c] **1** [of politician, policy] 支持者 [zhīchí zhě] **2** [of team] 追随者 [zhuīsuí zhě]

suppose [sə'pəuz] VT 认为 [rènwéi] ▶ **I suppose** 我想 ▶ **it was worse than she'd supposed** 事情比她想像的要糟 ▶ **I don't suppose she'll come** 我想她不会来 ▶ **he's about sixty, I suppose** 我想他大概60岁 ▶ **I suppose so/not** 我看是/不是这样 ▶ **suppose he was right** 假定他是对的 ▶ **he is supposed**

to do it (duty) 他应该做的 ▶ **he's supposed to be an expert** 人们以为他是个专家

supposedly [sə'pəʊzɪdlɪ] ADV 据称 [jùchēng]

supposing [sə'pəʊzɪŋ] CONJ 假使 [jiǎshǐ]

suppress [sə'prɛs] VT 1 [+ religion] 禁止 [jìnzhǐ]; [+ revolt] 镇压 [zhènyā] 2 [+ information, publication] 封锁 [fēngsuǒ] 3 [+ feelings] 抑制 [yìzhì] 4 [+ yawn, laugh, sneeze] 忍住 [rěnzhù]

supreme [su'pri:m] ADJ 1 (in titles) 最高的 [zuìgāo de] 2 (great) 极度的 [jídù de]

Supt, (ESP US) **Supt.** (POLICE) ABBR (= superintendent) 警长 [jǐngzhǎng]

surcharge ['sɜ:tʃɑ:dʒ] N [c] 附加费 [fùjiā fèi]

○ **sure** [ʃʊə(r)] I ADJ 1 (definite, convinced) 有把握的 [yǒu bǎwò de] ▷ How can you be sure? 你怎么这么有把握？ 2 (reliable) [+ remedy] 有效的 [yǒuxiào de]; [+ sign] 准确无误的 [zhǔnquè wúwù de] ▷ She has a sure grasp of social issues. 她对社会问题掌握得准确无误。 3 ▶ **to be sure to do sth** (certain) 肯定做某事 [kěndìng zuò mǒushì] ▷ Kids are sure to love crawling through the tunnel. 孩子们肯定喜欢爬隧道。 II ADV ▶ **she sure is pretty** (ESP US: inf) 她确实很漂亮 [tā quèshí hěn piàoliang] ▶ **to make sure that...** (take action) 保证… ▷ Make sure that you follow the instructions carefully. 你一定要仔细按照说明书做。 ▷ You must make sure that you finish your work on time. 你必须保证按时完成工作。; (check) 查明… ▷ He looked in the bathroom to make sure that he was alone. 他看了看洗澡间，确定是否只有他一个人。▶ **sure!** (inf) (of course) 当然了！ ▶ **sure enough** 果然 ▶ **to be sure of (doing) sth** 有把握(做)某事 ▶ **that's for sure** 毫无疑问 ▶ **I'm sure of it** 我确信 ▶ **I'm not sure how/why/when** 我不能肯定如何/为什么/什么时候 ▶ **to be sure of o.s.** 有自信心

surely ['ʃʊəlɪ] ADV (for emphasis) 想必 [xiǎngbì]; (frm) (certainly) 肯定 [kěndìng] ▶ **surely you don't mean that!** 你肯定不是这个意思！ ▶ **slowly but surely** 缓慢而稳步地

surf [sɜ:f] I N [U] 拍岸的浪花 [pāi'àn de lànghuā] II VI 冲浪 [chōnglàng] III VT ▶ **to surf the Internet** 网上冲浪 [wǎngshàng chōnglàng] ▶ **to go surfing** 去冲浪

surface ['sɜ:fɪs] I N 1 [c] [of object] 表面 [biǎomiàn] 2 [c] (top layer) 表层 [biǎocéng] 3 [c] [of lake, pond] 水面 [shuǐmiàn] 4 [s] (of mind, emotions) 外表 [wàibiǎo] II VI 1 [fish, diver +] 浮出水面 [fúchū shuǐmiàn] 2 [news +] 被揭露 [bèi jiēlù]; [feeling +] 显露 [xiǎnlù] 3 (inf) (rise from bed) 起床 [qǐchuáng] III VT [+ road] 铺路 [pūlù] ▶ **on the surface** 在表面上

surfboard ['sɜ:fbɔ:d] N [c] 冲浪板 [chōnglàng bǎn]

surfing ['sɜ:fɪŋ] N [U] 冲浪 [chōnglàng] see also **surf**

surge [sɜ:dʒ] I N [c] 1 [(in demand, interest)] 急剧上升 [jíjù shàngshēng] 2 [(in flow)] 汹涌

[xiōngyǒng] 3 [of emotion] 一阵 [yīzhèn] ▶ **a surge of electricity** 电涌 II VI 1 [water +] 奔腾 [bēnténg] 2 [people, vehicles +] 涌 [yǒng] 3 [level, rate +] 急剧上升 [jíjù shàngshēng] 4 (liter) [emotion +] 翻腾 [fānténg] 5 (ELEC) 突然增加 [tūrán zēngjiā] ▶ **to surge forward** 蜂拥向前

surgeon ['sɜ:dʒən] N [c] 外科医师 [wàikē yīshī]

surgery ['sɜ:dʒərɪ] N 1 [U] (treatment) 外科手术 [wàikē shǒushù] 2 [c] (BRIT) (room) [of doctor, dentist] 诊所 [zhěnsuǒ] 3 [c] (BRIT) (also: **surgery hours**) [of doctor, dentist] 门诊时间 [ménzhěn shíjiān] 4 [c] (BRIT) [of MP etc] 接待时间 [jiēdài shíjiān]

surgical ['sɜ:dʒɪkl] ADJ 1 [+ instrument, mask etc] 外科手术用的 [wàikē shǒushù yòng de] 2 [+ treatment, operation] 外科的 [wàikē de]

surname ['sɜ:neɪm] N [c] 姓 [xìng]

surpass [sɜ:'pɑ:s] (frm) VT 超过 [chāoguò]

surplus ['sɜ:pləs] I N [c] ▶ **a surplus (of sth)** 过剩的(某物) [guòshèng de (mǒuwù)] II ADJ [+ stock, grain etc] 过剩的 [guòshèng de] ▶ **a trade surplus** 贸易顺差 ▶ **it is surplus to our requirements** (frm) 超过我们的需要

surprise [sə'praɪz] I N 1 [c] (unexpected event) 意想不到的事物 [yìxiǎng bùdào de shìwù] 2 [U] (astonishment) 诧异 [chàyì] II N [c] [+ visit, announcement etc] 出人意料的 [chūrén yìliào de] III VT 1 (astonish) 使感到意外 [shǐ gǎndào yìwài] 2 (catch unawares) 使震惊 [shǐ zhènjīng] ▶ **it came as a surprise (to me)** 这出乎(我的)意料 ▶ **to take sb by surprise** 使某人吃惊 ▶ **to my (great) surprise** 使我(很)惊奇的是 ▶ **it surprised me that...** 令我吃惊的是… ▶ **it wouldn't surprise me if...** 如果…我不会感到吃惊

surprised [sə'praɪzd] ADJ 惊讶的 [jīngyà de] ▶ **to be surprised to find/see sth** 真没想到会发现/看到某物 ▶ **to be surprised at sth** 对某事感到吃惊 ▶ **to be surprised that...** 对…感到惊讶

请勿将 **surprised** 和 **surprising** 混淆。在发生意外或异常情况时，可以说你感到 **surprised**。I'm surprised at your behaviour...I was surprised that it was so cold in August... **surprising** 的事物让人感到 **surprised**。A surprising number of customers complained...It's not surprising that she was disappointed when he didn't arrive.

surprising [sə'praɪzɪŋ] ADJ [+ situation, announcement] 出人意外的 [chūrén yìwài de] ▶ **it is surprising how/that...** 真没想到如此/是…

用法参见 **surprised**

surprisingly [sə'praɪzɪŋlɪ] ADV 出人意外地 [chūrén yìwài de] ▶ **(somewhat) surprisingly, he agreed** 他(有点)出人意外地同意了

surrender [sə'rɛndə(r)] I N 1 [c/U] (act) 投

降 [tóuxiáng] **2** [U] [of weapons] 交出 [jiāochū]
II VI 投降 [tóuxiáng] **III** VT **1** [+ weapons,
territory] 交出 [jiāochū] **2** [+ claim, right] 放弃
[fàngqì]

surrogate ['sʌrəgɪt] **I** N [c] 替代品 [tìdài pǐn]
II ADJ (substitute) 替代的 [tìdài de]

surround [sə'raund] VT **1** [walls, circumstances +]
围绕 [wéirǎo] **2** [police, soldiers +] 包围 [bāowéi]
▶ **to surround o.s. with people/things** 周围
都是人/物

surrounding [sə'raundɪŋ] ADJ 周围的
[zhōuwéi de]

surroundings [sə'raundɪŋz] NPL 环境
[huánjìng]

surveillance [sə:'veɪləns] N [U] 监视 [jiānshì]
▶ **under surveillance** 在监视下

survey [n 'sə:veɪ, vb sə:'veɪ] **I** N [c] **1** (ESP BRIT)
[of house] 查勘 [chákān] [美 = inspection]
2 [of land] 测量 [cèliáng] **3** (poll) 民意测验
[mínyì cèyàn] **II** VT **1** (ESP BRIT) [+ house] 查
勘 [chákān] [美 = inspect] **2** (examine, measure)
[+ land] 测量 [cèliáng] **3** (carry out survey on)
[+ people, organizations] 调查 [diàochá] **4** (look at)
[+ scene, work etc] 审视 [shěnshì]

surveyor [sə'veɪə(r)] N [c] **1** [of land] 勘测员
[kāncèyuán] **2** (BRIT) [of buildings] 房产检视
员 [fángchǎn jiǎnshìyuán] [美 = **structural
engineer**]

survival [sə'vaɪvl] **I** N [U] [of person, company]
生存 [shēngcún] **II** CPD [复合词] [+ course, kit,
guide] 救生 [jiùshēng]

survive [sə'vaɪv] **I** VI **1** [person, animal +] 幸
存 [xìngcún] **2** [custom +] 继续存在 [jìxù
cúnzài] **II** VT **1** (outlive) [+ person] 比…活得
长 [bǐ…huódé cháng] **2** [+ accident, illness etc]
从…中逃生 [cóng…zhōng táoshēng] ▶ **to
survive on £80 a week** 每周靠80英镑过活

survivor [sə'vaɪvə(r)] N [c] **1** [of illness, accident]
幸存者 [xìngcúnzhě] **2** [of incest, abuse] 生还者
[shēnghuánzhě] ▶ **the only survivor from the
1990 team** 1990年队伍的惟一幸存者

susceptible [sə'sɛptəbl] ADJ **1** ▶ **susceptible
(to)** [+ heat, injury] 易受的 [yìshòu de]; [+ flattery,
pressure] 易受…影响的 [yìshòu…yīngxiǎng de]
2 [+ person] 易受感动的 [yìshòu gǎndòng de]

suspect [adj, n 'sʌspɛkt, vb səs'pɛkt] **I** ADJ
可疑的 [kěyí de] **II** N [c] (in crime) 嫌疑犯
[xiányí fàn] **III** VT **1** [+ person] 怀疑 [huáyí]
2 [+ sb's motives etc] 质疑 [zhìyí] **3** (think) 猜想
[cāixiǎng] ▶ **to suspect sb of doing sth** 怀疑某
人做某事 ▶ **to suspect that...** 怀疑…

suspend [səs'pɛnd] VT **1** (hang) 悬挂 [xuánguà]
2 (delay, stop) 暂停 [zàntíng] **3** (from employment)
暂令停职 [zànlìng tíngzhí]

suspended sentence [səs'pɛndɪd-] N [c] 缓
刑 [huǎnxíng]

suspenders [səs'pɛndəz] NPL **1** (BRIT) 吊袜
带 [diào wàdài] [美 = **garters**] **2** (US) 背带

suspense [səs'pɛns] N [U] **1** (uncertainty) 焦
虑 [jiāolǜ] **2** (in novel, film etc) 悬念 [xuánniàn]
▶ **to keep sb in suspense** 使某人处于紧张状态

suspension [səs'pɛnʃən] N **1** [c/U] (from job,
team) 暂令停职 [zànlìng tíngzhí] **2** [U] (in car etc)
减震装置 [jiǎnzhèn zhuāngzhì] **3** [U] [of payment,
flight etc] 暂停 [zàntíng]

suspension bridge N [c] 吊桥 [diàoqiáo]

suspicion [səs'pɪʃən] N **1** [c/U] (about crime,
wrongdoing) 怀疑 [huáiyí] **2** [c/U] (distrust) 怀
疑 [huáiyí] **3** [c] (idea) 模糊的想法 [móhu de
xiǎngfǎ] **4** [s] (trace, hint) 一点儿 [yìdiǎnr] ▶ **to
be arrested on suspicion of murder** 因谋杀嫌
疑被逮捕 ▶ **to be under suspicion** 受到怀疑

suspicious [səs'pɪʃəs] ADJ **1** [+ look] 表示怀疑
的 [biǎoshì huáiyí de]; [+ nature] 多疑的 [duōyí
de] **2** [+ circumstances, death, package] 可疑的
[kěyí de] ▶ **to be suspicious of or about sb/sth**
对某人/某事起疑心

sustain [səs'teɪn] VT **1** [+ interest, growth, life
etc] 维持 [wéichí] **2** [+ person] 支撑 [zhīchēng]
3 (frm) [+ injury, loss, defeat] 遭受 [zāoshòu]

SUV N ABBR (= sports utility vehicle) 越野车
[yuèyě chē]

SW ABBR **1** (= south-west) 西南部 [xīnán bù]
2 (RAD) (= short wave) 短波 [duǎnbō]

swagger ['swægə(r)] **I** N [s] 昂首阔步
[ángshǒu kuòbù] **II** VI 大摇大摆 [dàyáo dàbǎi]

swallow ['swɔləu] **I** N [c] **1** (bird) 燕子 [yàn zi]
2 [of food, drink] 吞咽 [tūnyàn] **II** VT **1** [+ food,
drink, pills] 吞下 [tūnxià] **2** [+ story, statement] 轻
信 [qīngxìn] **III** VI 吞咽 [tūnyàn] ▶ **to swallow
one's pride** 放下架子
▶ **swallow up** VT **1** [+ money, resources] 耗尽
[hàojìn] **2** [+ company] 吞并 [tūnbìng]

swam [swæm] PT of **swim**

swamp [swɔmp] **I** N [c/U] 沼泽 [zhǎozé]
II VT (flood) 浸没 [jìnmò] ▶ **to be swamped
with sth** 某事多得难以招架

swan [swɔn] N [c] 天鹅 [tiān'é]

swap [swɔp] **I** N [c] 交换 [jiāohuàn] **II** VT
1 ▶ **to swap sth (for)** (exchange for) (以某物) 作
交换 [yǐ mǒuwù zuò jiāohuàn]; (replace with)
以…替代某物 [yǐ…tìdài mǒuwù] **2** [+ stories,
opinions] 交换 [jiāohuàn] ▶ **to do a swap (with
sb)** (与某人) 交换 ▶ **to swap places (with sb)**
(与某人) 换位子

swarm [swɔ:m] **I** N [c] [of bees, ants, people]
群 [qún] **II** VI **1** [bees, ants +] 成群地行
进 [chéngqún de xíngjìn] **2** [people +] 蜂拥
[fēngyōng] ▶ **to be swarming with** 挤满

sway [sweɪ] **I** VI [person, tree +] 摇摆 [yáobǎi]
II VT (influence) 动摇 [dòngyáo] **III** N ▶ **to hold
sway (over sb/sth)** 有支配 (某人/某物) 的力量
[yǒu zhīpèi (mǒurén/mǒuwù) de lìliàng]

Swaziland ['swɑ:zɪlænd] N 斯威士兰
[Sīwēishìlán]

swear [swɛə(r)] (pt **swore**, pp **sworn**) I VI (curse) 咒骂 [zhòumà] II VT (promise) 宣誓 [xuānshì]
▶ **to swear that...** (promise) 发誓…; (confirm) 起誓保证… ▶ **to swear to do sth** 宣誓做某事 ▶ **to swear an oath** 起誓 ▶ **to be sworn to secrecy/silence** 发誓要保守秘密/保持沉默
▶ **swear by** VT FUS [不可拆分] ▶ **I swear by it/them** 我极其信赖某事/他们 [wǒ jíqí xìnlài mǒushì/tāmen]
▶ **swear in** VT [+ person] 使宣誓就职 [shǐ xuānshì jiùzhí]

swear word N [C] 骂人的话 [màrén de huà]

sweat [swɛt] I N [U] 汗水 [hànshuǐ] II VI 出汗 [chūhàn] ▶ **to be in a (cold) sweat** (lit) 出了一身(冷)汗; (fig) 吓得出了一身(冷)汗

sweater ['swɛtə(r)] N [C] 毛衣 [máoyī]

sweatshirt ['swɛtʃə:t] N [C] 棉毛衫 [miánmáoshān]

sweatsuit ['swɛtsu:t] N [C] 运动服 [yùndòngfú]

sweaty ['swɛtɪ] ADJ 满是汗的 [mǎnshì hàn de]

Swede [swi:d] N [C] 瑞典人 [Ruìdiǎnrén]

swede [swi:d] (BRIT) N [C/U] 洋大头菜 [yáng dàtóu cài] [美 = **rutabaga**]

Sweden ['swi:dn] N 瑞典 [Ruìdiǎn]

Swedish ['swi:dɪʃ] I ADJ 瑞典的 [Ruìdiǎn de] II N [U] (language) 瑞典语 [Ruìdiǎnyǔ]

sweep [swi:p] (pt, pp **swept**) I N [C] 1 ▶ **the floor could do with a sweep** 地板该扫了 [dìbǎn gāi sǎo le] 2 (curve) 蜿蜒 [wānyán] 3 (range) 广度 [guǎngdù] II VT 1 (with brush) 扫 [sǎo] 2 (with hand) 拂去 [fúqù]; [+ one's hair] 掠 [luè] 3 [wind +] 吹 [chuī]; [water, crowd +] 冲 [chōng] 4 [eyes, lights +] 扫视 [sǎoshì] III VI 1 ▶ **to sweep in/out/past** [person +] 昂首阔步地进来/出去/走过 [ángshǒu kuòbù de jìnlái/chūqù/zǒuguò] 2 [hand, arm +] 挥舞 [huīwǔ] 3 [wind +] 吹 [chuī] ▶ **to sweep sth under the carpet** or **rug** (fig) 隐瞒某事
▶ **sweep aside, sweep away** VT 一扫而空 [yīsǎo érkōng]
▶ **sweep up** I VI 清扫 [qīngsǎo] II VT [+ dirt, rubbish etc] 扫去 [sǎoqù]

sweet [swi:t] I N (BRIT) 1 [C] (chocolate, mint etc) 糖果 [tángguǒ] [美 = **candy**] 2 [C/U] (pudding) 甜点 [tiándiǎn] [美 = **dessert**] II ADJ 1 (sugary) 甜的 [tián de] 2 (fragrant) 芳香的 [fāngxiāng de] 3 [+ sound] 悦耳的 [yuè'ěr de] 4 [+ air, water] 清新的 [qīngxīn de] 5 (kind) 和蔼的 [hé'ǎi de] 6 (inf) (cute) 可爱的 [kě'ài de] 7 [+ revenge] 令人满意的 [lìngrén mǎnyì de] ▶ **to smell/taste sweet** 闻/尝起来甜美 [wén/cháng qǐlái tiánměi] ▶ **sweet and sour** 糖醋

sweetcorn ['swi:tkɔ:n] N [U] 1 (BOT) 甜玉米 [tián yùmǐ] 2 (CULIN) 玉米粒 [yùmǐ lì]

sweeten ['swi:tn] VT 使变甜 [shǐ biàntián]

sweetener ['swi:tnə(r)] N [C] 1 (sugar substitute) 代糖 [dàitáng] 2 (fig) 甜头 [tiántou]

sweetheart ['swi:tha:t] N [C] 1 (boyfriend/girlfriend) 心上人 [xīnshàng rén] 2 (form of address) 亲爱的 [qīn'àide]

sweetness ['swi:tnɪs] N [U] (of food, drink) 甜 [tián]

swell [swɛl] (pt **swelled**, pp **swollen** or **swelled**) I VI 1 (also: **swell up**) [face, ankle etc +] 肿胀 [zhǒngzhàng] 2 (increase) [amount, size +] 增加 [zēngjiā] 3 (liter) (get louder) 变响亮 [biàn xiǎngliàng] II VT 使增加 [shǐ zēngjiā] III N [S] [of sea] 海面波浪 [hǎimiàn bōlàng] IV ADJ (US: inf) (excellent) 出色的 [chūsè de] ▶ **to swell with pride** (liter) 充满自豪

swelling ['swɛlɪŋ] N [C/U] 肿块肿胀 [zhǒngkuàizhǒngzhàng]

swept [swɛpt] PT, PP of **sweep**

swerve [swə:v] I N [C] (in car etc) 改变方向 [gǎibiàn fāngxiàng] II VI [car etc +] 突然转向 [tūrán zhuǎnxiàng] III VT [+ car etc] 使突然转向 [shǐ tūrán zhuǎnxiàng]

swift [swɪft] I ADJ 1 [+ recovery] 快速的 [kuàisù de]; [+ response, decision] 敏捷的 [mǐnjié de] 2 [+ stream, movement] 速度快的 [sùdù kuài de] II N [C] (bird) 褐雨燕 [hè yǔyàn] ▶ **to be swift to do sth** 迅速地做某事

swim [swɪm] (pt **swam**, pp **swum**) I VI 1 [person, animal +] 游水 [yóushuǐ] 2 (as sport) 游泳 [yóuyǒng] 3 (fig) [room +] 旋转 [xuánzhuǎn] II VT 1 [+ river etc] 游过 [yóuguò] 2 [+ distance] 游 [yóu] III N [C] ▶ **to go for a swim** 去游泳 [qù yóuyǒng] ▶ **to go swimming** 去游泳 ▶ **my head is swimming** 我头晕

swimmer ['swɪmə(r)] N [C] 1 游泳者 [yóuyǒng zhě] 2 (sportsperson) 游泳运动员 [yóuyǒng yùndòngyuán] ▶ **he's a good swimmer** 他是个游泳好手

swimming ['swɪmɪŋ] N [U] 游泳 [yóuyǒng]

swimming pool N [C] 游泳池 [yóuyǒng chí]

swimming trunks (BRIT) NPL 游泳裤 [yóuyǒng kù] [美 = **trunks**]

swimsuit ['swɪmsu:t] N [C] 游泳衣 [yóuyǒng yī]

swing [swɪŋ] (pt, pp **swung**) I N 1 [C] (in playground) 秋千 [qiūqiān] 2 [C] (movement) 摇摆 [yáobǎi] 3 [C] (in opinions etc) 剧变 [jùbiàn] 4 [U] (MUS) 强节奏爵士音乐 [qiáng jiézòu juéshì yīnyuè] II VT 1 [+ arms, legs] 摆动 [bǎidòng] 2 [+ vehicle etc] 使转向 [shǐ zhuǎnxiàng] III VI 1 [pendulum etc +] 晃动 [huàngdòng] 2 [door etc +] 转动 [zhuǎndòng] 3 [vehicle +] 转向 [zhuǎnxiàng] 4 [person +] 摇摆 [yáobǎi] 5 [opinions, attitudes +] 剧变 [jùbiàn] ▶ **a swing to the left** (POL) 改向左派 ▶ **to get into the swing of things** 积极投入某事 ▶ **to be in full swing** [party etc +] 正处于全盛时期 ▶ **to take a swing at sb/sth** (try to hit) 挥拳打某人/某物
▶ **swing at** VT FUS [不可拆分] (try to hit) 挥拳打 [huīquán dǎ]

swipe [swaɪp] I VT 1 (inf) (steal) 偷 [tōu]

2 (through machine) [+ card] 刷卡 [shuākǎ] **II** VI
▸ **to swipe at** 猛打 [měngdǎ] **II** N ▸ **to take a
swipe at sb/sth** (lit) 挥臂猛击某人/某物 [huībì
měngjī mǒurén/mǒuwù]; (fig) (criticize) 含沙射
影地攻击某人/某物 [hánshāshèyǐng de gōngjī
mǒurén/mǒuwù]

swirl [swə:l] **I** VI [water, leaves +] 打旋 [dǎxuàn]
II VT 使旋动 [shǐ xuándòng] **III** N [C] 打旋
[dǎxuàn]

Swiss [swɪs] (pl **Swiss**) **I** ADJ 瑞士的 [Ruìshì
de] **II** N [C] (person) 瑞士人 [Ruìshìrén]

switch [swɪtʃ] **I** N [C] **1** (for light, radio etc) 开关
[kāiguān] **2** (change) 转变 [zhuǎnbiàn] **II** VT
1 (change) 改变 [gǎibiàn] **2** (exchange) 调换
[diàohuàn] **III** VI (change) 转变 [zhuǎnbiàn]
▸ **to switch two things round** or **over** 交换两
样东西的位置
▸ **switch off I** VT [+ light, engine, radio etc] 关掉
[guāndiào] **II** VI (inf) (stop paying attention) 失
去兴趣 [shīqù xìngqù]
▸ **switch on** VT [+ light, engine, radio etc] 开启
[kāiqǐ]

switchboard ['swɪtʃbɔːd] N [C] 交换台
[jiāohuàn tái]

Switzerland ['swɪtsələnd] N 瑞士 [Ruìshì]

swivel ['swɪvl] **I** VI ▸ **to swivel round** 转动
[zhuǎndòng] **II** VT ▸ **to swivel sth round** 使某
物转动 [shǐ mǒuwù zhuǎndòng]

swollen ['swəulən] **I** PP of **swell II** ADJ
1 [+ ankle, eyes etc] 肿胀的 [zhǒngzhàng de]
2 [+ lake, river etc] 涨水的 [zhǎngshuǐ de]

swoop [swuːp] **I** N [C] **1** (by police, soldiers) 突
袭 [tūxí] **2** [of bird, aircraft] 飞扑 [fēipū] **II** VI
1 [bird, aircraft +] 突然下落 [tūrán xiàluò]
2 [police, soldiers +] 突袭 [tūxí] ▸ **in** or **at one fell
swoop** 一下子

swop [swɒp] N, VT = **swap**

sword [sɔːd] N [C] 剑 [jiàn]

swordfish ['sɔːdfɪʃ] (pl **swordfish**) N [C/U] 箭
鱼 [jiànyú]

swore [swɔː(r)] PT of **swear**

sworn [swɔːn] **I** PP of **swear II** ADJ ▸ **a sworn
statement** 宣誓证词 [xuānshì zhèngcí] ▸ **to
be sworn enemies** 不共戴天的仇敌

swum [swʌm] PP of **swim**

swung [swʌŋ] PT, PP of **swing**

syllable ['sɪləbl] N [C] 音节 [yīnjié]

syllabus ['sɪləbəs] (ESP BRIT) N [C] 教学大纲
[jiàoxué dàgāng] ▸ **on the syllabus** 含在教
学大纲内

symbol ['sɪmbl] N [C] **1** (sign) 象征
[xiàngzhēng] **2** (MATH, CHEM) 符号 [fúhào]
3 (representation) 标志 [biāozhì]

symbolic [sɪm'bɒlɪk], **symbolical**
[sɪm'bɒlɪkl] ADJ **1** [importance, value, gesture] 象
征性的 [xiàngzhēng xìng de] **2** [+ language,
representation] 象征主义的 [xiàngzhēng zhǔyì
de] ▸ **to be symbolic of sth** 是某物的象征

symmetrical [sɪ'mɛtrɪkl] ADJ 对称的
[duìchèn de]

symmetry ['sɪmɪtrɪ] N [C/U] 对称性 [duìchèn
xìng]

sympathetic [sɪmpə'θɛtɪk] ADJ
1 (understanding) 有同情心的 [yǒu tóngqíngxīn
de] **2** (likeable) [+ person, character] 意气相
投的 [yìqì xiāngtóu de] **3** (supportive) 赞同
的 [zàntóng de] ▸ **to be sympathetic to sth**
(supportive) 赞同某事; (understanding)
同情某事

sympathize ['sɪmpəθaɪz] VI ▸ **to sympathize
(with)** (express sorrow for) [+ person] (对⋯) 表示
同情 [duì⋯ biǎoshì tóngqíng]; (understand)
[+ sb's feelings] 体谅 [tǐliàng]; (support)
[+ organization, cause, idea] 支持 [zhīchí]

sympathy ['sɪmpəθɪ] **I** N [U] 同情心
[tóngqíng xīn] **II** sympathies NPL (support) 支
持 [zhīchí]; (condolences) 慰问 [wèiwèn] ▸ **to
have** or **feel sympathy for sb** 同情某人 ▸ **to
have sympathy with** [+ idea, attitude] 赞同
▸ **with deepest sympathy** 深表慰问 ▸ **to
come out in sympathy (with sb)** [workers +] 声
援(某人)

symphony ['sɪmfənɪ] N [C] 交响乐 [jiāoxiǎng
yuè]

symptom ['sɪmptəm] N [C] **1** (MED) 症状
[zhèngzhuàng] **2** (indication) 征兆 [zhēngzhào]

synagogue ['sɪnəgɔg] N [C] 犹太教堂 [yóutài
jiàotáng]

synchronize ['sɪŋkrənaɪz] **I** VT [+ watches,
movements] 使⋯在时间上一致 [shǐ⋯zài shíjiān
shang yīzhì] **II** VI ▸ **to synchronize with**
与⋯一致 [yǔ⋯yīzhì] ▸ **to synchronize sth with
sth** 使某物与某物一致

syndicate [n 'sɪndɪkɪt, vb 'sɪndɪkeɪt] **I** N [C] [of
people, businesses, newspapers] 辛迪加 [xīndíjiā]
II VT ▸ **to be syndicated (to)** [article +] 联网发
表 [liánwǎng fābiǎo]; [programme +] 联网播放
[liánwǎng bōfàng]

syndrome ['sɪndrəum] N [C] **1** (MED) 综合征
[zōnghé zhèng] **2** (fig) 种种表现 [zhǒngzhǒng
biǎoxiàn]

synonym ['sɪnənɪm] N [C] 同义词 [tóngyì cí]

synthetic [sɪn'θɛtɪk] **I** ADJ [+ material, chemical]
合成的 [héchéng de] **II** NPL ▸ **synthetics**
(fabrics etc) 合成纤维 [héchéng xiānwéi]

Syria ['sɪrɪə] N 叙利亚 [Xùlìyà]

Syrian ['sɪrɪən] **I** ADJ 叙利亚的 [Xùlìyà de]
II N [C] (person) 叙利亚人 [Xùlìyàrén]

syringe [sɪ'rɪndʒ] N [C] 注射器 [zhùshè qì]

syrup ['sɪrəp] N [U] **1** (in cooking) 糖浆
[tángjiāng] **2** (MED) 糖浆剂 [tángjiāng jì]
3 (also: **golden syrup**) 糖浆 [tángjiāng]

○ system ['sɪstəm] N [C] **1** (organization, set) 系统
[xìtǒng] ▷ a new administrative system 新的行政
系统 ▷ a computer system 电脑系统 **2** (method)
方法 [fāngfǎ] ▷ a simple filing system 简单的文件

归档方法 **3** (ANAT, LAW, MATH) 系统 [xìtǒng] ▷ the digestive system 消化系统 ▷ the legal system 法律系统 ▷ the decimal system 十进制 **4** (body) 身体 [shēntǐ] ▷ The strenuous exercise made great demands on her system. 艰苦的锻炼使她的身体付出很大的代价。▶ **the system** (government) 制度 ▶ **it was a shock to his system** 对他震动很大 ▶ **to get sth out of one's system** 把某事发泄出来

systematic [sɪstə'mætɪk] ADJ 有系统的 [yǒu xìtǒng de]

Tt

T, t [tiː] N [c/u] (letter) 英语的第二十个字母

ta [taː] (BRIT: inf) INT 谢谢 [xièxie]

tab [tæb] N [c] **1** (on drinks can) 拉环 [lāhuán] **2** (on garment) 标签 [biāoqiān] **3** (US) (bill) 账单 [zhàngdān] ▶ **to pick up the tab** (inf) 付账 ▶ **to keep tabs on** (inf) [+ person, sb's movements] 监视

table ['teɪbl] I N [c] **1** (piece of furniture) 桌子 [zhuōzi] **2** (chart) 表格 [biǎogé] II VT (BRIT) [+ motion, proposal etc] 提议 [tíyì] ▶ **to lay** or **set the table** 摆餐桌 ▶ **to clear the table** 清理餐桌 ▶ **to turn the tables on sb** 转而占了某人的上风

tablecloth ['teɪblklɔθ] N [c] 桌布 [zhuōbù]

table d'hôte [taːblˈdəut] N [c] 套餐 [tàocān]

table lamp N [c] 台灯 [táidēng]

table mat N [c] **1** (for plate) 桌垫 [zhuōdiàn] **2** (for hot dish) 盘垫 [pándiàn]

tablespoon ['teɪblspuːn] N [c] **1** (spoon) 餐匙 [cānchí] **2** (amount) 一餐匙的量 [yī cānchí de liàng]

tablespoonful ['teɪblspuːnful] N [c] 一餐匙的量 [yī cānchí de liàng]

tablet ['tæblɪt] N [c] **1** (MED) 药片 [yàopiàn] **2** (HIST) (for writing) 写字版 [xiězìbǎn] ▶ **a tablet of soap** (BRIT: frm) 一块肥皂

table tennis (SPORT) N [u] 乒乓球 [pīngpāngqiú]

tabloid ['tæblɔɪd] N [c] 小报 [xiǎobào] ▶ **the**

tabloids 各种小报 [gèzhǒng xiǎobào]

taboo [təˈbuː] I N [c] (religious, social) 禁忌 [jìnjì] II ADJ [+ subject, place, name etc] 忌讳的 [jìhuì de]

tack [tæk] I N [c] (nail) 图钉 [túdīng] II VT **1** (nail) 用图钉钉 [yòng túdīng dìng] **2** (stitch) 粗缝 [cūféng] III VI (NAUT) 抢风航行 [qiǎngfēng hángxíng] ▶ **to change tack, try a different tack** 改变方针 ▶ **to tack sth on to (the end of) sth** [+ note, clause] 把某事物附加到某事物的(末尾)

▶ **tack up** VT 粗缝 [cūféng]

tackle ['tækl] I N **1** [u] (for fishing) 用具 [yòngjù] **2** [u] (for lifting) 滑轮 [huálún] **3** [c] (FOOTBALL) 抢球 [qiǎngqiú]; (RUGBY) 擒抱 [qínbào] II VT **1** (deal with) [+ problem] 解决 [jiějué] **2** (challenge) [+ person] 坦诚面对 [tǎnchéng miànduì] **3** (FOOTBALL, RUGBY) 截球 [jiéqiú]

tacky ['tækɪ] ADJ **1** (sticky) 黏的 [nián de] **2** (pej) (cheap-looking) 俗气的 [súqì de]

tact [tækt] N [u] 机智 [jīzhì]

tactful ['tæktful] ADJ 老练的 [lǎoliàn de]

tactical ['tæktɪkl] ADJ **1** [+ move, withdrawal, error] 策略的 [cèlüè de] **2** (MIL) [+ weapons] 战术的 [zhànshù de]; [+ policy, bombing etc] 战略的 [zhànlüè de] ▶ **tactical voting** (BRIT) 策略性投票

tactics ['tæktɪks] NPL 策略 [cèlüè]

tactless ['tæktlɪs] ADJ 不得体的 [bù détǐ de]

tadpole ['tædpəul] N [c] 蝌蚪 [kēdǒu]

taffy ['tæfɪ] (US) N [u] 太妃糖 [tàifēitáng] [英=**toffee**]

tag [tæg] I N [c] **1** (label) 标签 [biāoqiān] **2** (electronic) 标签 [biāoqiān] II VT **1** (label) [+ object] 加标签于 [jiā biāoqiān yú] **2** (describe) [+ person] 把…称为 [bǎ…chēngwéi] ▶ **a price/name tag** 价格/姓名标签

▶ **tag along** VI 尾随 [wěisuí]

Tahiti [taːˈhiːtɪ] N 塔希提 [Tǎxītí]

tail [teɪl] I N [c] **1** [of animal] 尾巴 [wěiba] **2** [of plane] 尾部 [wěibù] **3** [of shirt, coat] 下摆 [xiàbǎi] II VT (follow) [+ person, vehicle] 尾随 [wěisuí] III **tails** NPL (formal suit) 燕尾服 [yànwěifú] ▶ **to turn tail (and run)** 掉头(逃跑) ▶ "**heads or tails?**" – "**tails**" "正面还是背面?" "背面"

▶ **tail off** VI **1** (in size, quality etc) 逐渐减少 [zhújiàn jiǎnshǎo] **2** (also: **tail away**) [voice +] 逐渐消失 [zhújiàn xiāoshī]

tailor ['teɪlə(r)] I N [c] **1** (person) 裁缝 [cáifeng] **2** (also: **tailor's**) 裁缝店 [cáifengdiàn] II VT ▶ **to tailor sth (to)** 修改某物(以适应) [xiūgǎi mǒuwù (yǐ shìyìng)]

tainted ['teɪntɪd] ADJ **1** [+ food, water, air] 被污染的 [bèi wūrǎn de] **2** (fig) [+ reputation etc] 被玷污的 [bèi diànwū de]

Tajikistan [taːdʒɪkɪˈstaːn] N 塔吉克斯坦

[Tǎjíkèsītǎn]

○**take** [teɪk] (*pt* **took**, *pp* **taken**) **I** VT **1** [+ *holiday, vacation*] 度 [dù]; [+ *shower, bath*] 洗 [xǐ]; [+ *decision*] 做 [zuò] **2** (*take hold of*) [+ *sb's arm etc*] 拿 [ná] ▷ *Let me take your coat.* 让我来拿你的外套吧。**3** (*steal*) 偷走 [tōuzǒu] ▷ *Someone's taken my pen.* 有人偷走了我的钢笔。**4** (*require*) [+ *effort, courage etc*] 需要 [xūyào] ▷ *It took a lot of courage to admit his mistake.* 他需要很大勇气去承认错误。**5** (*tolerate*) [+ *pain, criticism etc*] 忍受 [rěnshòu] ▷ *I can't take any more.* 我不能再忍受了。**6** (*hold*) [+ *passengers, spectators etc*] 容纳 [róngnà] ▷ *The new stadium can take about 8000 people.* 新的体育场大约可以容纳8000人。**7** (*accompany*) [+ *person*] 送 [sòng] ▷ *He offered to take her home in a taxi.* 他提出乘出租车送她回家。**8** [+ *prisoner*] 俘获 [fúhuò] ▷ *Marines went in, taking 15 prisoners.* 海军陆战队员进去了，俘获了15名犯人。**9** (*accept*) [+ *job, position*] 接受 [jiēshòu] ▷ *I eagerly took the job.* 我兴冲冲地接受了这份工作。**10** (*carry, bring*) [+ *object*] 携带 [xiédài] ▷ *Don't forget to take your umbrella.* 别忘了带雨伞。**11** (*travel along*) [+ *road*] 走 [zǒu] ▷ *Take the Chester Road out of town.* 走切斯特路出城。**12** [+ *car, train etc*] 乘坐 [chéngzuò] ▷ *She took the train to New York.* 她乘火车去纽约。**13** [+ *size*] 穿 [chuān] ▷ *What size do you take?* 你穿多大号？**14** [+ *time*] 花费 [huāfèi] ▷ *The sauce takes 25 minutes to prepare.* 做调味汁要花25分钟。**15** (*react to*) 看待 [kàndài] ▷ *How did he take the news?* 他怎样看待这个消息？ ▷ *No one took my message seriously.* 没有人认真看待我的讯息。**16** [+ *exam, test*] 参加 [cānjiā] ▷ *She's not yet taken her driving test.* 她还没考驾照。**17** [+ *drug, pill etc*] 服用 [fúyòng] ▷ *I took a couple of aspirins.* 我服下几片阿斯匹林。**18** (ESP BRIT) (*teach*) [+ *subject, class*] 教 [jiāo] ▷ *She took them for geography.* 她教他们地理。**19** (*study*) [+ *subject, course*] 修 [xiū] ▷ *I'm taking history at university.* 我在大学修历史。**II** VI (*have effect*) [*dye, injection, drug +*] 见效 [jiànxiào] ▷ *You need a few minutes for cortisone to take.* 你得等几分钟让可的松见效。**III** N [c] **1** (CINE) 镜头 [jìngtóu] ▷ *She had to do several takes to get it right.* 她拍了好几个镜头才得到满意的效果。**2** (*inf*) (*viewpoint*) 看法 [kànfǎ] ▷ *What's your take on this?* 你对这件事的看法是什么？ ▶ **to take sth from** [+ *drawer, box etc*] 把某物从…拿出来 ▶ **I take it that** 我的理解是… ▶ **take it or leave it** 接不接受随便 ▶ **to take sb for...** (*mistake*) 把某人误认为… ▷ *I took him for a doctor.* 我把他误认为是医生了。 ▶ **to take sb's hand, take sb by the hand/arm** 拉某人的手，牵某人的手/挽某人的胳膊 ▶ **to take sb for a walk** 带某人去散步 ▶ **to take it on** or **upon o.s. to do sth** 将做某事的责任揽到自己身上 ▶ **to take to doing sth** 开始有规律地做某事

▶ **take after** VT FUS [不可拆分] (*resemble*) 像 [xiàng] ▷ *He takes after his dad.* 他像他的爸爸。

▶ **take apart** VT (*dismantle*) [+ *bicycle, radio, machine*] 拆开 [chāikāi]

▶ **take away I** VT **1** (*remove*) 拿走 [názǒu] **2** (*carry off*) 带走 [dàizǒu] **3** (MATH) 减去 [jiǎnqù] ▷ *What's 35 take away 10?* 35减去10等于多少？**II** VI ▶ **to take away from** (*detract from*) 减损 [jiǎnsǔn]

▶ **take back** VT **1** (*return*) [+ *goods*] 退回 [tuìhuí] **2** (*retract*) [+ *one's words*] 收回 [shōuhuí]

▶ **take down** VT **1** (*write down*) 记录 [jìlù] **2** (*dismantle*) [+ *wall, fence etc*] 拆除 [chāichú]

▶ **take in** VT **1** (*deceive*) [+ *person*] 蒙骗 [mēngpiàn] ▷ *I wasn't going to be taken in by his charm.* 我不会被他的魅力所蒙骗。**2** (*understand*) 明白 [míngbái] ▷ *Robert took it all in without needing explanations.* 罗伯特没用任何解释就全明白了。**3** (*include*) 容纳 [róngnà] ▷ *The university has expanded to take in the school of art.* 为了容纳艺术学院，大学进行了扩张。**4** [+ *lodger*] 留宿 [liúsù] **5** [+ *orphan, refugee, stray dog*] 收容 [shōuróng] **6** [+ *dress, waistband*] 改窄 [gǎizhǎi]

▶ **take off I** VI **1** (*aircraft*) 起飞 [qǐfēi] **2** (*also:* **take o.s. off**) (*go away*) 动身 [dòngshēn] ▷ *They took off for a weekend in the country.* 他们动身去乡下度周末。**II** VT **1** (*time from work*) 休假 [xiūjià] ▷ *She took two days off work.* 她休了两天假。**2** [+ *clothes, glasses, make-up*] 脱下 [tuōxià] **3** (ESP BRIT) (*imitate*) [+ *person*] 模仿 [mófǎng]

▶ **take on** VT **1** (*undertake*) [+ *work, responsibility*] 承担 [chéngdān] ▷ *Don't take on any more responsibilities.* 不要再承担更多的责任了。**2** [+ *employee*] 雇用 [gùyòng] ▷ *The company has taken on more staff.* 公司雇用了更多员工。**3** (*compete against*) 与较量 [yǔ…jiàoliàng] ▷ *I knew I couldn't take him on.* 我知道自己没法跟他较量。**4** (*develop*) 越来越显示出 [yuèláiyuè xiǎnshìchū] ▷ *His writing took on a greater intensity.* 他的写作越来越显示出深度。

▶ **take out** VT **1** (*invite*) [+ *person*] 邀请 [yāoqǐng] ▷ *He took her out for a meal.* 他邀请她出去吃饭。**2** (*remove*) [+ *tooth*] 拔除 [báchú] **3** [+ *loan, mortgage, licence etc*] 取得 [qǔdé]

▶ **take out on** VT ▶ **to take one's anger/feelings out on sb** 向某人发泄怒气/情感 [xiàng mǒurén fāxiè nùqì/qínggǎn]

▶ **take over** VT **1** [+ *business, country*] 接管 [jiēguǎn] **2** [+ *job*] 接手 [jiēshǒu] ▷ *His widow has taken over the running of the company.* 他的遗孀接手经营这家公司。**II** VI ▶ **to take over from sb** 从某人手中接管 [cóng mǒurén shǒuzhōng jiēguǎn]

▶ **take to** VT FUS [不可拆分] **1** (*like*) 喜欢上 [xǐhuan shang] ▷ *I immediately took to Alan.* 我立刻喜欢上了艾伦。**2** (*begin*) 开始常做 [kāishǐ chángzuò] ▷ *He's recently taken to fishing.* 他最近开始常去钓鱼。

▸ **take up** I VT **1** (start) [+ hobby, sport] 开始 [kāishǐ] **2** [+ job] 从事 [cóngshì] **3** (occupy) [+ time, space] 占用 [zhànyòng] ▷ I won't take up any more of your time. 我不会占用你更多的时间。 **4** (deal with) 着手处理 [zhuóshǒu chǔlǐ] ▷ He intends to take up the proposal with the prime minister. 他打算与首相着手处理该提议。**5** (continue) [+ task, story] 继续 [jìxù] ▷ David was taking up where he had left off. 戴维接着上次中断的地方继续。**6** (shorten) [+ hem, garment] 改短 [gǎiduǎn] II VI (befriend) ▸ **to take up with sb** 开始和某人鬼混 [kāishǐ hé mǒurén guǐhùn] ▸ **to take sb up on an offer** 接受某人提出的建议

takeaway ['teɪkəweɪ] (BRIT) N [c] **1** (shop, restaurant) 外卖店 [wàimàidiàn] [美=**takeout**] **2** (food) 外卖 [wàimài] [美=**takeout**]

taken ['teɪkən] I PP of **take** II ADJ ▸ **to be taken with sb/sth** (attracted to) 被某人/某事迷住 [bèi mǒurén/mǒushì mízhù]

takeoff ['teɪkɔf] N [c] [of plane] 起飞 [qǐfēi]

takeout ['teɪkaut] (US) N [c] **1** (shop, restaurant) 外卖店 [wàimàidiàn] [英=**takeaway**] **2** (food) 外卖 [wàimài] [英=**takeaway**]

takeover ['teɪkəuvə(r)] N [c] **1** (of company) 接管 [jiēguǎn] **2** (of country) 占领 [zhànlǐng]

takings ['teɪkɪŋz] (BRIT: COMM) NPL (from sales) 营业收入 [yíngyè shōurù]

talc [tælk] N [U] (also: **talcum powder**) 爽身粉 [shuǎngshēnfěn]

tale [teɪl] N [c] **1** (story) 故事 [gùshì] **2** (account) 传闻 [chuánwén] ▸ **to tell tales** [child +] 打小报告

talent ['tælnt] N [c/U] 才能 [cáinéng] ▸ **to have a talent for sth** 在某事上有天分

talented ['tæləntɪd] ADJ [+ person, actor etc] 有才能的 [yǒu cáinéng de]

○ **talk** [tɔːk] I N **1** [c] (prepared speech) 讲话 [jiǎnghuà] ▷ a talk on careers abroad 关于海外事业发展的讲话 **2** [U] (conversation) 谈话 [tánhuà] ▷ I won't have that kind of talk at the table! 我不会在餐桌上进行这类谈话的! **3** [U] (gossip) 谣言 [yáoyán] ▷ There is talk that the president may be deposed. 有谣言说总统可能被罢免。**4** [c] (discussion) 交谈 [jiāotán] ▷ I want to have a long talk with her. 我想跟她长谈一次。II VI **1** (speak) 说话 [shuōhuà] **2** (chat) 聊 [liáo] ▷ We talked for hours. 我们聊了几个小时。**3** (give information) 招供 [zhāogòng] ▷ They'll talk, they'll name me. 他们会招供的，他们会供出我的。**4** (gossip) 说闲话 [shuō xiánhuà] ▷ We don't want the neighbours to talk. 我们不想让邻居说闲话。III VT [+ politics, sport etc] 谈论 [tánlùn] ▷ Let's talk business. 咱们谈论正事吧。IV **talks** NPL (POL ETC) 会谈 [huìtán] ▸ **to give a talk** 作讲座；[+ politician] 发表讲话 ▸ **to talk to or with sb** 跟某人讲话 ▸ **to talk about sth** 谈论某事 ▸ **talking of...** 谈到…

▸ **talk down** VT (denigrate) 贬低 [biǎndī]

▸ **talk into** VT ▸ **to talk sb into (doing) sth** 说服某人做某事 [shuōfú mǒurén zuò mǒushì]

▸ **talk out of** VT ▸ **to talk sb out of (doing) sth** 说服某人不做某事 [shuōfú mǒurén bù zuò mǒushì]

▸ **talk over, talk through** VT [+ problem etc] 仔细商讨 [zǐxì shāngtǎo]

▸ **talk up** VT (exaggerate) 夸耀 [kuāyào]

talkative ['tɔːkətɪv] ADJ 健谈的 [jiàntán de]

talk show (TV, RAD) N [c] **1** (US) 脱口秀 [tuōkǒuxiù] [英=**chat show**] **2** (discussion programme) 访谈节目 [fǎngtán jiémù]

tall [tɔːl] ADJ 高的 [gāo de] ▸ **how tall are you?** 你有多高? ▸ **he's 6 feet tall** 他6英尺高 ▸ **a tall order** 苛求

用法参见 **high**

tambourine [tæmbə'riːn] N [c] 铃鼓 [línggǔ]

tame [teɪm] I ADJ **1** [+ animal, bird] 驯服的 [xùnfú de] **2** (fig) [+ story, party] 乏味的 [fáwèi de] II VT [+ animal, bird] 驯养 [xùnyǎng]

tamper ['tæmpə(r)] VI ▸ **to tamper with sth** 乱动某物 [luàndòng mǒuwù]

tampon ['tæmpɔn] N [c] 月经棉栓 [yuèjīng miánshuān]

tan [tæn] I N [c] (also: **suntan**) 晒黑的肤色 [shàihēi de fūsè] II VI **1** [person +] 晒黑 [shàihēi] III VT [+ hide, animal skin] 鞣 [róu] IV ADJ (colour) 黄褐色的 [huánghèsè de] ▸ **to get a tan** 晒黑

tandem ['tændəm] N [c] 双人脚踏车 [shuāngrén jiǎotàchē] ▸ **in tandem (with)** (与…)紧密配合

tangerine [tændʒə'riːn] I N [c] (fruit) 红橘 [hóngjú] II ADJ (colour) 橘红的 [júhóng de]

tangle ['tæŋgl] I N [c] [of branches, knots, wire] 缠结 [chánjié] II VT ▸ **to be/get tangled (up)** 乱成一团 [luànchéng yī tuán] ▸ **in a tangle** [wires, string etc +] 乱成一团；(fig) 错综复杂

tank [tæŋk] N [c] **1** (MIL) 坦克 [tǎnkè] **2** (for petrol, water) 箱 [xiāng] **3** (also: **fish tank**) 缸 [gāng]

tanker ['tæŋkə(r)] N [c] **1** (ship) 油轮 [yóulún] **2** (truck) 油罐车 [yóuguànchē] **3** (RAIL) 运油火车 [yùnyóu huǒchē]

tanned [tænd] ADJ [+ skin, person] 晒黑的 [shàihēi de]

tantrum ['tæntrəm] N [c] 发脾气 [fā píqì] ▸ **to have a tantrum** [child +] 耍脾气 ▸ **to throw a tantrum** [adult +] 发脾气

Tanzania [tænzə'nɪə] N 坦桑尼亚 [Tǎnsāngníyà]

Tanzanian [tænzə'nɪən] I ADJ 坦桑尼亚的 [Tǎnsāngníyà de] II N [c] (person) 坦桑尼亚人 [Tǎnsāngníyàrén]

tap [tæp] I N [c] **1** (ESP BRIT) (on sink, pipe etc) 龙头 [lóngtóu] [美=**faucet**] **2** (gentle blow) 轻敲 [qīngqiāo] II VT **1** (hit gently) 轻拍 [qīngpāi]

2 [+ *resources, energy*] 利用 [lìyòng] **3** [+ *telephone*] 窃听 [qiètīng] ▶ **on tap** (*inf*) (*resources, information*) 现成的; (*beer*) 扎啤

tap-dancing ['tæpdɑːnsɪŋ] N [U] 踢踏舞 [tītàwǔ]

tape [teɪp] I N **1** [U] (*in cassette etc*) 带 [dài] **2** [c] (*cassette*) 磁带 [cídài] **3** [U] (*adhesive*) 胶带 [jiāodài] **4** [c/U] (*for tying*) 绑带 [bǎngdài] **5** [c] (*tag*) (*on clothes*) 标签 [biāoqiān] II VT **1** (*record*) 录制 [lùzhì] **2** (*attach*) 贴 [tiē] ▶ **tape up** VT (*fasten with tape*) 捆扎 [kǔnzā]

tape measure N [c] 卷尺 [juǎnchǐ]

tape recorder N [c] 录音机 [lùyīnjī]

tapestry ['tæpɪstrɪ] N **1** [c/U] (*on wall*) 挂毯 [guàtǎn] **2** [c] (*liter*) 多彩景象 [duōcǎi jǐngxiàng]

tar [tɑː] N [U] **1** (*on road etc*) 沥青 [lìqīng] **2** (*in cigarettes*) 焦油 [jiāoyóu]

target ['tɑːgɪt] I N [c] **1** (*of missile etc*) 目标 [mùbiāo] **2** (*fig*) (*of criticism, abuse*) 对象 [duìxiàng] **3** (*aim*) 目标 [mùbiāo] II VT **1** (*attack*) [+ *troops etc*] 瞄准 [miáozhǔn] **2** (*try to solve*) [+ *problem*] 尽力解决 [jìnlì jiějué] **3** (*criticize*) [+ *person*] 抨击 [pēngjī] **4** [+ *audience, market*] 把…作为目标 [bǎ…zuòwéi mùbiāo] ▶ **to be on target** [*project, work, sales* +] 按计划进行

tariff ['tærɪf] N [c] **1** (*tax*) 关税 [guānshuì] **2** (BRIT: *frm*) (*in hotel, restaurant*) 价目 [jiàmù]

tarmac® ['tɑːmæk] I N [U] **1** (BRIT) (*on road*) 沥青碎石路面 [lìqīng suìshí lùmiàn] [美= **blacktop**] **2** (AVIAT) ▶ **the tarmac** 柏油路面 [bǎiyóu lùmiàn] II VT (BRIT) [+ *road*] 用柏油铺 [yòng bǎiyóu pū]

tarpaulin [tɑːˈpɔːlɪn] N [c/U] 油布 [yóubù]

tarragon ['tærəgən] N [U] 龙蒿 [lónghāo]

tart [tɑːt] I N [c] **1** (*cake*) 果馅饼 [guǒxiànbǐng] **2** (BRIT: *inf!*) (*prostitute*) 妓女 [jìnǔ] II ADJ (*bitter*) 酸的 [suān de] ▶ **tart up** (BRIT: *inf*) VT [+ *room, building*] 艳俗地装饰 [yànsú de zhuāngshì] ▶ **to tart o.s. up** (*inf*) 打扮

tartan ['tɑːtn] I N [c/U] 苏格兰方格呢 [Sūgélán fānggéní] II ADJ [+ *rug, scarf etc*] 苏格兰方格的 [Sūgélán fānggé de]

TARTAN

是一种有图案的厚羊毛布料，其图案是由不同宽度和颜色的直线条条垂直交叉组成。**tartan** 用来做 **kilt** ——一种苏格兰成年男子和男孩子在正式场合穿的特别的短裙。这种布料起源于 **Highlands** (苏格兰高地)——即苏格兰群山连绵的西北部。在那里，**tartan** 被作为反抗英国王室的标志，并因此在1747年至1782年期间被禁用。不同的颜色和图案代表着苏格兰的不同地区。

tartar(e) sauce ['tɑːtə-] N [U] 塔塔沙司 [tǎtàshāsī]

task [tɑːsk] N [c] **1** 任务 [rènwù] ▶ **to take sb to task** (*rebuke, scold*) 责备某人

taste [teɪst] I N **1** [U] (*sense*) 味觉 [wèijué] **2** [c] (*flavour*) 味道 [wèidao] **3** [c] (*sample*) 尝试 [chángshì] **4** [s] (*fig*) [*of suffering, freedom etc*] 体验 [tǐyàn] **5** [U] (*choice, liking*) 品位 [pǐnwèi] II VT **1** (*get flavour of*) 尝 [cháng] **2** (*test, detect*) 品尝 [pǐncháng] III VI ▶ **to taste of/like sth** 有/像某物的味道 [yǒu/xiàng mǒuwù de wèidao] ▶ **to develop** *or* **acquire a taste for sth** 养成对某物的爱好 ▶ **to have good/bad taste** 品好/差 ▶ **to be in good/bad taste** [*remark, joke* +] 格调高雅/低俗 ▶ **to taste delicious/bitter** 尝起来好吃/苦

tasteful ['teɪstful] ADJ [+ *clothes, furnishings*] 高雅的 [gāoyǎ de]

tasteless ['teɪstlɪs] ADJ **1** [+ *food*] 无味的 [wúwèi de] **2** [+ *remark, joke*] 不雅的 [bùyǎ de] **3** [+ *furniture, decor etc*] 低俗的 [dīsú de]

tasty ['teɪstɪ] ADJ [+ *food*] 味美的 [wèiměi de]

tattered ['tætəd] ADJ **1** [+ *clothes*] 褴褛的 [lánlǚ de] **2** (*fig*) [+ *hopes*] 潦倒的 [liáodǎo de]

tatters ['tætəz] N ▶ **to be in tatters** [*clothes* +] 破烂的 [pòlàn de]; [*plan, relationship* +] 千疮百孔的 [qiān chuāng bǎi kǒng de]

tattoo [təˈtuː] I N [c] **1** (*on skin*) 纹身 [wénshēn] **2** (BRIT) (*military display*) 军乐队表演 [jūnyuèduì biǎoyǎn] II VT ▶ **to tattoo sth on sth** 将某物纹刺在某处 [jiāng mǒuwù wéncì zài mǒuchù]

taught [tɔːt] PT, PP *of* **teach**

taunt [tɔːnt] I VT [+ *person*] 讥笑 [jīxiào] II N [c] (*insult*) 侮辱 [wǔrǔ] ▶ **to taunt sb with/about sth** 用/就某事嘲弄某人

Taurus ['tɔːrəs] N **1** [U] (*sign*) 金牛座 [Jīnniú Zuò] **2** [c] (*person*) 金牛座的人 [Jīnniú Zuò de rén] ▶ **I'm (a) Taurus** 我是金牛座的

taut [tɔːt] ADJ [+ *skin, thread etc*] 紧绷的 [jǐnbēng de]

⊕ **tax** [tæks] I N [c/U] (*on goods, income etc*) 税 [shuì] II VT **1** [+ *earnings, goods etc*] 对…征税 [duì…zhēngshuì] **2** (*test*) [+ *person, memory, patience*] 考验 [kǎoyàn] ▷ *That question really taxed him.* 那个问题对他真是个考验。 ▶ **before/after tax** 税前/后 ▶ **free of tax** 免税的

taxation [tækˈseɪʃən] N [U] **1** (*system*) 税制 [shuìzhì] **2** (*money paid*) 税额 [shuì'é]

tax-free ['tæksfriː] ADJ 免税的 [miǎnshuì de]

taxi ['tæksɪ] I N [c] 出租车 [chūzūchē] II VI [*plane* +] 滑行 [huáxíng]

taxi driver N [c] 出租司机 [chūzū sījī]

taxi rank (BRIT) N [c] 出租车候客站 [chūzūchē hòukèzhàn] [美= **taxi stand**]

taxi stand (US) N [c] 出租车候客站 [chūzūchē hòukèzhàn] [英= **taxi rank**]

taxpayer ['tækspeɪə(r)] N [c] 纳税人

[nàshuìrén]

TB N ABBR (= *tuberculosis*) 肺结核 [fèijiéhé]

tbc ABBR (= *to be confirmed*) 有待确认 [yǒudài quèrèn]

tea [tiː] N [C/U] **1** (*drink*) 茶 [chá] **2** (*dried leaves*) 茶叶 [cháyè] **3** (BRIT) (*evening meal*) 晚饭 [wǎnfàn] ▶ **(afternoon) tea** (BRIT) (下午) 茶 ▰用法参见 **meal**

○ TEA
●
● 英国人和美国人喝的茶大多是红茶。通常
● 茶里要加牛奶,可能还加糖,当然也可以
● 在茶里只放一小片柠檬。花草茶 (**herbal**
● **tea**),如薄荷或甘菊茶,正风行起来。tea
● 还可以指下午小餐,通常有三明治、蛋
● 糕,还有茶。在英国的一些地方,**tea** 还
● 可以指晚上的正餐。

---

tea bag N [C] 袋茶 [dàichá]

tea break (BRIT) N [C] 茶点时间 [chádiǎn shíjiān] [美= **coffee break**]

teach [tiːtʃ] (*pt, pp* **taught**) I VT **1** ▶ **to teach sb sth, teach sth to sb** 教某人某事,将某事教给某人 [jiāo mǒurén mǒushì, jiāng mǒushì jiāogěi mǒurén] **2** (*in school*) [+ *pupils, subject*] 教 [jiāo] **3** (*educate*) 教育 [jiàoyù] II VI (*be a teacher*) 教书 [jiāoshū] ▶ **to teach sb to do sth/ how to do sth** 教某人做某事/怎样做某事

teacher ['tiːtʃə(r)] N [C] 教师 [jiàoshī]

teaching ['tiːtʃɪŋ] N [U] (*job*) 教学 [jiàoxué] II **teachings** NPL 教导 [jiàodǎo]

tea cloth (BRIT) N [C] 擦拭布 [cāshìbù] [美= **dishcloth**]

teacup ['tiːkʌp] N [C] 茶杯 [chábēi]

tea leaves NPL 茶叶 [cháyè]

○ team [tiːm] N [C] **1** (*of people, experts, horses*) 组 [zǔ] ▷ *a team of scientists* 一组科学家 **2** (SPORT) 队 [duì]

　▶ **team up** VI 合作 [hézuò] ▶ **to team up with sb** 与某人合作

teamwork ['tiːmwəːk] N [U] 协力合作 [xiélì hézuò]

teapot ['tiːpɔt] N [C] 茶壶 [cháhú]

tear¹ [tɛə(r)] (*pt* **tore**, *pp* **torn**) I N [C] (*rip, hole*) 裂口 [lièkǒu] II VT **1** (*rip*) 撕裂 [sīliè] **2** (*remove violently*) 扯 [chě] III VI **1** (*become torn*) 撕破 [sīpò] **2** (*rush*) 飞奔 [fēibēn] ▶ **to tear sth to pieces** *or* **to bits** *or* **to shreds** [+ *paper, letter, clothes*] 把某物撕成片{或}小块{或}条 ▶ **to tear sb to pieces** (*fig*) 与某人激烈争吵

　▶ **tear along** VI [*driver, vehicle +*] 疾驰 [jíchí]
　▶ **tear apart** VT **1** (*upset*) [+ *person*] 使心神不安 [shǐ xīnshén bù'ān] **2** (*divide*) [+ *group of people*] 使分裂 [shǐ fēnliè]

　▶ **tear away** VT ▶ **to tear o.s. away (from sth)** 强迫自己离开(某事物) [qiǎngpò zìjǐ líkāi (mǒushìwù)]

　▶ **tear down** VT [+ *building, statue*] 拆除 [chāichú]
　▶ **tear off** VT [+ *clothes*] 脱掉 [tuōdiào]
　▶ **tear up** VT [+ *sheet of paper, cheque*] 撕毁 [sīhuǐ]

tear² [tɪə(r)] N [C] (*when crying*) 眼泪 [yǎnlèi] ▶ **to be in tears** 哭泣 ▶ **to burst into tears** 哭起来

tearful ['tɪəful] ADJ [+ *person, face*] 含泪的 [hánlèi de]

tear gas N [U] 催泪弹 [cuīlèidàn]

tease [tiːz] I VT 逗弄 [dòunong] II N [C] (*person*) 爱开玩笑的人 [ài kāi wánxiào de rén]

teaspoon ['tiːspuːn] N [C] (*spoon, amount*) 茶匙 [cháchí]

teaspoonful ['tiːspuːnful] N [C] 一茶匙的量 [yī cháchí de liàng]

teatime ['tiːtaɪm] (BRIT) N [U] 茶点时间 [chádiǎn shíjiān]

tea towel (BRIT) N [C] 擦拭布 [cāshìbù] [美= **dish towel**]

technical ['tɛknɪkl] ADJ **1** [+ *problems, advances*] 技术的 [jìshù de] **2** [+ *terms, language*] 专业的 [zhuānyè de] **3** [+ *skills, ability etc*] 专业技能的 [zhuānyè jìnéng de]

technically ['tɛknɪklɪ] ADV **1** [+ *advanced, demanding*] 科技地 [kējì de] **2** (*strictly speaking*) 严格说来 [yángé shuōlái]

technician [tɛk'nɪʃən] N [C] 技师 [jìshī]

technique [tɛk'niːk] N **1** [C] (*method*) 手法 [shǒufǎ] **2** [U] (*skill*) 技术 [jìshù]

technological [tɛknə'lɔdʒɪkl] ADJ 工艺的 [gōngyì de]

technology [tɛk'nɔlədʒɪ] N [C/U] 工艺学 [gōngyìxué]

teddy (bear) ['tɛdɪ(-)] N [C] 玩具熊 [wánjùxióng]

tedious ['tiːdɪəs] ADJ 乏味的 [fáwèi de]

tee [tiː] N [C] (GOLF) 球座 [qiúzuò] ▶ **tee off** VI (GOLF) 开球 [kāiqiú]

teem [tiːm] VI ▶ **to be teeming with** [+ *visitors, tourists etc*] 充满 [chōngmǎn]

teen [tiːn] ADJ (*teenage*) 青少年的 [qīngshàonián de] *see also* **teens**

teenage ['tiːneɪdʒ] ADJ [+ *children, fashions etc*] 十几岁的 [shíjǐsuì de]

teenager ['tiːneɪdʒə(r)] N [C] 青少年 [qīngshàonián]

teens [tiːnz] NPL ▶ **to be in one's teens** 在少年时代 [zài shàonián shídài]

tee-shirt ['tiːʃəːt] N = **T-shirt**

teeth [tiːθ] NPL *of* **tooth**

teetotal ['tiː'təutl] ADJ [+ *person*] 滴酒不沾的 [dījiǔ bùzhān de]

tel. ABBR (= *telephone number*) 电话号码 [diànhuà hàomǎ]

telecommunications ['tɛlɪkəmjuːnɪ'keɪʃənz] N [U] 电信 [diànxìn]

telegram ['tɛlɪgræm] N [C] 电报 [diànbào]

telegraph pole ['tɛlɪgrɑːf-] N [C] 电话线杆 [diànhuà xiàngān]

telephone ['tɛlɪfəun] I N 1 [U] (system) 电话 [diànhuà] 2 [C] (piece of equipment) 电话 [diànhuà] II VT, VI 打电话 [dǎ diànhuà] ▶ to be on the telephone (talking) 正在打电话; (BRIT) (connected to phone system) 装电话

telephone box (BRIT) N [C] 电话亭 [diànhuàtíng] [美= phone booth]

telephone call N [C] 电话 [diànhuà] ▶ to make a telephone call 打电话

telephone book, telephone directory N [C] 电话簿 [diànhuàbù]

telephone number N [C] 电话号码 [diànhuà hàomǎ]

telesales ['tɛlɪseɪlz] N [U] 电话销售 [diànhuà xiāoshòu]

telescope ['tɛlɪskəup] N [C] 望远镜 [wàngyuǎnjìng]

televise ['tɛlɪvaɪz] VT 电视播放 [diànshì bōfàng]

television ['tɛlɪvɪʒən] N 1 [C] (also: television set) 电视机 [diànshìjī] 2 [U] (system) 电视 [diànshì] 3 [U] (business) 电视业 [diànshìyè] ▶ to be on television [programme +] 由电视播放; [person +] 上电视

television programme N [C] 电视节目 [diànshì jiémù]

⊙**tell** [tɛl] (pt, pp **told**) I VT 1 (inform) ▶ to tell sb sth 告诉某人某事 [gàosù mǒurén mǒushì] ▷ They told us the news. 他们告诉了我们这个消息。2 (relate) [+ story, joke] 讲 [jiǎng] ▷ Will you tell me a story? 你能给我讲个故事吗? 3 (distinguish) ▶ to tell sth from sth 把某物和某物区分开 [bǎ mǒuwù hé mǒuwù qūfēn kāi] 4 (know) 确定 [quèdìng] ▷ I couldn't tell what they were thinking. 我不能确定他们在想什么。5 (reveal) 表明 [biǎomíng] ▷ The facts tell us that this is not true. 事实向我们表明这不是真的。II VI (have an effect) 影响 [yǐngxiǎng] ▷ The late nights were beginning to tell on my health. 熬夜开始影响我的健康了。▶ to tell sb to do sth 指示某人做某事 ▶ to tell sb that... 告诉某人说… ▶ to tell sb about or of sth 给某人讲述某事 ▶ to tell the time 看时间 ▶ (I) tell you what... (inf) (我) 提议… ▶ to do as one is told 按吩咐做事

▶ **tell apart** VT (distinguish) 分辨出 [fēnbiàn chū]

▶ **tell off** VT ▶ to tell sb off 斥责某人 [chìzé mǒurén]

▶ **tell on** VT FUS [不可拆分] (inf) (inform against) 揭发 [jiēfā]

teller ['tɛlə(r)] (US) N [C] (in bank) 出纳员 [chūnàyuán]

telly ['tɛlɪ] (BRIT: inf) N [C/U] 电视 [diànshì] ▶ on telly 在电视上播放 ▶ to watch telly 看电视 [美= TV]

temp [tɛmp] I N [C] 临时雇员 [línshí gùyuán] II VI 做临时工 [zuo línshígōng]

temper ['tɛmpə(r)] I N [C/U] 脾气 [píqì] II VT (frm) (moderate) 使缓和 [shǐ huǎnhé] ▶ to be in a good/bad temper 情绪好/坏 ▶ to lose one's temper 发怒 ▶ to have a bad temper 脾气坏

temperament ['tɛmprəmənt] N [C/U] 性情 [xìngqíng]

temperamental [tɛmprə'mɛntl] ADJ 1 [+ person] 喜怒无常的 [xǐnù wúcháng de] 2 [+ car, machine] 时好时坏的 [shíhǎo shíhuài de]

temperature ['tɛmprətʃə(r)] N 1 [C/U] [of place] 气温 [qìwēn] 2 [U] [of person] 体温 [tǐwēn] ▶ to have or be running a temperature 发烧 ▶ to take sb's temperature 测某人的体温

temple ['tɛmpl] N [C] 1 (building) 庙宇 [miàoyǔ] 2 (at side of head) 太阳穴 [tàiyángxué]

temporarily ['tɛmpərərɪlɪ] ADV 临时地 [línshí de]

temporary ['tɛmpərərɪ] ADJ 临时的 [línshí de] ▶ temporary secretary/teacher 临时秘书/代课教师

tempt [tɛmpt] VT 诱使 [yòushǐ] ▶ to tempt sb into doing sth or to do sth 诱使某人做某事 ▶ to be tempted to do sth 受到引诱去做某事

temptation [tɛmp'teɪʃən] N [C/U] 诱惑 [yòuhuò]

tempting ['tɛmptɪŋ] ADJ 诱人的 [yòurén de]

⊙**ten** [tɛn] NUM 十 [shí] ▶ tens of thousands 好几万

tenant ['tɛnənt] N [C] 房客 [fángkè]

tend [tɛnd] I VT 1 (frm) [+ plants, crops] 看护 [kānhù] 2 (frm) [+ sick person] 照料 [zhàoliào] II VI 1 ▶ to tend to do sth 倾向于做某事 [qīngxiàng yú zuò mǒushì] 2 ▶ to tend towards sth 趋于某事 [qū yú mǒushì] 3 ▶ to tend to sb/sth 照料某人/某事物 [zhàoliào mǒurén/mǒushìwù]

tendency ['tɛndənsɪ] N [C] 倾向 [qīngxiàng] ▶ a tendency to do sth 做某事的倾向

tender ['tɛndə(r)] I ADJ 1 (loving) [+ person, care] 温柔的 [wēnróu de] 2 (sore) [+ arm, leg etc] 有触痛的 [yǒu chùtòng de] 3 [+ meat, vegetables] 嫩的 [nèn de] 4 [+ age] 年幼的 [niányòu de] II N [C] (COMM) (offer) 投标 [tóubiāo] III VT (frm) [+ offer, resignation, apology] 提出 [tíchū] ▶ to tender for sth (COMM) 为某事投标 [wèi mǒushì tóubiāo] ▶ to put in a tender (for) (参加某项) 投标 ▶ to put work out to tender (BRIT) 对工程进行招标

tendon ['tɛndən] N [C] 腱 [jiàn]

tenner ['tɛnə(r)] (BRIT: inf) N [C] (ten pounds) 10英镑 [shí yīngbàng]; (ten-pound note) 面值10英镑的钞票 [miànzhí shí yīngbàng de chāopiào]

tennis ['tɛnɪs] N [U] 网球运动 [wǎngqiú yùndòng]

tennis ball N [C] 网球 [wǎngqiú]
tennis court N [C] 网球场 [wǎngqiúchǎng]
tennis match N [C] 网球赛 [wǎngqiúsài]
tennis player N [C] 网球手 [wǎngqiúshǒu]
tennis racket N [C] 网球拍 [wǎngqiúpāi]
tenor ['tɛnə(r)] N 1 [C] (MUS) 男高音歌手 [nán gāoyīn gēshǒu] 2 [S] *of speech, reply etc* 大意 [dàyì]
tenpin bowling ['tɛnpɪn-] (ESP BRIT) N [U] 十柱保龄球 [shí zhù bǎolíngqiú]
tense [tɛns] I ADJ 1 [+ *person, smile, period, situation*] 紧张的 [jǐnzhāng de] 2 [+ *muscle*] 紧绷的 [jǐnbēng de] II N [C] (LING) 时态 [shítài] III VT, VI (*also*: **tense up**) (*tighten*) 绷紧 [bēngjǐn]
tension ['tɛnʃən] N 1 [C/U] (*of situation*) 紧张的局势 [jǐnzhāng de júshì] 2 [U] (*of person*) 焦虑 [jiāolǜ] 3 [U] (*between ropes, wires*) 张力 [zhānglì]
tent [tɛnt] N [C] 帐篷 [zhàngpeng]
tentative ['tɛntətɪv] ADJ 1 [+ *person*] 犹豫不决的 [yóuyù bù jué de] 2 [+ *step, smile*] 试探性的 [shìtànxìng de] 3 [+ *conclusion, agreement, plan*] 暂定的 [zàndìng de]
tenth [tɛnθ] NUM 1 (*in series*) 第十 [dì shí] 2 (*fraction*) 十分之一 [shífēn zhī yī] *see also* **fifth**
tent peg N [C] 帐篷桩 [zhàngpeng zhuāng]
tent pole N [C] 帐篷支柱 [zhàngpeng zhīzhù]
tepid ['tɛpɪd] ADJ 1 [+ *liquid*] 微温的 [wēiwēn de] 2 (*fig*) [+ *reaction, applause*] 不热烈的 [bù rèliè de]
○**term** [tə:m] I N [C] 1 (*word, expression*) 词语 [cíyǔ] ▷ *a term of abuse* 骂人的词语 2 (*period*) 期间 [qījiān] ▷ *Blair's second term of office as Premier* 布莱尔作为首相的第二个任期 3 (*at school, university*) 学期 [xuéqī] II VT (*call*) 将…称作 [jiāng…chēngzuò] ▷ *The press termed the visit a triumph.* 媒体称这次访问非常成功。 III **terms** NPL (*conditions*) [*of agreement, treaty etc*] 条款 [tiáokuǎn] ▶ **in simple/economic terms** 简单/就经济而言 ▶ **in terms of the climate/economy** 就气候/经济而言 ▶ **on easy terms** (COMM) 以分期付款方式 ▶ **in the short/long term** 短/长期 ▶ **to think/talk in terms of doing sth** 就做某事的角度来考虑/说 ▶ **to be on good terms** 关系好 ▶ **to be on good terms with sb** 与某人关系好 ▶ **on equal** *or* **the same terms** 按同样条件 ▶ **to come to terms with sth** 接受某事为事实
terminal ['tə:mɪnl] I ADJ [+ *disease, patient*] 晚期的 [wǎnqī de] II N [C] 1 (COMPUT) 终端 [zhōngduān] 2 (ELEC) 接头处 [jiētóuchù] 3 (COMM) (*for oil, ore etc*) 储备区 [chǔbèiqū] 4 (*at airport*) 终点站 [zhōngdiǎnzhàn]
terminally ['tə:mɪnlɪ] ADV ▶ **terminally ill** 病入膏肓的 [bìng rù gāo huāng de]
terminate ['tə:mɪneɪt] I VT 1 (*frm*) [+ *discussion etc*] 终结 [zhōngjié] 2 [+ *contract, pregnancy*] 终止 [zhōngzhǐ] II VI [*contract* +] 终止 [zhōngzhǐ]

▶ **this train terminates in…** (*frm*) 本次列车的终点站是…
termini ['tə:mɪnaɪ] NPL *of* **terminus**
terminology [tə:mɪ'nɔlədʒɪ] N [C/U] 术语 [shùyǔ]
terminus ['tə:mɪnəs] (*pl* **termini**) N [C] (*for buses, trains*) 终点站 [zhōngdiǎnzhàn]
Ter(r). ABBR (= *terrace*) 地 [dì]
terrace ['tɛrəs] I N [C] 1 (BRIT) (*row of houses*) 成排的房屋 [chéngpái de fángwū] 2 (*patio*) 平台 [píngtái] 3 (AGR) 梯田 [tītián] II **terraces** NPL (BRIT: SPORT) ▶ **the terraces** 球场看台 [qiúchǎng kàntái]
terraced ['tɛrəst] ADJ 1 [+ *house*] 成排的 [chéngpái de] 2 [+ *garden*] 梯状的 [tīzhuàng de]
terrain [tɛ'reɪn] N [C/U] 地势 [dìshì]
terrible ['tɛrɪbl] ADJ 1 [+ *accident, winter*] 可怕的 [kěpà de] 2 (*very poor*) 糟糕的 [zāogāo de] 3 (*inf*) (*awful*) 糟透的 [zāotòu de]
terribly ['tɛrɪblɪ] ADV 1 (*very*) 非常 [fēicháng] 2 (*very badly*) 差劲地 [chàjìn de]
terrier ['tɛrɪə(r)] N [C] (*dog*) 活泼的小狗 [huópo de xiǎo gǒu]
terrific [tə'rɪfɪk] ADJ 1 (*very great*) [+ *amount, thunderstorm, speed*] 惊人的 [jīngrén de] 2 (*wonderful*) [+ *time, party, idea etc*] 极好的 [jíhǎo de]
terrified ['tɛrɪfaɪd] ADJ 吓坏的 [xiàhuài de] ▶ **to be terrified of sth** 被某事吓破胆
terrify ['tɛrɪfaɪ] VT 使惧怕 [shǐ jùpà]
terrifying ['tɛrɪfaɪɪŋ] ADJ 令人害怕的 [lìng rén hàipà de]
territorial [tɛrɪ'tɔ:rɪəl] I ADJ [+ *waters, boundaries, dispute*] 领土的 [lǐngtǔ de] II N [C] (BRIT: MIL) 英国义务兵 [Yīngguó yìwùbīng]
territory ['tɛrɪtərɪ] N 1 (*land*) 领土 [lǐngtǔ] 2 (*fig*) 范围 [fànwéi]
terror ['tɛrə(r)] N [U] (*great fear*) 恐惧 [kǒngjù] ▶ **in terror of sth** 对某事胆战心惊 ▶ **to have a terror of (doing) sth** 害怕(做)某事
terrorism ['tɛrərɪzəm] N [U] 恐怖主义 [kǒngbù zhǔyì]
terrorist ['tɛrərɪst] I N [C] 恐怖分子 [kǒngbù fènzǐ] II ADJ 恐怖分子的 [kǒngbù fènzǐ de]
○**test** [tɛst] I N [C] 1 (*trial, check*) 试验 [shìyàn] ▷ *a nuclear test* 核试验 2 [*of person, courage etc*] 判断标准 [pànduàn biāozhǔn] ▷ *The test of any civilised society is how it treats its minorities.* 对于任何文明社会的判断标准是它怎样对待少数民族。 3 (MED) 检验 [jiǎnyàn] ▷ *a blood test* 验血 4 (CHEM) 化验 [huàyàn] ▷ *They carried out tests on the water.* 他们对水域进行验。 5 (SCOL) 测验 [cèyàn] 6 [*of intelligence*] 测验 [cèyàn] ▷ *an intelligence test* 智力测验 7 (*also*: **driving test**) 驾驶考试 [jiàshǐ kǎoshì] II VT 1 (*try out*) 试验 [shìyàn] ▷ *The drug was tested on gorillas.* 药品在大猩猩身上进行了试验。 2 (MED) 检测 [jiǎncè] ▷ *They tested her blood type.* 他们检测了她的血型。 3 (SCOL) 测试 [cèshì] ▷ *I will test you*

on your knowledge of French. 我要测试一下你的法语. ▶ **to put sth to the test** 将某事物加以考验 ▶ **to test water for impurities** 测试水的纯度

testicle ['tɛstɪkl] N [c] 睾丸 [gāowán]

testify ['tɛstɪfaɪ] I VI 1 (LAW) 作证 [zuòzhèng] II VT (LAW) ▶ **to testify that...** 证实… [zhèngshí...] ▶ **to testify to sth** [person +] 证实某事 [zhèngshí mǒushì]; [fact +] 证明某事 [zhèngmíng mǒushì]

testimony ['tɛstɪmənɪ] N [c/U] 1 (LAW) 证词 [zhèngcí] 2 ▶ **to be (a) testimony to sth** 是对某事物的(一个)证明 [shì duì mǒushìwù de (yī gè) zhèngmíng]

test match (BRIT: CRICKET, RUGBY) N [c] 国际锦标赛 [guójì jǐnbiāosài]

test tube N [c] 试管 [shìguǎn]

tetanus ['tɛtənəs] (MED) N [U] 破伤风 [pòshāngfēng]

text [tɛkst] I N 1 [U] (*written material*) 正文 [zhèngwén] 2 [c] (*book*) 课本 [kèběn] 3 [c] (*also:* **text message**) 手机短信 [shǒujī duǎnxìn] II VT (*on mobile phone*) 发短消息 [fā duǎnxiāoxi]

textbook ['tɛkstbuk] N [c] 课本 [kèběn]

textile ['tɛkstaɪl] I N [c] 纺织品 [fǎngzhīpǐn] II **textiles** NPL (*industries*) 纺织厂 [fǎngzhīchǎng]

text message N [c] 短信 [duǎnxìn]

text messaging [-'mɛsɪdʒɪŋ] N [U] 发短信 [fā duǎnxìn]

texture ['tɛkstʃə(r)] N [c/U] [of cloth, skin, soil] 质地 [zhìdì]

Thai [taɪ] I ADJ 泰国的 [Tàiguó de] II N 1 [c] (*person*) 泰国人 [Tàiguórén] 2 [U] (*language*) 泰语 [Tàiyǔ]

Thailand ['taɪlænd] N 泰国 [Tàiguó]

○**than** [ðæn, ðən] I PREP 1 (*in comparisons*) 比 [bǐ] ▷ *She's taller than her husband.* 她比丈夫高. ▷ *We've got less than three weeks.* 我们只有不到3周的时间了. ▷ *This year my salary is more than twice what it was last year.* 我今年的薪水是去年的两倍多. II CONJ 比 [bǐ] ▷ *He loves her more than she loves him.* 他比她爱得深. ▶ **it's smaller than a matchbox** 它比一个火柴盒还小 ▶ **more/less than Paul** 比保罗多/少 ▶ **more than 20** 多于20 ▶ **more than once** 不止一次 ▶ **she's older than you think** 她比你想的年纪要大 ▶ **I'd rather stay in than go out** 我宁可呆在家里而不愿出去

○**thank** [θæŋk] VT [+ person] 感谢 [gǎnxiè] ▶ **thank you (very much)** (非常)感谢你 ▶ **no, thank you** 不,谢谢你 ▶ **thank God, thank Goodness, thank heavens** 感谢上帝 ▶ **to thank sb for (doing) sth** 感谢某人(做)某事 ▶ **I don't need any help, thank you** 我自己来,谢谢你

thankful ['θæŋkful] ADJ ▶ **to be thankful (for sth)** 感激(某事) [gǎnjī (mǒushì)] ▶ **to be thankful that/to be...** 庆幸…

thankfully ['θæŋkfəlɪ] ADV 幸亏 [xìngkuī] ▶ **thankfully, there were few victims** 幸亏受害者不多

thanks [θæŋks] I NPL 感谢 [gǎnxiè] II INT (*inf*) 谢谢 [xièxie] ▶ **to give sb one's thanks** (*frm*) 向某人表示感谢 ▶ **many thanks, thanks a lot** 多谢 ▶ **no, thanks** 不了,谢谢 ▶ **thanks to sb/sth** 多亏某人/某事

Thanksgiving (Day) ['θæŋksgɪvɪŋ(-)] (US) N [c/U] 感恩节 [Gǎn'ēnjié]

⊙ **THANKSGIVING**

每年11月的第4个星期四是 **Thanksgiving** (感恩节),是美国一个重要的全国性节日,对于每个家庭也是一个值得庆祝的日子. 感恩节是为了纪念第一批到达北美大陆的英国定居者— **pilgrims** (英国清教徒). 感恩节名字的由来可以追溯到1621年,清教徒们为了第一次丰收而向上帝表示感谢. 传统的感恩节大餐以烤火鸡为主菜,以 **pumpkin pie** 为甜点.

○**that** [ðæt] (*demonstrative adj, pron:* pl **those**) I ADJ 那 [nà] ▶ **that man/woman/book** 那个男人/女人/那本书 ▶ **that place** 那个地方 ▶ **that one** 那一个 ▶ **that one over there** 那边的那个 II PRON 1 (*demonstrative*) 那 [nà] ▶ **who's/what's that** 那是谁/那是什么? ▶ **is that you?** 是你吗? ▶ **I prefer this to that** 两相比较,我更喜欢这个 ▶ **will you eat all that?** 你会把那个都吃完吗? ▶ **that's my house** 那是我的房子 ▶ **that's what he said** 那是他所说的 ▶ **that is (to say)** 也就是(说) ▶ **that's it** (*finished*) 就这样; (*exactly*) 没错 ▶ **that's that** 就这样了 2 (*relative*) …的 […de] ▶ **the girl that came in** 进来的那个女孩 ▶ **the man that I saw** 我见过的那个男的 ▶ **the woman that you spoke to** 和你说过话的那个女的 ▶ **all that I have** 我所有的一切 ▶ **the day that he came** 他来的那天 III CONJ 引导宾语从句的关系代词 ▶ **he thought that I was ill** 他以为我病了 ▶ **it's interesting that you should agree** 有趣的是你竟然同意了 ▶ **I'm so happy that I could sing for joy** 我高兴得唱起了歌 IV ADV (*so*) 如此 [rúcǐ] ▶ **that much/bad/high** 如此多/糟糕/高

thatched [θætʃt] ADJ [+ roof, cottage] 茅草屋顶的 [máocǎo wūdǐng de]

thaw [θɔː] I N 1 [c] [of ice, snow] 解冻 [jiědòng] 2 [s] (*fig*) (*in relations*) 缓和 [huǎnhé] II VI 1 [ice, snow +] 融化 [rónghuà] 2 (*fig*) [relations +] 缓和 [huǎnhé] III VT 1 (*also:* **thaw out**) [+ frozen food] 解冻 [jiědòng] 2 (*fig*) [+ atmosphere, relations] 缓

和 [huánhé] ▶ **it's thawing** (weather) 雪化了

the [ðiː, ðə] DEF ART **1** 定冠词，用于指代已知的人或物 ▶ **the man/girl/house/book** 男人/女孩/房子/书 ▶ **the men/women/houses/books** 男人/女孩/房子/书 ▶ **the yellow dress, not the green one** 那件黄色的衣服，不是绿色的 ▶ **the Germans and the French** 德国人和法国人 ▶ **the history of France** 法国史 ▶ **I haven't the time/money** 我没钱/时间 ▶ **the best solution** 最好的解决方案 ▶ **to play the piano/violin** 弹钢琴/拉小提琴 ▶ **the age of the computer** 计算机时代 ▶ **I got it from the teacher** 我从老师那儿得来的 ▶ **I'm going to the butcher's/the cinema** 我要去肉店/电影院 ▶ **can you give it to the nurse?** 你能把它交给那位护士吗？ **2** (adjective forming uncount noun) 用于形容词前表示不可数的一类物；(forming plural noun) 用于形容词前构成复数，表示一类人或物 ▶ **to attempt the impossible** 尝试不可能的事 ▶ **the rich and the poor** 穷人和富人 **3** (in dates, decades) 表示具体时间 ▶ **the fifth of March** 3月5日 ▶ **the nineties** 90年代 **4** (in titles) 用于称谓中 ▶ **Elizabeth the First** 伊丽莎白一世 ▶ **Peter the Great** 彼得大帝 **5** (in comparisons) ▶ **the faster he works, the more mistakes he makes** 他工作得越快，犯的错误就越多 [tā gōngzuò de yuèkuài, fàn de cuòwù jiù yuèduō] ▶ **the more I look at it the less I like it** 我越看越不喜欢 ▶ **two dollars to the pound** 两美元兑换一英镑

theatre, (US) **theater** ['θɪətə(r)] N **1** [c] (building) 剧院 [jùyuàn] **2** [U] (entertainment) 戏剧 [xìjù] **3** [c] (MED) (also: **operating theatre**) 手术室 [shǒushùshì] **4** [c] (US) (also: **movie theater**) 电影院 [diànyǐngyuàn] [英=**cinema**] ▶ **to go to the theatre** 去看戏

theatrical [θɪ'ætrɪkl] ADJ **1** [+ event, production, performance] 戏剧的 [xìjù de] **2** (fig) [+ gesture, behaviour] 矫揉造作的 [jiǎo róu zào zuò de]

theft [θɛft] N [c/u] 盗窃 [dàoqiè]

their [ðɛə(r)] ADJ **1** (of men, boys, mixed group) 他们的 [tāmen de] ▷ **Their children grew up in the countryside.** 他们的孩子在乡间长大。; (of women, girls) 她们的 [tāmen de] ▷ **The girls went out with their boyfriends.** 女孩们和她们的男朋友们一起出去了。; (of things, animals) 它们的 [tāmen de] ▷ **The trees shed their leaves every autumn.** 这些树每年秋天都落叶。 **2** (his or her) 他/她的 [tā/tā de] ▷ **Does anyone need any help with their homework?** 谁做家庭作业需要帮助？

theirs [ðɛəz] PRON **1** (of men, boys, mixed group) 他们的 [tāmen de]; (of women, girls) 她们的 [tāmen de]; (of animals) 它们的 [tāmen de] **2** (his or hers) 他/她的 [tā/tā de] ▷ **I don't know whose handkerchief it is. Somebody must have left theirs.** 我不知道那是谁的手帕。一定是谁把它落在这儿了。 ▶ **it's theirs** 是他们/她们的 ▶ **a friend of theirs** 他们/她们的一个朋友

them [ðɛm, ðəm] PRON **1** (plural referring to men, boys, mixed group) 他们 [tāmen]; (referring to women, girls) 她们 [tāmen] ▷ **I'll phone them later.** 我过一会儿给他们/她们打电话。 ▷ **If you see your parents, do give them my best wishes.** 如果你见到你的父母，一定代我向他们问好。 ▷ **Not them again.** 又是他们/她们。 ▷ **I was at school with them.** 我和他们/她们是校友。; (referring to things and animals) 它们 [tāmen] ▷ **He took off his glasses and put them in his pocket.** 他摘下眼镜，把它们放进口袋。 **2** (singular) (him or her) 他/她 [tā/tā] ▷ **If anyone phones, please tell them I'm out.** 如果有人打电话，告诉他/她我出去了。

theme [θiːm] N [c] **1** [of speech, article, book etc] 主题 [zhǔtí] **2** (MUS) 主旋律 [zhǔxuánlǜ]

theme park N [c] 主题公园 [zhǔtí gōngyuán]

themselves [ðəm'sɛlvz] PL PRON **1** (referring to men, boys, mixed group) 他们自己 [tāmen zìjǐ]; (referring to girls, women) 她们自己 [tāmen zìjǐ] ▷ **Have they hurt themselves?** 他们/她们伤了自己吗？ ▷ **They all enjoyed themselves.** 他们/她们都玩得很开心。 ▷ **They cooked the meal themselves.** 他们/她们自己做的饭。 ▷ **They only care about themselves.** 他们只关心自己。; (referring to animals) 它们自己 [tāmen zìjǐ] ▷ **Cats wash themselves.** 猫自己清洗自己。 **2** (emphatic referring to men, boys, mixed group) 他们本人 [tāmen běnrén]; (referring to women, girls) 她们本人 [tāmen běnrén] ▷ **They themselves live in London.** 他们/她们本人住在伦敦。 **3** (singular) (himself or herself) 他/她自己 [tā/tā zìjǐ] ▷ **Anyone who has a problem should deal with it themselves.** 任何人有问题都应该自己解决。 ▶ **by themselves** (unaided) 他/她们独立地 ▷ **They built the house by themselves.** 他/她们自己盖了房子。; (alone) 他/她们独自地 ▷ **They live by themselves.** 他们/她们自己住。

then [ðɛn] I ADV **1** (at that time) (past) 当时 [dāngshí] ▷ **Life was simpler then.** 当时的生活较为简单。; (future) 那时 [nàshí] ▷ **I'm coming up on Friday so I'll see you then.** 我星期五会来的，那就那时见吧。 **2** (after that) 之后 [zhīhòu] ▷ **He thought a bit and then answered.** 他想了一会儿之后答应了。 ▷ **I'll give him a call and then we'll know what's happening.** 我给他打个电话，之后我们就会知道是什么事了。 **3** (therefore) 就是 [jiùshì] ▷ **This, then, is what you must do.** 这就是你要做的。 II ADJ 当时的 [dāngshí de] ▷ **the then president** 当时的总统 ▶ **by then** 到那时 ▶ **from then on** 从那时起 ▶ **before then** 在那

之前 ▶ **until then** 直到那时 ▶ **since then** 自从那时 ▶ **but then** (however) 不过 ▶ **well/OK then** 好吧 ▶ **if... then...** 如果…就…

theology [θɪˈɒlədʒɪ] N [U] 神学 [shénxué]

theoretical [θɪəˈrɛtɪkl] ADJ **1** [+ explanation, subject] 理论的 [lǐlùn de] **2** [+ possibility, risk] 假设的 [jiǎshè de]

theory [ˈθɪərɪ] N [C/U] 理论 [lǐlùn] ▶ **in theory** 就理论而言

therapist [ˈθɛrəpɪst] N [C] 治疗专家 [zhìliáo zhuānjiā]

therapy [ˈθɛrəpɪ] N [U] 治疗 [zhìliáo] ▶ **to be in therapy** 接受治疗

⊙ **there** [ðɛə(r)] ADV (referring to place, pointing, indicating) 那儿 [nàˈr] ▶ **they've lived there for 30 years** 他们在那儿住了30年 ▶ **he went there on Friday** 他是星期五去那儿的 ▶ **is Shirley there please?** (on telephone) 请问雪莉在吗？ ▶ **it's over there** 在那边 ▶ **it's in/down there** 就在那边 ▶ **put it in/down there** 就把它放在那边 ▶ **that book there** 在那边的那本书 ▶ **there he is!** 他在那儿呐！ ▶ **there you are** (offering something) 给你 ▶ **that's what it's there for** 那就是它存在的原因 ▶ **there is/there are** 有 ▶ **there has been an accident** 发生了一个事故 ▶ **there are 3 of them** 他们中有3个 ▶ **hello there, hi there** 你好啊 ▶ **there!** 嘿！ ▶ **there, there** (comforting) 好了，好了

请勿将 **there**，**their** 和 **they're** 混淆。 **there** 表示某事物的存在，引起对某事物的注意，或表示某事物在某地或将要到达某地。There is nothing to be afraid of...There she is...I'll meet them there later. **their** 表示某物属于上文提到的某人或某物，或与上文提到的某人或某物有关。They walked their dog together every day...It wasn't their fault that they were late. **they're** 是 they are 的缩略形式。They're nice people.

thereabouts [ˈðɛərəˈbauts] ADV ▶ **or thereabouts** (place) 或其附近 [huò qí fùjìn]; (amount) 大约如此 [dàyuē rúcǐ]

thereafter [ðɛərˈɑːftə(r)] (frm) ADV 此后 [cǐhòu]

thereby [ˈðɛəbaɪ] (frm) ADV 因此 [yīncǐ]

therefore [ˈðɛəfɔː(r)] ADV 因此 [yīncǐ]

there's [ˈðɛəz] = **there is, there has**

thermal [ˈθəːml] ADJ **1** [+ springs, baths] 温的 [wēn de] **2** [+ power, insulation] 热量的 [rèliàng de] **3** [+ underwear] 保暖的 [bǎonuǎn de] **4** [+ paper, printer] 热敏的 [rèmǐn de]

thermometer [θəˈmɒmɪtə(r)] N [C] 温度计 [wēndùjì]

Thermos® [ˈθəːməs] N [C] (also: **Thermos flask**) 保温瓶 [bǎowēnpíng]

thermostat [ˈθəːməustæt] N [C] 恒温器 [héngwēnqì]

⊙ **these** [ðiːz] I PL ADJ (demonstrative) 这些 [zhèxiē] II PL PRON 这些 [zhèxiē] ▶ **these ones are cheaper than those ones** 这些比那些便宜 ▶ **these days** 目前 ▶ **which are better? these or those?** 哪些更好？这些还是那些？

thesis [ˈθiːsɪs] (pl **theses** [ˈθiːsiːz]) N [C] **1** (for degree) 论文 [lùnwén] **2** (argument) 论点 [lùndiǎn]

⊙ **they** [ðeɪ] PL PRON **1** (referring to men, boys, mixed group) 他们 [tāmen] ▷ They haven't arrived yet. 他们还没到。; (referring to women, girls) 她们 [tāmen] ▷ They're pretty girls. 她们是漂亮的女孩。; (referring to animals, things) 它们 [tāmen] ▷ They are healthy animals. 它们是健康的动物。 **2** (in generalizations) 人们 [rénmen] ▷ They say that there are plenty of opportunities. 人们都说有很多机会。 **3** (he or she) 他/她 [tā/tā] ▷ If anyone has any problems they can come to Mary for help. 如果谁有任何问题，可以向玛丽寻求帮助。

they'd [ðeɪd] = **they had, they would**

they'll [ðeɪl] = **they shall, they will**

they're [ðɛə(r)] = **they are**

they've [ðeɪv] = **they have**

thick [θɪk] ADJ **1** [+ slice, line, book, clothes etc] 厚的 [hòu de] **2** [+ sauce, mud, fog] 浓的 [nóng de] **3** [+ forest, hair etc] 浓密的 [nóngmì de] **4** (BRIT: inf) (stupid) 笨的 [bèn de] ▶ **it's 20 cm thick** 有20厘米粗 ▶ **thick and fast** 席卷而来 ▶ **in the thick of it** 深陷某事 ▶ **through thick and thin** 在任何情况下

thicken [ˈθɪkn] I VI **1** [sauce etc +] 变稠 [biànchóu] **2** [crowd etc +] 聚集 [jùjí] II VT [+ sauce etc] 使变稠 [shǐ biànchóu] ▶ **the plot thickens** 事情变得复杂了

thickness [ˈθɪknɪs] N [C/U] **1** [of rope, wire] 厚度 [hòudù] **2** (layer) 层 [céng]

thief [θiːf] (pl **thieves** [θiːvz]) N [C] 贼 [zéi]

任何将他人物品未经许可就据为己有的人，都可被叫做 **thief**。**robber** 是指用暴力的手段，或以暴力相威胁，将他人的物品据为己有，例如抢劫银行或商店等。**burglar** 是指入室抢劫者。

thigh [θaɪ] N [C] 大腿 [dàtuǐ]

thin [θɪn] I ADJ **1** [+ slice, line, book, material etc] 薄的 [báo de] **2** [+ soup, sauce] 稀的 [xī de] **3** [+ person, animal] 瘦的 [shòu de] **4** [+ hair] 稀疏的 [xīshū de] **5** [+ crowd] 少的 [shǎo de] II VT (also: **thin down**) [+ sauce, paint] 使变稀 [shǐ biànxī] III VI (also: **thin out**) [crowd, vegetation +] 减少 [jiǎnshǎo] ▶ **thin on the ground** 寥寥无几的 ▶ **his hair is thinning** 他的头发变得稀疏了

⊙ **thing** [θɪŋ] I N [C] **1** 事 [shì] ▷ A strange thing happened. 发生了一件很奇怪的事。 **2** (physical object) 物品 [wùpǐn] ▷ A baby's not a thing. It's a human being! 婴儿不是物品，是人！ **3** (matter, subject, anything) 事情 [shìqíng] ▷ Don't bother me with little things like that. 别用那些小事烦我。 ▷ Don't you worry about a thing. 别担心

任何事。II **things** NPL 1 (belongings) 东西
[dōngxi] ▷ I like my own things around me. 我喜
欢我的东西都在我旁边。2 (in general) 情形
[qíngxíng] ▷ How are things going? 情形如何？
▶ **the thing is...** 是这样… ▶ **for one thing** 一
则 ▶ **the best thing would be to...** 最好的方式
是… ▶ **first thing (in the morning)** （早晨）头
件事 ▶ **last thing (at night)** （晚上）最后做
的事 ▶ **to have a thing about** (inf) (like) 喜爱;
(dislike) 厌恶 ▶ **to do one's own thing** (inf) 自
由行事 ▶ **you lucky/silly thing** (inf) 你这个幸
运的/傻人

●**think** [θɪŋk] (pt, pp **thought**) I VI 1 (reflect) 思
考[sīkǎo] ▷ He thought for a moment, but said
nothing. 他思考了一会，没说什么。2 (reason)
想[xiǎng] ▷ People didn't think this way 20 years
ago. 人们20年前不这么想。II VT 1 (be of the
opinion, believe) 认为[rènwéi] 2 (believe) 以
为[yǐwéi] ▷ How old do you think I am? 你以
为我多大？3 (reflect) 想[xiǎng] ▷ "What are
you thinking?" "I am thinking how lovely you look".
"你在想什么？" "我在想你是多么好看。"
4 (conceive, imagine) 想出[xiǎngchū] III N
▶ **to have a think about sth** 考虑某事[kǎolù
móushì] ▶ **to think of** (reflect upon) 想着; (recall)
记起; (show consideration for) 考虑; (conceive of)
想到 ▶ **what do you think of...?** 你认为…怎么
样？▶ **to think about sth/sb** 想着某事物/某
人 ▶ **I'll think about it** 我要考虑一下 ▶ **to
think of doing sth** 考虑做某事 ▶ **to think
highly of sb** 看重某人 ▶ **to think nothing of
doing sth** 认为做某事没什么了不起 ▶ **to
think aloud** 自言自语 ▶ **think again!** 别想！
▶ **he is thought to have survived** 人们认为他
活了下来 ▶ **I think so/not** 我想是/不是的
▶ **think back** VI 1 **to think back (to sth)** 回想
起(某事)[huíxiǎng qǐ (mǒushì)]
▶ **think over** VT [+ offer, suggestion] 仔细考虑
[zǐxì kǎolù]
▶ **think through** VT 全面考虑[quánmiàn
kǎolù]
▶ **think up** VT [+ plan, scheme, excuse] 想出
[xiǎngchū]

thinking ['θɪŋkɪŋ] N [U] 1 (ideas) 想法[xiǎngfǎ]
2 (thought) 思考[sīkǎo] ▶ **to my (way of)
thinking** 依我看来

third [θəːd] I NUM 1 (in series) 第三[dì sān]
2 (fraction) 三份[sānfèn] II N 1 [U] (AUT) (also:
third gear) 第三挡[dì sāndǎng] 2 [c] (BRIT:
UNIV) (degree) 学位考试最低及格成绩 ▶ **a
third of** 三分之一 see also **fifth**

thirdly ['θəːdlɪ] ADV 第三[dì sān]

third party insurance (BRIT) N [U] 第三方
保险[dì sān fāng bǎoxiǎn]

Third World I N ▶ **the Third World** 第三世界
[Dì Sān Shìjiè] II ADJ [+ country, debt] 第三世界
的[Dì Sān Shìjiè de]

thirst [θəːst] N 1 [c/u] (feeling) 口渴[kǒukě]

2 [U] (condition) 干渴[gānkě] ▶ **a thirst for...**
[+ success, learning etc] 对…的渴望

thirsty ['θəːstɪ] ADJ 渴的[kě de] ▶ **gardening
is thirsty work** 园艺是辛苦的工作

●**thirteen** [θəː'tiːn] NUM 十三[shísān] see also
fifteen

thirteenth [θəː'tiːnθ] NUM 第十三[dì shísān]
see also **fifth**

thirtieth ['θəːtɪɪθ] NUM 第三十[dì sānshí]

●**thirty** ['θəːtɪ] NUM 三十[sānshí] see also **fifty**

○

this [ðɪs] (pl **these**) I ADJ 1 (demonstrative) 这
[zhè] ▶ **this man** 这个男人 ▶ **this house**
这座房子 ▶ **this one is better than that
one** 这个比那个好
2 (with days, months, years) 这个[zhège]
▶ **this Sunday/month/year** 这个星期
天/月/今年
II PRON 这个[zhège] ▶ **who's/what's
this?** 这是谁/什么？▶ **this is where I live**
这是我住的地方 ▶ **this is how you do it** 你
应该这么做 ▶ **this is what he said** 这是他
所说的 ▶ **this is Janet** (in introduction) 这是
珍妮特; (on telephone) 我是珍妮特 ▶ **like
this** 像这个一样的
III ADV (demonstrative) ▶ **this much/high/
long** 这么多/高/长[zhème duō/gāo/
cháng] ▶ **it was about this big** 它大约有这
么大 ▶ **we can't stop now we've gone this
far** 我们已经走了这么远了，停不下来了

thistle ['θɪsl] N [c] 蓟[jì]

thongs [θɔŋz] (US) NPL (open shoes) 夹趾拖鞋
[jiāzhǐ tuōxié] [英=**flip-flops**]

thorn [θɔːn] N [c] 刺[cì]

thorough ['θʌrə] ADJ 1 [+ search, investigation etc]
彻底的[chèdǐ de] 2 [+ knowledge, research] 详尽
的[xiángjìn de] 3 (methodical) [+ person] 细致的
[xìzhì de] 4 (complete) 完全的[wánquán de]

thoroughly ['θʌrəlɪ] ADV 1 [examine, study +] 全
面地[quánmiàn de] 2 [wash, search +] 彻底地
[chèdǐ de] 3 (very, very much) 十分地[shífēn de]
▶ **I thoroughly agree** 我完全同意

●**those** [ðəuz] I PL ADJ 那些[nàxiē] II PL PRON
那些[nàxiē] ▶ **those people/books** 那些人/书
▶ **I prefer those ones to these** 与这些相比我更
喜欢那些 ▶ **are those yours?** 那些是你的吗？

●**though** [ðəu] I CONJ (although) 虽然[suīrán]
▷ Though he hadn't stopped working all day, he
wasn't tired. 虽然一整天都在工作，他却不累。
II ADV 但是[dànshì] ▷ It's not easy, though. 但
是不容易啊。▶ **even though** 尽管

though 和 although 都用在从句中，
引出某个意外的情况或跟另一事实形
成对照的情况。though 不用于非常
正式的英语中。Though he was noisy
and sometimes arrogant, I quite liked
him...It was certainly not paper, though

it looked very much like it...Although she said she was hungry, she refused food and drink...The street is much the same, although there are some rather smart new shops. **even though** 可用于强调令人吃惊的事实。She wore a fur coat, even though it was a very hot day. **as though** 通过对比或解释的方式来描述某个情形。He looked at me as though I was a total stranger...The furniture looked as though it had come out of somebody's attic. **though** 也可以表示 'however' 的含义。但这种用法非常不正式。At weekends, though, the atmosphere changes...He was dressed neatly, though.

⊙**thought** [θɔːt] I PT, PP of think II N 1 [c] (idea) 想法 [xiǎngfǎ] ▷ The thought never crossed my mind. 我从来没有这种想法。**2** [U] (reflection) 沉思 [chénsī] ▷ She frowned as though deep in thought. 她皱着眉头好像陷入深深的沉思。**3** [U] (way of thinking) 观点 [guāndiǎn] ▷ This school of thought argues that depression is best treated with drugs. 这个学术派的观点认为抑郁最好用药物治疗。**4** [c] (intention) 念头 [niàntou] ▷ Her one thought was to get back to Derek. 她惟一的念头是回到德里克身边。III **thoughts** NPL (opinions) 看法 [kànfǎ] ▷ Tom disclosed his thoughts on Britain. 汤姆透露了他对英国的看法。▶ **after much thought** 经慎重考虑后 ▶ **to give sth some thought** 琢磨某事

thoughtful ['θɔːtful] ADJ **1** (deep in thought) 深思的 [shēnsī de] **2** (considerate) 体贴的 [tǐtiē de]

thoughtless ['θɔːtlɪs] ADJ (inconsiderate) [+ behaviour, words, person] 不体贴的 [bù tǐtiē de]

⊙**thousand** ['θaʊzənd] NUM ▶ **a** or **one thousand** 一千 [yī qiān] ▶ **thousands of** 许许多多 ▷ thousands of dollars 许多美元

thousandth ['θaʊzəntθ] NUM (in series) 第一千 [dì yī qiān]

thrash [θræʃ] VT **1** (hit) 鞭打 [biāndǎ] **2** (inf) (defeat) 击溃 [jīkuì]
  ▶ **thrash about, thrash around** VI 乱冲乱撞 [luànchōng luànzhuàng]
  ▶ **thrash out** VT (inf) [+ problem, differences] 推敲 [tuīqiāo]

thread [θrɛd] N **1** [c/U] (yarn) 线 [xiàn] **2** [c] [of screw] 螺纹 [luówén] **3** [c] (of story, account) 思路 [sīlù] II VT **1** [+ needle] 穿 [chuān] **2** (join with string) 串 [chuàn] ▶ **to thread one's way between/through** 小心翼翼地穿过

threat [θrɛt] N [c/U] (danger) 威胁 [wēixié] ▶ **to make a threat (against sb)** 威胁(某人) ▶ **to be under threat (of/from sth)** 受到(某物)的威胁 ▶ **a threat to sth** 对某物的威胁

threaten ['θrɛtn] I VI [storm, danger +] 似将发生 [sì jiāng fāshēng] II VT **1** (make a threat against) [+ person] 威胁 [wēixié] **2** (endanger)

[+ life, livelihood etc] 使受到威胁 [shǐ shòudào wēixié] ▶ **to threaten sb with a knife/gun** 用刀/枪威胁某人 ▶ **to be threatened with imprisonment/extinction** 受到监禁/覆灭的威胁 ▶ **to threaten to do sth** (promise) 扬言做某事; (seem likely) 可能发生某事

threatening ['θrɛtnɪŋ] ADJ [+ behaviour, person, letter] 威胁的 [wēixié de]

⊙**three** [θriː] NUM 三 [sān] see also five

three-dimensional [θriːdɪ'mɛnʃənl] ADJ **1** [+ object] 三维的 [sānwéi de] **2** [+ film, picture, image] 立体的 [lìtǐ de]

three-piece suite ['θriːpiːs-] (ESP BRIT) N [c] 三件一套的沙发 [sānjiàn yī tào de shāfā]

three-quarters [θriː'kwɔːtəz] I NPL 四分之三 [sìfēn zhī sān] II ADV ▶ **three-quarters full/empty** 四分之三满/空 [sìfēn zhīsān mǎn/kōng] III PRON 四分之三 [sìfēn zhī sān] ▶ **three-quarters of an hour** 45分钟

threshold ['θrɛʃhəʊld] N [c] **1** [of building, room] 门槛 [ménkǎn] **2** (fig) (on scale) 限度 [xiàndù] ▶ **to be on the threshold of** (fig) 正处在…的开端

threw [θruː] PT of throw

thrift shop (US) N [c] 慈善商店 [císhàn shāngdiàn] [英 = charity shop]

thrifty ['θrɪftɪ] ADJ [+ person] 节俭的 [jiéjiǎn de]

thrill [θrɪl] I N [c] (excitement) 兴奋 [xīngfèn] II VI ▶ **to thrill at/to sth** 因某事而兴奋 [yīn mǒushì ér xīngfèn] III VT [+ person, audience] 使兴奋 [shǐ xīngfèn] ▶ **to give sb a thrill** 使某人兴奋 ▶ **a thrill of anticipation/surprise** 一阵期望/惊奇 ▶ **to be thrilled with sth/to do sth/that...** 对于某事/做某事/…感到兴奋

thriller ['θrɪlə(r)] N [c] (novel, play, film) 惊险 [jīngxiǎn]

thrilling ['θrɪlɪŋ] ADJ [+ performance, news etc] 令人兴奋的 [lìng rén xīngfèn de]

thriving ['θraɪvɪŋ] ADJ [+ business, community] 繁荣的 [fánróng de]

throat [θrəʊt] N [c] **1** (gullet) 咽喉 [yānhóu] **2** (neck) 脖子 [bózi] ▶ **to clear one's throat** 清清嗓子 ▶ **to have a sore throat** 嗓子疼

throb [θrɔb] I N [s] **1** [of heart] 悸动 [jìdòng] **2** [of pain] 一跳跳的疼 [yī tiàotiào de téng] **3** [of engine, music] 振动 [zhèndòng] II VI **1** [head, foot etc +] 一跳一跳地疼 [yī tiàotiào de téng] [heart +] 悸动 [jìdòng] **3** [engine, music +] 振动 [zhèndòng]

throne [θrəʊn] N [c] **1** (chair) 宝座 [bǎozuò] **2** (fig) 皇位 [huángwèi]

throng [θrɔŋ] I N [c] (crowd) 大群 [dàqún] II VT [people +] [+ streets, beaches etc] 蜂拥而至 [fēngyōng ér zhì] III VI ▶ **to throng to/into/around** 拥向/入/在周围 [yōng xiàng/rù/zài zhōuwéi]

⊙**through** [θruː] I PREP **1** [+ place] 穿过 [chuānguò] ▷ The rain poured through a hole in the *roof.* 雨在屋顶上穿了一个洞。**2** (*throughout*) [+*time*] 整个 [zhěnggè] ▷ *trips for older people all through the year* 整year都为老年人安排的旅行 **3** (*coming from the other side of*) 穿过 [chuānguò] ▷ *They could hear music through the walls of the house.* 他们能听到音乐穿墙而来。**4** (*by means of*) 通过 [tōngguò] ▷ *They were opposed to change through violence.* 他们反对通过暴力变革。**5** (*because of*) 由于 [yóuyú] ▷ *The discovery of adrenalin came about through a mistake.* 由于一个错误导致了肾上腺素的发现。**II** ADV **1** (*in space*) 穿过 [chuānguò] ▷ *We decided to drive straight through to Birmingham.* 我们决定开车直接去伯明翰。**2** (*in time*) 整个 [zhěnggè] ▷ *hard work right through the summer* 持续了整个夏天的辛苦工作 **III** ADJ [+*ticket, train*] 直达的 [zhídá de] ▶ **(from) Monday through Friday** (US) (从) 周一到周五 [英=**to**] ▶ **to be through** (*on telephone*) 被接通 ▷ *You're through.* 已为您接通。▷ *You're through to the accounts department.* 已为你接到会计部。▶ **to be through with sb/sth** 与某人断绝往来/再也不做某事 ▶ "**no through road**" (BRIT) "此路不通" ▶ "**no through traffic**" (US) "此路不通"

throughout [θruː'aut] **I** PREP **1** [+*place*] 遍及 [biànjí] **2** [+*time*] 贯穿 [guànchuān] **II** ADV **1** (*everywhere*) 全部 [quánbù] **2** (*the whole time*) 始终 [shǐzhōng]

throw [θrəu] (*pt* **threw**, *pp* **thrown** [θrəun]) **I** N [c] 投掷 [tóuzhì] **II** VT **1** (*toss*) [+*stone, ball etc*] 丢 [diū] **2** (*place carelessly*) 扔 [rēng] **3** [+*person*] 抛 [pāo] **4** [+*one's head, arms etc*] 甩 [shuǎi] **5** [*horse*+] [+*rider*] 摔出 [shuāichū] **6** [+*fit, tantrum*] 发作 [fāzuò] **7** (*fig*) (*confuse*) 惊扰 [jīngrǎo] ▶ **to throw one's energy/money into sth** 把大量的精力/金钱投入某事 ▶ **to throw o.s. into sth** 积极投入某事 ▶ **to throw o.s. somewhere** 重重地倒在某处 ▶ **to be thrown in(to) jail** *or* **prison** 被投入监狱 ▶ **to be thrown into turmoil/confusion** 陷入混乱/迷惑 ▶ **to throw open** [+*doors, windows*] 使大开着; [+*debate*] 使公开 ▶ **to throw a party** (*inf*) 开个派对
▶ **throw about, throw around** (*inf*) VT (*fig*) [+*money*] 挥霍 [huīhuò]
▶ **throw away** VT **1** [+*rubbish*] 扔掉 [rēngdiào] **2** [+*opportunity*] 错过 [cuòguò]
▶ **throw in** VT (*inf*) (*include*) 免费供应 [miǎnfèi gōngyìng]
▶ **throw off** VT (*get rid of*) 摆脱 [bǎituō]
▶ **throw out** VT **1** [+*rubbish*] 扔掉 [rēngdiào] **2** (*from team, organization*) 赶走 [gǎnzǒu] **3** [+*case, request*] 否决 [fǒujué]
▶ **throw up** (*inf*) VI (*vomit*) 呕吐 [ǒutù]

thru [θruː] (US) = **through**

thrush [θrʌʃ] N **1** [c] (*bird*) 画眉鸟 [huàméiniǎo] **2** [U] (MED) 鹅口疮 [ékǒuchuāng]

thrust [θrʌst] (*pt, pp* **thrust**) **I** N **1** [U] (TECH) 推力 [tuīlì] **2** [c] (*push*) 猛推 [měngtuī] **3** [s] (*impetus*) 要点 [yàodiǎn] **II** VT **1** [+*person, object*] 猛推 [měngtuī] **2** [+*hand, sword*] 戳 [chuō]

thud [θʌd] **I** N [c] 砰的一声 [pēng de yī shēng] **II** VI 砰然作响 [pēngrán zuòxiǎng]

thug [θʌg] N [c] 暴徒 [bàotú]

thumb [θʌm] **I** N [c] (*on hand*) 大拇指 [dàmǔzhǐ] **II** VT ▶ **to thumb a lift/ride** 搭便车 [dā biànchē] ▶ **to give sb/sth the thumbs down** (*inf*) 不同意某人/某事 ▶ **to give sb/sth the thumbs up** (*inf*) 同意某人/某事
▶ **thumb through** VT FUS [不可拆分] [+*book, magazine*] 翻阅 [fānyuè]

thumbtack ['θʌmtæk] (US) N [c] 图钉 [túdīng] [英=**drawing pin**]

thump [θʌmp] **I** N [c] **1** (*blow*) 重击 [zhòngjī] **2** (*sound*) 砰的一声 [pēng de yī shēng] **II** VT **1** (ESP BRIT: *inf*) (*hit*) [+*person*] 揍 [zòu] **2** [+*object, table*] 撞击 [zhuàngjī] **III** VI **1** ▶ **to thump on sth** 撞击某物 [zhuàngjī mǒuwù] **2** [*heart etc*+] 砰砰作响 [pēngpēng zuòxiǎng]

thunder ['θʌndə(r)] **I** N [U] **1** (*in sky*) 雷 [léi] **2** (*fig*) [*of guns, waterfall etc*] 隆隆声 [lónglóngshēng] **II** VI **1** ▶ **it was thundering** 打雷了 [dǎléi le] **2** [*guns, train etc*+] 轰隆作响 [hōnglóng zuòxiǎng] **III** VT (*shout*) 大嚷大叫 [dà rǎng dà jiào] ▶ **to thunder past** [*train etc*+] 像雷电一样通过

thunderstorm ['θʌndəstɔːm] N [c] 雷雨 [léiyǔ]

Thu. ABBR (= *Thursday*) 星期四 [xīngqīsì]

Thur(s). ABBR (= *Thursday*) 星期四 [xīngqīsì]

Thursday ['θəːzdɪ] N [c/U] 星期四 [xīngqīsì]
see also **Tuesday**

thus [ðʌs] (*frm*) ADV **1** (*therefore*) 因此 [yīncǐ] **2** (*in this way*) 就这样 [jiù zhèyàng]

thwart [θwɔːt] VT **1** [+*person, plans*] 阻挠 [zǔnáo]

thx ABBR (= *thanks*) 谢谢 [xièxie]

thyme [taɪm] N [U] (*herb*) 百里香 [bǎilǐxiāng]

tick [tɪk] **I** N [c] **1** (ESP BRIT) (*mark*) 勾号 [gōuhào] [美=**check**] **2** [c] [*of clock*] 嘀嗒声 [dīdāshēng] **3** [c] (ZOOL) 扁虱 [biànshī] **4** [c] (BRIT: *inf*) (*moment*) 一刹那 [yīchànà] **5** (BRIT: *inf*) (*credit*) ▶ **to buy sth on tick** 赊账购买某物 [shēzhàng gòumǎi mǒuwù] **II** VI [*clock, watch*+] 嘀嗒作响 [dīdā zuòxiǎng] **III** VT (ESP BRIT) [+*item on list*] 打勾 [dǎgōu] [美=**check off**] ▶ **what makes him tick?** (*inf*) 什么使他成为这个样子的?
▶ **tick away, tick by** VI [*clock, time, seconds*+] 时间嘀嗒流逝 [shíjiān dīdā liúshì]
▶ **tick off** VT **1** (ESP BRIT) [+*item on list*] 打勾 [dǎgōu] [美=**check off**] **2** (BRIT: *inf*) (*scold*) 责骂 [zémà] **3** (US: *inf*) (*annoy*) 使厌烦 [shǐ yànfán]
▶ **tick over** VI [*business etc*+] 照常进行 [zhàocháng jìnxíng]

ticket ['tɪkɪt] N **1** [c] (for public transport, theatre, raffle etc) 票 [piào] **2** [c] (AUT) (also: **parking ticket**) 违章停车罚单 [wéizhāng tíngchē fádān] **3** [c] (price label) 标价牌 [biāojiàpái] **4** [s] (US: POL) 候选人名单 [hòuxuǎnrén míngdān]

ticket barrier N [c] (automatic) 检票口 [jiǎnpiàokǒu]

ticket collector N [c] (on train, bus) 检票员 [jiǎnpiàoyuán]

ticket inspector N [c] (on train, bus) 查票员 [chápiàoyuán]

ticket machine N [c] 售票机 [shòupiàojī]

ticket office N [c] 售票处 [shòupiàochù]

tickle ['tɪkl] I VT **1** [+ person] 挠 [náo] **2** (fig) (amuse) 逗乐 [dòulè] II VI [feather, hair etc +] 发痒 [fāyǎng]

ticklish ['tɪklɪʃ] ADJ **1** [+ person] 怕痒的 [pàyǎng de] **2** [+ problem, decision, issue etc] 棘手的 [jíshǒu de]

tide [taɪd] N **1** [c] (in sea) 潮汐 [cháoxī] **2** [s] (fig) [of events, fashion, opinion] 趋向 [qūxiàng]
▸ **high/low tide** 涨/落潮
▸ **tide over** VT (with loan etc) 渡过 [dùguò]

tidy ['taɪdɪ] I ADJ **1** [+ room, desk, person] 整洁的 [zhěngjié de] **2** (inf) [+ sum, profit] 可观的 [kěguān de] II VT (also: **tidy up**) [+ room, house etc] 整理 [zhěnglǐ]
▸ **tidy away** VT 整理 [zhěnglǐ]
▸ **tidy up** VT, VI 整理 [zhěnglǐ]

tie [taɪ] N **1** (clothing) 领带 [lǐngdài] **2** (string etc) 带子 [dàizi] **3** (link) 联系 [liánxì] **4** (ESP BRIT: SPORT) (match) 淘汰赛 [táotàisài] **5** (draw) (in competition) 平局 [píngjú] II VT **1** (also: **tie up**) [+ shoelaces etc] 扎 [zā] **2** (also: **tie together**) [+ ropes etc] 拴 [shuān] **3** (link) 紧密相关 [jǐnmì xiāngguān] III VI ▸ **to tie (with sb)** (SPORT ETC) (与某人) 打成平局 [(yǔ mǒurén) dǎchéng píngjú] ▸ **to tie sth in a bow/knot** 将某物打成蝴蝶结/打结 ▸ **to tie string/ribbon around sth** 把绳/丝带绕着某物打结
▸ **tie down** VT (fig) (restrict) [+ person] 束缚 [shùfù] ▸ **to tie sb down to a date/price** 为某人定死日期/价钱
▸ **tie in** VI ▸ **to tie in with** 与⋯相符 [yǔ⋯xiāngfú]
▸ **tie up** VT **1** [+ parcel etc] 捆绑 [kǔnbǎng] **2** [+ dog] 拴 [shuān] **3** [+ person] 捆绑 [kǔnbǎng] **4** (settle) [+ arrangements, deal etc] 了结 [liǎojié] ▸ **to be tied up** (inf) (busy) 忙得不可开交

tier [tɪə(r)] N [c] **1** [of stadium etc] 排 [pái] **2** [of cake] 层 [céng]

tiger ['taɪgə(r)] N [c] 老虎 [lǎohǔ]

tight [taɪt] I ADJ **1** (not loose) [+ string, skin, cloth] 紧绷的 [jǐnbēng de] **2** (compact) 紧密的 [jǐnmì de] **3** (firm) [+ hold, grip] 紧的 [jǐn de] **4** (close-fitting) [+ shoes, clothes] 紧身的 [jǐnshēn de] **5** (sharp) [+ bend] 急转的 [jízhuǎn de]

6 (strict) [+ budget, schedule] 紧张的 [jǐnzhāng de]; [+ security, controls] 严格的 [yángé de] **7** (scarce) [+ money] 短缺的 [duǎnquē de] **8** (inf) (stingy) 小气的 [xiǎoqì de] **9** (inf) (drunk) 醉了的 [zuìle de] II ADV (hold, squeeze, shut +) 紧紧地 [jǐnjǐn de] ▸ **to be packed tight** [suitcase +] 塞满; [people +] 靠紧

tighten ['taɪtn] I VT **1** [+ rope, strap] 拉紧 [lājǐn] **2** [+ screw, bolt] 弄紧 [nòngjǐn] **3** [+ grip, security, rules etc] 加紧 [jiājǐn] II VI **1** [grip +] 握紧 [wòjǐn] **2** [rope, strap etc +] 拉紧 [lājǐn]
▸ **tighten up** VT [+ screw, bolt] 弄紧 [nòngjǐn]

tightly ['taɪtlɪ] ADV **1** (firmly, tautly) [grasp, cling, close, seal +] 紧紧地 [jǐnjǐn de] **2** (closely) [knit +] 紧密地 [jǐnmì de] **3** (rigorously) [control, regulate +] 严格地 [yángé de] ▸ **a tightly knit community** 内部联系密切的社区

tights [taɪts] (BRIT) NPL 连裤袜 [liánkùwà] [美 = **pantyhose**]

tile [taɪl] N [c] **1** (on roof) 瓦 [wǎ] **2** (on floor, wall) 砖 [zhuān] II VT [+ floor, bathroom etc] 给⋯铺砖 [gěi⋯pūzhuān]

till [tɪl] I N [c] (BRIT) (in shop etc) 收银台 [shōuyíntái] [美 = **cash register**] II VT (cultivate) [+ land, soil] 耕种 [gēngzhòng] III PREP, CONJ = until

tilt [tɪlt] I VT **1** [+ object] 翘起 [qiàoqǐ] **2** [+ part of body] 仰起 [yǎngqǐ] II VI **1** [+ object] 倾斜 [qīngxié] **2** [part of body +] 抬起 [táiqǐ] III N [c] (slope) 倾斜 [qīngxié] ▸ **(at) full tilt** 全速地

timber ['tɪmbə(r)] (BRIT) N [U] (material) 木料 [mùliào] [美 = **lumber**]

○ time [taɪm] I N **1** [U] 时间 [shíjiān] ▷ a period of time 一段时间 ▷ I haven't got much time. 我没太多时间。**2** [U] (by clock) 时候 [shíhou] ▷ during my time in Toronto 我在多伦多的时候 **3** [c] (day) 时期 [shíqí] ▷ in these difficult times 在这困难时期 **4** [s] (by clock) 时间 [shíjiān] ▷ I will see you at the same time next week. 下星期和你在同一时间见面。**5** [c] (occasion) 次 [cì] ▷ the last time I saw her 我最后一次见到她 **6** [U] (MUS) 节拍 [jiépāi] II VT **1** (measure time of) 计时 [jìshí] ▷ He timed his speech. 他对自己的演讲进行了计时。▷ They timed his rate of breathing. 他们计算他呼吸的频率。**2** (fix moment for) [+ visit etc] 定 [dìng yú] ▷ They timed the attack for six o'clock. 他们定于6点发动攻击。▸ **it is time for sth/to do sth** 是做某事的时候 ▸ **to have a good/bad time** 度过一段愉快/不愉快的时光 ▸ **to spend time** 花时间 ▸ **to spend one's time doing sth** 花时间做某事 ▸ **three times a day** 一日三次 ▸ **three times the size of sth** 某物大小的3倍 ▸ **four at a time** 一次4个 ▸ **for a time** 好一段时间 ▸ **all the time** 总是 ▸ **for the time being** 暂时 ▸ **from time to time** 偶尔 ▸ **time after time, time and again** 一次次 ▸ **at one time** (in the past) 曾经 ▸ **at the same time** (nevertheless) 然而; (simultaneously)

同时 ▶ **at times** (*sometimes*) 有时 ▶ **in time** (*eventually*) 到时 ▶ **to be in time** (MUS) [*singers, dancers etc +*] 合拍 ▶ **in time (for)** 正好赶上 (…) ▶ **in a week's/month's time** 一周/月以后 ▶ **in no time, in next to no time** 立刻 ▶ **it's about time… or it's high time…** 早就该… ▶ **the best/worst film of all time** 有史以来最好/最差的电影 ▶ **any time** 任何时候 ▶ **on time** 准时 ▶ **once upon a time** 很久以前 ▶ **to be 30 minutes behind time/ahead of time** 晚了/提前30分钟 ▶ **by the time he arrived** 到他到达时 ▶ **5 times 5 is 25** 5乘5等于25 ▶ **what time is it?, what's the time?** 几点了? ▶ **to ask sb the time** 问某人时间 ▶ **time off** (*from work*) 休假 ▶ **to have a hard time** 受苦受难 ▶ **time's up!** 时间到了! ▶ **to have no time for sth** (*fig*) 没有时间关注某事 ▶ **in one's own (good) time** (*without being hurried*) 从容地 ▶ **in** *or* (US) **on one's own time** (*out of working hours*) 业余时间 ▶ **to take one's time** 慢慢来 ▶ **to take time** 需要时间 ▶ **to be behind the times** 落伍 ▶ **to be ahead of** *or* **before one's time** 领先于某人的时代 ▶ **to time sth well/badly** 把某段时间计划得好/糟糕 ▶ **to be timed to happen** 定于发生

timeless ['taɪmlɪs] ADJ 永恒的 [yǒnghéng de]

time limit N [c] 期限 [qīxiàn]

timely ['taɪmlɪ] ADJ [+ arrival, reminder] 及时的 [jíshí de]

time out (US: SPORT) N [c] 休场 [xiūchǎng] [英= **stoppage**]

timer ['taɪmə(r)] N [c] 定时器 [dìngshíqì]

timetable ['taɪmteɪbl] N [c] **1** (BRIT: RAIL ETC) 时刻表 [shíkèbiǎo] [美= **schedule**] **2** (BRIT: SCOL) 课程表 [kèchéngbiǎo] [美= **class schedule**] **3** (*programme of events*) 计划表 [jìhuàbiǎo]

time zone N [c] 时区 [shíqū]

timid ['tɪmɪd] ADJ [+ person, animal] 胆小的 [dǎnxiǎo de]

timing ['taɪmɪŋ] N [U] **1** (*skill*) 时间把握 [shíjiān bǎwò] **2** [of announcement] 时间安排 [shíjiān ānpái]

tin [tɪn] N **1** [U] (*metal*) 锡 [xī] **2** [c] (BRIT) (*can*) 罐 [guàn] [美= **can**] **3** [c] (*container*) (*for biscuits, tobacco etc*) 听 [tīng] **4** [c] (BRIT) (*for baking*) 锡盒 [xīhé] [美= **pan**]

tinfoil ['tɪnfɔɪl] N [U] (*foil*) 锡纸 [xīzhǐ]

tingle ['tɪŋgl] **I** VI (*when circulation returns, with cold*) 刺痛 [cìtòng]; (*with excitement*) 激动起来 [jīdòng qǐlái] **II** N ▶ **a tingle of excitement** 一阵兴奋 [yī zhèn xīngfèn]

tinker ['tɪŋkə(r)] **I** VI ▶ **to tinker with sth** 随意乱修某物 [suíyì luànxiū mǒuwù] **II** N [c] **1** (*pot mender*) 补锅匠 [bǔguōjiàng] **2** (BRIT: *infl*) (*gipsy*) 浪人 [làngrén]

tinned [tɪnd] (BRIT) ADJ [+ food] 罐装的 [guànzhuāng de] [美= **canned**]

tin opener [-əupnə(r)] (BRIT) N [c] 开罐器 [kāiguànqì] [美= **can opener**]

tint [tɪnt] **I** N [c] **1** (*colour*) 淡色 [dànsè] **2** (*for hair*) 染色 [rǎnsè] **II** VT [+ hair] 染 [rǎn]

tinted ['tɪntɪd] ADJ [+ hair, spectacles, glass] 泛…色的 [fàn…sè de]

tiny ['taɪnɪ] ADJ 极小的 [jíxiǎo de] ▶ **a tiny bit** 微乎其微

tip [tɪp] **I** N [c] **1** [of branch, paintbrush etc] 顶端 [dǐngduān] **2** (*protective on umbrella, walking stick*) 尖端 [jiānduān] **3** (*to waiter etc*) 小费 [xiǎofèi] **4** (BRIT) (*for rubbish*) 弃置场 [qìzhìchǎng] **5** (BRIT) (*for coal*) 堆 [duī] **6** (*advice*) 提示 [tíshì] **II** VT **1** [+ waiter] 给…小费 [gěi…xiǎofèi] **2** (*pour*) 倒出 [dàochū] **3** (*also: tip over*) (*overturn*) 翻转 [fānzhuǎn] **4** (*predict*) [+ winner etc] 猜测 [cāicè] **5** (*tilt*) [+ object, part of body] 倾斜 [qīngxié] **III** VI (*also: tip over*) [object, part of body +] 倾斜 [qīngxié] ▶ **the tip of the iceberg** (*fig*) 冰山一角
▶ **tip off** VT [+ person] 提醒 [tíxǐng]

tiptoe ['tɪptəʊ] VI 踮着脚走 [diǎnzhe jiǎo zǒu] ▶ **on tiptoe** 踮着脚走

tire ['taɪə(r)] **I** N (US) = **tyre II** VT (*also: tire out*) (*make tired*) 使疲劳 [shǐ píláo] **III** VI (*become tired*) 疲劳 [píláo] ▶ **to tire of sth** 对某事感到厌倦了

tired ['taɪəd] ADJ 累的 [lèi de] ▶ **to be tired of (doing) sth** 厌倦于 (做) 某事

请勿将 **tired** 与 **tiring** 混淆。如果你 **tired**,说明你感到疲劳,需要休息。*Do you mind if I sit down? I'm feeling very tired.* **tiring** 的任务或旅途让人感到 **tired**。*Looking after young children is very tiring…I went to bed early after the long and tiring journey.*

tiresome ['taɪəsəm] ADJ 讨厌的 [tǎoyàn de]

tiring ['taɪərɪŋ] ADJ [+ work, day etc] 令人疲劳的 [lìng rén píláo de]

用法参见 **tired**

tissue ['tɪʃu:] N **1** [U] (ANAT, BIO) 组织 [zǔzhī] **2** [c] (*paper handkerchief*) 纸巾 [zhǐjīn]

tissue paper N [U] 绵纸 [miánzhǐ]

tit [tɪt] N [c] **1** (*infl*) (*breast*) 乳房 [rǔfáng] **2** (*bird*) 山雀 [shānquè] ▶ **tit for tat** 以牙还牙

title ['taɪtl] N **1** [c] [of book, play etc] 标题 [biāotí] **2** [c] (*rank*) 称号 [chēnghào] **3** [c] (SPORT) 冠军 [guànjūn] **4** [U] (LAW) (*right*) ▶ **title to** 所有权 [suǒyǒuquán]

T-junction ['ti:'dʒʌŋkʃən] N [c] 丁字路口 [dīngzì lùkǒu]

to [tu:, tə] **I** PREP **1** (*direction*) 到 [dào] ▶ **to France/London/school/the station** 去法国/伦敦/学校/车站 ▶ **we went to a party last night** 我们昨晚去参加了一个聚会 ▶ **the road to Manchester** 通往曼彻斯特的路

2 (as far as) ▸ **from here to London** 从这儿到伦敦 [cóng zhèr dào Lúndūn] ▸ **to count to ten** 数到10

3 (position) 向 [xiàng] ▸ **to the north/south** 朝北/南 ▸ **to the left/right** 向左/右 ▸ **nailed/stuck to the wall** 钉/粘在墙上

4 (in time expressions) ▸ **it's five/ten/a quarter to five** 差5分/10分/一刻5点 [chà wǔfēn/shífēn/yíkè wǔ diǎn]

5 (for, of) 的 [de] ▸ **the key to the front door** 前门的钥匙 ▸ **a letter to his wife** 给他妻子的一封信 ▸ **she is secretary to the director** 她是主管的秘书

6 (indirect object) ▸ **to give sth to sb** 给某人某物 [gěi mǒurén mǒuwù] ▸ **to talk to sb** 对某人说 ▸ **I sold it to a friend** 我把它卖给了一个朋友 ▸ **you've done something to your hair** 你打理了你的头发 ▸ **it was clear to me that...** 对我来说这显而易见…; (after noun) (involving) ▸ **damage to sth** 对某物的损害 ▸ **a danger to sb** 对某人的危险 ▸ **repairs to sth** 对某物的修理

7 (towards) ▸ **to be friendly/kind/loyal to sb** 对某人友好/仁慈/忠实 [duì mǒurén yǒuhǎo/réncí/zhōngshí]

8 (in relation to) ▸ **30 miles to the gallon** 每加仑可行30英里 [měi jiālún kě xíng sānshí yīnglǐ] ▸ **A is to B as C is to D** A与B的关系就像C与D的关系 ▸ **three goals to two** 3比2

9 (purpose, result) ▸ **to come to sb's aid** 来帮某人的忙 [lái bāng mǒurén de máng] ▸ **to sentence sb to death** 判某人死刑

10 (indicating range, extent) ▸ **from... to...** 从…到…[cóng…dào…] ▸ **everything from seeds to vegetables** 从种子到蔬菜的每样东西 ▸ **from May to September** 从5月到9月

11 (with) ▸ **to enter to the sound of drums** 随着鼓声进入 [suízhe gǔshēng jìnrù] **II WITH VERB 1** (simple infinitive) 与原形动词一起构成动词不定式 ▸ **to go/eat** 走/吃 ▸ **to want/to try to do sth** 想/试着做某事

2 (with vb omitted) 用来代替动词不定式或不定式短语, 避免重复 ▸ **I don't want to** 我不想 ▸ **you ought to** 你应该

3 (in order to) 为了 [wèile] ▸ **I did it to help you** 我这么做是为了帮你 ▸ **measures to help developing nations** 用以帮助发展中国家的措施

4 (equivalent to relative clause) 用作定语 ▸ **I have things to do** 我有事要做 ▸ **he has a lot to lose** 他要失去很多

5 (after adjective etc) 用于某些动词、名词、形容词后构成不定式 ▸ **to be ready to go** 准备走 ▸ **it's great to see you** 见到

你太好了 ▸ **too old/young to do sth** 年纪太大/太小以至于不能做某事 ▸ **it's too heavy to lift** 它太重了根本提不动 ▸ **to be old/young enough to do sth** 到了做某事的年龄/足够年轻做某事

6 (and) ▸ **he awoke/arrived to find that everyone had gone** 他醒来/到了发现大家都走了 [tā xǐnglái/dàole fāxiàn dàjiā dōu zǒule]

III ADV ▸ **to push/pull the door to** 把门掩上 [bǎ mén yǎnshang] ▸ **to and fro** 来来回回地

toad [təud] N [c] 蟾蜍 [chánchú]

toadstool ['təudstu:l] N [c] (CULIN) 毒菌 [dújūn]

toast [təust] **I** N **1** [U] (CULIN) 烤面包 [kǎomiànbāo] **2** [c] (drink) 祝酒 [zhùjiǔ] **II** VT **1** (CULIN) (+ bread etc) 烤 [kǎo] **2** (drink to) 为…祝酒 [wèi…zhùjiǔ] ▸ **a piece** or **slice of toast** 一片烤面包 ▸ **to drink a toast to sb** 为某人干杯

toaster ['təustə(r)] N [c] 烤面包机 [kǎo miànbāo jī]

tobacco [tə'bækəu] N [U] 烟草 [yāncǎo]

tobacconist's (shop) [tə'bækənɪsts-] N [c] 烟草店 [yāncǎodiàn]

toboggan [tə'bɔgən] N [c] 平底雪橇 [píngdǐ xuěqiāo]

⊙ **today** [tə'deɪ] **I** ADV **1** 今天 [jīntiān] ▷ I hope you're feeling better today. 我希望你今天感觉好些。 **2** (at the present time) 现在 [xiànzài] ▷ This is the best translation available today. 这是现存的最好的翻译。 **II** N [U] **1** 今天 [jīntiān] ▷ Today is Thursday. 今天星期四。 **2** (the present time) 现今 [xiànjīn] ▷ the Africa of today 现今的非洲 ▸ **what day is it today?** 今天星期几？ ▸ **a week ago today** 上星期的今天 ▸ **today is the 4th of March** 今天是3月4日 ▸ **today's paper** 今天的报纸

toddler ['tɔdlə(r)] N [c] 学步的小孩 [xuébù de xiǎoháir]

toe [təu] N [c] **1** (of foot) 脚趾 [jiǎozhǐ] **2** (of shoe, sock) 脚趾处 [jiǎozhǐchù] ▸ **big/little toe** 大/小脚趾 ▸ **to toe the line** 听从命令

TOEFL ['təufəl] N ABBR (= Test of English as a Foreign Language) 托福 [Tuōfú]

toenail ['təuneɪl] N [c] 脚指甲 [jiǎozhǐjiǎ]

toffee ['tɔfɪ] N **1** [U] (BRIT) (substance) 太妃糖 [tàifēitáng] [美= **taffy**] **2** [c] (sweet) 乳脂糖 [rǔzhītáng]

⊙ **together** [tə'gɛðə(r)] ADV **1** (with each other) 一起 [yìqǐ] ▷ We went on long bicycle rides together. 我们一起骑了很长一段时间的自行车。 **2** (in the same place) 在一起 [zài yìqǐ] ▷ The trees grew close together. 这些树长拢在一起。 **3** (at the same time) 同时 [tóngshí] ▷ Three horses crossed the finish line together. 3匹马同时越过终点线。 **4** (in a group) 合在一起 [hé zài yìqǐ] ▷ Mix the ingredients together thoroughly. 把这些原料充分

地合在一起。**5** (combined) 加起来 [jiā qǐlái] ▷ *The two opposition parties together won 29 per cent of the vote.* 两个反对党加起来赢得29%的选票。 ▸ **together with** 连同

Togo ['təʊgəʊ] N 多哥 [Duōgē]

toilet ['tɔɪlət] I N [c] **1** (apparatus) 抽水马桶 [chōushuǐ mǎtǒng] **2** (BRIT) (room) 卫生间 [wèishēngjiān] [美=**bathroom**] II CPD [复合词] [+ kit, accessories etc] 厕所 [cèsuǒ] ▸ **to go to the toilet** (ESP BRIT) 上厕所

toilet bag (BRIT) N [c] 洗漱包 [xǐshùbāo]

toilet paper N [U] 卫生纸 [wèishēngzhǐ]

toiletries ['tɔɪlətrɪz] NPL 卫生用品 [wèishēng yòngpǐn]

toilet roll N [c/U] 卫生卷纸 [wèishēng juǎnzhǐ]

token ['təʊkən] I N [c] **1** (sign) 象征 [xiàngzhēng] **2** (instead of money) 代金券 [dàijīnquàn] II ADJ [+ strike, payment, gesture] 象征性的 [xiàngzhēngxìng de] ▸ **by the same token** 同样

told [təʊld] PT, PP of **tell**

tolerable ['tɔlərəbl] ADJ **1** (bearable) 可忍受的 [kě rěnshòu de] **2** (frm) (fairly good) 相当好的 [xiāngdāng hǎo de]

tolerant ['tɔlərnt] ADJ 宽容的 [kuānróng de] ▸ **to be tolerant of** 对…宽容

tolerate ['tɔləreɪt] VT **1** [+ pain, noise etc] 忍受 [rěnshòu] **2** (accept) 容忍 [róngrěn]

toll [təʊl] I N [c] **1** [of casualties, accidents] 伤亡人数 [shāngwáng rénshù] **2** (on road, bridge) 通行费 [tōngxíngfèi] II VI [bell +] 鸣响 [míngxiǎng] ▸ **the work took its toll on us** 这工作让我们受尽折磨

toll-free ['təʊlfriː] (US: TEL) I ADJ [+ number] 免费的 [miǎnfèi de] [英=**Freephone®**] II ADV ▸ **to call toll-free** 拨打免费电话 [bōdǎ miǎnfèi diànhuà]

tomato [tə'mɑːtəʊ] (pl **tomatoes**) N [c/U] 西红柿 [xīhóngshì]

tomato sauce (CULIN) N [U] (ketchup) 西红柿酱 [xīhóngshì jiàng]

tomb [tuːm] N [c] 坟墓 [fénmù]

tombstone ['tuːmstəʊn] N [c] 墓碑 [mùbēi]

tomorrow [tə'mɔrəʊ] I ADV **1** 明天 [míngtiān] **2** (in the future) 未来 [wèilái] II N **1** [U] 明天 [míngtiān] **2** [c/U] (future) 将来 [jiānglái] ▸ **a week tomorrow, tomorrow week** 下星期的明天 ▸ **the day after tomorrow** 后天 ▸ **tomorrow morning** 明天早晨

ton [tʌn] N [c] **1** (BRIT) 英吨 [yīngdūn] **2** (US) (also: **short ton**) 美吨 [měidūn] **3** (metric ton) 公吨 [gōngdūn] ▸ **tons of** (inf) 大量的

tone [təʊn] I N **1** [c] [of sound] 音质 [yīnzhì] **2** [c] [of voice] 腔调 [qiāngdiào] **3** [s] [of speech, article etc] 基调 [jīdiào] **4** [c/U] [of colour] 色调 [sèdiào] **5** [s] (TEL) 声音 [shēngyīn] II VT (also: **tone up**) [+ muscles] 增强 [zēngqiáng]

▸ **tone down** VT **1** [+ criticism etc] 缓和 [huǎnhé] **2** [+ colour, flavour] 调和 [tiáohé] ▸ **tone in with, tone with** (ESP BRIT) VT FUS [不可拆分] 搭配 [dāpèi]

Tonga [tɔŋgə] N 汤加 [Tāngjiā]

tongs [tɔŋz] NPL 夹子 [jiāzi]

tongue [tʌŋ] N **1** [c] (ANAT) 舌头 [shétou] **2** [U] (CULIN) 口条 [kǒutiáo] **3** [c] (frm) (language) 语言 [yǔyán] ▸ **tongue in cheek** 毫无诚意的

tonic ['tɔnɪk] N **1** [U] (also: **tonic water**) 奎宁水 [kuíníngshuǐ] **2** [c/U] (MED) 滋补品 [zībǔpǐn] **3** [c] (fig) (boost) 有兴奋作用的东西 [yǒu xīngfèn zuòyòng de dōngxi]

tonight [tə'naɪt] ADV, N 今晚 [jīnwǎn]

tonsil ['tɔnsl] N [c] 扁桃体 [biǎntáotǐ] ▸ **to have one's tonsils out** 切除扁桃体

tonsillitis [tɔnsɪ'laɪtɪs] N [U] 扁桃腺炎 [biǎntáoxiànyán]

○**too** [tuː] ADV **1** (excessively) 太 [tài] ▷ *It was too far to walk.* 要是走路就太远了。**2** (also) 也 [yě] ▷ *You're from Brooklyn? Me too!* 你从布鲁克林来？我也是！**3** (for emphasis) 并且 [bìngqiě] ▷ *We did learn to read, and quickly too.* 我们确实学会了阅读，并且学得很快。▸ **too bad!** 很遗憾！▸ **I'm not too happy with it** 我对此并不是很高兴 ▸ **all too well/recently, only too well/recently** 好/近得不能再好/近

▨用法参见 **also**

took [tʊk] PT of **take**

tool [tuːl] N [c] **1** (implement) 用具 [yòngjù] **2** (fig) 工具 [gōngjù] **3** (pej) (person) 爪牙 [zhǎoyá]

tool box N [c] 工具箱 [gōngjùxiāng]

tool kit N [c] 工具包 [gōngjùbāo]

tooth [tuːθ] (pl **teeth**) N [c] **1** (ANAT) 牙齿 [yáchǐ] **2** [of comb, saw, zip] 齿 [chǐ] ▸ **to have a tooth out** or (US) **pulled** 拔牙 ▸ **to brush one's teeth** 刷牙

toothache ['tuːθeɪk] N [c/U] 牙痛 [yátòng] ▸ **to have toothache** 牙痛

toothbrush ['tuːθbrʌʃ] N [c] 牙刷 [yáshuā]

toothpaste ['tuːθpeɪst] N [c/U] 牙膏 [yágāo]

toothpick ['tuːθpɪk] N [c] 牙签 [yáqiān]

○**top** [tɔp] I N **1** [c] [of mountain, building, tree, stairs] 顶部 [dǐngbù] **2** [c] [of page] 顶端 [dǐngduān] ▷ *Go back to the top of the page.* 回到本页的顶端。**3** [c] [of cupboard] 顶层 [dǐngcéng] **4** [c] [of surface, table] 表面 [biǎomiàn] **5** [s] (ESP BRIT) [of street] 尽头 [jìntóu] **6** [c] (lid) [of box, jar, bottle] 盖子 [gàizi] **7** [s] [of table, league] 榜首 [bǎngshǒu] **8** [c] (AUT) (also: **top gear**) 最高挡 [zuì gāodǎng] **9** [c] [blouse etc] 上衣 [shàngyī] II ADJ **1** [+ shelf, step, storey, marks] 最高的 [zuìgāo de] **2** [+ executive, golfer etc] 顶级的 [dǐngjí de] ▸ **top speed** 全速 III VT **1** (be first in) [+ poll, vote, list] 获第一名 [huò dìyī míng] **2** (exceed) [+ estimate, speed etc] 超过 [chāoguò] ▷ *US investments here topped fifty million dollars.* 美

国的投资超过5000万美元。▸ **at the top of the stairs/page/street** 在楼梯/页面的顶端/街道的尽头 ▸ **at the top of the list** 居于榜首 ▸ **to get to the top** (*in profession etc*) 取得高层地位 ▸ **on top of** (*above*) 在…上面 ▷ *She laid her hand on top of his.* 她把手放在他的手上。; (*in addition to*) 除…之外 ▷ *700 jobs are being cut on top of the 2000 that were lost last year.* 除了去年2000人失去工作之外，又有700个工作职位被削减。▸ **to get on top of sth** (*fig*) 圆满地处理某事 ▸ **from top to bottom** 彻底 ▸ **from top to toe** (BRIT) 从头到脚 ▸ **at the top of one's voice** 扯着嗓子叫喊 ▸ **to be/go over the top** (BRIT: *inf*) 过分 ▸ **top priority** 最优先 ▸ **to be or come top** 独占鳌头

▸ **top up** VT **1** [+ *drink*] 加满 [jiāmǎn] **2** [+ *salary, loan*] 增加 [zēngjiā]

top hat N [C] 大礼帽 [dà lǐmào]

topic ['tɔpɪk] N [C] 话题 [huàtí]

topical ['tɔpɪkl] ADJ [+ *issue, question*] 热门的 [rèmén de]

topless ['tɔplɪs] ADJ [+ *bather, waitress, dancer*] 袒胸的 [tǎnxiōng de]

topping ['tɔpɪŋ] (CULIN) N [C/U] 配料 [pèiliào]

topple ['tɔpl] I VT [+ *government, leader*] 推翻 [tuīfān] II VI (*also*: **topple over**) [*person, object* +] 翻倒 [fāndǎo]

torch [tɔːtʃ] N [C] **1** (BRIT) (*electric*) 手电筒 [shǒudiàntǒng] [美= **flashlight**] **2** (*with flame*) 火把 [huǒbǎ]

tore [tɔː(r)] PT *of* **tear**[1]

torment [n 'tɔːmɛnt, vb tɔː'mɛnt] I N [C/U] 折磨 [zhémó] II VT **1** [*feelings, guilt* +] 折磨 [zhémó] **2** (*annoy*) 折磨 [zhémó] ▸ **in torment** 在折磨中

torn [tɔːn] I PP *of* **tear**[1] II ADJ ▸ **to be torn between** 在两者中游移不定 [zài liǎngzhě zhōng yóuyí bùdìng]

tornado [tɔː'neɪdəu] (*pl* **tornadoes**) N [C] 飓风 [jùfēng]

torpedo [tɔː'piːdəu] (*pl* **torpedoes**) N [C] 鱼雷 [yúléi]

torrent ['tɔrnt] N [C] **1** (*flood*) 急流 [jíliú] **2** (*fig*) ▸ **a torrent of abuse/questions** 一片谩骂/成堆的问题 [yī piàn mànmà/chéngduī de wèntí]

torrential [tɔ'rɛnʃl] ADJ [+ *rain*] 滂沱的 [pāngtuó de]

tortoise ['tɔːtəs] N [C] 乌龟 [wūguī]

torture ['tɔːtʃə(r)] I N [U] **1** 酷刑 [kùxíng] **2** (*torment*) 折磨 [zhémó] II VT **1** 对…施以酷刑 [duì…shīyǐ kùxíng] **2** (*torment*) 使痛苦 [shǐ tòngkǔ]

Tory ['tɔːrɪ] (BRIT: POL) I ADJ 保守党的 [Bǎoshǒudǎng de] II N [C] 保守党党员 [Bǎoshǒudǎng dǎngyuán]

toss [tɔs] I VT **1** 扔 [rēng] **2** [*wind, sea* +] [+ *boat etc*] 使颠簸 [shǐ diānbǒ] **3** [+ *salad*] 拌 [bàn] **4** [+ *pancake*] 抛起使翻转 [pāoqǐ shǐ fānzhuǎn]

II N **1** ▸ **with a toss of her head** 她把头往后一仰 [tā bǎ tóu wǎnghòu yī yǎng] **2** ▸ **to decide sth by the toss of a coin** 抛硬币决定某事 [pāo yìngbì juédìng mǒushì] ▸ **to toss a coin** 掷硬币 ▸ **to toss one's head** 一摆头 ▸ **to win/lose the toss** (SPORT) 掷硬币占上风/落下风 ▸ **I don't give a toss** (BRIT: *inf*) 我不在乎 ▸ **to toss and turn** (*in bed*) 辗转反侧

▸ **toss up** VI 掷硬币决定 [zhì yìngbì juédìng]

⊕**total** ['təutl] I ADJ **1** [+ *number, workforce, cost etc*] 总的 [zǒng de] **2** (*complete*) [+ *failure, wreck, stranger*] 完全的 [wánquán de] II N [C] (*sum of money, number*) 总数 [zǒngshù] ▷ *The companies have a total of 1776 employees.* 公司总共有1776名员工。II VT **1** (*add up*) 加起来 [jiā qǐlái] ▷ *Votes cast for each candidate will be totalled.* 每个候选人的选票要被加起来。**2** (*add up to*) 总计 [zǒngjì] ▷ *1980 revenues totalled 18 billion dollars.* 1980年税收总计180亿美元。▸ **in total** 总共

totalitarian [təutælɪ'tɛərɪən] ADJ [+ *regime, state*] 极权主义的 [jíquán zhǔyì de]

totally ['təutəlɪ] ADV **1** [*agree, destroy* +] 完全地 [wánquán de] **2** [+ *different, new*] 绝对地 [juéduì de]

touch [tʌtʃ] I N **1** [U] (*sense of touch*) 触觉 [chùjué] **2** [C] (*contact*) 触摸 [chùmō] **3** [C] (*detail*) 修饰 [xiūshì] II VT **1** (*with hand, foot*) 触摸 [chùmō] **2** (*tamper with*) 瞎搞 [xiāgǎo] **3** (*make contact with*) 碰到 [pèngdào] **4** (*move*) (*emotionally*) 感动 [gǎndòng] **5** (*use, consume*) 碰过 [pèngguò] III VI (*be in contact*) 接触 [jiēchù] ▸ **a personal touch** 独特的方法 ▸ **to put the finishing touches to sth** 对某事物做最后的润色 ▸ **a touch of frost/flu** etc 些微的霜/有点儿感冒{等} ▸ **to be out of touch** 落伍的 ▸ **to be/keep in touch with sth** 与某事保持联系 ▸ **to be/keep in touch (with sb)** (与某人) 保持联系 ▸ **to get in touch with sb** 与某人联系 ▸ **to lose touch (with sb)** (与某人) 失去联系

▸ **touch down** VI [*aircraft* +] 着陆 [zhuólù]

▸ **touch on** VT FUS [不可拆分] (*mention*) 提及 [tíjí]

▸ **touch up** VT (*paint*) 修饰 [xiūshì]

touchdown ['tʌtʃdaun] N **1** [C/U] [*of aircraft, spacecraft*] 着陆 [zhuólù] **2** [C] (SPORT) 触地得分 [chùdì défēn]

touched [tʌtʃt] ADJ (*emotionally*) 感动的 [gǎndòng de]

touching ['tʌtʃɪŋ] ADJ (*moving*) [+ *scene, story etc*] 使人感动的 [shǐrén gǎndòng de]

touchline ['tʌtʃlaɪn] (SPORT) N [S] 边线 [biānxiàn]

touch-sensitive ['tʌtʃ'sɛnsɪtɪv] ADJ [+ *screen*] 触摸感应的 [chùmōgǎnyìng de]

touchy ['tʌtʃɪ] ADJ **1** [+ *person*] 敏感的 [mǐngǎn de] **2** [+ *subject*] 棘手的 [jíshǒu de]

tough [tʌf] ADJ **1** (*strong, hard-wearing*)

[+*material*] 坚韧的 [jiānrèn de] **2** [+*meat*] 老的 [lǎo de] **3** [+*person, animal*] (*physically*) 强壮的 [qiángzhuàng de] **4** (*mentally*) 顽强的 [wánqiáng de] **5** (*difficult*) [+*task, problem, way of life*] 艰辛的 [jiānxīn de] **6** [+*time*] 倒霉的 [dǎoméi de] **7** (*firm*) [+*stance, negotiations, policies*] 严格的 [yángé de] **8** (*rough*) 无法无天的 [wú fǎ wú tiān de] ▸ **tough (luck)!** 倒霉！

tour ['tʊə(r)] **I** N [c] **1** (*journey*) 旅行 [lǚxíng] **2** [*of town, factory, museum*] 观光 [guānguāng] **3** (*by pop group, sports team etc*) 巡回表演 [xúnhuí biǎoyǎn] **II** VT [+*country, city etc*] 观光 [guānguāng] ▷ *The Prime Minister toured the poorest area of Liverpool.* 首相巡视了利物浦最贫穷的地区。▸ **to go on a tour of** [+*museum etc*] 去游览…; [+*region*] 去…旅行 ▸ **to go/be on tour** [*pop group, theatre company etc* +] 进行巡回演出

tour director (US) N [c] 导游 [dǎoyóu]

tour guide N [c] 导游 [dǎoyóu] [美= **tour director**]

tourism ['tʊərɪzm] N [U] 旅游业 [lǚyóuyè]

tourist ['tʊərɪst] **I** N [c] 游客 [yóukè] **II** CPD [复合词] [+*season, attraction*] 旅游 [lǚyóu] ▸ **the tourist trade** 旅游业

tourist office N [c] 旅游咨询处 [lǚyóu zīxúnchù]

tournament ['tʊənəmənt] N [c] 锦标赛 [jǐnbiāosài]

tow [təʊ] **I** VT [+*vehicle, trailer*] 拖 [tuō] **II** N (AUT) ▸ **to give sb a tow** 帮某人拖车 [bāng mǒurén tuōchē] ▸ **to have sb in tow** (*inf*) 带着某人 ▸ **"on** *or* (US) **in tow"** (AUT) "被拖着" ▸ **tow away** VT [+*vehicle*] 拖走 [tuōzǒu]

○**toward(s)** [tə'wɔːd(z)] PREP **1** (*in direction of*) (*lit*) 朝着 [cháozhe] ▷ *He saw his mother running toward(s) him.* 他看见妈妈朝着他跑来。; (*fig*) 向着 [xiàngzhe] ▷ *the trend toward(s) couples living together rather than marrying* 向着同居而不结婚方向发展的趋势 **2** (*with regard to*) 对于 [duìyú] ▷ *There has been a change of attitude toward(s) science.* 对于科学有态度上的转变。**3** (*near*) 接近 [jiējìn] ▷ *Their home was toward(s) the top of the hill.* 他们的家接近山顶。**4** (*as contribution to*) 为 [wèi] ▷ *He gave them £20,000 toward(s) a house.* 他为他们的房子捐助两万英镑。**5** (*in time*) 接近 [jiējìn] ▷ *towards the end of the year* 接近年底时

towel ['taʊəl] **I** N [c] 毛巾 [máojīn] **II** VT [+*hair*] 用毛巾擦 [yòng máojīn cā] ▸ **to throw in the towel** (*fig*) 认输 ▸ **to towel o.s. dry** 用毛巾擦干自己

towelling ['taʊəlɪŋ] N [U] (*fabric*) 毛巾布 [máojīnbù]

tower ['taʊə(r)] **I** N [c] 塔 [tǎ] **II** VI [*building, mountain* +] 耸立 [sǒnglì] ▸ **to tower above** *or* **over sb/sth** 比某人/某物高得多

tower block (BRIT) N [c] 高楼大厦 [gāolóu dàshà]

○**town** [taʊn] N **1** [c] 城镇 [chéngzhèn] **2** [U] (*one's home town*) 家乡 [jiāxiāng] ▷ *She left town.* 她离开了家乡。▸ **to go to town** (*fig*) 以极大的精力去做 ▸ **in town** 在市中心 ▸ **to be out of town** 出城

town centre (BRIT) N [c] 市中心 [shì zhōngxīn]

town hall (BRIT) N [c] 市政厅 [shìzhèngtīng]

tow rope ['təʊrəʊp] N [c] 拖绳 [tuōshéng]

tow truck (US) N [c] (*breakdown lorry*) 拖车 [tuōchē]

toxic ['tɒksɪk] ADJ [+*fumes, waste etc*] 有毒的 [yǒudú de]

toy [tɔɪ] **I** N [c] 玩具 [wánjù] **II** CPD [复合词] [+*train, car etc*] 玩具 [wánjù] ▸ **toy with** VT FUS [不可拆分] **1** [+*object, food*] 心不在焉地摆弄 [xīn bù zài yān de bǎinòng] **2** [+*idea*] 漫不经心地考虑 [màn bù jīngxīn de kǎolǜ]

toyshop ['tɔɪʃɒp] N [c] 玩具店 [wánjùdiàn]

trace [treɪs] **I** N [c] **1** (*sign*) [*of substance*] 痕迹 [hénjì]; [*of person*] 踪迹 [zōngjì] **2** (*small amount*) ▸ **a trace of** 微量的 [wēiliàng de] **II** VT **1** (*draw*) [+*picture*] 描摹 [miáomó] **2** (*with finger*) 勾画 [gōuhuà] **3** (*also*: **trace back**) [+*development, progress etc*] 追溯 [zhuīsù] **4** (*locate*) [+*person, letter*] 追踪 [zhuīzōng]; [+*cause*] 探究 [tànjiū] ▸ **to vanish** *or* **disappear without trace** 消失得无影无踪

track [træk] **I** N [c] **1** (*path*) 小径 [xiǎojìng] **2** [*of bullet etc*] 轨迹 [guǐjì] **3** [*of suspect, animal*] 足迹 [zújì] **4** (RAIL) 轨道 [guǐdào] **5** (*on tape, record*) 曲目 [qǔmù] **6** (SPORT) 跑道 [pǎodào] **II** VT (*follow*) [+*animal, person*] 追踪 [zhuīzōng] ▸ **to keep/lose track of sb/sth** 掌握/跟不上某人/某物的动态 ▸ **to be on the right track** (*fig*) 方向正确 ▸ **track down** VT [+*prey, criminal*] 追踪到 [zhuīzōng dào]

tracksuit ['træksuːt] (BRIT) N [c] 运动服 [yùndòngfú] [美= **sweatsuit**]

tractor ['træktə(r)] N [c] 拖拉机 [tuōlājī]

○**trade** [treɪd] **I** N **1** [U] (*buying and selling*) 贸易 [màoyì] **2** [c] (*skill, job*) 谋生之道 [móushēng zhī dào] **3** [c] (*specific kind of work*) 行业 [hángyè] ▸ **the book trade** 图书业 **II** VI (*do business*) 做生意 [zuò shēngyì] **III** VT **1** (*exchange*) ▸ **to trade sth (for sth)** (ESP US) 用某物交换(某物) [yòng mǒuwù jiāohuàn (mǒuwù)] ▸ **to trade with** [+*country, company*] 与…进行贸易 ▸ **to trade in** [+*merchandise*] 从事业 ▸ **trade in** VT [+*old car etc*] 以旧换新 [yǐ jiù huàn xīn]

trademark ['treɪdmɑːk] N [c] 商标 [shāngbiāo]

trader ['treɪdə(r)] N [c] 商人 [shāngrén]

tradesman ['treɪdzmən] (*pl* **tradesmen**) N [c]

1 (*workman*) 工匠 [gōngjiàng] **2** (*shopkeeper*) 小业主 [xiǎoyèzhǔ]

trade union (ESP BRIT) N [c] 工会 [gōnghuì] [美= **labor union**]

trading ['treɪdɪŋ] N [U] 交易 [jiāoyì]

tradition [trə'dɪʃən] N [c/U] 传统 [chuántǒng]

traditional [trə'dɪʃənl] ADJ [+ *costume, music, method etc*] 传统的 [chuántǒng de]

traffic ['træfɪk] I N [U] **1** (*vehicles*) 交通 [jiāotōng] **2** [*in drugs etc*] 非法交易 [fēifǎ jiāoyì] **3** (*air traffic, sea traffic etc*) 航行 [hángxíng] II VI ▸ **to traffic in** [+ *liquor, drugs*] 贩卖 [fànmài]

traffic circle (US) N [c] 转盘 [zhuànpán] [英= **roundabout**]

traffic jam N [c] 交通阻塞 [jiāotōng zǔsè]

traffic lights NPL 红绿灯 [hónglǜdēng]

traffic warden (ESP BRIT) N [c] 交通管理员 [jiāotōng guǎnlǐyuán]

tragedy ['trædʒədɪ] N [c/U] **1** (*disaster*) 极大的不幸 [jídà de bùxìng] **2** (THEAT) 悲剧 [bēijù]

tragic ['trædʒɪk] ADJ **1** [+ *death, consequences, accident*] 悲惨的 [bēicǎn de] **2** (THEAT) [+ *play, hero etc*] 悲剧的 [bēijù de]

trail [treɪl] I N [c] **1** (*path*) 小路 [xiǎolù] **2** [*of footprints etc*] 串 [chuàn] II VT **1** (*drag*) [+ *scarf, coat, fingers*] 拖 [tuō] **2** (*follow*) [+ *person, animal*] 跟踪 [gēnzōng] III VI **1** (*drag*) [*scarf, coat, fingers +*] 拖曳 [tuōyè] **2** (*move slowly*) 拖着步子走 [tuōzhe bùzi zǒu] **3** (*in game, contest*) 落后 [luòhòu] ▸ **to be on the trail of sb/sth, be on sb's trail** 追踪某人/某物
▸ **trail away, trail off** VI [*sound, voice +*] 渐弱至无声 [jiànruò zhì wúshēng]

trailer ['treɪlə(r)] N [c] **1** (AUT) 拖车 [tuōchē] **2** (US) (*caravan*) 房式拖车 [fángshì tuōchē] [英= **caravan**] **3** (CINE, TV) 预告片 [yùgàopiàn]

trailer park (US) N [c] 活动住房停放处 [huódòng zhùfáng tíngfàngchù] [英= **caravan site**]

train [treɪn] I N [c] **1** (RAIL) 火车 [huǒchē] **2** [*of dress*] 裙裾 [qúnjū] II VT **1** (*teach skills to*) 培训 [péixùn] **2** [+ *dog*] 训练 [xùnliàn] **3** [+ *athlete*] 培养 [péiyǎng] **4** (*educate*) [+ *mind*] 开发 [kāifā] **5** [+ *plant*] 给⋯整枝 [gěi⋯zhěngzhī] ▸ **to train sth on sb/sth** [+ *camera, hose, gun etc*] 把某物对准某人/某物 [bǎ mǒuwù duìzhǔn mǒurén/mǒuwù] III VI **1** (*learn a skill*) 受训练 [shòu xùnliàn] **2** (SPORT) 锻炼 [duànliàn] ▸ **train of thought** 思路 ▸ **a train of events** 一系列的事件

trained [treɪnd] ADJ **1** [+ *worker, teacher*] 经专门训练的 [jīng zhuānmén xùnliàn de] **2** [+ *animal*] 驯化的 [xùnhuà de] ▸ **to the trained eye** 经专业眼光鉴定

trainee [treɪ'niː] N [c] **1** (*apprentice*) 受训者 [shòuxùnzhě] **2** (*in office, management job*) 实习生 [shíxíshēng]

trainer ['treɪnə(r)] N [c] **1** (SPORT) 教练 [jiàoliàn] **2** (BRIT) (*shoe*) 运动鞋 [yùndòngxié] [美= **sneaker**] **3** [*of animals*] 驯兽师 [xùnshòushī]

training ['treɪnɪŋ] N [U] **1** (*for occupation*) 培训 [péixùn] **2** (SPORT) 训练 [xùnliàn] ▸ **to be in training for sth** (SPORT) 为某事进行训练

training course N [c] 培训班 [péixùnbān]

trait [treɪt] N [c] 特性 [tèxìng]

traitor ['treɪtə(r)] N [c] 叛徒 [pàntú]

tram [træm] (BRIT) N [c] (*also:* **tramcar**) 有轨电车 [yǒuguǐ diànchē] [美= **streetcar**] ▸ **to go by tram** 乘有轨电车去

tramp [træmp] I N **1** (*vagrant*) 流浪者 [liúlàngzhě] **2** (ESP US: *inf, pej*) (*woman*) 荡妇 [dàngfù] II VI (*walk slowly*) 踏 [tà] III VT [+ *town, streets*] 踏遍 [tàbiàn]

trample ['træmpl] I VT **1** [+ *grass, plants*] 践踏 [jiàntà] **2** [+ *person*] 踩 [cǎi] II VI ▸ **to trample on** 践踏在 [jiàntà zài] ▸ **to trample on sb's feelings** 伤害某人的感情

trampoline ['træmpəliːn] N [c] 蹦床 [bèngchuáng]

trance [trɑːns] N [c] 恍惚 [huǎnghū] ▸ **to be in/go into a trance** 在/陷入迷睡状态

tranquil ['træŋkwɪl] ADJ 宁静的 [níngjìng de]

tranquillity, (US) **tranquility** [træŋ'kwɪlɪtɪ] N [U] 安谧 [ānmì]

tranquillizer, (US) **tranquilizer** ['træŋkwɪlaɪzə(r)] N [c] 镇静剂 [zhènjìngjì]

transaction [træn'zækʃən] N [c] (*piece of business*) 交易 [jiāoyì]

transatlantic ['trænzət'læntɪk] ADJ **1** [+ *trade, phone-call, flight etc*] 跨越大西洋的 [kuàyuè Dàxīyáng de] **2** (BRIT) (*American*) 大西洋彼岸的 [Dàxīyáng bǐ'àn de]

transcript ['trænskrɪpt] N [c] [*of tape, notes*] 讲稿 [jiǎnggǎo]

transfer [n 'trænsfə(r), vb træns'fəː(r)] I N **1** [c/U] [*of money, documents etc*] 转移 [zhuǎnyí] **2** [c/U] [*of employee*] 调任 [diàorèn] **3** [c/U] (POL) [*of power*] 移交 [yíjiāo] **4** [c] (SPORT) 转会 [zhuǎnhuì] **5** [c] (BRIT) (*picture, design*) 转印 [zhuǎnyìn] [美= **decal**] II VT **1** [+ *employee*] 调任 [diàorèn] **2** [+ *money, documents etc*] 转移 [zhuǎnyí] **3** (POL) [+ *power, ownership*] 移交 [yíjiāo] ▸ **by bank transfer** 通过银行转账 ▸ **to transfer the charges** (BRIT: TEL) 收费转移

transform [træns'fɔːm] VT [+ *person, situation etc*] 完全改变 [wánquán gǎibiàn] ▸ **to transform sb/sth into** 使某人/某事变成

transformation [trænsfə'meɪʃən] N [c/U] 改变 [gǎibiàn] ▸ **transformation into sth** 改变成某事物

transfusion [træns'fjuːʒən] N [c/U] (*also:* **blood transfusion**) 输血 [shūxuè]

transit ['trænzɪt] I N **1** ▸ **in transit** (*people*) 在途中 [zài túzhōng]; (*things*) 运送中 [yùnsòng zhōng] **2** [U] (US) 运输 [yùnshū] II ADJ [+ *area,* building] 中转的 [zhōngzhuǎn de]

transition [træn'zɪʃən] N [C/U] 过渡 [guòdù] ▸ **transition from/to sth** 从/向某事物过渡

translate [trænz'leɪt] VT 1 [+ word, book etc] 翻译 [fānyì] 2 (convert) 转化 [zhuǎnhuà] ▸ **to translate a book from English into French** 把一本书从英语翻译成法语

translation [trænz'leɪʃən] N 1 [C] (text) 译文 [yìwén] 2 [U] (act of translating) 翻译 [fānyì] ▸ **to read sth in translation** 读某物的译文

translator [trænz'leɪtə(r)] N [C] 译者 [yìzhě]

transmission [trænz'mɪʃən] N 1 [U] (of information, disease) 传播 [chuánbō] 2 [C] (TV, RAD) (broadcast) 播送 [bōsòng] 3 [U] (act of transmitting) 播出 [bōchū] 4 [C/U] (AUT) 传动装置 [chuándòng zhuāngzhì]

transmit [trænz'mɪt] VT 1 [+ message, signal] 发送 [fāsòng] 2 (frm) [+ disease] 传播 [chuánbō] 3 (TV, RAD) [+ programme] 播出 [bōchū]

transmitter [trænz'mɪtə(r)] (TV, RAD) N [C] 发射机 [fāshèjī]

transparent [træns'pærnt] ADJ 1 [+ blouse, plastic] 透明的 [tòumíng de] 2 (fig) [+ lie, pretence] 显而易见的 [xiǎn ér yì jiàn de]; [+ costs, activity] 清楚的 [qīngchǔ de]

transplant [vb træns'plɑːnt, n 'trænsplɑːnt] I VT 1 (MED) [+ organ] 移植 [yízhí] 2 (move) 使迁移 [shǐ qiānyí] 3 [+ plant] 移栽 [yízāi] II N 1 [C/U] (MED) (operation) 移植 [yízhí] 2 [C] (MED) (organ) 移植器官 [yízhí qìguān] ▸ **to have a heart/liver transplant** 进行心脏/肝脏移植

transport [n 'trænspɔːt, vb træns'pɔːt] I N [U] 1 [of people, goods] 运输 [yùnshū] 2 (transportation) 交通工具 [jiāotōng gōngjù] II VT (move) 运送 [yùnsòng] ▸ **to have one's own transport** 有自己的交通工具 ▸ **public transport** (ESP BRIT) 公共交通 ▸ **Department of Transport** (BRIT) 交通部

transportation ['trænspɔː'teɪʃən] N [U] 1 (US) (transport) 运输 [yùnshū] 2 (means of transport) 交通工具 [jiāotōng gōngjù] ▸ **Department of Transportation** (US) 交通部

transvestite [trænz'vestaɪt] N [C] 爱穿着异性衣物的人 [ài chuānzhuó yìxìng yīwù de rén]

trap [træp] I N [C] 1 (for animals) 陷阱 [xiànjǐng] 2 (trick) 圈套 [quāntào] 3 (carriage) 双轮马车 [shuānglún mǎchē] II VT 1 [+ animal] 诱捕 [yòubǔ] 2 (trick) [+ person] 诱导 [yòudǎo] 3 (confine) (in bad marriage etc) 使陷入 [shǐ xiànrù] 4 (in building etc) 困住 [kùnzhù] 5 (capture) [+ gas, water, energy] 使不泄漏 [shǐ bù xièlòu] ▸ **to set** or **lay a trap for sb** 为某人设陷阱 ▸ **to trap one's finger in the door** 某人的手指被门夹了一下

trash [træʃ] N [U] 1 (US) 废物 [fèiwù] [英= **rubbish**] 2 (pej) (nonsense) 胡说八道 [hú shuō bā dào]

trash can (US) N [C] 垃圾桶 [lājitǒng] [英=

(dust) bin]

trauma ['trɔːmə] N [C/U] 创伤 [chuāngshāng]

traumatic [trɔː'mætɪk] ADJ 创伤的 [chuāngshāng de]

travel ['trævl] I N [U] (travelling) 旅行 [lǚxíng] II VI 1 [person +] 前往 [qiánwǎng] 2 [light, sound, news +] 传播 [chuánbō] III VT [+ distance] 走过 [zǒuguò] IV **travels** NPL 游历 [yóulì] ▸ **news travels fast** 消息传得快 ▸ **this wine doesn't travel well** 这酒不宜长途运输

travel agency N [C] 旅行社 [lǚxíngshè]

travel agent N [C] 1 (shop, office) 旅行中介 [lǚxíng zhōngjiè] 2 (person) 旅行代理人 [lǚxíng dàilǐrén]

traveller, (US) **traveler** ['trævlə(r)] N [C] 1 旅行者 [lǚxíngzhě] 2 (BRIT) (gypsy) 漂泊者 [piāobózhě]

traveller's cheque, (US) **traveler's check** N [C] 旅行支票 [lǚxíng zhīpiào]

travelling, (US) **traveling** ['trævlɪŋ] I N [U] 行程 [xíngchéng] II CPD [复合词] [+ circus, exhibition] 巡回 [xúnhuí] ▸ **travelling expenses** 旅费

travel insurance N [U] 旅行保险 [lǚxíng bǎoxiǎn]

travel rep N [C] 全陪导游 [quánpéi dǎoyóu]

travel sick ADJ 晕车/船/机的 [yùnchē/chuán/jī de]

travel sickness N [U] 晕车/船/机症 [yùnchē/chuán/jī zhèng]

tray [treɪ] N [C] 1 (for food, drink) 托盘 [tuōpán] 2 (on desk) 文件盘 [wénjiànpán]

treacherous ['trɛtʃərəs] ADJ 1 [+ person] 不忠的 [bù zhōng de] 2 [+ ground, conditions, current] 危险的 [wēixiǎn de]

treacle ['triːkl] (BRIT) N [U] (also: black treacle) 糖浆 [tángjiāng] [美= molasses]

tread [trɛd] (pt **trod**, pp **trodden**) I N 1 [S] (footstep) 脚步声 [jiǎobùshēng] 2 [C/U] [of tyre] 轮胎面 [lúntāimiàn] II VI 走 [zǒu] ▸ **to tread carefully** (fig) 小心行事 ▸ **tread on** VT FUS [不可拆分] 踩上 [cǎishang]

treasure ['trɛʒə(r)] I N 1 [U] (gold, jewels etc) 宝藏 [bǎozàng] 2 [C] (inf) (person) 宝贝 [bǎobèi] II VT (value) [+ object, memory, friendship] 珍惜 [zhēnxī] III **treasures** NPL 珍品 [zhēnpǐn]

treasurer ['trɛʒərə(r)] N [C] 财务总管 [cáiwù zǒngguǎn]

treasury ['trɛʒərɪ] N ▸ **the Treasury,** (US) **the Treasury Department** 财政部 [cáizhèngbù]

treat [triːt] I N [C] 1 (gift, present) 待遇 [dàiyù] 2 (luxury) 礼遇 [lǐyù] II VT 1 (behave towards) [+ person, object] 对待 [duìdài] 2 (MED) [+ patient, illness] 医治 [yīzhì] 3 (TECH) [+ substance, material] 处理 [chǔlǐ] ▸ **to treat sth as a joke** 把某事当作笑话 ▸ **to treat sb for a wound/injury** 给某人治疗伤口/伤处 ▸ **to treat a substance/material with sth** 用某物

处理某种物质/材料 ▶ **to treat sb to sth** 用某物款待某人 ▶ **to treat o.s. to sth** 使自己享受某物

treatment ['tri:tmənt] N 1 [U] (attention) 对待 [duìdài] 2 [C/U] (MED) 治疗 [zhìliáo] ▶ **to have** or **receive treatment for sth** (MED) 因某病接受治疗

treaty ['tri:tɪ] N [C] 条约 [tiáoyuē]

treble ['trebl] I ADJ 1 (triple) 三倍的 [sānbèi de] 2 (MUS) [+ instrument] 高音 [gāoyīn]; [+ voice, part] 高音部 [gāoyīnbù] II N [C] 1 (singer) 高音歌手 [gāoyīn gēshǒu] 2 (on hi-fi, radio etc) 高音部 [gāoyīnbù] III VT 使成三倍 [shǐ chéng sānbèi] IV VI 增至三倍 [zēng zhì sānbèi] ▶ **to be treble the amount/size of sth** 是某物数量/大小的三倍

tree [tri:] N [C] 树 [shù]

trek [trɛk] I N [C] 跋涉 [báshè] II VI 徒步穿越 [túbù chuānyuè]

tremble ['trembl] VI 1 [voice +] (with fear etc) 颤抖 [chàndǒu] 2 [body +] (with fear, cold etc) 战栗 [zhànlì] 3 [ground, trees +] 抖动 [dǒudòng]

tremendous [trɪ'mendəs] ADJ 1 (enormous) [+ amount, success etc] 极大的 [jídà de] 2 (excellent) 极棒的 [jíbàng de]

trench [trentʃ] N [C] 1 沟 [gōu] 2 (in battlefield) 战壕 [zhànháo]

trend [trend] N [C] 1 (tendency) 趋势 [qūshì] 2 (fashion) 潮流 [cháoliú] ▶ **a trend towards/away from (doing) sth** (做)某事/背离某事的倾向 ▶ **to set a trend** 领导潮流

trendy ['trendɪ] (inf) ADJ [+ idea, person, clothes, place] 时髦的 [shímáo de]

trespass ['trespəs] VI ▶ **to trespass on** 擅入 [shànrù] ▶ **"no trespassing"** "禁止擅入"

trial ['traɪəl] I N [C/U] 1 (LAW) 审理 [shěnlǐ] 2 [of machine, drug etc] 试验 [shìyàn] II **trials** NPL (ordeal) 麻烦 [máfan] ▶ **horse trials** 马术比赛 ▶ **trial by jury** 陪审团审理 ▶ **to be sent for trial** 送审 ▶ **on trial** (LAW) 受审; (on approval) 试验 ▶ **by trial and error** 反复试验

trial period N [C] (for employee, product) 试用期 [shìyòngqī]

triangle ['traɪæŋgl] N [C] 1 (MATH) 三角 [sānjiǎo] 2 (MUS) 三角铁 [sānjiǎotiě]

triangular [traɪ'æŋgjulə(r)] ADJ 三角形的 [sānjiǎoxíng de]

tribe [traɪb] N [C] 部落 [bùluò]

tribunal [traɪ'bju:nl] N [C] 特别法庭 [tèbié fǎtíng]

tribute ['trɪbju:t] N [C/U] 赞赏 [zànshǎng] ▶ **to be a tribute to sth** 归功于某事 ▶ **to pay tribute to sb/sth** 对某人/某事表示敬意

trick [trɪk] I N [C] 1 (by conjuror) 戏法 [xìfǎ] 2 (deception) 伎俩 [jìliǎng] 3 (skill, knack) 诀窍 [juéqiào] 4 (CARDS) 一圈牌 [yī quān pái] II VT (deceive) 耍花招 [shuǎ huāzhāo] ▶ **to play a trick on sb** 对某人耍花招 ▶ **a trick of the light**

光引起的幻觉 ▶ **that should do the trick** (inf) 这应该奏效 ▶ **to trick sb into doing sth** 用计诱使某人做某事

trickle ['trɪkl] I VI 1 [water, tears, blood +] 一滴滴地流 [yī dīdī de liú] 2 [people, things +] 相继走 [xiāngjì zǒu] II N [C] [of water, blood] 细流 [xìliú]

tricky ['trɪkɪ] ADJ [+ job, problem] 棘手的 [jíshǒu de]

tricycle ['traɪsɪkl] N [C] 三轮车 [sānlúnchē]

trifle ['traɪfl] I N 1 [C] (small detail) 琐事 [suǒshì] 2 [C/U] (CULIN) 水果蛋糕 [shuǐguǒ dàngāo] II ADV ▶ **a trifle long/short** 有点长/短 [yǒudiǎn cháng/duǎn] III VI ▶ **to trifle with sb/sth** 耍某人/不重视某事 [shuǎ mǒurén/bù zhòngshì mǒushì]

trigger ['trɪgə(r)] I N [C] 1 [of gun] 扳机 [bānjī] 2 [of bomb] 导火索 [dǎohuǒsuǒ] 3 (cause) 诱因 [yòuyīn] II VT 1 [+ alarm, bomb] 启动 [qǐdòng] 2 (also: **trigger off**) [+ reaction, riot] 引发 [yǐnfā]

trim [trɪm] I ADJ 1 [+ garden area] 整齐的 [zhěngqí de] 2 [+ figure, person] 苗条的 [miáotiáo de] II N 1 [C] (haircut) 修剪 [xiūjiǎn] 2 [C/U] (decoration) (on clothes) 镶边 [xiāngbiān]; (on car) 饰边 [shìbiān] III VT 1 [+ cut] [+ hair, beard] 剪短 [jiǎnduǎn] 2 (decorate) ▶ **to trim (with)** (以…)装饰 [(yǐ…)zhuāngshì] 3 (NAUT) [+ sail] 整帆 [zhěngfān] ▶ **to keep in (good) trim** 保持身体健康

▶ **trim off** VT 除去 [chúqù]

trimmings ['trɪmɪŋz] NPL 1 (CULIN) 花色配菜 [huāsè pèicài] 2 [of pastry etc] 边角料 [biānjiǎoliào]

Trinidad and Tobago ['trɪnɪdædntə'beɪgəu] N 特立尼达和多巴哥 [Tèlìnídá hé Duōbāgē]

trio ['tri:əu] N 1 (MUS) [of musicians] 三重奏 [sānchóngzòu] 2 (MUS) (composition) 三重奏曲 [sānchóngzòu qǔ] 3 (group of three) 三人组 [sānrénzǔ]

trip [trɪp] I N [C] 1 (journey) 出行 [chūxíng] 2 (outing) 外出 [wàichū] II VI 1 (also: **trip up**) (stumble) 绊倒 [bàndǎo] 2 (liter) (walk lightly) 轻快地走 [qīngkuài de zǒu] III VT (also: **trip up**) (cause to fall) 把…绊倒 [bǎ…bàndǎo] ▶ **to go on a trip** 外出旅行

▶ **trip over** VT FUS [不可拆分] [+ stone, root etc] 绊倒 [bàndǎo]

▶ **trip up** I VI 1 = **trip** 2 (fig) (make a mistake) 出差错 [chū chācuò] II VT 1 = **trip** 2 (fig) (cause to make a mistake) 使犯错 [shǐ fàncuò]

　用法参见 **journey**

triple ['trɪpl] I ADJ 三部分的 [sān bùfen de] II ADV ▶ **triple the distance/size** 三倍的距离/尺寸 [sānbèi de jùlí/chǐcùn] III VT 使增至三倍 [shǐ zēng zhì sānbèi] IV VI 三倍于 [sānbèi yú]

triplets ['trɪplɪts] NPL 三胞胎 [sānbāotāi]

tripod ['traɪpɔd] N [C] (for camera, telescope) 三脚架 [sānjiǎojià]

triumph ['traɪʌmf] I N 1 [C] (great achievement) 巨大的成功 [jùdà de chénggōng] 2 [U] (satisfaction) 得意 [déyì] II VI ▶ to triumph (over) 1 [+ problem, disability etc] 胜(过) [shèng (guò)] 2 [+ opponent] 战胜 [zhànshèng]

triumphant [traɪʌmfənt] ADJ [+ person, team] 得胜的 [déshèng de]; [+ wave, return] 凯旋的 [kǎixuán de]

trivia ['trɪvɪə] NPL 琐事 [suǒshì]

trivial ['trɪvɪəl] ADJ 琐碎的 [suǒsuì de]

trod [trɒd] PT of **tread**

trodden [trɒdn] PP of **tread**

trolley ['trɒlɪ] N [C] 1 (BRIT) (for luggage, in supermarket) 手推车 [shǒutuīchē] [美=cart] 2 (BRIT) (table on wheels) 茶具车 [chájùchē] [美=cart] 3 (BRIT) (in hospital) 有轮子的病床 [yǒu lúnzi de bìngchuáng] [美=gurney] 4 (US) (vehicle) 电车 [diànchē] [英=tram]

trombone [trɒm'bəʊn] N [C] 长号 [chánghào]

troop [tru:p] N [C] 1 [of people, animals] 群 [qún] 2 [of soldiers] 队 [duì] II VI ▶ to troop in/out 结队进/出 [jiéduì jìn/chū] III **troops** NPL (MIL) 部队 [bùduì]

trophy ['trəʊfɪ] N [C] (cup, shield etc) 奖品 [jiǎngpǐn]

tropical ['trɒpɪkl] ADJ [+ rainforest, disease, climate] 热带的 [rèdài de]

trot [trɒt] I N [S] 1 [of person] 小步快跑 [xiǎobù kuàipǎo] 2 [of horse] 小跑 [xiǎopǎo] II VI [horse, person +] 小步快跑 [xiǎobù kuàipǎo] ▶ on the trot (BRIT: inf) (in succession) 一个接一个地 [yīgè jiē yīgè de] ▶ trot out (inf) VT [+ excuse, information] 重复 [chóngfù]

trouble ['trʌbl] I N 1 [C/U] (difficulties, bother, effort) 麻烦 [máfan] 2 [S] (problem) 问题 [wèntí] 3 [U] (unrest) 骚乱 [sāoluàn] II VT 1 (worry) 使担忧 [shǐ dānyōu] 2 (disturb) 打扰 [dǎrǎo] III VI ▶ to trouble to do sth 费心做某事 [fèixīn zuò mǒushì] IV **troubles** NPL 忧虑 [yōulù] ▶ to be in trouble (with police, authorities) 惹麻烦; [ship, climber etc +] 陷入困境 [xiànrù kùnjìng] ▶ to have trouble doing sth 做某事有困难 ▶ what's the trouble? 怎么了? ▶ the trouble is... 问题是… ▶ stomach/back trouble 胃部/背部毛病 ▶ it's no trouble! 没问题! ▶ to go to the trouble of doing sth, take the trouble to do sth 不辞劳苦地做某事 ▶ please don't trouble yourself 不麻烦您了

troubled ['trʌbld] ADJ 1 [+ person] 焦虑的 [jiāolù de] 2 [+ place, times] 多事的 [duōshì de]

troublemaker ['trʌblmeɪkə(r)] N [C] 闹事者 [nàoshìzhě]

troublesome ['trʌblsəm] ADJ [+ child etc] 烦人的 [fánrén de]; [+ injury, cough etc] 麻烦的 [máfan de]

trough [trɒf] N [C] 1 (for feeding animals) 槽 [cáo] 2 (fig) (low point) 低谷 [dīgǔ] ▶ a trough of low

pressure (MET) 低压槽

trousers ['traʊzəz] NPL 裤子 [kùzi] [美=pants] ▶ a pair of trousers 一条裤子

trout [traʊt] N 1 [C/U] 鳟鱼 [zūnyú] 2 [U] (food) 鳟鱼肉 [zūnyú ròu]

trowel ['traʊəl] N [C] 1 (garden tool) 小铲子 [xiǎo chǎnzi] 2 (builder's tool) 瓦刀 [wǎdāo]

truant ['tru:ənt] I N 1 ▶ to play truant 逃学 [táoxué] 2 [C] (pupil) 逃学学生 [táoxuéshēng] II VI 逃学 [táoxué]

truce [tru:s] N [C] 休战 [xiūzhàn] ▶ to call a truce 宣布休战

truck [trʌk] N 1 [C] (ESP US) 卡车 [kǎchē] [英=lorry] 2 [C] (BRIT: RAIL) 货车 [huòchē] 3 ▶ to have no truck with sb/sth 拒不与某人打交道/参与某事 [jù bù yǔ mǒurén dǎ jiāodào/cānyù mǒushì]

truck driver (ESP US) N [C] 卡车司机 [kǎchē sījī] [英=lorry driver]

true [tru:] ADJ 1 [+ story, motive, feelings] 真实的 [zhēnshí de] 2 (genuine, typical) 真正的 [zhēnzhèng de] 3 (accurate) [+ likeness] 准确的 [zhǔnquè de] ▶ it is true that... …是真的 ▶ to come true [dream, prediction +] 实现 ▶ to hold true 适用 ▶ to be true to sb 对某人忠诚 ▶ to be true to sth (to idea, cause) 忠于某事 ▶ true to form 一如既往 ▶ true to life 逼真的

truly ['tru:lɪ] ADV 1 (genuinely) 确实地 [quèshí de] 2 (for emphasis) 相当地 [xiāngdāng de] 3 (truthfully) 的确地 [díquè de] ▶ yours truly (in letter) 您忠诚的

trumpet ['trʌmpɪt] N [C] 小号 [xiǎohào]

trunk [trʌŋk] I N [C] 1 [of tree] 树干 [shùgàn] 2 [of elephant] 象鼻 [xiàngbí] 3 (case) 箱子 [xiāngzi] 4 (US) (of car) 后备箱 [hòubèixiāng] [英=boot] 5 (frm) [of person] 躯干 [qūgàn] II **trunks** NPL (also: **swimming trunks**) 游泳裤 [yóuyǒngkù]

trust [trʌst] I N 1 [U] (have confidence in) [+ person] 信任 [xìnrèn] 2 [C] (FIN) 信托 [xìntuō] 3 [C] (BRIT) (also: **trust hospital**) 由政府出资独立经营的医院 II VT 1 (have confidence in) [+ person] 信任 [xìnrèn] 2 (consider reliable) [+ legs, voice etc] 信赖 [xìnlài] 3 [+ sb's judgement, advice] 相信 [xiāngxìn] ▶ sb's trust in sb 某人对某人的信任 ▶ a position of trust 重任 ▶ to take sth on trust [+ advice, information] 未经证实就相信某事 ▶ to hold sth in trust (LAW) 受托保管某物 ▶ to trust sb to do sth 信任某人做某事 ▶ to trust sb with sth 把某物托付给某人 ▶ to trust (that)... (frm) (hope) 相信…

trusted ['trʌstɪd] ADJ [+ friend, advisor] 可靠的 [kěkào de]

trusting ['trʌstɪŋ] ADJ [+ person, nature] 相信别人的 [xiāngxìn biérén de]

trustworthy ['trʌstwɜ:ðɪ] ADJ [+ person] 可靠的 [kěkào de]

truth [tru:θ] (pl **truths** [tru:ðz]) N 1 [U] (facts)

事实 [shìshí] **2** [U] (*truthfulness*) 真实性 [zhēnshíxìng] **3** [C] (*principle*) 真理 [zhēnlǐ]

truthful ['truːθful] ADJ **1** [+ *person*] 诚实的 [chéngshí de] **2** [+ *answer, account*] 如实的 [rúshí de]

○**try** [traɪ] **I** N [C] **1** 尝试 [chángshì] ▷ *It's worth a try.* 这值得一试。**2** (RUGBY) 触球 [chùqiú] **II** VT **1** (*attempt*) 试 [shì] ▷ *I tried a different approach to the problem.* 我试着用不同的方法来解决这个问题。**2** (*test*) 尝试 [chángshì] ▷ *I've tried herbal cigarettes but I don't like them.* 我尝试过草烟但不喜欢。**3** (LAW) [+ *case, person*] 审理 [shěnlǐ] **4** [+ *person, place*] 试 [shì] ▷ *Have you tried the local music shops?* 你试过当地的音乐商店吗? **III** VI (*make effort*) 努力 [nǔlì] ▷ *You can do it if you try.* 如果你努力就能够做到。

▶ **to have a try at sth, give sth a try** 尝试做某事 ▶ **to try to do sth, try doing sth** 尽力做某事 ▶ **to try one's best or hardest to do sth** 尽最大的能力做某事

▶ **try on** VT [+ *dress, hat, shoes*] 试穿 [shìchuān]

▶ **to try it on (with sb)** (BRIT: *inf*) 试探 (某人)

▶ **try out** VT (*test*) 试验 [shìyàn]

trying ['traɪɪŋ] ADJ **1** [+ *person*] 难对付的 [nán duìfu de] **2** [+ *experience, situation*] 令人厌烦的 [lìng rén yànfán de]

T-shirt ['tiːʃəːt] N [C] 短袖衫 [duǎnxiùshān]

tub [tʌb] N [C] **1** (*container*) 缸 [gāng] **2** (US) 浴缸 [yùgāng] [英=**bath**]

tube [tjuːb] N [C] **1** (*pipe*) 管子 [guǎnzi] **2** [C] (*container*) 筒 [tǒng] **3** (BRIT) ▶ **the tube** (*underground*) 地铁 [dìtiě] [美=**subway**] **4** (US: *inf*) ▶ **the tube** (*television*) 电视 [diànshì] [英= **the box**] ▶ **to travel by tube** 乘地铁

tuberculosis [tjubəːkju'ləusɪs] N [U] 肺结核 [fèijiéhé]

tube station (BRIT) N [C] 地铁站 [dìtiězhàn]

tuck [tʌk] **I** VT (*put*) 夹 [jiā] **II** N [C] (SEWING) 褶 [zhě]

▶ **tuck away** VT (*store*) 妥善保存 [tuǒshàn bǎocún] ▶ **to be tucked away** (*building etc*) 隐蔽起来

▶ **tuck in** VT **1** [+ *clothing*] 塞进 [sāijìn] **2** [+ *child*] 给…盖好被子 [gěi…gàihǎo bèizi] **II** VI (BRIT: *inf*) (*eat*) 尽情吃 [jìnqíng chī]

▶ **tuck into** (BRIT: *inf*) VT FUS [不可拆分] [+ *meal*] 大吃 [dàchī]

▶ **tuck up** (BRIT) VT [+ *invalid, child*] 给…盖好被子 [gěi…gàihǎo bèizi]

tuck shop (BRIT) N [C] 糖果铺 [tángguǒpù]

Tue(s). ABBR (= *Tuesday*) 星期二 [xīngqī'èr]

Tuesday ['tjuːzdɪ] N [C/U] 星期二 [xīngqī'èr] ▶ **it is Tuesday 23rd March** 今天是3月23号,星期二 ▶ **on Tuesday** 在星期二 ▶ **on Tuesdays** 每个星期二 ▶ **every Tuesday** 每逢星期二 ▶ **every other Tuesday** 隔周星期二 ▶ **last/next Tuesday** 上个/下个星期二 ▶ **the following Tuesday** 下个星期二

▶ **Tuesday's newspaper** 星期二的报纸 ▶ **a week/fortnight on Tuesday** 一周/两周后的星期二 ▶ **the Tuesday before last** 上上个星期二 ▶ **the Tuesday after next** 下下个星期二 ▶ **Tuesday morning/afternoon/evening** 星期二早晨/下午/晚上

tug [tʌg] **I** VT 拉 [lā] **II** VI ▶ **to tug at** 拉 [lā] **III** N **1** ▶ **to give sth a tug** 猛拽某物 [měngzhuài mǒuwù] **2** [C] (*ship*) 拖船 [tuōchuán]

tuition [tjuː'ɪʃən] N [U] **1** 教学 [jiàoxué] **2** (*fees*) 学费 [xuéfèi]

tulip ['tjuːlɪp] N [C] 郁金香 [yùjīnxiāng]

tumble ['tʌmbl] **I** N [C] 跌倒 [diēdǎo] **II** VI [*person, object +*] 滚落 [gǔnluò]; [*water +*] 翻滚 [fāngǔn]; [*prices, levels +*] 跌 [diē] ▶ **to have** or **take a tumble** 跌跤

▶ **tumble to** (*inf*) VT FUS [不可拆分] ▶ **he tumbled to the fact that...** 他突然明白事实是… [tā tūrán míngbai shìshí shì…]

tumble dryer (BRIT) N [C] 滚筒干衣机 [gǔntǒng gānyījī] [美=**dryer**]

tumbler ['tʌmblə(r)] N [C] (*glass*) 平底玻璃杯 [píngdǐ bōlibēi]

tummy ['tʌmɪ] (*inf*) N [C] 肚子 [dùzi]

tumour, (US) **tumor** ['tjuːmə(r)] (MED) N [C] 肿瘤 [zhǒngliú]

tuna ['tjuːnə] N [C/U] (*also*: **tuna fish**) 金枪鱼 [jīnqiāngyú]

tune [tjuːn] **I** N [C] (*melody*) 曲调 [qǔdiào] **II** VT **1** (MUS) [+ *instrument*] 调 [tiáo] **2** [+ *engine, machine*] 调试 [tiáoshì] **3** [+ *radio, TV*] 调台 [tiáotái] ▶ **to be in/out of tune** [*instrument +*] 调子正确/不正确; [*singer +*] 合/跑调 ▶ **to be in/out of tune with** (*fig*) 与…协调/不协调 ▶ **to change one's tune** 突变态度 ▶ **to the tune of 10,000 pounds** 最大限额到1万镑

▶ **tune in** VI (RAD, TV) 收听/看 [shōutīng/kàn]

▶ **tune up** VI [*musician, orchestra +*] 调音 [tiáoyīn]

tunic ['tjuːnɪk] N [C] 无袖上衣 [wúxiù shàngyī]

Tunisia [tjuː'nɪzɪə] N 突尼斯 [Tūnísī]

Tunisian [tjuː'nɪzɪən] **I** ADJ 突尼斯的 [Tūnísī de] **II** N [C] (*person*) 突尼斯人 [Tūnísīrén]

tunnel ['tʌnl] **I** N [C] **1** 隧道 [suìdào] **2** (*in mine*) 坑道 [kēngdào] **II** VI 挖地道 [wā dìdào]

turbulence ['təːbjuləns] N [U] 猛烈而不稳定的水流/气流 [měngliè ér bù wěndìng de shuǐliú/qìliú]

turf [təːf] **I** N **1** [U] (*grass*) 草坪 [cǎopíng] **2** [C] (*square of grass*) 草皮 [cǎopí] **II** VT [+ *area*] 铺 [pū]

▶ **turf out** (BRIT: *inf*) VT [+ *person*] 赶走 [gǎnzǒu]

Turk [təːk] N [C] 土耳其人 [Tǔ'ěrqírén]

Turkey ['təːkɪ] N 土耳其 [Tǔ'ěrqí]

turkey ['təːkɪ] N **1** [C] (*bird*) 火鸡 [huǒjī] **2** [U] (*meat*) 火鸡肉 [huǒjī ròu]

Turkish ['təːkɪʃ] **I** ADJ 土耳其的 [Tǔ'ěrqí de] **II** N [U] (*language*) 土耳其语 [Tǔ'ěrqíyǔ]

Turkmenistan ['təːkmɛnɪstɑːn] N 土库曼斯

坦 [Tǔkùmànsītǎn]

turmeric ['tɜːmərɪk] (CULIN) N [U] 姜黄 [jiānghuáng]

turmoil ['tɜːmɔɪl] N [S/U] 混乱 [hùnluàn] ▶ **in turmoil** 处于混乱状态

☉ **turn** [tɜːn] I N [c] 1 (change) 转变 [zhuǎnbiàn] ▷ every twist and turn in government policy 政府政策的每一次扭动 2 (in road) 转弯 [zhuǎnwān] 3 (performance) 表演 [biǎoyǎn] ▷ a comedy turn 喜剧表演 4 (in game, queue, series) 机会 [jīhuì] ▷ He stood in the queue waiting his turn. 他排队等着轮到他。5 (BRIT: inf): MED) 发病 [fābìng] ▷ Mrs Reilly is having one of her turns. 瑞利夫人的病发作了。II VT 1 [+ part of body] 转动 [zhuàndòng] ▷ He turned his head left and right. 他把头左右转动。2 [+ object] 调转 [diàozhuǎn] ▷ She turned the bedside chair to face the door. 她把床边的椅子转向门口。3 [+ handle, key] 转动 [zhuàndòng] 4 [+ page] 翻 [fān] 5 (shape) [+ wood, metal] 打制 [dǎzhì] III VI 1 (rotate) [object, wheel +] 旋转 [xuánzhuǎn] ▷ The cog wheels started to turn. 齿轮开始旋转。2 (change direction) [person +] 转身 [zhuǎnshēn] ▷ He turned abruptly and walked away. 他突然转身走开了。3 [vehicle +] 转向 [zhuǎnxiàng] ▷ You come over a bridge and turn sharply to the right. 你走到桥边然后扭直向右转。4 (become sour) [milk +] 变质 [biànzhì] ▶ **to take a turn for the worse** [situations, relations +] 恶化 [èhuà] ▶ **"no left turn"** "禁止左转" ▶ **it's my turn to...** 轮到我做… ▶ **to take turns** or **to take it in turns (to do sth)** 轮流做(某事) ▶ **in turn** (one after the other) 轮流; (then, afterwards) 依次 ▶ **turn of events** 事态变迁 ▶ **it gave me quite a turn** (inf) 吓了我一大跳 ▶ **at the turn of the century/year** 在世纪/新年之交 ▶ **to do sb a good turn** 帮某人大忙 ▶ **to turn forty** 满40岁 ▶ **to turn grey** [person, hair +] 变灰白 ▶ **to turn green/blue etc** 变绿/蓝[等] ▶ **to turn nasty** 变糟

▶ **turn against** VT FUS [不可拆分] 转而反对 [zhuǎnér fǎnduì]

▶ **turn around** VI = **turn round**

▶ **turn away** I VI 放弃 [fàngqì] II VT 1 [+ applicants] 拒绝 [jùjué] 2 [+ business] 放弃 [fàngqì]

▶ **turn back** I VI 往回走 [wǎnghuí zǒu] II VT [+ person, vehicle] 掉头 [diàotóu]

▶ **turn down** VT 1 [+ request, offer] 拒绝 [jùjué] 2 [+ heat, sound] 调低 [tiáodī] 3 [+ bedclothes] 垂放 [chuífàng]

▶ **turn in** I VI (inf) (go to bed) 睡觉 [shuìjiào] II VT [+ oneself] (to police) 自首 [zìshǒu]; [+ sb else] (to police) 告发 [gàofā]

▶ **turn into** I VT FUS [不可拆分] 变成 [biànchéng] ▷ The water turns into steam. 水变成了蒸汽。II VT 使变成 [shǐ biànchéng] ▷ Don't turn a drama into a crisis. 别把戏剧变成闹剧。

▶ **turn off** I VI (from road) 拐弯 [guǎiwān] II VT

1 [+ light, radio, tap etc] 关 [guān] 2 [+ engine] 关掉 [guāndiào]

▶ **turn on** I VT 1 [+ light, radio, tap etc] 打开 [dǎkāi] 2 [+ engine] 发动 [fādòng] II VT FUS [不可拆分] [+ person] 攻击 [gōngjī]

▶ **turn out** I VT [+ light, gas] 关掉 [guāndiào] II VI [voters etc +] 到场 [dàochǎng] ▶ **to turn out to be** (prove to be) 原来是 ▶ **to turn out well/badly** 结果很好/很糟

▶ **turn over** I VI [person +] 翻身 [fānshēn] II VT 1 [+ object, page] 翻转 [fānzhuǎn] 2 (give) 移交 [yíjiāo] ▷ He had refused to turn over funds that had belonged to Potter. 他拒绝移交属于伯特的款项。▶ **to turn sth over to** (change function of) 把某物改变成

▶ **turn round**, **turn around** I VI 1 [person, vehicle +] 调转 [diàozhuǎn] 2 (rotate) 转动 [zhuǎndòng] II VT [person, vehicle +] 调头 [diàotóu]

▶ **turn to** I VT FUS [不可拆分] 1 [+ page] 翻到 [fāndào] 2 [+ person] 求助于 [qiúzhù yú] II VT [+ attention, thoughts] 转到 [zhuǎndào] ▷ We turn now to the British news. 我们现在转到英国新闻。

▶ **turn up** I VI 1 (arrive) [person +] 露面 [lòumiàn] 2 (be found) [lost object +] 出现 [chūxiàn] II VT 1 [+ collar, sleeves] 竖起 [shùqǐ] 2 [+ radio, heater etc] 开大 [kāidà] 3 [+ hem] 改短 [gǎiduǎn]

turning ['tɜːnɪŋ] N [c] (in road) 拐弯 [guǎiwān]

turning point N [c] 转弯处 [zhuǎnwānchù]

turnip ['tɜːnɪp] N [c/U] 萝卜 [luóbo]

turnout ['tɜːnaut] N [c] [of people, voters etc] 全部参与人(数) [quánbù cānyùrén (shù)]

turnover ['tɜːnəuvə(r)] N [c/U] 1 (COMM) (amount of money) 营业额 [yíngyè'é] 2 (COMM) [of staff] 人事变动率 [rénshì biàndònglǜ] 3 (CULIN) 糖三角 [tángsānjiǎo] ▶ **there is a rapid turnover in staff** 人员变动很快

turn signal (US) N [U] 指示器 [zhǐshìqì] [英= **indicator**]

turnstile ['tɜːnstaɪl] N [c] 旋转栅门 [xuánzhuǎn shānmén]

turn-up ['tɜːnʌp] N [c] 1 (BRIT) (on trousers) 卷边 [juǎnbiān] [美= **cuff**] 2 ▶ **that's a turn-up for the books!** (inf) 真是意想不到的事! [zhēnshì yìxiǎng bù dào de shì!]

turquoise ['tɜːkwɔɪz] I N [c] (stone) 绿松石 [lǜsōngshí] II ADJ [+ colour] 青绿色的 [qīnglǜsè de]

turtle ['tɜːtl] (BRIT) N [c] 龟 [guī] [美= **sea turtle**]

tusk [task] N [c] [of elephant, boar etc] 长牙 [chángyá]

tutor ['tjuːtə(r)] I N [c] 1 (BRIT: SCOL) 助教 [zhùjiào] 2 (private tutor) 家庭教师 [jiātíng jiàoshī] II VT (teach) 教 [jiāo]

tutorial [tjuː'tɔːrɪəl] N [c] 辅导课 [fǔdǎokè]

tuxedo [tʌk'siːdəu] (US) N [C] 男式晚礼服 [nánshì wǎnlǐfú] [英= **dinner jacket, DJ**]

TV N ABBR (= *television*) 电视 [diànshì] ▸ **on TV** 在电视上播放 ▸ **to watch TV** 看电视

tweed [twiːd] I N [C/U] 粗花呢 [cūhuāní] II ADJ [+ *jacket, skirt*] 粗花呢的 [cūhuāní de]

tweezers ['twiːzəz] NPL 镊子 [nièzi] ▸ **a pair of tweezers** 一把镊子

twelfth [twɛlfθ] NUM **1** (*in series*) 第十二 [dì shí'èr] **2** (*fraction*) 十二分之一 [shí'èr fēn zhī yī]

◎ **twelve** [twɛlv] NUM 十二 [shí'èr] ▸ **at twelve (o'clock)** (*midday*) 中午12点; (*midnight*) 凌晨零点 *see also* **five**

twentieth ['twɛntιιθ] NUM 第二十 [dì èrshí]

◎ **twenty** ['twɛntι] NUM 二十 [èrshí] ▸ **twenty-one** 二十一 *see also* **fifty**

twenty-four-seven, 24/7 ['twɛntιfɔːsɛvn] (*inf*) ADV 夜以继日地 [yè yǐ jì rì de] ▸ **to do sth twenty-four-seven** 夜以继日地做某事

◎ **twice** [twaɪs] ADV 两次 [liǎngcì] ▸ **twice as much/long as** 多/长至两倍 ▸ **twice a week** 一周两次 ▸ **she is twice your age** 她年纪比你大一倍

twig [twɪg] I N [C] 嫩枝 [nènzhī] II VI (BRIT: *inf*) (*realize*) 明白 [míngbai] III VT (BRIT: *inf*) (*realize*) 恍然大悟 [huǎngrán dà wù]

twilight ['twaɪlaɪt] N [U] **1** (*evening*) 黄昏 [huánghūn] **2** (*light*) 暮色 [mùsè]

twin [twɪn] I ADJ **1** [+ *sister, brother*] 孪生的 [luánshēng de] **2** [+ *spires, towers etc*] 成双的 [chéngshuāng de] II N [C] **1** (*person*) 双胞胎 [shuāngbāotāi] **2** (*also:* **twin room**) 双人房 [shuāngrénfáng] III VT (BRIT) [+ *towns etc*] ▸ **to be twinned with** 与…结对子 [yǔ…jié duìzi]

twin beds NPL 成对的单人床 [chéngduì de dānrénchuáng]

twinkle ['twɪŋkl] I VI [*star, light, eyes* +] 闪烁 [shǎnshuò] II N [s] 光芒 [guāngmáng]

twin room N [C] 双人房 [shuāngrénfáng]

twirl [twəːl] I VT 使旋转 [shǐ xuánzhuǎn] II VI **1** (*twist*) 缠绕 [chánrào] **2** (*move round and round*) 转圈 [zhuànquān] III N ▸ **to do a twirl** 转一圈 [zhuàn yī quān]

twist [twɪst] I N [C] **1** (*action*) 拧 [nǐng] **2** (*in road, track etc*) 弯曲处 [wānqūchù] **3** (*in coil, flex etc*) 螺旋状 [luóxuánzhuàng] **4** (*in story*) 转变 [zhuǎnbiàn] II VT **1** (*turn*) 扭 [niǔ] **2** (*turn the ends of*) 使成螺旋状 [shǐ chéng luóxuánzhuàng] **3** (*injure*) [+ *ankle etc*] 扭伤 [niǔshāng] **4** [+ *sb's arm, hand etc*] 扭 [niǔ] **5** (*turn*) [+ *object*] 扭转 [niǔzhuǎn] **6** (*fig*) [+ *meaning, words*] 曲解 [qūjiě] III VI **1** [*road, river* +] 盘旋 [pánxuán] **2** [*arm, leg etc* +] 扭曲 [niǔqū]

twit [twɪt] (*inf*) N [C] 笨蛋 [bèndàn]

twitch [twɪtʃ] I N [C] 抽动 [chōudòng] II VI [*muscle, body* +] 颤动 [chàndòng]

◎ **two** [tuː] NUM 二 [èr] ▸ **two by two, in twos** 两两成群 ▸ **to put two and two together** (*fig*) 根据事实推断 *see also* **five**

two-percent milk [tuːpəˈsɛnt-] (US) N [U] 半脱脂奶 [bàn tuōzhīnǎi] [英= **semi-skimmed (milk)**]

TXT (TEXTING) ABBR = **text**

type [taɪp] I N **1** [C] (*category, example*) 种类 [zhǒnglèi] **2** [C] (*sort, kind*) 类型 [lèixíng] **3** [C] [*person* +] 型 [xíng] **4** [U] (TYP) 字体 [zìtǐ] II VT, VI 打字 [dǎzì]
▸ **type into** VT 录入 [lùrù]
▸ **type up** VT 打印 [dǎyìn]

typewriter ['taɪpraɪtə(r)] N [C] 打字机 [dǎzìjī]

typhoid ['taɪfɔɪd] N [U] 伤寒 [shānghán]

typhoon [taɪˈfuːn] N [C] 台风 [táifēng]

typical ['tɪpɪkl] ADJ [+ *behaviour, weather etc*] 典型的 [diǎnxíng de] ▸ **typical of** 典型的 ▸ **that's typical!** 一向如此!

typically ['tɪpɪklɪ] ADV **1** (*generally*) 通常地 [tōngcháng de] **2** (*very*) [+ *English, Chinese etc*] 典型地 [diǎnxíng de] **3** (*as usual*) 向来 [xiànglái]

typing ['taɪpɪŋ] N [U] 打字 [dǎzì]

typist ['taɪpɪst] N [C] 打字员 [dǎzìyuán]

tyre, (US) **tire** ['taɪə(r)] N [C] 轮胎 [lúntāi]

tyre pressure, (US) **tire pressure** N [C] 轮胎气压 [lúntāi qìyā]

Uu

U, u [juː] N [c/u] (letter) 英语的第二十一个字母

UFO N ABBR (= unidentified flying object) 不明飞行物 [bùmíng fēixíngwù]

Uganda [juːˈɡændə] N 乌干达 [Wūgāndá]

Ugandan [juːˈɡændən] I ADJ 乌干达的 [Wūgāndá de] II N [c] (person) 乌干达人 [Wūgāndárén]

ugly [ˈʌɡlɪ] ADJ 1 [+ person, dress, building] 丑陋的 [chǒulòu de] 2 (unpleasant) [+ situation, incident] 令人不快的 [lìng rén bùkuài de]

UHT ADJ ABBR (= ultra-heat treated) 超高温处理 [chāogāowēn chǔlǐ]

UK N ABBR (= United Kingdom) ▶ the UK 大不列颠及北爱尔兰联合王国 [Dàbùlièdiān jí Běi'ài'ěrlán Liánhéwángguó]

Ukraine [juːˈkreɪn] N ▶ (the) Ukraine 乌克兰 [Wūkèlán]

Ukrainian [juːˈkreɪnɪən] I ADJ 乌克兰的 [Wūkèlán de] II N 1 [c] (person) 乌克兰人 [Wūkèlánrén] 2 [u] (language) 乌克兰语 [Wūkèlányǔ]

ulcer [ˈʌlsə(r)] N [c] 溃疡 [kuìyáng]

ultimate [ˈʌltɪmət] I ADJ 1 (final) [+ aim, success, result] 最终的 [zuìzhōng de] 2 (greatest) [+ responsibility, authority] 最大的 [zuìdà de] II N ▶ the ultimate in luxury etc 最奢华{等}之物 [zuì shēhuá {děng} zhī wù]

ultimately [ˈʌltɪmətlɪ] ADV 1 (finally) 最终地 [zuìzhōng de] 2 (basically) 根本地 [gēnběn de]

ultimatum [ʌltɪˈmeɪtəm] (pl **ultimatums** or **ultimata** [ʌltɪˈmeɪtə]) N [c] 最后通牒 [zuìhòu tōngdié] ▶ to give sb an ultimatum 给某人下最后通牒

ultrasound [ˈʌltrəsaʊnd] N 1 [c] (also: **ultrasound scan**) 超声 [chāoshēng] 2 [u] (sound waves) 超声波 [chāoshēngbō]

ultraviolet [ˈʌltrəˈvaɪəlɪt] ADJ [+ rays, light, radiation] 紫外的 [zǐwài de]

umbrella [ʌmˈbrɛlə] I N [c] 1 伞 [sǎn] 2 (fig) ▶ under the umbrella of 在…的庇护下 [zài…de bìhù xià] II ADJ 1 [+ group, organization] 包罗万象的 [bāoluó wànxiàng de] 2 [+ term, word] 集合的 [jíhé de]

umpire [ˈʌmpaɪə(r)] I N [c] (TENNIS, CRICKET) 裁判员 [cáipànyuán] II VT [+ game] 当…的裁判 [dāng…de cáipàn]

UN N ABBR (= United Nations) ▶ the UN 联合国 [Liánhéguó]

unable [ʌnˈeɪbl] ADJ ▶ to be unable to do sth 不能做某事 [bùnéng zuò mǒushì]

unacceptable [ʌnəkˈsɛptəbl] ADJ 不能接受的 [bùnéng jiēshòu de] ▶ it is unacceptable for ministers to tell lies 部长撒谎是不能接受的

unaccompanied [ʌnəˈkʌmpənɪd] ADJ 1 [+ child] 无人陪同的 [wúrén péitóng de] 2 [+ voice, instrument] 无伴奏的 [wú bànzòu de]

unaccustomed [ʌnəˈkʌstəmd] ADJ 1 ▶ to be unaccustomed to sth 对某事不习惯 [duì mǒushì bù xíguàn] 2 (unusual) 不寻常的 [bù xúncháng de] ▶ to be unaccustomed to doing sth 不习惯做某事

unanimous [juːˈnænɪməs] ADJ [+ decision] 一致同意的 [yīzhì tóngyì de] ▶ to be unanimous in sth/in doing sth 一致同意某事/做某事

unarmed [ʌnˈɑːmd] ADJ 无武装的 [wú wǔzhuāng de] ▶ unarmed combat 徒手搏击

unattended [ʌnəˈtɛndɪd] ADJ [+ luggage etc] 无人看管的 [wúrén kānguǎn de] ▶ to leave sth/sb unattended 单独留下某物/某人

unattractive [ʌnəˈtræktɪv] ADJ 1 [+ person, character] 没有魅力的 [méiyǒu mèilì de] 2 [+ building, place] 乏味的 [fáwèi de] 3 [+ prospect, idea] 讨厌的 [tǎoyàn de] ▶ to be unattractive to sb [plan, idea +] 对某人没有吸引力

unauthorized [ʌnˈɔːθəraɪzd] ADJ 1 [+ visit, use] 未经批准的 [wèijīng pīzhǔn de] 2 [+ version, biography] 未经授权的 [wèijīng shòuquán de]

unavailable [ʌnəˈveɪləbl] ADJ 1 [+ product, book] 不可获得的 [bùkě huòdé de] 2 [+ person] 联系不上的 [liánxì bù shàng de] ▶ to be unavailable for comment 无法发表评论

unavoidable [ʌnəˈvɔɪdəbl] ADJ [+ delay, job losses etc] 不可避免的 [bùkě bìmiǎn de]

unaware [ʌnəˈwɛə(r)] ADJ ▶ to be unaware of sth 不知道某事 [bù zhīdào mǒushì] ▶ to be unaware that... 没有意识到…

unawares [ʌnəˈwɛəz] ADV ▶ to catch or take sb

unawares 使某人吃惊 [shǐ mǒurén chījīng]

unbearable [ʌn'bɛərəbl] ADJ **1** [+ heat, pain] 难以忍受的 [nányǐ rěnshòu de] **2** [+ person] 不能容忍的 [bùnéng róngrěn de] ▶ **to become unbearable** [heat, pain, life +] 变得难以忍受

unbeatable [ʌn'biːtəbl] ADJ **1** [+ person, team] 难以战胜的 [nányǐ zhànshèng de] **2** [+ price, value, quality] 无与伦比的 [wú yǔ lún bǐ de]

unbelievable [ʌnbɪ'liːvəbl] ADJ **1** 不可信的 [bùkěxìn de] **2** (amazing) 难以置信的 [nányǐ zhìxìn de] ▶ **it is unbelievable that...** ···真是难以置信

unbias(s)ed [ʌn'baɪəst] ADJ [+ person, opinion] 公正的 [gōngzhèng de]

unborn [ʌn'bɔːn] ADJ [+ child] 未出生的 [wèi chūshēng de]

unbreakable [ʌn'breɪkəbl] ADJ 不易打碎的 [bùyì dǎsuì de]

unbutton [ʌn'bʌtn] VT [+ coat, shirt etc] 解开···的纽扣 [jiěkāi···de niǔkòu]

uncalled-for [ʌn'kɔːldfɔː(r)] ADJ [+ remark, criticism etc] 无理由的 [wú lǐyóu de]

uncanny [ʌn'kænɪ] ADJ [+ resemblance, ability, feeling] 异乎寻常的 [yìhū xúncháng de] ▶ **it's uncanny** 这真怪异

uncertain [ʌn'səːtn] ADJ [+ future, outcome] 不确定的 [bù quèdìng de] ▶ **to be uncertain about sth** 对某事心无定数 ▶ **to be uncertain how/whether to do sth** 拿不准该如何做某事/是否要做某事 ▶ **it's uncertain whether...** 是否···仍无法确定 ▶ **in no uncertain terms** 毫不含糊地

uncertainty [ʌn'səːtntɪ] N [U] (confusion) 不确定 [bùquèdìng]

unchanged [ʌn'tʃeɪndʒd] ADJ 未改变的 [wèi gǎibiàn de]

uncivilized [ʌn'sɪvɪlaɪzd] ADJ **1** (lit) [+ country, people] 未开化的 [wèi kāihuà de] **2** (fig) [+ person, behaviour, hour] 无教养的 [wú jiàoyǎng de]

uncle ['ʌŋkl] N [c] (father's older brother) 伯父 [bófù]; (father's younger brother) 叔父 [shūfù]; (father's sister's husband) 姑父 [gūfù]; (mother's brother) 舅父 [jiùfù]; (mother's sister's husband) 姨父 [yífù]

unclear [ʌn'klɪə(r)] ADJ **1** [+ reason, implications] 不清楚的 [bù qīngchǔ de] **2** [+ instructions, answer] 含糊的 [hánhu de] ▶ **it is** or **remains unclear whether...** 是否···仍不确定 ▶ **to be unclear about sth** 对某事不甚明了

uncomfortable [ʌn'kʌmfətəbl] ADJ **1** (physically) [+ person] 不舒服的 [bù shūfu de]; [+ chair, room, journey] 不舒适的 [bù shūshì de] **2** (uneasy) [+ person] 不安的 [bù'ān de] **3** (unpleasant) [+ situation, fact] 不利的 [bùlì de]

uncommon [ʌn'kɔmən] ADJ 罕见的 [hǎnjiàn de]

unconditional [ʌnkən'dɪʃənl] ADJ [+ love, acceptance, surrender] 无条件的 [wú tiáojiàn de]

unconscious [ʌn'kɔnʃəs] I ADJ **1** (not awake) 失去知觉的 [shīqù zhījué de] **2** (not deliberate) 无意识的 [wú yìshí de] **3** (unaware) ▶ **unconscious of** 未察觉的 [wèi chájué de] II N ▶ **the unconscious** 潜意识 [qiányìshí] ▶ **to knock/beat sb unconscious** 把某人打昏过去

uncontrollable [ʌnkən'trəuləbl] ADJ **1** [+ person] 不受管束的 [bùshòu guǎnshù de] **2** [+ temper, laughter] 控制不住的 [kòngzhì bùzhù de]

unconventional [ʌnkən'venʃənl] ADJ [+ person, behaviour] 反传统的 [fǎn chuántǒng de]

uncover [ʌn'kʌvə(r)] VT **1** (remove covering from) 露出 [lòuchū] **2** (discover) [+ plot, evidence] 发现 [fāxiàn]

undecided [ʌndɪ'saɪdɪd] ADJ **1** [+ person] 犹豫不决的 [yóuyù bùjué de] **2** [+ question] 未决定的 [wèi juédìng de] ▶ **to be undecided about sth** 对某事拿不定主意

undeniable [ʌndɪ'naɪəbl] ADJ [+ fact, evidence] 不可否认的 [bùkě fǒurèn de]

⊙under ['ʌndə(r)] I PREP **1** (beneath) 在···下面 [zài···xiàmian] ▷ the cupboard under the sink 在水槽下面的橱柜 **2** (less than) [+ age, price] 不到 [bùdào] ▷ He's still under 18. 他还不到18岁。 **3** (according to) [+ law, agreement] 根据 [gēnjù] ▷ Equal pay for men and women is guaranteed under English law. 根据英格兰法律,应保证男女同工同酬。 **4** [+ sb's leadership] 在···的领导下 [zài···de lǐngdǎo xià] ▷ China under Chairman Mao 毛主席领导下的中国 **5** [+ chapter, heading etc] 在···[zài···zhōng] ▷ It's filed under letter C. 它被归在字母C中。 II ADV **1** [go, fly etc +] 从下面 [cóng xiàmian] **2** (in age, price etc) 以下 [yǐxià] ▷ children aged 12 and under 12岁及以下的儿童 ▶ **she writes under the name Jan Hunt** 她以简·亨特这个名字写东西

under-age [ʌndər'eɪdʒ] ADJ [+ person] 未成年的 [wèi chéngnián de] ▶ **under-age drinking/sex** 未成年人的饮酒/性行为

underbush ['ʌndəbuʃ] (US) N [U] 下层灌木丛 [xiàcéng guànmùcóng] [英 = undergrowth]

undercover [ʌndə'kʌvə(r)] I ADJ [+ operation, work, agent] 秘密的 [mìmì de] II ADV [work +] 暗中的 [ànzhōng de]

underdone [ʌndə'dʌn] ADJ 半生不熟的 [bàn shēng bù shú de]

underestimate [vb ʌndər'ɛstɪmeɪt, n ʌndə r'ɛstɪmət] I VT [+ importance, amount, person] 低估 [dīgū] II N [c] 低估 [dīgū]

undergo [ʌndə'gəu] (pt **underwent,** pp **undergone**) VT [+ surgery, test, treatment, training] 经受 [jīngshòu]

undergraduate [ʌndə'grædjuɪt] I N [c] 本科生 [běnkēshēng] II CPD [复合词] [+ course, *degree etc*] 本科 [běnkē]

underground ['ʌndəgraund] I N ▸ **the underground 1** (BRIT) (*railway*) 地铁 [dìtiě] [美 = **subway**] **2** (POL) 地下组织 [dìxià zǔzhī] II ADJ [+ *car park, cables, newspaper, activities*] 地下的 [dìxià de] III ADV **1** (*below ground*) 在地下 [zài dìxià] **2** (*secretly*) 秘密地 [mìmì de]

undergrowth ['ʌndəgrəuθ] (BRIT) N [U] 下层灌木丛 [xiàcéng guànmùcóng] [美 = **underbush**]

underline [ʌndə'laɪn] (BRIT) VT **1** [+ *word, sentence*] 在…下面划线 [zài…xiàmian huàxiàn] [美 = **underscore**] **2** (*emphasize*) 强调 [qiángdiào] [美 = **underscore**]

undermine [ʌndə'maɪn] VT [+ *sb's confidence, authority*] 逐渐削弱 [zhújiàn xuēruò]

underneath [ʌndə'ni:θ] I ADV **1** (*below*) 在下面 [zài xiàmian] **2** (*fig*) (*at heart*) 心底里 [xīndǐlǐ] II PREP **1** (*below*) 在…下面 [zài…xiàmian] **2** (*fig*) 在…背后 [zài…bèihòu] III N ▸ **the underneath** 底部 [dǐbù]

underpants ['ʌndəpænts] NPL 内裤 [nèikù]

underpass ['ʌndəpɑːs] N [C] **1** (*for pedestrians*) 地下通道 [dìxià tōngdào] **2** (*road under motorway*) 高架桥下通道 [gāojiàqiáo xià tōngdào]

underscore [ʌndə'skɔː(r)] VT **1** (*highlight*) 强调 [qiángdiào] **2** (*with line*) [+ *word, phrase etc*] 在…下面划线 [zài…xiàmian huàxiàn]

undershirt ['ʌndəʃəːt] (US) N [C] 贴身内衣 [tiēshēn nèiyī] [英 = **vest**]

underside ['ʌndəsaɪd] N [C] 底面 [dǐmiàn]

underskirt ['ʌndəskəːt] (BRIT) N [C] 衬裙 [chènqún]

ↂ **understand** [ʌndə'stænd] (*pt, pp* **understood**) VT [+ *speaker, sb's words, meaning*] 明白 [míngbai]; [+ *foreign language*] 懂 [dǒng]; [+ *book, subject, behaviour*] 理解 [lǐjiě] ▷ *They are too young to understand what is going on.* 他们太年轻，无法理解所发生的一切。▷ *His wife doesn't understand him.* 他的妻子不理解他。▸ **to understand that...** (*believe*) 获悉… ▸ **he is understood to be in Italy** 人们认为他在意大利 ▸ **to make o.s. understood** 将自己的意思表达清楚

understandable [ʌndə'stændəbl] ADJ 可以理解的 [kěyǐ lǐjiě de] ▸ **it is understandable that...** …是可以理解的

understanding [ʌndə'stændɪŋ] I ADJ 通情达理的 [tōngqíng dálǐ de] II N [C/U] **1** (*knowledge*) 了解 [liǎojiě] **2** [U] (*sympathy*) 同情 [tóngqíng] **3** [C] (*agreement*) 协定 [xiédìng] **4** [U] (*trust*) 相互理解 [xiānghù lǐjiě] ▸ **to come to an understanding with sb (about sth)** (就某事)和某人达成协议 ▸ **to have an understanding of sth** 对某事有一定的了解 ▸ **on the understanding that...** 条件下

understate [ʌndə'steɪt] VT 轻描淡写 [qīng miáo dàn xiě]

understatement ['ʌndəsteɪtmənt] N [C/U] 轻描淡写的陈述 [qīng miáo dàn xiě de chénshù]

understood [ʌndə'stud] I PT, PP *of* **understand** II ADJ **1** (*agreed*) 取得同意的 [qǔdé tóngyì de] **2** (*implied*) 不言而喻的 [bù yán ér yù de] ▸ **it is understood that...** 不言而喻的是…

undertake [ʌndə'teɪk] (*pt* **undertook**, *pp* **undertaken**) VT [+ *task, job*] 承担 [chéngdān] ▸ **to undertake to do sth** (*frm*) 保证做某事

undertaker ['ʌndəteɪkə(r)] (BRIT) N [C] 丧事承办人 [sāngshì chéngbànrén] [美 = **mortician**]

undertaking ['ʌndəteɪkɪŋ] N [C] (*task*) 任务 [rènwù] ▸ **to give an undertaking to do sth** 承诺做某事 ▸ **to give an undertaking that...** 承诺…

underwater ['ʌndə'wɔːtə(r)] I ADV [*swim etc* +] 在水下 [zài shuǐxià] II ADJ [+ *exploration, camera etc*] 水下的 [shuǐxià de]

underway [ʌndə'weɪ] ADJ 在进行中的 [zài jìnxíng zhōng de] ▸ **to get underway** 开始

underwear ['ʌndəweə(r)] N [U] 内衣 [nèiyī]

underworld ['ʌndəwəːld] N ▸ **the underworld 1** (*criminal*) 黑社会 [hēishèhuì] **2** (MYTH) 阴间 [yīnjiān]

undesirable [ʌndɪ'zaɪərəbl] ADJ [+ *person, effects, behaviour*] 不良的 [bùliáng de] ▸ **it is undesirable that...** …令人不快

undisputed ['ʌndɪs'pjuːtɪd] ADJ **1** [+ *fact*] 无可置疑的 [wú kě zhìyí de] **2** [+ *champion*] 无可争辩的 [wú kě zhēngbiàn de]

undo [ʌn'duː] (*pt* **undid**, *pp* **undone**) VT **1** [+ *shoelaces, knot, buttons, trousers*] 解开 [jiěkāi] **2** (*spoil*) [+ *work*] 使无效 [shǐ wúxiào] **3** [+ *damage*] 消除 [xiāochú]

undone [ʌn'dʌn] I PP *of* **undo** II ADJ **1** [+ *work, tasks etc*] 未做的 [wèizuò de] **2** [+ *shoelaces, zip, button*] 松开的 [sōngkāi de] ▸ **to leave sth undone** 未完成某事 ▸ **to come undone** [*shoelaces, zip, button +*] 开了; [*blouse, dress +*] 解开了 ▷ *His shoelaces came undone.* 他的鞋带开了。

undoubtedly [ʌn'dautɪdlɪ] ADV 毋庸置疑地 [wúyōng zhìyí de]

undress [ʌn'drɛs] I VI 脱衣服 [tuō yīfu] II VT 脱去…的衣服 [tuōqù…de yīfu]

unearth [ʌn'əːθ] VT **1** [+ *remains, treasure etc*] 发掘 [fājué] **2** [+ *secrets, evidence*] 发现 [fāxiàn]

uneasy [ʌn'iːzɪ] ADJ **1** (*worried*) 不安的 [bù'ān de] **2** (*fragile*) [+ *peace, truce, relationship*] 令人不安的 [lìng rén bù'ān de] ▸ **to be uneasy about sth** 为某事忧虑

unemployed [ʌnɪm'plɔɪd] I ADJ [+ *person*] 失业的 [shīyè de] II NPL ▸ **the unemployed** 失业者 [shīyèzhě]

unemployment [ʌnɪm'plɔɪmənt] N [U] 失

业 [shìyè]

unequal [ʌnˈiːkwəl] ADJ 1 [+ lengths, amounts] 不同的 [bùtóng de] 2 [+ system, situation] 不平等的 [bù píngděng de] ▶ to be/feel unequal to sth (frm) 不胜任某事/感觉难以胜任某事

UNESCO [juːˈnɛskəʊ] N ABBR (= United Nations Educational, Scientific and Cultural Organization) 联合国教科文组织 [Liánhéguó Jiàokēwén Zǔzhī]

uneven [ʌnˈiːvn] ADJ 1 [+ teeth, road, surface] 高低不平的 [gāodī bùpíng de] 2 [+ breathing] 乱的 [luàn de]; [+ rate] 有差异的 [yǒu chāyì de] 3 (inconsistent) [+ performance] 不稳定的 [bù wěndìng de]

unexpected [ʌnɪksˈpɛktɪd] ADJ 意外的 [yìwài de]

unexpectedly [ʌnɪksˈpɛktɪdlɪ] ADV 意外地 [yìwài de]

unfair [ʌnˈfɛə(r)] ADJ [+ system, situation, act, person] 不公平的 [bù gōngpíng de] ▶ to be unfair to sb 对某人不公平 ▶ it's unfair that... …是不公平的 ▶ it is unfair to generalize 笼统地概括是不公平的 ▶ to gain an unfair advantage 获取不正当的利益

unfaithful [ʌnˈfeɪθful] ADJ [+ husband, wife] 不忠的 [bùzhōng de] ▶ to be unfaithful to sb 对某人不忠

unfamiliar [ʌnfəˈmɪlɪə(r)] ADJ [+ place, person, subject] 陌生的 [mòshēng de] ▶ to be unfamiliar to sb 对某人来说不熟悉 ▶ to be unfamiliar with sth 不熟悉某事

unfashionable [ʌnˈfæʃnəbl] ADJ [+ clothes, ideas] 过时的 [guòshí de]; [+ place] 不流行的 [bù liúxíng de]

unfasten [ʌnˈfɑːsn] VT 1 [+ strap, belt, button, clothes] 解开 [jiěkāi] 2 [+ lock, latch] 打开 [dǎkāi]

unfavourable, (US) **unfavorable** [ʌnˈfeɪvrəbl] ADJ 1 [+ conditions, impression] 不利的 [bùlì de] 2 [+ review, reaction] 不赞同的 [bù zàntóng de] ▶ to be unfavourable to sb [terms, conditions +] 不利于某人

unfinished [ʌnˈfɪnɪʃt] ADJ 未完成的 [wèi wánchéng de] ▶ unfinished business 未做完的事情

unfit [ʌnˈfɪt] ADJ (physically) 不太健康的 [bù tài jiànkāng de] ▶ to be unfit for sth/to do sth 不胜任某事/不适合做某事 ▶ unfit for work 身体不佳无法工作 ▶ unfit for human consumption 不宜给人食用

unfold [ʌnˈfəʊld] I VT [+ sheet, map] 展开 [zhǎnkāi] II VI [situation, story, facts +] 展现 [zhǎnxiàn]

unforgettable [ʌnfəˈɡɛtəbl] ADJ 难忘的 [nánwàng de]

unfortunate [ʌnˈfɔːtʃənət] ADJ 1 (unlucky) [+ person, accident] 不幸的 [bùxìng de] 2 (regrettable) [+ event, remark] 令人遗憾的 [lìng

rén yíhàn de] ▶ it is unfortunate that... 不幸的是…

unfortunately [ʌnˈfɔːtʃənətlɪ] ADV 可惜 [kěxī]

unfounded [ʌnˈfaʊndɪd] ADJ [+ allegations, fears] 没有根据的 [méiyǒu gēnjù de]

unfriendly [ʌnˈfrɛndlɪ] ADJ 1 [+ person] 不友善的 [bù yǒushàn de] 2 [+ behaviour, remark] 不友好的 [bù yǒuhǎo de] ▶ to be unfriendly to sb 对某人不友好

unfurnished [ʌnˈfəːnɪʃt] ADJ [+ house, flat] 无家具设备的 [wú jiājù shèbèi de]

ungrateful [ʌnˈɡreɪtful] ADJ 不领情的 [bù lǐngqíng de]

unhappiness [ʌnˈhæpɪnɪs] N [U] 不幸 [bùxìng]

unhappy [ʌnˈhæpɪ] ADJ 1 [+ person] 愁苦的 [chóukǔ de] 2 (unfortunate) [+ accident, event] 不幸的 [bùxìng de] 3 [+ childhood] 悲惨的 [bēicǎn de] ▶ to be unhappy about or with sth (dissatisfied) 对某事不满

unhealthy [ʌnˈhɛlθɪ] ADJ 1 [+ person] 身体不佳的 [shēntǐ bùjiā de] 2 [+ place, diet, lifestyle] 不利于健康的 [bù lìyú jiànkāng de] 3 [+ interest] 不健康的 [bù jiànkāng de]

unheard-of [ʌnˈhəːdɒv] ADJ 1 (unknown) 无先例的 [wú xiānlì de] 2 (exceptional) 前所未闻的 [qián suǒ wèi wén de]

unhelpful [ʌnˈhɛlpful] ADJ 1 [+ person] 不予帮助的 [bù yǔ bāngzhù de] 2 [+ advice] 无用的 [wúyòng de] ▶ to be unhelpful to sb [person +] 对某人毫无帮助; [situation, system +] 对某人是无益的

unhurt [ʌnˈhəːt] ADJ 没有受伤的 [méiyǒu shòushāng de] ▶ to escape unhurt 安然逃脱

unhygienic [ˈʌnhaɪˈdʒiːnɪk] ADJ 不卫生的 [bù wèishēng de]

unidentified [ʌnaɪˈdɛntɪfaɪd] ADJ 无法识别的 [wúfǎ shíbié de]

uniform [ˈjuːnɪfɔːm] I N [C/U] 制服 [zhìfú] II ADJ 1 (regular) [+ length, width etc] 统一的 [tǒngyī de] 2 (similar) [+ objects] 相同的 [xiāngtóng de] 3 [+ result, rise, growth] 一致的 [yīzhì de] ▶ in uniform 穿着制服

unify [ˈjuːnɪfaɪ] VT 使统一 [shǐ tǒngyī]

unimportant [ʌnɪmˈpɔːtənt] ADJ 微不足道的 [wēi bù zú dào de]

uninhabited [ʌnɪnˈhæbɪtɪd] ADJ [+ area, island, house etc] 无人居住的 [wúrén jūzhù de]

unintentional [ʌnɪnˈtɛnʃənəl] ADJ 无心的 [wúxīn de]

○**union** [ˈjuːnjən] I N 1 [U] (unification) 合并 [hébìng] ▷ We are working for the union of the two countries. 我们正为这两个国家的合并而努力。2 [C] (also: trade union) 工会 [gōnghuì] II CPD [复合词] [+ activities, representative etc] 协会 [xiéhuì]

Union Jack N [C] 英国国旗 [Yīngguó guóqí]

unique [juːˈniːk] ADJ 1 (individual) [+ number, pattern etc] 独一无二的 [dú yī wú èr de] 2 (distinctive) [+ ability, skill, performance] 罕有的 [hǎnyǒu de] ▶ to be unique to sb/sth 某人/某物独有的

unisex [ˈjuːnɪsɛks] ADJ [+ hair salon, clothing] 不分男女的 [bù fēn nánnǚ de]

unit [ˈjuːnɪt] N [c] 1 (single whole) 单位 [dānwèi] 2 (group, centre) 小组 [xiǎozǔ] 3 (measurement) 单位 [dānwèi] 4 (machine) 部件 [bùjiàn] 5 (section) [of furniture etc] 组合件 [zǔhéjiàn] 6 (MIL) 分队 [fēnduì] 7 (in course book) 单元 [dānyuán]

unite [juːˈnaɪt] I VT [+ people, party] 使联合 [shǐ liánhé] II VI [people, party +] 联合行动 [liánhé xíngdòng]

united [juːˈnaɪtɪd] ADJ 1 [+ group] 和睦的 [hémù de] 2 [+ effort] 共同的 [gòngtóng de] 3 (POL) [+ country] 统一的 [tǒngyī de] ▶ to be united in sth [+ desire, belief, dislike] 在某事上保持一致 ▶ to be united on sth [+ issue, need] 就某事达成一致 ▶ to be united against sb/sth 团结起来对抗某人/某事

United Arab Emirates [-ˈɛmɪrɪts] NPL ▶ the United Arab Emirates 阿拉伯联合酋长国 [Ālābó Liánhé Qiúzhǎngguó]

United Kingdom N ▶ the United Kingdom 大不列颠及北爱尔兰联合王国 [Dàbùlièdiān Jí Běiʾàiěrʾlán Liánhé Wángguó]

United Nations N ▶ the United Nations 联合国 [Liánhéguó]

United States (of America) N ▶ the United States (of America) 美利坚合众国 [Měilìjiān Hézhòngguó]

unity [ˈjuːnɪti] N [U] 1 (solidarity) 团结 [tuánjié] 2 (unification) 统一 [tǒngyī]

Univ. ABBR (= university) 大学 [dàxué]

universal [juːnɪˈvəːsl] ADJ 普遍的 [pǔbiàn de]

universe [ˈjuːnɪvəːs] N [c] 宇宙 [yǔzhòu]

○**university** [juːnɪˈvəːsɪti] I N [c/U] 大学 [dàxué] ▶ to go to university 上大学 II CPD [复合词] [+ student, professor, education, year] 大学 [dàxué]

unjust [ʌnˈdʒʌst] ADJ [+ action, treatment, society, law] 不公正的 [bù gōngzhèng de]

unkind [ʌnˈkaɪnd] ADJ 刻薄的 [kèbó de] ▶ to be unkind to sb 对某人刻薄 ▶ it is unkind to make fun of people 取笑他人是不友好的 ▶ it was unkind of him to say that 他那么说是不友好的

unknown [ʌnˈnəun] I ADJ 1 [+ fact, number] 未知的 [wèizhī de] 2 [+ writer, artist] 名不见经传的 [míng bù jiàn jīngzhuàn de] 3 (unidentified) [+ person] 陌生的 [mòshēng de] II N 1 [c] (person) 无名小卒 [wúmíng xiǎozú] 2 [s] (thing) 未知事物 [wèizhī shìwù] ▶ he was unknown to me 我不认识他 ▶ unknown to me, he... 不为我所知, 他… ▶ it is not unknown for

travellers to forget their passports 旅客忘带护照的事并不少见 ▶ an unknown quantity 一个未知数 ▶ fear of the unknown 对未知事物的恐惧

unlawful [ʌnˈlɔːful] ADJ 非法的 [fēifǎ de]

unleaded [ʌnˈlɛdɪd] I ADJ 无铅的 [wúqiān de] II N [U] 无铅燃料 [wúqiān ránliào]

unleash [ʌnˈliːʃ] VT [+ feeling, force etc] 激起 [jīqǐ]; [+ missile] 发射 [fāshè]

unless [ʌnˈlɛs] CONJ 除非 [chúfēi] ▶ unless otherwise stated 除非另有说明

unlike [ʌnˈlaɪk] I ADJ (not alike) 不相似的 [bù xiāngsì de] II PREP 1 (in contrast to) 与…相反 [yǔ…xiāngfǎn] 2 (different from) 不同于 [bùtóng yú] 3 (not typical of) 无…的特征 [wú…de tèzhēng]

unlikely [ʌnˈlaɪklɪ] ADJ 1 未必会发生的 [wèibì huì fāshēng de] 2 [+ combination, circumstances] 不大可能的 [bùdà kěnéng de] ▶ in the unlikely event that... 万一有…情况 ▶ in the unlikely event of anything going wrong 万一有事不顺 ▶ it is unlikely that... …是不大可能的 ▶ he is unlikely to win 他获胜的希望不大

unlimited [ʌnˈlɪmɪtɪd] ADJ [+ supply, resources] 无限制的 [wú xiànzhì de]; [+ money, travel] 无限量的 [wú xiànliàng de]

unlisted [ˈʌnˈlɪstɪd] ADJ 1 (US: TEL) [+ person, number] 未列入电话簿的 [wèi lièrù diànhuàbù de] [英= ex-directory] 2 (ECON) 不上市的 [bù shàngshì de]

unload [ʌnˈləud] VT 1 [+ objects] 卸 [xiè] 2 [+ car, lorry etc] 从…上卸货 [cóng…shang xièhuò]

unlock [ʌnˈlɔk] VT [+ door, car, suitcase] 开 [kāi]

unlucky [ʌnˈlʌki] ADJ 1 [+ person] 不幸的 [bùxìng de] 2 [+ object, number] 不吉利的 [bù jílì de] ▶ he was unlucky enough to lose his wallet 他丢了钱包, 真是太倒霉了 ▶ we were unlucky not to win 真不走运, 我们没赢

unmarried [ʌnˈmærɪd] ADJ 未婚的 [wèihūn de]

unmistak(e)able [ʌnmɪsˈteɪkəbl] ADJ 明显的 [míngxiǎn de]

unnatural [ʌnˈnætʃrəl] ADJ 1 (not normal) 反常的 [fǎncháng de] 2 (not sincere) 做作的 [zuòzuo de] ▶ it is not unnatural that... …是很正常的 ▶ it is unnatural to keep the sexes apart 将两性分开是不合人情的 ▶ it would be unnatural for two people to agree all the time 要两个人总是意见一致是不正常的

unnecessary [ʌnˈnɛsəsəri] ADJ 不必要的 [bù bìyào de] ▶ it was unnecessary to do anything 什么都不必做

unnoticed [ʌnˈnəutɪst] ADJ ▶ it went or passed unnoticed 没有人察觉 [méiyǒu rén chájué]

unofficial [ʌnəˈfɪʃl] ADJ 1 [+ estimate, report] 非官方的 [fēi guānfāng de] 2 [+ strike] 未经工会同意的 [wèijīng gōnghuì tóngyì de]

unpack [ʌnˈpæk] I VI 开包 [kāibāo] II VT

[+ suitcase, bag] 打开…取出东西 [dǎkāi…qǔchū dōngxi]

unpaid [ʌnˈpeɪd] ADJ **1** [+ bill, tax] 未支付的 [wèi zhīfù de] **2** [+ holiday, leave] 无薪的 [wúxīn de] **3** [+ work] 无报酬的 [wú bàochou de] **4** [+ worker] 无酬服务的 [wúchóu fúwù de]

unpleasant [ʌnˈplɛznt] ADJ [+ experience, task, situation, sensation] 使人不愉快的 [shǐ rén bù yúkuài de]; [+ person, manner] 令人讨厌的 [lìng rén tǎoyàn de] ▶ **to be unpleasant to sb** 跟某人过不去 ▶ **she's unpleasant to work with** 她很难一起共事 ▶ **it is very unpleasant to be criticized** 受到批评让人很不高兴

unplug [ʌnˈplʌg] VT 拔去…的插头 [báqù…de chātóu]

unpopular [ʌnˈpɒpjʊlə(r)] ADJ [+ person, decision] 不受欢迎的 [bù shòu huānyíng de] ▶ **to be unpopular with sb** 不受某人的欢迎 ▶ **to make sb/o.s. unpopular (with sb)** 使某人/自己不受(某人的)欢迎

unprecedented [ʌnˈprɛsɪdɛntɪd] ADJ **1** [+ decision, event, increase] 前所未有的 [qián suǒ wèi yǒu de] **2** [+ success] 空前的 [kōngqián de]

unpredictable [ʌnprɪˈdɪktəbl] ADJ [+ person, weather, result] 易变的 [yìbiàn de]

unprofessional [ʌnprəˈfɛʃənl] ADJ [+ attitude, conduct, act] 不专业的 [bù zhuānyè de]

unprotected [ˈʌnprəˈtɛktɪd] ADJ **1** (not defended) 不设防的 [bù shèfáng de] **2** (not covered) 无保护的 [wú bǎohù de] ▶ **unprotected sex** 无防范措施的性行为 ▶ **be unprotected from sth** 未经保护地暴露于某物

unqualified [ʌnˈkwɒlɪfaɪd] ADJ **1** [+ teacher, nurse etc] 不合格的 [bù hégé de] **2** (complete) [+ disaster, success, support] 完全的 [wánquán de] ▶ **to be unqualified for** 不能胜任 ▶ **to be unqualified to do sth** 没资格做某事

unravel [ʌnˈrævl] **I** VT **1** [+ string, wool] 解开 [jiěkāi] **2** [+ mystery, truth] 弄清 [nòngqīng] **II** VI [mystery, puzzle +] 明朗 [mínglǎng]

unreal [ʌnˈrɪəl] ADJ **1** (artificial) 假的 [jiǎ de] **2** (bizarre) 离谱的 [lípǔ de]

unrealistic [ˈʌnrɪəˈlɪstɪk] ADJ [+ person, expectation, idea, view] 不切实际的 [bù qiè shíjì de] ▶ **it is unrealistic to expect that...** 指望…是不切实际的

unreasonable [ʌnˈriːznəbl] ADJ **1** [+ person, attitude] 无理的 [wúlǐ de] **2** [+ decision, price, amount] 不合理的 [bù hélǐ de] ▶ **it is unreasonable to expect that...** 指望…是荒谬的 ▶ **it is not unreasonable that...** …并不过分

unrelated [ʌnrɪˈleɪtɪd] ADJ **1** [+ incident, cause] 不相关的 [bù xiāngguān de] **2** [+ people] 无亲缘关系的 [wú qīnyuán guānxì de] ▶ **unrelated to sth** 和某物无关 ▶ **unrelated to sb** 和某人无亲缘关系的

unreliable [ʌnrɪˈlaɪəbl] ADJ **1** [+ person, firm] 不可信赖的 [bù kě xìnlài de] **2** [+ machine, method] 不可靠的 [bù kěkào de]

unrest [ʌnˈrɛst] N [U] 动荡 [dòngdàng]

unroll [ʌnˈrəʊl] VT 展开 [zhǎnkāi]

unruly [ʌnˈruːlɪ] ADJ **1** [+ child, behaviour] 任性的 [rènxìng de] **2** [+ hair] 不服帖的 [bù fútiē de]

unsafe [ʌnˈseɪf] ADJ **1** (in danger) [+ person] 不安全的 [bù ānquán de] **2** (dangerous) [+ machine, bridge, conditions] 危险的 [wēixiǎn de] **3** (BRIT: LAW) [+ conviction] 不成立的 [bù chénglì de] ▶ **it is unsafe to play here** 在这儿玩不安全 ▶ **the car was unsafe to drive** 开这辆车不安全 ▶ **unsafe to eat/drink** 食用/饮用不安全 ▶ **unsafe sex** 无防范措施的性行为

unsatisfactory [ˈʌnsætɪsˈfæktərɪ] ADJ 令人不满意的 [lìng rén bù mǎnyì de]

unscrew [ʌnˈskruː] VT [+ lid, cap] 旋开 [xuánkāi]

unsettled [ʌnˈsɛtld] ADJ **1** [+ person] 不安的 [bù ān de] **2** [+ situation, future] 不稳定的 [bù wěndìng de] **3** [+ question, argument, issue etc] 未解决的 [wèi jiějué de] **4** [+ weather] 易变的 [yìbiàn de]

unsettling [ʌnˈsɛtlɪŋ] ADJ 使人不安的 [shǐ rén bù ān de]

unshaven [ʌnˈʃeɪvn] ADJ [+ man, face] 胡子未刮的 [húzi wèi guā de]

unskilled [ʌnˈskɪld] ADJ **1** [+ worker] 不熟练的 [bù shúliàn de] **2** [+ work, job] 无需特殊技能的 [wúxū tèshū jìnéng de]

unstable [ʌnˈsteɪbl] ADJ **1** [+ ladder] 不牢固的 [bù láogù de] **2** [+ government, situation] 不稳固的 [bù wěngù de] **3** [+ person] 反复无常的 [fǎnfù wú cháng de] **4** (CHEM, PHYS) [+ substance] 不稳定的 [bù wěndìng de]

unsteady [ʌnˈstɛdɪ] ADJ **1** [+ step, voice] 不平稳的 [bù píngwěn de] **2** [+ person] 摇晃的 [yáohuàng de] **3** [+ ladder etc] 不稳固的 [bù wěngù de] ▶ **to be unsteady on one's feet** 走路摇摇晃晃

unsuccessful [ʌnsəkˈsɛsful] ADJ **1** [+ attempt, application] 失败的 [shībài de] **2** [+ person, applicant] 不成功的 [bù chénggōng de] ▶ **to be unsuccessful in or at doing sth** 做某事没有成功

unsuitable [ʌnˈsuːtəbl] ADJ **1** [+ place, time, clothes] 不适宜的 [bù shìyí de] **2** [+ candidate, applicant] 不合适的 [bù héshì de] **3** [+ friend, husband, partner] 不相称的 [bù xiāngchèn de] ▶ **to be unsuitable for sth/for doing sth** 不适于某事/做某事 ▶ **to be unsuitable for sb** 对某人不合适

unsure [ʌnˈʃʊə(r)] ADJ 没有把握的 [méiyǒu bǎwò de] ▶ **to be unsure about sth** 对某事没有把握 ▶ **to be unsure of o.s.** 对自己缺乏信心

unsympathetic [ˈʌnsɪmpəˈθɛtɪk] ADJ **1** (uncaring) 无动于衷的 [wú dòng yú zhōng de] **2** (unlikeable) 冷淡的 [lěngdàn de] ▶ **to be unsympathetic to(wards) sth** 对某事不表同情

untidy [ʌnˈtaɪdɪ] ADJ **1** [+ room] 不整洁的 [bù zhěngjié de] **2** [+ person, appearance] 邋遢的 [lātā de]

untie [ʌnˈtaɪ] VT **1** [+ rope, knot] 解开 [jiěkāi] **2** [+ prisoner, dog] 松开 [sōngkāi] **3** [+ sb's hands, feet] 给…松绑 [gěi…sōngbǎng]

○**until** [ənˈtɪl] **I** PREP 直到…时 [zhídào…shí] ▷ They didn't find her until the next day. 他们直到第二天才找到她。**II** CONJ 到…为止 [dào…wéizhǐ] ▷ She waited until he had gone. 她一直等到他走为止。▶ **until now** 直到现在 ▶ **not until now** 直到现在才 ▶ **until then** 届时 ▶ **not until then** 直到那时…才

untrue [ʌnˈtruː] ADJ 不正确的 [bù zhèngquè de] ▶ **it is untrue that...** …与事实不符 ▶ **it would be untrue to say that...** 说…就不对了

unused¹ [ʌnˈjuːzd] ADJ 闲置的 [xiánzhì de]

unused² [ʌnˈjuːst] ADJ ▶ **to be unused to sth/ to doing sth** 不习惯某事/做某事 [bù xíguàn mǒushì/zuò mǒushì]

unusual [ʌnˈjuːʒəl] ADJ **1** 不寻常的 [bù xúncháng de] **2** (distinctive) 与众不同的 [yǔ zhòng bùtóng de] ▶ **it's unusual to see someone so tall** 难得见到这么高的人

unusually [ʌnˈjuːʒəlɪ] ADV 异乎寻常地 [yìhū xúncháng de]

unveil [ʌnˈveɪl] VT **1** [+ statue, plaque] 为…揭幕 [wèi…jiēmù] **2** [+ plan] 透露 [tòulù]

unwanted [ʌnˈwɒntɪd] ADJ **1** [+ clothing, animal] 没人要的 [méirén yào de] **2** [+ child, pregnancy] 不想要的 [bù xiǎngyào de]

unwelcome [ʌnˈwɛlkəm] ADJ **1** [+ guest] 不受欢迎的 [bù shòu huānyíng de] **2** [+ news] 讨厌的 [tǎoyàn de] ▶ **to feel unwelcome** 感到不受欢迎

unwell [ʌnˈwɛl] ADJ ▶ **to feel/be unwell** 觉得/身体不适 [juéde/shēntǐ bùshì]

unwilling [ʌnˈwɪlɪŋ] ADJ ▶ **to be unwilling to do sth** 不愿做某事 [bùyuàn zuò mǒushì]

unwind [ʌnˈwaɪnd] (pt, pp **unwound**) **I** VT [bandage, scarf etc] 解开 [jiěkāi] **II** VI (relax) 放松 [fàngsōng]

unwise [ʌnˈwaɪz] ADJ **1** [+ decision, choice] 愚蠢的 [yúchǔn de] **2** [+ person] 不明智的 [bù míngzhì de] ▶ **it would be unwise to expect too much** 期望过多是不明智的 ▶ **to be unwise enough to do sth** 做某事真是傻

unwittingly [ʌnˈwɪtɪŋlɪ] ADV 无意地 [wúyì de]

unwrap [ʌnˈræp] VT 打开…的包装 [dǎkāi…de bāozhuāng]

unzip [ʌnˈzɪp] VT 拉开 [lākāi]

○**up** [ʌp] **I** PREP **1** (to higher point on) [+ hill, slope, ladder, stairs] 沿…向上 [yán…xiàngshàng] ▶ **he went up the stairs/the hill/the ladder** 他上了楼/山/梯子 **2** (along) [+ road, river] 沿着 [yánzhe] ▶ **a bus came/went up the road** 一辆公共汽车沿着路开过来/去 **3** (at higher point on) [+ hill, ladder, tree] 在…高处 [zài…gāochù]; [+ road] 在…高远处 [zài…gāoyuǎnchù]; [+ river] 在…上游 [zài…shàngyóu] ▶ **the cat was up a tree** 猫在树上 ▶ **they live further up the street** 他们住在这条街那边儿

II ADV **1** (towards higher point) 往上 [wǎngshàng] ▶ **the lift only goes up to the 12th floor** 电梯只到12层楼以上 ▶ **to pace up and down** 走来走去 **2** (at higher point) 高高地 [gāogāo de] ▶ **up in the sky** 在天上 ▶ **up here/there** 这/那上面 ▶ **up above** 再往上 **3** ▶ **to be up** (be out of bed) 起床 [qǐchuáng]; (be at an end) [time +] 结束 [jiéshù]; (be on the increase) [price, level, amount +] 上升 [shàngshēng] ▶ **what's up?** (inf) 怎么了? ▶ **what's up with him?** 他怎么了? **4** (to/in the north) 在/向北方 [zài/xiàng běifāng] ▶ **he often comes up to Scotland** 他常北上去苏格兰 ▶ **how long are you staying up here?** 你在那儿住了多久了? **5** (approaching) ▶ **to go/come/run up (to sb)** (朝某人) 走过/过来/跑去 [(cháo mǒurén) zǒuguò/guòlái/pǎoqù] **6** ▶ **up to** (as far as) 直到 [zhídào]; (in approximations) 多达 [duōdá] ▶ **the water came up to his knees** 水到他的膝盖了 ▶ **I can spend up to £100** 我可以花到100英镑 ▶ **up to 100 people** 多达100人 **7** ▶ **up to** or **until** 直到 [zhídào] ▶ **I'll be here up to** or **until 5.30 pm** 我会一直呆到下午5点30分 ▶ **up to now** 直到现在 **8** ▶ **it is up to you** (to decide) 随便你 (决定) [suíbiàn nǐ (juédìng)] **9** ▶ **to be up to sth** (inf) (be doing) 忙于做某件坏事 [máng yú zuò mǒu jiàn huàishì] ▶ **what is he up to?** 他在搞什么鬼? **10** ▶ **to be up to sth** (adequate for) [+ task] 足够某事 [zúgòu mǒushì]; [+ standard] 达到某事 [dádào mǒushì] ▶ **his work is not up to the required standard** 他的工作未能达到要求的标准 ▶ **to be up to doing sth** 胜任做某事 **11** ▶ **to feel up to sth/to doing sth** 感到能胜任某事/感到有力气做某事 [gǎndào néng shèngrèn mǒushì/gǎndào yǒu lìqì zuò mǒushì] **12** (in other expressions) ▶ **to be up against sb/sth** 面临某人/某事 [miànlín mǒurén/mǒushì] ▶ **to be up for discussion** 即将讨论

III VT (*increase*) 增加 [zēngjiā]
IV VI (*inf*) ▸ **she upped and left** 她突然起身离开了 [tā tūrán qǐshēn líkāi le]
V NPL ▸ **ups and downs** (*in life, career*) 起起伏伏 [qǐqǐ fúfú] ▸ **we all have our ups and downs** 我们都有盛衰浮沉

up-and-coming [ˌʌpənd'kʌmɪŋ] ADJ [+ *actor, musician, company*] 有前途的 [yǒu qiántú de]

upbringing ['ʌpbrɪŋɪŋ] N [c] 教养 [jiàoyǎng]

update [*vb* ʌp'deɪt, *n* 'ʌpdeɪt] I VT [+ *records, information*] 更新 [gēngxīn] II N [c] 最新信息 [zuìxīn xìnxī] ▸ **to update sb on sth** 告知某人某事最新动态

upfront [ʌp'frʌnt] I ADJ **1** [+ *person*] 坦率的 [tǎnshuài de] **2** (*advance*) [+ *charge, cost*] 提前支付的 [tíqián zhīfù de] II ADV [*pay, charge* +] 提前地 [tíqián de] ▸ **to be upfront about sth** 对某事很坦率 ▸ **to be upfront about being gay/divorced** *etc* 公开表示自己是同性恋/已离婚{等}

upgrade [*vb* ʌp'greɪd, *n* 'ʌpgreɪd] I VT **1** [+ *computer* etc] 使升级 [shǐ shēngjí] **2** [+ *employee*] 提升 [tíshēng] II N [c] 升级 [shēngjí] ▸ **to upgrade sth/sb to sth** 将某物升级为某物/将某人升为某职 ▸ **an upgrade to sth** 提升到某个等级

upheaval [ʌp'hi:vl] N [c] 剧变 [jùbiàn]

uphill ['ʌp'hɪl] I ADJ **1** [+ *climb, journey*] 上坡的 [shàngpō de] **2** (*fig*) [+ *task*] 艰难的 [jiānnán de] II ADV [*walk, push* +] 往坡上 [wǎng pōshang] ▸ **an uphill struggle** *or* **battle (to do sth)** (做某事的)艰苦奋斗

uphold [ʌp'həʊld] (*pt, pp* **upheld**) VT [+ *law, principle, decision*] 维护 [wéihù]

upholstery [ʌp'həʊlstərɪ] N [U] 软垫 [ruǎndiàn]

upkeep ['ʌpki:p] N [U] **1** [*of building, place*] 维护 [wéihù] **2** [*of person, service*] 供养 [gōngyǎng]

upload [ʌp'ləʊd] VT 上载 [shàngzài]

upmarket [ʌp'mɑ:kɪt] (BRIT) ADJ [+ *product, hotel*] 高档的 [gāodàng de] [美 = **upscale**]

upon [ə'pɒn] (*frm*) PREP 在…上面 [zài…shàngmian] ▸ **upon doing sth** 在做某事之时 ▸ **Christmas/the football season is upon us** 圣诞节/足球赛季就要来了 ▸ **row upon row/layer upon layer of** 一排排的/一层层的…

upper ['ʌpə(r)] I ADJ **1** [+ *floor, deck, shelf*] 上层的 [shàngcéng de] **2** [+ *lip*] 上面的 [shàngmian de] **3** [+ *part*] 较高的 [jiàogāo de] **4** [+ *arm, back, body*] 上部的 [shàngbù de] II N [c] [*of shoe*] 鞋帮 [xiébāng] ▸ **the upper sixth** (BRIT: SCOL) 中学七年级(英国中学教育的最后一年,在此期间,学生参加大学升学资格的考试)

upper class I N ▸ **the upper class(es)** 上流社会 [shàngliú shèhuì] II ADJ (*also*: **upper-class**) 上流社会的 [shàngliú shèhuì de]

upright ['ʌpraɪt] I ADJ **1** (*vertical*) [+ *freezer, vacuum cleaner*] 立式的 [lìshì de] **2** (*honest*)

[+ *person*] 正直的 [zhèngzhí de] II ADV [*sit, stand* +] 挺直地 [tǐngzhí de] III N [c] (ARCHIT) 垂直的构件 [chuízhí de gòujiàn] ▸ **to remain upright** 保持直立

uprising ['ʌpraɪzɪŋ] N [c] 起义 [qǐyì]

uproar ['ʌprɔ:(r)] N [U] **1** (*shouting*) 喧嚣 [xuānxiāo] **2** (*protest*) 骚乱 [sāoluàn] ▸ **an uproar over** *or* **about sth** 因某事引起的骚乱

upscale ['ʌpskeɪl] (US) ADJ [+ *product, hotel*] 高档的 [gāodàng de] [英 = **upmarket**]

upset [*vb* ʌp'sɛt, *n* 'ʌpsɛt] (*pt, pp* **upset**) I VT **1** (*make unhappy*) [+ *person*] 使苦恼 [shǐ kǔnǎo] **2** (*knock over*) [+ *glass* etc] 打翻 [dǎfān] **3** (*disturb*) [+ *routine, plan*] 打乱 [dǎluàn] II ADJ **1** (*unhappy*) 心烦意乱的 [xīnfán yìluàn de] **2** [+ *stomach*] 不舒服的 [bù shūfu de] III N ▸ **to have/get a stomach upset** (BRIT) 感到肠胃不适 [gǎndào chángwèi bùshì] ▸ **to be upset about sth** 为某事感到烦恼 ▸ **to get upset** (*sad*) 感到难过; (*offended*) 感到生气

upside down [ʌpsaɪd-] I ADV [*hang, hold, turn* +] 上下颠倒地 [shàngxià diāndǎo de] II ADJ 上下颠倒的 [shàngxià diāndǎo de] ▸ **to turn a place upside down** 把某地方翻得乱七八糟 ▸ **to turn sb's life** *or* **world upside down** 把某人的生活搞得天翻地覆

upstairs [ʌp'stɛəz] I ADV **1** [*be* +] 在楼上 [zài lóushang] **2** [*go* +] 往楼上 [wǎng lóushang] II ADJ [+ *window, room*] 楼上的 [lóushang de] III N [s] [*of building*] 楼上 [lóushang]

up-to-date ['ʌptə'deɪt] ADJ **1** (*modern*) 最新的 [zuìxīn de] **2** (*well-informed*) 掌握最新信息的 [zhǎngwò zuìxīn xìnxī de] ▸ **to keep up-to-date (with sth)** 跟上(某事的)最新发展 ▸ **to keep sb up-to-date (with** *or* **on sth)** 为某人提供(关于某事的)最新信息 ▸ **to keep sth up-to-date** 不断更新某物

uptown ['ʌptaʊn] (US) I ADV **1** [*be* +] 在市镇外围的住宅区 **2** [*go* +] 去市镇外围的住宅区 II ADJ 住宅区的 [zhùzháiqū de]

upward ['ʌpwəd] I ADJ 向上的 [xiàngshàng de] II ADV = **upwards** ▸ **upward of** (*more than*) 多于…

upwards ['ʌpwədz] ADV 向上 [xiàngshàng]

uranium [juə'reɪnɪəm] N [U] 铀 [yóu]

Uranus [juə'reɪnəs] N 天王星 [Tiānwángxīng]

urban ['ə:bən] ADJ [+ *area, development*] 城市的 [chéngshì de]

urge [ə:dʒ] I N [c] 冲动 [chōngdòng] II VT **1** ▸ **to urge sb to do sth** 怂恿某人做某事 [sǒngyǒng mǒurén zuò mǒushì] **2** ▸ **to urge caution** 强调要谨慎 [qiángdiào yào jǐnshèn] ▸ **to have an urge to do sth** 强烈地想要做某事 ▸ **an urge for revenge** 复仇的强烈欲望 ▸ **urge on** VT 激励 [jīlì]

urgency ['ə:dʒənsɪ] N [U] [*of task*] 紧迫 [jǐnpò] ▸ **a note of urgency** (*in voice*) 急迫的语气 ▸ **sense of urgency** 紧迫感 ▸ **as a matter of**

urgency 作为紧急事件

urgent ['əːdʒənt] ADJ **1** [+ letter, message etc] 紧急的 [jǐnjí de] **2** [+ need, voice] 急迫的 [jípò de]

urinal ['juərɪnl] N [c] 小便池 [xiǎobiànchí]

urinate ['juərɪneɪt] VI 排尿 [páiniào]

urine ['juərɪn] N [U] 尿 [niào]

URL (COMPUT) N ABBR (= Uniform Resource Locator) 统一资源定位符 [tǒngyī zīyuán dìngwèiqì]

urn [əːn] N [c] **1** (pot) 瓮 [wèng] **2** (for ashes) 骨灰瓮 [gǔhuīwèng] **3** (also: **tea urn**) 茶水壶 [cháshuǐhú]

Uruguay ['juərəgwaɪ] N 乌拉圭 [Wūlāguī]

Uruguayan [juərə'gwaɪən] **I** ADJ 乌拉圭的 [Wūlāguī de] **II** N [c] (person) 乌拉圭人 [Wūlāguīrén]

US N ABBR (= United States) ▸ **the US** 美国 [Měiguó]

○ **us** [ʌs] PRON 我们 [wǒmen] ▷ They need us. 他们需要我们。▷ He brought us a present. 他带给我们一份礼物。▷ He lives with us. 他和我们住在一起。

USA N ABBR (= United States of America) ▸ **the USA** 美国 [Měiguó]

○ **use** [n juːs, vb juːz] **I** N **1** [U/S] (using) 使用 [shǐyòng] ▷ the use of artificial drugs 人造药品的使用 **2** [c/U] (purpose) 用途 [yòngtú] ▷ Metal detectors have many uses. 金属探测器有很多用途。**3** [c] [of word] 用法 [yòngfǎ] ▷ Old uses of some words are dying out. 一些词的旧用法正逐渐消失。**II** VT **1** [+ object, tool] 使用 [shǐyòng] **2** [+ word, phrase] 应用 [yìngyòng] **3** (pej) [+ person] 利用 [lìyòng] **4** (also: **use up**) [+ supply] 用完 [yòngwán] ▷ You've used all the ice cubes. 你用掉了所有的冰块。▸ **to be in use** 正被使用 ▸ **to go out of use** 不再被使用 ▸ **to be of use (to sb)** (对某人)有用 ▸ **to make use of sth** 利用某物 ▸ **it's no use** 没用的 ▸ **it's no use arguing/crying** etc 吵/哭[等]是没用的 ▸ **what's the use** 有什么用呢! ▸ **to be no use (to sb)** (对某人)毫无用处 ▸ **to have a use for sth** 用得着某物 ▸ **to have the use of sth** 使用某物 ▸ **she used to do it** 她过去是这么做的 ▸ **I didn't use to** or **I used not to worry so much** 我过去不这么焦虑 ▸ **to be used to sth/to doing sth** 习惯于某事/做某事 ▸ **to get used to sth/to doing sth** 开始习惯于某事/做某事

▸ **use up** VT 用完 [yòngwán]

used [juːzd] ADJ **1** [+ tissue, glass, envelope] 用过的 [yòngguò de] **2** [+ car] 旧的 [jiù de]

useful ['juːsful] ADJ 有用的 [yǒuyòng de] ▸ **to be useful to** or **for sb** 对某人有用的 ▸ **to be useful for sth/doing sth** 对某事/做某事有帮助的 ▸ **it's useful to keep a diary** 写日记很有助益 ▸ **it would be useful for us to have more information** 得到更多的信息会对我们很有用 ▸ **to come in useful** 有帮助

useless ['juːslɪs] ADJ **1** (unusable) 无用的 [wúyòng de] **2** (pointless) 徒劳的 [túláo de] **3** (inf) (hopeless) 无能的 [wúnéng de] ▸ **it's useless to complain** 抱怨是无用的 ▸ **to be useless at sth/at doing sth** (inf) 对某事/做某事非常差劲

user ['juːzə(r)] N [c] **1** [of product, service] 使用者 [shǐyòngzhě] **2** (consumer) [of petrol, gas etc] 用户 [yònghù]

user-friendly ['juːzə'frendlɪ] ADJ 易于使用的 [yìyú shǐyòng de]

USS N ABBR (= United States Ship) 美国军舰 [Měiguó Jūnjiàn]

usual ['juːʒuəl] ADJ [+ time, place etc] 惯常的 [guàncháng de] ▸ **as usual** (as normally happens) 像往常一样; (just the same) 像平常一样 ▸ **warmer/colder than usual** 比平常暖和/冷 ▸ **it is usual to tip waiters** 给侍者小费是很平常的

usually ['juːʒuəlɪ] ADV 通常地 [tōngcháng de]

utensil [juː'tensl] N [c] 用具 [yòngjù] ▸ **cooking/kitchen utensils** 烹饪/厨房用具

utility [juː'tɪlɪtɪ] N **1** (also: **public utility**) 公共设施 [gōnggòng shèshī] **2** [U] (frm) (usefulness) 效用 [xiàoyòng]

utilize ['juːtɪlaɪz] (frm) VT 利用 [lìyòng]

utmost ['ʌtməust] **I** ADJ 极度的 [jídù de] **II** N ▸ **to do one's utmost (to do sth)** 竭尽全力(做某事) [jiéjìn quánlì (zuò mǒushì)] ▸ **of the utmost importance** 最重要的

utter ['ʌtə(r)] **I** ADJ (total) [+ amazement, nonsense, fool] 绝对的 [juéduì de] **II** VT (liter) [+ sounds, words] 说 [shuō]

utterly ['ʌtəlɪ] ADV (totally) 全然 [quánrán]

U-turn ['juː'təːn] N [c] **1** (when driving) U形转弯 [U xíng zhuǎnwān] **2** (fig) 彻底转变 [chèdǐ zhuǎnbiàn] ▸ **to do a U-turn** (in vehicle) 180度掉头; (fig) 彻底转变

Uzbek ['ʌzbɛk] **I** ADJ 乌兹别克的 [Wūzībiékè de] **II** N **1** [c] (person) 乌兹别克人 [Wūzībiékèrén] **2** [U] (language) 乌兹别克语 [Wūzībiékèyǔ]

Uzbekistan [ʌzbɛkɪ'staːn] N 乌兹别克 [Wūzībiékè]

V¹, v [viː] N [C/U] (letter) 英语的第二十二个字母

V² (TEXTING) ABBR (= very) 很 [hěn]

v. ABBR **1** (= versus) 对 [duì] **2** (= volt) 伏特 [fútè]
3 (= verse) 诗 [shī]

vacancy ['veɪkənsɪ] N [C] (job) 空缺 [kòngquē];
(hotel room) 空房 [kōngfáng] ▶ "no vacancies"
"客满" ▶ have you any vacancies? (hotel) 你
们有空房吗?

vacant ['veɪkənt] ADJ **1** [+ seat, bathroom] 空
着的 [kòngzhe de] **2** [+ look, expression] 茫然的
[mángrán de] **3** [+ job] 空缺的 [kòngquē de]

vacate [və'keɪt] (frm) VT [+ house, seat] 空出
[kōngchū]; [+ job] 辞去 [cíqù]

vacation [və'keɪʃən] N [C] **1** (ESP US) 休假
[xiūjià] [英 = holiday] **2** (at university etc) 假期
[jiàqī] ▶ to take a vacation 休假 ▶ to be/go
on vacation 在/去度假

vaccinate ['væksɪneɪt] VT ▶ to vaccinate sb
(against sth) 给某人接种疫苗(预防某疾病)
[gěi mǒurén jiēzhòng yìmiáo (yùfáng mǒu
jíbìng)]

vaccination [væksɪ'neɪʃən] N **1** [U]
(immunization) 疫苗接种 [yìmiáo jiēzhòng]
2 [C] (injection) 预防针 [yùfángzhēn] ▶ a
vaccination against smallpox/tetanus 天花疫
苗接种/破伤风预防针

vaccine ['væksiːn] N [C/U] 疫苗 [yìmiáo]

vacuum ['vækjum] I N [C] **1** 真空 [zhēnkōng]
2 (fig) 空白 [kòngbái] II VT [+ room, carpet etc]
用吸尘器打扫 [yòng xīchénqì dǎsǎo]

vacuum cleaner N [C] (also: vacuum) 真空吸
尘器 [zhēnkōng xīchénqì]

vagina [və'dʒaɪnə] N [C] 阴道 [yīndào]

vague [veɪg] ADJ **1** [+ memory, idea] 不清楚的 [bù
qīngchǔ de]; [+ shape, outline] 模糊的 [móhu de];
[+ talk, instructions] 含糊的 [hánhu de] **2** (evasive)
[+ person, promise] 含糊其辞的 [hánhu qící de]
3 (distracted) [+ person, look] 茫然的 [mángrán
de] ▶ I haven't the vaguest idea 我一无所知

vaguely ['veɪglɪ] ADV **1** (unclearly) 含糊地
[hánhu de] **2** (evasively) 闪烁其辞地 [shǎnshuò
qící de] **3** (slightly) 略微地 [lüèwēi de]

vain [veɪn] ADJ **1** (conceited) [+ person] 自负的
[zìfù de] **2** (useless) [+ attempt, action, hope] 徒劳
的 [túláo de] ▶ in vain 徒然 ▶ to die in vain
白白死去

Valentine's Day ['væləntaɪnz-] N [C/U] 情人
节 [Qíngrénjié]

valiant ['væljənt] ADJ 勇敢的 [yǒnggǎn de]

valid ['vælɪd] ADJ **1** [+ ticket, document] 有效的
[yǒuxiào de] **2** [+ argument, reason] 令人信服的
[lìng rén xìnfú de]

valley ['vælɪ] N [C] 山谷 [shāngǔ]

valuable ['væljuəbl] I ADJ **1** [+ jewels,
painting etc] 贵重的 [guìzhòng de] **2** (useful)
[+ lesson, contribution] 有价值的 [yǒu jiàzhí de]
II **valuables** NPL 贵重物品 [guìzhòng wùpǐn]

valuation [vælju'eɪʃən] N [C] [of house etc] 估
价 [gūjià]

○**value** ['væljuː] I N **1** [C/U] (financial worth)
价值 [jiàzhí] **2** [U] (importance) 重要性
[zhòngyàoxìng] ▷ The value of this experience
should not be underestimated. 这次经历的重要性
不应被低估。 **3** [U] (worth in relation to price) 价
格 [jiàgé] ▷ Both offer excellent value at around
£50 for a double room. 对一间双人房双方都报
出50英镑左右的优惠价格。II VT **1** (assess
the worth of) 给…估价 [gěi…gūjià] ▷ jewellery
valued at around $10,000 估价在1万美元左右的
珠宝 **2** (appreciate) 重视 [zhòngshì] ▷ She genuinely values
his opinion. 她确实很重视他的看法。III **values**
NPL (principles, beliefs) 价值观念 [jiàzhí
guānniàn] ▶ value for money 物有所值 ▶ to
lose (in) value [currency, property +] 贬值 ▶ to
gain (in) value [currency, property +] 升值 ▶ to be
of value to sb 对某人有益

valued ['væljuːd] ADJ 受重视的 [shòu
zhòngshì de]

valve [vælv] N [C] (in pipe, tube) 阀 [fá]; (in heart,
vein) 瓣膜 [bànmó]

vampire ['væmpaɪə(r)] N [C] 吸血鬼 [xīxuèguǐ]

van [væn] N [C] **1** (AUT) 厢式运货车 [xiāngshì
yùnhuòchē] **2** (BRIT: RAIL) 铁路货车厢 [tiělù
huòchēxiāng]

vandal ['vændl] N [C] 蓄意破坏公物者 [xùyì
pòhuài gōngwùzhě]

vandalism ['vændəlɪzəm] N [U] 蓄意破坏公物
的行为 [xùyì pòhuài gōngwù de xíngwéi]

vandalize ['vændəlaɪz] VT 肆意毁坏 [sìyì huǐhuài]

vanilla [və'nɪlə] N [U] 香草 [xiāngcǎo]

vanish ['vænɪʃ] VI **1** [person, aircraft +] 消失 [xiāoshī] **2** (cease to exist) [tradition, system, species +] 灭绝 [mièjué]

vanity ['vænɪtɪ] N [U] 虚荣 [xūróng]

vapour, (US) **vapor** ['veɪpə(r)] N [C/U] 蒸汽 [zhēngqì]

variable ['vɛərɪəbl] I ADJ **1** (likely to change) [+ mood, quality, climate] 易变的 [yìbiàn de] **2** (able to be changed) [+ temperature, height, speed] 可变的 [kěbiàn de] II N [C] **1** (MATH) 变量 [biànliàng] **2** (factor) 可变因素 [kěbiàn yīnsù]

variant ['vɛərɪənt] N [C] 变体 [biàntǐ]

variation [vɛərɪ'eɪʃən] N **1** [C/U] (in price, level, amount) 变动 [biàndòng] **2** [C] [of plot, musical theme etc] 变化 [biànhuà]

varied ['vɛərɪd] ADJ **1** (diverse) [+ opinions, reasons] 各种各样的 [gèzhǒng gèyàng de] **2** (full of variety) [+ career, work, diet] 丰富多彩的 [fēngfù duōcǎi de]

variety [və'raɪətɪ] N **1** [U] (diversity) 多样性 [duōyàngxìng] **2** [S] (range) [of objects] 若干 [ruògān] **3** [C] (type) 种类 [zhǒnglèi] ▶ **a wide variety of...** 种类繁多的… ▶ **for a variety of reasons** 由于种种原因

various ['vɛərɪəs] ADJ **1** (several) 不同的 [bùtóng de] **2** (different) 各种各样的 [gèzhǒng gèyàng de]

varnish ['vɑ:nɪʃ] I N [C/U] 清漆 [qīngqī] II VT 给…涂清漆 [gěi...tú qīngqī] ▶ **to varnish one's nails** 给指甲涂指甲油

vary ['vɛərɪ] I VT (make changes to) [+ routine, diet] 更改 [gēnggǎi] II VI (be different) [amount, sizes, colours +] 有差异 [yǒu chāyì] ▶ **to vary with** [+ weather, season, age etc] 随…而变化

vase [vɑ:z, US veɪs] N [C] 花瓶 [huāpíng]

Vaseline® ['væsɪli:n] N [U] 凡士林 [Fánshìlín]

vast [vɑ:st] ADJ **1** [+ area] 广阔的 [guǎngkuò de] **2** [+ knowledge] 渊博的 [yuānbó de] **3** [+ expense] 巨额的 [jù'é de]

VAT [vi:eɪ'ti:, væt] (BRIT) N ABBR (= value added tax) 增值税 [zēngzhíshuì]

vault [vɔ:lt] I N [C] **1** (tomb) 地下墓室 [dìxià mùshì] **2** (in bank) 保险库 [bǎoxiǎnkù] **3** [of roof] 拱顶 [gǒngdǐng] II VT (also: **vault over**) 跃过 [yuèguò]

VCR N ABBR (= video cassette recorder) 录像机 [lùxiàngjī]

VD N ABBR (= venereal disease) 性病 [xìngbìng]

VDT (US) N ABBR (= visual display terminal) 视频显示装置 [shìpín xiǎnshì zhuāngzhì] [英 = **VDU**]

VDU (BRIT) N ABBR (= visual display unit) 视频显示装置 [shìpín xiǎnshì zhuāngzhì] [美 = **VDT**]

veal [vi:l] N [U] 小牛肉 [xiǎoniúròu]

veer [vɪə(r)] VI **1** [vehicle +] 突然转向 [tūrán zhuǎnxiàng] **2** [wind +] 转向 [zhuǎnxiàng]

vegan ['vi:gən] I N [C] 纯素食主义者 [juésùshí zhǔyìzhě] II ADJ 纯素食主义者的 [juésùshí zhǔyìzhě de]

vegetable ['vɛdʒtəbl] I N [C] 蔬菜 [shūcài] II CPD [复合词] [+ oil, dish] 蔬菜 [shūcài]

vegetarian [vɛdʒɪ'tɛərɪən] I N [C] 素食者 [sùshízhě] II ADJ [+ diet, restaurant etc] 素的 [sù de]

vegetation [vɛdʒɪ'teɪʃən] (frm) N [U] 植物 [zhíwù]

veggieburger ['vɛdʒɪbə:gə(r)] N [C] 素食汉堡包 [sùshí hànbǎobāo]

vehement ['vi:ɪmənt] ADJ 激烈的 [jīliè de]

vehicle ['vi:ɪkl] N [C] **1** (car, bus etc) 机动车 [jīdòngchē] **2** (frm) (means) 工具 [gōngjù]

veil [veɪl] N [C] **1** (covering) 面纱 [miànshā] **2** (fig) [of secrecy, silence] 掩盖 [yǎngài]

vein [veɪn] N [C] **1** (in body) 静脉 [jìngmài] **2** [of leaf] 叶脉 [yèmài] **3** [of metal, mineral] 矿脉 [kuàngmài] **4** (mood, style) 风格 [fēnggé]

Velcro® ['vɛlkrəu] N [U] 尼龙搭扣 [Nílóngdākòu]

velocity [vɪ'lɔsɪtɪ] N [C/U] 速度 [sùdù]

velvet ['vɛlvɪt] I N [C/U] 天鹅绒 [tiān'éróng] II ADJ 天鹅绒的 [tiān'éróng de]

vending machine ['vɛndɪŋ-] N [C] 自动售货机 [zìdòng shòuhuòjī]

vendor ['vɛndə(r)] N [C] **1** (in street) 小贩 [xiǎofàn] **2** (LAW) [of house, land] 卖主 [màizhǔ]

Venezuela [vɛnɛ'zweɪlə] N 委内瑞拉 [Wěinèiruìlā]

Venezuelan [vɛnɛ'zweɪlən] I ADJ 委内瑞拉的 [Wěinèiruìlā de] II N [C] (person) 委内瑞拉人 [Wěinèiruìlārén]

vengeance ['vɛndʒəns] N [U] 报复 [bàofù] ▶ **to do sth with a vengeance** 加倍努力地做某事

venison ['vɛnɪsn] N [U] 鹿肉 [lùròu]

venom ['vɛnəm] N [U] **1** [of snake, insect] 毒液 [dúyè] **2** (fig) (bitterness) 怨恨 [yuànhèn]

vent [vɛnt] I N [C] (for air, smoke etc) 孔 [kǒng] II VT [+ feelings, anger] 发泄 [fāxiè] ▶ **to give vent to** [+ feelings, anger] 发泄

ventilate ['vɛntɪleɪt] VT 使通风 [shǐ tōngfēng]

venture ['vɛntʃə(r)] I N [C] 探险 [tànxiǎn] II VT [+ opinion, sentence] (frm) 冒昧地表示 [màomèi de biǎoshì] III VI 冒险前往 [màoxiǎn qiánwǎng] ▶ **business venture** 企业 ▶ **to venture to do sth** 冒险做某事 ▶ **to venture into sth** 大胆尝试某事

venue ['vɛnju:] N [C] 举行场所 [jǔxíng chǎngsuǒ]

Venus ['vi:nəs] N (planet) 金星 [Jīnxīng]

verb [və:b] N [C] 动词 [dòngcí]

verbal ['və:bl] ADJ **1** [+ skills, translation etc] 语言的 [yǔyán de] **2** [+ attack] 口头的 [kǒutóu de] **3** (LING) 动词的 [dòngcí de]

verdict ['və:dɪkt] N [C] **1** (LAW) 裁定 [cáidìng]

2 (opinion) 定论 [dìnglùn] ▶ **a verdict of guilty/ not guilty** 有罪/无罪的裁定

verge [vɜːdʒ] N [c] **1** (BRIT) [of road] 路边草带 [lùbiān cǎodài] **2** ▶ **to be on the verge of sth/of doing sth** 即将发生某事/即将做某事 [jíjiāng fāshēng mǒushì/jíjiāng zuò mǒushì]
▶ **verge on** VT FUS [不可拆分] 濒临 [bīnlín]

verify ['vɛrɪfaɪ] VT 证实 [zhèngshí] ▶ **to verify that...** 证实⋯

versatile ['vɜːsətaɪl] ADJ **1** [+ person] 多才多艺的 [duōcái duōyì de] **2** [+ substance, machine] 多功能的 [duōgōngnéng de]

verse [vɜːs] N **1** [U] (poetry) 诗 [shī] **2** [c] [of poem, song] 诗节 [shījié] **3** [c] (in bible) 节 [jié]
▶ **to write in verse** 用韵文写

version ['vɜːʃən] N [c] **1** [of book, design] 版本 [bǎnběn] **2** [of event, incident] 说法 [shuōfǎ]

versus ['vɜːsəs] PREP 与⋯相对 [yǔ⋯xiāngduì]; (in competition) 对 [duì]

vertical ['vɜːtɪkl] **I** ADJ 垂直的 [chuízhí de] **II** N ▶ **the vertical** 垂直方向 [chuízhí fāngxiàng]

○**very** ['vɛrɪ] **I** ADV **1** 很 [hěn] ▷ **a very good idea** 一个很好的主意 **2** ▶ **the very end/beginning** 最终/一开始 [zuìzhōng/yì kāishǐ] **II** ADJ ▶ **those were his very words** 那就是他的原话 [nà jiùshì tā de yuánhuà] ▶ **the very thought (of it) alarms me** 一想起(它)就让我惊恐不安 ▶ **at the very least** 至少 ▶ **very well** (agreeing) 那好吧 ▶ **very much so** 确实如此 ▶ **very little** 极少的 ▶ **there isn't very much (of...)** (⋯)不太多了 ▶ **I like him very much** 我非常喜欢他

vessel ['vɛsl] (frm) N [c] **1** (boat) 轮船 [lúnchuán] **2** (container) 容器 [róngqì]

vest [vɛst] **I** N [c] **1** (BRIT) (underwear) 汗衫 [hànshān] [美 = **undershirt**] **2** (US) (waistcoat) 马甲 [mǎjiǎ] [英 = **waistcoat**] **II** VT (frm)
▶ **to be vested with sth** 被赋予某物 [bèi fùyǔ mǒuwù] ▶ **to be vested in sb** 被给予某人

vet [vɛt] **I** N [c] **1** (ESP BRIT) (veterinary surgeon) 兽医 [shòuyī] [美 = **veterinarian**] **2** (US: inf) (veteran) 老兵 [lǎobīng] **II** VT (BRIT) (check) 审查 [shěnchá]

veteran ['vɛtərn] **I** N [c] [of war] 老兵 [lǎobīng] **II** ADJ [+ MP, campaigner] 经验丰富的 [jīngyàn fēngfù de]

veterinarian [vɛtrɪ'nɛərɪən] (US) N [c] 兽医 [shòuyī] [英 = **vet, veterinary surgeon**]

veterinary ['vɛtrɪnərɪ] ADJ 兽医的 [shòuyī de]

veterinary surgeon (frm) (BRIT) N [c] 兽医 [shòuyī] [美 = **veterinarian**]

veto ['viːtəu] (pl **vetoes**) **I** N [c] 否决 [fǒujué] **II** VT 否决 [fǒujué] ▶ **power of veto** 否决权 ▶ **to put a veto on** 禁止

VHF (RAD) N ABBR (= very high frequency) 特高频 [tègāopín]

via ['vaɪə] PREP **1** [+ place] 经由 [jīngyóu] **2** (by means of) 通过 [tōngguò]

viable ['vaɪəbl] ADJ 可行的 [kěxíng de]

vibrate [vaɪ'breɪt] **I** VI 震颤 [zhènchàn] **II** VT 使震动 [shǐ zhèndòng]

vibration [vaɪ'breɪʃən] N **1** [U] (movement) 震动 [zhèndòng] **2** [c] (instance) 颤动 [chàndòng]

vicar ['vɪkə(r)] N [c] 教区牧师 [jiàoqū mùshī]

vice [vaɪs] N **1** [c] (moral fault) 恶习 [èxí] **2** [U] (criminal activities) 毒品色情犯罪 [dúpǐn sèqíng fànzuì] **3** [c] (BRIT) (tool) 老虎钳 [lǎohǔqián] [美 = **vise**]

vice-chairman [vaɪs'tʃɛəmən] N [c] 副主席 [fùzhǔxí]

vice president N [c] **1** (POL) 副总统 [fùzǒngtǒng] **2** [of club] 副会长 [fùhuìzhǎng]

vice versa ['vaɪsɪ'vɜːsə] ADV 反之亦然 [fǎnzhī yìrán]

vicinity [vɪ'sɪnɪtɪ] N ▶ **in the vicinity (of)** 在 (⋯) 附近 [zài (⋯) fùjìn]

vicious ['vɪʃəs] ADJ **1** [+ attack, blow] 剧烈的 [jùliè de] **2** [+ person, dog] 凶残的 [xiōngcán de] **3** [+ words, look, letter] 恶毒的 [èdú de]

victim ['vɪktɪm] N [c] [of accident etc] 受害者 [shòuhàizhě] ▶ **to be the victim of** [+ attack etc] 成为⋯的受害者

victimize ['vɪktɪmaɪz] VT 欺负 [qīfu]

victor ['vɪktə(r)] (liter) N [c] 胜利者 [shènglìzhě]

Victorian [vɪk'tɔːrɪən] **I** ADJ **1** [+ house, furniture etc] 维多利亚时代的 [Wéiduōlìyà Shídài de] **2** (old-fashioned) [+ values etc] 古板守旧的 [gǔbǎn shǒujiù de] **II** N [c] (person) 维多利亚时代的人 [Wéiduōlìyà Shídài de rén]

victorious [vɪk'tɔːrɪəs] ADJ 胜利的 [shènglì de]

victory ['vɪktərɪ] N [c/U] 胜利 [shènglì] ▶ **to win a victory over sb** 击败某人获胜

video ['vɪdɪəu] **I** N **1** [c] (film) 录像 [lùxiàng] **2** [U] (system) 录像 [lùxiàng] **3** [c] (cassette) 录像带 [lùxiàngdài] **4** [c] (ESP BRIT) (machine) 录像机 [lùxiàngjī] [美 = **VCR**] **II** CPD [复合词] [+ equipment etc] 录像 [lùxiàng] **III** VT (ESP BRIT) 录下 [lùxià] [美 = **tape, videotape**]

video camera N [c] 摄像机 [shèxiàngjī]

video game N [c] 电子游戏 [diànzǐ yóuxì]

video recorder N [c] 录像机 [lùxiàngjī]

video shop (BRIT) N [c] 录像带租赁店 [lùxiàngdài zūlìndiàn]

videotape ['vɪdɪəuteɪp] **I** N [c/U] 录像带 [lùxiàngdài] **II** VT (record) 录 [lù]

vie [vaɪ] (frm) VI ▶ **to vie (with sb) (for sth/to do sth)** (与某人)争夺(某物)/争(做某事) [(yǔ mǒurén) zhēngduó (mǒuwù)/zhēng (zuò mǒushì)]

Vietnam ['vjɛt'næm] N 越南 [Yuènán]

Vietnamese [vjɛtnə'miːz] (pl **Vietnamese**) **I** ADJ 越南的 [Yuènán de] **II** N **1** [c] (person) 越南人 [Yuènánrén] **2** [U] (language) 越南语 [Yuènányǔ]

○**view** [vjuː] **I** N [c] **1** (from window, hilltop etc) 景

色 [jǐngsè] **2** (*outlook*) 见解 [jiànjiě] **3** (*ability to see sth*) 看 [kàn] ▷ *They pushed forward for a better view.* 他们用力朝前挤，想看得清楚些。**4** (*opinion*) 看法 [kànfǎ] ▷ *his views on women* 他对女人的看法 **II** VT **1** (*frm*) (*look at*) 看 [kàn] **2** (*consider*) 看待 [kàndài] ▷ *How do you view the matter?* 你如何看待这件事？▸ **to block sb's view** 挡住某人的视线 ▸ **on view** (*in museum etc*) 在展出 ▸ **in full view (of)** (⋯) 全都看得见的 ▸ **to take the view that…** 认为⋯ ▸ **in view of the weather/the fact that…** 考虑到天气/⋯这个事实 ▸ **in my view** 在我看来 ▸ **with a view to…** 是为了⋯

viewer ['vjuːə(r)] N [C] (*of TV*) 观众 [guānzhòng]

viewpoint ['vjuːpɔɪnt] N [C] **1** (*attitude*) 角度 [jiǎodù] **2** (*place*) 观察位置 [guānchá wèizhi]

vigilant ['vɪdʒɪlənt] ADJ 警惕的 [jǐngtì de]

vigorous ['vɪɡərəs] ADJ **1** [+ *exercise*] 充满活力的 [chōngmǎn huólì de] **2** [+ *campaign, action*] 积极的 [jījí de]

vile [vaɪl] ADJ **1** (*offensive*) [+ *behaviour, language*] 可恶的 [kěwù de] **2** (*unpleasant*) [+ *weather, food, temper*] 极坏的 [jíhuài de]

villa ['vɪlə] N [C] **1** (*in countryside*) 乡间别墅 [xiāngjiān biéshù] **2** (*in town*) 市郊独立的别墅 [shìjiāo dúlì de biéshù]

village ['vɪlɪdʒ] N [C] 村庄 [cūnzhuāng]

villager ['vɪlɪdʒə(r)] N [C] 村民 [cūnmín]

villain ['vɪlən] N [C] **1** (*scoundrel*) 恶棍 [ègùn] **2** (*in novel, play etc*) 反面人物 [fǎnmiàn rénwù] **3** (*BRIT*) (*criminal*) 职业罪犯 [zhíyè zuìfàn]

vindictive [vɪn'dɪktɪv] ADJ [+ *person, action*] 报复性的 [bàofùxìng de]

vine [vaɪn] N [C] **1** (*producing grapes*) 葡萄藤 [pútáoténg] **2** (*in jungle*) 藤本植物 [téngběn zhíwù]

vinegar ['vɪnɪɡə(r)] N [C/U] 醋 [cù]

vineyard ['vɪnjɑːd] N [C] 葡萄园 [pútáoyuán]

vintage ['vɪntɪdʒ] **I** N [C] (*of wine*) 酿造年份及产地 [niàngzào niánfèn jí chǎndì] **II** ADJ **1** [*wine*] 上等的 [shàngděng de] **2** [*car, aeroplane*] 古老而享有声誉的 [gǔlǎo ér xiǎngyǒu shēngyù de] **3** [+ *comedy, performance etc*] 经典的 [jīngdiǎn de] ▸ **the 1970 vintage** (*of wine*) 1970年产的葡萄酒

vinyl ['vaɪnl] N [U] **1** (*material*) 乙烯基 [yǐxījī] **2** (*records*) 唱片 [chàngpiàn]

viola [vɪ'əulə] N [C] 中提琴 [zhōngtíqín]

violate ['vaɪəleɪt] (*frm*) VT **1** [+ *law, agreement*] 违背 [wéibèi] **2** [+ *peace, privacy*] 侵犯 [qīnfàn] **3** [+ *tomb*] 亵渎 [xièdú]

violation [vaɪə'leɪʃən] N [C/U] **1** [*of agreement, law*] 违反 [wéifǎn] **2** [*of tomb*] 亵渎 [xièdú] ▸ **in violation of** [+ *rule, law*] 违背

violence ['vaɪələns] N [U] **1** 暴力 [bàolì] **2** (*liter*) (*strength*) 猛力 [měnglì]

violent ['vaɪələnt] ADJ **1** [+ *person, crime*] 暴力的 [bàolì de] **2** [+ *death, explosion*] 猛烈的

[měngliè de] **3** [+ *opposition, pain, emotion*] 强烈的 [qiángliè de]

violet ['vaɪələt] **I** ADJ [+ *light, glow, sky*] 紫罗兰色的 [zǐluólánsè de] **II** N [C] (*flower*) 紫罗兰 [zǐluólán]

violin [vaɪə'lɪn] N [C] 小提琴 [xiǎotíqín]

violinist [vaɪə'lɪnɪst] N [C] 小提琴手 [xiǎotíqínshǒu]

VIP [viːaɪ'piː] N ABBR (= *very important person*) 要人 [yàorén]

virgin ['vəːdʒɪn] **I** N [C] 处女 [chǔnǚ] **II** ADJ [+ *snow, forest*] 原始的 [yuánshǐ de]

Virgo ['vəːɡəu] N **1** (*U*) (*sign*) 处女座 [Chǔnǚ Zuò] **2** [C] (*person*) 处女座的人 [Chǔnǚ Zuò de rén] ▸ **I'm (a) Virgo** 我是处女座的

virtual ['vəːtjuəl] ADJ **1** 实际上的 [shíjìshang de] **2** (*COMPUT*) 虚拟的 [xūnǐ de] ▸ **it's a virtual certainty/impossibility** 这实际上是件已确定的事/不可能的事

virtually ['vəːtjuəlɪ] ADV 事实上 [shìshíshang] ▸ **it is virtually impossible** 事实上这是不可能的

virtual reality N [U] 虚拟现实 [xūnǐ xiànshí]

virtue ['vəːtjuː] N **1** [U] (*moral correctness*) 美德 [měidé] **2** [C] (*good quality*) 优点 [yōudiǎn] **3** [C] (*advantage*) 优势 [yōushì] ▸ **by virtue of** (*frm*) 由于

virus ['vaɪərəs] (*MED*, *COMPUT*) N [C] 病毒 [bìngdú]

visa ['viːzə] N [C] 签证 [qiānzhèng]

vise [vaɪs] (*US*) N = **vice**

visibility [vɪzɪ'bɪlɪtɪ] N [U] **1** 能见度 [néngjiàndù] **2** (*fig*) (*prominence*) 瞩目 [zhǔmù]

visible ['vɪzəbl] ADJ **1** (*able to be seen*) 可见的 [kějiàn de] **2** (*fig*) (*noticeable*) 明显的 [míngxiǎn de]

vision ['vɪʒən] N **1** [U] (*sight*) 视力 [shìlì] **2** [C] (*hope for the future*) 想像 [xiǎngxiàng] **3** [C] (*in dream etc*) 幻象 [huànxiàng]

○ visit ['vɪzɪt] **I** N [C] **1** (*to person*) 拜访 [bàifǎng] **2** (*to place*) 访问 [fǎngwèn] **II** VT **1** [+ *person*] 拜访 [bàifǎng] **2** [+ *place*] 游览 [yóulǎn] ▸ **to pay sb a visit** 拜访某人 ▸ **on a private/official visit** 进行私人性/官方的访问

▸ **visit with** (*US*) VT FUS [不可拆分] 拜访 [bàifǎng]

visiting hours ['vɪzɪtɪŋ-] NPL (*in hospital*) 探视时间 [tànshì shíjiān]

visitor ['vɪzɪtə(r)] N [C] **1** (*to city, country*) 游客 [yóukè] **2** (*to person, house*) 来客 [láikè]

visitor centre, (*US*) **visitor center** N [C] 游客中心 [yóukè zhōngxīn]

visual ['vɪzjuəl] ADJ 视觉的 [shìjué de]

visualize ['vɪzjuəlaɪz] VT **1** (*imagine*) 设想 [shèxiǎng] **2** (*envisage*) 想像 [xiǎngxiàng]

vital ['vaɪtl] ADJ **1** (*essential*) 至关重要的 [zhìguān zhòngyào de] **2** (*full of life*) [+ *person*] 有活力的 [yǒu huólì de] ▸ **it is vital to…/that…**

对…/…是至关重要的 ▶ **to be of vital importance (to sb/sth)** (对某人/某事)极其重要 ▶ **vital organs** 重要器官

vitality [vaɪ'tælɪtɪ] N [U] (liveliness) 生命力 [shēngmìnglì]

vitamin ['vɪtəmɪn, US vaɪtəmɪn] I N [c] 维生素 [wéishēngsù] II CPD [复合词] [+ pill, supplement] 维生素 [wéishēngsù]

vivid ['vɪvɪd] ADJ 1 [+ description, memory] 生动的 [shēngdòng de] 2 [+ colour, light] 鲜艳的 [xiānyàn de] ▶ **a vivid imagination** 生动的想象力

V-neck ['viːnɛk] N [c] 1 (also: **V-neck sweater**) V领衫 [V lǐng shān] 2 (collar) V字领 [V zì lǐng]

vocabulary [vəʊ'kæbjʊlərɪ] N 1 [c/U] [of person] 词汇量 [cíhuìliàng] 2 [c] [of language] 词汇 [cíhuì]

vocal ['vəʊkl] ADJ 1 (lit) 嗓音的 [sǎngyīn de] 2 (fig) (outspoken) 直言不讳的 [zhíyán bù huì de]

vocation [vəʊ'keɪʃən] N [c] 职业 [zhíyè]

vocational [vəʊ'keɪʃənl] ADJ [+ training, course, skills] 职业的 [zhíyè de]

vodka ['vɔdkə] N [c/U] 伏特加酒 [fútèjiā jiǔ]

vogue [vəʊg] N ▶ **the vogue for** …的新潮流 […de xīncháoliú] ▶ **to be in vogue** 正在流行 ▶ **to come into vogue** 开始流行

voice [vɔɪs] I N [c] 1 嗓音 [sǎngyīn] 2 (opinion) 意见 [yìjiàn] II VT [+ opinion, anger, concern] 表达 [biǎodá] ▶ **in a loud/soft voice** 大声地/柔声地 ▶ **to have a voice in sth** 对某事有发言权 ▶ **to give voice to** [+ doubt, wish etc] 表露 ▶ **the active/passive voice** 主动/被动语态

voice mail N [U] 语音留言 [yǔyīn liúyán]

void [vɔɪd] I N [c] 1 (space) 空间 [kōngjiān] 2 (fig) (emptiness) 空虚 [kōngxū] II ADJ (invalid) [+ vote, contract] 无效的 [wúxiào de] ▶ **to be void of sth** (frm) 缺乏某物

vol. ABBR (= **volume**) 册 [cè]

volatile ['vɔlətaɪl] ADJ 1 [+ situation] 不稳定的 [bù wěndìng de] 2 [+ person, temper] 多变的 [duōbiàn de] 3 (TECH) [+ liquid, substance] 易挥发的 [yì huīfā de]

volcano [vɔl'keɪnəʊ] (pl **volcanoes**) N [c] 火山 [huǒshān]

volleyball ['vɔlɪbɔːl] N [U] 排球 [páiqiú]

volt [vəʊlt] N [c] 伏特 [fútè]

voltage ['vəʊltɪdʒ] N [c/U] 电压 [diànyā] ▶ **high/low voltage** 高压/低压

volume ['vɔljuːm] N 1 [c] [of object, gas etc] 体积 [tǐjī] 2 [c] [of sales, traffic] 量 [liàng] 3 [c] (frm) (book) 卷 [juàn]; (in series) 册 [cè] 4 [U] (sound level) [of TV, radio, stereo] 音量 [yīnliàng] ▶ **volume one/two** [of book] 第一/二册 ▶ **the**

way she looked at him spoke volumes 她看他的眼神意味深长

voluntarily ['vɔləntrɪlɪ] ADV 主动地 [zhǔdòng de]

voluntary ['vɔləntərɪ] ADJ 1 (not compulsory) 自愿的 [zìyuàn de] 2 [+ work, worker] 志愿的 [zhìyuàn de] 3 [+ organization] 自愿的 [zìyuàn de]

volunteer [vɔlən'tɪə(r)] I N [c] 1 (unpaid worker) 志愿者 [zhìyuànzhě] 2 (helper) 自愿参加者 [zìyuàn cānjiāzhě] 3 (to army etc) 志愿兵 [zhìyuànbīng] II VT (frm) [+ information, explanation] 主动提供 [zhǔdòng tígōng] III VI (for army etc) 自愿 [zìyuàn] ▶ **to volunteer to do sth** 自愿做某事

vomit ['vɔmɪt] I N [U] 呕吐物 [ǒutùwù] II VT [+ blood etc] 吐 [tù] III VI 呕吐 [ǒutù]

○ **vote** [vəʊt] I N [c] 1 选票 [xuǎnpiào] 2 ▶ **the vote** (votes cast) 选票总数 [xuǎnpiào zǒngshù]; (right to vote) 选举权 [xuǎnjǔquán] ▷ **They captured 13 per cent of the vote.** 他们获得了百分之十三的选票。 ▷ **Women have had the vote for over fifty years.** 妇女获得选举权已有五十多年了。 II VT ▶ **to vote Labour/Green etc** 投票给工党/绿党{等} [tóupiào gěi gōngdǎng/lǜdǎng {děng}] III VI 投票 [tóupiào] ▶ **to cast one's vote** 投票 ▶ **to put sth to the vote** 将某事交付表决 ▶ **to take a vote on sth** 就某事进行表决 ▶ **to vote to do sth** 投票决定做某事 ▶ **to vote yes/no to sth** 投票赞成/反对某事 ▶ **to be voted chairman etc** 被投票选为主席{等} ▶ **to vote for sb** 投某人票 ▶ **to vote for/against sth** 投票支持/反对某事 ▶ **to vote on sth** 投票表决某事

voter ['vəʊtə(r)] N [c] 选举人 [xuǎnjǔrén]

voting ['vəʊtɪŋ] N [U] 选举 [xuǎnjǔ]

voucher ['vaʊtʃə(r)] N [c] 代金券 [dàijīnquàn]

vow [vaʊ] I N [c] 誓言 [shìyán] II VT ▶ **to vow to do sth** 发誓做某事 [fāshì zuò mǒushì] ▶ **to take or make a vow to do sth** 立誓要做某事 ▶ **to vow that...** 立誓…

vowel ['vaʊəl] N [c] 元音 [yuányīn]

voyage ['vɔɪɪdʒ] I N [c] 航行 [hángxíng] II VI (frm) 航行 [hángxíng]

vulgar ['vʌlgə(r)] ADJ 1 (rude) [+ person, joke, gesture] 粗俗的 [cūsú de] 2 (tasteless) [+ decor, design] 庸俗的 [yōngsú de]

vulnerable ['vʌlnərəbl] ADJ 1 [+ person] 易受伤的 [yì shòushāng de] 2 [+ position, target] 脆弱的 [cuìruò de] ▶ **to be vulnerable to sth** 易受某物伤害

vulture ['vʌltʃə(r)] N [c] 1 秃鹫 [tūjiù] 2 [+ person] 乘人之危者 [chéng rén zhī wēi zhě]

Ww

W, w¹ ['dʌblju:] N [C/U] (letter) 英语的第二十三个字母

W² ABBR **1** (= west) 西方 [xīfāng] **2** (ELEC) (= watt) 瓦 [wǎ]

waddle ['wɔdl] VI (duck, fat person +) 摇摇摆摆地行走 [yáoyáo bǎibǎi de xíngzǒu]

wade [weɪd] VI **1** (in water, mud) ▸ **to wade across/through sth** 跋涉而过某地 [báshè ér guò mǒudì] **2** (fig) ▸ **to wade through** [+ book, report] 吃力地看完 [chīlì de kànwán]
▸ **wade in** VI 插手 [chāshǒu]

wading pool ['weɪdɪŋ-] (US) N [C] 浅水池 [qiǎnshuǐchí] [英= **paddling pool**]

wafer ['weɪfə(r)] N [C] (biscuit) 威化饼 [wēihuà bǐng]

waffle ['wɔfl] I N **1** [C] (CULIN) 蛋奶烘饼 [dànnǎi hōngbǐng] **2** [U] (empty talk) 空话 [kōnghuà] II VI (also: **waffle on**) 胡扯 [húchě]

wag [wæg] I VT **1** [+ finger] 摇动 [yáodòng] **2** [+ tail] 摇 [yáo] II VI [tail +] 摇 [yáo]

wage [weɪdʒ] I N [C] (also: **wages**) 工资 [gōngzī] II VT [+ war, campaign] 发动 [fādòng] ▸ **a day's wages** 一天的工资 ▸ **to wage war (against** or **on sth)** (对某事)开战

wage packet (ESP BRIT) N [C] 工资袋 [gōngzīdài]

wager ['weɪdʒə(r)] I N [C] 赌注 [dǔzhù] II VT 以…为赌注 [yǐ…wéi dǔzhù] ▸ **I'll wager that...** (inf) 我打赌…

wagon, (ESP BRIT) waggon ['wægən] N [C]

1 (horse-drawn) 四轮运货马车 [sìlún yùnhuò mǎchē] **2** (BRIT: RAIL) 货车 [huòchē] ▸ **to be on the wagon** (inf) 戒酒

wail [weɪl] I N [C] **1** [of person] 嚎啕声 [háotáoshēng] **2** [of siren] 呼啸声 [hūxiàoshēng] II VI **1** [person +] 嚎啕 [háotáo] **2** [siren +] 呼啸 [hūxiào] III VT 哀诉 [āisù]

waist [weɪst] N [C] **1** 腰 [yāo] **2** [of clothing] 腰身 [yāoshēn]

waistcoat ['weɪskəut] (BRIT) N [C] 马甲 [mǎjiǎ] [美= **vest**]

○ **wait** [weɪt] I VI 等待 [děngdài] II N [C] (interval) 等待时间 [děngdài shíjiān] ▷ There was a long wait. 等待时间很长。▸ **to wait for sb/sth** 等候某人/某物 ▸ **there was a letter waiting for me** 有封信等我去取 ▸ **I can't wait** or **I can hardly wait to tell her** 我等不及要告诉她 ▸ **it can wait** 这可以过会儿再说 ▸ **wait a minute!** 等一下！▸ **"repairs while you wait"** "修补，立等可取" ▸ **to keep sb waiting** 让某人等着 ▸ **to lie in wait for sb** 埋伏着等待某人
▸ **wait around, wait about** VI ▸ **to wait around** or **about for sth** 无所事事地等待某事 [wúsuǒ shìshì de děngdài mǒushì]
▸ **wait behind** VI 留下来等候 [liúxiàlái děnghòu]
▸ **wait on** VT FUS [不可拆分] (in restaurant, hotel etc) 侍候 [shìhòu]
▸ **wait up** VI 熬夜等待 [áoyè děngdài] ▸ **don't wait up for me** 不要熬夜等我

waiter ['weɪtə(r)] N [C] 男服务员 [nán fúwùyuán]

waiting list ['weɪtɪŋ-] N [C] 等候者名单 [děnghòuzhě míngdān] ▸ **to be on the waiting list (for sth)** 被列于(某事的)等候者名单

waiting room ['weɪtɪŋ-] N [C] 等候室 [děnghòushì]

waitress ['weɪtrɪs] N [C] 女服务员 [nǚ fúwùyuán]

waive [weɪv] VT **1** [+ rule, fee] 取消 [qǔxiāo] **2** [+ right] 放弃 [fàngqì]

wake [weɪk] (pt **woke, waked,** pp **woken, waked**) I VT (also: **wake up**) 唤醒 [huànxǐng] II VI (also: **wake up**) 醒来 [xǐnglái] III N [C] **1** (for dead person) 守灵 [shǒulíng] **2** [of boat] 尾波 [wěibō] ▸ **in the wake of sth** 紧随某事而来 ▸ **to follow in sb's wake** 紧随某人 ▸ **to leave sth in one's wake** 走后留下某物
▸ **wake up** I VT 唤醒 [huànxǐng] II VI 醒来 [xǐnglái] ▸ **to wake up to sth** 意识到某事

waken ['weɪkn] VT, VI = **wake**

Wales [weɪlz] N 威尔士 [Wēi'ěrshì] ▸ **the Prince of Wales** 威尔士王子

○ **walk** [wɔːk] I N **1** [C] 散步 [sànbù] **2** [S] (gait) 步态 [bùtài] **3** [C] (route) 散步场所 [sànbù chǎngsuǒ] II VI 走 [zǒu] III VT **1** [+ distance] 走 [zǒu] **2** [+ dog] 遛 [liù] ▸ **it's 10 minutes' walk**

from here 从这儿走有10分钟的路程 ▶ **to go for a walk** 去散步 ▶ **to slow to a walk** 放慢速度改为步行 ▶ **people from all walks of life** 各界人士 VI ▶ **to walk in one's sleep** 梦游 ▶ **I'll walk you home** 我陪你走回家

▶ **walk off with** (inf) VT FUS [不可拆分] **1** (steal) 顺手拿走 [shùnshǒu názǒu] **2** (win) [+ prize] 轻易赢得 [qīngyì yíngdé]

▶ **walk out (of sth)** 退出 (某事) [tuìchū (mǒushì)] **2** ▶ **to walk out (on sb)** 离开 (某人) [líkāi (mǒurén)] **3** (strike) 罢工 [bàgōng]

walker ['wɔːkə(r)] N [c] 散步者 [sànbùzhě]

walkie-talkie ['wɔːkɪ'tɔːkɪ] N [c] 步话机 [bùhuàjī]

walking ['wɔːkɪŋ] N [U] 步行 [bùxíng] ▶ **it's within walking distance** 只有几步路

walking stick N [c] 手杖 [shǒuzhàng]

Walkman® ['wɔːkmən] N [c] 随身听 [suíshēn tīng]

walkway ['wɔːkweɪ] N [c] 人行道 [rénxíngdào]

wall [wɔːl] N [c] **1** [of building, room] 墙 [qiáng] **2** (around city) 城墙 [chéngqiáng]; (around garden, field) 围墙 [wéiqiáng] **3** (side) [of tunnel, cave] 内壁 [nèibì]; [of stomach, artery] 壁 [bì] ▶ **to go to the wall** (inf) 破产

▶ **wall in** VT 用墙围住 [yòngqiáng wéizhù]

Wall Street N 华尔街 [Huáěrjiē]

wallet ['wɔlɪt] N [c] 钱包 [qiánbāo]

wallpaper ['wɔːlpeɪpə(r)] I N [c/U] **1** 墙纸 [qiángzhǐ] **2** (COMPUT) 桌面 [zhuōmiàn] II VT 糊墙纸于 [hú qiángzhǐ yú]

walnut ['wɔːlnʌt] I N **1** [c] (nut) 核桃 [hétao] **2** [c] (also: **walnut tree**) 胡桃树 [hútáoshù] **3** [U] (wood) 胡桃木 [hútáomù] II CPD [复合词] [+ desk, table etc] 胡桃 [hútáo]

walrus ['wɔːlrəs] (pl **walrus** or **walruses**) N [c] 海象 [hǎixiàng]

waltz [wɔːlts] I N [c] (music) 圆舞曲 [yuánwǔqǔ]; (dance) 华尔兹舞 [huá'ěrzīwǔ] II VI **1** (dance) 跳华尔兹舞 [tiào huá'ěrzīwǔ] **2** (inf) ▶ **to waltz in/off** etc 大摇大摆地走进/离开 [等] [dàyáo dàbǎi de zǒujìn/líkāi [děng]]

wand [wɔnd] N [c] (also: **magic wand**) 魔杖 [mózhàng]

wander ['wɔndə(r)] I VI **1** (roam) 漫游 [mànyóu]; (because lost) 迷失 [míshī] **2** [mind, thoughts +] 恍惚 [huǎnghū] II VT [+ streets, countryside] 在…闲逛 [zài…xiánguàng] III N [s] 漫步 [mànbù] ▶ **to wander off/away** 走失/走散 ▶ **to have** or **go for** or **take a wander** 出去逛逛

wane [weɪn] I VI **1** [moon +] 亏缺 [kuīquē] **2** [interest, influence etc +] 减弱 [jiǎnruò] II N ▶ **to be on the wane** 日益衰落 [rìyì shuāiluò]

want [wɔnt] I VT **1** (wish for) 想要 [xiǎngyào] **2** (inf) (need) 需要 [xūyào] II N [s] (frm) (lack) ▶ **want of** 缺乏 [quēfá] III **wants** NPL (needs)

需求 [xūqiú] ▶ **to want to do sth** 想要做某事 ▶ **to want sb to do sth** 希望某人做某事 ▶ **to want sth done** 要别人把某事做好 ▶ **your hair wants cutting/washing** 你的头发要剪剪/洗洗了 ▶ **you want to be more careful** (inf) 你要多加小心 ▶ **you're wanted on the phone** 有你的电话 ▶ **he is wanted by the police** 他被警察通缉 ▶ **"cook wanted"** "招聘厨师" ▶ **if you want** 如果你乐意的话 ▶ **to want out** (inf) (of deal etc) 想退出 ▶ **to want in** (inf) (on deal etc) 想参加入 ▶ **for want of** 因为缺乏

wanted ['wɔntɪd] ADJ [+ criminal, man] 受通缉的 [shòu tōngjī de]

war [wɔː(r)] N [c/U] **1** (fighting) 战争 [zhànzhēng] **2** (fig) (competition) 战争 [zhànzhēng] ▷ a trade/price war 一场贸易/价格战 ▶ **to be at war (with sb)** (与某人) 进行战争 ▶ **to go to war** 开战 ▶ **to make war on sb/sth** 向某人/某事开战 ▶ **a war on drugs/crime** 毒品/犯罪的斗争 ▶ **war of words** 口诛笔伐

ward [wɔːd] N [c] **1** (in hospital) 病房 [bìngfáng] **2** (POL) (district) 行政区 [xíngzhèngqū] **3** (LAW) (child) 被监护人 [bèi jiānhùrén]

▶ **ward off** VT [+ threat, danger] 防止 [fángzhǐ]; [+ attacker] 避开 [bìkāi]

warden ['wɔːdn] N [c] **1** (in park, game reserve) 管理员 [guǎnlǐyuán] **2** (at jail) (BRIT) 看守 [kānshǒu]; (US) 监狱长 [jiānyùzhǎng] [英= **governor**] **3** (BRIT) (at youth hostel) 舍监 [shèjiān]

wardrobe ['wɔːdrəub] N **1** [c] (cupboard) 衣橱 [yīchú] **2** [c] (clothes) 衣服 [yīfu] **3** [U] (CINE, THEAT) 戏装 [xìzhuāng]

warehouse ['wɛəhaus] N [c] 仓库 [cāngkù]

warfare ['wɔːfɛə(r)] N [U] 战争 [zhànzhēng]

warhead ['wɔːhɛd] N [c] 弹头 [dàntóu]

warm [wɔːm] I ADJ **1** [+ meal, soup, water] 温热的 [wēnrè de]; [+ day, weather] 暖和的 [nuǎnhuo de] **2** [+ clothes, blankets] 保暖的 [bǎonuǎn de] **3** [+ applause, welcome] 热情的 [rèqíng de] **4** (friendly) [+ person] 友爱的 [yǒu'ài de] II VT 使暖和 [shǐ nuǎnhuo] ▶ **it's warm** 天很暖和 ▶ **are you warm enough?** 你觉得够暖和吗? ▶ **to keep warm** 保暖 ▶ **to keep sth warm** [+ food] 使某物保温; [+ building, house etc] 使某物保持温暖 ▶ **with my warmest thanks** 顺致我最诚挚的谢意 ▶ **to warm one's hands/feet** 暖暖手/脚 ▶ **to warm to sb/sth** 对某人/某事产生好感

▶ **warm up** I VI **1** [room, weather +] 暖起来 [nuǎn qǐlái]; [water, food etc +] 变热 [biànrè] **2** [athlete, pianist etc +] 热身 [rèshēn] **3** [engine, photocopier etc +] 预热 [yùrè] II VT **1** [+ food] 加热 [jiārè] **2** [+ person] 使暖起来 [shǐ nuǎn qǐlái]

🔲 用法参见 **hot**

warmly ['wɔːmlɪ] ADV **1** [welcome, greet, applaud +] 热情地 [rèqíng de] **2** [dress, wrap up +] 暖和地 [nuǎnhuo de]

warmth [wɔːmθ] N [U] **1** (of fire) 温暖
[wēnnuǎn] **2** (of clothing, blanket) 暖和
[nuǎnhuo] **3** (friendliness) 热情 [rèqíng] ▶ **we
huddled together for warmth** 我们挤在一
起取暖

warm-up ['wɔːmʌp] N [c] **1** (SPORT) 热身活
动 [rèshēn huódòng] **2** (fig) (rehearsal) 预演
[yùyǎn] ▶ **a warm-up match** or **game** 一场
热身赛

warn [wɔːn] I VT ▶ **to warn sb that** 警告某
人… [jǐnggào mǒurén…] II VI ▶ **to warn of sth**
警告提防某事 [jǐnggào dīfáng mǒushì] ▶ **"War
may break out," he warned** "战争可能会爆
发," 他警告道 ▶ **to warn sb not to do sth** 告
诫某人不要做某事 ▶ **to warn sb of sth** 警告
某人某事 ▶ **to warn sb against sth** 告诫某人
提防某事 ▶ **to warn against doing sth** 告诫
不准做某事

warning ['wɔːnɪŋ] N **1** [c] (action, words, sign)
警告 [jǐnggào] **2** [c/U] (notice) 预兆 [yùzhào]
▶ **to give sb a warning** 给某人一个警告 ▶ **let
this be a warning to you** 让这事成为你的鉴诫
▶ **without (any) warning** (suddenly) 出人意料
地; (without notice) 毫无征兆地

warrant ['wɔrnt] I N [c] **1** (for arrest) 逮捕
令 [dàibǔlìng] **2** (also: **search warrant**) 搜查
令 [sōuchálìng] II VT (merit) 应受到 [yīng
shòudào]

warranty ['wɔrəntɪ] N [c] 担保 [dānbǎo]
▶ **under warranty** 在质保期内

warrior ['wɔrɪə(r)] N [c] 战士 [zhànshì]

warship ['wɔːʃɪp] N [c] 军舰 [jūnjiàn]

wart [wɔːt] N [c] 疣 [yóu]

wartime ['wɔːtaɪm] I N ▶ **in wartime** 在战时
[zài zhànshí] II ADJ 战时的 [zhànshí de]

wary ['wɛərɪ] ADJ ▶ **to be wary (of sb/sth)** 提
防 (某人/某事) [dīfáng (mǒurén/mǒushì)] ▶ **to
be wary about** or **of doing sth** 对做某事很谨慎

was [wɔz] PT of **be**

wash [wɔʃ] I VT **1** (+ clothes, dishes, paintbrush)
洗 [xǐ] **2** (carry) ▶ **to be washed ashore/out
to sea** etc 被冲到岸边/冲向大海 [等] [bèi
chōngdào ànbiān/chōngxiàng dàhǎi [děng]]
II VI **1** (person +) 洗净 [xǐjìng] **2** (sea, waves etc +)
▶ **to wash over/against sth** 冲过/拍打某物
[chōngguò/pāidǎ mǒuwù] III N **1** (clean) 洗
[xǐ] **2** [s] (of ship) 涡流 [wōliú] ▶ **to wash one's
face/hands/hair** 洗脸/手/头发 ▶ **to wash
one's hands of sth/sb** 洗手不干某事/断绝与
某人的关系 ▶ **to wash sth out of sth** 将某物
从某物上冲掉 ▶ **to have a wash** 洗一下 ▶ **to
give sth a wash** 洗一洗某物 ▶ **to be in the
wash** 正在洗
  ▶ **wash away** VT (+ bridge, building, village etc) 冲
  走 [chōngzǒu]
  ▶ **wash down** VT **1** (with wine, lager etc) (+ food)
  吞下 [tūnxià] **2** (clean) (+ wall, path) 冲洗
  [chōngxǐ]

▶ **wash off** VI, VT 洗掉 [xǐdiào]
▶ **wash out** I VI (dye, colour +) 洗褪色 [xǐ tuìsè];
(dirt, stain +) 洗掉 [xǐdiào] II VT (+ tank, bucket
etc) 刷洗 [shuāxǐ]
▶ **wash up** I VI **1** (BRIT) (wash dishes) 洗餐具 [xǐ
cānjù] **2** (US) (have a wash) 洗一洗 [xǐyīxǐ] II VT
1 (BRIT) (+ plates) 洗 [xǐ] **2** (onto land) 把…冲上
岸 [bǎ…chōngshàng àn]

washbasin ['wɔʃbeɪsn] N [c] 脸盆 [liǎnpén]

washcloth ['wɔʃklɔθ] (US) N [c] 毛巾 [máojīn]
[英= **face cloth, flannel**]

washer ['wɔʃə(r)] N [c] (on tap etc) 垫圈
[diànquān]

washing ['wɔʃɪŋ] N [U] **1** (dirty) 待洗衣物 [dàixǐ
yīwù] **2** (clean) 洗好的衣物 [xǐhǎo de yīwù]
▶ **to do the washing** 洗衣服

washing line (BRIT) N [c] 晾衣绳
[liàngyīshéng]

washing machine N [c] 洗衣机 [xǐyījī]

washing powder (BRIT) N [c/U] 洗衣
粉 [xǐyīfěn] [美= **soap powder, laundry
detergent**]

washing-up [wɔʃɪŋ'ʌp] (BRIT) N [U] 待洗餐
具 [dàixǐ cānjù] [美= **dirty dishes**] ▶ **to do the
washing-up** 洗餐具 [美= **wash the dishes**]

washing-up liquid (BRIT) N [U] 洗洁剂 [xǐjié
jì] [美= **dishwashing liquid**]

washroom ['wɔʃrum] N [c] 盥洗室
[guànxǐshì]

wasn't ['wɔznt] = **was not**

wasp [wɔsp] N [c] 黄蜂 [huángfēng]

waste [weɪst] I N **1** [s/U] (of resources, food,
money) 浪费 [làngfèi] **2** (rubbish) 废料 [fèiliào]
II ADJ (+ material) 废的 [fèi de] III VT (+ money,
energy, time) 浪费 [làngfèi]; (+ opportunity) 失去
[shīqù] IV **wastes** NPL (land) 荒地 [huāngdì]
▶ **what a waste!** 真可惜！▶ **it's a waste of
money** 这是白费钱 ▶ **it's a waste of time** 这
是浪费时间 ▶ **you're wasting your time** 你是
在浪费时间 ▶ **to go to waste** 浪费掉 ▶ **to lay
waste (to) sth** 毁坏某物
  ▶ **waste away** VI 消瘦下去 [xiāoshòu xiàqù]

waste ground (BRIT) N [U] 荒地 [huāngdì]

wastepaper basket ['weɪstpeɪpə-] (BRIT) N
[c] 废纸篓 [fèizhǐlǒu]

⊙watch [wɔtʃ] I N [c] **1** (wristwatch) 手表
[shǒubiǎo] **2** (guards) 警卫 [jǐngwèi] **3** (spell of
duty) 值班 [zhíbān] II VT **1** (look at) (+ people,
objects) 注视 [zhùshì]; (+ match, programme, TV)
看 [kàn] **2** (spy on, guard) 监视 [jiānshì] **3** (pay
attention to) 关注 [guānzhù] **4** (be careful of) 留
意 [liúyì] III VT ▶ 注视 [zhùshì] ▶ **to keep watch**
放哨 ▶ **to keep a close watch on sb/sth** 密切
注意某人/某事 ▶ **on watch** 放哨 ▶ **to be
under watch** 被监视 ▶ **to watch sb do/doing
sth** 看着某人做某事 ▶ **watch what you're
doing/how you drive** 小心你在做的事/小
心驾驶 ▶ **watch it!** (inf) 当心！

▶ **watch for, watch out for** VT FUS [不可拆分] 留心 [liúxīn]

▶ **watch out** VI 提防 [dīfang] ▶ **watch out!** (inf) 小心！

▶ **watch out for** VT FUS [不可拆分] = **watch for**

watchdog ['wɔtʃdɒg] N [C] (authority) 监察人员 [jiānchá rényuán]

watchstrap ['wɔtʃstræp] N [C] 表带 [biǎodài]

◐ **water** ['wɔːtə(r)] I N [U] 水 [shuǐ] II VT [+ plant] 给…浇水 [gěi…jiāoshuǐ] III VI 1 [eyes +] 流泪 [liúlèi] 2 [mouth +] 流口水 [liú kǒushuǐ] IV **waters** NPL (area of water) 水域 [shuǐyù] ▶ a drink of water 一杯水 ▶ to pass water 小便 ▶ the water's edge 水边 ▶ in British waters 在英国海域

▶ **water down** VT 1 [+ drink, paint] 搀水冲淡 [chānshuǐ chōngdàn] 2 [+ article, proposal] 使缓和 [shǐ huǎnhé]

watercolour, (US) **watercolor** ['wɔːtəkʌlə(r)] I N [C] (painting) 水彩画 [shuǐcǎihuà] II **watercolours** NPL (paints) 水彩颜料 [shuǐcǎi yánliào]

watercress ['wɔːtəkrɛs] N [U] 水田芥 [shuǐtiánjiè]

waterfall ['wɔːtəfɔːl] N [C] 瀑布 [pùbù]

watering can ['wɔːtərɪŋ-] N [C] 喷壶 [pēnhú]

watermelon ['wɔːtəmɛlən] N [C] 西瓜 [xīguā]

waterproof ['wɔːtəpruːf] ADJ 防水的 [fángshuǐ de]

water-skiing ['wɔːtəskiːɪŋ] N [U] ▶ **to go water-skiing** 去滑水 [qùhuáshuǐ]

water sports NPL 水上运动 [shuǐshang yùndòng]

watery ['wɔːtəri] ADJ 1 (thin) [+ coffee, soup etc] 稀的 [xī de] 2 (resembling water) [+ liquid, substance, discharge etc] 水状的 [shuǐzhuàng de] 3 [+ eyes] 眼泪汪汪的 [yǎnlèi wāngwāng de] 4 (pale) [+ light] 淡淡的 [dàndàn de]

watt [wɔt] N [C] 瓦 [wǎ] ▶ a 100-watt lightbulb 一只100瓦的灯泡

wave [weɪv] I N [C] 1 [of hand] 挥动 [huīdòng] 2 (on water) 波浪 [bōlàng] 3 (RAD) 波 [bō] 4 (in hair) 卷曲 [juǎnqū] 5 [of emotion, panic, anger] 高涨 [gāozhàng]; [of violence, attacks, strikes] 风潮 [fēngcháo] II VI 1 (gesture) 挥手示意 [huīshǒu shìyì] 2 [branches, grass +] 摆动 [bǎidòng]; [flag +] 飘动 [piāodòng] III VT 1 (motion with) [+ hand] 挥 [huī]; [+ flag, handkerchief] 挥动 [huīdòng] 2 (brandish) [+ weapon, gun, spear] 挥舞 [huīwǔ]; [+ letter, newspaper, photo] 晃动 [huàngdòng] ▶ **to give sb a wave** 向某人挥挥手 ▶ **the pain came in waves** 痛感阵阵袭来 ▶ **to wave to/at sb** 对/向某人挥手 ▶ **to wave goodbye to sb, wave sb goodbye** 向某人挥手告别 ▶ **he waved me away/over** 他挥手让我离开/过来

▶ **wave aside** VT [+ suggestion, objection] 对…置之不理 [duì…zhì zhī bù lǐ]

wavelength ['weɪvlɛŋθ] N [C] (RAD, PHYS) [of light, sound] 波长 [bōcháng] ▶ **to be on the same wavelength** 和谐融洽

waver ['weɪvə(r)] VI 1 [voice +] 颤抖 [chàndǒu]; [flame, shadow +] 摇曳 [yáoyè] 2 [feeling +] 动摇 [dòngyáo] 3 (hesitate) [person +] 犹豫不决 [yóuyù bùjué]

wavy ['weɪvi] ADJ 1 [+ line] 波浪式的 [bōlàngshì de]; [+ hair] 卷曲的 [juǎnqū de]

wax [wæks] I N 1 (in candles, polish) 蜡 [là] 2 (earwax) 耳垢 [ěrgòu] II VT [+ floor, car] 给…打蜡 [gěi…dǎlà] III VI [moon +] 渐圆 [jiànyuán]

◐ **way** [weɪ] I N 1 [C] (route) 路 [lù] ▷ A man asked me the way to St Paul's. 有一个人问我去圣保罗教堂的路怎么走。 2 [C] (path, access) 路线 [lùxiàn] ▷ This is the way in. 这是进来的路线。 3 [S] (distance) 距离 [jùlí] ▷ We've a fair way to go yet. 我们还颇有一段距离要走。 4 [C] (direction) 方向 [fāngxiàng] ▷ Which way did she go? 她朝哪个方向去了？ 5 [C] (manner) 方式 [fāngshì] ▷ Do you like the way he dealt with the problem? 你喜欢他处理这个问题的方式吗？ ▷ She smiled in a friendly way. 她友好地笑了笑。 6 [C] (method) 方法 [fāngfǎ] ▷ different ways of cooking fish 不同的烹调鱼的方法 II ADV (far, a lot) 远远地 [yuǎnyuǎn de] ▷ He was way behind. 他远远落在了后面。 ▷ We'll have to decide way in advance. 我们得早早地提前作决定。 III **ways** NPL (habits) 习俗 [xísú] ▶ "**which way?**" – "**this way**" "往哪边？" "这边" ▶ **on the way** 在路上 ▶ **to be on one's way** 在途中 ▶ **to fight one's way through a crowd** 费劲地挤过人群 ▶ **to keep out of sb's way** 别去惹某人 ▶ **it's a long way away** 离这儿很远 ▶ **all the way/most of the way/half the way** 完全地/大部分地/一半地 ▶ **to go out of one's way to do sth** 不辞辛苦地做某事 ▶ **to be in the way** 挡道的 ▶ **out of the way** (finished) 解决掉的; (secluded) 偏远的 ▶ **to lose one's way** 迷路 ▶ **under way** (activity, project etc) 在进行中 ▶ **the way back** 回去的路 ▶ **to make way for sb/sth** 让位 (给某人/某物) ▶ **to get one's (own) way, have one's (own) way** 自主行事 ▶ **to give way** (break, collapse) 倒塌; (stop resisting) 屈服 ▶ **the right/wrong way up** (BRIT) 正面/反面朝上 ▶ **the wrong way round** (BRIT) 刚好相反 ▶ **he's in a bad way** (inf) 他健康状况不佳 ▶ **you can't have it both ways** 你不能两者兼得 ▶ **to have a way of doing sth** 善于做某事 ▶ **in a way** 在某种程度上 ▶ **in some ways** 在某些方面 ▶ **no way!** (inf) 没门！ ▶ **by the way...** 顺便提一下 ▶ "**way in**" (BRIT) "入口" ▶ "**way out**" (BRIT) "出口" ▶ "**give way**" (BRIT) "减速让车" ▶ **way of life** 生活方式 ▶ **do it this way** 这么做 ▶ **I had no idea you felt that way (about it)** 我不知道你(对这事)是那样想的

WC (BRIT) N ABBR (= water closet) 厕所 [cèsuǒ]

◐ **we** [wiː] PL PRON 我们 [wǒmen] ▷ We live in

London. 我们住在伦敦。

weak [wiːk] ADJ **1** [+ person, muscle, back etc] 虚弱的 [xūruò de]; [+ heart, voice, eyesight] 衰弱的 [shuāiruò de]; [+ object, material] 易坏的 [yìhuài de] **2** (morally) [+ person] 懦弱的 [nuòruò de] **3** (ECON) [+ currency, pound, dollar etc] 疲软的 [píruǎn de] **4** (poor) [+ performance] 差的 [chà de]; [+ position] 软弱的 [ruǎnruò de] **5** (not convincing) [+ argument, evidence] 不充分的 [bù chōngfèn de] **6** (low-strength) [+ tea, coffee, substance etc] 淡的 [dàn de] **7** [+ smile] 淡淡的 [dàndàn de]

weaken ['wiːkn] I VI (resolve, person +] 变得优柔寡断 [biànde yōuróu guǎ duàn]; [+ influence, power +] 变弱 [biàn ruò] II VT [+ person] 使虚弱 [shǐ xūruò]; [+ institution] 削弱 [xuēruò]

weakness ['wiːknɪs] N **1** [c] (frailty) 虚弱 [xūruò] **2** [U] [of system, method] 薄弱 [bóruò]; [of economy, currency, market] 疲软 [píruǎn]; [of sound, signal] 微弱 [wēiruò] **3** [c] (problem) 缺点 [quēdiǎn] ▶ to have a weakness for sth 特别偏爱某物

wealth [wɛlθ] N [c] **1** (riches) 财富 [cáifù] **2** (prosperity) 富裕 [fùyù] **3** ▶ a wealth of... 大量的… [dàliàng de…]

wealthy ['wɛlθɪ] I ADJ 富有的 [fùyòu de] II NPL ▶ the wealthy 富人 [fùrén]

weapon ['wɛpən] N [c] **1** (lit) 武器 [wǔqì] **2** (fig) 手段 [shǒuduàn]

wear [wɛə(r)] (pt wore, pp worn) I N [U] **1** (use) 使用 [shǐyòng] **2** (damage) 磨损 [mósǔn] **3** (clothing) ▶ evening/beach wear 晚装/沙滩装 [wǎnzhuāng/shātānzhuāng] II VT [+ clothes, shoes] 穿着 [chuānzhe]; [+ spectacles, jewellery] 戴着 [dàizhe] III VI (become shabby) 磨损 [mósǔn] ▶ to wear one's hair up/long/loose etc 把头发梳上去/留着长发/松散着头发 [等] ▶ to wear a hole in sth 在某物上磨出一个洞 ▶ I can't decide what to wear 我拿不定主意该穿什么 ▶ to wear well 经久耐用 ▶ to wear thin [material +] 磨薄; [excuse, joke +] 渐失效力; [patience +] 快磨没了
▶ wear away I VT 使磨损 [shǐ mósǔn] II VI 磨损 [mósǔn]
▶ wear down I VT **1** [+ heel] 使磨薄 [shǐ móbáo] **2** [+ person] 使精疲力竭 [shǐ jīng pí lì jié]
▶ wear off VI 逐渐消失 [zhújiàn xiāoshī]
▶ wear on VI 消逝 [xiāoshì]
▶ wear out I VT **1** [+ shoes, clothing] 穿破 [chuānpò] **2** (tire) (inf) 使疲乏 [shǐ pífá] II VI 耗尽 [hàojìn]

weary ['wɪərɪ] I ADJ (tired) 疲劳的 [píláo de] II VI ▶ to weary of sb/sth 厌烦某人/某事 [yànfán mǒurén/mǒushì] ▶ to be weary of sb/sth 厌倦某人/某事

weasel ['wiːzl] N [c] 鼬 [yòu]

weather ['wɛðə(r)] I N [U] 天气 [tiānqì] II VT **1** [+ crisis] 经受住 [jīngshòu zhù] **2** [+ wood, rock] 使经风历雨 [shǐ jīng fēng lì yǔ] III VI 褪色 [tuìsè] ▶ what's the weather like? 天气怎么样? ▶ under the weather 不舒服 ▶ to weather the storm 经受住风暴的袭击

weather forecast N [c] 天气预报 [tiānqì yùbào]

weatherman ['wɛðəmæn] (pl **weathermen**) N [c] 天气预报员 [tiānqì yùbàoyuán]

weave [wiːv] (pt wove, pp woven) I VT [+ cloth] 织 [zhī]; [+ basket] 编 [biān] II VI (pt, pp weaved) ▶ to weave in and out of/among 在…中穿插出/在…中迂回行进 [zài…zhōng chuānjìn chuānchū/zài…zhōng yūhuí xíngjìn] III N [c] 织法 [zhīfǎ]

web [wɛb] N [c] **1** [of spider] 网 [wǎng] **2** [of paths] 网 [wǎng]; (of reasons, lies) 一套 [yī tào] **3** ▶ the Web 互联网 [hùliánwǎng] ▶ on the Web 在互联网上

web page N [c] 网页 [wǎngyè]

website ['wɛbsaɪt] N [c] 网址 [wǎngzhǐ]

wed [wɛd] (pt wed, pp wedded or wed) I VT 与…结婚 [yǔ…jiéhūn] II VI 结婚 [jiéhūn]

we'd [wiːd] = we had, we would

Wed(s). ABBR (= Wednesday) 星期三 [xīngqīsān]

wedding ['wɛdɪŋ] N [c] 婚礼 [hūnlǐ]

wedding anniversary N [c] 结婚纪念日 [jiéhūn jìniànrì]

wedding day N [c] 婚礼日 [hūnlǐrì]

wedding dress N [c] 婚纱 [hūnshā]

wedding ring N [c] 结婚戒指 [jiéhūn jièzhǐ]

wedge [wɛdʒ] N [c] **1** (under door etc) 三角木 [sānjiǎomù] **2** [of cheese, cake etc] 楔形 [xiēxíng] **3** (tool) 楔子 [xiēzi] II VT **1** ▶ to wedge sth open/shut 顶住某物使之开着/关着 [dǐngzhù mǒuwù shǐ zhī kāizhe/guānzhe] **2** (push) ▶ to wedge sth in sth 将某物楔入某物 [jiāng mǒuwù xiērù mǒuwù] ▶ to be wedged (in) between 被紧紧地夹在…中间 ▶ to drive a wedge between 在…之间挑拨离间

Wednesday ['wɛdnzdɪ] N [c/U] 星期三 [xīngqīsān] see also **Tuesday**

wee [wiː] I ADJ (SCOTTISH) 很小的 [hěnxiǎo de] II VI (BRIT: inf) 撒尿 [sāniào] III N [c] (BRIT: inf) **1** (urine) 尿 [niào] **2** (act) 撒尿 [sāniào] ▶ to have a wee (BRIT: inf) 去小便

weed [wiːd] I N [c] **1** (plant) 杂草 [zácǎo] **2** (inf, pej) (person) 孱弱的人 [chánruò de rén] II VT [+ garden] 给…除杂草 [gěi…chú zácǎo]
▶ weed out VT 淘汰 [táotài]

weedkiller ['wiːdkɪlə(r)] N [c/U] 除草剂 [chúcǎojì]

⊙ week [wiːk] N [c] **1** 星期 [xīngqī] ▷ I had a letter from my mother last week. 上星期我收到一封我母亲的信。 **2** (working week) 工作周 [gōngzuòzhōu] ▷ workers on a three-day week 实行3天制工作周的工人 **3** (Monday to Friday) ▶ the week 工作日 [gōngzuòrì] ▶ this/next/last week 本/下/上周 ▶ once/twice a week

一周一次/两次 ▶ **in two weeks' time** 在两周后 ▶ **a week today/on Friday** 下星期的今天/下星期五 ▶ **during the week** 在工作日期间

weekday ['wiːkdeɪ] N [c] 工作日 [gōngzuòrì] ▶ **on weekdays** 在工作日

weekend [wiːk'ɛnd] N [c] 周末 [zhōumò] ▶ **at the weekend** 在周末 ▶ **this/next/last weekend** 这个周末/下周末/上周末

weekly ['wiːklɪ] I ADV 每周 [měizhōu] II ADJ [+ newspaper, magazine] 每周一期的 [měizhōu yīqī de]; [+ payment, meeting, visit etc] 按周的 [ànzhōu de] III N [c] 1 (newspaper) 周报 [zhōubào] 2 (magazine) 周刊 [zhōukān]

weep [wiːp] (pt, pp **wept**) I VI 1 (person) 哭泣 [kūqì] 2 [wound +] 渗出液体 [shènchū yètǐ] II N [c] ▶ **to have a weep** 大哭一场 [dàkū yī chǎng]

weigh [weɪ] I VT 1 [+ parcel, baby, flour] 称…的重量 [chēng…de zhòngliàng] 2 (consider) [+ evidence, facts, risks etc] 权衡 [quánhéng] II VI ▶ **she weighs 50kg** 她的体重为50公斤 [tāde tǐzhòng wéi wǔshí gōngjīn] ▶ **how much do you weigh?** 你有多重？ ▶ **to weigh on sb** 使某人心情沉重 ▶ **to weigh anchor** 起锚
▶ **weigh down** VT 1 (physically) 压垮 [yākuǎ] 2 (with worry, problems) ▶ **to be weighed down with** or **by sth** 深受某事重压之苦 [shēnshòu mǒushì zhòngyā zhīkǔ]
▶ **weigh out** VT 称出 [chēngchū]
▶ **weigh up** (ESP BRIT) VT [+ evidence, alternatives] 掂量 [diānliang]; [+ person] 评价 [píngjià]

weight [weɪt] I N 1 [u] 重量 [zhòngliàng] 2 [c] (heavy object) 重物 [zhòngwù] 3 [c] (for scales) 砝码 [fǎmǎ] 4 [c] (problem, responsibility) 重压 [zhòngyā] II VT ▶ **to be weighted in favour of sb/sth** 设置得有利于某人/某事 [shèzhì de yǒulì yú mǒurén/mǒushì] III **weights** NPL (in gym) 举重器械 [jǔzhòng qìxiè] ▶ **sold by weight** 按分量出售 ▶ **to lose weight** 体重减轻 ▶ **to put on weight** 体重增加 ▶ **to throw one's weight behind sth/sb** 全力支持某事/某人 ▶ **to pull one's weight** 做好本分工作
▶ **weights and measures** 度量衡
▶ **weight down** VT 压住 [yāzhù]

weightlifting ['weɪtlɪftɪŋ] N [u] 举重 [jǔzhòng]

weir [wɪə(r)] N [c] 堰 [yàn]

weird [wɪəd] ADJ [+ object, situation, effect] 奇特的 [qítè de]; [+ person] 古怪的 [gǔguài de]

welcome ['wɛlkəm] I ADJ [+ visitor, news, change etc] 受欢迎的 [shòu huānyíng de] II N [c] 欢迎 [huānyíng] III VT 1 [+ visitor, speaker etc] 欢迎 [huānyíng] 2 [+ news, change etc] 欢迎 [huānyíng] ▶ **welcome to Beijing!** 欢迎到北京来！ ▶ **to make sb (feel) welcome** 使某人（感到）受欢迎 ▶ **to be welcome to do sth** 欢迎做某事 ▶ **"thank you" – "you're welcome!"** "谢谢你。" "别客气！" ▶ **to give sb a warm**

welcome 热烈欢迎某人

weld [wɛld] I VT 焊接 [hànjiē] II N [c] 焊接点 [hànjiēdiǎn] ▶ **to weld sth to sth** 将某物同某物结合起来

welder ['wɛldə(r)] N [c] 焊工 [hàngōng]

welfare ['wɛlfeə(r)] I N [u] 1 (well-being) 幸福 [xìngfú] 2 (US) (social aid) 福利救济 [fúlì jiùjì] [英= **social security**] II CPD [复合词] [+ system, services] 福利的 [fúlì de]

welfare state N ▶ **the welfare state** 福利国家 [fúlì guójiā]

⊙ **well** [wɛl] I N [c] 1 (for water) 井 [jǐng] 2 (oil well) 油井 [yóujǐng] II ADV 1 (to a high standard) 好 [hǎo] ▷ **She speaks French well.** 她法语说得好。2 (completely) 充分地 [chōngfèn de] ▷ **Mix all the ingredients well.** 将所有的配料充分混合。▷ **I don't know him well.** 我不是很了解他。3 (emphatic with adv, adj, phrase) 很 [hěn] ▷ **The film is well worth seeing.** 这部电影很值得一看。III ADJ (healthy) 身体好的 [shēntǐ hǎo de] ▷ **He's not very well.** 他身体不太好。IV VI [tears +] 涌上 [yǒngshàng] V INT 唔 [ńg] ▷ **Well! I don't know what to say to that.** 唔，我不知道对此该怎么说什么。▶ **to do well** [person +; business +] 进展顺利 ▶ **well done!** 棒极了！ ▶ **well done** [+ meat] 煮得老的 ▶ **he did as well as he could** 他尽可能做得好 ▶ **how well do you know him?** 你对他有多了解？ ▶ **as well** (in addition) 也 ▶ **X as well as Y** (in addition to) 除了Y还有X ▶ **you might** or **may as well tell me** 你还是告诉我吧 ▶ **you may** or **could well be right** 你很可能是对的 ▶ **it's just as well** 幸好 [hǎo] ▶ **well and truly** 确实地 ▶ **I don't feel well** 我觉得不舒服 ▶ **get well soon!** 早日康复！ ▶ **well, as I was saying...** 那么，像我刚才所说的… ▶ **oh well** 噢，那好吧
▶ **well up** VI [tears, emotions etc +] 涌上 [yǒngshàng]

we'll [wiːl] = **we will, we shall**

well-behaved ['wɛlbɪ'heɪvd] ADJ 行为端正的 [xíngwéi duānzhèng de]

well-being ['wɛl'biːɪŋ] N [u] 康乐 [kānglè]

well-built ['wɛl'bɪlt] ADJ [+ person] 体格健美的 [tǐgé jiànměi de]

well-dressed ['wɛl'drɛst] ADJ 穿着考究的 [chuānzhuó kǎojiù de]

wellington ['wɛlɪŋtən] (ESP BRIT) N [c] (also: **wellington boot**) 橡胶长统靴 [xiàngjiāo chángtǒngxuē] [美= **rubber boot**]

well-known ['wɛl'nəun] ADJ [+ person] 有名的 [yǒumíng de]; [+ fact, brand] 众所周知的 [zhòng suǒ zhōu zhī de] ▶ **to be well-known for sth** 因某事而著名 ▶ **it is well-known that...** …是众所周知的
用法参见 **famous**

well-off ['wɛl'ɔf] ADJ 富裕的 [fùyù de]

well-paid ['wɛl'peɪd] ADJ [+ person] 报酬优厚的 [bàochóu yōuhòu de]; [+ job] 高薪的 [gāoxīn de]

welly ['wɛlɪ] (BRIT: *inf*) N [c] 橡胶长统靴
[xiàngjiāo chángtǒngxuē] [美= **rubber boot**]

Welsh [wɛlʃ] I ADJ 威尔士的 [Wēi'ěrshì de]
II N [U] (*language*) 威尔士语 [Wēi'ěrshìyǔ]
III NPL ▶ **the Welsh** 威尔士人 [Wēi'ěrshìrén]

Welshman ['wɛlʃmən] (*pl* **Welshmen**) N [c] 威
尔士男子 [Wēi'ěrshì nánzǐ]

Welshwoman ['wɛlʃwumən] (*pl*
Welshwomen) N [c] 威尔士女子 [Wēi'ěrshì
nǚzǐ]

went [wɛnt] PT *of* **go**

wept [wɛpt] PT, PP *of* **weep**

were [wə:(r)] PT *of* **be**

we're [wɪə(r)] = **we are**

weren't [wə:nt] = **were not**

○ **west** [wɛst] I N **1** [U/s] (*direction*) 西方 [xīfāng]
2 ▶ **the West** (POL) 西方国家 [xīfāng guójiā]
II ADJ 西部的 [xībù de] III ADV 向西 [xiàng
xī] ▶ **the west of Ireland** 爱尔兰西部 ▶ **to the
west** 以西 ▶ **the west wind** 西风 ▶ **west of
…** 以西 ▷ It's 15 miles or so west of Oxford. 它位于
牛津以西15英里左右。

western ['wɛstən] I ADJ **1** (GEO) 西部的 [xībù
de] **2** (POL) 西方国家的 [xīfāng guójiā de]
II N [c] 西部影片 [xībù yǐngpiàn]

West Indian I ADJ 西印度群岛的 [Xīyìndù
Qúndǎo de] II N [c] 西印度群岛人 [Xīyìndù
Qúndǎorén]

West Indies [-'ɪndɪz] NPL ▶ **the West Indies**
西印度群岛 [Xīyìndù Qúndǎo]

westward(s) ['wɛstwəd(z)] ADV 向西
[xiàngxī]

wet [wɛt] I ADJ **1** [+ *person, clothes*] 湿的 [shī de];
[+ *paint, cement, glue*] 未干的 [wèigān de]
2 (*rainy*) [+ *weather, day*] 多雨的 [duōyǔ de]
II N [c] (BRIT: POL) 采取自由主义的保守党
成员 III VT (*dampen*) 把…弄湿 [bǎ…nòngshī]
▶ **soaking wet** 湿透了 ▶ **to get wet** 弄湿 ▶ **to
get sth wet** 把某物弄湿 ▶ **his face was wet
with tears** 他泪流满面 ▶ **"wet paint"** "油漆
未干" ▶ **wet blanket** 扫兴的人 ▶ **to wet one's
pants** or o.s. 尿裤子 ▶ **to wet the bed** 尿床

wet suit N [c] 紧身潜水衣 [jǐnshēn qiánshuǐyī]

we've [wi:v] = **we have**

whack [wæk] VT 猛击 [měngjī]

whale [weɪl] N [c] 鲸 [jīng]

wharf [wɔ:f] (*pl* **wharves** [wɔ:vz]) N [c] 码头
[mǎtóu]

○ **what** [wɔt] I PRON **1** (*interrogative subject, object,
object of prep*) 什么 [shénme] ▶ **what is
happening?** 发生了什么事? ▶ **what is it?**
那是什么? ▶ **what are you doing?** 你在干
什么? ▶ **what are you talking about?** 你
在说什么? ▶ **what?, what did you say?** 什
么? ▶ **what about me?** 那我呢? ▶ **what
about going to a movie?** 去看电影怎么

样?
2 (*in indirect questions/speech subject, object*)
什么 [shénme] ▶ **do you know what's
happening?** 你知道发生了什么事吗?
▶ **tell me what he said** 告诉我他说了什么
3 (*relative*) 所…的 [suǒ…de] ▶ **I saw what
was on the table** 我看见了桌上的东西
▶ **what you say is wrong** 你所说的是错的
II ADJ **1** (*interrogative, in indirect questions/
speech*) 什么 [shénme] ▶ **what time is it?**
几点了? ▶ **what size is this shirt?** 这件
衬衫是几码的? ▶ **what number do I dial?**
我要拨什么号码? ▶ **what books do you
need?** 你需要什么书?
2 (*in exclamations*) 多么 [duōme] ▶ **what a
mess!** 真是一团糟! ▶ **what a lovely day!**
多么好的天气啊! ▶ **what a fool I am!** 我
真是个傻子!
III INT (*disbelieving*) 什么 [shénme]
▶ **what, no coffee!** 什么, 没咖啡了!

对某人或某事物的外表或外形特征进行
提问时, 应该用 **what** 或 **like** 引导的
问句, 而不能用 **how** 引导的问句。例
如, *How is Susan?*, 可以用来询问 Susan
的健康状况。如果想知道她的外貌, 则
应问 *What does Susan look like?* 如果想了
解她的个性, 可以问 *What is Susan like?*

whatever [wɔt'ɛvə(r)] I ADJ (*any*) 任何的
[rènhé de] II CONJ (*no matter what*) 无论什么
[wúlùn shénme] III ADV (*whatsoever*) 任何
[rènhé] IV PRON **1** (*indicating vagueness*) 不论什
么 [bùlùn shénme] **2** (*what*) 究竟什么 [jiūjìng
shénme] **3** ▶ **do whatever is necessary/you
want** 做任何必要的/你想做的事情 [zuò rènhé
bìyào de/nǐ xiǎngzuò de shìqing] ▶ **whatever
happens** 无论发生什么 ▶ **no reason
whatever** 没有任何原因 ▶ **nothing whatever**
根本没有什么

whatsoever [wɔtsəu'ɛvə(r)] ADV = **whatever**

wheat [wi:t] N [c] 小麦 [xiǎomài]

wheel [wi:l] I N **1** 轮 [lún] **2** (*also*: **steering
wheel**) 方向盘 [fāngxiàngpán] **3** (*on ship*) 舵
轮 [duòlún] II VT 推 [tuī] III VI ▶ **to wheel
around** 猛地转过身 [měng de zhuǎnguò shēn]
▶ **at the wheel** 正在开车

wheelbarrow ['wi:lbærəu] N [c] 独轮车
[dúlúnchē]

wheelchair ['wi:ltʃɛə(r)] N [c] 轮椅 [lúnyǐ]

wheel clamp (BRIT) N [c] 车轮固定夹 [chēlún
gùdìngjiā] [美= **Denver boot**]

wheeze [wi:z] I VI 气喘 [qìchuǎn] II N [c]
(BRIT: o.f., *inf*) (*scheme*) 巧妙主意 [qiǎomiào
zhǔyì]

○ **when** [wɛn] I ADV (*interrogative*) 什么时候
[shénme shíhou] ▶ **when did it happen?**
什么时候发生的?

II PRON (*relative*) ▶ **the day when** 当…的那一天 [dāng…de nà yī tiān]
III CONJ 1 (*in time clauses*) 当…时 [dāng…shí] ▶ **when you've read it, tell me what you think** 当你读过之后，告诉我是怎么想的 ▶ **be careful when you cross the road** 过马路时要当心 ▶ **that was when we needed you** 那是我们需要你的时候 ▶ **she was reading when I came in** 当我进来时她正在阅读 ▶ **I know when it happened** 我知道什么时候发生的 2 (*whereas*) 而 [ér] ▶ **you said I was wrong when in fact I was right** 你说我是错的而事实上我是对的 3 (*considering*) 既然 [jìrán] ▶ **why did you buy that when you can't afford it?** 既然买不起为什么还要买？

whenever [wɛnˈɛvə(r)] I CONJ 1 (*any time that*) 无论何时 [wúlùn héshí] 2 (*every time that*) 每当 [měidāng] 3 (*showing uncertainty*) 任何什么时候 [rènhé shénme shíhou] II ADV 随便什么时候 [suíbiàn shénme shíhou]

where [wɛə(r)] I ADV (*in or to what place*) 在哪里 [zài nǎli] ▷ Where's Jane? 简在哪儿？ II CONJ 1 (*the place in which*) 哪里 [nǎli] ▷ Do you know where he is? 你知道他在哪里吗？ ▷ People looked to see where the noise was coming from. 人们想弄清噪音是从哪里传来的。 2 (*relating to phase*) 在…阶段 [zài…jiēduàn] ▷ The government is at a stage where it is willing to talk. 政府正处于乐于进行会谈的阶段。 ▷ That's where you're wrong! 那就是你的错误所在！ 3 (*whereas*) 然而 [rán'ér] ▷ Sometimes a teacher will be listened to, where a parent might not. 有时老师的话听得进去，而父母的可能就不行了。 ▶ **where are you from?** 你是哪里人？ ▶ **where will it all end?** 到哪儿才是个头？ ▶ **this is where…** (*lit*) 这是…的地方；(*fig*) 这是…之处 ▶ **where possible** 如有可能的话

whereabouts [adv wɛərəˈbauts, n ˈwɛərəbauts] I ADV 在哪里 [zài nǎli] II N ▶ **the whereabouts of sb/sth** 某人的下落/某物的所在 [mǒurén de xiàluò/mǒuwù de suǒzài]

whereas [wɛərˈæz] CONJ 而 [ér]

whereby [wɛəˈbaɪ] ADV ▶ **a system whereby we…** 我们借以…的一种制度 [wǒmen jièyǐ…de yī zhǒng zhìdù]

wherever [wɛərˈɛvə(r)] I CONJ 1 (*no matter where*) 无论在哪里 [wúlùn zài nǎli] 2 (*not knowing where*) 不管在哪里 [bùguǎn zài nǎli] II ADV (*showing surprise*) 究竟在哪里 [jiūjìng zài nǎli] ▶ **sit wherever you like** 你喜欢坐哪儿就坐哪里

whether [ˈwɛðə(r)] CONJ 是否 [shìfǒu] ▷ I can't tell whether she loves me or she hates me. 我搞不清她是爱我还是恨我。 ▶ **I don't know whether to accept or not** 我不知道是接受还是不接受 ▶ **whether we like it or not** 无论

我们喜欢与否 ▶ **it's doubtful whether…** 是否…还不肯定

which [wɪtʃ] I ADJ 1 (*interrogative singular*) 哪个 [nǎge]; (*plural*) 哪些 [nǎxiē] ▶ **which picture do you want?** 你要哪幅画？ ▶ **which books are yours?** 哪些书是你的？ ▶ **which one/ones?** 哪个/些？ ▶ **which one of you did it?** 你们中的哪个人做的？ 2 (*in indirect questions/speech singular*) 哪个 [nǎge]; (*plural*) 哪些 [nǎxiē] ▶ **he asked which book I wanted** 他问我要哪本书 3 (*relative*) ▶ **in which case** 在这种情况下 [zài zhèzhǒng qíngkuàng xià] ▶ **by which time** 到那时为止 II PRON 1 (*interrogative subject, object*) 哪个 [nǎge] ▶ **which of these is yours?** 这些中的哪个是你的？ ▶ **which of you are coming?** 你们中的哪些人会来？ ▶ **which do you want?** (*singular*) 你要哪个？; (*plural*) 你要哪些？ 2 (*in indirect questions/speech subject, object*) 哪个 [nǎge] ▶ **ask him which of the models is the best** 问他哪种型号是最好的 ▶ **tell me which you want** (*singular*) 告诉我你要哪个; (*plural*) 告诉我你要哪些 ▶ **I don't mind which** 哪个都行 3 (*relative subject, object*) …的那个 […de nàge…] ▶ **the shot which you heard/which killed him** 你听到的那一枪/杀死他的那一枪 ▶ **the chair on which you are sitting** 你正坐着的那把椅子 ▶ **he said he knew, which is true** 他说他知道，事实的确如此 ▶ **after which** 在那以后

whichever [wɪtʃˈɛvə(r)] I ADJ (*any… that*) 无论哪个 [wúlùn nǎge] II PRON 1 (*no matter which*) 无论哪个 [wúlùn nǎge] 2 (*specifying*) …的那一个 […de nà yīgè] ▶ **whichever way you look at it** 无论你以何种方式看待它

while [waɪl] I N [s] 一会儿 [yīhuìr] ▷ a book that I read a little while ago 我不久前刚看的一本书 II CONJ 1 (*at the same time as*) 当…的时候 [dāng…de shíhou] ▷ While I was in London she was in Paris. 当我在伦敦的时候，她在巴黎。 2 (*during the time that*) 在…时 [zài…shí] ▷ Someone opened the door while he was making his speech. 在他演讲时有人打开了门。 3 (*although*) 虽然 [suīrán] ▷ While I'm very fond of him, I don't actually want to marry him. 虽然我很喜欢他，但我真的不想嫁给他。 4 (*but*) 而 [ér] ▷ The first two services are free, while the third costs £35. 头两次服务是免费的，而第3次要花费35镑。 ▶ **for a while** 有一会儿 ▶ **in a while** 过一会儿 ▶ **all the while** 一直

▶ **while away** VT 消磨 [xiāomó] ▷ They whiled away the hours telling stories. 他们以讲故事消磨时间。

whilst [waɪlst] CONJ = while

whim [wɪm] N [C] 一时的兴致 [yīshí de xìngzhì] ▸ **on a whim** 一时心血来潮 ▸ **at the whim of** 由…随心所欲地

whimper ['wɪmpə(r)] I N [C] 呜咽声 [wūyèshēng] II VI 呜咽 [wūyè] ▸ **without a whimper** (without complaining) 一声不吭地

whine [waɪn] I N [C] **1** [from person, animal] 哀鸣 [āimíng] **2** [of engine, siren] 呜呜声 [wūwūshēng] II VI **1** [person, animal +] 哀叫 [āijiào] **2** [engine, siren +] 发呜呜声 [fā wūwūshēng] **3** (complain) 发牢骚 [fā láosāo] ▸ **to whine about sth** 没完没了地抱怨某事

whip [wɪp] I N [C] **1** (for hitting) 鞭子 [biānzi]; (riding crop) 马鞭 [mǎbiān] **2** (POL) (person) 组织秘书 [zǔzhī mìshū] II VT **1** (hit) [+ person, animal] 鞭打 [biāndǎ] **2** (beat) [+ cream, eggs] 搅打 [jiǎodǎ] **3** (snatch) ▸ **to whip sth out/off/away** 猛地掏出/脱下/拿走 [měng de tāochū/tuōxià/názǒu] **4** ▸ **to whip sb into hysteria/a frenzy** 煽动得某人歇斯底里/如痴如狂 [shāndòng de mǒurén xiēsīdǐlǐ/rú chī rú kuáng]
▸ **whip up** VT **1** [+ cream] 搅打 [jiǎodǎ] **2** (inf) [+ meal, dress] 迅速做好 [xùnsù zuòhǎo] **3** [+ support, hatred, hysteria etc] 煽动 [shāndòng]

whipped cream [wɪpt-] N [U] 泡沫奶油 [pàomò nǎiyóu]

whirl [wə:l] I VT 使旋转 [shǐ xuánzhuǎn] II VI [snow, leaves etc +] 回旋 [huíxuán]; [dancer, object +] 旋转 [xuánzhuǎn] III N [S] [of activity, pleasure] 一连串 [yī liánchuàn] ▸ **her mind or head is in a whirl** 她的思绪一片纷乱 ▸ **to give sth a whirl** (inf) (try) 试一试某事
▸ **whirl around** I VI **1** (turn) 猛地转身 [měng de zhuǎnshēn] **2** (move) [dancer +] 旋转起舞 [xuánzhuǎn qǐwǔ]; [snow, leaves etc +] 飞旋 [fēixuán] II VT 使旋转 [shǐ xuánzhuǎn]

whisk [wɪsk] I N [C] 打蛋器 [dǎdànqì] II VT [+ cream, eggs] 搅打 [jiǎodǎ] ▸ **to whisk sb away or off** 飞快地把某人送走

whiskers ['wɪskəz] NPL [of animal] 须 [xū]; [of man] 髯 [rán]

whisky, (US) whiskey ['wɪskɪ] N [C/U] 威士忌酒 [wēishìjì jiǔ]

whisper ['wɪspə(r)] I N [C] **1** 低语 [dīyǔ] **2** (liter) [of wind, leaves] 沙沙声 [shāshāshēng] II VI 低语 [dīyǔ] III VT 悄声说出 [qiāoshēng shuōchū] ▸ **to say sth/speak in a whisper** 小声说某事/小声说话 ▸ **to whisper sth to sb** 低声对某人说某事

whistle ['wɪsl] I VI **1** [person +] (melodiously) 吹口哨 [chuī kǒushào]; (in surprise) 吹了声口哨 [chuīleshēng kǒushào]; (in surprise) 吹了声口哨 [zhuànmíng] **2** [kettle, train +] 鸣笛 [míngdí] **3** [bullet +] 呼啸而行 [hūxiào ér xíng] II VT [+ tune] 用口哨吹出 [yòng kǒushào chuīchū] III N [C] **1** (device) 哨子 [shàozi] **2** (sound) 口哨声 [kǒushàoshēng]

○**white** [waɪt] I ADJ **1** 雪白的 [xuěbái de]; [+ wine] 白的 [bái de] **2** (with milk) [+ coffee] 加奶的 [jiānǎi de] **3** [+ person] (racially) 白种人的 [báizhǒngrén de]; (with fear, anger, illness etc) 苍白的 [cāngbái de] II VT **1** [U] (colour) 白色 [báisè] ▷ A woman dressed in white came up to me. 一位身穿白色衣服的女子朝我走来。 **2** [C] (person) 白人 [báirén] **3** [C/U] [of egg] 蛋白 [dànbái] **4** [C] [of eye] 眼白 [yǎnbái] III **whites** NPL (washing) 白色衣物 [báisè yīwù] ▸ **to go white** (with fear, anger, illness etc) 脸色变得煞白; (lose hair colour) [person, hair +] 头发变白

white coffee (BRIT) N [C/U] 加奶咖啡 [jiānǎi kāfēi]

White House N ▸ **the White House** 白宫 [Báigōng]

whitewash ['waɪtwɒʃ] I N **1** [U] (paint) 白涂料 [bái túliào] **2** [C/U] (cover-up) 粉饰 [fěnshì] **3** [C] (inf: SPORT) 得零分的惨败 [dé língfēn de cǎnbài] II VT **1** (paint) 粉刷 [fěnshuā] **2** (cover up) 粉饰 [fěnshì]

whiting ['waɪtɪŋ] (pl **whitings** or **whiting**) N [C/U] 牙鳕 [yáxuě]

whittle ['wɪtl] VT ▸ **to whittle sth down/away** 削减/消耗某物 [xuējiǎn/xiāohào mǒuwù]

whizz [wɪz] VI ▸ **to whizz past (sth)** 飕飕地飞过 (某ц) [sōusōu de fēiguò (mǒuwù)]

WHO N ABBR (= World Health Organization) ▸ **the WHO** 国际卫生组织 [Guójì Wèishēng Zǔzhī]

○**who** [hu:] PRON **1** (interrogative subject, object, object of prep) 谁 [shéi] ▸ **who is it?** 是谁? ▸ **who's there?** 是谁? ▸ **who are you?** 你是谁? ▸ **who did you call?** 你给谁打电话了? ▸ **who did you discuss it with?** 你和谁讨论了? **2** (in indirect questions/speech subject, object, after preposition) 谁 [shéi] ▸ **I told her who I was** 我告诉了她我是谁 ▸ **can you tell me who lives here?** 你能告诉我谁住在这儿吗? ▸ **tell me who you invited** 告诉我你邀请了谁 ▸ **I don't know who he gave it to** 我不知道他把它给了谁 **3** (relative subject, object) …的那个… […de nàge…] ▸ **the girl who came in** 进来的那个女孩 ▸ **the man who met in Sydney** 我们在悉尼遇到的那个男子 ▸ **my cousin who lives in New York** 我住在纽约的表亲 ▸ **Nicole, who you've met, is getting married** 你所见过的那个尼科尔，就要结婚了

whoever [hu:'ɛvə(r)] PRON **1** (the person who) 谁 [shéi] **2** (anyone) 无论谁 [wúlùn shéi] **3** (no matter who) 不管什么人 [bùguǎn shénme rén] **4** (in questions) (who) ▸ **whoever told you that?** 那事究竟是谁告诉你的? [nàshì jiūjìng shìshéi gàosù nǐ de?]

whole [həʊl] I ADJ 1 (*entire*) (*lit*) 整个的 [zhěnggè de] ▷ *We spent the whole summer in Italy.* 我们整个夏天都是在意大利过的。; (*fig*) (*emphatic*) 完全的 [wánquán de] ▷ *a whole new way of doing business* 一个全新的商业运作方式 **2** (*unbroken*) 完整的 [wánzhěng de] ▷ *He swallowed it whole.* 他把它完整地吞了下去。 II N 1 [c] (*entirety*) 整体 [zhěngtǐ] **2** ▶ **the whole of sth** 某物的全部 [mǒuwù de quánbù] ▶ **the whole (of the) time** 所有的时间 ▶ **the whole lot (of it)** 全部 ▶ **the whole lot (of them)** 全部 ▶ **as a whole** 整个看来 ▶ **on the whole** 大体上

wholefood(s) ['həʊlfuːd(z)] NPL (ESP BRIT) 天然食品 [tiānrán shípǐn]

wholeheartedly [həʊl'hɑːtɪdlɪ] ADV [*agree, support etc* +] 全心全意地 [quán xīn quán yì de]

wholemeal ['həʊlmiːl] (BRIT) ADJ [+ *bread, flour, pasta*] 全麦的 [quánmài de]

wholesale ['həʊlseɪl] I N [c] 批发 [pīfā] II ADJ 1 [+ *price, market*] 批发的 [pīfā de] **2** (*widespread*) 大规模的 [dàguīmó de] III ADV [*buy, sell* +] 以批发价 [yǐ pīfàjià]

wholesome ['həʊlsəm] ADJ 1 [+ *food*] 健康的 [jiànkāng de] **2** (*innocent*) 健康向上的 [jiànkāng xiàngshàng de]

wholewheat ['həʊlwiːt] ADJ = **wholemeal**

wholly ['həʊlɪ] ADV 完全地 [wánquán de]

whom [huːm] (*frm*) PRON 1 (*interrogative*) 谁 [shéi] **2** (*relative*) 所…的那个… [suǒ…de nàge…] ▶ **whom did you see?** 你见到谁了？ ▶ **to whom did you give it?** 你把它给谁了？ ▶ **tell me from whom you received it** 告诉我你从谁那儿得来的 ▶ **the man whom I saw/to whom I spoke** 我见到的/我跟他说过话的那个男人 ▶ **her brother, whom you've met, is a gifted pianist** 你所见过的她哥哥，是位有天赋的钢琴家

whore [hɔː(r)] (*inf, pej*) N [c] 娼妓 [chāngjì]

whose [huːz] I ADJ 1 (*interrogative*) 谁的 [shéi de] **2** (*relative*) …的 […de] II PRON 谁的 [shéi de] ▶ **whose is this?** 这是谁的？ [zhèshì shéi de?] ▶ **whose are these?** 这些是谁的？ ▶ **whose book is this/coats are these?** 这本书是谁的/这些外套是谁的？ ▶ **whose tent did you borrow?** 你借了谁的帐篷？ ▶ **the woman whose car was stolen** 汽车给偷走的那个女的 ▶ **Jane Smith, whose voice you liked so much, is performing live** 简·史密斯—她的嗓音为你所喜欢—正在做现场表演 ▶ **I know whose it is** 我知道这是谁的

why [waɪ] I ADV 为什么 [wèishénme] ▶ **why is he always late?** 为什么他总是迟到？ ▶ **why not?** 为什么不呢？ ▶ **why not do it now?** 为什么不现在做呢？ ▶ **I don't know why** 我不知道为什么 ▶ **can you tell me the reason why?** 你能告诉我为什么吗？ II CONJ 为什么 [wèishénme] ▶ **I wonder why he said that** 我想知道他为什么那么说 ▶ **the reason why he did it** 他那么做的原因 ▶ **that's not the reason why I'm here** 那不是我在这儿的原因 III INT (*expressing surprise, shock, annoyance*) 嗯 [ńg]; (*explaining*) 那么 [nàme] ▶ **why, it's you!** 呦，是你呀！ ▶ **why, that's impossible!** 嗯，那是不可能的！ ▶ **"I don't understand" "why, it's obvious!"** "我不明白""嗨，这是显而易见的！"

wicked ['wɪkɪd] ADJ 1 (*evil*) [+ *person*] 邪恶的 [xié'è de]; [+ *act, crime*] 罪恶的 [zuì'è de] **2** (*mischievous*) [+ *smile, sense of humour*] 顽皮的 [wánpí de] **3** (*inf*) (*terrible*) 可怕的 [kěpà de]

wicket ['wɪkɪt] N [c] 1 (*stumps*) 三柱门 [sānzhùmén] **2** (*area*) 三柱门之间的场地 [sānzhùmén zhījiān de chǎngdì] ▶ **to take a wicket** 使一个击球员出局

wide [waɪd] I ADJ 1 [+ *road, river, area etc*] 宽 [kuān de] **2** [+ *range, variety, publicity, choice etc*] 广泛的 [guǎngfàn de] II ADV ▶ **to open sth wide** [+ *window, mouth*] 张大某物 [zhāngdà mǒuwù] ▶ **to go wide** [*shot etc* +] 打偏 ▶ **how wide is it?** 它有多宽？ ▶ **it's 3 metres wide** 它有3米宽

widely ['waɪdlɪ] ADV 1 [*differ, vary* +] 大大地 [dàdà de]; [*travel* +] 范围广地 [fànwéi guǎng de] **2** [+ *spaced, separated*] 相距远地 [xiāngjù yuǎn de] **3** [+ *believed, known*] 广泛地 [guǎngfàn de] ▶ **to be widely read** 博览群书

widen ['waɪdn] I VT 1 [+ *road, river etc*] 拓宽 [tuòkuān] **2** [+ *experience, horizons etc*] 扩展 [kuòzhǎn] **3** [*gap, difference etc*] 扩大 [kuòdà] II VI 1 [*road, river etc* +] 变宽 [biànkuān] **2** [*gap, difference etc* +] 扩大 [kuòdà]

wide open ADJ [+ *eyes, mouth*] 大张的 [dàzhāng de]; [+ *window*] 大开的 [dàkāi de]

widespread ['waɪdspred] ADJ [+ *use, practice, belief, feeling*] 分布广的 [fēnbù guǎng de]; [+ *support, opposition*] 普遍的 [pǔbiàn de]

widow ['wɪdəʊ] N [c] 寡妇 [guǎfù]

widowed ['wɪdəʊd] ADJ 丧偶的 [sàng'ǒu de]

widower ['wɪdəʊə(r)] N [c] 鳏夫 [guānfū]

width [wɪdθ] N 1 [c/u] 宽度 [kuāndù] **2** [c] (*in swimming pool*) 池宽 [chíkuān] ▶ **it's 7 metres in width** 它的宽度为7米

wield [wiːld] VT 1 [+ *sword, knife*] 持 [chí] **2** [+ *power, influence*] 行使 [xíngshǐ]

wife [waɪf] (*pl* **wives**) N [c] 妻子 [qīzi]

wig [wɪg] N [c] 假发 [jiǎfà]; (*worn in court*) 假发套 [jiǎfàtào]

wiggle ['wɪgl] I VT, VI 扭动 [niǔdòng] II N [c] 扭动 [niǔdòng]

wild [waɪld] I ADJ 1 [+ *animal, plant*] 野生的 [yěshēng de] **2** (*uncultivated*) [+ *area*] 荒芜的 [huāngwú de] **3** [+ *weather, sea*] 暴风雨

的 [bàofēngyǔ de] **4** [+ person, behaviour] 狂野的 [kuángyě de] **5** (inf) (angry) 愤怒的 [fènnù de] **6** [+ idea, guess] 随便的 [suíbiàn de] **7** [+ applause, cheers] 狂热的 [kuángrè de] **II** N ▸ **in the wild** 在野生状态下 [zài yěshēng zhuàngtài xià] **III** **the wilds** NPL 偏僻地区 [piānpì dìqū] ▸ **to run wild** 毫无管束 ▸ **I'm not wild about it** (inf) 我对此无多大兴趣 ▸ **the audience went wild** 观众变得非常狂热

wilderness ['wɪldənɪs] N [c] 荒野 [huāngyě]

wildlife ['waɪldlaɪf] N [U] 野生动物 [yěshēng dòngwù]

wildly ['waɪldlɪ] ADV **1** [applaud, cheer +] 狂热地 [kuángrè de] **2** [wave, shake +] 剧烈地 [jùliè de] **3** (very) [+ different, successful, optimistic etc] 极度地 [jídù de] **4** (very much) [vary, fluctuate +] 极大地 [jídà de]

will [wɪl] **I** AUX VB **1** (forming future tense) ▸ **I will call you tonight** 我今晚会给你打电话的 [wǒ jīnwǎn huì gěi nǐ dǎ diànhuà de] ▸ **what will you do next?** 下面你要做什么? ▸ **will you do it? yes I will/no I won't** 你会做吗? - 是的, 我会的/不, 我不会 ▸ **I will have finished it by tomorrow** 我明天前可以做完 **2** (in conjectures, predictions) 该是 [gāishì] ▸ **he'll be there by now** 他现在该到了 ▸ **that will be the postman** 那准是邮差 ▸ **he will have left by now** 他现在一定已经离开了 **3** (in commands, requests, offers) ▸ **will you be quiet!** 你安静点! [nǐ ānjìng diǎn!] ▸ **will you help me?** 你帮帮我好吗? ▸ **will you have a cup of tea?** 你要来杯茶吗? **4** (be prepared to) 会 [huì] ▸ **I won't put up with it!** 我不会容忍它的! **5** (characteristic behaviour) 会 [huì] ▸ **it will dissolve in water** 它会溶解在水中 **6** (emphatic annoyance) 总是 [zǒngshì] ▸ **he will leave the gate open** 他总是开着门 **II** VT ▸ **to will sb to do sth** 用意志力促成某人做某事 [yòng yìzhìlì cùchéng mǒurén zuò mǒushì] ▸ **he willed himself to go on** 他尽力使自己继续 **III** N **1** (volition) 意志 [yìzhì] ▸ **she lost her will to live** 她失去了活下去的意志 ▸ **against his will** 违背他的意愿 **2** (testament) 遗嘱 [yízhǔ] ▸ **to make a will** 立遗嘱

willing ['wɪlɪŋ] ADJ **1** ▸ **to be willing to do sth** 愿意做某事 [yuànyì zuò mǒushì] **2** (enthusiastic) 热切的 [rèqiè de] **3** [+ helper, participant etc] 积极肯干的 [jījí kěngàn de] ▸ **to show willing** 表现得乐意

willingly ['wɪlɪŋlɪ] ADV 乐意地 [lèyì de]

willingness ['wɪlɪŋnɪs] N [c] **1** (readiness) 愿意

[yuànyì] **2** (enthusiasm) 热切 [rèqiè]

willow ['wɪləu] N **1** [c] (tree) 柳树 [liǔshù] **2** [U] (wood) 柳木 [liǔmù]

willpower ['wɪl'pauə(r)] N [U] 意志力 [yìzhìlì]

wilt [wɪlt] VI 枯萎 [kūwěi]

win [wɪn] (pt, pp **won**) **I** N [c] 胜利 [shènglì] **II** VT **1** [+ game, fight, argument, election] 在…中获胜 [zài…zhōng huòshèng] **2** [+ prize, medal] 赢得 [yíngdé]; [+ support, popularity, order] 获得 [huòdé] **III** VI 获胜 [huòshèng] ▸ **win over** VT [+ person] 争取过来 [zhēngqǔ guòlái] ▸ **win round** (BRIT) VT = **win over**

wince [wɪns] **I** VI 咧嘴 [liězuǐ] **II** N [c] 咧嘴 [liězuǐ]

wind¹ [wɪnd] **I** N **1** [c/U] 风 [fēng] **2** [U] (flatulence) 肠胃气胀 [chángwèi qìzhàng] **3** [U] (breath) 呼吸 [hūxī] **II** VT 使呼吸困难 [shǐ hūxī kùnnan] ▸ **into** or **against the wind** 逆风 ▸ **to get wind of sth** (inf) 听到某事的风声 ▸ **the wind (section)** (MUS) 管乐器(部) ▸ **to break wind** 放屁

wind² [waɪnd] (pt, pp **wound**) **I** VT **1** ▸ **to wind sth around sth** [+ rope, bandage] 把某物绕在某物上 [bǎ mǒuwù rào zài mǒuwù shang] **2** [+ watch, clock, toy] 给…上发条 [gěi…shàng fātiáo] **II** VI ▸ **to wind through/uphill** etc 蜿蜒穿过/上坡等 [wānyán chuānguò/shàngpō děng] ▸ **wind down** VT **1** [+ window] 摇下 [yáoxià] **2** (cut back) [+ activity] 逐步减少 [zhúbù jiǎnshǎo] ▸ **wind up** **I** VT **1** [+ watch, clock, toy] 给…上发条 [gěi…shàng fātiáo] **2** [+ window] 摇上 [yáoshàng] **3** [+ firm] 停业 [tíngyè] **4** [+ meeting, discussion] 结束 [jiéshù] **5** (BRIT: inf) (tease) 哄骗 [hǒngpiàn]; (annoy) 烦扰 [fánrǎo] **II** VI 告终 [gàozhōng]

windfall ['wɪndfɔːl] N [c] **1** (money) 意外收获 [yìwài shōuhuò] **2** (apple) 落果 [luòguǒ]

winding ['waɪndɪŋ] ADJ [+ road, river] 蜿蜒的 [wānyán de] ▸ **a winding staircase** 盘旋式楼梯

wind instrument [wɪnd-] N [c] 管乐器 [guǎnyuèqì]

window ['wɪndəu] N [c] **1** (in house, building) 窗户 [chuānghu]; (in shop) 橱窗 [chúchuāng]; (in car, train) 窗 [chuāng] **2** (pane) 窗玻璃 [chuāng bōli] **3** (COMPUT) 视窗 [shìchuāng]

window box N [c] 窗台花箱 [chuāngtái huāxiāng]

window cleaner N [c] 擦窗工人 [cāchuāng gōngrén]

window pane N [c] 窗玻璃 [chuāng bōli]

windowsill ['wɪndəusɪl] N [c] 窗台 [chuāngtái]

wind power ['wɪnd-] N [U] 风力 [fēnglì]

windscreen ['wɪndskriːn] (BRIT) N [C] 挡风玻璃 [dǎngfēng bōlí] [美=**windshield**]

windscreen wiper [-waɪpə(r)] (BRIT) N [C] 挡风玻璃雨刮器 [dǎngfēng bōlí yǔguāqì] [美=**windshield wiper**]

windshield ['wɪndʃiːld] (US) N [C] 挡风玻璃 [dǎngfēng bōlí] [英=**windscreen**]

windshield wiper [-waɪpə(r)] (US) N [C] 挡风玻璃雨刮器 [dǎngfēng bōlí yǔguāqì] [英=**windscreen wiper**]

windsurfing ['wɪndsɜːfɪŋ] N [U] 帆板运动 [fānbǎn yùndòng]

windy ['wɪndɪ] ADJ [+ weather, day] 有风的 [yǒufēng de] ▶ **it's windy** 今天风很大

wine [waɪn] I N [C/U] **1** (from grapes) 葡萄酒 [pútáojiǔ] **2** (from other fruits etc) 果酒 [guǒjiǔ] II VT ▶ **to wine and dine sb** 以酒宴款待某人 [yǐ jiǔyàn kuǎndài mǒurén]

wine bar N [C] 酒吧 [jiǔbā]

wine glass N [C] 酒杯 [jiǔbēi]

wine list N [C] 酒水单 [jiǔshuǐdān]

wing [wɪŋ] I N [C] **1** [of bird, insect] 翅膀 [chìbǎng]; [of aeroplane] 机翼 [jīyì] **2** [of building] 侧楼 [cèlóu] **3** [of organization] 派系 [pàixì] **4** (BRIT) [of car] 挡泥板 [dǎngníbǎn] [美=**fender**] II the wings NPL (THEAT) 舞台的侧面 [wǔtái de cèmiàn]

winger ['wɪŋə(r)] N [C] 边锋 [biānfēng]

wing mirror (BRIT) N [C] 侧视镜 [cèshì jìng] [美=**sideview mirror**]

wink [wɪŋk] I N [C] [of eye] 眨眼 [zhǎyǎn] II VI **1** [person +] 眨眼 [zhǎyǎn] **2** [light +] 闪烁 [shǎnshuò] ▶ **to give sb a wink, wink at sb** 向某人眨了眨眼

winner ['wɪnə(r)] N [C] 获胜者 [huòshèngzhě]

winning ['wɪnɪŋ] ADJ **1** [+ team, entry] 获胜的 [huòshèng de]; [+ shot, goal] 致胜的 [zhìshèng de] **2** (attractive) [+ smile, personality] 迷人的 [mírén de] see also **winnings**

winnings ['wɪnɪŋz] NPL 赢得的钱 [yíngdé de qián]

winter ['wɪntə(r)] I N [C/U] 冬季 [dōngjì] II VI 过冬 [guòdōng] ▶ **in (the) winter** 在冬季

wipe [waɪp] I VT **1** (dry, clean) 擦 [cā] **2** (remove) 擦去 [cāqù] **3** (erase) [+ tape] 抹掉 [mǒdiào] II N [C] ▶ **to give sth a wipe** 把某物擦一擦 [bǎ mǒuwù cā yī cā] ▶ **to wipe one's nose** 擦鼻子
▶ **wipe away** VT [+ tears] 擦去 [cāqù]; [+ mark] 除去 [chúqù]
▶ **wipe off** VT 擦掉 [cādiào]
▶ **wipe out** VT (destroy) [+ city, population, wildlife] 消灭 [xiāomiè]
▶ **wipe up** VT 把…擦干净 [bǎ…cā gānjìng]

wire ['waɪə(r)] I N **1** [C/U] (metal) 金属丝 [jīnshǔsī] **2** [C] (ELEC) (uninsulated) 电线 [diànxiàn]; (insulated) 电缆 [diànlǎn] **3** [C] (ESP US) (telegram) 电报 [diànbào] II VT **1** (US) (with telegram) 发电报给 [fā diànbào gěi]

2 (also: **wire up**) ELEC) [+ building] 给…布线 [gěi…bùxiàn]; [+ appliance, plug] (put cables in) 给…接线 [gěi…jiēxiàn]; (connect) 给…连线 [gěi…liánxiàn]

wiring ['waɪərɪŋ] N [U] 线路 [xiànlù]

wisdom ['wɪzdəm] N [U] [of person] 智慧 [zhìhuì]; [of action, remark] 明智 [míngzhì]

wisdom tooth (pl **wisdom teeth**) N [C] 智齿 [zhìchǐ]

wise [waɪz] ADJ [+ person] 睿智的 [ruìzhì de]; [+ action, remark] 明智的 [míngzhì de] ▶ **I'm none the wiser** 我仍然糊里糊涂 ▶ **it would be wise to do it now** 现在去做这件事应是明智之举
▶ **wise up** (inf) VI ▶ **to wise up to sth** 了解某事 [liǎojiě mǒushì]

wish [wɪʃ] I N [C] 愿望 [yuànwàng] II VT 但愿 [dànyuàn] ▶ **to make a wish** (silently) 默默地许愿; (out loud) 大声地许愿 ▶ **we have no wish to cause problems** 我们并不想引起麻烦 ▶ **best wishes** (on birthday, promotion etc) 良好的祝愿 ▶ **with best wishes** (in letter) 好好 ▶ **give her my best wishes** 代我向她致意 ▶ **to wish to do sth** 想要做某事 ▶ **to wish sb goodbye/good night** 向某人告别/道晚安 ▶ **to wish sb well** 祝某人一切顺利 ▶ **to wish sth on sb** 想让某事发生在某人身上 ▶ **to wish for sth** 渴望某物

wishful ['wɪʃful] ADJ ▶ **wishful thinking** 痴心妄想 [chī xīn wàng xiǎng]

wistful ['wɪstful] ADJ 憧憬的 [chōngjǐng de]

wit [wɪt] I N **1** [U] (wittiness) 风趣 [fēngqù] **2** [C] (person) 风趣的人 [fēngqù de rén] **3** [U] (sense) 领悟力 [lǐngwùlì] II wits NPL (intelligence) 才智 [cáizhì] ▶ **to be at one's wits' end** 智穷计尽 ▶ **to have one's wits about one** 保持头脑清醒

witch [wɪtʃ] N [C] 女巫 [nǚwū]

○

with [wɪð, wɪθ] PREP **1** (together with, at the house of) 和…在一起 [hé…zài yīqǐ] ▶ **I was with him** 我和他在一起 ▶ **I'll be with you in a minute** 请稍等 ▶ **we'll take the children with us** 我们会带着孩子们的 ▶ **mix the sugar with the eggs** 把糖和鸡蛋混在一起 ▶ **we stayed with friends** 我们和朋友们呆在一起 ▶ **a waiter came round with some wine** 服务员拿着酒过来了 ▶ **I'm with you** (inf) (I understand) 我明白你的意思 ▶ **to argue/fight/compete with sb** 与某人争论/斗争/竞争

2 (indicating feature, possession) 有 [yǒu] ▶ **a room with a view** 能观景的房间 ▶ **the man with the grey hair/blue eyes** 戴着灰帽子/有蓝眼睛的男人

3 (indicating manner) 带着 [dàizhe] ▶ **with tears in her eyes** 眼睛里含着泪水地 ▶ **with a sigh/laugh** 叹了口气/笑着地 ▶ **she stood with her hands on her hips** 她

又着腰站着

4 (*indicating means, substance*) 用 [yòng]
▶ **to walk with a stick** 拄着拐杖走 ▶ **you can open the door with this key** 你可以用这把钥匙开门 ▶ **he was covered with bruises/mud** 他满身淤伤/泥巴 ▶ **to fill sth with water** 在某物里装满水

5 (*indicating cause*) ▶ **red with anger** 气得涨红了脸 [qìde zhànghónglé liǎn] ▶ **to shake with fear** 怕得发抖 ▶ **he spent a week in bed with flu** 他因为流感卧病在床一星期

6 (*in relation to*) 后接 **with** 的动词，例如 ▶ **to deal with, to cope with** 参阅动词。▶ **to be bored/pleased with sth/sb** 因某事/某人而觉得闷/高兴 [yīn mǒushì/mǒurén ér juéde mèn/gāoxìng] ▶ **to deal/cope with sth** 对付/应付某事 ▶ **to have a problem with money** 在经济上有麻烦

7 (*according to*) 随着 [suízhe] ▶ **it will improve with time** 会随着时间而改进

withdraw [wɪθˈdrɔː] (*pt* **withdrew**, *pp* **withdrawn**) I VT **1** (*take away*) [+ *object*] 抽回 [chōuhuí] **2** (*frm*) (*take back*) [+ *offer*, *remark*] 收回 [shōuhuí] **3** ▶ **to withdraw money** (*from bank*) 提款 [tíkuǎn] II VI **1** [*troops* +] 撤回 [chèhuí] **2** (*from activity, organization*) 退出 [tuìchū] **3** (*from room*) 离开 [líkāi] ▶ **to withdraw into o.s.** 变得孤僻

withdrawal [wɪθˈdrɔːəl] N **1** [C/U] (*removal*) [*of troops*] 撤退 [chètuì]; [*of offer, remark*] 收回 [shōuhuí]; [*of services*] 撤销 [chèxiāo] **2** [U] (*from activity, organization*) 退出 [tuìchū] **3** [C/U] (FIN) [*of money*] 提款 [tíkuǎn] **4** [U] (MED) (*following addiction*) 戒毒期 [jièdú qī] **5** [U] (PSYCH) (*uncommunicative behaviour*) 社交冷漠 [shèjiāo lěngmò]

withdrawn [wɪθˈdrɔːn] I PP *of* **withdraw** II ADJ 性格内向的 [xìnggé nèixiàng de]

wither [ˈwɪðə(r)] VI **1** [*flower, plant* +] 枯萎 [kūwěi] **2** (*become weak*) 衰败 [shuāibài] ▶ **wither away** VI 消亡 [xiāowáng]

withhold [wɪθˈhəʊld] (*pt, pp* **withheld**) VT [+ *money, aid*] 拒给 [jùgěi]; [+ *permission*] 不给 [bùgěi]; [+ *information, facts*] 拒绝提供 [jùjué tígōng]

◊within [wɪðˈɪn] I PREP **1** [+ *place*] 在⋯里面 [zài⋯lǐmiàn]; [+ *society, organization*] 在⋯内部 [zài⋯nèibù]; [+ *person*] 在⋯内心 [zài⋯nèixīn] **2** [+ *time, distance*] 在⋯之内 [zài⋯zhīnèi] **3** [+ *limit, budget*] 在⋯限度以内 [zài⋯xiàndù yǐ'nèi] II ADV (*in place, area, object*) 在里面 [zài lǐmiàn]; (*in society, organization*) 在内部 [zài nèibù] ▶ **within reach (of sb)** 在(某人)伸手可及的地方 ▶ **within sight (of sth)** 在看得到(某物)的地方 ▶ **within the week** 在本周内 ▶ **within a mile of sth** 在离某地不出一英里的地方 ▶ **within an hour of his arrival** 在他到达后一小时内 ▶ **within the law** 合法的

◊without [wɪðˈaʊt] PREP 没有 [méiyǒu] ▶ **without a coat** 未穿外套 ▶ **without speaking** 不曾说话 ▶ **it goes without saying** 这不消说 ▶ **without anyone knowing** 不为人知地

withstand [wɪθˈstænd] (*pt, pp* **withstood**) VT 经受住 [jīngshòu zhù]

witness [ˈwɪtnɪs] I N [C] (*gen, also in court*) 目击者 [mùjīzhě]; (*to document*) 联署人 [liánshǔrén] II VT **1** (*see*) [+ *event*] 目击 [mùjī]; (*fig*) (*experience*) 经历 [jīnglì] **2** (*confirm*) [+ *signature*] 联署 [liánshǔ] ▶ **witness for the prosecution** 控方证人 ▶ **witness for the defence** 辩方证人 ▶ **to be (a) witness to sth** 为某事的目击者 ▶ **to bear witness to sth** 表明某事 ▶ **to witness to sth** 为某事作证

witty [ˈwɪtɪ] ADJ 诙谐的 [huīxié de]

wives [waɪvz] NPL *of* **wife**

wizard [ˈwɪzəd] N [C] **1** (*with magical powers*) 男巫 [nánwū] **2** (*inf*) (*expert*) 奇才 [qícái]

wk ABBR (= **week**) 星期 [xīngqī]

WKND (TEXTING) ABBR (= **weekend**) 周末 [zhōumò]

WLTM ABBR (= **would like to meet**) 想结识 [xiǎng jiéshí]

wobble [ˈwɒbl] VI [*object, table, jelly* +] 摇晃 [yáohuàng]; [*person, knees* +] 颤抖 [chàndǒu]

woe [wəʊ] I N [U] (*sorrow*) 悲哀 [bēi'āi] II **woes** NPL (*misfortunes*) 不幸 [bùxìng]

woke [wəʊk] PT *of* **wake**

woken [ˈwəʊkən] PP *of* **wake**

wolf [wʊlf] (*pl* **wolves** [wʊlvz]) I N [C] 狼 [láng] II VT (*inf*) (*also*: **wolf down**) 狼吞虎咽地吃下 [lángtūn hǔyàn de chīxià]

◊woman [ˈwʊmən] (*pl* **women**) N [C] 妇女 [fùnǔ] ▶ **young woman** 年轻女子 ▶ **woman doctor/friend** 女医生/女性朋友

womb [wuːm] N [C] 子宫 [zǐgōng]

women [ˈwɪmɪn] NPL *of* **woman**

won [wʌn] PT, PP *of* **win**

wonder [ˈwʌndə(r)] I N **1** [C] (*miracle*) 奇迹 [qíjì] **2** [U] (*awe*) 惊奇 [jīngqí] II VT ▶ **to wonder whether/why** etc 想知道是否/为什么{等} [xiǎng zhīdào shìfǒu/wèishénme {děng}] III VI 感到奇怪 [gǎndào qíguài] ▶ **it's a wonder that...** 奇怪的是⋯ ▶ **(it's) no/little/small wonder that...** (这)难怪⋯ ▶ **to work or do wonders** 创造奇迹 ▶ **to wonder about sth** 对某事感到疑惑 ▶ **to wonder at sth** 对某事感到诧异 ▶ **I wonder if you could help me** 不知你是否可以帮我

wonderful [ˈwʌndəful] ADJ 绝妙的 [juémiào de] ▶ **it's wonderful to see you** 见到你真是太好了

won't [wəʊnt] = **will not**

wood [wʊd] N **1** [U] 木材 [mùcái] **2** [C] (*forest*) 树林 [shùlín]

wooden [ˈwʊdn] ADJ **1** [+ *object*] 木制的 [mùzhì

de] **2** (fig) [+ performance, actor] 呆板的 [dāibǎn de]

woodwind ['wudwɪnd] ADJ [+ instrument] 木管乐器的 [mùguǎn yuèqì de] ▶ **the woodwind (section)** (MUS) 木管乐器(部)

woodwork ['wudwɜːk] N [U] **1** (craft) 木工手艺 [mùgōng shǒuyì] **2** (wooden parts) 木制品 [mùzhìpǐn]

wool [wul] N [U] 羊毛 [yángmáo] ▶ **to pull the wool over sb's eyes** 蒙骗某人

woollen, (US) **woolen** ['wulən] ADJ 羊毛的 [yángmáo de]

woolly, (US) **wooly** ['wulɪ] ADJ **1** [+ socks, hat etc] 羊毛的 [yángmáo de] **2** (confused) [+ ideas, person] 糊涂的 [hútu de]

○ **word** [wɜːd] I N **1** [c] 词 [cí] **2** [s] (promise) 诺言 [nuòyán] **3** [U/s] (news) 消息 [xiāoxi] II VT 措辞 [cuòcí] ▶ **what's the word for "pen" in French?** "钢笔"这个词在法语里怎么说? ▶ **word for word** (verbatim) 一字不变地; (in translation) 逐字地 ▶ **to put sth into words** 用语言表达某事 ▶ **not a word** 一句话也不 ▶ **in a word** 简而言之 ▶ **in other words** 换句话说 ▶ **to have a word (with sb)** (和某人) 谈谈 ▶ **to have words (with sb)** (和某人) 争论 ▶ **I'll take your word for it** 我相信你说的话 ▶ **by word of mouth** 口头地 ▶ **a word of warning/thanks etc** 警告/感谢[等]的话 ▶ **the last word** 定论 ▶ **in so many words** 直截了当地 ▶ **to break one's word** 食言 ▶ **to give sb one's word** 对某人许下承诺 ▶ **to keep one's word** 遵守诺言 ▶ **to send word of sb/sth** 转告某人/某事的消息 ▶ **to leave word (with sb/for sb) that...** (通过某人/给某人)留个口信儿…

wording ['wɜːdɪŋ] N [U] 措辞 [cuòcí]

word processing [-'prəusesɪŋ] N [U] 文字处理 [wénzì chǔlǐ]

word processor [-prəusesə(r)] N [c] **1** (machine) 文字处理器 [wénzì chǔlǐqì] **2** (software) 文字处理软件 [wénzì chǔlǐ ruǎnjiàn]

wore [wɔː(r)] PT of **wear**

○ **work** [wɜːk] I N **1** [U] (tasks, duties) 事情 [shìqing] ▷ I must go, I've got loads of work to do. 我得走了，我有一大堆事情要做。 **2** [U] (job) 工作 [gōngzuò] ▷ The work of a doctor is very interesting and varied. 医生的工作非常有趣而且丰富多彩。 **3** [U] (place) 工作场所 [gōngzuò chǎngsuǒ] **4** [c] (ART, LITER) 作品 [zuòpǐn] ▷ Chopin's works 萧邦的作品 II VI **1** (have job, do tasks) 工作 [gōngzuò] ▷ She works for a drug company. 她在一家药品公司工作。 ▷ We were working 24 hours a day. 我们曾一天工作24小时。 **2** (function) [mechanism, machine +] 运行 [yùnxíng] ▷ The new machine is working well. 新机器运行良好。 ▷ The traffic lights weren't working. 红绿灯坏了。 **3** (take effect) [medicine etc +] 见效 [jiànxiào] ▷ How long does a sleeping pill take to

work? 一颗安眠药要多长时间开始见效? **4** (be successful) [idea, method +] 起作用 [qǐ zuòyòng] ▷ 95% of these diets do not work. 95%的这些减肥食谱都不起作用。 III VT **1** (shape) [+ clay, wood, leather etc] 加工 [jiāgōng] **2** (exploit) [+ mine] 开采 [kāicǎi]; [+ land] 耕种 [gēngzhòng] **3** (operate) [+ machine] 操作 [cāozuò] **4** (cause) [+ miracle] 创造 [chuàngzào] ▷ I can't work miracles, you know. 你要知道，我不能创造奇迹。 IV **works** NPL (activities) 作业 [zuòyè] see also **works** ▶ **to set to work** or **start work (on sth)** 着手做(某项工作) ▶ **to be at work (on sth)** 在做(某项)工作 ▶ **to go to work** 去上班 ▶ **to be out of work** 失业 ▶ **to have no work** 没有工作 ▶ **to have your work cut out** 面临艰巨的任务 ▶ **to work hard** 努力工作 ▶ **to work on the principle that...** 按照…原则行事 ▶ **to work one's way to the top** 费力地一点点爬到高职 ▶ **to work loose** [part, knot +] 渐渐变松 ▶ **to work sth into sth/work sth in** [+ substance] 将某物和进某物/将某物和进去

▶ **work off** VT [+ energy, anger] 发泄 [fāxiè]

▶ **work on** VT FUS [不可拆分] **1** (busy o.s. with) 从事于 [cóngshì yú] **2** (try to influence) [+ person] 设法说服 [shèfǎ shuōfú]

▶ **work out** I VI **1** (SPORT) 锻炼 [duànliàn] **2** (progress) [job, plans etc +] 发展 [fāzhǎn] II VT [+ answer, solution] 努力找出 [nǔlì zhǎochū]; [+ plan, details] 制订出 [zhìdìng chū] ▶ **it works out at 100 pounds** 算下来达100磅 ▶ **I can't work out why...** 我弄不懂为什么…

▶ **work up** VT [+ courage, enthusiasm] 激发 [jīfā] ▶ **to get worked up (about sth)** (对某事) 很激动

○ **worker** ['wɜːkə(r)] N [c] (employed person) 工人 [gōngrén] ▷ The dispute affected relations between management and workers. 这场争端影响到管理层和工人的关系。 ▶ **a hard/good worker** 工作努力/良好的人 ▶ **factory/postal/health etc worker** 工厂工人/邮政/医疗工作者{等}

work experience N [U] 工作经历 [gōngzuò jīnglì]

workforce ['wɜːkfɔːs] N [c] (of region, country) 劳动力 [láodònglì]; (of company) 职工总数 [zhígōng zǒngshù]

○ **working** ['wɜːkɪŋ] I ADJ **1** [+ person, population, mother] 在职的 [zàizhí de] **2** [+ life, clothes] 工作的 [gōngzuò de]; [+ hours, conditions, practice] 工作上的 [gōngzuòshang de] **3** (moving) [+ part] 运行的 [yùnxíng de] **4** (functioning) [+ model] 发挥机能的 [fāhuī jīnéng de] **5** (temporary) [+ title, definition] 暂行的 [zànxíng de] II **workings** NPL (of device, brain) 运转 [yùnzhuǎn]; (of institution) 运作 [yùnzuò] ▶ **to have a working knowledge of sth** 具有足够运用的某方面的知识 ▶ **to have a good working relationship with sb** 和某人有良好的工作关系

working class I N ▶ **the working class(es)** 工

人阶级 [gōngrén jiējí] **II** ADJ (*also:* **working-class**) 工人阶级的 [gōngrén jiējí de]

working day (ESP BRIT) N [C] (*not holiday*) 工作日 [gōngzuòrì]; (*working hours*) 工作时间 [gōngzuò shíjiān]

working week (ESP BRIT) N [C] 工作周 [gōngzuòzhōu]

workman ['wəːkmən] (*pl* **workmen**) N [C] 劳动者 [láodòngzhě]

workout ['wəːkaut] N [C] 锻炼 [duànliàn] ▶ **to go for a workout** 去健身

work permit N [C] 工作许可证 [gōngzuò xǔkězhèng]

workplace ['wəːkpleɪs] N [C] 工作场所 [gōngzuò chǎngsuǒ]

works [wəːks] (*pl* **works**) (BRIT) N [C] **1** (*factory*) 工厂 [gōngchǎng] **2** (*inf*) ▶ **the works** 相关的所有事物 [xiāngguān de suǒyǒu shìwù]

worksheet ['wəːkʃiːt] N [C] 工作表 [gōngzuòbiǎo]

workshop ['wəːkʃɔp] N [C] **1** (*building*) 车间 [chējiān] **2** (*session*) 专题研讨会 [zhuāntí yántǎohuì]

workstation ['wəːksteɪʃən] N [C] **1** (*desk*) 工作台 [gōngzuòtái] **2** (*computer*) 工作站 [gōngzuòzhàn]

work surface N [C] 厨房橱柜上的操作面

worktop ['wəːktɔp] (BRIT) N [C] 厨房橱柜上的操作面 [美= **countertop**]

○ **world** [wəːld] **I** N **1** (*earth*) ▶ **the world** 世界 [shìjiè] ▷ *in many parts of the world* 在世界的许多地方 **2** [C] (*planet*) 星球 [xīngqiú] **3** [C] (*everyday existence*) 生活 [shēnghuó] ▷ *It was as if my world had collapsed.* 这就好像我的生活已经崩溃了。 **4** [C] (*sphere*) 界 [jiè] ▷ *The world of football is very competitive.* 足球界竞争很激烈。 **II** CPD [复合词] [+ *champion, record, power, authority*] 世界 [shìjiè]; [+ *tour*] 环球 [huánqiú] ▶ **all over the world** 全世界 ▶ **to think the world of sb** 非常看重某人 ▶ **what in the world is he doing?** 他究竟在做什么？ ▶ **it'll do you a** or **the world of good** (inf) 这会对你大有好处 ▶ **out of this world** (inf) 无与伦比的 ▶ **World War One/Two** 第一次/第二次世界大战

World Cup (FOOTBALL) N ▶ **the World Cup** 世界杯足球赛 [Shìjièbēi Zúqiúsài]

worldwide ['wəːld'waɪd] **I** ADJ 世界范围的 [shìjiè fànwéi de] **II** ADV 在全世界 [zài quán shìjiè]

World-Wide Web [wəːld'waɪd-] N ▶ **the World-Wide Web** 万维网 [Wànwéiwǎng]

worm [wəːm] N [C] **1** (*also:* **earthworm**) 蚯蚓 [qiūyǐn] **2** (COMPUT) 蠕虫病毒 [rúchóng bìngdú] **II** VT 给…驱肠虫 [gěi…qū chángchóng] ▶ **to have worms** 患有寄生虫病 ▶ **to worm one's way into sth** [+ *position*] 费尽心机地钻入某处; [+ *sb's affections*] 千方百计地获取某事 ▶ **to worm sth out of sb** 从某人口中

慢慢探出某事

worn [wɔːn] **I** PP *of* **wear** **II** ADJ [+ *carpet, shoe, patch, brakes etc*] 用旧的 [yòng jiù de]

worn-out ['wɔːnaut] ADJ **1** (*damaged*) [+ *object*] 破旧的 [pòjiù de] **2** (*exhausted*) [+ *person*] 疲惫不堪的 [píbèi bù kān de]

worried ['wʌrɪd] ADJ 闷闷不乐的 [mènmèn bù lè de] ▶ **to be worried about sth/sb** 担心某事/某人 ▶ **to be worried that...** 担心…

worry ['wʌrɪ] **I** N **1** [U] (*feeling of anxiety*) 忧虑 [yōulù] **2** [C] (*cause of anxiety*) 担心 [dānxīn] **II** VT 使担心 [shǐ dānxīn] **III** VI 担心 [dānxīn] ▶ **to worry about** or **over sth/sb** 担心某事/某人

worrying ['wʌrɪɪŋ] ADJ 令人担心的 [lìng rén dānxīn de]

worse [wəːs] **I** ADJ (*comparative of bad*) 更坏的 [gènghuài de] **II** ADV (*comparative of badly*) 更糟地 [gèngzāo de] **III** N [U] 更坏的事 [gènghuài de shì] ▶ **to get worse** 逐渐恶化 ▶ **to go from bad to worse** 每况愈下 ▶ **you could do worse (than to...)** (做…)还是不错的 ▶ **a change for the worse** 向更坏方向的转变 ▶ **he is none the worse for it** 他并未因此怎么样 ▶ **so much the worse for you!** 那你就更加不妙！

worsen ['wəːsn] **I** VT 使变得更坏 [shǐ biàn de gènghuài] **II** VI 变得更坏 [biàn de gènghuài]

worse off ADJ **1** (*financially*) 收入变少的 [shōurù biànshǎo de] **2** (*not as good*) 变得更糟糕的 [biàn de gèng zāogāo de] ▶ **he is now worse off than before** (in situation) 他现在的情况比以前更糟糕

worship ['wəːʃɪp] **I** N [U] 礼拜 [lǐbài] **II** VT **1** [+ *god*] 敬奉 [jìngfèng] **2** (*adore*) [+ *person, thing*] 崇拜 [chóngbài] ▶ **Your Worship** (BRIT) (*to mayor*) 阁下; (*to judge*) 法官大人

worst [wəːst] **I** ADJ (*superlative of bad*) 最坏的 [zuì huài de] **II** ADV (*superlative of badly*) 最糟地 [zuì zāo de] **III** N [S/U] 最坏的事 [zuì huài de shì] ▶ **at worst** 在最坏的情况下 ▶ **if the worst comes to the worst** 如果最坏的事情发生 ▶ **at one's worst** 在最糟糕的状态下

worth [wəːθ] **I** N [U] 价值 [jiàzhí] **II** ADJ ▶ **to be worth £50** 值50英镑 [zhí wǔshí yīngbàng] ▶ **it's worth it** 这是值得的 ▶ **how much is it worth?** 它值多少钱？ ▶ **400 dollars' worth of damage** 价值400美元的损失 ▶ **50 pence worth of apples** 50便士的苹果 ▶ **it would be worth your while to do something about the problem** 花工夫处理这个问题是值得的 ▶ **it would be (well) worth doing...** (很)值得做…

worthless ['wəːθlɪs] ADJ 毫无价值的 [háowú jiàzhí de]

worthwhile ['wəːθ'waɪl] ADJ [+ *activity*] 值得做的 [zhídé zuò de]; [+ *cause, job*] 有价值的 [yǒu jiàzhí de] ▶ **it might be worthwhile to write to them** 给他们写信是值得的

worthy [wəːðɪ] ADJ **1** (*respectable*) [+ *person*] 可敬的 [kějìng de]; [+ *motive, goal*] 高尚的

[gāoshàng de] **2** (*deserving*) [+ *winner, successor*] 相称的 [xiāngchèn de] ▶ **to be worthy of sth/sb** (*deserving of*) 值得某物/配得上某人; (*reminiscent of*) 和某物/某人相称的

O

would [wud] AUX VB **1** (*conditional tense*) ▶ **I would love to go to Italy** 我很愿意去意大利 [wǒ hěn yuànyì qù Yìdàlì] ▶ **you would never guess that...** 你永远猜不到… ▶ **I'm sure he wouldn't do that** 我确定他不会那么做的 ▶ **if you asked him he would do it** 如果你要求的话他会做的 ▶ **if you had asked him he would have done it** 如果你问过他的话，他早就会做了
2 (*in offers, invitations, requests*) ▶ **would you like a biscuit?** 你要来块饼干吗？[nǐ yào lái kuàn bǐnggān ma?] ▶ **would you ask him to come in?** 你要叫他进来吗？ ▶ **would it be all right if I sat down?** 我可以坐下吗？ ▶ **he asked me if I would go with him** 他问我是否愿意和他一起去
3 (*be willing to*) ▶ **she wouldn't help me** 她不愿意帮助我 [tā bù yuànyì bāngzhù wǒ] ▶ **she wouldn't behave** 她不会老老实实的 ▶ **the door wouldn't open** 门是打不开的 ▶ **I wish you would tidy your room** 但愿你会收拾你的房间
4 (*in indirect speech*) ▶ **he said he would be at home later** 他说他晚点儿会在家的 [tā shuō tā wǎndiǎnr huì zàijiā de] ▶ **she asked me if I would be angry if...** 她问我如果…我是否会生气
5 (*used to*) ▶ **he would spend every day on the beach** 他以前天天都呆在沙滩上 [tā yǐqián tiāntiān dōu dāi zài shātān shang]
6 (*conjecture*) ▶ **you wouldn't know him** 你一定认不出他的 [nǐ yīdìng rèn bù chū tā de] ▶ **it would have been midnight** 可能已经是半夜了
7 (*emphatic annoyance*) 老是 [lǎoshi] ▶ **it would have to snow today!** 今天又得下雪！▶ **you would say that, wouldn't you!** 你会那么说，是不是！
8 (*insistence*) ▶ **I didn't want her to, but she would do it** 我不想她这么做，但她会的 [wǒ bù xiǎng tā zhème zuò, dàn tā huì de]

wouldn't ['wudnt] = would not

wound¹ [waund] PT, PP of **wind²**

wound² [wu:nd] **I** N [c] (伤口 [shāngkǒu] **II** VT **1** (*physically*) 使受伤 [shǐ shòushāng] **2** (*emotionally*) 伤害 [shānghài] ▶ **to be wounded in the leg/arm** etc 腿部/手臂 {等} 受伤

wove [wəuv] PT of **weave**

woven ['wəuvn] PP of **weave**

WPC (BRIT) N ABBR (= **woman police constable**) 女警官 [nǚ jǐngguān]

wrap [ræp] **I** N [c] (*shawl*) 披肩 [pījiān]; (*cape*) 斗篷 [dǒupéng] **II** VT **1** (*cover*) 包 [bāo] **2** ▶ **to wrap sth around sth/sb** [+ *paper, scarf, cloth* etc] 用某物把某物/某人裹起来 [yòng mǒuwù bǎ mǒuwù/mǒurén guǒ qǐlái]; [+ *arms, legs* etc] 用某物紧紧缠绕着某物/某人 [yòng mǒuwù jǐnjǐn huánràozhe mǒuwù/mǒurén] ▶ **under wraps** [+ *plan, scheme*] 保密
▶ **wrap up I** VI (*warmly*) 穿得暖和 [chuān de nuǎnhuo] **II** VT **1** (*pack*) 包起来 [bāo qǐlái] **2** (*complete*) [+ *deal, agreement*] 完成 [wánchéng]

wrapper ['ræpə(r)] N [c] **1** (*on food, goods*) 包装纸 [bāozhuāngzhǐ] **2** (BRIT) [*of book*] 书皮 [shūpí]

wrapping paper ['ræpɪŋ-] N [U] (*brown*) 牛皮纸 [niúpízhǐ]; (*gift wrap*) 包装纸 [bāozhuāngzhǐ]

wreath [ri:θ] (pl **wreaths** [ri:ðz]) N [c] **1** (*funeral wreath*) 花圈 [huāquān] **2** (*garland*) 花环 [huāhuán]

wreck [rɛk] **I** N [c] **1** (*wreckage*) [*of vehicle, ship*] 残骸 [cánhái] **2** (US) (*accident*) 事故 [shìgù] [英= **crash**] **3** (*inf*) (*person*) 憔悴的人 [qiáocuì de rén] **II** VT **1** (*ruin*) [+ *equipment, room* etc] 毁坏 [huǐhuài]; [+ *process, life, chances, marriage*] 破坏 [pòhuài] **2** (*sink*) [+ *ship*] 使失事 [shǐ shīshì] **3** (*destroy*) [+ *car, building*] 摧毁 [cuīhuǐ]

wreckage ['rɛkɪdʒ] N [S/U] [*of car, plane, ship* etc] 残骸 [cánhái]; [*of building*] 废墟 [fèixū]

wren [rɛn] N [c] 鹪鹩 [jiāoliáo]

wrench [rɛntʃ] **I** N **1** [c] (*tool*) 扳手 [bānshǒu] **2** [s] (*tug*) 猛扭 [měngniǔ] **3** [s] (*sadness*) 痛苦 [tòngkǔ] **II** VT **1** (*pull*) ▶ **to wrench sth away/out** etc 猛力将某物挣开/拔出 {等} [měnglì jiāng mǒuwù zhèngkāi/báchū {děng}] **2** (*injure*) [+ *arm, back, ankle* etc] 扭伤 [niǔshāng] ▶ **to wrench sth from sb** 从某人手里抢走某物 ▶ **to wrench sth open** 用力扭开某物 ▶ **to wrench o.s. free** 用力挣脱

wrestle ['rɛsl] VI **1** ▶ **to wrestle (with sb)** (SPORT) (和某人) 摔跤 [(hé mǒurén) shuāijiāo]; (*fight*) (和某人) 打架 [(hé mǒurén) dǎjià] **2** ▶ **to wrestle with sth** [+ *problem, issue, question*] 努力解决某事 [nǔlì jiějué mǒushì]; [+ *conscience*] 与某事做苦苦挣扎 [yǔ mǒushì zuò kǔkǔ zhēngzhá]

wrestler ['rɛslə(r)] N [c] 摔跤选手 [shuāijiāo xuǎnshǒu]

wrestling ['rɛslɪŋ] N [U] 摔跤 [shuāijiāo]

wretched ['rɛtʃɪd] ADJ **1** (*miserable*) 悲惨的 [bēicǎn de] **2** (*bad*) 糟糕的 [zāogāo de] **3** (*expressing irritation*) (*damned*) 讨厌的 [tǎoyàn de] **4** (*unhappy*) ▶ **to be wretched** 感到苦恼 [gǎndào kǔnǎo]

wriggle ['rɪgl] **I** VI (*also*: **wriggle about**) 扭动 [niǔdòng] **II** VT [+ *one's toes, fingers*] 扭动 [niǔdòng] **III** N [c] 扭动 [niǔdòng]
▶ **wriggle out of** VT FUS (不可拆分) (*inf*) ▶ **to wriggle out of sth/of doing sth** 摆脱某事/做

某事 [bǎituō mǒushì/zuò mǒushì]

wring [rɪŋ] (pt, pp **wrung**) VT 1 [+ neck] 扭 [niǔ]
2 ▸ **to wring one's hands** (lit) 扭绞双手 [niǔjiǎo shuāngshǒu]; (fig) 无能为力 [wú néng wéi lì]
3 ▸ **to wring sth out of sb** 千方百计从某人处索取某物 [qiān fāng bǎi jì cóng mǒurén chù suǒqǔ mǒuwù]
▸ **wring out** VT [+ cloth etc] 绞干 [jiǎogān]

wrinkle ['rɪŋkl] I N [C] (on skin) 皱纹 [zhòuwén]; (in paper, cloth etc) 褶皱 [zhězhòu]
II VT [+ forehead] 皱起 [zhòuqǐ] III VI (skin +) 起皱纹 [qǐ zhòuwén]; (paint, paper etc +) 有皱痕 [yǒu zhòuhén] ▸ **to wrinkle one's nose (at sth)** (对某事) 皱鼻子

wrinkled ['rɪŋkld] ADJ [+ skin, face] 布满皱纹的 [bùmǎn zhòuwén de]; [+ person] 满脸皱纹的 [mǎnliǎn zhòuwén de]; [+ clothing, fabric, paper] 起皱的 [qǐzhòu de]

wrist [rɪst] N [C] 手腕 [shǒuwàn]

○**write** [raɪt] (pt **wrote**, pp **written**) I VT 1 (note down) [+ address, number etc] 写下 [xiěxià]
2 (compose) [+ letter, note] 写 [xiě] **3** (create) [+ novel, music etc] 创作 [chuàngzuò] **4** (also: **write out**) [+ cheque, receipt, prescription] 开 [kāi]
II VI 写字 [xiězì] ▸ **to write sb a letter, write a letter to sb** 给某人写信 ▸ **to write to sb** 写信给某人
▸ **write away** VI ▸ **to write away for sth** [+ information] 发信索要某物 [fā xìn suǒyào mǒuwù]; [+ goods] 函购某物 [hángòu mǒuwù]
▸ **write down** VT 记下 [jìxià]
▸ **write in** VI 发函 [fāhán]
▸ **write into** VT ▸ **to write sth into sth** [+ contract, agreement] 把某事写入某物 [bǎ mǒushì xiěrù mǒuwù]
▸ **write off** I VT 1 [+ debt, money] 注销 [zhùxiāo] **2** [+ person] 把…看作不存在 [bǎ…kàizuò bù cúnzài] **3** [+ plan, project] 取消 [qǔxiāo] **4** (BRIT) (wreck) [+ vehicle] 报废 [bàofèi] II VI ▸ **to write off for sth** [+ information] 写信索要某物 [xiě xìn suǒyào mǒuwù]; [+ goods] 函购某物 [hángòu mǒuwù]
▸ **write out** VT 1 [+ list, name and address, report] 写下 [xiěxià] **2** (copy out) 誊写 [téngxiě] **3** [+ cheque, receipt etc] 开 [kāi]
▸ **write up** VT [+ minutes, report, findings] 把…整理成文 [bǎ…zhěnglǐ chéngwén]; [+ event, visit

etc] 详细记述 [xiángxì jìshù]

write-off ['raɪtɔf] N [C] 报废物 [bàofèiwù]
writer ['raɪtə(r)] N [C] 1 (author) 作家 [zuòjiā] **2** [of report, document etc] 作者 [zuòzhě]
writing ['raɪtɪŋ] N [U] 1 (sth written) 文字 [wénzì] **2** (handwriting) 笔迹 [bǐjì] **3** (style) 文风 [wénfēng] **4** (activity) 写作 [xiězuò] ▸ **in writing** 以书面形式
writing paper N [U] 信纸 [xìnzhǐ]
written ['rɪtn] PP of write
wrong [rɔŋ] I ADJ 1 (inappropriate) [+ choice, action, decision] 不恰当的 [bù qiàdàng de]; [+ person, equipment, kind, job] 不合适的 [bù héshì de] **2** (incorrect) [+ answer, information, report] 错误的 [cuòwù de] **3** (unsatisfactory) 不好的 [bù hǎo de] **4** (morally bad) 不道德的 [bù dàodé de] II ADV (incorrectly) [do, spell etc +] 错误地 [cuòwù de] III N 1 [C] (injustice) 不公 [bùgōng] **2** [U] (evil) 邪恶 [xié'è] IV VT (treat unfairly) 冤枉 [yuānwang] ▸ **you've got it wrong** 你搞错了 [+ answer +] 是错的; [person +] (about sth) 弄错的; (in doing, saying sth) 搞错了 ▸ **to be wrong to do sth** [person +] 做某事是不对的 ▸ **it is wrong to steal, stealing is wrong** 偷窃是不道德的 ▸ **what's wrong?** 出了什么事？ ▸ **what's wrong with you?** 你怎么了？ ▸ **there's nothing wrong** 没问题 ▸ **to go wrong** [plan +] 失败; [machine +] 发生故障 ▸ **where did I go wrong?** 我错在哪里了？ ▸ **to be in the wrong** 做错
wrongful ['rɔŋful] ADJ 不正当的 [bù zhèngdàng de]
wrongly ['rɔŋli] ADV 1 (incorrectly) [answer, translate, spell, believe +] 错误地 [cuòwù de] **2** (by mistake) [diagnose, identify +] 错误地 [cuòwù de] **3** (unjustly) [accuse, imprison +] 不公正地 [bù gōngzhèng de] **4** (inappropriately) [+ dressed, arranged] 不恰当地 [bù qiàdàng de] ▸ **she supposed, wrongly, that...** 她错误地假定…
wrong number N [C] ▸ **you've got the wrong number** 你打错了 [nǐ dǎcuò le] ▸ **it was a wrong number** 这个电话号码是错的
wrote [rəut] PT of write
wrung [rʌŋ] PT, PP of wring
WWW (COMPUT) N ABBR (= World-Wide Web) 万维网 [Wànwéiwǎng]

Xx

X, x [ɛks] N [C/U] (letter) 英语的第二十四个字母

XL ABBR (= extra large) 特大号 [tèdàhào]

Xmas ['ɛksməs] N ABBR (= Christmas) 圣诞节 [Shèngdànjié]

X-ray ['ɛksreɪ] I N [C] 1 (ray) X射线 [X shèxiàn] 2 (photo) X光照片 [X guāng zhàopiàn] II VT 用X光检查 [yòng X guāng jiǎnchá] ▶ to have an X-ray 作一次X光检查 ▶ to take an X-ray of sth 对某物做X光检查

xylophone ['zaɪləfəun] N [C] 木琴 [mùqín]

Yy

一度的 [yī nián yī dù de] **2** [+ *rate, income etc*] 一年的 [yī nián de] **II** ADV **1** (*once a year*) 一年一次地 [yī nián yī cì de] **2** (*every year*) 每年地 [měinián de] ▶ **twice yearly** (*as adv*) 一年两次地; (*as adj*) 一年两次的

yearn [jəːn] VI ▶ **to yearn for sth** 渴望某事 [kěwàng mǒushì] ▶ **to yearn to do sth** 渴望做某事

yeast [jiːst] N [U] 酵母 [jiàomǔ]

yell [jɛl] **I** N [C] 叫喊 [jiàohǎn] **II** VI 叫喊 [jiàohǎn] **III** VT 叫喊着说 [jiàohǎnzhe shuō] ▶ **to let out a yell** 大喊一声 ▶ **to yell at sb** (*scold*) 对某人大喊大叫

✪ **yellow** [ˈjɛləʊ] **I** ADJ 黄色的 [huángsè de] **II** N [C/U] 黄色 [huángsè] **III** VI 变黄 [biànhuáng]

Yellow Pages® NPL ▶ **the Yellow Pages®** 黄页电话号码簿

Yemen [ˈjɛmən] N 也门 [Yěmén]

Yemeni [ˈjɛmənɪ] **I** ADJ 也门的 [Yěmén de] **II** N [C] (*person*) 也门人 [Yěménrén]

✪ **yes** [jɛs] **I** ADV **1** (*replying to question*) 是的 [shìde] **2** (*contradicting*) 不 [bù] ▷ *"That isn't possible." – "Oh yes it is!"* "那是不可能的。" – "不，是可能的！" **II** N [C] **1** (*vote*) 赞成 [zànchéng] **2** (*answer*) 是 [shì] **3** (*person*) 投赞成票者 [tóu zànchéngpiàozhě] ▶ **to say yes** 同意

✪ **yesterday** [ˈjɛstədɪ] **I** ADV 昨天 [zuótiān] ▷ *She left yesterday.* 她昨天走的。 **II** N [U] 昨天 [zuótiān] ▶ **all day yesterday** 昨天一整天 ▶ **the day before yesterday** 前天 ▶ **yesterday morning/afternoon** 昨天上午/下午

✪ **yet** [jɛt] **I** ADV **1** (*up to now*) (*with negative*) 还 [hái]; (*in questions*) 已经 [yǐjīng] ▷ *They haven't finished yet.* 他们还没完工。 ▷ *Have you written to him yet?* 你已经写信给他了吗？ **2** (*now*) (*in negatives*) 还 [hái] ▷ *He hasn't arrived yet.* 他还没来呢。 ▷ *Don't get up yet.* 先别起床。 **3** (*still*) 仍然 [réngrán] ▷ *There may yet be time.* 仍有时间。 **II** CONJ 然而 [rán'ér] ▶ **not just yet** 现在不 ▶ **the best yet** 迄今最好的 ▶ **as yet** 迄今为止 ▶ **a few days yet** 还有几天 ▶ **to have yet to do sth** 还没做某事 ▶ **yet another** 又一个 ▶ **yet again** 又一次

yew [juː] N [C] (*tree*) 紫杉 [zǐshān] **2** [U] (*wood*) 紫杉木 [zǐshānmù]

yield [jiːld] **I** N [C] **1** (AGR) 产量 [chǎnliàng] **2** (COMM) 利润 [lìrùn] **II** VT **1** (*give up*) [+ *control, responsibility*] 让出 [ràngchū] **2** (*produce*) [+ *harvest*] 出产 [chūchǎn]; [+ *results, profit*] 产生 [chǎnshēng] **III** VI **1** (*surrender*) ▶ **to yield (to sth)** 屈服 (于某事) [qūfú (yú mǒushì)] **2** [*door, lock +*] 弯曲 [wānqū] **3** (US) (*in car etc*) 让路 [rànglù] [英 = **give way**] ▶ **a yield of 5%** 5%的利润

YMCA N ABBR (= *Young Men's Christian Association*) (*hostel*) 由基督教青年会运营的供

Y, y [waɪ] N [C/U] (*letter*) 英语的第二十五个字母

Y (TEXTING) ABBR (= *why*) 为什么 [wèishénme]

yacht [jɔt] N [C] **1** (*sailing boat*) 帆船 [fānchuán] **2** (*luxury craft*) 游艇 [yóutǐng]

yachting [ˈjɔtɪŋ] N [U] 帆船驾驶运动 [fānchuán jiàshǐ yùndòng]

yard [jɑːd] N **1** [C/U] (*paved area*) 院子 [yuànzi] **2** [C] (US) (*garden*) 庭院 [tíngyuàn] [英 = **garden**] **3** (*measure*) 码, 长度单位。一码等于3英尺或0.9144米 ▶ **builder's yard** 建筑工地

yarn [jɑːn] N **1** [U] (*thread*) 纱线 [shāxiàn] **2** [C] (*inf*) (*tale*) 奇谈 [qítán]

yawn [jɔːn] **I** VI 打呵欠 [dǎ hēqiàn] **II** N [C] 呵欠 [hēqiàn]

yd ABBR (= *yard*) 码, 长度单位。一码等于3英尺或0.9144米

✪ **yeah** [jɛə] (*inf*) ADV 是的 [shìde]

✪ **year** [jɪə(r)] N [C] **1** 年 [nián] **2** (SCOL, UNIV) 学年 [xuénián] **3** (COMM) 年度 [niándù] **4** [*of wine*] 年份 [niánfèn] ▶ **in the year 2000** 在2000年 ▶ **every year** 每年 ▶ **this year** 今年 ▶ **last year** 去年 ▶ **next year** 明年 ▶ **a or per year** 每年 ▶ **all year round** 一年到头 ▶ **year in, year out** 年复一年 ▶ **he's 8 years old** 他8岁 ▶ **an eight-year-old child** 一个8岁的小孩 ▶ **I hadn't seen him for** or **in years** 我有好多年没见他了 ▶ **we lived there for years** 我们住在那儿有好多年了

yearly [ˈjɪəlɪ] **I** ADJ **1** [+ *event, meeting etc*] 一年

男子住宿的旅馆

yob [jɔb] (BRIT: inf, pej) N [c] 粗俗的男人 [cūsú de nánrén]

yoga ['jəʊgə] N [U] 瑜珈 [yújiā]

yog(h)urt ['jəʊgət] N 1 [c/U] (substance) 酸奶 [suānnǎi] 2 [c] (also: pot of yoghurt) 一盒酸奶 [yī hé suānnǎi]

yolk [jəʊk] N [c/U] 蛋黄 [dànhuáng]

⊘ you [juː] PRON 1 (singular) 你 [nǐ]; (plural) 你 们 [nǐmen] ▷ Do you know her? 你/你们认识她 吗？▷ I like you. 我喜欢你/你们。▷ I'll send you the photos when I've got them. 我拿到照片后会 寄给你/你们的。▷ I gave it to you. 我把它给 你/你们了。▷ It's for you. 是给你/你们的。2 (in generalizations) (one) 任何人 [rènhérén] ▷ You can't put metal dishes in a microwave. 金属制的碟 子不能用于微波炉。▶ you never know 谁知道

you'd [juːd] = you had, you would

you'll [juːl] = you will, you shall

⊘ young [jʌŋ] I ADJ 幼小的 [yòuxiǎo de] II the young NPL (people) 年轻人 [niánqīngrén]; (of animal) 幼仔 [yòuzǎi] ▶ a young man 一个小 伙子 ▶ a young lady 一位少女 ▶ my younger brother/sister 我的弟弟/妹妹 ▶ the younger generation 年轻一代 ▶ in my younger days 在我年轻的时候

youngster ['jʌŋstə(r)] N [c] 小孩 [xiǎohái]

⊘ your [jɔː(r)] ADJ (of one person) 你的 [nǐ de]; (of more than one person) 你们的 [nǐmen de] ▷ your house 你/你们的房子 ▷ Have you cleaned your teeth? 你/你们刷牙了吗？

请勿将 **your** 和 **you're** 混淆。**your** 是 指与正在和你谈话的人相关，或从属于 他们的某事物。Is that your brother?... Your spelling is terrible. **your** 也可用来泛 指与人有关的事物。I've heard that diets can be bad for your health. **you're** 是 you are 的缩略形式。If you're not well, you should go to bed.

you're [jʊə(r)] = you are

用法参见 **your**

yours [jɔːz] PRON (of one person) 你的 [nǐ de]; (of more than one person) 你们的 [nǐmen de] ▶ is this yours? 这是你/你们的吗？▶ a friend of yours 你/你们的一个朋友 ▶ yours sincerely/

faithfully 你真挚的/忠实的 ▶ yours (in letter) 谨上

yourself [jɔː'sɛlf] PRON 1 你自己 [nǐzìjǐ] ▷ Have you hurt yourself? 你伤到自己了吗？▷ Did you paint the room yourself? 你自己粉刷了房间？ ▷ Buy yourself something nice. 给你自己买点好东 西。▷ Be honest with yourself. 你得正视自己。 2 (emphatic) 你本人 [nǐběnrén] ▷ So you yourself live in London, do you? 那你本人住在伦敦，是吗？ 3 (you) 你 [nǐ] ▷ an intelligent person like yourself 像你一样有智慧的人 ▶ by yourself (unaided) 独立地 ▷ Did you make the cake by yourself? 你自 己一个人做了蛋糕?; (alone) 独自地 ▷ Do you live by yourself? 你独自一人住吗？

yourselves [jɔː'sɛlvz] PL PRON 1 你们自己 [nǐmen zìjǐ] ▷ Have you hurt yourselves? 你们伤到 自己了吗？▷ Did you paint the house yourselves? 你们自己粉刷了房子？▷ Buy yourselves something nice. 给你们自己买点好东西。 2 (emphatic) 你们本人 [nǐmen běnrén] ▷ So you yourselves live in London, do you? 那你们本人住在 伦敦，是吗？3 (you) 你们 [nǐmen] ▷ intelligent people like yourselves 像你们一样有智慧的人 ▶ by yourselves (unaided) 独力地 ▷ Did you make the cake by yourselves? 你们自己做了蛋糕?; (alone) 独自地

youth [juːθ] I N 1 [U] (young days) 青少年 时期 [qīngshàonián shíqī] 2 [U] (being young) 年轻 [niánqīng] 3 [c] (young man) 男青年 [nánqīngnián] II the youth NPL 青年人 [qīngniánrén] ▶ in my youth 在我的青年时代

youth club N [c] 青年俱乐部 [qīngnián jùlèbù]

youthful ['juːθfʊl] ADJ [+ appearance, enthusiasm etc] 年轻的 [niánqīng de]; [+ indiscretion] 不成 熟的 [bù chéngshú de]

youth hostel N [c] 青年招待所 [qīngnián zhāodàisuǒ]

you've [juːv] = you have

YR (TEXTING) ABBR (= your) 你的 [nǐ de]

yr ABBR (= year) 年 [nián]

YWCA N ABBR (= Young Women's Christian Association) (hostel) 由基督教青年会运营的供 女子住宿的旅馆

Zz

[美 = zipper] II VT (also: zip up) 拉…的拉链
[lā…de lāliàn]

zip code (US) N [C] 邮政编码 [yóuzhèng biānmǎ] [英 = post code]

zipper ['zɪpə(r)] (US) N [C] 拉链 [lāliàn] [英 = zip]

zit [zɪt] (inf) N [C] (pimple) 青春痘 [qīngchūndòu]

zodiac ['zəʊdɪæk] N ▶ the zodiac 黄道十二宫图 [huángdào shí'èr gōng tú]

zone [zəʊn] N [C] (area) 地带 [dìdài]

zoo [zu:] (pl zoos) N [C] 动物园 [dòngwùyuán]

zoology [zu:'ɒlədʒɪ] N [U] 动物学 [dòngwùxué]

zoom [zu:m] VI 1 ▶ to zoom past/along 疾驰而过/沿…疾驰 [jíchí ér guò/yán…jíchí] 2 ▶ to zoom in (on sth/sb) (PHOT, CINE) (对准某物/某人) 拉近镜头 [(duìzhǔn mǒuwù/mǒurén) lājìn jìngtóu]

zucchini [zu:'ki:nɪ] (pl zucchini or zucchinis) (US) N [C/U] 绿皮密生西葫芦 [lǜpí mìshéng xīhúlu] [英 = courgette]

Z, z [zɛd, US zi:] N [C/U] (letter) 英语的第二十六个字母

Zambia ['zæmbɪə] N 赞比亚 [Zànbǐyà]

Zambian ['zæmbɪən] I ADJ 赞比亚的 [Zànbǐyà de] II N [C] (person) 赞比亚人 [Zànbǐyàrén]

zeal [zi:l] N [U] 热情 [rèqíng]

zebra ['zi:brə] N [C] 斑马 [bānmǎ]

zebra crossing (BRIT) N [C] 斑马线 [bānmǎxiàn]

zero ['zɪərəʊ] (pl zero or zeroes) I N 1 [U/C] (number) 零 [líng] 2 [U] (nothing) 没有 [méiyǒu] ▷ Visibility at the city's airport came down to zero. 这个城市机场的能见度降为零。 II ADJ 为零的 [wéilíng de] ▶ 5 degrees below zero 零下5度 ▶ zero in on VT FUS [不可拆分] 瞄准 [miáozhǔn]

zest [zɛst] N 1 [U] (enthusiasm) 热忱 [rèchén] 2 [U/S] (excitement) 兴趣 [xìngqù] 3 [U] (of orange, lemon) 外皮 [wàipí] ▶ zest for life 对生命的热情

zigzag ['zɪgzæg] I N [C] 弯弯曲曲的线条 [wānwān qūqū de xiàntiáo] II VI 曲折前进 [qūzhé qiánjìn]

Zimbabwe [zɪm'bɑ:bwɪ] N 津巴布韦 [Jīnbābùwéi]

Zimbabwean [zɪm'bɑ:bwɪən] I ADJ 津巴布韦的 [Jīnbābùwéi de] II N [C] (person) 津巴布韦人 [Jīnbābùwéirén]

zinc [zɪŋk] N [U] 锌 [xīn]

zip [zɪp] I N [C] (BRIT) (fastener) 拉链 [lāliàn]

Language
in
Action

Chinese
in
Action

GREETINGS

▼ MEETING PEOPLE

- It is very important to use the appropriate form of greeting in China. As with other cultures, the way that you greet somebody will depend on whether you know them or whether they are a stranger. The most common greeting is:

  你好 (nǐ hǎo), or
  您好 (nín hǎo)

- The form 您好 (nín hǎo) is more formal and should be used when you want to show particular respect.

- Chinese people show great respect for the wisdom and experience of their elders. The senior people present will usually initiate the greetings, and you should greet the oldest, most senior person before any others.

▼ SOME TYPICAL GREETINGS

你好! (nǐ hǎo)	Hello!
嗨! (hāi)	Hi!
喂! (wèi)	Hello! (usually on the phone)
早上好! (zǎoshang hǎo)	Good morning!
早! (zǎo)	Morning!
最近身体怎么样? (zùijìn shēntǐ zěnmeyàng)	
	How have you been?
还不错，谢谢 (hái bùcuò, xièxie)	
	Fine, thanks.
好久不见!最近还好吗? (hǎojiǔ bù jiàn! zuìjìn hái hǎo ma?)	
	Long time no see! How are you doing?
很好，谢谢，你怎么样? (hěn hǎo, xièxie, nǐ zěnmeyàng)	
	Very well, thank you, and you?
挺好的，多谢。(tǐng hǎo de, duōxiè)	
	Fine, thanks.
棒极了! (bàng jí le)	Great!
一般。(yībān)	So-so.

▼ CHINESE NAMES

- Chinese family names are placed first, followed by the given name. For instance, in the name "Zhao Li," "Zhao" is the family name, "Li" the given name. Family names usually consist of one syllable, whereas given names can have either one or two syllables.

- Chinese people call their close friends and family members by their given names. For example, "Ma Wenli" may be addressed by close friends as "Wenli."

- In formal situations you should address Chinese people by their family name or full name and the appropriate courtesy title. Unlike English, professional, social, and family titles always follow the name:

  > Mr. Liu would be 刘先生 (Liú xiānsheng)
  >
  > Mr. Li Nan 李楠先生 (Lǐ Nán xiānsheng)
  >
  > Mrs. Liu 刘夫人 (Liú fūrén)
  >
  > Miss Liu 刘小姐 (Liú xiǎojiě)
  >
  > Ms. Liu 刘女士 (Liú nǚshì)
  >
  > Dr. Ma would be 马医生 (Mǎ yīshēng)
  >
  > Professor Xu would be 徐教授 (Xú jiàoshòu)

- Chinese people will often address people by their surname followed by their job title, for example

  > 叶主任 (Yè zhǔrèn) Director Ye
  >
  > 林老师 (Lín lǎoshī) Teacher Lin

- Most Chinese women continue using their maiden names even after marriage, but they may indicate their marital status by using 太太 (tàitai) or 夫人 (fūrén) with their maiden name.

- 小姐 (xiǎojiě) is a polite and common form of address for a woman. An older woman can be addressed as 大姐 (dàjiě).

- If you want to address a group of people formally – for example, at a meeting – you say 女士们先生们 (nǚshìmen xiānshengmen) meaning 'Ladies and Gentlemen' (or just 女士们 ('Ladies') or 先生们 ('Gentlemen') if the group is not mixed).

- When you are not sure about someone's name or title, you should address him or her as 先生 (xiānsheng) (Sir) or 女士 (nǚshì) (Madam) or 小姐 (xiǎojiě) (Miss).

▼ INTRODUCTIONS

让我把你介绍给我的朋友们。 (ràng wǒ bǎ nǐ jièshào gěi wǒ de péngyoumen) *Let me introduce you to my friends.*

我想让你认识一下我的丈夫。 (wǒ xiǎng ràng nǐ rènshi yīxià wǒ de zhàngfu) *I'd like you to meet my husband.*

请允许我介绍一下到场的嘉宾。 (qǐng yǔnxǔ wǒ jièshào yīxià dàochǎng de jiābīn) *Please allow me to introduce these distinguished guests.*

这是珍妮特。 (zhè shì Zhēnnítè) *This is Janet.*

In response:

很高兴见到您。 (hěn gāoxìng jiàndào nín) *Pleased to meet you.*

嗨，你好。 (hāi, nǐ hǎo) *Hi, how are you doing?*

您好。(nín hǎo) *How do you do?*

- If you want to attract the attention of someone you do not know – for example, in the street or in a shop – you say 劳驾 (láojià).

▼ PARTING

- The most common way to say goodbye to someone is 再见(zàijiàn). Other alternatives are 回见 (huíjiàn) and 再会 (zàihuì).

再见！(zàijiàn) *Goodbye!*
再会！(zàihuì) *Bye!*
7点见。(qīdiǎn jiàn) *See you at seven.*
晚安！(wǎn'ān) *Good night!*
明天见！(míngtiān jiàn) *See you tomorrow!*
星期一见！(xīngqīyī jiàn) *See you on Monday!*
"回见！" "好，再会" (huíjiàn – hǎo, zàihuì) *'See you later.' – 'Okay, bye.'*

▼ BUSINESS CARDS

- Business/name cards are frequently used in business circles in China and will almost always be exchanged when meeting someone for the first time on business.

- Cards should be held in both hands when they are being offered or received. When receiving another person's card, you should take the time to look at it attentively before putting it away.

寰宇进出口有限责任公司

王长海　总经理

地址：北京市和平路15号
邮编：100082
电话：+8610 64446666
传真：+8610 64446688
E-mail: wangchanghai@huanyu.com

Huan Yu Import & Export Co. Ltd.

Wang Changhai　General Manager

Address: No. 15 Heping Road, Beijing, China
Zip Code: 100082
Tel: +8610 64446666
Fax: +8610 64446688
E-mail: wangchanghai@huanyu.com

TELEPHONE

▼ MAKING A PHONE CALL

- When Chinese people make a phone call, they ask for the person they wish to speak to by name. It is not the Chinese caller's habit to give their own name first when making or receiving a call.

- When answering the telephone the standard response upon picking up the receiver is 喂 (wèi).

- When giving telephone numbers, Chinese speakers normally read out the numbers one by one so that:

  020 7900 0283 would be read:

  零二零　七九零零　零二八三
  líng'èrlíng qijiǔlínglíng líng'èrbāsān

- When making a phone call, you might want to say:

喂？(wèi) *Hello?*
请问…在吗？(qǐngwèn…zài ma) *Could I speak to … please?*
是…吗？(shì…ma) *Is that …?*
我怎么拨外线电话？(wǒ zěnme bō wàixiàn diànhuà) *How do I make an outside call?*
…的区号是多少？(…de qūhào shì duōshao) *What is the code for … ?*
我5分钟后打回来。(wǒ wǔ fēnzhōng hòu dǎ huílái) *I'll call back in 5 minutes.*
他回来时，可否让他给我回电话？(tā huílái shí, kěfǒu ràng tā gěi wǒ huí diànhuà)
Could you ask him to call me when he gets back?
对不起，我拨错号了。(duìbuqǐ,wǒ bōcuò hào le) *Sorry, I must have dialled the wrong number.*
电话掉线了。(diànhuà diàoxiàn le) *We were cut off.*
线路很不清楚。(xiànlù hěn bù qīngchu) *This is a very bad line.*

- You might hear:

请讲。(qǐng jiǎng) *Speaking.*
请问您是哪位？(qǐngwèn nín shì nǎ wèi) *Who's speaking?*
请问您找哪位？(qǐngwèn nín zhǎo nǎ wèi) *Who would you like to speak to?*
请别挂断。(qǐng bié guàduàn) *Please hold (the line).*
没人接听。(méi rén jiētīng) *There's no reply.*
电话占线。(diànhuà zhànxiàn) *The line is engaged (Brit) or busy (US).*
请问您是哪位？(qǐngwèn nín shì nǎ wèi) *Who shall I say is calling?*
您要留言吗？(nín yào liúyán ma) *Would you like to leave a message?*

TELEPHONE

▼ AN EXAMPLE CONVERSATION

您好，这里是北京饭店。
Hello, Beijing Hotel.

请转二零一六房间分机，我找张先生。
Please could you put me through to room number 2016? I'd like to speak to Mr. Zhang.

好的，请稍等。
Hold on one moment, please.

他不在，您能帮我给他捎个话吗？
He doesn't seem to be in at the moment. Can I leave a message?

当然可以。
Of course.

请让他给约翰·史密斯回电话，电话号码是零零四四二零七三零六三八九二。
Could you ask him to call John Smith back? The phone number is 00442073063892.

好的。
Okay.

▼ USEFUL TELEPHONE VOCABULARY

打电话 (dǎ diànhuà) *make a phone call*
电话号码 (diànhuà hàomǎ) *phone number*
分机号码 (fēnjī hàomǎ) *extension number*
市话 (shìhuà) *local call*
长途电话 (chángtú diànhuà) *national call*
国际长途电话 (guójì chángtú diànhuà) *international call*

CORRESPONDENCE

▼ PERSONAL LETTERS

● Starting and ending a personal letter

Opening lines:

亲爱的妈妈: *Dear Mum*

小强: *Dear Xiao Qiang*

Closing lines:

祝身体健康! *Take care!*

祝万事如意! *All the best*

● Sample letter

> ***i*** Note the use of a colon after the recipient's name.

婷婷:

　　好久没给你写信了。近来还好吗? 最近工作忙吗? 你是否还在上夜校?

　　我工作还很忙, 天天加班。但老板对我很好, 晚上经常开车顺路送我回家。过两天公司放假, 准备和同事一起去旅游。

　　先写到这儿吧, 有空给你打电话。

　　祝
万事如意!

毛毛

2004年2月4日

> ***i*** The date should be written after your signature.

● Useful expressions

真高兴收到你的来信。 *It was lovely to hear from you.*

对不起, 没能及时给你回信, 只因… *Sorry I didn't reply sooner but …*

代我向…问好。 *Give my regards to …*

东东谨祝一切安好。 *Dong Dong sends his best wishes.*

盼早日回信。 *Looking forward to hearing from you.*

CORRESPONDENCE

▼ FORMAL LETTERS

● Starting and ending a formal letter

Opening lines:

致启者: *Dear Sir or Madam*

致有关人: *To whom it may concern*

Closing lines:

敬上 *Regards*

此致 敬礼! *Yours sincerely*

● Sample letter

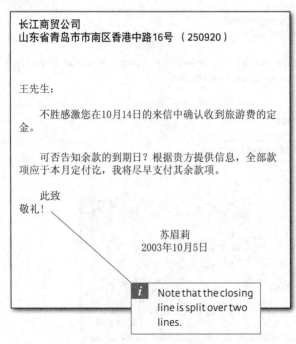

长江商贸公司
山东省青岛市市南区香港中路16号 （250920）

王先生:

　　不胜感激您在10月14日的来信中确认收到旅游费的定金。

　　可否告知余款的到期日？根据贵方提供信息，全部款项应于本月定付讫，我将尽早支付其余款项。

　　此致
敬礼!

苏眉莉
2003年10月5日

> *i* Note that the closing line is split over two lines.

● Useful expressions

现答复您⋯的来信。*In reply to your letter of …*
有关⋯ *With reference to …*
收到您⋯来信不胜感激。*Thank you for your letter of …*
我们荣幸地通知您⋯ *We are pleased to inform you that …*
我们很遗憾地通知您⋯ *We regret to inform you that …*
为⋯致信给您。*I am writing to you to …*
如需详情，尽请与我联系。*If you require any further information, please do not hesitate to contact me.*
切盼回复。*I look forward to hearing from you.*

▼ **ADDRESSING AN ENVELOPE IN CHINESE**

• You should start in the upper left hand corner with the addressee's post code. The address is written in the middle of the envelope, followed by the name of the addressee.

• Note that the address is written in the order:
> province, city
> street, house number
> addressee's name

• The sender's address and name, followed by their postcode, should be written in the lower right hand corner of the envelope.

• **Sample envelope**

i   Addressee's postcode

310000

浙江 杭州
定安路99号3幢1单元201室
张鹏收

北京长安路37号 王露
100018

i   Sender's address, name and postcode

CORRESPONDENCE

▼ E-MAIL

● E-mail is becoming very popular in China, but it is important to check that the person you are writing to actually uses it. Many Chinese executives and officials have an e-mail address but do not check their mail very regularly.

● Business e-mails should be brief but not too familiar or chatty.

● **Sample e-mail**

◀ 回复	▶▶ 转发	✎ 写信	⬚⬛ 收件箱	▭ 收信

收件人： lili@cmail.com.cn
抄送：
主题：拓展产品系列讨论会

王经理：

　　根据近期的市场调研，我公司的彩电产品系列目前有些滞后于市场的发展需要，为提高企业竞争力，建议召开一次讨论会，共同商讨、制定相应措施。

　　会议时间暂定为2004年6月2日星期三下午2:00，地点在公司二楼小会议室。请通知相关人员准时参加。

　　如有问题，请尽早回复。

　　此致

敬礼!

张 力

收件人：	To:
抄送：	Cc:
主题：	Subject:

▼ APPLYING FOR A JOB

● When applying for a job in China, the general principles of covering letters, CVs and interview etiquette should be followed.

● Your CV should be no longer than three pages.

▼ SAMPLE COVERING LETTER

尊敬的人事部经理：

　　从2004年5月22日的《中国青年报》招聘版上获悉贵公司国际部需要一名英语专业应届毕业生。我深感自己符合招聘广告上的各项要求，特申请这一职位。

　　我将于2004年6月获得北京技术大学文科硕士学位，并于7月份毕业，所学专业为商务英语。我本科阶段的专业为科技英语。多年对英语的专门研究使自己具有扎实的英语基本功，顺利通过了英语专业四级和八级考试，并且在TOEFL和GRE考试中也获得了较高的分数。

　　在校期间，除了认真完成学业外还积极参加各种实践、实习活动。我分别在惠普（中国）公司和中国技术进出口公司进行了实习，在工作过程中学以致用，进一步提高了英语水平，锻炼了处理实际问题的能力，增强了团队配合的意识。

　　读研究生之前，我在青岛贸促会全职工作的一年中，参加了多次贸易谈判，并参与组织了两届大型国际贸易洽商会，工作得到了领导和同事的一致肯定。

　　贵公司在外贸界很有声誉，欣闻你们的招聘信息，我郑重地递交简历一份（随信附上），如蒙给予面试机会，将不胜感激。

联系地址：北京技术大学外贸英语系 （100008）
手机：13503321245

　　此致

敬礼!

李　明
2004年5月23日

▼ **SAMPLE CV**

个人简历

求职意向: 外贸公司、外企、国家机关及其他能发挥个人潜力的机构
姓名: 李明 性别: 男
出生年月: 1979年9月1日 健康状况: 良好
毕业院校: 北京技术大学 专业: 外贸英语
电子邮件: liming@yahoo.com.cn 联系电话: 010-87656666,
通信地址: 北京技术大学外贸英语系 13503321245
邮编: 100008

教育背景:

2001年9月—2004年7月 北京技术大学 外贸英语专业 文科硕士学位
1997年9月—2000年7月 北京技术大学 科技英语专业 文科学士学位

外语水平:

英语
* 基本技能: 听、说、读、写、口笔译能力
* 标准测试: 国家英语专业四、八级;TOEFL;GRE
法语
* 基本技能: 听、说、读、写、翻译能力

计算机水平:

编程、操作应用系统、网络、数据库

获奖情况:

1999年 北京市"优秀大学生"称号
1997年9月—2000年7月 一等奖学金

实践与实习:

2001年7月—2001年8月 惠普(中国)公司口、笔译工作
2003年5月—2004年5月 中国技术进出口公司

工作经历:

2000年7月—2001年8月 山东省青岛市贸易促进委员会

个性特点:

性格开朗,脚踏实地,乐于助人,善与人沟通

最喜欢的话:

有志者, 事竟成

> *i* CVs often include a proverb as an expression of a salient feature of the applicant's personality.

证明人:

王成 硕士论文导师 010-68997543
田刚 山东省青岛市贸易促进委员会主任 0532-6789432

NUMBERS

▼ CARDINAL NUMBERS

0	零 (líng)		24	二十四 (èrshísì)
1	一 (yī)		25	二十五 (èrshíwǔ)
2	二 (èr)		30	三十 (sānshí)
3	三 (sān)		31	三十一 (sānshíyī)
4	四 (sì)		40	四十 (sìshí)
5	五 (wǔ)		50	五十 (wǔshí)
6	六 (liù)		60	六十 (liùshí)
7	七 (qī)		70	七十 (qīshí)
8	八 (bā)		80	八十 (bāshí)
9	九 (jiǔ)		90	九十 (jiǔshí)
10	十 (shí)		100	一百 (yībǎi)
11	十一 (shíyī)		101	一百零一
12	十二 (shí'èr)			(yībǎi líng yī)
13	十三 (shísān)		212	二百一十二
14	十四 (shísì)			(èrbǎi yīshí'èr)
15	十五 (shíwǔ)		1,000	一千 (yīqiān)
16	十六 (shíliù)		1,001	一千零一
17	十七 (shíqī)			(yīqiān líng yī)
18	十八 (shíbā)		2,500	二千五百
19	十九 (shíjiǔ)			(èrqiān wǔbǎi)
20	二十 (èrshí)		100,000	十万 (shíwàn)
21	二十一 (èrshíyī)		1,000,000	一百万 (yībǎi wàn)
22	二十二 (èrshí'èr)		1,000,000,000	十亿 (shíyì)
23	二十三 (èrshísān)			

▼ ORDINAL NUMBERS

1st	第一 (dì-yī)		15th	第十五 (dì-shíwǔ)
2nd	第二 (dì-èr)		20th	第二十 (dì-èrshí)
3rd	第三 (dì-sān)		50th	第五十 (dì-wǔshí)
4th	第四 (dì-sì)		100th	第一百 (dì-yībǎi)
5th	第五 (dì-wǔ)		101st	第一百零一
6th	第六 (dì-liù)			(dì-yībǎi líng yī)
7th	第七 (dì-qī)		110th	第一百一十
8th	第八 (dì-bā)			(dì yībǎi yīshí)
9th	第九 (dì-jiǔ)		1,000th	第一千 (dì-yīqián)
10th	第十 (dì-shí)			

▼ FRACTIONS AND PERCENTAGES

½	二分之一 (èr fēn zhī yī)		0.5	零点五 (líng diǎn wǔ)
⅓	三分之一 (sān fēn zhī yī)		3.5	三点五 (sān diǎn wǔ)
¼	四分之一 (sì fēn zhī yī)		6.89	六点八九 (liù diǎn bājiǔ)
⅔	三分之二 (sān fēn zhī èr)		10%	百分之十 (bǎi fēn zhī shí)
			100%	百分之百 (bǎi fēn zhī bǎi)

DATE

▼ DAYS OF THE WEEK

星期一 (xīngqīyī)	Monday
星期二 (xīngqī'èr)	Tuesday
星期三 (xīngqīsān)	Wednesday
星期四 (xīngqīsì)	Thursday
星期五 (xīngqīwǔ)	Friday
星期六 (xīngqīliù)	Saturday
星期日 (xīngqīrì)	Sunday

▼ MONTHS OF THE YEAR

一月 (yīyuè)	January
二月 (èryuè)	February
三月 (sānyuè)	March
四月 (sìyuè)	April
五月 (wǔyuè)	May
六月 (liùyuè)	June
七月 (qīyuè)	July
八月 (bāyuè)	August
九月 (jiǔyuè)	September
十月 (shíyuè)	October
十一月 (shíyīyuè)	November
十二月 (shí'èryuè)	December

▼ TALKING ABOUT THE DATE

今天几号?	What's the date today?
今天星期几?	What day is it today?
今天是2004年1月20日。	It's the 20th of January 2004.
在20日	on 20th
1月1日	the first of January
在2月	in February
在2005年	in 2005
在十九世纪	in the nineteenth century
在九十年代	in the nineties

▼ WHEN?

今天	today
昨天	yesterday
明天	tomorrow
前天	the day before yesterday
后天	the day after tomorrow
昨天上午/下午/晚上	yesterday morning/afternoon/evening
明天上午/下午/晚上	tomorrow morning/afternoon/evening
第二天	the next day
每个星期六	every Saturday
下周日	next Sunday
上周二	last Tuesday

TIME

▼ WHAT TIME IS IT?

几点了? (jǐ diǎn le?)

1点
(yī diǎn)

1点15分 / 1点一刻
(yī diǎn shíwǔ fēn / yī diǎn yīkè)

1点25分
(yī diǎn èrshíwǔ fēn)

1点30分 / 1点半
(yī diǎn sānshí fēn / yī diǎn
bàn)

1点45分 / 2点差一刻
(yī diǎn sìshíwǔ fēn /
liǎng diǎn chà yī kè)

1点50分 / 2点差10分
(yī diǎn wǔshí fēn /
liǎng diǎn chà shí fēn)

上午9点 / 晚上9点
(shàngwǔ jiǔ diǎn /
wǎnshang jiǔ diǎn)

中午12点 / 凌晨零点
(zhōngwǔ shí'èr diǎn /
língchén líng diǎn)

▼ USEFUL EXPRESSIONS

几点开始? What time does it start?
20分钟后 in twenty minutes
大约在8点钟 at around eight o'clock
上午 in the morning
下午 in the afternoon
傍晚 in the evening

English
in
Action

▼ 姓名和称谓

姓名

在说英语的国家中，姓名是由父母取的 *first name*（名字)和父母双方或一方的 *surname*（姓氏)组成。*forename* 即 *first name*。

> ℹ️ 许多人还有 *middle name*（中名)。*middle name* 也是由父母取的，通常用缩略形式，而不用全称。*middle name* 用缩略形式在美国尤为常见：*John F Kennedy*。*Christian name*（教名)是指基督徒给孩子取的名字。

姓名缩写

initials（姓名缩写)是由某人的 *first name, middle name* 和 *surname* 的第一个字母的大写形式组成。例如，如果某人的全名是 *Elizabeth Margaret White*，她的姓名缩写即为 *EMW*。在某些商务和银行业环境中，她可以自称或被称为：*E.M. White*。
作者的姓名通常用 *initials*：*J.K. Rowling, E.M. Forster*。

先生、夫人等

如果某人不是你的朋友，你可以用头衔加姓氏礼貌地称呼他。*Mr*（先生)用于男士的姓氏前。已婚女士被称为 *Mrs*（夫人)，未婚女士使用 *Miss*（小姐)或 *Ms*（女士)。

> *Mr Nichols can see you now.*（用于办公室会话)

人们有时也用这种比较礼貌的方式称呼比自己年长的人。

> *We'd better let Mrs Townsend know.*
> *Perhaps you should invite Mr Thomson as well.*

> ℹ️ 过去，已婚的女性总是改用夫姓。如今，一些女性婚后仍延用自己的姓氏。如果不清楚一位女士是否已婚，可使用称呼 *Ms*。一些较年轻的女性更倾向于使用 *Ms*，而不是 *Mrs* 或 *Miss*，但是较年长的女性则不喜欢使用 *Ms* 这一称呼。

知名人士

一般只用姓氏来称呼作家、作曲家、艺术家和其他知名人士。

> *the works of Shakespeare*
> *the paintings of Van Gogh*

昵称

人们常用 *nickname*，名字的非正式形式，来称呼他人，在会话中更是如此。许多名字都有约定俗成的简短形式。例如，如果某人的名字是 *James*，人们可以称他为 *Jamie*, *Jim* 或 *Jimmy*。

日常交流

▼ 称呼他人

称呼不认识的人

- 如果你想引起某个不认识的人的注意 —— 比如，在大街上或在商店里 —— 通常说 *Excuse me*。

  Excuse me. You've dropped your scarf.
  Excuse me. I think I'm next.

- 在现代英语中，*Mr*，*Mrs*，*Miss* 和 *Ms* 作为头衔，只用在姓氏前，而不能单独使用。*gentleman* 或 *lady*，*sir* 或 *madam* 也都不能单独用来称呼不认识的人。*sir* 或 *madam* 通常是商店中的工作人员用于招呼顾客时才用的礼貌性称呼。

> *i* 在正式的场合称呼一群人 —— 例如，开会时 —— 可用 *ladies and gentlemen*。如果是性别单一的一群人，可以只称呼 *ladies* 或 *gentlemen*。
> *Good evening, ladies and gentlemen.*

称呼认识的人

- 如果你知道对方的姓氏，你可用头衔（通常是 *Mr*，*Mrs* 或 *Miss*）加姓氏称呼他们。这种用法相当正式。初次见面，或在电话中与你不认识的人交谈时，你会使用这种称呼方式。

  Thank you, Mr Jones.
  Goodbye, Dr Kirk

- 在英国、美国、澳大利亚等国的工作场所中，人们通常直呼名字，甚至对老板也是如此。在学校里，学生通常用 *Mr*，*Mrs* 或 *Miss* 加上姓氏称呼老师。在许多日常会话中，除非你想特别指明说话的对象，否则根本不用提及对方的姓名。

  What do you think, John?
  Are you going to the meeting with the new Finance Director?

> ⚠ 在 *Mr*，*Mrs* 和 *Miss* 后，只能加姓氏，而绝对不能加名。

▼ 问候

与人打招呼

- 与人打招呼通常用 hello。这个词既非太正式，又不会太随便，适用于大多数场合。在 hello 的后面，通常加上对方的名字或寒暄的话。

  'Hello, Tina.' — 'Hello. How are you today?'

  Hello, John. Had a good day?

- hi 或 hiya是更为随便的问候方式，在年轻人中以及美式英语中尤为常用。

  Hiya, Tommy. How are you doing?

- 若要以正式方式问候他人，所用的词要视一天里的具体时间而定。

  中午12点钟之前说 good morning。

  Good morning, Mr Wright. How are you today?

  中午12点钟和6点钟之间说 good afternoon，6点之后人们说 good evening。

  Good afternoon. Could I speak to Ms Duff, please?

  Good evening. I'd like a table for four, please.

在拨打正式电话，以及与政府官员、商界人士等会面时，通常使用这些问候形式。

> ⚠ 只有晚间与人告别，或当自己或他人上床睡觉之前，才能说 good night。它不能用来问候别人。
> good day 在英式英语中是一种已经过时，并且相当正式的说法，但在美式英语和澳大利亚英语中仍较为常见。

- 如果某人说 How are you?，你可以简单地回答 Very well, thank you. 或 Fine, thanks.。你也可以礼貌地反问一声 How are you?，或更随便些 And you?。

  'Hello, John. How are you?' — 'Fine, thanks, Mark. And you?'

- 在见面问候或告别时显得热情而有礼貌，人们有时说 Nice to see you.。

  'Hello, it's nice to see you again. How are you?' – 'Nice to see you too, Mr Bates.'

日常交流

特别的日子

- 在某人的生日见到其人时，可以说 *Happy Birthday!* 或 *Many happy returns!*。

- 在圣诞节见到别人时，可以说 *Merry Christmas!* 或 *Happy Christmas!*。

- 在新年，你可以祝愿人们 *Happy New Year!*。

分别

- 与人分别时，说 *goodbye*。这种表达方式有点正式。

  'Goodbye, John,' Miss Saunders said.

- *bye* 是更常用的告别方式，而且比较随便。

  See you about seven. Bye.

- *bye-bye* 的语气更加随便，它用于关系密切的亲戚和朋友之间，以及向小孩子道别时。

  Bye-bye, dear. See you tomorrow.

> **i** 道晚安时，可以用 *goodnight* 或 *night*。
> *Well, I must be going. Night, John.*
> *I'm off to bed. Goodnight, everyone.*

- 如果你认为很快能再次见到对方，可以说 *See you later.*。

  'See you later.' – 'Okay, bye.'
  See you on Monday.

- 许多讲美式英语的人会用 *have a nice day* 向他们不太熟识的人道别。例如，在商店或酒店中工作的人员会对顾客这样说。

> ⚠ 在现代英语中，*good morning*，*good afternoon* 和 *good evening* 不用于告别。

> **i** 在正式场合，比如商务会议，人们通常用握手以示问候或道别。在不太正式的场合下表示问候或道别，男士们也会握手，或者，互相轻拍后背或肩膀，而女士们则常常亲吻女性或男性亲友。在问候或道别时，你也可以只用上述表达方式而不使用任何肢体动作，如握手、拍肩或是亲吻。

▼ 自我介绍和介绍他人

自我介绍

● 与陌生人初次见面，在自我介绍时，可以告诉对方你的姓名或介绍你是谁。你需要先说 hello 或其他客套的话。

> 'Hello. I'm Harry,' said the boy.
> 'I don't think we've met, have we? Are you visiting?' – 'Yes, I'm Peter Taylor.'

● 如果想显得正式些，则说 May I introduce myself?。

> May I introduce myself? I'm Dr Anderson.

> **i** 初次见面说 How do you do?，是一种极为正式，并且已经过时的表达方式。正确的回答也应是 How do you do?。
> 'I'm Nigel Jessop. How do you do?' – 'How do you do? I'm Alison Vere.'

介绍他人

● 在介绍从未谋面的人相互认识时，说 This is ...。介绍时，使用何种姓名形式可以视场合的正式程度而定（见第2页）。

> This is Shirley , Mr McKay. Shirley, this is Mr McKay.

● 如果需要正式些，则说 I'd like to introduce ...。

> Mr Anderson, I'd like to introduce my wife.

● 比较随意的介绍某人的方式是 I don't think you know ..., do you?。

> 'I don't think you know Ann, do you?' – ' No, I don't think we've met. How are you?'

⚠ 用手指指着别人介绍是很无礼的行为。但是，可以用手指指着物品或指示方向。

对介绍的应答

● 当你被介绍给对方后，你们双方都互道 hello。

> 'Francis, this is James.' – 'Hello, Francis. How are you?'

● 如果双方都很年轻，而且不是在很正式的场合，可以说 hi。

> 'Jan, this is my boyfriend Jeff.' – 'Hi, Jeff.'

▼ 邀请

邀请某人做某事

● 通常，礼貌地邀请某人做某事，应说 *Would you like to ...?*。

> *Would you like to come to my party on Saturday?*
> *Well, would you like to comment on that, Tessa?* (在会议或讨论中)

● 另一种礼貌的邀请形式是，祈使句与 *please* 连用。这种形式多由处于主导位置的一方使用。

> *Please help yourself to a drink.*
> *Sit down, please.*

● 也可用 *How would you like to ...?* 或 *Why don't you ...?* 间接地邀请某人，或用以 *how about* 开头的问句邀请。

> *How would you like to come and work for me?*
> *Why don't you come to the States with us in November?*
> *How about coming to stay for a few days?*
> *How about some lunch?*

> *i* 如果应邀到某人家中做客，通常要带小礼物，比如鲜花或蛋糕。如被邀请就餐，大多数人会顺便带一瓶酒。主人通常会当面打开礼物。

回应邀请

● 如果接受邀请，就说 *thank you*。如果更加随便的话，就说声 *thanks*。

> *'You could borrow our tent if you'd like.' – 'Thank you. I'll come round and pick it up some time.'*

也可加一句 *Yes, I'd love to.* 或 *I'd like that very much.*。

> *'Won't you join me for lunch?' – 'Thanks, I'd like that very much.'*

● 如果拒绝邀请，不愿拜访某人或随某人去某地，则说 *I'm sorry, I can't.*。如果想解释原因，则用 *I'm afraid ...* 或 *I'd like to but ...*，再加上原因。

> *'Can you come and spend the day with me on Sunday?' – 'Oh, I'm sorry. I can't.'*
> *'We're having a party on Saturday. Can you come?' – 'I'm afraid I'm busy.'*
> *'Would you like to stay for dinner?' – 'I'd like to but I can't tonight.'*

▼ 感谢他人

表示感谢

● 如果别人刚刚为你做了某事，或送给你某物，表示感谢的常用方式是说 thank you，或更随意地说声 thanks。

> 'Don't worry. I've given you a good reference.' – 'Thank you, Mr Dillon.'
> 'There's your receipt.' – 'Thanks.' (在商店)

● 人们常常加上 very much 以加强语气。

> 'Here you are.' – 'Thank you very much.'

你也可以说 Thanks a lot. (但不能说 Thank you a lot. 或 Thanks lots.)。

> 'I'll ring you tomorrow morning.' – 'OK. Thanks a lot.'

● 如果需要解释为何感谢对方，则说 Thank you for … 或 Thanks for …。

> Thank you for the earrings, Dad.
> Thanks for helping out.

在信中感谢某人（见第19页），一般都说 Thank you for …。

> Dear Madam, Thank you for your letter of 5 June.

在正式的商务信函中，可以用 I am grateful for …。

> I am grateful for your prompt reply to my request.

如果是给朋友的信，则用 Thanks for …。

> Thanks for writing.

> ℹ️ 你会听到一些讲英式英语的人说 cheers 或 ta 表示感谢，这是非正式的表达方式。

如果某人请你吃东西，表示拒绝时，可以说 No, thank you. 或 No, thanks. (不能只说 Thank you.)。

> 'Would you like a coffee?' – 'No, thank you.'

如何回答感谢

● 如果某人因你帮忙而表示感谢，则应回答 That's all right. 或 That's OK.。

> 'Thank you, Charles.' – 'That's all right, David.'

如果想显得既礼貌又友好，可以说 It's a pleasure. 或 Pleasure.。

> 'Thank you very much for talking to us about your research.' – 'It's a pleasure.'

▼ 道歉

致歉

● 如果打扰了某人或麻烦了某人，有多种道歉方式。最常用的是 sorry 或 I'm sorry。

> *'Stop that, you're giving me a headache.' – 'Sorry.'*
> *Sorry I'm late.*

可以在 I'm sorry 中加上副词 very，so，terribly 或 extremely，加强语势。

> *I'm very sorry if I worried you.*
> *I'm terribly sorry but I have to leave.*

> **i** 当不小心做了某事，例如踩了某人的脚，可以说 sorry 或 I'm sorry。讲美式英语的人则说 excuse me。

● 当打搅了某人或打断了某人的工作时，用 Excuse me, I'm sorry to disturb you.。这是礼貌的道歉方式。

> *Excuse me for disturbing you at home.*
> *I'm sorry to disturb you but I need your signature.*

● 如果想请某人让一下路，或想同陌生人讲话时，可以用 excuse me。一些说美式英语的人则会说 pardon me。

> *Excuse me, but is there a good restaurant near here?*
> *Excuse me, do you mind if I squeeze past you?*
> *Pardon me, Sergeant. I wonder if you'd do me a favor?* (美)

● 如果因需要做某事而不得不离开片刻，例如在商务环境中，或与不太熟识的人在一起时，也可以说 Excuse me。

> *Excuse me for a moment. I have to make a telephone call.*

> **i** 如果做了令人尴尬或失礼的事时，譬如打饱嗝、打嗝、打喷嚏或吃东西时发出声音，应该道歉。人们通常会说 excuse me 或 I beg your pardon。

接受道歉

● 接受道歉通常有固定的表达形式，例如 That's okay.，Don't worry about it.，或 It doesn't matter.。

> *'I'm sorry.' – 'That's okay.'*
> *'I apologize for what I said.' – 'Don't worry about it.'*
> *'I'm sorry to ring so late.' – 'I'm still up. It doesn't matter.'*

▼ 请某人重复所说过的话

● 让某人重复所说的话时，通常用固定的简短表达方式，例如Sorry?，I'm sorry?，或 Pardon?。这些都是非正式的说法。

> 'Have you seen the guide book anywhere?'
> 'Sorry?'
> 'The guide book.' (英)

在美式英语中，通常用 Excuse me? 或 Pardon me?。

> 'How old is she?'
> 'Pardon me?'
> 'I said how old is she?' (美)

● 也可用 wh- 开头的特殊疑问词，核对对方所说过的部分内容。

> 'Can I speak to Nick, please?'
> 'Who?'
> 'Nick.'
> 'We're going to Spain in April.'
> 'Where?'
> 'Spain.'

> ⚠ 当与不太熟识的人说话时 —— 例如，在电话中 —— 使用稍长一些的表达形式，譬如 I'm sorry, I didn't quite catch that. 或 I'm sorry, would you mind repeating that, please?。
>
> > 'What about tomorrow at three?'
> > 'I'm sorry, would you mind repeating that, please?'
> > 'I said, what about meeting tomorrow at three?'

ENGLISH IN ACTION

10

▼ 许可

请求许可

● *Can I ...?* 用于请求许可做某事。

> *Can I put the heating on? I'm cold.*

Could I ...? 更礼貌些。若要显得愈加礼貌，例如在电话中或在商务环境中，则加上 *please*。

> *Could I stay at your place for a bit, Rob?*
> *Good afternoon. Could I speak to Mr Duff, please?*

● 用 *Would it be all right if I ...?* 或 *Would it be all right to ...?* 一类的表达形式，比较间接地请求许可。

> *Would it be all right if I used your phone?*
> *Would it be all right to take one of these brochures?*

在不太正式的情况下，可以说 *Is it okay if I ...?*

> *Is it okay if I smoke?*

更加礼貌的方式是说 *Do you mind if I ...?* 或 *Would you mind if I ...?*。

> *Do you mind if we speak English?*
> *Would you mind if I just asked you a few questions?*

> **i** 在英国和美国，许多人不喜欢别人抽烟，所以当在某人家中做客或与他人外出时，在抽烟前先征求对方许可是非常礼貌的做法。

准许某人的请求

● 在非正式的场合，可以只说 *OK* 或 *all right*。

> '*Could I have a word with you, please?*' – '*OK.*'

● *sure* 语气稍微强些，且用于美式英语。

> '*Can I go with you?*' – '*Sure.*'

● *of course* 和 *by all means* 比较正式，语气也较强。

> '*Could I make a telephone call?*' – '*Of course.*'
> '*Can I come too?*' – '*By all means.*'

拒绝请求

● 拒绝某人请求最常用的方式是用 *Sorry*，*I'm sorry* 或 *I'm afraid not* 等，然后解释原因。

> '*Could I see him for a few minutes?*' – '*I'm sorry, you can't. He's very ill.*'

11

▼ 同意和不同意

寻求赞同

● 反问句可以用来询问某人是否同意自己的说法。使用反问句，通常是期望他人同意自己的观点。

> *That's an extremely interesting point, isn't it?*
> *The film was really good, wasn't it, Andy?*
> *Property in London is quite expensive, isn't it?*

● 在表示喜欢或不喜欢某事，或认为某事是对是错后，可以用反问句 *don't you?* 寻求对方的赞同。代词 *you* 重读。

> *I love these shoes, don't YOU?*
> *I think it would be best if I left, don't YOU?*

表示同意

● 表明赞同某人或某事最简单的方式，是说 *yes*。人们常常用 *mm* 来代替 *yes*。

> *'You like jazz, don't you?' – 'Yes.'*
> *'She's a bit strange, isn't she?' – 'Mm.'*

可以在 *yes* 后面加上适当的动词形式。

> *'I was really rude to you at the party.' – 'Yes, you were.'*

也可以在 *yes* 后面跟一个反问句。

> *'That car's fantastic!' – 'Yes, it is, isn't it?'*

⚠ 如果对某个带有否定词的陈述表示同意，应说 *no* 而不是 *yes*。
> *'She's not a very nice person.' – 'No.'*

● 在表示同意某事是事实时, 可以用以下表达方式 *That's right.*, *That's true.* 或 *True.*。

> *'I'll have more to spend then.' – 'Yes, that's true.'*

> **i** *I agree* 是相当正式的表达方式。
> > *'The whole thing's a disaster.' – 'I agree.'*

● 当某人说出他所喜欢的事物或他的想法时，可以用 *So do I.* 或 *I do too.* 来表明自己同意他的观点。

> *'I find that amazing.' – 'So do I.'*
> *'I love champagne.' – 'Yes, I do too.'*

如果对某人带有否定的观点表示同意时，则可以说 *Neither do I.* 或 *I don't either.*。

> *'I don't like him.' – 'Neither do I.'*

- 可以用 *absolutely* 这样的表达方式来表示完全同意，语气强烈。

    'I thought her performance was brilliant.' – 'Absolutely.'

    如果表示同意，但并不完全同意某人的观点时，可以说 *I suppose so.* 或 *I suppose not.*。美式英语用 *I guess so.*。

    'Some of these places haven't changed a bit.' – 'I suppose not.' (英)

> *i* 你会发现，说英语国家的人们常运用面部表情、手势或其他肢体动作，来强调同意或不同意，或发表看法。其中最常见的是，上下点头表示同意或允许某人做某事，左右摇头表示不同意或不允许做某事。

表示不同意

- 人们通常避免说 *no*，不直接表示完全不赞同，以此显得比较礼貌。人们用 *I don't think so.* 和 *Not really.* 等表达方式使不赞同的话听上去更柔和些。

    'You'll change your mind one day.' – 'Well, I don't think so.'
    'That sort of holiday must be really expensive.' – 'Well, not really.'

- 人们常常先说 *yes* 或 *I see what you mean*，然后再用 *but* 引出表示反对的观点。

    'It's a very clever book.' – 'Yes, perhaps, but I didn't like it.'

- 在正式场合，可以使用以下任何一种表达方式：

'She was a brilliant prime minister.' – 'I totally disagree.'
'University education can divide families.' – 'I can't go along with that.'
'We ought to be asking the teachers what they think.' – 'With respect, shouldn't you be asking the students too?'

▼ 反应

有几种对听到和看到的事作出反应的方式表达。

感叹句

- 感叹句常用来表达对某事的反应。

    Wonderful!
    Oh dear!
    That's awful!

- 有时用 *how* 和 *what* 引出感叹句。*how* 一般与形容词连用，并且形容词后没有其他句子成分。

    'He never rang, even though he said he would.' – 'How strange!'

what 用于名词前。如果用单数可数名词，则必须在 *what* 后面加不定冠词 *a*(或 *an*)。

    'I can't come on Saturday. I've got to work.' – 'What a shame!'
    What an awful thing to say!

13

表示惊奇或感兴趣

● 表示惊奇可以用 *Really?*，或其他简短的固定表达方式，譬如*good heavens*。

> *'It only takes 35 minutes to get into town from my house.' – 'Really?'*
> *Good heavens, is that the time?*

⚠ *Good God* 和 *My God* 是相当常见的表达方式，语气强烈。因为这可能会冒犯信仰宗教的人，所以应该慎用。

● 反问句可用于表示惊奇或感兴趣。

> *'He goes swimming every day.' – 'Does he?'*

● *that's* ... 或 *how* ... 可与形容词连用，例如 *strange* 或*interesting*，用于表示惊奇或感兴趣。

> *'He said he hated the place.' – 'How strange! I wonder why.'*
> *'They both say they saw a light in the sky.' – 'How interesting.'*

表示愉快

● 可以用 *That's great.* 或 *That's wonderful.* 等表示对某个情形或某人所说的话感到高兴。

> *'I've booked the flights.' – 'Oh, that's great.'*

● 你也可单独使用形容词，例如*Wonderful.*。

> *'We can give you an idea of what the final price would be.' – 'Wonderful.'*

表示如释重负

● *Oh good.* 或 *That's all right then.* 用于表达听到某事感到松了口气。

> *'I think he'll understand.' – 'Oh good.'*
> *'Are the earrings all right?' – 'They're perfect.' – 'Good, that's all right then.'*

● 也可以说 *That's a relief.* 或*What a relief!*。

> *He didn't seem to notice. – 'Well, that's a relief.'*

● *thank God* 或 *thank goodness* 之类的表达方式可用于表示如释重负。

> *Thank God you're safe!*
> *'I've found your passport.' – 'Thank goodness for that.'*

表示恼怒

● 可以用 *Oh no!* 来表示恼怒。也可以说 *That's a nuisance.* 或 *What a nuisance.*。

> *'I don't know if we'll make it to the airport in time.' – 'Oh no!'*
> *'I'm sorry. He's just left.' – 'What a nuisance!'*

⚠ 你可能会听到有人用骂人的话表示恼怒，但你不能这么说，因为，听上去特别粗鲁无礼。

表示失望或忧虑

- 可以用 *Oh dear.*，*That's/What a pity.* 或 *That's/What a shame.* 来表达失望、烦乱之情。

  Oh dear. I wonder where they are.

  'I'm leaving New York tomorrow.' – 'That's a shame.'

- 如果非常心烦，则说 *Oh no!*。

  'John's had a nasty accident.' – 'Oh no! What happened?'

表示同情

- 当某人告诉你发生在他们身上不好的事情时，可以说 *Oh dear.*。

  'It was pouring with rain.' – 'Oh dear.'

  也可以用 *how* 加一个恰当的形容词。

  'We couldn't even see the stage.' – 'Oh, how annoying.'

  也可以说 *What a pity.* 或 *What a shame.*。

  'The journey took us four hours.' – 'What a shame.'

- *I'm sorry to hear that.* 显得比较正式。

  'I was ill last week.' – 'I'm sorry to hear that.'

- 如果所发生的事情非常严重，可以说 *I'm so sorry.* 或 *That's terrible.*。

  'You remember my sister? Well, she died last month.' – 'I'm so sorry.'

  'I've just lost my job.' – 'That's terrible.'

  如果某人未能做成某事，你可以说 *Bad luck.* 或 *Hard luck.*，暗示失败并非他们的过错。

  'I failed my driving test again.' – 'Oh, bad luck.'

ENGLISH IN ACTION

信件和电话

▼ 写信该如何开头和结尾

给公司或组织机构的信件

称谓	结束语
Dear Sir	
Dear Madam	Yours faithfully (英)
Dear Sir or Madam	Yours truly (美)
Dear Sirs (英)/Gentlemen (美)	

如果是非常正式的信件，或不知道收信人的姓名，对男士用 Dear Sir，对女士则用 Dear Madam。如果不确定收信人的性别，写 Dear Sir or Madam 是最保险的。如果是写给公司而不是个人时，在英式英语中用 Dear Sirs，在美式英语中用 Gentlemen。

写给已知姓名的个人正式信件

称谓	结束语
Dear Ms Roberts	Yours sincerely (英)
Dear Dr Jones	Sincerely yours/Yours truly (美)
Dear Professor Honeyford	

结尾可用下列表达方式，显得不那么正式：

Yours
Kind regards
(With) best wishes

给朋友或熟人的信件

称谓	结束语
Dear Jeremy	All the best
Dear Aunt Jane	Love (from)
Dear Granny	Lots of love (from)
Hi Josh	All my love

男士给男士写信时，不常用 Love，All my love 和 Lots of love，而多用 Yours，Best wishes 或 All the best 一类的表达方式。

电子邮件

尽管有时也需要用电子邮件发送正式信函，但是，当人们写电子邮件时，普遍比写信要随意。信件的开头和结尾方式同样适用于电子邮件。

信件和电话

> *i* 人们在给关系亲密的朋友或男/女朋友写信或电子邮件时，往往在落款后加几个 X。X代表吻。

▼ 英国地址

Ms S Wilkins
10 Osprey Close
Guildford
Surrey
GL4 2PX ◄

> *i* 邮政编码写在城市名称或地区名称的下面。

Nicola Thornbury
64 Newbridge Gardens
Bristol
BS7 4BT

▼ 美国地址

Mark Smith
968 Michigan St
Seattle WA 98060-1024 ◄
USA

> *i* 邮政编码写在城市名称和州名之后，州名用缩略形式。

- 寄往海外的信件通常要写发件人的地址。发件人的地址写在信封的背面，并在地址前加注 sender 或 from。

- 称呼通常由收信人的头衔、名字的首字母及姓氏组成：

Ms S Wilkins
Dr. P Smith

- 如果是非正式书信，可以只写收信人的名和姓：

Sarah Wilkins

- 如果收信人是已婚的夫妇，通常只写男方名字的首字母：

Mr and Mrs G T Black

▼ 给朋友的电子邮件

| ◀ reply | ▶▶ forward | ✎ compose | 📭 inbox | 📧 get mail |

To:	gemma@net.co.uk
From:	gordon@onemo.net
Subject:	Concert next week
cc:	
bcc:	

> ℹ 电子邮件 (gemma@net.co.uk) 的英文读法为:
> gemma **at** net **dot** co **dot** uk

Hi Gemma

I've just bought the new album by 'The Roads', and it's brilliant! I've got a spare ticket to a concert they're giving in Edinburgh next Wednesday evening, so I hope you can make it.

See you soon!

Gordon

▼ 商业电子信函

| ◀ reply | ▶▶ forward | ✎ compose | 📭 inbox | 📧 get mail |

| To:kevin.morrison@unt.com |
| From:charles.stimpson@unt.com |
| Subject:Budget meeting |
| cc: |
| bcc: |

Following on from our phone conversation this morning, the Budget meeting will now be held on Wednesday at 10 a.m. in the South Meeting Room. I hope that you can attend.

Charles

ENGLISH IN ACTION

重点词组

To	收件人	Send	发送
From	发件人	Forward	转发
Subject	主题	Reply	答复发件人
Cc	抄送	Compose	撰写
Bcc	密件抄送	Delete	删除
Attachment	附件		

▼ 感谢信（英式）

> **i** 在非正式信件中，地址和日期写在右上角，或只写日期。参见第45页日期的写法。

41 Mallard Crescent
Leeds
LS6 9BR

► 2 January 2003

Dear Tom and Lucy

Thank you for the lovely Christmas presents you sent me. The scarf is beautiful and the book is just what I wanted. As you know, J K Rowling is my favourite author.

I hear you're off to Spain soon. I'm so envious! I haven't got any holidays planned, but I'm going to London next weekend to see my aunt and uncle.

Thanks again for the presents, and have a great time in Spain. Don't forget to send me a postcard!

Lots of love

Carolyn

ENGLISH IN ACTION

重点词组

可以用下列方式开头：
It was lovely to hear from you.
Thanks for your letter.
Sorry I haven't written sooner.
It was great to see you last weekend/week/Monday.

可以用下列方式结尾：
Write soon.
Look forward to seeing you soon.
Give my regards to Sally.
Julia sends you a big hug.

▼ 给笔友的信

14 Glebe Avenue
Bristol
BR6 7AL

14 August 2003

Dear Xiao Ming

I'm so excited to have a Chinese pen pal! I'm hoping to learn lots about your country and the way you live from your letters.

I thought I would start by telling you a few things about myself. I'm 14 years old and live with my mum and dad and my little sister, Jenny, in a city in the south of England. Our house has three bedrooms and a big garden. We have two cats who are quite old now and sleep all the time. My best friend, Jack, lives next door.

My school isn't far from the house, so I can walk there when it isn't raining. My favourite subjects are languages and geography. I'd like to learn to speak a few words in Chinese. Can you teach me something?

What sorts of things do you like doing in your spare time? I like playing on the computer and watching football. Mum says I should get more exercise!

Please write back soon and tell me all about yourself and your family. I can't wait to hear from you!

All the best

Nick

● 重点词组

I'm hoping to …
… a few things about myself/you …
What sorts of things … ?
I can't wait to hear from you

1386 Pine Boulevard
Los Angeles, California
20015

May 25, 2003

> **i** 以英式风格写信的人，在*Dear*...后面加逗号或不加任何标点。以美式风格写信的人，则在*Dear*...后面加冒号。参见第2页有关姓名和头衔的内容。

Dear Julia:

How are things? I'm sorry I haven't written earlier but I've been so busy moving into my new apartment.

It's my birthday on June 14 and I'm having a party to celebrate. Can you come? It starts at 7 p.m. and will probably end around midnight. There'll be food but please bring a bottle! If you'd like to stay the night, I have plenty of room and it will give us a chance to catch up on each other's news.

I hope you'll be able to come and look forward to hearing from you soon.

Love

Marie

▼ 酒店预订函(英式)

26 Guanghua Road
Chaoyang District
Beijing 100027
China

Mrs Elaine Hudson
Manager
Poppywell Cottage
Devon
DV3 9SP

23rd June 2003

Dear Mrs Hudson

> **i** 在商务信函的右上角，写上发信人自己的地址，但不要写发信人的姓名。日期紧跟在收信人地址的下一行。在信纸的左上角，通常在日期的下一行，写上收信人的姓名和 / 或职务头衔。如果使用带信头的信纸，日期写在收信人地址的上一行上或下一行，或写在信纸的右上角。参见第45页有关日期的写法。

My sister stayed with you last year and has recommended your guest house very highly.

I would like to reserve a room for one week from 18th–24th August. I would be very grateful if you would let me know how much this would be for two adults and two children and whether you have a room free between these dates.

Yours sincerely
Ming Li

▼ 投诉信（美式）

323 Florida Grove Rd
Hopelawn
New Jersey
NJ 08851

Railroad Inc.
43 Abbeyhill Drive
Hopelawn
New Jersey
NJ 08952

November 27, 2003

Dear Sir or Madam:

I traveled from Atlantic City to New York on one of your trains last Thursday November 20 and am writing to let you know that I am very dissatisfied with the service you are providing.

The train was not only one hour late leaving Atlantic City it lost a further 30 minutes en route. The heating did not appear to be working and there was no restaurant car. I feel that your customers are paying very high prices for tickets to travel on your trains but are receiving a very unsatisfactory level of service. I have been very reluctant to take my car into the city and have no wish to add to the general congestion and pollution but you can be sure that I will be driving from now on.

Yours truly

Michael Pentangeli

▼ 英式工作申请函

CURRICULUM VITAE

Name: **Sarah Williamson**
Address:11 North Street, Barnton, NE6 2BT
Telephone: 01294 476230
E-mail: sarah@metalcomp.co.uk
Date of birth: 2 February 1970
Nationality: British

Qualifications

BA (Hons) in Business Studies (2.1), University of Newby,1991–1995
3 A-levels: Economics (A), German (B), Mathematics (C)
7 GCSEs: English Language, Mathematics, Physics, Biology, French, German, Geography

Employment

1997–present: *Sales and Marketing Executive*, Metal Company plc, Barnton
1995–1997:   *Marketing Assistant*, Metal Company plc

Other skills

- Computer literate (Word for Windows, Excel)
- Good working knowledge of German
- Full, clean driving licence

Interests

- Travel (have travelled extensively throughout Europe and North America)
- Sailing
- Running marathons (New York 1999, Glasgow 2002)

Referees

Mrs Susan Beattie
Sales and Marketing Director
Metal Company plc
Barnton
NE4 3KL

Dr John Findlay
Department of Business Studies
University of Newby
Newby
NE13 2RR

▼ 工作申请书（英式）

11 North Street
Barnton
NE6 2BT

Director of Human Resources
Clifton Manufacturing Ltd
Firebrick House
Clifton
MK45 6RB

17 January 2003

Dear Sir or Madam

Re: Job Reference 685Z

With reference to your advertisement in the Guardian of 16 January, I wish to apply for the position of Marketing Manager in your company.

I am currently employed as a Sales and Marketing Executive for the Metal Company in Barnton, where my role is maintaining and developing links with our customers within the UK and producing material for marketing purposes.

I am interested in this position as it offers an opportunity to apply my sales and marketing skills in a new and challenging direction. I enclose my curriculum vitae for your consideration. Please do not hesitate to contact me if you require any further details.

Yours faithfully

Sarah Williamson

▼ 美式工作申请函

RÉSUMÉ

Name: Lisa Brown
Address: 110 West 92nd Street
           New York
           New York 10025
Telephone: 1-212-873-4150
E-mail: lisa.brown@skynet.com

Education
University of Pennsylvania, 1992–1994
Master of Arts in Business

Cornell University, 1987–1991
Bachelor of Arts in History, Magna Cum Laude

Employment
1997–present: General Sportswear Company, New York, New York: *Export Sales Co-ordinator:*
Sell the entire range of sportswear products to all key German accounts. Negotiate terms with all German customers, and conduct regular sales trips to Germany.

1994–1997: Brooklyn Candy Company, Brooklyn, New York: *Sales Representative:*
Sold the entire range of products to all key national and French accounts. Increased domestic sales by 24% in the fiscal year 1997.

Skills
• Fluent German. Working knowledge of French, Spanish, and Italian.
• Negotiating.
• Selling.
• Familiarity with many computer programs.
• Typing at 65 words per minute.

References
References available upon request.

▼ 工作申请书（美式）

110 West 92nd Street
New York, New York
10025

Mr. John Smith
Personnel Director
Thomas International Corporation
53 Madison Avenue
New York, New York
10016

January 17, 2003

Dear Mr. Smith

With reference to your advertisement in the New York Times of January 25, I wish to apply for the position of Export Sales Manager in your company.

I am currently employed as an Export Sales Co-ordinator with General Sportswear Company, have almost ten years of experience in sales and marketing, and am responsible for all sales to the German market. I speak fluent German, and have a working knowledge of French, Spanish, and Italian. I feel that my skills and experience would be great assets for your company in this position.

I enclose my résumé for your reference, and am available for an interview at any time. Please feel free to contact me if you require any further information.

Thank you for your time and consideration.

Sincerely

Lisa Brown

ENGLISH IN ACTION

信件和电话

▼ 打电话

接通

● 下列表达可以帮助你找到正确的电话号码：

What is the dialling code for Liverpool?（英式）
What is the area code for Los Angeles?（美式）
What is the number for directory enquiries?（英式）
What is the number for directory assistance?（美式）
I want to make a reverse-charge call to London.（英式）
I want to make a collect call to London.（美式）
How do I get an outside line?

开始通话

接听电话

● 接听电话时，通常先说 *hello*，或使用比较正式的问候方式（参见第4页）。如果当时你在工作，可以给出自己的姓名，所在部门或公司的名称，或给出电话号码或分机号码。参见第41页，如何报电话号码。

Hello?
Hello, Li Xin speaking.
Good morning, Lotus Blossom Hotel. Can I help you?
Eight six nine two three five seven. Hello?

如何问候接听电话的人

● 当对方接听电话并致以问候后，打电话的人通常也要问候对方，然后说 *It's …* 或 *This is …* 以表明自己的身份。

Oh, hello. It's Mei Rong here.
Hello. This is Rong.

结束通话

● 可以用第5页中任何一种告别方式结束通话。也可以说 *Speak to you soon.* 或 *Thanks for ringing.*。

在办公室

要求接通某人

● 如果你知道联络对方的姓名或分机号码，或想转接到某个特定部门，可以使用下列的短语。

Hello. Could I speak to Susan, please?
Hello. Is Paul there, please?
Could you put me through to Dr Henderson, please?
Can I have extension 5443, please?

● 如果你认为自己知道接听电话的人是谁，则可以问 *Is that …?*。

如果正是其人，对方则回答 *Speaking.*。

> '*Hello. Is that Emma?*' – '*Speaking.*'

接线员或秘书可能会说…

● 如果是与接线员或秘书通话，他们可能会使用以下表达方式：

> *Who shall I say is calling?*
> *Hold the line, please.*
> *Hold on, I'll see if she's in.*
> *I'll just get him.*
> *One moment, please.*
> *I'm putting you through now.*
> *Dr Jackson is on another line. Do you want to hold?*
> *There's no reply.*
> *I'm sorry. Mr Green isn't here at the moment.*
> *Would you like to leave a message?*

留言

● 如果想找的人不在，你可以留言，告知晚些时候会再打，或者让别人转告，请他回电话。

> *Could I leave a message, please?*
> *I'll call back in half an hour.*
> *Would you ask him to call me when he gets back?*

通话故障

● 如果无法接通想拨打的号码，可以用下列惯用语解释问题所在：

> *I can't get through.*
> *Their phone is out of order.*
> *I can't get a signal here.*
> *I must have dialled the wrong number.*
> *We were cut off.*

● 也有可能无法听清对方的话：

> *We've got a crossed line.*
> *This is a very bad line.*
> *The line is breaking up.*

录音留言

● 录音留言在英国和美国非常普遍，在大型公司或组织里就更加常见。无人接听电话时就会听到：

> *Your call is in a queue and will be answered shortly.*
> *All our operatives (美) are busy at the moment. Please hold the line.*
> *Please replace the handset and try again.*
> *The number you are calling is engaged (英)/busy (美). Please try again later.*

The number you have dialled has not been recognized.
Please hold the line while we try to connect you.

● 人们通常也会在家中的电话答录机上录下个人留言，以下是告知拨打电话的人何时开始录音的标准方式：

Please speak after the tone (英)/*beep* (美).

▼ 手机短信

随着手机的出现, 一种新的短信 "语言" 诞生了, 并且因其迅捷、有趣, 尤其受到年轻人的青睐。它的特点是, 根据类似的发音, 采用简短的拼写方式：例如, *U* 代表 *you*, *R* 代表 *are*, *d8* 代表 *date* 以及 *2nite* 代表 *tonight*。新的表达方式总是不断地出现。

2 = to	**SUM1** = someone
2DAY = today	**THX** = thanks
2MORO = tomorrow	**TTFN** = ta ta *or* bye for now
2NITE = tonight	**TTYL** = talk to you later
2U = to you	**TXT** = text
4 = for	**U** = you
B = be	**V** = very
B4 = before	**WAN2** = want to
COZ = because	**WIV** = with
CU = see you	**XLNT** = excellent
D8 = date	**WKND** = weekend
EZ = easy	**W/O** = without
GR8 = great	**WUD** = what are you doing?
H8 = hate	**Y** = why
L8R = later	**YR** = your
LOL = laugh out loud/lots of love	
LV = love	
M8 = mate	
MSG = message	
NE = any	
NE1 = anyone	
OIC = oh I see	
PLS = please	
PPL = people	
R = are	
RN = right now	
RU = are you	
RUOK = are you OK?	
S/O = someone	
S/TH = something	

THX 4 THE MSG.
XLNT NEWS! CU AT
THE WKND THEN.
LOL JAMES

ENGLISH IN ACTION

▼ 大写字母

● 大写字母用于句子的第一个单词, 或某人所说的原话的第一个单词:

We went to the theatre yesterday.
Then our friends said, "We're going."

● 下列单词的第一个字母也必须大写:

– 人名或机构名:

Miss Helen Perkins from Price Waterhouse

– 书名、电影名和戏剧名 (但其间常用短词不用大写, 比如of, the 和 and):

Johnny Depp's new film, Pirates of the Caribbean

– 地名:

He was born in India in 1941.
I'm going to Edinburgh tomorrow.

– 日期、月份和节日名称:

The trial continues on Monday.
It was mid-December and she was going home for Christmas.

– 表示来自或在某个特定国家或地方的人、物、事件的名词和形容词:

the Germans and the British   a French poet
the Californian earthquake

– 作为商标的产品的名称:

a secondhand Volkswagen
a new Hoover

– 用于某人名字前的头衔:

President Bush
King Henry II

– 代词I:

I thought I was alone.

● 下列大写字母和小写字母均可:

– 表示方向的单词, 例如 north 和 southeast:

I'm from the north/North of England.

– 表示年代的单词:

music from the seventies/Seventies

– 不带人名的头衔:

a great prime minister/Prime Minister

拼写和标点

▼ 表示所属关系的撇号

● 撇号(')用于表示某物属于某人。它加在单数名词、代词或人名后,其后跟s。

my friend's house   *someone's house*   *Helen's house*

> ⚠️ ● 在以 s 结尾的名词的复数形式后加撇号。
>
> *our friends' houses (= the houses of our friends)*
>
> ● 撇号不用于构成物主代词: *yours, hers, ours* 和 *theirs*。也不用于构成名词复数: *apples, cars*。
>
> ● 以英语为母语的人也会被这些规则弄糊涂。在果蔬店或市场小摊上,你经常可以看到诸如 *tomatoe's* 或 *orange's* 这样的拼写,而不是 *tomatoes* 或 *oranges*。有时这种错误的用法被幽默地称为"果蔬店老板的撇号"。

▼ 动词缩写形式中的撇号

● 撇号用于单词的缩写形式中,表示一个或多个字母已经被省略。它常用于 *be, have, shall, will* 和 *would* 等词的缩写形式前:

I'm terribly sorry. (= I am)
I'll come round about seven. (= I will)
It's really hot today. (= It is)

● 当 not 与前面的动词连写时,撇号也用于 *n* 和 *t* 之间:

I can't see a thing. (= I cannot)
I don't like him very much. (= I do not)
I wouldn't do that if I were you. (= I would not)

● 你有时会发现撇号用在表示年份或年代的两个数字前:

souvenirs from the '68 campaign (= 1968)
the clothes we used to wear in the '60s and '70s (= 1960s and 1970s)

▼ 何时用连字符

● 连字符(-)用于连接构成一个形容词的两个或多个单词之间。只有当形容词位于被它所形容的名词前时,才使用连字符。当形容词位于名词之后时,连字符省略。

a twentieth-century painter
a step-by-step guide to giving up smoking
a stained-glass window
a painter from the twentieth century
the stained glass above the door

● 一些表示家庭成员的常用名词,书写时使用连字符:

mother-in-law   father-in-law   parents-in-law

sister-in-law brother-in-law

如果一个名词是由多个词构成, 而且第一部分只有一个字母, 也应使用连字符:

X-ray T-shirt

- 从21到99的数字, 书写时通常带有连字符, 不以 a 开头的分数也用连字符:

  sixty-two people
  one-third of those interviewed
  three-quarters of the company's senior management

- 前缀用于以大写字母开头的单词前时, 往往后加连字符:

  a wave of anti-British feeling
  anti-American protesters

- 连字符用于表示有关联的两个国家或团体的形容词之间, 或表示往返于两地之间:

  Swedish-Norwegian relations
  the New York-Montreal train

> **i**　在印刷文本中, 当一个完整的单词在一行中写不下, 而得断开写到下一行时, 在断词的行末使用连字符, 表示该单词转至下一行。

⚠️　许多由多个词构成的名词、动词和形容词, 书写时使用连字符。为确定单词的拼写, 你应该查阅字典英语部分的相关词条:

　　non-smoker push-up self-confidence
　　absent-minded short-lived

▼ 基本拼写规则

这些基本拼写规则旨在帮助你拼写新词或难词。

双写辅音字

- 以元音开头的词尾, 例如 -ance, -ence, -ing, -er 或 -ed, 加在以单元音加一个辅音结尾的词后时, 如果重音落在单词的最后一个音节上, 或单词只有一个音节时, 双写辅音。(在下列例子中, 重读音节用横线标出)

  *ad<u>mit</u> + ance = admi**tt**ance*
  *be<u>gin</u> + ing = begi**nn**ing*
  *stop + ed = sto**pp**ed*
  *run + er = ru**nn**er*

- 以元音开头的词尾加在以一个元音 +l 或 +p 结尾的词后, 不论重音落在哪个音节, 通常双写 l 或 p。

  *cancel + ation = cance**ll**ation*
  *dial + ing = dia**ll**ing*
  *ful<u>fil</u> + ed = fulfi**ll**ed*

kidnap + *er* = *kidna**pp**er*
slip + *ing* = *sli**pp**ing*

⚠ 词尾 *-ful* 总是拼写成一个 l，而词尾 *-fully* 则总是拼写成两个 l。

    grateful – gratefully
    careful – carefully
    beautiful – beautifully

以不发音的 e 结尾的词

● 当以元音开头的词尾，例如 *-ible, -able, -ing, -ed, -er* 或 *-ity*，加在以不发音的 e 结尾的词后时，省略 e。

    response + *ible* = *responsible*
    value + *able* = *valuable*
    fascinate + *ing* = *fascinating*
    secure + *ity* = *security*
    fame + *ous* = *famous*
    nice + *est* = *nicest*

⚠ 当以元音开头的词尾加在以 *-ce* 或 *-ge* 结尾的词后时，保留 e。这是为了保持 c 或 g 仍发清音。

    notice + *able* = *noti**ce**able*
    change + *able* = *chan**ge**able*
    outrage + *ous* = *outra**geo**us*

● 在英语中，许多副词以 *-ly* 结尾。如果 *-ly* 加在以辅音字母加 *-le* 结尾的形容词后，形容词词末的 *-e* 省略。

    gentle + *ly* = *gently*
    idle + *ly* = *idly*
    subtle + *ly* = *subtly*

在以 –y 结尾的词后加词尾

● 当词尾加在以辅音 *-y* 结尾的词后时，y 通常变成 i：

    carry + *es* = *carries*
    early + *er* = *earlier*
    lovely + *est* = *loveliest*
    beauty + *ful* = *beautiful*
    crazy + *ly* = *crazily*

ENGLISH IN ACTION

⚠ 但是, 加 -ing 时, y 不变成 i 。

> *carry + ing = carrying*
> *try + ing = trying*

像 *dry* 和 *shy* 这样的单音节形容词, 结尾的 y 通常不变。

> *dry + ness = dryness*
> *shy + ly = shyly*

以 –y 结尾的名词复数

● 以辅音 + y 结尾的单词的复数, 先变 y 为 i 再加 -es :

> *story + es = stories*
> *quality + es = qualities*
> *spy + es = spies*

● 以一个元音 + y 结尾的单词, 其复数通过加 -s 构成:

> *donkey + s = donkeys*
> *holiday + s = holidays*
> *boy + s = boys*

以 –s, -x, -z, -sh 或 –ch 结尾的单词

以 -s, -x, -z, -sh, 或 -ch 结尾的名词, 其复数通过加 -es 构成。以这些字母或字母组合结尾的动词, 其第三人称单数形式也同样由加 -es 构成。

名 词	动 词
bus + es = buses	*fuss + es = fusses*
mass + es = masses	*pass + es = passes*
fox + es = foxes	*mix + es = mixes*
buzz + es = buzzes	*buzz + es = buzzes*
rash + es = rashes	*diminish + es = diminishes*
match + es = matches	*reach + es = reaches*

以 –c 结尾的单词

● 当以 e 或 i 开头的词尾加在以 c 结尾的单词后时, c 后加一个 k, 以保持 c 仍发浊音:

> *mimic + k + ed = mimicked*
> *picnic + k + ing = picnicking*

- 以 *-ic* 结尾的形容词, 其副词形式是加 *-ally* 而不是 *-ly* :

  artistic – artistically
  automatic – automatically
  specific – specifically

> *i* 词尾 *-ally* 的发音同 *-ly*。

以 **-ous/-ary** 结尾的形容词

- 英语中, 许多形容词以 *-ous* 或 *-ary* 结尾。在英式英语中, 当 *-ous* 或 *-ary* 加在以 *-our* 结尾的单词后时, *-our* 变成 *-or*。

  glamour + ous = glamorous
  honour + ary = honorary
  humour + ous = humorous

-ie- 或 -ei-?

- 有时很难记住发音 /iː/ 的字母排列顺序。基本规则是, i 在 e 之前, 但当 i 和 e 的组合在 c 之后时, i 在 e 之后, 但也有一些例外:

  i 在 e 之前 。

  believe field piece relief thief

  e 在 i 之前

  ceiling conceited deceive receipt receive

▼ 难拼写的单词

下面是许多人认为很难拼写的单词列表:

  accommodation(英)/*accommodations*(美)
  address
  alcohol
  autumn
  awkward
  beautiful
  committee
  confident
  disappointment
  doubt
  embarrass
  foreign

government
handkerchief
independent
island
lightning
necessary
occasion
opportunity
precede
proceed
professor
pronunciation
psychiatrist
recommend
sandwich
science
sign
succeed
suspicious
tomorrow
vegetable
vehicle
Wednesday

ENGLISH IN ACTION

▼ 英式英语和美式英语的拼写差异

英式英语和美式英语的拼写，有一些非常常见的区别，多数情况下可以通过规则掌握。最重要的规则列出如下：

-our 和 -or

英式英语中以 *-our* 结尾的单词在美式英语中拼作 *-or*。

英式英语	美式英语
behaviour	*behavior*
flavour	*flavor*
neighbour	*neighbor*

-re 和 -er

英式英语中以 *-re* 结尾的单词在美式英语中拼作 *-er*。

英式英语	美式英语
centre	*center*
litre	*liter*
theatre	*theater*

-ae-/-oe- 和 -e-

某些英式英语中含有 -ae- 或 -oe- 的单词在美式英语中只拼作一个 e。

英式英语	美式英语
anaesthetic	*anesthetic*
diarrhoea	*diarrhea*
manoeuvre	*maneuver*

-oul- 和 -ol-

● 英式英语中带有 -oul 拼写的单词在美式英语中拼作 -ol。

英式英语	美式英语
mould	*mold*
moult	*molt*
smoulder	*smolder*

双写辅音

● 在美式英语中, 当一个词尾加在双音节单词后, 而该双音节单词的最后一个音节不重读时, 不双写 l。

	英式英语	美式英语
cancel + ed	*cancelled*	*canceled*
jewel + er	*jeweller*	*jeweler*
travel + ing	*travelling*	*traveling*

● 一些单词在英式英语中含有双辅音但在美式英语中是单辅音。

英式英语	美式英语
carburettor	*carburetor*
jewellery	*jewelry*
programme	*program*
tranquillize	*tranquilize*
woollen	*woolen*

⚠ 若最后一个音节重读, 不论在英国英语还是美国英语中, 最后的辅音都要双写。

	英式英语	美式英语
admit + ed	*admitted*	*admitted*
admit + ing	*admitting*	*admitting*

有些动词, 例如 *appal, distil, enrol* 和 *fulfil*, 在英式英语中, 其基本形式和带 -s 的形式只有一个单辅音, 但在美式英语中是双辅音。

英式英语	美式英语
appal	*appall*
appals	*appalls*

-iz- 和 –is-

●英语中的许多动词, 例如 *criticize – criticise* 和 *organize – organise*, 以及由它们派生的名词, 例如 *organization – organisation*, 可以拼写成 -iz- 或 -is-。英式英语中, 两种拼法都是正确的, 但在美式英语中, -iz- 是惟一正确的拼写形式。

英式英语	美式英语
apologize apologise	*apologize*
emphasize emphasise	*emphasize*
recognize recognise	*recognize*

●在英式英语中以 -yse 结尾的动词, 在美式英语中拼作 -yze。

英式英语	美式英语
analyse	*analyze*
paralyse	*paralyze*

i 为避免麻烦, 你可以全部使用 -ze- 形式, 但下列单词是例外, 它们必须拼作 -is-。

advertise	*disguise*	*revise*
advise	*exercise*	*supervise*
comprise	*franchise*	*surprise*
despise	*improvise*	*televise*
devise	*promise*	

重要单词的不同拼写形式

英式英语	美式英语
analogue	*analog*
axe	*ax*
catalogue	*catalog*
cheque	*check*
defence	*defense*
dialogue	*dialog*
disk	*disc*
grey	*gray*

英式英语	美式英语
licence（名词）	*license*（名词）
（动词都拼作 *license*）	
offence	*offense*
practise（动词）	*practice*（动词）
（名词都拼作 *practice*）	
pretence	*pretense*
pyjamas	*pajamas*
sceptical	*skeptical*
speciality	*specialty*
storey	*story*
tyre	*tire*

ENGLISH IN ACTION

数字

▼ 基数

下列的数字称作基数。根据此表，你可以知道如何构成其他数字。数字可用作形容词（用于名词前，有时也称作限定词）或代词（用于代替名词）。

0	nought(英)/naught(美), zero, nothing, oh	100	one hundred/a hundred
1	one	101	one hundred and one/
2	two		a hundred and one
3	three	102	one hundred and two/
4	four		a hundred and two
5	five	110	one hundred and ten/
6	six		a hundred and ten
7	seven	120	one hundred and twenty/
8	eight		a hundred and twenty
9	nine	200	two hundred
10	ten	300	three hundred
11	eleven	400	four hundred
12	twelve	500	five hundred
13	thirteen	1000	one thousand/
14	fourte en		a thousand
15	fifteen	1001	one thousand and one/
16	sixteen		a thousand and one
17	seventeen	1010	one thousand and ten/
18	eighteen		a thousand and ten
19	nineteen	1100	one thousand one hundred
20	twenty	1200	one thousand two hundred
21	twenty-one	1500	one thousand five hundred
22	twenty-two	2000	two thousand
23	twenty-three	5000	five thousand
24	twenty-four	10,000	ten thousand
25	twenty-five	20,000	twenty thousand
26	twenty-six	100,000	one hundred thousand/
27	twenty-seven		a hundred thousand
28	twenty-eight	150,000	one hundred and fifty thousand/
29	twenty-nine		a hundred and fifty thousand
30	thirty	1,000,000	one million/a million
40	forty	2,000,000	two million
50	fifty	1,000,000,000	one billion/a billion
60	sixty		
70	seventy		
80	eighty		
90	ninety		

▼ 重点短语

She's fifteen (years old).

on page two hundred and fifty-six

two plus seven are nine

eight minus two are six

hundreds of years

the two women

all five candidates

two small children

Fifteen people were missing.

Five of the children came with their father.

in fives

They sold the house for £150,000.

数字

- **one** 作为数字用在名词前，强调只有一个事物，或用于表示表达的精确性。当谈论一个团体中的特定一员时也用 one。否则，就用 a。

  There was only one gate into the palace.
  One member said that he would never vote for such a proposal.
  A car came slowly up the road.

- 数字0有如下几种表达方式：

  在温度、税率、利率中，用 *zero*
  It was fourteen below zero when they woke up.
  在小数点前，用 *nought*(英式)/*naught*(美式)
  nought point eight nine (0.89)
  表示计算，在口语中用 *nothing*
  five minus five is nothing
  当一个一个地报数字，或在小数点后时，用 oh 或字母 o
  point oh eight nine (.089)
  在体育比分中，用 *nil*
  England beat Germany one-nil.

- 介于999和100的数字通常用阿拉伯数字表示。当朗读或写成单词时，在英式英语中，百位数和十位数之间用 and 连接，而在美式英语中，省略 and。

  261 → *two hundred and sixty-one* (英)
  two hundred sixty-one (美)

- 介于1000和9999之间的数字，逗号通常放在第1个数字后：1,526

- 有时以空格代替逗号：15 000 1 986 000

- 当大于 9999 的数字写成阿拉伯数字时，通常在右起第3位数字前加逗号，在右起第6位数字前加逗号，依次类推，从而把数字分成3个数字一组的几组：15,000 1,986,000

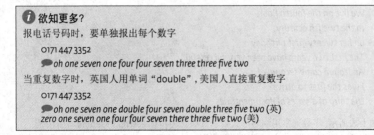

ⓘ 欲知更多？

报电话号码时，要单独报出每个数字

  0171 447 3352
  💬 *oh one seven one four four seven three three five two*

当重复数字时，英国人用单词 "double"，美国人直接重复数字

  0171 447 3352
  💬 *oh one seven one double four seven double three five two* (英)
  zero one seven one four four seven there three five two (美)

数字

▼ 序数词

序数词用于表明某物在一个系列或序列中所处的位置, 可以用作形容词(用于名词前, *the* 或 *her* 一类的限定词之后)、代词(代替名词), 或副词(在谈论赛跑或其他比赛时, 与某些动词连用, 比如*come* 或 *finish*)。大多数分数的分母用序数词表示。

1st	first	26th	twenty-sixth
2nd	second	27th	twenty-seventh
3rd	third	28th	twenty-eighth
4th	fourth	29th	twenty-ninth
5th	fifth	30th	thirtieth
6th	sixth	31st	thirty-first
7th	seventh	32nd	thirty-second
8th	eighth	40th	fortieth
9th	ninth	41st	forty-first
10th	tenth	42nd	forty-second
11th	eleventh	50th	fiftieth
12th	twelfth	60th	sixtieth
13th	thirteenth	70th	seventieth
14th	fourteenth	80th	eightieth
15th	fifteenth	90th	ninetieth
16th	sixteenth	100th	hundredth
17th	seventeenth	101st	hundred and first
18th	eighteenth	102nd	hundred and second
19th	nineteenth	103rd	hundred and third
20th	twentieth	110th	hundred and tenth
21st	twenty-first	200th	two hundredth
22nd	twenty-second	1000th	thousandth
23rd	twenty-third	2000th	two thousandth
24th	twenty-fourth	10,000th	ten thousandth
25th	twenty-fifth	1,000,000th	millionth
		1,000,000,000th	billionth

We live on the fourth floor.
in the twelfth century
on her twenty-first birthday
The first two years have been very successful.
An Italian came second.
I was the first to arrive.
the third of a series of documentaries

● 如上表所示, 序数词常用缩略形式表示, 1加 *st* 为 *first*, 2加 *nd* 为 *second*, 3加 *rd* 为 *third*, *fourth* 到 *ninth* 分别用相应的基数词加 *th* 表示 —— 例如, *6th*。这些缩写形式在日期中尤为常用。

数字

● 10 以上不是 10 的倍数的序数词, 由基数词加序数词构成, 之间用连字符分开。

my thirty-third birthday
on the fifty-sixth floor
our forty-fifth wedding anniversary

> **i** 楼房的第一层, 在英式英语中被称为 ground floor, 在美式英语中则被称为 first floor。在英式英语中, 再往上的一层为 first floor, 在美式英语中则为 second floor。

▼ 分数、小数和百分数

1/2	a half
1/3	a third
1/4	a quarter
1/5	a fifth
1/6	a sixth
1/10	a tenth
2/3	two-thirds
5/8	five-eigths
0.5	(nought) point five (英)/(naught) point five (美)
3.5	three point five
6.89	six point eight nine
10%	ten per cent (英)/ten percent (美)
100%	one hundred per cent (英)/one hundred percent (美)

● 除了 half (一半) 和 quarter (四分之一) 以外, 分数的分母用序数词表示。

four and a half centuries
a mile and a half below the surface
The state produces a third of the nation's oil.
More than two-thirds of the Earth is water.

● 分数的分子通常可以用不定冠词 a。

The country spends over a fifth of its budget on education.

正式用语和书面语中, 或需要强调数量时, 用 one。

one quarter of the total population

● 分子大于 1 时, 通常要加连字符。

the first two-thirds of this century
He's due at the office in three-quarters of an hour.

星期和日期

▼ 星期

Monday	星期一	Saturday	星期六
Tuesday	星期二	Sunday	星期日
Wednesday	星期三		
Thursday	星期四		
Friday	星期五		

What day <u>is it</u> today? <u>It's</u> Thursday.
Why didn't you come to the meeting <u>on</u> Wednesday?
I'm usually here <u>on</u> Mondays and Fridays.
Deliveries <u>usually</u> arrive <u>on a</u> Thursday.
The attack took place <u>last</u> Thursday.
Talks are likely to start <u>next</u> Tuesday.
We meet here <u>every</u> Saturday morning.
I'll be away <u>from</u> Monday <u>to</u> Friday.
I'll need an answer <u>by</u> Monday.
We're having a party on <u>the last</u> Sunday <u>in</u> May.

▼ 月份

January	一月	July	七月
February	二月	August	八月
March	三月	September	九月
April	四月	October	十月
May	五月	November	十一月
June	六月	December	十二月

● 月份前用介词 in。

It always snows <u>in</u> January.
I flew to London <u>in early</u> March.
It happened <u>in late</u> May, and the apple trees were in bloom.
He spent two weeks with us <u>in</u> July 1993.

> ⚠ next（下一个）或 last（上一个）加月份，前面不用介词 in。
> *Staff were on strike <u>last</u> June.*
> *I don't know where I'll be <u>next</u> November.*

● 某月中的具体日子前用介词 on。

His exhibition opens <u>on 5 February</u> (英)/February 5 (美).
The trial will begin <u>on August the twenty-second</u>.

> 在英国，一学年分为三个 terms (学期)，夏季有长假期，圣诞节和复活节各有一个较短的假期。在美国，一学年分为两个 semesters (学期)，十月、四月以及圣诞节和复活节都会放假。

星期和日期

▼ 季节

Spring	春季	Autumn(英)/Fall(美)	秋季
Summer	夏季	Winter	冬季

- 季节前的介词用 in。

  In winter the nights are extremely cold.
  It's nice to get away in the spring.
  We met again in the spring of 1977.

  ⚠ next(下一个)或 last(上一个)加上季节，前面不用介词 in。
  The final report is due out next autumn(英)/fall(美).
  I was supposed to go last summer.

▼ 日期的写法

- 书写日期有几种不同的方式：

13 September	September 13
13th September	September 13th

- 上面的例子是书信中日期的书写方式。美国人通常把月份放在最前面。

- 若想给出年份，则将年份放在最后。如果将日放在月后，则用逗号将年份与日期分开。

  13th September 2004 (in a letter)
  My date of birth is 13 September 1957.
  I was born on September 13th, 1957.

- 也可按如下所示的方式，将日期完全用数字表达。数字形式常常用于信或表格的上部。在英国，日放在最前面。

  13/9/57 或 *13.9.57*

- 在美国，月份放在日之前。

  9/13/57 或 *9.13.57*

▼ 日期的读法

- 即使日期是用基数词表示，也要读作序数词。

  September 13 读作 *September the thirteenth*(英)

- 若月放在表示日的数字之后，月份前要加介词 of。

  13 September 读作 *the thirteenth of September*

  > ℹ 在以上两种情况下，美国人通常都读作 September thirteenth。

- 若所指的月份很明确, 就可省略月份。

    'What's the date today?' – 'It's the twelfth.'

▼ 年的读法

- 读年份时一般分成两部分。例如:

    1957 读作 *nineteen fifty-seven*
    1860 读作 *eighteen sixty*

    以"20-" 开头的年份 —— 例如, 2003 和 2010 —— 可以读作 *two thousand and …*。例如:

    2003 读作 *two thousand and three*
    2010 读作 *two thousand and ten*

    以"20-" 开头的年份也可以分成两部分读, 例如:

    2020 可读作 *twenty twenty*
    2004 可读作 *twenty oh four*

- 以"-00" 结尾的年份, 可将第二部分读作 *hundred*。例如:

    1900 读作 *nineteen hundred*

    人们常常写 the year 2000, 而不是仅仅写成 2000。人们通常将其读作 *the year two thousand*。

- 以"01-09" 结尾的年份有两种读法。例如:

    1807 可以读作 *eighteen oh seven* 或 *eighteen hundred and seven*。

▼ 年代和世纪

- 1970 –1979 可以读作 *the nineteen seventies*, 或非正式的读法为 *the seventies*。

    the 1960s 读作 *the (nineteen) sixties*
    the 1970s 读作 *the (nineteen) seventies*

- 说到 20 世纪的年代时, 不必指出世纪。例如, 1920s 可以读作 *the twenties*。它可以写作 the '20s, the 20s 或 the Twenties。

⚠ 1400 –1499 称作 the fifteenth century (15世纪), 而不是 "the fourteenth century" (14世纪)。这非常合逻辑, 因为 1 世纪是指从 1 年 —— 公元纪年的开始 —— 到 99 年。我们现在正处于 21 世纪 (2000-2099)。

- 世纪还可以写作序数词, 例如, the 20th century。

时间

▼ 几点了?

It's one o'clock

It's a quarter past one (英)
It's a quarter after one (美)
It's one fifteen

It's half past one (英)
It's half after one (美)
It's one thirty

It's a quarter to two (英)
It's a quarter of two (美)
It's one forty-five

Its twenty-five past one (英)
It's twenty-five after one (美)
It's one twenty-five

It's ten to two (英)
It's ten of two (美)
It's one fifty

It's 13 minutes to two (英)
It's 13 minutes of two (美)
It's one forty-seven

⚠ o'clock 只用在表示整点的时间后。例如, 可以说 five o'clock, 但不能说 "ten past five o'clock" 或 "a quarter past five o'clock"。

● 可以用 minutes 表示5分钟以内的时间, 或精确地表示时间。

It was twenty-four minutes past ten.
We left home at exactly five minutes to ten.

● 从以上例子可知, 可以用小时加过了多少分钟来表示时间。

7.35 可以读作 *seven thirty-five* 或 *twenty-five minutes to eight*。

● 在整点后未必一定用 o'clock。人们常常只用数字。

I used to get up every morning at six.

● 如果过整点的分钟数小于10, 许多人在分钟数前用 o, 读作 oh。例如:

10.07 可以读作 *ten oh seven* 或 *ten seven*。

时间

注意, 在写时间时, 英国人在小时后加圆点, 譬如: 10.07。而美国人多用冒号: 7:35。

● 若所指的钟点很明确, 在介词 past 或 to 之后不必加钟点。

    'What time is it?' – 'Twenty-five past.'
    'What time does the train leave?' – 'I think it's at quarter to.'

问时间	回答
What time is it?	*It's nearly ten past twelve.* (英)
	It's nearly ten after twelve. (美)
What's the time now?	*It's three o'clock exactly.*
What time do you make it?	*I make it four twenty-seven.*
Do you have the time (on you)?	*Yes, it's half past nine.*
Can you tell me the time?	*Yes, it's nearly quarter to eight.*

相关用语
Mary left at three and caught the bus.
The students must leave their rooms by nine o'clock this morning.
He was home by six for dinner.
She was busy until three o'clock, when she had to meet her parents.
I've been awake since four.
Did you see the eleven o'clock news?

04:00	16:00
four in the morning 4 a.m.	four in the afternoon 4 p.m.

09:00	21:00
nine in the morning 9 a.m.	nine in the evening 9 p.m.

12:00	
twelve in the morning midday 12 a.m. noon	

● 可以加 a.m. (代表 ante meridiem, 拉丁语, 表示 "中午之前") 表示午夜到中午之间的时间。同样, p.m. (代表 post meridiem, 表示 "中午之后") 表示中午到午夜之间的时间。这些缩写通常不用于对话中, 而且从不与 o'clock 连用。

    The doors will be opened at 10 a.m.
    He finally got home at 11.30 p.m., having set out at 6 a.m.

▼ 与时间有关的惯用语

● 时间表达法中经常用到名词词组

yesterday
today
tomorrow

yesterday {
    morning
    afternoon
    evening
last night

tomorrow {
    morning
    afternoon
    evening
    night

last {
    Friday
    week
    month
    year

next {
    Friday
    week
    month
    year

the day before yesterday
the day after tomorrow
the previous day
the day before
the next day
the following day
the day after
the week before last
the week after next
a week on Thursday (下周二起的一个星期)

> ⚠ 表示时间的词或短语不与介词at, in 或 on连用。
> One of my friends wrote to me today.
> So, you're coming back next week?

● 表示时间的词或短语常常与动词的一般现在时或现在进行时连用, 表示将来会发生的事情。

    The plane leaves tomorrow morning.
    They're coming next week.

ENGLISH IN ACTION

时间

▼ 定期发生的事

every	hour day Saturday week month year etc	on	Saturdays Tuesdays and Fridays etc

every other	day week month year etc	every	two three etc	hours days weeks etc

once	an hour a day etc	once every	week month 2 weeks etc

twice three times four times etc	an a	hour day week month etc

The nurse comes in to see him every day.
He has driving lessons on Mondays and Fridays.
We wrote to each other every other day.
The Olympics are held every four years.
The group meets once a week.
It only rains here once every five or ten years.
The medicine should be taken three times a day.

▼ 与时间连用的介词

AT

● at 用于:

► 表示钟点的时间:at eight o'clock, at three fifteen
► 宗教节日:at Christmas, at Easter
► 用餐时间:at breakfast, at lunchtimes
► 具体的较短的一段时间:at night, at the weekend, at weekends, at half-term

IN

● in 用于:

► 季节:in winter, in the spring
► 年份、年代和世纪:in 1985, in the year 2000, in the thirties, in the nineteenth century
► 月份:in July, in December
► 一天中的各时段:in the morning, in the evenings

▸ 较长的一段时间: in wartime, in the holidays

● in 也可用于表示某事将要发生在将来的某个时间段期间或之后。

I think we'll find out in the next few days.

ON

● on 用于:

▸ 星期: on Monday, on Tuesday morning, on Sunday evenings

▸ 特殊的日子: on Christmas Day, on my birthday

▸ 具体日期: on the twentieth of July, on June 21st, on the twelfth

DURING/OVER

● during 和 over 表示某事发生在某个特定的时间段中的某个时候, 或贯穿于整个时间段。

I saw him twice during the holidays.
Will you stay here over Christmas?

FROM ...TO ...

● from ... to ... 表示某段时间从开始到结束的整段时间。

The building is closed from April to June.
We had no rain from March to October.

也可用 till 或 until 代替 to。

The ticket office will be open from 10 a.m. until 1 p.m.
They were working from dawn till dusk.

BY

● by 表示 "不迟于"。

By eleven o'clock, Brody was back in his office.
Can we get this finished by tomorrow?

SINCE/FOR/AGO

● for 可与任何时态的动词连用, 表示某事持续发生或不发生了多长时间, 具体指一段时间时也用 for。

He didn't speak for a long time.
I will be in London for three weeks.
I've lived here for nine years.

● since 用于现在完成时或过去完成时, 表示某事从何时开始发生。

Marilyn has lived in Paris since 1984.
I had eaten nothing since breakfast.

● ago 用于一般过去时, 表示某事是在距离说话时间多久前发生的。

We saw him about a month ago.
John's wife died five years ago.

⚠ ago 常与时间段连用。ago 不与现在完成时连用。不能说 "We have seen him about a month ago."。

度量衡

> **i** 英国沿用两种度量系统:"公制"系统,如中国所使用的,和"英制"(非公制)系统。公制系统是官方系统,用途广泛。但英制系统仍用于度量人的身高和体重、酒吧饮品,显示在路标上的距离和某些体育运动,譬如板球、足球和马术等。在美国,公制系统除了在军事、医学和科学领域外,并不太常用。

● 每种系统都有自己的度量单位名词,如下所示。缩写形式在括号中给出。若用公制单位,就用十进制数字表示:1.69 metres (读作 one point six nine metres),4.8 kilograms (读作 four point six kilograms)。

● 对于非公制单位,常用分数形式:6 ¾ inches (读作 six and three quarter inches),1 ½ tons of wheat (one and a half tons of wheat)。

长度

公制

1 kilometre (km)	=	1000 metres	=	0.6214 miles
1 metre (m)	=	100 centimetres	=	1.094 yards
1 centimetre (cm)	=	10 millimetres	=	0.394 inches

非公制

1 mile	=	1760 yards	=	1.609 kilometres
1 yard (yd)	=	3 feet	=	0.914 metres
1 foot (ft)	=	12 inches	=	30.48 centimetres
1 inch (in)	=	25.4 millimetres		

> **i** 符号 ' 有时用于表示英尺;符号 " 表示英寸。例如,3'6"表示3英尺6英寸。
> ● 单数形式 foot 和复数形式 feet 都可与数字连用。
> *The room is almost 20 foot long.*

面积

公制

1 square kilometre (km²)	=	100 hectares	=	0.386 square miles
1 hectare (ha)	=	100 ares	=	2.471 acres
1 are (a)	=	100 square metres	=	119.6 square yards
1 square metre (m²)	=	1.196 square yards		

非公制

1 square mile	=	640 acres	=	2.59 square kilometres
1 acre	=	4840 square yards	=	0.405 hectares
1 square yard	=	9 square feet	=	0.836 square metres
1 square foot	=	144 square inches	=	929.03 square centimetres
1 square inch			=	6.452 square centimetres

度量衡

重量

公制

1 tonne	=	1000 kilograms	=	19.688 hundredweight
1 kilogram (kg)	=	1000 grams	=	2.205 pounds
1 gram (g)	=	1000 milligrams		

非公制

1 ton	=	20 hundredweight	=	1.016 tonnes
1 hundredweight (cwt)	=	8 stone	=	50.8 kilograms
1 stone (st)	=	14 pounds	=	6.356 kilograms
1 pound (lb)	=	16 ounces	=	454 grams

> ***i*** 有时 kilo (公斤) 可以代替 kilogram, metric ton (公吨) 代替tonne。

容量

公制

1 decalitre (dal)	=	10 litres	=	2.2 gallons (2.63 US gallons)
1 litre (l)	=	100 centilitres	=	1.76 pints (2.1 US pints)
1 centilitre (cl)	=	10 millilitres	=	0.018 pints (0.021 US pints)

非公制

1 gallon (gal)	=	4 quarts	=	4.546 litres
1 quart (qt)	=	2 pints	=	1.136 litres
1 pint (pt)	=	20 fluid ounces	=	56.8 centilitres
1 fluid ounce (fl oz)	=	28.4 millilitres		

> ***i*** 在美式英语中, metre 和 litre 拼写为 meter (米) 和 liter (公升)。
>
> ● 美国非公制容量度量单位不同于英国。一美制品脱等于0.833英制品脱, 相当于 16美制液量盎司。

提问	回答
How tall is he?	*He's about six feet / foot tall.*
How high is the Shanghai TV Tower?	*It's 468 metres* (英)*/meters* (美) *high.*
How far is it to Glasgow from here?	*It's about fifteen miles.*
How much do you weigh? ⎤	*I'm / I weigh twelve stone four*
What weight are you? ⎦	(英), *I'm / I weigh 68 pounds* (美).
You're about ten and a half stone, aren't you? (英)	*I'm a little heavier than that.*

度量衡

● 下列形容词和相应的介词短语可用于表示尺寸的度量单位名词后。

- *long/in length*
- *deep/in depth*
- *high/in height*
- *tall*
- *thick/in thickness*
- *wide/in width*

The room is almost 20 foot long.
I need a piece of wood two foot six long.
The water was 2 metres deep.
Each layer is 6 metres thick.
He was five foot seven tall.
The island is about 25 miles long by 12 miles wide.

---

i 在英国, a pint 单独使用时, 常指一品脱啤酒。a half 也可以单独使用, 指酒吧里的半品脱饮品。a quarter 单独使用时, 指四分之一磅的物品, 譬如蔬菜等。
He's gone out to the pub for a pint.
I'll have a half of lager.
A quarter of mushrooms, please.

货币

▼ 英国货币

- 英国的货币单位为英镑, 1英镑等于100便士。

- 英镑的符号为 £, 写在数字之前。字母 p 代表便士, 写在数字之后。
    £40 读作 *forty pounds*
    60p 读作 *sixty pence or sixty p (pronounced /piː/)*
    £2.50 读作 *two pounds fifty or two fifty*

i	在日常生活中, 人们常用一些非正式的说法, 表示不同面值的纸币和硬币。

美式英语		英式英语	
penny	1 cent	*quid*	£1
nickel	5 cents	*fiver*	£5
dime	10 cents	*tenner*	£10
quarter	25 cents	*ton*	£100
Buck	$1	*grand*	£1000

- 美国的货币单位为美元, 1美元等于100美分。

- 美元的符号为 $, 写在数字之前。字母 c 代表美分, 写在数字之后。
    $40 读作 *forty dollars*
    60c 读作 *sixty cents*
    $2.50 读作 *two dollars fifty cents*

提问	回答
How much is that?	*That's four seventy-eight, please.*
How much is it to park?	*Two dollars twenty cents.*
How much will it cost?	*It'll cost you about a hundred pounds.*
Do you have any change?	*I'm sorry, I don't.*
Do you have change for five pounds?	*Yes, I can give you five pound coins.*

国家、语言和货币

- 下表列出了世界上人口超过750,000 的大多数国家的名称。

- 形容词 (ADJ) 一列的词条，表示来自某国或与某国有关的事物。人民 (people) 一列的词条，表示某个国家的人。人民 (people) 的表示方法通常与表示国籍的形容词 (ADJ) 是一样的，故不重复列出。例如，Belgian (比利时的) 的表示国家或来自某个国家的人。人民称为 Belgian (比利时人)。

- 人民 (people) 一列中，前面有定冠词 the 的的词条只能用作复数。以 -man 结尾的词条只能用来指男性；以 -woman 结尾的词条只能指女性。

> **i** 当心别冒犯了别人！Great Britain，或 Britain是一个地理名词，指包括英格兰、威尔士和苏格兰在内的政治的岛。 the United Kingdom是一个政治名词，包括英格兰、威尔士、苏格兰和北爱尔兰。 尽管苏格兰、威尔士、爱尔兰分别有自己的议会，但他们和英格兰一起，都从属于这个议会。苏格兰人、爱尔兰人和威尔士人都不是英格兰人，如果你称他们为"英格兰人"或来自英格兰，对他们是一种冒犯。不列颠群岛 (the British Isles) 也是一个地理名词，指包括英伦岛、爱尔兰岛及其附近小岛在内的所有岛屿。但是，爱尔兰和英国是一个独立的国家，首都是都柏林。
> the United States of America, America, the USA 和 the US 都用于指同一个国家。然而，必须得谨用America，因为它实际上是整个美洲大陆。加拿大、墨西哥等国家的人会认为他们也是America的一部分。

国家		形容词	人民	语言	货币
Afghanistan	阿富汗	Afghan, Afghani		Pashto, Dari	afghani
Albania	阿尔巴尼亚	Albanian		Albanian	lek
Algeria	阿尔及利亚	Algerian		Arabic, French	Algerian dinar
America	美国	American		English	US dollar
Angola	安哥拉	Angolan		Portuguese	new kwanza
Argentina	阿根廷	Argentine, Argentinian		Spanish	Argentinian Peso
Armenia	亚美尼亚	Armenian		Armenian	dram
Australia	澳大利亚	Australian		English	Australian dollar
Austria	奥地利	Austrian		German	euro (previously schilling)
Azerbaijan	阿塞拜疆	Azeri, Azerbaijani		Azeri	manat

56

国家	形容词	人民	语言	货币
Bangladesh 孟加拉国	Bangladeshi		Bengali	taka
Belarus 白俄罗斯	Belarussian		Belorussian, Russian	Belarussian rouble
Belgium 比利时	Belgian		Flemish, French	euro (previously franc)
Benin 贝宁	Beninese, Beninois		French, Fon	CFA franc
Bhutan 不丹	Bhutanese		Dzongkha, Nepali	ngultrum
Bolivia 玻利维亚	Bolivian		Spanish, Quechua, Aymara	boliviano
Bosnia and Herzegovina 波斯尼亚和黑塞哥维那	Bosnian, Herzegovinian		Bosnian, Croatian, Serbian	convertible marka
Botswana 博茨瓦纳	Botswanan		English, Setswana	pula
Brazil 巴西	Brazilian		Portuguese	real
Britain 英国	British	Briton, the British	English	pound sterling
Bulgaria 保加利亚	Bulgarian		Bulgarian	lev
Burkina Faso 布基纳法索	Burkinabé		French, Mossi	CFA franc
Burundi 布隆迪	Burundi	Burundian	Kirundi, French	Burundi franc
Cambodia 柬埔寨	Cambodian		Khmer	new riel
Cameroon 喀麦隆	Cameroonian		French, English	CFA franc
Canada 加拿大	Canadian		English, French	Canadian dollar
Central African Republic 中非共和国	Central African		French, Sango	CFA franc
Chad 乍得	Chadian		French, Arabic, Sara, Sango	CFA franc
Chile 智利	Chilean		Spanish	Chilean peso
China 中国	Chinese	the Chinese	Chinese	yuan
Colombia 哥伦比亚	Colombian		Spanish	Colombian peso

国家、语言和货币

国家		形容词	人民	语言	货币
Congo, Democratic Republic of	刚果民主共和国	Congolese		French	Congolese franc
Congo, Republic of	刚果共和国	Congolese		French	CFA franc
Costa Rica	哥斯达黎加	Costa Rican		Spanish	colón
Côte d'Ivoire	科特迪瓦	Ivorian		French	CFA franc
Croatia	克罗地亚	Croat, Croatian		Croatian	Croatian kuna
Cuba	古巴	Cuban		Spanish	Cuban peso
Cyprus	塞浦路斯	Greek Cypriot, Turkish Cypriot		Greek, Turkish	Cypriot pound, Turkish lira
Czech Republic	捷克共和国	Czech		Czech, Slovak	koruna
Denmark	丹麦	Danish	Dane	Danish	Danish krone
Dominican Republic	多米尼加共和国	Dominican		Spanish	Dominican peso
East Timor	东帝汶	East Timorese		Tetum	US dollar
Ecuador	厄瓜多尔	Ecuadorean		Spanish, Quechua	US dollar
Egypt	埃及	Egyptian		Arabic	Egyptian pound
El Salvador	萨尔瓦多	Salvadoran, Salvadorean		Spanish	Salvadoran colón
Eritrea	厄立特里亚	Eritrean		Tigre, Kunama	nakfa
Estonia	爱沙尼亚	Estonian		Estonian	kroon
Ethiopia	埃塞俄比亚	Ethiopian		Amharic	birr
Finland	芬兰	Finnish	Finn	Finnish, Swedish	euro (previously markka)
France	法国	French	Frenchman, Frenchwoman, the French	French	euro (previously franc)

国家、语言和货币

国家		形容词	人民	语言	货币
Gabon	加蓬	Gabonese		French, Fang	CFA franc
Gambia, The	冈比亚	Gambian		English	dalasi
Georgia	格鲁吉亚	Georgian		Georgian, Russian	lari
Germany	德国	German		German	euro (previously Deutschmark)
Ghana	加纳	Ghanaian		English, Akan	new cedi
Great Britain	大不列颠及北爱尔兰联合王国	British	Briton, the British	English	pound sterling
Greece	希腊	Greek		Greek	euro (previously drachma)
Guatemala	危地马拉	Guatemalan		Spanish	quetzal
Guinea	几内亚	Guinean		French	Guinean franc
Guinea-Bissau	几内亚比绍	Guinea Bissauan		Portuguese, Creole	CFA franc
Guyana	圭亚那	Guyanese, Guyanan	the Guyanese	English	Guyanese dollar
Haiti	海地	Haitian		French, Creole	gourde
Honduras	洪都拉斯	Honduran		Spanish	lempira
Hungary	匈牙利	Hungarian		Hungarian	forint
Iceland	冰岛	Icelandic	Icelander	Icelandic	krona
India	印度	Indian		Hindi, English	Indian rupee
Indonesia	印度尼西亚	Indonesian		Bahasa Indonesia	Indonesian rupiah
Iran	伊朗	Iranian		Farsi	Iranian rial
Iraq	伊拉克	Iraqi		Arabic, Kurdish	Iraqi dinar
Ireland, Republic of	爱尔兰共和国	Irish	Irishman, Irishwoman, the Irish	Irish, English	euro (previously punt)
Israel	以色列	Israeli		Hebrew, Arabic	new Israeli shekel

国家、语言和货币

国家		形容词	人民	语言	货币
Italy	意大利	Italian		Italian	euro (previously lira)
Jamaica	牙买加	Jamaican		English	Jamaican dollar
Japan	日本	Japanese	the Japanese	Japanese	yen
Jordan	约旦	Jordanian		Arabic	Jordanian dinar
Kazakhstan	哈萨克斯坦	Kazakh, Kazakhstani		Kazakh, Russian	tenge
Kenya	肯尼亚	Kenyan		Kiswahili, English	Kenyan shilling
Kuwait	科威特	Kuwaiti		Arabic	Kuwaiti dinar
Kyrgyzstan	吉尔吉斯斯坦	Kyrgyzstani, Kyrgyz		Kyrgyz	som
Laos	老挝	Lao, Laotian		Lao, Laotian	new kip
Latvia	拉脱维亚	Latvian		Latvian	lat
Lebanon	黎巴嫩	Lebanese	the Lebanese	Arabic, French	Lebanese pound
Lesotho	莱索托	Lesothan, Basotho	Mosotho, Basotho	Sesotho, English	loti
Liberia	利比里亚	Liberian		English	Liberian dollar
Libya	利比亚	Libyan		Arabic	Libyan dinar
Lithuania	立陶宛	Lithuanian		Lithuanian	litas
Luxembourg	卢森堡	Luxembourg	Luxembourger	French, German, Luxemburgian	euro (previously Luxembourg franc, Belgian franc)
Macedonia	马其顿	Macedonian		Macedonian	denar
Madagascar	马达加斯加	Malagasy		French, Malagasy	Malagasy franc
Malawi	马拉维	Malawian		English, Chichewa	Malawian kwacha
Malaysia	马来西亚	Malaysian		Malay	ringgit
Maldives	马尔代夫	Maldivian		Divehi	rufiyaa

国家、语言和货币

国家	形容词	人民	语言	货币
Mali 马里	Malian		French, Bambara	CFA franc
Malta 马耳他	Maltese	the Maltese	Maltese, English	Maltese lira
Mauritania 毛里塔尼亚	Mauritanian		French, Arabic	ouguiya
Mauritius 毛里求斯	Mauritian		English, Creole	Mauritian rupee
Mexico 墨西哥	Mexican		Spanish	New Mexican peso
Moldova 摩尔瓦多	Moldovan		Moldovan, Romanian, Russian	leu
Mongolia 蒙古共和国	Mongol, Mongolian		Khalkha, Mongolian	tugrik
Morocco 摩洛哥	Moroccan		Arabic, Berber	Moroccan dirham
Mozambique 莫桑比克	Mozambican		Portuguese	metical
Myanmar 缅甸	Myanmar		Burmese	kyat
Namibia 纳米比亚	Namibian		Afrikaans, English	Namibian dollar
Nepal 尼泊尔	Nepalese	the Nepalese	Nepali	Nepalese rupee
Netherlands, The 荷兰	Dutch	Dutchman, Dutchwoman, the Dutch	Dutch	euro (previously guilder)
New Zealand 新西兰	New Zealand	New Zealander	English, Maori	New Zealand dollar
Nicaragua 尼加拉瓜	Nicaraguan		Spanish	gold cordoba
Niger 尼日尔	Nigerien		French	CFA franc
Nigeria 尼日利亚	Nigerian		English, Hausa, Yoruba, Ibo	naira
North Korea 朝鲜	North Korean		Korean	North Korean won
Norway 挪威	Norwegian		Norwegian	Norwegian krone
Oman 阿曼	Omani		Arabic	Omani rial

61

国家、语言和货币

国家		形容词	人民	语言	货币
Pakistan	巴基斯坦	Pakistani		Urdu, English, Punjabi	Pakistani rupee
Panama	巴拿马	Panamanian		Spanish	balboa
Papua New Guinea	巴布亚新几内亚	Papua New Guinea		Pidgin, English, Motu	kina
Paraguay	巴拉圭	Paraguayan		Spanish, Guaraní	guaraní
Peru	秘鲁	Peruvian		Spanish, Quechua	nuevo sol
Philippines, The	菲律宾	Filipino, Philippine	Filipino, Filipina (women only), Philippine	Filipino, English	Philippine peso
Poland	波兰	Polish	Pole	Polish	zloty
Portugal	葡萄牙	Portuguese	the Portuguese	Portuguese	euro (previously escudo)
Puerto Rico (US)	波多黎各 (美)	Puerto Rican		Spanish, English	US dollar
Romania	罗马尼亚	Romanian		Romanian	leu
Russia	俄罗斯	Russian		Russian	rouble
Rwanda	卢旺达	Rwandan		Kinyarwanda, French, English	Rwandan franc
Saudi Arabia	沙特阿拉伯	Saudi, Saudi Arabian		Arabic	Saudi riyal
Senegal	塞内加尔	Senegalese	the Senegalese	French	CFA franc
Serbia and Montenegro	塞尔维亚和黑山	Serb, Serbian or Montenegrin	Serb, Montenegrin	Serbo-Croation	new dinar
Sierra Leone	塞拉利昂	Sierra Leonean		English	leone
Singapore	新加坡	Singapore, Singaporean	Singaporean	Malay, Chinese, Tamil, English	Singapore dollar
Slovakia	斯洛伐克	Slovak		Slovak	koruna
Slovenia	斯洛文尼亚	Slovenian, Slovene		Slovenian	tolar

国家、语言和货币

国家	形容词	人民	语言	货币
Somalia 索马里	Somali		Somali, Arabic	Somali shilling
South Africa 南非	South African		Afrikaans, English, Bantu	rand
South Korea 韩国	South Korean		Korean	South Korean won
Spain 西班牙	Spanish	Spaniard, the Spanish	Castilian Spanish	euro (previously peseta)
Sri Lanka 斯里兰卡	Sri Lankan		Singhalese, Tamil, English	Sri Lankan rupee
Sudan 苏丹	Sudanese	the Sudanese	Arabic	Sudanese dinar
Swaziland 斯威士兰	Swazi		English, Siswati	lilangeni
Sweden 瑞典	Swedish	Swede	Swedish	Swedish krona
Switzerland 瑞士	Swiss	the Swiss	German, French, Italian	Swiss franc
Syria 叙利亚	Syrian		Arabic	Syrian pound
Tajikistan 塔吉克斯坦	Tajik		Tajik, Uzbek, Russian	somoni
Tanzania 坦桑尼亚	Tanzanian		Swahili, English	Tanzanian shilling
Thailand 泰国	Thai		Thai	baht
Togo 多哥	Togolese		French, Ewe	CFA franc
Trinidad and Tobago 特立尼达和多巴哥	Trinidadian, Tobagoan		English	Trinidad and Tobago dollar
Tunisia 突尼斯	Tunisian		Arabic, French	Tunisian dinar
Turkey 土耳其	Turkish	Turk	Turkish, Kurdish, Arabic	Turkish lira
Turkmenistan 土库曼斯坦	Turkmen		Turkmen, Russian	manat
Uganda 乌干达	Ugandan		English, Luganda, Swahili, Luo	Ugandan shilling
Ukraine 乌克兰	Ukrainian		Ukrainian, Russian	hryvni
United Arab Emirates 阿联酋	Emirian		Arabic	Emirian dirham

国家、语言和货币

国家	形容词	人民	语言	货币
United Kingdom 大不列颠及北爱尔兰联合王国	British	Briton, the British	English	pound sterling
United States of America 美利坚合众国	American		English	US dollar
Uruguay 乌拉圭	Uruguayan		Spanish	Uruguayan peso
Uzbekistan 乌兹别克斯坦	Uzbek		Uzbek, Russian	sum
Venezuela 委内瑞拉	Venezuelan		Spanish	bolívar
Vietnam 越南	Vietnamese	the Vietnamese	Vietnamese	new dông
Yemen 也门	Yemeni		Arabic	yemeni rial
Zambia 赞比亚	Zambian		English	Zambian kwacha
Zimbabwe 津巴布韦	Zimbabwean		English, Shona	Zimbabwean dollar